1 MONTH OF
FREE
READING

at

www.ForgottenBooks.com

By purchasing this book you are eligible for one month membership to ForgottenBooks.com, giving you unlimited access to our entire collection of over 1,000,000 titles via our web site and mobile apps.

To claim your free month visit:
www.forgottenbooks.com/free995014

ISBN 978-0-260-96652-0
PIBN 10995014

For support please visit www.forgottenbooks.com

THE

PARLIAMENTARY DEBATES

(AUTHORISED EDITION),

FOURTH SERIES.

COMMENCING WITH THE FIFTH SESSION OF THE TWENTY-SIXTH PARLIAMENT

OF THE

UNITED KINGDOM OF GREAT BRITAIN AND IRELAND.

62 VICTORIÆ.

VOLUME LXXII,

COMPRISING THE PERIOD FROM

THE THIRTY-FIRST DAY OF MAY

TO

THE NINETEENTH DAY OF JUNE

1899.

PRINTED AND PUBLISHED,

UNDER CONTRACT WITH HER MAJESTY'S STATIONERY OFFICE,

BY

WYMAN AND SONS, LIMITED, FETTER LANE, LONDON.

1899.

TABLE OF CONTENTS

TO

VOLUME LXXII.

SEVENTH VOLUME OF SESSION.

COMMONS: WEDNESDAY, 31st MAY 1899.

PRIVATE BILL BUSINESS.

Page

Woodhouse and Conisbrough Railway (Abandonment) Bill—Lords
. Amendment considered, and agreed to   1

South Staffordshire Stipendiary Justice Bill—Read the third time, and
passed   1

Belfast and Northern Counties Railway Bill—As amended, considered;
Amendments made; Bill to be read the third time   1

Bootle Corporation Bill—As amended, considered; to be read the third
time   1

Barton-on-Sea Water Bill [Lords]—Read a second time, and committed ...   2

Glasgow Corporation (Gas and Water) Bill [Lords]—Read a second
time, and committed   2

Glasgow Corporation (Tramways, &c.) Bill [Lords]—Read a second time,
and committed...   2

Liverpool Overhead Railway Bill [Lords]—Read a second time, and
committed   2

London Hospital Bill [Lords]—Read a second time, and committed   ...   2

Mid-Kent Gas Bill [Lords]—Read a second time, and committed   2

Oldham Corporation Bill [Lords]—Read a second time, and committed   ...   2

South Hants Water Bill [Lords]—Read a second time, and committed   ...   2

Stockton and Middlesbrough Water Bill [Lords]—Read a second time,
and committed...   3

May 31.]   *Page*

Waterford and Central Ireland Railway Bill—Read a second time.

    Ordered, That the Bill be committed to the Committee on the Great
    Southern and Western, and Waterford, Limerick and Western
    Railway Companies Amalgamation, and Great Southern and Western
    Railways Bills   3

    Ordered, that the orders made on 14th March in respect of the Great
    Southern and Western, and Waterford, Limerick, and Western
    Railway Companies Amalgamation Bill, and the Great Southern and
    Western Railway Bill, be applicable to the Waterford and Central
    Ireland Railway Bill.—(*Mr. Molloy.*)   3

Electric Lighting Provisional Orders (No. 2) **Bill**—Read the third time,
and passed   3

Electric Lighting Provisional Orders (No. 5) **Bill**—Read the third time,
and passed   3

Electric Lighting Provisional Orders (No. 6) **Bill**—Read the third time,
and passed   3

Electric Lighting Provisional Orders (No. 8) **Bill**—Read the third time,
and passed   3

**Housing of the Working Classes Provisional Order (Borrowstoun-
ness) Bill**—Read a second time, and committed   3

PETITIONS.

BOROUGH FUNDS ACT, 1872—Petition from Kidderminster, for alteration of
Law ; to lie upon the Table   3

Education of Children Bill—Petitions in favour ;—From Sheffield ;—and
Federation of School Boards of the West Riding of the County of York ;
to lie upon the Table   3

Elementary Education (New Bye-Laws) Bill—Petition from Federation
of School Boards of the West Riding of the County of York, in favour ;
to lie upon the Table   4

GROUND RENTS (TAXATION BY LOCAL AUTHORITIES)—Petitions in favour ;—
From Workington ; and, School Board for London ; to lie upon the Table   4

Mines (Eight Hours) Bill—Petition of the Mining Association of Great
Britain, against ; to lie upon the Table.   4

Mines (Eight Hours) Bill—Petitions in favour ;—From Graig Gadbys ;
Merthyr Tydvil ;—Tunnel Pit ;—Cwmaman ;—Cwmbach ;—Plymouth ;—
Hill of Beath ;—Rosebank ; Court Herbert ;—Donibristle ; Balgonie ;—
Wellwood ;—West Wemyss ; Cannock Chase (four) ;—Hednesford (two) ;
Cannock ;—Chase Terrace ; Hazel Slade ;—Chasetown ; Gentleshow ;—
Glynea ;—Point of Ayr ;—Hamilton ;—Kenmuishill ;—Kimberley ;—and
Bonytloy Collieries ; to lie upon the Table ... ...   ₹

Public Health Acts Amendment Bill—Petitions in favour,—From Cambridge ;—and Tettenhall ; to lie upon the Table   4

May 31.]　　　　　　　　　　　　　　　　　　*Page*

Sale of Intoxicating Liquors on Sunday Bill—Petitions in favour ;—From
Brailes ;—Silvertown ;—Leeds ;—Tidal Basin ;—Custom House ;—Honing ;
Lingdale ;—Aldershot ;—Dartmouth ;—Paignton ;—and Torquay (four) ;
to lie upon the Table ...　　...　　...　　...　　...　　...　　...　　...　　4

Telegraphs (Telephonic Communication, &c.) Bill—Petition from Liverpool, against ; to lie upon the Table ...　　...　　...　　...　　...　　...　　4

VACCINATION ACTS, 1867 TO 1898—Petition from Wandsworth and Clapham,
for alteration of Law ; to lie upon the Table　　...　　...　　...　　...　　4

RETURNS, REPORTS, &c.

INLAND REVENUE (PROSECUTIONS UNDER GAME LAWS)—Return (presented
19th May) to be printed. (No. 223.)　　...　　...　　...　　...　　...　　∗

FEE GRANT (SCOTLAND)—Return presented,—relative thereto (ordered 15th
May ; *Mr Caldwell*), to lie upon the Table, and to be printed. (No. 224.)...　　5

TRADE REPORTS (ANNUAL SERIES)—Copies presented,—of Diplomatic and
Consular Reports, Annual Series, Nos. 2272 to 2278 (by Command) ; to lie
upon the Table...　　...　　...　　...　　...　　...　　...　　...　　...　　5

DISEASES OF ANIMALS ACTS, 1894 AND 1896—Copy presented,—of Order, dated
18th May, 1899, No. 5944, revoking Order, No. 5920, which prohibited
the conveyance of animals by the steamship "Hindustan" (by Act) ; to lie
upon the Table...　　...　　...　　...　　...　　...　　...　　...　　...　　5

LIGHT RAILWAYS ACT, 1896—Copy presented,—of Order made by the Light
Railway Commissioners, and modified and confirmed by the Board of Trade,
authorising the construction of a Light Railway in the Isle of Sheppey and
County of Kent, between Queenborough Station and Leysdown (Sheppey
Light Railway Order, 1898) (by Command) ; to lie upon the Table　　...　　5

LIGHT RAILWAYS ACT, 1896—Copy presented,—of Order made by the Light
Railway Commissioners, and modified and confirmed by the Board of Trade,
authorising the construction of Light Railways in the Counties of Glamorgan and Brecon, between Vaynor, Dowlais, and Merthyr Tydfil (Merthyr
Tydfil Light Railway Order, 1899) (by Command) ; to lie upon the Table　　5

LIGHT RAILWAYS ACT, 1896—Copy presented,—of Order made by the Light
Railway Commissioners, and modified and confirmed by the Board of Trade,
authorising the construction of Light Railways in the County of Middlesex
from Uxbridge to Hanwell (London United Tramways, Limited (Light
Railway Extensions) Order, 1898) (by Command) ; to lie upon the Table...　　5

GAS AND WATER WORKS FACILITIES ACT, 1870—Copy presented,—of Report
by the Board of Trade as to dispensing with the consents of the Sevenoaks
Rural District Council and the Hildenborough Parish Council in the case
of the Tonbridge Gas Provisional Order (by Act) ; to lie upon the Table ;
and to be printed. (No. 225.)　　...　　...　　...　　...　　...　　...　　6

HARWICH HARBOUR—Copy presented,—of Abstract of the Accounts of the Receipts
and Expenditure of the Harwich Harbour Conservancy Board from the time
of their incorporation down to and inclusive of the 31st March, 1899, &c.
(by Act) ; to lie upon the Table, and to be printed. (No. 226.)　　...　　...　　6

PARLIAMENTARY PAPERS.

(WHITSUNTIDE RECESS.)

The following Papers presented by command of Her Majesty during the Whitsuntide Recess, were delivered to the Librarian of the House of Commons during the Recess, pursuant to the Standing Order of the 14th August, 1896:—

TRADE REPORTS (ANNUAL SERIES)—Copies of Diplomatic and Consular Reports, Annual Series, Nos, 2265 to 2271 6

FISHERY BOARD (SCOTLAND)—Copy of Seventeenth Annual Report, being for 1898, Part II. (Report on the Salmon Fisheries.) 6

EAST INDIA (EXAMINATIONS FOR THE CIVIL SERVICE)—Copy of Regulations for Examinations for the Civil Service of India 6

LOCAL TAXATION (ROYAL COMMISSION)—Copy of Minutes of Evidence, Vol. III. 7

WINE DUTIES—Copy of Correspondence with the Colonial Office respecting the increase in the Wine Duties ... • 7

BRITISH SOUTH AFRICA COMPANY (BECHUANALAND RAILWAY)—Copy of correspondence with Mr. C. J. Rhodes relating to the proposed extension of the Bec uanaland Railway. Ordered, that the said Papers do lie upon the Table. h... 7

PAPER LAID UPON THE TABLE BY THE CLERK OF THE HOUSE—Inquiry into Charities (County of Flint).—Further Return relative thereto (ordered 5th May, 1897 ; *Mr. Grant Lawson*) ; to be printed. (No. 227.) 7

ELECTRIC LIGHTING PROVISIONAL ORDERS—Copy ordered, "of Memorandum stating the nature of the proposals contained in the Provisional Order included in the Electric Lighting Provisional Orders (No. 16) Bill."—(*Mr. Ritchie.*)—Copy presented accordingly ; to lie upon the Table, and to be printed. (No. 228. 7

ELECTRIC LIGHTING PROVISIONAL ORDERS—Copy ordered, "of Memorandum stating the nature of the proposals contained in the Provisional Orders included in the Electric Lighting Provisional Orders (No. 17) Bill."—(*Mr. Ritchie.*)—Copy presented accordingly ; to lie upon the Table, and to be printed. (No. 229.) 7

ELECTRIC LIGHTING PROVISIONAL ORDERS—Copy ordered, "of Memorandum stating the nature of the Proposals contained in the Provisional Orders included in the Electric Lighting Provisional Orders (No. 18) Bill."—(*Mr. Ritchie.*)—Copy presented accordingly ; to lie upon the Table, and to be printed. (No. 230.) ... ... — ... ...

ELECTRIC LIGHTING PROVISIONAL ORDERS—Copy ordered, "of Memorandum stating the nature of the Proposals contained in the Provisional Orders included in the Electric Lighting Provisional Orders (No. 19) Bill."— (*Mr. Ritchie.*) Copy presented accordingly ; to lie upon the Table,and to be printed. (No. 231.) ... ...

May 31.]   Page

PUBLIC BUSINESS.

Education of Children Bill—Considered in Committee   8

CLAUSE 1.

Amendment proposed—

> In page 1, line 6, after the word ' hundred,' to insert the words ' and five.' "
> (*Mr. George Whiteley.*)

DISCUSSION :—

Mr. Tomlinson (Preston) ...	10	Sir F. S. Powell	12
Sir F. S. Powell (Wigan)...	11	Colonel Pilkington (Lancashire, Newton)	12

Question put, "That the words ' and five ' be there inserted."

The Committee divided :—Ayes, 10 ; Noes, 163—(Division List No. 160.)

Amendment proposed—

> In page 1, line 7, to leave out the word ' twelve,' and insert the words
> "eleven years and six months.' "—(*Mr. George Whiteley.*)

DISCUSSION :—

Mr. Wylie (Dumbartonshire)	16	Sir A. Hickman (Wolverhampton,	
Mr. Tennant (Berwickshire)	18	W.)	23
Mr. Tomlinson (Preston) ...	18	Mr. J. Wilson (Durham, Mid)	23
Viscount Cranborne (Roches-		Mr. Arnold (Halifax)	24
ter)	19	Mr. George Whiteley	24
Mr. Middlemore (Birming-		The Vice President of the Com-	
ham, N.)	20	mittee of Council on Education	
Colonel Mellor (Lancashire,		—(Sir John Gorst, Cambridge	
Radcliffe)	20	University)	24
Sir Albert Rollit (Islington,		Mr. Tomlinson	24
S.)	21	Mr. George Whiteley	24
Colonel Pilkington (Lanca-			
shire, Newton)	22		

Question put—"That the word 'twelve' stand part of the Clause."

The Committee divided :—Ayes, 177 ; Noes 18.   (Division List, No. 161.)

Amendment proposed—

> " In Clause 1, page 1, line 6, after ' shall,' to insert ' except where any
> bye-laws under the Elementary Education Acts,1870 to 1897, shall from time to
> time otherwise provide.' "—(*Mr. Tomlinson.*)

Question proposed :—"That those words be there inserted."

DISCUSSION :—

Mr. Jeffreys (Hants, N.)...	27	Mr. Tomlinson	28
Sir F. S. Powell	27	Sir Albert Rollit	29
Mr. Robson (South Shields)	27	Captain Pretyman (Suffolk, Wood-	
Mr. Gibson Bowles (Lynn		bridge)	29
Regis)	28		

Amendment, by leave, withdrawn.

Amendment proposed—

     " In page 1, line 12, at the end to add the words, 'Provided also that the local authority for any rural district, may, by bye-law for any parish within their district, fix 13 years as the minimum age for exemption from school attendance in the case of children to be employed in agriculture, and that in such parish such children over 11 and under 13 years of age who have passed the standard fixed for partial exemption from school attendance by the bye-laws of the local authority shall not be required to attend school more than 250 times in any year. Such bye-law shall have effect as a bye-law made under Section 74 of the Elementary Education Act, 1870, and all Acts amending the same. The local authority shall be the local authority fixed by Section 7 of the Elementary Education Act, 1876.' "—(*Mr. Robson.*)

DISCUSSION :—

Sir William Hart Dyke		*Mr. Jeffreys*	35
(*Kent, Dartford*) ...	33	*Mr. Yoxall* (*Nottingham, W.*) ...	36
Major Rasch (*Essex, S.E.*)...	34		

Amendment proposed to the proposed Amendment—

     " In line 1. to leave out the words 'local authority for any rural district,' in order to insert words 'county council of any county.' "—(*Captain Bethell.*)

DISCUSSION :—

Sir John Gorst	37	*Mr. Grant Lawson* (*York,*	
		N.R., Thirsk)	38

Amendment to the proposed Amendment, by leave, withdrawn.

Amendment proposed to the proposed Amendment—

     " In line 1, to leave out the word 'rural.' "—(*Mr. George Whiteley.*)

DISCUSSION :

Captain Pretyman... ...	39	*Mr. Robson*	41
Mr.Cripps(*Gloucester,Stroud*)	40	*Viscount Cranborne*	41
Sir John Lubbock (*London*		*Mr. Grant Lawson*	41
University)	40	*Mr. Tomlinson*	41
Sir John Gorst	40	*Major Rasch*	41

Question, " That the word stand part of the Amendment," put and negatived.

Amendment proposed to the proposed Amendment—

     " In line 3, to leave out the words 'to be employed in agriculture,' in order to insert the words 'not employed in any factory or workshop.' " - (*Mr. George Whiteley.*)— instead thereof.

DISCUSSION :—

Mr. George Whiteley ...	42	*Sir John Gorst*	42
Viscount Cranborne ...	42		

Question put, " That the words 'to be employed in agriculture' stand part of the proposed Amendment."

The Committee divided :—Ayes, 245 ; Noes, 26. (Division List, No. 162.)

Amendment proposed—

     " In line 4, after 'agriculture' to add " any operations connected therewith.' "—(*Mr. Galloway.*)

Amendment negatived.

Amendment proposed—

"In line 6, to leave out all after ' shall,' and insert, ' be entitled to a certificate or certificates of exemption from attendance for any period or periods not exceeding three months in all during any one year, if it be shown to the satisfaction of the local authority that the child will obtain suitable employment during the periods of exemption, and if, in the opinion of the local authority, the child has made good attendance prior to such period.' "—(*Mr Giles.*)

DISCUSSION :—

Mr. Grey (West Ham, N.) 46   *Captain Pretyman*   47
Colonel Lockwood (Essex,   *Sir John Gorst*   48
Epping)   47

Question proposed, " That the words proposed to be left out stand part of the clause."

Amendment negatived.

Amendment proposed—

"In Clause 1, page 1, line 12, at end, to add, ' Provided also that a child shall be entitled to obtain partial exemption from school attendance, on attaining the age of twelve years, if such child has made three hundred attendances in not more than two schools during each year for five preceding years whether consecutive or not.' "—(*Mr. Rutherford.*)

DISCUSSION :—

Sir John Gorst   48   *Mr. George Whiteley*   48

Amendment agreed to.

Amendment proposed—

"After the words last inserted, to add the words ' provided also that if it is shown to the satisfaction of the local educational authority that the earnings of any child above the age of 11 years are necessary, by reason of the poverty of the parents, to the maintenance of the said child, the said educational authority may in such cases grant a certificate exempting such child from the operation of this Act."—(*Colonel Mellor.*)

DISCUSSION :—

Mr. Robson   50   *Mr. Duckworth (Lancashire, Mid-*
Colonel Mellor   51   *dleton)*   53
Sir J. Gorst   51   *Mr. Grant Lawson*   53
Mr. Tomlinson   51   *Mr. Seton-Karr (St. Helens)*   ...   54
Mr. George Whiteley   ...   51   *Mr. Herbert Whiteley*   ...   54
Mr. Robson   52   *Colonel Pilkington*   55
Mr. George Whiteley   ...   52   *Mr. Seton-Karr*   56
Colonel Mellor   52

The Committee divided :—Ayes 63 ; Noes 229.—(Division List, No. 163.)

Question proposed, " That Clause 1, as amended, stand part of the Bill."

DISCUSSION :—

Mr. G. Whiteley   59

MR. ROBSON rose in his place, and claimed to move, " That the Question be now put."

Question put, " That the Question be now put."

The Committee divided :—Ayes 263 ; Noes 26.—(Division List No. 164.)

May 31.]   *Page*

Question, "That Clause 1, as amended, stand part of the Bill," put accordingly, and agreed to.

Committee report Progress : to sit again upon Wednesday next.

Fine or Imprisonment (Scotland and Ireland) (*re-committed*) **Bill**— Considered in Committee, and reported without Amendment. Bill read the third time, and passed   63

Metropolis Management Acts Amendment (Bye-Laws Bill) [Lords.]— Read a second time, and committed for to-morrow   63

Seats for Shop Assistants (England and Ireland) Bill—Read a second time, and committed for Friday   63

METROPOLITAN SEWERS AND DRAINS—Bill to amend the Metropolis Management Act with respect to Sewers and Drains, ordered to be brought in by Mr. James Stuart and Mr. John Burns   63

Public Health Acts Amendment Bill—Dr. Clark, Dr. Farquharson, Dr. Fox, Mr. Galloway, Mr. Heath, Sir Alfred Hickman, Mr. Hobhouse, Mr. Brynmor Jones, Sir Francis Sharp Powell, Sir Albert Rollit, Mr. T. W. Russell, Mr. Schwann, Mr. J. G. Talbot, Mr. Whitmore, and Mr. Henry J. Wilson nominated Members of the Select Comitteee on the Public Health Acts Amendment Bill. Ordered, That the Committee have power to send for persons, papers, and records. Ordered That five be the quorum. —(*Sir William Walrond.*)   63

Metropolitan Sewers and Drains Bill—To Amend the Metropolis Management Act with respect to Sewers and Drains. Presented, and read the first time ; to be read a second time upon Wednesday next, and to be printed. (Bill 223.)   64

PUBLIC PETITIONS COMMITTEE—Fifth Report brought up, and read ; to lie upon the Table, and to be printed   64

Adjourned at ten minutes before Six of the clock.

LORDS : THURSDAY, 1ST JUNE 1899.

PRIVATE BILL BUSINESS.

The LORD CHANCELLOR acquainted the House that the Clerk of the Parliaments had laid upon the Table the Certificates from the Examiners that the Standing Orders applicable to the following Bills have been complied with :—Electric Lighting Provisional Order (No. 14) [Lords] ; Gas and Water Orders Confirmation [Lords] ; Tramways Orders Confirmation (No. 1) [Lords] ; Tramways Orders Confirmation (No. 3) [Lords]   65

And the Certificate that the further Standing Orders applicable to the following Bill have been complied with : Shirebrook and District Gas. The same were ordered to lie upon the Table   65

Gas Light and Coke Company Bill—Read the second time, and committed : The Committees to be proposed by the Committee of Selection   65

June 1.]   *Page*

Great Central Railway Bill—Read the second time, and committed : The
Committee to be proposed by the Committee of Selection   65

**South Eastern and London, Chatham, and Dover Railway Companies
Bill**—Read the second time, and committed :   The Committee to be proposed by the Committee of Selection   65

South-Eastern Railway Bill—Read the second time, and committed :   The
Committee to be proposed by the Committee of Selection   65

Great Northern Railway Bill [Lords].—Read the third time, and passed, and
sent to the Commons   65

Sunderland Corporation Bill [Lords]—Read the third time, and passed, and
sent to the Commons   66

Crowborough District Water Bill—Read the third time, with the Amendments; further Amendments made ; Bill passed, and returned to the
Commons   66

**Leith Harbour and Docks Bill, South Staffordshire Stipendiary Jus-
tices Bill**—Brought from the Commons ; read the first time ; and referred to the Examiners   66

Metropolitan Water Companies Bill—Returned from the Commons with
the Amendments agreed to   66

Burley-in-Wharfedale Urban District Water Bill — Returned from
the Commons with the Amendments agreed to   66

Nuneaton and Chilvers Coton Urban District Council Water Bill—
Returned from the Commons with the Amendments agreed to   66

Woodhouse and Conisbrough Railway (Abandonment) Bill—Returned
from the Commons with the Amendments agreed to   66

Pilotage Provisional Order Bill—The Chairman of Committees informed
the House that the opposition to the Bill was withdrawn ; the Order made
on the 12th of May last discharged ; and Bill committed to a Committee
of the whole House   66

Electric Lighting Provisional Order (No. 9) Bill [Lords]—Committed
to a Committee of the whole House to-morrow   66

Electric Lighting Provisional Orders (No. 10) Bill [Lords]—Committed
to a Committee of the whole House to-morrow   66

Electric Lighting Provisional Orders (No. 11) Bill [Lords]—Committed
to a Committee of the whole House to-morrow   66

**Education Department Provisional Order Confirmation (Liverpool)
Bill** [Lords]—Committed to a Committee of the whole House on Monday
next   ...   .   —   67

**Education Department Provisional Order Confirmation (London)
Bill**—Committed.   The Committee to be proposed by the Committee of
Selection   67

Gas Orders Confirmation (No. 1) Bill [Lords]—Committed to a Committee
of the whole House   67

June 1.]   *Page*

Gas Orders Confirmation (No. 2) Bill [Lords]—Committed. The Committee to be proposed by the Committee of Selection   67

Water Orders Confirmation Bill [Lords]—Committed to a Committee of the whole House   67

Electric Lighting Provisional Orders (No. 14) Bill [Lords]—To be read the second time to-morrow   67

Gas and Water Orders Confirmation Bill [Lords]—To be read the second time to-morrow   67

Tramways Orders Confirmation (No. 1) Bill [Lords]—To be read the second to-morrow   67

Tramway Orders Confirmation (No. 3) Bill [Lords]—To be read the second time to-morrow   67

Electric Lighting Provisional Orders (No. 5) Bill (No. 101)— Brought from the Commons ; read the first time ; to be printed ; and referred to the Examiners   67

Electric Lighting Provisional Orders (No. 5) Bill (No. 102)—Brought from the Commons; read the first time ; to be printed ; and referred to the Examiners   67

Electric Lighting Provisional Orders (No. 6) Bill (No. 103)—Brought from the Commons; read the first time; to be printed ; and referred to the Examiners   67

Electric Lighting Provisional Orders (No. 8) Bill (No. 104)—Brought from the Commons; read the first time; to be printed; and referred to the Examiners   68

Local Government Provisional Orders (No. 3) Bill (No. 105)—Brought from the Commons; read the first time; to be printed ; and referred to the Examiners   68

RETURNS, REPORTS, &c.

The LORD CHANCELLOR acquainted the House that the following Papers, having been commanded to be presented to this House by Her Majesty, had been so presented on the following dates by delivery to the Clerk of the Parliaments, pursuant to Order of the House of the 17th February, 1896, *viz.* :—

1. Trade Reports—(Annual Series) : No. 2663, Germany (Hamburg) ; No. 2664, Russia (Batoum and District) ; No. 2265, Russia (Taganrog) ; No. 2266, Netherlands (Amsterdam) ; No. 2267, Western Pacific (Tonga) ; No. 2268, Italy (Genoa and District) ; No. 2269, Greece (Ionian Islands) ; No. 2270, Turkey (Salonica) ; No. 2271, Switzerland (May 25) ; No. 2272, Germany (The Grand Duchy Baden) ; No. 2273, Turkey (Tripoli) ; No. 2274, Italy (Elba) ; No. 2275, Paraguay ; No. 2276, France (Saigon etc.) ; No. 2277, Japan ; No. 2278, Spain (Canary Islands) (May 31st)   ...   68

2. Wine Duties— Correspondence respecting the increase in the wine duties   68

June 1.] *Page*

3. British South Africa Company—Correspondence with Mr. C. J. Rhodes relating to the proposed extension of the Bechuanaland Railway 68

4. Local Taxation (Royal Commission)—Minutes of evidence: Volume III. 68

The same were ordered to lie on the Table.

FISHERIES (SCOTLAND)—.Seventeenth Annual Report of the Fishery Board for Scotland, being for the year 1898; Part II. Report on Salmon Fisheries 69

EDUCATION DEPARTMENT (SOUTH-WESTERN DIVISION)—General Report for the year 1898, by A. Rankine, Esq., Chief Inspector 69

COLONIES (ANNUAL) No. 260.—Niger (West African Frontier Force); Reports for 1897-98 69

LIGHT RAILWAYS ACT, 1896.—Orders made by the Light Railway Commissioners and modified and confirmed by the Board of Trade authorising the construction of—

1. Light railways in the counties of Glamorgan and Brecon between Raynor, Dowlais, and Merthyr Tydfil.

2. A light railway in the Isle of Sheppey and County of Kent between Queenborough Station and Leysdown.

3. Light railways in the county of Middlesex from Uxbridge to Hanwell. 69

Presented (by command), and ordered to lie on the Table.

INDIA (EXAMINATIONS).—Regulations for examinations for the Civil Service of India 69

GAS AND WATER WORKS FACILITIES ACT, 1870.—Report by the Board of Trade as to dispensing with the consents of the Sevenoaks Rural District Council and the Hildenborough Parish Council in the case of the Tonbridge Gas Provisional Order 69

GAS COMPANIES (METROPOLIS).—Accounts of the Metropolitan Gas Companies for the year 1898 69

HARWICH HARBOUR.—Abstract of accounts of receipts and expenditure of Harwich Harbour Conservancy Board, to 31st day of March, 1899; with report on proceedings, etc. 69

DISEASES OF ANIMALS ACTS, 1894 AND 1896.—Order dated the 18th of May, 1899, No. 5944, revoking Order No. 5920, which prohibited the conveyance of animals by the ss. *Hindustan* 69

POLLING DISTRICTS (COUNTY OF CARNARVON).—Order made by the County Council of Carnarvon dividing into two parts the Permorfa polling district of the county 70

FACTORY AND WORKSHOP (WHITE LEAD FACTORIES).—Special rules with regard to the employment of persons in white lead factories 70

PUBLIC RECORDS (ADMIRALTY DEPARTMENT).—Fifth Schedule containing a list and particulars of classes of documents which have been removed from the office of the Commissioners for executing the office of Lord High Admiral of the United Kingdom of Great Britain and Ireland, and deposited in the Public Record Office, but which are not considered of sufficient public value to justify their preservation therein; laid before the House (pursuant to Act), and ordered to lie on the Table 70

PETITION.

Municipal Corporations (Borough Funds) Act, 1872.—Petition for amendment of ; of the Urban District Council of Budleigh Salterton, in the County of Devon ; read, and ordered to lie on the Table **70**

Jones's Divorce Bill [H.L.]—Amendment reported (according to order), and Bill to be read the third time To-morrow **70**

Anchors and Chain Cables Bill—Motion made, and Question proposed—

       "That this Bill be now read a second time."—(*The Earl of Dudley*)   ...   **70**

     Question put, and agreed to.

     Bill read the second time (according to Order), and committed to a Committee of the whole House **71**

Infectious Diseases (Notification) Act (1889) Extension Bill—Read the third time (according to Order) ; an Amendment made ; Bill passed, and returned to the Commons **71**

Fine or Imprisonment (Scotland and Ireland) Bill—Brought from the Commons ; read the first time ; and to be printed. (No. 100.)   ...   **71**

       House adjourned at twenty minutes before Five of the clock.

COMMONS, THURSDAY, 1st JUNE 1899.

PRIVATE BILL BUSINESS.

Private Bills [Lords]. (Standing Orders not previously inquired into complied with.) Mr. Speaker laid upon the Table Report from one of the Examiners of Petitions for Private Bills, that, in the case of the following Bills, originating in the Lords, and referred on the first reading thereof, the Standing Orders not previously inquired into, and which are applicable thereto, have been complied with, viz. :—Bexhill and St. Leonards Tramroads Bill ; Bury Corporation Water Bill ; Church Stretton Water Bill ; Furness Railway Bill ; Gainsborough Urban District Council (Gas) Bill ; Great Yarmouth Water Bill ; Humber Conservancy Bill ; Leigh-on-Sea Urban District Council Bill ; Loughborough Corporation Bill ; Paisley and Barrhead District Railway Bill ; Port Talbot Railway and Docks Bill ; Salford Corporation Bill ; Wakefield Corporation Bill. Ordered, that the Bills be read a second time   ...   **72**

Private Bills [Lords]. (No Standing Orders not previously inquired into applicable.) Mr. Speaker laid upon the Table Report from one of the Examiners of Petitions for Private Bills, That, in the case of the following Bills, originating in the Lords, and referred on the First Reading thereof, no Standing Orders not previously inquired into are applicable, viz. :—Colonial and Foreign Banks Guarantee Fund Bill ; Hampstead Church (Emmanuel West End) Bill ; Mersey Docks and Harbour Board (Finance) Bill ; St. Neot's Water Bill ; Stretford Gas Bill ; Wick and Pulteney Harbours Bill. Ordered, that the Bills be read a second time **72**

June 1.]   *Page*

PROVISIONAL ORDER BILLS. (STANDING ORDERS APPLICABLE THERETO
COMPLIED WITH.)—Mr. Speaker laid upon the Table Report from one
of the Examiners of Petitions for Private Bills, That, in the case
of the following Bills, referred on the First Reading thereof, the
Standing Orders which are applicable thereto have been complied with,
viz. : — Local Government Provisional Order (Housing of Working
Classes) Bill ; Local Government Provisional Orders (Gas) Bill ; Local
Government Provisional Orders (No. 4) Bill ; Local Government Pro-
visional Orders (No. 6) Bill ; Local Government Provisional Orders
(No. 7) Bill ; Local Government Provisional Orders (No. 8) Bill ; Pier and
Harbour Provisional Orders (No. 2) Bill. Ordered, That the Bills be
read a second time To-morrow   73

PROVISIONAL ORDER BILLS (NO STANDING ORDERS APPLICABLE)—Mr.
Speaker laid upon the Table Report from one of the Examiners of
Petitions for Private Bills, That, in the case of the following Bills, referred
on the first reading thereof, no Standing Orders are applicable, viz :—Local
Government (Ireland) Provisional Order (No. 1) Bill ; Local Government
Provisional Orders (No. 5) Bill ; Local Government Provisional Orders
(Poor Law) Bill. Ordered, that the Bills be read a second time To-morrow   73

PRIVATE BILLS [LORDS] (STANDING ORDERS NOT PREVIOUSLY INQUIRED
INTO NOT COMPLIED WITH).—Mr. Speaker laid upon the Table Report
from one of the Examiners of Petitions for Private Bills, That, in the case
of the following Bill, originating in the Lords, and referred on the first
reading thereof, the Standing Orders not previously inquired into, and
which are applicable thereto, have not been complied with, viz.—

Mersey Docks and Harbour Board (Pilotage) Bill [Lords].—Ordered,
that the Report be referred to the Select Committee on Standing Orders   73

Belfast Corporation Bill.—Read the third time, and passed   73

Cambridge University and Town Gas Bill [Lords]; **Glastonbury Water
Bill** [Lords]; **Queen's Ferry Bridge Bill** [Lords].—Read a third time
and passed, with Amendments   73

Hull, Barnsley, and West Riding Junction Railway and Dock Bill
[Lords]; **St. Albans Gas Bill** [Lords].—As amended, considered ; to be
read the third time   74

London Water (Purchase) Bill.—Order of the day for the second reading
read   74

Motion made and Question proposed—
   " That the Order of the Day for the second reading be dischrnged."—
   (*Mr. Stuart.*)

DISCUSSION :—

   Mr. *Whitmore* (*Chelsea*) ...   74   Mr. *Stuart* (*Shoreditch, Hoxton*)...   75
   Mr. *Bartley* (*Islington, N.*)   75   Mr. *Boulnois* (*Marylebone, E.*)...   75

Question put, and agreed to.

Order for Second Reading discharged, and Bill withdrawn.

Friends' Provident Institution Bill [Lords] **(Stamp Duties)**—Committee
to consider of authorising the imposition of certain Stamp Duties upon
certain Memorials under any Act of the present Session relating to the
Friends' Provident Institution (Queen's Recommendation signified), To-
morrow...   77

Local Government (Ireland) Provisional Order (No. 4) Bill—To confirm a Provisional Order of Local Government Board for Ireland relating to Dean's Grange Joint Burial Board District, ordered to be brought in by Mr. Attorney-General for Ireland and Mr. Solicitor-General for Ireland   77

Local Government (Ireland) Provisional Order (No. 4) Bill— "To confirm a Provisional Order of the Local Government Board for Ireland relating to the Dean's Grange Joint Burial Board District," presented accordingly, and read the first time ; to be referred to the Examiners of Petitions for Private Bills, and to be printed. [Bill 324.]...   77

PETITIONS.

BOROUGH FUNDS ACT, 1872—Petition from Todmorden, for alteration of Law ; to lie upon the Table   78

Local Government (Scotland) Act (1894) Amendment Bill—Petition from Monifieth, in favour ; to lie upon the Table   78

London Government Bill—Petition from Croydon, for alteration ; to lie upon the Table   78

Mines (Eight Hours) Bill—Petitions in favour ;—from Soothill Wood ;— Cwm Colling ;—Oakengates ;—Altham ;—and West Kiveton Collieries ; to lie upon the Table   78

Private Legislation Procedure (Scotland) Bill—Petitions in favour ;— from Aberdeen ;—and Ardrossan ; to lie upon the Table   78

Public Health Acts Amendment Bill—Petition from Kingston-upon-Hull, in favour ; to lie upon the Table   78

Sale of Intoxicating Liquors on Sunday Bill—Petitions in favour ; —from St. Germans ;—Westleton ;—Walpole ;—Chebsey ;—and, Rochdale ; to lie upon the Table   78

RETURNS, REPORTS, &c.

ELEMENTARY SCHOOLS (CHILDREN WORKING FOR WAGES)—Return presented,—relative thereto [ordered 28th April, 1898 ; *Mr. Spicer*] ; to lie upon the Table, and to be printed. [Fo. 205.]   78

EAST INDIA (EXAMINATIONS FOR THE CIVIL SERVICE)—Copy presented,— of Regulations for Examinations for the Civil Service of India [by Act] ; to lie upon the Table   78

GAS COMPANIES (METROPOLIS)—Copy presented,—of Accounts of the Metropolitan Gas Companies for the year 1898 [by Act] ; to lie upon the Table, and to be printed. [No. 206.]   78

POLLING DISTRICTS (CARNARVON)—Copy presented,—of Order made by the County Council of Carnarvon dividing into two parts the Penmorfa Polling District of the County [by Act] ; to lie upon the Table   79

FACTORY AND WORKSHOP ACTS (WHITE LEAD FACTORIES)—Copy presented, of Special Rules with regard to the employment of persons in White Lead Factories [by Act] ; to lie upon the Table   79

SUPREME COURT OF JUDICATURE (IRELAND) ACT, 1877--Copy presen:' d,— of Four Orders in Council dated 13th May, 1899, giving effect to the Rules of Court under The Local Government (Ireland) Act 1898 [by Act] ; to lie upon the Table   79

QUESTIONS.

TRAINING OF VOLUNTEER OFFICERS—Question, Sir Howard Vincent (Sheffield, Central); Answer, The Under Secretary of State for War (Mr. G. Wyndham, Dover)   79

THE ARMENIAN PRELACY—Question, Mr. Stevenson (Suffolk, Eye); Answer, The Under Secretary of State for Foreign Affairs (Mr. St. John Brodrick, Surrey, Guildford)   80

COMMERCIAL EDUCATION—Question, Sir Howard Vincent (Sheffield, Central); Answer, The Secretary to the Local Government Board (Mr. T. W. Russell, Tyrone, S.)   80

CLAPHAM SORTING OFFICE—Question, Mr. Steadman (Tower Hamlets, Stepney); Answer, The Secretary to the Treasury (Mr. R. W. Hanbury, Preston)   81

THE PUNJAUB WAR AND THE TIRAH CAMPAIGN—Question, Mr. H. D. Green (Shrewsbury); Answer, The Under Secretary of State for War (Mr. G. Wyndham, Dover)   81

THE ANGLO-AMERICAN COMMISSION—Question, Sir Edward Gourley (Sunderland); Answer, The Under Secretary of State for Foreign Affairs (Mr. Brodrick, Surrey, Guildford)...   81

RUSSIAN CLAIMS IN CHINA—Question, Mr. Provand (Glasgow, Blackfriars); Answer, The Under Secretary of State for Foreign Affairs (Mr. Brodrick, Surrey, Guildford)   82

INSTRUCTION IN POOR LAW SCHOOLS—Question, Mr. James Stuart (Shoreditch, Hoxton); Answer, The Secretary of Local Government Board (Mr. T. W. Russell, Tyrone, S.)   82

THE COMPTROLLER AND AUDITOR-GENERAL—Question, Mr. McKenna (Monmouth, N.); Answer, The First Lord of the Treasury (Mr. A. J. Balfour, Manchester, E.)   83

REDEMPTION OF IRISH TITHE RENT-CHARGE—Question, Mr. William Moore (Antrim, N.); Answer, The Chief Secretary for Ireland (Mr. G. W. Balfour, Leeds, Central)   84

BELFAST (PUBLIC MEETINGS)—Question, Mr. Dillon (Mayo, E.); Answer, The Chief Secretary for Ireland (Mr. G. W. Balfour, Leeds, Central)   ...   85

BUSINESS OF THE HOUSE—Questions, Mr. Channing (Northampton, E.); Mr. Caldwell (Lanark, Mid); Mr. Warner (Stafford, Lichfield); Answer, The First Lord of the Treasury (Mr. A. J. Balfour, Manchester, E.)   86, 87

NEW MEMBER SWORN.

Sir George Augustus Pilkington, knight, for South West Lancashire (Southport Division)   87

June 1.]   *Page*

PUBLIC BUSINESS.

BELFAST (PUBLIC MEETINGS)—Motion for the Adjournment of the House ... 87

Motion made and Question proposed—
"That this House do now adjourn."—(*Mr. Dillon.*)

The Chief Secretary for Ireland, *Mr. G. W. Balfour* (Leeds, Central) ... 95

Question put.

The House divided : Ayes, 73 ; Noes, 125. (Division List, No. 165.)

SUPPLY—[11TH ALLOTTED DAY]—Considered in Committee.

CIVIL SERVICE AND REVENUE DEPARTMENT ESTIMATES, 1899-90.

REVENUE DEPARTMENTS.

1. Motion made and Question proposed—
"That a sum not exceeding £5,522,885 be granted to Her Majesty to defray the charges necessary for the salaries and expenses of the Post Office, the Post Office Savings Banks, Annuities and Securities, and the collection of Post Office revenue."

DISCUSSION :

Mr. Steadman (*Tower Hamlets, Stepney*) 99	*The Secretary to the Treasury* (*Mr. Hanbury, Preston*) ...	103

Motion made, and Resolution proposed—
"That item A (salaries) be reduced by £100, in respect of the salary of the Postmaster-General."—(*Mr. Steadman.*)

DISCUSSION :—

Captain Norton (*Newington, W.*) 104	*Mr. Monk* (*Gloucester*)	114
Sir W. Cameron Gull (*Devonshire, Barnstaple*) ... 106	*Mr. Hanbury* ... ... *Mr. Maddison*	115 115
Mr. Spicer (*Monmouth Boroughs*) 108	*Mr. Pickersgill* (*Bethnal Green, S.W.*)... ... ... *Mr. Hanbury*	116 116
Mr. Ascroft (*Oldham*) ... 109	*Captain Norton*	120
Mr. Maddison (*Sheffield, Brightside*) 111	*Mr. Hanbury* ... ... *Sir W. Cameron Gull*	120 121
The Secretary to the Treasury (*Mr. Hanbury, Preston*)... 113	*Mr. Hanbury* ... ... *Mr. Ascroft*	121 122
Mr. Maddison 114	*Mr. Hanbury*	122

Question put.

The Committee divided : Ayes, 107 ; Noes, 158. (Division List No. 166.)

Original Question again proposed.

Motion made, and Question proposed—
"That Item A (Salaries) be reduced by £100, in respect of the salary of the Postmaster-General."—(*General Laurie.*)

DISCUSSION :—

Dr. Clark (*Caithness*) ... 125	*The Secretary to the Treasury* (*Mr. Hanbury, Preston*) ...	126
Mr. Humphreys Owen (*Montgomery*) 126	*General Laurie* (*Pembroke and Haverfordwest*)	127

Motion, by leave, withdrawn.

June 1.]   *Page*

Original Question again proposed.

DISCUSSION :—

Colonel Welby (Taunton) ...	127	*Mr. E. Robertson (Dundee)*	...	128
Mr. Dillon (Mayo, East) ...	128	*The Secretary to the Treasury (Mr.*		
Sir James Fergusson (Man-		*Hanbury, Preston)* ...	...	128
chester, N.E.)	128	*Mr. Dillon*		129

Question put, and agreed to.

2. £570,915, to complete the sum for Post Office Packet Service.

3. £2,338,390, to complete the sum for the Post Office Telegraphs.

DISCUSSION :—

Sir J. Blundell Maple		*Sir J. Blundell Maple*		132
(Camberwell, Dulwich) ...	130	*Captain Bethell (York E.R., Hol-*		
The Secretary to the Treasury		*derness)*		132
(Mr. Hanbury, Preston)	131			

Vote agreed to.

4. Motion made, and Question proposed—

"That a sum, not exceeding £496,600, be granted to Her Majesty, to complete the sum necessary to defray the Charge which will come in course of payment during the year ending on the 31st day of March, 1900, for the salaries and expenses of the Customs Department."

Motion made, and Question proposed—

"That Item B (Port Establishments) be reduced by £100 in respect of Salaries, etc."—(*Mr. Gray*.)

DISCUSSION :—

The Secretary to the Treasury		*Mr. H. S. Samuel (Tower Ham-*		
(Mr. Hanbury, Preston)...	134	*lets, Limehouse)*	...	149
Mr. Gray (West Ham, N.)	134	*Sir F. Evans (Southampton)*	...	150
Mr. Hanbury	142	*Mr. C. H. Wilson (Hull, W.)*	...	151
Mr. Gray	145	*Mr. Hanbury*	...	151
Mr. Hanbury	146	*Mr. Havelock Wilson* ...	...	152
Mr. Ryder (Gravesend) ...	147	*Mr. Gray*	...	153
Mr. Steadman (Tower Ham-		*Mr. Dalziel (Kirkcaldy)*...	...	154
lets, Stepney)	148	*Mr. Hanbury*	...	155
Mr. Hanbury	148	*Mr. Dalziel*	...	155

Question put.

The Committee divided : Ayes, 57 ; Noes, 90.   (Division List No. 167.)

Original Question put, and agreed to.

SUPPLY [19TH MAY].

Resolutions reported :—

CIVIL SERVICES AND REVENUE DEPARTMENTS ESTIMATES, 1899–1900.

CLASS VI.

"5. £287,628, to complete the sum for Superannuations and Retired Allowances.

"6. £2,130, to complete the sum for Merchant Seamen's Fund Pensions.

"7. £785 to complete the sum for Miscellaneous Charitable and other Allowances.

Resolutions to be reported To-morrow ; Committee to sit again To-morrow.

CLASS II.

"2. That a sum, not exceeding £9,446, be granted to Her Majesty, to complete the sum necessary to defray the Charge which will come in course of payment during the year ending on the 31st day of March 1900, for the Salaries and Expenses of the Office of the Commissioners in Lunacy in England."

"3. That a sum, not exceeding £67, be granted to Her Majesty, to complete the sum necessary to defray the Charge which will come in course of payment during the year ending on the 31st day of March 1900, for the Salaries and Expenses of the Mint, including the expenses of Coinage."

"4. That a sum, not exceeding £9,274, be granted to Her Majesty, to complete the sum necessary to defray the Charge which will come in course of payment during the year ending on the 31st day of March 1900, for the Salaries and Expenses of the National Debt Office."

"5. That a sum, not exceeding £14,300, be granted to Her Majesty, to complete the sum necessary to defray the Charge which will come in course of payment during the year ending on the 31st day of March 1900, for the Salaries and Expenses of the Public Record Office."

"6. That a sum, not exceeding £13, be granted to Her Majesty, to complete the sum necessary to defray the Charge which will come in course of payment during the year ending on the 31st day of March 1900, for the Salaries and Expenses of the Establishment under the Public Works Loan Commissioners."

"7. That a sum, not exceeding £26,884, be granted to Her Majesty, to complete the sum necessary to defray the Charge which will come in course of payment during the year ending on the 31st day of March 1900, for the Salaries and Expenses of the Department of the Registrar General of Births, &c., in England."

"8. That a sum, not exceeding £36,393, be granted to Her Majesty, to complete the sum necessary to defray the Charge which will come in course of payment during the year ending on the 31st day of March 1900, for the Salaries and Expenses of the Office of the Commissioners of Her Majesty's Works and Public Buildings."

Resolutions agreed to.

ADJOURNMENT.

Motion made, and Question, "That this House do now adjourn."—(*Sir William Walrond*)—put, and agreed to.

House adjourned accordingly at a quarter before Ten of the clock.

LORDS : FRIDAY, 2ND JUNE, 1899.

NEW PEER.

The Marquess of Exeter—Sat first in Parliament, after the death of his father   161

PRIVATE BILL BUSINESS.

Portsmouth Corporation Bill [Lords]—The Chairman of Committees informed the House that the opposition to the Bill was withdrawn : The Orders made on the 27th of February and the 18th of May last discharged ; and Bill committed   161

North-Eastern and Hull and Barnsley Railways (Joint Dock) Bill [Lords]—The Queen's consent signified ; and Bill reported from the Select Committee with Amendments   161

June 2.]   Page

North-Eastern Railway Bill [Lords]—The Queen's consent signified ; and
Bill reported from the Select Committee with Amendments   161

Coalville Urban District Gas Bill [Lords]—Commons Amendments considered, and agreed to...   161

Kensington and Notting Hill Electric Lighting Bill—Read the second
time, and committed ; the Committee to be proposed by the Committee of
Selection   161

Midland and South-Western Junction Railway Bill—Read the second
time, and committed   161

Cobham Gas Bill [Lords]—Read the third time, an Amendment made,
Bill passed, and sent to the Commons   161

All Saints' Church (Cardiff) Bill [Lords].—Read the third time, and
passed, and sent to the Commons   161

**Weston-super-Mare, Clevedon, and Portishead Tramways Com-
pany (Light Railway Extensions) Bill** [Lords].—Read the third
time, and passed, and sent to the Commons...   162

Whitehaven Corporation Bill.—Read the third time, and passed, and sent
to the Commons   162

**Birmingham, North Warwickshire, and Stratford-upon-Avon
Railway Bill** [Lords].—Read the third time, and passed, and sent to the
Commons   162

Grosvenor Chapel (London) Bill [Lords].—Read the third time, and
passed, and sent to the Commons   162

Moss Side Urban District Council (Tramways) Bill [Lords].—Read the
third time, and passed, and sent to the Commons   162

Stretford Urban District Council (Tramways) Bill [Lords].—Read the
third time, and passed, and sent to the Commons   162

Withington Urban District Council (Tramways) Bill [Lords].—Read the
third time, and passed, and sent to the Commons   162

Belfast Corporation Bill.—Brought from the Commons ; read the first time,
and referred to the Examiners   162

Cambridge University and Town Gas Bill [Lords].—Returned from
the Commons agreed to, with Amendments...   162

Glastonbury Water Bill [Lords].—Returned from the Commons agreed to,
with Amendments : the said Amendments considered, and agreed to   ...   162

Queen's Ferry Bridge Bill [Lords].—Returned from the Commons agreed
to, with Amendments : the said Amendments considered, and agreed to ...   162

Electric Lighting Provisional Orders (No. 14) Bill [Lords].—Read the
second time, (according to Order)   162

Gas and Water Orders Confirmation Bill [Lords].—Read the second time,
(according to Order)   162

Tramways Orders Confirmation (No. 1) **Bill** [Lords].—Read the second time, (according to Order) 163

Tramways Orders Confirmation (No. 3) **Bill** [Lords].—Read the second time, (according to Order) 163

Jones's Divorce Bill [Lords].—Read the third time (according to Order), and passed, and sent to the Commons 163

PETITIONS.

MUNICIPAL CORPORATIONS (BOROUGH FUNDS) ACT, 1872.—Petition for Amendment of ; of Mayor, &c., of Kidderminster ; read, and ordered to lie on the Table 163

COMPULSORY VACCINATION.—The LORD CHANCELLOR (the Earl of Halsbury) : My Lords, I have to present a Petition from the Guardians of the Poor of the Wandsworth and Clapham Union, in the County of London, and in doing so I am bound to say that I entirely differ from the reasoning with which they prefer their request, and also from the request itself, which is for the abolition of any form of compulsory vaccination. Petition read, and ordered to lie on the Table 163

RETURNS, REPORTS, ETC.

TREATY SERIES, No. 12 (1899).—Accession of Japan to the Industrial Property Convention of 20th March, 1883 163

TRADE REPORTS—ANNUAL SERIES.—No. 2279. Tunis (Trade and general progress, 1898-99). No. 2280. China (Ichang). No. 2281. China (Amoy) 163

CAPE OF GOOD HOPE (OBSERVATORY).—Report of the Astronomer at the Cape of Good Hope Observatory to the Lords Commissioners of the Admiralty, for the year 1898. Presented (by command), and ordered to lie on the Table 163

SUPERANNUATION—TREASURY MINUTES.—(1) Dated 19th May 1899, declaring that James Mills, turner, Royal Gun Factory, War Department ; and (2) dated 24th May 1899, declaring that Charles Brading, fitter, Royal Laboratory, War Department ; were appointed without Civil Service certificates through inadvertence on the part of the head of their Department 164

NATIONAL DEBT (SAVINGS BANKS).—Balance-sheet setting forth the assets and liabilities of the Commissioners for the Reduction of the National Debt, in respect of trustee savings banks, on 20th November 1898 ... 164

SUPREME COURT OF JUDICATURE ACT (IRELAND), 1877.—Four Orders in Council, dated 13th May, 1899, giving effect to Rules of Court under the Local Government (Ireland) Act, 1898. Laid before the House (pursuant to Act), and ordered to lie on the Table 164

Parish Councillors (Tenure of Office) Bill.—Read the third time (according to Order), with the Amendment, and passed, and returned to the Commons 164

Sea Fisheries Bill [Lords].—A Bill to amend the law relating to sea fisheries was presented by the Earl of Camperdown (for the Lord Heneage) ; read the first time ; to be printed ; and to be read the second time on Thursday next. (No. 106.) 164

Congested Districts (Scotland) Act Amendment Bill—Order of the day for the Second Reading read.—(*The Secretary for Scotland, Lord Balfour of Burleigh.*) Bill read the second time (according to Order), and committed to a Committee of the whole House on Monday next...   ...   **164**

THE SOUDAN EXPEDITION, 1898.—PROPOSED GRANT TO LORD KITCHENER OF KHARTOUM.—Message from the Queen: Delivered by the Lord Chancellor, and read by his Lordship, as follows:

"Her Majesty, taking into consideration the eminent services of Major-General Lord Kitchener of Khartoum, G.C.B., K.C.M.G., in planning and conducting the recent expedition into the Soudan, and being desirous, in recognition of such services, to confer some signal mark of Her favour upon him, recommends to the House of Lords that She should be enabled to grant Lord Kitchener the sum of thirty thousand pounds."

Ordered, that the said Message be taken into consideration on Monday next **166**

House adjourned at twenty minutes before Five of the clock.

COMMONS: FRIDAY, 2ND JUNE, 1899.

PRIVATE BILL BUSINESS.

Private Bills (Lords).—(STANDING ORDERS NOT PREVIOUSLY INQUIRED INTO COMPLIED WITH.)—MR. SPEAKER laid upon the Table Report from one of the Examiners of Petitions for Private Bills, That, in the case of the following Bill, originating in the Lords, and referred on the First Reading thereof, the Standing Orders not previously inquired into, and which are applicable thereto, have been complied with, viz. :

Brighton Marine Palace and Pier Bill (Lords).—Ordered, That the Bill be read a second time...   ...   .   **167**

Provisional Order Bills.—(STANDING ORDERS APPLICABLE THERETO COMPLIED WITH.)—Mr. SPEAKER laid upon the Table Report from one of the Examiners of Petitions for Private Bills, That, in the case of the following Bills referred on the First Reading thereof, the Standing Orders which are applicable thereto have been complied with, viz. :

Electric Lighting Provisional Orders (No. 16) **Bill ; Local Government (Ireland) Provisional Orders** (No. 2) **Bill.**—Ordered, that the Bills be read a second time upon Monday next **167**

Brigg Urban District Gas Bill.—Lords Amendments considered, and agreed to **167**

South-Eastern and London, Chatham, and Dover Railway Companies (New Lines) Bill.—Read the third time, and passed **167**

Norfolk Estuary Bill [Lords].—Read the third time, and passed, without Amendment **167**

June 2.]   *Page*

London and North-Western Railway (New Railways) Bill.—As
Amended, considered; two Clauses added; an Amendment made; Bill
to be read the third time   167

**Derby Corporation Water Bill, Leicester Corporation Water Bill,
and Sheffield Corporation (Derwent Valley) Water Bill.**—Ordered,
That it be an instruction to the Committee on the Derby Corporation
Water Bill, the Leicester Corporation Water Bill, and the Sheffield Corporation (Derwent Valley) Water Bill, that they have power, if they think
fit, to consolidate the said Bills or any part or parts thereof respectively
into one or more Bills.—(*Sir John Brunner.*)   167

Local Government (Ireland) Provisional Order (No. 1) Bill.—Read a
second time, and committed   168

**Local Government Provisional Order (Housing of Working Classes)
Bill.**—Read a second time, and committed....   168

Local Government Provisional Orders (Gas) Bill.—Read a second time,
and committed   168

Local Government Provisional Orders (No. 4) Bill.—Read a second time,
and committed   168

Local Government Provisional Orders (No. 5) Bill.—Read a second time,
and committed   168

Local Government Provisional Orders (No. 6) Bill.—Read a second time,
and committed   168

Local Government Provisional Orders (No. 7) Bill.—Read a second time,
and committed   168

Local Government Provisional Orders (No. 8) Bill.—Read a second time,
and committed...   168

Local Government Provisional Orders (Poor Law) Bill.—Read a second
time, and committed   168

Pier and Harbour Provisional Orders (Poor Law) Bill.—Read a second
time, and committed   168

Broughty Ferry Gas and Paving Order Bill [Lords].—Reported, without
Amendment [Provisional Order confirmed]; Report to lie upon the Table;
Bill to be read the third time upon Monday next   168

**Education Department Provisional Orders Confirmation (Aberavon,
&c.) Bill** [Lords].—Reported, without Amendment [Provisional Orders
confirmed]; Report to lie upon the Table; Bill to be read the third time
upon Monday next   168

City and Brixton Railway Bill—Reported, with Amendments; Report to
lie upon the Table, and to be printed   168

Arbroath Corporation Gas Bill [Lords].—Reported, without Amendment; Report to lie upon the Table, and to be printed; Bill to be
read the third time   169

Dumbarton Burgh Bill [Lords].—Reported, with Amendments; Report to
lie upon the Table, and to be printed   169

Kew Bridge Bill [Lords].—Reported, without Amendment; Report to lie upon the Table, and to be printed; Bill to be read the third time ... 169

Jones's Divorce Bill [Lords].—Read the first time; to be read a second time 169

Great Northern Railway Bill [Lords].—Read the first time; and referred to the Examiners of Petitions for Private Bills 169

Sunderland Corporation Bill [Lords]. —Read the first time; and referred to the Examiners of Petitions for Private Bills 169

Friends' Provident Institution Bill [Lords] **(Stamp Duties).**—(Considered in Committee.)

Resolved, That it is expedient to authorise the imposition of the following Stamp Duties upon certain Memorials under any Act of the present Session relating to the Friends' Provident Institution :—For and upon the first Memorial enrolled of the names of the persons who shall be deemed held and taken to be Trustees of the Institution, or of any special fund of the Institution, the sum of five pounds; and upon every other such Memorial in which the name of any person shall for the first time be inserted as a Trustee of the Institution the sum of five pounds.—*(Dr. Farquharson.)* Resolution to be reported upon Monday next 169

RETURNS, REPORTS, ETC.

Sinking Funds—Account presented,—of the Commissioners for the Reduction of the National Debt, showing the amount received and applied in the year ended 31st of March, 1899, in respect of the Old and New Sinking Funds [by Act]; to lie upon the Table and to be printed. (No. 237.) ... 169

National Debt (Savings Banks)—Copy presented,—of Balance Sheet, setting forth the Assets and Liabilities of the Commissioners for the Reduction of the National Debt in respect of Trustee Savings Banks on the 20th November, 1898 (by Act); to lie upon the Table, and to be printed. (No. 208) 170

Superannuation Act, 1884—Copies presented,—of Treasury Minutes declaring that the undermentioned Persons were appointed to the Offices set against their names without a Civil Service Certificate, through inadvertence on the part of the Heads of their Departments, viz., James Mills, Turner, Royal Gun Factory, War Department, dated 19th May, 1899; Charles Brading, Fitter, Royal Laboratory, War Department, dated 24th May, 1899 (by Act); to lie upon the Table 170

Parliamentary Returns—Copy presented,—of Treasury Minute, dated 29th May, 1899, directing the discontinuance of the annual account, under the Savings Banks Moneys Act, 1863, of assets and liabilities of the National Debt Commissioners in respect of Trustee Savings Banks (by Act); to lie upon the Table 170

Aldershot (Sewage Farm and Dairy)—Copy presented,—of Report on the condition of the Aldershot Camp Sewage Farm, and of the Dairy maintained upon it (by Command); to lie upon the Table 170

Colonial Reports (Annual)—Copy presented,—of Report, No. 260 (Niger, West African Frontier Force. Reports for 1897-8) (by Command); to lie upon the Table... 170

Sugar Bounties, Etc.—Return presented,—relative thereto (ordered 27th April; *Mr. Seale-Hayne*); to lie upon the Table, and to be printed. (No. 209) 170

CAPE OF GOOD HOPE OBSERVATORY—Copy presented,—of Report of the
Astronomer to the Lords Commissioners of the Admiralty for the year
1898 (by Command) to lie upon the Table **171**

TREATY SERIES (No. 12, 1899)—Copy presented,—of Accession of Japan to
the Industrial Property Convention of 20th March, 1883 (by Command) ;
to lie upon the Table **171**

TRADE REPORTS (ANNUAL SERIES)—Copies presented,—of Diplomatic and
Consular Reports, Annual Series, Nos. 2279 to 2281 (by Command) ; to lie
upon the Table...   ...   .   **171**

PROSECUTION OF OFFENCES ACT, 1879 AND 1884—Address for "Return showing
the working of the Regulations made in 1886 for carrying out the Prosecution of Offences Acts, 1879 and 1884, with statistics setting forth the
number, nature, cost, and results of the proceedings instituted by the
Director in accordance with those Regulations from the 1st day of January,
1898, to the 31st day of December, 1898 (in continuation of Parliamentary
Paper, No. 204, of Session 1898)."—(*Mr. Jesse Collings.*) **171**

DEATHS FROM WINDOW CLEANING ACCIDENTS—Address for "Return showing
approximately the number of Coroners' Inquests in the County of London
during the five years ended 31st day of December, 1898, in cases in which
persons were killed by falling from windows while engaged in cleaning
them."—(*Mr. Provand*) **171**

Lunacy Bill [Lords]—Read the first time ; to be read the second time upon
Monday, 12th June, and to be printed. (Bill 225) **171**

THE SOUDAN EXPEDITION 1898 : PROPOSED GRANT TO LORD KITCHENER
OF KHARTOUM :

VICTORIA R.

Her Majesty, taking into consideration the eminent services of Major-
General Lord Kitchener of Khartoum, G.C.B., K.C.M.G., in planning and
conducting the recent Expedition into the Soudan, and being desirous, in
recognition of such services, to confer some signal mark of her favour upon
him, recommends to her faithful Commons that she should be enabled to
grant Lord Kitchener the sum of £30,000.
Balmoral, 1st June, 1899.

Ordered, That Her Majesty's Most Gracious Message be referred to the
Committee of Supply.—(*Mr. Balfour*) **172**

MESSAGE FROM THE LORDS—That they have agreed to,—Infectious
Disease (Notification) Act (1889) Extension Bill, with an Amend-
ment ; Crowborough District Water Bill, with Amendments. That
they have passed a Bill, intituled, "An Act to dissolve the
marriage of Charlotte Jane Jones, the wife of Robert Colvill
Jones, with the said Robert Colvill Jones, and to enable her to marry
again ; and for other purposes." [Jones's Divorce Bill [Lords.] Also, a
Bill, intituled, "An Act to confer further powers upon the Great Northern
Railway Company." [Great Northern Railway Bill [Lords.] And, also, a
Bill, intituled, "An Act to enable the Mayor, Aldermen, and Burgesses of
the Borough of Sunderland to construct additional Tramways in and adja-
cent to the borough ; and for other purposes." [Sunderland Corporation
Bill [Lords] **172**

BILL INTRODUCED.

TRUSTEE SAVINGS BANKS—Bill to amend the Trustee Savings Banks Act, ordered to be brought in by Sir Albert Rollit, Mr. Campbell, and Mr. Ure 172

Trustee Savings Banks Bill—"To amend the Trustee Savings Banks Acts"; presented accordingly, and read the first time; to be read a second time upon Monday next, and to be printed. (Bill 230.) 172

PETITIONS.

BOROUGH FUNDS ACT, 1872—Petitions for alterations of law;—from Horncastle;—Tredegar;—Nantyglo;—and, Abertillery; to lie upon the Table 173

Building Feus and Leases (Scotland) Bill—Petition from Addington, against; to lie upon the Table 173

County Councillors (Qualification of Women) (Scotland) Bill—Petition from Haddington, against; to lie upon the Table... 173

Crofters' Holdings (Scotland) Act (1886) Amendment Bill—Petition from Haddington, against; to lie upon the Table... 173

Ecclesiastical Assessment (Scotland) Bill—Petition from Haddington, in favour; to lie upon the Table 173

Education (School Attendance) (Scotland) Bill—Petition from Haddington, for alteration; to lie upon the Table 173

Executors (Scotland) Amendment Bill—Petition from Haddington, in favour; to lie upon the Table 173

Fine or Imprisonment (Scotland and Ireland) Bill—Petition from Haddington, in favour; to lie upon the Table 173

FOREIGN SUGAR—Petition of the Royal Jamaica Society of Agriculture and Commerce and Merchants' Exchange, for imposition of countervailing duties; to lie upon the Table 173

GROUND RENTS (TAXATION BY LOCAL AUTHORITIES)—Petition from Ashton-in-Makerfield, in favour; to lie upon the Table 173

Ground Values (Taxation) (Scotland) Bill—Petition from Haddington, against; to lie upon the Table 173

Local Government (Scotland) Act (1894) Amendment Bill—Petition from Drainie, in favour; to lie upon the Table 174

Local Government (Scotland) Bill—Petitions, in favour;—From Elgin;—and, Haddington; to lie upon the Table 174

Mines (Eight Hours) Bill—Petitions in favour;—From Cefn Brithda;—Cwmtillery (two);—New Tredegar;—Vivian;—Tillery;—Burnbank;—Garswood;—Tenghenith;—Darranddu;—Gyfelach;—St. George;—Dunvant;—Primrose;—;—Weig Fawr;—Elba;—Fforest Fach;—Hindley Green;—Henwain Pit;—Lower Deep Pit;—Griffin Pit (No. 2);—Clydach;—Coal Brook Vale;—North Blaina;—and, Griffin Pit (No. 3) Collieries; to lie upon the Table 174

June 2.]   *Page*

Parish Churches (Scotland) Bill--Petition from Haddington, in favour;
to lie upon the Table   174

Poor Law Officers' Superannuation (Scotland) Bill--Petition from
Haddington, in favour; to lie upon the Table   174

Private Legislation Procedure (Scotland) Bill--Petitions in favour;—
from Dalkeith;—and Haddington; to lie upon the Table...   174

Public Libraries (Scotland) Acts Amendment Bill—Petition from
Haddington, in favour; to lie upon the Table   174

Roman Catholic University in Ireland—Petition from London, for
establishment; to lie upon the Table   174

Sale of Intoxicating Liquors on Sunday Bill—Petitions in favour;—
From Dorking —Hayle;—Spitalfields;—Kingsclere Woodlands;—Pilton;
—Kemton Mandeville;—and, Somerton; to lie upon the Table   174

Small Tenants (Scotland) Bill—Petition from Haddington, against; to
lie upon the Table   174

Succession (Scotland) Bill.—Petition from Haddington, for alteratión; to lie
upon the Table   175

Teinds (Scotland) Bill.—Petitions in favour;—From Elgin —and, Haddington; to lie upon the Table   175

Town Councils (Scotland) Bill.—Petitions in favour;—From Partick;—
and, Stornoway; to lie upon the Table   175

Trout Fishing Annual Close Time (Scotland) Bill.—Petition from Haddington, in favour; to lie upon the Table   175

QUESTIONS.

Provisional Order Bills.—Question, Mr. Lloyd-George (Carnarvon);
Answer, The Secretary to the Local Government Board (Mr. T. W. Russell,
Tyrone, S.)   175

Russian Cargoes for Ta-lien-Wan—Question, Sir Edward Gourley
(Sunderland); Answer, The Under Secretary of State for Foreign Affairs
(Mr. Brodrick, Surrey, Guildford)   175

British Traders at Canton—Question, Mr. Hatch (Lancs., Gorton); Answer,
The Under Secretary of State for Foreign Affairs (Mr. Brodrick, Surrey,
Guildford)   176

Sierra Leone—Question, Mr. Hedderwick (Wick Burghs); Answer, The
Secretary of State for the Colonies (Mr. J. Chamberlain, Birmingham,
W.):   176

Aldershot Sewage Farm—Question, Mr. J. G. Talbot (Oxford University);
Answer, The Under Secretary of State for War (Mr. G. Wyndham,
Dover)...   177

Civil Service Pay Deductions—Question, Captain Norton (Newington,
W.); Answer, The Financial Secretary to the Treasury (Mr. R. W.
Hanbury, Preston)   177

June 2.]   *Page*

FATALITIES AMONG RAILWAY SERVANTS—Question, Mr. Channing (North-ampton, E.); Answer, The President of the Board of Trade (Mr. C. T. Ritchie, Croydon)   178

THE KHARTOUM PRISONERS—Question, Mr. Pirie (Aberdeen, N.); Answer, The Under Secretary of State for Foreign Affairs (Mr. Brodrick, Surrey, Guildford)   178

FEVER AMONG THE SOUDANESE TROOPS—Question, Mr. Pirie (Aberdeen, N.); Answer, The Under Secretary of State for Foreign Affairs (Mr. Brodrick, Surrey, Guildford)   179

IRISH LIGHTS—Question, Mr. William Allan (Gateshead); Answer, The President of the Board of Trade (Mr. C. T. Ritchie, Croydon)....   180

QUEEN'S BIRTHDAY CELEBRATION AT SOUTHSEA—Question, Mr. Gibson Bowles (Lynn Regis); Answer, The Under Secretary of State for War (Mr. G. Wyndham, Dover)   181

LEVEL CROSSINGS—DESBOROUGH RAILWAY FATALITY—Question, Mr. Channing (Northampton, E.); Answer, The President of the Board of Trade (Mr. C. T. Ritchie, Croydon)   181

SOUTH AFRICAN REPUBLIC—THE KILLING OF MR. EDGAR—Question, Mr. Griffith (Anglesea); Answer, The Secretary of State for the Colonies (Mr. J. Chamberlain, Birmingham, W.)   182

FRENCH CLAIMS ON CHINA—Question, Sir Edward Sassoon (Hythe); Answer, The Under Secretary of State for Foreign Affairs (Mr. Brodrick, Surrey, Guildford)   183

INLAND REVENUE—STAMPING OF ADVERTISEMENT ORDERS—Question, Mr. Hazell (Leicester); Answer, The Chancellor of the Exchequer (Sir M. Hicks-Beach, Bristol, W.)   183

ROYAL COMMISSION ON INDIAN EXPENDITURE—Question, Sir Mancherjee Bhownaggree (Bethnal Green, N.E.); Answer, The Secretary of State for India (Lord George Hamilton, Middlesex, Ealing) ... ·   184

INDIAN SUGAR TRADE—Question, Captain Sinclair (Forfar); Answer, The Secretary of State for India (Lord George Hamilton, Middlesex, Ealing)...   185

BUSINESS OF THE HOUSE—Questions, Captain Sinclair (Forfar), Mr. Boulnois (Marylebone, E.), Mr. J. Morley (Montrose), Mr. J. Dillon (Mayo, E.), Sir W. Lawson (Cumberland, Cockermouth), Mr. J. Redmond (Water-ford), Captain Pretyman (Suffolk, Woodbridge), Mr. Drage (Derby); Answers, The First Lord of the Treasury (Mr. A. J. Balfour, Man-chester, E.)   185

PUBLIC BUSINESS.

SUPPLY [12TH ALLOTTED DAY].—Considered in Committee.

CIVIL SERVICES AND REVENUE DEPARTMENTS ESTIMATES, 1899–1900.

CLASS II.

Motion made, and Question proposed -

... "That a sum, not exceeding £132,732, be granted to Her Majesty, to complete the sum necessary to defray the Charge which will come in course of payment during the year ending on the 31st day of March, 1900, for the Salaries and Expenses of the Local Government Board."

Motion made, and Question proposed—
    "That Item A (Salaries) be reduced by £100, in respect of the Salary of the President of the Local Government Board."—(*Mr. Pickersgill.*)

DISCUSSION :—

	Page		Page
The President of the Local Government Board (Mr. Chaplin, Lincolnshire, Sleaford)	193	Mr. Chaplin	208
		Sir Walter Foster	208
		Mr. Labouchere (Northampton)	209
Mr. Pickersgill (Bethnal Green, S.W.)	196	Mr. Chaplin	213
		Mr. Labouchere	213
Mr. Channing (Northampton, E.)	198	Sir William Harcourt (Monmouthshire, W.)	215
Mr. Chaplin	199	Mr. Bayley (Derbyshire, Chesterfield)	215
Mr. Channing	199	Mr. Chaplin	216
Mr. Chaplin	205	Mr. Bayley	216
Mr. Channing	205	Mr. Dillon (Mayo, E.)	216
Mr. Hazell (Leicester)	206	Mr. Labouchere	217
Sir Walter Foster (Derby, Ilkeston)	206	Mr. Channing	218
		Dr. Clark (Caithness)	218

Original Question again proposed.

The Committee divided ; Ayes, 59 ; Noes, 190.   (Division List No. 168.)

Motion made, and Question proposed—
    "That Item A (Salaries) be reduced to £500, in respect of the Salary of the President of the Local Government Board."—(*Sir Albert Rollit.*)

DISCUSSION—

	Page		Page
Mr. Gray (West Ham, N.)	223	The President of the Local Government Board (Mr. Chaplin, Lincolnshire, Sleaford)	227
Lord E. Fitzmaurice (Wilts, Cricklade)	224		
Mr. Bartley (Islington, N.)	225	Sir Albert Rollit (Islington, S.)	228
Sir F. S. Powell (Wigan)	225	Mr. Chaplin	228
Sir Walter Foster (Derby, Ilkeston)	226	Mr. Gray	228
General Laurie (Pembroke and Haverfordwest)	227	Mr. Mendl (Plymouth)	231

Motion by leave withdrawn.

Original Question again proposed.

Motion made, and Question proposed—
    "That Item A (Salaries) be reduced by £50, in respect of the Salary of the President of the Local Government Board."—(*Mr. Samuel Smith.*)

DISCUSSION :—

	Page		Page
Mr. Flower (Bradford, West)	239	Mr. Middlemore (Birmingham, N.)	254
Mr. William Jones (Carnarvon, Arfon)	242	Mr. Dillon (Mayo, East)	254
Mr. Drage (Derby)	244	The President of the Local Government Board (Mr. Chaplin, Lincolnshire, Sleaford)	256
Mr. Trevelyan (York, W. R., Elland)	247		
Mr. Hazell (Leicester)	248	Mr. Samuel Smith (Flintshire)	258
Mr. T. W. Russell (Tyrone, S.)	248	Mr. Chaplin	258
Dr. Clark (Caithness)	249	Mr. Flower	260
Mr. Lowles (Shoreditch, Haggerston)	250	Mr. Chaplin	260
Lord E. Fitzmaurice (Wilts, Cricklade)	251	Mr. Flower	261
		Mr. Chaplin	262

Motion, by leave, withdrawn.

Original Motion again proposed.

Discussion :—

Mr. Lloyd-George (Carnarvon, etc.)	265	Mr. Lloyd-George	... ...	268
Mr. Griffith-Boscawen (Kent, Tunbridge)	267	Mr. Griffith-Boscawen	... ...	268

Motion made, and Question proposed :—

"That Item A (Salaries) be reduced by £150, in respect of the Salary of the President of the Local Government Board."—(Mr. Griffith-Boscawen.)

Discussion :—

Lord E. Fitzmaurice (Wilts, Cricklade)	271	The President of the Local Government Board (Mr. Chaplin, Lincolnshire, Sleaford)	278
Mr. J. G. Talbot (Oxford University)	273	Mr. Stevenson (Suffolk, Eye)	279
Mr. J. H. Roberts (Denbighshire, W.)	274	Colonel Milward (Warwick, Stratford-on-Avon)	280
Mr. T. W. Russell (Tyrone, S.)	276	Mr. Chaplin	281
Mr. Lloyd-George (Carnarvon, etc.)	276	Mr. Havelock Wilson (Middlesbrough)	282
Mr. T. W. Russell	276	Mr. Chaplin	283

It being Midnight, the Chairman left the Chair to make his Report to the House.

Committee report progress ; to sit again on Monday next.

SUPPLY [1st June].—Resolutions reported—

CIVIL SERVICES AND REVENUE DEPARTMENTS ESTIMATES, 1899-1900.

REVENUE DEPARTMENTS.

"1. That a sum, not exceeding £5,552,885, be granted to Her Majesty to complete the sum necessary to defray the Charge which will come in course of payment during the year ending on the 31st day of March, 1900, for the Salaries and Expenses of the Post Office Services, the Expenses of Post Office Savings Banks, and Government Annuities and Insurances, and the Collection of the Post Office Revenue."

Mr. Crilly (Mayo, N.) 284

Vote agreed to.

"2. That a sum, not exceeding £570,915, be granted to Her Majesty, to complete the sum necessary to defray the Charge which will come in course of payment during the year ending on the 31st day of March, 1900, for the Expenses of the Post Office Packet Service."

Mr. Havelock Wilson (Middlesbrough) 285

Vote agreed to.

"3. That a sum, not exceeding £2,338,390, be granted to Her Majesty, to complete the sum necessary to defray the Charge which will come in course of payment during the year ending on the 31st day of March, 1900, for the Salaries and Working Expenses of the Post Office Telegraph Service."

"4. That a sum, not exceeding £496,600, be granted to Her Majesty, to complete the sum necessary to defray the Charge which will come in course of payment during the year ending on the 31st day of March, 1900, for the Salaries and Expenses of the Customs Department."

CLASS VI.

" 5. That a sum, not exceeding £287,628, be granted to Her Majesty, to complete the sum necessary to defray the Charge which will come in course of payment during the year ending on the 31st day of March, 1900, for Superannuation, Retired Compensation, and Compassionate Allowances and Gratuities under sundry Statutes, for Compassionate Allowances and Gratuities awarded by the Treasury, and for the Salaries of Medical Referees."

" 6. That a sum, not exceeding £2,130, be granted to Her Majesty, to complete the sum necessary to defray the Charge which will come in course of payment during the year ending on the 31st day of March, 1900, for certain Pensions to Masters and Seamen of the Merchant Service, and to their Widows and Children."

" 7. That a sum, not exceeding £785, be granted to Her Majesty, to complete the sum necessary to defray the Charge which will come in course of payment during the year ending on the 31st day of March, 1900, for certain Miscellaneous Charitable and other Allowances."

Resolutions agreed to.

Imbecile (Training Institutions) Bill—Order of the Day for the Second Reading read.

Mr. Round (Essex, Harwich)   288

Adjourned at twenty-five minutes after Twelve of the clock.

LORDS: MONDAY, 5TH JUNE 1899.

PRIVATE BILL BUSINESS.

THE LORD CHANCELLOR acquainted the House that the Clerk of the Parliaments had laid upon the Table the Certificates from the Examiners that the Standing Orders applicable to the following Bills have been complied with :—Electric Lighting Provisional Orders (No. 3) ; Electric Lighting Provisional Orders (No. 4) ; Electric Lighting Provisional Orders (No. 12) ; Electric Lighting Provisional Orders (No. 13) ; Electric Lighting Provisional Orders (No. 15) ; Tramways Orders Confirmation (No. 2). Also the Certificate that no Standing Orders are applicable to the following Bill :—Metropolitan Common Scheme (Harrow Weald) Provisional Order. Also the Certificates that the further Standing Orders applicable to the following Bills have been complied with :—West Middlesex Water ; Fishguard and Rosslare Railways and Harbours ; Aire and Calder Navigation ; Dublin Corporation (Markets) ; East London Water ; Great Western and Great Central Railway Companies ; London, Brighton and South Coast Railway (Various Powers) ; Manchester Corporation (General Powers) ; Milton Creek Conservancy ; North Pembrokeshire and Fishguard Railway ; Uxbridge and Rickmansworth Railway ; South Staffordshire Stipendiary Justice. Also the Certificates that no further Standing Orders are applicable to the following Bills :—Cork Corporation (Finance) ; Redditch Gas. And also the Certificate that the further Standing Orders applicable to the following Bill have not been complied with : Baker Street and Waterloo Railway. The same were ordered to lie on the Table 289, 290

Watermen's and Lightermen's Acts Amendment Bill [Lords]—Witnesses ordered to attend the Select Committee   290

Yorke Estate Bill- -Committed for Thursday next   290

June 5.] Page

Buenos Ayres and Pacific Railway Company Bill—Committee to meet on Thursday next 290

Caledonian Railway (General Powers) Bill—Committee to meet on Thursday next 290

Lisburn Town Commissioners Bill—Committee to meet on Thursday next 290

Shirebrook and District Gas Bill—Read 2a, and committed 290

South Eastern and London Chatham, and Dover Railway Companies (New Lines) Bill—Brought from the Commons, read a first time, and referred to the Examiners 290

Education Department Provisional Order Confirmation (Liverpool) Bill—House in Committee (according to order); Bill reported without amendment ; Standing Committee negatived ; and Bill to be read the third time to-morrow 290

Pilotage Provisional Order Bill—House in Committee (according to order) ; Bill reported without amendment ; Standing Committee negatived ; and Bill to be read the third time to-morrow 290

Maryport Harbour Bill ; Watermen's and Lightermen's Acts Amendment Bill ; Workington Corporation Water Bill ; Great Eastern Railway (General Powers) Bill ; Southport and Lytham Tramroad Bill ; Southport Tramways Bill ; North Staffordshire Railway Bill ; London and South Western Railway Bill—Report from the Committee of Selection, That the Lord Erskine be proposed to the House as a member of the Select Committee in the place of the Viscount Powerscourt ; read and agreed to ... 290, 291

RETURNS, REPORTS, &c.

China No. 2 (1899)—Correspondence between Her Majesty's Government and the Russian Government with regard to their respective railway interests in China : Presented (by command), and ordered to lie on the Table 291

Parliamentary Returns Act, 1869 (Trustee Savings Bank)—Treasury Minute, dated 29th May, 1899, directing the discontinuance of the return annually laid before Parliament, pursuant to the sixth section of the Savings Banks Moneys Act, 1863, showing the assets and liabilities of the National Debt Commissioners in respect of Trustee Saving Banks : Laid before the House (pursuant to Act), and ordered to lie on the Table ... 291

NEW BILL.

Reformatory Schools Amendment Bill—A Bill to amend the law with regard to reformatory schools was presented by the Lord Leigh ; read 1a, to be printed ; and to be read a second time on Thursday next [No. 107] 291

Congested Districts (Scotland) Act Amendment Bill—House in Committee (according to order) ; Bill reported without amendment ; Standing Committee negatived ; and Bill to be read the third time To-morrow ... 291

Soudan Campaign 1898 ; Proposed Grant to Lord Kitchener of Khartoum—(*The Prime Minister and Secretary of State for Foreign Affairs*) 292

Postponed till Thursday.

House adjourned at Twenty-five minutes before Five of the clock.

COMMONS: MONDAY, 5TH JUNE 1899.

PRIVATE BILL BUSINESS.

PROVISIONAL ORDER BILLS (STANDING ORDERS APPLICABLE THERETO COMPLIED WITH)—Mr. Speaker laid upon the Table Report from one of the Examiners of Petitions for Private Bills, That in the case of the following Bills, referred on the First Reading thereof, the Standing Orders which are applicable thereto have been complied with, viz. :—Electric Lighting Provisional Orders (No. 17) Bill ; Electric Lighting Provisional Order (No. 18) Bill ; Electric Lighting Provisional Orders (No. 19) Bill ; Local Government (Ireland) Provisional Order (Housing of Working Classes) Bill ; Local Government (Ireland) Provisional Orders (No. 3) Bill ; Local Government Provisional Orders (No. 10) Bill ; Local Government Provisional Orders (No. 11) Bill ; Local Government Provisional Orders (No. 12) Bill ; Local Government Provisional Orders (No. 14) Bill. Ordered, That the Bills be read a second time To-morrow 292, 293

PROVISIONAL ORDER BILLS (NO STANDING ORDERS APPLICABLE)—Mr. Speaker laid upon the Table Report from one of the Examiners of Petitions for Private Bills, That, in the case of the following Bills, referred on the First Reading thereof, no Standing Orders are applicable, viz. :—Local Government Provisional Order (No. 13) Bill ; Local Government Provisional Orders (No. 9) Bill ; Military Lands Provisional Order Bill. Ordered, That the Bills be read a second time To-morrow... 293

Belfast and Northern Counties Railway Bill (Queen's Consent Signified) —Read the third time, and passed 293

Bootle Corporation Bill—Read the third time, and passed 293

Hull, Barnsley, and West Riding Junction Railway and Dock Bill— Read the third time, and passed, with an Amendment 293

St. Albans Gas Bill—Read the third time, and passed, with Amendments ... 293

Birkenhead Corporation Bill—As amended, considered ; an Amendment made ; Bill to be read the third time 293

West Gloucestershire Water Bill—As amended, considered ; to be read the third time 293

Woking Water and Gas Bill—As amended, considered ; to be read the third time 293

Friends' Provident Institution Bill (Stamp Duties)— Resolution reported :

> "That it is expedient to authorise the imposition of the following Stamp Duties upon certain Memorials under any Act of the present Session relating to the Friends Provident Institution :—
>
> > For and upon the first memorial enrolled of the names of the persons who shall be deemed held and taken to be Trustees of the Institution, or of any special fund of the Institution, the sum of Five Pounds ; And upon every other such Memorial in which the name of any person shall for the first time be inserted as a Trustee of the Institution the sum of Five Pounds."

Resolution agreed to.

Ordered, That it be an instruction to the Committee on the Friends Provident Institution Bill, That they have power to make provision therein pursuant to the said Resolution.—(*Dr. Farquharson*) 294

Dundee Gas, Tramways, and Extension Bill (changed to " Dundee Gas, Street Improvements, and Tramways Bill."
Motion made and Question proposed—

"That Standing Orders 204 and 235 be suspended, and that the Bill be now read a second time."—(*Dr. Farquharson.*)

DISCUSSION :—

Mr. John Ellis (*Nottingham, Rushcliffe*) 294
Dr. Farquharson (*Aberdeenshire, W.*) 294

Mr. James Lowther (*Kent, Thanet*) 294
Mr. T. W. Russell (*Tyrone, S.*) 295

Question put and agreed to.

Bill accordingly read a second time, and committed.

Wishaw Water Bill [Lords]—Ordered, that Standing Orders 204 and 235 be suspended, and that the Bill be now read a second time.—(*Dr. Farquharson*); Bill accordingly read a second time, and committed 295

Great Southern and Western and Waterford, Limerick, and Western Railway Companies Amalgamation, Great Southern and Western Railway and Waterford and Central Ireland Railway Bills—Ordered, that the Order [14th March] that all petitions of County Councils under the provisions of the Local Government (Ireland) Act, 1898, against the Bills, be presented seven clear days before the meeting of the Committee, and that the petitioners praying to be heard by themselves, their counsel, or agents, or witnesses be heard against the Bills, be suspended in the case of the petition of the County Council of the County of Cork against the Great Southern and Western and Waterford, Limerick, and Western Railway Companies Amalgamation Bill, and that the said petition be referred to the Select Committee on the said Bills, and that the petitioners be heard by their counsel, agents, or witnesses against the said Bill.—(*Mr. J. F. X. O'Brien*) 295

Broughty Ferry Gas and Paving Order Bill [Lords]—Read the third time, and passed, without Amendment 295

Education Department Provisional Orders Confirmation (Aberavon, &c.) Bill [Lords]—Read the third time, and passed, without Amendment 295

Electric Lighting Provisional Orders (No. 16) Bill—Read a second time, and committed 296

Local Government (Ireland) Provisional Orders (No. 2) Bill—Read a second time, and committed 296

PETITIONS.

Building Feus and Leases (Scotland) Bill—Petition from Aberdeen, against; to lie upon the Table 296

Cemeteries Rating Bill—Petition from St. Pancras, for alteration; to lie upon the Table 296

Cheap Trains Bill—Petition from St. Pancras, in favour; to lie upon the Table 296

Ecclesiastical Assessments (Scotland) Bill—Petition of the General Assembly of the Church of Scotland, in favour; to lie upon the Table ... 296

June 5.]   *Page*

Executors (Scotland) Amendment Bill—Petition from Aberdeen, in
favour ; to lie upon the Table   296

Grocers' Licences (Scotland) Abolition Bill—Petition from Leith, in
favour ; to lie upon the Table   296

Ground Values (Taxation) (Scotland) Bill—Petition from Aberdeen,
against ; to lie upon the Table   296

Metropolis Management Acts Amendment (Bye-Laws) Bill—Petition
from St. Pancras, for alteration ; to lie upon the Table   296

Mines (Eight Hours) Bill—Petitions in favour ;—from Sinby ;—Bretby ;—
Donisthorpe ;—Alloa and Devon ;—Alva ;—Clackmannan ;—Tillicoultry ;—
and, Cadley Hill Collieries ; to lie upon the Table   296

Money Lending Bill—Petition from Leith, in favour ; to lie upon the
Table   296

Poor Law Relief (Disfranchisement)—Petitions for alteration of Law ;—
from Keighley ; and, Hunslet ; to lie upon the Table   297

Roman Catholic University of Ireland—Petitions against establishment ;
From Helensburgh ;—and, Alexandria ; to lie upon the Table   297

Sale of Intoxicating Liquors on Sunday Bill—Petitions in favour ;—from
Petersfield ;—Tre-y-ddol ;—Lincoln ;—and, Nottingham ; to lie upon the
Table   297

Seats for Shop Assistants (England and Ireland) Bill—Petition from
Glasgow, for extension of provisions to Scotland ; to lie upon the Table...   297

Succession (Scotland) Bill—Petition from Aberdeen, against ; to lie upon
the Table   297

Town Councils (Scotland) Bill—Petitions from Kirkintilloch, in favour ;
to lie upon the Table...   297

RETURN PRESENTED.

China (No. 2, 1899)—Copy presented,—of Correspondence between Her
Majesty's Government and the Russian Government with regard to their
respective Railway interests in China [by Command] ; to lie upon the
Table   297

Infectious Disease (Notification) Act (1888) Extension Bill—Lords'
Amendment to be considered forthwith ; considered, and agreed to   ..   297

QUESTIONS.

Labour in Jam Factories—Questions, Mr. Hedderwick (Wick Burghs) ;
Mr. Tennant (Berwickshire) ; Answers, The Secretary of State for the
Home Department (Sir Matthew White Ridley, Lancs, Blackpool)   ...   297

American and Canadian Affairs—Question, Sir Charles Dilke (Gloucester,
Forest of Dean) : Answer, The Under Secretary of State for Foreign
Affairs (Mr. Brodrick, Surrey, Guildford)   299

June 5.] *Page*

THE PHŒNIX PARK MURDERERS—Question, Mr. James Lowther (Kent, Thanet); Answer, The Chief Secretary for Ireland (Mr. G. W. Balfour, Leeds, Central) 299

COUNTY COURT FEES—Question, Sir Charles Dilke (Gloucester, Forest of Dean); Answer, The Secretary to the Treasury (Mr. Hanbury, Preston) 299

THE DUM-DUM BULLET—Questions, Mr. Dillon (Mayo, E.); Colonel Milward (Warwick, Stratford-upon-Avon); Answers, The Secretary of State for India (Lord George Hamilton, Middlesex, Ealing) 300

THE DUM-DUM BULLET—Question, Mr. Channing (Northampton, E.); Answer, The Under Secretary of State for War (Mr. Wyndham, Dover)... 301

POSTAL DELIVERIES IN DORSETSHIRE—Question, Colonel Welby (Taunton); Answer, The Secretary to the Treasury (Mr. Hanbury, Preston) 302

THE PARLIAMENTARY DEBATES CONTRACT—Questions, Sir Charles Cameron (Glasgow, Bridgeton); Mr. R. G. Webster (St. Pancras, East); Mr. Channing (Northampton, E.); Answers, The Secretary to the Treasury (Mr. Hanbury, Preston) 303

IRELAND—NATIONAL SCHOOL TEACHERS AS GUARDIANS—Question, Mr. Tully (Leitrim, S.); Answer, The Chief Secretary for Ireland (Mr. G. W. Balfour, Leeds, Central) 304

AGRICULTURAL GRANTS IN ROSCOMMON AND LEITRIM—Question, Mr. Tully, (Leitrim, S.); Answer, The Chief Secretary for Ireland (Mr. G. W. Balfour, Leeds, Central) 305

TRANSVAAL AFFAIRS—Question, Mr. Bryn Roberts (Carnarvonshire, Eifion); Answer, The Secretary of State for the Colonies (Mr. J. Chamberlain, Birmingham, W.) 305

THE PARLIAMENTARY DEPOSITS BILL—Question, Mr. Tomlinson (Preston); Answer, The Attorney General (Sir Richard Webster, Isle of Wight) ... 306

PEERS AND PARLIAMENTARY ELECTIONS—Question, Mr. James Lowther Answer, The First Lord of the Treasury (Mr. A. J. Balfour, Manchester, E.) 307

THE PEACE CONFERENCE—Question, Mr. Dillon, (Mayo, E.); Answer, First Lord of the Treasury (Mr. A. J. Balfour, Manchester, E.) 308

IRELAND—EMERGENCY MEN CARRYING FIREARMS—Question, Mr. Austin (Limerick, W.); Answer, The Chief Secretary for Ireland (Mr. G. W. Balfour, Leeds, Central) 308

PUBLIC BUSINESS.

PERSONAL EXPLANATION.

Mr. Dillon (Mayo, E.) ... 309   The First Lord of the Treasury (Mr. A. J. Balfour, Manchester, E.) 310

PRIVILEGE.

INTERFERENCE OF PEERS IN THE ELECTION FOR THE SOUTHPORT DIVISION OF LANCASHIRE.

Motion made, and Question proposed—

"That it having been represented to this House that the Duke of Devonshire and the Lord Bishop of Liverpool did severally infringe the liberties and privileges of this House by concerning themselves in the election of a member to represent the Southport Division of the county of Lancashire in the House of Commons, a Select Committee be appointed to inquire into the alleged breaches of privilege."—(Mr. James Lowther.)

June 5.]   *Page*

DISCUSSION :—

Sir Wilfrid Lawson (Cumberland,   *First Lord of the Treasury (Mr. A. J.*
Cockermouth) 315   *Balfour, Manchester, E.)* 315
                                   Mr. James Lowther (Kent, Thanet) ... 316

Question put—

The House divided :—Ayes, 86 ; Noes, 231. (Division List No. 169.)

THE SOUDAN EXPEDITION, 1898.—Proposed Grant to Lord Kitchener of
Khartoum.—MESSAGE FROM HER MAJESTY TO THE HOUSE OF LORDS
DELIVERED BY THE LORD CHANCELLOR.

Motion made, and Question proposed—

     "That the action of the Lord Chancellor in presenting to the House of
Lords a Message from Her Majesty, recommending that she should be
enabled to grant to Lord Kitchener a sum of £30,000, is a departure from
ancient constitutional precedents, contrary to the usage of Parliament, and a
gross breach of the privileges of this House, inasmuch as the Message
attributes to the House of Lords a power of initiating money grants which
alone appertains to the House of Commons, instead of concurring in those
grants."—*(Mr Swift MacNeill.)*

DISCUSSION :—

     Mr. Channing (Northampton, E.)   321   *Sir Henry Campbell-Bannerman*
     First Lord of the Treasury (Mr.   *(Stirling Burghs)* 323
     A. J. Balfour, Manchester, E.)   322   *Mr. Dillon (Mayo, E.)* ... 324

Motion, by leave, withdrawn.

MESSAGE FROM THE LORDS :—That they have agreed to : Parish Councillors
(Tenure of Office) Bill with an Amendment ; Amendments to Coalville
Urban District Gas Bill [Lords], Glastonbury Water Bill [Lords], Queen's
Ferry Bridge Bill [Lords], without Amendment. 325

That they have passed a Bill intituled "An Act for supplying with gas the
parish of Cobham, in the County of Surrey, and adjacent places."
[Cobham Gas Bill [Lords] 325

Also, a Bill, intituled "An Act to authorise the sale of the church of All
Saints', Tyndall Street, in the county borough of Cardiff, with the site
thereof, and the application of the proceeds of sale to the provision of
a new church ; and for other purposes." [All Saints' Church (Cardiff) Bill
[Lords] 325

Also, a Bill, intituled, " An Act to empower the Weston-super-Mare, Clevedon,
and Portishead Tramways Company to construct light railways in the
county of Somerset ; and for other purposes. [Weston-super-Mare,
Clevedon, and Portishead Tramways Company (Light Railway Extensions)
Bill [Lords] 325

Also, a Bill, intituled, " An Act to confer further powers on the Corporation of
Whitehaven with respect to their water and electric lighting undertakings,
to extend the borough of Whitehaven, to consolidate the rates of the
borough and simplify the collection thereof ; and for other purposes."
[Whitehaven Corporation Bill [Lords] 325

Also a Bill, intituled, " An Act to empower the Birmingham, North Warwickshire, and Stratford-upon-Avon Railway Company to make new railways
in the counties of Worcester and Warwick ; and for other purposes."
[Birmingham, North Warwickshire, and Stratford-upon-Avon Railway
Bill [Lords] 325

June 5.]

Page

Also, a Bill, intituled, "An Act for the abolition of the perpetual curacy of the consecrated chapel, called 'Grosvenor Chapel,' in the parish of Saint George, Hanover Square, in the county and diocese of London, and for vesting the said chapel in the rector of the said parish ; and for other purposes." [Grosvenor Chapel (London) Bill [Lords] 325

Also, a Bill, intituled, "An Act to empower the Urban District Council for the district of Moss Side to work any tramway for the time being belonging to or leased by them ; and for other purposes." [Moss Side Urban District Council (Tramways) Bill [Lords] 326

Also, a Bill, intituled, "An Act to empower the Urban District Council for the district of Stretford to work any tramway for the time being belonging to or leased by them ; and for other purposes." [Stretford Urban District Council (Tramways) Bill [Lords] 326

And, also, a Bill, intituled, "An Act to empower the Urban District Council for the district of Withington to work any tramway for the time being belonging to or leased by them ; and for other purposes." [Withington Urban District Council (Tramways) Bill [Lords] 326

Cobham Gas Bill [Lords] ; All Saints' Church (Cardiff) Bill [Lords] ; Weston-super-Mare, Clevedon, and Portishead Tramways Company (Light Railway Extensions) Bill [Lords]; Whitehaven Corporation Bill [Lords] ; Birmingham, North Warwickshire, and Stratford-upon-Avon Railway Bill [Lords] ; Grosvenor Chapel (London) Bill [Lords] ; Moss Side Urban District Council (Tramways) Bill [Lords] ; Stretford Urban District Council (Tramways) Bill [Lords] ; Withington Urban District Council (Tramways) Bill [Lords] Read the first time, and referred to the Examiners of Petitions for Private Bills ... ... · 326

Jones' Divorce Bill [Lords].—Ordered, That a Message be sent to the Lords, to request that their Lordships will be pleased to communicate to this House, Copies of the Minutes of Evidence and Proceedings, together with the Documents deposited, in the case of Jones' Divorce Bill [Lords] ; and that the Clerk do carry the said Message 326

Ordered,—That it be an Instruction to the Select Committee on Divorce Bills, that they do hear Counsel and examine Witnesses for Jones' Divorce Bill [Lords], and also that they do hear Counsel and examine Witnesses against the Bill, if the Parties concerned think fit to be heard by Counsel and produce Witnesses.—(Mr. Attorney-General.) 327

SUPPLY.

(MESSAGE FROM HER MAJESTY [GRANT TO LORD KITCHENER]).

In the Committee.

Queen's Message [2nd June] read.

Motion made, and Question proposed—

"That a sum, not exceeding £30,000, be granted to Her Majesty, to be issued to Major-General Lord Kitchener of Khartoum, G.C.B., K.C.M.G., as an acknowledgment of his eminent services in planning and conducting the recent Expedition in the Soudan."—(The First Lord of the Treasury.)

DISCUSSION :—

Sir Hy. Campbell-Banner-
man (Stirling Burghs) ... 332
Mr. J. Morley (Montrose
Burghs) 338
Mr. Arnold-Forster (Bel-
fast, W.) 340
Sir F. Dixon Hartland
(Middlesex, Uxbridge) ... 340
Mr. J. Morley 340
The First Lord of the
Treasury (Mr. A. J. Bal-
four, Manchester, E.) ... 342
Mr. J. Morley 342
Mr. A. J. Balfour ... 342
Mr. J. Morley 343
Mr. A. J. Balfour ... 343
Mr. J. Morley 343
Mr. Dillon (Mayo, E.) ... 344
Mr. J. Morley 344
Sir J. Fergusson (Man-
chester, N.E.) 345
Mr. J. Morley 345
Mr. A. J. Balfour ... 345
Mr. J. Morley 349
Mr. A. J. Balfour ... 349
Mr. C. P. Scott (Lancashire,
Leigh) 350
Lord Chas. Beresford (York) 359
Mr. J. Morley 362

Lord Chas. Beresford 362
Mr. Labouchere (Northamp-
ton) 364
Lord Chas. Beresford 369
Mr. Labouchere 369
Mr. Atherley-Jones (Durham,
N.W.) 372
Mr. Lees Knowles (Salford, W.) ... 374
Mr. Pirie (Aberdeen, N.)... 377
The Under Secretary of State for
Foreign Affairs (Mr. St. John
Brodrick, Surrey, Guildford) ... 381
Mr. Pirie 381
Mr. Vicary Gibbs (Herts, St.
Albans)... 382
Mr. C. P. Scott 384
Mr. Vicary Gibbs... 384
Sir Wilfrid Lawson (Cumberland,
Cockermouth) 385
Sir A. Acland-Hood (Somerset,
Wellington) 388
Mr. Dillon 390
Col. Saunderson (Armagh, N.) ... 394
Mr. Swift MacNeill (Donegal, S.) ... 395
Col. Saunderson 396
Mr. R. Wallace (Edinburgh, E.)... 398
Mr. Arnold-Forster 400
Mr. Swift MacNeill 401
Mr. Sydney Gedge (Walsall) ... 402

Question put.

The Committee divided: Ayes, 393; Noes, 51. (Division List No. 170.)

Resolution to be reported to-morrow; Committee to sit again on Wednesday.

House adjourned at ten minutes after Twelve of the clock.

LORDS: TUESDAY, JUNE 6TH, 1899.

ROYAL ASSENT.—COMMISSION :—The following Bills received the Royal Assent:—Solicitors; Supreme Court (Appeals); Public Libraries (Scotland) Acts Amendment; Metropolitan Water Companies; Education Department Provisional Order Confirmation (Swansea); Metropolitan Police Provisional Order; Local Government Provisional Orders (No. 1); St. Andrews Burgh Provisional Order Confirmation; Rushden and Higham Ferrers District Gas; Ilford Urban District Council (Rates); Aberdeen Harbour; Herne Bay Water; Walton-on-Thames and Weybridge Gas; Crowborough District Gas; St. David's Water and Gas; Clay Cross Water; Glasgow District Subway; Loughborough and Sheepshed Railway; Dublin Improvement (Bull Alley Area); Bristol Floods Prevention; Perth Water, Police, and Gas; Vale of Glamorgan Railway; Wallasey Tramways and Improvements; Northern Assurance Company; Tenterden Railway; Surrey Commercial Docks; Horsforth Urban District Council (Water); Burley-in-Wharfedale Urban District Water; Nuneaton and Chilvers Coton Urban District Council Water; Woodhouse and Conisbrough Railway (Abandonment); Coalville Urban District Gas; Glastonbury Water; Queen's Ferry Bridge 410

PRIVATE BILL BUSINESS.

THE LORD CHANCELLOR acquainted the House that the Clerk of the Parliaments had laid upon the Table the Certificates from the Examiners that
the further Standing Orders applicable to the following Bills have been
complied with: London, Chatham, and Dover Railway; Leith Harbour and
Docks; Belfast Water. And also the Certificate that the further Standing
Orders applicable to the following Bill have not been complied with:
Belfast Corporation. The same were ordered to lie on the Table...   ...   410

Baker Street and Waterloo Railway Bill—Examiner's Certificates of non-
compliance with the Standing Orders referred to the Standing Orders
Committee on Monday next   410

Belfast Corporation Bill—Examiner's Certificates of non-compliance with
the Standing Orders referred to the Standing Orders Committee on
Monday next   410

London, Brighton, and South Coast Railway (Pensions) Bill—Committee
to meet on Thursday next   410

Shotley Bridge and Consett District Gas Bill—Committee to meet on
Friday next   410

Transvaal Mortgage Loan and Finance Company Bill [Lords]—Reported
with Amendments   410

Ayr Burgh Bill—Read a second time and committed   410

Lowestoft Water and Gas Bill [Lords]—Read a third time, and passed, and
sent to the Commons   411

North-Eastern and Hull and Barnsley Railways (Joint Dock) Bill
[Lords]—Read a third time, and passed, and sent to the Commons   ...   411

North Eastern Railway Bill [Lords]—Read a third time, and passed, and
sent to the Commons   411

Ilford Gas Bill—Read a third time, with the Amendments; further Amendments made; Bill passed, and returned to the Commons   411

Wolverhampton Tramways Bill [Lords]; Wolverhampton Corporation Bill
[Lords]; South Staffordshire Tramways Bill [Lords]; Fishguard Water and
Gas Bill; Barry Railway Bill; Lancashire and Yorkshire Railway (Various
Powers) Bill; Rhondda Urban District Council Bill; Wetherby District
Water Bill; Edinburgh Corporation Bill—Report from the Committee of
Selection, That the following Lords be proposed to the House to form the
Select Committee for the consideration of the said Bills, viz. :—D. North-
umberland (chairman), E. Bradford, L. Clonbrock, L. Clanwilliam (E.
Clanwilliam), L. Crawshaw : agreed to; and the said Lords appointed
accordingly: The Committee to meet on Thursday next, at Eleven of the
clock: and all petitions referred to the Committee, with leave to the
petitioners praying to be heard by counsel against the Bills to be heard
as desired, as also counsel for the Bills   411

Belfast and Northern Counties Railway Bill—Brought from the
Commons; read the first time, and referred to the Examiners   412

Bootle Corporation Bill—Brought from the Commons; read the first time,
and referred to the Examiners   412

June 6.] Page

Broughty Ferry Gas and Paving Order Bill [Lords]—Returned from the Commons agreed to 412

Educational Department Provisional Orders Confirmation (Aberavon, Etc.) Bill [Lords]—Returned from the Commons agreed to ... 412

Norfolk Estuary Bill [Lords]—Returned from the Commons agreed to ... 412

χ**Brigg Urban District Gas Bill**—Returned from the Commons with the Amendments agreed to 412

χ **Infectious Disease (Notification) Act (1889) Extension Bill**—Returned from the Commons with the Amendment agreed to 412

Hull, Barnsley and West Riding Junction Railway and Dock Bill [Lords]—Returned from the Commons agreed to, with an Amendment ... 412

St. Albans Gas Bill [Lords]—Returned from the Commons agreed to, with Amendments 412

Jones' Divorce Bill [Lords]—Message from the Commons for copy of the minutes of evidence taken before this House; together with the proceedings and the documents deposited in the case : Ordered, to be communicated, with a request that they may be returned 412

Education Department Provisional Order Confirmation (Liverpool) Bill [Lords]—Read the third time according to order, and passed, and sent to the Commons 412

Pilotage Provisional Order Bill—Read the third time (according to order), and passed 413

Electric Lighting Provisional Orders (No. 3) Bill—Read a second time according to order, and committed : The Committee to be proposed by the Committee of Selection 413

Electric Lighting Provisional Orders (No. 4) Bill—Read a second time, according to order, and committed to a Committee of the Whole House on Thursday next... 413

Electric Lighting Provisional Orders (No. 12) Bill [Lords]—Read a second time, according to order 413

Electric Lighting Provisional Orders (No. 13) Bill [Lords]—Read a second time, according to order 413

Electric Lighting Provisional Orders (No. 15) Bill [Lords]—Read a second time, according to order 413

Tramways Orders Confirmation (No. 2) Bill [Lords]—Read a second time, according to order 413

RETURNS, REPORTS, ETC.

RAILWAY AND CANAL TRAFFIC ACT, 1888 (SECTION 31)—Sixth Report by the Board of Trade of proceedings under Section 31 of the Act, including proceedings upon complaints made under Section 1 of the Railway and Canal Traffic Act, 1894 413

IRISH LAND COMMISSION (JUDICIAL RENTS)—Return for the month of November, 1898 413

ALDERSHOT (SEWAGE FARM AND DAIRY)—Report on the condition of the Aldershot Camp Sewage Farm, and of the dairy maintained upon it; Presented by command, and ordered to lie on the Table 413

MERCHANT SHIPPING ACT, 1894—Order in Council of 19th May, 1899, authorising an increase in the clerical establishment of the Commissioners of Northern Lighthouses, and in the salary of Mr. William Coats, accountant and cashier to the Commissioners 413

SUPREME COURT OF JUDICATURE AMENDMENT ACT, 1875—Order in Council of 19th May, 1899, amending the Order in Council of 28th July, 1893, so far as it relates to the South-Eastern Circuit 414

GREENWICH HOSPITAL ACTS, 1865-1869—Order in Council of 19th May, 1899, authorising the grant of a special gratuity to Mrs. Lynch 414

COLONIAL PROBATES ACT, 1892—Order in Council of 19th May, 1899, applying the Colonial Probates Act, 1892, to the Colony of Queensland ... 414

INTERMEDIATE EDUCATION (IRELAND)—Rule made by the Intermediate Education Board for Ireland appointing the places at which examinations for 1899 shall be held 414

INDIA (PROGRESS AND CONDITION)—Statement exhibiting the moral and material progress and condition of India during the year 1897-98 : Thirty-fourth number. Laid before the House (pursuant to Act), and ordered to lie on the Table 414

PETITION.

MUNICIPAL CORPORATION (BOROUGH FUNDS) ACT, 1872—Petition for Amendment of ; of Urban District Council of Leadgate ; read, and ordered to lie on the Table 414

Prevention of Corruption Bill [Lords] SECOND READING—Order of the Day for the Second Reading read 414

Moved—

" That the Bill be now read 2a."—(*The Lord Russell of Killowen.*)

DISCUSSION—

Lord Bishop of London	...	416	Lord Russell of Killowen	...	427
The Marquess of Londonderry		419	The Marquess of Londonderry	...	427
The Lord Chancellor (The			Lord Russell of Killowen	...	428
Earl of Halsbury)	...	421	The Marquess of Londonderry	...	428
The Lord Bishop of Win-			Lord Russell of Killowen	...	428
chester	...	...	422		

On Question agreed to ; Bill read a second time accordingly and committed to a Committee of the whole House on Thursday next.

Marriages Validity Bill [Lords]—Order of the Day for the Second Reading read. 429

THE LORD BISHOP OF LONDON : My Lords, in consequence of a communication which I have received this morning from the Lord Chancellor of Ireland, I would ask leave to withdraw the Order for the Second Reading 429

Order discharged ; Bill withdrawn.

June 6.]

Farnley Tyas Marriages Bill—Read a second time (according to order) and committed to a Committee of the whole House on Thursday next ... 429

Congested Districts (Scotland) Act Amendment Bill [Lords]—Read a third time (according to order) and passed ; and sent to the Commons ... 429

House adjourned at twenty-five minutes after Five of the clock.

COMMONS : TUESDAY, 6TH JUNE, 1899.

ROYAL ASSENT—Message to attend the Lords Commissioners.

The House went, and, being returned,

MR. SPEAKER reported the Royal Assent to a number of Bills (see first item in House of Lords report this day ; *ante*, page 409).

PRIVATE BILL BUSINESS.

PRIVATE BILLS [Lords]—STANDING ORDERS NOT PREVIOUSLY INQUIRED INTO COMPLIED WITH)—MR. SPEAKER laid upon the Table Report from one of the Examiners of Petitions for Private Bills, that, in the case of the following Bills, originating in the Lords, and referred on the First Reading thereof, the Standing Orders, not previously inquired into, and which are applicable thereto, have been complied with, viz. :—

Great Northern Railway Bill [Lords]—Ordered, That the Bill be read a second time 430

Sunderland Corporation Bill [Lords]—Ordered, That the Bill be read a second time 430

Arbroath Corporation Gas Bill [Lords]—Read the third time, and passed without Amendment 430

Kew Bridge Bill [Lords]—Read the third time, and passed, without Amendment 430

London and North Western Railway (New Railways) Bill—Read the third time, and passed. [New Title.] 430

Bexhill and St. Leonards Tramroads Bill [Lords]—Read a second time and committed... 430

Bury Corporation Water Bill [Lords]—Read a second time and committed 430

Church Stretton Water Bill [Lords]—Read a second time, and committed 430

Colonial and Foreign Banks Guarantee Fund Bill [Lords]—Read a second time and committed 430

Gainsborough Urban District Council (Gas) Bill [Lords]—Read a second time, and committed 430

Great Yarmouth Water Bill [Lords]—Read a second time, and committed 430

June 6.]   *Page*

Hampstead Church (Emmanuel West End) Bill [Lords]—Read a second time, and committed   430

Humber Conservancy Bill [Lords]—Read a second time, and committed ...   430

Leigh-on-Sea Urban District Council Bill [Lords]—Read a second time, and committed...   430

Mersey Docks and Harbour Board Finance Bill [Lords]—Read a second time, and committed   431

Port Talbot Railway and Docks Bill [Lords]—Read a second time and committed   431

Salford Corporation Bill [Lords]—Read a second time, and committed ...   431

Stretford Gas Bill [Lords]—Read a second time, and committed   431

Wakefield Corporation Bill [Lords]—Read a second time, and committed   431

Wick and Pulteney Harbours Bill [Lords]—Read a second time and committed   431

Great Southern and Western and Waterford, Limerick, and Western Railway Companies Amalgamation, Great Southern and Western Railway, and Waterford and Central Ireland Railway Bills— Ordered, that the Order [14th March] that all Petitions of County Councils under the provisions of the Local Government (Ireland) Act, 1898, against the Bills, presented seven clear days before the meeting of the Committee be referred to the Committee, and that the petitioners praying to be heard by themselves, their counsel, or agents, or witnesses be heard against the Bills be suspended in the case of the Petition of the County Council of Queen's County against the Great Southern and Western Railway Bill, and that the said Petition be referred to the Select Committee on the said Bills, and that the petitioners be heard by their counsel, agent, or witnesses against the said Bill.—(*Mr. J. F. X. O'Brien.*)   431

Bradford Tramways and Improvement Bill—Petition for additional Provision ; referred to the Examiners of Petitions for Private Bills ...   431

Electric Lighting Provisional Orders (No. 17) Bill—Read a second time, and committed   431

Electric Lighting Provisional Order (No. 18) Bill—Read a second time, and committed   432

Electric Lighting Provisional Orders (No. 19) Bill—Read a second time, and committed   432

Local Government (Ireland) Provisional Order (Housing of Working Classes) Bill—Read a second time, and committed   432

Local Government (Ireland) Provisional Orders (No. 3) Bill—Read a second time, and committed   432

Local Government Provisonal Orders (No. 9) Bill—Read a second time, and committed   432

Local Government Provisional Orders (No. 10) Bill—Read a second time, and committed   432

Local Government Provisional Orders (No. 11) Bill—Read a second time,
and committed 432

Local Government Provisional Orders (No. 12) Bill—Read a second time,
and committed 432

Local Government Provisional Orders (No. 13) Bill—Read a second time,
and committed 432

Local Government Provisional Orders (No. 14) Bill—Read a second time,
. and committed 432

Military Lands Provisional Order Bill—Read a second time, and committed 432

PRIVATE BILLS GROUP (J)—Sir Henry Fletcher reported from the Committee
on Group J. of Private Bills, That the parties promoting the Airdrie and
Coatbridge Water Bill [Lords] had stated the evidence of John Motherwell Alston, Town Clerk, Coatbridge, was essential to their case ; and it
having been proved that his attendance could not be procured without the
intervention of the House, he had been instructed to move that the said
John Motherwell Alston do attend the said Committee To-morrow at
half-past Eleven of the clock ; Ordered, That John Motherwell Alston do
attend the Committee on Group J. of Private Bills To-morrow, at half-
past Eleven of the clock 432

Blackpool Improvement Bill—Reported from the Select Committee on
Police and Sanitary Regulations Bills, with Amendments 433

Darwen Corporation Bill—Reported from the Select Committee on Police
and Sanitary Regulations Bills, with Amendments ; Ordered, That the
Report do lie upon the Table, and be printed 433

PETITIONS.

GROUND RENTS (TAXATION BY LOCAL AUTHORITIES)—Petitions in favour :—
From West Bridgford ;—Greenock ;—Askington ;—Sheerness ;—Ryde
(four) ;—Chapel en le Frith ;—St. James's ;—Llanrhystyd ;—Gravesend ;—
Motherwell ;—Rothbury ;—and, Working Men's Club and Institute
Union, Limited ; to lie upon the Table 433

Mines Eight Hours Bill—Petition from Manor Pit Colliery, in favour ; to
lie upon the Table 433

POOR LAW RELIEF DISFRANCHISEMENT—Petition from West Ham, for alteration of Law ; to lie upon the Table 433

Private Legislation Procedure (Scotland) Bill—Petition from Aberdeen,
in favour ; to lie upon the Table 433

Registration of Firms Bill—Petition from Aberdeen, in favour ; to lie upon
the Table 433

Telegraphs (Telephonic Communication, &c.) Bill—Petition from Aberdeen, against ; to lie upon the Table... 433

Workmen's Compensation Act (1897) Amendment Bill—Petition from
Aberdeen, against ; to lie upon the Table 433

RETURNS, REPORTS, &c.

IRISH LAND COMMISSION (JUDICIAL RENTS)—Copy presented,—of Return of
Judicial Rents during the month of November, 1898 [by Command]; to
lie upon the Table 434

INTERMEDIATE EDUCATION (IRELAND)—Copy presented,—of Rule made by
the Intermediate Education Board for Ireland appointing the places at
which Examinations shall be held for 1899 [by Act]; to lie upon the
Table 434

RAILWAY AND CANAL TRAFFIC ACTS, 1888 AND 1894—Copy presented,—
of Sixth Report by the Board of Trade of Proceedings under Section 31
of The Railway and Canal Traffic Act, 1888, including Proceedings upon
Complaints made under Section 1 of The Railway and Canal Traffic Act,
1894 [by command]; to lie upon the Table... 434

VOLUNTARY SCHOOLS ASSOCIATIONS—Return presented,—relative thereto
[ordered 24th March; Sir Francis Powell]; to lie upon the Table, and
to be printed. [No. 210.] 434

COLONIAL PETROLEUM ACT, 1892—Copy presented,—of Order in Council of
the 19th May, 1899, applying the Act to the Colony of Queensland [by
Act]; to lie upon the Table 434

MERCHANT SHIPPING ACT, 1894—Copy presented,—of Order in Council of
the 19th May, 1899, authorising an increase in the Clerical Establishment
of the Commissioners of Northern Lighthouses, and in the salary of Mr.
William Coats, accountant and cashier to the Commissioners [by Act]; to
lie upon the Table 434

SUPREME COURT OF JUDICATURE AMENDMENT ACT, 1875—Copy presented,
—of Order in Council of 19th May, 1899, amending the Order in Council
of 28th July, 1893, so far as it relates to the South-Eastern Circuit [by
Act]; to lie upon the Table 434

GREENWICH HOSPITAL ACTS, 1865 AND 1869—Copy presented,—of Order
in Council 19th May, 1899, authorising the grant of a special gratuity to
Mrs. Lynch [by Act]; to lie upon the Table 435

EAST INDIA (PROGRESS AND CONDITION)—Copy presented,—of Statement
exhibiting the Moral and Material Progress and Condition of India during
the year 1897-8. Thirty-fourth Number [by Act]; to lie upon the
Table 435

TREATY SERIES (No. 13, 1899)—Copy presented,—of Accession of Japan to the
International Union for the Protection of Literary and Artistic Works,
15th July 1899 [by Command]; to lie upon the Table 435

QUESTIONS.

ROYAL NAVAL RESERVE—Question, Sir Edward Gourley (Sunderland);
Answer, The First Lord of the Admiralty (Mr. G. J. Goschen, St. George's,
Hanover Square) 435

CUSTOMS OFFICIALS—Question, Mr. Steadman (Tower Hamlets, Stepney);
Answer, The Secretary to the Treasury (Mr. Hanbury, Preston) 436

June 6.] *Page*

POST OFFICE—CLERKS' SALARIES—Question, Mr. Yoxall (Nottingham, W.);
Answer, The Secretary to the Treasury (Mr. Hanbury, Preston) 437

AMERICAN MAIL SERVICE—Question, Sir John Leng (Dundee); Answer, The
Secretary to the Treasury (Mr. Hanbury, Preston) 437

IRELAND—COUNTY COURT OFFICERS—Question, Mr. Ingledew (Kildare, N.);
Answer, The Secretary to the Treasury (Mr. Hanbury, Preston) 438

NATIONAL SCHOOL TEACHERS—Question, Mr. Macaleese (Monaghan, N);
Answer, The Chief Secretary for Ireland (Mr. G. W. Balfour, Leeds,
Central) 438

LOCAL GOVERNMENT (IRELAND) ACT; ORDERS AND RULES UNDER—
Question, Mr. Tully (Leitrim, S.); Answer, The Chief Secretary for
Ireland (Mr. G. W. Balfour, Leeds, Central) 439

MIGRATION OF POPULATION—Question, Dr. Robert Ambrose (Mayo, W.)—
Answer, The Chief Secretary for Ireland (Mr. G. W. Balfour, Leeds,
Central) 439

BRITISH NEW GUINEA PAPERS—Question, Sir John Lubbock (London University); Answer, The Secretary of State for the Colonies (Mr. J. Chamberlain, Birmingham, W.) 440

ANGLO-AMERICAN COMMISSION—Question, Sir Edward Gourley (Sunderland);
Answer, The Secretary of State for the Colonies (Mr. J. Chamberlain,
Birmingham, W.) 440

IMPERIAL INSTITUTE—Question, Mr. Hogan (Tipperary, Mid); Answer, The
Secretary of State for the Colonies (Mr. J. Chamberlain, Birmingham, W,) 441

WEST INDIES—FRUIT STEAMERS LOCAL DUTIES—Question, Mr. Lawrence
(Liverpool, Abercromby); Answer, The Secretary of State for the Colonies
(Mr. J. Chamberlain, Birmingham, W.) 441

WAR OFFICE—NETHERAVON HOUSE, WILTS—Question, Mr. Goulding (Wilts,
Devizes); Answer, The Under Secretary of State for War (Mr. G.
Wyndham, Dover) 442

SALISBURY PLAIN—Questions, Mr. Thomas Bayley (Derbyshire, Chesterfield),
Mr. Gibson Bowles (Lynn Regis); Answers, The Financial Secretary to
the War Office (Mr. Powell-Williams, Birmingham, S.) 442

BARRACK AND MILITARY WORKS LOAN BILL—Question, Mr. Buchanan
(Aberdeenshire, E.); Answer, The Under Secretary of State for War
(Mr. G. Wyndham, Dover) 443

PUNJAUB WAR AND TIRAH CAMPAIGN MEDALS—Question, Mr. H. D. Greene
(Shrewsbury); Answer, The Secretary of State for India (Lord George
Hamilton, Middlesex, Ealing) 443

INDIAN CONFECTIONERY TRADE—Question, Mr. Maclean (Cardiff); Answer,
The President of the Board of Trade (Mr. C. T. Ritchie, Croydon) ... 443

PUBLIC BUSINESS.

Finance Bill---(As amended, considered)—

A Clause (Amendment of s. 4 of The Finance Act, 1894, restricting the
exemptions thereby given to non-lineals from the principle of aggregation,
and extending certain exemptions to persons taking benefits under separate
disposition)—(*Lord Alwyne Compton*)—brought up, and read the first time 444

June 6.]
·*Page*

Motion made and Question proposed—
"That the Clause be read a second time."

DISCUSSION—

The Chancellor of the Exchequer (Sir M. Hicks-Beach, Bristol, W.) ... 447	Lord Alwyne Compton (Bedfordshire, Biggleswade) 452	
Sir H. Campbell-Bannerman (Stirling Burghs) ... 449	Mr. Gibson Bowles 452	
Mr. Gibson Bowles (Lynn Regis) 450	Sir M. Hicks-Beach 454	
Mr. Haldane (Haddington) 451	Mr. Gibson Bowles 454	
	Sir M. Hicks-Beach 455	
	Mr. James Lowther (Kent, Thanet) 456	
	Mr. Labouchere (Northampton) ... 457	

Motion and clause, by leave, withdrawn.

Amendment proposed in new Clause 3 (inserted in Committee), line 6, after the word "enumerated," to insert the words "and tested."—(*Mr. Chancellor of the Exchequer.*)

Question proposed—
"That those words be there inserted."

DISCUSSION—

Mr. Lough (Islington, W.) 458	Mr. Caldwell (Lanark, Mid) ... 459	
The Chancellor of the Exchequer (Sir M. Hicks-Beach, Bristol, W.) ... 458	Sir H. H. Fowler (Wolverhampt, E) 459	
	Sir M. Hicks-Beach 459	
Sir H. Campbell-Bannerman (Stirling Burghs) ... 458	Sir H. Campbell-Bannerman ... 459	
	Sir M. Hicks-Beach 460	

Debate adjourned till Thursday.

Bill as amended to be printed. [Bill 227.]

London Government Bill—As amended, considered.

New Clause—

"No person shall be eligible as borough councillor who holds any office the salary of which is paid either wholly or partly out of the funds provided either directly or indirectly out of the rates or out of the county fund. It shall be the duty of every new borough council formed under this Act by the incorporation of a single parish to take effectual measures for the care and preservation of all vestry minutes, rate books, valuation books, maps, and all other records belonging to the civil parish, and in cases when a new borough council is formed by the incorporation of several parishes or district boards, it shall be the duty of the new borough council to collect the records belonging to the said parishes and district boards, and to take measures for their preservation. And it shall be lawful for any new borough council to expend money out of the rates for the preparation and printing of inventories and calendars of such documents which may be deemed to be of historical or public interest."—(*Mr. Moon.*)

brought up, and read the first time.

Motion made, and Question proposed—
"That the clause be read a second time."

DISCUSSION :—

The First Lord of the Treasury (Mr. A. J. Balfour, Manchester, E.) 461	Mr. Bryce (Aberdeen) 461	

June 6.]   *Page*

Motion and Clause, by leave, withdrawn.

New Clause—

"If any question arises, or is about to arise, as to whether any power, duty, or liability is or is not transferred by or under this Act to the council of any metropolitan borough, or any property is or is not vested in any such council, that question, without prejudice to any other mode of trying it, may, on the application of the council, be submitted for decision to the High Court in such summary manner as, subject to any rules of Court, may be directed by the Court; and the Court, after hearing such parties and taking such evidence (if any) as it thinks just, shall decide the question."—(*Mr. Pickersgill.*)

brought up, and read the first time.

Motion made and Question proposed—

"That the clause be now read a second time."

The Solicitor-General (Sir R. B. Finlay, Inverness Burghs) 462

Question put and agreed to.

Clause read the first and second time, and added.

Amendment proposed—

"In Clause 1, page 1, line 20, after 'administrator,' to insert 'and to establish and incorporate a council for each of the boroughs so formed.'"—(*Mr. Solicitor-General.*)

Question proposed—

"That those words be there inserted."

DISCUSSION :—

Mr. Sydney Buxton (Tower Hamlets, Poplar) ...	463	Col. Hughes (Woolwich) ...	...	463
The First Lord of the Treasury (Mr. A. J. Balfour, Manchester, E.) ...	463	Mr. Pickersgill (Bethnal Green, S.W.)	...	464
		Mr. A. J. Balfour	...	464

Question put and agreed to.

Other Amendments made.

Amendment proposed—

"In Clause 1, page 1, line 21, to leave out Sub-section (b)."—(*Mr. Solicitor-General.*)

DISCUSSION :—

Col. Hughes (Woolwich) ...	464	Sir H. H. Fowler (Wolverhampton, E.)	470
The First Lord of the Treasury (Mr. A. J. Balfour, Manchester, E.) ...	464	Mr. Cohen (Islington, E.) ...	473
Mr. Courtney (Cornwall, Bodmin)	464	Mr. Labouchere (Northampton) ...	473
Mr. E. Boulnois (Marylebone, E.)	467	Mr. Carvell Williams (Nottingham-shire, Mansfield)	474
		Mr. Heywood Johnson (Sussex, Horsham)	475

Question put—

The House divided.—Ayes, 196 ; Noes, 161. (Division List No. 171.)

Amendment proposed—

"In page 2, lines 5 and 6, to leave out the words 'that number being divisible by three.'"—(*Mr. Pickersgill.*)

June 6.]   *Page*

Question proposed—

" That the words proposed to be left out stand part of the Bill."

DISCUSSION :—

The Solicitor-General (Sir R. B. Finlay, Inverness Burghs)	479	Mr. Steadman (Tower Hamlets, Stepney)	480
		Mr. Lough (Islington, W.) ...	481
Mr. Sydney Buxton (Tower Hamlets, Poplar) ...	480	Sir E. Clarke (Plymouth) ...	482
		Mr. Banbury (Camberwell, Peckham)	482

The House divided.—Ayes, 245 ; Noes, 89. (Division List No. 172.)

Amendment.

Amendment proposed—

"In Clause 2, page 2, line 33, to leave out from ' purpose' to ' make' in line 34."—(*Mr. Sydney Buxton.*)

Question proposed—

" That the words proposed to be left out stand part of the clause."

DISCUSSION :—

The First Lord of the Treasury (Mr. A. J. Balfour, Manchester, E.) ...	486	Mr. Stuart (Shoreditch, Hoxton) ...	487

Amendment negatived.

Amendment proposed—

" In Clause 2, page 2, line 37, at end to add (c) — At the first election of aldermen after the passing of this Act any six councillors may agree in nominating one person as alderman, and thereupon such person shall be declared elected as alderman, and the six councillors nominating him shall have no further part in such election ; and that every subsequent triennial election of aldermen any twelve councillors may agree in nominating one person as alderman, and thereupon such person shall be declared elected as alderman, and the twelve councillors nominating him shall have no further part in such election. '"—(*Mr. Courtney.*)

Question proposed—

" That those words be there inserted."

The First Lord of the Treasury (Mr. A. J. Balfour, Manchester, E.) 488

Question put, and negatived.

Amendment proposed—

" In page 2, line 37, at the end of Clause 3, to insert the words, ' (d) A person shall be qualified to be elected as alderman in any metropolitan borough who is qualified to be elected as councillor in the same or any other metropolitan borough."—(*Mr. Courtney.*)

Question proposed—

" That those words be there inserted."

DISCUSSION :—

The First Lord of the Treasury (Mr. A. J. Balfour, Manchester, E.) · ...	490	Sir J. Brunner (Cheshire, Northwich)	491
Lord Hugh Cecil (Greenwich)	490	Mr. E. A. Goulding (Wilts, Devizes)	492
		Captain Norton (Newington, W.)	492
Mr. Stuart (Shoreditch, Hoxton)	490	Mr. Banbury (Camberwell, Peckham)	492
		Mr. Kimber (Wandsworth) ...	492
Sir E. Clarke (Plymouth)	491	Mr. J. Lowles (Shoreditch, Haggerston)	493

Question put.

The House divided.—Ayes, 67 ; Noes, 139. (Division List No. 173.)

Amendment proposed—

" In page 3, line 24, after the words ' town clerk,' to insert the words ' and shall be the town clerk within the meaning of the Acts relating to the registration of electors.' "—*(Mr. Solicitor-General.)*

Question proposed—

" That those words be there inserted."

Amendment proposed to the proposed Amendment—

" After the word ' and ' to insert the words ' he or the registration officer appointed by the borough council as hereinafter provided.' "—*(Mr. James Stuart.)*

Question proposed—

" That those words be there inserted in the proposed Amendment."

DISCUSSION :—

Mr. John Burns (Battersea)	497	*The Attorney-General (Sir Richard Webster, Isle of Wight)*	...	498
Mr. R. G. Webster (St. Pancras, E.)	498			

Amendment to the proposed Amendment, by leave, withdrawn.

Amendment agreed to.

Clause 4 :—

Amendment proposed—

" In Clause 4, line 21, to insert ' or do not, within six months after application made, give their sanction.' "—*(Captain Jessel.)*

Question proposed—

" That those words be there inserted."

DISCUSSION :—

The Attorney-General (Sir Richard Webster, Isle of Wight)...	500	*The Solicitor-General (Sir R. B. Finlay, Inverness Burghs)* ...		501
Mr. Stuart (Shoreditch, Hoxton)	500			

Question put, and agreed to.

Clause 6 :—

Amendment proposed—

" In page 5, line 32, to leave out sub-section (6), of Clause 6."—*(Mr. Pickersgill.)*

Question proposed—

" That the words proposed to be left out stand part of the Bill."

DISCUSSION :—

The Solicitor-General (Sir R. B. Finlay, Inverness Burghs)...	502	*Mr. McKenna (Monmouth, N.)* ...		504
		Sir F. S. Powell (Wigan) ...		505
Mr. Sydney Buxton (Tower Hamlets, Poplar) ...	503	*Mr. Stuart (Shoreditch, Hoxton)*...		505
		Sir E. Clarke (Plymouth) ...		506
Mr. Lowles (Shoreditch, Haggerston)	504			

Question put—

The House divided :—Ayes, 141 ; Noes, 57. (Division List, No. 174.)

June 6.] *Page*

Amendment proposed—

"In page 6, line 12, after the word 'order' to insert the words, 'provided that, at any interval of not less than five years, the London County Council and the borough council may revise and alter the amount of the contribution, or, in default of agreement, the Local Government Board may, on the application of either party, if it think fit, revise and vary the existing arrangement.'" —(*Mr. Sydney Buxton.*)

Question proposed—

"That those words be there inserted."

The First Lord of the Treasury (*Mr. A. J. Balfour, Manchester, E.*) 509

Amendment, by leave, withdrawn.

Other Amendments made.

Amendment proposed—

"In page 6, line 28, to leave out the word 'report,' in order to insert the word 'submit.'" —(*Mr. Pickersgill.*)

instead thereof :—

Question proposed—

"That the word 'report' stand part of the Bill."

DISCUSSION :—

The Solicitor-General (*Sir R. B. Finlay, Inverness Burghs*) 510	*Mr. Lowles* (*Shoreditch, Haggerston*) 511
Mr. Stuart (*Shoreditch, Hoxton*) 511	*The First Lord of the Treasury* (*Mr. A. J. Balfour, Manchester, E.*) 511

Question put and agreed to.

Amendment negatived.

Amendment proposed—

"In page 7, line 1, after the word 'parish,' to insert the words, 'it shall be constituted a parish for the purposes of assessment, and for the making, levy, and collection of rates, and.'" —(*Mr. Cripps.*)

Question proposed—

"That those words be there inserted."

DISCUSSION :—

The Attorney-General (*Sir Richard Webster, Isle of Wight*) 513	*The First Lord of the Treasury* (*Mr. A. J. Balfour, Manchester, E.*) 514
Sir Edward Clarke (*Plymouth*) 514	

Amendment, by leave, withdrawn.

Amendment proposed—

"In page 7, line 23, after the word 'borough' to insert the words, 'and of churchwardens of every parish within their borough except in so far as these relate to ecclesiastical purposes.'" —(*Mr. James Stuart.*)

Question, "That those words be there inserted," put, and negatived.

Other amendments made.

Amendment proposed—

" In page 8, line 5, after the word 'clerk' to insert the words, ' upon such date or within such period as the Local Government Board may prescribe, so that all the rates collected in a metropolitan borough from any person may be included in one demand note.' "—(*Mr. Pickersgill.*)

Question proposed—

" That those words be there inserted."

Amendment, by leave, withdrawn.

Other Amendments made.

Amendment proposed—

" In page 8, line 33, to leave out the words ' where the whole of a Poor Law union is within one borough.' "—(*Mr. Cripps.*)

Question proposed—

" That the words proposed to be left out stand part of the Bill."

DISCUSSION :—

The Attorney-General (Sir   Mr. Stuart (Shoreditch, Hoxton) ... 519
Richard Webster, Isle of
Wight)   518

Amendment, by leave, withdrawn.

Other Amendments made.

Amendment proposed—

" In page 10, line 40, after the word 'borough' to insert the words 'notwithstanding the inclusion of the parish in the first schedule to this Act.' "—(*Mr. Bousfield.*)

Question proposed—

" That those words be there inserted."

The First Lord of the Treasury (Mr. A. J. Balfour, Manchester, E.)   ... 520

Question put, and negatived.

Amendment proposed—

" To leave out the words relating to population, in order to insert 'is part.' "—(*Mr. Bousfield.*)

The First Lord of the Treasury (Mr. A. J. Balfour, Manchester, E.)   ... 521

Amendment agreed to.

Amendment proposed—

" In page 11, line 33, at the end of line 17, to insert the words—

' If, under or by virtue of the provisions of this Act, or of any Order in Council made in pursuance thereof, any parish or place maintaining its own poor shall be divided into two or more parishes or portions of parishes, such division shall not destroy the settlements which poor persons may have therein at the date of such division, but every person who has at the date of such division a settlement in any parish or place divided as aforesaid shall be deemed to be settled in the new parish which shall contain the house or other place or places in which the settlement, acquired or derived by such person, shall have been gained. Provided always that no such settlement as aforesaid shall be retained if it was gained under or by virtue of a residence partly in one of the new parishes and partly in another.

' If, under or by virtue of the provisions of this Act, or of any Order in Council made in pursuance thereof, any parish or place maintaining its own poor shall be divided into two or more parishes or portion of parishes, such division shall not destroy a status of irremovability acquired by virtue of a residence in the union of which the divided parish shall have formed part or consisted, but such status of irremovability shall be deemed to have been acquired in the parish which shall contain the house or other place in which the person having such status of irremovability shall be resident at the time when such division shall take place, or if he shall then be in receipt of relief in the parish which shall contain the house or other place in which he was resident at the time of becoming chargeable.' "—(*Captain Chaloner.*)

Question proposed—

"That those words be there inserted."

The First Lord of the Treasury (Mr. A. J. Balfour, Manchester, E.) ... 522

Amendment, by leave, withdrawn.

Amendment proposed—

"In page 12, line 30, after the word 'churchwarden,' to insert the words 'or sidesman.'"—*(Mr. Tomlinson.)*

Question proposed—

"That the words 'or sidesman' be there inserted."

Amendment, by leave, withdrawn.

Amendment proposed—

"In page 12, lines 32 and 33, to leave out the words 'the inhabitants of the parish,' in order to insert the words, 'Such inhabitants of the parish as shall have obeyed that rubric of the Book of Common Prayer which is printed at the end of the Order of the Administration of the Holy Communion, and which requires that every parishioner shall communicate at the least three times in the year, of which Easter is to be one.'"—*(Lord Hugh Cecil.)*

The First Lord of the Treasury (Mr. A. J. Balfour, Manchester, E.) ... 526

Question proposed—

"That the words 'the inhabitants of' stand part of the Bill."

It being Midnight, the Debate stood adjourned.

Debate to be resumed on Thursday.

QUESTION.

RIOTING IN BELFAST—Question, Mr. Dillon (Mayo, E.); Answer, The Chief Secretary for Ireland (Mr. G. W. Balfour, Leeds Central).

Adjourned at Twenty minutes after Twelve of the clock.

COMMONS.—WEDNESDAY, 7TH JUNE, 1899.

PRIVATE BILL BUSINESS.

City and Brixton Railway Bill—As amended, considered ; to be read the third time 537

Godalming Corporation Water Bill—As amended, to be considered upon Tuesday next 537

London County Council (General Powers) Bill—As amended, to be considered upon Tuesday next 537

London Improvements Bill—As amended, considered ; to be read the third time 537

June 7.]

Stockport Corporation Bill—As amended, considered ; to be read the third time   537

Brighton Marine Palace and Pier Bill [Lords]—Read a second time, and committed   537

Furness Railway Bill [Lords]—Read a second time, and committed   ...   537

Paisley and Barrhead District Railway Bill [Lords]—Read a second time, and committed...   537

STANDING ORDERS.

Ordered, That so much of the Standing Order No. 91 as fixes five as the quorum of the Select Committee on Standing Orders be read, and suspended   537

Ordered, That, for the remainder of the Session, three be the quorum of the Committee—(*Mr John Ellis.*)...   537

PETITIONS.

Borough Funds Act (1872)—Petition from Mytholmroyd, for alteration of law ; to lie upon the Table   537

Education of Children Bill—Petitions in favour ;—From Burton-on-Trent, and Wolverhampton ; to lie upon the Table   538

Ground Rents (Taxation by Local Authorities)—Petitions in favour ;— From Burton-on-Trent and Wolverhampton ; to lie upon the Table ...   538

Local Government (Scotland) Act (1894) **Amendment Bill**—Petition from Row, in favour ; to lie upon the Table   538

Mines (Eight Hours) Bill—Petitions in favour ;—From Dysart Colliery, and Dannikier ; to lie upon the Table   538

Parish Churches (Scotland) Bill—Petition of the General Assembly of the Church of Scotland, in favour ; to lie upon the Table   538

Poor Law Officers' Superannuation (Scotland) Bill—Petitions in favour ; —From Angus, and Stirling ; to lie upon the Table   538

Private Legislation Procedure (Scotland) Bill—Petition from Airdrie, in favour ; to lie upon the Table   538

Rating of Machinery Bill—Petition of the Mining Association of Great Britain, against ; to lie upon the Table   538

Sale of Intoxicating Liquors on Sunday Bill—Petitions in favour ;—From Sheffield, London, Bolton, Barnsley, Pendleton, and Ashton-under-Lyne ; to lie upon the Table   538

Telegraphs (Telephonic Communication, &c.) Bill—Petition from Bristol, against ; to lie upon the Table   538

June 7.]   *Page*

Telegraphs (Telephonic Communication, &c.) Bill—Petition from Todmorden, for alteration ; to lie upon the Table   538

Town Councils (Scotland) Bill—Petition from Airdrie, in favour ; to lie upon the Table   538

RETURNS, REPORTS, &c.

EAST INDIA (PROGRESS AND CONDITION)—Paper [presented 6th June] to be printed [No. 211.]   539

NATIONAL PORTRAIT GALLERY—Copy presented,—of Forty-second Annual Report of the Trustees of the National Portrait Gallery (1899) [by Command] ; to lie upon the Table   539

SUPERANNUATION ACT, 1884—Copy presented,—of Treasury Minute, dated 30th May, 1899, declaring that James Muspratt, auxiliary postman, London Post Office Department, was appointed without a Civil Service certificate through inadvertence on the part of the Head of his Department [by Act] ; to lie upon the Table   539

PUBLIC WORSHIP REGULATION AND CHURCH DISCIPLINE—Return presented, relative thereto [Ordered 23rd February—*Mr. Sydney Gedge*] ; to lie upon the Table, and to be printed...   539

PUBLIC BUSINESS.
SERVICE FRANCHISE BILL.

(In the Committee.)

Clause 1 :—

Amendment proposed—

"In page 1, line 6, to leave out from the word 'employment' to the word 'he,' in line 8."—(*Mr. McKenna.*)

Sir J. Blundell Maple (*Camberwell, East Dulwich*)   540

Question put, "That the words proposed to be left out stand part of the Clause."

The Committee divided :—Ayes, 40 ; Noes, 58. (Division List, No. 175.)

Clause, as amended, agreed to.

DISCUSSION :—

Mr. Duncombe (*Cumberland, Egremont*)   541   *Sir Charles Dilke* (*Gloucester, Forest of Dean*)   541
Mr. McKenna (*Monmouth, N.*)   541

Clauses 2 and 3 agreed to.

Bill reported ; as amended, to be considered upon Wednesday next   ...   541

EDUCATION OF CHILDREN BILL.

(IN THE COMMITTEE.)

DISCUSSION .—

Mr. George Whiteley (*Stockport*) 542   *Mr. James Lowther* (*Kent, Thanet*)   542

Amendments ruled "Out of order."

Intoxicating Liquors (Sunday Closing) Bill.—Second Reading ; order for Second Reading read.

Motion made and Question proposed—" That the Bill be now read a second time."—(*Mr. Tritton.*)

DISCUSSION :—

Mr. Colville (*Lanarkshire, N.E.*)	544	Mr. James Lowther	...	545
Mr. James Lowther (*Kent, Thanet*)	545	Mr. Nussey (*Pontefract*)	...	550
Mr. T. W. Russell (*Tyrone, S.*)	545			

Amendment proposed—

  " To leave out from the word ' That,' to the end of the Question, in order to add the words ' no Bill to restrict the sale of intoxicating liquors on Sunday is satisfactory unless it embodies the principle of local option.' "—(*Mr. Nussey.*)

Question proposed, "That the words proposed to be left out stand part of the Question."

DISCUSSION :—

Mr. Warner (*Stafford, Lichfield*)	551	Mr. Galloway (*Manchester,*		
Mr. Sydney Gedge (*Walsall*)	553	*S.W.*)	...	557
Sir Wilfrid Lawson (*Cumberland,*		Sir Wilfrid Lawson	...	558
Cockermouth)	553	Mr. Galloway	...	558
Mr. Sydney Gedge	554	Mr. Davitt (*Mayo, S.*) ...	...	561
Mr. Tritton (*Lambeth, Nor-*		Mr. Galloway	...	561
wood)	556	Mr. Gibson Bowles (*Lynn Regis*)		561
Mr. Sydney Gedge	556	Sir Wilfrid Lawson	...	562
Mr. Samuel Young (*Cavan,*		Mr. Gibson Bowles	...	562
E.)	556	Mr. Davitt	...	563
Sir Wilfrid Lawson ...	557	Mr. Gibson Bowles	...	563
Mr. Samuel Young ...	557			

Motion made, and Question proposed—

  " That the Debate be now adjourned."—(*Mr. Galloway.*)

  Sir J. Leese (*Lancashire, Accrington*) 566

Question put.

  The House divided—Ayes, 95 ; Noes, 85—(Division List, 176.)

Debate to be resumed upon Wednesday next.

Wine and Beerhouse Acts Amendment Bill—Second Reading.

  Order for Second Reading read.

Motion made, and Question proposed—

  " That the Bill be now read a second time."—(*Mr. Lloyd-George.*)

DISCUSSION :—

Mr. James Lowther (Kent, Thanet) 567
Sir Wilfrid Lawson (Cumberland, Cockermouth) ... 569
Mr. James Lowther ... 569
Mr. Courtney (Cornwall, Bodmin)... 571
Mr. Edmund Robertson (Dundee) 572
The Under Secretary to the Home Office (Mr. Jesse Collings, Birmingham, Bordesley) 574
Mr. Gibson Bowles (Lynn Regis) 575
Mr. Jesse Collings 575
Mr. J. H. Roberts (Denbighshire, W.) 575
Mr. Banbury (Camberwell, Peckham) 577
Mr. Warner (Staffordshire, Lichfield) 578
Sir James Fergusson (Manchester, N. E.) 579
Mr. Dalziel (Kirkcaldy Burghs)... 580
Mr. Jesse Collings 581
Mr. Dalziel 581
Mr. Richards (Finsbury, E.) ... 582
Mr. Evershed (Staffordshire, Burton) 583

Amendment proposed—

"To leave out the word 'now,' and at the end of the Question to add the words 'upon this day three months.'"—(Mr. Tomlinson.)

Question proposed—

"That the word 'now' stand part of the question."

Question put—

The House divided :—Ayes, 138 ; Noes, 183.—(Division List, No. 177.)

Main Question, as amended, put, and agreed to.

Second Reading put off for three months.

Succession Scotland Bill (Second Reading.)—Order for Second Reading read.

Motion made, and Question proposed—
"That the Bill be now read a second time."

DISCUSSION :—

The Lord Advocate (Mr. A. Graham Murray, Buteshire) 591
Mr. Banbury (Camberwell, Peckham) 591

It being half-past Five of the clock, the Debate stood adjourned.

Debate to be resumed on Wednesday, 21st June.

PRIVATE BILL BUSINESS.

Ordered that Mr. Henry Plews do attend the Committee on the Great Southern and Western, and Waterford, Limerick, and Western Railway Companies Amalgamation, and the Great Southern and Western Railway Bills to-morrow, at Twelve of the clock.

PUBLIC PETITIONS COMMITTEE.—Sixth Report brought up and read ; to lie upon the Table, and to be printed.

Adjourned at twenty-five minutes before Six o'clock.

LORDS : THURSDAY, 8TH JUNE, 1899.

NEW PEER.

The Lord Monson—Sat first in Parliament after the death of his brother.

PRIVATE BILL BUSINESS.

Owens College, Manchester Bill [Lords].—Report of Her Majesty's Attorney-General received, and ordered to lie on the Table 593

North-West London Railway Bill—Committee to meet on Monday next 593

Ayr Burgh Bill—Committee to meet on Thursday next 593

Brooke's Park (Londonderry) Bill—Committed for Tuesday next ... 593

Nottingham Corporation Bill—The CHAIRMAN OF COMMITTEES informed the House that the opposition to the Bill was withdrawn ; the Order made on the 28th of April last discharged ; and Bill committed 593

Cambridge University and Town Gas Bill [Lords]—Commons Amendments considered, and agreed to 593

St. Albans Gas Bill [Lords]—Commons Amendments considered, and agreed to 593

Hull, Barnsley, and West Riding Junction Railway and Dock Bill [Lords]—Commons Amendments considered, and agreed to 593

Wolverhampton Tramways Bill [Lords]—Report from the Select Committee : That the Committee had not proceeded with the consideration of the Bill, no parties having appeared in opposition thereto ; read, and ordered to lie on the Table : The Orders made on the 13th of March and Tuesday last discharged ; and Bill committed 593

Maryport Harbour Bill [Lords]—Report from the Select Committee : That it is not expedient to proceed further with the Bill ; read, and ordered to lie on the Table 594

Buenos Ayres and Pacific Railway Company Bill [Lords]—Reported, with Amendments 594

Lisburn Town Commissioners Bill—Reported, with Amendments ... 594

London, Brighton, and South-Coast Railway (Pensions) Bill—Reported, with Amendments 594

Yorke Estate Bill [Lords]—Reported, with Amendments 594

West Middlesex Water Bill—Read the second time, and committed : The Committee to be proposed by the Committee of Selection 594

Aire and Calder Navigation Bill—Read the second time, and committed : The Committee to be proposed by the Committee of Selection 594

June 8.]   *Page*

Cork Corporation (Finance) Bill—Read the second time, and committed ...   594

East London Water Bill.—Read the second time, and committed : The Committee to be proposed by the Committee of Selection...   594

Great Western and Great Central Railway Companies Bill.—Read the second time, and committed : The Committee to be proposed by the Committee of Selection   594

London, Brighton, and South Coast Railway (Various Powers) Bill—Read the second time, and committed : The Committee to be proposed by the Committee of Selection   594

Manchester Corporation (General Powers) Bill—Read the second time, and committed : The Committee to be proposed by the Committee of Selection   595

South Staffordshire Stipendiary Justice Bill—Read the second time, and committed...   595

Redditch Gas Bill—Read the second time, and committed   595

Milton Creek Conservancy Bill—Read the second time, and committed : The Committee to be proposed by the Committee of Selection   595

North Pembrokshire and Fishguard Railway Bill—Read the second time, and committed for Monday next   595

Uxbridge and Rickmansworth Railway Bill—Read the second time, and committed   595

Owen's College, Manchester Bill—Read the second time (according to Order)   595

Great Grimsby Street Tramways Bill [Lords]—Read the third time ; Amendments made ; Bill passed, and sent to the Commons   595

London and North-Western Railway (New Railways) Bill—Brought from the Commons ; read the first time ; and referred to the Examiners   595

Arbroath Corporation Gas Bill [Lords]—Returned from the Commons agreed to   595

Kew Bridge Bill [Lords]—Returned from the Commons agreed to   595

Brynmawr and Western Valleys Railway Bill.—Report from the Committee of Selection, That the following Lords be proposed to the House to form the Select Committee for the consideration of the said Bills : (viz.) M. Bristol, E. Bathurst, E. Camperdown (chairman), L. Seaton, L. Shute (*V. Barrington*) :—Gas Orders Confirmation (No. 2) Bill [Lords] ; Education Department Provisional Order Confirmation (London) Bill [Lords] ; Stockport Corporation Water Bill ; Stockport District Water Bill ; Scunthorpe Urban District Gas and Water Bill ; Goole Urban District Council Bill ; South-Eastern and London, Chatham, and Dover Railway Companies Bill ; South-Eastern Railway Bill. Agreed to ; and the said Lords appointed accordingly : The Committee to meet on Tuesday next, at Eleven o'clock ; and all petitions referred to the Committee, with leave to the petitioners praying to be heard by counsel against the Bills to be heard as desired, as also counsel for the Bills.   595–596

RETURNS, REPORTS, ETC.

EDUCATION DEPARTMENT.—Report to Committee of Council on Education of the proceedings of the Charity Commissioners for England and Wales under the Endowed Schools Acts, 1869–1889, for the year 1898 ...　　...　596

TRADE REPORTS (ANNUAL SERIES.)—No. 2282. Brazil (Bahia); No. 2283. France (Nice and District); No. 2284. Brazil (Rio de Janeiro); No. 2285. Denmark (Iceland); No. 2286. Turkey (Beirut and the coast of Syria) ...　596

TREATY SERIES, No. 13 (1899.)—Accession of Japan to the International Union for the protection of literary and artistic works, 15th July, 1899 ...　596

NATIONAL PORTRAIT GALLERY.—Forty-second Annual Report of the Trustees of the National Portrait Gallery (1899)　　...　　...　　...　　...　　...　596

SOUTH AFRICAN REPUBLIC.—Further Correspondence relating to the claim of the South African Republic for damages on account of the Jameson raid. Presented [by Command], and ordered to lie on the Table ...　　...　596

SUPERANNUATION ACT, 1884—Treasury Minute, dated May 30, 1899, declaring that James Muspratt, auxiliary postman, London, Post Office Department, was appointed without a Civil Service certificate through inadvertence on the part of the head of his Department. Laid before the House (pursuant to Act), and ordered to lie on the Table ...　　...　　...　　...　597

PETITION.

AGRICULTURAL RATES ACT, 1896—Petition for amendment of; of Tithe-owning Clergy of England and Wales, read, and ordered to lie on the Table ...　　...　　...　　...　　...　　...　　...　　...　　...　　...　597

QUESTION.

SOUTH AFRICAN REPUBLIC—BLOEMFONTEIN CONFERENCE—Question, The Earl of Camperdown; Answer, The Under Secretary of State for War (The Earl of Selborne)　　...　　...　　...　　...　　...　　...　　...　　...　597

THE SOUDAN CAMPAIGN, 1898—Moved—

　　"That Standing Order No. XXI. be considered in order to its being suspended for this day's sitting."—(*The Marquess of Salisbury.*)

On Question, agreed to, and ordered accordingly.

Moved—

　　"That the consideration of the Queen's Message and the Motion for according the thanks of this House to the forces engaged in the recent operations in the Soudan have precedence of the Orders of the Day."—(*The Marquess of Salisbury*).

On Question, agreed to, and ordered accordingly.

　　DISCUSSION :

The Prime Minister and Secretary of State for Foreign Affairs (The Marquess of Salisbury) ... 600	*The Earl of Kimberley* 600	
	The Marquess of Salisbury ... 600	

Her Majesty's most gracious Message of Friday last considered (according to
Order): Then a humble Address of thanks and concurrence ordered
nemine dissentiente to be presented to Her Majesty thereupon: The said
Address to be presented to Her Majesty by the Lords with White Staves.

RESOLUTION :—

   The Prime Minister and Secretary of State for Foreign Affairs (the Marquess of Salisbury), the Earl of Kimberley   602

Resolved, *nemine dissentiente*, That the thanks of this House be given to Major-
General Lord Kitchener of Khartoum, G.C.B., K.C.M.G., for the
distinguished skill and ability with which he planned and conducted the
campaign on the Nile of 1896-97-98, which culminated in the battle of
Omdurman, the capture of Khartoum, and the overthrow of the power of
the Khalifa.

That the thanks of this House be given to Major-General Sir A.Hunter, K.C.B.,
D.S.O.; Major-General Sir H. M. L. Rundle, K.C.B., C.M.G., D.S.O.,
R.A.; Major-General Sir W. F. Gatacre, K.C.B., D.S.O.; Major-General
the Hon. N. G. Lyttelton, C.B.; Major-General A. G. Wauchope,
C.B., C.M.G.; Major and Brevet Colonel SirF. R. Wingate, K.C.M.G., C.B.,
D.S.O., R.A.; Lieutenant-Colonel and Brevet Colonel C. J. Long, R.A.;
Major and Brevet Colonel J. G. Maxwell, D.S.O.; Major and Brevet
Colonel H. A. Macdonald, D.S.O.; Lieutenant-Colonel D. F. Lewis, C.B.;
Major and Brevet Lieutenant-Colonel J. Collinson, C.B.; Commander
C. R. Keppel, C.B., D.S.O., R.N.; and to the other Officers and Warrant
Officers of the Navy, the British and the Egyptian Army, and the Royal
Marines, for the energy and gallantry with which they executed the
services which they were called upon to perform ;

That this House doth acknowledge and highly approve the gallantry, discipline,
and good conduct displayed by the Petty Officers, Non-commissioned
Officers, and Men of the Navy, the British and the Egyptian Army, and
Royal Marines during the campaign ;

That the thanks of this House be given to Lieutenant-General Sir Francis
Grenfell, G.C.B., G.C.M.G., for the support and assistance which he
afforded to the forces employed in the operations in the Soudan ;

That this House doth acknowledge, with admiration, the distinguished valour,
devotion, and conduct of those other Officers and Men who have perished
during the campaign in the Soudan in the service of their country, and
feels deep sympathy with their relatives and friends ;

Ordered that the Lord Chancellor do communicate the said resolutions to
General Lord Kitchener of Khartoum and to Lieutenant-General Sir
Francis Grenfell, and that General Lord Kitchener of Khartoum be requested by the Lord Chancellor to communicate the same to the several
other officers referred to therein   609

Sea Fisheries Bill [Lords]—(Second Reading.)—Order of the Day for the
Second Reading read.

   Lord Heneage   610

Moved—

   " That the Bill now be read a second time."

DISCUSSION :—

   The Secretary of State for Scot-   Lord Heneage   612
   land (Lord Balfour of
   Burleigh)   611

On Question, agreed to.

Bill read a second time (according to Order), and committed to a Committee of the whole House on Thursday, the 22nd instant.

Reformatory Schools Amendment Bill [Lords]—(Second Reading.) Order of the Day for the Second Reading read.

    Lord Leigh   612

Moved—
    "That the Bill now be read a second time."

DISCUSSION :—
    Lord James of Hereford   ...   614   *Lord Norton*   614

On Question, agreed to.

Bill read a second time (according to Order), and committed to a Committee of the whole House on Monday next.

Prevention of Corruption Bill [Lords]—House in Committee (according to Order): Bill reported without Amendment : Standing Committee negatived : Amendments made : Bill re-committed to a Committee of the whole House ; and to be printed as amended. (No. 108.)

Farnley Tyas Marriages Bill [Lords]—House in Committee (according to Order): Bill reported without Amendment : Standing Committee negatived : and Bill to be read a third time To-morrow.

QUESTION.

THE APPOINTMENT OF AN ADDITIONAL JUDGE—Question, Lord Russell of Killowen ; Answer, The Lord Chancellor   617

House adjourned at twenty minutes before Six of the clock.

COMMONS, THURSDAY, 8TH JUNE, 1899.

MESSAGE FROM THE LORDS—That they have agreed to :—Pilotage Provisional Order Bill, with Amendment ; Ilford Gas Bill, with Amendments   ...   618

    That they have passed a Bill, intituled, "An Act to amend the Congested Districts (Scotland) Act, 1897." [Congested Districts (Scotland) Act Amendment Bill [Lords]...   618

    Also, a Bill, intituled, "An Act to confirm a Provisional Order made by the Education Department under the Elementary Education Acts, 1870 to 1893, to enable the School Board for Liverpool to put in force the Lands Clauses Acts." [Education Department Provisional Order Confirmation (Liverpool) Bill [Lords] i   618

    Also, a Bill, intituled, "An Act to confirm further powers on the Lowestoft Water and Gas Company in connection with their water undertaking ; and for other purposes." [Lowestoft Water and Gas Bill [Lords]   618

June 8.]   *Page*

Also, a Bill, intituled, "An Act for enabling the North-Eastern Railway Company and the Hull, Barnsley, and West Riding Junction Railway and Dock Company to make a dock and railways at Hull ; and for other purposes." [North-Eastern and Hull and Barnsley Railways (Joint Dock) Bill [Lords]   618

And, also, a Bill, intituled, "An Act to confer additional powers upon the North-Eastern Railway Company for the construction of new railways and other works and the acquisition of additional lands ; and for transferring to the Company the North Holderness Light Railway Company ; and for other purposes." [North-Eastern Railway Bill [Lords]   618

Jones's Divorce Bill [Lords]--That they do communicate Minutes of Evidence and Proceedings taken upon the Second Reading of Jones's Divorce Bill, as desired by this House, with a request that the same may be returned   618

PRIVATE BILL BUSINESS.

Private Bills [Lords]—(STANDING ORDERS NOT PREVIOUSLY INQUIRED INTO COMPLIED WITH)—Mr. SPEAKER laid upon the Table Report from one of the Examiners of Petitions for Private Bills, that, in the case of the following Bill, originating in the Lords, and referred on the First Reading thereof, the Standing Orders not previously inquired into, and which are applicable thereto, have been complied with, viz. :—Totland Water Bill [Lords]—Ordered, That the Bill be read a second time   619

All Saints' Church (Cardiff) Bill [Lords]—Motion made, and Question proposed—

"That it be an Instruction to the Examiners of Petitions for Private Bills, to whom the Bill is referred, that they do inquire and report as to whether Standing Order No. 3 (notices by advertisement) has or has not been complied with."—(*Mr. D. A. Thomas.*)

DISCUSSION :—

Mr. J. W. Lowther (Cumberland, Penrith) ... 621		*Sir E. Hill (Bristol, S.)...* ...	623
Mr. D. Brynmor Jones (Swansea District) ... 622		*Mr. Maclean (Cardiff)* ...	623

Motion, by leave, withdrawn.

West Gloucestershire Water Bill—Read the third time, and passed   ...   624

Woking Water and Gas Bill—Read the third time, and passed...   ...   624

Dumbarton Burgh Bill [Lords]—As amended, considered ; Amendments made ; Bill to be read the third time   624

Sheffield Corporation Markets Bill—As amended, considered ; Amendments made ; Bill to be read the third time...   624

Railway Bills (Group 8)—Mr. A DE TATTON EGERTON reported from the Committee on Group 8 of Railway Bills ;—That, for the convenience of parties, the Committee had adjourned till Monday, the 19th of June, at half-past Eleven of the clock. Report to lie upon the Table...   624

June 8.]   .   *Page*

STANDING ORDERS—Resolution reported from the Committee—

    "That, in the case of the Mersey Docks and Harbour Board (Pilotage) Bill [Lords], the Standing Orders ought to be dispensed with : That the parties be permitted to proceed with their Bill."

    Resolution agreed to   624

Police and Sanitary Regulations Bills—Ordered, That Joseph Parry and John James Lackland do attend the Select Committee on Police and Sanitary Regulations Bills To-morrow, at Twelve of the clock   624

Education Department Provisional Order Confirmation (Liverpool) Bill [Lords]—Read the first time ; referred to the Examiners of Petitions for Private Bills, and to be printed. [Bill 228.]   625

Lowestoft Water and Gas Bill [Lords]—Read the first time ; and referred to the Examiners of Petitions for Private Bills   625

North-Eastern and Hull and Barnsley Railways (Joint Dock) Bill [Lords]—Read the first time ; and referred to the Examiners of Petitions for Private Bills   625

North-Eastern Railway Bill [Lords]—Read the first time ; and referred to the Examiners of Petitions for Private Bills   625

PETITIONS.

POOR LAW RELIEF (DISFRANCHISEMENT)—Two Petitions from Cardiff, for alteration of Law ; to lie upon the Table   625

RETURNS, REPORTS, &c.

SOUTH AFRICAN REPUBLIC—Copy presented,—of further correspondence relating to the claim of the South African Republic for damages on account of the Jameson Raid [by Command] ; to lie upon the Table   ...   625

EDUCATION (ENGLAND AND WALES) (ENDOWED SCHOOLS ACTS)—Copy presented,—of the Report of the proceedings of the Charity Commissioners for England and Wales, under the Endowed Schools Acts, 1869 to 1889, for the year 1898 [by Command] ; to lie upon the Table...   625

TRADE REPORTS (ANNUAL SERIES)—Copies presented,—of Diplomatic and Consular Reports, Annual Series, Nos. 2282 to 2286, [by Command] ; to lie upon the Table   626

Papers laid upon the Table by the Clerk of the House :—

    1. Inquiry into Charities (County of Carmarthen),—Further Return relative thereto [ordered 10th February, 1898 ; [*Mr. Grant Lawson.*]; to be printed. [No. 213.]

    2. Charitable Endowments (West Riding of the County of York), Charitable Endowments (Bradford), Inquiry into Charities (Parish of Halifax, including County Borough of Halifax), Inquiry into Charities (City of Sheffield), Leeds (Inquiry into Charities), Huddersfield County Borough (Charities),—Further Returns relative thereto [ordered 10th August 1894, 13th May, 1896, 8th February, 1897 ; 8th April 1897, 29th July, 1897 ; [*Mr. Francis Stevenson* and *Mr. Grant Lawson*]; to be printed. [No. 214.]   626

June 8.] Page

WORKMEN'S TRAINS—Return ordered, "showing (1) the number of Workmen's Trains running on all Railways in Great Britain; (2) the distance run and the fares charged on each particular Train; and (3) the Return to be prepared as that issued by the Board of Trade dealing with London Railways in 1897."—(*Mr. Woods.*) 626

EXPERIMENTS ON LIVING ANIMALS—Address for "Return showing the number of Experiments performed on Living Animals during the year 1898, under Licences granted under the Act 39 and 40 Vic. c. 77, distinguishing Painless from Painful Experiments (in continuation of Parliamentary Paper, No. 215, of Session 1898)."—(*Mr. Jesse Collings.*) 626

ARMY (LENGTH OF SERVICE AND AGES OF MEN IN EACH UNIT)—Address for "Return with respect to all Infantry Regiments to which one or more Battalions have been added; the Return also to show the number of men of the First Class Army Reserve recalled to, and serving with, the Colours in each Battalion of such Regiments (in continuation of Return [C. 8757])."—(*Mr. Arnold Forster.*) 626

ARMY (LENGTH OF SERVICE AND AGES OF MEN IN NEW BATTERIES OF ROYAL ARTILLERY)—Address for "Return showing the number of Men serving in each of the newly-formed Batteries or Companies of the Royal Artillery, with the Age and Length of Service of the Men."—(*Mr. Arnold Forster.*) 627

EAST INDIA (MILITARY BULLET)—Address for "Copy of Reports on the Military Bullet now in use in India."—(*Lord George Hamilton.*)... ... 627

MALTA (POLITICAL CONDITION)—Address for "Copy of a Despatch addressed to the Secretary of State for the Colonies by Sir Arthur Lyon Fremantle, late Governor of Malta, dated 29th December, 1898, on the political condition of Malta; and of all recent Correspondence relative to the same."—(*Mr. M'Iver.*) 627

QUESTIONS.

THE MUSCAT INCIDENT—Question, Sir Charles Dilke (Gloucester, Forest of Dean); Answer, The Under Secretary of State for Foreign Affairs (Mr. Brodrick, Surrey, Guildford) 627

EXEMPTION OF FOREIGN CONSULS FROM TAXATION—Question, Mr. Dillon (Mayo, E.); Answer, The Under Secretary of State for Foreign Affairs (Mr. Brodrick, Surrey, Guildford) 627

RUSSIA AND BRITISH LOAN CONTRACTS IN CHINA—Question, Lord Charles Beresford (York); Answer, The Under Secretary of State for Foreign Affairs (Mr. Brodrick, Surrey, Guildford) 628

RUSSIAN RAILWAY CONCESSIONS IN PERSIA—Question, Mr. Maclean (Cardiff); Answer, The Under Secretary of State for Foreign Affairs (Mr. Brodrick, Surrey, Guildford) 628

BRITISH INTEREST IN THE PERSIAN GULF—Question, Mr. Maclean (Cardiff); Answer, The Under Secretary of State for Foreign Affairs (Mr. Brodrick, Surrey, Guildford) 629

RUSSIAN TAXES ON ENGLISH COMMERCIAL TRAVELLERS—Question, Mr. Bill (Staffordshire, Leek); Answer, The Under Secretary of State for Foreign Affairs (Mr. Brodrick, Surrey, Guildford) 629

June 8.]   Page

TONGA—Question, Mr. Hogan (Tipperary, Mid.); Answer, The Under Secretary of State for Foreign Affairs (Mr. Brodrick, Surrey, Guildford)   ...   630

MANCHURIAN RAILWAYS—Question, Mr. Lambert (Devon, South Molton); Answer, The Under Secretary of State for Foreign Affairs (Mr. Brodrick, Surrey, Guildford)   630

THE YANG-TSZE VALLEY—Question, Mr. Lambert (Devon, South Molton); Answer, The Under Secretary of State for Foreign Affairs (Mr. Brodrick, Surrey, Guildford)   630

BRITISH OFFICERS AT OMDURMAN—Question, Mr. C. P. Scott (Lancashire, Leigh); Answer, The Under Secretary of State for Foreign Affairs (Mr. Brodrick, Surrey, Guildford)   631

FUTURE MILITARY OPERATIONS IN THE SOUDAN—Question, Mr. C. P. Scott, Lancashire, Leigh); Answer, The Under Secretary of State for Foreign Affairs (Mr. Brodrick, Surrey, Guildford)   631

THE PATRIOTIC FUND—Question, Mr. Spicer (Monmouth Boroughs); Answer, The Under Secretary of State for War (Mr. G. Wyndham, Dover)   ...   631

ELECTRIC MOTORS IN THE NAVY—Question, Sir Fortescue Flannery (Yorkshire, Shipley); Answer, The First Lord of the Admiralty (Mr. G. J. Goschen, St. George's, Hanover Square)   632

WATER TUBE BOILERS—Question, Sir J. Fergusson (Manchester, N.E.); Answer, The First Lord of the Admiralty (Mr. G. J. Goschen, St. George's, Hanover Square   633

LIFE ASSURANCE IN THE UNITED KINGDOM—Question, Mr. Boulnois (Marylebone, E.); Answer, The President of the Board of Trade (Mr. Ritchie, Croydon)   633

BLACKHEAD LIGHTHOUSE—Question, Captain Donelan (Cork, E.); Answer, The President of the Board of Trade (Mr. Ritchie, Croydon)   634

SIGNALMEN ON THE NORTH-EASTERN RAILWAY—Question, Sir Fortescue Flannery (Yorkshire, Shipley); Answer, The President of the Board of Trade (Mr. Ritchie, Croydon)   634

NEWBIGGIN-BY-THE-SEA FISHERIES—Question, Mr. Fenwick (Northumberland, Wansbeck); Answer, The President of the Board of Trade (Mr. Ritchie, Croydon)   635

SCOTTISH EDUCATION DEPARTMENT CIRCULARS—Question, Mr. Crombie, (Kincardineshire); Answer, The Lord Advocate (Mr. A. Graham Murray, Buteshire)   635

BRITISH COLUMBIA AND THE JAPANESE—Question, Mr. Hogan (Tipperary, Mid.); Answer, The Secretary of State for the Colonies (Mr. Chamberlain, Birmingham, W.)   636

SOUTH AFRICAN REPUBLIC—THE BLOEMFONTEIN CONFERENCE—Questions, Mr. Drage (Derby), Mr. Dillon (Mayo, E.), Mr. Philip Stanhope (Burnley), Mr. C. P. Scott (Lancashire, Leigh), Mr. Maclean (Cardiff), and Sir H. Campbell-Bannerman (Stirling Burghs); Answers, The Secretary of State for the Colonies (Mr. J. Chamberlain, Birmingham, W.), and the First Lord of the Treasury (Mr. A. J. Balfour, Manchester, E.)   636

June 8.]   *Page*

BATHING FATALITY AT ALDERSHOT—Question, Mr. Jeffreys (Hants, N.); Answer, The Under Secretary of State for War (Mr. G. Wyndham, Dover) 640

MILITARY PRISONS—Question, Dr. Farquharson (Aberdeenshire, W.); Answer, The Under Secretary of State for War (Mr. G. Wyndham, Dover) ... 640

THE METROPOLITAN POLICE—Question, Captain Norton (Newington, W.); Answer, The Secretary of State for the Home Department (Sir M. White-Ridley, Lancashire, Blackpool) 640

ALLAHABAD HIGH COURT — LADY BARRISTERS — Question, Mr. Herbert Roberts (Denbighshire, W.); Answer, The Secretary of State for India (Lord George Hamilton, Middlesex, Ealing) 641

LEGAL EDUCATION IN INDIA—Question, Sir William Wedderburn (Banff-shire); Answer, The Secretary of State for India (Lord George Hamilton, Middlesex, Ealing) 641

PASTEUR INSTITUTE FOR INDIA—Question, Sir William Wedderburn (Banff-shire); Answer, The Secretary of State for India (Lord George Hamilton, Middlesex, Ealing) 643

MINERAL RIGHTS IN HYDERABAD STATE—Question, Sir Andrew Scoble (Hackney, Central); Answer, the Secretary of State for India (Lord George Hamilton, Middlesex, Ealing) 643

INDIAN SUGAR TRADE—Question, Captain Sinclair (Forfar); Answer, The Secretary of State for India (Lord George Hamilton, Middlesex, Ealing) . 644

SAVINGS BANK INQUIRY—Question, Sir John Leng (Dundee); Answer, The Chancellor of the Exchequer (Sir Michael Hicks-Beach, Bristol, W.) ... 644

TEA ADULTERATION—Question, Sir Fortescue Flannery (Yorkshire, Shipley); Answer, The First Lord of the Admiralty (Mr. Goschen, St. George's, Hanover Square) 645

IRELAND—RIOTING AT COOKSTOWN—Question, Mr. Dillon (Mayo, E.); Answer, The Chief Secretary for Ireland (Mr. G. W. Balfour, Leeds, Central) ... 646

IRISH LAND COMMISSION, COUNTY CAVAN—Question, Mr. Young (Cavan, E.); Answer, The Chief Secretary for Ireland (Mr. G. W. Balfour, Leeds, Central) 647

IRISH LAND COMMISSION—COURT VALUERS—Question, Mr. Young (Cavan, E.); Answer, The Chief Secretary for Ireland (Mr. G. W. Balfour, Leeds, Central) 647

IRISH INDUSTRIAL SCHOOLS—Question, Captain Donelan (Cork, E.); Answer, The Chief Secretary for Ireland (Mr. G. W. Balfour, Leeds, Central) ... 648

ASSISTANT LAND COMMISSIONERS, IRELAND—Question, Captain Donelan (Cork, East); Answer, The Chief Secretary for Ireland (Mr. G. W. Balfour, Leeds, Central) 648

IRISH EMIGRATION TO AMERICA—Question, Captain Donelan (Cork, East); Answer, The Chief Secretary for Ireland (Mr. G. W. Balfour, Leeds, Central) 649

LAND PURCHASE ACTS—Question, Mr. Young (Cavan, E.); Answer, The Chief Secretary for Ireland (Mr. G. W. Balfour, Leeds, Central) 650

June 8.]   *Page*

THE AGRICULTURAL GRANT, COUNTY KILDARE—Question, Mr. Carew
(Dublin, College Green) ; Answer, The Chief Secretary for Ireland (Mr.
G. W. Balfour, Leeds, Central)   650

IRISH LOCAL GOVERNMENT ORDERS—Question, Mr. Dillon (Mayo, E.) ;
Answer, The Chief Secretary for Ireland (Mr. G. W. Balfour, Leeds,
Central)   651

CORK COUNCIL CONTRACTS—Question, Mr. Tully (Leitrim, S.) ; Answer, The
Chief Secretary for Ireland (Mr. G. W. Balfour, Leeds, Central) ...   652

AGRICULTURAL GRANT, COUNTY ROSCOMMON)—Question, Mr. Tully (Leitrim,
S.) ; Answer, The Chief Secretary for Ireland (Mr. G. W. Balfour, Leeds,
Central)   652

BELFAST STREET RIOTS—Questions, Captain Donelan (Cork East) and Mr.
McCartan (Down S.) ; Answer, The Chief Secretary for Ireland (Mr. G. W.
Balfour Leeds, Central)   653

LOCAL GOVERNMENT ELECTION EXPENSES—Question, Mr. Macaleese (Monaghan,
N.); Answer, The Chief Secretary for Ireland (Mr. G. W. Balfour, Leeds,
Central)   656

THE METROPOLITAN VOLUNTEERS' "MARCH PAST"—Question, Sir Howard
Vincent (Sheffield, Central) ; Answer, The First Commissioner of Works
(Mr. Akers-Douglas, Kent, St. Augustine's)...   657

HOUSES OF PARLIAMENT.—SUGGESTED PROVISION OF AN AMBULANCE—
Question, Mr. Tomlinson (Preston) ; Answer, The First Commissioner
of Works (Mr. Akers-Douglas, Kent, St. Agustine's)   657

RETIRED OFFICERS AND CIVIL EMPLOYMENT IN PUBLIC DEPARTMENTS—
Question, Captain Norton (Newington W.) ; Answer, Mr. Anstruther (St.
Andrews Burghs)   657

TELEGRAPHIC DELAYS—Question, Mr. Ascroft (Oldham) ; Answer, Mr.
Anstruther (St. Andrews Burghs)   658

THE "MANDAT-POST" SYSTEM—Question, Mr. Bill (Staffordshire, Leek) ; Answer, Mr. Anstruther (St. Andrews Burghs)   659

THE MONEY LENDING BILL—Question, Mr. Ascroft (Oldham) ; Answer, The
First Lord of the Treasury (Mr. A. J. Balfour, Manchester, E.)   659

BUSINESS OF THE HOUSE—Questions, Mr. Crombie (Kincardineshire), Mr.
Channing (Northampton, E.), Sir H. Campbell-Bannerman (Stirling
Burghs), and Sir Charles Cameron (Glasgow, Bridgeton) ; Answers, The
First Lord of the Treasury (Mr. A. J. Balfour, Manchester, E.)   660

MUNICIPAL TRADING COMMITTEE—Question, Mr. Bartley (Islington, N.) ;
Answer, The First Lord of the Treasury (Mr. A. J. Balfour, Manchester, E.) 66₁

PUBLIC BUSINESS.

Undersized Fish Bill—

The President of the Board   Mr. Gibson Bowles (Lynn Regis)   661
of Trade (Mr. Ritchie,
Croydon)   661

Bill "to provide against the Destruction of Undersized Fish," ordered to be brought in by Mr. Ritchie.

Bill "to provide against the Destruction of Undersized Fish," presented accordingly, and read the first time ; to be read a second time upon Monday next, and to be printed. [Bill 229.]

Parish Councillors (Tenure of Office) Bill—Lords' Amendment to be considered forthwith ; considered, and agreed to   663

THE SOUDAN EXPEDITION, 1896-7-8.

(THANKS OF THE HOUSE.)

Motion made and Question proposed—

"That the thanks of this House be given to Major-General Lord Kitchener of Khartoum, G.C.B., K.C.M.G., for the distinguished skill and ability with which he planned and conducted the campaign on the Nile of 1896-7-8, which culminated in the battle of Omdurman, the capture of Khartoum, and the overthrow of the power of the Khalifa."—*Mr. Balfour.*

DISCUSSION :—

Sir H. Campbell-Bannerman (Stirling Burghs) ... 667		Mr. Davitt (Mayo, S.) 668	
Dr. Farquharson (Aberdeenshire, W.) 667		Mr. Dillon (Mayo, E.) 668	

Question put.

The House divided—Ayes, 321 ; Noes, 20. (Division List, No. 178.)

1. Resolved, That the thanks of this House be given to Major-General Lord Kitchener of Khartoum, G.C.B., K.C.M.G., for the distinguished skill and ability with which he planned and conducted the campaign on the Nile of 1896-7-8, which culminated in the Battle of Omdurman, the capture of Khartoum, and the overthrow of the power of the Khalifa.

Motion made, and Question proposed—

"That the thanks of this House be given to :—Major-General Sir Archibald Hunter, K.C.B., D.S.O. ; Major-General Sir Henry MacLeod Leslie-Rundle, K.C.B, C.M.G, D.S.O, R.A. ; Major-General Sir William Forbes Gatacre, K.C.B., D.S.O. ; Major-General the Hon. Neville Gerald Lyttelton, C.B. ; Major-General A. G. Wauchope, C.B., C.M.G. ; Major and Brevet-Colonel Sir Francis Reginald Wingate, K.C.M.C., C.B., D.S.O., R.A. ; Lieutenant-Colonel and Brevet-Colonel C. J. Long, R.A. ; Major and Brevet Colonel J. G. Maxwell, D.S.O. ; Major and Brevet-Colonel H. A. MacDonald, D.S.O. ; Lieutenant-Colonel D. F. Lewis, C.B. ; Major and Brevet Lieutenant-Colonel J. Collinson, C.B. ; Captain C. R. Keppel, C.B., D.S.O., R.N. ; and to the other Officers and Warrant Officers of the Navy, the British and the Egyptian Army, and the Royal Marines, for the energy and gallantry with which they executed the services which they were called upon to perform."—(*Mr. A. J. Balfour.*)

DISCUSSION :—

Dr. Farquharson (Aberdeenshire, W.) 673		Mr. Davitt 680	
Mr. Davitt (Mayo, S.) ... 674		Mr. A. J. Balfour 680	
The First Lord of the Treasury (Mr. A. J. Balfour, Manchester, E.) 675		Mr. Channing 681	
		Mr. Dillon (Mayo, E.) 682	
		Major Rasch (Essex, S.E.) ... 685	
Mr. Davitt... 675		Mr. H. J. Wilson (York, W.R., Holmfirth) 686	
Mr. Channing (Northampton, E.)... ... 676			
		Mr. Bryn Roberts (Carnarvonshire, Eifion) 686	
Mr. A. J. Balfour... ... 678			
Dr. Farquharson 679		Mr. Lees Knowles (Salford, W.) 688	
Mr. A. J. Balfour... ... 679			

Question put.

The House divided—Ayes, 347 ; Noes, 18. (Division List, No. 179.)

2. Resolved, That the thanks of this House be given to Major-General Sir Archibald Hunter, K.C.B., D.S.O. ; Major-General Sir Henry MacLeod Leslie-Rundle, K.C.B., C.M.G., D.S.O., R.A. ; Major-General Sir William Forbes Gatacre, K.C.B., D.S.O. ; Major-General the Hon. Neville Gerald Lyttelton, C.B. ; Major-General A. G. Wauchope, C.B., C.M.G. ; Major and Brevet Colonel Sir Francis Reginald Wingate, K.C.M.G., C.B., D.S.O., R.A. ; Lieutenant-Colonel and Brevet Colonel C. J. Long, R.A. ; Major and Brevet Colonel J. G. Maxwell, D.S.O. ; Major and Brevet Colonel H. A. MacDonald, D.S.O. ; Lieutenant-Colonel D. F. Lewis, C.B. ; Major and Brevet Lieutenant-Colonel J. Collinson, C.B.; Captain C. R. Keppel, C.B., D.S.O., R.N. ; and to the other Officers and Warrant Officers of the Navy, the British and the Egyptian Army, and the Royal Marines, for the energy and gallantry with which they executed the services which they were called upon to perform **694**

Motion made, and Question put—

"That this House doth acknowledge and highly approve the gallantry, discipline, and good conduct displayed by the Petty Officers, Non-commissioned Officers, and Men of the Navy, the British and the Egyptian Army, and the Royal Marines during the campaign."—(*Mr. Balfour*.)

The House divided ; Ayes, 355 ; Noes, 16. (Division List, No. 180.)

3. Resolved,—That this House doth acknowledge and highly approve the gallantry, discipline, and good conduct displayed by the Petty Officers, Non-commissioned Officers, and Men of the Navy, the British and the Egyptian Army, and the Royal Marines during the campaign **697**

Motion made, and Question proposed—

"That the thanks of this House be given to Lieutenant-General Sir Francis Grenfell, G.C.B., G.C.M.G., for the support and assistance which he afforded to the forces employed in the operations in the Soudan."—(*Mr. Balfour*).

Mr. Davitt (*Mayo, S.*) **697**

Question put, and agreed to.

Resolved,—That the thanks of this House be given to Lieutenant-General Sir Francis Grenfell, G.C.B., G.C.M.G., for the support and assistance which he afforded to the forces employed in the operations in Soudan - - - - - - - - - - - - - - **697**

Motion made, and Question proposed—

"That this House doth acknowledge, with admiration, the distinguished valour. devotion, and conduct of those other officers and men who have perished during the campaign in the Soudan in the service of their country, and feel deep sympathy with their relatives and friends."—(*Mr. Balfour*).

DISCUSSION :—

Lord Charles Beresford (*York*) **697**	*The First Lord of the Treasury* (Mr. A. J. Balfour, Manchester, E). **698**	
Mr. Dillon (*Mayo, E.*) ... **698**		

Question put, and agreed to.

5. Resolved,—That this House doth acknowledge, with admiration, the distinguished valour, devotion, and conduct of those other officers and

June 8.]　　　　　　　　　　　　　　　　　　　　　　　　　　　　*Page*

men who have perished during the campaign in the Soudan in the service
of their country, and feel deep sympathy with their relatives and friends.—
(*Mr. Balfour*)　-　-　-　-　-　-　-　-　-　-　-　-　- 699

Ordered,—That the said resolutions be transmitted by Mr. Speaker
to Major-General Lord Kitchener of Khartoum, G.C.B., K.C.M.G., and
that he be requested to communicate the same to the several officers and
men referred to therein.—(*Mr. Balfour*)　-　-　-　-　-　-　- 699

London Government Bill—Order read, for resuming adjourned Debate
on Amendment proposed [6th June] on consideration of the Bill, as
amended :—

" And which Amendment was, in page 12, lines 32 and 33, to leave out the
words ' the inhabitants of the parish,' it order to insert the words ' such inhabitants of the parish as shall have obeyed that rubric of the Book of Common
Prayer which is printed at the end of the Order of the Administration of the
Holy Communion, and which requires that every parishioner shall communicate
at the least three times in the year, of which Easter is to be one.'"—(*Lord Hugh
Cecil.*)

Question again proposed—

"That the words ' the inhabitants of ' stand part of the Bill."

Discussion Resumed :—

Mr. Carvell Williams (Notts, Mansfield)	...	...	699	*Mr. Gedge (Walsall)* ...	...	702
				Mr. Harwood (Bolton) ...	...	702
Mr. Vicary Gibbs (Herts, St. Albans) ...	...	...	701	*Lord Hugh Cecil (Greenwich)*	...	703

Amendment, by leave, withdrawn.

Amendment proposed—

" In page 12, line 33, after the words last inserted, to insert the words ' who
shall declare themselves bona fide members of the Church of England.' "—
(*Mr. Talbot.*)

Question proposed, " That those words be there inserted."

Discussion :—

The First Lord of the Trea-sury (Mr. A. J. Balfour, Manchester, E.)...	...	704	*Viscount Cranborne (Rochester)*...	...	705
			Mr. J. G. Talbot (Oxford Univer-sity) ...	... ...	706
Mr. Vicary Gibbs (Herts, St. Albans) ...	...	705			

Question put, and negatived. Other Amendments made.

Amendment proposed—

" In Clause 26, page 15, line 27, at end, to insert—' Provided that the
borough council may, if it thinks fit, take into account continuous service under
any authority or authorities to which this Act refers, in order to calculate the
total period of service of any officer entitled to compensation under this Act.' "—
(*Mr. W. F. D. Smith.*)

Question proposed, " That these words be there inserted."

The First Lord of the Treasury (Mr. A. J. Balfour, Manchester, E.) 707

Question put, and agreed to.

Further Amendment proposed—

"(2) Sub-sections 4 and 7 of Section 89 of the Local Government Act, 1894, shall apply to the existing officers affected by this Act, as if references in those sub-sections to the borough council, and all expenses incurred by the borough council in pursuance of those sub-sections shall be paid out of the general rate."—(*Mr. Solicitor-General.*)

Question proposed, "That those words be there inserted."

DISCUSSION :—

Mr. Stuart (Shoreditch, Hoxton) 707	The Solicitor-General (Sir R B. Finlay, Inverness Burghs) ... 708
Mr. John Burns (Battersea) 708	

Amendment agreed to.

Amendment proposed—

"In Schedule 1, page 18, to leave out lines 10 and 11, and insert the words, 'The area consisting of the Parliamentary Division of Whitechapel, consisting of all the areas included in the Whitechapel District Board of Works, together with the Parliamentary Division of St. George's-in-the-East (including Wapping).' "—(*Sir Samuel Montagu.*)

Question proposed—

"That the words proposed to be left out to the word 'Limehouse,' in line 11, stand part of the Bill."

DISCUSSION :—

Mr. H. S. Samuel (Tower Hamlets, Limehouse) ... 710	Mr. Lowles (Shoreditch, Haggerston) 711
Mr. Sydney Buxton (Tower Hamlets, Poplar) ... 710	Mr. Stuart (Shoreditch, Hoxton)... 712
Lord Hugh Cecil (Greenwich) 710	Mr. Herbert Robertson (Hackney, S.) 712
Mr. Steadman (Tower Hamlets, Stepney) ... 710	The Solicitor-General (Sir R. B. Finlay, Inverness Burghs) ... 713
The First Lord of the Treasury (Mr. A. J. Balfour, Manchester, E.) 711	Mr. Steadman 714

Question put.

The House divided—Ayes, 133 ; Noes, 55. (Division List, No. 181.)

Other Amendments made.

Amendment proposed—

"In Schedule 1, page 18, to leave out lines 14 and 15, and insert 'The area consisting of the parishes of St. George the Martyr, Christ Church, St. Saviour, Southwark, and Newington.' "—(*The Solicitor-General.*)

Mr. Sydney Buxton (Tower Hamlets, Poplar) ... 715	The Solicitor-General (Sir R. B. Finlay, Inverness Burghs) ... 715

Amendment agreed to.

Other Amendments made.

Mr. Stuart (Shoreditch, Hoxton) 716

June 8.]　　　　　　　　　　　　　　　　　　　　　　　　　Page

Amendment proposed—

　　"In page 18, line 30, to add, 'and including the Collegiate Church of St. Peter, Westminster, and the Liberty of the Rolls.'"—(The Solicitor-General.)

Question, "That these words be there inserted," put, and agreed to.

Mr. Stuart (Shoreditch, Hoxton) 716	The Solicitor-General (Sir R. B. Finlay, Inverness Burghs) ... 717

Other Amendments made.

Another Amendment proposed—

　　"In page 19, column 2, line 20, before the word 'subject,' to insert the words, 'subject to bye-laws and regulations made by the County Council and.'"—(Mr. James Stuart.)

Question proposed, "That those words be there inserted."

The Solicitor-General (Sir R. B. Finlay, Inverness Burghs) 717

Amendment, by leave, withdrawn.

Amendments proposed—

　　"In Schedule 2, page 19, column 2, line 23, after 's. 100,' to add, 'and s. 101'; and in Schedule 2, page 19, column 2, line 23, after 's. 100,' add, 'subject to the requirement that borough council shall send annually to county council a copy of the register.'"—(Mr. Stuart, for Captain Sinclair.)

The Solicitor-General (Sir R. B. Finlay, Inverness Burghs) 717	Mr. Stuart (Shoreditch, Hoxton)... 717

Amendment, by leave, withdrawn.

Attention called to the fact that there were not 40 Members present. House counted, and 40 Members being present, Debate resumed.

Amendment proposed—

　　"In page 20, to leave out lines 26 and 27."—(Sir John Dickson-Poynder.)

Question proposed, "That the words proposed to be left out stand part of the Bill."

DISCUSSION :—

Mr. Pickersgill (Bethnal Green, S.W.) 721	The Solicitor-General (Sir R. B. Finlay, Inverness Burghs) ... 725
Mr. Lowles (Shoreditch, Haggerston) 722	Mr. Causton (Southwark, W.) ... 726
	Colonel Hughes (Woolwich) ... 726
Mr. Stuart (Shoreditch, Hoxton) 723	Mr. John Burns (Battersea) ... 727
	Sir J. Dickson-Poynder (Wilts, Chippenham) 728

Amendment, by leave, withdrawn.

Amendments proposed—

　　"In Schedule 2, page 20, to leave out lines 26 and 27; and to leave out lines 28 to 30."—(Mr. Pickersgill.)

The First Lord of the Treasury (Mr. A. J. Balfour, Manchester, E.) 730	Col. Hughes (Woolwich)... ... 730
	Mr. Sydney Buxton (Tower Hamlets, Poplar) 730

Amendments, by leave, withdrawn.

Other Amendments made.

Bill to be read the third time upon Tuesday next

June 8.] *Page*

Finance Bill—Order read, for resuming Adjourned Debate on Amendment proposed (6th June) on consideration of the Bill, as amended :—

And which Amendment was—

"In page 2, line 27, after the word 'enumerated,' to insert the words, 'and tested.'"—(*Mr. Chancellor of the Exchequer.*)

Question again proposed, "That those words be there inserted."

Question put, and agreed to.

Other Amendments made.

Amendment proposed—

"In page 5, line 27, after the word 'form,' to insert the words 'but does not include any County Council or Municipal Corporation bills repayable not later than twelve months from their date, or any overdraft at the bank or other loan raised for a merely temporary purpose for a period not exceeding twelve months.'"—(*Mr. Chancellor of the Exchequer.*)

Question proposed, "That those words be there inserted."

Mr. J. P. Smith (*Lanark, Partick*) 731

Amendment proposed to the proposed Amendment—

"In line 2, after the word 'bills,' to insert the words 'of exchange or promissory notes.'"—(*Mr. Caldwell.*)

Question proposed, "That those words be inserted [in the proposed Amendment."

The Chancellor of the Ex-   Mr. Caldwell (*Lanark, Mid*) ... 732
chequer (Sir M. Hicks-
Beach, Bristol, W.) ... 732

Amendment to the proposed Amendment, by leave, withdrawn.

Original Question again proposed.

Amendment proposed to the proposed Amendment—

"In line 3, after the word 'raised,' to leave out the words 'for a merely temporary purpose'"—(*Sir Charles Cameron.*)

Question proposed, "That the words proposed to be left out stand part of the proposed Amendment."

The Chancellor of the Ex-   Sir Charles Cameron (*Glasgow,*
chequer (Sir M. Hicks-   *Bridgeton*) 733
Beach, Bristol, W.) ... 733

Amendment to the proposed Amendment, by leave, withdrawn.

Words inserted.

Amendment proposed—

"In page 5, line 22, after the word 'called,' to insert the words, 'But provided that the duty under this section shall be paid by a local authority only once in respect of the exercise by them of borrowing powers, and shall not be paid in respect of money reborrowed by them to replace money borrowed which may have been paid off otherwise than by means of a statutory sinking fund.'"—(*Sir Charles Cameron.*)

Question proposed, "That those words be there inserted."

The Solicitor-General (*Sir R. B. Finlay, Inverness Burghs*) 734

Question put.

The Committee divided—Ayes, 69 ; Noes, 168. (Division List, No. 182.)

Another Amendment made.

Bill to be read the third time upon Tuesday next.

Colonial Loans Fund Bill—Considered in Committee.

(In the Committee.)

Clause 1 :—

Question proposed, " That Clause 1 stand part of the Bill."

DISCUSSION :—

Mr. Caldwell (Lanark, Mid)	736	Mr. Dalziel (Kirkcaldy Burghs)...	741
Mr. Dillon (Mayo, E.) ...	737	Mr. Davitt (Mayo, S.)	742
The Chancellor of the Exchequer (Sir M. Hicks-Beach (Bristol, W.) ...	739	Mr. Bartley (Islington, N.) ...	743
		Mr. Hedderwick (Wicks Burghs).	743
		Mr. Caldwell	744
Mr. Sydney Buxton (Tower Hamlets, Poplar) ...	740	Sir John Leng (Dundee) ...	744
		Sir M. Hicks-Beach	745
Mr. Dillon...	740	Mr. Weir (Ross and Cromarty)...	745

It being Midnight, the Chairman left the Chair to make his Report to the
House 746

Committee report progress ; to sit again upon Monday next.

SUPPLY REPORT [5TH JUNE].

Message from Her Majesty (Grant to Lord Kitchener),—Resolution
reported—

" LORD KITCHENER OF KHARTOUM.

" That a sum, not exceeding £30,000, be granted to Her Majesty, to be
issued to Major-General Lord Kitchener of Khartoum, G.C.B., K.C.M.G.,
as an acknowledgment of his eminent services in planning and conducting the
recent Expedition in the Soudan."

Resolution agreed to 747

Education of Children Bill—As amended, considered ; to be read the third
time on Wednesday next 747

Seats for Shop Assistants (England and Ireland) Bill—Considered in
Committee 747

(In the Committee.)

Clause 1 :—

Sir James Fergusson (Manchester, N.E.)	747	Mr. Caldwell (Lanark, Mid.) ...	748
		Mr. Tomlinson (Preston) ...	748

Committee report progress ; to sit again To-morrow.

Experiments on Living Animals—Return presented relative thereto
[Address 8th June ; Mr. Jesse Collings] ; to lie upon the Table, and to be
printed. [No. 215.] 748

Adjourned at ten minutes after Twelve of the clock.

LORDS : FRIDAY, 9TH JUNE 1899.

PRIVATE BILL BUSINESS.

The LORD CHANCELLOR acquainted the House that the Clerk of the Parliaments
had laid upon the Table the Certificate from the Examiners that the
further Standing Orders applicable to the following Bill have been complied
with :—South-Eastern and London, Chatham, and Dover Railway Companies (New Lines). And also the Certificate that the Standing Orders
applicable to the following Bill have been complied with :—Local Government Provisional Orders (No. 3). The same were ordered to lie on the
Table 749

Cardiff Railway Bill—Committee to meet on Tuesday next... 749

Fishguard Water and Gas Bill—Report from the Select Committee, that the Committee had not proceeded with the consideration of the Bill, the opposition thereto having been withdrawn ; read, and ordered to lie on the Table : The Orders made on the 18th of April and Tuesday last discharged ; and Bill committed 749

Barry Railway Bill—Report from the Select Committee, that the Committee had not proceeded with the consideration of the Bill, the opposition thereto having been withdrawn ; read, and ordered to lie on the Table ; the Orders made on the 25th April and Tuesday last discharged ; and Bill committed 749

South Staffordshire Tramways Bill [Lords].—Report from the Committee of Selection, that the Lord Cheylesmore be proposed to the House as a member of the Select Committee on the said Bill in the place of the Earl of Bradford ; read, and agreed to 749

Wolverhampton Corporation Bill [Lords].—Report from the Committee of Selection, that the Lord Cheylesmore be proposed to the House as a member of the Select Committee on the said Bill in the place of the Earl of Bradford ; read, and agreed to 750

Lancashire and Yorkshire Railway (Various Powers) Bill—Report from the Committee of Selection, that the Lord Cheylesmore be proposed to the House as a member of the Select Committee on the said Bill in the place of the Earl of Bradford ; read, and agreed to... 750

Rhondda Urban District Council Bill—Report from the Committee of Selection, that the Lord Cheylesmore be proposed to the House as a member of the Select Committee on the said Bill in the place of the Earl of Bradford ; read, and agreed to 750

Wetherby District Water Bill—Report from the Committee of Selection, that the Lord Cheylesmore be proposed to the House as a member of the Select Committee on the said Bill in the place of the Earl of Bradford ; read, and agreed to 750

Edinburgh Corporation Bill—Report from the Committee of Selection, that the Lord Cheylesmore be proposed to the House as a member of the Select Committee on the said Bill in the place of the Earl of Bradford ; read, and agreed to 750

Shotley Bridge and Consett District Gas Bill—Reported with Amendments 750

Dublin Corporation (Markets) Bill—Read the second time, and committed ; the Committee to be proposed by the Committee of Selection 750

London, Chatham, and Dover Railway Bill—Read the second time, and committed 750

Leith Harbour and Docks Bill—Read the second time, and committed ; the Committee to be proposed by the Committee of Selection 750

Belfast Water Bill—Read the second time, and committed 751

West Gloucestershire Water Bill—Brought from the Commons ; read the first time, and referred to the Examiners 751

Woking Water and Gas Bill—Brought from the Commons ; read the first time, and referred to the Examiners 751

June 9.]   *Page*

Electric Lighting Provisional Orders (No. 14) Bill [Lords]—Order for Committee read   751

Gas and Water Orders Confirmation Bill [Lords]—Order for Committee read   751

Tramways Orders Confirmation (No. 1) Bill [Lords]—Order for Committee read   751

     The Earl of Morley   ... 751   *The Secretary of State for Scotland (Lord Balfour of Burleigh)*   752

Bills committed to a Committee of the whole House.

Tramways Order Confirmation (No. 3) Bill [Lords]—Committed: The Committee to be proposed by the Committee of Selection....   752

Metropolitan Common Scheme (Harrow Weald) Provisional Order Bill—Read the second time (according to Order), and committed to a Committee of the Whole House on Monday next   753

Electric Lighting Provisional Orders (No. 1) Bill [Lords]—House in Committee (according to Order): Bill reported without Amendment: Standing Committee negatived; and Bill to be read the third time on Monday next   753

Electric Lighting Provisional Orders (No. 4) Bill—House in Committee (according to Order): Bill reported without Amendment: Standing Committee negatived; and Bill to be read the third time on Monday next   ...   753

Electric Lighting Provisional Orders (No. 9) Bill [Lords]—House in Committee (according to Order): Bill reported without Amendment: Standing Committee negatived; and Bill to be read the third time on Monday next   753

Electric Lighting Provisional Orders (No. 10) Bill [Lords]—House in Committee (according to Order): Amendments made: Standing Committee negatived; the Report of Amendments to be received on Monday next   ...   753

Electric Lighting Provisional Orders (No. 11) Bill [Lords]—House in Committee (according to Order): Bill reported without Amendment: Standing Committee negatived; and Bill to be read the third time on Monday next   753

RETURNS, REPORTS, ETC.

Wages of Domestic Servants (Board of Trade, Labour Department)—Report on the money wages for indoor domestic servants: Presented (by Command), and ordered to lie on the Table   753

Arundel Port—Account and Report for 1898-99: Delivered (pursuant to Act), and ordered to lie on the Table   753

PETITIONS.

Vaccination Acts—Petition for repeal of compulsory clauses in; of Guardians of the Poplar Union; read, and ordered to lie on the Table   754

Vaccination Act, 1898—Petition for repeal; of Guardians of the Bridport Union; read, and ordered to lie on the Table.   754

X**Parish Councillors (Tenure of Office) Bill**—Returned from the Commons with the Amendment agreed to   754

June 9.] *Page*

Trawlers' Certificates Suspension Bill—Report from the Select Committee (with proceedings of the Committee) made, and to be printed. (No. 109.) Bill reported with Amendments, and committed to a Committee of the whole House on Monday next; and to be printed as amended. (No. 110.) 754

Summary Jurisdiction Act (1879) Amendment Bill—To be read the second time on Monday the 26th instant.—(*The Lord Penrhyn.*) 754

Lincolnshire Coroners Bill [Lords]—Read the third time (according to Order), and passed, and sent to the Commons 754

Farnley Tyas Marriages Bill—Read the third time (according to Order), and passed 754

House adjourned at forty minutes after Four of the clock, to Monday next, at forty-five minutes after Ten of the clock.

COMMONS: 9TH JUNE 1899.

PRIVATE BILL BUSINESS.

PRIVATE BILLS [Lords]—(STANDING ORDERS NOT PREVIOUSLY INQUIRED INTO COMPLIED WITH)—Mr. SPEAKER laid upon the Table Report from one of the Examiners of Petitions for Private Bills, That, in the case of the following Bills, originating in the Lords, and referred on the First Reading thereof, the Standing Orders not previously inquired into, and which are applicable thereto, have been complied with, viz.:—Cobham Gas Bill [Lords]; Moss Side Urban District Council (Tramways) Bill [Lords]; Stretford Urban District Council (Tramways) Bill [Lords]; Weston-super-Mare, Clevedon, and Portishead Tramways Company (Light Railway Extensions) Bill [Lords]; Whitehaven Corporation Bill [Lords]; Withington Urban District Councils (Tramways) Bill [Lords]—Ordered, That the Bills be read a second time 755

PRIVATE BILLS [Lords]—(NO STANDING ORDERS NOT PREVIOUSLY INQUIRED INTO APPLICABLE)—Mr. SPEAKER laid upon the Table Report from one of the Examiners of Petitions for Private Bills, That, in the case of the following Bill, originating in the Lords, and referred on the First Reading thereof, no Standing Orders not previously inquired into are applicable, viz.:—Grosvenor Chapel (London) Bill [Lords]—Ordered, That the Bill be read a second time... 755

PROVISIONAL ORDER BILLS—(STANDING ORDERS APPLICABLE THERETO COMPLIED WITH)—Mr. SPEAKER laid upon the Table Report from one of the Examiners of Petitions for Private Bills, That, in the case of the following Bill, referred on the First Reading thereof, the Standing Orders which are applicable thereto have been complied with, viz.:—Local Government (Ireland) Provisional Orders (Housing of Working Classes) (No. 2) Bill—Ordered, That the Bill be read a second time upon Monday next 755

PROVISIONAL ORDER BILLS—(NO STANDING ORDERS APPLICABLE)—Mr. SPEAKER laid upon the Table Report from one of the Examiners of Petitions for Private Bills, That, in the case of the following Bill, referred on the First Reading thereof, no Standing Orders are applicable, viz.:—Local Government (Ireland) Provisional Order (No. 4) Bill—Ordered, That the Bill be read a second time upon Monday next 756

PRIVATE BILLS—PETITION FOR ADDITIONAL PROVISION—(STANDING ORDERS NOT COMPLIED WITH)—Mr. SPEAKER laid upon the Table Report from one of the Examiners of Petitions for Private Bills, That, in the case of the Petition for additional Provision in the following Bill, the Standing Orders have not been complied with, viz. :—Bradford Tramways and Improvement Bill—Ordered, That the Report be referred to the Select Committee on Standing Orders   756

Crowborough District Water Bill—Lords' Amendments considered, and agreed to   756

Brompton and Piccadilly Circus Railway Bill—As amended, considered ; to be read the third time   756

Jones's Divorce Bill [Lords]—Read a second time, and committed...   ...   756

Loughborough Corporation Bill [Lords]—Read a second time, and committed   756

Housing of the Working Classes Provisional Order (Borrowstounness) Bill—Reported, without Amendment [Provisional Order confirmed]. Report to lie upon the Table. Bill to be read the third time upon Monday next   756

Local Government (Ireland) Provisional Order (No. 1) Bill—Reported, without Amendment [Provisional Order confirmed]. Report to lie upon the Table. Bill to be read the third time upon Monday next   757

Local Government Provisional Orders (Housing of Working Classes) Bill—Reported, without Amendment [Provisional Orders confirmed] ; Report to lie upon the Table. Bill to be read the third time upon Monday next   757

Local Government Provisional Orders (Poor Law) Bill—Reported. without Amendment [Provisional Order confirmed] ; Report to lie upon the Table. Bill to be read the third time upon Monday next   757

Local Government Provisional Orders (No. 5) Bill—Reported, without Amendment [Provisional Orders confirmed] ; Report to lie upon the Table. Bill to be read the third time upon Monday next   757

Local Government Provisional Orders (No. 8) Bill—Reported, with Amendments [Provisional Orders confirmed] ; Report to lie upon the Table. Bill, as amended, to be considered upon Monday next   757

Pier and Harbours Provisional Orders (No. 1) Bill—Reported with Amendments (Provisional Orders confirmed) ; Report to lie upon the Table. Bill, as amended, to be considered upon Monday next   757

London County Council (Money) Bill—Reported, with Amendments ; Report to lie upon the Table   757

Hastings and St. Leonards Gas Bill [Lords]—Reported, with Amendments ; Reports to lie upon the Table, and to be printed   757

Derby Corporation Tramways, &c., Bill—Reported, with Amendments ; Reports to lie upon the Table, and to be printed   758

Skipton Urban District Gas Bill [Lords]—Reported, with Amendments ; Reports to lie upon the Table, and to be printed   758

Lowestoft Promenade Pier Bill—Reported, with Amendments ; Reports to lie upon the Table, and to be printed   758

London Hospital Bill [Lords]—Reported, without Amendments; Report to lie upon the Table. Bill to be read a third time   758

Stockton and Middlesbrough Water Bill [Lords]—Reported, without Amendment; Report to lie upon the Table, and to be printed. Bill to be read the third time   758

Friends' Provident Institution Bill [Lords]—Reported, with an Amendment; Report to lie upon the Table   758

Infant Orphan Asylum Bill [Lords]—Reported, without Amendment; Report to lie upon the Table. Bill to be read the third time   758

Aberdeen Corporation Bill [Lords]—Reported, with Amendments; Report to lie upon the Table, and to be printed   758

Mid-Kent Gas Bill [Lords]—Reported with Amendments; Report to lie upon the Table, and to be printed.   758

Walker and Wallsend Union Gas (Electric Lighting) Bill.—Reported, with Amendments; Report to lie upon the Table, and to be printed ...   758

Electric Lighting Provisional Orders (No. 7) Bill.—Reported, without Amendment; Report to lie upon the Table. Bill to be read the third time upon Monday next   758

PRIVATE BILLS (GROUP B.)—Sir John Brunner reported from the Committee on Group B of Private Bills, "That for the convenience of parties, the Committee had adjourned till Wednesday next, at half-past Eleven of the clock." Report to lie upon the Table   759

Great Southern and Western and Waterford, Limerick, and Western Railway Companies Amalgamation and other Bills.—Ordered, "That the parties appearing before the Select Committee on the Great Southern and Western and Waterford, Limerick and Western Railway Companies Amalgamation and other Bills have leave to print the Minutes of the evidence taken before the Committee day by day from the clerk's copy, if they think fit."—(*Sir Robert Penrose Fitzgerald.*)   759

MESSAGE FROM THE LORDS.—That they have agreed to. Amendment to—Hull, Barnsley, and West Riding Junction Railway and Dock Bill [Lords] Amendments to—Cambridge University and Town Gas Bill [Lords].—St. Albans Gas Bill [Lords]—Without Amendment   759

That they have passed a Bill, intituled, " An Act to authorise the Great Grimsby Street Tramways Company to extend their tramways; and for other purposes."—[Great Grimsby Street Tramways Bill [Lords]   759

Great Grimsby Street Tramways Bill [Lords].—Read the first time; and referred to the Examiners of Petitions for Private Bills   759

PETITIONS.

BOROUGH FUNDS ACT, 1872.—Petition from Denholme, for alteration of law; to lie upon the Table.   759

GROUND RENTS (TAXATION BY LOCAL AUTHORITIES.)—Petition from Rochdale, in favour; to lie upon the Table   759

Local Government (Scotland) Act Amendment (1894) Bill—Petition from Paisley, in favour; to lie upon the Table   760

Local Government (Scotland) Act (1894) Amendment (No. 2) Bill—Petition from Paisley, against; to lie upon the Table   760

June 9.]   *Page*

Local Government (Scotland) Bill—Petition from Aberdeen, for alteration ; to lie upon the Table   760

Mines Eight Hours Bill—Petition in favour ; from Cymmer, and Llanbradach ; to lie upon the Table   760

PARLIAMENTARY FRANCHISE—Petition from Greenwich, for extension to women ; to lie upon the Table   760

Private Legislation Procedure (Scotland) Bill—Petition from Aberdeen, in favour ; to lie upon the Table   760

Public Health Acts Amendment Bill—Petition from Congleton, in favour ; to lie upon the Table   760

ROMAN CATHOLIC UNIVERSITY IN IRELAND—Petition from Paisley, against establishment ; to lie upon the Table   760

Sale of Food and Drugs Bill—Petitions for alteration ;—from Leith, and Aberdeen ; to lie upon the Table   760

Sea Fisheries Regulation (Scotland) Act (1895) Amendment Bill—Petition from Aberdeen, against ; to lie upon the Table   760

Small Tenants (Scotland) Bill—Petition from Aberdeen, in favour ; to lie upon the Table   760

Town Council (Scotland) Bill—Petitions in favour ;—from Newburgh, and Nairn ; to lie upon the Table...   760

TUBERCULOSIS (RECOMMENDATIONS OF ROYAL COMMISSION)—Petition from Edinburgh, for legislation ; to lie upon the Table   760

VACCINATION ACTS, 1867 TO 1898—Petition from Reading, for alteration of law ; to lie upon the Table   761

RETURNS, REPORTS, ETC.

BOARD OF TRADE (LABOUR DEPARTMENT) (WAGES OF DOMESTIC SERVANTS) Copy presented,—of Report on the Money Wages of Indoor Domestic Servants [by Command] ; to lie upon the Table   761

PUBLIC WORKS LOAN BOARD—Copy presented,—of Twenty-Fourth Annual Report (for 1898-9), with Appendices [by Act] ; to lie upon the Table, and to be printed. [No. 216]   761

TREATY SERIES (No. 14, 1899).—Copy presented,—of Withdrawal of Montenegro from the International Union for the Protection of Literary and Artistic Works [by Command] ; to lie upon the Table   761

Paper laid upon the Table by the Clerk of the House :—

     1. Arundel Port,—Copy of the Annual Report and General Account of the Commissioners of Arundel Port for period from 25th March, 1898, to 25th March, 1899 [by Act]   761

     2. Public Records (Court of Exchequer),—Copy of Second Schedule containing a List and Particulars of Classes of Documents, which formerly were or ought to have been in the Office of the King's or Queen's Remembrancer of the Exchequer, or of the Clerk appointed to take charge of the Port Bonds or Coast Bonds, and which are now in, but are not considered of sufficient public value to justify their preservation in the Public Record Office   761

June 9.]   *Page*

LOCAL AUTHORITIES (ENGLAND, WALES, AND IRELAND) TECHNICAL EDUCA-
TION—Return ordered, "showing the extent to which, and the manner in
which, Local Authorities in England, Wales, and Ireland have applied or
are applying funds to the purposes of Technical Education (including
Science, Art, Technical, and Manual Instruction) during the years 1897-8
and 1898-9, under the following Acts: Local Taxation (Customs and
Excise) Act, 1890; Technical Instruction Act, 1889 and 1891; Welsh
Intermediate Education Act, 1889; and Public Libraries and Museums
Act."—(*Sir John Gorst.*) **761**

METROPOLITAN WATER COMPANIES (ACCOUNTS).—Return ordered, "of the
Accounts, as they are respectively made up, of the Metropolitan Water
Companies and the Staines Reservoirs Joint Committee to the 30th day
of September and the 31st day of December, 1898 (in continuation of
Parliamentary Paper, No 346, of Session 1898.)"—(*Mr. T. W. Russell.*) ...   **762**

PRIVATE LEGISLATION PROCEDURE (SCOTLAND) (EXPENSES).—Committee to
consider of authorising the payment, out of moneys to be provided by
Parliament, of any remuneration, allowances, and expenses that may
become payable under any Act of the present session to provide for
improving and extending the Procedure for obtaining Parliamentary
Powers by way of Provisional Orders in matters relating to Scotland
(Queen's Recommendat on signified), upon Monday next.—(*Sir William
Walrond.*)   ...   .¡. **762**

NEW WRIT.

NEW WRIT FOR EDINBURGH (SOUTH DIVISION)—In the room of Robert
Cox, esquire, deceased.—(*Sir William Walrond*) **762**

QUESTIONS.

FOREIGN SERVICE MESSENGERS—Question, Sir Charles Dilke (Gloucestershire,
Forest of Dean); Answer, The Under Secretary of State for Foreign
Affairs (Mr. Brodrick, Surrey, Guildford) **762**

THE MOST FAVOURED NATION CLAUSE IN TREATIES WITH THE UNITED
STATES—Question, Colonel Milward (Stratford-upon-Avon); Answer,
The Under Secretary of State for Foreign Affairs (Mr. St. John Brodrick,
Surrey, Guildford) **763**

FOREIGN SUGAR BOUNTIES—Question, Sir Howard Vincent (Sheffield, Central);
Answer, The Under Secretary of State for Foreign Affairs (Mr. St. John
Brodrick, Surrey, Guildford) **763**

THE ARMENIAN MASSACRES—Question, Colonel Denny (Kilmarnock Burghs);
Answer, The Under Secretary of State for Foreign Affairs (Mr. St. John
Brodrick, Surrey, Guildford)...   ...   .   **763**

IRELAND LOAN FUND BOARD—Questions, Mr. James O'Connor (Wicklow,
W.) and Mr. Doogan (Tyrone, E.); Answer, The Chief Secretary for
Ireland (Mr. G. W. Balfour, Leeds, Central) **764**

IRISH SALMON FISHERIES—Question, Mr. Seton-Karr (St. Helens); Answer,
The Chief Secretary for Ireland (Mr. G. W. Balfour, Leeds, Central)   ...   **765**

PAY OF IRISH RESIDENT MAGISTRATES—Questions, Mr. McCartan (Down, S.),
Mr. Davitt (Mayo, E.), and Mr. William Johnston (Belfast, S.); Answer,
The Chief Secretary for Ireland (Mr. G. W. Balfour, Leeds, Central)   ...   **767**

IRISH LAND VALUATIONS—Question, Captain Donelan (Cork, E.); Answer, The
Chief Secretary for Ireland (Mr. G. W. Balfour, Leeds, Central)...   ...   **768**

June 9.] *Page*

NEW RATING SYSTEM IN IRELAND—Question, Mr. Tully (Leitrim, S.);
Answer, The Chief Secretary for Ireland (Mr. G. W. Balfour, Leeds,
Central) 768

PRISON APPOINTMENTS—Question, Mr. Graham (St. Pancras, W.); Answer,
The Secretary of State for the Home Department (Sir M. White Ridley,
Lancashire, Blackpool) 769

FATAL ACCIDENT TO A DOCK LABOURER AT GARSTON—Question, Mr. M'Gee
(Louth, S.); Answer, The Secretary of State for the Home Department
(Sir M. White Ridley, Lancashire, Blackpool) 769

THE PETROLEUM BILL—Question, Mr. Tully (Leitrim, S.); Answer, The
Secretary of State for the Home Department (Sir M. White Ridley, Lancashire, Blackpool) 770

EMOLUMENTS OF LIGHTHOUSE KEEPERS—Question, Mr. Nicol (Argyll); Answer, The President of the Board of Trade (Mr. C. T. Ritchie, Croydon)... 770

YOUGHAL RIFLE RANGE—Question, Captain Donelan (Cork, E.); Answer, The
Under Secretary of State for War (Mr. George Wyndham, Dover) ... 771

LADYSMITH BARRACKS—Question. Mr. Buchanan (Aberdeenshire, E.);
Answer, The Under Secretary of State for War (Mr. George Wyndham,
Dover 771

PRESBYTERIAN SERVICES FOR TROOPS IN INDIA—Question, Mr. Hedderwick
(Wicks Burgh); Answer, The Secretary for India (Lord George Hamilton,
Middlesex, Ealing) 772

PENSIONS TO SCOTTISH SCHOOL TEACHERS—Question, Mr. Buchanan (Aberdeenshire, E.); Answer, The Lord Advocate (Mr. A. G. Murray, Buteshire) 772

MOUNTJOY POSTAL ARRANGEMENTS—Question, Mr. Doogan (Tyrone, E.);
Answer, The Financial Secretary to the Treasury (Mr. Hanbury,
Preston) 773

LURGAN POST OFFICE—Question, Mr. McGhee (Louth, S.) Answer, The Financial Secretary to the Treasury (Mr. Hanbury, Preston) 774

POSTMAN'S PAY—Question, Mr. Giles (Cambridge, Wisbech); Answer, The
Financial Secretary to the Treasury (Mr. Hanbury, Preston) 774

DUBLIN TELEGRAPHISTS' HOURS OF DUTY—Mr. Davitt (Mayo, S.); Answer,
The Financial Secretary to the Treasury (Mr. Hanbury, Preston) ... 775

ADULTERATED TEA—Question, Mr. Carew (Dublin, College Green); Answer,
The Financial Secretary to the Treasury (Mr. Hanbury, Preston) ... 775

LICENCES FOR TRADESMEN'S CARTS AND VANS—Question, Mr. Giles (Cambridge, Wisbech); Answer, The Financial Secretary to the Treasury (Mr.
Hanbury, Preston) 776

THE CHINA SQUADRON—Question, Mr. Hedderwick (Wicks Burghs); Answer,
The First Lord of the Admiralty (Mr. G. T. Goschen, St. George's, Hanover Square) 776

Colonial Loans Fund Bill—Statement, The First Lord of the Treasury
(Mr. A. J. Balfour, Manchester, E.) Question, Mr. Dillon (Mayo, E.);
Answer, The First Lord of the Treasury (Mr. A. J. Balfour, Manchester,
E.) 777

PUBLIC BUSINESS.

SUPPLY [13TH ALLOTTED DAY].

(In the Committee.)

CIVIL SERVICES AND REVENUE DEPARTMENTS ESTIMATES, 1899-1890.

CLASS II.

Motion made, and Question proposed—

"That a sum, not exceeding £49,482, be granted to Her Majesty, to complete the sum necessary to defray the charge which will come in course of payment during the year ending on the 31st day of March, 1900, for the salaries and expenses of the Department of Her Majesty's Secretary of State for Foreign Affairs."

DISCUSSION :—

Sir Charles Dilke (Gloucester, Forest of Dean) 778

The Under Secretary of State for Foreign Affairs (Mr. Brodrick, Surrey, Guildford) 77

Motion made, and Question proposed—

"That Item A (Salaries) be reduced by £100, in respect of the salary of the Secretary of State."—(*Sir Charles Dilke.*)

DISCUSSION :—

Lord Charles Beresford (York) 784

The Secretary of State for the Colonies (Mr. J. Chamberlain, Birmingham, W.) ... 787

Lord Charles Beresford ... 787

The First Lord of the Admiralty (Mr. Goschen, St. George's, Hanover Square) 788

Lord Charles Beresford ... 788

Under Secretary of State for Foreign Affairs (Mr. Brodrick, Surrey, Guildford) ... 792

Lord Charles Beresford ... 792

Mr. Brodrick 800

Mr. Hedderwick (Wick Burghs) 813

Mr. Brodrick 814

Sir E. Grey (Northumberland, Berwick) ... 814

Sir E. Sassoon (Hythe) ... 824

Mr. Joseph Walton (York, W. R., Barnsley) ... 828

Mr. Bill (Staffordshire, Leek) ... 839

Mr. Macdona (Southwark, Rotherhithe) 840

Mr. Moon (St. Pancras, N.) ... 842

Mr. Harwood (Bolton) 843

Earl Percy (Kensington, S.) ... 845

Mr. Provand (Glasgow, Blackfriars) 853

Mr. Yerburgh (Chester) 859

Mr. Brodrick 859

Mr. Yerburgh 860

The Chancellor of the Exchequer (Sir M. Hicks-Beach, Bristol, W.) 864

Mr. Labouchere (Northampton) ... 865

Mr. Keswick (Surrey, Epsom) ... 867

Mr. Barlow (Somerset, Frome) ... 868

Mr. MacIvor (Liverpool, Kirkdale) 872

Mr. J. A. Pease (Northumberland) 872

It being Midnight, the Chairman left the Chair to make his Report to the House.

The Committee report progress ; to sit again upon Monday next.

Seats and Shop Assistants (England and Ireland) Bill—Considered in Committee, and reported, without Amendment ; Bill read the third time, and passed 876

Adjourned at five minutes after Twelve of the clock.

LORDS: MONDAY, 12TH JUNE 1899.

PRIVATE BILL BUSINESS.

The LORD CHANCELLOR acquainted the House that the Clerk of the Parliaments had laid upon the Table the Certificates from the Examiners, that the further Standing Orders applicable to the following Bills have been complied with : Belfast and Northern Counties Railway ; Bootle Corporation. The same were ordered to lie on the Table 877

STANDING ORDERS COMMITTEE—Report from, That the Standing Orders not complied with in respect of the Baker Street and Waterloo Railway Bill ought to be dispensed with and the Bill allowed to proceed, provided the names of the Great Central Railway Company and of the Waterloo and City Railway Company be struck out 877

That the Standing Orders not complied with in respect of the Belfast Corporation Bill ought to be dispensed with and the Bill allowed to proceed, provided Clause 23 be struck out 877

Read, and agreed to.

Stockport Corporation Water Bill—A witness ordered to attend the Select Committee 877

Caledonian Railway (General Powers) Bill [Lords]—The Queen's consent signified ; and Bill reported, with Amendments 877

Aberdeen Joint Passenger Station Bill [Lords]—Reported, with Amendments 877

North Pembrokeshire and Fishguard Railway Bill—Reported, without Amendments 877

North-West London Railway Bill—The Queen's consent signified ; and Bill reported, with Amendments 878

Lancashire and Yorkshire Railway (Various Powers) Bill—Report from the Select Committee, That the Committee had not proceeded with the consideration of the Bill, the opposition thereto having been withdrawn ; read, and ordered to lie on the Table : the Orders made on the 25th of April and Tuesday last discharged ; and Bill committed 878

Wetherby District Water Bill—Report from the Select Committee, That the Committee had not proceeded with the consideration of the Bill, the opposition thereto having been withdrawn ; read, and ordered to lie on the Table ; the Orders made on the 25th of April and Tuesday last discharged ; and Bill committed 878

West Highland Railway Bill [Lords]—Commons Amendments considered, and agreed to 878

Transvaal Mortgage Loan and Finance Company Bill [Lords]—Read the third time, and passed, and sent to the Commons 878

Crowborough District Water Bill—Returned from the Commons with the Amendments agreed to 878

Electric Lighting Provisional Orders (No. 14) Bill [Lords] ; **Gas Orders Confirmation (No. 1) Bill** [Lords]; **Gas and Water Orders Confirmation Bill** [Lords] ; **Water Orders Confirmation Bill** [Lords]—House to be in Committee To-morrow 878

Metropolitan Common Scheme (Harrow Weald) Provisional Order Bill—House in Committee (according to Order) ; Bill reported, without Amendment ; Standing Committee negatived ; and Bill to be read the third time To-morrow   879

Electric Lighting Provisional Orders (No. 1) Bill [Lords]—Read the third time (according to Order), and passed   879

Electric Lighting Provisional Orders (No. 4) Bill—Read the third time (according to Order), and passed   879

Electric Lighting Provisional Orders (No. 9) Bill [Lords] ; **Electric Lighting Provisional Orders (No. 11) Bill** [Lords]—Read the third time (according to Order), and passed, and sent to the Commons   ...   879

Electric Lighting Provisional Orders (No. 10) Bill [Lords]—Amendments reported (according to Order), and Bill to be read the third time To-morrow   879

Report from the Committee of Selection, that the following Lords be proposed to the House to form the Select Committee for the consideration of the said Bills; viz.—D. Bedford (Chairman), D. Marlborough, E. Dartmouth, E. Windsor, L. Bolton :—Electric Lighting Provisional Orders (No. 3) Bill ; Central Electric Supply Bill ; Central London Railway Bill ; Charing Cross, Euston, and Hampstead Railway Bill ; Kensington and Notting Hill Electric Lighting Bill ; Midland Railway Bill ; Gas Light and Coke Company Bill ; London, Brighton, and South Coast Railway (Various Powers) Bill. Agreed to ; and the said Lords appointed accordingly : The Committee to meet on Thursday, the 22nd instant, at Eleven o'clock ; and petitions referred to the Committee, with leave to the petitioners praying to be heard by counsel against the Bills to be heard as desired, as also counsel for the Bills   879

RETURNS, REPORTS, &c.

TREATY SERIES: No. 14 (1899)—Withdrawal of Montenegro from the International Union for the protection of Literary and Artistic Works...   ...   880

DISEASES OF ANIMALS ACT, 1894—Returns as regards Ireland for the year ended 31st December, 1898   880

ELECTRIC LIGHTING ACTS, 1882 AND 1888—Special Reports by the Board of Trade under Section 1 of the Electric Lighting Act, 1888 : I. City of London Electric Lighting ; II. Gateshead Electric Lighting. Presented (by Command), and ordered to lie on the Table   880

PUBLIC RECORDS (COURT OF EXCHEQUER)—Second Schedule of classes of documents which formerly were, or ought to have been, in the Office of the King's or Queen's Remembrancer, of the Exchequer, or the Clerk appointed to take charge of the Port Bonds or Coast Bonds, and which are now in, but are not considered of sufficient public value to justify their preservation in, the Public Record Office   880

PUBLIC WORKS LOAN BOARD—Twenty-fourth Annual Report for 1898-99, with Appendices. Laid before House (pursuant to Act) and ordered to lie on the Table   880

QUESTION.

IRELAND—INCITEMENT TO CRIME—M'HALE *v.* SULLIVAN—Question, The Lord Coleridge ; Answers, The Lord Chancellor, and The Earl of Arran ...   880

Reformatory Schools (Amendment) Bill [Lords]—Committee.

    Clause 1:—

        Lord James of Hereford   ...   888   *Lord Leigh*   888

    Bill reported, without Amendment; and re-committed to the Standing Committee.

Isolation Hospitals (Amendment) Bill [Lords]—House to be in Committee on Thursday, the 22nd instant   888

Trawlers' Certificates Suspension Bill [Lords]—House in Committee (according to Order): The Amendments proposed by the Select Committee made; Standing Committee negatived; The Report of Amendments to be received on Friday next   888

Manchester Canonries Bill [Lords]—A Bill to amend Section 20 of the Parish of Manchester Division Act, 1850—Was presented by the Earl Egerton (for the Lord Bishop of Manchester): read the first time; to be printed; and to be read the second time on Thursday, the 22nd instant. (No. 111.)   888

Youthful Offenders Bill [Lords]—A Bill to amend the law relating to youthful offenders, and for other purposes connected therewith, was presented by the Lord James; read the first time; to be printed; and to be read the second time on Monday next. (No. 112.)   889

Seats for Shop Assistants (England and Ireland) Bill—Brought from the Commons; read the first time; and to be printed. (No. 113.)   ...   889

        House adjourned at five minutes past Five of the clock.

COMMONS: MONDAY, 12th JUNE, 1899.

PRIVATE BILL BUSINESS.

PRIVATE BILLS (STANDING ORDER 62 COMPLIED WITH)—Mr. SPEAKER laid upon the Table Report from one of the Examiners of Petitions for Private Bills, That in the case of the following Bill, referred on the First Reading thereof, Standing Order No. 62 has been complied with, namely :—Millwall Dock Bill. Ordered, That the Bill be read a second time...   889

PRIVATE BILLS [Lords] (STANDING ORDERS NOT PREVIOUSLY INQUIRED INTO COMPLIED WITH)—Mr. SEPAKER laid upon the Table Report from one of the Examiners of Petitions for Private Bills, That in the case of the following Bills, originating in the Lords, and referred on the First Reading thereof, the Standing Orders not previously inquired into, and which are applicable thereto, have been complied with, viz. :—All Saints' Church (Cardiff) Bill [Lords]; Lowestoft Water and Gas Bill [Lords]. Ordered, That the Bills be read a second time   889

Birkenhead Corporation Bill [Lords]—Read the third time, and passed, with Amendments. [New Title.]   889

City and Brixton Railway Bill—Read the third time, and passed   890

Dumbarton Burgh Bill [Lords]—Read the third time, and passed, with Amendments   890

London Improvements Bill (Queen's Consent signified); Sheffield Corporation Markets Bill; Stockport Corporation Bill—Read the third time, and passed   890

June 12.]   *Page*

Blackpool Improvement Bill—As amended, considered ; to be read the third time   890

Dublin Corporation Bill—As amended, to be considered To-morrow   ...   890

Great Northern Railway Bill [Lords]; **Sunderland Corporation Bill** [Lords]—Read a second time, and committed   890

Electric Lighting Provisional Orders (No. 7) Bill; Housing of the Working Classes Provisional Order (Borrowstounness) Bill; Local Government (Ireland) Provisional Order (No. 1 Bill); Local Government Provisional Order (Housing of Working Classes) Bill; Local Government Provisional Orders (No. 5) Bill; Local Government Provisional Orders (Poor Law) Bill. Read the third time, and passed   890

Local Government Provisional Orders (No. 8) Bill; Pier and Harbour Provisional Orders (No. 1) Bill.—As amended, considered ; to be read the third time To-morrow   890

Local Government (Ireland) Provisional Orders (Housing of Working Classes) (No. 2) Bill.—Local Government (Ireland) **Provisional Order (No. 4) Bill.**—Read a second time, and committed   890

Electric Lighting Provisional Order (No. 20) Bill.—To confirm a Provisional Order made by the Board of Trade, under the Electric Lighting Acts, 1882 and 1888, relating to the City of London, ordered to be brought in by Mr. Ritchie and Mr. Hanbury. Ordered, that Standing Order 193A be suspended, and that the Bill be now read the first time.—(*Mr. Ritchie*)...   891

Electric Lighting Provisional Order (No. 20) Bill.—To confirm a Provisional Order made by the Board of Trade, under the Electric Lighting Acts, 1882 and 1888, relating to the City of London, presented accordingly, and read the first time ; to be referred to the Examiners of Petitions for Private Bills, and to be printed. (Bill 230.)   891

Mersey Docks and Harbour Board (Pilotage) Bill (Lords)—Report (8th June) from the Select Committee on Standing Orders read. Ordered, that the Bill be read a second time.—(*Dr. Farquharson.*)   891

PETITIONS.

GROUND RENTS (TAXATION BY LOCAL AUTHORITIES)—Petitions in favour ;— From Wakefield, and Ealing, to lie upon the Table   891

Local Government (Scotland) Act (1894) Amendment Bill.—Petition from Elgin, in favour ; to lie upon the Table   891

Mines (Eight Hours) Bill—Petition from Kilburn, in favour ; to lie upon the Table   891

Parish Councils Association (Scotland) Bill—Petition from Greenock, in favour ; to lie upon the Table...   891

Poor Law Officers' Superannuation (Scotland) Bill—Petition from Greenock, against ; to lie upon the Table   891

POOR LAW RELIEF (DISFRANCHISEMENT)—Petition from Reading, for alteration of Law ; to lie upon the Table   891

POOR LAW (SCOTLAND) ACTS—Petition from Greenock, for alteration of Law ; to lie upon the Table...   892

June 12.] *Page*

Private Legislation Procedure (Scotland) Bill—Petitions in favour; From Elgin, Forfar, Kirkcudbright, and Perth; to lie upon the Table ... 892

Sale of Intoxicating Liquors on Sunday Bill—Petitions in favour; From Manchester, Rochester, and Newcastle; to lie upon the Table ... 892

SALE OF INTOXICATING LIQUORS TO CHILDREN—Petition from Brierfield, for alteration of Law; to lie upon the Table 892

Sea Fisheries Regulation (Scotland) Act (1895) Amendment Bill— Petition from Aberdeen, against; to lie upon the Table 892

Town Councils (Scotland) Bill—Petition from Aberdeen, against; to lie upon the Table 892

Trout Fishing Annual Close Time (Scotland) Bill—Petition from Forfar, in favour; to lie upon the Table 892

VACCINATION ACTS, 1867 TO 1898—Petition from Daventry, for alteration of Law; to lie upon the Table 892

RETURNS, REPORTS, &c.

ELECTRIC LIGHTING ACTS, 1882 AND 1888 — Copies presented,—of Special Reports by the Board of Trade under Section 1 of The Electric Lighting Act, 1888 :—(1) City of London Electric Lighting; (2) Gateshead Electric Lighting; [by Command]; to lie upon the Table 892

DISEASES OF ANIMALS ACTS, 1894 AND 1896 (IRELAND)—Copy presented,— of Return, in pursuance of the Acts as regards Ireland for the year 1898 [by Command]; to lie upon the Table 892

CHANNEL ISLANDS (CROWN RIGHTS)—Return ordered, "of Revenues drawn from the Crown Rights in the Channel Islands in each year during the last five years, distinguishing for each Island separately the Amount received from Tithes, from Fines on Transfer of Property, from Seigneurial Dues, and from other sources; and stating the Cost of Collection, the several Payments made for Local Purposes, and the Net Amount paid into the Exchequer."—(*Sir Charles Dilke.*) 893

MESSAGE FROM THE LORDS—That they have agreed to—Farnley Tyas Marriages Bill, without Amendment. That they have passed a Bill, intituled, "An Act to constitute the Divisions of Lincolnshire separate Counties for all the purposes of the Coroners Acts." [Lincolnshire Coroners Bill [Lords.] 893

QUESTIONS.

TRADE IN THE RUSSIAN EMPIRE—Question, Sir Howard Vincent (Sheffield, Central); Answer, The Under Secretary of State for Foreign Affairs (Mr. Brodrick, Surrey, Guildford) 893

THE DISTRESSED ARMENIANS—Question, Mr. Samuel Smith (Flintshire); Answer, The Under Secretary of State for Foreign Affairs (Mr. Brodrick, Surrey, Guildford) 894

CRIMPING IN THE UNITED STATES—Question, Colonel Denny (Kilmarnock Burghs); Answer, The Under Secretary of State for Foreign Affairs (Mr. Brodrick, Surrey, Guildford)... 894

NAVIGATION OF MERCHANT VESSELS—Question, Mr. Havelock Wilson (Middlesbrough); Answer, The President of the Board of Trade (Mr. Ritchie, Croydon) 895

SCOTTISH UNIVERSITIES—Question, Mr. Crombie (Kincardineshire); Answer,
The Lord Advocate (Mr. A. G. Murray, Buteshire)   896

ORPHAN HOMES OF SCOTLAND—Question, Sir Charles Cameron (Glasgow,
Bridgeton); Answer, The Lord Advocate (Mr. A. G. Murray, Buteshire)   896

ATTACK BY BRITISH SOLDIERS ON A RANGOON WOMAN—Question, Mr.
Davitt (Mayo, S.); Answer, The Secretary of State for India (Lord
George Hamilton, Middlesex, Ealing)   896

ASSAM TEA PLANTATIONS—Question, Mr. Schwann (Manchester, N.); Answer,
The Secretary of State for India (Lord George Hamilton, Middlesex,
Ealing)...   897

LIQUOR TRADE IN THE MADRAS PRESIDENCY—Question, Mr. Samuel Smith
(Flintshire); Answer, The Secretary of State for India (Lord George
Hamilton, Middlesex, Ealing)   897

DIVINE SERVICE IN GOVERNMENT FACTORY CHAPELS—Question, Mr. Channing
(Northampton, E.), and Mr. Carvell Williams (Notts., Mansfield); Answer,
The Under Secretary of State for War (Mr. Wyndham, Dover)   898

TROOPS AT ALDERSHOT—Question, Major Rasch (Essex, S.E.); Answer, The
Under Secretary of State for War (Mr. Wyndham, Dover)   899

SCHOOL ACCOMMODATION AT BETHNAL GREEN—Question, Mr. J. G. Talbot
(Oxford University); Answer, The Vice-President of the Committee of the
Council on Education (Sir J. Gorst, Cambridge University)   900

WORKING-CLASS DWELLINGS AT BETHNAL GREEN—Question, Mr. J. G.
Talbot (Oxford University); Answer, The Secretary of State for the
Home Department (Sir M. White Ridley, Lancashire, Blackpool)...   ...   900

UNQUALIFIED DISPENSERS—Question Major Rasch (Essex, S.E.); Answer,
The Vice President of the Committee of the Council on Education (Sir J.
Gorst, Cambridge University)   901

SCHOOL TEACHERS SUPERANUATION—Question, Mr. Bill (Staffordshire, Leek);
Answer, The Secretary of State for the Home Department (Sir M. White
Ridley, Lancashire, Blackpool)   901

IRELAND—INDUSTRIAL SCHOOLS ACT—Question, Colonel M'Calmont (Antrim,
E.); Answer, The Chief Secretary for Ireland (Mr. G. W. Balfour, Leeds,
Central)   901

GLIN DISTRICT SCHOOL—Question, Mr. Austin (Limerick, W.); Answer, The
Chief Secretary for Ireland (Mr. G. W. Balfour, Leeds, Central)   902

IRISH NATIONAL TEACHERS EXAMINATIONS—Question, Mr. Davitt (Mayo, S.);
Answer, The Chief Secretary for Ireland (Mr. G. W. Balfour, Leeds,
Central)   902

LAND VALUATION AT SLIGO—Question, Mr. P. A. M'Hugh (Leitrim, N.);
Answer, The Chief Secretary for Ireland (Mr. G. W. Balfour, Leeds,
Central)   903

THIN POSTCARDS FOR COMMERCIAL PURPOSES—Question, Sir Reginald
Hanson (London); Answer, The Financial Secretary to the Treasury (Mr.
Hanbury, Preston)   904

THE EAST CENTRAL DISTRICT POST OFFICE STAFF—Question, Mr. M'Ghee
(Louth, S.); Answer, The Financial Secretary (Mr. Hanbury, Preston) ...   904

NEWBLISS POST OFFICE MESSENGER—Question, Mr. Macaleese (Monaghan,
N.); Answer, The Financial Secretary to the Treasury (Mr. Hanbury,
Preston)   904

June 12.] *Page*

LIMERICK SORTING CLERKS—Question, Mr. Patrick O'Brien (Kilkenny) ; Answer, The Financial Secretary to the Treasury (Mr. Hanbury Preston) ... 905

STATE AID FOR THE BLIND—Question, Mr. Patrick O'Brien (Kilkenny) ; Answer, The Secretary of State for the Home Department (Sir M. White Ridley, Lancashire, Blackpool) 906

CASTLETOWN, BEREHAVEN PIER—Question, Mr. Patrick O'Brien, Kilkenny ; Answer, The Chief Secretary for Ireland (Mr. G. W. Balfour, Leeds, Central) 906

THE VICAR OF ST. MICHAEL'S, SOUTHAMPTON—Question, Mr. Samuel Smith, (Flintshire) ; Answer, The First Lord of the Treasury (Mr. A. J. Balfour, Manchester, E.) 907

SOUTH AFRICAN REPUBLIC—THE BLOEMFONTEIN CONFERENCE—Question, Mr. Galloway (Manchester, S.W.) ; Answer, The First Lord of the Treasury (Mr. A. J. Balfour, Manchester, E.)· 907

BUSINESS OF THE HOUSE—Questions, Sir Charles Cameron (Glasgow, Bridgeton), Mr. Gibson Bowles (Lynn Regis), Mr. Channing (Northampton, E.), Mr. Bartley (Islington, N.), and Mr. James Lowther (Kent, Thanet) ; Answers, The First Lord of the Treasury (Mr. A. J. Balfour, Manchester, E.) ... 907

PUBLIC BUSINESS.

Private Legislation Procedure (Scotland) (Expenses)—Considered in Committee.

Motion made and Question proposed—

"That it is expedient to authorise the payment, out of moneys to be provided by Parliament, of any remuneration, allowances, and expenses that may become payable under any Act of the present Session to provide for improving and extending the procedure for obtaining Parliamentary powers by way of Provisional Orders in matters relating to Scotland."—(*Sir William Walrond.*)

Amendment proposed—

"To leave out the word 'remuneration.'"—(*Mr. Thos. Shaw.*)

Question proposed, "That the word 'remuneration' stand part of the Resolution."

DISCUSSION :—

The Lord Advocate (Mr. A. G. Murray, *Buteshire*)	909	Mr. J. P. Smith (*Lanark, Partick*)	910
Dr. Clark (*Caithness*) ...	909	Mr. Channing (*Northampton, E.*)	910

Amendment, by leave, withdrawn.

Original Question put, and agreed to.

Resolved, That it is expedient to authorise the payment, out of moneys to be provided by Parliament, of any remuneration, allowances, and expenses that may become payable under any Act of the present Session to provide for improving and extending the procedure for obtaining Parliamentary powers by way of Provisional Orders in matters relating to Scotland.

Resolution to be reported To-morrow.

Private Legislation Procedure (Scotland) Bill—Committee.

Order for Committee read.

"That it be an instruction to the Committee that they have power to extend
the scope of the Bill to include the remainder of the United Kingdom."—(*Capt.
Sinclair.*)

DISCUSSION :—

Mr. Buchanan (*Aberdeen-shire, E.*) 913	Sir H. Campbell-Bannerman (*Stirling Burghs*) 914	
The Lord Advocate (*Mr. A. G. Murray, Buteshire*) ... 914	Mr. Dalziel (*Kirkcaldy*)... ... 916	
	Mr. Lloyd-George (*Carnarvon*) ... 916	

Question put, and negatived.

BILL CONSIDERED IN COMMITTEE.

Clause 1 :—

Amendment proposed—

"In page 1, line 6, to leave out 'public authority or.'"—(*Mr. Edmund
Robertson.*)

Question proposed, "That the words 'public authority or' stand part of
the clause."

DISCUSSION :—

The Lord Advocate (*Mr. A. G. Murray, Buteshire*) 919	Sir H. Campbell-Bannerman (*Stirling Burghs*) 920
Mr. Cripps (*Gloucestershire, Stroud*) 919	Mr. A. G. Murray 920
	Dr. Clark (*Caithness*) 920

Amendment, by leave, withdrawn.

Amendment proposed—

"In page 1, line 6, after 'authority,' to insert the words, 'other than a
public authority seeking powers inconsistent with, or in addition to, the
general law."—(*Mr. Cripps.*)

Question proposed, "That those words be there inserted."

DISCUSSION :—

The Lord Advocate (*Mr. A. G. Murray, Buteshire*) ... 922	Mr. Stuart Wortley (*Sheffield, Hallam*) 926
Mr. J. P. Smith (*Lanarkshire, Partick*) 924	Mr. Ure (*Linlithgow*) 926
Mr. Cripps (*Gloucester, Stroud*) 924	Mr. Jeffreys (*Hants, N.*) ... 927
Sir H. Campbell-Bannerman (*Stirling Burghs*)... ... 925	Mr. Cripps 927
	The First Lord of the Treasury (*Mr. A. J. Balfour, Manchester, E.* 928

Amendment, by leave, withdrawn.

Amendment proposed—

"In page 1, line 6, to leave out 'or persons.'"—(*Dr. Clark.*)

Question proposed, "That the words 'or persons' stand part of the
clause.

The Lord Advocate (*Mr. A. G. Murray, Buteshire*) 930

Amendment, by leave, withdrawn.

Amendment proposed—

"In page 1, line 6, after 'persons,' to insert 'other than railway companies.'"—(*Mr. Cripps.*)

Question proposed, "That those words be there inserted."

DISCUSSION :—

The Lord Advocate (*Mr. A. G. Murray, Buteshire*) ...	931	Mr. Caldwell	936
Mr. Caldwell (*Lanarkshire, Mid*)	931	Mr. Hedderwick (*Wicks Burghs*)	936
Mr. Renshaw (*Renfrewshire, W.*)	932	Mr. Edmund Robertson (*Dundee*)	937
Mr. Robert Wallace (*Perth*)	934	Mr. Dalziel (*Kirkcaldy Burghs*)...	937
Mr. Cripps (*Gloucester, Stroud*)	934	Mr. J. P. Smith (*Lanarkshire, Partick*)	937
Mr. Bryce (*Aberdeen*) ...	935	Mr. Colville (*Lanark, N.E.*) ...	938
		Dr. Clark (*Caithness*)	938
		Sir H. Campbell-Bannerman (*Stirling Burghs*)	938

Amendment, by leave, withdrawn.

Amendment proposed—

"In page 1, line 9, to leave out the words 'at present.'"—(*Mr. Caldwell.*)

Question proposed, "That the words 'at present' stand part of the clause."

The Lord Advocate (*Mr. A. G. Murray, Buteshire*) 939

Question put, and agreed to.

Amendment proposed—

"In page 1, line 10, to leave out the word 'shall,'and insert the word 'may' instead thereof."—(*Mr. Parker Smith.*)

Question proposed, "That the word 'shall' stand part of the clause."

DISCUSSION :—

The Lord Advocate (*Mr. A. G. Murray, Buteshire*) ...	940	Mr. Soutter (*Dumfriesshire*) ...	943
Sir Charles Cameron (*Glasgow, Bridgeton*)... ...	941	Dr. Farquharson (*Aberdeenshire, W.*)	944
Mr. Crombie (*Kincardineshire*)	941	Mr. Buchanan (*Aberdeenshire, E.*)	944
Mr. A. G. Murray ...	942	Dr. Clark (*Caithness*)	945
Mr. Caldwell (*Lanarkshire, Mid*)	942	Mr. Robert Wallace (*Perth*) ...	945
Mr. Thomas Shaw (*Hawick Burghs*)	942	Mr. A. G. Murray	945
	943	Mr. Caldwell	946
		Mr. Gibson Bowles (*Lynn Regis*)	946
		Dr. Clark	947

Question put.

The Committee divided :—Ayes, 196 ; Noes, 80. (Division List, No. 183.)

Amendment proposed—

"In page 1, line 11, to leave out from the word 'by' to the end of the clause, and add the words 'Private Bill, according to the existing practice of Parliament, unless and until there is opposition to the Bill, in which case only the procedure established by this Act shall apply' instead thereof."—(*Mr. Edmund Robertson.*)

Question proposed, "That the words proposed to be omitted to the words 'a provisional,' in line 12, stand part of the clause."

June 12.] Page

DISCUSSION :—

The Lord Advocate (Mr. A.
  G. Murray, Buteshire) ... 952
Mr. Thorburn (Peebles and
  Selkirk) 953
Dr. Clark (Caithness) ... 953
Sir Mark Stuart (Kirkcud-
  bright) 953

Mr. Dalziel (Kirkcaldy Burghs)... 954
Mr. Edmund Robertson (Dundee) 954
Dr. Clark 955
Captain Sinclair (Forfar) ... 955
Mr. J. P. Smith (Lanarkshire,
  Partick) 956

Question put.

The Committee divided :—Ayes, 146 ; Noes, 56. (Division List, No. 184.)

Amendment proposed—
  "In page 1, line 12, to leave out the words 'a provisional' and insert
'an.'"—(Mr. J. P. Smith.)

Question proposed, 'That the words 'a provisional' stand part of the
clause."

Mr. Caldwell (Lanarkshire,
  Mid) 957

The Lord Advocate (Mr. A. G.
  Murray, Buteshire) 957

Amendment, by leave, withdrawn.

Amendment proposed—
  "In page 1, line 21, after the word 'advertisement' to insert words 'in at
least two newspapers circulating in the locality interested.'"—(Mr. Dalziel.)

Question proposed, "That those words be there inserted.

The Lord Advocate (Mr. A. G.
  Murray, Buteshire) ... 958

Mr. Dalziel (Kirkcaldy Burghs)... 959

Amendment, by leave, withdrawn.

Amendment proposed—
  "In Clause 1, page 1, line 24, to leave out 'prescribed' and insert 'required
by Standing Orders.'"—(Mr. Caldwell.)

Question proposed, "That the word 'prescribed' stand part of the
clause."

DISCUSSION :—

The Lord Advocate (Mr. A. G.
  Murray, Buteshire) ... 959
Mr. J. P. Smith (Lanark-
  shire, Partick) 959
Mr. Caldwell (Lanarkshire,
  Mid) 959
Mr. Thomas Shaw (Hawick
  Burghs) 960
Mr. A. G. Murray ... 960

Mr. Thomas Shaw 960
Dr. Clark (Caithness) 961
Mr. J. P. Smith 962
Mr. A. G. Murray 963
Mr. Alexander Cross (Glasgow,
  Camlachie) 963
Dr. Clark 964
Mr. Caldwell 964

Question put.

The Committee divided :—Ayes, 130 ; Noes, 55. (Divisional List, No.
185.)

Amendment proposed—
  "In page 1, to leave out Clause 1."—(Dr. Clark.)

Question proposed, "That Clause 1, as amended, stand part of the
Bill."

June 12.] *Page*

Discussions—

Sir Charles Cameron (Glasgow, Bridgeton) 968		Mr. Caldwell (Lanark, Mid.) ... 969	
Mr. Souttar (Dumfriesshire) 968			

Question put.

The Committee divided:—Ayes, 175; Noes, 62. (Division List, No. 186.)

Clause 2 :—

Amendment proposed—

"In page 2, line 2, after the word 'Commons,' to insert the words, 'and two Members of each House of Parliament appointed at the beginning of each session in manner provided by Standing Orders shall be a Standing Joint Committee of the two Houses of Parliament."—(*Dr. Clark.*)

Question proposed, "That those words be there inserted."

Discussion :—

The Lord Advocate (Mr. A. G. Murray, Buteshire) ...	Mr. J. P. Smith	980
	Mr. Dillon (Mayo, E.)	980
Mr. Caldwell (Lanark, Mid)	974	Mr. Hedderwick (Wick Burghs)	981
Mr. Richards (Finsbury, E.)	975	Mr. Stuart Wortley (Sheffield,	
Dr. Clark (Caithness) ...	975	Hallam)	982
Sir H. Campbell-Bannerman		Dr. Clark	982
(Stirling Burghs) ...	976	Colonel Denny (Kilmarnock	
Mr. Cripps (Gloucestershire,		Burghs)	983
Stroud)...	977	Mr. Dalziel	983
Mr. A. G. Murray ...	978	Mr. A. G. Murray ...	984
Mr. Edmund Robertson		Sir H. Campbell-Bannerman ...	984
(Dundee)	978	The First Lord of the Treasury	
Mr. Dalziel (Kirkcaldy		(Mr. A. J. Balfour, Man-	
Burghs)	979	chester, E.)	985
Mr. Cochrane (Ayrshire, N.)		Mr. Cripps	988
Sir H. Campbell-Bannerman		Sir H. Campbell-Bannerman ...	988
Mr. A. G. Murray ...	977	Mr. A. J. Balfour	989
Mr. Souttar (Dumfriesshire)	980		

Motion made, and Question, "That the Chairman do report Progress, and ask leave to sit again," put, and agreed to. Committee report Progress; to sit again upon Thursday 989

Trout Fishing Annual Close Time (Scotland) Bill [Lords]—Second Reading—Order for Second Reading read 989

Motion made, and Question proposed—

"That the Bill be now read a Second time."

Mr. Dalziel (Kirkcaldy Burghs) 989

It being Midnight, the Debate stood adjourned. Debate to be resumed upon Thursday.

Lunacy Bill [Lords]—Order for the Second Reading read—(*The Secretary to the Local Government Board, Mr. T. W. Russell, Tyrone, S.*) : Thursday.

DISCUSSION :—

... *Mr. Channing (Northamp-*   *Mr. John Burns*   991
    ton, E.)   990
    The Secretary to the Local
    Government Board (Mr. T.
    W. Russell, Tyrone)   ...   990

Second Reading deferred till Thursday.

Baths and Washhouses Acts (Amendment) Bill—Order for Second
Reading read—*(Mr. Bigwood, Middlesex, Brentwood)*...   991

DISCUSSION :—

    Mr. Caldwell (Lanark, Mid.)   992   *Mr. John Burns (Battersea)*   ...   992
Second Reading deferred till Thursday.

Adjourned at ten minutes after Twelve of the clock.

LORDS: TUESDAY 13TH JUNE 1899.

NEW PEER.

The Duke of Beaufort sat first in Parliament after the death of his father.

PRIVATE BILL BUSINESS.

The LORD CHANCELLOR acquainted the House that the Clerk of the
Parliaments had laid upon the Table the Certificate from the Examiners
that the further Standing Orders applicable to the following Bill have
been complied with: Woking Water and Gas—And also the Certificate that
the Standing Orders applicable to the following Bill have been complied
with : Electric Lighting Provisional Orders (No. 2.) The same were
ordered to lie on the Table   993

Edinburgh Corporation Bill—A witness ordered to attend the Select
Committee   993

Southport Tramways Bill [Lords]—Report from the Select Committee,
That the promoters do not intend to proceed further with the Bill ;
Ordered that the Bill be not further proceeded with   993

**Rhondda Urban District Council Bill ; Workington Corporation
Water Bill** [Lords]—Reported from the Select Committee with Amendments   993

Brooke's Park (Londonderry) Bill [Lords] ; **Cardiff Railway Bill**—
Reported with Amendments   993

Kensington and Notting Hill Electric Lighting Bill—The Chairman of
Committees informed the House that the Opposition to the Bill was withdrawn ; The Orders made on the 2nd instant and yesterday discharged ;
and Bill committed for Friday next   993

Watermen's and Lightermen's Acts Amendment Bill [Lords]—Report
from the Select Committee, That it is not expedient to proceed
further with the Bill ; read, and ordered to lie upon the Table   994

June 13.] *Page*

South-Eastern and London, Chatham, and Dover Railway Companies (New Lines) Bill—Read the second time, and committed: the Committee to be proposed by the Committee of Selection 994

Buenos Ayres and Pacific Railway Company Bill [Lords]; **Yorke Estate Bill** [Lords]—Read the third time, and passed, and sent to the Commons 994

City and Brixton Railway Bill; London Improvements Bill; Sheffield Corporation Markets Bill; Stockport Corporation Bill —Brought from the Commons, read the first time, and referred to the Examiners 994

Birkenhead Corporation Bill [Lords]—Returned from the Commons agreed to, with Amendments 994

Dumbarton Burgh Bill [Lords]—Returned from the Commons agreed to, with Amendments: The said Amendments considered, and agreed to ... 994

Metropolitan Common Scheme (Harrow Weald) Provisional Order Bill—Read the third time (according to Order), and passed 994

Electric Lighting Provisional Orders (No. 10) Bill [Lords]—Read the third time (according to Order), and passed, and sent to the Commons ... 994

Gas Orders Confirmation (No. 1) Bill [Lords]; **Water Orders Confirmation Bill** [Lords]—House in Committee (according to Order): Amendments made: Standing Committee negatived: The Report of Amendments to be received on Thursday next 994

Electric Lighting Provisional Orders (No. 14) Bill [Lords]—House in Committee (according to Order): Bill reported without Amendment: Standing Committee negatived; and Bill to be read the third time on Thursday next... 995

Gas and Water Orders Confirmation Bill [Lords]—House in Committee (according to Order); Amendments made: Standing Committee negatived: The Report of Amendments to be received on Thursday next 995

Electric Lighting Provisional Orders (No. 12) Bill [Lords]; **Electric Lighting Provisional Orders (No. 13) Bill** [Lords]; **Electric Lighting Provisional Orders (No. 15) Bill** [Lords]—Committed to Committee of the whole House on Thursday next 995

Tramways Orders Confirmation (No. 2) Bill [Lords]—Committed: The Committee to be proposed by the Committee of Selection... 995

Electric Lighting Provisional Orders (No. 2) Bill—To be read the second time on Thursday next—(*The Earl of Dudley*.) 995

Electric Lighting Provisional Orders (No. 7) Bill (No. 114); Housing of the Working Classes Provisional Order (Borrow-Stounness) Bill (No. 115); Local Government (Ireland) Provisional Order (No. 1) Bill (No. 116); Local Government Provisional Order (Housing of Working Classes) Bill (No. 117); Local Government Provisional Order (No. 5) Bill (No. 118); Local Government Provisional Orders (Poor Law) Bill (No. 119)—Brought from the Commons, read the first time, to be printed, and referred to the Examiners 995

London, Brighton, and South Coast Railway (Pensions) Bill; Lisburn Town Commissioners Bill, now **Lisburn Urban District Councils Bill** —Read the third time, with the Amendments, and passed, and returned to the Commons 996

RETURNS, REPORTS, ETC.

SOUTH AFRICAN REPUBLIC—Papers relating to the complaints of British subjects in the South African Republic   996

EXPLOSIVES—I. (Explosion of carbo-gelatine at factory near Faversham,) Report to the right hon. the Secretary of State for the Home Department, by Colonel A. Ford, C.B., Her Majesty's Chief Inspector of Explosives, on the circumstances attending an explosion of carbo-gelatine in course of manufacture, which occurred at the factory of the Cotton Powder Company, at Uplees Marshes, near Faversham, on the 5th of May, 1899. II. (Explosion of Percussion Caps at factory at Streetly, near Birmingham.) Report to the right hon. the Secretary of State for the Home Department, by Major A. Cooper-Key, R.A., Her Majesty's Inspector of Explosives, on the circumstances attending an explosion of percussion caps in course of manufacture at the factory of the Birmingham Metal and Munitions Company, Limited, at Streetly, near Birmingham, on the 11th of April, 1899. Explosive Act, 1875—Twenty-third Annual Report of Her Majesty's Inspector of Explosives.—Presented, by command, and ordered to lie on the Table   996

CERTIFIED INEBRIATE REFORMATORIES (RULES FOR MANAGEMENT)—Rules made with the approval of the Secretary of State for the Home Department for the domestic management of the certified inebriate reformatory at Horfield in the County of Gloucester   996

Laid before the House (pursuant to Act), and ordered to lie on the Table.

QUESTION.

ESTATE DUTY.

The Chairman of Committees (The Earl of Morley) ... 997	The Lord Chancellor (The Earl of Halsbury) 1000
Lord Stanley of Alderley ... 1000	

House adjourned at five minutes before Five of the clock.

COMMONS: TUESDAY 13TH JUNE 1899.

PRIVATE BILL BUSINESS.

PRIVATE BILLS (Lords).

(Standing Orders not previously inquired into complied with.)

MR. SPEAKER laid upon the Table Report from one of the Examiners of Petitions for Private Bills, That, in the case of the following Bills, originating in the Lords, and referred on the First Reading thereof, the Standing Orders not previously inquired into, and which are applicable thereto, have been complied with, viz. :—Great Grimsby Street Tramways Bill [Lords]; North Eastern and Hull and Barnsley Railways (Joint Dock) Bill [Lords]; North Eastern Railway Bill [Lords]. Ordered, that the Bills be read a second time.   1002

Brompton and Piccadilly Circus Railway Bill — Queen's Consent signified. Read the third time, and passed   1002

Infant Orphan Asylum Bill [Lords]; **London Hospital Bill** [Lords]; **Stockton and Middlesbrough Water Bill** [Lords]. Read the third time, and passed, without Amendment   1002

Darwen Corporation Bill—As amended, considered ; to be read the third time   1002

Godalming Corporation Water Bill (by Order)—Order for consideration, as amended, read.

Motion made, and Question proposed—

"That the Order for the Consideration of the Bill, as amended, be deferred till Thursday next."—(*Dr. Farquharson.*)

DISCUSSION :—

Mr. Duncombe (Cumberland, Egremont) 1003	*Mr. Gibson Bowles (Lynn Regis)* 1003
The Secretary to the Local Government Board (Mr. T. W. Russell, Tyrone) ... 1003	*The Under Secretary of State for Foreign Affairs (Mr. Brodrick, Surrey, Guildford)* 1004
	Mr. Stuart (Shoreditch, Hoxton) 1004

Question put.

The House divided :—Ayes, 168 ; Noes, 34. (Division List, No. 187).

Order for consideration, as amended, deferred till Thursday.

London County Council (General Powers) Bill—(By Order.) Order for consideration, as amended, read   1005

Motion made, and Question proposed, "That the Bill be now considered."

Amendment proposed—

"To leave out the words 'now considered,' in order to add the words 're-committed to the former Committee with respect to Clause 10 (Acquisition of Site of Spitalfields Market by agreement), and Clause 25 (Act not to authorise taking twenty houses of persons of the labouring class in any parish).'"—(*Mr. Alexander Hargreaves Brown.*)

Question, "That the words 'now considered' stand part of the Question," put, and negatived ; words added.

Main Question, as amended, put, and agreed to.

Bill re-committed to the former Committee in respect of Clause 10 (Acquisition of Site of Spitalfields Market, by agreement), and Clause 25 (Act not to authorise taking twenty houses of persons of the labouring class in any parish) 1006

Dublin Corporation Bill—(By Order.) Order for consideration, as amended, read   1006

Motion made, and Question proposed,

"That the Bill be now considered."—(*Mr. John Redmond.*)

Amendment proposed—

"To leave out the word 'now,' and, at the end of the Question, to add the words, 'upon this day three months.'"—(*Mr. Carson.*)

Question proposed, "That the word 'now' stand part of the Question."

DISCUSSION :—

Mr. Johnson-Ferguson (Lei-cestershire, Loughborough) . 1022
Mr. Fison (York, W. R., Doncaster) 1031
Colonel Saunderson (Armagh, N.) 1032
Mr. Dillon (Mayo, E.) ... 1035
Colonel Saunderson ... 1035
The Secretary to the Local Government Board (Mr. T. W. Russell, Tyrone, S.) 1035

Mr. William Redmond (East Clare) 1038
Colonel Saunderson 1039
Mr. Bartley (Islington, N.) ... 1039
Mr. William Moore (Antrim, N.) 1040
Mr. Duncombe (Cumberland, Egremont)... 1044
Mr. T. M. Healy (Cork, N.) ... 1044

Question put.

The House divided :—Ayes, 291 ; Noes, 129. (Division List, No. 188.)

Main Question put, and agreed to.

Bill, as amended, considered ; to be read the third time.

Ionian Bank Bill. (By Order.) Order for Second Reading read.

The Financial Secretary to the Treasury (Mr. Hanbury, Preston) 1053

Bill read a second time and committed.

St. Neots Water Bill. [Lords]. (By Order). (Order for Second Reading read) 1053

Motion made, and Question proposed—

"That the Second Reading of the Bill be deferred till Monday."—(*Mr. J. W. Lowther.*)

Mr. Duncombe (Cumberland, Egremont) 1053
Mr. J. W. Lowther (Cumberland, Penrith) ... 1053

Second Reading deferred till Monday next.

Totland Water Bill (Lords)—Read a second time and committed 1054

Local Government Provisional Orders (No. 8) Bill; Pier and Harbour Provisional Orders (No. 1) Bill—Read the third time, and passed ... 1054

STANDING ORDERS.—Resolution reported from the Committee—

"That in the case of the Bradford Tramways and Improvement Bill, Petition for additional Provision, the Standing Orders ought to be dispensed with : That the parties be permitted to introduce their additional Provision, if the Committee on the Bill think fit."

Resolution agreed to 1054

MESSAGE FROM THE LORDS—That they have agreed to, Electric Lighting Provisional Orders (No. 1) Bill ; Electric Lighting Provisional Orders (No. 4) Bill. Amendments to West Highland Railway Bill [Lords] without Amendment 1054

That they have passed a Bill, intituled, "An Act to confirm a Provisional Order made by the Board of Trade under the Electric Lighting Acts, 1882 and 1888, relating to Clontarf." [Electric Lighting Provisional Order (No. 9) Bill [Lords.] 1054

Also, a Bill, intituled, "An Act to confirm certain Provisional Orders made by the Board of Trade under the Electric Lighting Acts, 1882 and 1888, relating to East Retford, Failsworth, Pemberton, Stourbridge, Swinton and Pendlebury, and Wednesbury." [Electric Lighting Provisional Orders (No. 11) Bill (Lords).] 1055

And, also, a Bill, intituled, " An Act for enabling the Transvaal Mortgage, Loan, and Finance Company, Limited, to arrange with the holders of their founders' shares, for sub-dividing shares, and creating certain preferences; and for other purposes." [Transvaal Mortgage, Loan, and Finance Company Bill [Lords.] 1055

Electric Lighting Provisional Order (No. 9) Bill [Lords.]—Read the first time; referred to the Examiners of Petitions for Private Bills, and to be printed. [Bill 231.] 1055

Electric Lighting Provisional Orders (No. 11) Bill [Lords]—Read the first time; referred to the Examiners of Petitions for Private Bills, and to be printed. [Bill 232.] 1055

Transvaal Mortgage Loan, and Finance Company Bill [Lords]— Read the first time; and referred to the Examiners of Petitions for Private Bills 1055

PETITIONS.

Borough Funds Act, 1872—Petition from Bethesda, for alteration of Law; to lie upon the Table 1055

Elementay Education (Voluntary Schools)—Petition from Tranmere, for alteration of Law; to lie upon the Table 1055

Ground Rents (Taxation by Local Authorities)—Petition from Huddersfield, in favour; to lie upon the Table 1055

Liquor Traffic Local Veto (Scotland) Bill—Petition from Blackford, in favour; to lie upon the Table 1055

Local Government (Scotland) Act (1894) Amendment Bill—Petition from Polmont, in favour; to lie upon the Table 1055

Public Health Acts Amendment Bill—Petition from Plymouth, in favour; to lie upon the Table 1056

Sale of Intoxicating Liquors on Sunday Bill—Petition from Nottingham, in favour; to lie upon the Table 1056

Vivisection—Petition from London, for prohibition; to lie upon the Table ... 1056

RETURNS, REPORTS, &c.

Army (Special Pensions)—Copy presented,—of return for the year ended 31st of March, 1899, of Pensions specially granted under Articles 730, 1170, and 1207 of the Army Pay Warrant [by Command]; to lie npon the Table 1056

South African Republic—Copy presented,—of Papers relating to the Complaints of British Subjects in the South African Republic [by Command]; to lie upon the Table 1056

Explosives—Copy presented,—of Twenty-third Annual Report of Her Majesty's Inspectors of Explosives, being for the year 1898 [by Command]; to lie upon the Table 1056

EXPLOSIONS (UPLEES MARSHES, FAVERSHAM)—Copy presented,—of Report by Colonel A. Ford, C.B., Her Majesty's Chief Inspector of Explosives, on the circumstances attending the destruction and explosion of carbo-gelatine in course of manufacture, which occurred at the factory of the Cotton Powder Company, at Uplees Marshes, near Faversham, on the 5th May, 1899 [by Command]; to lie upon the Table 1056

EXPLOSIONS (STREETLY, BIRMINGHAM)—Copy presented,—of Report by Major A. Cooper-Key, R.A., Her Majesty's Inspector of Explosives, to the right hon. the Secretary of State for the Home Department, on the circumstances attending an explosion of percussion caps in course of manufacture at the factory of the Birmingham Metal and Munitions Company, Limited, at Streetly, near Birmingham, on the 11th April, 1899 [by Command]; to lie upon the Table 1056

INEBRIATE REFORMATORIES (RULES FOR MANAGEMENT)—Copy presented,— of Rules, made with the approval of the Secretary of State for the Home Department, for the Domestic Management of the certified Inebriate Reformatory at Horfield, in the county of Gloucester [by Act]; to lie upon the Table 1057

MERCHANT SHIPPING, 1898—Copy ordered, " of Tables showing the Progress of British Merchant Shipping."—(*Mr. Ritchie.*) Copy presented accordingly; to lie upon the Table; and to be printed. (No. 217.) 1057

ELECTRIC LIGHTING PROVISIONAL ORDERS—Copy ordered, " of Memorandum stating the nature of the Proposals contained in the Provisional Order included in the Electric Lighting Provisional Order (No. 20) Bill."—(*Mr. Ritchie.*) Copy presented accordingly; to lie upon the Table, and to be printed. (No. 218.) 1057

COMPANIES (WINDING UP)—Return ordered, " of the names of all the companies registered in England which were ordered to be wound up by the Court, or which passed resolutions for winding up voluntarily, during the year ending the 31st day of December, 1896, showing the names and addresses of the liquidators, and giving the following particulars, viz.: (1) the amount of paid-up capital, distinguishing the amount paid up in cash and the amount issued as paid up otherwise than for cash; (2) the estimated amount of probable loss arising on each of the above-named classes of shares, respectively; (3) the estimated amount of probable loss to unsecured or partially secured creditors; (4) the names of companies going into liquidation during the year 1896 on which no losses to shareholders or creditors are estimated as probable."—(*Mr. Charles M'Arthur.*) 1057

BILLS INTRODUCED.

DRAINAGE SEPARATION—Bill to enable Local Authorities to deal separately with the sewage and drainage of their districts, ordered to be brought in by Mr. Stephens, Sir John Lubbock, Sir Walter Foster, Sir William Priestley, Mr. John Burns, Mr. Bigwood, Mr. Cripps, Mr. Lawson Walton, Dr. Ambrose, and Mr. Brynmor Jones 1057

REGISTRATION OF ELECTORS (ENGLAND)—Bill to amend the Law regarding the Registration of Electors in England, ordered to be brought in by Mr. R. G. Webster, Sir Edward Gourley, Major Rasch, Mr. Vaughan-Davies, and Mr. Pierpoint 1058

DRAINAGE SEPARATION BILL—" To enable Local Authorities to deal separately
with the sewage and drainage of their districts," presented, and read the
first time ; to be read a second time upon Wednesday, 21st of June, and
to be printed. (Bill 233.) 1058

REGISTRATION OF ELECTORS (ENGLAND) BILL—" To amend the Law regarding the Registration of Electors in England," presented, and read the first
time ; to be read a second time upon Monday, 3rd of July, and to be
printed. (Bill 234.) 1058

QUESTIONS.

LONGFORD MILITIA—Question, Mr. J. P. Farrell (Cavan, W.) ; Answer, The
Under Secretary of State for War (Mr. Wyndham, Dover)   1058

SALISBURY PLAIN—Question, Mr. Thomas Bayley (Derbyshire, Chesterfield) ;
Answer, The Financial Secretary to the War Office (Mr. J. Powell
Williams, Birmingham, S.) 1059

CEYLON LAND ORDINANCES—Question, Mr. Schwann (Manchester, N.) ;
Answer, The Secretary of State for the Colonies (Mr. J. Chamberlain,
Birmingham, W.)   1059

THE TRANSVAAL : THE BLOEMFONTEIN CONFERENCE—Questions, Mr. Ellis J.
Griffith (Anglesey), and Mr. Labouchere (Northampton) ; Answers, The
Secretary of State for the Colonies (Mr. J. Chamberlain, Birmingham, W.) 1059

ALLEGED ARMING THE BOERS IN NATAL—Question, Sir Alfred Hickman
(Wolverhampton, W.) ; Answer, The Secretary of State for the Colonies
(Mr. J. Chamberlain, Birmingham, W.)   1061

POLITICAL RIGHTS OF UITLANDERS—Questions, Sir Ellis Ashmead-Bartlett
(Sheffield, Ecclesall), Mr. C. P. Scott (Lancashire, Leigh), Mr. Swift
MacNeill (Donegal, S.) ; Answers, The Secretary for the Colonies (Mr.
J. Chamberlain, Birmingham, W.) 1061

THE PACIFIC CABLE—Question, Mr. Hogan (Tipperary, Mid) ; Answer, The
Secretary of State for the Colonies (Mr. J. Chamberlain, Birmingham, W.) 1063

MAURITIUS SUGAR INDUSTRY—Question, Mr. W. Holland (Yorkshire, W.R.,
Rotherham) ; The Secretary of State for the Colonies (Mr. J. Chamberlain,
Birmingham, W.)   1063

WEST AFRICAN LIQUOR TRAFFIC—Question, Captain Sinclair (Forfarshire) ;
Answer, The Secretary of State for the Colonies (Mr. J. Chamberlain,
Birmingham, W.)   1063

TONGA—Question, Mr. Hogan (Tipperary, Mid) ; Answer, The Under Secretary of State for Foreign Affairs (Mr. Brodrick, Surrey, Guildford)   ... 1064

THE ALASKAN BOUNDARY QUESTION —Question, Mr. Hogan (Tipperary,
Mid) ; Answer, The Under Secretary of State for Foreign Affairs (Mr.
Brodrick, Surrey, Guildford)...   1064

TURKISH LOAN, 1885—Questions, Mr. Dillon (Mayo, E.), and Mr. Pierpoint,
(Warrington) ; Answers, The Under Secretary of State for Foreign Affairs
(Mr. Brodrick, Surrey, Guildford) 1064

RUSSIA IN CHINA—Question, Sir Ellis Ashmead-Bartlett (Sheffield, Ecclesall) ;
Answer, The under Secretary of State for Foreign Affairs (Mr. Brodrick,
Surrey, Guildford) 1065

PROHIBITION OF RICE EXPORTS FROM NANKING—Question, Mr. Provand
(Glasgow, Blackfriars) ; Answer, The Under Secretary of State for Foreign
Affairs (Mr. Brodrick, Surrey, Guildford) 1065

IRISH LIGHTS—MAIDEN ROCKS, LARNE—Question, Mr. Field (Dublin, St.
Patrick); Answer, The President of the Board of Trade (Mr. Ritchie,
Croydon)   1066

BRITISH SOLDIERS AT RIO DE JANEIRO—Question, Mr. Hogan (Tipperary,
Mid) ; Answer, The President of the Board of Trade (Mr. Ritchie, Croydon) 1066

BUENOS AYRES CATTLE TRADE—Question, Mr. Field (Dublin, St. Patrick) ;
Answer, The President of the Board of Agriculture (Mr. W. H. Long,
Liverpool, West Derby)   1067

NEW WINE DUTIES—Question, Mr. Lambert (Devon, South Molton) ; Answer,
The Chancellor of the Exchequer (Sir M. Hicks-Beach, Bristol, W.)   ... 1068

THE BAWNBOY LETTER CARRIER—Question, Mr. J. P. Farrell (Cavan, W.) ;
Answer, The Financial Secretary to the Treasury (Mr. Hanbury,
Preston)   1068

LOUGH RYNN LETTER DELIVERIES—Question, Mr. Tully (Leitrim, S.) ;
Answer, The Financial Secretary to the Treasuryy (Mr. Hanbury,
Preston)   1068

BELFAST POST OFFICE STAFF—Question, Mr. Schwann (Manchester, N.) ;
Answer, The Financial Secretary to the Treasury (Mr. Hanbury,
Preston)   1069

SCOTTISH SECONDARY AND TECHNICAL SCHOOLS—Question, Mr. Buchanan
(Aberdeenshire, E.) ; Answer, A Junior Lord of the Treasury (Mr.
Anstruther, St. Andrews Burgh)   1069

KERRY COUNTY COUNCIL—Question, Mr. Field (Dublin, St. Patrick) ;
Answer, The Chief Secretary for Ireland (Mr. G. W. Balfour, Leeds,
Central)   1070

ULSTER AND CONNAUGHT NATIONAL SCHOOL TEACHERS—Question, Mr. Field
(Dublin, St. Patrick) ; Answer, The Chief Secretary for Ireland (Mr. G.
W. Balfour, Leeds, Central) 1070

INTERMEDIATE EDUCATION IN IRELAND—Question, Mr. Field (Dublin, St.
Patrick) ; Answer, The Chief Secretary for Ireland (Mr. G. W. Balfour,
Leeds, Central)   1071

LONGFORD COUNTY COUNCIL COLLECTOR—Questiop, Mr. J. P. Farrell (Cavan,
W.) ; Answer, The Chief Secretary for Ireland (Mr. G. W. Balfour, Leeds,
Central)   1071

LONGFORD AND THE AGRICULTURAL GRANT—Question, Mr. J. P. Farrell
(Cavan, W.) ; Answer, The Chief Secretary for Ireland (Mr. G. W. Balfour,
Leeds, Central)   1072

QUEEN'S ISLAND WORKMEN, BELFAST—Question, Mr. Dillon (Mayo, E.) ; Answer,
The Chief Secretary for Ireland (Mr. G. W. Balfour, Leeds, Central)   ... 1073

WESTPORT COMMISSIONERS — Question, Dr. Robert Ambrose (Mayo, W.);
Answer, The Chief Secretary for Ireland (Mr. G. W. Balfour, Leeds,
Central)   1074

DUBLIN POLICE CLOTHING—Question, Mr. Crilly (Mayo, N.) ; Answer, The
Chief Secretary for Ireland (Mr. G. W. Balfour, Leeds, Central) 1074

June 13.]   *Page*

DOMINICK O'DONNELL OF GLENGAD—Question, Mr. Crilly (Mayo, N.); Answer,
The Chief Secretary for Ireland (Mr. G. W. Balfour, Leeds, Central)   ... 1074

EXTRA POLICE AT BELMULLET—Question, Mr. Crilly (Mayo, N.); Answer,
The Chief Secretary for Ireland (Mr. G. W. Balfour, Leeds, Central)   ... 1075

LOCAL GOVERNMENT IN WEST CAVAN—Question, Mr. J. P. Farrell (Cavan, W.);
Answer, The Chief Secretary for Ireland (Mr. G. W. Balfour, Leeds,
Central)   1075

MULLINGAR ASYLUM BOARD JOINT COMMITTEE.—Question, Mr. J. P. Farrell
(Cavan, W.); Answer, The Chief Secretary for Ireland (Mr. G. W. Balfour,
Leeds, Central)   1076

ANNALY ESTATE, COUNTY LONGFORD—Question, Mr. J. P. Farrell (Cavan, W.);
Answer, The Chief Secretary for Ireland (Mr. G. W. Balfour, Leeds,
Central)   1076

ROSCOMMON AND THE AGRICULTURAL GRANT—Question, Mr. Tully (Leitrim S.);
Answer, The Chief Secretary for Ireland (Mr. G. W. Balfour, Leeds,
Central)   1077

BUSINESS OF THE HOUSE—Question, Sir Charles Dilke (Gloucester, Forest of
Dean); Answer, The First Lord of the Treasury (Mr. A. J. Balfour,
Manchester, E.)   1078

NEW WRIT

For the Burgh of Edinburgh (East Division)—in the room of Robert Wallace,
esquire, deceased.—(*Mr. Herbert Gladstone.*) 1078

Local Government Bill—Order for Third Reading read.

PUBLIC BUSINESS.

Motion made, and Question proposed—

"That the Bill be now read a third time."

Mr. Duncombe (Cumberland, Egremont)   1080

Amendment proposed—

"To leave out the words 'now read the third time,' in order to add the
words 'recommitted in respect of Clause 2.'—(*Mr. Elliot*)—instead thereof."

Question proposed, "That the words 'now read the third time' stand part
of the Question."

DISCUSSION :—

The Chancellor of the Exchequer *(Sir M. Hicks-Beach, Bristol, W.)* ... 1080	*Mr. R. G. Webster (St. Pancras, E.)* 1085
Earl Percy (Kensington, S.) 1082	*Mr. Labouchere (Northampton)* 1086
Sir H. Campbell Bannerman (Stirling Burghs) ... 1084	*Mr. Elliot (Durham City)* ... 1086

Question put, and agreed to.

Main Question put, and agreed to.

Bill accordingly read the third time, and passed.

June 13.]   *Page*

Finance Bill—Read the third time, and passed 1086

PLUMBERS' REGISTRATION.

Mr. Lees Knowles (Salford, W.) 1087

Notice taken that 40 Members were not present; House counted and 40 Members not being present—

House adjourned at Eight of the clock.

COMMONS : WEDNESDAY, 14TH JUNE 1899.

PRIVATE BILL BUSINESS.

Ilford Gas Bill—Lords Amendments considered, and agreed to 1089

Friends' Provident Institution Bill [Lords]; **Lowestoft Promenade Pier Bill**; **Mid-Kent Gas Bill** [Lords]; **Skipton Urban District Gas Bill** [Lords]—As amended, considered; to be read the third time ... 1089

Cobham Gas Bill [Lords]; **Grosvenor Chapel (London) Bill** [Lords]; **Moss Side Urban District Council (Tramways) Bill** [Lords]; **Stretford Urban District Council (Tramways) Bill** [Lords]; **Weston-Super-Mare, Clevedon, and Portishead Tramways Company (Light Railway Extensions) Bill** [Lords]—Read a second time, and committed 1089

Whitehaven Corporation Bill [Lords]; **Withington Urban District Council (Tramways) Bill** [Lords]—Read a second time, and committed 1089

PRIVATE BILLS (GROUP B)—Ordered, that William Jaffray do attend the Committee on Group B of Private Bills this day 1089

PETITIONS.

Ground Values (Taxation) (Scotland) Bill—Petition from Motherwell, in favour; to lie upon the Table 1090

INEBRIATES ACT, 1898—Petition from Rochdale, for alteration of Law; to lie upon the Table 1090

Local Government (Scotland) Act (1894) Amendment Bill—Petitions in favour—From Ardrossan, and Cathcart; to lie upon the Table ... 1090

Parish Councils Association (Scotland) Bill—Petition from Motherwell, in favour; to lie upon the Table 1090

Private Legislation Procedure (Scotland) Bill—Petition from Motherwell, in favour; to lie upon the Table 1090

Sale of Intoxicating Liquors on Sunday Bill—Petitions in favour—From Liverpool; Brettenham; Penrith (three); Carlisle; Talkin; Kirkoswald; Meal Bank; Siddick; Skirwith; Blencarn; Whitehaven (eig t); Yosthwaite; Wetherall; Walton; Parton (two); Moor Row; Crosby; Ivegill; Hutton End; Kirkbride; Dearham; Flimby; Stainton; Renwick; Newbiggin; Ainstable; Gilsland; Ormathwaite; Low Seaton; Workington (two); Distington; St. Bees; Calthwaite; Blencowe; Plumpton; Wigton; Cleator; Great Broughton; Carlisle; Great Salkeld; Applethwaite; Portinscales; Gamblesby; Blyth; Langwathby; Lazenby; Allonby; Maybrary; Mealsgate; Haverigg; Millom; Thelkeld; Brigham; and Lincoln; to lie upon the Table 1090

June 14.]   *Page*

Shops (Early Closing) Bill—Petition from Motherwell, in favour; to lie
upon the Table   1090

Small Houses (Scotland) Bill—Petition from Motherwell, in favour; to lie
upon the Table   1090

Teinds (Scotland) Bill—Petition of the Society of Solicitors of Elginshire,
in favour; to lie upon the Table   1090

Town Councils (Scotland) Bill—Petition from Motherwell, in favour; to lie
upon the Table   1091

Trout Fishing Annual Close Time (Scotland) Bill—Petition from
Motherwell, in favour; to lie upon the Table   1091

Workmen's Houses Tenure Bill—Petition from Motherwell, in favour; to
lie upon the Table   1091

RETURNS, REPORTS, &c.

CHARITY COMMISSION (WELSH INTERMEDIATE EDUCATION ACT (1889)—Copy
presented—of Report of the Charity Commissioners of their Proceedings
under the Welsh Intermediate Education Act, 1889 [by Command]; to
lie upon the Table   1091

NORTH SEA FISHERMEN—Return presented—relative thereto [ordered 23rd
of February]—(*Mr. Herbert Robertson*)—to lie upon the Table, and to be
printed. (No. 219.) 1091

RAILWAYS—Copy presented,—of Report by the Board of Trade on Applications
made during the year 1898 under the Railway Companies' Powers Act,
1864, and of the Proceedings of the Board of Trade with respect thereto
[by Act]; to lie upon the Table, and to be printed. (No. 220.) 1091

MUNICIPAL CORPORATIONS (NEW CHARTERS) (SMETHWICK)—Copy presented,
of Charter of Incorporation of the Borough of Smethwick, dated 12th of
June, 1899, [by Act]; to lie upon the Table   1091

ELECTRIC LIGHTING PROVISIONAL ORDERS—Copy ordered, "of Memorandum
stating the nature of the Proposals contained in the Provisional Orders
included in the Electric Lighting Provisional Orders (No. 9) Bill;
Electric Lighting Provisional Orders (No. 10) Bill; Electric Lighting Provisional Orders (No. 11) Bill; Electric Lighting Provisional Orders
(No. 12) Bill; Electric Lighting Provisional Orders (No. 13) Bill; Electric
Lighting Provisional [Orders (No. 14) Bill; Electric Lighting Provisional
Orders (No. 15) Bill."—(*Mr. Ritchie.*) Copy presented accordingly; to lie
upon the Table, and to be printed. (No. 221).   1091

PUBLIC BUSINESS.

Lincolnshire Coroners Bill [Lords]—Read the first time; to be read a second
time on Monday next, and to be printed. (Bill 234)   1092

Education of Children Bill—Order for third reading read ...   .

Motion made and Question proposed—

" That the Bill be now read the third time."—(*Mr. Robson.*)

Amendment proposed—

" To leave out the word ' now,' and at the end of the Question to add the
words ' upon this day three months.' "—(*Mr. Seton-Karr.*)

Question proposed, " That the word ' now ' stand part of the Question."

DISCUSSION :—

Mr. George Whiteley, (Stockport) 1097
Mr. Duckworth (Lancashire, Middleton) 1101
Sir F. S. Powell (Wigan)... 1106
Mr. Tomlinson (Preston) ... 1109
Mr. Yoxall (Nottingham, West) 1111
Major Rasch (Essex, S.E.) 1114
Mr. Samuel Smith (Flintshire) 1115
Mr. Hobhouse (Somerset, E.) 1116
Mr. Schwann (Manchester, N.) 1117
Mr. J. H. Johnson (Sussex, Horsham) 1120
Mr. Harwood (Lancashire, Bolton) 1121

Mr. James Kenyon (Lancashire, Bury)... 1125
Mr. Duncombe (Cumberland, Egremont)... 1127
Mr. James Kenyon 1127
Mr. Maddison (Sheffield, Brightside) 1128
The Vice-President of the Committee of Council on Education (Sir J. Gorst, Cambridge University) 1131
Sir William Harcourt (Monmouthshire, W.) 1132
Colonel Mellor (Lancashire, Radcliffe)... 1133

Question, "That the word 'now' stand part of the Question," put, and agreed to.

Main Question put, and agreed to.

Bill read the third time, and passed.

Service Franchise Bill—(As amended, considered.)

New clause—

"All enactments and all orders made in pursuance of the Registration Acts which relate to the registration of persons entitled to vote in respect of a lodger qualification shall relate with the necessary variations and alterations of precepts, notices, lists, and other forms to persons qualified to vote under the service franchise."—(*Sir C. Dilke.*)

Brought up, and read the first time.

Motion made, and Question proposed, "That the clause be read a second time."

DISCUSSION :—

Sir J. Blundell Maple (Camberwell, Dulwich) ... 1138
Mr. T. M. Healy (Louth, N.) 1138
Mr. Robert Wallace (Perth). 1141

Captain Norton (Newington, W.). 1142
The Solicitor-General (Sir R. B. Finlay, Inverness Burghs) ... 1143

Question put.

The House divided :—Ayes, 139 ; Noes, 184. (Division List, No. 189.)

Mr. T. M. Healy (Louth, N.) 1147

Amendment proposed—

"In page 1, line 6, after the word 'employment,' to insert the words, 'and the dwelling-house is not inhabited by any person under whom such man serves in such office, service, or employment.' "—(*Sir Blundell Maple.*)

Question proposed, "That those words be there inserted."

DISCUSSION :—

Sir Charles Dilke (Gloucestershire, Forest of Dean) ... 1147
Mr. Robert Wallace (Perth) . 1148
Sir J. Blundell Maple (Camberwell, Dulwich) ... 1149
Mr. Robert Wallace ... 1149
The Solicitor-General (Sir R.B. Finlay, Inverness Burghs). 1151

Mr. Asquith (Fife, E.)... ... 1152
Mr. T. M. Healy (Louth, N.) ... 1152
Serjeant Hemphill (Tyrone, N.) . 1154
Mr. Abel Thomas (Carmarthen, E.) 1154
Mr. Clancy (Dublin Co., N.) ... 1154

Motion made, and Question put—
"That the Debate be now adjourned."

The House divided :—Ayes, 139 : Noes, 187. (Division List No. 190.)

Question again proposed—
"That those words be there inserted."

Debate arising, and it being after half-past Five of the clock, Mr. Speaker proceeded to interrupt the business.

Whereupon Sir Blundell Maple rose in his place, and claimed to move, "That the Question be now put."

Question put—
"That the Question be now put."

The House divided :—Ayes, 185 ; Noes, 143. (Division List, No. 191.)

Question put accordingly.

The House divided :—Ayes, 171 ; Noes, 154. (Division List, No. 192.)

Further proceeding on consideration, as amended, adjourned till To-morrow.

And, it being Six of the clock, Mr. Speaker adjourned the House without Question put.

Adjourned at Six of the clock.

LORDS : THURSDAY, 15TH JUNE 1899.

PRIVATE BILL BUSINESS.

The LORD CHANCELLOR acquainted the House that the Clerk of the Parliaments had laid upon the Table the Certificate from the Examiners that the further Standing Orders applicable to the following Bill have been complied with—London and North-Western Railway (New Railways) 1165

Also, the Certificate that no further Standing Orders are applicable to the following Bill—West Gloucester Water 1165

And, also, the Certificate that the further Standing Orders applicable to the following Bill have not been complied with—London and North-Western Railway Bill (Additional Powers) 1165

The same were ordered to lie on the Table.

Shirebrook and District Gas Bill ; South Staffordshire Stipendiary Justice Bill ; Nottingham Corporation Bill ; Wolverhampton Tramways Bill (Lords.)—Committee to meet To-morrow 1165

Brynmawr and Western Valleys Railway Bill ; Edinburgh Corporation Bill ; South Staffordshire Tramways Bill (Lords)—Reported from the Select Committee, with Amendments 1165

South-Eastern Railway Bill—Report from the Select Committee, That the Committee had not proceeded with the consideration of the Bill, the opposition thereto having been withdrawn ; read, and ordered to lie upon the Table ; The orders made on the 1st and 8th instant discharged ; and Bill committed... 1165

June 15.] *Page*

Belfast Corporation Bill; Baker Street and Waterloo Railway Bill—
Read the second time, and committed; The Committees to be proposed
by the Committee of Selection 1166

Belfast and Northern Counties Railway Bill—Read the second time,
and committed 1166

Bootle Corporation Bill—Read the second time, and committed; The
Committee to be proposed by the Committee of Selection 1166

North Pembrokeshire and Fishguard Railway Bill—Read the third time
and passed 1166

Shotley Bridge and Consett District Gas Bill—Read the third time,
with the Amendments, and passed, and returned to the Commons ... 1166

Brompton and Piccadilly Circus Railway Bill—Brought from the Commons; read the first time; and referred to the Examiners ... 1166

Infant Orphan Asylum Bill [Lords]; **London Hospital Bill** [Lords];
Stockton and Middlesbrough Water Bill [Lords];—Returned from
the Commons agreed to 1166

X **Ilford Gas Bill**—Returned from the Commons with the Amendments agreed
to 1166

Tramways Orders Confirmation (No. 1) Bill [Lords];—House to be in
Committee To-morrow 1166

Education Department Provisional Order Confirmation (London) Bill
[Lords];—Reported from the Select Committee with Amendments, and
committed to a Committee of the whole House 1166

**Local Government Provisional Orders (No. 8) Bill (No. 125); Pier and
Harbour Provisional Orders (No. 1) Bill (No. 126)**—Brought from
the Commons; read the first time; to be printed; and referred to the
Examiners 1166

Gas Orders Confirmation (No. 1) Bill [Lords]; **Water Orders Confirmation Bill** [Lords]; **Gas and Water Orders Confirmation Bill**
[Lords];—Amendments reported (according to Order), and Bills to be read
the third time To-morrow 1167

Electric Lighting Provisional Orders (No. 14) Bill [Lords];—Read the
third time (according to Order), and passed and sent to the Commons ... 1167

Electric Lighting Provisional Orders (No. 12) Bill [Lords]; **Electric
Lighting Provisional Orders (No. 13) Bill** [Lords]; **Electric
Lighting Provisional Orders (No. 15) Bill** [Lords.]—Committee of
the whole House (which stands appointed for this day) put off till To-
morrow 1167

Electric Lighting Provisional Orders (No. 2) Bill—Read the second time
(according to Order), and committed to a Committee of the whole House
To-morrow 1167

RETURNS, REPORTS, &c.

CHURCH OF ENGLAND (CONFESSIONAL BOXES)—Return respecting: Laid
before the House pursuant to Address of the 3rd of March last, and to
printed. (No. 121.) 1167

FISHERY BOARD FOR SCOTLAND—Reports on the state of the markets for
Scottish herrings on the Continent and in the United States of America... 1167

June 15.]   *Page*

ARMY (SPECIAL PENSIONS)—Return for the year ended 31st March, 1899,
    of Pensions specially granted under Articles 730, 1170, and 1207 of the
    Army Pay Warrant 1167

TRADE REPORTS (ANNUAL SERIES) : No. 2287, Chile (Valparaiso and District) ;
    No. 2288, Brazil (Pernambuco and District) ; No. 2289, Trade of Malaga
    and District   1168

TRADE REPORTS (MISCELLANEOUS SERIES) No. 504, Commercial Education in
    the United States ; No. 505, Agricultural Education in France   1168

WELSH INTERMEDIATE EDUCATION ACT, 1889—Report of the Charity Com-
    missioners for England and Wales—Presented (by Command), and ordered
    to lie on the Table   1168

RAILWAYS COMPANIES' POWERS ACT, 1864—Report by the Board of Trade on
    applications made during the year 1898 under the Railways Companies'
    Powers Act, 1864, and of the proceedings of the Board of Trade with
    respect thereto...   1168

MUNICIPAL CORPORATIONS (INCORPORATION OF SMETHWICK)—Charter of
    Incorporation of the borough of Smethwick, dated 12th June, 1899. Laid
    before the House (pursuant to Act), and ordered to lie on the Table   ... 1168

PETITIONS.

Board of Education Bill [Lords]—Petition in favour of : of the Clerical and
    Lay Members of the Synod of the Diocese of Salisbury ; read, and ordered
    to lie on the Table   1168

Elementary Education (Defective and Epileptic Children) Bill [Lords]
    A Bill to make better provision for the elementary education of defective
    and epileptic children in England and Wales ; was presented by the Earl
    Waldegrave (for the Lord President, D. Devonshire) ; read the first time ;
    and to be printed. (No. 120.)   1168

Education of Children Bill (No. 123) ; London Government Bill
    (No 124)—Brought from the Commons ; read the third time ; and to be
    printed 1168

Finance Bill—Brought from the Commons ; read the first time ; to be
    printed ; and to be read the second time To-morrow—(*The Lord Privy Seal,
    V. Cross*)—and Standing Order No. 39 to be considered in order to its
    being dispensed with. (No. 122.)   1169

QUESTIONS.

MALTESE NOBILITY—Question, Viscount Sidmouth ; Answer, The Under Secre-
    tary of State for the Colonies (The Earl of Selborne)   1169

LONDON GOVERNMENT BILL—Question, The Earl of Kimberley ; Answer, The
    Lord Privy Seal (Viscount Cross)   1169

House adjourned at Twenty-five minutes before Five of the clock.

COMMONS: THURSDAY, 15TH JUNE 1899.

PRIVATE BILL BUSINESS.

Private Bills [Lords]—(Standing Orders not previously inquired into complied with).

MR. SPEAKER laid upon the Table Report from one of the Examiners of Petitions for Private Bills—That, in the case of the following Bill, originating in the Lords, and referred on the First Reading thereof, the Standing Orders not previously inquired into, and which are applicable thereto, have been complied with, viz. :—

Clyde Navigation Bill [Lords]—Ordered—That the Bill be read a second time 1170

Provisional Order Bills [Lords]—(Standing Orders applicable thereto complied with).

MR. SPEAKER laid upon the Table Report from one of the Examiners of Petitions for Private Bills—That, in the case of the following Bill, originating in the Lords, and referred on the First Reading thereof, the Standing Orders which are applicable thereto have been complied with, viz. :— ... 1170

Education Department Provisional Order Confirmation (Liverpool) Bill [Lords]—Ordered—That the Bill be read a second time To-morrow ... 1170

Blackpool Improvement Bill—Read the third time, and passed 1170

Godalming Corporation Water Bill (By Order)—As amended, considered.

    Amendment proposed—

        " In Clause 54, page 28, to leave out Sub-section 8, and insert: ' (8) And any balance remaining in any year shall be divided between the area of the borough and the area outside the borough within the water limits in the proportion of the water rents collected from each of those two areas during each year. The proportion belonging to the outside area shall be applied in reduction of the water rents of the outside area, and the proportion belonging to the area of the borough shall be applied at the discretion of the Corporation either in reduction of the water rents within the area of the borough or carried to the general district fund.' "—(*Mr Brodrick.*)

    Question proposed, " That Sub-section 8 stand part of the clause."

    DISCUSSION :—

Mr. *Schwann* (*Manchester, N.*)	...	... 1172	Mr. *J. W. Lowther* (*Cumberland, Penrith*)...	... 1173

    Question put, and negatived.

    Question, " That those words be here inserted," put, and agreed to.

    Bill to be read a third time.

Dublin Corporation Bill.—Ordered, That Standing Order 207 be suspended, and that the Third Reading of the Dublin Corporation Bill be taken To-morrow, though opposed.—(*Mr. T. M. Healy.*)... 1174

Bradford Tramways and Improvement Bill.—Reported, with Amendments; Report to lie upon the Table, and to be printed 1174

Airdrie and Coatbridge Water Bill [Lords]. Reported, with Amendments; Report to lie upon the Table... 1174

MESSAGE FROM THE LORDS.

That they have agreed to—

Metropolitan Common Scheme (Harrow Weald) Provisional Order Bill, without Amendment 1174

London, Brighton, and South Coast Railway (Pensions) Bill 1174

Lisburn Urban District Council Bill—(changed from "Lisburn Town Commissioners Bill"), with Amendments 1174

Amendments to Dumbarton Burgh Bill [Lords], without Amendment ... 1174

That they have passed a Bill, intituled, "An Act to confirm certain Provisional Orders made by the Board of Trade, under the Electric Lighting Acts, 1882 and 1888, relating to Camborne, Dukinfield, Fenton, Finchley, Shipley, and Swinton." (Electric Lighting Provisional Orders (No. 10) Bill [Lords.] 1174

Also, a Bill, intituled, "An Act for authorising the Buenos Ayres and Pacific Railway Company, Limited, to prepare and carry into effect a scheme or schemes of arrangement with their shareholders, or with any class or classes of shareholders; and to increase and consolidate its capital; and for other purposes." (Buenos Ayres and Pacific Railway Company Bill. [Lords]. 1174

And, also, a Bill, intituled, "An Act to give effect to a compromise of opposing claims affecting certain estates of the late Sir James Cockburn, 7th Baronet, deceased, situate in the Counties of Pembroke, Cardigan, and Carmarthen, and in the City and County of London." (Yorke Estate Bill. [Lords] 1174

Electric Lighting Provisional Orders (No 10) Bill [Lords.] Read the first time; referred to the Examiners of Petitions for Private Bills, and to be printed. (Bill 235.) 1175

Buenos Ayres and Pacific Railway Company Bill [Lords].

Yorke Estate Bill. [Lords]. Read the first time; and referred to the Examiners of Petitions for Private Bills 1175

PETITIONS.

Companies Acts Amendment Bill.—Petition from Redhill and Reigate, against; to lie upon the Table 1175

Local Government (Scotland) Act (1894) Amendment Bill.—Petitions in favour; From Montrose; and Arbroath; to lie upon the Table 1175

POOR LAW AMENDMENT (SCOTLAND) ACT, 1845—Petition from Arbroath, for alteration of law; to lie upon the Table.

RETURNS, REPORTS, &c.

FISHERY BOARD (SCOTLAND)—Copy presented,—of Reports on the State of the Markets for Scottish-cured Herrings on the Continent, and in the United States of America [by Command]; to lie upon the Table.

TRADE REPORTS (ANNUAL SERIES)—Copies presented,—of Diplomatic and Consular Reports, Annual Series, Nos. 2287 to 2289 [by Command]; to lie upon the Table.

QUESTIONS.

MOUNTAIN ARTILLERY—Question, Capt. Pretyman (Suffolk, Woodbridge) ;
Answer, The Under Secretary of State for War (Mr. Wyndham,
Dover) 1175

ROYAL ARSENAL, WOOLWICH—Question, Mr. Steadman (Tower Hamlets,
Stepney) ; Answer, The Financial Secretary to the War Office (Mr. J.
Powell Williams, Birmingham, S.   1176

RIOTS IN MADRAS PRESIDENCY—Questions, Sir Mancherjee Bhownaggree
(Bethnal Green, N.E.), and Mr. Dillon (Mayo, E.) ; Answers, The Secretary
of State for India (Lord George Hamilton, Middlesex, Ealing.)   1176

THE FRANCAISE IN INDIA—Question, Sir William Wedderburn (Banffshire) ;
Answer, The Secretary of State for India (Lord George Hamilton, Middlesex, Ealing)   1177

BOMBAY CIVIL AND CRIMINAL PROCEDURE—Question, Sir William Wedderburn ; Answer, The Secretary of State for India (Lord George Hamilton,
Middlesex, Ealing)   1178

COOPERS HILL COLLEGE—Question, Sir Seymour King (Hull, Central) ;
Answer, The Secretary of State for India (Lord George Hamilton, Middlesex, Ealing)   1178

THE ARMENIAN ARCHBISHOP AND BISHOPS—Question, Mr. Stevenson (Suffolk,
Eye) ; Answer, The Under Secretary of State for Foreign Affairs (Mr.
Brodrick, Surrey, Guildford) 1179

TURKISH LOAN OF 1855—Question, Mr. Dillon (Mayo, E.) ; Answer, The
Under Secretary of State for Foreign Affairs (Mr. Brodrick, Surrey,
Guildford)   1179

THE ANSAHS, OF ASHANTI—Question, Mr. J. A. Pease (Northumberland,
Tyneside) ; Answer, The Secretary of State for the Colonies (Mr. J.
Chamberlain, Birmingham, W.)   1180

WEST AFRICAN LIQUOR TRAFFIC—Mr. W. F. Lawrence (Liverpool, Abercromby) ; Answer, The Secretary of State for the Colonies (Mr. J.
Chamberlain, Birmingham, W.)   1181

FALSE TRANSVAAL REPORTS—Question, Mr. Bryn Roberts (Carnarvonshire,
Eifion) ; Answer, The Secretary of State for the Colonies (Mr. J. Chamberlain, Birmingham, W.)   1182

" ANTI-BRITISH " PROPAGANDA—Questions, Sir Ellis Ashmead-Bartlett
(Sheffield, Ecclesall), and Mr. Swift MacNeill (Donegal, S.) ; Answers,
The Secretary of State for the Colonies (Mr. J. Chamberlain, Birmingham,
W.)   1182

SHUNTING FATILITY ON THE CHATHAM AND DOVER RAILWAY—Question, Mr.
Maddison (Sheffield, Brightside) ; Answer, The President of the Board
of Trade (Mr. Ritchie, Croydon)   1183

BEER MATERIALS COMMITTEE—Question, Sir Cuthbert Quilter (Suffolk, Sudbury) ; Answer, The Chancellor of the Exchequer (Sir M. Hicks-Beach,
Bristol, W.)   1183

METROPOLITAN STREET OBSTRUCTIONS—Question, General Laurie (Pembroke
and Haverfordwest) ; Answer, The Under Secretary for the Home
Office (Mr. Jesse Collings, Birmingham, Bordesley)   1184

June 15.] *Page*

NATURALISATION CERTIFICATES.—Question, Mr. Swift MacNeill (Donegal, S.) ; Answer, The Under Secretary for the Home Office (Mr. Jesse Collings, Birmingham, Bordesley) 1185

ECCLESIASTICAL JUDGES.—Question, Mr. Charles McArthur (Liverpool, Exchange) ; Answer, The Under Secretary for the Home Office (Mr. Jesse Collings, Birmingham, Bordesley) 1186

BRITISH ARTISTS AND THE PARIS EXHIBITION—Question, Mr. Courtney (Cornwall, Bodmin) ; Answer, The Financial Secretary to the Treasury (Mr. Hanbury, Preston) 1186

ASSISTANTS TO SUB-POSTMASTERS—Question, Mr. Steadman (Tower Hamlets, Stepney) ; Answer, The Financial Secretary to the Treasury (Mr. Hanbury, Preston 1187

CENTRAL TELEGRAPH STAFF, LONDON—Question, Mr. M'Ghee (Louth, S.) ; Answer, The Financial Secretary to the Treasury (Mr. Hanbury, Preston) 1187

IRELAND—THE BAGOT ESTATE—Question, Mr. Hayden (Roscommon, S.) ; Answer, The Chief Secretary for Ireland (Mr. G. W. Balfour, Leeds, Central) 1188

IRISH COUNTY INFIRMARIES—Question, Mr. T. M. Healy (Louth, N.) ; Answer, The Chief Secretary for Ireland (Mr. G. W. Balfour, Leeds, Central) 1188

PENALTIES FOR CARRYING FIREARMS IN IRELAND—Question, Mr. T. M. Healy (Louth, N.) ; Answer, The Chief Secretary for Ireland (Mr. G. W. Balfour, Leeds, Central) 1189

THE ROSSMORE ESTATE—Question, Mr. Macaleese (Monaghan, S.) ; Answer, The Chief Secretary for Ireland (Mr. G. W. Balfour, Leeds, Central) ... 1190

IRISH LOCAL GOVERNMENT FINANCE—Question, Mr. Swift MacNeill (Donegal, S.) ; Answer, The Chief Secretary for Ireland (Mr. G. W. Balfour, Leeds, Central) 1191

AGRICULTURAL GRANT TO COUNTY DONEGAL—Questions, Mr. Swift MacNeill (Donegal, S.), and Mr. T. M. Healy (Louth, N.) ; Answers, The Chief Secretary for Ireland (Mr. G. W. Balfour, Leeds, Central)... 1192

NEWCASTLE, WEST (LIMERICK) CREAMERY—Question, Mr. Austin (Limerick, W.) ; Answer, The Chief Secretary for Ireland (Mr. G. W. Balfour, Leeds, Central) 1193

IRISH INTERMEDIATE EDUCATION—Question, Mr. William Johnston (Belfast, S.) ; Answer, The Chief Secretary for Ireland (Mr. G. W. Balfour, Leeds, Central) 1194

DISTURBANCES AT COOKSTOWN—Question, Mr. Doogan (Tyrone, E.) ; Answer, The Chief Secretary for Ireland (Mr. G. W. Balfour, Leeds, Central) ... 1194

IRISH LAND PURCHASE—Question, Mr. Young (Cavan, E.) ; Answer, The Chief Secretary for Ireland (Mr. G. W. Balfour, Leeds, Central) 1195

DISTRICT INSPECTOR MEEHAN—Question, Mr. J. P. Farrell (Cavan, W.) ; Answer, The Chief Secretary for Ireland (Mr. G. W. Balfour, Leeds, Central) 1195

LONGFORD AND THE AGRICULTURAL GRANT—Question, Mr. J. P. Farrell, (Cavan, W.) ; Answer, The Chief Secretary for Ireland (Mr. G. W. Balfour, Leeds, Central) 1196

June 15.]   *Page*

RIOTING IN BELFAST—Question, Mr. Dillon (Mayo, E.); Answer, The Chief
    Secretary for Ireland (Mr. G. W. Balfour, Leeds, Central)...   1197

CLERKS OF IRISH UNIONS—Question, Mr. Tully (Leitrim, S.); Answer, The
    Chief Secretary for Ireland (Mr. G. W. Balfour, Leeds, Central) 1197

BUSINESS OF THE HOUSE—Questions, Mr. J. P. Farrell (Cavan, W.), and Captain
    Donelan (Cork, E.); Answers, The First Lord of the Treasury (Mr. A. J.
    Balfour, Manchester, E.)   1198

PUBLIC BUSINESS.

INDIAN TARIFF ACT, 1899.

Motion made, and Question proposed—

> " That an humble Address be presented to Her Majesty, praying that Her
> Majesty will be pleased to disallow the Indian Tariff Act, 1899.")—(*Sir Henry
> Fowler.*)

DISCUSSION :—

The Secretary of State for India (Lord George Hamilton, Middlesex, Ealing) 1201
Sir Howard Vincent (Sheffield, Central) 1219
The Secretary of State for the Colonies (Mr. J. Chamberlain, Birmingham, W.)... 1220
Mr. J. M. Maclean (Cardiff) 1222
The First Lord of the Treasury (Mr. A. J. Balfour, Manchester, E.) 1223
Mr. J. M. Maclean   ... 1223
Lord George Hamilton   ... 1224
Mr. J. M. Maclean   ... 1224
Lord George Hamilton   ... 1236
Mr. Lough (Islington, W.)... 1251

Sir Lewis McIvor (Edinburgh, W.) 1258
Mr. L. R. Holland (Tower Hamlets, Bow)   1269
Mr. Wylie (Dumbartonshire)   ... 1275
Sir Charles Cameron (Glasgow, Bridgeton)   1278
Mr. Courtney (Cornwall, Bodmin) 1283
Mr. J. Chamberlain   ... 1291
Sir H. H. Fowler (Wolverhampton, E.) 1303
Mr. J. Chamberlain   1304
Mr. J. M. Maclean   1304
Mr. J. Chamberlain   1304
Sir H. Campbell-Bannerman (Stirling Burghs)   1307
Sir Edward Clarke (Plymouth) ... 1311
Sir H. Campbell-Bannerman   ... 1311

Question put—

The House divided :—Ayes, 152; Noes, 293. (Division List No. 193.)

PRIVATE LEGISLATION PROCEDURE (SCOTLAND) [EXPENSES]—Resolution
reported—

> "That it is expedient to authorise the payment, out of moneys to be pro-
> vided by Parliament, of any remuneration, allowances, and expenses that may
> become payable under any Act of the present Session to provide for improv-
> ing and extending the procedure for obtaining Parliamentary powers by way
> of Provisional Orders in matters relating to Scotland."

Resolution agreed to.

Baths and Wash Houses Acts Amendment Bill—Read a second time,
and committed for Monday next.

House adjourned at twenty minutes after Twelve of the clock.

LORDS: FRIDAY, 16TH JUNE 1899

PRIVATE BILL BUSINESS.

London and North-Western Railway (Additional Powers) Bill—
Examiner's Certificate of non-compliance with the Standing Orders referred
to the Standing Orders Committee on Thursday next 1317

Kensington and Notting Hill Electric Lighting Bill; Shirebrook
and District Gas Bill; South Staffordshire Stipendiary Justice
Bill; Nottingham Corporation Bill; Wolverhampton Tramways
Bill [Lords]—Reported with Amendments 1317

Fishguard Water and Gas Bill; Wetherby District Water Bill; South-
Eastern Railway Bill. Committee to meet on Monday next 1317

Barry Railway Bill; Lancashire and Yorkshire Railway (New Railways) Bill; Lancashire and Yorkshire Railway (Various Powers)
Bill—Committee to meet on Friday next 1317

Birkenhead Corporation Bill [Lords]—Commons Amendments considered,
and agreed to 1317

Owen's College (Manchester) Bill [Lords]—Committed forthwith; reported,
with Amendments 1317

Woking Water and Gas Bill—Read the second time, and committed ... 1317

Brooke's Park (Londonderry) Bill [Lords]—Read the third time, and passed,
and sent to the Commons 1317

Blackpool Improvement Bill; Darwen Corporation Bill; Dublin Corporation Bill—Brought from the Commons; read the third time, and
referred to the Examiners 1317

Great Central Railway Bill—The Chairman of Committees informed the
House that the opposition to the Bill was withdrawn: the Order made on
the 1st instant discharged; and Bill committed 1317

Tramways Orders Confirmation (No. 2) Bill [Lords]; Tramways Orders
Confirmation (No. 3) Bill [Lords]; West Middlesex Water Bill;
Aire and Calder Navigation Bill; East London Water Bill;
Milton Creek Conservancy Bill; Great Western Railway Bill;
Great Western and Great Central Railway Companies Bill—
Report from the Committee of Selection, That the following Lords be
proposed to the House to form the Select Committee for the consideration
of the said Bills; (viz.), E. Spencer (chairman), V. Falmouth, L. Boston,
L. Crofton, L. Sudley (E. Arran); agreed to: and the said Lords
appointed accordingly: The Committee to meet on Thursday next, at
Eleven o'clock; and all petitions referred to the Committee, with leave to
the petitioners praying to be heard by counsel against the Bills to be
heard as desired, as also counsel for the Bills 1317

Gas Orders Confirmation (No. 1) Bill [Lords]; Water Orders Confirmation Bill [Lords]; Gas and Water Orders Confirmation Bill
[Lords]—Read the third time (according to Order), and passed, and sent
to the Commons 1318

Electric Lighting Provisional Orders (No. 12) Bill [Lords]; Electric
Lighting Provisional Orders (No. 15) Bill [Lords]; Electric
Lighting Provisional Orders (No. 2) Bill—House in Committee
(according to Order): Bills reported without Amendment: Standing
Committee negatived; and Bills to be read the third time on Monday
next 1319

Tramways Orders Confirmation (No. 1) Bill [Lords]—House in Committee . (according to Order) : Amendments made ; Standing Committee negatived ; the Report of Amendments to be received on Monday next 1319

Electric Lighting Provisional Orders (No. 3) Bill; Central Electric Supply Bill; Central London Railway Bill; Charing Cross, Euston, and Hampstead Railway Bill; Midland Railway Bill; Gas Light and Coke Company Bill; London, Brighton, and South Coast Railway (Various Powers) Bill—Report from the Committee of Selection, that the Lord Brougham and Vaux be proposed to the House as a member of the Select Committee on the said Bills in the place of the Duke of Bedford ; and that the Lord Brougham and Vaux be chairman of the said Committee ; read, and agreed to 1319

North Staffordshire Railway Bill [Lords]; **London and South-Western Railway Bill** [Lords]—Report from the Committee of Selection, that the Lord Amherst of Hackney be proposed to the House as a member of the Selelt Committee on the said Bills in the place of the Lord Farnham ; read, and agreed to 1319

RETURNS, REPORTS, &c.

MERCHANT SEAMEN'S FUND—Account of the receipt and expenditure under the Seamen's Fund Winding-up Act, from 1st January to 31st December, 1898 ; laid before the House (pursuant to Act), and ordered to lie on the Table 1319

London Government Bill.—To be read the second time on Tuesday next. (*The Lord President, The Duke of Devonshire*) 1320

Finance Bill (Second Reading)—Order of the Day for the Second Reading read. Read the second time (according to Order) ; Committee negatived ; Then Standing Order No. XXXIX. considered (according to Order), and dispensed with : Bill read the third time, and passed 1320

Trawlers' Certificate, Suspension Bill [Lords]—Amendments reported (according to Order) ; further Amendments made ; and Bill to be read the third time on Thursday next 1320

Elementary Education (Defective and Epileptic Children) Bill [Lords] —To be read the second time on Tuesday next 1320

QUESTIONS.

INDENTURING IN WESTERN AUSTRALIA—Question, The Lord Stanley of Alderley and the Marquess of Ripon ; Answer, The Under Secretary of State for the Colonies (The Earl of Selborne) 1320

THE LONDON GOVERNMENT BILL—THE EARL OF KIMBERLEY 1328

The Prime Minister and Secretary of State for Foreign Affairs (*The Marquess of Salisbury*) 1327

House adjourned at Five of the clock.

COMMONS: FRIDAY, 16TH JUNE, 1899.

PRIVATE BILL BUSINESS.

Darwen Corporation Bill; Dublin Corporation Bill (By Order)—
Read the third time and passed   1328

**Derby Corporation (Tramways, &c.) Bill; London County Council
(Money) Bill**—As amended, considered ; to be read the third time   ... 1328

Glasgow Corporation Telephones Bill (By Order); Second Reading
deferred till Friday, June 30th   1328

**Education Department Provisional Order Confirmation (Liverpool)
Bill** [Lords]—Read a second time and committed...   1328

RAILWAY BILLS (GROUP 8).

Greenock and Port Glasgow Tramways Bill—Ordered, that Robert
Cook, John Daniel Clink, John Cameron, Daniel M'Arthur Erskine, and
Hugh M'Master do attend the Committee on Group 8 of Railway and
Tramway Bills upon Monday next, at half-past Eleven of the clock—(*Mr.
James William Lowther*)   1328

Kingscourt, Keady, and Armagh Railway Bill.

Mr. T. M. Healy (*Louth, N.*)   1329

**Local Government Provisional Orders (No. 2) Bill; Local Govern-
ment Provisional Orders (No. 7) Bill**—Reported with Amendments
(Provisional Orders confirmed) ; Report to lie upon the Table ; Bill, as
amended, to be considered upon Monday next   1329

**Local Government (Ireland) Provisional Orders (No. 2) Bill; Local
Government (Ireland) Provisional Orders (No. 3) Bill**—Reported,
without Amendment (Provisional Orders confirmed) ; Report to lie upon
the Table ; Bills to be read the third time upon Monday next   1329

Military Lands Provisional Orders Bill—Reported, with an Amendment
(Provisional Orders confirmed) ; Report to lie upon the Table ; Bill, as
amended, to be considered upon Monday next   1329

Electric Lighting Provisional Orders (No. 16) Bill—Reported, with
Amendments ; [Provisional Orders confirmed] ; Report to lie upon
the Table ; Bill, as amended, to be considered upon Monday next   ... 1330

**Electric Lighting Provisional Order (No. 18) Bill; Electric Lighting
Provisional Orders (No. 19) Bill**—Reported, without Amendment ;
[Provisional Order confirmed] ; Report to lie upon the Table ; Bills to be
read the third time upon Monday next   1330

Bexhill and Rotherfield Railway Bill; Inverness Harbour Bill
[Lords]—Reported, with Amendments ; Reports to lie upon the Table, and
to be printed 1330

Wishaw Water Bill [Lords]—Reported, without Amendment ; Report to
lie upon the Table, and be printed 1330

Barton-on-Sea Water Bill [Lords]—Reported, with Amendments ; Report
to lie upon the Table, and to be printed   1330

June 16.]   *Page*

Colonial and Foreign Banks Guarantee Fund Bill [Lords]—Reported, with Amendments ; Report to lie upon the Table 1330

Glasgow Corporation (Gas and Water) Bill [Lords] ; **Gainsborough Urban District Council (Gas) Bill** [Lords] ; **Dundee Gas, Street Improvements, and Tramways Bill** [Lords] ; **Lanarkshire (Middle Ward District) Water Bill** [Lords] ; **Liverpool Overhead Railway Bill** [Lords]—Reported, with Amendments ; Reports to lie upon the Table, and to be printed 1330

Local Government Provisional Order (No. 13) Bill—Reported (Provisional Order not confirmed) ; Report to lie upon the Table 1330

Worcestershire County Council Bill—Reported, with Amendments ; Report to lie upon the Table, and to be printed 1331

Jones's Divorce Bill [Lords]—Reported, from the Select Committee on Divorce Bills, without Amendment ; Report to lie upon the Table ; Bill to be read a third time 1331

Jones's Divorce Bill [Lords]—Ordered, That the Minutes of Evidence and Proceedings in the House of Lords on the Second Reading of Jones's Divorce Bill, together with the Documents deposited in the case, be returned to the House of Lords ; and that the Clerk do carry the same.—(*Mr. Solicitor-General*) 1331

Derby Corporation Water Bill ; **Leicester Corporation Water Bill** ; **and Sheffield Corporation (Derwent Valley) Water Bill, Consolidated into the " Derwent Valley Water Bill "**—Reported, with Amendments ; Report to lie upon the Table, and to be printed 1331

Message from the Lords—That they have agreed to Finance Bill, North Pembrokeshire and Fishguard Railway Bill, without Amendment ; Shotley Bridge and Consett District Gas Bill, with Amendments 1331

That they have passed a Bill, intituled, " An Act to confirm certain Provisional Orders made by the Board of Trade under the Electric Lighting Acts, 1882 and 1888, relating to Crayford, Halesowen, Handsworth, Lye and Wollescote, and Lymington." [Electric Lighting Provisional Orders (No. 14) Bill.] [Lords] 1331

Electric Lighting Provisional Orders (No. 14) Bill [Lords]—Read the first time ; referred to the Examiners of Petitions for Private Bills, and to be printed. (Bill 237.) 1331

PETITIONS.

Liquor Traffic Local Veto (Scotland) Bill—Petition from Dumfries and Maxwelltown, in favour ; to lie upon the Table 1331

Local Authorities Servants' Superannuation Bill—Petition from Sheffield, in favour ; to lie upon the Table 1332

Local Government (Scotland) Act (1894) Amendment Bill—Petitions in favour, from Dundee, and Beath ; to lie upon the Table 1332

Local Government (Scotland) Act (1894) Amendment (No. 2) Bill—Petition from Dundee, against ; to lie upon the Table 1332

Poor Law Relief (Disfranchisement)—Petition from Holbeach, for alteration of Law ; to lie upon the Table 1332

Private Legislation Procedure (Scotland) Bill—Petition from St. Andrews, in favour ; to lie upon the Table 1332

Sale of Intoxicating Liquors on Sunday Bill—Petitions in favour, from Sawbridgeworth, Great Yarmouth, and Wisbech ; to lie upon the Table   1332

RETURNS, REPORTS, &c.

MERCHANT SEAMEN'S FUND—Account presented,—of the Receipt and Expenditure under the Seamen's Fund Winding-up Act from 1st January to 31st December, 1898 [by Act] ; to lie upon the Table, and to be printed. (No. 222)   1332

APPOINTMENTS OPEN TO RETIRED SOLDIERS—Return ordered, "showing the number of appointments which would be open to reserve and retired Soldiers under the heads enumerated as suitable in Appendix to Report of Select Committee on Retired Soldiers' and Sailors' Employment, 1895 ; the number of Soldiers now holding such appointments ; and the number of vacancies which have occurred in such appointments since December, 1895, in the following form :—

Employment.	Number of men employed under each head.	Number of ex-Soldiers employed.	Number of Vacancies which have occurred since 31st day of December 1895.

—(*Colonel Long*)   1332

PUBLIC INCOME AND EXPENDITURE—Return ordered, "of Net Public Income and Net Public Expenditure under certain specified heads, as represented by Receipts into and Issues out of the Exchequer from 1869-70 to 1898-9, inclusive) in continuation of Parliamentary Paper, No. 344, of Session 1898)."—(*Sir Henry Fowler*)   1333

LOCAL GOVERNMENT(IRELAND) ACT, 1898 (METHOD OF DETERMINING AMOUNTS TO BE TAKEN AS HAVING BEEN RAISED IN STANDARD YEAR)—Copy ordered, "of Memorandum respecting the method adopted in determining the amounts of poor rate and county cess to be taken as having been raised during the standard financial year under Section 49 of the Local Government (Ireland) Act, 1898."—(*Mr. Gerald Balfour.*)—Copy presented accordingly ; to lie upon the Table, and to be printed. (No. 232.)   1333

SHOP HOURS ACT (1892) AMENDMENT.—Bill to amend the Shop Hours Act, 1892, ordered to be brought in by Mr. Steadman, Sir Charles Dilke, and Mr. Woods   1333

Shop Hours Act Amendment Bill—" To amend the Shop Hours Act, 1892," presented accordingly, and read the first time ; to be read a second time upon Wednesday, 28th June, and to be printed. (Bill 238.)   1333

FIRE BRIGADES.—Ordered, That Mr. Alfred Thomas be discharged from the Select Committee on Fire Brigades.—Ordered, that Mr. William Jones be added to the Committee.—(*Mr. Munro Ferguson*)   1333

QUESTIONS.

MOUNTAIN AND GARRISON ARTILLERY.—Question, Mr. Arnold-Forster (Belfast, W.); Answer, The Under Secretary of State for War (Mr. Wyndham, Dover) 1333

RECRUITS' RATIONS—Question, Mr. Hayden (Roscommon, S.); Answer, The Under Sercetary of State for War (Mr. Wyndham, Dover) 1334

EDWARD LYNCH'S PENSION—Question, Mr. Hayden (Roscommon, S.); Answer, The Under Secretary of State for War (Mr. Wyndham, Dover) 1334

THE CONNAUGHT RANGERS AT MEERUT—Question, Mr. Herbert Roberts (Denbighshire, W.); Answer, The Secretary of State for India (Lord G. Hamilton, Middlesex, Ealing) 1335

OUTRAGE BY BRITISH SOLDIERS AT RANGOON—Questions, Mr. Henry Roberts (Denbighshire, W.), Mr. Davitt (Mayo, S.), Mr. Dillon (Mayo, E.), and Mr. Swift MacNeill (Donegal, S.); Answers, The Secretary of State for India (Lord George Hamilton, Middlesex, Ealing) 1335

CALCUTTA MUNICIPAL BILL—Question, Mr. Herbert Roberts (Denbighshire, W.); Answer, The Secretary of State for India (Lord George Hamilton, Middlesex, Ealing) 1336

KURDISH ATROCITIES IN ARMENIA—Question, Mr. Schwann (Manchester, N.); Answer, The Under Secretary of State for Foreign Affairs (Mr. Brodrick, Surrey, Guildford) 1337

THE TRANSVAAL OATH OF ALLEGIANCE—Question, Mr. Bryn Roberts (Carnarvonshire, Eifion); Answer, The Secretary of State for the Colonies (Mr. J. Chamberlain, Birmingham, W.) 1337

ANTI-BOER PROPAGANDA—Question, Mr. Swift MacNeill (Donegal, S.); Answer, The Secretary of State for the Colonies (Mr. J. Chamberlain, Birmingham, W.)... 1338

THE NEWFOUNDLAND FISHERIES—Questions, Sir T. Gibson-Carmichael (Edinburgh, Mid-Lothian) and Mr. Gibson Bowles (Lynn Regis); Answers, The Secretary of State for the Colonies (Mr. J. Chamberlain, Birmingham, W.) 1338

ORPHAN HOMES OF SCOTLAND—Question, Sir Charles Cameron (Glasgow, Bridgeton); Answer, The Lord Advocate (Mr. A. Graham Murray, Buteshire) 1338

SCOTCH EDUCATION GRANT—Question, Dr. Clark (Caithness); Answer, The Lord Advocate (Mr. A. Graham Murray, Buteshire) 1339

CASE OF SARAH HALE—Question, Mr. Steadman (Tower Hamlets, Stepney); Answered privately by the Secretary of State for the Home Department (Sir M. White Ridley, Lancashire, Blackpool) 1339

THE NEW ECCLESIASTICAL JUDGE—Question, Lord Balcarres (Lancashire, Chorley); Answer, The Under Secretary of State for the Home Department (Mr. Jesse Collings, Birmingham, Bordesley)... 1340

NATIONAL DEBT ANNUITIES—Question, Mr. J. P. Smith (Lanark, Partick); Answer, The Chancellor of the Exchequer (Sir M. Hicks-Beach, Bristol, W.) 1340

THE INNISKEEN RAILWAY ACCIDENT—Question, Mr. Macaleese (Monaghan, N.); Answer, The President of the Board of Trade (Mr. Ritchie, Croydon) 1341

ALLEGED OUTRAGE ON THE GREAT WESTERN RAILWAY—Question, Mr. Schwann (Manchester, N.); Answer, The President of the Board of Trade (Mr. Ritchie, Croydon) 1341

SCOTTISH LIGHTHOUSE KEEPERS—Question, Dr. Clark (Caithness); Answer, The President of the Board of Trade (Mr. Ritchie, Croydon) 1342

CIRCULAR POSTAGE—Question, Mr. Edward Barry (Cork Co., S.); Answer, The Financial Secretary to the Treasury (Mr. Hanbury, Preston)... ... 1342

THE MOY POSTMASTERSHIP—Question, Mr. William Johnston (Belfast, S.); Answer, The Financial Secretary to the Treasury (Mr. Hanbury, Preston) 1343

COST OF POSTCARDS—Question, Mr. Flavin (Kerry, N.); Answer, The Financial Secretary to the Treasury (Mr. Hanbury Preston) 1343

FERRYBANK POSTMASTERSHIP—Question, Mr. Patrick O'Brien (Kilkenny); Answer, The Financial Secretary to the Treasury (Mr. Hanbury, Preston) 1344

SUB-POSTMASTERS' PAY—Question, Mr. Patrick O'Brien (Kilkenny); Answer, The Financial Secretary to the Treasury (Mr. Hanbury, Preston)... ... 1344

DUBLIN POSTMAN'S GRIEVANCES—Question, Mr. Patrick O'Brien (Kilkenny); Answer, The Financial Secretary to the Treasury (Mr. Hanbury, Preston) 1345

SUPERIOR APPOINTMENTS IN THE IRISH POST OFFICE—Question, Mr. Patrick O'Brien (Kilkenny); Answer, The Financial Secretary to the Treasury (Mr. Hanbury, Preston) 1346

BERKHAMSTED NATIONAL SCHOOLS—Question, Mr. Trevelyan (York, W.R., Elland); The Vice-President of the Committee of Council on Education (Sir J. Gorst, Cambridge University) 1347

SOUTH KENSINGTON MUSEUM (ART BRANCH)—Question, Mr. Maurice Healy (Cork); Answer, The Vice-President of the Committee of Council on Education (Sir John Gorst, Cambridge University) 1347

MEAT INSPECTION AT LIVERPOOL—Question, Mr. Patrick O'Brien (Kilkenny); Answer, The President of the Local Government Board (Mr. Chaplin, Lincolnshire, Sleaford) 1348

STATE AID FOR THE BLIND—Question, Mr. Patrick O'Brien (Kilkenny); Answer, The President of the Local Government Board (Mr. Chaplin, Lincolnshire, Sleaford) 1348

PUBLIC VACCINATION AT READING—Question, Mr. Palmer (Reading); Answer, The President of the Local Government Board (Mr. Chaplin, Lincolnshire, Sleaford) 1349

KILDARE STREET LIBRARY—Question, Mr. Patrick O'Brien (Kilkenny); Answer, The Chief Secretary for Ireland (Mr. G. W. Balfour, Leeds, Central) 1350

ROYAL COLLEGE OF SCIENCE, DUBLIN—Question, Mr. Patrick O'Brien (Kilkenny); Answer, the Chief Secretary for Ireland (Mr. G. W. Balfour, Leeds, Central) 1350

MONAGHAN UNION MEDICAL OFFICER—Questions, Mr. Macaleese (Monaghan, N.) and Mr. T. M. Healy (Cork); Answers, The Chief Secretary for Ireland (Mr. G. W. Balfour, Leeds, Central)... 1350

REVISED VALUATIONS—Question, Mr. Edward Barry (Cork Co., S.); Answer, The Chief Secretary for Ireland (Mr. G. W. Balfour, Leeds, Central) ... 1352

AGRICULTURAL GRANT FOR ROSCOMMON—Question, Mr. Hayden (Roscommon, S.); Answer, The Chief Secretary for Ireland (Mr. G. W. Balfour, Leeds, Central)   1352

BALROTHY COUNTY CESS—Question, Mr. Clancy (Dublin Co., N.); Answer, The Chief Secretary for Ireland (Mr. G. W. Balfour, Leeds, Central)   ... 1353

CELTIC LANGUAGE IN IRISH SCHOOLS—Question, Mr. Flavin (Kerry, N.); Answer, The Chief Secretary for Ireland (Mr. G. W. Balfour, Leeds, Central)   1354

TITHE RENT CHARGE REDEMPTION IN IRELAND—Question, Mr. Smith Barry (Huntingdonshire, Huntingdon); Answer, The Chief Secretary for Ireland (Mr. G. W. Balfour, Leeds, Central)...   1354

FAIR RENTS IN COUNTY CAVAN—Question, Mr. J. P. Farrell (Cavan, W.); Answer, The Chief Secretary for Ireland (Mr. G. W. Balfour, Leeds, Central)   1355

PROMOTION IN THE ROYAL IRISH CONSTABULARY—Question, Mr. J. P. Farrell (Cavan, W.); Answer, The Chief Secretary for Ireland (Mr. G. W. Balfour, Leeds, Central)   1356

SANITARY WORKS IN CASTLEREA AND BALLAGHADEREEN—Question, Mr. Hayden (Roscommon, S.); Answer, The Chief Secretary for Ireland (Mr. G. W. Balfour, Leeds, Central)   1357

FEVER IN THE OUGHTERARD UNION—Question, Mr. Patrick O'Brien (Kilkenny); Answer, The Chief Secretary for Ireland (Mr. G. W. Balfour, Leeds, Central)   1357

FISH TRAFFIC ON RAILWAYS—Question, Mr. Patrick O'Brien (Kilkenny); Answer, The Chief Secretary for Ireland (Mr. G. W. Balfour, Leeds, Central)   1358

ILLEGAL FISHING IN IRELAND—Question, Mr. Patrick O'Brien (Kilkenny); Answer; The Chief Secretary for Ireland (Mr. G. W. Balfour, Leeds, Central)   1358

COUNTY CAVAN MAGISTRACY—Question, Mr. J. P. Farrell (Cavan, W.); Answer, The Chief Secretary for Ireland (Mr. G. W. Balfour, Leeds, Central)   1359

CHAIRMAN OF IRISH TOWN COMMISSIONERS—Question, Mr. Maurice Healy (Cork); Answer, The Chief Secretary for Ireland (Mr. G. W. Balfour, Leeds, Central)   1360

STEAM TRAWLING OFF HOWTH—Question, Mr. Clancy (Dublin Co., N.); Answer, The Chief Secretary for Ireland (Mr. G. W. Balfour, Leeds, Central)   ... 1360

LORD DILLON'S ESTATE.—Question, Mr. T. M. Healey (Louth, N.); Answer, The Chief Secretary for Ireland (Mr. G. W. Balfour, Leeds, Central)   ... 1361

PUBLIC BUSINESS.

SUPPLY [14TH ALLOTTED DAY].

In the Committee.

CIVIL SERVICES AND REVENUE DEPARTMENTS ESTIMATES, 1899–1900.

CLASS IV.

Motion made, and Question proposed—

"That a sum, not exceeding £701,861, be granted to Her Majesty to complete the sum necessary to defray the Charge which will come in course of payment during the year ending on the 31st day of March, 1900, for Public Education in Scotland, and for Science and Art in Scotland."

DISCUSSION :—

The Lord Advocate (Mr. A. G. Murray, Buteshire) ... 1363
Mr. Thomas Shaw (Hawick Burghs) 1374
Mr. Renshaw (Renfrew, W.) 1382
Mr. Haldane (Haddington) 1388
Colonel Denny (Kilmarnock Burghs) 1391
Mr. Bryce (Aberdeen, S.) ... 1394
Sir Mark Stewart (Kirkcudbright) 1400
Mr. Crombie (Kincardineshire) 1402

Mr. J. P. Smith (Lanark, Partick) 1406
Captain Sinclair (Forfar) ... 1412
Mr. Weir (Ross and Cromarty) ... 1415
Captain Sinclair 1415
Sir Wm. Wedderburn (Banffshire) 1417
Mr. A. G. Murray 1419
Sir Wm. Wedderburn 1417
Mr. Monro Ferguson (Leith Burghs) 1422
Mr. Caldwell (Lanarkshire, Mid) 1424

Motion made, and Question proposed—

> "That a sum, not exceeding £701,411, be granted for the said service."—(*Sir Charles Cameron.*)

DISCUSSION :—

The Lord Advocate (Mr. A. G. Murray, Buteshire) ... 1432
Sir Charles Cameron (Glasgow, Bridgeton) 1433
Mr. A. G. Murray · ... 1433
Mr. Colville (Lanarkshire, N.E.) 1434
Mr. Hedderwick (Wick Burghs) 1435
Mr. Renshaw (Renfrew, W.) 1437

Mr. Thomas Shaw (Hawick Burghs) 1438
Sir John Kinloch (Perthshire, E.). 1438
Dr. Clark (Caithness) 1439
Mr. Thomas Shaw 1441
Mr. Alex. Cross (Glasgow, Camlachie) 1441
Mr. A. G. Murray 1442
Mr. McLeod (Sutherland) ... 1442
Mr. Weir (Ross and Cromarty) ... 1442

Question put.

The Committee divided :—Ayes, 46 ; Noes, 103.   (Division List, No. 194.)

Original Question again proposed.

DISCUSSION RESUMED :—

The Lord Advocate (Mr. A. G. Murray, Buteshire) ... 1443
Dr. Clark (Caithness) ... 1450
Mr. A. G. Murray ... 1450
Mr. Caldwell (Lanarkshire, Mid.) 1451

Mr. A. G. Murray 1451
Sir John Kinloch (Perthshire, E.) 1452
Mr. A. G. Murray 1452
Captain Sinclair (Forfar) ... 1452

It being Midnight, the Chairman left the Chair to make his Report to the House.

Committee report progress, to sit again on Monday next.

Adjourned at five minutes after Twelve of the clock.

LORDS: MONDAY, 19TH JUNE, 1899.

PRIVATE BILL BUSINESS.

The LORD CHANCELLOR acquainted the House that the Clerk of the Parliaments had laid upon the Table the Certificates from the Examiners that the Standing Orders applicable to the following Bills have been complied with, viz. :—Electric Lighting Provisional Orders (No. 5); Electric Lighting Provisional Orders (No. 6); Housing of the Working Classes Provisional Order (Borrowstounness); Local Government Provisional Order (Housing of Working Classes) 1453

Also the Certificates that no further Standing Orders are applicable to the following Bills :—Local Government (Ireland) Provisional Order No. 1); Local Government Provisional Orders (Poor Law) 1453

And, also, the Certificates that the further Standing Orders applicable to the following Bills have been complied with :—Sheffield Corporation Markets; City and Brixton Railway; London Improvements; Stockport Corporation; Lincoln and East Coast Railway and Dock. The same were ordered to lie upon the Table 1453

Great Eastern Railway (General Powers) Bill [Lords]—The Queen's consent signified; and Bill reported from the Select Committee with Amendments 1453

Wetherby District Water Bill—Reported with Amendments 1453

South-Eastern Railway Bill—The Queen's consent signified; and Bill reported with Amendments 1454

Southport and Lytham Tramroad Bill [Lords]—Reported from the Select Committee, with Amendments 1454

North Staffordshire Railway Bill [Lords]—The Queen's consent signified; and Bill reported from the Select Committee, with Amendments 1454

West Gloucestershire Water Bill—Read the second time, and committed 1454

Caledonian Railway (General Powers) Bill [Lords]: **Aberdeen Joint Passenger Station Bill** [Lords]; **South Staffordshire Tramways Bill** [Lords]—Read the third time, and passed, and sent to the Commons 1454

Cardiff Railway Bill; **Rhondda Urban District Council Bill**—Read the third time, with the Amendments, and passed, and returned to the Commons 1454

Lowestoft Promenade Pier Bill; **Godalming Corporation Water Bill**—Brought from the Commons; read the third time; and referred to the Examiners 1454

Jones's Divorce Bill [Lords]—Minutes of Evidence and Proceedings before this House on the Second Reading, together with the documents deposited in the case, returned from the Commons 1454

Education Department Provisional Order Confirmation (London) Bill [Lords]—House to be in Committee on Thursday next 1454

Local Government Provisional Orders (No. 3) Bill—To be read the second time on Thursday next—(*The Lord Harris*) 1454

Electric Lighting Provisional Orders (No. 5) Bill; **Electric Lighting Provisional Orders (No. 6) Bill**—To be read the second time To-morrow —(*The Earl of Dudley*) 1455

Tramways Orders Confirmation (No. 2) Bill [Lords]; Tramways Orders Confirmation (No. 3) Bill [Lords]; West Middlesex Water Bill; Aire and Calder Navigation Bill; East London Water Bill; Milton Creek Conservancy Bill; Great Western Railway Bill; Great Western and Great Central Railway Companies Bill —Report from the Committee of Selection, that the Earl of Mansfield be proposed to the House as a member of the Select Committee on the said Bills, in the place of the Viscount Falmouth ; read, and agreed to ... 1455

Electric Lighting Provisional Orders (No. 12) Bill [Lords] —Read the third time (according to Order), and passed, and sent to the Commons 1455

Electric Lighting Provisional Orders (No. 13) Bill (Lords)— House in Committee (according to Order) ; Amendments made ; Standing Committee negatived ; the Report of Amendments to be received To-morrow 1455

Electric Lighting Provisional Orders (No. 15) Bill [Lords]—Read the third time (according to Order), and passed, and sent to the Commons ... 1455

Electric Lighting Provisional Orders (No. 2) Bill—Read the third time (according to Order), and passed 1455

Tramways Orders Confirmation (No. 1) Bill [Lords]—Amendments reported (according to order), and Bill to be read the third time To-morrow 1455

RETURNS, REPORTS &c.

Education (Scotland)—Minute of the Committee of Council on Education in Scotland, dated 15th June, 1899, amending the terms of Paragraph 5 of the Minute of 27th April, 1899, providing for the distribution of the sum available for Secondary or Technical (including Agriculture) Education under Section 2, Sub-section (4) of the Local Taxation Account (Scotland) Act, 1898 1456

Army (Military Works)—Approximate estimate of expenditure for the year 1899-1900 under existing loans 1456

Colonies (Annual)—No. 261. Jamaica. Annual Report for 1897–98 (for Report for 1896-97, see No. 225) 1456

Railways (Continuous Brakes)—Return by railway companies of the United Kingdom for the six months ending 31st December, 1898 ... 1456

Trade Reports (Annual Series)—No. 2290. Japan (Yokohama and District). No. 2291: Persia (Azerbaijan). No. 2292: Africa (Congo trade returns). Presented (by Command), and ordered to lie on the Table 1456

Public Records (Treasury)—Schedule containing a list and particulars of classes of Treasury documents which have been deposited in the Public Record Office, but which are not considered of sufficient public value to justify their preservation therein ; laid before the House (pursuant to Act), and Ordered to lie on the Table 1456

PETITION.

London Government Bill—Petition for Amendment of ; of the Vestry of the Parish of St. George, Hanover Square, London ; read, and Ordered to lie on the Table 1456

Anchors and Chain Cables Bill—House to be in Committee on Thursday next 1457

June 19.]   *Page*

Education of Children Bill—To be read the third time on Friday, the 30th instant. (*The Viscount Knutsford.*) 1457

Public Libraries Bill [Lords]—Lord WINDSOR: My Lords, I understand that the Local Government Board object to several of the clauses in this Bill, and therefore I ask leave to postpone the Second Reading in the hope that some modification may be made which will remove these objections. Order of the Day for Second Reading read, and discharged... 1457

Youthful Offenders Bill [Lords]—Second Reading; Order of the Day for the Second Reading read.

Moved, "That the Bill be now read the second time. (*Lord James of Hereford.*)

DISCUSSION—

Lord Leigh 1462	*Lord James of Hereford* ... 1465
Lord Norton 1463	*Lord Leigh* 1466

On Question, agreed to.

Bill read the second time accordingly, and committed to a Committee of the whole House on Tuesday, the 27th instant.

BILL INTRODUCED.

Light Load Line Bill [Lords].—A Bill to supplement the law relating to load lines on merchant ships was presented by the Lord Muskerry; read the first time; to be printed; and to be read the second time on Monday the 26th instant. (No. 127) 1466

QUESTION.

THE ROYAL ACADEMY—Question, The Lord Stanley of Alderley; Answer, The Prime Minister and Secretary of State for Foreign Affairs (The Marquess of Salisbury) 1466

House adjourned at forty minutes after Five of the clock.

COMMONS: MONDAY, 19TH JUNE, 1899.

NEW WRIT—New Writ for the County of York, West Riding (Osgoldcross Division), in the room of Sir John Austin, Baronet (Chiltern Hundreds).— (*Mr. William M'Arthur.*) 1474

PRIVATE BILL BUSINESS.

PRIVATE BILLS—[Lords]—(STANDING ORDERS NOT PREVIOUSLY INQUIRED INTO COMPLIED WITH.)—Mr. SPEAKER laid upon the Table Report from one of the Examiners of Petitions for Private Bill, That, in the case of the following Bills, originating in the Lords, and referred on the First Reading thereof, the Standing Orders not previously inquired into, and which are applicable thereto, have been complied with, viz.—Buenos Ayres and Pacific Railway Company Bill [Lords]; Transvaal Mortgage, Loan, and Finance Company Bill [Lords]. Ordered, That the Bills be read a second time 1474

PRIVATE BILLS [Lords]—(NO STANDING ORDERS APPLICABLE)—MR. SPEAKER laid upon the Table Report from one of the Examiners' of Petitions for Private Bills, That, in the case of the following Bill, originating in the Lords, and referred on the First Reading thereof, no Standing Orders are applicable, viz. **Yorke Estate Bill** [Lords]. Ordered, That the Bill be read a second time   1474

PROVISIONAL ORDER BILLS—(STANDING ORDERS APPLICABLE THERETO COMPLIED WITH)—MR. SPEAKER laid upon the Table Report from one of the Examiners of Petitions for Private Bills, That, in the case of the following Bill, referred on the First Reading thereof, the Standing Orders which are applicable thereto have been complied with, viz.: Electric Lighting Provisional Order (No. 20) Bill ; Ordered, that the Bill be read a second time to-morrow   1474

PRIVATE BILL [Lords] (STANDING ORDERS NOT PREVIOUSLY INQUIRED INTO NOT COMPLIED WITH)—Mr. SPEAKER laid upon the Table Report from one of the Examiners of Petitions for Private Bills, that, in the case of the following Bill, originating in the Lords, and referred on the First Reading thereof, the Standing Orders not previously inquired into, and which are a plicable thereto, have not been complied with, viz., Birmingham, NorthpWarwickshire, and Stratford-upon-Avon Railway Bill [Lords]. Ordered, that the Report be referred to the Select Commitee on Standing Orders 1475

London, Brighton, and South Coast Railway (Pensions) Bill ; Lisburn Urban District Bill—Lords' Amendments considered, and agreed to   1475

Friends' Provident Institution Bill [Lords]—Read the third time, and passed, with an Amendment 1475

Lowestoft Promenade Pier Bill—(Queen's Consent signified).   Read the third time, and passed   1475

Skipton Urban District Gas Bill [Lords]—Read the third time, and passed, with Amendments   1475

Godalming Corporation Water Bill—Read the third time, and passed ... 1475

Mid Kent Gas Bill [Lords]—Read the third time, and passed, with Amendments 1475

Aberdeen Corporation Bill [Lords]—As amended, considered ; Amendments made ; Bill to be read the third time   1475

Hastings and St. Leonards Gas Bill [Lords]—As amended, considered ; to be read the third time   1476

Walker and Wallsend Union Gas (Electric Lighting) Bill —As amended, considered ; Amendments made ; Bill to be read the third time   1476

All Saints' Church (Cardiff) Bill [Lords]—To be read a second time upon Thursday   1476

Great Grimsby Street Tramways Bill [Lords] ; **Lowestoft Water and Gas Bill** [Lords] ; **Mersey Docks and Harbour Board (Pilotage) Bill** [Lords] ; **Millwall Dock Bill** ; **North-Eastern and Hull and Barnsley Railways (Joint Dock) Bill** [Lords] ; **North-Eastern Railway Bill** [Lords]—Read a second time, and committed   1476

St. Neots Water Bill [Lords]—(By Order).   Read a second time, and committed 1476

June 19.]   *Page*

London County Council (General Powers) Bill — Ordered, That the Minutes of Evidence taken before the Committee on the Great Eastern Railway Bill, in the Session of 1887, be referred to the Committee on the London County Council (General Powers) (re-committed) Bill.—(*Dr. Farquharson*) 1476

Electric Lighting Provisional Orders (No. 18) Bill ; Electric Lighting Provisional Orders (No. 19) Bill ; Local Government (Ireland) Provisional Orders (No. 2) Bill ; Local Government (Ireland) Provisional Orders (No. 3) Bill—Read a third time, and passed 1476

Electric Lighting Provisional Orders (No. 16) Bill ; Local Government Provisional Orders (No. 2) Bill; Local Government Provisional Orders (No. 7) Bill; Military Lands Provisional Order Bill—As amended, considered ; to be read the third time To-morrow... 1477

Harrow and Uxbridge Railway Bill ; Bristol Gas Bill [Lords]— Reported, with Amendments ; Reports to lie upon the Table, and to be printed 1477

MESSAGE FROM THE LORDS—That they have agreed to—Amendments to Birkendead Corporation Bill [Lords]—Without Amendments 1477

That they have passed a Bill, intituled, " An Act to confirm certain Provisional Orders made by the Board of Trade under The Gas and Water Works Facilities Act, 1870, relating to Alton (Hants) Gas, Bedworth Gas, Elstree and Boreham Wood Gas, Limavady Gas, and Well ng oroug Gas." [Gas Orders Confirmation (No. 1) Bill [Lords] ... i.. b ...h 1477

Also, a Bill, intituled, " An Act to confirm certain Provisional Orders made by the Board of Trade under The Gas and Water Works Facilities Act, 1870, relating to Burnham and District Water, Harpenden Water, Maidstone Water, Stourbridge Water, and Tilehurst, Pangbourne, and District Water." [Water Orders Confirmation Bill [Lords] 1477

Also, a Bill, intituled, " An Act to confirm certain Provisional Orders made by the Board of Trade under The Gas and Water Works Facilities Act, 1870, relating to Herne Bay Gas, Hoylake and West Kirby Gas and Water, Tonbridge Gas, and York Town and Blackwater Gas " [Gas and Water Orders Confirmation Bill [Lords] 1477

And, also, a Bill, intituled, " An Act for conferring powers upon the trustees of the will of the late James Hood Brooke to acquire Gwyn's Grounds, Londonderry, and lay out the same as a public park ; and for other purposes." [Brooke's Park (Londonderry) Bill. [Lords.] 1477

Gas Orders Confirmation (No. 1) Bill [Lords.]—Read the first time ; referred to the Examiners of Petitions for Private Bills, and to be printed. [Bill 239.] 1478

Water Orders Confirmation Bill [Lords]—Read the first time ; referred to the Examiners of Petitions for Private Bills, and to be printed. [Bill 240.] 1478

Gas and Water Orders Confirmation Bill [Lords]—Read the first time ; referred to the Examiners of Petitions for Private Bills, and to be printed. [Bill 241.] 1478

Brooke's Park (Londonderry) Bill [Lords]—Read the first time, and referred to the Examiners of Petitions for Private Bills 1478

PETITIONS.

Church Discipline Bill.—Petition from Nottingham, in favour ; to lie upon the Table   1478

Liquor Traffic Local Veto (Scotland) Bill.—Petition from Nottingham, in favour ; to lie upon the Table   1478

Local Government (Scotland) Act (1894) Amendment Bill—Petitions in favour : from Wick and Brechin ; to lie upon the Table 1478

Poor Law Amendment (Scotland) Act, 1845—Petition from Bothwell, for alteration of Law ; to lie upon the Table   1478

Private Legislation Procedure (Scotland Bill.—Petitions in favour : from Brechin, Astruther, Easter, and Crail ; to lie upon the Table   1478

Sale of Intoxicating Liquors on Sunday Bill.—Petitions in favour : From Walton, Glastonbury, Street, Parbrook, Aller, Long Sutton, and Preston (three) ; to lie upon the Table   1478

Town Council (Scotland) Bill.—Petition from Selkirk, in favour ; to lie upon the Table   1479

RETURNS, REPORTS, &c.

Trade Reports (Annual Series)—Copies presented,—of Diplomatic and Consular Reports, Annual Series, Nos. 2290 to 2292 (by Command) ; to lie upon the Table   1479

Colonial Reports (Annual)—Copy presented,—of Report No. 261 (Jamaica, Annual Report for 1897-8) (by Command) ; to lie upon the Table   ... 1479

Railways (Continuous Brakes)—Copy presented,—of Return by Railway Companies of the United Kingdom for the six mouths ending the 31st December, 1898 (by Command) ; to lie upon the Table   1479

London County Council—Copy presented,—of Returns relating to the Council up to 31st March, 1899, with Estimate of Expenditure for the year ending 31st March, 1900 (by Act) ; to lie upon the Table, and to be printed. (No. 233)   1479

Superannuation Act, 1887—Copy presented,—of Treasury Minute, dated 8th June, 1899, granting to Mr. Alfred Edgar Clay, Second Division Clerk in the Money Order Office, General Post Office, a Retired Allowance under the Act (by Act) ; to lie upon the Table   1479

Education (Scotland)—Copy presented,—of Minute of the Committee of Council of Education in Scotland, dated 15th June, 1899, amending the terms of Paragraph 5 of the Minute of 27th April, 1899, providing for the distribution of the sum available for Secondary or Technical (including Agricultural) Education, under Section 2, Sub-section (4), of The Local Taxation Account (Scotland) Act, 1898 (by Command) ; to lie upon the Table   1479

Army (Military Works)—Copy presented,—of Approximate Estimate of Expenditure for the year 1899-1900 under existing Loans (by Command) ; to lie upon the Table 1479

Paper laid upon the Table by the Clerk of the House—

Public Records (Treasury)—Copy of Schedule of Documents (of the Treasury, which are not considered of sufficient public value to justify their preservation in the Public Record Office (by Act)   1480

ARMY RIFLE RANGES—Address for "Return of the Rifle Ranges which have
been closed to the firing of full-charge ammunition since the issue of the
Lee-Metford rifle, and of new ranges approved during the same period."—
(*Mr. Frederick Wilson.*)   1480

QUESTIONS.

ADMIRALTY CONTRACTS—Question, Mr. Edmund Robertson (Dundee) ; Answer,
The Secretary to the Admiralty (Mr. Macartney, Antrim, S.)   1480

THE GUARDS' LOST STORES—Question, Sir James Fergusson (Manchester, N.E.);
Answer, The Financial Secretary to the War Office (Mr. J. Powell-
Williams, Birmingham, S.)   1481

THE GUERNSEY MILITIA—Questions, Major Rasch (Essex, S.E.), and Mr. R.
G. Webster (St. Pancras, E.) ; Answers, The Financial Secretary to the
War Office (Mr. J. Powell-Williams, Birmingham, S.)   1481

THE METROPOLITAN VOLUNTEER REVIEW—Question, General Russell (Cheltenham) ; Answer, The Financial Secretary to the War Office (Mr. J. Powell
Williams, Birmingham. S.)   1481

JOSEPH DENISTON (LATE OF THE 10TH FOOT)—Question, Mr. J. P. Farrell
(Kerry, S.) ; Answer, The Financial Secretary to the War Office (Mr. J.
Powell-Williams, Birmingham, S.)   1482

CORK MILITARY DISTRICT CONTRACTS—Question, Captain Donelan (Cork, E.);
Answer, The Financial Secretary to the War Office (Mr. J. Powell-Williams,
Birmingham, S.)   1482

FIGHTING ON THE TURCO-SERVIAN FRONTIER—Question, Mr. Stevenson
(Suffolk, Eye) ; Answer, The Under Secretary of State for Foreign Affairs
(Mr. Brodrick, Surrey, Guildford)   1483

SIR W. GARSTON'S REPORT ON THE SOUDAN—Question, Mr. J. E. Ellis (Nottingham, Rushcliffe) ; Answer, The Under Secretary of State for Foreign
Affairs (Mr. Brodrick, Surrey, Guildford)   1484

SOUTH AFRICAN REPUBLIC—THE MURDER OF MRS. APPLEBE—Question,
Mr. William Johnston (Belfast, S.) ; Answer, The Secretary of State for
the Colonies (Mr. J. Chamberlain, Birmingham, W.)   1484

THE KILLING OF MR. EDGAR BY A BOER POLICEMAN—Question, Mr.
Duncombe (Cumberland, Egremont) ; Answer, the Secretary of State for
the Colonies (Mr. J. Chamberlain, Birmingham, W.)   1485

THE JAMESON RAID—Question, Mr. C. P. Scott (Lancashire, Leigh) ; Answer,
The Secretary of State for the Colonies (Mr. J. Chamberlain, Birmingham,
W.)   1485

PROMOTION IN THE PRISON SERVICE—Question, Mr. Lough (Islington, W.);
Answer, The Secretary of State for the Home Department (Sir M. White
Ridley, Lancashire, Blackpool)   1485

GLASGOW BAKERY DISPUTE—Question, Sir Charles Cameron (Glasgow, Bridgeton) ; Answer, The Lord Advocate (Mr. A. G. Murray, Buteshire)   ... 1486

ABERDEEN CEMETERY SCANDAL—Question, General Russell (Cheltenham);
Answer, The Lord Advocate (Mr. A. G. Murray, Buteshire)   1486

THE DAY SCHOOL CODE—Question, Viscount Cranborne (Rochester); Answer.
The Vice-President of the Committee of Council on Education (Sir J.
Gorst, Cambridge University)   1487

CARMARTHEN CHARITIES—Question, Mr. Lloyd Morgan (Carmarthen);
Answer, The Parliamentary Charity Commissioner (Mr. Grant Lawson
(York, N.R., Thirsk) 1487

HYDE PARK LIGHTING—Question, Gen. Russel (Cheltenham); Answer, The
First Commissioner of Works (Mr. Akers-Douglas, Kent, St. Augustines) 1488

FINTONA SUNDAY MAILS—Question, Mr. Dillon (Mayo, E.); Answer, The
Financial Secretary to the Treasury (Mr. Hanbury, Preston)   1489

NORTH KERRY POSTAL ARRANGEMENTS—Question, Mr. Flavin (Kerry, N.);
Answer, The Financial Secretary to the Treasury (Mr. Hanbury, Preston) 1489

BELFAST POST OFFICE STAFF—Question, Mr. MacAleese (Monaghan, N.);
Answer, The Financial Secretary to the Treasury (Mr. Hanbury, Preston) 1490

DUNDALK POSTMASTERSHIP — Question, Mr. MacAleese (Monaghan, N.);
Answer, The Financial Secretary to the Treasury (Mr. Hanbury, Preston) 1490

BALLYMAHON POSTAL ARRANGEMENTS—Question, Mr. Hayden (Roscommon,
S.); Answer, The Financial Secretary to the Treasury (Mr. Hanbury,
Preston)   1491

MAIL TRAIN DELAYS AT LIMERICK JUNCTION—Question, Mr. Flavin (Kerry,
N.); Answer, The Financial Secretary to the Treasury (Mr. Hanbury,
Preston)   1491

ENNISKILLEN POST OFFICE—Question, Mr. Jordan (Fermanagh, S.); Answer,
The Financial Secretary to the Treasury (Mr. Hanbury, Preston)   ... 1492

WEST CAVAN TRAMWAYS—Question, Mr. J. P. Farrell (Kerry, S.); Answer,
The Financial Secretary to the Treasury (Mr. Hanbury, Preston)   ... 1492

LANESBOROUGH POSTAL ARRANGEMENTS—Question, Mr. Hayden (Roscommon,
S.); Answer, The Financial Secretary to the Treasury (Mr. Hanbury,
Preston)   1493

BALLYDUFF POSTAL ARRANGEMENTS—Question, Mr. Flavin (Kerry, N.);
Answer, The Financial Secretary to the Treasury (Mr. Hanbury,
Preston)   1494

IRISH SCHOOL TEACHERS' PENSION FUND—Question, Mr. Flavin (Kerry, N.);
Answer, The Chief Secretary for Ireland (Mr. G. W. Balfour, Leeds,
Central)   1494

IRISH GUARDIANS AND LABOURERS' COTTAGES—Question, Mr. Gibney (Meath,
N.); Answer, The Chief Secretary for Ireland (Mr. G. W. Balfour, Leeds,
Central)   1495

CARRYING FIREARMS IN IRELAND—Question, Mr. Hayden, Roscommon, S.);
Answer, The Chief Secretary for Ireland (Mr. G. W. Balfour, Leeds,
Central)   1495

TYRONE COUNTY COUNCIL RATE COLLECTOR—Question, Mr. Hemphill
(Tyrone, N.); Answer, The Chief Secretary for Ireland (Mr. G. W.
Balfour, Leeds, Central)   1496

June 19.]   *Page*

JUDICIAL RENTS IN IRELAND—Question, Mr. Flavin (Kerry, N.); Answer, The Chief Secretary for Ireland (Mr. G. W. Balfour, Leeds, Central)   ... 1496

DEATH OF ANNE FINEGAN CORMARY—Question, Mr. MacAleese (Monaghan); , Answer, The Chief Secretary for Ireland (Mr. G. W. Balfour, Leeds, Central)   1497

SYLVESTER DWYER—Question, Mr. Flavin (Kerry, N.); Answer, The Chief Secretary for Ireland (Mr. G. W. Balfour, Leeds, Central)   1498

RAILWAY COMMUNICATION IN DONEGAL—Question, Mr. T. D. Sullivan (Donegal, W.); Answer, The Chief Secretary for Ireland (Mr. G. W. Balfour, Leeds, Central)   1499

MULLINGAR ASYLUM—Question, Mr. J. P. Farrell (Kerry, S.); Answer, The Chief Secretary for Ireland (Mr. G. W. Balfour, Leeds, Central)...   ... 1499

GUN LICENCES IN IRELAND—Question, Mr. J. P. Farrell (Kerry, S.); Answer, The Chief Secretary for Ireland (Mr. G. W. Balfour, Leeds, Central)   1499

STEAM TRAWLING OFF THE DUBLIN COAST—Question, Mr. Clancy (Dublin Co., N.); Answer, The Attorney-General for Ireland (Mr. Atkinson, Londonderry, N.) 1500

THE BOARD OF EDUCATION BILL—Questions, Mr. Stevenson (Suffolk, Eye) and Colonel Lockwood (Essex, Epping); Answer, The First Lord of the Treasury (Mr. A. J. Balfour, Manchester, E.)   1500

THE TELEPHONE BILL—Question, Sir Charles Cameron (Glasgow, Bridgeton); Answer, The First Lord of the Treasury (Mr. A. J. Balfour, Manchester, E.)   ...   .   '...   ... 1501

THE LAKES OF KILLARNEY—Questions, Mr. Lough (Islington, E.), and Mr. Swift MacNeill (Donegal, S.); Answer, The First Lord of the Treasury (Mr. A. J. Balfour, Manchester, E.) 1501

CYPRUS—Question, Mr. Pierpoint (Warrington); Answer, The First Lord of the Treasury (Mr. A. J. Balfour, Manchester, E.)   1502

HOME OFFICE VOTE—Question, Mr. Tennant (Berwickshire); Answer, The First Lord of the Treasury (Mr. A. J. Balfour, Manchester, E.) 1502

BARRACKS LOAN BILL—Question, Mr. Buchanan (Aberdeenshire, E.); Answer, The First Lord of the Treasury (Mr. A. J. Balfour, Manchester, E.)   ... 1502

PUBLIC BUSINESS.

BUSINESS OF THE HOUSE (GOVERNMENT BUSINESS) :—

Motion made, and Question proposed—

> " That for the remainder of the Session Government business do have precedence on Tuesday and Wednesday, and that the provisions of Standing Order 56 be extended to all the days of the week."—(*Mr. A. J. Balfour.*)

DISCUSSION—

Sir H. Campbell-Bannerman (*Stirling Burghs*) ... 1505
Sir Charles Dilke (*Gloucester, Forest of Dean*) ... 1507
Mr. Dillon (*Mayo, E.*) ... 1508
Sir Blundell Maple (*Camberwell, Dulwich*) 1511
Mr. Bryce (*Aberdeen, S.*) ... 1512
Mr. Galloway (*Manchester, S.W.*) 1512
Mr. Reckitt (*Lincolnshire, Brigg*) 1513
Mr. Gibson Bowles (*Lynn Regis*) 1514
Mr. Edmund Robertson (*Dundee*) 1516
Mr. William Johnston (*Belfast, S.*) 1516
Mr. Swift MacNeill (*Donegal, S.*) 1517
Captain Sinclair (*Forfarshire*) 1518
Mr. Coghill (*Stoke-upon-Trent*) 1519
Mr. Channing (*Northampton, E.*) 1519

Mr. Carvell Williams (*Nottingham, Mansfield*) 1520
Mr. Labouchere (*Northampton*) ... 1520
Mr. J. E. Ellis (*Nottinghamshire, Rushcliffe*) 1522
Mr. Arthur J. Moore (*Derry City*) 1522
The First Lord of the Treasury (*Mr. A. J. Balfour, Manchester, E.*) 1523
Mr. Dillon 1525
Mr. A. J. Balfour 1525
Mr. Reckitt 1526
Mr. A. J. Balfour 1526
Mr. Swift MacNeill 1527
Mr. A. J. Balfour 1527
Sir H. Campbell-Bannerman ... 1527
Mr. A. J. Balfour 1527
Mr. Tennant (*Berwickshire*) ... 1527
Mr. A. J. Balfour 1527
Mr. Galloway 1528
Mr. A. J. Balfour 1528
Mr. Wallace (*Perth*) 1528

Question put.

The House divided :—Ayes, 250 ; Noes, 119. (Division List No. 195.)

Private Legislation Procedure (Scotland) Bill—Considered in Committee.

(In the Committee.)

Clause 2 :—

Amendment again proposed—

"In page 2, line 2, after the word 'Commons' to insert the words 'and two Members of each House of Parliament appointed at the beginning of each Session in manner provided by Standing Orders shall be a Standing Committee of the two Houses of Parliament.'"—*Dr. Clark.*

Question again proposed, "That those words be there inserted."

DISCUSSION :—

The Lord Advocate (*Mr. A. G. Murray, Buteshire*) ... 1531

Sir H. Campbell-Bannerman (*Stirling Burghs*) 1533
Dr. Clark (*Caithness*) 1533

Amendment by leave withdrawn.

Amendment proposed—

"In page 2, line 3, to leave out from 'shall' to end of clause, and insert, 'if the two Houses of Parliament think fit so to order prescribe all matters of practice and procedure which will enable them to take into consideration the draft Order, and to report thereon to the Secretary for Scotland."—(*Mr. Cripps.*)

Question proposed, "That the words proposed to be left out stand part of the clause."

June 19.]   *Page*

DISCUSSION :—

Mr. A. G. Murray ... 1534	*Mr. Edmund Robertson (Dundee)* 1534
Mr. J. E. Ellis (Notts, Rush-cliffe) 1534	*Mr. A. G. Murray* 1535

Amendment, by leave, withdrawn.

The Amendment suggested by the Lord Advocate put, and agreed to.

Amendment proposed—

    " In page 2, line 13, to leave out ' or mainly.' "—(*Mr. Moulton.*)

Question proposed, "That the words ' or mainly ' stand part of the clause."

    Mr. A. G. Murray   1536

Amendment put, and negatived.

Amendment proposed—

    " In page 2, line 13, after ' Scotland,' to insert, ' or do not raise any question of policy or principle not previously determined by Parliament."—(*Dr. Clark.*)

Question proposed, "That those words be there inserted."

    Mr. A. G. Murray   1536

Amendment, by leave, withdrawn.

The Amendment suggested by the Lord Advocate put and agreed to.

Amendment proposed—

    " In page 2, line 13, after ' Scotland,' to insert, ' or effect a change in the general law.' "—(*Mr. J. P. Smith.*)

Question proposed, "That those words be there inserted."

DISCUSSION :—

Mr. Cripps (Gloucester, Stroud) 1537	*Mr. Stuart-Wortley (Sheffield, Hallam)* 1537
Mr. Caldwell (Lanarkshire, Mid) 1537	*Mr. A. G. Murray* 1538

Question put, and negatived.

Amendment proposed—

    " In page 2, line 13, after ' Scotland,' to insert, ' or which raise any such question of policy or principle.' "—(*The Lord Advocate.*)

Question, "That those words be there inserted," put and agreed to.

Amendment proposed—

    " In page 2, line 22, to leave out ' that notices published and served and."—(*Captain Sinclair.*)

Question proposed, "That the words proposed to be left out stand part of the clause."

DISCUSSION :—

Mr. A. G. Murray ... 1538	*Mr. A. G. Murray* 1539
Mr. Cripps... 1538	

Amendment, by leave, withdrawn.

Amendment proposed—

    " In page 2, line 26, to leave out from the word ' Parliament' to the end of the clause."—(*Mr. Cripps.*)

Question proposed, "That the words proposed to be left out stand part of the clause."

June 19.] *Page*

DISCUSSION :—

Sir Charles Cameron (Glasgow, Bridgeton) 1540
Dr. Clark (Caithness) ... 1540
Mr. A. G. Murray ... 1540
Sir F. S. Powell (Wigan)... 1541
Mr. Renshaw (Renfrew, W.) 1541
Mr. J. E. Ellis (Notts, Rushcliffe) 1541
Mr. A. G. Murray... ... 1542
Mr. J. E. Ellis 1542
Mr. Cripps 1542

Mr. Souttar (Dumfriesshire) ... 1542
Mr. A. G. Murray 1543
Mr. Cripps 1543
Sir Charles Cameron 1543
Mr. Robert Wallace (Perth) ... 1543
Mr. Caldwell 1544
Mr. Courtney (Cornwall, Bodmin) 1544
Mr. Cripps 1545
Mr. Courtney 1545
Dr. Clark 1546

Question put.

The Committee divided :—Ayes, 206 ; Noes, 72. (Division List, No. 196.)

Question proposed, " That Clause 2, as amended, stand part of the Bill."

Mr. Edmund Robertson 1547

Question put, and agreed to.

Clause, as amended, agreed to.

Clause 3 :—

Amendment proposed—

" In page 2, leave out lines 31 and 32, and insert, ' If the Chairmen report in favour of.' "—(*Mr. Parker Smith.*)

Question proposed, " That lines 31 and 32 stand part of the clause."

DISCUSSION :—

Mr. A. G. Murray... ... 1549
Mr. Cripps 1549

Mr. Caldwell 1549
Mr. J. P. Smith 1550

Question put, and agreed to.

Amendment proposed—

" In page 2, line 37, to leave out from 'shall' to 'direct,' in line 30."—(*Mr. Thomas Shaw.*)

Question proposed, " That the words proposed to be left out stand part of the clause."

DISCUSSION :—

Mr. A. G. Murray ... 1550
Mr. Edmund Robertson ... 1550
Mr. A. G. Murray ... 1551
Mr. Caldwell 1551
Mr. Courtney 1551

Mr. Renshaw 1552
Sir H. Campbell-Bannerman ... 1552
Mr. A. G. Murray 1553
Mr. Thomas Shaw 1553

Amendment, by leave, withdrawn.

Amendment proposed—

" In page 3, line 1, to leave out ' Commissioners,' and insert, ' a Joint Committee of the two Houses of Parliament appointed by the Standing Joint Committee.' "—Dr. Clark.

Question proposed, " That the word ' Commissioners ' stand part of the clause."

DISCUSSION—

Mr. A. G. Murray ... 1554
Sir Charles Cameron ... 1556
Sir H. Campbell-Bannerman 1558
Mr. Stuart-Wortley ... 1559
Sir Charles Cameron ... 1559
Mr. Crombie (Kircardineshire) 1560

Sir Charles Cameron 1560
Mr. Crombie 1560
Mr. Dalziel (Kirkcaldy Burghs)... 1561
Mr. A. G. Murray 1561
Captain Sinclair (Forfar) ... 1562

Amendment, by leave, withdrawn.

Clause 3, as amended, agreed to.

Clause 4 :—

Amendment proposed—

" In page '3' line 13, to leave out the words ' a panel,' and insert the word ' panels' instead thereof."—(*Sir Charles Cameron*.)

Question proposed, " That the words ' a panel ' stand part of the clause."

DISCUSSION :—

Mr. A. G. Murray	... 1564	*Mr. Caldwell*	... ...	... 1566
Mr. Dalziel	 1565			

The Committee divided :—Ayes, 135 ; Noes, 48. (Division List, No. 197.)

Amendment proposed—

" In page 3, line 18, to leave out from the first ' The ' to ' Scotland,' in line 19, and insert, ' Committee of Selection of either House.' "—(*Mr. Caldwell*.)

Question proposed, " That the words proposed to be left out stand part of the clause."

DISCUSSION :—

Sir Charles Cameron	... 1567	*Mr. Thomas Shaw*	...	... 1569
Mr. A. G. Murray	... 1568	*Dr. Clark*	... ...	... 1569

Amendment, by leave, withdrawn.

An Amendment made.

Amendment proposed—

" In page 3, line 20, to leave out ' shall,' and insert ' may if they consider it necessary. ' "—(*Sir Charles Cameron*).

Question proposed, " That the word ' shall ' stand part of clause."

DISCUSSION :—

Mr. A. G. Murray	... 1570	*Dr. Clark*	... ...	... 1570
Sir Charles Cameron	... 1570	*Mr. Caldwell*	... ...	... 1570

Amendment, by leave, withdrawn.

Amendment proposed—

" In page 3, line 20, to leave out ' 25 ' and insert ' 10.' "—(*Sir H. Campbell-Bannerman.*)

Question proposed, " That ' 25 ' stand part of the clause."

DISCUSSION :—

Mr. A. G. Murray	... 1571	*Mr. A. G. Murray*	...	... 1572
Sir H. Campbell-Bannerman	1571			

Question put and negatived.

Question, " That ' 20 ' be there inserted," put, and agreed to.

An Amendment made.

Amendment proposed—

" In page 3, line 22, to leave out the word ' five,' and insert the word ' two.' "—(*Mr. Thomas Shaw.*)

Question proposed, " That the word ' five ' stand part of the clause."

June 19.]   *Page*

DISCUSSION :—

    Mr. J. P. Smith 1572   *Mr. A. G. Murray* 1573

    Sir John Leng (Dundee) ... 1573   *Sir Charles Cameron* 1574

Question put.

The Committee divided :—Ayes, 149 ; Noes, 69. (Division List, No. 198.)

Clause, as amended, agreed to.

Clause 5 :—

Amendment proposed—

    " In page 3, line 31, to leave out the words 'Secretary for Scotland acting jointly with the Chairmen,' and insert the words, 'Committees of Selection of the Houses of Lords and Commons respectively.' "—(*Sir Charles Cameron.*)

Question proposed, " That the words proposed to be left out stand part of the clause."

DISCUSSION :—

    Mr. A. G. Murray   ... 1576   *Mr. Cripps* 1578

    Mr. Thomas Shaw 1577   *Sir Charles Cameron*   ... 1579

    Dr. Clark 1577   *Mr. Hedderwick*...   1579

    Sir H. Campbell-Bannerman 1577   *Sir Charles Dalrymple (Ipswich)* 1580

    Mr. A. G. Murray   ... 1578

Question put.

The Committee divided :—Ayes, 157 ; Noes, 82. (Division List, No. 199.)

Amendment proposed—

    " In page 3, line 33, to leave out from ' Orders,' to ' to act,' in line 34, and insert, ' appoint three persons being Members of either House of Parliament, or persons whose names are on the panel.' "—(*The Lord Advocate.*)

Question proposed, " That the words proposed to be left out stand part of the clause."

DISCUSSION—

    Mr. Thomas Shaw 1583   *Mr. Dillon (Mayo, E.)* 1584

    Mr. A. G. Murray...   ... 1583

    Sir H. Campbell-Bannerman 1583

    The First Lord of the Trea-

    sury (Mr. A. J. Balfour,

    Manchester, E.)...   ... 1584

Amendment proposed to the proposed Amendment—

    " To leave out all the words after ' panel,' in order to insert the words, ' and in the event of the Chairman selecting the panel and their not appearing to serve on the panel.' "—(*Mr. Caldwell.*)

Question proposed, " That those words be there inserted in the proposed Amendment."

DISCUSSION—

    Mr. A. G. Murray   ... 1585   *Mr. A. J. Balfour*   1586

    Sir H. Campbell-Bannerman 1585

Amendment to the proposed Amendment, by leave, withdrawn.

Original Amendment again proposed.

DISCUSSION :—

    Sir Charles Cameron   ... 1586   *Mr. A. G. Murray*   1586

Amendment put, and agreed to.

June 19.]   *Page*

Amendment proposed—

     "In page 3, line 35, at end, to insert, 'Any casual vacancy among the Commissioners or in the office of Chairman of the Commissioners caused by death, resignation, or disqualification, or inability to give attendance, such resignation or inability to give attendance, such resignation or inability to attend being certified by a writing under the Commissioner's hand, addressed to the Secretary for Scotland, shall be filled up by the Secretary for Scotland by appointing a Member of either House or a member of the panel.'"—(*The Lord Advocate.*)

Question proposed—"That those words be there inserted."

     Sir Chas. Cameron 1586

Question put, and agreed to.

Amendment proposed—

     "In page 3, line 36, leave out Sub-section (2), and insert: 'If it shall happen that all or any of the Commissioners so appointed are not Members of either House of Parliament, there shall be paid to such of the Commissioners as are not Members of either House of Parliament such remuneration for their services as the Treasury shall determine.'"—(*The Lord Advocate.*)

Agreed to.

Amendment proposed—

     "To leave out Sub-section 3."—*Mr. J. P. Smith.*

Question proposed, "That Sub-section 3 stand part of the clause."

Discussion :—

Commd. Bethell (York, E.R., Holderness)	...	1587	*Mr. Dillon*	...	...	... 1588
Mr. A. G. Murray...	...	1587	*Mr. Cripps*	...	...	... 1588
Mr. Dalziel	...	1587	*Mr. Caldwell*	...	...	... 1588
			Mr. Dalziel	...	...	... 1588

Amendment agreed to.

Other Amendments made.

Amendment proposed—

     "In page 4, line 7, after 'Order,' add providing that this will not disqualify Scottish Members of either House of Parliament from acting on Committees which deal with Orders which they have no local or personal interest.'"—*Mr. Crombie.*)

Question Proposed, "That those words be there added."

     Mr. Jonathan Samuel (Stockton) 1588

Question put, and agreed to.

Clause 5, as amended, agreed to.

Clause 6 :—

Amendment proposed.

     "In page 4, line 10, after 'place' to insert 'in Scotland.'"—(*Mr. Thomas Shaw.*)

Question proposed, "That those words be there inserted."

Amendment proposed to the proposed Amendment—

     "After the word 'in' to insert 'the locality in.'"—(*Mr. Caldwell.*)

Question proposed, "That those words be there inserted in the proposed Amendment."

     Mr. A. G. Murray 1589

June 19.]   *Page*

Question put, and negatived.

Original Amendment put, and agreed to

Other Amendments made.

Clause 6, as amended, agreed to.

Clause 7 :— ·

Amendment proposed—

   " In page 4, line 31, to leave out all the words from the beginning of the
clause, to the word ' after,' in line 32."—(*Mr. Thomas Shaw*)

Question proposed, " That the words proposed to be left out stand part of the
clause."

DISCUSSION :—

Mr. A. G. Murray	... 1591	*Dr. Clark*	... ...	... 1593
Dr. Clark ...	... 1592	*Mr. Hobhouse (Somerset, E.)*		... 1593
Mr. Caldwell ...	... 1592	*Mr. A. G. Murray*	...	... 1593
Mr. Cripps ...	... 1592	*Mr. Thomas Shaw*	...	... 1594

It being Midnight, the Chairman left the Chair to make his Report to the
House.

Committee report Progress ; to sit again To-morrow.

Baths and Washouses Acts Amendment Bill—Considered in Com-
mittee ...   .

(In the Committee.)

Clause 1 :—

Committee report Progress ; to sit again this day 1595

Regulation of Railways Bill—Order for Second Reading read, and dis-
charged ; Bill withdrawn   1595

MILITARY WORKS (MONEY)—Committee to consider of authorising the issue,
out of the Consolidated Fund, of such sums as may be required for the
purpose of Military Works and Services (Queen's Recommendation signi-
fied), upon Wednesday.—(*Mr. Wyndham*)   1595

Adjourned at ten minutes after Twelve of the clock.

THE

PARLIAMENTARY DEBATES

(*AUTHORISED EDITION*)

IN THE

FIFTH SESSION OF THE *TWENTY-SIXTH PARLIAMENT* OF THE
UNITED KINGDOM OF *GREAT BRITAIN* AND *IRELAND*, APPOINTED
TO MEET THE 7TH FEBRUARY 1899, IN THE 62ND YEAR OF THE REIGN OF

HER MAJESTY QUEEN VICTORIA.

PART I.]　　SEVENTH VOLUME OF SESSION 1899.

An Asterisk (*) at the commencement of a Speech indicates revision by the Member.

HOUSE OF COMMONS.

Wednesday, 31st May 1899.

MR. SPEAKER took the Chair at
Twelve of the Clock.

PRIVATE BILL BUSINESS.

WOODHOUSE AND CONISBROUGH
RAILWAY (ABANDONMENT) BILL.
　Lords amendment considered, and
agreed to.

SOUTH STAFFORDSHIRE STIPEN-
DIARY JUSTICE BILL.
　Read the third time, and passed.

BELFAST AND NORTHERN COUNTIES
RAILWAY BILL.
　As amended, considered ; Amendments
made ; Bill to be read the third time.

BOOTLE CORPORATION BILL.
　As amended, considered ; to be read
the third time.

VOL. LXXII.　[FOURTH SERIES.]

BARTON-ON-SEA WATER BILL [Lords].
Read a second time, and committed.

GLASGOW CORPORATION (GAS AND
WATER) BILL [Lords].
Read a second time, and committed.

GLASGOW CORPORATION (TRAMWAYS,
&c.) BILL [Lords].

Read a second time, and committed.

LIVERPOOL OVERHEAD RAILWAY
BILL [Lords].
Read a second time, and committed.

LONDON HOSPITAL BILL [Lords].
Read a second time, and committed.

MID-KENT GAS BILL [Lords].
Read a second time, and committed.

OLDHAM CORPORATION BILL [Lords].
Read a second time, and committed.

SOUTH HANTS WATER BILL [Lords].
Read a second time, and committed.

A

STOCKTON AND MIDDLESBROUGH WATER BILL [Lords].

Read a second time, and committed.

WATERFORD AND CENTRAL IRELAND RAILWAY BILL.

Read a second time.

Ordered, that the Bill be committed to the Committee on the Great Southern and Western, and Waterford, Limerick and Western Railway Companies Amalgamation, and Great Southern and Western Railway Bills.

Ordered, that the orders made on 14th March in respect of the Great Southern and Western, and Waterford, Limerick, and Western Railway Companies Amalgamation Bill, and the Great Southern and Western Railway Bill, be applicable to the Waterford and Central Ireland Railway Bill.—(*Mr. Molloy.*)

ELECTRIC LIGHTING PROVISIONAL ORDERS (No. 2) BILL.

Read the third time, and passed.

ELECTRIC LIGHTING PROVISIONAL ORDERS (No. 5) BILL.

Read the third time, and passed.

ELECTRIC LIGHTING PROVISIONAL ORDERS (No. 6) BILL.

Read the third time, and passed.

ELECTRIC LIGHTING PROVISIONAL ORDERS (No. 8) BILL.

Read the third time, and passed.

HOUSING OF THE WORKING CLASSES PROVISIONAL ORDER (BORROWSTOUNNESS) BILL.

Read a second time, and committed.

PETITIONS.

BOROUGH FUNDS ACT, 1872.

Petition from Kidderminster, for alteration of Law; to lie upon the table.

EDUCATION OF CHILDREN BILL.

Petitions in favour;—from Sheffield;—and Federation of School Boards of the West Riding of the County of York; to lie upon the Table.

ELEMENTARY EDUCATION (NEW BYE-LAWS) BILL.

Petition from Federation of School Boards of the West Riding of the County of York, in favour; to lie upon the Table.

GROUND RENTS (TAXATION BY LOCAL AUTHORITIES).

Petitions in favour;—From Workington; and, School Board for London; to lie upon the Table.

MINES (EIGHT HOURS) BILL.

Petition of the Mining Association of Great Britain, against; to lie upon the Table.

MINES (EIGHT HOURS) BILL.

Petitions in favour; — From Graig Gadbys; Merthyr Tydvil;—Tunnel Pit;—Cwmaman; — Cwmbach;—Plymouth;—Hill of Beath; — Rosebank; — Court Herbert; — Donibristle; — Balgonie; — Wellwood;— West Wemyss;— Cannock Chase (four);—Hednesford (two);—Cannock;—Chase Terrace;—Hazel Slade;—Chasetown; Gentleshow;—Glynea;—Point of Ayr; — Hamilton; — Kenmuishill;—Kimberley;—and, Bonyfloy Collieries; to lie upon the Table.

PUBLIC HEALTH ACTS AMENDMENT BILL.

Petitions in favour;—From Cambridge;—and, Tettenhall; to lie upon the Table.

SALE OF INTOXICATING LIQUORS ON SUNDAY BILL.

Petitions in favour;—From Brailes;—Silvertown;— Leeds;— Tidal Basin;—Custom House;—Honing;—Lingdale;—Aldershot; — Dartmouth;—Paignton;—and, Torquay (four); to lie upon the Table.

TELEGRAPHS (TELEPHONIC COMMUNICATION, &c.) BILL.

Petition from Liverpool, against; to lie upon the Table.

VACCINATION ACTS, 1867 TO 1898.

Petition from Wandsworth and Clapham, for alteration of Law; to lie upon the Table.

INLAND REVENUE (PROSECUTIONS UNDER GAME LAWS).

Return [presented 19th May] to be printed. [No. 223.]

FEE GRANT (SCOTLAND).

Return presented,—relative thereto [ordered 15th May; *Mr Caldwell*]; to lie upon the Table, and to be printed. [No. 224.]

TRADE REPORTS (ANNUAL SERIES).

Copies presented,—of Diplomatic and Consular Reports, Annual Series, Nos. 2272 to 2278 [by Command]; to lie pon the Table.

DISEASES OF ANIMALS ACTS, 1894 AND 1896.

Copy presented,—of Order, dated 18th May, 1899, No. 5944, revoking Order, No. 5920, which prohibited the conveyance of animals by the steamship "Hindustan" [by Act]; to lie upon the Table.

LIGHT RAILWAYS ACT, 1896.

Copy presented,—of Order made by the Light Railway Commissioners, and modified and confirmed by the Board of Trade, authorising the construction of a Light Railway in the Isle of Sheppey and county of Kent, between Queenborough Station and Leysdown (Sheppey Light Railway Order, 1898) [by Command]; to lie upon the Table.

LIGHT RAILWAYS ACT, 1896.

Copy presented,—of Order made by the Light Railway Commissioners, and modified and confirmed by the Board of Trade, authorising the construction of Light Railways in the counties of Glamorgan and Brecon, between Vaynor, Dowlais, and Merthyr Tydfil (Merthyr Tydfil Light Railway Order, 1899) [by Command]; to lie upon the Table.

LIGHT RAILWAYS ACT, 1896.

Copy presented,—of Order made by the Light Railway Commissioners, and modified and confirmed by the Board of Trade, authorising the construction of Light Railways in the County of Middlesex from Uxbridge to Hanwell (London United Tramways, Limited (Light Rail-way Extensions) Order 1898) [by Command]; to lie upon the Table.

GAS AND WATER WORKS FACILITIES ACT, 1870.

Copy presented,—of Report by the Board of Trade as to dispensing with the consents of the Sevenoaks Rural District Council and the Hildenborough Parish Council in the case of the Tonbridge Gas Provisional Order [by Act]; to lie upon the Table, and to be printed. [No. 225.]

HARWICH HARBOUR.

Copy presented,—of Abstract of the Accounts of the Receipts and Expenditure of the Harwich Harbour Conservancy Board from the time of their incorporation down to and inclusive of the 31st March, 1899, &c. [by Act]; to lie upon the Table, and to be printed. [No. 226.]

———

PARLIAMENTARY PAPERS (*WHITSUNTIDE RECESS*).

———

The following Papers, presented by command of Her Majesty during the Whitsuntide Recess, were delivered to the Librarian of the House of Commons during the Recess, pursuant to the Standing Order of the 14th August, 1896 :—

TRADE REPORTS (ANNUAL SERIES).

Copies of Diplomatic and Consular Reports, Annual Series, Nos. 2265 to 2271.

FISHERY BOARD (SCOTLAND).

Copy of Seventeenth Annual Report, being for 1898, Part II. (Report on Salmon Fisheries).

EAST INDIA (EXAMINATIONS FOR THE CIVIL SERVICE).

Copy of Regulations for Examinations for the Civil Service of India.

LOCAL TAXATION (ROYAL COM-
MISSION).

Copy of Minutes of Evidence, Vol. III.

WINE DUTIES.

Copy of Correspondence with the Colonial Office respecting the increase in the Wine Duties.

BRITISH SOUTH AFRICA COMPANY (BECHUANALAND RAILWAY).

Copy of correspondence with Mr. C. J. Rhodes relating to the proposed extension of the Bechuanaland Railway.

Ordered, That the said Papers do lie upon the Table.

PAPER LAID UPON THE TABLE BY THE CLERK OF THE HOUSE.

Inquiry into Charities (County of Flint),—Further Return relative thereto [ordered 5th May 1897; [*Mr. Grant Lawson*]; to be printed. [No. 227.]

ELECTRIC LIGHTING PROVISIONAL ORDERS.

Copy ordered, "of Memorandum stating the nature of the proposals contained in the Provisional Order included in the Electric Lighting Provisional Orders (No. 16) Bill."—(*Mr. Ritchie.*)

Copy presented accordingly; to lie upon the Table, and to be printed. [No. 228.]

ELECTRIC LIGHTING PROVISIONAL ORDERS.

Copy ordered, "of Memorandum stating the nature of the proposals contained in the Provisional Orders included in the Electric Lighting Provisional Orders (No. 17) Bill."—(*Mr. Ritchie.*)

Copy presented accordingly; to lie upon the Table, and to be printed. [No. 229.]

ELECTRIC LIGHTING PROVISIONAL ORDERS.

Copy ordered, "of Memorandum stating the nature of the Proposals contained in the Provisional Orders included in the

Electric Lighting Provisional Orders (No. 18) Bill."—(*Mr. Ritchie.*)

Copy presented accordingly; to lie upon the Table, and to be printed. [No. 230.]

ELECTRIC LIGHTING PROVISIONAL ORDERS.

Copy ordered, "of Memorandum stating the nature of the Proposals contained in the Provisional Orders included in the Electric Lighting Provisional Orders (No. 19) Bill."—(*Mr. Ritchie.*)

Copy presented accordingly; to lie upon the Table, and to be printed. [No. 231.]

PUBLIC BUSINESS.

EDUCATION OF CHILDREN BILL.

Considered in Committee.

(In the Committee.)

CLAUSE 1.

MR. GEORGE WHITELEY (Stockport): The first Amendment I have put down upon the Paper provides, if carried, that the operation of this Bill shall be postponed until 1905. I am not in any way wedded to that time, and if the hon. Member in charge of the Bill will accept my Amendment, the date may be made 1903 instead of 1905. I shall be quite willing to accept the figures 1903, and not delay the Committee by moving the Amendment. It appears to me that the hon. Member is not willing, and therefore it is my duty to proceed. My reasons for postponing the operation of the Bill are manifold. In the first place this Bill creates an entirely new state of affairs. New arrangements will have to be made throughout all the factories and workshops in almost every kind of employment throughout the United Kingdom. Work that has been carried on without difficulty in the past will be temporarily disorganized, and the internal economy of every business in which half-timers are employed at the present time will have to be reconstructed. I may point out with regard to Lancashire that the number of half-timers attached to factories and workshops is 66,000, and out of that number 48 per cent. are employed in the cotton trade itself. It is perfectly true that the whole of those 31,000 are not half-timers between the ages of 11 and 12, but undoubtedly a considerable proportion of them are. If they are all withdrawn at one fell swoop by a wave of the magic wand of the hon. Gentleman who brings in this Bill, great difficulty will ensue. Take, for instance, rink spinning, for in that class of work there are a large number of small half-timers, whose business it is to put the empty bobbins on the spindles and remove them when filled. Their little fingers are best adapted for this work, and if those children are suddenly withdrawn it will be some time before the trade is enabled to adapt itself to the new position of affairs. This is a time when it is absolutely necessary that steps should be taken by all those of us who own mills to meet this difficulty, and adapt ourselves to the new change which is about to take place. Take, again, the loom weavers, more particularly where the looms are of narrow carriage. All those employ two half-timers, one in the morning and one in the afternoon, and without the assistance of those half-timers that work will be seriously impeded. If the half-timer is under 12 years of age, you are going to prevent him carrying on his work in the way in which he is accustomed to deal with it, and so earn the wage he has hitherto earned. The fullest consideration should be given by the Committee to this question. Of course honourable Members who do not come from the counties where this work is carried on naturally do not see the importance which we attach to this question; but the result of this change will be to strain the cotton industry, and, that being so, it ought to be done in a gradual manner. There is no necessity to hurry. It is not so many years, in the recollection of most Members of this House, since the age of half-timers was raised from 10 to 11. There is no doubt that some time is required to adapt ourselves to this change, and what I press upon the House is that we should have a few years given to us to do so. It is a far-reaching matter and a question of grave import-

ance to a very large number of people, and it is not a matter that ought to be passed through this House without very full consideration. If the object is attained and this Bill is carried, and you ultimately raise the age of half-timers, I am entitled to argue that a system which has grown up amongst us in the factories, will not, if it is allowed to exist a few years longer, work that untold measure of harm that is suggested. The question whether the half-time system is injurious is a matter that we shall be able to deal with afterwards, but, even if it were injurious and detrimental to the health and education of the children, it is a system that has, at any rate, lasted so long that it is not necessary in making this change that it should be hurried. I therefore, in moving my Amendment that this Bill shall not come into operation until 1905, am only asking for an extension of time in order that we may be enabled to meet the difficulties, and carry on our business with the least possible dislocation owing to the changes that this Bill will create.

Amendment proposed: On page 1, line 6, after the word " hundred," to insert the words " and five "—(*Mr. George Whiteley*).

Question proposed: " That the words ' and five ' be there inserted."

*MR. TOMLINSON (Preston): I have an amendment on somewhat similar lines to that which has been moved by the hon. Member for Stockport, and as it is possible that I may not have an opportunity of moving it I would like to say a few words upon this. In putting down my amendment I had not in my mind quite those considerations on which my hon. friend has supported his amendment. I had not so much in my mind the special difficulties that might arise in carrying on satisfactorily the Lancashire industries. What I wished to do was to give the Education Department a little more time to accommodate itself to this change which is suggested. No doubt there are a great many in this House who look upon the half-time system as one which ought to be terminated ; but I think it is, or may be made, a good system. The tendency of education at the present time is totally to dissociate education from the work the children will have to do in after life. When children have passed their standards and left their schools they in a few years forget nearly everything which they have learned. If we could maintain some association between education and the work which the children will have to perform later in life we shall have done something to interest them in education whilst they are beginning to learn the business which they have to follow. Now, it appears to me that this disassociation between the future work and the education which the children are receiving is a serious reproach to the Education Department. If this Bill is passed the Education Department ought to have ample time to infuse a more practical spirit into its educational system. If you go beyond the fundamental rules of reading, writing, and arithmetic you at once get into a region where in the majority of cases what is taught is of no practical benefit to the children. If the half-time system is carried on properly it does conjoin the work which the children have to perform in after life with the education they are pursuing at the same time. If we are to abolish the system then we must adapt ourselves to the changed circumstances that must ensue, and in order to give time to the Educational Department to infuse a more practical spirit into elementary education I shall support the amendment of my hon. friend.

*Sir F. S. POWELL (Wigan): I have taken the greatest interest in this subject from my earliest years. As a clergyman's son I passed much of my youth in the neighbourhood of factories, and I in my later years find myself in much the same position. I sympathise with these people, and I desire to promote their prosperity. I cannot help contrasting the position of our factory hands with the position of those engaged in similar industries abroad. I do not want my argument to refer to foreign competition, which may be pressed too far, but what I do desire to see is the advancement of our own workpeople. What I see when I am abroad, sometimes in manufacturing towns, sometimes in the cantons of Switzerland, and sometimes on the breezy uplands of the Black Forest, is crowds of children flocking to school, and I want to know what the children here have done that they are not to have the same advantages. What have the parents of these children done that they are not

to have the same advantages as the parents on the Continent? What has the British nation done that we are not to have the same advantages as other nations? I find in the Education Report issued last year, the most valuable document of its kind that we have, that in Switzerland such great importance is attached to education that the legislation of the country will not allow any child to go into the factory until he is 14 years of age. The comparison is steadily against our people. It will injure our production—

*THE CHAIRMAN: Order, order! The hon. Member must remember that the general question is not now under discussion. The question is whether the Bill shall come into operation next year or five years hence.

*Sir F. S. POWELL: My hon. friend in moving his Amendment said the present condition of affairs has lasted so long that this matter need not be hurried, I say that it has lasted far too long. Thirty years of recorded time has gone by since the age of the half-timer had reached 10. Surely the time has now come to move forward a step, and I hope we shall take the step firmly, surely, and speedily. As a Lancashire Member I desire to say that one Lancashire Member at least does desire to advance education, and he does not desire to hear, on this occasion, what he heard so much of when the Education Bill of 1897 was passed, that Lancashire was behind, was in arrear, and was retarding progress, those remarks ought not to be made without justice, and I do not desire to hear them made at all.

COLONEL PILKINGTON (Lancashire, Newton): If you compare the working classes on the uplands of the Black Forest or those of Switzerland with those of this country, you will also find that the Members of Parliament here are representing the best interests of the working classes of Lancashire. The reason why they urge as strongly as they do that every consideration that it is possible to give should be given to this matter, is because they are not only pleading the cause of the manufacturers but they are also pleading the cause of the children. In the industries that have been alluded to there is a career for the whole life of the operative, boy and man, and the question is when the child should put his step upon the first rung of the ladder, and it is, in our opinion, a question which deserves most careful attention. The point which I wish to urge is that the time given by this Bill is much too short. There is no doubt a great deal of work that will have to be done, and there will have to be a great deal of trouble taken in reorganising the plan upon which these industries are carried on. It is all very well for people not engaged in trade, who are not under the stress and difficulties of trade, to deal with this question in a philanthropic way, but those who are engaged in those industries are face to face with the difficulty, and as I think know best what is best for the industry where this difficulty centres. Everybody in this House must know perfectly well that this system has been working for many years. You will interfere with the organisation of business, which will be very much disorganised, and everybody will agree with me that the utmost time and consideration ought to be given to the change which is going to be made. From the centres of industry no agitation has come at all for the change that is suggested ; the agitation has come from the elementary teachers encouraged by the Vice-President of the Education Council, and there are a great many people in Lancashire who do not believe in it. I venture to ask both sides of this House with all respect to consider very carefully the great interests they now propose to touch, and to touch very closely. Home Rulers surely have some principle of Home Rule which they apply to places other than Ireland ; surely Home Rule should be conceded to Lancashire, which is deeply interested in this question of training up the children. These industries are keeping the country going, and supplying it with the sinews of war, and if this change is suddenly made you will hamper and destroy them. In conclusion, I ask that the extension of time which is asked for by the Amendment may be granted, and unless it is I can only assure the House that these industries will be greatly and dangerously disorganised.

The Committee divided :—Ayes, 10 ; Noes, 163—(Division List No. 160).

AYES.

Ascroft, Robert
Cross, Herb. S. (Bolton)
Hornby, Sir William Henry
Howorth, Sir Henry Hoyle
Kemp, George

Leese, Sir Jos. F. (Accrington)
Maden, John Henry
Pilkington, Richard
Rutherford, John
Whiteley, H. (Ashton-und'-L.)

TELLERS FOR THE AYES—
Mr. George Whiteley and
Mr. Tomlinson.

NOES.

Abraham, William (Rhondda)
Allan, William (Gateshead)
Allen, W.(Newc.-und'r-Lyme)
Anstruther, H. T.
Arnold-Forster, Hugh O.
Ashton, Thomas Gair
Asquith, Rt. Hon. H. H.
Austin, M. (Limerick, W.)
Bainbridge, Emerson
Baker, Sir John
Banes, Major George Edward
Bethell, Commander
Birrell, Augustine
Blake, Edward
Blundell, Colonel Henry
Bond, Edward
Broadhurst, Henry
Brunner, Sir John Tomlinson
Bullard, Sir Harry
Burns, John
Burt, Thomas
Buxton, Sydney Charles
Caldwell, James
Cameron, Sir Charles (Glas.)
Cameron, Robert (Durham)
Campbell-Bannerman, Sir H.

Causton, Richard Knight
Cawley, Frederick
Channing, Francis Allston
Clark, Dr. G. B. (Caithness-sh.)
Clough, Walter Owen
Coghill, Douglas Harry
Colville, John
Corbett, A. Cameron (Gl'sg'w)
Cornwallis, Fiennes Stan. W.
Crombie, John William
Dalrymple, Sir Charles
Dilke, Rt. Hon. Sir Charles
Douglas, Charles M. (Lanark)
Drage, Geoffrey
Duckworth, James
Dyke, Rt. Hon. Sir W. Hart
Edwards, Owen Morgan
Engledew, Charles John
Evans, Sir Francis H. (S'ton)
Farquharson, Dr. Robert
Ferguson, R. C. Munro (Leith)
Finlay, Sir Robert Bannatyne
FitzGerald,Sir Robert Penr'se-
Fitzmaurice, Lord Edmond
Fitz Wygram, General Sir F.
Flower, Ernest

Fry, Lewis
Galloway, William Johnson
Giles, Charles Tyrrell
Goddard, Daniel Ford
Godson, Sir Augustus Fred'ck
Gold, Charles
Goldsworthy, Major-General
Gorst, Rt. Hn. Sir John Eldon
Gourley, Sir E. Temperley
Gray, Ernest (West Ham)
Grey, Sir Edward (Berwick)
Griffith, Ellis J.
Gull, Sir Cameron
Gurdon, Sir W. Brampton
Haldane, Richard Burdon
Harwood, George
Hayne, Rt. Hon. Chas. Seale-
Hazell, Walter
Hedderwick, Thomas C. H.
Helder, Augustus
Hickman, Sir Alfred
Hobhouse, Henry
Holland, W. H. (York, W. R.)
Horniman, Frederick John
Hutton, Alfred E. (Morley)
Hutton, John (Yorks, N. R.)

Jacoby, James Alfred
Jeffreys, Arthur Frederick
Jenkins, Sir John Jones
Johnstone, Heywood (Sussex)
Jones, D. Brynmor (Swansea)
Jones, Wm. (Carnarvonshire)
Kitson, Sir James
Knowles, Lees
Lafone, Alfred
Langley, Batty
Lawrence, Sir E. Durn'g- (Cor.)
Lawson, John Grant (Yorks.)
Lawson, Sir W. (Cumb'land)
Leng, Sir John
Lockwood, Lieut.-Col. A. R.
Logan, John William
Lucas-Shadwell, William
Lyell, Sir Leonard
M'Arthur, William (Cornwall)
M'Ghee, Richard
M'Iver, Sir L. (Edinburgh, W.)
M'Kenna, Reginald
Maddison, Fred
Mappin, Sir Frederick Thorpe
Mellor, Colonel (Lancashire)
Mendl, Sigismund Ferdinand
Middlemore, J. Throgmorton
Monk, Charles James
Montagu, Sir S. (Whitechapel)

Morgan, J. Lloyd (Carmarthen)
Morgan, W. P. (Merthyr)
Morley, Charles (Brecon-hire)
Morley, Rt. Hon. J. (Montrose)
Moss, Samuel
Nussey, Thomas Willans
O'Connor, J. (Wicklow, W.)
O'Connor, T. P. (Liverpool)
Oldroyd, Mark
O'Malley, William
Orr-Ewing, Charles Lindsay
Palmer, George W. (Reading)
Paulton, James Mellor
Pease, Alfred E. (Cleveland)
Pease, Joseph A. (Northumb.)
Perks, Robert William
Pirie, Duncan V.
Platt-Higgins, Frederick
Powell, Sir Francis Sharp
Provand, Andrew Dryburgh
Purvis, Robert
Pym, C. Guy
Randell, David
Rasch, Major Frederic Carne
Reid, Sir Robert Threshie
Richardson, J. (Durham, S. E.)
Rickett, J. Compton
Russell, T. W. (Tyrone)
Scott, C. Prestwich (Leigh)

Shaw, Charles Ed. (Stafford)
Sidebotham, J. W. (Cheshire)
Smith, Samuel (Flint)
Soames, Arthur Wellesley
Spicer, Albert
Steadman, William Charles
Stuart, James (Shoreditch)
Sullivan, Donal (Westmeath)
Talbot, Rt. Hn. J. G. (Oxf. U.)
Tennant, Harold John
Wallace, Robert (Perth)
Walton, Joseph (Barnsley)
Warner, Thomas C. T.
Warr, Augustus Frederick
Whittaker, Thomas Palmer
Williams, John C. (Notts)
Wilson, Charles H. (Hull)
Wilson, Henry J. (York, W.R.)
Wilson, J. (Durham, Mid.)
Wilson, John (Falkirk)
Wilson, John (Govan)
Woodhall, William
Woodhouse, Sir J. T. (H'dsfld.)
Woods, Samuel
Wylie, Alexander
Yerburgh, Robert Armstrong
Yoxall, James Henry
TELLERS FOR THE NOES—Mr.
   Robson and Mr. Kenyon.

MR. GEORGE WHITELEY: I now beg to move to substitute for the word "twelve" the words "eleven years and six months." The Bill proposes to raise the age to 12. There is always a time in the age of a child when it is able to become a half-timer after the age has elapsed. If you fix 11 years and 6 months, practically the age of 12 will be arrived at, and your object will be attained. But the child will be competent to the work before reaching the age. There is nothing magical about the word twelve. One often hears an expression of the opinion that we were pledged by our representative at the Berlin Conference to raise the age of half-timers to 12, and the argument that has been put forward since is that, whether we are in favour of it or not, the pledge having been given we ought to act up to it with honour. But, in the first place, was any pledge given at the Conference in favour of raising the age of half-timers, and, if so, by whom was it given? Was it given by the Minister of Education, and, if so, in what capacity? Did he act as the direct representative of the British Ministry, and was he instructed by the Government to agree? If he was, the question arises as to whether any Government or Minister generally of this country has the right in any shape or form to make such a pledge. I think no such pledge was given, and all I say is,

let us have a fair field and no favour. If you fix 12 years of age as the time, it means really 12 years and some months, and the child is able to work full time at the age of 13, so that fixing the age at 12 will result in doing away with half-timers altogether. If that is what you are trying to do, why do you not have the courage of your opinion and put a clause into the Bill to that effect, and not try to do it indirectly by a side-wind. Give us 11 years and six months now, and insert a clause in your Bill that the age should advance automatically, so that in a few years you will have the age that you put down here. I think if you do that you will make the Bill a good deal more palatable.

Amendment proposed: In page 1, line 7, to leave out the word "twelve," and insert the words "eleven years and six months"—(*Mr. George Whiteley*).

Question proposed: "That the word 'twelve' stand part of the Clause."

MR. WYLIE (Dumbartonshire): I object to the Amendment of the hon. Member for Stockport. I have given notice of an Amendment that the age shall be raised to 13, but owing to information I have received from the Education Department, which leads me to believe that it is not practicable, I have decided to withdraw that Amendment. The reason for my objection is that raising the age will conduce to the physical and educational advantage of the children. The only practical difference of opinion between the supporters and opponents of this Bill is as to whether the country can afford this or not. The question is not very great. The great economical factor is the saving of time and labour by machinery and scientific combination. This country has taken the lead in industrial pursuits, and so great has been our combination of these advantages that it is calculated that the labour of six English workmen is equal to that of 24 Germans or French, 32 Austrians, 50 Spaniards, 75 Italians, or 82 Portuguese; and the accumulated wealth and wages in this country are proportionately greater. Under these circumstances, who shall venture to say that the country cannot afford to give its children proper education, or that it should lag behind other Continental Powers? In no country in the world so much as in England has so great advantage been taken of labour saving appliances, and no country is better able to afford a proper education for her children. I have come into close contact not only with the hon. Members of this House who represent Lancashire, but also with the employers and the operatives of the country. I have the highest opinion of their intelligence, and there is a very great deal in what they say. It is this: "What Lancashire thinks to-day England thinks to-morrow." No Scotch Member has taken part in the Debate on the second reading, with the exception of the right hon. Gentleman the Member for Fife, and my excuse for intervening now, if excuse be needed, must be the effect which this Bill will have upon the Scotch Bill of a similar character which has yet to come before the House. Scotch Members showed their opinion very forcibly in the division on the second reading of the Bill, when 44 of them voted for it and only three against it. I think it is a sound policy to give children a good elementary education such as they could receive by staying at school till the age of 12 or 13. If the age limit were raised to 12 it would, I believe, remove the stigma which attaches to this country of not having fulfilled the engagement we entered into at the Berlin Conference; it would partially remove the reproach that though we are the wealthiest nation in the world we lag behind many of our poorer neighbours, and it would diminish the number of the ignorant, depraved, and feeble in this country.

MR. TENNANT (Berwickshire): Those of us who are Scotchmen as well as those who are Scotch Members will welcome the remarks of the hon. Member who has just sat down. There are one or two matters which I do not think have been dwelt upon with sufficient force in this House with regard to the raising of the age. What is the industrial position at the present moment? In England you have total or partial exemption at 11, but a child is not allowed to be employed in a factory until it is 13. The result of this is, that you have a gap which my honourable friend the Member for South Shields is endeavouring to diminish by one year, but even if this Bill passes into law, that gap would still remain. The remarks made by the Vice President of the Council on the subject not very long ago must be still fresh in the memory of the House. But I do not wish to dwell upon the details which he gave on that occasion; I wish rather to remind honourable Members of what the condition of affairs is. In Scotland we are even worse off than the people are in England, because the age at which a child is exempt from school attendance is 10 instead of 11. I am aware that my honourable friend the Member for Forfarshire has a Bill which seeks to raise the age from 10 to 11, but even if that Bill passes, and this Bill passes, you will have an unequal state of things. I think it is of the utmost importance that we should in future, even if we cannot at the present moment, endeavour to bridge over a hiatus which I venture to say does more harm than any want in the legislation of this country.

* MR. TOMLINSON: I think that it is the greatest misfortune that there should be a gap between the time when a child leaves school and the time when he begins some occupation. One of the worst results of that system is that children take up desultory employment instead of applying themselves to some kind of regular occupation. The object of the amendment is not to prevent that system from being put an end to, but to preserve the half-time system which bridges over the gap. The great advantage of the half-time system is that it enables children to begin to learn to work while their education is still going on. It is because I think that this Bill will tend to break down the half-time system that I desire to support the amendment.

VISCOUNT CRANBORNE (Rochester): There is no question that a great deal of money is wasted on education, because education does not go on long enough. If there is to be any progress in that direction, the only chance you have to make it is by combining education with industry. The essential idea of the Evening Continuation School system is that you carry on education even when a child has begun to work. Whether, in detail, the half-time system is right or wrong, it is a step in the right direction. It may be, as the House thought on the Second Reading of this Bill, that the age is too low now, but the principle is right, and the only principle upon which progress is possible is the combination of the two elements of child-life—education and industry. The only chance you have of progress in education is to permit parents to allow their children to work during a part of their education. The question then arises as to whether you have the right to limit the power of parents to determine whether their children shall be employed or not. You have that right if you can show that it is bad for the children, but no inquiry has yet been made, and, until an inquiry has been made, and it has been proved that it is injurious to the children, the wishes of the parents ought to be respected. I deny the contention that, as a general rule, the parents are anxious to oppress their children. The parents may be wrong in their views as to what is best for their children; but in the vast majority of cases they have the interests and advancement of their children at heart. Therefore, before any alteration is made in the half-time system, it should be established that it is bad for the children educationally and physically. I do not believe that it is bad for the children physically. Those great factories in which children work are carefully looked after from the sanitary point of view; the strain on the children at work is not so great as the strain on the children at school, and I am of opinion that the

mental strain in the school is more likely to injure their health than the physical strain at work. It has not been proved that the half-time system is bad from the point of view of education. Therefore, though I hope my hon. Friend will withdraw the Amendment, I shall feel bound to support him if he goes to a division.

MR. MIDDLEMORE (Birmingham, N.): I think the noble Lord is certainly inaccurate in one of his remarks. What we maintain in connection with this Bill is that those who are now parents have themselves been brought up under a bad system, and under a far worse system than their children. I would remind the Committee that at the Berlin Conference we were definitely pledged to do the very thing that this Bill proposes to do, and I should have thought after that fact there was nothing further to be said in the matter. But whether the Bill is passed by the present Government or not, it will be passed by the succeeding Government. We cannot fight against time in this matter. The noble Lord has spoken about the health of the children. I believe that all medical opinion right through the country is dead against the half-time system. Moreover, there is not a medical man in this House who does not oppose it. One medical authority has said that every month the children are taken from the workshop and placed in the school would be a distinct gain to their health. Parliament has no more sacred charge committed to it than the charge of the child life of this country, and if it now determines to save 50,000 children from the dangers of the workshop, it will do one of the best strokes of business it has ever done. If the Bill passes through Committee to-day, the 31st of May will be a red letter day in the Parliamentary calendar.

* COLONEL MELLOR (Lancashire, Radcliffe): I desire to endorse the remarks of the noble Lord the Member for Rochester. With regard to the Amendment itself, I think it would have been as well if my hon. friend the Member for Stockport would not press it to a division, but holding the views I do on the half-time question, I shall feel bound to support it if he does. The constant assertion has been indulged in

Mr. Tomlinson.

by the Press, and by people outside, and on public platforms, that the condition of life of the half-timers of Lancashire is one which is directly inimical to their health. As one who has had perhaps a greater experience on the subject than any other Member of the House, I wish to say that the objections which formerly undoubtedly existed in the mills to half-time labour have to a large extent ceased, and if children must work at all at the age of 11, 12, or 13 years in doors, there is no employment in this country where they work under better or more healthy conditions than in the modern cotton mills of Lancashire. I have taken the liberty of sending to members copies of a few photographs. One is a group of 12 half-timers, and the other is a group of over-lookers numbering 27, in a mill in my constituency. I have in every case given in the height, weight, chest measurement, and periods of sickness of the children and the men, and I undertake to say that in no condition or class of life or labour could you find other children or men who have passed through the half time period with less injury than they have. Of the 27 men 20 of them have had no sickness that they can remember, and they began to work, not at the age of 11 years, but at 9. I mention this to disabuse members of the idea that half-time labour is as injurious as it has been represented. I was not present at the debate on the second reading of the Bill, but I read the speech of the honourable Member for the Middleton Division (Mr. Duckworth). The honourable Member was once a half-time worker, and the position to which he has now reached is one that reflects upon him the highest credit. The physique of the honourable Member is a splendid testimony of the healthiness of the half-time system and to the value of the combination of education with industrial training.

* Sir ALBERT ROLLIT (Islington, S.): I desire to say only one or two words upon the remarks made by the noble Lord, who has raised, in very moderate and able terms, an important question of principle. I quite agree that if you can combine industrial training with general education it is most desirable to do so, and hence our advocacy at all times of continuation schools ; but the question of age goes to the very root of this matter. If you remove a child from school at too

early an age, you cannot possibly ever recover the time, and waste must ensue. On this point I agree with the noble Lord in saying that if we can show that by such removal or exemption you injure the education of the child itself, then the arguments in favour of this Bill are irresistible. I have had a large amount of experience among Yorkshire and Lancashire institutions in relation to technical, commercial, and secondary training, and I say that the one great and universal regret in connection with these institutions is that the want of primary education renders it very difficult to inculcate technical and commercial instruction. It is the want of general information that is felt, and, therefore, if you lessen the education given in earlier years, you prevent that technical instruction, which is of such paramount importance to this country. I heard my honourable Friend the Member for Stockport say something about our being pledged to Germany and to other countries at the Berlin Conference. It is not a question of being pledged, it is a question of what is to the interest of our own country ; and I think anyone who has studied the course of commercial competition in these days must know that it is largely the educational advantage held by Germany which has given her the commercial and industrial position she holds to-day. In Germany primary education was commenced with the century under her great Minister Stein ; it was commenced in this country as a State system only a quarter of a century ago ; and that is the cause to a large extent of the comparative position we occupy to-day. What other countries have given to their children should also be given to the children of this country, for the sake both of themselves individually, and of the nation as a whole.

Colonel PILKINGTON: Representing one of the Lancashire divisions, I feel that this is a most important question. Feeling strongly as I do that to raise the age from 11 at all is a mistake, I shall certainly support the Amendment of my hon. friend the Member for Stockport. We are in many cases fighting for an industry, and fighting for the people of Lancashire ; and therefore I shall certainly follow him into the Lobby. I have listened with very great attention to the speech of the noble lord, and it seems to me that we are deciding this question on very imperfect information as to health or as to anything else. If we draw the string too tight, we shall have nothing like evasion of the Act by the large manufacturers, but there will pro bably be evasions in hundreds of thousands of cases in which it will be very difficult to note what is being done by a child under 12 years of age. For these reasons I advocate that the age should be increased at the present time merely to 11½ years.

* Sir A. HICKMAN (Wolverhampton, W.): It appears to me that this Bill would not be complete without a provision for finding food for those children who are prevented from earning their own livelihood or from assisting their parents in the amount of wages earned.

Mr. J. WILSON (Durham, Mid.): Give their fathers more wages.

* Sir A. HICKMAN: A very good suggestion, no doubt, but perhaps the hon. Member will point out how that can be done.

Mr. J. WILSON (Durham, Mid.): I will do so in a moment if the hon. Member will allow me.

*Sir A. HICKMAN: The hon. Member can do so when I sit down. Something has been said about technical education, but the great defect in technical education is that it is not of a practical character. But these children who are half-timers are receiving what I consider to be certainly the most practical technical education, for they are actually learning the work which is to fit them afterwards to earn their own livelihood. The returns show that only about one child in 300 leaves school at the age of 12, so that it is not a very crying evil, and this small percentage consists probably of the very children upon whom com-

pulsory attendance would press most hardly. Surely in this matter it is better to go by degrees, and not to move in advance of public opinion. The Amend-ment offers the promoters a fair compromise, and that being so I think they ought to accept it.

Mr. ARNOLD (Halifax): Before the Committee proceed to the division, I should like to say a word on behalf of the parents. They resent that a hard and fast line should be drawn, and that they should be left without any discretion at all. The bulk of the parents are opposed to strict legislation on the point.

Mr. GEORGE WHITELEY: Will the Vice-President inform the Committee whether this country is or is not pledged in any way whatever as a result of what was done by the Berlin Conference?

The VICE-PRESIDENT OF THE COMMITTEE OF COUNCIL ON EDUCATION (Sir John Gorst): The British Government pledged itself, amongst the other Governments of Europe, that it was desirable that the minimum age for working in factories and work-shops should be 12.

*Mr. TOMLINSON: I would ask the right hon. Gentleman how it has happened, then, that no Government has thought it its duty to take steps to redeem that pledge?

Mr. GEORGE WHITELEY: I would point out to the Committee that that is no pledge whatever. It is merely an expression of opinion.

Question put.

The Committee divided:—Ayes, 177; Noes, 18—(Division List No. 161).

AYES.

Abraham, William (Rhondda)
Allan, William (Gateshead)
Allen, W. (Newc.-under-Lyme)
Anson, Sir William Reynell
Anstruther, H. T.
Ashton, Thomas Gair
Atherley-Jones, L.
Austin, M. (Limerick, W.)
Baker, Sir John
Banes, Major George Edward
Billson, Alfred

Birrell, Augustine
Blake, Edward
Blundell, Colonel Henry
Bond, Edward
Bowles, Capt. H. F. (Middlesex)
Broadhurst, Henry
Brunner, Sir John Tomlinson
Bullard, Sir Harry
Burns, John
Burt, Thomas
Buxton, Sydney Charles

Caldwell, James
Cameron, Robert (Durham)
Campbell, Rt. Hn. J. A. (Glasg.)
Campbell-Bannerman, Sir H.
Carmichael, Sir T. D. Gibson-
Caunton, Richard Knight
Cawley, Frederick
Channing, Francis Allston
Clark, Dr. G. B. (Caithness-sh.)
Clough, Walter Owen
Coghill, Douglas Harry

Colonel Pilkington.

Cohen, Benjamin Louis
Colomb,SirJohnCharlesReady
Colston, Chas. Edw. H.Athole
Colville, John
Corbett, A.Cameron(Glasgow)
Crombie, John William
Dalrymple, Sir Charles
Dilke, Rt. Hon. Sir Charles
Douglas, Charles M. (Lanark)
Drage, Geoffrey
Duckworth, James
Duncombe, Hon. Hubert V.
Dyke, Rt. Hon. Sir Wm. Hart
Edwards, Owen Morgan
Eagledew, Charles John
Esmonde, Sir Thomas
Evans, Sir F. H. (South'ton)
Farquharson, Dr. Robert.
Ferguson, R. C. Munro (Leith)
Finlay, Sir Robert Bannatyne
Fisher, William Hayes
Fitzmaurice, Lord Edmond
Fitz Wygram, General Sir F.
Flower, Ernest
Fry, Lewis
Galloway, William Johnson
Garfit, William
Gedge, Sydney
Goddard, Daniel Ford
Godson, Sir Augustus Fredk.
Gold, Charles
Goldsworthy, Major-General
Gorst, Rt. Hon. Sir J. Eldon
Gourley, Sir. E. Temperley
Gray, Ernest (West Ham)
Greville, Hon. Ronald
Grey, Sir Edward (Berwick)
Griffith, Ellis J.
Gull, Sir Cameron
Gurdon, Sir Wm. Brampton
Haldane, Richard Burdon
Harwood, George
Hayne, Rt. Hon. Ch. Seale-
Hazell, Walter
Heaton, John Henniker
Hedderwick, Thos. Ch. H.
Helder, Augustus
Henderson, Alexander
Hobhouse, Henry

Holland,Wm. H. (York,W.R.)
Horniman, Frederick John
Hutton, Alfred E. (Morley)
Hutton, John (Yorks, N.R.)
Jacoby, James Alfred
Jenkins, Sir John Jones
Johnstone, Heywood (Sussex)
Jones, David Brynmor (Swan.)
Jones, Wm. (Carnarvonshire)
Kitson, Sir James
Knowles, Lees
Lafone, Alfred
Langley, Batty
Lawrence, Sir E. D.- (Corn.)
Lawson, John Grant (Yorks.)
Lawson, Sir Wilfrid (Cumber.)
Leng, Sir John
Lloyd-George, David
Loder, Gerald Walter Erskine
Logan, John William
Long, Col. C. W. (Evesham)
Lowe, Francis William
Lucas-Shadwell, William
Lyell, Sir Leonard
M'Arthur, Chas. (Liverpool)
M'Ghee, Richard
M'Iver,Sir L. (Edinburgh,W.)
M'Kenna, Reginald
Maddison, Fred.
Mappin, Sir Frederick Thorpe
Mendl, Sigismund Ferdinand
Middlemore, J. Throgmorton
Monk, Charles James
Montagu, Sir S. (Whitechapel)
Morgan, J. Lloyd (Carm'rth'n)
Morley, Charles (Breconshire)
Morley,Rt.Hon. J. (Montrose)
Morton, A. H. A. (Deptford)
Moss, Samuel
Nussey, Thomas Willans
O'Connor, J. (Wicklow, W.)
O'Connor, T. P. (Liverpool)
Oldroyd, Mark
O'Malley, William
Orr-Ewing, Charles Lindsay
Palmer, G. Wm. (Reading)
Paulton, James Mellor
Pease, Alfred E. (Cleveland)
Pease, Joseph A. (Northumb.)

Perks, Robert William
Pirie, Duncan V.
Platt-Higgins, Frederick
Powell, Sir Francis Sharp
Pretyman, Ernest George
Provand, Andrew Dryburgh
Purvis, Robert
Pym, C. Guy
Randell, David
Rasch, Major Frederic Carne
Reid, Sir Robert Threshie
Rickett, J. Compton
Robertson, Herbert (Hackney)
Rollit, Sir Albert Kaye
Round, James
Russell, T. W. (Tyrone)
Shaw, Charles Edw. (Stafford)
Sinclair, Capt. J. (Forfarshire)
Soames, Arthur Wellesley
Souttar, Robinson
Spicer, Albert
Steadman, William Charles
Stuart, James (Shoreditch)
Sullivan Donal (Westmeath)
Talbot, Rt. Hn.J.G. (Oxf'd U.)
Tennant, Harold John
Wallace, Robert (Perth)
Walton, Joseph (Barnsley)
Warner, Thos. Courtenay T.
Warr, Augustus Frederick
Whittaker, Thomas Palmer
Williams,John Carvell (Notts)
Wilson, Charles Henry (Hull)
Wilson, H. J. (York, W. R.)
Wilson, John (Durham, Mid.)
Wilson, John (Falkirk)
Wilson, John (Govan)
Wilson, Jos. H. (Middlesbro')
Woodall, William
Woodhouse,SirJ.T.(Hudders.)
Woods, Samuel
Wortley, Rt.Hon.C.B. Stuart-
Wylie, Alexander
Yerburgh, Robert Armstrong
Yoxall, James Henry

TELLERS FOR THE AYES—
  Mr. Robson and Mr.
  Kenyon.

NOES.

Arnold, Alfred
Ascroft, Robert
Coddington, Sir William
Cranborne, Viscount
Cross, H. Shepherd (Bolton)
Giles, Charles Tyrrell
Hickman, Sir Alfred
Hornby, Sir William Henry

Howorth, Sir Henry Hoyle
Jeffreys, Arthur Frederick
Kemp, George
Leese, Sir J. F. (Accrington)
Maden, John Henry
Mellor, Colonel (Lancashire)
Seton-Karr, Henry
Sidebotham, J. W. (Cheshire)

Tomlinson, Wm. Ed. Murray
Whiteley, H. (Ashton-u.-L.)

TELLERS FOR THE NOES—
  Mr. George Whiteley and
  Mr. Pilkington.

*MR. TOMLINSON : I wish to move as an Amendment, to insert after the word "shall" in line seven the words "except where any bye-laws under the Elementary Education Acts, 1870 to 1897, shall from time to time otherwise provide." The object is to give some latitude to the local authorities in applying the provisions of the Bill. It seems to me quite alien to English habits to adapt the same cast iron system of administration to all parts, instead of easing the burden wherever possible. I would only propose to give latitude within certain reasonable limits, but I hold that the very fact that the local authorities have the power of modifying the application of the Bill would act in the direction of developing their energies in carrying out these duties. I do not think it is an unreasonable thing to allow these bodies the latitude I suggest.

Amendment proposed : In Clause 1, page 1, line 6, after "shall," to insert "except where any bye-laws under the Elementary Education Acts, 1870 to 1897, shall from time to time otherwise provide."—(*Mr. Tomlinson.*)

Question proposed : "That those words be there inserted."

Mr. JEFFREYS (Hants, N.) : This is a proposal to give local authorities a certain option. Honourable Members opposite are very fond of local option, and I, for one, do not see why the authorities who represent the parents should not have the power of altering the school age in order to meet the requirements of particular districts. It cannot be said that children engaged in agricultural work are following an unhealthy occupation. On the contrary, the work is healthy, and therefore if the local authorities have the power of judging what is best for them with regard to age, no harm can be done. I think it would be rather unwise not to accept the amendment. It is frequently the case that parents summoned before local magistrates for not sending their children to school are let off very lightly, and, indeed, they willingly pay the fine because they know the children's earnings much more than cover it.

*Sir F. S. POWELL : One of the greatest obstacles to educational progress in this country is the extremely low standard mentioned in the bye-laws, and I have noticed some very emphatic words in educational inspectors' reports upon this subject. I very much regret that this proposal has been made, as I certainly fear, that if this discretion is given to local authorities, it will have a tendency to destroy the effects of the Bill.

Mr. ROBSON (South Shields): It is impossible for me to accept the Amendment. Its object, as I understand, is to enable local educational authorities to lower the standard set up by Parliament. That is rather opposed to the current of all our legislation on this subject, for our efforts have hitherto been directed to induce the local authorities to come up to that standard. I doubt very much if any local authorities will avail themselves of the Amendment, if carried, in order to fix an age below that appointed by the Act. Does the hon. Member think he will achieve his object by his Amendment ? I think I can show him good reasons for not pressing it to a division. The words of the Amendment are that the Act shall apply except where any bye-law under the Elementary Education Acts, 1870—1897, shall otherwise provide. Has the hon. Member tried the experiment of reading the whole of the clauses, so as to get at the meaning of these words ? If he does, he will find there are already bye-laws under the Education Acts, made upon the basis of 11 as the minimum age for leaving school. Under this Act 12 will be made the minimum school age, and therefore, in future, if the Amendment is accepted, 12 would be the minimum age, except in cases where the existing bye-laws say it shall be 11. That is a very fair point for consideration, and I would respectfully suggest to the hon. Member that it would be well for him at any rate to defer his proposal until the Report stage.

Mr. GIBSON BOWLES (Lynn Regis): I should like to ask the hon. Gentleman opposite whether he has correctly read the Amendment. It seems to me that it provides for future, rather than for existing, bye-laws. Our sympathies are all with education, but I do not think it is wise to lay down too hard and fast a rule. I would give local option to the authorities, and I therefore heartily support the Amendment.

Sir J. GORST : Perhaps I may be allowed to say that under the existing Education Acts, the local authorities have no power to make any bye-laws fixing an age standard. All they can do is to fix an educational standard, and therefore, in my opinion, the Amendment, if carried, would be quite inoperative. The hon. Member had better postpone it till later.

*Mr. TOMLINSON : I do not follow the right hon. Gentleman in that. If we empower the local authorities to make these bye-laws it surely would be possible, the principle having been once accepted, to provide words making it operative.

Mr. Tomlinson.

I do not think the objection of my hon. Friend the Member for Wigan really applies to my Amendment; as he really objects to allowing local authorities to permit children to leave school before they have passed a certain standard.

*SIR ALBERT ROLLIT: Surely this is an unheard of proposal. If passed it would have the effect of virtually abrogating the provisions of the Bill. There would, practically, be no national age standard at all. I hope the Committee will not depart from the principles which at present govern our educational policy by fixing the age limit in Parliament, and giving this discretion to local authorities; and I therefore trust that the Amendment will be strenuously opposed.

CAPTAIN PRETYMAN (Suffolk, Woodbridge): I, too, hope that the Amendment will not be pressed. It is putting too great a strain on many of us, to ask us to vote for it.

*MR. TOMLINSON: I do not propose to press the Amendment to a division, and will therefore ask leave to withdraw it.

Amendment, by leave, withdrawn.

MR. ROBSON: I beg now to move to add the following words at the end of the clause:

"Provided also that the local authority for any rural district may, by by-law for any parish within their district, fix 13 years as the minimum age for exemption from school attendance in the case of children to be employed in agriculture, and that in such parish such children over 11 and under 13 years of age who have passed the standard fixed for partial exemption from school attendance by the by-laws of the local authority shall not be required to attend school more than 250 times in any year. Such by-law shall have effect as a by-law made under Section 74 of the Elementary Education Act, 1870, and all Acts amending the same. The local authority shall be the local authority fixed by Section 7 of the Elementary Education Act, 1876."

The object of this Amendment is to secure that in agricultural districts the children shall give two winters to school, instead of one winter and one summer. It empowers the local authority to extend the school age from 12 to 13. The Amendment is entirely optional, and it is open to the rural districts, if they are so disposed, to ignore it altogether. I hope

that they will not, and on the contrary I think that they will act upon it. It is an attempt to apply the principle of summer work and winter schooling which prevails in Germany and Switzerland. The high school age, which obtains in those countries under this system, is not merely acceptable, but it is popular, and those countries would never have reached their present educational supremacy but for the principle which I propose to embody in this Amendment. I know that some of my hon. friends have supposed that in putting this Amendment forward, I am making a concession to the agricultural interest at the cost of the principle of the Bill. But I venture to think that those who have studied it will entertain a different view. It does not at all contract the operation of the Bill, nor is this the first time on which the principle has been raised in connection with it. There are those who have devoted years to the advocacy of some change of this sort, and their reason for doing so is that they have observed the great difficulty of enforcing the present compulsory system in rural districts. Had I brought forward this Bill without seeking, in some practical way, to deal with this difficulty, I should have been much to blame. Hon. Members have, perhaps, scarcely realised the serious degree to which our compulsory system has failed in the rural districts. Its enforcement depends entirely on local vigilance and on public opinion, and undoubtedly that opinion is strongly opposed to the exercise of compulsion at those seasons of the year when a child can profitably be employed on the land. An examination of the returns of school attendance in rural districts shows how lax has been the enforcement of the law. Looking down the last returns I note that, whereas one school had been open 338 times, the attendances of various children had averaged from 54 to 64, while a little judicious inquiry has brought to light the fact that some of the children had been actually employed on the land, illegally, by members of the School Board for that district. In another school, out of 422 possible attendances, the returns show 22, 65, 78, and 98 attendances, while no summons for irregular attendance has been taken out for four years. The principle of recognising the difference between factory and agricultural labour has worked with good effect in both Germany and Switzerland, and I do not see why it should not act equally well in this country. After all, the Amendment may well be described as one enabling compulsion to be exercised, when it can be efficacious, in rural districts. Remember, I am not giving away the principle of the Bill; I am simply taking, in the 13th year, the time given up in the 12th, and it must be borne in mind that in the later year the brain of the child will have become more receptive. I think the Amendment is an indispensable step towards filling up the fatal gap which now exists between the age at which a child leaves school, and the earliest age at which he can be got hold of for the purposes of higher education. Hitherto the agriculturists of England have been the most inveterate opponents of a high school age; they, rather than Lancashire, have blocked the way of progress in this respect. In foreign countries agriculturists are more in favour of a higher school age than people in towns. In Germany and Switzerland we have instances in which the school age runs up to 16 years, and they want to get higher. The motive of that is only partly educational; in Germany and Switzerland, as in England, the agricultural boy is in a great hurry to get away from school in order to run to the nearest town and enter the first mill or shop, but if we had a higher school age accompanied by summer work, we keep the boy on the land until he has learned something of it, and we give him a start in what is the most natural of all employments. That is the reason why, in all the countries of Europe where a high educational standard is insisted upon, we have this principle prevailing in rural districts almost without exception. The reason why it is insisted upon is not only a national and philanthropic one, but because the rural districts have a very sound material interest in it. It is to their advantage that a boy should learn the trade of the land on which he was born, and on which he may possibly remain. It is to the interest of everybody that there should be fair play to every inducement which will stop the steady flow of agricultural children from the villages to the towns. It is as much to the interest of the towns as it is to the interest of the country districts. If the agricultural districts of England appreciate the force of this argument, we shall have them demanding

Mr. Robson,

a still higher school age. Since my agricultural friends have discovered the virtue of this Amendment, I am astonished to find how many have said, "You may carry up the age to 14 with that Amendment"; and I think we may be able to oblige them later. Those who have hitherto been the enemies of a high school age will in future be its most effective allies. I would wish to ask the indulgence of the Committee to refer to a very important detail in the Amendment, namely, the number of attendances. When I first drafted the Amendment I put down 300 attendances, and it was argued with a great deal of force and with very good evidence that in putting down that number I was not making much of a concession, and that in fact without my Amendment at all, supposing the Bill stood in its original form, the probabilities were that agricultural children would only attend about 300 times between the ages of 11 and 12. An Amendment has been put down by my hon. Friend, the Member for North Hants, fixing the number at 200 attendances. I think I went a little too high, but I think my hon. Friend has gone a great deal too low, and, having taken the advice of those who could speak with authority and experience on educational affairs, I was advised that all the purposes of my Amendment would be well met if I put the number at 250 attendances, which represents about half the year. I hope my hon. friends, more particularly on this side of the House, will observe that by giving 250 attendances in each of the two extra years, agricultural children will thereby get 25 per cent. more education than borough children. It will be accepted, as far as I can learn, as meeting the special necessities of the agricultural districts, and I venture to hope that the figure which I now suggest, and which I ask your permission to insert, is one which will save discussion on this Amendment.

Amendment proposed, in page 1, line 12, at the end, to add the words:

"Provided also that the local authority for any rural district may, by bye-law for any parish within their district, fix thirteen years as the minimum age for exemption from school attendance in the case of children to be employed in agriculture, and that in such parish such children over eleven and under thirteen years of age who have passed the standard fixed for partial exemption from school attendance by the bye-laws of the local authority shall not be required to attend school more than two hundred and fifty times in any year.

"Such bye-law shall have effect as a bye-law made under section seventy-four of The Elementary Education Act, 1870, and all Acts amending the same.

"The local authority shall be the local authority fixed by section seven of The Elementary Education Act, 1876."—(*Mr. Robson.*)

Question proposed.

"That those words be there added."

*Sir WILLIAM HART DYKE (Kent, Dartford): I have listened with pleasure to the excellent statement of the hon. and learned Gentleman. There is no doubt, at the first blush and the first examination of these proposals, that they are essentially a new development of our educational system. To my mind they are none the worse for it, if they are in the right direction, and although we have had many disquisitions as to the benefit or otherwise of the half-time system, we have now at all events before us, a concrete case for discussion and a very important one, which I venture to think will have a very considerable bearing on the educational future of this country. I rise to support the Amendment heartily. I support it from every point of view, not only as one much mixed up with educational affairs, but also from my own knowledge of village rural life. Educationally, socially and otherwise, I think it is a step in the right direction. The great thing we have to consider after all is the success of this proposed change, and if we only could secure that, we ought all to go into the lobby to support it. I think there are many chances in favour of its complete success. What will be the effects on the child, the parent and the State? First, let us take the child upon whom the experiment is to be made. The condition of the child in an agricultural village, whatever the agricultural industry surrounding him may be, whether it be corn growing or fruit growing, is at present most hazardous and uncertain. He never knows when he may be called into the field to scare away rooks or hustled suddenly into school. The amendment removes at once this terrible uncertainty, and in addition gives the child a chance of two more years of school life, not spread over the year in the present haphazard fashion, but restricted to certain periods. That

will be of great advantage to the child. With regard to the parent, I believe the Amendment will remove an immense cause of continual friction between the parent and the school attendance officer. Many of the parents have to struggle for existence in rural districts, and this Amendment, if worked well, will have regard to their feelings, instincts, and if you like their prejudices. At present the parents have the school attendance officer always at their elbow. The present Amendment will give them a clear period of the year in which allowance will be made for their children's absence from school, and it will enable them to make clear and definite arrangements for their children's education, and also for their being enabled to earn money. As regards the State, I believe the amendment will be valuable not only to the cause of education in general, but it will remove the large amount of friction and difficulty which now exists between the central department and the rural districts. I am bound to say that in rural districts I have found the strongest objection to any idea of the over-education of children. I remember once attending a meeting to open a large school in a district in England, and I was attacked on the platform because I advocated technical education. Again, this scheme would overcome the enormous amount of prejudice now existing. Parents and children would know what demands were made upon them, and the employer would also know when he could count on getting labour on his farm. I believe it would be of great advantage to our farmers to know when they could command such labour. It is most important to remove the friction which exists between parents and school attendance officers. I know, from my own personal knowledge, that a woman and her children in Kent can earn during the fruit-picking season from 30s. to 35s. a week. It can easily be understood how any family earning that amount can defy the school attendance committee, and pay the fines imposed for non-attendance. I hope this Bill will pass, and believing that it will do much for the future of elementary education in this country, I will give this amendment my most hearty support.

MAJOR RASCH (Essex, S.E.): I never thought that I should have the honour of addressing this Committee in favour of the

B

proposal of a higher school age in rural districts on this particular day of the year. But my honourable and learned Friend the Member for South Shields has so re-organised his proposal that it is possible for us to find salvation in his views, and do our best to support him. I also imagine that the proposal is acceptable to the Vice-President of the Council, who, I find, has not shown himself so hostile to agricultural interests as I thought he was. As I understand the proposal, it is that children are to be allowed to go to school in the winter and to pick up some useful education in the summer. In the opinion of many of us in agricultural districts, the raising of the age of compulsory attendance has gone far enough. What we have to contend against in the Eastern Counties is not so much low prices, high rates, and foreign competition, as the dearth of agricultural labour and the depopulation of the rural districts. I am not exaggerating when I say there are many towns in the Eastern Counties where the population is less than it was in the time of the Stuarts, and still less than in the Middle Ages. A neighbour of my own had recently to give up his farm because he could not get labour; and the dearth of labour is caused by forcing the pace of education. One of my constituents, owing to the impossibility of getting labour, has been forced—it sounds rather absurd—to milk his cows with a gas engine. I am sorry for the cows, but it is absolutely the case. Agricultural labour has gone up something like 20 per cent, and things are much worse in the agricultural districts than they were five years ago. We had the Agricultural Rating Act, but if you take half-a-crown out of one pocket of a man and put sixpence into another pocket, he does not gain any moral or material benefit. At the risk of incurring the epithet which the honourable Member for Fife in one of his highly elaborated witticisms threw at our heads the other day, of being a "Tony Lumpkin," I have ventured to lay before the Committee my views, which are also the views of my constituents, as to the absolute state of the case with reference to the depopulation of the rural districts.

MR. JEFFREYS : I do not like the age being raised, but as the House, on the Second Reading of the Bill, decided that it should be raised, I fear that we

Major Ruschl

must make the best of it. I am glad the hon. and learned Member has proposed this Amendment. After what has been said, not only by him, but also by my right hon. Friend the Member for Dartford, and my hon. and gallant Friend the Member for South-East Essex, I think the Committee will see there is a great deal of unanimity on this question. As the Amendment originally stood, I thought we were getting nothing in the way of a concession, and I therefore put down another Amendment. In the model bye-laws issued by the Department under Section 74 of the Elementary Education Act, it is stated that children between the ages of 11 and 13 years of age, who shall be beneficially employed to the satisfaction of the local authority, shall not be obliged to attend school for more than 150 attendances in each year, and when I put down 200 attendances I was therefore giving 50 more than were already allowed. But, as the hon. Gentleman considers that 250 is a reasonable number, I will not move my Amendment. I may qualify what I have said, however, by hoping that we shall not, next year, or in successive years, be forced to raise the age. We are gradually creeping up. A few years ago it was 10 years, now it is 11, and this Bill proposes to make it 12. I am afraid education is incurring the hostility not only of the farmers but also of the working classes of this country, for many labouring men object to the enforced attendance at school of children who are able to earn a little. I only hope the Amendment will, as suggested, keep the children on the land instead of their flocking to the towns as at present. If it does that, agriculturists will put up with the extra year.

MR. YOXALL (Nottingham, W.) : I am very loth to disturb the unanimity of the Committee, but I venture to think that, in his desire to be conciliatory, my honourable and learned Friend has gone too far. The normal number of attendances is 420, and the Education Department declines to give a grant to any school not open 400 times in the year. My honourable Friend proposed to reduce the number to 300 attendances, but when he further reduces it to 250 I feel bound to make a protest, and to say that if a chance is offered me I shall divide against the proposal.

CAPTAIN BETHELL (York, E. R., Holderness) : The Amendment having received the support of my right honourable Friend the Member for Dartford, I would wish to suggest an Amendment in detail. The honourable and learned Gentleman proposes that the local authority for any rural district may have power to fix the minimum age. I wish to suggest to the Committee that it would be better that the County Council of any county should exercise the power. The County Council would exercise it more impartially, and would consider the demands of any portion of the area concerned. Its members are drawn from varying classes, and from a much wider area, and, I think, for that reason alone, it would be the better authority. But, above all, I would suggest to the Vice-President that the House of Commons has accepted the proposal that County Councils should have a great deal to do with educational questions in the future. The authority proposed to be wielded under the Amendment is legislative, and not administrative, and I would suggest that it would be better wielded by the County Council than by the local authorities. I do not know what arguments induced the honourable and learned Member to put in " the local authority for any rural district," but I hope he will be good enough to consider the arguments I have urged. I would also be glad if the Vice-President would give his views, especially with reference to the second consideration. The Amendment I propose to move is to leave out " the local authority for any rural district," and to substitute the words " the County Council of any county." It might be said that agriculturists are obstinate with reference to education, but educationalists also sometimes display obstinacy and dogmatism.

Amendment proposed to the proposed Amendment, in line 1, to leave out the words " local authority for any rural district," in order to insert words " county council of any county."—*(Captain Bethell.)*

Question proposed :

" That the words proposed to be left out stand part of the proposed Amendment."

SIR J. GORST : I hope my honourable and gallant Friend will not press this Amendment. I naturally had some share in the authorship of the Bill of 1896, and I was extremely favourable to the county council as the educational authority ; but this is a very burning question, and if it is introduced into the discussion on this Bill I am afraid we have no chance of getting through our labours before the end of the session ; I therefore hope my honourable and gallant Friend will take the authority as it exists in the Bill, and not raise the general question of educational authority.

* MR. GRANT LAWSON (York, N.R Thirsk) : I also join in the appeal to the honourable and gallant Member not to press the Amendment. In many county councils the agricultural members are in a very small minority, and would not be able to make their influence felt.

CAPTAIN BETHELL : In deference to the views of the Vice-President I will not press the Amendment.

Amendment to the proposed Amendment by leave withdrawn.

Original Question again proposed.

MR. GEORGE WHITELEY : I move that the word " rural " in the first line of this Amendment be omitted. In order to make clear to the Committee the object of my proposal, I may say that I intend to move later to omit the words " to be employed in agriculture " in order to insert " not employed in any factory or workshop." I do not move my Amendment in any hostile spirit to the agricultural interest. In my humble judgment the original Amendment is not only an attempt but a too successful attempt to square the agricultural Members, and those of us who are not occupied in that industry or connected with it are to be the Jonahs to be thrown overboard. I was very much interested in the speech of the honourable and gallant Member for South-east Essex, because when I moved the rejection of the second reading of this measure he was my seconder. What a state of backsliding has now occurred ! He informed us in his speech of a few interesting facts. He told us of one farmer who had to milk his cows with a gas engine. I am glad it was not a water engine. He informed us he had found salvation in the Amendment proposed by the honourable and learned Member for South Shields, but I think his position is not one in which to rejoice. The object of my Amendment is to extend the operation of the honourable and learned gentleman's Amendment to all half-timers, not half-timers under the Factories and Workshops Act. It practically admits all half-timers at the age of 11 provided they have made attendances to the very small number of 250. The half-timers not included in the Factories and Workshops Act number 55,000, and if they were subdivided I think I would not be very long in estimating that half of them are employed in agriculture and the other half employed in other occupations which do not come under the Factories and Workshops Act. There is a demand for the services of these children at certain periods, and they may be able to earn a pittance which would be a very great benefit to their parents and themselves. Take the boys employed in country-houses during the three months in the autumn. They are employed as errand boys and in connection with shooting. Why should every other class of boy be excluded from the Amendment in order that the agricultural boy should be included? If my honourable friend sees his way to adopt this Amendment it would apply not only to agricultural children but also to children employed in occupations other than in factories and workshops. I venture to press this Amendment and I shall certainly take it to a division.

Amendment proposed to the proposed Amendment: In line 1, to leave out the word "rural."—(*Mr. George Whiteley*).

Question proposed:
"That the word 'rural' stand part of the proposed Amendment:"

CAPTAIN PRETYMAN: I hope we shall not further discuss this particular Amendment, as it was not before us on the Second Reading. On the general question, we quite recognise that the honourable and learned Gentleman is anxious to meet the necessities of agriculturists—

*THE CHAIRMAN: The honourable Member must confine himself to the Amendment which has been moved to the Amendment.

CAPTAIN PRETYMAN: As regards this particular Amendment I think there are objections to it. In order to make it

Mr. George Whiteley.

operative at all, we must give sufficient inducement to school attendance committees to adopt it. The honourable and learned Member who moved the Amendment said it would increase the amount of education in rural districts by 25 per cent. But will the school attendance committees be given a sufficient inducement to bring this Act into operation? I think it is extremely doubtful. The honourable and learned Member seems to assume that under this Amendment children will be able to attend school in winter, and be absent in summer—

*The CHAIRMAN: Order, order! The honourable Member is not now discussing the Amendment to omit the word "rural."

CAPTAIN PRETYMAN: I will state my arguments on the original Amendment.

MR. CRIPPS (Gloucester, Stroud): I only wish to raise a technical point. Does the honourable and learned Member mean by the words "rural district" the Rural District Council? because if so he will exclude a large number of farmers. What are technically called urban districts very often contain large rural areas, and it certainly seems to me that the retention of the word "rural" would limit the effect of the Amendment beyond what is intended by the honourable and learned Member.

SIR JOHN LUBBOCK (London University): I venture to suggest to the honourable Member for Stockport that he should not press the consideration of his Amendment at the present moment, but that he should ask the Vice-President to give it consideration before the next stage of the Bill. I am so anxious that the Bill should pass that I hope the question of the number of attendances will not be re-opened. The Clause may not be exactly ideal, but it is something of a compromise which my honourable and learned Friend in charge of the Bill has very wisely put down to meet honourable Members on this side, and which seems to be generally acceptable. I should think it is not necessary to press the matter further.

SIR J. GORST: I think that the word "rural" is really not necessary, as long as we keep the word "agriculture" further on in the Amendment.

MR. ROBSON : I was about to rise for the purpose of making an observation which has, however, been now sufficiently made by the Vice-President. I think the word "rural" might be omitted.

VISCOUNT CRANBORNE : The omission of "rural" will put us in a difficulty when we get, later on in the Clause, to the words "employed in agriculture." If the word "rural" is left out, it will be an extremely difficult matter to determine who will be held to be engaged in agriculture, and it will be necessary to provide some definition as to what the words really mean. I am not at liberty to discuss that now, but it opens a very wide question. I would suggest to the honourable and learned Gentleman that, if the proposal should be workable at all, the word "rural" is to be kept in.

MR. GRANT LAWSON : My noble friend who has just spoken has forgotten the distinction which has been already made in the Act of 1896. I only wish to say on the Amendment that, if an agriculturist has the misfortune to live in an urban district, that is no reason why we should abandon him.

*MR. TOMLINSON : It has been put to me as a very great hardship that girls are not allowed to go on half time for the purpose of assisting the domestic work of the household. Education carried beyond a certain point tends to unfit girls for domestic duties, and domestic life, and if a system could be adopted by which girls could devote half their time to learning domestic habits which would probably be most necessary for them in after life, whilst carrying on their education with the other half, it would be conferring on them a very great benefit.

MAJOR RASCH : The honourable Member for Stockport has just reproved me for supporting the Amendment. My position is absolutely the same whenever agricultural interests are concerned. We have often asked for bread and have been offered a stone, and have been lucky if the stone were not cast at our heads. We have had this Amendment offered to us; it will be of some practical use to us, and we are not ashamed to accept it.

Question, "That the word 'rural' stand part of the Amendment," put and negatived.

Amendment proposed to the proposed Amendment : In line 3, to leave out the words "to be employed in agriculture," in order to insert the words "not employed in any factory or workshop"—(*Mr. George Whiteley*)—instead thereof.

Question proposed,

"That the words 'to be employed in agriculture' stand part of the proposed Amendment."

MR. GEORGE WHITELEY : I quite agree that the word "rural" is not necessary at all; but the words I now propose will make the Amendment much more workable. It will create less friction and difficulty, and will enable a large class of children during the summer months to earn full wages instead of half-time wages as at present. I appeal to the honourable and learned Member as to whether he cannot accept the Amendment.

VISCOUNT CRANBORNE : I would ask my right honourable friend the Vice-President of the Council what is his conception of the word "agriculture" in this connection. We are engaged in passing an Act of Parliament, and we have got to be exact. I suppose it will be the duty of the magistrates to say what children are or are not engaged in agriculture. I wish to know what would be the advice of the Vice-President as to the interpretation of the word. For example, would driving a herd to market be agriculture ; if so, would helping to keep the beasts in order in the market place be agriculture ; would feeding chickens be agriculture ; and if not, why not? I want to know where the honourable and learned gentleman would draw the line ; I think an Act of Parliament ought to be precise, and ought to give more guidance as to what it means. I would ask my right honourable friend, whose business it will be to administer this Act, or who at any rate will have to give advice in its administration, to say what he considers to be the meaning of the word "agriculture."

SIR J. GORST : If Parliament should pass the scheme in its present form it would be for the magistrates to determine what is meant by "agriculture." As to

the illustrations which have been given
by the noble Lord, I should think most
judges would very easily determine that
such operations were connected with
agriculture. If there is any doubt about

it, the matter can be referred to the High
Court.

Question put—

The Committee divided:—Ayes, 245;
Noes, 26. (Division List, No. 162.)

AYES.

Abraham, William (Rhondda)
Allan, William (Gateshead)
Allen, W. (Newc. under Lyme)
Allison, Robert Andrew
Anson, Sir William Reynell
Anstruther, H. T.
Arnold-Forster, Hugh O.
Ashton, Thomas Gair
Atkinson, Rt. Hon. John
Baillie, Jas. E. B. (Inverness)
Baker, Sir John
Banbury, Frederick George
Banes, Major George Edward
Barlow John Emmott
Bayley, Thomas (Derbyshire)
Bemrose, Sir Henry Howe
Bethell, Commander
Bhownaggree, Sir M. M.
Biddulph, Michael
Bill, Charles
Billson, Alfred
Birrell, Augustine
Blake, Edward
Blundell, Colonel Henry
Boulnois, Edmund
Broadhurst, Henry
Brunner, Sir John Tomlinson
Bullard, Sir Harry
Burns, John
Burt, Thomas
Buxton, Sydney Charles
Caldwell, James
Cameron, Sir Chas. (Glasgow)
Cameron, Robert (Durham)
Campbell, Rt. Hn. J. A. (Glas.)
Campbell-Bannerman, Sir H.
Carew, James Laurence
Carmichael, Sir T. D. Gibson-
Carvill, Patrick G. Hamilton
Causton, Richard Knight
Channing, Francis Allston
Clark, Dr. G. B. (Caithness-sh.)
Clough, Walter Owen
Coghill, Douglas Harry
Collings, Rt. Hon. Jesse
Colomb, Sir John C. Ready
Colston, Chas. E. H. Athole
Colville, John
Corbett, A. C. (Glasgow)
Cornwallis, F. Stanley W.
Cotton-Jodrell, Col. E. T. D.
Cranborne, Viscount
Crilly, Daniel
Cripps, Charles Alfred
Crombie, John William
Currie, Sir Donald
Dalbiac, Colonel Philip Hugh
Dalrymple, Sir Charles
Dickson-Poynder, Sir John P.
Dilke, Rt. Hon. Sir Charles
Dillon, John
Disraeli, Coningsby Ralph
Dorington, Sir John Edward

Douglas, Charles M. (Lanark)
Drucker, A.
Duckworth, James
Duncombe, Hon. Hubert V.
Dunn, Sir William
Dyke, Rt. Hon. Sir W. Hart
Edwards, Owen Morgan
Engledew, Charles John
Esmonde, Sir Thomas
Evans, Samuel T. (Glam.)
Evans, Sir F. H. (South'ton)
Farquharson, Dr. Robert
Ferguson, R. C. Munro (Leith)
Finch, George H.
Finlay, Sir Robert Bannatyne
Fisher, William Hayes
Fison, Frederick William
Fitzmaurice, Lord Edmond
FitzWygram, General Sir F.
Flower, Ernest
Fry, Lewis
Garfit, William
Giles, Charles Tyrrell
Gladstone, Rt. Hn. H. J.
Godson, Sir Augustus Fdk.
Gold, Charles
Gorst, Rt. Hn. Sir John E.
Gourley, Sir Edward T.
Gray, Ernest (West Ham)
Greene, Henry D. (Shrewsb'y)
Grey, Sir Edward (Berwick)
Griffith, Ellis J.
Gull, Sir Cameron
Gunter, Colonel
Gurdon, Sir Wm. Brampton
Haldane, Richard Burdon
Hardy, Laurence
Hare, Thomas Leigh
Harwood, George
Hayne, Rt. Hn. Ch. Seale-
Hazell, Walter
Hedderwick, Thomas C. H.
Helder, Augustus
Hoare, Samuel (Norwich)
Hobhouse, Henry
Holland, W. H. (York, W. R.)
Horniman, Frederick John
Houston, R. P.
Howard, Joseph
Howorth, Sir Henry Hoyle
Hughes, Colonel Edwin
Humphreys-Owen, Arthur C.
Hutton, Alfred E. (Morley)
Hutton, John (Yorks, N. R.)
Jacoby, James Alfred
Jeffreys, Arthur Frederick
Jenkins, Sir John Jones
Johnson-Ferguson, Jabez Ed.
Johnstone, Heywood (Sussex)
Jolliffe, Hon H. George
Jones, D. Brynmor (Swansea)
Jones, Wm. (Carnarvonshire)
Kenyon, James

Kitson, Sir James
Knowles, Lees
Labouchere, Henry
Lafone, Alfred
Langley, Batty
Laurie, Lieut.-General
Lawrence, Sir E. Durning-(Cor)
Lawson, John Grant (Yorks.)
Lawson, Sir W. (Cumb'land)
Leng, Sir John
Llewelyn, Sir Dillwyn-(Swan.)
Lloyd-George, David
Loder, Gerald W. Erskine
Logan, John William
Long, Col. Ch. W. (Evesham)
Lorne, Marquess of
Lough, Thomas
Lowe, Francis William
Loyd, Archie Kirkman
Lucas-Shadwell, William
Lyell, Sir Leonard
M'Arthur, Charles (Liverp'l)
M'Arthur, William (Corn'l),
M'Ewan, William
M'Ghee, Richard
M'Iver, Sir Lewis (Edin. W.)
M'Leod, John
Maddison, Fred
Mappin, Sir Fredk. Thorpe
Mendl, Sigismund Ferdinand
Middlemore, John Throgm't'n
Milward, Colonel Victor
Molloy, Bernard Charles
Monk, Charles James
Montagu, Sir S. (Whitechapel)
Morgan, J. Lloyd (Carmart'n)
Morgan, W. Prit'h'd (Merth'r)
Morley, Charles (Breconshire)
Morley, Rt. Hon. J. (Montr'e)
Morrison, Walter
Morton, A. H. A. (Deptford)
Morton, Ed. J. C. (Devonport)
Moss, Samuel
Myers, William Henry
Nicol, Donald Ninian
Norton, Capt. Cecil William
Nussey, Thomas Willans
O'Connor, Jas. (Wicklow, W.)
O'Connor, T. T. (Liverpool)
Oldroyd, Mark
Orr-Ewing, Charles Lindsay
Palmer, Sir C. M. (Durham)
Palmer, Geo. Wm. (Reading)
Paulton, James Mellor
Pease, Alfred E. (Cleveland)
Pease, H. Pike (Darlington)
Pease, Joseph A. (Northumb.)
Philipps, John Wynford
Phillpotts, Captain Arthur
Pickersgill, Edward Hare
Pierpoint, Robert
Pirie, Duncan V.
Platt-Higgins, Frederick

Sir J. Gorst.

Powell, Sir Francis Sharp
Pretyman, Ernest George
Price, Robert John
Priestley, Briggs (Yorks.)
Purvis, Robert
Randell, David
Rasch, Major Frederic Carne
Redmond, J. E. (Waterford)
Richardson, J.(Durham, S.E.)
Rickett, J. Compton
Roberts, John H. (Denbighs.)
Robertson, Herbert (H'ckney)
Rollit, Sir Albert Kaye
Russell, T. W. (Tyrone)
Saunderson, Rt. Hon. Col. E.J.
Scoble, Sir Andrew Richard
Shaw, Charles Edw. (Stafford)
Sinclair, Capt. J. (Forfarshire)
Smith, James P'rk'r(Lanarks.)
Smith, Samuel (Flint)

Soames, Arthur Wellesley
Spencer, Ernest
Spicer, Albert
Steadman, William Charles
Stevenson, Francis S.
Stuart, James (Shoreditch)
Sullivan, Donal (Westmeath)
Talbot, Lord E. (Chichester)
Talbot,Rt.Hn. J. G.(Oxf'd.U.)
Tennant, Harold John
Thomas, A. (Glamorgan, E.)
Thornton, Percy M.
Usborne, Thomas
Wallace, Robert (Perth)
Walton, J. Lawson (Leeds, S.)
Walton, Joseph (Barnsley)
Warner, Thos. Courtenay T.
Warr, Augustus Frederick
Weir, James Galloway
Whitmore, Charles Algernon

Whittaker, Thomas Palmer
Williams, J. Carvell (Notts.)
Willox, Sir John Archibald
Wilson, Charles Henry (Hull)
Wilson, Hy. J. (York,W. R.)
Wilson, John (Durham, Mid.)
Wilson, John (Falkirk)
Wilson, John (Govan)
Wilson, Jos. H. (Middlesbro')
Woodall, William
Woodhouse,SirJ.T.(Hudersf'd)
Woods, Samuel
Wortley, Rt. Hn.C. B. Stuart-
Wylie, Alexander
Yerburgh, Robert Armstrong
Yoxall, James Henry

TELLERS FOR THE AYES—
Mr. Robson and Colonel
Lockwood.

NOES.

Arnold, Alfred
Ascroft, Robert
Bowles, T. G. (King's Lynn)
Cawley, Frederick
Cross, H. Shepherd (Bolton)
Fergusson,Rt.Hn.SirJ.(Man)
FitzGerald, Sir Rt. Penrose-
Galloway, William Johnson
Gedge, Sydney
Greville, Hon. Ronald

Heaton, John Henniker
Henderson, Alexander
Hickman, Sir Alfred
Hornby, Sir William Henry
Leese, Sir J. F. (Accrington)
Lubbock, Rt. Hon. Sir John
Maclean, James Mackenzie
Maden, John Henry
Mellor, Colonel (Lancashire)
Pilkington, Richard

Rothschild, Hn. Lionel Walter
Rutherford, John
Seton-Karr, Henry
Sidebotham, J. W. (Cheshire)
Tomlinson, Wm. Ed. Murray
Whiteley,H.(Asht'n-und'r-L.)

TELLERS FOR THE NOES—
Mr. George Whiteley, and
Sir William Coddington.

MR. GALLOWAY (Manchester, S.W.): I beg to move, in line 4, after "agriculture," to add "or any operations connected therewith." The words I suggest seem to me to make the clause more workable, and they will cover all the cases mentioned by the noble Lord. In effect, my proposal will widen the scope of the Amendment.

Amendment negatived.

*MR. GILES (Cambridge, Wisbech): My object in placing upon the paper the Amendment which stands in my name was to give expression and effect to the resolutions passed by the Isle of Ely County Council and numerous other public bodies against the Bill. I am very anxious, and I am sure a great many honourable Members in this House are also anxious—not that education should be retarded, but improved; and on behalf of the agriculturists of North Cambs. I repudiate the idea that farmers are against education itself. What they desire is that education and employment should go hand in hand. I should be disposed to withdraw my Amendment if I thought the number of attendances would be fixed at 250 instead of 300,

and if I thought such a proposal would be accepted by honourable Members opposite. (Opposition cries of "Yes.") If that is so, I shall withdraw my Amendment, for I feel that the concession which the honourable Member for South Shields has made is a very great one to the agriculturists; his Amendment in their favour has my hearty support, and I believe it will be one means of making education more popular in the rural districts.

Amendment proposed, in line 6, to leave out all after "shall," and insert

"be entitled to a certificate or certificates of exemption from attendance for any period or periods not exceeding three months in all during any one year, if it be shown to the satisfaction of the local authority that the local authority that the child will obtain suitable employment during the periods of exemption, and if, in the opinion of the local authority, the child has made good attendance prior to such period."—(*Mr. Giles.*)

Question proposed, "That the words proposed to be left out stand part of the Clause."

*MR. GRAY (West Ham, N.): With regard to this Amendment, I should like to make one observation. I am heartily in favour of its principle, and I am certain it will work well, but I desire to ask the Vice-President of the Council whether he can furnish some estimate of the number of attendances now actually made by children who have passed the exemption standard. I want to see how this standard of 250 attendances will compare with the attendances made now by children under similar conditions. I want to draw attention to a practical difficulty which is, that there is no provision that these 250 attendances shall be made. There is no guarantee that these attendances will ever be made, and I should like to know if they are not made, what steps the Education Department can take to bring any local authority to book which does not secure that the children in its district makes the stipulated number of attendances.

COLONEL LOCKWOOD (Essex, Epping): I value this measure and this Amendment not so much for the benefit which it will confer upon the rural districts, but because it recognises for the first time in the history of the educational movement that there is to be a difference drawn between children in the country districts and children in the urban districts.

CAPTAIN PRETYMAN: The average age now is about 11 years and 6 months at which a child leaves school, and exemption begins when the child has attained a certain age. The minimum age is 11, and it is proposed to raise it to 12. The Amendment says—

"Shall not be required to attend school more than 250 times in any year."

I suppose the honourable Member means a school year. It may happen that in October a child at 11 years and 6 months old passes the standard which entitles him to exemption, and that child will have made the 250 attendances which he has to make under this Amendment. He will, therefore, become free to work during the months of November, December, January and February. That child will have very little benefit indeed, whereas another child would be able to be away for the whole time. I think it is right, and in the interest of the community, that children should be allowed to follow a healthy outdoor occupation during the

Mr. Gray.

period they are attending school. This is a Bill which I agreed with in principle, and which I am anxious to see passed into law. We must, however, remember that this is an adoptive Amendment, and if it is to be adopted by the local authorities it must be workable, and I think it would be in the interests of the country districts. Difficulties may of course arise which will require to be discussed and be considered by the Education Department, and I think it is very unfortunate that a measure of this sort could not be taken up by the Education Department. This Amendment raises difficult and complicated points which I hope the honourable Member who has introduced the Bill, and the Vice-President of the Council, will most carefully consider between this and the Report stage. If this is done I think it will be a most valuable measure for all concerned.

SIR J. GORST: It would scarcely be possible within the limits of the time at the disposal of the Committee to discuss the details of the operation of the Amendment. I may say that this Amendment has been carefully considered by the experienced officials of the Education Department who are conversant with the working of the Education Acts, and, without entering into detail, I may say that it is their opinion that this particular Amendment is workable; and that by the bye-laws that will be made under it the general intentions of the Committee in passing this Amendment can no doubt be carried into effect.

Question put, Amendment negatived. Amendment proposed—in Clause 1, page 1, line 12, at end, to add,—

"Provided also that a child shall be entitled to obtain partial exemption from school attendance on attaining the age of twelve years if such child has made three hundred attendances in not more than two schools during each year for five preceding years whether consecutive or not."—(*Mr. Rutherford.*)

SIR J. GORST: The Government are willing to accept this Amendment.

MR. GEORGE WHITELEY: The existing law provides that a child shall pass a certain standard of education; if you withdraw that child before it obtains that certificate you are deemed to be acting in contravention of the existing Act, and you are liable to a penalty. It seems to me that there is some difficulty with regard to the proposition of my honourable friend, and unless the section I have referred to is repealed difficulties may ensue.

Amendment agreed to.

*Colonel MELLOR: I may explain very shortly the object of the Amendment I now rise to move. I think that where the local authority are satisfied as to the poverty of the parents they should have power to enable a child to be allowed to work half time. The honourable and learned gentleman assures me that the present Act gives all the protection needed for poor families, the number of which he appears to think is very small. I believe, however, that these very poor parents exist in greater numbers than honourable Members opposite suppose. The result of my inquiries and the investigations I have made lead me to believe that this Act, unless some saving clause of this kind is introduced, may be made the means of cruelty and of injustice also. I, for one, have always been in favour of raising the age of children, provided that some provision is made for meeting such difficult cases as are contemplated by my Amendment. On this question I go much further than the National Union of Teachers, for I have advocated the extension of the principle of compulsion not only until 13 years of age, but in evening schools until the age of 16. After 13 a child should only be allowed to work the whole day up to 16 on condition that a limited number of attendances at a night school up to that age was insisted upon. Under the present system I believe that a great proportion of the money we spend on education is so much money wasted, and I believe that unless our system of elementary education is followed up at the night schools it will be little use, and our expectations will never be realised. I must, therefore, press my proposal to a division, although if it can be shown that my contention is wrong I will withdraw my proposition, because I do not want to obstruct the passing of this Bill, which I believe will be, on the whole, the means of doing great good to the children.

Amendment proposed, after the words last inserted, to add the words :

"Provided also, that if it is shown to the satisfaction of the local educational authority that the earnings of any child above the age of 11 years are necessary, by reason of the poverty of the parents, to the maintenance of the said child, the said educational authority may in such cases grant a certificate exempting such child from the operation of this Act :"—*(Colonel Mellor)* :—

Question proposed, "That those words be there added."

MR. ROBSON : In a very few words I hope I shall be able, satisfactorily, to meet the point raised by the honourable Member who has moved this Amendment. I gather that he accepts the statement of the law which I submitted by reference to a well known authority, where it has been laid down that the poverty of the parents is a reasonable excuse under the Education Act of 1870 for the absence of the child from school and his presence at work. There seems to be an idea that there is an unconditional law of compulsion in England, but that is not so. There is a law of compulsion, but it depends upon the absence of a reasonable excuse, and the poverty of the parents has always been held to be a reasonable excuse. The words of the Bill are much more elastic and suitable than either of the two Amendments to deal with poor parents. The honourable Member raises a further point ; he refers to the Factory Acts, and he wishes to know how they will affect the case of poor parents. Now the Factory Acts forbid a child to work during the whole time up to the age of 13, but they do allow him to work half-time up to the age of 13, provided that a certificate of exemption from school attendance is obtained. The honourable Member says it may be that the educational authorities will not be able to force the child to go to school between the ages of 11 and 13, and he asks will a child be still able to do so under the Factory Acts between the ages of 11 and 13 ? Under the Factory Acts a child can go to the factory at the age of 11, after my Bill passes, if there is a reasonable excuse for its exemption from school attendance, provided it produces a certificate of exemption from the education authority. That authority, in the case of a poor child, cannot force the parents to send it to school, and in such a case the education authority would desire that the child should go to the factory. It would be to the advantage of the education authority, in such a case, to give a certificate at 11 years of age, by which the child would not only be able to absent itself from school but could go straight to the factory. I hope the honourable Member will accept my assurance on this point. The view I have expressed I have arrived at after a very careful consideration of the law, and I trust that he will withdraw his Amendment.

*COLONEL MELLOR: I should like to have the views of the Vice-President of the Council on this point.

SIR J. GORST: I could not put the case more clearly than the honourable Member opposite has done, for his views are entirely in accordance with those of the Education Department. If the honourable Member himself had not risen, I was prepared to say that the Amendment of my honourable friend, though good in principle, was quite unnecessary, because, under the existing law, everything he seeks to carry out by this Amendment is already provided for.

*COLONEL MELLOR: If the local authority has power, notwithstanding this Act, to allow children to work, it also has power to prevent children working. That being so, it appears to me that the Bill is quite as unnecessary as the Amendment.

*MR. TOMLINSON: If this Bill passes without this Amendment there will be no power to allow a child to go half-time in a factory, though he may be allowed to take up desultory employment.

MR. GEORGE WHITELEY: I withdrew my Amendment earlier in the discussion because I felt that this matter would be fully discussed at this stage, for I look upon this as a very important Amendment indeed. I do not at all agree with the argument of the honourable Member opposite that all the necessary provision is made by the existing law. If it is provided for, what harm can there be in introducing this Amendment, the effect of which will be to make the point clear? Why does the honourable Member opposite object to having the thing made perfectly clear?

Mr. Robson.

MR. ROBSON: I do not wish to introduce this Amendment, because it would be more disadvantageous to poor parents than the existing law. The Amendment would require the poor parents to make a declaration of pauperism in order to gain an advantage which they already possess in a more suitable form under the existing law.

MR. GEORGE WHITELEY: Representing here a Lancashire constituency, I am going to do my best in the interests of the Lancashire industry. I do not think we ought to be pressed to withdraw any Amendment which we think is fair and just, and we do not regard this Amendment in the light which the honourable Member opposite has thrown upon it. The Amendment has all the elements which should recommend it to the Committee, and there never was a more reasonable Amendment drafted. In cases where the poverty is really so great that the parents cannot properly maintain a child, such child should be permitted to go to work. There are, no doubt, cases existing where the father may be ill, and the mother is obliged to remain at home to look after him. In such a case the work of a child is of great importance, although some honourable Members opposite apparently think that half-a-crown a week is not much to bring in. Such a sum, however, is of very great importance in the conduct of such a household to secure the means of livelihood. Are we going to say that a child shall not be allowed to work under any circumstances whatever? I think the honourable Member in charge of this Bill, with his great majority, ought not to oppose this Amendment, and thus render our position a difficult and disagreeable one. As he is strong, so he ought to be merciful, and he ought to withhold his "bowels of compassion" somewhat. I do press this point, and I hope the honourable Member will press his Amendment to a division, for it is a most important one, and will have a very far-reaching effect.

* COLONEL MELLOR: I am afraid I cannot accept the interpretation of the law on this subject which the hon. and learned Member in charge of the Bill has just put before the Committee. I may state, for the information of the Committee,

that I put the hon. Member's views on this point before a thoroughly competent authority, who for years past has had the duty of administering the Education Acts, and with the permission of the Committee I will read what he says on this subject.

"Local authorities may (as Mr. Robson stated to you) in case of poverty grant exemption from attendance at school under Bye-law 2 at any age, and allow employment of any kind, other than that under the provisions of the Factory and Workshops Acts. But a certificate can not be given under Bye-law 5b, under any circumstances, till eleven years of age has been attained, and the required standard of education passed, and so employment under any of the Labour Acts is debarred, however poor a family may be. If you raise the age the power of the local authority will be curtailed accordingly."

The object of my Amendment is to correct this disability where factory labour is concerned, and as at present advised I feel that I must press it to a division.

MR. DUCKWORTH (Lancashire, Middleton): I should have voted for the Amendment if I had not felt that the ordinary law of the land was adequate, but feeling assured that that is so, I think it is the crux of the whole affair. But although it may have been the law of the land, I believe it has not been generally known, and has certainly not been understood to be the law in Lancashire. After this discussion it will be understood that, by the ordinary law of the land, exemptions can be made, and it will be known that the poverty of the parents is a reasonable excuse why a child should go half-time to school. I do not, therefore, see any necessity for this Amendment.

MR. GRANT LAWSON: I desire to know whether the local authority is barred from initiating a prosecution in cases where poverty is known to exist, or whether it would be necessary for the parent to be prosecuted before the law will enable him to obtain exemption for a child on the ground of poverty.

MR. SETON-KARR (St. Helens): I should like to state briefly what my views are on this matter. So far, I am not quite clear in my own mind as to whether the effect of this Amendment is met by the existing law. The right honourable Gentleman has practically said "those are my sentiments." I want a clear explanation from the right honourable Gentleman as to the operation of the present law, and I want to know whether it does really meet the point of this Amendment. I am in doubt about it, and it is a very important point, and unless I can get a clear explanation from the right honourable Gentleman on this point, I for one shall vote for this Amendment if it goes to a division. I think this House has gone quite far enough already in preventing parents from enjoying the legitimate fruits of the labour of their children. I cannot account for the extraordinary and feverish anxiety displayed by some honourable Members opposite in endeavouring to rush this Bill through this afternoon. I am not very much in love with the Bill at all, because I think it goes a little too far——

*THE CHAIRMAN: Order, Order. The honourable Member is now discussing the principles of the Bill, and he must confine himself to the Amendment.

MR. SETON-KARR: I do attach great importance to a practical explanation by the right honourable Gentleman, and I trust that he will give it to us.

MR. HERBERT WHITELEY (Ashton-under-Lyne): I do not speak for the purpose of offering undue or factious opposition. I think that this is an Amendment which, in the interest of the Bill itself, the promoter would do well to accept. He says that this Amendment would not make the right of exemption more obvious to the people of the country than the existing law ; but I assure him that that is not the case. I speak from intimate experience, and I do not believe that it is understood in the least among the working people that they can get exemption for their children by pleading poverty. I urge the honourable Member to let this provision come in and make the point clear to all. The mere fact of its being put in the Bill will emphasise the law as it exists.

COLONEL PILKINGTON : I would support the opinion expressed by the honourable Member who has just sat down. It seems to me to cover the ground entirely. If the Amendment is on all fours with the law, why cannot it be accepted and put into the Bill ? My experience is the same as that of my honourable friend who has just spoken, that the present state of the law is not understood, at any rate in Lancashire. The magistrates and the Committees of the Local Authorities do not act upon it. In practice they say that no person, whether pleading poverty or not, will be allowed to send children into the factory until they attain the age of 12. To do away with that misunderstanding, I appeal to the honourable Member in charge of the Bill to accept the Amendment, because I believe that without it the Act would be absolutely unworkable, and poor people would not be able to send their children to the factory in a straightforward way.

MR. SETON-KARR : Before the Committee go to a division I wish to point out that we have not received any definite statement as to the existing law. The honourable Member who introduced the Bill first said that the object of the Amendment was provided for by the existing law, and in that he was supported by the Vice-President ; but when challenged upon the point he said the Amendment proposed to do something to which he objected. My point is that these statements are contradictory, and I want some definite statement on the subject.

The Committee divided :—Ayes 63 ; Noes 229.—(Division List No. 163.)

AYES.

Arnold, Alfred	Gedge, Sydney	Maclean, James Mackenzie
Ascroft, Robert	Gibbs, Hon. V (St. Albans)	Maden, John Henry
Bemrose, Sir Henry Howe	Giles, Charles Tyrrell	Melville, Beresford Valentine
Bethell, Commander	Gilliat, John Saunders	Monk, Charles James
Biddulph, Michael	Godson, Sir Augustus Fredk.	Nicol, Donald Ninian
Bigwood, James	Greville, Hon. Ronald	Pilkington, Richard
Bill, Charles	Gunter, Colonel	Pym, C. Guy
Blundell, Colonel Henry	Hare, Thomas Leigh	Rutherford, John
Boulnois, Edmund	Hickman, Sir Alfred	Scoble, Sir Andrew Richard
Bowles,T.Gibson(King's Lynn	Hornby, Sir William Henry	Seton-Karr, Henry
Brown, Alexander H.	Howorth, Sir Henry Hoyle	Sidebotham, J. W. (Cheshire)
Bullard, Sir Harry	Jackson, Rt. Hon. Wm. Lawies	Spencer, Ernest
Cawley, Frederick	Jolliffe, Hon. H. George	Tomlinson, W. E. Murray
Clarke, Sir Edward (Plym'th)	Kemp, George	Usborne, Thomas
Coddington, Sir William	Kenyon, James	Whiteley, H.(Ashton-und.-L.)
Cox, Irwin Ed. B. (Harrow)	Knowles, Lees	Wilson, John (Falkirk)
Cross, H. Shepherd (Bolton)	Lafone, Alfred	Wylie, Alexander
Dixon-Hartland, Sir F. Dixon	Laurie, Lieut.-General	
Duckworth, James	Lawson, John Grant (Yorks.)	TELLERS FOR THE AYES—
Fergusson,Rt.Hn.SirJ.(Man.)	Leese, Sir J. F. (Accrington)	Colonel Mellor and Mr.
Finch, George H.	Llewelyn, Sir D.- (Swansea)	George Whiteley.
Fison, Frederick William	Loder, Gerald Walter E.	
Galloway, William Johnson	Long, Col. C. W. (Evesham)	
Mr. Herbert Whiteley.		

NOES.

Abraham, William (Rhondda)
Allan, William (Gateshead)
Allen,W.(Newc.-under-Lyme)
Allison, Robert Andrew
Anstruther, H. T.
Arnold-Forster, Hugh O.
Ashton, Thomas Gair
Asquith, Rt. Hn. Herbert H.
Atherley-Jones, L.
Atkinson, Rt. Hon. John
Austin, M. (Limerick, W.)
Baillie,James E. B.(Inverness)
Bainbridge, Emerson
Baker, Sir John
Banes, Major George Edward
Barlow, John Emmott
Bayley, Thomas (Derbyshire)
Bhownaggree, Sir M. M.
Billson, Alfred
Birrell, Augustine
Bond, Edward
Bowles,Capt.H.F.(Middlesex)
Broadhurst, Henry
Brunner, Sir John Tomlinson
Burns, John
Burt, Thomas
Buxton, Sydney Charles
Caldwell, James
Cameron, Sir Charles (Glasg.)
Cameron, Robert (Durham)
Campbell, Rt. Hn. J.A.(Glasg.)
Campbell-Bannerman, Sir H.
Carew, James Laurence
Carmichael, Sir T. D. Gibson-
Carvill,Patrick Geo.Hamilton
Causton, Richard Knight
Channing, Francis Allston
Clark, Dr.G.B.(Caithness-sh.)
Clough, Walter Owen
Coghill, Douglas Harry
Cohen, Benjamin Louis
Collings, Rt. Hon. Jesse
Colston, Chas. Edw. H.Athole
Colville, John
Corbett,A.Cameron(Glasgow)
Cornwallis,FiennesStanleyW.
Cotton-Jodrell, Col. E. T. D.
Crilly, Daniel
Crombie, John William
Dalbiac, Colonel Philip Hugh
Dalrymple, Sir Charles
Dickson-Poynder, Sir John P.
Dilke, Rt. Hon. Sir Charles
Dillon, John
Disraeli, Coningsby Ralph
Douglas, Charles M. (Lanark)
Drucker, A.
Duncombe, Hon. Hubert V.
Dunn, Sir William
Dyke, Rt. Hn. Sir William H.
Edwards, Owen Morgan
Engledew, Charles John
Evans, S. T. (Glamorgan)
Evans, Sir F. H. (South'ton)
Farquharson, Dr. Robert
Ferguson, R. C. M. (Leith)
Finlay, Sir R. Bannatyne
Fisher, William Hayes
FitzGerald, Sir R. Penrose-
Fitzmaurice, Lord Edmond

FitzWygram, General Sir F.
Flower, Ernest
Fry, Lewis
Garfit, William
Gibbs, Hn. A.G. H. (City Lond.
Gladstone, Rt. Hn. Herbert J.
Goddard, Daniel Ford
Gold, Charles
Goldsworthy, Major-General
Gordon, Hon. John Edward
Gorst, Rt. Hn. Sir J. Eldon
Goulding, Edward Alfred
Gourley, Sir E Temperley
Gray, Ernest (West Ham)
Green, W D. (Wednesbury)
Grey, Sir Edward (Berwick)
Gull, Sir Cameron
Gurdon, Sir W. Brampton
Hardy, Laurence
Hayne, Rt. Hn. C. Seale-
Heaton, John Henniker
Hedderwick, Thomas C. H.
Helder, Augustus
Henderson, Alexander
Hoare, Samuel (Norwich)
Hobhouse, Henry
Holland,Wm. H (York,W.R.)
Horniman, Frederick John
Houston, R. P.
Howard, Joseph
Hubbard, Hon. Evelyn
Hughes, Colonel Edwin
Humphreys-Owen, Arthur C.
Hutton, Alfred E. (Morley)
Hutton, John (Yorks, N.R.)
Jacoby, James Alfred
Jenkins, Sir John Jones
Johnson-Ferguson, Jabez E.
Johnstone, Heywood (Sussex)
Jones, D. Brynmor (Swansea)
Jones, Wm. (Carnarvonshire)
King, Sir Henry Seymour
Kitson, Sir James
Labouchere, Henry
Langley, Batty
Lawrence, Sir E. D.- (Corn.)
Lawson, Sir W. (Cumberland)
Leng, Sir John.
Lloyd-George, David
Lockwood, Lt.-Col. A. R.
Logan, John William
Lorne, Marquess of
Lough, Thomas
Lowe, Francis William
Loyd, Archie Kirkman
Lubbock, Rt. Hon. Sir John
Lucas-Shadwell, William
Lyell, Sir Leonard
M'Arthur, Charles (Liverpool)
M'Arthur, William (Cornwall)
M'Ewan, William
M'Ghee, Richard
M'Iver, Sir L. (Edinburgh,W.)
M'Leod, John
Maddison, Fred.
Mappin, Sir Fredk. Thorpe
Mendl, Sigismund Ferdinand
Middlemore, John. T.
Mildmay, Francis Bingham
Milward, Colonel Victor

Molloy, Bernard Charles
Montagu, Sir S.(Whitechapel)
Moon, Edward Robert Pacy
Morgan,J.Lloyd(Carmarthen)
Morgan,W.Pritchd.(Merthyr)
Morley, Charles (Breconshire)
Morley, Rt. Hn. J. (Montrose)
Morrison, Walter
Morton, ArthurH.A.(Deptf'd)
Morton, Edw.J.C.(Devonport)
Moss, Samuel
Myers, William Henry
Norton, Capt. Cecil William
Nussey, Thomas Willans
O'Connor, Arthur (Donegal)
O'Connor, Jas. (Wicklow, W.)
O'Connor, T. P. (Liverpool)
Oldroyd, Mark
O'Neill, Hon. Robert Torrens
Orr-Ewing, Charles Lindsay
Palmer, Sir Chas.M.(Durham)
Palmer, GeorgeWm.(Reading)
Paulton, James Mellor
Pease, Alfred E. (Cleveland)
Pease,HerbertPike(Darlingt'n
Pease, Joseph A. (Northumb.)
Perks, Robert William
Philipps, John Wynford
Phillpotts, Captain Arthur
Pickersgill, Edward Hare
Pierpoint, Robert
Pirie, Duncan V.
Powell, Sir Francis Sharp
Price, Robert John
Priestley, Briggs (Yorks.)
Priestley,SirW.Overend(Edin
Provand, Andrew Dryburgh
Purvis, Robert
Randell, David
Rasch, Major Frederic Carne
Redmond, John E. (Waterf'rd)
Richardson, J. (Durham, S.E.)
Rickett, J. Compton
Roberts, John Bryn (Eifion)
Roberts, John H. (Denbighs.)
Robertson, Edmund (Dundee)
Robertson, Herbert(Hackney)
Rollit, Sir Albert Kaye
Rothschild, Hn. Lionel Walt'r
Russell, T. W. (Tyrone)
Scott, Chas. Prestwich (Leigh)
Shaw, Charles Edw. (Stafford)
Sinclair,Capt. John(F'rf'rsh'e)
Smith, James Parker (L'n'rks)
Smith, Samuel (Flint)
Soames, Arthur Wellesley
Souttar, Robinson
Spicer, Albert
Steadman, William Charles
Stevenson, Francis S.
Stuart, James (Shoreditch)
Sullivan, Donal (Westmeath)
Talbot, Lord E. (Chichester)
Talbot,Rt.Hn.J.G.(Ox.Univ.)
Tennant, Harold John
Thomas,Abel (Carmarthen,E.)
Thomas, A. (Glamorgan, E.)
Thornton, Percy M.
Tritton, Charles Ernest
Wallace, Robert (Perth)

Walton, J. Lawson (Leeds, S.) | Williams,JohnCarvell(Notts.) | Woods, Samuel
Walton, Joseph (Barnsley) | Willox, Sir John Archibald | Yerburgh, Robert Armstrong
Warner, Thomas Courtenay T. | Wilson, Charles Henry (Hull) | Yoxall, James Henry
Warr, Augustus Frederick | Wilson, Henry J.(York,W. R.) |
Weir, James Galloway | Wilson, John (Durham, Mid.) | TELLERS FOR THE NOES.—
Wentworth, Bruce C. Vernon- | Wilson, John (Govan) | Mr. Robson and Mr. Ban-
Whitmore, Charles Algernon | Woodall, William | bury.
Williams, Colonel R. (Dorset) | Woodhouse,SirJ.T.(Huds'f'ld) |

Question proposed—

" That clause 1, as amended, stand part of the Bill."

MR. GEORGE WHITELEY: I now move to leave out Clause 1. It is an entirely different clause from what it was at the beginning of the afternoon's debate. I think in its new form it deserves the most careful scrutiny of the House, and I do not think we should evade that duty. If the hon. Member in charge of the Bill will accept my motion and reject the clause, I will abstain from any further opposition——[*laughter*]—I cannot understand the laughter of the honourable Members. The opposition which I have offered to the clause has been actuated by no other feeling than that of the interests of the constituents I represent. The clause proposes to raise the age of half-timers to 12 years, and I consider that in the highest degree undesirable. I want to ask whether there has been any demand for the change proposed from the employers of the country, from the working classes, from the children which it seeks to befriend, or from any great body of the public. ["Yes."] This Committee knows that there has been no demand whatever for such a Bill as this. [An honourable Member :—"Question".] My honourable Friend says "Question." This is a very great question, which will have to be very fully debated in the House. There has been no demand for the Bill from the employers, because they are aware that it would disorganise their business.

There has been no demand for it from the working classes, because they are perfectly well contented that their children should be brought up in the same manner as they themselves have been brought up. They are desirous that their children should enter upon work and should be able to earn money as they themselves did, and gain experience in their early years. There has been no demand for the Bill from the children of the country, for every Member acquainted with children knows that the children of working families at the present time eagerly look forward to the period when they can leave school and earn some money. I would say that if this Bill were to be decided upon by those who know best the whole subject of debate, it would be lost by a very large majority. The Bill has been demanded by one section of the community, and one section alone: by the National Union of School Teachers. The *Cotton Factory Times*, in an article the other day, says that this Bill means misery and suffering to widows and orphans, and that the agitation in support of it has been carried on only to put money in the pockets of the schoolmasters. The whole question has been pressed on the House by the National Union of School Teachers, who would like to lead the House captive, bound hand and foot, on this matter. That is an undignified position for the House to be in—

MR. ROBSON rose in his place, and claimed to move, " That the Question be now put."

Question put—
"That the Question be now put.'

The Committee divided :—Ayes 263 ;
Noes 26.—(Division List No. 164.)

AYES.

Abraham, William (Rhondda)
Aird, John
Allan, William (Gateshead)
Allan,W. (Newc. under Lyme)
Allison, Robert Andrew
Anstruther, H. T.
Arnold-Forster, Hugh O.
Ashton, Thomas Gair
Asquith, Rt. Hn. Herbert Hy.
Atherley-Jones, L.
Atkinson, Rt. Hon. John
Austin, M. (Limerick W.)
Baillie, Jas. E. B. (Inverness)
Bainbridge, Emerson
Baker, Sir John
Banbury, Frederick George
Banes, Major George Edward
Barlow, John Emmott
Bayley, Thomas (Derbyshire)
Beaumont, Wentworth C. B.
Bemrose, Sir Henry Howe
Bhownaggree, Sir M. M.
Biddulph, Michael
Bigwood, James
Bill, Charles
Billson, Alfred
Birrell, Augustine
Blundell, Colonel Henry
Bolton, Thomas Dolling
Bond, Edward
Bowles, Capt. H. F. (Midd'x.)
Broadhurst, Henry
Brown, Alexander H.
Brunner, Sir John Tomlinson
Bullard, Sir Harry
Burns, John
Burt Thomas
Buxton, Sydney Charles
Caldwell, James
Cameron, Sir Chas. (Glasgow)
Campbell, Rt. Hn. J. A. (Glas.
Campbell-Bannerman, Sir H.
Carmichael, Sir T. D. Gibson-
Causton, Richard Knight
Cawley, Frederick
Channing, Francis Allston
Clarke, Sir Ed. (Plymouth)
Clough, Walter Owen
Coghill, Douglas Harry
Cohen, Benjamin Louis
Collings, Rt. Hon. Jesse
Colston, Ch. Ed. H. Athole
Colville, John
Corbett, A. Cameron (Glas.)
Cornwallis, Fiennes, S. W.
Cotton-Jodrell, Col. Ed. T. D.
Crombie, John William
Dalbiac, Col. Philip Hugh
Dalrymple, Sir Charles
Dickson-Poynder, Sir John P.
Disraeli, Coningsby Ralph
Dorington, Sir John Ed.
Douglas, Charles M. (Lanark)
Drucker, A.
Duckworth, James
Duncombe, Hon. Hubert V.
Dunn, Sir William

Dyke, Rt. Hn. Sir Wm. Hart
Edwards, Owen Morgan
Esmonde, Sir Thomas
Evans, Sir Sam. T. (Glamorg.)
Evans, Sir F. H. (South'ton)
Farquharson, Dr. Robert
Ferguson, R. C. Munro (Leith)
Finch, George H.
Finlay, Sir Robert Bannatyne
Fisher, William Hayes
Fison, Frederick William
Fitzmaurice, Lord Edmond
Fitz Wygram, General Sir F.
Flower, Ernest
Fry, Lewis
Garfit, William
Gedge, Sydney
Gibbs, Hn.A.G.H. (C. of Lon.)
Giles, Charles Tyrrell
Gilliat, John Saunders
Gladstone, Rt. Hon. H. J.
Goddard, Daniel Ford
Gold, Charles
Goldsworthy, Major-General
Gordon, Hon. John Edward
Gorst, Rt. Hon. Sir J. Eldon
Gourley, Sir Edw. Temperley
Gray, Ernest (West Ham)
Green,Walfrd D. (Wedn'sb'y)
Gretton, John
Greville, Hon. Ronald
Grey, Sir Edward (Berwick)
Gunter, Colonel
Gurdon, Sir Wm. Brampton
Hall,,Rt. Hon. Sir Charles
Hardy, Laurence
Hare, Thomas Leigh
Harwood, George
Hayne, Rt. Hn. Charles Seale.
Heaton, John Henniker
Hedderwick, Thomas C. H.
Helder, Augustus
Henderson, Alexander
Hoare, Samuel (Norwich)
Hobhouse, Henry
Holland, W. H. (York, W. R.)
Horniman, Frederick John
Houston, R. P.
Howard, Joseph
Hubbard, Hon. Evelyn
Hughes, Colonel Edwin
Humphreys-Owen, Arthur C.
Hutton, John (Yorks. N.R.)
Jackson, Rt. Hn. Wm. Lawes
Jacoby, James Alfred
Jenkins, Sir John Jones
Johnson-Ferguson,Jabez Edw.
Johnstone, Heywood (Sussex)
Joliffe, Hon. H. George
Jones, D. Brynmor (Swansea)
Jones, Wm. (Carnarvonshire)
Kenyon, James
King, Sir Henry Seymour
Kitson, Sir James
Knowles, Lees
Labouchere, Henry
Lafone, Alfred

Langley, Batty
Laurie, Lieut.-General
Lawrence, Sir E.Durning-(Cor
Lawson, John Grant (Yorks.)
Lawson, Sir W. (Cumberland)
Leng, Sir John
Llewelyn,Sir Dillwyn-(Swan.)
Lockwood, Lt.-Col. A. R.
Loder, Gerald Walter Erskine
Logan, John William
Long, Col. C. W. (Evesham)
Lorne, Marquess of
Lough, Thomas
Lowe, Francis William
Loyd, Archie Kirkman
Lubbock, Rt. Hon. Sir John
Lucas-Shadwell, William
Lyell, Sir Leonard
Lyttelton, Hon. Alfred
Maclure, Sir John William
M'Arthur, Charles (Liverpool)
M'Arthur, William (Cornwall)
M'Ewan, William
M'Kenna, Reginald
M'Leod, John
Maddison, Fred.
Manners, Lord Edward W. J.
Mappin, Sir Frederick Thorpe
Mendl, Sigismund Ferdinand
Middlemore, J. Throgmorton
Mildmay, Francis Bingham
Milward, Colonel Victor
Molloy, Bernard Charles
Monk, Charles James
Montagu, Sir S. (Whitechapel)
Moon, Edward Robert Pacy
Morgan, J. Lloyd (Carm'rthen)
Morley, Charles (Breconshire)
Morley, Rt. Hn. J. (Montrose)
Morton, A. H. A. (Deptford)
Morton, E. J. C. (Devonport)
Moss, Samuel
Myers, William Henry
Nicol, Donald Ninian
Norton, Capt. Cecil William
Nussey, Thomas Willans
O'Connor, Arthur (Donegal)
O'Connor, T. P. (Liverpool)
Oldroyd, Mark
O'Neill, Hon. Robert Torrens
Orr-Ewing, Charles Lindsay
Palmer, Sir Ch. M. (Durham)
Palmer, Geo. Wm. (Reading)
Paulton, James Mellor
Pease, Alfred E. (Cleveland)
Pease, Her. Pike (Darlington)
Pease, Joseph A. (Northumb.)
Pender, Sir James
Perks, Robert William
Philipps, John Wynford
Phillpotts, Captain Arthur
Pickersgill, Edward Hare
Pierpoint, Robert
Pirie, Duncan V.
Platt-Higgins, Frederick
Powell, Sir Francis Sharp
Price, Robert John

Priestley, Briggs (Yorks.)
Priestley, Sir W. O. (Edin.)
Provand, Andrew Dryburgh
Purvis, Robert
Pym, C. Guy
Randell, David
Rasch, Major Frederic Carne
Richardson, J. (Durham, S.E.)
Rickett, J. Compton
Roberts, John Bryn (Eifion)
Roberts, John H. (Denbighs)
Robertson, Edmund (Dundee)
Robertson, Herbert (Hackney)
Rollit, Sir Albert Kaye
Rothschild, Hon. Lionel W.
Russell, T. W. (Tyrone)
Scoble, Sir Andrew Richard
Scott, Chas. Prest. (Leigh)
Shaw, Charles Ed. (Stafford)
Sidebotham, J. W. (Cheshire)
Skewes-Cox, Thomas

Smith, Jas. Parker (Lanarks.)
Soames, Arthur Wellesley
Souttar, Robinson
Spencer, Ernest
Spicer, Albert
Steadman, William Charles
Stevenson, Francis S.
Stuart, James (Shoreditch)
Sullivan, Donal (Westmeath)
Sutherland, Sir Thomas
Talbot, Lord E. (Chichester)
Talbot, Rt. Hn. J.G. (Oxf'd U.)
Tennant, Harold John
Thomas, A. (Carmarthen, E.)
Thomas, Alf. (Glamorgan, E.)
Thornton, Percy M.
Tritton, Charles Ernest
Vincent, Col. Sir C. E. Howard
Wallace, Robert (Perth)
Walton, J. Lawson (Leeds, S.)
Walton, Joseph (Barnsley)

Warner, Thos. Courtenay T.
Warr, Augustus Frederick
Weir, James Galloway
Wentworth, Bruce C. Vernon-
Williams, Colonel R. (Dorset)
Williams, J. Carvell (Notts.)
Wilson, Charles Henry (Hull)
Wilson, Hy. J. (York, W. R.)
Wilson, John (Durham, Mid.)
Wilson, John (Falkirk)
Wilson, John (Govan)
Wilson, Jos. H. (Middlesboro')
Woodall, William
Woodhouse, Sir J.T. (Hudders.
Woods, Samuel
Wortley, Rt. Hon. C. B. Stuart-
Wylie, Alexander
Yoxall, James Henry
TELLERS FOR THE AYES—
Mr. Robson and Sir Lewis
M'Iver.

NOES.

Arnold, Alfred
Boulnois, Edmund
Bowles, T. G. (King's Lynn)
Clark, Dr. G. B. (Caithness.)
Coddington, Sir William
Cross, H. Shepherd (Bolton)
Dixon-Hartland, Sir F. Dixon
FitzGerald, Sir Rob. Penrose-
Galloway, William Johnson
Gibbs, Hn. Vicary (St. Albn's)

Goulding, Edward Alfred
Hatch, Ernest Fredk. Geo.
Hickman, Sir Alfred
Hornby, Sir William Henry
Howorth, Sir Henry Hoyle
Kemp, George
Maclean, James Mackenzie
Maden, John Henry
Mellor, Colonel (Lancashire)
Melville, Beresford Valentine

Pilkington, Richard
Rutherford, John
Seton-Karr, Henry
Tomlinson, Wm. E. Murray
Whiteley, H. (Ashton-und'r-L.
Whitmore, Charles Algernon

TELLERS FOR THE NOES—Mr.
George Whiteley and Mr.
Ascroft.

Question, "That Clause 1, as amended, stand part of the Bill," put accordingly, and agreed to.

And, it being after half-past Five of the clock, the Chairman left the Chair to make his Report to the House.

Committee report Progress : to sit again upon Wednesday next.

FINE OR IMPRISONMENT (SCOTLAND AND IRELAND) BILL. *(re-committed)*

Considered in Committee, and reported, without amendment. Bill read the third time, and passed.

METROPOLIS MANAGEMENT ACTS AMENDMENT (BYE-LAWS) BILL [LORDS].

Read a second time, and committed for to-morrow.

SEATS FOR SHOP ASSISTANTS (ENGLAND AND IRELAND) BILL.

Read a second time, and committed for Friday.

METROPOLITAN SEWERS AND DRAINS.

Bill to amend the Metropolis Management Act with respect to Sewers and Drains, ordered to be brought in by Mr. James Stuart and Mr. John Burns.

PUBLIC HEALTH ACTS AMENDMENT BILL.

Dr. Clark, Dr. Farquharson, Dr. Fox, Mr. Galloway, Mr. Heath, Sir Alfred Hickman, Mr. Hobhouse, Mr. Brynmor Jones, Sir Francis Sharp Powell, Sir Albert Rollit, Mr. T. W. Russell, Mr. Schwann, Mr. J. G. Talbot, Mr. Whitmore, and Mr. Henry J. Wilson nominated Members of the Select Committee on the Public Health Acts Amendment Bill.

Ordered—That the Committee have power to send for persons, papers, and records.

Ordered—That Five be the quorum— *(Sir William Walrond.)*

METROPOLITAN SEWERS AND DRAINS BILL.

To Amend the Metropolis Management Act with respect to Sewers and Drains. Presented, and read the first time ; to be read a second time upon Wednesday next, and to be printed. [Bill 223.]

PUBLIC PETITIONS COMMITTEE.

Fifth Report brought up, and read ; to lie upon the table, and to be printed.

BUSINESS OF THE HOUSE.

MR. GRAY : I am anxious to know which branch of the Inland Revenue estimates will be taken to-morrow.

*A LORD of the TREASURY (MR. ANSTRUTHER, St. Andrews Burghs) : I think it has been generally understood that the Post Office Estimates will be the first Order to-morrow.

Adjourned at ten minutes before Six o'clock.

HOUSE OF LORDS.

Thursday, 1st June 1899.

PRIVATE BUSINESS.

THE LORD CHANCELLOR acquainted the House that the Clerk of the Parliaments had laid upon the Table the Certificates from the Examiners that the Standing Orders applicable to the following Bills have been complied with :

ELECTRIC LIGHTING PROVISIONAL ORDERS (No. 14) [Lords].

GAS AND WATER ORDERS CONFIRMATION [Lords].

TRAMWAYS ORDERS CONFIRMATION (No. 1) [Lords].

TRAMWAYS ORDERS CONFIRMATION (No. 3) [Lords].

And the Certificate that the further Standing Orders applicable to the following Bill have been complied with :

SHIREBROOK AND DISTRICT GAS.

The same were ordered to lie upon the Table.

GAS LIGHT AND COKE COMPANY BILL.

Read 2*a*, and committed : The Committees to be proposed by the Committee of Selection.

GREAT CENTRAL RAILWAY BILL.

Read 2*a*, and committed : The Committees to be proposed by the Committee of Selection.

SOUTH - EASTERN AND LONDON, CHATHAM, DOVER RAILWAY COMPANIES BILL.

Read 2*a*, and committed : The Committees to be proposed by the Committee of Selection.

SOUTH-EASTERN RAILWAY BILL.

Read 2*a*, and committed : The Committees to be proposed by the Committee of Selection.

GREAT NORTHERN RAILWAY BILL [Lords].

Read 3*a*, and passed, and sent to the Commons.

SUNDERLAND CORPORATION BILL [Lords].

Read 3*a*, and passed, and sent to the Commons.

CROWBOROUGH DISTRICT WATER BILL.

Read 3*a*, with the amendments ; further amendments made ; Bill passed, and returned to the Commons.

LEITH HARBOUR AND DOCKS BILL, SOUTH STAFFORDSHIRE STIPENDIARY JUSTICE BILL.

Brought from the Commons ; read 1a ; and referred to the Examiners.

METROPOLITAN WATER COMPANIES BILL.

Returned from the Commons with the Amendments agreed to.

BURLEY-IN-WHARFEDALE URBAN DISTRICT WATER BILL.

Returned from the Commons with the Amendments agreed to.

NUNEATON AND CHILVERS COTON URBAN DISTRICT COUNCIL WATER BILL.

Returned from the Commons with the Amendments agreed to.

WOODHOUSE AND CONISBROUGH RAILWAY (ABANDONMENT) BILL.

Returned from the Commons with the Amendment agreed to.

PILOTAGE PROVISIONAL ORDER BILL.

The Chairman of Committees informed the House that the opposition to the Bill was withdrawn ; the order made on the 12th of May last discharged ; and Bill committed to a Committee of the whole House.

ELECTRIC LIGHTING PROVISIONAL ORDER (No. 9) BILL [Lords].

Committed to a Committee of the whole House to-morrow.

ELECTRIC LIGHTING PROVISIONAL ORDERS (No. 10) BILL [Lords].

Committed to a Committee of the whole House to-morrow.

ELECTRIC LIGHTING PROVISIONAL ORDERS (No. 11) BILL [Lords].

Committed to a Committee of the whole House to-morrow.

C

EDUCATION DEPARTMENT PROVISIONAL ORDER CONFIRMATION (LIVERPOOL) BILL [Lords].

Committed to a Committee of the whole House on Monday next.

EDUCATION DEPARTMENT PROVISIONAL ORDER CONFIRMATION (LONDON) BILL [Lords].

Committed. The Committee to be proposed by the Committee of Selection.

GAS ORDERS CONFIRMATION (No. 1) BILL [Lords].

Committed to Committee of the Whole House.

GAS ORDERS CONFIRMATION (No. 2) BILL [Lords].

Committed: The Committee to be proposed by the Committe of Selection.

WATER ORDERS CONFIRMATION BILL [Lords].

Committed to a Committee of the whole House.

ELECTRIC LIGHTING PROVISIONAL ORDERS (No. 14) BILL [Lords].

To be read 2*a* to-morrow.

GAS AND WATER ORDERS CONFIRMATION BILL [Lords].

To be read 2*a* to-morrow.

TRAMWAYS ORDERS CONFIRMATION (No. 1) BILL [Lords].

To be read 2*a* to-morrow.

TRAMWAYS ORDERS CONFIRMATION (No. 3) BILL [Lords].

To be read 2*a* to-morrow.

ELECTRIC LIGHTING PROVISIONAL ORDERS (No. 5) BILL, (No. 101)

Brought from the Commons; read 1ᵃ; to be printed; and referred to the Examiners.

ELECTRIC LIGHTING PROVISIONAL ORDERS (No. 5) BILL, (No. 102.)

Brought from the Commons; read 1ᵃ; to be printed; and referred to the Examiners.

ELECTRIC LIGHTING PROVISIONAL ORDERS (No. 6) BILL, (No. 103.)

Brought from the Commons; read 1ᵃ; to be printed; and referred to the Examiners.

ELECTRIC LIGHTING PROVISIONAL ORDERS (No. 8) BILL, (No. 104.)

Brought from the Commons; read 1ᵃ; to be printed; and referred to the Examiners.

LOCAL GOVERNMENT PROVISIONAL ORDERS (No. 3) BILL, (No. 105.)

Brought from the Commons; read 1ᵃ; to be printed; and referred to the Examiners.

REPORTS, RETURNS, &c.

THE LORD CHANCELLOR acquainted the House that the following papers having been commanded to be presented to this House by Her Majesty had been so presented on the following dates by delivery to the Clerk of the Parliaments, pursuant to Order of the House of the 17th February, 1896, viz. :

1. Trade Reports—(Annual Series):
   No. 2263. Germany (Hamburg);
   No. 2264. Russia (Batoum and District);
   No. 2265. Russia (Taganrog);
   No. 2266. Netherlands (Amsterdam);
   No. 2267. Western Pacific (Tonga);
   No. 2268. Italy (Genoa and District);
   No. 2269. Greece (Ionian Islands);
   No. 2270. Turkey (Salonica);
   No. 2271. Switzerland (May 25);
   No. 2272. Germany (the Grand Duchy Baden);
   No. 2273. Turkey (Tripoli);
   No. 2274. Italy (Elba);
   No 2275. Paraguay;
   No. 2276. France (Saigon, etc.);
   No. 2277. Japan;
   No. 2278. Spain (Canary Islands) (May 31);

2. Wine Duties—Correspondence respecting the increase in the wine duties;

3. British South Africa Company—Correspondence with Mr. C. J. Rhodes relating to the proposed extension of the Bechuanaland Railway;

4. Local Taxation (Royal Commission) —Minutes of Evidence: Volume III.

The same were ordered to lie on the Table.

FISHERIES (SCOTLAND).

Seventeenth Annual Report of the Fishery Board for Scotland, being for the year 1898 ; Part II. Report on Salmon Fisheries.

EDUCATION DEPARTMENT (SOUTH-WESTERN DIVISION).

General Report for the year 1898, by A. Rankine, Esq., Chief Inspector.

COLONIES (ANNUAL)—No. 260.

Niger (West African Frontier Force) ; Reports for 1897-98.

LIGHT RAILWAYS ACT, 1896.

Orders made by the Light Railway Commissioners and modified and confirmed by the Board of Trade authorising the construction of—

1. Light railways in the counties of Glamorgan and Brecon between Vaynor Dowlais and Merthyr Tydfil ;
2. A light railway in the Isle of Sheppey and county of Kent between Queenborough Station and Leysdown ;
3. Light railways in the county of Middlesex from Uxbridge to Hanwell ;

Presented (by command), and ordered to lie on the Table.

INDIA (EXAMINATIONS).

Regulations for examinations for the Civil Service of India.

GAS AND WATER WORKS FACILITIES ACT, 1870.

Report by the Board of Trade as to dispensing with the consents of the Sevenoaks Rural District Council and the Hildenborough Parish Council in the case of the Tonbridge Gas Provisional Order.

GAS COMPANIES (METROPOLIS).

Accounts of the Metropolitan Gas Companies for the year 1898.

HARWICH HARBOUR.

Abstract of accounts of receipts and expenditure of Harwich Harbour Conservancy Board, to 31st day of March, 1899 ; with report on proceedings, &c.

DISEASES OF ANIMALS ACTS, 1894 AND 1896.

Order, dated the 18th day of May, 1899, No. 5944, revoking Order No. 5920, which prohibited the conveyance of animals by the ss. "Hindustan."

POLLING DISTRICTS (COUNTY OF CARNARVON).

Order made by the County Council of Carnarvon dividing into two parts the Penmorfa polling district of the county.

FACTORY AND WORKSHOP (WHITE LEAD FACTORIES).

Special rules with regard to the employment of persons in whitelead factories.

PUBLIC RECORDS (ADMIRALTY DEPARTMENT).

Fifth Schedule containing a list and particulars of classes of documents which have been removed from the office of the Commissioners for executing the office of Lord High Admiral of the United Kingdom of Great Britain and Ireland, and deposited in the Public Record Office, but which are not considered of sufficient public value to justify their preservation therein.

Laid before the House (pursuant to Act), and ordered to lie on the Table.

MUNICIPAL CORPORATIONS (BOROUGH FUNDS) ACT, 1872.

Petition for amendment of ; of the Urban District Council of Budleigh Salterton, in the County of Devon ; read, and ordered to lie on the Table.

JONES'S DIVORCE BILL [H.L.].

Amendment reported (according to order), and Bill to be read 3ᵃ to-morrow.

ANCHORS AND CHAIN CABLES BILL.

Motion made and Question proposed—

"That this Bill be now read a second time." —(*The Earl of Dudley.*)

THE PARLIAMENTARY SECRETARY TO THE BOARD OF TRADE (THE EARL OF DUDLEY): My Lords, this is a little Bill which passed through the House of Commons without any discussion at all. It is practically a Consolidation Bill. At present the law relating to the testing of anchors and chain cables is contained in three Acts of Parliament, which are somewhat conflicting and confusing, and it is therefore difficult to obtain convictions under the Acts. This Bill consolidates those Acts and simplifies the Law. The only new provision is contained in Clause 15, which deals with the issue of bogus certificates. It has been pointed out to the Board of Trade that certain firms are in the habit at present of putting marks on their anchors and chain cables in such a manner as to resemble the marks put upon them when tested under the auspices of the Board of Trade. We do not desire to prevent private testing, but we do wish, when articles are so tested, that marks should not be put upon them of a confusing and misleading character. I beg to move the Second Reading of this Bill.

Question put and agreed to.

Bill—Read 2ª (according to order) and committed to a Committee of the Whole House.

INFECTIOUS DISEASE (NOTIFICATION) ACT (1889) EXTENSION BILL.

Read 3ª (according to order); an amendment made; Bill passed, and returned to the Commons.

FINE OR IMPRISONMENT (SCOTLAND AND IRELAND) BILL.

Brought from the Commons; Read 1ª; and to be printed. (No. 100.)

House adjourned at twenty minutes before Five o'clock till To-morrow, a quarter past Four o'clock.

HOUSE OF COMMONS.

Thursday, 1st June 1899.

MR. SPEAKER took the Chair at Three of the clock.

PRIVATE BILL BUSINESS.

PRIVATE BILLS [Lords].

(Standing Orders not previously inquired into complied with.)

Mr. Speaker laid upon the Table report from one of the Examiners of Petitions for Private Bills, that, in the case of the following Bills, originating in the Lords, and referred on the first reading thereof, the Standing Orders not previously inquired into, and which are applicable thereto, have been complied with, viz.—

BEXHILL AND ST. LEONARDS TRAM-ROADS BILL [Lords].

BURY CORPORATION WATER BILL [Lords].

CHURCH STRETTON WATER BILL [Lords.]

FURNESS RAILWAY BILL [Lords].

GAINSBOROUGH URBAN DISTRICT COUNCIL (GAS) BILL [Lords].

GREAT YARMOUTH WATER BILL [Lords].

HUMBER CONSERVANCY BILL [Lords].

LEIGH-ON-SEA URBAN DISTRICT COUNCIL BILL [Lords].

LOUGHBOROUGH CORPORATION BILL [Lords].

PAISLEY AND BARRHEAD DISTRICT RAILWAY BILL [Lords].

PORT TALBOT RAILWAY AND DOCKS BILL [Lords].

SALFORD CORPORATION BILL [Lords].

WAKEFIELD CORPORATION BILL [Lords].

Ordered, That the Bills be read a second time.

PRIVATE BILLS [Lords].

(No Standing Orders not previously inquired into applicable).—Mr. Speaker laid upon the Table Report from one of the Examiners of Petitions for Private Bills, That, in the case of the following Bills, originating in the Lords, and referred on the First Reading thereof, no Standing Orders not previously inquired into are applicable, viz. :—

COLONIAL AND FOREIGN BANKS GUARANTEE FUND BILL [Lords].

HAMPSTEAD CHURCH (EMMANUEL, WEST END) BILL [Lords].

MERSEY DOCKS AND HARBOUR BOARD (FINANCE) BILL [Lords].

ST. NEOT'S WATER BILL [Lords].

STRETFORD GAS BILL [Lords].

WICK AND PULTENEY HARBOURS BILL [Lords].

Ordered, that the Bills be read a second time.

PROVISIONAL ORDER BILLS.

(Standing Orders applicable thereto complied with).—Mr. Speaker laid upon the Table Report from one of the Examiners of Petitions for Private Bills, That, in the case of the following Bills, referred on the First Reading thereof, the Standing Orders which are applicable thereto have been complied with, viz. :—

LOCAL GOVERNMENT PROVISIONAL ORDER (HOUSING OF WORKING CLASSES) BILL.

LOCAL GOVERNMENT PROVISIONAL ORDERS (GAS) BILL.

LOCAL GOVERNMENT PROVISIONAL ORDERS (No. 4) BILL.

LOCAL GOVERNMENT PROVISIONAL ORDERS (No. 6) BILL.

LOCAL GOVERNMENT PROVISIONAL ORDERS (No. 7) BILL.

LOCAL GOVERNMENT PROVISIONAL ORDERS (No. 8) BILL.

PIER AND HARBOUR PROVISIONAL ORDERS (No. 2) BILL.

Ordered, That the Bills be read a second time to-morrow.

PROVISIONAL ORDER BILLS.

(No Standing Orders applicable).

Mr. Speaker laid upon the Table Report from one of the Examiners of Petitions for Private Bills, that, in the case of the following Bills, referred on the first reading thereof, no Standing Orders are applicable, viz.—

LOCAL GOVERNMENT (IRELAND) PRO-VISIONAL ORDER (No. 1) BILL.

LOCAL GOVERNMENT PROVISIONAL ORDERS (No. 5) BILL.

LOCAL GOVERNMENT PROVISIONAL ORDERS (POOR LAW) BILL.

Ordered, that the Bills be read a second time to-morrow.

PRIVATE BILLS [Lords].

(Standing Orders not previously inquired into not complied with.)

Mr. Speaker laid upon the Table Report from one of the Examiners of Petitions for Private Bills, that, in the case of the following Bill, originating in the Lords, and referred on the first reading thereof, the Standing Orders not previously inquired into, and which are applicable thereto, have not been complied with, viz.—

MERSEY DOCKS AND HARBOUR BOARD (PILOTAGE) BILL [Lords].

Ordered, that the Report be refered to the Select Committee on Standing Orders.

BELFAST CORPORATION BILL.

Read the third time, and passed.

CAMBRIDGE UNIVERSITY AND TOWN GAS BILL [Lords].
GLASTONBURY WATER BILL [Lords].
QUEEN'S FERRY BRIDGE BILL [Lords].
Read the third time, and passed, with Amendments.

HULL, BARNSLEY, AND WEST RIDING JUNCTION RAILWAY AND DOCK BILL [Lords].

ST. ALBANS GAS BILL [Lords].

As amended, considered ; to be read the third time.

LONDON WATER (PURCHASE) BILL.

Order of the day for the SECOND READING read.

MR. STUART (Shoreditch, Hoxton) : Before the House proceeds to discuss the Second Reading of this Bill, I wish to say that as the Royal Commission which is considering this question has not yet reported, it is almost impossible to come to a decision in regard to this Bill while that Commission is sitting. I move to discharge the Order for the Second Reading.

Motion made and Question proposed,

" That the Order of the Day for the Second Reading be discharged."—(*Mr. Stuart.*)

*MR. WHITMORE (Chelsea) : I have a motion on the Paper for the direct rejection of this Bill, and I confess that I should have been rather glad if it had been convenient to move that motion, and ask the House to reject this Bill on Second Reading on the grounds of general policy. I cannot however but be content with the motion of the hon. Gentleman opposite for the withdrawal of this Bill, but I wish to take formal notice of what he has said. He stated that it would be impossible for this House to come to a satisfactory decision pending the issuing of the report of the Royal Commission. Personally, I cordially agree with that view, and I only wish the hon. Member and his friends had come to that decision some time ago. If my hon. friend's argument has any force now, it had greater force last autumn, when the County Council resolved to promote their scheme of Water Bills in this Session of Parliament. The Royal Commission is now sitting, and it is notorious that the Report of the Royal Commission will not be presented to Parliament in sufficient time for legislation to take effect this year. This fact was pointed out to the hon. Gentleman opposite and his friends, but they disregarded that objection, and proceeded to introduce their gigantic scheme, a portion of which is now before us. I think it would have been indeed well if the hon. Member and his friends had seen before how absurd and how futile it was to present to Parliament such a scheme while the Royal Commission was sitting to decide the essential points which were dealt with in this Bill. What has happened? Fears have been unnecessarily excited upon this subject, and a great problem which ought to have been solved as quickly as possible has been brought into the arena of politics. I do not wish now to dwell on the past, and I welcome what the hon. gentleman has said. I welcome the fact that he recognises that practically it would be impossible for this House to come to any decision upon this great question until the Royal Commission has reported. I gather from that statement that the hon. Member and his friends attach great importance to the Report of that Commission, and I hope when this question next comes before the House it will be found in the shape of a Bill not promoted by the majority of the London County Council actuated by party motives, but as an authoritative measure introduced by the Government and based upon the Report of the Royal Commission.

MR. BARTLEY (Islington, N.): I desire to draw attention to the fact that the unfortunate London ratepayer has had to pay very heavily for all this. The London County Council bring these Bills forward at enormous expense, and then they find out, as the hon. Member opposite has said, that it is advisable that the measures should be withdrawn pending the report of the Commission. It must be borne in mind that the smaller ratepayers now are very heavily taxed, and this is not the first time this sort of thing has happened, and I protest against this unnecessary and extravagant expenditure.

MR. STUART: An imputation has been put upon my conduct by the hon. Member opposite, otherwise I had no intention of raising a debate in this House. It must not be in any way inferred by the hon. Gentleman and his friends that my withdrawal of this Bill is in any way an undertaking that the Report of the Royal Commission will be accepted by my friends or by myself. Our position is perfectly clear as to this Bill, and perfectly harmonious with itself. When the

Royal Commission was appointed I made the statement that I thought it was a very unfortunate thing, and that it would have the effect of a large number of concessions being granted to the companies, and that it would result in absolutely putting a stop to any purchase Bills being proceeded with while the Commission was sitting, and that has turned out to be the case. Following that line, we introduced no purchase Bills in 1898, when so many concessions were given to the Water Companies. I entirely object to the statement of the hon. Member that at the beginning of this Session or at the end of last year it was generally known that the Commission would not report for another year. In February I moved that the question should be put forward to a certain date in order that we might give the Commission a chance of reporting earlier. It is perfectly clear that the Report will not be in the hands of Members for some time, and that it will be then too late to be dealt with in connection with this Bill. This Bill has been withdrawn in deference to the wishes of the House, and I have taken a course which I think every Member of the House must desire. Under circumstances of great difficulty I have endeavoured to keep this Bill so that it might wait until the Royal Commission has reported. That, I think, is a very proper motive. If this Commission had reported within a reasonable time, as we hoped it would have done by keeping this Bill before the House, we should have saved a whole year's delay, which is of extreme importance. This delay is not due to my action, but entirely to the action of the Government in appointing this Commission, which now stands in the way of any such Bill as this being proceeded with. It is quite clear that if proceeded with we could not arrive at a decision. I hope I have made my position clear to the hon. Gentleman and to the House.

MR. BOULNOIS (Marylebone, E.): It is a great pity that my hon. friend did not take the advice given him when the County Council were considering the question of these purchase Bills, to the effect that it would be absurd for the Council to bring in a Bill until the Royal Commission had reported upon the questions which would be submitted to them. Everyone knew perfectly well that the

Royal Commission could not by any possibility report in time for this Session. They have not reported, and I think it is within the knowledge of almost everyone that the question which is before the Royal Commission is so enormous and deals with so many interests that it would have been practically impossible for them to present any Report to this House in time for legislation this Session. It is reasonable and quite expected that after the evidence which the Royal Commission will receive has been concluded they will take some time to consider their Report, and I shall not be at all surprised if it is two or three months before we see it. I feel rather strongly upon this subject, because, besides the cost to the ratepayers, which has already been alluded to, I think some consideration should also be shown to the Water Companies, who have been very much harassed during this Session, and have had to incur very considerable expense in the matter. I can only say that, in my opinion, this Bill was premature, and I am only surprised that the promoters of it have kept it alive so long, for they must have known that the moment they brought it before the House it would receive its quietus.

Question put and agreed to.

Order for Second Reading discharged, and Bill withdrawn.

FRIENDS PROVIDENT INSTITUTION BILL [Lords] (STAMP DUTIES).

Committee to consider of authorising the imposition of certain Stamp Duties upon certain Memorials under any Act of the present Session relating to the Friends Provident Institution (Queen's Recommendation signified), To-morrow.

LOCAL GOVERNMENT (IRELAND) PROVISIONAL ORDER (No. 4.)

Bill to confirm a Provisional Order of the Local Government Board for Ireland relating to the Dean's Grange Joint Burial Board District, ordered to be brought in by Mr. Attorney General for Ireland and Mr. Solicitor General for Ireland.

LOCAL GOVERNMENT (IRELAND) PROVISIONAL ORDER (No. 4) BILL.

"To confirm a Provisional Order of the Local Government Board for Ireland relating to the Dean's Grange Joint Burial Board District," presented accordingly, and read the first time ; to be referred to the Examiners of Petitions for Private Bills, and to be printed. [Bill 324.]

PETITIONS.

BOROUGH FUNDS ACT, 1872.

Petition from Todmorden, for alteration of Law ; to lie upon the Table.

LOCAL GOVERNMENT (SCOTLAND) ACT (1894) AMENDMENT BILL.

Petition from Monifieth, in favour ; to lie upon the Table.

LONDON GOVERNMENT BILL.

Petition from Croydon, for alteration ; to lie upon the Table.

MINES (EIGHT HOURS) BILL.

Petitions in favour : from Soothill Wood ;—Cwm Colling ;—Oakingates ;—Altham ;—and, West Kiveton Collieries ; to lie upon the Table.

PRIVATE LEGISLATION PROCEDURE (SCOTLAND) BILL.

Petitions in favour ;—from Aberdeen ; —and, Ardrossan ; to lie upon the Table.

PUBLIC HEALTH ACTS AMENDMENT BILL.

Petition from Kingston-upon-Hull, in favour ; to lie upon the Table.

SALE OF INTOXICATING LIQUORS ON SUNDAY BILL.

Petitions in favour ;—from St. Germans ; Westleton ;—Walpole ;— Chebsey ;—and, Rochdale ; to lie upon the Table.

ELEMENTARY SCHOOLS (CHILDREN WORKING FOR WAGES).

Return presented,—relative thereto [ordered 28th April 1898 ; *Mr. Spicer*] ; to lie upon the Table, and to be printed. [No. 205.]

EAST INDIA (EXAMINATIONS FOR THE CIVIL SERVICE).

Copy presented,—of Regulations for Examinations for the Civil Service of India [by Act] ; to lie upon the Table.

GAS COMPANIES (METROPOLIS).

Copy presented,—of Accounts of the Metropolitan Gas Companies for the year 1898 [by Act] ; to lie upon the Table, and to be printed. [No. 206.]

POLLING DISTRICTS (CARNARVON).

Copy presented,—of Order made by the County Council of Carnarvon dividing into two parts the Penmorfa Polling District of the County [by Act]; to lie upon the Table.

FACTORY AND WORKSHOP ACTS (WHITE LEAD FACTORIES).

Copy presented,—of Special Rules with regard to the employment of persons in White Lead Factories [by Act]; to lie upon the Table.

SUPREME COURT OF JUDICATURE (IRELAND) ACT, 1877.

Copy presented,—of Four Orders in Council dated 13th May, 1899, giving effect to the Rules of Court under The Local Government (Ireland) Act 1898 [by Act]; to lie upon the Table.

QUESTIONS.

TRAINING OF VOLUNTEER OFFICERS.

SIR HOWARD VINCENT (Sheffield, Central): I beg to ask the Under Secretary of State for War, why Officers of the Volunteer Force are not allowed the privilege of sergeants and privates of training themselves for the Country's service with regiments near which civil duties may call them away from the head quarters of their own corps: and, if, having regard to the deficiency of officers in the Force, the Secretary of State will consider the re-adjustment of this inequality, and at the same time review the conditions under which the refundment of the equipment allowance granted to officers passing school are required from regiments.

THE UNDER SECRETARY OF STATE FOR WAR (MR. G. WYNDHAM, Dover): Officers are required to perform their drills with their own corps, as it is their duty to instruct and guide the men under their command and for this purpose a personal knowledge of them is indispensable. The Secretary of State is not prepared to remit this obligation, nor to relax the conditions upon which the outfit allowance is granted.

SIR HOWARD VINCENT: I beg to give notice that at the earliest opportunity I will call attention to the hardship arising from this arrangement.

THE ARMENIAN PRELACY.

MR. STEVENSON (Suffolk, Eye): I beg to ask the Under Secretary of State for Foreign Affairs whether Her Majesty's Government will represent to the Sultan the injury done to the Armenian archbishop and bishops, who are forcibly detained in the monastery of St. James at Jerusalem without trial, and without knowing for what offences they have been exiled from their dioceses: And, whether, seeing that those prelates are men of high character, the Secretary of State will communicate on the subject with the Powers which are parties to Articles 61 and 62 of the Berlin Treaty.

*THE UNDER - SECRETARY OF STATE FOR FOREIGN AFFAIRS (MR. ST. JOHN BRODRICK (Surrey, Guildford): Inquiries are being made as to the position of these prelates, and I am afraid I cannot at present make any statement with regard to them.

COMMERCIAL EDUCATION.

SIR HOWARD VINCENT: I beg to ask the Vice-President of the Committee of Council on Education, who represented this country at the recent Conference convened by the Italian Government upon Commercial Education, and when his report will be published; and if, in connection with the proposed scheme for establishing the University of London in the Imperial Institute, it will be possible for Her Majesty's Government to make it a condition with the Senate of the University that the University shall establish a Chair of Commercial Education and grant diplomas of knowledge in commercial science, bearing in mind that the United Kingdom possesses no Schools of Commerce similar to those at Paris, Antwerp, Leipzig, Vienna, Moscow, and other Continental centres.

THE SECRETARY TO THE LOCAL GOVERNMENT BOARD (MR. T. W. RUSSELL, TYRONE, S.) (FOR SIR J. GORST): Captain Abney represented this country. His report is in course of preparation. It is not possible to say when it will be published. The Government cannot at present interfere with the scheme for establishing the University of London, which has been entrusted by Parliament to a Commission.

CLAPHAM SORTING OFFICE.

MR. STEADMAN (Tower Hamlets, Stepney): I beg to ask the Secretary to the Treasury, as representing the Postmaster General, whether the duties of the four postmen whose places are vacant at Clapham Sorting Office, now being performed by casuals, will be allotted to the assistant postmen (ex-Army men) who have passed the Civil Service examination and been waiting seven months for the appointment.

THE SECRETARY TO THE TREASURY (MR. R. W. HANBUBY, Preston): The vacancies referred to will not be allotted to ex-Army Assistant Postmen, as there are many ex-Telegraph Messengers with prior claims still to be provided for. I may explain that at the time the arrangement was made for giving 50 per cent. of the postmen's places to reserve men, it was also stipulated that certain telegraph messengers who entered the service before April, 1897, and who were of a certain age, should have a prior claim over the others. These claims are not yet worked out, but they soon will be.

THE PUNJAUB WAR AND THE TIRAH CAMPAIGN.

MR. H. D. GREENE (Shrewsbury): I beg to ask the Under Secretary of State for War, whether medals and clasps for service in the last Punjaub War and the Tirah Campaign, 1897-8, have been issued to Officers and men of the Bengal Staff Corps entitled thereto ; and, if not, what is the cause of the delay, and when the distribution will take place.

MR. WYNDHAM : I understand that the Secretary of State for India will be prepared to answer this question to-morrow.

THE ANGLO - AMERICAN COMMISSION.

SIR EDWARD GOURLEY (Sunderland): I beg to ask the Secretary of State for the Colonies if he will be good enough to inform the House whether the Anglo-American Commission is to re-assemble ; if so, when ? Can he state the nature and extent of the differences alleged to exist between the American and Canadian members of the Commission ; and whether the whole or any portion of the points at issue are to be referred to arbitration ?

*MR. BRODRICK : The Commission adjourned until 2nd August. Negotiations are still proceeding, and it is impossible to make any statement at present.

RUSSIAN CLAIMS IN CHINA.

MR. PROVAND (Glasgow, Blackfriars) : I beg to ask the Under Secretary of State for Foreign Affairs whether, within a few days after signing the recent railway agreement of 28th April last between this country and Russia, the Russian Minister at Pekin made a demand on the Chinese Government for a concession for a branch railway from a point on the Trans-Manchuria Railway to Pekin, so as to connect Port Arthur and Pekin ; whether the Chinese Government refused this demand ; whether our representative at Pekin has conveyed to the Chinese Government an assurance given by Count Muravieff to our Ambassador at St. Petersburg that Russia had not demanded a concession, but only made a friendly request that China should concede in principle the right to build such a railway when applied for by Russian subjects ; whether our Government knew of the intention of Russia to make this demand or friendly request when they signed the railway agreement of 28th April ; and whether all the papers connected with this matter will be laid upon the table of the House before the Foreign Office Estimates come up for consideration ?

MR. BRODRICK : The answer to questions 1 and 2 is in the affirmative. . As regards the remaining questions, communications have been and are passing between the two Governments. I hope to present papers relating to the Northern Railway before the Foreign Office Vote is discussed next week ; but it will not be possible to include those relating to the subject matter of this question, which is still under discussion.

INSTRUCTION IN POOR LAW SCHOOLS.

MR. JAMES STUART (Shoreditch, Hoxton) : I beg to ask the President of the Local Government Board whether he has received a letter from the Guardians of the Poor of Shoreditch, bringing under his notice the subject of elementary education in Poor Law schools and its severance from the Education Department, and asking that the education in Poor Law schools should be placed under the Education Department ; whether he is prepared to take any steps to carry out this wish ; and what reply he has given to the Guardians of Shoreditch. I may also ask, at the same time, whether he has taken any steps to carry out the recommendation of the Poor Law Schools Committee in reference to placing the education of the children in the metropolitan Poor Law schools under the inspection of the Education Department ; and, if not, what are the difficulties which stand in the way ; and whether such obstacles require legislation for their removal.

MR. T. W. RUSSELL (for MR. H. CHAPLIN): I will answer the two questions of the hon. Member together. As regards the first, I have received a letter from the Shoreditch Board of Guardians on this subject. A reply has not at present been sent, as the matter is receiving my consideration. As regards the second question, I communicated with the Education Department with reference to the recommendation of the Poor Law Schools Committee that Poor Law Schools should be inspected by inspectors of that Department so far as the education work in the schools is concerned. The Education Department, however, felt a difficulty in assenting to this arrangement, unless the inspection of the schools was transferred to them in its entirety, including not only the education given in the schoolroom but also the boarding and other arrangements. In this I was unable to concur. Pending the settlement of the question temporary arrangements have been made for the inspection of the schools. Legislation would probably be necessary in connection with any transfer of duties in this matter.

THE COMPTROLLER AND AUDITOR-GENERAL.

MR. M'KENNA (Monmouth, N.): I beg to ask the First Lord of the Treasury whether Mr. Mills is shortly about to retire from the post of Comptroller and Auditor-General ; whether any promise of appointment to this post has been made in anticipation of the retirement of Mr. Mills ; and whether there is any foundation for the statement that the Government contemplate appointing a gentleman who has had no previous connection with the Exchequer and Audit Department, and who has had no training or experience appropriate to the important duties exercised by the Comptroller and Auditor-General.

THE FIRST LORD OF THE TREASURY (MR. A. J. BALFOUR, Manchester E.): I do not feel called upon to make any statement in regard to an appointment to a place not yet vacant ; but when the time comes and the appointment is made I shall, of course, accept all the responsibility.

REDEMPTION OF IRISH TITHE RENT-CHARGE.

MR. WILLIAM MOORE (Antrim, N.): I beg to ask the Chief Secretary to the Lord Lieutenant of Ireland if he is aware that the Irish Land Commission had, prior to the Land Act of 1896, no power to compulsorily redeem tithe rent-charge issuing out of an estate sold by them ; that it became the practice to sell the estate to the occupying purchasers indemnified against the payment of the tithe rent-charge, and to retain so much of the purchase money as would when invested yield sufficient income to meet the tithe rent-charge so accruing ; that the Act of 1896, not being retrospective, gave no relief in relation to prior proceedings ; if he could see his way to inform the House in how many cases the Land Commission are still retaining part of the purchase money of estates in order to meet the liability to tithe rent-charge, and the total amount of moneys so retained ; and whether he is prepared to afford the owners of such funds so retained by way of indemnity facilities to vary the tithe rent-charge, though no longer entitled to an estate in the lands, or to compulsorily redeem such tithe rent-charge so as to liberate the balance of the indemnity fund after such redemption.

*THE CHIEF SECRETARY FOR IRELAND (MR. G. W. BALFOUR, Leeds Central): The facts of the case are not quite correctly set forth in the first paragraph ; but the matter is somewhat too complicated to explain within the limits of an answer to a question. With regard to the second paragraph, it is believed that the case of the Marquis of Bath was the only one in which a fund was retained in Court to provide for the payment of Tithe Rent Charge which the lands were liable and sold subject to, but with an indemnity against, such liability. There is a considerable number of cases in which the redemption moneys of tithes redeemed have not been allocated by reason of the obstacles arising from the decision in the Marquis of Bath's Estate and the existence of superior interests ; but to compile a return of these cases would occupy much time, and involve the examination of the Estate Accounts and Records in the cases of all Estates in which there were retainers upon funds to credit. In answer to the third paragraph, Tithe Rent Charge not redeemed would, under the Bill recently introduced, be automatically varied, and I presume it would be for the Commission to consider whether, if the Tithe Rent Charge were reduced, any part of the indemnity fund might properly be released.

BELFAST (PUBLIC MEETINGS).

MR. DILLON (Mayo, E.) : I beg to ask the Chief Secretary to the Lord Lieutenant of Ireland whether his attention has been drawn to the proceedings at the Custom House steps in Belfast on Sunday 20th May, when a man named James Davies was killed in the course of a riot which sprang from those proceedings ; whether he is aware that for many weeks language of a most provocative character has been used at the meetings held at these steps on Sunday afternoons, that charges of a most filthy character have been made against Roman Catholic nuns by a man named Ballantine, also that an attack on a Roman Catholic convent in Belfast was made by a mob the week before last ; whether his attention has been drawn to the statement of the coroner of Belfast, at the inquest on Davies, that the evidence had shown that Mr. Ballantine was a man totally unfitted to preach the Gospel ; that if there was one thing which would excite religious feeling and bitterness in the city it was the attack made on the nuns and the nunnery in the Cranlin Road ; and, with reference to the statement made by Mr. Ballantine that the deaths were not registered, more insulting language could not have been used—not only was immorality suspected,

but murder also ; and also to the statement of the jury in their verdict that the authorities should take more active measures to preserve the peace at the Custom House steps on Sunday ; and, what steps the Irish Government propose to take to put a stop to these incitements to violence. I desire further to ask the Chairman a question of which I have sent him private notice, viz., whether the language insulting to Catholic priests and nuns used on Sunday May 21 at the Custom House steps was repeated by Mr. Trew on last Sunday evening ; whether there have been any serious disturbances in consequence ; how many police were present last Sunday, and whether the right hon. Gentleman intends to draft extra police into Belfast for next Sunday.

*MR. G. W. BALFOUR: I have only just received notice of the additional Question just put to me by the hon. Gentleman. I am not aware whether the insulting language referred to was repeated last Sunday ; and I do not think it necessary to provide extra police for next Sunday, neither can I say at the moment how many policemen were on duty last Sunday. In regard to the question on the Paper, my attention has been directed to the proceedings at the Custom House steps in Belfast on Sunday, the 21st, on which occasion a man named James Davies received injuries which resulted in his death the following day. The Government have received from the coroner copies of the depositions of the witnesses examined at the inquest held on Thursday last touching the death of Davies, and of the finding of the coroner's jury. The statements in the second and third paragraphs are substantially correct, except that, as regards the alleged attack by a mob on a Roman Catholic convent in Belfast, the police have no information of any such attack and have no reason to believe that such an attack was made. The depositions have only reached me to-day, and the question of taking further action is now under consideration.

BUSINESS OF THE HOUSE.

MR. CHANNING (Northampton, E.) : I beg to ask the First Lord of the Treasury what Supply will be taken tomorrow, and whether Orders of the Day Nos. 3 and 5 will be taken to-night ?

Mr. A. J. BALFOUR: As to-night is one of the allotted days for Supply, I shall take nothing to-night but Supply. As regards to-morrow, the first vote taken will be the vote for the Local Government Board.

MR. CALDWELL (Lanark, Mid.): And next week?

MR. A. J. BALFOUR: On Monday we shall discuss the vote for Lord Kitchener. On Tuesday, as at present advised, I propose to take the London Government Bill or the Finance Bill. That may be open to alteration to-morrow.

MR. WARNER (Stafford, Lichfield): What will be the second Order on Monday?

MR. A. J. BALFOUR: I cannot say yet. I do not know whether we shall be fortunate enough to get through the Lord Kitchener discussion at an early hour or not.

NEW MEMBER SWORN.

Sir George Augustus Pilkington, knight, for South - West Lancashire (Southport Division).

BELFAST (PUBLIC MEETINGS).

MOTION FOR THE ADJOURNMENT OF THE HOUSE.

MR. DILLON, member for East Mayo rose in his place, and asked leave to move the adjournment of the House for the purpose of discussing a definite matter of urgent public importance, viz., "the persistent holding of disorderly and riotous public meetings in the City of Belfast, and the grave danger to the public peace resulting from these proceedings, and from the inaction of the executive"; but the pleasure of the House not having been signified, Mr. Speaker called on those members who supported the motion to rise in their places, and not less than forty members having accordingly risen:—

MR. DILLON: In reply to a question I put to him just now, the Chief Secretary stated that the depositions forwarded to him in connection with an inquest held in the city of Belfast on Friday last have only just reached him, and he apparently gave that as a reason for his not having made up his mind as to the action which he ought to take in regard to the meetings on the Custom House steps at Belfast and the general condition of the city. That is a very strange attitude for a responsible Minister of the Crown to take up, and it becomes still more strange when he states he does not intend to draft any extra police force into the city to ensure that public liberty is safeguarded. What are the facts? On Sunday week, the 21st May, in pursuance of an evil custom which has been in force for years, meetings were being held on the Custom House steps and addressed by rival preachers; the result was that a riot took place, and in the rush of the crowd a man named James Davies was knocked down, sustaining injuries which soon after culminated in his death in hospital. The inquest was held on the 25th May, and the evidence adduced showed that on the occasion three meetings were in progress—one conducted by Mr. Galbraith, a temperance preacher, on behalf of a society called the Christian Endeavourers, and a second by a Mr. Ballantine who claimed to represent the orthodox Protestants. At the inquest evidence was given which he would like to draw attention to. Mr. Galbraith in his evidence was asked as to the language used by Mr. Ballantine. Let me read exactly what occurred, as reported. Mr Galbraith was asked:—

"Coming to last Sunday, did he make use of any observation to which you took exception?—Oh, yes; he made several observations.

"Give us some of them?—The principal one was the remark that in the nunnery on the Crumlin Road births occurred which were not registered, and deaths also.

"You heard him say that?—Yes I heard him distinctly say that.

"What did you infer from that?—I would infer that the nuns had given birth to children which they murdered, and also that the coroner hadn't been doing his duty when those deaths were left unrecorded. Your Honour, that is the inference I took. I am speaking on my oath.

"Don't you know as a matter of law that both births and deaths must be registered?—I can't say, sir; I'm not very well up in law.

"You addressed your meeting on the subject —what was the nature of your remarks, can you say?—'A nation's curse.'

"Was your discourse directed upon Mr. Ballantine's remarks? What did you say?—I said that, as a citizen and a Protestant, I protested that such statements should be made at such a time; that the remark was entirely unchristian, and calculated to embitter the feelings between Protestants and Roman Catholics. That was what I said, so far as my memory serves me.

"Did you incite the crowd to remove him from the steps and prevent him speaking?—No; I said to them to do nothing about the steps that would bring discredit and disgrace to the city of Belfast.

"As a result of these remarks made by him did anything happen?—Not just then. He also said that the wall of the convent was knocked down in order to let the priests go in at night.

This was the language used in the hearing of the people in a whole row of Catholic houses. Was it not enough to set men's blood on fire? Then the Witness was further examined by the Coroner as follows:—

"The Coroner: Did you hear him say anything about Christian Endeavourers going to hell?—I held my meeting under the auspices of the C.E. I had a C.E. badge on, and it was the badge that attracted his attention. He said—in fact he named my name—that Christian Endeavourers were all taking the power out of God's hands. He also asked what was the difference between the Roman Catholics. I may say that I worship in a Methodist church, the pastor of which is a converted Roman Catholic, the Rev. P. L. Donovan. That was the meaning of the remark he made to the crowd. He said all these people were going to hell straight.

"The Coroner: Did you consider that that was preaching the gospel of peace?—I did not, sir."

Having disposed in this manner of the Roman Catholics, he denounced in similar terms the Presbyterians, Methodists, and Christian Endeavourers. I am prepared for scepticism on this point, and I certainly cannot understand any responsible Minister of the Crown tolerating such language. What was the police evidence? —Let me read it—

Constable Joseph Deasy, Glengall Street Barracks, said he was on duty at the Custom House steps on Sunday evening last. He saw Galbraith and Ballantine there addressing meetings. Portions of Mr. Ballantine's remarks was that the Methodists and Presbyterians were all going ——

The Coroner: Then he included the Presbyterians too?—He did. He also said something about the Endeavourers.

The Coroner: That was not very courteous to the strangers. Did he consign the Catholics there too?—No, I didn't hear him.

Sergeant Magee: You were a considerable distance from him—on the outskirt of the crowd?—I was.

Did Mr. Galbraith take exception to any of these remarks?—He did.

Did you hear what he said?—I did. He asked the crowd—" Is there any Protestant —Methodist or any other denomination— going to stand up and listen to that man?" or words to that effect.

The result of that was, I believe, that a considerable portion of the audience rushed at Mr. Ballantine?—Yes.

You have some experience of the meetings there?—Yes, I have been there for the last six months.

What is the conduct of the crowd attending those meetings generally?—Very bad, generally.

Have the police been obliged to escort people for their own protection out of the crowd by bringing them to the barracks, putting them on trams, &c.?—Yes, on several occasions. On last Sunday week we had several. Twice I saw people turned out cut and bleeding.

Would you say as to the subject of the discourses are they religious or political?—More religious than political.

The Coroner: I'm afraid there's not much religion in them.

Sergeant Magee: And are they insulting occasionally to different religious denominations?—Yes, from the Lord Mayor down— especially Mr. Ballantine.

The Coroner: In your opinion, sergeant, are these meetings on the steps calculated to lead to a breach of the peace?—They are, sir; on some occasions we have great trouble in preserving order, especially when Catholics are passing there.

But most important of all is the Coroner's summing up. The Coroner (Mr. Finegan) occupies a responsible position. He was for many years Conservative agent for the county Down, and is one of the most respected men in Ireland. I, therefore, attach especial importance to his views. What was it he said? I will read it:

" Could they conceive anything more calculated to foster and intensify that animosity than the words used by that so-called preacher of the Gospel, words which he himself admitted he did use, namely, that in the Convent on the Crumlin Road no deaths or births were registered. What was the only meaning of those words but an accusation against the nuns of that convent of immorality, and murder to conceal their immorality? That was the naked meaning of the words, used without a shadow of foundation, by a man who posed as a Gospel teacher for five-and-twenty years. He could conceive nothing more scandalous than such an accusation made without the slightest foundation against a community of ladies whom he, from his official position, knew were doing incalculable good in their city. Not content with this, he, with Christian charity, which he measured by his own standard, consigned Methodists and Presbyterians to perdition, and included with them even the strangers and visitors who were enjoying their hospitality that week, the members of the Christian Endeavour Convention. He thought the time had arrived when steps should be taken by the high officials of this country to put a stop to those speakers who thus provoked breaches of the peace in their city, and provoked it, too, standing upon the very property of the Government."

And this was language used on the property of the Government.

"The jury found a verdict according to the medical evidence. They had not sufficient evidence to show by whom the death was caused. They were of opinion that the authorities should take more active measures to preserve the peace at the Custom House steps on Sunday."

That occurred on 21st May, and one would suppose that the Executive Government of Ireland would have done something in the interval to see that decent order was maintained. They knew what had been going on the previous Sunday, and that the same class of thing had been going on for six months. But what did they do? On the following Sunday— that is, last Sunday— at the same place where this poor man was killed, and within two days after the inquest had been held upon him, another gentleman turned up, a preacher of the Gospel. A friend of mine, whose name I can give if necessary, writes me to the following effect on the 29th May :—

" Referring to my letter of 27th regarding the conduct at Custom House steps, Belfast, yesterday Trew repeated what Ballantine had said the previous Sunday about the immoral relations between priests and nuns, and said very likely Finegan (the coroner) had himself a latch-key for the back door of the convent."

That was the language of a Christian apostle! Then—this is important, because it bears out absolutely all I have said in regard to the Belfast mob—

"he then referred to the coming demonstration, and said the rebels would be kept to the slums, but the anti-demonstration would make the soldiers and police keep the city of Belfast proper for them, they would march where they chose and show that they were the masters of Belfast. The constabulary sports are to be held next Saturday. He advises them as Protestants not to support them, but on Saturday they would assemble and march to the grounds where the sports are to be held, for what purpose he did not exactly specify. But previous to this he said he understood amongst other flags over the tents on the ground there would be a green flag, 'and I promise you that flag will come down more quickly than the police ran down the Shankill Road last June.'"

That was a reference to the occasion when the mob hunted the police down the Shankill Road, and when three policemen were carried to the hospital after a furious riot.

"He then proceeded to deliberately incite to murder. Here are his words :—'Now, there

Mr. Dillon.

are a number of rebel bands coming from Dublin and other places for the rebel demonstration. Some will come on Saturday evening and some on Sunday evening. The train leaves Dublin at 5.20 and arrives at the Great Northern Railway here at 9 o'clock, and I hope you will be there to give them a hot reception.'"

Is that language which, in a city like Belfast, ought to be used? One of the reasons why I have moved the adjournment of the House is that such language has been allowed. Are these murderous ruffians— for that is the only appropriate word to employ—to be permitted to lie in wait at the Great Northern Railway station to attack the Nationalists? Is there any decent pretext why the authorities should not prevent these things?

" Surely the Government will send an extra force of police. The town is seething with excitement. The result of not sending extra police would be that more than half the men on ordinary beat duty in the streets would be drawn away, whereas in every portion of the town they would require to be doubled, and in some places trebled. This is an important point, and should be strongly urged. At all these times there occur very bad cases of assault in many parts of the city owing to the want of sufficient police patrols. I omitted to state that Trew wound up by a furious tirade upon the police, the result of which was a furious onslaught on the policemen present, and for a length of time there was furious rioting, the mob throwing stones in the most desperate manner at the police, and the police repeatedly charged."

Seven or eight men were arrested and brought up before the magistrates next morning, when the police-sergeant gave evidence as to Trew's presence in the mob, and that 800 men pursued two men a great distance amid continuous volleys of stones. Brave Belfast men! One thing I am entitled to ask, and that is, What measures are the Government going to take for the preservation of the peace on Sunday and on Monday next? On the Monday there is to be a great Nationalist demonstration in Belfast. It was announced to take place four weeks ago. As they did last year, the organisers have left the order of route to the discretion of the magistrates of Belfast. They are going to follow the route so laid down, avoiding the Protestant quarters. Last week, under the inspiration of the gentleman whose language I have quoted, a counter demonstration was organised, and the intention is announced that they will traverse Belfast, not by a route fixed by the Magistrates, but at their own sweet will, so that the "rascally rebels" are to be kept to the slums. More than that, they have chosen a route so that they will cross a main avenue up which, a few minutes before, the Nationalists will be marching. Is it to be tolerated that this Orange mob are to be permitted to march hither and thither in every direction for the purpose of exciting a riot? It is not because I am speaking for the Nationalists of Belfast that I take this step. The Nationalists of Belfast have on many occasions done things of which I disapproved. Once they maintained a riot for weeks against odds. But is that civilisation? Ought not any Government to be ashamed who will not secure the right of the people of Belfast to walk in peace through the streets of their own city? When I remind the House of what occurred last year, it will be admitted that I am justified in the action I have taken to-day. I then went down to Belfast to a Nationalist demonstration. I must acknowledge the most creditable and courageous language used by the hon. Member for South Belfast, who denounced the proceedings of his own friends, and condemned any interference with the Nationalist demonstration. The Nationalists, he said, have as good a right to walk through the streets of Belfast as the Orangemen, and he said he would spend a month in gaol in order to vindicate their right to march through the streets of Belfast. Well, till last year, no riots had taken place for years. It is no answer to my argument to say, 'Why don't the Nationalists give up their meetings?' I reply, 'Why don't the Orangemen give up their meetings?' Why should the citizens of this free country give up their rights in deference to the threats of a scoundrel like that whose language I have quoted? They have as good a right to meet as any citizens of this country, so long as they conduct themselves decently and conform to the regulations. It is idle to speak of the Nationalists being responsible. It is the business of the Government not to allow these Orangemen to put down the Nationalist meeting announced three weeks ago, and to maintain the peace, and I have a right to demand that the Government should do so. Well, last year I was informed that if I went to Belfast I would be murdered. Several letters to that effect were sent to me. And other Nationalists were warned that if they went there they would not come out alive. However, I went to Belfast and found that the magistrates had laid down the route of the Catholic procession. But in deference to the threats of the mob the magistrates altered the route of the procession, and acting on my advice the Nationalists consented to the change, and at the last moment they had, consequently, to alter all their arrangements. What was the result? There were more than 10,000 men in the line of procession and an enormous multitude at the sides. The police force was utterly inadequate, but the Protestant mob were afraid to attack the procession for two reasons—first, because the Catholics were more numerous, and, second, because the fighting iron men were at work. When the procession was over the Nationalists went home peaceably, but hours afterwards the iron men joined the Protestant mob, and they attacked the police so furiously that 103 policemen had to be carried to the hospital, where their wounds were dressed. At the time the attack was made on the police, there was not a sign of the Catholic demonstration. The mob of Belfast warned the executive Government that they would not allow any extra police to be brought in, and the unfortunate police force were utterly insufficient to cope with the enormous fighting crowd sweeping through the streets. Order was not restored until the military appeared, and then they cheered the military and shook hands with them. Now, is this going to be repeated on Monday next? Are the police of Belfast to be hammered by these ruffians without any reinforcements, or is the Government going to bring in such an overwhelming force as will teach these people once and for all that they must keep the peace, and behave like civilized human beings, or stand the consequences? They are a very bad mob on both sides, and a Protestant mob, like all disorderly mobs, do very cowardly things, as I have shown from the extract I have read. The worst thing that an executive Government ever did if they wished to keep the peace, was to put into the minds of the Orange mob at Belfast that they were afraid of them. If Mr. Trew and Mr. Ballantine are to be allowed to lay down the law to the magistrates of Belfast and the executive Government, then you may prepare for a very lively time in Belfast.

Motion made and Question proposed—
"That this House do now adjourn"—(*Mr. Dillon*).

THE CHIEF SECRETARY FOR IRELAND (Mr. G. W. BALFOUR, Leeds, Central): The hon. Member for East Mayo has moved the adjournment of the House to call attention to what he calls a matter of public urgency, which I take to be, the language used by a Mr. Ballantine on the Custom House steps, Belfast, on Sunday. But the hon Member did not confine himself to that matter. He has devoted the larger part of his speech to events which happened last year, and events which may possibly happen on Monday next. I will deal very shortly with what I understand to be the pith of the matter to which the hon. Gentleman called attention in moving the adjournment of the House. In reply to a question by the hon. Member I stated that the subject was being considered by me. I have only received the depositions of the Coroner this morning in connection with the loss of life that has taken place in consequence of the disturbance at the Customs House. The hon. Member says he moved the adjournment of the House in order to bring pressure to bear upon the Government with regard to the forthcoming meeting at Belfast. Sir, I do not think that the hon. Member is likely to influence the Government by his speech, nor are we likely to be helped by the interposition of the hon. Member in the character of a supporter of law and order. As to the language used by Mr. Ballantine, I think that even the language of the hon. Member himself is hardly stronger than the occasion needed, when the hon. Member says that Mr. Ballantine is the representative of the Orthodox Church in Ireland. Sir, I feel quite sure that the number of persons in Belfast who sympathise with the outrageous language used by Mr. Ballantine must be small indeed. But holding that view as I do, I am not prepared to say now what course it would be wise and proper for the Government to take. I must have time to deal with the matter. I am communicating with the authorities on the other side of St. George's Channel in order to enable the Government to fully consider the matter. I have only had the opportunity of considering the depositions taken by the coroner this morning, after my return from a holiday, and, therefore, I am not now, on a motion for the adjournment, going to give a different answer from what I have given already to a question put by the hon. Member. In connection with the events of last Sunday, six men have been condemned to different periods of imprisonment. The hon. Member has complained with reference to the disturbances and riots of last year—in which he was a leader, if not a prominent member—that the Government have not brought a sufficient force of police into Belfast. I would remind him that a Commission inquired into the riots of 1886, and investigated all the details, and reported that it was not desirable to draft police from the surrounding districts into the city, because doing so would be provocative of more harm than good. The magistrates and the Government have subsequently deemed it advisable to employ both the military and the police for the preservation of the peace, and this they did last year when the two processions took place. But I am happy to say that Mr. Trew has, acting on the advice of my hon. friend the Member for South Belfast, agreed to abandon the counter-demonstration. I can assure the hon. Member for East Mayo that the Government are fully alive to the difficulties of the position, and will take steps to deal with any disturbance that may arise.

Question put—

The House divided :—Ayes, 73 ; Noes, 125 (Division List No. 165).

AYES.

Allan, William (Gateshead)
Allison, Robert Andrew
Austin, M. (Limerick, W.)
Bainbridge, Emerson
Baker, Sir John
Barlow, John Emmott
Bayley, Thomas (Derbyshire)
Billson, Alfred
Blake, Edward
Broadhurst, Henry
Caldwell, James
Cameron, Sir Chas. (Glasgow)
Cameron, Robert (Durham)
Carew, James Laurence
Channing, Francis Allston
Clark, Dr. G. B (Caithness-sh)
Colville, John
Crombie, John William
Douglas, Charles M. (Lanark)
Duckworth, James
Engledew, Charles John
Esmonde, Sir Thomas
Farquharson, Dr. Robert
Fox, Dr. Joseph Francis
Goddard, Daniel Ford
Gold, Charles

Gourley, Sir E. Temperley
Hedderwick, Thomas C H.
Holland, W. H. (York, W.R.)
Humphreys-Owen, Arthur C.
Jones, William (Carnarvons.)
Labouchere, Henry
Langley, Batty
Lawson, Sir Wilfrid (Cumb.)
Leese, Sir J. F. (Accrington.)
Leng, Sir John
Lough, Thomas
Lyell, Sir Leonard
MacAleese, Daniel
M'Ewan, William
M'Ghee, Richard
M'Leod, John
Maddison, Fred.
Maden, John Henry
Morgan, J Lloyd Carmarthen
Morton, E. J. C. (Devonport.)
Norton, Capt. Cecil William
O'Brien, James F. X. (Cork)
Oldroyd, Mark
Pickersgill, Edward Hare
Pilkington, SirG.A.(Lan. SW)
Pirie, Duncan V.

Priestley, Briggs (Yorks.)
Redmond, J. E. (Waterford)
Reid, Sir Robert Threshie
Roberts, J. H. (Denbighs.)
Shaw, Charles E. (Stafford)
Steadman, William Charles
Stevenson, Francis S.
Stuart, James (Shoreditch)
Sullivan, Donal (Westmeath)
Tennant, Harold John
Thomas, A. (Glamorgan, E.)
Trevelyan, Charles Philips
Walton, J. Lawson (Leeds S.)
Walton, Joseph (Barnsley)
Warner, Thomas Courtenay T.
Williams, John Carvell (Notts
Wilson, John (Durham, Mid.)
Wilson, John (Govan)
Woodhouse,SirJ.T. (Hddsf'd.)
Woods, Samuel
Yoxall, James Henry

TELLERS FOR THE AYES—
Mr. Dillon and Mr. James
O'Connor.

NOES.

Ascroft, Robert
Atkinson, Rt. Hon. John
Balfour, Rt.Hn.A.J.(Manch'r)
Balfour,RtHnGeraldW.(Leeds
Banbury, Frederick George
Bartley, George C. T.
Barton, Dunbar Plunket
Beach, W W Bramston (Hants.)
Beresford, Lord Charles
Bethell, Commander
Bill, Charles
Blakiston-Houston, John
Blundell, Colonel Henry
Boulnois, Edmund
Bowles, T.Gibson(King'sLynn
Brassey, Albert
Brodrick, Rt. Hon. St. John
Brown, Alexander H.
Bullard, Sir Harry
Campbell,Rt.Hn.JA(Glasgow
Chaplin, Rt. Hon. Henry
Cochrane, Hon. Thos.H.A.E.
Coghill, Douglas Harry
Collings, Rt. Hon. Jesse
Colomb,SirJohnCharlesReady
Courtney, Rt. Hon.LeonardH.
Cripps, Charles Alfred
Cubitt, Hon. Henry
Curzon, Vicount
Dalbiac, Colonel Philip Hugh
Dalrymple, Sir Charles
Dorington, Sir John Edward
Doughty, George
Douglas, Rt. Hon. A. Akers-
Drage, Geoffrey
Duncombe, Hon. Hubert V.
Fardell, Sir T. George
Fellowes,Hon.AilwynEdward
Fergusson,Rt.Hn.SirJ.(Mane'r
Finlay, Sir Robert Bannatyne
Fisher, William Hayes
Fitzmaurice, Lord Edmond
Flannery, Sir Fortescue

Flower, Ernest
Galloway, William Johnson
Garfit, William
Gibbons, J. Lloyd
Gray, Ernest (West Ham)
Greene,HenryD.(Shrewsbury)
Gretton, John
Greville, Hon. Ronald
Hamilton,Rt.Hn.Lord George
Hanbury, Rt. Hon. R. Wm.
Harcourt, Rt. Hon. Sir Wm.
Hayne, Rt. Hon. C. Seale-
Heath, James
Heaton, John Henniker
Helder, Augustus
Hoare, Edw. B. (Hampstead)
Hoare, Samuel (Norwich)
Hornby, Sir William Henry
Houston, R. P.
Howell, William Tudor
Hozier, Hon. Jas. H. Cecil
Jackson, Rt. Hon. W. Lawies
Jenkins, Sir John Jones
Jessel, Capt. Herbert Merton
Johnstone, Heywood (Sussex)
Kenyon, James
Knowles, Lees
Lafone, Alfred
Laurie, Lieut.-General
Lawrence SirE.Durning-(Corn
Lawson, John Grant (Yorks.)
Llewelyn,SirDillwyn-(Swnsea
Lockwood, Lt.-Col. A.R.
Loder, Gerald Walter Erskine
Long,ColCharlesW. (Evesham
Long, Rt. HnWalter(Liverpool
Macartney, W. G. Ellison
Maclure, Sir John William
M'Iver,SirLewis(Edinboro',W
Meysey-Thompson, Sir H. M.
Milward, Colonel Victor
Monk, Charles James
Moore, William (Antrim, N.)

Morton, Arthur H.A.Deptford
Murray, RtHnAGraham(Bute
Myers, William Henry
Nicol, Donald Ninian
Nussey, Thomas Willans
Orr-Ewing, Charles Lindsay
Palmer, Sir C. M. (Durham)
Pease, H. Pike (Darlington)
Pilkington,R. (Lancs Newton
Platt-Higgins, Frederick
Priestley,SirW.Overend(Edin
Pryce-Jones, Lt.-Col. Edward
Purvis, Robert
Pym, C. Guy
Rankin, Sir James
Rasch, Major Frederic Carne
Rollit, Sir Albert Kaye
Rothschild,Hon.LionelWalter
Russell, T. W. (Tyrone)
Ryder, John Herbert Dudley
Samuel, Harry S. (Limehouse)
Sassoon, Sir Edward Albert
Scoble, Sir Andrew Richard
Seton-Karr, Henry
Sidebotham, J. W. (Cheshire)
Stanley, Henry M. (Lambeth)
Stanley, Lord (Lancs.)
Talbot, Lord E. (Chichester)
Tomlinson,Wm. Edw. Murray
Tritton, Charles Ernest
Valentia, Viscount
Warr, Augustus Frederick
Webster, R. G. (St. Pancras)
Welby, Lieu.-Col. A. C. E.
Williams,JosephPowell-(Birm
Willox, Sir John Archibald
Wilson, John (Falkirk)
Wodehouse, Rt Hon E R (Bath
Wyndham, George

TELLERS FOR THE NOES—
Sir William Walrond and
Mr. Anstruther.

SUPPLY [11TH ALLOTED DAY].

Considered in Committee.

(In the Committee.)

CIVIL SERVICE AND REVENUE DEPART-
MENTS ESTIMATES, 1899-90.

REVENUE DEPARTMENTS.

1. Motion made and Question proposed—

"That a sum not exceeding £5,522,885
be granted to Her Majesty to defray the
charges necessary for the salaries and expenses
of the Post Office, the Post Office Savings
Banks, Annuities and Securities, and the
collection of Post Office revenue."

MR. STEADMAN (Stepney): I rise
for the purpose of directing the attention
of the Committee to the dissatisfaction
which exists in every department of the
Post Office service, in order to try if
possible to secure what I consider a very
reasonable demand, viz., the appointment of a Committee composed of Members of this House, to go into the various
grievances of the Post Office employees.
On the discussion on the Amendment on
this subject which was moved to the
Address, the Secretary to the Treasury
stated that a Departmental Committee
had reported, as had also another Committee, composed of himself and the
Postmaster-General, and that therefore
no further Committee was necessary or
required. But I should like to point out
that both these Committees were unsatisfactory to the employees. It stands
to reason that a Departmental Committee composed of officials, which contained only one impartial member—a
Member of the House of Lords—could
not be satisfactory to the 160,000 male
and female employees in the Post Office
service. I know that the Secretary to
the Treasury stated that Members of
this House had no technical knowledge
of the work of the Post Office. That is
quite true. I do not presume to have
any technical or practical knowledge of
the various departments of the Post Office.
Members of this House may not have
the technical knowledge possessed by
Mr. Carden and other heads of departments, yet it does not follow that if
these gentlemen appeared before an independent committee, composed of Members of this House, they might not be
able to make their defence more clear
and definite than they have hitherto

done. The Secretary to the Treasury
also stated that a telegraphist was not
any more than a typewriter. He gives
his own case away, because in a later
part of his speech, he himself says that
no work is more complicated than the
work of the Post Office. If the work is
complicated and technical, it must require
great skill. If it does not require great
skill, it cannot be of that complicated
character which the Secretary to the
Treasury admits it is. The best reply to
the statement that a telegraphist is no
more than a typist is the reply of
practical men who have knowledge of
the subject. Dr. Walmsley, C.E., says:—

"I do not agree with Mr. Hanbury's statement. The whole idea of offering additional
advantages to the operators who qualify in a
scientific examination proves that the work
requires a knowledge of applied science."

Professor Jefferson, who has an intimate
knowledge of telegraphy since 1873, says:

"I am of opinion that the work requires far
more technical skill than that of a typewriter.
I can personally vouch for the fact that the
efficiency of telegraphists has greatly increased
of late years."

Mr. Preece and other scientific men have
expressed a similar opinion. We are told
that the telegraphist is apprenticed, and
learns his trade, practically at the expense
of the State. In the first place, the
telegraphist starts as a lad of fifteen or
sixteen years. He has to give five
years' service to the State, and receives only a very few shillings a week,
and after five years he gets the magnificent salary of 21s. a week. Is that
apprenticeship at the expense of the
State? Thousands of lads are apprenticed
to British employers, and not only learn
their trade, but receive a salary quite
equal to that paid to the lads in the Post
Office, and after five or seven years they
are not asked to accept a wage of 21s. a
week. They demand and receive the
minimum wage fixed by their trade
union, and agreed to by the employers.
The lads in the Post Office no more learn
their trade at the expense of the State
than thousands of other lads apprenticed
to private employers. They get an
increment of £6 per annum, and as the
result of a conference between the
Postmaster - General and the Secretary to the Treasury they are
allowed a double increment on condition that they learn to perform
extra duty in the shape of sorting; but
the restrictions are so strong at the

present moment that 40 per cent. of the employees in the Post Office are not receiving the double increment. Look at the sweating that goes on. An advertisement was issued a short time ago for two practised sorting and telegraph clerks at Cambridge, with a knowledge of postal work, and expected to be educated young men, and they were offered the magnificent salary of 16s. a week, which works out at the rate of 4d. per hour. I now come to the case of the postmen. They are allowed, as a result of the Tweedmouth Committee, to get six stripes instead of three. They have to wait five years between each stripe, so that before a man can reach the maximum, he has to be in the service thirty years with an unblemished character. For the least trifling thing the officials put the postmen back, so that very few live to receive even four stripes. One case to which I might refer was that of a rural postman who, in the course of his round, had to go through a private farm road to deliver letters at the farm house. One day, when he was half way up the road, he met a person whom he thought was a servant at the farm, to whom he handed the letter which he had to deliver. For this he was reported to the post office. At this time his stripe was almost due, and the result was that instead of securing his stripe in March last he must now wait until 1902. If he makes one mistake between this and then I suppose he will be put still further back. Many postmen now are only in receipt of two or three stripes where they ought to be in receipt of the maximum. Another case to which I might refer was a case of H. C. Simmons, a postman who was transferred from Helensburgh, in Scotland, to Sutton, in Surrey. At the time he was transferred he was entitled to a stripe, and the postmaster at Helensburgh actually paid him 5s. 10d. due as stripe money. On his transfer he applied to the postmaster at Sutton for his stripe. That gentleman, however, knew nothing about the matter, and up to the present time the man has not received his stripe. The next case is the case of a mail-cart postman in the rural districts. In the course of his speech the Secretary to the Treasury said that the average allowed for horses and carts was 20s. and 23s. a week, but the information I have shows that the amount was 8s. and 11s. a week respectively, and in one case, where there

was a vacancy, it cost the Government £3 a week for the loan of a horse and cart. With reference to Christmas boxes, it was said that the Post Office did not take that into consideration when fixing wages, but Mr. Lewin Hill, in his evidence before the Tweedmouth Commission, gave quite another version; whilst in their findings the Committee said if they had seen their way to do away with the system of Christmas boxes in favour of some better system they would certainly have done so. Not only in the Telegraph department and among the postmen, but among the clerks and engineers, discontent exists in the postal service. Complaints are made that there is a larger number of men employed on the unestablished staff than are employed on the establishment. Some have been employed for 15 years, and when they apply to be put on the establishment they are told there are no vacancies. Another important point is the right of combination. These men have a number of organisations in existence, but what is the use of organisations if the heads of them are not recognised by the department? I am sorry that the name of Mr. Cleary has been imported into the discussion, because the retiring Secretary to the Treasury, I am sure, would not wilfully misinform the House, with reference to that gentleman; but whoever was responsible for the information with which the right hon Gentleman was supplied undoubtedly misled him. Mr. Cleary was never refused admission at the Trades Union Congress at Belfast. His credentials were very closely examined and were accepted as satisfactory, and from that time to the present the sorters have always been represented at the Congresses. They have now, I believe, elected Mr. Cleary to represent them at Plymouth. There are two plans of action which these men can adopt: they can strike, and they can appeal to this House for justice. The state of things now is entirely altered from the state of things which existed in 1894 at the time of the postmen's strike; men now in every department have their organisation which represents the great majority of the people there, and if they strike they paralyse the whole postal system. The right hon. Gentleman shakes his head, but if the telegraphists went out to-morrow they could not be replaced. God forbid that I should advocate that they should go out on strike ; I have never advocated a strike in my life ; but, while I think that if a man cannot get his just demands he is entitled to strike, I look for the time to come when these men will be able to get justice from this House, and strikes will be done away with. All these organisations right through the departments have their coaches and organisers ; true, they are not yet directly represented here in this House, but they have friends here who are prepared to take up their quarrels. Mr. Lewin Hill, after retiring on a very good pension, denounced these men and said they ought to be disfranchised, but I doubt if any Government would follow the suggestion. They have every right to the franchise, but the intimidation which they have to put up with is simply scandalous.

THE SECRETARY TO THE TREASURY (MR. HANBURY, Preston): If the hon. Gentleman will give me the names with regard to this, the matter shall be inquired into.

MR. STEADMAN : Hitchcock is one name. Look at the case of Mr. Rash, whose increment was at first stopped because he was an official of the men's organisation. Now that he has got his increment they are watching him about as if he was a felon instead of an honest workman employed by the State.

MR. HANBURY : This is a well-known case, which has been very carefully inquired into, and I can assure the hon. Gentleman that he is entirely mistaken in the statement which he has just made to the Committee.

MR. STEADMAN : I am only going on the facts which have been placed at my disposal. I accept the explanation of the right hon. Gentleman, and I am pleased to hear that it is not so. I hope the Secretary to the Treasury will concede what these men are asking, which is simply for an opportunity of appearing before a Committee composed of Members of this House in order that they may state their grievances. I know the right hon. Gentleman has already stated that two Committees have been appointed to consider this question, and he further asked what guarantee was there that this new Committee would satisfy the Post

Mr. Steadman.

Office employees. My opinion is that they will be satisfied with this Committee, and there will be an end to the matter. If this is not done, they will go on agitating until the Committee is appointed, and it might just as well be appointed first as last. If the men have no case, so much the worse for the men, and so much the better for the Government. Seeing that these men are the faithful servants of Her Majesty's Government, and bring into the revenue three or four million sterling per annum, I think they are worthy of the just consideration of this House, and I move that item A be reduced by £100, in respect of the salary of the Postmaster-General.

Motion made and resolution proposed—

"That item A (salaries) be reduced by £100, in respect of the salary of the Postmaster-General."—(*Mr. Steadman.*)

*CAPTAIN NORTON (Newington, W.): I desire to speak for a few moments on this question, because I feel that if the right hon. gentleman—who we all acknowledge to be one of the most fair-minded men who ever sat on that bench —would consent to this inquiry he would not only be making his own path smoother, but would be doing a great public service. These officials do not feel that they have been treated with justice, and it is most galling to Members of this House to be approached and constantly assailed by these demands for justice by members of the Postal Department and of the Telegraph Department, who complain that they have not received justice at the hands of the Government. Now the right hon. gentleman, when dealing with this subject last year, endeavoured to show that the telegraphists were men who were not performing work of such a skilful character as had been made out. These men are placed in charge of delicate apparatus. They are supposed not only to understand it, but also to be able to detect faults and put them right. They have now to perform duties which, when they first entered the service, were done by skilled officers, and, therefore, it cannot be contended that they are not performing labour of a very high-class character. They are men who must have not only mental quickness but physical dexterity, and they have to do their labour under great pressure. They claim that they are treated on a par with those who perform

a class of work which is not quite of such a high order. These men perform very difficult duties, which require considerable experience to enable them to perform. With regard to these five years' men the Tweedmouth Committee was asked to recommend that these men should receive from 24s. to 28s. per week, and they consider that the whole question has been evaded, and in this way. They have allowed an employee after twenty-one years of age to have an increment yearly of some £6, if he learns sorting, and further on another increment of another £6, but this does not meet the question in any way. These men have to pass a special examination, and to prove that this test is not a farce I may say that only 46 per cent. of the candidates succeed in passing the examination. These men have to prepare for this examination in their own time, and what they were given to expect they would obtain by the Tweedmouth Commission they have not yet obtained. The other class who, I think, have a certain grievance are the operators, who complain that they are debarred from obtaining the maximum rate of £190 per annum. These men entered the service in view of the statement placed before them by the Civil Service Commissioners, and they were given to understand that they had a prospect of rising to £190 per annum. What is the answer which the right hon. Gentleman gives to that? It is that owing to a system of classification being done away with, and the first and second class being amalgamated, a special class has been formed, and the men can obtain promotion to that class. But the difficulty of getting into that class is so great that practically the majority of the men remain at a maximum of £160 per year, whereas they were led to believe that they could attain a maximum of £190. Now a man has to serve something like twenty years before he can obtain the sum of £160, and, therefore, promotion is practically impossible. In Liverpool the time for promotion is about 17 years for men in the Postal Department, compared with some 27 for the telegraphists. The telegraphists are, in this respect, placed in a worse position than the men in the Postal Department, although it is admitted that they perform work of a slightly superior character. The Tweedmouth Commission recommended that the want of uniformity of the work should be

no barrier to promotion. It has been argued with respect to the telegraphists that there is no market value of labour to go by, but it is well known that the men employed by the Eastern Telegraph Company perform practically the same work. They must be men of a slightly higher class and superior as operators, but they are able to obtain £204 per annum, and the average service for that salary is some 19 years. Therefore, the Government treat their public servants unfairly as compared with the outside labour market. Now I come to the question of finality. If a Committee were now appointed I think it would lead to the closing of the whole question. I think it is degrading not only to the Government, but also to the Members of this House, to be constantly assailed in regard to these grievances in many instances by our own constituents. I do not believe that I have any constituents connected with the telegraph departments, but many hon. Members have been approached by these men, who demand what they believe to be just and proper. I am compelled to admit that the right hon. Gentleman met the men very fairly on what is known as the Norfolk-Hanbury Commission, and I think the right hon. Gentleman himself will agree with me that on that Commission I gave him loyal support. In the interests of the House and of the public service this matter should be placed at rest at once. I have always spoken in defence of public servants in this House, and I believe that they are being unfairly treated. It is well known that they have not the same power of combination as other men have in the outside world. Therefore, it is due to these men that their position should be investigated by Members of this House. If after investigation has taken place and justice has been done by this House, further agitation takes place, the right hon. Gentleman knows that he will have no more cordial supporter than myself. I am confident that this concession will not only give satisfaction to the men concerned, but also to the service generally.

Motion made, and Question proposed—

"That Item A (Salaries) be reduced by £100 in respect of the salary of the Postmaster-General."—(*Mr. Steadman*).

SIR W. CAMERON GULL (Devonshire, Barnstaple): There are just two or three points to which I desire to allude. The first is the principle by which the wages of postmen in county towns are fixed. I believe there are five different scales granted to postmen, and their wages are fixed in some cases according to the population of the town in question. That is a very clear and distinct principle, but now, apparently, another principle is being introduced, and that is the cost of living, which is one of very considerable difficulty. The Post Office, apparently, are not now dealing with the wages of postmen either on the one principle or on the other. In a case which I brought before the authorities some time ago, on the principle of population, the postmen were entitled to a much higher scale of wages; and another case had been brought to the notice of the authorities where it was shown that the cost of living entitled the postmen to the higher scale, and there the case was met by the argument that the population of the district was not sufficient. Therefore, as far as the Post Office is concerned, we get a sort of see-saw—one district asks for a higher rate, and we are told that the population is not sufficient; another district asks for a higher rate, and we are told that the cost of living there does not warrant it. I hope the right hon. Gentleman will state on what principle these matters are settled. I think the most convenient one is the rate fixed by the population, without going into the question of the cost of living, which must be a very difficult question to settle. Then there is the question of providing more late letter-boxes on the trains. All the mail trains carry in certain carriages a late letter-box, which always there, but in the remote country districts we have no such facilities. We have been asking for some time for late letter-boxes to be attached to the trains from Ilfracombe to Barnstaple, and we have been told that it is quite impossible, and that late letter-boxes cannot be put on these trains unless there is someone in charge of them. I pointed out that on another branch, from Torrington to Barnstaple, there was a late letter-box, but we were told that it never ought to have been there, and that it was quite impossible to grant another. The reason given seems to me to be perfectly extraordinary, for it is that there is nobody to look after them. Now, if all the letter-boxes in the country look

Sir W. Cameron Gull.

after themselves, surely a late letter-box can do the same. A very large sum of money is given by the public for gratuities to guards and other non-Post Office servants for looking after mail bags and parcels, and if it is only a question of the safe custody of these boxes, I think it is very easy, by granting a small extra sum of money, to see that these boxes are adequately protected, and it would be undoubtedly a great convenience if a late letter-box could be attached to these trains. This would be very convenient to the outlying districts, where there is very often only a short space of time to answer letters before the mail goes, and the extra hour or so which a late letter-box would give them would be a very great convenience indeed. I hope the right hon. Gentleman will do his best to see if this can be done.

MR. SPICER (Monmouth Boroughs): I do not wish to weary the Committee with going over the details of these difficulties in connection with many of the employees of the Post Office. I desire to associate myself with the remarks of my hon. friend, the Member for West Newington. I listened in the earlier part of the Session with great interest to the Secretary to the Treasury, when he declined a Committee of Inquiry, and since then, though I thought at the time he had made out a good case, I have taken some trouble to inquire into the different answers given to many of his statements, and I confess the more I have gone into the matter the more I have come to the conclusion that this matter will never be properly settled until there has been an inquiry by Members of this House. After all, in these days of labour disputes, I maintain that the greater portion of these disputes would not reach the painful position they do if employees felt they had always the right of approach to their own principals, whether those principals are the heads of private firms or of great limited companies. So, I say, in connection with any long-standing dispute going on in any Government Department, after all, if it is impossible to come to a satisfactory solution of the question by a discussion between the employees and the heads of the Departments, and then with the representatives of those Departments in this

House—then I maintain those employees have a right to appeal to the Members of this House to look into the question by appointing a Committee. Though I give the Secretary to the Treasury full credit for having done all he can in this matter, I feel confident that sooner or later this Committee will have to be appointed. It may not be appointed during this Parliament, but it will be, I am quite sure, in some future Parliament, and by that time a great deal of real damage in the way of discipline will have been effected. I shall support the motion for a reduction unless the right hon. Gentleman is willing to grant this inquiry, which, in the interests of the public service, must be given sooner rather than later.

Mr. ASCROFT (Oldham): I regret that the hon. Member who has moved the reduction has not thought fit to demand a Committee to inquire not only into the wages of postmen, but also into the administration and management of the Post Office itself. I feel satisfied that we do not get the full value for the money we spend in the Post Office, and if it were run on businesslike lines we should have far less complaints made. I have good reasons for supporting this amendment, for my constituents have petitioned the Postmaster-General, and their petition has been refused. I understand that the salaries of the postmen are based upon the population. Now the constituency which I represent has 203,000 people in it, and the salaries you pay the postmen there run from 22s. or 24s. to a maximum of 26s. At Cardiff, Derby, Wolverhampton, and Sunderland, which are far smaller places than my constituency, the full maximum is 28s. A memorial from my constituency has been presented, and the prayer of it has been declined. We are asking for an inquiry by the House of Commons into this and other questions. There was a cheer raised when reference was made to the postmen bothering the Members of this House, but that was the only way which the postmen have of getting their grievances remedied. I only regret that the office of Postmaster-General is not represented directly in this House, so that we might go more fully into these questions and thresh them out. There is another question, and a very important question. Every Member of this House is aware that every sub-postmaster and postmistress has to enter into a guarantee, and to get that guarantee they have to go to an Insurance Company and pay a premium, which is, considering the smallness of the amount, a very considerable item. Last year, on behalf of a number of my constituents, I approached the Postmaster-General and submitted to him a scheme for the purpose of forming an association of postmasters to guarantee the members of that association at a small premium, and we were led to believe that if we were financially strong, and on business lines, we should receive the same treatment as other associations. We formed ourselves into that company, and we were prepared with some thousand pounds which we offered to invest in Consols if he would only allow us to insure by means of bonds the members of our association. That was refused on most curious grounds, namely, that we had not sufficient members, neither had we sufficient capital. The Postmaster-General had forgotten what had been the habit and custom of himself and all previous Postmaster-Generals during the last twenty years. I find on referring to the Post Office figures, that in 1887 a society assured the Postmaster-General against the dishonesty of 5,451 sub-postmasters; the liability was £1,025,000, and the whole of the funds of that society were no more than £2,571. The risk was not great, and the whole amount of defalcations amounted to only £147 13s. 7d. Each year followed on pretty nearly the same basis till 1897, when the same Society, which had then £17,754, assured an amount of £6,500,000, and the whole defalcations were £1,246. Taking the whole of the statistics in relation to the defalcations during the last year, I think they amounted to 1 in 400, but the amounts have been exceedingly small, ranging from £37 to £54. I submit that, under these circumstances, an association of postmasters who bind themselves together for insuring honesty and preventing loss to the Post Office ought to be met in a much more kindly manner than they were met by the Postmaster-General, and I only hope his representative will have this question inquired into, and when I come before him with some of these members of the association we may have a different result than that which we have had up to the present time.

MR. MADDISON (Sheffield, Brightside): I desire to support this reduction, because I think the inquiry asked for is one which the Government ought to grant. I quite agree with what the hon. Member for Stepney said with respect to strikes, and more especially with regard to postal employees. I have long come to the conclusion that men employed by the State who have an opportunity of first appealing to the responsible Government and then to the Members of this House ought not to have it both ways. Of course they cannot be in the same position as private employees who are dealing with a single firm, and it should be remembered that State employment has its disadvantages as well as its advantages. One of the disadvantages is that it is riddled through and through and permeated with officialism, and it is almost impossible—although we have such an eminently fair-minded gentleman at the head of affairs as the Secretary to the Treasury—for those men to put their grievances before him or the Postmaster-General in a way that will give them a chance, I won't say of fair play, but of that investigation which is necessary to come to a just conclusion. It is no indictment of the right hon. Gentlemen to say that he is necessarily in the hands of the permanent officials, for that is a necessity of the case. He cannot inquire himself, except through an official medium, and when we have cases put before us on the authority of very reliable men where intimidation and other injustices have been perpetrated under the system of which these men complained, I say that these employees have no other alternative but to appeal to the Members of this House. For my part, I have always had some hesitation in taking up the cases of men employed by the State, because undoubtedly there is a sort of notion that, because they are employed by the State, they can make such demands as they like, because they are paid out of a very full Treasury. I know that every halfpenny of that money comes out of the general taxation of the country, and I agree that we are here as guardians of the public purse. The right hon. Gentleman has never denied that we are here as the guardians of these men's interest, and it has not been shown that the public interest is of greater importance than the interest of these men, who do so much for the prosperity of the country.

I therefore appeal to the right hon. Gentleman to grant a Committee of this House. We do not want an official inquiry, but what is needed is that Members of Parliament, responsible to their consciences and to their constituencies, should sit on that Committee, and with the assistance of the Department decide these various cases which are causing so much discontent in the service. In this case we want a non-official Committee, although I confess that I do not think such an inquiry will put an end to disputes in the future. I wish to call attention to what I think is a great scandal in connection with the postal service, and that is the insanitary condition of many of the postal buildings. Now, I know that the chief medical officer of the Department declared before the Tweedmouth Committee that anything affecting the health of the men with regard to their duties, or any insanitary conditions of the Post Office buildings, would be reported to him at once by the local medical officer, whose duty it was to point out what in his opinion required to be remedied. That is a sort of answer which settles everything in the official mind. What more need of inquiry into the insanitary condition of Post Offices can there be, when the chief medical officer deliberately, and on his own responsibility, declares that all cases of insanitation are reported to him by the local medical officers and would therefore be attended to? What are the facts? The Tweedmouth Committee, as the right hon. Gentleman knows very well, scheduled 182 postal offices, and the condition of 69 of these was condemned. When we remember that there are over 20,000 postal buildings in the country, and that only a small proportion of these were scheduled, is it not an enormous percentage that was proved to be insanitary? Does it not go a long way to show that you want much more than a mere declaration from the medical officer of health, however high his position may be? I would just like to refer to one or two of the offices in which this great nation does its business. Take Grimsby. I do not know whether it is called an important place—no doubt the people of Grimsby think it is—but what is the condition of the Post Office there? It consists of a building, or buildings, which were formerly used as a grocer's shop, a butcher's shop, a confectioner's shop, and a barber's shop, which is I suppose thrown in to give it dignity. The instrument room used by the telegraphists is made up of what used to be the bedrooms. The ceilings are low, and a few small windows are the only means of ventilation. This is the wretched concern in which the Government business is carried on, and I say it is a disgrace to this great nation that men should have to perform their arduous duties in such a hovel. Come to another town, Preston, with which the right hon. Gentleman is, no doubt, well acquainted, seeing that it is his own constituency. There the lavatory——

Mr. HANBURY: I may at once state that a new Post Office is being erected, and all this will be remedied.

Mr. MADDISON: But how long will it be before that is done?

Mr. HANBURY: The work is in hand now.

Mr. MADDISON: However that may be, it does not affect my point. (A laugh.) I must say that I am surprised that a postal reformer, of all people in the world, should laugh when I am endeavouring to point out that men are being killed by the conditions under which they are called upon to fulfil their duties. Now, in the Preston Post Office the dining-room is only separated from the lavatory by a lath and plaster partition, and offensive smells are so often noticeable that clerks are compelled, at times, to leave their dinners unfinished. What about the local medical officer? Why does he not report the case to the chief medical superintendent? No doubt in the new Post Office things may be different, but what is to be done until the new office is ready? In dozens of offices a similar state of affairs exists, if not worse, and why is it? Simply because the Government put a ring fence around their offices and keep out the ordinary sanitary authorities. Why should they not allow these offices to come under the Factory and Workshops Act? Why not allow the inspectors to go into these offices? The Home Office is a department of the Government, and we all know it has done great service to the health and general well-being of the work-people of this country. I ask, then, and surely it is a pertinent ques-

tion, why they do not allow the Acts to apply and thus ensure that the offices are kept sweet and clean and fit for people to work in. Why should they be exempted from the regulations which private employers are forced to observe? We are sometimes twitted with claiming special privileges for State workmen, but here we are only asking that they shall be put on an equality with the employees of private firms. I suppose the right hon. gentleman will give us the usual stereotyped answer, as he did when the case of Mr. Ash was brought before him. He knows very well that in that case Mr. Ash made a complaint which was set aside. He also knows that in the very same office the operators have complained, and that their complaints were contemptuously ignored until the Committee reported that the very place as to which the complaints were made was practically in the condition they alleged, and was incommodious and insanitary. Therefore I do submit to the right hon. Gentleman that this is a question he should take into his serious consideration. It is not merely a matter for inquiry; it is one for prompt action on common-sense lines.

*The CHAIRMAN: I must inform the hon. Member that the question of the sanitary condition of Post Offices should be raised on the Vote for Public Buildings. It cannot properly be raised on this Vote.

Mr. MADDISON: I had thought it might be so, but the only way to test it was to proceed, and as you kindly allowed me to go on, I came to the conclusion that I must be in order. Of course, Sir, your mandate is supreme, and I bow at once to it. I will only say, in conclusion, I hope the right hon. Gentleman will give us the inquiry for which we are asking.

Mr. MONK (Gloucester): I wish to say one or two words with regard to the desire of the employees of the Post Office for the appointment of a Committee to consider their grievances. I supported the Amendment to the Address moved by the hon. Member for Stepney, and I see no reason to regret the vote I then gave. On the contrary, I must say I think it very undesirable that alleged grievances should be allowed to seethe below the surface. They cause grave discontent in the public service, and I am sure that if my right hon. friend would consent to the appointment of a Committee of this House it would have a very good and salutary effect. I do not wish to bring forward any grievances on this occasion, but I do make this appeal to my right hon. friend.

MR. HANBURY: My hon. friend the Member for Gloucester has appealed to me to grant this Committee on the ground that there are grievances which are seething below the surface. Now, I should say that of all grievances connected with any State Department, these are the very grievances to which that remark would least apply. This is the third or fourth time on which an appeal for the appointment of a Committee of the House of Commons has been brought before the House itself. We have had this question threshed out periodically once or twice every Session. There has been the fullest opportunity given for stating all the grievances, and I should think that every Member of this House who has listened to the Debates on the Post-Office service must know these alleged grievances by heart at the present moment. Not only have we had speech after speech on the subject, but we have been flooded with pamflet after pamflet and post-card after post-card. I cannot, therefore, agree with my hon. friend that these are grievances which are seething below the surface. What has happened in this case case? The hon. Member for Newington appeals for finality. We had an explanation from the hon. Member for Sheffield as to that, when he said he had no doubt that if this Committee were appointed it would remove certain current grievances, but he felt certain that new ones would arise at once.

MR. MADDISON: I did not say at once. I said after a considerable time.

MR. HANBURY: Well, I will venture to say at once, from experience. The result would be that we should have a House of Commons Committee sitting practically every Session, and that is the finality the hon. Member has undertaken on behalf of those for whom he spoke. The hon. Member also said that if the Committee sat it would close the discus-

Mr. Monk.

sion, as they would accept its verdict. But exactly the same promise has been given on previous occasions. There was an agitation on the very points we are now discussing. Those points have been under discussion four or five or six years, and the very same points were raised at the time when the Tweedmouth Committee was appointed. When that Committee was appointed, and when the names were read out in this House, there was a unanimous chorus of approval, and everybody who had been agitating said, "It's exactly the sort of Committee we want." (Mr. PICKERSGILL: No.) I believe one Member, the hon. Member for Bethnal Green, did object.

MR. PICKERSGILL: I was not alone.

MR. HANBURY: The hon. Member was very nearly alone. He is fond of being in a minority, and he certainly was in a minority on that occasion. Again the same promise was made when the inquiry was held by the Duke of Norfolk and myself. That inquiry, it will be remembered, was suggested by the right hon. Baronet the Member for the Forest of Dean. He said, "The discussion of these matters in the House is not the best way out of the difficulty, and that if the Tweedmouth Committee have left grievances without redress, would it not be better for the Postmaster-General and the Secretary to the Treasury to sit together, so that both departments shall be represented in any decision that may be come to?" The suggestion was at once carried into effect, and further than that, we also agreed that any Members of Parliament who were interested in the matter should sit with us and be allowed to ask questions. We got most valuable assistance from some hon. Members. So far as finality was concerned we had a distinct understanding before the Committee sat, and before the Conference was held, that the decisions come to should be accepted. Now, were the decisions come to at these two inquiries in any way adverse to the claims of the Post Office officials? Were they stinted or illiberal? The Tweedmouth Committee, on the contrary, after a most searching inquiry—an inquiry presided over by Lord Tweedmouth, a most impartial man, and held before officials well qualified by technical and financial knowledge to deal with the matter—made proposals, the result of which was that nearly £300,000 a year was added to the salaries of the staff of the Post Office. That was a very considerable addition. There were certain points reserved by the Tweedmouth Committee which apparently they were not sure came within the scope of their reference, or as to which they had not sufficient information. Well, the Duke of Norfolk and myself practically re-opened the whole inquiry. We allowed anybody who liked to come before us, we saw the men themselves, and consequently any gaps that might have been left open by the Tweedmouth Committee were, I think, thoroughly filled up. What did we do? We added practically another £100,000 a year to the £300,000 granted on the recommendation of the Tweedmouth Committee. Nobody, therefore, can say that these men have not had a fair hearing, or that a large addition has not been made to their salaries. After all, what are the grievances brought forward to-night? Can anybody say that the hon. Member for Stepney has practically shown in his speech any real grievance whatever? He mentioned one or two small cases, but, after all, what are they as compared with an enormous staff of nearly 200,000 men? I say with regard to that large staff that you can hardly draw a comparison between it and the ordinary staff of a private firm. The vastness of its numbers makes a great difference, and while I am far from saying that a civil department of this kind ought to be necessarily amenable to the same sort of discipline as exists in the Army, I do say that the same principles are at work, and a somewhat stringent discipline is really required. I think that any Member who has a case of anything like oppression brought under his notice is perfectly justified, and is, in fact, doing right, in bringing it before either the Postmaster-General or myself, or even before the House. But the case which was raised by the hon. Member for Stepney was one in regard to which I felt it my duty to interrupt him in his remarks, and to assure him that he was absolutely misinformed as to the facts. No doubt it is right there should be an appeal to this House, but it is a gross abuse of that right of appeal for hon. Members to plead the cases of individual members of the staff, in order to get for them additional salaries. It is perfectly

legitimate to bring forward statements on behalf of large classes of men. The House has already got abundant information with regard to the details of this case, and has been called into council as to the proper steps to be taken. It will be noted that the hon. Member for Stepney did not go into any details whatever on the question of wages; he merely hinted, and I do not think he did more than that, that we were paying rates below what would be paid in outside services. It is somewhat difficult, no doubt, to draw a comparison between what the Post-office pays and what is paid by private firms. But I will give one comparison, at any rate, and I think it is the only one possible. A few years ago we took over from the National Telephone Company the employees, principally women, who were engaged on the trunk wires, and I venture to say that, counting in the pensions we now pay them, these people are receiving from 30 to 40 per cent. larger salaries than when they were in the employment of the company. Hon. Members who draw comparisons between servants of the State and others are too apt to forget the great facilities Post Office servants get, such as constant employment, large pensions, good holidays, for which they are paid, and large sick pay and sick leave. If these are added together it will be found that the Post Office are paying wages considerably above the level of those paid by outside employers. The hon. Member for Stepney was only able to bring forward three cases of grievance, and two of them concern stripes. After five years' unblemished service a postman is entitled to a stripe, which means extra pay of 1s. a week. The hon. Member complained that a rural messenger did not receive a stripe because, instead of delivering a letter to the house to which it was addressed, he gave it to somebody whom he met some distance from the house. I can conceive no greater offence on the part of a postman. The very thing he is paid to do is to deliver letters at houses to which they are addressed. The second case was that of a man who, having served five years with an unblemished character, has not received his stripe. The man has only to bring the matter before the Postmaster-General, or before the ordinary officials of the Post Office, and he will receive his stripe in due course. The third case was that of a rural postman in Scotland who, in the opinion of the hon. Member, receives an insufficient allowance for a horse and cart he has to provide. I cannot believe there is any case in which only 11s. a week is allowed, and certainly not a case in which only 8s. is allowed, and I feel sure the hon. Member has been imposed upon. Then the hon. Member complains that certain engineers who had served a given number of years are not yet on the established staff. The reply on that head is that in the Post Office, as in other branches of the public service, the established places are limited. The hon. Gentlemen passed on to what he called the right of combination. Does the hon. Member deny that there is the fullest right of combination amongst Post Office officials? They can combine for any purpose they like, and they have full right of access to the Postmaster-General himself. The only limitation imposed by the Postmaster-General is that the combination must consist of *bona fide* servants in his Department, and not of outsiders, and I think that is a most wise and salutary precaution. The Duke of Norfolk has refused, as every Postmaster-General has refused, to listen to complaints which do not come from his own men, but which are worked up for them by outside agitators. Does it not seem rather absurd that a staff of 200,000 men should have to go outside their own ranks in order to find a fit person to represent their views? I should like to say one further word with regard to this application for a Committee of this House. Why should we have it at all? Let me speak with perfect frankness about this thing. We have already had two Committees; we have also had a great deal of pressure brought to bear upon Members. That pressure is becoming almost intolerable. The hon. Member for Newington posed as the just judge, and said, "I am weary of all this agitation; let us try and put an end to it." Well, I am not weary of the agitation. So long as I am satisfied, as I am now, that everything has been done that ought to be done for the men, I will not yield to agitation. The whole thing has been thoroughly thrashed out and dealt with fairly; and if the hon. Member is weary of agitation, well, all I can say is that I do not envy the man who takes that view of things.

Mr. Hanbury.

*CAPTAIN NORTON: The right hon. Gentleman misinterprets me. I did not say I was weary of agitation. I said it was positively degrading, both to the House and to hon. Members individually, that year by year those complaints of a large number of Government officials were brought before us. These men were labouring under the idea that they were not receiving justice, and that the two Committees which investigated their case were, practically speaking, packed Committees. The belief of these men is that their case was investigated largely by higher officials, and their feeling is that these higher officials are against them in the matter; and their opinion is that this House will give them justice.

THE CHAIRMAN: The hon. and gallant Member is exceeding the limits of a personal explanation.

MR. HANBURY: I say at once that I do myself believe that, considering everything, and that full inquiry has already been held, the only advantage these men could derive from a House of Commons Committee would be that the agitation and pressure, now distributed over the whole House, would be focussed and concentrated upon the Select Committee. I, for one, am not prepared to grant a Committee of that kind. Now, passing from that, I come to the question raised by my friend the hon. Member for Barnstaple, namely, the princip'e upon which postmen's wages are paid. I was glad to hear that he supported the view which has always been taken by the Treasury, that the wages of postmen should depend on the population of the town or district in which they live. That roughly affords a test of the cost of living. Unless you are to go into the special circumstances of every locality throughout the United Kingdom, this rough-and-ready rule is the best test, and it has been found to work well. No doubt the hon. Member for Oldham made the complaint that the postmen in that town were not being paid as highly as he thought they should be. I know the interest which the hon. Member has in his constituents, but at the same time he was not able to prove that these men were not being paid according to the population scale. The hon. Member thought that as some concession had been made in Cardiff and Wolverhampton a similar concession should be made to Oldham. I am always opposed to these special concessions. We ought to adhere to the rough-and-ready principle which I have explained. The hon. Member for Barnstaple raised a further question as to travelling letter-boxes on trains. The answer given him by the Department seems to have been that there was no Post Office official in charge. After all, it is a question of expense. No doubt if there were a sufficient number of letters to justify it, it might pay the Post Office to put a man in charge. But the hon. Member went beyond that, and spoke as if the letters could take care of themselves. That might be the case, no doubt, if the letters were going from one point to another; but if they had to be handed out at intermediate stations it would be necessary to have a man in charge.

SIR W. CAMERON GULL: There are exactly the same number of intermediate stations between Torrington and Barnstaple as between Bideford and Barnstaple.

MR. HANBURY: If that were the case there ought to be a man in charge. I think the Post Office ought to consult, so far as it can, public convenience. All these concessions made by the Post Office not only add to the public convenience, but, I am satisfied, bring in fresh business and a handsome return. I will

see how far it is possible to meet the case of my hon. Friend, but it is utterly impossible to put Post Office officials on such duty unless there is a certain amount of business to warrant the charge. My hon. friend the Member for Oldham has spoken about the scheme of an Association of sub-postmasters formed for the purpose of finding the guarantees required by the Post Office. He gave his case away, I think, when he admitted that there was not sufficient capital, and not a sufficient number of members of the Association.

MR. ASCROFT: What I said was that that was the argument of the Postmaster-General.

MR. HANBURY: If the hon. Member will give me the number of the members of the Association, and where these men can be found, I will see what can be done. Then there was the case raised by the hon. Member for Sheffield as to Post Office buildings. I cannot go into all the details, but I am very much obliged to him for having brought it forward. A new Post Office is reported to be necessary at Preston, and therefore I cannot be accused of having perpetrated a job in that case. If I can do anything to meet the convenience of Sheffield I shall do it.

Question put.

The Committee divided. Ayes, 107; Noes, 158. (Division List No. 166).

AYES.

Allan, William (Gateshead)
Allen, Wm (Newc.under Lyme)
Allison, Robert Andrew
Ambrose, Robert
Austin, M. (Limerick, W.)
Baker, Sir John
Barlow, John Emmott
Bayley, Thomas (Derbyshire)
Beaumont, Wentworth C.B.
Billson, Alfred
Birrell, Augustine
Broadhurst, Henry
Brunner, Sir John Tomlinson
Burt, Thomas
Caldwell, James
Cameron, Sir Charles (Glasgow)
Carew, James Laurence
Carmichael, Sir T. D. Gibson-
Cawley, Frederick
Channing, Francis Allston
Clark, Dr. G. B. (Caithness-sh.)
Clough, Walter Owen
Colville, John
Dalbiac, Colonel Philip Hugh

Dalziel, James Henry
Dillon, John
Douglas, Charles M. (Lanark)
Drucker, A.
Duckworth, James
Dunn, Sir William
Engledew, Charles John
Esmonde, Sir Thomas
Evans, Samuel T. (Glamorgan)
Evans, Sir Francis H. (South'ton)
Farquharson, Dr. Robert
Goddard, Daniel Ford
Gourley, Sir Edw. Temperley
Griffith, Ellis J.
Gurdon, Sir W. Brampton
Harwood, George
Hayne, Rt. Hon. C. Seale-
Hazell, Walter
Hedderwick, Thomas C. H.
Holland, W. H. (York, W. R.)
Humphreys-Owen, Arthur C.
Jenkins, Sir John Jones
Jones, William (Carnarvons.)
Kearley, Hudson, E.

Langley, Batty
Lawson, Sir W. (Cumb'land)
Leese, Sir J. F. (Accrington)
Leng, Sir John
Lloyd-George, David
Lough, Thomas
MacAleese, Daniel
M'Dermott, Patrick
M'Ewan, William
M'Kenna, Reginald
Maddison, Fred
Maden, John Henry
Mendl, Sigismund Ferdinand
Monk, Charles James
Montagu, Sir S. (Whitechapel)
Moss, Samuel
Norton, Capt. Cecil William
Nussey, Thomas Willans
O'Brien, James F. X. (Cork)
O'Connor, Arthur (Donegal)
O'Connor, James (Wicklow, W.
O'Connor, T. P. (Liverpool)
Oldroyd, Mark
Pease, Alfred E. (Cleveland)

Pickersgill, Edward Hare
Pilkington,SirGeo.A LancsSW
Priestley, Briggs (Yorks.)
Rickett, J. Compton
Roberts, John Bryn (Eifion)
Roberts, John H. (Denbighs.)
Robson, William Snowdon
Rollit, Sir Albert Kaye
Shaw, Charles Edw. (Stafford)
Smith, Samuel (Flint)
Souttar. Robinson
Spicer, Albert
Stevenson, Francis S.

Strauss, Arthur
Stuart, James (Shoreditch)
Sullivan, Donal (Westmeath)
Tennant, Harold John
Thomas,Alfred(Glamorgan,E.
Trevelyan, Charles Phillips
Tritton, Charles Ernest
Wallace, Robert (Perth)
Walton,JohnLawson(Leeds,S.
Weir, James Galloway
Whittaker, Thomas Palmer
Williams,JohnCarvell(Notts.)
Wilson, Charles Henry (Hull)

Wilson, Henry J. (York,W.R.)
Wilson, John (Durham, Mid)
Wilson, John (Falkirk)
Wilson, John (Govan)
Woodhouse, SirJ.T.(H'ddersˈd
Woods, Samuel
Wylie, Alexander
Young, Samuel (Cavan, East)
Yoxall, James Henry

TELLERS FOR THE AYES —
Mr. Steadman and Mr.
Ascroft.

NOES.

Atkinson, Rt. Hon. John
Bailey, James (Walworth)
Balfour, Rt.Hn A.J.(Manchˈr)
Balfour, RtHnGerald W(Leeds
Banbury, Frederick George
Bartley, George C. T.
Barton, Dunbar Plunket
Beach, Rt.Hn.SirM.H.(Bristol)
Beckett, Ernest William
Begg, Ferdinand Faithfull
Bethell, Commander
Biddulph, Michael
Bill, Charles
Blakiston-Houston. John
Blundell, Colonel Henry
Boulnois, Edmund
Bowles,T-Gibson (King'sLynn
Brassey, Albert
Campbell,Rt.Hn.JA (Glasgow
Carson, Rt. Hon. Edward
Chamberlain,J.Austen)Worcˈr
Chaplin, Rt. Hon. Henry
Charrington. Spencer
Coddington, Sir William
Coghill, Douglas Harry
Cohen, Benjamin Louis
Collings, Rt. Hon. Jesse
Colomb,SirJohnCharlesReady
Courtney,Rt. Hon. Leonard H
Cubitt, Hon. Henry
Curzon, Viscount
Dalrymple, Sir Charles
Davies, Sir H. D. (Chatham)
Dickson-Poynder, Sir John P.
Digby, John K D. Wingfield-
Disraeli, Coningsby Ralph
Dorington, Sir John Edward
Doughty, George
Douglas, Rt. Hon. A. Akers-
Douglas-Pennant, Hon. E. S.
Drage, Geoffrey
Duncombe, Hon. Hubert V.
Fardell, Sir T. George
Fellowes, Hon. Ailwyn Edw.
Ferguson,Rt.Hn.SirJ.(Mˈncˈr
Finch, George H.
Finlay, Sir Robert Bannatyne
Fisher, William Hayes
FitzGerald,SirRobert Penrose-
Fitz Wygram, General Sir F.
Flannery, Sir Fortescue
Forster, Henry William
Foster, Colonel (Lancaster)
Foster, Harry S. (Suffolk)

Galloway, William Johnson
Garfit, William
Gibbons, J. Lloyd
Gibbs,Hn A.G.H (City ofLon)
Gibbs, Hon. Vicary(St.Albans)
Gilliat, John Saunders
Goldsworthy, Major-General
Gordon, Hon. John Edward
Goschen, George J. (Sussex)
Goulding,Edward Alfred
Gray, Ernest (West Ham)
Greville, Hon. Ronald
Gull, Sir Cameron
Gunter, Colonel
Hamilton,Rt. Hn. Lord George
Hanbury, Rt. Hon. RobertWm.
Heath, James
Heaton, John Henniker
Helder, Augustus
Hermon-Hodge, R. Trotter
Hill, Arthur (Down, West)
Hill, Sir E. Stock (Bristol)
Hoare, E. Brodie (Hampstead)
Hornby, Sir William Henry
Houston, R. P.
Howell, William Tudor
Hozier, Hon. J. H. Cecil
Hubbard, Hon. Evelyn
Johnstone, Heywood (Sussex)
Jolliffe, Hon. H. George
Kemp, George
Kimber, Henry
King, Sir Henry Seymour
Knowles, Lees
Lafone, Alfred
Laurie, Lieut.-General
Lawrence, Sir E. D. (Corn.)
Lawrence, W. F. (Liverpool)
Lawson, John Grant (Yorks.)
Leigh-Bennett, Henry Currie
Llewelyn, Sir Dillwyn- (Swan)
Loder, Gerald Walter Erskine
Long, Col. Chas W. (Evesham)
Long, Rt. Hn. W. (Liverpl.)
Lowe, Francis William
Lubbock, Rt. Hon. Sir John
Macartney, W. G. Ellison
Maclure, Sir John William
M'Iver, Sir Lewis (Edin., W.)
Manners, Lord Edwd. Wm. J.
Maple, Sir John Blundell
Martin, Richard Biddulph
Meysey-Thompson, Sir H. M.
Mildmay, Francis Bingham

Montague, Hn. J. S. (Hants)
Moon, Edward Robert Pacy
Moore, William (Antrim, N.)
Morton, A. H. A. (Deptford)
Murray, Rt. Hn. A. G. (Bute)
Myers, William Henry
Nicol, Donald Ninian
Northcote, Hn. Sir H. Stafford
Orr-Ewing, Charles Lindsay
Palmer, Sir C. M. (Durham)
Pender, Sir James
Pierpoint, Robert
Pilkington,R.(Lancs, Newton)
Platt-Higgins, Frederick
Powell, Sir Francis Sharp
Priestley, Sir W. O. (Edin.)
Pryce-Jones, Lt.-Col. Edward
Purvis, Robert
Rankin, Sir James
Robertson, Herbert (Hackney)
Rothschild, Hon.LionelWalter
Russell, T. W. (Tyrone)
Rutherford, John
Ryder, John Herbert Dudley
Samuel, Harry S. (Limehouse)
Savory, Sir Joseph
Sidebotham, J. W. (Cheshire)
Smith,JamesParker(Lanarks)
Stanley, Hon. A. (Ormskirk)
Stanley, Henry M. (Lambeth)
Stanley, Lord (Lancs.)
Talbot, Lord E. (Chichester)
Thornton, Percy M.
Tomlinson,Wm. Edw. Murray
Usborne, Thomas
Valentia, Viscount
Vincent,Col. Sir C.E. Howard
Ward,Hon. Robert A.(Crewe)
Warr, Augustus Frederick
Webster,SirR. E.(IsleofWight)
Welby, Lieut.-Col. A C. E.
Wentworth, Bruce C. Vernon-
Whiteley, H. (Ashton-u -L.)
Whitmore, Charles Algernon
Williams, J Powell- (Birm.)
Willox, Sir John Archibald
Wodehouse,Rt.Hn.E.R.(Bath)
Wortley, Rt Hon.C. B.Stuart-
Wyndham, George

TELLERS FOR THE NOES—Sir
William Walrond and Mr.
Anstruther.

Original Question again proposed.

GENERAL LAURIE (Pembroke and Haverfordwest): The matter I wish to bring before the Committee is absolutely different from that which has just been disposed of. It is a public complaint, at any rate a complaint by a section of the public amongst my constituents in Pembroke Dock, as to the delay in postal deliveries owing to the insufficiency of the staff and the inadequacy of the accommodation in the Post Office there. I would not have brought up the case before the Committee in this way, but my constituents have by petition and otherwise brought it before the Department over and over again without avail. They take the view that it is not a reasonable thing that a delivery of letters should be so drawn out that the postman takes two hours to cover one street of continuous houses. I do not know what the people of London would think if the postmen were two hours going their rounds here. The Department frankly own that their men are not able to keep up with their work, but when asked to increase the staff they say that there is no accommodation. When again asked to increase the accommodation, we are again told that the matter has been under consideration for some time, and that some day when the accommodation is increased they will increase the staff, and satisfy the inhabitants with a better service. These replies, though courteous, are so vague and unsatisfactory that I felt bound to place the motion in my name on the paper, and unless I get a satisfactory answer I shall be constrained to press it.

Motion made and Question proposed—

"That Item A (Salaries) be reduced by £100, in respect of the salary of the Postmaster-General."—(*General Laurie.*)

DR. CLARK (Caithness): Seeing that we are making a large profit by the Post Office, the department ought to do something to increase their staff, so as to give facilities to the general public, especially in small villages and country districts. I understand that the Postmaster-General has been doing something in this direction. Personally I have been compelled to bring before the Department several cases in which a daily delivery is required in my own constituency. It is desirable when the right hon. Gentleman replies that he should state what the Post Office is doing to secure a daily delivery everywhere throughout the country.

MR. HUMPHREYS-OWEN (Montgomery): It appears to me that the policy of the Post Office in relation to remote and sparsely populated districts is one which requires to be altered. Many complaints have been made on this account in my own constituency, and in other thinly populated parts of Wales. I admit that the Post Office officials when I have brought these cases before them have treated me with the utmost civility, and raised most agreeable expectations, but these expectations have never been fulfilled. I always understood that what stands in the way of postal reforms is not so much the inability of the Post Office to carry them out, as their inability to induce the Treasury to relax its hold on the public purse. Everybody knows that if you want to induce a population to settle in the country the first thing necessary is to provide postal and telegraphic communication with the rest of the world. I hope the right hon. Gentleman will commune with himself in his double capacity as representative of the Treasury and of the Post Office, and persuade himself as representing the Treasury to grant to himself as representing the Post Office increased postal and telegraphic facilities, which tend so much to add to the conveniences of country life.

MR. HANBURY: I think the hon. Member for Montgomery was a little hard on the Treasury. If he will look at the state of the Post Office and Telegraphic services now compared with a few years ago, he will find how great is the improvement that has been made. The question of a daily delivery was raised by the hon. Member for Caithness. I believe it is a fact that in some of the more remote districts of Scotland we have not yet been able to carry out a daily delivery; but, of course, we are going steadily forward with the work, and I hope that very soon the whole of the country will be so served. I should say that three-fourths of the whole country have been already accommodated with a daily delivery, and the Department hopes that, within a time measured by months, there will be daily deliveries everywhere. In the meantime, if the hon. Member will quote any specific case in his district, I will see what can be done to improve the service. In regard to the case mentioned by my hon. and gallant friend the Member for Pembroke, of delay in the delivery of letters, that, I understand, is attributed to the shortness of the staff, and that again depends on the accommodation for the staff, for of course we must have accommodation for sorting the letters. I can promise my hon. and gallant friend that the addition to the accommodation in the existing premises will not be indefinitely delayed, and that within four months —which is not a very long time for a Government department—the additional accommodation will be provided.

GENERAL LAURIE: We have had many promises from the Department for many years, and they have had no result. But under the circumstances I accept the promise of the right hon. Gentleman, and with the consent of the House I will withdraw my motion.

Motion by leave withdrawn.

Original Question again proposed.

*COLONEL WELBY (Taunton): There is a question I should like to ask the right hon. Gentleman in regard to a grievance of old non-commissioned officers in the service of the Department who are employed as overseers and telegraph messengers. I understand that they have been told that they are not to be promoted to the post of assistant inspector. That tells in every case upon them in regard to the increment in their salaries, and places them in an invidious position as regards those who have not served in the Army. I am further informed that they have been told that they cannot receive any promotion after the age of 40. If a man enters the Army at twenty-four years of age, and serves for twenty-one years, he will then be six years over the time for promotion under this rule. The wish of the War Office is to get non-commissioned officers to re-engage and to serve for a period of twenty-one years, but if the public Departments put a bar to their promotion at the age of forty it will tend to prevent non-commissioned officers from re-engaging. I beg therefore to ask the right hon. Gentleman to consider whether it is not possible to extend the limit to the age of forty-five

Mr. Hanbury.

or forty-six. I would also ask the right hon. Gentleman whether it would not be possible to publish and put in the library of the House of Commons the regulations in respect of the Post Office officials, their pay, and their retiring allowance.

MR. DILLON (Mayo, East): The hon. and gallant Member has made a complaint on behalf of old non-commissioned officers in the Department. I have to make a complaint in an opposite direction, a complaint which represents a widespread and increasing feeling in the country. I have to protest against the system of giving discharged soldiers and non-commissioned officers employment in the Government Departments of the State in preference to civilians. It is neither just nor fair to the ordinary civilian that he should be forced to make way for an increasing number of soldiers and non-commissioned officers.

*SIR JAMES FERGUSSON (Manchester, N.E.): I do not wish to go into the general question raised by the hon. Member for Mayo, but as regards the employment of old non-commissioned officers to keep the telegraph boys in order, which was instituted when I was at the Post Office, it is rather hard on men who have served well in the Army for a certain number of years that they should thereby be disqualified for holding superior appointments in public Departments for which they are peculiarly fitted. They are tried and trustworthy men, and it is, *prima facie*, a mistake that men of that description should be debarred from rising above the position of overseers of telegraph boys to the position of assistant inspectors or inspectors.

MR. E. ROBERTSON (Dundee): This question is new to me, and I rise to suggest to my right hon. friend that he should, in his reply, tell us as nearly as he can what the offices are in regard to which preference is given to non-commissioned officers in the Army, and in particular I should like to ask him to say whether a corresponding preference is given to telegraph messengers.

MR. HANBURY: The hon. and gallant Member introduced this question as if it were a new matter. I do not think it can be, or I should have heard of it. Certainly there have been no new regulations made, to my knowledge, within the last three or four years. If my hon. and gallant Friend will ask a question in the House about it, or see me privately, I will give him the fullest information that I can. Of course, I have not the details before me at the present moment, and all I can say in reply to my hon. Friend opposite is that a certain number of places as postmen are reserved for men who have served with the colours. The rule is that 50 per cent. of the postmen's places are reserved for soldiers and sailors, and, I believe, militiamen, and 50 per cent. for ex-telegraph messengers. I agree that it might be useful if the House had fuller knowledge of these regulations than it has at the present moment, and I will see whether the suggestion of my hon. and gallant Friend can be carried out. I may say generally, speaking for myself at any rate, that I am not able to entirely agree with the suggestion of the hon. Member for Mayo. I think we ought to find places in the public Departments for those who have served the country well with the colours, both in the Army and Navy, and we are steadily trying to bring about that change with regard to postmen. I will go further and say, those men ought not to have lower wages because they have a pension. A man who has earned his pension ought to have his pension and pay at the same time. The effect of reserving 50 per cent. of the postmen's places for old soldiers and 50 per cent. for ex-telegraph messengers has been to a large extent to disorganise the telegraph messenger service; but I am of opinion that as many positions as postmen ought to be reserved for the Army as the Army can find men thoroughly qualified to take those places. The Army may, however, help the Post Office by inducing boys from the Duke of York's School and the Royal Hibernian School to become telegraph messengers, and then to join the Army and become postmen in their turn. In that way those boys would have an assured career in the Army and the postal service, and that would be an advantage both to the Army and to the postal service.

MR. DILLON: I rise to repeat my protest against the employment on a considerable scale of Army and Navy men in public Departments. I think it is monstrous that the public Departments of this country should be turned into recruiting departments for the services of the country. The Army and Navy ought to take care of themselves. The business of great civil Departments is to do the work of the country. It is a totally new departure to make these Departments recruiting agencies. It is quite possible that a majority in the House might adopt the policy, but it has never been deliberately adopted in all its bearings to the full knowledge of the House, and possibly, if carried to the extent indicated in the speech of the right hon. Gentleman, the time will come when a reaction will set in. I have had bitter complaints made to me on behalf of civilians who have rendered good and faithful service to the Post Office, and who naturally expected to be appointed permanent postmen when vacancies arose. In consequence, however, of these new regulations, they were informed that all the posts were practically for men who had served in the Army or Navy. After the statement of the right hon. Gentleman it is perfectly clear that that is the actual state of the case. Now the right hon. Gentleman makes a further proposal that the telegraph service is to be used as a recruiting agency. That is a very extraordinary proposal, and ought to be opposed. For my part, so far from thinking the hon. and gallant Member is justified in asking for further concessions for the Army, I think the Department has gone much too far in that direction.

Question put and agreed to.

" 2. £570,915, to complete the sum for Post Office Packet Service."

" 3. £2,338,390, to complete the sum for Post Office Telegraphs."

SIR J. BLUNDELL MAPLE (Camberwell, Dulwich): I rise to call the attention of the Committee to the greatly increased expenditure in the maintenance of the postal telegraphic services. I think there is a great waste of money in this branch of the service. For instance, some private wires have been attached to my place of business by the Post Office. I have had an estimate from the National Telephone Company to supply the service at half the cost. As the Post Office refuse to amend their charge, a change is being made, and the Post Office are taking down all their posts and wires for two miles and a half. I should not have called attention to this matter but for the fact that the same thing is going on in other parts of the country, and also in my own neighbourhood I think that to lose business in this way shows very bad management on the part of the Post Office, and I should like to have a promise from the Secretary to the Treasury that he will cause inquiry to be made into this matter.

MR. HANBURY: I do not think it is necessary to make inquiries, because I know the facts perfectly well. The monopoly of the Post Office does not extend to wires, whether telegraph or telephone, between houses or properties belonging to private individuals. The service my hon. Friend refers to is not essentially part of the Post Office work at all. In regard to such services, they would come into competition, not only with the National Telephone Company, but with any private individual who likes to start a company for setting up these wires; and as the Post Office has plenty of public work of its own to do, it has been recently rather unwilling to extend the system of private wires where the distances are comparatively short, and where it is possible there may be very keen competition. The private wires we are perhaps willing to extend are the longer ones. For instance, we are now, I believe, laying private wires between London and Edinburgh. I cannot undertake that the Post Office will go farther than they have gone already. Within the last month or two we have made very considerable reductions in our charges for private wires, if the persons using them will undertake to use them for another five years. I do not know whether the wires to which my hon. Friend refers come within that category. We do not intend to enter into competition with a public company, and I cannot undertake that we shall go any further than we have already gone. We have reduced the charges on those wires to a certain extent, and if the right hon. Gentleman is not content with the charge we make I can only say that he must go to the National Telephone Company. We are certainly not going to enter into a cutting competition with the company.

SIR J. B. MAPLE: I am afraid the right hon. Gentleman does not quite recognise the point that these wires have been put up now for some five years, and

Sir J. Blundell Maple.

that the Post Office is not only throwing money away by not reducing its prices, but it is actually taking down all the posts and tackle, which is a great expense; and it does seem to me to be a ridiculous thing to say that the charges to which I have referred are not worth saving.

CAPTAIN BETHELL (York E. R., Holderness): What I really think we ought to ask the right hon. Gentleman is whether, instead of pulling them down, it might not be possible to sell them; and, secondly, whether it is not possible to stop the disgraceful waste of money that has been and is going on.

MR. HANBURY: I contradict absolutely that a waste of money has taken place. What my hon. Friend complains of is that unless the Post Office grants him the same terms for these wires as the terms adopted by the National Telephone Company he will not continue the connection. It is quite clear that that cannot be done. We must have a fixed tariff, and we have already made considerable reductions. If he does not like to pay our terms, it appears to us better to remove the wires.

Vote agreed to.

4. Motion made, and Question proposed—

"That a sum, not exceeding £496,600, be granted to Her Majesty, to complete the sum necessary to defray the charge which will come in course of payment during the year ending on the 31st day of March, 1900, for the salaries and expenses of the Customs Department"

*MR. GRAY (West Ham, N.): In the year 1890, upon this Vote, a discussion was initiated on the grievances of the various grades of Customs officers. The Chancellor of the Exchequer of that day, who is now the First Lord of the Admiralty, agreed at the time to institute an inquiry into the allegations which had been brought forward as to the general condition of the service. And as my excuse for bringing up this subject again I should just like to refer to the words of the right hon. Gentleman the present First Lord of the Admiralty. The right hon. Gentleman urged that good faith should be kept with these officers in order that they should have no reason to complain that the terms on which they entered the service had been changed to their detriment. I contend that the terms of their service have been changed, greatly to their detriment, and they have a good cause of complaint with which to come to this House. As a result of the debate in 1890 the then Chancellor of the Exchequer and the Financial Secretary of that day (Mr. Jackson) entered into a prolonged inquiry, the outcome of which was a Treasury Minute which was promulgated in 1891. That minute gave almost universal satisfaction through the whole of the Customs service; and now, if I may, I shall point out to the Committee how this applies to this vote, and how it is that we are making allegations against Her Majesty's Treasury. These men are the officers responsible for the collection of £22,000,000, the product of the import duty on all dutiable goods coming into Great Britain. The number of officers is not large, although the duty is an exceedingly important one. Fifteen hundred men of various grades in the service take charge of the whole of these matters, from the moment that the imported goods come into the port to the time when they pass out through the bonded warehouses to the merchants to whom they are consigned. Now, in 1890 these officers made certain complaints. They alleged that promotion was delayed, that the duty which they were performing was not such as they were entitled to expect when they entered their service; they alleged that changes in their duties were being made to their disadvantage, that work which had been performed by officers of higher grade was being shifted on to the shoulders of men with lower qualifications, and that there was an insufficiency of staff to safeguard the revenues of the country. There were two or three other charges as to which the Chancellor of the Exchequer and the Financial Secretary were unable to agree, but so far as the charges which I have enumerated are concerned they admitted that the officers had made good the charges brought forward in the House. Consequently the Treasury recommended the Customs Board to make certain changes in the service which would do away with these complaints. The recommendations, in the main, were such as to give contentment in the service, and it was concluded by the officers that a new bargain had been entered into between them and their employers. They were prepared to execute their part of the con-

tract faithfully, and they naturally looked to the Treasury to perform theirs. Now, having examined the complaints from these officers, I have come to the conclusion that there has been a gross breach of faith on the part of the Government, and especially upon that part which is known as the Customs Board. I fully recognise, of course, the difficulties that may ensue if one too readily lends one's ear to complaints made by any portion of the Civil Service. Therefore I have tried for the last two or three years to avoid bringing this subject under the notice of the Committee. I have tried private negotiations with the Financial Secretary to the Treasury, and I have to record that I am thankful for the courtesy that I have always received, and I can only regard the information which has been supplied to him from other sources as misleading. The highest grade officers on out-door work are the collectors. There are very few of these offices, and they are looked upon as the prizes of the profession, and are watched with keen anxiety by those officers who are a grade below. The next is the grade of surveyor, who receives a minimum of £350 per annum, rising to a maximum of £500. In the first place these latter gentlemen complain that the promotion to the rank of out-door collector had been stayed. The Chancellor of the Exchequer admitted very fully the complaint, and arranged that there should be an increase in the number of officers employed in the higher grades, and particularly that those collectorships should be open to the surveyors. The surveyors realised that from that date they would have a chance of getting a collectorship. Now, although that minute is eight years old, not one appointment to a collectorship from a surveyorship was made until last year. Two years ago I addressed a question on the subject to the Treasury, and the reply I got was most unsatisfactory. The Treasury fully admitted that a promise was made, but it was not expedient from the point of view of the Government to carry that promise out.

*Mr. HANBURY: To carry what out?

*Mr. GRAY: The promise that the collectorships should be open to the surveyors. During that time a number of men, from age, have been retired from the service who have been led while they were in to expect promotion through the clause inserted in the Treasury minute. It was also said that in order to improve the condition of affairs that there should be re-created a certain number of surveyors of the first class. It was said that they would create a more rapid promotion from the second and the third grade of surveyors. In 1892, when the minute was promulgated, there were 53 officers of higher grade, and in 1898 there were only 42. There has been a reduction in this portion of the service, and in the higher ranks of the service extensive reductions have been made, while in the lower ranks great increases have been made. All this may be desirable and in the interests of the public service. It may be desirable that the strictest economy should prevail, but you can carry economy so far as to endanger the efficiency of the service, and I allege now that it has been carried to such a length as not only to endanger the efficiency of the department but to result in a very great loss. My second complaint is, that all the second and third class officers have lost that promotion which they should have had if the first-class surveyors had been re-created. The loss to the surveyors is a loss to the officers below them, and a number of men in the first-class surveyor class being reduced instead of increased has resulted in the first-class examining officers losing their chance of promotion. Their complaint, however, is of a somewhat different character; how it has arisen is not quite known, but these out-door officers are engaged in the particular work of measuring up the casks, estimating the amount of spirit they contain, and the amount of duty which the Treasury ought to receive. They are men exposed to all kinds of weather, who are out both night and day, and whose hands have lost the skill for writing essays and answering questions on paper, and who are consequently no longer able to compete in the examination room with the young men of twenty or twenty-five years of age who have come straight from their schools, and who have crammed up the work from books and papers, but who are wholly without that practical experience which is so necessary for this business. That is the complaint that they brought

Mr. Gray.

up, and the Chancellor of the Exchequer of that day dealt with it by saying that the examinations for this part of the service should be no longer of a literary character, but of a practical character. It was pointed out that neither under the nominative nor the competitive system did the service obtain the men fitted to discharge the duties of this office, and in the future, instead of having a competitive examination, it was said that the persons who desired to go in for this office should be called to London, where they could be subjected to a practical vivâ voce examination. That was an eminently satisfactory solution. It was practical work; the men had not to write essays and make up fancy accounts. They had to find actual quantities and go through everyday work. What happened? Within the first two years following the issue of the minute this promise was distinctly broken and violated. The men were put through an examination, largely of a literary character, with the result that the men from the schools who were ready to write essays as to the way in which you ought to gauge a cask, but who could not do the practical work, got these positions. After two years the complaints resulted in the abolition of this examination; but the mistake having been made, a certain number of these young men were placed over the heads of the older men of practical experience; and once there it is extremely difficult to remedy the mistake which has been committed. Year after year they have gone on, and older men who should have been sent to the top of their grade are standing 53 places lower down than they ought to be. When the time comes to compete for the surveyorships, these men will step forward, and the old men, the practical men, who have all the skill, will lose all possibility of receiving any chance of obtaining one of the prizes of the profession to which they are justly entitled, and to which the Treasury minute admitted their right of claim. I suggest that the claims of these old men who have suffered, not through any fault of their own, but through the manner in which the Customs Board has carried out the recommendations which the Treasury placed in their hands—I suggest the fault is one which must be remedied, even though it may be difficult. These men have lost 53 chances to which they are entitled, and therefore the younger men ought not to feel aggrieved if these positions are increased by 53 more. These men might well be added to that grade of service, and that would in some measure recompense them for the loss which they have sustained owing to the way in which the minute of 1891 was carried out. Now, prior to this inquiry, which was held by the right hon. Gentleman who is now First Lord of the Admiralty, in 1890, it was alleged by the officers that many important duties which ought to be discharged by men of ripe experience were being placed in the hands of young and inexperienced persons. This refers particularly to the important work of import gauging. I ask the attention of the Committee to this phase, because if it were not so serious the explanations given would be extremely amusing. The First Lord of the Admiralty agreed and set forth in the Minute that in future the important work of import gauging, which had hitherto been performed by first or second class examining officers, should in the future be fulfilled, so far as possible, by first-class examiners only. Since the date of the writing of the Minute the clause has never been carried out. The work of import gauging is still being carried on by second-class examining officers and the assistant-examining officers. I brought that matter before the Commissioners, and their explanation is that the phrase "important work of gauging" does not apply to the whole, but only to the more important portions of it. They say it is ridiculous that a first-class examining officer should be made to gauge cheap wine, especially claret, that they are only expected to gauge the more important wine. I am very much surprised that such an explanation should be given, because in the report a little further on the same duty is described, the same class of officers is referred to, and there is no distinction drawn between cheap and expensive wine. Again and again throughout the pages of this Minute a promise is made to these men by a State Department that a certain class of work shall in future be discharged by particular officers in order to increase the rates of promotion for men in the lower grades. For two years a private confidential interpreting Minute existed between the Treasury and the Customs Board, of which the men had no knowledge whatever. They saw casks of wine still gauged by men of the second class, and they wondered why the work was not discharged by higher grade men. But the whole of the time there existed this interpreting Minute, to the effect that those who signed it never meant what they attached their names to. I am told—I hope it is no breach of etiquette to mention it—that the secretary who wrote the Minute did not accurately represent those who subsequently signed it. That is a very lame excuse for any Department to put before the House of Commons as a justification for what, to my mind, is defrauding men of what they were led to expect. I am not setting forth any new claim for these men, I am not asking for any increase in their salaries, and I am not taking up the usual line of asking that the men should be allowed to break their contract. My own contention is that this document constitutes a contract between the men and the Department, and I care not whether it was clumsily drawn by a secretary or whether those who signed it neglected to carefully examine its clauses. It has been signed by Ministers of State, and every word of it ought to be interpreted as an ordinary man would interpret it, and its operation should not be restricted in a sense never intended. I may point out that this work of import gauging is one requiring great skill, dexterity, and long years of practice. For the purposes of the State it is as important that cheap wines should be as accurately gauged as expensive wines, because on the gauging depends the amount of duty the merchant has to pay. The principle is exactly the same, and this Minute laid down in the most explicit manner that this work was to be discharged by first-class examining officers, in order that those below them might enjoy the opportunity of promotion. I shall listen with no little curiosity to the defence which the Secretary of the Treasury may now bring forward. The Customs Board themselves admit that they do not retain the work of import gauging for first-class officers alone, but they allege that it is absurd to suggest that the work of gauging light clarets should be reserved for first-class officers. I have ventured to dwell on this particular phase of the question, but it would be easy to show that it is only one cause of the discontent which runs through the whole of this important State

Department, and a discontented class of servants is not likely to render efficient service to the State. I will now pass to another question. The great complaint made by the men is that the rate of promotion is slower than they were entitled to expect. Again and again it was stated in the Minute that while the Treasury could not undertake to increase the salaries, they would undertake to improve the rate of promotion, and therefore *inter alia* the Minute laid down that each branch of the service should have attached to it a sufficient margin of officers of that class to meet the vacancies arising from sickness and leave of absence. The men of the lower ranks had been for years, were during the time of the Minute, and are still, called upon in the most unwarrantable fashion to discharge the more important duties of officers of a superior grade without receiving the emoluments attached to that particular grade. It would be absurd to suggest that it would be possible to do without the system of "acting" altogether. In the smaller ports men may reasonably be called upon, daily if you will, to discharge the duties of the higher ranks, but I allege, and I think I can prove, that this system of "acting" is going on all over the country to a most unwarrantable extent. In London and the provinces men of inferior grade are called upon, at a minute's notice, to discharge not for a day, or a week, or a month, but for even greater periods, the duties of officers who are sick. Take Mount Pleasant office for example. I am prepared to give the names, places, and times. In Mount Pleasant, where nearly the whole of the Postal import duty is collected, a first-class examining officer has been acting as surveyor for six weeks straight off. This is not a small port a couple of hundred miles away from the central office. The amusing part of it is that if a man in receipt of £70 a year is away sick, they will send to a neighbouring station for a man of the same class to fill his place, but when a man is absent who is in receipt of £400 a year it is naturally cheaper to employ a man of £250 to discharge his duties, and save the expense which would be attached to increasing the staff of that particular depôt. That may be to the interests of the Exchequer, but it is not to the interest of the taxpayer in the long run, because a

Mr. Gray.

man so employed becomes discontented, and some of the men are not fit for the duty. A special promise was made with regard to Liverpool, but it has never been fulfilled. The following are the number of days worked in the port of Leith by inferior officers in superior positions :--January 105, February 69, March 63, April 41, May 53, July 62, December 65, in addition to which there were parts of days, together making up nearly 12 days. For a port of that character this is a most unwarrantable exercise of the system of "acting." In other ports of the country the same thing is going on. In district after district there are unreasonable claims on young men to discharge the duties of older and more responsible officers. I believe the Secretary of the Treasury has admitted that the principle of acting ought not to be carried on to an unreasonable extent, and the whole question therefore is, what can be described as unreasonable? I cannot come to any other conclusion, after a most careful study of the Minute, and also a study of the system, that "acting" is carried on to an unwarrantable extent. The explanation to my mind is that there is competition between the Excise and Customs Departments as to which can collect the largest amount of revenue at the smallest amount of cost, and the consequence is that year after year, although the Customs revenue has increased, the cost of the service is decreasing. I am inclined to think if the Secretary of the Treasury will carry his investigations not a very great distance, he will find that this system has resulted not in the collection of a larger amount of revenue, but of a much smaller amount than would be secured if the service were sufficiently manned. With regard to the Assistants, their claim is not based on the Treasury Minute, for the sufficient reason that that class was not in existence when the Minute was issued. They asked the Treasury to institute certain reforms in their conditions of service, rates of pay, and promotion, and, oddly enough, the Treasury acceded to all their claims, but instead of applying the remedy to the men already in the service who asked for these improvements, it was applied only to new entrants to the service. What is the result? You have sitting at the same desk, in the same office, two men—

one with four years' service and a salary of £70 5s., the other with four days' service and a salary of £70. The latter has had no service ; he is only a young fellow who has just passed his examinations, but under the new conditions he gets £70 as his initial salary. The other man has four years' service, but before he joined this particular grade he was discharging two classes of duty, one of a comparatively important character, the other of a comparatively unimportant character. In the new class which has been constituted he drops the unimportant work, and is discharging nothing but the important work. That is the first year of their comradeship. After the seventh year the newcomer is getting £100, whereas the other must labour 12 or 13 years before he reaches that level. Such an arrangement is manifestly unjust. I apologise to the Committee for having elaborated these grievances at such great length, but I believe I am justified, not only because of the complaints on the part of the men, but also because, owing to the inadequate staff, there is being practised very extensive fraud on Her Majesty's Revenue. The men declare, and I have no reason to doubt them, that this is the sort of thing that goes on day by day. A cargo of high-class wines or spirits arrives at the docks ; it is immediately taken charge of by a first-class examining officer ; it is gauged and ullaged, and its strength is determined and registered. It is then transferred to a bonded warehouse, where it is locked up in charge of a bonded warehouseman and a representative of the Customs Board. What takes place to secure that no leakage occurs a Surveyor of Customs goes into the bonded warehouse, consults the register of casks, and asks that the particular cask be produced. Now there are not sufficient officers of this class to allow the officer to wait until the particular cask he asks for is brought up. Having called for the cask, he is off to some other duty and may not be back for five hours. Meantime the cask is tampered with, and the loss which was going on has been made good, and the officer is deceived. In its turn that particular cask will be dealt with to make up the loss in others. I may be told that this is a fanciful picture, but is it not a fact that within the last few months, at one port alone, no less than ten thousand gallons of spirits escaped in this way, involving duty to the Crown of over £7,000 ? I would ask whether in the neighbourhood of the docks in that port it was not possible to purchase 2d. worth of good spirits in the streets from unlicensed persons, and the Customs officers did not discover the fraud until after an employee had been dismissed. Who had to pay the piper ? The bonded warehouse hands over bonds to the Treasury for, I think, £5,000. That was not sufficient to cover the loss in this case, and the Treasury had to put into force an old Act of Parliament by which they compelled the warehouse to pay the full duty. That occurred through an inadequate staff of Customs officers. In two other ports spirits have been leaking away to the extent of several hundreds of pounds of duty during the last twelve months, in what manner it is absolutely impossible to determine, because the Customs Board have not at their disposal a sufficient staff of officers to go round and take stock in the warehouses. I am not asking that the salaries of these men be increased, because I do not take the view that having entered into a contract that contract should be broken. But while I take that stand in defence of the Treasury, I am bound to take an equal stand in defence of the men. Many of them live in my own constituency, and they have made me familiar with their complaints, and I think the Board of Customs have so far offered no adequate defence. I appeal to the Secretary of the Treasury to look into the matter himself. I have the utmost confidence in his fairness, and if he be left alone and not fettered by any permanent official who may receive a bonus if they can get the Estimates cut down, I should be prepared to leave the case in his hands. I had hope of urging the appointment of a Committee of Enquiry, but I prefer that the Secretary of the Treasury should be judge and jury at the same time, because I am confident he will deal with the question fairly. I move that the vote be reduced by £100.

Motion made and Question proposed—

    " That Item B (Port Establishments) be reduced by £100 in respect of Salaries, etc." (*Mr. Gray.*)

*Mr. HANBURY : I think the hon. Member for North West Ham has made a very unfair attack upon the permanent officials. Who are these permanent officials who have received the bonuses of which he spoke, and what reason has he to suppose that they are less fair in trying to deal with a matter of this kind than I am? The whole speech of my hon Friend is a speech practically in favour of more rapid promotion in this branch of the Customs service. That is the whole gist of his remarks from beginning to end. He first complains that the terms of the Goschen Minute have not been carried out with regard to the promotion of surveyors to collectorships. As far as I understand the Goschen Minute, the idea was that a certain number of surveyors should be appointed to collectorships, that there should be no gulf between the grades, and that it should be possible for surveyors to be appointed as collectors in certain ports. That has occurred certainly in one case quite recently, and my hon. Friend must know that in a great number of cases the salaries of surveyors are very much in excess of the salaries of collectors. The hon. Member has dealt with the question of the number of surveyors, and he very fairly says that that number in relation to the number of junior officers to a great extent governs the rapidity of promotion. But he also says that there has been a reduction in the number of higher grade officers since 1892. That statement is, however, misleading. The total number of surveyors' posts, or their equivalents, since the Goschen Minute has undoubtedly been increased. I do not say that decreases have not taken place, but the statistics of my hon. Friend evidently refer only to the port of London, where, naturally, they have decreased, because there was not sufficient work for them to do. Nevertheless, the number of surveyors elsewhere has been increased, and all these places are open to men in the lower grade, whether they belong to London or to other ports. Therefore, the number of places open to them has not been decreased in any way by the reduction in the port of London. I have been asked if there was not a distinct promise of a permanent increase in the first and second class surveyors in the port of London. That was not so, for it was simply said that there should be a temporary increase pending the promotion of certain third-class surveyors, and my point is that the promise as to London has been carried out, and the promise as to pro-

Mr. Hanbury.

motion has also been carried out. Although the surveyors all over the country have been reduced by eight, this has been only a nominal decrease, because the number of equivalent posts has been increased by nine or ten. It should also be remembered that the first-class examining officers, which is the class immediately next to the surveyors, are actually getting the same maximum salary as was being obtained by seventeen of the surveyors at the time of the Goschen Minute. The hon. Member said that the number of places for junior appointments has also been very largely increased, but that is not the fact. The comparison that has been made by my hon. Friend, or by those who advised him, is a comparison based upon the estimates of 1890-91, and in those estimates a peculiar mistake occurred. It had been intended to cut down the second class by 200, and the result was that in the estimates the number put down as intended to serve during that year was 617 as against 860. As a matter of fact that policy was not carried out, and the number actually on the staff during that year was not 617 but 816. That entirely alters the calculation of my hon. Friend, and the proportion of surveyors and examining officers first class to the lower classes is exactly the same now as it was at the time of the Goschen Minute. Then the hon. Member complains that a large amount of work is being done by the second-class examining officers which ought to be done by the first-class officers; but if the former were transferred it would have the effect of increasing the number of the higher grade, and, indirectly, increasing the pensions. I agree with the hon. Member that the language of the Minute is not as perfect as it possibly might be, but it is better to interpret that Minute by the language of the person who drew it up, and my right hon. Friend, the present First Lord of the Admiralty, on the very first day when this Minute had to be interpreted, said that in his view only important work should be given to the first-class examining officers. Surely that was in accordance with common sense. I do not suppose that even my hon. Friend wants to create posts for men, or to pay salaries higher than the character of the work which they have actually got to do. What is the difference between these two classes? The second class have to gauge the cheaper wines, whereas the work of the first-class examining officers is that of gauging the dearer wines, and more especially spirits. Why is it that the inferior officers gauge the inferior wines, while the first-class officers have to gauge the higher class of wines? One reason is that the responsibility is greater; and I understand that there is less difference between the casks containing light French wines, so that less skill in gauging is required. In regard to spirits and dearer wines that is not the case, more especially in regard to spirits, which come in all kinds of casks and shapes, and a man has to be an expert to gauge the different shapes and different forms of these casks. I think, therefore, there is a great difference between the work of the two classes. The hon. Member next referred to the system of "acting," and I perfectly agree with him that it is possible to carry this practice too far. It is, however, an advantage for one of a lower grade to discharge the duties of a higher position, and act as substitute in the absence of his superior officer, because that better qualifies him for promotion. I find the same thing going on in the Post Office, where I have known men "acting" for a year at a time, and that is grossly unfair. I cannot help thinking, however, that it is perfectly fair to apply it to the Customs service. I am surprised to find that the cases quoted by my hon. Friend were not very long ones, and he quoted a case which he thought was one of great hardship, where a man had been "acting" for six weeks. I do not think that was a hardship, and if that is one of the worst cases, then I cannot think that the practice prevails to the extent which the hon. Member thinks it does. The hon. Member complains that under the Goschen Minute there was an arrangement by which the men pass from the second class of examining officers to the first class by competitive examination, but that was found to be somewhat too favourable to the younger officers, and a system was substituted by which the men practically went up by seniority if they passed a qualifying examination. The hon. Member said that he wanted to see the Goschen Minute carried out literally, but his great complaint now is that the Goschen Minute is carried out.

MR. GRAY: The Goschen Minute laid it down that the Chancellor of the

Exchequer, having seen the advantage of this form of examination, decided to introduce it in the Customs service, and what I complained of was that the two subsequent examinations were a violation of that clause.

*MR. HANBURY: I do not think that my hon. Friend's contention is correct, because it has never been brought to my knowledge that this examination was not in accordance with the Treasury Minute of Mr. Goschen. I now come to the last point, which is that of assistants of Customs. The hon. Member complains that there are men acting as assistants of Customs some of whom have had four years' service, and yet others who have only had one year of service are getting exactly the same pay. When I heard that statement I asked the hon. Member if he meant the same service, for he knows very well that the old class of outdoor officers performed not only the duties now discharged by assistants, but also those which are assigned to the watcher class; and therefore their work was of a mixed nature, and was not, on an average, as high as that of the present assistants. Two or three years ago the new class of assistants was appointed to do the superior work, and the men to whom reference has been made were held to be qualified to pass into that class at their existing salaries, although they were higher than the minimum of that class. The complaint of my hon. Friend is that these men, who had been performing work of a mixed nature for three or four years before their appointment, are now receiving the same salaries in the new class as the men who entered it upon its formation without previous service. Is there anything unreasonable in that? I confess that I see no hardship in it at all. If my hon. friend had been able to show that they had been performing the same duties throughout their service, then the case would have been different. Then there is the question of "frauds." That matter has not been brought before my notice, and I am somewhat inclined to think that my hon. Friend has somewhat exaggerated the facts of the case. The impression put upon my mind was that we ought to have some more efficient system of dealing with these matters, and if the hon. Gentleman, who apparently has some means of getting into touch

with persons able to give information, will enable the authorities to communicate with them with the same readiness and promptitude, it will be of considerable assistance. I hope, therefore, that we may count upon his services.

MR. RYDER (Gravesend) : I wish the Committee to extend to me the kindness and consideration it always grants to a Member of this House who addresses it for the first time. I have to call attention to certain grievances suffered by the officers of Customs. There are three classes of men—examining officers, preventive officers, and boatmen. It is to the case of preventive officers I propose to refer. They have practically three grievances, which come under the heads of salary, promotion, and Sunday pay. The evidence given before the Ridley Commission showed the importance of the duties performed by these men. Let me give a few statistics on the question of pay. In the London branch an officer commences with a salary of £110, as against £90 paid in the Water guard branch. The examining officer rises by an annual increment of £7 10s. to a maximum of £220. In the Water guard the annual rise is £5, and the maximum £150. The number of second class officers in the examining branch is 56, and they have 329 superior appointments. In the Water guard branch they get only 59 superior appointments, and of these only 42 go up to a maximum of £200. Beyond this the examining officers have practically no Sunday duty or night duty, and they very seldom do 48 hours per week. The Water guard men work from 53 to 84 hours per week, and have a good deal of night and Sunday work, for which they get no pay whatever. I think these men are correct in saying that they are suffering under certain hardships. Under a Treasury Minute of 1891 it was directed that preventive officers' duties should be performed by examining officers. I do suggest that, if the Secretary to the Treasury is unable to meet their claims

Mr. Hanbury

in their entirety, he should at any rate allow them to commence at a salary of £100, and to rise by an increment of £7 10s. to a maximum of £210 ; that they should get 7s. per day for Sunday duty, and that the upper section appointments should be increased to, say, 80 or 90. I think you will then have a body of men who are contented. The Committee are quite aware of the importance of the duties performed by these men, and must know how necessary it is to employ men above reproach.

MR. STEADMAN : I rise for the purpose of calling attention to the rate of pay given to Customs watchers. This body of men have taken the place of men who, some little time ago, were in receipt of a salary of £100 per annum, full pay in sickness and on holidays, and pensions and uniform. Now, they began at 19s. a week, which represented 4¾d. per hour. Since they have been made permanent men, however, their wages have been raised to 21s. per week, but as they work 54 hours they are only getting 4½d. per hour. Their position is one of great responsibility, and all they ask for is an increase of 3s. per week, rising by annual increments of £2 12s. per annum, up to 28s. per week. Seeing that they have taken the place of officers who were receiving £100 per year and other emoluments, I do think they are entitled to some consideration at the hands of the Secretary to the Treasury. I would also like to put in an appeal on behalf of the boatmen whose case is to be brought forward by the honourable Member for Limehouse.

*MR. HANBURY : The honourable Member seems to be under a misapprehension as to the salary of the men who have been replaced by the Customs watchers. These watchers have only succeeded to the inferior work of the officers for whom they were substituted. The original class has been divided into two classes, and these watchers are doing the inferior part of the work. The honourable member says they work nine hours per day, but that is only a matter of calculation, for out of that they are allowed an hour for meals. The chief complaint, however, was on the point of wages, and the honourable Member is not satisfied with the 21s. they receive; he has set up the ideal of 24s. as a living wage. These men's wages have already been raised from 19s. to 21s., but, in addition, they get considerable advantages, which bring their earnings very near, if not above, 24s. Then, it should be borne in mind that 24s. is advocated as the wage of a perfectly able-bodied man, whereas a large number of these men are pensioners, and it is quite possible that they are not able-bodied. And again, although nominally they are employed nine hours, their average period of working is, I am told, only seven hours, and it is not very hard work. What I want to impress on the honourable gentleman is this, that if he says 24s. is a wage which ought to be paid, then 21s., with all the various advantages they get, and which an outsider would not get, is certainly equal to the 24s. The men, for instance, get a fortnight's holiday in the year, and they also receive sick pay, and bearing in mind that they do not do a full eight hours per day I think they should be satisfied with the remuneration given them.

Mr. H. S. SAMUEL (Tower Hamlets, Limehouse): I desire to enlist the sympathy of the Secretary to the Treasury for the grievances of the Customs boatmen. These men are really examining officers, and their duty is to go over all ships which arrive in port. Their grievances principally relate to salary, employment on Sunday, hours of work, and, in the case of the London men, travelling expenses. In regard to salary, they commence at £55 a year, rising by 30s. for a certain number of years, and then by 50s. a year until the maximum sum of £80 is reached. It therefore takes them fifteen years to reach the maximum salary, which

is a very long period indeed. I know that there are some cases in which the maximum salary has been raised from £80 to £85, but in these cases they are no longer paid seizure money, and overtime is now hardly ever required. In many instances instead of being better off they are now worse off than before. I ask the right honourable Gentleman to see whether their salaries could not be improved. The complaint as to Sunday labour is, that while in most departments the men are paid time and a half for Sunday labour, all that the Customs boatmen get is £5 a year, and they are liable for duty on every Sunday. Some of the men, indeed, get no money for Sunday labour. I consider that a hardship, and I ask the right honourable Gentleman to look into the question. Then as to travelling expenses, boatmen who are moved from one port to another receive travelling expenses; but when the boatmen in London are moved from one station to another they get no expenses to cover the cost of the removing of their homes. It is possible to say that London is one port, but then, in the estimation of the House and the Government, London is an aggregation of cities, and the men who are compelled to move their homes from one of these cities to another ought to have their expenses paid by the Department. As to the hours of work on the London stations, the men want them changed from the four-deck-watch system to the three-deck-watch system. I hope the right honourable Gentleman will lend a sympathetic ear to the petition for the redress of these grievances.

Sir F. EVANS (Southampton): I am anxious also to appeal to the right honourable Gentleman for these men. They are, in my opinion, very underpaid. I would go further than the right honourable Gentleman who has just spoken. I have to see constantly many of these men at work, I know what their work is, and the responsibility which is thrown upon them, and I hold that their pay is quite inadequate. We know the many temptations that are put in their way and the corruption which has followed in other countries. Let us take care that we do not by underpaying them put temptations in their way, when they have wives and families to support. These men are called Customs boatmen, but, except in London, they do no boating. If you go down to Southampton or Greenock you never see them in a boat. It would be much better if they could be called assistant preventive officers, which they really are, and that some addition should be made to their salary adequate to their work, to the responsibility of their position, and to a just appreciation of the temptations that are coming in their way. In granting this the Treasury would do well for themselves as well as for the men.

MR. C. H. WILSON (Hull, West): I know there is a great amount of dissatisfaction amongst this highly respectable body of men, who have really important duties to perform. The rate of wages throughout the country is tending upwards, and their rate of pay is totally inadequate. I would suggest that the maximum salary should be raised to £100, and that the yearly increment should be so raised as to enable the men to reach the maximum in 11 years instead of 15.

*MR. HANBURY: We know something of the dissatisfaction amongst the Customs boatmen, but the books of my right honourable Friend the Patronage Secretary are so overladen with applications for these positions that he has been obliged to refuse to receive any further applications. That is *primâ facie* an indication of the enormous competition there is to enter the service, and a rough-and-ready test of whether or not the men are fairly treated. My honourable Friend raises the point of responsibility, but

Sir F. Evans.

these men are always acting under the supervision of preventive officers. The question of the wages of Customs boatmen and preventive officers generally was thoroughly gone into by the present First Lord of the Admiralty and my right honourable Friend the Member for Leeds, who was then Secretary to the Treasury in 1891. The salaries were then considerably increased, and there was no contention here that the decision arrived at as the result of the enquiry had not been properly carried out, or that the promises made to the men had not been fulfilled. We have not only to look at the pay these men get, but the promotions they have received. The promotions of the boatmen have been considerably increased since the Water guard and preventive duties have been separated from the ordinary warehousing and other duties. At certain of the smaller places the boatmen get very considerable allowances in addition to their pay, for they practically act as preventive officers. As to Sunday work, it is absolutely necessary that we should have a certain number of these men on duty on Sunday. The question is whether they are properly paid for what they do; £5 a year was added to the maximum salary in order to meet this Sunday duty, and the men knew when they entered the service that the £85 included seven days' work, if they were called upon to do Sunday duty. With regard to the travelling expenses of the men in London I do think that there is a case for inquiry, and I promise to look into it.

MR. HAVELOCK WILSON (Middlesbrough): I am exceedingly sorry that the right honourable Gentleman has adopted the course he has in regard to the classing of these men. If they are not paid for their service as they ought to be, it is quite possible for smuggling to go on wholesale. The men have long hours of labour, and the pay they receive is very small indeed. They are a hard working body of men, and·I trust that the right honourable Gentleman will reconsider the matter; otherwise I for one shall be prepared to go to a division.

*MR. GRAY : I cannot allow the challenge of the Secretary to the Treasury to pass unnoticed. I understood him to insinuate in the last phrase of his speech that I was in touch with the men who were responsible for the fraud. [MR. HANBURY was understood to take exception to this.] Then I am afraid the language of the Secretary to the Treasury is a little like the language of the Treasury Minute –- expressed in somewhat unusual English — it was certainly open to the interpretation I placed upon it. With regard to the position of the examining officers, notwithstanding what the Secretary to the Treasury has asserted, their position is worse now than it was at the time the Treasury Minute was passed. I have explained again and again that it is most fallacious to take the averages of the two or three years before the Minute and the two or three years after, because promotions were delayed pending the inquiry, and therefore on both sides of the inquiry the first year or two ought to be eliminated. If he will take the three or four years before the inquiry, and the three or four years subsequent to the inquiry, I think he will find that in every branch of the service the rate of promotion is absolutely slower now than it was before the inquiry, and therefore the promises have not been kept. I am placed in this position, I have all the arguments on my side, and the right honourable Gentleman has all the voting strength from the dining-room and elsewhere on his, and hence I hesitate to go to a Division. I shall, however, bring the matter forward on every available opportunity until it has been satisfactorily

dealt with. Meanwhile, I must express my deep regret that the Secretary to the Treasury has not met me in a more generous spirit.

MR. DALZIEL (Kirkcaldy): I only rise to express my surprise at the easy manner in which the honourable Gentleman is satisfied. He has raised a subject to-night that we have had before the House almost every Session for the last five or six years. He has got no satisfaction whatever, except the old stereotyped official statement, which means nothing; and the question will be put off for another year, and nothing more will be done. Now, Sir, I represent a considerable number of men who are interested in this question. Whether the honourable Gentleman goes to a Division or not, I shall certainly go to a Division, and I hope to have his support. We have had facts produced here to-night which show beyond all doubt that there is a pressing and urgent grievance so far as these men are concerned, but it is not a new grievance. The right honourable Gentleman knows the grievance just as well as we do. He could have made a speech to-night which would have thrilled the House, if only he had been sitting on the other side. We miss his eloquence, but admire his impartiality. The Government is supposed to be the champion of short hours and big wages. Where is the eight hours movement now? I think this is a case in which the right honourable Gentleman should have gone a little farther than the mere official promise to look into it. But the right honourable Gentleman is worked too hard already. The question is not going to be dealt with; it is going to be shelved. The Debate is going to be closed to-night, and nothing more will be done until next year, because we have had the promise to look into the question until we are tired of it.

*MR. HANBURY : I have not promised to look into it.

MR. DALZIEL : Then the matter is even worse than I anticipated, and we have no alternative but to take the opinion of the House upon it. The honourable Gentleman who has just sat down says the numerical strength is against us. Well, I have seen some rather funny Divisions during the dinner hour, and if the honourable Member will only induce his friends to come into our lobby, we may be able to place a very powerful case before the right honourable Gentleman.

Question put.

The Committee divided :—Ayes 57 ; Noes 90.—(Division List No. 167.)

AYES.

Allan, William (Gateshead)
Atherley-Jones, L.
Baker, Sir John
Barlow, John Emmott
Bayley, Thomas (Derbyshire)
Billson, Alfred
Brunner, Sir John Tomlinson
Caldwell, James
Carew, James Laurence
Carvill, Patrick Geo. Hamilton
Cawley, Frederick
Clark, Dr. G. B. (Caithness-sh.)
Clough, Walter Owen
Colville, John
Orilly, Daniel
Dillon, John
Doughty, George
Duckworth, James
Evans, Sir Francis H. (South'ton
Farquharson, Dr. Robert
Gourley, Sir E. Temperley

Gray, Ernest (West Ham)
Gurdon, Sir W. Brampton
Harwood, George
Hazell, Walter
Humphreys-Owen, Arthur C.
King, Sir Henry Seymour
Leng, Sir John
Lloyd-George, David
MacAleese, Daniel
M'Dermott, Patrick
M'Leod, John
Maddison, Fred
O'Connor, T. P. (Liverpool)
Oldroyd, Mark
Pickersgill, Edward Hare
Priestley, Briggs (Yorks.)
Rickett, J. Compton
Round, James
Samuel, Harry S. (Limehouse)
Spicer, Albert
Steadman, William Charles

Sullivan, Donal (Westmeath)
Sutherland, Sir Thomas
Thomas, David Alfred (Merthyr
Thornton, Percy M.
Wallace, Robert (Perth)
Warr, Augustus Frederick
Weir, James Galloway
Whittaker, Thomas Palmer
Williams, John Carvell (Notts
Wilson, Charles Henry (Hull)
Wilson, Frederick W. (Norfolk
Wilson, Henry J. (York, W.R.
Wilson, John (Durham, Mid)
Wilson, Jos H (Middlesbrough
Yoxall, James Henry

TELLERS FOR THE AYES—
Mr. Ryder and Mr. Dalziel.

NOES.

Arnold, Alfred
Bailey, James (Walworth)
Balfour, Rt Hon G. W. (Leeds)
Banbury, Frederick George
Bartley, George C. T.
Barton, Dunbar Plunket
Bethell, Commander
Biddulph, Michael
Blakiston-Houston, John
Blundell, Colonel Henry
Brodrick, Rt. Hon. St. John
Bullard, Sir Harry
Chamberlain, J Austen (Worc'r
Chaplin, Rt. Hon. Henry
Charrington, Spencer
Clare, Octavius Leigh
Cochrane, Hon. Thos. H. A. E.
Cohen, Benjamin Louis
Collings, Rt. Hon. Jesse
Colston, Chas. Edw. H. Athole
Corbett, A C (Glasgow)
Cripps, Charles Alfred
Curzon, Viscount
Dalrymple, Sir Charles

Davies, Sir H. D. (Chatham)
Douglas, Rt. Hon A. Akers-
Duncombe, Hon. Hubert V.
Fellowes, Hon. Ailwyn E
Field, Admiral (Eastbourne)
Finlay, Sir Robert Bannatyne
Fisher, William Hayes
Forster, Henry William
Foster, Colonel (Lancaster)
Garfit, William
Gibbs, Hon. V. (St. Albans)
Giles, Charles Tyrrell
Gilliat, John Saunders
Godson, Sir Augustus Fred.
Goldsworthy, Major-General
Gordon, Hon. John Edward
Goschen, George J. (Sussex)
Goulding, Edward Alfred
Green, Walford D (Wednesbury
Hamilton, Rt. Hon. Lord George
Hanbury, Rt. Hon. Robert Wm.
Heath, James
Hermon-Hodge, Robert Trotter
Houston, R. P,

Howell, William Tudor
Jenkins, Sir John Jones
Jolliffe, Hon H. George
Kemp, George
Knowles, Lees
Laurie, Lieut.-General
Lawrence, Sir E Durning-(Corn
Lawson, John Grant (Yorks.)
Leigh-Bennett, Henry Currie
Llewelyn Sir Dillwyn (Swansea
Loder, Gerald Walter Erskine
Long, Rt Hn Walter (Liverpool)
Lowe, Francis William
Lowles, John
Lucas-Shadwell, William
Macartney, W. G. Ellison
Macdona, John Cumming
M'Iver, Sir Lewis (Edinb'h, W
Moon, Edward Robert Pacy
Moore, William (Antrim, N.)
Morrison, Walter
Murray, Rt Hn A Graham (Bute
Nicol, Donald Ninian
Pilkington, Rich (Lanc Newton

Platt-Higgins, Frederick
Pollock, Harry Frederick
Priestley, Sir W. Overend (Edin
Purvis, Robert
Robertson, Herbert (Hackney
Russell, T. W. (Tyrone)
Sidebotham, J. W. (Cheshire)
Skewes-Cox, Thomas

Smith, James Parker (Lanarks
Stanley, Lord (Lancs.)
Strauss, Arthur
Tomlinson, Wm. Edw. Murray
Usborne, Thomas
Webster, Sir R E (Isle of Wight
Williams, Joseph Powell-(Birm
Willox, Sir John Archibald

Wilson, John (Falkirk)
Wyndham, George

TELLERS FOR THE NOES—
    Sir William Walrond and
    Mr. Anstruther.

Original Question put, and agreed to.

CLASS VI.

5. £287,628, to complete the sum for Superannuations and Retired Allowances.

6. £2,130, to complete the sum for Merchant Seamen's Fund Pensions.

7. £785, to complete the sum for Miscellaneous Charitable and other Allowances.

Resolutions to be reported To-morrow ; Committee to sit again To-morrow.

SUPPLY [19TH MAY].

Resolutions reported :—

CIVIL SERVICES AND REVENUE DEPARTMENTS ESTIMATES, 1899-1900.

REVENUE DEPARTMENTS.

1. "That a sum, not exceeding £1,316,232, be granted to Her Majesty, to complete the sum necessary to defray the Charge which will come in course of payment during the year ending on the 31st day of March 1900, for the Salaries and Expenses of the Inland Revenue Department."

CLASS II.

2. "That a sum, not exceeding £9,446, be granted to Her Majesty, to complete the sum necessary to defray the Charge which will come in course of payment during the year ending on the 31st day of March 1900, for the Salaries and Expenses of the Office of the Commissioners in Lunacy in England."

3. "That a sum, not exceeding £67, be granted to Her Majesty, to complete the sum necessary to defray the Charge which will come in course of payment during the year ending on the 31st day of March 1900, for the Salaries and Expenses of the Mint, including the Expenses of Coinage."

4. "That a sum, not exceeding £9,274, be granted to Her Majesty, to complete the sum necessary to defray the Charge which will come in course of payment during the year ending on the 31st day of March 1900, for the Salaries and Expenses of the National Debt Office."

5. "That a sum, not exceeding £14,300, be granted to Her Majesty, to complete the sum necessary to defray the charge which will come in course of payment during the year ending on the 31st day of March 1900, for the Salaries and Expenses of the Public Record Office."

6. "That a sum, not exceeding £13, be granted to Her Majesty, to complete the sum necessary to defray the Charge which will come in course of payment during the year ending on the 31st day of March 1900, for the Salaries and Expenses of the Establishment under the Public Works Loan Commissioners."

7. "That a sum not exceeding £26,884, be granted to Her Majesty, to complete the sum necessary to defray the Charge which will come in course of payment during the year ending on the 31st day of March 1900, for the Salaries and Expenses of the Department of the Registrar General of Births, &c. in England."

8. "That a sum not exceeding £36,393, be granted to Her Majesty, to complete the sum necessary to defray the Charge which will come in course of payment during the year ending on the 31st day of March 1900, for the Salaries and Expenses of the Office of the Commissioners of Her Majesty's Works and Public Buildings."

Resolutions agreed to.

ADJOURNMENT.

Motion made, and Question, "That this House do now adjourn,"—(*Sir William Walrond*)—put, and agreed to.

House adjourned accordingly at a quarter before Ten of the clock.

HOUSE OF LORDS.

Friday, 2nd June 1899.

NEW PEER.

The Marquess of Exeter—Sat first in Parliament, after the death of his father.

PRIVATE BUSINESS.

PORTSMOUTH CORPORATION BILL [Lords].

The Chairman of Committees informed the House that the opposition to the Bill was withdrawn: The orders made on the 27th of February and the 18th of May last discharged; and Bill committed.

NORTH-EASTERN AND HULL AND BARNSLEY RAILWAYS (JOINT DOCK) BILL [Lords].

The Queen's consent signified; and Bill reported from the Select Committee with amendments.

NORTH-EASTERN RAILWAY BILL [Lords].

The Queen's consent signified; and Bill reported from the Select Committee with amendments.

COALVILLE URBAN DISTRICT GAS BILL [Lords].

Commons Amendments considered, and agreed to.

KENSINGTON AND NOTTING HILL ELECTRIC LIGHTING BILL.

Read 2a, and committed; the Committee to be proposed by the Committee of Selection.

MIDLAND AND SOUTH-WESTERN JUNCTION RAILWAY BILL.

Read 2a, and committed.

COBHAM GAS BILL [Lords].

Read 3a, an Amendment made, Bill passed, and sent to the Commons.

ALL SAINTS' CHURCH (CARDIFF) BILL [Lords].

Read 3a, and passed, and sent to the Commons.

WESTON - SUPER - MARE, CLEVEDON, AND PORTISHEAD TRAMWAYS COMPANY (LIGHT RAILWAY EXTENSIONS) BILL [Lords].

Read 3a, and passed, and sent to the Commons.

WHITEHAVEN CORPORATION BILL.

Read 3a, and passed, and sent to the Commons.

BIRMINGHAM, NORTH WARWICKSHIRE, AND STRATFORD-UPON-AVON RAILWAY BILL [Lords].

Read 3a, and passed, and sent to the Commons.

GROSVENOR CHAPEL (LONDON) BILL [Lords].

Read 3a, and passed, and sent to the Commons.

MOSS SIDE URBAN DISTRICT COUNCIL (TRAMWAYS) BILL [Lords].

Read 3a, and passed, and sent to the Commons.

STRETFORD URBAN DISTRICT COUNCIL (TRAMWAYS) BILL [Lords].

Read 3a, and passed, and sent to the Commons.

WITHINGTON URBAN DISTRICT COUNCIL (TRAMWAYS) BILL [Lords].

Read 3a, and passed, and sent to the Commons.

BELFAST CORPORATION BILL.

Brought from the Commons; read 1a; and referred to the Examiners.

CAMBRIDGE UNIVERSITY AND TOWN GAS BILL [Lords.]

Returned from the Commons agreed to, with amendments.

GLASTONBURY WATER BILL [Lords].

Returned from the Commons agreed to, with amendments: The said amendments considered, and agreed to.

QUEEN'S FERRY BRIDGE BILL [Lords].

Returned from the Commons agreed to with amendments: The said amendments considered, and agreed to.

ELECTRIC LIGHTING PROVISIONAL ORDERS (No. 14.) BILL [Lords].

Read 2a (according to order).

GAS AND WATER ORDERS CONFIRMATION BILL [Lords].

Read 2a (according to order).

F

TRAMWAYS ORDERS CONFIRMATION
(No. 1) BILL [Lords].
Read 2*a* (according to order).

TRAMWAYS ORDERS CONFIRMATION
(No. 3) BILL [Lords].
Read 2*a* (according to order).

JONES'S DIVORCE BILL [H.L.].

Read 3*a* (according to order), and passed, and sent to the Commons.

PETITIONS, REPORTS, ETC.

MUNICIPAL CORPORATIONS (BO-ROUGH FUNDS) ACT, 1872.

Petition for Amendment of ; of Mayor, &c., of Kidderminster ; read, and ordered to lie on the Table.

COMPULSORY VACCINATION.

*THE LORD CHANCELLOR (the EARL of HALSBURY): My Lords, I have to present a petition from the Guardians of the Poor of the Wandsworth and Clapham Union, in the County of London, and in doing so I am bound to say that I entirely differ from the reasoning with which they prefer their request, and also from the request itself, which is for the abolition of any form of compulsory vaccination.

Petition read, and ordered to lie on the Table.

TREATY SERIES, No. 12 (1899).

Accession of Japan to the Industrial Property Convention of 20th March 1883.

TRADE REPORTS—ANNUAL SERIES.

No. 2279. Tunis (Trade and general progress, 1898-99).
No. 2280. China (Ichang).
No. 2281. China (Amoy).

CAPE OF GOOD HOPE (OBSERVA-TORY).

Report of the Astronomer at the Cape of Good Hope Observatory to the Lords Commissioners of the Admiralty, for the year 1898.
Presented (by command), and ordered to lie on the Table.

SUPERANNUATION — TREASURY MINUTES.

(1) Dated 19th May, 1899, declaring that James Mills, turner, Royal Gun Factory, War Department ; and,

(2) Dated 24th May, 1899, declaring that Charles Brading, fitter, Royal Laboratory, War Department ;

were appointed without Civil Service certificates through inadvertence on the part of the head of their Department.

NATIONAL DEBT (SAVINGS BANKS).

Balance-sheet setting forth the assets and liabilities of the Commissioners for the Reduction of the National Debt in respect of trustee savings banks on 20th November, 1898.

SUPREME COURT OF JUDICATURE ACT (IRELAND) 1877.

Four Orders in Council, dated 13th May, 1899, giving effect to Rules of Court under the Local Government (Ireland) Act, 1898.

Laid before the House (pursuant to Act) and ordered to lie on the Table.

PARISH COUNCILLORS (TENURE OF OFFICE) BILL.

Read 3*a* (according to order), with the amendment, and passed, and returned to the Commons.

SEA FISHERIES BILL [H.L].

A Bill to amend the law relating to sea fisheries was presented by the Earl of Camperdown (for the Lord Heneage) ; read 1*a* ; to be printed ; and to be read 2*a* on Thursday next. (No. 106).

CONGESTED DISTRICTS (SCOTLAND) ACT AMENDMENT BILL.

SECOND READING.

Order of the day for the second reading read.

*THE SECRETARY FOR SCOTLAND (Lord BALFOUR of BURLEIGH) : My Lords, it will be within the recollection of your Lordships that two years ago an Act was passed which constituted a Congested Districts Board for Scotland, and under which certain powers were given to the Board for expending a sum of money which Parliament had set apart for the purposes of the Act. Those powers, of course, are the only ones under which the Board can work, and the experience of the year and a-half's working which we have had has shown us that in some respects they do not confer all the powers which we would like to be able to exercise. It is obviously inexpedient for us to enter upon any enterprise which we are not sure we have the right to carry through in all its developments, and the object of this small Bill, which I now ask your Lordships to read a second time, is in some respects to extend the powers which are given to the Board by the principal Act. The chief object of the Bill is to enable the Board to give grants-in-aid to various localities within the congested districts in aid of practical education. As your Lordships are probably aware, a new Code of Education in Scotland has been promulgated this year, part of the policy of which has been to give large grants from the Imperial funds for this class of work. We do not aim at definite trade teaching, but, on the other hand, we recognise that if the children in these districts are to be made useful citizens, we cannot confine their education wholly to book-work. What we desire to aim at is to develop all their faculties, and by means of practical work to cultivate their faculties of observation and of manual dexterity. Under the Code which I have just mentioned liberal grants are offered to localities which meet the conditions laid down. I am sure your Lordships will consider that it is a sound principle upon which to work that Imperial funds should not be given as a rule except in response to corresponding activity and expenditure on the part of the localities, and there is certainly no intention on my part to in any way cast discredit upon what I have described as a sound principle. I will further say that so far as much the larger portion of the districts in Scotland are concerned, there will, I believe, be no sort of difficulty in their coming forward and meeting the conditions upon which these grants are offered. They know the value of practical education, and they have therefore every inducement to put their hands into their pockets, and to do their part; but in those Highland and poor districts to which the work of the Congested Districts Board is confined the conditions are different. They have the fewest openings for practical education, and yet they are precisely the very districts which cannot contribute out of their own resources to gain the advantages which are offered from the Imperial funds, and one of the chief objects we want to serve by this Bill is to help those poor districts to meet the conditions laid down, and, where we find it necessary, to give them funds which will enable them to obtain the Code

grant. We trust that in this way we shall be able to elicit a real, practical interest in these matters, and to get the local authorities to start and manage these schools. The Board are absolutely unanimous that this policy is a right one. Since it has been indicated publicly we have had many representations in favour of it; I believe I may say that all those who have communicated with me have expressed themselves in favour of this policy. I have every hope, if your Lordships will pass this Bill, that it will not encounter opposition in another place, and I ask your Lordships now to give it a second reading.

Bill read 2a (according to order), and committed to a Committee of the whole House on Monday next

THE SOUDAN EXPEDITION, 1898.

PROPOSED GRANT TO LORD KITCHENER OF KHARTOUM.

Message from the Queen—Delivered by the Lord Chancellor, and read by his Lordship, as follows :

Her Majesty, taking into consideration the eminent services of Major-General Lord Kitchener of Khartoum, G.C.B., K.C.M.G., in planning and conducting the recent expedition into the Soudan, and being desirous, in recognition of such services, to confer some signal mark of Her favour upon him, recommends to the House of Lords that She should be enabled to grant Lord Kitchener the sum of thirty thousand pounds:

Ordered, that the said message be taken into consideration on Monday next.

House adjourned at twenty minutes before Five o'clock to Monday next, a quarter past Four o'clock.

HOUSE OF COMMONS.

Friday, 2nd June 1899.

PRIVATE BUSINESS.

PRIVATE BILLS [Lords].

(Standing Orders not previously inquired into complied with.)

MR. SPEAKER laid upon the Table Report from one of the Examiners of Petitions for Private Bills, That, in the case of the following Bill, originating in the Lords, and referred on the First Reading thereof, the Standing Orders not previously inquired into, and which are applicable thereto, have been complied with, viz. :—

BRIGHTON MARINE PALACE AND PIER BILL [Lords].

Ordered, That the Bill be read a second time.

PROVISIONAL ORDER BILLS.

(Standing Orders applicable thereto complied with.)

Mr. Speaker laid upon the Table Report from one of the Examiners of Petitions for Private Bills, That, in the case of the following Bills, referred on the First Reading thereof, the Standing Orders which are applicable thereto have been complied with, viz. :—

ELECTRIC LIGHTING PROVISIONAL ORDERS (No. 16) BILL.

LOCAL GOVERNMENT (IRELAND) PROVISIONAL ORDERS (No. 2) BILL.

Ordered, That the Bills be read a second time upon Monday next.

BRIGG URBAN DISTRICT GAS BILL.

Lords Amendments considered, and agreed to.

SOUTH-EASTERN AND LONDON, CHATHAM, AND DOVER RAILWAY COMPANIES (NEW LINES) BILL.

Read the third time, and passed.

NORFOLK ESTUARY BILL [Lords].

Read the third time, and passed, without Amendment.

LONDON AND NORTH-WESTERN RAILWAY (NEW RAILWAYS) BILL.

As Amended, considered ; two Clauses added ; an Amendment made ; Bill to be read the third time.

DERBY CORPORATION WATER BILL, LEICESTER CORPORATION WATER BILL, AND SHEFFIELD CORPORATION (DERWENT VALLEY) WATER BILL.

Ordered, That it be an instruction to the Committee on the Derby Corporation Water Bill, the Leicester Corporation Water Bill, and the Sheffield Corporation (Derwent Valley) Water Bill, that they have power, if they think fit, to consolidate the said Bills or any part or parts thereof respectively into one or more Bills.—(*Sir John Brunner.*)

LOCAL GOVERNMENT (IRELAND) PROVISIONAL ORDER (No. 1) BILL,

Read a second time, and committed.

LOCAL GOVERNMENT PROVISIONAL ORDER (HOUSING OF WORKING CLASSES) BILL.

Read a second time, and committed.

LOCAL GOVERNMENT PROVISIONAL ORDERS (GAS) BILL.

Read a second time, and committed.

LOCAL GOVERNMENT PROVISIONAL ORDERS (No. 4) BILL.

Read a second time, and committed.

LOCAL GOVERNMENT PROVISIONAL ORDERS (No. 5) BILL.

Read a second time, and committed.

LOCAL GOVERNMENT PROVISIONAL ORDERS (No. 6) BILL.

Read a second time, and committed.

LOCAL GOVERNMENT PROVISIONAL ORDERS (No. 7) BILL.

Read a second time, and committed.

LOCAL GOVERNMENT PROVISIONAL ORDERS (No. 8) BILL.

Read a second time, and committed.

LOCAL GOVERNMENT PROVISIONAL ORDERS (POOR LAW) BILL.

Read a second time, and committed.

PIER AND HARBOUR PROVISIONAL ORDERS (No. 2) BILL.

Read a second time, and committed.

BROUGHTY FERRY GAS AND PAVING ORDER BILL [Lords].

Reported, without Amendment [Provisional Order confirmed] ; Report to lie upon the Table.

Bill to be read the third time upon Monday next.

EDUCATION DEPARTMENT PROVISIONAL ORDERS CONFIRMATION (ABERAVON, &c.) BILL [Lords].

Reported, without Amendment [Provisional Orders confirmed] ; Report to lie upon the Table.

Bill to be read the third time upon Monday next.

CITY AND BRIXTON RAILWAY BILL.

Reported, with Amendments ; Report to lie upon the Table, and to be printed.

ARBROATH CORPORATION GAS BILL
[Lords].

Reported, without Amendment; Report to lie upon the Table, and to be printed.

Bill to be read the third time.

DUMBARTON BURGH BILL [Lords].

Reported, with Amendments ; Report to lie upon the Table, and to be printed.

KEW BRIDGE BILL [Lords].

Reported, without Amendment ; Report to lie upon the Table, and to be printed.

Bill to be read the third time.

JONES' DIVORCE BILL [Lords].

Read the first time ; to be read a second time.

GREAT NORTHERN RAILWAY BILL
[Lords].

Read the first time ; and referred to the Examiners of Petitions for Private Bills.

SUNDERLAND CORPORATION BILL
[Lords].

Read the first time ; and referred to the Examiners of Petitions for Private Bills.

FRIENDS PROVIDENT INSTITUTION BILL [LORDS] [STAMP DUTIES].

Considered in Committee.

(In the Committee.)

Resolved, That it is expedient to authorise the imposition of the following Stamp duties upon certain Memorials under any Act of the present Session relating to the Friends Provident Institution :—

For and upon the first Memorial enrolled of the names of the persons who shall be deemed held and taken to be Trustees of the Institution, or of any special fund of the Institution, the sum of five pounds ; and upon every other such Memorial in which the name of any person shall for the first time be inserted as a Trustee of the Institution the sum of five pounds.—(*Dr. Farquharson.*)

Resolution to be reported upon Monday next.

SINKING FUNDS.

Account presented,—of the Commissioners for the Reduction of the National Debt, showing the amount re-ceived and applied in the year ended 31st March, 1899, in respect of the Old and New Sinking Funds [by Act] ; to lie upon the Table and to be printed. [No. 207.]

NATIONAL DEBT (SAVINGS BANKS).

Copy presented,—of Balance Sheet setting forth the Assets and Liabilities of the Commissioners for the Reduction of the National Debt in respect of Trustee Savings Bank on the 20th November, 1898 [by Act] ; to lie upon the Table, and to be printed. [No. 208.]

SUPERANNUATION ACT, 1884.

Copies presented, — of Treasury Minutes declaring that the under-mentioned Persons were appointed to the Offices set against their names without a Civil Service Certificate, through inadvertence on the part of the Heads of their Departments, viz., James Mills, Turner, Royal Gun Factory, War Department, dated 19th May, 1899 ; Charles Brading, Fitter, Royal Laboratory, War Department, dated 24th May, 1899 [by Act] ; to lie upon the Table.

PARLIAMENTARY RETURNS.

Copy presented,—of Treasury Minute, dated 29th May, 1899, directing the discontinuance of the annual account, under the Savings Banks Moneys Act, 1863, of assets and liabilities of the National Debt Commissioners in respect of Trustee Savings Banks [by Act] ; to lie upon the table.

ALDERSHOT (SEWAGE FARM AND DAIRY).

Copy presented,—of Report on the condition of the Aldershot Camp Sewage Farm and of the Dairy maintained upon it [by Command] ; to lie upon the Table.

COLONIAL REPORTS (ANNUAL).

Copy presented,—of Report, No. 260 (Niger, West African Frontier Force. Reports for 1897-8) [by Command] ; to lie upon the Table.

SUGAR (BOUNTIES, &c.)

Return presented,—relative thereto [ordered 27th April ; Mr. Seale-Hayne] ; to lie upon the Table, and to be printed. [No. 209.]

CAPE OF GOOD HOPE OBSERVATORY.

Copy presented,—of Report of the Astronomer to the Lords Commissioners of the Admiralty for the year 1898 [by Command]; to lie upon the Table.

TREATY SERIES (No. 12, 1899).

Copy presented,—of Accession of Japan to the Industrial Property Convention of 20th March, 1883 [by Command]; to lie upon the Table.

TRADE REPORTS (ANNUAL SERIES).

Copies presented, of Diplomatic and Consular Reports, Annual Series, Nos. 2279 to 2281 (by command); to lie upon the table.

PROSECUTION OF OFFENCES ACT, 1879 and 1884.

Address for "Return showing the working of the Regulations made in 1886 for carrying out the Prosecution of Offences Acts, 1879 and 1884, with statistics setting forth the number, nature, cost, and results of the proceedings instituted by the Director in accordance with those Regulations from the 1st day of January 1898 to the 31st day of December 1898 (in continuation of Parliamentary Paper, No. 204, of Session 1898)."—(*Mr. Jesse Collings.*)

DEATHS FROM WINDOW CLEANING ACCIDENTS.

Address for "Return showing approximately the number of Coroners' Inquests in the county of London during the five years ended 31st day of December 1898 in cases in which persons were killed by falling from windows while engaged in cleaning them."—(*Mr. Provand.*)

LUNACY BILL [*LORDS*].

Read the first time; to be read a second time upon Monday, 12th June, and to be printed. [Bill 225.]

THE SOUDAN EXPEDITION 1898.
PROPOSED GRANT TO LORD KITCHENER OF KHARTOUM.

THE FIRST LORD OF THE TREASURY (Mr. A. J. BALFOUR, Manchester, E.), at the Bar, acquainted the House that he had a Message from Her Majesty to this House, signed by Her Majesty's own hand, and he presented the same to the House; and it was read by Mr. Speaker (all the Members of the House being uncovered), and is as followeth:—

VICTORIA R.

Her Majesty, taking into consideration the eminent services of Major-

General Lord Kitchener of Khartoum, G.C.B., K.C.M.G., in planning and conducting the recent expedition into the Soudan, and being desirous, in recognition of such services, to confer some signal mark of her favour upon him, recommends to her faithful Commons that she should be enabled to grant Lord Kitchener the sum of thirty thousand pounds.

Balmoral.
1st June, 1899.

Ordered, That Her Majesty's Most Gracious Message be referred to the Committee of Supply.—(*Mr. Balfour.*)

MESSAGE FROM THE LORDS.

That they have agreed to,—
Infectious Disease (Notification) Act (1889) Extension Bill, with an Amendment:—
Crowborough District Water Bill, with Amendments.

That they have passed a Bill, intituled, "An Act to dissolve the marriage of Charlotte Jane Jones, the wife of Robert Colvill Jones, with the said Robert Colvill Jones, and to enable her to marry again; and for other purposes." [Jones Divorce Bill [*Lords.*]

Also, a Bill, intituled, "An Act to confer further powers upon the Great Northern Railway Company." [Great Northern Railway Bill [*Lords.*]

And, also, a Bill, intituled, "An Act to enable the Mayor, Aldermen, and Burgesses of the borough of Sunderland to construct additional Tramways in and adjacent to the borough; and for other purposes." [Sunderland Corporation Bill [*Lords.*]

BILLS INTRODUCED.

Trustee Savings Banks,—Bill to amend the Trustee Savings Banks Acts, ordered to be brought in by Sir Albert Rollit, Mr. Campbell, and Mr. Ure.

Trustee Savings Banks Bill,—"to amend the Trustee Savings Banks Acts," presented accordingly, and read the first time; to be read a second time upon Monday next and to be printed. [Bill 226.]

PETITIONS, REPORTS, &c.

BOROUGH FUNDS ACT, 1872.

Petitions for alterations of law ;—from Horncastle ;— Tredegar ; — Nantvglo ;—and, Abertillery ; to lie upon the Table.

BUILDING FEUS AND LEASES (SCOTLAND) BILL.

Petition from Haddington, against ; to lie upon the Table.

COUNTY COUNCILLORS (QUALIFICATION OF WOMEN) (SCOTLAND) BILL.

Petition from Haddington, against ; to lie upon the Table.

CROFTERS' HOLDINGS (SCOTLAND) ACT (1886) AMENDMENT BILL.

Petition from Haddington, against ; to lie upon the Table.

ECCLESIASTICAL ASSESSMENTS (SCOTLAND) BILL.

Petition from Haddington, in favour ; to lie upon the Table.

EDUCATION (SCHOOL ATTENDANCE) (SCOTLAND) BILL.

Petition from Haddington, for alteration ; to lie upon the Table.

EXECUTORS (SCOTLAND) AMENDMENT BILL.

Petition from Haddington, in favour ; to lie upon the Table.

FINE OR IMPRISONMENT (SCOTLAND AND IRELAND) BILL.

Petition from Haddington, in favour ; to lie upon the Table.

FOREIGN SUGAR.

Petition of the Royal Jamaica Society of Agriculture and Commerce and Merchants' Exchange, for imposition of countervailing duties ; to lie upon the Table.

GROUND RENTS (TAXATION BY LOCAL AUTHORITIES).

Petition from Ashton-in-Makerfield, in favour ; to lie upon the Table.

GROUND VALUES (TAXATION) (SCOTLAND) BILL.

Petition from Haddington, against ; to lie upon the Table.

LOCAL GOVERNMENT (SCOTLAND) ACT (1894) AMENDMENT BILL.

Petition from Drainie, in favour ; to lie upon the Table.

LOCAL GOVERNMENT (SCOTLAND) BILL.

Petitions in favour ;—From Elgin ;—and, Haddington ; to lie upon the Table.

MINES (EIGHT HOURS) BILL.

Petitions in favour ; — From Cefn Brithda ; — Cwmtillery (two) ; — New Tredegar ; — Vivian ; — Tillery ; — Burnbank ;—Garswood ;— Tenghenith ;— Darranddu ; — Gyfelach ; — St. George ;—Dunvant ; — Primrose ; — Weig Fawr ;—Elba ;—Fforest Fach ;—Hindley Green ;—Henwain Pit ;—Lower Deep Pit ;—Griffin Pit (No. 2) ; — Clydach ; — Coal Brook Vale ;—North Blaina ;—and, Griffin Pit (No. 3) Collieries ; to lie upon the Table.

PARISH CHURCHES (SCOTLAND) BILL.

Petition from Haddington, in favour ; to lie upon the Table.

POOR LAW OFFICERS' SUPERANNUATION (SCOTLAND) BILL.

Petition from Haddington, in favour ; to lie upon the Table.

PRIVATE LEGISLATION PROCEDURE (SCOTLAND) BILL.

Petitions in favour ;—From Dalkeith ;—and, Haddington ; to lie upon the Table.

PUBLIC LIBRARIES (SCOTLAND) ACTS AMENDMENT BILL.

Petition from Haddington, in favour ; to lie upon the Table.

ROMAN CATHOLIC UNIVERSITY IN IRELAND.

Petition from London, for establishment ; to lie upon the Table.

SALE OF INTOXICATING LIQUORS ON SUNDAY BILL.

Petitions in favour ;—From Dorking ;—Hayle ;—Spitalfields ;—Kingsclere Woodlands ;—Pilton ;— Kemton Mandeville ;—and, Somerton ; to lie upon the Table.

SMALL TENANTS (SCOTLAND) BILL.

Petition from Haddington, against ; to lie upon the Table.

SUCCESSION (SCOTLAND) BILL.

Petition from Haddington, for alteration ; to lie upon the Table.

TEINDS (SCOTLAND) BILL.

Petitions in favour ;—From Elgin ;—and, Haddington ; to lie upon the Table.

TOWN COUNCILS (SCOTLAND) BILL

Petitions in favour ;—From Partick ;—and, Stornoway ; to lie upon the Table.

TROUT FISHING ANNUAL CLOSE TIME (SCOTLAND) BILL.

Petition from Haddington, in favour ; to lie upon the Table.

QUESTIONS.

PROVISIONAL ORDER BILLS.

MR. LLOYD GEORGE (Carnarvon): With regard to the Provisional Order Bills which were in the Paper to-day, may I suggest that it would be for the convenience of the House if the same procedure was followed as in the case of other Bills, and the names inserted instead of the numbers ? I wished, for instance, to know whether one of the Orders in to-day's paper refer to Rhyl.

THE SECRETARY TO THE LOCAL GOVERNMENT BOARD (Mr. T. W. Russell, Tyrone, S.): No. The Rhyl order is not contained in any of the Bills before the House.

RUSSIAN CARGOES FOR TA-LIEN-WAN.

SIR EDWARD GOURLEY (Sunderland) : I beg to ask the Under Secretary of State for Foreign Affairs, if he can inform the House whether British vessels (flying the British flag) are, under existing Russian regulations, permitted to carry cargoes of grain or other lawful merchandise from Black Sea Russian ports to Ta-lien-wan ; and whether the carrying trade from Russian ports will be limited to ships flying the Russian flag when the Trans-Siberian railway is ready for traffic or open to ships of all nations ?

THE UNDER SECRETARY OF STATE FOR FOREIGN AFFAIRS (Mr. ST. JOHN BRODRICK, Surrey, Guildford) : By referring to page 134 of the Blue-Book China No. 1, 1899, the honourable Member will see that the Russian Chargé d'Affaires at Pekin

informed Her Majesty's Minister on 23rd June, 1898, that Ta-lien-wan could not be considered a " port effectivement ouvert " until the establishment of a Customs service similar to that existing at other ports opened by Treaty, and that a declaration to that effect would have to be made to the Representatives of the Treaty Powers. Her Majesty's Government are awaiting such a communication from the Russian Government. No regulation has as yet been issued by the Russian Government confining the carrying trade between Russian ports and Ta-lien-wan to Russian ships.

BRITISH TRADERS AT CANTON.

*MR. HATCH (Lancs., Gorton) : I beg to ask the Under Secretary of State for Foreign Affairs, whether the Chinese authorities at Canton have objected to the establishment by Messrs. Banher and Company, British subjects resident there, of business premises in the native city of Canton ; whether Messrs. Banher and Company in establishing such premises are acting within treaty rights ; and, such being the case, whether Her Majesty's Government have taken any steps to ensure the enforcement of such rights ?

*MR. BRODRICK : A British subject named Banker having intimated towards the end of last year his desire to open a piece goods shop in the native city of Canton, the Viceroy requested Her Majesty's Consul to order Banker to close it, basing his opposition on the 3rd section of the Chefoo Convention. The Consul in reply pointed out that the section in question was abrogated by the Additional Article signed in 1885, and stated that he was informing Mr. Banker that he was at liberty to pursue his business, but that, in the event of the two Governments subsequently deciding that the area of exemption from likin was to be confined to the foreign concessions, he would be liable to the payment of likin.

SIERRA LEONE.

MR. HEDDERWICK (Wick Burghs): I beg to ask the Secretary of State for the Colonies when the report of Sir David Chalmers upon the origin of the troubles in the hinterland of Sierra Leone will be laid upon the Table of the House.

The SECRETARY OF STATE FOR THE COLONIES (Mr. J. CHAMBERLAIN, Birmingham, W.): As I have already stated, I sent the report to Sir F. Cardew for his observations. I have now received these and am considering them with the report. Both documents are very lengthy, and some considerable delay has taken place in printing them. No time will be lost in coming to a conclusion on the numerous questions raised, but I am sorry to say it is not possible for me to fix a date for laying the Papers on the Table, although I hope they will be ready in a fortnight or three weeks.

MR. HEDDERWICK: Will the report be laid on the Table before the Colonial vote is taken ?

MR. J. CHAMBERLAIN: I do not think any date has as yet been fixed for the Colonial vote. It is always a matter of arrangement between the two sides of the House.

ALDERSHOT SEWAGE FARM.

MR. J. G. TALBOT (Oxford University): On behalf of the hon. Member for North Hants I beg to ask the Under Secretary of State for War whether he has received the report of the medical officer appointed by the War Office to inspect the Camp Sewage Farm at Aldershot. And, whether it is still proposed to supply the troops with milk from this farm.

The UNDER SECRETARY OF STATE FOR WAR (MR. G. WYNDHAM, Dover): The report has been received, and will be laid on the table of the House to-day. There has been no question of supplying the troops with this milk as part of their rations. The question has been whether they should be prohibited from purchasing it. Dr. Andrewes' report contains nothing which would warrant such a prohibition. It does, however, suggest one improvement in the arrangement of the farm, the cost of which is now being investigated.

CIVIL SERVICE PAY DEDUCTIONS.

CAPTAIN NORTON (Newington, W.): I beg to ask the Secretary of the Treasury, whether, in view of the fact that the granting of retired pay to an officer represents the conclusion of a bargain between an officer and the service he has left, in view, further, of the fact that the amount received by the Treasury from deductions made from the pay of retired officers of the Army and Navy employed in the Civil Service is so comparatively small, amounting to some £3,600 a year, he will secure officers in the possession of what is admittedly their own, and allow them to hold, without deduction from the salary, any appointments they may be fortunate enough to obtain in the Civil Service ; and, whether he is aware that the deductions made from the pay of officers retired from the Army or Navy who are employed in the Civil Service, compared with the total amount received of effective and non-effective pay, vary from 90 per cent. to about 2 per cent.

The FINANCIAL SECRETARY TO THE TREASURY (Mr. R. W. HANBURY, Preston): I have already explained that any change in the present practice would require fresh legislation. I cannot find any instance in which the amount of deduction approaches 90 per cent. The usual deduction is 10 per cent. The deduction of (roughly) 2 per cent. to which the hon. Member refers is explained by the fact that, under Rule 4, the total emoluments of an officer may not be reduced by abatement to less than £400 per annum.

FATALITIES AMONG RAILWAY SERVANTS.

MR. CHANNING (Northampton, E.): I beg to ask the President of the Board of Trade what has been the number of railway servants killed by accidents in which the movement of vehicles used exclusively on railways was concerned in the year 1898 ; and, what has been the number of such fatal accidents investigated in 1898 by inspectors or sub-inspectors of the Board of Trade.

The PRESIDENT OF THE BOARD OF TRADE (Mr. C. J. RITCHIE, Croydon): The number of railway servants killed in 1898 was 490. The number of fatal accidents inquired into was 116.

THE KHARTOUM PRISONERS.

MR. PIRIE (Aberdeen, N.): I beg to ask the Under Secretary of State for Foreign Affairs whether he has obtained information from the Egyptian Government as to the number of Europeans and Egyptians released by the capture of Khartoum ; and if he can give the same to the House, stating their various nationalities, and the number of men and women respectively.

*MR. BRODRICK: We have received the following statement from Lord Cromer of the number of prisoners released subsequently to the Battle of Omdurman :—

INCLOSURE 1 IN No. 1.

STATEMENT OF NUMBER OF PRISONERS RELEASED AFTER THE BATTLE OF OMDURMAN.

1. Government prisoners, military and civilian, in Omdurman, mostly Egyptians and Turks (approximate)   8,676
2. Government prisoners, military and civilian, in the Soudan, other than Omdurman, mostly Egyptians and Turks (approximate)..   1,324
3. Christian prisoners in Omdurman, other than Copts   ...   213
4. Coptic prisoners in Omdurman   562
5. Abyssinian refugees in Omdurman   272

Total (approximately) ... 11,047
Subtract 193 Copts, who were Government employees, and are included in paragraphs 1 and 2...   193

Approximate total of Soudan refugees who were released by Government after the Battle of Omdurman   ... 10,854

There were 177 Christian and 36 Jew prisoners found in Omdurman after the Battle, who may be divided as follows, according to nationality :—

Austrians	... 2	women out of total	4
Greeks	... 45	,, ,,	94
Italians	... 6	,, ,,	12
Cypriots	... 4	,, ,,	10
Armenians	... 1	,, ,,	4
Syrians	... 23	,, ,,	50
English (Lupton Bey's family)	... 3	,, ,,	3
Jews	... 18	,, ,,	36
			213

FEVER AMONG THE SOUDANESE TROOPS.

MR. PIRIE: I beg to ask the Under Secretary of State for Foreign Affairs whether the epidemic of cerebro-spinal fever is still prevalent among the Native troops in the Soudan ; and what are the latest reports as to their health and mortality.

*MR. BRODRICK: We have heard no more on the subject since my answer to the honourable Member's Question on 14th April, when I stated that the epidemic was abating.

IRISH LIGHTS.

MR. WILLIAM ALLAN (Gateshead): I beg to ask the President of the Board of Trade when the new lighthouse and fog signal are to be erected on the Black Head, Ireland ; and, when is a new lighthouse to be erected at the Maiden Rocks, Ireland.

MR. RITCHIE: I am informed by the Commissioners of Irish Lights that a site has been obtained for the new lighthouse and fog signal on the Black Head, and that the work will be proceded with at at once. No proposal for a new lighthouse at the Maiden Rocks is before the Board of Trade.

MR. W. ALLAN: Is the right hon. Gentleman aware that the present lighthouse is 70 years old?

MR. RITCHIE: I do not know its age.

QUEEN'S BIRTHDAY CELEBRATION AT SOUTHSEA.

MR. GIBSON BOWLES (Lynn Regis): I beg to ask the Under Secretary of State for War whether, after considerable preparations had been made for the celebration of Her Majesty's birthday on the 24th May at Southsea, the general in command of the troops, in consequence of the falling of a slight shower of rain, ordered the flag to be hauled down and the parade to be cancelled ; whether he can say if the parade was thus cancelled in consequence of an apprehension of the damage that might have been done, either to the men's uniforms or to their arms by rain ; and, if not, what the reason was for the cancelling of the parade and the disappointment of the numerous spectators who had come by train and otherwise to see it ; and, whether he is aware that, in spite of the rain, a detachment from H.M.S. "Excellent," of 900 officers and men, with six field guns, came to and remained on the ground, re-hoisted the flag, went through various evolutions, fired a *feu de joie*, and returned to H.M.S. "Excellent."

MR. WYNDHAM : The Queen's Birthday parade was countermanded in view of heavy rain falling at the time when the troops were parading. At 11.20 the rain ceased, but owing to the distribution of the troops in widely separate quarters it would then have been impossible to effect a concentration in time.

LEVEL CROSSINGS.—DESBOROUGH RAILWAY FATALITY.

MR. CHANNING (Northampton, E.): I beg to ask the President of the Board of Trade why the Board of Trade did not send a representative to attend the inquest, held at Desborough on Thursday, 25th May, on two persons killed at the level crossing at Desborough Station on Saturday, 20th May, although the coroner specially adjourned the inquest from Saturday to the following Thursday to enable the Board to be represented ; whether he has considered the rider appended to their verdict by the jury blaming the Midland Railway Company for not providing an official to warn passengers crossing, and for not providing a safe means of crossing at this station ; whether he is aware that on Tuesday, 23rd May, about a dozen people were exposed to serious risk from an express train while crossing the line at the same place ; whether an inquiry will be held by an Inspector of the Board of Trade ; and, whether he will now bring in legislation giving powers to the Board of Trade to make compulsory orders to supply footbridges or subways when necessary ?

THE PRESIDENT OF THE BOARD OF TRADE (Mr. RITCHIE, Croydon): The Board of Trade do not send representatives to attend inquests unless the coroner applies for the appointment of an assessor under Section 8 of the Regulation of Railways Act, 1871. No application was made by the Coroner. The Board of Trade have communicated with the Midland Railway Company with regard to the rider to the verdict of the Coroner's Jury. I was not aware of the occurrence to which the hon. Member refers as having taken place on the 23rd ultimo. If necessary an inquiry will be held by one of the Board's inspectors. I do not propose to introduce any legislation on the subject.

MR. CHANNING : Do I understand the right hon. Gentleman to say that an inquiry will be held into the amount of risk at this special crossing, or will it be into the accident itself ?

MR. RITCHIE : Not into the accident. That is not necessary, having regard to the evidence given before the coroner's inquest. The inquiry to which I refer is in respect of the risk to which people are exposed from express trains, having regard to the fact that there is no bridge over the line.

MR. CHANNING : Will that inquiry be held ?

MR. RITCHIE : I have told the hon. Gentleman it will be held if necessary. We are in communication with the railway company on the subject, and I cannot yet say definitely one way or the other.

MR. CHANNING : The right honr Gentleman has implied that a coroner must make application in the specific form set out in section 8 of the Act of 1871. I should like to ask him whether the letter of which I have a copy here, and which was sent to the Board of Trade by the coroner, explaining that he had specially adjourned the inquest of five days in order to admit of the Board of Trade being represented, is not sufficient for the purpose ?

MR. RITCHIE : Certainly not. Before a Board of Trade Inspector is sent to an inquest, a request to that effect must be made by the coroner. The letter to which the hon. Gentleman refers was not a request at all. It was simply a statement that the inquest had been adjourned so that, if the Board of Trade thought it necessary, they could send an inspector. The Board of Trade did not think it necessary. No application was made under the Act.

SOUTH AFRICAN REPUBLIC.—THE KILLING OF MR. EDGAR.

MR. GRIFFITH (Anglesey): I beg to ask the Secretary of State for the Colonies whether an application has been made to the Government of the South African Republic for compensation to Mrs. Edgar, the wife of Mr. Edgar, who was recently killed by a policeman at Johannesburg; and, if so, what reply has been received to such application?

MR. J. CHAMBERLAIN: Mrs. Edgar has asked Her Majesty's Government to apply to the Government of the South African Republic for compensation to her and her child for the death of her husband. The matter is under consideration. No application has been made.

FRENCH CLAIMS ON CHINA.

*SIR EDWARD SASSOON (Hythe): I beg to ask the Under Secretary of State for Foreign Affairs whether he is aware that the French Consul at Chungking, under the guise of a demand for compensation for losses arising from missionary troubles, is officially pressing for exclusive mining rights in certain districts of Szechuen province on both sides of the Yangtze river; and, whether it is the intention of Her Majesty's Government to take any action in the matter?

*MR. BRODRICK: Recent reports received from our Consul at Chungking allude to endeavours on the part of a French firm to secure a kerosine concession, but make no mention of any application for mining rights. It would not be open to the French to obtain exclusive rights. The Anglo-French Declaration of 1898 provides that any advantages conceded to either Great Britain or France in Yunnan and Szechuen shall, as far as rests with them, be extended and rendered common to both Powers. Her Majesty's Consul at Chungking will be asked to report on the question.

INLAND REVENUE.—STAMPING OF ADVERTISEMENT ORDERS.

MR. HAZELL (Leicester): I beg to ask Mr. Chancellor of the Exchequer whether his attention has been called to a decision of Mr. Commissioner Kerr in the City of London Court, on 3rd January last, in reference to the stamping of written orders for advertisements; whether it appeared that the Commissioner objected to such an order being used as evidence because it had not been stamped with a sixpenny stamp, being a contract above the value of £5, and in consequence the plaintiff was non-suited

with costs; whether the Commissioner is correctly reported to have stated that the Inland Revenue Commissioners advised that all such contracts ought to be stamped, and that, in fact, a £10 penalty had been exacted from several suitors recently; whether he is aware that it is not the custom to stamp such orders; and, whether he can promote legislation exempting such orders from stamp duty?

THE CHANCELLOR OF THE EXCHEQUER (Sir MICHAEL HICKS-BEACH, Bristol, W.): My attention has been called to the case referred to. From the terms of the question it may be gathered that the plaintiff produced the order as evidence of a contract. That being so, it ought, on the plaintiff's own showing, to have been stamped as an "agreement," and under Section 14 of the Stamp Act, 1891, the Court could not admit it as evidence of a contract, except on payment of the Stamp Duty and the prescribed penalty. As regards legislation, none seems necessary. An order, *quâ* order, does not require a stamp; but if the order is given under such circumstances as to constitute it a memorandum of an agreement, or is relied upon as evidence of a contract, then it ought to be stamped as an agreement.

ROYAL COMMISSION ON INDIAN EXPENDITURE.

SIR MANCHERJEE BHOWNAG-GREE (Bethnal Green, N.E.): I beg to ask the Secretary of State for India whether he has received any reply to the letter addressed by him on the 15th ult. to the Secretary of the Royal Commission on Indian Expenditure, regarding the long delay that had occurred in the submission of its Report; and, if so, will he state its contents to the House?

THE SECRETARY OF STATE FOR INDIA (LORD GEORGE HAMILTON, Middlesex, Ealing): I have received some personal replies from individual members of the Commission, but I am not yet in a position to give the general sense of the Commissioners. As regards the draft Report, I am informed that, of the three portions of which it is composed, two have already been circulated, or are in the act of being circulated for the approval of the Commission.

SIR M. BHOWNAGGREE: Is there any likelihood of the report being issued before the end of the Session.

LORD GEORGE HAMILTON: That is a question I cannot answer.

INDIAN SUGAR TRADE.

CAPTAIN SINCLAIR (Forfar): I beg to ask the Secretary of State for India whether he is now in a position to give the House the complete figures of the exports and imports of sugar from and into India for the year ending 31st March 1899, distinguishing raw sugar from refined.

LORD GEORGE HAMILTON: The exports of sugar from India in tee year ending 31st March 1899 (including re-imported sugar) were as follows:—Raw, 289,668 cwts.; refined, 208,899 cwts. The imports for the same period were as follows:—Raw, 312,778 cwts.; refined, 3,764,910 cwts.

CAPTAIN SINCLAIR: I beg to ask the Secretary of State for India whether he can give particulars of the exports of refined sugar from India to Ceylon during the past few years; and whether the refined sugar so exported is native-refined or a re-export of foreign-refined.

LORD GEORGE HAMILTON: On page 110 of the recent Countervailing Duties Blue Book the hon. Member will find two tables giving details of Indian sugar exports to Ceylon and other countries. The tables distinguish between refined and unrefined sugar. All the sugar shown in the two tables 36 and 37 is Indian sugar. The re-exports of foreign refined sugar from India to Ceylon were small, and so were not shown separately in the Blue-book.

ORDER OF BUSINESS.

CAPTAIN SINCLAIR: I beg to ask the First Lord of the Treasury when he proposes to take Scotch Estimates, and, in particular, the Scotch Education vote?

MR. A. J. BALFOUR: Perhaps it will be convenient for hon. Gentlemen representing Scotland to fix this day fortnight as the day for taking Scotch Supply. Next Friday, as they are aware, is allocated to the Foreign Office Vote.

MR. BOULNOIS (Marylebone, E.): When will the London Government Bill be next taken?

MR. BALFOUR: I shall put the London Government Bill as the first Order for Monday, simply in order to avoid Monday, which will be devoted to discussing in Committee of Supply the Vote to Lord Kitchener, being counted as an allotted day under the Supply Rule. But immediately the Order is called on I shall postpone it, and I propose to take it second on Tuesday, and if not on Tuesday, I shall take it as the first Order on Thursday.

MR. J. MORLEY (Montrose, &c): I believe we are right in assuming that the Government, in reference to the proposed Vote to Lord Kitchener, does not intend to proceed by way of Bill, but by some method—which I confess I do not quite myself understand—by which a Vote can be procured by a mere resolution in Committee?

MR. A. J. BALFOUR: It is hardly a resolution in Committee. It is a Vote in Committee of Supply. The precedent followed is that of 1874, when a sum of money was voted by this House to Lord Wolseley. The alternative method of proceeding by Bill, which was adopted in 1884, seems to be more cumbrous, and might lead to prolonged and quite unnecessary discussion, and would not in effect have any different result from a Vote in Committee of Supply. It is necessary that I should adopt this technical device of putting the London Government Bill down first, otherwise one of the days allocated to Supply would be exhausted on this Vote, and that would, I think, be a misuse of the rule.

MR. J. MORLEY: It does not come up in the Estimates in any other form?

MR. A. J. BALFOUR: It is an Estimate; it will be passed in Committee of Supply, and there will be a Report stage.

MR. DILLON (Mayo, E.): Am I correct in saying that the Government stated, at an early period of this Session, that this Vote would be granted by way of Bill?

Mr. A. J. BALFOUR: No; I think not. I have always contemplated this procedure.

Sir W. LAWSON (Cumberland, Cockermouth): Will it be possible for the right hon. Gentleman to make his statement on behalf of this grant in Committee?

Mr. A. J. BALFOUR: Yes, sir.

Mr. J. REDMOND (Waterford): I wish to ask the right hon. Gentleman whether any arrangement has been come to as to the time for taking the Irish estimates. I have reason to believe that at the commencement of the week after next some important Irish business will be before the House, which will necessitate a large attendance of Irish members, and if the Irish estimates can be taken at the same time it would be a very great convenience.

Mr. A. J. BALFOUR: The date to which the hon. Gentleman refers has already been allocated to Scotland. I will, however, inquire whether any arrangement can be arrived at which will be agreeable to both parties. I shall be very glad to meet the general views.

Captain PRETYMAN (Suffolk, Woodbridge): What will be the first Order on Tuesday?

Mr. A. J. BALFOUR: The first Order on Tuesday will be the Finance Bill.

Mr. DRAGE (Derby): When will the Small Houses Bill be taken?

Mr. A. J. BALFOUR: I cannot give any forecast at present. It will depend on the progress made with the London Government Bill.

SUPPLY [12TH ALLOTTED DAY].

Considered in Committee.

(In the Committee.)

CIVIL SERVICES AND REVENUE DEPARTMENTS ESTIMATES, 1899–1900.

CLASS II.

Motion made, and Question proposed—

" That a sum, not exceeding £132,732, be granted to Her Majesty, to complete the sum necessary to defray the charge which will come in course of payment during the year ending on the 31st day of March, 1900, for the salaries and expenses of the Local Government Board."

*Mr. PICKERSGILL (Bethnal Green, S.W.): I wish to call attention to the administrative action of the right hon. Gentleman the President of the Local Government Board in regard to vaccination. I do not intend to dwell upon the violent and unconstitutional language that has been made use of to applicants for exemption certificates, whose only offence is that they have desired to exercise the right which the High Court of Parliament has granted to them, beyond to say that it is noteworthy that language of that kind has not been indulged in since the session began. The gravamen of my complaint against the Local Government Board and the right hon. Gentleman is this: that he has by his action encouraged vaccination officers to flout their employers and paymasters, the boards of guardians. There has been, as I shall show, a distinct change in the relations between boards of guardians and vaccination officers — a change entirely due to the action of the right hon. Gentleman. Prior to the recent action of the right hon. Gentleman the relations between them were governed by a general order, dated October, 1874, which prescribed that the guardians should in cases of default of vaccination cause proceedings to be taken, and for that purpose should give directions authorising the vaccination officers to institute and conduct them. There was no doubt as to the construction to be put on the terms of that order; the guardians might either give special directions in each individual case, or such general directions as would enable the officer to initiate the proceedings without first referring to them. Thus, while it was within the competency of boards of guardians if they chose to give general directions, yet, in the absence of such directions, it was the duty of the officer to lay each individual case before the guardians, and take their directions upon it. That order was acted upon for a quarter of a century—until the right hon. Gentleman came upon the scene. Now let me call attention to the terms of the order for which the right hon. Gentleman is responsible. It is dated the 18th October last, and provides that at the end of seven days after the expiration of six months from the birth of the child the vaccination officer shall give to the parent notice to vaccinate the child, and if that notice is not duly complied with it will become the duty of the vaccination officer to take proceedings under the Act of 1871 for the enforcement of the law. This new order, it will be seen, gives the go-by entirely to the board of guardians: it says the duty shall be independently exercised by the vaccination officer under the Vaccination Act, 1871, although the order of 1874, which gave the control to the guardians was issued three years after the Act of 1871 became law. Now, the contention that the vaccination officer is independent of the board of guardians in these proceedings is an entirely new contention. It has originated with the right hon. Gentleman, and for 25 years before his intervention the Local Government Board interpreted the law in an opposite sense and declared that the vaccination officers should look to the board of guardians for instructions to prosecute.. I refer to the Keighley case in 1875. It is inconceivable that the Local Government Board should have taken the extreme step of sending the Keighley Board of Guardians to prison if there had then prevailed at the Local Government Board the contention the Board now makes, that the vaccination officer can take proceedings altogether independent of the board of guardians. One of these authorities is so recent that I quote it because of the significancy of the date. I refer to what is called the Reading letter, indited by the Local Government Board in January, 1898. At that time a vaccination officer wrote to the Local Government Board asking if he should prosecute defaulting parents in spite of the directions of the board of guardians to the contrary. The reply was that he was to obey the board of guardians. The date of that letter is significant, because the right hon. Gentleman says in explanation of the change of policy, that he relies on the decision of the Queen's Bench in the case of Bramble and Lowe. Now that case was decided in 1897, and six months after we have the Local Government Board giving the same instructions which had been given for 25 years, viz., that the vaccination officer must obey the board of guardians. Let me say a word in regard to the Bramble and Lowe case. The right hon. Gentleman has entirely misunderstood, or at all events misstated, the effect of the decision of the Queen's Bench Division. Bramwell and Lowe is no authority for the proposition that the vaccination officer can prosecute without the sanction of the board of guardians. In Bramble and Lowe the guardians had given the vaccination officer concerned a general authority to institute and conduct proceedings against all persons in default under the Vaccination Acts. If they gave this general authority to prosecute all persons, that was equivalent to giving authority to prosecute in every individual case ; and therefore they were only carrying out the old instructions under the Act of 1874, that the guardians, if they choose, might give a general authority to their officers. So that the Bramble and Lowe case does not help the right hon. Gentleman. This question as to the relations between the vaccination officer and his guardians was raised last year in the discussion on the Vaccination Bill. I, myself, raised it. I had upon the Paper a clause which would have made the matter perfectly clear. The clause was as follows :—

"Notwithstanding anything contained in the Vaccination Acts, no parent or other person having the custody of a child shall be prosecuted for neglecting or refusing to vaccinate such child unless and until the sanction of the guardians has been obtained for such prosecution."

I proposed that clause, but withdrew it in consequence of the pledge which was given by the right hon. Gentleman opposite. I will remind the committee what that pledge was. I quote from *Hansard.* The right hon. Gentleman said—

"I am very sorry that the hon. Member thought it necessary to move this clause."

Then he refers to something which he had said before, and he adds—

"What I stated then was altogether out of date after what I stated this afternoon. Since the debate of last night I have quite recognised the fact that the administration of a compulsory vaccination law would be neither necessary nor desirable."

That seems tolerably clear in itself, but if anything were required to clinch the matter it was supplied by the speeches following the declaration of the right hon. Gentleman. For instance, my hon. friend, the Member for Shoreditch, who immediately followed, thought that the declaration made by the right hon. Gentleman sufficiently met the case, and he suggested that the amendment should be withdrawn. Thereupon followed my hon. friend the member for Northampton, who was not altogether satisfied, and pointed out, as was indeed perfectly true, that although, as we understood, the pledge would bind the right hon. gentleman personally, it would not bind his successors. The hon. member for Northampton said at the close of his speech—

"We have got what we want, but at the same time I think that if this clause were carried it would simply embody in the Bill the pledge which the right hon. Gentleman has given us."

Then the hon. member for Caithness said—

"We have got the pledge of the President of the Local Government Board that he will not do anything to interfere with the relations between the vaccination officers and the guardians—that he will not put it into force."

These statements sufficiently show how the House understood the pledge of the right hon. Gentleman. The right hon. Gentleman was present; he accepted the interpretation which we all on this side of the House put upon his declaration, and therefore I thought I was justified in withdrawing my amendment, and I did withdraw it. There can be no doubt that the right hon. Gentleman has misled the House of Commons, unintentionally of course. But the invariable practice of the House has been that in a cases where a Minister of the Crown has misled the House of Commons, however unintentionally, the Minister of the Crown should be held to be bound by the pledge in the sense in which the House understood it, and on which the House acted. Before I pass from this point I desire to refer to another matter not so important, but still sufficiently important. That is the question of the circulation of pro - vaccination papers by the Boards of Guardians. Quite recently the right hon. Gentleman has informed the Boards of Guardians that they are entitled to circulate at the pu l c expense pamphlets issued by the Jenner Society. What is the Jenner Society? It is an association whose publications have been recently described by no mean authority — Lord Grimthorpe —

Mr. Pickersgill.

as "controversial fireworks," and as publications "more likely to defeat than to promote the object the society have in view." Well, I certainly do not object to the circulation of the pamphlets of the Jenner Society on the ground that they are likely to injure the cause of anti-vaccination; but I do object to the circulation at the public expense of these worthless and misleading publications. I say it is not the business of a public Department to boom a private association and to circulate its publications at the public cost. It is most objectionable and may easily degenerate into a great public scandal. This question was discussed when the Vaccination Bill was before the House last year. There was a clause in that Bill to the effect that any Local authority might incur expense in diffusing information as to the advantages of vaccination, but the overwhelming preponderance of the opinion of the House was against public expenditure being incurred for any such purpose. A Division was taken upon that, and the clause was defeated by 270 to 49. In these circumstances I have called attention to these matters, and in order to do so effectively I have moved the reduction of the salary of the right hon. Gentleman. It seems to me that the present condition of things is intolerable; that Boards of Guardians should be compelled to appoint and to pay a vaccination officer who, the moment he is appointed, can flout his employers. That appears to me to be reducing local self-government to an absurdity. There are other incidental disadvantages attaching to the present condition of things. As the vaccination officers are paid by fees, they have a direct pecuniary interest in promoting prosecutions. That is most undesirable, and is really returning to the old system of common informers, only under more aggravated circumstances. Another incidental disadvantage is the strained relations that are created between the guardians and the vaccination officers. The former refuse legal assistance to the latter, and the consequence is that the vaccination officers rush into court unprepared, their summonses are dismissed, and an easy popular triumph is achieved by the class of persons whom hon. gentlemen opposite denounce and whom they desire to discourage. It is impossible to exaggerate the extreme inconvenience arising from the present condition of things, which is entirely due to the action of the right hon. Gentleman. It is not due to any change in the law, but is simply the result of Departmental action for which the right hon. Gentleman is responsible. It is that action of which I now complain. I beg, therefore, to move the reduction of the vote.

Motion made, and Question proposed—

"That Item A (Salaries) be reduced by £100, in respect of the Salary of the President of the Local Government Board."— (*Mr. Pickersgill.*)

THE PRESIDENT OF THE LOCAL GOVERNMENT BOARD (MR. CHAPLIN, Lincolnshire, Sleaford): As the hon. Gentleman has thought fit to charge me with having misled Parliament, I think, perhaps, it is right that I should reply to the statement that he has made without delay. In the first place, I would refer to one of the small points that he has raised, in order to clear that out of the way. The hon. Member complains that the Local Government Board sanctioned expenditure for the circulation of literature in order to promote vaccination throughout the country, and that, he says, is a most improper practice, and an entirely new one.

*MR. PICKERSGILL : I did not say it was entirely new.

MR. CHAPLIN : Then I fail to see exactly what point there is in the hon. Member's remark. It has been the practice of the Local Government Board for the last 20 years or more to give a sanction of this kind. The sanction is given under Section 28 of the Vaccination Act of 1867, and as I believe that the effect of this practice has been to promote vaccination, and not, as the hon. member says, to interfere with it, I see no reason whatever to alter the practice in this respect. The hon. Gentleman proceeded at great length and in much detail to give to the House his version of the history of the prosecutions connected with the present position of vaccination officers in regard to the various boards of guardians. The gravamen of his complaint against me is that I have done all I can to teach the vaccination officers to flout the guardians. He says that, under the order of 1867, it was the duty of the vaccination officers to take their instruc-

VOL. LXXII.   [FOURTH SERIES.]

tions from the guardians, and for 25 years that was the invariable practice until I came on the scene and intervened. And why did I intervene, or, rather, why did someone else intervene ? A case was tried. The hon. Member will have his opinion, and he will allow me to have mine. He will allow me also to remind him, as I have told him repeatedly in the House before, that that opinion is supported by that of the law officers of two different Governments. It was the Law Courts which intervened in 1897, and the judgment was that the power of the officers to institute proceedings was given by Act of Parliament, and that they did not require any special directions. Now comes the question of the amendment which the hon. Member alleges was withdrawn by him upon a specific pledge by myself.

*MR. PICKERSGILL : Certainly.

MR. CHAPLIN : I recollect perfectly well what happened upon that occasion. On the 19th of July the Government made a concession with regard to the case of conscientious objectors which everybody will perfectly recollect, and on the following day (Wednesday) the hon. Member moved his amendment. On that day, also, I made a statement explaining the grounds upon which I consented to the concession which the Government had made, and, as far as I can remember, if was received by gentlemen on that side of the House with a general chorus of approval, and far too flattering things were said with regard to the attitude taken by me on that occasion. During the interval for lunch, exactly the same thing happened in the lobby. Hon. Gentleman after hon. Gentleman came up to me and congratulated me upon the position we had taken, expressing themselves perfectly satisfied. But that was not all. The Paper was still crowded with amendments, and they intimated their intention to take them off forthwith. There was one exception, and that was the hon. Member for Bethnal Green.

*MR. PICKERSGILL : That is not so.

MR. CHAPLIN : I do not think there was an amendment of the smallest importance moved, and I do not think there was one pressed to a Division.

G

*MR. PICKERSGILL: Mine was not pressed to a Division.

MR. CHAPLIN: I very well remember what happened. The hon. Member for the Harborough Division, the hon. Member for Shoreditch, and the hon. Member for Leicester addressed to me some kindly observations, and said, "We will do all we can to get the hon. Member for Bethnal Green to withdraw his amendment," and when we came back from luncheon there was a good deal of conversation going on upon the opposite benches, and I presume they were trying to persuade the hon. Member that the amendment was altogether unnecessary. Apparently, however, it was without effect, because when we resumed our sitting the hon. Member moved his amendment, and as soon as his amendment was moved I got up and replied declining altogether to accept it. I had already explained either that morning or the night before to the hon. Member what was the law on the subject, and as I have been challenged I think it is only fair that I should take the liberty of reminding the House of what was stated on the subject between the hon. Member and myself. Speaking of myself, the hon. Member made this observation—

"He now says not under this Bill, and that is just the point. It is not under the powers given by this Bill. It is under the powers of the Act of 1874; where the guardians did not prosecute to his satisfaction he intended to authorise the vaccination officers to initiate prosecutions, not only on the authority of their employers, the guardians, but in the face of their distinct resolutions to the contrary."

That was the charge made against me by the hon. Member. I replied:

"I do not think my hon. friend could have been in the Committee when I made my reply to that point. I pointed out to the Committee that the power and duty of the vaccination officers were imposed upon them by Act of Parliament, and not by regulations, and that it was under the Act of Parliament that they would have to perform their duty."

Well, then he made a further observation, in which I think he was equally incorrect, and I proceeded—

"The hon. Gentleman is entirely mistaken; the case has been submitted to law officers of two different Governments, and it has also been tried in the Court of Queen's Bench, and it was there decided that the power and duty

of the vaccination officers to institute prosecutions was given under an Act of Parliament without any instructions whatever."

Well, that was my interpretation of the law, which I believe to have been absolutely correct, and having given that version of the law I declined to accept the amendment of the hon. Member, as he knows perfectly well. After that the hon. Member withdrew his amendment. Now he comes forward and says he withdrew his amendment on an assurance given by me. Sir, I absolutely deny that I gave any assurance whatever of any sort or kind upon the subject. Why should I have done so? I did not care twopence whether he withdrew his amendment or not. I believe I am speaking the truth when I say that he was urged before the debate began by many of his own friends, or by some of his own friends to withdraw it.

*MR. PICKERSGILL: I am sorry to interrupt the right hon. Gentleman, but his constant statements of what occurred between myself and my friends are the reverse of the facts. Many of my hon. friends, conspicuously the hon. Member for Northampton, strongly objected to my withdrawing the amendment, and were really very angry with me because I did withdraw it.

MR. CHAPLIN: It is a matter of perfect indifference to me whether the hon. Member withdrew the amendment or not, for it is perfectly certain that he would have been defeated by an enormous majority. In the second place, I want to point out that I cannot have given the assurance which he supposes I gave, because any interference on my part with the proceedings of the vaccination officers as regards prosecutions would have been entirely superfluous and ineffectual. The hon. Member says that he relies on my speech on the point. The answer to that is very simple and very complete. I was shown an extract from a paper a day or two ago, in which it was stated that the report of the speech cannot have been inaccurate because it was corrected by myself. On that point I must say that the speech was never corrected. It was wholly inaccurate from beginning to end. It so happened during those debates I had such complaints to make of the persistent inaccuracy of the reports that I desired my secretary to communicate with the responsible authority on the subject. I believe every one of my speeches, or nearly every one, was marked with an asterisk, indicating that I had corrected it. I corrected one speech, and only one, and that was the speech after the concession had been made with regard to the conscientious objector. Not only that, but I have a letter of apology from the responsible authority expressing his great regret that the speech which has been referred to by the hon. Member was marked with an asterisk. It was never corrected at all, although it appears in the volume of *Hansard* as if it were What did I say upon that occasion? I cannot now give the exact words, but the effect was that after the very great concession made by the Government on the question, the speech of the hon. Member appeared to me to be altogether out of date, and that in my opinion the amendment was, in view of the concession, uncalled for and unnecessary, and on that ground I declined to accept it. In fact, that concession, in my view, and certainly in the view of nine Members out of ten on that side of the House, was everything that was necessary. That was shown by the speech made by another very ardent anti-vaccinationist, if he will forgive me for calling him so, the hon. Member for Northampton, who the same afternoon expressed his appreciation of the speech of the President of the Local Government Board. He urged that we should not go on splitting hairs on this matter, but that the declaration of the First Lord of the Treasury that there should be no going behind a man's conscientious objection should be carried out. That was evidently the expression of the general feeling on that side of the House on that afternoon. This is the very simple explanation of what occurred, and I am bound to say that I think the hon. Member has very greatly distorted it, unintentionally, I am quite sure. With all respect, I contend that it would have been quite impossible for any Minister in charge of a Bill to be more open in connection with this particular branch of the question than I was during the whole of those debates. There was no obligation on my part on the second reading of the Bill to tell the House what I had in my mind with regard to the future on this particular subject. I saw an observation in the Press that I blurted it out by mistake, and that I made a great blunder in doing so. As a matter of fact, I did it inten-

tionally in order that the House should be aware what I had in my mind on this particular subject. Having made this statement to the House, and having warned them what was before them, I had a majority of over 10 to 1 in favour of the second reading of the Bill. It is certainly not my fault that any misunderstanding has occurred. It is the fault of the hon. Member himself and those who agree with him if they did not understand the position. Then, passing from that subject, the hon. Member complains that it is to the direct interest of the vaccination officers under the present system to make as many vaccinations as they can. That may appear intolerant to the hon. Member and others who are anxious to do everything in their power to prevent vaccination. But to us it is the reverse of intolerance, and one of its great advantages is that it has the effect of promoting vaccination. I am thankful to believe—and it is a matter of great congratulation, although it may be very distasteful to some hon. Gentlemen opposite—that under the Act of last year vaccination is growing more steadily and to a greater extent than for many years past. We look upon it, of course, from totally opposite points of view. I desire to do everything in my power to promote vaccination; the hon. Member and some of his friends desire to do everything in their power to prevent it. That is the real issue between us, and that is the source of the complaint made against me. With regard to the particular charge of the hon. Member, nothing could have been more open than my attitude on the subject. I should think it would have been one of the greatest mistakes I ever made in my life if I did not refuse to accept the amendment moved by the hon. Member on the occasion to which he has referred.

*MR. CHANNING (Northampton, E.): I do not think I need offer any apology to the right hon. Gentleman for intervening in this debate in support of the reduction moved by my hon. friend. There are some points in the reply of the right hon. Gentleman which we must accept absolutely, but at the same time there are other points which I think the right hon. Gentleman will not quarrel with me if I deal with at the present moment. I should like to say a word with regard to the point raised by my hon. friend as to the authorisation to boards of guardians to distribute the literature of the Jenner Society. I think the right hon. Gentleman quite misapprehended the point made by my hon. friend, which was that the House of Commons having decided against this course on the Report stage of the Vaccination Bill, it was therefore improper on the part of the Local Government Board to authorise a course which the House of Commons had condemned. With regard to the main question, so far as I have been able to follow the right hon. Gentleman's quotations, I think they are taken from the preceding day's debate. He dealt rather lightly with the proceedings of the day on which my hon. friend's amendment was moved. I can confirm most fully my hon. friend's statement regarding the impression produced by the speech of the right hon. Gentleman upon myself, upon my hon. friend the Member for Shoreditch who followed him, and upon other Members on this side of the House, viz., that he frankly recognised what I think he ought to have taken from the Royal Commission, that in future vaccination was to be a voluntary and not a compulsory proceeding. The right hon. Gentleman has not denied the particular words which seem to me to have produced—of course I accept his disclaimer — the impression that he had acquiesced in the view that vaccination was to be voluntary, and not compulsory.

MR. CHAPLIN : It is now.

*MR. CHANNING : Not in the sense contemplated by the amendment of my hon. friend, which was that there should be local option, and that the local authorities should retain the discretion left in their hands for 25 years with regard to these prosecutions.

MR. CHAPLIN : I declined, at the commencement of my speech, to accept the amendment.

*MR. CHANNING : The governing and decisive words to which I wish to refer are as follows—

"Since the debate of last night, I have quite recognised the fact that a compulsory administration of the Vaccination Law would be neither necessary nor desirable."

Mr. Channing.

Those words seem to me absolutely decisive with regard to this question, and many Members on this side of the House met the right hon. Gentleman frankly and cordially during the discussions, under the impression that he was dealing with the question in the broad spirit indicated in the report of the Royal Commission. I do not think that the general impression produced upon the House by the right hon. Gentleman's speech can be seriously contested. I do not care to attack the right hon. Gentleman very fiercely in a personal sense on this matter. In the conduct of the Bill upstairs he certainly showed a conciliatory spirit in meeting Amendments, and the main ground of the complaint now brought before the House is that the right hon. Gentleman did substantially recognise the situation last July, but that the forces surrounding him had brought about a change in his attitude, the result of which is the extraordinary Order issued last October by the Local Government Board, which completely altered the relations of the Local Government Board and the boards of guardians throughout the country, and altered fundamentally the administration of the Vaccination Act. In referring to the case of Bramwell and Low, the right hon. Gentleman has omitted an essential point. The Board of Guardians in that case had passed a resolution previously to the effect that there should be no prosecutions n the Union, which I believe was the Union of Ipswich, and the vaccination officer who brought the case against Low alleged that he had special authority for instituting the prosecution, and vested his claim on the fact that the Board had rescinded the previous resolution against prosecutions, and had issued this order authorising him to prosecute. That was the point that was taken, and his whole case was the case which has been invariably recognised by the Local Government Board hitherto, that the authority was in the guardians. Looking at the decision and the *obiter dicta* of Mr. Justice Wright in that case, I have the impression that if the case went to a higher court there might be something else said upon that question. Then with regard to the general question, I hold in my hand a return of the number of conscientious objection certificates taken out under the Act during the last few months up to the close of last year. Those returns cover 230,000 children. The right hon. Gentleman said just now very hopefully that he thought the Bill had led to a great many more vaccinations taking place; but he is certainly labouring under a misapprehension if he thinks that 230,000 represents all the children unvaccinated in this country. In Leicester there are nearly 80,000 unvaccinated children, but only 9,885 certificates were taken out. In my own constituency some 7,000 certificates have been taken out, in two unions, but if the right hon. Gentleman wishes to find the approximate number of children there who are not vaccinated, he must in estimation multiply the number by four or five, and even then he may find himself well under the mark. That would be a fair measure of the real opposition. But what I mainly desire on behalf of my constituents is to enter an emphatic protest against the change in the administration of the law through the issue of this order—a change which we believe to be absolutely illegal. As my friend stated with great force, there is a regular concatenation of evidence. The rights of boards of guardians to decide whether prosecutions or not should be instituted has been recognised for at least 24 years. The right hon. Gentleman the President of the Board of Trade, who was President of the Local Government Board in the previous Administration, said in 1888, in reference to the general order of 1874, that it was not binding on boards of guardians, but that it was merely a communication, and that it rested with the boards of guardians to take their own course. Again, on the 5th of July, he said the Local Government Board could not interfere in the exercise by the guardians of their powers; that "the enforcement of the Vaccination Act is committed to an elective tribunal, and they must use their own discretion in the matter." The original Evesham letter was issued by a Conservative Administration, and the replies were also made by a Conservative President of the Local Government Board. And the right hon. Gentleman who now holds the position up till January last adopted the same views in the matter. In answer to a question I put to the right hon. Gentleman with regard to a letter written by the Board at that time to the Reading vaccination officer, and the reply that "it

would be contrary to the Board's practice to advise an officer of the guardians without reference to the guardians in a matter in which the guardians have jurisdiction," he said that it was the decision in the case of Bramwell and Low which made him alter his views. And so the present Order says that within seven days after the six months have expired the vaccination officer shall take proceedings. There can be no answer to the statement that the discretionary power of the boards of guardians had been recognised for many years, but I want to drive this question home because it really raises one of the most important issues of practical politics in the near future. What is the right hon. Gentleman going to do with his order? Does he mean business? Is he going down into my constituency to prosecute the parents of these 5,000 or 10,000 children who are not vaccinated, who decline to take out conscientious objection certificates under the clause? In the Oundle Union there have been recently several prosecutions. That is a Union where only a few obections have been lodged. Were those prosecutions instituted by the board of guardians or the Local Government Board? That has been done where the opposition is weak. The right hon. Gentleman knows very well that there are unions throughout the country where people will not consent to have their children vaccinated, where many of them refuse to take out conscientious objection certificate at all. The reason is perfectly plain. During the two or three months up to September 12th the poorer parents of Northamptonshire contributed in fees nearly £1,000, which went to the relief of the rates. That is a thing which I do not for one moment think was ever intended. It was never intended to impose a fine upon the people. We have boards of guardians who refuse to and will not prosecute. I think before the discussion comes to an end we are entitled to know whether the right hon. Gentleman means business by this Order, and whether he intends to force vaccination officers all over the country to prosecute, or whether he is going to take the advice of the Royal Commission, which expressed the opinion in the strongest terms that it would be neither wise nor statesmanlike to override the decision of the boards of guardians. There are one or two other points I wish to refer to. In the first place, the right hon. Gentleman expressed the opinion that the additional cost to the rates of the country, in connection with the new vaccination procedure, would be exceedingly small. Taking the number of children at 950,000, the cost of the vaccination officer and public vaccinator under the old system was 2s. per head. Under the new arrangement it will be 7s. per head, which represents no less an addition of nearly a quarter of a million sterling to the union rates for carrying out this policy. This is keenly felt, especially in districts like my own, where the expenses have been practically nominal for many years past, and where an incubus of £200 or £300 is piled upon the rates for a purpose which the people, by their votes, have expressed a desire not to have imposed upon them. Whatever the reply of the right hon. Gentleman may be upon the general broad issue which we raise—as to the right of the local authorities as against the Local Government Board to control these prosecutions, I have to bring before him certain other points connected with his administration. He accepted in Committee an amendment to exclude any form of compulsory vaccination of children in hospitals and workhouses under the age prescribed by the Act, but this has been violated both by the right hon. Gentleman and by the hospital and workhouse authorities. In the first place in his Order, the right hon. Gentleman instructed the public vaccinator that, in the cases of infants in workhouses and hospitals, the offer to vaccinate should be made at the end, not of the fourth month, but of the second month. And when I complained of this distinction in correspondence with the Local Government Board, he declined to assimilate the law in regard to children in and out of workhouses. Does it not seem monstrous to apply one standard to poor children in workhouses and infirmaries, and another to children elsewhere? I have brought before him a large number of cases where children have been vaccinated two or three weeks after birth, and I have drawn special attention to cases in St. Pancras Workhouse, where the age of vaccination has ranged from eight days to twenty-three days, and to one case in Queen Charlotte's Hospital, where a child only two days old was vaccinated. I quite recognise the wish of the right hon.

Mr. Channing.

Gentleman to prevent these things. I know he has expressed disapproval of this early vaccination, but I think I have a right, after his acceptance of that amendment in Committee, to ask him to deal with this question more effectively in the near future. There are many specific grievances with which he ought to deal. In one notorious case a vaccination officer entered a cottage and, without the presence or consent of the parent, deliberately re-vaccinated a two-year old child, instead of the infant to whom the notice referred. That occurred in the Ross Union, and I think the right hon. Gentleman should express a strong opinion to the Ross Board of Guardians on the matter. Again, numerous cases have occurred in which the Public Vaccinator has ignored the provision requiring 24 hours' notice, and without the consent of the parents, they have effected the vaccination of hundreds of children by terrorism of nurses and others in charge. I could quote one case at Oldbury where the Public Vaccinator vaccinated without notice, and I have, too, a number of cases from the county of Sussex. Further there have been repeated instances of refusals, on the part of the magistrates, to recognise serious illness or even death of other children in the same family resulting from vaccination, as an adequate reason for non-vaccination. The right hon. Gentleman will remember that, at his request, I agreed not to press an amendment defining that as a specific ground, because he said his general concession covered the whole matter, and that such a provision would no longer be necessary. There have further been cases in which the conscientious objector's certificate has been held to be invalid because it has not been sent to the Vaccination Officer within seven days as prescribed by the Act. Several prosecutions have taken place in which parents have been fined on that ground. There was a case too in which a parent was refused a certificate by a stipendiary magistrate, although a previous child had been seriously ill. He was prosecuted before an ordinary bench of magistrates and fined 20s. and costs, or a month's imprisonment. That was at Gillingham, in Kent. Many parents complain that they have been compelled to pay for producing the birth certificates of children, and one was actually fined when he presented the notice of the registrar, which, I believe, contains the date of the birth of the child. He was on that occasion refused his certificate. The charge for these certificates is often 3s. 6d. Other cases have occurred in which parents ordered by the magistrates to procure birth certificates have been unable to obtain exemption, because the Court has not again sat until after the child has passed the age fixed by the Act, and consequently the right to the certificate has lapsed. These matters, however, are all subsidiary to the main issue I have raised, viz., that the right to decide these matters should rest solely with the board of guardians. This was the position which we understood to be accepted by the Government at Reading election and at other places, yet now the right hon. Gentleman has issued an Order directing the vaccination officers to proceed to institute prosecutions without any reference to the board of guardians whatever.

MR. CHAPLIN: I gave no such instruction whatever. I merely stated what the law was.

MR. CHANNING: The instructions are specific, and there is not a word with reference to the boards of guardians being consulted in any way. The vaccination officer is explicitly instructed to prosecute at once after the child is 6 months old. The order, beyond doubt, is opposed to the procedure of 30 years, and overrides the rights which are claimed by more than 600 boards of guardians throughout the country. We say that this is an illegal and unconstitutional usurpation of the rights of local authorities on the part of the right hon. Gentleman. We acquit him of all personal responsibility for it, because we believe it to be the result of pressure put upon him in certain quarters. That pressure has placed him in an unpleasant position, but he will occupy a still more unpleasant

one if the Order is not withdrawn, seeing that it will bring him into regular warfare with the men of Leicestershire and Northampton.

MR. HAZELL (Leicester): I consider it is my duty to say a few words as to the feeling of my constituents in Leicester on this question. If the right hon. Gentleman imagines that the Act of last year has finally settled the matter, he is greatly mistaken. The great majority of parents in Leicester would not go before a magistrate. No complaints, as far as I know, have been made in Leicester as to the conduct of the magistrates. They have not insulted the people. Indeed, every facility has been given the people to make declarations, but the fact remains that they will not go before a magistrate. We have had a very learned disquisition as regards the right of the Local Government Board to overrule the wishes of the boards of guardians. Let us suppose that the right hon. Gentleman is quite correct in his exposition of the law, and that the case has been carried to the highest court of appeal. The fact remains that in Leicester the conflict between the Local Government Board and the board of guardians, which affects the good feeling that ought to exist between a Government Department and the local authority, would still continue. During recent years only 1 per cent. of the children in Leicester have been vaccinated, and the people are quite satisfied with being as they are. They are determined, at all events, that the views of the Local Government Board on this matter shall not prevail. If the right hon. Gentleman considers that it is practicable to enforce his views on the local Board of Guardians, there are difficulties in the way which it would be very hard to foresee and disagreeable to contemplate. I strongly urge upon the right hon. Gentleman not to force his views on this matter.

*SIR WALTER FOSTER (Derby, Ilkeston): I should like to say a few words on this question, because the right hon. Gentleman will remember that when we were in Committee last year I specially discussed the position and powers of the vaccination officers. I must say that when the Order was issued at the end of last year by the

Local Government Board I was obliged to regard it as, at least, unfortunate. The right hon. Gentleman is perfectly right in the position he has taken up in reference to what his intention was in the debate which occurred on the 19th July last. There is no doubt the right hon. Gentleman intended to maintain the law as it exists, and to take up his stand on the interpretation of the law which the law courts had given him, and which has been backed up by the law officers of two successive Administrations. He could, therefore, hardly do anything else. But I admit that when the right hon. Gentleman made the remarks which he did to my hon. friend the Member for Bethnal Green who moved the amendment, I thought the days of vigorous compulsion were at an end. That was the impression I received from his speech; but it was not the impression, I have no doubt now, that he intended to convey. But the remarkable thing is that before the debate I appealed to my hon. friend behind me in the strongest way not to take up the time of the House in moving his amendment. My hon. friend the Member for Bethnal Green refused my request, but afterwards was so satisfied with the speech of the right hon. Gentleman in the debate that he withdrew his amendment, thus showing that he clearly misunderstood the purport of the speech of the President of the Local Government Board. While we acquit the right hon. Gentleman of all intention to mislead the House, I must say the issue of the circular at the close of the year was, at all events, unfortunate. And for this reason: we have a number of vaccination officers appointed by the boards of guardians, and receiving their payments from the boards of guardians, these officers would in the future perform their most difficult duties without reference to the authorities who appoint them, and who pay them their salaries. The result of that must be that these vaccination officers would be placed in a most intolerable position. While remaining the servants of the boards of guardians, they will be pursuing a certain line of action without reference to, and possibly contrary to, the policy and wishes of the boards who appoint and pay them. The result will be that the vaccination officers will not be able to do their work, in such places as Leicester or North-

Sir W. Foster.

ampton, with any comfort or success. But that is not the only possible difficulty. It may happen that boards of guardians will cease to appoint vaccination officers, and so we may have vaccination falling into greater neglect than ever. I should like to know what the right hon. Gentleman will do if any boards of guardians refuse to appoint vaccination officers, and defy the Local Government Board?

MR. CHAPLIN: They nearly all have.

*Sir Walter FOSTER: But what action is the right hon. Gentleman prepared to take with regard to those who do not so appoint vaccination officers? Has the right hon. Gentleman a definite line of policy when the difficulty arises? Setting aside this question, I want to congratulate the right hon. Gentleman on the statement he has been able to make as to the success of the Act. That statement must be reassuring to the country, and to the House, that the policy carried out last year was, after all, the right policy for promoting vaccination. I have received evidence myself from medical men in various parts of the country that there has been a larger amount of vaccination during the last few months than in the same number of months for many preceding years. I believe, however, that the result would have been greater, and that we should have had an infinitely larger amount of vaccination, had it not been for the very stupid attitude of the Press and of the magistrates in this matter. The magistrates in some places had acted with stupidity, because they did not carried out the law in the spirit intended by Parliament. When the clause was under discussion last year I pointed out that its peculiar form admitted of a great variety of administrative procedure, and would consequently bring the Act into disrepute. Unfortunately, the press took up the case generally over the country, and there was a great deal of wild writing which induced the magistrates to raise difficulties in granting certificates. The action of the magistrates kept alive the agitation which the clause was intended to allay, and I believe if a wiser course had been adopted, and if these certificates had been granted more easily, we should have had a much greater amount of vaccination performed under the Act. I am satisfied that as time passes we shall have a great deal of the arrears of vaccination made up under the Act. But I believe that this would have been done more readily if the right hon. Gentleman had accepted my proposal that every medical man should be regarded as a public vaccinator. There are one or two other points to which I wish to call attention. In the first place, I think the policy, carried out in some places, of prosecuting people who fail to send in certificates of exemption within seven days, is unnecessarily irritating. Another point is that the right hon. Gentleman should discourage, by every means in his power, the vexatious requirement that a man must be obliged to present a certificate of the birth of his child when he applies for exemption. That is a serious impediment to the working of the Act. A man who earns only £1 per week cannot afford to pay 2 or 3 shillings for the two certificates. Again, I hold that it is the duty of the Local Government Board to prevent prosecutions being made when the plea of insanitary surroundings is put in. My hon. friend behind me quoted a case of a man who was fined 20s. with the alternative of a month's imprisonment because he refused to have his child vaccinated when diphtheria was prevalent in the neighbourhood. That was an intolerable hardship and an injustice. I hope that the right hon. Gentleman will, throughout the administration of the Act, do all he can to lessen the causes of irritation in the working of the Act, and so promote the consumption of calf lymph, which is being used to such a large extent for vaccination.

MR. LABOUCHERE (Northampton): We all look with the most friendly feeling to the right hon. Gentleman the President of the Local Government Board, but it appears to me that it was under something like false pretences that he received the blessings that were rained down upon him last Session. We accepted him, as we are told another was accepted in Heaven, as a repentant sinner. But, far from being a repentant sinner, it now appears that the right hon. Gentleman has repented of repenting, and has gone back entirely to the error of his ways. The right hon. Gentleman tells us that if the Amendment of the hon. Member for Bethnal Green had been submitted to the test of a vote it would not have been

carried. Now, how in the name of wonder does he know whether it would have been carried or not? He might as well say that, if all the horses nominated had run in the Derby, Flying Fox would not have won, and Holocauste would have won but for his accident.

AN HON. MEMBER: So he would.

MR. LABOUCHERE: I am very glad he did not, for I backed Flying Fox. Be that as it may, the right hon. Gentleman cannot tell us with assurance that the amendment would not have passed. We really do believe that if my hon. friend the Member for Bethnal Green had persevered with his amendment we had a very fair chance of carrying it. The right hon. Gentleman has alluded to the speech he made on that occasion. He says he would not give a pledge that he would not enforce the law, and would not allow prosecutions without the consent of the Boards of Guardians. But it is a very remarkable thing that, as a matter of fact, all the speakers who heard him, and who made speeches after him, were under the impression that the right hon. Gentleman actually did say what he is reported to have said. So that the illusion extended not only to the Reporters' Gallery, but to these benches. I do not see the Solicitor General in his place, but the Solicitor General, in a short speech he made on that occasion, confirms the view that the right hon. Gentleman said that the vaccination officers would not be allowed to prosecute without the consent of the board of guardians. My hon. friend the Member for Caithness said on the same day—

"The clause we have adopted only applies to the 29th and 31st clauses of the Act of 1867."

My hon. friend's contention was that the pledge had been given in regard to the Act, but that it was possible there might be prosecutions [in regard to the Acts of 1871 and 1874. My hon. friend in raising this point said—

"Here we have obtained the pledge of the President of the Local Government Board that he would not prosecute under the Act of 1867."

My hon. friend continued :—

"The clause we have adopted only applies to the 29th and 31st Clauses of the Act of 1867. It does not apply to the Act of 1871 at all. Under the Act of 1874, which this clause practically abolishes, the Local Government

Board have got power to make rules, orders, and regulations with regard to the proceedings to be taken by the guardians or their officers for the enforcement of the Acts of 1867 and 1871. The clause you have adopted only affects the Act, of 1867, and we have got the pledge of the President of the Local Government Board that he would not do anything to interfere with the relations between the vaccination officers and the guardians, that he would not put it into force. Now, the right hon. Gentleman may not always be in that position. The next President of the Local Government Board may not take that view in regard to the matter. The point raised by the hon. Gentleman below me goes further, and I should like to have the Solicitor General's view of the matter."

That was, that having received an assurance that the President of the Local Government Board would not put in force any rights he had acquired by the Act of 1867, to insist on the vaccination officers prosecuting without the authority of the board of guardians, whether it was possible for him to use that power under the Acts of 1871 and 1874. Now, what does the Solicitor General say? He does not for a moment repudiate the position taken by my hon. friend the Member for Caithness, that the President of the Local Government Board had said that he would not use the power under the Act of 1867; but he says—

"I think there can be no prosecution except under section 29 of the Act of 1867. No other prosecution is possible."

Therefore, we stand on this, that we on this side of the House, and the Solicitor General sitting by the side of the right hon. Gentleman, were under the impression that the President of the Local Government Board had agreed not to use his powers under the Act of 1867. The Solicitor General went out of his way to tell us that if the right hon. Gentleman did not use it under that Act he could not use it under the Acts of 1871 and 1874. It was under these circumstances that the hon. Member for Bethnal Green withdrew his amendment. Now, the right hon. Gentleman the President of the Local Government Board says that the law of 1867 allows prosecutions by vaccination officers without the permission of the board of guardians. That is true, but the right hon. Gentleman knows that the law had slept for twenty-five years. It was dead. Then he tells us, "I did not make any particular order on the subject," whereupon my hon. friend the Member for East Northamptonshire read out the order which he issued at the end of last year. It is as clear as possible that the right hon. Gentleman sent out that order after making this pledge to the House. He revived the law of 1867, and he tells the vaccination officers that they are to prosecute without the consent or approval of the board of guardians. I think that is a great mistake. All we claim is that the parents and guardians of children should have the right to decide whether the child should be vaccinated or not. If you keep up this turmoil and trouble by the Local Government Board ordering the vaccination officers to prosecute without the permission of the board of guardians, you are invading the whole system of local self government. I have the honour to represent a constituency which takes a very strong view on the subject. It is one of the centres of anti-vaccination; but, notwithstanding, they do not take small-pox. They get on uncommonly well without vaccination. I agree entirely with the remark of my hon. friend that if you perpetually invade the rights of local authorities in this matter, if you keep up continuously this turmoil, you will make it not only a question whether vaccination is a good or a bad thing, but whether a man is to be forced to have his children vaccinated at all. It must be admitted that many persons who have come to exercise the right given them by law, and who seriously object to the vaccination of their children, have very frequently been insulted by the magistrates. I do hope that the President of the Local Government Board will keep his eye on these magistrates, and, if this thing is not stopped, that he will make an example of one of them, and have him struck off the roll. Whatever a magistrate's view may be of the question, he has no right to tell a man that he is a fool, or an idiot, when he comes forward to claim the right given him by law. I hope the right hon. Gentleman will issue an order in regard to the powers of the vaccination officers, and leave the power of prosecution to the boards of guardians, as was done for twenty-five years past.

MR. CHAPLIN : The hon. Member who has just sat down has asked me to withdraw my order.

Mr. Labouchere.

MR. LABOUCHERE: Yes.

MR. CHAPLIN: He thinks that if I give up my order the guardians will revert to the old position, which they occupied for twenty-five years. Sir, they will do absolutely nothing of the kind. What was the order, and what was our course in regard to it? The circular letter in which we imposed the order was to this effect:

"Having regard to the decision of the Queen's Bench in the case referred to, and with the opinions given by the law officers of the Crown, the Board have not inserted any provision in the order imposing any duty either on the guardians or on the vaccination officer as regards the institution and conduct of proceedings. The power and duty of treating such proceedings are vested in the vaccination officer under the Vaccination Acts passed prior to the Act of last Session without any order from the Board, or direction in regard to it."

Then, some hon. Members have relied on one paragraph in the Order which is to this effect:—

"If that notice is not duly complied with within the time specified therein, it will become the duty of the Vaccination Officer under the Vaccination Acts to take proceedings for the enforcement of the law."

These are not instructions from us; they are merely an intimation, in accordance with the usual practice of the Local Government Board, as to what is the duty under the Acts of Parliament of the parties concerned. When hon. Members ask me to revert to the old practice, what is it that they ask me to do?

MR. LABOUCHERE: Withdraw the circular.

MR. CHAPLIN: Withdraw fiddle-sticks! The only thing I could do would be to re-insert in my order the old regulation which was in the old orders, and which has been already adjudged by the courts to be superfluous and ineffectual. Is it reasonable that I should be asked to take such a course? Sir, I am extremely sorry that this misunderstanding arose. The only way in which it could have arisen is this. The hon. Member for Bethnal Green, has taken a very prominent part in the discussion of this particular question. I had always given him credit, at all events, that he had made himself master of the position; but it is quite clear that he has never done so; he has never understood the position of affairs; otherwise, after I had said as plainly as a man could say that I declined to accept his amendment, he would have known that certain other things followed as a matter of course. The hon. Member for East Northamptonshire quoted in support of his view the statement made by the hon. Member for Caithness, who said that I had promised that I would do absolutely nothing whatever to interfere with the relations between the guardians and the vaccination officers. Well, I have done absolutely nothing; I have left them on one side altogether. The Board have not inserted any provision in the order imposing any duty either on the board of guardians or the vaccination officer as regards the institution of proceedings. Then, I am asked to keep my eye on the magistrates, and strike them off the roll. The Local Government Board have nothing whatever to do with that, and I can hardly think the hon. Gentleman was serious in his suggestion. Any complaints of the conduct of magistrates in relation to vaccination certificates should be addressed to the Home Office, and any complaint of vaccination under unsanitary conditions will have careful examination by the Local Government Board. As to the vaccination of workhouse children under the age of two months, I have not the particulars with me at the present moment, but I am under the impression that no objection or opposition whatever was made by the parents of those children, who were perfectly acquainted with what was going on, and although I quite agree that, as a general rule, so far as I am advised, under ordinary circumstances it is not advisable that children should be vaccinated at so early an age, there has been nothing in the circumstances which have occurred to call for active interference on the part of the Local Government Board or for any re-consideration of the Order. An hon. Member has enlarged upon the enormous number of children going unvaccinated now in various parts of the country, and asked me what I was going to do as to this Order. Sir, out of 640 boards of guardians in the country I am thankful to say that there have never been more than some half-dozen or a dozen Boards who have made difficulties, and all of these, with two or three exceptions, have been either settled or are on the eve of settlement. It was for that reason that I regret, more than I can say, the kind of speeches which have been made by a limited number of hon. Gentlemen in this House to night, because the only effect of those speeches going forth to the world can be, although I hope they will not have much effect when the guardians know their duty, to increase whatever difficulties there have been. What I shall do is to perform the duties which Parliament has imposed upon me, to the very best of my ability, without fear or favour, of course avoiding—I should be very foolish if I did not—anything that would cause irritation ; at the same time I shall do my utmost to promote vaccination. I shall do, in fact, in the future exactly what I have done in the past. I have received the report of the Board's medical inspectors as to the increase or decrease of vaccination in eleven different unions—West Bromwich, Maidstone, Lambeth, Fulham, St. Olave's (Southwark), Holborn, Whiteehapel, St. Saviour's (Southwark), Paddington, Stoke-on-Trent, and the County of Glamorgan. In the first quarter of 1898 the number of vaccinations in those eleven Unions was 3,744 ; in the first quarter of 1899 there were 6,614 vaccinations, a net increase of 77 per cent. So far as it goes, I have every reason to hope and believe that that may be taken as a fair indication of what is going on in other parts of the country. What I conceive to be my duty is to do everything in my power to promote an increase of vaccination throughout the country, similar to that which is going on in those eleven unions.

SIR W. HARCOURT (Monmouthshire, W.) : I think the statement of the right hon. Gentleman is most satisfactory. I have always thought that there was a good deal of exaggerated alarm on the subject. But the figures which the right hon. Gentleman has just given must have satisfied him, as well as the House and the country, how much better the amended Bill was than the Bill originally introduced.

MR. BAYLEY (Derbyshire, Chesterfield) : I rise for the purpose of asking the right hon. Gentleman one question. I am sorry to say that, in listening to his speech very carefully this afternoon, I have not been able to understand for one moment what the Local Government Board are proposing to do in the future.

Mr. Chaplin.

Is the custom of the last thirty years to be enforced or not ? That is a perfectly simple question, and one that the House has a perfect right to have a straightforward, clear, and definite reply upon.

MR. CHAPLIN : You have had a definite reply.

MR. BAYLEY : Well, then, I am so very dense that I cannot understand it, and I do not think it was understood on this side of the House. Will the right hon. Gentleman give us a clear "Yes," or "No" as to whether the custom of the last thirty years is going to be altered, or are the Government going to put in force what is said to be the law ?

MR. CHAPLIN : I have already told you that it has been ruled illegal by a Court, and I have no power to interfere.

MR. BAYLEY : Then, when is the right hon. Gentleman going to enforce the law upon different Boards of Guardians, and when is he going to enforce it in Leicester ? Is he going to enforce it in any constituency ? There have been many changes in the Vaccination Bill of last year, and I think, if the right hon. Gentleman will enforce it in any one of those constituencies where it is not enforced to-day, there will be a considerable change of front again on this question. But do I understand that in Leicester the law, as the right hon. gentleman has given it to us to-day, will be enforced by the Local Government Board ? Will they prosecute and pay the money for prosecutions ? Is the right hon. Gentleman going to be in earnest on this question ? If he is not, he had better tell us ; if he is, let him begin the campaign. Meanwhile, I should like to know if he is really determined, whether he means to commit the Board of Guardians of Leicester to prison because they won't find money to pay a vaccination officer.

MR. DILLON (Mayo, E.) : The hon. Member who has just sat down seemed to think that the Local Government Board would be compelled to imprison the Guardians of Leicester and of other districts if they did not obey them. I have a suggestion to make to the Local Government Board if they are placed in that position, and that is, to adopt the Irish system. In

Ireland, if a Board of Guardians does not do its duty, paid Guardians are sent down to take their places. I should be very glad to see this system adopted, because I believe, if it were adopted in England, we should be able to get rid of it in Ireland.

Mr. LABOUCHERE: I do think we ought to have an answer to the question put by my hon. friend the Member for Chesterfield, for it really is the whole crux of the position. Suppose that in a constituency there are no prosecutions, either on the part of the Board of Guardians or of the vaccination officer in the case of persons who are not vaccinated, what is the action that the right hon. Gentleman proposes to take? For 25 or 30 years the Local Government Board did not interfere. They left the matter entirely to the localities. Is it the intention of the right hon. Gentleman to continue to act on these lines, or does he intend, when the Guardians do not give their consent to a prosecution, to order the vaccination officer to give his consent? When neither the Board of Guardians nor the vaccination officer is prepared to prosecute, is it the intention to order a prosecution on behalf of the Local Government Board?

Mr. CHANNING: May I supplement that question by another, which I think the right hon. Gentleman will find it absolutely necessary to give a clear answer to? What will happen if the vaccination officer declines to carry out or institute any prosecution?

Dr. CLARK (Caithness): I should like, as a further question, to ask the right hon. Gentleman, whom the vaccination officer is to obey if the Board of Guardians are not in favour of prosecutions and the Local Government Board are. At present a vaccination officer has to give security that he will obey the directions of the Local Government Board, as well as of the Board of Guardians who appoint him and pay him. All prosecutions mean money, and, unless the Board of Guardians provide it recourse will have to be made to the Local Government Board. I do not think the Local Government Board have any fund which could be used for this specific purpose.

The Committee divided; Ayes, 59; Noes, 190. (Division List No. 168).

AYES.

Allan, William (Gateshead)
Allison, Robert Andrew
Barlow, John Emmott
Bayley, Thomas (Derbyshire)
Beaumont, Wentworth C. B.
Billson, Alfred
Burns, John
Burt, Thomas
Cameron, SirCharles(Glasgow)
Clark, Dr. G.B.(Caithness-sh.)
Colville, John
Dalziel, James Henry
Davies,M.Vaughan-(Cardigan
Duckworth, James
Dunn, Sir William
Esmonde, Sir Thomas
Goddard, Daniel Ford
Gourley,SirEdwardTemperley
Gurdon,Sir WilliamBrampton
Holland, Wm. H.(York,W.R.)
Humphreys-Owen, Arthur C.

Jones, William (Carnarvons.)
Labouchere, Henry
Langley, Batty
Lawson, Sir Wilfrid (Cumb)
Lyell, Sir Leonard
MacAleese, Daniel
M'Leod, John
Maddison, Fred
Mendl, Sigismund Ferdinand
Molloy, Bernard Charles
Montagu, Sir S (Whitechapel)
Morton, E J. C. (Devonport)
Norton, Capt. Cecil William
O'Brien, James F. X. (Cork)
O'Connor, Arthur (Donegal)
O'Connor,James (Wicklow,W.
Oldroyd, Mark
Palmer, Sir C. M (Durham)
Paulton, James Mellor
Pease, Alfred E. (Cleveland)
Priestley, Briggs (Yorks.)

Roberts, John Bryn (Eifion)
Roberts, John H. (Denbighs.)
Smith, Samuel (Flint)
Soutter, Robinson
Spicer, Albert
Steadman, William Charles
Tennant, Harold John
Trevelyan, Charles Philips
Walton, Joseph (Barnsley)
Weir, James Galloway
Whittaker, Thomas Palmer
Williams, JohnCarvell(Notts.
Wilson, Charles Henry (Hull)
Wilson, FrederickW(Norfolk)
Wilson, Henry J.(York,W.R.)
Wilson, John (Govan)
Wilson, JosH(Middlesbrough)

Tellers for the Ayes—
Mr. Pickersgill and Mr. Channing.

NOES.

Acland-Hood,Capt.SirAlex.F.
Arnold-Forster, Hugh O.
Atkinson, Rt. Hon. John
Austin, Sir John (Yorkshire)
Bailey, James (Walworth)
Baker, Sir John
Balcarres, Lord
Balfour, Rt. Hn. G.W.(Leeds).
Banbury, Frederick George
Bartley, George C. T.
Barton, Dunbar Plunket
Beach,Rt.Hn.SirMH.(Bristol)

Beach,WWBramston(Hants.)
Beckett, Ernest William
Bethell, Commander
Bhownaggree, Sir M. M.
Birrell, Augustine
Blakiston-Houston, John
Blundell, Colonel Henry
Boscawen, Arthur Griffith-
Bowles,T.Gibson(King's Lynn
Butcher, John George
Caldwell, James
Campbell,Rt.Hn.JA(Glasgow

Carmichael, Sir T. D. Gibson-
Cecil, Evelyn (Hertford, East)
Cecil, Lord Hugh (Greenwich)
Chamberlain,Rt.Hon.J.(Birm.
Chamberlain,JAusten(Worc'r
Chaplin, Rt. Hon. Henry
Clough, Walter Owen
Coddington, Sir William
Coghill, Douglas Harry
Collings, Rt. Hon. Jesse
Colston, Chas. Edw. H.Athole
Corbett, A.Cameron(Glasgow)

Cornwallis, FiennesStanley W.	Hatch, Ernest Frederick Geo.	Pease, Herbert Pike(Darlingt'n
Courtney, Rt.Hn. Leonard H.	Hayne, Rt Hon. Charles Seale-	Phillpotts, Captain Arthur
Cox, Irwin Edward B. (Harrow	Heath, James	Pierpoint, Robert
Cranbourne, Viscount	Hedderwick, Thomas Chas. H	Pilkington, Rich(LancsNewt'n
Cripps, Charles Alfred	Helder, Augustus	Platt-Higgins, Frederick
Crombie, John William	Hill, Arthur (Down, West)	Powell, Sir Francis Sharp
Cubitt, Hon. Henry	Hill, Sir Edward Stock(Bristol	Pretyman, Ernest George
Curran, Thomas B. (Donegal)	Hoare, Edw Brodie(Hampstead	Priestley, SirW.Overend (Edin
Curzon, Viscount	Hoare, Samuel (Norwich)	Pryce-Jones, Lt.-Col. Edward
Dalbiac, Colonel Philip Hugh	Hobhouse, Henry	Purvis, Robert
Dalrymple, Sir Charles	Hornby, Sir William Henry	Rasch, Major Frederic Carne
Digby, John K. D. Wingfield.	Howard, Joseph	Ritchie, Rt. Hon. C. Thomson
Dixon-Hartland, Sir F. Dixon	Hozier, Hon. James Henry Cecil	Rollit, Sir Albert Kaye
Dorington. Sir John Edward	Hubbard, Hon. Evelyn	Rothschild, Hon. Lionel Walter
Doughty, George	Hutton, John (Yorks. N.R.)	Russell, T. W. (Tyrone)
Douglas, Rt. Hon. A. Akers-	Jackson, Rt. Hon. Wm. Lawies	Rutherford, John
Douglas-Pennnnt, Hon. E. S.	Jolliffe, Hon. H. George	Ryder, John Herbert Dudley
Drage, Geoffrey	Kennaway, Rt. Hon. Sir John H	Samuel, Harry S. (Limehouse)
Drucker, A.	Knowles, Lees	Seely, Charles Hilton
Duncombe, Hon. Hubert V.	Laurie, Lieut-General	Seton-Karr, Henry
Farquharson, Dr. Robert	Lawrence, Sir E. D - (Corn)	Sidebotham, J. W. (Cheshire)
Fellowes, Hon. AilwynEdward	Lawrence, W. F. (Liverpool)	Smith, JamesParker(Lanarks.
Ferguson, R. C. Munro (Leith)	Lawson, John Grant (Yorks.)	Stanley, Henry M. (Lambeth)
Ferguson, RtHonSirJ(Manc'r	Leng, Sir John	Stanley, Lord (Lancs.)
Finch, George H.	Llewelyn, Sir Dillwyn-(Swan	Stewart, SirMarkJ.M'Taggart
Finlay, Sir Robert Bannatyne	Loder, Gerald W. Erskine	Sullivan, Donal (Westmeath)
Fisher, William Hayes	Long, Col. C. W. (Evesham)	Sutherland, Sir Thomas
Fitzmaurice, Lord Edmond	Long, Rt. Hn. W. (Liverpool)	Talbot, Rt. Hn. J.G.(Oxf'dUniv
Fitz Wygram, General Sir F.	Lowe, Francis William	Thornton, Percy M.
Flannery, Sir Fortescue	Lowles, John	Tomlinson, Wm. Edw Murray
Flower, Ernest	Lubbock, Rt. Hon. Sir John	Tritton, Charles Ernest
Foster, Harry S. (Suffolk)	Lucas-Shadwell, William	Ure, Alexander
Fox, Dr. Joseph Francis	Macartney, W. G. Ellison	Valentia, Viscount
Garfit, William	Macdona, John Cumming	Wallace, Robert (Perth)
Gedge, Sydney	M'Arthur, Charles (Liverpool)	Webster, SirR.E (IsleofWight
Gibbons, J. Lloyd	M'Ewan, William	Welby, Lieut.-Col. A.C.E.
Gibbs, Hon. Vicary(St Albans)	M'Iver, Sir L. (Edinburgh, W.)	Whiteley, H. (Ashton-under-L
Giles, Charles Tyrrell	Middlemore. J. Throgmorton	Williams, Colonel R. (Dorset)
Gilliat, John Saunders	Milward, Colonel Victor	Willliams, J. Powell- (Birm.)
Goldsworthy, Major-General	Monk, Charles James	Wilson, John (Falkirk)
Gordon, Hon. John Edward	Moon, E. Robert Pacy	Wodehouse, RtHonE.R.(Bath)
Goschen, George J. (Sussex)	Morgan, J L. (Carmarthen)	Wolff, Gustav Wilhelm
Gray, Ernest (West Ham)	Morrison, Walter	Woodall, William
Green, WalfordD(Wednesbury	Morton, A H.A. (Deptford)	Wortley, Rt. Hon. C.B. Stuart-
Greene, W.Raymond-(Cambs.)	Muntz, Philip A.	Wylie, Alexander
Gretton, John	Murray, Rt Hn. A. G. (Bute)	Wyndham, George
Greville, Hon. Ronald	Murray, Charles J. (Coventry)	Young, Samuel (Cavan, East)
Gunter, Colonel	Myers, William Henry	Younger, William
Halsey, Thomas Frederick	Nicol, Donald Ninian	
Hamilton, Rt Hon LordGeorge	O'Connor, T. P. (Liverpool)	TELLERS FOR THE NOES.—
Hanbury, Rt.Hon.Robert Wm	O'Neill, Hon. Robert Torrens	Sir William Walrond and
Hardy, Laurence	Orr-Ewing, Charles Lindsay	Mr. Anstruther.
Hare, Thomas Leigh	Parkes, Ebenezer	

Original Question again proposed.

SIR ALBERT ROLLIT (Islington, S.) : I wish to draw the attention of the Committee to the varying character and restricted length of the repayment of loans for municipal and other public works. I had hoped it would have been possible to avoid any motion on the subject, and that the question of my hon. friend would have received a more favourable reply. Unfortunately the reply only referred to the inability of the Local Government Board to increase the length of the terms, and apparently refused to give that consideration which municipal and other local authorities urgently desire. That reply struck me as being inconsistent with the remarks of the Chancellor of the Exchequer on the Finance Bill, because the right hon. Gentleman then stated that he hoped to be able at no distant date to give better terms for the repayment of these loans, and he spoke with regret of the apparent indisposition of Municipal Corporations to avail themselves to the extent be would have wished of the assistance of the Government in relation to loans generally. One great difficulty, undoubtedly, has been that the terms of repayment have been onerous and have prohibited Corporations from using those facilities as much as they otherwise would be disposed to do. I quite admit that some difficulties arise which are not entirely within the control of the right hon. Gentleman. There are various Acts of Parliament which prescribe different periods of repayment, and various departments prescribe different terms for the loans which they authorize for public works. I hope that, at some early date, instead of the gross anomalies and absurdities which now exist some better and more logical system can be created, under which public bodies will know exactly what they may expect with reference to this question. But although these difficulties exist, I venture to say that, except perhaps in the case of tramways, which are under the jurisdiction of the President of the Board of Trade, and with the exception of what may be determined by Act of Parliament, the President of the Local Government Board has the chief discretion in this matter, and it rests with him to say what length of repayment shall be laid down. I should like to direct attention to the fact that the Act of Parliament which gives this discretion has, I think, by long course of practice, been given rather a restricted interpretation. The Act says that the public authority may determine what the length of the term of repayment shall be, and that then it shall obtain the sanction of the Local Government Board. It seems to me that the rational interpretation of the Act is that the local authority should determine the time which the repayment should cover, and ask the sanction of the Local Government Board. That would be local government in the true sense of the term. Instead of that, however, the Board has acted on a different principle. It must be admitted that there are different terms, and great variations in practice. If a loan is granted through a Bill in Parliament, the term may be as long as sixty years; if under the Public Health Act, fifty years; and if an application is made by the Local Government Board under the Municipal Corporations Act, the term is only thirty years. That generally is the practice. Take two cases in point. If you take a piece of moorland for a watershed you may have a term possibly of 100 years. If on the other hand you apply to the Board of Trade for a site for a tram depôt in the centre of a populous town, you are limited by the provisions of the department to some thirty years.

That is an inequality most difficult to defend. What is the result of that system ? Suppose the money in each case was £100,000 there would be a very considerable difference in the annual repayments. Take another case in which I think the Local Government Board has exercised its discretion unwisely. In one of the boroughs it was decided to repave certain streets with wood in the very best possible manner, including that part covered by the tram lines. It was also resolved to pave the side walks at the same time. The Board of Trade gave a period of thirty years ; yet the Local Government Board, for the parts outside the tram lines, and also for the side walks, limited the period of repayment to fifteen years. That differential system cast a considerably greater burden on the ratepayers. The period of repayment should be proportioned to the life of the work for which the loan is granted. The contention of the persons concerned in the instance I have given was that the part within the tram lines was the one to suffer most from traffic, and that the other parts would only be little affected ; yet the term of repayment in the first case was double what it was in the second. I am also informed that there is one class of work of the very highest importance, both from the social and economic point of view, which has been very materially impeded by the action of the Local Government Board, and that is the housing of the working classes. The desire on the part of municipalities in those cases is to provide on the most reasonable terms for those who are unable to obtain house accommodation, and yet, owing to the rapidity of repayment, the present generation is compelled to pay a very high rate. Everyone will admit that the Local Government Board has an important function to fulfil which is not to be overlooked. It rests with the Board to protect posterity from any undue burden being imposed on it by the present generation. All we ask, in view of the inequalities and anomalies between the department and Acts of Parliament, is that there should be some uniform and reasonable system ; and, above all, that where modern public works, which are generally of a substantial character, are constructed for the benefit of the community, the department should have fair regard for the probable length of life of such works. Rightly or wrongly, there is a very strong feeling among all classes of local authorities that the discretion of the department has not been exercised as well as it might be. I trust that what the Chancellor of the Exchequer said on the Finance Bill will be remembered by the President of the Local Government Board, and that inducements will be offered to corporations to avail themselves of the financial assistance which can be given to them, and which is valuable not only to the corporations, but also as a means of investment. I beg to move the reduction of the vote by £500.

Motion made and Question proposed,

"That Item A (Salaries) be reduced to £500, in respect of the salary of the President of the Local Government Board."—(*Sir Albert Rollit.*)

*MR. GRAY (West Ham, N.): I wish strongly to emphasise the appeal of my hon. friend. The decision of the Local Government Board has had a baneful influence on the progress of works in the borough which I represent. A few years ago the Board of Guardians of West Ham applied to the Local Government Board for permission to raise a loan in order to purchase land and erect buildings for an infirmary. They were informed that the Board had no power to extend the period of repayment beyond 35 years. An Act was passed by this House giving the Board power to extend the period to 60 years, but when the Board of Guardians applied for those terms they were told that the loan on land must be repaid in 40 years, and that on buildings in 30 years. Oddly enough, the borough authorities came to Parliament at the same time, and by a private Bill obtained permission to raise a loan to be repaid in 60 years, double the period allowed to the Guardians by the Local Government Board for the loan on buildings. It seems to me that, while some general line of action should be adopted by the various Departments concerned, the rule should not be too rigidly enforced in new communities such as West Ham, which in thirty years has grown from a few thousands to a population of over a quarter of a million. All our loans are outstanding, and it is unreasonable that the taxation for their repayment should fall entirely on the present generation. I quite agree

Sir A. Rollit.

that we should have some regard for the burdens which we impose on posterity, but I think also that we should have regard also for the present generation. In fixing the date for the repayment of loans regard should be had for the conditions of the community concerned. In a borough recently incorporated, with a rapidly growing population, it is necessary to erect infirmaries, schools, and other public buildings, and it is unreasonable to compel the present generation to pay for them.

LORD E. FITZMAURICE (Wilts, Cricklade): I wish to add a word about the borrowing powers of county councils, which depend upon the well-known clauses of the Local Government Act, 1888, taken in connection with the Local Loans Act. I believe that the result of these clauses taken together is that the county councils cannot borrow under any circumstances for a period of more than 20 years. Now, I am not an advocate for a very lengthy period, but I think a cast-iron rule is a mistake, although there is a tendency to put a little too much upon posterity. I think 30 years, considering the character of some of the buildings, is too short a term. There is no grievance with regard to the loans for main roads and pavements, and I do not think any loans for that purpose ought to exceed 30 years. The matters for which county councils borrow are chiefly for the erection of lunatic asylums, police stations, and matters connected with the constabulary. Owing to the number of lunatics sent into asylums, there is a growing tendency, which cannot be avoided, to contract loans for the purpose of enlarging asylums, and I think 30 years is rather a short period in regard to matters of that kind. In almost every county town in England the accommodation provided for the county police no longer supplies the requirements of modern ideas, and the county councils have to contract a considerable debt to make provision for the county constabulary. Therefore I think it is rather a grievance that we should have a cast-iron rule fixing the period at 30 years. I am inclined to think that it can be fairly argued that there ought to be discretionary power in such cases, where the President of the Local Government Board thinks that the buildings contemplated are of such a substantial character that a longer period is justifiable, to grant a longer term to the county council.

MR. BARTLEY (Islington, N.): I think there is a great deal to be said on the other side of the question. One of the serious dangers of modern times is the great increase in the borrowing tendency of local bodies. I think we ought to lay it down that the present generation should, within a reasonable time, pay for these improvements. There has been a very great change during the last 20 or 30 years, because formerly localities had to pay 4½ per cent. interest for these loans, and now they get them for very little over 3 per cent. Therefore they have borrowed the money to very great advantage, and the amount which they have to pay in interest makes a very large difference in the amount that has to be paid each year for the repayment of these loans. Although I should not say that the period of thirty years ought never to be exceeded, I should be very sorry indeed to see more latitude given in this matter. Many localities are now borrowing enormous sums of money—very properly, in most cases—but in doing so they ought to be prepared at the time to pay a large proportion of the cost of those loans. It is quite true that people change their notions of what is required, and it has been said that the county police stations are not up to the standard at which they ought to be. It is quite possible that in another thirty or forty years another change may take place, and the people may then think that the present stations are not good enough. I think we should be prepared to encourage local bodies to pay off these loans within thirty years in nearly all cases, and I should regret to see anything done to secure momentary popularity which would make borrowing more easy. I hope the right hon. Gentleman will not be too lenient, and not give way on this question.

*SIR F. S. POWELL (Wigan): I think that upon this occasion we ought to consider the subject with thoughtfulness and with care. I feel quite sure that to limit the time unduly would be to hinder progress by preventing localities from carrying out great improvements. We should have regard, in all cases, to the nature of the works, and I think anyone who has observed the short life of many of these works will feel that a short time ought to

be fixed for the repayment of the money borrowed. We have not only to consider the life of the work, but also the change of fashion. Many of the works may now be up to date, but in the course of a few years they may become old-fashioned and antiquated. They may be like the machinery in a textile factory, which may be perfectly good but yet out of date, and has to make way for better machinery. The same thing applies to public works, and that is a consideration which we should bear carefully in mind. Then we have to consider the probable life of a community, for some of them last only about thirty or forty years as a town, and then they often return to their rural condition through the failure of their industry. I have known places in Lancashire which in my boyhood were country districts, but became centres of industry, and now, the minerals being exhausted, have again become country districts. I should be extremely sorry to see the term made so limited as to hinder progress, but at the same time I think it is unwise to postpone a payment which must be made sooner or later, and which unless care is taken may become most oppressive and injurious to a coming generation.

*SIR WALTER FOSTER: I can quite understand the desire of the right hon. Gentleman not to extend the period of loans generally, considering the enormous amount of the local indebtedness of this country. But there are some points in which a little leniency might be exercised. Take the case of a rural district where there is the greatest possible difficulty in obtaining any action by local authorities for sanitary purposes because they are frightened by any increase in the rates. Scores of small urban and rural districts are in a condition which is a disgrace and a danger to the whole nation. We shall never get rid of that state of things unless we enable the local authorities to carry out sanitary works under more easy conditions. I should not myself be disinclined to see some central method of dealing with these questions, although I am afraid that this is not likely to be done. I think the right hon. Gentleman would be wise, in dealing with loans for the water supply and for sanitary purposes in such areas as I have alluded to, if he would extend, as far as possible, the period for repayment. In such cases as these it is not only the community which is likely to be endangered, but even the whole nation may be injured by the neglect of a particular locality. If that state of things can be avoided by the extension of the period of repayment for a loan, a benefit will be conferred upon the community at large.

GENERAL LAURIE (Pembroke and Haverfordwest) : My view is that if communities are determined to be extravagant they ought to pay for it, and pay for it within a limited period. Very often—as in cases with which I have been associated—it is not the local authorities who are extravagant, but the Local Government Board, who insist upon them being extravagant. Take the case of my own borough. The Local Government Board has, no doubt most wisely, insisted that they should sewer and lay on fresh water supplies into the borough. That is, therefore, not their extravagance, for it is done by the direction of the Local Government Board. The occupier has to meet the rates, but he is, in many cases, simply a leaseholder, and it is hard to make him bear the burden of great permanent improvements, because he undertakes when he leases the ground and puts the houses on it that he will pay all the taxes. When new taxes are sprung on a community by the Local Government Board, the occupiers are called upon to meet the whole of the expense if the loan is to be paid within a limited period, and not spread over the whole tenure of their lease ; a state of things which they never contemplated at the time when the lease was taken. In such cases I think the time should be much more extended than it is at present, and the occupier should not be burdened with the whole cost of the improvements.

MR. CHAPLIN : I desire to remind hon. Members who have spoken that in these matters the Local Government Board are the trustees for posterity, or in other words, for the future ratepayers of the country, and we are obliged in our discretion to take such action in these matters as appears to us, at all events, to be fair to all the interests and all the parties who are concerned. I have given the greatest attention to the matters which have been placed before me, and after considering as carefully as I could all the various points of view which have

Sir W. Foster.

been submitted to my consideration, I came to the conclusion that the Local Government Board should go more in the direction of the views stated by my hon. friend the Member for Islington. With regard to the period mentioned for loans with respect to the purchase of land, my hon. friend is mistaken, for almost invariably the practice of the Local Government Board is, in sanctioning loans for the purchase of land, to allow a period of fifty years for its repayment. Therefore, I heard with some surprise the statement which fell from my hon. friend.

SIR ALBERT ROLLIT : Perhaps the right hon. Gentleman will permit me to say that if I was mistaken I was misinformed. My information came from one of the town clerks affected, who has been in communication with the Local Government Board.

MR. CHAPLIN : Then, the hon. Member for West Ham called my attention to a case which had occurred only the other day, in which he said some land had been purchased for an infirmary, and that while the town council had been able to borrow money for purposes other than for the purchase of land at a period of sixty years, in this case the Board of Guardians only allowed thirty years.

*MR. GRAY : I said that thirty years was the period which the Board of Guardians could borrow for under the sanction of the Local Government Board for the buildings.

MR. CHAPLIN : Some expectations appear to me to have been aroused by the Act to which my hon. friend referred, which was passed in the year 1897. Previously to that time it was quite true that in the purchase of land the Guardians would not have been able to obtain a loan for a period of more than thirty years. In that respect they were placed at a great disadvantage as compared with other local authorities. That Act extended the period, with a view of placing boards of guardians on a similar footing with regard to the purchase of land as other authorities. It appears to have been the expectation and consequence of that Act that wider and more general changes were to have been made with regard to the periods for loans borrowed. I do not think that I need to go into the various questions raised by my hon. friend, except in one particular instance, and that is allowing a period of 30 years in the case of wood pavements. My own experience is that to allow 30 years for the laying down of wood pavements would be an extraordinary time, because the paving would perish long before the repayment of the loan was completed. I could not sanction any proposal of that kind. My hon. friend raised another question with which, as far as my own feelings are concerned, I have some sympathy, and that is the question of loans for the erection of workhouses and accommodation for the aged and deserving poor. But there is another side to that question. It must be remembered that the repair and maintenance of such buildings becomes more expensive every year, and the ratepayers of the future will have to find the money for maintaining and extending the accommodation, as well as the interest on the loan. I think the House ought not to forget that a change of circumstances very often in these days involves great expenditure, and very often expensive alterations have to be made. Even at the present moment there is a great demand for better accommodation in the workhouses in various parts of the country for the aged poor, and claims in this direction may have to be made at no distant period upon the ratepayers of this country. If we were to extend the period for the repayment of loans for such purposes to 50 or 60 years, which I think has been suggested, we should have one generation of ratepayers paying for the new and the old accommodation as well, and I cannot help thinking that that would be a most unfair arrangement. There is also this consideration—that the shorter the period the more it will act as a check upon extravagance, and certainly when you consider how enormously the loans borrowed by local authorities are increasing by leaps and bounds every day, I do think that we ought not very willingly to part with any check upon extravagance of that kind. It has been pointed out from the benches behind me that this expenditure is often incurred under the instructions and the insistence of the Local Government Board itself. I acknowledge that, for sanitary purposes, it is the duty sometimes of the Local Government Board to give instructions of that kind. But even then it is impossible for the Local Government Board to supervise all the details of expenditure for this purpose. But, even in such cases, where it may have required the erection of certain buildings or accommodation, it is very desirable that there should be as much inducement as possible for the local authority to confine the expenditure within the smallest limits they possibly can, consistently with the due performance of the work. Having regard to the great increase in the indebtedness of the local authorities throughout the country, and having regard to all those other considerations to which I have alluded, I am not disposed, and I should be most reluctant, to meet the views of hon. Gentlemen with regard to the extension of the period for repayment, in the interest of the ratepayers of the future, or to proceed in the direction in which they ask me to proceed. The hon. Member opposite urged that in regard to sanitary matters some concessions might be made ; but, when I come to consider the various purposes for which sanitary expenditure is incurred, and the different times allowed for the loans for different purposes, I cannot think that there is any great necessity in this case for a change, or that improvements are prevented because the periods for repayment are not extended. The question of sewage was mentioned, but in such a case as that we have discretionary power to allow forty years, and I do not think that that period is so short as to prevent wise and necessary improvements being carried out which would otherwise be accomplished. My hon. friend complained that the County Councils were not allowed more than thirty years for the erection of lunatic asylums, police-stations, and matters of that kind. He thought there was no grievance in regard to the main roads, but in these cases my hon. friend thinks that the period might be increased. I should say that, generally speaking, the arguments I have endeavoured to put forward with regard to workhouses and accommodation for the aged poor apply in exactly the same degree to the case of lunatic asylums, and I am more disposed in that direction to be lenient. I am very sorry indeed that it should fall to my lot or that I should conceive it to be my duty to resist a demand made by so many hon. Members representing various constituencies, but for the general reasons which I have stated I have come to the conclusion that it would be contrary to the public interest to concede their demand, and therefore I cannot accede to the proposal of my hon. friend.

*MR. MENDL (Plymouth) : I very much regret that such a cast-iron rule in regard to local loans should exist. The case to which the hon. Member for West Ham referred was the case of a new community which has grown up in a generation and had all its loans outstanding ; but the community I represent is a very old community which is now being transformed into a new town. In consequence of the conditions on which the local loans are obtained and repaid, that new town is being built up at the sole expense of the present ratepayers. Whole streets are being pulled down and rebuilt, and water works, etc., are being erected at their expense. The natural result of a system of this kind is to discourage any Local Committee from improving an old town. It is a matter of very great regret that the right hon. Gentleman is not able to hold out some hope that some alteration might be made in the existing system of repayment of local loans, as the natural result of it is to discourage local progress in consequence of the unfair burden imposed upon existing ratepayers by the cost of permanent improvements being thrown entirely on them.

Original question again proposed. Motion by leave withdrawn.

MR. SAMUEL SMITH : I beg to move the reduction of the salary of the President of the Local Government Board by £100, in order to call the attention of the Committee to the administration of the barrack schools for pauper children under the present Poor Law system. I wish to specially remind the Committee that the Poor Law Schools Committee issued what is a most important report on the extremely unwholesome character of the barrack school system. My object in bringing the matter before the Committee to-night is to spur on the Local Government Board and to spur on the Boards of Guardians to carry out the broader policy of the recommendations of the Committee. That Committee was presided over by Mr. Mundella, and contained a number of well-known gentlemen, and altogether was a very strong and competent Committee to deal with the question of

Mr. Chaplin.

pauper children. I will ask now permission to lay before the Committee a few facts with regard to this matter. The Committee was limited to the Metropolitan Schools, containing some 17,000 pauper children, but I believe it may be taken as substantially representing all the pauper schools of the country. The condition is worse in London because the schools are larger, but the vices of this system of training are obvious everywhere. The conclusion the Committee came to was that the system was an extremely expensive one, and an extremely unwholesome one. The herding vast numbers of children together in large institutions has a deadly effect on health and character ; it produces worse results than when children are brought up even in the poorest homes. The Committee give a number of recommendations for the suppression of this system altogether. It was shown that the average cost for 17,000 pauper children was £29 5s. 6d. per head, or 11s. per child a week ; that is to say, the cost of bringing up a pauper child is about half the income of an average working class family containing six or seven persons. At the Hanwell school the cost ran up per child to as much as £42 15s. 2d. The cost of that enormous institution was £177,000. That, in any case, is a wasteful expense in the highest degree. But that in itself would not matter so much if the system were not such a bad one. I do not think there is a philanthropist who does not agree that to herd fifteen hundred children together in an institution where they are only known by numbers is anything but injurious to the health of these children. The rate of mortality is far higher than that of the poorest families in the metropolis. Infectious diseases are never absent from these institutions. Ophthalmia is a constant scourge ; there are times when as many as 20 per cent. of the children are ill at a time ; in some of the schools all the children have been visited with this plague at one time or another, and great numbers of them have their eyes weakened for life ; they go out into the world heavily handicapped from this cause alone. The report of one of the medical officers shows that you cannot have a number of children herded together without mischief of this kind occurring. He says—

"In the schools as conducted at present, with the exception of Hanwell, every child loses its education directly it gets ophthalmia. The attack often lasts for months in greater or less severity, during the whole of which time the child ceases to have any mental training or to be subjected to the school discipline. Although in some cases the time that active eye mischief is present is comparatively short, the eye may remain unhealthy, or in a state that necessitates isolation during many months. Throughout this period the children must spend their days in the room or airing yard of the isolation ward. They have for companions only other children afflicted in the same way; they are cut off from their friends, from their games in the field, from their walks in the country, from their work in the school or in the shop; if able to read they have no opportunity, and they are not ill enough to interest others. Thus, in the milder cases the restrictions necessary for preventing the spread of the malady constitute a much greater immediate evil for the affected children than does the disease itself."

But this is not the only disease prevalent in these schools; ringworm and skin-diseases are also very common, and the average health of the children is very low indeed. That seems to be a terrible condition of things, and although everybody knows that it is practically true, still the system is going on, and nothing whatever has been done to improve it. The Report on the education of the children is also very unsatisfactory; the standard attained is very much below that of ordinary elementary schools. The inspection is not by the ordinary class of inspectors subject to the requirements of the Code, but by a special class under the Local Government Board. The Report of the Commission states:

" The information we have obtained, confirmed as it has been by our personal observation and examination, has convinced us that, in many of these particulars, the Poor Law Schools of the Metropolis are far below the standard usually attained, age for age, by the children in public elementary schools."

The schools are not under the Education Department, but the Local Government Board. But worst of all in my opinion is the evil, the demoralising effect on character, especially in the case of girls, of the life of the schools. There is only one opinion among all the witnesses as to the deadening effect of this herding of masses of children without love or affection. I should like to quote two or three proofs of this. Miss Whitworth has acted for several years as Secretary for that admirable Society, the Metropolitan Association for Befriending Young Servants. She gives a list of these faults:

" Rudeness, sullenness, violence, destructive-ness, carelessness, idleness, obstinacy, and a curious ignorance of common things."

This witness also alludes to another trait in the character of the girls. They are unable, she says, to face any difficulty, and they are in despair at a small trouble.

" A girl only thinks she would 'like to be dead,' or to commit suicide or something, when she gets into a minor trouble or difficulty. Perhaps she is put upstairs for a half-day, and she says she will never do anything again as long as she lives, and will never be seen alive again; that kind of thing is very common; the inability to face difficulty comes from never having had any difficulties to face; a girl in school has so few difficulties, she does not know what it is to have survived them, and she thinks she cannot survive them."

" This failing is attributed by the witness to the fact that the children have everything done for them at the school, and that they necessarily lead a mechanical and routine life. The following is the testimony of a lady who has worked for twelve years amongst workhouse girls:—

" In district school girls, with scarcely an exception, I have found very strongly marked what I think is a great characteristic of the girls brought up in such large schools - intense obstinacy and sullenness. . . . I do not remember a single instance of exactly the same kind of temper among the other girls, the greater number of whom come from very poor homes; their fathers dock labourers, and large families living in one or two rooms. I do feel most strongly that family life, even among the very poor, has an entirely different effect on the character of a child from life in a large school."

Dr. Barnardo is also a gentleman who has had vast experience of this subject. He has passed through his hands altogether 11,000 children. His evidence before the Commission is of immense value. With regard to the girls he says:—

" The mental condition of the girls has been a source of great amazement to me, their dulness and incapacity, and especially the animalism of their tempers. I have had some of these cases which have been the most perplexing I have ever had in all my experience, and I have been compelled to reject most of these girls as unfitted for emigration. I did so with great regret, but there was no hope of my being able eventually to emigrate them. I do not know whether a topic of this sort may be usefully introduced here; but I am bound to say that evil habits are much more prevalent than, I think, the public have any conception of in all Poor Law establishments of a barrack class in which girls are aggregated."

Now, I particularly ask the Committee to listen to this sentence:—

" Very few girls come from Poor Law institutions who have not, apparently, been more or less contaminated. When these children were sent down to our village home, or to our other homes, the facts crept out in a few days in their own communications with other girls in the cottage. Our small cottages gave us so much more opportunity of finding the evil out much more quickly than would have otherwise been the case."

I do not think that anyone will deny the substantial truth of what I stated. These facts are admitted on all hands, and although this Report was issued five or six years ago, this scandalous condition of things is still going on.

MR. CHAPLIN : No, no ; it is not.

MR. SAMUEL SMITH : I believe there has been one change. There is the Sutton school, containing 1,500 children, and I believe a scheme is now in progress for removing some of that great mass of children. But the great bulk of the schools, which contain 52,000, are still in the same condition that they were five years ago. How long are we going to be before we alter it ? The way in which we are wedded to this system has sometimes made me think that there must be some persons interested in these large establishments where such large numbers of children are herded together because of the difficulty there is to change their habits. I cannot doubt that one of the chief obstacles to the adoption of a more humane system is the class of officials who draw good salaries, and the persons interested in the contracts given to them for feeding and clothing the children. I noticed the other day a scheme for building large numbers of cottage homes, but they are to be built in large villages, and the cost of each house would come to £200. For that you could build a first-class workman's house. The Guardians will not move unless we can move public opinion in this House, and the only reason that I raise the question here to-night is in order to let the public know what is being done. Now, what I propose to do is to suggest that some of the recommendations of the Committee which reported five years ago should be carried out. The principal recommendation of the Committee was to board out the children in respectable working class homes, as is done in every country but this—as is done in Scotland with such excellent results, where the number of pauper children disappear, because they are brought up with other children, and so lose their pauper taint. The total number of children boarded out now in this country is 2,000 out of the 52,000, in

addition to which there are 4,000 boarded out with other unions. Another recommendation is that these children should be separated from the penal class as much as possible. They should be brought up in a healthy home, in God's ordinance, which is the only way to bring them up. One of the rules of the Local Government Board is that no child can be boarded out at a greater cost than 4s. a week. In the pauper school they cost 11s. a week, but to be boarded out they must not cost more than 4s. Just consider what an absurd limit that is. Is it not better to board them out for 5s. or 6s. or 8s. per week rather than keep them in these barrack schools at a cost of 11s. per week ? I have one quotation which I would like to give to the House as to the advantage of home training —

"One advantage to the child of boarding out is that it provides home training and allows development of personal affections. Of course the home training is what has made our English working classes as good as they are. Home training involves a great many things which perhaps men know less of than women ; it is the small details of every-day home life that bring out the character of a child, and that, as it grows up, enable it, though unconsciously, to develop self-dependence, resourcefulness, thriftiness ; it learns by the example of its elders. This is a perfectly unconscious influence, and no amount of teaching by direct information could give a child that particular class of experience which it gets in the every-day home life—the rubs and frictions that come from brothers and sisters and elders and youngsters ; the self-denial that it sees its parents going through when times are bad, the happiness when times are better ; the need of forethought ; the dependence for success on industrious habits ; the value of money and clothes — from all these the boarded-out child learns and realises what the life that is coming to it will be. Then there is another thing, home life draws out the personal affections, and I think it is one of the most terrible things in workhouses or in very large schools that a child who can elsewhere be trained, up to a certain age, through its affections has that particular item in its human character perfectly undeveloped, and I believe that is the reason that so many of them in after life fall. I am not speaking against the officers of the schools. I think they do good work as far as they can, but it is a sheer impossibility that they can do what can only be done in the ordinary everyday home.

" Then another point is that they are educated in a family of mixed ages and both sexes, which is most important. Of course, it is impossible in a large school or in a large workhouse to allow the boys and girls to mix together, and they never see each other from one year's end to another. This is a serious drawback in after life, especially with girls ;

they have not been accustomed to receive the respect which a boy ought to give to a girl in his own cottage home, they do not know how to treat boys, they have never seen them; consequently they do not know how to treat young men, nor do the young men know how to treat the girls when they meet them."

Next to the system of boarding out, I would put Cottage Homes. By Cottage Homes I do not mean a large village of twenty or thirty houses, which results in many hundreds of children being brought together, but the Cottage Homes like those of the Sheffield Union, where twenty or thirty children are put under the care of a kind motherly house-mother, and the children attend the public schools of the place, and live as natural a life as possible. I desire to separate the children from everything which contains the least pauper taint. The last thing to which I wish to call the attention of the Committee is a method of which I have myself very great experience, and that is emigration, and I say, of all the means at our disposal, that is the best way of disposing of pauper or deserted children. I have had very considerable experience of this system, and have been a party to the emigration of 3,000 poor children from Liverpool to Canada. These were not Poor Law children, but rather waifs and strays and the really destitute; but they had not the name of pauper children, which is such a brand of inferiority in Canada. These children get on far better in Canada than is possible in this old and crowded country. They easily find there homes in the houses of yeoman farmers, where they live with the family, and are often adopted, and the vast majority do well in after-life. One great advantage is that they are entirely cut off from their degraded relatives in this country, who constantly get hold of the pauper children when they come out of the institutions and drag them back to vice and misery. Here we have an overplus of children; every channel is choked up. In Canada there is a large free channel; but instead of seeing that system increase it is steadily diminishing. At one time the Board of Guardians of Liverpool used to emigrate 400 children a year, and now it is 78. No doubt there are difficulties in the way, little trifling expenses of £1 here and £1 there, which the guardians cannot see their way to pay; but in reality it is a great economy. You send these children for a six months'

training; you pay them about £10 a head, allow them their passage money to Canada; the whole thing can be done for £15, or £20 at the outside, instead of £300. Looking at it from an economic point of view, there does seem to be an enormous saving in treating the children in this way, and I cannot understand the practice in this country in regard to it. When I blame the guardians they say it is the fault of the Local Government Board, and when I speak to the Local Government Board upon the subject they lay the blame upon the boards of guardians. In Canada we have 5,000,000 of people with unlimited territory; in crowded London we have 6,000,000 of people and multitudes of children; and yet nothing is done to make use of this grand channel for the disposition of our pauper children. A great portion of these workhouse children are children of parents who have contracted the taste for drink, which they have transmitted to their descendants, and in their surroundings in this country they have become drunkards. But we have thousands of these children, who have been sent to Canada, who have grown up to manhood and womanhood free from temptation, and have remained all their lives total abstainers. Surely, when the House is aware of the enormous advantages of this system, they ought to bring pressure to bear on the Local Government Board and the boards of guardians to look better after these poor children. It is very hard to see why reforms of this kind are so slow of being adopted in England. I believe we require legislation to bring power to bear on backward boards of guardians, and to stop vicious parents taking their children from school and tramping about the country with them, because the children in the process acquire vicious habits and are continually thrown upon the rates. They deal far more summarily in America with these vicious parents. The children are by law taken out of the hands of vicious parents, and put under the control of trustees up to the age of 18 and 21, and so saved from continuing the vicious lives to which their parents are condemned. We require something of the kind in this country, but we are so dreadfully jealous of the rights of parents that we have hitherto refused to interfere with their rights over their unhappy offspring. I hope that one result of this debate will be that something will be done by the Local Government Board in regard to the treatment of pauper children more encouraging than in the past.

Motion made and Question proposed,

"That Item A (Salaries) be reduced by £50, in respect of the salary of the President of the Local Government Board." — (*Mr. Samuel Smith.*)

MR. FLOWER (Bradford, West) : I rise to ask the President of the Local Government Board for some information as to the policy he desires to adopt in substitution for the system of barrack schools. The right hon. Gentleman stated that the Sutton school is to be closed ; but I should like to know when, and to what purpose that very large building is to be devoted. I express the hope that that building will not be devoted to children who may be described as feeble-minded and defective. Apart from the future of the buildings, what is the policy of the Department in regard to the future of the children in these large schools ? The right hon. Gentleman has spoken of the comparative failure of the boarding-out system. I am afraid that for that failure a certain amount of blame is to be attached to the Department. Only two of the unions connected with the Sutton school— Woolwich and Camberwell—have availed themselves of the boarding-out system, and that to a very limited extent. The plan of the Local Government Board of building blocks to accommodate sixty children is one which requires more complete experiment than it has yet obtained before it should be sanctioned to any large degree. The block system is undoubtedly better than the barrack system, but it is open to the chief objection to the barrack system—namely, the creation of an artificial atmosphere around the children. Probably you will obtain a higher percentage in regard to sanitation, health, ophthalmia, etc.; yet you cannot from an ethical or educational standpoint regard these blocks of houses as being at all an adequate or advisable way of dealing with the children. I would like to know from the right hon. Gentleman whether his Department had really decided to sanction the proposal of the Stepney Board of Guardians to expend no less than £10,500 on the

Mr. Samuel Smith.

purchase of land in Essex on which to erect blocks of cottages for 250 children which are at present in the Sutton schools. If the Stepney Board of Guardians had pursued a similar course to that adopted by the Whitechapel Board of Guardians they might have found that they could have reduced the number of children to be dealt with by 40 or 50 per cent. An even more dangerous departure is, I understand, contemplated by the Poplar Board of Guardians, who propose to found a whole village of pauper children at a minimum cost of £100,000. And Greenwich and Dulwich, I understand, also propose to go in for large blocks. I would suggest to my right hon. friend that, in sanctioning the building of these blocks of schools, he is taking a step which in the event of failure it would be exceedingly difficult for him to redress. If you once have these large blocks of buildings erected, you have them on your hands for all time to come, and it would be impossible, however unfavourable the results may be, to effect any change or reform, at any rate for many years to come. The great difficulty about the boarding-out system advocated by my hon. friend the Member for Flintshire is that of securing suitable foster parents and adequate inspection. In regard to the difficulties of inspection I am not quite sure that the remedy does not lie with the Local Government Board themselves. If they had carried out the recommendation of their own Departmental Committee they would have appointed several lady inspectors, instead of one only. The duties of inspection have not been carried out with much discretion or tact. Obviously you do not encourage working people to come forward and express their willingness to act as foster parents if they are to be treated by the inspectors as "persons to be found out." There has, however, never been a case in which boarding-out has proved a failure in the Australian colonies, and I do not believe myself that the difficulties I have mentioned are insurmountable if properly dealt with. In large industrial communities, such as Woolwich—which is building blocks of houses, each to accommodate sixty children—it would be absolutely absurd to say that you could not get forty respectable working men and their wives to undertake the care of these children. I feel quite confident that with greater stimulus from my right hon.

friend a great deal may be done in encouraging and developing the boarding-out system. Now, sir, the hon. Gentleman advocated another method of dealing with these children—a method of which I also am largely in favour—and that was the principle of scattered homes. This principle has passed the experimental stage, and has been a great success at Bradford, Bath, and Sheffield. The system, of course, is that the houses should respectively accommodate fifteen children—I believe that is the number at Sheffield, but the Sheffield Guardians think it rather excessive. I would rather see ten children in each home, and they should attend the public elementary school and participate in what may be called the general child life of the community. They lose in that way the taint of pauperism which I am afraid, if once attached to a child, clings to it all through its life. I think the Local Government Board would do well to help forward as far as they can those boards of guardians who are prepared to adopt the scattered home system. I am afraid that they have not done so altogether. I am afraid with regard, for example, to Camberwell that they have not exhibited that appreciation of the enterprise that that Board of Guardians has displayed in relation to the scattered homes of their pauper children. I pass from that to another matter to which the hon. Member has alluded, viz., tramps. On that head I think no blame is to be attached to the Local Government Board, because both the President and his Department have given a sympathetic help to a proposal which has been before Parliament for the last three years for increasing the powers of boards of guardians to deal with vagrant children. That that Act has not become law is no fault of the Government, or of the President of the Local Government Board. I am afraid the source of the evil is to be traced to the occupants of the benches opposite. But if the Government can see their way to bring in a Bill of their own to deal with this question upon similar lines, I believe they would find it would be generally welcomed. I feel sure it would be enthusiastically received on this side, and I feel sure many hon. Members opposite would give it their support. I have seen a statement made to the effect that children of the tramp class number no fewer than

50,000. That statement is probably a little high; but it would not, I think, be beyond the mark to say that the number would be somewhere between 30,000 and 50,000. The figures appear to be mounting up at an alarming rate. As a member of the London School Board I have frequently come across cases of this particular tramp class. We have, for example, a lady visitor now in the Tower Hamlets district whose special business it is to look after the children of this class, who are to be found either in the casual wards of a workhouse or in a common lodging-house. The Bill to which I refer would give guardians the power, when they are called upon, to retain their hold of these children until they are able to earn their own livelihood.

* MR. WILLIAM JONES (Carnarvonshire, Arfon): I wish to call attention to one point, and it is the system of education in Poor Law schools. I find that a recommendation of the Poor Law Schools Committee Report pointed out the desirability of more trained teachers. I consider the teachers to be a most important factor in any school, and I should like to know what orders of the Local Government Board have been issued, or what steps have been taken, to improve the teaching and obtain more trained teachers in these schools. I find on looking at the statistics of these schools that there are 172 teachers employed, of whom only 60 are trained. The rest are partially trained, but most of them are untrained. The few who are partially trained obtain Queen's scholarships. But there are a great number who have no qualifications for teaching at all, and who would not be recognised by the Education Department. There are those who hold a certificate by the Local Government Board. We know that the Local Government Board is not an educational authority, and the certificate represents a much lower standard of qualification than that of the Education Department. Why should these children, simply because they are pauper children, be taught by teachers who are not trained, and who simply hold a certificate without any educational qualification attached to it whatever? I say there is need of a higher standard. A standard has been recommended over and over again by the Commissioners, and I should like to know what has been done towards advancing the recommendations by the Local Government Board. We need a higher standard both in the interests of the scholar and the teacher. In the interests of the children, to begin with, because all children, and particularly those of the poorer classes, and of the very poorest, ought to receive the best possible education calculated to form capable citizens from the best possible teachers. Again, teachers in all departments of public service should stand on the same footing, and should be able to pass freely from the service of Poor Law authorities to that of other school managers. Of course, no one wishes to disregard the claims and interests of all competent teachers now on the staff, but wherever vacancies occur the Local Government Board should see that those vacancies are filled not by incompetent teachers, not by those who get certificates sanctioned by the Local Government Board, but by teachers qualified under the Education Department. Some of the teachers are mere drudges. I will read a portion of a letter written by a certificated Poor Law teacher to the *Schoolmaster* of the 12th November, 1898, giving an idea of a Poor Law teacher's daily life :—

" Rise at 7 a.m., take children in dining hall to breakfast at 7.30 a.m., leave hall at 8 a.m. (teachers' breakfast), school at 9 a.m. till 12 a.m. ; take children in dining hall for dinner till 12.35 or 12.40 (teachers' dinner), school at 2 p.m. to 4.30 p.m. ; take children in hall at 6 p.m. to 6.30 p.m. to supper, hear prayers and see children to bed at 7.30 p.m. or later."

I say that that kind of life makes a teacher a mere drudge, gives him no varied interest in life, does not widen his intellectual outlook, and provides him with no chance of mixing with his fellow-men. In eleven schools the teachers are resident on the premises, but in nine others I am glad to say they live out of school and so come in contact with their fellow-men. The plan gives more freedom and freshness to the teachers, and enables them to become more efficient instructors. The remedy for the present state of things is to send all the children out of these inefficient schools to public elementary schools, and I earnestly press on the President of the Local Government Board and his staff the desirability of transferring these Poor Law schools to the Education Department. In several districts the guardians are already sending the children from these workhouse schools

Mr. William Jones.

to elementary schools. In Stoke when the workhouse children attended the Board schools it was found that their education was of a very low standard indeed, and they were very much behind the other children in the schools. In Ipswich, not long ago, there was a proposal to send the girls of St. John's Home to a public elementary school, and when a guardian objected, one of the others— himself a workhouse boy in the forties —stated that he was in favour of sending the girls to a public elementary school, and he added that since the boys of the Home had gone out to school they had become much brighter. All the guardians, with the exception of one—a lady — voted in favour of the girls also being sent out to school. I trust the Local Government Board will recommend every board of guardians to act similarly. Poverty is not a crime but a misfortune, and we should in the interests of civilisation and humanity do our best to remove these children from the stigma and taint of pauperism, and that can be partially done by placing them in schools where they will enjoy free intercourse with other children drawn from all classes of the community.

**Mr. DRAGE (Derby) : As one of those who have been urging on the Local Government Board the desirability of better education for pauper children, I should like to point out that great reforms have been accomplished the last few years. In the first place the staff of the Board has been considerably increased and many of the abuses which obtained in times past were really largely due to an insufficient staff and to want of proper accommodation for the staff. The right hon. gentleman has by means of circulars and by the action of his department carried out reforms in reference to nursing and other details. He has also constituted in the Children's Committee of the Metropolitan Asylums Board a new authority to remove certain classes of children from Poor Law schools. It is very hard to convey to the Committee the enormous difficulties attending what appears the apparently simple operation of breaking up one of these barrack schools. Many hon. Members are aware of the enormous difficulty of obtaining from the various local authorities in the metropolis the

necessary agreement. There is one institution in connection with the Poor Law system which has rendered excellent service, and the work of which has been much encouraged by the right hon. Gentleman. I refer to the training ship "Exmouth," and now when there is an outcry for more sailors for the Navy and the mercantile marine it is pleasing to direct attention to the figures which the right hon. Gentleman has been able to give with reference to that institution. I would ask the right hon. Gentleman whether he would consider the desirability of stationing other ships either at Grays or around the coast under the same superintendence and the same committee. There are, however, one or two abuses of which we have to complain from year to year, and to which I wish to direct the attention of the right hon. Gentleman. First of all there was the question of the children of vagrants, called "ins and outs," whose education is broken off when they leave the workhouses. The right hon. Gentleman has been asked to introduce a bill to deal with it, but what I desire to point out is that there have been several decisions by the metropolitan magistrates that such children can be dealt with under Section 14 of the Industrial Schools Act, 1866, merely on the ground that their parents are not providing them with education. If the right hon. Gentleman cannot introduce a Bill this session I would urge him to make known to metropolitan and country boards of guardians that there is an existing provision under which the children of vagrant parents can be dealt with. Such children coming into and going out of workhouses are a moral and physical disadvantage to the children with whom they associate; they discourage the teachers, and are themselves as regards their parents a scandal to the country. I am well aware of the reforms which the right hon. Gentleman has carried out, but I would wish to ask him whether he is going to give any further accommodation for Poor Law children now in the workhouses in the metropolis. The Poor Law Commissioners and their successors have, since 1841, been never tired of calling attention to the result of bringing up children in workhouses in London in the midst of poverty. Children in London workhouses are worse off than children in country workhouses, and

no provision is made for their proper accommodation and education. Again, as the committee is aware, such children have often to be protected from their parents when they get situations, and what I desire further to ask is whether the right hon. Gentleman will extend the power of inspection at present possessed by the Girls' Friendly Society, which does the work of the Metropolitan Association for Befriending Young Servants in the provinces. In 1897 no less than 2,686 girls—all Poor Law children—were looked after by the London society, and what I ask is that the right hon. Gentleman, through the Local Government Board, should use his influence on behalf of the sister society in the provinces with unions which do not now permit lady visitors. I may remind the Committee, as showing the admirable action of these societies, that whereas many years ago one girl in five returned to the workhouse in a pitiable condition, probably to remain there for the rest of her life, the proportion has now been reduced to one in fifty-two, and if permission similar to that given to the town society were extended to the country society a great advantage would be gained. In connection with the emigration of boys and girls to the colonies I would earnestly ask the right hon. Gentleman whether he could not in some way meet the views which have been expressed on that subject. There is only one other matter to which I desire to refer, and that the position of the canal boat children. It is one of the anomalies of our present adminstration that these children are now partly under the inspection of the Local Government Board and partly under that of the Education Department. The result is that they are practically left without any education at all. A very short Act of Parliament or a more stringent adminis- tration of the existing law would lead those children from a life of almost certain vagrancy into a condition of moral and physical improvement, and I earnestly press the matter on the attention of the right hon. Gentleman. The question of the enormous increase of vagrancy in recent years is one which will, no doubt, engage the earliest atten. tion of the right hon. Gentleman in the near future. The number of vagrants was larger last year, in 1898, than it has ever been since 1858, with one exception.

A question arises upon this point, upon which more than once I have pressed the right hon. Gentleman, under the Bill passed by Her Majesty's Government in 1882—whether he cannot promote continuity and uniformity of administration in the Vagrancy Act. When this has been done, as in Liverpool and elsewhere, we have had a great diminution in vagrancy. I wish to ask the attention of the Committee to one subject more, namely, that though we have had exhaustive inquiries into this subject by two Committees, so far as I am aware there has not been in this House the slightest opportunity given for discussing the reports of the two Committees which have considered the question of the unemployed. It is a matter which is bound to come up again with increasing urgency, and I do press upon the Committee that now is the time, when trade is steadily increasing, to cope with this difficulty. I respectfully urge that the recommendations of the last Committee upon the subject, that local organisations for thrift and charity should combine with the local boards of guardians, is one which offers the most practical and satisfactory solution, not only of the problem of the unemployed, but that of old age and poverty of every form.

MR. TREVELYAN (York, W.R., Elland): I wish to draw attention to the practice of allowing the children of the Sutton barrack schools, on Derby Day, to beg coins from passers - by. This matter has already been brought under the notice of the right hon. Gentleman, but it would seem that he has determined to do nothing to put an end to the practice. We hope that the determination is not irrevocable. The circumstances are these :—On Derby Day it is the practice, and it has been for twenty years, to permit the children at these schools to be drawn up in a field near by, with banners flying and band playing, for the purpose of attracting the attention of those who are going down to the racecourse. They collect a large sum of money in the course of the day. Personally I have no particular objection to their receiving money from those going down to see the Derby ; I would object quite as much if the money came from people going to a cricket match or a Church congress. What we do object to is that children should be permitted to

Mr. Drage.

beg. They are of a poor and sordid origin, and it is only too likely that, even without this incitement and example, they would take to begging methods of life when they leave the schools. It is suggested, as a reason for not putting an end to the practice, that the money is devoted to giving the children a treat at the Crystal Palace. No one would wish to deprive the children of that treat, but I would suggest that there are other ways in which money could be raised for the purpose, either by private subscription, or by the Local Government Board permitting the expenditure of public money to the small extent which would be necessary to give the children a day's holiday. I hope the right hon. Gentleman will consider whether he cannot stop this encouragement of begging propensities in the children, and for the future prohibit the practice.

MR. HAZELL : I wish to draw attention to the expenditure going on in connection with certain orphan schools. We know that the system of large barrack schools has been condemned, yet in spite of that condemnation by experts, considerable sums are still being expended upon them. How is it that a sum of £6,000 is to be expended on a new infant school at Hanwell, and that, at Marylebone, £12,000 is to be spent, in spite of the statement of the right hon. Gentleman that he is unfavourable to any further development of the system ?

*MR. T. W. RUSSELL : I do not think my hon. friend will find that any expenditure which has been sanctioned for these schools has been sanctioned for the purpose of providing any further accommodation. It is only to provide for alterations which could not be avoided, and which are necessary in the interests of the children already in the school. My right hon. friend said, two or three years ago, that he would sanction no expenditure involving any enlargement of the schools.

MR. HAZELL : Still, the fact remains that, as I understand, some thousands of pounds are to be spent in building new infant schools. There is another point I wish to touch upon. The system of barrack schools is a very wasteful one. Take the case of food. There is a rigid rule that each child shall have exactly the same amount of food, and the result is that, while one child gets more than he can eat, another does not have enough. Miss Davenport Hill has shown the enormous waste of food which goes on, and, I believe, the Bethnal Green Board of Guardians, last November, took the trouble to ascertain the extent of the waste. They weighed all the food given out and all left, and they found a waste of 190 gallons of bread and meat, while in three weeks, in December, they discovered a waste of 178 gallons of milk alone. The present system of barrack schools is notoriously expensive as well as inefficient, and I should like to emphasise what has been said as to the boarding out of pauper children. It is well known that the cost of boarding them out is a great deal less than the cost of keeping them in barrack schools. In Scotland 84 per cent. of the pauper children are boarded out, while in England only 5 per cent. are boarded out. There is this great difficulty, however, that unless the foster parents are care fully selected, and the children carefully inspected, their last state is worse than the first. I have had considerable experience of boarding out children for a limited period. I am connected with Committees which send 50,000 or 60,000 children to the country in the summer months in cottage homes, and that experience leads me to the conviction that all these pauper children should be sent to the country the whole year round. Of course, there are many villages where the house accommodation is so limited, and so bad, that no children could be boarded out to any good purpose; but, on the other hand, there are villages where the accommodation is good, and where the surroundings are wholesome from a moral, social, and education point of view. We are thankful for the limited amount of progress that has been made in this direction by the Local Government Board, but we ask that it should be continued and extended to a much greater degree.

DR. CLARK : There are two items on this vote to which I have a very strong objection. The first is the educational part. I have always thought it ridiculous that the Local Government Board should grant low grade certificates which nobody will accept. This matter ought to be in the hands of the Education Department, and pauper children ought to be placed in the same condition as other children, and their teachers ought to be as competent as the teachers of the Board Schools. In fact, a lot of work is done by the Local Government Board which ought to be done by the Education Department. I have had a little experience of the Scotch boarding-out system. I was a member of the parochial board of one of the largest parishes in Scotland, which sends four members to Parliament, and all the children there were boarded out. I went out over and over again to inspect the children, and found in every case they were happy and comfortable, and became, in fact, the foster children of the foster parents, bore their name, and very often took charge of the old women in their declining years as if they were their own mothers. Ninety per cent. of the pauper children in Scotland are boarded out, and the system has been thoroughly successful in every direction. You take away the children from their early associations, place them where nobody knows whether they are pauper children or not, give them a home training, and afford them ten times a better chance of succeeding in after life than under the English system. My hon. friend the Member for Flintshire has spoken of ophthalmia and contagious diseases spreading among the children in the barrack schools. Twenty years ago I was medical officer for Norwood, and I saw plenty of the effects and physical evils of the barrack school system ; but these were nothing to the moral evils. All you do under the English system is to breed a pauper class, and to take away all the elements of character which might be useful to the children in after life. I know not how long we are going to keep up this terrible system in England, the evils of which are admitted in every debate we have had for years in this House. We all agree that the boarding-out system is the best, but practically nothing is done. I hope we shall have a double Division—a Division against the Education Department on the vote, and a Division on the whole estimate.

MR. LOWLES (Shoreditch, Haggerston): The constituency I have the honour to represent have a magnificent establishment 10 or 15 miles from London, and there, I venture to say, the cottage · home system will compare favourably with the boarding out system referred to by the hon. Gentleman who has just spoken. The Local Government Board ought to have the credit that they have encouraged the cottage home system for pauper children. I have gone down to see these children within the last 10 days, and have seen them undergoing physical exercise which would have done credit to the best Board Schools. I admit that the old barrack system was very bad, but the method of the cottage home system, encouraged by the Local Government Board, is bearing splendid fruit, and the children are receiving the highest possible training to fit them for the struggle in life. Many of the parents of the children of the poorer parts of London regard with envy the training which these children get in the cottage homes. I have not enquired into the certificates which the teachers in these homes hold, but I have seen the training which they give to the children, and it is most exemplary.

LORD E. FITZMAURICE: I think we will all agree that whatever the outcome of this debate may be, we are discussing one of the most important and interesting questions which could be discussed in this House—one far more important than those which have excited a great deal of feeling and have commanded a larger attendance, for we are discussing what is to be the future of those who, to use a popular phrase, are called the submerged tenth. We have heard to-night a great deal of the children in large barrack schools. I quite agree with the hon. Member for Flintshire in what he has said in regard to this subject, and we are all indebted to him for bringing up this question. But we must always bear in mind that barrack schools are mostly connected with the metropolis and certain other centres of population, such as Liverpool, Manchester, Leeds, etc. We must not assume, in talking of children in barrack schools, that we are speaking necessarily of the whole pauper children in the country, because there are large numbers of children who are not, and never will be, or can be, sent to these barrack schools. In the past there has been a difficulty in dealing with these children in any other way. The barrack

schools were founded originally from the most excellent and philanthropic motives, but, like many other experiments, they have not worked out in the manner that was hoped. If you take an ordinary union in the rural districts, or in small country towns, you find that very few pauper children find their way into these large barrack schools, and that they have been boarded out or sent to cottage homes. The conclusion that this discussion seems to me to bring us to certainly coincides with my experience, namely, that there is no universal scheme to be found for the education and future training of the pauper child. You must adapt your machinery according to your circumstances, for the machinery which may be good for crowded centres in the metropolis and in our great provincial cities is not necessarily the best for the other districts which have been described. In reality, if this question is ever to be dealt with in any thorough going manner, it must be dealt with as a rule by a careful study of individual districts, and, I might almost say, of individual cases. I recollect, that some years ago there was in one of the reports of the Local Government Board a very able and interesting report written by Mr. Wodehouse, who occupied a position in the Local Government Board. That report showed that we must not rush away with the conclusion that the training of these children in pauper schools is always and invariably a failure. In that report Mr. Wodehouse quoted a great number of cases, drawn from the records of the Local Government Board, where boys who had been educated in pauper schools had succeeded in obtaining a most useful education, and had done exceedingly well afterwards in whatever career they had followed, either in this country or in foreign countries. But, if I may speak from my imperfect recollection of a report that I read some years ago, he pointed out in that report that there was great difficulty in connection with the education of the girls, and, so far as I recollect, he also pointed out that the best cases came from the smaller workhouse schools, where a larger amount of individual care would be given to each individual case, rather than from those barrack schools, which have, on the whole, received, and I think rightly received, the condemnation of my hon. Friend the member for Flint,

Mr. Lowles.

and also of the Committee which so carefully examined the whole matter some years ago. But we must bear this in mind : that while it is easy to condemn, for unanswerable reasons, the organisation of these barrack schools, it is not equally easy to see what you are to do with the enormous mass of children who are congregated in these schools. They are numbered by thousands. Close these schools to-morrow, and what are you going to do with these children the day after to-morrow? It is impossible to shoot them all into Canada or Australia, or to have their education conducted by a boarding-out committee. I think we ought to thank the right hon. Gentleman opposite for having appointed another lady inspector to visit the boarding-out children. The appointment, I believe, has been very carefully made, and the lady appointed is, I have every reason to think, doing admirable work. But more appointments are required. Then there is the question of cottage homes. I live not a great distance from the city of Bath, which has been mentioned to-night, and there I am informed that the system of cottage homes is working exceedingly well. In other cases we hear that some of these cottage homes are falling back to the very system which has been made the principal charge against barrack schools, viz., that you are simply reducing barrack schools in one place in order to restore them in a slightly modified shape in another. I do not commit myself to any assertion as to whether this is correct or not; I only mention it to show that the matter is one which can only be solved by the most extreme care in individual cases. The conclusion I would venture to urge is that the remedy for the evils which affect this large and unfortunate class of pauper children who are so deserving of our sympathy is not to be found in any one set of cut-and-dried measures. You must look to boarding-out where you can form a suitable boarding-out committee and appoint efficient inspectors. Many cases can be dealt with effectually by emigration. Under exceptional circumstances you may still be able to deal advantageously with the children in schools connected with workhouses; and others you may deal with in those cottage homes which are, as it were, a combination of school and home. I think that this debate will in any case have been useful,

and that we shall all feel that we owe a debt of gratitude to the hon. Member for Flint for having raised this question ; and I have no doubt that year after year, in proportion as this question continues to receive attention, we shall find that we have gradually removed that large class of pauper children who are now so heavy a tax upon our resources and upon the ratepayers of the country.

MR. MIDDLEMORE (Birmingham, N.): In the speech to which we have just listened many salient points have been touched upon, and there is no one here who could not learn something from it. I have some knowledge of the schools to which the right hon. Gentleman has referred, and, as to barrack schools, I think he touched precisely upon the right point in saying that we must be guided in our appreciation or condemnation of a school by the surrounding circumstances My own experience is that large schools are very useful when we get as schoolmasters men who devote themselves thoroughly to the work, whose character is a daily inspiration to children, and who are able to make a school a great moral and intellectual institution. But I think as a rule cottage homes are far better, because they are smaller, and because the selection of a good superintendent is far easier than the selection of a really powerful man. The boarding-out system requires good arrangement. Although the Local Government Board do not select the managers of the barrack schools they certainly do select people to visit Canada to inspect the boarding-out system there and they generally select men who know as much about Canada as they know about Heaven. These persons have sent home some extremely ridiculous reports In Canada everything depends upon the *personnel*. You want first-class visitors, because you have to overcome the objection of the people to receive these children. My experience of them is that many of them are so " wooden" and stupid that they would far rather receive children direct from the streets than from the ordinary workhouse schools. The whole matter, in my opinion, depends upon the *personnel* of the managers

MR. DILLON : There can be no doubt whatever that this question of the education of pauper children is one of the most important subjects that ever came under the consideration of this House, because if we are ever in this country to make a serious effort to do away with the curse of pauperism, which I conceive to be one of the greatest reproaches of modern civilisation, and the peculiar characteristics of which are that it seems to increase in proportion to the enormous increase of wealth, the position we must first attack is that of the pauper children. I take a very particular interest in this subject, because it is a burning question in Ireland, and because I think if we were let alone we are in process of teaching the people of this country how to deal with this subject. I contend that upon this particular question of our pauper children we are far ahead of this enormously wealthy country. The noble Lord towards the end of his very interesting speech touched upon what seemed to me to be one of the most hopeful and promising methods of dealing with this whole question, and that is the substitution for the present system of bringing up those unhappy children of the industrial school system. I have always held, from the time I first gave any attention to this great problem, that it is immoral, and, in fact, criminal, for any community to keep children in workhouses who cannot under any circumstances, or in any degree, be responsible for the unfortunate position in which they are placed. It is the duty of the State to rescue them from the circumstances in which they are brought into the world, and to give them every chance of becoming honest and self-supporting citizens. This great and wealthy country has failed in its duty by leaving those children in barrack schools and Poor Law schools under circumstances which hamper them in the struggle for existence, and they are sent forth at the very out-start of their young lives, devoid of the spirit of self-respect. But even if they receive a decent education in Poor Law schools, they go forth branded with the brand of pauperism. The noble Lord spoke of a few cases which came under his own notice, of children taken from Poor Law schools and sent to industrial schools. That was where all those children should be sent. I do not say we should have a cast-iron system. There might be cases in which the children might be boarded out where there would be

Mr. Dillon.

an excellent committee, and where the rural population was of such a character as to lend itself to a boarding-out-system. I believe that system is a great success in Scotland. There you have a class of small homes and good living people, whose family affections are so strong that they can absorb those children into their own families. There are districts where the boarding-out system is cruel, because the population is not of the character which could bear the boarding-out of children, and where some other system must be devised; and where that is the case, the proper direction to take for the administration of those children is the development of the industrial school system to such an extent as would absorb all the children, and separate them by a gulf from those unhappy creatures who must be accommodated in workhouses. That I believe to be practicable and not a difficult plan to carry out. We in Ireland were carrying it out, but we were accused of evading the law. Perhaps we were evading the law, but we were doing so in the cause of Christian charity, and with most marvellous results. We got, no doubt, into the industrial schools in Ireland large bodies of children who in this country, by a more strict interpretation of the law, would be sent to barrack schools or Poor Law schools. In my opinion all the children who are unprovided for, and who are sent under the present law which prevails in this country into poor houses, ought to be accommodated in industrial schools, and it is because I believe, and strongly believe, that it is in this direction mainly, perhaps, not solely, that the remedy must be found for this great and crying evil, that I have been induced to say a few words in this discussion.

MR. CHAPLIN : Everyone will acknowledge the importance of this subject, and I have no complaint to make as to the manner in which it has been presented to the Committee. We have necessarily had a somewhat discursive debate, but I think I will be consulting the convenience of the Committee if I reply to one or two minor points which have been raised, and then deal with the general case. The hon. Member for the Elland division complained of the action of the Local Government Board in permitting school children to present themselves on the road to Epsom to the view of passers-by, and of the fact that sometimes in their good nature the passers-by flung small coins to the children. It is argued that this is extremely demoralising to the children, and I have been asked to use my authority to put an end to that proceeding. I am sorry to differ from the hon. Member, but I see nothing whatever discreditable in the proceeding. The children do not beg; nothing of the kind is permitted. All that happens is that the children assemble to watch the passers-by in train and carriage going down to Epsom, and some of the passengers fling pennies and sixpences to the children, which in the course of a year amount to a not inconsiderable sum, which is invariably expended in giving the children an outing at the seaside or elsewhere   That is a proceeding which nothing would induce me, as President of the Local Government Board, to prevent, even if it cost me my salary. With regard to the education of Poor Law children, many hon. Gentlemen have argued that it is very improper, and in their opinion very undesirable, that the education of these children as regards standard and teachers should be less in any respect than the education given to children in public elementary schools. I am not disposed to disagree with that statement myself, and as far as the Local Government Board is concerned it has done all it can to meet the views expressed on that point. We have put ourselves in communication with the Education Department, and we have told them that we are perfectly ready to hand over the inspection of the education of these Poor Law children to them; but difficulties have arisen in connection with the subject over which I have no control, and there the matter remains at present. So far as the Local Government Board is concerned, we are prepared and ready to put the inspection of the education of these children in the hands of the Education Department. The hon. Member who introduced the motion, and who moved the reduction of my salary—I am glad to say by an insignificant amount — commenced by referring to the report of the Committee which was appointed to investigate the whole question connected with the Poor Law schools of the metropolis. He dealt at some length with the recommendations of the Committee, and he referred to the condemnation of the barrack schools, with

which I entirely agree. We have had two or three exhaustive debates on this subject already, and there is absolutely no difference of opinion between us. But then the hon. Member went on to say: "Here are all these evils put before the House over and over again, and practically nothing whatever has been done." As to that I must differ from him. As I have been challenged on the point, it will be my duty to state as briefly as I can what really has been done with regard to the partial adoption of the recommendations contained in the report of the Committee to which he has referred. As soon as I succeeded to the charge of the Local Government Board, one of the first duties I undertook was to enquire into this question, and the conclusion I came to was that the proposal in the report of the Committee recommending that the charge of the Poor Law schools in the metropolis should be put into the hands of an entirely new Department was one which it would be unwise and injudicious to adopt. I arrived also at the conclusion that with regard to certain classes of children—children suffering from various diseases and infirmities—it was very desirable that they should all be treated by·one central authority, instead of being treated in different districts; and we proceeded to take measures to do that, the central authority selected for the purpose, after a great deal of consideration, being the Metropolitan Asylums Board. The great complaint of the hon. Member is the barrack system. The barrack system has grown up out of the five metropolitan school districts. The hon. Member says we have done nothing in this matter. Since I have been at the Local Government Board, of those five districts we have dissolved two. These things are not to be dissolved in a moment, with all the arrangements which they have for educating pauper children, and all the moneys they have expended in building and one thing and another. Considering the time that we have been at the Local Government Board, it is going too far to say that we have done nothing.

MR. SAMUEL SMITH: I do not say that.

MR. CHAPLIN: The hon. Member has said over and over again "practically nothing has been done." I will tell him what has been done. I speak of the five unions of the South Metropolitan District, comprising the Unions of Camberwell, Greenwich, St. Olave's, Stepney, and Woolwich. By the dissolution of that district 2,841 children had been provided for: 692 in Camberwell, 801 Greenwich, 670 in St. Olave's, 326 in Stepney, and 352 children at Woolwich. I do not say that all these arrangements have been completed at present, but very considerable progress has been made, as the Committee will perceive in a moment. With regard to Camberwell, we have sanctioned the purchase of twenty scattered homes, which are to contain fifteen children; so at once there is provision made for 300 children out of that 692. In addition to that, there is to be a central Cottage Home adjacent, to provide for 200 more. The site for this home has been approved by the Local Government Board, and it is a site having buildings upon it which can be adapted to this purpose. That provides for 500 children, and leaves 192 still to be provided for. Upon that subject we are in communication at this moment with the Board of Guardians as to how they will provide for these. They propose to do that by the purchase of ten more scattered homes, each to contain fifteen children. In Greenwich we have 801 children, and the guardians there propose to buy, to begin with, six freehold houses for separate homes in Culvert Road, each house to contain ten children, and then they propose to purchase 65 acres of land for Cottage Homes. This land is situated at a place called Sidcup. The remainder is to be provided for by boarding out. With regard to St. Olave's, there are 670 children to be provided for. The guardians there have proposed to purchase sites for their accommodation, but the price asked for the land is so extremely high, £357 an acre, that we have asked for further explanations as to the kind of site, and the Board of Trade has not yet given its sanction for the purchase of that land. Then we have Stepney, with 326 children; they are asking now for permission to purchase a site in Essex on which to provide for Cottage Homes, with 15 in each house, and they have provided for the remaining 260 children by proposing to make four blocks containing 60 children each. The purchase of this site has been approved by the Local Government Board, and the plans are being prepared at this present moment. With

Mr. Chaplin.

regard to the merits of scattered homes, blocks, and cottage homes, it will be more convenient, perhaps, if I express my views upon that at a later stage in the evening. With regard to the Union of Woolwich, where 352 children are to be provided for, the purchase of a site of 31 acres of land at Plumstead has been authorised by the Local Government Board, and it is proposed to accommodate the children by building small blocks to contain 40 children each, and some will be provided for in detached homes containing fifteen each. I have not seen the plans of these yet, but we are informed that we may expect them almost directly. The hon. Member says that we have done nothing, but I think that he will admit at all events that some progress has been made for providing for the children in that particular Union. But we also have to provide for a special class. Five classes of children are to be taken charge of in future by the Metropolitan Asylums Board — ophthalmic children, 800; children suffe ing from ringworm, 400; convalescent children, 360; children defective in intellect, 60; and remand children, 273.

MR. FLOWER: Is that table up to date?

MR. CHAPLIN: I believe so. Then, with regard to the ophthalmic children, two sites have been acquired—one at Brentwood, in Essex, and one at Swanley, in Kent—on which schools are to be built for their accommodation. It is proposed to establish the children suffering from ringworm in the girls' school at Banstead, which will accommodate them extremely well. This property has recently been acquired by the Metropolitan Asylums Board. In regard to convalescents, there has been provided a home at Herne Bay for 134, a home at Margate for 91, and arrangements are being made for the accommodation of 100 at another place. For children who are mentally defective, two houses, one of which is at Peckham, have been provided, which will accommodate 20 each, and provision is to be made for the others; and for remands one house has been bought at Camberwell and another will be purchased at Hampstead which will accommodate 50 each. The difficulty which has arisen with regard to this class of children is that they must be within reasonable reach of the Court to which the children will have to be brought back. That difficulty has been surmounted by an agreement between the guardians and the Metropolitan Asylums Board and the police by which they will undertake to convey them to the Court when required. The school managers of the district have agreed to sell to the Metropolitan Asylums Board their property at Sutton and Banstead, and in that way I think we have satisfactorily disposed of the state of things under which the barrack system flourished in the past. We have also provided accommodation at other places. I come now to some other questions which have been raised in this discussion, and in particular to the system of "boarding-out." It is a practice I have adopted myself, and the Local Government Board have no objection to it; on the contrary we have always advocated it. It has been pointed out that there are two great difficulties in connection with this question; the difficulty of proper inspection and the difficulty of getting good foster parents. With regard to the first we have been rather blamed, but I am not altogether my own master in this matter, and when I ask for more inspectors there is always a fight with another portion of the Government. But we have an additional staff of inspectors, and, so far as I am concerned, I must say that I am in utter ignorance as to the way in which these inspectors have been guilty of failure or neglect of duty. I believe I am correct in saying -that they have performed their duties with satisfaction to us. With regard to the question of scattered homes, the Committee will perceive, by the permission we have given to the district of Camberwell, that there is no disinclination whatever on the part of the Local Government Board to give that system a fair trial. It has been suggested by one hon. Member that it has been tried with complete success at Bedford, Bath, and Sheffield.

Mr. FLOWER : I expressly excepted Sheffield.

Mr. CHAPLIN : I am sorry I did not hear that, because with regard to Sheffield we have some very unsatisfactory reports indeed. What I do want to impress upon the House is this, that if we have not been able to accept all the propositions that have been made with regard to the future of these children, it is because a very grave responsibility rests upon us. For my part, I can conceive nothing more unhappy, or more to be commiserated, in regard to some poor unfortunate child than that it should be relegated to some scattered home, free altogether from inspection, where it might possibly be living unhappily, and, as often might be the case, where it was unkindly treated, and regarded solely as something out of which a profit ought to be made, rather than that the child should be brought up with advantage to itself. But human nature is human nature after all, and unless these people are most carefully watched something of that kind is sure to happen ; and I think the Committee will understand that if the Local Government Board do not jump at these proposals as some hon. Members think we ought to do, it is because we do not want to relegate these poor little souls to homes of that kind. For my own part, after a very careful personal inspection of many of these homes, I have always regarded the cottage home system with great favour. Something has been said in the course of this debate about industrial training, and the necessity for promoting it amongst these children. I do not think there is anything which ought to be fostered more than that, for it is a real way of educating these children so as to give them an opportunity of making provision for themselves in after life. Industrial training is most carefully attended to at these cottage homes, and, if the hon. Gentleman had seen the actual results of the training at some of the cottage homes under the control of the South Metropolitan School Managers, I think he would be most agreeably surprised, and he would be led to form the opinion which I hold myself, that there is a great deal to be said for the system of keeping these children in cottage homes. Another question has been raised upon which the conduct of the Local Government Board has been very much criticised. We have been condemned in some quarters because we have sanctioned provision being made for the children who have been displaced by the closing of the South Metropolitan Schools District under the block system. Under that system the number of children under one management is to be limited to 300, and they are to be accommodated in different blocks of not more than 60 in each. I confess that, as a general rule, I should have preferred cottage homes wherever they are possible, although I have seen some very remarkable instances of success in connection with the block system. The girls school at Banstead was conducted on that principle, and I never saw in my life an establishment which filled me with more admiration, and which appeared to me to be better conducted, or which produced better practical results, which is the very best test of the successful management of an institution of that kind, There you have a number of children to provide for, and your great object ought to be to bring them up at your school so that they would be able to provide for themselves happily and comfortably in after life. In this institution, after the very closest and most careful examination of what was going on, I asked the lady manager if, when these children left her, she could get good places for them, and she replied, "I have not the slightest difficulty in the world; in fact, I cannot keep pace with the demand; everybody wants the girls from my establishment." She told me that the year before last she had received over 1,000 applications for girls as servants, and she was not able to supply more than 150. I want to know if you can have a more successful bringing up of Poor Law children than that? In the face of that fact, and also in the face of the statement made by the boards of guardians, that not only did they prefer the blocks, but that they also found that their expenditure would be very considerably less than it would be by the provision of cottage homes, I came to the conclusion that I should have no right, and should not be justified, in forcing upon them my own particular view in the face of all they had said to me, and in the face of such results as I have described which had followed as a result of the block system. But there is also this to be said—that I might have had very considerable difficulty in enforcing my views upon them if they had rejected them. It is quite true that I could have refused my sanction to any plans or proposals to which I objected, but the result of that would have been to have brought us to an absolute deadlock. The hon. Member for Bradford has asked me when the Sutton schools will be closed. In reply, I may say that they will be closed as soon as the new accommodation is provided. How

soon that will be it is not in my power to say, but I may tell the hon. Member this —that I never lose an opportunity of pressing upon all parties concerned the necessity of providing for this new accommodation at as early a date as possible. With regard to emigration, I may say that the Local Government Board do all in their power to further that system, and we never refuse our assistance to an application for emigration from any board of guardians in the country unless it be under circumstances which we think might be dangerous or injurious to the child. We are, however, obliged to insist upon a certain condition with regard to inspection up to the age of 16, and we insist that there should be an inspection every year. The Canadian Government have objected to the cost of this, which, in consequence, falls upon the guardians, and probably it is owing to this—to my great regret—that emigration to Canada has fallen off in number during the last year. Still, in my judgment, that is far better than that the children should go out to Canada as emigrants to be taken into service in distant parts of the Dominion without due safeguards, and every word that I use with regard to children and their dangerous position in scattered homes tells with ten times greater force with regard to children emigrating to Canada. I think, to the best of my ability, I have dealt with all the various questions which have been raised—or certainly with most of them—in the course of the debate upon this question, and I can only assure the Committee that this subject which we have been engaged in discussing this afternoon is not only one of which I recognise the extreme importance, but, as has been pointed out by the noble Lord, it is one in which I take a deep personal interest myself. I can also assure hon. Gentlemen that, so far as it rests with me, nothing shall be wanting on my part to secure the better education and the welfare of these children. There are two matters which had almost escaped my memory—one was with regard to the question of vagrant children. Perhaps I may remind the Committee that my hon. friend the Member for Bradford, with the full knowledge and support of the Local Government Board, introduced a Bill on this subject last year which would have had a very considerable effect upon this question. It was, unfortunately,

Mr. Chaplin.

stopped by the action of the hon. Gentleman opposite, the Member for Bethnal Green, but the Government, if it is possible to find time, will introduce a Bill on that subject which will no doubt be founded upon the Bill of the hon. Member, and I hope it may have some considerable effect in enabling us to solve that question. There is one other matter which, for the moment, escaped my memory, and that is the question raised by my hon. friend the Member for Derby, who spoke of the great advantages of the training which is to be enjoyed by Poor Law children on the training-ship "Exmouth." With that I entirely agree, and I doubt very much if among all the different forms of education for Poor Law children there is one which is more successful than the education given upon that ship. It performs a double purpose. We are a great naval nation, and our supremacy throughout the world in every quarter of the globe depends upon our Navy, and our Navy depends upon our having a sufficient number of seamen. Therefore, when our Poor Law children are sent, as they are at the present moment, on training ships, a double purpose is fulfilled. Children are brought up there more happily, more healthily, and under circumstances more desirable perhaps than any other system of Poor Law education; while, at the same time, it trains a race of sailors who may be most useful to their country in after life. My hon. friend appeals to me to do my utmost to extend that system. That is my desire, and it is also my intention, and I hope no distant time may elapse before we may have, not one, but many ships performing a similar duty and working under similar conditions. I thank the Committee for allowing me to dwell at so much length upon this question, which was so exhaustively debated upon a former occasion, and I hope that, to the best of my ability, I have dealt with nearly all the questions put before me.

MR. SAMUEL SMITH: I beg to ask leave to withdraw my motion for the reduction of the Vote.

Motion by leave withdrawn.

Original question again proposed.

MR. LLOYD-GEORGE (Carnarvon &c.): I wish to call attention to a question which I have already pressed on the Local Government Board. I should like to know whether the right hon. Gentleman is now prepared to take some steps to put into operation the clause of the Local Government Act of 1888 which empowers him to delegate certain functions of his Board to the county councils. This question has been very carefully considered by the county councils individually and by the County Councils Association, and the latter body has drafted a scheme and submitted it to the Local Government Board. That scheme has been considered by a Committee appointed by the right hon. Gentleman himself to consider the arrears of work. The Local Government Board has, year by year, had an increasing amount of work cast upon it by legislation, and, to show the importance of this matter, the scheme of the County Councils Association proposes to delegate something like 112 powers, mostly exceedingly trivial, to the county councils. These powers include the question of altering the boundaries of parishes, of fixing the names of district councils, and of deciding on the tolls and dates of fairs, and similar small matters. I think all these powers could very well be delegated to the county councils. Boundary questions, for instance, take up a lot of the time of the Local Government Board, and as the chiefs of the staff find it quite impossible to give attention to insignificant little matters of purely local moment, although of importance to the parish, they are neglected. The departmental committee proposed to meet the difficulty of coping with the work by increasing the clerical staff. That, I suggest, is not the way to deal with it, for in that case the duties would be left in the hands of inexperienced persons, who would be unable to grasp those principles which make efficient administrators of local affairs. Seeing that this Act was passed eleven years ago, is it not time that something was done in this matter? I know it is very difficult to persuade a Department to rid itself of any portion of its work. But is not this rather a matter for a Committee of the House of Commons than for a departmental committee? May I suggest to the right hon. Gentleman that a Parliamentary Committee might be appointed with a view to developing some scheme for putting this clause into operation. Again, I may suggest that if, in parts of England, there are difficulties in the way, owing to the position of non-county boroughs, the experiment might well be tried in other parts where such difficulties are non-existent. Wales certainly offers such a field. Welsh county councils are practically unanimous in desiring the proposed change, and if the experiment were tried there and proved successful, then it could be extended to the rest of the country. As to the case of non-county boroughs, I don't know whether there is any real difficulty beyond that raised by the official element—by, for instance, the town clerks. I think that if it were left to the county councils themselves they would promptly give effect to the clause.

*Mr. GRIFFITH-BOSCAWEN (Kent, Tunbridge): I wish to call attention to a matter which has excited a good deal of interest in the country. It is one concerning the administration of the Poor Law, and it affects the question of adequate religious ministration in workhouses. There can be no doubt there has been a determined attempt to prevent the appointment of workhouse chaplains, and in consequence a large number of the inmates of our unions are deprived of the proper means of spiritual support and help. I complain, first, of the failure of boards of guardians in a great many unions to appoint chaplains; and, secondly, of the failure of the Local Government Board to carry out the law on this point. I may remind the Committee that by the Poor Law Act, 1834, the Poor Law Commissioners, whose successors are the Local Government Board, were empowered to appoint paid officers, and these were defined to include clergymen. The Act did not lay it down definitely that a clergyman or chaplain should be appointed in every case, but four years after it was passed the Poor Law Commissioners issued a circular in which they said it was the duty of boards of guardians to appoint chaplains in every case. They said, in effect, the Commissioners think such an appointment is in all cases necessary: first of all for the superintending of the moral and religious state of the inmates generally; secondly, for the direction of the religious instruction of the children; and thirdly, for the administration of spiritual counsel to the aged, infirm, and sick. In the year 1847 the Poor Law Board issued a general order that no chaplain, whenever a vacancy occurred, was to be

Mr. Lloyd-George.

appointed without the consent of the Bishop. Therefore it is established that under the existing law it is the duty of every board of guardians to appoint a chaplain for every workhouse. It is very important that that should be done to provide for the spiritual health and comfort of these poor people. That has been the law ever since the Act of 1834 was passed; but, as a matter of fact, the law is constantly evaded. I find from the Poor Law Report of last year that there are 650 unions, with 674 workhouses; but there are only 571 chaplains, and therefore it is clear that there are over a hundred workhouses without any chaplain at all.

Mr. LLOYD-GEORGE: Does that include voluntary chaplains?

*Mr. GRIFFITH-BOSCAWEN: I am speaking of the paid and regularly appointed chaplains. In Lancashire there are ten workhouses out of twenty-three without chaplains, in the West Riding of Yorkshire twenty-one out of thirty-five, and in Cornwall out of thirteen unions there is no chaplain at all. I can appreciate the point of the hon. Member opposite that there are volunteer chaplains or other means by which spiritual ministrations may be given to the paupers; but I submit that that is not a proper fulfilling of the spiritual work of the workhouses. A clergyman should be duly appointed to devote his whole time to the work, and if that is not done the law is evaded. I go further and say that there are several instances where no provision whatever has been made for religious ministrations in the workhouses. Take, for instance, the case of Nottingham, where there was no chaplain for ten months, and the inspector complained that the inmates were dying without any religious ministration at all. In the following year the master of the workhouse made a similar complaint; and no provision from that day to this has ever been made for the inmates of that workhouse who belong to the Church of England, although they are in a large majority. It is true that a clergyman from a neighbouring parish has been allowed to come in at four o'clock on Sunday afternoon to give religious ministration, but that is the hour when able-bodied inmates go out for exercise. What has happened in the case of the Nottingham Union has happened in many other cases. I do not wish to treat this matter in any sectional spirit;

but I say that, owing to the failure of the guardians to appoint chaplains, and the failure of the Local Government Board to carry out the law, we are running a very great risk that in these workhouses no adequate or proper religious ministrations are provided at all. Moreover, in a considerable number of cases boards of guardians have made direct infractions of the law. At Nottingham, for instance, instead of a clergyman of the Church of England, a Dissenting layman was appointed. No doubt every provision is made to secure religious liberty, but the law contemplates the appointment of a chaplain of the Church of England, and ministers of all denominations are quite properly allowed to visit the workhouses.

AN HON. MEMBER : On the cheap.

*Mr. GRIFFITH-BOSCAWEN : By the rules of the Poor Law Board ministers of all religious denominations are allowed to go into the workhouses to give ministrations to the members of their own creed and to instruct the children ; but what I am complaining of is that in a great many cases the boards of guardians have made special provision for various religious bodies, and have directly excluded all provision for the members of the Church of England. I will take the case of Abergavenny, in the county of Monmouth. Here a clergyman of the Church of England applied to have the right to come into the workhouse, without any remuneration, to have service on Sunday, and Holy Communion on Easter Day, but he was not allowed to do so unless he would consent to join in a rota with other ministers of different creeds. At the same time when a Roman Catholic priest made a similar application he was allowed to do so. I ask why these religious disabilities are placed on the members of the Church of England, who are in the vast majority, when special privileges are given to the ministers of other creeds. I say that it is the duty of the Local Government Board to make inquiry, and if the law is broken to see, at all events, that no further disability is placed on the ministers of the Church of England. Let me give another case. It has been distinctly laid down that ministers of various creeds may go into workhouses and give ministration to those who belong to their creed. Nobody is compelled to attend any

service which is not of his particular denomination. But there are various cases where the children of Church of England parents in workhouses have been compelled to go to what are called undenominational services. In South Shields, for instance, all the children have been compelled to attend the service of a body called the Sunday School Union—an undenominational body. The matter was brought before the Local Government Board, and that Board rather characteristically stated that they hoped the Churchmen interested would not press the case. The case was pressed, and the Board wrote a letter in which it was stated that there was no evidence that the children were compelled to attend a religious service not of their own creed, because, they said, the service was not religious. A similar case occurred at St. Asaph, where the children were compelled to attend an undenomonational service. There the Local Government Board took a very different line, and wrote a letter in which they laid it down that even although the service might be called undenominational, if it was given by any minister of any denomination it would be regarded as a service of that denomination, and that therefore the opinion of the Board was that the action of the Board of Guardians was not in accordance with the intention of the Act. I ask, Is it fair to Church of England parents that their children should be compelled to be sent to services to which they do not give their assent ? I will give another instance. At St. Albans all the children in the workhouse have been compelled to attend Dissenting services in the Union chapel. The Local Government Board in this case acted with greater bravery, and ordered that the children who were on the Church of England register should not be compelled to attend the service. The Board of Guardians, however, refused to carry out the order of the Local Government Board, although only one of the children was a Dissenter, all the rest belonging to the Church of England. I do not want to deal with this matter in any narrow or bigoted spirit, but I say we are running great danger. We are running very great danger of two things—first, of compelling the children of Church of England parents, contrary to all their principles of religious liberty, to attend services which are disapproved of by the parents, and, secondly, by the failure to appoint chaplains, of providing, in many cases, no sufficient religious instruction for these inmates. I venture to think this is a matter which demands the prompt attention of the Local Government Board. Not only is it the law that there should be chaplains appointed in workhouses, but it is also the law that there should be chaplains appointed in prisons for convicts. In the case of workhouses the matter is left to the board of guardians and the Local Government Board. In the case of prisons it is left to the Home Office. I have shown that in the case of workhouses the law is rarely carried out at all, and the conditions under which chaplains have to work are often unsatisfactory. Every single prison is provided for, whereas a great number of workhouses are not provided for at all. I venture to think that the results which have been obtained, and obtained quietly, without any sectional animosity, in our prison and convict establishments ought to be obtained also in the workhouses.

Motion made, and Question proposed :

"That Item A (Salaries), be reduced by £150, in respect of the Salary of the President of the Local Government Board."—(*Mr Griffith-Boscawen.*)

Lord E. FITZMAURICE : I do not desire to follow my hon. friend on the opposite side of the House into the various questions of detail with regard to the appointment of chaplains which he has raised, because each turns upon the particular facts of the case which are known to him ; but I am anxious to say something with regard to the very important matter which was raised by my friend the Member for Carnarvon Boroughs—I mean in regard to the various proposals which have been made from time to time to try and carry out the clause of the Local Government Act of 1888, which proposed to delegate a considerable amount of the powers of the Local Government Board, in matters of detail, to the county councils. There can be no doubt that that proposal at the time excited a very wide feeling of interest in the country. I recollect very well the interest it excited on this side of the House. I was not a Member at the time that this Bill passed into law, but I know there was no portion of the Bill which excited so great an amount of interest as that clause. The year after it became law, a Committee of this House was appointed to examine the question, and a Provisional

Mr. Griffith-Boscawen.

Order was presented by the Local Government Board, and laid on the table of this House, proposing to carry out the terms of the clause in question, and it was referred to that Committee, which, if I recollect rightly, was presided over by Mr. Stansfeld, who had been President of the Local Government Board, and possessed a knowledge of local government law second to no man in the country. A strong opposition had just begun to show itself for the first time, and the Government thought it wise to withdraw the Provisional Order. Subsequently the County Councils Association, hoping that these passions—if I may call them so—would subside, brought forward a very carefully prepared scheme. Communications followed between the Local Government Board and the County Councils Association and the association representing non-county boroughs, and the result was the appointment of a Departmental Committee. There, I regret to say, these difficulties again arose. They were found not to have diminished by time, but, on the contrary, to have increased, because a considerable number of Acts of Parliament were passed conferring fresh powers on the county councils, and with regard to nearly all of these matters questions of difference—greater or less, according to circumstances—arose between the county councils and the non-county boroughs, and in nearly all those cases, I regret to say, those differences have continued, and hardly in one of them has a satisfactory settlement been arrived at. The Committee was presided over by Sir John Hibbert, for many years a Member of this House, and Secretary to the Local Government Board on one occasion, and Secretary to the Treasury on another ; and if there was one man in the country who could have brought these difficulties to a satisfactory termination Sir John Hibbert was that man. But his efforts, and the efforts of the Committee over which he presided, were entirely ineffective ; and the result is that the matter remains exactly where it did. My hon. friend has made a suggestion, which may be a practicable one. He says that in Wales these differences between the county councils and the non-county boroughs are not so acute as they are, unfortunately, in England, and possibly a delegation of powers might be made to a particular county or group of counties in the hope that conviction might be carried to the minds of the non-county boroughs. I believe that the suspicions of the non-county boroughs are founded upon nothing, and are really matters of prejudice. Suspicions are excited, articles are written in local newspapers, an ancient borough is assured that the county council desires to control its liberties, when really no such idea is entertained. However unreasonable all these suspicions, there they are, and they are a most serious matter. I am not going to complain of the action of the Local Government Board, knowing as I do these difficulties, because hitherto they have failed to solve this exceedingly difficult problem, and here I must add that there is another difficulty which has not yet been mentioned. The Local Government Board, Sir John Hibbert stated only yesterday at a meeting of the County Councils Association, was rather inclined to intimate to the county councils that as several of these questions were sanitary matters, the fact that such a very small number of the county councils of England had appointed medical officers of health was one reason why the Local Government Board might well hesitate to confer large powers in regard to sanitary matters. The county councils have the remedy in regard to that matter in their own hands. I have in my own county quite recently had to fight this question of the appointment of a medical officer of health, and it has been carried to a successful issue. If the county councils wish to put themselves right with the public they should appoint medical officers of health, and thereby deprive non-county boroughs of one solid argument which they have made against the delegation of these powers by the Local Government Board.

MR. J. G. TALBOT (Oxford University): I wish to emphasise in a very few words the complaint which my hon. friend the Member for Tonbridge has made as to the treatment of some of the poorer inhabitants of the country who are obliged to end their days in workhouses. It is a strange thing that, after having successfully laboured for many years to remove religious disabilities, we should have arrived at a time when religious disabilities are imposed on one denomination only, viz., the Church of England. I will illustrate what I mean by the case of South Shields. In the South Shields Union, all the children (including Church of England children) attend an undenomi-

national service. Although there are 600 inmates, the Guardians refuse to appoint and pay a chaplain, and there is no Church of England service on Sundays. According to the *South Shields Daily Gazette,* at the undenominational service for the children—

"No religious teaching is introduced, no child is compelled to attend . . . . no creed or dogma or religious teaching of any kind is placed before the children at these meetings."

I suppose some persons who have studied this question will look upon this state of things as a judgment upon the Church of England for what, no doubt, was a grievous mistake on her part in former days, when she denied to others the liberties which she herself enjoyed. The conditions have remarkably changed now, but I do not see that that is any reason for acquiescing in what must be acknowledged to be an act of real injustice. It seems that now members of the Church of England in workhouses are the only people who do not receive religious ministrations from chaplains of their denomination. Members of the Church of England will not be satisfied until the religious grievance as to chaplains is removed, and if not removed by the action of the Local Government Board other steps must be taken.

MR. J. H. ROBERTS (Denbighshire, W.): I regret very much that the shadow of religious controversy which falls upon these subjects has manifested itself in the discussion upon the question of the administration of the poor law schools in this House this evening. My desire is to emphasise the importance of the question which has been raised by my hon. friend. It seems to me that the Committee does not sufficiently realise the position of the Local Government Board in this matter and the work it performs. The hon. Gentleman opposite said the amount of arrears was simply appalling. Reference has been made to the Departmental Committee of 1896, which issued two reports, one in 1897 and one in June last year. I do not want to weary the Committee with many statistics, but I would just lay before them one or two striking figures bearing on the subject. The report of the Committee referred to the enormous extent in which the work had increased during the two or three years mentioned. In 1895 the department received and registered 119,000 letters, and in 1896 the amount was 168,000. The Committee also pointed out that the number of enquiries had increased in 1896 to double the amount it was in 1885. In 1885 there were 2,000,000 inquiries, in 1896 6,000,000. All these figures prove that the work in all departments during the last ten or fifteen years has more than doubled itself. It was pointed out that the arrears were greatest in the Public Health Department, and that at the end of 1896 there there were more than 100 cases awaiting enquiry, cases unallotted to the inspectors. The Committee recommended a reorganisation of the staff, and went on to say that it would cost a great deal of money, but that they thought that if the country obtained prompt attention to the work it would not grudge the extra amount. I doubt whether any reorganisation will effectually cope with the largely increased duties. The second report, June, 1898, referred to the more important question of the devolution of powers on the county councils. I hardly think the reason given by the Committee when they say they cannot recommend any scheme is a sufficient one. They point to the fact that the Provisional Order Bill of 1889 was discussed by the Committee upstairs, and was opposed by the opinion of the parties generally, and that they think this opposition has not abated, but that there still continues a certain amount of opposition to the devolution of these powers to the county councils. There are, at all events, three different circumstances which give to Wales a strong case to have these powers tried within its boroughs. First of all, all the Welsh county councils have asked for a devolution of the powers ; secondly, the Welsh county councils have had considerable experience of this Act ; thirdly, the circumstances of Wales are different in many respects to those of the rest of the country generally, and there is no doubt the country is ripe for this devolution. In conclusion, I will simply remind the Committee of a few words used by the right hon. Gentleman the Member for Wolverhampton in the debate on this question last year. He said—

"Devolution is one of the first questions which ought to engage the attention of the Local Government Board, but I do not think a Departmental Committee is the best tribunal to which it could be referred, but that it should be referred to a Committee of the whole House."

Mr. Herbert Roberts.

I think it is a great pity such a valuable instruction should be allowed to rust for want of additional powers. I am glad to express my appreciation of the sympathetic reply given on this question by the right hon. Gentleman the President of the Local Government Board last year and to-night. I trust that during the last twelve months he has had time and opportunity to acquire further information as to the desirability of making this transfer of powers to the county councils, and that he will to-night be able to give us a statement to that effect.

*Mr. T. W. RUSSELL : I served upon the Departmental Committee to which reference has been made, and that is the reason why I have been asked to reply to the observations made by my hon. friend on the other side. My hon. friend said he thought that a Departmental Committee was not the proper method by which to consider this question, and he suggested that a Committee of the whole House of Commons would have done the work better. I wish to point out to him that he has had both a Departmental Committee and a Committee of the House of Commons.

Mr. LLOYD-GEORGE : The Committee of the House of Commons considered a special scheme.

*Mr. T. W. RUSSELL : The first thing that I wish to impress on the Committee is that so far as the Local Government Board is concerned it has been in complete sympathy with the county councils. Everybody knows how we are overburdened with work, and no one knowing anything about the Local Government Board, and feeling the pressure there, could fail to have great sympathy with the proposal to transfer work to county councils or to any other body capable of dealing with it. In less than a year after the passing of the Act of 1888 a Provisional Order was made not only for the transference of work from the Local Government Board to the County Council, but also work from the Board of Trade and the Home Office. The Bill for the confirmation of the Order, after second reading, went upstairs to a Select Committee, who heard evidence upon the subject, but that Bill was so bitterly opposed that the Committee came to the conclusion and reported that in their opinion it opened up

questions which were beyond their power, and that the Bill must be abandoned. The real difficulty which the Committee had to consider was the bitter hostility of the non-county boroughs to any transfer of powers to the county councils. The Departmental Committee was appointed originally to inquire into the organisation of the Local Government Board, and it was only after they had been sitting for some time that the reference to them was extended so as to include this question of devolution. The Committee then took into consideration the question as to how far it was possible to devolve on county councils certain duties discharged by the Local Government Board. A scheme was submitted, and we examined witnesses from the County Councils' Association, from non county boroughs, and from urban districts, some of the latter having populations greater than many boroughs. The Committee found from the outset that instead of this feeling of hostility on the part of non-county boroughs having disappeared, if anything, it had become intensified in the interim. Sir John Hibbert then suggested as a compromise, and the Committee were prepared to recommend that the non-county boroughs should be at liberty to elect between the Local GovernmentBoard and the county councils. The witnesses would not listen even to that mild proposal, and speaking for 110 non-county boroughs and a large number of urban districts they told the Committee that they would prefer to be under the central authority rather than the county councils. It is not too much to say that every member of the Departmental Committee looked with favour on the principle of transfer, but in face of the hostility of the witnesses they were driven to the conclusion that it would be unwise to proceed further. The Committee were impressed all through with the idea that they were not appointed originally to deal with the question. In their report they state—

"Having carefully considered the whole question, we have come to the conclusion that the opposition which prevented the passage of the Bill has in no way abated, and the hostility of non-county boroughs and urban councils to the transfer of powers to the county councils, and their preference for the central authority was declared by the witnesses examined more strongly even than in 1889."

The Department then set itself to find what business it could reasonably divest itself of without legislation, and only to-day I revised an order about to be issued by the Local Government Board, handing over to boards of guardians and other authorities entire control of no less than 6,000 appointments. So far as we could we have carried out the intention of the Committee, and it was not the fault of the Committee or of the Local Government Board that the question of transfer was not more favourably considered. As to the proposal that devolution should be tried with Welsh County councils only, we have been advised that under section 10 any transfer which took place must be general to the whole of the county councils in England and Wales. With regard to the reorganisation of the staff, some rather hard words had been said about the Treasury, but I am glad to say, so far as the recommendations of the Departmental Committee were concerned, they were all accepted at once by the Treasury, and the Local Government Board got all the Committee recommended. Very great changes have taken place since then. The staff of engineers has been largely increased, and the number of auditors has also been increased, and although I am not able to say that the whole of the arrears have been cleared off, the most of them have gone, and the Department is now in a fairly workable condition, and the delay so long complained of has practically ceased to exist.

Mr. CHAPLIN: Two speeches have been delivered by the hon. Members for Oxford and Tunbridge, to which I am bound in duty to make a reply. I make no complaint that they have raised the question they did, because I am sure we are all animated by the most sincere desire for the religious welfare of the inmates of our workhouses, and that the Church of England should certainly not be placed under any special disability in regard to the holding of services in workhouses. I cannot, however, go as far as my right hon. friend the Member for Oxford University, who said that the time was now near when the Church of England would be the only denomination whose religious ceremonies were excluded from workhouses. Nor is that borne out by the statement made by the hon. Member for Tunbridge, who pointed out that out of 670 workhouses over 500 have chaplains of their own. The hon. Member gave a number of cases in support of his views, including that of Nottingham, which occurred as long ago as 1882, but I am net in a position to-night to deal with the details he has raised. The regulations cited by the hon. Member are true, but they have never been enforced by legal process since 1887. The remedy of the Local Government Board is by mandamus or by appointing a chaplain ourselves, but it has not been necessary to do so. What happens in the great majority of cases where there is no chaplain is that either the Church service is performed voluntarily by the vicar of the parish or a neighbouring clergyman, or the inmates have full permission to leave the workhouse to attend divine service. My hon. friend asks me to enforce the appointment of a chaplain in every case; but what I have sought to do myself has been to secure the performance of divine service by other means rather than by a harsh enforcement of the law, which I cannot help thinking, especially in districts largely peopled by Nonconformists, would give rise to bitter religious animosity. Generally, I think since I have been responsible my efforts have been attended with not altogether unfavourable results. I have, as a matter of fact, two or three cases in hand at the present moment, but I have every hope that I shall succeed in bringing them shortly to a satisfactory determination. In any event I can assure my hon. friends that I warmly sympathise with them when they say that the Church of England ought not to be placed under any special disability. There is no difference of opinion on that point, and they may be assured that I shall resist by every means in my power any attempt in that direction.

* Mr. **STEVENSON** (Suffolk, Eye): I desire to ask the right hon. Gentleman a question somewhat similar to a question which has been already discussed. I have no doubt that the work imposed at present on the Local Government Board is practically overwhelming. There are two remedies. One is that the Department should no longer be overworked and undermanned, and the other is that there should be a certain devolution on the lines suggested by two Committees. It might be asked also whether there is not a certain amount of work now being done by the Board which might well be abolished. One instance occurred in my own constituency within the last three years in

which the Local Government Board undertook certain work which involved the local expenditure of money which occupied a very considerable amount of time, and was really unnecessary. A parish sought an extension of its boundaries, and wanted £400 to enable it to purchase additional land for a burial ground, and the Parish Council passed a resolution to that effect. The parish gave its assent, and the matter was brought before the County Council. Then in a few months an inspector was sent down by the Home Office. The Local Government Board thought it necessary to send a second inspector in addition to the one sent by the Home Office. When you have two Departments like the Local Government Board and the Home Office almost in the same building, surely it is possible for some communication to take place between them, and some arrangement made by which one of them might have sent down. The effect of that course not being pursued was that the parish had to bear the cost of both inquiries. It was not a large parish, but there were two inquiries, one of which was wholly unnecessary, and which might have been avoided by a little judicious management. Upon a former occasion I called the attention of the President of the Local Government Board to this matter, and he made a sort of half-promise that the question should be looked into. A similar case occurred in the county of Norfolk, and in other counties similar occurrences have taken place. What I wish to know is whether some arrangement cannot be made for cases of this kind, and whether one inspector cannot be sent down on behalf of both Departments.

*Colonel MILWARD (Warwick, Stratford-upon-Avon): I am very much obliged to the hon. Member who has just sat down, because the question he has raised was the very point I wished to call attention to. I have been particularly requested to bring this question before the House because a vast number of really unnecessary inquiries take place by the officers of the Local Government Board. I asked for a Return showing how many inquiries had taken place, but the Assistant-Secretary informed me that the Local Government Board had at present more important things to attend to than to satisfy me in that direction. In every measure passed by this House dealing with

Mr. Chaplin.

county, parish, and district councils we only throw more absolute power into the hands of the Local Government Board and its inspectors. The particular cases I wish to allude to occurred in Warwickshire, and one of them was the provision of sewerage and water for a small parish, Alveston, containing about 1,000 inhabitants. In this case no less than five inquiries were held by inspectors, and four of those inquiries were held by different inspectors. Most people would think that when a particular inspector goes to one place the same inspector should be sent there again, but in this case out of five inquiries four of them were held by different inspectors. In another case, in a still smaller village of some 200 or 300 inhabitants, the necessity arose for a supply of water to the priest's house and to the Roman Catholic school. Now this water supply could have been obtained by an expenditure of about £20, and in this case I believe two inquiries were held. Not only are these constant inspections and inquiries held by the Local Government Board, but we all know that the county councils are almost daily holding inquiries all over the kingdom, and scarcely a single meeting passes at the County Council with which I am connected without two or three inquiries being ordered. Surely it is possible to classify these inquiries. No doubt the President of the Local Government Board will say that they are statutory inquiries, but it ought to be possible to classify the inquiries and to hold many of them in one centre. I only hope, now that attention has been called to the fact that small localities are put to considerable expense by the holding of these inquiries into perfectly trivial matters, that something will be done to throw the expense of them upon those persons who insist upon holding them, if they are unable to prove their case. At all events steps should be taken to have the inquiries less frequently, and less inspectors should be employed by the Local Government Board, who are constantly travelling about the country to hold the statutory inquiries.

MR. CHAPLIN: In reply to the hon. Gentleman opposite with regard to the cases in which double inquiries are held by the Home Office and the Local Government Board, I may say that this question has not escaped my attention. I have been in communication with the Home Office with a view to putting an end to that state of things as far as possible, and I believe my right hon. friend contemplates introducing a Bill on the subject which will enable us to avoid these double inquiries taking place. With regard to what has been said by my hon. friend the Member for Stratford-upon-Avon, the Local Government Board have quite recently issued a minute, which is intended to limit the number of inquiries made by the Local Government Board as much as possible. I agree with the hon. Member that inquiries have been held occasionally in cases where they were not necessary, but in most of these cases we have not altogether had a free hand, because in a number of instances we are compelled by statute to hold these inquiries, and we have no option whatever. The hon. Gentleman thinks the difficulty might be got over by what he calls classification, and by making a number of the inquiries by one inspector from one centre. That expedient has also been considered by the Local Government Board, but after full deliberation and carefully weighing the matter in every respect the conclusion was come to by those best able to form an opinion on the subject that such a proposal, so far from mitigating or lessening the labours of the Local Government Board, would tend rather to increase them, and no good would be obtained by making a change in the direction suggested by the hon. Member. I now desire to make an appeal to hon. members opposite to allow this Vote to be taken to night. I know that the hon. Member for Middlesbrough has risen more than once this evening, but if he will allow this Vote to be taken now he will have an opportunity of making his observations on the Report stage. I do appeal to him and other hon. Members who desire to speak to allow this Vote to be taken now.

MR. HAVELOCK WILSON (Middlesbrough): I should have been very pleased indeed to give way in response to the appeal made by the right hon. Gentleman, but seeing that I have waited ever since half-past six this evening, and have made many efforts to get an opportunity of speaking, I hardly think I can accede to the wishes of the right hon. Gentleman. I have made several efforts to get the Board of Trade to enforce the law with regard to the accommodation of seamen on board ship. I may say that I have almost entirely despaired of getting the President of the Board of Trade to enforce the law with regard to seamen's accommodation. I think the President of the Board of Trade is almost past redemption, and I intend now to see what the President of the Local Government Board will do, as I think he is not so much subject to the pressure of the shipowning community, and if I can once convince him that he has the power to insist upon the law being carried out in reference to seamen, I think he will have no hesitation in carrying out that law. Now, the port sanitary authorities have full control in all ports over the sanitation and the accommodation which is provided for seamen on board ship, and I do believe that if the port sanitary authorities were left to their own discretion with regard to these matters they would insist upon the law being carried out; but, unfortunately, the Board of Trade will not allow the port sanitary authorities to do their duty in this respect. I believe that in many cases the officers of the port sanitary authorities have complained that ships have not had the proper amount of accommodation for seamen on board, and the Board of Trade have objected to them interfering in the matter. Now, I want to make an appeal to the right hon. Gentleman opposite. I believe that he has the power to insist upon every seaman on board ships in British ports having the proper accommodation. I want to ask the right hon. Gentleman to take upon himself the duty of insisting upon the law being enforced. We know perfectly well that many of the vessels belonging to the P. and O. Company which come into the port of London from time to time have not the proper amount of accommodation for the crews on board. They have not the 72 cubic feet, for in many cases they have only 60 cubic feet. It is within the power of the right hon. Gentleman and his officials to insist upon the law being enforced, and I do urge upon him the necessity of having the law enforced in a proper manner. I do not wish to detain the House at any length at this late hour. There are several matters I intend to bring forward, but as it is near the hour for adjourning I will bring them up on the Report stage. There is one other question, with regard to the rating of machinery. I find that there are a number of unions which are

Mr. Havelock Wilson.

not enforcing the law with regard to the proper rating of machinery.

MR. CHAPLIN : I do again appeal to the hon. Member to now allow this Vote to be taken, for he will have a chance of again raising the matter on the Report stage.

Mr. HAVELOCK WILSON : Then I will give way, and adopt the course suggested by the right hon. Gentleman.

Mr. WEIR (Ross and Cromarty) : I have several matters to bring before the House, and I cannot wait until the Report stage.

It being midnight, the Chairman left the chair to make his report to the House.

Committee report progress ; to sit again on Monday next.

SUPPLY (1st June).

Resolutions reported—

CIVIL SERVICES AND REVENUE DEPARTMENTS ESTIMATES, 1899-1900.

REVENUE DEPARTMENTS.

1. "That a sum, not exceeding £5,552,885, be granted to Her Majesty to complete the sum necessary to defray the charge which will come in course of payment during the year ending on the 31st day of March, 1900, for the salaries and expenses of the Post Office Services, the expenses of Post Office Savings Banks, and Government annuities and insurances, and the collection of the Post Office revenue."

MR. CRILLY (Mayo, N.) : I desire to offer a protest against the treatment meted out to competent Irish officials in the General Post Office in Dublin. I think nobody in this House will deny that these civil servants who have spent a great many years in the service are very capable officers. We find that men in the Dublin Post Office who have been attached to the staff for the greater part of their official lives are denied, when vacancies arise, admittance to the higher offices in that department. I know myself that there is a very great deal of dissatisfaction existing in the Post Office at Dublin at the present time on account of the persistent way in which these Irish officials are denied admission to the higher · offices in the Dublin Post

Office Those hon. Members who have been in this House for years, and who have watched the way in which these higher offices in Ireland are filled up when they become vacant, know that a vicious system of promotion exists in all the Civil Service departments of Ireland, and we have in the Post Office in Dublin a concrete example of the system to which I have referred. Let me point out to the House that since 1892 many English officials have been brought over to Ireland to fill these offices at the expense of Irish servants who have been in the Post Office for many years. Since the beginning of 1892 ten English officials have been appointed to situations in the General Post Office in Dublin which carry salaries varying from · £350 to £1,200 per annum. Under this condition of affairs I think Irishmen have a legitimate right to complain, and certainly the officials of the Dublin Post Office have a right to vehemently protest against this unfair and ungenerous treatment to which they have been subjected during a long course of years. I understand from what I can gather that an important position in the Dublin Post Office is about to become vacant, and it is a situation carrying with it a very high salary. I trust that when this case arises the old policy will be reversed, and that the Postmaster-General will see his way to reward some Irish official with this position, so that Irish officials in this department in Ireland may have an incentive to do their duty zealously and faithfully. I have not much hope that the system will be changed all of a sudden, but I cannot allow the Report stage of this Vote to be taken without offering the protest which I now make.

Vote agreed to.

2. "That a sum, not exceeding £570,915, be granted to Her Majesty, to complete the sum necessary to defray the charge which will come in course of payment during the year ending on the 31st day of March, 1900, for the Expenses of the Post Office Packet Service."

Mr. HAVELOCK WILSON : I desire to call the attention of the Secretary to the Treasury, while the Post Office Steam Packet Vote is under the consideration of the House, to the rate of wages paid to the men on board the steamships which are under contract with Her Majesty's Government. For some considerable time I have been urging complaints with regard to the wages paid by the companies who tender for the Post Office Packet Service. There is the Peninsular and Oriental Company, with regard to which I have endeavoured to force the President of the Board of Trade to do his duty in reference to the men employed in this service, but up to the present time my efforts have been fruitless. I now venture to make an appeal to the right hon. Gentleman who has charge of this packet service to see if he will endeavour to make some alteration in regard to this question. There was a resolution passed in this House in 1891 which stipulated that in all contracts between ship-owners and others for Government work the tabulated rate of wages should be paid. I contend that the Peninsular and Oriental Company do not pay a fair rate of wages to their sailors and firemen on board their ships. In addition to this, the Peninsular and Oriental Company are breaking the law with regard to the provision of accommodation for seamen. The law says that each seaman employed on board ship shall have 72 cubic feet of accommodation, but this company do not provide that for their seamen. It is the old story, and no doubt the right hon. Gentleman by this time will be quite tired of listening to the same old story, but I shall keep on repeating it until the Government Department see that the law is carried out as it ought to be. The right hon. Gentleman has an opportunity of enforcing the law by giving notice to the Peninsular and Oriental Company that, unless they are prepared to give their seamen the proper amount of accommodation which they ought to have, the company will not get any contracts from the Government. It is in the power of the right hon. Gentleman to do that, and I trust he will take that course. In addition to that, I would like him also to say that the seamen shall receive a fair rate of wages. We are told that they are paid the rate of wages which are current in India ; but the contracts are not made in India, but in this country, and I contend that according to the fair wages resolution this company ought to pay the rate of wages which is current in this country. I wish to enter my protest against the manner in which this particular company has carried on its business. The manner in which this company—which receives some £400,000 from the Government for carrying mails, and other subsidies, every year—carries on its business is very unfair to traders, for they carry cargo at a much less rate from the Continent to this country than they do from this country to the Continent, and there is a difference in some cases of about 25 per cent. Now the Government encourage this company, which is unfair both to traders and seamen, and I appeal to the right hon. Gentleman to see if something cannot be done to remedy this state of things. I do not intend to detain the House any longer, but I do hope that the appeal which I have made will have some effect.

Vote agreed to.

3. "That a sum, not exceeding £2,338,390, be granted to Her Majesty, to complete the sum necessary to defray the charge which will come in course of payment during the year ending on the 31st day of March, 1900, for the Salaries and Working Expenses of the Post Office Telegraph Service."

4. "That a sum, not exceeding £496,600, be granted to Her Majesty, to complete the sum necessary to defray the charge which will come in course of payment during the year ending on the 31st day of March, 1900, for the Salaries and Expenses of the Customs Department."

Class VI.

5. "That a sum, not exceeding £287,628, be granted to Her Majesty, to complete the sum necessary to defray the Charge which will come in course of payment during the year ending on the 31st day of March, 1900, for Superannuation, Retired, Compensation, and Compassionate Allowances and Gratuities under sundry Statutes, for Compassionate Allowances and Gratuities awarded by the Treasury, and for the Salaries of Medical Referees."

6. "That a sum, not exceeding £2,130, be granted to Her Majesty, to complete the sum

necessary to defray the charge which will come in course of payment during the year ending on the 31st day of March, 1900, for certain Pensions to Masters and Seamen of the Merchant Service, and to their Widows and Children."

7. "That a sum, not exceeding £785, be granted to Her Majesty, to complete the sum necessary to defray the charge which will come in course of payment during the year ending on the 31st day of March, 1900, for certain Miscellaneous Charitable and other Allowances."

Resolutions agreed to.

IMBECILE (TRAINING INSTITUTIONS) BILL.

Order of the day for the second reading read.

*Mr. ROUND (Essex, Harwich): I venture to ask the House to pass the second reading of this Bill, the object of which is to exempt from rates these institutions which are supported by voluntary contributions, and which only concern five Unions. I hope the House will consent, for I am not aware of opposition to it. I may say that there are many precedents for this measure. Such institutions are now exempted from Imperial taxation, and all I desire is to extend that exemption to local taxation. In Ireland they have been exempted by statute.

Mr. CALDWELL (Lanark, Mid.) objecting, the second reading was deferred till Wednesday next.

Adjourned at twenty-five minutes after Twelve o'clock till Monday next.

HOUSE OF LORDS.

Monday, 5th June 1899.

PRIVATE BILL BUSINESS.

The LORD CHANCELLOR acquainted the House that the Clerk of the Parliaments had laid upon the Table the Certificates from the Examiners that the Standing Orders applicable to the following Bills have been complied with :

ELECTRIC LIGHTING PROVISIONAL ORDERS (No. 3).

ELECTRIC LIGHTING PROVISIONAL ORDERS (No. 4).

ELECTRIC LIGHTING PROVISIONAL ORDERS (No. 12).

ELECTRIC LIGHTING PROVISIONAL ORDERS (No. 13).

ELECTRIC LIGHTING PROVISIONAL ORDERS (No. 15).

TRAMWAYS ORDERS CONFIRMATION. (No. 2).

Also the Certificate that no Standing Orders are applicable to the following Bill :

METROPOLITAN COMMON SCHEME (HARROW WEALD) PROVISIONAL ORDER.

Also the Certificates that the further Standing Orders applicable to the following Bills have been complied with :

WEST MIDDLESEX WATER.

FISHGUARD AND ROSSLARE RAILWAYS AND HARBOURS.

AIRE AND CALDER NAVIGATION.

DUBLIN CORPORATION (MARKETS).

EAST LONDON WATER.

GREAT WESTERN AND GREAT CENTRAL RAILWAY COMPANIES.

LONDON, BRIGHTON & SOUTH COAST RAILWAY (VARIOUS POWERS).

MANCHESTER CORPORATION (GENERAL POWERS).

MILTON CREEK CONSERVANCY.

NORTH PEMBROKESHIRE AND FISHGUARD RAILWAY.

UXBRIDGE AND RICKMANSWORTH RAILWAY.

SOUTH STAFFORDSHIRE STIPENDIARY JUSTICE.

Also the Certificates that no further Standing Orders are applicable to the following Bills :

CORK CORPORATION (FINANCE).

REDDITCH GAS.

And also the Certificate that the further Standing Orders applicable to the following Bill have not been complied with :

BAKER STREET AND WATERLOO RAILWAY.

The same were ordered to lie on the Table.

WATERMEN'S AND LIGHTERMEN'S ACTS AMENDMENT BILL.

Witnesses ordered to attend the Select Committee.

YORKE ESTATE BILL.

Committed for Thursday next.

BUENOS AYRES AND PACIFIC RAILWAY COMPANY BILL.

CALEDONIAN RAILWAY (GENERAL POWERS) BILL.

LISBURN TOWN COMMISSIONERS BILL.

Committee to meet on Thursday next.

SHIREBROOK AND DISTRICT GAS BILL.

Read 2a, and committed.

SOUTH-EASTERN AND LONDON, CHATHAM, AND DOVER RAILWAY COMPANIES (NEW LINES) BILL.

Brought from the Commons, read 1a, and referred to the Examiners.

EDUCATION DEPARTMENT PROVISIONAL ORDER CONFIRMATION (LIVERPOOL) BILL.

PILOTAGE PROVISIONAL ORDER BILL.

House in Committee (according to order) : Bills reported without amendment : Standing Committee negatived ; and Bills to be read 3a to-morrow.

MARYPORT HARBOUR BILL.
WATERMEN'S AND LIGHTERMEN'S ACTS AMENDMENT BILL.

K

WORKINGTON CORPORATION WATER BILL.

GREAT EASTERN RAILWAY (GENERAL POWERS) BILL.

SOUTHPORT AND LYTHAM TRAMROAD BILL.

**SOUTHPORT TRAMWAYS BILL.
NORTH STAFFORDSHIRE RAILWAY BILL.**

LONDON AND SOUTH-WESTERN RAILWAY BILL.

Report from the Committee of Selection, That the Lord Erskine be proposed to the House as a member of the Select Committee in the place of the Viscount Powerscourt ; read, and agreed to.

China, No. 2. (1899)—Correspondence between Her Majesty's Government and the Russian Government with regard to their respective railway interests in China : Presented (by command), and ordered to lie on the Table.

Parliamentary Returns Act, 1869 (Trustee Savings Bank)—Treasury Minute, dated 29th May, 1899, directing the discontinuance of the return annually laid before Parliament, pursuant to the sixth section of the Savings Banks Moneys Act, 1863, showing the assets and liabilities of the National Debt Commissioners in respect of Trustee Savings Banks : Laid before the House (pursuant to Act), and ordered to lie on the Table.

NEW BILL.

REFORMATORY SCHOOLS AMENDMENT BILL.

A Bill to amend the law with regard to reformatory schools was presented by the Lord Leigh ; read 1a ; to be printed ; and to be read 2a on Thursday next.

(No. 107.)

CONGESTED DISTRICTS (SCOTLAND) ACT AMENDMENT BILL.

House in Committee (according to order) : Bill reported without amendment : Standing Committee negatived ; and Bill to be read 3a To-morrow.

SOUDAN CAMPAIGN 1898.

PROPOSED GRANT TO LORD KITCHENER OF KHARTOUM.

The PRIME MINISTER AND SECRETARY OF STATE FOR FOREIGN AFFAIRS (The MARQUESS of SALIS-

BURY) : My Lords, I wish to give notice that it is my intention on Thursday to move a vote of thanks to the Forces occupied in the recent campaign in Egypt, and I think it would, perhaps, be more convenient to take the consideration of Her Majesty's Message with respect to Lord Kitchener at the same time. There are reasons why, perhaps, it would be desirable that we should take the Message into consideration at that time. Of course, your Lordships are aware that our action is somewhat formal, and, therefore, I propose to postpone until Thursday the consideration of Her Majesty's Gracious Message.

> House adjourned at Twenty-five
> minutes before Five o'clock,
> till To-morrow, Three o'clock.

HOUSE OF COMMONS.

Monday, 5th June 1899.

PRIVATE BILL BUSINESS.

PROVISIONAL ORDER BILLS (Standing Orders applicable thereto complied with).

Mr. Speaker laid upon the table Report from one of the Examiners of Petitions for Private Bills, That in the case of the following Bills, referred on the First Reading thereof, the Standing Orders which are applicable thereto have been complied with, viz. :—

ELECTRIC LIGHTING PROVISIONAL ORDERS (No. 17) BILL.

ELECTRIC LIGHTING PROVISIONAL ORDER (No. 18) BILL.

ELECTRIC LIGHTING PROVISIONAL ORDERS (No. 19) BILL.

LOCAL GOVERNMENT (IRELAND) PROVISIONAL ORDER (HOUSING OF WORKING CLASSES) BILL.

LOCAL GOVERNMENT (IRELAND) PROVISIONAL ORDERS (No. 3) BILL.

LOCAL GOVERNMENT PROVISIONAL ORDERS (No. 10) BILL.

LOCAL GOVERNMENT PROVISIONAL ORDERS (No. 11) BILL.

LOCAL GOVERNMENT PROVISIONAL ORDERS (No. 12) BILL.

LOCAL GOVERNMENT PROVISIONAL ORDERS (No. 14) BILL.

Ordered, That the Bills be read a second time To-morrow.

PROVISIONAL ORDER BILLS (NO STANDING ORDERS APPLICABLE).

Mr. Speaker laid upon the Table Report from one of the Examiners of Petitions for Private Bills, That, in the case of the following Bills, referred on the First Reading thereof, no Standing Orders are applicable, viz. :

LOCAL GOVERNMENT PROVISIONAL ORDER (No. 13) BILL.

LOCAL GOVERNMENT PROVISIONAL ORDERS (No. 9) BILL.

MILITARY LANDS PROVISIONAL ORDER BILL.

Ordered, That the Bills be read a second time To-morrow.

BELFAST AND NORTHERN COUNTIES RAILWAY BILL (QUEEN'S CONSENT SIGNIFIED).

Read the third time, and passed.

BOOTLE CORPORATION BILL.

Read the third time, and passed.

HULL, BARNSLEY, AND WEST RIDING JUNCTION RAILWAY AND DOCK BILL.

Read the third time, and passed, with an Amendment.

ST. ALBANS GAS BILL.

Read the third time, and passed, with Amendments.

BIRKENHEAD CORPORATION BILL.

As amended, considered ; An Amendment made ; Bill to be read the third time.

WEST GLOUCESTERSHIRE WATER BILL.

WOKING WATER AND GAS BILL.

As amended, considered ; to be read the third time.

FRIENDS' PROVIDENT INSTITUTION BILL (STAMP DUTIES).

Resolution reported :

"That it is expedient to authorise the imposition of the following Stamp Duties upon certain Memorials under any Act of the present Session relating to the Friends Provident Institution :—

For and upon the first Memorial enrolled of the names of the persons who shall be deemed held and taken to be Trustees of the Institution, or of any special fund of the Institution, the sum of Five Pounds ;

And upon every other such Memorial in which the name of any person shall for the first time be inserted as a Trustee of the Institution the sum of Five Pounds."

Resolution agreed to.

Ordered, That it be an Instruction to the Committee on the Friends Provident Institution Bill, That they have power to make provision therein pursuant to the said Resolution.—(*Dr. Farquharson.*)

DUNDEE GAS, TRAMWAYS, AND EXTENSION BILL (changed to "DUNDEE GAS, STREET IMPROVEMENTS, AND TRAMWAYS BILL").

Motion made and Question proposed : " That Standing Orders 204 and 235 be suspended, and that the Bill be now read a second time."—(*Dr. Farquharson.*)

*MR. JOHN ELLIS (Nottingham, Rushcliffe) : Will the hon. Gentleman give some reason for his motion ? These Orders have been drawn with very great care, and they provide that a certain time should be allowed for notice. I think this practice of moving the suspension of the Standing Orders is one that requires being made with much caution.

DR. FARQUHARSON (Aberdeenshire, West) : I understand the reason is that the promoters of the Bill made a mistake in not having given notice in time before the holidays.

MR. J. ELLIS : Is anyone damnified by it ?

MR. JAMES LOWTHER (Kent, Thanet) : As a member of the Standing Orders Committee, I join the hon. Member in saying that care ought to be taken that motions of this kind should not be too repeatedly made. Of course the Standing Orders Committee take into consideration cases such as are here referred to. When it is represented to them that in consequence of the holidays parties would be prejudiced, the Committee is in the habit of granting indulgence.

*MR. T. W. RUSSELL (Tyrone, S.) : This Motion has the approval of the Chairman of Committees, and the House may be perfectly certain that no one is damnified by it.

Question put and agreed to.

Bill accordingly read a second time, and committed.

WISHAW WATER BILL [Lords].

Ordered, that Standing Orders 204 and 235 be suspended, and that the Bill be now read a second time. — (*Dr. Farquharson.*)

Bill accordingly read a second time, and committed.

GREAT SOUTHERN AND WESTERN AND WATERFORD, LIMERICK, AND WESTERN RAILWAY COMPANIES AMALGAMATION, GREAT SOUTHERN AND WESTERN RAILWAY, AND WATERFORD AND CENTRAL IRELAND RAILWAY BILLS.

Ordered, that the Order [14th March] that all petitions of County Councils under the provisions of the Local Government (Ireland) Act, 1898, against the Bills, be presented seven clear days before the meeting of the Committee, be referred to the Committee, and that the petitioners praying to be heard by themselves, their counsel, or agents, or witnesses be heard against the Bills, be suspended in the case of the petition of the County Council of the County of Cork against the Great Southern and Western and Waterford, Limerick, and Western Railway Companies Amalgamation Bill, and that the said petition be referred to the Select Committee on the said Bills, and that the petitioners be heard by their counsel, agent, or witnesses against the said Bill.—(*Mr. J. F X. O'Brien.*)

BROUGHTY FERRY GAS AND PAVING ORDER BILL [Lords].

Read the third time, and passed, without amendment.

EDUCATION DEPARTMENT PROVISIONAL ORDERS CONFIRMATION (ABERAVON, &c.) BILL [Lords].

Read the third time, and passed, without amendment.

ELECTRIC LIGHTING PROVISIONAL ORDERS (No. 16) BILL.

Read a second time, and committed.

LOCAL GOVERNMENT (IRELAND) PROVISIONAL ORDERS (No. 2) BILL.

Read a second time, and committed.

PETITIONS.

BUILDING FEUS AND LEASES (SCOTLAND) BILL.

Petition from Aberdeen, against; to lie upon the Table.

CEMETERIES RATING BILL.

Petition from St. Pancras, for alteration ; to lie upon the Table.

CHEAP TRAINS BILL.

Petition from St. Pancras, in favour; to lie upon the Table.

ECCLESIASTICAL ASSESSMENTS (SCOTLAND) BILL.

Petition of the General Assembly of the Church of Scotland, in favour; to lie upon the Table.

EXECUTORS (SCOTLAND) AMENDMENT BILL.

Petition from Aberdeen, in favour; to lie upon the Table.

GROCERS' LICENCES (SCOTLAND) ABOLITION BILL.

Petition from Leith, in favour; to lie upon the Table.

GROUND VALUES (TAXATION) (SCOTLAND) BILL.

Petition from Aberdeen, against; to lie upon the Table.

METROPOLIS MANAGEMENT ACTS AMENDMENT (BYE-LAWS) BILL.

Petition from St. Pancras, for alteration ; to lie upon the Table.

MINES (EIGHT HOURS) BILL.

Petitions in Favour,—From Sinby ;— Bretby ; — Donisthorpe ; — Alloa and Dev n ;— Alva ;— Clackmannan ;—Tillicoultry ;—and, Cadley Hill Collieries ; to lie upon the Table.

MONEY-LENDING BILL.

Petition from Leith in favour; to lie upon the Table

POOR LAW RELIEF (DISFRANCHISE-MENT.

Petitions for alteration of Law ;—From Keighley ; and, Hunslet ; to lie upon the Table.

ROMAN CATHOLIC UNIVERSITY OF IRELAND.

Petitions against establishment ;—From Helensburgh ;—and, Alexandria ; to lie upon the Table.

SALE OF INTOXICATING LIQUORS ON SUNDAY BILL.

Petitions in favour ;—From Peters-field ; — Tre-y-ddol ; — Lincoln ; — and, Nottingham ; to lie upon the Table.

SEATS FOR SHOP ASSISTANTS (ENG-LAND AND IRELAND) BILL.

Petition from Glasgow, for extension of provisions to Scotland ; to lie upon the Table.

SUCCESSION (SCOTLAND) BILL.

Petition from Aberdeen, against ; to lie upon the Table.

TOWN COUNCILS (SCOTLAND) BILL.

Petition from Kirkintilloch, in favour ; to lie upon the Table.

RETURN PRESENTED.

CHINA (No. 2, 1899).

Copy presented,—of Correspondence be-tween Her Majesty's Government and the Russian Government with regard to their respective Railway interests in China [by Command] ; to lie upon the Table.

INFECTIOUS DISEASE (NOTIFICATION) ACT (1889) EXTENSION BILL.

Lords' Amendment to be considered forthwith : considered, and agreed to.

QUESTIONS.

LABOUR IN JAM FACTORIES.

MR. HEDDERWICK (Wick Burghs) : I beg to ask the Secretary of State for the Home Department whether he is aware that jam factories are kept going, exempt from the provisions of the Fac-tories Acts, for six months in the year, by being used for the curing of fish and other like purposes as soon as the period of exemption for the fruit trade has expired ; whether his attention has been drawn to the fact that a crowd of country girls was imported by a jam factory with-out any provision having been made for their accommodation, and that in conse-quence the girls arriving went where they could find a roof to cover them, many being taken into houses of ill-fame ; and whether he will cause inquiry to be made into all the circumstances of the case.

*THE SECRETARY OF STATE FOR THE HOME DEPARTMENT (Sir MAT-THEW WHITE RIDLEY, Lancs., Blackpool): The first paragraph of the question relates to facts which have long been well known to my Department and which I attempted to deal with in a Bill last Session. I have seen in the *Fortnightly Review* for last month a statement to the effect of the second paragraph ; but it was put forward as a mere rumour without names, dates, or other means of identification. In these circumstances and in view of the fact that the provision of lodging accom-modation for workpeople is a matter outside the Factory Acts, I do not see that an inquiry by my Department is possible.

MR. HEDDERWICK : I beg to ask the Secretary of State for the Home Department whether he is aware that for many months in the year children of thirteen years of age and upwards are kept at work in jam factories from 6 o'clock in the morning till 10 and 11 o'clock at night, and are required to carry weights which sometimes amount to 'about a hundredweight ; also that the damp heat in such factories rises frequently to 90 deg., and is productive of colds, bron-chitis, pneumonia, and consumption : and whether he proposes to take any steps in the matter.

*SIR M. WHITE RIDLEY : In answer to the hon. Member I may remind him that last year I introduced a Bill which would have brought jam factories fully within the sanitary provisions of the Factory Acts, and would have enabled me to limit the excessive hours of labour. I think some such legislation is desirable, and I have already said so several times this Session.

MR. TENNANT (Berwickshire) : May I ask the right hon. Gentleman whether he will endeavour to pass the Bill this year ?

*Sir M. WHITE RIDLEY: That question should be addressed to the Leader of the House, but, as I have said, I have a Bill on the subject ready.

AMERICAN AND CANADIAN AFFAIRS.

*Sir CHARLES DILKE (Gloucester, Forest of Dean): I beg to ask the Under Secretary of State for Foreign Affairs whether the understanding among the delegates at the recent Conferences between the Governments of the United Kingdom, the Dominion of Canada, and the United States has not prevented an official statement on the subject of the negotiations by the Ministry of the Dominion; and whether Her Majesty's Government look forward to being able to make any statement to the House upon the matter in the course of the present session. The Government have caused to be published a statement which in part answers this question, but perhaps the right hon. Gentleman may like to add something to that.

*The UNDER SECRETARY of STATE for FOREIGN AFFAIRS (Mr. St. John Brodrick, Surrey, Guildford): I have nothing to add, except that the Government hope to be in a position to make a statement to the House before the close of the Session.

THE PHŒNIX PARK MURDERERS.

Mr. JAMES LOWTHER (Kent, Thanet): I beg to ask the Chief Secretary to the Lord Lieutenant of Ireland whether there is any truth in the rumour that several of the criminals convicted of the murder of Lord Frederick Cavendish and Mr. Thomas Henry Burke are about to be set at liberty.

The CHIEF SECRETARY for IRELAND (Mr. G. W. Balfour, Leeds, Central): There is now only one convict undergoing sentence in connection with the murders of Lord Frederick Cavendish and Mr. Burke. The consideration of his position is for the Lord Lieutenant, and I have nothing to add to the reply given by His Excellency, and published in the Press, to the petition presented to him by the Corporation of Dublin on the 7th April last.

COUNTY COURT FEES.

*Sir CHARLES DILKE: I beg to ask the Secretary to the Treasury whether, in connection with the proposed reduction of county court fees, his attention has been called to a report of the Incorporated Law Society, dated 1895 ; and whether, in fixing the fees charged in County courts, regard is had to making the county courts self-supporting, a principle not applied to the High Court.

*The SECRETARY to the TREASURY (Mr. Hanbury, Preston): I have seen the report mentioned in the first paragraph. The total expenditure of the Supreme Court is (roughly) £632,000. But it is generally accepted as a constitutional doctrine that the courts and judges should be supplied gratis to the suitor by the State. If £199,000 be deducted in respect of rent and the salaries and pensions of the judges, there remains a balance of £433,000 representing other expenditure. The fee revenue (including the Land Registry) amounts to £417,000 ; which would leave a deficit of £16,000. But the Supreme Court must also be credited with the annuity of £92,000 a year, which was established in 1869 as the equivalent of interest on the Suitors' Fee Funds, which converts this deficit of £16,000 into a net surplus of £76,000 per annum. The county courts, on the other hand, show a net deficit of £19,000 per annum. The total expenditure upon them amounts to £598,000 per annum, which gives a balance of £439,000 when £159,000 is deducted in respect of rent and judges' salaries and pensions. As against this outlay the fee revenue only amounts to £420,000.

THE DUM-DUM BULLET.

Mr. DILLON (Mayo, East): I beg to ask the Secretary of State for India who is responsible for the use of the Dum-Dum bullet by British troops in India.

*The SECRETARY of STATE for INDIA (Lord George Hamilton, Middlesex, Ealing): I stated, in reply to a question put to me by the hon. Member in this House on March 24, 1898, that these bullets were issued by order of the Government of India, that no further sanction for their issue was necessary, and that no such sanction was either asked for or given ; but that Her Majesty's Government were fully informed as to the proceedings of the Government of India, and saw no reason for questioning their propriety. I may add that the reason for the issue of this bullet was that experience had shown that the bullet previously in use did not adequately protect the troops using it. As at present advised, I see no reason for modifying the opinion which I then expressed. But I may add that since last autumn the Government of India have had a new pattern of bullet under trial, and I was informed in reply to an inquiry about two months ago that those trials were not complete, but that they would be proceeded with and reported on as soon as possible.

MR. DILLON : Will the noble Lord kindly state whether he will be willing to lay before the House, before the new bullet is adopted, the opinion of medical experts as to the effects of the bullet ?

*LORD G. HAMILTON : There were experiments made in connection with the old bullet, and it was on the strength of those experiments that the bullet now in use was adopted.

MR. DILLON : But the result of those experiments was never communicated to the House of Commons. This is becoming a very serious question now. When I pressed the noble Lord on a previous occasion he refused me information as to the Dum-Dum bullet, and I wish to know now—and I think it a reasonable question—whether he can undertake and will undertake to communicate to the House of Commons the results of the experiments now being tried with the new bullet, before it is adopted for the Indian troops.

*LORD G. HAMILTON : I am not aware that I ever refused, on a previous occasion, to give the reports that were then asked for, and if the hon Member wishes to have them I will lay them before the House.

COL. MILWARD (Warwick, Stratford-upon-Avon) : May I ask the Secretary of State whether the Dum-Dum bullet contains any explosive substance, or whether it is not composed of a leaden nose and a nickel base, instead of the nickel nose and leaden base of the Lee-Metford bullet ?

MR. SPEAKER : Order, order. The hon. Member is entering into a debate on the merits of the subject.

Mr. CHANNING : I beg to ask the Under Secretary of State for War

whether, in view of the decisive condemnation of the use of the Dum-Dum bullet by the Peace Conference at the Hague, Her Majesty's Government will take into consideration the advisability of discontinuing the use of this bullet in wars with semi-civilised or savage people, as well as with those nations who are parties to the Conference ?

*The UNDER SECRETARY OF STATE FOR WAR (Mr. WYNDHAM, Dover) : I would ask leave to refer the hon. Member to the First Lord's reply to a later question on the Paper.

POSTAL DELIVERIES IN DORSET-SHIRE.

COLONEL WELBY (Taunton) : I beg to ask the Secretary to the Treasury, as representing the Postmaster - General, whether he is aware that the villages of Mere, Zeals, Bourton, and Buckhorn Weston, adjoining Gillingham, where there is a head post office and a railway station on the main South-Western line to Exeter, are in the postal delivery of Bath, distant more than 20 miles in a direct line : whether he can see his way to rearranging the Gillingham and Bath deliveries so as to give these and neighbouring villages the full benefits of being situated near a main line of railway ; and whether he can see his way to placing in the library of the House of Commons maps of the United Kingdom coloured to show the areas of the different rural postal deliveries.

*Mr. HANBURY : These villages are all in the postal delivery of Bath. To transfer them to the postal delivery of Gillingham might improve the communication with the districts served by the London and South-Western Railway, but would possibly impair the communication with the districts served by the Great Western Railway with which they have long been in direct communication, and it may be that a larger number of letters would be delayed than would be accelerated. The night mail service to and from Gillingham has, however, recently been placed upon a more secure footing than formerly, and inquiry shall be made as to the expediency of serving the places in question from Gillingham. The Post Office is not in possession of any maps coloured to show the areas of the different rural postal deliveries ; and it would be a work of much complexity to prepare such maps; which would, moreover, stand in need of constant correction, and would be unintelligible without further information which cannot be given on a map.

THE PARLIAMENTARY DEBATES CONTRACT.

SIR CHARLES CAMERON (Glasgow, Bridgeton): I beg to ask the Secretary to the Treasury whether any change has been made in the arrangements for printing the official Parliamentary Debates; and when Members may expect their reports to be issued with reasonable promptitude.

MR. R. G. WEBSTER (St. Pancras, East): I would like at the same time to ask the Secretary to the Treasury whether he is aware that the cause of the delay in the publication of the Reports of the Parliamentary Debates of this Session is the fact that the reporters of the Parliamentary corps are largely in arrears of salary; and if any fresh arrangements are now being made to carry the work out in a businesslike manner.

*MR. HANBURY: I will answer these questions together. I learned on the day on which the House rose before Whitsuntide of the disputed arrears of payment to reporters—which, it appeared, had contributed to the delay in issuing the reports. In consequence of this delay I gave instructions to the Controller of the Stationery Office to cancel at once the existing contract if any report was still in arrear on Wednesday last, the day the House reassembled; to make arrangements for a new contract; and to warn the existing contractor accordingly. A new contract commenced on Wednesday last, on the same conditions in all respects as that which had been cancelled. The conditions, as I have satisfied myself, are such as to allow a reasonable profit to the contractor. The reports for days between April 30 and May 5 are in the hands of the late contractor, and all that is possible has been done by the Stationery Office to hasten their publication. His sureties have been informed of their liability for the consequences of the delay. The reports of the 5th and up to the 19th May will be published at once by the new contractors, Messrs. Wyman, who have already large printing contracts. As regards all other reports subsequent to that of May 19th the new contractor will be required to carry out all the provisions of the contract strictly and punctually.

MR. CHANNING (Northampton, E.): May I ask, in connection with that answer, whether the proofs of reports taken between May 5 and May 19 will be at once forwarded to Members, if that has not been done already?

*MR. HANBURY: Oh, yes, certainly.

MR. R. G. WEBSTER: I should like to know whether the right hon. Gentleman, taking into consideration the fact that the discussion on the report stage of the London Government Bill shortly comes on, will tell us whether we are to take *The Times* report as official, or, if not, what report we are so to take.

The question was not answered.

IRELAND—NATIONAL SCHOOL TEACHERS AS GUARDIANS.

MR. TULLY (Leitrim, S): I beg to ask the Chief Secretary to the Lord Lieutenant of Ireland whether he can state on what grounds the Commissioners of National Education have refused to pay to Mr. Kenny, national teacher, Ballinameen, North Roscommon, the moneys at present due to him, and have prohibited him from acting as Poor Law guardian and district councillor in Boyle Union, to which position he was elected, although in other parts of Ireland national teachers have been frequently elected as Poor Law guardians and served as such; and, whether he will direct that there will be no further interference by the National Board with Mr. Kenny in the office to which he has been elected in Boyle Union.

MR. G. W. BALFOUR: The Commissioners have withheld salary from Mr. Kenny, National School teacher, pending his disconnecting himself with the offices of Poor Law guardian and district councillor in Boyle Union, to which he had been recently elected. They consider that the holding of such offices by a teacher of a National school is inconsistent with the proper observance of their rules requiring teachers "to abstain from controversy," and prohibiting them from taking any part in elections except by voting. If any teachers of National schools have held the position of Poor Law guardians, as alleged, it was without the sanction or knowledge of the Commissioners.

AGRICULTURAL GRANTS IN ROS-COMMON AND LEITRIM.

MR. TULLY: I beg to ask the Chief Secretary to the Lord Lieutenant of Ireland if he can state the amount fixed as the agricultural grant to the County Roscommon, and also to the county Leitrim, the amount of the excluded charges in the case of each county, and the details of these excluded charges?

MR. G. W. BALFOUR: The yearly amount of the Agricultural Grant to the County Roscommon is £18,534. The Grant to the County Leitrim is £10,291 10s. The amount of the Excluded Charges in the County Roscommon is £3,300, and in the County Leitrim, £5,489. The Excluded Charges consist of (1) Special expenses levied on a contributory place under the Public Health Acts or enactments directing expenses to be levied as expenses under these Acts; (2) Railway Charges; (3) Navigation and Drainage Charges; (4) Relief of Distress Charges; (5) Malicious Injury Charges.

MR. TULLY: Can the right hon Gentleman say whether there are any Drainage Charges?

MR. G. W. BALFOUR: This includes Drainage Charges.

TRANSVAAL AFFAIRS.

MR. BRYN ROBERTS (Carnarvonshire, Eifion): I beg to ask the Secretary of State for the Colonies whether he is aware that Mr. D. P. Faure, in a letter appearing in the *South African News* of 8th May, states that 1s. was paid for every signature to the Johannesburg petition, and that not twenty-one dozen out of the signatories would be willing to forfeit their nationality in order to obtain the franchise; whether Mr. Faure is the gentleman who was selected by Lord Rosmead to act as interpreter between the Colonial Office and the Transvaal delegates at the London Convention in 1884; whether he can state what steps were taken by Sir Alfred Milner to ascertain the genuineness of the petition; and whether he will instruct Sir Alfred Milner in future to refuse, in accordance with precedent, to receive any petition dealing with the internal affairs of the South African Republic?

The SECRETARY OF STATE FOR THE COLONIES (MR. J. CHAMBERLAIN, Birmingham, W.): Mr. Faure did make the two statements referred to in the first two paragraphs, but I do not know what authority he had for either. He was selected as an interpreter in 1884. The genuineness of the signatures to the Uitlanders' petition has been verified by affidavits. The answer to the fourth part of the question is in the negative.

MR. BRYN ROBERTS: Will the right hon. Gentleman say by whose affidavits the genuineness of the signatures is verified?

MR. J. CHAMBERLAIN: I do not think it would be giving the hon. Gentleman any valuable information if I gave the names of the persons who made the affidavits; but they were the persons who collected the signatures.

MR. BRYN ROBERTS: The right hon. Gentleman stated on a previous occasion that Sir Alfred Milner had satisfied himself in the matter. Did Sir Alfred Milner make the affidavit; and, if not, how did he ascertain the genuineness of the signatures?

MR. J. CHAMBERLAIN: That seems to me to be hardly a serious question; but Sir Alfred Milner has satisfied himself, and has come to the conclusion that the signatures are authentic. It is, of course, a matter of opinion, and, if the hon. Member takes a different view, I do not wish to deprive him of it.

MR. BRYN ROBERTS: I simply wished to know the grounds on which Sir Alfred Milner based his convictions.

THE PARLIAMENTARY DEPOSITS BILL.

MR. TOMLINSON (Preston): I beg to ask Mr. Attorney General whether his attention has been called to the Parliamentary Deposits Bill; and whether, considering that the Parliamentary Deposits and Bonds Act was promoted and carried by the Government of the day, he will use his influence with the Government to induce them to make this Bill a Government measure?

The ATTORNEY GENERAL (Sir RICHARD WEBSTER, Isle of Wight): I am acquainted with the provisions of the

Parliamentary Deposits Bill to which my hon. and learned friend refers. In my opinion it is certainly a Bill which ought to pass, but I cannot say more in the matter.

PEERS AND PARLIAMENTARY ELECTIONS.

MR. JAMES LOWTHER : I beg to to ask the First Lord of the Treasury whether his attention has been called to a published letter, dated 22nd May, purporting to have been addressed by the Duke of Devonshire to an elector in the Southport Division of Lancashire in support of one of the candidates then contesting that constituency, for which a new writ was moved upon 12th May ; also to a letter to a similar effect alleged to have been written by the Bishop of Liverpool ; and, if the said letters be genuine, what action he proposes to take with a view either to the enforcement or repeal of the Sessional Order passed at his instance at the beginning of this Session, in which it is declared to be a high infringement of the liberties and privileges of the Commons for any peer, prelate, or other lord of Parliament to concern himself in the election of Members to serve for the Commons in Parliament ; and whether, in view of the repeated disregard of the said Sessional Order by Cabinet Ministers and other leading Peers countenanced openly in a recent instance by Members of the House of Commons of long standing, including the Chancellor of the Exchequer and the First Lord of the Admiralty, he proposes any longer to recommend the retention of an Order which, as he himself has stated, this House is powerless to enforce.

THE FIRST LORD OF THE TREASURY (Mr. A. J. BALFOUR, Manchester, E.) : As regards the letters to which my right hon. friend refers, I know nothing about them, and consequently do not know whether they were or were not private letters addressed to individuals. I presume, however, that they were, and if they were I do not think they would contravene the Sessional Order laid down by the House. That, however, is a matter on which I am no greater authority than my right hon. friend. As regards the general question, I have two or three times explained to the House the opinions I myself hold, and I do not think it necessary to repeat those opinions.

THE PEACE CONFERENCE.

MR. DILLON : I beg to ask the First Lord of the Treasury whether a resolution prohibiting the use of the Dum-Dum bullet was passed at Commission No. I. of the Peace Conference on 1st June ; whether this resolution was opposed by the British delegate ; and whether he can undertake that the British delegates will be instructed not to oppose this resolution in the General Conference. I also beg to ask the First Lord of the Treasury whether he can state what attitude was taken by the British delegate in Commission No. I. of the Peace Conference on the question of dropping explosives from balloons.

MR. A. J. BALFOUR : In answer to both these questions, I have to say that the members of the Conference have agreed that their proceedings shall be conducted in secret, except in so far as regards communications which are made with their consent to representatives of the Press on the spot. Her Majesty's Government cannot, under these circumstances, make any communication as to the instructions given to or the attitude taken by the British delegates.

IRELAND—EMERGENCY MEN CARRYING FIREARMS.

MR. AUSTIN (Limerick, W.) : May I ask the Chief Secretary to the Lord Lieutenant of Ireland whether his attention has been called to the case of an emergency man named Thomas Crawford, in the employment of the representatives of the late Surgeon O'Grady, who was on the 15th May arrested for drunkenness near the town of Abbeyfeale, county Limerick, and for firing a loaded revolver, with the result that a man named Ahearn was wounded in the hand ? Is he aware that Crawford was fined 20s. for being drunk, and only 2s. 6d. for firing his revolver, by the magistrates sitting in petty sessions at Abbeyfeale ? Is Crawford still permitted to carry loaded firearms ? And can he inform the House upon what grounds did the magistrates refuse the application of Mr. Ahearne's solicitor for informations against Crawford ?

*MR. G. W. BALFOUR : The facts are substantially as stated in the question, except that there is no evidence that Mr. Ahearn was wounded in the hand as a result of the discharge of the revolver. He made no complaint in the matter until the 17th of May, and the head constable of police who then examined his hand could find no trace of recent injury. What was pointed out as the alleged wound was a perfectly healed scar. I presume the magistrates refused to send the case for trial because they did not consider that the scar was caused by Crawford. The police took possession of Crawford's revolver on the 15th of May, and Government have since ordered the revocation of his licence to keep firearms.

PERSONAL EXPLANATION.

MR. DILLON : I desire, sir, with your permission, to say a few words in the nature of a personal explanation. Last Friday I asked the First Lord of the Treasury whether I was correct in stating that, in my recollection, the Government had at an earlier date in the Session declared their intention of submitting a Bill in Parliament for the grant to Lord Kitchener of Khartoum. The right hon. Gentleman on that occasion declared that I was incorrect, and that the Government had made no such statement, and that he had all through expressed his intention of proceeding according to the arrangement now proposed. I think I am entitled to try to prove that my memory was accurate, and I would point out that on February 17 last I put a question to the Chancellor of the Exchequer, the first reference made during the present Session, I think, to the proposed grant. I asked the Chancellor of the Exchequer whether it was proposed to ask the House to vote any sum to Lord Kitchener in respect of the battle of Omdurman, and, if so, when the Vote would be taken ; and I also asked whether the procedure would be by Bill or by Vote. The Chancellor of the Exchequer answered :

" Yes, sir ; we shall ask the House of Commons to vote a sum of £30,000, which will probably be invested in the purchase of an annuity for Lord Kitchener of Khartoum. I think the procedure must be by Bill, and it will be taken at an early date."

I think I am entitled to call the attention of the First Lord of the Treasury to two subsequent occasions on which the matter was referred to, for it will be in the memory of the House that he said that he had in his mind all along the proceeding by Vote in Committee of Supply. On the 20th February

the hon. Member for East Clare asked the First Lord of the Treasury at what date the Bill for giving Lord Kitchener £30,000 would be introduced ; and the First Lord replied :

" I am afraid 1 cannot give an answer to the question at present. As the hon. Gentleman knows, I rather hoped to begin the ordinary legislative work of the Session to-day. That hope has been disappointed, and the ordinary work cannot now begin until Thursday. If the hon. Gentleman will ask the question on Thursday, I will endeavour to answer him."

Whereupon the hon. Gentleman the Member for East Clare said he would put the question on Thursday. On the 23rd February the hon. Member for Kilkenny asked the following question, on behalf of the hon. Member for East Clare :

" When the Bill to grant £30,000 to Lord Kitchener will be introduced."

The First Lord of the Treasury replied :

" I cannot give a definite answer to this question, but I will undertake to give a week s notice before any steps in the matter are taken by the Government."

I do not for one moment insinuate, nor do I believe, that the First Lord of the Treasury had any intention of deceiving the House of Commons, but the House is entitled to get the information which it asked for. I am also entitled to prove that the Chancellor of the Exchequer, in reply to a question, declared that the procedure would be by way of Bill, and not by Vote in Committee of Supply ; and I think I have established the fact that I was right.

MR. A. J. BALFOUR : As the hon. Member has appealed to me, I gladly recognise that there is some justification for the view he took. It is, however, the fact that I had forgotten the particular questions and answers to which he has referred. It is also the fact that it was desired that the question should be dealt with in Committee of Supply by way of a Vote, rather than by a Bill. There were, no doubt, precedents which seem to be in favour of proceeding by Bill rather than by Vote, but investigations show that the precedents as a whole point to the procedure by Vote in Committee of Supply. As I am on my legs, it may be convenient for the House to know that on Thursday next I shall propose a resolution embodying the thanks of this House to the officers and men engaged in the Soudan campaign.

PRIVILEGE.

INTERFERENCE OF PEERS IN THE ELECTION FOR THE SOUTHPORT DIVISION OF LANCASHIRE.

MR. JAMES LOWTHER : I rise for the purpose of calling the attention of the House to a question of privilege. In answer to a question, I elicited from the First Lord of the Treasury the statement that he had no knowledge of the letters to which my question referred. Now, I have, unfortunately, during the present Session had occasion more than once to call the attention of the House to breaches deliberately made of the Sessional Order regarding the interference of Peers in Parliamentary elections. But the case which I desire now very briefly to submit to the House differs in one very important point from others which have been raised. When I raised other questions of this character I was told that until the issue of the writ the House had not been in the habit of taking any cognisance of breaches of the Sessional Order. I never admitted myself that there was any ground for the differentiation. I never admitted that the mere fact of the writ issuing or not took away any force from the Sessional Order passed every year. With the permission of the House I shall read a short extract from one of the letters, and the whole of the other letter, which is very short. The letter of the Duke of Devonshire was not, as my right hon. friend surmised, a private letter, but was obviously written to be published. It is addressed apparently to a perfect stranger, and could have been written for no other purpose than being printed. It appeared in one of the local newspapers, which stated :

"The following reply has been received by a Southport Unionist, who called the Duke of Devonshire's attention to the reasons urged by and on behalf of a few Southport Liberal Unionists for not on this occasion considering it their paramount duty to oppose the Home Rule candidate."

The reply is dated Lismore Castle, May 22 ; and I may say in passing that the writ for the Southport election was issued ten days before, although I myself attach no importance whatever to the argument that the breach of privilege depends on whether the interference is before or after the issue of the writ. The letter runs :

"Sir,—I have received your letter of the 19th inst., and am sorry to hear that there is any difference of opinion among Liberal Unionists at Southport as to the duty of giving their support to Mr. Balfour. . . . The present demoralisation and powerlessness of the Opposition are, in my opinion, most inadequate reasons for supporting a candidate whose return would, in however small a degree, tend to resuscitate the unfortunate Home Rule proposals which were rejected at the last General Election."

Then, sir, the Bishop of Liverpool wrote the following letter to a Churchman in Southport :

"Dear Sir,—I answer your question without any hesitation. If I had a vote for Southport, I should certainly not give it to any candidate who was in favour of Home Rule for Ireland."

I need hardly say that I heartily sympathise with every word contained in those letters. I feel also bound to add that I myself consider that both the Duke of Devonshire and the Bishop of Liverpool were perfectly right in writing those letters ; but, as the right hon. Gentleman told me on a previous occasion that the fact of the alleged breach of privilege being committed before the issue of the writ prevented his taking notice of it, I desire to emphasise the fact that such an answer would not hold good at the present moment. Now, sir, it is not for the House to deal in a legislative capacity with this question. It is not for me to express an opinion as to whether the Order is wise or foolish ; the duty before the House is a judicial duty. We have to interpret our Order upon judicial lines, and it is to that point that I shall endeavour to confine myself. It is necessary, no doubt, from a judicial standpoint that both sides of the question should be placed before the House, and, very briefly, I shall endeavour to do so. It is a matter of notoriety that every Prime Minister during the last quarter of a century has set this Order at defiance, and consequently we must not judge harshly the noble duke and the bishop if they may think that they were perfectly justified in adopting this course. They no doubt remembered that Lord Beaconsfield, when Prime Minister of England, set this Order at defiance, and Lord Salisbury and Lord Rosebery also set it at defiance. But there have been recent cases brought before the House, every one of which, I think, shows that this House is not in earnest in its desire to enforce the Order. The Lord Chancellor, who is, as we know, the head of the law, threw his great weight into the scale in favour of the proceeding in question not being a breach of the law, and consequently the

Duke of Devonshire and the Bishop of Liverpool may feel called upon, in reply, to quote that high authority in favour of their contention. When I speak of the Duke of Devonshire I must remind the House that this is not a case, any more than the others to whom I have recently drawn attention, of an obscure peer. My right hon. friend the Leader of the House has imagined me spending a great part of my time in endeavouring to rake up cases of this sort. I can assure the right hon. Gentleman that, so far from that being the case, I have declined to bring before the House numerous cases which have been mentioned to me. I have always gone on the principle that my right hon. friend the member for Dartford (Sir W. Hart Dyke) so pithily put when he said that I had gone to the top of the tree to find the fish. The Duke of Devonshire cannot be stated to be an obscure peer any more than the Lord Chancellor or those other peers I have mentioned in connection with this Sessional Order. The Duke of Devonshire will be remembered in the House of Commons as an old Parliamentary hand. He is not merely a leader at this moment of one of the recognised parties in the State, but he was for some years an acknowledged leader when the party opposite was in opposition, and he is one of the highest authorities on Parliamentary procedure. I must also point out that the noble Duke has had some considerable experience in the interpretation of this very Sessional Order. It will be remembered that a complaint was made by the right hon. Gentleman the Member for West Monmouth, that he went down to Derby, the county of which the noble Duke was Lord Lieutenant, and delivered a speech of an electioneering character, and we are aware that at Darlington, after the issue of the writs from the Crown Office for the general election of 1895, a very able speech was delivered by the noble Duke on current topics which had been submitted to the electorate, with the candidate for Darlington by his side. Therefore, sir, I feel justified in saying that the case of the Duke of Devonshire is one which, if passed over, as I hope it will be, by this House, will finally and indelibly emphasise the opinion of the House that the right hon. Gentleman the First Lord of the Treasury was correct when he said that this Order was a sham

and a farce. Sir, I quoted my right hon. friend on a previous occasion, and I will not do so again. But I think it right to point out that my right hon. friend is not alone in his opinion amongst his colleagues as to this being a sham and a farce. If it is desired to enforce this obsolete Order, the least my right hon. friend can do is to lend his countenance as far as he can to the maintenance of the Order. But what did we find the other day when I called attention to the case of the Lord Chancellor and of other peers? We find that some twenty Members of the House of Commons themselves took part in the proceedings. They were not obscure or young Members. They were headed by my hon. friend the Father of the House of Commons, who, for upwards of forty years has had experience of Parliamentary ruling. A gentleman who was present tells me that the Lord Chancellor was moved into the chair by one of the oldest Members of this House, the First Lord of the Admiralty, and the proposition was seconded by the Chancellor of the Exchequer. These are two high Parliamentary authorities, and certainly old hands. I found them here thirty-four years ago when I first entered the House, and one was a Cabinet Minister very shortly after that time. Therefore, sir, I need not detain the House further than by calling my right hon. friend's attention to another great authority upon this subject—Lord James. Lord James, another of the Cabinet colleagues of my right hon. friend, is perhaps one of the greatest authorities living on election law, and he took a very active part in all the legislation regulating elections in this country for many years. I hold in my hand a report of a speech of his delivered in this House, in which he said—

"The resolution we pass every year is an obsolete and a meaningless resolution, and the time will come—next Session, I hope—when the House of Commons will have to say whether the period has not arrived when we should cease altogether to go through this form of protesting without foundation, and without having the power to give any effect to our protests. The resolution does not add to the dignity of the House or to the protection of its Members."

Now I have shown that the Duke of Devonshire has on more than one occasion proved that he takes an enlightened view of this absurd obsolete Order, and that being so I place the matter now in the hands of the House. I have no desire to anticipate the commencement of the next Session. but if I am in a position to do so I shall feel it my duty to afford the House an opportunity once and for all of getting rid of this absurd and meaningless Order· Meanwhile I shall put myself in order by moving a Resolution.

Motion made, and Question proposed—

" That it having been represented to this House that the Duke of Devonshire and the Lord Bishop of Liverpool did severally infringe the liberties and privileges of this House by concerning themselves in the election of a member to represent the Southport Division of the county of Lancashire in the House of Commons, a Select Committee be appointed to inquire into the alleged breaches of privilege."—(*Mr. James Lowther.*)

SIR WILFRID LAWSON (Cumberland, Cockermouth): I will not detain the House for more than a moment, but I feel it my duty to say a few words in support of the proposition. I do not think that anybody can say that the present state of affairs is satisfactory. In public or private life the most contemptible of all characters is the swaggerer, and I think it is a bit of swagger on our part to affirm a resolution, threatening all sorts of pains and penalties, which we have not the slightest power to carry out.

MR. A. J. BALFOUR : My right hon. friend, if perseverance deserves reward, is certainly predestined, after, I suppose, a long series of similar speeches, to succeed in his endeavour. This, I think, is the third or fourth time in the course of the present Session in which he has brought the same matter before the House in substantially the same speech, and really the importunate widow is not in it with my right hon. friend. I confess I am unwilling to imitate my right hon. friend ·in one respect. Doubtless he has less reason to regret the necessary repetitions which these discussions force upon him, but I myself have personally the strongest

objection to repeating the same arguments more than a certain number of times. I have really nothing to add to the reasons which induced me to advise the House on a previous occasion, as I advise it now, ˙not to take any formal action in regard to these matters. Whether a court of law—if the matter could be referred to it—would decide that the two letters read by my right hon. friend are breaches of the Standing Order or not I am unable to say ; but of one thing I am certain, and that is, that the Standing Order is not without effect, and great effect. It conduces to the abstention of Members of the other House from our electoral contests, which would not occur if the Order were repealed. It is not, therefore, a mere empty form. Whether it is desirable to exclude the House of Lords from entering into our electoral affairs is another matter. I do not know whether my right hon. friend would agree with me on that point—I rather think he would not ; but he has not raised it now, though he threatens to raise it next Session. It was raised last Session, and the Session before the last, and the Session before that, and so on back into the indefinite past, whenever the Sessional Order came up for discussion. In the meantime I strongly advise the House not to take any steps with regard to these letters, and although, perhaps, it may be less relevant to the point of order, I do not advise the House now any more than in the past to make any change in the Standing Order which would have more far-reaching and wide-spreading results than my right hon. friend anticipates.

MR. JAMES LOWTHER : After the renewed assurance of my right hon. friend that peers can do what they like, I will not proceed any further in the matter. (Cries of " Divide, divide.")

Question put.

The House divided : Ayes, 86. Noes, 231. (Division List No. 169.)

AYES.

Allan, William (Gateshead)
Allen, W. (Newc. under Lyme)
Allison, Robert Andrew
Ambrose, Robert
Atherley-Jones, L.
Austin, M. (Limerick, W.)
Bainbridge, Emerson
Baker, Sir John
Barlow, John Emmott
Bartley, George C. T.
Bayley, Thomas (Derbyshire)
Billson, Alfred
Blake, Edward
Bowles, T. Gibson (King's Lynn)
Brunner, Sir John Tomlinson
Buchanan, Thomas Ryburn
Burns, John
Caldwell, James
Cameron, SirCharles(Glasgow)
Curran, Thomas (Sligo, S.)
Dilke, Rt. Hon. Sir Charles
Dillon, John
Disraeli, Coningsby Ralph
Donelan, Captain A.
Doogan, P. C.
Duckworth, James
Duncombe, Hon. Hubert V.
Evans, Sir Francis H. (S'ton.)
Farquharson, Dr. Robert
Galloway, William Johnson

Gourley, SirEdwardTemperley
Hayne, Rt. Hon. CharlesSeale-
Heaton, John Henniker
Hedderwick, Thomas C. H.
Holland, Wm. H. (York, W. R.)
Jones, Wm. (Carnarvonshire)
Kearley, Hudson E.
Kinloch, SirJohnGeorgeSmyth
Labouchere, Henry
Lambert, George
Langley, Batty
Lloyd-George, David
Lough, Thomas
MacAleese, Daniel
MacDonnell, Dr. M. A(Q'n'sCo)
MacNeill, John Gordon Swift
M'Cartan, Michael
M'Ghee, Richard
M'Hugh, E. (Armagh, S.)
M'Kenna, Reginald
M'Laren, Charles Benjamin
Montagu, Sir S. (Whitechapel)
Morton, Edw.J.C.(Devonport)
Norton, Capt. Cecil William
Nussey, Thomas Willans
O'Brien, James F. X. (Cork)
O'Connor, T. P. (Liverpool)
Palmer, Sir Chas. M.(Durham)
Perks, Robert William
Pilkington, SirG. A.(LancS.W.)

Pirie, Duncan V.
Priestley, Briggs (Yorks.)
Robertson, Edmund (Dundee)
Scott, Charles Prestwich
   (Leigh)
Smith, Samuel (Flint)
Souttar, Robinson
Stanhope, Hon. Philip J.
Steadman, William Charles
Stevenson, Francis S.
Strachey, Edward
Sullivan, Donal (Westmeath)
Thomas, A. (Glamorgan, E.)
Tully, Jasper
Ure, Alexander
Walton, Joseph (Barnsley)
Warner, Thomas Courtenay T.
Wedderburn, Sir William
Weir, James Galloway
Wharton, Rt. Hon. J. Lloyd
Williams, J. C. (Notts.)
Wilson, Charles Henry (Hull)
Wilson, John (Govan)
Wilson, J. H. (Middlesbrough)
Woods, Samuel
Young, Samuel (Cavan, East)
Yoxall, James Henry
TELLERS FOR THE AYES—
   Mr. James Lowther (Kent)
   and Sir Wilfrid Lawson.

NOES.

Allhusen, AugustusHy.Eden
Allsopp, Hon. George
Anson, Sir William Reynell
Arnold, Alfred
Arnold-Forster, Hugh O.
Arrol, Sir William
Ashton, Thomas Gair
Atkinson, Rt. Hon. John
Austin, Sir John (Yorkshire)
Bagot, Capt. JoscelineFitzRoy
Bailey, James (Walworth)
Baird, John George Alexander
Baldwin, Alfred
Balfour, Rt. Hon. A.J. (Manch'r.
Balfour, Rt. Hn. G.W. (Leeds)
Barry, Rt. Hn. A.H.S.-(Hunts)
Bathurst, Hon. Allen Benj.
Beach, Rt Hn Sir M H(Bristol)
Beaumont, Wentworth C. B.
Begg, Ferdinand Faithfull
Beresford, Lord Charles
Bhownaggree, Sir M. M.
Biddulph, Michael
Blundell, Colonel Henry
Bond, Edward
Brassey, Albert
Brodrick, Rt. Hon. St. John
Brookfield, A. Montagu
Bryce, Rt. Hon. James
Bullard, Sir Harry
Burt, Thomas
Buxton, Sydney Charles
Campbell, Rt.Hn.JA(Glasg'w)
Campbell, J. H. M. (Dublin)
Campbell-Bannerman, Sir H.
Carlile, William Walter
Cavendish, R. F. (N. Lancs.)
Cayzer, Sir Charles William

Cecil, Evelyn (Hertford, East)
Chamberlain, Rt.Hn.J. (Birm)
Chamberlain, J. A. (Wor'r.)
Channing, Francis Allston
Chaplin, Rt. Hon. Henry
Chelsea, Viscount
Cochrane, Hon. Thos. H. A. E.
Coddington, Sir William
Coghill, Douglas Harry
Cohen, Benjamin Louis
Collings, Rt. Hon. Jesse
Colville, John
Cook, Fred. Lucas (Lambeth)
Courtney, Rt.Hon.LeonardH.
Cox, Irwin Edward B(Harrow)
Crombie, John William
Curzon, Viscount
Dalbiac, Colonel Philip Hugh
Davies, M. V.- (Cardigan)
Denny, Colonel
Dickson-Poynder, Sir John P.
Digby, John K. D. Wingfield-
Dorington, Sir John Edward
Douglas, Rt. Hon. A. Akers-
Douglas, Charles M. (Lanark)
Douglas-Pennant, Hon. E. S.
Drage, Geoffrey
Drucker, A.
Elliot, Hon. A. R. Douglas
Engledew, Charles John
Fardell, Sir T. George
Fellowes, Hon. Ailwyn E.
Ferguson, R. C. Munro (Leith)
Fergusson, Rt.Hn.Sir J. (Mtr.)
Field, Admiral (Eastbourne)
Finch, George H.
Finlay, Sir Robert Bannatyne
Fisher, William Hayes

Fison, Frederick William
Fitzmaurice, Lord Edmond
Flannery, Sir Fortescue
Foster, Colonel (Lancaster)
Fowler, Rt. Hon. Sir Henry
Fry, Lewis
Gedge, Sydney
Gilliat, John Saunders
Goddard, Daniel Ford
Gold, Charles
Goldsworthy, Major-General
Gordon, Hon. John Edward
Gorst, Rt. Hn. Sir John Eldon
Goschen, George J. (Sussex)
Graham, Henry Robert
Green, Walford D. (Wedn'b'y)
Grey, Sir Edward (Berwick)
Gurdon, SirWilliam Brampton
Halsey, Thomas Frederick
Hamilton, Rt.Hn.Lord George
Hanbury, Rt.Hn.RobertWm.
Hardy, Laurence
Hare, Thomas Leigh
Hatch, Ernest Frederick Geo.
Helder, Augustus
Hill, Arthur (Down, West)
Hill, SirEdwardStock (Bristol)
Hoare, E. Brodie (Hampstead)
Hoare, Samuel (Norwich)
Hobhouse, Henry
Horniman, Frederick John
Houldsworth, Sir Wm. Henry
Houston, R. P.
Howard, Joseph
Hozier, Hon.JamesHenryCecil
Hubbard, Hon. Evelyn
Hutton, John (Yorks., N.R.)
Jackson, Rt. Hon. Wm. Lawies

Jessel,CaptainHerbertMerton
Johnson-Ferguson,Jabez Edw.
Jolliffe, Hon. H. George
Jones, D. Brynmor (Swansea)
Kemp, George
Kennaway,Rt.Hon.SirJohnH.
Kimber, Henry
Knowles, Lees
Lafone, Alfred
Laurie, Lieut.-General
Lawrence,SirE.Durning-(Corn
Lawson, John Grant (Yorks.)
Lecky,Rt.Hon.WilliamEdw.H
Leng, Sir John
Llewellyn, Evan H. (Somerset)
LlewelynSirDillwyn (Swansea
Lockwood, Lt.-Col. A. R.
Loder, Gerald Walter Erskine
Long,Col.CharlesW.(Evesham
Long,Rt.Hn. Walter(Liverp'l)
Lowe, Francis William
Lowther,RtHnJW(Cum'land)
Loyd, Archie Kirkman
Lyell, Sir Leonard
Macartney, W. G. Ellison
Macdona, John Cumming
Maclean, James Mackenzie
M'Calmont, H. L. B. (Cambs.)
M'Calmont,Col.J.(Antrim,E.)
M'Ewan, William
M'Iver,SirLewis(EdinburghW
Malcolm, Ian
Manners,LordEdward Wm. J.
Mappin, Sir Frederick Thorpe
Maxwell,Rt. Hon.SirHerbertE
Mellor, Colonel (Lancashire)
Melville, Beresford Valentine
Middlemore, J. Throgmorton
Mildmay, Francis Bingham
Milward, Colonel Victor

Moon, Edward Robert Pacy
Morgan,J.Lloyd(Carmarthen)
Morley,RtHonJohn(Montrose
Morrison, Walter
Morton,ArthurH.A.(Deptford
Murray, Rt. Hon. A. G. (Bute
Murray, Charles J. (Coventry)
Myers, William Henry
Northcote, Hon.SirH.Stafford
Oldroyd, Mark
Paulton, James Mellor
Pease, H. Pike (Darlington)
Pease, Joseph A. (Northumb.)
Pickersgill, Edward Hare
Pierpoint, Robert
Platt-Higgins, Frederick
Powell, Sir Francis Sharp
Pretyman, Ernest George
Purvis, Robert
Pym, C. Guy
Quilter, Sir Cuthbert
Rankin, Sir James
Ridley, Rt. Hon. Sir M. W.
Ritchie, Rt. Hon. C. Thomson
Roberts, John Bryn (Eifion)
Robertson, Herbert(Hackney)
Rothschild,Hn. Lionel Walter
Russell,Gen.F.S.(Cheltenham
Russell, T.W. (Tyrone)
Rutherford, John
Ryder, John Herbert Dudley
Sassoon, Sir Edward Albert
Saunderson,Rt.Hn.ColEdw.J.
Scoble, Sir Andrew Richard
Seely, Charles Hilton
Sharpe, William Edward T.
Sidebottom, Wm. (Derbysh.)
Simeon, Sir Barrington
Sinclair, Capt J. (Forfarshire)
Soames, Arthur Wellesley

Stanley,Hn. Arthur(Ormskirk
Stanley, Edward J.(Somerset)
Stanley, Henry M. (Lambeth)
Stanley, Lord (Lancs.)
Stock, James Henry
Strutt, Hon. Charles Hedley
Sturt,Hon. Humphry Napier
Talbot, Lord E. (Chichester)
Tennant, Harold John
Thomas, David A. (Merthyr)
Thorburn, Walter
Tomlinson, Wm. Edw.Murray
Trevelyan, Charles Philips
Usborne, Thomas
Valentia, Viscount
Vincent,Col.Sir C. E. Howard
Wallace, Robert (Edinburgh)
Wallace, Robert (Perth)
Wanklyn, James Leslie
Ward, Hon Robert A. (Crewe)
Warr, Augustus Frederick
Webster, R. G. (St. Pancras)
Webster, Sir R.E.(I. ofWight)
Welby, Lieut.-Col. A. C. E.
Whiteley,H.(Ashton-under-L.
Whitmore, Charles Algernon
Williams, Col. R. (Dorset)
Williams, J. (Powell-(Birm.)
Wilson-Todd, Wm.H.(Yorks.)
Wolff, Gustav Wilhelm
Woodall, William
Wortley, Rt.Hon.C.B.Stuart-
Wylie, Alexander
Wyndham, George
Wyvill, Marmaduke D'Arcy
Yerburgh, Robert Armstrong
Younger, William
TELLERS FOR THE NOES—
  Sir William Walrond and
  Mr. Anstruther.

PRIVILEGE.

MESSAGE FROM HER MAJESTY TO THE HOUSE OF LORDS, DELIVERED BY THE LORD CHANCELLOR.

MR. J. G. SWIFT MACNEILL: I wish to direct the attention of the House at the first available moment to what I conceive to be a gross breach of the privileges of this House, and to put myself in order I will read the resolution which I intend to submit to the House. I shall not detain the House five minutes, and then we shall hear what the First Lord of the Treasury has to say, and I wish him a happy deliverance. The resolution is this:—

"That the action of the Lord Chancellor in presenting to the House of Lords a message from Her Majesty recommending that she should be enabled to grant to Lord Kitchener a sum of £30,000 is a departure from ancient constitutional precedent; is contrary to the usage of Parliament; and is a gross breach of the privilege of this House, inasmuch as the message attributes to the House of Lords the power of initiating money grants, which alone appertains to the House of Commons, instead of concurring in these grants."

That is absolutely flagrant. The first authority that I would like to quote to the House is Sir Erskine May, and I will only quote two sentences. He says, "The responsibility discharged by the House of Lords in the granting of supplies for the service of the time is concurrence, and not initiation." I need not remind the House that, though this is the Queen's message, it is in reality a message for which the Ministers are responsible. The message to the House of Lords in this case is identical in words to that received by this House, as if there were a concurrent and co-ordinate jurisdiction, which there is not. We are told that this message is identical with the message which came to the House in reference to Sir Garnet Wolseley in 1874; but in that case there was a message conveyed to the House of Lords, as in Kitchener's case, with this difference—Her Majesty, taking into consideration the eminent services of Major-General Sir Garnet Wolseley in conducting the Ashantee campaign, and desiring to confer some signal mark of her favour, "recommends to the House of Lords to concur" with the House of Commons in enabling Her Majesty to grant to Sir Garnet Wolseley £30,000. Those were also the terms that were adopted in 1841 and in 1857, when in similar cases the House of Lords was asked to concur. We have the words of Mr. Speaker Onslow, who said Ministers had always sent these messages to both Houses, but the distinction of the wording was that the initiation in making the grant of money is to be only with the Commons, as is done in the Speech from the Throne. I put this matter before the House as a matter for its observation, and I think it is a gross breach of privilege. With these words I beg to move the Resolution and bring it up to the chair.

Motion made, and Question proposed—

"That the action of the Lord Chancellor in presenting to the House of Lords a Message from Her Majesty, recommending that she should be enabled to grant to Lord Kitchener a sum of £30,000, is a departure from ancient constitutional precedents, contrary to the usage of Parliament, and a gross breach of the privileges of this House, inasmuch as the Message attributes to the House of Lords a power of initiating money grants which alone appertains to the House of Commons, instead of concurring in those grants."—(*Mr. Swift MacNeill.*)

Mr. CHANNING (Northampton): I think my hon. friend is amply justified in the course he has taken in bringing this matter before the House. A difference in the form of words may be a matter of serious importance, and it certainly does seem to me that the difference between a direct invitation to the House of Lords to enable the Queen to carry out a grant of a certain sum of money, and a message to the House of Lords to concur with this House in so doing, is a very grave difference indeed, and one which amply justifies my hon. friend in moving his resolution. The proper course for the Government in this matter would clearly have been to proceed by a Resolution, base a Bill upon the Resolution, and send the Bill to the House of Lords. At any rate there is a vast and vital difference between the resolution in 1874 and the present one. I beg to second the Resolution.

*Mr. SPEAKER: I am in very great doubt whether I should allow this matter to be brought before the House as a question of privilege at all. My reason for being in doubt is that it is in any case necessary that the House of Lords should

take some action for the purpose of enabling the grant to be made. The Queen by her Message asks the House of Lords to enable her to make such a grant. What the hon. Member is now doing is to ask the House to assume that the message is to be interpreted as asking the House of Lords to act in a way in which they are not entitled to act, and contrary to the privilege of this House, although the language is consistent with a request to that House to act only in a constitutional way. I am, however, very anxious not to take upon myself the responsibility of a decision where there is any ground for suggesting that the matter may be one involving a question of privilege for the judgment of the House. The only point is whether the word "concur," which could be read into the message by implication, ought to have been expressly used. I may point out on the question of precedent that in 1883, when motions were made for grants by way of pensions to Lord Alcester and Lord Wolseley, two resolutions were submitted to the House of Lords, in one of which the word "concur" was used, and in the other left out, and the same words were used in the latter Resolution as on the present occasion.

Mr. A. J. BALFOUR: I was not aware that the hon. Member was going to raise this point. I understand that he makes two allegations—one that the course pursued by the Lord Chancellor and presumably by the House of Lords is contrary to the precedents and practice of Parliament; and the other that it is a breach of the privileges of this House. Sir, I challenge both those statements. Take the second point first. Mr. Speaker has already pointed out that the concurrence of the House of Lords and the action of the House of Lords is absolutely necessary to enable this grant to be given. It is a pure assumption on the part of the hon. Gentleman, which he does not himself seriously hold—an assumption which none of us hold, and an assumption which not a single person in this House believes to be true—that the House of Lords, in the case of the grant to Lord Kitchener, are going to violate those ancient constitutional usages which are divided between the two Houses of Parliament in different measures, the responsibility arising from the passing of the Finance Acts. So much for the point of substance. On the point

L

of form, it is only necessary that I should repeat to the House what has already been indicated by Mr. Speaker—namely, that so high a constitutional authority as Mr. Gladstone, a statesman who was never supposed to be oblivious of the constitutional privileges of the House of which he was so long a distinguished ornament. In the time of Mr. Gladstone the following resolution was brought down to the House, and was read to the House by the Leader of the House, in that case Lord Granville. The message was :—

"VICTORIA R.

"Her Majesty, taking into consideration the important services rendered by Garnet Joseph Lord Wolseley, general in Her Majesty's Army, in the course of the recent expedition to Egypt, and being desirous to confer some signal mark of her favour for those distinguished services, recommends the House of Lords to enable Her Majesty to make provision to secure for the said Garnet Joseph Lord Wolseley and his next surviving male heir the sum of £2,000 per annum."

On the constitutional point the words I have read out are precisely on all fours with the gracious message which the Lord Chancellor, on Friday last, read out in the House of Lords. Whereas it is clear that there, is on the one hand, no substantial invasion of our privileges intended by the House of Lords, so it is equally plain, on the other hand, that what they have done is in no sense contrary to tradition, or precedent, or the usage of Parliament. I hope, under these circumstances, the hon. Gentleman will not think it necessary to press his motion to a Division, and that he will permit the House to proceed to the discussion which it is anxiously waiting for.

SIR H. CAMPBELL-BANNERMAN (Stirling Burghs): I think we are indebted to my hon. friend for bringing this matter forward (Ministerial cries of "Oh, oh!" and laughter). Although some hon. Members opposite appear to differ from me on this point, I am sure the Leader of the House does not differ from me. I am sure we are indebted to my hon. friend for having turned his watchful eye upon the minutiæ of the proceedings in another place. I conceive that the main point which he had in view has been substantially gained by the right hon. Gentleman the Leader of the House having formally disclaimed the slightest intention to depart from

former precedents and usage in this matter. It is unfortunate, from the point of view of those of us who take a rigid view of the relations between the two Houses in this matter, that there is a precedent containing the very words which are now complained of, because otherwise we might have had some justification in discerning an insidious attempt on the part of the right hon. Gentleman opposite to exalt the other House of Parliament at the expense of this. But after the assurance of the right hon. Gentleman, and after his being able to adduce a precedent coming from an unimpeachable source for the words which are now being used, I trust my hon. friend will be content with the substantial victory he has gained, and not put the House to any further trouble.

MR. DILLON : I rose for the purpose of stating that, while asking my hon. friend not to put the House to the trouble of a Division, I do not accept the First Lord of the Treasury's statement that there is a precedent for what is now being done. If I am rightly informed, the precedent he alluded to was on an occasion when the Message was made the foundation of a Bill, and if that be true it is no precedent whatever. Many years ago, in the days of Mr. Speaker Onslow, in order to settle these disputes, it was agreed and clearly set forth that the two Houses should enact on the same day, but that the Message in each House should be in different terms, and it was on that specific understanding that the two Houses came to an agreement. And now the right hon. Gentleman seeks to establish a proposition that it is in accordance with precedent that what has been clearly set forth is to be departed from, and that the two Messages to the two Houses are to be in identical words. I hold that this procedure is not in accordance with precedent. This is a distinct breach of the privileges of this House, and it is only because I know that the House desires to go on with the actual question before it that I urge my hon. friend not to press his motion to a Division.

MR. J. G. SWIFT MACNEILL : Having regard to the circumstances of the case, I will withdraw my motion, and accept the moral triumph.

Motion, by leave, withdrawn.

MESSAGE FROM THE LORDS.

That they have agreed to—Parish Councillors (Tenure of Office) Bill with an Amendment.

Amendments to Coalville Urban District Gas Bill [Lords], Glastonbury Water Bill [Lords], Queen's Ferry Bridge Bill [Lords], without Amendment. That they have passed a Bill intituled "An Act for supplying with gas the parish of Cobham, in the county of Surrey, and adjacent places." [Cobham Gas Bill [Lords].

Also, a Bill, intituled "An Act to authorise the sale of the church of All Saints', Tyndall Street, in the county borough of Cardiff, with the site thereof, and the application of the proceeds of sale to the provision of a new church; and for other purposes." [All Saints' Church (Cardiff) Bill [Lords].

Also, a Bill, intituled "An Act to empower the Weston-super-Mare, Clevedon, and Portishead Tramways Company to construct light railways in the county of Somerset; and for other purposes." [Weston-super-Mare, Clevedon, and Portishead Tramways Company (Light Railway Extensions) Bill [Lords].

Also, a Bill, intituled, "An Act to confer further powers on the Corporation of Whitehaven with respect to their water and electric lighting undertakings, to extend the borough of Whitehaven, to consolidate the rates of the borough and simplify the collection thereof; and for other purposes." [Whitehaven Corporation Bill [Lords].

Also, a Bill, intituled, "An Act to empower the Birmingham, North Warwickshire, and Stratford-upon-Avon Railway Company to make new railways in the counties of Worcester and Warwick; and for other purposes." [Birmingham, North Warwickshire, and Stratford-upon-Avon Railway Bill [Lords].

Also, a Bill, intituled, "An Act for the abolition of the perpetual curacy of the consecrated chapel, called 'Grosvenor Chapel,' in the Parish of Saint George, Hanover Square, in the county and diocese of London, and for vesting the said chapel in the rector of the said parish; and for other purposes." [Grosvenor Chapel (London) Bill [Lords].

Also, a Bill, intituled, "An Act to empower the Urban District Council for the district of Moss Side to work any tramway for the time being belonging to or leased by them; and for other purposes." [Moss Side Urban District Council (Tramways) Bill [Lords].

Also, a Bill, intituled, "An Act to empower the Urban District Council for the district of Stretford to work any tramway for the time being belonging to or leased by them; and for other purposes." [Stretford Urban District Council (Tramways) Bill [Lords].

And, also, a Bill, intituled, "An Act to empower the Urban District Council for the district of Withington to work any tramway for the time being belonging to or leased by them; and for other purposes." [Withington Urban District Council (Tramways) Bill [Lords].

COBHAM GAS BILL [Lords].

ALL SAINTS' CHURCH (CARDIFF) BILL [Lords].

WESTON - SUPER - MARE, CLEVEDON, AND PORTISHEAD TRAMWAYS COMPANY (LIGHT RAILWAY EXTENSIONS) BILL [Lords].

WHITEHAVEN CORPORATION BILL [Lords].

BIRMINGHAM, NORTH WARWICKSHIRE, AND STRATFORD-UPON-AVON RAILWAY BILL [Lords].

GROSVENOR CHAPEL (LONDON) BILL [Lords].

MOSS SIDE URBAN DISTRICT COUNCIL (TRAMWAYS) BILL [Lords].

STRETFORD URBAN DISTRICT COUNCIL (TRAMWAYS) BILL [Lords].

WITHINGTON URBAN DISTRICT COUNCIL (TRAMWAYS) BILL [Lords].

Read the first time; and referred to the Examiners of Petitions for Private Bills.

JONES' DIVORCE BILL [Lords].

Ordered,—That a Message be sent to the Lords, to request that their Lordships will be pleased to communicate to this House, Copies of the Minutes of Evidence and Proceedings, together with the Documents deposited, in the case of Jones' Divorce Bill [Lords]; and that the Clerk do carry the said Message.

Ordered,—That it be an Instruction to the Select Committee on Divorce Bills, that they do hear Counsel and examine Witnesses for Jones' Divorce Bill [Lords], and also that they do hear Counsel and examine Witnesses against the Bill, if the Parties concerned think fit to be heard by Counsel and produce Witnesses.—(*Mr. Attorney General.*)

SUPPLY.

(Message from Her Majesty [Grant to Lord Kitchener]),—considered in Committee :—

(In the Committee.)

Queen's Message [2nd June] read.

THE FIRST LORD OF THE TREASURY (MR. A. J. BALFOUR, Manchester, E.): Mr. Lowther, in the earlier hours of last September the whole country was in a mood of anxious, if hopeful, expectation. It was known that the long drama of the Soudan, extending for sixteen years, was visibly and surely drawing to a close. That drama is one on which we cannot look back with unmingled satisfaction. It has been marked by some great disasters, by some barren successes, but by one tragic event which has stamped itself indelibly in the hearts and memories of the people of these islands ; and the question, Sir, connected with this great drama was of what character would be the final catastrophe. We knew that the enemy whom we had to meet was far superior to us in numbers ; that in point of courage and daring they were not inferior to any fighting troops that the world has ever seen; that they fought with the great advantages accruing to the fact that they were in their own country, and that we were divided from our military base by many miles of country and great difficulties. The question, therefore, which we asked ourselves, not without some pardonable anxiety, was whether t e superior arms, superior organisation, and the superior strategy of our own forces enabled us to bring this long controversy to a final and triumphant issue. Sir, the fact that the mid-day sun on the 2nd of September saw finally and for ever the power of Mahdism crushed was due, above all others, to the genius of the man whom we desire to-day to honour and reward. Mr. Lowther, I hope that no hon. Gentleman will this afternoon allow the course which he proposes to take upon this Vote to be warped or modified by any view which he may entertain upon the question of the policy of the Government in advancing from Wady Halfa to Khartoum. On that policy sharp differences have divided us in the past. Those differences are not yet healed, and I do not anticipate that the division of judgment which has shown itself in the course of many sharp debates can be expected to die out until history gives some final verdict upon the policy which we have thought it right to pursue. No man, Sir, by the vote he gives to-night, will in any way prejudice the views which he may take upon these broad questions of policy, and I venture respectfully to submit to the Committee that not only would the discussion of questions of controversy such as these to which I have referred, if permitted, interfere with our unanimity on the present occasion and deprive our action of something of its grace, but I would submit also that it is on the worst possible precedent and example so far as the relations between the civil and military powers are concerned. Sir, those who would withhold from a successful general his merited reward, not on the ground of military incompetence or incapacity, but on the ground that he was carrying out a policy of which they disapprove, are, in effect, saying to him, and to the gallant soldiers who supported him, " You have endured hardships ; you have faced death ; you have gone on an expedition where defeat meant instantaneous destruction or slavery, of which instantaneous destruction would have been by far a more happy lot. All this you have done ; you have done it with courage, competence, and perseverance, and you have done it to the best of your ability ; we are proud of the skill which you have shown, but you have done it in a cause of which we disapprove, and, because we disapprove of it, therefore we withhold from you the reward which on other grounds you have so honourably and justly earned." An argument like that requires our soldiers to mix themselves up with questions of policy. It compels them to consider not merely whether they are to obey orders, but what the orders are which they are required to obey ; and though we live in a country so happily circumstanced and with constitutional traditions so deeply based that we can hardly conceive even the interference on the part of the military power with the authority of the civil power, yet if such a thing were possible the course I am commenting upon would be the very course to bring it about. For a country in which the Army seriously concerns itself in questions of policy is a country on the verge of a military despotism. If, therefore, as I conceive, the one question before the Committee on the present occasion is a question of military merit, then I venture to say that on this question the country has long made up its mind, and months ago has given an authoritative decision. My mind goes back to the great banquet held in the Mansion House, I think in the early days of November, at which Lord Salisbury, Lord Rosebery and the right hon. Gentleman the member for Monmouthshire all vied with each other in giving praise, lavish praise, but not excessive praise, to the hero of Omdurman. Exploits which are praised alike by Lord Salisbury, Lord Rosebery and the right hon. Gentleman the Member for Monmouthshire are exploits which seem to me to have no critics in any quarter of this House, and in no section of the country. I know not where objection is to come from if these three gentlemen are agreed. But, sir, has the lapse of time and the calmer criticism which is born of that lapse of time, made any modification of our views on this subject? I trow not. I think it has strengthened rather than diminished the estimate which all competent critics have formed of the great series of operations which had their culmination on the 2nd September, to which I have referred. I do not propose to make any comparison between the exploits of Lord Kitchener and his army and the exploits which have adorned the annals of this country in times past. Such comparisons may be misleading; they are almost certain to be barren. It would be sufficient if we concentrate our attention to-day upon the difficulties which Lord Kitchener had to face, and the manner in which he surmounted them. Now, what was the problem with which Lord Kitchener had to deal? He had to deal with an enemy posted in a country nearly 1,400 miles from his base at Cairo—a distance comparable to that which separates Paris from St. Petersburg. He had to deal with this enemy posted in their own country, knowing, as I have said, that they were superior, and must be superior in numbers to any force that he could bring against them. He was in a country absolutely barren of all supplies of any sort or kind or description on which an army can subsist, except only water, and then only so long as the army kept within near reach of the Nile. The forces with which he had to carry out this stupendous military operation were in part composed of the Egyptian army, which had only fifteen years before practically given themselves up without a blow to be massacred by the enemy against which Lord Kitchener was leading them. So great was the prestige of the Dervish force, so great their acknowledged superiority in war, that practically as soon as the forces of Egypt under Hicks Pasha met the forces of the Khalifa, practically there was no battle, but only a dreadful and terrible massacre. That, Sir, was the problem that Lord Kitchener had to solve; that was the problem which, in fact, he did solve with a less expenditure of men and a less expenditure of money than, I venture to say, has ever been made on any similar occasion in the history of military operations of this, or perhaps any other civilised community. Other generals—and these are the greatest whose exploits history has recorded—have done their great deeds with an army which was ready to their hands. Lord Kitchener had in part to create the army with which he worked, for he was one of those eminent organisers who from the very beginning made the Egyptian Army what it is to-day from what it was in the time of Hicks Pasha. And, again, other generals have shown perhaps their greatest skill in using to the best advantage their lines of communication, for the proper use of lines of communication is, I suppose, part of the art of war; but Lord Kitchener not only had to use to the best advantage his long line of communication, he had in great part to create it. And as he was in part the creator of the army, so he was in large measure the creator of that railway without which the Soudan could either not have been reconquered at all, or could not have been reconquered without an expenditure of blood and treasure which it is terrible even to contemplate. We must not contemplate the services of Lord Kitchener merely as the victor at Atbara, the victor at Omdurman, as the successful general in a few great combats, as the brilliant leader of a brief military expedition. No, Sir. There is a famous phrase used of a great Frenchman, that he. was the "organiser of victory." Lord Kitchener combined in his own person that organisation of victory of which I speak, and also carried out all those military operations by which victory was ultimately secured. He organised the victories, he won them; and of those two great feats I venture to think that the organisation was perhaps the greater. Whoso would realise what it is that Lord Kitchener has done for the Soudan, for Egypt, and for England, should not think of him merely, or chiefly, as he was before the fortified lines at Atbara or in the open plain near Omdurman. They should think of him through those long months and years of patient, arduous, anxious preparation. They should think of him as the man whose foresight never was at fault, who never turned his eye from the objective which he had in view, who immersed himself with an unwearied and almost superhuman industry in every detail which could secure the final triumph, who never, even amid the utmost complexity of detail, allowed himself to lose sight of the final object towards which every measure was intended to converge. He had the art of extracting from every shilling of public money every halfpenny it was worth, and of extracting from every one of the distinguished men under his command all that they were capable of doing. Sir, that requires something more than untiring industry. It requires a genius for managing men, and for inspiring them with confidence—a genius without which, I venture to think, all the art of war to be learned from books is so. much waste paper. Lord Kitchener showed, in addition to these great qualities, a reticent caution which never for a moment permitted him to precipitate the action at the appropriate moment, and the decisive courage which never allowed that moment to pass unfruitfully used. That, Sir, I venture to think, in dealing with such an enemy, and in such a country, constitutes the highest qualities of a soldier which could very well be demanded from any general on whom we bestow our confidence. Sir, it is true, of course, that alone and un-aided, by his single merit and by his own right arm, those great triumphs for Egypt, for England, and for civilisation could not have been won. It is true that the states-manship of Lord Cromer, the brilliant administrative abilities of the officers

Mr. A. J. Balfour.

whom he collected around him, the great soldierly qualities of the generals under his command, to whom, I trust, the House will unanimously on Thursday next vote their thanks—that the disciplined resolu-tion of the Egyptian forces, the cheerful daring of the Soudanese, and last but not least the great fighting qualities of the men of his own race—all contributed to the final consummation. But the men of whom I have thus spoken in not unde-served praise would, I think, themselves be the first to admit that in all this expedition Lord Kitchener was the moving spirit, that Lord Kitchener was the animating soul, and that he, above all others who were engaged in these great and extended operations, has deserved from this House and from the country some mark of the gratitude of the nation. Feeling, therefore, that I am only carry-ing out, in the first place, the wishes of the House, and, in the second place, the wishes of my countrymen, I beg now to move, in accordance with the notice given on Friday.

Motion made, and Question proposed—

"That a sum, not exceeding £30,000, be granted to Her Majesty, to be issued to Major-General Lord Kitchener of Khartoum, G.C.B., K.C.M.G., as an acknowledgment of his eminent services in planning and conducting the recent Expedition in the Soudan."—(*The First Lord of the Treasury.*)

*Sir HENRY CAMPBELL-BANNER-MAN (Stirling Burghs): Mr. Lowther, I rise for the purpose of saying on my own behalf, and on the part of my political friends, that we fully share the estimate of Lord Kitchener's services which the right hon. Gentleman the First Lord of the Treasury has so eloquently expressed. In his conduct of the long series of operations which culminated in the cap-ture of Omdurman and the occupation of the region of the Upper Nile Lord Kitchener's grasp of the difficulties to be encountered, the skill and foresight with which he formed his plans, the alternating boldness and caution with which he carried them into execution deserved and attracted the admiration of the world. He was engaged in warfare with a fanatical adversary who carries bravery to the pitch of recklessness, and who is unsurpassed in his own methods of fighting—methods which are in a peculiar degree trying to the bravest and best disciplined forces. He was acting in

a climate pernicious to the health and depressing to the spirits of Europeans, in a country, as the right hon. Gentleman has described to us, practically barren of supplies, and at a long and ever-lengthening distance from his own base. The complete success which, under these conditions, he achieved constitutes one of the most brilliant pages in the history of British arms. Mr. Lowther, Lord Kitchener deserves all the honours that have been conferred upon him by his Queen and by his country, and he deserves the grateful recognition of this House. But when we speak of Lord Kitchener it will, of course, be understood that we do not imply that the merit is all his. In passing this Vote we should be giving expression to our grateful recognition and admiration of the services of those, whether his own countrymen or of African race, who fought and endured under him, and of the distinguished officers who advised and assisted him. And I would go further and say that we ought to include in our warmest gratitude, and to give perhaps a larger share of the tribute of our praise than is sometimes given to them, those British officers who, through many years of patient hope and effort, have been creating and building up the Egyptian Army, and, what is much more important and much more difficult, have been breathing into that army the spirit of self-confidence and solidarity without which any army is of little use. In honouring Lord Kitchener, therefore, we are setting the seal of our approbation upon all those patient labours as well as on those brilliant exploits, and we do so with one mind and one voice. Now, I would gladly stop here, but we cannot shut our eyes to the fact that there are some reasons adduced for our not passing this Vote, at any rate in the full measure in which it is proposed. And perhaps it is only right—although the right hon. Gentleman has, no doubt with great propriety from his point of view, hesitated to anticipate objections that may be raised—perhaps it is only right that I, from another side of the House, and from another point of view, should refer briefly in anticipation to these objections. If I thought that my silence would have any effect in inducing the House to pass a unanimous vote I should sit down at once. And yet perhaps it is better that I should, against my will, undertake the somewhat difficult

duty of meeting an enemy who has not yet, from no fault of his own, appeared in the field. So far as I can gather from what has appeared in the Press and from other sources, there are two circumstances, or sets of circumstances, which are alleged to militate against this Vote being passed without opposition. The first of these is the incident of the disentombment of the remains of the Mahdi, and their dispersal under circumstances which involve something like ignominy attempted to be put on his memory. Well, I believe for my part that there has been no wavering in the honest judgment of British opinion upon this matter from the first day until now. The news, when it was received in this country, struck us all with a shock, and with something like horror. We could hardly believe that such a thing had been done, and now at this cool distance of time, in the absence of any explanation, and being unable at the same time to see what explanation can possibly be offered, we still remain regarding it with condemnation and continue to deplore it. So far as I have seen, all that can be said in favour of it is that it was necessary to destroy and to obliterate that which would have been a focus of fanaticism and discontent among the population of the region for which we have become responsible. That may be asserted, but even among those who are best acquainted and most familiar with what are called Eastern notions there is by no means a unanimous opinion on the subject. And let me point out to the Committee that the Mahdi was a false prophet, and not likely to be held in much veneration by the greater part of the Mussulman world, but no doubt held in veneration in his own part of the world. But he was something more than that; he was our enemy. He was a bitter enemy of the domination of Egypt, and we stand largely in the place of Egypt, and by the side of Egypt, in the matter. And on that account there was, in our treatment of his tomb and of his remains an element, an air of vindictiveness, which surely was unworthy of this country. I make every allowance for this political desire to do away with a focus of fanaticism and discontent. But still it remains that there was a cruel outrage performed, what in all civilised countries would be considered a cruel outrage and, I cannot help adding, a gross blunder. If ever there was a case where an act may be considered to be worse than a crime—to be a blunder—it was this. It is singular how often, as any one of us may observe, it is not the most exalted aspect of a case which is most forced on our minds. It is the humbler and more familiar aspect, and this act seems to me to have been an infraction not only of sound policy, but of good feeling and good taste, I would even say of good manners. If I were to explain to the House exactly how it strikes me I would employ an illustration which I hesitate to use because it may be thought hardly equal to the dignity and seriousness of the debate. I recall to my mind a picture drawn by a man who had a singular knowledge of human nature—the late John Leech—in which he represented a fine lady sitting in a room with two children playing in a corner. The little girl complains to her mother of the conduct of her brother. "Is he not wicked, mamma?" she says; "he is swearing." "My dear," says the mother, "it is worse than wicked, it is vulgar." I believe that that is an exact illustration of the sort of feeling with which we regard what has happened on this occasion, as far as we understand it, and subject to the explanations which may come from the bench opposite. But although I have this strong feeling as to this particular event —although I reprobate it in as strong a way as I have stated—yet it appears to me that it would be a most exaggerated and fantastic view of the matter if we were to set a detached, isolated, and comparatively unimportant event—however much we reprobate it in itself—against the whole mass of labours and risks and successes which attach to Lord Kitchener and those who served under him. Therefore, although sharing the strong feeling entertained in many quarters in regard to this particular occurrence, I do not see any reason for altering my opinion as to the vote which is now before the Committee. But the second of the objections 'which are held to justify hesitation in assenting to this vote is perhaps of a more serious kind. It relates to the treatment of the wounded during the campaign and after the battle. As to this there has been much conflicting evidence, and for my part I candidly say that I give most weight to the evidence which clears our soldiers of complicity in anything inhuman or cruel. I do not say that from any desire to huddle up or hide

Sir H. Campbell-Bannerman.

away an unpleasant topic; but because of my belief in their temper and character and in the moral influences which sway their conduct. But there has been, as far as I am aware, no material evidence against the British regiments employed, and the wild stories which circulated at first have been disproved or have been withdrawn. But it is alleged that the Sudanese battalions did commit excesses of cruelty upon the wounded on the field of battle. Now, undoubtedly there is great danger of uncivilised troops practising in battle, and especially at the close of the battle, those savage methods of warfare to which, in a wilder state, they are habituated. That is the case; and it may be—for we have no full information on the subject— that there were unnecessary excesses committed at Omdurman to some extent. Then the best use to which we can put that fact is to impress upon those responsible—whether civilians or soldiers—if they wish to preserve our national name free from stain, if they wish to prevent a degradation in the tone of our own Army which co-operates with these troops, if they wish to satisfy the universal sentiment of the British people, the urgent duty to see that precautions are taken against the recurrence of any such danger in future. Do not let us deceive ourselves. War is war, and war means carnage in every case. But wars conducted between savage tribes or against savage tribes mean excessive carnage, and probably retaliatory carnage, to an extent that must be abhorrent to every humane and civilised mind. The only justification for our being in that region of the world at all is that we bring to it, slowly and lamely it may be, and in circuitous ways, civilisation and peaceful development. Let it be an instruction to all our officers, while leaving them perfect freedom of action—because it is they only who know the difficulties, as it is they only who incur the risks, of the situation— let us impress upon them that they should conduct their operations as nearly as possible according to the rules of civilised warfare; and let us see that those officers are numerous enough and have authority enough to repress the natural barbarism of those whom they are obliged to use as instruments under them. These are the views which I have formed from all that I have seen and read and heard of what occurred in this campaign. I have dealt with the subject imperfectly, because I cannot anticipate what may be said either in attack or defence on the matter. But I have laid down some general considerations; and I conclude by saying that, from these general considerations I see in neither of the criticisms which have been applied to this vote anything of such proportion or gravity as can be set against the undoubted claim of Lord Kitchener to our grateful recognition; and therefore I shall support, and cordially support, the vote before the Committee.

Mr. J. MORLEY (Montrose Burghs): With much that has been said by the First Lord of the Treasury and by my right honourable friend I am glad to find myself in very considerable concurrence. The First Lord of the Treasury stated that in September we were watching the close of the great Soudan drama which had attracted attention and even absorbed it for so many years. I wish—and it is the only remark that I will make on this aspect of the matter—I could believe that we had seen the fall of the curtain on the fifth act of the Soudan tragedy. But here is another point on which I am in absolute agreement with the right honourable Gentleman—to-night is not an occasion when we can justifiably enter upon considerations of policy in any aspect whatever. In all that the right honourable Gentleman said on that branch of the matter I fully agree. Whatever we may think of that policy, Lord Kitchener was the instrument—the able and powerful instrument—of a policy imposed upon him by the Government of this country and by this House; and therefore, whatever we think of that policy ought not to, and cannot, stand in the way of our appreciation of Lord Kitchener's military merits. Upon the question of military merits it would be ridiculous for me to offer any opinion, and I do not propose to do so. I accept from those who are competent to pronounce on military matters all that has been said by the right honourable Gentleman; though perhaps the reference to Carnot as the great organiser of victory was a little overdrawn. But I will not dwell on that point. Now, I hope the House of Commons—which, after all, is an assembly that loves fair play and manliness—will believe that to nobody in the Committee could it be more disagreeable than to me to use any language or take up any attitude which might seem to deprive an act of grace of some of its

graciousness. But there are other things to think about besides graciousness; and in my judgment the topic referred to and dwelt upon by my right honourable friend is one of those topics which, as he admits, cannot escape notice and criticism in the Committee to-night. Upon that point I dare say I shall find myself obliged to dissent from the majority of the Committee; but I believe the majority of the Committee will agree that their praise of Lord Kitchener would be worthless if they were not willing to hear points of criticism and objection. The topic to which my right honourable friend began by referring was the destruction of the tomb of the Mahdi, and the exhumation and dispersion of the Mahdi's remains. From the rather impatient manner in which in some quarters my right honourable friend's introduction of that topic was listened to, some honourable Members would appear to have forgotten what my right honourable friend reminded them of—the extraordinary feeling of shock and disgust which was aroused. [Cries of "No."] The honourable Gentlemen who say "No" forget that from no quarter was there more disgust, more vividly expressed, than from some of their honourable friends below the gangway. The honourable Member for Leamington the other day made a speech in which he regarded what had been done with disapproval. It was in consequence of the demonstration of feeling in the House and the country that the Government applied to Lord Cromer to send his own views and to send Lord Kitchener's defence and justification of what had occurred. I want to argue this matter in a way which will not offend anyone; but we must recognise that upon this House there is no responsibility, among all those which weigh upon us, which weighs more heavily than the responsibility of supervising and keeping a strict and vigilant watch upon what is done by our agents abroad. Years ago an eminent public writer said that the Government ought to support its agents, in difficulties always, in errors sometimes, in crimes never. I am not going to argue that I would describe this particular transaction as criminal; but I do regard it, not as one of those errors into which a wise and good man may accidentally fall, but as one of those errors against which this House is called upon by its most supreme duty to register an emphatic and formal protest. I do not belong to the school—if school there be—which would deal out honours and emoluments to good public servants with a grudging and parsimonious hand, and I am not one of those who are not inclined to make allowances for men called upon to take important decisions in moments of emergency. On the contrary, I will make all allowance for men in positions of that kind; but this was evidently not such an occasion. I want to ask the Committee and the First Lord of the Treasury whether they hold that there is no kind of military action for which the plea of political necessity is not a good defence. Is there no kind of military action which could impair the title of such an eminent man as Lord Kitchener to a special mark of honour from this House? That cannot be contended, and I will give an illustration, and it shall be an African illustration. It has often been alleged that in the Congo State there is a resort to cannibal forces—that the Government of the Congo State employs, or has employed, cannibals to make war on the enemies of that Government. I will not insult the First Lord of the Treasury by asking him whether if it had been brought home to a British general that he had employed cannibal forces, he would propose that this House should give a mark of special honour to such a general. I am not going for a moment to embark the House on a discussion upon a discriminating scale of outrages upon humanity or upon natural piety, but I can suppose that to a Belgian, at all events, the exhumation of a dead enemy's remains is quite as inhuman, quite as great a violation of natural piety, as the employment of cannibal forces. I do not say that is my opinion, but I think I can imagine a Belgian making it a fair defence. He would say, "We are engaged in a great civilising and humanising task; in the execution of that task the resort to cannibal forces is indispensable; in the execution of that task what is indispensable is justifiable," and therefore his syllogism is concluded in his own favour. I do not say that, but the Committee will agree with me that there are military acts which no plea of political necessity can possibly justify. Let us look for a moment at what this plea of political necessity on the papers amounts to. The first authority quoted is Lord Cromer. I have no wish whatever to disparage the authority of Lord Cromer, but I would

Mr. J. Morley.

point out that all Lord Cromer can know upon the political necessity of this act must be from representations made to him by the military authorities. He was there himself for a very short time—but he committed himself to the view that there was a political necessity for the destruction of the tomb. I would ask the Committee to listen to another authority, who is not inferior to Lord Cromer nor to Lord Kitchener himself upon this matter. That is a gentleman well known by the name of Slatin Pasha, or, as he is now, Sir Rudolph Slatin. I see to-day that Sir Rudolph Slatin has slightly changed his view, but in an interview which he had in March with a representative of some London newspaper—(cries of "Name")—the London *Echo*. That is a detail; but, be that as it may, the authenticity of the interview is not disputed. "May we take it," Slatin Pasha was asked, "that the desecration of the Mahdi's tomb, about which so much has been said in England, is likely to give the last blow to the religious faith of the people in the creed of the dead prophet?" Sir Rudolph paused a moment before answering. "I don't think," he said slowly, "that the interference with the bones of the Mahdi was a necessary act." Therefore, when the Committee naturally is very much affected by the authority of Lord Cromer, pray let it bear in mind that Slatin Pasha, whose authority is higher than Lord Cromer's, expresses dissent from his view—higher as to the frame of mind of the people who lived there.

Mr. ARNOLD-FORSTER (Belfast, W.).—I beg to ask for the name of the correspondent.

Mr. J. MORLEY.—It is not a question of correspondent; it is a long interview.

SIR F. DIXON-HARTLAND (Middlesex, Uxbridge): Does Slatin Pasha admit it?

Mr. J. MORLEY: It is not denied at all. I have already stated to the Committee that my attention has been called to a statement of Slatin Pasha's in which he rather withdraws from that position, but not I think categorically. I am not going to press that point further. But look at Lord Kitchener's own position, and this is, after all, the pith of the matter. It is the only aspect of the case which I shall at all attempt to present prett fully to the Committee. Lord Kitchener says, in the despatch which he telegraphed to Lord Cromer in consequence of the rise of feeling in this House, that he destroyed the tomb for two reasons. These two reasons may, for all I know, have been perfectly good ones. The first is that it was politically advisable, considering the state of the country, that the Mahdi's tomb, which was the centre of pilgrimage and fanatical zeal, should be destroyed. The second reason, which he had not mentioned before, is that the tomb was in a dangerous condition, owing to the damage done by shell-fire and might have caused loss of life. I am not going myself to dwell on the destruction of the tomb, but Lord Kitchener mentions later that:—

"In consequence of advice given to me after the taking of Omdurman, by Mahometan officers, it would be better to have the body removed, as otherwise many of the more ignorant people of Kordofan would consider the sanctity with which they surrounded the Mahdi prevented us from doing so."

I may just call attention to one rather remarkable circumstance, namely, that this so-called "removal" was taken apparently not because Lord Kitchener thought it a political necessity, not because Lord Cromer thought it a political necessity, but because Mahometan officers thought it was politically advisable. Therefore, when you come to testing the authority upon which this revolting proceeding took place, do pray bear in mind that it was on the authority of Mahometan authorities. Has it come to this, then, that on a matter affecting our standard of civilisation this House is to take the standard from Mahometan officers? I have no prejudice against Mahometans, but I confess I think it would mark a deterioration of the highest principles that have animated public life in this country for a very long time if that is to be accepted which hon. Gentlemen opposite seem to desire. The Mahdi set a better example. I do not know whether any right hon. Gentleman on the front bench will put me right, but I am told, and I believe it is true, that Sir Herbert Stewart, who met his death in the expedition of 1885, was buried in the Mahdi's territory, and that the remains of Sir Herbert Stewart are to this day absolutely intact. Therefore, the Mahdi and his people paid some respect and veneration to the tomb of a brave enemy, which I deplore Lord Kitchener did not think it necessary to do. Let the Committee test the political necessity. It may have been politically advisable to make a deep impression on the ignorant people of Kordofan, as these Mahometan officers said. It is rather remarkable that they are not supposed to have been impressed by the Maxim guns, or by the slaughter, or by the vast exhibition of British power and energy. But this removal of the remains of their own dead prophet was to make an impression. If that is so, a very plain question arises. If the object was to impress the minds of these people, why was the operation conducted in stealth?

Mr. A. J. BALFOUR: No.

Mr. J. MORLEY: The right hon. Gentleman, I am sure, is well informed, and he says it was not conducted in stealth. Then all the reports I have had access to—and I have consulted all that are available—are misleading on that point. But here Slatin Pasha remains exactly where he was. He, at all events, like the rest of the public, conceived that this operation was done secretly. I should be glad if some member of the Government would by-and-by explain how far I am mistaken on that point. What Slatin Pasha said was this—

"The wrong thing about it was that it was done secretly. If it was held desirable to do this the emirs and sheikhs who still believed in the Mahdi should have been summoned, and then, with the utmost publicity, and in the presence of all, the bones might have been removed from the tomb and buried elsewhere, showing them that their prophet was nothing but an ordinary man. But to do the thing secretly was a great mistake."

I do not dwell on the phrase "removal." It is a smooth and almost elegant expression for what really happened. And here I do not think there is one gentleman in this House—I am certain not one soldier —who will get up and say that he approves or that he does not disapprove and even abhor the actual proceeding taken, whether there was a valid political necessity or not, of mutilating the body of the Mahdi. (Ministerial cries of "There was no mutilation.") Was his head not cut off? (Cheers.)

Mr. A. J. BALFOUR: No.

MR. J. MORLEY: What does Lord Kitchener mean when he says, "When I left Omdurman for Fashoda I ordered the destruction of the tomb. This was done in my absence, the Mahdi's bones being thrown into the Nile"? Surely, then, there was mutilation. "The skull only was preserved." I should be only too glad if the Government are able to say that the head was not severed from the body.

MR. A. J. BALFOUR: I understand the right hon. Gentleman to suppose, on the strength of the phrase which he has just read out, that the head was severed from the rest of the remains with which it was connected; but, as a matter of fact, there was a mere collection of bones which had fallen to pieces by natural processes before exhumation took place.

MR. J. MORLEY: This is a gruesome topic! Yes, but you are not to escape gruesome topics if your commanders indulge in gruesome proceedings. If there was no deliberate mutilation—and, of course, I accept that and am heartily glad to accept it—I have no desire to blacken anybody's character—it cannot be denied that on Lord Kitchener's own assurance "the skull of the Mahdi was preserved and handed over to me for disposal." I think the act of digging up the remains of a dead enemy and dispersing them—and that is not denied—and the appropriation as a kind of trophy, a horrible trophy, of the skull of your dead enemy is one of those things I need not discuss. It has happened in history in two or three cases, I can only recall two or three, or perhaps four. The French Revolutionists in their frenzy went to the Church of St. Lazare and fired into the tombs of the Kings and threw their bones to the winds. The Kings of France did not perhaps deserve much better. One of them, and the greatest of them, had himself perpetrated an act of this kind, because at a monastery—with the teaching of which he happened to disagree—an exhumation was carried out to the tune of 3,000 corpses. So Louis XIV. did not get worse treatment than he meted out to others. Then our own journals contain a famous order of the House directing that the carcases of Oliver Cromwell and others should be taken from their graves. ("Hear, hear" from the Irish benches.) I can understand our friends from Ireland objecting to put up a statue to Oliver Cromwell, but I am amazed that they should think it is a good thing to take up his carcase.

MR. DILLON: If the right hon. Gentleman alludes to me, I did not say it was a good thing. I thought it a good exemplification of the savage temper of this House in those days.

MR. J. MORLEY: Now I have one or two questions which the Government, in vindication of Lord Kitchener himself, must answer. When Lord Kitchener left Omdurman for Fashoda, what instructions did he leave behind? Did he order the casting of the remains into the Nile? Did he direct the body to be decently interred elsewhere? When the skull was handed over, was it carried off as a trophy? Where was it carried to? Lord Cromer says it is now buried at Wady Halfa. When? Was the reinterment in consequence or not of the feeling shown in this House and the country? Sir, the House may think these are slight incidents. I venture to think it will be a very bad day for this House and the country when such ignoble proceedings are treated in this House as trivial and when it is felt that they require no justification. This is the question—and here is where I venture, with the utmost reluctance, to differ from my right hon. friend who sits near me—Is this House or not to have an opportunity of protesting against this ignoble proceeding? I do not at all call a perfunctory parenthesis a protest on the part of the House. We want something more than that. You send your soldiers to civilise savages. Take care the savages do not barbarise your soldiers. What is more important a great deal, take care that the maxims, standards, and feelings of this House are not barbarised. The more you extend your Empire—and the Colonial Secretary will be the first man to agree with me—the more need is there, the more imperative is it, that this House should exact from its agents abroad the same standards of conduct which we exact at home; and it will be a bad day indeed if we have one conscience for the mother country and another conscience for all that vast territory over which your eye does not extend. We must be slow in entrusting power far away from our control and observation. We must strongly insist that that power shall be used in conformity with our own principles of humanity. When I used some language—which I abide by—on this transaction the right hon. Member for Manchester rebuked 'me. It was a kind of rebuke, I fancy, that was heard in a neighbouring country, or has been for some months past, when anyone ventured to criticise the General Staff.

SIR J. FERGUSSON (Manchester, N.E.): What I complained of was that the right hon. Gentleman condemned Lord Kitchener when he had been told inquiries were being made.

MR. J. MORLEY: We were not then assured of Lord Kitchener's share in the transaction, and I expressly disclaimed any wish to censure Lord Kitchener on that occasion. So the right hon. Baronet is completely wrong. I do not know whether many will agree with me or not, but this is an occasion, in my view, if ever there was an occasion, when, in a form that cannot be mistaken, this House should show it is capable of expressing what I believe to be, and I·believe you will find to be, the real voice of the conscience of this country and those who send us here; and it is because I think that, and think it most profoundly, that I for one, whatever others may do, must say "No" to this Vote.

MR. A. J. BALFOUR: .,I rather hesitate to rise again so soon after addressing the House, but the right hon. Gentleman has put some questions to me. He has appealed to me, as representing the Government, for some view of the transactions to which he has referred—transactions, I may say, which, in my judgment, whatever view the House may take of them, have been thrown into most undue and disproportionate prominence by the course which the right hon. Gentleman has thought it fit to take. Let us at once agree that the idea that any British officer, with our concurrence or approval, direct or indirect, should use his power to execute vengeance upon a dead enemy is absolutely repulsive to all the instincts of civilised men, whether they be soldiers or civilians. But I do not believe that the element of vengeance entered in the smallest degree into the motive or action of Lord Kitchener, or coloured with even the faintest colouring the policy which, on public grounds and

public grounds alone, he thought it his duty to follow. The right hon. Gentleman talked—and I have heard some people talk elsewhere—as if the Mahdi was a man against whom Lord Kitchener was fighting, as if he was the general conducting the force we had opposed and defeated, and, the general of our enemy having been killed, vengeance was taken on his dead remains. I need not remind the Committee that the Mahdi had been dead twelve years, and that, as far as I know, Lord Kitchener had never been brought into military conflict with him. He did not represent the military element against which we were fighting, though he did represent the superstition which lay at the base of that military force. Let me add, to make the case with regard to vengeance complete, that I believe the Mahdi's family, his son-in-law, and other relatives, have been treated by Lord Kitchener and the British authorities with the utmost consideration, and if vengeance had been his motive and animating impulse he would not have associated the action to which the right hon. Gentleman objects with the treatment of those most nearly connected with the dead false prophet. The right hon. Gentleman has fallen into error on another point. He believes the operation was secret. I am informed, on the contrary, that it was done publicly, and that publicity was an essential part of the policy which originally prompted it, and that it was deliberately carried out—I believe there were British officers present —but it was deliberately carried out, by Lord Kitchener's orders, by the native officers and men of the Soudanese regiments. The reason they were selected for the duty was in order that they might know and transmit the knowledge throughout the length and breadth of the Soudan that the Mahdi was after all not the Heaven-sent prophet they imagined him to be, but belonged to a temporary, false, and dying creed. The right hon. Gentleman has criticised not only the motives of Lord Kitchener, but the strength of the considerations which induced him to take the course he did take. It is difficult, perhaps impossible, for us sitting here comfortably in an English June to estimate the political and religious considerations which animate the savage superstitions of the black population of the Soudan, but I desire to remind the House of what, I think, they have forgotten—of the army of occupation, the 20,000 men whom Lord Kitchener took with him to Omdurman and Khartoum, about a third only were British troops, and that third had to be immediately removed. You practically left, and intended to leave—it was your policy to leave—at Khartoum no more white men than were necessary to command your native levies. Of whom did those native levies consist ?   In part of Egyptian I believe, were re- largely Soudanese ; were largely com- one time of their

military transactions of the campaign. This handful of British officers were going to be left alone in the midst of this vast and seething mass of native Soudanese, who, up to the very eve of the day when the last of these trans- actions took place had been fanatical and devoted followers of Mahdism. Was it not the first duty of the man responsible for the safety of these officers that he should, if possible, cut at the very root of that fanatical superstition which had been the strength of Mahdism for fifteen or sixteen years ? The right hon. Gentleman, among others, may think that the means were ill contrived to attain the end, but that it was a matter of first necessity that the end should be attained no hon. Member who understands the real position in the Soudan then and now can possibly doubt.   Recollect that, though we had destroyed, as a fighting body, the vast array of 60,000 men shattered outside Omdurman, there re- mained in Kordofan, Darfur, and else- where in the Soudan garrisons of the Khalifa the vast tribes who had been devoted followers of the Mahdi, and who were wavering in their allegiance to the Khalifa. Lord Kitchener was of opinion, and I believe is of opinion, that had he not pursued the course he did pursue these tribes, instead of throwing in their lot with us and accepting our rule, would have continued to follow Mahdism, with consequences, not to this country only, but to Egypt and the Soudan, which will

Mr. A. J. Balfour.

suggest themselves to the mind of every man who has followed the history of the great Nile basin during the last 20 years. This great fabric of the Mahdist tyranny rested on two bases.   In the first place it had a military basis of armed strength, brutal and unceasing cruelty and tyranny, which never for a moment relaxed its grip ; and, on the other hand, it rested on the super- stitious belief of a most superstitious population in the supernatural character of the prophet who had brought this phase of Mahometanism into being.   We shattered the first of these foundations at Ferkeh, at Atbara, and Omdurman ; we shattered it at a cost of many valuable lives of our own countrymen and allies, we shattered it at the cost of an appall- ing slaughter—appalling but necessary slaughter—of those arrayed against us ; and is Lord Kitchener to be blamed because he destroyed the other founda- tion of Mahdism, without inflicting a wound on a single individual—without, so far as I know, doing anything which can be described as hurting the religious convictions of any human being—without battle, without slaughter, without inflicting death, pain, suffering, or loss upon anyone ? If it be true, as Lord Kitchener believed and believes, that the course he then took— a course not dictated by vengeance or hostility to a dead foe, but a course simply intended to preserve the future of the Soudan from that which had been its curse in the past—if he is right in sup- posing that that policy did produce its effect, and that it is owing to that policy that at this moment Darfur and Kordofan are faithful to British and Egyptian rule, and that at this moment the Khalifa, instead of making fresh head and leading new troops against our men, finds himself the leader of a rapidly diminishing body of discouraged followers—if, I say, that was the result, will any man get up here and blame him ? It is very easy, it is a very simple matter, in the name of civilisation and morality, and in the security of Britain, with the ease and con- ditions of civilised life around us, to blame one who in a critical moment took a decision of which you disapprove. You have no responsibility now for the safety of the English officers to whom you com- mitted the charge of the Soudan ; it is not on your shoulders the blame would fall if by a recrudescence of this blood- thirsty superstition all these men had been sacrificed.   Recollect, there is but a step from the recrudescence of Mahdism to the absolute destruction of every white man from north to south of the Soudan. That was the problem Lord Kitchener had to face. All that could be done by successful fighting, by brilliant feats of arms, by undaunted courage, had been done, and for the moment the forces of the Khalifa were shattered and flying. He had still to deal with that more subtle malady chronic in the Soudan—the superstitious malady which easily believes in the prophetic mission of some bloodthirsty pretender to religious eminence, a belief which, when it once gains head, can only be crushed, as we have crushed it, at a vast cost of life, labour, and money. I can hardly imagine the right hon. Gentleman the member for Montrose having to take a decision in face of the living reality with which he had to deal; but if I can imagine the right hon. Gentleman being told after the fall of Khartoum that he had to choose between the disinterment of the Mahdi's body on the one hand and with it the destruction of the superstition which the Mahdi created over a vast area of the Soudan, and, on the other hand, a possible recrudescence of the difficulties from which we have suffered so much, and as a consequence of those difficulties the probable destruction of men of our own blood and country who had served us long and well, and whom we had left there in the midst of an alien population to bring to them the blessings of peace and civilisation—if, I say, I could conceive the right hon. Gentleman having to decide then and there what line he would take, I greatly doubt whether his policy would have widely differed from that Lord Kitchener adopted.

Mr. J. MORLEY: I would have returned the remains to the ground.

Mr. A. J. BALFOUR: The right hon. Gentleman says he would have put the remains in the ground again, and possibly that might have been a better course; but let it be remembered, when the right hon. Gentleman talks as if these bones had been tossed with every circumstance of ignominy into the first receptacle that could be found for them, that that was not the case. There were no circumstances of ignominy, and from such information as I have obtained I learn that no such impression of ignominy was pro-

duced on the native population. I believe that anything in the nature of cremation, which to other ideas would probably have been more desirable, would have been regarded by them as the last insult that could have been offered, but as I am informed what was actually done had no such result. But, after all, the distinction does not appear to be so great as the right hon. Gentleman supposes, and even were it greater than it is are we in a debate intended to do honour and confer reward for long years of faithful, responsible, and anxious service, carried out under unexampled difficulties with unexampled skill, to dwell at this disproportionate length upon what, even in the corrected view of the right hon. Gentleman, would appear to have been a mere error of judgment? I hope I have in the argument I have developed said something which will not only bring back the discussion to its true proportion, but will also show that in the course he adopted Lord Kitchener was animated by none of those mean, contemptible motives too rashly, and surely most foolishly, attributed to him. Sir, rightly or wrongly—as I believe, rightly —he took a general survey of the whole situation in the Soudan as he found it, and, with the tremendous responsibility on his shoulders of seeing that the lives of our officers left there in command of Soudanese troops were not again to be sacrificed as too many lives have in the past been sacrificed, he took a decision, not one, I well believe, agreeable to himself, but dictated by a high sense of his duty to the country he served and to the country of which he was the conqueror. I hope that the right hon. Gentleman, who I fully recognise has performed a task which to himself must have been extremely disagreeable with all moderation, will feel that enough has been said upon this topic and that we may with every advantage now proceed to the termination of the discussion and a decision on the Vote.

Mr. C. P. SCOTT (Lancashire, Leigh): If there is one thing more deplorable than another in connection with the perpetration of these barbarities by an army commanded by a British general, that is that they should be defended by the Leader of the House. The excuse which has been made amounts to this, that because we were making use of barbarous instruments we therefore must have recourse to barbarous methods. The country ought, in view of the further use of Soudanese troops, to know that such is the consequence of the employment of savage troops in the service of the British Government. The leader of the Opposition has admitted that there are two grave matters which we ought justly to consider in connection with this Vote: one, the treatment of the tomb and body of our dead enemy, and the other the treatment of our wounded enemies on the field of battle. My right hon. friend has said, and justly said, that as far as the British troops are concerned no very grave charges of inhumanity had been brought against them. I hold and believe that that is the case, although there were isolated cases of inhumanity, established on their own testimony, as some of them have written letters on the subject which have been published in this country. I think that even in these isolated cases things were done which we must all regret. But there is a far graver question, and that is the conduct of those native troops on whom we largely relied in this campaign and upon whom we have apparently come to entirely rely in order to hold the country. No one can suppose that this is a pleasant subject to raise in this House, or that anyone would raise it out of lightness of heart or from any political or party motive; and the leader of the House will do me the justice to believe that in speaking of it I am not actuated by any such motives. But the House is entitled to know, so far as can be known, what did happen in regard to this grave, this terrible matter. I do not pretend to be able to lay the whole facts before hon. Members—it is quite impossible for any private person to do so—and all I can attempt to establish is that there is a strong case for inquiry, and that, in face of the facts they already knew, the House should not be asked to confer a signal mark of honour and favour in respect of the conduct of the campaign until it has caused the matter to be sifted to the very bottom. It is admitted on all hands that the wounded were killed in the course of the battle of Omdurman, as probably they have been killed in every battle in the Soudan since we have been engaged with this savage and relentless enemy. No rational man would for a moment contend that in no circumstances is it justifiable

Mr. C. P. Scott.

to kill a wounded man. If a wounded man has arms and is resisting, or shows clearly that he intends to resist, he is a combatant just like any other, and must be treated as such ; but when the wounded were killed, not because they had weapons and showed that they intended to use them, but simply because they were lying in the way of advancing troops, then that is taking a very great and terrible responsibility, and it is a matter which needs to be hedged round with the greatest possible care and precaution by the commander of the force, who must make the utmost possible effort to let the troops understand clearly what is expected of them, to prevent them going beyond the border-line of what is an extremely slippery slope, and who must also take care that there is a sufficient supply of officers thoroughly instructed in their duty to restrain the very unruly and barbarous material under their command. Was that done on this occasion ? Sufficient proof that it was not done can be brought before the House. When I some time ago asked what orders were given I was informed that no orders were given on that occasion different from those given on other occasions. That does not carry us very much further, and we have not been able to learn what were the orders or what was exactly expected of the officers and of the troops. We ought to know. I believe it is the fact that no general order was given in regard to the treatment of the wounded. That has been stated by General Gatacre, and that fact is part of my complaint. An order ought to have been given, remembering the troops that were employed and what had occurred on previous occasions. But that some orders were given was proved by statements in the private letters of our own soldiers, and although I am not prepared to take the word of these men—many of whom are not men of education, and are not used to weigh their words very carefully—as to the exact nature of the order, this, at least, emerges as absolutely certain, that even our own soldiers did not understand clearly that they were to discriminate, as they ought to discriminate, between a wounded enemy who was dangerous and another who was not. The House should remember that the letters from which I am about to quote extracts were written, not for any ulterior purpose, but simply as representing the impression produced upon our troops by the orders they had received. Lieutenant Fison, presumably a man of education, wrote :

"Previous to the advance the Sirdar had issued orders that all wounded dervishes passed over had to be killed."

Private Pendlebury, of the Lancashire Fusiliers, wrote :

"The order was to bayonet every one, dead or alive, as we passed them."

Private Barlow, of the same regiment, wrote :

"As we advanced we were ordered to kill all the wounded that we met."

Then a soldier, in his diary, published in the *Birmingham Argus*, said—

"The order was given that all wounded dervishes met with were to be shot or bayoneted " ;

while the *Chronicle* thus quoted a letter from a private soldier :

"Before the battle began they gave the order out, and as we advanced they were lying underneath the bushes. You ought to have seen the men bayonet them."

The *Westminster Gazette* quoted the following from a soldier's private letter—

"After the battle we advanced over the battlefield, when we had to walk over the dead and wounded enemy. All the enemy who were wounded were quickly bayoneted."

From such perfectly spontaneous testimony the House must conclude that at least there was a very considerable negligence, a very considerable want of precision, a very marked want of forethought, on the part of those who should have thought of the wounded on the battlefield. I hope the time will never come when the House will idly treat this matter, and think that because we are waging war with barbarous enemies, who would give no quarter if they were victorious, we should treat them when they are defeated after their own barbarous methods and refuse them the privileges we would grant to a civilised enemy in similar circumstances. I am willing not only to admit but to claim that there were on the part of our own troops many cases of signal humanity, and that many dervishes who showed that they had thrown away their weapons were allowed to pass harmless through the British lines; but that fact does not do away with the other evidence of acts which all must regret. But what was the impression produced upon the native troops by the orders that were given, and what was their conduct ? If

it is the case that we are to depend almost exclusively upon these black troops, the conduct of these men in the field becomes a very serious matter, and so also does the question of how they are to be restrained from pursuing their natural instincts of brutality and barbarism. As to their conduct at the battle of Omdurman, the only evidence obtainable is that of officers and correspondents who were present. The first that I will quote is Mr. Cross, who died shortly afterwards from the effects of enteric fever in the Soudan. He was a very brave and very trustworthy witness. Mr. Stevens, in his book on the Soudan campaign, has described him as "quiet, gentle, patient, brave, sincere—the type of an English gentleman." Such a man was not likely to bear false witness in a matter in which the reputation of his own country was concerned. But he said :

"It was about 8.15 when the fight at the zareba was over, and about nine o'clock orders were given for the zareba to be opened and a general advance made in the direction of Omdurman. One of the chief features of this advance was the conduct of the black camp followers, who hurried out in front of the lines and hastily looted the dead and wounded. They took good care that the latter were soon numbered with the former. It was a shameful sight to see them shooting down the stricken dervishes at such close quarters that many of the bodies were set on fire, and the smell of burning flesh was added to the horrors of the battlefield. So careless were they in their shooting that one ran as much risk of being shot by them during the advance as by the enemy. At least four men in the Warwicks were struck by these reckless shooters, who continued their grisly task throughout the day, stripping off the jibbehs, rifling the pockets, and gathering sheaves of spears and swords. Many a jibbeh which will be exhibited in triumph after this campaign has been bought at the price of the life of a wounded man. In a few cases a revolver was necessary in self-defence, but the wholesale slaughter that was carried on by the blacks was indefensible."

That statement relates only to the black camp followers, but some precautions ought to have been taken to keep these in hand and prevent their bloodthirsty and brutal instincts bringing discredit on the army. I asked a question on this matter, and was promised an answer, but none has been given, Lord Kitchener having never referred to that part of the subject. If, however, it is only a matter of camp followers it would be a comparatively small matter, but I am sorry to say that is very far from being the case. Mr. Maxwell, the special correspondent, after describing what happened immediately after the repulse of the attack on the zareba, said :

"Some of the Sirdar's Soudanese were cautiously making their way across the field of battle, their duty being one which, however hateful it may seem to the theoretical humanitarians, warfare against a savage horde like the followers of the Khalifa makes imperative. There is no need to dwell on such incidents, as the Sirdar's black troops were doing what had to be done to make a safe path across the scene of conflict."

Then Mr. Charles Williams, one of the most cool-headed and most experienced of correspondents, included in his telegram to the *Chronicle* describing the battle a passage which was deliberately struck out by the censor. Mr. Williams subsequently wrote :—

" A most material passage in my description of the affray—for one must sacrifice all sense of proportion to call the affair of September 2nd a battle—was suppressed without the slightest intimation of the fact being communicated to me. When I am asked, therefore, why I omitted such a striking incident, it is necessary to explain that I did not. After the first phase of the fight the Sirdar, with his staff, moved to the right, and I accompanied them. . . . While I was going on a staff officer of the British division called out to me, 'Come along ; we're off to Omdurman.' So I started by a short cut to join the British division, a few minutes before the dervishes made their second attack, which so seriously threatened Macdonald's brigade. I witnessed this from a commanding position on the hill. But in reaching that position I had crossed a portion of the slaughter-ground in the first phase, and had witnessed within a few yards of me the way in which native soldiers were killing all the dervishes wounded in that part of the field, because some of the wounded had thrown spears or javelins at the troops. Moved by indignation (though at Abu Klea I had a spear thrown at myself, and the man who threw it had his head blown off by a Grenadier Guardsman) I was about to appeal to some senior officer, for I saw no British executive officer with the Gippies, when a medical officer advised me to retire, as the bullets were flying about recklessly. My description of the scene was excessively mild —but it was suppressed. I do not say the slaughter after the fight was wholly unprovoked. I do say it was excessive, and ought to have been checked."

There was only one other statement I will read to the House. It fills in the details of the occurrence. It is an extract from a private letter, and I shall be glad to give the name of the writer to the Leader of the House if he desires it, as proof of my good faith. The letter was not written for publication, but it was sent to a friend by the writer, who

Mr. C. P. Scott.

was present throughout with the native brigades. He said :

" After attack on zareba the fire zone was scattered with dead and dying dervishes. When the force advanced in *échelon* of brigades from the left the British brigades happened to pass over ground which was practically clear of bodies, but the natives of Maxwell's brigade, whom I accompanied, marched in a broadish formation (column of double companies) across that part of the ground where the attack had been most of all pressed home. . . . I rode out of the zareba, just ahead of this native brigade, in order to look at some of the dervishes. I trotted out slowly, but immediately found myself under a heavy fire from these men in my rear, and, turning round, I saw that the front ranks of Maxwell's brigade, in a fairly well-preserved formation, were shooting independently—*i.e.* each man shooting as he thought good—at dead and dying dervishes. I turned round, and came in circuitously behind the ranks, and went across the field with them till I was sick. Men dropped out of the ranks here and there and potted men who were dying and then striped them. They as a rule before stripping them both shot and bayoneted them, to make sure they were dead. If any heap of dervishes was in the way, four or five men would fire a volley before approaching it. One or two of the wounded screamed and crawled up and begged to be let off, and that was excruciatingly heart-rending to see, because the Soudanese then jabbed them, with a noisy laugh. I stopped about fifteen to twenty minutes, and I must have seen a great many men killed like that in that time. Behind the ranks came a fringe of camp followers, who were shooting and looting everywhere, and who positively made it dangerous to be anywhere near them. They overburdened themselves with all sorts of loot, which they dragged off the dead dervishes. I saw no single live dervish at any point within 300 or 400 yards of the ground over which Maxwell's brigade advanced after they had passed by. I talk solely of what happened under my own nose, and I only speak of those things of the occurrence of which I am as positive as that I breathe. You may say that it was necessary for the safety of the advancing troops. That is a matter for discussion. I only mention the fact that from about 8.15 to about 9 practically the whole of the front ranks of Maxwell's brigade, with whom I was, were engaged close by me in shooting and bayoneting every wounded man they saw ; that I saw some fall out of the ranks to do so, and driven back, non-commissioned officers swearing at them, &c., and that behind there was a crowd of excited camp followers doing what I have said. I left these natives at about 8.40 and rode eastwards towards the river. The shooting went on just as much for the next twenty minutes at least some half-mile to my right rear, but I was not actually with them then.

" After the second phase of the battle, which you know about, I was with Lewis's brigade. These were formed at one time at right angles to Macdonald's. Subsequently the two brigades were in line, with their backs towards the river, and in that formation they advanced westwards, when the attack had been repelled, for a distance of about 1½ mile. All this ground was thickly covered with dead and dying dervishes. I accompanied Lewis's brigade. I was shoulder to shoulder between two battalions, who were deployed in the firing line throughout. There was no conceivable reason for excitement or angry ferocity on the part of the men. They had never been in any danger so long as they went on shooting, and they knew it. Therefore there was no excuse for the way they behaved when we passed over the ground when everything was over. When there were thick clumps of bodies (as there were repeatedly) in our way the regiments were halted and made to fire a volley. Except for that, I heard no order to kill the wounded. It wasn't necessary, for these men—and I noticed the 15th battalion especially—fell out of the ranks in order to stalk wounded dervishes, and crept up behind them and potted them in the small of the neck. Officers swore, but the men saw red and wouldn't stop—paid no attention. I saw an officer hit a man with the flat of his sword for this. I went and kicked one myself back into the ranks, because it wasn't tolerable to see. This went on till about twelve o'clock, and then the order to cease fire was given. I don't speak of any other brigades, because I was only close with these two at those times, and it was not possible to give evidence which is absolutely indubitable in every detail unless you are quite close."

Now I venture to say, after such a narrative with regard to the conduct of these troops, no one could possibly defend deeds of that kind. Everybody must regret such conduct, and everybody must feel that things of this kind could only happen if the whole of our Sudanese warfare was thoroughly rotten, and if the general in charge of the troops had given up any attempt to restrain this kind of excesses. At any rate, I think that this House, before it is called upon to give the Vote which it is now asked to give, is entitled to have these matters sifted to the bottom, that it is entitled to know who is responsible for these things, and to have some assurance, in the words of the Leader of the Opposition, that every possible precaution will be taken in the future that unhappy events of this kind shall not happen again. There is one other matter which I think is almost as painful as the treatment of the wounded upon the battlefield, and that is the failure to bring them adequate succour when the battle was over. I am aware that something was done, but it was quite insufficient, to bring succour to the wounded. Lieutenant Churchill has described how, three days after the battle, he went over the field and found these

wretched wounded men crawling down at the rate of some 300 or 400 yards a day, and crawling across the river without anyone to help them. Even a week after that, he went on to the battlefield again, and there some of these wretched men were still suffering these agonies. I think that is a terrible state of things, for these men were not just a few here and there isolated cases, but the correspondents who went out a week after the battle saw hundreds of these poor men on the banks of the river crawling about and trying to get what little shelter they could find, and they were doing their best to sustain life. Considering that a single steamer would have sufficed to have brought all these men to Omdurman, I think it is deplorable that a steamer was not set aside for this purpose, and that a more systematic and organised effort was not made to bring these men back and properly provide for them. I asked the Under Secretary of State for Foreign Affairs whether he considered that these men should be treated on the same terms as the wounded soldiers of civilised armies, and whether the convention as to the conduct of war did not provide that the wounded of all nations should be brought in. The right hon. Gentleman replied that as much as possible should be done in that direction, but my complaint is that it was not done in this case. Many of the steamers I know were wanted for other purposes, but I think the claims of humanity ought to have come before these other necessities, and at least one of the steamers might have been spared to bring succour to these miserable men. I should not have taken advantage of this occasion to bring forward this subject, and I should have been glad to have brought it forward earlier upon the Supplementary Estimates for the service in the Soudan, but I was told that it could not then be raised because Lord Kitchener was not paid out of those Estimates; and I was told that this was the stage when the matter might be brought forward, because Lord Kitchener, as the Sirdar, was paid out of Egyptian and not out of British money. I think I have at least shown that there is matter here for the gravest possible consideration of this House. We are probably now only at the beginning and not at the end of our Soudanese troubles. I believe that we are probably at the beginning of a series of conflicts with savage enemies as fierce probably as those we were engaged in upon this occasion. This is of vital importance in the future when we are employing troops which are not our own, and not animated by the traditions of the British Army, and which are probably very much under-officered by white officers. Therefore it is of the most vital consequence that steps should be taken which will render it impossible that things of this kind shall happen again. I shall perhaps be told that I am attacking the honour of the British Army, but I do not think that the honour of the British Army has anything to fear from an investigation of the facts as to what was done on this occasion, or upon any other occasion. I do think, however, that we should take great care that nothing shall be done at any future time which may bring discredit upon our arms. I claim that none of us, at least on this side of the House, are called upon to vote for this grant until this matter has been sifted to the bottom, and until it has been shown that we have some guarantee that the deeds which followed the battle of Omdurman will not occur in the future.

*LORD CHARLES BERESFORD (York): I am at a loss to conceive why my right hon. friend the Leader of the House wants to close this debate so soon. This question has excited great interest in the country, and not only that, but it is a question which affects the honour of the British Army. I should have thought, therefore, that my right hon. friend would have rather encouraged the debate on this matter so as to have thoroughly cleared up the question; and if the debate goes on I feel perfectly certain that Lord Kitchener will be found to have done the right thing in regard to this question. Now the two points which I should like to touch upon, and which are interesting the country so much, are these: Was it necessary to disentomb the Mahdi, and was the disentombment done in an honourable manner? With regard to the second point, I quite agree with my right hon. friend the Leader of the House that it might have been done in a very much better manner. For my part, I should like to have seen the remains not only taken away and buried somewhere else, but taken away with some sort of ceremony and respect for the dead, which sentiments everybody ought to hold. That is the point which woke up the British public.

because the chivalry of our country does not like to think that the remains of a man who had fought against us have been treated with some sort of spite. Then there is another point, and it is as to the manner in which the disentombment was carried on. I was very glad to hear the right hon. Gentleman say that there was no silence or secrecy about it, but that it was done publicly by the men under Lord Kitchener's command. As far as the act of disentombment is concerned, I am certain that every military and naval man deplores the way in which it was done, for it was not done according to our own traditions of English chivalry. Now as to the point whether it was necessary. Remember, Lord Kitchener, as I understand it, gave the order for the disentombment of the Mahdi, and I hold most strongly that Lord Kitchener was absolutely right in giving that order, and I will endeavour to show the Committee why, if hon. Members will be good enough to listen to me. Lord Kitchener gave the order for the disentombment, but he did not see it carried out, and I say that they did not carry it out on the lines which the British people desire that it should be carried out. Lord Kitchener, however, takes the full responsibility, and by so doing he adopts the old chivalrous method of our military people—he takes the full responsibility of all that happened, although he had absolutely no connection with the way in which it was carried out. I believe that Lord Kitchener just as much regrets the way in which his orders were carried out as everybody else does who has studied the question. Now, as to the point of necessity. The disentombment of the Mahdi's remains was necessary simply to secure that there should be no revival of that religious fanaticism which undoubtedly would have occurred if the Government had allowed the Mahdi's remains to remain where they were. In the East, when once the Mahometan people make a holy place, or make a saint of one of their leaders, his tomb becomes a place to which they go for the purpose of raising fanaticism in the times that may follow, and everybody knows that that is the case. Now I wish to take, most respectfully, issue with the right hon. Gentleman the Member for Montrose upon this point. I say this with great respect and with great earnestness that, so far as I can judge from the right hon. Gentleman's writings and by his teachings, he is no judge of religious fanaticism whatever. I say this with respect because, as I understand what he has written, he does not regard religious fanaticism as anything that can ever be powerful, because he says himself that he does not understand the question at all. That being so I cannot accept the right hon. Gentleman as a guide as to what should be done to check this religious fanaticism. With regard to the reason why Lord Kitchener disentombed the Mahdi, the First Lord of the Treasury has already pointed out that half his army were old Mahdists, and that was a very important point. Remember that these men and the Mahometan officers serving under Lord Kitchener were the men who went to Lord Kitchener and proved to his satisfaction that unless this false religion and this false prophet were proved to be false these risings would continue, and they told him that the only way he could prove it was by disentombing the Mahdi. They pointed out to Lord Kitchener that they would have the greatest difficulty in the future in governing the Soudan if this were not done, because fanaticism must be revived. Then as to the tribes. Lord Kitchener has not had very easy work—and he is not going to have very easy work—in governing all these tribes. Most of these tribes I knew myself in the Soudan, and they have all been nearly decimated under the banner of Mahdism. You may say that the Mahdi did not do it, but the Khalifa decimated them in the name of the teachings of the Mahdi, and all these tribes would naturally wish that it should be proved that the Mahdi himself was a false prophet, and that could only be done by disentombing him. On the one side I entirely sympathise with the right hon. Gentleman's views in respect to the treatment of the dead ; but, after all, it is only a theory and a sentiment. On the other side, however, you have the hard practical fact that this fanaticism would rise again if this was not done, because the people told Lord Kitchener so, and they would not have told him so had they any doubt in their own minds as to whether in the future this man might not be regarded as a saint in this holy place. There is nothing in history that I have ever read that can exceed the horrors and the terrors that went on in the Soudan before the brilliant victory at Omdurman. There

was only one man in history who even approached the atrocity, the bloodshed, and the murders that went on in the Soudan under the direction of the Mahdi and the Khalifa, and under the guise and religion of the Mahdi, and that man was Ibrahim Pasha. The right hon. Gentleman the Member for Montrose does not believe in the power of religious fanaticism——

Mr. J. MORLEY : The noble Lord cannot have read my writings, or else he would have seen that fanaticism was one of the things I have written most about.

*Lord CHARLES BERESFORD : I understood the right hon. Gentleman to argue that religious fanaticism was so absurd that he could not admit its power, but I am not a literary man. Let me give an instance of religious fanaticism which occurred when I was in the Soudan. There was a great sheikh captured, and he was brought into the presence of a distinguished general who questioned him about the Mahdi. The general said to him, "Is this man a man of God ?" "Certainly," replied the sheikh. "And how do you know ?" asked the general, and the sheikh answered, "Because he performed miracles." "Does he ?" asked the general. "What miracles has he performed lately ?" "Well, he came down to Khartoum and he wanted to go to Omdurman and he had no boat. He prayed, and an alligator came up out of the Nile and carried him to Omdurman." "And did you see it ?" asked the general. "Oh, no," replied the sheikh ; "but all the people told me, and they saw it." That man actually believed this story. But there is a comic side to this question, for the general happened to have a glass eye, and he said to the sheikh, "If I take out one of my eyes, throw it up in the air, catch it, and put it back again, don't you think I ought to be a Mahdi ?" "Yes," said the sheikh. The general took out his glass eye, threw it up, caught it as it was falling, and put it back again, and the sheikh fell on his knees before him and said, "God is great : you must be the Mahdi." I quote this as an illustration of what I mean by religious fanaticism. Now, the right hon. Gentleman opposite is in a very peculiar position in regard to this question, and he ought to be consistent. The right hon. Gentleman is a trustee of the British

Museum, and there can be no such object lesson with regard to the desecration of tombs than there is in the British Museum, for there are mummies not only of distinguished kings, but of people who were worshipped and prayed to as gods in the old days, and the right hon. Gentleman as a trustee of the museum, is more or less responsible for that state of things. I wish to carry out this matter to its logical conclusion. Suppose, a thousand years hence, another right hon. Gentleman of the same views as the right hon. Gentleman opposite may be in the same position; he would think nothing of having dug up the Mahdi, and bringing home to the British Museum those remains for everybody to look at. I do think the right hon. Gentleman ought to be consistent about this question. If you dig up a man who may have been buried some two or three thousand years ago, you may preserve his skull as a relic of the past; but if you dig up the remains of the Mahdi, you are doing a thing that is atrocious. With regard to what Lord Kitchener did, I feel perfectly certain that he did the right thing. He was noble and big about it; it was not done in the way that he wished it to be done; but he gave the order and he took upon himself the whole and absolute responsibility for everything that was done. My right hon. friend the Leader of the House also mentioned the question of revenge. How could there be any question of revenge? It was a question of sheer political necessity for the future administration of the Soudan. If we wanted to be revengeful, why did we not imprison the Mahdi's two sons? We took them prisoners, but Lord Kitchener gave them land and liberty because he wished to show that he did not desire to exhibit vengeance but sympathy for them, and thus show respect for the man who had ruled the country for so many years. In some respects I am sorry that this question has been brought forward in the way it has, although I believe that the more it is discussed the better will people see that nothing has been done which is discreditable to the great General we had out there. By his conduct of the operations in the Soudan Lord Kitchener has not only commanded the admiration of all of us, but he has also commanded the respect of every single nation in Europe, for he has shown himself to be a brilliant administrator and a most

Lord Charles Beresford.

uncommonly good financier. For these reasons I am sorry that there should have been one word brought forward with regard to his qualifications for the graceful act that this House is asked to make towards him. On the other hand, I am very glad indeed that the subject has been brought forward, and although I differ from my right hon. friend the First Lord of the Treasury as to the advisability of fully and thoroughly debating this question, I believe that the more it is debated the more credit and the more respect will be given to the great General who upheld our honour in the Soudan.

MR. LABOUCHERE (Northampton): Hon. Gentlemen opposite appear to imagine that the opposition on this side of the House to the Vote is due solely to certain acts that were done by Lord Kitchener. I am free to confess that if the wounded at Omdurman had been well treated, and if we had never heard one word about the Mahdi's tomb and the Madhi's body, I would have voted against this grant. It seems to be thought that up to the present time, when a grant has been proposed for some successful General, it has always been accepted with acclamation by the House. That is a mistake. In the case of the grants to Sir Beauchamp Seymour, afterwards Lord Alcester, and to Lord Wolseley, I challenged a Division upon them, and had a small measure of support on this side of the House. Will any hon. Gentleman tell me why, in the name of goodness, when a public servant belonging to the Army or Navy fulfils his duty efficiently, a Vote of public money is granted to him? Why is a grant never offered to men in the Civil Service? Can hon. Gentlemen opposite tell me of one single case in which any great statesman or prominent civil servant has been granted, during this century, a Vote of money for exceptional services? And yet there have been statesmen who have done acts for the benefit of the country compared to which the deeds of naval and military men were small. Take Egypt, for instance, where Lord Cromer has distinguished himself for as many years as Lord Kitchener, and has done quite as great service to the country; and yet no one has suggested that Lord Cromer should be given a grant of £30,000. (Cries of "Divide.") Unless the closure is put on, we mean to carry on this discussion for some time, and hon. Members opposite may safely go away to dinner, and put themselves out of their misery. I can perfectly understand that in such a case as the battle of Waterloo or the battle of Trafalgar, on which the fate of the entire nation might depend, you might vote the victorious general or admiral a sum of money; but that is one of the exceptions that prove the rule. I have no feeling against Lord Kitchener, but I contend that no such element entered into the Soudan campaign. Besides, there was not that equality between the combatants which is necessary to make a great, important, and serious victory. The First Lord of the Treasury has praised Lord Kitchener, and I am quite willing to agree to everything he said in regard to Lord Kitchener's military capacity. But I ask, does the First Lord suppose that we are so poor in generals, that if the task had been given to one of many other generals he could not have done it equally well and effectually as Lord Kitchener? I want to point out that it was not by the efforts or by the genius of Lord Kitchener that this victory was effected, but because he had the men and the means at his disposal. The task was not exceedingly difficult from a military point of view. His objective was Omdurman; he had time and means at his disposal; he went forward with his army; he encountered no serious military resistance all the time; and naturally he arrived at his objective point. I have always observed that when some deed of arms has been done the Government which is in power at the time invariably takes an exaggerated view of it, because they consider that if the deed of arms is creditable it reflects some special honour on themselves. Lord Kitchener has already been largely benefited by what has occurred. He has been made a peer, which is a distinction I do not myself appreciate, although he may; he has had promotion, and he will, whatever credit due to him, have a good billet. We were told that the whole Army will rejoice at Lord Kitchener getting this money; but it does seem to me that, if you have an army that suffered largely from the climate and disease, you would do far better to give something to the widows and orphans of the soldiers who died, or to those who survive but whose con-

stitution has been wrecked. This habit of giving grants of money to successful generals is exceptional to this country. In no other country would it be done. Take America, for instance. Admiral Dewey has covered himself with honour, and I saw recently in an American newspaper that a subscription had been organised for him; but there has been no idea or thought of the United States Government proposing a vote of money for him. Take, again, Major Marchand; the French Government do not intend to reward Major Marchand by a money grant. But by marching without an army through a country peopled by vast numbers of savage tribes he performed a more distinguished feat than Lord Kitchener did marching with his army to Omdurman. ["Oh! Oh!"] The result may not have been greater, but he did more. It seems to me he is a very brave man. If hon. Gentlemen opposite cannot hear the name of Major Marchand without murmuring, I will take the name of the hon. Member for Lambeth. I hold that that hon. Gentleman did a greater deed by advancing through all those forests, with a few men under him, to the relief of Emin Pasha, than Lord Kitchener did in advancing on Omdurman. ["Oh! Oh"] Well, that is my opinion. On general grounds I should oppose this grant, and I am perfectly consistent in doing so, because I have opposed grants before now to men equally distinguished. But undoubtedly there are special reasons why Lord Kitchener's grant should be opposed. There is the case of the wounded. My hon. friend behind me read extracts from the newspapers in regard to the killing of the wounded Dervishes. It was stated that if they had not been killed they would themselves have killed those who came to help them. The number of those who were killed is exceedingly remarkable. If we acquit the English soldiers of killing the wounded, yet there were a large number of savages in the army who killed the wounded whenever they got the chance. Major Stuart-Wortley, a distinguished officer, wrote an article in *Scribner's Magazine* in regard to the operations of the Arab Irregulars which he commanded. These Arabs were ordered by the Sirdar to clear the west bank of the Nile in order to enable a battery of howitzers to shell the Mahdi's tomb, and to clear the way for the entry into Omdurman. How did these Arab Irregulars conduct themselves? When about 500 yards from the mud houses they halted, and after a few minutes resumed the advance, firing all the while. Then they rushed into the houses and slaughtered every soul in them. That was not an account by newspaper correspondents, but by the commander himself. The fact is that this is a constant practice in African wars; and it is one of the reasons why so many of us on this side of the House specially object to those African wars. My right hon. friend the Leader of the Opposition said he hoped that what occurred at Omdurman would be a lesson to our officers, and that in future there would not be the same destruction of wounded men. I expressed that hope in regard to the Matabele campaign; but in vain. I asked "Where are the wounded?" and could get no reply. The real reason was that all the wounded had been killed. Until this House takes very serious notice of what goes on in these wars, our officers will find it difficult to restrain savages. While you employ savages abominable atrocities will take place. I think it would have been much better if the Mahdi's tomb had not been destroyed. It is not the habit of modern nations to destroy any monument of the enemy. When Blucher, on the occupation of Paris by the Allies, after Waterloo, wrote orders to blow up the Bridge of Austerlitz, the Duke of Wellington interfered to prevent it. Then, about the body of the Mahdi. The First Lord said that the head was not decapitated. Very likely the head was not cut off: I understand it was simply taken from a quantity of bones, and that the rest of the bones were thrown into the Nile. The right hon. Gentleman says that was done decorously. But I cannot understand how you can take up a lot of bones decorously, and throw them into the river. My right hon. friend quoted the case of Cromwell, and the Irish Members on that occasion said that the English Government were quite right. The only case I remember which is exactly on all fours with that of the Mahdi is that of Thomas à Becket. At that time there was a change of religion, and there had been large pilgrimages to certain shrines. What did that unmitigated ruffian Henry VIII. do?—["Order, order"]—I confess that I did not think anybody would complain if I called Henry VIII. an unmitigated

Mr. Labouchere.

ruffian. Hon. Gentlemen opposite do not like us going on with this debate; but the longer we go on the better it will be, because we will bring home to the country what actually did take place. Well, Henry VIII. ordered the tomb of Thomas à Becket to be desecrated, and his remains thrown to the winds. Every historian—even Mr. Froude, who had a passion for Henry VIII.—disapproved of that action. Since those other ruffians, the cavaliers of Charles II., rifled Cromwell's tomb there has been no case of political desecration in this country. If hon. Gentlemen refer to *The Times* of this morning they will see letters protesting against and denouncing the desecration which has taken place in a certain parish in Southwark, because certain corpses have been taken up to be buried elsewhere. That shows how strong is the opinion in this country in regard to these matters. I say again it was a most unsoldierly act on the part of Lord Kitchener to desecrate the tomb of the Mahdi, and to destroy his remains. ["Oh! oh!"] Whether necessary or unnecessary, it was an unsoldierly act. I knew when I said that it was an unsoldierly act a good many hon. Gentlemen would say "Oh! oh!" I laid the trap for them. But I suppose they would accept General Wolseley as a proper specimen of a soldier, and Sir Henry Brackenbury. In 1873-74 General (then Sir Garnet) Wolseley advanced to take Coomassie. His military secretary, Sir H. Brackenbury, published an official narrative of what took place. When the army reached Coomassie there was a discussion as to whether it was desirable to blow up and to destroy the monuments of the old kings of Coomassie; and Sir Henry goes on to say that "the rifling of the tombs of the dead, even though these dead were the savage ancestors of a barbarous king, is an act that does not appeal to the instinct of a true soldier." That is the opinion of a gentleman who, I think, has as good an idea as to what a good soldier is as any gentleman on that side of the House. There is nothing new in this. It has been the opinion of civilisation for years and years. Charles V. was a soldier, and what did he say when it was proposed to destroy the bodies of the Reformers? He said: "I do not fight with the dead; I fight with the living," and he would not have anything to do with such a thing. What are the pleas that are put forward for this destruction of the Mahdi's remains? The First Lord of the Treasury told us that Lord Kitchener held that there would be pilgrimages to the tomb, and that the cult of the Mahdi would continue unless these remains were scattered to the winds. I should imagine myself that this action with regard to the remains would strengthen " public opinion " against us. The First Lord of the Treasury also said that it was absolutely necessary, because we were leaving white soldiers there, and that it was to protect their lives that we put an end to the Mahdi's remains. Now, does anyone suppose that, if the people of the Soudan were not frightened by the execution we did on them, they would be prevented from breaking out into rebellion simply because of the fact that the remains of the Mahdi had been thrown away and his tomb rifled? The noble Lord the Member for York said that Lord Kitchener had nobly and honestly taken upon himself the responsibility for that which he was not in reality responsible for.

*Lord CHARLES BERESFORD: What I said was that Lord Kitchener had taken the responsibility of giving the order, although he was not responsible for the way in which it was carried out. The way in which it was carried out must have been as repugnant to his feelings as to those of the hon. Gentleman.

Mr. LABOUCHERE : The noble Lord comes here and tells us that Lord Kitchener privately told him ——

*Lord CHARLES BERESFORD : I assure the hon. Member that Lord Kitchener has never told me anything at all. I said so distinctly. I did not know he was in England.

Mr. LABOUCHERE : I thought the noble Lord said so. But the noble Lord has used as an argument that, although Lord Kitchener officially says he was responsible for the way the orders were carried out, he was not in reality responsible. He must have heard that from someone. Lord Kitchener has taken the full responsibility in respect to all that was done, and he rightly did so, for as General he was responsible for all that occurred. In any case we must remember that the Mahdi was not a common man. He was a great ruler, imagining himself to be a prophet. He was the Sovereign of that country for a considerable number of years. He had driven out the Egyptians from the country, and put himself at the head of those men who, Mr. Gladstone said, were " brave men, rightly struggling to be free." As to his pretensions to be a prophet, I do not much believe in prophets myself, but he must have been regarded by his people as a national hero, and although his government was bad he was a patriot, and not only his immediate adherents but the country must have been indignant at the way his remains were treated. The noble Lord the Member for York said that the Mahdi was a scoundrel and a barbarian ; but he should remember that this scoundrel and barbarian had built up a great city in his reign in which there were 10,000 people, not in any way connected with the Soudan, pursuing their avocations without let or hindrance. The desecration of the tomb of the Mahdi is an individual act for which Lord Kitchener is responsible, and if we vote this sum of money to him we shall make the country responsible for it. That is why I object to the Vote. I object to it on general grounds, and as an outrage on every sanction of modern civilisation. I have no doubt some Liberals will leave the House without voting, and that some will vote with the Government; but I do hope that there will be found a sufficient number of Liberals who will vote against the grant in order that it may be shown that the Liberals as a party are against it. The First Lord of the Treasury answered several questions put to him by my right hon. friend the Member for Montrose, but he did not answer the questions, When was it that the skull of the Mahdi was handed over, whether it was carried off as a trophy, and, if so, where to, when was it buried at Wady Halfa, and was that in consequence of the disgust and indignation excited in England? The right hon. Gentleman did not answer these questions. Wady Halfa is 1,400 miles from Omdurman, and we ask that the matter should be investigated and some explanation given as to how the skull appeared at a place 1,400 miles from where it was taken. Was it given to Lord Kitchener, was it in his possession for some time, or was it given to somebody else ?

Mr. A. STANLEY (Lancashire, Ormskirk): My only excuse for rising at this time of the evening, when the most important business of the day is coming on, is that I think I am the only Member of this House who has had the rather questionable pleasure of being at Omdurman, and of having inspected the Mahdi's tomb with the Sirdar himself, although the Mahdi from no fault of his own is no longer there. Moreover, I should have felt ashamed of myself had I sat here and listened silently to accusations being made against gallant British and Egyptian officers, amongst whom I have lived for four or five years, and many of whom I am proud to regard as my friends. I was afraid when I came to the House that I might have been betrayed into offending against proper rules by the accusations brought. I am glad to say, however, that there is no need for that, because the accusations, so far as I have heard them, remarkably resemble nonsense. The right hon. Gentleman who first protested talked about what cannibals might have done under certain conditions, and what Belgian officers might have done. He also quoted the opinion of Slatin Pasha as having more weight than the opinions of Lord Cromer and Lord Kitchener combined. The right hon. Gentleman has inveighed against the Sirdar for following the advice of his Mahometan officers in the disposal of the Mahdi's body; but surely the right hon. Gentleman has forgotten that for no inconsiderable portion of his life Slatin Pasha was a Mahometan himself. Now, Sir, the arguments about the wounded, and about the bones of the Mahdi, have been repeated *ad nauseam*, and I do not propose to say anything more about them. The question I desire to put to the Committee is, Did the Sirdar as a general do what he was asked to do? The task set before him was to retrieve the Soudan from the most shameful tyranny which has ever existed. He had to do that with the least possible loss of life and treasure to his own side. Did the Sirdar do that, or did he not? I say unhesitatingly that he did, and that by his decisive action at a most critical point in the world's history he did more to maintain the peace of the world than a dozen Peace Conferences. He showed that in the cause of justice England's right hand had not lost its strength nor her brain its cunning. I do not think it is going too far to say that by the success of the British and Egyptian Army on that occasion he showed that England was prepared for all emergencies, and that if she wanted peace, as she now desires, she was strong enough to enforce it. Sir, I have said that at this period of the evening I do not wish to detain the Committee very long; my only claim to speak is that I speak in the name of many of those who take a most lively interest in this debate, but are not here to speak for themselves. I may speak, I think, in the name of the small band of English soldiers and civilians who, in thirteen short years, have raised Egypt from the gutter and put it on an equality with the most prosperous nations of the world. It is in their name, Sir, that I ask the Committee to listen to me when I beseech them to unite as one man to inscribe upon the glorious roll of English heroes a name which will, I am sure, gather glory in years to come and be no less respected than those which precede it on the roll. I ask, Sir, that there may be no division, but that we may elect as one man to inscribe on England's roll of glory the name of Kitchener of Khartoum.

Mr. ATHERLEY-JONES (Durham, N.W.): Sir, I should not like to give a silent vote on this question. I quite recognise, and fully appreciate, many of the excuses which may be justly urged for some of the things which in calm moments we deplore the necessity of doing, but which are the necessary accessories of war. But, passing over those acts of inhumanity which are essential to all warfare, I am bound to say that I am unable to follow my political chief in the vote which I shall give this evening. Sir, I have listened, and anxiously listened, to the speeches which have been made this evening, to see if I could find some way of recording my vote, however humble, in recognition of the undoubtedly gallant services of a distinguished public servant. But, although the apologists have been many, and although the apologies have been diverse and manifold, I have been unable to find any sufficient vindication for the action which is abhorrent to the conscience of civilised mankind, the desecration of the tomb of the Mahdi. It was urged by the not undistinguished son of a very distinguished man, who, if he had been in this House now, would have been the first, I feel convinced, from my observation of his character, to have repudiated and stigmatised in just language this action on the part of the chief of the Egyptian Army—it was urged by Mr. Winston Churchill, in a speech which he made in the Midlands the other day, that Lord Kitchener was not responsible himself for this barbarity, but by an act of chivalry took upon himself the responsibility in order to stand by his comrades. Now, I have known, in the history of military achievements, cases in which a general officer has thought it right to shield the error or mistake of a subordinate; but I have never yet read of a general officer who took upon himself, in the interests of the profession to which he belonged, to be an apologist for an actual wrong. If Lord Kitchener had repudiated the act, what would have been the result? It would have been the act of an individual Englishman. Lord Kitchener's vindication of that act, his acceptance of the responsibility of it, transforms the act of an individual Englishman into a deliberate act of the English nation, unless the English nation, by its Parliamentary representatives, seizes this opportunity to repudiate the act. But why is it that these officers, when Lord Kitchener is responsible for the mode of operation of removing the Mahdi's remains, have not thought fit to step forward and vindicate the character of their chief by saying that the chief gave the order to remove the body, but did not give the order for the desecration to be carried out in the way in which it was? No, Sir, I do not think that that contention, supported by the high authority of the noble Lord who spoke from the other side of the House, can be accepted. The second line of defence which has been adopted is, that there were reasons of public policy why this course should be adopted. I believe that there has been no crime committed by a foreign Power which has not been justified by contemporaries on the plea of public necessity; but for my part, I can only say that—whatever may be the judgment in the heat of the moment and in the enthusiasm, perhaps, of the adventure with which that particular deed is associated—cold, calm criticism will refuse to see those grounds of public policy which should be adequate for such an act. What is the ground of public policy upon which this act was committed? It is said that you prevent a recrudescence of Mahdism by holding up to the fanatical followers of the Mahdi the illusion of the idol which they have hitherto worshipped. Sir, to my mind there may be another motive. There may be a motive which is stronger even than religious fanaticism, and that is, vengeance for the outrage which has been inflicted upon their chosen leader and religious chief. Is that a justification? Are we not strong enough; are we not sufficiently great and powerful as a nation, having put down our foot, to withstand a fanatical force? Is it not an indication of weakness to the fanatical followers of the Mahdi that we have to destroy two or three of their religious chiefs in order to prevent the necessity of having to cross swords with them a second time? Now, Sir, although public policy may be successfully urged—I mean public policy from the low, narrow, and sordid standpoint in which it has been urged to-day—there is a higher public policy, and that public policy is, to maintain the standard of civilisation and humanity which ought to belong to this country. I cannot help asking myself, when it is our boast that we go forth to conquer these savage tribes to bring to them the blessings of religion, to tame their ferocity, and raise them up to a higher moral standard—I cannot help asking myself what they will think of our boasted civilisation and its pioneers when they know that that religion countenances body-snatching and the desecration of tombs. Therefore, although it is with great pain and reluctance that I shall record my vote against the grant of this money for what is otherwise so well deserved, I feel not the smallest shrinking in the performance of my duty, and I hope that those who are true to the traditions of English Liberalism and the great principles of humanity and civilisation will take the same course.

*MR. LEES KNOWLES (Salford, W.): I merely wish to add a few words to this debate, because, like my hon. friend who has spoken behind me, I, too, was in Egypt at the time of the campaign, and heard a great deal about what took place. The hon. Member for the Leigh division has quoted numerous extracts from newspaper reports and also from private letters. He quoted, to begin with, a letter from a lieutenant who, I am sorry to say, has since died, and whose explanation with regard to the correspondence cannot therefore be obtained; he quoted also extracts from letters written by numerous private soldiers. I do not think much of them, and I do not think the correspondents of newspapers, especially in Egypt, loved Lord Kitchener. When I was in Cairo I came in contact with several of them, and they seemed to think they ought to be permitted to run riot over the camp, and see everything that was going on at the front. I think, therefore, that any information from such sources ought to be taken *cum grano*. With regard to the privates, they would surely not get full information about an action which extended over a large area of country. Hon. Gentlemen opposite seem to be most anxious to decry the merits of our military brethren, and to wish to prove to the hilt this charge of cruelty. I will not allude to the so-called desecration of the Mahdi's tomb; that has been sufficiently dealt with already. But so long as the Mahdi was treated with veneration and superstition it was absolutely desirable that his bones should be scattered to the winds. I look upon that not as a matter of revenge at all, but as a matter of necessity. That I conceive to be the main ground of defence. Revenge has been described by Bacon as a kind of wild justice, and he went on to say:

"Some, when they take revenge, are desirous that the party should know whence it cometh; this is the more generous. For the delight seemeth to be not so much in doing the hurt, as in making the party repent.'

But let me allude for a moment to the second charge, namely, the alleged cruelty on the battlefield. Now, as home testimony is not always estimated at its highest value, let us go for evidence abroad. I will take the evidence of two foreign military *attachés*, representing on the staff of the Sirdar two great civilised military nations, Germany and Italy. The German *attaché* wrote a letter, which appeared in the *Times* of January 16th, absolutely refuting the charges. Last December, as I was returning home from abroad, I met Major Luigi Calderari, of the 40th Infantry Regiment, the Italian *attaché*. I had a long conversation with him, and asked him particularly with regard to the alleged cruelties on the part of the Anglo-Egyptian Army on the battlefield. He repudiated the idea of any such charge, and later, seeing that this question was

Mr. Lees Knowles.

being worked up for political reasons—because I must say that I cannot but think that this cry about the desecration of the Mahdi's tomb and the alleged cruelty on the battlefield has been raised chiefly for political reasons—I wrote to him and asked him if he would allow me to quote the conversation, or, at all events, would put in writing that which he had said to me, in order that I might not misrepresent him in any way. He did so, and he has supported absolutely the despatches to which allusion has been made to-night. And what did he say? He said this:

"I am very glad to have an opportunity to put in writing what I stated to you verbally in Milan as to the manner in which the Dervish prisoners at the battle of Omdurman were treated, and to deny in the most absolute way that any cruelty was practised towards the prisoners. I rode on the field of battle in various directions, and everywhere I saw hundreds of wounded lying alive, notwithstanding that the ground had already been traversed by the Anglo-Egyptian troops. I happened to be for a while at the head of the troops in their advance after the attack on the zareba had been repulsed, and then again I was able to convince myself that the wounded were not in any way molested. If an occasional wounded man was killed it was only in legitimate defence, because, as is well known, it is a custom with these peoples to pretend to be dead and then to fire on the enemy as he passes, or, worse still, to ask for water and help and then treacherously to kill those who are succouring them. I do not write these things in order to defend Lord Kitchener: he is so far above such accusations that merely to waste words in denying them would be an insult to him. I can only repeat that I am very happy that an opportunity presents itself for me to give a denial to statements which are untrue. It was, moreover, my duty to do so, especially as some Italian newspapers have copied and republished such statements."

I may perhaps be allowed to quote two lines from our military Poet-Laureate, Rudyard Kipling, in which he describes the Dervish as "Fuzzy-Wuzzy," who is

"All 'ot sand and ginger when alive,
And generally shammin' when 'e's dead."

These are the men with whom our regulars have to deal, and I am quite sure that, so far as my information goes, there never was any cruelty at all with regard to the wounded on the battlefield. All this outcry is not genuine. It is not what is called in Lancashire "jannock," it is not real. There is a political ring about it, and the opposition to the Vote is, in my judgment, simply initiated with the object of obtaining a political cry. We have always had Gordon on our consciences and in our hearts, and Gordon has been avenged at last. (Opposition cheers.) I will withdraw the word "avenged." Gordon was the last man who would have wished for vengeance. I would rather say that rapine and torture have been crushed out of the Soudan by such men as Wolseley and Kitchener.

*MR. PIRIE (Aberdeen, N.): The First Lord of the Treasury has stated that we who stay at home are placed in a very invidious position to judge the actions of men who bear the brunt and are exposed to the hardships of a campaign. It is, no doubt, a fact that those who follow my right hon. friend the Member for Montrose will have the imputation—a false imputation—cast on them of niggardliness, and of adopting a cheeseparing policy ; but although, for this reason, such a course is a hard and a difficult one, it is, to my mind, the course dictated by duty. I have listened very carefully to the whole of this debate, and I have heard nothing but praise for the organisation, the economy, and completeness with which the work was carried out, and I hope the whole House will be unanimous in the vote of thanks which will be proposed next Thursday to the general, the officers, and the men who took part in it. I look, however, upon this request for a grant as giving an opportunity as much for a criticism of the Government as of the individual to whom we are asked to vote the money. If any honour is done to a general officer commanding, he regards it as an honour to the army composing the expedition, and from them it is extended to the Government which organised the expedition, and in the same way condemnation and criticism of the individual must also extend to the Government. I believe that, apart from the question of policy, the whole spirit animating the Government since the news of the Soudan victory reached this country constitutes one of the strongest arguments in opposition to this Vote. I think the Government have lost all sense of proportion in this matter, and to this complete loss of proportion, and the corresponding excess of praise which has been meted out to the expedition, is traceable to a great extent the opposition which has been displayed this afternoon.

The First Lord of the Treasury took some pains to defend Lord Kitchener's action as regards the Mahdi's body as not having been animated by any spirit of revenge. In my opinion that is entirely beside the mark. The First Lord of the Treasury would be entirely right if there were any such accusation, but no one has accused Lord Kitchener of being animated by a mere spirit of paltry revenge against the Mahdi ; even to imagine such an accusation against a British general is somewhat derogatory to a true soldierly instinct. But where I find fault is that, owing to the action of Lord Kitchener, and the exaggerated importance and praise bestowed on the expedition, and the way in which—to employ a word felicitously used the other day with regard to Empire—the expedition was "boomed' by the Government, the nation has been impregnated with the spirit that the outcome and result of the expedition had been "Gordon avenged," which is a very different thing from any personal feeling of revenge between Lord Kitchener and the Mahdi. That spirit has been far too prevalent in this country, and I think it is the duty of this House to do what it can to disabuse the nation of it. It is a lowering and a false spirit of the right conception of war. There are two ways from which this point may be looked at : one from the political point of view, to which I attach very little importance ; the other from the moral point of view, which is far more important. As regards the first point, I will dismiss it by merely saying that ignorant and unscrupulous people throughout the country, with whom any means are justifiable to influence votes, should remember that at the time of the fall of Khartoum the Duke of Devonshire and the right hon. Gentleman the Member for West Birmingham were Members of the then Government, and also that the Soudan Expedition of 1885 was required to be recalled owing to the Pendjeh incident. We should then hear less of the cry "Gordon avenged." On the moral side of the question I have a much greater quarrel with the Government. I think anything that encourages that cry, and some public men have made use of the very words, is lowering the conception of war. To show the extent to which it has permeated the nation, the sister of the great man about whom the cry was raised had to write to the Press repudiating it, and stating that her brother would have been the last man to have approved or tolerated it. Surely, such an incident is a matter for shame to any right-thinking nation. It might have been more excusable had the force against whom we waged this so-called war been a foe more worthy of ourselves. For many years, since 1870, certain of us have been casting reflections upon a neighbouring nation for harbouring a spirit of revenge against a former foe. It would be well if we could sometimes see ourselves as others see us. If this neighbouring nation does harbour a spirit of revenge, it is against her equal, instead of, as was our case, against a foe comparatively contemptible and beneath our notice. I think very likely why such a spirit exists is due to the fact that now for two generations this nation has not known what real war is, and I hope it will be many more generations before she does; but all the more important is it to keep a high level of soldierly feeling. It is instructive to go back through those generations, to either the Crimean war or the Indian Mutiny, and to see the proportion in which the men who waged those wars were rewarded by this House. In connection with the Crimean war, I think I am right in saying not one peerage was conferred. Lord Raglan died during the progress of the war, and no successor of his was ennobled. The men who bore the brunt and stress of the Indian Mutiny were comparatively unrewarded. Lord Clyde, it is true, was ennobled and received a life pension, but it came out of the Indian Exchequer, and it is a moot point whether Lord Kitchener, being in the pay of Egypt, the Egyptian Exchequer ought not to be asked to find the money for the grant. Since these two wars we have been pursuing a progressive course as regards rewards. We have been almost prostituting honours, and it seems to me that the less worthy the foe the greater the reward. It is because I feel it our duty to check this system, and believe that unless it is checked we will go on from bad to worse, that I for one will vote with my right hon. friend the Member for Montrose. The unchivalrous action of Lord Kitchener in destroying the Mahdi's tomb brings the expedition down to the same low level as a punitive expedition against, for instance, the King of Benin and has lowered its whole tone.

Mr. Pirie.

I gladly join in praise of the manner in which the expedition was carried on as regards our loss being at a minimum; but the blunders with regard to our own wounded at Atbara and Omdurman, and the hospitals at Alexandria, should not be glossed over, and it would be better if the chiefs of the Army showed a greater readiness to censure when fault has to be found on big issues. This debate has divided itself into two main questions, the treatment of the wounded dervishes and the disentombment of the Mahdi's remains. I would not be doing my duty, and it is a duty which I do gladly, if I did not state that I differ from the views of my hon. friends with reference to the treatment of the wounded dervishes. I think the House ought to recognise that war cannot be waged with white gloves, and, with some slight experience of Soudanese fighting, I say that any British general would have been wrong to have risked the life of one of his soldiers even if it were necessary to clear the ground of the wounded enemy; and I say, as this question is attracting attention, that it is the history of these Soudanese fights that before many hours the ground occupied by the Soudanese is taken possession of by the British, as a rule very early in the day. The British have to advance, and if they are exposed to, say, a dropping fire from the Soudanese wounded, the British general is entitled to clear the ground, even if he has to sacrifice the enemy. If the people of this country are shocked, as they naturally must be, by such action in waging war against uncivilised savages, the better for the country that the necessary horrors of such wars should be realised, and I hope it will have that effect. It has also been said that we employed an unusually large number of Soudanese soldiers, and that therefore, perhaps, the horrors must have been greater than they otherwise would. With that I agree, and the lesson this outcry will teach will be that greater need of control must be exercised over the Soudanese troops; but on the whole question of the wounded I join with those who [are vindicating Lord Kitchener, where, however, no vindication ought to be required, as he did nothing that was not necessary. Now I come to his action with regard to the Mahdi's body. I must say I cannot defend that action in any way. The noble and gallant Member for York seems to think that it is a sufficient excuse that the Mahdi's reign was one of unexampled savagery and barbarity. If that is the case, I would ask hon. Members to remember the answer given by the Under-Secretary for Foreign Affairs last Friday as regards the number of foreigners who lived in Khartoum during the whole of the Mahdi's reign.

*MR. BRODRICK : The hon. Gentleman only asked me how many prisoners had been released.

*MR. PIRIE : But the admission was that upwards of 11,000 alien men and women lived in Khartoum during the whole of the Mahdi's reign, and the right hon. Gentleman differentiated between what he called first-class Government prisoners and another class employed in Government work. When we see Italians, Greeks, Syrians, and other foreigners living in Khartoum, I think it is an answer to the argument that the Mahdi's tomb had been destroyed because of the fanatical population. I look upon the defence of this action as an aggravation, and I think it would have been nobler and would have redounded more to the credit of. the Government and the nation if they acknowledged that a mistake had been made, and bravely faced the consequences. From another aspect I cannot see how we Liberals can support this vote. We are pledged to do away with the existing power of the House of Lords. In the opinion of my constituents the existence of the House of Peers is a direct obstacle to the freedom, prosperity and progress of this country, and I am in complete accord with that opinion myself. That being so, I fail to see how I can hold that opinion and at the same time support a grant which will subsidise and perpetuate a peerage. It would have been more logical to have obtained the grant before giving the peerage. I would remind the Committee of the great danger of this constant increase in rewards and honours of this sort, and I hope it will be remembered that this system must be checked. Let me read to the Committee an extract which ought to be taken to heart by both parties. In Condorcet's "Life of Turgot," a book described by John Stuart Mill as "one of the wisest and noblest of lives, delineated by one of the wisest and noblest of men," Condorcet writing of his friend says :

"Turgot never bestowed a patent, no medals or other minor orders by which the art of the charlatan seeks to reward vanity. His object was to encourage, not to corrupt, and he believed that in all his transactions it was the duty of a statesman to reform mankind and not to strengthen their failings, even though it might be possible to derive temporary advantage from their weaknesses."

It would also be useful to go back to the last occasion on which the House discussed a similar grant, and I will quote what the late Lord Randolph Churchill stated on the subject of the Sir Garnet Wolseley Annuity Bill in 1883. He said it was his intention to support the second reading of the Bill, because he understood the Leader of the Opposition expressed his intention of supporting the Prime Minister, but he was bound to say that if the Leader of the Opposition had seen his way to have voted against the Government he, and some members below the gangway, would be prepared to strengthen his hands. That is an opinion with which I entirely agree. I associate myself with my right hon. friend the Member for Montrose in opposing this Vote. I will put one question to the Committee. The whole nation admires the character and life of General Gordon, and all I ask is, Would Gordon have acted in the same way as Lord Kitchener with regard to the Mahdi's tomb ? There is only one answer—he would not.

*MR. VICARY GIBBS (Herts, St. Albans) : The hon. Member who has just sat down has stated that the campaign is regarded as one of vengeance, especially in connection with the death of Gordon. None of us can forget the circumstances under which General Gordon died, and, although that page cannot be blotted from our memories by the noble and distinguished conduct of Lord Kitchener, we are grateful to the man who has given us something to set in the balance. We have no feeling of satisfied vengeance, but we have a feeling of gratitude, and when hon. Gentlemen opposite speak so warmly about their sense of duty in opposing this Vote, I think we are entitled quite as fully to express our gratitude, and we believe, as the hon. Member believes, that in introducing the apparently irrelevant issue

of the House of Lords, he is doing his duty to his constituents, that we also are representing our constituents when we say that we give this Vote from our hearts, and with the greatest pleasure and most complete conviction that in doing so we are pleasing and satisfying those whom we represent. Various grounds have been attempted on which to oppose this Vote. The broad ground was that taken by the hon. Member for Northampton, who says we have not had value for our money. He will find very few to support him in that view. There will also, I conceive, be little sympathy in the country for the men who have greedily swept together every libel they could gather against their countrymen fighting their battles abroad. The hon. Member for Aberdeen went so far as to say that we had gone on and on in the prostitution of honour. I consider language of that kind monstrous when it is applied to the man to whom we are expressing our thanks to-day. But I must thank the hon. Member for disassociating himself from the charge with reference to the treatment of the wounded, and I am glad that a man who has held Her Majesty's commission has declined to join in it. I have no knowledge of military matters, but it only requires common sense to know that in the heat of battle you cannot control every single camp follower. No one supposes camp followers are the kind of people whom you would ask to stay a week with you in the country, and it is monstrous to attempt to take away the character of Lord Kitchener because camp followers may or may not have committed excesses on the field of battle, and from a man who considers this Vote a prostitution of honour we have the assurance that clearing the ground of the wounded, sooner than risk our own soldiers, is justifiable and proper, and conduct of which no general officer need be ashamed. I think it has been made perfectly clear to the people of this country that all proper humanity was shown and all proper care taken. Anyone who had listened to the speech of the hon. Member for the Leigh Division of Lancashire could not have failed to come to the conclusion that there had been wanton and cruel destruction of the wounded, and yet a few sentences later he tells us that 3,000 or 4,000 Dervishes were crawling about on the field. Why were they not murdered

Mr. Vicary Gibbs.

also? The second statement appears to be contrary to the first.

Mr. C. P. SCOTT: I only referred to that portion of the field over which the two native battalions passed. Of course, there were a number of wounded left in other parts of the field.

*Mr. VICARY GIBBS: I accept the hon. Member's explanation of what he said, but I will point out that from his own account this destruction of the wounded was only partial, and I fully believe it was only done where it was considered essential to the safety of our own soldiers, and only in isolated cases. I will turn for a moment to this question of the desecration of the Mahdi's tomb. Upon this point I cannot share the view of hon. Gentlemen opposite, because I think the life of one single child is worth a wilderness of dead ruffians. We have been told, on excellent authority, that it is in the interest of the safety and security of this country in the future that that tomb should have been desecrated, and for my part I am very much obliged to the man or the men who desecrated it. Hon. Members opposite talked as if it was an extraordinary thing to disentomb a body, but when the St. Pancras Railway Station was made thousands of tombs were desecrated, for the convenience of the living. If thousands of the tombs of respectable Englishmen in London are to be desecrated for the convenience of those now living, why should we object to desecrate one tomb in the Soudan, when it is done for the safety and security of the faithful servants of this Empire who are serving us abroad when it is a question in which their lives are involved? It seems perfectly ludicrous to draw a comparison between the safety and security of English soldiers, and the question of sentiment which is involved in the desecration of the Mahdi's tomb. The hon. Member for Northampton sought to draw an invidious contrast between Sir Garnet Wolseley's action at Coomassie and the action of Lord Kitchener in this case. He said that Sir Garnet Wolseley had declined to disturb the tombs of the ancient kings of Coomassie. But the hon. Member for Northampton must know perfectly well that there is absolutely no comparison to be made between the two cases. The desecration of the Mahdi's tomb was done not for the purpose of punishing anybody, not for the purpose of private vengeance or of public vengeance, but for the safety and security of that country which we are morally bound by the action we have taken·to do everything in our power to keep sound and secure. When we come to consider these facts I do think we may brush aside such a controversy as to whether the decomposed bones of the Mahdi ought to have been thrown into the river or buried somewhere else, or as to what has become of his head. Personally, I really think that I should be indifferent myself what happens to these bones after this human machine ceases to work. As I am indifferent as to what happens to these bones of mine, I am still more indifferent as to what happens to a bloody ruffian who is now fortunately dead.

SIR WILFRID LAWSON (Cumberland, Cockermouth): A great deal has been said this evening about the Mahdi's tomb, but I never expected to hear such a long defence in this House of body-snatching as I have heard to-night. If it was bad to cut off the Mahdi's head, surely it was a great deal worse to go into the Soudan and kill 10,000 people at the battle of Omdurman. It appears to me to be very horrible to invade a country like this and cut down these people without rhyme or reason, and it seems infinitely worse than cutting off the head of a man who has been dead for some years. But I am not going to attack Lord Kitchener, because he was only carrying out the orders of the nation. He was not to blame for all he did, whether bad or good, for the nation was responsible, and as a humble member of the nation I think I am entitled to give my opinion upon it. The whole point with regard to this question is—is it desirable, beneficial, and creditable that we should vote this large sum of public money for this purpose? As I said before, I do not think that Lord Kitchener is to blame for what he did. He effected the object he had in view. He lost very few men in capturing Khartoum, and he did it very cheaply. That seems to be the reason why credit has been bestowed upon him in all the speeches I have read—that is, how very cheaply he killed these men. He performed a feat which had never been done before in battle, for he killed more men

than had ever been killed before in the same time. Mr. Charles Williams, who is one of the oldest and best known war correspondents we have, gave a very vivid description of the slaughter, and the net total came out at 10,800 killed within four hours. It must be remembered that the battle did not last more than four hours, and there were several intervals. Nothing like this slaughter has ever been recorded before. I am at a loss to know what we are going to vote this money for. I am ready to admit that the proceedings in the Soudan gave immense delight to a very large number of British newspaper editors, poets, City aldermen, and distinguished statesmen, and these I admit form an influential section of the community. These proceedings gave immense delight to those people who considered that this battle was the finest thing that had been done for generations. Lord Rosebery has stated that this campaign was more far-reaching and beneficent in its results than any which history has recorded, and it has added lustre to the memorable name of British arms. What we did was to shoot down people at a long range to which they could not reply, and that is looked upon as one of the greatest achievements of British arms. If Lord Rosebery is right, then I feel a little nervous and anxious, because we are getting enormous armies and navies together, and they must be to fight somebody, and I wonder what will happen when we fight with somebody who can fight, and not those poor Dervishes. What will happen when we fight with the Russians, the Chinese, and the Japanese altogether? In my opinion Lord Kitchener has already been rewarded, for he has been called up to the House of Lords to sit there along with bishops and brewers, and that is a great honour. After all, in this matter Lord Kitchener only did his duty, and it was a duty for which he was engaged, and I do not see why we should give Lord Kitchener this money. I think it is a bad system, for it is only blood money. I believe there were some 10,000 people killed, and you are proposing to give him £30,000; therefore he gets £3 per head for every man killed. Why should this blood money be paid, and why should Lord Kitchener have this gift? Because a soldier has done his duty, why·should he be put upon this pedestal above·all other public servants? Why don't you, when a judge conducts a

N

case with great skill, ask for a Vote of money for him? If a bishop gives a brilliant charge to his clergy, why don't you ask for a Vote for the bishop? A Cabinet Minister works a Bill through this House the same as the President of the Local Government Board did the Vaccination Bill, but you do not give him anything. When a fireman goes to a great fire and performs some heroic deed, you do not vote him any money, although the deed he performs in my opinion is more glorious than the deeds of war. I should like to discuss for a moment whether this is such a magnificent victory as it is supposed to be. What is there glorious about it, and what were the reasons for undertaking this expedition? I hardly know the real reason, because I have heard so many. We were told at first that the Khalifa might come down upon Egypt. Lord Cromer said a few months before the expedition was undertaken that there never was a time when there was so little danger to the people of Egypt. Of course, if ever you want to persuade people to vote money you can do it by putting in a word or two about slavery. But why don't you stop slavery at Zanzibar? The next reason given was, to stop the cruelty of the Khalifa, and that sounds a grand thing. If you are going to stop cruelty, why didn't you stop the cruelty of the Sultan? I am trying to find out why this money is to be voted, and what is the glory and the honour of this victory. If it was to put down cruelty committed by the Khalifa, was it not more cruel still to shoot them down and leave them to die in misery on the desert? We have heard something to-night about avenging Gordon's death, and Lord Rosebery said that by our victory we had paid off a debt which for thirteen years had been near the heart and conscience of every Englishman. The Chaplain at Windsor once stated that for every drop of English blood that had been shed at Khartoum rivers of blood of those who slew Gordon would flow. I would rather be a heathen than a Christian like that. I think that from that point of view this expedition has not been satisfactory, for what is it we have conquered? Lord Cromer says in his report that the Soudan is a great howling desert. What trade are we going to get out of this place? I have been driven to the conclusion that the reason for undertaking

Sir Wilfrid Lawson.

this campaign at all was that we were ashamed of the great scandal of our remaining in Egypt and of breaking our pledges to other European Powers. We wanted some excuse for staying a little longer, and so we invaded the country of the Khalifa, and we said that now that Egypt had got the Soudan back again we would remain there to protect the two countries. To carry out this policy we invaded the Soudan and slaughtered and mutilated some 30,000 people. We have had numerous banquets where statesmen have poured out streams of maudlin bunkum in honour of this policy, for which we are called upon to grant this Vote. I confess that I do not think there is anything noble at all about our proceedings in the Soudan, for they are about as ignoble as they can possibly be, for this kind of Imperialism is nothing more than organised selfishness. I read the other day some lines which are applicable to the Jingoes. They are:

> Of all the human family
> I love myself the best;
> Kind Providence take care of me,
> And Sambo take the rest.

This is not the opinion of the Little Englander. I say that this policy is nothing more than sordid selfishness, and it will end in the degradation and ultimate destruction of all the nations which yield to it. It is because it is proposed to-night to endorse this kind of Imperialism that I shall give this Vote my most strenuous opposition.

Sir A. ACLAND-HOOD (Somerset, Wellington): I shall neither follow the hon. Gentleman who has just sat down in his endeavour to find salvation in the Mahdi's tomb, nor shall I attempt to deal with his criticisms of Lord Rosebery. One of the charges against Lord Kitchener is that he has polluted the pure waters of the Nile by throwing in it the body of the Mahdi, which may probably have given that river its peculiar brown tinge. I only wish to say a few words to-night in defence of that Service to which I am proud to belong, and in defence of my own comrades who served in that campaign. There are two charges against Lord Kitchener. The first is that of the desecration of the Mahdi's tomb and the throwing of the Mahdi's body into the Nile. The second charge is the treatment of the wounded after the battle of Omdurman. As regards the first charge, the hon. Member for Northampton gave the Committee an illustration of Lord Wolseley's behaviour at Coomassie, where he told us that in that case the general in command did not allow the tomb of the kings to be disturbed. I might perhaps remind the hon. Gentleman that the result of that was that we had to have another expedition. But, after all, the whole of this matter is one of common sense. I would ask the right hon. Gentleman the Member for Montrose to look at this matter from a common-sense point of view, and I would ask him if he would rather have his throat cut or allow these bones to be thrown in the Nile ? As regards the charge brought against British soldiers of killing the wounded Dervishes on the battlefield, I have seen wounded Soudanese, after a brother officer has given them water, turn round and shoot the man who gave them that water. I would ask the hon. Member for the Leigh Division, and others who have spoken on behalf of the wounded Dervishes, what they would do if, after they had taken water to these Dervishes on the field of battle, they turned round and shot at them. I have seen that myself, and if some hon. Members opposite would go and see things for themselves on the field of battle I am sure they would hold a different opinion. When we consider that the Government of which the right hon. Gentleman the Member for West Monmouth was a Member are responsible for the whole of this war, they must take the blame for all these atrocities which have happened in the Soudan, for the blame does not rest upon Lord Kitchener, or the present Government, but it rests upon the party opposite and their friend the Mahdi.

Mr. DILLON: I rejoice to say that upon a question of this kind the voice of Ireland will be given by a decisive majority against this Vote. The voice of the majority of the Irish Members has always been on the side of justice and right, and had it not been for the Irish vote you would have had very few great reforms in this century. There is one point on which I most heartily agree with the First Lord of the Treasury. In his opening remarks, in eloquent and powerful language, he pointed out to the Committee that in discussing this question we were not entitled to consider the merits of the policy on which this expedition was based. He pointed out—I think with absolute truth—that Lord Kitchener and the officers

and men who served under him were not entitled to ask whether the policy was a justifiable one or not. They were soldiers, and they were bound to obey. If I were an English Member, and if it were simply a question of the skill and gallantry with which this expedition was carried out—no matter how much I condemned it—I should vote in support of this Vote. When I listened to the eloquent language used by the First Lord of the Treasury, when he drew a picture of the sad condition of this country, my memory was carried back to a day of great excitement in this land, when the Commander-in-Chief stated that if he was ordered by the Government and the Queen to keep the peace against the Loyalists of Ireland, he would rather break his sword than obey those orders. I only hope that the First Lord of the Treasury will apply the same principles, without fear and favour, to Ireland as he is now applying to the Soudan. If it were only a question of the merits of the policy, I would vote in favour of this grant; but there is something to be said with regard to the conduct of Lord Kitchener after the battle. Even in the ranks of hon. Members who sit behind the Government there has been manifested a wide divergence of opinion on this question, and the hon. and gallant Member for York declared that every man in England—whether civil or military—was disgusted and horrified at the method by which the Mahdi's tomb was desecrated. He stated that he had had no communication with Lord Kitchener, but he declared it to be his conviction that Lord Kitchener, while he gave the order for the removal of the Mahdi's body and the destruction of the tomb, was in no other way responsible for the method by which the remains of the Mahdi were outraged, and he expressed the greatest possible regret for the circumstances which attended that act ; and that regret is evidently shared by a considerable number of hon. Members who sit on the Government benches. But in the second speech of the First Lord of the Treasury there was not a single word of regret. On the contrary, he declared that he had no regret to express ; and he seemed to think that everything that was done in connection with the outrage upon the remains of the Mahdi, the desecration of his tomb, and the disposal of his remains was not only necessary, but was also decently and properly done. In that respect the right hon. Gentleman differs *toto cœlo* from the Member for York and the hon. Member for the Leigh Division, who expressed their compassion for those who would be called upon to defend this act in the House. We did not want to wait long for another instance of considerable divergence of opinion on this occasion, because one hon. Member got up and expressed his gratitude to Lord Kitchener for having given this country some revenge for the death of Gordon ; and it is idle after that for the First Lord of the Treasury and the noble Lord the Member for York to deny that there are numbers of men on the opposite benches who looked with pleasure on the desecration of the Mahdi's tomb because they looked upon it as a piece of vengeance for the death of Gordon,and that is a common-place in this country and this House. I am pretty familiar with the writings and the life of Gordon, a man for whom I always had the greatest respect, and it is enough to make him turn in his grave at the insult levelled at him, whose whole life was founded on the teachings of the Founder of his religion. I hold that the right hon. Gentleman the Member for Montrose is discharging a public duty in protesting against the proceedings of which complaint is made. I have no doubt that the right hon. Gentleman will be defeated, and that the money will be voted. Yes, but the value of the protest will not pass away, and many a man who votes for this grant will, as an Englishman, feel humiliated at the acts which have been done in the name of this country. At all events, I am glad to know that the name of Ireland will be free from any complicity in this business. It seems to me there has been great cruelty and oppression, and I speak on this matter with some knowledge. We, having suffered from the same evil, have learned to sympathise with the oppressed, and we are not ashamed to come here and say so. The treatment of the Mahdi's tomb has been so fully treated that I do not propose to travel over the ground again, but I do ask the Committee to consider one aspect of this question, and that is this— the chief and only defence which has been offered to-night for the destruction of the Mahdi's tomb and the throwing of the remains into the Nile with ignominy is that the Mahdi was a prophet in the eyes of his people, and that his tomb might be the centre of reverence and superstition. If that argument were logically followed it would lead to a very

Mr. *Dillon.*

strange conclusion. If we are ever to accept the principle, which I thought was consigned to the evil past, that because we differ from people and regard their convictions and faiths and beliefs as superstitious, we are entitled to outrage and degrade the tombs of the men whose memories the people venerate, we will travel upon a road which promises to lead to strange conclusions indeed. You are going to arrogate to yourselves the right to destroy and desecrate all tombs in India which may incite fanaticism. India is not without its fanaticism. You had fanatical risings there a few years ago. Do you believe that the Indian saints are any better than the Mahdi ? If you carry this policy to extremities we may be led into further difficulties. A letter written to *The Times* by the Marquis of Northampton points out that because the Mahdi was regarded by the orthodox Mussulmans as a heretic, then it was a necessity, for which we must take the responsibility, that his tomb should be destroyed in order to put a stop to the fanaticism of the Soudanese. It appears to me from all the arguments that have been urged that you are attempting to establish the position that in dealing with savage peoples you are justified in having recourse to any measures which your military commanders recommend as necessary. The hon. Member for Leamington said the other day that we ought to have recourse to all methods of civilised warfare in these matters ; if we have not, we shall be dragged by irresistible compulsion to this position, that we are to crush and humiliate and break the spirit of the people with whom we have to deal. That is the spirit which is given expression to to-night. I do not forget that we too have our sacred places, to which we at times make pilgrimages. What would be said for the Mahometans if they desecrated and destroyed those holy places ? In this respect the Mahometans put us to shame, for, although they do not believe in the teachings of the Founder of Christianity, because He is venerated by a great section of the human race they also venerate Him. I also believe—I am convinced— that on the field of Omdurman there was an unnecessary, brutal, and wholesale slaughter of the wounded, and I was struck by the contradiction of Lord Kitchener to the charge brought forward. The contradiction given by Lord Kitchener was no contradiction at all, and there is no doubt that the troops under his command, whether British, Egyptian, or Soudanese, had wantonly killed many wounded. He said he hardly thought it likely that the men who brought the charges would find an exponent of their views in Parliament ; but if they did he categorically denied that the troops under his command did any such thing. The contradiction was too much, because it was idle to deny that the troops did kill the wounded. It is a well-known fact that in all these Soudanese battles it has been the habit to kill the wounded. There was no more humane man than Gordon himself ever sent out by the people of this country, and I have read in two works that he was always of opinion that this evil might be remedied. He said, "If you go to help them, these people will try and kill your men. " (Cheers from the Government benches.) Yes, that is so ; what is the use of denying it ? Of course, they have all been killed, you cannot have it both ways. My point is, What is the use of sending home a telegram saying that the wounded have not been killed when, as a matter of fact, they all have been killed? You may talk as you please about going into countries like the Soudan under the idea of bringing civilisation to them. You do not do so. The Leader of the Opposition gave it as his opinion that nothing was gained by the unnecessary horrors of these expeditions and these battles. You have been at it now 25 years, and you have not brought civilisation yet. You have turned a comparatively peaceful country into a desert waste. At all events, whatever its condition at one time, there has been ten times the loss of life, misery, degradation, and horror of every kind, since Europeans set their feet in that country under the prostituted name of Christianity, carrying in their train murder, rapine, whisky, disease, and—the Bible. That is the civilisation you have given them. I must do this justice, however, to the men responsible for the present Government. Certainly, we do not hear from them that they are carrying on these wars for the purpose of spreading Christianity. They are carrying them on for the extension of trade, and it is mockery and hypocrisy to say that the object of these wars is the good of these unhappy races and the spread of Christianity, for every act done has been in direct opposition to the principles enunciated by the Founder of that religion.

COLONEL SAUNDERSON (Armagh, N). As the hon. Member for East Mayo has spoken on behalf of one section of the Irish, I may be allowed to say a word on behalf of the other Irish.

MR. SWIFT MacNEILL : The Anglo-Irish.

COLONEL SAUNDERSON : Which I think in the division lobby will show a majority. The hon. Member for East Mayo has made a speech strongly deprecative of the action of Great Britain in Egypt.

MR. DILLON : The Soudan I said.

COLONEL SAUNDERSON: The hon. Gentleman has made very many speeches in which he has for many years depreciated the action of Great Britain in all parts of the world, especially in Ireland. The two heroes the hon. Gentleman and his friends appeared to admire most in recent years are the Mahdi and Wolf Tone, the reason being that the Mahdi had fought against Great Britain and Wolf Tone hated Great Britain, and was also usually drunk. The hon. Gentleman was tremendously shocked at the unburying of the Mahdi's remains. What is there horrible in that ? I remember not so very long ago that a section of the Irish people who sympathised with the hon. Gentleman desired to show their hatred for a gentleman who was the head of the police in Ireland, and they took up his wife's remains and threw them into a river. My memory may fail me, but I do not remember that the hon. Member then rose in his place and called down the denunciations of all Christian men on this abominable act. The Christianity of the hon. Member seems to be somewhat sporadic in its character. To my mind, the shooting of a so-called landgrabber, the houghing of a cow, or injuring a dumb beast, is fifty times worse than the digging up of the remains of a dead fanatic. I pass from the remarks of the hon. Member, and desire to say a word or two on the more serious aspect of the case as put forward by the right hon. Gentleman the Member for Montrose. I listened to his speech to-night, and as I listened compared it with the speech he delivered on the 25th of May, which to my mind explained the object of the speech of to-night. In the speech of the 25th of May the right hon. Gentleman brought a bill of indictment against the Government and summoned them before the bar of civilised opinion. In that speech, in order that we might judge the Vote we are discussing to-night, he read numerous letters giving an account of all the abominable cruelty and tyranny we practised. If it is true, as has been alleged, that the British are bloodthirsty and revengeful and deal cruelly with these native races, then one would expect them to be universally hated by the native races.

Mr. SWIFT MacNEILL: So you are.

Colonel SAUNDERSON: I venture to say that the hon. Member who makes the statement has never been in Africa.

Colonel Saunderson.

Mr. SWIFT MacNEILL: I have been in Africa.

Colonel SAUNDERSON: Then I am sorry the hon. Member did not remain there. I have been all over these countries, and I ask anyone who has ever visited this country to look at the relations which exist in South Africa between the natives and the British. The whole of the black races are on the British side and they hate the Boers. The right hon. Gentleman the Member for Montrose seemed to say that he should deal all round with the black races as he should deal with the white. I at once deny that. The ordinary black you meet with in Africa is a man with the intelligence of a child and the passions of a man. In dealing with a child you restrain him until his intellect has grown sufficiently to guide him. If he were to try that on the Upper Congo, what would he find? The first thing the natives would do would be to fatten him and then eat him. Then as to Egypt, see what the tyrannical British have done there. We have been masters of the Soudan for some time, and we intend to remain so; we are in Egypt, and intend to remain there; and what have we done? We have raised up out of the wretched people an army to which it is a credit to belong, soldiers worthy to stand by our own men. What about the Soudanese? We have only to think of them at Omdurman under British officers. So long as a nation can always produce the right man at the right time, that nation is on the rising grade. We, thank God, are on the rising grade. We are told that the whole country was shocked at this terrible act of desecration. I can only speak for myself, and I was not in the least shocked at the desecration of the tomb of the Mahdi. On the contrary, I thought it one of the wisest acts that ever was done. I do not say it was done in the right way. I think it ought to have been carried out with more ceremony, not out of respect for the memory of the Mahdi, whose acts were not calculated to inspire affection—who as a bloodthirsty tyrant has left a record which will never be forgotten—but because I think it would have been a wise thing to attract the universal attention of the inhabitants of the Soudan, in the neighbourhood of Omdurman, to the fact that we had conquered the Mahdi's country, and had taken the bones of the false prophet out of their tomb and scattered them to the winds. The right honourable Gentleman the Member for Montrose Burgh drew a terrible picture of our men taking up the corpse of the Mahdi and cracking off his head. This has had a terrible effect on the Liberal and Radical Federation. (Laughter, and an honourable Member: "Where's the joke?") I should look upon it as a joke if the hon. Member's head was cut off. I certainly think it would have been better, for the sake of the peace of the Soudan, if as much notoriety as possible could have been given to what I look upon as having been a very wise proceeding. It was our duty, having taken the country, to ensure its peace. Anybody who knows anything about the Mahometan world is aware that if we had allowed a sort of Mecca to grow up about Omdurman we should have seen a recrudescence of disturbance which would inevitably have led to a vast expenditure of life and money. I admit that the taking up of a dead man's bones and the scattering of them was a very unfortunate necessity—a thing one would not choose to do; and, from what I know of Lord Kitchener, it was a thing which, if he had not believed it to be an imperative necessity, he would not have done. He realised, knowing the country as he did, and knowing the nature and character of the Mahometans, that to leave there a centre of fanaticism for a fanatical population to dwell upon would have been an act of insanity. I not only think it was a wise thing to dig up the remains of the Mahdi, but I hope the tomb itself will be rased to the ground, and nothing of it left. The idea that Lord Kitchener, who knocked the Mahdi's army into a cocked hat, was animated by a spirit of revenge, is preposterous. Can anybody be foolish enough to believe that he would have revenged himself on the dead bones of a man he had never seen? The idea of revenge could never have entered into the head of Lord Kitchener or any other man with a grain of sense. It was done for the purpose of establishing peace in the Soudan, and, so far as it was done for that object, it merits the approval of this country; and I hope the maudlin sentimentality that has been showered over this act will be dissipated to the winds by the common-sense of the British people. We must remember the task we are performing in Africa. We are not there simply founding colonies, we are creating an Empire, and in doing that I believe we are fulfilling a noble destiny. We are bringing into the Dark Continent civilisation; we shall also bring peace and prosperity, and the nations of the world will do well to learn that it is a dangerous and sometimes a fatal thing to get in the way of a nation that is fulfilling its destiny.

Mr. R. WALLACE (Edinburgh, E.): The case against the argument of my right hon. friend has been a restatement of the tyrant's plea of necessity. But, however calculated to be useful as a matter of order Lord Kitchener's expedient might have been, it was an expedient which ought never to have been put in force. There are times when you must draw a line, and say that whatever may be gained, or whatever may be lost, across that line we must not go. I should like to ask whether the country can afford to give this grant of money. I do not think we can. I listened most carefully to the discussions on the Finance Bill, and it seemed to me that we are not able to pay our way as we go along, and that we are compelled to have recourse to the proverbial old stocking in which we have been making provision for a rainy day. If we pass this Vote we shall have to make another excursion to the garret in search of the old stocking, and take out of it a much larger sum than appears on the face of this Vote. If you are going to pay Lord Kitchener for taking Omdurman, you will have to give the army something as well, because the army, even from Lord Kitchener's own testimony, did half the work. If it had not been for the bravery of the officers and soldiers there would not have been nearly so many Dervishes killed. Dervishes, fighting in defence of their faith and their fatherland, are, I understand, tolerably formidable enemies, but our brave soldiers did not mind that. They knew that if they once got behind their killing machinery they could mow down these ridiculous enthusiasts like ninepins, at 900 and even 1,000 yards distance; and they did it bravely and splendidly. As has been rightly said, they killed more men per minute than have been killed in any previous war. In short, "it was a glorious victory," and are these men to get nothing? When the working classes, out of whose pockets a very large portion of this grant must come, consider this Vote, they will not like the differential treatment of the General and the men. "This is just the old story over again," they will say— "the aristocratic head official gets every-

Mr. R. Wallace.

thing, while the poor man who risks his life and does the work gets nothing." *——

MR. ARNOLD-FORSTER: I should like to say just a few words before this debate concludes, and to briefly refer to the speech of the right honourable Gentleman the Member for Montrose. I regret that the right honourable Gentleman should have thought it his duty to make the speech which he has made. The harm that is done by speeches of that kind is difficult to estimate; and it is the more dangerous because the attack is by inuendo and not direct. The essence of the charge is now withdrawn, and with regard to the question of policy the right honourable Gentleman says that Lord Cromer's opinion is not of the first importance. Why? Because he has not been in the Soudan. But is not the opinion of Lord Cromer as valuable, if not more valuable, than that of any other man in Egypt or out of it? The right honourable Gentleman did not cite the opinion of Lord Kitchener himself, and I can hardly imagine, next to that of Lord Cromer, an opinion more valuable than Lord Kitchener's. As to the question of policy, that should not have been dealt with in the language generally associated with great political crimes. We are conscious

---

*At this point the hon. Member was apparently seized with momentary faintness. "His voice faltered, he could not read his notes or find his eye-glass, nor could he drink, or even hold in his hands the glass of water that was passed to him from the front Opposition bench. He sat down abruptly, and, after a painful pause, Mr. Arnold-Forster continued the debate."—(*The Times*). Mr. Wallace was removed to Westminster Hospital, where he expired at two o'clock on the morning of the 6th June—within three hours of his rising to address the House. The cause of death is stated to have been cerebral congestion.

of the danger to this country of allowing our people to get out of hand. We have known it for centuries, and have for centuries been providing every safeguard against the evil it might do; and no nation in the world, I assert, has succeeded so well or so far in this respect as we have. It is hard, when we know what our people are doing and refraining from doing, that their efforts should be minimised by such an unfortunate speech as that of the right honourable Gentleman opposite.

Mr. SWIFT MacNEILL: I should have liked very much to reply to the speech of the Member for North Armagh, but I must pay some regard to the lateness of the hour and the patience of honourable Members. With regard to the desecration of the Mahdi's body, I submit that we have no right to do what is morally wrong, even if it be politically right. England is supposed to be the elevator of nations, but in her actions towards other nations she takes a lower tone, and in this matter it is proposed to sanction a foul and disgusting outrage. It grieves me to think I am in opposition to Lord Rosebery in this matter. Lord Rosebery thinks we ought to give Lord Kitchener £30,000 on becoming a peer. I always thought it was those who received the peerages who paid. The proposed grant—£30,000—was exactly the sum of Mr. Hooley's cheque which he thought would work miracles and make him one of the gentlemen of England—a member of the Carlton Club. I am not going through the various reasons which have been given in justification of this grant. I can only say that the desecration of the Mahdi's body is a denial by a professedly Christian nation of the immortality of the soul. It is very much to be re-

VOL. LXXII.   [Fourth Series.]

gretted that Lord Kitchener did not recollect and follow the words and example of Charles V., who, when urged by Catholic advisers to wreck vengeance on the tomb of Luther, replied, " I war not with the dead, but with the living."

Mr. SYDNEY GEDGE (Walsall): I desire to call the attention of the Committee and the Government to the action of Lord Kitchener with regard to Christian missions. He desires the best interests of the Soudanese, and has raised £100,000 to found an Educational College in memory of General Gordon. He has, however, excluded from the subjects taught that which was the root of Gordon's strength, the mainspring of his actions, and what he most of all desired to give to the nations --namely, the Christian religion. For the establishment of a mission the funds have been subscribed and the men are ready to go, but Lord Kitchener has forbidden them to enter Khartoum, through fear, it is believed, of complications with the French. I expect that that danger has probably by this time passed away. It has been stated in the newspapers that Cardinal Vaughan is organising a Roman Mission which is to take the place of the Italian priests who had been expelled, and it seems to be time to remove the embargo on Protestant missions, and not to follow the mistaken, cowardly policy of the East India Company of excluding missions for many years, only to find that in the Mutiny the Christian converts saved India for England. I hope that the attention of the Government will be given to the subject.

Question put.

The Committee divided :—Ayes, 393 ; Noes, 51. (Division List No. 170.)

O

AYES.

Acland-Hood, Capt. Sir A. F.
Aird, John
Allan, William (Gateshead)
Allen, W. (Newc. under Lyme)
Allhusen. A. Henry Eden
Allsopp, Hon. George
Anson, Sir William Reynell
Arnold, Alfred
Arnold-Forster, Hugh O.
Arrol, Sir William
Ashton, Thomas Gair
Asquith, Rt. Hon. H. Henry
Atkinson, Rt. Hon. John
Austin, Sir John (Yorkshire)
Bagot, Capt. J. FitzRoy
Bailey, James (Walworth)
Baird, John G. Alexander
Balcarres, Lord
Baldwin, Alfred
Balfour, Rt Hn A J (M'nch'r)
Balfour, Rt. Hn. G. W (Leeds)
Banbury, Frederick George
Barnes, Frederic Gorell
Barry, RtHnAHSmith-(Hunts
Bartley, George, C. T.
Barton, Dunbar Plunket
Bathurst, Hon Allen Benjamin
Beach, RtHn Sir M. H.(Bristol)
Beach, W W Branston (Hants)
Beaumont, Wentworth C. B.
Beckett, Ernest William
Begg, Ferdinand Faithfull
Bentinck, Lord Henry C.
Beresford. Lord Charles
Bethell, Commander
Bhownaggree, Sir M. M.
Biddulph, Michael
Bigwood, James
Bill, Charles
Billson, Alfred
Birrell, Augustine
Blakiston-Houston, John
Blundell, Colonel Henry
Bond, Edward
Bonsor, Henry Cosmo Orme
Boulnois, Edmund
Bowles,Capt H.F. (Middlesex)
Brassey, Albert
Brodrick, Rt. Hon. St. John
Brookfield, A. Montagu
Brown, Alexander H.
Brunner, Sir John Tomlinson
Bryce, Rt. Hn. James
Buchanan, Thomas Ryburn
Bullard, Sir Harry
Burdett-Coutts, W.
Butcher, John George
Buxton, Sydney Charles
Caldwell, James
Campbell, J. H. M. (Dublin)
Campbell-Bannerman, Sir H.
Carlile, William Walter
Causton, Richard Knight
Cavendish, R. F. (N. Lancs.)
Cavendish, V.C.W.(Derbysh.)
Cayzer, Sir Charles William
Cecil, Evelyn (Hertford, East)
Cecil, Lord Hugh (Greenwich)

Chaloner, Captain R. G. W.
Chamberlain, Rt. Hn.J(Birm)
Chamberlain, J. A. (Worc'r)
Chaplin. Rt. Hon. Henry
Charrington, Spencer
Chelsea, Viscount
Clare, Octavius Leigh
Clarke, Sir E. (Plymouth)
Clough, Walter Owen
Cochrane, Hon. T. H. A. E.
Coddington, Sir William
Coghill, Douglas Harry
Collings, Rt. Hon. Jesse
Colston, C. E.. H. Athole
Compton, Lord Alwyne
Cook, F. L. (Lambeth)
Cooke, C. W. R. (Hereford)
Corbett, A. C. (Glasgow)
Cornwallis, F. Stanley W.
Cotton-Jodrell.-Col. E. T. D.
Cox, Irwin E. B. (Harrow)
Cripps, Charles Alfred
Crombie, John William
Cubitt, Hon. Henry
Curzon, Viscount
Dalbiac, Colonel Philip Hugh
Dalkeith, Earl of
Dalrymple, Sir Charles
Davenport, W. Bromley-
Davies, Sir H. D. (Chatham)
Davies, M.Vaughan-(Cardigan
Denny, Colonel
Dickson-Poynder, Sir John P.
Digby, John K. D. Wingfield-
Disraeli, Coningsby Ralph
Dixon-HartlandSirFredDixon
Dorington, Sir John Edward
Douglas, Rt. Hon. A. Akers-
Douglas, Charles M. (Lanark)
Douglas-Pennant, Hon. E. S.
Doxford, William Theodore
Drage, Geoffrey
Duckworth, James
Duncombe, Hon. Hubert V.
Dunn, Sir William
Dyke, Rt. HonSirWilliamHart
Egerton, Hon. A. de Tatton
Elliot, Hon. A. Ralph Douglas
Engledew, Charles John
Evans, Saml. T. (Glamorgan)
Evans,SirFrancisH(South'ton)
Evershed, Sydney
Fardell, Sir T. George
Farquharson, Dr. Robert
Fellowes, Hon.AilwynEdward
Ferguson, R. C.Munroe(Leith)
Fergusson,RtHn.SirJ(Mane'r)
Field, Admiral (Eastbourne)
Finch, George H.
Finlay, Sir Robert Bannatyne
Firbank. Joseph Thomas
Fisher, William Hayes
Fison, Frederick William
FitzGerald,SirRobertPenrose-
Fitzmaurice, Lord Edmond
Fitz Wygram, General Sir F.
Flannery, Sir Fortescue

Fletcher, Sir Henry
Flower, Ernest
Folkestone, Viscount
Forster, Henry William
Foster, Colonel (Lancaster)
Foster, Harry S. (Suffolk)
Fowler, Rt. Hon. Sir Henry
Fry, Lewis
Galloway, William Johnson
Garfit, William
Gedge, Sydney
Gibbs,Hn.AG H(CityofLond.)
Gibbs,Hon.Vicary(St.Albans)
Giles, Charles Tyrrell
Gilliat, John Saunders
Godson,SirAugustusFrederick
Gold, Charles
Goldsworthy, Major-General
Gordon, Hon. John Edward
Gorst,Rt. Hon. Sir John Eldon
Goschen,Rt HnGJ(S.George's)
Goschen, George J. (Sussex)
Goulding, Edward Alfred
Graham, Henry Robert
Grey, Ernest (West Ham)
Green, Walford D. (Wednes.)
Greene,Henry D. (Shrewsb'y.)
Gretton, John
Greville, Hon. Ronald
Grey, Sir Edward (Berwick)
Griffith, Ellis J.
Hall, Rt.Hon.Sir Charles
Halsey, Thomas Frederick
Hamilton, Rt.Hon. Lord Geo.
Hanbury,Rt. Hon. RobertWm.
Hanson, Sir Reginald
Hardy, Laurence
Hare, Thomas Leigh
Harwood, George
Hatch, Ernest Frederick Geo.
Heath, James
Heaton, John Henniker
Hedderwick, Thomas C. H.
Helder, Augustus
Henderson, Alexander
Hermon-Hodge,RobertTrotter
Hickman, Sir Alfred
Hill, A. (Down, West)
Hill, Sir E. S. (Bristol)
Hoare, E. B. (Hampstead)
Hobhouse, Henry
Holland, Hon Lionel R. (Bow)
Holland, W. H. (York W.R.)
Hornby, Sir William Henry
Horniman, Frederick John
Houldsworth, Sir W. Henry
Houston, R. P.
Howard, Joseph
Howorth, Sir Henry Hoyle
Hozier, Hon. J. H. Cecil
Hubbard, Hon. Evelyn
Hutchinson, Capt. G. W. G.-
Hutton, John (Yorks. N.R)
Jackson, Rt.Hn. Wm. Lawies
Jacoby, James Alfred
Jebb, Richard Claverhouse
Jenkins, Sir John Jones
Jessel, Capt. Herbert Merton

Johnson-Ferguson,JabezEdw.
Johnstone, Heywood (Sussex)
Jolliffe, Hon. H. George
Jones,DavidBrynmor(Swans'a

Kearley, Hudson E.
Kemp, George
Kennaway, Rt. Hn. Sir J. H.
Kenyon, James
Keswick, William
Kimber, Henry
Kinloch, Sir J. George Smyth
Kitson, Sir James
Knowles, Lees

Lambert, George
Laurie, Lieut.-General
Lawrence, Sir E. D. (Corn.)
Lawrence, Wm. F. (Liverpool)
Lawson, John Grant (Yorks.)
Lecky,RtHonWilliamEdw.H.
Lees, Sir Elliott (Birkenhead)
Leese,SirJosephF.(Accrington
Leighton, Stanley
Llewellyn, Evan H.(Somerset)
Llewelyn,SirDillwyn(Swansea
Long,Col.CharlesW.(Evesham
Long,Rt. HnWalter (Liverpool
Lopes, Henry Yarde Buller
Lorne, Marquis of
Lowe, Francis William
Lowles, John
Lowther, RtHonJames (Kent)
Loyd, Archie Kirkman
Lubbock,Rt. Hon. Sir John
Lucas-Shadwell, William
Lyell, Sir Leonard
Lyttelton, Hon. Alfred

Macartney, W. G. Ellison
Macdona,John Cumming
MacIver, David (Liverpool)
Maclean, James Mackenzie
Maclure, Sir John William
M'Arthur, Charles (Liverpool)
M'Arthur, William (Cornwall)
M'Calmont, H. L. B. (Cambs.)
M'Calmont, Col. J. (Antri,mE
M'Iver, Sir Lewis (Edinb'h, W
M'Kenna, Reginald
M'Killop, James
M'Laren, Charles Benjamin
Malcolm, Ian
Manners, Lord Edward Wm.J.
Maple, Sir John Blundell
Marks, Henry Hananel
Martin, Richard Biddulph
Maxwell,Rt.Hon.SirHerbertE
Melville, Beresford Valentine
Meysey-Thompson, Sir H. M.
Middlemore, John T.
Milbank, Sir P. C. John
Mildmay, Francis Bingham
Milner, Sir Frederick George
Milward, Colonel Victor
Montagu, Hon. J. S. (Hants.)
Moon, Edward Robert Pacy
More, R. Jasper (Shropshire)
Morgan, Hn. F. (Monm'thsh.)
Morgan, W. P. (Merthyr)
Morley, C. (Breconshire)
Morrison, Walter
Morton, A. H. A. (Deptford)
Morton, E. J. C. (Devonport)
Moulton, John Fletcher
Muntz, Philip A.

Murray, Rt. Hn. A. G. (Bute)
Murray, C. J. (Coventry)
Myers, William Henry

Newark, Viscount
Newdigate, Francis A.
Nicol, Donald Ninan
Northcote, Hon. Sir H. S.
Nussey, Thomas Willans

Oldroyd, Mark
O'Neill, Hon. Robert Torrens
Orr-Ewing, Charles Lindsay

Palmer,Sir CharlesM(Durham
Palmer, George Wm. (Reading
Parkes, Ebenezer
Paulton, James Mellor
Pearson, Sir Weetman D.
Pease, Alfred E. (Cleveland)
Pease,Herbert Pike(Darling'n
Pease, Joseph A. (Northumb.)
Pender, Sir James
Penn, John
Perks, Robert William
Phillpotts, Captain Arthur
Pierpoint, Robert
Platt-Higgins, Frederick
Pollock, Harry Frederick
Powell, Sir Francis Sharp
Pretyman, Ernest George
Priestley,Sir W.Overend(Edin
Pryce-Jones, Lt.-Col. Edward
Purvis, Robert

Quilter, Sir Cuthbert

Rankin, Sir James
Rasch, Major Frederic Carne
Reid, Sir Robert Threshie
Richardson, Sir T. (Hartlep'l)
Rickett, J. Compton
Ridley, Rt. Hon. Sir M. W.
Ritchie, Rt Hon. C. T.
Robertson, H. (Hackney)
Robson, William Snowdon
Rothschild, Hon. L. Walter
Round, James
Royds, Clement Molyneux
Russell, Gen. F S (Chelt'nhm)
Russell, T. W. (Tyrone)
Rutherford, John
Ryder, J. H. Dudley

Samuel, H. S. (Limehouse)
Sandys, Liet.-Col. T. Myles
Sassoon, Sir Edward Albert
Saunderson, Rt. Hn. Col.E.J.
Savory, Sir Joseph
Scoble, Sir Andrew Richard
Seely, Charles Hilton
Seton-Karr, Henry
Sharpe, William Edward T.
Shaw, Charles E. (Stafford)
Simeon, Sir Barrington
Sinclair, Capt. J. (Forf'rshire)
Skewes-Cox, Thomas
Soames, Arthur Wellesley
Stanley, Hon. A. (Ormskirk)
Stanley, E. J. (Somerset)
Stanley, H. M. (Lambeth)
Stanley, Lord (Lancashire)
Stevenson, Francis S.
Stewart, Sir M. J. M'T.
Stock, James Henry
Stone, Sir Benjamin

Strutt, Hon. Charles Hedley
Sturt, Hon. Humphry Napier

Talbot, Lord E. (Chichester)
Talbot,Rt.HnJG(Oxf'dUniv.)
Tennant, Harold John
Thomas,Abel (Carmarthen,E.)
Thomas,Alfred (Glamorgn,E.)
Thomas, D. Alfred (Merthyr)
Thorburn, Walter
Thornton, Percy M.
Tomlinson, Wm. Edw.Murray
Trevelyan, Charles Philips
Tritton, Charles Ernest

Valentia, Viscount
Verney, Hon.Richard Greville
Vincent, Col.Sir C.E. Howard

Wallace, Robert (Perth)
Walton, J. Lawson (Leeds, S.)
Wanklyn, James Leslie
Ward, Hn. Robert A. (Crewe)
Warner,Thomas CourtenayT.
Warr, Augustus Frederick
Webster, R. G. (St. Pancras)
Webster,SirR. E.(IsleofWight
Welby, Lieut.-Col. A.C.E.
Wentworth, Bruce C. Vernon-
Wharton,Rt. Hon. John Lloyd
Whiteley,H.(Ashton-under-L.
Whitmore, Charles Algernon
Williams, Colonel R. (Dorset)
Williams,JosephPowell-(Birm
Willox,Sir John Archibald
Wilson, Charles Henry (Hull)
Wilson,FrederickW.(Norfolk)
Wilson, John (Falkirk)
Wilson-Todd,Wm.H.(Yorks.)
Wodehouse,Rt.Hon.ER(Bath)
Wolff, Gustav Wilhelm
Woodhouse,SirJT(Huddersf'd
Wortley,Rt.Hon.C.B. Stuart-
Wylie, Alexander
Wyndham, George
Wyndham-Quin, Major W.H.
Wyvill, Marmaduke D'Arcy
Yerburgh, Robert Armstrong
Younger, William

TELLERS FOR THE   AYES—
Sir William Walr   and
Mr. Anstruther.   ond

NOES.

Allison, Robert Andrew
Ambrose, Robert
Atherley-Jones, L.
Austin, M. (Limerick, W.)

Bayley, Thomas (Derbyshire)
Bolton, Thomas Dolling
Broadhurst, Henry
Burt, Thomas
Cameron, Sir C. (Glasgow
Channing, Francis Allston
Crilly, Daniel
Curran, Thomas (Sligo, S.)

Davitt, Michael
Dilke, Rt. Hon. Sir Charles
Dillon, John
Donelan, Captain A.
Doogan, P. C.

Ellis, John Edward

Farrell, Thomas J. (Kerry, S.)
Fenwick, Charles

Labouchere, Henry
Lawson, Sir Wfd. (Cumb'land)
Lewis, John Herbert

MacAleese, Daniel
MacNeill, John Gordon Swift
M'Cartan, Michael
M'Dermott, Patrick
M'Ghee, Richard
Morley, Rt. Hn. J. (Montrose)

O'Brien, James F. X. (Cork)
O'Connor, J. (Wicklow, W.)
O'Connor, T. P. (Liverpool)
O'Malley, William

Pickard, Benjamin
Pickersgill, Edward Hare
Pirie, Duncan V.

Priestley, Briggs (Yorks.)

Richardson, J. (Durham, S.E.)
Roberts, John Bryn (Eifion)
Samuel, J. (Stockton on Tees)
Smith, Samuel (Flint)
Souttar, Robinson
Stanhope, Hon. Philip J.
Steadman, William Charles
Sullivan, Donal (Westmeath)

Tully, Jasper

Wedderburn, Sir William
Williams, John Carvell (Notts.)
Wilson, John (Durham, Mid.)
Wilson, J. H. (Middlesbrough)
Woods, Samuel

TELLERS FOR THE NOES—
Mr. Scott and Mr. Henry J.
Wilson.

It being after Midnight, the Chairman left the chair to make his Report to the House.

Resolution to be reported to-morrow. Committee to sit again upon Wednesday.

House adjourned at ten minutes after Twelve of the clock.

HOUSE OF LORDS.

Tuesday, June 6th 1899.

ROYAL ASSENT.

COMMISSION.

The following Bills received the Royal Assent:

Solicitors.

Supreme Court (Appeals).

Public Libraries (Scotland) Acts Amendment.

Metropolitan Water Companies.

Education Department Provisional Order Confirmation (Swansea).

Metropolitan Police Provisional Order.

Local Government Provisional Orders (No. 1).

St. Andrew's Burgh Provisional Order Confirmation.

Rushden and Higham Ferrers District Gas.

Ilford Urban District Council (Rates).

Aberdeen Harbour.

Herne Bay Water.

Walton-on-Thames and Weybridge Gas.

Crowborough District Gas.

St. David's Water and Gas.

Clay Cross Water.

Glasgow District Subway.

Loughborough and Sheepshed Railway.

Dublin Improvement (Bull Alley Area).

Bristol Floods Prevention.

Perth Water, Police, and Gas.

Vale of Glamorgan Railway.

Wallase Tramways and Improvements. y

Northern Assurance Company.

Tenterden Railway.

Surrey Commercial Docks.

Horsforth Urban District Council (Water).

Burley-in-Wharfedale Urban District Water.

Nuneaton and Chilvers Coton Urban District Council Water.

Woodhouse and Conisbrough Railway (Abandonment).

Coalville Urban District Gas.

Glastonbury Water.

Queen's Ferry Bridge.

PRIVATE BILL BUSINESS.

THE LORD CHANCELLOR acquainted the House that the Clerk of the Parliaments had laid upon the Table the Certificates from the Examiners that the further Standing Orders applicable to the following Bills have been complied with:

LONDON, CHATHAM, AND DOVER RAILWAY.

LEITH HARBOUR AND DOCKS.

BELFAST WATER.

And also the Certificate that the further Standing Orders applicable to the following Bill have not been complied with:

BELFAST CORPORATION.

The same were ordered to lie on the Table.

BAKER STREET AND WATERLOO RAILWAY BILL.

Examiner's Certificates of non-compliance with the Standing Orders referred to the Standing Orders Committee on Monday next.

BELFAST CORPORATION BILL.

Examiner's Certificates of non-compliance with the Standing Orders referred to the Standing Orders Committee on Monday next.

LONDON, BRIGHTON, AND SOUTH-COAST RAILWAY (PENSIONS) BILL.

Committee to meet on Thursday next.

SHOTLEY BRIDGE AND CONSETT DISTRICT GAS BILL.

Committee to meet on Friday next.

TRANSVAAL MORTGAGE LOAN AND FINANCE COMPANY BILL [H.L.].

Reported with amendments.

AYR BURGH BILL.

Read 2a, and committed.

P

LOWESTOFT WATER AND GAS BILL
[H.L.].

Read 3a, and passed, and sent to the Commons.

NORTH - EASTERN AND HULL AND BARNSLEY RAILWAYS (JOINT DOCK) BILL [H.L.].

Read 3a, and passed, and sent to the Commons.

NORTH - EASTERN RAILWAY BILL [H.L.].

Read 3a, and passed, and sent to the Commons.

ILFORD GAS BILL,

Read 3a with the amendments ; further amendments made ; Bill passed, and returned to the Commons.

WOLVERHAMPTON TRAMWAYS BILL [H.L.].

WOLVERHAMPTON CORPORATION BILL [H.L.].

SOUTH STAFFORDSHIRE TRAMWAYS BILL [H.L.].

FISHGUARD WATER AND GAS BILL.

BARRY RAILWAY BILL.

LANCASHIRE AND YORKSHIRE RAILWAY (VARIOUS POWERS) BILL.

RHONDDA URBAN DISTRICT COUNCIL BILL.

WETHERBY DISTRICT WATER BILL.

EDINBURGH CORPORATION BILL.

Report from the Committee of Selection, That the following Lords be proposed to the House to form the Select Committee for the consideration of the said Bills ; (viz.),

D. Northumberland (chairman),

E. Bradford,

L. Clonbrock,

L. Clanwilliam (E. Clanwilliam),

L. Crawshaw.

Agreed to ; and the said Lords appointed accordingly : The Committee to meet on Thursday next, at Eleven of the clock ; and all petitions referred to the Committee, with leave to the petitioners praying to be heard by counsel against the Bills to be heard as desired, as also counsel for the Bills.

BELFAST AND NORTHERN COUNTIES RAILWAY BILL.

Brought from the Commons ; read 1a ; and referred to the Examiners.

BOOTLE CORPORATION BILL.

Brought from the Commons ; read 1a ; and referred to the Examiners.

BROUGHTY FERRY GAS AND PAVING ORDER BILL [H.L.].

Returned from the Commons agreed to.

EDUCATIONAL DEPARTMENT PROVISIONAL ORDERS CONFIRMATION (ABERAVON, ETC.) BILL [H.L.].

Returned from the Commons agreed to.

NORFOLK ESTUARY BILL [H.L.].

Returned from the Commons agreed to.

BRIGG URBAN DISTRICT GAS BILL.

Returned from the Commons with the amendments agreed to.

INFECTIOUS DISEASE (NOTIFICATION) ACT (1889) EXTENSION BILL.

Returned from the Commons with the amendment agreed to.

HULL, BARNSLEY AND WEST RIDING JUNCTION RAILWAY AND DOCK BILL [H.L.].

Returned from the Commons agreed to, with an amendment.

ST. ALBANS GAS BILL [H.L.].

Returned from the Commons agreed to, with amendments.

JONES'S DIVORCE BILL [H.L.].

Message from the Commons for copy of the minutes of evidence taken before this House ; together with the proceedings and the documents deposited in the case: Ordered to be communicated, with a request that they may be returned.

EDUCATION DEPARTMENT PROVISIONAL ORDER CONFIRMATION (LIVERPOOL) BILL [H.L.].

Read 3a (according to order), and passed, and sent to the Commons.

PILOTAGE PROVISIONAL ORDER BILL.

Read 3a (according to order), and passed.

ELECTRIC LIGHTING PROVISIONAL ORDERS (No. 3) BILL.

Read 2a (according to order), and committed : The Committee to be proposed by the Committee of Selection.

ELECTRIC LIGHTING PROVISIONAL ORDERS (No. 4) BILL.

Read 2a (according to order), and committed to a Committee of the Whole House on Thursday next.

ELECTRIC LIGHTING PROVISIONAL ORDERS (No. 12) BILL [H.L.].

Read 2a (according to order).

ELECTRIC LIGHTING PROVISIONAL ORDERS (No. 13) BILL [H.L.].

Read 2a (according to order).

ELECTRIC LIGHTING PROVISIONAL ORDERS (No. 15) BILL [H.L.].

Read 2a (according to order).

TRAMWAYS ORDERS CONFIRMATION (No. 2) BILL [H.L.].

Read 2a (according to order).

RETURNS, REPORTS, ETC.

RAILWAY AND CANAL TRAFFIC ACT, 1888 (SECTION 31).

Sixth Report by the Board of Trade of proceedings under section 31 of the Act, including proceedings upon complaints made under section 1 of the Railway and Canal Traffic Act, 1894.

IRISH LAND COMMISSION (JUDICIAL RENTS).

Return for the month of November 1898.

ALDERSHOT (SEWAGE FARM AND DAIRY).

Report on the condition of the Aldershot Camp Sewage Farm, and of the dairy maintained upon it.

Presented (by command), and ordered to lie on the Table.

MERCHANT SHIPPING ACT, 1894.

Order in Council of 19th May 1899, authorising an increase in the clerical establishment of the Commissioners of Northern Lighthouses, and in the salary of Mr. William Coats, accountant and cashier to the Commissioners.

SUPREME COURT OF JUDICATURE AMENDMENT ACT, 1875.

Order in Council of 19th May 1899, amending the Order in Council of 28th July 1893, so far as it relates to the South-Eastern Circuit.

GREENWICH HOSPITAL ACTS, 1865–1869.

Order in Council of 19th May 1899, authorising the grant of a special gratuity to Mrs. Lynch.

COLONIAL PROBATES ACT, 1892.

Order in Council of 19th May 1899, applying the Colonial Probates Act, 1892, to the Colony of Queensland.

INTERMEDIATE EDUCATION (IRELAND).

Rule made by the Intermediate Education Board for Ireland appointing the places at which examinations for 1899 shall be held.

INDIA (PROGRESS AND CONDITION).

Statement exhibiting the moral and material progress and condition of India during the year 1897–98 : Thirty-fourth number. Laid before the House (pursuant to Act), and ordered to lie on the Table.

PETITION.

MUNICIPAL CORPORATION (BOROUGH FUNDS) ACT, 1872.

Petition for amendment of ; of Urban District Council of Leadgate ; read, and ordered to lie on the Table.

PREVENTION OF CORRUPTION BILL. [H.L.]

SECOND READING.

Order of the Day for the Second Reading read.

LORD RUSSELL OF KILLOWEN : My Lords, having explained the principles and provisions of the Bill at considerable length on the occasion of its introduction, I do not intend, in moving its

Second Reading, to delay your Lordships by making more than a very few observations. The Bill has not only been largely discussed in the Press, but it has also been very generally considered by the Chambers of Commerce, the Trade Associations, and the various Co-operative Associations throughout the country, and there has been a unanimous opinion expressed by these various authorities in favour of the principle of the Bill, and I would go further, and say, in favour of a stringent measure to enforce the principle of this Bill. This is not merely an opinion which has been expressed apart from the opportunity of seeing the Bill itself, because the Bill has been widely circulated by myself amongst the Chambers of Commerce, and the opinions they have expressed have been arrived at after consideration of the actual provisions of the Measure. I do not desire that your Lordships should understand that in all the details of the Bill these various bodies agree, but the great majority of them have expressed a general approval of the Bill as it stands. I have myself been in communication with representatives of certain interests that might be supposed to be affected by the Bill if it became Law—persons representing Bankers, Insurance Companies, and Solicitors. I have listened to the representations they have made, and have very little doubt that in Committee I shall be able to make such alterations in the Bill as will meet any just objections they may be inclined to put forward to its provisions. In moving the Second Reading of the Bill, I will conclude by stating the course I propose to take if, as I should hope I may anticipate, your Lordships give the Bill a Second Reading this evening. I intend to put it down for the Committee stage on Thursday; and, inasmuch as it would be much more convenient that the Bill should go before a Committee, whether a Select Committee or a Grand Committee, to be considered in detail, with all the Amendments printed—and I may mention that the number of Amendments which I have to propose is not inconsiderable —I shall propose on Thursday to recommit the Bill *pro formâ*, in order that it may be reprinted with the Amendments. I now beg to move that the Bill be read a second time.

Moved—

"That the Bill be now read 2*a*."—*The Lord Russell of Killowen.*

Lord Russell.

*THE LORD BISHOP OF LONDON: My Lords, this Bill, as the Preamble states, is for the purpose of putting a stop to a practice which is producing great evils by corrupting the morals of the community, and from that point of view I cannot abstain from taking a great interest in the Bill, and from expressing the hope that it will successfully pass through your Lordships' House. If the Bill was concerned solely with what is called commercial morality, I should not have ventured to address the House upon it; but it concerns all pecuniary dealings between man and man. It deals with a practice which taints almost everything men are able to do one with another. It deals with a mischief, the principle of which is that no money is to be passed from one person to another without some of it sticking to the fingers of everyone who touches it. Such a principle as that, which meets with mute and tacit acceptance by society, really constitutes a very great danger, and prevents us from trusting even those who are in our most intimate employment; it prevents them, when they wish to be strictly honest, from entirely succeeding, and it removes the basis of confidence which it is so desirable to maintain in all the dealings which we have one with another. If this practice only extended to the matter of gratuities passing between one person and another upon every transaction that took place, though it might be exceedingly undesirable, yet it might not be entirely reprehensible. There was a time, I believe, when even the occupants of the Judicial Bench received gratuities from those whom they tried; and, though it might be urged that if they received them impartially from both parties, and decided the case according to the evidence, no particular harm was done, I think it will be admitted that the practice was not one calculated to promote honourable dealings between the parties. Even the passing of gratuities is exceedingly undesirable; but it is impossible that the evil can stop short there. Gratuities rapidly give an opportunity for blackmailing, which is one of those incidents of ordinary life to which we must all feel a deep-seated objection. The process by which blackmailing is reached is a very simple one. For instance, the representative of a firm doing business with another firm on a tolerably large scale may get a letter from the principal foreman suggesting that a subscription to a philanthropic object would be greatly welcomed. The subscription is given, and then the area of subscriptions rapidly extends. Clubs, feasts, festivals, athletic sports, and every pursuit of the employees of the firm which receives goods are brought forward as deserving of support in one form or another, and eventually a period is reached when the communications become of a somewhat more personal character, and when a postscript is attached giving the private address of the writer. That is the beginning of an indication that, unless a gratuity is given immediately to the correspondent, some objection will be taken to the goods that are supplied, and the commercial transaction may be brought to an end. It is obvious that the existence of a state of things such as this is destructive of all morality between man and man. I have been informed of a case that is still worse, where a foreman received from a firm a whole sheaf of postal orders with the request that they might be distributed among foremen of other firms, accompanied by written instructions as to the way in which the recipients were to pick holes and find fault with the goods supplied by another firm which the first firm meant to cut out in the trade. I need not enlarge upon the report of the London Chamber of Commerce, which supplies an adequate number of instances in which the principle of gratuities rapidly develops into blackmail. I suppose we are all agreed as to the great evil of these illicit secret payments, but I can quite understand that there may be some differences of opinion whether or no the practice can be stopped by legislation. I take a high view both of the functions and possibilities of legislation. It is quite true that men cannot be made virtuous by Act of Parliament, but at least temptations can be removed from their path, and it can be made more possible for men to be virtuous than vicious. One function of the law, at all events, is that it should express the public conscience, and so break down corrupt conventions. There is nothing more difficult or more important than to break down the conventions of society when they become corrupt. It is very hard for an individual to resist them by himself, or to raise an isolated voice against them ; and it is only when he has something to support him that he can really hope to succeed in escaping from them. These conventions cannot be attacked by legislation until they have reached a point at which they are ready

to fall, and on this question of corrupt practices I venture to think that conventions of trade have reached a point when they are ready to fall if a sufficient impulse is given to them. There are many who are groaning under them, and who only require some such support as this Bill, if passed, will give them to enable them to free themselves. Trade custom in itself is very hard to contend against. It is not so much a regulation or a habit as an atmosphere in which ordinary morality has often to be abandoned, frequently with a sigh on the part of those who abandon it. There are, however, many who long to get back to that ordinary morality which in their private life they can afford to practise, but which they are compelled to put on one side in their commercial life. How are they to do so ? If a man says to one who asks him to consent either to give or to receive an illicit commission, "You are asking me to do a dishonourable act," the answer is, "If you want to keep your honour you should not come here." If he says, "You ask me to do an illegal act," the answer is, "What does it matter, there is no penalty ?" But when he is in a position to say, "You are asking me to commit a misdemeanour for which you and I can be imprisoned," the position becomes entirely different. It is by the introduction of that position, and by giving that support, that a corrupt convention can be broken down, evil habits abandoned, and a new start made. The great force of law, after all, lies ,in its power of isolation, tracing an offence back to its causes, and onwards to its consequences. It is useless to say that the law has not succeeded in the past. The law has succeeded. A representative of a great firm to whom I was talking on this subject told me that in his dealings with foreign countries he was compelled to give bribes to obtain orders, and in dealing with firms in this country gratuities had also to be given. "But," he added, "there is one class of the community—those who bear Her Majesty's Commission—in dealing with whom there is no suggestion of a gratuity." There is, therefore, one class above suspicion. An Act of Parliament has been passed to enforce upon public bodies the same standard as that which prevails amongst those who hold Her Majesty's Commission ; and I venture to think the time has arrived when that Act should be extended universally, when the whole community deserves the same protection, and when the same sentiment of honour may be encouraged in the mind of everybody, because they have behind them the law which explains and enforces the true meaning of their actions, and gives them the necessary stimulus to be true to what, in their own hearts, they know to be right, and to stand up for uprightness in their dealings one with another. No doubt the provisions of the Bill will meet with close criticism, but the acceptance of its principle will, I am quite sure, be welcomed by the sound majority of the commercial world, who will feel their hands strengthened in resisting the tyranny of the petty dishonesty which at present weaves its meshes around them in a way which it is exceedingly difficult for them to overcome without such help as this Bill provides.

THE MARQUESS OF LONDONDERRY : My Lords, I cannot but think that this Bill is one that should be only alluded to and supported or opposed by those whom I may call legal experts on this somewhat complicated question ; but I am quite sure we all welcome the admirable speech which has just been delivered by the right reverend Prelate, who has touched upon the question from a moral and thoroughly practical point of view. I confess that, under these circumstances, I feel considerable diffidence in rising to address your Lordships on this question, and, indeed, I should not do so but for the fact that I have the honour to be a member of a most important Chamber of Commerce—the Chamber of Commerce of the City of Belfast—the members of which watch with a very jealous eye all measures that come before Parliament, and do me the great honour of asking me to criticise or put forward their views when any measure in which they are interested comes before your Lordships' House. The Belfast Chamber of Commerce have taken considerable interest in this Bill, and, like all rightthinking business men, they regard its object as most laudable. At the same time, they would feel greatly obliged to the noble and learned Lord in charge of the Bill if he could see his way in Committee to make some slight alterations which would meet their views. As I understand, this Bill was originally recommended to the noble and learned Lord

Bishop of London.

opposite, and, consequently, to your Lordships' House, by the Chamber of Commerce of the City of London. The Bill, as it then stood, was closely considered by the Chamber to which I have the honour to belong, and some of its provisions did not meet with their approval. They consequently issued a draft on first reading that Bill, and in that draft they protested against a provision which appeared in one of the clauses to the effect that every case of undisclosed commission or inducement should be deemed to be corrupt and, *ipso facto*, punishable. Since that draft was issued a considerable change has been made in the provision referred to, and it has been amended in such a way that no consideration given or offered to any agent, by any person having business relations with the principal of such agent, shall be deemed to have been corruptly given or offered when it is proved that the principal had given his consent thereto, or that the consideration was not calculated or intended, and had no tendency, to corrupt the agent by inducing him to do or to leave undone something contrary to his duty, or by creating any other undue influence on the mind of the agent. The Belfast Chamber of Commerce welcome the change in Clause 3, which has been made under the auspices of the noble and learned Lord the Lord Chief Justice. But there are two clauses in the Bill which they think will work harshly and unjustly – I allude to Clauses 7 and 8, which the Belfast Chamber of Commerce consider of somewhat too wide and drastic a character. They consider that there might be greater leniency shown in certain cases between a donor and a recipient, and that there should be a difference made between persons between whom fiduciary relations exist and those between whom no such relations exist. They also consider that hard cases might arise under these clauses, and that persons might be injuriously affected who had no intention to carry on their business except in a *bonâ fide* manner. In a report sent to me examples have been given to show that it would be possible for recommendations to be given in a perfectly *bonâ fide* manner to employ a doctor or solicitor, or to patronise a particular establishment ; but apparently under the Bill any gift or advantage conferred in recognition of such friendly offices, even a return of similar recommendations, might be treated as a criminal offence. The Belfast Chamber of Commerce speak in the highest possible terms in support of the provisions of the Bill dealing with the giving to agents of false or misleading accounts or receipts, and they consider these very excellent provisions. There is one other point upon which the Belfast Chamber of Commerce offer a suggestion, and it is that prosecutions under this Bill, when it becomes an Act, should, so far as Ireland is concerned, be instituted by the Attorney-General for Ireland. They are of opinion that if a provision to that effect were inserted frivolous objections would not be raised, and they consider that it would be the means, to a great extent, of avoiding the blackmailing of innocent people. I know quite well that these are questions which should be dealt with in Committee, and I feel that I owe your Lordships an apology for having brought under your attention so many details at this stage of the Bill; but, as a member of an important Chamber of Commerce, I felt it my duty to bring before the House the opinions of the Chamber upon the Bill, so as to give the noble and learned Lord who is in charge of it an opportunity of thinking over the suggestions, and, I hope, eventually acquiescing in them.

THE LORD CHANCELLOR (the EARL of HALSBURY): My Lords, I should be very sorry indeed to utter a discordant note, and I suppose if it were put in an abstract form nobody would deny that there ought to be punishment for bribing an agent to betray his principal. The only observation I have to make has been in a measure anticipated by the noble Marquess, and it is that several of the provisions of the Bill might be misunderstood, and possibly might work injustice by operating in a direction quite the contrary to what is intended. It is unnecessary to go further into criticisms of this sort, not only because this is not the period for criticism on particular clauses, but also because the noble and learned Lord the Lord Chief Justice has intimated that he himself intends to move amendments which your Lordships will be able to consider. May I say generally that when we are all agreed that something has to be done and that very drastic measures are demanded, it is sometimes the most dangerous condition into which a Legislature can get, because it is very

Marquess of Londonderry.

likely then to do a great deal more than it intends by reason of the feeling that something must be done. The inevitable result is that a reaction sets in against what it is desirable and proper to do. Although I have said this by way of caution, I heartily agree with the general object of the Bill. I think there is a considerable demand for it. I confess for myself that, regarding our Acts of Parliament as perhaps the most well-founded portions of our history —I think it has been remarked that it is almost certain they will be accepted as absolute verities by future generations—I do think the preamble of the Bill is a little too sweeping in its allegations of corruption and immorality. The preamble states that—

"Whereas secret commissions in various forms are prevalent to a great extent in almost all trades and professions, and in some trades the said practice has increased and is increasing: And whereas the said practice is producing great evils, by corrupting the morals of the community, and by discouraging honest trade and enterprise, and it is expedient to check the same and other kindred malpractices, by making them criminal."

We need not, I think, stamp our century with the imputation that the whole of our morals are being corrupted by this system. I do not know that a preamble is of very much consequence to any Act of Parliament, but I do hope that my noble and learned friend will not be too much enamoured of the language of the preamble to render it necessary for us to stamp this century in the way this preamble does. On the part of Her Majesty's Government, I have to say that they welcome this Bill, and are not in the least disposed to oppose its second reading.

*THE LORD BISHOP of WINCHESTER: My Lords, although my right rev. brother the Bishop of London has already addressed to your Lordships words which we should all have been sorry to lose, I hope your Lordships will not feel it inappropriate that something further should be said from this bench on a matter which so closely concerns the moral well-being of the community. Bishops and clergy are specially concerned in this matter, not merely as those who have a supreme interest in the morals of the people, but because, from the circumstances of their life-work, they have of necessity a special knowledge on the subject which is not possessed by all your Lordships. The ordinary life of the parish clergyman brings him in contact with those in the lower grades of industrial life. They come to him, not as to an employer, not as to a politician, but as to a personal friend, whose advice they seek and to whom they open their hearts; and it would be very easy for anyone who has had this experience to give your Lordships case after case in which, against their will, men, and perhaps women, have lost their self-respect by having to fall in with these trade customs, from which they cannot escape. The testimony of working men on this subject is, so far as I know, practically unanimous as to the way in which their particular trades are corrupted under this system. In the not inconsiderable correspondence which I have been engaged in on this subject, one man after another bears testimony to this fact, that the present alienation of large bodies of workmen from the ordinary ministrations of religion and the observance of public worship is due, in no small measure, to the fact that they feel it would be hypocritical to appear as religious men when in their trade and ordinary life they are reluctantly but constantly engaged in doing things which are contrary to such public profession. I am sure, therefore, that the bishops and clergy throughout the land will give a cordial welcome to the Bill the second reading of which the Lord Chief Justice has just moved. May I venture to say that I am specially thankful for the quarter from which the Bill has come. I try to picture sometimes to myself what would have been the comments which would have been made on the Bill had it emanated from the members of the episcopal bench. We should have heard of the fantastic, unpractical, utopian ideas of the clergy, living up in a balloon and out of touch with the ordinary commercial conditions of public life and trade. But, fortunately, the Bill comes to us from a source which none dares thus to decry. It comes to us on the motion of the Lord Chief Justice of England, who told us, in his opening remarks on the subject, that he spoke from much experience, largely professional and in part judicial, as to the evils, the magnitude of which it is impossible to exaggerate. The noble and learned Lord has been supported throughout by Sir Edward Fry, than whom no man is more entitled to deal with questions of this

Bishop of Winchester.

kind. They are supported by practically all the chambers of commerce throughout the land, and one has only to be very briefly in communication with those whose affairs bring them into contact with the questions with which this Bill deals to find how general is the approval of it. One man who occupies a position which gives him wide and varied knowledge of the commercial world writes:

    " The evil aimed at is so great and so mischievous that I think the advantage of any chance of checking it far outweighs the possible inconvenience or even hardship which might arise in some really innocent cases. '

Five or six years ago a Church society with which I have the honour to be connected, a society which interests itself specially in social problems, issued a large number of inquiries to employers of labour and men of business with reference to the difficulty, if any, experienced by them in reconciling the principles of the highest honesty and probity with the ordinary transactions in which they were daily engaged. The result of these inquiries was seen in the melancholy monotony of the replies. So much information was given by the Lord Chief Justice on the matter that it would be mere repitition were I to quote the answers received, but I could easily do so if desired. There is one answer, however, which I should like to read to the House, as representing the drift of many others and because it concerns closely a good many of those who sit in your Lordships' House. The writer, speaking of the difficulty which he, as a veterinary surgeon, experienced with regard to the acceptance of bribes by the various coachmen and others with whom he had to do business, says:

    "I never give these bribes. But if there be any necessity for it, that is the fault of the so-called 'better classes.' They may not like being robbed, but they would rather be robbed than bothered."

When the veterinary surgeon who was pressed for these bribes went to the employer he was told that it was no doubt unfortunate, but it could not be helped, and that it was a pity he had raised the question. Now, my Lords, under the existing law, what can we expect such a man to do? There is, it seems to me, a deep pathos in the position of people, hating the system and longing to get rid of it, but feeling that unless they are prepared to forfeit their daily bread, it is simply impossible to give it up, inasmuch as a few dishonest folk can make it exceedingly hard for so many. A curious object lesson as to the view of working men upon the matter can be seen in the growth of the Co-operative Wholesale Society. It is part of the working of a trade movement which now reaches some £60,000,000 per annum, and the getting rid of this bribery system is one of the motives which has instigated these men to found the Wholesale Society. They contend that they were bound to do so if they were to fall back on what they call the principles of the Rochdale pioneers of 50 years ago—fundamental honesty in trade. On the general policy of this Bill my correspondence shows that there are practically only two lines of objection taken. The first is that the details are unworkable, and in regard to that a good deal may require consideration, but that is an objection which I am very ready to leave in the hands of those who are primarily responsible for the Bill. But there is another objection of which not much has been heard in these debates, though it has been loudly proclaimed outside. There are certainly not a few people who think that our competition with foreign traders will be affected if this Bill becomes law. I again venture to quote a private letter from one who has had experience all over the world in mercantile affairs, and who says :

"If this Bill became law we should have to face a loud and logical outcry about driving trade away from this country. It is certain that business without bribery is practically impossible with such countries as Russia, Spain, China, South America . . . British trade is not self-contained, and this question of commissions is as international as the question of disarmament."

That is a question upon which, as regards its technical side, I am incapable of expressing an opinion, but I fall back on the general principle which underlies all legislation, or attempted legislation, of this kind—the principle that in the long run "honesty is the best policy." My Lords, either the Bill is likely to have some effect in stopping bribery or it is not. If not, let us oppose it by all means as a useless Bill, but do not let us bring in the totally different question of foreign competition. If, on the other hand, we feel that we are by passing this Bill likely to check in some degree an admitted evil, will anyone have the face to say that we

ought to abstain from doing so lest, if we are successful, we might in some degree interfere with our foreign trade ? The success of English trade throughout the world has been due to the excellence of our goods ; and, secondly, to the honesty of our merchants. I do not know how many of your Lordships have read the extremely interesting Blue Book which was published last year, containing a summary by the Board of Trade of the reports of foreign consuls as to the increase or decrease of British trade in different parts of the world. One learned from that Blue Book, amongst many other things, that where British trade is being ousted by other trade it appears to be, first, in cases where cheapness, and nothing but cheapness, is the consideration, and, secondly, in cases where ingenious adaptation to the peculiar wants of customers has been more readily adopted by our rivals on the Continent than by ourselves ; but where quality is what is wanted English trade is able to hold its ground. I should wish on this point to quote two authorities, one of them public, and one private. In the report to which I have referred it is stated, speaking of the competition of Russia in cheap sewing machines, that—

"It may be difficult to draw the line between cheap and trumpery articles, but it is something that the word 'English' applied (in Russia) to goods or materials usually means the best that man can make."

Such testimony, coming from an official source, is surely of high value. Again, to quote from a private letter, the head of one of the leading firms in the cotton trade writes :

"The possession of trade marks that are known to and prized by the natives is exceedingly valuable, and merchants who have them will not hesitate to spend any amount of money on their protection from imitation or infringement. What makes them valuable is the fact that goods on which they appear are known to be right. The mark sells the goods, but the goods must first of all have earned their reputation. Thirty years ago we began consigning to China, really in order to get rid of our surplus production. For a long time we did the business at a loss. The goods were new to the market and had to be sold for what they would fetch ; but they were honest stuff . . . . and they never varied in quality. Gradually the Chinese grew familiar with the marks. They found the goods bearing those marks could be thoroughly depended upon, and now they order them in large quantities, paying us our price for them."

We may lose that reputation if we compete with other nations in the pitiable expedient of bribery and corruption, and once lost that reputation will never be regained. Ten years ago, on the initiative of Lord Randolph Churchill, a Bill was passed for preventing corruption on the part of the servants of public companies. I believe the testimony is unanimous that that Act, after ten years working, has been found to be productive of enormous good, and that the abuses against which it was aimed have been far less prevalent. If anyone will refer to the debate in both Houses of Parliament on the occasion of the introduction of that Bill, he will find that when the complaint was made, " Why stop with the servants of public companies ? " the reply was, " We are proceeding one step at a time. Before very long, if it proves successful, the provisions of the Bill will be extended." I venture to think that the time has now come when that step, to which those who introduced the Bill ten years ago wisely looked forward, should be taken. I support the second reading of the Bill on all these grounds, but most of all on the ground that it is our bounden duty to help the helpless against a system which is daily to a larger extent entangling men and women who would fain be free, and by depriving them of their self-respect is inflicting a deadly injury upon English life.

LORD RUSSELL OF KILLOWEN : My Lords, the friends of this Bill have, I think, every reason to be satisfied with the course the discussion has taken, and the observations I propose to make to your Lordships will be of the briefest kind. So far as the speeches that have been made are concerned, I have to thank the two right rev. Prelates for the valuable contributions they have made to the debate in support of this Bill. With regard to the criticisms made by the noble Marquess opposite, in his capacity as president of the Belfast Chamber of Commerce, I have to say two things. I shall endeavour, in the Amendments I propose to submit, to give effect to some of those criticisms, but to one of them I cannot give my assent ; on the contrary, I shall feel obliged strongly to oppose it ; that is, the suggestion that this Bill should be put in operation only in prosecutions to be instituted by the Attorney-General.

THE MARQUESS OF LONDON-DERRY : In Ireland.

Bishop of Winchester,

LORD RUSSELL OF KILLOWEN : Whether in Ireland, or in England, or by the Lord Advocate in Scotland, the admission of such a provision would, I believe, render the Bill practically nugatory. I am willing to consider the suggestion made by the noble and learned Earl on the Woolsack, whether leave from some judicial authority should not be considered a necessary precedent to a prosecution, but that is a different matter. I confess to a feeling of regret that the noble Marquess addressed your Lordships in his character as president of the Belfast Chamber of Commerce rather than——

THE MARQUESS OF LONDON-DERRY : I am not president at the present moment. I am only a member of the Belfast Chamber of Commerce.

LORD RUSSELL OF KILLOWEN : I regret that the noble Marquess addressed your Lordships in his character as a member of the Belfast Chamber of Commerce rather than in his important character as a great coalowner in the North of England, because, if my information is not very misleading, the noble Lord could give us very useful information on the subject, which would tend to make your Lordships feel that a Bill of this kind, and a very stringent Bill indeed, on the lines indicated is absolutely called for. I thank the noble and learned Earl the Lord Chancellor for the spirit in which he made his criticism, and it probably will relieve his mind if I inform him, in reference to his desire for historical accuracy in the preamble, that the preamble is taken *verbatim et literatim* from a paragraph in the report of the London Chamber of Commerce. I may also add that, inasmuch as I do not myself approve of any preambles in Acts of Parliament, I intend to move an Amendment to omit the preamble altogether. May I again inform the House the course I propose to take, subject to your Lordships' agreeing to the Second Reading to-night ? I intend to put the Bill down for Committee stage on Thursday, but merely for the formal purpose of having it re-committed, so that it may come before any Committee your Lordships may decide to refer it to with the full Amendments which I shall propose in print.

On Question, agreed to ; Bill read a second time accordingly, and committed to a Committee of the whole House on Thursday next.

MARRIAGES VALIDITY BILL [Lords].

Order of the Day for the Second Reading read.

THE LORD BISHOP OF LONDON : My Lords, in consequence of a communication which I have received this morning from the Lord Chancellor of Ireland, I would ask leave to withdraw the Order for the Second Reading.

Order discharged ; Bill withdrawn.

FARNLEY TYAS MARRIAGES BILL.

Read a second time (according to order, and committed to a Committee of the whole House on Thursday next.

CONGESTED DISTRICTS (SCOTLAND) ACT AMENDMENT BILL [Lords].

Read a third time (according to order), and passed ; and sent to the Commons.

> House adjourned at twenty-five minutes after Five of the clock, to Thursday next, at fifteen minutes after Four of the clock.

HOUSE OF COMMONS.

Tuesday, 6th June 1899.

ROYAL ASSENT.

Message to attend the Lords Commissioners.

The House went, and, being returned,

MR. SPEAKER reported the Royal Assent to a number of Bills (see first item in House of Lords report this day ; *ante*, page 409).

PRIVATE BILL BUSINESS.

PRIVATE BILLS [Lords].

Standing Orders not previously inquired into complied with.

MR. SPEAKER laid upon the Table Report from one of the Examiners of Petitions for Private Bills, that, in the case of the following Bills, originating in the Lords, and referred on the First Read-

ing thereof, the Standing Orders, not previously inquired into, and which are applicable thereto, have been complied with, viz. :—

GREAT NORTHERN RAILWAY BILL [Lords].

SUNDERLAND CORPORATION BILL [Lords].

Ordered, That the Bills be read a second time.

ARBROATH CORPORATION GAS BILL [Lords].

Read the third time, and passed without Amendment.

KEW BRIDGE BILL [Lords].

Read the third time, and passed, without Amendment.

LONDON AND NORTH WESTERN RAILWAY (NEW RAILWAYS) BILL.

Read the third time, and passed. [New Title].

BEXHILL AND ST. LEONARDS TRAMROADS BILL [Lords].

Read a second time, and committed.

BURY CORPORATION WATER BILL [Lords].

Read a second time, and committed.

CHURCH STRETTON WATER BILL [Lords].

Read a second time, and committed.

COLONIAL AND FOREIGN BANKS GUARANTEE FUND BILL [Lords].

Read a second time, and committed.

GAINSBOROUGH URBAN DISTRICT COUNCIL (GAS) BILL [Lords].

Read a second time, and committed.

GREAT YARMOUTH WATER BILL [Lords].

Read a second time, and committed.

HAMPSTEAD CHURCH (EMMANUEL, WEST END) BILL [Lords].

Read a second time, and committed.

HUMBER CONSERVANCY BILL [Lords].

Read a second time, and committed.

LEIGH-ON-SEA URBAN DISTRICT COUNCIL BILL [Lords].

Read a second time, and committed.

MERSEY DOCKS AND HARBOUR BOARD (FINANCE) BILL [Lords].

Read a second time, and committed.

PORT TALBOT RAILWAY AND DOCKS BILL [Lords].

Read a second time, and committed.

SALFORD CORPORATION BILL [Lords].

Read a second time, and committed.

STRETFORD GAS BILL [Lords].

Read a second time, and committed.

WAKEFIELD CORPORATION BILL [Lords].

Read a second time, and committed.

WICK AND PULTENEY HARBOURS BILL [Lords].

Read a second time, and committed.

GREAT SOUTHERN AND WESTERN AND WATERFORD, LIMERICK, AND WESTERN RAILWAY COMPANIES AMALGAMATION, GREAT SOUTHERN AND WESTERN RAILWAY, AND WATERFORD AND CENTRAL IRELAND RAILWAY BILLS.

Ordered, that the Order [14th March] that all Petitions of County Councils under the provisions of the Local Government (Ireland) Act, 1898, against the Bills, presented seven clear days before the meeting of the Committee be referred to the Committee, and that the petitioners praying to be heard by themselves, their counsel, or agents, or witnesses be heard against the Bills be suspended in the case of the petition of the County Council of Queen's County against the Great Southern and Western Railway Bill, and that the said petition be referred to the Select Committee on the said Bills, and that the petitioners be heard by their counsel, agent, or witnesses against the said Bill.—(*Mr. J. F. X. O'Brien.*)

BRADFORD TRAMWAYS AND IMPROVEMENT BILL.

Petition for additional Provision; referred to the Examiners of Petitions for Private Bills.

ELECTRIC LIGHTING PROVISIONAL ORDERS (No. 17) BILL.

Read a second time, and committed.

ELECTRIC LIGHTING PROVISIONAL ORDER (No. 18) BILL.

Read a second time, and committed.

ELECTRIC LIGHTING PROVISIONAL ORDERS (No. 19) BILL.

Read a second time, and committed.

LOCAL GOVERNMENT (IRELAND) PROVISIONAL ORDER (HOUSING OF WORKING CLASSES) BILL.

Read a second time, and committed.

LOCAL GOVERNMENT (IRELAND) PROVISIONAL ORDERS (No. 3) BILL.

Read a second time, and committed.

LOCAL GOVERNMENT PROVISIONAL ORDERS (No. 9) BILL.

Read a second time, and committed.

LOCAL GOVERNMENT PROVISIONAL ORDERS (No. 10) BILL.

Read a second time, and committed.

LOCAL GOVERNMENT PROVISIONAL ORDERS (No. 11) BILL.

Read a second time, and committed.

LOCAL GOVERNMENT PROVISIONAL ORDERS (No. 12) BILL.

Read a second time, and committed.

LOCAL GOVERNMENT PROVISIONAL ORDER (No. 13) BILL.

Read a second time, and committed.

LOCAL GOVERNMENT PROVISIONAL ORDERS (No. 14) BILL.

Read a second time, and committed.

MILITARY LANDS PROVISIONAL ORDER BILL.

Read a second time, and committed.

PRIVATE BILLS (GROUP J).

Sir Henry Fletcher reported from the Committee on Group J of Private Bills, That the parties promoting the Airdrie and Coatbridge Water Bill [Lords] had stated the evidence of John Motherwell Alston, town clerk, Coatbridge, was essential to their case; and it having been proved that his attendance could not be procured without the intervention of the House, he had been instructed to move that the said John Motherwell Alston do attend the said Committee To-morrow at half-past Eleven of the clock.

Ordered, That John Motherwell Alston do attend the Committee on Group J of

Private Bills To-morrow, at half-past Eleven of the clock.

BLACKPOOL IMPROVEMENT BILL.

Reported from the Select Committee on Police and Sanitary Regulations Bills, with Amendments.

DARWEN CORPORATION BILL.

Reported from the Select Committee on Police and Sanitary Regulations Bills, with Amendments.

Ordered, That the Reports do lie upon the Table, and be printed.

PETITIONS.

GROUND RENTS (TAXATION BY LOCAL AUTHORITIES).

Petitions in favour;— From West Bridgford ;— Greenock ;— Askington ;— Sheerness ;—Ryde (four) ;—Chapel en le Frith ;— St. James's ;— Llanrhystyd ;— Gravesend ;—Motherwell ;—Rothbury ;— and, Working Men's Club and Institute Union, Limited ; to lie upon the Table. ·

MINES (EIGHT HOURS) BILL.

Petition from Manor Pit Colliery, in favour ; to lie upon the Table.

POOR LAW RELIEF (DISFRANCHISE- MENT).

Petition from West Ham, for alteration of Law ; to lie upon the Table.

PRIVATE LEGISLATION PROCEDURE (SCOTLAND) BILL.

Petition from Aberdeen, in favour ; to lie upon the Table.

REGISTRATION OF FIRMS BILL.

Petition from Aberdeen, in favour ; to lie upon the Table.

TELEGRAPHS (TELEPHONIC COMMU- NICATION, &c.) BILL.

Petition from Aberdeen, against ; to lie upon the Table.

WORKMEN'S COMPENSATION ACT (1897) AMENDMENT BILL.

Petition from Aberdeen, against ; to lie upon the Table.

RETURNS, REPORTS, &c.

IRISH LAND COMMISSION (JUDICIAL RENTS).

Copy presented,—of Return of Judicial Rents during the month of November, 1898 [by Command] ; to lie upon the Table.

INTERMEDIATE EDUCATION (IRELAND).

Copy presented,—of Rule made by the Intermediate Education Board for Ireland appointing the places at which Examina- tions shall be held for 1899 [by Act] ; to lie upon the Table.

RAILWAY AND CANAL TRAFFIC ACTS, 1888 AND 1894.

Copy presented,—of Sixth Report by the Board of Trade of Proceedings under Section 31 of The Railway and Canal Traffic Act, 1888, including Proceedings upon Complaints made under Section 1 of The Railway and Canal Traffic Act, 1894 [by Command] ; to lie upon the Table.

VOLUNTARY SCHOOLS ASSOCIATIONS.

Return presented,—relative thereto [ordered 24th March ; Sir Francis Powell] ; to lie upon the Table, and to be printed. [No. 210.]

COLONIAL PETROLEUM ACT, 1892.

Copy presented,—of Order in Council of the 19th May 1899, applying the Act to the Colony of Queensland [by Act] ; to lie upon the Table.

MERCHANT SHIPPING ACT, 1894.

Copy presented,—of Order in Council of the 19th May 1899, authorising an increase in the Clerical Establishment of the Commissioners of Northern Light- houses, and in the salary of Mr. William Coats, accountant and cashier to the Commissioners [by Act] ; to lie upon the Table.

SUPREME COURT OF JUDICATURE AMENDMENT ACT, 1875.

Copy presented,—of Order in Council of 19th May 1899, amending the Order in Council of 28th July 1893, so far as it relates to the South-Eastern Circuit [by Act] ; to lie upon the Table.

GREENWICH HOSPITAL ACTS, 1865 AND 1869.

Copy presented,—of Order in Council 19th May 1899, authorising the 'grant of a special gratuity to Mrs. Lynch [by Act]; to lie upon the Table.

EAST INDIA (PROGRESS AND CONDITION).

Copy presented,—of Statement exhibiting the Moral and Material Progress and Condition of India during the year 1897-8. Thirty-fourth Number [by Act]; to lie upon the Table.

TREATY SERIES (No. 13, 1899).

Copy presented, — of Accession of Japan to the International Union for the Protection of Literary and Artistic Works, 15th July 1899 [by Command]; to lie upon the Table.

QUESTIONS.

ROYAL NAVAL RESERVE.

SIR EDWARD GOURLEY (Sunderland): I beg to ask the First Lord of the Admiralty whether it is his intention to ask Parliament this or next Session to amend the Act limiting the enrolling of seamen for the Royal Naval Reserve to 30,000 men, for the purpose of increasing the number of first and second class seamen, and also of stokers and firemen; can he state the approximate number of permanent officers, engineers, and men that will be needed to complete the manning of the whole of the ships now in commission, as well as those that will be ready for the pennant at the close of the current financial year; and whether, in conjunction with the Lords of the Admiralty, he has formed any approximate estimate of the number of men of all ranks that will be needed for reserve purposes in the event of war; if so, will he give the numbers.

THE FIRST LORD OF THE ADMIRALTY (MR. G. J. GOSCHEN, St. George's, Hanover Square): The hon. Member has seen my proposals for this year, to which I have nothing to add, and he must allow me to put off until next year my statement as regards future Estimates. In reply to the second question, it is impossible to state in advance what the composition of the fleet in commission will be at the close of the current financial year. My answer to the third question is that the number of men of all ranks needed for reserve purposes in the event of war will, of course, depend on the nature of the war, and I am not prepared to make a statement on the subject.

CUSTOMS OFFICIALS.

MR. STEADMAN (Tower Hamlets, Stepney): I beg to ask the Secretary to the Treasury will he explain why Customs watchers who act as lockers at bonded warehouses, a duty done by the established out-door officers, are compelled to do nine hours a day all the year round, while the established officers only do eight hours a day in summer and seven hours in winter; whether, seeing that the salaries of out-door officers are £100 per annum, while the wages of watchers are 21s. a week, he will explain the method adopted in calculating the daily hours of duty of Customs watchers, which is now said to be only seven hours a day; and whether he will state the number of hours worked per day (based on a similar calculation) by the established out-door officers; whether, out of a total of 343 watchers now employed in the Customs Department of the Port of London, only forty were previous to 1896 liable to work from 6 a.m. to 6 p.m.; whether their wages were the same as now, 21s. a week, while the remainder were paid 19s. a week for an eight hours' day in summer and seven hours in winter, the overtime payment being 8d. per hour; whether the former were paid overtime before and after 6 a.m. and 6 p.m. each day, and the latter before and after 8 a.m. in summer and 9 a.m. in winter and 4 p.m. each day, regardless of the number of hours worked during the week; and whether overtime was only paid previous to 1896 after seventy-two hours' duty each week.

*THE SECRETARY TO THE TREASURY (MR. HANBURY, Preston): Watchers who act as lockers at bonded warehouses are not compelled to serve nine hours a day all the year round. Their hours vary from seven to nine, including meal time, according to the season of the year and the business of the particular warehouse. Very few outdoor officers are now serving as lockers or in any other capacity, and they are an expiring class. The salaries of outdoor officers are not £100. Second class outdoor officers receive £55 rising by £3 to £80, and first-class outdoor officers receive £85 rising by £3 to £100. £100 is therefore the maximum and not the normal salary of the class. The daily hours of duty of Customs watchers are not said to be only seven. I informed the hon. Member on 18th of April that "the minimum average number of hours a day, based on a recent week's work, was seven"—that is, that (with one slight exception) no individual watcher averaged less than seven hours' attendance per day during that week. The actual ordinary attendance (excluding overtime) of the established outdoor officers during the same week averaged 7½ hours per day. The facts stated in the third paragraph are correct. In the fourth paragraph the hon. Member presumably refers to the 40 men specified in paragraph 3. If so, overtime was paid after 12 hours' attendance on any one day (which is not the same as paying it after 72 hours' attendance in any one week).

POST OFFICE—CLERKS' SALARIES.

MR. YOXALL (Nottingham, W.): I beg to ask the Secretary to the Treasury, as representing the Postmaster-General, what is the correct maximum salary for the clerks' class at 54s. per week offices, the officers of which class are employed entirely upon supervising and technical duties in the Postal Service.

MR. HANBURY: The maximum salary for clerks at all provincial offices —irrespective of the wages of the rank and file—is determined by the number of established officers, and has no necessary relation to the maximum wages of the rank and file. At the few offices where the rank and file have a maximum of 54s. a week the maximum salary of the clerks at present ranges from £160 to £175 a year.

AMERICAN MAIL SERVICE.

SIR JOHN LENG (Dundee): I beg to ask the Secretary to the Treasury if he will explain why the Return relating to the American Mail Service, ordered 27th February, has not yet been issued.

MR. HANBURY: The preparation of this Return involved some correspondence

with the United States Post Office and a considerable amount of clerical labour, so that there has been no undue delay in compiling it. It was presented on the 4th ult., ordered to be printed on the 5th, and will be in the hands of Members one day this week.

IRELAND—COUNTY COURT OFFICERS.

MR. ENGLEDEW (Kildare, N.): I beg to ask the Secretary to the Treasury if he has completed the arrangements in regard to the vouching of the grant for clerical assistance to the various county court officers in Ireland; and, if the arrangements are completed, would he lay upon the Table copies of the various circulars issued in connection therewith, and at the same time furnish a Return showing the amount now being paid out of the grant to the various officers, together with the amounts paid to them as on the 1st day of April, 1897.

*MR. HANBURY: Yes Sir; the arrangements are completed, and I will furnish a return of the allowances payable on 1st April, 1897, and now; and also a memorandum of the arrangements adopted for vouching the expenditure of the county court officers in Ireland, within the limit of the fixed allowances.

NATIONAL SCHOOL TEACHERS.

MR. MACALEESE (Monaghan, N.): I beg to ask the Secretary to the Treasury whether there are in the service of the Board of National Education in Ireland numerous second-class teachers who only receive third-class salaries; can he explain upon what principle this system is sanctioned by the Board of National Education; and will he undertake to communicate with the Commissioners of National Education in Ireland with a view to seeing that teachers are paid the full salaries attaching to their classification.

*THE CHIEF SECRETARY FOR IRELAND (MR. G. W. BALFOUR, Leeds, Central): At the request of my right hon. friend I will answer this question. There are many teachers ranking in second class who receive but third class salary under the Board's rules, namely, principal teachers the average attendance at whose schools is less than 30 pupils, and assistant teachers who are entitled only to third class salary as such. After five years' service, however, the assistant teachers receive under the Education Act of 1892 a bonus which nearly equalises their emoluments with the salary of second class. Those arrangements are based on the principle of fixing remuneration in proportion to the duties and responsibilities of the recipient. The Commissioners do not recognise the claim that teachers should under all circumstances be paid the full salaries attaching to their classification.

MR. MACALEESE: May I ask the right hon. Gentleman whether the same system obtains in this country?

*MR. G. W. BALFOUR: I am afraid I cannot answer that question.

LOCAL GOVERNMENT (IRELAND) ACT; ORDERS AND RULES UNDER.

MR. TULLY (Leitrim, S.): I beg to ask the Chief Secretary to the Lord Lieutenant of Ireland whether there have been complaints from the officials and members of the new county and district councils and also from the public as to the difficulty in procuring copies of the rules and regulations issued by the Privy Council and Local Government Board from time to time for the transaction of their business; and whether he will direct that copies of the Orders in Council and Local Government Board Orders will be put on sale to the public at the same time that they are put in force under the Local Government (Ireland) Act, 1898.

*MR. G. W. BALFOUR: The Orders in Council referred to have all been issued as Parliamentary papers, and copies can be procured through any bookseller. No complaints have been received as to the alleged difficulty in obtaining copies of these Orders in Council. Copies of the Orders issued by the Local Government Board are sent to every local body affected by the Orders, and to any member of the general public *bonâ fide* concerned who makes an application for a copy. It is proposed ultimately to print both the Orders in Council and Local Government Board Orders of a permanent character in one volume for presentation to Parliament.

MIGRATION OF THE POPULATION.

DR. ROBERT AMBROSE (Mayo, W.): I beg to ask the Chief Secretary for Ireland whether his attention has been drawn to a resolution of the Mayo County Council, passed unanimously at their meeting 20th May, in which they state that, in order to prevent the periodical recurrence of famine, and to render unnecessary the annual migration of large numbers of the adult male and female population of county Mayo, and thereby save them from the risk of a disaster such as befel the people of Achill a few years ago, in which a large body of them were drowned, it is necessary that compulsory powers be given to the County Council to acquire for purposes of migration and enlargement of holdings such lands as are available for such purposes in county Mayo; and whether, in view of such a resolution, passed unanimously by such a representative body as the County Council of Mayo, he will without delay introduce legislation to meet the views of that body.

*MR. G. W. BALFOUR: The reply to the first paragraph is in the affirmative, and to the second in the negative.

BRITISH NEW GUINEA PAPERS.

SIR JOHN LUBBOCK (London University): I beg to ask the Secretary of State for the Colonies whether he will publish the appendices and papers referred to in the Annual Report for 1897-98 on British New Guinea (C. 9046 26) recently issued, especially those relating to scientific subjects, referred to on pp. 75-77 of the Report, and designated by Sir W. MacGregor as of considerable interest and of much importance; and whether he will encourage the preparation of such Reports in future by affording facilities for their publication for the benefit of scientific research.

THE SECRETARY OF STATE FOR THE COLONIES (MR. J. CHAMBERLAIN, Birmingham, W.): The papers referred to are all published in Queensland, and copies are regularly furnished by my department to the various learned societies to whom they are likely to be of interest. It is the usual practice to publish any reports of general interest or utility not already published elsewhere.

ANGLO-AMERICAN COMMISSION.

SIR EDWARD GOURLEY: I beg to ask the Secretary of State for the Colonies if he will be good enough to inform the House whether the Anglo-American Commission is to re-assemble; if so, when: can he state the nature and extent of the differences alleged to exist between the American and Canadian members of the Commission; and whether the whole or any portion of the points at issue are to be referred to arbitration.

MR. J. CHAMBERLAIN : In reply to the first two questions I have nothing to add to the answers given by the Under Secretary of State for Foreign Affairs. Before the Commission adjourned proposals and counter proposals were made by the British and United States Commissioners for referring the question of the Alaska boundary to arbitration, but they had been unable to agree as to the arbitral tribunal and the terms of reference. Negotiations on this question are still proceeding between Her Majesty's Government and the United States Government.

IMPERIAL INSTITUTE.

MR. HOGAN (Tipperary, Mid.): I beg to ask the Secretary of State for the Colonies whether the conferences in reference to the future of the Imperial Institute are now concluded; and, if so, whether there is any objection to stating the general results or recommendations that have been arrived at.

MR. J. CHAMBERLAIN : Satisfactory progress has been made with the negotiations, and a definite proposal is now before the Senate of the University and the Council of the Institute. If, as is hoped, the replies of the two bodies are favourable, the result will be communicated to the House.

WEST INDIES—FRUIT STEAMERS—LOCAL DUTIES.

MR. LAWRENCE (Liverpool, Abercromby): I beg to ask the Secretary of State for the Colonies whether he can now state when the contemplated fruit steamers may be expected to commence running between the West India Islands and this country ; and when the return re Local Colonial Duties on Rum will be laid upon the Table.

MR. J. CHAMBERLAIN : (1) I am not yet able to fix a date for the commencement of this service. (2) Some of

the Colonies have not yet furnished the information required for completing the Return. When they have done so the Return will be laid without delay.

WAR OFFICE—NETHERAVON HOUSE, WILTS.

MR. GOULDING (Wilts., Devizes): I beg to ask the Under Secretary of State for War, with regard to the fact that Netheravon House, Wilts., which has been recently purchased by the Government for War Office purposes, is still untenanted, whether, in view of the disastrous results to the parish which will arise from the principal mansion not being inhabited, the Secretary of State for War will take immediate action to procure its early occupation.

*THE UNDER - SECRETARY OF STATE FOR WAR (Mr. WYNDHAM, Dover): Every effort has been and will be made by the War Department to obtain a tenant for Netheravon House.

SALISBURY PLAIN.

MR. THOMAS BAYLEY (Derbyshire, Chesterfield): I beg to ask the Financial Secretary to the War Office whether, in the Return No. 150, of 1899, which was ordered by the House in February last and distributed in May, of the gross and net rentals of property at Salisbury Plain purchased by the War Department, the column headed "present rental" gives in all cases the actual rental paid to the proprietor of the land at the time of purchase, or whether in any cases the amount of rental in that column represents a nominal rental which in practice was reduced by an allowance of, in some cases, as much as 20 per cent. reduction on the nominal rent.

*THE FINANCIAL SECRETARY TO THE WAR OFFICE (Mr. POWELL WILLIAMS, Birmingham, S.): The Return contains the rentals paid under the various agreements, but what reduction has been customary from those rentals I am not able to say without further reference. Perhaps the hon. Gentleman will put the question down again.

MR. THOMAS BAYLEY : I will do so.

MR. GIBSON BOWLES (King's Lynn): Have any tenants failed to pay the reduced rent to the War Office ?

Q

*MR. POWELL WILLIAMS : Some of them claim to receive from the War Office a reduction similar to that which they formerly received.

MR. GIBSON BOWLES : Was that taken into account in the price ?

*MR. POWELL WILLIAMS : No, I think not.

BARRACKS AND MILITARY WORKS LOAN BILL.

MR. BUCHANAN (Aberdeenshire, E.): I beg to ask the Under Secretary of State for War when the Barracks and Military Works Loan Bill will be introduced.

*MR. WYNDHAM : I hope to bring in a Bill at an early date.

PUNJAUB WAR AND TIRAH CAMPAIGN MEDALS.

MR. H. D. GREENE (Shrewsbury): I beg to ask the Secretary of State for India whether medals and clasps for service in the last Punjaub War and the Tirah Campaign, 1897-8, have been issued to officers and men of the Bengal Staff Corps entitled thereto ; and, if not, what is the cause of the delay, and when the distribution will take place.

THE SECRETARY OF STATE FOR INDIA (LORD GEORGE HAMILTON, Middlesex, Ealing): The medals and clasps granted for the operations on the Punjaub frontier in 1897-98 have been in course of distribution since last summer. Any delay which may have occurred is due to the medal rolls not having been promptly submitted.

INDIAN CONFECTIONERY TRADE.

MR. MACLEAN (Cardiff): I beg to ask the President of the Board of Trade whether he can now give the correct figures showing the quantity and value of exports of British confectionery, and of re-exports of foreign and colonial confectionery of all kinds to India ?

THE PRESIDENT OF THE BOARD OF TRADE (MR. C. T. RITCHIE, Croydon): I have communicated with the Customs on this subject, but I am informed that it would not be possible to compile from the records available in that Department a trustworthy return of the nature desired.

FINANCE BILL.

As amended, considered.

*LORD ALWYNE COMPTON (Beds, Biggleswade): I beg to move the following new clause :—

> The proviso at the end of section four of The Finance Act, 1894, shall be repealed, and the following proviso inserted in lieu thereof :—
>
> Provided that any property so passing in which the deceased never had an interest, or which under a disposition not made by the deceased passes immediately on the death of the deceased to some person other than a person taking an interest in property passing at the death of the deceased of which the deceased was competent to dispose, shall not be aggregated with any other property but shall be an estate by itself, and the estate duty shall be levied at the proper graduated rate on the principal value thereof ; but if any benefit under a disposition not made by the deceased is reserved or given to a person taking an interest in property passing at the death of the deceased of which the deceased was competent to dispose, such benefit shall be aggregated with property of the deceased for the purpose of determining the rate of estate duty."

This new clause which I propose to add to the Bill seeks to remedy an injustice which, I contend, is contained in Clause 4 of the Finance Act of 1894. It is practically the same as an Amendment which I moved last year, but in it I have endeavoured to meet the criticisms by which I was upon that occasion met, and I hope I have succeeded in doing so. If the House will permit me, I will endeavour to show, as briefly and clearly as possible, what is the injustice of which we complain, and what is the remedy which I seek to apply. It is true that Clause 4 of the Finance Act of 1894 gives exemption in certain cases where property passes on a man's death from its being aggregated with free property in his own possession, but in the proviso which I seek to repeal there is an exception to that exemption in respect of lineal ancestor, lineal descendant, husband, or wife. That sounds rather paradoxical, perhaps, but let us look at it in this way. Take the case of a man who dies, having settled property in which he has merely a life interest. He also has free property of his own—that is, property which he is free to dispose of, say, for instance, to the extent of £100,000. The settled property passes to his eldest son on his death, but as the law stands at present the whole of the property, settled or free, is aggregated. Thus the younger children who succeed to but a small portion of the personal estate, it may be, have to pay the whole rate of duty as upon the settled estate and upon the free property aggregated together. That constitutes, to my mind, a hardship—at least, it is regarded as a hardship by those upon whom the burden has fallen. I do not expect to get very much sympathy in the matter, particularly from hon. Members opposite, for I know that their view of the matter is that if a man succeeds to anything at all it is fair that he should pay a heavy rate of duty upon it. But that is not my only point. Take the case of the same man ; he also has £100,000, and suppose that he has no sons at all, and that the property passes either to his collaterals or to strangers, under the law as it now stands it is not aggregated at all. That is illogical, unfair, and perfectly unsound, and is absolutely opposed to every principle of the succession and legacy duties ever since those duties have been invented, inasmuch as the strangers and the collaterals in succeeding to the same property are paying a less tax than the lineal descendants. Now I am not aware whether the draftsman of this clause knew what would be the effect of the words he used ; but of one thing I am quite certain, and that is that the author of the Bill himself, the right hon. Gentleman the Member for West Monmouth, did not dream what the effect would be, for when last year I brought up the subject he said that the exemption for which Section 4 provided was only intended to operate in cases where there was no connection between the deceased and the persons to whom the property passed. May I take the case again of the same man with £100,000. Supposing that he has no children, the estate will not be aggregated to pay the full rate of the high estate duty, and his brother who succeeds to the whole settled property and the free property will escape aggregation. That is the injustice of which I complain. I hope that this new clause, which stands in my name, will be accepted, because it will remove that injustice, and the younger children and the wife will derive the benefit from the property which the deceased has power to dispose of and which he naturally wishes to give to them. Their

property will escape aggregation with the larger settled property which goes to the elder son. As there must always be a *quid pro quo* in these matters, I am prepared to present to the Chancellor of the Exchequer brothers and collaterals. Under my clause the brothers and the collaterals or the strangers who obtain both settled property and free property —there having been no children—will be aggregated, and only the wife or the younger children will escape. Of course, I know that several criticisms have been levelled against the clause as it stands. Certain Members opposite say that the Finance Act of 1894 should not be touched at all. My answer to that is that whatever they may feel in regard to the Act, I am certain that they do not care to see an injustice done, and that if once an injustice is proved they will seek to remedy it. I think I have proved my case that there is an injustice, and I ask their sympathy and assistance in getting this injustice removed. There arises the question of the loss to the Revenue which this exemption would cause. I have examined the matter most closely, and I cannot see that any great loss would fall on the Chancellor of the Exchequer. The bulk of the property which a man leaves must be either settled property or free property. Suppose a man left a million of free property to his children, all that would be aggregated and pay the full rate. In the same way if he left settled property the eldest son would not escape aggregation ; the only loss would be in the case of the younger children and the wife, who would succeed to some small portion of the man's free property. Supposing that a millionaire leaves £100,000 of his property free, dividing it amongst his four younger sons, or £25,000 to each, it would be aggregated and pay the 8 per cent. duty. But under my clause they would only pay 4½ per cent. If six millionaires died in the year the loss would only be £21,000, while from the settled property the revenue would receive £480,000. That seems a very small loss to remedy a great injustice. I also ask a little assistance from hon. Members on this side of the House. I beg them to remember that when this Act was introduced Members on this side of the House fought it most desperately, and it was talked about on every platform at the last General Election. And I appeal also to the

Chancellor of the Exchequer. I hope that some of my logic has penetrated his armour, and that he will be able to agree to my request. I do not profess to have a legal mind, and it is quite possible that the wording of the clause may not be quite satisfactory, but I trust that he will admit the principle of the clause. I beg to move the new clause standing in my name.

A Clause (Amendment of s. 4 of The Finance Act, 1894, restricting the exemptions thereby given to non-lineals from the principle of aggregation, and extending certain exemptions to persons taking benefits under separate disposition)—(*Lord Alwyne Compton*)—brought up, and read the first time :—

Motion made and Question proposed— "That the Clause be read a second time."

*THE CHANCELLOR OF THE EXCHEQUER (Sir M. HICKS BEACH, Bristol, W.): One of the main principles of the Act of 1894 was that all property passing on the death of a deceased person should be aggregated for the purposes of estate duty. It was found impossible in practice by the Government which passed that Act to carry out that principle completely, because it was felt that where property passing on the death of a deceased person included property in which he had no interest, or which he was never at any time competent to dispose of, and which passed to complete strangers—that it would be unfair to aggregate that property with property passing to lineals for the purposes of determining estate duty, and thus entail a higher estate duty on wife, husband, son, or daughter as compared with that which they ought to pay on property passing to them. And therefore the Act as it stands departs from the great principle of the estate duty, which is to have no reference to the person to whom the property passes, but to have reference solely to the property which passes at death of the deceased ; and it provides that where property in which the deceased never had any interest, or which he was not competent to dispose of, passes to non-lineals or to strangers, then in that case it will not be aggregated with the rest of the estate for the purposes of the estate duty. The hon. and learned Gentleman the Member for Dumfries Burghs, when this matter

Lord Compton.

was raised last year by my noble friend, pointed out that no doubt to some extent this was a relief to lineals, for the result was that the rate of estate duty was less from this non-aggregation. But my noble friend very fairly said that that did not remove the grievance of lineals, because *inter se* they still had to pay the rate of duty on the whole of the property passing to them at death, although the main bulk of the property would pass to the elder son, and a very small portion pass to the younger children, on which the younger children would have to pay a high rate of duty. My noble friend endeavoured last year to remedy this grievance. Well, I think he felt that the proposal he made would not satisfactorily effect his desires, and I know that he has devoted very much consideration to the clause which he has just moved. In fact, I think any one who listened to the speech he has just delivered will recognise that he has gone into the minutiæ of a complicated subject with great ability and energy. But I am bound to say—and my noble friend is aware of the fact—that the clause as it stands, if embodied in the law, would not carry out his wishes, because, although it would remedy some grievances, it would effect other grievances even greater than those which he seeks to remedy. He proposes to take away with one hand a certain amount from the Revenue, and to give a considerable amount with the other hand. Having had this matter investigated during the last three weeks very carefully by the Board of Inland Revenue, I do not think the net loss to the Revenue would be very serious. But there would be grievances effected in certain cases, which my noble friend and the hon. Member for Woodbridge who sits beside him are aware of, and which I am quite sure neither of them would desire to inflict. Now I have a proposal to make to my noble friend. If the right hon. Gentleman the Member for West Monmouth and the hon. and learned Member for the Dumfries Burghs were here to-day, I think they would admit that this question of aggregation is not at present in a satisfactory condition ; they would admit that there is ground for the complaint my noble friend has made, and that some endeavour should be made to remedy that complaint, without at the same time causing other sources of complaint and of loss to the

Revenue. Now, if my noble friend will not press this clause to-day, what I propose is this. The question is most complicated and most difficult. It is one which if the House would be good enough to take my advice they would not attempt to deal with without inquiry. I would propose that in the course of the autumn a Departmental Committee should be appointed to consider this subject, on which I should be extremely glad to have the services of my noble friend and of other hon. Members who are interested in this matter. We must endeavour to thresh the matter out and arrive at some result, which may be embodied in legislation next year, which will remedy this grievance without causing any great loss to the Revenue or creating other grievances.

Sir H. CAMPBELL-BANNERMAN (Stirling Burghs): I believe that there are in the House a few Members who think that they understand this subject, but are there any Members who really in their conscience could declare that they do understand the question? I am not so sure but that there are two gentlemen sitting next each other on the Opposition bench—the noble Lord and the hon. Member for Woodbridge—who understand it; and the hon. Member for King's Lynn, who knows everything; and there are my hon. and learned friends, the Members for Dumfries and Haddington, the ex-Chancellor of the Exchequer, and the right hon. Gentleman who at present holds that office. A good many of these authorities—certainly all on this side of the House—are absent to-day. Far be it from me to intervene in a matter which I cannot say I really understand. But the right hon. Gentleman has made a proposal which appears to me to be exceedingly discreet and wise. There is a danger, in the administration of this most intricate law, of harshness towards individuals, and also a danger of affecting the interests of the State. The right hon. Gentleman, as I understand it, proposes that there shall be a Departmental Committee, or a body of that kind, to inquire into the working of aggregation, and to report what amendment that Committee would recommend on the present practice. I have had an opportunity of knowing to some extent the opinion of the author of the Act, my right hon. friend the Member for West Monmouth, and, although I am not entitled to speak in his name, I understand he will have no objection to an inquiry into the matter. Of course the inquiry is to affect not the principle but the working of the provision which carries the principle into effect. That being so, I think I can assure the right hon. Gentleman that the opinion on this side of the House, very unworthily represented by me, is in favour of the proposal of the right hon. Gentleman for a Committee.

Mr. GIBSON BOWLES (Lynn Regis): I am very much obliged to the right hon. Gentleman the Leader of the Opposition for the compliment he has paid me that I know everything. I know perfectly well that under certain circumstances and on some occasions I can be as ignorant as the Leader of the Opposition himself. I have, I admit, taken some trouble in regard to this question of aggregation. As to the particular point referred to by my noble friend, it is one of the grievances called "hard cases." It is not a very large grievance and it exists in a very few limited number of instances. If my noble friend's clause were adopted it would, undoubtedly, not have any great effect on the Revenue. While it would relieve to some extent a hardship, it would bring in further revenue in another direction. But I think it is extremely dangerous to deal with an Act of this sort piecemeal and by way of meeting hard cases as they arise. If you have to deal with it you should deal with principles, and modify them where you can. I will not enlarge upon the Amendment of my noble friend, because I presume, that, after the concession made by the Chancellor of the Exchequer, he will not press it. What I say, however, is that the Chancellor of the Exchequer has bowels of compassion for some of the hard cases under this Act, but for others he seems to have none. The case of aggregation I fully admit is one of the difficulties of the Act. I have made a calculation, and have arrived at the conclusion, and I believe I am right, that instead of there being, as was intended under the Act, one aggregation of all property, there are no less than 19 aggregations and segregations of property, and so, instead of having one rate, you have 19 different rates; therefore no doubt aggregation in itself and by itself is a very proper subject for inquiry, but it is not the only subject for inquiry. If the right hon. Gentleman is going to inquire into one of the hardships which he thinks may be included in this Act, there are others which require attention. There is the assumption that everything a man has in his life is supposed to be a fraud under the Act. There is the assumption under which you give your wife a ring, and die within twelve months, and your wife has to pay duty on all the rest of the property. Then again, if a man gives a reduction of 25 per cent. in the rent to his tenants, duty has to be paid on the 25 per cent. because it is a gift. I could name half a dozen hardships and I therefore trust that if a Departmental Committee is to be appointed it will not be restricted to the question of aggregation.

MR. HALDANE (Haddington): I have listened with attention to the speech of the hon. Member for King's Lynn. The clause of the noble Lord is one which deals with a subject which I agree is a very intricate one. Aggregation under the Finance Act is simple enough where it is a case merely of two estates belonging to the same testator passing at death. There it is a plain enough principle to treat them as one. But when you come to two estates passing upon the testator's death, one of which has not been his own, you get to a much more difficult question of justice. It may often be very unfair to tax on the aggregate footing. There are other cases in which it may be apparent that such taxation should take place, and the difficulty is to find the true principle. Now, as the law at present stands it is very defective. If an estate not belonging to the testator passes to one son on his death, and another estate to another son, there is aggregation. It may be a very small estate or a very big estate, and that may be a real injustice; because the duty is not, as is generally the case with the testator's property, taken out of the bulk of the testator's property before it passes to the beneficiary; the whole burden in that case may fall upon one very ill able to bear it. Take another instance. Property passes on a testator's death to his brother, part of it under the testator's own will, and part of it under an outside settlement. There is no aggregation. . . . . as wrong as the other is . . . . . yet both arise under the law of the existing Act. The amendment of the noble Lord has much to

Mr. G. Bowles.

commend it, but in this proposal every reform in so difficult a field wants great consideration. The suggestion of a Committee which has been made by the Chancellor of the Exchequer seems to me to be a very proper one, and a suggestion to which Members on this side of the House should accede. Speaking for myself, I have only one view of what is right with regard to this matter, and that is, while being ready to strengthen the Act in order to carry out its principle, to be ready equally to pare off all the minor injustices—sometimes, I admit, galling—arising from the application which has been made of a novel principle in an Act which is without exact precedent.

LORD ALWYNE COMPTON: In moving the clause I had no intention of going behind the Act. I am perfectly confident that the more the matter is scrutinised the more clearly will it be established that there is an injustice, and as an inquiry has been promised by the Chancellor of the Exchequer I beg to withdraw the Amendment.

Motion and clause, by leave, withdrawn.

MR. GIBSON BOWLES: At the present time, as hon. Members are no doubt aware, the principle of the Act is that the first duty shall be charged upon the principal value, but in the case of agricultural property there is a special proviso which provides that the principal value shall not exceed 25 times the annual value as assessed. The annual value is arrived at by a severe process of deduction. There are deductions for tithes, insurance, rates, management, and rents—in fact, for every conceivable charge on land; and the absolutely irreducible minimum which is left, multiplied by 25, is the principal value to be taxed. That proviso was introduced by the First Lord of the Treasury, the intention of the proviso being clearly shown by the following short extract from the right hon. Gentleman's speech:

"The main object of my Amendment is to secure that the owners of agricultural land, which is practically, or very nearly, unsaleable, shall pay upon the value which such land will fetch in the open market. Of course I admit that 25 years' purchase is probably far too much for a great deal of the agricultural land of the country."

There are three ways of dealing with this question. You may either remove the proviso and leave agricultural land to be treated on its real principal value, or you may say—and I think this is the method to which I should give preference—that twenty-five years, instead of being the maximum, should be the minimum. Then there is the third method, which I now propose to the House, and that is, to extend to other land beside agricultural land the advantages given to that particular land. I do not think it right that an estate which brings in net £1,000 a year should only pay on £25,000 value. Would a gentleman who has an estate worth £1,000 a year be prepared to take £25,000 for it ? I doubt very much whether he would take £40,000 or £50,000 ; and if there were special advantages attaching to it he might ask £60,000, £70,000, £80,000, or even £90,000. I therefore think there is a specially favourable estimate given to agricultural land, which I think should be extended to other land. Take an example. Two very interesting Returns have been presented to the House with regard to the purchase of land by the War Office on Salisbury Plain. They are not absolutely correct—neither gross nor net rental is correct. We have heard to-day from the Under Secretary of State for War that the gross rentals are not correct because the farmers are claiming the deductions which they have had for years, part of which are not included. Therefore any deduction I draw from the Returns would be rather less favourable than they appear. I only propose to draw one moral from the figures, and that is, that the gross rental is admittedly higher than the rental the farmers have paid. The Commissioners of Inland Revenue tell us that the average number of years' purchase on which they have been getting duty on the gross annual value is, in the case of agricultural property, between 16 and 17 ; in the case of house property—*i.e.*, leasehold, no doubt—between 15 and 16 ; and in the case of ground rents about 27, so that there is an enormous difference. The gross rental in the return is £9,429, and if we multiply it by 17 it will give the value of the whole property at about £160,000. The War Office paid £476,000 for it, and therefore it comes to this, that while the selling price in the market is £476,000, estate duty is only paid on £160,000. Then, if the net rental of £6,316 is multiplied by 25, it gives £157,000. There again there is a very vast difference between the sum on which duty is paid and the actual price of the estate. I think it is right that agricultural land should have these advantages, but I hold also that other classes of land should have the same advantages. I have never ceased in my opposition, not to the death duties, for I regard them as an excellent form of taxation, but to the false principle and the exaggerated rates of duty imposed by the Finance Act of 1894. But if the principle of the Act is to remain, if the rates of the duty under it are to be charged, then let us all be tarred with the same brush as regards personal property, agricultural property, and urban landed property. The reason is that I know perfectly well that if I get everybody tarred with the same brush they will be more ready to join with me in securing Amendments. My difficulty always has been to get the assent of the country gentlemen to the improvement of this Act. They will not assist me because they are taxed so lightly under this 25 years' arrangement ; but if I can get all the duty put up to the same rate, then I think they will not be able to wrap themselves in their mantle of 25 years and hold themselves disinterested. It is a very great advantage when we wish to have a bad law repealed to put it in force as far as possible, and it is on that principle that I should like to see a bad law made a little more harsh where it presses least. The Amendment which I propose to move would extend to other land the provisions which now apply to agricultural land. I can hardly expect its ready acceptance by my right hon. friend the Chancellor of the Exchequer. In fact, I rather expect his opposition, because he told the House he meant to resist whatever I propose in reference to the death duties.

*Sir M. HICKS BEACH: No, no !

Mr. GIBSON BOWLES : Let me quote my right hon. friend's words :

"I have resisted the insidious proposal of the hon. Member for King's Lynn, and, whatever he says, I shall continue to resist him, because I know that his object is to destroy the Act, not legitimately, but by evasions which will prevent its working."

I have never suggested evasions, but I have proposed Amendments. My right hon. friend says he will always resist my proposals, but he accepted half a dozen of them in the Act of 1896, although he did not think it necessary to inform the House that they were my suggestions. I do not expect that my present proposal will be accepted, but I put it forward for consideration, and the reasons I have given in support of it are not without a certain amount of cogency.

New Clause (extension of special method of valuation of agricultural property to other landed property)—(*Mr. Gibson Bowles*)—brought up, and read the first time.

Motion made, and Question proposed— "That the Clause be read a second time."

*SIR M. HICKS BEACH : The hon. Member's speech is a singular argument in favour of the proposal he has made to the House. He started with the assumption that agricultural land had an unfair advantage in taxation by the proviso in the Finance Act. The hon. Member's original proposal on the Paper was that instead of 25 years being the maximum, it should be the minimum at which agricultural land should be valued. What he really desires is to increase the number of years' purchase at which agricultural land is assessed for the purpose of the death duties, and his argument tended in that direction because he based it on the price given by the War Office for the land recently purchased on Salisbury Plain for manœuvring purposes. When land is purchased under compulsory powers by a Government Department from owners who do not wish to sell, it is not likely that it will be obtained at a low value. It would be absurd to assess for taxation the land generally throughout the country on such a basis. The hon. Member says he thinks the law as it stands is inequitable. What did he say when this very proviso was under discussion? He said it was a concession on the part of the Government, and he went on to point out that the Government had driven rather a hard bargain, as the number of years' purchase of agricultural land was taken at 25 as a maximum, but that so high a figure had never been taken up to the present in regard to agricultural land. Therefore the hon. Member at the time

Mr. G. Bowles,

did not think it unfair or inequitable to assess agricultural land more lightly than any other class of land or property, Now he desires, by his proposal, not to increase the rate at which agricultural land may be assessed, but to extend a low rate of assessment to other classes of realty. In the first place, I would say, in regard to house property, that there is absolutely no reason for the proposal. House property must necessarily be subject to very large deductions for repairs in assessing its annual value for the purpose of death duties or anything else. I find that the highest average number of years' purchase at which house property has been valued in the course of the last five years for death duty is a little over eighteen years on the net value, which is lower than the average on agricultural land, so that if the proviso of the hon. Member were applied to house property it would have no practical effect, while it would draw a most invidious distinction between freehold and leasehold house property, and I think he will see that himself. But when we come to another head of realty, viz., ground rents, I must venture to say that this proviso would be entirely inapplicable. Ground rents are not too heavily taxed, in my opinion—I have never thought otherwise—for death duty purposes, for the simple reason that they are not liable to the kind of deductions to which the ordinary ownership of real property, such as houses and agricultural land, is liable. I hope I have said enough to convince the House that the proposal of my hon. friend is unnecessary and impracticable.

MR. JAMES LOWTHER (Kent, Thanet) : My hon. friend the Member for King's Lynn, on questions of this nature, is regarded as a very competent authority, and I could hardly believe my eyes when I read the suggestions in his first clause. I need hardly assure him that I would rather endeavour to forget what is past, and to believe that he placed his clause on the paper simply for the purpose of illustration. My hon. friend talks about an irreducible minimum in connection with the value of agricultural landed property. If my hon. friend had any practical experience he would know differently. We all find that what we thought was an irreducible minimum last year is from various causes still further reduced this year. Then, my hon. friend makes no distinction between the case of an estate determined in accordance with an Act of Parliament depriving owners of their land without their consent and that of land disposed of in the open market. I am sorry my hon. friend has so far fallen away from his sphere of usefulness, and I am sorry also to take exception to another line of argument he employed. He talked of the death duties as a very sound source of Revenue, subject to the restrictions which he himself would place upon them. I think they are a very objectionable means of raising Revenue, and I have always held that view. My hon. friend's authority is high—I say it in no sarcastic spirit—no one knows the system and principles of taxation better than he does, but he has not added to his authority by that statement. I have no objection to relief being given to the taxpayer if it be put forward on a fair and thorough basis, but I do not understand when my hon. friend proposes his clause that that is his intention. I think it will have the effect of weakening the slight concession made to agricultural land, and I hope on this ground that he will not press the matter.

Mr. LABOUCHERE (Northampton): I understand, from what fell from the hon. Member for King's Lynn, that certain lands have been sold to the War Office on Salisbury Plain, and that this land would amount, roughly speaking, to £150,000. These lands, I understand, have been sold for something like £400,000. The Chancellor of the Exchequer says we must take into consideration the fact that something was paid for disturbance. I believe 10 per cent. was paid for disturbance, and that would be in all £165,000. Consequently the landowners are gaining too great an advantage from the present state of the death duties. Admitting that they have been sold at a fair price, as a matter of fact, landowners at the present moment only pay between one-third and one-half of what other persons with money have to pay for death duties. If that is so, I can only say that landowners gain an undue advantage as against personal property, and the sooner that state of things is altered the better it will be for the community.

Motion and clause, by leave, withdrawn.

Amendment proposed, in new Clause 3 (inserted in Committee), line 6, after the word "enumerated," to insert the words "and tested."—(*Mr. Chancellor of the Exchequer.*)

Question proposed—
"That those words be there inserted."

Mr. LOUGH (Islington, W.): I desire to point out that we have not seen these clauses before, and we do not know anything about the changes proposed in the Finance Bill which we are considering. The right hon. Gentleman is now proposing an Amendment which we have never seen before. I venture to say that if the right hon. Gentleman will give the matter consideration he will come to the conclusion that we ought to have the Bill printed as it now stands, and let us see it in its new form before he asks us to proceed with it.

*Sir M. HICKS BEACH: I omitted in the first instance to move that the Bill should be reprinted, and afterwards I forgot the matter; but this clause which I desire to amend is the clause imposing the duty on bottled spirits. I should be very happy to read it.

Mr. LOUGH: We cannot take it in like that, because we have not measured carefully the effect of this Amendment.

Sir H. CAMPBELL-BANNERMAN: The right hon. Gentleman has, I dare say, explained very fully the meaning of this Amendment. At the same time I must appeal not only to his sense of fairness, but also to his recollection of the ordinary proceedings of the House, whether it is not an extraordinary thing to ask us to discuss this Finance Bill without having had the Bill reprinted with the Amendments inserted in it in Committee. I venture to say that a first-class Bill of this kind should have been reprinted, because the Bill was very substantially amended in Committee. There were great changes made in the rates chargeable on wines and spirits, and there was a long Amendment inserted by the hon. Member for Staffordshire. I notice on the Paper that there is a series of important Amendments by the right hon. Gentleman, and I think he will readily see what sort of position we are in. Surely we ought to have the Bill before us after going through Committee, as it issued from that stage, before we are invited to consider any further Amendments upon it. I do not think it would be unreasonable to adjourn the consideration of this Bill until Thursday, in order that we might have the Bill reprinted.

MR. CALDWELL (Lanark, Mid.): In order to give effect to the contention put forward I will move "that the consideration of this Bill be postponed." The Chancellor of the Exchequer knows perfectly well that the Bill will pass on Thursday if it is taken up then, and the right hon. Gentleman must admit the reasonableness of the claim for delay.

SIR H. H. FOWLER (Wolverhampton, E.): I beg leave to second the adjournment, and I appeal to the Chancellor of the Exchequer to accept it, because otherwise a very dangerous precedent may be set. The House has very strict rules in reference to financial matters, and the Chancellor of the Exchequer, I am sure, would not like to weaken our control in regard to financial legislation. A great many important changes, and certainly a very important new clause, was introduced, which I did not quite understand, by the hon. Member for West Staffordshire. We have not seen the Bill printed in its amended form, and we have not had an opportunity of putting down any Amendment. As a matter of principle, as well as propriety, I appeal to the Chancellor of the Exchequer to postpone the Bill. The London Government Bill is the next order, and we can get on with that. We will give every facility for the passing of this Bill, but I think we ought to maintain the absolute freedom of the House in dealing with financial matters.

*SIR M. HICKS BEACH: I really think that I have some grounds of complaint, for, although I assumed that the Bill would be reprinted, no notice was given me that objection would be taken to proceeding with the Bill because it has not been reprinted. If this matter had been mentioned to me yesterday——

SIR H. CAMPBELL-BANNERMAN: But we did not know until this morning.

Sir H. Campbell-Bannerman.

*SIR M. HICKS BEACH: There have not been such important changes in the Bill as hon. Members seem to think, although some changes were made in the wine and spirit duties. However, I do not wish to force the matter on the House, and as the Bill has not been printed I will consent to the debate being adjourned.

Debate adjourned till Thursday.

Bill, as amended, to be printed.   [Bill 227.]

LONDON GOVERNMENT BILL.

As amended, considered.

MR. MOON (St. Pancras, N.): I think that the attitude of those who have oft-times the control of public records is hardly so sympathetic as it should be, and they do not take that care and interest in them which they should. I think, therefore, that the Amendment I have on the Paper is necessary, especially the last portion empowering new borough councils to spend money in the proper registration of their records.

*MR. SPEAKER: Order, order! The hon. Member cannot move the last portion, as it clearly involves a charge upon the rates.

MR. MOON: Then I beg to move the first portion of the clause down to the word "for their preservation."

New clause—

"No person shall be eligible as borough councillor who holds any office the salary of which is paid either wholly or partly out of funds provided either directly or indirectly out of the rates or out of the county fund. It shall be the duty of every new borough council formed under this Act by the incorporation of a single parish to take effectual measures for the care and preservation of all vestry minutes, rate books, valuation books, maps, and all other records belonging to the civil parish, and in cases when a new borough council is formed by the incorporation of several parishes or district boards, it shall be the duty of the new borough council to collect the records belonging to the said parishes and district boards, and to take measures for their preservation. And it shall be lawful for any new borough council to expend money out of the rates for the preparation and printing of inventories and calendars of such documents which may be deemed to be of historical or public interest."—(*Mr. Moon.*)

brought up, and read the first time.

Motion made, and Question proposed—

" That the clause be read a second time."

THE FIRST LORD OF THE TREASURY (MR A. J. BALFOUR, Manchester E.) : I am in hearty sympathy with my hon. friend. I think indeed, a question has already been put to me in the House on the general subject, and that I have given a specific answer. I do not think it would be desirable to attempt to deal with the preservation of ancient records in a clause of this kind, simply in reference to the case of London, and not in reference to the country at large. I think it is true that all over the country we have a very imperfect record of historic documents, and probably the people who are day by day in occupation of their office do not devote that attention and money that is required in order to keep in order valuable and historic documents which throw a very useful light upon the past. I do not think that anything will be gained for the object which my friend has in view by adopting even only the words he is allowed to move. He cannot move the latter part of his proposed Amendment because that would be out of order, and with regard to the other portion I think the whole matter is amply safeguarded by present legislation. The whole subject is at present under investigation, and a Report will shortly be represented upon which practical steps will, probably, be taken, applying to the whole of the country.

MR. BRYCE (Aberdeen, S.): After the observation made by the right hon. Gentleman I do not propose to support the Amendment. I hear with great pleasure the assurance of the right hon. Gentleman, and, as he realises the importance of the matter and is only deterred from dealing with it by the fact that it should be dealt with comprehensively, I hope that when he does deal with the matter, having regard to the great importance of the question, he will precede any step which he intends to take by having a systematic inquiry.

MR. MOON : I beg leave to withdraw the clause.

Motion and clause, by leave, withdrawn.

MR. PICKERSGILL (Bethnal Green, S.W.): The object of the Amendment I have placed upon the Paper is to provide an easy, expeditious and cheap method of dealing with any questions of law that may arise with reference to this Bill. The proposed clause is merely a reproduction of Clause 8, which was put into the Local Government Acts of 1888 and 1894. In both cases, but especially as regards the Act of 1888, that clause has been largely availed of and has been found very useful. I do not think anyone can object to the clause, because it does not make this mode of raising a question exclusive, but merely provides that it shall be raised in accordance with the precedent I have referred to. I beg to move the clause.

New clause—

" If any question arises, or is about to arise, as to whether any power, duty, or liability is or is not transferred by or under this Act to the council of any metropolitan borough, or any property is or is not vested in any such council, that question, without prejudice to any other mode of trying it, may, on the application of the council, be submitted for decision to the High Court in such summary manner as, subject to any rules of Court, may be directed by the Court ; and the Court, after hearing such parties and taking such evidence (if any) as it thinks just, shall decide the question."—(*Mr. Pickersgill.*)

brought up and read the first time.

Motion made and Question proposed—

" That the clause be now read a second time."

THE SOLICITOR - GENERAL (Sir R. B. FINLAY, Inverness Burghs): I doubt whether this clause will be as necessary as the one in the Acts of 1888 and 1894 ; at the same time I have no objection to it whatever.

Question put and agreed to.

Clause read the first and second time, and added.

SIR R. B. FINLAY : The Amendment I now propose is a drafting Amendment, and at the same time rests upon the principle which I understood the House and Committee adopted, namely, that the whole of the county outside the City is to be comprised in the Schedule of the Bill. That being so, the wording of the section is not very applicable to the case, and this Amendment is merely to make it applicable.

Amendment proposed—

" In Clause 1, page 1, line 20, after 'administrator,' to insert ' and to establish and incorporate a council for each of the boroughs so formed.' "—(*Mr. Solicitor-General.*)

Question proposed—

" That those words be there inserted."

MR. SYDNEY BUXTON (Tower Hamlets, Poplar): The object of these Amendments taken altogether is to get rid of any friction that is likely to arise in the creation of areas outside London. That is one of the objects for which the Bill was introduced, and I am bound to say that the most extraordinary state of things that was ever seen in this House occurred on the last evening of this discussion, when we had about 17 areas scheduled in the Bill, and the right hon. Gentleman the First Lord of the Treasury cut and carved out the rest of London at his own sweet will. What was done was done, I am glad to say, in a very satisfactory manner, and I do not propose to oppose this Amendment. I am glad now that there is so little left for the Commissioners to deal with, and I think we ought to ask the Government whether, under the circumstances, it is necessary to appoint special Commissioners.

MR. A. J. BALFOUR: It seems to me the hon. Gentleman is rather hard to please. He first congratulates the Government on carving up the boroughs, and then he objects to the way in which it is done. The arrangement has been eminently successful. It was impossible to lay down a hard and fast proposition, and I think we have approached the limit of perfection as nearly as poor human nature can be expected to approach it. We may confidently expect that when the Schedule does appear it will embrace nearly all London. I think this Amendment should be accepted.

*COLONEL HUGHES (Woolwich): The whole of London is included, except, perhaps, Stoke Newington.

MR. A. J. BALFOUR: We have arranged for that.

*COLONEL HUGHES: If that is to be a separate borough, I think it ought to be so decided.

MR. PICKERSGILL: The Solicitor-General said that his Amendment was to adapt the Bill to the Schedule. The Schedule is not complete, and I do not think there is anything relating to the way in which Stoke Newington is to be dealt with. That being so, I do think the Committee is entitled to ask the Government now how they intend to proceed in that matter.

MR. A. J. BALFOUR: I should suggest that that should be reserved till we reach the Schedule, when it will be open to hon. Members to discuss this matter and modify the Schedule; in which case we shall have to remodel the Bill.

Question put and agreed to.

Other Amendments made.

Amendment proposed—

" In Clause 1, page 1, line 21, to leave out sub-section (b)."—(*Mr. Solicitor-General.*)

*COLONEL HUGHES: I want to know what is going to be done in Stoke Newington. I do not see how such cases as Stoke Newington can be dealt with if this sub-section is taken out. If Stoke Newington, with a population of only 30,000 or 40,000, is to be made into a borough, why should not Plumstead, with a population of 62,000, have the same privileges?

MR. A. J. BALFOUR: My hon. friend will, I think, see that if I complied with his desire I would be gradually dragged into a most inconvenient discussion on the Schedule. My hon. friend will have full opportunity on the Schedule of explaining his views in regard to Stoke Newington and Plumstead, and I very earnestly hope that he will reserve to that occasion any controversial matter he may desire to bring forward.

Amendment agreed to.

MR. COURTNEY (Cornwall, Bodmin): In discussing this question of the eligibility of women to serve as aldermen or councillors in the new borough councils, I hope that the House will remain in the same good temper which prevailed when the subject was under discussion on a former occasion. I believe it is admitted on all hands that it is necessary that in the Bill this question should be settled by express words. As the Bill now stands there are various opinions as to what it effects. Some hold that women are clearly eligible to sit as councillors, but not as aldermen ; while others hold that women are not only eligible to sit as councillors and aldermen, but are eligible even to become mayors. I think it is well to dismiss the question altogether of the interpretation of the Bill as it stands, and to decide expressly whether women shall be eligible to sit as councillors and aldermen. These councils which we are now creating will take over with very little alteration the work of the existing vestries. It may be that in the future that work will be enlarged, and I shall be glad to see every opportunity seized to increase the scope of the work ; but I do not think that the work will be seriously enlarged for some time. Now, on the vestries as at present constituted women sit. They are eligible to be elected, and they are elected. I find there is a large concurrence of opinion from those who have had practical experience of the work of women on vestries that there is much appropriate work for them to do, which cannot be discharged with equal qualifications and ability by the male members of the councils. The most important work of the new borough councils for a long time will be sanitary work ; and in relation to the provision of sanitation, the revision of existing deficiencies, suggestions for the amendment of sanitary legislation, and, above all, sanitary inspection and supervision, women have shown themselves in the vestries to be pre-eminently qualified. I am aware that in some vestries—at least in one vestry—a motion has been carried against the admission of women to the councils. We should take that for what it is worth ; but against the significance attached to the fact that the adverse motion had been carried by a majority in the Kensington Vestry, I would put this circumstance, that even while the Bill has been passing through the House there have been elections to the vestries all over London, and that a woman has been elected to sit in that particular vestry, and in the case of other vestries women have been elected. The electors therefore have attested their desire that women should be eligible to sit in vestries and councils. When the House considers the character

of vestry work, the experience we have had of women sitting on the vestries, and this happy state of opinion on the part of the electors, that they at least desire that women should remain eligible, would it not be a very strong action on the part of the House to declare that, although they had been eligible and had served with usefulness, and even with distinction, in the past, they should be no longer eligible ? I can scarcely believe that a majority in this House will, under these circumstances, take away the franchise and the eligibility which have been found to be a valuable element in the constitution of the vestries. We now come to the question of aldermen, which is a different question, because hitherto the vestries have had no aldermen. There are several Members in this House who object to aldermen altogether, but we cannot enter on that question now, since the House has decided to accept the principle that aldermen are to form part of the new boroughs. But the question arises whether women as well as men should be eligible to serve as aldermen. Now I hold that the work to be discharged justifies the eligibility of women as aldermen as much as councillors. There is this difference only between the two cases. Women as councillors might have to undergo contested elections, whereas women as aldermen will obtain their position by the co-option of the elected members of the council. I could conceive many Members objecting to women having to face the exigencies and experiences of a contested election, but that argument, whatever it is worth, does not at all apply to women being declared eligible to serve as aldermen. Many are quite ready to have women as aldermen who would hesitate to have them as councillors, and I cannot see any possible reason why those who want women to be councillors can object to women being aldermen. My proposal goes no further than that. Some desire that women should be eligible as mayors, but I make no such proposition. There is one substantial reason why the line should be drawn at mayors, and that is, that the mayors of the new councils will be *ex officio* justices of the peace. Now, what reason is there why women who are now eligible as vestrywomen and councillors should not be aldermen ? The only reason alleged, that I know of, is the suggestion that if this provision is introduced into the constitution of the metropolitan boroughs it will be necessary to carry their eligibility into all the municipal boroughs throughout the length and breadth of the country. I see no necessity for carrying that eligibility further than is now proposed, unless it is found that the experiment now suggested works well, and if it works well I do not know why it should not be so extended. But the reason for adopting the proposal here is, it is something that stands by itself, and does not require that the experiment should be carried further than it is now proposed to be carried. The question of the boroughs in the country may be considered in the future if the experience of London warrants making the same proposal in respect to these country boroughs. I beg to propose the Amendment standing in my name.

Amendment proposed—

"In page 2, line 2, by inserting after the word 'councillors,' the words 'and no person shall be disqualified by sex or marriage for being elected or being an alderman or a councillor.'"—(*Mr. Courtney.*)

Question proposed—

"That those words be there inserted."

*Mr. E. BOULNOIS (Marylebone, E.): I do not at all quarrel with the decision which has placed my right hon. friend in front of me, because he has put the issue before the House in a form which, if different from mine, is, at all events, a definite issue, and one on which the House can come to a decision, and set the matter at rest. The House will recollect that the question whether women should be eligible as councillors, aldermen, or mayors was practically left at the close of the debate in the state precisely where it was when the Bill was introduced. There were three Divisions taken in Committee, each contradicting the other, and the whole question was left in a hopeless tangle from which my right hon. friend the Leader of the House promised to extricate it on the Report stage. I should like to remind the House that on the Second Reading of the Bill the First Lord of the Treasury, in answer to a question, said there was no doubt that under the Bill women could sit as councillors, but that there was considerable doubt as to whether they could sit as mayors or aldermen.

Mr. Courtney.

But I am anxious that they should not sit either as councillors or aldermen. I am aware that the action which I have taken in this matter is not approved of by that portion of the fair sex which set up a claim to be on an equality with men in most things, if not in all, and who are everlastingly proclaiming to the world their rights and their wrongs. On the other hand, I feel satisfied in my own mind that if the House were to reject the proposal before it the bulk of the women in the country would be glad. The proposal to drag them and their sisters into municipal and political warfare—because it must come to this—is not regarded with favour by the great majority of women throughout the country. I read with some interest the report of a meeting held the other day by the Women's Liberal Federation, at which one of the speakers, a woman, denounced as "venomous persons" those who are opposed to the women's franchise. I am bound to assume I am one of those "venomous persons" whom these ladies would like to see out of Parliament; and I have no doubt my punishment will come in due course when the Government sees fit to dissolve Parliament. My right hon. friend the Member for Bodmin has said that women are eminently qualified to undertake the duties which would be imposed on the councils of these new boroughs. He alluded to only one duty, the supervision of sanitation. But I should like to ask my right hon. friend, what do women know about building operations, street and road-making, drain-making, sewer-inspection, rate-making, and the assessment of houses? I could enumerate an infinity of other duties which, it is clear to my mind, a woman cannot discharge. It is true, I admit, that women already sit on some of the metropolitan vestries, and my right hon. friend says they have served with distinction. Well, that is not my experience. I could count on my fingers the women who sit on vestries in the metropolis, and my experience is that they are failures, and, in addition to that, they are practically nonentities. — ["Oh! oh!" and "Hear! hear!"]—I quite understand that those hon. Members who are in favour of the right hon. Gentleman's proposition object to my describing these women as "failures" and "nonentities," but that is, of course, my personal opinion. We do not want these ladies on the borough councils. I believe the majority of the Members who desire to see this Bill effective want to have men elected on these new councils who have business capabilities, who have been trained to public life, and who would bring to bear on the deliberations and decisions of these councils practical experience. I am aware that women sit on boards of guardians throughout the country, and am perfectly willing to admit that they do very good service on these boards. There are duties in connection with the working of boards of guardians which women can very properly undertake, especially amongst the women and children in the work-houses, and on the outdoor roll. But, because on some of these bodies women are doing good service, is that any good reason why they should be admitted to other spheres where, in my view, they would be altogether out of place? I venture to say that, if their claim to sit on the new borough councils is admitted, and the House this evening says by its vote that they shall be eligible for these councils, their ambition will lead them to still higher flights. They will want the Parliamentary franchise, and even other higher privileges. At the risk of pro-ducing another shudder in the breast of the Leader of the House, I must repeat that if the House grants the privilege to women of sitting as councillors or alder-men in these councils, there is no logical reason whatever for excluding them here-after from the House of Commons itself. At a meeting which was held in London within the last few days of a great number of ladies who are in favour of this privilege being accorded to them, and where some gentlemen more or less prominent in Parliament were present, the hon. Baronet the Member for Cocker-mouth made a characteristic speech, in which he said that the House of Commons was a curious body (which we all admit, of course)—that one day it passed a law against gambling, and the next day it adjourned for the Derby. And the hon. Baronet went on to say that if women sat in Parliament they would do nothing so inconsistent as that. He added that women were as fit as males were to sit in Parlia-ment. Sir Arthur Arnold, at the same meeting, said he believed strongly that the office of Archbishop of Canterbury should be open to women. I think that reduces the matter almost to an absurdity. So that if the women themselves do not aspire to priestly office, there are some men who would claim that for them. If we admit women as councillors to the new boroughs, it is prac-tically impossible to exclude them from the offices of aldermen and mayor. All I can say is that if in addition to the House allowing women to sit as coun-cillors they also allow that they should be eligible as mayors and aldermen, then the whole thing will be reduced to an absurdity and a farce. I only know one case where a woman has been elected as a mayor, and that was in New Zealand, where women have the franchise and other privileges. I hold in my hand a letter in which it is stated:—

" There has been only one Lady Mayor in New Zealand. She was Mrs. Yates, and she held office in the town of Onehunga, near Auckland, in the year 1894. The proceedings at her local Council were often ill-tempered and disorderly, and though she has since asked the ratepayers to re-elect her they have not done so."

Well, I do not want myself to see an imitation of that kind in this country. The great argument which I venture to use against women being admitted is that they do not at present sit on the provincial municipali-ties, nor on the London County Council; but I cannot for a moment believe that the House of Commons, having admitted women into active public life in the borough councils, could deny them the privilege of sitting in provincial munici-palities. For my part, I sincerely hope that the House will come to a definite issue upon this subject, and that they will re-solve that women are not entitled to be either councillors, aldermen, or mayors.

*SIR H. H. FOWLER (Wolverhampton, E.): I hope the House will allow me to say a word or two on this question, because I can claim some responsibility for the legislation which at present pre-vails with reference to the rural districts, the urban districts, and London, because I think it was by the Act of 1894 that all these steps were taken. There is no doubt this question with reference to the posi-tion of women requires to be dealt with rather more straightforwardly than it has been by this House. There has been a desire, perhaps not an unnatural desire having regard to some considerations, to shirk the question, and the House has adopted a variety of methods from time to time of postponing anything like a straightforward decision upon the question, which, after all, is of great importance; and I think it is due to the country and to the House of Commons, if the House has views, whether they be adverse or favourable, that they should state them in the open. I would draw a line in the first instance, in what I have to say to-night, between administrative and legislative work. The first step in what is called the enfranchisement of women, but what I would rather call the first step in the State availing itself of the services of women, was in the constitution of school boards, and I do not think that anybody who has served on school boards and knows anything of the working of school board education would deny the fact that the presence of women on school boards has been of very great value with reference to female education. Personally, I go so far as to say that I do not think a school board is properly constituted unless there is a woman upon that school board. And I am satisfied that, strong as men may be, and wise as men may be, they never will be able to get that control over female education which an efficient school board ought to have unless they are assisted by ladies in carrying out the administration. Well, Sir, when I went to the Local Government Board I found that there was a considerable difference of legal opinion as to whether women were capable of being elected on boards of guardians. The Local Government Board had avoided, I think under legal advice, giving any very definite opinion upon this question, but I felt so strongly on the point that I issued a circular to the various boards of guardians strongly recommending the election of women on boards of guardians. I agree with every word the hon. Gentleman has just uttered with reference to the great value—I may say the inestimable value—of women upon boards of guardians. So long as you have pauper children, and so long as you have pauper women, you are bound to have women placed in a position of responsibility and control with reference to the management of workhouses and the relief of the poor. The next important step was when, in the Act of 1894, we extended the powers, or rather altered the constitution, of boards of guardians, and made them, in fact, rural councils, reconstructing the whole system of urban councils at the same time. I do not remember that there

Sir H. H. Fowler.

was any strong debate upon the subject, but at all events Parliament affirmed the principle that women might be upon parish councils, rural district councils, boards of guardians, and urban councils; and it is a narrow line dividing urban district councils from municipal boroughs. But by that Act the whole system of urban district elections was applied to London vestries, who then were the responsible local authorities in London. We are now asked to say that what we did in 1894 was wrong, when women were allowed to serve on the vestries like those of Paddington, Islington, &c., and that women are not competent to serve on those new bodies which are to have the duties of the original authorities. When we are asked to make a change such as this, the *onus probandi* is upon those who ask that that change may be made. The first question is, Has the election of women been a failure? I do not think the evidence that the hon. Gentleman who has just sat down has given is at all conclusive upon that point. He has been rather severe on the qualifications of the ladies, and on the manner in which they discharge their duties. So far as I have been able to form an opinion, they have discharged their duties with great efficiency and success, and to the advantage of the health of the people of London, who, with almost unanimity, will welcome the presence of women on these new governing bodies. Under these circumstances, I think we should prefer that a very strong case should be made out before we reject services which have been already rendered with efficiency and success. My right hon. friend the Member for Bodmin would exclude women from the office of mayor, recognising that there must be a line drawn somewhere in reference to the extent of female public work. I am bound to tell the House that women are eligible as chairmen of urban district councils, though the House accepted my suggestion specifically prohibiting women from becoming magistrates during their term of office. I now come to a point on which I should like to speak very plainly. While I advocate most strongly the presence of women on these administrative bodies, while I believe they are capable of rendering the greatest service to boards of guardians, urban councils, and district councils, and, I believe, to the councils in London, I am not prepared to go further in that direction. I am prepared, in fact, to steadfastly and persistently oppose any attempt to convert women either into mayors, or magistrates, or archbishops, or heads of police, or generals in the Army, or Members of Parliament. I believe that what the right hon. Gentleman the First Lord of the Treasury said on the last occasion when this question came before the House represented the opinion of a vast majority of the people of this country and all sides of politics, viz., that the presence of ladies in this House would on public grounds be intolerable. I think we ought to talk plainly on this point. While we advocate that the fullest scope should be given to female efficiency and female assistance in public work, we ought not to keep in the background that it is our firm and unalterable determination not to proceed in a direction that would render Parliament ridiculous and the administration of public affairs in this country impossible. I think it right to say plainly, intending as I do to support the motion of my right hon. friend the Member for Bodmin, that I do not regard this as a link in a long chain of events leading to something else. There is a line to be drawn, beyond which I do not believe the people of the country will ever go; but that is no reason why London should be deprived of the great advantage of services rendered by ladies in local administration.

Mr. COHEN (Islington, E.): As a matter of right and justice, and in the interests of making these new borough councils as successful as the vestries which they are going to supersede, I earnestly hope that this House will by a very large majority pass this Amendment.

Mr. LABOUCHERE (Northampton): I, like my right hon. friend the Member for Wolverhampton, am logical in these matters. I have voted on all occasions not only against women being members of councils and of the House of Commons, but against them having votes at all, and I always contemplate doing so as long as I have the honour of being a Member of this House. At the present moment you do not allow women to sit on municipal bodies in the country. Why, then, should an exception be made in the case of London? If you admit women in London, the precedent would be followed

in the provinces, and the next step would be a claim for women to sit in the House of Commons. I can see the thin end of the wedge in this proposition. Let hon. Members be firm. Let them be men. I will yield to none in my admiration for women. Woman is the right person, provided she is in her right place. There are some who have not been successes as members of their own sex, and who like to muddle and meddle in politics in the hope that they may be successes as men. Although there are weak men on the Opposition side of the House, I am glad to see stalwarts on the other side. The majority of women will not approve of this proposal. The few women who come forward and make a great noise are never supported by their own sex. The right hon. Member for Bodmin was not logical, because he himself does not propose that women should be eligible for the office of mayor. He passed that point over insidiously with a long joke. Can the right hon. Gentleman promise that he will always vote against women being eligible for the office of mayor or for membership to the House of Commons? I hope the House will decide that in the important councils of the nation men, and men only, shall sit.

*Mr. CARVELL WILLIAMS (Nottinghamshire, Mansfield): Hon. Members opposite have made a distinguished convert in the hon. Member who has just spoken.

Mr. LABOUCHERE: I beg my hon. friend's pardon. I was opposed to women having votes before half the hon. Gentlemen opposite were born.

*Mr. CARVELL WILLIAMS: Yes, but the hon. Member, who is supposed to be a great Radical, has used the most familiar of Tory arguments against all reform. It is that if something were conceded something else would be forthwith demanded. My hon. friend is affrighted at the prospect of women sitting in this House. The First Lord of the Treasury says that the idea is intolerable, but I will venture on this prediction—that if the time arrives when the electors of this country desire to send women to this House the right hon. Gentleman will look upon this question in a very different light. Hon. Members opposite admit that the services of women on school boards and boards of guardians have been valuable. Let me remind the House that there was a time when the appearance of women on those boards was quite a novelty, and when the prediction was freely indulged in that their presence would be injurious. That feeling has now entirely disappeared, and no one wishes to exclude them from those boards. The principle on which I should decide all these questions is the principle of freedom—freedom on the part of those who aspire to positions of public importance, and freedom on the part of the constituencies to send whom they please to Parliament or to other public bodies. The proposal to exclude women is, in my opinion, one that would be unjust to the women of this country and injurious to the country as a whole.

MR. HEYWOOD JOHNSTONE (Sussex, Horsham): Surely if the people wish to be represented by women, and if they think that their interests would be served by women representatives on the newly created boroughs, they should be permitted to have them. No woman would be compelled to serve or to come forward as a candidate. We recognise that women can fill very useful positions, and I shall certainly vote for this Amendment, which puts it in the power of the electors themselves to choose whether they will or will not be represented by women. But, apart from that, I should vote for this Amendment on the grounds of humanity. If I know anything of the history of municipal life, I am inclined to think that the newly created boroughs will celebrate their incorporation by banquets to which Members of this House will probably be invited, and it is very desirable that they should have the guiding hand of women in these matters. I sincerely hope that women will be elected to the borough councils, believing, as I do, that they will discharge good and serviceable work.

Question put—

The House divided. Ayes, 196 ; Noes, 161. (Division List No. 171.)

AYES.

Allan, William (Gateshead)	Corbett, A. Cameron (Glas'w)	Hatch, Ernest Frederick G.
Allen, Wm. (New. under Lyme)	Courtney, Rt. Hon. L. H.	Hayne, Rt. Hon. Charles S.
Ambrose, Robert	Crombie, John William	Heath, James
Anson, Sir William Reynell	Curran, Thomas B. (Donegal)	Heaton, John Henniker
Arnold-Forster, Hugh O.	Curran, Thomas (Sligo, S.)	Hedderwick, Thomas C. H.
Ashton, Thomas Gair	Curzon, Viscount	Hickman, Sir Alfred
Asquith, Rt Hon Herbert Henry	Dalrymple, Sir Charles	Hoare, Edw. B. (Hampstead)
Atherley-Jones, L.	Dalziel, James Henry	Hobhouse, Henry
Austin, Sir John (Yorkshire)	Davies, M. Vaughan-(Cardigan	Holden, Sir Angus
Austin, M. (Limerick, W.)	Davitt, Michael	Holland, Hon. L. R. (Bow)
Baird, John Geo. Alexander	Denny, Colonel	Holland, W. H. (York, W. R.)
Baker, Sir John	Dilke, Rt. Hon. Sir Charles	Horniman, Frederick John
Balfour, Rt. Hn. A. J. (Man'r)	Dillon, John	Hughes, Colonel Edwin
Balfour. Rt Hn. G. W. (Leeds)	Doogan, P. C.	Jacoby, James Alfred
Barlow, John Emmott	Douglas, C. M. (Lanark)	Johnson-Ferguson, Jabez Edw.
Barton, Dunbar Plunket	Drucker, A.	Jones, Wm. (Carnarvonshire)
Bayley, Thomas (Derbyshire)	Duckworth, James	Kennaway, Rt. Hon. Sir John H.
Begg, Ferdinand Faithfull	Dunn, Sir William	Kimber, Henry
Bentinck, Lord Henry C.	Ellis, John Edward	Kinloch, Sir John George Smyth
Bhownaggree, Sir M. M.	Evans, Sir F. H. (South'ton)	Lawson, John Grant (Yorks.)
Billson, Alfred	Evershed, Sydney	Lawson, Sir W. (Cumb'land)
Birrell, Augustine	Farquharson, Dr. Robert	Leng, Sir John
Bousfield, William Robert	Fenwick, Charles	Lewis, John Herbert
Brunner, Sir John Tomlinson	Ferguson, R. C. M. (Leith)	Llewelyn, Sir D. (Swansea)
Bryce, Rt. Hon. James	Finlay, Sir Robert B.	Lloyd-George, David
Buchanan, Thomas Ryburn	Firbank, Joseph Thomas	Long, Col. C. W. (Evesham)
Bullard, Sir Harry	Fisher, William Hayes	Lopes, Henry Yarde Buller
Burns, John	Fison, Frederick William	Lough, Thomas
Burt, Thomas	FitzGerald, Sir Robert P.-	Lubbock, Rt. Hon. Sir John
Butcher, John George	Fitzmaurice, Lord Edmond	Lucas-Shadwell, William
Buxton, Sydney Charles	Fowler, Rt. Hon. Sir Henry	Lyell. Sir Leonard
	Fry, Lewis	MacAleese, Daniel
Caldwell, James	Galloway, William Johnson	MacNeill, John Gordon Swift
Cameron, Sir Chas. (Glasgow)	Gladstone, Rt. Hn. Herbert J	M'Arthur, William (Cornwall)
Campbell, J. H. M. (Dublin)	Goddard, Daniel Ford	M'Cartan, Michael
Campbell-Bannerman, Sir H.	Gold, Charles	M'Ghee, Richard
Carvill, Patrick G Hamilton	Gorst, Rt. Hon. Sir John E.	M'Iver, Sir Lewis (Edin. W.)
Causton, Richard Knight	Goulding, Edward Alfred	M'Kenna, Reginald
Cawley, Frederick	Gourley, Sir Edward T.	M'Killop, James
Channing, Francis Allston	Graham, Henry Robert	Maddison, Fred.
Clough, Walter Owen	Haldane, Richard Burdon	Montagu, Hn. J. S. (Hants.)
Coghill, Douglas Harry	Harwood, George	Montagu, Sir S. (Whitechapel

Mr. Carvel Williams.

Morley, Rt. Hn. J. (Montrose.)
Morton, A. H. A. (Deptford)
Morton, Edw. J. C. (Dvnpt.)
Moulton, John Fletcher
Newdigate, Francis Alexander
Northcote, Hon. Sir H. S.
Norton, Capt. Cecil William
Nussey, Thomas Willans
O'Brien, James F. X. (Cork)
O'Connor, J. (Wicklow,W.)
O'Connor, T. P. (Liverpool)
Pease, H. P. (Darlington)
Pender, Sir James
Pickard, Benjamin
Pickersgill, Edward Hare
Pirie, Duncan V.
Price, Robert John
Purvis, Robert
Reid, Sir Robert Threshie
Richardson, J. (Durham, S.E.)
Robertson, Edmund (Dundee)
Robson, William Snowdon
Rollit, Sir Albert Kaye
Royds, Clement Molyneux
Russell, Gen. F. S. (Chelten'm)

Russell, T. W. (Tyrone)
Samuel, J. (Stockton on Tees)
Shaw, Charles Edw. (Stafford)
Shaw, Thomas (Hawick B.)
Simeon, Sir Barrington
Sinclair, Capt. J. (Forfarshire)
Smith, Samuel (Flint)
Spencer, Ernest
Stanhope, Hon. Philip J.
Stanley, Henry M. (Lambeth)
Steadman, William Charles
Stevenson, Francis S.
Strauss, Arthur
Strutt, Hon. Charles Hedley
Sullivan, Donal (Westmeath)
Talbot,Rt.Hn.J.G.(Oxf'dUniv
Tennant, Harold John
Thomas,Abel (Carmarthen,E.)
Thomas,Alfred(Glamorgan,E.)
Thomas, David A. (Merthyr)
Thornton, Percy M.
Trevelyan, Charles Philips
Tritton, Charles Ernest
Walton, John L. (Leeds, S.)
Warr, Augustus Frederick

Wedderburn, Sir William
Weir, James Galloway
Whiteley, George (Stockport)
Whitmore, Charles Algernon
Whittaker, Thomas Palmer
Williams, JohnCarvell(Notts.)
Willox, Sir John Archibald
Wills, Sir William Henry
Wilson, Charles Henry (Hull)
Wilson, Fred. W. (Norfolk)
Wilson, Hen. J. (York, W.R.)
Wilson, John (Durham, Mid.)
Wilson, John (Govan)
Woodall, William
Woodhouse, SirJ.T.(Hudd'f'd)
Wortley, Rt. Hn. C. B. Stuart-
Wylie, Alexander
Wyndham, George
Wyvill, Marmaduke D'Arcy
Young, Commander(Berks,E.)
Young, Samuel (Cavan, East)
TELLERS FOR THE AYES—
  Mr. Heywood Johnstone
  and Mr. Cohen.

NOES.

Acland-Hood, Capt.SirAlex.F.
Anstruther, H. T.
Arrol, Sir William
Atkinson, Rt. Hon. John
Bagot,Capt.Josceline FitzRoy
Bailey, James (Walworth)
Balcarres, Lord
Barnes, Frederic Gorell
Barry,RtHnAH.Smith-(Hunts
Bathurst, Hn. Allen Benjamin
Beach,Rt.Hn.SirM.H.(Bristol)
Beaumont, Wentworth C. B.
Beckett, Ernest William
Blundell, Colonel Henry
Bolton, Thomas Dolling
Bonsor, Henry Cosmo Orme
Bowles,T.Gibson (King'sLynn
Brassey, Albert
Broadhurst, Henry
Brodrick, Rt. Hon. St. John
Brookfield, A. Montagu
Campbell,Rt Hn.J.A.Glasgow
Cavendish, R. F. (N. Lancs.)
Cavendish, V. C. W.(Derby.)
Cayzer, Sir Charles William
Chaloner, Captain R. G. W.
Chamberlain, Rt. Hn. J.(Birm.
Chamberlain,J.Austen(Worc'r
Chaplin, Rt. Hon. Henry
Charrington, Spencer
Clarke, Sir Edward (Plymouth
Cochrane, Hon. Thos. H. A. E.
Coddington, Sir William
Collings, Rt. Hon. Jesse
Cook, Fred. L. (Lambeth)
Cooke, C. W. R. (Hereford)
Cripps, Charles Alfred
Cubitt, Hon. Henry
Dalbiac, Colonel Philip Hugh
Dalkeith, Earl of
Dickson-Poynder, Sir J. P.
Digby, John K. D. W.-
Dixon-Hartland, Sir Fredr D.
Donelan, Captain A.
Douglas, Rt. Hon. A Akers-
Doxford, William Theodore
Duncombe, Hon. Hubert V.

Elliot, Hon. A. Ralph D.
Engledew, Charles John
Evans, S. T. (Glamorgan)
Fardell, Sir T. George
Fellowes, Hon. Ailwyn E.
Finch, George H.
Fitz Wygram, General Sir F.
Flannery, Sir Fortescue
Fletcher, Sir Henry
Flower, Ernest
Folkestone, Viscount
Foster, Colonel (Lancaster)
Garfit, William
Gibbons, J. Lloyd
Gibbs,HnAGH (City of Lond.
Gibbs, Hon. V. (St. Albans)
Godson, Sir Augustus F.
Goldsworthy, Major-General
Goschen,RtHnG.J.(StGeorge's
Goschen, George J. (Sussex)
Gretton, John
Gunter, Colonel
Gurdon, Sir Wm. Brampton
Hall, Rt. Hon. Sir Charles
Halsey, Thomas Frederick
Hamilton, Rt. Hon. Lord Geo.
Hanbury, Rt. Hon. R. Wm.
Hardy, Laurence
Hare, Thomas Leigh
Henderson, Alexander
Hermon-Hodge, R. Trotter
Hornby, Sir William Henry
Howard, Joseph
Howell, William Tudor
Hozier, Hon. Jas. Henry Cecil
Hubbard, Hon. Evelyn
Hutchinson, Capt. G. W. G.-
Hutton, John (Yorks. N.R.)
Jenkins, Sir John Jones
Jessel, Capt. Herbert Merton
Jolliffe, Hon. H. George
King, Sir Henry Seymour
Kitson, Sir James
Knowles, Lees
Labouchere, Henry
Laforc, Alfred
Lambert, George

Laurie, Lieut.-General
Lawrence, Wm. F. (Liverpool)
Llewellyn, E. H. (Somerset)
Lockwood, Lt.-Col. A. R.
Loder, Gerald Walter Erskine
Long, Rt. Hn. W. (Liverpool)
M'Donnell,Dr.M.A.(Queen'sC
MacIver, David (Liverpool)
Maclure, Sir John William
M'Calmont, H. L. B. (Cambs.)
M'Ewan, William
Malcolm, Ian
Maple, Sir John Blundell
Mappin, Sir Frederick Thorpe
Marks, Henry Hananel
Melville, Beresford Valentine
Meysey, Thompson, Sir H. M.
Mildmay, Francis Bingham
Milward, Colonel Victor
Moon, Edward Robert Pacy
More,Robt.Jasper(Shropshire)
Morgan,Hn.Fred(Monm'thsh.
Murray, Rt. Hn. A. G. (Bute)
Myers, William Henry
Nicol, Donald Ninian
Palmer, Sir C. M. (Durham)
Palmer, George W. (Reading)
Platt-Higgins, Frederick
Powell, Sir Francis Sharp
Pretyman, Ernest George
Priestley, Sir W. O. (Edin.)
Pym, C. Guy
Quilter, Sir Cuthbert
Richards, Henry Charles
Richardson, Sir T. (Hartlep'l)
Rickett, J. Compton
Ridley, Rt. Hon. Sir M. W.
Ritchie, Rt. Hon. Chas. T.
Robertson, Herbert (Hackney)
Rothschild, Hon. Lionel W.
Ryder, John Herbert Dudley
Samuel, Harry S. (Limehouse)
Savory, Sir Joseph
Scoble, Sir Andrew Richard
Sharpe, William Edward T.
Sidebottom, T. H. (Stalybr.)
Stanley, Edw. J. (Somerset)

R 2

Stanley, Lord (Lancs.)
Stewart, Sir Mk. J. M'Taggart
Stock, James Henry
Talbot, Lord E. (Chichester)
Thorburn, Walter
Tomlinson, Wm. Edw. Murray
Tully, Jasper
Valentia, Viscount

Vincent, Col. Sir C. E. Howard
Walrond, Rt. Hn. Sir Wm H.
Wanklyn, James Leslie
Warner, Thomas Courtenay T.
Webster, R. G. (St. Pancras)
Wharton, Rt. Hn. John Lloyd
Williams, Colonel R. (Dorset)
Williams, Jos. Powell- (Birm.

Wilson, John (Falkirk)
Wilson-Todd, Wm. H. (Yorks.)
Wodehouse, Rt. Hn. E. R (Bath)
Wolff, Gustav Wilhelm

TELLERS FOR THE NOES—
Mr. Boulnois and Mr. Banbury.

MR. PICKERSGILL : The Amendment I have to move is—

"To leave out in Clause 2, page 2, lines 5 and 6 the words ' that number being divisible by three.'"

In the debate on this question in Committee the Government found itself obliged to make a concession, which provided that any representation sent to the Local Government Board by a borough council supported by a two-thirds majority in favour of triennial elections would be considered. Whatever the rule is, it ought to be uniform over the whole of London ; and by the omission which I propose triennial elections could be obtained. I have no doubt that a substantial majority on the newly created councils will be in favour of triennial elections, but it is not reasonable to suppose that, having regard to the severity of the conditions, all the councils will pass the necessary resolution. It would be absurd to have triennial elections in one district and annual elections in another, and I hope the Government will favourably consider the Amendment I now move.

Amendment proposed—

"In page 2, lines 5 and 6, to leave out the words ' that number being divisible by three.'"—(*Mr. Pickersgill*).

Question proposed—

"That the words proposed to be left out stand part of the Bill."

SIR R. B. FINLAY : The proposal made by the hon. and learned Member is, I take it, to leave out these words in order afterwards to insert other words providing for triennial elections over London. When this matter was discussed in Committee a certain solution was arrived at, and I have come to the conclusion that it is better, after considering the views of hon. Members on both sides, that we should adhere to that arrangement.

MR. SYDNEY BUXTON : The House will remember that there was a considerable feeling in favour of triennial elections, and ultimately the Government made the proposal now in the Bill. As far as Ip am concerned I am prepared to adhere to that compromise. I quite agree that the wording may require some alteration, and I hope the Government will accept an Amendment I propose to move in regard to it. If proper option is given to adopt triennial elections, they will be universally adopted, and therefore the desire we have in our minds will be achieved.

MR. STEADMAN (Tower Hamlets, Stepney) : I rise to support the Amendment moved by my hon. and learned friend the Member for Bethnal Green. I am aware of the compromise arrived at when the Bill was discussed in Committee, but although the borough councils may vote by a two-thirds majority in favour of triennial elections, representations must afterwards be made to the Local Government Board for their consideration. I believe the same provision was made in the Local Government Act of 1894. Previous to that Act, the elections for Poor Law guardians in London took place annually, but the moment the boards of guardians had the opportunity for deciding whether they should have annual or triennial elections, they universally decided in favour of the latter. There we have a practical illustration of the feeling in London on this question ; and, that being so, why should we not at once make provision in the Bill for triennial elections, without putting the borough councils to the cost of deciding for themselves, when we know by past experience what their opinions will be ? There is another important point attached to this Amendment. The chief object of this Bill is to induce the electors to take an interest in local affairs. In the year 1900 this Bill will come into operation. In November we shall have the first elections for the new boroughs, and in the same month we shall have the elections for the London School Board. In March, 1901, we shall have the London County Council elections ; in the following month the elections for boards of guardians in London, and possibly in the summer we may have Parliamentary elections, and if this Bill is allowed to stand in its present form we may have in November of that year also the annual elections for the borough councils ; so that in 1901 we shall have certainly three, and possibly four, elections. When we ask the people to vote in such a number of elections, they will tell us that they are sick and tired of voting. The School Board, the London County Council, and the new borough councils are bodies of such an important character that we are anxious for the electorate of London to take an interest in their election by voting. My own experience in these local matters is that where you have a constant recurrence of elections you cannot get the people to take an interest in them, and for that reason I will support the Amendment.

Mr. LOUGH (Islington, W.) : These numerous elections are very expensive, and the benefit conferred by this Amendment would be very much appreciated in the divisions referred to. Upon this point I desire to claim the attention of the House, because I am sure that this matter requires more consideration than has yet been given to it. The clause deals with the number of councillors which shall be allotted to each ward. Take my particular division. It has five wards, and the number for each ward are to be selected having regard to rateable value and population. That would be extremely difficult, but we might get over it. But mark the other condition—that the selection of the number must be divisible by three. It must be either three, six, or nine, and you cannot have four, five, seven, eight, or ten. It is hard enough to observe the conditions with regard to population and rateable value, but when you divide by three you put a burden upon the people which will prove to be very onerous. This is no fancied argument, and I hope the right hon. Gentleman, who has all through adopted a conciliatory attitude, will give it careful consideration. The Solicitor-General was not very strong in opposing this Amendment, and he approached it in the way which he generally adopts when he wants to draw a little more opinion from the House. In every ward you prevent a number of

councillors that might be suitable, because the number must be divided by three. Everyone is agreed that in most of these divisions the triennial system will be adopted. We are now trying to ride both horses as the Bill stands, and therefore I would ask the right hon. Gentleman to give this proposal his careful consideration.

*Sir E. CLARKE (Plymouth) : I hope my right hon. friend will not be induced by compliments passed upon his conciliatory disposition to abandon what is really an important part of this Bill by accepting what is a very unreasonable and a somewhat ungracious Amendment. The question was fully argued when the subject of triennial elections was discussed, and strong opinions were expressed on both sides. I hold myself a very strong opinion in favour of annual elections, and, as so much has been said about a larger public interest being aroused by triennial elections, I cannot help remembering the mischief that has been done by the constant intervention of political organisation. There is really nothing in the objection that has just been made, and which my right hon. friend is so solemnly exhorted to take into consideration. The boundaries will be fixed with due regard to population and rateable value in such proportion as will make them fairly equal. The Government made a great concession by inserting a clause under which it was left to the borough council to have an opportunity of addressing the Local Government Board, when that application represented the opinion of a majority of the whole council, to have the election once in three years. That was a considerable concession. It was a compromise which has been frankly accepted by the hon. Member for the Tower Hamlets, and surely it is very unreasonable, under the cover of compliments, to endeavour now to upset this decision.

Mr. BANBURY (Camberwell, Peckham) : I was very strongly in favour of triennial elections when the question came up, but in view of the fact that the Government made a concession in Committee in favour of triennial elections, I feel it my duty upon this occasion to support the Government.

The House divided : Ayes, 245 ; Noes, 89. (Division List No. 172.)

AYES.

Acland-Hood, Capt.Sir Alex.F.
Anson, Sir William Reynell
Arnold-Forster, Hugh O.
Arrol, Sir William
Asquith, Rt. Hn. Herbert Hen.
Atkinson, Rt. Hon. John
Austin, Sir John (Yorkshire)
Bagot, Capt. J. FitzRoy
Bailey, James (Walworth)
Baird, John George A.
Balcarres, Lord
Balfour, Rt.Hn.A.J.(Manch r)
Balfour, Rt. Hn. G.W.(Leeds)
Banbury, Frederick George
Barnes, Frederic Gorell
Barton, Dunbar Plunket
Bathurst, Hon. Allen B.
Beach, Rt Hn Sir M. H. (Bristol)
Beckett, Ernest William
Begg, Ferdinand Faithfull
Bentinck, Lord Henry C.
Beresford, Lord Charles
Bethell, Commander
Blundell, Colonel Henry
Boulnois, Edmund
Bousfield, William Robert
Bowles, T. G. (King's Lynn)
Brassey, Albert
Brookfield, A. Montagu
Bryce, Rt. Hon. James
Bullard, Sir Harry
Burt, Thomas
Butcher, John George
Buxton, Sydney Charles
Campbell, Rt Hn J.A.(Glasgow
Campbell, J. H. M. (Dublin)
Campbell-Bannerman, Sir H.
Cavendish, R. F. (N. Lancs.)
Cavendish, VCW(Derbyshire)
Cawley, Frederick
Cecil, Evelyn (Hertford, East)
Cecil, Lord Hugh (Greenwich)
Chaloner, Captain R. G. W.
Chamberlain, Rt.Hn.J.(Birm.
Chamberlain, J. A (Wore'r)
Chaplin, Rt. Hon. Henry
Clarke, Sir Edw. (Plymouth)
Clough, Walter Owen
Cochrane, Hon. T. H. A. E.
Coghill, Douglas Harry
Cohen, Benjamin Louis
Collings, Rt. Hon. Jesse
Cook, Fred. Lucas (Lambeth)
Cooke,C.W.Radcliffe(Heref'd)
Corbett,A.Cameron (Glasgow)
Courtney, Rt. Hn. Leonard H.
Cripps, Charles Alfred
Cubitt, Hon. Henry
Curzon, Viscount
Dalbiac, Colonel Philip Hugh
Dalkeith, Earl of
Dalrymple, Sir Charles
Denny, Colonel
Dickson-Poynder, Sir John P.
Digby, John K. D. Wingfield-
Dilke, Rt. Hon. Sir Charles
Dixon-Hartland, Sir Fred. D.
Douglas, Rt. Hon. A. Akers-
Doxford, William Theodore
Drucker, A.
Duncombe, Hon. Hubert V.
Elliot, Hon. A. RalphDouglas
Evans, Samuel T.(Glamorgan)
Evershed, Sydney

Fardell, Sir T. George
Fellowes, Hon Ailwyn Edw.
Finch, George H.
Finlay, Sir Robert Bannatyne
Firbank, Joseph Thomas
Fisher, William Hayes
Fison, Frederick William
FitzGerald, Sir Robert Penrose-
Fitzmaurice, Lord Edmond
Fitz Wygram, General Sir F.
Flannery, Sir Fortescue
Fletcher, Sir Henry
Flower, Ernest
Folkestone, Viscount
Foster, Colonel (Lancaster)
Fowler, Rt. Hon. Sir Henry
Fry, Lewis
Galloway, William Johnson
Garfit, William
Gedge, Sydney
Gibbons. J. Lloyd
Gibbs,Hn.A.G.H.(CityofLond
Giles, Charles Tyrrell
Godson, Sir Augustus Fred'k
Goldsworthy, Major-General
Gordon, Hon. John Edward
Gorst, Rt. Hon. Sir J. Eldon
Goschen,Rt.Hn.G.J.(St.Geo's)
Goschen, George J. (Sussex)
Goulding, Edward Alfred
Gretton, John
Haldane, Richard Burdon
Hall, Rt. Hon. Sir Charles
Halsey, Thomas Frederick
Hamilton, Rt. Hon. Lord Geo.
Hanbury,Rt. Hon. Robert W.
Hardy, Laurence
Hatch, Ernest F. George
Hayne, Rt. Hon. Chas. Seale-
Heath, James
Heaton, John Henniker
Hermon-Hodge, Robert T.
Hoare, E. Brodie (Hampstead)
Holland, Hon. L. R. (Bow)
Holland, W. H. (York, W. R.)
Howard, Joseph
Howell, William Tudor
Hozier, Hon. J. Henry Cecil
Hubbard, Hon. Evelyn
Hughes, Colonel Edwin
Hutchinson,Capt.G.W. Grice-
Hutton, John (Yorks, N.R.)
Jessel, Capt. Herbert Merton
Johnson-Ferguson, Jabez E.
Johnstone, Heywood (Sussex)
Jolliffe, Hon H. George
Kearley, Hudson E.
Keswick, William
Kimber, Henry
King, Sir Henry Seymour
Knowles, Lees
Lafone, Alfred
Lambert, George
Laurie, Lieut.-General
Lawrence, W. F. (Liverpool)
Lawson, John Grant (Yorks.)
Llewellyn, E. H. (Somerset)
Llewelyn, Sir D-(Swansea)
Lockwood, Lt.-Col. A. R.
Loder, Gerald Walter Erskine
Long, Rt. Hn. W. (Liverpool)

Lopes, Henry Yarde Buller
Lowles, John
Lowther, Rt. Hon. J. (Kent)
Lubbock, Rt. Hon. Sir John
Lucas-Shadwell, William
MacIver, David (Liverpool)
Maclure, Sir John William
M'Arthur, Charles (Liverpool)
M'Arthur, William (Cornwall)
M'Calmont, H. L. B.(Cambs.)
M'Calmont, Col. J. (Antrim, E.
M'Ewan, William
M'Iver. Sir L. (Edinburgh,W.
M'Killop, James
Malcolm, Ian
Manners, Lord Edw. Wm. J.
Maple, Sir John Blundell
Mappin, Sir Frederick Thorpe
Marks. Henry Hananel
Melville. Beresford Valentine
Meysey-Thompson, Sir H. M.
Middlemore, J. Throgmorton
Mildmay, Francis Bingham
Milward, Colonel Victor
Moon, Edward Robert Pacy
More,Robt.Jasper Shropshire)
Morgan,Hn.Fred.(Monm'ths.)
Morrell, George Herbert
Morton, Ar. H. A. (Deptford)
Muntz, Philip A.
Murray, Rt. Hn. A. G. (Bute)
Myers, William Henry
Newdigate, Francis Alexander
Nicol, Donald Ninian
Palmer, Geo. Wm. (Reading)
Parkes, Ebenezer
Pender, Sir James
Penn, John
Platt-Higgins, Frederick
Powell, Sir Francis Sharp
Pretyman, Ernest George
Price, Robert John
Priestley, Sir W. O. (Edin.)
Purvis, Robert
Quilter, Sir Cuthbert
Richards, Henry Charles
Richardson, Sir T. (Hartlep'l)
Ridley, Rt. Hn. Sir Matt. W.
Ritchie, Rt. Hon. C. Thomson
Robertson, Herbert(Hackney)
Rollit, Sir Albert Kaye
Rothschild, Hn. Lionel Walter
Round, James
Royds, Clement Molyneux
Russell, T. W. (Tyrone)
Rutherford, John
Ryder, John Herbert Dudley
Scoble, Sir Andrew Richard
Sharpe, William Edward T.
Sidebottom, T. H. (Stalybr.)
Simeon, Sir Barrington
Smith, Hon. W.F.D. (Strand)
Spencer, Ernest
Spicer, Albert
Stanhope, Hon. Philip J.
Stanley, Edw. J. (Somerset)
Stanley, Henry M. (Lambeth)
Stanley, Lord (Lancs.)
Stewart, Sir M. J. M'Taggart
Stock, James Henry
Stone, Sir Benjamin
Strauss, Arthur

Strutt, Hon. Charles Hedley

Talbot, Lord E. (Chichester)
Talbot, Rt. Hn.J.G.(Ox. Uni)
Tennant, Harold John
Thorburn, Walter
Thornton, Percy M.
Tomlinson, W. Edw. Murray
Tritton, Charles Ernest
Valentia, Viscount
Vincent, Col. Sir. C. E. H.

Wanklyn, James Leslie.
Warr, Augustus Frederick
Webster, R. G. (St. Pancras)
Webster, SirR.E.(I. of Wight)
Wharton, Rt. Hon. J. Lloyd
Whiteley,George (Stockport)
Whitmore, Charles Algernon
Williams, Col. R. (Dorset)
Williams, Joseph P.- (Birm.)
Willox, Sir John Archibald
Wilson, John (Falkirk)

Wilson-Todd, W. H. (Yorks.)
Wodehouse, RtHnE.R. (Bath)
Wortley,·Rt. Hon. C. B. S.-
Wylie, Alexander
Wyndham, George
Wyvill, Marmaduke D'Arcy

Young, Commander (Berks,E.)

TELLERS FOR THE AYES—Sir William Walrond and Mr. Anstruther.

NOES.

Abraham,William(Cork,N.E.)
Allan, William (Gateshead)
Allen, Wm.(Newc.underLyme
Ambrose, Robert
Ashton, Thomas Gair
Baker, Sir John
Barlow, John Emmott
Beaumont, Wentworth, C. B.
Billson, Alfred
Bolton, Thomas Dolling
Broadhurst, Henry
Brunner, Sir John Tomlinson
Buchanan, Thomas Ryburn
Burns, John
Caldwell, James
Cameron,SirCharles(Glasgow)
Carvill, PatrickGeo Hamilton
Channing, Francis Allston
Charrington, Spencer
Dalziel, James Henry
Davies, M. V.- (Cardigan)
Davitt, Michael
Dillon, John
Donelan, Captain A.
Doogan, P. C.
Douglas, C. M. (Lanark)
Duckworth, James
Dunn, Sir William
Fenwick, Charles
Ferguson, R. C. Munro (Leith)
Goddard, Daniel Ford

Gold, Charles
Gourley, Sir Edward T.
Gurdon, Sir William B.
Harwood, George
Hedderwick, Thomas C. H.
Holden, Sir Angus
Holland, W. H. (York, W. R.)
Horniman, Frederick John
Jacoby, James Alfred
Kinloch, Sir John George S.
Kitson, Sir James
Langley, Batty
Lawson, Sir W. (Cumberland)
Leng, Sir John
Lewis, John Herbert
Lloyd-George, David
Lough, Thomas
Lyell, Sir Leonard
MacAleese, Daniel
MacDonnell, DrMA(Queen'sC
MacNeill, John Gordon Swift
M'Cartan, Michael
M'Ghee, Richard
M'Kenna, Reginald
Maddison, Fred.
Montagu, Sir S. (Whitech'l)
Morton, E. J. C. (Devonport)
Norton, Capt. Cecil William
Nussey, Thomas Willans
O'Brien, J. F. X. (Cork)
O'Connor, T. P. (Liverpool)

Palmer, Sir C. M. (Durham)
Pickard, Benjamin
Richardson, J. (Durham, S.E.)
Rickett, J. Compton
Robson, William Snowdon

Samuel, J. (Stockton on Tees)
Shaw, Charles Edw. (Stafford)
Shaw, Thomas (Hawick B.)
Sinclair, Capt. J. (Forfarshire)
Smith, Samuel (Flint)
Sullivan, Donal (Westmeath)

Thomas, Abel(Carmarthen,E.)
Thomas, A. (Glamorgan, E.)
Trevelyan, Charles Philips
Tully, Jasper
Wedderburn, Sir William
Weir, James Galloway
Whittaker, Thomas Palmer
Williams, John C. (Notts.)
Wills, Sir William Henry
Wilson, Charles Henry (Hull)
Wilson, Fredk. W. (Norfolk)
Wilson, H. J. (York, W.R.)
Wilson, John (Durham, Mid.)
Wilson, J. H. (Middlesbrough)
Woodhouse,SirJ.T.(H'dd'rsf'd
Young, Samuel (Cavan, East)
TELLERS FOR THE NOES—Mr. Pickersgill and Mr. Steadman.

Other Amendments made.

MR. SYDNEY BUXTON : This clause was practically taken from the Local Government Act of 1894, and the words I now move to omit are words which do not find any place in that Act. They seem to me to restrict the possibility of boroughs having full liberty to adopt the annual system. In an extreme case, if a certain proportion of the 70 members were to stay away they could prevent the adoption of the system of triennial elections. I am afraid that if these words are left in they might put considerable difficulties in the way of the adoption of this provision. I hope, therefore, that the Government will accept this Amendment.

Amendment proposed—

"In Clause 2, page 2, line 33, to leave out from 'purpose' to 'make' in line 34."—(*Mr. Sydney Buxton.*)

Question proposed—

"That the words proposed to be left out stand part of the clause."

MR. A. J. BALFOUR : I trust the House will retain the Bill as it now stands. I ought to say that at the time this clause was adopted I expressed grave apprehensions at the determination which the London Members had arrived at to adopt a system which certainly could not prove acceptable if extended to the provinces. But the general opinion was so strong among London Members that I made a concession, and we arrived at a compromise which was this—that the councils themselves should have practically the power of adopting the triennial system in preference to the annual system, but it should be done only on the condition that a distinct and absolute majority were in favour of it. It will be observed that if the hon. Member's Amendment is carried and the words in the Bill to which he objects are left out, it would be possible for one-third of the Members to make this great change. That would not be carrying out the intention of the House, and I trust that the hon. Gentleman will not insist upon a division.

MR. STUART (Shoredich, Hoxton): I should be glad if the right hon. Gentleman could see his way to adopt this Amendment, but I rise to call his attention to another point upon which I will not make a motion, but which is closely associated with this question, and which the right hon. Gentleman may see his way to deal with in another place. It bears upon triennial elections, and the point is that it would be extremely in the interests of London electors generally if, wherever a triennial election was ordered by the Local Government Board, it could be ordered for the year 1900, or one of the three years dating therefrom.

Amendment negatived.

MR. COURTNEY: The Amendment I now beg to move is one which was submitted to the House in Committee, and after a slight discussion I withdrew it. The object of the Amendment is very simple. We all know that the experience of municipal contests shows that the power of appointing aldermen has often been abused, first of all by the wire-pullers of the party securing the election of all the aldermen, and then by those aldermen joining in the election of subsequent aldermen. The Amendment I propose is very simple in its operation, and will insure the election of aldermen by the minority to an extent corresponding to the position which that minority holds. It can best be explained by an example. A council should never exceed 60 members, so that with the aldermen one in 10 the council should never exceed 70. The common council of 60 comes to elect its aldermen, and under the present system the majority of 31 could elect the whole 10 aldermen, thus converting a majority of 2 in the entire council into a majority of 12. Now, what I propose is that in the first election, where 60 will have to elect 10 aldermen, that when 6 of the councillors join together they shall be able to nominate one alderman, and that all those six councillors shall immediately retire from taking any other part in the election. The result of that would be, that if there was a majority of 14— that is to say, if the council was com-

posed of 36 members on the one side and 24 on the other, the 36 would elect 6 aldermen, and the 24 four, which would give each side proportionate representation. Under the present system the experience in many of our boroughs has shown us that the election of aldermen has been a matter of great jealousy, and this has also been the case in the London County Council. In the London County Council a simple majority have always had the power of electing the whole of the aldermen. By this alteration it would limit the number which the majority of a council have power to elect, and give a choice to the minority. The matter is so simple that nobody could pretend to misunderstand it, and the machinery is so simple that it could not go wrong. It would secure the end which we all have in view, which is the addition to the members of the council of an entirely new element, and it would be a simple means of solving what is acknowledged to be a difficult and delicate question, and one which raises an undesirable feeling at the beginning of the career of every council.

Amendment proposed—

"In Clause 2, page 2, line 37, at end to add—

(c) 'At the first election of aldermen after the passing of this Act any six councillors may agree in nominating one person as alderman, and thereupon such person shall be declared elected as alderman, and the six councillors nominating him shall have no further part in such election; and that every subsequent triennial election of aldermen any twelve councillors may agree in nominating one person as alderman, and thereupon such person shall be declared elected as alderman, and the twelve councillors nominating him shall have no further part in such election.' "—(*Mr. Courtney*)

Question proposed—

"That those words be there inserted."

MR. A. J. BALFOUR: I see no reason for altering the view which I expressed on a former occasion at an earlier stage of the Bill that this Amendment should not be accepted. I agree with my right hon. friend that his scheme has the great advantage of being exceedingly simple, and I do not think that there would be any practical difficulty in the way of its working properly. I also agree that it has the great merit of preventing the election of aldermen being used as a machinery in favour of any particular party, but whether it will secure that the councils will obtain a better class men as aldermen I gravely doubt. The practical result will be that a party of six councillors who would vote, or who would meet together to select their alderman, might exercise their choice in favour of individuals for whom no party would be responsible in its collective capacity. On the whole, I am disposed to think that the responsibility which must attach to the organised action of a party must produce better results than the relatively irresponsible action of groups of six gentlemen who would like to elect their own friends. On these grounds I feel constrained to adhere to my former decision, and if my right hon. friend thinks it necessary to divide the House I shall feel obliged to go into the lobby against him.

Question put, and negatived.

Mr. COURTNEY: The Bill as it stands provides that, to be qualified to act as an alderman in a borough, a man must be qualified for election to the county council in that particular borough. My desire is to enlarge that qualification so as to extend it to any one who is qualified to be elected as a councillor for any metropolitan borough and enable him to act as an alderman in any other metropolitan borough. Why should we limit the choice of the electors to nominate an alderman, seeing that the aldermen are chosen by the electors and, of course, would be responsible to them? Persons who are qualified to be elected as aldermen elsewhere surely should be qualified to be elected as aldermen in any particular borough. It is well known that in some parts of the City there are men who have peculiar qualifications for this work who would not be eligible as the Bill now stands. In the interest of the freedom of voice of the electors, I think this would be a great benefit, while on the other hand no harm could be done by it. It simply enlarges the power of choice, and if that is extended it will only be used in the rarest of cases. I beg to move the Amendment.

Amendment proposed—

" In page 2, line 37, at the end of Clause 3, to insert the words, '(d) A person shall be qualified to be elected as alderman in any metropolitan borough who is qualified to be elected as councillor in the same or any other metropolitan borough.'"—(*Mr. Courtney.*)

Question proposed—

" That those words be there inserted,"

Mr. A. J. BALFOUR: Perhaps I might remind this House of what occurred with regard to this matter on a previous occasion. When this question was brought forward, I did my best to induce the House to accept the proposal, but the House, after by no means a brief discussion, came to the conclusion that it would not be an improvement to the Bill. I do not wish to withdraw from the position that I then took up, and under the same circumstances I should take the same course again. I would suggest to my right hon. friend that it is hardly worth while to divide the House again upon the subject.

Lord H. CECIL (Greenwich): I hope the House will see its way to accept this Amendment. It is quite true that it was raised on another occasion, but it is an Amendment of great importance, and since that time many representatives may have changed their opinions upon it. The kind of man who would make a good alderman might very well live in another part of, London and still by reason of his business connection have a very real interest in a particular district. He might have a real capacity for public business and an earnest desire to interest himself in that borough. So far as I can see I cannot discover any reason why this Amendment should not be accepted. It will only be applied in cases where there are very strong reasons for going outside the borough, and surely you are not going to say by statutory enactment that a borough shall not be able to go outside to elect its aldermen, when by so doing they might find ideal men to fit the position.

Mr. STUART: I should have been content to give a silent vote on this matter if there had been a desire to discuss the question. I am against it for the reasons that this proposal is against the whole principle of local government in England. The only exception is that of the London School Board, in which, no doubt, there was a reason for breaking the precedent, as what was desired in that case was to get experts in education on the Board. So far as this Bill is concerned, there is no necessity for going outside the area of the borough. I gave the whole argument against this proposal on a previous occasion, and therefore there is no reason for entering into it now. The boroughs of London do not ask for aldermen, and have expressed general dissatisfaction at the idea that they are going to be put upon them, and if you are going now to allow aldermen to be elected from the outside you will create greater dissatisfaction than already exists.

* SIR E. CLARKE: I see no reason why the Amendment should not be accepted at once if what the hon. Gentleman who has just sat down has suggested is all that can be said against it. The only argument which he appears to have adduced is that if you go outside the boroughs the electors may elect the wrong man. I am sorry he has so little faith in the electors. It may be that there are persons who by long residence or business were once connected with the borough, although they now live elsewhere, who on their retirement from business are taking great interest in public life. Yet, as the Bill now stands, you would refuse any such persons, although the borough councils might recognise that if they could obtain this experience and this knowledge that he would be just the person to be desired.

SIR J. BRUNNER (Cheshire, Northwich): I desire to call attention to a fact which must be obvious to everybody who studies the reorganisation of large businesses of the present day. In the manufacturing parts of London large businesses are being turned into and worked by limited companies. Now, if this Amendment is not carried the man whose interest is entirely centred in the locality in which his business is will find himself debarred from any share of management in public affairs. All these are good business men, and yet they will be excluded from any share of local government. I desire to support the Amendment.

MR. E. A. GOULDING (Wilts, Devizes): Various arguments have been used in favour of the Amendment. It has been put that it would afford rich men, or single men who want some purpose in life, an opportunity of doing service to the East End districts. Again, it was said that it would enable business men, who could not give time to work a contested election, to be brought in as aldermen. Now we are told that it is a scheme to bestow upon the East End of

London the patronage of men from Chelsea and the West End, who would come to the East to air their fads. We have seen the evil of that system in the case of certain aldermen in the London County Council, who were brought in not because of their knowledge of municipal affairs but because of their political services. I most sincerely hope the same canker will not be introduced in the new municipalities, and I trust that the hon. Member will not press his Amendment to a division. The matter was decided in Committee in a very large House, and the vast majority of the London Members voted against the scheme of the Amendment.

CAPTAIN NORTON (Newington, W.): Surely the reply to what has fallen from the hon. and learned Member for Plymouth as to those who are so very anxious to serve in certain areas, in which they have large interests and in which they have lived in former times, is that an outlay of £10 will give them a qualification to enable them to sit on the borough council.

*MR. BANBURY (Camberwell, Peckham): If this Amendment is not carried, the new boroughs will, I think, be debarred from choosing some men as alderman who are eminently suited for that position. I have a striking instance in my own constituency of this. The gentleman in question is not of my way of thinking; he was a Progressive member of the London County Council, and served the district well. But his business has been turned into a limited liability company, and he does not now reside in the district. Therefore, unless this Amendment is carried, this gentleman, who has been connected with the place for twenty-five years and who is thoroughly capable of being an alderman, will be prevented from serving the district in which he is so much interested.

*MR. KIMBER (Wandsworth): The main argument on which the Amendment was decided against in Committee was that every man who is a councillor or an alderman is put in the position of administering the funds of the locality, and should be, at least, one of those who contribute to these funds. The plea about hardship to a man who converts his business into a limited liability has no place against the argument, for the double reason that when

Mr. Stuart,

a man is going to convert himself into a limited liability company he should think of what effect it will have ; and in the second place, if he wants to retain his qualification as a ratepayer, it is very easy for him to retain some of the property in his own hands. In all the arguments of the hon. Gentleman the mover of the Amendment, or of those who followed him on the same side, not a shadow of answer was given to the statement that it would induce irresponsible persons to come into the councils from the outside and squander the money to which they had not contributed. Moreover, if an outsider were allowed to be elected, a man who lived, perhaps, on the other side of the street down the centre of which ran the boundary of the borough might be co-opted to the borough council, and there urge the expenditure of money upon that very street to the benefit of his property, although he would not pay a penny of the rates for it. One of the great objects of the Bill is to enable localities to manage themselves in local affairs ; but if the Amendment is carried there is no reason why certain carpet-baggers, whose strings are pulled by political associations, should not be elected all over London into half a dozen con-tituencies to work for these politicals associations.

*MR. J. LOWLES (Shoreditch, Hagger-ston): I voted against this Amendment in Committee, but I confess I have since changed my mind. I am still opposed to the principle of the Amendment, but,

looking upon the matter from a purely practical, utilitarian point of view, I think it should be adopted. There is, for instance, the chairman of the Shore-ditch Board of Guardians, one of the best administrators and exponents of the Poor Law that the borough ever had. He is non-resident and would be disqualified, as the Bill stands, from serving on the borough council. My hon. friend who shares with me the representation of Shoreditch knows perfectly well that many of the leading businesses in that borough have been turned into a limited companies—not for bogus purposes, but for expansion—and their owners would now be rendered ineligible. The best men from a purely local point of view, who spend nineteenths of their time and their money freely in the locality, and who know better than most men what the needs of the public are, would be excluded from taking part in local government. I con fess frankly that that would be a great mistake, and I hope that on this occasion the House will reverse its judgment, and give the borough councils the permissive . power to elect men—not political carpet-baggers—but men who are part of the real life of the district, and are best quali-fied to represent the district, although for the reasons stated they may be technically not on the rate board in dividually.

Question put.

The House divided. Ayes, 67 ; Noes, 139. (Division List No. 173).

AYES.

Anstruther, H. T.	Fisher, William Hayes	Murray, Rt. Hn. A. G. (Bute
Arrol, Sir William	Flannery, Sir Fortescue	Pierpoint, Robert
Atkinson, Rt. Hon. John	Garfit, William	Price, Robert John
Balfour, Rt. Hn. A. J. (Manch'r)	Gibbs, Hn. A. G. H. (CityofLond	Rickett, J. Compton
Balfour, Rt. Hn. G.W. (Leeds)	Gordon, Hon. John Edward	Ritchie, Rt. Hon. C. Thomson
Banbury, Frederick George	Gorst, Rt. Hon. Sir John Eldon	Sharpe, William Edward T.
Barnes, Frederic Gorell	Hayne, Rt. Hon. Charles Seale-	Sidebottom, T. H. (Stalybr.)
Beach, Rt. Hn. Sr. M. H. (Bristol	Hill, SirEdwardStock (Bristol)	Smith, Hon. W. F. D. (Strand)
Bethell, Commander	Horniman, Frederick John	Talbot, Rt. Hn. J. G. (Ox. Univ.
Bigwood, James	Howard, Joseph	Tomlinson, Wm Edw. Murray
Blundell, Colonel Henry	Hubbard, Hon. Evelyn	Trevelyan, Charles Philips
Brookfield, A. Montagu	Hughes, Colonel Edwin	Tritton, Charles Ernest
Bryce, Rt. Hon. James	Knowles, Lees	Webster.SirR. E. (IsleofWight
Bullard, Sir Harry	Lafone, Alfre l	Whitmore, Charles Algernon
Cecil, Lord Hugh (Greenwich)	Lewis, John Herbert	Williams, JohnCarvell(Notts.)
Chaloner, Captain R. G.W.	Long, Rt. Hn. Walter (Liverp'l)	Willox, Sir John Archibald
Chaplin, Rt. Hon. Henry	Lowles, John	Wortley, Rt. Hn. C. B. Stuart-
Charrington, Spencer	Macdona, John Cumming	Wyndham, George
Cohen, Benjamin Louis	MacIver, David (Liverpool)	Young, Commander(Berks, E.)
Corbett, A. Cameron (Glasgow)	M'Killop, James	
Cornwallis, Fiennes S. W.	Manners, Lord Edw. Wm. J.	TELLERS FOR THE AYES—
Courtney, Rt. Hon Leonard H.	Middlemore, J. Throgmorton	Sir Edward Clarke and Sir
Doxford, William Theodore	Morton, A. H. A. (Deptford)	John Brunner.
Finlay, Sir Robert Bannatyne	Muntz, Philip A.	

Mr. Kimber.

NOES.

Allan, William (Gateshead)
Austin, Sir John (Yorkshire)
Austin, M. (Limerick, W.)
Bailey, James (Walworth)
Balcarres, Lord
Barton, Dunbar Plunket
Bathurst, Hon. Allen Benj.
Beckett, Ernest William
Bhownaggree, Sir M. M.
Billson, Alfred
Boulnois, Edmund
Bousfield, William Robert
Broadhurst, Henry
Burns, John
Caldwell, James
Campbell, J. H. M. (Dublin)
Carvill, Patrick G. Hamilton
Cawley, Frederick
Chamberlain, J. A. (Worc'r)
Channing, Francis Allston
Clough, Walter Owen
Cochrane, Hon. T. H. A. E.
Coghill, Douglas Harry
Collings, Rt. Hon. Jesse
Cook, Fred. Lucas (Lambeth)
Cooke, C. W. R. (Hereford)
Cripps, Charles Alfred
Curran, Thomas (Sligo, S.)
Curzon, Viscount
Dalbiac, Colonel Philip Hugh
Dalkeith, Earl of
Dalrymple, Sir Charles
Donelan, Captain A.
Doogan, P. C.
Douglas, Rt. Hon. A. Akers-
Drucker, A.
Duncombe, Hon. Hubert V.
Evans, Samuel T. (Glamorgan
Fellowes, Hon. Ailwyn Edw.
Fenwick, Charles
Finch, George H.
Firbank, Joseph Thomas
Flower, Ernest
Forster, Henry William
Foster, Colonel (Lancaster)
Gibbons, J. Lloyd
Goddard, Daniel Ford
Godson, Sir Augustus Fredk.

Goldsworthy, Major-General
Greville, Hon. Ronald
Gurdon, Sir Wm. Brampton
Hamilton, Rt. Hn. LordGeorge
Hanbury, Rt. Hn. Robert Wm.
Harwood, George
Heath, James
Heaton, John Henniker
Hermon-Hodge, R. Trotter
Hoare, Ed. Brodie(Hampstead
Holland, Wm. H.(York,W.R.)
Howell, William Tudor
Hutchinson,Capt.G.W. Grice-
Jenkins, Sir John Jones
Jessel, Capt. Herbert Merton
Kearley, Hudson E.
Keswick, William
Kimber, Henry
Lambert, George
Lawson, John Grant (Yorks.)
Leese, Sir Jos. F. (Accrington)
Leng, Sir John
Llewellyn,EvanH. (Somerset)
Llewelyn,SirDillwyn-(Sw'ns'a
Lucas-Shadwell, William
Lyttelton, Hon. Alfred
MacAleese, Daniel
Maclure, Sir John William
M'Arthur, Charles (Liverpool)
M'Ghee, Richard
M'Kenna, Reginald
Maddison, Fred.
Maple, Sir John Blundell
Mellor, Colonel (Lancashire)
Milward, Colonel Victor
Montagu, Sir S.(Whitechapel)
More,Robt.Jasper(Shropshire)
Morgan,Hn.Fred.(Monm'thsh.
Morrell, George Herbert
Morton, Edw. J. C.(Devonp't
Nicol, Donald Ninian
Norton, Capt. Cecil William
O'Connor,James(Wicklow,W.
Pease, Joseph A. (Northumb.)
Penn, John
Phillpotts, Captain Arthur
Pickard, Benjamin
Pickersgill, Edward Hare

Powell, Sir Francis Sharp
Pryce-Jones, Lt. Col. Edward
Purvis, Robert
Richards, Henry Charles
Richardson,SirThos.(Hartlep'l
Ridley,Rt. Hn.SirMatthewW.
Robertson, Herbert (Hackney)
Russell, T. W. (Tyrone)
Samuel, Harry S. (Limehouse)
Samuel, J. (Stockton on Tees)
Scoble, Sir Andrew Richard
Seton-Karr, Henry
Shaw, Thomas (Hawick B.)
Simeon, Sir Barrington
Smith, Samuel (Flint)
Stanley, Lord (Lancs.)
Steadman, William Charles
Stock, James Henry
Stone, Sir Benjamin
Stuart, James (Shoreditch)
Sullivan, Donal (Westmeath)
Thomas, David A. (Merthyr)
Thornton, Percy M.
Tully, Jasper
Usborne, Thomas
Valentia, Viscount
Walrond, Rt. Hon. SirWm.H.
Walton, Joseph (Barnsley)
Warr, Augustus Frederick
Webster, R. G. (St. Pancras)
Wedderburn, Sir William
Weir, James Galloway
Wharton, Rt.Hon.John Lloyd
Whiteley, H.(Ashton-under-L
Whittaker, Thomas Palmer
Williams, J. Powell- (Birm.)
Wilson, Fred. W. (Norfolk)
Wilson, Henry J.(York,W.R.)
Wilson, John (Durham, Mid.)
Wilson, John (Falkirk)
Wilson,Jas.H.(Middlesbrough
Woods, Samuel
Wylie, Alexander

TELLERS FOR THE NOES—
  Mr. Goulding and Mr.
  Marks.

SIR R. B. FINLAY: I beg to move an Amendment providing that the duties in connection with registration should be discharged by the town clerk. In the boroughs generally the duties of registration are thrown on the town clerks and overseers. In London there is no town clerk at present, and the duties of registration are discharged by persons who ordinarily perform the duties of returning officer and are named by the Sheriff. The object of the Amendment is to make it clear that in the boroughs the duties relating to registration shall be discharged by the town clerks on the borough council.

Amendment proposed—

"In page 3, line 24, after the words 'town clerk, to insert the words, 'and shall be the town clerk within the meaning of the Acts relating to the registration of electors.'"—(*Mr. Solicitor-General.*)

Question proposed—

"That those words be there inserted."

MR. STUART: I have an Amendment on the paper providing that registration matters may be dealt with by the town clerk or his assistant. I do not want my Amendment to be ruled out of order by the passage of the Solicitor-General's, and therefore probably I shall be in order if I were to move that in the Amendment proposed by the Solicitor-General, after the words "town clerk" the words "or his deputy" should be inserted. It might possibly happen that the town clerk may take a strong political line, and consequently not be trusted in respect to the transaction of registration business, and I therefore suggest that the words "or his deputy" should be added. I do not wish to go outside the right hon. Gentleman's arrangement or compromise. It seems to me his object is to get personal responsibility in respect to the making up of the register, and if this Bill creates the town clerk a responsible authority, as it does, we should get out of a very serious difficulty if we put in the words "or a registration officer appointed by the borough council for that purpose." I do not wish to weaken the right hon. Gentleman's compromise. I accept it; but I propose to get out of the difficulty connected with it by substituting for the town clerk the town clerk or his deputy.

Amendment proposed to the proposed Amendment—

"After the word 'and,' to insert the words 'he or the registration officer appointed by the borough council as hereinafter provided.'" —(*Mr. James Stuart.*)

Question proposed—

"That those words be there inserted in the proposed Amendment."

*Mr. JOHN BURNS (Battersea): It seems to me that the First Lord of the Treasury, in making the town clerk supremely responsible in these matters, has done everything we could reasonably hope for. The greater includes the less, and the town clerk, having been made responsible for the voters' list and the overseers' work, would necessarily be responsible for any deputy appointed to discharge a section of the work. I have no fear that the town clerk will allow political gerrymandering to sway him to any material extent; but if inclined to be operated on in that direction, the loss he would incur by being found out, and the penalty he would have

to pay, would be so great that, apart from inclination, there would be a tremendous deterrent. May I point out to the hon. Member for Shoreditch that economy and efficiency are opposed to such a multiplicity of officials. If the responsibility for all those duties is fixed on the town clerk, I believe the money will be saved to the ratepayers, and if the First Lord of the Treasury could suggest some means by which polling officers should have less than the two guineas a day they now receive, I should strongly support him.

Mr. R. G. WEBSTER (St. Pancras, E.): I entirely agree with the observations of the hon. Member for Battersea, and I sincerely hope that the town clerk, when appointed, will be like Cæsar's wife —above suspicion. I did not put down any Amendment, such as I did to the London County Council Bill, making town clerks ineligible to sit in this House, because it was pointed out to me that it would be unnecessary, because these gentlemen would probably not be amenable to political influences. I thoroughly support the proposal of the Solicitor-General. I think it is necessary for us to give these powers exclusively to town clerks, and it is very desirable that they should be solely responsible and that there should be no devolution to anybody else.

The ATTORNEY-GENERAL (Sir RICHARD WEBSTER, Isle of Wight) I hope the House will not accept this Amendment. In the first place, I do not think it necessary, or that it is based on a right principle, because it picks out one particular part of the duties which would fall on the town clerk and gives him special authority to appoint a deputy to discharge them. I have been anticipated by the hon. Member for Battersea in many of my objections to this Amendment. My own opinion is that some words may be necessary to enable the borough councils to give the town clerks assistance by way of deputy or otherwise, but the responsibility for the work should in my judgment remain with the town clerk.

Amendment to the proposed Amendment, by leave, withdrawn.

Amendment agreed to.

Clause 4 :—

* CAPTAIN JESSEL (St. Pancras, S.) : As the House knows, sanction must be given by the London County Council, or for certain purposes by the Local Government Board, for loans to local bodies. The Vestry of St. Pancras, which is in the division I represent, complain very much of the time taken by the London County Council in sanctioning loans. If the House will permit me, I will give one or two examples. In December, 1892, a loan of £30,000 for an electric installation was asked for. Of that sum £15,400 was received in March, 1894, and the remainder was not paid till January, 1895. A period of three years elapsed before we got all the loan. On another occasion we applied for a loan in November, 1895, but only got £6,540 in January, 1897, and £2,945 in June of the same year. Delay in that case was owing to the London County Council going into the whole of the past expenditure. On another occasion a loan was asked for in July, 1897, but the greater portion of it was not paid till March, 1898. The delay in this case, again, was caused by the inquiry made by the London County Council into the expenditure and valuing up of the mains, which I maintain is not necessary in order to get the sanction for the loan. The last occasion was in May, 1898, when a loan of £23,000 was applied for. £12,000 was received on 16th March, and the balance is waiting at the present moment. The result of this is that the Vestry of St. Pancras has been obliged to borrow money from the bankers at the rate of 4 per cent., whereas the London County Council could have got it for

The Attorney-General.

them at 2¾ per cent. I complain that, at present, the London County Council mix up the question of sanctioning the loan with the question of lending the money, and I maintain that the two are entirely different questions. If the Amendment is accepted by the House, it will result in advantage to the borough councils and to the London County Council itself, and for this reason : In the first place, they could always refuse if they think it right, in which case there would be a prompt appeal ; and, in the second place, the London County Council would not be granting money for works already completed. I beg to move the Amendment standing in my name.

Amendment proposed—

" In Clause 4, line 21, to insert ' or do not, within six months after application made, give their sanction.' "—*(Captain Jessel.)*

Question proposed—

" That those words be there inserted."

SIR RICHARD WEBSTER : For the reason given by the hon. Gentleman I think this a reasonable Amendment, as I understand there have been considerable delays. I think six months is long enough in all probability. If any question of real necessity arises the Local Government Board would consider the matter.

MR. STUART : The Attorney-General knows very little about the relations of the local authorities, and the speech of the hon. Member for St. Pancras has been so confused that he has been greatly misled. There have been upwards of 400 loans made by the London County Council to the local authorities, and I do not believe, except in the three instances to which the hon. and gallant Member referred, has there been any complaint whatever with respect to the sanctioning of the loans. I want to point out that there is a difference between asking for the sanction of a loan for a parish and getting the money. Now, what the whole of this clause refers to is not the providing of the money by the London County Council, but the sanctioning of the loan. The first step which has to be taken is to settle whether the local body is justified in requiring the loan for the purpose stated, and that has to be inquired into. When that is done, and the decision given favourably, the local authority can go and ask for the loan. If they take it from the London County Council they get it at 2¾ per cent. There is no proof whatever, so far as sanctioning the loan is concerned, that there has been any delay at all ; but if there was delay there was very good reason for it. I regard the suggestion that the London County Council must give their sanction to loans within six months, or that then the matter will be taken out of their hands, as an insult to the London County Council. As I have said, if the London County Council delay longer than six months in giving their sanction, there is a right good reason for it. Under these circumstances I do trust that there will not be an endeavour made on the part of any person in this House to attach any stigma to the London County Council in this matter.

Sir R. B. FINLAY : I can assure the hon. Gentleman and the House that there is no desire to attach the slightest stigma to the County Council in this matter. No part of the business of the London County Council is better done than that relating to loans. The hon. Gentleman has not given any reason why we should not accept this Amendment. If we provide that in the case of a refusal there shall be an appeal from the London County Council to another authority, it is obviously necessary that there should be the same appeal to the Local Government Board if assent is not given within six months.

Question put, and agreed to.

Clause 6 :—

Mr. PICKERSGILL : I beg to move to omit Sub-section 6. This sub-section gives power to the borough councils to promote and oppose Bills in Parliament, and it seems to me to be a matter of such extreme importance that I propose to appeal from the judgment of the Committee to the judgment of the House. This clause touches a side of the Bill which, I think, has not perhaps received sufficient attention from the House — I mean the financial side. There can be no doubt that one effect of this Bill will be to undoubtedly increase expenditure and to raise the rates.

Mr. CRIPPS : To promote economy.

Mr. PICKERSGILL : The Bill will raise the rates directly, because it proposes to transfer the discharge of central functions from the central to the local body. I also think its inevitable effect will be to promote expense indirectly. If I am right in this, then I say it would be most unwise to open such a flood-gate of expenditure as this sub-section would do. It seems to me that the form of expenditure which is grudged more than any other is expenditure upon litigation, whether it be in courts of law or in Parliament, because, in these cases, whoever wins, the public has to pay the costs on both sides. Of course, I know very well that litigation, in the sense in which I use the term, is inevitable, but surely it is only common sense to restrain it within as narrow limits as possible. My case against this clause is, that there is no necessity for it, and that, as the law stands, the borough councils will have quite sufficient powers for the promotion of their own interests. It may be said in theory that this clause puts all on an equal footing. As a matter of fact it does not. It will place the poorer districts of the metropolis at a serious disadvantage compared with the richer districts. You may say that the law courts are open to all. But the man with the longer purse has the advantage, and what applies in the case of individual litigants applies equally to public bodies who indulge in litigation. I do think, having regard to the importance of this question, we are justified in appealing to the House to omit the sub-section.

Amendment proposed—

"In page 5, line 32, to leave out sub-section (6), of Clause 6."—(*Mr. Pickersgill.*)

Question proposed—

"That the words proposed to be left out stand part of the Bill."

Sir R. B. FINLAY : I hope that the House will take the same view as that adopted by the majority of the Committee on this question. It is perfectly right and reasonable that the same powers should be conferred on these borough councils in the metropolis as are enjoyed by all the town councils throughout the country. Of course, the County Council may deal with Bills relating to the metropolis as a whole, but there may be many matters affecting the health or comfort of the inhabitants of a particular district in regard to which it is desirable that the borough council should have the power of promoting or opposing Bills, or of enforcing their rights by legal procedure.

MR. SYDNEY BUXTON : I regret that the First Lord of the Treasury is absent, because he might have been induced by the arguments of my hon. friend to have met us in regard to this matter. This really is the last blot on the Bill in connection with the position which the borough councils will hold against the County Council. The Solicitor - General has argued this question on the analogy of the large borough councils in the country, but these metropolitan borough councils can never be in the same position in regard to their internal relations as the large boroughs throughout the country. We know that for years past—in fact, ever since the London County Council has been in existence — the County Council has promoted Bills for the benefit of all parts of London, and there has been no objection found on the part of the vestries themselves. I think the onus lies on the Government, and those who propose the change, to show that the system which has prevailed up to the present moment has not been successful. I believe that in every case in which the vestry—which is practically now the borough council — has had a desire to have some legal question promoted by the London County Council that question has been promoted and carried through by the County Council to the satisfaction of the local body. I think, therefore, that as regards the actual working of the scheme we ought to have some argument from the Solicitor-General, or from the Attorney-General, to show that it has not been successful, and has not worked properly, and that, therefore, there is some reason for the change. I think there is considerable force in the remark with regard to the cost of these powers. Unfortunately the cost of promoting Bills in Parliament under the present system is an expensive one. Since it came into existence the County Council has had to expend a sum of £20,000 or £30,000 in this direction. I look, therefore, with some trepidation at the probable expense which will be involved when we have 20 or 30 borough councils promoting their own bills. It is perfectly true, as has been said, that the cost will fall heavily on the poorer districts, and that

Sir R. B. Finlay.

the richer boroughs will be able to promote their Bills with greater advantage, because they will have plenty of funds to draw upon, whereas the poorer districts, with equal interests involved, will not be able to carry them through. I think also we ought to look on the matter from the point of view of the House of Commons itself, and I must say I view with great trepidation the large amount of time that will be devoted by this House to the consideration of these Bills. That is a practical difficulty which I really think the Government have not given sufficient attention to.

MR. LOWLES : I hope the Government will retain the clause as it is. I am really astonished at the jealousy manifested by the London County Council throughout the whole proceedings in connection with this Bill. I can only conceive that the object of the hon. Gentleman who has just sat down is to enable the County Council to keep its grip over the local authorities. I venture to say that if the local authorities are left to themselves we shall not have that reckless expenditure in promoting Bills which has been predicted by the hon. Gentleman opposite. Where purely local interests would require power under the section it would be usefully and rightfully used. I therefore hope the House will resist the proposal, which has been made entirely in the interests of the London County Council.

*MR. McKENNA (Monmouth, N.) : Whether this Amendment be accepted or not, the members of the various borough councils can promote Bills in Parliament. Their only risk, if the Amendment is carried, is that if their Bill is unsuccessful they will have to bear the cost themselves. In every case where there is a legitimate and proper demand for a Bill by a borough council, they can get their measure through the General Powers Bill of the County Council. It is only when there is strong opposition that any difficulty is likely to arise. If the members of the borough council introduce a measure not acceptable to the general feeling of London, they will do so at their own risk, and that risk will be that a Committee of this House might refuse them costs. There could be no real hardship, because the arbiters in every case would be a Committee of this House. All the Amendment proposes is to give that Committee the power of deciding whether the promotion of a Bill by a borough council was wanton and reckless, and that if it were the members of the council ought to pay the costs themselves. The general power the London County Council now has to include in its Bill any proposal put forward by a borough gives every opportunity to the boroughs to get cheaply what they require.

*Sir F. S. POWELL (Wigan): I have some experience in the working of the Borough Funds Act, which provides a most salutary check, and, although some change in the machinery may be desirable, I am perfectly sure that until we have that improvement we ought to retain the Act as it stands. The functions of the new councils will be executive and administrative, not legislative. The object of the Act is to check the tendency to promote legislation and to indulge in wasteful expenditure. I believe it protects the interests of the subject, and I therefore suggest the importance of retaining it.

Mr STUART: I do not think that my hon. colleague in the representation of Shoreditch has any right to say that the London County Council regards this Bill in the spirit of jealousy. I appeal to the First Lord of the Treasury as to whether I, for one, as largely representing the London County Council in this House, have not done my very best to amend this Bill in a non-partisan spirit. That is shown by Amendments suggested by myself and by others having been adopted by the right hon. Gentleman. When the Bill first came before the House I ventured to say it was a disintegrating Bill. It has ceased largely, but not wholly, to be a disintegrating Bill. There still remain disintegrating clauses in the Bill, but this is the most disintegrating clause of all. It appears to me that if we grant these powers we shall be taking a great step towards the disintegration of London. London is one, and ought to be regarded by this House as one. That we have maintained throughout the whole of this discussion. There is no advantage that I can see in any way whatever in allowing these different portions of London to act

on their own account in this House. Their interests are too much combined and united to make that desirable or useful. The clause is a bad one, and part of the old spirit in which the Bill was framed— viz., of opposition to the unity of London —a spirit, however, which the discussions on this Bill have largely caused to evaporate.

Sir E. CLARKE: I really cannot allow the statement just made to pass unchallenged. The hon. Member said that this clause remains in the Bill in antagonism to the London County Council. He talks about the Bill as a disintegrating Bill, and he says that he and his friends have been insisting on the unity of London. There is a certain amount of truth in that. They have been seeking to secure for one body which they represent authority over all parts of London. They have in that contention, as far as this Bill is concerned, absolutely failed, and I do not accept for a moment the claim they are making now inside and outside the House, that they have been supporting the Bill and sympathising with its objects. They have been defeated in this sense, that the House recognised, on the second reading, and recognises now, that London is not one, but a collection of places entitled to have separate municipal existence and authority apart from the authority and interference of the London County Council. The object of this Bill has, I think, been to put the London County Council in its proper place, and when it passes I think the hon. Member and his friends will be obliged to admit outside, if not here, that very much has been done in spite of them to give proper municipal life to London

Question put.

The House divided: Ayes, 141; Noes, 57. (Division List, No. 174.)

AYES.

Arrol, Sir William
Atkinson, Rt. Hon. John
Balcarres, Lord
Balfour, Rt.Hn.A.J.(Manch'r)
Balfour, Rt.Hn.G. W. (Leeds)
Banbury, Frederick George
Barton, Dunbar Plunket
Bathurst, Hon. Allen B.
Beach,Rt.Hn.SirM.H.(Bristol)
Beckett, Ernest William
Bethell, Commander
Bhownaggree, Sir M. M.
Blundell, Colonel Henry
Bousfield, William Robert
Brodrick, Rt. Hon. St. John
Brookfield, A. Montagu
Bullard, Sir Harry
Cecil, Lord Hugh (Greenwich)
Chaloner, Captain R. G. W.
Chamberlain, J. A. (Worc'r)
Chaplin, Rt. Hon. Henry
Charrington, Spencer
Clarke, SirEdward(Plymouth)
Clough, Walter Owen
Cochrane, Hon. Thos. H. A.E.
Coghill, Douglas Harry
Cohen, Benjamin Louis
Collings, Rt. Hon. Jesse
Cooke,C.W.Radcliffe(Heref'd)
Corbett, A.Cameron(Glasgow)
Cornwallis,FiennesStanleyW.
Cripps, Charles Alfred
Curzon, Viscount
Dalrymple, Sir Charles
Denny, Colonel
Douglas, Rt. Hon. A. Akers-
Doxford, William Theodore
Drucker, A.
Duncombe, Hon. Hubert V.
Fardell, Sir T. George
Fellowes, Hon. Ailwyn Edw.
Field, Admiral (Eastbourne)
Finlay, Sir Robert Bannatyne)
Fisher, William Hayes
Flannery, Sir Fortescue
Flower, Ernest
Foster, Colonel (Lancaster)
Garfit, William

Gedge, Sydney
Gibbons, J. Lloyd
Gibbs, Hn.A.G H.(C. of Lond.
Giles, Charles Tyrrell
Godson, Sir Augustus Fredk.
Goldsworthy, Major-General
Gordon, Hon. John Edward
Gorst, Rt. Hon. Sir J. Eldon
Goulding, Edward Alfred
Greene, H. D. (Shrewsbury)
Greville, Hon. Ronald
Hamilton, Rt. Hon. Lord G.
Hanbury, Rt. Hn. Robert W.
Hanson, Sir Reginald
Heath, James
Heaton, John Henniker
Hermon-Hodge, R. Trotter
Hill, Sir Edw. Stock (Bristol)
Hoare, E. Brodie (Hampstead)
Howell, William Tudor
Hubbard, Hon. Evelyn
Hughes, Colonel Edwin
Hutchinson, Capt.G.W.Grice-
Jessel, Capt. Herbert Merton
Johnstone, Heywood (Sussex)
Knowles, Lees
Lafone, Alfred
Lawson, John Grant (Yorks.)
Llewelyn,SirDillwyn-(Sw'ns'a
Long, Rt.Hn.Walter(Liverp'l)
Lopes, Henry Yarde Buller
Lowles, John
Lowther, Rt. Hon. Jas. (Kent)
Loyd, Archie Kirkman
Lucas-Shadwell, William
Macdona, John Cumming
MacIver, David (Liverpool)
M'Arthur, Charles (Liverpool)
M'Killop, James
Maple, Sir John Blundell
Marks, Henry Hananel
Martin, Richard Biddulph
Mellor, Colonel (Lancashire)
Middlemore, J. Throgmorton
Milner, Sir Frederick George
Milward, Colonel Victor
More, Robt. J. (Shropshire)
Morrell, George Herbert

Morton, A. H. A. (Deptford)
Muntz, Philip A.
Murray, Rt. Hn. A. G (Bute)
Murray, Charles J. (Coventry)
Parkes, Ebenezer
Percy, Earl
Phillpotts, Captain Arthur
Pierpoint, Robert
Platt-Higgins, Frederick
Powell, Sir Francis Sharp
Pryce-Jones, Lt.-Col. Edward
Purvis, Robert
Richardson, Sir T. (Hartlep'l)
Ridley, Rt. Hon. Sir M. W.
Ritchie, Rt. Hon. Chas. T.
Robertson, Herbert(Hackney)
Russell, T. W. (Tyrone)
Samuel, Harry S. (Limehouse)
Saunderson,Rt. Hn. Col. E. J.
Sooble, Sir Andrew Richard
Seton-Karr, Henry
Sharpe, William Edward T.
Sidebottom, T. H. (Stalybr.)
Simeon, Sir Barrington
Smith, Hon. W.F.D. (Strand)
Stanley, Lord (Lancs.)
Stock, James Henry
Stone, Sir Benjamin
Talbot,Rt.Hn.J.G.(OxfdUniv
Thornton, Percy M.
Tomlinson, Wm. Edw.Murray
Tritton, Charles Ernest
Usborne, Thomas
Valentia, Viscount
Warr, Augustus Frederick
Webster, R.G. (St. Pancras)
Webster, Sir R. E.(I.ofWight)
Whiteley,H.(Ashton-under-L)
Williams, J. Powell- (Birm.)
Willox, Sir John Archibald
Wilson, John (Falkirk)
Wilson,J.W.(Worcestersh,N.)
Wylie, Alexander
Wyndham, George
Young, Commander(Berks,E.)
TELLERS FOR THE AYES—
  Sir William Walrond and
  Mr. Anstruther.

NOES.

Allan, William (Gateshead)
Atherley-Jones, L.
Austin, Sir J. (Yorkshire)
Barlow, John Emmott
Billson, Alfred
Broadhurst, Henry
Burns, John
Buxton, Sydney Charles
Caldwell, James
Cawley, Frederick
Curran, Thomas (Sligo, S.)
Davies, M. V.- (Cardigan)
Davitt, Michael
Dilke, Rt. Hon. Sir Charles
Dillon, John
Donelan, Captain A.
Doogan, P. C.
Douglas, C. M. (Lanark)
Evans, S. T. (Glamorgan)
Evershed, Sydney

Fenwick, Charles
Goddard, Daniel Ford
Gurdon, Sir William B.
Hedderwick, Thomas Chas. H.
Holland, W. H. (York, W.R.)
Horniman, Frederick John
Jones, W. (Carnarvonshire)
Lawson, Sir W. (Cumb'land)
Leng, Sir John
Lewis, John Herbert
Lloyd-George, David
MacAleese, Daniel
M'Cartan, Michael
M'Ghee, Richard
M'Kenna, Reginald
Montagu, Sir S. (Whitechapel)
Morton, E. J. C. (Devonport)
Norton, Capt. Cecil William
O'Connor, T. P. (Liverpool)
Price, Robert John

Provand,Andrew Dryburgh
Rickett, J. Compton
Samuel, J. (Stockton-on-Tees)
Shaw, Thomas (Hawick, B.)
Steadman, William Charles
Sullivan, Donal (Westmeath)
Thomas, David A. (Merthyr)
Trevelyan, Charles Philips
Tully, Jasper
Walton, Joseph (Barnsley)
Weir, James Galloway
Whittaker, Thomas Palmer
Williams, John C. (Notts.)
Wilson, Fred. W. (Norfolk)
Wilson, H. J. (York, W. R.)
Wilson, John (Durham, Mid.)
Wilson, J. H. (Middlesbrough)
TELLERS FOR THE NOES—Mr.
  Pickersgill and Mr. James
  Stuart.

MR. SYDNEY BUXTON : The Amendment I now propose relates to the financial basis between the London County Council and the new borough councils, and it is one which the right hon. Gentleman the First Lord of the Treasury said he would consider before the Report stage. I do not want to enter into the arguments with which I troubled the House upon the last occasion, but it does seem to me necessary that we should provide for some sort of revision. Under these circumstances, I will ask the right hon. Gentleman to take this into his favourable consideration, although I do not wish to press it unduly upon him.

Amendment proposed—

"In page 6, line 12, after the word 'order,' to insert the words, 'provided that, at any interval of not less than five years, the London County Council and the borough council may revise and alter the amount of the contribution, or, in default of agreement, the Local Government Board may, on the application of either party, if it think fit, revise and vary the existing arrangement.'"—(*Mr. Sydney Buxton.*)

Question proposed—

"That those words be there inserted."

MR. A. J. BALFOUR : I am afraid that the words of the hon. Gentleman opposite will hardly do, because they divorce too obviously the responsibility of expenditure from the responsibility of management. If the local authority is ready to take over the duties, it should, no doubt, be ready to take over the expenditure which is associated with those duties, and which is necessary to carry those duties into effect. If I could find a thoroughly satisfactory form of words which would make it possible to have a revision in those cases in which public necessity requires an immense extension of the duties originally made the subject of agreement, I should be very glad to consider it. I can well imagine cases in which some power of going back over the original decision would be desirable in the public interest, although I confess that the words of this proposal are rather vague, and I do not think that we could accept the suggestion of the hon. Member. There is, of course, still time in another place to insert words which would meet the case, and I shall be glad to consider them if the hon. Member can think of a satisfactory form of words.

MR. SYDNEY BUXTON : Under the circumstances I will not press my Amendment.

Amendment, by leave, withdrawn.

Other amendments made.

MR. PICKERSGILL : The object of the Amendment I now beg to move has been discussed before, and when it was mentioned in Committee the Leader of the House advanced one objection to it, and, so far as my memory serves me, one objection only. He said that it would be inconvenient in reference to the administration of sanitary law, because in those cases it was sometimes necessary, at all events, to take action upon an emergency. Seeing that there was considerable force in that objection, I have met it by the consequential Amendment which stands in my name. I propose by a subsequent Amendment to exempt from the requirement of approval any Committee appointed for the purpose of the Public Health Act. I do, therefore, hope this will not be opposed by the Government. There are two precedents for this—one is that of the municipal corporations, and the other the district councils. As these precedents are on our side, I think I have fairly met the objection of the right hon. Gentleman opposite, and I trust that he will consent to adopt this Amendment.

Amendment proposed—

" In page 6, line 28, to leave out the word 'report,' in order to insert the word 'submit.'"—(*Mr. Pickersgill.*)

instead thereof :—

Question proposed—

"That the word 'report' stand part of the Bill."

SIR R. B. FINLAY : I hope the House will not accept this Amendment, which will require, with the one exception mentioned in a subsequent Amendment, that the act of every committee shall be submitted to the council. Surely the provision of the Bill as it stands is much more reasonable, for it provides that :

"Every committee shall report their proceedings to the council, but to the extent to which the council so direct the act and proceedings of the committee shall not require the approval of the council."

I fail to see what sense there is in confining that power to one particular class of cases.

S 2

MR. STUART: The arrangement under the Bill proposes to give a certain power to these metropolitan municipalities which does not exist in any other committee, either on county councils or municipalities. It is a great pity that you should enable a body to shuffle off its responsibilities upon committees. I shall support this amendment, because I believe it will bring the law in London in uniformity with the law which is in force in other places.

MR. LOWLES: From my own observations I can only say that the committees already existing do very good work in this regard, and take great interest in it. The only check upon their work is that they are subordinate to the local governing body themselves, and to take away the check is a very dangerous thing. By this Bill the power of revision by the Council by whom they are appointed will be done away with, and I think to take away such a wholesome check will be very dangerous indeed.

MR. A. J. BALFOUR: Our point is that if this Amendment is carried, it will throw a great deal of unnecessary labour on the council. On the other hand, under the clause as it stands the possibility of abuse is reduced to a minimum, because when a committee is suspected of abusing its powers it can be dispossessed of those powers at a moment's notice by the body to which it is subordinate.

MR. LOWLES: Under this clause?

MR. A. J. BALFOUR: Yes. And under the circumstances I am sure that my hon. friend will feel that no independent body is set up which can set its parent body at defiance.

Question put and agreed to.

Amendment negatived.

MR. CRIPPS: I propose now to move the Amendment standing in my name at the beginning of the Paper. The object of my Amendment is simply to introduce a scheme which would be of great convenience in dealing with the difficult and complex subject of rating, and would not affect the incidence of rating either as regards individuals or areas. What I seek to do is to make the borough the unit for assessment purposes, for making the levy, and for the collection of rates, as against the parish which is the unit at the present time. What the Government have done in Sub-section 10 is to make the duties of the overseer vest in the council of the borough, which is not only clumsy but is in itself an absurdity, because although the borough council is made the overseer of each parish in its area, the parish is kept alive as a rating unit. My proposal is that, instead of having this complex machinery, instead of making the borough council the overseer, we should have one overseer for the borough unit, and that for rating purposes it should be constituted a parish. It is not only a question of machinery; it goes outside; it is also a matter of expense. It goes over the whole borough, and you can afford to have the work properly done, and then it can be supervised by the council. I hope the House will appreciate what I mean. You want a borough unit, and you want to know whether property is being assessed at a proper amount. The best way to arrive at that is to take the larger entity, and give the overseer a skilled assistant, through whom the work can be properly done. It is a great advantage to have a larger rather than a smaller entity. If you deal with the matter on this principle you get greater simplification and far greater certainty in every assessment, and that is the matter with which we have to deal. As I shall not have another opportunity of speaking on this subject, allow me to say a word as to the objection raised by the Solicitor-General on the last occasion. He suggested that my scheme might interfere in some way with the liabilities of various areas throughout the borough. I would point out that this does not deal with any question of the kind. All we are doing here is to find out the best basis of assessment.

Amendment proposed—

"'In page 7, line 1, after the word 'parish,' to insert the words, 'it shall be constituted a parish for the purposes of assessment, and for the making, levy, and collection of rates, and.' "—(*Mr. Cripps.*)

Question proposed—

"That those words be there inserted."

Sir RICHARD WEBSTER: I recognise at once the clearness and ability with which my hon. and learned friend has stated his case; and, although I do not pretend to have the experience which he has had on the Royal Commission, this is a subject that I have a very great experience of. I quite agree if some scheme could be arrived at whereby for rating, valuation, and all other purposes, the borough could be made one parish it would be a great help; but it is not possible to do that in the way he proposes. The difficulties in the way are almost insuperable. We have to deal with the question of a borough comprising more than one parish, and we shall also have to deal with a parish which is in more than one union. I hope my hon. friend will not misunderstand me. I am pointing out that the simple amendment which he proposes to put into this Bill will not be sufficient to bring about the uniformity which he desires to obtain. I am not so clear upon this, but I think there would be considerable difficulty in the question of the equalisation of rates, unless you had certain consequential amendments put in, because at present the equalisation of rates is arrived at by means of population, and not by boroughs. We have approached this question with the object of seeing whether, either by a clause by itself or by some amendment in the Bill, some such scheme as that which my hon. friend suggests could be adopted; but I am afraid there are great difficulties in the way. It is not because we do not sympathise with his Amendment that we do not adopt it, but because the consequential amendments would be so serious. I am not sure whether all that the hon. Gentleman desires to be done in this Bill could be accomplished by his Amendment, even if it were agreed to; and, at the same time, we are not in a position to accept it without grave consideration as to its effect on existing Acts of Parliament.

Sir EDWARD CLARKE: My hon. and learned friend has made a very sympathetic speech in reply to the Amendment of the hon. and learned Gentleman the Member for Stroud, whose object was to make, for the purpose of assessment, the borough a unit. My hon. and learned friend said he sympathised with that object, and, no doubt, in that respect he is in accord with all other Members of this House. The subject is a complex one, and I only rise because the Attorney-General, at the end of his speech, said that there was a possibility of constructing a scheme by which this object could be carried into effect. We are all of us agreed that the object which the hon. and learned Member has is a good object, and one which it is desirable to carry out. I would, therefore, ask if it is not possible that, between this stage and the discussion of the matter in another place, certain amendments might be made in this clause which would effectuate that object.

Mr. A. J. BALFOUR: I entirely admit that my hon. and learned friend who has just sat down, and the hon. and learned Gentleman who moved the Amendment, have not misconstrued the views of the Government when they say that we regard the object with most sympathetic interest; but the real difficulty is that we cannot make the area of the borough coincide with the area for assessment until we have brought the union area into coincidence with the borough area. There is machinery for doing that under the Local Government Act, and I hope that by that machinery gradually, but not less effectually, the end which my hon. and learned friend, in common with the Government, has in view will be carried into effect. To do it directly and immediately by a provision in this Bill introduced in another place is more than I am in a position to promise, the difficulties involved being so considerable. If it can be done nobody will rejoice more than myself and the other members of the Government who are responsible for this measure.

Mr. CRIPPS: Having regard to what has been said by the First Lord of the Treasury and the Attorney-General, I will not press my Amendment.

Amendment, by leave, withdrawn.

Amendment proposed—

" In page 7, line 23, after the word 'borough' to insert the words, 'and of churchwardens of every parish within their borough except in so far as these relate to ecclesiastical purposes.'"—(*Mr. James Stuart.*)

Question, " That those words be there inserted," put, and negatived.

Other Amendments made.

Amendment proposed—

" In page 8, line 5, after the word 'clerk' to insert the words, 'upon such date or within such period as the Local Government Board may prescribe, so that all the rates collected in a metropolitan borough from any person may be included in one demand note.'"—(*Mr. Pickersgill.*)

Question proposed, " That those words be there inserted."

Amendment, by leave, withdrawn.

Other Amendments made.

MR. CRIPPS: I beg to move an amendment in Clause 12 providing that in all cases, whether the Poor Law union is one borough or not, the assessment committee shall be appointed by the borough council instead of by the board of guardians. This will bring the Bill into conformity with the recommendations of the Local Taxation Committee. I am anxious to anticipate an objection that may be raised based on the Attorney General's last argument. He suggested that we should have overlapping of union areas. That is no difficulty whatever. At the present moment throughout London we have an assessment not only for unions and certain Poor Law areas, but also for Imperial purposes; and it is one of the greatest advantages of assessment in the metropolis that it it available for Imperial as well as for local purposes. Supposing we have an assessment good enough for Imperial purposes and sound and just in itself, what does it matter whether the area over which the assessment committee have authority provides the basis of the assessment or not? At present we have not got the areas of local government coincident with the areas of the spending authorities, and I venture to prophesy they will not be for 100 years. If the Attorney-General's argument holds good, we may postpone the whole question of rating reform. If the basis of assessment is fair and sound, it is wholly immaterial whether it is made by the spending authority or not. That is done every day in London as regards our Imperial taxation, and also with regard to certain matters of local duties, and there is not the slightest reason why we should postpone rating reform until the spending areas are coincident with the local government areas. This matter was especially recommended by the Royal Commission on Local Taxation. It is an admirable and necessary reform, and does not require any consequential amendment. The Attorney General is thoroughly conversant with all rating questions, and I hope he will be able on behalf of the Government to accept this great reform, which will not in any way be affected by the bogey, if I may say so, of the overlapping union areas. I beg to move.

Amendment proposed—

" In page 8, line 33, to leave out the words 'where the whole of a Poor Law union is within one borough.'"—(*Mr. Cripps.*)

Question proposed—

" That the words proposed to be left out stand part of the Bill."

SIR RICHARD WEBSTER: It is quite impossible at this particular stage to accept this Amendment, as the Government have gone as far as they ought in this direction already. Apart from the difficulty of overlapping, which is much more serious than my hon. and learned friend thinks, his Amendment would dispossess the guardians of their right to appoint the assessment committees in all cases, even where the areas were not conterminous with the borough or controlled by the borough authorities. I do not see any uniformity of assessment or other advantage that would be obtained in that case. We have accepted my hon. and learned friend's principle as far as we possibly can by making it apply in analogous cases, and we are not prepared to accept this Amendment.

MR. LOUGH: I have got the same Amendment on the paper, and I am very sorry that the Attorney-General has not seen his way to deal with it more sympathetically. I would direct the attention of the Government to a further proviso I have put down, which,

I think, would meet the objection of the Attorney-General. It is as follows: "Provided that where the boundaries of one or more unions are not conterminous with the area of a borough, a scheme under this Act shall settle any question arising over such overlapping of areas." This really would settle the whole matter. Let us have a scheme under the Act which would settle any difficulty suggested by the Attorney-General. The right hon. Gentleman is anxious to preserve the authority of the board of guardians in this matter, but the primary object of the board of guardians is to relieve the poor. Why, then, should they have anything to say to assessment? It is a duty which could far more appropriately be given over to the borough councils, and I believe that if my proviso were considered by the Government it would be seen that every difficulty would be met by it. The Attorney-General says that he has accepted the principle of the hon. and learned Member's amendment in all cases where the Poor Law union is conterminous with the borough. In Islington we are all right, as the Poor Law union and the borough cover exactly the same area. Therefore I am quite unselfish in this matter, and I really put down my proviso to meet the objections raised by the Attorney-General. It would enable us to adopt a uniform system in London, and would be a great improvement on the clause as it stands.

MR. A. J. BALFOUR: I think the hon. Gentleman must know that no scheme under this Bill could possibly meet the difficulty, as it could not alter either the area of taxation or the power of taxation. The difficulty arises from the fact that the most important rates which the ratepayers have to pay are the rates raised by the Poor Law guardians. There is no ground for dispossessing the existing assessment committees, and the only way to get over the difficulty is to make the unions conterminous to the boroughs. That is an object to be attained gradually. There is power in existence to enable it to be gradually obtained, but it cannot be obtained in any rough and ready manner under this Bill.

Amendment, by leave, withdrawn.

Other Amendments made.

Amendment proposed—

"In page 8, line 38, after the word 'unions,' to insert the words 'and the town clerk shall be the clerk to such assessment committee.'"— (*Colonel Hughes.*)

Question—

"That those words be there inserted,"

put, and *negatived*.

Other Amendments made.

MR. STUART: I appeal to the Attorney-General and to the Solicitor-General to accede to the Amendment I now rise to move, because I submit it will accomplish the object which I have in view. We have a large number of local Acts in operation in London, and these will have to be repealed. I think we ought to secure that all these Acts should be repealed by one statute. As the Attorney-General well knows, the difficulty of laying your hands on these Acts and knowing whether they exist or not is very great. I am sure that this proposal I am making is a very practical one, but I will not press my Amendment if I can get some satisfactory assurance that the matter will be considered.

Amendment proposed—

"In page 10, line 14, to leave out paragraph (e), of sub-section (1), of Clause 15."—(*Mr. James Stuart.*)

Question proposed—

"That the words proposed to be left out stand part of the Bill."

SIR RICHARD WEBSTER: I would remind the hon. Member opposite that the Bill follows exactly the precedent of the last Local Government Act. It is absolutely necessary in every Bill of this kind to consider the number of local Acts, to modify them and repeal 'hem in some way, and there are a larg number of local Acts which will have to be dealt with. It would be convenient, no doubt, that these should be embodied in one statute, and I will consider what can be done in this direction. But there are other considerations which might make such a course very inconvenient, for some of them have a very wide application. I agree that there should be some convenient method provided of getting at the Act, and I assure the hon. Gentleman that I will not overlook the point. I think he will see, however, that we cannot possibly omit the sub-section altogether.

MR. STUART : After what the hon. and learned Gentleman has said, I ask leave to withdraw my Amendment.

Amendment, by leave, withdrawn.

Other Amendments made.

*MR. BOUSFIELD (Hackney, N.): I am still in the dark as to what the Government propose to do under the Bill in regard to the district which I represent. I have acknowledged in Committee before the courtesy which I have received from the First Lord of the Treasury, and the great consideration he gave to the matter. The conclusion which the right hon. Gentleman came to has certainly pleased one part of my division very well, but it has displeased the other part. It so happens that Stoke Newington is the only district which stands outside the Bill, and which has not been scheduled. What I propose to insert is a provision the object of which is to make it quite clear that the question of dividing a parish, for the purpose of transferring part of it for local purposes from one area to another, is still within the competence of the Boundary Commission, and may be done, notwithstanding the fact that the area has been scheduled. I have in mind the portion of Hackney which is in my division. I represent North Hackney, which is made up of Stoke Newington and a portion of the parish of Hackney. I pointed out how one part of my division was to be joined with South Hornsey, and the Government were good enough to give way so far. There then still remains the question as to whether the other portion of my division should go with it, and all I desire is to make it quite clear that this matter has been left open. I quite recognise that I cannot ask this House to come to a final decision upon such a point when there is a conflict of opinion ; but I do ask the Government to recognise that they should not come to an adverse

Sir Richard Webster.

decision on this point, but still leave the matter open. I ask that these words may be inserted in order that the question may be left open for the Boundary Commissioners to decide and to adjust the boundary. It is agreed on all hands that wherever it is possible it is important that the boundary of the new municipal boroughs should be conterminous with the boundary of the Parliamentary borough, and I wish the Commissioners to be left free to decide between the differences in local opinion in following out that principle. It is eminently desirable that you should have the right sort of spirit in local boroughs, and that it should not be divided for parliamentary purposes. I do not ask the Government for a decision on this matter at this moment ; all I ask is that it may be shown on the face of the Bill that this is a matter which will have to be hereafter determined. I beg to move the Amendment standing in my name.

Amendment proposed—

"In page 10, line 40, after the word 'borough' to insert the words 'notwithstanding the inclusion of the parish in the first schedule to this Act.' "—(*Mr. Bousfield.*)

Question proposed—

"That those words be there inserted."

MR. A. J. BALFOUR : I can heartily sympathise with my hon. friend in respect to the hot water in which he finds himself, because I myself, though I do not represent London, have got into hot water also over the question of areas and boundaries which cannot be settled. My hon. friend suggests an Amendment which has no other object than to enable the parish of Hackney to be cut in two. We have already decided that it shall not be cut in two, and therefore I think it is superfluous to introduce in the clause an Amendment intended to facilitate an arrangement which we do not intend to promote. I hope the Amendment will not be passed.

Question put, and negatived.

MR. BOUSFIELD : As to the Amendment I now rise to move, this is a matter in which I hope to meet a better fate than I experienced in the last Amendment I proposed. There was, no doubt, a strong opinion in South Hornsey before the matter came before this House that the insular part of South Hornsey must come into Stoke Newington, but there is a difficulty in arriving at a correct estimate of the population. Since then South Hornsey has considered its position, and, finding it must partly come in, desires to come in as a whole. What the Government should do now, having got the voice of the inhabitants of South Hornsey upon the matter, is simply to insert in the schedule "South Hornsey and Stoke Newington." I do not know whether the First Lord of the Treasury has considered that, or it might be dealt with in the alternative, and South Hornsey added to the rest of the County of London.

Amendment proposed, to leave out the words relating to population, in order to insert " is part."—(*Mr. Bousfield.*)

MR. A. J. BALFOUR: After the statement made by my hon. friend, I see no reason why the Amendment should not be accepted.

Amendment agreed to.

*CAPTAIN CHALONER (Wilts, Westbury): The Amendment which stands in my name has been framed with a view to prevent a danger which, in the opinion of the Executive Council of the Union of Poor Law Associations of England and Wales exists in regard to this Bill—a danger which would affect not only London but the whole of the United Kingdom. Under a case tried last year, under the Local Government Act, 1888, between the parish of St. Saviour's and the Dorking Union, it was decided that where a parish was subdivided into two or more parishes the Poor Law settlements were extinguished in the divided parishes. We are advised that the same thing would happen under the present Bill. We therefore appeal to Her Majesty's Government to accept this Amendment, to avert what we think a real danger. If this is impossible, I hope, at any rate, that the right hon. Gentleman will give me an assurance, either

that he is satisfied that our fears are ungrounded or that something will be effected to prevent harm being done.

Amendment proposed—

" In page 11, line 33, at the end of line 17, to insert the words—

'If, under or by virtue of the provisions of this Act, or of any Order in Council made in pursuance thereof, any parish or place maintaining its own poor shall be divided into two or more parishes or portions of parishes, such division shall not destroy the settlements which poor persons may have therein at the date of such division, but every person who has at the date of such division a settlement in any parish or place divided as aforesaid shall be deemed to be settled in the new parish which shall contain the house or other place or places in which the settlement acquired or derived by such person, shall have been gained. Provided always that no such settlement as aforesaid shall be retained if it was gained under or by virtue of a residence partly in one of the new parishes and partly in another. 'If, under or by virtue of the provisions of this Act, or of any Order in Council made in pursuance thereof, any parish or place maintaining its own poor shall be divided into two or more parishes or portions of parishes, such division shall not destroy a status of irremovability acquired by virtue of a residence in the union of which the divided parish shall have formed part or consisted, but such status of irremovability shall be deemed to have been acquired in the parish which shall contain the house or other place in which the person having such status of irremovability shall be resident at the time when such division shall take place, or if he shall then be in receipt of relief in the parish which shall contain the house or other place in which he was resident at the time of becoming chargeable.' "—(*Captain Chaloner.*)

Question proposed—

" That those words be there inserted."

MR. A. J. BALFOUR: I think my hon. and gallant friend was perfectly justified in bringing this matter forward. It does appear that there are cases where parishes were divided —not under the Act of 1888—and where the evil which my friend fears had actually occurred and the Poor Law settlement has been destroyed. If that were a possible result of this Bill, I agree it must be carefully guarded against. But I do not think my hon. and gallant friend need be alarmed. As a matter of fact there is power given in this Bill to provide, by scheme, against that danger, and it has been the practice of the Local Government Board, acting under the Act of 1888, whenever a parish is divided, to take care that the settlement is not thereby destroyed. I can assure my hon. friend that every care and precaution shall be taken, by scheme, to prevent the result which he very justly says would be most disastrous if it occurred. It is neither necessary nor desirable to introduce into this Bill this very elaborate Amendment, and perhaps my hon. friend will be content to take from me the assurance that the question will be considered, and that, in so far as parishes are divided under this Bill, schemes shall be provided so that settlements shall not thereby be destroyed.

*CAPTAIN CHALONER: After that assurance, I beg leave to withdraw the Amendment.

Amendment, by leave, withdrawn.

MR. CLOUGH (Portsmouth): The object of the next Amendment standing in my name is to bring the Inner and the Middle Temple into line with the rest of the City under the new arrangements. These have been generally considered extra-parochial ; they are not a parish by themselves, but have been generally considered as within the City. The Assessment of the Inner Temple and the Middle Temple is, in point of fact, made under the provisions of Clause 59 of the Metropolis Act of 1855, by the Assessment Committee of the Corporation of London, and they could, if they wished, be represented on the committee. Their present assessment value, though not rateable value, is : Inner Temple, £23,483, and Middle Temple, £14,500. There are other four Inns of Court—Lincoln's Inn, Gray's Inn, Staple's Inn, and Furnival's Inn, which were under the Metropolis Act of 1855 put on Schedule C by themselves. Whenever any question of rating arises there is always a difficulty in regard to making them pay their ratio, and hitherto the City has never been able to get them to pay 'the Consolidated and Sewers Rates, though they do, in fact, pay the Police Rates—

MR. BOUSFIELD: I rise to a point of order. Is this Amendment within the scope of the Bill?

Mr. A. J. Balfour..

MR. SPEAKER: I think the Amendment would make places rateable which are not now rateable.

MR. CLOUGH: That is my intention.

MR. SPEAKER: That cannot be done under this Bill.

Amendment ruled out of order.

Amendment proposed—

"In page 12, line 30, after the word ' churchwarden,' to insert the words ' or sidesman.' "—(*Mr. Tomlinson.*)

Question proposed—

"That the words ' or sidesman ' be there inserted."

Amendment, by leave, withdrawn.

LORD HUGH CECIL (Greenwich): It is consolatory to me to reflect that the Amendment I now rise to move is not one which is likely to raise much discussion, for no one could conceive a more inopportune moment to raise a contested point. I hope, late though the hour be, that there may be some exercise of forbearance while I try to compress my remarks into as brief a compass as possible. The Bill removes from the ecclesiastical vestries all civil powers and authorities. There remains to them, therefore, nothing but the authority relating to Church affairs, which is safeguarded under Clause 21. There is, therefore, what may be called a disestablishment of the Church in regard to local matters. It follows that when Church affairs have to be dealt with it is only right and reasonable that the body to deal with Church affairs under the Act should be, not the body of public citizens at large, but the body of Church members. The next question is, Who are the Church members ? More than one answer has been given to that question, but my answer is that those only ought to exercise authority in Church matters, among the laity, who are by the law of the Church communicant members. I think there is no dispute about the meaning of the rubric referred to in the Amendment ; all parties in the Church are agreed on that. In point of law there can be no doubt that it would be decidedly improper to allow that those who disobey the law of the Church should exercise government within the Church. It would seem to me a very fatal thing to do. Then comes the further matter, Is it an expedient course? It is very often reasonably complained that the laity of the Church of England have not that share of influence that ought properly to belong to them. I think that if the true cause of that want of influence were carefully sought, it would be found in the fact that the laity are an indeterminate body. It is very difficult to know what the Church of England really thinks, but supposing this Amendment is carried that difficulty will be in a large measure removed; we shall have a number of bodies all entitled to speak in the name of the laity of the Church. I do not think that there is anything which would weigh with the House on the other side except the argument that this is a revival of the old principle of the Test Act. But I do not think it is at all reasonable to say that this proposal contains the same principle as the Test Act. What person who is not a communicant is at all likely to meddle with the ecclesiastical vestries? I do not conceal from the House that the motive I have in moving the Amendment is to face that most difficult question, what is a lay member of the Church of England.

Amendment proposed—

" In page 12, lines 32 and 33, to leave out the words 'the inhabitants of the parish,' in order to insert the words, 'Such inhabitants of the parish as shall have obeyed that rubric of the Book of Common Prayer which is printed at the end of the Order of the Administration of the Holy Communion, and which requires that every parishioner shall communicate at the least three times in the year, of which Easter is to be one.' "—(*Lord Hugh Cecil.*)

Question proposed—

" That the words 'the inhabitants of' stand part of the Bill."

MR. A. J. BALFOUR : I will not enter into the argument with my noble friend as to whether the Amendment is open to the objection often brought against the Test Act, but I will ask him whether he cannot imagine cases in which the administration of some office carrying with it local authority, dignity, and some small measure of local power would give rise to contention wholly unworthy of religion. My noble friend does not conceal from the House that his chief motive for bringing forward the Amendment is, I will not say to raise a discussion, but to turn men's attention to the problem of what constitutes a lay member of the Church of England, with a view, not to the local government of London, but to some future measure under which increased authority may be given to the laity of the Church. I am one of those who desire that the laity should have greater influence in matters ecclesiastical, and no doubt whenever, if ever, the ideal which I entertain on the subject takes practical shape, no question of greater importance can come up for discussion. But, Sir, I would make two observations upon the suggestion of my noble friend. One is that the definition of a layman in the Church of England is far more rigid than the definition which has been found satisfactory in the case of the Church of Scotland, even in a matter so important as that of the choice of a minister. The second observation that I would make to my noble friend is that from his own point of view this surely is a most inopportune and inexpedient moment to choose for discussing a question which we should approach in a mood different perhaps from that in which we have discussed the secular problems which have occupied us to-night. It is surely unwise to ask the House to divert its mind from questions of assessment, questions of rating, questions of area, and all the other important problems connected with the London Government Bill, and suddenly to come to a determination upon a question avowedly brought before us, not for the purpose of dealing with any problem of London government, but apparently with the object of preparing the way for some ecclesiastical reform. Nothing can exceed the importance of the question raised by the Amendment; but why should we be required to come, under most unfavourable circumstances, to a decision—which must affect and prejudice any further discussion which the House may have on some future occasion—in dealing with a Bill which only by accident in one corner, in one stray fragment, touches in some remote degree the ancient ecclesiastical constitution of the country?

"It being Midnight, the Debate stood adjourned.

Debate to be resumed on Thursday.

QUESTION.

RIOTING IN BELFAST.

MR. DILLON (Mayo, E.): Before the House adjourns, I desire to ask the Chief Secretary for Ireland for some information as to what occurred in the City of Belfast last night. It will be within the recollection of hon. Members that last week I felt it my duty to call the

Mr A. J. Balfour.

attention of the House and of the Irish Minister to the deliberate organisation of riot and disorder in the City of Belfast which had been going on for several weeks. I then pointed out to the Chief Secretary that if he pursued the course which he pursued under similar circumstances last year with regard to the threats, a similar condition of disorder and scandalous riot would probably take place. The Chief Secretary, in reply, took upon himself the whole of the responsibility of preserving the peace of the City of Belfast on Sunday and Monday last. He said that the Government of Ireland were fully aware of the gravity of the situation, and were determined that peace should be preserved. I desire to draw the attention of the House to the fact that in the present instance there was no question of being taken by surprise, because for weeks the Government had been warned that riot and disorder would occur. In spite, however, of the statement of the Chief Secretary and of the warning which was given to the Government, there was last night in Belfast scandalous and violent rioting. I desire to emphasise one point in particular. I took the liberty of pointing out last week to the Chief Secretary that it was idle to expect, according to my experience, to preserve the peace of the City effectively, with an insufficient police force, by the action of the military alone. In dealing with a riotous mob the military are very ineffective. They cannot arrest anyone, and all they can do is to charge with fixed bayonets or fire, and that is not a proper way, except in the very last extremity, to protect the police. Now what occurred? Yesterday a large National procession took place in Belfast. Shortly before half-past six a disturbance, unfortunately similar to that of last year, broke out on the Old Lodge Road. The affair originated at Alton Street, where there is a Nationalist arch, and ended in an attack on the police. Stones of all sizes were hurled at the police, and District-inspector Hurst, seeing that affairs were getting serious, blew his whistle, unsheathed his sword, and ordered a charge. The police charged the mob, which was 250 strong, and it fled up the Lodge Road. The police were outdistanced, and stopped about one hundred yards up the road. Stones then began to fly again, and the crash of broken windows was to be heard. The mob remained above the Baths, shying stones for a while, but no person was injured. A detachment of the Dragoon Guards arrived immediately afterwards, and galloped up the road, the crowd dispersing into the side streets. The military turned four hundred yards up the street and walked down, but the crowd, during the absence of the military up the road, stoned eight policemen who were stationed at the corner of Upper Townsend Street. Two ornamental plate-glass windows in the public-house of Edward O'Neill were shattered, and another public-house was also damaged. The Dragoons continued to parade the street, and about seven o'clock the police made a charge under military protection, and arrested three men at the corner of Broadbent Street. They were quickly surrounded by an escort of the cavalry, under Sergeant M'Donald, and removed to Brown Square Barracks. The charges preferred against them were riotous behaviour, and the prisoners gave the names of William Henry Telford, Boyd Street; William Marshall, Tyne Street, Ballymacarrett; and Alexander Harrison, Dickson Street, Grosvenor Road. Meanwhile the stoning at Woodford Street and other points was kept up vigorously, and many of the windows in Brown's Square Barracks were broken. Several more persons were injured, and the *Telegraph* reporter received a severe blow on the knee from a falling stone. About eight o'clock the cavalry at Townsend Street were withdrawn to scatter a mob on the Old Lodge Road, and, reinforcements being at hand, the crowd on the Shankhill had a clear passage to the police barracks; and they attacked it vigorously. Hundreds of stones were hurled at the windows, but the few police who were about remained in shelter, and no person was injured. Head-constable Buick had assistance telephoned for from the barracks, and District-inspector Hurst, coming up with twenty men, called out the reserves in the barracks. The whole force, along with the reinforcement of cavalry, then charged up the Shankhill, the mob scattering in all directions. The mob retreated to Dover Street, and the original military cordon returning from the Old Lodge Road, the cavalry force was augmented to the number of fifty troopers. The sight of this imposing force of the cavalry awed the crowd, who remained quiet for some time, no police being in sight. On the Old Lodge Road several wild scenes took place, and the police had to charge frequently. At eight o'clock a force of Rifles arrived at the barracks and took up a position in Brown's Square, to which several men who had been arrested on the Lodge Road were now conveyed under a strong police escort. At ten minutes past eight the City Commissioner, who was accompanied by Mr. Seddall, drove up from North Street and had a consultation with the authorities on the spot. The laxity of the police had been condemned so far, and stern measures, it is stated, will be taken, if the rioting continues. The Rifles were wheeled into the

Shankhill with fixed bayonets, awaiting orders. The rioting in Upper Townsend Street and Sherbrook Street now became fierce, and a terrible attack was made on the police who had been up the Old Lodge Road. A number of constables had to run for all they were worth down Sherbrook Street. Several constables were injured, but repeated charges by the horsemen scattered the rioters, though only for a few minutes. Quiet was no sooner comparatively restored on the Shankhill than terrible rioting broke out on the Lodge Road. A crowd in Stanhope Street stoned the Nationalist party vigorously, and about 20 police got sandwiched between them and received severe treatment. Pavers were torn up by the women, who along with the men on both sides hurled them to such an extent that for ten minutes the air was black with missiles. The police, shut in between both parties, were badly injured, and they were powerless to either charge or escape. They tried to make their way into Arnon Street by a side thoroughfare, but were repulsed by the crowds who ran after them. Scarcely a window in Stanhope Street escaped, and many heads were cracked by the showers of stones. Matters were so serious that a company of the Rifles were sent for and advancing up Lime Street wheeled into the Lodge Road and charged the Protestant mob with fixed bayonets several hundred yards. On the way back to their starting place the crowd stoned the police with renewed vigour. Sergeant M'Manus, of Glenrave Street, was cut off, and several women went up to within a few yards of them and hurled pavers at them. The Rifles then charged the Catholic crowd in Stanhope-street, and there rowdies pelted the military vigorously, but the Protestant mob left them alone. The police had disappeared for the time being, but the next thing heard was the bugle of a detachment of

Mr. Dillon.

Dragoons, which rang out the charge, and instantly the red-coats came in sight, and galloped down the Old Lodge Road, the crowd retired into the side streets. Additional Rifles were now despatched to the scene, and charge after charge was made in the side streets. The Riot Act by this time had been read, and matters were assuming a very serious aspect. The police were chased from Stanhope Street, and when again reinforced by the infantry made a charge, and one arrest was made, the prisoner being removed to Brown's Square by ten constables, under Mr. M'Ardle, D. I. At nine o'clock a detachment of Rifles marched into Brown's Square, and orders having been given, they loaded their rifles, and faced up the Shankhill, prepared for any eventualities. Immediately afterwards Constable Norton, one of the wounded policemen in Stanhope Street, was assisted into the barracks with a badly injured leg and arm. He almost fainted on the way to the barracks, and once he got inside his injuries were attended to. It subsequently transpired that the reading of the Riot Act took place near Agnes Street, where a crowd of some 14,000 people had assembled, and so threatening was their attitude that Major Gregg read the Act. O'Neill's premises, already referred to, were badly wrecked by another mob earlier in the evening, and before the Rifles charged with their bayonets. At 9.30 matters looked a little easier ; but the streets were still guarded by soldiers. The prisoners so far are still detained in Brown's Square Barracks, and will not be taken to the Central Station till the trouble subsides. At 9.30 the Shankhill Road presented a scene such as even at its worst experiences has seldom, if ever, been eclipsed. Cordons of police and infantry, with fixed bayonets, and dragoons cut off access at every available point, while detachments of cavalry were constantly moving up and down the thoroughfare, keeping the crowds in motion. There seemed to be riot in the very air, and from the most unexpected quarters showers of stones and other missiles were being every moment hurled wherever a police constable chanced to put in an appearance. To crown all, and add to the confusion, dense volumes of smoke intensified the growing darkness. Some dozens of chimneys had been purposely set on fire, showers of burnt paper making it only too clear that the simultaneous outbreaks were no mere coincidence. Now, I ask again, is that a condition of things that ought to be tolerated in a civilised country and after full warning? This kind of thing went on for several hours, and I have heard a rumour about an hour or two ago that a military officer who was struck has since died. Now, I say that in view of what occurred in the House last week, and of the constant repetition of these scandalous scenes, and of the well-known fact, particularly in the present instance, that these riots were organised and meetings held for weeks previously for the avowed intention of getting up these riots, it is a disgrace and scandal that the Irish Government are not better able to preserve the peace of the city. The Shankhill Road and the Old Lodge Road have been turned into a veritable pandemonium. What I specially complain of is that the police were again and again hunted down and driven into the fight before the military came to their aid. This is a monstrous and outrageous thing, and is calculated to inflame and encourage the riotous spirit which has so often disgraced Belfast. I do not wish to be misunderstood. I have not, on this or on a previous occasion, come before the House appealing for protection for the Catholics of Belfast. They are well able to protect themselves, but every citizen of Belfast, Catholic or Protestant, Methodist or Presbyterian, is entitled to the protection of the law. I ask the Chief Secretary if he has any further information, and in particular whether it is true that the military officer who was struck has since died.

THE CHIEF SECRETARY FOR IRELAND (Mr. G. W. BALFOUR, Leeds, Central): I have no information to the effect that the military officer in question has since died. With regard to the general question, the hon. Member appears to be under the extraordinary delusion that the police are to be expected not merely to suppress riots, but also attempts at riots. You might just as well expect the police not merely to check crime, but even to prevent crime from the outset. Such a claim is perfectly absurd, and the hon. Member must know it to be so.

MR. DILLON: Not at all.

MR. G. W. BALFOUR: All the precautions which could be taken were taken, and it is impossible in a city like Belfast absolutely to prevent any attempt at rioting. When rioting breaks out, all that the authorities and the police can do is to take adequate measures to suppress it, and in this case such measures were taken. Considering the extreme tension prevailing in such a place as Belfast, I have heard that all the authorities, the military as well as the police, did their duty in an admirable way, and prevented what might have been a very serious riot, resulting in serious loss of life. The responsibility for these disturbances rests with those who got up the processions last year, and this year, knowing perfectly well what the result would be on the peace of this city. As to the occurrences of last evening, I say that as far as I am aware no rioting has taken place. A telegram sent by the Commissioner at 8.30 says:

"City remains in its normal state; I will wire at 10 p.m."

At 10 o'clock a telegram was received stating:—

"City continues quiet, and, as far as I can judge, no danger of rioting to-night."

Adjourned at twenty minutes after Twelve o'clock.

HOUSE OF COMMONS.

Wednesday, 7th June 1899.

PRIVATE BUSINESS.

CITY AND BRIXTON RAILWAY BILL.
As amended, considered; to be read the third time.

GODALMING CORPORATION WATER BILL.
As amended, to be considered upon Tuesday next.

LONDON COUNTY COUNCIL (GENERAL POWERS) BILL.
As amended, to be considered upon Tuesday next.

LONDON IMPROVEMENTS BILL.
As amended, considered; to be read the third time.

STOCKPORT CORPORATION BILL.
As amended, considered; to be read the third time.

BRIGHTON MARINE PALACE AND PIER BILL [Lords].
Read a second time, and committed.

FURNESS RAILWAY BILL [Lords].
Read a second time, and committed.

PAISLEY AND BARRHEAD DISTRICT RAILWAY BILL [Lords].
Read a second time, and committed.

STANDING ORDERS.

Ordered, That so much of the Standing Order No. 91 as fixes five as the quorum of the Select Committee on Standing Orders be read, and suspended.

Ordered, That, for the remainder of the Session, three be the quorum of the Committee.—(*Mr. John Ellis.*)

PETITIONS.

BOROUGH FUNDS ACT, 1872.
Petition from Mytholmroyd, for alteration of law; to lie upon the Table.

VOL. LXXII.   [FOURTH SERIES.]

EDUCATION OF CHILDREN BILL.
Petitions in favour;—From Burton-on-Trent;—and, Wolverhampton; to lie upon the Table.

GROUND RENTS (TAXATION BY LOCAL AUTHORITIES).
Petitions in favour;—From Burton-on-Trent; and, Wolverhampton; to lie upon the Table.

LOCAL GOVERNMENT (SCOTLAND) ACT (1894) AMENDMENT BILL.
Petition from Row, in favour; to lie upon the Table.

MINES (EIGHT HOURS) BILL.
Petitions in favour;—From Dysart Colliery;—and, Dannikier; to lie upon the Table.

PARISH CHURCHES (SCOTLAND) BILL.
Petition of the General Assembly of the Church of Scotland, in favour; to lie upon the Table.

POOR LAW OFFICERS' SUPERANNUATION (SCOTLAND) BILL.
Petitions in favour;—From Angus;—and, Stirling; to lie upon the Table.

PRIVATE LEGISLATION PROCEDURE (SCOTLAND) BILL.
Petition from Airdrie, in favour; to lie upon the Table.

RATING OF MACHINERY BILL.
Petition of the Mining Association of Great Britain, against; to lie upon the Table.

SALE OF INTOXICATING LIQUORS ON SUNDAY BILL.
Petitions in favour;—From Sheffield; — London; — Bolton; — Barnsley; — Pendleton;—and, Ashton-under-Lyne; to lie upon the Table.

TELEGRAPHS (TELEPHONIC COMMUNICATION, &c.) BILL.
Petition from Bristol, against; to lie upon the Table.

TELEGRAPHS (TELEPHONIC COMMUNICATION, &c.) BILL.
Petition from Todmorden, for alteration; to lie upon the Table.

TOWN COUNCILS (SCOTLAND) BILL.
Petition from Airdrie, in favour; to lie upon the Table.

T

RETURNS, REPORTS, &c.

EAST INDIA (PROGRESS AND CONDITION).

Paper [presented 6th June] to be printed. [No. 211.]

NATIONAL PORTRAIT GALLERY.

Copy presented, — of Forty-second Annual Report of the Trustees of the National Portrait Gallery (1899) [by Command]; to lie upon the Table.

SUPERANNUATION ACT, 1884.

Copy presented,—of Treasury Minute, dated 30th May, 1899, declaring that James Muspratt, Auxiliary Postman, London, Post Office Department, was appointed without a Civil Service Certificate through inadvertence on the part of the Head of his Department [by Act]; to lie upon the Table.

PUBLIC WORSHIP REGULATION AND CHURCH DISCIPLINE.

Return presented, — relative thereto [ordered 23rd February; Mr. Sydney Gedge]; to lie upon the Table, and to be printed. [No. 212.]

SERVICE FRANCHISE BILL.

Considered in Committee.

(In the Committee.)

Clause 1 :—

MR. McKENNA (Monmouth, N.) : The object of the Amendment standing in my name is to extend the scope of the Bill. At present no person is eligible for the service franchise if the person under whom he serves inhabits the qualifying premises, and in consequence shop assistants who reside in their master's house are disqualified if the master also lives in the same house, but not if he lives away. Another anomaly of the present law is that by converting his business into a limited company the master enables his assistants to qualify, in spite of the fact that he inhabits the same premises. The proposed Amendment would cure this defect. It would also get rid of the uncertainty which now exists as to whether the sergeant or other officer of the police who lives in the police barracks is a person under whom the police serve in such a sense as to disqualify. This is a point which has not yet been decided by the courts, and it is quite conceivable that it might be decided in such a way as to practically lead to the disqualification of all the police. I beg to move the Amendment.

Amendment proposed—

" In page 1, line 6, to leave out from the word 'employment,' to the word ' he,' in line 8."—(*Mr. McKenna.*)

Question proposed—

" That the words proposed to be left out stand part of the clause."

SIR BLUNDELL MAPLE (Camberwell, East Dulwich) : The hon. Gentleman does not seem to recognise that this Bill is to clear away certain difficulties which have arisen owing to the decision of the judges in regard to the service franchise. The hon. Member is perfectly right when he says that if a master lives in a particular house the men-servants are not entitled to vote. It is impossible to leave out the words mentioned in this Amendment unless you further extend the franchise, and therefore I am unable to accept it.

Question put.

The Committee divided :— Ayes, 40 ; noes, 58. (Division List, No. 175.)

AYES.

Anstruther, H. T.	Gedge, Sydney	Mount, William George
Arrol, Sir William	Goldsworthy, Major-General	Nicol, Donald Ninian
Barnes, Frederic Gorell	Gorst, Rt. Hon. Sir J. Eldon	Powell, Sir Francis Sharp
Bond, Edward	Hanson, Sir Reginald	Purvis, Robert
Bullard, Sir Harry	Helder, Augustus	Rothschild, Hon. Lionel W.
Cavendish, V. C. W. (Derbys.)	Kenyon, James	Russell, T. W. (Tyrone)
Douglas, Rt. Hon. A. Akers-Drage, Geoffrey	Lawrence, W. F. (Liverpool)	Stone, Sir Benjamin
Egerton, Hon. A. de Tatton	Lawson, John Grant (Yorks.)	Usborne, Thomas
Fardell, Sir T. George	Lees, Sir Elliott (Birkenhead)	Welby, Lieut.-Col. A. C. E.
Finlay, Sir Robert Bannatyne	Lopes, Henry Yarde Buller	Whiteley, George (Stockport)
Firbank, Joseph Thomas	Lowther, Rt. Hon. J. (Kent)	Wilson, John (Falkirk)
FitzGerald, Sir R. Penrose-	Maclure, Sir John William	TELLERS FOR THE AYES—
Fletcher, Sir Henry	M'Killop, James	Sir Blundell Maple and Mr.
Folkestone, Viscount	Middlemore, J. Throgmorton	Harry Samuel.

NOES.

Allan, William (Gateshead)
Allen, W.(Newc.-under-Lyme)
Beaumont, Wentworth C. B.
Billson, Alfred
Broadhurst, Henry
Brunner, Sir John Tomlinson
Burt, Thomas
Caldwell, James
Cameron, Sir Charles (Glasg.)
Colville, John
Davitt, Michael
Dilke, Rt. Hon. Sir Charles
Dillon, John
Doogan, P. C.
Duckworth, James
Ellis, John Edward
Farquharson, Dr. Robert
Fenwick, Charles
Goddard, Daniel Ford
Gold, Charles
Gurdon, Sir Wm. Brampton

Harwood, George
Healy, Thomas J. (Wexford)
Hedderwick, Thomas C. H.
Holland, W. H. (York, W. R.)
Jacoby, James Alfred
Jones, Wm. (Carnarvonshire)
Lawson, Sir Wilfrid(Cumb'l'd)
Leng, Sir John
Lyell, Sir Leonard
MacAleese, Daniel
M'Cartan, Michael
M'Ghee, Richard
Maddison, Fred
Montagu, Sir S.(Whitechapel)
Morgan, J. Lloyd(Carmarthen)
Morley, Charles (Breconshire)
Morris, Samuel
Norton, Capt. Cecil William
Nussey, Thomas Willans
O'Brien, James F. X. (Cork)
O'Brien, Patrick (Kilkenny)

Richardson, J. (Durham, S.E.)
Rickett, J. Compton
Roberts, John H. (Denbighs.)
Robson, William Snowdon

Samuel, J. (Stockton on Tees)
Shaw, Thomas, (Hawick B.)
Smith, Samuel (Flint)
Steadman, William Charles
Stevenson, Francis S.
Sullivan, Donal (Westmeath)
Trevelyan, Charles Philips
Warner, Thomas Courtenay T.
Williams, JohnCarvell(Notts.)
Wilson, Henry J.(York, W. R.)
Wilson, John (Durham, Mid.)
Young, Samuel (Cavan, East)

TELLERS FOR THE NOES—
   Mr. M'Kenna and Mr.
   Lloyd-George.

Clause, as amended, agreed to.

After the announcement of the figures,

MR. DUNCOMBE (Cumberland, Egremont) presented himself at the Table, and, addressing the Chairman, said : I was in the Aye Lobby, and the tellers left the door before I was counted.

*THE CHAIRMAN : The hon. Member ought to have stated that before the numbers were announced.

MR. McKENNA : There will be a further opportunity of moving Amendments, and, as undoubtedly hon. Members opposite are not here in their natural strength, I do not propose to move any further Amendments of mine.

*SIR CHARLES DILKE (Gloucester, Forest of Dean) : I propose to follow the same course. The Amendments which have been carried extend the Bill, and an alteration of its whole framework will be necessary.

Clauses 2 and 3 agreed to.

Bill reported ; as amended, to be considered upon Wednesday next.

EDUCATION OF CHILDREN BILL.

Considered in Committee.

(In the Committee.)

*THE CHAIRMAN : The three new clauses standing in the name of the hon.

Member for Stockport are out of order. They are drawn in such a way that they could not be accepted as Amendments to this Bill. They are in effect Amendments of the Factory Acts.

MR. GEORGE WHITELEY (Stockport) : I respectfully submit that th second of my proposed clauses does not in any way deal with the Factory Acts, although I admit frankly that the third one does. The second clause merely exempts from this Act a certain trade, but if the Chairman rules that I am out of order I shall be out of court.

MR. JAMES LOWTHER (Kent, Thanet) : On a point of order, I wish to know whether it would be possible for me to extend the exception to persons engaged in agriculture.

*THE CHAIRMAN : The exception of persons employed in agriculture has already been inserted in the Bill. I have given the best consideration I can to the matter, and I think the hon. Member's clause as drawn is on the wrong side of the line, and therefore I cannot accept it.

MR. GEORGE WHITELEY : I am sorry I have gone over the line ; but I think, after your ruling, Sir, I will withdraw both clauses, and submit them in a different form on the Report stage.

INTOXICATING LIQUORS (SUNDAY CLOSING) BILL.

(Second Reading.)

Order for Second Reading read.

MR. TRITTON (Lambeth, Norwood): I have been called upon most unexpectedly to move the second reading of this Bill, which I confess I thought I would have very little chance of commending to the House of Commons this afternoon. The Bill which has been committed to my charge has been drawn after a long and careful consideration by the Church of England Temperance Society. I venture to say no subject at the present moment exercises more the minds of a large number of earnest men and women in this country than the question of some restriction of the hours during which public-houses are open in England. The right hon. Gentleman the Secretary for the Colonies said in 1894 that Sunday closing was—

"a question which had probably excited more interest and had brought to its support more influence than any other, unless it be the reduction of public-houses."

In 1897 the right hon. Baronet the Home Secretary, speaking in the House of Commons, said:

"There is a great amount of popular feeling on the side of Sunday closing. . . . This object is dear to the hearts of earnest men, who believe that by total prohibition on Sunday they may not only improve the keeping of Sunday in England, but may at the same time remove many of those extra causes of intemperance which may be supposed to occur in an interval of leisure such as Sunday should be."

The Bill which I have the honour to present to the House of Commons is not a Sunday Closing Bill. It is a Bill to restrict the sale of intoxicating liquors on Sunday. The first clause says:

"Subject to any order made under this Act, all premises in which intoxicating liquor is sold by retail shall be closed during the whole of Sunday, Christmas Day, and Good Friday."

The second clause is as follows:

"The licensing authority for the time being empowered by law to grant licences for the sale of intoxicating liquor may make an order permitting licensed premises in their licensing district, or in any part thereof, to be open on Sunday, Christmas Day, or Good Friday, during such time or times as they may by the order prescribe, not exceeding in the whole *two hours* on any such day, for the sale of intoxicating liquor for consumption off the premises only, and may make an order varying or revoking any previous order."

I am not an advocate of total Sunday closing myself. It is desirable we should proceed gradually, and I believe this Bill is one which will meet with the approval of many who, though interested in the temperance question, do not see their way to advocate Sunday closing, and I hope we shall secure their votes for this measure. The subject is one to which I have devoted myself for many years, and in which I take the very greatest interest. I urge this Bill on the House, firstly, on behalf of the publicans themselves; secondly, on behalf of large numbers of public-house employees throughout the land who do not know the blessing of a Sunday's rest; and thirdly, because I believe it is a step in the right direction towards securing some check on intemperance, which is a blot on our national escutcheon. I most earnestly appeal to the House to let this modest Bill pass. It is in accordance with the feelings of a large number, not only of clergymen but of devoted men and women throughout the country, who are grieved at the terrible evil of intemperance which disgraces our land. Let it go to a Committee upstairs. We have not a great deal of work to do this session, and I appeal to the Government—I am sure I shall not appeal in vain to the Parliamentary Secretary to the Local Government Board, the only occupant of the Treasury bench, as his zeal in the cause is well known—but I appeal to the Government to let this Bill be read a second time, and passed into law. I venture to think that in days to come, when other Members occupy these benches, it will be said with great credit to this Conservative and Unionist Government that it used the great majority the country gave it to pass into law a measure which cannot fail to be the greatest possible blessing not only in the present day but for all generations.

Motion made and Question proposed—

"That the Bill be now read a second time."
—(*Mr. Tritton.*)

MR. COLVILLE (Lanarkshire, N.E.): I rise to support very cordially the second reading of this Bill. Arguments are not needed, and I merely wish to say that for the last forty-five years we have enjoyed in Scotland the blessing of Sunday closing, and it has been universally admitted that it has acted not only in the interests of the publicans and all engaged in the trade, but has been an unmixed blessing to all classes of the community.

MR. JAMES LOWTHER: I rise for an opposite purpose to that stated by the hon. Member. I wish to place before the House the peculiar position in which it is now placed. We have a Bill before us which has been unexpectedly brought under our notice. I do not, of course, blame my hon. friend in any shape or form. He has followed a perfectly straightforward course, as everyone who knows him would expect. But we now find ourselves called on to deal with a measure of extreme importance, and one on which great public feeling has always been exhibited as long as I can recollect, and the Treasury bench is empty with the exception of one occupant. Has the Parliamentary Secretary to the Local Government Board any mandate from his colleagues to convey their views on this subject to the House?

MR. T. W. RUSSELL (Tyrone, S.): None at all. I am on the Treasury bench because matters affecting the Local Government Board appear on the Order Paper, and I have no intention of dealing with other matters.

MR. JAMES LOWTHER: Quite so. My hon. friend bears out my statement. He is here to discharge his own duty and to attend to a particular question, but he is not in a position to speak for his colleagues or to afford the House any guidance as to the views of Her Majesty's Government on a subject of such importance as that now before us. I am glad to see that my hon. friend has now been relieved from his solitary position, and that he has been joined by my right hon. friend the Under Secretary for the Home Department. I would ask my right hon. friend if he has come to state the views of the Government to the House, and if he can assure us that this matter has been fully considered by the Cabinet, or if he can present the views of the Secretary of State for the Home Department. We are all of us approaching this subject under very peculiar conditions. A Royal Commission appointed by this Government is, I believe, at this very moment charged with the consideration of this subject, although I feel doubtful as to how far I am justified in saying that the

Royal Commission is still sitting. I observe that the Chairman of that Commission has publicly declared that the Commission is dissolved, and he has stated that in virtue of the power conferred upon him by the Commission he declared it to be dissolved. How that announcement stands from a legal point of view I hesitate to express any opinion upon. I am inclined to think it is absolutely *ultra vires*, and consequently has no effect. But even assuming that view to be incorrect, and that the Royal Commission is discharged from further consideration of the subject, it would be very unfortunate for the House, without any official authority or guidance whatever, to attempt to deal with so important a subject. The question of the hours at which intoxicating liquors shall be retailed on Sundays is one of the most difficult problems which a Royal Commission could undertake. I have seen a draft of the rival reports of this Commission, and they reveal a very extraordinary conflict of opinion, though I am not aware that any exact official announcement has yet been made upon this subject. The hon. Member for Cockermouth would be in favour of making short work of this question, not only on Sundays, but upon any other day, and upon this subject I do not think that the hon. Member has ever drawn any distinction between one day and another. According to my hon. friend's view it is a most mischievous and injurious trade, which ought not to be merely limited to a certain number of hours, but should be absolutely extinguished for ever. That is the view which the hon. Member for Cockermouth has persistently advocated for many years. I doubt whether the Members of this House have had an opportunity of studying the report of the Royal Commission which has been appointed, and I do not think any Member or any authoritative section of the House would care to rush pell-mell into a decision upon this thorny subject. With reference to the Bill itself, I am bound to admit that I did not regard it as a probable subject to be considered to-day, nor had I regarded it as a Bill which was likely to be taken this Session. Therefore my hon. friend in that respect shares my surprise. The promoter of this Bill does not give us a memorandum or epitome, as some promoters have done, and I think he was wise in not doing that, because on the face of it the measure shows pretty well what his intentions are. My hon. friend proposes that public-houses shall be closed on Sunday without any recommendation from the Executive or without any report from the Royal Commission. Besides this, he proposes to allow the licensing authority to discharge duties which have never been confided to any licensing authority before. The Bill provides that the sale of intoxicating liquors on a Sunday shall be confined to two hours, and only for consumption off the premises. I am not going to find fault with that on its merits. There is a good deal to be said in favour of meeting the views of a very large number of people who have not the luxury which a cellar affords, and who are dependent upon the nearest licensed house for the beer which they consume at their meals. Therefore I am not disposed to find fault with my hon. friend for having afforded greater facilities for the consumption of intoxicating liquors off the premises. I fail to see, on the other hand, what provision my hon. friend has made for that very interesting personage the *bona fide* traveller. He is a person of whom we have heard a great deal in our time. He very often performs a very arduous journey, and he is sometimes supposed to hail from a place not very far outside the area of his own parish. I presume that my hon. friend desires to guard against the spurious traveller, but I think the case of the *bona fide* traveller is one which ought to be seriously regarded by Parliament. I represent myself a constituency where the *bona fide* traveller looms very largely—probably few hon. Members are aware of the great number of attractions in the district which I have the honour to represent. Therefore I make no apology to the House for drawing attention to the very grave inconvenience and the gross injustice which a measure of this kind would inflict upon a vast number of persons for whose convenience and comfort Parliament ought to have some regard. That being so, I think I am entitled to ask how he can expect the House of Commons—practically without notice, and in face of the circumstances to which I have already drawn attention—to give a second reading to a Bill dealing with so complicated and controversial a subject. The hon. Gentleman opposite, upon the Service Franchise Bill, waived the right

Mr. James Lowther.

which he undoubtedly possessed of pressing the advantage he had gained. I am not going to make this suggestion to my hon. friend, and if he will take my advice he will avail himself of the opportunity he has got; but I hope he will avail himself of it in true Parliamentary fashion by not attempting to gloss over the undoubted difficulties which surround this subject, for it is a very thorny and difficult question. I do not think myself that the Royal Commission would be wasting their time if they were to listen to the suggestions which my hon. friend has to make. As far as I can judge, I think the time of that Commission has been very largely wasted, and I do not think that the result of its labours, whenever that result is forthcoming, will redound very largely to the credit of those concerned. I am quite aware that a great deal of that result is due to the system adopted by the authorities. The plan of appointing on a judicial inquiry a certain number of bigoted partisans on either side, and then bringing an equivalent number of persons supposed to have a well-balanced mind, is pernicious to a degree. I have no hesitation in saying that a large number of the members of the Royal Commission, though they are very valuable as witnesses, are in the wrong place.

MR. SPEAKER: Order, order! The hon. Member will not be in order in discussing the way in which the Commission is composed, or the manner the matter was conducted before the Royal Commission, before it has reported.

MR. JAMES LOWTHER: I am glad that I am relieved from the difficulty of trying to give an account of the proceedings before the Commissioners. As you very properly pointed out, the least said about them the better. I gather that I have the assent of my hon. friend to this; he recognises the desirability and the necessity of expounding a scheme, which so far has never been done before. My hon. friend has studied this question in all its bearings for a great many years, but he has never identified himself with the extreme views held by some upon this subject. There has been a marked distinction between the moderate spirit which has actuated my hon. friend and those which have been advocated by some who hold more extreme views, who call his Bill half-hearted, and look upon him as a turn-coat. But they are wrong in doing so, because he has disassociated himself from the more extreme views, and he never has associated himself with the extremists who desire to annihilate such a large industry. As to the further clauses of the Bill, I hoped that my hon. friend would have relieved me from the necessity of endeavouring to expound them. I think it is usual for those urging the acceptance of a Bill upon the House to discharge that duty. My hon. friend proposes to adopt for his purpose the provisions of the Licensing Acts; and, supposing that it is right for us to deal with the matter at all, that is a very reasonable course to be pursued. Therefore I shall not detain the House by going through the subsidiary clauses of the Bill. The fact remains that the House would be adopting an absolutely unprecedented course in reading a Bill of this kind a second time on this occasion; a Bill dealing with such great interests; a scheme for shutting up every refreshment house in the country, so far as consumption on the premises is concerned, without so far as I can see any provision whatever for recognising hotels, although it may perhaps appear by reference to some existing Act. So far as I can see, my hon. friend would shut up, so far as the *bona fide* travelling public are concerned, every hotel and licensed house in the country. As regards hotels, there is a very great distinction between the refreshment houses used by the wealthy and those used by the poor, and I have always contended that legislation of this kind is for the most part essentially class legislation. My friend has absolved himself from that extreme reform, but I cannot see that he contemplates any preferential treatment as regards hotels. The law distinctly recognises such a distinction being made, and possibly by some reference there may be some Act embodied in this Bill which will carry out this idea. So far as the Bill itself is concerned it appears upon the face of it that it would be a very crude measure, not accompanied by any of those necessary safeguards either to the trade concerned or to the community at large, of which hitherto the promoters of all measures of this kind have availed themselves. The House would be well advised to decline to deal with this matter at all. Under the circumstances, I do not wish to put my hon. friend in a position of diffi-culty by moving that this Bill be read a second time six months hence, which would be the natural conclusion of my remarks. I would much rather leave it to my hon. friend to reconsider his position under the circumstances, in order that he may have an opportunity of withdrawing the measure.

MR. NUSSEY (Pontefract): We all recognise, I think—no matter what our views may be upon the temperance question, whether we are in favour of any particular measure or not—the necessity of some reform. We all desire to promote the real temperance of this country, and any such measure must have the support of this House; but there is always the danger that upon such a question as this we may legislate before the time is ripe for such legislation. I do not think any Bill which is brought before this House can be successful unless it has the full authority of the people behind it, and that being so I now propose to devote my attention to the second clause of the Bill. If I understand this Bill correctly, the second clause proposes the partial closing of public-houses on Sunday. It proposes that they may open for two hours every Sunday if in the opinion of the licensing authority it is expedient; but what I suggest is that the licensing authority, as at present constituted, is not in touch with the feeling of the people in the locality on that question. I do not see how any Member of this House can know whether a public-house in a particular district should be open for a particular time only. It is impossible to legislate in advance of local public opinion in such a matter as this; and unless you have the people with you, the police with you, and the magistrates with you, it is useless decreeing that all public-houses shall be closed on Sunday. I would much rather place this question in the hands of the people themselves, in the hands of those who use public-houses, and who have every right to use them in a fair and proper manner. We on this side of the House, who profess to trust the people, do not see why we should not give them full power over this as over other matters. I think, myself, that if the people had a right to control the public-houses there would be better beer and better whisky and a larger measure of temperance. It seems to me that the motion which I hope to move is essentially a popular one, and drafted on popular lines, and therefore I shall move, "That no Bill to restrict the sale of intoxicating liquors on Sunday would be satisfactory unless it embodies the principle of local option." That will satisfy even the aspirations of my hon. friend the Member for Cockermouth. He can have no logical objection to local option on Sundays, if he advocates it for the rest of the week. Then there is the fact that the Royal Commission has not yet reported, and I would also point out that this Bill is exciting a great deal of interest in the country, and that it comes here most unexpectedly on a Wednesday afternoon, on the eve of the report of the Royal Commission. Till we have that report I do think it would be better not to proceed with this Bill in its present form, but to put the whole question into the hands of the people. With that remark I beg to move my Amendment.

Amendment proposed—

"To leave out from the word 'That,' to the end of the question, in order to add the words 'no Bill to restrict the sale of intoxicating liquors on Sunday is satisfactory unless it embodies the principle of local option.'"— (*Mr. Nussey.*)

Question proposed—

"That the words proposed to be left out stand part of the question."

MR. WARNER (Stafford, Lichfield): I beg to second the Amendment, although it does not exactly express my views on this Bill. Although I am in favour of temperance, and of every sort of legislation that can really conduce to temperance, I must say there are restrictions in this Bill which would work very seriously against the comfort of the working classes of this country. The point I object to most is that those depraved beings like myself who like a glass of beer, and who have not the opportunity of storing it, cannot get their beer on Sunday unless the licensing authority gives them leave. The licensing authorities vary in different places. I have no confidence in the "great unpaid" as being proper judges of when working men who like their beer should get it. I daresay they are very good judges of how much is good for the working men, but at the same time a little must be left to the feeling of those who want to drink beer. We ought to allow

Mr. Nussey.

these to have some control over the hours of Sunday closing. I do not think any Bill will be satisfactory which goes to such an extent against the feelings of the working men, because in most places it would annoy them by cutting off their dinner beer and supper beer on Sundays. I quite recognise that something must be done towards preventing a great many public-houses becoming drinking shops on Sunday. I do not say in all cases, but in certain cases, they do a considerable amount of harm, which by legislation might be controlled. The first necessity, however, is to get the people to back up the proposed legislation. In America, where much temperance legislation had been passed of which the people did not thoroughly approve, the result was that the law was broken to an enormous extent. I think that any Bill that deals with this subject at all ought to go into the question of preventing children going into public-houses. It may be said that that question is outside Sunday closing; but I believe it is of even greater importance than Sunday closing, that the country is ready for such a measure, and that the people would support it to their utmost. We are on the verge of getting a report, or several reports, from the Royal Commission which has been considering the licensing question for three years. It is said these reports will be issued next week, and therefore I think to-day is about the most inopportune of the whole year when such a measure as this could have been brought forward. When the reports of the Royal Commission are fully considered, we should get a better Bill, that would be approved of not only by the Royal Commission itself, but by the large majority of the gentlemen opposite, and one very much more satisfactory than any mere Bill for Sunday closing or local option. I think in the near future the Unionist Government will be obliged to deal with temperance legislation, so as to reduce intemperance, and do some good without annoying and irritating a large portion of our labouring population. I dissociate myself entirely from those who are opposed to temperance legislation, and I would not for one moment, if I thought any good could come from it, and that drunkenness would really be stopped by it, have voted against this Bill. I think that the Amendment is a very wise one, and that the people of the district should have some power to say whether there should be Sunday closing or not. The licensing authorities are not sufficiently in touch with the people to justify their being entrusted with un-limited power.

*Mr. SYDNEY GEDGE (Walsall): There is one reason why we should not read this Bill a second time. If it becomes law it will not affect any of us in this House. We shall be interfering with the comforts and necessities of a large body of Her Majesty's subjects, in the happy consciousness that we ourselves shall not be interfered with at all. That is beyond all contradiction. No one in this House is in the habit of frequenting public-houses on Sunday to have his refreshment, and to meet and have social intercourse with his mates. He has his own house, his own wine and beer cellar, and if the Bill becomes law his freedom will not be interfered with in any way. There are many reasons against the Bill becoming law. This is not the first time I have felt it my duty to oppose similar legislation ;.but I always do it with regret, for I desire the object aimed at as heartily as the promoters of such legislation do. I can even go as far as to say that if I really believed that this Bill would con-siderably diminish drunkenness I should be very much disposed to vote for it. But I do not believe that it would have that effect. I think what is proposed is illogical. This Bill deals generally with what are called intoxicating liquors. It treats all liquors alike—the fiery spirits, the strong adulterated gin, the innocent claret, and the refreshing beer, or even choice cider, so cordially and so strongly recommended to us by one hon. Member of this House. It makes no distinction between them all; no matter how in-finitesimal the proportion of alcohol in them, they are at once called intoxicating liquors. I can understand the logical position of those, like the hon. Baronet the Member for Cockermouth, who con-sider it exceedingly wrong to drink any liquor at all——

Sir WILFRID LAWSON (Cumber-land, Cockermouth): I rise to order. I never made any such statement.

Mr. SYDNEY GEDGE: Of course I withdraw the statement on the assurance of the hon. Baronet; but from the public

action of the hon. Baronet, notwithstanding the very good tempered and vivacious way he has of airing his views, I certainly got the impression that he thought all alcoholic liquors were bad, and that the manufacture should be stopped.

Sir WILFRID LAWSON: I am sorry to interrupt again ; but I never said anything of the kind.

*Mr. SYDNEY GEDGE: Then the manufacture is not wrong, the drinking is not wrong, but the sale is wrong. Whatever the hon. baronet may say, there are those who hold the view that alcohol does such an infinite amount of mis-chief that it ought not to be manufactured or sold. That is a logical position. But it is illogical for people to say, "We do not want to close public-houses on week days. All we desire is to close them entirely on Sunday." There are others who say that it is wrong for a man to take a moderate amount of refreshment on Sunday which he enjoys on week-days ; and the argument is that Sunday is a sacred day. Nobody would go further than myself in advocating the claims of Sunday as a sacred day, and a day to be devoted to rest. It would be perfectly logical to contend that every-thing should be prohibited by law which interferes with the day of rest —railways, newspapers, the sale of tobacco and cigars, the opening of public-houses, and so on. But I see no logic in permit-ting trains to be run, newspapers, tobacco, cigars, &c., to be sold on Sunday, and in preventing the sale of drinks because they have a proportion of alcohol in them. Why do you not prohibit all these things ? Because they are for the public convenience, and if they were pro-hibited no one would stand such an in-terference with liberty. It is said by some that the results would be so excellent that we ought to prohibit the sale on Sunday. I doubt whether the result would be so excellent. It would arouse in the breast of those who desire drink a determination to have it at all hazards. It is alleged that statistics show that in districts where Sunday closing prevails there is less drunkenness than in those districts where the public-houses are open. But I remember a learned Queen's Counsel, who supported a similar bill, admitting in this House that these statistics are utterly unreliable; and a little consideration shows that that must be the case. A man goes to a public-house, he drinks too much, creates a disturbance on his way home, is arrested, and appears in statistics. But suppose the public-houses are closed; the man sends for all the drink he wants, either on the Saturday night or on the Sunday during the two hours which the promoters of this Bill are good enough to allow the public-houses to be open. The drink is brought to his house, and is partaken of, not only by himself, but by his family. We have had a good deal of evidence to show that the result is very fatal to the sobriety, not only of himself, but of his children. I know from private sources which I can thoroughly trust, from a lady who has done a great deal of work among the poor in Cardiff, that as the result of Sunday closing in the town there has been an increase of drinking and its fearful effects. That seems to me a very strong reason against this measure. Though the Bill permits the local authority to open the house for a few hours during the day, they might not do so. The magistrates might say that they were not disposed to open the public-houses on the Sunday, when the State has closed them. We must remember that there are a large number of unmarried workmen who, as a rule, have only a bedroom, and no place to sit in, except the common room of a public-house. And there are a large number of highly respectable workmen who, from the dearness of rent, are unable to have a separate room where they can entertain their mates and discuss where better wages can be obtained, and the like. Are these men to be driven to the corners of the streets in all weathers, because the only common room open to them is closed? Then again, look at the number of clubs which have been founded, and which it is impossible to close—not bogus clubs, but genuine clubs, Radical clubs, Conservative clubs, and Unionist clubs, all of them with bars for the sale of drink. These clubs are frequently used to escape the licensing laws and the police laws; the members get intoxicating drink late at night and on Sundays, and this has led to an increase in drunkenness. It is far better, I think, that those disposed to take too much should take the liquor under the supervision of the police, and with proper regulations, than that they should be driven to form clubs for the purpose. I myself would punish drunkenness wher-

Mr. Sydney Gedge.

ever it occurs. I would punish a man for getting drunk in his own house, just as I would punish a man for torturing a cat in his own house. In regard to the Bill before the House, from the first account we had of it from my hon. friend I thought that for once I might support such a Bill. But when I read it through, especially the second clause, I found it was really a Bill for the total closing of public-houses on Sunday.

MR. TRITTON: The hon. Member accuses me of not being quite straightforward in my description of the Bill, but I have to inform him that I read out the whole of the first and second clauses.

*MR. SYDNEY GEDGE: I did not for a moment suggest that the hon. Member gave a mistaken notion of the Bill. It is a Bill for the total closing of public-houses on Sunday except to those who go to fetch their refreshment. A Bill of this kind would merely create annoyance, and cause a man who is poor to be treated in a different way from his neighbour who is better off. If the people honestly wish to close public-houses on Sunday, they can do so by not frequenting them. If publicans wish to close, they are at liberty to do so; but they are afraid that, if they do, their customers will go on week days to houses which open on Sundays. They should do what they believe to be right, and take the consequences. To legislate for their protection is demoralising. There is want of logic in the Bill; the good results we all desire could not be obtained by it; it would create unfairness and inconvenience; and I, therefore, cannot support either the second reading or the Amendment.

MR. SAMUEL YOUNG (Cavan, E.): This Bill has come upon us with surprise to-day. I read it for the first time a few minutes ago, and could scarcely find out whether it was a Bill for the total closing of public-houses on Sunday or whether it gave authority to the licensing authority to open the houses for the off-sale of liquor. As a member of the Royal Commission, I do not know if I have a right to speak on this subject at all; but I think it would be very advisable not to proceed further with the Bill, at any rate until the House has full information in regard to the various questions that arise as to the opening and closing of public-houses on Sundays and weekdays. In a few days, probably, the report of the Royal Commission will be issued, and until you have that report there is no use considering the matter in this crude and ill-constructed form. If the Amendment before the House is carried, the Royal Commission will have been sitting for three years to no purpose. In regard to local veto they have not given such a recommendation, nor have they given any recommendation in regard to total closing on Sunday.

SIR WILFRID LAWSON: I rise to a point of order. Is the hon. Member entitled to divulge the findings of a Royal Commission that has not yet reported ?

*MR. SPEAKER: It would be contrary to the practice of the House for an hon. Member to state what are the views of a Royal Commission of which he is a member, and which has not yet reported to Her Majesty.

MR. SAMUEL YOUNG: I bow to the ruling of the Chair. I may be permitted to say that this Bill does not apply to Ireland, Scotland, and Wales, and I have no objection to leave the English people to discuss the whole matter. On its merits, the Bill is of a most absurd construction. I think the House should wait until they get the authoritative report of the findings of the Royal Commission, and they would then be in a better position to deal with the whole question.

MR. GALLOWAY (Manchester, S.W.): Few of us thought that this Bill would be reached to-day, and some of us have only seen it since we entered the House. We are, therefore, at a disadvantage in considering it. That is one reason why the House should not come to a decision on this question to-day ; another reason is that the report of the Royal Commission of 24 members, which will be issued in a day or two, should be first considered. I think the House would do well if, instead of voting either for the Amendment or the second reading of the Bill, the debate were adjourned ; and before I sit down I shall, with the permission of the Chair, move that the debate be now adjourned. The first observation that occurred to me in listening to the speech of the mover of the Amendment was that he claimed that they on that side of the House represent the Temperance Party. I admit that the hon. Baronet the Member for Cocker-

mouth has led a party which is known as the Temperance Party ; but I entirely deny that they have a monopoly of the desire to promote temperance, or that they have a special claim to call themselves the Temperance Party.

SIR WILFRID LAWSON: Hear, hear !

MR. GALLOWAY: I am glad that the hon. Baronet admits that. Instead of bandying this about as a party question, we should deal with it on broad grounds. The promotion of the cause of temperance is not a party question, and we would do far more for the interests of the temperance cause if we treated it on non-party lines. I agree with the adage that it is no use attempting to make people sober by Act of Parliament. The hon. Member who moved the Amendment said himself that no measure could achieve success if it was not backed up by the people. If that is so, has there been any desire expressed by the people of the country for this Bill ? I deny that there has been. I have received many letters from so-called temperance reformers of the wildest character. When the Scottish Local Veto Bill was coming on I had a letter from one eminent temperance leader asking me to vote for it because, he said, the Bill would bring about a sober Sunday for England ! Why, the Bill did not even apply to England ! Legislation proposed in this House is not considered by these people on its merits, but from a fanatical point of view. Now, I entirely deny that in this country we have a drunken Sunday, and I protest most emphatically against such an aspersion being put on the working classes. They are not drunken on Sunday or any other day of the week. I admit there is a certain amount of deplorable drunkenness and crime produced from drunkenness ; but, I ask, are you going to make people sober or decrease the consumption of alcohol by Act of Parliament ?

SIR WILFRID LAWSON: Certainly.

MR. GALLOWAY: I would ask what possible ground there is for such an assertion ? What possible data can be produced, what argument can be used, in favour of that statement ? Does the hon. Member assert that the working classes of this country are such a weak-kneed set of people that because a public-house door is open they cannot pass it without going in ? I must say I cannot take so low and mean a view of the people as that. But if the argument be true, the proper way to deal with such a state of affairs is not by closing the public-houses, but by doing everything you can to strengthen the moral courage of the people. It is not by a measure of this kind, or by Acts of Parliament of any kind, that you are going to promote the cause of temperance reform in the country. I believe much more could be done in the cause of temperance if some system were found whereby the alcoholic liquors sold in public-houses were not of the raw, rotten, and bad character they now are. There is no doubt that some of the spirits sold in public-houses in large towns are unfit for human consumption. Coming to the details of the Bill, the first clause provides that public-houses shall be closed on Sunday, Christmas Day, and Good Friday; but the second clause allows the licensing authority the power of leaving open the public-houses for two hours if so desired. Now, there are some who have a respect for the licensing authorities as at present constituted. Some of these authorities, I admit, are particularly good, and do their administrative work in a manner that reflects credit on themselves. But there are other authorities who do not deal with the questions brought before them from a judicial point of view, but from their own point of view, leaving out of consideration the real justice of the case. I remember well discussing this matter with a magistrate in the city of Manchester, who told me that he went to every Licensing Session, and voted regularly against every licence. He believed he was acting for the best, but it is monstrous for a man holding views like that to be allowed to act in a judicial capacity. If that is the way in which the Sunday exemptions are to be given, what would happen? It would become a question of which party had a majority on the licensing authority. And if the magistrates who represent the views of hon. Members on this side of the House were in a minority, they would immediately come to the Minister responsible for the appointment of magistrates, and bring pressure to bear for the appointment of a sufficient number of magistrates to give them a majority. We all know what happened at Manchester, where the appointments were made for party purposes. What happened at Manchester was that after these gentlemen were put upon the bench the whole

Mr. Galloway.

of the licensing policy of the city of Manchester was entirely reversed. I do not say that the appointment of these gentlemen was contrary to the practice which was previously adopted, but that was the result, and it is deplorable that those whose duty it is to administer justice in this country should be appointed for party purposes, and should be put on the bench to carry out the views of any particular section of the community. If the working of this Bill were to bring about or accentuate that state of things, it would be bad from all points of view. Clause 3 refers to the provisions of the Licensing Acts of 1872 and 1874. Now, the judges of this land have complained many times that Acts of Parliament do not state exactly what they mean, and they have to look up other Acts in order to see what is meant. As far as I can understand this clause, I suppose it is intended to exclude clubs. Some hon. Members have doubts whether these words do exclude clubs. If this Bill passes without alteration, I can quite understand what an excellent means it will be for the expenditure of money, testing whether clubs are included or not. If my hon. friend intends to exclude clubs, it will be better to have it stated clearly in the Bill. For my part, I admit that there may be a great deal to be said in favour of treating clubs upon a different basis from public-houses, although I have always looked upon this as class legislation of the worst possible description. If it is right that the working man's club should be closed on Sunday, I cannot see why the clubs which the rich men frequent should not be treated in the same way. I admit that, on account of the constitution of some clubs, there should not be the same regulations as apply to public-houses, which are frequented by people of a different character, and whose ways and means of life are not of the same intellectual standard. As a matter of abstract justice, I have never been able to understand why you should treat a public-house upon one basis and a club upon another basis altogether different. If you admit the principle that you are going to treat a club on a different basis to a public-house, then there is no reason whatsoever why working people should not form themselves into clubs, and use them as public-houses, and thereby avoid altogether the object which my hon. friend has in view in bringing forward this Bill. The last remark which I desire to make is on Clause 5, which says that the Bill shall not apply to Scotland, Ireland, or Wales. I presume that Wales is excluded because they have, practically, Sunday closing there already. As a supporter of the Act of Union, I think it is a pity that national measures of this kind do not treat the whole of the United Kingdom upon the same basis.

*MR. DAVITT (Mayo, S.) : We will accept it for Ireland.

MR. GALLOWAY : I do not know what particular authority the hon. Member has to speak on behalf of Ireland. I have always held, and still hold, that in legislation of this kind we ought to be placed on all fours in all parts of the United Kingdom. We are in the position of not having received the report of the Royal Commission which has been sitting for three years considering this question, and we do not know what their recommendations may be, for we have had no opportunity of considering the evidence which was given before that Commission. Therefore a more inopportune time than this to consider this question could hardly have been selected. Under these circumstances I beg to move the adjournment of the Debate.

MR. GIBSON BOWLES (King's Lynn): I beg leave to second this motion. A question of this importance should not be dealt with by a "snap" debate, for it involves nothing less than the liberties of the people of England. My belief is that the people of England believe that it is better to have liberty with drunkenness than slavery with temperance, and that it is better to have liberty with disease than slavery with health. That is the question really involved in this Bill, and it is of such importance, and has come on so suddenly, without opportunities to adequately discuss the matter, that I do not think it should be discussed in this casual way in the absence of the leaders of both parties. It is a very serious question, and it is much more serious than appears on the surface. Let me say one word as to the temperate man. We are called upon to admire the temperate man ; but what is he ? Why, he is a poor, pale-blooded, infirm, unenergetic man, without generosity and without perseverance. Was Moses a temperate man, or

Martin Luther, or Napoleon, or any man who was any good in this world ? No ! Those men had great courage and energetic convictions, and they all took, on proper occasions, a certain amount of alcoholic nourishment. I do not know whether, on the motion for adjournment, I should be in order in going into the merits of the Bill. Temperance advocates themselves are an illustration of intemperance itself, for of all the intemperate people in this world there are none so intemperate as they are. They are not content themselves with their own form of temperance, but they would impose their Puritanical tyranny on their countrymen, assuming, as the promoters of this Bill do assume, that we all abuse our opportunities for refreshment. They do not ask whether a man abuses liquor or not, but they assume that he is going to abuse it. The modern history of this question and the facts of the present day do not justify any more of these nauseating Puritanical attacks on the liberties of the people of England.

SIR WILFRID LAWSON : I rise to order. I desire to know if the hon. Gentleman is in order in discussing this question on a motion for adjournment.

MR. SPEAKER : No new question has yet been put before the House, and the hon. Member is in order.

MR. GIBSON BOWLES : I think the hon. Baronet opposite ought to be obliged to you, Mr. Speaker, for telling him what are the elementary rules of debate. I say that all the facts of this day prove, and increasingly prove day by day, that no such special interference with the liberties of the English people is required in the cause of temperance. I am a student of my fellow-countrymen, and I do declare most solemnly in this House that to-day temperance is making most fearful strides among the population. When I was young I remember well that nothing could be obtained at a railway station except alcoholic refreshment, which was generally beer or spirits. But now every railway station refreshment room is overflowing, I was going to say with milk and honey, but at least with milk and mineral waters. The poor pale glass of whisky is out of date, and modest drunkenness dare not show her face. So true is this, that drunkenness is almost extinct in this country. I do declare that in this country I never see a drunken man. It is only when I cross the Channel or the Tweed that I come across an example of that almost extinct animal the drunken man; and it is a most remarkable thing that in the only countries where I see drunken men this Bill does not apply. I should like to ask the twelve great statesmen—whose names will live in history and which appear on the back of this Bill—what are they about when they bring in a Bill which is to apply tyranny in England in the name of temperance, where it is not required, at the same time leaving out of the measure Scotland and Ireland where it is required most?

MR. DAVITT: We have got Sunday closing in Ireland.

MR. GIBSON BOWLES: Yes, but have you got temperance in Ireland?

MR. DAVITT: Yes, we have, and we boast the noblest temperance reformer of this century.

MR. GIBSON BOWLES: If that is so, then it is the most striking example possible of the absolute ineffectiveness of temperance work, because there is no country in the universe where temperance reformers have had their efforts crowned with so small a success as in Ireland. I am in favour myself of refreshment, but it should be occasional and small. If a man became drunk and disorderly, I would curtail his liberty only when he interfered with the liberty of others; but if he got drunk in a quiet and orderly manner in his own house I would not interfere with him, and I would

"let him play the fool in his own house,"

as Hamlet says. I do believe that all these attempts to impose what is miscalled temperance upon the English people, to prevent them being able to go into public-houses because it is assumed that they will get drunk, are destined to fail, and I believe every one of these twelve eminent statesmen whose names appear on the back of this Bill will find when the next General Election comes round that the attacks they have made upon the liberties of the English people will be very seriously and warmly resented. Now, what is it that this Bill deals with? It does not deal with drunkenness gener-

ally, but only with one particular occasion for getting drunk, providing you wish to. Those who have travelled in the East know the great convenience of what are known as guest-houses. Well, the public-house is the guest-house of England, as its name implies, and it is the only one left open to the poor man. The rich man has his club, and he has also his hotel, which is an expensive refuge not open to the poor man. The public-house is so named because it is a house of public entertainment, and this is where these intemperate temperance Puritans make a mistake. They assume that a man only goes into a public-house in order to get drunk; that is an entirely unwarranted assumption, which is disproved almost by everybody who frequent public-houses. Public-houses are open to all, and people frequent them in order to obtain reasonable refreshment; and it is perfectly outrageous, because one in a thousand happens to overstep the moderate limit, to call upon this House to close the whole of our public-houses altogether. In my opinion the Amendment is almost worse than the Bill itself, because it suggests, I am informed, local option. I am not afraid to say that I am dead against either Sunday closing or local option. Upon one occasion, when I was contesting an election for a small town in the Midlands, I was interviewed by a temperance deputation. They asked me, "Are you in favour of local option and the closing of public-houses on Sunday?" I replied, "What is the good of asking me those questions; you know you are all Radicals and you mean to vote against me." They replied, "Oh, no, we put temperance before all things, and if you will satisfy us on the temperance question we shall be quite prepared to vote for you." I told them that I was against Sunday closing and local option, and that I was in favour of a little moderate drunkenness—I think I called it hilarity; at any rate, it is that sort of exhilaration which the hon. Baronet opposite gets from drinking a glass of pure water. There are people who are capable of getting drunk with their own speeches, and I believe some people can get drunk upon tea. As for myself, I was never drunk in my life. All I desire is that we should realise things as they actually are. No matter whether we are at leisure or engaged in social meetings, we all take a certain amount of

Mr. Gibson Bowles.

exciting food or liquor to exhilarate us, and to whip up the sluggish flow of our spirits to make us proper companions for the friends we meet. All our enjoyments are based upon the consumption of a certain amount of exciting food or liquor. The right hon. baronet opposite, probably, gets exhilarated on a mutton chop or porridge——

MR. SPEAKER : Order, order ! The hon. Member is travelling very far from the Amendment.

MR. GIBSON BOWLES : I will at once bring my remarks to a close. All I wish to say now is that the whole social arrangements of this country are based upon the taking of a moderate amount of refreshment, and this Bill proposes to make a difference in that respect with regard to those who wish to obtain that refreshment. On those grounds I most strongly object to the Bill, and I second and support the motion of my hon. friend for the adjournment of the Debate, because I think that this is a far more important question than it appears to be. It is a question which involves the liberty of the people of England, and therefore it is one which should be discussed when the occupants of the front benches are present.

Motion made and Question proposed—

"That the Debate be now adjourned."— (*Mr. Galloway.*)

SIR J. LEESE (Lancashire, Accrington): I should not have interfered in this Debate if the hon. Member for Manchester had not made special reference to certain statements of mine. But before I take any notice of his criticisms I should like to say that I regard this ——

*MR. SPEAKER : Order, order ! The only question now before the House is whether the Debate should now be adjourned.

SIR J. LEESE: Perhaps I may be allowed to say that this is a very serious question, and I do not think that the Debate upon it ought to be adjourned at this stage. I should regret extremely that the consideration of this Bill should now be postponed, because it contains a principle of the greatest possible importance.

Question put.

The House divided : Ayes, 95 ; Noes, 85. (Division List 176.)

AYES.

Acland-Hood,Capt.SirAlex.F.
Anstruther, H. T.
Ascroft, Robert
Austin, M. (Limerick, W.)
Bailey, James (Walworth)
Balcarres, Lord
Baldwin Alfred
Barnes, Frederic Gorell
Bathurst,Hn.AllenBenjamin
Blundell, Colonel Henry
Bowles,T.Gibson(King'sLynn
Brookfield, A. Montagu
Bullard, Sir Harry
Chaloner, Captain R.G.W.
Coddington, Sir William
Cohen, Benjamin Louis
Collings, Rt. Hon. Jesse
Cornwallis,FiennesStanleyW.
Dalbiac, Colonel Philip Hugh
Douglas-Pennant, Hon. E. S.
Doxford, William Theodore
Drucker, A.
Duncombe, Hon. Hubert V.
Fisher, William Hayes
FitzGerald, Sir Rt. Penrose-
Flannery, Sir Fortescue
Fletcher, Sir Henry
Flower, Ernest
Folkestone, Viscount
Foster, Colonel (Lancaster)
Gibbons, J. Lloyd
Gold, Charles
Goldsworthy, Major-General

Goulding, Edward Alfred
Gray, Ernest (West Ham)
Gretton, John
Hare, Thomas Leigh
Hermon-Hodge, R. Trotter
Hickman, Sir Alfred
Hornby, Sir William Henry
Howell, William Tudor
Hutchinson, Capt. G. W. G.-
Jenkins, Sir John Jones
Kemp, George
Kenyon, James
Lawson, John Grant (Yorks.)
Lecky, Rt. Hon. Wm. E. H.
Loder, Gerald Walter Erskine
Lopes, Henry Yarde Buller
Loyd, Archie Kirkman
Lucas-Shadwell, William
MacAleese, Daniel
M'Iver, Sir L. (Edinburgh,W.)
Maple, Sir John Blundell
Marks, Henry Hananel
Milbank, Sir Powlett C. J.
Morgan, Hn. F. (Monm'tbsh.)
Morrell, George Herbert
Morris, Samuel
Morrison, Walter
Morton, A. H. A. (Deptford)
Mount, William George
Murray, Rt. Hn. A. G. (Bute)
Newdigate, Francis Alex.
O'Brien, Patrick (Kilkenny)
Phillpotts, Captain Arthur

Pretyman, Ernest George
Purvis, Robert
Rankin, Sir James
Redmond, John E. (Waterf'rd)
Richards, Henry Charles
Richardson, Sir T. (Hartlep'l)
Robertson, Herbert(Hackney)
Rothschild, Hn. Lionel Walt'r
Royds, Clement Molyneux
Russell, Gen. F.S. (Chelt'nh.)
Rutherford, John
Samuel, H. S. (Limehouse)
Sassoon, Sir Edward Albert
Scoble, Sir Andrew Richard
Seely, Charles Hilton
Sharpe, William Edward T.
Stone, Sir Benjamin
Tully, Jasper
Usborne, Thomas
Vincent, Col. Sir C. E. H.
Walrond, Rt. Hn. Sir Wm. H.
Webster, R. G. (St. Pancras)
Whiteley, George (Stockport)
Whitmore, Charles Algernon
Williams, Jos. Powell-(Birm.)
Wilson-Todd, W. H. (Yorks.)
Wodehouse, Rt. Hn. E. (Bath)
Wortley, Rt. Hn.C. B. Stuart-
Wyvill, Marmaduke D'Arcy

TELLERS FOR THE AYES—
Mr. Galloway and Mr. Young.

Mr. Gibson Bowles.

NOES.

Allan, William (Gateshead)
Allen, W. (Newc. under Lyme)
Arrol, Sir William
Bagot, Capt. J. FitzRoy
Barlow John Emmott
Bayley, Thomas (Derbyshire)
Billson, Alfred
Birrell, Augustine
Broadhurst, Henry
Buchanan, Thomas Ryburn
Burt, Thomas
Caldwell, James
Cameron, Sir C. (Glasgow)
Cawley, Frederick
Clough, Walter Owen
Crombie, John William
Davitt, Michael
Doogan, P. C.
Duckworth, James
Fenwick, Charles
Firbank, Joseph Thomas
Goddard, Daniel Ford
Gourley, Sir Edw. Temperley
Grey, Sir Edward (Berwick)
Gurdon, Sir W. Brampton
Hayne, Rt. Hn. C. Seale-
Heath, James
Hedderwick, Thomas C. H.
Holland, Wm. H (York, W. R.)
Howard, Joseph

Jacoby, James Alfred
Kitson, Sir James
Lambert, George
Langley, Batty
Lawrence, Wm. F. (Liverp'l)
Lawson, Sir W. (Cumberland)
Leese, Sir J. F. (Accrington)
Leng, Sir John
Lloyd-George, David
Lowther, Rt Hon. J. (Kent)
Lyell, Sir Leonard
M'Ghee, Richard
M'Kenna, Reginald
M'Killop, James
Maddison, Fred.
Molloy, Bernard Charles
Morley, Charles (Breconshire)
Norton, Capt. Cecil William
Nussey, Thomas Willans
O'Brien, James F. X. (Cork)
Oldroyd, Mark
Pease, Alfred E. (Cleveland)
Pease, Joseph A. (Northumb.)
Philipps, John Wynford
Pickard, Benjamin
Richardson, J. (Durham, S.E.)
Rickett, J. Compton
Roberts, John H. (Denbighs)
Robertson, Edmund (Dundee)
Robson, William Snowdon

Russell, T. W. (Tyrone)
Samuel, J. (Stockton-on-Tees)
Shaw, Thomas (Hawick B.)
Stewart, Sir J. M'Taggart
Strutt, Hon. Charles Hedley
Stuart, James (Shoreditch)
Sullivan, Donal (Westmeath)
Tennant, Harold John
Thorburn, Walter
Tomlinson, Wm. Edw. Murray
Trevelyan, Charles Philips
Walton, Joseph (Barnsley)
Warner, Thos. Courtenay T.
Wedderburn, Sir William
Weir, James Galloway
Williams, J. Carvell (Notts.)
Willox, Sir John Archibald
Wilson, John (Durham, Mid.)
Wilson, John (Falkirk)
Wilson, John (Govan)
Wilson, J.W.(Worcestersh.N.)
Wolff, Gustav Wilhelm
Woodhouse, Sir J.T.(Hudders.
Woods, Samuel
Yoxall, James Henry

TELLERS FOR THE NOES—
Mr. Tritton and Mr. Colville.

Debate to be resumed upon Wednesday next.

WINE AND BEERHOUSE ACTS AMENDMENT BILL.

SECOND READING.

Order for Second Reading read.

MR. LLOYD-GEORGE (Carnarvon): I beg to move the second reading of this Bill. It is a measure which is supported on both sides of the House, and its object is to amend the Beerhouse Acts so as to simply place beerhouse licences on exactly the same footing as ordinary licences for the sale of beer and spirits.

Motion made and Question proposed—

"That the Bill be now read a second time."

MR. JAMES LOWTHER: I confess that I am placed in a rather peculiar position in having again to trespass upon the time of the House in dealing with a subject which is very much like the one discussed in a Bill which has already been under our consideration to-day. Unlike the promoter of the other Bill to which I have alluded, the hon. Gentleman has furnished us with a memorandum, which is extremely useful to people like myself, for it informs me what the particular objects are which the Bill has in view. The memorandum says that the object of this Bill is to interfere in a hostile sense with what has been long recognised by Parliament as a vested interest. I do not think that is denied. The object of this Bill is to give to the licensing justices the same discretion in dealing with beer and cider houses that they now possess in regard to fully licensed houses and other places of refreshment, and this Bill is to place them in a different position, so far as the law is concerned, to that which they occupy now. I deprecated earlier in the day the attempt to deal with this subject until the Royal Commission which is now considering the question has issued its report, and it is not necessary for me to repeat what I have said before. But there is in this Bill a very great distinction between the two measures with regard to vested interest. Parliament designedly gave to these beerhouses a vested interest, and placed them in such a position that the renewal of their licences was wholly outside the discretion of the licensing justices. I have heard a good deal of argument in years past upon this question, and it is not necessary to go into detail. I believe it was the object of the Legislature in dealing with these beerhouses to discourage the consumption of stronger drink by encouraging the consumption of milder beverages. There is no doubt that the national taste, whether for good or evil, has very largely changed; and the taste for beer has, relatively, hardly kept pace with the taste for stronger drinks. As the law at present stands, the owners of these beer licences possess a vested interest, which, under this Bill, it is sought to remove. I think it is unwise to attempt to remove a vested interest without that degree of consideration which it is impossible for this measure to receive this afternoon. I put this question upon the higher ground that this is a specific vested interest created by Parliament which we are now asked to disturb. I refer to the opinion of Sir Harry Poland, who is acquainted with the Licensing Acts in all their aspects. He was a practising barrister and was engaged as Prosecutor by the Treasury. His practical experience in his profession has been supplemented by the position he occupies as chairman of one of the largest licensing benches in London. With reference to this very question, he says that the Beer Acts of 1830, 1834, and 1840 covered the "off" and "on" licences up to 1869. In 1828 it was thought to encourage the drinking of beer as against spirits, and it was provided that any man could have a licence from the Excise for beer without going to the magistrates for approval. In 1830 that law was enacted. These licences were obtained as a right up to 1834; then it was found that the persons put into the beerhouses were not real tenants but merely nominees; and in order to prevent that, the Act of 1840 was passed, and it was provided that no licence to sell beer or cider should be given to any person not a resident occupier or owner.

SIR WILFRID LAWSON: May I ask what the right hon. Gentleman is quoting from?

MR. JAMES LOWTHER: I am quoting from the First Report of the Royal Commission on the Liquor Licensing Laws, presented to Parliament by command of Her Majesty. The hon. Gentleman was quite right in asking the question, but I am not a retailer of the illicit gossip which has been going round recently as to the alleged intentions of the Royal Commission. I take no cognisance

of any gossip of that kind; and I confine myself entirely to the documents presented to Parliament by command of the Queen. Sir Harry Poland proceeds with regard to the licences obtained as of right from the Excise under the Acts of 1834 and 1840, and states that such licences could only be refused by the magistrates on one of the four grounds mentioned in Section E; and that the Legislature recognised that they were entitled to carry on a lawful trade in which they had embarked their capital. Coming from such a great and unique authority, I think Sir Harry Poland's opinion ought to have great weight with the House. We are now asked to take this matter out of the hands of the Royal Commission at the suggestion of private Members, without any official guidance, and I think such a recognised authority as my right hon. friend the Member for Bodmin will admit that that is a step which the House should be very chary in adopting. We are asked to interfere with a vested interest, and knowing the high character and sense of justice of my right hon. friend the Member for Bodmin, who has made himself responsible for this Bill, I turn it over to find the compensation clause, but there is no such clause in it. Perhaps my right hon. friend was prevented by his position as a private Member from making any motion which would involve taxation. That may be the reason why there is no compensation clause in the Bill, but at any rate we are asked to interfere with a vested interest at the instance of private Members, without any provision whatever for compensation. There are only four grounds under which these licences can be taken away under the existing law— viz., character, disorderly conduct, previous bad character, and want of accommodation. The Bill is an invasion of the general principle which has, as a rule, always guided legislation. That principle, which even those who have contravened it have made a show of complying with, is that the possessor of every right or interest shall have equitable compensation in the event of that right or interest being invaded. The Bill provides that the justices shall have full and complete control over these houses, which they never had before. I am glad to see my right hon. friend the Under Secretary of State for the Home Department in his place, with his usual devotion to duty, and I hope he will be in a position to state what course the Government think it advisable that the House should adopt in the very peculiar circumstances in which we are placed. No doubt the fact that the Royal Commission has not yet reported may be used against the Bill, but I hope my right hon. friend will go further, and that he will be prepared to express his regret at this assault on vested interests unaccompanied by some kind of compensation. It is an act of legislative injustice, and I think we ought to have some sort of explanation from the Government. I am unwilling to conclude by proposing to postpone further action on the part of the House, although it may appear to be a natural Amendment following the remarks I have been allowed to make. I should, however, like to hear some explanation, and after the course which the House has adopted with regard to the previous Bill, it is by no means improbable that reasons may suggest themselves for deferring the consideration of this Bill for some period, during which we may hear the Report of the Royal Commission and an announcement of the policy of Her Majesty's Government on the whole question.

MR. COURTNEY (Cornwall, Bodmin): My right hon. friend the Member for Thanet appeared to pick up information as he went along. He seems to know a great deal more about the subject now than he did before, although he was not very accurate in the beginning. It is quite true that in 1830 an Act was passed which allowed beerhouses to be set up irrespective of the control of the magistrates. The operation of that Act showed that it was much abused, and in 1840 an amending Act was passed. Even, however, with the restrictions in the latter Act, these beerhouses became largely a public nuisance, and in 1869 an Act was passed in order to control as much as possible the evil effects that arose from them. My right hon. friend has developed a most extraordinary theory of vested interest in this matter. In 1840 Parliament curtailed the vested interest in these houses ; in 1869 it did not create a vested interest, but it put conditions on the exercise of that interest. In that year Parliament brought these houses for the first time under the control of the magistrates, to the extent of the four causes which have been mentioned.

Mr. James Lowther.

It did not create a vested interest. It was a limitation of interest, and the mere fact that Parliament did that showed that it claimed to have that right. The present Bill does not propose that the magistrates should have the unlimited right of putting down these houses. If that were suggested, there might have been something in the argument of my right hon. friend. All that the Bill proposes is that the magistrates shall have the same discretion with respect to the licences granted before 1869 as it has with reference to the licences granted since that year. It puts these licences under the same discretion as ordinary public-houses. Reference has been made to the Royal Commission. I am not going to say anything about the Commission, or what it may or may not recommend, but every authority, before the Licensing Commission was established, sought to bring these comparatively few houses, which were in existence before 1869, under the same magisterial control that applies to hotel licences and ordinary licences whether before or since 1869. To refuse to give this magisterial discretion is to say that Parliament is powerless. It is said that the Bill of 1869 created a vested interest. Parliament in what it did that year affirmed that the opinion of the magistrates should be invoked in the control of these houses. The Bill before the House is very simple, and has been supported by county bench after county bench throughout the country, who ask that power may be given them to deal with the miserable pest-houses in their neighbourhoods, which they cannot now control. On behalf of the magistrates and of their liberty of action, I appeal to the House to consider this Bill.

MR. EDMUND ROBERTSON (Dundee): Hon. Members who have been in the House this afternoon will agree that the right hon. Gentleman the Member for Thanet has discharged with great ability the duty which fell upon him so unexpectedly of opposing two Bills of a very intricate character. I do not complain so much of the absence of the representatives of the Treasury Department as I do of the absence of the law officers of the Crown. This Bill confessedly involves a very intricate point of law, and it would be to the advantage of the discussion if we could have heard from the Attorney-General or the Solicitor-General what the law really is, and what the bearing of this

Bill will be. I have listened carefully to what has been said by my right hon. friend the Member for Bodmin on the question of vested interest. I have also listened to the right hon. Gentleman the Member for Thanet, and I must confess that I have come to the conclusion that he has established a case of interference with what is in effect a vested interest, which, in accordance with the ordinary practice of Parliament, could not be taken away without compensation ; and I am not convinced by the speech of my right hon. friend the Member for Bodmin that that is not the case. Section 19 of the Act of 1869 says, with respect to the licences now under consideration, that it shall not be lawful for the justices to refuse an application for a certificate for the sale of beer except on one or more of the grounds specified. My right hon. friend the Member for Bodmin talked lightly of the interference which this Bill proposes ; but the Bill proposes to repeal Section 19 of the 1869 Act, and it goes further and states that—

"Notwithstanding anything in the Acts mentioned or in Acts now in force, the licensing justices shall be at liberty to refuse a certificate for any licence for the sale of beer or cider on any ground appearing to them sufficient."

That appears to me to be absolutely putting it within the discretion of the justices to control licences which at the present moment are not empowered to interfere with except on certain specified grounds. In that way the Bill does touch a vested right, and the extension of the powers of the magistrates may result in the vested right being taken away ; and if it be a valuable right, the only principle on which Parliament can deal with it is by compensation. But is it a valuable right ? That is a point on which I should have desired some information from the law officers of the Crown. I presume it is a valuable right, because, like all other licences, it is in the nature of a monopoly, and I would appeal to my hon. friends who advocate temperance reform to take care lest they may be taking a most dangerous step by confusing between licences which are a vested and a valuable right and licences which, although a valuable, are not a vested right. It is in my opinion dangerous for them to confuse, as my right hon. friend the Member for Bodmin did, beerhouse with ordinary public-house licences, which are not a vested right at all. What is the real

difficulty in all these matters ? Why are the licences of beer-houses a valuable right ? Simply because of the infatuated policy Parliament has pursued for generations, in insisting in making the duty on licences so small as to be only an infinitesimal part of their value. If the duties were made higher, then, although licences might be a vested, they would not be a valuable right in the sense that is taken objection to. What chance is there of getting reforms like that ? I have been appealing to the Chancellor of the Exchequer in this, as in former sessions, to give us on the authority of his Department information as to what is the difference between the duty on licences and the annual value of the licences. If we had that information it would then be seen how many millions a year of public money are squandered because of the ridiculously low duties on licences. That is the view which I venture to put before the House on this question. I must adhere to my statement, until I am enlightened by either the right hon. Gentleman on the Treasury Bench or by the law officers of the Crown, that there are good grounds for the rejection of the Bill. The only way to deal with the question is to level up the duties on all licences to their annual value.

The UNDER SECRETARY to the HOME OFFICE (Mr. Jesse Collings, Birmingham, Bordesley) : Of course hon. Members are quite right in taking advantage of the opportunity which has been given them of discussing this somewhat intricate subject. But hon. Members have asked what is the position of the Government as regards this Bill. I should have thought that any Member of Parliament, and especially my right hon. friend the Member for Bodmin, must know what is the inevitable position of the Government with regard to this measure, and others of a similar character. The Government, three years ago, with general approval, appointed a Royal Commission to inquire into the working of the licensing laws, and that Commission has spared no effort in order to obtain information, not only on the particular point of the licensing question now before the House, but on that question as a whole. It is on the eve of presenting its Report, and giving us the result of its inquiries and deliberations ; and is it to be supposed that the Government would now be prepared to pre-judge that Report on any particular point by expressing a decided opinion or any opinion on this Bill, or any other Bill of a similar character, affecting the inquiry which they themselves had insti-tuted? If I were to ask my right hon. friend the Member for Bodmin, as a mem-ber of the former Administration, would any Government, after having appointed a Royal Commission of such impor-tance, give an opinion a few days before the Report of that Commission was received on a point which had been referred to it, I think he would only give one answer; and I venture to challenge him as to whether it would be even courteous to that important Commission if the Govern-ment were to pronounce an opinion, or even to discuss the question, before they had the valuable results of its delibera-tions. My right hon. friend the Member for Thanet asked what were the opinions of the Government with regard to com-pensation and other matters. I have not seen the Report of the Royal Commission, but I take it that the question of compen-sation is very likely to figure largely in it, and is it to be expected that the Government would now offer opinions which would forestall the mature conclu-sions of the Commission? Not a single point has been raised this afternoon which has not been the subject of a vast amount of labour on the part of the Commission. With reference to the intricate point dis-cussed so ably by my right hon. friends, I have no doubt, judging from the evidence which has been given before the Commis-sion, that light will also be thrown on it.

MR. GIBSON BOWLES : What about the Bill? How are we going to vote?

MR. JESSE COLLINGS : I must leave that to the superior judgment—for it is a superior judgment—of my hon. friend. He knows better than anybody else what course to take; but with regard to this Bill, or any Bill of a similar character, the Government cannot, under the circum-stances, express any opinion.

*MR. J. H. ROBERTS (Denbighshire, W.) : I personally doubt the propriety of referring to the details of the evidence given before a Commission which has not yet reported, but as the right hon. Gentleman opposite has read the evidence

Mr. Jesse Collings.

of Sir Harry Poland, I should like to remind the House that Sir Harry Poland stood almost alone in the opinion he expressed, and that the overwhelming evidence given on this particular point was strongly in favour of the Bill now being discussed. The second point to which I desire to allude is the unanimity of opinion in favour of this Bill which was expressed, long before the Com-mission was appointed, by those really responsible for the administration of the licensing laws. We cannot have a better opinion in regard to a question of this character than the opinion of the justices responsible for the administra-tion of the law, and I would like to state one or two facts in regard to the unanimity which prevails on this point. Resolutions have been passed in favour of this Bill by no less than 21 quarter sessions in England and Wales, 18 being unanimous; by 11 city benches, 10 being unanimous; and by 48 benches of borough justices, 34 being unanimous. In addition, very strong approval of the Bill has been expressed by a large number of county councils and standing joint committees throughout the country. I very much doubt whether there is a single Bill which has ever been before the Committee which has had behind it such an overwhelming support from those authorities primarily connected with the administration of the law to be affected by the Bill. There is one more point to which I desire to allude, and that is the question of compensation which has been raised more than once this afternoon. Speaking for myself, I am inclined to think that the statement of my right hon. friend the Member for Bodmin was absolutely convincing upon this point. From 1830 onwards he traced the history of this question, step by step, and laid it before the House in such a lucid manner that it should be impossible for anyone to have a doubt in future with regard to it. Dealing with the speech of the hon. Member for Dundee, I am not quite sure whether the vigorous expression of opinion he gave in regard to it represents the opinion of his colleagues; I believe it is only his personal opinion. But, apart from this important question of compen-sation, whatever may be the Report of the Royal Commission—and I am not going to suggest what it is going to be—it seems to me that in addition to the Acts which have been laid before the

House by the right hon. Gentleman opposite, there is the all-important fact which ought to be remembered, namely, that legislation subsequent to 1859 is quite as much in favour of the views he holds upon the question as the legislation at the time spoken of. I do not know whether hon. Members recollect what took place in this House in 1884, when the right hon. Gentleman the present President of the Board of Trade himself passed a Bill through this House dealing with "off" beer licences, and effecting that which it is the object of the present Bill to effect in regard to beerhouses; but I do say that if it was right in 1882 to pass an Act of that character without making compensation, it is equally equitable to do the same thing in the present Bill. I hope this Bill will not be treated from a political standpoint. I desire to echo in the strongest possible way what has been already said more than once to-day, namely, that we must endeavour, whatever our political views may be, to combine before any substantial progress is made in temperance reform, and believing as I do that this is absolutely a non-party question, and that the Bill represents the views of almost all the justices of this country who are primarily responsible for the administration of the law, I hope that we shall take the second reading without any party consideration.

MR. BANBURY (Camberwell, Peckham): The hon. Member for Dundee began his speech by lamenting the absence of the law officers of the Crown. I was rather inclined to agree with him that we had lost something by their absence, but he gave us such an able exposition of the Bill that I think we have lost nothing. His point seemed to be so unanswerable that I was rather inclined not to get up, but allow the House to go to a division upon the subject; but, as the hon. Member who has just sat down has made one or two observations about this not being a political subject, I think I should like to say a few words upon it. Those of us who have listened to the hon. Member for Dundee must have been convinced that people holding these licences have invested their money in them on the faith of an Act of Parliament. In that respect they differ from the ordinary holder of ordinary licences of public-houses, because he knows very well when he purchases the licence that there is a possibility of his being

deprived of it. That is a condition of most investments, but it is not a condition which attaches in this case, as has been clearly shown. An hon. Member says this is not a political question. It is not a political question. It is a question of right or wrong; it is a question of taking away something a licensed holder has because certain people think the cause of temperance may be advanced. The cause of temperance is a very good cause. I should be very loth to do anything which would in any way tend to prevent sobriety prevailing in the land. Intemperance is a very great danger to any State. But, on the other hand, I hope you will not tamper with the rights of property in order to further temperance reform. The hon. Member for Dundee has said that it was always understood that if a vested right was a valuable right it should not be taken away without compensation. If it is a monopoly it is a valuable right. No monopoly would be a right unless it was valuable, and I think we may be quite certain that these people would not retain their licences unless they made something out of them. Now I do not wish to allude to the Royal Commission. My right hon. friend has said that it is not right to prejudge the evidence which they may bring forward or the conclusions at which they may arrive. But it is very evident that, should the Royal Commission arrive at a conclusion which is detrimental to public-house proprietary, their recommendations may make those licences very valuable assets, of which people should not be deprived without proper compensation. I am afraid that I have but weakly shown what seem to me to be strong grounds for rejecting this Bill; but I hope that every Member of this House will pause long before he commits himself to the second reading of this Bill.

MR. WARNER (Stafford, Lichfield): There are other reasons than the fear of interfering with vested rights—which the House has a perfect right to deal with in the interests of the community—which incline me to look with disfavour on the Bill. For my part, I object to giving the magistrates any more power over the licensing question than they have at the present moment, and I think that the whole liquor question, including that branch of it, would be better dealt with as a whole. But I do protest against the way in which we have been treated by the representatives of Her Majesty's Government. They have sat silent for three parts of this debate, and then the right hon. Gentleman the UnderSecretary for the Home Department gets up and shelters himself behind the Royal Commission. Of course, we know that Her Majesty's Government has faith in Royal Commissions; but, unfortunately, we have not that faith on this side of the House. In common courtesy to this House, ought he not to have got up at once when this Debate began and moved the adjournment, instead of simply allowing it to go on, and saying that for the present the Government could not express an opinion, as there was a Commission sitting upon the question ?

SIR JAMES FERGUSSON (Manchester, N.E.): I think that this question is too important to be disposed of by flippant allusions to the Government or the magistrates. In the last forty or fifty years the magistrates have done much to reduce the excessive number of licences. I cannot help remembering what has taken place in this House over a pretty long period of years in respect to this question. I recollect the important discussion which took place in 1857 upon the very question which we are now discussing, when Lord Cranbrook made his first great reputation in this House by a speech on the Beer Bill. He introduced a Bill which was intended to place licences of beerhouses on the same footing as fully licensed houses. The Bill was of a somewhat drastic character. It was in advance of public opinion, and this House declined to accept it. At the same time, although that Bill was defeated by a small majority, it was understood that the Government of the day would deal with the question itself. I do not think any special legislation took place until 1869, and it is worth the while of hon. Members to refer to the speech made by Mr. Hardy. It was a very exhaustive and comprehensive speech, in which he demonstrated the great evils that accrued from beer licences in the country, the low character of many of the houses, and the urgent need, in the interests of morality and the welfare of the working classes, of reducing the number of those houses and of raising the character of those that remained. But, as I have said, nothing

Mr. Warner.

has been done, and up to this day licences to sell beer can be obtained by simple application to the Inland Revenue authorities. That cannot be a satisfactory state of things. I myself was, many years ago, chairman of a Royal Commission to inquire into a certain branch of the licensing question, namely, the grocers' licences in Scotland. We took evidence and made recommendations of a much wider character than were incidental to the subject, and we found that there was a great evil to be remedied. I agree quite with the hon. Member for Dundee that the only effectual cure for the existence of low-class houses entrusted with licences would be to raise the value of the licences ; and I have no doubt an expedient could be found by which compensation could be made to those houses which were extinguished out of the increased receipts of the licence duty. I do not think it can be denied that public-houses and the majority of beer and spirit licences should be subjected to much stricter regulation than is imposed upon them. I think the very slightest consideration of the subject must show that it is not one which can be dealt with in a hasty and partial manner. I do not know why a reference to the Royal Commission need excite the ridicule of the House. The question has been referred to a Commission composed of small numbers, and I think a Commission of small numbers is more likely to come to a satisfactory conclusion than a large body. Meanwhile, I do not know whether it will be possible to make any alteration of the law without having regard to the evidence given before that Commission, and the recommendations made.

MR. DALZIEL (Kirkcaldy Burghs): We have had an interesting Debate this afternoon. There are two points which have been raised. This first is that the Bill interferes with vested interests, and the second is that we ought to await the report of the Royal Commission. I venture to say, with all respect to the hon. Gentleman who has just sat down, that the first objection has not been proved. There are no particular vested interests in beerhouse licences granted since 1869, and I see no reason why licences before that year should be placed on a different footing. Then, Sir, there is another reason given by the right hon. Gentleman the Under Secretary. There is one advantage which we have when the Under-Secretary speaks, and that is that he is always clear, though he is not always convincing. I have listened to his speech with some interest because I have a recollection that some years ago he treated the subject in a different way. According to his speech to-day we must wait for the Royal Commission.

MR. JESSE COLLINGS: The Government say so, not I.

MR. DALZIEL: Then, Sir, that makes my point all the more important. Whether as Leader of the House or as private Member, the right hon. Gentleman's opinions are far too well founded to change, irrespective of the side on which he may sit. I always read the speeches of the right hon. Gentleman with great interest; and therefore when he made a statement to-day about the folly of going to a division on this question before the Royal Commission had reported I thought of another policy he had recommended some years ago. There was an interesting little Bill in 1894 before the House on old age pensions, and the right hon. Gentleman gave to the House the advantage of his opinions upon that Bill. The second reading took place just on the eve of the report of the Royal Commission, and what did he say in reply to the suggestion of the Government that we should wait for the Royal Commission's report? He said:

"He hoped the second reading of the Bill would not be deferred until the Royal Commission's Report, as that would mean the hanging up of the question !for another year ; it was an urgent question, at any rate so far as the initial steps were concerned, and he hoped, therefore, that the hon. Member would carry the Bill to a division. He (Mr. Collings) should vote with a better heart, and with more pleasure than he thought he had felt with regard to any vote he had ever recorded in his life."

I am sure the right hon. Gentleman will be obliged to me for reminding him of that declaration, because it is an important justification for the vote I am going to give to-day. I do not know whether the right hon. Gentleman is satisfied upon that point, but I have many more. I am not going to trouble him with the quotation of many opinions, I think I have given my best; but I will give him one more, if he is still unconvinced, which I am sure will have some weight—the opinion of the

right hon. Gentleman the Colonial Secretary, whose absence we deplore, because had he been here I am sure he would have given him his advice. The Secretary for the Colonies spoke at that time as member of the Royal Commission that was just about to report. Speaking on the Bill he said :

"We were dealing with a subject which was quite right for legislation, and with regard to which he thought it would be a great advantage not only to the public at large but also to members of the Royal Commission that some indication of the feeling of that House should be given."

That is our case to-day. We want to give the Royal Commission, even at this late hour, some indication as to what the opinion of the House really is.

MR. RICHARDS (Finsbury, E.): While the House has greatly enjoyed the collection of ancient speeches which the hon. Member has just presented, I hope he will not forget not only that circumstances alter cases, but also that there is a great difference between old age pensions and the abolition of privileges which have existed for 40 or 50 years. The right hon. Gentleman the Under Secretary of State for the Home Department, in the speech which has been quoted, described, and I think rightly described, the question of old age pensions as an urgent one. I venture to describe it as an urgent one still, and to say that only a small number of very estimable but somewhat fanatical persons would describe a question affecting the alteration of the licensing law as an urgent or even an important question. But I protest most strongly against this attempt to interfere with the small licence-holders. We hear a great deal from the other side of the House about big brewers and tied houses. This Bill affects the little man. You are asked to take from the little men privileges which they enjoy, because the majority of small beerhouses are not tied houses. ("Oh!") I adhere to what I said. I know an attempt is being made to make them tied houses, but I say unhesitatingly that the majority of these houses in the country—and I have had great experience on the subject in one of the counties of England—are not tied houses. I know that in London there has been an attempt, and is an attempt, to secure to a larger extent than has hitherto prevailed the principle of tied houses by buying up small beerhouses. With the greatest respect to the right hon. Gentleman the Member for Bodmin, I venture to say that the opinion of Sir Harry Poland on licensing law is at least of equal value to that of the right hon. Gentleman ; and he clearly points out that these beerhouses are a vested interest. What does this Bill do ? I am constantly hearing, outside the House and inside, that it is the publican who is to be evicted and compensated, and not the brewer, the shareholder, or the capitalist ; but this Bill attacks the smallest man of the whole of this great trade or machinery, and practically turns him out into the street. I venture to say that the law as it exists at present is very unjust. While the magistrate who holds shares in a railway company is unable to adjudicate in his own division in matters in which that company is concerned because he is "an interested person," every teetotal advocate, every gentleman who has been put upon the bench for no other reason than that he is an opponent of the licensing interest, or for political services rendered to his party, sits on the licensing committees. These are the people who have carried, practically unanimously, the resolutions in favour of extending their own power. They are, therefore, the resolutions of interested parties—not interested pecuniarily, but in other ways. What I would venture to suggest to the House is that the Debate should now be adjourned. I think we have had enough surprises this afternoon, and I therefore beg to move the adjournment of the Debate.

*MR. SPEAKER : I cannot accept it at this hour of the afternoon. If the motion had been made at an early stage, and before the Bill had been fully discussed, it might have been different ; but I cannot accept it at this stage, when there is a prospect of an early division.

MR. EVERSHED (Staffordshire, Burton) : I cannot help thinking that it would be unfair and unwise on the part of this House to come to a decision on the Bill which has come before us in such an unexpected manner. I admit at once that there is something anomalous in the state of the law affecting beerhouses and other licensed properties. I can only say that whenever this House, if I am a Member of it, comes to deal with a question which gives greater facility to the securing of

Mr. Richards.

justice to publicans, and which in any way advances the cause of temperance, I shall vote for it. But I am bound to confess that, as far as temperance is concerned, I shall draw the line at the point where the liberty of the subject is in any way affected. So far as this Bill is concerned, I venture to think that it cannot be very satisfactory even to the promoters, even if they pass it this afternoon, because it comes before us in such an unexpected manner. I venture to say that neither the right hon. Gentleman opposite who represents the Government nor hon. Members on this side of the House had any idea that this question would come up. If we pass this Bill without compensation to those from whom we take property, all I can say is that the country will not have much respect for the decision arrived at. I venture to say that there is no pressing hurry in this matter. A Royal Commission is about to report. These small houses are as well conducted as any other licensed property. They serve the poorer class of this country, and great harm would be done to that class if this subject were disposed of hurriedly. I quite understand that there can be no reason why a hurried vote should be taken now, and I certainly think that this matter can be left until the Commission which is now sitting has made its Report.

*MR. TOMLINSON (Preston) : The time has come when it seems desirable that the issue should be put before this House in a definite and concrete form, and I propose to conclude my remarks by moving an Amendment that this Bill shall be read a second time this day three months. It is quite clear, although some hon. Members do not seem to know what the provisions of the Act of 1869 are, that it is a question of justice. It appears to me that no one could come to the conclusion that this Bill was just who understood the provisions of the Act of 1869. The hon. Member for the Lichfield Division evidently does not appreciate the scheme of that Act. It is common knowledge now that the intention of that Act was that in future there should be no fresh grant of Excise beerhouse licences, and that all licences, whether of beerhouses or houses where other intoxicating liquors were sold, should in future come under the control of the magistrates. That was entirely a new departure. Previous to that time anybody who could get a licence from the Excise could retail beer, and it was felt that if all existing licences of that kind were put under the control of the magistrates the men who had obtained them, and had by carrying on their business acquired a valuable privilege, would be put into an inferior position. In 1869 Parliament had regard to vested interests and vested rights, and it was not thought right that Parliament should take away without compensation that which they had granted. Consequently licences then existing were preserved under the conditions on which they had been granted. Section 4 of the Act provided for the extinction in future of fresh licences by enacting that no licences or renewals of licences should be granted' except on the production of a certificate. Section 6 provided a form of the certificate, which should remain in force for one year. The object of granting the certificate was to preserve the right which the holders of the Excise licences had acquired under the Act of 1869. This Bill seeks to put these licences on the same footing as licences granted by the magistrates, which would place them in an inferior position in point of stability to that which they at present hold. The result of the Act of 1869 was to give that value to beerhouses which has enabled the brewers to have that hold upon them that they have now, and it is under that Act that the tied house system has grown up. When the licensing laws come to be discussed the tied house question will be one of the great questions which will have to be dealt with. That is one of the drawbacks to the Act of 1869, but the wisdom of that policy is not now in contention. What we have to deal with on the Bill is a question of justice. Are we now to take away without compensation rights which were given by Parliament in 1869? Only one hon. Member in the debate has justified that. He said Parliament had impaired some of the rights reserved by the Act of 1869 by the Act of 1884; but I cannot help thinking that there must have been some exceptional ground for the treatment then accorded to certain licences. But, if not, I decline, because Parliament committed an error in 1884, to commit an error now. That

being so, I beg to move that this Bill be read a second time this day three months.

Amendment proposed—

"To leave out the word 'now,' and at the end of the question to add the words 'upon this day three months.'"—(*Mr. Tomlinson.*)

Question proposed –

"That the word 'now' stand part of the question."

*MR. H. LEWIS (Flint Boroughs): This Bill has been on the Order Book for to-day for the last two months and I do not think that it lies in the mouth of any hon. Member to complain that this question has come on unexpectedly. The Bill is not a party measure, and has been introduced by hon. Members on both sides of the House. All over the country resolutions have been passed in favour of the Bill. The courts of quarter sessions in the most important counties and the licensing benches in the largest towns have passed resolutions in favour of it. They have done so because they have no power to interfere with these beerhouses on several grounds which apply to fully licensed houses. Supposing a beerhouse is insanitary, or devoid of proper sanitary accommodation, the licence cannot be interfered with or taken away; nor can the magistrates interfere if it is conducted in an objectionable manner, or if it is not required to meet the wants of the neighbourhood in which it is situated. Therefore it is not surprising that benches of magistrates, without distinction of political colour, have supported this Bill. The question of compensation which some hon. Members have sought to raise upon this Bill has been settled definitely by a Conservative Government, and I commend the Bill to the support of a large number of hon. Gentlemen on either side of this House who wish to take some step in the direction of licensing reform.

SIR W. HOULDSWORTH (Manchester, N.W.): I have come to the conclusion that there is almost an unanimous opinion that these houses, under proper conditions, should be placed under the jurisdiction of the magistrates, and I think the argument brought forward by the hon. Gentleman opposite has brought that out. All this debate comes to is a question of compensation, and I do not think that that comes in at all. This Bill has been spoken of as if it was an

X

abolition bill, which it is not. If this Bill passes there would be no alteration whatever, so far as the beerhouses are concerned, so long as the magistrates in their discretion issued the licences. If at any time the justices exercised their discretion and put down some of these beerhouses, then they would have compensation in the ordinary way. If compensation is given under a new Act after the Report of the Royal Commission, or by the will of the House, these beerhouses will participate in that compensation in precisely the same way as any other licensed houses. The only thing we have to consider is whether it is desirable to put these houses on the same footing as other licensed houses, and I have no hesitation in saying, in my opinion, it will be most desirable to do so.

Question put.

The House divided : Ayes, 138 ; noes, 183 (Division List, No. 177).

AYES.

Allan, William (Gateshead)
Allen, Wm. (New. u. Lyme)
Arrol, Sir William
Baird, John George Alexander
Baker, Sir John
Barlow, John Emmott
Beaumont, Wentworth C. B.
Biddulph, Michael
Billson, Alfred
Birrell, Augustine
Blake, Edward
Bolitho, Thomas Bedford
Bolton, Thomas Dolling
Broadhurst, Henry
Brown, Alexander H.
Buchanan, Thomas Ryburn
Burns, John
Burt, Thomas
Caldwell, James
Cameron, Sir Chas. (Glasgow)
Campbell-Bannerman, Sir H.
Cawley, Frederick
Channing, Francis Allston
Colville, John
Courtney, Rt. Hon L. H.
Crombie, John William
Dalziel, James Henry
Davies, M. V. - (Cardigan)
Davitt, Michael
Denny, Colonel
Digby, John K. D. Wingfield-
Doogan, P. C.
Duckworth, James
Dunn, Sir William
Evans, Sir F. H. (South'ton)
Fenwick, Charles
Ferguson, R. C. Munro (Leith)
Fitzmaurice, Lord Edmond
Fowler, Rt. Hon. Sir Henry
Gladstone, Rt. Hon. H. J.
Gourley, Sir Edward T.
Gurdon, Sir Wm. Brampton
Hayne, Rt. Hn. Charles Seale-
Hobhouse, Henry
Holland, W. H. (York, W. R.)
Horniman, Frederick John
Howard, Joseph

Humphreys-Owen, Arthur C.
Jacoby, James Alfred
Jenkins, Sir John Jones
Jones, D. Brynmor (Swansea)
Jones, Wm. (Carnarvonshire)
Kay-Shuttleworth, Rt Hn Srt U.
Kennaway, Rt. Hon. Sir J. H.
Kinloch, Sir John George S.
Kitson, Sir James
Labouchere, Henry
Lambert, George
Langley, Batty
Laurie, Lieut.-General
Lawson, Sir W. (Cumberland)
Leng, Sir John
Lloyd-George, David
Lucas-Shadwell, William
Lyell, Sir Leonard
M'Arthur, William (Cornwall)
M'Ghee, Richard
M'Kenna, Reginald
M'Killop, James
M'Laren, Charles Benjamin
Maddison, Fred.
Mappin, Sir Fredk. Thorpe
Martin, Richard Biddulph
Molloy, Bernard Charles
Montagu, Sir S. (Whitechapel)
Morgan, J. Lloyd (Carmarthen)
Morgan, W. Pritchd. (Merthyr)
Morley, Charles (Breconshire)
Morton, Edw. J.C. (Devonport)
Moulton, John Fletcher
Nussey, Thomas Willans
Oldroyd, Mark
Orr-Ewing, Charles Lindsay
Palmer, Sir C. M. (Durham)
Parkes, Ebenezer
Paulton, James Mellor
Pease, Alfred E. (Cleveland)
Pease, Herbert Pike (Darlingt'n
Pease, Joseph A. (Northumb.)
Pease, Sir Joseph W. (Durham)
Philipps, John Wynford
Pickard, Benjamin
Price, Robert John
Provand, Andrew Dryburgh

Richardson, J. (Durham, S.E.)
Rickett, J. Compton
Roberts, John H. (Denbighs.)
Robson, William Snowdon
Round, James
Samuel, J. (Stockton-on-Tees)
Scott, Chas. Prestwich (Leigh)
Shaw, Thomas (Hawick B.)
Sinclair, Capt J. (Forfarshire)
Smith, Samuel (Flint)
Souttar, Robinson
Spicer, Albert
Steadman, William Charles
Stephens, Henry Charles
Stewart, Sir M. J. M'Taggart
Stirling-Maxwell, Sir John M.
Strutt, Hon. Charles Hedley
Sullivan, Donal (Westmeath)
Talbot, Rt. Hn. J.G. (Ox. Univ.)
Tennant, Harold John
Thomas, A. (Carmarthen, E.)
Thomas, Alf. (Glamorgan, E.)
Thomas, D. Alfred (Merthyr)
Trevelyan, Charles Philips
Tritton, Charles Ernest
Wallace, Robert (Perth)
Walton, Joseph (Barnsley)
Webster, R. G. (St. Pancras)
Weir, James Galloway
Williams, Colonel R. (Dorset)
Williams, J. Carvell (Notts.)
Willox, Sir John Archibald
Wills, Sir William Henry
Wilson, Charles Henry (Hull)
Wilson, Hy. J. (York, W. R.)
Wilson, John (Durham, Mid.)
Wilson, John (Falkirk)
Wilson, John (Govan)
Wilson, Jos. H. (Middlesbro')
Woodall, William
Woodhouse, Sir J.T. (H'dd'rsf'd)
Woods, Samuel
Wylie, Alexander
Yoxall, James Henry
TELLERS FOR THE AYES—
  Mr. Herbert Lewis and Sir
  William Houldsworth.

NOES.

Acland-Hood, Capt. Sir A. F.
Anstruther, H. T.
Ascroft, Robert
Atkinson, Rt. Hon. John
Bailey, James (Walworth)
Baldwin, Alfred
Sir W. Houldsworth.

Banbury, Frederick George
Barnes, Frederic Gorell
Barry, Rt Hn A H Smith-(Hunts
Beach, Rt Hn Sir M H (Bristol)
Begg, Ferdinand Faithfull
Bethell, Commander

Blundell, Colonel Henry
Bond, Edward
Bonsor, Henry Cosmo Orme
Bowles, T. G. (King's Lynn)
Brassey, Albert
Brodrick, Rt. Hon. St. John

Brookfield, A. Montagu
Brymer, William Ernest
Bullard, Sir Harry
Burdett-Coutts, W.
Butcher, John George
Campbell, Rt. Hn. J. A. (Glasg.
Carew, James Laurence
Cecil, Evelyn (Hertford, East)
Chaloner, Captain R. G. W.
Chamberlain, J. A. (Worc'r)
Charrington, Spencer
Cochrane, Hon. Thos. H. A. E.
Coddington, Sir William
Cohen, Benjamin Louis
Collings, Rt. Hon. Jesse
Compton, Lord Alwyne
Cook, Fred. Lucas (Lambeth)
Cooke, C. W. Radcliffe (Heref'd)
Cornwallis, Fiennes Stanley W.
Cripps, Charles Alfred
Cross, Herb. Shep. (Bolton)
Cubitt, Hon. Henry
Dalbiac, Colonel Philip Hugh
Dalkeith, Earl of
Davies, Sir H. D. (Chatham)
Dickson-Poynder, Sir John P.
Disraeli, Coningsby Ralph
Dixon-Hartland, Sir F. Dixon
Douglas, Rt. Hon. A. Akers-
Douglas-Pennant, Hon. E. S.
Doxford, William Theodore
Drage, Geoffrey
Drucker, A.
Dyke, Rt. Hon. Sir Wm. Hart
Egerton, Hon. A. de Tatton
Evershed, Sydney
Fergusson, Rt. Hn. Sir J (Manc'r
Finch, George H.
Firbank, Joseph Thomas
Fisher, William Hayes
FitzGerald, Sir Robert Penrose-
FitzWygram, General Sir F.
Flower, Ernest
Folkestone, Viscount
Foster, Colonel (Lancaster)
Foster, Harry S. (Suffolk)
Galloway, William Johnson
Garfit, William
Gibbs, Hn. A. G. H (City of Lond.
Gibbs, Hn. Vicary (St. Albans)
Gilliat, John Saunders
Godson, Sir Augustus Fredk.
Gold, Charles
Goldsworthy, Major-General
Gordon, Hon. John Edward
Goschen, George J. (Sussex)

Goulding, Edward Alfred
Greene, H. D. (Shrewsbury)
Greene, W. R. (Cambs.)
Gretton, John
Greville, Hon. Ronald
Gunter, Colonel
Hall, Rt. Hon. Sir Charles
Hanson, Sir Reginald
Hare, Thomas Leigh
Hatch, Ernest Fredk. Geo.
Heath, James
Heaton, John Henniker
Helder, Augustus
Hickman, Sir Alfred
Hill, Sir Edw. Stock (Bristol)
Hoare, E. Brodie (Hampstead)
Hoare, Samuel (Norwich)
Kemp, George
Kenyon, James
Kimber, Henry
King, Sir Henry Seymour
Knowles, Lees
Lawson, John Grant (Yorks.)
Lees, Sir Elliott (Birkenhead)
Llewellyn, Evan H. (Somerset)
Llewellyn, Sir Dillwyn- (Swan.)
Lockwood, Lt.-Col. A. R.
Loder, Gerald Walter Erskine
Lopes, Henry Yarde Buller
Lorne, Marquess of
Lowther, Rt. Hon. Jas. (Kent)
Loyd, Archie Kirkman
Lubbock, Rt. Hon. Sir John
MacAleese, Daniel
Macdona, John Cumming
MacIver, David (Liverpool)
Maclean, James Mackenzie
Maclure, Sir John William
M'Arthur, Charles (Liverpool)
M'Calmont, H. L. B. (Cambs.)
M'Cartan, Michael
M'Iver, Sir Lewis (Ed'nb'gh, W.
Malcolm, Ian
Manners, Lord Edw. Wm. J.
Maple, Sir John Blundell
Marks, Henry Hananel
Milbank, Sir Powlett Chas. J.
Milward, Colonel Victor
More, Robt. Jasper (Shropshire)
Morgan, Hn. Fred. (Monm'thsh
Morrell, George Herbert
Morris, Samuel
Morton, Arthur H. A. (Deptford
Mount, William George
Muntz, Philip A.
Murray, Rt. Hn A Graham (Bute

Myers, William Henry
Newdigate, Francis Alexander
O'Brien, Patrick (Kilkenny)
Penn, John
Percy, Earl
Powell, Sir Francis Sharp
Pretyman, Ernest George
Pryce-Jones, Lt.-Col. Edward
Purvis, Robert
Quilter, Sir Cuthbert
Rankin, Sir James
Rasch, Major Frederic Carne
Redmond, J. E. (Waterford)
Richardson, Sir Thos. (Hartlep'l
Robinson, Brooke
Rothschild, Hon. Lionel W.
Rutherford, John
Sassoon, Sir Edward Albert
Scoble, Sir Andrew Richard
Seely, Charles Hilton
Seton-Karr, Henry
Sharpe, William Edward T.
Shaw, Charles Edw. (Stafford)
Sidebottom, T. H. (Stalybr.)
Simeon, Sir Barrington
Spencer, Ernest
Stanley, Hon. A. (Ormskirk)
Stanley, E. J. (Somerset)
Stanley, H. M. (Lambeth)
Stanley, Lord (Lancashire)
Stock, James Henry
Stone, Sir Benjamin
Talbot, Lord E. (Chichester)
Thorburn, Walter
Thornton, Percy M.
Tully, Jasper
Usborne, Thomas
Verney, Hon. Richard G.
Vincent, Col. Sir C. E. Howard
Walrond, Rt. Hon. Sir W. H.
Warner, Thomas Courtenay T.
Welby, Lieut.-Col. A. C. E.
Wentworth, Bruce C. V.-
Whiteley, H. (Ashton-und.-L.)
Whitmore, Charles Algernon
Williams, Joseph P.- (Birm.)
Wilson-Todd, W. H. (Yorks.)
Wodehouse, Rt Hn ER (Bath)
Wyndham, George
Wyndham-Quin, Major W. H.
Wyvill, Marmaduke D'Arcy
Young, Com. (Berks, E.)
Young, Samuel (Cavan. East)
TELLERS FOR THE NOES—
 Mr. Tomlinson and Mr.
 Duncombe.

Main Question, as amended, put, and agreed to.

Second Reading put off for three months.

SUCCESSION (SCOTLAND) BILL (SECOND READING).

Order for Second Reading read.

MR. THOMAS SHAW (Hawick Burghs): The main object of this Bill is to abolish the law of primogeniture in Scotland. All reasonable men who are not actuated by prejudice are in favour of the principle of this measure. The law of primogeniture is an anachronism which cannot be defended on any social or political ground, and one that has too long survived on the Statute Book. That being so, I beg to move the second reading of this Bill.

Motion made, and Question proposed—

"That the Bill be now read a second time."

*THE LORD ADVOCATE (Mr. A. G. MURRAY, Buteshire): Whatever may be said about the law of primogeniture, I think the House generally will agree that it has lasted so long that it should not be done to death at a quarter past five on a Wednesday afternoon. This Bill does a lot of other things besides doing away with the law of primogeniture, and will make a considerable change in the position and rights of husbands, wives, and children with respect to heritable property. It goes on with a clause by which it abolishes the possibility of making entails in Scotland. (Hear, hear.) The hon. Gentleman says "Hear, hear," but I doubt very much whether he has considered what the practical result of the provision would be. While it would leave a man power to tie up his property by deed so far as any property is concerned, so far as the Finance Act is concerned, it would place the unfortunate Scotchman in an infinitely worse position than his English brother. I only mentioned this fact to show that legislation at 5.15 on a Wednesday afternoon is not very safe work, and I do not think my hon. friend can believe seriously that we can take this Bill at such an hour. There are also other considerations of another kind. The House will remember what I attempted to suggest so far as Scotland is concerned. Anyone who wishes to leave his heritable property between his children can do so, if he is so minded. There is no popular force of feeling behind this Bill, and what I venture to say is that when you are going to make a general change in the laws of succession which have been in force a long time, and are well understood, it is a matter which requires very grave consideration. And I may also point out that it is a matter which ought to be taken up by the responsible Government of the day, and not put forward by a private Bill. I am not complaining that it has been brought forward by a private Bill, but I do say the House can scarcely be expected to pass such a Bill at this time of the day. I beg to move the Bill be read a second time this day six months.

MR. BANBURY (who was very imperfectly heard) was understood to say : Whether or not the law of primogeniture ought to be abolished is a matter which requires great consideration. It seems to me that this Bill, if passed, is going to

alter a law which has been in existence for centuries. (Cries of "Divide.") Hon. Members cry "Divide." As I said before, this Bill, if passed, is going to alter a law which has been in existence for centuries ; and after a debate of three minutes, when a Member gets up who does not often trouble the House, to express his views upon the subject, hon. Members cry "Divide"—

It being half-past five of the clock, the Debate stood adjourned.

Debate to be resumed on Wednesday, 21st June.

PRIVATE BILL BUSINESS.

GREAT SOUTHERN AND WESTERN, AND WATERFORD, LIMERICK, AND WESTERN RAILWAY COMPANIES AMALGAMATION, AND THE GREAT SOUTHERN AND WESTERN RAILWAY BILLS.

Sir Robert Penrose-Fitzgerald reported from the Select Committee on the Great Southern and Western Railway and other Bills, that the parties promoting the Great Southern and Western, and Waterford, Limerick, and Western Railway Companies Amalgamation, and the Great Southern and Western Railway Bills had stated that the evidence of Mr. Henry Plews, general manager of the Great Northern Railway (Ireland), Amiens Street Terminus, Dublin, was essential to their case ; and it having been proved that his attendance could not be procured without the intervention of the House, he had been instructed to move that the said Henry Plews do attend the said Committee to-morrow, at twelve of the clock.

Ordered, that Mr. Henry Plews do attend the Committee on the Great Southern and Western, and Waterford, Limerick, and Western Railway Companies Amalgamation, and the Great Southern and Western Railway Bills to-morrow, at twelve of the clock.

PUBLIC PETITIONS COMMITTEE.

Sixth report brought up and read ; to lie upon the table, and to be printed.

[Adjourned at twenty-five minutes before Six o'clock.

HOUSE OF LORDS.

Thursday, 8th June 1899.

NEW PEER.

The Lord Monson—Sat first in Parliament after the death of his brother.

PRIVATE BILL BUSINESS.

OWENS COLLEGE, MANCHESTER, BILL [Lords].

Report of Her Majesty's Attorney-General received, and ordered to lie on the Table.

NORTH-WEST LONDON RAILWAY BILL.

Committee to meet on Monday next.

AYR BURGH BILL.

Committee to meet on Thursday next.

BROOKE'S PARK (LONDONDERRY) BILL.

Committed for Tuesday next.

NOTTINGHAM CORPORATION BILL.

The Chairman of Committees informed the House that the opposition to the Bill was withdrawn ; the order made on the 28th of April last discharged ; and Bill committed.

CAMBRIDGE UNIVERSITY AND TOWN GAS BILL [Lords].

Commons Amendments considered, and agreed to.

ST. ALBANS GAS BILL [Lords].

Commons Amendments considered, and agreed to.

HULL, BARNSLEY, AND WEST RIDING JUNCTION RAILWAY AND DOCK BILL. [Lords.]

Commons Amendments considered, and agreed to.

WOLVERHAMPTON TRAMWAYS BILL [Lords].

Report from the Select Committee : That the Committee had not proceeded with the consideration of the Bill, no parties having appeared in opposition

thereto ; read, and ordered to lie on the Table : The orders made on the 13th of March and Tuesday last discharged ; and Bill committed.

MARYPORT HARBOUR BILL [Lords].

Report from the Select Committee : That it is not expedient to proceed further with the Bill ; read, and ordered to lie on the Table.

BUENOS AYRES AND PACIFIC RAILWAY COMPANY BILL [Lords].

Reported with Amendments

LISBURN TOWN COMMISSIONERS BILL.

Reported with Amendments.

LONDON, BRIGHTON, AND SOUTH-COAST RAILWAY (PENSIONS) BILL.

Reported with Amendments.

YORKE ESTATE BILL [Lords].

Reported with Amendments.

WEST MIDDLESEX WATER BILL.

Read 2ª, and committed : The Committee to be proposed by the Committee of Selection.

AIRE AND CALDER NAVIGATION BILL.

Read 2ª, and committed : The Committee to be proposed by the Committee of Selection.

CORK CORPORATION (FINANCE) BILL.

Read 2ª, and committed.

EAST LONDON WATER BILL.

Read 2ª, and committed : The Committee to be proposed by the Committee of Selection.

GREAT WESTERN AND GREAT CENTRAL RAILWAY COMPANIES BILL.

Read 2ª, and committed : The Committee to be proposed by the Committee of Selection.

LONDON, BRIGHTON, AND SOUTH COAST RAILWAY (VARIOUS POWERS) BILL.

Read 2ª, and committed : The Committee to be proposed by the Committee of Selection.

MANCHESTER CORPORATION (GENE-
RAL POWERS) BILL.

Read 2ª, and committed : The Committee to be proposed by the Committee
of Selection.

SOUTH STAFFORDSHIRE STIPEN-
DIARY JUSTICE BILL.

Read 2ª, and committed.

REDDITCH GAS BILL.

Read 2ª, and committed.

MILTON CREEK CONSERVANCY BILL.

Read 2ª, and committed : The Committee to be proposed by the Committee
of Selection.

NORTH PEMBROKESHIRE AND FISH-
GUARD RAILWAY BILL.

Read 2ª, and committed for Monday
next.

UXBRIDGE AND RICKMANSWORTH
RAILWAY BILL.

Read 2ª, and committed.

OWEN'S COLLEGE, MANCHESTER
BILL.

Read 2ª (according to order).

GREAT GRIMSBY STREET TRAMWAYS
BILL [Lords].

Reading 3ª ; Amendments made ; Bill
passed, and sent to the Commons.

LONDON AND NORTH-WESTERN RAIL-
WAY (NEW RAILWAYS) BILL.

Brought from the Commons ; read 1ª ;
and referred to the Examiners.

ARBROATH CORPORATION GAS BILL
[Lords].

Returned from the Commons agreed
to.

KEW BRIDGE BILL [Lords].

Returned from the Commons agreed
to.

BRYNMAWR AND WESTERN VALLEYS
RAILWAY BILL.

Report from the Committee of Selection,
That the following Lords be proposed to
the House to form the Select Committee
for the consideration of the said Bills ;
(viz.)—

M. Bristol,
E. Bathurst,
E. Camperdown (chairman),
L. Seaton,
L. Shute (*V. Barrington*) ;

GAS ORDERS CONFIRMATION (No. 2)
BILL [Lords].

EDUCATION DEPARTMENT PROVI-
SIONAL ORDER CONFIRMATION
(LONDON) BILL [Lords].

STOCKPORT CORPORATION WATER
BILL.

STOCKPORT DISTRICT WATER BILL.

SCUNTHORPE URBAN DISTRICT GAS
AND WATER BILL.

GOOLE URBAN DISTRICT COUNCIL
BILL.

SOUTH-EASTERN AND LONDON, CHAT-
HAM, AND DOVER RAILWAY COM-
PANIES BILL.

SOUTH-EASTERN RAILWAY BILL.

Agreed to ; and the said Lords appointed
accordingly : The Committee to meet on
Tuesday next, at Eleven o'clock ; and all
petitions referred to the Committee, with
leave to the petitioners praying to be
heard by counsel against the Bills to be
heard as desired, as also counsel for the
Bills.

RETURNS, REPORTS, ETC.

EDUCATION DEPARTMENT.

Report to Committee of Council on
Education of the proceedings of the
Charity Commissioners for England and
Wales under the Endowed Schools Acts,
1869-1889, for the year 1898.

TRADE REPORTS (ANNUAL SERIES).

No. 2282. Brazil (Bahia) ;
No. 2283. France (Nice and District) ;
No. 2284. Brazil (Rio de Janeiro) ;
No. 2285. Denmark (Iceland) ;
No. 2286. Turkey (Beirut and the coast
of Syria).

TREATY SERIES, No. 13 (1899).

Accession of Japan to the International
Union for the protection of literary and
artistic works, 15th July, 1899.

NATIONAL PORTRAIT GALLERY.

Forty-second Annual Report of the
Trustees of the National Portrait Gallery
(1899).

SOUTH AFRICAN REPUBLIC.

Further correspondence relating to the
claim of the South African Republic for
damages on account of the Jameson raid.

Presented (by command), and ordered to lie on the Table.

SUPERANNUATION ACT, 1884.

Treasury Minute, dated May 30, 1899, declaring that James Muspratt, auxiliary postman, London, Post Office Department, was appointed without a Civil Service certificate through inadvertence on the part of the head of his department. Laid before the House (pursuant to Act), and ordered to lie on the Table.

PETITION.

AGRICULTURAL RATES ACT, 1896.

Petition for amendment of; of Tithe-owning Clergy of England and Wales, read, and ordered to lie on the Table.

QUESTIONS.

SOUTH AFRICAN REPUBLIC—BLOEM-FONTEIN CONFERENCE.

THE EARL OF CAMPERDOWN: My Lords, seeing the noble Earl, the Under Secretary for the Colonies, in his place, I wish to ask him whether he is in a position to give any information to the House with regard to the negotiations which have recently taken place between Sir Alfred Milner and the President of the Transvaal Republic.

THE UNDER-SECRETARY OF STATE FOR THE COLONIES (THE EARL OF SELBORNE): My Lords, it is unfortunately true that the Conference has broken up without any result, and a new situation has thus been created. President Kruger has rejected the proposals for a settlement offered by Sir Alfred Milner, and the alternative suggested by him was considered by Sir Alfred Milner, and is now considered by Her Majesty's Government, as entirely inadequate. Her Majesty's Government have not yet received the Memorandum which Sir Alfred Milner informs them he has communicated to the Press on the subject of the Conference. Her Majesty's Government understood that this Memorandum would be telegraphed by Reuter verbatim to this country, but owing to some unexplained cause it has not yet arrived. I am therefore unable to say whether the statement

of the Government of the South African Republic, which has been published in the meantime, agrees in all respects with Sir Alfred Milner's account. Her Majesty's Government understand that the discussion turned mainly on the question of the franchise. Sir Alfred Milner was of opinion that the exclusion of the Uitlanders from representation was the root of the difficulties which has arisen, and that it was desirable, if possible, to come to an arrangement on this point before dealing with other questions in dispute between the two Governments. Sir Alfred Milner asked that the franchise should be given to all naturalised aliens who have resided five years in the country, with retrospective effect, and a fair amount of representation be conceded to the new population. President Kruger's proposal was substantially as follows: First, that aliens who were resident in the country before 1890 might naturalise and have the full franchise in two years' time; secondly, that the bulk of the Uitlanders might be naturalised in two years' time and might receive the franchise five years later—that is to say, in seven years from the present time. Between the period of naturalisation and that of receiving the franchise they would have to abandon their present nationality and would have no rights of nationality in the Transvaal. The President also attached to his offer certain conditions as to a pecuniary qualification, and the proof of possession of civil rights in the country from which the alien had come. It is not clear whether the further condition that a majority of two-thirds of the burghers would be required to confirm the possession of the franchise would be insisted upon. The President agreed that three members might be added to the representation of the mining districts, thus giving to them five members out of a total of 31. According to these proposals, no change whatever would take place for two years, and then only in the case of a small majority of the Uitlanders who had resided eleven years in the Transvaal. The whole of these proposals were made subject to an agreement by this country to refer all differences with the Transvaal to the arbitration of a foreign Power. Sir Alfred Milner considered these proposals as altogether inadequate, and further informed the President that Her Majesty's Government would not consent to the intervention of any foreign Power in disputes between themselves and the Government of the South African Republic. The President also asked for the incorporation of Swaziland, but does not appear to have pressed this claim. He also demanded that the question of an indemnity for the Jameson raid should be settled, and was informed by Sir Alfred Milner that the British South Africa Company had agreed, in a despatch which was then on its way, that, while protesting against the amount of the claim sent in as altogether unreasonable, they would nevertheless consent to submit to arbitration the amount of damages for any material injury suffered by the Transvaal in consequence of the Jameson raid. The question of the dynamite monopoly was touched upon, but, in view of the failure to come to an agreement with regard to the franchise, it was reserved for further discussion between the two Governments. I have to add that the despatch in response to the petition of the Uitlanders to the Queen, which was sent to the High Commissioner before the invitation to the Conference was received from the President of the Orange Free State, and which has been held back pending the result of the Conference, will now be communicated to the Government of the South African Republic, and, as soon as they have received it, will be laid on the Table with other papers, including the petition of the Uitlanders to the Queen, and the counter-petition of other Uitlanders to the Government of the South African Republic.

THE SOUDAN CAMPAIGN, 1898.

Moved—

"That Standing Order No. XXI. be considered in order to its being suspended for this day's sitting."—(*The Marquess of Salisbury.*)

On Question, agreed to, and ordered accordingly.

Moved—

"That the consideration of the Queen's Message and the Motion for according the thanks of this House to the forces engaged in the recent operations in the Soudan have precedence of the Orders of the Day."—(*The Marquess of Salisbury.*)

On Question, agreed to, and ordered accordingly.

THE PRIME MINISTER AND SECRETARY OF STATE FOR FOREIGN AFFAIRS (the MARQUESS OF SALISBURY): My Lords, the first motion which I have to submit to you is that Her Majesty's Gracious Message with reference to Lord Kitchener of Khartoum be taken into consideration. It does not appear to me that any arguments will be needed to commend this course to your Lordships. Lord Kitchener has received from Her Majesty the high honour of a seat in this House, in recognition of his great achievements, and the honour that has been paid to him throughout the length and breadth of the land is a sufficient proof that the people of this country entirely associate themselves with the action of Her Majesty in conferring that honour upon him. But, if that honour was to be paid, it is in accordance with precedent, and I think obviously suitable and proper, that some means should be provided for maintaining the dignity thus conferred. It has been done so frequently, and, so far as this House is concerned, so entirely without protest or without difference of opinion, that I think I may, without further preface, move that this House will be ready to concur with the other House of Parliament in making a provision in accordance with the terms of Her Majesty's Gracious Message.

THE EARL OF KIMBERLEY: My Lords, I need scarcely assure your Lordships that I most cordially concur in the motion that has been made by the noble Marquess opposite, and I shall follow his example in not, on this occasion, attempting to pronounce a eulogy on the conduct of Lord Kitchener, because we have all of us, I think, repeatedly expressed our opinion very strongly on the subject, and I do not suppose that upon the main question of the reward which is proposed to be conferred on Lord Kitchener there will be any difference of opinion. But, while I say that, I feel myself compelled to make an allusion to one discordant note, and that is the feeling which has been excited by the manner in which the body of the Mahdi was disposed of. For my part I wish to say, and I am sure I shall have the sympathy of everyone here present, that I have no feeling whatsoever specially for the Mahdi. On the contrary, I conceive as wholly pernicious his appearance as a false prophet; and if

I make any remarks on this subject, it is only upon the general feeling which I believe to be shared by most people, if not by all, that it is necessary to be extremely careful in dealing with any question which affects the dead. We all, I think, feel that with the dead we can have no war; but in the present circumstances it appears to have been thought—and I am not at all inclined to contest the opinion of those who were on the spot, and were best able to form an opinion—that it was absolutely necessary to remove the tomb where the Mahdi had been interred, to prevent the possibility of its becoming afterwards a focus of discontent and a rallying point for any who might still feel any sympathy with the Mahdi and his disciples. It is not upon that ground that I make the observation which I feel compelled to make on this occasion. But I think that, after making every allowance for the reasons to which I have alluded, it is a matter for some regret that the way in which the remains of the Mahdi were disposed of was not entirely consonant with our feelings with regard to the disposal of the dead. It is a subject which is very distasteful to me to allude to, and I am not at all disposed to pursue it on this occasion. Neither do I wish to be supposed to be strongly condemning the proceedings which were sanctioned by the distinguished officer whose services we all recognise. But I felt it to be my duty, my painful duty, to make this simple observation; and, after saying that, I repeat that, notwithstanding the feelings which I entertain, in common with a good many other people, on this particular subject, I do most cordially and most heartily concur in any honour we can bestow on Lord Kitchener on this occasion. I therefore willingly support the motion of the noble Marquess.

THE MARQUESS OF SALISBURY: My Lords, perhaps it would be proper that I should make one or two remarks in reference to the observations which have fallen from the noble Earl, and which were distinguished by great moderation and good taste. So far as Lord Kitchener was responsible for what was done, I am unable to agree with the noble Earl. I believe that certain steps had to be taken with a view to the possibility of the revival of a fanatical feeling in the country. There is reason to believe that what Lord Kitchener ordered to be done was not quite rightly interpreted by those who carried it out, and he was at a distance when it was carried out. Into that question I need not enter, but I would entreat the House to remember that these questions, however deeply we feel upon them, are not questions of ethics; they are not even questions of policy; they are questions of taste, and taste varies in different countries at different times. There have been occasions even in this country when bodies have been dug up, to show opinions entertained at the time, and in a neighbouring country it has been still more abundantly done. If Lord Kitchener, when he was thinking, as he was bound to think, of the opinions of the vast populations that surrounded him, forgot for the moment the opinions that might prevail in London, we cannot blame him. I believe he did what he thought was necessary on the occasion for destroying this baneful superstition, and in that object at least we all of us must heartily sympathise.

Her Majesty's most gracious Message of Friday last considered (according to order): Then an humble Address of thanks and concurrence ordered *nemine dissentiente* to be presented to Her Majesty thereupon: The said Address to be presented to Her Majesty by the Lords with White Staves.

THE MARQUESS OF SALISBURY: My Lords, I now have to propose to you a motion which I believe is in accordance with strict precedent on similar occasions, and which I am sure has never been more heartily adopted than it will be on the present occasion. If I may be permitted, I will read the motion to the House. Its terms are as follow:

"That the thanks of this House be given to Major-General Lord Kitchener of Khartoum, G.C.B., K.C.M.G., for the distinguished skill and ability with which he planned and conducted the Campaign on the Nile of 1896-97-98, which culminated in the Battle of Omdurman, the capture of Khartoum, and the overthrow of the power of the Khalifa;

That the thanks of this House be given to—

Major-General Sir A. Hunter, K.C.B., D.S.O.;

Major-General Sir H. M. L. Rundle, K.C.B., C.M.G., D.S.O., R.A.;

Major-General Sir W. F. Gatacre, K.C.B., D.S.O.;

Major-General the Hon. N. G. Lyttelton, C.B. ;

Major - General A. G. Wauchope, C.B., C.M.G. ;

Major and Brevet Colonel Sir F. R. Wingate, K.C.M.G., C.B., D.S.O., R.A. ;

Lieutenant-Colonel and Brevet Colonel C. J. Long, R.A. ;

Major and Brevet Colonel J. G. Maxwell, D.S.O. ;

Major and Brevet Colonel H. A. Macdonald, D.S.O. ;

Lieutenant-Colonel D. F. Lewis, C.B. ;

Major and Brevet Lieutenant-Colonel J. Collinson, C.B. ;

Commander C. R. Keppel, C.B., D.S.O., R.N. ;

and to the other Officers and Warrant Officers of the Navy, the British and the Egyptian Army, and the Royal Marines, for the energy and gallantry with which they executed the services which they were called upon to perform ;

That this House doth acknowledge and highly approve the gallantry, discipline, and good conduct displayed by the Petty Officers, Non-commissioned Officers, and Men of the Navy, the British and the Egyptian Army, and Royal Marines during the campaign ;

That the thanks of this House be given to Lieutenant-General Sir Francis Grenfell, G.C.B., G.C.M.G., for the support and assistance which he afforded to the forces employed in the operations in the Soudan ;

That this House doth acknowledge, with admiration, the distinguished valour, devotion, and conduct of those other Officers and Men who have perished during the campaign in the Soudan in the service of their country, and feels deep sympathy with their relatives and friends."

My Lords, some fourteen years ago, about this time of the year, standing in this place, I had to move a similar vote of thanks to General Viscount Wolseley and the officers and men who had served with him in the Egyptian campaign. But the circumstances then were very different. It was necessary to point out and to dwell upon the fact that great merit and devotion had been shown by the British officers and men in carrying out the duties which were assigned to them, though the result of their efforts was not success. It was no blame of theirs that the result was not success ; it was a combination of circumstances which it is now unnecessary to unravel. But we felt that the want of success then was no detraction to the great merits they had shown, or to the gratitude which their services would demand and receive from the country. Now we have a different task to perform. We have, indeed, to

bring before you equal merit, equal valour, equal skill and tenacity, but the whole has been crowned with a splendid success. Yet, let us not forget that, to the exertions of Lord Wolseley, and those who served under him in two Egyptian campaigns, it is due that the door was opened to the subsequent operations of which Lord Kitchener was the head, and that the brilliant campaigns—brilliant, though one of them was unsuccessful—with which Lord Wolseley was associated prepared the way for Lord Kitchener, and may claim a part of the lustre which has been shed upon his head. As the noble Earl has justly said, this is a worn-out subject. We have all listened to, and taken part in repeating, the praises which are due to the Sirdar, and, as those praises have been echoed and thoroughly accepted by his countrymen, there is now little more to be said. He will remain a striking figure, not only adorned by the valour and patriotism which all successful generals can show, but with the most extraordinary combination of calculation, of strategy, of statesmanship, which it has ever fallen to any general in those circumstances to display. His means were limited. The grotesque financial arrangements under which the Egyptian Exchequer lives prevented him from transgressing a very modest limit in the expenditure he was authorised to incur. He had all the difficulties to a certain extent—the unknown and untried difficulties—attaching to a campaign whose objective was a city which no white army had ever visited before, and he was fighting with an enemy vastly superior in numbers to his own forces, animated by a fanaticism which gives more powerful impulse for warlike qualities than probably any other, however high the motive, by which soldiers can be actuated. He had before him natural difficulties of a character which made it uncertain how far it would be within his means to overcome them, and with those difficulties he succeeded in winning a brilliant though not bloodless battle, but a battle which shattered in one moment the evil power that for so many years had brooded over those districts of Africa. It was a very wonderful achievement ; but, as I say, he was guided by the knowledge which others who had gone before him had gained, and he was not limited in point of time, as we know was the case with the last expedition. He took exactly the time that was necessary for his work, he made precisely the preparations which that work required, he expended upon it exactly the military strength which it demanded, and his victory came out with absolute accuracy, like the answer to a scientific calculation. I am glad that in making this motion I am not to speak of Lord Kitchener's merits alone. No doubt they were enormous, transcendent, and they have been fully recognised by his Sovereign and by his countrymen; but there is in all warlike history too much tendency to attach the whole merit of every campaign entirely to the leader by whom it was won. In this case he had singular assistance. The British troops, upon whose strength and steadfastness some unwise persons had cast doubt, showed that never in their history were they so stout and vigorous, even in the presence of the most formidable foe. He was supported to an unprecedented extent by the resources of science. The gunboats, which he himself largely designed, and which were conducted with great gallantry and skill, contributed no small amount to the victory; and the construction of the railway, in the circumstances under which it was undertaken, was a marvellous effort of individual energy and skill on the part of the well-known engineer who undertook it, and also shows to what a lofty point the material and scientific progress of English industry has reached. These were all very remarkable circumstances. Perhaps I am inclined to attach to Lieutenant Girouard's work a very conspicuous position among these great achievements; but to my mind that which was most wonderful of all was the brilliant and unfailing conduct of the Egyptian troops. I say this because I can remember the debates we used to have many years ago about the impossibility of inducing them to undertake the slightest amount of military exertion or even face the smallest warlike risk. It is one of the worst circumstances we have to lament in connection with these wars. I do not see my noble friend Lord Northbrook in his place, but I remember he used a phrase at which we rather laughed at the time, but which was a very prudent remark. He told us that the Egyptian troops were magnificent soldiers if only they would stand. That very lamentable defect ruined all their other qualities. When the enemy came

upon them they did not even resist. They threw away their weapons and allowed themselves to be slaughtered without resistance. It was a fearful condition of things, but the wonderful thing is that proper training, proper government, fair consideration, and great military skill, exercised by British officers, have made those men who were mere sheep equal to any native troops in the world; they have given them a strength of discipline, an absolute trust in their officers, which has made their conduct on the field of battle splendid to behold. Therefore I am glad that this vote of thanks includes General Grenfell, because it is very largely to his exertions and his guidance that this great reform in the character of the Egyptian soldiers is due. We ought not, while we exult in the victory achieved, to forget by how much patient labour and how much skilful training he brought the Egyptian troops up to the point where they could make to us the return—the splendid return—they have made. I will not, my Lords, trouble you further, but I will only just notice these two things. This campaign —I do not want to touch any question of policy — will, I believe, by its result largely increase British fame and influence all over the world, and largely strengthen the outworks of our Empire. This result has been gained by the exercise, in a very unusual and conspicuous degree, of two of the qualities by which we believe our race is adorned, and which largely contributed to the success and power we have achieved. The first is the great industrial progress, the enormous power over the forces of nature, which we have used for commercial purposes and improved year by year, but which now, to an extent never done before, we have shown to have been one of the most potent weapons that a skilful general can wield. The other is that it has brought out that quality which is the real secret of the domination of this country over such vast millions of uncultivated people. Our officers have the power—not merely one or two men, but almost all our officers either in India or in Egypt—to an extent which, I think, has never yet been given to any race in the world, of inducing men of a lower race to attach themselves absolutely to their officers who govern them, to repose in them the most complete confidence and trust, to obey them without question, and to follow them into any danger. It is this splendid influence of often a handful of officers over vast masses of men of other races, which has enabled us to rear up that vast empire, so far out of proportion to the numerical strength which we can bring to support it, but which we have been able to make and to defend by the strength of those vast multitudes of other races whom our officers have had this singular and marvellous power of governing, training, and attaching. I do not think it has ever been shown in a more distinguished form than in the force, cohesion, and excellence they have given to the Egyptian troops ; but they have only produced qualities which they have always shown, and which they show no signs of losing—qualities which have erected, and which, I trust, will maintain for many generations yet to come, the power and influence of the Empire of the Queen.

THE EARL OF KIMBERLEY : My Lords, the noble Marquess, in the extremely interesting speech which we have just listened to, has left me very little to say. I concur with all that he has said, but I am most struck with the latter part of his speech. I feel, as he does, that what we have most reason to be proud of is the manner in which we have reorganised, not only the Government, but I might almost say the people of Egypt. It seems to me that this is a subject which we do well to dwell upon, because the strength and the safety of our Empire—I mean outside this country—over the vast numbers of, as we regard them, less civilised peoples, rests entirely, I may say, upon the moral qualities possessed by those who lead them. I may perhaps be allowed to wander slightly from the immediate subject of our discussion when I mention the name of Lord Cromer. It is only due to Lord Cromer—though on an occasion like this he could not, of course, be included in the Vote which we are about to pass—to say that it has been by his statesmanlike conduct, his indefatigable industry, his calm, quiet, patient perseverance, that the organisation of Egypt as we now see it has been attained. Without that I do not think even the abilities of Lord Kitchener could have produced the results which we are celebrating to-day. The striking conclusion at which we have been able to arrive is

The Marquess of Salisbury.

that by means of these admirable young officers—for many of them are very young officers—we are able to make use of large populations which, perhaps, without our leading would never have attained to that warlike demeanour which the noble Marquess has so justly commended in the Egyptians. I am tempted to repeat a very small but striking anecdote told to me not long ago which referred to one of our great fights in India during the time of the Mutiny. An old officer told me the story. During a very hot engagement a young English officer was killed, and the commanding officer remarked to a Sikh subardar—a non-commissioned officer of high rank—how deeply he regretted the loss of this officer, and added : " But even that loss we can well sustain when we have men like you who we know can be trusted in all circumstances." " Yes," was the reply, " that may be ; we can fight, and fight well, but we want your young men to lead us." That has been the secret of our success. In celebrating what Lord Kitchener has achieved, the noble Marquess has justly dwelt upon the extraordinary skill with which he made all the preparations which ended in his brilliant achievement ; and it seems to me that that is perhaps the most remarkable part of the whole achievement. I believe, myself, that those who dwell upon the history of great military operations will find in the past history of the world that the greatest and most successful commanders have been those who have known best the secret of long, careful, and complete preparation before they ventured on the great campaigns which they succeeded in. That is the example which Lord Kitchener has shown to us, and it is for that he well deserves the special honour which we bestow upon him to-night. But, as the noble Marquess says, it is not the leader only ; and it is remarkable to reflect that the power and influence of our officers should have so transformed the Egyptian troops that they were worthy to stand by the side of British soldiers. One cannot help making this reflection. I suppose that all of us in the abstract would desire to avoid war ; we all of us desire peace ; but there are circumstances in which I believe that war may even elevate a nation ; and in this present instance I believe it has been a matter of great good fortune to the Egyptian people that the occasion has arisen where they have been able to show that they are capable of standing firmly before the enemy, because, whatever we may say, the greatness of nations will always rest on their being ready and willing to face great dangers when they are threatened; and the fact that the Egyptians have shown these qualities against their enemies must give us a much higher opinion of them, and must tend not only to raise their own opinion of themselves, but to give them a confidence which probably nothing else would ever impart to them. My Lords, I really should be guilty of wasting your time if I were to attempt to repeat what the noble Marquess has so well said. All I will add is this: I do not believe that there is a more pleasing and a more honourable task for Parliament, representing the nation, to perform, than that it should meet to offer a grateful tribute of admiration to those of our countrymen who in distant lands face great dangers and achieve great successes for the Empire to which we belong.

Resolved, *nemine dissentiente*, That the thanks of this House be given to Major-General Lord Kitchener of Khartoum, G.C.B., K.C.M.G., for the distinguished skill and ability with which he planned and conducted the campaign on the Nile of 1896-97-98, which culminated in the battle of Omdurman, the capture of Khartoum, and the overthrow of the power of the Khalifa.

That the thanks of this House be given to—

> Major-General Sir A. Hunter, K.C.B., D.S.O. ;
>
> Major-General Sir H. M. L. Rundle, K.C.B., C.M.G., D.S.O., R.A. ;
>
> Major-General Sir W. F. Gatacre, K.C.B., D.S.O. ;
>
> Major-General the Hon. N. G. Lyttelton, C.B. ;
>
> Major-General A. G. Wauchope, C.B., C.M.G. ;
>
> Major and Brevet Colonel Sir F. R. Wingate, K.C.M.G., C.B., D.S.O., R.A. ;
>
> Lieutenant - Colonel and Brevet Colonel C. J. Long, R.A. ;
>
> Major and Brevet Colonel J. G. Maxwell, D.S.O. ;

> Major and Brevet Colonel H. A. Macdonald, D.S.O. ;
>
> Lieutenant-Colonel D. F. Lewis, C.B.;
>
> Major and Brevet Lieutenant-Colonel J. Collinson, C.B. ;
>
> Commander C. R. Keppel, C.B., D.S.O., R.N. ;

and to the other Officers and Warrant Officers of the Navy, the British and the Egyptian Army, and the Royal Marines, for the energy and gallantry with which they executed the services which they were called upon to perform ;

That this House doth acknowledge and highly approve the gallantry, discipline, and good conduct displayed by the Petty Officers, Non-commissioned Officers, and Men of the Navy, the British and the Egyptian Army, and Royal Marines during the campaign ;

That the thanks of this House be given to Lieutenant-General Sir Francis Grenfell, G.C.B., G.C.M.G., for the support and assistance which he afforded to the forces employed in the operations in the Soudan ;

That this House doth acknowledge, with admiration, the distinguished valour, devotion, and conduct of those other Officers and Men who have perished during the campaign in the Soudan in the service of their country, and feels deep sympathy with their relatives and friends ;

Ordered that the Lord Chancellor do communicate the said resolutions to General Lord Kitchener of Khartoum and to Lieutenant-General Sir Francis Grenfell, and that General Lord Kitchener of Khartoum be requested by the Lord Chancellor to communicate the same to the several other officers referred to therein.

SEA FISHERIES BILL [Lords].

SECOND READING.

Order of the Day for the Second Reading read.

LORD HENEAGE : My Lords, I hope I shall not be thought discourteous to your Lordships if in a very few words I ask you to give a Second Reading to this Bill, because when I moved its Second Reading last year I went very thoroughly into the whole history of the Bill. Your Lordships have already passed this Bill through all its stages in four successive sessions. The Bill is the outcome of the

Report of the Select Committee of the House of Commons, which was moved for by the late Government in 1893, to take into consideration resolutions which have been come to by the Sea Fisheries Association and by a number of international conferences held during the previous ten years. In 1896 and 1897 the Board of Trade passed the Bill through all its stages in this House, and it was sent down to the House of Commons, but on each occasion failed to get through that House. Last year I had the honour of introducing the Bill, and having, as I thought, ascertained that the Government were not going to bring in a Bill during the present session, I have put it down again, and I now ask your Lordships to give it a Second Reading. I am anxious that the Bill should, if possible, pass this session. It is a Bill which the present President of the Board of Trade stated three years ago it would be a disgrace to any Government not to do their best to pass, and I trust that in the present session I shall not only be able to get the Bill through your Lordships' House, but that the Government will give us some assistance in passing it into law in another place.

Moved, that the Bill now be read 2ª."

THE SECRETARY FOR SCOTLAND (Lord BALFOUR OF BURLEIGH): My Lords, in the unavoidable absence of the noble Earl the Parliamentary Secretary to the Board of Trade (the Earl of Dudley), I have been asked to state the view which Her Majesty's Government hold as to the proper procedure in regard to this Bill. The noble Lord has correctly stated that the House has passed a similar Bill upon other occasions. The Board of Trade are unable to regard the whole of the provisions of this Bill with satisfaction, and more particularly they think that some of the provisions of the second clause go in advance of what is necessary at the present time. I do not rise to oppose the Second Reading of the Bill, but to inform the House that the Government have prepared a measure of their own, which, I believe, is being introduced into the other House of Parliament at the present time, dealing with this subject; and I would venture to suggest to the noble Lord that if we pass the Second Reading of this Bill to-day he should not ask the House to make any further pro-

Lord Heneage.

gress with the measure until, at any rate, we see what chance the Bill introduced by the Government has of passing the other House of Parliament. If that Bill should pass the other House, as we have every reason to hope it will, when it comes here it will be a fair matter for consideration on the part of the noble Lord, and of the House generally, which of the two Bills will be the better to pass. I venture to suggest, under the circumstances, that if to-night we give this Bill a Second Reading, the noble Lord should come under the obligation not, in the meantime, at any rate, to proceed further with the measure in this House.

LORD HENEAGE: My Lords, I perfectly accept what has been said by the noble Lord opposite. I had no knowledge of the intention of the Government to bring in a Bill dealing with this subject. I am perfectly prepared to withdraw my Bill at any time after it has secured a Second Reading, if the Bill which the Government are about to introduce meets the case.

On Question, agreed to.

Bill read 2ª (according to order), and committed to a Committee of the whole House on Thursday, the 22nd instant.

REFORMATORY SCHOOLS AMEND-
MENT BILL [Lords].
[SECOND READING.]

Order of the Day for the Second Reading read.

*LORD LEIGH: My Lords, the Bill which I am now asking your Lordships to read a second time is a very simple one. Its object is to amend the Act which I had the honour of introducing into this House in 1893. Your Lordships are fully aware that until 1893 it was obligatory for magistrates to send all children committed to a reformatory in the first instance to the gaol. It was owing to the fact that I considered this practice objectionable in the highest degree that I introduced a Bill in 1893 giving the magistrates the power of using their discretion in the matter; but I regret that the Bill—it is now an Act of Parliament—did not go far enough. I desire that it should be made compulsory, and not permissive, for magistrates to send all children direct to the school. Although the

Act of 1893 is permissive, it has effected a great deal of good, and I believe it has had the result of inducing many magistrates to send boys direct to the reformatory, instead of, as formerly, allowing them to reach the reformatory through a prison. I hold in my hand a return which I have received from the Inspector of Reformatories, which says that in England, during the last year, out of the 1,170 boys and girls who were committed to prison, no fewer than 926 were sent to school direct, showing, I think, that the feeling of the magistrates generally is tending towards doing what I want to see done. In Scotland, out of 242 committals, no fewer than 227 were sent direct to school. If you put these two together you will find that there were no fewer than 1,153 children out of 1,412 sent direct to the reformatories. But what has become of the 259 children who were sent to prison? In my opinion it is most objectionable that there should be two forms of committal. Under the present system you may have boys in the same reformatory who were first sent to prison, but who were no worse than the other boys who were sent direct to the school; and the fact of sending the lads to prison is calculated to create a very bad feeling among them. My noble and learned friend the Chancellor of the Duchy of Lancaster, whom I am glad to see in his place to-day, told me recently of a case, which I fear is not an uncommon one, of a little boy of eleven years of age who had been sent to a reformatory for fourteen days for merely throwing stones. I should like to ask how many of your Lordships in your school days refrained from throwing stones. For myself, I confess that I have thrown many, but I did not suffer imprisonment for it. I feel very strongly on this point, and I think it is remarkable that this is the only country in Europe which compels children to qualify for the reformatory through a gaol. I hope I may live to see the day, and that it will not be far distant, when no boy under fifteen or sixteen years of age will be sent to prison, except under very peculiar circumstances. I have often spoken to the superintendent of the reformatory schools in my own county, and he has told me that the boys committed to gaol before going to the reformatory have always proved the hardest to reform. I sincerely believe, if it were made compulsory to send children direct to reformatories,

that the percentage of reformations, which at this moment is about 90 per cent., would be considerably larger and that there would scarcely be a boy who, on his discharge from a reformatory, would not be able to earn his livelihood. As an old visiting magistrate of many years' standing, and chairman of a reformatory in my own county, I heartily thank the Government for having improved the circumstances under which boys are admitted into gaols at the present time, and for adopting classification. But they have not done enough. They must repeal the old Act, and not allow any boy to be sent to gaols except, as I have said, under very peculiar circumstances. It has been asked, "What harm does it do to send boys to gaol first?" I contend that it does a great deal of harm. The boys so sent retain the gaol mark, which tends to debar them from securing that employment which otherwise they might obtain. Under the circumstances, I hope your Lordships will give the Bill a Second Reading.

Moved, "That the Bill be now read 2ª."

LORD JAMES OF HEREFORD: My Lords, I am desired, on behalf of the Home Office, to say that the Government cordially supports the proposal of my noble friend. It is due to the noble Lord to say that he has taken an active part and shown a practical interest in this question. In 1893 he introduced a Bill similar to the one he is now submitting, but at that time it was thought that it would be better to allow the power of sending direct to the reformatory to be at the discretion of the magistrates. Since that time a Departmental Committee has met and recommended the very measure which the noble Lord now submits to you. Further than that, in a Bill to be introduced on the part of the Government in a few days, it is proposed to insert a provision to prevent children being sent to gaol except under peculiar circumstances. The Bill of the Government will be closely identical with that of my noble friend, but I think the honour ought to remain with him of having introduced this beneficial reform, and, so far as they can do so, the Government will render him every assistance in carrying the Bill.

*LORD NORTON : My Lords, I thoroughly agree with the principle of this Bill—namely, that children convicted of crime should be punished otherwise than in common prisons. At the same time, children convicted more than once must not be allowed to go unpunished, and in some cases they may have to be dealt with in the same way as adult prisoners. The Act of 1893, which this Bill proposes to amend, provides that in lieu of punishment children convicted of crime a second time may be merely sent to reformatory schools. The sooner the idea of treating these schools as a means of punishment is got rid of the better. To treat schools as prisons is one of the greatest blunders we could possibly fall into. A penal school, if such a thing were possible, would be a monstrosity of the greatest cruelty and mischief, and I can conceive of nothing that would have a worse effect than treating a child differently to an adult by continuing his punishment over a number of years, and stamping him as a criminal for the whole of his childhood. A child who commits a crime should be adequately punished, but when, as an after treatment, he is sent to school he should not be branded as a criminal. Reformatories are considered penal institutions because they are under the Home Office, but they are as agreeable schools as any in the country. There is practically no difference between reformatory schools and industrial schools, and they are treated indiscriminately by magistrates. The reformatory school, even if it were intended as such, cannot be made penal treatment, and I hope that treating these schools as penal institutions will be avoided altogether when we deal next year with the detail of the Education Department. I shall endeavour, when this matter comes before the House, and I hope I shall be successful, to get these schools, both reformatory and industrial, transferred from the Home Office to the Education Department, to which they properly belong. I speak on this matter with some authority. I introduced the first Acts, both with regard to reformatory schools and industrial schools, and I have devoted considerable attention to their administration for half a century. When I first suggested to Parliament that it was a mistake to treat these schools as penal institutions, I was told that everyone was against me, but the various Royal Commissions of inquiry who have discussed the subject have gradually come round to my view on the

Lord Norton.

subject. Lord Aberdare's Commission proposed bringing reformatories partially under the Education Office. The last Commission came entirely to my opinion, and the Chairman—Sir Godfrey Lushington—signed a special Report, opposed to these schools being treated in any sense as penal institutions, and recommending that they should be part of the education system. In all these schools technical is given in addition to intellectual instruction, and in this respect they are in advance of other national schools throughout the country. Therefore, if any change is to be made, it should be to make other publicly aided schools more like them, and to place them all equally under the Department to which they ought to belong. Children who have committed crimes cannot, however, be relieved of punishment by these schools being put on a proper footing and cleared altogether of their penal character. They must be adequately punished, and then sent either to a reformatory or to their homes. I recollect very well that some years ago Sir William Harcourt, who was then Home Secretary, came to see my own reformatory in the neighbourhood of Birmingham, and he asked: "Have none of these children decent homes?" Hearing that some had received a reply in the affirmative, he expressed his surprise that they were not, after punishment, sent home, when they would have to attend National schools; and I agree with the right hon. Gentleman that only those children should be sent to a reformatory who have not decent homes to which to go. I wish both the Act which this Bill is intended to amend, and the Bill itself, were differently worded in order that their object should be made quite clear. It is certainly an important thing to prevent children convicted of crime being punished in common prisons. That is the true object of this Bill, but as drafted it will not achieve that result. The only enacting clause in the Bill—and in my opinion there is nothing more dangerous than one-clause Bills—reads as follows:

"The Reformatory Schools Act, 1893, shall be read and have effect as if the following proviso were added at the end of Section 1, that is to say: 'Provided that where the offender is ordered to be sent to a certified reformatory school he shall not in addition be sentenced to penal servitude or imprisonment.'"

As a matter of fact, the offender is never sent to a reformatory school, and in addition, but as a preliminary, sentenced to imprisonment ; so that the Bill, as it stands, proposes to provide against a thing that is never done. The Bill does not carry out the important object it has in view ; which, however, magistrates may be hoped to make it do.

On Question, agreed to.

Bill read a second time (according to order), and committed to a Committee of the whole House on Monday next.

PREVENTION OF CORRUPTION BILL [Lords].

House in Committee (according to order): Bill reported without amendment : Standing Committee negatived : Amendments made : Bill re-committed to a Committee of the whole House ; and to be printed as amended. (No. 108.)

FARNLEY TYAS MARRIAGES BILL [Lords].

House in Committee (according to order): Bill reported without amendment : Standing Committee negatived ; and Bill to be read 3ª To-morrow.

QUESTION.

THE APPOINTMENT OF AN ADDITIONAL JUDGE.

LORD RUSSELL OF KILLOWEN : My Lords, I beg to ask the noble and learned Earl the Lord Chancellor whether Her Majesty's Government have considered and are prepared to give effect to the urgent representations made to the Lord Chancellor, by (amongst others) the Incorporated Law Society and the Council of the Bar of England, as to the necessity for the appointment of additional Judges. I hope the noble and learned Earl will find it convenient to answer the Question.

THE LORD CHANCELLOR : My Lords, my answer to the first part of the Question is that Her Majesty's Government have considered the Question, and, under the circumstances, they have considered it right to agree to the appointment of an additional Judge to be added to the Equity Division.

House adjourned at twenty minutes before Six o'clock, till To-morrow, a quarter past Four o'clock.

HOUSE OF COMMONS.

Thursday, 8th June 1899.

MESSAGE FROM THE LORDS.

They have agreed to :—

Pilotage Provisional Order Bill, without Amendment.

Ilford Gas Bill, with Amendments.

That they have passed a Bill, intituled "An Act to amend the Congested Districts (Scotland) Act, 1897." [Congested Districts (Scotland) Act Amendment Bill [Lords].

Also, a Bill, intituled, "An Act to confirm a Provisional Order made by the Education Department under the Elementary Education Acts, 1870 to 1893, to enable the School Board for Liverpool to put in force the Lands Clauses Acts." [Education Department Provisional Order Confirmation (Liverpool) Bill [Lords].

Also, a Bill, intituled, "An Act to confer further powers on the Lowestoft Water and Gas Company in connection with their water undertaking ; and for other purposes." [Lowestoft Water and Gas Bill [Lords].

Also, a Bill, intituled, "An Act for enabling the North Eastern Railway Company and the Hull, Barnsley and West Riding Junction Railway and Dock Company to make a dock and railways at Hull ; and for other purposes." [North Eastern and Hull and Barnsley Railways (Joint Dock) Bill [Lords].

And, also, a Bill, intituled, "An Act to confer additional powers upon the North Eastern Railway Company for the construction of new railways and other works and the acquisition of additional lands ; and for transferring to the company the North Holderness Light Railway Company ; and for other purposes." [North Eastern Railway Bill [Lords].

Jones Divorce Bill [Lords] — That they do communicate Minutes of Evidence and Proceedings taken upon the Second Reading of Jones' Divorce Bill, as desired by this House, with a request that the same may be returned.

PRIVATE BILL BUSINESS.

———

PRIVATE BILLS [Lords].

Standing Orders not previously inquired into complied with.

MR. SPEAKER laid upon the Table Report from one of the Examiners of Petitions for Private Bills, that, in the case of the following Bill, originating in the Lords, and referred on the first reading thereof, the Standing Orders not previously inquired into, and which are applicable thereto, have been complied with, viz.:—

TOTLAND WATER BILL [Lords].

Ordered, That the Bill be read a second time.

ALL SAINTS' CHURCH (CARDIFF) BILL [Lords].

MR. D. A. THOMAS (Merthyr-Tydvil): It is only necessary to detain the House a very short time in order to explain the Motion which appears on the Paper in my name. The Bill to which my Motion refers is called the "All Saints' Church (Cardiff) Bill," and it has passed the House of Lords. It has not yet been read a second time in this House, and, in fact, I take the opportunit of bringing up my Motion before they Bill comes on for second reading. My contention is that the Standing Orders of the House have not been complied with in this case. Hon. Members know that the Standing Orders provide in the case of Private Bills that notice should be given in October or November setting forth the objects of the Bill to be brought in, with a short explanation at the head of the notice describing the main objects of the Bill. I do not want to go into the merits of the Bill, but I may say that the objects of the Bill are to sell the present parish church called All Saints, and to devote the funds partly to the building of a new church and partly towards the present church of Dewi Sant, and to substitute as parish church for the church about to be sold the church about to be built. In the notices published in the *Gazette* and in the local newspapers in November last, it was stated at the head that it was proposed that the church called the New Church of Dewi Sant, the Welsh Church of the parish of All Saints' should be constituted the parish church in place of the church it is proposed to sell. Now, the Bill itself provides for something very different indeed. Had it not been for what I regard as the very material changes between the objects as set forth in the notices and the objects provided for in the Bill, I suppose there would have been very little opposition to the Bill. The Bill itself provides, not that the church of Dewi Sant should be substituted as the parish church, but that the new church proposed to be built should be the parish church. Clause 10 provides that "The new church (to be built) should, on and after its consecration, for all purposes, take the place of and be in substitution for, the old church." I contend that the notices given in November last were distinctly misleading, and that a complete change of policy occurred between the time of giving the notices and the introduction of the Bill. The Bill in due course came before the Examiners, and they reported that the Standing Orders were compiled with; and I understand that there is no appeal against the decision of the Examiners. The only way to get out of the difficulty, it appears to me, is to refer the Bill back to them. I do not believe that this would cause any delay, because they will be able to report in a few days, and the Bill has not yet been put down for a second reading in this House. I do not wish to attach the smallest suspicion of blame to the Examiners. If I had been one of them I would have committed exactly the same mistake. Nor do I want to ascribe any blame to the Parliamentary agents of the promoters of the Bill, who are a firm of very high standing. But I cannot free myself from suspicion of doubt as to the action of the promoters. A friend of mind told me that in January he heard rumours that a change of policy had occurred, but, on inquiring, he was assured that the church of Dewi Sant was to be made the parish church. I say deliberately that the notices given of this Bill were distinctly misleading, and have, in fact, misled the people of Cardiff.

Motion made and Question proposed—

"That it be an Instruction to the Examiners of Petitions for Private Bills, to whom the Bill is referred, that they do inquire and report as to whether Standing Order No. 3 (notices by advertisement) has or has not been complied with."—(*Mr. D. A. Thomas.*)

*MR. J. W. LOWTHER (Cumberland, Penrith): The view taken by the hon. Member for Merthyr Tydvil in this case has my warmest sympathy, although I am afraid I cannot recommend the House to accept the motion which he has just made. The case, in a few words, is simply this: that under the notices which were given of this Bill it was proposed, amongst other things, to "constitute the new church dedicated to Dewi Sant, situate in Howard Gardens, in the said parish of All Saints', the Parish Church of the Parish and District Chapelry of All Saints' in substitution for the existing Church of All Saints, and to make all such provisions and confer all such powers as may be necessary for accomplishing that object." In the short title of the notice which was given, this phrase occurs: "Constitution of the New Church of Dewi Sant as Parish Church." I think that that is a wholly misleading notice, and I can quite understand that the inhabitants of Cardiff, seeing that notice of the Bill, thought that the Welsh church of Dewi Sant was to be constituted the parish church; that that fell in with their views, and that they, therefore, would not take further objection. They did not do what perhaps they ought to have done—send for a copy of the Bill, or at any rate inspect the Bill at the Private Bill Office of the House of Commons. It is only recently that they have discovered the omission in the Bill itself of provisions to carry out what was in the notice. It seems to me, as I have said, that the notice was very misleading, and that the public were led to expect that certain things would appear in the Bill. But when the Bill came to this House not only does this provision not occur, but the very opposite occurs—that the new church to be built is to be the parish church of the parish of All Saints'. So much on the merits of the case. Then comes the question of procedure. Now, although I have not a very strong feeling on the matter, I think it would not be a very wise thing to send the Bill back to the Examiners. It must be a matter of common knowledge that very often the notices go considerably beyond what is afterwards contained in the Bill. You cannot, under certain circumstances, expect that the Bill shall contain everything that is in the notice. There are numerous cases in which notices drawn in November must contain proposals which, by the time the Bill reaches this House, it is obvious cannot be carried out. And, therefore, we cannot say that because a Bill does not carry out every particular in the notice there has been a non-compliance with the Standing Orders. If the Bill went back to the Examiners they would only report that, though in certain respects it did not carry out all that was in the notice, there has not been non-compliance with the Standing Orders. To send it back, moreover, would cause a great deal of delay and a very considerable amount of expense. Exception to the notices should also have been taken at an earlier stage, in the other House. For these reasons I do not ask the House to take that step on a question of procedure. When the Bill comes before the House there will be an opportunity to excise or amend the clause to which the hon. Member objects, and to insert the proposal that the church of Dewi Sant shall be the parish church. To that no technical objection can be taken. The hon. Member's case will not be prejudiced by waiting till that time, and therefore I should suggest that the House should not pass the motion standing in the hon. Member's name, but reserve to itself the right to amend the Bill in Committee.

MR. D. BRYNMOR JONES (Swansea District): I do not think that the case is quite met by the course suggested by the Chairman of Committees. If we get the Bill sent back to the Examiners they will have to report that the Standing Orders have not been complied with. In Sir Erskine May's, "Parliamentary Practice," it is said that "in preparing a Bill for deposit the promoters should be careful that no provisions are inserted which are not sufficiently alluded to in the notices." Our complaint is that in the notices there was no sufficient indication that the Bill would propose that the new church would be the parish church. It was quite the contrary. The notice was that the existing Welsh church of Dewi Sant should be the parish church. But when the Bill is laid on the Table of the House it turns out that another church is to be made the parish church, the new church of All Saints, in which the English services are to be carried on. The case comes back to the general proposition I have read. In the notice in November no sufficient indication was given that it was intended to make the new All Saints' Church the parish church, and therefore we ask that the Bill should be sent back to the Examiners, and that they should report whether the rule has been complied with.

SIR E. HILL (Bristol, S.): It is not my intention to offer any remarks upon the technical objection as to the sufficiency of the notice, but I wish to state that which I think the House ought to know, and which probably is the cause of the terms of the original notice not being in exact accordance with the Bill. The church of Dewi Sant is a church built by the subscriptions of those who thought that the Welsh-speaking population of the whole of Cardiff should possess a church in which their own language was used. The Welsh-speaking population of All Saints' is a very small and diminishing quantity. Under these circumstances it would have been impossible to carry out the terms of the notice without destroying what the hon. Member opposite has rightly described as a thorough Welsh church, inasmuch as, as soon as it becomes the parish church, the services must necessarily be held in the language of the great majority of the parishioners.

MR. SPEAKER: Order, order. I think the hon. Member is going into a question which does not arise upon the instruction.

MR. MACLEAN (Cardiff): I quite agree with the view expressed by the Chairman of the Committee of Ways and Means. The House of Lords has passed this Bill, but it is still open to consideration by this House. How, therefore, can the public suffer any loss by anything that has been overlooked by the House of Lords? Hon. Members will have ample opportunity, when the Bill is brought forward, of correcting it.

MR. D. A. THOMAS: After what has fallen from the Chairman of Ways and Means I do not propose to press my motion to a division.

Motion by leave withdrawn.

Mr. D. Brynmor Jones.

WEST GLOUCESTERSHIRE WATER BILL.

Read the third time, and passed.

WOKING WATER AND GAS BILL.

Read the third time, and passed.

DUMBARTON BURGH BILL [Lords].

As amended, considered; to be read the third time.

SHEFFIELD CORPORATION MARKETS BILL.

As amended, considered; Amendments made; Bill to be read the third time.

RAILWAY BILLS (GROUP 8).

Mr. A. DE TATTON EGERTON reported from the Committee on Group 8 of Railway Bills; That, for the convenience of parties, the Committee had adjourned till Monday 19th June, at half past Eleven of the clock.

Report to lie upon the Table.

STANDING ORDERS,

Resolution reported from the Committee—

"That, in the case of the Mersey Docks and Harbour Board (Pilotage) Bill [Lords], the Standing Orders ought to be dispensed with: —That the parties be permitted to proceed with their Bill."

Resolution agreed to.

POLICE AND SANITARY REGULA-TIONS BILLS.

Sir STAFFORD NORTHCOTE reported from the Select Committee on Police and Sanitary Regulations Bills; That the parties opposing the Warrington Corporation Bill had stated that the evidence of Joseph Parry, civil engineer, of Liverpool, and John James Lackland, civil engineer, of St. Helens, was essential to their case; and it having been proved that their attendance could not be procured without the intervention of the House, he had been instructed to move that the said Joseph Parry and John James Lackland do attend the said Committee to-morrow, at Twelve of the clock.

Ordered, That Joseph Parry and John James Lackland do attend the Select Committee on Police and Sanitary Regulations Bills to-morrow, at Twelve of the clock.

EDUCATION DEPARTMENT PROVISIONAL ORDER CONFIRMATION (LIVERPOOL) BILL [Lords].

Read the first time ; Referred to the Examiners of Petitions for Private Bills, and to be printed. [Bill 228.]

LOWESTOFT WATER AND GAS BILL [Lords].

Read the first time ; and referred to the Examiners of Petitions for Private Bills.

NORTH-EASTERN AND HULL AND BARNSLEY RAILWAYS (JOINT DOCK) BILL [Lords].

Read the first time ; and referred to the Examiners of Petitions for Private Bills.

NORTH-EASTERN RAILWAY BILL [Lords].

Read the first time ; and referred to the Examiners of Petitions for Private Bills.

PETITIONS.

POOR LAW RELIEF (DISFRANCHISEMENT).

Two Petitions from Cardiff, for alteration of Law ; to lie upon the Table.

RETURNS, REPORTS, &c.

SOUTH AFRICAN REPUBLIC.

Copy presented,— of further correspondence relating to the claim of the South African Republic for damages on account of the Jameson Raid [by Command] ; to lie upon the Table.

EDUCATION (ENGLAND AND WALES) (ENDOWED SCHOOLS ACTS).

Copy presented,—of Report of the proceedings of the Charity Commissioners for England and Wales, under the Endowed Schools Acts, 1869 to 1889, for the year 1898 [by Command] ; to lie upon the Table.

TRADE REPORTS (ANNUAL SERIES).

Copies presented,—of Diplomatic and Consular Reports, Annual Series, Nos. 2282 to 2286 [by Command] ; to lie upon the Table.

Papers laid upon the Table by the Clerk of the House :—

1. Inquiry into Charities (County of Carmarthen),—Further Return relative thereto [ordered 10th February 1898 ; [*Mr. Grant Lawson*]; to be printed. [No. 213.]

2. Charitable Endowments (West Riding of the County of York), Charitable Endowments (Bradford), Inquiry into Charities (Parish of Halifax, including County Borough of Halifax), Inquiry into Charities (City of Sheffield), Leeds (Inquiry into Charities), Huddersfield County Borough (Charities),— Further Returns relative thereto [ordered 10th August 1894, 13th May 1896, 8th February 1897, 8th April 1897, 29th July 1897 ; [*Mr. Francis Stevenson* and *Mr. Grant Lawson*] ; to be printed. [No. 214.]

WORKMEN'S TRAINS.

Return ordered, "showing (1) the number of Workmen's Trains running on all Railways in Great Britain ; (2) the distance run and the fares charged on each particular Train ; and (3) the Return to be prepared as that issued by the Board of Trade dealing with London Railways in 1897."—(*Mr. Woods.*)

EXPERIMENTS ON LIVING ANIMALS.

Address for "Return showing the number of Experiments performed on Living Animals during the year 1898, under Licences granted under the Act 39 and 40 Vic. c. 77, distinguishing Painless from Painful Experiments (in continuation of Parliamentary Paper, No 215, of Session 1898)."—(*Mr. Jesse Collings.*)

ARMY (LENGTH OF SERVICE AND AGES OF MEN IN EACH UNIT).

Address for "Return with respect to all Infantry Regiments to which one or more Battalions have been added ; the Return also to show the number of men of the First Class Army Reserve recalled to, and serving with, the Colours in each Battalion of such Regiments (in continuation of Return [C. 8757])."—(*Mr. Arnold-Forster.*)

ARMY (LENGTH OF SERVICE AND AGES OF MEN IN NEW BATTERIES OF ROYAL ARTILLERY).

Address for "Return showing the number of Men serving in each of the newly formed Batteries or Companies of the Royal Artillery, with the Age and Length of Service of the Men."—(*Mr. Arnold-Forster.*)

EAST INDIA (MILITARY BULLET).

Address for "Copy of Reports on the effect of Military Bullet now in use in India."—(*Lord George Hamilton.*)

MALTA (POLITICAL CONDITION).

Address for "Copy of a Despatch addressed to the Secretary of State for the Colonies by Sir Arthur Lyon Fremantle, late Governor of Malta, dated 29th December, 1898, on the political condition of Malta; and of all recent Correspondence relative to the same."—(*Mr. M'Iver.*)

———

QUESTIONS.

———

THE MUSCAT INCIDENT.

*SIR CHARLES DILKE (Gloucester, Forest of Dean): I beg to ask the Under Secretary of . State for Foreign Affairs whether the discussion of local details in relation to the Muscat incident has sufficiently closed to allow of the presentation of the Papers to Parliament.

*THE UNDER SECRETARY OF STATE FOR FOREIGN AFFAIRS (Mr. BRODRICK, Surrey, Guildford): I am afraid the discussion of local details is not yet closed, and we cannot lay Papers at present.

EXEMPTION OF FOREIGN CONSULS FROM TAXATION.

MR. DILLON (Mayo, E.): I beg to ask the Under Secretary of State for Foreign Affairs what are the immunities and privileges (if any) in regard to the exemption from personal taxation enjoyed by the Consuls representing foreign countries in different portions of the Empire;

and are the same immunities and privileges allowed to all Consuls, whether paid by salary or by fees.

*MR. BRODRICK: Consuls of foreign states enjoy no special privileges or immunities, as a matter of right, in the Queen's Dominions. In the United Kingdom foreign Consuls are, however, exempted in practice, as a matter of courtesy, from payment of income tax on their official salaries, but not from other taxes.

RUSSIA AND BRITISH LOAN CONTRACTS IN CHINA.

LORD CHARLES BERESFORD (York): I beg to ask the Under Secretary of State for Foreign Affairs whether the protest presented on 24th July by the British Minister at Pekin to the Tsung-li-Yamen, in which it was stated that England would not tolerate any interference of another Power with the British loan contract entered into freely by the Chinese Government, especially referred to the demand made by Russia at Pekin, on 11th June, 1898, and 19th July, 1898, that the portion of the line to be built should not be mortgaged to the British bondholders, and that no foreign control should be permitted even in case of default, both of which points were included in the preliminary contract between the Chinese Government and a British corporation on 7th June, 1898; and, whether the Foreign Office subsequently insisted on the British corporation withdrawing from the agreement the clauses objected to by Russia, despite the British Minister's statement that England would tolerate no interference in the matter.

*MR. BRODRICK: The negotiations concerning the Northern Railways loans are detailed at length in the Blue-book, and must be considered in connection with the negotiations for a general settlement proceeding at the time. The British corporation was consulted, and agreed to the arrangements made upon which their capital was successfully raised.

RUSSIAN RAILWAY CONCESSIONS IN PERSIA.

MR. MACLEAN (Cardiff): I beg to ask the Under Secretary of State for Foreign Affairs when the agreement giving Russia priority of railway concessions in Persia expires; and what steps Her Majesty's Government propose taking, at the expiration of this agreement, to place England on an equal footing with Russia as regards the construction of railways in Persia.

*MR. BRODRICK: No public announcement has been made as to the agreement in question, and it would be inexpedient for Her Majesty's Government to make a declaration as to their intentions.

BRITISH INTERESTS IN THE PERSIAN GULF.

MR. MACLEAN: I beg to ask the Under Secretary of State for Foreign Affairs whether, in view of the concessions granted to German capitalists for the construction of a railway through Asia Minor and Mesopotamia to Bagdad, Her Majesty's Government will notify the Porte that English interests in the trade of the Persian Gulf make it necessary for any line that may be hereafter constructed from Bagdad to Bussora and the Gulf to be entrusted to English capitalists.

*MR. BRODRICK: I am afraid I cannot make any statement as to the intentions of Her Majesty's Government in this matter, but we are fully alive to the necessity of maintaining British interests in the Persian Gulf.

RUSSIAN TAXES ON ENGLISH COMMERCIAL TRAVELLERS.

*MR. BILL (Staffordshire, Leek): I beg to ask the Under Secretary of State for Foreign Affairs whether the Russian Government has lately imposed a tax of 50 roubles on English commercial travellers carrying on their business in Russia; and also a tax of 500 roubles, or over £50, on the firms which they represent; and whether Her Majesty's Ambassador at St. Petersburg has been instructed to make representations to the Russian Government against such charges as calculated to check the development of trade between that country and England.

*MR. BRODRICK: The reply to the two questions in the first paragraph is in the affirmative. There are, however, several points in regard to which the precise manner in which the new law will be applied is open to doubt, and upon these points Her Majesty's Ambassador has been instructed to ask for explana-

tions, before it can be decided whether Her Majesty's Government would be warranted in making any representations against the proposed charges.

TONGA.

MR. HOGAN (Tipperary, Mid.): I beg to ask the Under Secretary of State for Foreign Affairs whether he is now in a position to make his promised statement in reference to the recent visit of H.M.S. "Tauranga" to Tonga, the interviews of Captain Stewart with King George, and the further responsibilities, if any, incurred by Her Majesty's Government in connection with this native kingdom.

*MR. BRODRICK: This agreement involves no liability on the part of Her Majesty's Government, and it is therefore not thought desirable to publish it.

MANCHURIAN RAILWAYS.

MR. LAMBERT (Devon, South Molton): I beg to ask the Under Secretary of State for Foreign Affairs if the clause in the Anglo-Russian Agreement, that the Russian Government is at liberty to support concessions for a railway from the main Manchurian line in a south-westerly direction, implies that the British Government will offer no objection to the construction of a railway joining Peking with the main Manchurian line.

*MR. BRODRICK: The clause referred to in the Anglo-Russian Agreement does not, in the opinion of Her Majesty's Government, cover the question of railway communication with Peking.

THE YANG-TSZE VALLEY.

MR. LAMBERT: I beg to ask the Under Secretary of State for Foreign Affairs if any consent has been given by China, Russia, or any country to the geographical definition of the Yang-tsze Valley as being the provinces bordering the Yang-tsze River and the provinces of Honan and Chekiang; and whether the Government has got inserted in any railway concessions obtained by foreign Powers in China a proviso guarding British goods from differential treatment or preferential rates, as suggested by Lord Salisbury's despatches of the 24th September last.

*MR. BRODRICK : The valley or basin of the Yang-tsze has been defined as stated in the question, and this definition was communicated to the Russian Government, but there has been no occasion to invite the assent of the Powers to it. As will be seen from the papers just presented, the Russian Government considered the question of railway rates as too technical for insertion in a preliminary agreement, and that it should be settled between the two Governments when the time came for its necessary consideration. Her Majesty's Government will, of course, use their best efforts to prevent British goods being subjected to differential treatment on Chinese railways.

BRITISH OFFICERS AT OMDURMAN.

MR. C. P. SCOTT (Lancashire, Leigh) : I beg to ask the Under Secretary of State for Foreign Affairs whether he can state what was the number of British officers present with each battalion of native troops at the Battle of Omdurman ; and whether care will be taken in any future operations in the Soudan that the proportion of British officers to native troops shall be kept to the full standard.

*MR. BRODRICK : The number of British officers in Soudanese battalions is five, in Egyptian battalions four. It is not now possible to say what number of these were present with each battalion at the Battle of Omdurman, but battalions are kept complete or very nearly so to the above establishments. It is, of course, not possible on a campaign to secure that all officers will be present at an engagement.

FUTURE MILITARY OPERATIONS IN THE SOUDAN.

MR. C. P. SCOTT : I beg to ask the Under Secretary of State for Foreign Affairs whether further military operations on a considerable scale are to be undertaken in the Soudan in the autumn ; and, if so, whether they are to be carried out entirely by means of native troops, or whether British troops will also be employed.

*MR. BRODRICK : It is impossible for me to make any statement as to whether military operations may be necessary in the Soudan next autumn or not. Nor has any question arisen as to the nature of troops to be employed.

THE PATRIOTIC FUND.

MR. SPICER (Monmouth Boroughs) : I beg to ask the Under Secretary of State for War whether he is aware that the Patriotic Fund Commissioners have declined to re-admit a widow named Frances Lewis, of Newport (Mon.), who, as the wife of Patrick Driscoll, 1st Battalion, 1st Regiment of Foot, was two years in the Crimea, and underwent many of the hardships of that campaign ; and whether the decision will be reconsidered, seeing that she is now aged, again a widow, and almost absolutely dependent on the ratepayers.

*THE UNDER SECRETARY OF STATE FOR WAR (Mr. G. WYNDHAM, Dover) : The case of Mrs. Lewis has been carefully considered by the Patriotic Fund Commissioners, and in view of the fact that there is not only no evidence of the death of her second husband, Charles Wilmott, but that the certificate of her third marriage has been unmistakably tampered with, they are unable to re-admit her to the list of recipients of the fund.

ELECTRIC MOTORS IN THE NAVY.

SIR FORTESCUE FLANNERY : I beg to ask the First Lord of the Admiralty whether an order has been issued, or is in contemplation, withdrawing from the engineering branch the control of the various electrical motors, and placing these complicated machines in charge of lieutenants ; and whether it is contemplated that the necessary duty of overhauling and repairing the motors shall be performed by the engineering branch.

THE FIRST LORD OF THE ADMIRALTY (Mr. G. J. GOSCHEN, St. George's, Hanover Square) : No change in the present Regulations as to the charge of electric motors is contemplated. In 1898 the torpedo officer, or where none is borne the gunnery officer, was made responsible for electric motors. Before that time electric motors were not specially mentioned in the Regulations, as there were scarcely any in the Service, but in the few cases in which they were fitted it was the practice for the torpedo officer to take charge of them. The motors are kept in repair by the torpedo staff.

WATER-TUBE BOILERS.

SIR J. FERGUSSON (Manchester, N.E.): On behalf of the hon. Member for West Belfast, I beg to ask the First Lord of the Admiralty when, and in what form, it will be convenient to him to present to the House the promised statement with regard to the performance of the water-tube boilers on board Her Majesty's ships.

MR. GOSCHEN: Every effort is being made to complete the statement as soon as possible, but in view of the large amount of current work in the office the preparation necessarily takes some time. It is not practicable to explain in an answer to a question the form in which the information will be given, but I shall be glad to show it to the hon. Member. It will be, generally speaking, a continuation of the Return No. 234 of 1895.

LIFE ASSURANCE IN THE UNITED KINGDOM.

MR. BOULNOIS (Marylebone, E.): I beg to ask the President of the Board of Trade whether the Board is obtaining Returns under the 3rd, 4th, 5th, and 6th schedules of the Life Assurance Companies Act, 1870, from those members of Lloyd's and others who have issued policies of insurance upon human life within the United Kingdom: and whether such persons who have begun such business since the passing of the Act have been required to make the deposit of £20,000 specified in the 3rd section thereof.

THE PRESIDENT OF THE BOARD OF TRADE (Mr. RITCHIE, Croydon): I can only give the hon. Member the same answer as I gave to the similar question asked by him on the 12th July, 1897. The Board of Trade have no information that any member of Lloyd's or other individual has issued or incurred any liability under such policies except as a member of a life assurance office.

MR. BOULNOIS: May I be allowed to hand the right hon. Gentleman copies of such policies which I hold in my hand?

MR. RITCHIE: Yes, I shall be glad if the hon. Gentleman will give me any information he can.

BLACKHEAD LIGHTHOUSE.

CAPTAIN DONELAN (Cork, E.): On behalf of the hon. Member for South Down, I beg to ask the President of the Board of Trade, with reference to the erection of the new lighthouse at Blackhead, county Antrim, whether he is aware of the danger involved in delaying to secure from the tenants and occupiers possession of the lands upon which it is proposed to construct the lighthouse there; whether, considering the increasing value of land in the vicinity of Whitehead, which is adjacent to the place, a fair and liberal offer will be made to the tenants for their interest in the holdings required; and if he can say about what date the work is likely to be commenced.

MR. RITCHIE: As stated by me on 2nd June, in reply to the hon. Member for Gateshead, a site has been obtained for the new lighthouse on the Blackhead. I am informed by the Commissioners of Irish Lights that the site can be entered upon at once. The Board of Trade have no power to make any suggestion as regards the amount to be paid to the tenants, which, in case of disagreement, will be determined by arbitration in manner provided by statute. I understand that tenders for the buildings will be invited very shortly, but I have no information as to the date upon which the work is likely to be actually commenced.

SIGNALMEN ON THE NORTH-EASTERN RAILWAY.

MR. FORTESCUE FLANNERY (Yorks, Shipley): I beg to ask the President of the Board of Trade if he will state to the House how many signal boxes on the North-Eastern Railway exist in which signalmen are on duty 12 hours consecutively without any relief: and whether the Board of Trade is taking steps, in the interest of the safety of the travelling public, to discourage such long hours of continuous labour in positions where concentrated attention to duty is essential for the safety of passengers.

MR. RITCHIE: The Board have not the information asked for in the first paragraph of the question. In cases under the Regulation of Railways Act, 1893, the Board discourage continuous twelve-hour shifts in signal boxes. The amount of work to be done by signalmen varies largely, and the case of nearly every box must be considered on its merits.

SIR FORTESCUE FLANNERY: Will the right. hon. Gentleman take any steps to obtain the information referred to in the first paragraph?

MR. RITCHIE: We have no power to compel the company to give the information, but if the hon. Member wishes it I will see what can be done.

NEWBIGGIN-BY-THE-SEA FISHERIES.

MR. FENWICK (Northumberland, Wansbeck): I beg to ask the President of the Board of Trade whether his attention has been drawn to the fact that property of the value of £110, belonging to the fishermen of Newbiggin-by-the-Sea, in the county of Northumberland, was destroyed last week by trawlers operating within the recognised limit; and whether, seeing that these offences occur with great frequency, he is prepared to take any further steps to prevent the inshore fishing industry on the north-east coast being wilfully destroyed by the illegal operations of these trawlers.

MR. RITCHIE: I have received no information as to the alleged destruction of fishing gear at Newbiggin, but the matter was referred to at the annual Fishery Conference on the 6th instant. Trawling within this district is prohibited by bye-law made by the Northumberland Sea Fisheries Committee, and it is for that body to take such steps as may be necessary to enforce their own bye-law.

SCOTTISH EDUCATION DEPARTMENT CIRCULARS.

MR. CROMBIE (Kincardineshire): I beg to ask the Lord Advocate, whether he will furnish Members desiring it with copies of the circulars of the Education Department which have been issued since the publication of last year's report, so that they may be in their hands before the discussion of Scotch Estimates.

*THE LORD ADVOCATE (MR. A. GRAHAM MURRAY, Buteshire): The circulars issued by the Department in the course of a year are numerous, and several of them have reference only to unimportant details of routine business.

All that are of general interest are on sale, and may be obtained at small cost, and it has never therefore been considered necessary to have them printed and distributed as Parliamentary papers. In any case the request could not be complied with before Friday of next week.

BRITISH COLUMBIA AND THE JAPANESE.

MR. HOGAN (Tipperary, Mid.): I beg to ask the Secretary of State for the Colonies whether recent enactments by the Legislature of the Province of British Columbia in reference to the immigration of Japanese have been disallowed at the instance of Her Majesty's Government; and, if so, upon what grounds.

THE SECRETARY OF STATE FOR THE COLONIES (MR. J. CHAMBERLAIN, Birmingham, W.): Certain laws enacted by the Legislature of the Province of British Columbia imposing disqualifications on Japanese have been disallowed by the Government of Canada at the instance of Her Majesty's Government on the ground that they were offensive to a friendly Power.

SOUTH AFRICAN REPUBLIC—THE BLOEMFONTEIN CONFERENCE.

MR. DRAGE (Derby): I beg to ask the Secretary of State for the Colonies whether he is in a position to make any statement to the House with regard to the Conference at Bloemfontein.

The following questions on the same subject also appeared on the paper:—

MR. DILLON: To ask the Secretary of State for the Colonies when he expects to be able to lay upon the table papers in reference to recent negotiations with the Government of the Transvaal.

MR. DILLON: To ask the Secretary of State for the Colonies whether he is in a position to make a statement as to the result of the Conference between President Kruger and Sir A. Milner.

MR. PHILIP STANHOPE (Burnley): To ask the Secretary of State for the Colonies when he will make a full statement as to the causes of the failure of the Conference between President Kruger and Sir Alfred Milner; and whether he will undertake that, pending the presentation to Parliament of the official reports of the proceedings of the Conference, Her Majesty's Government will proceed with no action tending to the possible rupture of diplomatic relations between this country and the Government of the Transvaal.

Mr. C. P. SCOTT : To ask the Secretary of State for the Colonies whether he will cause to be printed and at once circulated to Members copies of the Outlanders' petition received some weeks since from the Transvaal, and also of the counter-petition.

Mr. J. CHAMBERLAIN : It is un-fortunately true that the Conference has broken up without any result, and a new situation has thus been created. Presi-dent Kruger has rejected the proposals for a settlement offered by Sir Alfred Milner, and the alternative suggested by him was considered by Sir Alfred Milner, and is now considered by Her Majesty's Government, as entirely inadequate. I have not yet received the Memorandum which Sir Alfred Milner informs us he has communicated to the Press on the subject of the Conference. He under-stood that this memorandum would be telegraphed by Reuter verbatim to this country, but owing to some unexplained cause it has not yet arrived. I am there-fore unable to say whether the state-ment of the Government of the South African Republic which has been pub-lished in the meantime agrees in all respects with Sir Alfred Milner's ac-count. I understand that the discussion turned mainly on the question of the franchise. Sir Alfred Milner was of opinion that the exclusion of the Uit-landers from representation was the root of the difficulties which have arisen, and that it was desirable, if possible, to come to an arrangement on this point before dealing with other questions in dispute between the two Governments. Sir Alfred Milner asked that the franchise should be given to all naturalised aliens who have resided five years in the country, with retroactive effect, and a fair amount of representation be con-ceded to the new population. President Kruger's proposal was substantially as follows : First, that aliens who were resident in the country before 1890 might naturalise and have the full fran-chise in two years' time ; secondly,

that the bulk of the Uitlanders might be naturalised in two years' time, and might receive the franchise five years later—that is to say, in seven years from the present time. Between the period of naturalisation and that of receiving the franchise they would have to aban-don their present nationality, and would have no rights of nationality in the Transvaal. The President also attached to his offer certain conditions as to a pecuniary qualification, and the proof of possession of civil rights in the country from which the alien had come. It is not clear whether the further condition, that a majority of two-thirds of the burghers would be required to confirm the possession of the franchise, would be insisted upon. The President agreed that three members might be added to the representation of the mining districts, thus giving to the five members out of a total of thirty-one. According to these proposals no change whatever would take place for two years, and then only in the case of a small minority of the Uitlanders who had resided eleven years in the Transvaal. The whole of these proposals were made subject to an agreement by this country to refer all differences with the Transvaal to the arbitration of a foreign Power. Sir Alfred considered these proposals as altogether inadequate, and further in-formed the President that Her Majesty's Government would not consent to the intervention of any foreign Power in dis-putes between themselves and the Government of the South African Re-public. The President also asked for the incorporation of Swaziland, but does not appear to have pressed this claim. He also demanded that the question of an indemnity· for the Jameson raid should be settled ; and was informed by Sir Alfred Milner that the British South Africa Company had agreed, in a despatch which was then on its way, that, while protesting against the amount of the claim sent in as altogether un-reasonable, they would nevertheless consent to submit to arbitration the amount of damages for any material injury suffered by the Transvaal in con-sequence of the Jameson raid. The question of the dynamite monopoly was touched upon, but, in view of the failure to come to an agreement with regard to the franchise, it was reserved for further discussion between the two Governments.

I have to add that the despatch in answer to the petition of the Uitlanders to the Queen, which was sent to the High Commissioner before the invitation to the Conference was received from the President of the Orange Free State, and which had been held back pending the result of the Conference, will now be communicated to the Government of the South African Republic, and as soon as they have received it will be laid on the Table with other papers, including the petition of the Uitlanders to the Queen, and the counter-petition of other Uitlanders to the Government of the South African Republic.

MR. MACLEAN : May I ask the right hon. Gentleman if he will include in those Papers the instructions he gave to Sir Alfred Milner for his guidance at the Conference ?

MR. J. CHAMBERLAIN : No, Sir ; that will not come into the present Blue-book. A subsequent Blue-book will have to be published as soon as we get the full report of the Conference, and that will contain all the instructions I gave.

MR. DILLON : I wish to point out that the right hon. Gentleman has not fully answered my question as to when he expects to lay on the Table the Papers relating to the Transvaal. I understood the right hon. Gentleman to say that he will lay immediately the despatches and reply to the Uitlanders' petition, and that further Papers will be laid at a later date. I venture to urge on the right hon. Gentleman the view that a situation has now arisen when the Government ought to lay before the House all the Papers relating to the negotiations which they propose at any time to communicate to the House.

MR. J. CHAMBERLAIN : The Government cannot lay Papers on the Table until they get them. I cannot possibly receive the full despatches containing what has taken place at the Conference for about three weeks. As soon as I get them I propose to lay them on the Table.

SIR H. CAMPBELL-BANNERMANN (Stirling Burghs) : I presume the Colonial Office Vote will not be taken before these Papers are received ?

THE FIRST LORD OF THE TREASURY (Mr. A. J. BALFOUR, Manchester, E.) : No, Sir ; I think that would be expedient.

BATHING FATALITY AT ALDERSHOT.

MR. JEFFREYS (Hants, N.) : I beg to ask the Under Secretary of State for War whether he is aware that Private D. Jackson, of the 2nd Black Watch, was drowned whilst bathing in the canal at Aldershot on 28th May, and that there were no appliances for saving life in the vicinity ; and whether proper bathing places will be established for the use of the soldiers at Aldershot.

*MR. WYNDHAM : I regret to say that a soldier of the Royal Highlanders was drowned in the canal, notwithstanding the praiseworthy efforts of a comrade to save him. The man was bathing contrary to orders, as the bathing season had not commenced. When bathing is permitted, certain hours are specified and picquets with the necessary apparatus for saving life are detailed at three bathing places. I may add that money is taken in this year's Estimates for the provision of a swimming bath at Aldershot.

MR. JEFFREYS : May I ask whether last week the weather was not hot enough for bathing at Aldershot ?

*MR. WYNDHAM : This private was drowned, I am sorry to say, on Sunday, the 28th May.

MILITARY PRISONS.

DR. FARQUHARSON (Aberdeenshire, W.) : I beg to ask the Under Secretary of State for War when the Annual Report of the Inspector-General of Military Prisons will be presented to the House.

*MR. WYNDHAM : I hope to present this Report before the end of the month.

THE METROPOLITAN POLICE.

CAPTAIN NORTON : I beg to ask the Secretary of State for the Home Department whether he can state if any difficulty is experienced at the present time in obtaining an adequate supply of suitable recruits for the ranks of the Metropolitan Police ; and by what number that force is short of its established strength.

*The SECRETARY OF STATE FOR THE HOME DEPARTMENT (SIR M. WHITE RIDLEY, Lancs., Blackpool) : The answer to the first paragraph is in the negative. It is necessary, in order to provide a margin for temporary augmentations, to keep the force below its authorised strength, and it is at the present moment 285 short ; but this includes a recently authorised augmentation of 100 men for whom recruiting has not yet commenced. The actual deficit therefore is 185, which is below the average of the past seven years. These figures take no account of the 75 men now being trained in the preparatory class.

ALLAHABAD HIGH COURT—LADY BARRISTERS.

MR. HERBERT ROBERTS (Denbighshire, W.) : I beg to ask the Secretary of State for India whether his attention has been drawn to the unsuccessful application of Miss Sorabji for permission to plead before the Allahabad High Court ; whether he is aware that the lady referred to has taken law honours at Oxford and has passed the LL.B examination of the Bombay University, and has complied with all the necessary regulations ; and whether he will state the grounds upon which she is prevented from practising before the High Courts of India.

THE SECRETARY OF STATE FOR INDIA (Lord GEO. HAMILTON, Middlesex, Ealing) : I am aware that Miss Sorabji applied to the High Court for permission to practise as a pleader, and that the Court, which has an absolute discretion in the matter under Letters Patent, refused its assent to her application. I do not know what honours Miss Sorabji may have taken at Oxford or elsewhere, nor do I know the grounds of the Court's refusal ; but I think it probable that in was on account of her sex, which would equally have debarred her from practising in any court of law in this country.

LEGAL EDUCATION IN INDIA.

SIR WILLIAM WEDDERBURN (Banffshire) : I beg to ask the Secretary of State for India whether he is aware that the control of legal education in Calcutta is wholly in private hands, the Government Presidency College having no law department, and the four private colleges teaching up to the full course of the University law degree ; and whether he will state upon what grounds the Bombay Government have now decided to pursue a different policy, and consider it not advisable that the control of higher legal education in Bombay should be wholly or partially in private hands.

LORD GEORGE HAMILTON : The facts are as stated in the first paragraph of the question. The grounds on which the Bombay Government decided that the control of higher legal education should not in Bombay be allowed to pass to private institutions are thus stated in a letter from that Government of the 1st September, 1898 :—

"In the opinion of this Government it is inadvisable to allow the control of higher legal education to pass to private institutions, for the administration of the law is undoubtedly a part of the general administration of the country, and in spite of the fundamental dissociation of law from politics there is a distinct danger of the perversion of legal instruction to political uses."

SIR WILLIAM WEDDERBURN : I beg to ask the Secretary of State for India whether for the last few years the Bombay Government have contributed nothing to the support of the Government Law School, but on the contrary have made a yearly profit of about Rs.8,000 from the fees paid by the students, and have now resolved to raise these fees ; whether he is aware that the Bombay Government refused to sanction the affiliation of the proposed private College of Law on the ground that they desired to improve the Government School by means of these enhanced fees, and were therefore unwilling that students should be diverted to another institution ; and whether this prevention of the establishment of a private College of Law has been sanctioned by the Government.

*LORD GEORGE HAMILTON : It is a fact that the fees received at the Government Law School at Bombay have during recent years exceeded the expenditure, but I doubt whether the average excess has been so much as Rs.8,000 ; in 1896-97 it was only Rs.3,190. It is also true that the Bombay Government have resolved to raise the fees ; but this is not to make a profit out of fees, but to make the new organisation self-supporting. I answered the second and third paragraphs of the question in my reply to the hon. Member's question of the 16th May last. The question of the fees had nothing to do with the refusal of the Bombay Government to sanction the application of the private institution to the Bombay University.

*Sir WILLIAM WEDDERBURN: Will the noble lord ascertain from the Bombay Government which of the contradictory reasons they rely upon for preventing the establishment of this private college?

*Lord GEORGE HAMILTON: No, sir, I can add nothing to my answer.

PASTEUR INSTITUTE FOR INDIA.

Sir WILLIAM WEDDERBURN: I beg to ask the Secretary of State for India whether his attention has been drawn to the proceedings of the Central Committee of the Pasteur Institute, held on the 15th April last, at the office of the Director-General, Indian Medical Service, at Simla (the Director-General himself in the chair), when it was proposed to ask the Government to make a grant for a Pasteur Institute, and to place it under a Government medical officer; whether this committee has been formed with the sanction of Government; and whether it is proposed to grant them the assistance asked for.

*Lord GEORGE HAMILTON: (1) I have seen a newspaper report of the meeting of the Pasteur Institute Committee to which the question refers. (2) The Government of India are, I believe, aware of the formation and proceedings of the committee; but I ascertained some weeks ago that they had not decided on their course of action. They hoped, however, to deal with the subject during the present summer.

MINERAL RIGHTS IN HYDERABAD STATE.

Sir ANDREW SCOBLE (Hackney, Central): I beg to ask the Secretary of State for India whether his attention has been called to certain prospectuses of the Godaveri Estates, Limited, and the Godaveri Valley Collieries, Limited, purporting to deal with mining and other rights in the Zemindari of Ramangavaram and Mullur, in Hyderabad State; and whether the Zemindar has power to give a lease of the mineral rights on his estate.

*Lord GEORGE HAMILTON: My attention has been called to these prospectuses, which appear to have been issued in London for the purpose of exploiting a concession alleged to have been granted by one Mathu Krishnam, Zemindar of Ramangavaram and Mullur, in the Warangal District of Hyderabad State. The Government of His Highness the Nizam brought the matter to the notice of the Government of India, and reported that they had nothing to do with this alleged concession; and that, inasmuch as no Zemindar has the right to lease minerals to an English Company without their consent and that of the Government of India, any contract purporting to deal with mining rights which may have been made by the Zemindar is null and void.

INDIAN SUGAR TRADE.

Captain SINCLAIR (Forfar): I beg to ask the Secretary of State for India if he will be good enough to state the quantities of sugar, raw and refined, entering India during the year 1898-9, specifying in each case the countries of origin.

*Lord GEORGE HAMILTON: The trade returns for March, 1899, give the following figures as the imports of sugar into India during the year 1898-99:—

Refined Sugar.

From Austria-Hungary	1,063,737 cwt.
,, Germany	413,971 ,,
,, Mauritius	1,793,607 ,,
,, China	185,682 ,,
,, Java	162,500 ,,
,, Straits Settlements	75,656 ,,
,, Other countries	69,757 ,,
Total	3,764,910 cwt.

Unrefined Sugar.

| From all countries | 312,778 cwt. |

I have as yet received no details regarding the countries from which this unrefined sugar came. It may be added that 167,644 cwt. of foreign refined sugar were re-exported from India during the year.

SAVINGS BANK INQUIRY.

Sir JOHN LENG (Dundee): I beg to ask Mr. Chancellor of the Exchequer if he can state to what kind of committee the proposed inquiry into the financial relations of the State to savings banks will be referred, and the scope of the reference.

THE CHANCELLOR OF THE EX-CHEQUER (Sir M. HICKS BEACH, Bristol, W.) : I have fulfilled the intention I expressed of consulting with several hon. Members who have taken a special interest in this subject; and a strong opinion has been expressed to me by some whose views I feel bound to respect that such a matter ought not to be referred to a Select Committee without a definite indication of the views of the Government. There would also be some difficulty in constituting a Committee at this time of the year, as some Members whose services I should much like to secure are already engaged on other work. I intend, therefore, to institute certain preliminary inquiries, with the assistance, I hope, of someone with practical knowledge of the working of savings banks ; and I hope to base on them a proposal which may be considered by a Select Committee early next session. This will not involve any real delay, as no legislation could in any case take place this year.

TEA ADULTERATION.

SIR FORTESCUE FLANNERY: I beg to ask Mr. Chancellor of the Exchequer if his attention has been called to a statement in the Press, that a quarter of the caper teas and half of the dust teas now imported should be confiscated under the Food and Drugs Act of 1875, by reason of their containing 20 per cent. of earthy matter and sand ; whether he will explain the nature of the precautions taken by the Customs Department in London for the detection of such adulteration, and whether the number of samples analysed could be increased with advantage: and, whether, having regard to the fact that the descriptions of tea above named are for the most part consumed by the humbler classes least able to protect themselves against adulteration, he will increase the staff of inspectors especially allocated to the duties of sampling and analysis of caper and dust teas.

MR. GOSCHEN: My attention has been called to this matter. The Board of Customs have, in view of representations made to them by certain firms and of statements in the Press, ordered a full inquiry to be made. It is not easy, within the limits of an answer to a

question, to explain the precautions taken by the Board for the detection of the adulteration of tea ; but I shall be happy, if the hon. Member wishes it, to supply him with particulars. The Board of Customs, as at present advised, do not consider that there is any need for altering the existing regulations, but if, as a result of the investigation now in progress, it should appear advisable to make such alterations or to increase the number of tea inspectors, the necessary steps will be taken at once. Meantime a circular has been issued to the tea inspectors directing them to administer the existing regulations with special care.

SIR FORTESCUE FLANNERY: When will the inquiry be held?

MR. GOSCHEN: It has already been begun.

IRELAND—RIOTING AT COOKSTOWN.

MR. DILLON: I beg to ask the Chief Secretary to the Lord Lieutenant of Ireland whether he is aware that on the 21st April last, while a private meeting of the Irish National Foresters, of Cookstown, was being held in their own hall, an attack was made on the hall, and the windows smashed, by an Orange drumming party ; and will he explain why the police were not present while the attack on the hall was going on, why no arrests were made, and why no one has been prosecuted.

*THE CHIEF SECRETARY FOR IRELAND (MR. G. W. BALFOUR, Leeds, Central) : I am aware of the occurrence referred to in the first paragraph. After the drumming party had marched through the streets it halted opposite the Foresters' Hall and continued drumming, at the same time hooting and yelling. When the drumming party had passed it was found that four panes of glass in the hall had been broken. The damage is estimated at ten shillings. A party of police was present on the occasion, but they saw no windows broken when the drumming party was passing, and did not become aware of the fact until afterwards. This is accounted for by the noise caused by the crowd, which was a large one. Every possible inquiry has been made with the view of obtaining evidence against the persons concerned in the breaking of the windows, but so far without success.

IRISH LAND COMMISSION, COUNTY CAVAN.

MR. YOUNG (Cavan, E.): I beg to ask the Chief Secretary to the Lord Lieutenant of Ireland whether he is aware that the judgments in two sittings of the Sub-Commissioners held in Bailieborough, county Cavan, 7th and 8th March and 10th May, have not yet been communicated to the tenants; whether he is aware that this delay is disappointing to many of those who are offered and desire to purchase their holdings under the Land Act; and whether he can say at what time the decision of the Land Commission will be made known.

*MR. G. W. BALFOUR: Judgments have been delivered in a few of the cases heard at Bailieborough on the 7th and 8th March last. It is expected, however, that the decisions will be announced on the 24th instant in the remaining cases, as well as in a large number of the cases subsequently heard on the 10th ultimo at the same place. The inspection and office work necessary to complete these cases is being proceeded with as rapidly as possible. The Commissioners have no information on the subject referred to in the second paragraph of the question.

IRISH LAND COMMISSION, COURT VALUERS.

MR. YOUNG: I beg to ask the Chief Secretary to the Lord Lieutenant of Ireland whether he is aware that in those cases where landlords and tenants agree to fix fair rents on the report of two court valuators there is great delay in securing the valuation; that in many instances four months will elapse after applying to the Land Commission before there is a response; and whether there is any reason for this delay.

*MR. G. W. BALFOUR: There has been some delay in referring a number of the applications mentioned to the court valuers for inspection, but the delay has been unavoidable owing to the work in other districts in appeal cases, and it is expected that all such applications will have been referred to the valuers before the end of July.

IRISH INDUSTRIAL SCHOOLS.

CAPTAIN DONELAN: On behalf of the hon. Member for South Down, I beg to ask the Chief Secretary to the Lord Lieutenant of Ireland, with reference to the complaint of Mr. Fagan, inspector of industrial schools in Ireland, that the children now committed in Ireland are rather destitute than criminal, whether he is aware that the circulars sent from Dublin Castle discouraging the magistrates from making such committals has raised considerable indignation throughout the country; that the Industrial Schools (Ireland) Act provides that such destitute children are proper subjects for committal under this Act; and that out of 396 boys discharged from industrial schools in Ireland from 1894 to 1896 (both inclusive) 347 are found doing well, and 31 only re-convicted; and out of 49 girls 47 are doing well, and not one re-convicted; and, whether, considering the good results of the present system, the closing of some of the prisons in Ireland, and the reduction of the number of prisoners in several others, he will consider the advisability of withdrawing or modifying the Circular referred to.

*MR. G. W. BALFOUR: The words attributed to Mr. Fagan will be found in his last Annual Report on Reformatory and Industrial Schools in Ireland. These words should be read with the context, when it will appear that in using the word criminal the inspector meant not alone actual criminals, but waifs and potential criminals. The statistics quoted in the question refer not to industrial school cases, but to those of reformatory schools. There is no intention to withdraw or modify the Circular mentioned.

CAPTAIN DONELAN: Is the right hon. Gentleman aware that this new rule may possibly lead to the closing of some of these schools altogether?

MR. G. W. BALFOUR: It is not a new rule at all, and I have no reason to believe that it will lead to the closing of any schools.

ASSISTANT LAND COMMISSIONERS, IRELAND.

CAPTAIN DONELAN: I beg to ask the Chief Secretary to the Lord Lieutenant of Ireland whether the Irish Land Sub-Commission has been appointed for a fixed term of three years; whether this rule will apply to all future appointments; and, with what object has the change been made.

*MR. G. W. BALFOUR: Presumably the hon. Member refers to the Rule made by the Land Commission on the 13th March last, and which has been laid on the Table. That Rule provides that Temporary Assistant Commissioners appointed by the Lord Lieutenant after the date thereof and before the 31st day of March, 1902, shall hold office, subject to the provisions of the Land Act of 1881, up to and including the 31st day of March, 1902, save that where any such Temporary Assistant Commissioner has attained the age of 65 years he shall not be appointed or re-appointed for a continuous period greater than one year. It is clear from the wording of this Rule that its application is limited to appointments made before the date mentioned. The object of the Rule is to give as long a tenure of office to Temporary Assistant Commissioners as is consistent with the convenience of the Service.

IRISH EMIGRATION TO AMERICA.

CAPTAIN DONELAN: I beg to ask the Chief Secretary to the Lord Lieutenant of Ireland whether he is aware that Irish emigration to America continues upon an extensive scale, and has considerably increased this year as compared with the same period last year; and whether it is intended to take any steps to revive Irish industries with a view to provide Irish workers with employment in their own country.

*MR. G. W. BALFOUR: It is the fact that the number of emigrants from Ireland to the United States during the past five months is larger than the number in the corresponding period of 1898, in which year, however, the number of Irish emigrants was smaller than for many years back. But the number of emigrants from Ireland to the United States and other countries during the past five months is considerably less than the average numbers for the corresponding period in the ten years 1889 to 1898.

CAPTAIN DONELAN: Will the right hon. Gentleman appoint a Committee to inquire into the causes of this steady drain of the Irish population to foreign countries?

*MR. G. W. BALFOUR: I do not think there is any occasion for such a Committee. As far as I am able to judge, the number of emigrants from Ireland to America depends much more upon the state of trade in America than on any other cause.

LAND PURCHASE ACTS.

MR. YOUNG: I beg to ask the Chief Secretary to the Lord Lieutenant of Ireland, with reference to the unreasonable delay complained of by the tenants and owners of land in Ireland in carrying out the Land Purchase Acts (Ireland), whether his attention has been called to an estate in Chancery near Kingscourt; whether he is aware that a number of tenants on that estate have agreed with the landlords to purchase at a price already fixed, and have lodged with the Land Commission the usual affidavits under the Land Purchase Acts, and no court valuer has since been sent to inspect the holdings; and if he can state the cause of delay or say when the court valuer will come down to inspect these holdings.

*MR. G. W. BALFOUR: The hon. Member's question does not contain sufficient information to enable the particular estate referred to to be identified. If he will communicate with me on the subject I will cause further inquiry to be made.

THE AGRICULTURAL GRANT, COUNTY KILDARE.

MR. CAREW (Dublin, College Green): I beg to ask the Chief Secretary to the Lord Lieutenant of Ireland whether he has seen the statement of the Secretary of the Kildare County Council that a sum of £753 had been struck off the amount to which the Council were entitled under the Agricultural Grant, notwithstanding the fact that exceptional circumstances existed which should have increased rather than diminished the county's share of the grant; whether he is aware that the Local Government Board has failed in response to the application of the Secretary of the Council to afford any information as to the basis on which they calculated the amount of the grant; and whether he will order the required information to be given.

*MR. G. W. BALFOUR : The amount of the reduction made by the certificate of the Local Government Board was £289, not £753 as stated in the question. All exceptional circumstances were considered in this case. The information asked for by the County Council was not given, but I propose to lay on the Table of the House a general memorandum explaining the methods adopted by the Local Government Board in calculating the amount of the grant.

IRISH LOCAL GOVERNMENT ORDERS.

MR. DILLON : To ask the Chief Secretary to the Lord Lieutenant of Ireland, whether he can undertake to have the Orders in Council, General Orders, and Rules issued by the Local Government Board, and the Rule of Court in connection with the Local Government (Ireland) Act, collected in one volume and issued to Members before the vote for the Irish Local Government Board is taken.

*MR. G. W. BALFOUR : There are some cases in which the Local Government Board Orders referred to may require modification, and I would rather that they were not collected and printed in a permanent form until these cases have been considered. Apart from that, the collection, when completed, will form a bulky volume, and I do not think there is any chance that it can be printed in time for the Estimates.

MR. DILLON : I beg to ask the Chief Secretary to the Lord Lieutenant of Ireland whether the General Order in reference to collectors of the poor rate, recently issued by the Local Government Board, has been laid upon the table of the House ; and why it has not been circulated.

*MR. G. W. BALFOUR : The General Order has not been laid on the table of the House. Copies of it were sent to every county council and board of guardians in Ireland, and the Order can be procured through any bookseller. I shall be happy to supply the hon. Member with a copy if he so desires.

MR. DILLON : Does not the right hon. Gentleman consider that to be a bad practice ? Can he not undertake that General Orders of this character,

which bear directly on the administration of the Local Government Board, shall be circulated as a Parliamentary paper ?

*MR. G. W. BALFOUR : If the hon. Member will give me a list of the General Orders which he would like so dealt with, I will see if it can be carried out.

CORK COUNCIL CONTRACTS.

MR. TULLY (Leitrim, S.) : I beg to ask the Chief Secretary to the Lord Lieutenant of Ireland, whether the Local Government Board informed one of the Cork Councils early in the year that a director of a joint-stock company, which had a contract with the Council, could not be a member of the Council ; and whether, as Article 12, Sub-section 5 (c), of the Application of Enactments Order, 1898, provides that a shareholder of a company having a contract is not disqualified as a councillor, and as a director's interest is not greater than a shareholder's, he will direct the Local Government Board to issue fresh instructions on the subject.

*MR. G. W. BALFOUR : The Local Government Board have been unable to trace any case such as is referred to in the first paragraph, but if the hon. Member will supply me with further particulars I will have another search made. I may add that the point raised appears to be a legal one, and could not, therefore, be finally decided by an opinion of the Local Government Board, even if they expressed one.

AGRICULTURAL GRANT, COUNTY ROSCOMMON.

MR. TULLY : I beg to ask the Chief Secretary to the Lord Lieutenant of Ireland whether he can state the amount deducted as an excluded charge from the Agricultural Grant for the county Roscommon in respect of the Suck drainage charges ; whether he is aware that the Suck drainage charges are not charges in connection with navigation works under Drainage and Navigation (Ireland) Acts, 1842 to 1857, or any special Act whether public or local ; and whether he will have the Agricultural Grant to Roscommon increased in respect of this matter.

*MR. G. W. BALFOUR : The amount deducted as an excluded charge from the Agricultural Grant to Roscommon in respect of the Suck drainage charges is £100. As regards the second and third paragraphs, the Commissioner of Valuation is of opinion that the Suck Drainage Act of 1889, under which these charges arise, fairly comes within the description given in the latter part of Section 57, Sub-section 6, paragraph 1, of the Local Government Act, and therefore that these charges should be excluded from the benefit of the Agricultural Grant.

MR. TULLY: Can the right hon. Gentleman give me the details of the excluded charges?

*MR. G. W. BALFOUR: I have not the details here, but if the hon. Member will put down a question I will attend to it.

BELFAST STREET RIOTS.

CAPTAIN DONELAN: On behalf of the hon. Member for S. Down, I beg to ask the Chief Secretary to the Lord Lieutenant of Ireland whether his attention has been called to the meeting in Shaftesbury Avenue, Belfast, addressed by one of the Custom House steps preachers, on the 27th May last; whether he is aware that the men present there then marched through the City of Belfast, and when passing through Dougall Street stoned and smashed the windows and fixtures in the business houses of a number of Roman Catholics, and that they afterwards attacked and assaulted with stones or otherwise a number of the city police; and, whether he will take steps to have this practice prevented by the local authorities.

*MR. G W. BALFOUR: The facts are generally as stated in the question, except that it is not true that the mob on this occasion made an attack on the police, none of whom were injured. Proceedings have been instituted against 17 persons for obstruction and riotous behaviour, and the cases will be heard at the Belfast Petty Sessions Court on the 18th instant.

CAPTAIN DONELAN: On behalf of the hon. Member for South Down, I beg to ask the Chief Secretary to the Lord Lieutenant of Ireland whether his attention has been called to the report of the proceedings at the inquest upon the body of the old man Davies who died from injuries received at a so-called religious meeting at the Custom House steps, Belfast; whether a copy of the depositions taken thereat has been received by the authorities, and if a copy will be laid upon the Table of the House; whether he is aware that the depositions disclose that foul and filthy imputations were made by the evangelists disturbing the peace there upon the members of a Roman Catholic Sisterhood remarkable for their works of mercy and charity, respected by the whole community of Belfast, and very dear to the Roman Catholic citizens; also that the coroner's jury and the coroner condemned these open-air demonstrations as disgraceful and a menace to the public peace of the city; and what steps, if any, will be taken to prevent a recurrence of this danger.

*MR. G. W. BALFOUR: I replied to a question on this subject, addressed to me by the hon. Member for East Mayo, on Thursday last. I see no reason for laying a copy of the depositions taken at the inquest on the table of the House, but if the hon. Member so desires I will be happy to supply him with a copy. In answer to the last paragraph, I do not propose, in view of all the circumstances of the case, and after conferring with the local authorities in Belfast, to institute proceedings for the language used on the occasion mentioned, but the Government will certainly prosecute in the event of a repetition of such language in future.

CAPTAIN DONELAN: On behalf of the hon. Member for South Down, I beg to ask the Chief Secretary to the Lord Lieutenant of Ireland whether he is aware that an attack was made upon the Nationalist demonstration on its way home from the meeting at Hannahstown, near Belfast, on Sunday evening last; that stones were thrown by a mob; that a disturbance took place in the Old Lodge or Shankhill Roads, and near the Townsend Street Police Barracks; and that the house of a Roman Catholic publican was attacked in or near Upper Townsend Street. Whether any, and how many, persons have been arrested; and if he can give particulars as to the damage done to persons and property in Belfast during these riots.

*MR. G. W. BALFOUR: Upon the return journey of the Nationalist procession from Hannahstown on the 5th instant, when near Broadway on the Falls Road, a small crowd of the Protestant party assembled in a field and groaned and displayed party emblems. Some of the processionists left the procession and attacked them, both mobs throwing stones. They were at once dispersed by the police and military, and no one was injured. On the Old Lodge Road a mob of roughs of the Protestant party, who had collected to watch the return of some of the processionists, made a wanton attack with stones on the police. They then immediately dispersed. They shortly afterwards reassembled and threw stones at the house of a Roman Catholic publican named O'Neill, breaking all the glass in the windows. They were dispersed by the police and military, and three of them arrested. The place where this disturbance took place is about 300 yards from Brown's Square Barrack, on the Shankhill Road. The disturbance extended to the Shankhill Road and continued for about three hours, but the rioters were held in check from the outset by the military and the police, and very little damage was done to property. In all 47 persons were arrested for riotous conduct, stone throwing, etc. So far as the police are aware, no person was seriously injured. Six members of the Royal Irish Constabulary were wounded, though not seriously. Mrs. O'Neill, wife of the publican whose house was attacked, and two of her boys were injured by stones, and one of them is in hospital suffering from a broken nose. Accurate particulars regarding injury to property cannot yet be given, but at present it would appear that about £270 would cover the damage done.

MR. McCARTAN: I beg to ask the Chief Secretary to the Lord Lieutenant of Ireland whether the military were withdrawn from the streets of Belfast at a very early hour yesterday morning; and, if so, by whose orders was this done; and whether he can say anything further as to the injuries inflicted on the military magistrate Major Tobin, and give further particulars generally as to the riots.

*MR. GERALD BALFOUR: Early yesterday morning the Commissioner of Police satisfied himself that the services of the military were no longer required, and an intimation to that effect having been conveyed to the magistrates on duty with the military, the latter were withdrawn from the streets by degrees. The injury to Major Tobin was of a trivial character, and it never incapacitated him from the discharge of his duty as a military magistrate. Further information regarding the riots is given in my reply to the previous question of the hon. Member. The city has been quiet since Tuesday night, and the riots may now be regarded as virtually over.

LOCAL GOVERNMENT ELECTION EXPENSES.

MR. MACALEESE (Monaghan, N): I beg to ask the Chief Secretary to the Lord Lieutenant of Ireland whether he is aware that heavy election expenses have been caused by candidates putting themselves forward at the recent local government elections in Ireland for divisions where no possible chance existed of their being returned; and whether he will undertake to amend the Local Government (Ireland) Act to the extent of obliging any candidate who provokes a contest, and fails to secure at least a fourth of the votes of the electorate, to pay a moiety of the cost of such election.

*MR. G. W. BALFOUR: The amendment in the law suggested by the hon. Member is clearly one which, if adopted at all, should be of general application. I think, however, it will be found on consideration to be open to grave objections.

THE METROPOLITAN VOLUNTEER "MARCH PAST."

SIR HOWARD VINCENT (Sheffield, Central): I beg to ask the First Commissioner of Works if, having regard to the desire of officers commanding and other officers and members of provincial regiments of Volunteers to see the March Past of the Metropolitan Volunteers before Field-Marshal H.R.H. the Prince of Wales, K.G., on Saturday, 8th July, in commemoration of a similar Review held by His Majesty King George III. in 1799, he will be good enough to authorise or move H.R.H. the Ranger to authorise the erection of a stand near the saluting base, provided that the cost be guaranteed by the Institute of Commanding Officers of the Volunteer Force and the Council or the Major-General Commanding the Home District be responsible for the distribution of seats.

*THE FIRST COMMISSIONER OF WORKS (Mr. AKERS DOUGLAS, Kent, St. Augustine's): The preliminary arrangements are still under the consideration of the General Officer Commanding the Home District, and his proposals have not yet come before the Office of Works. Should the Review take place, it will no doubt be possible to give reasonable facilities for the erection of stands.

HOUSES OF PARLIAMENT— SUGGESTED PROVISION OF AN AMBULANCE.

MR. TOMLINSON (Preston): I beg to ask the First Commissioner of Works whether he will consider the desirability of providing an ambulance within the precincts of the House, to be ready for use in case of accident or sudden illness.

*MR. AKERS DOUGLAS: In reply to my hon. friend, I have to say that the matter appears to me to be outside my jurisdiction ; and I would refer him to the authorities of the House.

RETIRED OFFICERS AND CIVIL EMPLOYMENT IN PUBLIC DEPARTMENTS.

CAPTAIN NORTON: I beg to ask the Secretary to the Treasury if he can state whether the Return for the year ended the 31st March, 1898, of the Army and Navy officers permitted under Rule 2 of the regulations drawn up under Section 6 of the Superannuation Act of 1887 to hold civil employment of profit under public Departments contains a complete list of all officers so employed ; and whether he is aware that Case 4, on pages 28 and 29 of the above-mentioned Return represents that of an officer whose retired pay is £450 a year, and emoluments of civil employment £500, who does not draw retired pay, who is consequently serving for £50 a year, and that the deductions made from this officer's salary, compared with the total amount received of effective and non-effective pay, amounts to 90 per cent.

MR. ANSTRUTHER (St. Andrews Burghs) (for Mr. HANBURY): My right hon. friend has no reason to doubt the completeness of the Return in question.

The lists, however, are not in the first instance compiled at the Treasury. The officer referred to in the second paragraph was appointed Naval Assistant to the Hydrographer while still on the active list. After being placed on the retired list, he was retained in his civil employment under the provisions of the Order in Council of 18th May, 1870, which necessarily precluded him from drawing retired pay. The case is not an ordinary instance of deduction, as the officer was in receipt of the same emoluments both before and after retirement.

TELEGRAPHIC DELAYS.

MR. ASCROFT (Oldham): I beg to ask the Secretary to the Treasury whether his attention has been called to the extraordinary length of time taken in the transit of the following telegraphic messages to Oldham, between the 3rd and 18th of May: From Manchester, 48 minutes ; Eastbourne, 2 hours 2 minutes and 2 hours 12 minutes ; Crystal Palace, 2 hours 17 minutes ; London, 2 hours 14 minutes ; Cambridge, 2 hours 4 minutes ; Kennington Oval, 2 hours 4 minutes ; Bath, 2 hours 4 minutes ; Worcester, 2 hours 11 minutes ; House of Commons, 1 hour 40 minutes ; and Liverpool, 1 hour 19 minutes ; and whether there is any intention on the part of the postal authorities to give a through wire to Oldham from London, or in some other way remove the cause for the constant complaints that are made by supplying an efficient and effective telegraphic service.

MR. ANSTRUTHER (for MR. HANBURY): My hon. friend communicated with the Postmaster-General on the 24th ultimo respecting the delay sustained by the telegrams in question. The various cases are being investigated, and as soon as the inquiry is completed an explanation will be furnished to him. In regard to the question of a wire from London to Oldham, I fear I can only refer him to the answer given on the 15th ultimo.

MR. ASCROFT: I beg to ask the Secretary to the Treasury, as representing the Postmaster-General, whether he can give any explanation why a telegraphic message sent from London on the 31st May to Messrs. Bradbury and Co., of Oldham, took over one hour before it arrived at the Oldham Post-office ; whether he is aware that the systematic neglect of the postal authorities to grapple with the delay in transmitting messages to Oldham is resulting in considerable loss to the constituency ; and whether, if the postal authorities cannot remedy the evil without going to the expense of a separate wire, it is intended to do what is necessary in the interests of the public.

MR. ANSTRUTHER (for Mr. HAN-BURY): The Postmaster - General is unable to find any trace of the message to which the hon. Member refers, but if he will furnish him with the necessary particulars inquiry will be made. The Postmaster - General is not aware that there is any general· delay in the transmission of Oldham telegrams. The cases to which the hon. Member has drawn attention are of an exceptional nature. The matter is, however, being kept under review, and every effort will be made to avoid unnecessary delay.

THE "MANDAT-POSTE" SYSTEM.

MR. BILL (Staffordshire, Leek) : I beg to ask the Secretary to the Treasury, as representing the Postmaster - General, whether the attention of the Postmaster-General has been called to the mandat-poste system, for the transmission of money by post, which has been for many years in operation with great success in Switzerland and Germany ; and whether he will consider whether it would be desirable to give the system a trial in this country.

MR. ANSTRUTHER (for Mr. HAN-BURY : The question whether it is desirable to introduce into this country the money-card system in operation in some Continental countries is under the consideration of the Postmaster-General, and it is not possible at present to make any definite announcement on the subject.

THE MONEY-LENDING BILL.

MR. ASCROFT : I beg to ask the First Lord of the Treasury whether, in view of the fact that the Money-lending Bill was particularly referred to in the Queen's Speech, and that it has already been read the third time in the House of Lords, it is the intention of the Government to proceed with the measure this session ; and whether he can give any informa-

tion as to the date when it will be brought forward for discussion in this House.

CAPTAIN CHALONER (Wilts, West-bury) : I beg at the same time to ask the First Lord of the Treasury whether there is any prospect of his being able to proceed with the Money-lending Bill at an early date.

MR. A. J. BALFOUR : I am afraid that in the present situation of the business of the House I cannot make any accurate forecast which would enable me to answer my hon. friends' questions.

BUSINESS OF THE HOUSE.

MR. CROMBIE : I beg to ask the First Lord of the Treasury whether he can state definitely the day on which Scotch Supply will be taken.

MR. A. J. BALFOUR : I think I intimated I would take it to-morrow week. On Monday I propose to take the Private Bill Procedure (Scotland) Bill, on Tuesday the third readings of the London Government Bill and the Finance Bill, and Thursday I propose to allocate to the Vote of Censure, or the Motion to be proposed by hon. Gentlemen opposite, on the subject of the sugar duties.

MR. CHANNING (Northampton, E.): What Supply, if any, will be taken after the Foreign Office Vote to-morrow ?

MR. A. J. BALFOUR : I confess I have not considered that. If the hon. Member will communicate with me privately later I will endeavour to inform him.

SIR H. CAMPBELL-BANNERMAN (Stirling Burghs): I wish to ask the right hon. Gentleman if he can tell the House when the Naval Works Bill and the Military Loans Bill will be introduced. Both Bills were promised long ago.

MR. A. J. BALFOUR : I am anxious to produce them at an early date, and I hope no long delay will intervene before they are introduced. The Military Bill is almost ready for introduction, and may be expected in a day or two. The Naval Bill is not quite so well advanced, but I think it will be in the hands of Members before very long.

Sir CHARLES CAMERON (Glasgow, Bridgeton): I beg to ask the First Lord of the Treasury when it is proposed to proceed with the Telegraphs (Telephonic Communication, &c.) Bill.

Mr. A. J. BALFOUR: I regret that my right hon. friend the Secretary to the Treasury is not able to be in his place to-day, and I have not been able to communicate with him. Perhaps the hon. Gentleman will postpone the question till a later day.

MUNICIPAL TRADING COMMITTEE.

Mr. BARTLEY (Islington, N.): When will the Municipal Trading Committee be appointed ?

Mr. A. J. BALFOUR: I am afraid I cannot give any pledge at present.

UNDERSIZED FISH BILL.

The PRESIDENT of the BOARD of TRADE (Mr. Ritchie, Croydon): I beg to ask the leave of the House to introduce a Bill dealing with undersized fish. Its object is to prevent the destruction of immature fish, and I am sure the House will realise that it is a matter of importance to prevent the destruction of such fish, which has the effect of limiting our food supply. The Bill is based on the Report of the Select Committee on Sea Fisheries. A measure was introduced by us in the House of Lords in 1897, and it passed through that House, but came down to the House of Commons too late to be considered. The present Bill is somewhat similar, and will, I hope, be passed into law. Every year the Fishery Department have been urging on me the great necessity of introducing a Bill on this subject, because of the great injury caused by the destruction of undersized fish which is constantly going on. Similar representations have also been made to me by the representatives of sea fisheries, and by the Fishmongers' Company.

Mr. GIBSON BOWLES (King's Lynn): This is a Bill which has been introduced almost every year since I have had the honour of holding a seat in this House, and I feel bound to make one or

two remarks with reference to it. I believe this Bill is introduced under an entire misapprehension. I am perfectly convinced that fish in the sea, or even the fringe of them, cannot be touched by anything done by trawlers or lines; but however that may be, what I wish to impress on the House is the great ignorance which prevails as to the habits of fish, even among fishermen. No one can tell, for instance, why the herring come one year and not another. Consequently if this Bill is founded on the assumption that we know a great deal about fish and their habits, it is a very serious misapprehension indeed. The right hon. Gentleman has referred to the Sea Fisheries Committee of 1893. That Committee practically reported what I have just said, viz., that there was great ignorance with regard to the size of fish. I would ask leave to read a sentence from the Report of the Biological Society, of which the First Lord of the Treasury and the Secretary for the Colonies are vice-presidents, and it is therefore a very important society. On page 239 the Report states :

"A calm survey of the situation, however shows that the cry concerning the annual diminution of our fish supply has been dispelled by the institution of statistics ; that the alleged destruction of spawn has no basis in fact; that the destruction of immature fish is common to all classes of fishermen, and nowhere is proved to have resulted in the ruin of any sea fishery."

I fail to see the basis of the Bill, or any justification for it, either in the Report of the Committee of 1893 or in that of the Biological Society. Our fish supply is increasing, and has increased very largely during the last ten years, both in quantity and value. There is, however, one matter to which I wish to call attention, and that is the increasing importation of foreign fishermen who are not subject to these restrictions.

Mr. RITCHIE: Yes, they are in France and elsewhere.

Mr. BOWLES : I think the right hon. Gentleman is mistaken. He is supposed to have informed my right hon. friend the Member for Thanet that these restrictions would apply to foreign fishermen, but in my opinion what my right hon. friend wanted to know was whether these restrictions were applied to foreign fishermen in their own waters.

If they were he would support the Bill, otherwise he would not. I think that is manifestly fair. There is great difficulty in saying what are undersized fish. Fish are of all sizes, and a fish is not undersized because it is small, any more than a Shetland pony is undersized because it is smaller than a shire horse. Our knowledge in regard to these matters is very defective indeed, and it would be a very dangerous thing to legislate without further information. What I suggest is that this matter should be referred to a Select Committee, and if the evidence given before the Committee justifies it, and if the fishermen are found ready to cut their own throats by opposing undersized fish—which I do not admit are undersized at all, because small fish are the very best—then let the Bill be proceeded with. I reserve my opinion of the Bill until I have seen it ; but whatever the Bill may be, I hope it will be referred to a Select Committee.

Mr. RITCHIE : I have no objection to considering the hon. Member's suggestion.

Bill to provide against the Destruction of Undersized Fish, ordered to be brought in by Mr. Ritchie.

Bill " to provide against the Destruction of Undersized Fish," presented accordingly, and read the first time ; to be read a second time upon Monday next, and to be printed. [Bill 229.]

PARISH COUNCILLORS (TENURE OF OFFICE) BILL.

Lords' Amendment to be considered forthwith ; considered, and agreed to.

THE SOUDAN EXPEDITION, 1896-7-8.

(THANKS OF THE HOUSE.)

THE FIRST LORD OF THE TREASURY (Mr. A. J. BALFOUR, Manchester, E.) : It will not, I think, be necessary for me to trouble the House at any length in regard to the series of resolutions which I propose you should put, Mr. Speaker, from the chair, for on Monday last, to the best of my ability, I made a general survey of the campaign which culminated at Omdurman, and did my best to explain

Mr. Bowlec.

the difficulties which were inherent to that expedition, and the skill, success, and courage with which the Sirdar and all those who served under him contrived to surmount them. For similar reasons it will not be necessary for me to say anything at all about the first of these Resolutions, for the ground of it was entirely covered by the Debate on Monday, and the result of the Division which the House then took is a sufficient indication of what the opinion of this assembly is as to the merits of Lord Kitchener as a soldier and as a general. With regard to the remaining names mentioned in the Resolution, it is hardly necessary for me to do more than say one word, for they are writ large in the history of the campaign, and they are names familiar to all those who followed the fortunes of British and Egyptian arms from month to month and year to year, in the course of that arduous and protracted contest. It may suffice, therefore, if I remind the House that the first name on the list— that of Major-General Hunter—is that of a man who has for 14 years been connected with the organisation of the Egyptian Army. As much as any other man, perhaps, he is to be congratulated upon the degree of discipline and efficiency which that army has attained. In addition to these services, stretching far back into the past, I may remind the House that he was in high command at Ferkeh, Hafir, and Dongola, and was in chief command of the expedition which took Abu Hammad, an expedition which was remarkable for a forced march of, I think, six days under the blazing sun of a tropical summer, a feat of endurance not perhaps least remarkable among the feats of a similar kind of which we have a record. The next name is that of the Chief of the Staff—Major-General Sir H. M. L. Rundle, who, in his responsible capacity, did so much to organise the expedition, and who, like General Hunter, has long been honourably connected with the history of the Egyptian Army. Major-General Gatacre is known to all Englishmen in connection with the Chitral campaign. He was, in this campaign, the chief commander under Lord Kitchener at the battle of Atbara, and he commanded the British Division at the final and crowning triumph at Omdurman. The two next names on the list are those of the generals who commanded the two brigades of British troops—Major-General

Lyttelton and Major-General Wauchope. Sir, the British troops were but a third, or thereabouts, of the total force engaged on our side, but, as everybody will admit, though they were a relatively small fraction of the total force, they were an absolutely essential portion of it, and without the assistance of British troops it would have been insanity to have undertaken the final advance towards Khartoum, and any attempt to have made that advance without them would have been followed by signal disaster. The next name is that of Colonel Sir F. R. Wingate, who, I think, under ordinary circumstances and in an ordinary campaign would probably hardly appear in the list of those whom this House would desire to thank in connection with a successful expedition; at least I am not aware that the head of the Intelligence Department has on similar occasions been included on the list of officers whom this House has desired to honour by name. But, Sir, this expedition had many circumstances which sharply distinguish it from other expeditions in which this country has been engaged, and the part played by the Intelligence Department was so important and so critical that I think we are well advised to include specially and by name the most distinguished officer to whose labours in chief measure the efficiency of that department is due. I need hardly mention the Intelligence Department without at the same time mentioning a name which does not appear, and cannot appear upon this list. It is a name which I think everybody must have in their recollection when they turn their minds to the sources of information which enabled us to deal successfully with the power of the Madhi. That name, sir, is that of Slatin Pasha, whose dramatic history is familiar to all. Sir, I do not know that I need say anything in particular about the distinguished names which follow, which are those of the commanders of artillery and the brigade commanders of the Egyptians and the Soudanese. Their names are familiar to all; they are Colonel MacDonald and Colonel Lewis ; and perhaps it is only needful for me to remind the House that Colonel MacDonald had, by the fortune of war, an opportunity of showing perhaps the most brilliant tactical display of the battle of Omdurman, and of bearing an especially distinguished part in a contest

where all played their part well and manfully. Colonel Lewis, who also commanded a brigade at Omdurman, had the good luck some month or six weeks later to be the General in chief command at the brilliant battle of Rosieries, and though that battle is subsequent to the military operations with which these resolutions specially deal, it is not unfit that we should bear in mind that his services in the Soudan were not confined either to the battle at Omdurman or the previous work which he did in connection with Lord Kitchener's main force. The last name in this list is that of Commander Keppel. It is not often, I believe, that the Navy has proved itself an efficient ally of the Army at a distance of 1,400 miles from its native ocean ; but in this case, as is well known, this distinguished naval officer and those under him played an essential and practical part in the battle of Omdurman, and had their place in the British line, and in that position performed essential service to the British arms. I need not dwell upon the spirited and most useful performances which distinguished the naval forces at earlier periods. It is enough if I remind the House that at Omdurman they were an essential part of our commanding force, and they performed admirable services not only in the battle of Omdurman, but in connection with the taking of the city of Omdurman after the victory was won. There is one other name upon the list—that of Lieut.-General Sir Francis Grenfell. He had not the good fortune, which he so ardently desired, of himself taking any immediate and active part in the advance to Khartoum, but none the less he did great service in the part that was allotted to him, and I am glad to think that we are able to include his name in this list, because surely no man is more closely or honourably associated with the recovery of the Egyptian military force from the disasters which had reduced it to a nullity, and almost worse than a nullity, than the distinguished general whom I ask the House to include in the list of those whom they are going to thank by name. Sir, the last paragraph of this series of resolutions refers to those who, alas ! cannot be benefited by any action we can take, and who are beyond the reach of any thanks or praise from us. They did their duty, and died in the consciousness that they would earn by their death the gratitude of their countrymen, and I am glad that I have this opportunity of putting on permanent record our sense of their services, and of conveying to those who mourn them, not merely as public servants and devoted citizens, but as near relations and friends, our sense of the magnitude of the loss they have endured. I think it is not necessary that I should add anything more, and I beg now to move the Resolutions which stand in my name on the paper.

SIR H. CAMPBELL-BANNERMAN (Stirling Burghs): I rise for the purpose of seconding the Motion just made by the First Lord of the Treasury. On Monday last, like the right hon. Gentleman, but in the more modest measure which befits my position, I had the opportunity of expressing my opinion of the splendid qualities exhibited and the brilliant services rendered in this expedition by the General in chief command, by the officers who constituted his staff, and by the troops of all ranks who served under him. I will not occupy the time of the House by repeating anything I then said, but will merely say that I cordially and sincerely approve of these Resolutions, which give expression to the admiration and gratitude of the House of Commons.

SOUDAN EXPEDITION (THANKS OF THE HOUSE).

Motion made and Question proposed,

"That the thanks of this House be given to Major-General Lord Kitchener of Khartoum, G.C.B., K.C.M.G., for the distinguished skill and ability with which he planned and conducted the campaign on the Nile of 1896-7-8, which culminated in the battle of Omdurman, the capture of Khartoum, and the overthrow of the power of the Khalifa."—(*Mr. Balfour.*)

DR. FARQUHARSON (Aberdeenshire, West): I am very unwilling to stir up any opposition to the unanimity with which this Vote will be passed, and I yield to no one in my appreciation of the brilliant services which have been rendered; but I should be wanting in my duty to the profession to which I still have the honour to belong, and the Army Medical Department, if I failed to direct the

Mr. A. J. Balfour.

attention of the House to a conspicuous omission.

*MR. SPEAKER: Order, order! The hon. Gentleman cannot do that upon this Resolution. Any observation which he desires to make upon the point will come on the next Resolution.

MR. DAVITT (Mayo, S.): Any opposition to a motion of this kind, which will be accepted with unanimity by the great bulk of the British people, must appear an ungracious act upon my part. I acknowledge it frankly, and I assure the House that it is only with a deep sense of conscientiousness and as a matter of duty that I take this step. I am not responsible for that system of rule which compels me, an Irish Nationalist, to come here, where I find myself in opposition to the bulk of the British nation. I cannot agree to this Motion, for several reasons. In the first place, a very serious step has been taken in moving a vote of thanks to the Egyptian Army, which means that this House of Commons claims to exercise sovereign rights over a country believed by other Powers of Europe to be independent.

*MR. SPEAKER: Order, order! If the hon. Member is going to confine his remarks to the Egyptian Army, that will come on the next resolution.

MR. DILLON (Mayo, E.): On a point of order, Sir, are you going to put each Resolution separately, or are we going to discuss the resolutions as a whole; because a question will arise as to the conduct of the Soudanese troops?

MR. SPEAKER: They will be taken separately, and any question relevant to a particular Resolution must be raised upon that Resolution. Otherwise confusion may arise.

Question put.

The House divided: Ayes, 321; Noes, 20. (Division List No. 178.)

AYES.

Acland-Hood,Capt.SirAlex.F.
Allan, William (Gateshead)
Allen, W. (Newc.underLyme)
Allhusen, Augustus Henry E.
Allsopp, Hon. George
Anson, Sir William Reynell
Arnold, Alfred
Ascroft, Robert
Ashton, Thomas Gair
Atkinson, Rt. Hon. John
Austin, Sir John (Yorkshire)
Bagot, Capt. J. FitzRoy
Baillie,James E. B.(Inverness)
Baird, John George A.
Balcarres, Lord
Baldwin, Alfred
Balfour, Rt.Hn.A.J.(Manch'r)
Balfour, Rt. Hn. G.W.(Leeds)
Banbury, Frederick George
Barlow, John Emmott
Barnes, Frederic Gorell
Barry, Rt.Hn.A.H.S.-(Hunts)
Bartley, George C. T.
Barton, Dunbar Plunket
Beach,Rt.Hn.SirMH.(Bristol)
Begg, Ferdinand Faithfull
Bemrose, Sir Henry Howe
Bentinck, Lord Henry C.
Beresford, Lord Charles
Bethell, Commander
Bhownaggree, Sir M. M.
Biddulph, Michael
Billson, Alfred
Blakiston-Houston, John
Blundell, Colonel Henry
Bolitho, Thomas Bedford
Bond, Edward
Boulnois, Edmund
Broadhurst, Henry
Brodrick, Rt. Hon. St. John
Brookfield, A. Montagu
Brown, Alexander H.
Bryce, Rt. Hon. James
Brymer, William Ernest
Bullard, Sir Harry
Butcher, John George
Buxton, Sydney Charles
Caldwell, James
Campbell,Rt.Hn.J.A.(Glas.)
Campbell-Bannerman, Sir H.
Carlile, William Walter
Cavendish, R. F. (N. Lancs.)
Cavendish, V.C.W.(Derbysh.)
Cawley, Frederick
Cayzer, Sir Charles William
Cecil, Evelyn (Hertford, East)
Cecil, Lord Hugh (Greenwich)
Chaloner, Captain R. G. W.
Chamberlain, Rt.Hn.J.(Birm.)
Chamberlain, J. A. (Worc'r.)
Channing, Francis Allston
Charrington, Spencer
Chelsea, Viscount
Clarke, Sir Ed. (Plymouth)
Cochrane, Hon. Thos. H. A. E.
Coddington, Sir William
Coghill, Douglas Harry
Cohen, Benjamin Louis
Collings, Rt. Hon. Jesse
Colston, Chas. Edw. H.Athole
Colville, John

Compton, Lord Alwyne
Cooke,C.W.Radcliffe(Heref'd)
Cox, Irwin Edw. B. (Harrow)
Cranborne, Viscount
Cripps, Charles Alfred
Crombie, John William
Curzon, Viscount
Dalkeith, Earl of
Davies,SirHoratioD.(Chath'm
Davies,M.Vaughan-(Cardigan
Denny, Colonel
Dickson-Poynder, Sir John P.
Disraeli, Coningsby Ralph
Dorington, Sir John Edward
Doughty, George
Douglas, Rt. Hon. A. Akers-
Doxford, William Theodore
Duckworth, James
Dunn, Sir William
Elliot, Hon. A. Ralph Douglas
Fardell, Sir T. George
Farquharson, Dr. Robert
Fellowes, Hon. Ailwyn Edw.
Ferguson, R. C. M. (Leith)
Fergusson,Rt.Hn.SirJ.(Man)
Finch, George H.
Finlay, Sir Robert Bannatyne
Fisher, William Hayes
Fison, Frederick William
FitzGerald, Sir Rob. Penrose-
Fitzmaurice, Lord Edmond
Flannery, Sir Fortescue
Fletcher, Sir Henry
Flower, Ernest
Folkestone, Viscount
Foster, Sir Walter (Derby Co.
Fry, Lewis
Gedge, Sydney
Gibbons, J. Lloyd
Gibbs, Hn. A.G.H. (City Lond.
Gibbs,Hon.Vicary(St. Albans)
Giles, Charles Tyrrell
Gladstone, Rt. Hn. Herbert J.
Goddard, Daniel Ford
Godson, Sir Augustus Fredk.
Gold, Charles
Goldsworthy, Major-General
Gordon, Hon. John Edward
Gorst, Rt. Hn Sir John E.
Goschen,RtHn G.J. (St. Geo's
Goschen, George J. (Sussex)
Goulding, Edward Alfred
Gourley,SirEdwardTemperley
Graham, Henry Robert
Green,Walfrd D. (Wedn'sb'y)
Griffith, Ellis J.
Gunter, Colonel
Gurdon,Sir WilliamBrampton
Hall, Rt. Hon. Sir Charles
Halsey, Thomas Frederick
Hamilton,Rt.Hon.LordGeorge
Hardy, Laurence
Hare, Thomas Leigh
Harwood, George
Hatch, Ernest Frederick Geo.
Hayne, Rt.Hon.CharlesSeale-
HedderwickThomasCharlesH
Helder, Augustus
Hickman, Sir Alfred
Hill,Rt.Hn.A.Staveley(Staffs.
Hill, Arthur (Down, West)

Hill, Sir EdwardStock(Bristol
Hoare,EdwBrodie(Hampstead
Hoare, Samuel (Norwich)
Hobhouse, Henry
Holland,Hon. Lionel R. (Bow)
Hornby, Sir William Henry
Horniman, Frederick John
Howard, Joseph
Howell, William Tudor
Hubbard, Hon. Evelyn
Humphreys-Owen, Arthur C.
Hutchinson, Capt. G. W. G.-
Hutton, John (Yorks., N.R.)
Jacoby, James Alfred
Jebb, Richard Claverhouse
Jeffreys, Arthur Frederick
Jessel, Capt. Herbert Merton
Johnson-Ferguson,Jabez Edw.
Johnstone, Heywood (Sussex)
Jolliffe, Hon. H. George
Jones, D. Brynmor (Swansea)
Kearley, Hudson E.
Kenyon, James
Kimber, Henry
King, Sir Henry Seymour
Kinloch, Sir John George S.
Kitson, Sir James
Knowles, Lees
Lafone, Alfred
Lambert, George
Laurie, Lieut.-General
Lawson, John Grant (Yorks.)
Lecky, Rt. Hn. William E. H.
Leese, Sir J. F. (Accrington)
Leighton, Stanley
Leng, Sir John
Llewelyn, Sir D.- (Swansea)
Lloyd-George, David
Lockwood, Lt.-Col. A. R.
Loder, Gerald Walter E.
Long, Col. C. W. (Evesham)
Long, Rt. Hon. W. (Liverpool)
Lopes, Henry Yarde Buller
Lorne, Marquess of
Lough, Thomas
Lowe, Francis William
Lowther, Rt. Hon. J. (Kent)
Lowther,Rt.Hn.J.W.(Cumb'd)
Lucas-Shadwell, William
Lyell, Sir Leonard
Lyttelton, Hon. Alfred
Macartney, W. G. Ellison
Macdona, John Cumming
MacIver, David (Liverpool)
Maclure, Sir John William
M'Arthur, Charles (Liverpool)
M'Calmont, H. L. B. (Cambs.)
M'Iver, Sir L. (Edinburgh, W.)
M'Killop, James
M'Laren, Charles Benjamin
Manners, Lord Edward W. J.
Mappin, Sir Frederick Thorpe
Mellor, Colonel (Lancashire)
Mellor, Rt. Hn. J. W. (Yorks.)
Melville, Beresford Valentine
Mendl, Sigismund Ferdinand
Middlemore, J. Throgmorton
Mildmay, Francis Bingham
Milward, Colonel Victor
Monk, Charles James
Montagu, Sir S. (Whitechapel)

Moon, Edward Robert Pacy
Moore, William (Antrim, N.)
Morgan, Hn. F. (Monm'thsh.)
Morgan,WPritchard (Merthyr
Morley, Charles (Breconsh.)
Morton, ArthurH.A.(Deptf'd)
Morton, E. J. C. (Devonport)
Moulton, John Fletcher
Mount, William George
Murray, Rt. Hn. A. G. (Bute)
Murray, Charles J. (Coventry)
Newdigate, Francis Alexander
Nicol, Donald Ninian
Norton, Capt. Cecil William
Nussey, Thomas Willans
Oldroyd, Mark
O'Neill, Hon. Robert Torrens
Orr-Ewing, Charles Lindsay
Parkes, Ebenezer
Paulton, James Mellor
Pease, Alfred E. (Cleveland)
Pease, Joseph A. (Northumb.)
Percy, Earl
Perks, Robert William
Pierpoint, Robert
Platt-Higgins, Frederick
Pretyman, Ernest George
Pryce-Jones, Lt.-Col. Edward
Purvis, Robert
Pym, C. Guy
Quilter, Sir Cuthbert
Rankin, Sir James
Rasch, Major Frederic Carne
Reckitt, Harold James
Richardson, J.(Durham, S.E.)
Richardson, Sir T. (Hartlep'l)
Ridley, Rt. Hon. Sir M. W.
Ritchie, Rt. Hon. Chas. T.

Roberts, John H. (Denbighs.)
Robertson,Herbert (Hackney)
Robinson, Brooke
Rollit, Sir Albert Kaye
Rothschild,Hon. LionelWalter
Round, James
Royds, Clement Molyneux
Russell, T. W. (Tyrone)
Rutherford, John
Ryder, John Herbert Dudley
Samuel, Harry S.(Limehouse)
Samuel, J. (Stockton on Tees)
Sassoon, Sir Edward Albert
Scoble, Sir Andrew Richard
Scott, Chas. Prestwich(Leigh)
Seely, Charles Hilton
Seton-Karr, Henry
Sharpe, William Edward T.
Shaw, Charles Ed. (Stafford)
Shaw, Thomas (Hawick, B.)
Shaw-Stewart,M.H.(Renfrew)
Simeon, Sir Barrington
Sinclair, Capt. J. (Forfarshire)
Smith, James Parker (L'n'rks)
Smith, Hon. W. F. D. (Strand)
Soames, Arthur Wellesley
Spicer, Albert
Stanley, Hon. A. (Ormskirk)
Stanley, Edward J. (Somerset)
Stanley, Henry M.(Lambeth)
Stanley, Lord (Lancashire)
Stevenson, Francis S.
Stirling-Maxwell, Sir J. M.
Stone, Sir Benjamin
Strachey, Edward
Sturt, Hon. Humphrey N.
Tennant, Harold John
Thomas, A. (Glamorgan, E.)

Thomas, David A. (Merthyr)
Thorburn, Walter
Thornton, Percy M.
Tollemache, Henry James
Tomlinson, W. E. Murray
Trevelyan, Charles Philips
Tritton, Charles Ernest
Ure, Alexander
Usborne, Thomas
Valentia, Viscount
Vincent, Col. Sir C. E. H.
Wallace, Robert (Perth)
Walton, Joseph (Barnsley)
Warr, Augustus Frederick
Wedderburn, Sir William
Wharton, Rt. Hon. John L.
Whiteley, George (Stockport)
Williams, Colonel R. (Dorset)
Williams, Joseph P.- (Birm.)
Willox, Sir John Archibald
Wilson, John (Govan)
Wilson, J. W. (Worces'e, N.)
Wilson-Todd, W. H. (Yorks.)
Wodehouse,Rt.Hn.E.R.(Bath)
Wolff, Gustav Wilhelm
Woodall, William
Wortley, Rt. Hon. C. B. S.-
Wyndham, George
Wyndham-Quin, Maj. W. H.
Young, Comm'nd'r (Berks,E.)
Younger, William
Yoxall, James Henry

TELLERS FOR THE AYES—
  Sir William Walrond and
  Mr. Anstruther.

NOES.

Austin, M. (Limerick, W.)
Curran, Thomas (Sligo, S.)
Dillon, John
Doogan, P. C.
Fenwick, Charles
Healy, Thomas. J. (Wexford)
Lawson, Sir W. (Cumberland)
MacAleese, Daniel

M'Ghee, Richard
Morris, Samuel
O'Brien, James F. X. (Cork)
O'Brien, Patrick (Kilkenny)
O'Connor, T. P. (Liverpool)
Roberts, John Bryn (Eifion)
Steadman, William Charles
Sullivan, Donal (Westmeath

Tully, Jasper
Wilson, H. J. (York, W. R.)
Wilson, John (Durham, Mid.)
Woods, Samuel

TELLERS FOR THE NOES—Mr.
  Davitt and Mr. James
  O'Connor.

1. Resolved, That the thanks of this House be given to Major-General Lord Kitchener of Khartoum, G.C.B., K.C.M.G., for the distinguished skill and ability with which he planned and conducted the campaign on the Nile of 1896-7-8, which culminated in the Battle of Omdurman, the capture of Khartoum, and the overthrow of the power of the Khalifa.

Motion made, and Question proposed—

"That the thanks of this House be given to:—

Major-General Sir Archibald Hunter, K.C.B., D.S.O. ;

Major-General Sir Henry MacLeod Leslie Rundle, K.C.B., C.M.G., D.S.O., R.A. ;

Major-General Sir William Forbes Gatacre, K.C.B., D.S.O. ;

Major-General the Hon. Neville Gerald Lyttelton, C.B.;

Major-General A. G. Wauchope, C.B., C.M.G. ;

Major and Brevet Colonel Sir Francis Reginald Wingate, K.C.M.G., C.B., D.S.O., R.A. ;

Lieutenant-Colonel and Brevet Colonel C. J. Long, R.A. ;

Major and Brevet Colonel J. G. Maxwell, D.S.O. ;

Major and Brevet Colonel H. A. Mac-Donald, D.S.O. ;

Lieutenant-Colonel D. F. Lewis, C.B. ;

Major and Brevet Lieutenant-Colonel J. Collinson, C.B. ;

Captain C. R. Keppel, C.B., D.S.O., R.N. ;

and to the other Officers and Warrant Officers of the Navy, the British and the Egyptian Army, and the Royal Marines, for the energy and gallantry with which they executed the services which they were called upon to perform."—(*Mr. A. J. Balfour.*)

Dr. FARQUHARSON : I should like to direct the attention of the House to an omission in this list, which, from my point of view, is important, and to be deeply regretted. While I appreciate the services of the distinguished officers mentioned in the Resolution, I do not see in the list the name of a man to whom I think a great portion of the success of the campaign is due, namely, Surgeon-General Taylor, whose distinguished and admirable conduct of the medical part of the service called forth the emphatic admiration of his chief. I do not propose to move anything, but I think it my duty to raise a protest against this omission. I understand there is no precedent for the inclusion of medical officers in such a vote of thanks ; but I should have thought the House might have made a precedent. I hope the omission was not made in deference to the foolish bogie about combatants and non-combatants. There was a notion in the old days that the officers were combatants, but that the medical officers were not so ; but now we know that in campaigns the doctors are called upon to expose themselves as much as, if not more than, other officers, and the distinction has been practically abolished. I hope that in any answer that may be made to me that will not be brought up again. It is practically admitted that success in modern warfare depends largely on engineering skill and medical science. I know that Lord Kitchener would be the first to recognise the great services rendered by the medical officers throughout the campaign and in the action in Omdurman, for in his despatch he gave a noble and generous tribute to the medical officers. His lordship said :

"The medical arrangements were so conducted as to afford the maximum of comfort with the minimum of suffering."

I do not think that any higher compliment than that could be paid by a commanding officer. Not only do the medical officers take a full share in the risk of battle, but when the actual campaign is over, when the fighting has terminated, and the other officers have retired to their tents, the doctors' work is practically beginning. They have to sit up long hours treating the sick and the suffering and wounded through perils and dangers. We should also remember that, when the ambulance work is over, they are fre-

quently called upon to fight pestilence. I emphatically say that the medical officers in this campaign accomplished their work with skill, bravery, and success, under a variety of the most unpromising conditions, and I express my disappointment that the name of not one of these medical officers appears in this Motion. It is unfortunate, because by a wise provision of the Secretary for War medical officers have now been given definite rank ; and it is a great misfortune, when their services have been so singularly successful, and when it is important that our Army Medical Department should be made more popular in the medical schools, that this recognition was not given. I want to know why this inclusion was not made, and I hope it may yet be done.

*Mr. DAVITT : I cannot support this Resolution for many reasons. First, there is no expression of regret, either in the terms of the Motion or in the speech of the right hon. Gentleman, for the killing of the wounded, on the orders of these officers, at the battle of Omdurman. I feel that their action towards helpless enemies on the field of battle was a disgrace to our modern civilisation, and yet we are asked, lower down in this Resolution, to declare that the conduct of the officers and men in this respect was worthy of admiration. I would not be an Irishman if I could give my assent for a moment to the laudatory terms of the Motion to the officers and men to which I have referred. We are called upon to vote this thanks for the mowing down by machinery of thousands of people who, whatever were their faults, never inflicted any injury or injustice upon my country. Hon. Members may laugh, but I am not aware that they have ever even thought in their wildest moments of desert warfare of invading the shores of England, and I cannot understand how, for the killing of thousands of these people by machinery while helpless on the field of battle, we are asked now to give these officers and soldiers this meed of praise. Sir, what were the casualties at this so-called great battle of Omdurman ? What was the real bravery for which this Vote is to be given ? I find, according to the statements made by correspondents who were on the field of battle, that there were about 100 Anglo-Egyptian soldiers killed. I am sorry—as sorry as any hon. Member opposite—for the families of those men who died on the field of battle in carrying out a policy for which they were not responsible. But at the same time my sympathies go out to the widows and children, and the tens of thousands of the poor Soudanese who lost at that battle their bread-winners. I say that the loss on the Anglo-Egyptian side was so trivial that it takes away altogether from the action at Omdurman the character of a real battle. There is one regrettable fact about this whole discussion which I deeply regret, and that is the studied silence of the speakers on both sides of the House with reference to the desperate bravery of those savage warriors in defence of their country. Sir, there have been English soldiers and English statesmen who were not ashamed in this House to bear testimony to the bravery and courage shown by their foes on the battlefield. I say it detracts from the character of present-day statesmen and soldiers that not a single man was found in this House to bear testimony to the pluck and courage of these Soudanese warriors, which was recognised by the English war correspondents.

MR. A. J. BALFOUR: On the Vote to Lord Kitchener, I, in the very strongest way, paid a warm tribute to the extraordinary courage of the Dervishes.

HON. MEMBERS: Withdraw.

MR. DAVITT: I at once withdraw. I was not in the House at the time, I regret to say, when the right hon. Gentleman spoke. I was travelling from Belfast in order to take part in the Division against the Vote to Lord Kitchener. Had I heard the right hon. Gentleman make the statement I would have cheered it heartily, because I must recognise that no one, so far as my experience in this House goes, is ever more courteous and generous to his opponents than the right hon. Gentleman. Therefore, I shall pass over what I had intended to say if the right hon. Gentleman had not corrected me upon that one point. But, Sir, what was the conduct of the soldiers in the Anglo-Egyptian army as compared with the bravery and heroism displayed by the Dervishes? I do not want to go over the ground travelled the other night by some hon. Members; I do not wish to bring up gruesome details. But we do know that the Dervish wounded

Mr. Davitt.

were slaughtered while lying helpless on the battlefield at Omdurman, and after this horrible slaughter I find, from the testimony given by one Corporal Rawlinson in a letter sent to his relatives in Wales, and published in the *Morning Leader* of January 12, 1899, that the Soudanese and Egyptian soldiers went into the city of Omdurman and slaughtered women and children. ("Oh!") According to this corporal several children were tossed on the bayonets of Soudanese soldiers under British and Egyptian officers. ("Oh!") Well, I do not accuse hon. Members of making mockery of this —I am sure they would protest against this as much as I do; their jeering so, I understand, signifies that they do not believe this statement. (Ministerial cheers.) Yes, but I am not the witness. I give you the name of the corporal who made the statement, and, to his credit be it said, it caused a feeling of unutterable disgust in his mind. Well, Sir, we are called to vote praise to men who have been capable of performing acts of cowardly barbarism of this kind. Sir, I for one will not support this Motion. I oppose it as an Irishman, simply because it would be impossible for me to condone in any way the killing of helpless wounded foes on the battlefield of Omdurman, or to support, directly or indirectly, the conduct of Soudanese and Egyptian soldiers under the orders of British officers in perpetrating nameless outrages inside the city after the battle was over.

*MR. CHANNING (Northamptonshire, E.): It is with the utmost reluctance and only from a sense of duty that any one would enter on the topics raised by my hon. friend the Member for Mayo. I cannot but think that the point might have been more properly raised on the next Resolution, that relating to the conduct of the troops, as I do not think the officers are responsible for some of the things that occurred. I voted against the grant to Lord Kitchener on Monday, not because I did not recognise his splendid services in organising the Egyptian Army and in carrying out the work began by a friend of mine on the opposite side of the House, whose friendship I much valued—the late Colonel Duncan. We are glad that the Egyptian Army has been made so efficient, and recognise the splendid services of Lord Kitchener and of the officers named in the resolution in carrying out this campaign. I, for one, feel the most profound doubt as to whether any justification could be offered for the charge that any officer, whether Lord Kitchener or an officer below him, could be found guilty of any formal order or any direct authorisation for the butchery of the wounded that occurred after the battle. The reason why I gave my vote against the grant on Monday, and the reason why I feel so profoundly on this occasion, is that I do think it is a national duty to face such facts as were laid before the House by my hon. friend the Member for the Leigh Division of Lancashire on Monday night, making up a body of evidence as to which there can be no doubt, to which no answer whatever has been given in these debates, and which is not seriously challenged by anyone, making it certain that terrible acts were committed on that battlefield, and have been committed again and again in these Soudanese campaigns. I do think it would be a cowardly neglect of duty, while expressing our warmest thanks to the officers who have carried out their duty nobly and effectively, if we were not to make an effort to make such acts as these impossible in the future. I am not going into the evidence adduced by my hon. friend the Member for the Leigh Division, but I should like to read a few words from the book of Major De Cosson, a distinguished officer who served under Sir Gerald Graham in the Suakim Campaign in 1885, and, upon these specific points, ask the First Lord of the Treasury whether those words do not justify us in asking that there should be some further inquiry into the conduct of these campaigns, so that, as far as possible, we should introduce the principles of Christianity and humanity into every detail of warfare as far as possible. In his book on the campaign of 1885, Major De Cosson says:

"One thing has troubled my mind much, and that is the knowledge that some of the enemy's wounded have been shot in cold blood, though I could scarcely credit it of English troops; but it was unfortunately too true, and I was told by those I could not doubt that the same thing was repeated during the skirmishes with the convoys, and that even an officer had been seen to empty his revolver at a man writhing on the ground. It is most painful for me to allude to the subject, but I do so that we may never have to reproach ourselves with anything of the kind again."

And then he says that in acts of self-defence the killing of even wounded men who attack those who are living may be justifiable. No sane man could dispute that fact. Then he goes on to say:

"It should be the earnest endeavour of every civilised Power to introduce as much humanity as possible into its treatment of a fallen adversary, even though their chivalry may occasionally cost a life. . . . Such acts should be rendered impossible by the most stringent regulations promulgated throughout the length and breadth of the land, and I feel that it is only necessary to allude to the matter for the remedy to be found."

This is the opinion of a British officer which confirms the view I have laid before the House. It may be urged that it is impossible, and that the wounded will act with treachery, but I would venture to lay before the House the remarkable evidence given by Mr. Winston Churchill as to the way in which Lord Tullibardine, to his infinite honour, went among the wounded and gave them water, without a single one of them seeking to injure him. I say that that is a proof that if you meet these poor creatures in a Christian and generous spirit, if you convince them that you do not intend to deny them quarter, they will not inflict any injury; and this will prove the advisability of introducing a higher standard into our warfare with them. To his honour, Lord Kitchener, after the battle of Atbara, gave the order that if the enemy would throw down their arms and raise their hands, they were at once to be passed through the ranks to the rear, and actually some of these men were enlisted in Lord Kitchener's army and loyally served at the battle of Omdurman. That shows that a higher standard of warfare can be introduced into these campaigns by treating these savage tribesmen with humanity. I hope the opportunity will not be lost of enforcing that lesson upon those who have the conduct of these campaigns in the future, so that the horrible events on that ghastly field of Omdurman shall never be repeated, and that England will not tolerate such conduct as has been complained of towards the wounded.

MR. A. J. BALFOUR: Before dealing with the more important topic raised, and unfortunately raised, by the hon. Member who has just spoken, I must say one word in answer to the hon. Member for West Aberdeen. He has reproached us for not having included, in the list of those who are thanked by name, some member of that great and distinguished profession to which he belongs. Sir, I can assure him that this omission does not indicate on our part any desire to underrate the eminent services rendered in war as well as in peace by the medical profession. But, Sir, the hon. Gentleman will feel with me that in these lists of names you must have some principle, you must draw a line in some place, and it is inevitable that beyond that line there will be names of men whose special services we should be glad to recognise. On that principle one name that I personally should like to see in the list is that of Lieutenant Girouard, who did such distinguished service in organising the railway. But, Sir, we have gone on the principle that you should not go below the rank of general of brigade, or some rank equivalent to that. We have included generals of divisions, all generals of brigades, naval officers commanding, and commanding officers of artillery, who practically do rank as generals of brigade, and there we have stopped. It would be impossible to add to the list without making it enormously, inconveniently, and impossibly lengthy. We have proceeded as near as we can in letter and spirit according to precedent, and while I entirely recognise the value of the services of many departmental officers, without whose assistance neither this nor any expedition could have been successfully conducted, I do not think it can be said that we convey any slight upon a great profession, or make an omission which we ought to have avoided, by not specially including these officers.

DR. FARQUHARSON: May I point out that I referred to the name and rank of Surgeon-Major Taylor?

MR. A. J. BALFOUR: Yes, but I am not talking of the rank in the Army List; I am talking of the actual work done in the field. Some of it, I think, was done by captains and majors, but on the field of battle they had, of course, the practical rank of general of brigade. Now, Sir, I leave that comparatively uncontroversial topic for the one raised by the hon. Gentleman the Member for Mayo, and by the hon. Member for East Northamptonshire.

Mr. A. J. Balfour.

The Member for Mayo does not profess, and has never professed, any interest for or sympathy with British soldiers, the British Army, or British institutions. He virtually comes here, I had almost said as an enemy of our country.

MR. DAVITT: Of the Government of Ireland.

MR. A. J. BALFOUR: I do not in the least wish to press the matter too far, but the hon. Gentleman has with perfect candour—and I must say always with tact and moderation, considering the substance of his speeches, for the form of his speeches is somewhat in contrast to their occasional substance—he has always let us clearly understand that, after all, a British success gave him no satisfaction, and that a British reverse would not break his heart. But, Sir, I do regret that the hon. Gentleman should have thought it necessary to cast perfectly unwarranted aspersions on the character for honour and humanity of British officers. I am sure that, as he stated that British officers had given orders that the wounded should be killed, he believes it.

MR. DAVITT: I believe it on the testimony of Englishmen who were on the spot, and who gave their evidence in English newspapers.

MR. A. J. BALFOUR: Well, I can assure the hon. Gentleman that it is my firm belief there never was a legend more absolutely devoid of any species of foundation, and I do not believe the most critical examination could extract a scintilla of evidence showing any condition of things so horrible as that in the story to which the hon. Gentleman has too easily given credence. Then he was followed by the hon. Gentleman the Member for East Northamptonshire, whose speech I confess I liked much less than that of the hon. Gentleman the Member for Mayo. The hon. Member for Mayo was perfectly frank; he spoke in a sense and in a degree, as I indicated, as an enemy; he spoke plainly and openly. The hon. Gentleman the Member for East Northamptonshire thought it desirable and appropriate to read out some story of what happened in 1885, and he told us that it is our business to see that such proceedings never occurred again. Of course, it is our business to see that the laws of humanity are preserved, in war as well as in peace. No doubt that is our duty, and neither we in this House nor the generals and officers of the Army have ever for a moment thought it was not a duty which we and they should earnestly and sedulously pursue. But to suggest, as the hon. Gentleman the Member for East Northamptonshire has suggested, that our soldiers are inhumane, and that our officers do nothing to discourage or to temper their inhumanity, is truly to put a libel upon a great and honourable profession, which, although no doubt the work of destruction is its primary business, has always had the tradition of carrying out its duties in a manner as consistent with the diminution of human suffering as is possible.

*Mr. CHANNING: The right hon. Gentleman has wholly misrepresented what I said. I quoted a well-known and very distinguished British officer who served in the campaign of 1885, and I gave his opinion as to these facts rather than my own. I expressly excluded, in the beginning of my speech, any belief in the responsibility of the officers for the acts which unfortunately took place.

Mr. A. J. BALFOUR: I can assure the hon. Gentleman that I have no desire to misrepresent him. I judged from the general tone and tenour of his speech. If I judged him unjustly, I am sorry for it, and I am glad that he should have an opportunity of explaining that in rising to carry out what he justly described as a most painful task he did not, at all events, intend to cast any slur on the officers and men of the British Army. I have only one word more to say about this question of the wounded. I believe the whole of these legends have been exploded by a multitude and host of eye-witnesses. But, of course, it is the fact—nobody has ever disguised it or pretended to disguise it—that there have been wounded in these battles who have, though wounded, remained combatants, and, being combatants, had to be treated as combatants. The laws of civilised warfare are sometimes represented as if they stated that the wounded were always to be spared. The laws of

civilised warfare are that non-combatants are always to be spared, and it would be impossible to carry on war under any principles by which one side was allowed to fight and the other side had its hands tied behind its back. Sir, the hon. Gentleman tells us that his evidence goes to show that any attempt to help these poor, unfortunate, wounded men on the field of battle was never made impossible by any hostile action on their part.

*Mr. CHANNING: I did not say that at all; I said that Lord Tullibardine's experience showed that it was not always the case.

Mr. A. J. BALFOUR: No, it certainly was not always the case—I quite grant that. But that is not the point; the point is, if you show, as I am told is the fact, that there were wounded who had to be killed, were they ever killed except in self-defence? As long as the wounded are combatants they must be treated as combatants, and, disguise it as we may, that is the inevitable result of war. The fact that in civilised battle such incidents are never heard of is because in civilised battle a wounded man always is a non-combatant. For my own part, I think the humane attempts of our men, the humane and persistent attempts of men like Lord Tullibardine and others, to carry succour and assistance to these poor wounded soldiers, though they knew that in doing so they carried their lives in their hands and ran the risk of a treacherous attack from the very men whom they attempted to assist, speak volumes for the humanity of that Army which hon. Members in their speeches have so cruelly traduced. I earnestly hope, Sir, under these circumstances, that neither the speech of the hon. Gentleman the Member for Mayo nor that of the hon. Member for East Northamptonshire will move a single Gentleman in this House to abstain from recording his vote of thanks and giving his assent to the resolution which you, Sir, have just read from the Chair.

Mr. DILLON: It was not to be expected that the cause we advocate in this House would be a popular one, and the most we can ask for, and, I think, have a right to expect, is that the great majority who are bound to vote in favour of this Resolution will give a fair hearing to the reply to the speech made by the right hon. Gentleman. Sir, what is it that has been alleged ? And what is the evidence upon which the charge has been made ? It has not been alleged by any-one, as the right hon. Gentleman sought to make it appear, that the charge is made against the whole body of officers in the British Army, or even the Egyptian Army. No such charge was ever made, and when the right hon. Gentleman triumphantly instanced the case of Lord Tullibardine and other officers who humanely, and unquestionably at the risk of their lives, offered assistance to some of those wretched wounded men, he undoubtedly did allude to facts which reflected infinite credit on Lord Tullibardine and other officers on that occasion. I have not the slightest doubt that they acted as humane and civilised soldiers ought to act. The charge has not been made by Irishmen, but by British soldiers and officers who took part in the campaign and were eye-witnesses, according to their statements, of what they stated. The charge that has been made is, substantially, that of the 16,000 men estimated to be wounded at the battle of Omdurman the great ma-jority were ruthlessly slaughtered after the battle. ("Oh!") Of course I am no eye-witness. I have no knowledge—did I ever pretend to have any knowledge ? —of these unhappy things, except what I derive, in common with the public of this country, from the evidence afforded by the letters of British soldiers and offi-cers published in the newspapers, and the evidence of military correspondents. The right hon. Gentleman did not seek to deny for a moment that a great many of the wounded were slaughtered. Everybody who is not a fool admits that on a field of battle, particularly when engaged in war with such people as the Dervishes, a certain number of the wounded have to be killed. But my conviction is that certainly the Soudanese—to an enormous extent, and to a much less extent the British troops—went out of their way to seek the wounded and kill them. Now I have the strongest objection to this Reso-lution because it includes an expression of thanks to the Soudanese troops. Sir, I have read with much interest an article written on the subject by Major-General Gatacre. That officer served for a long time in India.

and most successfully conducted the operations against the plague in India, and it was only when he was re-moved in the ordinary course of duty that difficulties arose. I am informed that he is an extremely humane man, and a man who undoubtedly has had great ex-perience of savage warfare. He, very naturally, defends the British officers, but in the course of his article he does not attempt to deny that the Soudanese did commit most painful atrocities ; and, after all, it must be remembered that we have the authority of Gordon him-self, who had a long experience of wars in the Soudan, that it was a fixed practice to give no quarter on either side. It is not very much to be wondered at that the Egyptian troops did commit dreadful atrocities, all the more, perhaps, because several tribes had old scores to wipe off. What I object to in this Resolution is that, without any expression of regret from the Government, without any pro-mise of inquiry to satisfy the conscience of this country, and without any indica-tion that there is even a doubt as to the transactions with reference to the wounded, we are called upon to vote the thanks of this House, not only to the British troops, but also to the Soudanese and Egyptian troops — the forces of a foreign country. Under those circumstances I, for one, will vote against this Resolution. The right hon. Gentleman endeavoured to make the case against my hon. friend the Member for South Mayo that he spoke on this question as an enemy of the British power, and that he would rejoice in a British defeat if it occurred ; but I have endeavoured to address myself to the question simply from the point of view of humanity, whatever my feelings towards British power may be. It may be—I think it is—that from the peculiar position we Irish Members hold in this House we are the most impartial. [Laughter.] Do you pretend to be im-partial ? You know perfectly well you are not. It is very hard for Englishmen to sit in judgment on their own victorious officers and troops, and to have any con-sideration for their defeated enemy. You are not quite so generous a people as that, and it is therefore no harm that there should be men in this House who can feel even for those savage tribes, who are God's creatures, and have a right to, at least, humane and merciful treatment, and to be looked upon as human beings, and not as noxious animals, as those who are sent to fight them too often come to regard them. I wish that the effect of this debate and the debate on Monday will be to moderate and temper the savagery of war. Although this is on a totally different branch of the subject, I desire also to support the contention put forward by the hon. Member for West Aberdeenshire. Why should not the names of the officers of mercy who accompany the army be joined in the vote of thanks to the combatant officers? It would be a good thing, if these votes of thanks are to be passed at all, that they should include the names of some men whose duty it was to save life, while thanking those whose duty it was to destroy life; and, belonging myself to the same profession, I desire to concur entirely with the view of the hon. Member that these votes should record the names of representatives of the healing and merciful side of war, and that we should register our conviction that, while war may be necessary, yet it is to civilised nations, or ought to be, a horrible evil, and that the moment victory is won it ought to be the duty of every soldier to help to succour and assuage the sufferings of those who have fallen by the strength of his right arm.

MAJOR RASCH (Essex, S.E.): It is difficult to see for what section of the public the hon. Member for East Northampton-shire holds his brief. It seems to me that they are the people who in the last century would have prosecuted Warren Hastings and Clyde, who twenty years ago would have attacked General Eyre, and, later, the men who won Rhodesia for the British Empire. They are the people who always find Englishmen in the wrong all over the world, and find foreigners right. They have friends in every country in which this nation has enemies. They are the people who wish to support, and did support, the reverend gentleman who talked at the Conference at Birmingham about the "filthy rags of Imperial policy." They rejoice in the name of "Little Englanders"; all the same they do not disdain the use of the Army and Navy when they want to bolster up a political party in the country. They sent Gordon to Khartoum, and deserted him when he got there. They sent Lord Wolseley up the Nile, and when he came back they had very little thanks for him.

They were ready to use the Sirdar, but having used him they throw him away like a squeezed orange. All I can say is I hope the hon. Member for East North-amptonshire will take a division; if he does he will probably have a greater record than even that achieved by my hon. friend the Member for King's Lynn the other night.

*MR. H. J. WILSON (York W. R., Holmfirth): I desire to make an appeal to the First Lord of the Treasury. There are two things about which we are all agreed—one is the bravery of the English officers and soldiers wherever they are, and the other that the vast majority of them are naturally humane men. Notwithstanding what the First Lord of the Treasury has said, I want to put it to him that all the stories referred to have not been exploded. I desire to support the appeal of my hon. friend the Member for East Northamptonshire (who does not deserve the language which has been applied to him) that there ought to be searching investigation into the matter. The proceedings of fourteen years ago, which have been referred to, throw a great light on this question, because the misbehaviour of the black troops then should show that these events were not unforeseen. If not unforeseen, precautions ought to be taken against them; and if such precautions were not taken, how then can we support this vote of thanks? I have here an account worse than anything that has yet been read. It bears every evidence of authenticity, and it shows how officers were implicated. I will not read it, but I will take the liberty of sending it to the First Lord of the Treasury in support of the plea of my hon. friend. I can assure him that nobody would be more thankful than we should if these stories could be entirely refuted; but if these methods of war are considered necessary, let us know who says so, and in any case let us know what has been done and who is responsible. Until this has been done I am obliged to vote, by my conscience, against all the Resolutions except the last.

MR. BRYN ROBERTS (Carnarvon-shire, Eifion): It may appear somewhat ungracious to vote against this resolution, and I desire to explain why I am compelled to do so. In the first place, I have all along felt strongly opposed to the passing, in modern times, of resolutions of this kind after every sort of campaign. I had almost said that this was a prostitution of the usages and functions of this House. I do not think that "prostitution" is the correct word—it is too strong a term; but I do think that we are passing these resolutions on very much too trivial occasions. It is far better we should reserve them for some great occasion. This House formerly never dreamt of passing a resolution of this kind except on an occasion, such as Waterloo or Trafalgar, which was equivalent to the saving of the Empire. Then the thanks of the House were given, and so important was it regarded that history recorded the fact as exceptional. But now every small campaign, if it happens to be successful —and it always is—is brought before this House, and we have a peerage given for such a matter as the bombardment of Alexandria. I object altogether to that; we ought not to throw away such an important honour, and, of course, it lessens the honour when it is given on every occasion. Suppose we were engaged in war with a European Power, with an army equal in numbers to our own and equally equipped; suppose we won a brilliant victory, which saved the reputation and possibly the existence of this country, what honour would there be left for the General who achieved such a feat? None, except to persuade the reigning monarch to go on his bended knees and hand over his crown. I am unwilling to believe the stories of cruelty on the part of our officers and men; but we must bear in mind that English officers and men have the weaknesses of humanity, and they may, on occasion, in the excitement of the moment, have allowed their feelings to carry them further than they ought. But where we find letters published in the local Press from private soldiers, in which the names of the men are given, and in which it is stated that the wounded were killed, and that it was done by order, it is a very serious thing indeed. I do not believe for a moment that it was done by order, but these men were evidently under the impression that it was. A private in the Lancashire Fusiliers writes:

"As we advanced we were ordered to kill all the wounded we met."

A corporal of the Grenadier Guards writes:

"We had to march with orders to kill all."

A soldier who was present at the battle writes:

"The ground was strewn with bodies, and

Mr. Bryn Roberts.

the order was given that all the wounded Dervishes were to be shot or bayoneted."

A private in the 2nd Fusiliers says that the order was conveyed to bayonet everyone, dead or alive. General Gatacre and Lord Kitchener have denied that any such order was given, and I accept their denial, but some inquiry ought to be made as to how came such an impression to be so general among the troops. Until some inquiry is made and the character of our men completely cleared, I certainly will not join in this Vote of thanks.

*Mr. LEES KNOWLES (Salford, W.) I have received a letter which appears to me to be a complete answer to the statement which has been made by the hon. Members opposite. It will be remembered that two foreign military attachés accompanied the Anglo-Egyptian Army. One represented Germany, and he wrote a letter, which appeared in *The Times* on the 16th of January, refuting these calumnies. The other, Major Luigi Calderari, represented the great military nation of Italy. Last December I had the honour of meeting him a few days after his return from the Soudan, and he was full of praise of our magnificent Anglo-Egyptian Army. He had been with the Staff, and therefore in a position to be able to see everything that went on. He subsequently wrote me the following letter, which I read in the House on Monday night, but as many hon. Members were not then present it may be desirable to read it again:—

"Caserta, February 28th, 1899.

"Dear Mr. Lees Knowles,—I am very glad to have an opportunity to put in writing what I stated to you verbally in Milan as to the manner in which the Dervish prisoners at the battle of Omdurman were treated, and to deny in the most absolute way that any cruelty was practised towards the prisoners. I rode on the field of battle in various directions, and everywhere I saw hundreds of wounded lying alive, notwithstanding that the ground had already been traversed by the Anglo-Egyptian troops. I happened to be for a while at the head of the troops in their advance after the attack on the zariba had been repulsed, and then again I was able to convince myself that the wounded were not in any way molested. If an occasional wounded man was killed it was only in legitimate defence, because, as is well known, it is a custom with these peoples to pretend to be dead and then to fire on the enemy as he passes, or, worse still, to ask for water and help, and then treacherously to kill those who are succouring them. I do not write these things in order to defend Lord Kitchener: he is so far above such accusations that merely to waste words in denying them would be an insult to him. I can only repeat that I am very happy that an opportunity presents itself for me to give a denial to statements which are untrue. It was, moreover, my duty to do so, especially as some Italian newspapers have copied and republished such statements.

"Believe me, etc., etc., etc.,
"LUIGI CALDERARI."

That, I think, is an important letter, and adds considerably towards the refuta-

tion of these calumnies. Coming from a foreigner, it may be appreciated by hon. Gentlemen from Ireland.

Question put.

The House divided : Ayes, 347 ; noes 18. (Division List, No. 179.)

AYES.

Acland-Hood, Capt. Sir A. F.
Allan, William (Gateshead)
Allen, W.(Newc. under Lyme)
Allhusen, Augustus Henry E.
Allsopp, Hon. George
Anson, Sir William Reynell
Arnold, Alfred
Ascroft, Robert
Ashton, Thomas Gair
Asquith, Rt. Hon. Herbert H.
Atherley-Jones, L.
Atkinson, Rt. Hon. John
Austin, Sir John (Yorkshire)
Bagot, Capt. J. FitzRoy
Bailey, James (Walworth)
Baillie, Jas. E. B. (Inverness)
Baird, John George Alexander
Balcarres, Lord
Baldwin, Alfred
Balfour, Rt.Hn.A.J.(Manch'r)
Balfour, Rt.Hon.G.W.(Leeds)
Banbury, Frederic George
Barnes, Frederic Gorell
Barry, Rt. Hn.A.H.S.-(Hunts)
Bartley, George C. T.
Barton, Dunbar Plunket
Beach, Rt. Hn.SirM.H.(Bristol
Beach, W. W. Bramston(Hants)
Beaumont, Wentworth C. B.
Begg, Ferdinand Faithfull
Bemrose, Sir Henry Howe
Bentinck, Lord Henry C.
Beresford, Lord Charles
Bethell, Commander
Bhownaggree, Sir M. M.
Billson, Alfred
Birrell, Augustine
Blakiston-Houston, John
Blundell, Colonel Henry
Bolitho, Thomas Bedford
Bond, Edward
Boulnois, Edmund
Bowles,Capt.H.F.(Middlesex)
Broadhurst, Henry
Brodrick, Rt. Hon. St. John
Brookfield, A. Montagu
Bryce, Rt. Hon. James
Brymer, William Ernest
Buchanan, Thomas Ryburn
Bullard, Sir Harry
Butcher, John George
Buxton, Sydney Charles
Caldwell, James
Campbell,Rt.Hn.JA(Glasgow
Campbell-Bannerman, Sir H.
Carlile, William Walter
Carson, Rt. Hon. Edward
Causton, Richard Knight
Cawley, Frederick
Cayzer, Sir Charles William
Cecil, Evelyn (Hertford, East)
Cecil, Lord Hugh (Greenwich)

Chaloner, Capt. R. G. W.
Chamberlain, Rt Hn J (Birm.)
Chamberlain,JAusten(Worc'r
Channing, Francis Allston
Chaplin, Rt. Hon. Henry
Charrington, Spencer
Chelsea, Viscount
Clough, Walter Owen
Cochrane, Hon. T. H. A. E.
Coddington, Sir William
Coghill, Douglas Harry
Cohen, Benjamin Louis
Collings, Rt. Hon. Jesse
Colston, Chas. Edw. H.Athole
Colville, John
Compton, Lord Alwyne
Cooke,C. W.Radcliffe(Heref'd)
Corbett, A.Cameron(Glasgow)
Cox, Irwin Ed. B. (Harrow)
Cranborne, Viscount
Cripps, Charles Alfred
Crombie, John William
Cross, Herb. Shepherd(Bolton)
Cubitt, Hon. Henry
Curzon, Viscount
Dalkeith, Earl of
Dalrymple, Sir Charles
Dalziel, James Henry
Davies,SirHoratioD. (Chath'm
Davies,M.Vaughan-(Cardigan
Denny, Colonel
Dickson-Poynder, Sir John P.
Disraeli, Coningsby Ralph
Dorington, Sir John Ed.
Doughty, George
Douglas, Rt. Hon. A. Akers-
Doxford, William Theodore
Duncombe, Hon. Hubert V.
Dunn, Sir William
Elliot, Hon. A. Ralph Douglas
Fardell, Sir T. George
Farquharson, Dr. Robert
Fellowes, Hon. Ailwyn Edw.
Ferguson, R. C. Munro (Leith)
Fergusson,Rt.Hn.SirJ.(Man.)
Finch, George H.
Finlay, Sir Robt. Bannatyne
Fison, Frederick William
FitzGerald, Sir Rbt. Penrose-
Fitzmaurice, Lord Edmond
FitzWygram, General Sir F.
Flower, Ernest
Folkestone, Viscount
Forster, Henry William
Foster, Colonel (Lancaster)
Foster, Sir W. (Derby Co.)
Fry, Lewis
Gedge, Sydney
Gibbons, J. Lloyd
Gibbs, Hn.A.G.H. (C. of Lon.)
Gibbs, Hon. V. (St. Albans)
Giles, Charles Tyrrell

Gilliat, John Saunders
Gladstone, Rt. Hon. H. J.
Goddard, Daniel Ford
Godson, Sir Augustus F.
Goldsworthy, Major-General
Gordon, Hon. John Edward
Gorst, Rt. Hon. Sir J. Eldon
Goschen, RtHnGJ(StGeorge's)
Goschen, George J. (Sussex)
Goulding, Edward Alfred
Gourley, Sir Edward T.
Graham, Henry Robert
Green, W D. (Wednesbury)
Greene, W. R.- (Cambs.)
Gretton, John
Griffith, Ellis J.
Gunter, Colonel
Gurdon, Sir William B.
Haldane, Richard Burdon
Hall, Rt. Hon. Sir Charles
Halsey, Thomas Frederick
Hamilton, Rt. Hon. Lord G.
Hardy, Laurence
Hare, Thomas Leigh
Hatch, Ernest Frederick Geo.
Hayne,Rt.Hon.CharlesSearle-
Heath, James
Hedderwick, Thomas C. H.
Helder, Augustus
Henderson, Alexander
Hermon-Hodge, Robert T.
Hickman, Sir Alfred
Hill, Rt. Hon. A. S. (Staffs)
Hill, Sir Edward S. (Bristol)
Hoare, E. Brodie (Hampstead)
Hoare, Samuel (Norwich)
Hobhouse, Henry
Holland, Hon. Lionel R. (Bow)
Hornby, Sir William Henry
Horniman, Frederick John
Houldsworth, Sir Wm. Henry
Howard, Joseph
Howell, William Tudor
Hozier, Hon. James Henry C.
Hubbard, Hon. Evelyn
Hughes, Colonel Edwin
Hutchinson,Capt. G. W.Grice-
Hutton, John (Yorks, N. R.)
Jackson, Rt. Hon. Wm.Lawies
Jacoby, James Alfred
Jebb, Richard Claverhouse
Johnson-Ferguson, JabezEdw.
Johnstone, Heywood (Sussex)
Jolliffe, Hon H. George
Kay-Shuttleworth,RtHnSirU.
Kearley, Hudson E.
Kenyon, James
Keswick, William
Kimber, Henry
King, Sir Henry Seymour
Kinloch,SirJohnGeorgeSmyth
Kitson, Sir James

Knowles, Lees
Lafone, Alfred
Lambert, George
Laurie, Lieut.-General
Lawrence, Wm. F. (Liverpool)
Lawson, John Grant (Yorks.)
Lecky, Rt. Hn. William Edw. H.
Lees, Sir Elliott (Birkenhead)
Leighton, Stanley
Leng, Sir John
Lewis, John Herbert
Llewelyn Sir Dillwyn (Swansea
Lockwood, Lt.-Col. A. R.
Loder, Gerald Walter Erskine
Long, Col. Charles W. (Evesham
Long, Rt. Hn. Walter (Liverp'l
Lopes, Henry Yarde Buller
Lorne, Marquess of
Lowe, Francis William
Lowther, Rt. Hn. J. (Kent)
Lubbock, Rt. Hon. Sir John
Lucas-Shadwell, William
Lyell, Sir Leonard
Lyttelton, Hon. Alfred
Macartney, W. G. Ellison
Macdona, John Cumming
MacIver, David (Liverpool)
Maclure, Sir John William
M'Arthur, Charles (Liverpool)
M'Arthur, William (Cornwall
M'Calmont, H. L. B. (Cambs.)
M'Iver, Sir L. (Edinburgh, W)
M'Kenna, Reginald
M'Killop, James
M'Laren, Charles Benjamin
Maple, Sir John Blundell
Mappin, Sir Frederick T.
Mellor, Colonel (Lancashire)
Mellor, Rt. Hn. J. W. (Yorks.
Melville, Beresford Valentine
Mendl, Sigismund Ferdinand
Middlemore, John T.
Milbank, Sir Powlett Chas. J.
Milward, Colonel Victor
Monk, Charles James
Montagu, Sir S. (Whitechapel
Moon, Edward Robert Pacy
Moore, William (Antrim, N.)
Morgan, Hn. F. (Monm'thsh.)
Morgan, W. P. (Merthyr)
Morton, Arthur H. A. (Deptf'd
Moulton, John Fletcher
Muntz, Philip A.
Murray, Rt. Hon. A. G. (Bute)
Murray, Charles J. (Coventry)

Newdigate, Francis Alexander
Norton, Capt. Cecil William
Nussey, Thomas Willans
Oldroyd, Mark
O'Neill, H. Robert Torrens
Parkes, Ebenezer
Paulton, James Mellor
Pease, A. E. (Cleveland)
Pease, H. Pike (Darlington)
Pease, Joseph A. (Northumb.)
Pender, Sir James
Penn, John
Percy, Earl
Perks, Robert William
Pierpoint, Robert
Pirie, Duncan V.
Pretyman, Ernest George
Price, Robert John
Priestley, Sir W. Overend (Edin
Pryce-Jones, Lt.-Col. Edward
Purvis, Robert
Pym, C. Guy
Rasch, Major Frederic Carne
Reckitt, Harold James.
Rentoul, James Alexander
Richardson, J. (Durham, S.E.)
Richardson, Sir T. (Hartlep'l)
Rickett, J. Compton
Ridley, Rt. Hon. Sir M. W.
Ritchie, Rt. Hon. C. Thomson
Roberts, John H. (Denbighs.)
Robertson, Herbert (H'ckney)
Robinson, Brooke
Rollit, Sir Albert Kaye
Rothschild, Hon. Lionel W.
Round, James
Royds, Clement Molyneux
Russell, T. W. (Tyrone)
Rydey, John Herbert Dudley
Samuel, Harry S. (Limehouse)
Samuel, J. (Stockton on Tees)
Seely, Charles Hilton
Seton-Karr, Henry
Sharpe, William Edward T.
Shaw, Charles Edw. (Stafford)
Shaw, Thomas (Hawick B)
Shaw-Stewart, M. H. (R'nfr'w)
Simeon, Sir Barrington
Sinclair, Capt. John (F'rfrsh'e)
Smith, Samuel (Flint)
Smith, Hon. W. F. (Strand)
Soames, Arthur Wellesley
Spicer, Albert
Stanley, Hon A. (Ormskirk)

Stanley Edward J. (Somerset)
Stanley, Henry M. (Lambeth)
Stanley, Lord (Lancs.)
Stephens, Henry Charles
Stevenson, Francis S.
Stewart, Sir M. J. M'Taggart
Stirling-Maxwell, Sir John M.
Stock, James Henry
Strachey, Edward
Strutt, Hon. Charles Hedley
Sturt, Hon. Humphry Napier
Talbot, Rt. Hn. J. G. (Oxf'd U.)
Tennant, Harold John
Thomas, Abel (Carmarthen, E.)
Thomas, A. (Glamorgan, E.)
Thorburn, Walter
Thornton, Percy M.
Tollemache, Henry James
Tomlinson, Wm. Ed. Murray
Trevelyan, Charles Philips
Tritton, Charles Ernest
Ure, Alexander
Usborne, Thomas
Valentia, Viscount
Vincent, Col. Sir C. E. Howard
Wallace, Robert (Perth)
Walton, Joseph (Barnsley
Warr, Augustus Frederick
Wedderburn, Sir William
Wentworth, Bruce C. Vernon-
Wharton, Rt. Hn. John Lloyd
Whiteley, H. (Ashton-und r-L.
Whitmore, Charles Algernon
Williams, Col. R. (Dorset)
Williams, Joseph P.- (Birm.)
Willox, Sir John Archibald
Wilson, J. (Durham, Mid.)
Wilson, John (Govan)
Wilson, J. W. (Worce-tsh. N.)
Wilson-Todd, W. H. (Yorks.)
Wodehouse, Rt Hn. E. R. (Bath)
Wolff, Gustav Wilhelm
Woodall, William
Woods, Samuel
Wortley, Rt. Hon. C. B. Stuart-
Wyndham, George
Wyndham-Quin, Major W. H.
Young, Commander (Berks, E.)
Younger, William
Yoxall, James Henry

TELLERS FOR THE AYES—
  Sir William Walrond and
  Mr. Anstruther.

NOES.

Carvill, Patrick Geo. Hamilton
Curran, Thomas (Sligo, S.)
Dillon, John
Doogan, P. C.
Lawson, Sir Wilfrid (Cumb'l'd)
MacAleese, Daniel
M'Ghee, Richard
Morris, Samuel

O'Brien, James F. X. (Cork)
O'Brien, Patrick (Kilkenny)
O'Connor, T. P. (Liverpool)
O'Malley, William
Pickard, Benjamin
Roberts, John Bryn (Eifion)
Steadman, William Charles
Sullivan, Donal (Westmeath)

Tully, Jasper
Wilson, Henry J. (York, W.R.)

TELLERS FOR THE NOES—
  Mr. Davitt and Mr. James
  O'Connor.

2. Resolved, That the thanks of this House be given to—

Major-General Sir Archibald Hunter, K.C.B., D.S.O. ;

Major-General Sir Henry Macleod Leslie Rundle, K.C.B., C.M.G., D.S.O., R.A. :

Major-General Sir William Forbes Gatacre, K.C.B., D.S.O. ;

Major-General the Hon. Neville Gerald Lyttelton, C.B. ;

Major-General A. G. Wauchope, C.B., C.M.G. ;

Major and Brevet Colonel Sir Francis Reginald Wingate, K.C.M.G., C.B., D.S.O., R.A. ;

Lieutenant-Colonel and Brevet Colonel C. J. Long, R.A. ;

Major and Brevet Colonel J. G. Maxwell, D.S.O. ;

Major and Brevet Colonel H. A. MacDonald, D.S.O. ;

LieutenantColonel D. F. Lewis, C.B. ;

Major and Brevet Lieutenant Colonel J. Collinson, C.B. ;

Captain C. R. Keppel, C.B., D.S.O., R.N. ;

and to the other Officers and Warrant Officers of the Navy, the British and the Egyptian Army, and the Royal Marines, for the energy and gallantry with which they executed the services which they were called upon to perform.

Motion made, and Question put—

" That this House doth acknowledge and highly approve the gallantry, discipline, and good conduct displayed by the Petty Officers, Non-commissioned Officers, and men of the Navy, the British and Egyptian Army, and the Royal Marines during the campaign."—(*Mr. Balfour*).

The House divided ; Ayes 355, Noes 16. (Division List No. 180).

AYES.

Acland-Hood,Capt.SirAlex.F.
Allan, William (Gateshead)
Allen, Wm. (New. u. Lyme)
Allhusen, Augustus Hy. E.
Allsopp, Hon. George
Anson, Sir William Reynell
Arnold, Alfred
Ascroft, Robert
Ashton, Thomas Gair
Asquith, Rt. Hon. Herbt. Hy.
Atkinson, Rt. Hon. John
Austin, Sir John (Yorkshire)
Bagot, Capt. J. FitzRoy
Bailey, James (Walworth)
Baillie, Jas. E. B. (Inverness)
Baird, John George Alexander
Balcarres, Lord
Baldwin, Alfred
Balfour, Rt. Hon. A. J. (Man)
Balfour,Rt. Hon.G.W. (Leeds)
Banbury, Frederick George
Barnes, Frederic Gorell
Barry, Rt.Hn.A.H.S.-(Hunts)
Bartley, George C. T.
Barton, Dunbar Plunket
Beach,RtHn.SirM H.(Bristol)
Beach, W. W. B. (Hants.)
Beaumont, Wentworth C. B.
Begg, Ferdinand Faithfull
Bemrose, Sir Henry Howe
Bentinck, Lord Henry C.
Beresford, Lord Charles
Bethell, Commander
Bhownaggree, Sir M. M.
Billson, Alfred
Birrell, Augustine
Blakiston-Houston, John
Blundell, Colonel Henry
Bolitho, Thomas Bedford
Bond, Edward
Boulnois, Edmund
Bousfield, William Robert
Bowles, Capt. H. F. (Middlx.)
Broadhurst, Henry
Brodrick, Rt. Hon. St. John
Brookfield, A. Montagu
Bryce, Rt. Hon. James

Brymer, William Ernest
Buchanan, Thomas Ryburn
Bullard, Sir Harry
Butcher, John George
Buxton, Sydney Charles
Caldwell, James
Cameron, Sir Chas. (Glasgow)
Campbell, Rt. Hon.J.A.(Glas.)
Campb-ll-Bannerman, Sir H.
Carlile, William Walter
Carmichael, Sir T. D. Gibson-
Carson, Rt. Hon. Edward
Causton, Richard Knight
Cawley, Frederick
Cayzer, Sir Charles William
Cecil, Evelyn (Hertford, East)
Cecil, Lord Hugh (Greenwich)
Chaloner, Captain R. G. W.
Chamberlain, Rt. Hn.J.(Birm.)
Chamberlain, J. A. (Worc'r.)
Chaplin, Rt. Hon. Henry
Charrington, Spencer
Chelsea, Viscount
Clough, Walter Owen
Cochrane, Hon. T. H. A. E.
Coddington, Sir William
Coghill, Douglas Harry
Cohen, Benjamin Louis
Collings, Rt. Hon. Jesse
Colston, Chas. E. H. Athole
Colville, John
Compton, Lord Alwyne
Cooke, C. W. R. (Hereford)
Corbett, A. C. (Glasgow)
Cranborne, Viscount
Cripps, Charles Alfred
Crombie, John William
Cross, H. Shepherd (Bolton)
Cubitt, Hon. Henry
Curzon, Viscount
Dalkeith, Earl of
Dalrymple, Sir Charles
Dalziel, James Henry
Davies, Sir H. D. (Chatham)
Davies, M. V. (Cardigan)
Dickson-Poynder, Sir John P.
Disraeli, Coningsby Ralph

Dixon-Hartland, Sir Fred. D.
Dorington, Sir John Edw.
Doughty, George
Douglas, Rt. Hon. A. Akers-
Doxford, William Theodore
Duckworth, James
Duncombe, Hon. Hubert V.
Dunn, Sir William
Elliot, Hon. A Ralph Douglas
Fardell, Sir T. George
Farquharson, Dr. Robert
Fellowes, Hon.AilwynEdward
Ferguson,R. C. Munro (Leith)
Fergusson,Rt.Hn.Sir J.(Man.)
Finch, George H.
Finlay, Sir Robert Bannatyne
Fisher, William Hayes
Fison, Frederick William
FitzGerald,SirRobertPenrose-
Fitzmaurice, Lord Edmond
FitzWygram, General Sir F.
Flower, Ernest
Folkestone, Viscount
Forster, Henry William
Foster, Colonel (Lancaster)
Foster, Sir Walter (Derby Co.)
Fry, Lewis
Gedge, Sydney
Gibbons, J. Lloyd
Gibbs, Hn.A.G.H.(C.ofLond.)
Gibbs, Hon. V. (St. Albans)
Giles, Charles Tyrrell
Gilliat, John Saunders
Gladstone, Rt. Hon. H. John
Goddard, Daniel Ford
Godson, Sir Augustus Freak.
Goldsworthy, Major-General
Gordon, Hon. John Edward
Gorst, Rt. Hon. Sir. J. Eldon
Goschen,Rt. Hn.G.J.(StG'rg's)
Goschen, George J. (Sussex)
Goulding, Edward Alfred
Gourley, Sir Edw. Temperley
Graham, Henry Robert
Gray, Ernest (West Ham)
Green, W. D. (Wednesbury)
Greene, W. Raymond-(Cambs)

Griffith, Ellis J.
Gunter, Colonel
Gurdon, Sir Wm. Brampton
Haldane, Richard Burdon
Hall, Rt. Hon. Sir Charles
Halsey, Thomas Frederick
Hamilton, Rt. Hon. Ld. Geo.
Hardy, Laurence
Hare, Thomas Leigh
Harwood, George
Hatch, Ernest Frederick Geo.
Hayne, Rt. Hon. Charles Seale-Heath, James
Hedderwick, Thomas C. H.
Helder, Augustus
Henderson, Alexander
Hermon-Hodge, Robert Trotter
Hickman, Sir Alfred
Hill, Rt. Hon. A. S. (Staffs.)
Hoare, Edw. Brodie (Hamps.)
Hoare, Samuel (Norwich)
Hobhouse, Henry
Hornby, Sir William Henry
Horniman, Frederick John
Houldsworth, Sir Wm. Henry
Howard, Joseph
Howell, William Tudor
Hozier, Hon. James Henry C.
Hubbard, Hon. Evelyn
Hughes, Colonel Edwin
Hutchinson, Capt. G. W. Grice-
Hutton, John (Yorks, N.R.)
Jackson, Rt. Hn. Wm. Lawies
Jacoby, James Alfred
Jebb, Richard Claverhouse
Johnson-Ferguson, Jabez Ed.
Johnstone, Heywood (Sussex)
Jolliffe, Hon. H. George
Jones, William (Carnarvons.)
Kay-Shuttleworth, Rt Hn. Sir U
Kearley, Hudson, E.
Kenyon, James
Kenyon-Slaney, Col. William
Keswick, William
Kimber, Henry
King, Sir Henry Seymour
Kinloch, Sir John Geo. Smyth
Kitson, Sir James
Knowles, Lees
Lafone, Alfred
Lambert, George
Laurie, Lieut.-General
Lawrence, W. F. (Liverpool)
Lawson, John Grant (Yorks.)
Lecky, Rt. Hon. Wm. E. H.
Lees, Sir Elliott (Birkenhead)
Leighton, Stanley
Leng, Sir John
Lewis, John Herbert
Llewelyn, Sir D.- (Swansea)
Lockwood, Lt.-Col. A. R.
Loder, Gerald W. Erskine
Long, Col. C. W. (Evesham)
Long, Rt. Hon. W. (Liverp'l)
Lopes, Henry Yarde Buller
Lorne, Marquess of
Lowe, Francis William
Lowther, Rt. Hon. J. (Kent)
Lowther, Rt. Hn J W(Cumb'l'd)
Lubbock, Rt. Hon. Sir John
Lucas-Shadwell, William
Lyell, Sir Leonard
Lyttelton, Hon. Alfred
Macartney, W. G. Ellison
Macdona, John Cumming

MacIver, David (Liverpool)
Maclure, Sir John William
M'Arthur, Charles (Liverpool)
M'Arthur, William (Cornwall)
M'Calmont, H. L. B. (Cambs.)
M'Iver, Sir L. (Edinb'rgh, W.)
M'Killop, James
M'Laren, Charles Benjamin
Maple, Sir John Blundell
Mappin, Sir Frederick Thorpe
Maxwell, Rt. Hon. Sir H. E.
Mellor, Colonel (Lancashire)
Mellor, Rt. Hon. J. W. (Yorks.)
Melville, Beresford Valentine
Mendl, Sigismund Ferdinand
Middlemore, J. Throgmorton
Milbank, Sir Powlett C. John
Mildmay, Francis Bingham
Milward, Colonel Victor
Monk, Charles James
Montagu, Hon. J. S. (Hants.)
Montagu, Sir S. (Whitechpl.)
Moon, Edward Robert Pacy
Moore, William (Antrim, N.)
More, R. Jasper (Shropshire)
Morgan, Hon. F. (Monm'thsh.)
Morgan, W. P. (Merthyr)
Morrell, George Herbert
Morton, A. H. A. (Deptford)
Moulton, John Fletcher
Muntz, Philip A.
Murray, Rt. Hn. A. G. (Bute)
Murray, Charles J. (Coventry)

Newdigate, Francis Alex.
Nicholson, William Graham
Nicol, Donald Ninian
Norton, Capt. Cecil William
Nussey, Thomas Willans

Oldroyd, Mark
O'Neill, Hon. Robert Torrens

Parkes, Ebenezer
Paulton, James Mellor
Pease, Alfred E. (Cleveland)
Pease, H. Pike (Darlington)
Pease, Joseph A. (Northumb.)
Pender, Sir James
Penn, John
Percy, Earl
Perks, Robert William
Pickard, Benjamin
Pierpoint, Robert
Pirie, Duncan V.
Powell, Sir Francis Sharp
Pretyman, Ernest George
Price, Robert John
Priestley, Sir W. O. (Edin.)
Pryce-Jones, Lt.-Col. Edward
Purvis, Robert
Pym, C. Guy

Rasch, Major Frederic Carne
Reckitt, Harold James
Richardson J. (Durham, S.E.)
Richardson, Sir T.(Hartlep'L)
Rickett, J. Compton
Ridley, Rt. Hn. Sir Matt. W.
Ritchie, Rt. Hon. C. Thomson
Roberts, John H. (Denbighsh.)
Robertson, Herbert (Hackney)
Robinson, Brooke
Robson, William Snowdon
Rollit, Sir Albert Kaye
Rothschild, Hon. Lionel Walter
Round, James

Royds, Clement Molyneux
Russell, Gen. F.S. (Cheltenh'm)
Russell, T. W. (Tyrone)

Samuel, Harry S. (Limehouse)
Samuel, J. (Stockton on Tees)
Seely, Charles Hilton
Seton-Karr, Henry
Shaw, Charles Edw. (Stafford)
Shaw, Thomas (Hawick B.)
Shaw-Stewart, M. H. (Renfrew)
Simeon, Sir Barrington
Sinclair, Capt. John (Forfarsh.)
Smith, Samuel (Flint)
Smith, Hon. W. F. D. (Strand)
Soames, Arthur Wellesley
Spicer, Albert
Stanley, Hon. A. (Ormskirk)
Stanley, Edw. Jas. (Somerset)
Stanley, Henry M. (Lambeth)
Stanley, Lord (Lancs.)
Steadman, William Charles
Stephens, Henry Charles
Stevenson, Francis S.
Stewart, Sir M. J. M'Taggart
Stirling-Maxwell, Sir John M.
Stock, James Henry
Stone, Sir Benjamin
Strachey, Edward
Strutt, Hon. Charles Hedley
Sturt, Hon. Humphry N.

Talbot, Rt. Hn. J. G. (Oxf'd. U.)
Tennant, Harold John
Thomas, A. (Carmarthen, E.)
Thomas, A. (Glamorgan, E.)
Thorburn, Walter
Thornton, Percy M.
Tollemache, Henry James
Tomlinson, Wm. E. Murray
Trevelyan, Charles Philips
Tritton, Charles Ernest

Ure, Alexander

Valentia, Viscount
Vincent, Col. Sir C. E. H.

Wallace, Robert (Perth)
Walton, J. Lawson (Leeds, S.)
Warr, Augustus Frederick
Wedderburn, Sir William
Wentworth, Bruce C. Vernon-
Wharton, Rt. Hon. John L.
Whiteley, George (Stockport)
Whitmore, Charles Algernon
Williams, Colonel R. (Dorset)
Williams, Jos. Powell-(Birm.)
Willox, Sir John Archibald
Wilson, John (Durham, Mid.)
Wilson, J. W. (Worcestersh. N.)
Wodehouse, Rt. Hn. E. R. (Bath)
Wolff, Gustav Wilhelm
Woodall, William
Woods, Samuel
Wortley, Rt. Hon. C. B. S.-
Wylie, Alexander
Wyndham, George
Wyndham-Quin, Major W. H.

Younger, William
Yoxall, James Henry

TELLERS FOR THE AYES—
  Sir William Walrond and
  Mr. Anstruther

NOES.

Austin, M. (Limerick, W.)	Morris, Samuel	Tully, Jasper
Curran, Thomas (Sligo, S.)	O'Brien, James F. X. (Cork)	Wilson, Hy. J. (York, W. R.)
Dillon, John	O'Brien, Patrick (Kilkenny)	
Doogan, P. C.	O'Connor, T. P. (Liverpool)	
Lawson, Sir W. (Cumb'land)	O'Malley, William	TELLERS FOR THE NOES—
MacAleese, Daniel	Roberts, John Bryn (Eifion)	Mr. Davitt and Mr. James
M'Ghee, Richard	Sullivan, Donal (Westmeath)	O'Connor.

3. Resolved,—That this House doth acknowledge and highly approve the gallantry, discipline, and good conduct displayed by the Petty Officers, Non-commissioned Officers, and men of the Navy, the British and the Egyptian Army, and the Royal Marines during the campaign.

Motion made, and Question proposed—

"That the thanks of this House be given to Lieutenant-General Sir Francis Grenfell, G.C.B., G.C.M.G., for the support and assistance which he afforded to the forces employed in the operations in the Soudan."—(*Mr. Balfour.*)

MR. DAVITT: I do not intend to divide the House upon either of the two remaining resolutions, because they do not raise the question upon which we desired to protest, more especially when one of these resolutions amounts to an expression of sympathy with those families who have lost their sons. I trust that in this connection the House will remember the family of an hon. Member of this House who was universally respected, and who died on Monday night in the performance of the manly duty of protesting against all this butchery.*

Question put and agreed to.

4. Resolved,—That the thanks of this House be given to Lieutenant-General Sir Francis Grenfell, G.C.B., G.C.M.G., for the support and assistance which he afforded to the forces employed in the operations in the Soudan.

Motion made, and Question proposed—

"That this House doth acknowledge, with admiration, the distinguished valour, devotion, and conduct of those other officers and men who have perished during the campaign in the Soudan in the service of their country, and feels deep sympathy with their relatives and friends."—(*Mr. Balfour.*)

LORD CHAS. BERESFORD (York): I wish to make a request to the Government, and, whether it will be complied with or not, I am sure I shall have the

* Refer to page 400 of this volume.

sympathy of the First Lord of the Treasury. It came to my knowledge, when a similar vote of condolence to the relatives of the men who were killed in the last Soudan campaign was passed in this House, that many of the widows and relatives of the men never knew at all that such a vote had been passed, as far as any official intimation was concerned, and they would not have known anything about it if I had not taken the trouble to write to them. I therefore ask the First Lord of the Treasury if he can see his way to order a memorandum to be sent to the relatives of those who fell in battle, in order that they may know that the gallantry of their relatives has been fully appreciated by the representatives of the country in this House. Many of them are very poor people, and they never see a newspaper at all, and a great many of them would have no idea that this vote has been passed unless they receive an intimation to that effect. I am sure that these poor people would greatly appreciate an official intimation that the devotion and gallantry of their relatives has been acknowledged in this House.

MR. DILLON: May I suggest that on future occasions when this House votes large sums of money, honours, distinctions, and sympathy with the relatives of those who fall in battle, the latter, who are often reduced to poverty by their loss, should receive a year or two's pay along with the resolution of sympathy.

MR. A. J. BALFOUR: I think the suggestion of my noble friend the Member for York is worthy of consideration. I do not know whether machinery exists for carrying out the suggestion, but I conjecture that no great difficulty need be found in doing so. On that point I can hardly pledge myself without consulting the officials concerned; but I can give the noble Lord the assurance that anything that can be done in the direction he has indicated will certainly be done.

Question put and agreed to.

5. Resolved,—That this House doth acknowledge, with admiration, the distinguished valour, devotion, and conduct of those other officers and men who have perished during the campaign in the Soudan in the service of their country, and feels deep sympathy with their relatives and friends.—(*Mr. Balfour.*)

Ordered,—That the said resolutions be transmitted by Mr. Speaker to Major-General Lord Kitchener of Khartoum, G.C.B., K.C.M.G., and that he be requested to communicate the same to the several officers and men referred to therein.—(*Mr. Balfour.*)

LONDON GOVERNMENT BILL.

Order read, for resuming adjourned Debate on Amendment proposed [6th June] on consideration of the Bill, as amended :—

"And which Amendment was, in page 12, lines 32 and 33, to leave out the words 'the inhabitants of the parish,' in order to insert the words 'such inhabitants of the parish as shall have obeyed that rubric of the Book of Common Prayer which is printed at the end of the Order of the Administration of the Holy Communion, and which requires that every parishioner shall communicate at the least three times in the year, of which Easter to be one.' "—(*Lord Hugh Cecil.*)

Question again proposed—

"That the words 'the inhabitants of' stand part of the Bill."

Debate resumed.

Mr. CARVELL WILLIAMS (Notts, Mansfield): While I very much admire the courage which the noble Lord has shown in bringing this matter forward, I must say I think there will be a general agreement on both sides of the House that in submitting this Amendment he has allowed his zeal to outrun his discretion. We are dealing with a Bill for the better government of this ancient metropolis, and the noble Lord calls on us to so shape the measure as to involve a re-construction of an ancient Church establishment. The noble Lord, in fact, seeks to make this a Disestablishment Bill ; but it is a piece of disestablishment beginning at the wrong end, for he proposes to disestablish, not the Church, but the parishioners. Further, he proposes not only to disfranchise all Nonconformists, but also a number—probably a majority—of members of the Church of England, who are non-communicants. What are the grounds on which the noble Lord makes this suggestion to the House ? First, he urges that it is only right and reasonable that a body which has to deal with Church affairs under the Act should be composed, not of the general public, but of Churchmen and communicating members of the Church. His second point was that it would be decidedly improper to allow those who disobeyed the law of the Church to exercise any government over Church matters. A very large number of Churchmen would stoutly deny both propositions of the noble Lord, but I would remind the noble Lord that these are not the principles on which the Church establishment in this country is based. He has to deal with facts as they are, and not as they ought to be. The parish church is the church of the parish and of all the inhabitants of the parish, and all inhabitants can claim the right of having free seats and of availing themselves of the services of the incumbent, whether they be communicants or not. Nonconformists, in common with Churchmen, can claim to be baptised, married, and buried with the Church's rites ; they have the right of electing churchwardens, and if they happen to be on the Parliamentary roll they have the right of deciding who shall, as their representatives in this House, act as supreme governors of the Church. Does the noble Lord intend this Amendment to be a beginning of a very much more extensive scheme ? Will he presently insist that no Minister of the Crown who does not communicate three times every year—once at Easter included—shall be allowed to administer the Church patronage in the hands of the Crown ? And then with regard to the large army of private patrons, will he insist that they all shall be communicants ? What is he going to do with this House ? Will he hereafter insist that none of us shall have a right to sit here and legislate for the Church unless we are communicants of that Church ? The noble Lord says the laity of the Church of England do not exercise their proper share of influence in relation to the affairs of the Church, and he suggests that the reason for their not doing so is that they are an indeterminate body. He proposes that they should cease to be indeterminate by depriving

Mr. A. J. Balfour.

them of their existing rights. He proposes to increase their interest in the affairs of the Church by banishing them from the parish church, unless they happen to be communicants of that church. The truth is this Amendment, in principle, seeks to convert the National Church into a sect, and not only into a sect but into a section of a sect. It proposes to make the Church as narrow as it can be made. I do not wonder that the noble Lord was haunted by the ghost of the Test and Corporation Acts—those infamous Acts, which were scathingly described by the poet Cowper as

> " Making the symbols of atoning grace
> An office key, a picklock to a place."

The noble Lord denies making the Communion a test in the same way as it was used in connection with the Test and Corporation Acts, but he proposes it as a qualification for entrance into the parish vestry, and thereby seeks to re-erect a barrier which the good sense and religion of the people of this country banished more than half a century ago. I have no doubt that the great majority of the members of the Church of England would strenuously object to the proposal of the noble Lord, and I am not surprised that the right hon. Gentleman the Member for Oxford University and the hon. Member for St. Albans were quick to dissociate themselves from the Motion, although they have put forward Amendments equally objectionable. The right hon. Gentleman the Member for Oxford University proposes to substitute for communicating a declaration of *bonâ fide* membership of the Church of England, while the Member for St. Albans supplies a double-shotted test, for he not merely requires a declaration——

Mr. VICARY GIBBS (Herts, St. Albans): Is the hon. Member in order in discussing my Amendment ?

Mr. SPEAKER: No. That Amendment can only be discussed in the event of the Amendment of the noble Lord being carried.

*Mr. CARVELL WILLIAMS: I am content with the fact that the Amendment of the hon. Member is on the Paper, and the House must draw its own conclusions from it. My view is that both the Amendments should be re-

jected, and I think it will be time enough for the noble Lord to come to this House with a proposition of this character when Churchmen themselves are agreed. There is another point, and that is what should constitute membership of the Church ? The noble Lord told us on a former occasion that he is anxious to maintain the independence of the Church and also its position as an Establishment. But the two things are incompatible, and the noble Lord knows that he will not secure their conjunction.

*Mr. SPEAKER: Order, order ! The hon. Member is now not merely discussing the general question of disestablishment, but he is also referring to a statement made in another Debate earlier in the session. He must confine himself to the Amendment.

*Mr. CARVELL WILLIAMS: I need not pursue that argument any further. I think I have said enough to prove the absolute futility of this discussion.

*Mr. GEDGE (Walsall): It seems to me there is no necessity whatever for this Amendment or any other Amendment. The inhabitants of the parish have hitherto had certain powers, partly ecclesiastical and partly secular, and I can see no reason why because the secular powers are now taken away the others should be taken away also. No doubt representative bodies will be appointed to deal with ecclesiastical matters. The only money they have to spend will be supplied by Churchmen. Those who pay the piper can also call the tune, and we may be quite sure that the inhabitants, unless in exceptional cases, will always elect Churchmen to attend to Church affairs. Without disparaging religious work done by Nonconformists, it has been the glory of the Church that she is answerable for all the parishioners. They all are entitled to her ministrations. I anticipate no danger whatever for the Church, and I cordially associate myself with what the hon. Member for Mansfield said as to the clergyman being the clergyman of the whole parish, and not of a section of the inhabitants.

Mr. HARWOOD (Bolton): Did I not know the undoubted earnestness of the noble Lord, I should have thought that he had brought forward this Amendment as a sort of grim joke, for it certainly carries us back to the days of the Inquisition and of the Star Chamber—times in our history which we would gladly forget. I regret that the matter has been brought forward. We know that all kinds of tests have been tried and have failed, and I do think that the re-imposition of this test would be a retrograde step of a most pitiful kind. I do not think the country has yet recovered from the shock inflicted upon it by the operation of the Act which turned a most sacred rite in the service of the Church into a mere qualification for voting power. The Church, in one sense, is a collection of those who are bound together by a common faith and a common love, and history teaches us that we have never been able to find any sure method of making such a faith. The Church of England is not a testing Church, and it has distinctly repudiated the idea of applying these tests as a final mark of membership.

*Mr. SPEAKER : Order, order ! The hon. Member is going beyond the scope of the Amendment.

Mr. HARWOOD : I will simply say, in conclusion, that those who glory in the Church will regard nothing with favour which is calculated to narrow the liberties of that Church, and I therefore trust that the noble Lord will withdraw his amendment.

Lord HUGH CECIL (Greenwich): I do not propose to put the House to the trouble of a division on this question, but, by permission of the House, I would like to express my dissent from the views of the hon. Member for Mansfield, and to state that I regard this purely as a matter of law, and not as any test of obedience.

Amendment, by leave, withdrawn.

*Mr. J. G. TALBOT (Oxford University) : Notwithstanding the criticisms which have come from the other side of the House, I will venture in a few words to ask the House to agree to the Amendment which stands in my name. I think I can show that my grounds for doing so are reasonable. My Amendment, which proposes to insert the words "who shall declare themselves *bonâ fide* members of the Church of England," ought not to offend the conscience of anyone or to

Mr. Harwood.

raise any bitter controversies. The framers of this Bill have distinctly raised the question of withdrawing Church matters from the jurisdiction of the new bodies which are to be established—this is shown by the words of this clause—and the only question is, by what sort of bodies shall they be administered in future. It surely cannot be considered fatuous, old-fashioned, or absurd that Churchmen should manage Church matters, and I think we are bound to secure the introduction into this Bill of words which shall enable them to do so. I do not know what view the Government may take of my Amendment, nor am I aware what is the opinion of the House upon it, but I do ask hon. Members not to be led astray by any plausible arguments, such as the allegation, true in a certain sense, that the Church is the Church of the whole nation. I only wish by moving this Amendment to show that we, as members of the Church of England, while anxious to acknowledge the service which the Government has done by preserving the management of the affairs of the Church from the control of the borough councils, are anxious to ensure that they shall be administered only by those who declare themselves to be Churchmen.

Amendment proposed—

"In page 12, line 33, after the words last inserted, to insert the words ' who shall declare themselves bonâ fide members of the Church of England."—(*Mr. Talbot.*)

Question proposed—

" That those words be there inserted."

The FIRST LORD of the TREASURY (Mr. A. J. BALFOUR, Manchester, E.) : I quite admit that this Amendment is not open to some of the objections urged against that of my noble friend the Member for Greenwich. But it is not a very opportune moment at which to discuss such questions as the reform of vestries. This Bill is a Bill for the reform of London municipal government. To make it a Bill for dealing with ecclesiastical matters would be throwing on our shoulders a burden which we neither desire to assume nor which ought to be thrust upon us on an occasion of this kind. On the abstract merits of the proposal I say nothing ; on the face of it the suggestion contained in the Amendment is an extremely plausible one. But any ecclesiastical reform of the vestries should take the shape of a measure applying to the whole country, and not to London alone. I am informed that the late Archbishop of Canterbury had very much at heart the question of the reform of the vestries, and I believe I am right in saying that what stopped all further procedure on his part in dealing with the question was the very problem touched on by my right hon. friend, namely, whether for vestry purposes the Church is to be regarded as a sect or as the Church of the whole nation. Is it practicable or tolerable that we should attempt to discuss, on such a Bill as this, a controversy we should find difficult enough successfully to tackle alone? While I do not complain of the action of my right hon. friend in moving the Amendment, I do protest that he has chosen a most improper time for raising this question.

Mr. VICARY GIBBS: My right hon. friend has rebuked those of us who have thought fit to intrude ecclesiastical matters into a debate on the London Government Bill. But this is the point I should like to draw attention to. It seems to be suggested that there is something inherently absurd and unreasonable in the proposition that the affairs of the Church of England, where they arise in connection with vestry business, should be managed by members of that Church. But surely it is not altogether unreasonable to bring before the House by means of this Amendment the fact that under the clause, as it now stands, persons who have no interest in the Church will be granted the power to interfere in purely ecclesiastical matters.

Viscount CRANBORNE (Rochester): In the few words I wish to say I would point out that the terms of this Amendment are much less rigid than those of the one proposed by my noble friend the Member for Greenwich. It was pointed out on a previous occasion by the First Lord of the Treasury that the test proposed in the last Amendment was stronger than that which prevailed in the Church of Scotland. But, as I understand the position in the Scottish Church, the members consist of communicants and those whom the body of Churchmen recognise as such, whereas the amendment proposes that a man who *bona fide* declares himself a Churchman will be accepted as such on his own word. I believe my

right hon. friend has stated that this Bill makes no change in the position of the Church in these matters. It is very evident that he ought to be the chairman for ecclesiastical purposes, yet under the scheme or method by which this clause will be carried out there is no guarantee of anything of that kind. Sooner or later this question must be faced; you cannot come up to the House of Commons and say that laymen are to have control over the Church of England, and not define what a layman is. One hon. Gentleman says that we must wait for a large Bill to deal with these matters; but will any Member of the Government or of the Front Opposition bench presume to foreshadow the time when we shall have a Bill to deal with ecclesiastical vestries? In the meantime the question has to be dealt with. Here is a simple example, which shows that this is the very opportunity, when we are reconstructing a public body which has exclusively to deal with Church matters, to take this matter into consideration. This is a very practical matter. Who ought to have control over Church matters? Why, evidently the Churchmen. The proposition before the House is a most reasonable one in my opinion, and it is for this reason that I cannot regret that my right hon. friend has proposed his Amendment. This proposal does not represent the view of a small body of Churchmen, but of the whole. There is no subject on which Churchmen as a whole agree so much as upon their having greater control over the Church.

*Mr. J. G. TALBOT: After the sympathetic reception which my proposal has had from my right hon. friend the First Lord of the Treasury, I beg to withdraw my Amendment. (Cries of "No, No.")

Question put and negatived. Other Amendments made.

Mr. W. F. D. SMITH (Strand, Westminster): I think the Amendment which stands in my name is desirable, because there are cases which may arise in which officers are simply transferred from the vestries to the borough councils, for whom they would perform the same work, and it is only fair that past services should be reckoned for the purposes of calculating the compensation to which they are entitled. With these remarks I beg to move the Amendment.

Amendment proposed—

"In Clause 26, page 15, line 27, at end, to insert—'Provided that the borough council may, if it thinks fit, take into account continuous service under any authority or authorities to which this Act refers, in order to calculate the total period of service of any officer entitled to compensation under this Act.'"—(*Mr. W. F. D. Smith.*)

Question proposed "That these words be there inserted."

MR. A. J. BALFOUR : The particular form in which the hon. Gentleman put his Amendment on a former occasion made it compulsory in its character, and thus rendered it obligatory for one municipality to pay for services performed for another municipality. The objection to such a clause was obvious. The hon. Member shows his appreciation of that fact here by making it voluntary. In this form it is not objectionable, and of course there are cases in which the change might be extremely hard upon the persons concerned. This proposal only gives the borough councils liberty to exercise the power, therefore I suggest to the House that we should accept this Amendment.

Question put and agreed to.

Further Amendment proposed.

THE SOLICITOR GENERAL (SIR R. B. FINLAY, Inverness Burghs): I think that one word of explanation as regards this Amendment is desirable. The object of it is to bring within the scope of the compensation clause the case of officers, such as registration officers whose powers and duties are not transferred by this Act. The duty of that class of officer has been transferred to the town clerk, and this Amendment is inserted to remove a doubt which may exist as to whether these persons come within the scope of the clause or not.

Amendment proposed, in page 15, after Sub-section (1), to insert—

"(2) Sub-sections 4 and 7 of Section 81 of the Local Government Act, 1894, shall apply to the existing officers affected by this Act, as as if references in those sub-sections to the district council were references to the borough council, and all expenses incurred by the borough council in pursuance of those sub-sections shall be paid out of the general rate."—(*Mr. Solicitor-General.*)

Question proposed, "That those words be there inserted."

MR. STUART (Shoreditch, Hoxton): After what has been said by the hon. and Mr. W. F. D. *Smith.*

learned Gentleman, I do not think any exception can be taken to the proposal. I only regret that the Solicitor-General was not able to put his Amendment down upon paper.

MR. JOHN BURNS (Battersea) : I go further, and say I see no reason whatever for the Amendment of the Solicitor-General. We have accepted the Amendment of the hon. Member for the Strand Division, and it seems to me that we have gone quite far enough. The Amendment of the Solicitor-General seeks to include officers who are not regularly employed, and who, because they are not regularly employed, are paid a higher rate of remuneration.

SIR R. B. FINLAY: At the end of the clause it runs—

"A scheme under this Act may make such provisions as may appear necessary for carrying this section into effect, and if necessary for determining the authority to whom any existing officer is to be transferred, and for applying the provisions of this section to any officer who suffers pecuniary loss by reason of anything in or done under this Act, although he is not transferred to a borough council."

To that I wish to add my Amendment. The object is not to bring in officers not regularly employed, but to remove a doubt which exists as to whether registration officers are officers in authority, and as such come within the scope of the compensation clause.

MR. JOHN BURNS: We are much indebted to the explanation of the hon. and learned Gentleman, but that does not remove my objection to this Amendment. We do not object to the registration officer who is constantly employed being brought within the scope of the clause, but I do trust that the clause will be so drawn that it will not include men who, because they have been precariously employed, have been paid a very much higher rate of remuneration than if they had been employed under the town clerk as permanent officials. I do protest against those registration officers who are only partially employed throughout the year being brought in. I regret that we accepted the Amendment of the hon. Member for the Strand Division, and I still more regret that the Solicitor-General is dipping his hand again into the public pocket. I strongly protest against it.

Amendment agreed to.

SIR SAMUEL MONTAGU (Tower Hamlets, Whitechapel): I hope the Committee will accept the Amendment I now rise to move. Since the Second Reading I have had many communications with my constituents, and, quite irrespective of party I find there is a universal opinion against the creation of this large municipality. They think that the municipality so created would be so large as to be unmanageable. Both Whitechapel and St. George's suffer from rack-renting and overcrowding, and have to be specially treated. At three meetings which were lately held by separate organisations unanimous votes have been passed against the proposal to have so large a municipality, and proposing as an alternative to unite the two Parliamentary boroughs of Whitechapel and St. George's. I find that there is no objection at all to this; that Mile End, Stepney, and Limehouse would be willing to be united into one borough, leaving Whitechapel and St. George's alone. The only case of difficulty is Wapping, which is a strip of land running round St. George's on the water side, which ought to be united with St. George's. It is in the Parliamentary borough, and ought to go into that division, but it is a very small area, containing less than 2,000 souls, and a rateable value of about £50,000. But as the feeling is so strong in favour of small boroughs, my friends are quite prepared in this case, if the Solicitor-General says that Wapping ought to remain with Limehouse, to waive its being included in St. George's. We are all in agreement that Mile End, Stepney, and Limehouse should go together, leaving Whitechapel and St. George's without Wapping as a separate municipality. I can assure the First Lord of the Treasury that there is no difference of opinion in this matter, either in St. George's or in the constituency which I represent. I have represented Whitechapel ever since it has been a Parliamentary borough, and as I do not intend to seek re-election after this Parliament, I have no further interest in the matter than to do what I consider my duty.

Amendment proposed—

"In Schedule 1, page 18, to leave out lines 10 and 11, and insert the words, 'The area consisting of the Parliamentary division of Whitechapel, consisting of all the areas included in the Whitechapel District Board of Works, together with the Parliamentary division of St. George's-in-the-East (including Wapping).'"—(*Sir Samuel Montagu.*)

Question proposed—

"That the words proposed to be left out to the word 'Limehouse,' in line 11, stand part of the Bill."

Mr. H. S. SAMUEL (Tower Hamlets, Limehouse) : The way in which the hon. Gentleman moves his Amendment entirely gets rid of my objection to it. My constituents have the very strongest objection to parting with the richest portion of the district of Limehouse. The population of Wapping is extremely small, and the rateable value extremely high, and if it were taken away it would mean a great increase of rates of Limehouse. The hon. Gentleman has now removed my objection, and is practically proposing the exact Amendment which I put down at the Committee stage of the Bill, when I proposed that the Poor Law districts of Mile End Old Town and Stepney should be joined together. From the first I have always objected to the creation of this large borough, and have always suggested that the best way to deal with the matter would be the formation of three boroughs of equal size. That being so, I accept the suggestion of the hon. Baronet, and I earnestly hope that the Government will agree to the suggestion which I believe is put before them with the unanimous assent of all the electors concerned.

Mr. SYDNEY BUXTON (Tower Hamlets, Poplar) : This particular scheme was put into the Bill conditionally, and subject to discussion and agreement when we came to this table. If the whole area were divided into two, having regard to population and rateable value, there would be two boroughs of almost equal size. I hope the Government will see their way to accept this Amendment.

Lord HUGH CECIL : I am loth to intervene in the discussion, but I feel confident that if the hon. Member for Bow and Bromley were here he would take a different view.

Mr. SYDNEY BUXTON : I did speak to the hon. Member for Bow and Bromley, and he said he was ready to accept the Amendment.

Mr. STEADMAN (Tower Hamlets, Stepney) : On the Committee stage of this Bill I moved an Amendment, and took some trouble to rake out some historical records in reference to Mile End. Seeing that it sends two Members to Parliament and four members to the London County Council, I thought it had a just claim on the First

Lord of the Treasury. But evidently my historical records had not the desired effect. On that occasion the First Lord of the Treasury laid down the principle that either the Tower Hamlets should be divided into two, or the whole thing should be referred to the Boundary Commission, but, seeing that he has made no provision in the Bill for the matter going to the Boundary Commission, the matter ought to be decided by the House. I may say that my own Vestry have passed a resolution in favour of the amalgamation of Limehouse and Mile End ; but if you look at the map you will see that that is not a good geographical area, because with the exception of the north-east of Wapping it is surrounded by St. George's-in-the-East. Therefore it would make a long straggling borough, and would be rather awkward to get at. That is the difficulty I am placed in in supporting the Amendment of the hon. Member. As the five parishes are now scheduled in the Bill, although they would make a very large borough, it would be a more uniform borough than the amalgamation of Mile End and Limehouse.

Mr. A. J. BALFOUR : Do I understand that the hon. Gentleman does not approve of the proposed division ?

Mr. STEADMAN : Well, it would make a very awkward borough.

Mr. A. J. BALFOUR : There are five Members representing this area in the House of Commons. Two have spoken strongly in favour of the new proposal, and I understand the other two take much the same view, while the fifth thinks that one division is better than two. I am very reluctant to diminish the size of the areas already agreed to. There must, of course, be a certain amount of objection to changes of this kind, and which cannot be entirely removed. As the House in Committee unanimously came to an agreement on the matter, and as the Members interested are not unanimous in any of the proposed changes, I think the House had better adhere to the original decision of the Committee.

*Mr. LOWLES (Shoreditch, Haggerston): I quite understood that the Government were prepared to accept the proposal. I believe that the proposed division is most acceptable to all parties

Mr. Steadman.

in the division, and I feel very strongly that there are many circumstances which justify it. The First Lord of the Treasury would be consulting the consensus of opinion on both sides of politics if he listened to the voice of the whole of the Members for the district, except the hon. Member for Stepney.

Mr. STUART : I hope that the First Lord of the Treasury will still favourably consider the division proposed. When he agreed to put the whole of these five boroughs in one division on the Committee stage, it was not by any means that that view prevailed in the Committee ; it was simply that hon. Members felt that something should be put in the Bill at that stage in order that the matter might be discussed. It has been very much discussed, and I venture to say there is more unanimity than the First Lord recognises in the desire to divide the area into two. The hon. Member for Stepney is the only Member of this House who has really said anything on the other side ; but I would point out that he himself is in favour of two boroughs, his only difficulty being that if Wapping is to be attached to Stepney it would not look well on the map. Then, I would point out that the hon. Member for Stepney admitted that his own representative Vestry is in favour of the proposal now before the House.

Mr. HERBERT ROBERTSON (Hackney, South): Several conversions seem to have taken place in regard to this matter, and the names of three hon. Gentlemen are mentioned as being converted to the division into two boroughs. The hon. Member for Mile End discussed this question with me over and over again. He was particularly keen as to this area being made one borough. Now we hear he has changed his mind. Then we are told that the hon. Member for Bow and Bromley had also changed his mind, but I found him very keen in having this large area made one borough. There is a great deal to be said as to the area nearest the City being very narrow and unworkable as a borough. I certainly had not the slightest idea that the Government had the intention of altering the area. I have heard distinct approval from people in the district of the arrangement the Government came to on the Committee stage of the Bill, and I have received no memorials from vestries or other public bodies against the proposal of the Government.

Sir R. B. FINLAY: I do not know why the hon. Member for Haggerston understood that this Amend-ment was to be accepted by the Government.

*Mr. LOWLES: A large deputation waited on the Government; I believed that they were given some encouragement.

Sir R. B. FINLAY: The deputation was received with courtesy, as usual, but the gentlemen seem to have jumped to the conclusion that the Government were going to accept this Amendment. We are told there is a general agreement on this proposal amongst the Members for the district, but it is unfortunate that some of these Gentlemen are absent. I cannot help thinking that, if these hon. Members entertained this view at all strongly, they would have been here to support it. We are in this difficulty, that we are asked to make a change of this kind without strong reasons of administrative con-

venience being adduced to the House for it. On the other hand, we have had some good reasons given the other way, which, to my mind, were convincing. If you look at the map it will be seen that, geographically speaking, the proposed division would be awkward. You would have Mile End and Limehouse, and then a long strip along the shore of the Thames which ought to belong to St. George's-in-the-East. That view was strongly presented to us by a deputation which was accompanied by the hon. Baronet who made this motion. Under these circumstances it is desirable that Wapping should belong to the other four districts, and the whole made into one borough.

Mr. STEADMAN: By leave of the House I may say I have no very strong feeling in this matter; and, seeing that I am in the minority, I am quite willing to withdraw any objection I have to the proposed division and to support the hon. Member for Whitechapel.

Question put—

The House divided: Ayes, 133; Noes, 55. (Division List No. 181.)

AYES.

Arnold, Alfred
Atkinson, Rt. Hon. John
Bailey, James (Walworth)
Baillie, Jas. E. B. (Inverness)
Balcarres, Lord
Balfour,'Rt.Hn.A.J.(Manch'r)
Balfour, Rt. Hn. G. W.(Leeds)
Barnes, Frederic Gorell
Bartley, George C. T.
Barton, Dunbar Plunket
Beckett, Ernest William
Begg, Ferdinand Faithfull
Blakiston-Houston, John
Blundell, Colonel Henry
Bousfield, William Robert
Brodrick, Rt. Hon. St. John
Cecil, Evelyn (Hertford, E.)
Cecil, Lord Hugh (Greenwich)
Chaloner, Captain R. G. W.
Chamberlain,Rt.Hn.J.(Birm.)
Chamberlain,J.Austen(Worc'r)
Chaplin, Rt. Hon. Henry
Clare, Octavius Leigh
Clarke, Sir Edw.(Plymouth)
Cochrane, Hon. Thos. H. A. E.
Coghill, Douglas Harry
Collings, Rt. Hon. Jesse
Colston, Ch. Ed. H. Athole
Cranborne, Viscount
Cross, H. Shepherd (Bolton)
Cubitt, Hon. Henry
Curran, Thomas B. (Donegal)
Curzon, Viscount
Dalkeith, Earl of
Dalrymple, Sir Charles

Davies, Sir H. D. (Chatham)
Dickson-Poynder, Sir John P.
Douglas, Rt. Hon. A. Akers-
Doxford, William Theodore
Drage, Geoffrey
Duncombe, Hon. Hubert V.
Fellowes, Hon. Ailwyn Edw.
Finlay, Sir Robert Bannatyne
Fisher, William Hayes
FitzGerald,SirRobertPenrose-
Folkestone, Viscount
Foster, Colonel (Lancaster)
Garfit, William
Gibbs, Hn.A.G.H.(C.ofLond.)
Gibbs, Hon. V. (St. Albans)
Godson, Sir Augustus F.
Goldsworthy, Major-General
Gordon, Hon. John Edward
Gorst, Rt. Hon. Sir Jo'n E.
Goulding, Edward Alfred
Gray, Ernest (West Ham)
Hardy, Laurence
Hatch, Ernest Frederick Geo.
Heath, James
Henderson, Alexander
Hermon-Hodge, Robert T.
Hill, Arthur (Down, West)
Hoare, Edw. Brodie (Hamps.)
Houston, R. P.
Howard, Joseph
Howell, William Tudor
Hubbard, Hon. Evelyn
Hughes, Colonel Edwin
Hutchinson, Capt. G.W.Grice-
Jebb, Richard Claverhouse

Jeffreys, Arthur Frederick
Jessel, Capt. Herbert Merton
Kemp, George
Keswick, William
King, Sir Henry Seymour
Lawrence, W. F. (Liverpool)
Lawson, John Grant (Yorks.)
Loder, Gerald Walter Erskine
Long, Rt. Bn. W. (Liverp'l.)
Lowe, Francis William
Lucas-Shadwell, William
Macartney, W. G. Ellison
Macdona, John Cumming
MacIver, David (Liverpool)
Maclure, Sir John William
M'Killop, James
Mellor, Colonel (Lancashire)
Milward, Colonel Victor
Monk, Charles James
Moon, Edward Robert Pacy
Moore, William (Antrim, N.)
Morgan, Hn. F. (Monm'thsh.)
Morrell, George Herbert
Morton, Arthur H. A.(Deptf'd)
Newdigate, Francis Alexander
Nicol, Donald Ninian
Pease, Herb. Pike(Darlington)
Penn, John
Percy, Earl
Pilkington, R.(Lancs Newton)
Priestley,SirWOverend(Edin.
Purvis, Robert
Rasch, Major Frederic Carne
Ridley, Rt. Hon. Sir Matt. W.
Ritchie, Rt. Hon. C. T.

Robertson, Herbert (Hackney)
Round, James
Russell, Gen. F.S(Cheltenham)
Russell, T. W. (Tyrone)
Savory, Sir Joseph
Sharpe, William Edward T.
Smith, Hon. W. F. D. (Strand)
Stanley, Lord (Lancs.)
Stewart, Sir M. J. M'Taggart
Stock, James Henry
Stone, Sir Benjamin

Strauss, Arthur
Strutt, Hon. Charles Hedley
Thorburn, Walter
Thornton, Percy M.
Tomlinson, Wm. Edw. Murray
Tritton, Charles Ernest
Valentia, Viscount
Wanklyn, James Leslie
Warr, Augustus Frederick
Wharton, Rt. Hon. John L.
Whiteley, H. (Asht'n-und'r-L.)

Williams, Colonel R. (Dorset)
Williams, J. Powell- (Birm.)
Wodehouse, Rt Hon E. R. (Bath)
Wylie, Alexander
Wyndham, George
Wyndham-Quin, Major W. H.

TELLERS FOR THE AYES— Sir William Walrond and Mr. Anstruther.

NOES.

Austin, Sir J. (Yorkshire)
Broadhurst, Henry
Buxton, Sydney Charles
Caldwell, James
Cameron, Sir Chas. (Glasgow)
Carvill, Patrick Geo. Hamilton
Charrington, Spencer
Colville, John
Crombie, John William
Curran, Thomas (Sligo, S.)
Davitt, Michael
Donelan, Captain A.
Doogan, P. C.
Evans, Samuel T. (Glamorgan)
Fenwick, Charles
Flower, Ernest
Gladstone, Rt. Hon. Herb. John
Goddard, Daniel Ford
Harwood, George
Hayne, Rt. Hon. Charles Seale-

Hedderwick, Thomas Charles H
Horniman, Frederick John
Jacoby, James Alfred
Lowles, John
MacAleese, Daniel
M'Dermott, Patrick
M'Ghee, Richard
Maddison, Fred.
Morgan, J Lloyd Carmarthen
O'Brien, Patrick (Kilkenny)
O Connor, James (Wicklow, W.
Oldroyd, Mark
Pease, Joseph A. (Northumb.)
Pickard, Benjamin
Pickersgill, Edward Hare
Power, Patrick Joseph
Price, Robert John
Richardson, J. (Durham, S.E.)
Rickett, J. Compton
Robson, William Snowdon

Samuel, Harry S. Limehouse)
Samuel, J. (Stockton-on-Tees)
Schwann, Charles E.
Shaw, Thomas (Hawick B.)
Smith, Samuel (Flint)
Steadman, William Charles
Sullivan, Donal (Westmeath)
Trevelyan, Charles Philips
Tully, Jasper
Wedderburn, Sir William
Weir, James Galloway
Williams, John Carvell (Notts.)
Wilson, Henry J. (York, W.R.)
Wilson, John (Durham, Mid)
Woods, Samuel

TELLERS FOR THE NOES— Sir Samuel Montagu and Mr. James Stuart.

Other Amendments made.

Amendment proposed—

" In Schedule 1, page 18, to leave out lines 14 and 15, and insert—' The area consisting of the parishes of St. George the Martyr, Christ Church, St. Saviour, Southwark, and Newington "—(*The Solicitor-General.*)

MR. SYDNEY BUXTON : I think the Solicitor-General should give some reason for this change.

SIR R. B. FINLAY : The alteration has been made for this reason. If anyone looks at the map he will see that this area forms a projecting tongue, which, in the Parliamentary Division, is in Bermondsey, and not with the rest of the parish along with Newington and West Southwark. It is admitted that it would be very inconvenient to divide the parish. A resolution has been sent to me which was passed by the vestry of Rotherhithe, St. Thomas' Board of Works, and the Vestry of Bermondsey, in support of the resolution passed by the Vestry of St. George the Martyr, in favour of the retention of that part of the borough. I hope that the House will not cut the area of the parish and the Poor Law Union in the way the original schedule will do.

Amendment agreed to.

Other Amendments made.

MR. STUART : We have passed a clause which says that every portion of the county of London shall be in some borough. Now, so far as I can make out, the Collegiate Church of St. Peter's, Westminster, is not so included.

SIR R. B. FINLAY : I have handed in an Amendment to meet that case. The reason why it was omitted before was that there was some question as to the right boundaries. I now beg to move that Amendment.

Amendment proposed—

" In page 18, line 30 to add ' and including the Collegiate Church of St. Peter, Westminster, and the Liberty of the Rolls.' "—(*The Solicitor-General.*)

Question, "That these words be there inserted," put and agreed to.

MR. STUART : I think there is another part of London that we have hung up, and that is the Tower. I think the Tower will have to be added to the Whitechapel district.

SIR R. B. FINLAY: I am very much obliged to the right hon. Gentleman. The matter will be considered.

Other Amendments made.

Another Amendment proposed—

"In page 19, column 2, line 20, before the word 'subject,' to insert the words 'subject to bye-laws and regulations made by the County Council and '"—(*Mr. James Stuart.*)

Question proposed—"That those words be there inserted."

SIR R. B. FINLAY: I had an interview with some persons of experience in regard to this matter. I am unable to see the necessity for these words, and I do not think any clear reasons were adduced in support of them. The matter will, however, be considered.

Amendment, by leave, withdrawn.

Amendments proposed—

"In Schedule 2, page 19, column 2, line 23, after 's. 100,' to add 'and s. 101'; and in Schedule 2, page 19, column 2, line 23, after 's. 100,' add 'subject to the requirement that borough council shall send annually to county council a copy of the register.'"—(*Mr. Stuart, for Captain Sinclair.*)

SIR R. B. FINLAY: The first of these Amendments is already dealt with by an Amendment made at my instance.

MR. STUART: As to the second Amendment, I do not see how, without it, the County Council can obtain a copy of the register.

SIR R. B. FINLAY: I hope the hon. Member will not press this. I do not see the necessity for the duplication of these registers. The register kept by the borough council may be inspected.

MR. STUART: I do not wish to press it, but I hope that the Solicitor-General will consider the matter when he is inquiring into other points.

Amendments, by leave, withdrawn.

SIR J. DICKSON-POYNDER (Wilts, Chippenham): I have to move to leave out lines 26 and 27 on page 20. It will be convenient, I think, that I should briefly call the attention of the House to the history of that portion of the Act with which we are now dealing, and which is embraced in the schedule of this Bill. Part III. is a consolidation of an Act which was passed by Lord Beaconsfield in 1851; but that Act, which was in vogue from 1851 to 1890, was seldom, if ever, brought into operation in the metropolis. It was framed by Lord Beaconsfield with the idea that if dwellings were required over and above those dwellings which were formerly acquired under Part I. and Part II., they should be acquired under Part III. There may have been individual instances here and there where Part III. was brought into operation, but, practically speaking, it was a dead letter from 1851 to 1890. In the year 1890, when there was a general consolidation of all the different Housing Acts, Lord Shaftesbury's Act came into operation. With the exception of one or two instances, between 1890 and now, Part III. has not been put into operation very much in the metropolis. It was exercised in the year 1893 on a considerably large scale for the acquisition of the Millbank Estate, and it was also put into operation in 1895 in what is known as the Falcon Court Improvement Estate. But in both these cases Part III. was exercised more in the sense of an addition to the scheme under Part I. and Part II. The House may know that the Millbank Estate, which is being rapidly developed, is to go to those persons who have been displaced, under the schemes known as Part I. in this Act, in other parts of London. Up to this point Part III. has been more or less excluded, and has not been brought into operation. Within the last few months, however, the London County Council and the Housing Committee of that body, recognising the extremely grave condition of affairs in London, the fearful state of congestion, the continuous increase of population, and the difficulty of accommodating the people, have taken what may be termed a new departure, and that a very drastic one. The result has been that the London County Council have committed themselves to a new and very extensive policy, which is not merely to continue to clear the areas and rebuild under Part I. of the Act on a large scale, and under a smaller scale under Part II., but, finding that they have been unable to replace entirely the number of people they have displaced under Part II., they have now committed themselves, for better or worse, to a very extensive exercise of Part III. of the Act. Part III. empowers a county council to purchase——

Attention called to the fact that there were not 40 members present. House counted, and 40 members being present, Debate resumed.

SIR J. DICKSON-POYNDER: Before 1890 every local authority that exercised Part III. had first to obtain the sanction of the Home Office. The Act of 1890 did away with that sanction, and every local authority which desires to exercise Part III. now is able to do so without asking any leave whatsoever. That Part enacts that local authorities may purchase land, but it is also laid down that the local authority, having purchased land, is obliged itself to build upon it, and to manage the buildings it erects. The reason why I move my Amendment is that I am quite sure, although in former years Part III. has not been much used, that it is now to be used considerably, and it is not in a properly equipped condition to enable it to be used to the benefit of the metropolis as a whole. If the indiscriminate purchase of land is to be carried out in London there should be further safeguards in one direction, and further extensions in another. With reference to safeguards, a Government authority should be called into requisition to give its sanction, both as regards the purchase of land, and also as to the plan of the buildings to be erected on it. There is, however, another important point in my humble opinion, which is that if this Part is to be exercised very largely throughout the metropolis there should be an extension allowed—namely that, having purchased the land, the local authority shall have full power to sell it as long as it is handed over to some company or society that is prepared to build working-class dwellings on it. In the case of Part I., a clearance having been made, the sanction of the Home Office has to be obtained before the local authority may build on it, and I should like some such regulation brought into operation with reference to Part III. If not, there will be in London in the future many districts in which land will be managed and controlled by the municipalities. In past legislation the principle has been laid down ˌthat it is not in the best interests of the metropolis, or of the private enterprise and industry which have made this country prosperous, that municipalities should have the control of property on a large scale in the metropolis. To such an extent has that principle been laid down that Part I. of the Housing Act provides that at the end of 10 years after the clearance, unless the sanction of the Home Office is obtained, the land must be sold by the municiʹality. Ten years have now nearly elapsed since the Act became law, and I hope the Government Department will stand firm and say that the land must go back to a private individual or to a society. There is great danger in front of us in working Part III. on an extensive scale. Land has enormously increased in value in the metropolis ; the price of building materials and labour has also enormously increased, and the result is that the officers of the London County Council have found out that it is practically impossible if land is purchased in the central portions of London to erect on it dwellings according to standard without finding a financial loss at the end. This is a very grave question, and, as I have said, the London County Council is committed to a very drastic policy in this direction. A very large section of its members in, their enthusiasm for meeting this great difficulty, are quite prepared to commit themselves to the principle— which is most dangerous and fallacious— that if you cannot build at a financial profit you should go to the rates for the deficit. That is undoubtedly the policy which the Progressive members of the London County Council contemplate. It is a policy against all the laws of political economy.

MR. STUART: The hon. Baronet has not adduced any proof of that statement.

SIR J. DICKSON-POYNDER: I can adduce my own knowledge of members of the Council who have considerable standing, and who advocate that policy.

MR. STUART: There is no ground for saying that that is the policy of the Progressive majority of the Council.

SIR J. DICKSON-POYNDER: I will not weary the House by entering into a controversy with the hon. Gentleman. If the London County Council exercise Part III. on an extensive scale, they will find it absolutely impossible to do it at a profit. The effect of the proposal in the Bill is that the thirty borough councils in London may have the opportunity of exercising Part III.—in other words, the power of buying land without the sanction of any Government Department, and of erecting dwellings on it. Until the law is amended, this is a very dangerous departure, and I would strongly urge on the Government, in the face of the great difficulties we have to meet, that before they insert Part III. in the London Government Act, they should remodel the Housing Act, especially on the point indicated. The County Council has a very clear and definite policy, which is to buy land in the outskirts of London in order that the people who have been displaced in the central portions may be housed. Particular attention is being given to the purchase of land in proximity to railway stations and tramways, to enable the working classes to get to their work. That policy can only be carried out by the central authority, and I think it is better that the general housing of London should be left in its hands. Even if the Government will not give way on this point, I would ask them to give some kind of pledge that Part III. of the Housing Act will be amended in the direction I have indicated.

Amendment proposed—

"In page 20, to leave out lines 26 and 27." —(*Sir John Dickson-Poynder*).

Question proposed, "That the words proposed to be left out stand part of the Bill."

MR. PICKERSGILL (Bethnal Green, S.W.): As the hon. Baronet has moved an Amendment which stands to my name, I would like to state why on reconsideration I decline to proceed with it. The question is a difficult one, and one on which it is quite possible that two opinions may be held. At present the London County Council has power under Part III. of the Housing Act to provide houses for the people, and the proposal in the Bill is, not that that power should be taken away from the County Council, but that while it remains with the Council concurrent power should be conferred on each of the new municipal bodies. From one point

of view that may be regarded as a somewhat dangerous proposal, but my point of view is different from that of the hon. Baronet. The difficulty I saw was that if the proposal were carried there would probably be a tendency in each district to provide dwellings for its own poor, and there would be less pressure on the central authority to carry out the power it now possesses. I am strongly of opinion that the provision of dwellings for the poor is a purpose the cost of which ought to fall on the whole of London. These poor are not the poor of Bethnal Green, or Battersea, or Shoreditch, but of London, and therefore the cost of making necessary provision for them ought to come out of the common purse. At one time I felt so strongly that I was inclined to vote against the proposal of the Government. There are, however, graver considerations on the other side. I do not desire to belittle the work of the County Council in regard to the Housing Act. The Council has undoubtedly done good work in clearing away rookeries, but it is only fair to say that it has done more in pulling down than building up. The Council has made provision for a considerable number of persons, yet it has not solved the great difficulty. It has not provided accommodation at a rent which a workman earning 20s. or 21s. a week can afford to pay. The housing question in London at present, I do not hesitate to say, is a gross scandal which earnestly presses for a satisfactory settlement. We have a condition of things under which a man in employment and earning fair wages has not been able to get accommodation, and has been obliged to send his family to the workhouse. That is a scandalous condition of things, and reflects the greatest discredit on the community. Considering that the question is a burning one, and in view of the communications that have reached me to the effect that the poorer localities of London desire to have this power, I decline to accept the responsibility of depriving them of the opportunity which the Government proposes to put in their way. For many reasons I shall support the Government proposal.

*MR. LOWLES: It is the first time, either by voice or vote, during the debates on this Bill, that I have supported any contraction of the powers to be conferred on the local authorities. I think the House ought to know that the hon. Baronet has the honour to be the chairman of the Housing of the Working Classes Committee of the London County Council, a position he fills with credit to himself and advantage to London, and he therefore speaks with special knowledge of the question. I myself was a member of the same committee for three years, and may claim some knowledge of the question also. It is proposed to give this power to the new boroughs, but you limit the exercise of it in each district strictly to its own area, thereby perpetuating the evil which the County Council is now trying to remove, namely the settling down of people in congested districts in the heart of London. The policy which the Council has pursued for years has been to get people to live out in the suburbs, and it has approached railway companies and has obtained possession of tramways in order to induce workmen to live where they can get better surroundings for their families. If we give these local authorities power to erect dwellings and limit its operation to their own districts, we will tempt them to buy land at exorbitant rates. Take that part of my constituency that adjoins the City. Every year land is becoming more valuable; small houses are being pulled down and are being replaced by warehouses which bring a larger revenue to the parish. I venture to say that an enthusiastic local body with perhaps Socialistic tendencies would disregard not only the loss of money but also the considerations of health in putting into force the power it is proposed to give to the municipal boroughs, and I therefore, in the interests of public health and from considerations of economy, support the amendment of the hon. Baronet.

MR. STUART: As I am interested largely in the County Council, I support the proposal in the Government Bill, because, at a meeting between the local authorities and the County Council, the Council, after a full consideration of the arguments brought forward by the local authorities, decided that it would be willing to concede to them the concurrent powers now included in the schedule. So far as I can speak for the County Council I say that it adheres to its undertaking.

Mr. Lowles.

That is the clear and simple position. It does not enter into the arguments; it is merely that, the arguments being considered on a previous occasion and a decision taken, the Council is prepared to abide by it. I admit the great respect in which the hon. Baronet opposite and his work are held by every member of the County Council, and although I differ from him on this particular I have the highest esteem for the work he is doing on the County Council. I must, however, take exception to the position which he incidentally took up with reference to the Progressive majority, and his suggestion that that majority would act in some remarkable manner. All I will say is that the hon. Baronet is himself chairman of the Housing Committee of the Council, and that is enough on that subject. The County Council has carried out Part III. with very considerable success and very considerable advantage to London. The hon. Baronet has pointed out the lines on which the Council is proceeding under his guidance, and I think there can be no hesitation in believing that the Council is endeavouring to house the poor of the metropolis under conditions acceptable to all parties in the Council, and to the views entertained throughout all parts of the metropolis generally. But we have had the representations of the local authorities before us, and, they being desirous of having this power, and the Council having decided to give it to them, that decision must be adhered to. I notice in all the Debates on questions of the transference of powers an underlying mistake. Many Members appear to assume that the new local authorities will be more Conservative and less Progressive than the County Council. I have no doubt that it will be found that their character will be very much the same, and that their method of dealing with the housing of the poor will be on very similar lines. That question is one of the most absolutely important questions for this metropolis, and the spirit in which the County Council is dealing with it is shown by the fact that whereas there is a great Progressive majority on the County Council, the hon. Baronet opposite is Chairman of the Housing Committee. I venture to believe that the new boroughs will deal with this question in a similar spirit, and I have as much confidence in putting the necessary power into their hands as I have in retaining it in the hands of the Council. I wish to support the proposal in the Bill on the main ground I have mentioned.

Sir R. B. FINLAY: I am sure that hon. Members on both sides of the House are thoroughly agreed as to the extreme importance of this question of the housing of the poor, and I am sure also that we all recognise the work which has been done in this direction by my hon. friend who moved the Amendment, and that he speaks with special knowledge on the subject. At the same time I cannot but feel that many of his arguments were directed to the point that the power given under the Housing of the Working Classes Act should be supplemented. There is a great deal of force in many of my hon. friend's observations, and I am perfectly certain they will receive careful consideration. But the question before the House is whether, under the Housing of the Working Classes Act in its present form, the power with reference to Part III. should not be extended to the borough councils. I would remind the House that this power is enjoyed by other municipal boroughs throughout the country, and I would ask why the metropolitan boroughs should not enjoy it also. There is very great cogency in one observation of the hon. Member who has just spoken, namely, that it was agreed at a conference between the local authorities and the County Council that this power should be extended to the borough councils. My hon. friend who moved the Amendment made some criticisms upon the policy of the County Council which I gather did not meet with acceptance in all parts of the House, but I would remind my hon. friend that whatever may be the policy of the majority of the County Council it does not at all follow that the policy of the borough councils will be the same. Under this Bill, when it becomes law, the power of exercising Part III. will only extend to the limit of each borough. My hon. friend said that it was desirable that those workmen should be provided with houses in the suburbs where they could easily go to and from their work. Of course, I recognise that it is very desirable, where it can be done, that we should find them accommodation so near a railway that they could get up to their work with convenience to themselves. But in many

2 C2

boroughs this is not always possible. Where they can do so, well and good; but under the circumstances, where they cannot, the borough council surely may be trusted only to put these powers in force within the borough where there is a legitimate demand for working men's houses within the borough. I do not think myself it would be abused, and I hope the House will agree to give these powers to the boroughs of London.

Mr. CAUSTON (Southwark, W.): I have great pleasure in hearing the right hon. Gentleman express his determination to give this power to the London boroughs. From time to time I have received communications from Judge Addison, of Southwark County Court, giving most harrowing descriptions of the trials that the people of South London have to undergo in respect to. want of dwellings. I think that the new local authorities ought to have power to deal with these matters if they so desire, because they know the local requirements and the difficulties which the working men have to contend with, especially those who have to go very early to their work. An hon. Member talks about the working classes being transported to the outskirts of London by railway. But when you talk of transporting the working classes, that means additional expense to them; and the working classes, or certain of them, such as the Borough Market and waterside labourers, are not remunerated by a very high wage, and when you ask them to go outside London by train or tram you impose on them an expense which they cannot bear. I think the local authorities should have power to deal with these matters even in the event of the County Council not seeing its way to do so, because they possess local knowledge which the County Council cannot be acquainted with.

*Colonel HUGHES: I should like to inform hon. Members that in the County of London there isplenty of room to build houses for double the population. There are numerous districts not yet covered where there is plenty of room. There are 3,006 acres at Plumstead, and there are other places, like Eltham, with 3,800 acres, where the population is only one and a-half persons per acre. As regards the remarks of the hon. Gentleman who has just sat down, I was before a magistrate to-day at the police-court—["Hear, hear"]—on business —and a man was brought before the magistrate charged with living with his wife and family in a disorderly house. The man said he was sorry that his children had to live in such a disreputable neighbourhood, but he was unable to find another house. In another case a man had to put his wife and family into the workhouse, where he paid for their maintenance, because he could not find a place in which to house them. In another case a woman was looking for apartments who had a child with her, and she was asked how many children she had, and she said, "I have one here and five in the churchyard," but when she got the apartments that same night there were six children there. Her statement was quite true, because while she went to look for apartments she left five children to play in the churchyard. That is the sort of subterfuge to which these people have to resort. We do want the County Council to build in these places where the population is only one and a half person per acre, but if they will not the borough councils can do it themselves, and do it cheaper than the London County Council; we can always get land that we want for our own benefit at a fair price, but directly the London County Council comes along the price goes up enormously. Then there is another thing: the people themselves do not like the barrack system which is adopted by the London County Council, which is undertaken at so large an expense; but you can build cottages in a borough like Woolwich, which has thirteen square miles. There is no difficulty. We have land there, and for the last ten years we have waited for the County Council to build municipal property. They have failed to do it, but in the last few months they begin to see that something ought to be done. The County Council will be able to undertake these buildings, outside boroughs without building land, which the local authority has not power to do; but the local authority can erect these small houses, which in their own knowledge are desirable, where they have land available within their own borough.

MR. JOHN BURNS: It is pleasing to note on all sides of the House a desire to

Colonel Hughes.

grapple with the housing problem, which is a most serious question. On this occasion I am a devoted supporter of the Government as against some supporters of the Government who sit below the gangway, who consider there is a serious risk in remitting to the local authority this power. I admit the risk, but I believe the housing problem is so serious that that risk must be incurred and undertaken. I believe that the Government have done wisely in putting into their Bill with regard to the housing problem a suggestion that the local authorities should have concurrently the same power as the London County Council enjoys. It seems to me that we ought to examine the argument of the hon. Baronet the Member for the Chippenham Division. It is true he was chairman of the Housing Committee, and he is to be congratulated on the congenial way in which he discharged his functions, but he has no mandate from his committee for the nervousness which he has shown to-night. He is under the impression that if the local authorities have these powers they will immediately embark in some wild scheme or other for which there is no justification. But these local authorities are very conservative in their views, and I think we can safely leave this power to them. When the hon. Member for Woolwich says that the County Council procedure is expensive, I venture to tell him that there is not another body in London, not even the Corporation, who could buy the immense number of acres of land which the County Council has bought within 12 miles of London at the price which it paid, which is £38 an acre. It is evident that something should be done to prevent the scandalous overcrowding both on the part of the local authority and the County Council, and I sincerely trust the Government will not listen to its supporters below the gangway, and I trust the borough councils will have the power which the Government desires to give them.

SIR J. DICKSON-POYNDER: After the observations which have fallen from hon. Members of this House, I beg leave to withdraw my Amendment.

Amendment, by leave, withdrawn.

Mr. PICKERSGILL: The last schedule in the Bill, I notice, gives the borough councils power to make bye-laws. Of course, borough councils would have power in the ordinary course to make bye-laws for a specific purpose, but the schedule which we are now considering is something quite different; it authorises them to make bye-laws for the good government of the borough, and it is at once obvious that these words are exceedingly vague. There is given to the thirty local authorities who are to be created by this Bill power to make bye-laws for the "good government" of the borough. It is true that they must not be in contradiction to the bye-laws of the County Council. So far so good. But there is nothing to prevent the bye-laws of one borough being absolutely contradictory to the bye-laws of another. It would be ridiculous to have a bye-law affecting one-half of a street and an absolutely contradictory bye-law the other half. There is a great tendency to make use of this power of making bye-laws for all purposes. The old Court of Queen's Bench was a great safeguard in this matter, but all that has now been completely changed, and the trend is quite the other way. At present it is safe to say that the Judges, instead of scrutinising very closely as they did in old days these particular matters, will sanction almost anything that comes before them in the shape of bye-laws. Considering how serious the result is, it is especially important from the point of view of the poorer parishes, considerably more than in the case of the rich, because a man of good circumstances, in the event of his breaking a bye-law, pays the fine, and there is the end of it, and the poor man earning perhaps a precarious livelihood is unable to do so, and goes to prison. No fewer than 75,000 persons are in prison now, not because they have committed a crime, but because they have done something for which the proper punishment is a fine, and they have not the money with which to pay. Under the circumstances I think you ought not to unduly extend this bye-law making power.

Amendments proposed, in Schedule 2, page 20, to leave out lines 26 and 27, and to leave out lines 28 to 30.—(*Mr. Pickersgill.*)

Mr. A. J. BALFOUR: I hope the hon. Gentleman will not persist in his Amendment. My objection, in the first place, is that we have in this Bill gone on the principle that the powers that are agreed to be transferred from the County Council to the borough councils shall be transferred under this Bill. I do not see that there is any real force in the objection made by the hon. Member. There are a great many cases in this country where there are two areas which are coterminous with each other and are not easily distinguished, which are under two separate systems, and all those boroughs have the power of making bye-laws. And yet it is said that such a principle would be inconsistent in connection with these boroughs in London. It is absurd to suggest that the borough of Poplar and of Mile End would require the same bye-laws as, for instance, say, Kensington. London north of the Thames and London south of the Thames have different circumstances to consider, and I think they should be allowed to decide the bye-laws which they require for themselves. What I have said applies rather to the first Amendment, but I hope what I have said is sufficient to enable the hon. Member to withdraw both his Amendments.

*Colonel HUGHES: The bye-laws must be sanctioned by the Local Government Board, and it is very much better that these borough councils should have the same powers as other boroughs have. They do not want to be under the County Council, they want to be under the laws of the country at large, and I think you may fairly leave it to the Local Government Board, and be quite satisfied that they will not allow bye-laws in contradiction to each other. The safeguards are quite sufficient.

Mr. SYDNEY BUXTON: When this question becomes merely a local matter, then I think you ought to have elasticity, and under the circumstances I cannot support my hon. friend's Amendments.

Mr. PICKERSGILL: Under the circumstances I do not press my Amendments.

Amendments, by leave, withdrawn.

Other Amendments made.

Bill to be read the third time upon Tuesday next.

FINANCE BILL.

Order read, for resuming Adjourned Debate on Amendment proposed (6th June) on consideration of the Bill, as amended :—

And which Amendment was—

"In page 2, line 27, after the word 'enumerated' to insert the words 'and tested.'"—(*Mr. Chancellor of the Exchequer.*)

Question again proposed, "That those words be there inserted."

Question put and agreed to.

Other Amendments made.

Amendment proposed—

"In page 5, line 27, after the word 'form,' to insert the words 'but does not include any County Council or Municipal Corporation bills repayable not later than twelve months from their date or any overdraft at the bank or other loan raised for a merely temporary purpose for a period not exceeding twelve months.'"—(*Mr. Chancellor of the Exchequer.*)

Question proposed, "That those words be there inserted."

MR. J. P. SMITH (Lanark, Partick): I think that no corporation could wish to keep raising money permanently in a matter of this sort. I would suggest that the words "for a period not exceeding twelve months" should be left out, although, under the circumstances, I will not move any Amendment.

MR. CALDWELL (Lanark, Mid.): I desire to point out that the Stamp Act refers to bills of exchange and promissory notes. In this Amendment you are not adopting any definition of the word "bills." I have no doubt whatever that the object which the Chancellor of the Exchequer has in view is that promissory notes shall be included as well as bills of exchange ; but under this short description by saying "corporation bills" it is not defined, and it has no corresponding term. It seems to me that there is a little ambiguity, and

in order to make it clear I would suggest to him that after the word "bills" he should add the words "of exchange or promissory notes."

Amendment proposed to the proposed Amendment—

"In line 2, after the word 'bills,' to insert the words 'of exchange or promissory notes.'"—(*Mr. Caldwell.*)

Question proposed, "That those words be inserted in the proposed Amendment."

*THE CHANCELLOR OF THE EXCHEQUER (Sir M. HICKS BEACH, Bristol, W.) : The hon. Member was good enough to call my attention to this point some little time ago, and I noticed that he had included in his Amendment the words "promissory notes." I thought I had convinced the hon. Member that the inclusion of these words is quite unnecessary, for I notice that, as his Amendment now stands on the paper, the words "promissory notes" are omitted. I have looked into the matter and taken the advice of the Inland Revenue, and I have been assured that these words are not only unnecessary, but that they would also be misleading. A promissory note is a loan raised for a period not exceeding twelve months, and consequently it is covered by these words.

*MR CALDWELL : Whilst I still think that it would be better to follow the phraseology of the Stamp Act, 1891, and use both terms—"bills of exchange and promissory notes," yet, having regard to the explanation just given by the Chancellor of the Exchequer, and which will appear on the Records of the House, that promissory notes are included in the term "bills," I ask leave to withdraw the Amendment.

Amendment to the proposed Amendment, by leave, withdrawn.

Original question again proposed.

SIR CHARLES CAMERON (Glasgow, Bridgeton): I think it is necessary to leave out the words "for a temporary purpose," because if money is temporarily applied to some permanent work the borrowing body might be called upon to pay duty twice upon the same money. I do not think it is the intention of the Chancellor of the Exchequer to tax these loans twice, and I have put down a couple of Amendments intended to obviate this. In other respects the Amendment is fairly satisfactory.

Amendment proposed to the proposed Amendment—

"In line 3, after the word 'raised' to leave out the words 'for a merely temporary purpose.'"—(*Sir Charles Cameron.*)

Question proposed, "That the words proposed to be left out stand part of the proposed Amendment."

*SIR M. HICKS BEACH: I believe that these words are necessary for the purpose of the clause, and if they were omitted it would be possible for a corporation to borrow for twelve months, and to continue that loan borrowing for an indefinite period of years and practically make it a permanent loan. I think the hon. Member will see that such a process would be very unfair.

SIR CHARLES CAMERON: I should like to know what is meant by "a merely temporary purpose." My constituents hold that the words might be held not to apply when the temporary loan is applied to permanent work.

*SIR M. HICKS BEACH: That is not so.

SIR CHARLES CAMERON: That being so I will not press this Amendment.

Amendment to the proposed Amendment, by leave, withdrawn.

Words inserted.

SIR CHARLES CAMERON: I do not think the Chancellor of the Exchequer will have any objection to my next Amendment, which simply makes the meaning of the clause more clear.

Amendment proposed—

"In page 5, line 22, after the word 'called' to insert the words: 'But provided that the duty under this section shall be paid by a local authority only once in respect of the exercise by them of borrowing powers, and shall not be paid in respect of money reborrowed by them to replace money borrowed which may have been paid off otherwise than by means of a statutory sinking fund.'"—(*Sir Charles Cameron.*)

Question proposed, "That those words be there inserted."

SIR R. B. FINLAY: I think the hon. Baronet will recognise what my right hon. friend said with regard to temporary loans. If these words are added they will introduce a totally new principle, which in practice would be most mischievous.

Question put.

The Committee divided: Ayes, 69; Noes, 168. (Division list No. 182.)

AYES.

Austin, Sir John (Yorkshire)
Bolton, Thomas Dolling
Broadhurst, Henry
Burns, John
Burt, Thomas
Caldwell, James
Causton, Richard Knight
Cawley, Frederick
Channing, Francis Allston
Clough, Walter Owen
Colville, John
Dalziel, James Henry
Davitt, Michael
Dillon, John
Doogan, P. C.
Evans, S. T. (Glamorgan)
Farquharson, Dr. Robert
Fenwick, Charles
Fitzmaurice, Lord Edmond
Foster, Sir W. (Derby Co.)
Fox, Dr. Joseph Francis
Gladstone, Rt. Hon. H. J.
Goddard, Daniel Ford
Griffith, Ellis J.

Harwood, George
Hayne, Rt. Hn. Charles Seale-
Hedderwick, Thomas Charles H
Horniman, Frederick John
Humphreys-Owen, Arthur C.
Jacoby, James Alfred
Jones, Wm. (Carnarvonshire)
Lawson, Sir W. (Cumb'land)
Leese, Sir J. F. (Accrington)
Leng, Sir John
MacAleese, Daniel
M'Arthur, Wm. (Cornwall)
M'Ghee, Richard
M'Kenna, Reginald
M'Laren, Charles Benjamin
Maddison, Fred
Montagu, Sir S. (Whitechapel)
Nussey, Thomas Willans
Oldroyd, Mark
Palmer, Geo. Wm. (Reading)
Pease, Alfred E. (Cleveland)
Pease, Joseph A. (Northumb.)
Philipps, John Wynford
Pickersgill, Edward Hare

Richardson, J. (Durham, S.E.)
Rickett, J. Compton
Robertson, Edmund (Dundee)
Robson, William Snowdon
Samuel, J. (Stockton-on-Tees)
Scott, Chas. Prestwich (Leigh)
Shaw, Thomas (Hawick B.)
Smith, Samuel (Flint)
Spicer, Albert
Stanhope, Hon. Philip J.
Strachey, Edward
Sullivan, Donal (Westmeath)
Trevelyan, Charles Philips
Weir, James Galloway
Whittaker, Thomas Palmer
Williams, John Carvell (Notts
Wilson, Henry J. (York, W.R.)
Wilson, John (Durham, Mid.)
Wilson, John (Govan)
Wilson, Jos H (Middlesbrough)
Yoxall, James Henry
TELLERS FOR THE AYES—
    Sir Charles Cameron and
    Mr. Provand.

NOES.

Acland-Hood, Capt. Sir A. F.
Anson, Sir William Reynell
Arnold, Alfred
Arnold-Forster, Hugh O.
Atkinson, Rt. Hon. John
Balcarres, Lord
Balfour, Rt.Hn.A.J.(Manch'r)
Balfour,RtHnGeraldW.(Leeds
Banbury, Frederick George
Barnes, Frederic Gorell
Bartley, George C. T.
Barton, Dunbar Plunket
Beach,Rt.Hn.SirM.H.(Bristol)
Beckett, Ernest William
Begg, Ferdinand Faithfull
Bentinck, Lord Henry C.
Bigwood, James
Billson, Alfred
Brodrick, Rt. Hon. St. John
Bullard, Sir Harry
Burdett-Coutts, W.
Carlile, William Walter
Cavendish, V.C.W.(Derbysh.)
Cecil, Evelyn (Hertford, E.)
Cecil, Ld. Hugh (Greenwich)
Chaloner, Captain R. G. W.
Chamberlain,Rt.Hn.J.(Birm.)
Chamberlain,J.Austin(Wore'r
Chaplin, Rt. Hon. Henry
Charrington, Spencer
Clare, Octavius Leigh
Clarke, SirEdward(Plymouth)
Cochrane, Hn. Thos. H. A. E.
Coghill, Douglas Harry
Cohen, Benjamin Louis
Collings, Rt. Hon. Jesse
Cook, Fred Lucas (Lambeth)
Corbett,A.Cameron(Glasgow)
Cotton-Jodrell, Col. Ed. T. D
Cox, Irwin Edw. B. (Harrow)
Cranborne, Viscount
Cubitt, Hon. Henry
Curzon, Viscount
Dalkeith, Earl of
Dalrymple, Sir Charles
Denny, Colonel
Dickson-Poynder, Sir John P.
Digby, John K. D. Wingfield-
Disraeli, Coningsby Ralph
Douglas, Rt. Hon. A. Akers-
Douglas-Pennant, Hon. E. S.
Duncombe, Hon. Hubert V
Dyke, Rt. Hn. Sir William H.
Fellowes,Hon.AilwynEdward
Fergusson,Rt.Hn.SirJ.(M'nc'r
Field, Admiral (Eastbourne)
Finch, George H.
Finlay, Sir Robert Bannatyne

Fisher, William Hayes
FitzGerald, Sir Robt. Penrose-
Flower, Ernest
Folkestone, Viscount
Foster, Colonel (Lancaster)
Foster, Harry S. (Suffolk)
Garfit, William
Gibbons, J. Lloyd
Gibbs,Hn.A.G.H.(City ofLon)
Gibbs, Hon. Vicary(St.Albans)
Giles, Charles Tyrell
Godson, Sir Augustus Fredk.
Goldsworthy, Major-General
Gordon, Hon. John Edward
Gorst, Rt Hn G J (St George's)
Goschen, George J. (Sussex)
Goulding, Edward Alfred
Gray, Ernest (West Ham)
Green, W. D. (Wednesbury)
Hamilton,Rt.Hn. Lord George
Hardy, Laurence
Hare, Thomas Leigh
Heath, James
Heaton, John Henniker
Henderson, Alexander
Hoare, Edw. B. (Hampstead)
Hoare, Samuel (Norwich)
Holland, Hon. L. R. (Bow)
Houston, R. P.
Howell, William Tudor
Hubbard, Hon. Evelyn
Jebb, Richard Claverhouse
Jeffreys, Arthur Frederick
Johnstone, Heywood (Sussex)
Kemp, George
Kennaway, Rt.Hon. Sir John
Kenyon-Slaney, Col. William
Kimber, Henry
Lawrence,W. F. (Liverpool)
Lawson, John Grant (Yorks.)
Lea, Sir T. (Londonderry)
Loder, Gerald Walter E.
Long, RtHnWalter(Liverpool)
Lucas-Shadwell, William
Macartney, W. G. Ellison
Macdona, John Cumming
MacIver, David (Liverpool)
Maclure, Sir John William
M'Arthur, Charles (Liverpool)
M'Calmont, H. L. B. (Cambs.)
M'Killop, James
Maxwell,Itt Hn.SirHerbertE.
Milbank, Sir Powlett C. John
Milward, Colonel Victor
Monk, Charles James
More, Robt. Jasper (Shropsh.
Morgan,HnFred.(Monm'thsh.
Morrell, George Herbert

Morton,ArthurH.A.(Deptford
Mount, William George
Murray,RtHnAGraham(Bute
Murray, Charles J. (Coventry)
Newdigate, FrancisAlexander
Nicol, Donald Ninian
Northcote, Hn. Sir H. Stafford
Orr-Ewing, Charles Lindsay
Pease, Herbert P. (Darling'n)
Penn, John
Phillpotts, Captain Arthur
Pilkington,R.(Lancs, Newton)
Platt-Higgins, Frederick
Priestley,SirW.Overend(Edin
Pryce-Jones, Lt.-Col. Edward
Purvis, Robert
Rankin, Sir James
Rasch, Major Frederic Carne
Ridley, Rt. Hon. SirMatt. W.
Ritchie, Rt. Hon. C. Thomson
Robertson, Herbert (Hackney)
Robinson, Brooke
Rothschild,Hon. LionelWalter
Round, James
Russell, Gen. F. S. (Chelt'h'm)
Russell, T. W. (Tyrone)
Sassoon, Sir Edward Albert
Sharpe, William Edward T.
Simeon, Sir Barrington
Smith, Jas. Parker (Lanarks.)
Stanley, Lord (Lancs.)
Stock, James Henry
Strutt, Hon. Charles Hedley
Talbot, Lord E. (Chichester)
Talbot,Rt.Hn.J.G.(Oxf'dUni.
Thornton, Percy M.
Tomlinson,Wm. Edw. Murray
Valentia, Viscount
Wanklyn, James Leslie
Warr, Augustus Frederick
Wharton, Rt. Hon.John Lloyd
Whiteley, H. (Ashton-u.-L.)
Williams, Colonel R. (Dorset)
Williams, Jos. Powell- (Birm.
Wilson,J.W.(Worcestersh.N.)
Wodehouse,Rt.Hn.E.R.(Bath
Wolff, Gustav Wilhelm
Wylie, Alexander
Wyndham, George
Wyndham-Quin, MajorW. H.
Younger, William

TELLERS FOR THE NOES—
Sir William Walrond and
Mr. Anstruther.

Another Amendment made.
Bill to be read the third time upon Tuesday next.

COLONIAL LOANS FUND BILL.

Considered in Committee.

(In the Committee.)

Clause 1 :—
Question proposed, "That Clause 1 stand part of the Bill."

*MR. CALDWELL (Lanark, Mid.): This clause practically contains the substance of the Bill. I therefore propose to take this opportunity of stating my objections to the measure. The clause confers the right to give loans to the Colonies, and it prescribes the whole regulations. I admit that according to the clause any loan to a colony must first of all receive the sanction and approval of Parliament. There must be a previous voting of the money. The objection which I take is practically to the Bill itself, in so far as it gives any facilities whatever for the Colonies to borrow money on the credit of the Imperial Exchequer. I object altogether to giving these facilities. I fear that if we thus become enormous creditors of the Colonies, we shall find it will not be beneficial to our relations with them, and it may turn out very greatly to our disadvantage. I may point out that this Bill leaves the amount of interest to be fixed by the Treasury, instead of deciding on the minimum, as is done in the case of loans to local authorities.

MR. DILLON (Mayo, E.) : The whole Bill is founded on this clause, and for my part I cannot find in any of the speeches which have been made by the Chancellor of the Exchequer any justification whatever for starting this new fund. The Bill proposes to create a new stock on exactly the same lines as the Local Loans Fund, and the stock will be placed on the market as a guaranteed stock bearing interest the amount of which is not fixed in the Bill, but which is to be fixed by the Treasury. When the right hon. Gentleman introduced this measure last year he said it was not only intended to be of assistance to the Colonies, but also to open up a new means of investment for Post Office Savings Banks deposits, and thus while they were helping the Colonies they would be aiding a class which they all desired to assist, viz., the thrifty, industrious people who deposited money in the Savings Banks. Now the real meaning of this is that, in order to keep up an expensive Savings Bank system, and to enable the Government to continue to pay a larger interest than can be earned under the present system of investment, a new stock is to be deliberately started. One of my chief objections to the Bill is based on that ground. Another is that you are starting machinery for lending money to the Colonies, as a result of which there will be a continuous pressure on the Chancellor of the Exchequer to lend improvidently. We all remember how, in the Debate last year, when it was alleged that the real object of this Bill was to

help the West Indian Colonies, the Chancellor of the Exchequer denied it. But the pressure of circumstances began to operate almost immediately, and it is already in contemplation to lend money to these Colonies under this Bill. If ever there was a period in the history of this country when the policy of lending money to the Colonies ought to be most jealously watched it is now. The extension of the Colonies has been so enormous, and the demands of the gentlemen popularly called Imperialists, inflationists, or extensionists are so excessive, that I confess I am inclined to look with great jealousy on any proposal for facilitating the lending of money to the Colonies. I asked the Chancellor of the Exchequer, on a former occasion, to what colonies this Bill would apply, and he indicated that it would apply to many African colonies, including Rhodesia, British Central Africa, East Africa—it may be the Soudan, but as to that I am not quite certain. However that may be, the prospect of opening up temptation to the Chancellor of the Exchequer to lend money freely to these African colonies appears to me to involve the adoption of a false policy and of a most vicious financial system. The Chancellor of the Exchequer told us that one good point about the Bill was that it gave Parliament a more efficient control over the finances of the colonies to which these loans were made, and he mentioned that there would be an annual and complete Return to this House on the same lines as that which embodied the loans to local authorities in this country. But I do not see the efficacy of these Returns at all, and therefore I do not look on that as in any way an argument in favour of the Bill. I think it would be far safer to continue the present system of making these loans. At present they are granted under special Acts, and in the long run many of them are wholly or partially remitted. I cannot see what the Chancellor of the Exchequer has to gain by devising machinery which will have the effect of applying pressure to the Treasury to grant loans more freely. If we are going to set up a new system, I would suggest that the money for these Colonial loans should be found, not by starting a new stock, but out of the cash at the disposal of the Commissioners of the National Debt. In any case the loans made under this Act will have to be a charge on the Consolidated Fund ultimately, and as any loss must eventually be borne by the taxpayers of this country, I think that the money might as well be advanced directly.

SIR M. HICKS BEACH (Bristol, W.): I have explained on several occasions, I am afraid without success in the case of the Member for East Mayo, the effect of this measure. But he certainly does not seem to realise the intent of the Bill. If its effect were to facilitate pressure upon the Chancellor of the Exchequer to make loans to the Colonies, I should never have proposed it. The safeguard of the Chancellor of the Exchequer in these matters is the fact that a loan made to the Colonies must obtain the assent of Parliament, and as under this Bill that provision is carefully inserted I do not think there is any ground for the hon. Member's alarm. What happens now is that if a Crown colony has good credit it goes into the market, through the Crown Agent, and obtains a loan. Anybody who chooses to look down the list of securities in the market can see that many of our Crown colonies have very good credit. The object of this Bill was, not that we may lend to what has been described as insolvent colonies, but that we may secure for the investors in our savings banks the chance of investment in the loans of the more solvent colonies. We may, of course, also lend to a colony which has not been so prosperous as other colonies. By the machinery proposed under the Bill the Colonies will be assisted by being able to obtain loans at a lower rate of interest, while there will be an advantage to this country in

Mr. Dillon.

providing for deposits in savings banks a better means of investment than Consols afford. I quite admit that the principle of this Bill is contained in the first clause, and that therefore the hon. Member had a perfect right to raise this Debate.

MR. SYDNEY BUXTON (Tower Hamlets, Poplar): As the Chancellor of the Exchequer says, we have already discussed the principle of this Bill, and if the remarks of my hon. friend had been directed against the measure introduced last year I should have entirely agreed with all he said. But this Bill is totally different; the objectionable features found in the last measure have now been removed, and there can be no practical objection to the present Bill. I do not see how this Bill would in any way either prevent or encourage loans to colonies. It is purely a machinery Bill. Any loan to a colony must first come in the form of a Bill before this House, where it will be discussed on its merits. Should this House agree to lend money to any particular colony, it surely would be an advantage to this country, as well as to the colony, that the loan should be made under a properly regulated system. I therefore feel bound to support this Bill.

MR. DILLON: I thoroughly understand that in each individual case of loans under this Bill the loan will have to be sanctioned by a separate Bill. But is the Chancellor of the Exchequer in earnest in saying it is seriously intended that these separate Bills shall be freely discussed? Do not we all know perfectly well that, 99 cases out of 100, when the Chancellor of the Exchequer of the day, with a great majority behind him, decides that such a Bill shall be brought in, the thing is practically done. My objection to this Bill is that it is no part of the business of the Government to bolster up an unsound banking system by making it a means of investment for funds that are accumulating beyond our present means of investment. That I may point out is the view of the *Economist* newspaper, which is one of the highest authorities on these questions. If the right hon. Gentleman desires to obtain good security outside the United Kingdom for the investment of Savings Bank money, why exclude India? I understand that it is excluded under this Bill, yet we know that India has a larger stock, and could therefore give greater relief than all the Crown colonies combined four or five times over. It seems to me absolutely logical and irresistible that if you are going to set up this new fund and look upon it as a desirable investment for your Savings Bank deposits, you must go on and consolidate the debt of all the Crown colonies, so as to reduce their interest. It is clear that to be of any effect this system must have large operation. The Bill contains within itself the germs of a great financial policy, and no one can see the extent to which it may be carried. It will, no doubt, enable the burdens of the Crown colonies to be enormously reduced, and I do not see why India should be debarred from sharing the benefits.

MR. DALZIEL (Kirkcaldy Burghs): I suppose that if this Bill is carried we shall have still another claim from the Government that they have done a great deal to knit more closely together the mother country and the Colonies. While I sympathise to a large extent with that desire on the part of the Government, I must say I do not think that this particular plan is calculated to have that effect. The policy of the Bill in the first place is to hold out a bait to our Colonies to the effect that they can obtain money from the mother country with less difficulty than in the past, and when I see the two front benches so unanimous upon the Bill I am inclined to look a little more closely into its merits. One point, I think, has not received sufficient attention.

The Chancellor of the Exchequer, in the course of the past year, has refused many applications for public funds; but his difficulties will be increased in the future if this Bill is passed, for under it you are practically setting yourselves up as a great money-lending institution. The result to the Colonies will be disappointing, for the poorer ones, which most require the loans, will find the greatest difficulty in providing the necessary guarantees. You will also run the risk of raising a rivalry among the Colonies as to the amount of credit to be guaranteed, and the inevitable result will be to interfere with the friendly relations which now exist. I am afraid that if you now pass this Bill you will on some future occasion be told that the passing of it was intended to sanction the principle of granting loans to colonies; and thus, therefore, we are now being asked to anticipate some decision which may have to be taken after 12 o'clock at night some years later, and we shall then be unable to discuss the question on its merits.

MR. DAVITT (Mayo, S.): I would support the Bill if I were satisfied that it would confer any real benefit on the Colonies. But from my own knowledge of the Colonies, and especially of Australia, I know they are already labouring under the disadvantage of having borrowed too much money. What they want in Australia and New Zealand is more population, and not more indebtedness.

SIR M. HICKS BEACH: This Bill will only apply to Crown colonies.

MR. DAVITT: Well, I say it is a bad policy to put temptation in the way of these colonies to borrow money. I think the better plan would be to lend this money to county councils in England and Ireland, and to give those bodies compulsory powers to buy agricultural land and place labourers upon it. That would, I believe, prove a very good investment.

MR. BARTLEY (Islington, N.): It seems strange that there should be any debate on a proposal of this kind, seeing that the object is to relieve the Chancellor of the Exchequer of his great difficulty in investing satisfactorily the Savings Bank deposits. This is a very small matter, and it would surely be as well to try the experiment.

*MR. HEDDERWICK (Wick Burghs): We are told we ought to support this Bill simply because it is a mere machinery Bill; and the Chancellor of the Exchequer has endeavoured to disarm opposition by informing us that even if be passed there will be a perfect check against possible abuse, inasmuch as before any loan could be granted under it a special Bill will have to be submitted to Parliament. Then what is the use of passing this Bill? Clearly the object of the Chancellor of the Exchequer is to facilitate the granting of loans. The Bill obviously holds out an inducement to any colony that wants a loan to apply for it. If we provide the Chancellor of the Exchequer with the machinery he desires, it will be much easier for him to grant a loan to any colony that may require one. I do not suppose the right hon. Gentleman would not insist on having substantial securities; but we must remember that securities have a marvellous way of ceasing to be substantial, and therefore I think it would be better to withhold from him the dangerous power for which he asks.

Mr. Davitt.

MR. CALDWELL: It may be true that before any loan is granted under this Bill another Bill will have to be passed; but my point is that the object of this Bill is to sanction the principle that the State is to provide loans out of Imperial funds in the manner prescribed by the Act. Once this Bill has been passed, when a Bill is brought in to sanction a particular loan it will be said that Parliament has already approved the principle, and we shall have hardly any chance of going into the merits of individual proposals, and I venture to assert that these Bills will be rushed through the House after midnight without practically any discussion. I should also like to point out that the Bill affords an opportunity of discriminating between one colony and another; and I venture to assert that when once you begin lending money to the Colonies you will open the door to all kinds of disputes, especially in regard to the amount of interest you charge. We know that in regard to local loans a large sum of money has to be written off yearly, because the authorities are unable to repay the amounts due to the Public Works Loan Commissioners. If they were not able to repay us, they would wish to be relieved. I do not know anything which would more readily bring the Colonies and the mother country into collision than by giving these financial preferences. It would breed dissatisfaction amongst every other colony which was asked to pay more interest than the favoured one.

SIR JOHN LENG (Dundee): It might be inferred from what has been said that our experience as Members of Parliament is that the Treasury of this country is always ready to throw away its money without careful examination. The arguments which have been adduced show, first, distrust of those who have the control of the finances of the Colonies; second, distrust of the Treasury, represented by the Chancellor of the Exchequer; and third, distrust of ourselves as Members of this House. I do not share the feeling of distrust in regard to any of these parties. Anyone who has paid attention to the present state of our finances, especially to the large sums of money accumulating in the savings banks, and to the increasing difficulty of handling that money and finding a safe and reasonable outlet for it, must see that the time has arrived when it is desirable that the Government should find new channels for investment. My only regret is that the Bill does not include India in its survey. If the experiment with the Crown colonies is tried and proves successful, it will encourage the Government to go further.

SIR M. HICKS BEACH: I appeal to the Committee to allow a division to be taken. We have already discussed the principle of the Bill when I moved the Resolution, and during the debate on the Second Reading. I do not complain that the Bill has been discussed to-night, but I hope we shall now come to a division.

MR. WEIR (Ross and Cromarty): I am not prepared to give a silent vote on this matter. I opposed a grant of £15,000 to Central Africa for making roads for men who are too indolent to make roads for themselves. I do not like the two front benches agreeing on this question. I have always found that something serious happens when this is the case. These loans, I fear, will be very much like the grants given away to the Northern Territories in Africa. It is said that each loan will be brought before Parliament; but what chance will we have of discussing them properly, if the front benches makes up their mind to back up any rotten colony? I admit that many of the colonies, like Canada and Australia, can borrow money at 3 per cent, and that their stock stands at over par; but are we, the British taxpayers, to provide money for these miserable bankrupt Crown colonies? I have too much regard for the poor people in the North and the starving crofters to agree to that, and I feel it my duty not to allow this Bill to pass in this House if I can help it. There has been a fall in Consols of 2 per cent. within the last few days. Is that in consequence of the Government scheme to furnish money to these bankrupt colonies? It is not so long since Consols stood at 113¼ and 114. Now I find to-day that they are down to 108¼. I cannot help thinking that that is in consequence of this Bill.

HON. MEMBERS: The Transvaal.

MR. WEIR: I do not think the Transvaal question has affected Consols at all. It is that investors are afraid that this country is going to guarantee these bankrupt colonies. I have no doubt that the bank deposits have gone up considerably, because people prefer to hold their money in hand rather than seek investments until they see what is going to happen. In regard to providing an outlet for the Savings Bank funds, if the Chancellor of the Exchequer is anxious there are many admirable facilities for their investment in our own country. Let the hon. Gentle man arrange a scheme to lend money to county councils. I know in the constituency I represent there are tens of thousands of acres of land which might be used by the people of the Highlands if the County Council had the chance of lending money to the people for developing the land. There would be a splendid security and Consols would again bound up to 114. Here are seas teeming with fish, not small fish, but large fish——

THE CHAIRMAN: The hon. Member is travelling very wide of the question before the House.

MR. WEIR: Well, I will confine myself to the Colonial Loans Fund. The Secretary for the Colonies said this was simply a machinery Bill. We do not want a machinery Bill, and I, for one, object most strongly to money being expended for the purpose of enabling these colonies providing roads——

It being midnight, the Chairman left the Chair to make his Report to the House.

Committee report progress; to sit again upon Monday next.

SUPPLY REPORT [5th June].

Message from Her Majesty (Grant to Lord Kitchener),—Resolution reported.

LORD KITCHENER OF KHARTOUM.

" That a sum, not exceeding £30,000, be granted to Her Majesty, to be issued to Major General Lord Kitchener of Khartoum, G.C.B., K.C.M.G., as an acknowledgment of his eminent services in planning and conducting the recent Expedition in the Soudan."

Resolution agreed to.

EDUCATION OF CHILDREN BILL.

As amended, considered ; to be read the third time upon Wednesday next.

SEATS FOR SHOP ASSISTANTS (ENGLAND AND IRELAND) BILL.

Considered in Committee.

(In the Committee.)

Clause 1 :—

SIR JAMES FERGUSSON (Manchester, N.E.): I wish to point out that this Bill is precisely the same as that for Scotland, which passed this House unanimously, but was rejected by the Lords because it was confined to Scotland. This Bill is brought in for the rest of the United Kingdom, and if the House is pleased to adopt it, I should be prepared, on behalf of the right hon. Baronet the Member for London University, to include Scotland in its scope.

MR. CALDWELL : I do not see why there should be the slightest difficulty in putting Scotland in the Bill.

MR. TOMLINSON (Preston): I move to report progress.

Committee report progress ; to sit again to-morrow.

EXPERIMENTS ON LIVING ANIMALS.

Return presented relative thereto [Address 8th June ; Mr. Jesse Collings]; to lie upon the Table, and to be printed. [No. 215.]

Adjourned at ten minutes after Twelve of the clock.

HOUSE OF LORDS.

Friday, 9th June 1899.

PRIVATE BILL BUSINESS.

THE LORD CHANCELLOR acquainted the House that the Clerk of the Parliaments had laid upon the Table the Certificate from the Examiners that the further Standing Orders applicable to the following Bill have been complied with:—

SOUTH - EASTERN AND LONDON, CHATHAM, AND DOVER RAILWAY COMPANIES (NEW LINES).

And also the Certificate that the Standing orders applicable to the following Bill have been complied with:—

LOCAL GOVERNMENT PROVISIONAL ORDERS (No. 3).

The same were ordered to lie on the Table.

CARDIFF RAILWAY BILL.

Committee to meet on Tuesday next.

FISHGUARD WATER AND GAS BILL.

Report from the Select Committee, That the Committee had not proceeded with the consideration of the Bill, the opposition thereto having been withdrawn; read, and ordered to lie on the Table: The orders made on the 18th of April and Tuesday last discharged; and Bill committed.

BARRY RAILWAY BILL.

Report from the Select Committee, that the Committee had not proceeded with the consideration of the Bill, the opposition thereto having been withdrawn; read, and ordered to lie on the Table; the orders made on 25th April and Tuesday last discharged; and Bill committed.

SOUTH STAFFORDSHIRE TRAMWAYS BILL [Lords].

Report from the Committee of Selection, that the Lord Cheylesmore be proposed to the House as a member of the Select Committee on the said Bill in the place of the Earl of Bradford; read, and agreed to.

WOLVERHAMPTON CORPORATION BILL [Lords].

Report from the Committee of Selection, that the Lord Cheylesmore be proposed to the House as a member of the Select Committee on the said Bill in the place of the Earl of Bradford; read, and agreed to.

LANCASHIRE AND YORKSHIRE RAILWAY (VARIOUS POWERS) BILL.

Report from the Committee of Selection, that the Lord Cheylesmore be proposed to the House as a member of the Select Committee on the said Bill in the place of the Earl of Bradford; read, and agreed to.

RHONDDA URBAN DISTRICT COUNCIL BILL.

Report from the Committee of Selection, that the Lord Cheylesmore be proposed to the House as a member of the Select Committee on the said Bill in the place of the Earl of Bradford; read, and agreed to.

WETHERBY DISTRICT WATER BILL.

Report from the Committee of Selection, that the Lord Cheylesmore be proposed to the House as a member of the Select Committee on the said Bill in the place of the Earl of Bradford; read, and agreed to.

EDINBURGH CORPORATION BILL.

Report from the Committee of Selection, that the Lord Cheylesmore be proposed to the House as a member of the Select Committee on the said Bill in the place of the Earl of Bradford; read, and agreed to.

SHOTLEY BRIDGE AND CONSETT DISTRICT GAS BILL.

Reported with Amendments.

DUBLIN CORPORATION (MARKETS) BILL.

Read 2ª, and committed: The Committee to be proposed by the Committee of Selection.

LONDON, CHATHAM, AND DOVER RAILWAY BILL.

Read 2ª, and committed.

LEITH HARBOUR AND DOCKS BILL.

Read 2ª, and committed: The Committee to be proposed by the Committee of Selection.

An Asterisk (*) at the commencement of a Speech indicates revision by the Member.

BELFAST WATER BILL.

Read 2ª, and committed.

WEST GLOUCESTERSHIRE WATER BILL.

Brought from the Commons; read 1ª, and referred to the examiners.

WOKING WATER AND GAS BILL.

Brought from the Commons; read 1ª, and referred to the Examiners.

ELECTRIC LIGHTING PROVISIONAL ORDERS (No. 14) BILL. [Lords.]

Order for Committee read.

GAS AND WATER ORDERS CONFIRMATION BILL. [Lords.]

Order for Committee read.

TRAMWAYS ORDERS CONFIRMATION (No. 1) BILL. [Lords.]

Order for Committee read.

THE CHAIRMAN OF COMMITTEES (The EARL of MORLEY): Before the House goes into Committee on the Electric Lighting Provisional Orders Bills I desire to call your Lordships' attention to the enormous number of Electric Lighting Provisional Orders this session. There are 19 Bills dealing with 90 Orders. Each Order consists of 36 pages, of which 30 contain common form clauses, and, from the great bulk which these Bills assume it will be seen how necessary it is that the Electric Lighting Orders (Common Form Clauses) Bill should be pressed forward in the other House. That Bill will obviate the necessity of introducing the common form clauses in all Provisional Orders. The examination of these statutes after they have received the Royal Assent involves great labour, not to speak of the enormous amount of printing which is necessitated. As soon as the Bills have received the Royal Assent every one of the Orders has to be most carefully examined, and I need not point out to your Lordships that the examination of the common form clauses is an absolute waste of time. Not only is the labour excessive, but great public inconvenience is caused, as the process of examining so many clauses delays the issue of the statutes to the public. There have been a good many complaints in recent years that the Statutes are not issued until late in the autumn. I would suggest to the Board of Trade, if they find it impossible to pass the Common Form Clauses Bill through Parliament this session, that in the coming session of Parliament they should group a large number of Orders of the same character in single Bills, and schedule the common form clauses at the end of each Bill.

THE SECRETARY FOR SCOTLAND (Lord BALFOUR OF BURLEIGH): My Lords, as I am temporarily representing the Board of Trade, owing to the absence of the noble Earl the Parliamentary Secretary, I say at once that the Board of Trade are deeply impressed with the strength of the case which the noble Earl the Chairman of Committees has put forward, and are in agreement with him as to the advantage of the course he suggests. I do not think anyone can doubt the desirability of adopting that course when they look at the great bulk which these Bills assume, and the noble Earl has laid them upon the Table of your Lordships' House as a very striking object lesson. I should not like, however, on behalf of the Board of Trade, to come under a definite obligation to press forward the Electric Lighting Orders (Common Form Clauses) Bill, because the more it is thought that the Government are bound to press forward that particular Bill, the more, I am afraid, some malicious persons may wish to place obstacles in its way; but it is the hope of the Board of Trade that the Bill will be passed this session if possible. If it is found impossible to get the Bill through this session, I think the alternative suggested by the noble Earl is one which is well worthy of consideration. I understand he has communicated privately with the Board of Trade in this direction, but in any case I have no hesitation in coming under an obligation to communicate with the officials of the Board of Trade with a view of having one of his suggestions carried into effect.

Bills committed to a Committee of the whole House.

TRAMWAYS ORDER CONFIRMATION (No. 3) BILL. [Lords.]

Committed: The Committee to be proposed by the Committee of Selection.

METROPOLITAN COMMON SCHEME (HARROW WEALD) PROVISIONAL ORDER BILL.

Read 2ª (according to order), and committed to a Committee of the Whole House on Monday next.

ELECTRIC LIGHTING PROVISIONAL ORDERS (No. 1.) BILL. [Lords.]

House in Committee (according to order): Bills reported without Amendment: Standing Committee negatived; and Bills to be read 3ª on Monday next.

ELECTRIC LIGHTING PROVISIONAL ORDERS (No. 4) BILL.

House in Committee (according to order): Bills reported without Amendment: Standing Committee negatived; and Bills to be read 3ª on Monday next.

ELECTRIC LIGHTING PROVISIONAL ORDERS (No. 9) BILL. [Lords.]

House in Committee (according to order): Bills reported without Amendment: Standing Committee negatived; and Bills to be read 3ª on Monday next.

ELECTRIC LIGHTING PROVISIONAL ORDERS (No. 10.) BILL. [Lords.]

House in Committee (according to order): Amendments made: Standing Committee negatived; the Report of Amendments to be received on Monday next.

ELECTRIC LIGHTING PROVISIONAL ORDERS (No. 11) BILL. [Lords.]

House in Committee (according to order): Bill reported without Amendment: Standing Committee negatived; and Bill to be read 3ª Monday next.

RETURNS, REPORTS, ETC.

WAGES OF DOMESTIC SERVANTS (BOARD OF TRADE, LABOUR DEPARTMENT).

Report on the money wages of indoor domestic servants: Presented (by command), and ordered to lie on the Table.

ARUNDEL PORT.

Account and Report for 1898-99: Delivered (pursuant to Act), and ordered to lie on the Table.

PETITIONS.

VACCINATION ACTS.

Petition for repeal of compulsory clauses in; of Guardians of the Poplar Union; read, and ordered to lie on the Table.

VACCINATION ACT, 1898.

Petition for repeal; of Guardians of the Bridport Union; read, and ordered to lie on the Table.

PARISH COUNCILLORS (TENURE OF OFFICE) BILL.

Returned from the Commons with the Amendment agreed to.

TRAWLERS' CERTIFICATES SUSPENSION BILL. [Lords.]

Report from the Select Committee (with proceedings of the Committee) made, and to be printed. (No. 109.) Bill reported with Amendments, and committed to a Committee of the whole House on Monday next; and to be printed as amended. (No. 110.)

SUMMARY JURISDICTION ACT (1879) AMENDMENT BILL.

To be read 2ª on Monday the 26th instant. (*The Lord Penrhyn.*)

LINCOLNSHIRE CORONERS BILL. [Lords.]

Read 3ª (according to order), and passed, and sent to the Commons.

FARNLEY TYAS MARRIAGES BILL.

Read 3ª (according to order), and passed.

House adjourned at forty minutes after Four o'clock, to Monday next, at forty-five minutes after Ten of the clock.

HOUSE OF COMMONS.

Friday, 9th June 1899.

PRIVATE BILL BUSINESS.

PRIVATE BILLS. [Lords.]

Standing Orders not previously inquired into complied with.

MR. SPEAKER laid upon the Table Report from one of the Examiners of Petitions for Private Bills, That, in the case of the following Bills, originating in the Lords, and referred on the First Reading thereof, the Standing Orders not previously inquired into, and which are applicable thereto, have been complied with, viz. :—

COBHAM GAS BILL. [Lords.]

MOSS SIDE URBAN DISTRICT COUNCIL (TRAMWAYS) BILL. [Lords.]

STRETFORD URBAN DISTRICT COUNCIL (TRAMWAYS) BILL. [Lords.]

WESTON - SUPER - MARE, CLEVEDON, AND PORTISHEAD TRAMWAYS COMPANY (LIGHT RAILWAY EXTENSIONS) BILL. [Lords.]

WHITEHAVEN CORPORATION BILL. [Lords.]

WITHINGTON URBAN DISTRICT COUNCILS (TRAMWAYS) BILL. [Lords.]

Ordered, that the Bills be read a second time.

PRIVATE BILLS. [Lords.]

No Standing Orders not previously inquired into applicable.

MR. SPEAKER laid upon the Table Report from one of the Examiners of Petitions for Private Bills, That, in the case of the following Bill, originating in the Lords, and referred on the First Reading thereof, no Standing Orders not previously inquired into are applicable, viz. :—

GROSVENOR CHAPEL (LONDON) BILL. [Lords.]

Ordered, That the Bill be read a second time.

PROVISIONAL ORDER BILLS.

Standing Orders applicable thereto complied with.

MR. SPEAKER laid upon the Table Report from one of the Examiners of Petitions for Private Bills, That, in the case of the following Bill, referred on the First Reading thereof, the Standing Orders which are applicable thereto have been complied with, viz. :—

LOCAL GOVERNMENT (IRELAND) PROVISIONAL ORDERS (HOUSING OF WORKING CLASSES) (No. 2) BILL.

Ordered, That the Bill be read a second time upon Monday next.

PROVISIONAL ORDER BILLS.

No Standing Orders applicable.

MR. SPEAKER laid upon the Table Report from one of the Examiners of Petitions for Private Bills, That, in the case of the following Bill, referred on the First Reading thereof, no Standing Orders are applicable, viz. :—

LOCAL GOVERNMENT (IRELAND) PROVISIONAL ORDER (No. 4) BILL.

Ordered, That the Bill be read a second time upon Monday next.

PRIVATE BILLS.

Petition for additional Provision.

Standing Orders not complied with.

MR. SPEAKER laid upon the Table Report from one of the Examiners of Petitions for Private Bills, That, in the case of the Petition for additional Provision in the following Bill, the Standing Orders have not been complied with, viz. :—

BRADFORD TRAMWAYS AND IMPROVEMENT BILL.

Ordered, That the Report be referred to the Select Committee on Standing Orders.

CROWBOROUGH DISTRICT WATER BILL.

Lords' Amendments considered, and agreed to.

BROMPTON AND PICCADILLY CIRCUS RAILWAY BILL.

As amended, considered ; to be read the third time.

JONES' DIVORCE BILL. [Lords.]

Read a second time, and committed.

LOUGHBOROUGH CORPORATION BILL. [Lords].

Read a second time, and committed.

HOUSING OF THE WORKING CLASSES PROVISIONAL ORDER (BARROW-STOUNNESS) BILL.

Reported, without amendment [Provisional Order confirmed]. Report to lie upon the table.

Bill to be read the third time upon Monday next.

LOCAL GOVERNMENT (IRELAND) PROVISIONAL ORDER (No. 1) BILL.

Reported, without Amendment [Provisional Order confirmed]; report to lie upon the Table.

Bill to be read the third time upon Monday next.

LOCAL GOVERNMENT PROVISIONAL ORDER (HOUSING OF WORKING CLASSES) BILL.

Reported, without Amendment [Provisional Orders confirmed]; report to lie upon the Table.

Bill to be read the third time upon Monday next.

LOCAL GOVERNMENT PROVISIONAL ORDERS (POOR LAW) BILL.

Reported, without Amendment [Provisional Order confirmed]; report to lie upon the Table.

Bill to be read the third time upon Monday next.

LOCAL GOVERNMENT PROVISIONAL ORDERS (No. 5) BILL.

Reported, without Amendment [Provisional orders confirmed]; report to lie upon the Table.

Bill to be read the third time upon Monday next.

LOCAL GOVERNMENT PROVISIONAL ORDERS (No. 8) BILL.

Reported, with Amendments [Provisional Orders confirmed]; report to lie upon the Table.

Bill, as amended, to be considered upon Monday next.

PIER AND HARBOUR PROVISIONAL ORDERS (No. 1) BILL.

Reported with Amendments (Provisional Orders confirmed); Report to lie upon the Table.

Bill, as amended, to be considered upon Monday next.

LONDON COUNTY COUNCIL (MONEY) BILL.

Reported, with Amendments; Report to lie upon the Table.

HASTINGS AND ST. LEONARDS GAS BILL. [Lords.]

Reported, with Amendments; Reports to lie upon the Table, and to be printed.*

DERBY CORPORATION TRAMWAYS, &c., BILL.

Reported with Amendments; Reports to lie upon the Table, and to be printed.*

SKIPTON URBAN DISTRICT GAS BILL. [Lords.]

Reported, with Amendments; Reports to lie upon the Table, and to be printed.

LOWESTOFT PROMENADE PIER BILL.

Reported, with Amendments; Reports to lie upon the Table, and to be printed.*

LONDON HOSPITAL BILL. [Lords.]

Reported, without Amendment; Report to lie upon the Table.

Bill to be read the third time.

STOCKTON AND MIDDLESBROUGH WATER BILL. [Lords.]

Reported, without Amendment; Report to lie upon the Table, and to be printed.

Bill to be read the third time.

FRIENDS' PROVIDENT INSTITUTION BILL. [Lords.]

Reported, with an Amendment; Report to lie upon the Table.

INFANT ORPHAN ASYLUM BILL. [Lords.]

Reported, without Amendment; Report to lie upon the Table.

Bill to be read the third time.

ABERDEEN CORPORATION BILL. [Lords.]

Reported, with Amendments; Reports to lie upon the Table, and to be printed.

MID-KENT GAS BILL. [Lords.]

Reported, with Amendments; Reports to lie upon the Table, and to be printed.

WALKER AND WALLSEND UNION GAS (ELECTRIC LIGHTING) BILL.

Reported, with Amendments; Reports to lie upon the Table, and to be printed.

ELECTRIC LIGHTING PROVISIONAL ORDERS (No. 7) BILL.

Reported—without Amendment; Report to lie upon the Table;

Bill to be read the third time upon Monday next.

PRIVATE BILLS (GROUP B).

SIR JOHN BRUNNER reported from the Committee on Group B of Private Bills—

"That, for the convenience of parties, the Committee had adjourned till Wednesday next, at half-past Eleven of the clock."

Report to lie upon the Table.

GREAT SOUTHERN AND WESTERN AND WATERFORD, LIMERICK, AND WESTERN RAILWAY COMPANIES AMALGAMATION AND OTHER BILLS.

Ordered—

"That the parties appearing before the Select Committee on the Great Southern and Western and Waterford, Limerick, and Western Railway Companies Amalgamation and other Bills have leave to print the Minutes of the Evidence taken before the Committee day by day from the Clerk's Copy, if they think fit."—(*Sir Robert Penrose-FitzGerald.*)

MESSAGE FROM THE LORDS.

That they have agreed to.

Amendment to—

HULL, BARNSLEY, AND WEST RIDING JUNCTION RAILWAY AND DOCK BILL. [Lords].

Amendments to—

CAMBRIDGE UNIVERSITY AND TOWN GAS BILL. [Lords.]

ST. ALBANS GAS BILL. [Lords.]

Without Amendment.

That they have passed a Bill, intituled, "An Act to authorise the Great Grimsby Street Tramways Company to extend their tramways; and for other purposes." [Great Grimsby Street Tramways Bill [Lords].

GREAT GRIMSBY STREET TRAMWAYS BILL. [Lords.]

Read the first time; and referred to the Examiners of Petitions for Private Bills.

PETITIONS.

BOROUGH FUNDS ACT, 1872.

Petition from Denholme, for alteration of law; to lie upon the Table.

GROUND RENTS (TAXATION BY LOCAL AUTHORITIES).

Petition from Rochdale, in favour; to lie upon the Table,

LOCAL GOVERNMENT (SCOTLAND) ACT AMENDMENT (1894) BILL.

Petition from Paisley, in favour; to lie upon the Table.

LOCAL GOVERNMENT (SCOTLAND) ACT (1894) AMENDMENT (No. 2) BILL.

Petition from Paisley, against; to lie upon the Table.

LOCAL GOVERNMENT (SCOTLAND) BILL.

Petition from Aberdeen, for alteration; to lie upon the Table.

MINES (EIGHT HOURS) BILL.

Petition in favour; from Cymmer; and, Llanbradach; to lie upon the Table.

PARLIAMENTARY FRANCHISE.

Petition from Greenwich, for extension to women; to lie upon the Table.

PRIVATE LEGISLATION PROCEDURE (SCOTLAND) BILL.

Petition from Aberdeen, in favour; to lie upon the Table.

PUBLIC HEALTH ACTS AMENDMENT BILL.

Petition from Congleton, in favour; to lie upon the Table.

ROMAN CATHOLIC UNIVERSITY IN IRELAND.

Petition from Paisley, against establishment; to lie upon the Table.

SALE OF FOOD AND DRUGS BILL.

Petitions for alteration;—from Leith;—and, Aberdeen; to lie upon the Table.

SEA FISHERIES REGULATION (SCOTLAND) ACT (1895) AMENDMENT BILL.

Petition from Aberdeen, against; to lie upon the Table.

SMALL TENANTS (SCOTLAND) BILL.

Petition from Aberdeen, in favour; to lie upon the Table.

TOWN COUNCIL (SCOTLAND) BILL.

Petitions in favour;—from Newburgh;—and, Nairn; to lie upon the Table.

TUBERCULOSIS (RECOMMENDATIONS OF ROYAL COMMISSION).

Petition from Edinburgh, for, legislation; to lie upon the Table,

VACCINATION ACTS, 1867 TO 1898.

Petition from Reading, for alteration of Law; to lie upon the Table.

RETURNS, REPORTS, ETC.

BOARD OF TRADE (LABOUR DEPART-MENT) (WAGES OF DOMESTIC SERVANTS).

Copy presented,—of Report on the Money Wages of Indoor Domestic Servants [by Command]; to lie upon the Table.

PUBLIC WORKS LOAN BOARD.

Copy presented,—of Twenty-fourth Annual Report (for 1898-9), with Appendices [by Act]; to lie upon the Table, and to be printed. [No. 216.]

TREATY SERIES (No. 14, 1899).

Copy presented,—of Withdrawal of Montenegro from the International Union for the Protection of Literary and Artistic Works [by Command]; to lie upon the Table.

Paper laid upon the Table by the Clerk of the House :—

1. Arundel Port,—Copy of the Annual Report and General Account of the Commissioners of Arundel Port for period from 25th March, 1898, to 25th March, 1899 [by Act].

2. Public Records (Court of Exchequer, —Copy of Second Schedule containing a List and Particulars of Classes of Documents, which formerly were or ought to have been in the Office of the King's or Queen's Remembrancer of the Exchequer, or of the Clerk appointed to take charge of the Port Bonds or Coast Bonds, and which are now in, but are not considered of sufficient public value to justify their preservation in the Public Record Office.

LOCAL AUTHORITIES (ENGLAND, WALES, AND IRELAND) TECHNICAL EDUCATION.

Return ordered, "showing the extent to which, and the manner in which, Local Authorities in England, Wales, and Ireland have applied or are applying funds to the purposes of Technical Education (including Science, Art, Technical, and Manual Instruction) during the years 1897-8 and 1898-9, under the following Acts : Local Taxation (Customs and Excise) Act, 1890; Technical Instruction Act, 1889 and 1891; Welsh Intermediate Education Act, 1889; and Public Libraries and Museums Act."—(*Sir John Gorst.*)

METROPOLITAN WATER COMPANIES (ACCOUNTS).

Return ordered, "of the Accounts, as they are respectively made up, of the Metropolitan Water Companies and the Staines Reservoirs Joint Committee to the 30th day of September and the 31st day of December, 1898 (in continuation of Parliamentary Paper, No. 346, of Session 1898.)"—(*Mr. T. W. Russell.*)

PRIVATE LEGISLATION PROCEDURE (SCOTLAND) (EXPENSES).

Committee to consider of authorising the payment, out of moneys to be provided by Parliament, of any remuneration, allowances, and expenses that may become payable under any Act of the present Session to provide for improving and extending the Procedure for obtaining Parliamentary Powers by way of Provisional Orders in matters relating to Scotland (Queen's Recommendation signified), upon Monday next.—(*Sir William Walrond.*)

NEW WRIT.

NEW WRIT FOR EDINBURGH (SOUTH DIVISION).

In the room of Robert Cox, esquire, deceased.—(*Sir William Walrond.*)

QUESTIONS.

FOREIGN SERVICE MESSENGERS.

*Sir CHARLES DILKE (Gloucester, Forest of Dean): I beg to ask the Under Secretary of State for Foreign Affairs whether the Secretary of State is acting on the recommendations, in respect to Foreign Service Messengers, contained in paragraph 20 of the final Report of the Ridley Commission.

*The UNDER SECRETARY OF STATE FOR FOREIGN AFFAIRS (Mr. BRODRICK, Surrey, Guildford): The

Secretary of State has reduced the salary for new appointments from £400 to £250, and proposes to raise the maximum age of appointment from 35 to 40 in accordance with the recommendations of the Royal Commission.

THE MOST FAVOURED NATION CLAUSE IN TREATIES WITH THE UNITED STATES.

COLONEL MILWARD (Stratford-upon-Avon) : I beg to ask the Under Secretary of State for Foreign Affairs whether the Treaties existing between the United States of America and the Governments of Austria-Hungary, Belgium, France, Germany, and Russia respectively contain what is known as the most favoured nation clause.

*MR. BRODICK : The treaties concluded by the United States with Austria, Belgium, and Russia contain the conditional most favoured nation articles. The treaty with Prussia contains an article according most favoured nation treatment to produce and manufactures in matters of import duties, &c. The treaty with France contains no most-favoured-nation article.

FOREIGN SUGAR BOUNTIES.

SIR HOWARD VINCENT (Sheffield, Central) : I beg to ask the Under Secretary of State for Foreign Affairs if the Belgian Government is taking any steps to obtain the consent of France and Russia to the abolition of the bounties upon the export of sugar, as desired by the other nations represented at the Conference last year at Brussels ; and if there is any hope of a successful issue to such efforts in the absence of penal legislation in the United Kingdom.

*MR. BRODRICK : The result of the negotiations in this direction, which were confided to the Belgian Government by the Sugar Bounty Conference of Brussels, have not yet been made known to Her Majesty's Government.

SIR HOWARD VINCENT : Will the Government make inquiries before the Vote is taken next Thursday ?

No answer was given,

THE ARMENIAN MASSACRES.

COLONEL DENNY (Kilmarnock Burghs) : I beg to ask the Under Secretary of State for Foreign Affairs whether he has had

any recent communication from Her Majesty's Ambassador at Constantinople in regard to the claims of British subjects on account of the Armenian massacres of August, 1896 ; whether he has heard that the United States Minister has obtained from the Sultan a promise that the American claims would be paid, also that the Turkish Government proposes to pay the American claims in connection with and through certain American firms with whom they are in negotiation for naval contracts ; and whether Her Majesty's Government will now influence the Sublime Porte so that the claims of British subjects may be settled without further loss of time.

*MR. BRODRICK : We have heard quite recently from Sir N. O'Conor on the subject. On the 23rd of May His Excellency again spoke to the Turkish Minister of Foreign Affairs very seriously and urged him to lose no time in informing the Sultan of his repeated representations. The answer to the second paragraph of the question is in the negative.

IRELAND—LOAN FUND BOARD.

MR. JAMES O'CONNOR (Wicklow, W.) : I beg to ask the Chief Secretary to the Lord Lieutenant of Ireland, is he aware that Mr. G. W. Young, late secretary to the Loan Fund Board of Ireland, has stated that the illegalities sanctioned by the Board amount to about £60,000, and that this sum is at present irrecoverable ; have the loan fund societies in Ireland been carried on under the authority of an Act of Parliament and under the control of a department in Dublin Castle ; have the Loan Fund Board in Dublin permitted these alleged violations of the law ; and does he propose to make any change in the constitution of the Board, by the insertion of a clause, or otherwise, in the Bill introduced by the Attorney-General for Ireland on the 6th of March last.

*THE CHIEF SECRETARY FOR IRELAND (MR. G. W. BALFOUR, Leeds, Central) : No such statement has been made by the late Inspector of Loan Funds as is referred to in the first paragraph. The loan fund societies in Ireland have been carried on under the provisions of an Act of Parliament and statutory rules made thereunder. They have not been carried on under the control of any Government department. A board called the Loan Fund Board, the members of which are nominated by the Lord Lieutenant, but over whose proceedings the Government have no control, exercises some powers of inspection and supervision over [the societies by whom loans are made. The Loan Fund Board has only power to dissolve a loan society which does not conform to the rules ; it has no other power over the proceedings of these societies. This power the Board has, I believe, exercised in some instances. The Bill referred to only aims at curing some legal defects in securities not regular in form, and does not deal with the general question. Any such clause as is suggested would be outside its scope.

MR. DOOGAN (Tyrone, E.) : May I ask whether, in view of the fact that the loss of this £60,000 will fall mostly on poor men, the Government will take any steps to recoup them ?

*MR. G. W. BALFOUR : I cannot hold out any hope that in the event of there being any deficiencies they will be made up by the Government.

MR. JAMES O'CONNOR : Is not the Bill introduced by the Attorney-General for Ireland intended to legalise certain transactions which, although not legal, were sanctioned or tolerated by the Local Government Board ?

*MR. G. W. BALFOUR : I have said that it is intended to deal with certain legal deficiencies.

IRISH SALMON FISHERIES.

MR. SETON-KARR (St. Helens) : I beg to ask the Chief Secretary to the Lord Lieutenant of Ireland whether he is aware that the fishery laws for the protection of salmon in the River Bann and in other Irish rivers are systematically evaded ; that the fixed railings in the salmon boxes in the River Bann at Coleraine are not lifted at the weekly close time ; and that it is the practice, when draughting for salmon in the River Bann, by means of a second net to constitute a fixed engine and leave no gaps ; whether he is aware that since the month of June has been included in the eel-fishing season thousands of salmon smelt are killed in the eel nets in the River Bann ; whether he will cause inquiry to be made into

these and other alleged illegal practices ; and whether, as there is a Bill now before this House entitled the Salmon Fisheries (Ireland) Acts Amendment Bill, which was unanimously agreed to and reported to this House by a Select Committee in 1892 after evidence thereon had been taken, the Government will give facilities for the discussion of the said Bill in this House this session.

*MR. G. W. BALFOUR : I am informed that the weekly close season is carefully observed not only on the River Bann, but also in other parts of the Coleraine Fishery district, and that openings are regularly made in the salmon boxes in order to allow a free passage for fish during the weekly close time. There are two draft nets used in the tidal parts of the river, one of which is shot after the other is hauled. This, I am told, is quite lawful, and does not cause an obstruction to the fish in anything more than the owners have a legal right to do. The nets are only used at times, and cannot at any time be used more than about 10 hours out of 24. · In the fresh water only one net is used at any one place. As regards the second and third paragraphs, I understand that salmon fry have been taken in eel nets in June. In June of last year a number of salmon fry were taken in the eel nets at Movanagher, and a number were dead. If the eel fishing is carried on at either Portna or Movanagher in June, the nets would kill all the fry that would come into them, and no care could save them owing to the shallow water and quick stream. At Toome eel fishery the water is deep and the current light, and with care fry can be taken and put back to the river alive, but not if there is a good quantity of eel. Two bailiffs are on the Toome eel fishery in June for the purpose of looking after the salmon fry while the eel nets are fishing, and inquiry will be made as to the quantity of fry that may be killed by eel nets during this month. I do not think it will be possible to give facilities for the discussion of the Bill mentioned in the last paragraph during the present session, and I may remind my hon. friend that the subject of the inland fisheries and fishery laws in Ireland is about to be inquired into by a Viceregal Commission.

MR. SETON-KARR : Arising out of the answer to the last paragraph, is the right hon. Gentleman aware that I have introduced that Bill every session for the past seven years; will he not under the circumstances consider the possibility of the giving facilities for discussing it this year?

*MR. G. W. BALFOUR: That does not rest with me.

PAY OF IRISH RESIDENT MAGISTRATES.

MR. McCARTAN (Down, S.) : I beg to ask the Chief Secretary to the Lord Lieutenant of Ireland whether his attention has been called to the resolution unanimously adopted by the Council of the Belfast Chamber of Commerce complaining of the inadequate emoluments of the two resident magistrates at present in charge of the city; whether he is aware that these two resident magistrates are men of good standing and experience at the Bar, and that, owing to the extension of the city boundaries, the amount of police court business has enormously increased, and that their salaries are much under the scale for Dublin, where the duties are considerably lighter; and whether, seeing that the Council have resolved that the scale in Belfast must be considerably raised if first-class men are to be attracted to the position, he will have the matter fully considered with the view of carrying out the feelings of the Chamber of Commerce and the citizens in this regard.

*MR. DAVITT (Mayo, E.): Before the right hon. Gentleman answers, may I ask whether in fact the salaries paid to Irish resident magistrates are not as a rule too high, considering the slight duties they have to perform, and are there not too many of these magistrates, considering the present crimeless condition of Ireland?

*MR. WILLIAM JOHNSTON (Belfast, S.) : Is it not a fact that this subject was brought under the right hon. Gentleman's notice by Members connected with Belfast a considerable time ago, and that he was favourably inclined to consider it, provided hon. Gentlemen opposite offered no opposition?

*MR. G. W. BALFOUR : Yes, it is the fact, as mentioned by the hon. Member for South Belfast, that this matter has been previously under my notice. My attention has been directed to the resolution referred to, but I am not prepared to admit that the case of the two resi-

dent magistrates at Belfast is exactly comparable with that of the divisional magistrates of Dublin. If the position of the resident magistrates at Belfast is to be improved legislation would be necessary for the purpose, and I should require to be assured that any measure dealing with the case would be treated as absolutely non-controversial by all sections before I could consent even to consider the question of introducing a Bill during the present session.

IRISH LAND VALUATIONS.

CAPTAIN DONELAN : On behalf of the hon. Member for South Down I beg to ask the Chief Secretary to the Lord Lieutenant of Ireland whether he can now say about what time the Sub-Commissioners in Ireland will be supplied with the valuations of lands and houses for the standard year in respect of the fair rent applications listed for hearing; and whether the same will be supplied by the Commissioners of Valuation in Ireland or at the request of the Land Commission, so as to save the tenants or owners from the expense and inconvenience of applying for certificates of valuation which will be comparatively useless to them afterwards.

*MR. G. W. BALFOUR : In continuation of my answer to the hon. Member's previous question of the 18th of May on this subject, I am informed that the certificates of valuation are being supplied to the Land Commission as required, and that certificates have been issued to the Commission in 3,100 cases to the present date. As regards the question of the cost of these certificates, I must refer the hon. Member to the statement made by me on the 12th May in reply to a similar question put by my hon. friend the Member for North Antrim.

NEW RATING SYSTEM IN IRELAND.

MR. TULLY (Leitrim, S.): I beg to ask the Chief Secretary to the Lord Lieutenant of Ireland whether the Land Commission have issued for the information of landlords and tenants making agreements for fair rents for the second statutory term instructions as to their liabilities for rates under the new rating system; and whether he can state if an agreement is binding on a landlord to allow his tenants half county cess under the second statutory term made since the 6th April last.

*MR. G. W. BALFOUR : The reply to the first paragraph is in the negative. Presumably the parties to an agreement would refer to the provisions of the Local Government Act and to the certificate as to poor rate and county cess published in the *Dublin Gazette* of 11th April, before executing the agreement. The precise meaning of the second paragraph is not quite clear to me, but I would refer the hon. Member to Section 52, Sub-section 2, of the Local Government Act of last year, which enacts that the occupier of a hereditament shall not be entitled to deduct from his rent any part of the poor rate, and any contract to the contrary respecting such deduction shall be void.

PRISON APPOINTMENTS.

MR. GRAHAM (St. Pancras, W.) : I beg to ask the Secretary to the Treasury whether there is any limit of age, and, if so, what limit, beyond which no prison official may be promoted to a deputy governorship, a fifth-class governorship, or to a clerkship in the Prison Department in the Home Office ; and are the competitive prison clerks, who paid a £3 examination fee, debarred at the age of forty-five from progressing in the customary course of promotion to clerkships in the Prison Department of the Home Office to fifth-class governorships, or to deputy governorships.

*THE SECRETARY OF STATE FOR THE HOME DEPARTMENT (Sir M. WHITE RIDLEY, Lancs., Blackpool) : I have been asked by my right hon. friend the Secretary to the Treasury to answer this question. It would be unusual, except under very special circumstances, to promote a prison official over the age of forty-five to any of these appointments. The appointments, as has been explained on previous occasions, are in the customary course of promotion only in the technical sense, that is to say, a fresh Civil Service certificate is not necessary. These posts require special qualifications, and are given by selection, and not by seniority or as a right of promotion.

FATAL ACCIDENT TO A DOCK LABOURER AT GARSTON.

MR. M'GHEE (Louth, S.) : I beg to ask the Secretary of State for the Home Department whether his attention has been called to the report of the proceedings at the coroner's inquest held at the Blackburn Arms, Garston, upon the dead body of a dock labourer, named Peter Mallor, who had been in the employ of the London and North-Western Railway Company, and assisting to load a steamer called the "Emerald," when he was killed by the falling on his head of a drum laden with caustic soda ; is he aware that the coroner reflected severely upon the employment of mere boys by this railway company at the time upon the "Emerald" ; and whether the hooks carrying the drum were defective, and had not previously been examined by any competent inspector ; and if, in the interests of the lives of the dock labourers and youths employed by this railway company, he will cause full inquiry to be made into the case, and surrounding circumstances.

*SIR M. WHITE RIDLEY : My attention has been called to the report of this case, and to the remarks made by the coroner. The matter is now being further investigated by officers of the Factory Department.

THE PETROLEUM BILL.

MR. TULLY : I beg to ask the Secretary of State for the Home Department whether he can state what day the Government will introduce their measure dealing with petroleum ; and whether it will deal with the question of the flash point, in accordance with the recommendation of the Select Committee that reported last year to the House.

*SIR M. WHITE RIDLEY : No, Sir, I am afraid I am not in a position to make any statement as to a petroleum Bill, either in respect of its introduction or its contents.

EMOLUMENTS OF LIGHTHOUSE KEEPERS.

MR. NICOL (Argyll) : I beg to ask the President of the Board of Trade if a reply has now been sent by the authorities to the petition of the lighthouse keepers of the United Kingdom for an increase of pay and other privileges ; and, if so, if he can state to the House the terms and effect of the reply.

THE PRESIDENT OF THE BOARD OF TRADE (MR. RITCHIE, Croydon) : A new scale of remuneration for lighthouse keepers, as proposed by the three lighthouse authorities, has been sanctioned by the Board of Trade, and I am informed by those authorities that a circular embodying the new scale is on the point of being issued. The details of the scale cannot be conveniently embodied in reply to a question, but I shall be happy to furnish my hon. friend with the particulars, in writing, if he desires it.

Mr. NICOL: Will the right hon. Gentleman have them printed?

Mr. RITCHIE: I hardly think that that is necessary. The particulars shall be distributed to those interested.

YOUGHAL RIFLE RANGE.

CAPTAIN DONELAN (Cork, E.): I beg to ask the Under Secretary of State for War whether he is aware that, in consequence of a recent breach in the sea embankment, the rifle range at Youghal, county Cork, has become flooded and practically useless; and whether the War Office will consider the desirability of co-operating with the local authorities and with the Great Southern and Western Railway Company, with a view to the execution of the necessary repairs.

*THE UNDER SECRETARY OF STATE FOR WAR (MR. G. WYNDHAM, Dover): It is a fact that the range cannot be used until the breach in the sea wall is repaired. Several authorities are interested in these repairs, which have already been attempted, but without success. A further report on the circumstances will be called for.

CAPTAIN DONELAN: Will the Department be prepared to make any contribution towards the cost of carrying out these repairs?

*MR. WYNDHAM: That is the very question which will be decided when we have the report. Several authorities are interested, and the allocation of the responsibility on each is a matter which will occupy our minds.

LADYSMITH BARRACKS.

MR. BUCHANAN (Aberdeenshire, East): I beg to ask the Under Secretary of State for War whether the British troops have been sent back from the Mooi river to Ladysmith, and what steps have been taken to improve the water supply and sanitary condition of the accommodation at Ladysmith.

*MR. WYNDHAM: These troops had been under canvas at an elevation of some 5,000ft. during the hot weather; they were moved back into huts at Ladysmith on the approach of the cold weather, when enteric fever is not prevalent. Fifty-three thousand pounds has been spent on improving the accommodation at Ladysmith, and the general officer commanding has been instructed to postpone other services in order to apply the largest possible sum to sanitary requirements at that station.

MR. BUCHANAN: Have they, then, been brought back to the same unhealthy quarters and huts from which they were removed in February?

*MR. WYNDHAM: Yes, but a large portion of this £53,000 has been spent on improving the sanitary condition of these very quarters, and the result of the expenditure will be reaped this year.

PRESBYTERIAN SERVICES FOR TROOPS IN INDIA.

MR. HEDDERWICK (Wick Burghs): I beg to ask the Secretary of State for India whether his attention has been drawn to a complaint that the Episcopalian chaplains attached to the Army in India object to Presbyterian services being conducted in the churches provided by Government for Her Majesty's troops, and that in consequence Scottish Presbyterian soldiers are compelled to worship in riding schools, theatres, and other even more unsuitable places; whether there is any foundation in fact for this complaint; and, if so, upon what grounds the exclusion of Presbyterian soldiers from the use of churches provided by Government for the purpose of worship is defended; and whether he has taken, or means to take, any steps to remove the grievance complained of.

THE SECRETARY OF STATE FOR INDIA (Lord GEORGE HAMILTON, Middlesex, Ealing): For some time past I have been in communication with the officials of the Scotch Church with a view of facilitating the use of existing buildings for divine service by Presbyterians in India. In consequence of representations which reached the Government of India, certain changes were made about a year ago in the rules which govern the use of Government churches. The tendency of those changes was to facilitate the use of such churches by denominations other than the Church of England. Since then, as I stated in this House on May 9, the only changes made in these rules have been (1) to define more accurately the religious bodies who may hold services in these churches, Presbyterians being expressly included; and (2) to make the final appeal, in case of difficulty, lie to the Metropolitan, whereas up to last summer the final decision lay with the Bishop of the diocese. No cases of difficulty or hardship under the new rules have as yet been reported to me, nor am I at present aware of any reason for taking action in the matter.

PENSIONS TO SCOTTISH SCHOOL TEACHERS.

MR. BUCHANAN: I beg to ask the Lord Advocate whether he will state the amount of the pension to be given to the teachers in Scotland whose services commenced before 1851, before they are called upon to exercise the option of applying for a pension.

THE LORD ADVOCATE (Mr. A. G. MURRAY, Buteshire): The Superannuation Act confers no special benefit on teachers who began work before 1851. A circular, explaining fully the conditions, has been sent to every teacher known to be in service, and the Department will, on application, inform a teacher of the approximate amount of his allowance if he accepts the Act.

MR. BUCHANAN: May I ask whether before a teacher is compelled to exercise his option as to whether he will retire or not, he will be informed of the amount of pension he is to get?

MR. A. J. MURRAY: Yes, if he takes his pension under the Act.

MOUNTJOY POSTAL ARRANGEMENTS.

MR. DOOGAN: I beg to ask the Secretary to the Treasury, as representing the Postmaster-General, whether he is aware that letters posted in Mountjoy Post Office, county Tyrone, after 9 a.m., do not arrive in the neighbouring county town of Dungannon till the following day; whether, in order to obviate the great inconvenience resulting from this long delay, which in some cases amounts to 24 hours, the residents of Mountjoy have petitioned the postal authorities for an evening collection similar to that which is in force in the adjoining districts of Arboe and Clonoe; and whether steps will be taken to grant the prayer of that petition, which up to the present has not been acceded to.

THE FINANCIAL SECRETARY TO THE TREASURY (Mr. HANBURY, Preston): It is the case that letters posted at Mountjoy, near Dungannon, after 9 a.m. do not arrive at Dungannon till the following day. The reason is that Mountjoy, not being on the homeward route of the postman, has not hitherto had an evening collection, the only collection being made by the postman when delivering at 9 a.m. Instructions have, however, now been given for an evening collection to be made at the Mountjoy Post Office.

LURGAN POST OFFICE.

MR. M'GHEE: I beg to ask the Secretary to the Treasury, as representing the Postmaster-General, with reference to the proposed building of a new post office at Lurgan, whether he can now state on what site the new building will be constructed; and, whether, considering the grave anxiety in Lurgan owing to the delay already involved, he can state about what date the erection of the building will be commenced, and what period will be allowed for the completion of the works.

MR. HANBURY: I regret to state that little progress has been made in this matter since I answered the hon. Member's question of the 8th ultimo. The Board of Public Works have not yet been able to design a suitable building, for erection on either of the two sites under consideration, the cost of which would not bring the total expenditure for site and building up to an amount far in excess of what the business would warrant.

POSTMEN'S PAY.

MR. GILES (Cambridge, Wisbech): I beg to ask the Secretary to the Treasury, as representing the Postmaster-General, whether the test applied by the Post Office authorities in determining whether the postmen in a district are entitled to a higher grade of pay is the cost of living in or the population of that district.

MR. HANBURY: Population is the first and principal test, but it is constantly modified by exceptional local circumstances, such as the high cost of living or high price of labour.

DUBLIN TELEGRAPHISTS' HOURS OF DUTY.

MR. DAVITT: I beg to ask the Secretary to the Treasury, as representing the Postmaster-General, whether, on Whit Monday, the telegraphists employed at 11, Regent Street (West Side) Post Office, who were on duty for eight consecutive hours, and forbidden to leave the building, were unable to obtain food or refreshment owing to the absence of the caterer; whether overtime is compulsory on the female telegraphists, owing to the office being shorthanded; and whether an hour's overtime per day is being exacted this week from some of these lady employees.

MR. HANBURY: At the Post Office at 21, Regent Street, to which it is presumed the hon. Member refers, only eight of the twenty-four telegraphists on duty on Whit Monday attended for as much as eight hours. It was by the general consent of the staff that the attendant was absent for that day, the staff having previously arranged to provide their own meals, as they wished the attendant to have a holiday, and none of them expressed any desire to leave the building for refreshment during the day. The office in question has its full staff. Overtime is compulsory on female telegraphists, as on all other Post Office servants, when necessity requires. During the Derby Week five telegraphists at this office voluntarily performed between them, during five days, seven hours extra duty in all, which was, of course, paid for extra at the authorised rate. No overtime is being exacted this week.

ADULTERATED TEA.

MR. CAREW (Dublin, College Green): I beg to ask the Financial Secretary to the Treasury whether he is aware that large importations of tea rejected by the Hamburg and New York Customs have recently been passed by the English Customs, and sold in London, although containing up to 20 per cent. of clay and sand, and unfit for human consumption; and whether, in view of the fact that the price of common teas has advanced 50 per cent., of which the poor are the largest consumers, the Government will insist on a more rigid inspection of all future importations to prevent a repetition of the fraud.

*MR. HANBURY: The Board of Customs have no means of testing the accuracy of the statement in the first paragraph. As was stated yesterday by my right hon. friend the Chancellor of the Exchequer, in reply to a similar question, a full inquiry is being made, and if it should appear advisable to alter the existing regulations or to increase the number of tea inspectors, the necessary steps will be taken at once. Meantime, a circular has been issued to the tea inspectors directing them to administer the existing regulations with special care.

LICENCES FOR TRADESMEN'S CARTS AND VANS.

MR. GILES: I beg to ask the Secretary to the Treasury whether he is aware that recently tradesmen in rural districts, especially builders and plumbers, have received notice from the collectors of taxes that they must take out licences for carts and vans used in the course of trade by reason of their sending and fetching their workmen in such carts and vans to and from the houses and places where their work was being performed, and that the Solicitor to the Board of Inland Revenue had expressed the opinion that workmen cannot be considered goods or burden in the course of trade or husbandry, within the meaning of 32 and 33 Vic., c 14, s. 19 (6); and whether, having regard to the fact that this practice has prevailed for a great many years, he will give instructions to the collectors of taxes not to exact the carriage duty on this account alone, or will take steps to amend the provisions of the Act.

*MR. HANBURY: There has been no change of practice in the matter as stated in the question, and the Act is 51 Vict., c. 8. The exemption of trade-carts extends only to vehicles which are constructed or adapted for use, and are used solely for the conveyance of goods or burden in the course of trade or husbandry. It has always been the view of the Board of Inland Revenue that workmen do not come within the meaning of the words "goods or burden." The proceeds of these licences are now, of course, paid over to the Local Taxation Account.

THE CHINA SQUADRON.

MR. HEDDERWICK: I beg to ask the First Lord of the Admiralty whether the summer cruise of Her Majesty's squadron, now in the China Seas, has been arranged; and, if so, whether Port Arthur and Talienwan are amongst the ports to be visited.

THE FIRST LORD OF THE ADMIRALTY (Mr. G. J. GOSCHEN, St. George's, Hanover Square): Yes, by the commander-in-chief of the station. The ports named by the hon. Member are not in the admiral's programme.

MR. HEDDERWICK: Will the right hon. Gentleman state the reason why these interesting ports are omitted?

MR. GOSCHEN: The commander-in-chief appears to have formed a programme which did not include these ports.

THE COLONIAL LOANS FUND BILL.

THE FIRST LORD OF THE TREASURY (Mr. A. J. BALFOUR, Manchester, E.): It might be convenient to the House if I state that I think we ought, on public grounds, to get through the stage of the Colonial Loans Bill which unfortunately was not finished last night at the earliest possible date. I must therefore put it first on Monday, although I hope it will only prevent us getting on with the Scotch Bill by a very short period.

MR. DILLON (Mayo, E.): Can the right hon. Gentleman give any indication as to what are the public grounds that necessitate any hurry in regard to this Bill?

MR. A. J. BALFOUR: I do not think I can answer that question, but my right hon. friend the Chancellor of the Exchequer is, I know, extremely anxious that the Bill should be got through for financial reasons.

MR. DILLON: He did not state them.

SUPPLY [13TH ALLOTTED DAY].

Considered in Committee.

(In the Committee.)

CIVIL SERVICES AND REVENUE DEPARTMENTS ESTIMATES, 1899-1900.

CLASS II.

Motion made, and Question proposed—
"That a sum, not exceeding £49,482, be granted to Her Majesty, to complete the sum necessary to defray the charge which will come in course of payment during the year ending on the 31st day of March, 1900, for the salaries and expenses of the Department of Her Majesty's Secretary of State for Foreign Affairs."

*SIR CHARLES DILKE (Gloucester, Forest of Dean): The reduction which I have to move in the salary of Lord Salisbury is based on a sad case, but a clear and grave case of neglect by the Government, and I propose to speak on one other question only before moving it. Last year I moved a reduction in the salary of the Secretary of State on account of matters which had occurred in the course of the previous twelve months. There had been developments in connection with Tunis, Siam, Madagascar, and China, all of which we wished to censure. An opinion was expressed that the Liberals were not agreed in their views on foreign policy; but every Liberal present voted for the reduction, which had the support of my right hon. friend the Member for West Monmouthshire. Since that time there has, no doubt, on the Address in reply to the Queen's Speech this year, been an attempt by my hon. friend the Member for Devonport (Mr. Kearley) again to raise the question of Madagascar. There has been a new Blue Book which justified his action, for it shows that no reply has been received from France to Lord Salisbury's remonstrance. But there is no new material. The matter was covered by the reduction which I moved last year. We attacked the Government with regard to it last year. The Blue Book of this year is virtually the same as the Blue Book of last year, for the whole matter has arisen from Lord Salisbury's neglect in 1890. We can add nothing to what we said last year, but we received no answer.

*THE UNDER-SECRETARY FOR FOREIGN AFFAIRS (Mr. BRODRICK, Surrey, Guildford): The arguments were very fully replied to.

SIR CHARLES DILKE: I do not think that an examination of *Hansard* will bear out that statement. We all agree that the principal events in foreign affairs which have lately happened, the choice of our representatives to the Hague, and the Mid-Africa delimitations, form a success for Lord Salisbury—a success to set against many failures. Relations with France are better, but there is the as yet unexplained incident of Muscat. The Muscat papers have virtually been refused to the House of Commons. The papers would not be damaging to the cause of peace, but they would be damaging to the Government. They are refused on the shallow pretext that "local details are still under discussion." The French Government has told its supporters that we expressed "profound regret" for something which they term an *inconvenance*—that is, "an unseemly or unbecoming act"—on whose part? We can all agree in regretting that we should be placed in the position which the Government, by refusing papers, seem to admit. The one subject upon which, in addition to that upon which I have to move the reduction, I wish to speak, but briefly—as I shall doubtless be followed by my noble friend, the Member for York, who has had unrivalled opportunities of forming opinions on the spot—is that of China, which is always with us. The recent arrangement with Russia is a very partial one, apparently a mere recognition of existing facts, leaving all dangerous matters where they were. It is exactly the agreement which, on the 12th of August of last year, was suggested by Mr. Lessar, the Russian Chargé d'Affaires, to the Leader of this House, and at first cold-shouldered by the Leader of this House. The Government have been riding two horses. The muddle between the policy of the "open door" and that of the Yang-tsze sphere has led to confusion which seems to have caused failure. On this point I think the House is really as unanimous as it was unanimous in previous debates with regard to the withdrawal of our ships from Port Arthur at a moment when a more general agreement with Russia might have been come to, more satisfactory than that which has been tardily made. My right hon. friend the Member for West Monmouthshire last year adopted and made his own upon this point all what he called the "very just criticism of the Member for Chester"—in other words, in the first place, criticism on the invitation to Russia to come to Port Arthur, without any arrangement with Russia at the time when one could have been made; and secondly, on the absurdity of the Yang-tsze scheme unless, which the Government do not intend, effective occupation of the Yang-tsze Valley should be brought about.

Sir. Charles Dilke.

A paper which supports the Government said the other day that, of the two policies, the integrity of China was gone, and the sphere policy had prevailed, but that all China was likely to become the Russian sphere ; and this, I confess, seems to me to be the net result of the Government policy. Its effect has certainly been a wonderfully rapid growth of Russian influence at Pekin, and all now see that the Chinese Empire, as we prophesied last year would be the case, is taking its place with Turkey and Persia among the fringe of empires under the protection of Russia which surround that Empire on the east and south and west. The now obvious exposure of the Chinese capital to Russian land attack is a curious commentary on the reasons which were given here for the occupation of Wei-hai-wei. I read in the "Naval Annual" for this year (a book which, on the whole, has always been friendly to the policy of the Admiralty) "Russia should be able to hold Manchuria," and, as I read the passage, whatever she can reach from Manchuria by land, "notwithstanding our command of the sea." I leave, however, the Government policy in China to my noble friend the Member for York and others, and pass at once to that matter which stands in such a position that a reduction on the vote is the only adequate means of expressing with regard to it what I feel. The story of the Waima incident is one of the strangest kind. In November, 1893, Colonel Ellis, commanding our forces in Sierra Leone, was warned by a confidential telegram from the Home Government that the French were near the frontier, and that he was to be careful. His letters home show that he was most careful, and that he wrote warning the French of his approach. On the 23rd December a French force attacked a force of the 1st West India Regiment and police. They killed Captain Lendy, D.S.O., Lieutenant Liston, Lieutenant Wroughton, one sergeant-major, four privates West India Regiment, two Sierra Leone police, and severely wounded fifteen non-commissioned officers and men and two police. The French lost one officer and two men killed, and a few wounded. On Christmas Day, 1893, Colonel Ellis wrote to the Government a letter published in the *London Gazette*, in which he said—

"That Waima is well within the sphere of British influence is, I think, beyond question."

And he added definite explanations which seemed to prove this. A letter from Colonel Ellis to the French commandant, also published in the *London Gazette*, and his letters home make it clear that Ellis had no doubt that Waima was within our sphere, and that the French, on consideration, did not assert that it was either French or Liberian. Colonel Ellis mentioned in his letters home that he had letters from the French commandant showing how very far the French had previously penetrated into the British sphere, and the fact is confirmed by a letter from Captain Lendy to his mother, written before the engagement, which she has. Colonel Ellis was knighted and died. On the 12th February, 1894, Lord Rosebery wrote to the mother of one of the officers killed that he was "determined" that the matter "shall be probed and examined to the uttermost." Before, however, making a formal demand on France for reparation the Government consulted the Astronomer Royal, and they also sent up surveying parties to the neighbourhood, whose work is mapped in Trotter's "Sources of the Niger." After two years inquiry and survey, Colonel Ellis's view was fully confirmed. When the payment of £10,000 was proposed as compensation to the French Missions in Uganda for action by Colonel Lugard, which had been approved and justified by the Government, some of us offered opposition on the ground that the Waima matter ought, at least, to be settled at the same time. We were beaten, and the money was paid over to the Cardinal Archbishop of Westminster to disburse among the French and Alsatian claimants: that is, this somewhat similar claim was dealt with and settled by itself. On the 18th March, 1898, I pressed with regard to this matter a question which was followed by a correspondence between the hon. Member for North Lambeth (Sir Henry M. Stanley) and the then Under Secretary of State, in which Mr. Curzon denied that the position of Waima was known at the time, but admitted that the former Government had, after full investigation, "included the question of compensation among the bases of discussion at the African Conference in Paris" in 1894-5. That Conference was held at the end of 1894 and beginning of 1895. If, as Mr. Curzon stated, the position of Waima was properly "determined" "in 1895," why, then, was the

matter not actively pressed after the determination in 1895? On the 1st April, 1898, the matter was mentioned by the Member for the Swansea district; on the 19th April I was informed that the frontier was not finally determined till 1896. On the 28th April I asked whether it was the case that compensation had distinctly been refused by France before the 15th September, 1895. This was denied by the Leader of the House; but the information is contained in a letter from Lord Dufferin, our then Ambassador in Paris, to the widow of one of the officers killed. On the 6th May, 1898, the senior Member for Portsmouth asked the Secretary of State for the Colonies a question on the subject, in the answer to which hope was held out that the matter would be settled, and a suggestion was made of temporary help pending settlement. Temporary help has been given in one case only, though not out of taxes. On the same day the Member for the Swansea district put another question to the Secretary of State for the Colonies, who confirmed the statement that the position of Waima was substantially known at the time of the incident, although not astronomically determined until 1895, or "finally determined" till 1896. On the 28th June, 1898, a question was asked by the Member for Chester (Mr. Yerburgh), when the Under-Secretary of State repeated that the matter was then included in general negotiations with France, and that, pending the result, a grant to the families of those slain was under consideration. No such grant was ever made, except the one advance just named of £100 from the Patriotic Fund. On the 14th July, 1898, there came a sudden change in the Government position, and that Government wrote to the French for compensation, treating the matter, not in connection with others, but as one apart. On the 21st July, in reply to the Member for the Leek Division of Staffordshire, the Government admitted this, but said that no reply had been received from France. No reply has been received, as I understand, up to the present time; yet the Uganda compensation has been paid. On the 1st August last year the hon. Member for Chester asked if a Supplementary Estimate, for the relief of the sufferers pending the settlement, could be proposed. The Under Secretary said that "should a Supplementary Vote be required, it would be asked for in that financial year." The financial year expired with last March, and nothing has been asked for, in spite of the need and of the promises. Coming to the present year, on the 13th February, the member for the Leek Division asked again with regard to compensation, and the present Under Secretary of State related a long story, ending "any case of urgency will be considered." Several of the cases are urgent. Nothing has been done in addition to the grant of £100 to one widow last year. On the 2nd March the hon. Member for Hampstead brought out the fact of the isolated treatment of this subject on the 14th July of last year, and of the receipt from France of no reply. But by this time the Government had come back again to the old position, and said that they were treating the matter in connection with other claims arising out of affairs in West Africa. On the 16th March the Member for the Wick Burghs, and on the 17th March the Member for the Swansea District, elicited the fact that the matter was before the law officers of the Crown. So that five and a-half years after the incident, and three years after the accurate determination of the facts, we have got as far as asking our own people what is our case. On the 23rd March the Member for the Leek Division discovered that no exact amount has ever been asked for from France, although France asked for a definite amount from us in the Uganda case; in other words, we have merely asked a vague question of France as to her willingness to pay compensation, to which, naturally, no reply has been returned. On the 24th March the Member for Chester discovered from the Government that the matter was not included in the recent African negotiations with France, but "is being dealt with separately." A more humiliating story was never placed before the House of Commons. I know nothing of the circumstances of the families of the native police, nor of those of the gallant non-commissioned officers and men of the West India regiment. The circumstances of the survivors left by the British officers killed are known to me. One of the mothers, aged seventy, has lost both her sons in Africa. The death of the one killed at Waima, a most distinguished officer of the Derbyshire regiment, has left that lady and

Sir. Charles Dilke.

her daughter alone in the world. Of the two other officers, one has left a widow and three children. They have received from the Government a nomination to Wellington, and £100, which went to pay the doctor's bills for the widow's premature confinement from shock and grief, but the lady is forced to eke out her income by sewing, the pension being insufficient. And the other mother, who is also a widow, has lost her only son. She has one other lady dependent upon her, who is earning her livelihood as a typewriter. These are cases of extraordinary hardship. But I am concerned with the blot upon the administration of the Foreign Office that its treatment of the matter has involved, and, having followed it closely since the time when the incident occurred, I feel that I have no alternative but to move the reduction, which I commend to the consideration of the House. The two matters that I have brought forward, that of Waima and that of China, are both examples of imbecility in the classical sense of that word : want of firmness of purpose, or distinct ideas clearly set before us. The energies of the Foreign Office have been too much taken up with Africa to enable the affairs of China to be properly dealt with. There was a time last year when the Foreign Office appeared to have set before itself the policy of alliances, specially intended to affect the Chinese situation—alliance with a military Power (Germany), alliance with the United States and with Japan. The most welcome, the policy of alliance with the United States, as we pointed out, is not a practical policy, for nobody in the United States desires a fighting or war alliance. The one thing necessary, however, above all, is clearness of foresight and of purpose, and that is what has been conspicuously wanting, especially in the case of China.

Motion made and Question proposed

"That Item A (Salaries) be reduced by £100. in respect of the salary of the Secretary of State."—(*Sir Charles Dilke.*)

LORD CHARLES BERESFORD (York): The right hon. Baronet has brought two cases before the Committee, and one I think I may describe as very humiliating—I refer to the Waima incident I should like to express my concurrence in the views of the right hon. Baronet on the matter. The facts of the case are these: The Government has acknowledged that these poor ladies do deserve some compensation, and they have asked the French Government to pay it. As far as I understand it, the French Government did not answer the letter for a very long time, and when eventually they did answer it they refused to pay anything. Three British officers were shot by French troops at a point twelve miles within our own boundaries—within our sphere of influence—and their widows and children can get no compensation. What a contrast between this case and the one in which our Government promptly paid £10,000 to the Uganda missionaries! And, above all, the Government sent out a Commission to find out the exact spot where the affair took place. It took two years to do its work. Why did they not send to the naval officer at the nearest station? He would have done the work in three days. I must say that what has occurred in this case would be a disgrace to any Government, whichever party might be in power. I now come to a question of great interest to the people of this country, and particularly to all connected with trade and commerce. I consider it to be one of the gravest problems this country has ever faced; it is a problem which requires immediate attention, and certainly wiser statesmanship than it has yet received. What is the problem? It is, that we have to secure our trade in that great country of China. This is a matter of vast importance to our working classes. Wherever we look we see that our markets are getting very circumscribed, thanks to the competition which we have to meet. It is not a question of territory that makes trade; it is one, rather, of population, and the population of China is enormous, exceeding 400,000,000. What is the struggle going on in China? It is a struggle between nations who want trade and nations who seek territory. Nations are represented by governments, and I say that the present Government are doing nothing whatever to secure or develop our trade with China. It may be suggested, in consequence of the remarks I am about to make, that I ought to belong to the Opposition. I do not think so by any means, but I do hope that my criticism will be most fair. One of the main things we are now suffering

from is the weakness of the Opposition. A weak Opposition means a weak Government, and a strong Opposition a strong Government. I do not propose to go into the reasons which brought us into our present position. I want to take things just as they are. I freely acknowledge that the Government have had a very difficult time in their foreign policy; they have had difficulties with many nations, but I maintain that most of these difficulties are now settled, and that this question of China ought to be brought prominently forward, and more ought to be done than is being attempted at present. Now, what are the dangers with regard to the future? One is in regard to the position of Russia in the North; and the other is that there is likely to be very shortly a rebellion in China. There have already been rebellions there, but that there will be some more very heavy rebellions in the near future I have not the slightest doubt. There are two policies, as the right hon. Baronet has pointed out —one is the policy of the open door and the other is the policy of spheres of influence. From what I can gather from Her Majesty's Government they have been bellowing very loudly for the open door, but they have been working all the time for the spheres of influence. What the have really been doing is drifting, and doing nothing at all. I have heard it said that the Government are deceiving the people, and I want to corroborate it by saying that they have deceived me. When I went out to China I was absolutely certain that the Government policy was that of the open door, and not only to keep the door open, but to put the house in order on the other side. When I get home again I find from the declarations of the Government that they are certainly working towards the policy of the spheres of influence, and against the open door. Why, the two things are imcompatible, and you must have either the one policy or the other or else you will drift on to the rocks as certain as possible. I maintain that the people of this country do not know the importance of our policy in China. We must take into consideration that our trade of this country amounts to a total of £970,000,000, and I quite understand that the commercial classes of this country would think, if we were to interfere in a strong measure or upon lines which might bring about war, that, for the sake of the £35,000,000 of trade which we do with China, we might jeopardise the whole of the £935,000,000 we do with other countries. But I do not agree with the argument at all. If we had begun to lose our trade in China this country would certainly have been in a worse position than now. Now, what does that £35,000,000 of trade with China mean?

THE SECRETARY OF STATE FOR THE COLONIES (MR. J. CHAMBERLAIN, Birmingham, W.): I think the noble lord said the trade of China was £970,000,000.

LORD CHAS. BERESFORD: No. I said that £970,000,000 was the total trade of the Empire. My point was that, taking the £35,000,000 from the total, it left £935,000,000 as the amount of trade we do with other countries, and those people who were interested in the larger sum might be disinclined to do anything which might jeopardise that trade by doing something with the object of protecting this £35,000,000. Now what does our trade with China represent? If I take the cost of the raw material and what the merchants provide, it will about represent the wages and rent of 350,000 people in this country. That, I think, is a very fair computation, and if I am not right I hope some hon. Gentleman with a more technical head than I have will correct me. With reference to the open door policy I maintain that the door is closed now. I maintain that directly you allowed the Russians to interfere with purely commercial enterprise, as they did in the case of the Shanghai-Kiang Railway, the open door was as effectively closed as if you had put a tariff on our goods. What happened? I asked my right hon. friend below me if all was true that I read in the Blue-book, for in that book it is perfectly clear that the British Minister told the Russian Minister at Pekin that the British Government would not tolerate any interference with the contract made between the British Corporation and the Chinese Government with regard to this railway. My hon. friend says that the British Corporation agreed to this interference; but they did nothing of the sort. The Corporation agreed because the Government told them to scratch out two clauses which the Russians ob-

Lord Charles Beresford.

jected to, and it was on that objection that our Minister said that the British Government would not tolerate any interference. I have said once or twice before—but it has been made out that I am wrong—that our treaties had been completely broken in China, and absolutely broken. I was told that I was altogether wrong, but if hon. Members can understand this book they will find on page 7, in Dispatch 14, from Mr. Balfour to Sir Charles Scott, that the First Lord of the Treasury himself says:

"An undoubted breach of our treaty rights with China is involved therein,"

that is to say, if the Russians persisted in this matter of interfering with commercial enterprises. Mr. Lessar said that he did not deny that what was contemplated constituted a breach of the treaty; but what was contemplated was carried out, and the Tien-tsin Treaty has been broken with regard to the Shanghai-Kiang Railway. Therefore we have no rights either in Shantung or Manchuria according to the treaties in force. That is absolutely so. By the treaty I have alluded to we were allowed to have those rights in Manchuria, but those rights have been absolutely nullified now, because Russia has told us that we must not go there. Now I come to the open door. Upon this policy the Government have certainly "taken in" one of their most energetic supporters. There was nobody so violent as the Chancellor of the Exchequer upon this point, for he was prepared to fight for the open door with great violence. The right hon. Gentleman said so in his speech. Now I come to my right hon. friend the Secretary for the Colonies, who was going to arm himself with a "long spoon," and he was all for the open door. Then I come to the First Lord of the Admiralty, who was more vigorous than anybody else over the open door.

*THE FIRST LORD OF THE ADMIRALTY (Mr. GOSCHEN, St. George's, Hanover Square): I never spoke about it.

LORD CHARLES BERESFORD: What did he do? Why, he came down here and asked the House to vote four battleships, four cruisers, and twelve torpedo boats. What for? Why, to protect our trade and commerce, and our trade and commerce cannot exist without the open door. Surely that is an argument on my side. Well, I do say that very big words were used, and I say that with regard to China we have seen them followed by very small deeds. It would have been better if the Government had done something in a strong, clear, and definite way which everybody could understand, than to have done nothing whatever. Now, the right hon. Baronet has made an allusion to a statement of mine, but I do not think that I ever used the word "alliance." I was very careful not to do it in America, because I knew that I should be metaphorically jumped on immediately. There has been no suggestion yet made to solve this problem of the future between China and this country. My suggestion was that the four countries—Great Britain, America, Japan, and Germany—should go to the Chinese and say: "We have got so much trade with you, and we will ask you to allow us to take over your army and we will put it right for you." It would be a Chinese Army with probably an Englishman at its head, but I do not see anything very absurd in that. I have only suggested that you should do in the case of the Chinese Army what you have already done with the Chinese Customs. You have a British man over the Customs, and why should you not have a British man over the army? I must say that, in speaking with members of other countries, I found both the Russians and the French were equally friendly towards my object. The mission I went out upon on behalf of the Associated Chambers of Commerce was to be as friendly and conciliatory as possible with everybody in that country, and I found that they all agreed with my proposal. I may be asked, why did I leave out France and Russia. I did so because I am a business man. France and Russia have no trade in China, and why should we ask them to come and help us to secure our trade? But even under this proposal France and Russia would be offered an equal opportunity to create trade, an opportunity which they do not possess now. It has been said that Germany would not join in this suggestion; but supposing I had not included Germany, all those people who oppose this scheme would have said this was a mischievous proposal, and that I wanted to get England, America, and Japan against the whole of Europe. The reason why I put

in Germany was that she has a trade there already, and I may inform the House that I have the most complete sympathy of the German merchants out there with the idea which I suggest. I do not know whether the Government has tried this suggestion with other countries. They know more about it than I do, and I imagine that they may have approached them. If they have, and these countries have proposed to join us, then the Government should let the people of China know this. I think we should do what we have always done before whenever we have had any of our interests in danger, that is, we should take the lead and then the other countries will be sure to follow. I am quite sure that the Americans will follow. But in Japan I got a most distinct intimation from many people that, if Great Britain led, Japan would certainly follow on this question. There is another point about the open door. Under the proposal I made it would not cost this country anything to leave the door open. The finances of China are ample. The Budget has already made provision for defence, and the arsenals and the army would also be amply provided for. If the money was expended as was intended, we would not have to pay a single shilling extra for getting this army into order. And it would give equality of opportunity to all nations. The open door would not cost this country one shilling. But I am absolutely certain that if we drift into spheres of influence we shall drift into war, on the face of it. Because if you go into spheres of influence you do away with the properly constituted Chinese authorities, and what are you going to put in their place? You will have to send troops there to maintain order and look after your trade. Now, let me refer to this precious Agreement. First of all I understand Russia proposed the Agreement. And what for? At the moment she proposed that Agreement there was a good deal of irritation in this country about the Shanghai-Newchwang Railway. Russia has extremely clever diplomatists, and they know that there is a magic word in this country, and that word is "peace," and they thought that if they put forward this Agreement it would be an Agreement on all questions, and that it would take in our own people immensely. They put forward the Agreement on account of the disturbance amongst our people, but they were astonished to find that our Foreign Office jumped at it with the greatest avidity. Russia by that Agreement forbade us to go to the north side of the Great Wall; but why didn't we, directly that Agreement was proposed to us, propose something that would be advantageous to ourselves? There were two things which would have been of great advantage to us. One was that Russia should not under any circumstances have put on preferential rates on the railways. The other was that a definite definition should be made of that part of the Yang-tsze country to which we were supposed to have some right. It would hardly be believed, but the Foreign Office never suggested these things at all, and it was not till a month afterwards that these things were suggested to Russia. It is again hardly to be believed that both these points were refused by Russia. There is a despatch in the Blue Book in which Lord Salisbury referred to what these spheres should be—the Yang-tsze and the provinces of Ho-nan and Che-kiang—but there is nothing whatever in regard to preferential rates. Then there is another point. Directly the Russians found we were so anxious to come to this agreement, they secured a great number of delays—everybody had something the matter with him, or someone had gone on holidays, or something of that sort. At any rate, they delayed answering the questions put to them, and, so far as I can make out, it was seven or nine months before the Agreement was signed. Now, why did Russia object to the insertion of these conditions? It was because, when the time comes when she is in a proper position to put on these preferential rates, she will do so. I should like to do away with all these questions of sentiment. We blame other countries for putting on protective tariffs. Why should they not? Other countries know their own affairs best. We have gone in for the open door and Free Trade, because it is best for our people and for our commerce. They put on their tariffs because it is best for them. If they did not put on their tariffs everyone of these countries would be over-run with English and American travellers, and they would not have a chance with us and the Americans at our own trade. At the same time we should do all we can to try and keep the door open wherever we can.

Lord Charles Beresford.

There is another point. My right hon. friend the Under Secretary for Foreign Affairs answers questions. Now, I object to the way he answers questions. Sometimes we really want an answer to the questions we put, but the way in which my right hon. friend answers them is much more suitable to the nursery than to the House of Commons. It is the way of the Foreign Office and some of their people whom I have met abroad. I met a gentleman, who was not the Minister at Pekin, but who was associated at Pekin with the Foreign Office. I said to him, "How very badly things are going on in China," and he replied, "Not at all; they are going on very well indeed."

*Mr. BRODRICK: Hear, hear.

LORD CHARLES BERESFORD: I said, "I have just read the Blue Book, and I have never read anything so shocking"; and he replied, "Oh! you Members of Parliament must know that there are a great number of matters that we don't put in the Blue Books." I said "You want me to believe that the Government put in the Blue Books everything against themselves and keep up their sleeve everything that tells for them." The Foreign Office appears to me like this sort of thing; that if London were occupied by the French, they would say it was the best thing under the circumstances. What I want to point out is that Lord Salisbury himself has been perfectly open about the matter. He has told us that there is nothing whatever in it, or words to that effect. I may say that he has laughed at the whole thing in a diplomatic way. Here is what Lord Salisbury himself says: "Her Majesty's Government cannot but note the scanty dimensions to which it has been reduced by these long negotiations." He knows perfectly that there is nothing in it, or in any other Agreement that Russia should think of making. Russia never made an Agreement yet except for her own advantage. She does not break the Agreement at once, but waits till the time is suitable. In saying this I do hope the Committee will not misunderstand me. I don't blame Russia one bit. We know what her policy is. But I do blame the people who are continually taken in by that policy. And they will be taken in again. Russian diplomatists are very clever, and they have a policy. They go across frontiers a long way, and whenever a remonstrance is made, the Russian general goes back, but he never goes back to where he came from, but remains a long way on the wrong side of the frontier. While Lord Salisbury was laughing at this question, the Cabinet were most triumphant; and when I heard the First Lord of the Admiralty bringing out all the advantages and benefits to trade and to the peace of the world, and all the other things that were going to come out of this Agreement, the tears came into my eyes. I must say that I agree with Lord Salisbury. I do not think that there is anything in that Agreement which is worth anything. In that Agreement, which we have signed, the Russians have a right to run a railway to the south-west of Pekin. We see in the Press—and I always believe the Press—that this is a fact, and that if Russia does run that railway it will compete with a railway in which British capital has been invested on the faith of Chinese assurances as well as those of our own Government that it would not be interfered with. If that railway is made I want to know what is to become of the large properties of the Pekin Syndicate, and what will become of all that English capital which has been invested there. Moreover, what will become of that country which is not designated the Yang-tsze region, which has no boundary, and about which no agreement has been come to with Russia? I hope the Government will put their foot down on this question if on nothing else. We gave over to Russia the Newchwang Railway, I suppose, for the sake of peace. Why should not Russia give in to us about the railway to Pekin? If the railway goes to Pekin, Russia must dominate the whole of China, and that would become a more serious question than anything else for this country. My own opinion is that if our Government would put their foot down over this question they would find that Russia would not make the railway. I believe that it is a very clever bit of diplomacy. I do not think they ever intended to make the railway, but that they imagined we would object to it, and that they would be able to say on some other occasion, "You see how we gave in when you objected to the railway to Pekin." Take the other point of policy which was conveyed in the term "spheres of influence." I object altogether to the proposal as to spheres of influence, and I shall oppose it with all

my might as long as I can. I believe that every man in China, every corporation and every single member of every commercial community—and they know their business there—would do everything they can to oppose the policy of spheres of influence, towards which the Government are most certainly drifting as fast as they can. And I will give some reasons for my position. If you have spheres of influence you cannot have everything. You will have to give up a large amount of your trade sooner or later. You cannot say to a nation, "That is your sphere of influence," and dictate to them what they are to do with it. We have never been able to do it yet. And you invite a hostile tariff if you go in for spheres of influence. Look at Madagascar, Indo-China, and other places, where they invariably put on a tariff against your trade. Let us see how our trade in China goes. Our total trade with China is 35 millions. Thirteen millions of these are with the provinces of Kwang-si and Kwang-tung, which are in the French sphere of influence; and $3\frac{1}{2}$ millions are with Manchuria, which we might as well at once acknowledge as Russian. There is no sentiment in this country which can drive the Russians out of Manchuria, but I believe there is a great and a growing sentiment that we should have a definite policy in China; that we should know what we intend to allow Russia to do, and what we intend to do ourselves. Under the sphere of influence policy we should lose Chifu, Tien-tsin, and Newchwang, the trade of which is seven millions sterling, equal to that of seven of the ports in the Yang-tsze Valley. That will give some sort of idea of what we stand to lose if we adopt the sphere of influence policy. There is even a greater objection than that. There is no doubt that with a sphere of influence we must have military occupation. I do not believe anyone in this Committee or even in this country wants to see one single acre added to the British Empire. That is the opinion on all sides of the Committee, and it is a common-sense opinion. Our Empire is too big now.

AN HON. MEMBER: No.

LORD CHARLES BERESFORD: Who says no? I will ask the hon. Member who says "No" a question. Supposing we had disturbances in the Cape and in

India, and that at the same time we had some bother with another country as we were likely to have had in France recently, those disturbances would not be naval but military questions; and, even if we had conscription, would we have enough of men to settle them? We would not. Therefore I maintain that our Empire is quite big enough—in fact, it is too big—already; and anything we can do to avoid adding to our spheres of influence or our domination of any character must be for the benefit of the Empire. There is one solution of the difficulty in China, and that is to manage the army on exactly the same lines as the Maritime Customs are managed. There is no difficulty in it whatever. On the question of men, the population of the provinces which we are supposed to have under our sphere of influence is 176 millions. We could send out at this moment about 30,000 troops, and that is all, unless the Reserve is called out. I daresay it may be said that I am unpatriotic. I was told that before, when I showed up the weakness of the Navy, when the only people who did not know about that weakness was our own. It is the same now with the Army. The argument is, "We must not do anything now, because we have so few men." Where will we be in five years? Russia will then have 140,000 men; we will have still 30,000. Will the Russians be able to dominate us? I think they will. Then about our sphere of influence. I find we have been claiming what we have not got. I found in Shanghai that the French settlement was called "French soil." When I went to visit the Viceroy of Nanking his Excellency asked my advice on certain questions in which the French were pressing him. I said; "I am only a commercial agent, but as your Excellency is good enough to ask my opinion, I will give it to you very frankly. Do not give the French anything. Balance the point. If you give this to the French you will put the Europeans in Shanghai on one side and the Chinese on the other; because the Chinese are certain to riot, and they will be right to riot." One of the proposals of the French was to turn a native burial ground into an abattoir. If a riot breaks out in the East you never know where it is going to stop. I was not uncivil to the French. I said that I did not believe the chivalrous French nation really meant it, and that

Lord Charles Beresford.

the demand was only an exuberance of feeling which obtains occasionally in all nations. What could the French do? They could not bombard Shanghai. I do not know whether the Viceroy took my advice or not, but all I know is that the French did not get anything, and that the French Consul said if it had not been for "*ce sacré* Beresford" he would have got all he wanted. Han-kau is in my humble opinion the most important city in China. It is the Chicago of the future. It will have the rail head from north to south, and it has got great waterways. Our interests in Hankau are very small compared with the interests of France and Russia. They got all they could. They have taken our property and put it into their own concessions, notwithstanding that our Foreign Office stated that no British property was to go into a Russian concession without the consent of the owners. But what about the property of Messrs. Greaves and Co., Messrs. Evans and Pugh, Mr. Jardine, and Mr. Sassoon? I said to Mr. Pugh, "Don't make a row about it, but you must be very ill and you must put on your night-clothes and be carried out by Cossacks, and you will see the British public will take the question up." (Laughter.) Hon. Members appear to think there is some joke in that, but I think that it is a very serious thing indeed, and I bring it forward to show that the Foreign Office and the Government are not taking those steps for the protection of British property which the owners have a right to expect. I was again asked my advice. I said, "Put a fence around your property" but the others said, "The Russians will pull it down." I said, "Let them pull it down 40 times; then you will have something to go on." I believe my advice was sound, and I hope my right hon. friend will tell us what happened to Mr. Pugh's property and the other properties. I should like to say a few words about the railway question. Everyone recognises that railways are the greatest civilising agencies any country can have. I should be delighted if other countries constructed railways in China, or anywhere else where we convey our trade, provided they did not put on a differential tariff. But let us remember this about Chinese railways. We talk about British railways in China. There is no such thing. There are railways in China which have been built with British capital, but they are Chinese railways under Chinese administration, Chinese responsibility, and Chinese protection. But the Russian railways are altogether different. They are put down avowedly for strategical purposes, and they are under Russian supervision, Russian administration, and Russian protection. That is a very different thing from the so-called British railways, and if we have trouble with Russia, it will be greatly to our disadvantage to have the railways in the position I have described. With regard to Northern China we have not a single atom of counterpoise to Russian influence, which is increasing every day. As I have already pointed out, Russia has refused to put in any clause stating that she will not put on differential rates on her railways, and it is absolutely child's play to imagine she will not when her position is strong enough. One word about the condition of China itself. There appears to be an opinion in this country that China is utterly and completely rotten. I entirely deny that. I was most careful to go around everywhere. I saw all the big people in China except two. I visited six out of eight Viceroys, and I lost no opportunity of paying my respects to every big man I could. I found that the Chinese people are an honest and hardworking and thrifty people. There is not a more honest lot of traders in any country in the world than in China. I went to all the banks and I asked questions, and every single banker said that the Chinaman's word was as good as his bond. It is the system that is corrupt, and it is the system that breeds corruption. Is there any man in this Committee who would govern 70, 40, or 20 millions of people for a salary of £180 a year? The officials must be paid somehow, and the system plays on one of the worst passions of the human race. There are many excellent, splendidly patriotic, and honest men in China, but they are obliged to squeeze by the system. And yet many of the Mandarins and Viceroys are poor, though many more are very rich. But it is the fault of the system, and to say that the Chinese as a nation are corrupt is not right, especially when it is said by as chivalrous a country as this generally is on questions of this character. As to the question of troops, the Chinese would

make a splendid army. Their acts of heroism are very creditable, and when they are paid and fed and clothed properly they stick to their commanders, and are absolutely fearless on the battlefield. If the Chinese Army were taken over, as I suggest, it would be as fine an army as any in the world. The idea that it would be difficult to put China right is not accurate. It would be easier to put it right than Japan, and I will tell you why. In Japan you have vested interests, feudal interests, and a religion. In China you have nothing of the kind. In China there are no vested interests. A Viceroy or a general is only three years in a position, and no one knows who is to succeed him. Again, there are no feudal interests whatever, and as for religion, the Chinese worship their ancestors, which is a religion that does not produce that fanaticism which other religions induce. Therefore, if we asked Russia and France to help us in recognising the Chinese Army exactly on the lines of the Maritime Customs, I believe it would be the salvation of China's power. There is one serious point with regard to China, and that is that in pursuing the policy we are pursuing now we shall be absolutely certain to drive China and Japan into the arms of Russia; and where shall we be then? That is the position we are certain to get into. The Chinese say to themselves, "Here are two great Powers, one who is not afraid to fight if necessary, and another who is." One of the Chinese Mandarins said to me: "Your country is like an old man who has made all his money and wants to keep it, and is afraid of running any risk by which he may lose it. Is it not better for us to throw ourselves into the arms of Russia, and trust her, rather than trust to you, our old friend, who are now trying to break us up?" What do the Government at this moment trust to? So far as I can make out they are trusting to the Peace Conference. I have a great respect for the theoretical part of the Peace Conference, but for the practical result I have none. The essential thing for Russia at the present moment is peace. Russia knew our country would take any step and make every effort in the direction of peace, and knew that we would go to the Peace Conference, and therefore it was that it was proposed. Why will not our people be practical, and instead of looking at theoretical sentiments look at the practical position? What has Russia done within a few weeks before the Peace Conference? In the last two years she has sent 22,000 troops through the Suez Canal to China, 22,000 more than she has brought back, and she has added 9,000,000 tons to her fleet. Here is the point — are we to believe all the assurances that are given to us by a country which cannot even keep the promises she makes to her own people? What is the case of Finland? The Finnish army is altogether 9,600, 5,600 with the colours and 4,000 in the reserve, and Russia promised that it should not be increased. Now it is to be run up to 125,000 in order to replace the troops that have gone out to Manchuria, and those which are going. The Coronation oath of 1889 promised that the Army should be increased no further, and that no Finnish troops were ever to be brought out of Finland. Now they are not only to serve in Russia, but Finland is to pay the whole of the expense, in spite of promises made in the Coronation oath of 1889. Let us look at the facts; we need not be rude, but let us look at the facts. What I think about the Government position is this. I quite admit that the problem is immense and very difficult, and I will work with all my heart and soul to keep the peace, but if we are going on as we are going on now we must drift into war, and when we do we shall find ourselves at a disadvantage. I think if we show true courage in this matter, and having stated our views are prepared to back them up, we shall have peace. I do not believe Russia can fight at this moment. That is my opinion. We do not want rashness, we want true courage, and if we attempt to tide over great difficulties, and do not attempt to solve them, we are certain to enlarge the difficulties. The Government can condemn my suggestions and my policy, but they cannot deny obvious facts with regard to Russia and our danger in China. We have had enough of this policy of drift, or what I may call a "pipe down" policy. We drifted into the Crimean war, the Egyptian war, and into the Soudan war. If the Government had only listened to the man in command then— I allude to General Gordon—we should have had none of the Soudan war, and none of the expenses which it has entailed. Let

Lord Charles Beresford.

us not drift into another Chinese war, let us have a definite policy, and let us have the policy put before the country itself with resolute courage. We need not be rude; things can be done in a conciliatory manner; but let us let other countries know what we are going to do, and then let us do it.

*Mr. BRODRICK: I do not think there will be any difference of opinion among members of the Committee as to the character of the speech we have just heard from my noble friend. We always listen to my noble friend with the greatest possible interest in this House. He has spoken this evening with his usual wit, with a great deal of imagination, and with an intimate knowledge, from his own standpoint, of the subject on which he has addressed us. I must say, on behalf of the Government, that I think we owe him some gratitude in this respect, that, unlike some Members who attack the Government—and I think we must treat my noble friend's speech as having been almost from first to last an attack, certainly one of criticism and attack—he endeavours to look at the question of China as a whole. He has a policy of his own, and is quite ready to take responsibility in regard to it. So far, we are entirely in favour of the way in which my noble friend has treated the subject, and we are grateful to him for the valuable statistical information he has compiled, and we feel that in his visit to China he did a great deal of good. First of all, he very much impressed the official classes with his own personality, and, secondly, he diffused around him, especially among the merchants—who, he told us, were very much in need of it—that cheerfulness and geniality which he always diffuses, whether he speaks in this House or outside. The cardinal point in my hon. friend's speech was the one item of commerce. My noble friend told us more than once in the course of his speech that he was making a commercial speech. I confess I thought that in many parts of his speech he was uncommonly near leaving the department over which my right hon. friend the President of the Board of Trade presides and calling in at the department of War. My noble friend made a fighting speech, full of strategy from beginning to end. He carried that out even in China, when he advised the man who was going to be evicted to put on his nightshirt and become ill. But he did in China exactly what he has done to-night. He arrived in China with the undoubted countenance and confidence of the Chambers of Commerce. He announced himself in every place that he visited as having come on a purely commercial mission. But the fighting spirit, the old Adam, is very strong in my noble friend. Before he had been in China four days he had begun upon the most crucial question he could attack. He arrived on October 16. He visited the Yamên on October 20, and, as he tells us in his admirably compiled work, four-fifths of his first conversation was entirely spent in advising the Yamên as to a complete reorganisation of their army. At their second meeting, apparently leaving all commercial questions on one side, they went into the question of reorganising the army, and the Yamên offered him 2,000 men to experiment upon. I notice that those 2,000 men were not those who were massed near the capital, but were in more or less distant provinces which they thought my noble friend was likely to go into after some period of time. By a natural sequence of thought he told them that the central Government was very weak, and might require to be supported. I have sometimes thought whether those conversations did not somewhat interfere with the commercial mission of my hon. friend. But in the East an army is not always considered from the point of view of defence from invaders, but is looked upon more as an admirable instrument for carrying on an arbitrary government comfortably within. (Hear, hear.) During the rest of his tour my noble friend gradually lost more and more of his commercial surroundings.

LORD CHARLES BERESFORD : No.

*MR. BRODRICK : When he arrived in the Yang-tsze Valley—I am sure he will not deny this—he was received with almost royal honours. He travelled in a Chinese man-of-war; he was saluted by the forts and by the fleets; the streets were kept clear for him by foot-soldiers; cavalry were massed for his reception; Viceroys received him bowing and with proper reverence for his exalted rank and the mission on which he had come. Through all this circumstance and pomp my noble friend went forward with all the consciousness of commercial predominance. The idea of certain Orientals is that the greater reception you give a man, the more cordially you agree to his advice, the sooner he will be apt to remove his somewhat dangerous personality from their district to that of somebody else. He received magnificent receptions. But I am afraid that, when he tells the Government that they have indulged in big words and have only got small results, I must retort on him that, although the reception of his advice was almost unlimited, the results which have come from it have hitherto been almost *nil.* And, although that does not in the least derogate from the position he has a right to take in this House, I think we must admit that in China my noble friend's mission, so far as the advancing of our trade is concerned, did not go very far. But he came back with a series of proposals which he desires the Government should discuss seriously. He says that capital is insecure in China. He tells us that the central Government must be supported and the army reorganised, that the open door must be kept open, and that these spheres of influence are of no use; and, above all, that in all this there is a great loss of British prestige. Now, Sir, what does my noble friend propose? I do not wish to occupy the House at great length, but what he proposes is practically a complete change of the whole government of China.

LORD CHARLES BERESFORD : I beg your pardon. I do not wish Great Britain to undertake the government of China, but the reorganisation of the military and police, so that there may be some security for our trade.

*MR. BRODRICK : Yes, but in his speeches elsewhere and the work he has contributed to literature, what he has asked for is not the reorganisation of the army and police only, but a reorganisation of the fiscal system of China. If there is any doubt about it, I can quote from his book. How are you to raise an army and carry on the police in all these districts which are not under control from Pekin? How can you reorganise the whole fiscal system, provide roads, posts, and telegraphs, unless you are going to take under your control the government of China? There are three ways of doing it—either by standing behind China and regulating her present Government; adopting my noble friend's plan, and joining other Powers in putting pressure on China; or taking the matter into our own hands. In his speech at Hong-kong the noble Lord said that in his view the future of China depended on an alliance between the United States, Germany, England, and Japan to preserve the integrity of China and the open door. Now he says France and Russia can join if they like. But he said Russia was not to be relied upon, and the policy of France was opposed to our own.

LORD CHARLES BERESFORD: So it is.

MR. BRODRICK: Now as regards the government of China through the Ya-mên. He says nothing is easier. His speeches teem with cases which show the weakness and inertness of the present Government in China. He tells us that the greater part of the administration in China is carried out by the Viceroys without regard to the central Government. The noble Lord said that in the war with Japan the Chinese Army was made up to a large extent of men armed with obsolete weapons and men for whom weapons could not be found. How are we to deal with these abuses unless we interfere in almost every portion of Chinese local and imperial life? Take the question of *likin*. If you are to adopt fiscal reforms in China, you must deal not only with the Customs, but with the *likin* at present exacted in the inland districts. Thanks to the efforts of Sir Claude Macdonald in getting the transit pass system enforced, goods coming from outside are, by one payment, free from the extortion to which they might be subject in the inland waters of China. It actually pays a Chinaman better at this moment on the Yang-tsze or the West river to export his goods and pay the cost of export and import, and pay duty both on export and import, and then pay the transit pass duty (12½ per cent.) rather than send them straight from one inland town to another paying the *likin*. To change this system would be to make a complete change in the whole fiscal system of provincial administration in China. I do not say it ought not to be attempted, but for foreigners to attempt it, and not the Chinese Government, would probably be an impossible operation; and when the noble Lord spoke of the Government of China two or three times as easy, as compared with Japan, I think he

Mr. Brodrick.

has not grasped the greatness of the problem with which he has to deal. What are the attempts you can make by means of other Powers? In the first place, what other Powers are you to invite? He spoke of Germany, the United States, and Japan. What inducements can you offer to a country like Germany to come into such an arrangement? If you could obtain a concert of all the Powers interested in China you might do a great deal. We have had experience of the concert of Europe in Crete. The House knows how long it has taken to obtain a general concert of the Powers in regard to the administration of Crete. Remember that any attempt of any kind in China must be made, as the noble Lord has pointed out, by Powers whose views are absolutely divergent, some having an interest in the "open door," others in obtaining a sovereignty over the spheres in which they have an interest. He does not believe in Russia and her policy, or France, but severely attacks them, and I think he is over-sanguine when he states the United States would join, since the only evidence we have from him here is that while in the United States he received no encouragement to believe they would join. Germany is one of the Powers that might have a great interest in China, but she has a much greater interest in not joining. To ask a Continental Power to join in an alliance for special operations in the East, from which her two nearest European neighbours are debarred by policy or some other reason, is in itself a most unwise operation. Surely the reply of Germany would be that her interest in Europe is a thousand times as great as any that she has in Asia, and she would not undertake any business in company with three Powers, two of whom, not being European Powers, are not able to influence to the same extent the course of European events. The noble Lord says he desires to see Great Britain use every effort to maintain the "open door." But if he wants it kept open I very much doubt whether he has shown absolute wisdom in so constantly pointing out the advantages we shall gain and the disadvantages other Powers must have by maintaining the open door. I think the policy of the open door, so long as we can make it good under the treaties, is one to which we must unflinchingly adhere. But, at the same time, if we want to obtain assistance in that respect, I am not sure that the open manner in which he speaks of it is the way to obtain it. We have only a third alternative—that Great Britain should undertake the task alone. He does not suggest that, but it has been suggested over and over again in this House that our representations to the Yamên should be treated as demands from which we cannot recede—that we alone of all Powers should press requests on the Yamên, which requests should be practically orders. If any other Power receives any advantage against which we protest, we are diplomatically beaten, but anything we ask must be granted. What position does that put us in ? It puts us in the position of claiming for ourselves what other Powers have, and for asking, not only concessions in the Yang-tsze Valley and basin—our special spheres of interest, but equal advantages throughout the rest of China. If we are to do that, we have to discover first how we are to retain these concessions when obtained. The first thing that would happen would be that an enormous force would be needed to occupy a railway being made against the will of a portion of the population. In Manchuria Russia supplies that force, because she has some 120,000 Russians there. How is it to be supposed we could maintain the necessary force to protect concessions throughout China ? We must act in this respect through the Yamên, if at all, and with the assent of the Chinese people. For us to attempt to govern China against the wishes of the Chinese people and with the open or occult hostility of other Powers interested in China, would be to undertake a responsibility which would be exhausting to the British Empire. It is asked, if we cannot control the Chinese Government, how can we secure that British interests all over China are not lost. The position in which we stand in regard to that I will state frankly. We cannot make the Yang-tsze Valley a province like Shantung or Manchuria, first, because it is infinitely larger, and, secondly, we are not prepared to undertake the immense responsibility of governing what is practically a third of China. If we do not do that, how then, it is asked, can you secure that you are not elbowed out completely ? My noble friend has told us that all the treaties under which we hold concessions have been absolutely broken, but I do not think he is correct. Of course the pre-

sence of a large Russian force in Manchuria may cause him to say that if Russia closes the door we shall not be able to reopen it, but up to this moment the Treaty of Tien-tsin has been observed, and no door has been shut. Our trade goes wherever it has gone before, and even to places where it formerly did not go ; and though my noble friend treats Russian promises as waste paper, we are bound to accept the assurances of Russian statesmen. No door has been closed, and, as regards access to the treaty ports in China, we hold the Chinese Government to the Treaty of Tien-tsin. We are ready to continue to do everything we diplomatically can to induce the Chinese Government to move forward for the benefit of the Chinese people. Upon this there will be no doubt in this country by those who have observed in the last eighteen months the immense amount of good that has been effected. New treaty ports have been opened, and we have promise of the inland waters being opened to steam navigation. In all cases where we have suffered loss from revolutionary movements we have been enabled to claim indemnity, and rioters have been punished, up to the last events in Hong-kong. It is therefore not to be assumed that diplomatic action in China is exhausted. The position as regards the Yang-tsze Valley is different. We have from the Chinese Government a promise not to alienate any portion of the provinces of the Yang-tsze to any foreign Power, and the Yang-tsze river is so far open that up to Nanking, 240 miles from the mouth, we are able to send, and are constantly sending, cruisers drawing up to 26 feet of water. Up to Han-kau, 600 miles from the mouth, we can and do send vessels drawing at high water 18½ feet and at low water 10 feet. We have fourteen vessels of various types and four cruisers available to proceed to Han-kau, a town that may in future become the Chicago of China. A thousand miles upward from the mouth of the river we can send gunboats drawing 6ft. of water, and even beyond that distance there is open water if we succeed in passing through the gorges. Although we are not prepared to police the inland parts of China, we are prepared to patrol the Yang-tsze river in order to protect our trade, and we are quite aware of the immense preponderance of British shipping and trade on the Yang-tsze. It is an essential part of the policy of the Government in the changes taking place in China that special protection for our trade in this region is assured, and we believe that that trade, large as it is, can be largely developed. At present it is hampered by every kind of restriction, and our efforts are directed to the removal of these difficulties. We are endeavouring to secure, and so far we have secured, that a full share of railway and mining concessions shall fall to British investors. Secondly, by means of transit passes we shall endeavour to provide that trade shall be free from undue taxation and exempted from *likin*. And thirdly, we are looking forward to the opening of inland waters besides the Yang-tsze and ports that are not now treaty ports to trade. In all these matters we must recognise the control of the Yamên, but that does not appear sufficient to properly protect our trade except in the large centres, and although we will not undertake to relieve the Yamên from the responsibility for the internal government of China, looking to the magnitude of the interests involved, we are not prepared to allow our trade to suffer. We propose, therefore, as regards the Yang-tsze Valley, to proceed as follows. We hold the Chinese Government to their undertaking not to alienate any of the provinces in the Yang-tsze basin to any other Power, and to permit the extension of the Burma railway into Yun-nan, which will connect us with Chunking, whenever British investors desire to make it—that is to say, whenever we demand the extension the Chinese Government will fulfil their pledge. We regard the improvement of the gorges of the Yang-tsze as a question, under arrangement with the Chinese Government, for British engineers. Experiments are shortly to be tried. We have at present three gunboats on the Yang-tsze river, besides such men-of-war as may be at Shanghai. We shall keep what force is considered necessary between I-chang and the mouth of the Yang-tsze, and we shall consider whether gunboats can be maintained above the gorge at I-chang. These measures will be purely precautionary, and it will be understood they are taken with the object of giving security to our merchants and traders. My noble friend has raised a very important question as

Mr Brodrick.

to how far we are diverging from the open door policy to the policy of spheres of influence. I, however, put the question rather differently, and I deny, on behalf of the Government, that we have abandoned the one policy or adopted the other; but I do say that I think the events of the last eighteen months should have taught any man who had studied what is going on in China that the method of carrying on operations and negotiations with foreign Powers interested in China by a duel in which the Yamên is the centre, receiving shots from both sides, is not altogether a desirable one. I do not think for a moment that we can regard the Yamên as a *quantité négligeable;* they are the Government of China in all matters concerning concessions to one Power or another, and it is necessary to go to them and take their authority; but I do think that the late recent Agreement with Russia, upon which my noble friend has been extremely severe, is not only a valuable Agreement but is in itself a happy augury for the future. My noble friend says Lord Salisbury had a diplomatic laugh at the Agreement, and said it had shrunk to modest dimensions, but knowing as I do how hard at work my noble friend has been since his return from China I am not surprised that he did not read the Blue Book with greater care. A few pages beyond he may see that Count Muravieff undertook an extension which has been carried out, and the expanded Agreement is that neither Power will ask for concessions in the sphere of the other or oppose a concession asked for by its neighbour. That is an important change, for it goes to the bottom of our policy and desire to come to terms with our opponents as to what is fair and just on both sides. Nobody supposes we can get a monopoly of the trade all over China; our object, like my noble friend's, is to secure our fair share. Beyond the Agreement which we have made with Russia, within the last few days English capitalists have, by Agreement with Germany, arranged for the construction of a railway to Chiukiang, which passes through the German sphere of influence and our own—Germany constructing that part of the railway in her sphere, and British capital constructing the more southern portion of the railway. Then we have the Agreement of 1896 with France in regard to the

Provinces of Szu-çhuan and Yun-nan. The object of that Agreement is to establish that the two Powers have the same interest, and we have agreed that there shall be no monopoly of concession, and that no concession shall be given which will keep out the other Power from trade or other advantages. Well, if we are to proceed by agreement and not by fighting, then I think we must put aside, to some extent, the policy of distrust. I do not deny that there has been distrust on both sides, and possibly legitimate distrust; at all events, we think so on our side. But is it desirable that every concession which is given to another Power, however remote from us, should be quoted in this House and out of it as a distinct loss of prestige on our part? That is the line which is taken up very often as regards these concessions, the results of which are often found to be absolutely different from the brief telegraphed summary which first reaches us. I believe that there is not only distrust on both sides, but the very feeling which animates the more interested of our fellow-countrymen in regard to what other Powers get in China is felt in regard to ourselves by other Powers, not only in respect of China, but of places almost all over the world. I read the foreign papers pretty closely, and I can say this, that you will hardly ever fail, in the course of a few days' reading, to find there the insinuation that, whether it is in Asia or Africa, wherever there is a scramble, we always manage to get the lion's share, not only in quantity, but we also generally contrive to get the tit-bits in quality. I am not sure, looking to the past history of Great Britain, that there is not some truth in that contention, and that from having been on the spot much earlier than other Powers, and having pushed our trade when trade was not so popular as it is now, we have obtained great advantages. But the past on either side is beyond recall, and if we are to have a new departure we must make it by dealing with doubtful questions in an amicable spirit, and by endeavouring to arrive at the conclusion that a fair compromise is not a bad bargain. In reference to what has fallen from my noble friend with regard to the railway proposed by Russia to Pekin, I do not think, although it has been stated in the papers that the Russian Government demanded a railway to

Pekin, that there is any truth in it, and I doubt whether any such demand has ever been made. But the Russian Government have a right, under their Agreement, to run railway branch lines in a south-westerly direction, if they can get such concession from the Yamén. Questions have been put to me on various occasions recently as to the effect of the railway connecting the Manchurian railway with Pekin, and the view which Her Majesty's Government would take of such an undertaking. I think I have made it sufficiently clear that Her Majesty's Government are inclined, as a general principle, to welcome any railways, by whomsoever established, or any operations on the inland waters of China which tend to open up China to the general trade and the commercial enterprise of the world. But the case of Pekin is undoubtedly different. Pekin is the seat of Government, and from Pekin edicts conveying utterances which are held to be semi-inspired are sent forth to nearly 400 millions of people. It would be certainly difficult for any of the Powers who are interested in China to acquiesce in the establishment in Pekin of a single great Power as a voice behind the Throne. Such a position would inevitably tend to the break up of China. It is obvious that if the edicts of Pekin were to be dictated by any one Power the tendency would be for the other Powers, who have spheres of influence, to turn those spheres of influence into spheres of sovereignty. This would be a result especially distasteful to Great Britain, which does not desire to obtain further territorial acquisition or a continental frontier, but which, at the same time, as we all know, has great commercial interests which we have no intention of surrendering. It is, therefore, in no spirit of jealousy, but simply in the general interest of China, that we must declare that we should be forced to advise the Chinese Government against any steps calculated to transfer the Government at Pekin to any other Power. Our position in this matter is very clear, because the issues are great. The proposal that has been offered to us this evening in my noble friend's speech might, if carried out, place us in that position to which I have referred; for if we were to control the army and the taxes we should not be far short of controlling the Government. But let me say one word before I sit down as to the difficulties which the Government have to face in dealing with this question. There is in this country great impatience at the delay, and a feeling which has found an echo in this House that the results achieved in China are very imperfect. I neither wonder at the one view nor cavil at the other. I think we ought to remember that Western methods are very different from those to which the Chinese are accustomed. You are dealing with superstitions and with the natural waste of energy of an Oriental Government which has undergone very little change in the course of many hundreds of years. You have mountains of prejudice to overcome and valleys of misgovernment to fill up, and in respect to this very policy which I have just sketched to the House it is one which ties our hands behind our backs. Consequently, there must be delays. In modern times there are two great Empires which have either broken up or are in the process of breaking up; the first has been dealt with by Europe, and the second has been dealt with by ourselves. In Turkey, for fifty years past, there has been held to be symptoms of inability on the part of Turkey to govern its provinces and to carry out the reforms which are demanded by Western civilisation. The Powers of Europe have addressed themselves to the task more than once or twice, and what has been the result? After 50 years some provinces have been detached from Turkey, but we can hardly say that the realms over which the Sultan bears sway are to-day administered in accordance with Western civilisation. We have ourselves experimented in a similar way with the great Empire of India, which is certainly not so extensive as China, has not so large a population, and is less homogeneous; but it is in some respects an easier task, because the complex nature of its population has made it more open to foreign invasion. In the course of some 140 years, however, we cannot see the end of our task in India, and there is still much to be desired there. Therefore I say, considering the great changes which have taken place in China not in 50 or 100 years or in 50 or 100 months, but in a period of much nearer 50 or 100 weeks since the first great change began when foreigners commenced to take any control of various spheres of influence in China—I do not think that what has been done since that time is a question either for impatience or still

Mr. *Brodrick.*

less for despair. On the contrary, I contend that the progress which has been made during the last 18 months is one calculated to give us confidence and hope. We have obtained the rights to open up the country, and we have also obtained from the Chinese Government the power to carry out extensions of our trade, and I hope that we shall not altogether waste our time and energy in struggles between the Powers who are carrying out this great work, but rather that we shall unite and work together not for the benefit of one country but for the benefit of all countries concerned. We have had very many other questions brought forward to-night, one of which has been a matter of severe comment by the right hon. Baronet the Member for the Forest of Dean. The right hon. Gentleman says that the incident of the slaughter of British soldiers at Waima was one in which we conspicuously failed, and for which we deserved the severest censure of the House of Commons. The right hon. Gentleman has continually applied to us such language in connection with Madagascar and also in connection with the minor difficulties we have had with the French Government. I notice that from time to time he has entirely ignored the replies which have been made to him on previous occasions. In the case of Madagascar, which was brought forward by him upon a previous occasion, the late Under Secretary for Foreign Affairs made him a very complete answer. Although I am not going to debate this question now, I may say that these difficulties have arisen out of arrangements which Lord Granville was responsible for making, and therefore, if these incidents are to be made points of attack between one Government and another, I say that the Government to which the right hon. Gentleman owes allegiance must bear its full share of responsibility. The right hon. Gentleman renewed all these attacks the other day on an occasion when I must say that I think his speech was positively grotesque. The right hon. Gentleman the Member for Montrose, speaking in the right hon. Gentleman's constituency, made a speech full of the highest anti-imperial sentiments, and complained of the number of questions raised in every part of the world, and urged the Government of Lord Salisbury not to be carried away by the entrancing vision of Imperialism. The right hon. Gentleman the Member for the Forest of Dean got up directly afterwards, and, by way of comment on his leader and colleague, proceeded to say that Lord Salisbury was not half Imperialist enough, and was constantly neglecting Imperial interests in all parts of the world. The right hon. Gentleman also said that if we had a more vigorous Foreign Minister we should occupy a better position than we do now. As to the point of which the right hon. Gentleman complains, I do not want it to be supposed for a moment that I speak with any want of sympathy with regard to this unfortunate assault made by the French, in pure ignorance, I believe, of the circumstances. But at the same time, without in any way admitting that they are not to blame, and without in the slightest degree detracting from what occurred, I will say that certainly nobody is less to blame than Lord Salisbury for compensation not having been given. The right hon. Gentleman himself stated that one suggestion after another had been made as to how the question should be treated—first, that we should deal with it as part of a general settlement, and, secondly, that it should be dealt with alone. Her Majesty's Government have, up to the last few days, been pressing this matter upon the attention of the Government of France, and we have the strongest hope that it will be brought to arbitration and duly settled. The fact that officers serving their country in West Africa have been subjected to attacks of that character, and have been killed, will hardly justify us in asking that their widows should be treated differently from those of other officers who have also been killed in action, because they were on duty at the time. We must consider what is fair and just, and if we can obtain from the French Government proper satisfaction for this unfortunate occurrence—I mean pecuniary satisfaction—we shall, of course, be only too glad to give the relatives of those officers the compensation which they seek.

Mr. HEDDERWICK (Wick Burghs): Will the right hon. Gentleman state the date of the last reply from the French Government?

*Mr. BRODRICK: We are now in communication with the French Government on the subject.

Mr. HEDDERWICK: Is it a year ago?

*Mr. BRODRICK: A great deal has been done by verbal communication and not by despatch, and I cannot give the exact date. The other questions touched upon by the right hon. Gentleman I may perhaps be excused from going into at this moment. He suggested that if the local details are under discussion in regard to Muscat, it is very curious that the foreign Office should not have been able to produce the papers. The local details are under discussion, and have been under discussion, as to what shall be done with regard to the coal store which the French desire to have in Muscat. The right hon. Gentleman knows that it is impossible to give the papers until the negotiations have been brought to an end. When they are brought to an end we shall be able to make a statement to the House. I am afraid that I have detained the Committee for too long a period, but in doing so I have had to travel over the whole of our policy in China. I can only say this, that we are most anxious to take Parliament into our confidence upon all questions relating to China. We know that it is a great strength to us to have the House of Commons behind us in this matter, and I trust that the House of Commons will appreciate the difficulties which we have to face, that they will not conceive it possible at the same time to treat amicably with foreign Powers and to begrudge them anything which they may obtain which may be of a valuable nature ; that they will not see in the concessions made in the nature of compromise that lack of courage which my noble friend suggests, but that they will credit us with resolutely pressing forward on a diplomatic course, but with sufficient support behind us, I think, from what has been achieved, to justify us in believing that in the future, by perseverance, by persistence, by watchfulness, and above all, by patience, we shall be able to preserve British commercial interests in China.

Sir E. GREY (Northumberland, Berwick): This debate, I am sure the Committee will feel, has already been sufficiently interesting, and there are probably other Members, with special knowledge on this important subject, who will greatly add to its interest. I shall not stand for very long between the Committee and those who wish to speak after me. Some things that the right hon. Gentleman opposite has said, I think, will make my task both a shorter and a pleasanter one than perhaps it would have been if he had been more reticent. I will first begin by expressing my obligation to the noble Lord the Member for York, both for his book and for his speech. Not that I agree with everything that he has written or has said, but he has brought into this question a brisk and keen interest which, I think, is thoroughly wholesome. In all these questions it is a great relief to have the drudgery of collecting statistics done by someone else, and the noble Lord has performed that drudgery and enabled us to have a most valuable book of reference at hand. I am glad to feel, too, that the right hon. Gentleman opposite, in the very important statement which he made with regard to the Government's view of what might be done in China, has made a great advance in definiteness upon anything we have heard before. It has been a much more definite and businesslike statement, and as far as it went it was, I think, entirely in the right direction. I understood the right hon. Gentleman to have reaffirmed again that a cardinal part of the policy of Her Majesty's Government is the independence of the Government at Pekin. I understood one part of his speech to be devoted to reaffirming that in set terms. Well, we are all agreed that that is very desirable ; but a condition of the independence of the Government at Pekin is that it should be able to keep order in its own country. If no other foreign country is to step in and exercise a predominant influence at Pekin, they must not have excuses for interference. But hardly a month passes without our hearing that some demand is made at Pekin for compensation by some foreign Power because the Chinese Government has not kept its local officials and populace under control in different parts of that great country. It is essential, if the Government at Pekin is to remain independent and grow stronger, that, though it may be difficult for it to adopt Western methods, it is absolutely necessary that it should learn to approach more to Western methods than it has yet done. And I cannot help

Sir E. Grey.

feeling that if the policy of the independence of the Chinese Government in its own house is to be preserved, it was rather unfortunate that the right hon. Gentleman should have to spend so much time in showing with great force the difficulties which attached to the policy advocated by the noble Lord the Member for York. The noble Lord has put forward as a policy the strengthening of the Government at Pekin, and he has stated a method by which he thinks it might be attained. The right hon. Gentleman pointed out with great force how difficult it would be to adopt these methods, and I fully recognise the great force there was in the criticism of the right hon. Gentleman as to some of the practical parts of the recommendations of the noble Lord. I assume that, though we cannot undertake obligations and responsibilities beyond a certain point, we should at any rate be perfectly ready to lend our advice and even to lend *personnel* to the Chinese Government if they would only ask for it and say that it was willing to make fair use of that advice and give a fair chance to such advisers as we lent. Apart from those points I differ entirely from the noble Lord with regard to the policy of having an agreement with Russia. I willingly recognise that in carrying out this agreement with Russia Her Majesty's Government have our sympathy, that we give them full credit for the earnestness that they have shown to bring the negotiations to some satisfactory conclusion, and I will go further and say that they have our sympathy in the trouble which they have evidently had in coming to any conclusion at all. The noble Lord the Member for York says this Agreement is not worth anything. I differ from that view entirely. He thinks it is not worth anything, because he thinks Russia will not keep that or any Agreement. Of course, if there is to be bad faith on the part of any Government with whom we are closely concerned in Chinese affairs, there will be trouble. But the Agreement does remove one chance of trouble ; it brings affairs to this point, especially if it is followed up by extending the scope of the Agreement to other matters—that if there is trouble, it is trouble entered upon deliberately by one of the two parties to the agreement. At least one of the dangers of which we have been most afraid is that of causing trouble between Russia and our own country in the Far East, and as the two Powers were drifting in the same direction, it would take very careful steering to avoid their coming into collision, and apparently there was no communication going on between them, no interchange of views as to what their respective courses were. The only way in which a collision in the Far East between Russia and ourselves can be avoided is by frank communication as to the course which each country believes it to be in its own interest to take. I believe that if frank communication takes place trouble will be avoided, because the interests of the two countries can be mutually reconciled. I therefore welcome this Agreement, not so much for what is contained within the four corners of it, but because it is the beginning of a policy of frank communication between the two countries, and because at last we are getting into the habit of discussing matters directly with each other instead of through the Government at Pekin, which must be an unsafe thing to do. But although the Government have my sympathy in the trouble that they have encountered, I think it is partly their own fault that they have had so much trouble, because in order to get an agreement with Russia you have to overcome prejudices naturally created, at any rate in a large section of Russian politicians, by 50 years of previous policy. You have to overcome that prejudice in order to bring them to an agreement at all, and you have to convince them first of all of our good faith, and to convince them that it is to their own interest to have an agreement. When our ships were at Port Arthur, as the right hon. Gentleman the Member for the Forest of Dean said to-night, and when the suggestion was first made that we should move our ships, we had the greatest opportunity that could possibly have been brought to us of persuading Russia, first of all, that we meant to deal fairly by her, and, next, that it was to her own interest to deal with us. That point, I know, has been made several times before, but it has never yet been answered. It has sometimes been misrepresented, as if we had urged that Her Majesty's Government should have kept the ships at Port Arthur, and should have told Russia that it was done in order to prevent her ever having an outlet to the sea. We never meant them to be used in that way. We

regarded this opportunity which came to us at Port Arthur as a great lever for removing the dead weight of suspicion, of reluctance, and of indecision which the Russians have shown towards us, and if you throw away a lever of that kind you find the task very much harder than it would otherwise have been and the results proportionately less. All through these negotiations there have been continual delays, but I do not think they are to be entirely attributed to suspicion. Some of the delays were due to genuine geographical ignorance on the part of those who were actively engaged in the negotiations on both sides. But if the Russians were suspicious, that was not very unnatural; because, as I understand, their object was that they should have a free hand in Manchuria, free from the interference of other Powers with their aims there. At the very time when we were pressing for a settlement with them on the point, we were also pressing a claim for a railway to be made by British capital to go into their sphere of interest in Manchuria. I am not surprised that when they found us advancing these two apparently inconsistent aims at the same time they should think that we had some ulterior object in view. The whole history of the case enforces what was well said, that the negotiations should be direct, and that we should not have two Powers, one and the other, bombarding Pekin, without entering into negotiations with each other; that they should not each have two opposite policies in mind, and that the actions of the representatives of each should be consistent. If I were to make a criticism as to the lesson to be learned by the Russian Government from the negotiations, I should say that it was that it should be more careful that the action taken by its representative at Pekin should correspond to the action at St. Petersburg. The policy of not letting the right hand know what the left is doing may be justifiable in certain circumstances; but it has been carried too far. But now that the British Government have shown their wish to discuss the matter in St. Petersburg, both the Governments should be careful that the action of their agents at Pekin should correspond with the action in St. Petersburg. I welcome that agreement both for its own sake and for what it promises in the future. As to our own special sphere of interest, the Yang-tsze region, we are all agreed that we do not wish to have more territorial responsibility in China—the responsibility of governing a vast extent of territory, and large masses of people. To my mind, one of the great dangers of spheres of interest is that they are so liable to bring with them direct obligations of a grave character, and that is why I especially welcome the policy of the Government in regard to the Yang-tsze. To patrol that great means of communication is within our power, without incurring any serious responsibility. It is likely to be more important and more effective, and to involve far less expense for the advancement of our rights in China, than the taking of Wei-hai-wei. I welcome these proposals of the Government, not merely because I believe they would be beneficial to British trade and British traders in the Yang-tsze region, but because the Government, in pursuing that line of policy, are giving us one of the best guarantees they can give that they are not pursuing a far more burdensome line of policy. Indeed, the Government have never made any secret that they are anxious to avoid territorial responsibility in China. But one thing occurs to my mind, and that is that we should not merely have a definition of the region of the Yang-tsze. If the Chinese have promised the non-alienation of that region, it is a concession that must not be made on paper only. If the Yang-tsze region is to remain the special happy hunting ground for British commerce, it is necessary that British capital should take advantage of the opportunities for investment offered by that region. What I have been a little afraid of is, that the Government have been devoting an undue amount of energy to other demands; that they are pressing for concessions in Kiang-Si—concessions in districts out of our reach, districts that are not approached by the river or waterway of the Yang-tsze, and where, if British capital were invested, and there were disturbances, we should find it difficult to obtain redress. Less effort should have been devoted to concessions further north, such as in the case of the Newchwang Railway, which caused a great deal of diplomatic inconvenience, and which certainly cannot lead to any very great development of commerce, except in that sphere of influence in the north in which Russia is to have a free hand. The importance of the railway concessions has not always been

Sir E. Grey.

admitted by Lord Salisbury in his speeches, and I think that there is some colour for the suggestion that Lord Salisbury has sometimes given the impression that we are exaggerating their importance. But, after all, railway concessions are important, for although the railways are not to be made at once, it is not likely to facilitate the making of the railways by urging that that is to be done by British capital alone. Then comes in the question of preferential rates. It appears from both the Blue Books that we have not made any great progress in regard to its settlement. I think on all these questions in regard to China that, although the Government have demurred to our criticism, we are entitled to say, considering everything that has happened hitherto, our criticism has not been exaggerated; but, on the contrary, has been exceedingly restrained. After all, this is not merely a battle of concessions. There has been a great change of late in the balance of influence and power in the Far East, and I have from time to time wondered how far the proposal which the right hon. Gentleman put before us to-night would have been accepted as satisfactory if we had been sitting on that side of the House, and the right hon. Gentleman had been sitting on the Opposition side of the House. I admit that many of the right hon. and hon. Gentlemen opposite were restrained in their criticism when the Liberal Government was in office; but I am afraid, Sir, that the state of incandescence to which some hon. Members on the other side would have been heated had we made an agreement of this kind with Russia, handing over Manchuria as their sphere of interest, would have been such that it would have been very difficult for their own leaders to appease them, even if they had made every effort in their power to do so. But we do not wish to make any criticism which would bring this China question into an active and prominent position in party politics. Only we have felt that the importance of the question made it necessary that the policy of the Government should be characterised, as the noble Lord the Member for York said, by clearness of thought and decisive action. And our uneasiness of late has been due to the fact that where the action of the Government has been decisive it has not been the result of clearness of thought. At the very moment when they were themselves anxious to enter on a policy of giving Russia a free hand in railway making, they took decisive action in regard to the Newchwang Railway ; but we do not consider that that was the result of any carefully thought out policy. Again, if they were anxious to make arrangements with Russia for an understanding, it was late in the day when they tried to obtain that understanding, and only after they had lost the best opportunity for doing so. The policy of the Government a year ago was to maintain not only the independence of China, but its integrity as well ; and yet, since then, very serious inroads have been made on the integrity of China. The very basis of this Agreement is an inroad on the integrity of China. Then there is the policy of the open door. That formerly included the right to press for concessions, but of late a certain amount of limitation has been put on it, and we have had to modify the right to press for such concessions in every part of the Chinese Empire. I confess I am not so hopeless as the noble Lord the Member for York in regard to the policy of the open door. I regret the noble Lord should have assumed that it is to the interest of Russia and France to have preferential tariffs in their spheres of influence. On the contrary, I do not believe that the experience of the French colonies shows that it is for their interest to have these high tariffs. Their experience has been that those high tariffs make any possession they obtain an expense to their own country. Although I do not see that it is possible to have anything like an alliance between the Powers interested in the Far East, there may come to be such a preponderance of opinion among them in favour of maintaining the open door in regard to tariffs as would lead to diplomatic pressure being brought to bear at Pekin to have portions of the Treaty of Tien-tsin applied in all parts of China. I consider the acquisition of Wei-hai-wei the most expensive part of the policy of the Government. Its acquisition was defended by Lord Salisbury not merely on naval grounds, but also, and even still more, on the ground that it would give moral courage to the Central Government at Pekin. I am still of opinion that the selection of Wei-hai-wei as a secondary naval base was wise, but I differ absolutely from the Government on the point that it would give moral

courage to the Central Government in Pekin. It has become perfectly apparent that it has not given that moral courage, and that it cannot do so, because it can never be regarded as a counterpoise to the consolidation of Russian power north of Pekin—a consolidation to which the new Agreement has given additional weight. Wei-hai-wei is occupied, and money is to be spent upon it, but it can never be a counterpoise to Russian influence in Pekin. All that the right hon. Gentleman has told us as to the plans of the Government about the patrolling the Yang-tsze River goes to prove that Wei-hai-wei is not the most satisfactory position which could have been chosen for practical purposes in respect to what is our great interest—the protection of British commerce in China. Well, we have had this anxiety with regard to what the Government has done, and we do not think that the best has been done ; we think that some valuable opportunities have been lost in the course of past events ; but I do welcome this Agreement with Russia for the sake of the relations between the two countries. I welcome what the right hon. Gentleman has told us to-night, as far as it goes, as a businesslike proposal, and one which is a considerable advance on, and more encouraging than, anything which has hitherto been heard of. In regard to the question of Madagascar, I think the right hon. Gentleman has gone too far in saying that Lord Salisbury's predecessors were responsible for what has taken place there. Right hon. and hon. Gentlemen are very apt to assume that the responsibility does lie on Lord Salisbury's predecessors for the present position of affairs in Madagascar. The recognition of the Protectorate took place in 1890. The right hon. Gentleman stated accurately that the notification of the Protectorate took place before 1890 ; but the recognition of the Protectorate had not taken place, and no action was taken in regard to it before 1890. The right hon. Gentleman is not entitled to assume that, because no protest had been made, Lord Salisbury was bound to make the bargain he did. My position is not that Lord Salisbury was wrong in recognising the Protectorate, but that the responsibility for the merits of the bargain in recognising the Protectorate is one that rests upon him and him alone, and that, with regard to what has happened since, the hands of succeeding Governments have been tied by the actual terms of the bargain Lord Salisbury made in 1890. A great deal of what the right hon. Gentleman said with reference to Waima appealed to me very strongly. It is undoubtedly a very hard case, and I would only say that, as far as we are concerned on this side of the House, the Government would have our sympathy and support in extending to it the most liberal treatment in their power. I know there have been great difficulties with regard to the case. I would like to raise again a point on this question which was referred to by the right hon. Baronet the Member for the Forest of Dean, in connection with the payment of £10,000 at the request of the French Government for losses sustained by French missionaries in Uganda. The right hon. Baronet criticised very strongly our action in making that payment without having got compensation for what had taken place in Waima. It fell to me to defend the payment of that £10,000, and I submit that when Her Majesty's Government undertook to pay the £10,000 to the French missionaries, instead of insisting upon the British East Africa Company paying it, they did so because they were dealing with the question, not on what they believed to be the strict and narrow ground of legal right, but because they wished to approach it on generous grounds. When I had to defend the action of the Government in this House, my defence was that there were two great countries, with very important questions and controversies between them, and it was not wise to haggle over smaller points ; that especially a case like this, where views differ, and it was a question of money payment, should be dealt with on broad and generous lines. I think the Government chose the better and more magnanimous part in paying the £10,000. I wish the French Government could have taken the same view ; and I hope, now that so much has been settled between the two Governments, the French Government may be able to isolate from their minds the payment of £10,000 which we made on their demand, though we were of opinion, and are still of opinion, that if the circumstances of the case had been strictly argued out, it was an exceedingly generous payment to have made. I trust that the result of this debate will be to impress upon the French Government how very similar, in the spirit in which it

Sir E. Grey.

may be treated, the claim with regard to Waima is to the claim they made on behalf of their own Catholic missionaries in Uganda.

*Sir E. SASSOON (Hythe): I am moved to interpose in the debate by the reflection that any contribution, however slender, by the humblest member of the Committee who happens to have some knowledge of China may be acceptable. I listened with unremitting interest and attention to the statement of the Under Secretary for Foreign Affairs in regard to China, and it certainly seems to me to be a great advance upon former statements of policy made by the Government. I was especially glad when the right hon. Gentleman said that Her Majesty's Government would strongly object to the removal of the capital from Pekin, and that they would hold the Chinese Government personally responsible for any alienation of territory in the Yang-tsze region. But I listened in vain for any statement as to whether my right hon. friend had in his mind any means of seeing that those engagements into which the Chinese Government have entered are to be fulfilled. Take the case of the Pekin and Hankow railway. While Her Majesty's Government were receiving assurances of non-alienation from the Chinese Government the present concessionaires of the railway cut in and obtain a contract for its construction in the very heart of our sphere of influence, and inferentially obtain exclusive rights over the whole of the land across which the railway would have to run. In regard to the revolt which took place in the Palace in Pekin, I deplore the countenance which was given by the famous tea party to the usurpation by the Dowager Empress of the Throne of the Emperor of China. If the information in our possession as to what was brewing fell short of enabling us to exercise some timely influence on behalf of the young Emperor, I submit that we ought certainly to have refrained from giving any colourable sanction to a *regime* which did not bode any good to China or to our own interests. I firmly believe that our Minister would have immensely increased his prestige and position if, cutting himself adrift from his colleagues in the Diplomatic body, he had abstained from acknowledging the machinations of an oligarchy mainly composed of corrupt and besotted reactionaries. I do not wish to minimise the signal services rendered by Sir Claude Macdonald when confronted by extreme difficulties. These difficulties he has surmounted by the exercise of undoubted skill, and tact, and resource. I believe, indeed, that Sir Claude Macdonald has done more for the interest of Great Britain in China than any other of our representatives. His opportune intercession in favour of Kung-Yi, the chief of the reform party in China, was the means of saving the life of that able man, a course that must redound to the credit and character of the British Envoy. The right hon. Baronet the Member for the Forest of Dean and the noble Lord the Member for York rather fell foul of Russia in the course of their speeches. They seemed to consider ill of its scope and probable effects. I frankly confess that a case might be made out for those who condemned Russia. I also admit that some economic or geographical causes in Russia, or, better still, the boundless ambition of many men in that country, might account for what has taken place. The ink was not dry on the compact between Great Britain and Russia in regard to China when proposals were made in Pekin which were in direct contradiction to the spirit of that Agreement. I say "spirit," because while we have engaged not to interrupt her schemes north of the Great Wall, for some occult reason or other a similar concession has not been made to us south of that Wall. I am inclined to ask the Under Secretary for Foreign Affairs how it is that that arises, and that the definition of the Yang-tsze region has been whittled down so much. What is the meaning which Her Majesty's Government attach to the word "basin"? Does it embrace all the territory watered by the Yang-tsze river itself, and its tributaries? My noble friend the Member for York has been good enough, in a speech characteristic of eloquence, to treat the Committee to the impressions he gathered during his distinguished commercial travels. He also presented us with an almost cut and dried scheme by which he expects to bring about the regeneration of China. It seems to me that the keystone of the edifice suggested by my noble friend is that we should enlist and mobi-

lise a solid phalanx of Chinese troops in order to prevent, I suppose, Russia or any other Power taking liberties with our rights in the Chinese Empire, or assailing India. I do not pretend to be able to say whether the latter contingency is chimerical, but I do say that with our present responsibilities in Egypt and elsewhere, my noble friend, with all his dash, will find it difficult to persuade the people of this country to undertake still further extensions and responsibilities in the manner he suggests. I hope that we are not destined yet awhile to witness a recrudescence of the state of feeling which Lord Salisbury 25 years ago described very aptly by the word "Mervousness." I should like to ask how the districts bordering on the Yang-tsze Valley stand. I take it that Russia, by means of the railway to Pekin, will be able to join with the French railway coming from the south-west of China, and running direct through the territory in which we are interested. The hon. Baronet opposite has also pointed out that no provision has been made against preferential rates or preferential treatment such as is certain to occur later on. I now turn to the other side of the shield. I congratulate Her Majesty's Government on the spirited effort they have made to secure—and very substantially to secure—British rights in other parts of China. The acquisition of Kowloon and Mirs Bay has immensely strengthened our naval and military position. Then again—I am sorry I differ from the hon. Baronet opposite—I think that the establishment of a port of arms at Wei-hai-wei as a counterpoise to the activity of another Power is another feather in the cap of Her Majesty's Government. The opening of another free port, and the vigorous stand made against the unjustifiable pretence of another Power in Shanghai are also matters on which the Government are to be congratulated. But all these would be eclipsed by any failure to uphold the integrity of the Yang-tsze Valley in its fullest sense. Already, as my noble friend has pointed out, there has been very serious attempts made to confiscate British owned property by the Russian and French consuls. At one port it was sought to confiscate property which was held and enjoyed ever since the port had been opened, and the right to which had never been questioned, but our Minister, with very considerable promptitude, went to the scene of these attempted depredations. Then, at Han-kau, which we are told is to be the Chicago of China, British merchants who had been established there for a whole generation have been interdicted from trading by Russia, and advised to move out of the settlement. Hon. Members who know anything of the fiscal system of Russia will not believe that British trade and enterprise in the whole of the north of China, or wherever Russian power is consolidated, will come in for anything but the shortest of shrifts, or have anything meted out to it but that preferential treatment to which I have alluded, and the effect of which will be to intercept all those advantages which the Treaty of Tien-tsin was designed to confer. You could drive a coach and six through that Treaty. I may mention one instance. The stipulation that Port Arthur should be reserved for the use of Russia and China is a distinct infraction of Article 52. That being the position, what is the remedy? The right hon. Baronet the member for the Forest of Dean spoke rather disparagingly of the prospects of an alliance between the three great Powers. The right hon. Baronet seems to think that it would not be to the interest of any of those Powers to enter into an alliance, or that they would be debarred by constitutional prescriptions. But the alliance I would respectfully urge the Government to enter into would be a defensive alliance. Those Powers have interests and rights in China, and if they are attacked they will be obliged to stand up for them. In my humble judgment a defensive alliance would have every prospect of duration. At any rate we cannot afford to ignore any consideration which would enable us to maintain our trade in the midst of all the rivalries which entangle the position in China. At present we appear, as far as China is concerned, to be in a state of suspended animation, or, perhaps more correctly, in a disembodied condition. Until the question of the Yang-tsze Valley is settled I would humbly urge the Government to stiffen their backs and to show the same leaven of grit and virility which they displayed with such conspicuous success in the North and on the West Coast of Africa, and even in China itself, when they made Count Muravieff withdraw his protest against the Newchwang loan, so that the

Sir E. Sassoon.

British flag may continue to be regarded as the symbol of liberty, security, and unrestricted freedom of trade.

*MR. JOSEPH WALTON (York W.R., Barnsley): It will not be necessary for me to occupy the time of the Committee by demonstrating that Her Majesty's Government have failed to carry out their announced policy in the Far East of upholding intact British treaty rights. The "open door" means, not only equal opportunities for general trade, but also equal opportunities to undertake commercial enterprises, whether the construction of railways or the development of mines. When Her Majesty's Government, unasked, conceded to Germany preferential rights in the great province of Shantung the open door was doomed, and then it became clear to everyone but to Her Majesty's Government that by this action they had made it inevitable that a similar concession must be granted to Russia in regard to Manchuria. I wish to refer to the recently concluded Anglo-Russian Agreement. Lord Salisbury, in his first public announcement of the conclusion of this Agreement, naturally minimised its importance, inasmuch as, in a telegram accepting the proposed Agreement in its general scope, on February 22nd, he remarks that "Her Majesty's Government cannot but note the scanty dimensions to which it has been reduced by these long negotiations." It is perfectly true that all parties in the country have strongly expressed the opinion that an agreement between Her Majesty's Government and the Russian Government in regard to China ought to be sought, and the announcement that such an agreement had been reached was hailed with satisfaction by the nation. When, however, the text of this Agreement was before us, we found that it was so limited in its scope that our satisfaction was greatly diminished. The object of this Agreement is stated to be "a sincere desire to avoid in China all cause of conflict where the interests of Great Britain and Russia meet, and to avert all causes of complications between them." I should like to examine the Agreement in order to see how far this most desirable object has been secured. In the first place Great Britain engages not to seek for her own account, or on behalf of British subjects, or of others, any railway concessions north of the Great Wall of China, and not to obstruct, directly or in-

directly, applications supported by the Russian Government for railway concessions in that region. In the second place, it is stated in the additional Note, that the present special Agreement is naturally not to interfere in any way with the right of the Russian Government to support, if it thinks fit, applications of Russian subjects or establishments for concessions for railways which, starting from the main Manchurian line, in a southwesterly direction, will traverse the region in which the Chinese line, terminating at Sin-ming-ting and Newchwang, is to be constructed. In reference to stipulation No. 1, I would draw the attention of Her Majesty's Government to the fact that in the earlier communications from the Russian Government leading up to the Agreement, all that Russia asked for was that England should undertake the same engagement in regard to Manchuria which Russia was prepared to give in regard to the Yang-tsze basin. I would ask why, in the Agreement concluded, the Russian sphere of concessions is defined as north of the Great Wall of China instead of simply as Manchuria, and whether this indicates that the Russian sphere is not to be regarded as limited to Manchuria. I would point out that, though we consider Corea as practically being an independent kingdom, the vagueness of the Agreement would appear to make it possible for Russia to contend in the future that geographically some portion, at any rate, of Corea is north of the Great Wall of China; and England has debarred herself in that area from undertaking commercial enterprises or supporting, directly or indirectly, the just claim of her natural allies the Japanese to preferential rights and privileges. This is an interpretation calculated to jeopardise the friendly relations and the co-operation of England and Japan in the Far East. Another serious defect in the Agreement is the absence of any exact definition of the limits, regarded as those of the Yang-tsze basin, which the Russian Government repeatedly stated it would be necessary to know before concluding the arrangement. In reply to a question which I put to the Under Secretary, the right hon. Gentleman said the Yang-tsze Basin comprised the provinces adjoining the Yang-tsze River and the provinces of Ho-nan and Che Kiang. To a second question as to whether Her Majesty's Government could

state exactly or approximately the point at which the Pekin-Hankau Railway would enter the basin of the Yang-tsze River I received the reply, "At the watershed of the Yang-tsze River." These two answers are clearly inconsistent, as it cannot for a moment be imagined that the boundary of the provinces to the north of the Yang-tsze River is identical with the line of the watershed of the river. What I therefore desire to ask the right hon. Gentleman is, whether the definition of the geographical limits of Manchuria and the Yang-tsze basin, as understood in the Anglo-Russian Agreement—which was to be fixed, on further examination, by a later Agreement—has yet been arrived at. Then with regard to the right of Russia to undertake the construction of railways starting from the main Manchurian line in a south-westerly direction. This stipulation cannot refer to railways north of the Great Wall, as in respect of that district the exclusive right of Russia to construct railways is clearly recognised in the first letter exchanged. The additional Note can, therefore, be only understood to apply to a district in China south of the Great Wall. And what I should like the Committee specially to notice is the fact that in the Agreement with Russia there is no understanding set forth calculated to avoid all cause of conflict where the interests of Great Britain and Russia meet in that enormous tract of territory in China stretching from the Great Wall southwards to the northern boundary of the Yang-tsze Basin. I hope, therefore, that we shall have a definite statement from the right hon. Gentleman as to what the arrangement really is in regard to this portion of the Chinese Empire. I would also ask the right hon. Gentleman how far in a south-westerly direction from the Manchurian Railway the right of Russia to construct railways is recognised. Already the Russo-Chinese Bank has constructed a railway 100 miles in length from Pekin southwards to Pao-ting; and the extension of that railway southwards to Cheng-ting is now proceeding. Russia has, again, the right to construct a line 140 miles westward to Tai-yuan-fu, and, according to repeated reports last year, also from that point a further line, about 330 miles long, to Si-ngan-fu, the capital of Shan-si, and a point, I may observe, only 200 miles north of the Yang-tsze river. The Russo-

Chinese Bank deny having made this application, but the Russian Government have made no denial. Russia will certainly desire to link up the railway system to which I have just referred with her Manchurian railways, and this means that she will not only dominate North China, but be placed practically in military occupation of the country southwards to the boundary of the Yang-tsze Basin. The importance of establishing herself at Singan-fu is apparent, when we remember that it is situated on the immemorial trade route to Central Asia, and it is the city which the Chinese Government have contemplated making the capital of China, if their position at Pekin becomes intolerable. I would further ask whether, in recognising the right of Russia to build railways in a south-westerly direction from her main Manchurian line, Her Majesty's Government did not obtain an assurance from Russia that the route of these lines should not be in such close proximity to the Pekin-Shanghai-Kwan-Niu-chwang line as would enable them to be in any sense competing lines for the traffic which would otherwise naturally come over the railway now being constructed with British capital. Her Majesty's Government sent special instructions last year to Sir Claude Macdonald to insist upon the insertion of provisions in all railway concessions securing equal treatment for British trade and British nationals. But I observe the Anglo-Russian Agreement contains no such provisions. This is the more unaccountable, inasmuch as Lord Salisbury telegraphed to Sir Claude Macdonald, on the 10th of September last, that preferential railway rates, or differential treatment, should of course be provided against in agreement with Russia in regard to railway concessions in Manchuria and the Yang-tsze region. I also find it stated in the Agreement that the two Governments have nowise in view to infringe in any way the sovereign rights of China or existing treaties. But I would point out to the Committee that, if ultimately territory in China be annexed by Russia, it will no longer be a part of the Chinese Empire ; and the rights which this country now enjoys under treaties entered into with the Chinese Government would be absolutely abrogated. I, therefore, ask the right hon. Gentleman whether any agreement has been arrived at with the Russian

Mr. Joseph Walton.

Government which will secure to each nation equal opportunities to trade in the spheres in which the preferential right of either nation has been recognised, not only so long as they remain integral parts of the Chinese Empire, but even after partition has taken place, should that come about. I think the Committee ought also to have some explanation of the support given by the British Legation at Pekin in sending a communication to the Yamén explaining that Russia had made no demand, but only a friendly request that China should concede in principle the right to build a railway to Pekin when applied for by Russian subjects. And I would draw the right hon. Gentleman's attention to the ridiculous position in which Her Majesty's Government were subsequently placed when the Russian Minister notified the Tsung-li-Yamén that—

"Russia is unable to regard Chinese wishes in the matter, and will send engineers to survey a line for connecting the Russian Manchurian Railway in the south-west to Pekin."

It seems to me that the China Correspondence (No. 2) just published, and the Notes exchanged between the United Kingdom and Russia with regard to their respective railway interests in China, most unfortunately demonstrate that Her Majesty's Government are still pursuing a policy of drift and of so-called "graceful concessions" which will result, in the long run, in serious injury to British commercial interests in Northern and Central China. A particularly humiliating diplomatic defeat is that sustained with regard to the conclusion of the Newchwang extension loan contract. On the 8th of August, 1898, Lord Salisbury informed the Chinese Minister that Russia had no right whatever to object to a mortgage loan being made by the Hong-kong and Shanghai Bank for the Newchwang Railway ; and he strongly advised China to pay no regard to the Russian Government's objection. And yet our Foreign Minister allowed himself to be driven to so completely abandon that position that the loan was concluded without any mortgage on that portion of the line north of the Great Wall. Such surrenders must of necessity entirely destroy the prestige and influence of this country with the Chinese Government. Perhaps I may be allowed to draw attention to what I consider is not an unimportant matter in connection with the negotiations which arose as to the New-chwang Extension Loan. I find that, after the negotiations had been proceeding for months, our representative in St. Petersburg had to admit his utter ignorance of the true locality of Si-nming-ting; and apparently no official map was in his possession showing distinctly the railway which was to be constructed by the proposed Newchwang Extension Loan; and it was only on reference to a map of Manchuria in Colquhoun's "China in Transformation" that our representative was enabled to ascertain the precise situation of Si-nming-ting. It is only fair to point out that a similar ignorance was displayed by the Russian officials. I only drew attention to this matter in order to venture the suggestion that it is high time our officials abroad were provided with the most complete maps, and the fullest information generally, whenever they have to conduct negotiations of so difficult and delicate a nature. In the correspondence just published between Her Majesty's Government and the Russian Government we have most startling evidence that Lord Salisbury, though he was a party to giving, unasked, to Germany preferential rights and privileges in the province of Shantung, did not seem at all anxious to secure similar rights and privileges for this country in the Yang-tsze Basin. In a letter to Sir Charles Scott on the 27th of February last, with reference to the proposal to limit the Agreement with Russia to simply imposing upon England and Russia the obligation of abstaining from opposing Russian and English railways in Manchuria and the Yang-tsze Basin respectively, Lord Salisbury stated :

"Her Majesty's Government, however, are not disposed to take any objection to the proposal, now made by Count Muravieff, on account of its more limited application. England and Russia will still each be bound to abstain from opposing railway projects of the other in its own sphere of interest, but they are not bound each to abstain from projecting railways of its own in the other's sphere of interest."

I must confess that I read these words with amazement. The only meaning they can bear is that Lord Salisbury had no objection to leave Russia free to undertake the construction of railways in the Yang-tsze Basin. It is true that he adds :

"This latter method of opposition is not one that is likely in either case to be adopted, but it cannot be said to impose any special disadvantage on Great Britain."

Having regard to the position thus taken up by Lord Salisbury in respect to the Yang-tsze Basin, the Committee is surely entitled to have from the right hon. Gentleman the Under Secretary of State for Foreign Affairs a clear and definite statement as to whether Her Majesty's Government claim any preferential rights or interests in the Yang-tsze Basin whatever, so that this country may know exactly where we are. As to Germany, the German Ambassador declared to Lord Salisbury that Germany had acquired "a special position" in Shantung, "whereas Great Britain, not having occupied any place in the Yang-tsze region, that region is still unreservedly open to German enterprise." In reply to a question in the House, the right hon. Gentleman stated that no further communication had been addressed to the German Government in regard to this matter. Unless an agreement be entered into, under which Germany will recognise the British nation as possessing similar preferential rights in the Yang-tsze Basin to those which we have conceded to Germany in Shantung, our interests cannot be regarded as by any means fully protected. It is most desirable that we should co-operate with Germany as far as possible in the Far East; but it would, I submit, be very foolish on our part to rely much on the assistance and support of Germany in China. It is obvious that Germany will not risk any conflict with Russia in the Far East which would expose her to attack on two frontiers in Europe, where she is situated between, so to speak, the hammer and the anvil, having Russia on her eastern and France on her western frontier. I do not know whether there is any truth in the rumour that the British Government are about to transfer Wei-hai-wei to Germany. I sincerely trust this report is well founded.

*MR. BRODRICK : No, Sir, there is no truth in the rumour.

*MR. WALTON : Well, I regret to hear it. I certainly had hoped it was true. Wei-hai-wei was taken, we were told, to restore the balance of power after Russia had seized Port Arthur, and to give courage to the Chinese Government at Pekin. But of what earthly use, I ask, will

Wei-hai-wei be to this country when Russia becomes practically in military occupation of North China, and probably of Pekin itself? I therefore earnestly hope that Her Majesty's Government will lose no time in getting rid of the white elephant of Wei-hai-wei, that they will abstain from spending money over it, and that they will, instead, take possession of some other position at or near the mouth of the Yang-tsze where our interests are predominant. Then, with regard to British commercial interests in the densely populated regions of Southern China, I have more than once called the attention of the Committee to the definite Agreement between the Governments of France and England, of January, 1896, under which each nation undertook to use its good offices to secure each for the other equal rights, privileges, and advantages for the prosecution of trade in the provinces of Yunnan and Szechuan. This Agreement appears to have been entirely disregarded by the French Government without, so far as the Committee have as yet been informed, any protest whatever having been made by Her Majesty's Government. A demand was certainly made upon the Chinese Government on the 25th of April, 1898, for an assurance, in writing, in regard to the provinces of Yunnan and Kwang-tung, similar to that given to France ; but, continuing the policy of drift which has so discredited British prestige in China, the right hon. Gentleman had to inform the House the other day that the assurance in writing had not yet been received, and was no longer being insisted on. A further important point, which may affect seriously British commercial interests in South China, is the position taken up by France with regard to the province of Kwang-si, in respect of which they have compelled the Chinese Government to enter into agreement as to non-alienation, ceding, or leasing. The right hon. Gentleman the Under Secretary for Foreign Affairs, in reply to a question I put to him, admitted that Her Majesty's Government had not addressed a similar demand to the Chinese Government, on the ground that the province of Kwang-si did not affect British interests in the same way as the province of Yunnan and Kwang-tung. I would, however, point out to the right hon. Gentleman that the merchants of Hong-kong take a view of the importance of

our commercial interests in Kwang-si which is diametrically opposed to that of the right hon. Gentleman. They declared to the noble and gallant Lord the Member for York that Great Britain ought to indicate clearly that the immense amount of British trade interests in the provinces of Kwang-tung and Kwang-si are such as to make it impossible for her ever to allow, under any conditions, prohibitive tariffs similar to those put on in Madagascar and Indo-China. With regard to that most interesting and also able work "The Break-up of China," by Lord Charles Beresford, perhaps I may be permitted to say how much, in my opinion, the whole nation is indebted to the noble Lord for having undertaken, in our commercial interests, the visit which he has recently made to China. The First Lord of the Treasury seemed somewhat amused that the noble Lord should have assumed the new rôle of a commercial emissary. For my part, however, I believe that, so far from having diminished the admiration with which he is regarded as a gallant and dashing naval officer, the noble Lord has increased his prestige, if possible, by the peaceful mission he undertook to promote the commerce of the country, and which has resulted in his giving to the world a mass of valuable commercial information, prepared in a manner so careful and lucid that it would do credit to any man entirely engaged in commercial affairs. In view of the opinion of the commercial men of Hong-kong, I ask whether Her Majesty's Government will not reconsider their decision to take no steps to uphold British commercial interests in the Province of Kwang-si. With regard to the great Province of Kwang-tung, the hinterland of Hong-kong, the position of affairs is exactly similar to that in reference to Yunnan ; and the opinion I have quoted of the commercial men at Hong-kong in respect to the extreme importance of upholding British commercial interests in Kwang-si applies with still greater force to Kwang-tung. I hope that the right hon. Gentleman, who did not favour the Committee with any information on this point when Chinese affairs were last under discussion, will now give the Committee some clear statement of what the Government policy is to be in regard to the upholding and safeguarding of British commercial interests in Southern China Surely in the

Mr. Walton.

ettlement of our outstanding differences with France some attempt has been made to come to an amicable and equitable agreement under which we shall be able to co-operate alongside of France in the development of Southern China on equal terms and conditions. As affecting the support which Italy may be expected to give us, if she secures a footing in China, I regret that Her Majesty's Government should have jeopardised the friendly relations between this country and our old traditional ally Italy by having handed over to France, so far as they could do it, the hinterland of Tripoli, to which the Italians have undoubtedly a superior claim. And I should like to know from the right hon. Gentleman what, if any, communication has passed between Her Majesty's Government and the Italian Government in regard to this matter. I am glad to see that Lord Salisbury—who minimised the value of railways in China, and expressed considerable doubt as to whether they would ever be constructed, and, if they were constructed, whether they would not prove a most unfortunate speculation—has now been driven to regard the question of the laying down of railways in that country as one of supreme importance, for I noticed the other day that the noble Lord said : " The politics of China are the politics of railways." This recognition by Lord Salisbury of the vital part that railways are going to play in the future of the Chinese Empire will, I trust, be followed by the adoption of a more energetic policy in securing that a fair proportion of them shall be constructed by British enterprise. It is well to bear in mind that, alone of all the nations seeking to acquire [rights and interests in China, Great Britain will permit other nations to trade in her special sphere on equal terms and conditions with herself. The knowledge, too, that there is not the remotest desire on the part of this country to interfere with the sovereign rights of China ought to have had the effect of making our influence with the Chinese Government at Pekin absolutely predominant, had not our prestige and influence been utterly destroyed by the diplomatic defeats that we have courted and suffered at the hands of other Powers. We were told in a formal and explicit manner last year, by Lord Salisbury, that

negotiations were proceeding for the reorganisation of the Chinese forces. It would be interesting to the Committee to know what has been the result of these negotiations. The question is When, if ever, does Her Majesty's Government intend to take some clear and definite action to prevent our being slowly but surely elbowed out of China ? The contrast between the energy of the Russians, French, and Germans, and their clear conception of what they want, with the supineness, irresolution, and total lack of a clear and consistent policy which has marked the dealings of our Government with a great crisis in the history of China, and of British interests in that country, is most humiliating. If ever we are to succeed in asserting the priority of British rights in the Yang-tsze Basin, there is not an hour to lose. In my opinion it is simply astounding, having regard to the fact that we were the pioneers in opening up trade with China, and that we have waged at least two warsat an enormous cost to maintain our right to trade there, that yet our Government have neither the enterprise nor the courage to move a single finger to enter into effective occupation of the rich Yang-tsze Basin. The great Yang-tsze River ought to have been surveyed by Her Majesty's Government right to its navigable limits, and a report not only presented, but the removal of obstructions to navigation should have been proceeded with long ago, in order that a flotilla of river gunboats might be placed upon that river to enable British trade to be carried on under proper protection, and also to assert our priority of claim to that region. I am glad to learn from the speech of the Under Secretary that Her Majesty's Government contemplate putting some gunboats on the Yang-tsze ; and on this point I speak feelingly, because, as a British subject, I shall look forward to having their protection when I make my intended expedition into Chung-King within the next six months. I am bound to admit that the statement of policy made in the speech ·of the right hon. Gentleman is a distinct step in advance, and so far as that is the case, though I speak from the Radical benches, I congratulate the right hon. Gentleman and the Government on having, even at the eleventh hour, become more alive to the serious dangers that face us in regard to our commercial interests in the great neutral market of China. We cannot afford to be driven out of that market, inhabited as it is by nearly a quarter of the world's population. I see no reason why we should not seek in a friendly fashion to work alongside with, and to co-operate with, all other Powers interested in opening up and developing that great Empire ; but at the same time it is our duty to maintain British rights, and to see that they are preserved to us in the future on equal terms with all other nations throughout the Chinese Empire.

*Mr. · BILL (Staffs., Leek): I rise to urge the Government to consider favourably the claims of the families of the officers killed at Waima. These officers lost their lives, not in what we may call the ordinary risks of their vocation, but in what I have seen described as an unfortunate accident that never should have happened. They were shot down by the troops of a friendly Power, whose susceptibilities we have always been ready to consider. These friendly troops were operating many miles within the British sphere. It is true that they were in pursuit of a foe common to both the English and the French, and it is equally correct that neither expedition was aware of the existence of the other ; but the leader of the French expedition, in his eagerness and recklessness, had overlooked the boundaries and had penetrated at one time to a point 58 miles from French territory. No doubt the responsibility for this slaughter rests upon his shoulders, and it does seem to me inexplicable that the French Government did not at once express its regret for the occurrence and offer an indemnity to the families of the slain officers. But five and a half years have elapsed and nothing has been done, and we do not even know if the French Government have given any reply to the formal demand addressed to them last July by the Foreign Office. What would the French have said had the position been reversed ? If our troops had gone 50 miles beyond our boundaries, and had slain three French officers, the whole of France would have rung with denunciations of this country. I do appeal most strongly to the right hon. Gentleman and the Government that they will not let this matter be protracted any longer. There are many Members on both sides of the House who take an interest in the question, and we

Mr. Walton.

are all agreed that it should be settled with the utmost despatch.

*Mr. MACDONA (Southwark, Rotherhithe): I would not have intruded on the present occasion but for the fact of the hon. Member for King's Lynn about twelve months ago having enabled me, by the tacit consent of this House, to pay a visit to China whilst Parliament was sitting. I am glad I went there, because my visit has disabused my mind of many of the prejudices which I entertained as to the country. One of those wrong impressions, held in common with a great many other people, was that the Chinese people had a great objection to railways. What appeared to be an insurmountable objection to railway construction in China was, of course, the worship which the Chinese paid to their ancestors. The bodies of these ancestors are distributed all over the country, and there is a great objection to interfering with them. But, after all, a Chinaman is an astute commercial man, and now that he finds that he can get a good price for his ancestor's body his objection to railways has disappeared, for at a fixed rate of five dollars each the ancestor's body has become a valuable asset, and when it has been removed from the route of one railway it has had a happy knack of turning up on the route of another projected line ready for sale again. A new state of affairs has of late grown up in China to that which has obtained for centuries past, and now there are great possibilities of opening up that magnificent country. We already possess something like 70 per cent. of the commerce with that country, and if we are not alive to our interests, if we are not firm in our policy with that nation, I very much fear from what I have seen that our trade in the future will not be as prosperous as it has been in the past. I was very glad indeed to hear the Under Secretary of State for Foreign Affairs tell us to-night that our sphere of influence in the Yang-tsze Valley is to be secured, and that British gunboats are to protect our interests along its course; and that other nations will not be allowed to alienate that territory to the exclusion of our trade. · Our object, and the object of the Government, must be to encourage trade · with · China. Whilst in China I received very great courtesy and kindness during my visit to Pekin · from our Minister there.

Sir Claude Macdonald, who has earnestly at heart the interests of this great empire. I should like to bear my ungrudging testimony to the hard work he has done, work which has so seriously affected his health, unfortunately. I quite agree with the remarks of the noble Lord the Member for York as to the marvellous industry, great perseverance, and energy displayed by the Chinese people in the development of their own trade. They work morning, noon, and night with unceasing toil and intelligent interest in their work, and certainly we ought to convert this industry on the part of this wonderful nation to our own commercial advantage. We have every facility for approaching them, for I have found that a great feeling of respect and attachment to this country permeates the Chinese mind. I came into contact with many of the Mandarins and other leading men in China during my visit there, and I found one of them—Chang-yen-Maw, a man of vast wealth, who holds a very exalted position, and who possesses a controlling influence in China at the present time— to be a man of wide sympathies and possessing a large-hearted tenderness for England and its people, whatever may be said of him to the contrary. I believe that if we only deal as openly with the Chinese as we do with other nations we shall largely increase our commercial strength in that country. Another point which has been brought out in this debate is the fact that Chinese can be made into magnificent soldiers and sailors. I have been to Wei-hai-wei, and have seen the tops of the vessels which were deliberately sunk by the Chinese themselves rather than surrender them to the enemy, and did what the noble Lord the Member for York, when he was in command of the "Condor" would have done had he been in the same position as the Chinese commander. It is well known that the admiral in command of the Chinese squadron, Admiral Ting, is a man of undaunted bravery, determined to fight to the very last, and it was only in consequence of direct instructions from Li Hung Chang, his chief on land, that he did not do so. I believe that the Chinese, properly drilled by English officers, properly fed and clothed, and capably led, will be found to make really good soldiers and sailors. In conclusion I can only express the hope that the Government will be firm in their determination to secure our trade in the Yang-tsze Valley and will run a British coast railway as far as they can from Shanghai to Hong-kong, securing the possession of British ports and British trade where they can be protected, if need be, by the British Navy.

*MR. MOON (St. Pancras, N.) : I think it is a great pity that the British Government and our Legation at Peking were not better informed of the events which were taking place in China. It is quite clear that the ordinary diplomatic staff of our Legation there can hardly have, during the short time that they are placed at this post, an opportunity of making themselves masters of the ins and outs of Chinese life. I am not prepared to propose a remedy, but probably some scheme for giving the Chinese Secretary higher rank and greater prestige, and giving him a greater number of Chinese retainers, would give the Legation an opportunity of obtaining that information the absence of which seems rather to have endangered our credit in allowing this *coup d'état* to take place, instead of supporting the reform party. I would say that the *coup d'etat* having taken place it would be just as well to make friends with the *de facto* ruler of China. But I think the Government and our Legation have failed to take the best step. Nevertheless the invitation to break down and remove the barrier which has hitherto been maintained by the Chinese Court against foreign ladies was one which they did not do amiss to accept. I agree with what has been said as to the Agreement effected by the exchange of Notes on the 28th of April last, seeing that it creates a sort of no man's land between the Yang-tsze basin on the south and the Russian sphere. With regard to that I think the Additional Note is specially unsatisfactory, as it seems to me to give Russia an invitation to pass through this no man's land. The last clause runs thus :

"The present special Agreement is naturally not to interfere in any way with the right of the Russian Government to support, if it thinks fit, applications of Russian subjects or establishments for concessions for railways, which, starting from the main Manchurian line in a south-westerly direction, would traverse the region in which the Chinese line terminating at Si-nmin-ting and Newchwang is to be constructed."

My right hon. friend the Under Secretary for Foreign Affairs yesterday, in answer to a question as to the meaning of the last clause, said it did not, in the opinion of Her Majesty's Government, cover the question of railway communications to Peking; but if it does not do so I am unable to attach any meaning to it at all. I fully sympathise with what my right hon. friend has said about the great difficulty of coping with the immensity of work which has been put upon the Foreign Office by the situation in China, as well as in other parts of the world. The Russians are in a very much more favourable position than England; their territory lies on the frontier of their own country, and Russians are on the frontier as soldiers and settlers, and they are more easily in touch with their new territories. They are not troubled either with a Parliament, or having having to make extra-Parliamentary speeches, and therefore they have a greater opportunity of dealing with any difficulties that may arise. It has been stated in this House by the First Lord of the Treasury, or by the Secretary of State for Foreign Affairs in another place, that the staff at the Foreign Office has not grown in proportion to the increase of work; and if I may say so, I, for one, if there were an increased estimate brought in, in order to permit an increase in the staff, should heartily support it.

MR. HARWOOD (Bolton): The keynote given by the noble Lord in his speech is commerce, and in the few remarks that I make I wish to speek from that standpoint, because the commerce with China nearly concerns the county from which I come. Most of the China trade is transacted in some form or other on the Manchester Exchange, and Lancashire is extremely interested in the development of the China trade. Everything which concerns that trade concerns us in a direct manner, and I am not ashamed to own that we look upon this matter from the point of view of £ s. d. I do not rise to condemn the Government's foreign policy, nor will I concur in any such condemnation. I think the one passion which Lord Salisbury possesses—if so cold a soul can be said to have any at all—is a passion for peace, and those who come from Lancashire will be very backward in condemning a policy which has been guided throughout by the desire to establish the peace of the world and maintain good relations with other

Mr. Moon.

nations. I venture to offer my humble expression of gratitude to Lord Salisbury and the Government for their great desire to preserve peace. Looking at this question from a commercial point of view—I have no right to speak for Manchester—as one who attends the Manchester Exchange, which is the centre of trade in Lancashire, I may have a better opportunity than the First Lord of the Treasury, who represents that city, of judging and feeling the general mind of Lancashire upon this point. As to the points raised by the noble Lord the Member for York as to the two policies, the open door and the possession of territory, we in Lancashire are still in favour of the policy of the open door, and I should like to point out to the Committee that the one policy is not equivalent to the other from the commercial point of view. Before the recent changes occurred we had free trade throughout the Chinese Empire, and it is very valuable to us as a matter of trade, because we have been shut out from so many other places. My experience as a member of the cotton trade is that we have been shut out from one place after another. Russia has shut us out, France has shut us out, and I deeply regret that the Government has allowed us to be shut out from the market of Tunis. This state of things cannot go on; we are bound to protest, not only for our own sake, but for the sake of the people who contribute so large a sum to the welfare of this country. Therefore, I say, you cannot balance the two policies of the open door and the preserved districts. Look at it from a trade point of view—the result of the spheres of influence is that our trade will be restricted to a market of 170,000,000 of people, rather than the 400,000,000 that inhabit China, with whom we should trade if we have the open door. This country cannot afford to be shut out from trading with half the large population of China. I have heard it said that the trade is not very large or important, but that is not the point which we have to consider. What we have to consider is not the present dimensions of the trade, but the prospect. We believe that in the future we shall do a greater trade in proportion to the population than we have ever done in the past; and it is not that we object to be shut out from the trade at this moment, but that we object to be shut out from the prospective trade. This point of view is one which may be fairly brought before the Committee and the country, and we in Lancashire feel it so strongly that if it comes to a question whether we shall have to go to war to keep the "open door," cruelly as we and all other persons would suffer by such a circumstance, I venture to tell the Under Secretary that if in the last necessity he is compelled to take that step we shall support him to the utmost of our power. I venture to make these few remarks because we feel very strongly in this matter. We are proud of our politics, proud of our Empire, proud of responsibility; but, above all, we are proud of our trade, and we shall object to the last to being shut out from any portion of our trading rights in the Chinese Empire.

*EARL PERCY (Kensington, S.): My principal object in intervening in this Debate to-night is to add a few words in support of what has fallen from the right hon. Baronet the Member for the Forest of Dean with regard to the claims of the relatives of those unfortunate officers who fell in the affair at Waima. I cannot say how deeply I regret the *non possumus* attitude which has been adopted by the Under Secretary, and I also regret that the claim put forward by the right hon. Baronet should have been given such a partisan character. I want at the outset to separate altogether what I may call the Imperial from the personal side of this question. The Imperial is no doubt an important—perhaps it is the most important—side of the question, but it is a side on which I wish only briefly to address the Government. To the ordinary onlooker the claim is so obvious and so legitimate that I regret that it should take our Government such a long time to receive satisfaction. Whatever may be the cause of the delay, I recognise fully that the Government has a right to say on this side of the subject that they, and they alone, are most competent judges of the methods to be adopted in securing the object which they assure us they have in view. But when we leave the Imperial side of the question and come to the personal we are on totally different ground. Upon the personal side of the question I think every Member of this House is not only capable, but is almost bound, to form an independent opinion on the facts before us. I must say that, after full considera-

tion of the facts which have been put before me, I do think that the wives of these officers have been treated very unhandsomely and very ungenerously. As I understand, only one of these ladies has received any compensation at all, and that a miserable pittance of £150, while both the other ladies have been told that they cannot have any compensation because they have other means of support. Now, Sir, the Government said that they were following the precedent usual in these matters, and that the case of these widows is parallel to that of the widows of officers who are killed in ordinary action in the performance of their duties. If that be the case, then I cannot understand why the Government is pressing for compensation from the French Government at all. The very fact that the Government are pressing for compensation is an admission that you have a grievance, and if that be the case those who are the principal sufferers have a prior claim to any satisfaction obtained. The more you emphasise the view that this was a pure accident, and that the French and English officers did not know on what territory they were meeting, and the more strongly you emphasise the fact that the geographical determination of Waima was at the time of the encounter uncertain, the more strongly you emphasise difference between the personal and Imperial aspect of the question. It seems to me that it is proved emphatically that if there is any claim for compensation at all it is the widows of those officers who ought to receive it. I do think there is ground for urging the Government as strongly as we can to take into serious consideration whether they cannot give to the relatives of the officers who were killed as liberal and as generous compensation as we should be expected to mete out as private employers to the relatives of those killed in our service. I want to make myself perfectly clear in the matter. I do not press this claim as a matter of charity. The right hon. Gentleman, in answer to a question some time ago, stated that, although the claims were still under the consideration of the French Government, the English Government were prepared to take into consideration the question of urgency in any particular case. I do not think this is a question of urgency at all; it is a question of moral justice. I think the Government are morally bound to provide compensation for these people on the grounds I have mentioned, and I feel sure that if they could see their way to come to this House and ask for an adequate grant they would soon find that the House of Commons was not disposed to offer any unnecessary objection, or to adopt an ungenerous attitude. Well, Sir, I should like, for one or two minutes, with the indulgence of the Committee, if I am not detaining them too long—["No!"]—to add one or two words in reference to the question of China. That is not a question on which, up to the present time, I have ventured to trouble the Committee with my own views, and I confess I should feel somewhat diffident to be called upon to contribute any very valuable contribution to Debates upon a subject which, up to the present moment, have done singularly little to elucidate the problem to be solved. The chief criticism which has been hitherto directed against the policy of the Government is the criticism which was reiterated to-night by the right hon. Baronet the Member for the Forest of Dean, and which, I think, may be summed up in the words employed by the right hon. Gentleman the Member for Berwick-on-Tweed last year, when he said that we should find our policy landed us between two stools—the policy of the open door on the one hand, and the policy of spheres of influence on the other. I cannot say that the criticism is of a very illuminating character. We all of us know that the Chinese Empire is at the present moment passing through a transition stage either of development or decay, and under these circumstances I think it is exceedingly difficult this evening to see how our policy can be more or less than a policy of transition. No one has suggested that the Government ought to go to war with other Powers in order to prevent the establishment of spheres of influence, and therefore the only practical problem that this House has now to solve is as to what steps to take in order to prevent those spheres of influence from becoming actual protectorates, or to prevent the open door being shut in our faces. Upon that point we have had no advice whatever from the right hon. Gentleman the Member for Berwick-on-Tweed, or from any of his supporters. At the most the suggestion is that we should come to some general agreement

Earl Percy.

with reference to this question with Russia. To-night the right hon. Gentleman expressed himself satisfied with that agreement. If that was the whole point of his complaint it was a very small one, and very easy to satisfy. I do not myself attach the slightest importance to the Russian Agreement. I do not think it offers the slightest guarantee to us for any of the matters that we have at heart. If it had been possible to secure by a general agreement with Russia the objects which we are really aiming at, then everybody knows that that agreement would have been secured long ago. If the aims of Russia in China and our own aims in China are mutually inconsistent, then I do not see the least use of perpetually urging the Government into playing a game where one party shows all his cards while the other keeps the best trumps up his sleeve. We all know that our desire is to obtain a general recognition of our sphere of influence. We all know that the German Minister pointed out the other day that we have not the courage, and are not likely to have the courage, to take steps to effect the occupation of that sphere of influence. No definition whatever of our sphere of influence in the Yang-tsze Valley has been included in the Russian Agreement. Therefore it seems to me that the points we now have to decide are, in the first place, what we intend to be the limit of our sphere of influence in the Yang-tsze Valley; secondly, what steps we intend to take in order to make our occupation of that sphere effective; and, in the third place, what are the limits beyond which any intrusion on the part of a foreign Power will be regarded as an unfriendly act. If the right hon. Baronet the Member for Berwick-on-Tweed or his colleagues had told us how far they were prepared to support Her Majesty's Government in undertaking additional obligations in China, I believe we should have advanced the subject a considerable length, because we should then have been in a position to confront Russia in the case of China as we confronted France in the case of Egypt, with a united national front. Now, Sir, as I understand it—I hope I am not detaining the Committee —["No!"]—only three possible or practicable policies with regard to China have been adumbrated. There is, in the first place, the policy of Her Majesty's Government, of which I am a hearty supporter. That policy I conceive to be the continuance of the distinction—which I do not think the right hon. Gentleman the Under Secretary of State for Foreign Affairs laid sufficient stress upon, for I hold it to be a very important distinction—between spheres of interest and spheres of influence. We are prepared to admit the principle that in its own sphere of interest each Power should be entitled to railway and mining concessions; but at the same time we maintain that all over China and in all these spheres the open door shall be kept for trade generally, and that no Power should be allowed to exercise pressure or coercion upon the central Government at Pekin. That policy has two advantages. In the first place it does not commit us to any immediate extension of our responsibilities; and in the second place, so long as China remains intact, we preserve the *status quo*. But I think the Government themselves will be the first to admit that that policy is of an essentially temporary character. The time must inevitably come when the Chinese Empire will fall into decay; and when Russia has concentrated all her forces along the northern frontier it will be idle to talk about the preservation of any sphere of influence. Then there is the policy of the noble Lord the Member for York, which seems to be nothing less than the assumption on the part of this country of the responsibility for a protectorate over the whole of China. The noble Lord wishes us to reorganise the military and naval defences of the empire and the whole administration of finance, and to generally bolster up the entire fabric—if possible, by international co-operation, and, failing that, by isolated intervention. He expressly points to the example of Egypt as an instance of isolated action on our part, in case of the failure of international co-operation. But he entirely ignores the fact that not only may Russia and the other Powers refuse to co-operate with us, but that they may offer the most strenuous opposition to any idea of isolated action. Therefore the policy of the noble Lord entirely falls to the ground unless he is prepared to assume responsibility infinitely greater than that which would be entailed by our having to defend some particular sphere of our own. He has the greatest objection to the policy of spheres of interest which may ultimately develop into spheres of influence. He asks us triumphantly what is to become of the rights of private concessionaires and bondholders in the event of the transformation of those spheres into actual facts? But he entirely forgets that those spheres are already a *fait accompli*, and it is only by obtaining some definite sphere of our own, the transformation of which into a Protectorate would inflict an injury on foreign Powers, which they are not prepared to face, that you can prevent such an eventuality. Then we have the theory of the hon. Member for Chester, which he has described as the policy of Egyptianising the Yang-tsze Kiang Valley; but if there is one thing more than another which would have condemned that policy I think it is the phrase he has chosen. There is really no analogy whatever between our position in Egypt and our position in China. Not only have we no control over the central government of China which we have over the central government of Egypt, but the geographical conditions of the country render the same method of defence impossible. Therefore it seems to me that the policy of the hon. Member for Chester also falls to the ground, unless he is prepared to contemplate the establishment of at least a fairly defensible frontier to the north of the Yang-tsze Valley. Now, Sir, although I am a strong supporter of our policy, and although I believe it is the only practicable policy, it is nevertheless one which may well be supplemented by steps which, if taken now, will prevent any misunderstanding and confusion in the future. By all means continue your amicable negotiations with Russia on the question of the continuation of the railway in China to Pekin. These are questions on which you may easily arrive at some *modus vivendi*. But at the same time I hope the Government will recognise that, although they cannot undo the harm which has been already done, at any rate they can prevent any misunderstanding of this kind occurring again, and ensure that whatever foreign railways have up to the present penetrated into our sphere of influence shall henceforth be unique specimens of their kind, and that within that sphere henceforward British enterprise alone shall have preferential rights. I do not pretend to have the advantage of any personal acquaintance with the internal geography of China, but I do not see why the Government should not say to any Power concerned that any intrusion on their part into the country south of the Hoangho will be regarded by ourselves as an unfriendly act and resented accordingly. That policy ought to secure the co-operation and support of every Power which desires to avert the disintegration and disruption of China. I confess that, so far as I have studied foreign politics, there is one feature of our policy on which I feel inclined to lay the greatest stress, and that is the desirability of our securing a firm, cordial, and lasting understanding with Germany. She is the only Power, both in the Near and the Far East, whose aims are at present, and must always be, practically identical with our own. We have been always talking, and talking again to-night, about the inevitable disruption and decay of Empires like Turkey and China. Well, Sir, I do not think they are likely to disappear, at any rate before Europe has undergone very considerable alteration. But, at all events, the external fact of the present situation is that, while Russia's object is almost openly to disintegrate and hasten the fall of the Chinese Empire, the policy of the other Empires is to prevent that action. The right hon. Gentleman the Under Secretary asked us just now what possible object Germany could have in coming to a definite arrangement with us. If you could show Germany that your whole object is directed simply to the maintenance of the strengthening of the Chinese Empire, I believe you would have her thorough support in any strong line of action that you chose to take in order to secure it. Lastly, there is the great advantage that you would come to a clear understanding both with the Governments of Turkey and China, that your watchword is friendly, hearty, consistent support of them, coupled with insistence, not merely suggestion of reforms; and that you do not intend, whether they like it or not, to give them the satisfaction of committing suicide. You may say that that is a policy which has been tried and met with disastrous failure. Sir, I do not think it is a policy which has been given a fair trial. I should like to see the Government make up their minds in Turkey, in Persia, and in China as to the precise points on which their Imperial interests are directly or indirectly touched, and, having done so, declare *urbi et orbi* to all whom it may concern that within the circle of those interests we intend to take any action which may

Earl Percy.

be necessary to safeguard them. Then, having made that declaration to Europe, you can go to China and say, "You may conduct your own government on any principles you please, but if disturbances arise either on the frontier or the Chinese Valley, or in the provinces which abut on the Yangtsze river, then those disturbances which directly or indirectly menace our own interests will be stopped by us." This is not a selfish policy. I am perfectly prepared to say that if you adopted that policy all round you would form those spheres of influence into agents for promoting the general welfare of the Empire. I believe that both in China and Turkey the one desire is to arrive at a cordial and friendly understanding with this country. The attitude of these countries at the present moment is this:

"We know perfectly well that the objects of England are far more coincident with our own than those of any other European nation; the only thing of which we are not sure is whether England attaches sufficient importance to those objects to justify us in incurring the enmity of other Powers."

It is therefore necessary that they should be placed in a position to deal with us directly, and that there should be correspondence between the Governments at Pekin and Constantinople on the one hand and with the Government in London on the other. In conclusion, I would only suggest that the policy I have indicated is no more than the policy to which we are already committed. You talk about assuming fresh responsibilities. To my mind you have already assumed responsibilities which cover the whole ground. At the present moment you are pledged to defend Turkey against any foreign combination, provided that she carries out reasonable reforms, and we are also pledged to defend China against any foreign combination, no matter what it may be, in all cases where any foreign nation puts pressure upon the Government at Pekin to refuse us concessions. What is the difference between that policy and the policy of saying, "You shall do so and so because it is to your own interest, and we will defend you whatever comes of it"? The only difference, to my mind, is that one is an open-handed and honest policy, and the other is a dishonest policy, which lays you open to the charge of hypocrisy. There is only one clear and honest attitude to take up, and I do not think the Government have any option in the matter. These spheres of influence have already been created, and unless you step in and create your own spheres of interest you will find the open door slammed in your face. My criticisms may not seem to be one essentially of support to the Government, but they are meant to be. It is for this reason, that the policy of Her Majesty's Government has recognised the fact—which I believe to be the true one—that not only are spheres of interest and the open door not incompatible, but absolutely identical and correlative ; and the only reason I have risen to-night is to urge upon the Government the necessity of carrying out that policy to its legitimate conclusion. I hope the Government will make up its mind, apart from any agreement with other nations, to lay down the limits of those spheres of influence, and declare at once that within those spheres of influence they do not intend to allow of any interference whatever.

*Mr. PROVAND (Glasgow, Black-friars) : I think this Debate, like those which have preceded it both last year and this year, has shown clearly that our sole interests in China which we desire to maintain are commercial, and that we have no intention whatever — so far as we have heard the opinion of those who have spoken on this subject in every part of the House—to promote any scheme of territorial aggrandisement. Even the noble Lord the Member for York —to whom we are indebted for the largest and most complete book on China, so far as commercial questions are con-cerned—places the question on a trading basis, and modestly calls himself a com-mercial agent. I think this shows that at last commercial matters are obtaining more attention in this House than they formerly did, and for a country that has always been largely governed by country gentlemen that is something to be thankful for. The right hon. Gentle-man the Under Secretary of State for Foreign Affairs, in his speech this evening, stated what had been done, and if he was more definite than formerly, it was merely because he had not to tell us of so many assurances which he had re-quired to accept, and which had not been, or would not be, observed by those who made them. On the other hand, he spoke,

as he always does, apologetically with regard to the past, and he was mildly optimistic in regard to the future. He had many things to explain with regard to the Blue Book and the Chinese papers, and he spoke very hopefully of the future. But in regard to actual results he had very little to say, because the gains were very few. The right hon. Gentleman said that we had received a full share of mining and railway concessions. I may say, in this respect, so has Belgium, which is a little country with no navy or army that the Chinese Government need fear. He also said that he had succeeded in inducing China to observe its pledge for the non-alienation of the Yang-tsze Valley. There would be very little difficulty indeed in inducing the Chinese Government to keep their promise in that respect, because we have no rights in the Yang-tsze Valley which are not common to all other nations. We have asked for no exclusive privileges there, for in that valley there is still the open door, which is as much open to every other country as it is to us. I think one of the most remarkable things which the right hon. Gentleman told us to-night was that the Tien-tsin Treaty had always been observed, and that no door had been closed. That was what the right hon. Gentleman said when he last addressed the House. I am very much surprised that he should say so, because the evidence shows that the Tien-tsin Treaty has not been observed, and that the doors that have been closed are very numerous. The basis of our trade with China is the Tien-tsin Treaty, and upon one clause— Article 54—which is usually known as the "most favoured nation" clause. That clause gives the British Government and British subjects free and equal participation in all privileges and advantages which have been or may be granted by the Emperor of China to any other Government or peo-ple. What has happened since that Treaty was signed ? France has taken possession of a large part of Southern China, and she has imposed duties against every country except herself. Japan has taken possession of Formosa, and has practi-cally done the same thing. Germany has taken possession of Shantung, and she has barred us from all mining and railway privileges in that province, and all com-mercial opportunities of every kind except such as she may not happen to want herself. And yet the right hon. Gentleman says that no door has been shut. It has not only been shut on us in Shantung, but the closing of it has been made in terms dictated to us from Berlin. In a despatch which was printed on the 4th of April last year our Ambassador at Berlin said, referring to Baron von Richtofen :

"His Excellency suggests a declaration to the following effect: that England formally declares to Germany that she has no intention, in establishing herself at Wei-hai-wei, of creating difficulties for Germany in Shantung, or of injuring or contesting her rights there, and more especially that in that province she will not establish railway communication."

That was not sufficient to satisfy Germany, because a few days afterwards the Ambassador wrote again to the right hon. Gentleman the First Lord of the Treasury, at that time in charge of our Foreign Office, in order to satisfy Count Hadzfeldt :

"It is specially understood that England will not construct any railroad communication from Wei-hai-wei or from any other point on the coast to the interior of the province of Shantung."

Therefore we not only closed that door, but we allowed Germany to state the terms on which the door should be closed. Again, take the railway agreement entered into only some few weeks ago with Russia. In that we practically agree that Russia shall close the door against ourselves so far as Manchuria is concerned. Now, how can any of these cases be reconciled with the principle of the most favoured nation clause, which was to secure our participation in all privileges, immunities and advantages which were given to any other country or might be given hereafter to any other country ? But, besides this, all these parts of China which have been already appropriated by other countries are now defined areas in which France, Japan, Germany, and Russia have exclusive rights, and we have been warned off in every case, and we can obtain no concession of any description except by their permission, and that will certainly not be given in regard to anything which they want themselves. On the other hand, the Yang-tsze Valley is open to everybody ; we have no exclusive rights there, nor could we say one word with reference to any mining or railway concessions being granted in the

Mr. *Provand.*

Yang-tsze Valley to any other country. In our dealings with Russia we have conducted our business without definiteness : whereas, on the other hand, Russia has clearly defined her policy. The result is that Russia has obtained many definite advantages, whereas we have obtained nothing at all. The Russian Agreement defines their rights in Manchuria as coming to the Great Wall, which is within about 50 miles of Pekin. Our agreement does not define the Yang-tsze Valley or that immense area of country between the Yang-tsze Valley and the Great Wall which has been spoken of as "no man's land." We may depend upon it that it will not be "no man's land" very long, and we shall find that some country has obtained rights there and we shall be excluded from it. Her Majesty's Government have stated that they do not consider the Russian Agreement covered a railway to Pekin ; but according to the telegrams from China it is stated distinctly that it is on the basis of that Agreement that Russia has asked for the concession of a railway to connect Port Arthur with Pekin. It certainly appears as if the statement of *The Times* correspondent was borne out by all that took place at the time. Our Government apparently knew nothing about Russia's intentions with regard to that railway ; or if so they surely would not enter into such an agreement if it was to be immediately set aside? There was a very extraordinary circumstance connected with our representative at St. Petersburg in connection with that Agreement The Russian Government informed him that they did not make any demand on the Chinese Government, but merely made a friendly request, which our representative communicated to the Government. at Pekin, and was answered to the effect that Russia had made the demand, and would not take any refusal. The papers in regard to this matter have not been laid upon the Table, and we shall not probably see them printed this session. When the question comes up again on the next China Debate no doubt we shall find that Russia has obtained everything she wants, and that she has paid no attention whatever to the Agreement signed only five weeks ago. What is going to be the result of this? Russia has gradually come down from the north, step by step, for generations, and she will very soon control all Northern China, and Pekin as well eventually. Tien-tsin is the gate of Manchuria and the port through which all the imports go which are sent to the north of the Great Plain, and there our tonnage was in 1896 represented by 1,250,000, whilst Russia was absolutely unrepresented by a single vessel. And yet the whole of Northern China is going to pass under the control of Russia. I know that I need not tender advice to the Government upon this question. It is only necessary for us to point out where they make mistakes, or express our approval where they are successful. If Russia does all these things while the Manchurian railroad is building, what will she do when it is finished? Naturally Russia will then be in a position to send as large an army as she pleases to Northern China, and there would be nothing to hinder her even taking possession of the Yang-tsze Valley, and we should be powerless to prevent her doing that. That point has been dealt with by other speakers in this House, and it certainly has been referred to many times by our Minister at Pekin. The right hon. Gentleman the Under Secretary of State for Foreign Affairs mentioned one circumstance which he said was always alluded to by speakers on this side, and that was that the Government lost prestige whenever a concession was given to any other country. But it is not on account of concessions to other countries that we have lost prestige. The fact is that we have been losing prestige for years in China under the government of both parties; but of all the series of diplomatic rebuffs we have received in China the most serious was sustained by us by the withdrawal of our men-of-war from Port Arthur and the abandonment of our rights in Shantung. Another reason for our loss of prestige was the acceptance of assurances from the Chinese Government and the representatives of other Governments which meant nothing at all, for they were merely given to satisfy our representative; many were not observed, and were never intended to be observed. Under the late Government we abandoned our claim to a portion of Southern China, and although the Chinese were under a signed Agreement with us not to give up that territory to any other country, yet in the very next year it was handed over to France. And what did we do in this matter? Why, nothing

at all. That was all done by the last Government, and I am speaking in no party sense in connection with these mistakes by the Foreign Office, because the last Government was no better than this Government in this respect. The only difference is that the present Government has had ten times more opportunities of making mistakes than its predecessors, and has taken advantage of them all. Our commercial policy in China has been neglected, and neither Government has made any serious attempt to secure our commercial interests. All these things have caused a great loss of prestige. Now, it is a very remarkable fact that while the Government policy is supposed to be dictated by the promotion of our commercial interests, there is amongst the commercial men of that country a feeling prevailing of the very deepest dissatisfaction at the way in which the possibilities of Chinese trade have been neglected for many years past. You could not find a dozen commercial men in China who would not blame both this and the last Government for their neglect of our real interests. I do not know whether the Government have ever taken advice from Chinese merchants, or from sources other than their strictly official channels. There is no doubt that the Government have been much more industrious of late, but their policy has been of little benefit to the commercial community. Take the much-lauded opening up of the Chinese waterways, which were spoken of in such glowing terms by the First Lord of the Treasury. It is idle to say that we have any waterway rights in China when the regulations and restrictions prevent us taking advantage of them. They have given something to us on paper, and taken it away from us in fact. I have had long business experience with China, and almost everything I have to say about the people is in their favour, for the Chinese merchants are honourable and enterprising, and that is quite as much as can be said for the commercial classes in any country under the sun. If we are to retain the trade we still have in China and increase it in proportion as commerce with China increases, then the Government must be firmer than it has been in the past in laying down a policy and maintaining it. If the Government fail to do this, we must inevitably lose the greater part of the trade which we have with China at the present time. The present Government, through their supineness and policy of drift, do not know to-day what their policy will be this day month, and that is the way our commercial interests in China have been dealt with. Unless this is changed, and a definite, clear, consistent, and firmer policy is adopted, which will command the respect of the Government at Pekin and the Powers represented there, we need not expect that we shall be able even to retain in China the commercial advantages which we have at the present moment.

*Mr. R. A. YERBURGH (Chester): I express my congratulations to the Government on their Agreement with Russia. I have had the honour, for some time, of advocating such an Agreement, for I believe it is the best way of securing the interest of this country in China. I do not lay great stress on the Agreement itself, for it is not a very extensive one; but I look upon it, not for what it gives at the present time, but rather for what it foreshadows in the future. I would like to ask the right hon. Gentleman the Under Secretary for Foreign Affairs whether I am right in understanding that he said that the Agreement gave Russia the right to construct a railway to Pekin?

*Mr. BRODRICK: No.

*Mr. YERBURGH: May I ask my right hon. friend what he did say?

*Mr. BRODRICK: Her Majesty's Government do not consider that by the Agreement Russia will be justified in making a railway to Pekin.

*Mr. YERBURGH: That is not an answer to my question. I want to know whether Her Majesty's Government think that the Agreement gives Russia the right to make a railway to Pekin.

*Mr. BRODRICK: The Agreement neither allows nor denies such a right.

Mr. Provand.

*Mr. YERBURGH: I understood the right hon. Gentleman to say that under the Agreement Russia would have a right to construct this railway to Pekin, and I was going to show that Russia could not possibly have any such right. If we look at page 90 of the Blue Book we see that the Note of Sir Charles Scott to Count Muravieff states:

"That the present special Agreement is naturally not to interfere in any way with the right of the Russian Government to support applications of Russian subjects for concessions for railways which, starting from the main Manchurian line in a south-westerly direction, would traverse the region in which the Chinese line terminating at Sinminting and Newchwang is to be constructed."

Well, there is a line already constructed as far as the Great Wall, and it is therefore obvious that Sir Charles Scott's Note cannot be construed as giving power to Russia to make a railway in the region between the Great Wall and Pekin, where no railway is to be constructed by the British Corporation. I would go even further than that. If the Memorandum of Count Muravieff, which will be found on page 84 of the Blue Book, is looked at, it will be found that it deals with the extension of the railway from the junction of Hsiao-hei-Sban to Sinminting, and with no other part of the line. It is pointed out that, while noting the assurances given in Sir Charles Scott's Memorandum, it must be clearly understood that the Imperial Government reserves to itself the right to support any application for railway concessions which Russian subjects may desire to obtain to the south-west of the main line towards Port Arthur, in the same region which is served by the line granted to the British and Chinese Corporation. I submit, then, that this additional Note, taken with the Memorandum, only gives Russia the right to construct a railway in the district between her main Manchurian line and the districts situated between Newchwang, Sinminting, or Hsiao-hei-Shan. We are extremely anxious to avoid any dispute with Russia, but as Russia has put in an application for a right to construct a railway to Pekin, we are face to face with the fact that that application may be pressed, and we are entitled to ask the Government what they intend to do should the claim be pressed. People have invested their money in the Newchwang railway extension largely on the strength of the Government having allowed its name to appear on the prospectus, and the Russian demand has placed the Government in a serious position, although I think it is not a position from which it is altogether impossible to escape. Manchuria was lost when Port Arthur was allowed to pass under Russian domination. Why should we fight for the shadow when we have given away the substance? Why should we support these railway extensions into the Russian spheres of influence? I think it would have been a better policy for the Government to have attempted to induce the parties to the Newchwang Concession and to this concession for the Chenting Taiyuan railway in Shansi, where we have very large interests, to make an exchange of their respective concessions. They would thus have got rid, once for all, of any intrusion into the Russian sphere of influence, and have confined operations to a region where Germany by an Agreement made with us has recognised that we have a sphere of railway interest. There is another point I should like to deal with in connection with our position in Northern China. I understood my right hon. friend to say that the policy of the Government was to keep any single Power from dominating Pekin. What does that mean? It means that you have deliberately to-night made yourselves responsible for checking the advance of Russia upon Pekin. And my right hon. friend added that the Government were opposed to the transference of the Imperial Court to any other part of China.

MR. BRODRICK : I never used the words "Imperial Court" at all. I said that the Government would advise the Chinese Government against the transference of the Chinese power from Pekin.

*MR. YERBURGH : I ask the Committee how, after we have given up Port Arthur and Manchuria, this country can oppose, with any chance of success, the predominance of Russia at Pekin. I listened with very great interest to the very admirable, able, and eloquent speech of my noble friend the Member for Kensington. He did me the honour of coupling my name with one of the three different policies which have been suggested with regard to China, namely, the Egyptianising the Yang-tsze region.

The noble Lord commenced by condemning the policy, but afterwards adopted it and extended it much further. He contended that there was no proper frontier of the Yang-tsze Valley, and that our sphere should therefore be extended up to the Yellow River. He would even go further than that; he would have Chinese troops to defend the region, and would build forts to defend the river. I therefore claim the noble Lord as a convert to the policy of Egyptianising the Yang-tsze region, which, combined with the policy of keeping the open door for general trade, is the policy which, when put forward last session, met with the severest criticism from the then Under Secretary for Foreign Affairs. Let us hope that the Government will make up their minds to Egyptianise the Yang-tsze region. What does that mean? It does not mean that you are to undertake the absolute control of the Yang-tsze region. I do not propose that for a moment. It means that you are to lend the Chinese Government men of capacity to assist them in reforming their finances, in establishing a commercial code, and in reorganising the forces of China. I believe I am right in saying that on the 17th of June last Lord Salisbury stated in the House of Lords that the proposition had been made to the Chinese Government that we should assist them in reorganising their army and navy, but that the difficulty was that the Chinese would not give a sufficiently independent position to our officers. If that difficulty had been met I take it that at the present time our officers would have been reorganising the Chinese navy and army. But what can be the objection to our officers reorganising the Chinese forces in the Yang-tsze Valley? It is not so large a scheme, and, perhaps, more feasible than Lord Salisbury's original proposition. It is well known that the Viceroys in the Yang-tsze region are in a more or less independent position, and that their connection with the central Government at Pekin is very loose. I believe there will be very little difficulty in getting the Viceroys in these provinces, if they were approached in the right way, to assist us in carrying through this reform. You need not undertake it all at once, but do it by slow degrees. An objection possibly might be that the cost would be too great. That is a very strong objection, but it could be met by a reform of the finances, for only about a sixth of the revenue of the provinces now reach the Imperial Exchequer. In regard to the general question, I think my noble friend has used language as to the conduct of affairs by the Government which is not altogether justifiable. He says that the Government have done nothing to develop or secure trade. I do not think anyone can bring that charge with any justification who has read the last Blue Book. There are in that Blue Book many instances of what the Government have done in the direction of developing and securing our trade interests. I need only quote in support of that the last annual report of the China Association. The Government have done a great deal in the past to support and develop the trade in China, and I have but to express the hope that they will not be weary in well-doing. If the Government are determined to continue to assist British enterprise as they have done in the last few months, if they will only have the courage to undertake these reforms in the Yang-tsze Valley, I do not think that any British Consul will have to write, as Consul Brennan had to write two or three years ago, that our pioneers in the treaty ports have been discouraged because they have received no effectual support from the Government. Let me turn for a moment to the Waima incident referred to by the right hon. Baronet the Member for the Forest of Dean. To me the position of affairs is most sad, and it is made more sad when only the other night we passed by universal consent a vote to Lord Kitchener for his successful operations in the Soudan. I think it is a shame that not a finger has been put forward to help the relatives of the murdered soldiers who have been left in penury and poverty. For six years their agony has been prolonged, and for three years the Government have known that justice was on their side; and yet the Government have done nothing. Last year a question was put to the then Under Secretary for Foreign Affairs as to whether the Government could not find any money for the use of these poor people until such time as compensation would be paid by the French Government, but still nothing has been done. I think it is inconceivably mean that the relatives of British soldiers who lost their lives in unfair combat should have received

Mr. Yerburgh.

no consideration from a British Government. I know there is a strong feeling on these benches in regard to this matter, and I do hope that the Government will see their way to give a more kindly and sympathetic consideration to this extremely distressing case.

*THE CHANCELLOR OF THE EXCHEQUER (Sir MICHAEL HICKS BEACH, Bristol, W.): I cannot speak on behalf of the Foreign Office, nor do I intend to enter into the history of the Waima case; but as that case has been before me in my position as Chancellor of the Exchequer I should just like to say a word or two with regard to it. My hon. friend has characterised the conduct of the Government as "inconceivably mean." Now, it is a very much easier thing, and a pleasanter thing, to do what I am sure the sympathies of all of us would desire, and to treat a case of this kind in a popular and liberal way. But one has to consider what the effect generally of such action would be. What are the circumstances in this particular case? These officers lost their lives in the discharge of their duty, as many other officers have done during the last three or four years. They left behind them near relatives in an unfortunate pecuniary position who suffered in that way heavily by their death. They lost their lives by what was unquestionably an accident. There is a regular system by which pensions or grants are given to the widows or near relatives of officers who have lost their lives in combat with the enemy on the field. Would it be right, and a principle that this House would desire to adopt, to treat the relatives of officers who have lost their lives in the discharge of their duty, by accident, better than the relatives of those officers who have lost their lives in the discharge of their duties in combat with the enemy? If you were once to adopt that principle it would be impossible to adhere to the rules which now govern the War Office in these matters. This is a case in which compensation has been demanded by the British Government from the French Government, but until the last few days we have had no real reason to suppose that the request for compensation would be favourably considered by the French Government. Therefore if we had granted to these unfortunate persons something by way of exceptional relief, we should have been treating them with exceptional favour as compared with the widows and the relatives of other officers who had lost their lives fighting in Egypt, the Soudan, or India without receiving similar compensation. I am happy to be able to say that very recently we have had reason to believe that this matter may be favourably considered by the French Government ; and it is possible that some terms of arbitration may be arranged. All I can say is this, that if that hope comes to fruition, if an arrangement is made, as I hope it may be, by which it is admitted that it is a case for arbitration, then I think the time will have arrived when we might consider the circumstances of these unfortunate persons, and ask the House to afford them some temporary relief.

MR. LABOUCHERE (Northampton): I have listened to the speeches that have been made in the course of this Debate, and as far as I can see the unfortunate Government has no friend in the House. Even hon. Members on the opposite side have taken exception to the main points of the Chinese policy that has been adopted ; and, being one of those who without respect of Party, are always prepared to support any Government which acts in a plain, sensible way with a view to establishing our commerce as far as possible by establishing peace abroad, I come forward and tender the Government my humble and sincere support. At the commencement of this Debate I think I saw in the gallery the distinguished representative of China in this country, but he has now gone away, and I am glad that he has left, because if he had stayed and listened to the speeches he would have thought that he had strayed into a den of thieves instead of the House of Commons. Because everybody who got up started a new theory for the cutting up and distributing of China between the various Powers. The Debate was commenced by the noble Lord the Member for York, and I have to congratulate him, because, although I do not agree with much that he said, there is one thing that I do agree with. The noble Member for York, not like me a poor civilian, but an eminent warrior, said he was against expansion. He may be called a Little Englander, but I do not think he will care for that—that

is a term which is applied by a foolish man to a wise one. It is a term that has been applied to Lord Salisbury, and if I may refer to so humble an individual, it has also been applied to me. I listened to the brilliant speech of the noble Lord the Member for South Kensington, which I do not agree with, in which he said we complained of the policy of the Government in China because it was a temporary policy. The policy is admittedly temporary at this moment, and it is the act of a wise Government to pursue a temporary policy, to look after our interests, and not pledge itself in any way. He was disposed not to treat with Russia, because he distrusted her ; that means that we must go to war with Russia. In order to do that we are to enter into an alliance with Germany, and the noble Lord seemed to consider that he had the Governments of all Europe in his pocket, as if Germany would enter into an alliance with us against Russia for that purpose. Germany would not enter into any such alliance. But the noble Lord went further and said that what we ought to do in China was, whatever comes, to tell the people we were ready to protect them, and whether they were attacked by France, Germany, or Russia, we would see they were not hurt. To do that we should have to have an Army not of 20,000, but of 2,000,000. Another hon. Member wished to Egyptianise the Yang-tsze Valley. He made a speech of very impressive character, and impressed upon us that what we were to do was to take into our possession a Chinese army and carry all before us in China. If the Government were to listen to such proposals as that, they would lose the confidence of the country in uncommonly short time. The Government have most unquestionably a very difficult task before them. What ought to be the aim of the Government ? They ought to do their best, without getting us into trouble with foreign countries, to maintain and extend so far as they can our trade with China. I am bound to say that in my opinion they have done this, and I do not see what else they could have done. Then, again, in the Yang-tsze Valley, which, as everybody knows, is divided by a great river, we are told that they have now gunboats on the river which can go up a thousand miles, and that they are patrolling the river and securing to us the commerce. We are further told that certain dredgings are taking place which will enable our gunboats to go further up, and this enables us to obtain all the commerce of that district and does not entail territorial expansion. We are told the treaty ports have been increased, and I am very glad to hear of it. We have heard also a good deal about the recent Treaty with Russia, and I congratulate the Government on having entered into that Treaty, and I am glad that they have given up the "long spoon" policy which was recommended by a colleague of the Government with regard to Russia. Nothing can now be done without our consent. We admit the Russians have a right to Manchuria, and that we are not going there. I do not quite understand the observation made by the Under Secretary just now that the Agreement with Russia did not justify that country in going to Pekin. I think, on the contrary, that Russia has expressly reserved a right to make railways wherever she pleases in a south-westerly direction from the Great Wall towards Pekin. I am most desirous to avoid lending advisers to the Chinese Government, because that would only lead to Russia doing the same thing, and ill blood would be bred between the two countries. The present Government, I quite admit, has a very difficult diplomatic task before it. At the present moment diplomacy is very difficult in any country where there is a free Press. The Press generally obtain all the news first, and very frequently obtain wrong news—I am now speaking of the daily Press. They get little scraps of information which are generally wrong, and build elaborate theories upon them. I entirely agree with Lord Salisbury when he said you must not form any conclusion as to the method of diplomacy pursued by the Government until it is completed. And I am bound to say, looking at his policy as a whole, it seems to have been a sound policy, getting as far as he can into agreement with Russia, and doing his best for the commerce of this country without compromising us with that or any other country.

*Mr. KESWICK (Surrey, Epsom): It appears to me that to give effect to the recommendations of the noble Lord the Member for York it would be absolutely necessary that we should establish a protectorate over the Empire

Mr. Labouchere.

of China. I do not think that it would be possible to give effect to his views in that way, and therefore we must be prepared to fall back and do that which is possible and practicable. There are some people who say and think that the Government have not done enough; but I do not see how they could have done more than they have without getting into trouble and producing a serious condition of things, which possibly we should not have approved of. It is not to war that I look for the universal observance of the Treaty of Tien-tsin, but it is to agreements entered into with other Powers. Our trade in China is very large, and capable of great extension, and the efforts of the Government in the opening of treaty ports and other ways have done a great deal towards extending it. Although the opening up of the inland waterways has been so far unsuccessful in the sense that the Customs arrangements have not been of such a satisfactory character as to allow inland navigation to be undertaken, I am encouraged by the fact that those ports are recognised as treaty ports, and all that is left to be done now is to make reasonable and suitable regulations. The future of China is, of course, speculative, but I fear that events are going so fast that it will be very difficult indeed to maintain our authority otherwise than by the united feeling of the whole of the country in support of the Government. There ought in this matter to be no party feeling, but an entire devotion to the best interests of commerce in China. If we can avoid taking territory, I hope it will be avoided. I fear, however, it will not, because we must protect our interests. But perhaps that may be possible without the acquisition of territory. I beg to support the policy of Her Majesty's Government.

*Mr. BARLOW (Somerset, Frome): I listened with very great interest to the remarks of the hon. Member for Chester. He expressed the hope that the Government would enter on a new and better course, and I inferred from the general tenour of his speech that he was not altogether pleased with the action of the Government. I noticed that when the hon. Gentleman recently spoke in Lancashire he studiously avoided saying anything about the action of the Government with regard to the present question.

Lancashire is a county very deeply interested in the Chinese question, and it is only fair to suppose that if the hon. Member had been able to say anything about the Government which he thought might commend them to the electors he would have said it. However, so far as my experience goes, the Government have been viewed with a great deal of suspicion in Lancashire, not only with reference to the Chinese question, but also in regard to the manner in which they have dealt with other questions in the East. I would not have intervened in this Debate had I not been interested in China for a number of years. I am not interested in China as the hon. Member for Northampton suggested some hon. Members were — as concessionaires, but I am interested as a merchant in China, and therefore I have a more abiding interest in the prospects of the country than perhaps other Members, who may be interested as concessionaries. There is no doubt there are huge undeveloped potentialities in China. A great deal has been done to secure our trade in various parts of the world, but I think that the present Government have to some extent sacrificed our interests in China, where we already had a firm foothold, and where there is a much greater prospect of speedy development than in some other parts of the world—Africa, for instance, of which we have heard a great deal during the present year. There is nothing more certain in connection with Eastern Asia, and particularly with China, than one fact, and that is if you lose prestige, if you give the impression that you are a declining Power, your influence and your trade are apt to depart from you, and I am sorry to say that from communications I have received from China, and from watching affairs very closely, that the policy of the present Government has given the idea to the natives of China that we are a declining Power. The noble Lord the Member for York said in his speech that there was an idea that we were like an old and wealthy man who was afraid to risk his money because he thought that if he risked it he might lose it ; that Russia, a much younger Power, was prepared to take greater risks and responsibilities, and that therefore it had advanced in recent years at a much more rapid rate than we had. I have no hostility to Russia. Russia has a settled purpose, and intends to carry it out to its

legitimate, and from its own point of view proper, conclusion. What I complain of is that if our Government have a settled purpose they have not made it clear to the residents in China, not only to the natives, but to the Europeans and the mercantile community. They think that the action of the Government means that English interests are being sacrificed, and that we will give way on any point when we are squeezed. That is not a course of policy which can secure us respect in the East or eventuate in our success. The prospect of the construction by Russia of a railway to Pekin is most likely to be prejudical to our interests and influence in China. It is possible, and indeed likely, that this will not impress the natives of China with our power, wisdom, or far-sightedness. Speaking from an experience extending over many years, it is my opinion that there is no nation in the East more reliable and trustworthy in its mercantile transactions than China. I would trust a Chinaman as soon as, and sooner than, any other native of the East to carry out any engagement he enters into, and therefore it is a very great mistake that this country should do anything that would prejudice or let slip our hold on a country where we have undoubtedly done a great deal, where we have most of the foreign trade in our hands, and where a conservative population were beginning to see that we have long been their friends. We have treated them fairly and well, and that population and its Government will not desert us unless convinced that we are unable to support them in their just demands against the undoubted interference of outsiders. I was sorry to hear the almost apologetic tone of the Under Secretary for Foreign Affairs with reference to affairs in China. Apology does not commend itself to the nations of the East. We must be strong if we want to secure their respect and obtain the.. support, and unless we are strong they will go to what they consider to be the rising star and the coming nation. I do not think that the way in which we allowed the Tien-tsin Treaty to be encroached upon is likely to secure us the respect or support of the natives of China. In that matter as in some others, the conduct and action of the Government have been reprehensible in mnay ways. The idea we have given in China is that we have been warned off by other Powers, and if they by our weakness secure the influence we had, the natives will begin to consider whether we are really strong, and whether these other nations—new comers—are not stronger and better able to defend an Empire which has very serious internal difficulties to deal with. The condition of China is a large, difficult, and intricate subject, but I am convinced that the present position which we occupy in China is not satisfactory to the people who know China, who have studied it on the spot, who know the peculiarities of its Government and the temperament of its people. There is a great and almost immeasurable trade to be obtained in China ; but we shall not obtain it, we shall not keep pace with other nations, if we do not show we are able to defend the rights we have obtained and that we are willing to take our full liability for the development of the resources of China. If we allow it to be seen that other countries can get concessions with reference to railways, and can have those railways managed by their own officials, while we allow our capital to go into China and to be managed by foreign people of one kind or another, as has been said in this Debate, then China will say, not unnaturally, from the Eastern point of view, that we are afraid to defend and stand up for our interests, and therefore we are not to be relied on to defend and promote its interest if it trusts in us. I have only spoken to-night in order, as far as it in my power lies, to warn the Members of this House of the unfavourable impression which the action of the Government has caused in China. Not a few hon. Members have been in China—I have been in some parts of the East myself—but it is very difficult for those who have not been in the East to realise to what an extent this feeling prevails. You may depend on it that a strong and reliable Government will be supported, cost what it may. The idea which obtains in China is that we are not definite, do not know what we want, and are turned away from our objects ; whereas other countries make up their minds as to what they want and get it. Nobody knows what we want, and nobody cares whether we get anything or not. That is not the way in which our commerce in China has been built up. Other forces and ideas have now come into play, and it is only by adapting ourselves to them that we can retain the

Mr. Barlow.

influence we have in China. Therefore I hope the Committee will do all in its power to assist the Government in taking up a strong, determined, and decided view that English interests in China must not be sacrificed ; that China must be supported in its legitimate demands and aspirations ; that English influence must be kept to the front, and not be allowed to lag behind in the race with other nations, which undoubtedly is getting keener for the new markets of the world. China presents great prospects for the future. It has a large, industrious, thrifty, and hard-working population, and it is in a country of that sort that we may expect the greatest expansion of trade in the future ; and unless we secure that expansion it will be impossible for the people of this country to maintain their position among the nations of the world. I speak not alone for Lancashire, but for other counties which have an indirect interest in the welfare of our producing community, and I say that it will be impossible for us to maintain our position when competition becomes keen unless the Government of the day, to whichever side it may belong, does what it can to support our legitimate influence and prestige in China, which I fear is sadly prejudiced at present.

Mr. MacIVER (Liverpool, Kirkdale): I wish to appeal to the Government to reconsider their decision with regard to the granting of compensation to the relatives of the unfortunate officers who were killed at Waima. I cannot help thinking that I am expressing the view of many hon. Members when I say that the Government ought not to wait until the French Government recognise their duty, but that they should do something themselves in the matter. Whatever difference of opinion may be expressed on other subjects, I believe there is no difference of opinion on this.

*Mr. J. A. PEASE (Northumberland, Tyneside): There is one subject to which I should like to draw the attention of the Committee. It has been already discussed during the present session, but it is a question which I, for one, will not allow to remain undebated as long as the institution of slavery remains under the British flag. At the present moment there are something like 350,000 slaves under the British flag in the Zanzibar Protectorate. The Government accepted the pledge of the late Government to free these slaves at the earliest possible moment, but up to the present have not carried it out. They find session after session an excuse for allowing this institution to remain. At the present rate of progress there are about 750 slaves annually freed in Pemba and Zanzibar, while on the mainland the Government have not taken any steps whatever to free the slaves employed there, and the Government, I know, assert that any slave can apply for his freedom, but I have evidence in my possession which shows that a great deal of pressure is placed upon the slave population to prevent them obtaining their freedom even through the courts. It is only recently that an individual employed in Pemba received an intimation from his superiors that his services were no longer required, and when one came to inquire into the reason it was found that it was attributed to the fact that he had endeavoured to secure justice for the slaves as against the Arab slave masters. There was a Debate a short time ago on the question of the retention of slaves by British subjects, and some doubt was expressed by hon. Members of this House as to whether it was legal for a British subject to administer a law allowing the detention of slaves. An Order in Council passed in 1877 applied the Indian Penal Code to the dominions of the Sultan of Zanzibar, and Section 370 of that Code enacts that whoever disposes of, accepts, or detains any person as a slave shall be liable, with or without a fine, to imprisonment for seven years. I hold that every one of Her Majesty's Ministers who are parties to the administration of the law with regard to slavery are really detainers of slaves and are morally guilty. All that is asked is that the Government should keep the pledge it gave to Parliament. In 1895 the First Lord of the Treasury stated that he would be glad to take any steps that could be reasonably taken. Four years have now elapsed, and practically no steps have been taken to liberate the slave population on the mainland. But a new interpretation has been placed on the law with regard to the abolition of the legal status of slavery. Hitherto, in the Indian Empire, it has always been interpreted as practically the same as the abolition of slavery itself; but in the East Coast Protectorate a different interpretation has been placed upon it, and the spirit in which the law is administered is indicated by the necessity imposed on a slave to go into the courts in order to obtain his freedom. The process is made difficult by the native officials, who themselves own a large number of slaves. The policy adopted by the Government with regard to the slave population has been to conciliate the Arab population rather than do justice to the slaves. The Government appear to me to have exaggerated the rights of the Mohammedan population, and as an illustration I might point to the fact that while no subject of the Sultan is allowed to inherit any slaves, unless he is the son of the owner, yet the present Sultan was permitted to inherit 30,000 slaves from the previous Sultan, although he is not a direct descendant. That shows the spirit in which the law is administered. I might also refer to a revolting case of cruelty which occurred in 1896, when a man placed a slave, for running away, in double irons, connected by a bar near the ankles, and to prolong his misery a cocoanut was given to him morning and evening. The miserable slave continued in the same spot, exposed to all kinds of weather, for seven months. The owner received a sentence of seven years' imprisonment, but the moment the judge's back was turned to come home on a holiday at the instance, I believe, of Sir Lloyd Mathews, the Sultan's Prime Minister, the Arab, who had almost killed the slave, was liberated from gaol. Such an act of so-called clemency was calculated, of course, to give encouragement to other Arabs to ill-treat their slaves. I object to the policy of the Government on this question on several grounds, but I object very strongly on the ground that they have made·an exception in favour of allowing the concubines of the Arab population to be exempt from the decree. I know the Foreign Office justify this on the ground that the children of concubines would become bastards if the concubines were allowed to take advantage of the decree. But no question of legitimacy or any alteration of connubial rights was raised. We desire to raise the moral tone of the home life of the Arab population. There are many concubines at present who are not slaves, and all the concubines of the Arab population should have the same opportunity of going into court to secure their freedom as other slaves.

It being midnight, the Chairman left the chair to make his report to the House.

Committee report progress ; to sit again upon Monday next.

SEATS FOR SHOP ASSISTANTS (ENGLAND AND IRELAND) BILL.

Considered in Committee, and reported, without Amendment ; Bill read the third time, and passed.

Adjourned at five minutes after Twelve o'clock till Monday next.

HOUSE OF LORDS.

Monday, 12th June 1899.

PRIVATE BILL BUSINESS.

The Lord Chancellor acquainted the House that the Clerk of the Parliaments had laid upon the Table the Certificates from the Examiners that the further Standing Orders applicable to the following Bills have been complied with :

BELFAST AND NORTHERN COUNTIES RAILWAY.

BOOTLE CORPORATION.

The same were ordered to lie on the Table.

STANDING ORDERS COMMITTEE.

Report from, That the Standing Orders not complied with in respect of the

BAKER STREET AND WATERLOO RAILWAY BILL

ought to be dispensed with and the Bill allowed to proceed, provided the names of the Great Central Railway Company and of the Waterloo and City Railway Company be struck out.

That the Standing Orders not complied with in respect of the

BELFAST CORPORATION BILL

ought to be dispensed with and the Bill allowed to proceed, provided Clause 23 be struck out.

Read, and agreed to.

STOCKPORT CORPORATION WATER BILL.

A witness ordered to attend the Select Committee.

CALEDONIAN RAILWAY (GENERAL POWERS) BILL. [Lords.]

The Queen's consent signified ; and Bill reported with Amendments.

ABERDEEN JOINT PASSENGER STATION BILL. [Lords.]

Reported with Amendments.

NORTH PEMBROKESHIRE AND FISH-GUARD RAILWAY BILL.

Reported without Amendments.

VOL. LXXII.   [FOURTH SERIES.]

NORTH-WEST LONDON RAILWAY BILL.

The Queen's consent signified ; and Bill reported with amendments.

LANCASHIRE AND YORKSHIRE RAILWAY (VARIOUS POWERS) BILL.

Report from the Select Committee, That the Committee had not proceeded with the consideration of the Bill, the opposition thereto having been withdrawn ; read, and ordered to lie on the Table : The orders made on the 25th of April and Tuesday last discharged ; and Bill committed.

WETHERBY DISTRICT WATER BILL.

Report from the Select Committee, That the Committee had not proceeded with the consideration of the Bill, the opposition thereto having been withdrawn ; read, and ordered to lie on the Table : The orders made on the 25th of April and Tuesday last discharged ; and Bill committed.

WEST HIGHLAND RAILWAY BILL. [Lords.]

Commons Amendments considered, and agreed to.

TRANSVAAL MORTGAGE LOAN AND FINANCE COMPANY BILL [Lords.]

Read 3°, and passed and sent to the Commons.

CROWBOROUGH DISTRICT WATER BILL.

Returned from the Commons with the Amendments agreed to.

ELECTRIC LIGHTING PROVISIONAL ORDERS (No. 14) BILL. [Lords.]

GAS ORDERS CONFIRMATION (No. 1) BILL. [Lords.]

GAS AND WATER ORDERS CONFIRMATION BILL. [Lords.]

WATER ORDERS CONFIRMATION BILL. [Lords.]

House to be in Committee To-morrow.

2 H

METROPOLITAN COMMON SCHEME (HARROW WEALD) PROVISIONAL ORDER BILL.

House in Committee (according to order); Bill reported, without amendment: Stonding Committee negatived; and Bill to be read 3ª To-morrow.

ELECTRIC LIGHTING PROVISIONAL ORDERS (No. 1) BILL [Lords.]

Read 3ª (according to order), and passed.

ELECTRIC LIGHTING PROVISIONAL ORDERS (No. 4) Bill.

Read 2ª (according to order), and passed.

ELECTRIC LIGHTING PROVISIONAL ORDER (No. 9) BILL. [Lords.]

ELECTRIC LIGHTING PROVISIONAL ORDERS (No. 11) BILL. [Lords.]

Read 3ª (according to order), and passed, and sent to the Commons.

ELECTRIC LIGHTING PROVISIONAL ORDERS (No. 10) BILL. [Lords.]

Amendments reported (according to order), and Bill to be read 3ª To-morrow.

———

Report from the Committee of Selection, that the following Lords be proposed to the House to form the Select Committee for the consideration of the said Bills; viz.—

D. Bedford (chairman),
D. Marlborough,
E. Dartmouth,
E. Windsor,
L. Bolton.

ELECTRIC LIGHTING PROVISIONAL ORDERS (No 3) BILL.

CENTRAL ELECTRIC SUPPLY BILL.

CENTRAL LONDON RAILWAY BILL.

CHARING CROSS, EUSTON, AND HAMPSTEAD RAILWAY BILL.

KENSINGTON AND NOTTING HILL ELECTRIC LIGHTING BILL.

MIDLAND RAILWAY BILL.

GAS LIGHT AND COKE COMPANY BILL.

LONDON, BRIGHTON, AND SOUTH COAST RAILWAY (VARIOUS POWERS) BILL.

Agreed to; and the said Lords appointed accordingly; The Committee

to meet on Thursday, the 22nd instant, at Eleven o'clock; and all petitions referred to the Committee, with leave to the petitioners praying to be heard by counsel against the Bills to be heard as desired, as also counsel for the Bills.

———

RETURNS, REPORTS, &c.

———

TREATY SERIES, No. 14 (1899).

Withdrawal of Montenegro from the International Union for the protection of Literary and Artistic Works.

DISEASES OF ANIMALS ACT, 1894.

Return as regards Ireland for the year ended 31st December 1898.

ELECTRIC LIGHTING ACTS, 1882 AND 1888.

Special Reports by the Board of Trade under Section 1 of the Electric Lighting Act, 1888 :—

I. City of London Electric Lighting

II. Gateshead Electric Lighting.

Presented (by command), and ordered to lie on the Table.

PUBLIC RECORDS (COURT OF EXCHEQUER).

Second Schedule of classes of documents which formerly were, or ought to have been, in the Office of the King's or Queen's Remembrancer, of the Exchequer, or of the Clerk appointed to take charge of the Port Bonds or Coast Bonds, and which are now in, but are not considered of sufficient public value to justify their preservation in, the Public Record Office.

PUBLIC WORKS LOAN BOARD.

Twenty-fourth Annual Report for 1898–99, with Appendices.

Laid before House (pursuant to Act) and ordered to lie on the Table.

———

QUESTION.

———

IRELAND—INCITEMENT TO CRIME— M'HALE *v.* SULLIVAN.

THE LORD CHANCELLOR (The EARL OF HALSBURY): The noble and learned Lord, Lord Coleridge, has given notice to call attention to the circumstances of the cases of the Queen *v.* Sullivan and M'Hale *v.* Sullivan, and to ask what steps Her Majesty's Government intend to take in the matter. This appears to refer to litigation which is still in existence, and from a letter in this morning's *Times*, signed by a gentleman who professes to have been one of the counsel in the case, it appears that there are proceedings still pending in the case, which may become the subject of a second trial, and be submitted to the decision of a Court. Under those circumstances the noble and learned Lord will probably agree with me that it is not desirable to break through the well accepted rule that no matter that is *sub judice* should be mentioned in this House or brought under any sort of public discussion.

*Lord COLERIDGE : My Lords, I may say at once that it would have been most improper on my part to have alluded to this subject in this House had I not already satisfied myself that no further proceedings in the matter would be taken. I satisfied myself on this point before I put my Notice down on your Lordships' Paper, and I have had a positive assurance—and I am authorised to state this—that all proceedings in the case of M'Hale *r.* Sullivan have been abandoned. I anticipate that there can therefore be no reason for any postponement of my Notice ; but if your Lordships think there is, I can only say that I do not know to what period your Lordships would desire to postpone the discussion.

The LORD CHANCELLOR : I understand from the Attorney-General for Ireland that no Rule for the discontinuance of the proceedings has been entered, and therefore there is a possibility of the case being tried again.

*Lord COLERIDGE : The people who have found the money with which the proceedings were maintained have assured me that the funds are exhausted. Apart from that, I am assured on good authority that all proceedings have been abandoned, and that there is no intention to resume them. Under these circumstances, I submit to your Lordships that I am entitled to call attention to these cases, without infringing the very proper rules for my guidance which the noble and learned Lord, the Lord Chancellor, has referred to. Unless I am stopped by

some Motion, I propose to proceed with my Notice, which is to call attention o the circum ances of the case of the Queen *v.* Sullivan, tried at the last Sligo Assizes, and the case of M'Hale *v.* Sullivan, tried at Dublin on 10th May and following days, both cases involving a charge against a member of the Royal Irish Constabulary of forgery and inciting to crime ; and to ask whether the said Sullivan is still a member of the Royal Irish Constabulary, and, if so, what steps Her Majesty's Government intend to take in the matter.

*The EARL OF ARRAN : Of course I take everything the noble and learned Lord has told us as being correct, and as the case is not to be retried I do not propose to move the Motion which I had intended to submit to your Lordships.

*Lord COLERIDGE : Then I take it, my Lords, there is no objection to my alluding to these cases. I have thought it my duty to do so, and I shall state the facts with the utmost brevity, and, I hope, with impartiality. For the last twelve months, in the County of Mayo, there has grown up an association which is called the United Irish League. It is not my business, nor is it my intention, to make any comments with regard to the League, its authors, its conduct, or its object. But it is necessary for me to allude to it to explain the case to which I desire to call the attention of this House. In Newport, a town in Mayo, there was a gentleman of the name of John M'Hale, who was the local president of the United Irish League. There was living at Westport an ignorant, unlettered man of the name of James Kelly, who was a member of the League. On the 14th of April James Kelly received through the post a letter in the following terms :

> "Newport, April 13, 1898.
> "2s. for drink.
> "Dear James Kelly,
> "As you are aware, Martin Kelly is going back to the bastard Stoney on Monday. Go with some of the boys and visit him, and tell him that if he works he will be sorry, and that he is working against our cause. It would be better to blacken your face. Do it to-morrow night, and watch the police. Other houses will be visited on the same night, so let Tiernan not be behind.
> "Yours truly,
> "JOHN M'HALE (Chairman).
> "Burn this for fear of danger. Don't bring any man but one you can trust."

No one can doubt, my Lords, that that was an incitement to crime. By whom was that letter written ? It is admitted on all hands, and has been admitted from the first, that the letter was not written by John M'Hale. By whom, then, was it written ? There was at Mulranney, a short distance off, a certain Sergeant Sullivan, who was a magnificent penman. He had, I believe, received prizes on account of his penmanship, and of his handwriting he was undoubtedly proud. Some people knew his handwriting well, and upon the receipt of this letter by James Kelly specimens of his handwriting were procured from various sources. These specimens, together with the forged letter, were sent to Mr. Gurrin, the well-known handwriting expert in London, and the gentleman who is always employed by the Home Government in criminal and other trials. The result of the comparison of these handwritings was that Mr. Gurrin came to the confident opinion that all the documents—the genuine documents and the forged document—were written by one hand. Armed with this evidence, a case was launched before the Petty Sessions at Westport. It was proved that the letter was received through the post; it was proved that John M'Hale had not written it ; it was proved that a man of the experience of Mr. Gurrin was of opinion that the letter submitted to him and the specimens —the undoubted and admitted specimens —of Sullivan's handwriting were written by the same hand. That was the case preferred before the justices, whose duty it was to see whether a *prima facie* case was made out, and, if so, to commit. I need hardly tell your Lordships that, in the absence of any other evidence than the evidence I have told you of, not only a *prima facie* but a conclusive case was made out. The magistrates, however, not only unanimously refused to commit, but at first wished to impound the document, so that it should never again pass into the hands of those who were prosecuting. This astonishing decision was, happily, in the latter part of it, not carried into effect. The magistrates ultimately, after argument—and I may say the person who appeared to prosecute was The MacDermott, a man of position in the profession, and a gentleman who had held the office of Attorney-General for Ireland—and after remonstrances, did give up the letter, but refused to commit, and in consequence it was determined that the

witnesses should be bound over to the next Assizes for the purpose of the charge being further investigated. On the 14th of July, at the Castlebar Assizes, a Grand Jury was impanelled and found a true bill against James Sullivan on three charges—libel, forgery, and inciting to crime. As is universal in Ireland, the Government took up the prosecution, and it was hoped and believed that The MacDermott, in whom those who were prosecuting had confidence, would be further employed to conduct the case. The Crown, however, refused to avail itself of the services of The MacDermott, and employed its own counsel. The case came on for trial on the 1st of December at Sligo, and then, my Lords, a most unprecedented scene was witnessed. Sligo is a county in which nine-tenths of the inhabitants are Roman Catholics, and there was witnessed the scene of the Crown on the one side and the defence upon the other combining together to strike every Roman Catholic off the panel. I would ask the noble Earl who, I believe, is going to reply to me, whether in his opinion the profession of the Roman Catholic faith disentitles a man to the discharge of his civic duties.

*THE EARL OF ARRAN : The noble and learned Lord is looking at me. I beg to inform him that I am not going to reply, on behalf of the Government, to his Question.

*LORD COLERIDGE : I understood that the noble Earl the Earl of Denbigh was going to reply. I want to ask whether noble Lords can wonder, in the presence of these facts, that the people of Sligo and the counties round, rightly or wrongly, believe that the object of the Crown in combining with the defence to prevent any Roman Catholic from being on the jury was that the prisoner should be acquitted and not convicted ? I do not say whether they were right or wrong, but I do say that in the presence of these facts it was a natural conclusion to arrive at. In the interval a remarkable thing happened. At the trial before the Justices at Westport a district inspector, of the name of Oulton, had been subpœnaed to produce the patrol book kept in the office of the Constabulary, and this book showed that on the evening of the 14th of April, the night on which the letter incited Kelly to commit a crime against the man Martin Kelly, an ambush was laid for an hour round the house of Martin Kelly in apparent anticipation of some outrage that might or would be likely to be committed. The patrol book showed that that took place for an hour. The report of Mr. Oulton's evidence was read by a constable of the name of Curtin, and on reading it he remembered that the entry in the patrol book as it appeared when it was produced by Oulton, the district inspector, was not the entry which appeared on the morning after it was made. He thereupon went and inspected the patrol book. He found that it had been altered, and it is admitted that the patrol book was altered, and altered by Sullivan. The alteration had the effect of making it appear that instead of the ambush being laid for three hours, as it was originally entered, it was an ambush of one hour. It was admitted that the book was altered, after the entry, by Sullivan. What was Curtin's duty? His duty was to make this known. If he had reported the matter to his immediate superior it would have been to Sullivan, but he did not do that. He waited for a few days until the district inspector—Oulton—visited the Constabulary. Curtin informed the prosecutors of what he had discovered, and reported the matter also to the district inspector. How was the report received? On the evening of the day on which Curtin had made this report to Oulton he was taken from the police office at Mulranney and banished to an island called Inniskear, 24 miles out into the Atlantic ocean. That was the way in which Constable Curtin was dealt with when he had the audacity and the temerity to say what he knew with regard to this case. Under these circumstances it could not be wondered at that the jury at Sligo did what was expected of them—they acquitted Sullivan, not only without hearing any evidence for the defence, but, in acquitting him, telling the learned judge that they had made up their minds to acquit him at a time before they had heard the evidence of Police-constable Curtin, which was material evidence in the case. Such was the slight indication which they gave of the impartiality of their minds in this matter. It is often thought advisable, ordinarily speaking, for the man who is acquitted to bring civil proceedings for malicious prosecution against the persons who prosecuted him; but in this case the facts were reversed, and the prosecutors, who had failed, brought an action for libel in Dublin, which was tried on the 10th of May, before Mr. Justice Andrews and a special jury. The same facts were then proved. Sullivan's defence was heard, and the matter was tried out to the utmost, squarely and fairly. Two points are worthy of notice. At the criminal trial some play was made by the defence by a suggestion that the handwriting of one of the witnesses for the prosecution bore similarities to the handwriting of the forged letter—and it was hinted that she might be the author. On the second occasion, when this matter was further investigated, this defence was tacitly abandoned. The evidence of Mr. Gurrin was forthcoming, and it was fortified by another expert witness, Mr. Price, who agreed with him. Not only was no expert evidence called to prove the slightest similarity between the handwriting of any of the witnesses and the handwriting of the forged letter, but there was no expert evidence called even to show that the forged letter was not written by the defendant Sullivan. The jury, after a long and patient trial, disagreed; ten were for the plaintiff M'Hale, and two for the defendant Sullivan. That, my Lords, is a short and brief account of the litigation in this case. I have thought it my duty to bring these facts to the attention of your Lordships' House. I, in common with your Lordships, wish to see in all civilised communities the law trusted and obeyed, and I say that if the law is administered in Ireland, or in any part of any civilised community, as it has been administered in the case of The Queen *v.* Sullivan, no man ought to wonder if the law, as so administered, has not the respect of the inhabitants of the country. Your Lordships will no doubt ask what I propose. I suggest that an independent inquiry—and I lay stress on the word "independent"—be held into this matter. Nothing less than an independent inquiry, I am sure, will satisfy the bulk of the people who live in the neighbourhood where these things have taken place, and I think nothing less ought to satisfy either Her Majesty's Government or your Lordships' House.

THE LORD CHANCELLOR: My Lords, I confess that I very much regret that the noble and learned Lord should have thought it right to raise this matter in your Lordships' House, seeing that it has not been raised in the House of Commons, where the Attorney-General for Ireland would have been present and would have been prepared to answer more perfectly than anyone in your Lordships' House can do for what has taken place. I protest against the last statement of the noble and learned Lord as to the division of the jury. I am not aware myself of any legal mode of obtaining such information as that. Here a man who has the misfortune to be a policeman in Ireland is accused of a criminal offence, and the whole object of the noble and learned Lord seems to show that the man was guilty, although he had been acquitted. Does the noble and learned Lord think that such action as that will commend itself to a civilised community? The Attorney-General for Ireland told me that he was perfectly satisfied that the verdict of the jury was right, and that for all that was done he was perfectly prepared to take the responsibility. Everything has been done by his direction, and he is perfectly prepared, when he himself can be heard, to defend his action throughout. There has been another trial in respect of the same matter in another court, and the noble and learned Lord suggests that the verdict was against the policeman; but the jury was discharged without agreeing upon a verdict, and further proceedings have been abandoned. The noble and learned Lord suggests that Her Majesty's Government should hold a new and independent investigation, but how is that to be done? What does the noble and learned Lord mean by an independent investigation? What objection was there to the civil trial, which the noble Lord himself said was fairly and squarely fought out? Did not the trial afford a method of ascertaining the facts? I have heard no suggestion from the noble and learned Lord that the matter was not capable of being investigated there, and because the jury disagreed the noble and learned Lord has made a speech, every word of which was an attempt to show the man was guilty. It seems to me that the noble and learned Lord has set a very bad example of the mode in which an impartial investigation should be conducted. If the parties are still of opinion that Sullivan is guilty, let them proceed. But the House has been informed that they will not proceed, and yet there is to be a dis-

The Lord Chancellor.

cussion of this sort, the whole object of which is to show that this man, who has been acquitted by one jury and in whose case another jury has disagreed, is guilty. If an investigation is to take place at all it ought to have been perfectly independent of such observations as those which have been made by the noble and learned Lord.

REFORMATORY SCHOOLS (AMENDMENT) BILL. [Lords.]

COMMITTEE.

House in Committee (according to Order).

Clause 1 :—

LORD JAMES OF HEREFORD: My Lords, to this clause, which is the only clause in the Bill, there is no objection in point of substance, but the Home Office take the view—with which, I must say, I coincide—that it will be absolutely necessary to amend the drafting. However, as this is only a question of form, I think the better way would be to allow the Bill to go through Committee, and then, perhaps, the noble Lord will move the alteration in the wording in the Standing Committee.

LORD LEIGH: I shall be much obliged to the noble and learned Lord if he will inform me what Amendment he would suggest, and I shall be quite willing to move it in the Standing Committee.

Bill reported without Amendment ; and re-committed to the Standing Committee.

ISOLATION HOSPITALS (AMENDMENT) BILL. [Lords.]

House to be in Committee on Thursday, the 22nd instant.

TRAWLERS' CERTIFICATES SUSPENSION BILL. [Lords.]

House in Committee (according to order): The Amendments proposed by the Select Committee made ; Standing Committee negatived : The Report of Amendments to be received on Friday next.

MANCHESTER CANONRIES BILL. [Lords].

A Bill to amend Section 20 of the Parish of Manchester Division Act, 1850— Was presented by the Earl Egerton (for the Lord Bishop of Manchester): read 1ᵃ ; to be printed ; and to be read 2ᵃ on Thursday, the 22nd instant. (No. 111.)

YOUTHFUL OFFENDERS BILL. [Lords.]

A Bill to amend the law relating to youthful offenders, and for other purposes connected therewith, was presented by the Lord James; read 1ᵃ; to be printed; and to be read 2ᵃ on Monday next. (No. 112.)

SEATS FOR SHOP ASSISTANTS (ENGLAND AND IRELAND) BILL.

Brought from the Commons; read 1ᵃ; and to be printed. (No. 113.)

House adjourned at five minutes past Five o'clock, till To-morrow, half-past Ten o'clock.

HOUSE OF COMMONS.

Monday, 12th June 1899.

PRIVATE BILL BUSINESS

PRIVATE BILLS (STANDING ORDER 62 COMPLIED WITH).

Mr. Speaker laid upon the Table Report from one of the Examiners of Petitions for Private Bills, That in the case of the following Bill, referred on the First Reading thereof, Standing Order No. 62 has been complied with, viz.:—

MILLWALL DOCK BILL.

Ordered, That the Bill be read a second time.

PRIVATE BILLS [Lords] (STANDING ORDERS NOT PREVIOUSLY INQUIRED INTO COMPLIED WITH).

Mr. Speaker laid upon the Table Report from one of the Examiners of Petitions for Private Bills, That in the case of the following Bills, originating in the Lords, and referred on the First Reading thereof, the Standing Orders not previously inquired into, and which are applicable thereto, have been complied with, viz:—

ALL SAINTS' CHURCH (CARDIFF) BILL. [Lords.]

LOWESTOFT WATER AND GAS BILL. [Lords.]

Ordered, That the Bills be read a second time.

BIRKENHEAD CORPORATION BILL. [Lords.]

Read the third time, and passed, with Amendments. [New Title.]

CITY AND BRIXTON RAILWAY BILL.

Read the third time, and passed.

DUMBARTON BURGH BILL. [Lords.]

Read the third time, and passed, with Amendments.

LONDON IMPROVEMENTS BILL (QUEEN'S CONSENT SIGNIFIED).

SHEFFIELD CORPORATION MARKETS BILL.

STOCKPORT CORPORATION BILL.

Read the third time, and passed.

BLACKPOOL IMPROVEMENT BILL.

As amended, considered; to be read the third time.

DUBLIN CORPORATION BILL.

As amended, to be considered To-morrow.

GREAT NORTHERN RAILWAY BILL. [Lords.]

SUNDERLAND CORPORATION BILL. [Lords.]

Read a second time, and committed.

ELECTRIC LIGHTING PROVISIONAL ORDERS (No. 7) BILL.

HOUSING OF THE WORKING CLASSES PROVISIONAL ORDER (BORROWSTOUNNESS) BILL.

LOCAL GOVERNMENT (IRELAND) PROVISIONAL ORDER (No. 1) BILL.

LOCAL GOVERNMENT PROVISIONAL ORDER (HOUSING OF WORKING CLASSES) BILL.

LOCAL GOVERNMENT PROVISIONAL ORDERS (No. 5) BILL.

LOCAL GOVERNMENT PROVISIONAL ORDERS (POOR LAW) BILL.

Read the third time, and passed.

LOCAL GOVERNMENT PROVISIONAL ORDERS (No. 8) BILL.

PIER AND HARBOUR PROVISIONAL ORDERS (No. 1) BILL.

As amended, considered; to be read the third time To-morrow.

LOCAL GOVERNMENT (IRELAND) PROVISIONAL ORDERS (HOUSING OF WORKING CLASSES (No. 2) BILL.

LOCAL GOVERNMENT (IRELAND) PROVISIONAL ORDER (No. 4) BILL.

Read a second time, and committed.

ELECTRIC LIGHTING PROVISIONAL ORDER (No. 20) BILL.

To confirm a Provisional Order made by the Board of Trade, under the Electric Lighting Acts, 1882 and 1888, relating to the City of London, ordered to be brought in by Mr. Ritchie and Mr. Hanbury.

Ordered, that Standing Order 193A be suspended, and that the Bill be now read the first time.—(*Mr. Ritchie.*)

ELECTRIC LIGHTING PROVISIONAL ORDER (No. 20) BILL.

To confirm a Provisional Order made by the Board of Trade, under the Electric Lighting Acts, 1882 and 1888, relating to the City of London, presented accordingly, and read the first time ; to be referred to the Examiners of Petitions for Private Bills, and to be printed. [Bill 230.]

MERSEY DOCKS AND HARBOUR BOARD (PILOTAGE) BILL. [Lords.]

Report [8th June] from the Select Committee on Standing Orders read.

Ordered that the Bill be read a second time.—(*Dr. Farquharson.*)

PETITIONS.

GROUND RENTS (TAXATION BY LOCAL AUTHORITIES).

Petitions in favour ;—From Wakefield ; —and Ealing ; to lie upon the Table.

LOCAL GOVERNMENT (SCOTLAND) ACT (1894) AMENDMENT BILL.

Petition from Elgin, in favour ; to lie upon the Table.

MINES (EIGHT HOURS) BILL.

Petition from Kilburn, in favour ; to lie upon the Table.

PARISH COUNCILS ASSOCIATION (SCOTLAND) BILL.

Petition from Greenock, in favour ; to lie upon the Table.

POOR LAW OFFICERS' SUPERANNUA-TION (SCOTLAND) BILL.

Petition from Greenock, against ; to lie upon the Table.

POOR LAW RELIEF (DISFRANCHISE-MENT).

Petition from Reading, for alteration of Law ; to lie upon the Table.

POOR LAW (SCOTLAND) ACTS.

Petition from Greenock, for alteration of Law ; to lie upon the Table.

PRIVATE LEGISLATION PROCEDURE (SCOTLAND) BILL.

Petitions in favour : From Elgin ;— Forfar ;— Kirkcudbright ;— and Perth ; to lie upon the Table.

SALE OF INTOXICATING LIQUORS ON SUNDAY BILL.

Petitions in favour—From Manchester ; —Rochester ;—and Newcastle ; to lie upon the Table.

SALE OF INTOXICATING LIQUORS TO CHILDREN.

Petition from Brierfield, for alteration of Law ; to lie upon the Table.

SEA FISHERIES REGULATION (SCOT-LAND) ACT (1895) AMENDMENT BILL.

Petition from Aberdeen, against ; to lie upon the Table.

TOWN COUNCILS (SCOTLAND) BILL.

Petition from Aberdeen, against ; to lie upon the Table.

TROUT FISHING ANNUAL CLOSE TIME (SCOTLAND) BILL.

Petition from Forfar, in favour ; to lie upon the Table.

VACCINATION ACTS, 1867 TO 1898.

Petition from Daventry, for alteration of Law ; to lie upon the Table.

RETURNS, REPORTS, &c.

ELECTRIC LIGHTING ACTS, 1882 AND 1888.

Copies presented,—of Special Reports by the Board of Trade under Section 1 of The Electric Lighting Act, 1888 :—
(1) City of London Electric Lighting ;
(2) Gateshead Electric Lighting ;
[by Command] ; to lie upon the Table.

DISEASES OF ANIMALS ACTS, 1894 AND 1896 (IRELAND).

Copy presented,—of Return, in pursuance of the Acts as regards Ireland for the year 1898 [by Command] ; to lie upon the Table.

CHANNEL ISLANDS (CROWN RIGHTS.)
Return ordered, "of Revenues drawn from the Crown Rights in the Channel Islands in each year during the last five years, distinguishing for each Island separately the Amount received from Tithes, from Fines on Transfer of Property, from Seigneurial Dues, and from other sources; and stating the Cost of Collection, the several Payments made for Local Purposes, and the Net Amount paid into the Exchequer."—(*Sir Charles Dilke.*)

MESSAGE FROM THE LORDS.

That they have agreed to—

Farnley Tyas Marriages Bill, without Amendment.

That they have passed a Bill, intituled, "An Act to constitute the Divisions of Lincolnshire separate Counties for all the purposes of the Coroners Acts." [Lincolnshire Coroners Bill] [Lords].

QUESTIONS.

TRADE IN THE RUSSIAN EMPIRE.

SIR HOWARD VINCENT (Sheffield, Central): I beg to ask the Under Secretary of State for Foreign Affairs if he is aware that the United States, France, and Germany are making every effort to profit by the coming reign of industrial activity in the Russian Empire; and, if he is now able to announce what steps Her Majesty's Government have at length decided to take to utilise for British capital and trade the friendly disposition thereto of His Imperial Majesty the Tsar and the Russian Government.

*THE UNDER SECRETARY OF STATE FOR FOREIGN AFFAIRS (Mr. BRODRICK, Surrey, Guildford): We have not seen any official reports to the effect mentioned by my hon. friend. No change has taken place since I answered my hon. friend's question a month ago which would enable me to add anything to the answer I then gave as to our commercial relations.

SIR HOWARD VINCENT: I shall take advantage of the earliest opportunity to call attention to the delay in the appointment of a commercial attaché at St. Petersburg.

THE DISTRESSED ARMENIANS.

MR SAMUEL SMITH (Flintshire): I beg to ask the Under Secretary of State for Foreign Affairs whether the Government will take into consideration the desirability of bringing under the notice of the International Congress, now assembled at the Hague, the distressed condition of the Armenians, with a view to concerted European action for their protection.

*MR. BRODRICK: Her Majesty's Government can take no action in the sense desired, as according to the terms of the invitation to the Conference such subjects are excluded from discussion.

CRIMPING IN THE UNITED STATES.

COLONEL DENNY (Kilmarnock Burghs): I beg to ask the Under Secretary of State for Foreign Affairs whether his attention has been called to the system of blackmail at present levied by the boarding masters and crimps at San Francisco, California, and Portland, Oregon, by which blood-money, amounting to £20 per head, is charged for the shipment of British seamen who have previously been induced to desert; whether he is aware that Consul J. Laidlaw, of Portland, Oregon, has stated in a despatch, dated 29th June, 1898, that a comprehensive Consular Convention should be concluded with the United States, giving the same exclusive jurisdiction as is now enjoyed by French and German Consuls, and should include powers to call upon the local authorities for the necessary assistance; whether Her Majesty's Government will endeavour to arrange such a Convention with the United States Government for the better protection of British shipmasters and seamen, and to abolish the system under which blood-money can be levied; whether he will inform the House of the exact terms of the Convention between the United States and France which the Consul's letter refers to; and whether Her Majesty's Government are prepared to take such steps as may be required to protect shipmasters and seamen in this matter.

*MR. BRODRICK: Attention has been called to the system which at present prevails in some ports of the United States with regard to the engagement of seamen. Reports on the subject, including that from Consul Laidlaw, to which reference is made, have been laid before Parliament. The Consular Convention between the United States and France will be found at p. 718 of vol. 55 of British and Foreign State Papers. Her Majesty's Government have under consideration what steps can be taken for the better protection of British shipmasters and seamen.

NAVIGATION OF MERCHANT VESSELS.

MR. HAVELOCK WILSON (Middlesbrough): I beg to ask the President of the Board of Trade whether his attention has been directed to the statement made by the crew of the s.s. *Pinner's Point*, in which they allege that during the passage of this vessel from the United Kingdom to the United States of America, in the month of May of this year, all the deck hands of this vessel, with the exception of the man at the wheel, were employed in discharging ballast from six in the morning till six in the evening ; whether he is aware that during the night this vessel was being navigated without a man on the look out, on the forecastle head or fore-deck ; and, whether, in view of the number of collisions that occur annually, involving serious loss of life and property, it is his intention to promote legislation at an early date with a view to preventing the possibility of vessels being navigated in such a dangerous manner.

THE PRESIDENT OF THE BOARD OF TRADE (Mr. RITCHIE, Croydon): My attention has not been directed to the statement referred to in the question, except by the hon. Member himself. Although the matter is not one in which the Board of Trade have any authority to interfere with the discretion of the master of a ship, unless he commits some offence under the Merchant Shipping Act, I have been in communication with the owners of the *Pinner's Point*, and I have been furnished with a statement signed by the master and chief officer, in which they emphatically deny that the vessel was ever left without a proper look-out, day or night, and this statement is confirmed by the boatswain and two A.B.'s. The master and chief officer also state that the ballast was not discharged until the steamer was approaching the American coast, and that for this work

the men received extra pay. I am not prepared to propose fresh legislation on the subject.

SCOTTISH UNIVERSITIES.

MR. CROMBIE (Kincardineshire): I beg to ask the Lord Advocate if he can state the number of male students in the various faculties of the four Scotch Universities during the years 1888 and 1898 respectively, and the number of female students in each faculty and University during the year 1898.

THE LORD ADVOCATE (MR. A. G. MURRAY, Buteshire): The Secretary for Scotland has obtained the information desired by the hon. Member from the Universities Courts, and will transmit it to him. It would not be convenient to give it in answer to a question.

ORPHAN HOMES OF SCOTLAND.

SIR CHARLES CAMERON (Glasgow, Bridgeton): I beg to ask the Lord Advocate whether he is aware that some 1,000 children of school age, inmates of the Orphan Homes of Scotland, on which over £200 of school rates were recently paid, have received no education for nearly two months, owing to the refusal of the School Board to receive them ; whether anything is being done to bring the present deadlock to an end ; and, whether the Scottish Education Department has taken any steps to enforce the law of Scotland as to the compulsory education of all children of school age.

MR. A. G. MURRAY: The legal questions connected with the matter referred to in the hon. Member's question are now under consideration, and it is therefore impossible for me at present to make any further statement regarding it.

ATTACK BY BRITISH SOLDIERS ON A RANGOON WOMAN.

MR. DAVITT (Mayo, S.): I beg to ask the Secretary of State for India whether certain British soldiers have been charged with an indecent assault upon a native woman at Rangoon ; whether such soldiers have been brought before any tribunal for this alleged crime ; and if any punishment has been inflicted for this outrage.

THE SECRETARY OF STATE FOR INDIA (LORD G. HAMILTON, Middlesex, Ealing): This matter has for some time past been occupying the attention of the Indian Government, with whom I have been in communication on the subject. I regret to say that it is true that an outrage was committed upon an elderly Burmese woman of unsound mind by a party of soldiers, who are said to have been under the influence of liquor. On appearance of police and a corporal the soldiers dispersed ; but one of them was arrested, and tried by jury on the 10th of May, but was acquitted on the ground that he was not proved to have committed or attempted the offence with which he was charged, and the Recorder concurred in the verdict. So far, no other person has been brought to trial ; but the Government of India are determined that the matter shall be thoroughly investigated, and that the culprits shall be brought to justice ; and they have impressed their views very strongly upon the civil and military authorities of Rangoon, who have undertaken that no effort shall be spared to bring the facts to light. Accordingly, a special Court of inquiry has been summoned to investigate and report upon the whole matter.

ASSAM TEA PLANTATIONS.

MR. SCHWANN : I beg to ask the Secretary of State for India when he will lay upon the Table of the House the Report on the Assam Tea Plantations, now for several years delayed in its presentation to Parliament.

LORD G. HAMILTON : I have not yet received the views of the Government of India on the subject of the Report to which the hon. Member's question refers, although in February last they hoped to be able to lay them before me at an early date. The matter with which the Report is concerned is a difficult and intricate one, but I will draw the Viceroy's attention to the desirability of expediting the submission of their opinions upon it.

MR. SCHWANN : Shall we get it before the end of the session ?

LORD G. HAMILTON : I doubt it, as the question is so complicated.

LIQUOR TRADE IN THE MADRAS PRESIDENCY.

MR. SAMUEL SMITH : I beg to ask the Secretary of State for India whether he is aware that three liquor shops have

been opened and still remain open in Brace Petta, one of the leading thoroughfares of the town of Bellary, in the Madras Presidency ; and that these three shops are very near each other, and situated in close proximity to Christian and Hindu places of worship, and on the only common road leading to the Cowl bazaar and the municipal high school in the fort ; whether a petition has been submitted to the Collector of Bellary by some of the leading residents in the immediate neighbourhood of the shops complaining of the nuisance caused by them, and praying for their removal ; and whether, having regard to the declared policy of the Government of India, as enunciated in their Dispatch, No. 29, of 4th February, 1890, he will give instructions for the closing of the said shops.

LORD G. HAMILTON : I have received no information on the subject of the first two clauses of the hon. Member's question. I do not propose to send any instructions to India on the matter, which is clearly one for the discretion of the authorities in India.

DIVINE SERVICE AT GOVERNMENT FACTORY CHAPELS.

*MR. CHANNING (Northampton, E.) : I beg to ask the Under Secretary of State for War whether he is aware that in the Government chapel at the Royal Small Arms Ordnance Factory at Enfield, the chaplain, the Reverend C. E. J. Carter, a member of the English Church Union, is in the habit of hiding the manual acts at the celebration of the Holy Communion, mixing water ceremonially with wine, elevating the consecrated elements, and burning candles in the day time, all of which practices have been judicially condemned by the Supreme Court in such cases ; further, that Mr. Carter celebrates Eucharists and Vespers for the dead, both services being without any authority within the Established Church of England ; and that a cross is illegally placed upon the re-table ; and whether the Secretary of State for War will take steps to secure the exclusion of illegal practices and unauthorised services from this and other chapels under his control.

*THE UNDER SECRETARY OF STATE FOR WAR (MR. WYNDHAM, Dover) : No complaint has been received from the persons using the chapel; and the Secretary of State does not feel called upon to interfere.

*Mr. CHANNING: I beg to give notice that I shall ask a further question on this matter.

Mr. CARVELL WILLIAMS (Notts, Mansfield): I beg to ask the Financial Secretary to the War Office what proportions of the sum of £565 4s. 5d., which appears from last year's Ordnance Factories Accounts to have been expended for "Divine Service," were allocated to the factories of Enfield, Waltham Abbey, Woolwich, and Birmingham respectively.

*Mr. WYNDHAM: The figures are as follows: Woolwich, £293 4s. 11d.; Enfield, £197 10s. 7d.; Waltham, £74 8s. 11d.; Birmingham, *nil.*

Mr. CARVELL WILLIAMS: I beg to ask the Under Secretary of State for War why there should be a Government chapel, with a chaplain, at the Royal Small Arms Ordnance Factory at Enfield, when in other Government establishments of the same character there is no such chapel or official.

*Mr. WYNDHAM: When the factory at Enfield was originated it was considered necessary, owing to the isolation of the buildings, to provide a chapel for spiritual ministrations to the workmen employed there.

TROOPS AT ALDERSHOT.

Major RASCH (Essex, S.E.): I beg to ask the Under Secretary of State for War what is the official strength at Aldershot; what were the numbers present on the Queen's Birthday parade; and how were the 5,000 men absent employed.

*Mr. WYNDHAM: The strength at Aldershot on 24th May amounted to 16,788 warrant officers, non-commissioned officers, and men, and of these 11,542 were present on parade. 1,563 men of the Royal Engineers, the Army Service Corps, and the Royal Army Medical Corps were engaged on their corps duties; the East Kent Volunteer Artillery, numbering 200, and the Northumberland Fusiliers, numbering 761, were not on parade, most of the latter being on furlough. There were 747 sick. The remaining absentees, to the number of about 2,000, were on guard and other station duties.

SCHOOL ACCOMMODATION AT BETHNAL GREEN.

Mr. J. G. TALBOT (Oxford University): I beg to ask the Vice-President of the Committee of Council on Education whether application has been made to the Department by the London School Board to sanction the erection of a new school in Wood Close, Bethnal Green; whether a new Board school is already being erected in Daniel Street, in the same neighbourhood; whether there is any need at the present time for increased school accommodation in this district, where the population is stationary and likely to decrease; and whether, under these circumstances, the Education Department will refuse their assent to the application of the London School Board.

The VICE-PRESIDENT of the COMMITTEE of the COUNCIL on EDUCATION (Sir J. GORST, Cambridge University): The reply to the first two questions is in the affirmative. The questions whether increased accommodation is required, and whether the population is likely to decrease, are now the subject of inquiry; and the sanction of the Education Department to the proposed school in Wood Street depends on the result of that inquiry.

WORKING-CLASS DWELLINGS AT BETHNAL GREEN.

Mr. J. G. TALBOT: I beg to ask the Secretary of State for the Home Department whether his attention has been called to various schemes of the London School Board for building new schools in the district of Bethnal Green, whereby a number of the dwellings of the working classes are to be removed; and whether sufficient accommodation has been provided for the persons so displaced; if not, whether he will take steps to ensure the enforcement of the law.

The SECRETARY of STATE for the HOME DEPARTMENT (Sir M. WHITE RIDLEY, Lancs., Blackpool): I am afraid that my right hon. friend's question is hardly definite enough to enable me to give a precise reply; but I am informed by the London School Board that in dealing with houses occupied by the labouring classes they have on all occasions paid due regard to the provisions of the Acts under which they are empowered to purchase such houses, and certainly I am not aware of any contraventions of the law in this respect.

Mr. J. G. TALBOT: Has the law been enforced in this particular district of London?

Sir M. WHITE RIDLEY: If any information is forwarded to me, I shall be pleased to communicate with the authorities.

UNQUALIFIED DISPENSERS.

Major RASCH: I beg to ask the Vice-President of the Council whether any provision has been made by which accidents resulting from mistakes made by unqualified dispensers in doctors' surgeries are brought to the notice of the Privy Council; and, if so, whose duty it is to report such cases, and is the Government in a position to state the number of such cases which have occurred during the past two years.

Sir J. GORST: The answer to this is in the negative. The General Medical Council are reported to have appointed a committee to consider the representations addressed to them by the Privy Council on the subject.

SCHOOL TEACHERS' SUPERANNUATION.

Mr. BILL (Staffs, Leek): I beg to ask the Secretary of State for the Home Department whether, as a superannuation system has been established for elementary school teachers, which includes those employed in reformatory and industrial schools, he will endeavour to procure the inclusion in some satisfactory pension scheme of the masters and matrons of those institutions.

Sir M. WHITE RIDLEY: When the Bill for establishing the superannuation system referred to was under consideration I consulted the Treasury to see whether it was possible to include the officers mentioned, but they did not feel justified in extending the State-aided pension scheme beyond certified teachers. I am afraid that I cannot see my way to reopening the question at present.

IRELAND–INDUSTRIAL SCHOOLS ACT.

Colonel M'CALMONT (Antrim, E.): I beg to ask the Chief Secretary to the Lord Lieutenant of Ireland whether powers now conferred on school boards in England could be extended to school attendance committees in Ireland, whereby, in cases where the attendance order of magistrates is not complied with and it has been shown that a child's home surroundings are objectionable, they should be empowered to bring such cases before the magistrates, with the object of having them dealt with under the provisions of the Industrial Schools Act.

The CHIEF SECRETARY FOR IRELAND (Mr. G. W. BALFOUR, Leeds, Central): There is a good deal to be said in favour of the proposal to which my hon. and gallant friend's question refers. Legislation, however, would be necessary to give effect to it, and I could not undertake to deal with the subject, at all events during the present session.

GLIN DISTRICT SCHOOL.

Mr. AUSTIN (Limerick, W.): I beg to ask the Chief Secretary to the Lord Lieutenant of Ireland why arrangements could not be made so as to have the tourist steamer plying between Kilrush and Tarbert proceed to Glin and Foynes to meet the train arriving at the latter place from Limerick at noon, so as to afford facilities for the conjoint unions to send on the children to the Glin District School, as also enabling the members of the board of management to attend regularly to the duties essential to the proper working of the institution.

Mr. G. W. BALFOUR: The contract between the Commissioners of Public Works and the Waterford Steamship Company, as the owners of the steamer referred to, is limited to the transit between Tarbert and Kilrush, and it would not be competent, therefore, for the Board of Works to require that the steamer should call at Glin as suggested. It is, of course, open to the authorities interested in the school to negotiate for this purpose with the Waterford Steamship Company.

IRISH NATIONAL TEACHERS' EXAMINATIONS.

Mr. DAVITT: I beg to ask the Chief Secretary to the Lord Lieutenant of Ireland how many second division of first class teachers applied this year to the Commissioners of National Education, Ireland, for admission to attend the July examination for first of first; and how many of these teachers are to be admitted; whether this number, in comparison with the former, is proportionately below the average for preceding years; and if so, can the Commissioners state why; what are the conditions necessary to entitle candidates for admission to the examination for the first division of first class; will he explain why this class of teachers have been kept in ignorance of their admission or non-admission for two months longer this year than heretofore; and whether, considering this prolonged delay, and the hardship inflicted on these teachers thereby, the Lord Lieutenant will advise the Commissioners to admit to the examination all those teachers who duly applied for entrance.

MR. G. W. BALFOUR: The number of applications referred to in the first paragraph was 134; permission to attend the examination was given in 78 of these. The proportion of admissions is higher this year than in previous years. Candidates for the first division of first class must be already in the second division of that class, and they may then obtain the higher grade either without examination after giving seven consecutive years of highly efficient service or by passing a special examination after three consecutive years of such service. Candidates proceeding under the revised programme have not been kept in ignorance of their admission longer this year than usual. In the case of those taking advantage of the recent concession to proceed for examination under the old programme this year, notice was unavoidably delayed pending the receipt of Treasury sanction. Permission to attend the examination is always contingent on the recommendation of the inspectors for efficiency in the schools, and the Commissioners cannot agree to any departure from this condition on the present occasion.

LAND VALUATION AT SLIGO.

MR. P. A. M'HUGH (Leitrim, N.): I beg to ask the Chief Secretary to the Lord Lieutenant of Ireland whether he is aware that the Sligo Corporation has asked the Commissioner of Valuation in Ireland for a valuation of all the land within their borough boundary, as distinguished from other rateable hereditaments, and that the Commissioner has replied saying he had no power to do what the Corporation asked; whether there is any public department in Ireland which can make such a valuation as is desired by the Sligo Corporation; and if so, how can it be put in motion in the particular case referred to; and is he aware that in towns which were not constituted urban

districts under the Local Government Act the lands are separately valued so that rates may be levied on plots of land even when the buildings on them are unoccupied.

MR. G. W. BALFOUR: The Sligo Corporation were informed by the Commissioner of Valuation that under the existing Statutes a revaluation for rating purposes of the land within the borough boundary was not feasible; but the existing valuation lists, of which they have a copy, set out separately the value of the land and other rateable hereditaments. The reply to the second paragraph is in the negative. As regards the third paragraph, lands are separately valued in all towns, whether urban districts or not.

THIN POST-CARDS FOR COMMERCIAL PURPOSES.

SIR REGINALD HANSON (London): I beg to ask the Secretary to the Treasury, as representing the Postmaster-General, whether any decision has yet been arrived at as to the provision of a large-sized thin inland post-card for commercial purposes.

THE FINANCIAL SECRETARY TO THE TREASURY (MR. HANBURY, Preston): The question is now under consideration, and I hope to be able to arrange for the provision of such a post-card.

THE EAST CENTRAL DISTRICT POST OFFICE STAFF.

MR. M'GHEE (Louth, S.): I beg to ask the Secretary to the Treasury, as representing the Postmaster-General, whether a reply can now be given to the petition forwarded to him in August, 1897, by the staff of the Eastern Central District Post Offices (countermen and telegraphists)?

MR. HANBURY: This memorial has now been answered. Among other points the memorialists asked for an increase in the number of superior appointments, and the number of overseers was increased on the 7th instant.

NEWBLISS POST OFFICE MESSENGER.

MR. MACALEESE (Monaghan, N.): I beg to ask the Secretary to the Treasury, as representing the Postmaster-General, if a recently appointed messenger to the Newbliss Post Office is paid the salary of 3s. 6d. a week; and, what are the duties this messenger has to perform, and upon what test was the salary of 3s. 6d. a week based.

Mr. HANBURY: There is no messenger employed at the Newbliss Post Office at the salary named. The Sub-Postmaster of Newbliss receives an allowance of 3s. a week to provide for the conveyance of certain mail bags between the post office and the railway station. Inquiry is being made as to the time occupied and the adequacy of the allowance.

LIMERICK SORTING CLERKS.

Mr. PATRICK O'BRIEN (Kilkenny): I beg to ask the Secretary to the Treasury, as representing the Postmaster-General, whether a decision has been arrived at by the Department whereby two acting sorting clerks at Limerick, with eight years' useful service, have been served with notice of dismissal owing to their inability to qualify in telegraphy at a very advanced age; whether this is to be understood as the final settlement of the case of the officials concerned; and will the Postmaster-General reconsider his decision, in view of the fact that the officials referred to entered the Post Office service under the disamalgamation scheme and were not called upon to learn telegraphy until they were 23 years old, and place those officers with such a lengthened connection with the Department on the establishment without the necessary telegraphic qualifications.

Mr. HANBURY: The acting sorting clerks referred to are those who were required, in accordance with the rules of the service, to qualify in telegraphy before being placed on the establishment; they were informed as far back as June, 1897, that they could not be retained in the service if they failed to qualify, Although they have since been granted further opportunities to qualify they have not become efficient in telegraphy, and have been definitely informed that their service as acting sorting clerks must be discontinued, but they have been offered nominations as postmen, which they have, however, declined. The eldest of these persons of "very advanced age" is 25. Other candidates under similar conditions with respect to age and service have been able to obtain the necessary qualifications, and there would be no justification for appointing the two officers in question without such qualifications. They have been treated with great consideration, and the case is now finally settled.

STATE AID FOR THE BLIND.

Mr. PATRICK O'BRIEN: On behalf of the hon. Member for Dublin (St. Patrick's) I beg to ask the Secretary of State for the Home Department whether his attention has been drawn to a meeting of the blind recently held in Dublin; and whether the Government intend to introduce a measure to provide State aid for the blind in Great Britain and Ireland similar to that provided by Continental Governments.

Sir M. WHITE RIDLEY: By the courtesy of the hon. Member I have seen a report of the recent meeting in Dublin of the National League of the Blind. The matter is not one which concerns specially my Department, and I am afraid I can only say that I am not aware that there is on the part of the Government any intention to introduce a measure such as that indicated.

CASTLETOWN BEREHAVEN PIER.

Mr. PATRICK O'BRIEN: On behalf of the hon. Member for St. Patrick's Division of Dublin, I beg to ask the Chief Secretary to the Lord Lieutenant of Ireland whether the Irish Board of Works have taken any steps with regard to the silting up by quarry owners of the pier at Castletown Berehaven; and whether he can state what has been done to preserve the pier in a condition suitable for the trade of the district and the shipment of fish.

Mr. G. W. BALFOUR: In November last the Board of Works caused this pier to be inspected, and directed the attention of the Grand Jury to the necessity of removing an accumulation of silt in the harbour. The Grand Jury at the March Assizes granted the sum of £100 for the purpose; inquiry will be made whether the work has been carried out. Inquiries made at the inspection in November tended to show that the silting did not arise from the action of the quarry owners, as alleged, but from the practice of depositing general rubbish along the foreshore, which was calculated to increase the rate at which silting would naturally take place at one side of the pier. The local authorities are, therefore, interested in preventing a continuance of this practice so far as possible. The duty of maintaining the pier in a condition suitable for its original purpose now rests with the County Council.

THE VICAR OF ST. MICHAEL'S, SOUTHAMPTON.

MR. SAMUEL SMITH : I beg to ask the First Lord of the Treasury whether he is aware that the Rev. J. W. J. J. Danbury, whom the Lord Chancellor has appointed to the vicarage of St. Michael's, Southampton, is a member of the Confraternity of the Blessed Sacrament; and that the wearing of sacrificial vestments and other illegal practices were notoriously in use at the church of which Mr, Danbury was the curate ; and whether, in view of the Resolution of the House of the 11th April, it is still possible to rescind this appointment.

THE FIRST LORD OF THE TREASURY (Mr. A. J. BALFOUR, Manchester, E.) : I understand the reverend gentleman to whom the hon. Member refers belongs to no association except the English Church Temperance Association.

SOUTH AFRICAN REPUBLIC—THE BLOEMFONTEIN CONFERENCE.

MR. GALLOWAY : I beg to ask the First Lord of the Treasury whether Her Majesty's Government have yet come to any decision with regard to, the new situation which has arisen in the Transvaal owing to President Kruger's rejection of the proposals for a settlement of the franchise question suggested by Sir Alfred Milner at the Bloemfontein Conference.

MR. A. J. BALFOUR : I have no statement to make upon Transvaal policy in addition to that which was made on Friday last by my right hon. friend the Secretary for the Colonies.

BUSINESS OF THE HOUSE.

SIR CHARLES CAMERON : I beg to ask the First Lord of the Treasury when it is proposed to proceed with the Telegraphs (Telephonic Communication, &c.) Bill.

Mr. A. J. BALFOUR : There are three or four questions with regard to public business in connection with Bills yet to come before the House, but I can make no statement at the present time in regard to these Bills, for, as the House

knows, the business for the week is fixed. To-day we take the Scotch Private Bill Procedure Bill ; to-morrow we shall take the Third Readings of the two Bills upon which the Report stage is finished, the London Government Bill and the Finance Bill ; Wednesday is a private members' day ; on Thursday we propose to take the discussion on the Indian Sugar Bounties ; and on Monday next, if the Scottish Private Bill Procedure Bill is not finished, we shall continue with it. It is also possible that on Monday I may have to ask the House to give us further facilities for Government business, and in making the request I shall make such a statement on business as I am able to do.

MR. GIBSON BOWLES (Lynn Regis) : What Supply will be taken on Friday ?

MR. A. J. BALFOUR : Scotch Estimates, beginning with the Education Vote.

MR. CHANNING : When will [the next stage of the Food and Drugs Bill be taken ?

MR. A. J. BALFOUR : That falls under the general category of questions to which I have already referred.

MR. BARTLEY (Islington, N.) : When does the right hon. Gentleman propose to take the Colonial Loans Fund Bill ?

MR. A. J. BALFOUR : I stated last week that I understood it was important that the Bill should be proceeded with to-day, and that it would, at the cost of some inconvenience, have to take precedence; but further consultation with my right hon. friend the Chancellor of the Exchequer has shown that it can be put off, and I will not make an abortive statement upon it now.

MR. JAMES LOWTHER (Kent, Thanet) : When is it intended to take the Undersized Fish Bill ?

MR. A. J. BALFOUR : It may be taken after Twelve o'clock.

PRIVATE LEGISLATION PROCEDURE (SCOTLAND) (EXPENSES).

Considered in Committee.

(In the Committee.)

Motion made and Question proposed—

" That it is expedient to authorise the payment, out of moneys to be provided by Parliament, of any remuneration, allowances, and expenses that may become payable under any Act of the present session to provide for improving and extending the procedure for obtaining Parliamentary powers by way of Provisional Orders in matters relating to Scotland."—(*Sir William Walrond.*)

MR. THOMAS SHAW (Hawick Burghs): I beg to move to omit the word "remuneration" from the Resolution. I am quite aware that this is only an enabling resolution, but I am anxious at the earliest moment to make it known what is the attitude I desire to take upon this Bill. I am not hostile to the principle of the Bill, but my objection is to setting up, by means of this measure, an extra-Parliamentary Commission of salaried officials. Without desiring to prejudge discussion of the Bill, I think its legitimate purpose would be met by confining the resolution to allowances and expenses.

Amendment proposed—

"To leave out the word 'remuneration.'"—(*Mr. Thos. Shaw.*)

Question proposed—

"That the word 'remuneration' stand part of the Resolution."

THE LORD ADVOCATE (Mr. A. G. MURRAY, Buteshire): I hope this will not be pressed. This Resolution merely enables the Committee to do certain things, and even if it is passed in its present form it will leave the situation precisely the same so far as the proposals of the Bill are concerned. When the Bill is in Committee it will be in order for my hon. and learned friend to move to strike out the clause which provides for the remuneration of certain of the Commissioners. It would be very inconvenient at this stage to discuss competing schemes.

DR. CLARK (Caithness): In all the Bills hitherto brought forward the proposal has been to have a paid Commission, but under this Bill the Commission will be partly paid and partly unpaid. If Members of either House sit on the Commission they are not to be paid, but all outsiders are to receive remuneration. I think this is a bad principle; they either all ought to be paid, or none should receive payment for the work done. In the past the Committee have done the work without payment, and, seeing how satisfactorily that principle has worked, I protest against setting up a paid Commission. I believe, however, that the Lord Advocate has on the Paper an Amendment which meets us half way, and under the circumstances I think it would be better to postpone the fight until we come to that Amendment.

MR. J. P. SMITH (Lanark, Partick): I understand that the Resolution provides not only for the remuneration of the Commissioners, but also for that of the clerks and other officials who will have to be paid whatever scheme may eventually be adopted; I hope, therefore, the Amendment will not be pressed.

MR. THOMAS SHAW: I beg to ask leave to withdraw it.

*MR. CHANNING (Northampton, E.): As an English Member, I wish to enter an emphatic protest against the proposal of this Bill to cheapen Private Bill procedure for Scotland by throwing part of the costs on the general taxpayer. Any scheme that may be adopted for that purpose should be applicable to the whole of the United Kingdom, and not merely to Scotland.

Amendment, by leave, withdrawn.

Original Question put and agreed to.

Resolved, That it is expedient to authorise the payment, out of moneys to be provided by Parliament, of any remuneration, allowances, and expenses that may become payable under any Act of the present session to provide for improving and extending the procedure for obtaining Parliamentary powers by way of Provisional Orders in matters relating to Scotland.

Resolution to be reported To-morrow.

———

PRIVATE LEGISLATION PROCEDURE (SCOTLAND) BILL.

COMMITTEE.

Order for Committee read.

CAPTAIN SINCLAIR (Forfar): I rise to move the Resolution which stands in my name, *i.e.*—

"That it be an instruction to the Committee that they have power to extend the scope of the Bill to include the remainder of the United Kingdom."

I wish to extend the benefits of this measure beyond the confines of Scotland. I desire that it may apply to the remainder of the United Kingdom. I do not think that this proposal is in any way in conflict with the principle of the Bill, for the Lord Advocate has told us that it can be so extended without any infringement of the principle embodied in it. I do not see anything in the circumstances of Scotland, or in the expression of Scottish opinion, to justify the limitation of such a measure as this to Scotland alone. The Bill confers no distinct enlargement of powers upon Scotland, and does not in any way interfere with the existing procedure in regard to Provisional Orders, but it does propose, practically, to place Scotch Private Bill legislation in the hands of people not connected with Parliament. I think it is exceedingly unfair to lay upon Scotland and Scottish opinion the responsibility for this measure. An attempt has been made to justify the application of this Bill to Scotland alone by pointing out that it is only from that country that a desire for it has come. Moreover, while you are adding nothing to the privileges of Scotland, you are directly taking away, by this Bill, the power of Parliament over legislation of this kind. You are saying that in future, instead of going to Parliament as hitherto for these powers, you must in the first instance go to the Secretary for Scotland. You are going to give no option whatever of making use of the new procedure or of proceeding under the old system. I do think that such option ought to be reserved to the promoters of Scottish Private Bills. You are making a serious change in the present system, and there is no doubt that these local inquiries will involve increased expense. It is, therefore unfair, that the whole responsibility for the change should be thrown upon public opinion in Scotland. The root of my objection to the Bill is its limitation to Scotland. I wish to rebut the claim which has been put forward that the expression of public opinion in Scotland has been sufficient to justify the making of this experiment in that country alone. Of the Scottish local authorities, which number from 200 to 300, there are only about 50 which have expressed any opinion at all on this measure, and I do not think that the expression of opinion at all justifies the proposal of the Government. Further, I

Captain Sinclair.

would like to point out that the Bill is extremely vague upon the most important and crucial points of its procedure. For instance, there is the question of the tribunal.

*MR. SPEAKER : Order, order ! The hon. Member is discussing the merits of the Bill as it applies to Scotland. That point does not arise at present. The question under debate is whether the Bill should be extended to the rest of the United Kingdom.

CAPTAIN SINCLAIR: It was not my intention to express any opinion on the merits of the tribunal. I only wanted to remind the House that this very crucial point has not been adequately dealt with. I believe that the Lord Advocate, representing the Government, has put down an Amendment in regard to this.

MR. SPEAKER : Order, order ! I must ask the hon. Member to keep to the Amendment.

CAPTAIN SINCLAIR : I am extremely sorry if, through ignorance or ineptitude, I have transgressed your ruling, Sir ; I only wished to point out the extremely vague character of the measure. I would ask hon. Members to notice that it places an increased burden on Scotland, while it gives no adequate relief to this country. It substitutes for the machinery which at present exists for dealing with Private Bill legislation a procedure which will be more costly, and which, at the same time, will afford very little relief to this House, to which, of course, the Commission will have to report all business of this kind. The question is whether the machinery you are setting up by this Bill can safely and properly be extended to the rest of the United Kingdom, and, while I am perfectly willing to see a system of devolution carried, I doubt whether this is machinery which can be safely extended. The whole burden of the report of the Joint Committee which thoroughly considered this subject in 1888 was that any scheme which should be brought forward dealing with Private Bill legislation should not be a piecemeal scheme, but should be one general and common in its application to the whole of the United Kingdom. In that way only can we do justice to the various interests of the different parts of the United Kingdom, and give this House that relief which should be not the least of the benefits of any measure of this kind. It is ridiculous to say that in Scotland there is any spontaneous demand for this measure, or any desire to have it as distinct from any other part of the United Kingdom. I have no wish, however, to defeat it. I only ask the House to seriously consider that it is proposing a great change, and I therefore beg to move the Instruction which stands in my name.

Motion made, and Question proposed—

"That it be an Instruction to the Committee that they have power to extend the scope of the Bill to include the remainder of the United Kingdom."—(*Captain Sinclair.*)

Mr. BUCHANAN (Aberdeenshire, E.): I desire to second the Instruction. I do so, first, on the ground that the grievance is the same whether in England, in Scotland, or in Ireland. That grievance, I take it, is the expense of the present system, and it is felt just as keenly by municipalities in remote parts of England and Ireland as it is in Scotland. The absence of local inquiry is also as strongly objected to, and the demand for it comes just as strongly from Ireland as it does from Scotland. Therefore, the grievance is the same, and the remedy is the same. My second point is that the bulk of the precedents in recent Parliamentary history have been in favour of general legislation on these matters, and it would not, therefore, be wise to limit to Scotland alone a proposal which should apply to the whole of the United Kingdom. In 1883, and again in 1888, when this question was discussed, it was generally agreed that the subject should be treated as one which concerned the whole of the United Kingdom, and it is only since then that Bills have been introduced dealing with Scotland alone. In 1892 the First Lord of the Treasury recognised the fact that the question was one which affected Ireland in an equal degree; and we have even had from the Lord Advocate himself, in the course of the Second Reading Debate on this Bill, a virtual admission of the principle for which I am contending, as he told us he agreed that this was a House of Commons question rather than a Scottish question. Upon the grounds, then, of the similarity of the grievance, and that precedents hitherto have been in the direction of not legislating for Scot-

land separately, I strongly urge the Government to agree to extend the provisions of this Bill to the rest of the United Kingdom. If the measure is a bad one, it should not apply to Scotland at all; and if it is a good one, why should not the rest of the kingdom have the benefit of it?

Mr. A. G. MURRAY: I think that both the hon. and gallant Member who moved the Instruction and the hon. Member who seconded it will recognise that I have always been very much in sympathy with a great many of the remarks which they have made, and I quite look forward to the time when it will be found that the procedure initiated by this Bill will have met with so much success in Scotland as to justify its adoption by the rest of the United Kingdom. As I said in my speech on the Second Reading, we have been careful to so cast the Bill as to enable us afterwards without difficulty to adapt its procedure to other parts of the kingdom. There is a very high authority for the proposition that there is a time for all things; but I do not think the time has yet arrived for extending this Bill as proposed by this Instruction. I do not know any course by which the Bill could be more effectively wrecked than by the passing of this Instruction. The idea of some reform of Private Bill procedure has long been in the forefront of discussion in Scotland; it has there occupied a practical position which it has not occupied in other parts of the United Kingdom. Perhaps I should make some little exception on behalf of Wales. But this I may say: the mind of the English people is not familiarised with the proposals contained in the Bill, and until that comes to pass I think hon. Members must be content to take what is admittedly to a certain extent an experiment in Scotland alone. That country is ready for this Bill, and I do not think that that can be said of any other part of the United Kingdom. I hope the two hon. Members, after the Bill has proved to be a success, will have the satisfaction of saying that Scotland has been the pioneer in this matter.

Sir H. CAMPBELL-BANNERMAN (Stirling Burghs): The right hon. Gentleman thinks apparently he is paying a compliment to Scotland by his action in this matter, when he declares that this is an experiment to be tried in Scotland for the benefit of the other portions of the United Kingdom. Whether it is called doing things piece by piece or is regarded as the insertion of the thin end of the wedge, at all events the proposals of the Government as embodied in the Bill are open to the observation that, on a matter which is common to the three kingdoms, one part has been selected for the experiment, and for no very obvious reason. The subject is a very large one, and ought not to be dealt with in a Bill exclusively relating to any particular part of the United Kingdom. There is, I think, from that point of view, some force in what my hon. friends have urged. But, while I have a great deal of sympathy with what they have said, I confess that I do not see that their arguments, after all, very strongly support the Instruction which we are discussing. The Motion before us is to extend the operation of this Bill to the rest of the United Kingdom. If my hon. friend had made the speech he has just delivered on the Motion for the Second Reading, and if he had then suggested that no Bill would be satisfactory which did not apply to all three parts of the United Kingdom, I could have understood his position. But he now desires to extend the operation of a Bill which he does not like to the rest of the United Kingdom, and although he and his colleagues may be quite justified in pointing out the disadvantages of the methods which the Government have chosen to adopt, I hardly think that they have made out a strong case for this Motion. No doubt there has been a strong desire in Scotland for action in this direction, but the difficulty has been as to the machinery to be decided upon. There are certain classes of people in Scotland who have acclaimed each of the successive Bills as almost the work of superhuman wisdom, and they have loudly denounced all those who have thought it necessary to point out the least fault. As to this particular Bill, let us hope that in the course of the discussion we may improve it and bring it into harmony with our desires to a greater extent than it is now. If we do so, ultimately we may extend the same system to the rest of the country. I am not at all sure that it is capable of that extension. There is another point, which is that in choosing Scotland as the field of experiment the Government have chosen the very quarter

Sir H. Campbell-Bannerman.

where there is less of this sort of business than elsewhere. The amount of this sort of legislation in Scotland is very small as compared with England, and in that respect this Bill can hardly be a very conclusive experiment. I notice that in the Convention of Royal Burghs, which have always been strong advocates of this new system of legislation, the best that has been said of it is that it would be well to take it with its faults, that it may be amended, and that at least we shall be able to see how it will work That is not very inspiring, I should imagine, for the supporters of the Bill. I can only express the hope that my hon. friend will allow us to get into Committee on the Bill in order that we may make the best measure we possibly can of it.

MR. DALZIEL (Kirkcaldy) : I confess I cannot understand why this Bill has been brought forward at all, and I am sure that if it had been intended to apply to the whole of the United Kingdom it would not have had a ghost of a chance. Still, I am glad it has been brought forward. But I am also glad that it does not apply to other parts of the United Kingdom. The principle of the Bill is good, and all Home Rulers are really in favour of it, because it embodies the principle of decentralisation. Our whole case in Scotland in regard to such questions as Local Veto, the land question, and other matters in which we are interested is that we should be dealt with separately, and therefore our position ought to be "a separate Bill for Scotland." If we can make the Bill good enough to be extended to the other parts of the United Kingdom, that is their business and not ours. There is good enough in the Bill to induce us to support the Government at the present stage, but when we get into Committee let us all do our best to harmonise the Bill according to our views.

MR. D. LLOYD-GEORGE (Carnarvon) : As a Member for a Welsh constituency, I must oppose this Instruction. This boon which it is sought to confer on the other nationalities of the United Kingdom is a boon for which they are not exceedingly eager, and there has been no expression of opinion in favour of it. The only argument in favour of the Instruction that I have heard of is that the Bill is such a very bad one that Scotland ought not to have a monopoly of its disadvantages, and that the other nationalities ought to take their share of the burden. I quite agree that it is a thoroughly bad Bill, and it is amazing to me how any Scotchmen can possibly support it. That, however, is a matter for Scotch Members themselves, and I would not have entered on the discussion had it not been for the suggestion that the Bill should be extended to Wales. I do not want this Bill to be extended to Wales, and I am sure there is not a parish council in the whole of Wales which would pass a resolution in support of it. I admit that there is a very crying grievance. The expense of Provisional Orders for water, gas, piers, &c., amount to several hundreds of pounds. The tariff is practically prohibitive. But that is not peculiarly a Scotch grievance ; it is a grievance that we want to redress in the House of Commons. Something has been said by the Lord Advocate in regard to the fact that the principle is good, and that there was as great a grievance in Wales to which the principle might at some future date be applied. There are a larger number of Private Bills and Provisional Orders from Wales this session than from the whole of Scotland ; but I do not think there is a single Welsh Member who has suggested that this is the way to deal with the grievance. There are two alternative plans for dealing with this question. The one is to constitute some sort of judicial tribunal. Well, that is a plan which would commend itself undoubtedly to several Members of the House, and there is a great deal to be said for it, for many of the questions to be decided in Provisional Orders are purely judicial. The alternative plan is to refer the matter to a democratic tribunal. But this Bill is neither the one thing nor the other ; it is a sort of mongrel half-breed measure. For my part, I cannot see how the Scotch Members can bring themselves to support the Bill ; but I venture to say that if the Instruction is carried the only result will be that every Welsh Member will devote the whole of his spare time to drawing up Amendments to the Bill in order to obstruct its passing through the House.

Question put, and negatived.

Bill considered in Committee.

(In the Committee.)

Clause 1 :—

Mr. EDMUND ROBERTSON (Dundee) : My object in moving the omission of the words " public authority or," in line 6 of page 1, is really to get some kind of. definition of the words " public authority." I do not know whether " public authority " has been already defined ; but it certainly has not been defined in the Bill itself, and I should be surprised to find it defined in the Interpretation Act. I would remind the Lord Advocate that there is this special reason for great care being taken on this point—namely, that by this Bill we are going to set up a subordinate legislative authority, whose decrees or orders are to have the effect of an Act of Parliament, but only if they have complied absolutely with the conditions laid down by the Bill. An order of theirs would be in the same position—a position that does not apply to anything in our present system—as an Act passed by a State Legislature stands to the Supreme Court of the United States. It might turn out after the lapse of ten or a dozen years that it was no statute at all because it did not comply with the conditions of the original Act. It might, in fact, prove to be absolutely *ultra vires.* For that reason, at this stage, we should be particularly careful that we are not laying down words which may upset what people have been taught to believe is, in effect, though not in form, a statutory law. Therefore I ask the Lord Advocate what it is he holds is meant by " public authority," and whether there are not other words which would more fully express the meaning. I have been asked, for instance, if a railway company is a public authority. I do not know whether it is . meant to be included in " public authority or persons." " Person " would be included under the Interpretation Act, because railway companies under that Act are incorporations, and " person " includes incorporations. " Person," as I understand it, is either natural or artificial, and an artificial " person " is an incorporation. But all other groups of human beings who are not incorporated are simply collections of individuals. The words " public authority " would appear to be surplusage, and I would suggest that it would be better to strike them out altogether. I beg to move.

Amendment proposed—

"In page 1, line 6, to leave out 'public authority or.'"—(*Mr. Edmund Robertson.*)

Question proposed—

"That the words 'public authority or' stand part of the clause."

Mr. A. G. MURRAY: I was a little bit puzzled in reading the Amendment of the hon. Member to know whether it was really a drafting Amendment or whether he wanted to raise a substantial question as to whether the Bill should or should not apply to any public authority. I now find that it is a drafting Amendment, and so viewing it I am somewhat indifferent on the matter. I think the word "person," in the singular, would be sufficient, because, with the aid of the Interpretation Act, either in its natural sense or as relating to a body corporate or incorporate, it would include every body. The object of the hon. Gentleman is that this Bill should apply to every body that has been hitherto, and is at present, able to apply to Parliament for leave to introduce a Private Bill.

Mr. EDMUND ROBERTSON: That is everybody.

Mr. A. G. MURRAY: Yes, that is everybody. The reason why the draftsman put "public authority or" into the Bill was that, as the hon. Member is aware, there has been a familiar cry against legislation by reference to other Acts as to what is intended, and the man in the street reading the word "person" might think for a moment that it did not include "public authority." Therefore it was more by way of indication than definition that the words "public authority" were included. The words, however, are not really necessary, as the word "person," in the singular, would cover everything desired. On the other hand, for the convenience of the ordinary individual the words "public authority or" would probably be more intelligible, and therefore the Bill has been framed in that way. If, however, there is a strong objection against them, I am perfectly willing that the words "public authority or" should go out.

Mr. CRIPPS (Gloucester, Stroud): I doubt very much whether the word "person" includes a body corporate in the sense of a local authority.

SIR H. CAMPBELL-BANNERMAN: It has been pointed out to me that there may be unfortunate entities who are neither "public authorities" under the Act nor "persons." For instance, there are Water Commissioners and River Navigation authorities. The Clyde Trustees is a large case, but there was also the Board of Navigation of the Forth, and after that large body ceased to exist there was at Alloa a Board of Navigation for the area between Stirling and Alloa. It has been pointed out to me that it is doubtful whether that body is a "public authority" in the proper sense of the term.

Mr. A. G. MURRAY: The 19th Section of the Interpretation Act states that in every Act passed after that Act the expression "person" includes any body or person corporate or incorporate; and, so far as I know, there is no body which is not corporate or incorporate.

DR. CLARK: I trust the hon. Member for Dundee will not press this Amendment, because if it is carried it will prevent the discussion of my Amendment, which is to omit the words "or persons," in order to limit the Bill to public authorities only. If we are to introduce a system of this kind tentatively, I think we ought to begin with the public authorities.

Mr. EDMUND ROBERTSON: The hon. Member asks me not to press my Amendment, in order that he may have an opportunity of moving his Amendment. I will not therefore proceed with it further.

Amendment, by leave, withdrawn.

Mr. CRIPPS: I beg to move—

"After 'authority' in page 1, line 6, to insert 'other than a public authority seeking powers inconsistent with, or in addition to, the general law.'"

The Amendment is a very important one, and I trust the First Lord of the Treasury and the Lord Advocate will consider it. As the Bill stands, any matter which can now be dealt with by Private Bill legislation comes under its provisions. What I propose is to prevent matters which are inconsistent with or an addition to the general law being dealt with. It is very important that this House should not delegate to any subordinate authority whatever the power of making any alteration in the general law. The matters which it is proposed to delegate include many important topics. During the recent discussions on the London Government Bill very many important questions were raised, and there is not one of them which could not be dealt with under this Bill. ' For instance, the criminal law might be altered as regards any municipality without' this House being able to decide one way or the other. It is a very important matter that this House should not give up its power to legislate to any other tribunal. The House has taken extra care in this direction in connection with sanitary matters, and appointed the Police and Sanitary Committee to report if any provision were introduced into a private Bill inconsistent with or extending the existing law. Then, again, with reference to franchise, proposed alterations might be relegated under the Bill to a Department—in this instance the Secretary of State for Scotland for the time being—and the same applies to difficulties that might arise between public interests on one side and private property on the other. Let me go further. Surely the Committee ought not to pass this clause in its present indefinite and indeterminate form. Let us ask ourselves if we intend to give an outside tribunal power to alter the general law. If we do not, we ought to make it clear now. We ought to say that it is inconsistent with our privileges and duties to delegate any such power to any such tribunal. What is the character of this proposed tribunal? Practically, as far as this House is concerned, it means the Secretary of State for Scotland. Of course, I am aware that the Chairmen of Committees have the power to decide whether a particular matter ought to be reserved, but that is no reason why we should delegate those powers to an outside tribunal. There are various matters connected with Private Bill legislation on which this House has more than once expressed its difference of opinion from that of the Chairmen. As this Bill stands many questions arising on unopposed Bills might be decided by the Secretary of State for Scotland, and by no one else, and his *fiat* would have the power of an Act of Parliament. Are we going to allow the criminal law to be altered in that way, or questions of fran-

chise and sanitary and rating questions? If not, then of course my Amendment ought to be accepted. Surely this House ought to distinguish carefully between judicial, administrative, and legislative questions. The proper duty of outside tribunals is administrative, and, although certain judicial and legislative work may incidentally be conferred upon them, they are not proper bodies for purely judicial business, and a great deal of Private Bill business is judicial. As far as legislation is concerned, we ought to keep that power in our own hands with reference to what may be extremely important points of principle. When this Bill was discussed on the Second Reading there was an opinion expressed on both sides of the House that the area within which we intended to delegate our legislative powers ought to be most clearly defined. But there is no definition in the Bill, and it seems to me to be one of the worst instances of the House not taking the care and trouble to find out what it intends to do, but simply leaving it to the Chairmen or to the outside tribunals to define for themselves instead of taking the definition from us. As to the question of devolution generally, I have always been in favour of proper devolution, and I have been misinterpreted more than once when it was said that I was in favour of the present system and opposed to any reform at all. It is, however, to my mind, a question of great importance whether this House should give up its privileges and decline to carry out its duties. Many important principles have been introduced in connection with Private Bill legislation. For the Amendment which I now move I ask the support of all who think that we ought to keep our legislative authority in our own hands, or clearly define what we intend to delegate to any outside authority.

Amendment proposed—

" In page 1, line 6, after ' authority,' to insert the words, ' other than a public authority seeking powers inconsistent with, or in addition to, the general law."—(*Mr. Cripps.*)

Question proposed—
" That those words be there inserted."

Mr. A. G. MURRAY: I think the hon. Member must feel that I cannot accept this Amendment. The practical reason against it has been very well put forward by the hon. Member for Dundee. If there were cases where something was proposed to be done absolutely different from the existing law, then the Chairman would say that they were matters which could not be determined by the tribunal, and that they should be reserved for consideration. But under the hon. Member's proposal, where the whole thing had been gone into and passed, an action might be raised in a court of law, and it might be contended that the Provisional Order was not worth the paper on which it was written, because it ought not to have gone before the tribunal at all. That is, I think, a very practical objection. We are really not touching the privileges of Parliament at all in this matter. The hon. Member will remember that if a Bill is opposed the parties can come up here and have the matter submitted to the Chairmen of Committees of the two Houses. What is the security at the present moment that something totally inconsistent with the general law is not introduced into a Private Bill?

MR. CRIPPS: The Police and Sanitary Committee was instituted for that very purpose.

MR. A. G. MURRAY: The Police and Sanitary Committee has nothing to do with opposed Bills unless it is discovered that they contain something inconsistent with the existing law. The Police and Sanitary Committee has no say in the matter at all, although if they had they would have taken the same view as the Scotch Office has taken. So far as this Bill is concerned, there is the same position upon the Report of the Government Department as there is in unopposed Bills. For all practical purposes I do not see any difference between the system to be set up by this measure, as to unopposed Bills, and the present system. I believe there is a proper check in this matter. I am not in favour of a subordinate tribunal introducing any matter inconsistent with Parliamentary procedure in unopposed measures, and I think we are safeguarded against any such contingency.

MR. CALDWELL (Lanark, Mid.): There is one important safeguard which is entirely overlooked. If any unopposed Bill comes before this House, there are the Second and Third Reading stages, and I

Mr. A. G. Murray.

have known Bills to be rejected which were practically unopposed because attention has been called by hon. Members to some important principle contained in them. What would be the effect of this measure? The Secretary for Scotland might pass a Provisional Order which would have the full effect of an Act of Parliament; it would never come before this House at all, and there would be no opportunity to call attention to its provisions. You make no provision whatever as to the Orders and central Instructions which are to have the effect of an Act of Parliament. You make no provision to have them laid upon the Table of this House, even after Twelve o'clock. You give all the power to the Secretary for Scotland, and there is nothing to prevent him passing Bills of the most drastic character. That is the difference between this procedure and the present system of dealing with Private Bills which are unopposed

MR. J. P. SMITH: The formal objection which the Lord Advocate raises to this Amendment is entirely without grounds. There are many things which ought not to be done at all here, among others the handing over of the duty of overlooking these measures to an outside authority, without having the safeguard of the general observation of Parliament upon them. The duty of the Chairmen of Committees and the Speakers' Counsel is to look through each Bill and see in what points it may alter the general law, and to bring such matters before the Unopposed Committee, who have to say whether that Bill shall come before the House or not. This House is extremely jealous of parting with these duties and relegating these matters to an outside tribunal. We have been extravagantly jealous of giving any fresh power, and now it appears to me that we are going to put all this power into the hands of the Secretary for Scotland. I think we ought to specifically and in terms reserve to ourselves the right to overlook these measures.

MR. CRIPPS: I would just like to say one or two words in respect of what was said by the Lord Advocate, because he appears to have failed to appreciate my argument. There is no question but that this House of Parliament does exercise some power over unopposed Bills. It is constantly exercised, and what I desire is that this House should keep that control, not in isolated cases, but in every case. If this Bill passes, these matters will be taken away from the cognisance of the House and put under the control of an outside tribunal, and the machinery will be administered by some outside court. Do not let it it be thought that you can give up by degrees your legislative authority without the power and prestige of this House suffering; that prestige is based on our having this authority, on our keeping our privileges, and exercising the duties which are entrusted to us. The most important authority entrusted to this House is undoubtedly legislative, and I suggest that the Lord Advocate or the First Lord of the Treasury should see that at a future stage of the Bill there should be some decision in order to show that we are not parting with our legislative authority on matters of general law. I cannot help thinking—though I do not wish to be disrespectful to the Lord Advocate—that the Committee will be led unconsciously astray if they allow the Bill to be passed in its present form, and give up their legislative authority on a most important point.

Sir H. CAMPBELL-BANNERMAN: I think the argument of my hon. and learned friend who has just sat down is a very strong justification for the position which some of us have assumed with regard to this matter, viz., that the House of Commons must not loosen its grip over Private Bill legislation, whether it be opposed or unopposed. It is obvious from the conversation which has passed that the danger is of substantial changes in legislation being introduced, perhaps unwittingly or in an underground manner, without the knowledge or assent of the House. The hon. and learned Gentleman spoke of the necessity of our doing something to maintain the prestige of Parliament. I do not care so much about the prestige of Parliament as the actual efficiency of Parliament in doing the work it is appointed to perform. Then, when I come to the words of the Amendment of my hon. friend the Member for Caithness, I think there is a good deal of force in what I understood the Lord Advocate to say, viz., that if you do insert these words it would give rise to any amount of wrangling and litigation afterwards on questions

as to whether this power is or is not inconsistent with, or in addition to, the general law. It seems to me to be almost impossible to find any definite words to convey what we mean, because there are always loopholes for different views to be taken of what is to be done. The only protection we can have is, while maintaining all the other machinery, to reserve to the House of Commons, which peculiarly represents the general interests of the community, its legislative authority in these matters.

*Mr. STUART WORTLEY (Sheffield, Hallam): It seems to me that the object my hon. and learned friend seeks to attain, would be best attained at a later stage of the Bill, when we proceed to the task of defining what are to be the powers of the Chairman of both Houses in respect of these matters. The right hon. Gentleman the Lord Advocate certainly surprised me—and I think some other Members of the House—when he described the present procedure as regards Bills containing proposals in excess of the general law, because the Sessional Order under which the Police and Sanitary Committee exists distinctly says that these Bills shall be committed to a special Committee if certain proposals exist in those Bills, and that independently of the existence or non-existence of opposition. We ought to be very careful that we do nothing whereby we sacrifice Parliamentary control.

Mr. URE (Linlithgow): It appears to me that the Amendment is open to three objections, one of which, at all events, seems to be fatal. In the first place, if it is carried, then public authorities will be precluded from taking advantage of the new procedure whenever the powers they seek are said to be in any particular inconsistent with the general law. But "persons" would not be so fettered. The proposed limitation would obviously not apply to "persons" at all. As the Amendment stands this would be the inevitable result; and therefore I am glad the Lord Advocate refused to give effect to an Amendment which would at least be an absurdity. In the second place, the hon. Member does not say what tribunal is to determine whether or not the powers sought are inconsistent with the general law. And this would result, possibly, in resort being made to a court of law to set aside an order after all the trouble and expense of securing it had been incurred. In the third place, the result of accepting the Amendment would be to shut out from the new procedure any Order, however important and extensive in its operation, if, in the opinion of some tribunal unnamed, it proposed, it may be in some small particular quite subordinate to its main purpose, to innovate upon the established law. Obviously, therefore, if the Bill is to be a really useful and valuable measure, the Amendment must be rejected.

MR. JEFFREYS (Hants, N.): I should like to warn the House against allowing any Committee to pass a Bill without reference to this House, because I am quite convinced that unless a particular clause in a Bill is opposed neither the Chairman of Committee nor the Members take the trouble to go into it at all. As I understand it, this Committee, consisting of Scotch Members, will pass these matters—and very important matters, too, to Scotland—and there will be no opportunity for this House to assert its legislative independence whatever. I hope, therefore, the Lord Advocate will provide an opportunity for bringing any Bill, whatever it may be, back to this House subsequently, so that if any alteration should be required the House may have an opportunity of making the necessary amendment. I think myself that it is a great change in our procedure to take away the legislative power of this House. I admit that there are many matters that might be satisfactorily conducted by Committees, but at the same time I do not like this House to lose touch of legislation altogether; and if the Lord Advocate can see his way to put in some Amendment that will bring the Bills back to this House, so that the House may have an opportunity of amending them where necessary, I think it would be well to introduce such an Amendment.

MR. CRIPPS: If the Lord Advocate will give the Committee an assurance that it is the intention of the Government to preserve as an ultimate resource the authority of this House when the general law is being altered, whether opposed or unopposed, I will at once withdraw the Amendment. If neither the Lord Advocate nor the First Lord of the Treasury will give us that assurance, I shall be

Mr. Ure.

bound to go to a Division, because I think the principle involved is one of great importance.

THE FIRST LORD OF THE TREASURY (MR. A. J. BALFOUR, Manchester, E.): I hope my hon. friend will not go to a Division. I agree that the matter is one of importance, but the method proposed by the hon. Gentleman is the very worst way to deal with it. Even those who most sympathise with the hon. Member must admit that he has raised the question in the wrong way and the wrong place. The matter must come up again on the second clause, and certainly the Government will be disposed to put in words to make it perfectly clear that one of the things which the Chairmen will have to do will be to see that if any new principle is raised that principle is referred to the House. Nobody is committed, neither my learned friend nor anybody else, by the withdrawal of the Amendment, but if the House or the Committee is eager to come to a decision that decision should be upon the second clause rather than upon the first.

MR. CRIPPS: After what the First Lord of the Treasury has said, I beg leave to withdraw the Amendment.

Amendment, by leave, withdrawn.

DR. CLARKE: I now move an Amendment to limit the subjects to be handed over to this Committee to the class of people who desire to have them so handed over, so that the Bill will not apply to those who are strongly opposed to it. According to the last Return, from 1887 to 1897, 297 Bills came before the House from Scotland, practically 30 per year. Of those, 92, or about one-third, were railway Bills, 57 were from insurance, tramway, water, and various other companies, Church funds, universities, and charities; 147 of the Bills came from local authorities, and local authorities have long been anxious to have local inquiries. They think local inquiries will be less expensive than inquiries held in London. I, for one, would be very glad to see this experiment again tried. It was tried forty years ago, and was a failure; and I am afraid that unless you modify your plans you will try it again and have another failure, because you will have local inquiries and local costs, and then you will have another fight and more costs here. Under these circumstances, why not permit the people who desire this change to have it? During ten years town councils and local authorities applied for 70 Bills; railway, docks, and similar companies, for 20; and the conforming Provisional Orders issued under various Acts were 15. Nearly all these were from local authorities, and if this Amendment were adopted you could begin the system by giving it to the people who are very anxious to have it and try it tentatively. Railway companies do not desire it; they think the inquiry here is much cheaper and more desirable than local inquiry; but people complain that town councillors, baillies, and provosts come up here as deputations at large cost when they are not required. For the last 20 years the agitation has been going on in Scotland to have local inquiry by local authorities for their purposes. The principle has been already adopted to a very large extent in three or four Acts which we have passed in the last ten years, in which sheriffs in Scotland have been empowered to do what previously was done only by this House. The principle of local inquiry is carried out more in Scotland than in England, and I do not at all object to its being carried out as far as possible, except that you must not, by giving these powers, change the law, unless with the sanction of this House. When you are beginning a great change of this kind, why not do it in conservative fashion—bit by bit—and then, if it be successful, and the railway and other companies discover that, after all, local inquiries are as efficient as and cheaper than the present system, it can be extended. When you are beginning such a system of devolution, you ought to begin with those who ask it, and not thrust it upon those who are opposed to it. I have never read any evidence that anyone except the local authorities desire the change, and if the Lord Advocate or the Government have such evidence I would be very glad to hear it. There was no such evidence brought before the Joint Committee of the Lords and Commons in 1888. The Lord Advocate has said that very often upstairs in our Committees the local people are wiped out, and are not considered. That is a reflection on the Committees of the House of Commons and the House of Lords, and I am not

at all certain that your new Committees will consider them more. The way in which Committees of both Houses have heard, not only witnesses, but also counsel, has been the wonder of all who have knowledge of it. I hope the Lord Advocate will accept this Amendment, and confine the Bill to the class of people who are desirous of having it. There is a further point to consider. The local authorities ask for Orders, not for private gain, but for public purposes; while all the other people that go for Orders do not want them for public purposes, but for private gain. Speculators in Scotland ought not to be placed in a different position from speculators in England, Wales, and Ireland. For public bodies who come for powers for public purposes which all can enjoy we ought to make the procedure as easy and as cheap as possible, but concessions and privileges should not be given to monopolists for private gain. A future Amendment will compel the Lord Advocate to have all these Orders made by him laid on the Table, and then we will be able to raise any question upon Orders which for any reason may not be satisfactory. This Amendment is merely to limit the Bill to the class of people who desire it, and I beg to move it.

Amendment proposed—

" In page 1, line 6, to leave out ' or persons.' "
—(*Dr. Clark.*)

Question proposed—

" That the words ' or persons ' stand part of the clause."

Mr. A. G. MURRAY : One great object of this Bill, as we very well know, is to cheapen Parliamentary procedure, but it is said it will cheapen it for persons who are well able to pay. No doubt there are persons who would like to go for a Private Bill, but are deterred by the expense in one year, and they do not come forward for several years afterwards. The Amendment would greatly limit the application of the Bill, and although, no doubt, roughly speaking, public bodies more than private individuals would take advantage of this procedure, yet there is really no reason for leaving private individuals out. Therefore I think the clause should stand as it is.

Dr. CLARK : I do not know much about the financial portion of the Bill, but I can see nothing in the Resolution which we have passed in the Committee to-day which will permit you to change unless ridiculous fees are being charged. Perhaps this will come up in another Amendment to make it permissive. I shall be very glad to further debate the matter then, so that perhaps it would be better to withdraw my Amendment now.

Amendment, by leave, withdrawn.

Mr. CRIPPS : There are only two points I need mention in moving this Amendment, to insert " other than railway companies." As far as railway companies are concerned, they desire convenience of procedure and cheapness. As regards the Light Railway Commissioners, as far as the schemes are small ones there is provision already made for dealing with them.

Amendment proposed—

" In page 1, line 6, after ' persons,' to insert ' other than railway companies.' "—(*Mr. Cripps.*)

Question proposed—

" That those words be there inserted."

Mr. A. G. MURRAY : This matter has very often been debated before. I certainly object to deal with railway companies as privileged bodies. There are plenty of representatives in this House who are fully aware of the merits of railway companies, and I have no doubt railway companies are quite certain of not being done any injustice. Railway questions are so far-reaching that I can scarcely conceive a railway Bill which would not, in the judgment of the Chairman, be more appropriate for a Private Bill than for this procedure. But, at the same time, there might be Bills of such a simple character that no big interests are involved, and such might go forward. I prefer to leave the Bill as it is, feeling quite certain that these questions of railway policy would never be sent down by these Committees, but would be dealt with by the House, as they ought to be.

Mr. CALDWELL : The case of railways is provided for in two different ways.

You have got certain important concessions as regards the management of the railway with reference to signals and other things, and with regard to the purchase of land, and I cannot conceive of any persons in Scotland who are anxious to promote a local railway not adopting the Light Railways Act procedure in order to construct a local line. When you come to deal with any railway, every other railway company at once feels interested in any possible extension, for they see in it the thin end of the wedge for increased competition. On these grounds, seeing that the whole consensus of opinion is entirely against including these railway schemes, and that no good object would be served, I think they should be excluded from this Bill during its experimental stage. If you find afterwards your system works well, arrangements can then be made to include these railway schemes ; but whilst things are in this experimental stage, and looking to the views which have been expressed on both sides of the House, I think we might fairly exclude them for the present.

*Mr. RENSHAW (Renfrew, W.) : Following the remarks made by the Lord Advocate, it seems to me that he admits that very few railway Bills will ever be dealt with under this Bill and by the new system ; but as the new system will apply to all these Bills in their earlier stages, at all events the promoters will have to go through the conditions laid down by this Bill, and they will certainly be affected to that extent. Their notices and all matters of that kind will be affected, and it will really make a change in regard to the manner in which the railway companies have to deal with the questions they wish to bring before Parliament. I remember the evidence which you, Mr. Lowther, and the Chairman of Committees in the House of Lords gave in Committee on Private Bill Procedure (Scotland) Bill, 1898. I do not remember what the precise number of Scotch Bills was, but I think it was something like 22, and in all the railway cases both Chairmen agreed that they would have to be dealt with by Parliament and not by the Commission. In answer to a question by myself, you, Mr. Lowther, gave the following evidence. Here is the question and answer :—

" (643.) I suppose you are actuated in that decision to some extent by the fact that it is exceedingly desirable that the railway questions should be dealt with on the same lines all over the United Kingdom?—Yes, partly that, and also because of the magnitude of these railways. I do not say that our decision would be the same in the case of a small railway asking for power to construct a small piece of line; but here we have the Caledonian, the Glasgow and South-Western, the Great North of Scotland, and the North British, three of whom run into England, and have stations in England, and have enormous connections and lines which are worked by them, and running powers over other lines and so forth, and therefore all sorts of interests are or may be affected in connection with those Bills, which I thought could be better dealt with here than they could be at a local inquiry."

The rig t. hon. Gentleman the Member for Bodmin also put the following question to the Earl of Morley, the Chairman of Committees in the House of Lords—

"(1368.) So that the proposed system under this Bill, you think, could not be applied to railways with any security?—No. I would almost suggest (but it is not a suggestion I make with absolute confidence) whether all railways might not be taken out of the Bill. I should not have made that suggestion if the Light Railways Act was not in operation. But, putting it only as a suggestion, would it not be sufficient to allow the smaller branches to be dealt with, if the promoters like, under the Light Railways Act, and take all the railways out of the Bill?"

Those were the views expressed by the two Chairmen in regard to this matter, and I think, from the point of view of simplifying procedure and of making it easier for those who are promoting Bills in regard to railway matters, and who have now two courses open to them—either to come under the Light Railways or come directly to this House—I think it is desirable that these railways should be excluded. I should certainly welcome the exclusion of railway Bills from the provisions of the Bill which we are now considering, because I do not believe that railway legislation ought to be dealt with separately, but ought to be dealt with as a whole and not simply as it affects the various parts of the United Kingdom. The conditions in regard to railway Bills ought to be the same for England, Ireland, and Scotland, and if a separate Commission deals with questions with regard to the working of our big railways in Scotland, I think difficulties might arise in regard to their operations with English companies which would be very undesirable, and would not be in the public interest.

MR. ROBERT WALLACE (Perth): I wish to join with other hon. Members in supporting the system recommended by the Government, and I should regret exceedingly to see the operation of the Bill cut down in any way. The first clause is quite general, and it deals with all public authorities and all kinds of subjects. If any limitation be necessary, let us have such limitation placed upon the second clause, and leave the first clause in its present form, so that either the authority or a private person may apply for this order. If you wish to have this qualified in some way, you have the opportunity to do it upon the second clause, when you set out the conditions upon which the Chairmen are to refuse to make these Orders. Why are the railway companies to be placed in any exceptional circumstances in regard to other companies or persons? If a railway company wish to pass some small measure and avoid the expense of coming to this House, why are they not to be allowed to take advantage of a Bill like this and obtain their Order in that way? I quite agree that, as a general rule, railway Bills will not come under the operation of this measure, because they are generally of such a magnitude that they will require to be dealt with by a Private Bill, and not by a Provisional Order; but there is a clause which protects and safeguards the interests of the railway companies, and I see no necessity in this clause for cutting down its operation, and I trust that the Government will stand by the clause as it is.

MR. CRIPPS: In moving this Amendment my view was that this House ought to keep its control over these matters. There are a great many matters affecting the public interest in regard to railway Bills which ought not to be taken away from the cognisance of this House. As has been pointed out, and as has been given in evidence before the Committee, nearly all these railway Bills affect not only Scotland, but also England. But, quite outside that, I would not allow any railway company to take these Bills without the control of this House. If you once allow this power to go outside of this House, we shall have no effective control as regards railway companies. What has this House done in this respect for the last 40 or 50 years? Why, it has had a contest with these railway companies, and the result has been that the House has put into railway Bills a large number of provisions in the public interest, and I want to preserve that power as against the railway companies, and I do not want them to have the power to go to the Secretary for Scotland or anyone else and ask him to give his consent to these schemes. When these concessions, which are of great value, are required the companies ought to be under an obligation to come to this House. Let me deal with the matter mentioned by the Lord Advocate. He asks, "Why do you want this, because, under any circumstances, these railway Bills will all be sent to this House?" If that is so, all we desire to do by this proposal is to make sure that our wishes are carried out. I believe a vast majority of the Members of this House are of the opinion that each railway Bill ought to be kept under our control. We ought to make that certain by legislation, but if you pass this Bill in its present form you have no further control. Under this Bill the Chairmen or the Secretary for Scotland might pass all these Bills without the slightest control by this House, and such measures might introduce new principles as regards the rates to be charged to any particular trade, and this House would have no power to deal with the matter at all. If the Committee is of opinion that these railway matters ought to come before the House, then the Amendment which I propose ought to be adopted.

MR. BRYCE (Aberdeen, S.): I think the persons who are brought here by the railway companies are those whom we have most of all to consider. The railway companies are able to bear the cost of coming to Parliament, but the people for whom we desire to cheapen this procedure are those persons who are compelled to come to Parliament to protect their own rights and interests when they are threatened by a railway company, and they are put to great expense in consequence. As regards many of the other arguments of the hon. Member for Stroud, they apply equally to other bodies as well as to railway companies. It is quite true that we part with some of our control, but the House has affirmed by the Second Reading of the Bill that it is agreeable to part with that control. I should say that upon the balance of the evidence upon the whole matter it is perfectly clear that all important railway Bills must be

Mr. Cripps.

sent here under the second clause of this Bill, and it is also clear that light railways will be obtained from the Light Railways Commissioners. Consequently there remains only a comparatively small number of cases, such as questions of small extensions of a railway system, which, if desirable, might be dealt with under this Bill. Therefore, the balance of argument appears to me to be in favour of the contention of the Lord Advocate.

MR. CALDWELL: It should be borne in mind that, as regards large railway Bills, everyone knows perfectly well that they must come before this House. I think it is a very unfortunate thing that the notices and advertisements provided by the Standing Orders are no longer to apply to a single railway Bill in Scotland, no matter how important, although that Bill must in the nature of things come before this House. Every Bill, however important, must go through this procedure and must have its notices and advertisements, and if you adopt the Amendment you avoid all that complication as to notices and advertisements between the procedure under the Bill and proceeding under the Standing Orders of the House. You are establishing a new precedent which is simply to be an experiment, but I think that every railway company, whether in Scotland, England, or Ireland, ought to be under the same law with regard to notices and advertisements, and the procedure ought to be uniform in all cases.

MR. HEDDERWICK (Wick Burghs): Upon this subject I find myself in agreement with my hon. friend the Member for Perth. It seems to me that a great deal of fuss is being made about a comparatively small matter. I do not deny that this Bill contains principles of great magnitude; but the operation of the measure will be very limited indeed. I do not suppose that there will be probably more than some 20 Bills affected if this measure be carried out in its entirety. I will state my views upon this point with extreme brevity. In my opinion, so long as an innovation upon the general law is guarded against, I see no reason why Bills of the character objected to by the hon. Member for Stroud should not be referred to the tribunal which is about to be set up by this Bill, always assuming that that tribunal is composed of a panel which has the confidence of this House. That is my opinion, and I hope that the Lord Advocate will resist this Amendment, and any other Amendment of a similar character which proposes to cut down the scope of this Bill. The people of Scotland know very well how to manage their own affairs ; and, if I may say so with respect, I think they can manage them better than people who are not in sympathy with them, and who have not the same knowledge of local affairs.

MR. EDMUND ROBERTSON : Before the House disposes of this Amendment I should like to say that I think the strongest argument is that which was mentioned in the concluding part of the last observation made by the hon. Member for Stroud, for I think there is a good deal of force in what he said. There may be such a thing as an unopposed railway Bill. I will ask my hon. friends who are opposing this Amendment whether they think it is desirable that an unopposed railway Bill should become law without this House intervening in any sort of way, possibly without any inquiry, and simply by the consent of the Secretary for Scotland and the Chairmen of Committees. It may seem that I am speaking now rather selfishly, and in the interests of an Amendment of mine lower down on the Paper, but my contention is that unopposed Bills ought to be excluded from this Bill altogether. I hope my hon. and learned friend will insert some provision to provide for what I consider is the strongest part of the case which he has laid before the Committee.

MR. DALZIEL : We are very desirous that these tribunals shall become more important and more powerful as time goes on, and while I do not want to shut the door against any railway company, I want to leave it open so that when the time comes when this system works well it will be possible to give greater powers. I cannot understand why my hon. friend should want unopposed Bills to come to this House. So far as I am concerned, I think the opinion in Scotland is that we want as many facilities as possible to get Bills through without coming before this House ; and I think this is a sound democratic principle.

MR. J. P. SMITH : There is one thing which detracts a great deal from the importance of this Amendment, and it is that nearly every railway Bill will not go through under this procedure, but will go to the Chairmen of Committees, and the ultimate control will be reserved for them. I agree that it is not satisfactory to cut out one particular class of Bills in the manner proposed by the Amendment, and I suggest to my hon. friend that the object which he has in view on the point he is raising might be better proposed on an Amendment which stands in my name, which gives the promoters of all Bills the option of coming before the House.

MR. COLVILLE (Lanark, N.E.) : There might be private individuals who would certainly object to having their cases dealt with in this way, and I am sure that this proposal would effect a very drastic change.

DR. CLARK : In regard to the question of cost, you do not consider at all the cases of poor persons who are compelled to come to this House to defend their interests, and who are dragged here by the action of the railway companies.

SIR H. CAMPBELL-BANNERMAN : I agree that the grievance is not so very great as far as the chief Scottish railway Bills are concerned, for they are nearly always opposed by one or other of the competing lines. Therefore I do not think, in this respect, there is much of a grievance to the general public so far as these railway schemes are concerned. I cannot, however, bring myself to vote for words which would absolutely shut out all railway Bills from the operation of this measure, for there might be some case arise in which it is conceivable that a railway company would not compete with or excite the opposition of any of the great Scottish railway companies.

MR. CRIPPS : Having regard to the course of the Debate, I will ask leave to withdraw my Amendment.

Amendment, by leave, withdrawn.

DR. CLARK : I do not wish to propose the Amendment which I have on the Paper, but I should like to ask the Lord Advocate why it is proposed to limit the clause to the right which we have at present, for there may be future rights.

MR. A. G. MURRAY: We only deal with the present when we define the scope of the Bill.

MR. CALDWELL: It might be held that there was a limited power here. I can conceive of certain things which Parliament does not deal with, and which are not dealt with by Private Bill legislation at the present moment. I think you ought to make the powers as wide and comprehensive as possible, and I move to leave out the words "at present." I would leave out the words "at present" so as to cover the future in the event of the powers under the Bill being extended by Parliament.

Amendment proposed—

"In page 1, line 9, to leave out the words 'at present.'"—(*Mr. Caldwell.*)

Question proposed—

"That the words 'at present' stand part of the clause."

Mr. A. G. MURRAY: It really cannot make the slightest difference.

Question put, and agreed to.

MR. J. P. SMITH: The object of my Amendment is to make the adoption of the procedure under the Bill optional. It is clear that there are many cases in which this Bill would be a great convenience, but there are a great many other cases in which it is confessed, on all hands, that it will not be suitable and that a return will have to be made to the present procedure. The question is, how you are going to decide these two classes of cases. According to the scheme of the Bill they are to be decided by the Chairmen of Committees. It seems to me that, in the first instance, at any rate, it would relieve a great deal of the complexity and difficulty if you were to leave the matter optional, and allow those who wanted to proceed by Private Bills to do so. Last year the strongest objection against this proposal was that it would deprive the new tribunal of its importance if you took away from it what would probably be the largest measures that could come before it. The evidence before the Select Committee last year went to show that under the Bill as it stands at present more than a third of the measures, comprising all the largest, would not go before

the new tribunal, but would be brought here under the present course of procedure, and that 8 out of the 21 Bills promoted last Session would have been kept here. Seeing that in most of the cases the views of the promoters of the Bill would correspond with the views of the Chairmen of Committees, that the Bill is suitable to be dealt with here, why not allow the promoters their choice from the first, and so avoid all complications, and different sets of notices and deposits? Another objection to making the scheme optional was the argument used by the right hon. Member for Aberdeen, who spoke on behalf of the small objector; but we know, as a fact, that large railway schemes, and other big improvement schemes in which the small objector is concerned, would certainly be brought here, and his position would remain exactly as it is at present. I think it would remove a great deal of the difficulty which besets the Bill if we began, at any rate, by making it optional. Moreover, we are accustomed to have optional schemes, and you would not have the risk of bringing under the new tribunal Bills that are not fitted for it. The Parliamentary Bills Committee of the Glasgow Corporation are strongly of opinion that the Bill should not be compulsory in the first instance, and that it should be in the option of the promoters to proceed by Private Bill procedure. Following the very frequent course of this House, we should begin by making the procedure optional, and then after some experience the question could be decided whether it was wise to make it compulsory. I therefore move that the word "may" be substituted for "shall."

Amendment proposed—

"In page 1, line 10, to leave out the word 'shall,' and insert the word 'may' instead thereof."—(*Mr. Parker Smith.*)

Question proposed—

"That the word 'shall' stand part of the clause."

MR. A. G. MURRAY: This matter was discussed both last year and the year before, and I do not think my opinion of it has ever wavered. The clause as it stands has been drawn entirely in the interest of the small objector. We were never under the hallucination that there would not be many Bills reserved for consideration by Committees in this House, and where the small objector will be constantly brought up to Westminster. That is a misfortune to the small objector, which, however, is inevitable. It is a principle of this Bill that there are certain subjects that ought to be proceeded with not by Provisional Order, but by Private Bill before this House; but there are other subjects that can be proceeded with by Provisional Order, and we would be giving up one of the greatest benefits of our measure if we allowed anyone who is strong enough to do it to avoid the Provisional Order, and to proceed by Private Bill.

SIR CHARLES CAMERON (Glasgow, Bridgeton): I have an Amendment to the same effect as that of the hon. Member for Partick, and I shall support him and go to a Division on the point. As to the small objector, the big corporation Bills will never come before this tribunal at all. The Bills that will come before it, as was stated by my hon. friend, will be very few. Not more than 12 measures would have come before the new tribunal last year, had this Bill been law. I imagine t at probably that number may be increased if a good tribunal can be set up; but the Bills to be brought before it will be small Bills. I had a conversation with the Chairman of the Light Railway Commission the other day, and he told me that they had got through 38 inquiries in 40 days. I myself should have a very strong objection to come before a tribunal such as is sketched out in the Bill as it stands. It is most important that at first, at any rate, the working of this Bill should be optional. During the Second Reading of the Bill, one of the strongest representations which I quoted in favour of making the Bill optional was that from the Faculty of Procurators in Glasgow, which is a body not influenced by Mr. Vary Campbell, and which can take an independent view on the subject.

MR. CROMBIE (Kincardineshire): I hope the Government will not consent to this Amendment. According to your own evidence, Mr. Lowther, before the Select Committee last year, only 60 per cent. of the present Bills would come under the new procedure proposed by the Bill; and if you are going to allow any corporation the option of proceeding by Private Bill, of what use will this Bill be? If the Bill is to be of any use at all

it is to compel corporations to adopt this cheaper method. I hope the Lord Advocate will make the tribunal a good tribunal.

MR. A. G. MURRAY: The hon. Baronet the Member for Bridgeton misread the evidence last year, when he said that out of the 21 Bills introduced only 12, according to his view, would be subject to the Provisional Order scheme. None of these Bills were corporation Bills.

MR. CALDWELL: It is perfectly true that corporations have promoted a number of Private Bills, but the Lord Advocate leaves out of view that corporations can proceed by Provisional Order under the present system. What is the procedure under the present system? There is the local inquiry, which costs practically nothing, as there are no agents. Then the Department to which the Bill belongs passes the Provisional Order, and it comes on here, where the Government Department is at the whole expense of carrying it through the House. The only expense ever incurred by the local authority is when there is opposition at the Committee stage. So completely successful has been the existing Provisional Order system that there has hardly been the rejection of a Provisional Order. Moreover, where they have been opposed in one House, they have very frequently not been opposed in the other. There could be nothing simpler or cheaper to the local authority than the powers under the present Provisional Order system. In England local authorities resort almost exclusively to that system, whereas in Scotland some have proceeded by Private Bill, when, according to the evidence of the Chairman of Committees, they might have proceeded under the present Provisional Order system. There is much misconception among the public in Scotland about this Bill. They believe that under this Bill local authorities will be able to get legislative powers cheaper than under the present system. The fact is that the process will be much dearer. Under this Bill they will have to pay fees in the local tribunal, as well as the fees in this House, and therefore this Bill, instead of being an advantage to corporations, will be a decided disadvantage. There is another important point that has to be borne in mind. Supposing

2 K

anyone comes to this House with a Bill, which is considered by a Committee and rejected; he can come in a succeeding session of Parliament and have the Bill remitted to a new Committee. By a very little alteration of the Bill he may get it passed, although it had been rejected by the former Committee. But under the procedure proposed by this Bill the Secretary for Scotland has full power. The principle of the Provisional Order must be approved of by the Secretary of Scotland first before he sends it to a Committee of his own selection. No one would have the remotest chance, therefore, of having his Bill re-considered.

MR. THOMAS SHAW: The Amendment would restrict the operation of the Bill in a most important particular, and I hope the Lord Advocate will stick to the Bill as it stands. The case which I personally want to protect is where a large corporation is dealing by Bill with a variety of interests, each of which is unable to defend itself before the Committees of this House or the House of Lords. In such a case, if the subject matter of the Bill is suitable for a Provisional Order, then the Provisional Order procedure ought surely to apply. That would be the more economical method. A second reason for the rejection of the Amendment is that under Section 2 of the Bill I find very careful provision is made for protecting the very cases aimed at by the Amendment. I think the value of the Bill would be diminished if we were to allow the option to promoters to proceed by Private Bill in all cases, for it would put the small objectors to great disadvantage.

MR. SOUTTAR (Dumfriesshire): I do not know whether hon. Members who stick by the word "shall," and absolutely refuse to consider the word "may," realise that they are depriving Scotland of the very ancient and valuable right of petitioning Parliament by Private Bills. It is a right which has been enjoyed for centuries, and has been of immense consequence. As we know, in early times that right was used by private individuals to oppose violence and oppression. It is now used largely by local authorities and commercial companies. It is a very valuable and precious right, and I cannot understand how Scotchmen are so willing to throw it away. The case is worse when

Mr. Caldwell.

we consider that this Bill applies to Scotland only. If Welshmen, Englishmen, and Irishmen were all to be tarred with the same brush, it would not matter so much. But if the Bill passes and the word "shall" is adhered to and "may" is refused, while Englishmen, Welshmen, and Irishmen retain their ancient privileges of being able to apply to Parliament for a Private Bill, Scotchmen will be precluded, and be forced to go in humble fashion to the Secretary for Scotland and ask his kind consent.

DR. FARQUHARSON (Aberdeenshire, W.): This Amendment raises an important constitutional principle, namely, the right of public bodies or private individuals to petition Parliament. Under this Bill, as it stands, the Secretary for Scotland is to be the ultimate court of appeal. Hon. Members who are familiar with the evidence given before the Select Committee last year must remember the very strong statement made by the Chairman of Committees on this point, who said:

"It is an entirely new thing to say to a man. 'You shall not petition the House of Commons.'"

And Lord Morley, speaking from his great experience as Chairman of Committees in the House of Lords, gave expression to sentiments equally strong and equally decided. It seems to me that, if there is really so strong a desire for the Bill as is said, the promoters need not fear its optional character. I hope my hon. friend will stick to his Amendment, and give us the pleasure of having a Division. We must remember that although, as stated in the Debate, this may be a very small Bill looking at it at first, it will have far-reaching consequences. Unless we take our stand now on principles, we shall have very little chance of having them adopted by the authorities later on. No doubt the Bill is an experiment, but it should be so framed as to render the experiment probably successful.

MR. BUCHANAN: The Lord Advocate has defended the measure on the ground that it is a tentative measure. If it were so, then the direction in which the Amendment goes is to make it of a tentative character. I object to the constituency I represent being made the object of an experiment.

With reference to the question of economy, if the Bill acts in the way that is expected and is the most economical method of procedure, corporations desiring to obtain powers will proceed by it. But if it is admitted that the Bill is purely experimental, I think an option should be left to the corporations of Scotland. I will support the Amendment, because I do not wish any disability to be put on Scotland which is not also put on England and Ireland.

DR. CLARK : If you pass the clause n its present form and also Clause 16, you take away all power to obtain Provisional Orders. Scotland occupies a very different position in connection with Provisional Orders from that of England, because it has a right to adopt by Provisional Order quite a number of things which English corporations cannot adopt by the same means, under the Burgh Police Act and also the Public Health Act of 1897. The Scotch corporations can acquire land by compulsion, can amalgamate burghs, and reconstruct their corporations as far as the number of councillors and wards is concerned, all by Provisional Order. In England those things can only be done through Parliament. Under this clause and Clause 16 you are taking that power away from us. You are taking away the cheap and easy method conferred on us by the Burgh Police Act and the Public Health Act, and you are giving us a more cumbersome and costly method. Why should we be compelled to accept what we do not require? I withdrew my Amendment some time ago in order to have a Division on this point, which will show whether we are going to compel people to give up a cheap and easy method for a costly and cumbersome one.

MR. ROBERT WALLACE : I wish to ask the Lord Advocate whether what my hon. friend has just said is really so or not. I understand by Section 16 that the present powers are conserved, and that the chief inquiry will still take place under the statute regulating Provisional Orders. My hon. friend says not, but I read the section entirely differently.

MR. A. G. MURRAY : The hon. Member is quite right. The powers as to Provisional Orders are kept intact, and the only question is whether we should substitute "may" for "shall."

MR. CALDWELL : The point is that if a local authority wishes to proceed by Provisional Order it would require to have the consent of the Government Department. Suppose, for instance, the Local Government Board refuses to give a Provisional Order on the terms desired by a corporation, the corporation can now come to this House with a Private Bill. It is obvious, therefore, that it is a great advantage to Scotch corporations that, if the Local Government Board, or any other Department, refuses to give them a Provisional Order, they can come to Parliament, but according to this Bill they will not be able to come to the House by Private Bill. They must go to the Secretary of State for Scotland, probably the very man who has refused to give them the Provisional Order. Of course if they can convince the Chairman of Committees, they might get their Bill through ; but supposing the Chairmen happened to belong to the same political party as the Secretary of State, there might be some doubt as to whether the corporations would get fair play. At present they will have the opportunity of getting the judgment of this House by a Private Bill, apart altogether from the opinion of the Secretary of State for Scotland, or of the Chairman of Committees of either House. We ought not to close the door, as this Bill does, to local authorities coming direct to petition this House.

MR. GIBSON BOWLES (Lynn Regis) : I think this discussion would really be far more germane to Clause 16. The question raised by this Bill and the method of treatment raised by the Amendment go to the very root of the rights of property in this country. It is a tremendous change in the procedure of this House in the application of laws to the rights of property. It is admitted it is an experimental measure, and if that be so surely it ought to be tried experimentally. If it does all that is claimed for it, it will not be refused by anybody, but people desiring to proceed under the old method should be allowed to do so. It would be very ill-advised to make it compulsory in all cases, and, for my part, I support the Amendment proposed by my hon. friend, and if necessary I shall vote with him.

DR. CLARK: I would ask the Lord Advocate what he means by Section 16. It reads as follows—

"Nothing contained in this Act shall affect the power of the Secretary for Scotland to make Provisional Orders under the provisions of any Act in force at the passing of this Act, or the procedure therein specified, save only that in the case of Provisional Orders which at present require confirmation by Parliament the provisions of Sections 7, 8, and 9 of this Act shall, with the necessary modifications,

apply as if they were contained in any Act in force as aforesaid."

But we can now apply to the Local Government Board under the Piers and Harbours Act, the Electric Lighting Act, and other statutes.

Question put.

The Committee divided : Ayes, 196 ; Noes, 80. (Division List No. 183.)

AYES.

Allhusen, Augustus Henry E.
Anson, Sir William Reynell
Archdale, Edward Mervyn
Arnold, Alfred
Arnold-Forster, Hugh O.
Asher, Alexander
Asquith, Rt. Hon. Herbert H.
Atkinson, Rt. Hon. John
Bailey, James (Walworth)
Balfour, Rt. Hon. A. J. (Man.)
Balfour,Rt.Hon.G W. (Leeds)
Banbury, Frederick George
Barnes, Frederic Gorell
Barton, Dunbar Plunkett
Bathurst, Hn. Allen Benjamin
Beach,Rt. Hn.SirMH (Bristol)
Begg, Ferdinand Faithfull
Bhownaggree, Sir M. M.
Bigwood, James
Blundell, Colonel Henry
Bolitho, Thomas Bedford
Bond, Edward
Brassey, Albert
Brodrick, Rt. Hon. St. John
Bryce, Rt. Hon. James
Bullard, Sir Harry
Burt, Thomas
Butcher, John George
Campbell-Bannerman, Sir H.
Cecil, E. (Hertford, East)
Cecil, Lord H. (Greenwich)
Chaloner, Captain R. G. W.
Chamberlain, J. A. (Worc'r)
Chaplin, Rt. Hon. Henry
Charrington, Spencer
Cochrane, Hon. T. H. A. E.
Coghill, Douglas Harry
Cohen, Benjamin Louis
Collings, Rt. Hon. Jesse
Colston, Chas. E. H. Athole
Colville, John
Cook, Fred. Lucas (Lambeth)
Corbett, A. C. (Glasgow)
Cornwallis, Fiennes S. W.
Courtney,Rt. Hon. Leonard H
Cranborne, Viscount
Crombie, John William
Cubitt, Hon. Henry
Curzon, Viscount
Dalbiac, Colonel Philip Hugh
Dalrymple, Sir Charles
Dalziel, James Henry
Davies, Sir H. D. (Chatham)
Digby, John K D. Wingfield-
Disraeli, Coningsby Ralph
Dixon-Hartland, Sir F. Dixon
Dorington, Sir John Edward
Douglas, Rt. Hon. A. Akers-

Doxford, William Theodore
Duncombe, Hon. Hubert V.
Elliot, Hon. A. Ralph D.
Fellowes, Hon. Ailwyn E.
Ferguson, R. C. M. (Leith)
Field, Admiral (Eastbourne)
Finlay, Sir Robert B.
Fisher, William Hayes
Fison, Frederick William
Fitzmaurice, Lord Edmond
Fletcher, Sir Henry
Foster, Colonel (Lancaster)
Foster, Harry S. (Suffolk)
Gedge, Sydney
Gibbons, J. Lloyd
Giles, Charles Tyrell
Gilliat, John Saunders
Gladstone, Rt. Hon. H. John
Goldsworthy, Major General
Gordon, Hon. John Edward
Gorst, Rt. Hon. Sir John E.
Goschen, RtHnGJ(StGeorge's)
Goschen, George J. (Sussex)
Goulding, Edward Alfred
Gray, Ernest (West Ham)
Gunter, Colonel
Hamilton,Rt.Hn.Lord George
Hanbury,Rt.Hon.RobertWm.
Hardy, Laurence
Hatch, Ernest Frederick Geo.
Hedderwick, Thomas C. H.
Henderson, Alexander
Hermon-Hodge, Robt. Trotter
Hickman, Sir Alfred
Hill, Arthur (Down, West)
Hoare, Samuel (Norwich)
Hobhouse, Henry
Howell, William Tudor
Howorth, Sir Henry Hoyle
Hutton, John (Yorks. N. R.)
Johnson-Ferguson,JabezEdw.
Johnston, William (Belfast)
Kay-Shuttleworth, RtHnSirU
Kemp, George
Kennaway, Rt. Hon. Sir J.H.
Kenyon-Slaney, Colonel Wm.
Kinloch, Sir J. Geo. Smyth
Knowles, Lees
Lawrence,SirE.Durning-(Corn
Lawson, John Grant (Yorks.)
Lecky, Rt. Hon. Wm. Edw.H.
Leigh-Bennett, Henry Currie
Llewellyn,Evan H. (Somerset)
Lockwood, Lt.-Col. A. R.
Long,Rt.Hn. Walter (Liverp'l)
Lowles, John
Loyd, Archie Kirkman
Macdona, John Cumming

M'Calmont,Col.J.(Antrim,E.)
M'Killop, James
Maple, Sir John Blundell
Middlemore, J. Throgmorton)
Mildmay, Francis Bingham
Milton, Viscount
Monk, Charles James
Montagu, Hn. J. S. (Hants)
More, Robt. Jasper (Shrops.)
Morgan, Hon. F.(Monm'thsh.)
Morley,RtHonJohn(Montrose
Morton, Arthur H.A. Deptford
Murray, RtHnAGraham(Bute
Murray, Charles J. (Coventry)
Newdigate, FrancisAlexander
Nicholson, William Graham
Nicol, Donald Ninian
Oldroyd, Mark
Peace,HerbertPikeDarlington
Percy, Earl
Pierpoint, Robert
Pilkington, R. (Lancs,Newton
Platt-Higgins, Frederick
Pretyman, Ernest George
Pryce-Jones,Lt.-Col.Edward
Purvis, Robert
Pym, C. Guy
Rasch, Major Frederic Carne
Ridley,Rt.Hn.SirMatthew W.
Ritchie,Rt. Hn.Chas.Thomson
Roberts, John Bryn (Eifion)
Robertson, Herbert, (Hackney
Rothschild,Hon.LionelWalter
Round, James
Russell, Gen. F.S.(Chelten'm)
Russell, T. W. (Tyrone)
Rutherford, John
Ryder, John Herbert Dudley
Savory, Sir Joseph
Sharpe, William. Edward T.
Shaw, Thomas (Hawick, B.)
Shaw-Stewart,M H.(Renfrew)
Sidebotham, J. W. (Cheshire)
Sidebottom, W. (Derbyshire)
Simeon, Sir Barrington
Smith, Hon. W. F. D. (St'nd)
Spicer, Albert
Stanley, H. M (Lambeth)
Stanley, Lord (Lancs.)
Stewart, Sir M. J. M'Taggart
Stock, James Henry
Stone, Sir Benjamin
Strauss, Arthur
Strutt, Hon. Charles Hedley
Sutherland, Sir Thomas
Talbot, Lord E. (Chichester)
Talbot,Rt. Hn.J.G.(Ox.Univ.)
Tennant, Harold John

Thorburn, Walter
Thornton, Percy M.
Tomlinson, Wm. Edw. Murray
Tritton, Charles Ernest
Ure, Alexander
Valentia, Viscount
Wallace, Robert (Perth)
Warde, Lieut.-Col. C. E. (Kent)
Webster, R. G. (St. Pancras)

Welby, Lieut.-Col. A. C. E.
Wentworth, Bruce C. Vernon.
Whiteley, George (Stockport)
Whitmore, Charles Algernon
Williams, Colonel R. (Dorset)
Williams, Joseph Powell-(Birm
Wodehouse, Rt. Hn. E. R. (Bath)
Wolff, Gustav Wilhelm
Wylie, Alexander

Wyndam, George
Wyndam-Quin, Major W. H.
Wyvill, Marmaduke D'Arcy
Young, Commander(Berks, E.)

TELLERS FOR THE AYES
Sir William Walrond and
Mr. Anstruther

NOES.

Austin, Sir John (Yorkshire)
Barlow, John Emmott
Bartley, George C. T.
Billson, Alfred
Birrell, Augustine
Bolton, Thomas Dolling
Bowles, T-Gibson (King'sLynn
Brunner, Sir John Tomlinson
Buchanan, Thomas Ryburn
Burns, John
Caldwell, James
Channing, Francis Allston
Clark, Dr. G. B. (Caithness-sh.)
Cripps, Charles Alfred
Curran, Thomas (Sligo, S.)
Davies, M. Vaughan-(Cardigan
Davitt, Michael
Dilke, Rt. Hon. Sir Charle
Dillon, John
Donelan, Captain A.
Doogan, P. C.
Dunn, Sir William
Evans, SamuelT. (Glamorgan)
Farquharson, Dr. Robert
Fenwick, Charles
Goddard, Daniel Ford
Gold, Charles
Griffith, Ellis J.

Hayne, Rt. Hon. C. Seale-
Healy, T. M. (N. Louth)
Hemphill, Rt. Hon. Chas. H.
Holden, Sir Angus
Holland, W. H. (York, W. R.)
Horniman, Frederick John
Joicey, Sir James
Lambert, George
Lawson, Sir Wilfrid (Cumb.)
Leng, Sir John
Lloyd-George, David
Loder, Gerald Walter Erskine
Logan, John William
Lough, Thomas
Lyell, Sir Leonard
Macaleese, Daniel
MacNeil, John Gordon Swift
M'Dermott, Patrick
M'Ewan, William
M'Ghee, Richard
M'Kenna, Reginald
M'Leod, John
Molloy, Bernard Charles
Morris, Samuel
Morton, E. J. C. (Devonport.)
Moss, Samuel
Moulton, John Fletcher
O'Brien, James F. X. (Cork)

O'Connor, James(Wicklow, W.
O'Malley, William
Palmer, SirCharlesM.(Durham
Powell, Sir Francis Sharp
Renshaw, Charles Bine
Richardson, J. (Durham, S.E.)
Rickett, J. Compton
Roberts, J. H. (Denbighs.)
Robertson, Edm. (Dundee)
Samuel, J. (Stockton-on-Tees)
Sinclair, Capt. J. (Forfarsh.)
Souttar, Robinson
Steadman, William Charles
Strachey, Edward
Sullivan, Donal (Westmeath)
Trevelyan, Charles Philips
Walton, J. Lawson (Leeds S.)
Wedderburn, Sir William
Whittaker, Thomas Palmer
Wilson, H. J. (York, W.R.)
Wilson, John (Durham, Mid.)
Wilson, John (Govan)
Woods, Samuel
Wortley, Rt. Hn. C.B. Stuart-

TELLERS FOR THE NOES —
Mr. Parker Smith and Sir
Charles Cameron.

MR. EDMUND ROBERTSON: I beg to move—

"In Clause 1, page 1, line 11, to leave out from 'by' to the end of the clause, in order to insert 'Private Bill according to the existing practice of Parliament, unless and until there is opposition to the Bill, in which case only the procedure established by this Act shall apply.'"

The object of this Amendment is to restrict the application of this Bill to opposed business. The principle of the Bill is simply to substitute for the inquiry now conducted at Westminster a local inquiry in the spot affected. That is the whole of the demand in Scotland. Legislation of this kind is founded on the notion that the inquiry at Westminster is by comparison with the local inquiry dear and dilatory. Accepting that as the principle of the Bill, all I propose is that it should be limited to the purpose for which it is demanded, and that we shall have a local inquiry only in cases where there is an inquiry now. There is no inquiry at present where the Bill is un-

opposed. Why, therefore, should we alter the existing practice in a matter in respect to which, from beginning to end of the whole controversy, there has not been the smallest atom of complaint? Has anybody ever heard from any responsible Scotch authority any complaint whatever on the ground of expense or delay in connection with the system adopted by this House and the other House in relation to Private Bills not contested? It seems to me that this Bill has failed to take account of the fundamental difference between opposed and unopposed business. It is simply with reference to opposed business that there is any complaint at all, and it is to opposed business that I venture to bring the Bill back. That is the object of the Amendment which I now propose. There is no need to disturb the existing system as regards unopposed Bills, and there has never been any demand for any change in it. I will add another consideration. Bills now unopposed in the sense of not being petitioned against by private parties may involve large questions of public interest. Under the system now proposed they will be withdrawn altogether from the cognisance of Parliament. I would ask the Lord Advocate what reason he can give for that proposal. I will mention one particular case. Two or three Sessions ago an unopposed Bill—a Cambrian Railway Bill—came before this House, and many hon. Members must remember that strong objection was taken to it on public grounds, the hon. Member for Aberdeen leading the opposition to the Bill on that occasion. What earthly reason can there be for taking away a Bill of this sort from the cognisance of the House and leaving it entirely to the two Chairmen of Committees and the Secretary of State for Scotland? It cannot be too often repeated that the demand in Scotland has been that a local inquiry should be substituted for an Imperial inquiry. I do not think the Committee is sufficiently impressed with the fact that of the Private Bills coming before Parliament year by year the large majority are unopposed. In the ten years ending 1897 there were 352 Private Bills from Scotland brought before Parliament. How many of these were opposed in one House or the other? The Return includes all cases where petitions were presented against Bills, although no opposition was offered afterwards, so that the number of opposed Bills as compared with unopposed Bills is really too large. Of the total number of Bills introduced only 168 were opposed, and 184 passed through both Houses without any opposition except such as was offered on the floor of this House, without any inquiry in Committee, and without expense or delay attributable to inquiry in this House. Why is not the present Bill confined to the 168 cases in which there was an inquiry, leaving both Houses of Parliament free to deal with the considerably larger number of cases in which there was no opposition and no inquiry? We have heard a great deal about railway Bills, but I have a Return here which entirely confirms the general conclusion I have drawn from the larger Return. In 1897 the total number of Private Bills sent up from Scotland was 39. Of these 17 were opposed in one House, 12 in both Houses, and 19 out of the 39 were unopposed. Of these 19 Bills no less than ten were railway

Mr Edmund Robertson.

Bills. It may be said that if my Amendment is accepted the scope of the Bill will be limited. That is true, but it is no answer to my proposal. By this Amendment you leave untouched the present procedure regarding unopposed Bills. It would involve, no doubt, a change in the structure of the Bill. We shall proceed as we proceed now up to the stage when opposition is offered, and then, and only then, should we begin by substituting a local inquiry for the existing inquiry. What I propose is absolutely consistent with the principle of the Bill. Nay more, it carries out the principle of the Bill better. It absolutely meets every demand made in Scotland for a change in the Private Bill system, and I venture to submit it to the consideration of the House and to ask the support of hon. Members from Scotland for it.

Amendment proposed—

" In page 1, line 11, to leave out from the word 'by,' to the end of the clause, and add the words ' Private Bill, according to the existing practice of Parliament, unless and until there is opposition to the Bill, in which case only the procedure established by this Act shall apply' instead thereof."—(*Mr. Edmund Robertson.*)

Question proposed—

" That the words proposed to be omitted to the words 'a Provisional,' in line 12, stand part of the clause."

MR. A. G. MURRAY : There is one assertion of the hon. Gentleman's at which I must say I was rather surprised. He said he had never heard any complaints about the expense of unopposed Bills.

MR. EDMUND ROBERTSON : I said I never heard any complaints of the system except as regards opposed Bills.

MR. A. G. MURRAY : A great many of us have heard complaints both long and loud as to the cost of unopposed Bills. No doubt fees form a great part of that expense, but they are not the whole of it. A firm of Parliamentary Solicitors has to be employed, in addition to the local solicitors, which means, of course, two separate sets of solicitors ; and I am sure my memory is not deceiving me when I say that one hon. Gentleman after another, on the Second Reading, referred to the enormous expense of unopposed Bills. The point of there being objection to the present system as entailing unnecessary expense and labour has, I think, bulked very largely in public opinion in Scotland. I submit it would really very much truncate this measure of reform if I were to accept this Amendment. It would, of course, have a far-reaching effect on the other provisions of the Bill, because it would turn the general theory of the Bill upside down. I cannot accept the Amendment, because if I did I would be really taking away from the people of Scotland half the benefit which they expect to get from this Bill, and I shall be surprised if that view is not supported by hon. Members.

MR. THORBURN (Peebles and Selkirk): I think the cost of unopposed Bills is one of the greatest and most crying evils complained of by the people of Scotland. Solicitors have first of all to be employed in Scotland, and then another set has to be employed in London, and the entire expense constitutes an evil which we should endeavour to cure.

DR. CLARK: The probability is that if this clause is retained in the Bill the cost of unopposed Bills will be greater. Glasgow and Aberdeen, and other parts of Scotland, will be exactly in the same position as they are now. They will have to employ a firm of solicitors in Edinburgh, who would charge more than Messrs. Beveridge or a few other firms in London. I happen to have had a great deal of litigation in Edinburgh and London, and I found that in London the costs were less than in Edinburgh. Under the new system you will not want a London Parliamentary agent, but you will want an Edinburgh one, and general experience has shown that the latter will want as much, if not more, than the former. I see no reason why the Amendment should not be accepted. Instead of getting what we asked for, we are getting a most revolutionary system which the Lord Advocate is endeavouring to carry through without any Amendment.

SIR MARK STEWART (Kirkcudbright): The hon. Member who moved the Amendment appears to be under a misconception with regard to the expense incurred on unopposed Private Bills. My experience is exactly the reverse of his. A few years ago it was my fortune to promote a Bill which was unopposed in every sense of the word, yet it cost something like £1,400 to get it through this House. That is a preposterous expense. Under the new system it will be necessary no doubt, to employ an Edinburgh agent; but what is that compared with the fees of this House? The Private Bill to which I have referred had, owing to several disasters, to be withdrawn, and it cost £400 to do it. That is a very good illustration of the cost of unopposed Private Bills. The sole object and aim of this Bill is to avoid expense. The hon. Gentleman who moved the Amendment is utterly mistaken, and I hope the Government will not give way in the matter.

MR. DALZIEL: I myself am inclined to sympathise more with the Government than with my hon. friends. They compare the cost between Edinburgh and London, and it has been said the cost is more in Edinburgh, but they should give some consideration to the fact that the money is spent in the country. I support the Government because when we have considered Scotch Private Bill legislation we have invariably attached importance to the question of unopposed Bills, and we have shown that under the present system the cost is immense and ought to be radically dealt with. We are setting up new machinery, and I look to the arena being widened, because I think we may be able to deal with other matters. Certainly on the present occasion we ought to include unopposed as well as opposed Bills.

MR. EDMUND ROBERTSON: May I be allowed to make clear what I have said with reference to the cost of unopposed Bills. I never said there were no complaints regarding the system. We all know there are. I have figures with reference to the cost of Bills promoted in 1897. One unopposed Bill cost in fees alone £237, and does anybody suppose that Scotland does not object to such an enormous expenditure? What I said was that the great demand on which this Bill was founded was the expense of the Westminster inquiry. I see nothing in the Bill which will alter the state of things as regards the expenditure on fees. The Lord Advocate has not shown us in what way any reduction will follow in that respect. Will he tell us where the preliminary proceeding is to take place? I see no reference to that in the Bill. Then, again, the two Chairmen have to take most important action, and I do not suppose we can avoid employing a London agent as well as an Edinburgh agent.

DR. CLARK: Let me bring two specific instances before the Committee. Three or four years ago there was a question of the union of two parishes in Edinburgh, and the local inquiry cost £3,500. Another question in which the Edinburgh Corporation was concerned was determined by arbitration, and the costs of the Corporation in that matter were £5,000. Those two cases support what I have previously stated, that an inquiry in Edinburgh is more expensive than an inquiry in London.

CAPTAIN SINCLAIR: It may be quite right to say that the new procedure will be cheaper than the old, but we have no facts or figures laid before us as to how that will be. It is perfectly true that in exceptional cases the cost of unopposed Bills is very considerable, but the fees of this House form the greater portion of the expense, and the point which seems to me to be before the Committee is, having regard to the question of fees, whether it is wise or not to remove unopposed Bills from the control of this House.

MR. J. P. SMITH: I think it would be a matter of very considerable importance if we had the rules of procedure to be prescribed under this Bill before we reach the Report stage. Of course, the Committee stage will show the form which the Bill itself will take.

Question put.

The Committee divided: Ayes, 146; Noes, 56. (Division List No. 184.)

AYES.

Allhusen, Augustus Hy. Eden
Archdale, Edward Mervyn
Arnold, Alfred
Asher, Alexander
Ashmead-Bartlett, Sir Ellis
Atkinson, Rt. Hon. John
Bagot, Capt. J. FitzRoy
Balfour, Rt. Hon. A. J. (Man.)
Balfour, Rt. Hon. G. W. (Leeds)
Barnes, Frederic Gorell
Bartley, George C. T.
Barton, Dunbar Plunket
Bathurst, Hon. Allen Benjamin
Beach, Rt. Hn. Sir M. H. (Bristol
Begg, Ferdinand Faithfull
Bhownaggree, Sir M. M.
Bigwood, James
Birrell, Augustine
Blundell, Colonel Henry
Bond, Edward
Brodrick, Rt. Hon. St. John
Bullard, Sir Harry
Butcher, John George
Cecil, Evelyn (Hertford, East)
Chaloner, Captain R. G. W.
Chamberlain, J Austen (Worc'r
Chaplin, Rt. Hon. Henry
Charrington Spencer
Cochrane, Hon. Thos. H. A. E.
Coghill, Douglas Harry
Cohen, Benjamin Louis
Collings, Rt. Hon. Jesse
Colston, Chas. Edw. H. Athole
Cook, Fred. Lucas (Lambeth)
Cranborne, Viscount
Cross, Alexander (Glasgow)
Cubitt, Hon. Henry
Curzon, Viscount
Dalbiac, Colonel Philip Hugh
Dalrymple, Sir Charles
Dalziel, James Henry
Davies, Sir Horatio D (Chatham
Denny, Colonel

Douglas, Rt. Hon. A. Akers-
Doxford, William Theodore
Duncombe, Hon. Hubert V.
Dyke, Rt. Hn. Sir William Hart
Elliot, Hon. A. Ralph Douglas
Fellowes, Hon. Ailway Edward
Ferguson, R.C. Munro (Leith)
Field, Admiral (Eastbourne)
Finlay, Sir Robert Bannatyne
Fisher, William Hayes
Foster, Colonel (Lancaster)
Foster, Harry S. (Suffolk)
Giles, Charles Tyrell
Gilliat, John Saunders
Goldsworthy, Major-General
Gordon, Hon. John Edward
Gorst, Rt. Hon. Sir John E.
Goschen, Rt. Hn. G. J. (St Geo.'s)
Goschen, George J. (Sussex)
Goulding, Edward Alfred
Gray, Ernest (West Ham)
Hamilton, Rt. Hn. Lord George
Hatch, Ernest Frederick Geo.
Hedderwick, Thomas C. H.
Henderson, Alexander
Hermon-Hodge, R. Trotter
Hill, Arthur (Down, West)
Howell, William Tudor
Hutton, John (Yorks. N.R.)
Jebb, Richard Claverhouse
Johnson, William (Belfast)
Kennaway, Rt. Hon. Sir. J. H.
Kenyon-Slaney, Col. William
Kinloch, Sir J. George Smyth
Knowles, Lees
Lawrence, Sir E Durning-(Corn
Lawson, John Grant (Yorks.)
Leigh-Bennett, Henry Currie
Long, Rt. Hon. W. Liv'rpool)
Lopes, Henry Yarde Buller
Lowles, John
Loyd, Archie Kirkman
Macdona, John Cumming

M'Arthur, Charles (Liv'rpool)
M'Calmont, Col. J. (Antrim, E)
M'Killop, James
Middlemore, J. Throgmorton
Mildmay, Francis Bingham
Milton, Viscount
Monk, Charles James
More, R. Jasper (Shropshire)
Morgan, Hn. F. (Moun'thsh.)
Morton, A. H. A. (Deptford)
Murray, Rt. Hn. A. G. (Bute)
Murray, Chas. J. (Coventry)
Newdigate, Francis Alexander
Nicholson, William Graham
Nicol, Donald Ninian
O'Neill, Hon. Robert Torrens
Pease, Herbt. Pike (Darlington
Pierpoint, Robert
Pilkington, R. (Lancs Newton)
Powell, Sir Francis Shary
Pretyman, Ernest George
Pryce-Jones, Lt.-Col. Edward
Purvis, Robert
Pym, C. Guy
Renshaw, Charles Bine
Ridley, Rt. Hon. Sir Matt. W.
Robertson, Herbert (Hackney)
Round, James
Russell, T. W. (Tyrone)
Ryder, John Herbert Dudley
Samuel, J. (Stockton-on-Tees)
Savory, Sir Joseph
Sharpe, William Edward T.
Sidebotham, J. W. (Cheshire)
Sidebottom, Wm. (Derbysh.)
Smith, Jas. Parker (Lanarks)
Stanley, Lord (Lancs.)
Stewart, Sir M. J. M'Taggart
Stock, James Henry
Stone, Sir Benjamin
Strutt, Hon. Charles Hedley
Sutherland, Sir Thomas
Tennant, Harold John

Thorburn, Walter
Thornton, Percy M.
Tomlinson, Wm. Edw. Murray
Tritton, Charles Ernest
Ure, Alexander
Valentia, Vicount
Wallace, Robert (Perth)

Warde, Lieut-Col. C. E. (Kent)
Webster, R. G. (St. Pancras)
Wentworth, Bruce C. Vernon-
Williams, Colonel R. (Dorset)
Williams, Joseph Powell-(Birm
Wolff, Gustav Wilhelm
Wylie, Alexander

Wyndham-Quin, Major W. H.
Wyvill, Marmaduke D'Arcy
Younger, Commander(BerksE.

TELLERS FOR THE AYES—
Sir William Walrond and
Mr. Anstruther.

NOES.

Austin, Sir John (Yorkshire)
Brunner, Sir John Tomlinson
Burns, John
Burt, Thomas
Caldwell, James
Cameron, SirCharles(Glasgow)
Channing, Francis Allston
Clark, Dr. G. B. (Caithness-sh.)
Collery, Bernard
Colville, John
Crombie, John William
Curran, Thomas (Sligo, S.)
Donelan, Captain A.
Doogan, P. C.
Dunn, Sir William
Evans, SamuelT.(Glamorgan)
Farquharson, Dr. Robert
Fenwick, Charles
Gladstone, Rt. Hn. Herbert J.
Goddard, Daniel Ford

Griffith, Ellis J.
Hayne, Rt. Hon. CharlesSearle-
Healy, Timothy M. (N.Louth)
Hemphill, Rt.Hon. Charles H.
Horniman, Frederic John
Kay-Shuttleworth, RtHnSirU
Lambert, George
Leng, Sir John
Lloyd-George, David
Macaleese, Daniel
M'Ghee, Richard
M'Laren, Charles Benjamin
M'Leod, John
Minch, Matthew
Molloy, Bernard Charles
Morley, Rt.Hon. J. (Montrose)
Morris, Samuel
Morton, E. J. C. (Devonport)
Moss, Samuel
Moulton, John Fletcher

Oldroyd, Mark
Richardson, J.(Durham, S. E.)
Rickett, J. Compton
Roberts, John Bryn (Eifion)
Robertson, Edmund (Dundee)
Scott, Chas. Prestwich (Leigh)
Shaw, Charles E. (Stafford)
Shaw, Thomas (Hawick B.)
Steadman, William Charles
Sullivan, Donal (Westmeath)
Trevelyan, Charles Philips
Wedderburn, Sir William
Whittaker, Thomas Palmer
Wilson, Hy. J. (York, W. R.)
Wilson, JohnJ.(Durham, Mid.)
Woods, Samuel

TELLERS FOR THE NOES—
Captain Sinclair and Mr.
Billson.

MR. J. P. SMITH: The Amendment which I have to submit regards the title of the Order. The Bill calls the Order a "Provisional" Order. I do not think "Provisional Order" would be quite the name for Orders issued by the Secretary for Scotland. I submit that "an Order" would be a far better title than "Provisional Order."

Amendment proposed—

"In page 1, line 12, to leave out the words 'a Provisional' and insert 'an.'"—(*Mr. J. P. Smith.*)

Question proposed—

"That the words 'a Provisional' stand part of the clause."

MR. CALDWELL: I think it is unfortunate that we should have the words "Provisional Order" introduced in this Bill. A Provisional Order, as it is understood in this House, is always confirmed by a Confirmation(Bill, and I therefore think it would be better if we could invent some other name in the present case, and thus save conflict with what are at present understood as Provisional Orders.

MR. A. G. MURRAY was understood to say that he thought the use of the word "Provisional" in the present case desirable.

Amendment, by leave, withdrawn.

MR. DALZIEL: I desire to move an Amendment, which I think the right hon. Gentleman will be able to accept, namely—

"In page 1, line 21, to insert after the word 'advertisement' 'in at least two newspapers circulating in the locality interested.'"

As the Bill stands it would be within the provision of the Act for the local authority or any promoter to simply print a Bill and stick it on a hoarding. Now, Sir, the custom has been with regard to Private Bills, and I believe it is the law at the present time, that you should publish them in one of the local papers circulating in the locality. I therefore beg to move the Amendment.

Amendment proposed—

"In page 1, line 21, after the word 'advertisement,' to insert words 'in at least two newspapers circulating in the locality interested.'"—(*Mr. Dalziel.*)

Question proposed—

"That those words be there inserted."

MR. A. G. MURRAY: I cannot accept the Amendment. We do not desire to put into the Act a matter which is purely one for the regulations. I have no doubt the regulations will be such as to preclude such modes of advertisement as the hon. Member has referred to, but I think it would be a mistake to make this one matter of advertisement a subject of the Bill.

MR. DALZIEL: I understand the right hon. Gentleman practically admits the point, and contemplates the introduction of regulations to provide for the insertion of advertisements as I propose. That being so, I will withdraw the Amendment.

Amendment, by leave, withdrawn.

Amendment proposed -

" In Clause 1, page 1, line 24, to leave out 'prescribed,' and insert 'required by Standing Orders.' "—(*Mr. Caldwell.*)

Question proposed—

" That the word ' prescribed ' stand part of the clause."

MR. A. G. MURRAY said he did not think any mischief could arise from the adoption of the wording of the Bill as it stood.

MR. J. P. SMITH : One of the matters complained of very much by the smaller corporations in regard to smaller Bills is the very great complexity of these notices, and it is one of the things which very much needs simplification. I would suggest that a much more effective way of meeting the difficulty than that proposed by the Amendment would be to give promoters the option of either going through a Provisional Order with a much more simple set of notices and advertisements for things that pass under this Act, or of having the more elaborate set of notices and advertisements which are a necessary condition in the case of a Bill before the House of Commons. I would ask the Lord Advocate whether he would not favourably consider an Amendment giving an alternative.

MR. CALDWELL : It is obvious that you could hardly have these notices made available for the Private Bills of a large railway company unless practically they were the notices prescribed by the Standing Order. You cannot make the proposed procedure do for Bills which are eventually to come to this House as Private Bills. Such a proposal would show absolute ignorance as to the procedure to be adopted. The procedure, notices, and advertisements must be such

Mr. A. G. Murray.

as would be required for the Acts of a railway company. Therefore you are going to make all the small undertakings practically undergo the same serving of notices and advertisements as to occupiers and owners as in the case of the larger undertakings. I do not see where the saving can come in.

MR. THOMAS SHAW : I desire to call the attention of the Lord Advocate to the effect of the statement he has made, which practically comes to this, that the preliminary advertisements should be equivalent in all respects to the procedure presented by Standing Orders in regard to Private Bills.

MR. A. G. MURRAY : The hon. Member has misunderstood my observation. The notice I was speaking of is limited to certain land proposed to be taken in the clause.

MR. THOMAS SHAW : May I point out that in Section 2, line 23, when to proceed by Provisional Order is declared to be impossible or inexpedient, then it is declared that the proposed Provisional Order should be subject to the Standing Orders as regards Private Bills. I suggest that " subject to the Standing Orders " should go out, and that it should be subject to such further advertisements as shall in the circumstances be considered necessary. I am entirely of the opinion that it would be most inexpedient in a Provisional Order of a comparatively trivial character to have it encumbered with the very heavy expense of newspaper advertisements and so on, simply because subsequently there might be a transmutation of the Order into a Private Bill. The important thing is to have the procedure cheap and prompt to begin with. We may then prescribe that if that event takes place such further advertisements as are necessary may be issued.

MR. A. G. MURRAY : I agree very much with what my hon. friend has said, but, of course, I dealt with the Amendment actually before me. I shall certainly note the observations which have been made. There are two suggestions—one contained in the Amendment on the Paper, and the other which has been made by my hon. friend. I would not like either of them in the Bill, because " under the Standing Orders " does not necessarily mean under the present Standing Orders ; it means the Standing Orders of the House of Commons, as those Standing Orders may be amended. It is perfectly obvious that if this Bill passes two things may happen —not only that we shall have to make General Orders under this Bill for this private legislation procedure, but also to a certain extent the Standing Orders of this House will have to be amended to meet the altered circumstances of the case, because it will be something they have not had to deal with before—viz., matters beginning under this procedure, and afterwards going on as Private Bills. Matters of great detail are not really appropriate for discussion in a deliberative body such as we are, and it would be very inappropriate to put such points in the Bill, but they will necessarily have to be considered. The present Amendment, however, would not mend matters at all, but rather make them worse. On the other hand, I am certainly prepared to give an undertaking to very carefully consider the suggestions which have been made.

DR. CLARK : I think, in addition to the General Orders which will be issued under Clause 15, we should have before us the modification of the present Standing Orders, so that we should be able to discuss the procedure next year when the Bill comes into operation. What we ought to do now is to determine upon one form or the other, either as shall be prescribed under the Standing Orders, or to adopt the optional form of the hon. Member for Partick, and give the suitors themselves the choice of beginning either under the cheaper form or under the old form. If it is a Bill which, either on account of its magnitude or otherwise, will probably come before the House, why should they not take the old form? It is certainly expensive and cumbersome, but if they so choose I do not see why we should not permit them. The best thing for the Lord Advocate to do would be to adopt the form suggested by my hon. friend, and then on the Report stage, or even later, he might be able to bring forward some other method. Nobody knows yet what kind of Orders will be drawn up by the Secretary for Scotland under Section 15 of the Bill, and it would be better that the petitioners should have the choice as to which procedure they will start under.

MR. CALDWELL : As to the rules which are to be laid before the Houses of Parliament, we know perfectly well that that means nothing. We will have no power whatever in regard to those rules. They will be brought on *en bloc* after Twelve o'clock at night ; there will be no opportunity of going into detail, and therefore this is the only point at which we can have any control over the procedure. The Lord Advocate has pointed out very clearly that there will have to be amendments of the Standing Orders of the House to meet the altered circumstances, and supposing my Amendment were carried, we could just prescribe that the procedure, the notices, and advertisements, should be as required by the Standing Orders, instead of having the Secretary for Scotland proceeding to make Orders under this Bill. The thing will be then prescribed by the Standing Orders of this House. It is very important that this House should retain power over the Standing Orders relating to what may come to be Bills promoted through this House. All matters as regards the preliminary procedure of Bills obviously must come, and ought to come, and ought never to go anywhere else than through this House. Why should we allow any outside authority whatever to determine the notices and advertisements to be served upon owners and occupiers, which this House requires should be done in the case of every private Bill that comes before the House? If you are going to make any modification, make a modification in accordance with the Standing Orders. It is quite competent under the Standing Orders to prescribe that certain notices shall be required in the case of all Bills that are ordered to come into this House as Private Bills, but let it be this House which prescribes the Standing Orders. If the hon. Member for Partick will press his Amendment to a Division I am willing to accept it, as the principle is the same ; but if not, I will go to a Division on mine.

MR. J. P. SMITH : I am very much obliged to the Lord Advocate for his promise to consider these matters, but I think we ought to ask him to put it more formally. This matter of notices is so important to those concerned in bringing forward Bills, that I think we are entitled to ask for some definite decision. If the Lord Advocate does not wish to decide at once, perhaps at the Report stage he will be able to give some decision. I think that would be sufficient, but certainly those who are bringing in Bills ought not to be hampered by a double set of advertisements and regulations. I submit that the suggestion I have made is the simplest manner of doing the thing. It may be taken for granted that the preliminaries enforced under this Bill will be more onerous than the House of Commons imposes upon this point.

MR. A. G. MURRAY: I am rather inclined to accept the suggestion of my hon. friend, but I do not wish to tie my hands at the present moment. I am not at all desirous of making the regulations, but I think the alternative of the hon. Member will find a proper place in the rules and regulations. If the hon. Member is satisfied with that, I am perfectly willing to give him an undertaking that we will consider by the Report stage whether we cannot at once make up our minds upon the matter and accept it.

MR. ALEXANDER CROSS (Glasgow, Camlachie): It appears to me that we are now debating an attempt to simplify this procedure, the success of which, as has been confessed in the Committee, largely depends upon details and not so much upon the general principle. If that be so, however much confidence I may have in the Scotch Office, I do not feel inclined to hand over to it the power which is here proposed. The rules will be brought up after Twelve o'clock, and necessarily will be subject to the most cursory examination. If we are to understand from the Lord Advocate that these rules are to come up for discussion on Report, that will be more satisfactory. It appears to me that it is essential in considering these matters that they should be simple and easily understood, even by those who are not lawyers.

MR. A. G. MURRAY: I do not quite understand what my hon. friend means. I have already said that I am perfectly willing to consider by the Report stage the Amendment which the hon. Member for Partick has suggested. As to the remarks about lawyers and the Scotch Office, neither of the two Chairmen of Committees as far as I know is a lawyer, nor is the Secretary for Scotland a lawyer, so where the lawyers come in I absolutely fail to see.

DR. CLARK: The hon. Member is confusing two things — the general regulations and the Standing Orders. At present it is determined by Standing Order, and always should be determined by Standing Order, what should be announced by public advertisement. The notices served upon owners, lessees, and occupiers are now determined by the Standing Order, and why should not that continue? Lastly, there is the question of deposit. Why should it change? There is no need to change it; it should be as prescribed by Standing Orders. The only point is that these regulations which are to be made under Section 15 will practically be made by the Scotch Office. We know that the Chairmen have other duties to attend to; they will be called in now and again, and the thing will be put, cut and dried, before them. But the whole work will be done in the Scotch Office—probably they will call in the Lord Advocate. All that my hon. friend the Member for Mid Lanark is contending for is that the conditions as to the important matters of advertising and the serving of notices upon the people affected, and as to deposits, shall be determined by Standing Order and not by anything that can be varied now and again as by regulation. These are matters for the Standing Orders of the House, and have been for centuries. The proposal in this clause is to take away from Parliament the right of discussing these alterations, because if you modify the Standing Orders they have to come before us, but if you have the two Chairmen and the Secretary for Scotland amending the Standing Orders in the form of regulations we will not be able to discuss or amend their proposals, because they will come up after Twelve o'clock, and whatever Government is in power they will keep sufficient Members here to carry them through. I think my hon. friend is perfectly right in his Amendment.

MR. CALDWELL: We are not speaking of the procedure prescribed by the General Orders. The point we are referring to is that, in the event of the Chairmen deciding that a proposal should proceed by Private Bill instead of under the procedure here proposed, the notices and advertisements shall be available as notices under the Private Bill procedure of this House. We decline to allow any outside authority to interfere and determine what the notices, advertisements and deposits shall be, in regard to what has to proceed through this House as a Private Bill. We must have those points determined by Standing Order, and not left at the disposal of an outside authority so far) as this House is concerned.

Question put.

The Committee divided : Ayes, 130 ; Noes, 55. (Division List No. 185.)

AYES.

Allhusen, Augustus Henry E.
Archdale, Edward Mervyn
Asher, Alexander
Ashmead-Bartlett, Sir Ellis
Atkinson, Rt. Hon. John
Bagot, Capt. J. FitzRoy
Balfour, Rt. Hn. G.W. (Leeds)
Barnes, Frederic Gorell
Bartley, George C. T.
Barton, Dunbar Plunket
Bathurst, Hon. Allen B.
Begg, Ferdinand Faithfull
Bhownaggree, Sir M. M.
Blakiston-Houston, John
Blundell, Colonel Henry
Bond, Edward
Bullard, Sir Harry
Chaloner, Captain R. G. W.
Chamberlain, J. A (Wore'r)
Chaplin, Rt. Hon. Henry
Charrington, Spencer
Cochrane, Hon. T. H. A. E.
Coghill, Douglas Harry
Cohen, Benjamin Louis
Collings, Rt. Hon. Jesse
Colston, Chas. E. H. Athole
Cook, Fred. Lucas (Lambeth)
Cornwallis, Fiennes Stanley W.
Cripps, Charles Alfred
Crombie, John William
Cubitt, Hon. Henry
Curzon, Viscount
Dalrymple, Sir Charles
Davies, Sir H. D. (Chatham)
Denny, Colonel
Douglas, Rt. Hon. A. Akers-
Doxford, William Theodore
Duncombe, Hon. Hubert V.
Dyke, Rt. Hon. Sir W. Hart
Elliot, Hon. A. Ralph Douglas
Fellowes, Hon Ailwyn Edw.
Field, Admiral (Eastbourne)
Finlay, Sir Robert Bannatyne
Fisher, William Hayes
Flower, Ernest

Foster, Colonel (Lancaster)
Foster, Harry S. (Suffolk)
Giles, Charles Tyrrell
Gilliat, John Saunders
Goldsworthy, Major-General
Gordon, Hon. John Edward
Gorst, Rt. Hon. Sir John Eldon
Goschen, George J. (Sussex)
Goulding, Edward Alfred
Gray, Ernest (West Ham)
Hamilton, Rt. Hn. Lord George
Hatch, Ernest Frederick Geo.
Hedderwick, Thos. Charles H.
Henderson, Alexander
Hermon-Hodge, R. Trotter
Hill, Arthur (Down, West)
Howell, William Tudor
Hutton, John (Yorks N.R.)
Jebb, Richard Claverhouse
Johnston, William (Belfast)
Kennaway, Rt. Hn. Sir John H.
Kenyon-Slaney, Col. William
Kinloch, Sir John Geo. Smyth
Knowles, Lees
Lawrence, Sir E. Durning-(Corn
Leigh-Bennett, Henry Currie
Long, Rt. Hn. Walter (Liverp'l)
Lopes, Henry Yarde Buller
Lowles, John
Loyd, Archie Kirkman
Macdona, John Cumming
M'Arthur, Charles (Liverpool)
M'Calmont, Col. J. (Antrim, E.)
M'Killop, James
Middlemore, J. Throgmorton
Milton, Viscount
Monk, Charles James
More, Robt. J. (Shropshire)
Morton, A. H. A. (Deptford)
Mount, William George
Murray, Rt. Hn. A. G. (Bute)
Newdigate, Francis Alexander
Nicholson, William Graham
Nicol Donald Ninian
O'Neill, Hon. Robert Torrens

Pease, Herbert P. (Darlington
Penn, John
Pierpoint, Robert
Pilkington, R. (Lancs. Newton)
Powell, Sir Francis Sharp
Pryce-Jones, Lt.-Col. Edward
Purvis, Robert
Pym, C. Guy
Renshaw, Charles Bine
Robertson, Herbert (Hackney)
Russell, T. W. (Tyrone)
Ryder, John Herbert Dudley
Savory, Sir Joseph
Sharpe, William Edward T.
Sidebotham, J. W. Cheshire)
Sidebottom, Wm. (Derbysh.)
Skewes-Cox, Thomas
Smith, James Parker (Lanark)
Stanley, Lord (Lancs.)
Stewart, Sir M. J. M'Taggart
Stock, James Henry
Stone, Sir Benjamin
Strutt, Hon. Chas Hedley
Thorburn, Walter
Thornton, Percy M.
Tomlinson, Wm. Edw. Murray
Tritton, Charles Ernest
Ure, Alexander
Valentia, Viscount
Wallace, Robert (Perth)
Wanklyn, James Leslie
Warde, Lieut.-Col. C. E. (Kent)
Webster, R. G. (St. Pancras)
Williams, Colonel R. (Dorset)
Williams, J. Powell- (Birm.)
Wolff, Gustav Wilhelm
Wylie, Alexander
Wyndham-Quin, Major W. H.
Wyvill, Marmaduke D'Arcy
Young, Commander (Berks, E.)

TELLERS FOR THE AYES—
Sir William Walrond and
Mr. Anstruther.

NOES.

Austin, Sir John (Yorkshire)
Billson, Alfred
Birrell, Augustine
Brunner, Sir John Tomlinson
Burns, John
Cameron, Sir Charles (Glasgow)
Clark, Dr. G. B. (Caithness-sh)
Cross, Alexander (Glasgow)
Curran, Thomas (Sligo, S.)
Dalziel, James Henry
Donelan, Captain A.
Doogan, P. C.
Dunn, Sir William

Evans, Samuel T. (Glamorgan)
Farquharson, Dr. Robert
Fenwick, Charles
Goddard, Daniel Ford
Griffith, Ellis J.
Hazell, Walter
Hemphill, Rt. Hon. Charles H.
Hogan, James Francis
Horniman, Frederick John
Kay-Shuttleworth Rt Hn Sir U.
Lawson, Sir Wilfrid (Cmb'land)
Leng, Sir John
Lloyd-George, David

Macaleese, Daniel
M'Ghee, Richard
M'Laren, Charles Benjamin
M'Leod, John
Minch, Matthew
Morley, Rt. Hn. John (Montrose
Morris Samuel
Morton, E. J. C. (Devonport)
Moss, Samuel
Oldroyd, Mark
O'Malley, William
Pirie, Duncan V.
Price, Robert John

Provand,Andrew Dryburgh	Shaw, Thomas (Hawick, B.)	Whittaker, Thomas Palmer
Rickett, J. Compton	Steadman, William Charles	Wilson, H. J. (York, W. R.)
Roberts, John Bryn (Eifion)	Sullivan, Donal (Westmeath)	Wilson, John (Govan)
Robertson, Edmund (Dundee)	Tennant, Harold John	Yoxall, James Henry
Samuel, J. (Stockton-on-Tees)	Trevelyan, Charles Philips	TELLERS FOR THE NOES—Mr.
Scott, Chas. Prestwich (Leigh)	Wedderburn, Sir William	Caldwell and Mr. Colville.

DR. CLARK : My object in moving to leave out Clause 1 has reference not only to the character of the clause, but also because I have put down a new clause, which I will move when it is reached, and which will carry out all the objects the Government state they desire, and all the objects that the people of Scotland had in view when they asked for the introduction of legislation of this kind. Under the new clause I propose that "where under the present practice any opposed Private Bill is referred to a Committee in either House of Parliament, every such Bill shall, from and after the passing of this Act, be referred to the Commissioners appointed under this Act." The first sub-section is practically similar to the Amendment proposed by the hon. Member for Dundee, that where there is no opposition, or if the opposition has been withdrawn, the Bill shall be dealt with as an unopposed Bill, according to the present practice. Then the next sub-section provides that the Report by the Commissioners shall be laid before either House of Parliament in which the Bill originated, and the procedure in the remaining stages shall follow the present practice. Under this plan there would be local inquiries by Commissioners, and their Report would be sufficient for the Committee stage in both Houses of Parliament. I cannot agree to Clause 1 as it stands at present, because it introduces a number of novelties which have never been asked for, and which are contrary to the practice of Parliament.

Amendment proposed—

"In page 1, to leave out Clause 1."— (*Dr. Clark.*)

Question proposed—

"That Clause 1, as amended, stand part of the Bill."

*SIR CHARLES CAMERON : I have heard the explanation of the Lord Advocate with reference to this clause and Clause 16, and I must confess that I cannot make head or tail of it. Under this clause a man wishing to get a Provisional Order under the Board of Trade—say for electric lighting—must present a petition to the Secretary for Scotland. He is forbidden to do anything else. Therefore he cannot apply to the Board of Trade, and, although by the subsequent clause all the powers of the Board of Trade are safeguarded, the right of initiating proceedings on the part of the applicant is by this clause taken away.

MR. SOUTTAR : I have pleasure in supporting my hon. friend in his Amendment. As the clause stands it is most injurious. It deprives Scotchmen of their ancient right to petition Parliament for a Private Bill, and that is a very great deprivation indeed. In the second place, it deprives Scotch Members of their right to legislate in regard to the affairs of their own country. It is true that Committees on Scotch Bills are not composed exclusively of Scotch Members, but we have always the right to call the action of these Committees in question, and that right will be lost. For my part, I fail to see, if the Bill becomes law, of what use it would be for Scotch Members to come to the House of Commons. It will not be because of Public Bills, because these are few and far between. It is true that it is proposed that the panel should include two Members of Parliament, and some of my friends seem to think that that is going to balance the evil effect of this clause. But I do not think the inclusion of two Members in the panel will in any sense take the place of Scotch supervision of Scotch Private Bill legislation. I think the clause, by putting the power into the hands of the Secretary for Scotland, really introduces Castle government into Scotland, and I cannot understand why my hon. friends, whom I generally esteem, can so readily accept such a provision. We have been for a long time opposed to Castle government in Ireland, and why should we approve of its introduction into Scotland? My hon. and right hon. friends think, perhaps, that at a later stage they will be able to so improve the Bill as to make it palatable; but the Bill as it stands is a bad Bill, and I support with all my heart the Amendment of my hon. friend the Member for Caithness.

MR. CALDWELL: This is a Bill that starts upon the principle of Home Rule. It is the first decisive attempt of the Government to devolve legislative powers on a body outside Parliament altogether. In so far as the Bill proceeds upon national lines, in so far as it separates Scotch business from Imperial business, and proceeds on the footing that Scotch business ought to be done in Scotland, in so far as it gives legislative power to a body in Scotland whose measures will have the effect of an Act of Parliament without coming to this House, I do not see how any Home Ruler could desire a more extensive programme than that. This clause acknowledges that purely Scotch business should not be dealt with by the Imperial Parliament. It is true that the business is confined to Private Bill legislation, but I would remind hon. Members that Private Bill legislation is co-extensive with Public Bill legislation. There was, for instance, the Glasgow Police Act, which modified in essential cases the general criminal law of Scotland so far as it applied to Glasgow. Then there are questions of taxation, and we might, if we had a Scotch Secretary of our own way of thinking, get the taxation of land values passed in Private Bill legislation. Practically, there is nothing we can get under the general public law which we cannot get under this Bill. It is very hard on us therefore to ask us to refuse a Home Rule measure of this kind, and

the lever which the Bill will give us. There are certain details of the Bill to which, of course, we object, but the Bill as a whole will give us a splendid lever. I remember, at the time when the Government introduced differential death duties on estates above £10,000, which were to pay 1 per cent. extra, it was said they were introducing the principle of graduation, which another Government would extend. The result was, that another Government did extend the principle of graduation. Again, when free education was introduced into Scotland, it was opposed on the ground that if it was introduced into Scotland it would be extended into England; and it was so extended to England. Depend upon it, every principle which we can get insinuated into a Bill for Scotland will be made a lever for extending it not only in Scotland, but in other parts of the United Kingdom. But the Bill has been brought forward under false pretences, so far as the local authorities are concerned, for its supporters insist that it will save expense to local authorities in promoting Private Bills. Nothing could be further from the case. The procedure will be much more expensive than under the present Provisional Order procedure. If you eliminate from this Bill the local authorities who ought to proceed under the present Provisional Order system, and if you also eliminate the case of railways in Scotland, you will have hardly anything left at all—three or four Bills of a general character, or the Bills of some private individuals who want to get certain monopolies. But if they want monopolies let them come here and have their case sifted, and let them pay for these monopolies. One great object we have in view in regard to police and sanitary matters is that we should have uniform legislation throughout the country. We have a Police and Sanitary Committee which deals with the whole of the United Kingdom. It is obvious that that Committee has far more experience and is better fitted to deal with such cases than three or four persons deciding on an isolated case. You are therefore throwing away the opportunity, if you pass this Bill in its present shape, of securing uniformity in police and sanitary legislation. The only reason why the Bill has been supported in Scotland is, that it has got a large support from the advocates in Parliament House in Edinburgh, who are, almost to a man, opposed to Home Rule in everything else.

*THE CHAIRMAN: The hon. Member is making a Second Reading speech. The question is, whether Clause 1 shall stand part of the Bill.

MR. CALDWELL: This measure is merely being promoted by those who have practically an influential interest in having a devolution of this kind. It is not a measure which is in the interest of the local authorities, for the present Private Bill and Provisional Order system is better and cheaper than that which the Bill provides.

Question put.

The Committee divided: Ayes, 175; Noes, 62. (Division List No. 186.)

AYES.

Allhusen, A. Henry Eden
Archdale, Edward Mervyn
Arnold, Alfred
Asher, Alexander
Ashmead-Bartlett, Sir Ellis
Atkinson, Rt. Hon. John
Austin, Sir John (Yorkshire)
Bagot, Capt. J. Fitzroy
Bailey, James (Walworth)
Baird, John George A.
Balfour, Rt.Hn.A.J.(Manch'r)
Balfour, Rt. Hn. G.W.(Leeds)
Banbury, Frederick George
Barnes, Frederic Gorell
Bartley, George C. T.
Barton, Dunbar Plunket
Bathurst, Hon. Allen B.
Beach, RtHnSirM. H. (Bristol)
Begg, Ferdinand Faithfull
Bhownaggree, Sir M. M.
Blakiston-Houston, John
Bond, Edward
Bullard, Sir Harry
Burt, Thomas
Butcher, John George
Campbell-Bannerman, Sir H.
Cavendish, VCW(Derbyshire)
Cecil, Evelyn (Hertford, East)
Chaloner, Captain R. G.W.
Chamberlain, J. A. (Worc'r)
Chaplin, Rt. Hon. Henry
Charrington, Spencer
Cochrane, Hon. Thos. H. A.E.
Coghill, Douglas Harry
Cohen, Benjamin Louis
Collings, Rt. Hon. Jesse
Colston, Chas. Edw. H. A.
Cook, Fred. Lucas (Lambeth)
Cornwallis, Fiennes S. W.
Cox, Irwin Edward B.
Cripps, Charles Alfred
Crombie, John William
Cross, Alexander (Glasgow)
Cubitt, Hon. Henry
Curzon, Viscount
Dalkeith, Earl of
Dalrymple, Sir Charles
Davies, Sir H. D. (Chatham)
Denny, Colonel
Dorington, Sir John Edward
Douglas, Rt. Hon. A. Akers-
Doxford, William Theodore
Duncombe, Hon. Hubert V.
Dyke, Rt. Hn. Sir William Hart
Elliot, Hon. A. Ralph Douglas
Fellowes, Hon. Ailwyn Edw.
Furguson,R. C. Munro (Leith)
Field, Admiral (Eastbourne)
Finlay, Sir Robert Bannatyne
Fisher, William Hayes

Flower, Ernest
Folkestone, Viscount
Foster, Harry S. (Suffolk)
Foster, Sir Walter (Derby Co.)
Gedge, Sydney
Gibbons, J. Lloyd
Giles, Charles Tyrrell
Gilliat, John Saunders
Gladstone, Rt. Hn. Herbert J.
Goldsworthy, Major-General
Gordon, Hon. John Edward
Gorst,Rt.Hon. Sir John Eldon
Goulding, Edward Alfred
Grey, Ernest (West Ham)
Gretton, John
Hamilton, Rt. Hon. Lord Geo.
Hatch, Ernest F. George
Hedderwick, Thomas C. H.
Helder, Augustus
Hemphill, Rt. Hon. C. H.
Henderson, Alexander
Howell, William Tudor
Hutton, John (Yorks, N.R.)
Jebb, Richard Claverhouse
Johnson, William (Belfast)
Kay-Shuttleworth,RtHnSir U
Kemp, George
Kennaway, Rt. Hn. Sir J. H.
Kenyon-Slaney, Col. William
Kinloch, Sir J. George Smythe
Knowles, Lees
Lawrence,SirE.Durning-(Corn
Lawson, John Grant (Yorks.)
Leese, Sir J. F. (Accrington)
Leigh-Bennett, Henry Currie
Llewellyn, E. H. (Somerset)
Lockwood, Lt.-Col. A. R.
Loder, Gerald Walter Erskine
Long, Rt. Hn. W. (Liverpool)
Lopes, Henry Yarde Buller
Lowles, John
Loyd, Archie Kirkman
Lyell, Sir Leonard
Macdona, John Cumming
M'Arthur, Charles (Liverpool)
M'Calmont,Col. J.(Antrim, E.
M'Killop, James
Mellor, Rt.Hn. J. W. (Yorks.)
Middlemore, J. Throgmorton
Milton, Viscount
Monk, Charles James
More,Robt.Jasper.Shropshire)
Morgan, Hn.Fred.(Monm'ths.)
Morley, Charles (Breconshire)
Morton, A. H. A. (Deptford)
Mount, William George
Muntz, Philip A.
Murray, Rt. Hn. A. G. (Bute)
Murray, Charles J. (Coventry)
Newdigate, FrancisAlexander

Nicholson, William Graham
Nicol, Donald Ninian
O'Neill, Hon. Robert Torrens
Orr-Ewing, Charles Lindsay
Pease, Herb. Pike(Darlington)
Penn, John
Pilkington,R. (Lancs Newton)
Pollock, Harry Frederick
Powell, Sir Francis Sharp
Pryce-Jones, Lt.-Col. Edward
Purvis, Robert
Pym, C. Guy
Rasch, Major Frederic Carne
Renshaw, Charles Bine
Ritchie, Rt. Hon. C. Thomson
Roberts, John Bryn (Eifion)
Robertson, Herbert(Hackney)
Round James
Russell,Gen.F.S.(Cheltenham
Russell, T. W. (Tyrone)
Ryder, John Herbert Dudley
Savory, Sir Joseph
Sharpe, William Edward T.
Shaw, Thomas (Hawick B.)
Sidebotham, J. W. (Cheshire)
Sidebottom, Wm. (Derbysh.)
Skewes-Cox, Thomas
Smith,JamesParker(Lanarks)
Stanley, Lord (Lancs.)
Stewart,SirMarkJ.M'Taggart
Stock, James Henry
Stone, Sir Benjamin
Strauss, Arthur
Strutt, Hon. Charles Hedley
Tennant, Harold John
Thorburn, Walter
Thornton, Percy M.
Tomlinson, Wm. Edw.Murray
Tritton, Charles Ernest
Ure, Alexander
Valentia, Viscount
Vincent, Col. Sir C. E. Howard
Wallace, Robert (Perth)
Wanklyn, James Leslie
Warde,Lieut.-Col.C.E. (Kent)
Wentworth, Bruce C. Vernon-
Whitmore. Charles Algernon
Williams, Colonel R. (Dorset)
Williams, Jos. Powell- (Birm.
Wodehouse,Rt.Hn.E.R.(Bath)
Wolff, Gustav Wilhelm
Wylie, Alexander
Wyndham-Quin, Maj. W. H.
Wyvill, Marmaduke D'Arcy
Young, Commander(Berks,E.)

TELLERS FOR THE AYES—
Sir William Walrond and
Mr. Anstruther.

NOES.

Barlow, John Emmott
Billson, Alfred
Birrell, Augustine
Brunner, Sir John Tomlinson
Burns, John
Cameron, Sir Charles (Glasgow)
Cameron, Robert (Durham)
Channing, Francis Allston
Clough, Walter Owen
Collery, Bernard
Colvil'e, John
Cummins, Andrew
Crilly, Daniel
Curran, Thomas (Sligo, S.)
Davitt, Michael
Dillon, John
Donelan, Captain A.
Doogan, P. C
Dunn, Sir William
Evans, S. T. (Glamorgan)
Farquharson, Dr. Robert
Fenwick, Charles

Ffrench, Peter
Goddard, Daniel Ford
Griffith, Ellis J.
Hayne, Rt. Hon. Chas. Seale-
Horniman, Frederick John
Joicey, Sir James
Lambert, George
Lawson, Sir Wilfrid (Cumb'land
Leng, Sir John
Lloyd-George, David
Logan, John William
Lough, Thomas
MacAleese, Daniel
M'Ghee, Richard
M'Laren, Charles Benjamin
M'Leod, John
Mendl, Sigismund Ferdinand
Morgan, J. L. (Carmarthen)
Morley, Rt. Hn. J. (Montrose.)
Morton, Edw. J. C. (Dvnpt.)
Moss, Samuel
Oldroyd, Mark

Pirie, Duncan V.
Price, Robert John
Provand, Andrew Dryburgh
Richards, Henry Charles
Rickett, J. Compton
Robertson, Edmund (Dundee)
Samuel, J. (Stockton on Tees)
Scott, C. Prestwich (Leigh)
Shaw, Charles Edw. (Stafford)
Sinclair, Capt. J. (Forfarshire)
Souttar, Robinson
Steadman, William Charles
Sullivan, Donal (Westmeath)
Trevelyan, Charles Philips
Whittaker, Thomas Palmer
Wilson, John (Durham, Mid.)
Wilson, John (Govan)
Yoxall, James Henry

TELLERS FOR THE NOES—
Dr. Clark and Mr. Caldwell.

Clause 2 :—

DR. CLARK : The Amendment which stands in my name on the Paper is taken from the last Bill introduced by the Government in 1892. It proposes that the determination of these matters should be not by the two Chairmen of the Committees, but by a standing Joint Committee of both Houses, composed of two peers and two commoners and the two Chairmen. The two peers and two commoners should be appointed every session, and every Provisional Order applied for should be sent to this Commission to be determined, and they should consider the procedure. In the present edition of the Bill this joint Committee is entirely dropped, and this work is relegated to the two Chairmen of the Committees. So far as the Chairman of Committees of this House is concerned, in my opinion he has quite enough to do. At the present time he is engaged all the morning on Private Bill work and all the evening in this House, and cannot be expected to give a great deal of time to this work. I much prefer the form proposed by the right hon. Gentleman in 1892, which gives us a body who will meet and discuss these matters.

Amendment proposed—

"In page 2, line 2, after the word 'Commons,' to insert the words 'and two Members of each House of Parliament appointed at the beginning of each session in manner provided by Standing Orders shall be a Standing Joint Committee of the two Houses of Parliament.'" —(Dr. Clark.)

Question proposed—

"That those words be there inserted."

MR. A. G. MURRAY : The hon. Member forgets that the scheme of the Bill of 1892 is radically different to the scheme of this Bill. The scheme of the Bill of 1892 was a scheme for Private Bills, and there was no radical change at all in the initial stages of those Bills. The Joint Standing Committee was then created in order to deal with the Bills in the House, and see whether, when they had got to the Committee stage, they should go down for local inquiry. The present Bill is not a Private Bill scheme at all, but a Provisional Order scheme, and it was thought right to reserve the control of this House over these matters. It is desirable that there should be somebody to determine what is fitted to be proceeded with as a Private Bill and what is fitted to be dealt with as a Provisional Order, and it was felt that the two Chairmen would be a proper tribunal for that purpose. There would be a great disadvantage in adding two Peers and two Members of this House to the tribunal, because a great deal would be done when Parliament is not sitting, and they would not be here. The two Chairmen, on the other hand, are obliged to be here in the Autumn to deal with Private Bill matters, and it is felt that they could do this work at the same time. I therefore do not propose to accept this Amendment.

MR. CALDWELL : The difference between this Bill and the Bill of 1892 is very small. True, that Bill was to deal with Private Bills, this is to deal with Provisional Orders ; but, call it whatever you like, it is the same thing, and the Provisional Order has the full effect of an Act of Parliament. The whole question which

2 L

the Joint Committee of 1892 had to determine was whether the Bill was one that should be relegated to local inquiry or not, and that is the scheme of the present Bill. The small changes in the Bill are immaterial. What is the effect of this tribunal? When a Conservative Government is in power the Chairman of Committees, the Secretary for Scotland, and the Chairman of the Committees of the House of Lords are Conservative, and they can say whether the Bill shall come to this House or not. They hold the strings, and the Secretary for Scotland can say " Refer it to me," and if he in his discretion sends it away we have no control over it whatever. There is a little difference if a Liberal Government is in power, because then, though the Chairman of Committee in this House and the Secretary for Scotland are Liberals, the Chairman of Committees in the House of Lords is a Conservative, and he has power to prevent such a thing being done. It is a strong order to deny the right of a Private Bill to come to this House and to relegate it to a Scotch tribunal. I think that matter ought to be determined by an impartial Committee.

MR. RICHARDS (Finsbury, E.): I thoroughly sympathise with my hon. friend the Member for Mid Lanark in the views he has put before the House. To my mind nothing is more unsatisfactory than the procedure with regard to Provisional Orders, as it amounts to nothing less than an attempt by permanent officials to smuggle through the House——

*THE CHAIRMAN: Order, order! I do not think that is quite the question that is now before the House.

MR. RICHARDS: Of course, if you rule that, Sir, I cannot go into it. I can only say I intend to support the hon. Member opposite, because in my opinion if the Bill is carried as it stands it will be clearly an injustice to Scotland, and so long as the Scotch people desire to take the opinions of Committees of this House it is not right of this or any other Government to attempt to deprive them of that constitutional right.

DR. CLARK: I am somewhat surprised that my Amendment is not accepted. I have taken that clause out of the Bill of 1892 which it was proposed to bring in after three years' consideration. The tribunal was proposed because it did

Mr. Caldwell.

not matter whether the initial stages of a Bill where taken at Edinburgh or Westminster, but it was thought proper that they should be determined by a Joint Standing Committee of this character, and that the matter should be considered by some independent Members. I believe that if the Government only express their willingness to appoint a Joint Committee of the two Houses they will get through this Bill to-night.

SIR H. CAMPBELL-BANNERMAN: In the course of this evening's discussion I said with regard to the Instruction that was moved before we got into Committee that I doubted whether there was full justification for the hope entertained by the Lord Advocate that this Bill would be found applicable to other parts of the United Kingdom besides Scotland. This was one of the points which I had in my mind when I said that, because here we are putting a great work and an immense responsibility upon the Chairmen of the two Houses. I may be told that the existing Chairmen have come before the Committee and said that they were willing and able to do this work, and I have no doubt that they would patriotically perform these duties if they were imposed upon them. But let us consider what the Chairman of this House has to do. He is the most laborious member of the House during the session, not excepting the Speaker himself, and during the autumn he is engaged to a very considerable extent in the preparatory steps of Private Bill business. Now we are going to ask him, together with the Chairman of the other House, to decide the very delicate question as to which of these proposals shall be dealt with as Private Bills and which shall be dealt with by way of Provisional Order. They are in effect to be the tribunal to deal with matters which will involve the employment of London agents, which rather disposes of some of the arguments, especially that rather fallacious argument of taking as much money for Scotland as you possibly can. I think if we consider the amount of work that this will impose upon the Chairmen, if the Bill is extended to the three kingdoms, we shall see very little prospect of this particular machinery being applied. I forget exactly the figures quoted, but there is a very small proportion of Scotch business before the House, and most of the Scotch Bills are unimportant—the most important are the railway Bills, which occupy a great deal of time. There are 145 Private Bills for England and 25 for Scotland, and supposing the same machinery is applied to the 145 as to the 25, we can form some opinion approximately of how heavy and difficult the duties which are laid upon the Chairman would be. After all, I think it is rather too much if we contemplate extending the provisions of this Bill to other parts of the kingdom. My hon. friend proposes to constitute a Joint Committee, and though his proposal may not be complete, it is one which would give a great relief to the Chairmen, and a tribunal which I think would be most satisfactory—it would introduce into that stage of the proceedings that control of Parliament which we desire to see so far as possible from first to last. The point which particularly struck me, and drew from me a few words earlier in the evening, was the alteration of the status of the two Chairmen. It is a very serious step to take, and I think they ought not to have this work imposed upon them if it can be avoided.

MR. CRIPPS: I believe if this proposal could be carried out it would be a distinct improvement in the Bill. But first of all, are we to understand that, at any time of the year when an application is made to proceed under the new Bill, the two Chairmen are then to be got together in order to investigate the importance of the measure under Clause 2? I do not think that is at all a practical proposal. I do not think the decision of the Chairmen in itself would be a sufficient guarantee that the rights of this House are preserved, because it is notorious that in many points in Private Bill legislation there is a great difference of opinion between the Chairman and the House. But if you have two Members from each House elected from time to time, you would get a true representation of the opinions of this House. As regards the present suggestion of only the two Chairmen, I certainly think the effect of this Bill would be to greatly increase the departmental power as against this House, and upon that point I am anxious to protect the power of this House. I cannot help coming to the conclusion that the increase which will be made will be really a departmental increase of power in the office of the Secretary for Scotland, and that is a thing we ought to guard

against. We ought to be at one upon this point, that we should preserve the legislative faculties of this House as far as possible.

MR. A. G. MURRAY: I should be glad if hon. Members who are so hostile to this Bill would do me the honour to read its clauses, as it is impossible to listen to the speeches made by hon. Members without discovering that they have not done so. If they look at the clause they will see that the Secretary for Scotland has nothing to do with it, and therefore it is ridiculous to say that the whole thing will fall into the hands of the Scotch Secretary. This is a Bill to the principle of which the House has agreed. The principle is that it is a Provisional Order Bill, and if hon. Members do not wish to wreck it they must face the fact that this is a Provisional Order Bill, and not a Private Bill Procedure Bill. I do not think that we can gain anything at all by the election of these hon. Gentlemen. In the ordinary course that would not add much to the control of the House, and there would be the other disadvantage that you would not be able to get hold of them after the rising of the House. Therefore you would not be able to proceed with any of these measures. You can get the two Chairmen together, and you have the benefit of getting their determinations during the months of October, November, and December upon these questions. As to whether they have time to do the work, both of them have said before a Select Committee that they have the time, and therefore the suggestion of adding two Members of this House, in my opinion, is an empty suggestion. Under the circumstances, I do not see my way to accept the Amendment.

MR. EDMUND ROBERTSON: I do not think the Lord Advocate has addressed himself to the most formidable argument against him. The Leader of the Opposition takes his stand on the immediate intention of the Government to extend the scheme and machinery of this Bill to the whole of the United Kingdom. Even if the Chairmen are willing and able to perform these duties with regard to Scotch Bills, they must recognise that if all the Private Bills that come before this House are to be considered by them they would not be able to deal with them. I have now the figures for the last seven years upon this question, and beginning with 1887 I find that the average annual number of English measures is 158, Irish 12, and Scotch 27. Is it reasonable to suppose that the Chairmen of both Houses will be able to undertake these duties with regard to them all ?

MR. DALZIEL : This is a point upon which I should like to ask the Lord Advocate to keep an open mind until the Report stage. Not one hon. Member who has spoken has opposed the Amendment; all have taken the same tone. This proposal is one which was introduced in the Bill of 1892 by the Leader of the House, and in face of the fact that there is no evidence of any need for change. I think the proposal which is put forward is a good one which ought to be accepted. Everybody has spoken in favour of the Amendment, and I put it to the Lord Advocate that if he wants the Bill to go through it can be only be got through by a give-and-take policy.

MR. COCHRANE (Ayrshire, N.) : The reason that I have not spoken up to now is that I considered that if this Bill passes this Amendment is not likely to give it the authority of law. The hon. Member says these words appeared in the Bill of 1892. But everybody knows that the Bill of 1892 was only intended to deal with the procedure on Private Bills, which it was intended to facilitate. If these Provisional Orders are to be brought up at any time of the year, it will throw the onus of considerable labour upon the Chairmen. Would it be more difficult to get two Members of the House of Lords and the House of Commons to assist them ? I myself do not see how we can expect the two Chairmen to do all this work themselves.

SIR H. CAMPBELL-BANNERMAN : I should like to supplement my statement by referring to the evidence of the Chairmen of Committees before the Select Committee. It is true they said that they could perform the duties which the Bill imposes upon them, but they stated that so long as their work was limited to Scotch or Irish Bills it could be done satisfactorily, whereas if it was to be extended to all Bills, including Welsh and English Bills, their work would be of a very difficult character. I hope that due weight will be given by the Government to that opinion.

MR. A. G. MURRAY : I am perfectly well aware of the evidence given before

Mr. Edmund Robertson.

the Select Committee, but sufficient unto the day is the evil thereof ; and when we find that the burden under this Bill presses too heavily upon the Chairmen, it will be time enough to consider this question. We should not do any good by considering it now.

MR. SOUTTAR : I wish to say, with regard to the answer given by the Lord Advocate, that it would be impossible to get two Members of the House of Commons and of the House of Lords to join this tribunal, that I do not think there is much in it—I think it would be quite easy, but there need not be any difficulty as to that. The salient point before the Committee in my opinion is this : that from the Chairmen's point of view this is a desirable Amendment. I think that for that reason the Chairmen themselves would be exceedingly glad that this Amendment should be accepted by the Government, and for my part I cannot see the slightest shadow of reason why they should refuse to accept it.

MR. J. P. SMITH : I cannot see why there is such a desperate hurry in getting these Provisional Orders through. I think it is of great importance that there should be more individuals concerned in the decision between the two Chairmen. You want to have more continuity in your position, and that continuity you will get if you have a small committee such as is suggested. It seems to be thought that a Chairman can be got hold of at any time during the summer recess or autumn. My own opinion has been that he was free during the recess to go wherever he pleased, and do whatever he pleased. I think therefore the decision of the Chairmen will necessarily have to be waited for during those months, but I do not see how any serious harm can come to the promoters.

MR. DILLON (Mayo, E.) : The arguments used in favour of this Amendment seem to be absolutely unanswerable. I can remember many occasions when a Chairman, even backed up by the opinion of the Committee, has been overruled by a large majority in the House itself. It is therefore a strong thing to urge that the House should be deprived of the power of review in the case of Private Bills, which may involve public issues of the greatest importance, and rely on the *ipse dixit* of the Chairmen of Committees. Irish Members naturally take a very great interest in this Bill, because we are promised some measure for Ireland to deal with the very same subject, and the Irish measure may be drawn somewhat upon the same lines as this Bill. I must confess that, although I am very anxious indeed to see some scheme devised by which the present inconvenience can be spared to Irish suitors and Scotch suitors also, as well as to the witnesses, I view these proposals for transferring the present jurisdiction for dealing with private Bills with the greatest possible suspicion. I confess from my own point of view the remedy to apply to these admitted grievances would be in a totally different direction. It would be some really representative local body sitting either in Edinburgh or Dublin. I think the hon. Member for Caithness is perfectly right in endeavouring to add to the Chairmen of the two Houses two independent Members of the two Houses. We all remember occasions again and again, when, under the cloak of a Private Bill, a matter of the utmost importance has been introduced, and it appears to me that the protection proposed to be given by this Amendment is quite reasonable and moderate.

*MR. HEDDERWICK : I desire to join in the forcible appeal that has been made to the Lord Advocate to reconsider his attitude with regard to this Amendment. I think it is much to be regretted that the Lord Advocate should show such an unyielding disposition in regard to Amendments which do not affect any vital part of his Bill. To pursue that course is not calculated to facilitate the passage of the measure. Now, Sir, there are some considerations which ought, I think, to weigh with the right hon. Gentleman. In the first place, I should like him to reflect upon the fact that the acceptance of the Amendment which is being proposed will in no wise affect the principle of his measure. In the second place this Amendment, which he has refused to consider, is an Amendment which has been approved by the right hon. Gentleman's own leader, the First Lord of the Treasury, and coming from such a source I should have thought it might have been treated with a little more respect than has been shown to it by the Lord Advocate. In the next place, the acceptance of this Amendment would satisfy the

feeling which has been very generally expressed, not only on this side of the House, but upon both sides—the feeling that there ought to be left to the House some remnant of control over measures which the House has hitherto fully and completely controlled. I am perfectly well aware from the expressions which have fallen from the Lord Advocate that he attaches no importance whatever to that feeling, but at the same time he cannot deny the existence of the feeling, and the fact that it has been very generally expressed ; and that being so, I think he would do well to reconsider his position.

*MR. STUART WORTLEY : I would have preferred a solution of the whole problem by a short Bill providing that a Committee on a Scotch Private Bill might sit at any time elsewhere than at Westminster. By the plan proposed in the present Bill the only security the House has that Private Bills shall be properly classified is the qualities of the Chairman so rightly exercised at present, and the objectional feature of the proposal is the new-fangled creation of a statutory officer outside the House, and over whom the only control the House would have would be by the supersession of its Chairman. I cannot see that any real or fundamental damage would be done to the Bill by associating two members with the Chairmen of the two Houses. I do not think that the important question of the classification of Bills should be left to officers selected in a circuitous manner and given a status novel to Parliamentary procedure.

DR. CLARK : During the hour and a half we have been discussing this Amendment only one Member has supported the Lord Advocate, *i.e.* my hon. friend the Member for North Ayrshire (Mr. Cochrane). We have been told that under the Bill of 1892 there was a different scheme, but the difference makes my Amendment all the more necessary. The fifth section of the 8th clause takes away the right of appeal to the House on the question of classification, for the Chairmen, with the sanction of the Secretary for Scotland, may refuse such an appeal. My hon. friend the Member for North Ayrshire opposes the Amendment because he thinks it will " dish " Home Rule for Scotland. Our idea, however, is that it will help Home Rule for Scotland. Unless we can get some stronger arguments against the proposal, I shall be compelled to go to a Division and take the feeling of the House.

Col. DENNY (Kilmarnock Burghs): I am opposed to any such power being given to the Chairmen as is proposed by this Bill, and I feel compelled to support the Amendment of the hon. Member for Caithness.

Mr. DALZIEL: I am sorry the learned Lord Advocate has shown so little disposition to meet the views of the critics of this Bill, as well as those of its supporters, because if he expects to carry this Bill in a reasonable time he will have to show a little more consideration for the arguments brought forward in favour of Amendments than he has to-night. We have had five speakers from the opposite side of the House, some of them Scotch Members, in favour of this Amendment, and we have only had the speech of one private Member in support of the Lord Advocate. I do not wish to under-rate the importance of the hon. Member for North Ayrshire, but he will excuse me if I say that he is in an official atmosphere. He is so close to the Treasury Bench that I cannot conceive the possibility of the hon. Member taking any view hostile to that of a Member who sits upon that bench. I see the right hon. Gentleman the Leader of the House has returned to his place, and I think it would be an advantage to know what are the reasons which have induced him to depart from his own proposal. I rather fancy, as the right hon. Gentleman has remained silent, that we have converted him, and I shall listen with interest to hear him defend his later position, because, after all, he is somewhat of a democrat, and he would be the last to argue, when there is practically a unanimous opinion in favour of an Amendment which raises a point to which we attach great importance, that that point should not have the fullest consideration. I beg, therefore, to appeal once again to the Lord Advocate. I think in the interests of the Bill he had better adopt the suggestion which I made some time ago, which was that he should leave the matter open and bring it forward again on Report, and see if he cannot do something to meet the unanimous expression of opinion to which the Committee has listened. The right hon. Gentleman has shown no disposition to concede anything, and I am rather afraid

Dr. *Hedderwick.*

that it will interfere with the speedy progress of this Bill.

Mr. A. G. MURRAY: My difficulty has been, first of all, with regard to the matter of time, because of the Chairmen being here in London in November and December, and they are in a very favourable position to give a decision upon the points put before them. This position would not be shared by private Members. My hon. and learned friend has asked why have we changed from the Bill of 1892? He forgets that this position with regard to the Chairmen is the position entirely approved by the Select Committee of last year. My principal difficulty is that a great many of the speeches have not really dealt with the question of whether private Members should be added so much as with the somewhat larger question of whether there is sufficient control by this House over the legislation here proposed. A great many Members have spoken as if, once the Chairmen have come to a determination that a particular subject should be dealt with as a Provisional Order, the matter disappeared from the control of this House altogether, and never came back to it. They always ignore the fact that it must come back. ("No.") Yes, if there is opposition it must come back, providing the opposition is not merely frivolous. I will consider whether there should not be some method of giving this House a still further control in all these matters, and also whether there may be any practicable way of adding some other Members besides the Chairmen for the consideration of this particular fact, treating it as a branch of what is really the larger question of the control of this House. I hope hon. Members will also consider that really time is the essence of the question.

Sir H. CAMPBELL-BANNERMAN: The right hon. Gentleman has shown a disposition to meet what was the general feeling of the Committee; but the promise he has made has not been quite so explicit as we desire. There has been a very strong case indeed made out. Not only have we had a number of Members on this side of the House desiring to have some Members of Parliament added to this Committee, but we have had the Member for the Kilmarnock Burghs intimate that it was deliberately accepted as a solemn necessity by all the Scotch Unionist Members of Parliament, and that there was an objection entertained to the proposal to confer these powers on the two Chairmen. In these circumstances I think the right hon. Gentleman might go a little further. Why should he not accept the Amendment of my hon. friend, subject to the opportunity of correcting or altering it on the Report stage ? That would be a more definite step to take. All that has been said has been not with any desire to wreck the Bill, as has been suggested, but with no desire except to make it as effective as possible for the purpose for which it is intended. We all know the immense difficulty in providing machinery for dealing with private legislation. The proof of that is the number of Bills which have been introduced again and again to this House and proved inadequate. This Bill is full of difficulties, and we wish to help the Lord Advocate, if he will allow us, out of those difficulties, and it is in that spirit I urge upon him to accept the Amendment.

MR. A. J. BALFOUR : No doubt it is perfectly true that this House has been year after year occupied with one variation after another of this one theme. No less than four Bills have been brought forward by different gentlemen—one of them by myself — attempting to deal with this problem. The right hon. Gentleman assumes for that reason that all these Bills have been of equal value. I am not quite sure that I agree with that. The truth is that this is a change in our procedure which may be carried out in many different ways ; and probably any one of those four ways which, after careful consideration, have been proposed is, if not quite as good, not very much worse than any other. But all ways are, no doubt, open to objection ; and I have noticed in dealing with these proposals that there is always some gentleman to be found on one side of the House or the other, and usually a gentleman from each side of the House, who has an alternative to suggest. The result is we lose ourselves in this perpetual balancing of alternatives, which, after all, do not differ much from one another, discussing then in immense detail, at a great cost of time, until the Bill is likely to be smothered. I trust the Committee will endeavour to avoid that danger which has proved so serious, and even fatal, to proposals which have preceded that which my right hon. friend

now has in charge. I am sorry I have not been able to listen to the whole discussion upon this present proposal—it is through no fault of mine—but I gather that all this anxiety, which has been expressed in different parts of the House, really arises from a fear—a natural fear, and, up to a certain point, a legitimate fear in my opinion—lest under the guise of reforming our Private Bill legislation we should permit the House to be deprived of real control not only over the details of this scheme or that scheme, but over the general principles of legislation which ought to govern not merely public Bills, but private Bills also. This is only one of a set of Amendments proposed by different gentlemen in different quarters of the House, all having the same object, namely, that of keeping the control which this House has over the private legislation of Scotland, or any other part of the United Kingdom, which may come under the scope of this Bill or any future Bill framed on like principles. I sympathise with that desire, and unless we allow our desire to see that object carried into effect smother and destroy what ought to be the governing principles of legislation of this land, namely, to reduce the cost, to reduce the trouble, and to prevent that great burden which some of these inquiries have necessitated, I see no objection to any reasonable provision being put into the Bill by which that object may be attained. But the Amendment before the House is not the best way for carrying it out. My right hon. friend has explained that if you insist that two unpaid unofficial Members should be here through October, November, and December——

SEVERAL HON. MEMBERS : No !

MR. CRIPPS : Bills must be deposited by December 21st.

MR. A. J. BALFOUR : We will not quarrel over the months ; it does not affect my argument whether it was November or December ; it is at any rate some months which are not in the session.

AN HON. MEMBER : Two days will be enough.

MR. A. J. BALFOUR : It may be, but it will be a tax upon either the Chairman of this House or the Chairman of the other House, or upon any Member who may have to deal with the matter, and to require unofficial and unpaid Members to attend in our holiday appears to me to be——

AN HON. MEMBER: There are legal Members of this House who are always in London in the late autumn, and who would be available.

MR. A. J. BALFOUR: I do not think the House wants a legal man. I think the House must be glad to have two private Members, who are not of the legal profession, who are quite willing to give their time in the public service. It is a serious thing to insist that it should be a necessary and integral part of our machinery that unpaid Members should be here out of session. That would be an objection which would be very serious, if not fatal. I would suggest as a far more complete alternative than anything that is done before a Bill goes to these local tribunals that this House should have a more complete control than it has under the Bill of the Government for dealing with the measure after it has left the local tribunal. I was very much struck by some arguments brought forward by my learned friend the Member for Stroud and others in the earlier part of the discussion, in which it was explained that there might be changes in our law introduced unknown to this House in unopposed Bills. That danger would not be prevented by the proposal before the House.

MR. CALDWELL: That is provided for afterwards.

MR. A. J. BALFOUR: My suggestion is that we should not try by this means simply to strengthen the Chairmen or the Members who are asked to do things which this House has never asked its Members to do before, but that we should endeavour to strengthen the grip which this House has upon proposed Private Bill legislation before it actually becomes law. If the Committee will let this Amendment slide, I will consult with my right hon. and learned friend whether some machinery of a far more effective character cannot be devised. The suggestion would not be open to the objection to asking Members to sit out of session and do unpaid work, and it would at the same time have the effect of carrying out the policy which I think the right hon. Gentleman opposite, the Leader

Mr. A. J. Balfour.

of the Opposition, has expressed his desire to see carried out, and it must meet the views of many English Members not interested in the details of Scotch legislation, but extremely anxious that the control of this House should not be lost of the general principles under which Private Bill legislation in this and all other parts of the United Kingdom ought to be conducted.

Mr. CRIPPS: If the Committee had all along been met in the sympathetic spirit of the First Lord of the Treasury, a great many of our difficulties would have been removed. I certainly should agree with him that if this Amendment did necessitate the attendance of Members of Parliament out of session to deal with work of this kind it would be a very strong objection. But there is no such necessity, because Bills are deposited by December 21st, as we all know. Probably this tribunal would want to consider this matter about twice a year, and that could be done about the time when Parliament met and when it rose—that is, about the beginning of February and the beginning of August—thus giving two periods in the year when the matters could be considered conveniently for all concerned. It is also very important that at the outset we should get a proper distinction made as to what matters should come before the House. I hope the First Lord of the Treasury will see that the objections to which he has referred do not really apply to this Amendment; but I must thank him for the sympathetic way in which he has dealt with the matter.

SIR H. CAMPBELL-BANNERMAN: We all fully recognise the way in which the right hon. Gentleman the Leader of the House has dealt with the subject, and we are grateful for the promise he has given with regard to the larger question of maintaining the control of Parliament over what may be important legislation contained in these private proposals. But that does not affect the particular proposal before the Committee, which is whether the tribunal to be composed to determine the initial question whether Bills should proceed in one way or in another should consist solely of the two Chairmen. We have urged many arguments against leaving the Chairmen to do this work alone. We have asked that two Members

—not chosen by the Party Whips, but appointed by the Committee of Selection or some other impartial body—should be put upon the tribunal as assessors or assistants to the two Chairmen. I do not think the right hon. Gentleman has met our proposals, and we are not content to leave the matter as it now stands. On the other hand, after the disposition which the Government has shown to meet us, I should regret very much having to go to a Division, and I would therefore suggest that we should now report Progress, and when we meet again next week at the same point in the Bill, the Government will have had time to consider the question and to see whether our desire can be carried into effect.

Mr. A. J. BALFOUR : I do not think any good would be gained by resisting the suggestion of the right hon. Gentleman, though I regret giving up even ten minutes of public time. I hope the House will consent, when we resume the discussion of this clause, to remember that what we have to deal with is the question of Parliamentary control. Whatever we decide, we shall do our best to meet the general views of the House.

Motion made, and Question,

" That the Chairman do report Progress ; and ask leave to sit again,"

put, and agreed to.

Committee report Progress ; to sit again upon Thursday.

TROUT FISHING ANNUAL CLOSE TIME (SCOTLAND) BILL. [Lords.]

SECOND READING.

Order for Second Reading read.

Motion made, and Question proposed-

" That the Bill be now read a second time."

MR. DALZIEL : This Bill has given rise to a very great deal of consideration. If the right hon. Gentleman intends now to proceed with the Second Reading, I think it is much too important a measure to be brought forward at a time when the House cannot possibly devote the attention to it which its importance demands. The Bill is bitterly opposed in certain parts of Scotland, although it may possess some good qualities, and there is a case of

some kind for the Bill. The result of the inquiry into this matter was of a very inconclusive character, and there was a general understanding that there should be further inquiry before any further legislation should be passed. Does the right hon. Gentleman intend to meet the generally expressed wish of those who are interested in the matter that there should be some further tribunal for the purpose of taking evidence ? The right hon. Gentleman is a fair man, and I am sure he does not wish to carry a measure which has given rise to so much opposition in different parts of Scotland. We know the advantage of taking care of the small trout, and in some parts of Scotland the present state of things is almost a crying scandal ; but, at the same time, the provisions of the Bill are such as to give rise to the reasonable suspicion that it is somewhat of a class measure. In this Bill there is to be no close time so far as private proprietors are concerned. My point is that if there is to be a close time at all it ought not to apply simply to places where our workmen get the pleasure of trout fishing, but it ought also to apply to lochs which are privately owned by Highland landlords and others throughout Scotland. I have spoken in order to give the right hon. Gentleman an opportunity of framing his answers to the questions which I thought it my duty to put to him in the interests of those who are concerned in the Bill——

It being midnight, the Debate stood adjourned.

Debate to be resumed upon Thursday.

LUNACY BILL [Lords].

Order for Second Reading read.

THE SECRETARY TO THE LOCAL GOVERNMENT BOARD (Mr. T. W. RUSSELL, Tyrone, S.) : Thursday.

MR. CHANNING : I should like to ask whether it is the intention of the Government to consider this, because we ought to have some notice. There are some very important changes suggested.

MR. T. W. RUSSELL : That question had better be directed to the Secretary of State for the Home Department.

2 M

Mr. JOHN BURNS (Battersea): May I appeal to the Under Secretary for the Home Department to put down this Bill at such a date as would enable the various local authorities throughout England and Wales who are interested in some of its provisions to suggest to him some simple but necessary Amendments which are contemplated. If any attempt is made to get it through to-night or to-morrow night, or any night this week, I should, in the interests of one district very much concerned in it, oppose it ; but, I believe, if he will consult the local authorities he may get the Bill through this session.

Second Reading deferred till Thursday.

BATHS AND WASHHOUSES ACTS (AMENDMENT) BILL.

Order for Second Reading read.

Mr. BIGWOOD (Middlesex, Brentford): This Bill merely provides that baths may be used for dancing and so on. In many districts the authorities have spent large sums of money for the purpose of putting up baths and washhouses under what is called the Adoptive Act, and they are very anxious indeed to make some use of them in the winter months. London already possesses that power, and I believe there is no objection to other authorities having the same.

Mr. CALDWELL : The use of public baths for the purpose of entertainments is a very important question ; we have purposely put a clause in the Act restricting such use, and until the matter can be discussed in the House in a proper way this Bill ought not to proceed.

Mr. JOHN BURNS : I do appeal to the hon. Member to withdraw his opposition to this Bill. It seems to me to be ridiculous that we should have, in many cases, a magnificent building absolutely empty for the four or five winter months, when with a piano therein we could get the boys and girls out of the streets and give them a course of physical drill with simple accompaniments, which ought charm the hon. Gentleman the member for a Lanarkshire constituency. I appeal to the hon. Member to add to his many legislative attainments by getting the credit of allowing this simple Bill to pass through.

Mr. CALDWELL : I object.

Second Reading deferred till Thursday.

Adjourned at ten minutes after
Twelve o'clock.

HOUSE OF LORDS.

Tuesday 13th June 1899.

NEW PEER.

The Duke of Beaufort sat first in Parliament after the death of his father.

PRIVATE BILL BUSINESS.

The Lord Chancellor acquainted the House that the Clerk of the Parliaments had laid upon the Table the Certificate from the Examiners that the further Standing Orders applicable to the following Bill have been complied with:

WOKING WATER AND GAS.

And also the Certificate that the Standing Orders applicable to the following Bill have been complied with:

ELECTRIC LIGHTING PROVISIONAL ORDERS (No. 2).

The same were ordered to lie on the Table.

EDINBURGH CORPORATION BILL.

A witness ordered to attend the Select Committee.

SOUTHPORT TRAMWAYS BILL. [Lords.]

Report from the Select Committee, That the promoters do not intend to proceed further with the Bill: Ordered that the Bill be not further proceeded with.

RHONDDA URBAN DISTRICT COUNCIL BILL.

WORKINGTON CORPORATION WATER BILL. [Lords.]

Reported from the Select Committee with Amendments.

BROOKE'S PARK (LONDONDERRY) BILL. [Lords.]

CARDIFF RAILWAY BILL.

Reported with Amendments.

KENSINGTON AND NOTTING HILL ELECTRIC LIGHTING BILL.

The Chairman of Committees informed the House that the opposition to the Bill was withdrawn: The orders made on the 2nd instant and yesterday discharged; and Bill committed for Friday next.

WATERMEN'S AND LIGHTERMEN'S ACTS AMENDMENT BILL. [Lords.]

Report from the Select Committee That it is not expedient to proceed further with the Bill: read, and ordered to lie on the Table.

SOUTH - EASTERN AND LONDON, CHATHAM, AND DOVER RAILWAY COMPANIES (NEW LINES) BILL.

Read 2ᵃ, and committed: the Committee to be proposed by the Committee of Selection.

BUENOS AYRES AND PACIFIC RAILWAY COMPANY BILL. [Lords.]

YORKE ESTATE BILL. [Lords.]

Read 3ᵃ, and passed, and sent to the Commons.

CITY AND BRIXTON RAILWAY BILL

LONDON IMPROVEMENTS BILL.

SHEFFIELD CORPORATION MARKETS BILL.

STOCKPORT CORPORATION BILL.

Brought from the Commons, read 1ᵃ, and referred to the Examiners.

BIRKENHEAD CORPORATION BILL. [Lords.]

Returned from the Commons agreed to, with Amendments.

DUMBARTON BURGH BILL. [Lords.]

Returned from the Commons agreed to, with Amendments: The said Amendments considered, and agreed to.

METROPOLITAN COMMON SCHEME (HARROW WEALD) PROVISIONAL ORDER BILL.

Read 3ᵃ (according to order), and passed.

ELECTRIC LIGHTING PROVISIONAL ORDERS (No. 10) BILL. [Lords.]

Read 3ᵃ (according to order), and passed, and sent to the Commons.

GAS ORDERS CONFIRMATION (No. 1) BILL. [Lords.]

WATER ORDERS CONFIRMATION BILL. [Lords.]

House in Committee (according to order); Amendments made: Standing Committee negatived: The Report of

Amendments to be received on Thursday next.

ELECTRIC LIGHTING PROVISIONAL ORDERS (No. 14) BILL. [Lords.]

House in Committee (according to order): Bill reported without Amendment: Standing Committee negatived; and Bill to be read 3ª Thursday next.

GAS AND WATER ORDERS CONFIRMATION BILL. [Lords.]

House in Committee (according to order): Amendments made: Standing Committee negatived: The Report of Amendments to be received on Thursday next.

ELECTRIC LIGHTING PROVISIONAL ORDERS (No. 12) BILL. [Lords.]

ELECTRIC LIGHTING PROVISIONAL ORDERS (No. 13) BILL. [Lords.]

ELECTRIC LIGHTING PROVISIONAL ORDERS (No. 15) BILL. [Lords.]

Committed to Committee of the whole House on Thursday next.

TRAMWAYS ORDERS CONFIRMATION (No. 2) BILL. [Lords.]

Committed: The Committee to be proposed by the Committee of Selection.

ELECTRIC LIGHTING PROVISIONAL ORDERS (No. 2) BILL.

To be read 2ª on Thursday next: (*The Earl of Dudley*).

ELECTRIC LIGHTING PROVISIONAL ORDERS (No. 7) BILL (No. 114).

HOUSING OF THE WORKING CLASSES PROVISIONAL ORDER (BORROWSTOUNNESS) BILL (No. 115).

LOCAL GOVERNMENT (IRELAND) PROVISIONAL ORDER (No. 1) BILL (No. 116).

LOCAL GOVERNMENT PROVISIONAL ORDER (HOUSING OF WORKING CLASSES) BILL (No. 117).

LOCAL GOVERNMENT PROVISIONAL ORDER (No. 5) BILL (No. 118).

LOCAL GOVERNMENT PROVISIONAL ORDERS (POOR LAW) BILL (No. 119).

Brought from the Commons, read 1ª, to be printed, and referred to the Examiners.

LONDON, BRIGHTON, AND SOUTH COAST RAILWAY (PENSIONS) BILL.

LISBURN TOWN COMMISSIONERS BILL,
now
LISBURN URBAN DISTRICT COUNCILS BILL.

Read 3ª, with the Amendments, and passed, and returned to the Commons.

RETURNS, REPORTS, ETC.

SOUTH AFRICAN REPUBLIC.

Papers relating to the complaints of British subjects in the South African Republic.

EXPLOSIVES.

I. (Explosion of Carbo-gelatine at Factory near Faversham.) Report to the right hon. the Secretary of State for the Home Department, by Colonel A. Ford, C.B., Her Majesty's Chief Inspector of Explosives, on the circumstances attending an explosion of carbo-gelatine in course of manufacture, which occurred at the factory of the Cotton Powder Company, at Uplees Marshes, near Faversham, on the 5th of May, 1899.

II. (Explosion of Percussion Caps at Factory at Streetly, near Birmingham.) Report to the right hon. the Secretary of State for the Home Department, by Major A. Cooper-Key, R.A., Her Majesty's Inspector of Explosives, on the circumstances attending an explosion of percussion caps in course of manufacture at the factory of the Birmingham Metal and Munitions Company, Limited, at Streetly, near Birmingham, on the 11th of April, 1899.

EXPLOSIVES ACT, 1875.

Twenty-third Annual Report of Her Majesty's Inspector of Explosives.

Presented (by command), and ordered to lie on the Table.

CERTIFIED INEBRIATE REFORMATORIES (RULES FOR MANAGEMENT.)

Rules made with the approval of the Secretary of State for the Home Department for the domestic management of the certified inebriate reformatory at Horfield in the county of Gloucester.

Laid before the House (pursuant to Act), and ordered to lie on the Table.

QUESTION.

ESTATE DUTY.

*The Chairman of Committees (The Earl of Morley), who had upon the Paper the following notice :

" To call attention to the fact that, on the succession to an estate registered in the Land Registry, the title of the successor, though he has paid all the estate duties due from him, is for all time endorsed with a notice that the estate is still subject to an indefinite liability for estate duty ; and to the effect which such an endorsement has on registered titles ; "

said : My Lords, I think I should explain that when I placed this notice upon the Paper of your Lordships' House I did so under a misapprehension. Latterly new rules have been introduced by my noble and learned friend on the Woolsack with regard to the registration of land, which really render my notice to a very large extent unnecessary ; but as it has been on the Paper for several days I think it is desirable that I should say a few words in explanation of the reason why I gave notice to call attention to this matter. It was quite by accident that I became aware of the mode in which indefinite liability for estate duty is, or has been up to quite recently, endorsed on registered titles. I found myself in the somewhat unusual position of succeeding to a property which had been registered in the Land Registry, and when I had produced to the Registrar the receipts from Somerset House showing that all the duties on the land which were then ascertainable had been paid, I assumed that my title would be a clear one, and that I would have all the advantages which are supposed to result from a registered title. I was somewhat surprised to find that, although I was registered with absolute title, and although I had paid all the duties then ascertainable, the following entry was inserted at the end of my title :

" The land is subject to such liability as may affect the same in respect of the estate duty on the decease of the owner."

This, it seems to me, is a very important matter, because it defeats the main object of registering titles, which is to give the owner of the land a clear title, and to facilitate a transfer. I inquired at once as to when this notice would be taken off, and was informed that it would never be taken off. I then made further inquiries as to the reason why it was placed on a registered title, and the explanation I received was this, that the Succession Duty Act of 1883 and the Finance Act of 1894 are so framed that they leave land charged in certain cases for estate duty over an unlimited period, and that that liability may very often arise, not from the will which creates the succession, but from extraneous circumstances which could never have entered into the head either of the testator or the successor, amongst other things the falling in of long leases or any increment to the deceased person's estate which may have come from sources which could not have been imagined at the time when the succession was created. Of course, this liability is increased by the fact that under the Finance Act of 1894 any such increment might affect the aggregation and consequently the rate of duty which would be paid upon the estate, and I was informed that no lapse of time whatever could free the holder of the title from this liability. The actual liability does not merely affect registered land, but it also affects unregistered land. Though this is a much wider question than the one to which I am calling the attention of your Lordships, which is confined entirely to registered titles, I ventured to suggest whether, from the point of view of public policy, there ought not to be some period at which an estate which has paid all ascertainable duties should be free from any further liability. I doubt very much whether the gain to the Exchequer is in any way commensurate with the vexation which a continuing liability causes, and the interference with the free and easy transfer of land which such a liability must inevitably produce. Although this is, as I have said, a much wider question, still I venture to call the attention of the noble and learned Lord on the Woolsack to it. I think it is a question which undoubtedly deserves consideration, from a public point of view, for the policy of Parliament now is to render land transfer as easy and as cheap as possible. For my own part, I attach very great importance to facilitating transfer, for I believe by this means we shall accomplish what seems to me, and what, I think, Parliament has admitted would be, a very useful object—we should by this means make a larger distribution of land possible. This is prevented at the present moment more by the expense, trouble, and delays consequent upon small transfers than by any other cause. This does not apply so much to large building estates, in respect of which it is generally easy to draw up a simple printed form of title and to convey the land cheaply and easily but in the case of rural estates ; the owner, who would often be glad to sell an acre or two of land round a village or large town, for the convenience of the people living in it, is debarred from doing so owing to the expense, trouble, and delay which he is put to being quite in-commensurate with the amount of money he would receive for the land. I venture to think this is a question which is well worthy of the consideration of your Lord-ships. With regard to registered land, the notice I have quoted to the House, which is endorsed on the titles, to the effect that the estate is still subject to an indefinite liability for estate duty, must obviously cast a taint on the title. At any rate, you do not get what you bargain for—namely, an absolutely clean title. Since I put the notice upon the Paper I have had a communication with the Registrar of the Land Registry, who has informed me that the Rules have been largely changed during the last year, and that amongst the new Rules which came into effect on the 1st January last the following finds a place :

" Where a notice of liability has been entered on the Register, it may be cancelled on the production of any such evidence as is mentioned in the preceding Rule."

The evidence mentioned in the preceding Rule is proof to the satisfaction of the Registrar that all duty payable in respect of such land by reason of the death of the proprietor has been paid and satis-fied. That to a large extent satisfies me, and if I had known that the Rule existed I should not have troubled the House with this notice. But there is one point to which I should like to call the atten-tion of the noble and learned Lord on the Woolsack. I put it to him whether the words " may be cancelled " ought not to be " shall be cancelled." At present it is no one's duty to cancel the notice. I cannot help thinking it should be the duty of the Registrar to cancel the notice after satisfactory evidence has been produced to him, showing that all the ascer-

The Earl of Morley.

tainable duties had been paid. That, at least, would be fair to owners of registered land, and would place them in the same position, so far as liability for duty goes, as the owners of unregistered land. If the Government can see their way to freeing all land, whether registered or not, from liability to duty after the efflux of a given period, of course that would solve the question to my mind in the most satisfactory way. I almost hope that if, as I believe, the Exchequer would lose a very trifling amount of money by so doing, that reform may be carried out. Failing that, however, such a small amendment as I have proposed in the Rules which have been so recently issued would meet the point I have in my mind, and I should be glad if the noble and learned Lord on the Woolsack would give me some encouragement to believe that that amendment will be adopted.

*LORD STANLEY OF ALDERLEY : My Lords, I desire to support the noble Earl in the action he has taken, and the views he has expressed. I would remind the noble and learned Lord on the Woolsack that one of his arguments in favour of the Bill establishing the Land Registry was that it would make land more saleable, but such will not be the case if, as the noble Earl has pointed out, on the succession to an estate registered in the Land Registry the title of the successor, though he has paid all the estate duties, is for all time endorsed with a notice that the property is still subject to an indefinite liability for duty. There is another danger, that of having to pay estate duties again if the receipts are lost, in this endorsement of a presump-tion that the estate is still liable. I have at this moment a dispute pending with the taxing authorities because with respect to a farm, the land tax of which had been redeemed in 1799, the land tax of 8s. 8d. on the tithe had, in 1860, been transferred to the farm, and since the Act of 1896, through the neglect of Somerset House to send lists of redeemed lands with their circular to the Land Tax Commissioners, the tax has been increased to £2 6s. 5d. in 1898, and to £1 19s. 6d. in 1899, and the Inland Revenue have refused to return it.

THE LORD CHANCELLOR (The EARL of HALSBURY): My Lords, my noble friend the Chairman of Committees has explained to your Lordships that the notice was placed on the Paper under a misapprehension ; and I ought to say, in justice to my noble friend, that he was really himself the author of the Rule which removed his objection, because some time ago my noble friend, who sat with me a considerable period on a Committee which went into the subject of the Land Register, was good enough to point out to me that, if what was called the Inland Revenue clause was insisted upon in its entirety, the result would be to stamp every transaction in the Land Registry with an unknown liability that would warn off everybody from dealing with the Registry. I have had some communication with my right hon. friend the Chancellor of the Exchequer, the result of which is the Rule my noble friend has read, and which seems to me to be enough, at all events for the present, to get rid of the difficulty. While the Inland Revenue were reluctant to release their hold over land out of which some profit might accrue, they were, however, reasonable enough to agree to this Rule. My noble friend the Chairman of Committees has taken the occasion to point out a defect I cannot deny. I agree with my noble friend that instead of leaving it in the discretion of the Registrar to erase the mark from the register, it would be better that it should be an obligation upon him. Certainly the Rule is meant to provide that it should be an obligation upon him. I cannot say that I disagree with my noble friend as to the policy of not insisting on the extreme rights of the Revenue, when the great importance of freeing the transfer of land is taken into consideration. I think it is very desirable that there should be some period of time at which it would be possible to remove absolutely any liability from land of which a purchaser for value, without notice, had become the possessor. That is only my own individual view, and I must not be understood to be committing my colleagues in any way on the subject. I can only say that in any future version of these Rules which I may be called upon to make I shall be very glad to see that the true intent and meaning of the Rule referred to shall be properly expressed, and shall not be left open to the criticism my noble friend has been good enough to pass upon it.

House adjourned at five minutes before Five o'clock, to Thursday next, half-past Ten o'clock.

HOUSE OF COMMONS.

Tuesday, 13*th June* 1899.

PRIVATE BILL BUSINESS.

PRIVATE BILLS. [Lords.]

(Standing Orders not previously inquired into complied with.)

MR. SPEAKER laid upon the Table Report from one of the Examiners of Petitions for Private Bills, That, in the case of the following Bills, originating in the Lords, and referred on the First Reading thereof, the Standing Orders not previously inquired into, and which are applicable thereto, have been complied with, viz. :—

GREAT GRIMSBY STREET TRAMWAYS BILL. [Lords.]

NORTH EASTERN AND HULL AND BARNSLEY RAILWAYS (JOINT DOCK) BILL. [Lords.]

NORTH EASTERN RAILWAY BILL. [Lords.]

Ordered, that the Bills be read a second time.

BROMPTON AND PICCADILLY CIRCUS RAILWAY BILL.

Queen's Consent signified.

Read the third time, and passed.

INFANT ORPHAN ASYLUM BILL. [Lords.]

LONDON HOSPITAL BILL. [Lords.]

STOCKTON AND MIDDLESBROUGH WATER BILL. [Lords.]

Read the third time, and passed, without Amendment.

DARWEN CORPORATION BILL.

As amended, considered ; to be read the third time.

GODALMING CORPORATION WATER BILL (by Order.)

Order for consideration, as amended, read.

Motion made, and Question proposed—

"That the Order for the Consideration of the Bill, as amended, be deferred till Thursday next."—(*Dr. Farquharson.*)

MR. DUNCOMBE (Cumberland, Egremont): I beg to protest against the postponement of this Bill again. It seems to me that the time has come to make more than a formal protest against these continual postponements. We really must make some effort to carry on the business of the House in accordance with the official programme. I think it is my duty, on behalf of private Members, to protest against the system of bringing us down here over and over again to consider private business, which has been put down by Order, and on a certain day, only to find that it has been postponed. I shall divide the House on the postponement of this Bill.

MR. T. W. RUSSELL (Tyrone, S.): The Bill has been postponed by consent of all parties, with a view to a possible conference, which will manifestly be for the convenience and interest of all the parties.

MR. GIBSON BOWLES (Lynn Regis): It may be for the convenience of the parties interested in the Bill to postpone it, but it is not at all for the convenience or the dignity of the House. In my opinion, after so much patience has been shown by my hon. friend, he owes it as a duty to himself and the House to go to a Division.

*THE UNDER SECRETARY OF STATE FOR FOREIGN AFFAIRS (Mr. BRODRICK, Surrey, Guildford): My hon. friend has been exceedingly patient, but very serious questions of principle are involved in this Bill, which ought to be carefully considered, and I do not think anything can be said against the postponement for a few days.

MR. STUART (Shoreditch, Hoxton): I am sure it would be very convenient for the business of the House if we were to insist absolutely in proceeding with a Bill when it is down by Order. But anyone who knows the House knows that very frequently a Bill on which there is a conflict of serious issues is settled out of Court, and the time of the House is greatly saved thereby in discussions that may arise here and also in Committee in another place. I sincerely hope that there will be no effort made to reverse the proceedings which have been adopted by this House for a long time under circumstances similar to those of this Bill.

Question put.

The House divided: Ayes, 168; Noes, 34. (Division List No. 187.)

AYES.

Ambrose, Robert	Commins, Andrew	Gurdon, Sir William Brampton
Arnold, Alfred	Courtney, Rt. Hon. Leonard H.	Halsey, Thomas Frederick
Arnold-Forster, Hugh O.	Cranborne, Viscount	Hammond, John (Carlow)
Arrol, Sir William	Crombie, John William	Hanbury, Rt. Hn. Robert W.
Ashton, Thomas Gair	Cubitt, Hon. Henry	Healy, Maurice (Cork)
Austin, M. (Limerick, W.)	Curzon, Viscount	Healy, Thomas J. (Wexford)
Bailey, James (Walworth)	Davies, M. V.- (Cardigan)	Healy, Timothy M. (N. Louth)
Baldwin, Alfred	Davitt, Michael	Hedderwick, Thomas Chas. H.
Barnes, Frederic Gorell	Digby, John K. D. Wingfield-	Helder, Augustus
Barry, Rt Hon A H S (Hunts)	Dilke, Rt. Hon. Sir Charles	Hemphill, Rt. Hon. Chas. H.
Barry, E. (Cork, S.)	Dillon, John	Hill, Sir E. Stock (Bristol)
Bartley, George C. T.	Disraeli, Coningsby Ralph	Hogan, James Francis
Barton, Dunbar Plunket	Donelan, Captain A.	Horniman, Frederick John
Bathurst, Hn. Allen Benjamin	Doogan, P. C.	Houldsworth, Sir Wm. H.
Bill, Charles	Elliot, Hon. A. Ralph Douglas	Jebb, Richard Claverhouse
Blake, Edward	Farquharson, Dr. Robert	Johnson-Ferguson, Jabez E.
Blundell, Colonel Henry	Farrell, James P. (Cavan, W.)	Johnston, William (Belfast)
Bond, Edward	Fenwick, Charles	Johnstone, Heywood (Sussex)
Brodrick, Rt. Hon. St. John	Finlay, Sir Robert Bannatyne	Jones, David B. (Swansea)
Brown, Alexander H.	FitzGerald, Sir Robert Penrose-	Jordan, Jeremiah
Buchanan, Thomas Ryburn	Flavin, Michael Joseph	Kenyon, James
Buxton, Sydney Charles	Fletcher, Sir Henry	Kilbride, Denis
Caldwell, James	Gedge, Sydney	Kinloch, Sir John George S.
Cameron, Robert (Durham)	Gibney, James	Knowles, Lees
Campbell, Rt. Hn. J A (Gl'sg'w)	Goddard, Daniel Ford	Langley, Batty
Cawley, Frederick	Gold, Charles	Lawrence, Sir E. D. (Corn.)
Coddington, Sir William	Goldsworthy, Major-General	Lawrence, Wm. F. (Liverpool)
Cohen, Benjamin Louis	Gordon, Hon. John Edward	Lawson, John Grant (Yorks.)
Collery, Bernard	Graham, Henry Robert	Lawson, Sir W. (Cumberland)
Collings, Rt. Hon. Jesse	Greene, Henry D. (Shrewsbury)	Lecky, Rt. Hon. W. Edw. H.
Colville, John	Gunter, Colonel	Leng, Sir John

Leaty, Thomas Richmond
Long,Col.Chas. W. (Evesham)
Lowther,Rt.Hn.J.W.(Cumb'd)
Lyell, Sir Leonard
MacAleese, Daniel
Macdona, John Cumming
MacDonnell,Dr.M.A.(Qu'nsC)
MacNeill, J. Gordon Swift
M'Arthur, Charles (Liverpool)
M'Ghee, Richard
M'Kenna, Reginald
Maddison, Fred.
Malcolm, Ian
Mellor, Colonel (Lancashire)
Mellor, Rt.Hon.J. W.(Yorks.)
Mendl, Sigismund F.
Middlemore, J. Throgmorton
Minch, Matthew
Monk, Charles James
Moon, Edward Robert Pacy
Moore, William (Antrim, N.)
Morley,Rt.Hon.J. (Montrose)
Morris, Samuel
Murnaghan, George
Nicol, Donald Ninian
Norton, Capt. Cecil William

O'Brien, James F. X. (Cork)
O'Connor, Jas.(Wicklow,W.)
O'Kelly, James
Oldroyd, Mark
Palmer, Geo. Wm. (Reading)
Paulton, James Mellor
Pilkington,R.(Lancs, Newton)
Platt-Higgins, Frederick
Powell, Sir Francis Sharp
Power, Patrick Joseph
Pryce-Jones, Lt.-Col. Edward
Rankin, Sir James
Rasch, Major Frederic Carne
Renshaw, Charles Bine
Richardson,J. (Durham, S.E.)
Robson, William Snowdon
Roche, John (East Galway)
Rothschild, Hn. Lionel Walter
Russell, T. W. (Tyrone)
Samuel, J. (Stockton on Tees)
Saunderson,Rt. Hn. Col. E. J.
Schwann, Charles E.
Seoble, Sir Andrew Richard
Sharpe, William Edward T.
Sidebotham, J. W. (Cheshire)
Smith,JamesParker(Lanarks)

Smith, Samuel (Flint)
Stewart Sir Mark J. McT.
Stone, Sir Benjamin
Stuart, James (Shoreditch)
Sullivan, Donal (Westmeath)
Sullivan, T. D. (Donegal, W.)
Tomlinson, Wm. Edw.Murray
Trevelyan, Charles Philips
Wallace, Robert
Webster, R. G. (St. Pancras)
Weir, James Galloway
Welby, Lieut.-Col. A. C. E.
Whitmore, Charles Algernon
Williams, J. Powell- (Birm.
Wills, Sir William Henry
Wilson,Hen. J. (York, W.R.)
Wilson, John (Durham, Mid.)
Wilson, John (Govan)
Wilson,J.W.(Worcestersh,N.)
Wodehouse,RtHn.E.R. (Bath)
Wyndham-Quin, Major W. H.
Wyvill, Marmaduke D'Arcy
Young, Samuel (Cavan, East
TELLERS FOR THE AYES—
  Mr. Radcliffe Cooke and
  Mr. Purvis.

NOES.

Aird, John
Allan, William (Gateshead)
Bayley, Thomas (Derbyshire)
Billson, Alfred
Bowles, T. G. (King's Lynn)
Carson, Rt. Hon. Edward
Ellis, John Edward
Firbank, Joseph Thomas
Fison, Frederick William
Garfit, William
Gourley, Sir E. Temperley
Gretton, John
Greville, Hon. Ronald

Howell, William Tudor
Howorth, Sir Henry Hoyle
Jacoby, James Alfred
Laurie, Lieut.-General
Lloyd-George, David
Loder, Gerald Walter E.
Lough, Thomas
Maclean, James Mackenzie
M'Calmont, Col. (Antrim, E.)
M'Killop, James
Marks, Henry Hananel
Molloy, Bernard Charles
Nussey, Thomas Willans

O'Neil, Hon. Robert Torrens
Palmer, Sir C. M. (Durham)
Roberts, J. H. (Denbighs.)
Strachey, Edward
Thornburn, Walter
Tully, Jasper
Wedderburn, Sir William
Wolff, Gustav Wilhelm

TELLERS FOR THE NOES—
  Mr. Duncombe and Colonel
  Dalbiac.

Order for consideration, as amended, deferred till Thursday.

LONDON COUNTY COUNCIL (GENERAL POWERS) BILL. (By Order.)

Order for consideration, as amended, read.

Motion made, and Question proposed—

"That the Bill be now considered."

Amendment proposed—

"To leave out the words 'now considered,' in order to add the words 're-committed to the former Committee with respect to Clause 10 (Acquisition of Site of Spitalfields Market by agreement) and Clause 25 (Act not to authorise taking twenty houses of persons of the labouring class in any parish).'" — (*Mr. Alexander Hargreaves Brown.*)

Question—

"That the words 'now considered' stand part of the Question."

Put, and negatived ; words added.

Main Question, as amended, put, and agreed to.

Bill recommitted to the former Committee in respect of Clause 10 (Acquisition of Site of Spitalfields Market, by agreement), and Clause 25 (Act not to authorise taking twenty houses of persons of the labouring class in any parish).

DUBLIN CORPORATION BILL. (By Order.)

Order for Consideration, as amended, read.

MR. JOHN REDMOND (Clare, E.): In moving that this Bill be now considered, I will not detain the House very long. But I think it is desirable that the main facts of this important measure should be put before the House at the commencement of the Debate. The question at issue in this Bill is one of such enormous and vital importance to the City of Dublin that I sincerely trust the House will carefully weigh every aspect of the question before it comes to a decision. The question may be stated in a nutshell. It is whether Dublin, the metropolis of Ireland, is to be permitted by Parliament to extend and develop itself as other great cities in the three kingdoms have been permitted, or whether it is to be for ever handicapped by the refusal of the application of those principles which, in similar circumstances, have been freely applied to scores of other great cities on this side of the channel. This Bill is bitterly opposed, as the House will find out in the course of the Debate, but I make the assertion that it is opposed not one whit more bitterly than were similar Bills in the past which dealt with English or Scotch cities, and I feel perfectly sure that when the House of Commons grasps the main facts of this case, it will not refuse the Bill a second reading. I propose to deal very briefly with the main objections which have been urged against the Bill up to the present, and which now will be urged over again in the course of this Debate. But before doing so I desire, very briefly indeed, to state to the House the main points which I urge in support of this measure. First of all, let me remind the House that this extension of the boundaries of the City of Dublin is no new question. In the year 1880, nearly 20 years ago, a Royal Commission was appointed to inquire into the whole of this subject. The Commission was a capable one. No one has ever accused it of not being a thoroughly impartial one. It held an extended inquiry, and took evidence from all classes of the population, and in the result it unanimously approved of the addition of the townships to the city, such as is now proposed. It may be asked, how can we explain the delay which has occurred since the finding of that Commission in 1880. I am not sure it is necessary for us to go into that question, but if it were necessary, it might be a fair thing to say that your system of governing Irish private business in this House, with its enormous expense and its attendant risk of matters being decided by people not acquainted with the facts and the locality, may possibly be the reason of this delay. However that may be, the finding of the Commission stands, and it is on record

Mr. John Redmond.

that there has been a unanimous decision in support of this measure. The position of the City of Dublin is absolutely unique, and it presents a stronger case for the annexation of these townships than ever came under the cognisance of Parliament. The area of the City of Dublin is strictly limited ; it is 3,807 acres, and the average of population per acre is something like 64. It is horribly congested in some of its districts. Let me remind the House that the average of population per acre in Bradford is only 20, in Sheffield 17, and in Hull 25. At present the Corporation of Dublin has no power to erect workmen's dwellings outside the city limits, and this very fact has the result that when there is land suitable and available for such a purpose, the knowledge that the Corporation cannot go outside inevitably raises the price to an absolutely prohibitive point. Again, from a sanitary point of view, the case in support of this Bill is overwhelming. It is of vital importance to have one central sanitary authority in all large centres of population. Yet the sanitary position of affairs in Dublin is absolutely intolerable. Three of the townships opposed to this amalagamation do not come under the Notification of Infectious Diseases Act, and the result is that under the present system virulent disease may be poured into the city. Dublin is now expending half a million sterling on a great scheme of main drainage. Three of these townships have practically no adequate or proper system of drainage, while the others have a most imperfect system which consists of discharging crude sewage at the mouth of the Liffey, with the result that every incoming tide drives that sewage up the river. Is it likely that the Corporation will allow their large expenditure to be nullified by the action of these two townships ? All precedents are in favour of this measure. Dublin is the only city of importance in the three kingdoms which has not had its area extended since 1840. Parliament has always acted on clearly defined principles with regard to these matters. Wherever the populations sought to be amalgamated have not grown really from one centre, where there has been no real business connection or community of interest, no doubt in the past claims of this kind have been refused ; but in such cases it was shown that there was absolutely no community of interest, and that each individual community was separate. But in such cases as I know of, where one population was merely the overflow of another, and where the manufactures, business, and commerce and interests were the same—in such cases, I say, the principle has been applied freely by Parliament of permitting this amalgamation. This has happened in the cases of many of the large towns of this country —in Southampton, Cheltenham, Manchester, Devonport, Plymouth, and Bristol, and a number of other cities— and I say respectfully to the House of Commons that it would be an unreasonable thing if, insisting as you do upon bringing Irish Private Bill legislation, at enormous cost, up to here in England, you refuse to apply the same principle to Irish Bills as you do to English and Scotch measures. No one can deny— it was not sought to be denied before the Committee—that the population in the townships is a mere overflow of Dublin itself. The community is practically the same. All the businesses, and manufactures, and commerce are in the City of Dublin, and it is a significant and interesting fact that every day the tramcars alone bring into the city from the suburbs, etc., 45,000 people. That is leaving out of account those who come by the suburban trains and on foot. This population, which comes every day from the suburbs to the city, is absolutely dependent upon the city for its business, for its support, and for its very existence, and it seems to me that it is a monstrous thing that this population does not at the present moment in any degree share the common burdens. I want the House for a moment to consider what are the main advantages that this population of the suburbs derives from its connection with the City of Dublin, and enjoys without making any contribution towards the cost. In these suburbs there is not a market of any sort. The markets are all in the city, but they are used by the suburbs, and surely it is an unreasonable thing to say that the suburbs shall have absolute immunity from any share in the expense. There are no baths or washhouses in the suburbs. These institutions are maintained at the cost of the city, and within the city boundaries. In all these townships running round Dublin there is only one library, and that is a small one, which hardly deserves the name; whereas the City of Dublin supplies magnificent libraries, supported at the cost of the city, and, of course, used by the inhabitants of the townships. I ought to say that down by the harbour there is a little technical school, but the great technical school is in the City of Dublin, and maintained by the city, and it is an interesting fact that one-third of the total number of pupils in that institution have been shown to come from Rathmines and Pembroke. Yet when asked to make a contribution these townships refuse to give one shilling. How about the hospitals? The city authorities contribute towards the hospitals within the city area a sum of about £6,000 annually. There is only one hospital outside the city. It is just outside the limits—about 50 yards or so without the boundary— and technically within one of the townships. Yet the Corporation of Dublin contributes towards its support three times the amount contributed by any township. These hospitals are, of course, availed of by the inhabitants of the townships. Therefore, I say it would be a monstrous thing if the present state of things were allowed to continue, and the townships were exempted. The same thing may be said as to the roads. The roads used by this vast population in coming in to their business are, of course, maintained by the city. It seems to me that these facts in themselves constitute an overwhelming case in support of the Bill. What are the main objections urged? First of all, we are told that the townships object. Of course the townships object to being obliterated. It is only human nature. It is a singular thing that no similar measure applying to England or Scotland was ever carried without being opposed by the inhabitants of the suburbs proposed to be included. But on this question I am not at all satisfied that the opposition of the townships is anything like unanimous. Recently, since the Bill passed in Committee, a great deal of attention naturally has been directed to it in Dublin and the suburbs, and it is interesting to see that within the last few days a memorial, signed by more than two-thirds of the electors of one of these townships, has been presented to the authorities, and memorials signed by 25 to 50 per cent. of the electors of other townships. It is true that the bodies which represent these townships object, but I would like to point out that although some time ago an undertaking was given that a plebiscite should be taken in each locality, that promise has not been carried out. I believe that at this moment the majority of the inhabitants of the townships are in favour of this measure. The next objection taken is that the townships are not having adequate representation on the new Corporation, and will not have their interests safeguarded. That was an objection which apparently weighed very heavily on the Committee, and to endeavour to meet it the Committee inserted in the Bill a provision giving the townships a representation greater than that to which they would be numerically entitled. In a Corporation of about eighty members I am informed the townships would be entitled to about sixteen members. The Committee have inserted in the Bill a provision that they are to have twenty-eight members. There is also another fact to be borne in mind in connection with this matter. At the present moment there are in the Corporation no less than fifteen members who reside and are the largest ratepayers in the townships, and who include some of the richest business men in Dublin. Is it to be supposed that these men would sacrifice their own interests or the interests of the townships in which they reside? Accordingly, therefore, the townships will be represented in the Corporation to the extent of about half its number of members. It seems to me that that disposes altogether of the fear that the interests of the townships would be sacrificed to the interests of the city. Then, again, the objection is taken that the first thing the new city would do would be to raise the rates and destroy the prosperity of the townships. I do not believe there is the slightest danger of that. As everyone knows, the valuation of the City of Dublin is ridiculously inadequate. That is not true of the townships, the valuation of which is, of course, more recent. It has been shown before the Committee that the valuation of the city is from 20 per cent. to 25 per cent. too low, and a calculation has been laid before the Committee that on a revaluation of the old area it would be possible to raise the sum required for the government of the new area by imposing a rate scarcely, if at all, larger than the rate paid at present by some of the townships. That question may, however, be left on one side, because

Mr. John Redmond.

the Committee strongly insisted and inserted a provision in the Bill that the new Corporation should not be allowed to raise the rates in Pembroke and Rathmines for ten years after the passing of the Bill. My information is that the usual limit in English cases where it has been put in at all has been five years; but in this Bill, in order to meet the fears and susceptibilities of the townships, ten years has been put in. In face of that, I fail to see what objection can be raised on the question of rating. Of course, there is another objection—I do not know whether I ought to mention it, because I am not sure whether it will be mentioned by the right hon. Gentleman opposite—the political objection. I hope the right hon. Gentleman will not mention it, because I am one of those who believe it is a misfortune to drag these political questions into matters of this sort. Is the right hon. Gentleman's case going to be that, forsooth, because the majority of the Corporation of Dublin are, not unnaturally, Nationalist, therefore they are to be treated on a different principle to every other city in England and Scotland, and that they are not to be trusted to deal fairly with their fellow-citizens? The right hon. Gentleman is an Irishman, and I hope he will not put forward any such contention. But if he does, I appeal confidently to the House of Commons —to men on that side as well as on this—not to listen to any such reason for rejecting a measure of this kind. If this measure is justified on the grounds I have mentioned, if it is for the benefit of the City of Dublin, if it is not for the injury of the townships, if it is in accordance with precedent and with the principle which has been applied to other cities, then I say it would be a disgraceful thing for the House of Commons to reject the Bill on the ground that the majority of the Corporation of Dublin happen to differ in their political opinions from the majority of the Members of this House, and I have too high an opinion of the fair-mindedness of individual Members to believe that any such reason as that will influence their decision. I ought to apologise for speaking so long, but I thought it right to put the main facts before the House at the commencement of the debate. In conclusion, I call upon the House to rest the case of Dublin on the same principle on which it rested the cases of other great cities which in recent years have had their boundaries extended under similar circumstances. I call on the House further to stand by the finding of its own Committee. This Bill has been adopted by a Committee, and while on this point I may say that nothing new came out before that Committee during the long dreary days of evidence. I do not think that the opponents of this Bill will be able to adduce one single new argument against it from the evidence given before the Committee. They had all their arguments and objections ready at the time of the Second Reading. I submit, if that be true, that their effort to destroy this Bill should have been made on the Second Reading. They allowed the Second Reading to go without Debate. The Bill then went before the Committee, and after the expenditure of thousands and thousands and thousands of pounds on behalf of all the people concerned, they come down here at this stage, after the Committee, and urge objections which were just as well known and just as apparent to them at the time of the Second Reading and before· any expense was incurred.

Mr. WILLIAM JOHNSTON (Belfast, S.): I wish to say why the Bill was not opposed on the Second Reading.

Mr. JOHN REDMOND: It is not worth while to interrupt now, as I am finishing, but one reason undoubtedly was, that none of the hon. Gentlemen now opposed to the Bill were present.

Mr. WILLIAM JOHNSTON: I was present.

Mr. JOHN REDMOND: Well, although the hon. Member is a host in himself, he is not sufficient to make a successful effort to defeat this Bill. Under these circumstances I sincerely trust the House will take a broad-minded and impartial view of this matter, and will pass the Bill by a large majority.

Motion made and Question proposed—
"That the Bill be now considered."—(*Mr. John Redmond.*)

Mr. CARSON (Dublin University): I think the last statement of the hon. and learned Member is one that is worthy of some observation. He asked what would appear to be a very pertinent question, viz., why, if we oppose this Bill now, we did not oppose it on the Second Reading. I think the question admits of a very simple answer. When I tell the House that this is a Bill for the extension of the boundaries of the City of Dublin, which now consists of about 3,800 acres, and that it is proposed by the Bill to add something like 18,000 acres, it will see that it was impossible for us who were interested in many parts of this Bill to know what case would be made before the Committee as to why certain portions of that 18,000 acres comprising nearly the whole of the County of Dublin were required. If we who are interested in the development of the townships were to oppose the Bill on the Second Reading we would be told that we were only dealing with 6,000 acres out of 18,000 acres, and we would be asked why should not the. Committee consider what portion of the remaining 12,000 acres ought to be added to the city, so that any opposition on our part would have been premature. Now that the Bill comes before the House, having passed the Committee, and having included the townships—which was our main objection—and when we know that the promoters of the Bill would accept no compromise which did not include the townships, then I say we are justified in asking the House to reject the Bill at this stage. It has been said that the Committee—which was a Committee of four—passed the Bill. That, in a sense, is true ; but I think the House ought to know that a Bill of such vital importance to the City and County of Dublin only passed by the casting vote of the Chairman, the Chairman under the circumstances voting twice. The Committee were evenly divided, and the preamble of the Bill was only passed by the casting vote of the Chairman. If one of the other Members who differed from him had been in the chair, the result would have been directly opposite. Therefore it is not exactly accurate to insist, as is often done, that the Bill has the entire sanction of the Committee at its back. The Bill proposes to add to the City of Dublin five separate townships in the suburbs of Dublin, which contain in all over 6,000 acres and have a population of between 70,000 and 80,000 people. Taking the extreme distance from one part to the other, it would be something like eight to ten miles, so that the House

will see that the interests of the outlying suburbs, separated as they are by
such a distance from north to south, have
absolutely nothing in common whatever.
Up to this they have had their separate
governments. In relation to these five
townships this Bill proposes to abolish
the five existing Corporations which have
been set up by Acts of Parliament—one
of them under an Act passed as far back
as 1847, which has been extended by a
number of succeeding Acts. That township contains about 32,000 inhabitants.
Pembroke Corporation has been in existence as a separate Corporation since
1863, and the remaining three have been
in existence since 1869, 1878, and 1867
respectively, the whole containing about
18,000 acres. It is a strong thing to say
that they should be abolished, but it is
especially strong—and here I differ entirely
from the hon. Gentleman who has just
addressed the House—to ask us to abolish
these Corporations when each and every
one of them objects to be annexed to the
City of Dublin. We are told that
all through England and Scotland it has
been the practice for great cities to take
in the areas adjoining them, but I doubt
whether a single case can be pointed out
where the inhabitants of the district
objected. The great cities always managed
to get on good terms with the suburbs.
Over and over again this House has
rejected proposals to annex outlying
municipalities when those municipal
bodies objected to be annexed. The
strongest case is Glasgow, where one
suburb was kept out for a long time,
although Glasgow is one of the best
governed cities of the day. The extraordinary part of the matter now before
the House is this, that of the five townships proposed to be annexed, each of
them appeared before the Committee and
objected. And when we are told by the
hon. and learned Member that he believes
the majority of the electors in these
townships are really in favour of this
annexation, I think it is a very strong
thing for him to say, for this reason—that
since the Dublin Corporation announced
that they were going to promote this
Bill we have had elections in the various
townships under the Local Government
Act passed a year ago, and the main
plank in the platform was annexation
or non-annexation to Dublin, and not one
of these townships is in favour of it
as at present governed. The Lord Mayor

Mr. *Carson.*

of Dublin offered himself as a candidate,
and he was rejected, and under the extended franchise set up by the Act of last
year all the old former Commissioners
were re-elected to the urban districts,
every one of them being absolutely
pledged to oppose this annexation. The
hon. and learned Gentleman tells us that a
large petition has been signed saying the
opposition has been withdrawn ; but it was
only sent down yesterday, it has been
largely signed by illiterates, and there is
no way of testing the signatures. The
Corporation of the Pembroke township
had the matter before it, and passed a
resolution that it would still oppose this
annexation. May I remind the House
that we are now discussing this question,
although only last year we confirmed, by
Act of Parliament, those public bodies,
and we are now asked, in this legislation
by a Private Bill, to put an end to these
municipal bodies, which have only been,
under the franchise of the Local Government Act, in existence a few months, and
throw the whole government of the City
of Dublin into a state of anarchy and
confusion. I may be asked why these
townships objected to be annexed by the
City of Dublin ; they did so because these
townships have grown up and flourished
and become prosperous under the excellent government to which they have
been subject from the first period of their
existence, and they now compare favourably with any great cities of the Empire.
Under these circumstances it is not
unnatural, and it is not surprising,
that the people who represent these
townships should ask to be left to govern
themselves. Take the case of Rathmines, where, at the present moment,
they have 21 representatives whose sole
business is to attend to the government of
Rathmines. Under this Bill they will
have eight members in a house of 90
members, who will not have to confine
their attention to the business of the particular township, but to the whole of the
city to which I have called attention.
Another thing is that in municipal affairs
each community desires to govern itself.
My hon. friend says that is a Home Rule
policy ; I should like to hear his sentiments as to putting an end to it. This
looks like an anti-Home Rule policy. But
the whole tendency of the people has
been, so far from extending areas, that
they should have a local government
conversant with their own local needs,

which can be looked after without their being complicated with other questions. I am not going into the political aspect of this case ; I have not the least intention of so doing, although a great deal might be said upon it. We have enough to do without touching that aspect at all. I should like to ask the House upon what is founded the claim of the Dublin Corporation to annex these townships, and I put the further question, and I ask those who support this Bill to mention a single advantage which will accrue to these various townships from this annexation by the City of Dublin. Viewing the whole of the evidence, all I can say is that they have not put forward one single advantage which would be gained by the townships being annexed to the City of Dublin. I know that in dealing with these questions the main ground put forward is that the portions to be annexed have been badly governed, but does anybody suggest that here ? I do not want to say anything against the Dublin Corporation, but I may make this comparison, that all these townships have been governed as well as Dublin, and in respect of many things they have been governed better. No justification for annexing them was given before the Committee, and Mr. Pember said this :

" Now, I say at once, we do not ask to bring in such places as Rathmines and Pembroke on account of their misgovernment, or on account of any special danger to Dublin therefrom ; that is not, in my judgment, the only or by any means the main reason for annexations of this kind. I quite admit that when you have misgovernment and consequent danger to the parent community it is a very great aggravation of the reasons for which you should bring them in, but the real theoretical reasons, the reasons of principle, remain beside, behind, and beyond all that."

Further on, on the same page, Mr. Pember says :

"I rely on what is now, I venture to say, a matter of well established principle, and that is that contiguous populations which have grown and spread from a common urban centre ought to be united for the purpose of municipal government."

(Cheers.) Yes, but where does he produce his instances in favour of that ? The only instances in which it has been done against the will of the municipality have been cases where there were charges of misgovernment. That is the strength of my case. Where a community is well governed and flourishing and prosperous, no advantage can be gained, and naturally they object to it. That is an overwhelming argument against it. Now gaining no advantage, what are the disadvantages ? They will have a great liability put upon them by the City of Dublin which it has previously incurred, their rates being far below the rates of that city. The first proposal in the Bill is that the property should be revalued, and the hon. and learned Member says that when it is revalued the valuation will be increased, and that means that the rates of the townships will go up, and with regard to the preferential rates for ten years the statement is beautifully misleading, because they will go and borrow money, and that money will have to be repaid, and the money with which to repay the loans will have to go upon the rates. What is the debt of the City of Dublin ? Very nearly two millions. And what is the debt of the whole of the five townships put together ? About £490,000.

An Hon. Member : What is the population ?

Mr. CARSON : About 80,000, and you are asked to put upon these townships a share of the £1,899,905 debt which has been incurred by the Corporation. One of these townships has power to borrow many thousands, which it has never been found necessary to exercise at all. If the Corporation take it over they can immediately exercise it, not for the benefit of the township for which it was given by Act of Parliament, but for the benefit of other parts of Dublin. Then there is another disadvantage. You have five townships with separate officers to look after the interests of the people—surveyors, inspectors, and various officers of the kind. All these people are to be dismissed the moment those five townships are abolished. It is said that they will get compensation under the Bill. They get some kind of compensation under the Bill, which will have to be borne by the townships just as well as by the city ; and then you will have the salaries of all the new officers, who will be elected by the Dublin Corporation in their own peculiar way, thrown just as much upon the townships as upon the city. Lastly, you will have these people, who have always objected to being made political bodies, made part of one of the strongest political institutions which exist in Ireland, namely, the Corporation of the City of Dublin. I do submit to the House that upon these grounds we have shown an overwhelming case why this Bill should not be allowed to pass this House, and why these townships should not be interfered with. Just let me say a word or two as regards the townships under the present system. In Rathmines, which was incorporated in 1847—and I would like to point out that those incorporations were passed without any protest whatever from the City of Dublin—the population at the time of incorporation was 9,640 ; at the present moment it is 32,000. In 1847 the rateable value was £40,000 ; at the present moment it is £140,000. Now, Sir, Rathmines, in every single particular, is absolutely independent of the Corporation of Dublin. The authorities gain nothing from them ; they ask nothing from them. They have no working arrangements with them of any kind ; and they are absolutely independent in every particular. Their water supply has been provided at a cost of £200,000, and they have spent considerable sums in obtaining the electric light. All these undertakings are proposed to be taken over by the Corporation, and instead, as I said before, of having these matters attended to by their own local representatives, all they will have will be a representation of eight out of 90 members, who will constitute the Corporation of Dublin under the new Bill. Passing to Pembroke, I find that it was incorporated in 1863. It then had a population of 13,000 ; it has now a population of 25,000. In 1863 the rateable valuation was £58,000 ; it is now £111,000. Since Pembroke was incorporated a township something like £1,000,000 has been spent on houses and on the improvement of the township, besides a large amount in electric lighting. The hon. and learned Member who moves that this Bill be considered spoke of the want of drainage in some of these townships. I think it is somewhat audacious of anybody speaking on behalf of the Dublin Corporation to mention in this House the drainage of any other Corporation. If there is one matter more than another which is an absolute disgrace to the Corporation of Dublin, it is the manner in which they have neglected the drainage of the city. Let me tell you something of the history of the drainage of the City of Dublin, and particularly in relation to Pembroke and

Mr. Carson.

Rathmines. As far back as 1871 a Committee sat with reference to the drainage of Dublin and the surrounding townships. In 1871 the Dublin Corporation were authorised to make a system of main drainage, not merely for Dublin but for the surrounding townships. What did they do ? Nothing. Pembroke and Rathmines, having waited for some years to see if anything would be done, came to this House and got a Bill to carry out their own main drainage at considerable expense. They spent upon main drainage something like £100,000, and those are two of the townships which you are now asked to annex. They have repaid by means of a sinking fund something like £14,000 or £15,000, and there has been no complaint of the drainage of Pembroke or Rathmines, while the drainage system of Dublin has stood where it was, and is only now being carried out after a lapse of some 28 years. And, Pembroke and Rathmines having got this system of drainage at enormous expense, you are now asked, by one provision of this Bill, to dissolve their Drainage Board and to permit the Corporation of the City of Dublin to take over this system of drainage which deals only with those two townships, and which has been erected for their own benefit. The Board, which has worked well since 1877, is also to be dissolved, and no doubt these townships will be asked to contribute, by the exercise of borrowing powers, to the drainage of the City of Dublin, which has been so long neglected. When the hon. and learned Member put forward this question of drainage I think it would have been well if he could have shown that the Dublin Corporation had put their own house in order before they came to say anything with regard to the drainage of these townships. The case of Clontarf is another case where the rateable value has increased enormously since they got their Bill of 1869. It has very nearly doubled, and the population has nearly trebled. As I said before, the fiercely contested question on the recent elections was, not whether the candidates were Unionist or Nationalist, but whether they were in favour of annexation or not. A candidate who came forward merely as a Unionist or Nationalist had not the least chance of getting on the Board. Therefore you have the position of all the townships objecting to this Bill, and all of them more or less increasing in their prosperity under the system of government which they have already. Why, then, should this Bill be passed? There can be no doubt that it would be for the benefit of the City of Dublin, but that is not sufficient for this House. Why should one corporation swamp five or six other corporations principally for the benefit of the one corporation? It is unprecedented to attempt any such task. But, after all, what has been, and what is, the tendency of legislation in this House? You have set up in England county councils, district councils, and parish councils, so that each locality may have the intelligence of its own representatives to see to the wants of that particular locality. Sir, that is exactly what you are asked to abolish in the present case. You are at the present moment, in relation to London, asked to set up municipalities in place of vestries. What is that except setting up the very townships that you are asked here by this Bill to destroy in Ireland? I submit that no case has been made out for annexation, and no case of advantage to the townships that you are asked to put an end to. Under these circumstances, I earnestly hope that the House will say that this is a matter that requires the very gravest consideration. I know that many Members are led away—and naturally and properly led away—by the fact that after this Bill has passed its Second Reading a Select Committee hears evidence. As I said before, this case is a very exceptional one in consequence of the great divergence of views of that Committee, and under those circumstances I hope the House will reject the Bill. I have only to say that my hon. friend the Member for South Dublin, who, at considerable inconvenience to himself, by reason of an accident which we all so much deplore, came down to the House yesterday when the Bill was down on the Paper—because his constituency, which is partly composed of Rathmines, is very much interested in this Bill—had undertaken to second my motion to reject the Bill; and I am sure the House will greatly regret to hear from the telegram I have just received from him, that he has met with another serious accident, and is unable to attend.

Amendment proposed—

"To leave out the word 'now,' and at the end of the Question to add the words 'upon this day three months.'"—(*Mr. Carson.*)

Question proposed—

"That the word 'now' stand part of the Question."

*MR. JOHNSON-FERGUSON (Leicester, Loughborough): As Chairman of the Committee that had this Bill before it, the responsibility rested on me of giving the casting vote which decided whether the preamble of the Bill should or should not be passed by the Committee, and I had better at once state the reasons which led me to take so responsible a step. The hon. Member who moved the consideration of this Bill reminded the House that nothing has been done in the way of extending the boundary of the City of Dublin since it was fixed in 1840. Prior to that time the portions of what are now the townships of Clontarf in the north and Pembroke in the south were included within the city boundary; but in 1840 these two districts were cut out of the city. Since that time the population of the city has very largely spread into the surrounding districts, and the five townships, or urban districts as we should know them in England, governed by councillors, have since been formed. On the north there are the townships of Clontarf and Drumcondra; on the west, New Kilmainham; and on the south, Rathmines and Rathgar, and Pembroke. At two points only the County of Dublin comes up to the boundary of the present City of Dublin, and the hon. Member for Dublin University seemed to forget that, except at these two very small points, these five townships practically cut off the county district which it was proposed to annex. It would be practically impossible for the Committee or this House to entertain the idea of annexing any portion of the county district to the city without at the same time including the townships within its boundary. In addition to that, these townships have been frequently spoken of as municipal bodies, but they are nothing of the sort. They are nothing more than urban districts as we know them in England, and under the Local Government Act of last year, their governing bodies have simply become urban district councils. What this Bill, in the form in which it passed its Second Reading, proposed to do was to extend the boundary of the City of Dublin so as to include, in the first place, these five townships, having an area of 6,100 acres, and a population in 1891 of

71,000, but now about 85,000. Then you have the county area, amounting to 7,500 acres, with a population in 1891 of 12,800, now about 14,000. Then there is what is known as "slob-land," extending to about 5,000 acres, being practically the estuary of the River Liffey, the whole of which is covered with water at high tide, and consists merely of sand-banks or mud-banks when the tide is out, and on which there is no population whatever. The Committee decided in the first place to strike out of the Bill that slob-land. That being under the control of the Port and Harbour Board, on which the Corporation of Dublin has a very large representation, the Committee considered it would be exceedingly undesirable to have two possibly conflicting authorities exercising control over land upon the proper management of which so largely depends the maintenance of the navigable channel of the River Liffey up to Dublin itself. They also struck out 6,000 acres of the area of the county which had been proposed to be annexed, because it was evident to the Committee that so far the population of the city of Dublin has not to any material extent spread on to those 6,000 acres. In the Bill in its present form it is proposed to add to the city the five townships and about 1,500 acres of land from the county lying between the townships of Drumcondra and New Kilmainham in the north, and New Kilmainham and Rathmines in the south. The population of these townships and the population of the county area which we propose should be annexed is practically the overflow of the City of Dublin. With the exception of the township of Kilmainham, the whole of the district we propose to annex is a residential district in which the well-to-do inhabitants of the City of Dublin come out to reside. Kilmainham, on the other hand, is mainly occupied with the works of the Great Southern and Western Railway, with a population of 7,000 persons engaged, more or less directly, with those works, while a very large proportion of the men engaged in these works live inside the City of Dublin, and go out in the morning to the works, returning to the city at night. In the second place, the township of Pembroke, though outside the boundary of the municipal City of Dublin, is inside the boundary of the Parliamentary City of Dublin. In the

third place, the whole of the area is at the present time subject to the same bridge tax as is the City of Dublin itself; and with the exception of Clontarf and about one half—the northern half—of the township of Drumcondra, it is under the control, and pays the rate towards the maintenance of the Metropolitan Police. With the exception of Rathmines, which has a separate water supply of its own, the whole of these districts derive their water supply from the City of Dublin. With the exception of Rathmines and Pembroke—which have a separate drainage scheme, which the hon. Member for Dublin University has alluded to, but to which I cannot give so high a character as he seems to do—the whole drainage of these districts, where it exists, flows in its crude state, either into the Liffey or on to the slob-lands. So far as New Kilmainham and the area of the county are concerned, it was clearly proved to the Committee that no scheme of main drainage could be introduced for those districts except in co-operation with the main drainage system of the City of Dublin; and so far as Clontarf and Drumcondra are concerned, it would be a much more costly undertaking to construct a separate main drainage scheme for them which, after filtering the sewage, would discharge a clear effluent into the sea, than it would be for them to join the main drainage system of the City of Dublin, which is now being constructed. The whole of these districts derive their supply of gas from works inside the City of Dublin. Then, I must differ from the hon. Member for Dublin University with respect to the indebtedness of the City of Dublin. According to the figures which were laid before the Committee, and which were never disputed, the indebtedness of the City of Dublin at the present moment is £1,562,000, of which about £720,000 was expended in the construction of the waterworks—a highly remunerative undertaking, the whole of which will be paid off within the next 45 years. In addition to that, the City of Dublin has an income derived from other sources than that of rates, of something like £80,000, of which £30,000 is derived from the rents of the Corporation property, an item which is rapidly increasing in value, and which was stated in evidence would in the course of three years, owing to the falling in of leases, yield to the city a clear annual rental of £37,000 a year. £30,000 of this income is derived from the sale of water by the Corporation for manufacturing purposes, £10,000 is derived from an annual payment from the Tramway Company in the City of Dublin for the use of the streets, while there is £10,000 derived from other sources. Lastly, I should like Members who sit for constituencies in England or Scotland— who are not familiar (as I myself was not) with the methods of valuation in Dublin— clearly to understand that the system with respect to valuation pursued in Ireland seems to be totally different from the system in this country. There seems to be no power of raising the valuation— in fact, it was given in evidence before the Committee that there is no power of raising the valuation of a property after it has once been valued, except a general valuation is taking place, or unless some important structural alteration is made in it. So that in the case of an old city, such as that of Dublin, while the valuation may fall if the property depreciates in value, it cannot be raised where the property increases in value. I took the responsibility of sending over to Dublin for Mr. Barton, Commissioner of Valuations, in Dublin Castle, and he gave it in evidence before the Committee that if a re-valuation takes place, as provided for in this Bill, the valuation of the City of Dublin itself would be raised by from 20 to 25 per cent., while that of the townships would be raised by from 10 to 15 per cent. Now, Sir, I also notice that the hon. Member for Dublin University stated that it was entirely contrary to the custom of this House to extend the boundary of cities in opposition to the wishes of the districts to be annexed. I entirely differ from him. I fully admit that some twenty years ago that was the custom of this House, but it certainly has not been the custom of the Committees upstairs for the last ten or fifteen years. In the case of Leamington, when it applied for powers to absorb the urban districts of Milverton and Lillington, that was contested before an Inquiry instituted by the Local Government Board, it was contested upon the Provisional Order upstairs, and I believe the contest was carried on even to the House of Lords. Southampton in precisely the same way, in the face of strenuous opposition, absorbed Shirley and Freemantle. In 1891 Cheltenham ab-

sorbed Charlton Kings and Leckhampton. There again it was fought with the utmost determination. In 1897 Plymouth absorbed Compton Giffard and some other urban districts surrounding it, while in the same year Bristol, having been defeated in 1895 in its efforts to extend its boundaries, got its Bill through Parliament, absorbing Stapleton and Horfield, with a population of between 70,000 and 80,000, although the Bill was fought right up to the House of Lords. In 1898 Devonport had a Bill granted it which included within it St. Budeaux and Penny Cross. We have had a very good example in this House within the last few weeks. Have we not in this House been engaged recently constituting a City of Westminster? Have hon. Members entirely forgotten the opposition to the Bill which was made by the Strand to its absorption inside the City of Greater Westminster. I hold here a circular—which was probably sent to every Member of this House—containing a list of twelve resolutions passed by different bodies within the last few months inside the Borough of the Strand, protesting against being included in the City of Greater Westminster, and in every case the objections urged against their absorption—and which were ignored by the House—were precisely the same objections as those which are now being urged by these townships against being included in this City of Greater Dublin, namely, the destruction of their self-government and the probability of their rates being materially enhanced. In every case where the House has to deal with these questions—or where a Committee upstairs has to deal with instances of this kind —what the Committee has had to decide is—are the circumstances of the case and are the arguments brought forward in support of the case sufficiently strong to justify them in overriding the opposition of the districts which it is proposed to annex. I certainly will not trouble the House with attempting to go through the evidence of the 71 witnesses, but there is the evidence of two gentlemen who came forward in support of this Bill, to which I wish to call the attention of the House, because these two gentlemen occupied exceptional positions. They cannot be considered in any way *ex parte* witnesses, and from the position which they occupy now—or have occupied in the past—they have had exceptional means of knowing what the circumstances of this particular case are. The first gentleman is Sir Francis MacCabe, who from 1878 to 1888 was the Inspector of the Dublin District under the Local Government Board of Ireland; and from 1888 to 1898 he was the Medical Commissioner of the Local Government Board of Ireland. I may summarise the evidence which he gave before us thus: that the Sanitary Staff of Dublin is one of the most efficient in the United Kingdom: that the maintenance of separate sanitary staffs for the five separate townships was both extravagant and inefficient, and that three out of the five townships had not even adopted the Notification of Infectious Diseases Act; and, lastly, he had no hesitation in saying that it is impossible for the sanitary condition, and therefore the health, of Greater Dublin to be made what it ought to be unless the whole district is merged in one city, and under the supervision of the Medical Officer of Health of Dublin, so as to have one uniform sanitary authority over the whole of that city. The other gentleman to whose evidence I wish to draw the attention of the House, is that of my hon. friend the Member for Tyrone, the Secretary to the Local Government Board of this country. I would summarise his evidence in these words. The reasons he urged for the extension of this boundary are (1) that the interest of the city and townships are common interests ; (2) that the present position under which the rich go out of the city and leave the poor to bear the burdens is essentially unjust to the City of Dublin; (3) that the rate of mortality is a scandal; (4) that the disposal of the sewage of the townships is a scandal ; and, lastly, that the maintaining of five or six different sanitary staffs leads to inefficient and extravagant expenditure. I wish to quote one or two extracts from his evidence, so that the House may hear the opinion of the hon. Member in his own words. He says :

" I do not know of a single interest that is not a common interest between the City of Dublin and these townships. That is the first reason why I am in favour of this amalgamation."

Then he was asked :

" I suppose this population to which you refer coming into the city in the morning and

going out of it again at night is a large population, and has increased during your own recollection since you have been resident?"

And he replied :

" Yes, decidedly ; very largely increased. That is my second reason for favouring the principle of annexation. I think that the present position of affairs is essentially unjust to the City of Dublin. The tendency for 30 years has been for the rich and the well-to-do classes to leave the city and to migrate to the townships. I do not complain of it. It was absolutely necessary that they should do so ; but the fact is as I have said, and it tells heavily against the interests of the city."

And then he goes on to describe what has taken place, and after giving an instance, he finishes with these words :

" I attribute it almost entirely to the fact that the poor have been left simply to stew in their own juice, and the rich and well-to-do have gone where forsooth they have lower rates, and these people are left to take care of themselves as best they can. It is deplorable "

Then he is asked this question :

" I suppose this part left behind contains almost all the poor ? "

And he answered :

" In the north side of the city that is almost so."

Then he is asked :

" Those are the artisans who work in Dublin and round about, I take it ? "

To which he replies :

" Yes ; and what is true of the Poor Law is true of other improvements in regard to the city, because the city is depleted of this class of people and of the resources and aid that they would bring to the city. Works of great improvement which ought to be carried out in Dublin cannot be undertaken because the rates are at a point where it is almost dangerous that they should be increased. To collect them would defeat their own ends. In the third place, I am quite convinced that the best interests of both the townships and the city are involved in the settlement of this question. I will take the case of the public health of Dublin. The public health of Dublin is at a very low ebb. I know that a great many people try to make it better than it is, but I have been behind the scenes, and I have proved this for myself, and I apply to the City of Dublin the same tests that I would apply to an English city of the Local Government Board. Typhoid is almost permanently resident in our midst. I affirm that. The infantile mortality of Dublin is a scandal. I know of no city in the United Kingdom where the infantile mortality is as high as in the City of Dublin, and if the Committee ask why that should be so my answer is plain. Take the main drainage of Dublin. '

He goes on to say—

"The reason why the main drainage of Dublin was not taken over 25 or 30 years ago has been absolutely the lack of money. It is for no other reason. The Dublin Corporation, I feel perfectly free to say, is not an ideal corporation from my standpoint, but I am firmly convinced that the Dublin Corporation would have tackled a scheme of main drainage 25 years ago but for the enormous cost involved in it and the poverty of the people in the main who are the ratepayers of Dublin. Now, if we have typhoid resident amongst us, and if this infantile mortality is, as I said, a scandal, and such as is to be found nowhere else, it is almost entirely due to two causes—the lack of main drainage and the very imperfect system of house drainage that we have. But these things I represent are due to want of funds, and the want of funds is largely due to the fact that the well-to-do have gone from our midst and left us to get on as best we may."

There is only one other extract which I will read. The hon. Member said :—

"If I were asked what the townships would gain by being annexed to the City of Dublin, I should state that I think they are in reality citizens of Dublin in everything but the duties of citizenship. That is my first answer. I say that they spend their day in Dublin ; they make their fortunes in Dublin ; they use the streets of Dublin ; they use all the institutions of Dublin ; and then they leave all these things to be kept up by people much poorer than themselves. I say that is a state of things which ought not to exist ; and instead of the townships asking what they are to get, I ask the question, What do they owe to the city where they make their fortunes, and which they use every day of their lives ? I say in everything but the upkeep of Dublin they are citizens."

I will not trouble the House with any further quotations from the evidence of my hon. friend. I do say this, that in the face of such evidence as that it requires the very strongest arguments on the part of the opponents of the Bill and the very strongest evidence to show that the evidence of my hon. friend and Sir Francis MacCabe is not to be relied on by the Committee. Now, let us see what the evidence of the opponents of the Bill was. I say that the opposition to it was mainly a rating opposition. Time after time I put this question to representative witnesses when they came before us, "Is it not in the main owing to the fear of increased rates that you are objecting ?" And the answer was almost in every case, "Yes, in the main it is." Now, how far is the evidence of my hon. friend borne out by witnesses on the opposition side ? Take the case of

Kilmainham. A Mr. Michael Flood, who came forward as a witness on behalf of the Urban Council of Kilmainham, stated that the township was in debt to the treasurer ; that where there was any drainage at all it was in a very bad state, and the drains go into the Liffey ; that the Notification of Diseases Act has not been adopted ; and that, though they make no payment whatever to the City of Dublin towards the hospitals, they send all their patients there when they have to be sent to a hospital at all. For Drumcondra Mr. H. Lindsay came forward, and his evidence was that the financial position of that township was very bad, and that the Government auditors' remarks were unfavourable to the township management. Mr. Petit, clerk to the Urban District Council, in cross-examination, said that the township was not provided with any sanitary appliance or oversight ; while Mr. J. Buckley, C.E., surveyor to the township, said that though they had a certain kind of filtration scheme, over 686 loads of sludge from tanks was allowed to accumulate for 12 months in the very centre of most thickly populated parts of the townships and no attempt had been made to clear it away, though repeated complaints had been made to the sanitary authorities. This is a question of rates. I see it is stated as an argument against the Bill, in a circular by one of the townships, that the rates of that township were only 3s. 6d., while those of the City of Dublin were 9s. 4d. That is incorrect, for it compares the whole rates of the city with the municipal and sanitary rates of the township. The position is this, that in the city the municipal rate is 6s. 4d. while in the townships it varies from 3s. 6d. to 4s. 10d. in the £, or an average of 4s. 6d. Allowing for the fact that under the re-valuation which will take place the valuation of the city will be raised 20 per cent., and the valuation of the townships 10 per cent., that would correspond to a rate of 5s. 2½d. for the city against 4s. 1d. in the townships, or a difference of about 1s. in the £1. Well, as the hon. Member for the City of Dublin has reminded the House, the Committee tried to deal with that by providing that in the case of the townships of Rathmines and Pembroke the rate should not exceed the present rate for a period of ten years, because we considered that, having constructed a main drainage system, though not by any means a perfect one, still they deserved more favourable treatment than the other townships; and that in the case of the other townships and the two county areas which are to be included with them the rate is not to exceed the present rate for a period of five years. Another objection which was taken to the inclusion was that under the scheme of the Bill the representation which was proposed to be given them was totally inadequate. We met that by dividing this area, after very great trouble, into seven wards, giving to each of these wards the same representation as the city wards—three councillors and one alderman to the ward —thus giving to the added area an aggregate representation of 28, as against 60 for the fifteen wards of the city. I venture to think that by that representation and by the method in which we dealt with the rating of the added area, we entirely met everything which may be considered a real grievance on the part of the opposing parties. When I look to the fact that the evidence of Sir Francis McCabe and my hon. friend the Member for Tyrone was of such a serious nature as I have read to the House, and seeing that during the whole of that inquiry the accuracy of my hon. friend's statements was never challenged, and that the facts which he brought before us were never in the slightest degree disproved, I venture to think that I had no other course open to me than to give my casting vote for the Bill.

*MR. FISON (York W. R., Doncaster): I was one of the Members of the Committee upstairs which for a long period heard witnesses and arguments on this case, and therefore desire briefly to address the House. I should like to say, in the first instance, that at the beginning of the inquiry, if I had any bias at all, it was a sentimental one in favour of allowing the City of Dublin to have a larger and more prosperous area. But after sitting on the Committee for 17 days, and hearing all the evidence, I came to the conclusion that the proposals of the promoters of the Bill were not really conducive to the good government of the district. The bias of my mind was changed by the evidence and arguments brought before us. We heard some ten thousand questions put and answered, and certainly I think it would be unfair

Mr. Johnson-Ferguson.

if I were not to say how much the Committee were indebted to the members of the Irish Bar on both sides for the great assistance they gave us. I do not wish to go over again the ground so ably traversed by the hon. and learned Member for Dublin University; but I would remind the House that this is a Bill for the inclusion of five townships and a large portion of the County of Dublin in the new area of the City of Dublin. Perhaps the strongest reason given for the proposal was that the City of Dublin is at present congested, that the City is unhealthy through that congested population, and that the population want more room. One eminent witness informed us that Dublin would not be a healthy place until 50,000 of the population had gone out of the present area. That, I think, is an exaggeration; but what I want to point out to the House is that the whole tendency of the promoters of this Bill was not to go in for a wider area of the county, but to go for the populous and wealthy areas of the townships. That will not be contradicted by anyone who followed the evidence. If you were to take Rathmines and Pembroke from the scope of the Bill, I believe the Corporation of Dublin would be scarcely inclined to go on with it. I do not think the House can put the opposition to the incorporation of the townships on the local authorities alone; for the inhabitants themselves are opposed to it. It is quite true, as an hon. Member opposite said, that a plebiscite was not taken, but that applies to both sides.

AN HON. MEMBER: There was one in the city.

*MR. FISON: On the other hand, there were no petitions in its favour. There was brought before the Committee on a late day a simple telegram from one of the smaller townships, saying that there was a feeling there in favour of the Bill. But I would call the attention of the House to the local elections which took place in January, in which annexation to the city was made a test question. These elections were held on a much more popular basis than was previously the case in Ireland. The electorate of Rathmines increased in January from 1,800 to 6,000. In every case the representatives carried at these elections in all the local bodies, irrespective of political party issues, were men pledged to resist this Bill. No evidence was submitted to us that there was even a substantial minority which was in favour of the Bill, and I do not think any better test than that could be given of the wishes of the inhabitants. It appears to me that the two largest townships—Rathmines and Pembroke—are really the key of the situation. Rathmines has a population of 32,000, and Pembroke of 25,000. There are 211 boroughs in England and Wales, of which 20 return Members to this House which have a less population than Rathmines; and 195 boroughs in England and Wales which have a less population than Pembroke. It is quite true that Pembroke and Rathmines are not municipal areas; but why draw a distinction between urban district councils—which you have only recently created—and municipal areas? These areas have governed themselves well in the past. I would ask the House to compare the way in which the City of Dublin has done its work with the way in which these townships have done their work. Rathmines has an independent water supply, and in 1893 the City of Dublin had to come to Rathmines to ask that township to help the city with its water supply. As to drainage, the story has been told how, in 1871, the Corporation obtained a Bill along with the townships for drainage purposes, how the Corporation refused to carry the scheme out, how Rathmines and Pembroke allowed their scheme to hang up for twelve months to permit of the Corporation coming in, and how the Corporation have even yet done nothing except to start their drainage scheme. I cannot agree entirely with what the hon. Member for Loughborough has said as to the excellence of that drainage scheme; but I think that the evidence showed that the joint drainage scheme of Rathmines and Pembroke is an excellent one. We are asked to deal, therefore, with two townships—one of which has been in existence for half a century and the other for 36 years—and both of which have managed their own affairs better than the City of Dublin. It would, I contend, be a very strong step to annex them to the City of Dublin against their wishes. We are told that differential rating would meet the case; but differential rating would be only a temporary remedy, and it would give opportunities to the City of Dublin to raise money, which all would eventually have to pay off. In regard to representation, it is true that this Bill gives a larger representation to the townships than formerly. There are 15 wards in the City of Dublin, with a representation of three councillors and an alderman, which gives 60 for the city; and it is proposed to add seven wards with an alderman and three councillors for each, or an aggregate of 28. I want to put it to the House if a town council of 60 has not managed its affairs as well as it ought to have done, how a council of 88 is to manage better. We are told that there are no precedents for the course we are taking, but I venture to say that there are no precedents whatever for including five townships in a city extension area when these townships were unanimously against it. There may no doubt have been precedents where the House has over-ridden the objections of townships, but these have been cases of bargain-making, where the townships were wanting to come in, but did not think the terms fair. There are no precedents, however, where so many townships were annexed totally against their wishes.

Col. SAUNDERSON (Armagh, N.): The House has derived a very erroneous impression of the state of affairs relating to the annexation of these townships to the City of Dublin if dependence is placed on the speeches of the hon. Gentlemen the Members for Waterford and Loughborough. These hon. Members have informed the House that they believe the majority of the people in these townships are in favour of annexation, but if they will believe that they will believe anything. Only two days ago there were meetings in several of the townships to consider the scheme, and the voting against it was as 14 to 1. In Rathmines the opposition to the Bill is quite unanimous, and in Clontarf it is also unanimous; and how the hon. and learned Gentleman has come to the conclusion that the majority of the people in these townships are in favour of annexation is a thing I cannot possibly understand. The hon. and learned Gentleman spoke of the want of public spirit on the part of these townships in not supporting the Dublin hospitals, and from that the House might be led to believe that the Dublin Corporation had the supervision of a certain number of hospitals in Dublin. But they have not the supervision of any hospitals in the City of Dublin, though they may subscribe to some of them. What struck me as a strange act of ingratitude on the part of the hon. and learned Gentleman was that he forgot to mention that on the Estimates every year a sum of £15,850 is voted by the Government for the Dublin hospitals.

Mr. DILLON (Mayo, E.) : That is in accordance with the Union compact.

COLONEL SAUNDERSON : At any rate, that leads us to believe that the financial relations between the two countries is satisfactory. I hold that no just cause for passing this measure has been made out by the City of Dublin. My hon. friend the Member for Tyrone, South, appears to think that the better classes in Dublin were disappearing, whereas the poorer classes were crowding into the city.

Mr. T. W. RUSSELL : What I said was that the rich had gone to the suburbs, and had left the poor behind to take care of themselves.

COLONEL SAUNDERSON : That strikes me as pretty much what I had said. I did not say that the hon. Member had said that the better classes had disappeared from the face of the earth, but that they had disappeared from the City of Dublin. I find from the census of 1891 that the professional and commercial classes had, compared with 1881, increased in Dublin to the number of 3,000, whereas the industrial classes, who I suppose are the working classes, had decreased by 7,500. The number of dwellings in Dublin had increased by 1,800. So that you have a decreasing industrial population, an increasing professional and commercial population, and likewise an increase in the number of houses, and I want to know how is this tremendous congestion of population, of which so much has been made, taking place in the City of Dublin ? I cannot help thinking that that argument of my hon. friend has not much weight. Now, the objections of the townships to join with the Corporation of Dublin are to my mind very well founded. The hon. Member for Waterford drew a tremendous picture of the sewage which is discharged into the sea outside Clontarf, but I wonder, when he mentioned sewage at all, he did not say

Colonel Saunderson.

that the main sewer of Dublin has always been the river Liffey. The Corporation of Dublin had a Bill pass through this House 20 years ago to carry out an improved system of drainage ; but what have they done ? Practically nothing. I am aware that at the present moment they are engaged in carrying out some works, but when they will be finished Heaven only knows. What the Corporation of Dublin really wants is more money. They have come to the very edge of their legal borrowing powers, and the only way in which additional funds can be procured is to increase the area of taxation by the annexation of these townships. But there are other objections which the House will easily understand on the part of these townships to be amalgamated with the Corporation of Dublin. The House will recognise at once that I would be the last man to introduce political considerations in a case of this kind ; but the objections taken by the townships to be incorporated with the City of Dublin are undoubtedly affected to a considerable extent by political considerations. There is no doubt of that. I consider these townships were amply justified in investigating the manner in which the business of the Corporation is conducted. In this hum-drum country over here, when you are about to choose officers to carry on the business of a Corporation, the first question you ask is whether the candidate understands anything about the business or the conduct of municipal affairs, and if he shows that he does, probably the man will be appointed ; but it is not so in Dublin. Let me remind the House that how the business of a Corporation is carried on has a very great interest of a pecuniary nature to the ratepayers. When an office in Dublin is vacant the last thing which ever apparently strikes the Corporation is to ask whether the candidate is fit for the post, or whether he understands the business of a Corporation. One of the great points in the City of Dublin apparently is to find out whether the candidate has been in gaol or not. If he can show that he has "done twenty years' time," or that he has been in gaol, no further questions are asked as to his capacity for understanding or managing municipal affairs. At present they are rather short of such candidates in Dublin, because just now they have only two ticket-of-leave men in the employment of the Corporation. It is absolutely necessary that this objection of the townships to incorporation with Dublin should be known. As I have said, there are only two ticket-of-leave men serving the Corporation at present, but there were more. How are these gentlemen elected? The House will understand that it is no very little objection on the part of the law-abiding and loyal townships to join a Corporation which carries on its business after this fashion. I will not go over the whole list, but let me take a few. There is Mr. Henry Campbell, a man whose great ability is known in this House. It does not appear that he knew much about municipal affairs. The *Freeman's Journal* at that time stated that there was something of an experiment in the appointment, an experiment which, for the sake of the people of Dublin, it hoped would have a successful issue. I do not think that these experiments commend themselves to the people of the townships. Then there is another case, that of a man named O'Brien. He is, I believe, a ticket-of-leave man, and is at present in the employment of the Corporation, his qualification apparently being that he was in prison. Still, that is not the sort of recommendation that is likely to be approved in the townships, and I think the House of Commons would object to a public servant being employed on such a ground. There was also another ticket-of-leave man, since dead, in the employ of the Corporation. His qualification was that he fired at a policeman, and on that qualification he was immediately made inspector of weights and measures. According to the ideas which obtain in Pembroke and Rathmines, that is a questionable reputation, and one which, in their opinion, did not fit him to be a very high official in the Corporation of Dublin. Another man was elected to a position, although he was in America at the time. He was sentenced to prison for 20 years, and that was sufficient to qualify him for the appointment. He was made sword-bearer. I need not proceed any further, but I think the people of Pembroke and Rathmines do not look at such cases with approval. They are law-abiding men, and they deal with the business of the townships purely on business principles, and the result is that they are opposed to this Bill, and we find Nationalists and Roman Catholics joining with Protestants against it. That cannot be denied; at any rate it may be denied, but its accuracy cannot be disputed. The townships say, "We never had a helping hand from this Corporation; they have opposed efforts of ours, fortunately unsuccessfully; we have worked out our own prosperity, and we have made the townships a credit to Dublin and to Ireland." I believe those townships show what Irishmen can do when they leave these wretched political questions aside. The people of the townships reason further. They say, "We are loyal men; we are in favour of the continuance of the Union, and we do not see why, against our will, you should throw us into the arms of this municipal octopus, which desires to swallow up our prosperity." The Corporation refused before the world to pass a vote of thanks on the occasion of the Queen's Jubilee—an occasion which ought to modify even the political rancour of Irishmen. The townships say, "Here is a Corporation carried on on strictly political grounds; it chooses men on political grounds, and if this Bill passes there will be a tremendous field for appointments, as the 20th section practically disestablishes, although it does not absolutely disendow, all holders of office. There will be rejoicing among all ticket-of-leave men in the country, as the Corporation is a sort of Greenwich Hospital for Nationalist wrecks." I think the townships are justified in resisting a proposal to swallow them up in a Corporation carried on on purely political grounds. I read a speech made some time ago by the hon. Member for East Clare, when he was seeking election as Lord Mayor of Dublin. That speech, if the hon. Member will permit me to say so, was, I thought, eminently to his credit. He said he would refuse to stand for the position of Lord Mayor of Dublin, or to support Home Rule, if he did not believe and expect that the minority would receive fair play.

Mr. WILLIAM REDMOND (East Clare): If the hon. and gallant Gentleman will permit me, I will explain what I did say. There was no question of standing for the position of Lord Mayor. What I did say was that I felt perfectly certain that the Corporation would give fair play to the minority, and that as far as I was personally concerned I would not have anything to do with any transaction which did not give the fullest possible fair play to the minority.

COLONEL SAUNDERSON : I think that was eminently to the credit of the hon. Member. But the Corporation of Dublin did not make him Lord Mayor; they only made him an alderman. A man who held such views would never be made Lord Mayor of Dublin, and I do not see why these townships, which now conduct their business on a purely businesslike footing, should be handed over to this political organisation, which, to my mind, in the past has shown itself eminently unable, and possibly unwilling, to manage its own affairs in a businesslike way, and which, if it gets the management of these townships, will certainly treat them in the same manner. The hon. Member for Loughborough has quoted some cases where legislation of a similar kind was carried out in this country, but he did not give any cases in which it was refused. He might have mentioned Glasgow, in connection with which Partick and Govan successfully opposed annexation. No instance has been attempted to be produced before this House of any great township, such as Rathmines, Rathgar, or Clontarf, being forced against its wish to join such a Corporation as Dublin; and believing as I do that if this Bill is passed, instead of adding to the prosperity of these townships, it will have an opposite effect, and that it is unfair to hand these townships over to a municipality which has proved so untrustworthy in the past, I hope the House will reject the Bill.

MR. BARTLEY (Islington, N.): I do not think anyone will accuse me of taking Home Rule views or of sympathising with the views of hon. Gentlemen opposite, but I have always held that we should treat Irish questions as English questions are treated, and that is the backbone of our position. I would ask the House, in spite of what my hon. and gallant friend has said, if there were a similar case in England or Scotland, where a large municipality, particularly such an important one as Dublin, was asking, on grounds of sanitation, or public health, and other reasons of an important character, for an extension of boundaries, and if the Bill had passed Committee, would the House throw it out? We know perfectly well it would not do that in the case of an English

Mr. William Redmond.

city, and I therefore protest against doing it in the case of an Irish city, above all in the case of the capital of Ireland.

MR. WILLIAM MOORE (Antrim, N.): Unlike a great many other Members who have addressed the House, I can claim to be a burgess of the City of Dublin, and an inhabitant of the area which hon. Gentlemen opposite say will benefit by this Bill. But although that area will be benefited, the change would be unjust to the townships, and it is therefore my duty to support my hon. and learned friend the member for the University of Dublin in his opposition. I was an interested spectator of the proceedings in the room upstairs when the hon. Member for Loughborough was Chairman of the Committee, and I should like to take this opportunity of dissociating myself from some of the criticisms which have appeared in the Irish papers on his conduct as Chairman. Although I differ from him and his conclusions, I do say, not in any feeling of impertinence, that he made an admirable Chairman. At the same time, that does not permit me to regard the decision of the Committee as any more than a decision obtained by the casting vote of the Chairman, and under such circumstances it is open to this House freely and impartially to decide whether that casting vote was properly or improperly given. The Committee had not, and the Chairman had not—I venture to say so respectfully—the entire circumstances before them. As my hon. and gallant friend has stated, a very large amount of the opposition against this Bill on the part of the townships arises from political distrust of the Corporation of Dublin; and when it was intended to produce before the Committee evidence on that point, and when it was suggested that the Dublin Corporation was guilty of political misconduct, the Chairman said that the Committee had no power or right to go into political questions. That, I think, was right. The proceedings might be interminable if such an area were opened for debate, but that does not prevent this House from taking such matters into consideration, and it is the first time that the townships of Dublin have had an opportunity of stating before the House one of their main objections to the scheme. We are asked, under this Bill, to destroy an active municipal life. Whether the bodies which carry on those duties outside the metropolis of Ireland are called Urban District Councils or Corporations makes very little difference. The only difference is that in one case the officer is called a town councillor, and in the other a councillor, and I make the hon. Member for Loughborough a present of the distinction. We have five municipalities, all actively carrying on their work to the satisfaction of their own inhabitants, and we are asked to take from them that power and to subject them to the tyranny and despotism of the Corporation of the City of Dublin, where only five Unionists are allowed to take part in municipal affairs. Counsel, in the address which was made for the Corporation of the City of Dublin before the Committee, persisted in saying that no accusation of misrule could be made against the townships, but such cannot be said of the Dublin Corporation. The Corporation is a g gant c political debating society, and i not i till after they have finished debating political questions will they turn their mind to the welfare of the citizens. From time to time the Corporation have, under an ancient right, appeared at the Bar of this House in support of some academic proposition like Home Rule, the relief of evicted tenants, or the release of the political prisoners; but have they ever approached this House in support of any single movement for the material prosperity of the country? Have the Corporation ever petitioned on behalf of Irish industries or the promotion of our fisheries; have they ever done any substantial thing outside the area of the purest party politics? That is the Corporation which is to deprive existing municipalities of the right to carry on their duties which they have performed to the satisfaction of those living under their government. Two-thirds of the rates of Dublin are paid by Unionists; they are able to return one Member of Parliament, but the wards are so gerrymandered that, as regards municipal government, they are only able to secure seven representatives. The Corporation have always devoted themselves to politics; they have rewarded political supporters with money contributed by Unionist ratepayers, and have neglected their proper business. While Rathmines and Pembroke were developing their drainage the Corporation did nothing. How does Dublin stand with regard to electric lighting? Hon. Gentlemen opposite will not contradict me when I say that Dublin is, as far as electric lighting is concerned, the worst lighted city in the three kingdoms. The Corporation have spent £98,000, and they have only 81 arc-lamps, or ten lamps in each of the eight streets lighted. It is absolutely impossible to obtain an electric lighting supply from the Corporation, and the money is absolutely thrown away. Reference has been made to a plebiscite. It is true that there was a plebiscite in Dublin. The Parnellite Corporation submitted the idea of swallowing these townships, and everyone in Dublin thought it would be to their advantage. When the Corporation came before the Committee, so anxious were they to carry the Bill that they deliberately, without any authority from the population, agreed to forego for ten years the rates which Pembroke and Rathmines were to pay before the plebiscite was taken. Either they were authorised or not; if they were authorised then the ten years provision is illusory; if they were not authorised the Bill is entirely different from that supported by the plebiscite. On every point concession after concession was offered by the Corporation, in such a way that the original principle of the Bill has been destroyed, and it is enough to make anyone suspicious of it. What is the real object of this Bill? Under the Public Health Act, as we all know, a municipality in Ireland has power to borrow to twice the extent of its annual valuation, and the borrowing power of the Dublin Corporation would amount to $1\frac{1}{2}$ millions. But they have already borrowed £1,700,000, and it is because their Exchequer is exhausted, and they want to replenish it, and for political reasons also, that they are so anxious to annex these townships. It is suggested that they want additional land to set up buildings for the industrial classes, but it was proved before the Committee that there are still 400 acres of land available for that purpose within the city, which is quite enough to keep them going for a good many years. Then the argument is used, because people come in from Rathmines and Pembroke to do business in the City of Dublin, that therefore they should be rated. I quite agree with that principle, but if they are to be rated they should be rated in their offices and warehouses in the city, and the fact that a man who lives in Pembroke should be rated any more than if he lived at Kingstown does not apply. You might as well tax an Irishman who comes to London and makes a profit here. Some hon. Members on the other side of the House may regard this matter as trifling, but I would assure the House that it is very important. If there were not a strong feeling in the matter, it is hardly likely we should have to-day such an unusually large representation in this House from all parts of Ireland. Time after time, before the Committee, the question was put as to the advantages which the townships would derive from the scheme, and it was jocularly remarked by one witness that they would have the honour and glory of belonging to the Municipality of Dublin. That is not an honour for which all of us in Ireland are ambitious. I would point out the deliberate unfairness of one of the sections. The Gas Company is the controlling influence in Dublin municipal politics. (Cries of " No "). Hon. Members may say " No," and they may have their reasons ; but I do know that the Gas Company has the right to supply Dublin at the rate of 3s. 5d. per 1,000 cubic feet, and that it charges the townships 4s. 6d. Now, it would be imagined as a matter of fair play that when the townships were dragged into this scheme they would share the same benefits as Dublin ; but Section 59 states that nothing contained in the Bill is to affect the rights and privileges of the Gas Company, the plain English of which is that, although the townships are dragged into the scheme, they will still have to pay 4s. 6d. That shows the spirit and the unfairness of the Bill, which are also indicated by the abject readiness of the Corporation to surrender all these concessions, such as the ten years' rating limit and the twenty-eight members representation, being well aware that these safeguards are utterly illusory. One of the instances which the hon. Member for Loughborough relied on was that of Bristol, but the hon. Member forgot to tell the House that Bristol has been up to the present day unable to annex Westbury - on - Trym, which is to all intents and purposes analogous to Rathmines and Pembroke. There is only one other matter I wish to touch upon. It is quite true that in the case of Belfast the boundaries were ex-

Mr. William Moore.

tended. But there is a great difference between the cases of Belfast and Dublin. Many years ago the authorities of Belfast saw that it might be fatal to the extension of that city if the adjoining townships were allowed to grow up. But in Dublin they allowed them to grow, and it is only when the Dublin Exchequer is practically exhausted that they show a desire to bring in the townships. It has been suggested by the hon. Member for Waterford that the same law should apply on both sides of the Irish Channel. I cordially endorse that ; but I would point out that you are proposing to do in Dublin the very reverse of what you are doing under the London Government Bill. Under the latter Bill you are creating separate municipalities, whereas in Dublin you are seeking to merge prosperous townships in the city.

MR. DUNCOMBE : I propose to support the Dublin Corporation in this matter, for I think it would be absolutely ridiculous for this House, which over and over again has supported the principle of local government for Ireland, to refuse, for political reasons, this demand on the part of the Corporation of Dublin.

MR. T. M. HEALY (Cork, N.) : The argument brought forward by the Member for Trinity College was that there were three Conservative divisions, and that it would be unwise to include these three divisions in the area of the City of Dublin. But there are six divisions affected by the proposal. The County Council of Dublin is Nationalist, Kilmainham is Nationalist, Clontarf and Drumcondra are Nationalist. Therefore, out of the six divisions three are Nationalist and three Conservative, but Pembroke will not long remain a Conservative division, because it will be Nationalist as soon as the Nationalists care to take the trouble of attending to the register. Rathmines will probably always remain Conservative. Therefore, when you are opposing this Bill on the ground of political prejudice, you must recollect that you are not opposing the Bill as a whole, which affects Nationalist equally with Conservative areas. It is most unfair, in regard to the capital of Ireland, that this House, having abolished its Parliament and otherwise curtailed its prosperity and influence, should now discuss this Bill on such grounds. Let any man consider what Dublin has already suffered by the Acts of the Imperial Parliament. Before 1800 Dublin was confined within its present municipal area. Dublin then enjoyed a Parliament, and in Sackville Street alone there were the residences of 40 peers. Her squares were inhabited by Commoners, and by the nobility and gentry of the island, but they all departed with the Union. First the nobility, and then the gentry left, and I remember well, Sir, the late Sir Herbert Stewart, who was killed at Abu Klea, furnishing an entire terrace of houses in London with the splendid decorative stones and chimney - pieces which he had quarried from out of these Dublin residences. They were some of the finest specimens of art, but they are now all gone, and what have remained? Only the premises of the merchants, with a few of their residences. The Borough Funds Act did not, when it passed this House, apply to Dublin. Before 1870 the work of private legislation was costly, and there were no citizens rich enough and public spirited enough to oppose the various measures by which the City of Dublin was robbed, and these little townships secured their privileges. In 1890 the tramways of Dublin were extended far out into the suburbs, but these suburbs are only imaginary divisions. These are the results of the rush for fresh air and more room, and the desire to avoid the taxation of the city. Now, Sir, what are the tests of a town? What are the tests by which we shall decide whether or not they shall be reckoned separate towns? These tests are its markets, its fairs, its amusements, its stock exchange, its courts of justice. Not one single one of these townships possesses one single attribute of this character. If Dublin were to be abolished, they would be abolished too. They are merely the excrescences of the city, and do not possess one single element of real urban life, and could not under any pretence be considered as separate entities. They are only divided from Dublin by a canal, and to call them separate areas is an absurdity. Dublin is the only city since Her Majesty the Queen came to the throne which has not extended its area. But, unfortunately, in the case of Dublin, its area has actually been reduced, and portions of these districts were actually at one time within the area of the City of Dublin. It is said that the Government of Ireland is a continuity, but I will, Sir, point out that so far back as 20 years ago a Royal Commission with a Conservative President, and with the present Chairman of the Local Government Board as one of its members, unanimously reported in favour of the very proposal now before the House; and in 1882 Lord Spencer promised to do by a Public Act what the Dublin Corporation are now seeking to do by a Private Bill. Now, how does this House treat the capital of England or of Scotland? Is it in the way it is now proposed to treat poor Dublin? Edinburgh has extended its boundaries, Glasgow has extended its boundaries, so have Londonderry and Belfast. In fact, every city in Great Britain has done so, and there has been no question of political prejudice. In regard to this very question of political prejudice, the City of Dublin has suffered more by the Act of Union than any other city in the three kingdoms. We are told that this House is competent to legislate for Ireland, that it is willing and anxious to do so sympathetically; you say, "True you are only 80 members, but there are 600 English members prepared to do you justice; but what are the conditions under which Ireland struggles in regard to public measures only? If we succeed in getting only one Act through we go home proud, but the conditions in regard to Private Bills are even worse. The Irish municipalities have to come here and litigate at an enormous cost before this House. A Bill is proposed, as in the present instance, to be read a second time. There is no objection taken to it. It is read a second time and sent to a Committee, whose verdict is understood shall influence the House in its final decision. There is no Irish representative on the Committee. The Member for Trinity College admits that he and his friends gambled on the verdict of the Committee, and it is only now when the verdict of the jury is in our favour that he comes forward and opposes it. That is, Sir, after the verdict of a jury on which no Irish Member sat, and a verdict has been arrived at after seventeen days' discussion, and in the course of which 17,000 questions have been asked, and after the Dublin Corporation has expended from £20,000 to £25,000, the hon. Member asks the House to reverse the decision. What justice is there in such proceedings? The people of Ireland, it is said, are very ignorant, are very stupid, and very uneducated; but the poorest man in Ireland, the most stupid and uneducated, will know how the rejection of a Bill of this kind, of this magnitude, supported as it is by the Local Government Board and its officials, how the rejection of it has been brought about by one of the Orange Members of the North of Ireland. Sir, I am amazed that a question of this great importance should be treated in this way by the hon. and gallant Member for North Armagh. He referred to the main drainage of Dublin. What has stopped this main drainage scheme? Why, it is because instead of having one authority to deal with there were no less than eight, and why should an unfortunate decayed corner of Dublin have taken upon its back this scheme of main drainage, involving, as it did, an expenditure of three-quarters of a million, without the townships contributing at all? We are told that Rathmines and Pembroke desired to carry out a scheme of drainage, but that Dublin opposed. No, Sir, what Dublin opposed was this. They opposed the delivery of the sewage into the mouth of the Liffey, where it would be washed back at every tide into the town to contaminate the whole town. It is said again that Rathmines has a water supply. Yes, at sixpence higher cost than Dublin; but it is unfiltered. But even unfiltered water ought to be good enough to put out a fire, but I read the other day that the great factory belonging to the eminent Conservative Member, Mr. Pym, and employing over 300 hands in Rathmines, caught fire and would have become a total loss if it had been left to the precious care of the two men and a boy who comprised the Rathmines Fire Brigade. There was no adequate fire brigade in Rathmines, and the Rathmines water would not squirt. I do not know whether it is the want of a filter or the want of pressure, but it was certain that but for the presence of the Dublin Brigade that factory would have been destroyed, and so it was the Dublin Fire Brigade was always coming to the rescue of these little townships, who paid nothing to the support of the brigade and who would be helpless without it. Then, there is the question of the repre-

Mr. T. M. Healy.

sentation. I have always been in favour of giving the Conservatives a greater representation on the Dublin Corporation than they now have. Five years ago in a Water Bill I engrafted a scheme of minority representation, but though it passed through this House, it was rejected in the House of Lords, that august body declaring that minority reports were not germane to water. Let me again remind the House of this fact, if political prejudice is brought forward against this measure, that every member of the Conservative party on the Dublin Corporation is in favour of this Bill, and some of them gave evidence before the Committee, while others were here yesterday trying to apply an antidote to the undignified lobbying of certain members of the other House, who for private reasons are opposing this Bill. I think they might very well wait to defend their personal interests until the Bill reaches the Second Chamber. The House, in conclusion, from every point of view is making a mistake if it rejects this Bill. It has been said that the Dublin Corporation has given positions to political prisoners. For myself, I was only in prison a very short time, but I look back upon that period as the proudest time of my life. I am very proud of having been in gaol for Ireland, prouder than I am of anything else in my career, and if the Corporation has taken pity upon a man who has suffered likewise, and sooner than he should die of hunger or tramp the streets, given him a small position, I see no reason why it should have been put forward as ground for opposing this Bill. Mr. O'Brien, the man referred to, has been given the charge of the baths and washhouses, and he was an old soldier, he was released by a Conservative Government so far back as 1877, and I really think that after 22 years there should be some Statute of Limitations. I am quite sure that if the Belfast Corporation appointed to some such office one of the Orangemen convicted and sent to prison in connection with the Belfast riots of 1886, or Mr. de Cobain when he comes out of prison, to some such office, we should not bring it forward as a ground for opposing a Bill of the Belfast Corporation. Again, Sir, may I point out that this Bill has been supported by the report of a Royal Commission, promised to be embodied in a Public Act by Lord Spencer, and surely in following such advice this House cannot be going wrong. Let me finally say this, the very smallest performances of the Dublin Corporation have been opposed by a narrow clique of this House and elsewhere. In 1890 the Chief Secretary gave Dublin the power to collect its own rates, but, notwithstanding the whole weight of Lord Salisbury, the Bill only passed the House of Lords by a majority of eight votes. It is a pure matter of party prejudice, but I caution this House, and I warn it—you cannot declare at the hust-

ings that you are willing to give Ireland everything, and now upon a narrow question of extension which you have granted to every large city in the United Kingdom, you will strike a greater blow at the Union than any that has been given by all the Ministries of the previous 90 years.

Question put.

The House divided : Ayes, 291 ; Noes, 129. (Division List No. 188.)

AYES.

Allan, William (Gateshead)
Allison, Robert Andrew
Ambrose, Robert
Arrol, Sir William
Ashmead-Bartlett, Sir Ellis
Ashton, Thomas Gair
Austin, M. (Limerick, W.)
Baldwin, Alfred
Barlow, John Emmott
Barry, E. (Cork, S.)
Bartley, George C. T.
Bayley, Thomas (Derbyshire)
Begg, Ferdinand Faithfull
Bigwood, James
Bill, Charles
Billson, Alfred
Blake, Edward
Bolitho, Thomas Bedford
Bolton, Thomas Dolling
Bond, Edward
Broadhurst, Henry
Brown, Alexander H.
Brunner, Sir John Tomlinson
Bryce, Rt. Hon. James
Buchanan, Thomas Ryburn
Burns, John
Burt, Thomas
Buxton, Sydney Charles
Caldwell, James
Cameron, Sir Chas. (Glasgow)
Cameron, Robert (Durham)
Campbell, Rt. Hn. J A (Glasgow
Campbell-Bannerman, Sir H.
Carew, James Laurence
Carvill, Patrick G. Hamilton
Causton, Richard Knight
Cawley, Frederick
Cayzer, Sir Charles William
Clancy, John Joseph
Clark, Dr. G. B. (Caithness-sh
Clough, Walter Owen
Coddington, Sir William
Coghill, Douglas Harry
Cohen, Benjamin Louis
Collery, Bernard
Commins, Andrew
Cook, Fred. Lucas (Lambeth)
Cooke, C. W. Radcliffe(Heref'd)
Corbet, William J. (Wicklow)
Corbett, A. Cameron(Glasgow)
Courtney, Rt. Hon. Leonard H.
Cranborne, Viscount
Crilly, Daniel
Crombie. John William
Cross, Alexander (Glasgow)

Cross, Herb. Shepherd(Bolton)
Cubitt, Hon. Henry
Curran, Thomas B. (Donegal)
Curran, Thomas (Sligo, S.)
Dalbiac, Colonel Philip Hugh
Dalkeith, Earl of
Dalrymple, Sir Charles
Dalziel, James Henry
Davies, SirHoratioD(Chatham
Davies, M.Vaughan-(Cardigan
Davitt, Michael
Denny, Colonel
Dickson-Poynder, Sir John P.
Dilke, Rt. Hon, Sir Charles
Dillon, John
Doogan, P. C.
Doughty, George
Drucker, A.
Duncombe, Hon. Hubert V.
Dunn, Sir William
Egerton, Hon. A. de Tatton
Elliot, Hn. A. Ralph Douglas
Fardell, Sir T. George
Farquharson, Dr. Robert
Farrell, James P. (Cavan, W.)
Farrell, Thomas J. (Kerry, S.)
Fenwick, Charles
Ferguson, R. C. Munro (Leith)
Fergusson, Rt.Hn.SirJ.(Manc'r
Ffrench, Peter
Field, William (Dublin)
Firbank, Joseph Thomas
Fitzmaurice, Lord Edmond
Fitz Wygram, General Sir F.
Flavin, Michael Joseph
Flower, Ernest
Foster, Harry S. (Suffolk)
Foster, Sir W. (Derby Co.)
Fowler, Rt. Hon. Sir Henry
Fox, Dr. Joseph Francis
Fry, Lewis
Gibbons, J. Lloyd
Gibney, James
Gladstone, Rt. Hon. H. John
Goddard, Daniel Ford
Gold, Charles
Gordon, Hon. John Edward
Gorst, Rt. Hon. Sir J. Eldon
Gourley, Sir Edw. Temperley
Gray, Ernest (West Ham)
Gretton, John
Greville, Hon. Ronald
Grey, Sir Edward (Berwick)
Griffith, Ellis J.
Gunter, Colonel

Gurdon, Sir Wm. Brampton
Haldane, Richard Burdon
Hammond, John (Carlow)
Harcourt, Rt. Hon. Sir Wm.
Harrington, Timothy
Hayden, John Patrick
Hayne, Rt. Hon. Charles Seale-
Healy, Maurice (Cork)
Healy, Thomas J. (Wexford)
Healy, Timothy M. (N.Louth)
Heaton, John Henniker
Hedderwick, Thomas C. H.
Helder, Augustus
Hemphill, Rt. Hon.CharlesH.
Hoare, E. Brodie (Hampstead)
Hobhouse, Henry
Hogan, James Francis
Holden, Sir Angus
Holland, W. H. (York, W. R.)
Horniman, Frederick John
Houldsworth, Sir Wm. Henry
Hutton, Alfred E. (Morley)
Jacoby, James Alfred
Jessel, Capt. Herbert Merton
Johnson-Fergusson, Jabez E.
Johnstone, Heywood (Sussex)
Joicey, Sir James
Jolliffe, Hon. H. George
JonesDavidBrynmor(Swansea
Jordan, Jeremiah
Kay-Shuttleworth,RtHnSirU
Kearley, Hudson E.
Kenyon, James
Kilbride, Denis
King, Sir Henry Seymour
Kinloch,SirJohnGeorgeSmyth
Kitson, Sir James
Knowles, Lees
Labouchere, Henry
Lambert, George
Langley, Batty
Laurie, Lieut.-General
Lawrence, W. F. (Liverpool)
LawsonSirWilfrid(Cumb'land
Leng, Sir John
Leuty, Thomas Richmond
Logan, John William
Lough, Thomas
Lowles, John
Lowther,RtHnJW(Cumb'land
Lloyd, Archie Kirkman
Lyell. Sir Leonard
MacAleese, Daniel
Macdona, John Cumming
MacDonnell,DrMA(Queen's C

MacIver, David (Liverpool)
Maclean, James Mackenzie
MacNeill, John Gordon Swift
M'Arthur, Charles (Liverpool)
M'Arthur, William (Cornwall)
M'Dermott, Patrick
M'Ghee, Richard
M'Kenna, Reginald
M'Killop, James
M'Leod, John
Maddison, Fred.
Mappin, Sir Frederick Thorpe
Marks, Henry Hananel
Mellor, Colonel (Lancashire)
Mellor, Rt. Hn. J. W.(Yorks.)
Mendl, Sigis und Ferdinand
Middlemore, J. Throgmorton
Minch, Matthew
Molloy, Bernard Charles
Monk, Charles James
Moon, Edward Robert Pacy
Morgan, J. L. (Carmarthen)
Morgan, W. P. (Merthyr)
Morley, Rt. Hon. J.(Montrose)
Morrell, George Herbert
Morris, Samuel
Morton, Ar. H. A. (Deptford)
Morton, E. J. C. (Devonport)
Moulton, John Fletcher
Murnaghan, George
Norton, Capt. Cecil William
Nussey, Thomas Willans
O'Brien, James F. X. (Cork)
O'Connor, J. (Wicklow, W.)
O'Connor, T. P. (Liverpool)
O'Kelly, James
Oldroyd, Mark
O'Malley, William
Palmer, Sir C. M. (Durham)
Palmer, G. Wm. (Reading)
Parnell, John Howard
Paulton, James Mellor
Perks, Robert William

Philipps, John Wynford
Pickard, Benjamin
Pickersgill, Edward Hare
Pierpoint, Robert
Pilkington,SirG.A.(L'nca.SW)
Pirie, Duncan V.
Platt-Higgins, Frederick
Pollock, Harry Frederick
Powell, Sir Francis Sharp
Power, Patrick Joseph
Price, Robert John
Priestley, Briggs (Yorks.)
Priestley, Sir W. O. (Edin.)
Provand, Andrew Dryburgh
Purvis, Robert
Quilter, Sir Cuthbert
Rasch, Major Frederic Carne
Reckitt, Harold James
Redmond, J. E. (Waterford)
Redmond, William (Clare)
Richardson, J. (Durham, S.E.)
Rickett, J. Compton
Roberts, John Bryn (Eifion)
Roberts, John H. (Denbighs.)
Robson, William Snowdon
Roche, John (East Galway)
Rothschild, Hon. Lionel W.
Royds, Clement Molyneux
Russell, T. W. (Tyrone)
Samuel, J. (Stockton-on-Tees)
Schwann, Charles E.
Scoble, Sir Andrew Richard
Scott, Chas. Prestwich (Leigh)
Seton-Karr, Henry
Shaw, Charles Edw. (Stafford)
Sinclair,Capt. John(Forfarsh.)
Smith, Jas. Parker (Lanarks.)
Smith, Samuel (Flint.)
Soames, Arthur Wellesley
Souttar, Robinson
Spicer, Albert
Stanhope, Hon. Philip J.
Stanley, Henry M. (Lambeth)

Steadman, William Charles
Stephens, Henry Charles
Stevenson, Francis S.
Stewart, Sir Mk. J. M'Taggart
Stone, Sir Benjamin
Strachey, Edward
Strauss, Arthur
Strutt, Hon. Charles Hedley
Stuart, James (Shoreditch)
Sullivan, Donal (Westmeath)
Sullivan, T. D. (Donegal, W.)
Tennant, Harold John
Thomas,Abel (Carmarthen,E.)
Thorburn, Walter
Thornton, Percy M.
Trevelyan, Charles Philips
Tully, Jasper
Wallace, Robert
Walton, John L. (Leeds, S.)
Wanklyn, James Leslie
Warde, Lieut-Col. C.E, (Kent)
Webster, R. G. (St. Pancras)
Wedderburn, Sir William
Weir, James Galloway
Whiteley,H.(Ashton-under-L)
Whittaker, Thomas Palmer
Williams, Colonel R. (Dorset)
Williams, John C. (Notts.)
Willox, Sir John Archibald
Wills, Sir William Henry
Wilson, Fred. W. (Norfolk)
Wilson, Henry J. (York, W.R.
Wilson, John (Durham, Mid)
Wilson, John (Govan)
Wilson, J.W. (Worcester, N.)
Woods, Samuel
Wyvill, Marmaduke D'Arcy
Young,Commander(Berks, E.)
Young, Samuel (Cavan, East)
Yoxall, James Henry

TELLERS FOR THE AYES—
Mr. Patrick O'Brien and
Captain Donelan.

NOES.

Aird, John
Allhusen, Augustus Henry E.
Allsopp, Hon. George
Anstruther, H. T.
Archdale, Edward Mervyn
Arnold-Forster, Hugh O.
Bagot, Capt. J. FitzRoy
Bailey, James (Walworth)
Banbury, Frederick George
Barnes, Frederic Gorell
Barry, Rt. Hn. A.H.S-(Hunts)
Bathurst, Hn. Allen Benjamin
Blakiston-Houston, John
Boulnois, Edmund
Bousfield, William Robert
Brookfield, A. Montagu
Brymer, William Ernest
Butcher, John George
Cavendish, V.C.W.(Derbysh.)
Cecil, Evelyn (Hertford, East)
Chaloner, Captain R. G. W.
Chamberlain, J. A. (Worc'r)
Charrington, Spencer
Clarke, Sir Edw. (Plymouth)
Colston, C. E. H. Athole
Cotton-Jodrell, Col. E. T. D.
Cripps, Charles Alfred
Cruddas, Wm. Donaldson
Curzon, Viscount

Digby, John K. D. Wingfield-
Disraeli, Coningsby Ralph
Dixon-Hartland, Sir. F. Dixon
Dorrington, Sir John Edward
Douglas, Rt. Hon. A. Akers-
Doxford, William Theodore
Drage, Geoffrey
Field, Admiral (Eastbourne)
Fisher, William Hayes
Fison, Frederick William
FitzGerald, Sir Robert P.-
Fletcher, Sir Henry
Folkestone, Viscount
Foster, Colonel (Lancaster)
Galloway, William Johnson
Garfit, William
Gibbs, Hn.A.G.H.(C. of Lond.
Giles, Charles Tyrrell
Gilliat, John Saunders
Goldsworthy, Major-General
Goschen, George J. (Sussex)
Goulding, Edward Alfred
Graham, Henry Robert
Hanson, Sir Reginald
Hardy, Laurence
Heath, James
Hermon-Hodge, Robert T.
Hill,SirEdwardStock (Bristol)
Hoare, Samuel (Norwich)

Hornby, Sir William Henry
Howell, William Tudor
Hozier, Hon. J. Henry Cecil
Hubbard, Hon. Evelyn
Hutchinson,Capt.G.W. Grice-
Hutton, John (Yorks. N.R.)
Jackson, Rt.Hon.Wm. Lawies
Jebb, Richard Claverhouse
Jenkins, Sir John Jones
Johnston, William (Belfast)
Kemp, George
Kenyon-Slaney, Col. William
Lawrence,SirE.Durning-(Corn
Lawson, John Grant (Yorks.)
Lecky, Rt. Hn. William E. H.
Lees, Sir Elliot (Birkenhead)
Llewellyn, E. H. (Somerset)
Loder, Gerald Walter Erskine
Long, Col. Chas. W. (Evesham)
Lubbock, Rt. Hon. Sir John
Macartney, W. G. Ellison
M'Calmont,Col.J.(Antrim, E.)
Malcolm, Ian
Maple, Sir John Blundell
Moore, William (Antrim, N.)
More, R. Jasper (Shropshire)
Morgan, Hn. F. (Monm'thsh.)
Morrison, Walter
Mount, William George

Murray,Col. Wyndham (Bath)
Newark, Viscount
Nicholson, William Graham
Nicol, Donald Ninian
Northcote, Hon. Sir H. S.
O'Neill, Hon. Robert Torrens
Orr-Ewing, Charles Lindsay
Penn, John
Percy, Earl
Pilkington,R.(Lancs. Newton)
Pretyman, Ernest George
Pryce-Jones, Lt.-Col. Edward
Rankin, Sir James
Renshaw, Charles Bine
Robertson, Herbert(Hackney)

Round, James
Russell,Gen. F S.(Cheltenham)
Rutherford, John
Ryder, John Herbert Dudley
Sandys, Lt.-Col. Thos. Myles
Seely, Charles Hilton
Sharpe, William Edward T.
Sidebotham, J. W. (Cheshire)
Sidebottom, William(Derbys.)
Simeon, Sir Barrington
Smith, Hon. W.F.D. (Strand)
Spencer, Ernest
Stanley, Lord (Lancs.)
Stirling-Maxwell, Sir John M.
Tomlinson, Wm. Edw. Murray

Tritton, Charles Ernest
Usborne, Thomas
Valentia, Viscount
Walrond, Rt. Hn. Sir Wm. H.
Welby, Lieut.-Col. A. C. E.
Wentworth, Bruce C. Vernon-
Whitmore, Charles Algernon
Williams, J. Powell- (Birm.)
Wolff, Gustav Wilhelm
Wortley, Rt. Hn. C.B. Stuart-
Wylie, Alexander
Wyndham-Quin, Major W. H.
TELLERS FOR THE NOES—
    Mr. Carson and Colonel
    Saunderson.

Main Question put, and agreed to.

Bill, as amended, considered ; to be read the third time.

IONIAN BANK BILL. (By Order.)

Order for Second Reading read.

THE FINANCIAL SECRETARY TO THE TREASURY (Mr. HANBURY, Preston) : It must be understood by the promoters that I can only allow this Bill to be read a second time on the distinct understanding that certain clauses shall be inserted at the initiative of the Treasury. The Bill does away altogether with the Stamp Duty, and the Estate Duty in certain cases, and that is a matter we must deal with.

Bill read a second time and committed.

ST. NEOTS WATER BILL [Lords]. (By Order.)

Order for Second Reading read.

Motion made and Question proposed—

"That the Second Reading of the Bill be deferred till Monday."—(*Mr. J. W. Lowther.*)

MR. DUNCOMBE : I object.

*MR. J. W. LOWTHER (Cumberland) : I appeal to my hon. friend not to press the objection. I may point out that, as a result of extending the time for the consideration of another Bill, the House is not now to be troubled with it, so there is sometimes a distinct advantage gained by postponement.

MR. DUNCOMBE : Of course, after that appeal, I withdraw my objection, but it must be understood that it is the last time I give way. The House ought

not to delay consideration of a Bill when a day has been definitely decided upon.

Second Reading deferred till Monday next.

TOTLAND WATER BILL [Lords].

Read a second time and committed.

LOCAL GOVERNMENT PROVISIONAL ORDERS (No. 8) BILL,

PIER AND HARBOUR PROVISIONAL ORDERS (No. 1) BILL,

Read the third time, and passed.

STANDING ORDERS.

Resolution reported from the Committee—

"That, in the case of the Bradford Tramways and Improvement Bill, Petition for additional Provision, the Standing Orders ought to be dispensed with :—That the parties be permitted to introduce their additional Provision, if the Committee on the Bill think fit."

Resolution agreed to.

MESSAGE FROM THE LORDS.

That they have agreed to—

Electric Lighting Provisional Orders (No. 1) Bill ;

Electric Lighting Provisional Orders (No. 4) Bill.

Amendments to—

West Highland Railway Bill [*Lords*] without Amendment.

That they have passed a Bill, intituled "An Act to confirm a Provisional Order made by the Board of Trade under the Electric Lighting Acts, 1882 and 1888, relating to Clontarf." [Electric Lighting Provisional Order (No. 9) Bill (*Lords.*).]

Also, a Bill, intituled, "An Act to confirm certain Provisional Orders made by the Board of Trade under the Electric Lighting Acts, 1882 and 1888, relating to East Retford, Failsworth, Pemberton, Stourbridge, Swinton and Pendlebury, and Wednesbury." [Electric Lighting Provisional Orders (No. 11) Bill (*Lords*).]

And, also, a Bill, intituled, "An Act for enabling the Transvaal Mortgage, Loan, and Finance Company, Limited, to arrange with the holders of their founders' shares, for sub-dividing shares, and creating certain preferences ; and for other purposes." [Transvaal Mortgage, Loan, and Finance Company Bill (*Lords*).]

ELECTRIC LIGHTING PROVISIONAL ORDER (No. 9 BILL). [Lords.]

Read the first time ; referred to the Examiners of Petitions for Private Bills, and to be *printed*. [Bill 231.]

ELECTRIC LIGHTING PROVISIONAL ORDERS (No. 11 BILL). [Lords.]

Read the first time ; referred to the Examiners of Petitions for Private Bills, and to be *printed*. [Bill 232.]

TRANSVAAL MORTGAGE, LOAN, AND FINANCE COMPANY BILL. [Lords.]

Read the first time ; and referred to the Examiners of Petitions for Private Bills.

PETITIONS.

BOROUGH FUNDS ACT, 1872.

Petition from Bethesda, for alteration of Law ; to lie upon the Table.

ELEMENTARY EDUCATION (VOLUNTARY SCHOOLS).

Petition from Tranmere, for alteration of Law ; to lie upon the Table.

GROUND RENTS (TAXATION BY LOCAL AUTHORITIES).

Petition from Huddersfield, in favour ; to lie upon the Table.

LIQUOR TRAFFIC LOCAL VETO (SCOTLAND BILL.

Petition from Blackford, in favour ; to lie upon the Table.

LOCAL GOVERNMENT (SCOTLAND) ACT (1894) AMENDMENT BILL.

Petition from Polmont, in favour ; to lie upon the Table.

PUBLIC HEALTH ACTS AMENDMENT BILL.

Petition from Plymouth, in favour ; to lie upon the Table.

SALE OF INTOXICATING LIQUORS ON SUNDAY BILL.

Petition from Nottingham, in favour ; to lie upon the Table.

VIVISECTION.

Petition from London, for prohibition ; to lie upon the Table.

RETURNS, REPORTS, &c.

ARMY (SPECIAL PENSIONS).

Copy presented,—of Return for the year ended 31st March, 1899, of Pensions specially granted under Articles 730, 1170, and 1207 of the Army Pay Warrant [by Command] ; to lie upon the Table.

SOUTH AFRICAN REPUBLIC.

Copy presented,—of Papers relating to the Complaints of British Subjects in the South African Republic [by Command] ; to lie upon the Table.

EXPLOSIVES.

Copy presented,—of Twenty-third Annual Report of Her Majesty's Inspectors of Explosives, being for the year 1898 [by Command] ; to lie upon the Table.

EXPLOSIONS (UPLEES MARSHES, FAVERSHAM).

Copy presented,—of Report by Colonel A. Ford, C.B., Her Majesty's Chief Inspector of Explosives, on the circumstances attending the destruction and explosion of carbo-gelatine in course of manufacture, which occurred at the factory of the Cotton Powder Company, at Uplees Marshes, near Faversham, on the 5th May, 1899 [by Command] ; to lie upon the Table.

EXPLOSIONS (STREETLY, BIRMINGHAM).

Copy presented,—of Report by Major A. Cooper-Key, R.A., Her Majesty's Inspector of Explosives, to the right hon. the Secretary of State for the Home Department, on the circumstances attending an explosion of percussion caps in course of manufacture at the factory of the Birmingham Metal and Munitions Company, Limited, at Streetly, near Birmingham, on the 11th April, 1899 [by Command]; to lie upon the Table.

INEBRIATE REFORMATORIES (RULES FOR MANAGEMENT).

Copy presented,—of Rules, made with the approval of the Secretary of State for the Home Department, for the Domestic Management of the certified Inebriate Reformatory at Horfield, in the county of Gloucester [by Act]; to lie upon the Table.

MERCHANT SHIPPING, 1898.

Copy ordered, "of Tables showing the Progress of British Merchant Shipping."—(*Mr. Ritchie.*)

Copy presented accordingly; to lie upon the Table, and to be printed. [No. 217.]

ELECTRIC LIGHTING PROVISIONAL ORDERS.

Copy ordered, "of Memorandum stating the nature of the Proposals contained in the Provisional Order included in the Electric Lighting Provisional Order (No. 20) Bill."—(*Mr. Ritchie.*)

Copy presented accordingly; to lie upon the Table, and to be printed. [No. 218.]

COMPANIES (WINDING UP).

Return ordered, "of the names of all the companies registered in England which were ordered to be wound up by the Court, or which passed resolutions for winding up voluntarily, during the year ending the 31st day of December 1896, showing the names and addresses of the liquidators, and giving the following particulars, viz.: (1) the amount of paid-up capital, distinguishing the amount paid up in cash and the amount issued as paid up otherwise than for cash; (2) the estimated amount of probable loss arising on each of the above-named classes of shares, respectively; (3) the estimated amount of probable loss to unsecured or partially secured creditors; (4) the names of companies going into liquidation during the year 1896 on which no losses to shareholders or creditors are estimated as probable."—(*Mr. Charles M'Arthur.*)

DRAINAGE SEPARATION.

Bill to enable Local Authorities to deal separately with the sewage and drainage

of their districts, ordered be brought in by Mr. Stephens, Sir John Lubbock, Sir Walter Foster, Sir William Priestley, Mr. John Burns, Mr. Bigwood, Mr. Cripps, Mr. Lawson Walton, Dr. Ambrose, and Mr. Brynmor Jones.

REGISTRATION OF ELECTORS (ENGLAND).

Bill to amend the Law regarding the Registration of Electors in England, ordered to be brought in by Mr. R. G. Webster, Sir Edward Gourley, Major Rasch, Mr. Vaughan-Davies, and Mr. Pierpoint.

DRAINAGE SEPARATION BILL.

"To enable Local Authorities to deal separately with the sewage and drainage of their districts," presented, and read the first time; to be read a second time upon Wednesday, 21st June, and to be printed. [Bill 233.]

REGISTRATION OF ELECTORS (ENGLAND) BILL.

"To amend the Law regarding the Registration of Electors in England," presented, and read the first time; to be read a second time upon Monday, 3rd July, and to be printed. [Bill 234.]

QUESTIONS.

LONGFORD MILITIA.

MR. J. P. FARRELL (Cavan, W.): I beg to ask the Under Secretary of State for War whether the decision of the War Office authorities to remove the Militia headquarters from Longford to Mullingar was come to by consultation with the officers of the regiment; whether it was owing to the difficulty of finding cadets for service with the regiment that the c ange was decided upon, and whether it ihnow final and irrevocable; and to what purpose is it intended to put the Artillery or Upper Barracks in Longford formerly occupied by these men.

*THE UNDER SECRETARY OF STATE FOR WAR (Mr. WYNDHAM, Dover): There is no intention of altering the decision in regard to the removal of the headquarters from Longford to Mullingar. The barracks at Longford are at present occupied by a field battery of Royal Artillery, pending the provision of a new barrack elsewhere.

SALISBURY PLAIN.

*MR. THOMAS BAYLEY (Derbyshire, Chesterfield): I beg to ask the Financial Secretary to the War Office whether, in the Return No. 150, of 1899, which was ordered by the House in February last and distributed in May, of the gross and net rentals of property at Salisbury Plain purchased by the War Department, the column headed " present rental " gives in all cases the actual rental paid to the proprietor of the land at the time of purchase, or whether in any cases the amount of rental in that column represents a nominal rental which in practice was reduced by an allowance of, in some cases, as much as 20 per cent. reduction on the nominal rent.

THE FINANCIAL SECRETARY TO THE WAR OFFICE (MR. J. POWELL WILLIAMS, Birmingham, S.): The figures shown in the column " present rental " of the Return referred to represent the actual rent on the 4th April, 1899, *i.e.*, the date on which the Return was rendered.

CEYLON LAND ORDINANCES.

MR. SCHWANN (Manchester, N.): I beg to ask the Secretary of State for the Colonies when he will distribute to Members the report of the Governor of Ceylon on the working of the Land Ordinances Act of 1897, in that island.

THE SECRETARY OF STATE FOR THE COLONIES (Mr. J. CHAMBERLAIN, Birmingham, W.): Papers relating to the Waste Lands Ordinances and Mr. Le Mesurier's complaints will be laid before the House as soon as they can be printed. The papers are somewhat voluminous, and there may be longer delay than I had contemplated, but the matter is being pressed forward as much as possible.

THE TRANSVAAL—THE BLOEMFON-TEIN CONFERENCE.

MR. ELLIS J. GRIFFITH (Anglesey): I beg to ask the Secretary of State for the Colonies whether he can state the cause of the delay in the transmission of Sir Alfred Milner's memorandum on the subject of the Bloemfontein Conference; and, if so, whether there is reason to believe that there was intentional interference with the prompt and regular despatch of such memorandum; can he state where the delay in the transmission of the message occurred; and whether he can explain the circumstances under which the representative of the Transvaal Government in Europe received information as to the proceedings at and the result of the Bloemfontein Conference before such information reached the Colonial Office.

MR. J. CHAMBERLAIN: Sir A. Milner's memorandum was at first communicated to Reuter's Agency, and was transmitted as a Press message, and not as a Government message. The delay in transmission was due to the partial interruption of the cable for repairs. I have no reason to believe that there was any intentional interference with its despatch. The message sent from the Transvaal was sent as a Government message, and so obtained priority. On learning that Reuter's message was delayed I instructed Sir A. Milner to have his memorandum sent as a Government message.

MR. LABOUCHERE (Northampton): I beg to ask the Secretary of State for the Colonies, whether his attention has been called to a statement made in a Reuter telegram on Friday last to the effect that Sir Alfred Milner had acknowledged that Mr. Kruger's request for arbitration by other than foreign Powers on all points of future difference under the Convention was reasonable: and, when the official documents which throw light on what took place will be published.

MR. J. CHAMBERLAIN: I have received the following explanation from Sir Alfred Milner in regard to the statement to which the hon. Member's question relates:

" The President's statement referred to is an inference from what I said which I consider was not justified, and which I immediately corrected. My position on the subject is correctly summed up in the words of my telegram of the 6th instant, viz. :—' Arbitration had been mentioned during the Conference along with other matters, but no definite proposal on the subject was before his Excellency at the moment. On some questions Her Majesty's Government clearly could not arbitrate, and on no question would they ever agree to arbitration by means of a foreign Government. At the same time there was a class of question about which Her Majesty's Government might agree to arbitrate if a suitable method could be found; if a proposal on that subject was submitted at any time it could be considered independently of any of the proceedings of this Conference. As already pointed out, His Excellency was not authorised to discuss this question, but any definite proposition which His Honour might make at any time would be submitted to the consideration of Her Majesty's Government. I distinctly stated that arbitration was not admissible on all questions of difference; and equally distinctly that on no question would arbitration by a foreign Power be admitted. As regards the President's position in the matter he never explained what he meant by arbitration, or made any definite proposal. On the other hand, I did certainly gather from the remark to which reference is made that he was prepared to abandon arbitration by foreign Powers."

Since the Conference President Kruger has submitted a proposal on the subject of arbitration which contemplates that the president of the arbitral tribunal should be the foreigner. The official documents connected with the Bloemfontein Conference will be published as soon as possible after they are received.

ALLEGED ARMING THE BOERS IN NATAL.

SIR ALFRED HICKMAN (Wolverhampton, West): I beg to ask the Secretary of State for the Colonies whether he has any information to the effect that the Transvaal Government has recently distributed arms and ammunition among the Boers in Natal, and is arming our own subjects against this country; and, if so, whether he will use his influence with the Natal Government to prevent this going on.

MR. J. CHAMBERLAIN: I have received no such information.

POLITICAL RIGHTS OF UITLANDERS.

SIR ELLIS ASHMEAD-BARTLETT (Sheffield, Ecclesall): I beg to ask the Secretary of State for the Colonies what steps Her Majesty's Government propose to take in order to put an end to the increasing danger to the public peace, and to the general commercial interest, caused by the refusal by the Boer Government of personal liberty and political rights to the Uitlanders of the Transvaal, who number over two-thirds of the white population.

MR. J. CHAMBERLAIN: I have already stated that Sir A. Milner has been instructed to have the despatch of Her Majesty's Government written in reply to the petition from British subjects in the Transvaal communicated to the Government of the South African Republic, and

a Blue Book containing this despatch and other papers will be laid on the Table to-day. Her Majesty's Government will wait for the despatches from the High Commissioner with full reports of the Conference before sending further instructions.

MR. C. P. SCOTT (Lancashire, Leigh): I beg to ask the Secretary of State for the Colonies what is the shortest time within which a foreigner coming to this country can actually exercise the franchise; and how this period compares with that proposed by Mr. Kruger for conferring the franchise on Uitlanders.

MR. J. CHAMBERLAIN said: A foreigner coming to this country can be naturalised after five years' residence in the United Kingdom. After naturalisation, if otherwise qualified, he can be registered and can exercise the franchise from the 1st of January after he is registered. If he completes the five years' residence and is naturalised just before the last day for sending in claims for registration, he can actually exercise the franchise within five years and about five months after coming to this country. The period within which it is proposed by President Kruger that a foreigner coming into the Transvaal may obtain the franchise appears to be seven years, namely two years before naturalisation and five years after naturalisation. But the proposal is only partially retro-active and foreigners who have lived in the Transvaal from before 1890 would still have to wait two-and-a-half years before obtaining the franchise, and foreigners whose residence began in or after 1890, and who have resided for two years or more, would have to wait five years.

MR. SWIFT MacNEILL (Donegal, S.): Is the right hon. Gentleman aware that in this country a certificate from the Secretary of State is necessary for legalising naturalisation, and the Secretary of State can withhold it at his discretion, without right of appeal, even if all other requirements are satisfied?

MR. J. CHAMBERLAIN: I have seen a statement to that effect in the papers. If the hon. Gentleman wants accurate information, however, as to the process of naturalisation, he had better apply to the Home Secretary.

2 P 2

MR. SWIFT MAC NEILL: I am refer-ring to the Statute of 1870.

THE PACIFIC CABLE.

MR. HOGAN (Tipperary, Mid.): I beg to ask the Secretary of State for the Colonies whether the proposals of Her Majesty's Government in reference to the construction of the Pacific Cable have now been revised; and, if so, whether he can give a general indication of the amended offer of co-operation with the Canadian and Australasian Governments.

MR. J. CHAMBERLAIN: The matter is still under discussion between Her Majesty's Government and the Colonial Governments concerned, and I am not yet in a position to make a statement.

MAURITIUS SUGAR INDUSTRY.

*MR. W. H. HOLLAND (York W.R., Rotherham): I beg to ask the Secretary of State for the Colonies if he can state whether there has been any diminution in the acreage under sugar in the Mauritius during the last five years; and, if so, to what extent.

MR. J. CHAMBERLAIN: It appears from the Blue Books for the years 1893–1897 (the last Blue Book we have) that the estimated acreage of cultivated lands on sugar estates in Mauritius was, in 1893, 71,000 arpents approximately; 1894, 114,000; 1895, 93,000; 1896, 52,000; 1897, 79,421. An arpent is about $1\frac{1}{20}$th of an acre. These figures show that there was a great increase in the estimated acreage of cultivated land between the years 1893 and 1894, a rapid decline between the years 1894 and 1896, and a partial recovery in the year 1897 which is the last year for which the figures are available.

WEST AFRICAN LIQUOR TRAFFIC.

CAPTAIN SINCLAIR (Forfar): I beg to ask the Secretary of State for the Colonies whether he can give to the House any information as to the results arrived at by the Brussels Conference on the West African Liquor Traffic; and when it is intended that the relative papers shall be laid before Parliament.

MR. J. CHAMBERLAIN: A Conven-tion was signed on the 8th June, and it will be communicated to the House as soon as possible. The papers relating to the matter will be laid before Parliament at an early date. I may add, in the meantime, that it involves a considerable increase of the duty on imported spirits.

TONGA.

MR. HOGAN: I beg to ask the Under Secretary of State for Foreign Affairs whether the agreement recently entered into practically amounts to a British Pro-tectorate over the Native Kingdom of Tonga; and whether the action of the captain of H.M.S. *Tauranga* was authorised by Her Majesty's Government or Her Majesty's High Commissioner for the Western Pacific?

*THE UNDER SECRETARY OF STATE FOR FOREIGN AFFAIRS (MR. BRODRICK, Surrey, Guildford): The answer to the first paragraph is in the negative. The action of the captain of the *Tauranga* was authorised by Her Majesty's Government.

THE ALASKAN BOUNDARY QUESTION

MR. HOGAN: I beg to ask the Under Secretary of State for Foreign Affairs whether Her Majesty's Government and the Government of the United States have now arrived at an understanding on the Alaskan boundary question.

*MR. BRODRICK: The answer to the hon. Gentleman's question is in the negative.

TURKISH LOAN, 1885.

MR. DILLON (Mayo, E.): I beg to ask the Under Secretary of State for Foreign Affairs whether the Convention for the conversion of the residue of the 4 per cent. Turkish Loan of 1885, which was signed in London 5th August, 1898, has yet been submitted to Parliament; and, if not, why not.

*MR. BRODRICK: I can only give a reply similar to that returned to a ques-tion on this subject on the 20th April: that as the negotiations are still incom-plete no statement can be made at present.

MR. DILLON: Does the right hon. Gentleman say that the statement in *The Times* of August 6th, that the Con-vention was signed on the previous day, is not true?

No answer.

Mr. PIERPOINT (Warrington): When does the right hon. Gentleman expect to be able to make a statement?

No answer.

RUSSIA IN CHINA.

Sir ELLIS ASHMEAD-BARTLETT: I beg to ask the Under Secretary of State for Foreign Affairs whether he can inform the House for what cause Her Majesty's Government by the recent Anglo-Russian agreement accepted the extension of the Russian sphere of interest up to the Great Wall of China, that is, close to Pekin.

*Mr. BRODRICK: No question arose in the Anglo-Russian Agreement of extending the Russian sphere of interest, but of defining the limits within which Her Majesty's Government would not apply for concessions or oppose them, if applied for by the Russian Government. The Great Wall of China forms a natural division, and is the boundary of Manchuria in the provinces of Mukdar.

Sir ELLIS ASHMEAD-BARTLETT: Am I to understand that the Russian sphere of interest has not been extended to the Great Wall of China?

*Mr. BRODRICK: I said the question of extending it did not arise in the Agreement.

PROHIBITION OF RICE EXPORTS FROM NANKING.

Mr. PROVAND (Glasgow, Blackfriars): I beg to ask the Under Secretary of State for Foreign Affairs whether the Viceroy of Nanking having recently prohibited the export of rice, the British Consul at Shanghai subsequently applied for permission to ship some to Wei-hai-Wei for the use of the garrison, but was refused; whether subsequently the Russian Consul peremptorily demanded permission to ship rice to Port Arthur, which demand was granted; and whether the request of the British Consul was then complied with.

*Mr. BRODRICK: We have no information confirmatory of the reports referred to by the hon. Member. At the instance of a British firm, who complained of the hardship entailed by the prohibition of the export of rice from Wuhu without sufficient notice, representations were made to the Chinese Government by Her Majesty's Chargé d'Affaires, in consequence of which instructions were sent to the Viceroy of Nanking to allow the export of all rice purchased prior to the date of the proclamation.

IRISH LIGHTS—MAIDEN ROCKS, LARNE.

Mr. FIELD (Dublin, St. Patrick): I beg to ask the President of the Board of Trade whether he can state how many applications, memorials, and requests have been made to the Irish Lights Board within the past ten years regarding the better marking of the Maiden Rocks, Larne, and the lighting of the beacon at the western entrance of Castletown, Berehaven; and, considering the numerous complaints by mariners and local bodies of the failure of the Irish Lights Board to provide proper warnings for mariners, both on the Maiden Rocks and the western entrance to Castletown, Berehaven, whether he will order a Board of Trade inquiry into the complaints regarding these two places against the Irish Lights Board.

The PRESIDENT of the BOARD of TRADE (Mr. Ritchie, Croydon): I am informed by the Commissioners of Irish Lights that they have received five applications, memorials, or requests in favour of the better marking of the Maiden Rocks. The Board understand that the question has been very fully considered by the Commissioners and by the Trinity House, who are of opinion that the existing arrangements are adequate for the present requirements of navigation. This view is confirmed by the opinion given to the Board of Trade by their nautical adviser. In particular, the Board are advised that the establishment of a fog signal in this locality would be of doubtful expediency. The Board of Trade have also received several memorials with respect to the lighting of the beacon at the western entrance of Castletown, Berehaven. As explained by me on former occasions, it is not thought desirable to encourage vessels to use the western channel, which is narrow and dangerous. I have no intention of ordering an inquiry into the complaints against the Commissioners of Irish Lights with respect to these two places.

BRITISH SAILORS AT RIO DE JANEIRO.

Mr. HOGAN: I beg to ask the President of the Board of Trade whether he has observed, at page 25 of the recently issued Consular Report on Rio de Janeiro, a reference to the evils that befall British sailors in that port through the traffic in drink carried on by boats licensed by the municipality ; and whether the representations made with a view to the suppression of this traffic have been successful.

MR. RITCHIE : Yes, Sir. My attention has been called to the passages referred to in the question. No further information has yet arrived from the Consul.

BUENOS AYRES CATTLE TRADE.

MR. FIELD : I beg to ask the President of the Board of Agriculture whether he is aware that the *Hindustan*, from Buenos Ayres to London (Deptford) with cattle, lost 155 bullocks out of 160, and 860 sheep out of 967, and that she was black-listed for 12 months from 23rd February, 1899 ; whether he can state the reason why the black-listing Order has been cancelled in three months ; and what has occurred since to enable the steamer to again carry live stock ?

*THE PRESIDENT OF THE BOARD OF AGRICULTURE (Mr. W. H. LONG, Liverpool, West Derby) : It is the case that the losses of the *Hindustan* on a voyage from the Argentine, in January last, were as stated in the question, and inasmuch as we considered that the losses were in part attributable to the fittings of the vessel we issued an Order prohibiting the carriage of cattle by her for a period of 12 months. We subsequently received assurances from the owners as to the future equipment of the vessel which justified us in withdrawing the prohibition Order, but the result of her voyages will be closely watched, and the owners have been warned that any recurrence of the losses may lead to the re-imposition of the Order.

MR. FIELD : Then the name of this vessel has been removed from the black list ?

*MR. W. H. LONG : Yes, because I have satisfied myself that the weather through which the vessel passed was of an exceptional character, and I have received definite assurances from the owners that steps will be taken to make the fittings more satisfactory.

NEW WINE DUTIES.

MR. LAMBERT (Devon, South Molton): I beg to ask the Chancellor of the Exchequer what amount of revenue he expects to derive from the new duty of 3d. per gallon on wine under 30 per cent. proof spirit.

*THE CHANCELLOR OF THE EXCHEQUER (Sir M. HICKS-BEACH, Bristol, W.) : About £127,000.

THE BAWNBOY LETTER CARRIER.

MR. J. P. FARRELL : I beg to ask the Secretary to the Treasury, as representing the Postmaster-General, whether he is aware that John Pinkman, a rural letter carrier in the Bawnboy sub-district, walks eight miles a day in his rounds, only receiving therefor the sum of 5s. 6d. per week ; on what scale is remuneration to these rural letter carriers fixed ; and will he consider the case with a view to improvement of salary.

THE FINANCIAL SECRETARY TO THE TREASURY (Mr. HANBURY, Preston) : The work of the rural postman referred to varies on different days of the week, and it is not clear from the particulars at present obtainable what average distance he walks daily. He receives a sum of 5s. 3d. a-week. The remuneration to messengers of this class is fixed at the rate of 4d. per hour in country districts. The Postmaster-General will consider the case of this postman, with a view of ascertaining whether any increase of his wages is justified. It may be found desirable to reduce his duties and assign some of them to other persons.

LOUGH RYNN LETTER DELIVERIES.

MR. TULLY (Leitrim, S.) : I beg to ask the Secretary to the Treasury, as representing the Postmaster-General, whether repeated complaints have been received from residents in Lough Rynn, county Leitrim, as to their letters being seriously delayed by being sent to Loughglynn, county Roscommon ; and if he can state what steps have been taken to remedy this matter.

MR. HANBURY : Several complaints have been received in regard to the missending of letters addressed to Lough Rynn. Instructions have been given with the view of ensuring the proper treatment of correspondence for Lough Rynn in future. The full address for the place is " Lough Rynn, Dromod R.S.O., co.

Leitrim," and the adoption of this address on all occasions would greatly facilitate the work of the sorters.

BELFAST POST OFFICE STAFF.

MR. SCHWANN : I beg to ask the Secretary to the Treasury, as representing the Postmaster-General, whether the Belfast Post Office authorities have made the minimum pay of each class the same as the maximum pay of the class below ; and, if so, whether this arrangement has received his sanction ; and, if not, would he take steps to increase the minimum of the higher classes, with retrospective action to September last, the date of the last revision.

MR. HANBURY : Under the last revision of the indoor force at Belfast the minimum of each class is the same as the maximum pay of the class below, except in the case of the class of clerks where the minimum is overlapped to the extent of 17s. a year by the maximum of the sorting clerks and telegraphists. The scales of pay are those authorised by the Treasury for the offices in the class into which Belfast falls. An officer who has been at the maximum of his scale for more than a year, on promotion enters the higher class at the minimum of the scale, plus one year's increment. If he has been at the maximum of his scale for less than a year he receives his first increment in the new class when that year has been completed. The Postmaster-General does not think it necessary to alter the scales as suggested.

SCOTTISH SECONDARY AND TECHNICAL SCHOOLS.

MR. BUCHANAN (Aberdeenshire, E.) : I beg to ask the Lord Advocate if he could state what are the higher class secondary and technical schools which come within the scope of paragraph 3 of the Minute of 27th April, 1899.

*THE JUNIOR LORD OF THE TREASURY (MR. ANSTRUTHER, St. Andrew's Burgh) (for the LORD ADVOCATE) : In the absence of my right hon. friend I am asked to say that it is impossible to give any exhaustive definition of the schools which come within the scope of the paragraph referred to, as each case must be judged on its own merits. But generally it may be said that the schools intended are those which come within the terms of Section 2 (1) (b) of the Educa-

tion and Local Taxation Act, 1892, and are not eligible to share in the Parliamentary Grant.

KERRY COUNTY COUNCIL.

MR. FIELD : I beg to ask the Chief Secretary to the Lord Lieutenant of Ireland whether any complaints have been made to the Local Government Board that contractors to the County Council of Kerry and District Council of Cahirciveen were members of these Boards ; whether contractors are disqualified by the Local Government Act of 1898 from being members of the councils to which they are contractors ; whether there is a difference in the law in case of a real and nominal contractor ; and, what steps have been taken by the Local Government Board to practically prevent real or nominal contractors from being members of the new Local Government bodies.

*THE CHIEF SECRETARY FOR IRLAND (MR. G. W. BALFOUR, Leed Central) : The reply to the first and second paragraphs is in the affirmative. Article 12 of the Application of Enactments Order of 22nd December, 1898, provides that a person shall not be qualified to be elected, or to sit, as member of a county or district council who is concerned by himself or his partner in any bargain or contract entered into with the council, or participates by himself or his partner in any such contract. A person acting in contravention of the provisions of this enactment is liable to a penalty not exceeding £20 for each occasion on which he acts, and it is further provided by Section 94 of the Act of last year that a person who incurs such a penalty shall for seven years be disqualified for being elected a member of any council. Save as to any question which may arise on the audit of the accounts, the Local Government Board have no jurisdiction in the matter. It is the duty of the parties interested, not of the Local Government Board, to institute proceedings for breach of the provisions of Article 12 of the Order referred to.

ULSTER AND CONNAUGHT NATIONAL SCHOOL TEACHERS.

MR. FIELD : I beg to ask the Chief Secretary to the Lord Lieutenant of Ireland whether his attention has been called to resolutions of managers of national schools in Ulster and Connaught, whereby they endeavour to prevent national teachers from belonging to a legal organisation and, whether, in view of the number of illiterates in Ireland, the Government intend to give the Irish local government bodies a share of control over the system of national education and the appointment and dismissal of Irish national teachers.

*MR. G. W. BALFOUR: I have referred this question to the Commissioners of National Education, who have informed me they have received no communication on the subject of the resolutions referred to. There is no intention on the part of the Government of giving local authorities a share of control over the appointment and dismissal of the teachers in Irish National schools, but it may be remarked that the Irish Education Act of 1892 vests in the county councils the power of bringing the compulsory clauses of the Act into operation within the areas of the rural districts of their respective counties, which seems to be the most direct means of coping with illiteracy.

INTERMEDIATE EDUCATION IN IRELAND.

MR. FIELD: I beg to ask the Chief Secretary to the Lord Lieutenant of Ireland whether he can state the terms of reference to the Viceregal Commission on Intermediate Education in Ireland; and whether those terms are at variance with those announced in the Session of 1898.

*MR. G. W. BALFOUR: In answer to the first paragraph, I would refer the hon. Member to the first Report of the Commissioners appointed to inquire into the system of Intermediate Education in Ireland. This Report was presented to Pariament last year. I do not know to what the second paragraph refers.

LONGFORD COUNTY COUNCIL COLLECTOR.

MR. J. P. FARRELL: I beg to ask the Chief Secretary to the Lord Lieutenant of Ireland will he explain why the Local Government Board have written to the Longford County Council that, unless they appoint one Jones to be a collector (he being an existing officer), any other person appointed by the council will have no power to collect rates, and any remuneration to him will be surcharged; whether he is aware that it is competent to the Council to retire Jones, according to the compensation scale laid down in the seventh schedule

of the Act; and whether he will lay the whole correspondence upon the Table of the House.

MR. G. W. BALFOUR: The secretary to the County Council, in a letter to the Local Government Board, asked what would be the result should the Council decline to appoint Mr. W. Jones (an existing officer willing to serve), and if they were to fill the vacancy by appointing an outsider. It was in reply to this inquiry that the Board stated that—

" If the council appoint a person as collector contrary to the provisions of Section 115, Subsection 10 of the Local Government Act, 1898, the appointment would be invalid, and the person appointed would have no legal authority to collect the rates, and any payments made to him would be surcharged."

This enactment provides that the scheme of a county council for the collection of the poor-rate

"shall not authorise the employment of officers not transferred to, or previously employed by, the council if sufficient existing officers have expressed their willingness to serve,"

and is not over-ridden by the 12th subsection, which regulates the compensation to the existing officers who cannot be provided for in the schemes. The correspondence is not of sufficient importance to lay on the Table of the House, but I will be happy to supply the hon. Member with a copy of it, should he so desire.

LONGFORD AND THE AGRICULTURAL GRANT.

MR. J. P. FARRELL: I beg to ask the Chief Secretary to the Lord Lieutenant of Ireland on what basis the allotment of the County Longford portion of the Agricultural Grant was fixed; what excluded charges (if any) were taken into account in fixing the amount for the half-year at £4,905 5s.; will he explain why it is that, although the figures on which this calculation was based have been asked for by the County Council, no reply has been vouchsafed; and will he see that the Local Government Board supply full information as desired.

*MR. G. W. BALFOUR: The basis on which the Agricultural Grant to Longford, as to other counties, was fixed, is defined in Sections 48, 49, 56 and 57 of the Act of last year. The excluded charges in the case of Longford consist of charges for malicious injuries, relief of distress, and special sanitary rates. They affected the Grant to the extent of about £90. The information asked for by the County Council was not given by the Local Government Board, but I propose, as already stated, to lay on the Table of the House a general Memorandum explaining the methods adopted in order to arrive at the basis on which the amounts of the Grant have been calculated.

QUEEN'S ISLAND WORKMEN, BELFAST.

MR. DILLON (Mayo, E.): I beg to ask the Chief Secretary to the Lord Lieutenant of Ireland whether he is aware that, on Friday last, in the Queen's Island, Belfast, a Roman Catholic workman was set on by a couple of hundred Protestant workmen and beaten severely; that the crowd dragged the Catholic to the water's edge, and, when he seized hold of a lamp with both hands to save himself from being thrown into the dock, he was kicked by several men on the abdomen and on the hands to make him relax his hold, and then thrown into the water, where he would have been drowned had he not been rescued by some men who were bathing; and, what steps the Government propose to take to put a stop to this state of things.

*MR. G. W. BALFOUR: The details in the first paragraph do not appear to be quite accurate. The man in question was a Protestant, although probably he was mistaken for a Roman Catholic, and his assailants were about twelve in number, who beat him with their fists, knocked him down, and kicked him, and finally threw him into the water. There has been, I regret to say, several other cases of gross and unprovoked assaults of a similar character in Belfast. In all of these cases the men assaulted are either ignorant of the names of their assailants or are unwilling to disclose them, but instructions have been given to the police to spare no pains in tracing the guilty parties and making them amenable.

MR. DILLON: Will the right hon. Gentleman station police inside these works, in order to prevent such abominable brutality, if the owners will not give assurances that it shall be stopped?

*MR. G. W. BALFOUR: I am afraid I cannot undertake to place policemen inside every factory in Belfast.

MR. DILLON: I am only speaking of the place where this man was thrown into the water.

WESTPORT COMMISSIONERS.

DR. ROBERT AMBROSE (Mayo, W.) I beg to ask the Chief Secretary to the Lord Lieutenant of Ireland if he is aware that the Westport Commissioners have petitioned the Local Government Board to constitute them an urban sanitary authority; and whether the Local Government Board have come to any decision in the matter.

MR. G. W. BALFOUR: A petition of the nature referred to has been received by the Local Government Board, who have given instructions for the holding of a local inquiry into the matter, pending which no decision will be come to.

DUBLIN POLICE CLOTHING.

MR. CRILLY (Mayo, N.) I beg to ask the Chief Secretary to the Lord Lieutenant of Ireland whether, seeing that the members of the Dublin Metropolitan Police are compelled to wear in summer the same heavy tunics and helmets that they wear in winter, arrangements can be made to extend to Dublin the rule which operates in London, permitting the use of a lighter police uniform in the summer months.

MR. G. W. BALFOUR: The question of lighter summer clothing for the Dublin Metropolitan Police has already engaged attention. It appears, however, that nothing can be done in the matter until the termination, in December next, of the existing clothing contracts. The matter will then be further considered by the Chief Commissioner of Police.

DOMINICK O'DONNELL, OF GLENGAD.

MR. CRILLY: I beg to ask the Chief Secretary to the Lord Lieutenant of Ireland, is he aware that Dominick O'Donnell, a landowner, is at present an inmate of the Belmullet Union; and, whether he is receiving any money from the Court of Chancery or from the receiver on his property at Glengad; if so will such money in future be paid to the local authorities for his maintenance in the said Union.

MR. G. W. BALFOUR: Mr. Dominick O'Donnell has been an inmate of the Belmullet Union Workhouse, but he is not there at present. He receives no allowance from the estate, it being wholly insolvent, though he occasionally receives small sums for expenses when giving assistance to the Court in the management of the property.

EXTRA POLICE AT BELMULLET.

MR. CRILLY: I beg to ask the Chief Secretary to the Lord Lieutenant of Ireland if he has received a resolution from the Belmullet Rural District Council protesting against the extra police force now stationed at Elly Bay Coastguard Station, Belmullet, and calling for their removal; and whether this request can be complied with; and, if not, can the reasons be stated why this extra police was established at Elly Bay.

MR. G. W. BALFOUR: The resolution referred to in the first paragraph has been received. The Council have been informed that it is not proposed, at present, to withdraw the force stationed at this place. The police there form portion of the ordinary police establishment of the county, and no expense is entailed to the district by their employment.

LOCAL GOVERNMENT IN WEST CAVAN.

MR. J. P. FARRELL: I beg to ask the Chief Secretary to the Lord Lieutenant of Ireland whether he is aware that great dissatisfaction exists in portions of West Cavan at the action of the Local Government Board in refusing to transfer the five divisions of Mulnalaghta, Scrabby, Loughdawn, Kilcogy, and Drumlummon from the Granard to the Cavan Union; whether several numerously signed petitions have been received by the Local Government Board asking them to assent to the change; whether he is aware that the County Council of Cavan has passed a resolution in its favour; and whether, in face of all this local feeling, the Local Government Board still persist in their refusal.

MR. G. W. BALFOUR: Several communications and petitions have been received by the Local Government Board in favour of the change suggested in the first paragraph. The Board have informed the applicants that they should bring the matter before the County Councils of Cavan and Longford, with a view to the making of a representation under Article 25, Paragraphs (1) (e) of the Application of Enactments Order of 22nd December last. Such a representation has been made by the Cavan County Council, and as it is believed the Longford County Council will also pass a resolution on the subject, the Board will defer, for the present, the consideration of the further action to be taken in the matter.

MULLINGAR ASYLUM BOARD JOINT COMMITTEE.

MR. J. P. FARRELL: I beg to ask the Chief Secretary to the Lord Lieutenant of Ireland whether he is aware that at its first meeting the Longford County Council passed a resolution protesting against the number of members allotted to county Longford upon the Joint Committee of the Mullingar Asylum Board; can he say whether the resolution which was forwarded to the Lord Lieutenant has been received; and, if so, why no reply has been given to it; and whether it will be considered with a view to increasing the number of members from five to seven members.

MR. G. W. BALFOUR: The resolution referred to in the first paragraph was received on the 26th April, and on the 28th April a reply was sent to the secretary to the County Council. The reply pointed out that the Lord Lieutenant, having decided that the Joint Committee of Management of the Asylum shall consist of 21 members to be appointed by the Councils of the counties of Longford, Meath and Westmeath, the proportion of the committee to be appointed by these counties had been calculated in accordance with the provisions of Section 9, subSection 7, of the Local Government Act of last year—namely, according to the average number of patients for the three years ended the 31st March, 1899, from the three mentioned counties, respectively.

ANNALY ESTATE COUNTY LONGFORD.

MR. J. P. FARRELL: I beg to ask the Chief Secretary to the Lord Lieutenant of Ireland can he now state what progress has been made in the matter of the purchase of the Annaly, county Longford,

Estate; how many of the tenants have purchased their holdings; and when may these tenants hope to have the vesting orders issued.

MR. G. W. BALFOUR: Applications for advances were received from 157 tenants to enable them to purchase their holdings on this estate. In 150 of these cases the advances were made in July of last year, and in the remaining seven cases the advances were made in January and February of this year. The Vesting Orders have long since been executed in all cases.

ROSCOMMON AND THE AGRICULTURAL GRANT.

MR. TULLY: I beg to ask the Chief Secretary to the Lord Lieutenant of Ireland whether he can state in detail the several amounts deducted from the Agricultural Grant as excluded charges in the county Roscommon, under the heading of Public Health Act charges, railway charges, Suck drainage charges, relief of distress charges, malicious injury charges, and navigation charges; whether he can give the same details as regards the county Leitrim; and whether, in the case of the county Roscommon, allowance was made for the fact that in the standard year a sum of £614 for bank interest, and of £604 for dog tax, was placed to the credit of the rates.

MR. G. W. BALFOUR: I can forward to the hon. Member, if he desires it, the amounts taken as raised for excluded charges in the Counties of Leitrim and Roscommon in the standard year, but it would be impossible without elaborate calculations to state the amount of deduction from the Agricultural Grant in respect of each of these charges. The calculations by which the amount of the Grant has been arrived at are very complicated and numerous, and I cannot undertake to go into details in each case. In calculating the amount to be deemed as having been raised as county cess during the standard year the Local Government Board made use of the audited abstracts of the county accounts, and all receipts, apart from county cess, were duly credited in determining the amount. The entry for dog tax in the accounts was £447, not £604, and allowance was made for the former amount when calculating the Grant. It does not appear from the accounts that any interest was allowed to the county by their Treasurer.

BUSINESS OF THE HOUSE.

*SIR CHARLES DILKE (Gloucester, Forest of Dean): I beg to ask the First Lord of the Treasury if he purposes before Tuesday, 20th June, to take Tuesdays; and, if so, whether the promised Bills relating to the amendment of the law on factories and regarding the taxation of clerical incomes will be introduced, and either printed or explained to the House before any such Motion for taking time for Government business is made.

THE FIRST LORD OF THE TREASURY (MR. A. J. BALFOUR, Manchester, E.): As I have already stated, I shall have on Monday to ask the House to give further facilities for Government business, and the right hon. Baronet will see that the details of the Bills he has mentioned, or any other Bills, have hardly any bearing on the request I shall have to make.

NEW WRIT.

For the Burgh of Edinburgh (East Division)—in the room of Robert Wallace, esquire, deceased.—(*Mr. Herbert Gladstone.*)

LONDON GOVERNMENT BILL.

Order for Third Reading read.

Motion made, and Question proposed—

"That the Bill be now read a third time."

MR. ELLIOT (Durham City): I beg to move the Amendment standing in my name, which is to re-commit the Bill in respect of Clause 2, and the main object for my doing so is that I feel most strongly upon this matter. Nothing would have induced me to bring the additional trouble upon my right hon. friend the Leader of the House which this re-committal must entail were it not that, after all, we are concerned in matter of extreme importance, and had it not been that the right hon. Gentleman showed us himself that he left to the House absolute liberty to deal with this matter. He left not only one or two stages to the House to decide, but the whole of the stages which it is competent for this House to consider. A word or two will be sufficient to bring to the recollection of the House the position in which we stood a few weeks ago. After having been told that the matter would come on on the Report stage in such a way that it could be dealt with, the fact remains that it was unexpectedly brought forward, and we were taken by surprise; no means were taken to get Members to the House—I blame no one, but merely state the facts—and we did not get, I submit, the real opinion of the House. I feel it is only right to appeal to a larger House, which will better reflect the true opinion of this House than the Division which took us by surprise a few nights ago. I am not a London Member, and those with whom I have spoken are not London Members. It is as a provincial Member that I venture to urge upon this House that the clause should be re-committed, in order to consider this principle which has been so recklessly accepted—a principle which will be applied to town councils and county councils throughout the length and breadth of England. Before going into the merits, I might just say that I am not one of those who attack the other sex on the ground that they are inferior to us. I number amongst my friends and acquaintances many women of ability and capacity, whose qualities would do credit to many of my male friends——

*Mr. SPEAKER: Order, order. The hon. Member will not be in order in discussing the whole question of the right of women to sit upon the council. The motion is that the Bill be re-committed in respect to a particular clause. If the Bill be re-committed then will be the time to discuss the whole question. The hon. Member can only argue now that another opportunity ought to be given to the House to consider the subject.

Mr. ELLIOT: I do not, of course, Sir, venture to dispute any ruling that you may lay down, but my contention is that the principle introduced into Clause 2 extends far beyond the London boroughs. It extends to town councils and county

councils, and although I do not want to trespass upon your ruling one iota, I do hope you will permit me to reason that if Clause 2 is accepted the municipalities throughout England will be greatly affected. I should have thought I might take that line.

*Mr. SPEAKER: The hon. Member follows what I said; he cannot discuss the question on its merits until he has succeeded in carrying the Motion.

Mr. ELLIOT: I feel that I am placed in a very embarrassing position, because I have taken some little trouble in this matter, and I feel now that I cannot say what I should like to say upon this occasion. I certainly did imagine that this would be an occasion when a general discussion would be taken; but if, as I understand, a general discussion may not be taken now, I must reserve what I have to say until we get into Committee, and simply move—

" That this Bill be re-committed in respect of Clause 2a."

Mr. DUNCOMBE (Cumberland, Egremont): After the ruling laid down by you, Sir, I shall also be relieved of the trouble that I have taken, and will simply second the Motion, and make any other remarks which I may have to make at another time.

Amendment proposed—

" To leave out the words 'now read the third time,' in order to add the words 're-committed in respect of Clause 2" — (*Mr. Elliot*).—instead thereof."

Question proposed—

" That the words 'now read the third time' stand part of the Question."

*THE CHANCELLOR OF THE EXCHEQUER (Sir M. HICKS-BEACH, Bristol, W.): I wish to intervene for a very few minutes to express my views on the Motion which my hon. friend has submitted for the consideration of the House. For many years, ever since I have had the honour of being a Member of this House, I have done the best in my power to oppose the grant of what are, in my opinion, erroneously called "women's rights." I have voted against the proposal with regard to the Parliamentary franchise, I have voted in the measure now before the House three times against women being councillors or aldermen; therefore I think my friend will see that my opinion on the merits of the question which he desires to discuss are entirely in accordance with his own. I do not attach the importance to this particular matter which my hon. friend does. I do not at all anticipate that if women are admitted to be aldermen and county councillors in London, that the whole system of county councils and borough councils in the United Kingdom will be affected. However that may be, the question immediately before us is whether the Bill should be re-committed. I will submit to my hon. friend some considerations which may induce him not to press the Motion. We have already had opportunities on three occasions of expressing our opinions by speech and vote upon this matter in the course of the progress of the Bill through the House; and I cannot help feeling that anyone who is so well informed as my hon. friend on the practice of the House may feel that there are not a few Members who, though generally somewhat indifferent to the merits of the question, would be very much disposed to oppose the re-committal of the Bill now it has reached its present stage. It is an absolutely unusual course for a Motion to be made for the re-committal of a Bill except by someone who is opposed to the measure; and when the measure is one which contains so many important provisions relating to perfectly different subjects, and has been so amply discussed as this Bill has been, I think there is additional ground against making what is a most inconvenient precedent by carrying a motion for the re-committal of the Bill. My hon. friend is likely to get on this ground a very much worse division than he might on the merits of the question. I feel very strongly that there is considerable objection, as I have said, for the reasons I have given, to the re-committal of the Bill. I am confident that that view is shared by many hon. Members on this side who would be ready enough, as I should be, if the issue could be fairly raised, to vote with my hon. friend; and

I would strongly urge him, from that point of view, not to press the matter further, but to let the Bill now proceed to its Third Reading. The measure will then go to another place, and we may again have cause to thank God that we have a House of Lords.

EARL PERCY (Kensington, S.): I am not in a position to-night to detain the House by recapitulating the arguments which I have already urged at a previous stage of the Bill, but I feel I must say one or two words in support of the motion of my hon. friend, in spite of the words which have fallen from the right hon. Gentleman the Chancellor of the Exchequer. Sir, we all recognise the very friendly treatment which the Chancellor of the Exchequer has given to this question; but I must confess, although he is a far better judge of expediency than I am, that I do not quite understand one of his arguments, which was, as I take it, that if we re-commit this Bill it will be open to discussion on every other important question which the Bill contains. Surely this question of the eligibility of women to sit on the councils can take place within the space of an hour. I am bound to say, considering the importance which many London Members attach to this point, that that is not a very large extension of Parliamentary time to ask of the Government. I know very well that it is a strong order to ask the Government to re-commit a Bill, and it can only be justified on two grounds—in the first place, that the point which we have to re-discuss is of sufficient importance, or, in the second place, that it did not receive fair and adequate treatment either in the Committee or on Report. Now, Sir, at the present stage, I only desire to say that some—in fact, the majority of—London Members are against the inclusion of women, so far as the opinion of London Members has been expressed in Committee, and that an overwhelming majority of Members think the inclusion of women will go very far to stultify the legislation of the present Bill. The only real objection which the Chancellor of the Exchequer has urged against the re-committal of the Bill is that it will be reconsidered in another place. Now, Sir, if I could be perfectly certain that the image of the lady aldermen would cross the mind of every one of the noble Lords in another place, then I might be able to rely upon the House of Lords to save us from the results of the discussion in Committee and the Report stage. But the manner in which the subject has been treated is so inadequate that I hope the House will be willing to give us another chance of discussing it. We have had several Divisions on the representation of women on these councils. We had, first, the Division which resulted in favour of the admission of women, which was taken in a thin House during the dinner hour, when almost every London Member was away. The second and third Divisions, which were unfavourable to the admission of women, were taken in a fuller House, when all the Members had returned. The result of those Divisions was summed up by the First Lord of the Treasury, when he said that the House of Commons had committed itself to an impossible and ridiculous position, and therefore must reserve the whole question for further consideration on the Report stage. Well, Sir, the Report stage was taken last Tuesday, and under conditions that entirely vitiate the conclusions at which the House of Commons arrived. The London Government Bill was put in the second place on the Paper, after the Finance Bill; and so unlikely did it appear that the discussion on the London Government Bill would be concluded before the close of Tuesday's debate that the First Lord of the Treasury expressly reserved Thursday for its consideration. Well, the Finance Bill, as it turned out, was completed at an early hour, and the question was raised for final decision at a time when most Members were taking

Earl Percy.

tea on the Terrace. I do not wish for a moment to accuse any Member of the Government of any complicity in this matter. On the contrary, we recognise, as the Chancellor of the Exchequer has said, that no one could have regretted the result of the Division more than he did, and I can imagine that in his own mind he saw battalions of women rushing through the breaches of his own Finance Bill. I do, however, think that the Government must accept responsibility for the totally unrepresentative character of the Division; and although I am perfectly willing to take the responsibility which attaches to me or to any other London Member for any lack of foresight on our part, at any rate against that has to be set the somewhat slipshod procedure on the part of the Government. I do not really believe that the decision arrived at is of much value on the general aspect of female suffrage. I have never argued the question from that point of view. But it is a question directly affecting London, and London alone, and it is a question which has been decided directly contrary to the opinions of the right hon. gentlemen who sit on the front Opposition bench, and directly contrary to the opinions of the vast majority of London Members. It has also been decided in a sense particularly opposite to the opinion of the London vestries themselves. Under these circumstances, if the motion is pressed to a Division, I shall certainly feel it my duty to support my hon. friend.

SIR H. CAMPBELL-BANNERMAN (Stirling Burghs): In the few words that I shall address to the House I shall confine myself entirely to the question before us. This is not an occasion on which to discuss the details of the London Government Bill, or the advantages or disadvantages of women sitting upon the councils. The question is whether it is a proper procedure to recommit the Bill on the grounds which have been advanced in support of it. Now, Sir, I venture to think that that is a Motion which is absolutely incapable of being supported by anyone who has regard to the practices and rules of the House. A Bill on the stage of the Third Reading has to be re-committed for some definite reason justifying that step being taken by the House, and that definite reason must surely be that some fault, some hiatus, some mistake, has been discovered which has to be amended before we proceed to the final stage. It is found, perhaps, that by accident one clause is inconsistent with another, or that something has been done which it is desirable to amend. Now we are asked to re-commit a Bill for the simple purpose of reversing a decision which has been taken upon one point of the Bill. I venture to say that that is an entirely novel and almost unprecedented proposal. The noble Lord who has just sat down endeavoured to make out that the decision was arrived at in an imperfect way, and under circumstances which invalidated its effect. We have been told that hon. Members were at tea on the Terrace. We cannot help that. But I have seldom seen an occasion in which a decision was come to by the House in a more formal or deliberate manner. I confess I am not deeply interested in the question one way or the other, but I protest against the power of recommitting a Bill being used for the pure and sole and simple purpose of reversing a decision at which the House has already deliberately arrived.

Mr. R. G. WEBSTER (St. Pancras, E.) I venture to say that the majority of the people of London have shown themselves opposed to women councillors. We have had a debate on justice to Ireland. Why should we not have justice to London? Justice is a word which is sometimes abused. We have been told that we ought to thank God that we have a House of Lords. I, for one, do thank God that we have a House of Lords. Take, for example, this question. It was decided on a snatch vote of the House of Commons, in which only 360 hon. Members gave a vote out of a total of 670. Therefore, I consider we are entitled to ask that the Bill should be recommitted. The opinion of the House on the question of whether women should be included on the new councils was taken on four occasions, and on two of those occasions the House decided that they should not be councillors and aldermen—[cries of "Divide]." Hon. Members are in a hurry to have their dinner. They shall go to dinner in due course. I sincerely hope the House of Lords will give us the opportunity of again considering the question.

Mr. LABOUCHERE (Northampton): As one of those who are opposed to women having this right, I do not intend, for technical reasons, to divide the House, and I do not see much use in further discussing the matter. The Chancellor of the Exchequer has adumbrated the idea that possibly we may have an opportunity later on. Well, Sir, I understand perfectly well what that means. I do not go so far as the Chancellor of the Exchequer, and say "Thank God we have a House of Lords." In fact, I entertain rather the reverse view on that subject. But under all the circumstances I think it would be better to leave the Lords and ladies to fight the matter out.

Mr. ELLIOT: After what the Chancellor of the Exchequer has said, it is quite clear that my object would be entirely defeated by going on with my Amendment. I look forward, with my right hon. friend, to a near and happy future, and beg now to be allowed to withdraw my Amendment.

Question put, and agreed to.

Main question put, and agreed to.

Bill accordingly read the third time, and passed.

FINANCE BILL.

Read the third time, and passed.

PLUMBERS' REGISTRATION.

MR. LEES KNOWLES (Salford, W.) who had on the paper the following Notice of Motion—

"To call attention to the registration of plumbers ; and to move, that it is desirable that the Government should introduce legislation dealing with the subject, and create a scheme for the national registration of plumbers,"

said : I wish to address the House upon a subject in which I have taken great interest for a considerable number of years—namely, the subject of the registration of plumbers. It is a subject which I think is of great public interest. In the first place, I should say that for many years past there has been a constant movement of apprentices from shops to shops, and consequently there has been less supervision on the part of the masters of these apprentices, who are thus not able to learn their work properly. It seems to me that if anyone fails in the ordinary occupations of life he thinks himself able to turn his hand to the plumbing trade. The consequence of that has been that there has been an immense amount of scamped work introduced into plumbing throughout the whole country. We had evidence of that before a Select Committee. For instance, we had the evidence of Mr. G. Davies, a foreman plumber, and Mr. G. Jennings, a member of the Institute of Mechanical Engineers, who gave before that Committee illustrations of scamped work——

Notice taken that 40 Members were not present ; House counted and 40 Members not being present——   .

The House was adjourned at Eight of the clock till To-morrow.

HOUSE OF COMMONS.

Wednesday, 14th June 1899.

PRIVATE BILL BUSINESS.

ILFORD GAS BILL.

Lords' Amendments considered, and agreed to.

FRIENDS' PROVIDENT INSTITUTION BILL. [Lords.]

LOWESTOFT PROMENADE PIER BILL.

MID-KENT GAS. [Lords.]

SKIPTON URBAN DISTRICT GAS BILL. [Lords.]

As amended, considered; to be read the third time.

COBHAM GAS BILL. [Lords.]

GROSVENOR CHAPEL (LONDON) BILL. [Lords.]

MOSS SIDE URBAN DISTRICT COUNCIL (TRAMWAYS) BILL. [Lords.]

STRETFORD URBAN DISTRICT COUNCIL (TRAMWAYS) BILL. [Lords.]

WESTON - SUPER - MARE, CLEVEDON, AND PORTISHEAD TRAMWAYS COMPANY (LIGHT RAILWAY EXTENSIONS) BILL. [Lords.]

Read a second time, and committed.

WHITEHAVEN CORPORATION BILL. [Lords.]

WITHINGTON URBAN DISTRICT COUNCIL (TRAMWAYS) BILL. [Lords.]

Read a second time, and committed.

PRIVATE BILLS (GROUP B.)

Sir JOHN BRUNNER reported from the Committee on Group B of Private Bills, that the parties promoting the Leicester Corporation Water Bill had stated that the evidence of William Jaffray, surveyor, &c., Matlock Bath, was essential to their case; and it having been proved that his attendance could not be procured without the intervention of the House, he had been instructed to move that the said William Jaffray do attend the said Committee this day.

Ordered, that William Jaffray do attend the Committee on Group B of Private Bills this day.

VOL. LXXII.   [FOURTH SERIES.]

PETITIONS.

GROUND VALUES (TAXATION) (SCOTLAND) BILL.

Petition from Motherwell, in favour; to lie upon the Table.

INEBRIATES ACT, 1898.

Petition from Rochdale, for alteration of Law; to lie upon the Table.

LOCAL GOVERNMENT (SCOTLAND) ACT (1894) AMENDMENT BILL.

Petitions in favour—From Ardrossan; —and, Cathcart; to lie upon the Table.

PARISH COUNCILS ASSOCIATION (SCOTLAND) BILL.

Petition from Motherwell, in favour; to lie upon the Table.

PRIVATE LEGISLATION PROCEDURE (SCOTLAND) BILL.

Petition from Motherwell, in favour; to lie upon the Table.

SALE OF INTOXICATING LIQUORS ON SUNDAY BILL.

Petitions in favour —From Liverpool; —Brettenham;—Penrith (three); - Carlisle; — Talkin; - - Kirkoswald; - - Meal Bank;—Siddick;—Skirwith; -Blencarn; —Whitehaven (eight); — Yosthwaite; Wetherall;— Walton; — Parton (two); Moor Row;—Crosby; -Ivegill; -Hutton End :—Kirkbride; —Dearham; - Flimby; —Stainton; —Renwick; - - Newbiggin; Ainstable;—Gilsland; —Ormathwaite; - - Low Seaton; — Workington (two); —Distington; — St. Bees; — Calthwaite; - Blencowe; — Plumpton; - - Wigton; — Cleator; — Great Broughton;—Carlisle; —Great Salkeld; — Applethwaite; Portinscales;—Gamblesby;—Blyth; - - Langwathby — Lazenby — Allonby; — Maybrary;— Mealsgate;— Haverigg; — Millom;—Thelkeld;— Brigham;— and, Lincoln; to lie upon the Table.

SHOPS (EARLY CLOSING) BILL.

Petition from Motherwell, in favour; to lie upon the Table.

SMALL HOUSES (SCOTLAND) BILL.

Petition from Motherwell, in favour; to lie upon the Table.

TEINDS (SCOTLAND) BILL.

Petition of the Society of Solicitors of Elginshire, in favour; to lie upon the Table.

2 Q

TOWN COUNCILS (SCOTLAND) BILL.

Petition from Motherwell, in favour; to lie upon the Table.

TROUT FISHING ANNUAL CLOSE TIME (SCOTLAND) BILL.

Petition from Motherwell, in favour; to lie upon the Table.

WORKMEN'S HOUSES TENURE BILL.

Petition from Motherwell, in favour; to lie upon the Table.

———

RETURNS, REPORTS, &c.

———

CHARITY COMMISSION (WELSH IN-TERMEDIATE EDUCATION ACT, (1889).

Copy presented—of Report of the Charity Commissioners of their Proceedings under The Welsh Intermediate Education Act, 1889 [by Command]; to lie upon the Table.

NORTH SEA FISHERMEN.

Return presented — relative thereto [ordered 23rd February]; Mr. Herbert Robertson; to lie upon the Table, and to be printed. [No. 219.]

RAILWAYS.

Copy resented,—of Report by the Board of p Trade on Applications made during the year 1898 under the Railway Companies' Powers Act, 1864, and of the Proceedings of the Board of Trade with respect thereto [by Act]; to lie upon the Table, and to be printed. [No. 220.]

MUNICIPAL CORPORATIONS (NEW CHARTERS) (SMETHWICK).

Copy presented,—of Charter of Incorporation of the Borough of Smethwick, dated 12th June, 1899 [by Act]; to lie upon the Table.

ELECTRIC LIGHTING PROVISIONAL ORDERS.

Copy ordered, " of Memorandum stating the nature of the Proposals contained in the Provisional Orders included in the- -

Electric Lighting Provisional Orders (No. 9) Bill;

Electric Lighting Provisional Orders (No. 10) Bill;

Electric Lighting Provisional Orders (No. 11) Bill;

Electric Lighting Provisional Orders (No. 12) Bill;

Electric Lighting Provisional Orders (No. 13) Bill;

Electric Lighting Provisional Orders (No. 14) Bill;

Electric Lighting Provisional Orders (No. 15) Bill."—(*Mr. Ritchie.*)

Copy presented accordingly; to lie upon the Table, and to be printed. [No. 221.]

———

LINCOLNSHIRE CORONERS BILL.
[Lords.]

Read the first time; to be read a second time upon Monday next, and to be printed. [Bill 234.]

———

EDUCATION OF CHILDREN BILL.

Order for Third Reading read.

Motion made and Question proposed—

" That the Bill be now read the third time."—(*Mr. Robson.*)

MR. SETON-KARR (Lancashire, St. Helens): I desire to offer a few observations on this Bill. In the first place, may I call attention to the somewhat unusual method adopted in carrying this Bill through the House, and to the somewhat indecent haste——[Cries of "Oh, oh!"]. Well, I think it is indecent haste. We only had one day to discuss the Second Reading, and one day for the Committee, while there was no opportunity for discussion on the Report stage. With all due deference to the hon. Member in charge of the Bill, I say it was not showing due respect to the House to take the Report stage after midnight, and now we are asked to finally pass the Bill without seeing in print the important alterations which have been made in it. The measure is described by the promoters as a " Bill for the better education of children." I yield to no man in my desire for further legislation calculated to improve the education of our children in our national elementary schools in order to better fit them for the battle of life. But will this Bill beneficially affect our children? I submit that it will not. Its scope is exceedingly small; it will only affect, I believe, something like 2 per cent. of the children in our elementary schools. It does not touch the real evil which is inherent in our system of national education. It rather does something to perpetuate it, for it may have the effect of compelling poor parents of half-timers to send their children to some less healthy and more arduous occupation. What was it one of our leading London papers, *The Morning Post*, said on this subject the other day? I will read it:

"More than a year ago the House of Commons called for a return of children who, while attending public elementary schools in England and Wales, are also engaged in labour. The belated report of the Education Department on the subject has just been published. The returns are avowedly incomplete; they are fragmentary, and in some degree misleading in the direction of optimism, and yet it must be said that they reveal such a scandalous condition of affairs as should not be allowed to exist for another year. Almost a hundred and fifty thousand children are confessed to be at work, earning wages, while putting in their full time at school. . . . One child works from five to eight in the morning, and then after school well into the evening; and another begins work at three in the morning, and is frequently working till nine at night. A child of six does a certain amount of stone-breaking in a Northumberland quarry; and one of eight in Yorkshire spends some time in brick-making, and so on. The details are sickening."

I endorse the observation that the details are sickening. And yet this Bill does not touch that great evil. It has absolutely nothing whatever to do with it. Why did not the hon. Member in charge of it take advantage of the opportunity to touch the larger question? Why did he merely deal with half-timers over eleven, when he might have dealt with the labour of children under eleven? It may be asked why we did not in Committee seek to amend what we considered to be a fundamental error of the Bill. Well, I think too much stress is laid on the mechanical and unpractical teaching in our elementary schools. It is assumed that the teaching there given is the best possible preparation for their future work in life. I submit that this is not the case at all. As a rule the children of a factory hand become in time factory hands, they have to earn their living by the sweat of their brow; and is it wise, then, to insist on a stereotyped system of education which in many cases does not fit them for the life they are bound to lead? A great distinction ought to be drawn between children under 11 and those over 11. Under that age is

the proper time for them to acquire the necessary standard of elementary education, yet this Bill does not prevent them being engaged in labour which will interfere with that education. It has never been proved that after attaining 11 years the work done by the half-timers affects their health. On the contrary, it does prepare them for their life in the future. It is frequently said that children who leave school at 12 years of age quickly forget everything they have learned. But is that their fault? Is it not rather the fault of the system? This Bill begins at the wrong end; it should protect the very young children, and not interfere with the half-timers. Has it been found that University education helps our young men who are seeking a livelihood at Klondyke or in the Australian wilds? Book-learning does not necessarily fit a child for the battle of life, while it is possible to inflict serious injury on a child by preventing it learning in time the practical business of life. What is the view of the glass-blowers on this question? At their instigation I opposed a clause in the Factory and Workshops Bill of 1895 which affected them. In a petition on the subject they say:

"We find it quite impossible to get all our boys 14 years of age or over, as there are about 1,500 or 1,600 boys employed in the glass trade of St. Helens who all have to work night-work in different turns or shifts. Thus it is quite necessary for us to catch them at 13, directly they have passed their standards and left the school, as it is much easier to train them to the work than if they have to wait a year, and in that time they either get into some other industry or are inclined to become loafers and will not work. This period of a year or two makes a very serious difference in the glass bottle trade. Our present hours of working in the glass bottle trade (which is one of the staple trades of St. Helens, employing over 2,000 men and boys) are 51 hours per week, alternately weekly day and night turns. The week that we are on the day turn we finish at 5 p.m. on the Friday and do not start till 5.30 p.m. on the following Monday, and thus we have an interval of about 72 hours. The week that we are on the night turn we always have an interval of 48 hours. We work in turns of three men and three boys, and in some cases four boys, and it is very important that they should always work together and that the boys should not be changed, otherwise our wages are lessened and the work made much harder. It is not our desire to increase the hours of working, but we ask that our boys of 13 or over who have passed their standards be allowed to work night turns as well as day, and so avoid the change of boys in turns every week. Under the Act of 1897 boys of 13 cannot be employed night turns, and consequently have to change sets in which they work every week, which is most injurious to those who have to take all night work, as above stated, and injurious to the effective and harmonious working of the turns and trade generally."

That, I think, supplies an illustration of my argument. It is possible that the legislation now asked for may have the same effect. Boys may be deprived of an opportunity of learning a good trade, they may be turned into loafers, and—although I do not lay much stress on this—the Bill may inflict injury on our trade, and help to drive it into the hands of foreign competitors. I submit this Bill may involve those dangers. I would wish to allude to the Amendment introduced by the hon. Member in charge of this Bill. I have been unable to get a printed copy of it, but I was present at the Debate, and remember something of it. The House will remember that the hon. Member made an exception in the case of boys between 11 and 13 employed in agriculture, which practically made them half-timers. The hon. Member's original Amendment was that they should not be required to attend school more than 300 times in any year, but he subsequently reduced the number to 250. I submit that 250 is too large. The maximum attendance of a full timer is 420 ; why, therefore, should the hon. Member take 250, which is more than half the maximum, as the number for half-timers ? I think the hon. Member was very unreasonable in not accepting the further Amendment moved by my hon. friend. But I wish to know why this exception only applies to country boys. I venture to think it is equally necessary to apply it to town boys. The exception applies to urban districts, but not to towns, and the boys must be employed in agriculture, though the Amendment does not say how long or in what way, which I think will lead to considerable confusion. Why should it not apply to town boys ? They have also to learn a trade and the business of life, and why should they have to wait for the opportunity until they are 12 ? It may be said that country boys lead a more healthy life, but that has never been proved. No doubt an open-air life conduces to health, but we cannot all live in the country, and it has never been proved that life in a mill is more unhealthy than life in an elementary school. At all events, it is an illogical Amendment, and

Mr. Seton-Karr.

I think the Amendment of my hon. friend the Member for Stockport ought to have been accepted, because the original Amendment draws a very unfair distinction between country boys and town boys. Let me allude to another minor difficulty. The Amendment applies only to boys employed in agriculture, but it does not say they must be so employed all the time. They may be only employed for a week in agriculture, and because of that week secure exemption, and be then employed in some other way. Take the case of the son of a gamekeeper. He would probably be going around with his father, setting traps and doing other kinds of work. Why should that boy, any more than the boy employed in agriculture, have to make a full attendance at school ? It may be very necessary for him to learn his trade, and why should the opportunity be postponed for a year ? The Bill is an anomaly and an injustice. I do not wish to detain the House, but I will say that in endeavouring to bring before it some of the reasons why I am opposed to this measure I have spoken from absolute conviction. I do not represent any cotton factory, but I happen to be chairman of a large Lancashire and Cheshire working men's federation, the members of which, absolutely unsolicited, have almost unanimously represented to me that they are hostile to this Bill. The feelings of these men ought to be respected. They know what they are about. Many thousands of Lancashire men resent the opinion that they cannot be trusted with the management of their own children, and they may bring that resentment home to hon. Members at the next General Election. These are some of the reasons why I think this is a mistaken Bill. I give full credit to the motives which actuate hon. Members who support it. I share their desire to benefit the children of this country, to increase their education, and to prevent their improper employment ; but this Bill does not do any good in that direction at all, and it may do a great deal of harm. I am perfectly aware that the Second Reading was carried by an enormous majority ; but large majorities are not always right.

Amendment proposed—

"To leave out the word 'now,' and at the end of the Question to add the words.' upon this day three months.'"—*(Mr. Seton-Karr).*

Question proposed, "That the word 'now' stand part of the Question."

Mr. GEORGE WHITELEY (Stockport): I do not desire, on the Third Reading of this Bill, to take up very much of the time of the House, for I fully recognise that, though in my judgment we have had all the arguments on our side, still the majority of the House must prevail. There is a special providence with big battalions, and I can only hope that the opposition we have undertaken has not gone to such a limit as would be deemed by any reasonable Member of the House to be perverse or factious. I readily and frankly acknowledge that, apart from the merits, if one had to follow the bent of one's natural inclination, it would be very much more preferable to appear as a supporter rather than as an opponent of this Bill. All the best instincts of human nature, all the sentiments of charity and sympathy and kindliness towards those who are unable to advocate their own case, impel us to support a children's Bill, and therefore I readily recognise and understand the opinion of the majority, and the promptness with which they allied themselves with the hon. Member who introduced the Bill. The House would not, in my opinion, be what it is if it were not influenced by such motives. But I am not altogether sure that the majority of the House in this discussion are really the true supporters of the cause of the children. What I want hon. Members to recognise, before we close this discussion, is that there is another side to this question for which very much can be said. I honestly say that I do not think that even at the eleventh hour hon. Members fully appreciate the conditions in the half-time constituencies, or the opinion of the public generally in those districts in this matter. I have perhaps taken a larger part in these Debates on the Bill than other Members representing these constituencies, and it may be, possibly, because of the paucity of my vocabulary that the case is in its present unsatisfactory condition. I have endeavoured to show that there is really no body of working public opinion at the back of this Bill. The employers are against it; the workmen are opposed to it, because they wish to bring up their children as they themselves were brought up; the children are opposed to it, because they look forward to the time when they can take their place for a few hours as important members of the family; and, generally speaking, there is no public opinion in favour of it. The only body of opinion in favour of it is undoubtedly, in my judgment, the National Union of Teachers. I challenge the hon. Member to give the opinion of any body of working men who have expert knowledge of the working of the half-time system in support of this Bill. The trade unions of Lancashire, where more half-time is worked than in the rest of the United Kingdom, are distinctly hostile to it. [Cries of "Not all."] Hon. Members say, "Not all." Hon. Members who know anything of the cotton industry—and the bulk of the half-timers work in the weaving sheds—know that all the weavers' trade unions are against the Bill. The arguments which have been advanced for the Bill have been few and have been dissipated. The children in the districts in which the half-time system most prevails compare favourably with the children in other districts and towns in the country. On the question of education I differ again from my hon. friends. They have shown no disparity whatever between Lancashire and the other towns. Of course, figures may be made to prove anything, but if one does happen to have recourse to figures on this particular point this is what they show. If you compare the School Grants of Lancashire with other counties, there are 27 counties which receive less on the average than Lancashire, while only 12 show a larger average. On the Second Reading I alluded to the intelligence of the people in those districts where half-time prevails. I challenge any hon. Member to say that the intelligence of the people where half-time is worked is lower than that in other parts of the country. I do not begrudge the preferential treatment that has been accorded by Government to agriculture. I venture to say that it is consistent with the chief characteristic of this Parliament, which has always placed agriculture first. I am heartily glad that even one section of the community is exempted from what I regard as an unnecessary Bill. But is it not almost absurd to suggest that you should enact that in the other counties of England the educational requirements, as represented by 250 attendances, should be sufficient to permit a child becoming a half-timer at 11, whereas in Lancashire and Yorkshire those educational requirements are not sufficiently met until a child is 12 years of age. I would venture to ask the House, in dealing with this matter of education, to consider what, to my mind, is a very important question, whether, to use a colloquial phrase, they are absolutely sure they have got hold of the right end of the stick in this matter. It seems to me that this step is a most important step, but, at the same time, it is a most dubious one; in fact, it is entirely a leap in the dark. In the future your educational system in the counties can only be described as an in-and-out running system. Two hundred and fifty attendances will be necessary in order to enable a child to become a half-timer, but those 250 attendances may be put in in 125 days, and all the rest of the year a child is free to do as he likes. My hon. friend has adopted this policy—in order to get his bacon streaky—of over-feeding his pig one day and starving it the next. Under this streaky education Bill you are going to cram your children for 125 days of the year, and then permit them to run wild. We all know that children easily assume and just as easily forget that which they have learned, unless their learning is continued to a later period of life. I venture to predict that this educational experiment of my hon. and learned friend will prove most unfortunate. I am almost glad that that will be so. I believe that a great many counties are suffering from the effects of education. In previous years a man who was not educated was perfectly willing to remain on the land tending the turnips or mangold wurtzel, and never aspired to any higher occupation. Now that you have educated the children they all desire to go to towns and obtain appointments as policemen, or as shop assistants, or in some other congenial occupation carried on in towns, where perhaps they will earn more wages. I am glad to hear that in relation to this assertion the National Union of Teachers are not having it all their own way. They have not cast their net wide enough to include all, because there are some who have escaped it. I think I have said enough to prove that neither does the intelligence, nor the education, nor the health suffer in the districts where the half-time system prevails. But there has been one argument, only one argument, placed before this House which, I think, carried weight, and it was the argument that has been

called the half-past five in the morning argument. That argument I endeavoured to meet by putting down on the Paper an Amendment doing away with all work for half-timers between 11 and 12 years of age before half-past eight in the morning. That Amendment was strongly opposed, but if it had been accepted by my hon. friend the Bill would have been more acceptable than it is at the present moment. But I cannot pass away from this part of the question without again citing to the House the result of the remarkable ballot taken on the question by the Weavers' Association. Of the 90,000 papers issued, 74,000 answers were received, and 66,000, or 89 per cent., were in favour of the present state of affairs. That fact ought to have great weight with hon. Members before they give their vote on the Third Reading. This House has the legal right, but I should like to know how far it has the moral right, to permit hon. Members sitting for constituencies who really have no interest whatever in the Bill and no expert knowledge of the half-time question to cram down the throats of Lancashire people legislation they do not like. We are told by folk who know nothing of the question that we are wasting the lives of the children for the sake of a system which ministers to the greed of miserly parents or the avarice of heartless capitalists, and that the only people who know anything of this question, the only people who are utterly and entirely unbiased in the matter, are the National Union of Teachers. I think this is a big assertion, in view of the ballot. There was another matter mentioned upon the Second Reading in debate which has not been pressed sufficiently upon the attention of the House, and that is the question of woman labour in our factories. The House knows perfectly well that although the death-rate statistics in the factory districts are not worse than in other parts of England, still they would be very much better if it were not for woman labour in the factories. I desire to press this point on the House as being of the utmost importance. The proper place for a woman, at all events during her child-bearing days, when she has a large family of small children—possibly a baby—is at home. In Lancashire, as in other parts of the country, the more you seek by legislation to remove from the revenue of the home even the smallest additional sum of money, as you are doing by destroying the half-time system, the more you are inevitably driving women back to the factories, and making them take their part in providing the daily bread for the family. To my mind this is a singularly unfortunate Bill. Most of the working class measures which have been introduced and carried in this House have been for the improvement and amelioration of the lot of the people, and have been supported by the working classes and trades unions. In the present case all these elements of support are wanting. You have no body of opinion at the back of you. You have no section of the community asking for this reform which knows anything of the textile movement. You have nothing but the National Union of Teachers. It cannot, even by a stretch of imagination, be called a burning question. It is a question which, as I have previously pointed out, is settling itself, and would settle itself in the course of a few years. I disapprove of the action of hon. Members in forcing the question down our throats, believing, as I do, that if it had only been allowed to settle itself by natural means, a good deal of the friction that has been aroused would never have existed at all. Personally I have no pecuniary interest in the cotton trade, and therefore I hope my action may be looked upon as an unselfish one. I believe the Bill to be unnecessary, impolitic, and unjust to a very large section of the community, and this being the last occasion we shall have of discussing this question I am pleased to have been able to raise my voice in this matter.

*Mr. DUCKWORTH (Lancashire, Middleton): I am sure no one would desire to charge the hon. Member for Stockport with want of zeal or want of ability in his opposition to this Bill. Whatever we may say as to his views on the matter, and however we may differ from him, we must all admire his determination to do all he possibly could to kill this Bill. He has struck it in the breast, he has stabbed it in the back, and he has knocked it on the head; and if it had not been for its catlike vitality I am sure the Bill would have been killed. We must all own that the hon. Member would not have taken the course he has in opposing this Bill if he had not conscientiously felt that he was doing what he believed to be right.

We all believe in his honesty, and we believe also in his straightforwardness and independence, for I have noticed that the hon. Member has been so independent as even to hold up to ridicule at times the Party to which he belongs. But I must confess that I am at a loss to understand why the hon. Gentleman, with his intelligence and his knowledge of Lancashire people and their work, can so persistently oppose th's Bill. I can only put it down to two things. One is his determined opposition to the teachers, and the other is that he must have a mandate from his constituency. I am not aware that he has pleaded that, but I cannot understand his action unless it be that he must really believe that his whole constituency, and perhaps some other constituencies in Lancashire, are very strongly opposed to this Bill. If that be so, it only lends colour to what I have heard said, that such towns as Stockport, Wigan, Ashton, and Stalybridge are about fifty years behind towns further north. I do not say that that is so, but I have heard it said, and this circumstance would give colour to that opinion. Let me state my own experience with reference to the constituency which I represent. During the Whitsuntide recess I was called upon to address what is called the "Four Hundred," and the council in connection with that constituency, which is a very extensive and enlightened constituency. I was expected to speak on this subject, in fact I was asked to explain the position I had taken up. I spoke in the afternoon to the council on general politics, and in the evening, at the public meeting, when about 400 people were present, I spent about fifty minutes in speaking on this subject alone. At both these meetings an unanimous vote of confidence in their Member was passed, and not a single question was asked me, or a single voice raised in opposition to the course I had taken. So that whatever force there may be in the arguments which have been used on the opposite side this morning as to the opposition of Lancashire, those arguments do not hold at all events so far as my constituency is concerned. I have received communications from several people on this subject. It has been argued that the trades unions are against this measure. I hold in my hand a resolution passed by the Trades Council of Rochdale, which reads as follows. The secretary says:

"Sir,—I am instructed by the members of the council to forward to you a copy of the resolution which was passed unanimously at the monthly meeting: 'That this council, being strongly of opinion that the age at which half-timers are allowed to commence work is too low, respectfully urges the Government to afford facilities for the passing of Mr. Robson's Half-Time Bill in the present session of Parliament.'"

I have also got a similar resolution from a Socialist organisation. They are very strongly in favour of this Bill.

"I am instructed," the secretary says, "by the council, as representative of the Socialists of the Middleton and Sowerby Parliamentary Divisions, to petition you with respect to Mr. Robson's Bill, at the Second Reading of which our Council considers you played a most commendable part. In the interests of the children and of education we hope you will persevere in the course you have adopted, and do all that lies in your power to assist in the passing of so desirable and humane a measure."

When I was in the North I took the opportunity of inviting to my own house the leaders of the trades organisations in our town and district. I will not say more as to the positions they occupy than that they are gentlemen who occupy the leading positions in our trades unions and councils. We went through these Amendments one by one, and talked them over as we sat around the table, and there was not a single Amendment that those gentlemen advised me to vote for except one. They were in favour of the Bill, and they urged me to advocate —as I have advocated—the passing of the measure. I think that that testimony clears away the arguments which have been used throughout the debate as to the strong opposition of Lancashire people. The hon. Member for Stockport knows very well that the opposition to the raising of the age from 11 to 12 is not so strong by a long way as was the opposition when the age was raised from 10 to 11, and he also knows very well that it will very soon pass away. He knows that even some of those who are so strongly in favour of retaining the age at 11 have spoken, in their personal and private capacity, in a very different way. That being so, I am sure the testimony I have given as to what I have heard when in Lancashire during the last two or three weeks will take the bottom out of the argument that the Lancashire people are strongly against the passing of this measure. On the Second Reading of this Bill emphasis was laid on the argument

Mr. Duckworth.

that it would disarrange or disorganise trade, and that it would harass employers. The hon. Member for Stockport knows— or if he does not know I can tell him— that in every case almost when old machines are taken out and new ones put in they are arranged to do without half-timers altogether. So that the employers themselves know that this system is passing away, that it is a remnant of a bygone age, and that the time has come when it ought not to be encouraged. I could give you employers by the score who have voluntarily done away with this half-time work. The noble Lord the Member for Rochester, on the Second Reading of this Bill, spoke in a very intelligent and very hopeful way. His opposition to it was that he had a fear that it would not answer the purpose that we claim for it, and he spoke about the money which we spend on education being, to a great extent, wasted. That is so. But why is it so? Simply because we do not give the children time to study; we do not give them time to get through what we expect them to get through. It is not a question of the teachers being over anxious to get results; it is because they know very well that the children, under the conditions of education to-day, have not sufficient time to study. Hence they are crammed, and the result is, as has been stated, that when the school years are over they are disgusted with schools; they are out of patience with all study, and they are very glad to get to work, or to play, or anything else they can do. Instead of children coming from elementary schools having had given to them a desire for study, an appetite for learning, they come away satiated with it, and they do not want to continue their studies. That ought not to be so—they ought to be ready, when they arrive at 14 years of age, to go on with their secondary education, and after that to go on to a technical school and prepare themselves for their duties in life. But they are not prepared to do this. The great complaint as to technical schools is that children come from elementary schools quite unprepared to commence their studies in the technical schools. The hon. Member for St. Helens has made a very singular address in the House this morning, but I should have thought that his own intelligence would have prevented him from making remarks such as he has made to-day. Surely he is under the old dispensation. I thought the Tory party had been educated. I remember when quite a young man, after the Franchise Bill had passed, Mr. Robert Lowe saying that we must educate our masters. Now we have an hon. Member of this House speaking disparagingly of education for the working-classes, and advocating that a child must only be educated to do the work that its father has done, and presumably that it must never go beyond what its father has done. That is a good old Tory doctrine, and we have not heard it for a long time. I thought it had died a natural death, and that our Conservative friends were in favour of having our children educated as much as possible. It appears, however, that the hon. Member for St. Helens is one of those who would be perfectly satisfied if a child were educated sufficiently to make a bow to certain persons or a curtsey when the parson or a squire passes by. I take it that that is not the feeling of hon. Members of the House, and I can assure the hon. Gentleman opposite that it is not the feeling of the great masses of this country. The teachers in our technical schools, the educationists throughout the country, and especially in the northern parts of the country where the industries of the country are carried on, all know perfectly well— and feel the importance of it—that it is necessary that the children who are to go to work in these days must be better educated than they have been in days gone by. We have been able to carry on a large trade in what I may call plain goods. As the hon. Member for Stockport knows very well, in years gone by, if a person could weave a calico piece he was considered proficient and all right; but we have to compete with people now who can do this work quite as well as we can ourselves. To make fancy goods requires a good deal of technical knowledge, which we shall have to cultivate if we want to keep abreast with the competition of foreign countries.

Mr. GEORGE WHITELEY: But the children don't learn fancy weaving at Board schools. They learn it at the mill.

*Mr. DUCKWORTH: No, no. The mind of the child is trained in the school, and it requires the training of the mind in order to obtain technical knowledge. I do not think that any Member of this House will plead that ignorance

is better than knowledge in anything— even if it is applied to pulling turnips, or the doing the things that have to be done by the children in agricultural districts. It is far better to have the minds of the children trained, and it is far behind the times to plead that ignorance is an advantage to a child; and I strongly protest against any such argument. I will not detain the House any longer, although there are several other things which I wished to say. I do hope that, now we have threshed this matter out to the extent that we have, the hon. Members will cease their opposition, and allow this Bill to pass.

*Sir F. S. POWELL (Wigan): I hope the House will allow me to submit some observations upon this occasion, although I occupied some time during the discussion of this measure in Committee. As reference has been made to the Borough of Wigan, I feel bound to say, although I did speak with much sincerity and some vigour in favour of the Bill, that I have received no protest against the remarks which I then made. On the other hand, I have received letter after letter in full sympathy with the course which I took and the views which I expressed in the Debate in Committee. I have heard—I must confess with some surprise—the speech made by my hon. friend the Member for St. Helens; and for the first time during many years in the Debates in Parliament I have heard education condemned as rather an injury than a benefit to those who have had the opportunity of taking advantage of it. I certainly think that such remarks come with very ill grace from a Lancashire Member; for we have in our County Palatine no less than two University Colleges—one in Liverpool and one in Manchester—and I venture to say that no man who has any acquaintance with Lancashire industries will deny the great benefits which have been conferred upon our county by these two magnificent institutions. The hon. Member made some reference to Lancashire parents as being very intelligent. As a Lancashire man I have always felt some diffidence in commenting upon such an observation; but I believe that the intelligence of the Lancashire operative is of a very high order, and one of my reasons for supporting this Bill is that, in my opinion, intelligence of that high order requires further opportunity of development. As a Lancashire man and as a Lancashire Member I still regard the standard of education in the schools as too low, although the standard is higher than it was some years ago. Another of my reasons for supporting this Bill is, that if children are prevented from going to work up to a certain age I feel quite sure that the standard of education must be raised. Not only this, but the children will be kept at school up to the school age fixed by the Bill, and they will be prevented from wasting their time in the streets. Reference has been made to the opinion of the operatives as being against the Bill. The hon. Member referred to one section —the Weavers' Union. Now I was present at a meeting where their representatives were heard, and there were two remarkable facts in connection with that Union, firstly, that those members of the Union who sent their children as half-timers at this early age were well-to-do parents and did not require the wages of their children for their support—and ·I was greatly impressed by what I heard upon that occasion ; secondly, the weavers who appeared were not the parents of the children referred to in the resolution. The great majority of them were not factory operatives at all, and gained their bread by other means. The hon. Member made a reference to some petition, or document, respecting labour in the glass works at St. Helens ; but the age he mentioned was a higher age than the one mentioned in the Bill, and therefore the remarks he made upon the subject were entirely irrelevant, and not appropriate to the discussion. I made some reference in a former Debate to the age on the Continent, and since then I have perused the Report of the Committee of the Council on Education for Scotland. Now, in Scotland there are 94,000 children between 11 and 12 years of age, and of that total 92 per cent. are at school. That is a most clear and absolute proof that in Scotland, at least, the parents who have regard to the welfare of their children keep them at school up to the age mentioned in this Bill. With regard to the woollen and worsted industries of Yorkshire, I have had some acquaintance in the interior working of the mills, both in Lancashire and Yorkshire, and I have no hesitation·in saying that, as regards the healthy condition of our factories, in consequence of the nature of the material used,

it is less satisfactory in Lancashire than in the worsted and woollen districts of Yorkshire. I have some statements here which the House will perhaps forgive me for reading. One is the testimony of the medical officer for the Borough of Wigan, who is also a member of the Wigan School Board. He says :

"I shall be sorry if there is an attempt made to exclude cotton factories from the operation of the Bill, for it is the children employed in cotton factories that will benefit most. My opinion, as a medical officer of health, and also as a general medical practitioner among these people, is that no child under twelve should be employed as a half-timer. I have seen the stunted growth, the swarthy, ill-looking appearance of many of these children, due in a great measure to the confinement and work in the mills. I can also speak as a member of our School Board, where people have to come before us for exemption of half-timers, and we invariably ask that the children shall be left longer at school. We have not many half-timers in Wigan, but it would be better if we had less."

Another medical friend of mine—Dr. Roocroft—who has had twenty years' experience in Wigan, writes to me as follows :

"With regard to raising the age of the factory workers, I have long felt that this ought to be done. After a somewhat extensive experience of nearly twenty years I can recall many instances where healthy and robust children, rapidly growing but not developed, have been taken from school and put to work. The result, in many cases, has been an arrest of development generally. Later I find that the circulatory, respiratory, and respiratory systems suffer, as instanced by anæmia, dyspepsia, constipation, and pulmonary tuberculosis. These diseases are induced, in my opinion, firstly, by throwing upon the child work at an early age, too early for the body to be over tired ; and secondly, by close confinement in hot, sometimes dusty and ill-ventilated places, coupled by the absence of exercise (play) in the open air, too long hours, and improper food."

I am grateful to the House for allowing me to read these letters, which are written by two highly distinguished medical practitioners. Now, Sir, if the House will bear with me, I wish to say that I do very greatly regret—as much as I regret anything in my Parliamentary life— that the opposition to this Bill has come from Lancashire, and from hon. Members sitting on this side of the House. I never presume to speak on behalf of Lancashire Members, but I do know from the Division lists the feeling of Lancashire Members. The vote on the Second

Reading of the Bill shows that the majority of the Lancashire Members were in favour of the Bill; and why should a section of them say that Lancashire is opposed to it? I have read the life of Lord Shaftesbury. We know what he says on the factory question. I can remember from my earliest years—I have mentioned it before, and I mention it again—the condition of these poor children, both in Lancashire and York-shire—their starved appearance, their deformed bandy legs, their other weak-nesses, and their want of development in accordance to their years. I myself believe that that condition of affairs amongst the parents is the great cause of the inferior condition of too many of the present generation, and I believe that you will not eradicate the result of this evil con-dition of things except you place the children under more favourable circum-stances. As a matter of fact, these children actually require more favourable conditions than other children. It has been the boast of the Conservative party that this factory legislation was specially their work. Can it be so said now? Who was it that raised the age of half-timers from 10 to 11? It was Mr. Acland, whose absence from this House I deeply lament. Why was it that that reform was delayed? I am grieved to confess that it came from some Members on these benches. And to-day, when I believe Parliament will take another step in advance, we cannot boast that this proposal was made by a Conservative Member. It is a gift from a distinguished and learned hon. Member on the other side of the House. That evil blot—for I contend it is an evil blot on the political history of our Party—cannot be obliterated; but I do appeal to my Lancashire friends that they should keep the record as clean as they can, and not oppose this Bill, even by one ad-verse vote; but, on the contrary, to give to the parents and the children of Lanca-shire a boon which has been too long delayed, but which, in my judgment, they eminently deserve.

Mr. TOMLINSON (Preston): I pro-test against the tone in which my hon. friend has alluded to the Lancashire Members, and also against the suggestion that those Lancashire Members who do not look upon the Bill as satisfactory hold views adverse to education. My belief is, and it is shared more largely out of the House than in it, that the best method of promoting education is to com-bine the initial stage of work with a continuance of education. Now, my hon. friend said something about the standard of exemption being too low. I should like to ask how this Bill is to increase or improve the standard? I do not want the standard of exemption to be made too low. I should like to see it raised. But that has nothing to do with this Bill. I hold that my objection to the principle of this Bill is a sound one, and that if we are to induce children to take an interest in their education, and to carry it on, we must not make a gap between education and the work they have to do in after life. My hon. friend spoke about the deformity of children in times past. That has nothing to do with the present state of things. The mills are well venti-lated, and the children are in good con-dition. I do not say that the present method is necessarily perfect; one might say that the method might be carried on much better. But it seems an extra-ordinary thing that all this should be said against half-timers, when this Bill itself introduces the half-time system in other spheres than the factory. Far more children will come under half-time by the raising of the age. It has been said that in Switzerland and other countries there are no half-timers, but it does not follow that that is a good system. I do not wish to press this point further, but only to deprecate the suggestion of my hon. friend, and to maintain that those Lan-cashire Members who know the feeling of their constituents, and who know something about the working of the half-time system in their constituencies, would not necessarily be improving the conditions of the education and work of those children by allowing this Bill to pass. I want to ask for some authoritative statement as to the views of the Govern-ment on this Bill. I think we ought to know something more of the views of the Government than we have yet obtained. The Bill has been brought in by a private Member, and we know that my right hon. friend the Vice-President of the Council is in favour of the principles of the Bill; but I would like to know what the Council for Education think of the Bill. It may be said that the Bill, as it stands, would not give much trouble to the Department; but do the Government intend to give it their support? And how do they intend to carry out the administration of the agricultural parts of it? What method will be taken or what Orders will be issued to see that agricultural pursuits alone are to be the basis of the half-time system in the future? What steps are to be taken to give it effect? I think that, considering the circumstances in which the Bill has been brought forward and the imputations made in some quarters against those who doubt the wisdom of this Bill, it was only right that I should have had the opportunity of making these observations. I protest against the idea that in the action I have taken against this Bill I am actuated by a desire to continue the employment of child labour. I oppose this measure on the ground, which I think a good one, that it prohibits a kind of child labour which leads up to a species of elementary education in the business which these children will have to carry on in after-life. Everybody must be acquainted with the fact that there are large numbers of children who leave school without the slightest idea of the pursuit which they are going to follow in after years. And the benefit of the half-time system is that it leaves these children time to contemplate what pursuit it is which they will follow, and allows them to begin to learn that pursuit.

*MR. YOXALL (Nottingham, West): I confess that this Bill would not remove the existence of child labour. We have heard that definitely from the hon. Member who has just sat down, and from the Member for Stockport. But in the meantime both concur in opposing a measure which would remove a small portion of child labour, and they object to us making a beginning with the partial abolition of child labour. I think that is rather inconsistent. From the hon. Member for Stockport we have a not less insidious attack on the Bill, but not a more accurate representation of the case. We were told by the hon. Member who has distinguished himself by opposing the Bill in the name of Lancashire that the public opinion of Lancashire was against it, and that there was no public opinion in favour of it. A more inaccurate statement was never made in this House, and that is saying a good deal. The outline of the proposal on which this Bill was based was drawn first of all by the respected Member

Mr. Tomlinson.

for Bury, and another distinguished Member—the Member for Bolton— speaking with more knowledge and in a greater representative position than the hon. Member for Stockport, was also associated with the proposal. The Bill in its first inception was due to these two hon. Members. Public opinion has been expressed again and again in Lancashire in favour of the Bill. The great majority of the organs of the press in Lancashire are in favour of it; the great majority of the working men of Lancashire are in favour of it; and every trades union in Lancashire but one, the weavers, is in favour of it.

MR. GEORGE WHITELEY: And that union is the only one which has half-timers.

*MR. YOXALL: What about the Spinners' Union? The Trades Union Congress for years have been asking for the abolition of the half-time system altogether. Every member of the Trades Union Council, except the member or members who represents the Weavers' Union, is in favour of this Bill; but we are told by the hon. Member opposite, with a coolness which would have been more suitable two days ago than to-day, that the only opinion in favour of this Bill is the opinion of the teachers. It has been suggested again and again that teachers have a great deal to gain by the Bill. As a fact, the teachers and the school managers and the school boards will lose pecuniarily by the passing of this Bill, because the school attendance for half-time counts for the purposes of grants as an attendance and a-half. Abolish the half-timers and you reduce the grant to the school, and the pecuniary incentive of the school managers and teachers will be diminished. I repudiate in the name of the teachers the insinuation that they have any private motive for pushing forward this measure. But one correct statement has been made by the hon. Member for Stockport, and that was that the teachers are not so satisfied with the Bill now as when it was introduced. I regret that it was ever necessary to have any compromise in this Bill. If the Government had done their duty, and had been consistent with their former proposals, and shown the least courage in this House, they would have said, "This is a Bill which carries out the pledges given in our name three years ago, and which must be carried in this form, and we will give facilities for its being carried without any compromise." If that had been done, the opposition of the Lancashire Members would have dropped to zero, and that of the agricultural Members would not be counted for much if the Government had been in earnest; but owing to the want of courage on the part of the Government it has been necessary for my hon. friend to introduce a clause with regard to the agricultural schools and agricultural children upon which I look with dread. We have the least efficient schools for farmers' sons and daughters of any country in Europe, and we have the least efficient and satisfactory system of elementary education for the labourers' sons and daughters, and every attempt that is made to improve the present condition is met with the opposition of the farmers, the farmers' friends, and the farmers' spokesmen in this House. They opposed this Bill unless some concession was made to enable children of eleven years of age to work on the land four or five months in the year, and that concession is given provided that during the remainder of the year the children go to school. I agree with the hon. Member for Preston, that before we adopt this particular clause on this point we ought to hear from the Government that when this concession is given they will insist upon some conditions which shall give them some return. I do not say that the compromise with regard to the agricultural schools will be bad; on the contrary, it may be good under certain conditions, but it depends entirely on the administration of the Education Department. Compulsory education in the rural districts now is about as ineffectual as it can possibly be, and unless some condition is made I fear that all we shall have done by this Bill will be to legalise what exists at present very largely —a certain amount of whole-time employment in the agricultural districts. Unless the Education Department steps in and insists that this concession shall only be made under conditions, I think that the object of this Bill will be perverted, and we shall have worse and less regular school attendances, and compulsory education will be less effective than it is now in the agricultural districts. It is a great danger, and can only be averted by the Education Department; but if the Government are not deterred by the agricultural members who sit behind them the concession may turn out to be a blessing in disguise. I apologise to the hon. and gallant Member opposite for daring to speak upon an agricultural question, but, nevertheless, I will say that the attitude of the farmers in opposing popular education is the most suicidal attitude that could be adopted. Better education is wanted in the agricultural districts, and I hope the hon. and gallant Member and his friends will endeavour to convince the farmers that if they obtain the services of the children on the land for certain months of the year, they must, in justice to the children, and in honourable keeping of a bargain, see to the best of their ability that the children attend school during the rest of the year. If there is a better tone adopted in the speeches of the agricultural Members of this House upon this question, it will go far to improve the chances of better education and to advance it. There are other countries besides this which were subject to agricultural depression, and the people of those countries escaped from that depression, not by reducing and annulling education, but by increasing it. It is the dulness of intellect, lack of adaptability, and want of flexibility on the part of the agricultural labourer that are in a great degree responsible for the depression. I was in a small market town in educated France from which £40,000 worth of eggs are exported to this country annually, and the landlord of the hotel to whom I spoke said he always understood that the English were a practical people; but that must be a mistake, because nothing was easier than to produce eggs for the market. Again, in Denmark, with the dairy produce which is exported to this country. That immense exportation is due to the better education of the people in that country and to nothing else. They attend not only primary but secondary schools, and many of them even agricultural colleges, and if we had better education in this country agriculture would revive in a like manner.

MAJOR RASCH (Essex, S.E.): The hon. Gentleman need not apologise for speaking on agricultural matters because he is not a farmer, any more than I need apologise for speaking upon this Bill because I am not a schoolmaster. He is as perfectly qualified to speak on this matter as on others. All that I wish to say is that I hope the House will not support the hon. Member for St. Helens in his motion for the rejection of this Bill. Personally, I opposed the Bill in its first stages, but I am now exceedingly glad that it has got to its present position. We know perfectly well we have obstructed this Bill. It was first possible we might have defeated it, but then we should have got a very much worse measure forced down our throats next year. This is a very serious matter for the agricultural interest, and we have to make the best of it. I wish to thank the hon. and learned Member for South Shields for having favourably considered the very reasonable proposals which we made to him some weeks ago. I am glad he thought fit to urge the House to temper the wind to the shorn lamb, and I congratulate him on the progress he has made with the Bill.

*Mr. SAMUEL SMITH (Flintshire): I also congratulate my hon. friend on having reached this stage of the Bill, for I believe no measure has ever passed this House with a more unanimous body of public opinion behind it. I have always been in favour of it, and have not the slightest fear of it; on the contrary, I believe it will do a great deal of good. One hon. Member has declared that there is no body of working-class opinion in favour of this Bill. But I formerly collected the opinions of the trade unions of this country on a proposal much more advanced, by a Bill to extend the school age to 14, with certain exemptions; and nine-tenths were in favour of the proposition to not merely extend the age for day attendance, but to make attendance at night schools compulsory up to the age of 15. The hon. Member for St. Helens argued that knowledge acquired at school was quickly forgotten. Of course, everyone knows that a system of cramming a child up to the age of 12 years, followed by a total absence from school afterwards, is calculated to have such results; and what we want to do is to persuade the people of this country of the essential fact that the child's mind is best formed between the ages of 12 and 15. What we want is regular attendance at evening schools for at least two years after leaving the day-school, and until we get that our education will remain a failure. With regard to the children in agricultural dis-

Major Rasch.

tricts, I congratulate my hon. and learned friend on what he has done. He secures, at any rate, that the children shall remain continuously at school for six or eight months, between the ages of 11 and 13, and that the exemption shall only apply during the period at which child-labour is useful in the fields. We want to keep the children in the rural districts, and it is good for their health that in the summer time they should be engaged in easy work in the fields. I certainly see no reason why we should not follow the example of Prussia, Switzerland, and other countries, and, while allowing exemption during the summer months, keep the education going in the winter until even 14 or 15 is reached. It is because that system is adopted in other countries that they are running us so hard in commercial competition.

*Mr. HOBHOUSE (Somerset, E.): Complaint has been made that so few voices have been raised in support of this Bill, but I am sure it is only owing to the exigencies of time that many other Members on this side of the House as well as on the other have not spoken in favour of the measure. As far as its factory provisions extend, there is one simple and sufficent justification for it. It is that no less than nine years ago, that this nation, in common with other European nations, pledged itself to this very important alteration in the status of children. [An hon. Member, "No."] Well, at any rate the British delegates at the Berlin Conference concurred in the resolution which was passed declaring the desirability of the change, and they did that with the consent of the Government of the day, at the head of which was the present Prime Minister. I venture to think that under these circumstances it would not have been surprising if the present Government had extended to this Bill a still more benevolent attitude than they have done. I should have been better pleased if they had themselves passed this Bill, and not left it to a private Member to gain the credit of redeeming what was almost a national obligation. I congratulate the hon. and learned Member on the ability he has shown in piloting the Bill through the House of Commons. I feel sure that the national conscience throughout the greater part of England revolts at seeing our children of tender years obliged to work in factories. With regard to the agricultural clauses, I confess I look upon them as a great experiment which is well worth trying, and I trust they will prove beneficial alike to employers, teachers, and children. Objection has been taken to prolonging what has been described as the mechanical and unpractical system of teaching in our schools. I earnestly hope that the Education Department will, now that this considerable change is being made in our educational system, take into consideration, especially as regards the agricultural districts, the desirability of making the education less unpractical, and giving it a more direct and useful bearing on our industrial life.

*MR. SCHWANN (Manchester, N.): Not only is my name on the back of the Bill, but for several years past I have always taken the opportunity at public meetings in my constituency to urge upon Lancashire the desirability of curtailing the work of children and enabling them to remain longer at school. The arguments which occur to me on this subject are connected with the health and the education of the children, and with the foreign competition which the industries of this country will have to meet. I have received several petitions and many letters in favour of this Bill, but up to the present I have not received a single line in condemnation of it. Being a Lancashire Member, and Manchester being practically the home of the Lancashire industries, I think it very probable that some of the manufacturers who are represented by the hon. Member for Stockport would have addressed a word of warning to me if they had any objection to the Bill. The question of health seems to me to deserve important consideration, and I think anybody who knows the Lancashire population must feel that it would be desirable if their physical conditions could be improved. An hon. Member has sent to Members of the House photographs of workers in Lancashire, and I think those photographs make out a case for the Bill in a most unmistakable manner. Lately a lady, the wife of the Agent-General of New Zealand, was in Manchester, and attended a public meeting, and she remarked to me upon the number of lads who attended the meeting. I told her that they were not lads, but were fathers of families who had been subjected to the conditions of half-

timers. I would not like to say that getting up in the morning at half-past five, as children, hurrying off in the cold to the mill, staying in a heated atmosphere, and coming out into the cold air again are the only elements affecting the health of the people. I believe that early marriages and hard work affect their stature. As my hon. friend the Member for Stockport has said that the health question is of no value, I will cite the opinion of Dr. Torrop, of Heywood, who probably has among his *clientèle* many factory workers. He says:

"I have no hesitation whatever in reiterating the opinion that without a shadow of doubt factory life is injurious to health. As I have put it before so I will put it again. The promising children of 10 degenerate into the lean and sallow young persons of 13, and so the process continues as they grow older until a whole population becomes stunted, and thus the conditions of life in the factory become a real source of danger to England's future."

These conditions, however, do not exist only in Lancashire. They exist also in Scotland, and in many other parts of England. Her Majesty's Chief Inspector of Factories, reporting upon work in the Dundee jute works, said:

"I do not think the decadence of child labour is to be deplored as far as the jute industry is concerned. If a jute spinner works hard the little shifter works harder. Often have I watched the latter continuously at work for long spells, rushing from one machine to another, perspiring copiously in the stifling heat. As I said in my last year's report, the typical Dundee half-timer is somewhat undersized and decidedly thin. These little creatures are diminutive when they commence work at 11 years of age, and the circumstances under which the majority of them labour are such that bodily growth is certainly not encouraged or fostered thereby."

With regard to the educational aspect of this question, I share the opinion that there is need for much improvement in our educational system. I am glad to see that the schoolmaster is abroad, and that he is specially abroad with reference to the education of the children. Mr. Bridges, of Oldham, who has been quoted before, said that of 300 boys who had taken scholarships in Oldham, only 40 were half-timers, and that it would be hopelessly cruel to put them in competition with children who spent the whole day in school. A good deal has been said about widows having to suffer by sending their children to school and losing the support they might otherwise bring them. So far as my experience goes, I am convinced that if there is one person who will not suffer her children to have any drawback either in education or in general well-being, it is a widow with young children. In some districts of Lancashire the people had lately been enjoying a holiday, and in Oldham the bankers had to make special arrangements to pay out from £40,000 to £50,000 or more, in cash, to the employees in the town to enable them to go to the seaside for their annual week's holiday at that season. Nobody objects to that, but rather rejoices that the wages in Lancashire are so good as to enable the people to put aside and draw out so large a sum. It is, however, rather astonishing that from those districts where large sums can be saved there should come complaints that the happiness of the home is going to be wrecked because two or three shillings per week are going to be dropped in some cases by curtailing the half-time system. Mr. Mawdsley, who represents as fully as anybody the general opinion of the cotton operatives of Lancashire, says he has lived in Lancashire and has watched the physical condition of the people too long to allow any child of his to become a half-timer. In regard to the argument that a certain dexterity in manipulating yarns is acquired by the children when they are young, I may remind the House that the hon. Member for Bolton rejected the argument with scorn, and I believe the hon. Member for Bury takes the same line. But I am going to cite the opinion of three gentlemen who are more qualified to express an opinion than they are. These gentlemen are Mr. Allan Gee, general secretary of the weavers and the textile workers; Mr. Ben Turner, general organiser of the weavers; and Mr. Drew, president of the Bradford textile operatives. Mr. Gee says there is nothing in the argument that it is necessary for children to go to work at the present age so as to acquire dexterity, Mr. Drew characterises it as a fairy tale, and Mr. Turner says it is nonsense. Having regard to the great competition and struggle with other nations that lie before us, I ask the House to take this small step, which not only will fulfil the pledge given at the Berlin Congress, but will be for the benefit of the nation at large. It is said that half-time is dying. I say "Let it die," and if we can accelerate the pace by

Mr. Schwann.

passing this Bill I think that is a consummation devoutly to be wished. I will conclude by quoting words which the right hon. Gentleman the Vice-President of the Council used at Berlin when pledging Great Britain to raise the age:

"We have confident hopes that millions of men, women, and children will derive from it a better future and an easier life, and that generations to come will be richer, stronger, and more virtuous, owing to the effects of the provisions of which the Conference has laid down the first outline."

I believe this Bill incorporates, although only to a small extent, what the right hon. Gentleman promised on that occasion, and I hope that if the Bill goes to a Division it will be carried by a large majority.

Mr. J. H. JOHNSTONE (Sussex, Horsham): The hon. and learned Member who has charge of this Bill is to be congratulated upon the good fortune which has attended his efforts—he is to be congratulated upon his success at the ballot, he is to be congratulated upon the skill and tact with which he has carried the Bill through its various stages, including the Report stage the other night, and he is to be congratulated upon having resisted the temptation to attempt to revise the Factory Acts, and remodel entirely our educational system. I think he has exercised a very wise discretion in dealing with one particular part of this important subject, and I think I may congratulate him, too—and that was the object of my rising this afternoon—upon the Amendment which was introduced into the Bill in the course of its progress through the House. I do not see any reason to deplore the introduction of that Amendment. It may have been due to some lack of moral courage on the part of the Government of the day—of that I know nothing; but for my part I regard this Amendment as a most useful and valuable concession to the agricultural interests of the country. It may not affect a large number of children to raise the educational age from eleven to twelve, because I fancy there are few school authorities in the country where the age limit is as low as eleven; but I am convinced of this, that the Amendment, which gives power to the school authorities to allow children employed in agriculture to become practically half-timers, is one which will be of great service in agricultural districts.

The difficulty at the present time in our agricultural districts is the difficulty of finding labour—it is an anxiety now; in a very short time it will be a very serious difficulty indeed—because the moment a child has left school, the moment a boy has completed what I may call his statutory education, he goes down to the station and becomes a booking clerk, a ticket collector, or a telegraph boy, or, at all events, he does not go on the land. His first object is to get away as fast as he can, and the result is that we have no young men coming on to take the place of the agricultural labourers who are passing away; no young men in the country who care to learn the trade of an agricultural labourer—because that trade does require a certain amount of skill—and the result is that farmers are not able to offer such good wages as they could give to men who thoroughly understand their business. It is my belief that if the young men in the country were to turn their minds a little more to learning the trade by which their fathers lived and became strong and healthy and happy men, they would make themselves able to earn wages far beyond anything that they can earn at the present time. If we are to keep strong, healthy, and industrious men on the land, we must be prepared to offer them more advantages than we give them at the present time, and I believe they would undoubtedly be able to command better wages if in their youth they were taught the trade or profession of agriculture in a practical way. For that reason I most heartily support this Bill, because in rural districts the young children will have a chance during several months of the year of learning the trade of an agricultural labourer, so that when they come to the age of 13 and leave school, they will be fitted to take their places on the farm, and be able to command wages which will compare favourably with what they could earn in other occupations, and thus they will not have the same inducement or the same temptation to go away from the land as they have at the present time. The result will be that we shall keep a good class of men on the land, and we shall see the houses in our villages filled with a prosperous, contented, and wage-earning peasantry.

MR. HARWOOD (Lancashire, Bolton): I propose to say one or two words in

reply to the remark of the hon. Member for Stockport, that no response has been made to the arguments which he brought forward at a previous stage of this Bill. On that occasion hon. Members in favour of the Bill imposed upon themselves a self-denying ordinance, because they wanted to insure the passage of the measure, and their silence was in no way due to any lack of arguments. As one who has been for many years an employer of short-timers, and has watched the system with some care, I feel that even I may have something to say worthy of the hon. Member's notice. There seems to be an impression in this House, and certainly in the press, that this Bill has been forced upon Lancashire, but I venture to say that that is a total misapprehension. I think the hon. Member in charge of the Bill will not object to my saying that it was generated in Lancashire, and had the fortunes of the ballot not declared otherwise, it would have been introduced by a Lancashire Member. While we have to be thankful that it has secured such an excellent pilot as the hon. Member for South Shields, we do not wish it to be forgotten that the main lines of the ship were laid down in the County Palatine. Much has been said about the feeling of Lancashire on the subject. Although we have been brought into constant contact with large numbers of men who employ half-timers, neither the hon. Member for Bury, who has taken so much interest in the Bill, nor myself have ever heard a word of protest, either in public or private, against the proposed change. I am quite sure that the employers recognise that in the natural course of events it is inevitable, and that it ought to be accepted in a spirit of true patriotism. The hon. Member for Stockport has often trotted out the result of the ballot among the weavers. We have been told that 77,000 voted against the proposed change. They are, however, only a comparatively small part of a body, which in its narrowest limits contains 314,000 members. But that is not all. There are between 500,000 and 600,000, none of whom, beyond the 77,000, have protested against the Bill. The spinners, too, are concerned, but they have made no protest at all, either in public or private. The hon. Member for Bury and I have met representative gatherings of trade unionist leaders, who have certainly made some representations respecting the raising of the half-time age, but their opposition, if opposition it can be called, has been of a feeble and half-hearted character. Many of these gentlemen have expressed to me personally their feelings to this effect : "The change is carried, and we shall adapt ourselves to it." But there is another gauge that the House can apply to the feeling with regard to the Bill, and that is the action of the operatives themselves in decreasing the number of half-timers. In 1891 the number was 173,000; in 1897 it had sunk to 110,000. Some hon. Members may, perhaps, ask why, under the circumstances, the system should not be left to die a natural death. The answer is because there are always people actuated by motives not shared by the majority, and there always comes a time when public opinion, sufficiently developed, should be backed by law. The hon. Member for Stockport has said that no facts have been brought forward showing the effects of the half-time system to be bad. It would not become me, as a millowner, to say that mills are not well ventilated and otherwise well arranged from a sanitary point of view. Nor could I say so with truth. At the same time, the fundamental conditions of the problem are such that work in mills is physically disadvantageous to children. What are the facts? Archdeacon Wilson, of Rochdale, who was formerly head-master of Clifton School, has for many years, as many hon. Members know, taken statistics relating to the health of children, both at schools and in the cotton mills; and what are his conclusions? While up to the age of 11 working-class boys and middle-class boys increase in height and weight on almost parallel lines, after that age the working-class boys fall off relatively both in height and weight. It is not simply the deflection of a curve, it is a distinct sweep; and in the case of the working-class boys the Archdeacon calls it the half-time curve. Between the ages of 11 and 13 the increase of height and weight in public school boys is double the augmentation in working-class boys. In other words, at the most important age, when the constitution is changing and the faculties are developing most rapidly, half-time children are subjected to a system which diminishes their natural increase by half. I do not wish to weary the House with statistics, but the hon. Member for Stock-

port has asked for them. The hon. Member for Stockport is a clever politician, and no doubt he asks this question about the effects of the half-time system because he knows it is difficult for a Lancashire man to answer. It is not easy for Lancashire Members to tell the House that their constituents are undersized. It is not wise for a Member to run his constituents down; but whatever risk may be involved I will speak the truth and say openly that in the manufacturing districts the physique of the people is distinctly below what it ought to be and what it is in other parts of the country. I was lately visited by an Australian politician, a relative of my own. I took him round my constituency, and he said that what struck him most was the smallness of the people. This gentleman was kind enough to add that he was also struck by their intelligent looks. The hon. Member for Stockport has asked whether Lancashire people are deficient in intelligence. I dare not say that they are. Their natural superiority has perhaps enabled them up to the present to countervail their disadvantages, but they have not had a fair chance. They will be far better when the half-time system, with its injury to health and education, is at an end. It is becoming worse every year in its effects on those who, following their parents, still cling to it. Those of us who know anything of machinery know that it is run much more quickly, is more complicated, and more extensive than it used to be, and the strain it places on the faculties of children is much greater that it was 20 years ago. It has been said that sending children to the mill early gives them technical training. That is a mistake. As a matter of fact, such training has ceased to be possible for children 11 years old, because the machines are so rapid and so large that millowners dare not put these youngsters to anything but sweeping up and attending generally. But there is another thing which I should like to tell the hon. Member. Personally, I have ceased to employ children under 12 years of age, and, after observation of the result, I have come to the conclusion that the extra year for the cultivation of the mind and the development of the body enables children to learn mill work better and more quickly. It was said in a previous Debate that farmers do not believe in education. I believe that state of mind has much to do with the wretched condi-

Mr. Harwood.

tion of English agriculture. What is wanted on the land is not so much money as brains. A celebrated artist, when asked what he mixed his colours with, replied, "Brains." I believe if English farming were mixed with more brains, it would be more prosperous. It must begin by the more stringent enforcement of elementary education, and by the multiplication of technical schools and colleges. Lancashire, at any rate, has discovered that intellectual training is good for trade. The people of that county have not continued this half-time system because they are greedy or hardhearted, but because they have grown up with it ; and the state of the Ministerial benches shows how Conservative they are, not only in politics but in other matters. Foreign competition is a great and increasing difficulty. If we are to hold our place in the world it must be primarily by the quality of our work. That quality depends on the development of the intelligence and the physical condition of the people, and, as a Lancashire Member and cotton spinner, I ask the House to pass the Bill, because in the end it will be a great boon to the trade of the country and of great advantage to the people.

Mr. JAMES KENYON (Lancashire, Bury): I have listened in the House to two or three Debates in which several experts on education on both sides have given their opinion, and I have listened to the speeches of the Vice-President of the Council on Education, and in almost every speech the burden of complaint has been that children are taken away from school too early. The unsatisfactory feature of the work of English education is that the children are taken away from school too soon. I am afraid that the half-time system is one of the factors in this matter. A child is at work in the mill at six o'clock in the morning, and in the afternoon of the same day he is expected to go to school and learn his lessons. Under these conditions a great many children are naturally sleepy, and, to put it mildly, are not in a fit condition to acquire the education that is offered to them. But there is also another factor in this question which deserves attention. The hon. Member for Bolton has pointed out that there are far fewer half-timers in this country now than formerly, and he quoted figures to establish his point. He was perfectly right, and I believe

that the parents who are now keeping their children at school and away from the mill are beginning to find out that the parents who allow their children to do half-time are hindering their children in their education very considerably. This is a point which I have pressed on my constituents, and it is a very important matter in the consideration of this question. It is unfair to the teachers of these schools, because you are asking them to do an impossible thing—to keep all the children in a line, and educate them as children ought to be educated. This is not a matter that applies only to England. I have received a letter from a friend in Germany, where the same complaint prevails, that all the classes in the school are overcrowded. What must it be in schools where the classes are not overcrowded, where there is a certain percentage of children attending school half the day only, and hindering the progress of the whole school ? My hon. friend the Member for Stockport has had a great innings in this matter as regards the number of speeches he has made as to what concerns Lancashire. The hon. Member has again quoted the figures of the ballot, but he has forgotten to tell the House that out of a membership of 85,000 of the Weavers' Union, 62 per cent. would be composed of young unmarried girls. They are not the parents of the half-timers. I would like to call the hon. Member's attention to what the secretary of one of the divisions of the Northern Counties Weavers' Union has said. He pointed out that the parents of these half-timers were mostly people in good positions—joiners, blacksmiths, mechanics, farmers—who could well afford to send their children to school, and had no reason to send them to the mill for the extra six months. I will give a typical instance of the condition of some of these parents. One has a family of eight children, each of whom goes to work as a half - timer. I suppose when the seventh and eighth child would be going half-time to the mill and half-time to the school, probably the income coming to that house would be £300 or £400 a year. This is the sort of capitalist who sends children to work half-time in the mill and half-time at school, depriving them of the education which they ought to have ; and the English taxpayer, who is providing a vast amount of money every year for the cost of education, has a right to see that this education is carried out in the best possible manner. The half-time system is a bad system as regards education, and the sooner it is entirely done away with the better. I can only congratulate my hon. and learned friend on the success he has so far achieved with the Bill, and I hope that in a few years from this time, at proper intervals—because we must not do these things too suddenly or all at once—the half-time system will be abolished entirely.

MR. DUNCOMBE rose in his place, and claimed to move, " That the Question be now put "; but Mr. Speaker withheld his assent, and declined then to put that Question.

MR. JAMES KENYON : One reason why I have had great pleasure in supporting this measure is that I am perfectly certain that 10, 15, or 20 years hence you will have to have a higher standard of education in the trading classes of this country. The technical schools are not doing that amount of good they ought to be doing, the reason being that the elementary education of the children is deficient. The whole complaint in my part of the country from the technical schools is that the boys come to learn different trades, but their elementary education in reading, writing, and arithmetic has not been properly attended to. In this respect the Bill of my hon. and learned friend will be a great improvement. It is a modest Bill ; it only means that the children will have to attend school another six months —surely not a very terrible departure. I am confident that if the House of Commons passes this Bill it will do a very great benefit indeed, not only to Lancashire but to the whole of the trading classes of this country. There has been some talk about the children not being able to learn their trade so well at the later age, and not being so amenable to discipline and instruction. I can only say that the experience of a number of friends of mine is that the boys will learn their trade just as well at 12 as at 11. The older children, as a rule, are much more likely to make less waste with the work than when they begin to learn the different processes at the earlier age. I think that that argument is really worth very little indeed. The rest which the children will get in the morning will help them in their education, and the raising of the standard of education will do an immense amount of

Mr. James Kenyon.

good to the technical schools of the country by sending the boys to them better taught elementarily, while the passage of the Bill through this House, and I hope through another place, will be a very great benefit, not only to Lancashire, but to the whole of this kingdom.

MR. MADDISON (Sheffield, Brightside) : I am sure the speeches we have heard from the hon. Member for Bolton and the hon. Member for Bury have given great encouragement to those of us who see in the development of our educational system the real hope of the future prosperity of our country. During this Debate we have heard a great deal about the attitude of the trades unions on this question of half-time. It is a fact that trades unions immediately interested in textile work have, so far as official votes are concerned, gone against this Bill. But the hon. Member for Bolton expressed the feeling which I believe exists in the minds of all the textile leaders— viz., that in their heart of hearts they welcomed this Bill, although they knew that through the half-time system, through lack of education, through this hereditary system growing up from father to son, it was very difficult indeed for them to put before their members in such a way as to convince them a question which affected the weekly revenue of their families. The best evidence you have that there was no heart in this opposition was found in the small number of men who came into the lobby during the Second Reading of the later stages of this Bill. Nobody knows better how to "lobby" than the trades union leaders of Lancashire, and the mere fact that very few came here is in itself very good evidence, of what their real opinion was. The trades unionists are constantly being told by employers that we are driving away trade from this country, and we in our way have tried to persuade and convince the workmen of the country that if they are to hold their own in the markets of the world they must give of their very best— that this is no mere capitalist plea, but that it is the bedrock of the industrial situation—that you must have an educated class of workmen, that you must have men who are not merely physically strong, but that they must be mentally vigorous as well. What do we see ? Here is a Bill which is as modest as any Bill of the kind could well be. It has to depend upon the fortune of the ballot ; when the

Second Reading was moved it was carried by an enormous majority, a decision which was come to without any guidance from the Leader of the House or from the Government as such ; it goes through its later stages, and we do not receive the slightest help from the Ministry——

SEVERAL HON. MEMBERS : The Vice-President !

MR. MADDISON : I was about to say so, if you will allow me to finish the sentence. We have had no support from the Leader of the House, and the only leading —and that has not been a very extended one—was from the right hon. Gentleman the Vice-President of the Council. What I feel, and what the country feels, is that this, the most important Bill of the session as I believe it to be, has not received, with that one exception, anything like the support that it ought to have received from the Government. I do not wish to continue this Debate at any length. I can only join with the hon. Member for Nottingham in his fears about the agricultural Amendment that the hon. and learned Member had to accept really as the price of his Bill. I do think that is an object lesson—that in the closing year of this century it should be necessary, in order to get a modest Bill of this sort through this House, for the promoter of it to make a compromise which at any rate the agricultural Members regarded as of such importance from their point of view that they withdrew their opposition. As their point of view is clearly not the point of view of the Bill itself, I cannot help feeling that there is some danger in it, and that danger is increased because there has been no response to the appeal of the hon. Member for Nottingham on the part of the Vice-President of the Council. He speaks with authority as an educational expert, and he has told the House that if the Education Department takes certain steps this Amendment may become not so dangerous, and he rightly asks the Vice-President of the Council to give the House some sort of assurance in that direction. The Vice-President has not done so. Personally, I am quite confident that so far as his influence is concerned he will do all that he possibly can in this direction, but we know that his influence is not always predominant, and that his policy does not always stamp the Education Department. I listened with

positive pain to the speech of the hon. Member for St. Helens, who told us, using that semi-pious language which generally accompanies the worst form of reaction, that Providence had destined the great mass of working people to go and work for their daily bread, and that therefore we ought to facilitate the time when the children could earn something for their parents. But has education no other value than that of wages ? It is this low conception of education, this mistaken notion of education, which is playing such mischief in our midst. When the nation realises that education is a national asset, when it understands that in our schools and by our school teachers we have the real making of the England of the future, it will not grudge, as it now does, almost every penny that is spent upon education, it will not grudge the child another year out of the factory ; but it will realise that in the making of brain, and in the giving of opportunity for muscles to be developed by play at the age when nature intended they should be, you are bringing up an intellectually and physically strong manhood, which in the severe years which face England will enable us to hold our own. But to have elaborate apologies for ignorance from one or two Members opposite is really deplorable. The almost absurd argument that this Bill would prevent young children from learning their trade has been entirely disposed of by the hon. Member for Bolton. I believe as firmly as any man in this House can in the proper apprenticeship of children, but if that apprenticeship is to be worth anything at all there must be years of careful preparation, and I stand up and repudiate with all the strength of which I am capable the unwarranted attack upon the National Union of Teachers with respect to this Bill. The trades unionists have long realised that the National Union of Teachers, and the teachers generally, are the best friends of the nation, and so far from being worthy of condemnation, I, for my part, couple them with the hon. Member for Bury, the hon. Member for Bolton, and the hon. and learned Member who has charge of this Bill, and say that the country owes a deep debt of gratitude to them for this small modicum of reform. In conclusion, I cannot help asking why Lancashire should be made an exception. How is it that it is only the Lancashire parent in the main who needs his child to go half-time to the mill ? Does the hon. Member for Stockport mean to say that Lancashire is an exceptionally poor part of the country ? Does he mean to say that the wages of the Lancashire operative are not sufficiently large to enable him to send his child to school, as the artisan of Sheffield, or Hull, or other cities and towns of the Kingdom does ? If he does maintain that, surely the remedy is not to dwarf the mind and body of the children, but that the trades unionists of whom he was speaking should turn their energies to better purpose, and see that their men get better wages, as their comrades in other parts of the country have done with great success. Although we have to watch the agricultural Amendment, and we cannot speak confidently of that, yet, nevertheless, with that unfortunate exception, I would express my thanks to the hon. and learned Member for the persistency and skill with which this Bill has been brought to its present stage. We shall always look back to the proceedings in connection with this Bill as in the main showing the House in its best light, as proving to us that employers of labour can get out of their narrow surroundings, that they can get out of the class circle in which they move, and look above and beyond mere profits, and that they can speak a word for those mute thousands who can have no champion in this House, who are silent in all such assemblies, and who are powerless and absolutely in the hands of those who are their parents. There are times when it is necessary for the State to even stand between the parent and the child, and if ever there was one the present is such an occasion.

THE VICE-PRESIDENT OF THE COUNCIL FOR EDUCATION (Sir J. GORST, Cambridge University) : It always seemed to me during the Debates on this Bill that its passage would be best promoted by abstaining from making speeches. But after what has been said by the hon. Member for Sheffield I think I must trouble the House. When what is called the agricultural Amendment was moved by the hon. Member for South Shields I did give an assurance to the House, on behalf of the Education Department, which I represent, which I did not think it would be necessary for me to repeat on this occasion. I said then that that Amendment had been most carefully considered by my

Mr. Maddison.

noble friend the Lord President of the Council and his advisers, that it was the opinion of the Education Department that that Amendment would work, and that under it it would be quite possible to ensure what the House desired—that the attendance of children employed in agriculture during the winter should be a real attendance, and their exemption from school attendance in the summer should really be made up by sufficient and proper attendance during the winter. I can only repeat that assurance now in the same words in which I gave it at the Committee stage of the Bill. As I am on my legs may I be allowed to congratulate most heartily the hon. and learned Member for South Shields on his success in carrying this extremely important Bill to its present stage. I hope he may have a long and successful Parliamentary career before him, but I am sure he will never, whatever may be his achievements in time to come, regret his name being associated with this measure, which I believe will be most important to the future of the community.

SIR W. HARCOURT (Monmouthshire, W.): I am sure the House has heard with great satisfaction the assurance of the right hon. Gentleman in answer to the appeal of the hon. Member for Nottingham. I am sure the House will never regret the afternoon of a day which it spent in giving what I hope will be a unanimous vote in support of the Bill we are now considering. I wish individually to associate myself with the congratulations the hon. Member for South Shields has already received for the zeal he has shown in introducing this Bill, and the judgment he has evinced in the conduct of the Bill. I am sure he desired as little as any of us to introduce, unnecessarily, controversial considerations in regard to this Bill, or any party feeling. This Bill has been the doing of the House of Commons. We have had what may well be called a soldiers' battle about this Bill, and it is all the better for it. Anyone who recollects the history of factory legislation, and to a great degree educational legislation, knows that that legislation has been the doing of private Members, and that private Members have advantages that Governments sometimes do not possess, because their promotion of measures of this kind arouses less party feeling and less controversy. I have listened this afternoon with the greatest satisfaction to what I must consider to be the voice of Lancashire, as expressed in the eloquent speech of the hon. Member for Wigan, and in the able and courageous speeches of the hon. Members for Bolton and Bury, and I venture to say that, according to my belief, they express the enlightened opinion of that great county. I have often spoken in this House and expressed my opinion as to the absolute inadequacy and inefficiency of the existing system of education in this country, especially its elementary education. In no part of the country is it more deficient —and I speak of that as having more personal knowledge of it—than in the agricultural districts. In my opinion, education in agricultural districts at this time is a disgrace to this country, when you' compare it with the education of countries which have less resources, and which might be expected to extract from their children what you would really almost call their life blood by putting them to work at an age too early, and removing them from the inestimable advantages of education. I must say I think it is a disgrace to this great and wealthy country that our elementary education should be what it is at present. In that respect, I have always desired to support to the utmost of my ability views which, I know, are entertained by the right hon. Gentleman the Vice-President of the Council, and I am confident that he will act upon those views. I hope this Bill is only the commencement of that which will be followed up, and must necessarily be followed up, by measures of the same description when the country has learnt that, so far from being a disadvantage, they are a great advantage to every class of the community. Therefore, Sir, I hope we shall by a unanimous vote pass the Bill of my hon. and learned friend, which will add at once, I believe, not only to the health, but to the wealth of this nation.

*Colonel MELLOR (Lancashire, Radcliffe): I do not rise in any spirit of hostility to this Bill, but only to ask the Vice-President of the Council if along with this Bill he will grant a certificate, so that after the Bill is passed—I hope by a unanimous vote—there may be a certificate granted which would enable local authorities to grant exemptions in the case of poor parents, those who, owing to distressed circumstances, cannot well afford to give up the earnings of half-timers after eleven years of age. I am assured by my hon. and learned friend who introduced the Bill that the law already provides for that exemption. Although I have been advised differently, I accept his assurance this afternoon; I only ask, seeing we have certificates for all manner of exemptions, that a certificate may be granted to the local authorities, so that those who are employed in Lancashire may know that they have an opportunity in the case of distressed circumstances of employing their children when eleven years of age. We are asked why Lancashire demands these exemptions; is Lancashire such an exceptionally poor county ? The reason is simply and solely that the textile trade of Lancashire affords to operatives in cotton mills an employment for children which is not afforded by any other trade in the country. We have been asked why does Leeds employ its half-timers when Huddersfield and Halifax have largely dispensed with them ? Simply because in Leeds, as in Lancashire, they can find methods of employment suitable for children, which will do the children no harm, which involve comparatively little fatigue, and at the same time carry on education to a period largely beyond the period of education over the country generally. In speaking at Leeds only the other day, the right hon. Gentleman the Member for Wolverhampton alluded to the fact that there are 1½ millions of children between the ages of eleven and fourteen in this country, and of those half a million are not on the register, and of those who are on the register only about 20 per cent. pass the fourth standard. The half-timers of Lancashire do not come into this category. The parents are compelled to send their children to school up to the age of thirteen years. Of all school children they are most regular in their attendance, because if they miss a half-day they are compelled by the law to go the whole of the next day. Nor are they behind in regard to the standards. We find that the half-timers of Lancashire do not leave school after the fourth standard, and that about five-sixths pass the fifth, sixth, and seventh standards. So that we have no right to say that the half-time system is so injurious to education as has been represented. We have been told, too, that the backwardness of children in regard to technical education is the result of the half-time system. This is entirely inaccurate.

Half-time children go to school till they are 13, fully a year longer than the general average of the children throughout the country. But that is not sufficient. Unless you can keep them in touch with education—and this is what I have urged all my life long—through night schools, until they are 15, 16, or 17 years of age, you will still have that fatal gap between the elementary day school and the technical school. Just one other point. We have heard about the poor Lancashire parents. I was asked by one of my own weavers:

"Have those gentlemen in London who passed the Second Reading of this Bill ever considered what would happen in the case of poor parents? I have been one myself, and I can speak from knowledge and experience. I am speaking of those who have five or six children, and perhaps only get £1 a week as weavers. Unless their children who are 11 years of age may go to work in the mills, it will mean that the mothers will go back to the mills to work, and of those two evils the latter will be much the greater."

I think that man was quite right. I hope the right hon. Gentleman will consider my point, and grant a certificate by which half-timers may, in the case of extreme poverty, be allowed to work in the mills at eleven years of age, as at present.

Question, "That the word 'now' stand part of the Question," put and agreed to.

Main Question put, and agreed to.

Bill read the third time, and passed.

SERVICE FRANCHISE BILL

(As amended, considered.)

*Sir CHARLES DILKE (Gloucester, Forest of Dean): With regard to the registration of voters, this Bill is left in a somewhat curious position by the Amendment which was accepted the other day. I see that it is the intention of the hon. Member who has charge of the Bill to attempt to reverse the decision which the Committee came to upon that occasion, and I shall—knowing that he is master of the battalions, although no doubt a stout resistance will be offered to that proposal—I shall not speak at length as I should otherwise have done, and I will confine myself to matters arising under the Bill as it originally stood. The hon. Baronet has placed in his Bill a provision as to which a good deal of attention has been called by Irish Members on former occa-

Colonel Mellor.

sions in connection with registration in Ireland. The words of that provision, I think, have been taken from a clause in the Representation of the People Act of 1884, which established the service franchise. If this new clause of mine is not accepted, we shall have to scrutinise very carefully the provisions a little lower down. But, apart from these words, the present system is one which is established under the Representation of the People Act, 1884. That is substantially still in force, although it has been somewhat modified. That system rests on a declaration which was put in in the year 1884 on the motion of the late Mr. Edward Stanhope, on behalf of the Gentlemen who now sit on the front bench and constitute the Government of the Conservative Party. It is the impression of some persons that the whole proceeding takes place under these words of Mr. Stanhope's; but that is not the case, for there is not only a form introduced by which an inquiry is made as to service, and a form is given, which is filled up, and then those persons are placed upon the list; but the overseers are also able to place persons on the service franchise entirely apart from the use of that form, and the revising barristers are able to transfer people from the ordinary list to the service franchise list, and *vice versâ.* A most extraordinary want of uniformity prevails throughout the country with regard to the extent to which these privileges are available. I will mention one extreme case, which is a striking one. In two divisions of Northumberland there are a large number of service voters, such as shepherds and persons of that class. In one of these divisions there are over 1,300 service voters on the register, while in the adjoining division there are but eight service voters on the register at all. That shows that in some cases the overseers place them on the list as they should do, whilst in other places they put them on as ordinary tenants. This practice is not very carefully scrutinised in court, because it does not affect the Parliamentary vote. Supposing that the Amendment of my hon. friend the Member for North Monmouth, which was carried the other day, should not be reversed, the case is stronger than if the Bill stands as it formerly stood, because that Amendment would affect persons who would be indistinguishable from the lodger class, except for the fact that they do not pay £10 a year, and the case for making them go through the same form as lodgers would be made all the stronger. But even under the Bill as it stands, without the Amendment of my hon. friend, we must remember how the service franchise is affected by the Bill itself. This Bill will introduce to the service franchise voters who are under the strictest discipline, such as persons who live in cubicles, and who are subject to the orders of some person who has the power of moving them about. Where you have militiamen living in a single room in cubicles it will be absolutely within the power of the sergeant or the staff-sergeant who has control of these men to break their occupation. By shifting a man— which he has the power to do by military discipline—from one cubicle to another, he prevents that man qualifying for a vote by occupation; whereas with another militiaman all he has to do is to leave him undisturbed, and that man will come on the register. This is a matter which ought to be very carefully scrutinised, because there are cases where this power may possibly be abused. There have been cases under the present law where this has happened, and it will be abused in the future. The Amendment which I have placed upon the paper is the only means which occur to me for meeting this difficulty, for it applies the fourth section of the Act of 1867 to this case. It makes the people claim as if they were lodgers, subject, of course, to the provisions of the Act of 1878, by which the old lodgers obtained a *primá facie* right. They do not have to attend unless they are objected to, and receive notice of such objection. I need hardly say that if a better way were suggested to the House I should very gladly withdraw this particular form of words; but I have taken the only words which occur to me, and I beg to move the new clause which stands in my name.

New clause—

"All enactments and all orders made in pursuance of the Registration Acts which relate to the registration of persons entitled to vote in respect of a lodger qualification shall relate with the necessary variations and alterations of precepts, notices, lists, and other forms to persons qualified to vote under the service franchise."—(*Sir C. Dilke.*)

Brought up and read the first time.

Motion made and Question proposed—
"That the clause be read a second time."

SIR J. BLUNDELL MAPLE (Camberwell, Dulwich) : I am sorry to have to oppose the introduction of this clause, but I consider that it would be greatly against the interests of the voter that he should have to go and make a claim for his vote. It seems to me that the right hon. Gentleman opposite, who desires that every man should have a vote, ought to try in every possible way to make it easy for a man to obtain a vote. I think if the service franchise voter has to go and ask for time off in order to substantiate his claim, it would be greatly to the detriment of that man obtaining a vote. As regards the words which were left out the other day, I am one of those who would be rather inclined to thank the hon. Gentleman on the other side for moving to leave out those words, because his action will strengthen my side from a party point of view. But the object of this Bill has not been at all to do that; it is simply to undo a decision of the Courts and correct the injustice that was done by the decision of the Lords of Appeal against the decision of Lord Justice Rigby, when he said that a dwelling-room must have walls right up to the ceiling. It is only for that purpose that this Bill has been brought forward. If the words I have alluded to are left out, then all our butlers and footmen and employees in hotels and in different businesses, where the owner lives upon the premises and can exercise an influence upon them, would be put on the register. I should not object to that, although it is a much further extension of the franchise than was contemplated in the Representation of the People Act of 1884. I know it will be a great gain to a certain Party if those words are left out, but I have treated this Bill as I believe it was right and proper I should treat it, and I have simply tried to get back the original intention of the Bill, and I do hope that my right hon. friend will not press this particular Instruction, because it will be necessary for us to oppose it.

MR. T. M. HEALY (Louth, N.) : I am sorry that the right hon. Baronet opposite has decided to oppose this Amendment, and I think the right hon. Gentleman the Member for the Forest of Dean has done a great public service in moving the introduction of this new clause. I am sure the right hon. Baronet opposite has no party intention or political end in view in bringing in this Bill, but I must look at it in the light in which it will affect Ireland. I take the case of the City of Derry. This Bill, if it is passed in its present form, will lose to the Nationalists the representation of the City of Derry and also North Tyrone, and probably another seat which I do not care to particularise. I think that the decision of the courts, which the hon. Baronet by his Bill is seeking to get rid of, was one of the most just decisions which was ever arrived at in a registration case. Suppose an employer in a large way of business has ten assistants, and they are living in a dormitory. At present they have not the franchise unless they each occupy a separate room. But what the right hon. Baronet opposite desires is this—that if they are put into cubicles they shall each have a vote. At the present time they must have a dividing line or partition, and they must have a roof or a ceiling over it. Now, I do not think it is a great deal to require that a person should occupy one room, and that there should be a ceiling over it. Take the case of a policeman who lives with other policemen at the station, and there is a plank between their beds. Under this Bill the inspector could claim a vote for every one of these policemen living in cubicles. What the Court said was that they must draw the line somewhere, and they decided that a " house " is not a bunk in which a policeman sleeps. I think that was a sound decision. Now, what does the hon. Baronet the Member for the Forest of Dean seek to do by his Amendment ? If this Bill is passed in its present shape, all that you will have to do in order to get votes for your shop assistants is to place them in a dormitory, and put between each of them a curtain, and then you can call it a cubicle or a room, and claim a vote for the person who occupies it. I really do not see why a chalk line drawn between the parties would not be sufficient. Why not let us have manhood suffrage at once ? Unless this Amendment is carried, let me tell the House what will happen. I take a man in the City of Derry who employs ten or twelve assistants, and suppose five of them are Catholics and five Protestants. That man can shift the Catholics about from bunk to bunk during the qualifying period

Mr. Healy.

in such a way that the Papists will lose their votes while the solid Protestants will have practically fixity of tenure in their bunks, and it is perfectly idle to contend that this kind of shifting will not go on unless this Amendment is carried. The hon. Baronet the Member for the Forest of Dean proposes that when you are giving the franchise under these exceptional conditions the person who is getting it shall make a claim and substantiate and prove that he has been in occupation for twelve months, and then the employer cannot shift out of it. I take also the case of the pensioners and places where soldiers live in barracks. Why, Sir, it would be possible for a partisan official to shift all the soldiers and all pensioners from one room to another according to their political opinions. It is well known in Ireland that politics and religion go hand in hand ; at all events, you can always tell a man's politics by his religion ; and unless some safeguard, such as the right hon. Baronet has suggested, is adopted you will really be leaving the door open to the most tremendous abuses. I feel sure that the hon. Baronet opposite only intended to enlarge the franchise, and there may be cases where the present law acts somewhat harshly. In my opinion, however, the present law as it has been administered in England and Ireland since the recent decision is on a sound and satisfactory basis, and ought not to be disturbed unless you are going to give the franchise generally and impartially to every citizen. This is not a measure really to give a vote to those who live in cubicles, but to give it to their employer, for it leaves the employer to determine which of his men shall have the vote, and it is not a wrong thing to ask that, at all events, the same precaution which you take in regard to lodgers who have the shifting franchise should be established in this case. Why do you require these precautions for the lodger ? The lodger remains in the same lodgings very often for years, and why is he to be put upon a lower basis than a man who occupies a cubicle, not by virtue of paying rent, but simply by virtue of the provision made for him by his employer ? The lodger pays money out of his own pocket for his occupation, and he has to come off year after year ; and so great is the abuse of the lodger franchise in Ireland that my hon. and learned friend opposite holds his seat by virtue of bogus lodger votes; and yet the precautions which you insist upon in the case of a lodger are deemed to be entirely unnecessary in the case of the service franchise, where an employer can shift men about like nine pins. I hope the right hon. Baronet will go to a Division on this Amendment, and I trust the general consequences of this Bill will be realised by the House, for I am afraid that this measure has not received the attention which it deserves. The hon. Baronet opposite is master of the situation, and I can only say that if this Bill passes without this Amendment I shall certainly move that it shall not apply to Ireland. I would respectfully ask him not to plunge us into a general discussion affecting the franchise and its application to Ireland, because I assure him that that would not lead to the progress of his Bill.

Mr. ROBERT WALLACE (Perth): I would point out that under the present law it is already in the power of the employer at the present time, by shifting a person from the room he occupies, to disfranchise him. Therefore it is not for that reason at all that I support the Amendment of my right hon. friend. I confess that I do not share the fears which have been expressed by so many hon. Members in regard to enfranchising those who occupy what have been called bunks or cubicles. It is perfectly true, as has been pointed out already, that for years these persons have had the franchise, until they were restrained by the Court of Appeal some 18 months ago. The hon. Baronet opposite does not seem to be aware that at the present time lodgers have not to attend the revision courts in order to make their claims, for the law was altered in this respect some years ago. They have now simply to make a claim accompanied by a declaration, and the reason why I support the clause of the right hon. Baronet is that I think it is most desirable, when you are introducing these new service voters upon your register, that you should make sure that they are really qualified, and you should insist upon it that they should make a declaration which, if false, would render them liable to punishment. That, I think, would be the effect of the operation of the Amendment of the right hon. Baronet the Member for the Forest of Dean. I think all of us are anxious that the register should exactly represent the *bona fide* electors of the district, and that

only those who are fully qualified should be upon the list, no matter which side they belong to. Therefore I think it is necessary that some such declaration should be made before these persons are placed upon the register. I am not sure that the Amendment is not much wider in its scope than the right hon. Baronet the Member for Forest of Dean intends. It says:

"All enactments and all orders made in pursuance of the Registration Acts which relate to the registration of persons entitled to vote in respect of a lodger qualification."

It applies all these enactments and orders to the persons who will be placed on the service franchise in future. I wish to ask my hon. and learned friend the Solicitor-General what the exact operation of those words will be, and whether, in fact, it might not cover the case of hardship described by the right hon. Baronet the Member for the Forest of Dean—that is, whether under the existing law a person who changes his rooms is entitled to claim as a lodger so long as he occupies other rooms in the same house. I want to ask my hon. and learned friend whether all the enactments and orders which apply to lodgers will also apply to the service franchise, and whether the effect of that would not be also to enable the service voter who has changed his occupation, as my hon. and learned friend has described, from one bunk to another, to claim by right of succession in the same way as lodgers. If that were so, and if the operation of the clause would bring in the right of succession as I have described it, then all the difficulties, I venture to suggest, of disfranchisement would absolutely disappear. It is for this reason, and not because I have the slightest desire, as everyone knows, to keep any of these voters off the list, that I support the clause of the right hon. Gentleman.

Captain NORTON (Newington, W.): I desire to support this Amendment because I wish to oppose this Bill as a whole, and one of my main reasons for doing so is that it will enlarge the franchise very unfairly. The effect of it is that it enlarges the franchise to the detriment of a great number of working men throughout London, while it places those who live in cubicles in an advantageous and privileged position.

*MR. SPEAKER: The hon. Member cannot argue against the principle of the Bill now; he must confine himself to the discussion of the clause which is before the House.

CAPTAIN NORTON : The Amendment of my right hon. friend will meet my objection to a certain extent, inasmuch as it will place the service voters on a better footing of equality. At the present moment, if a voter entitled to the service franchise is placed in the position in which the hon. Baronet seeks to place him, he would have an undoubted advantage over the lodger. It would be in the power of the employer to enfranchise or disfranchise any one of these individuals ; whereas a lodger, owing to the fact that he cannot obtain another room in the same house, and is obliged to go to another house, would thereby lose his vote. There are many warehouse assistants in London who, when they obtain a better position in their place of business, desire to move into a better class of lodging— men, so to speak, who have risen in the social status, but who would be deprived of the vote. The result of the Amendment would be to diminish to an appreciable extent the injustice which the hon. Baronet would do to a large number of men throughout the metropolis.

THE SOLICITOR - GENERAL (Sir R. B. FINLAY, Inverness Burghs) : I

cannot think this is a desirable Amendment, as it might have a disfranchising effect. Whereas at present it is the duty of the overseer to get returns in respect of those who are occupiers, and who ought to be put on the register, it would make it incumbent on every person to prepare a list, and send in a claim as if he were a lodger. That was not the intention of the Legislature when the service franchise was passed. We hear a good deal about legislation by reference, and another objection to the Amendment is that it would be one of the most effectual instances of legislation by reference I ever heard of. My hon. and learned friend opposite asked a question as to what the effect of the clause would be. If my hon. and learned friend is puzzled as to what the effect of the clause would be, anyone might be excused if he were puzzled. Until a particular case arose, and it was carefully looked into, it would be perfectly impossible to say what the effect of the Amendment would be. It professes to apply only to enactments relating to registration, but the question is extremely difficult and complicated, and it would be unwise to adopt the clause without further consideration.

Question put.

The House divided : Ayes, 139 ; Noes, 184. (Division List No. 189.)

AYES.

Abraham, William (Rhondda)
Allan, William (Gateshead)
Allen, Wm(Newc.under Lyme)
Allison, Robert Andrew
Ashton, Thomas Gair
Asquith, Rt. Hon. Herb. Hy.
Austin, M. (Limerick, W.)
Baker, Sir John
Barlow, John Emmott
Barry, E. (Cork, S.)
Bayley, Thomas (Derbyshire)
Billson, Alfred
Birrell, Augustine
Broadhurst, Henry
Brunner, Sir John Tomlinson
Bryce, Right Hon. James
Buchanan, Thomas Ryburn
Burns, John
Burt, Thomas
Buxton, Sydney Charles
Caldwell, James
Cameron, Robert (Durham)
Campbell-Bannerman, Sir H.
Carvill, Patrick G. Hamilton
Causton, Richard Knight
Cawley, Frederick
Clark, Dr. G. B. (Caithness-sh.)

Collery, Bernard
Colville, John
Commins, Andrew
Crombie, John William
Davies, M. Vaughan-(Cardigan
Davitt, Michael
Dillon, John
Donelan, Captain A.
Doogan, P. C.
Duckworth, James
Dunn, Sir William
Evans, Samuel T. (Glamorgan
Evans, Sir F. H. (South'ton)
Farrell, James P. (Cavan, W.)
Fenwick, Charles
Ferguson, R. C. Munro (Leith)
Ffrench, Peter
Fitzmaurice, Lord Edmond
Flavin, Michael Joseph
Foster, Sir W. (Derby Co.)
Gibney, James
Gladstone, Rt. Hn. Her. John
Goddard, Daniel Ford
Gold, Charles
Gourley, Sir Edw. Temperley
Gurdon, Sir Wm. Brampton
Hammond, John (Carlow)

Harcourt, Rt. Hon. Sir Wm.
Harwood, George
Hayden, John Patrick
Hayne, Rt. Hon. C. Seale-
Hazell, Walter
Healy, Thomas J. (Wexford)
Hedderwick, Thos. C. H.
Hemphill, Rt. Hon. Ch. H.
Holland, Wm. H. (York, W.R.)
Horniman, Frederick John
Hutton, Alfred E. (Morley)
Jacoby, James Alfred
Johnson-Ferguson, Jabez Edw.
Joicey, Sir James
Jones, David Brynmor (Swan.)
Jones, Wm. (Carnarvonshire)
Jordan, Jeremiah
Kay-Shuttleworth, Rt. H. Sir U.
Kearley, Hudson E.
Kinloch, Sir John George Smyth
Kitson, Sir James
Langley, Batty
Lawson, Sir W. (Cumb'land)
Leng, Sir John
Leuty, Thomas Richmond
Lewis, John Herbert
Lloyd-George, David

Lough, Thomas
Macaleese, Daniel
MacDonnell,DrM.A.(Q'n'sC.)
MacNeill, John Gordon Swift
M'Arthur, Wm. (Cornwall)
M'Ewan, William
M'Ghee, Richard
M'Kenna, Reginald
M'Leod, John
Maddison, Fred.
Maden, John Henry
Mellor, Rt. Hn. J. W. (Yorks)
Molloy, Bernard Charles
Morgan, J. Lloyd (Carm'rth'n)
Morrell, George Herbert
Morris, Samuel
Moss, Samuel
Norton, Captain C. W.
O'Brien, James F. X. (Cork)
O'Brien, Patrick (Kilkenny)
O'Connor, J. (Wicklow, W.)

O'Connor, T. P. (Liverpool)
Oldroyd, Mark
Palmer, Sir C. M. (Durham)
Paulton, James Mellor
Perks, Robert William
Pickard, Benjamin
Power, Patrick Joseph
Price, Robert John
Priestly, Briggs (Yorks)
Reckitt, Harold James
Richardson, J. (Durham, S.E.)
Rickett, J. Compton
Roberts, John Bryn (Eifion)
Robertson, Edmund (Dundee)
Samuel, J. (Stockton-on-Tees)
Schwann, Charles E.
Scott, Chas. Prestwich (Leigh)
Sinclair, Capt. J. Forfarshire)
Stevenson, Francis S.
Sullivan Donal (Westmeath)
Sullivan, T. D. (Donegal, W.)

Tennant, Harrold John
Thomas, A. (Glamorgan, E.)
Trevelyan, Charles Philips
Wallace, Robert
Walton, Joseph (Barnsley)
Wedderburn, Sir William
Weir, James Galloway
Whittaker, Thomas Palmer
Willams, John Carvell (Notts)
Wilson, H. J. (York, W. R.)
Wilson, John (Durham, Mid.)
Wilson, John (Govan)
Wilson, Jos. H. (Middlesbro')
Woods, Samuel
Young, Samuel (Cavan, East)
Yoxall, James Henry

TELLERS FOR THE AYES—
Sir Charles Dilke and Mr.
T. M. Healy.

NOES.

Aird, John
Allsopp, Hon. George
Anstruther, H. T.
Archdale, Edward Mervyn
Arnold, Alfred
Arrol, Sir William
Ashmead-Bartlett, Sir Ellis
Bagot, Captain J. Fitzroy
Bailey, James (Walworth)
Baird, John George Alex.
Baldwin, Alfred
Banbury, Frederick George
Barry, Rt. Hon. A. H.S.(Hunts
Barton, Dunbar Plunket
Beach,Rt. Hn.Sir M. H.(Bris.)
Bemrose, Si. Henry Howe
Bethell, Commander
Bhownaggree, Sir M. M.
Biddulph, Michael
Bill, Charles
Blakiston-Houston, John
Blundell, Colonel Henry
Bolitho, Thomas Bedford
Brookfield, A. Montagu
Brown, Alexander H.
Campbell, Rt.Hn.J.A.(Glasg.)
Cavendish,V. C. W.(Derbsh.)
Cecil, Evelyn (Hertford, E.)
Clarke, Sir Edward (Plym.)
Clough, Walter Owen
Coddington, Sir William
Coghill, Douglas Harry
Collings, Rt. Hon. Jesse
Colston, Chas. Edw. H.Athole
Cooke, C. W. R. (Hereford)
Corbett, A.Cameron(Glasgow)
Cornwallis, Fiennes S. W.
Courtney, Rt. Hon. L. H.
Cripps, Charles Alfred
Cross, H. Shepherd (Bolton)
Cruddas, William Donaldson
Curzon, Viscount
Dalbiac, Colonel Philip Hugh
Davies, Sir Horatio D. (Chat.)
Denny, Colonel
Dixon-Hartland, Sir F. Dixon
Donkin, Richard Sim
Doughty, George
Doxford, William Theodore
Drucker, A.

Duncombe, Hon. Hubert V.
Egerton, Hon. A. de Tatton
Elliot, Hon. A. R. Douglas
Fardell, Sir T. George
Field, Admiral (Eastbourne)
Finch, George H.
Finlay, Sir Robert Bannatyne
Firbank, Joseph Thomas
Fison, Frederick William
Fitz Wygram, General Sir F.
Flannery, Sir Fortescue
Fletcher, Sir Henry
Flower, Ernest
Folkestone, Viscount
Garfit, William
Gibbons, J. Lloyd
Giles, Charles Tyrrell
Gordon, Hon. John Edward
Goschen, George J. (Sussex)
Goulding, Edward Alfred
Graham, Henry Robert
Gray, Ernest (West Ham)
Gretton, John
Gunter, Colonel
Hanson, Sir Reginald
Hare, Thomas Leigh
Heath, James
Hickman, Sir Alfred
Hoare, E. B. (Hampstead)
Hoare, Samuel (Norwich)
Hobhouse, Henry
Houldsworth, Sir W. Henry
Howard, Joseph
Hozier, Hon. Jas. Henry Cecil
Hutchinson, Capt.G.W.Grice-
Jebb, Richard Claverhouse
Johnson, William (Belfast)
Kenyon, James
Kenyon-Slaney, Col. William
Kimber, Henry
King, Sir Henry Seymour
Knowles, Lees
Labouchere, Henry
Laurie, Lieut.-General
Lawrence,Sir E.Durn'g. (Cor.)
Lawson, John Grant (Yorks.)
Leigh-Bennett, Henry Currie
Llewellyn, E. H. (Somerset)
Llewellyn,SirDillywn-(Swan.)
Loder, Gerald Walter Erskine

Long, Col. C. W. (Evesham)
Long, Rt. Hn. W. (Liverpool)
Lopes, Henry Yarde Buller
Maclean, James Mackenzie
M'Arthur, Charles (Liverpool)
M'Killop, James
Malcolm, Ian
Marks, Henry Hananel
Mellor, Colonel (Lancashire)
Milward, Colonel Victor
Monk, Charles James
Moon, Edward Robert Pacy
More,Robt.Jasper(Shropshire)
Morgan,Hn.Fred(Monm'thsh.
Morrison, Walter
Morton, A. H. A. (Deptford)
Murray, Rt. Hn. A. G. (Bute)
Murray, Col.Wyndham (Bath)
Myers, William Henry
Newark, Viscount
Nicholson, William Graham
Nicol, Donald Ninian
Northcote, Hn. Sir H. Stafford
Orr-Ewing, Charles Lindsay
Parkes, Ebenezer
Parnell, John Howard
Pease, H. Pike (Darlington)
Percy, Earl
Pierpoint, Robert
Pilkington,R.(Lancs. Newton)
Powell, Sir Francis Sharp
Priestley, Sir W. O. (Edin.)
Pryce-Jones, Lt.-Col. Edward
Purvis, Robert
Rasch, Major Frederic Carne
Redmond, J. E. (Waterford)
Renshaw, Charles Bine
Rentoul, James Alexander
Robertson, Herbert (Hackney)
Rothschild, Hon. Lionel W.
Round, James
Russell,Gen.F.S.(Cheltenh'm)
Russell, T. W. (Tyrone)
Rutherford, John
Sassoon, Sir Edward Albert
Savory, Sir Joseph
Scoble, Sir Andrew Richard
Seely, Charles Hilton
Seton-Karr, Henry
Sharpe, William Edward T.

Shaw-Stewart,M.H.(Renfrew) | Tritton, Charles Ernest | Wodehouse, Rt.Hn E.R.(Bath
Sidebotham, J. W. (Cheshire) | Usborne, Thomas | Wolff, Gustav Wilhelm
Sidebottom, Wm. (Derbysh.) | Vincent, Col Sir C. E. Howard | Wylie, Alexander
Simeon, Sir Barrington | Walrond, Rt. Hon. SirWm.H. | Wyndham-Quin, Major W. H.
Smith, Jas. Parker (Lanarks.) | Warde, Lieut.-Col.C.E.(Kent) | Wyvill, Marmaduke D'Arcy
Spencer, Ernest | Warr, Augustus Frederick | Young, Commander (Berks,E.)
Stanley, Edw. Jas. (Somerset) | Webster, R. G. (St. Pancras) |
Stanley, Henry M. (Lambeth) | Wentworth, Bruce C. Vernon- |
Stirling-Maxwell, Sir John M. | Wharton, Rt. Hon.John Lloyd | TELLERS FOR THE NOES—
Stock, James Henry | Whitely, George (Stockport) | Sir Blundell Maple and
Stone, Sir Benjamin | Whiteley,H.(Ashton-under-L. | Captain Jessel.
Thornburn, Walter | Willox, Sir John Archibald |
Tomlinson, Wm. Ed. Murray | Wilson,J.W.(Worcestersh.N.) |

MR. T. M. HEALY (Louth, N.): I wish to move an Amendment limiting the application of the Bill, to England and Scotland.

*MR. SPEAKER: I think the Amendment of the hon. Member ought to come in at the end of the Bill.

MR. T. M. HEALY: In that case it would have to be in the form of a new clause, and I could not move it without notice.

*MR. SPEAKER: I think it might be moved as an Amendment to Clause 3.

SIR J. BLUNDELL MAPLE: The effect of the Amendment I now propose will be to put back the Bill into exactly the same position as it was when I introduced it, and before that little error, as I consider it, of my hon. friends opposite occurred last Wednesday, when they voted to omit the words which I propose to reinsert. By leaving out these words the spirit that pervaded the service franchise, ever since it was adopted by the late Mr. Gladstone, was entirely altered. The object of this Bill was simply to restore the franchise to certain classes of service employees, who were disfranchised by a decision of a Court of Appeal.

Amendment proposed—

"In page 1, line 6, after the word 'employment,' to insert the words 'and the dwelling-house is not inhabited by any person under whom such man serves in such office, service, or employment.'"—(*Sir Blundell Maple.*)

Question proposed—

"That those words be there inserted."

*SIR CHARLES DILKE: At the time of the introduction of the service franchise in 1884 the only objection taken to it by the Conservative Party was on this point, and it was made by the Leader of that Party. Sir Stafford Northcote in an extraordinarily short speech said :—

"Under this clause, if a Minister did not inhabit a public office assigned to him, the office-keeper would have a vote ; on the other hand, it would be that if a Minister occupied the house as a dwelling, the office-keeper would lose his vote."

Now, the absurdity which Sir Stafford Northcote pointed out on that occasion was again pointed out the other day, and we think the time has come to do away with these restrictions which are involved in the words the hon. Baronet proposed to put back in the Bill. I frankly confess that we designed by the Amendment moved last Wednesday to make such a hole in the existing complicated franchises as to make it certain that a broad and simple franchise would be speedily adopted. We shall certainly take the opinion of the House before we allow the decision of the House last Wednesday to be reversed, and if we are beaten it will show, I think, the hollowness of the pretence that this is a large extension of the franchise, and that we are in favour of a much fuller and simpler franchise.

MR. ROBERT WALLACE: In regard to this particular Amendment, I wish to point out to the hon. Baronet opposite that on the Second Reading I stated that whilst we could not but recognise that there was a grievance to be redressed, at the same time there was a danger that in striving to remedy that grievance we would probably introduce a greater anomaly than at present exists. I ventured to ask the hon. Baronet in charge of the Bill at the time of the Second Reading how he proposed to deal with the lodger question, and I got from him a pledge, which the hon. Baronet has perhaps forgotten, in regard to the subject matter of this very Amendment. I pointed out that in a large part of London, but especially in the warehouses established in the West Central district, the employees there resident were deprived of their service franchise owing to the fact that their employers, who resided ordinarily beyond the mileage limit, kept a bedroom in the warehouse for their occasional use. By that means the employers obtained for themselves an occupation franchise, but they deprived all those who were resident in these large blocks of buildings of the service franchise.

Sir J. BLUNDELL MAPLE: What I said at that time, and I say it now, was that if the hon. and learned Gentleman, or any other hon. Member, will bring forward a Bill to do away with that anomaly I would support it; but I cannot consent to deal with the matter in this Bill.

Mr. ROBERT WALLACE: I am far from charging the hon. Baronet with a breach of faith, but I did put this difficulty before him on the Second Reading, and I understood the hon. Baronet to say that he would strive to remedy it in connection with this Bill. I may have misapprehended him, of course. The clause as it stands would, it is true, remedy that which all recognise as an undoubted grievance. I am not speaking in any hostile spirit against the Bill, but I am most unwilling that a greater grievance should be raised by pressing the Amendment on this measure than the grievance which is proposed to be taken away. I shall point out how this difficulty arose. A list is made out at present of those who are occupiers of dwelling-houses in London, and the courts of law decided that part of a house or dwelling where the landlord was non-resident would come within the definition of the occupation franchise, and consequently all those who occupy different rooms in a house were put on the list as occupiers. But they stuck to the principle that as long as a landlord had a room in the house, and occupied it, there could be no other occupier, and that all the others resident in the house were simply lodgers. Now, may I point out to the House the effect of that decision. A lodger only obtains his vote on condition that he occupies a particular part of a house of a certain annual value. A great deal of misunderstanding arose from the fact that it was supposed that the lodger should pay £10 per annum. But nothing of the

kind is necessary. The lodger may either pay rent, or he may occupy his room or rooms under the condition of rendering services, and if his services are of the equivalent value of £10 a year, as long as he is not compelled by his contract to reside on the premises, he is entitled to the lodger franchise. I want to ask hon. Gentlemen opposite why they are going to select one particular class of lodgers and give them the franchise, and deprive all other lodgers of the franchise under the existing law. The lodgers you are selecting to give the franchise to are the class least suitable for the privilege. They are dependent, residing on the premises, and under the control of the employer, liable to be enfranchised or disfranchised at any moment by their employer; while the other lodgers whom you are excluding from the franchise are independent lodgers—in fact tenants, occupying their own room and under the control of no one. In the one case, you have full-grown men and women, married it may be, quite independent; in the other case you have youths of 21 or 22 years of age, absolutely dependent on their employers, and yet you select them for the franchise while you refuse the qualification to the others. It is for that reason that while this clause remains as it is it is impossible to support this part of the Bill. I do not know whether my hon. and learned friend the Solicitor-General would for one moment accept the Bill on behalf of the Government in the form it stands to-day. I am perfectly certain that, knowing my hon. and learned friend the Solicitor-General as a great lawyer, he will tell this House that to pass the Bill as it stands to-day is to destroy a qualification existing at present for the franchise. I ask, in all sincerity, is it not a great pity to tinker in this manner with the franchise? I am not referring to questions which are controversial; I am not discussing whether it is necessary to shorten the term of occupation, or the question of one man one vote, but I am simply pointing out to the Solicitor-General how, by two lines in this Bill, he could remove one of the greatest inequalities existing in regard to the franchise. He might introduce a provision something like this: that, as to all persons who occupy a part of any premises under circumstances in which, if the landlords or employers were not resident, they would be held to be inhabiting occupiers, the presence of the employers or landlords should not disqualify them from being registered. I say at once if anybody stays to consider the effect of this Amendment they will find this distinction ; as a question of law, lodgers' and occupiers' qualifications are precisely the same. Where the landlord resides in the basement the persons occupying the house are lodgers, but if the landlord controls his house in the same way but lives next door they are occupiers. I am quite sure the Solicitor-General would not defend this Amendment, and I ask him now to give us some assurance that he will introduce an Amendment on some such lines as I have suggested. If he does that he will receive the cordial support of all those who sit upon this side of the House.

SIR R. B. FINLAY: I am afraid I cannot do as the hon. Gentleman suggests, and I think I will leave that to my hon. and learned friend when he in his turn has to fill the position I now hold. I am personally in favour of re-introducing the words struck out in Committee, because to my mind the alteration made in Committee will have a very far-reaching effect, not in the way of a direct dealing with the subject, but by a side wind. The distinction between a lodger and an occupier may be shortly described in this way : where the landlord resides upon the premises in which a man lives the man is a lodger, and where he resides in a house in which the landlord does not live he is an occupier. Those who now have the service franchise get it as occupiers, not as lodgers, and if you provide that these also are to have the service franchise you must go further, and by a Parliamentary miracle convert every person who would be a lodger into an occupier, so that, by being an occupier, he may enjoy the franchise independently of his landlord. Under those circumstances a lodger, who now has to have an occupation of the value of £10, would enjoy the franchise as an occupier whatever the value of his occupation might be. I am not going to discuss a question of that kind. I have only risen for the purpose of pointing out how far-reaching the alteration was which was made in Committee, and to say that, individually, I intend to vote against the striking out of these words.

MR. ASQUITH (Fife, E.) : The objection we on this side have to the Bill in its present form is twofold : first, it is too far-reaching, and it does not deal directly with the subject, but deals with it by a side wind. This is a tinkering attempt to deal with a very small part of a very large question, which will produce not greater uniformity in the law, but give rise to a fresh set of anomalies and injustices. The object of this Bill is to reintroduce to the suffrage a class which may be called dependent voters, which is at present excluded by the decision of a court of law. I think that they ought to have the suffrage. It is impossible to separate this class of persons from the case of other persons. If you are going to allow those who, by virtue of fee, service, or employment occupy positions in the same shop, at which the landlord does not reside, to have the franchise, how can you deny the same privilege to persons occupying the same position in similar services because the employer does reside on the premises ? If you are going to deal with this question at all it must be dealt with by a more logical method. I am speaking I believe the universal opinion of this side of the House when I say, not that we oppose this Bill because it extends the franchise, but we oppose this Bill because it does not extend the franchise in the only way that it should be extended by getting rid of the lodger and occupier and giving every man who occupies an inhabited house an equal right to take part in the elections, in whichever character he occupies that house.

MR. T. M. HEALY : The Attorney-General of England has spoken in a very singular way of the decision of the House of Commons, from whom I take it we have a right to expect something in the shape of wisdom as a legislative body. He also forgets, curiously enough, that the decision he refers to, which distinguished between a lodger and an ordinary householder, was disputed by the Conservative Party of the day. The hon. and learned Member for Plymouth was counsel on the one side, and Lord Russell and Lord Herschell counsel on the other, and they contended for the view which we now take. Nobody referring to that decision can deny that it was quite against the Conservative view of that day. I remember that I applied to Lord Herschell to reverse the decision, but the argument then was of a different character. Mr. Gladstone's view was to let all the decisions stand and simply pass a general Act, and give the county franchise the same position which the borough franchise now enjoys. But let us consider what this Bill suggests. It suggests that these dependents shall have a right to a franchise which the honest working man, who pays for the room he occupies, will not have. The object of the Bill is to present to a large class of persons, assistants in shops, warders, attendants in asylums, hospitals, stablemen, gardeners, grooms, and policemen a right to vote. You give them a sort of shifting qualification according as their landlord shifts their bunks. At the moment the landlord comes to reside in the house they occupy they are to lose their right to vote. You are giving a groom or gardener two important rights that the working man has not got. He need not reside in a room, but only in a bunk, and a bunk need not be rated for the relief of the poor. We talk about manhood suffrage, but what about groomhood suffrage ? I protest against it. I do not think that it is a harsh requirement that a man should live in a room in order to have the franchise. If this Bill is passed you might put two sticks in the ground and sling a hammock between them, and then, swinging in your hammock, say, without rating and not occupying a room, you might enjoy the benefit of the franchise. It may be said to be an anomaly, but there it is. When Mr. Gladstone brought in this clause he was thought to be going very far, but he brought it in in a state of things then known to Parliament, and said the man must occupy a room. I look forward to the day when the courts will be occupied in defining the compartment of a room.

MR. SPEAKER: Order, order. The hon. Member is going into another part of the clause.

MR. T. M. HEALY: The immediate question before the House is whether the landlord should occupy the house or not. Really the whole thing covers itself with absurdity, and I respectfully say we ought to return to common-sense, namely, to the decision of the Committee last week. I do hope that the House will support the Committee in respect of the decision at which the Committee arrived last week.

*SERJEANT HEMPHILL (Tyrone, N.): As an Irishman, I must ask to be permitted to say a few words, and I do so because my hon. friend the Member for Louth said on a recent occasion that my seat was one of those which was threatened by this legislation. I assume, therefore, that this measure applies to Ireland, and that being so, I think I have a right to complain that it has been very inadequately discussed so far as the interest of Ireland is concerned. Every stage of it has been taken at a time when very few Irish Members were present, and the Bill, if passed, will have very far-reaching consequences. The House hardly realises how it will affect the general franchise of the country. I trust that this Amendment will not be carried, because the only redeeming feature of the Bill is that, as it now reads, it abolishes the distinction between the resident and non-resident employer. What difference can there be whether the employer resides on the premises or not ; will not the employee be equally fitted for the franchise, whether he, the master, lives on the premises or elsewhere ? Why should the employees of a man who may live in one of the great squares of the West End be placed in a better position than those of a man who is obliged to reside on the premises where he exercises his trade or business ? I cannot conceive anything more unfair. If it is considered right that the employees should have a right to vote, let them have it, but let the same principle be applied to all employees, irrespective of where the employer may reside.

MR. ABEL THOMAS (Carmarthen, E.): If you read the definition into these proposed words, you will see exactly what you are going to do. "Where a man himself inhabits any compartment of a house by virtue of any fee, service, or employment, and the compartment is not inhabited by anyone else "— that clearly means so long as the master does not share the compartment—"he shall have a vote," that is exactly what everybody wants to avoid, as I understand. If hon. Members will only read the Amendment with the definition, the whole matter is too clear for argument.

MR. CLANCY (Dublin Co., N.): This subject is, as I think, of very great importance, and certainly Irish Members have not had an opportunity of discussing

2 S

the Bill as it should be discussed. I was under the impression that the Bill was confined in its application to England, but as it has general application, and is quite as important to Ireland as to England, and as we have had no opportunity to discuss it, and we cannot hope to discuss it in five minutes, I shall be obliged to take up at least three times that amount of time in discussing this subject. I beg to move the adjournment of the Debate.

Motion made, and Question put—

"That the Debate be now adjourned."

The House divided: Ayes, 139; Noes, 187. (Division List No. 190.)

AYES.

Abraham, William (Rhondda)
Allan, William (Gateshead)
Allen, W.(Newc.-und'r-Lyme)
Allison, Robert Andrew
Ashton, Thomas Gair
Baker, Sir John
Barlow, John Emmott
Barry, E. (Cork, S.)
Bayley, Thomas (Derbyshire)
Billson, Alfred
Birrell, Augustine
Broadhurst, Henry
Buchanan, Thomas Ryburn
Burns, John
Burt, Thomas
Buxton, Sydney Charles
Caldwell, James
Cameron, Robert (Durham)
Cawley, Frederick
Clark, Dr. G. B. (Caithness-sh.)
Colville, John
Commins, Andrew
Crilly, Daniel
Crombie, John William
Curran, Thomas B. (Donegal)
Dalziel, James Henry
Davies, M. Vaughan-(Cardig'n)
Davitt, Michael
Dilke, Rt. Hon. Sir Charles
Dillon, John
Donelan, Captain A.
Doogan, P. C.
Duckworth, James
Dunn, Sir William
Evans, Samuel T. (Glamo'gn)
Evans, Sir F. H. (Southa'ton)
Farrel, James P. (Cavan, W.)
Fenwick, Charles
Ferguson, R. C. Munro (Leith)
Ffrench, Peter
Fitzmaurice, Lord Edmond
Flavin, Michael Joseph
Foster, Sir W. (Derby Co.)
Fox, Dr. Joseph Francis
Gibney, James
Gladstone, Rt. Hn. Herbert J.
Goddard, Daniel Ford
Gold, Charles

Gurdon, Sir W. Brampton
Hammond, John (Carlow)
Harcourt, Rt. Hon. Sir W.
Harwood, George
Hayne, Rt. Hon. Chas. Seale-
Hazell, Walter
Healy, Thomas J. (Wexford)
Healy, Timothy M. (N. Louth)
Hedderwick, Thomas C. H.
Hemphill, Rt. Hn. Charles H.
Holland, W. H. (York, W. R.)
Horniman, Frederick John
Hutton, Alfred E. (Morley)
Jacoby, James Alfred
Johnson-Ferguson, Jabez E.
Joicey, Sir James
Jones, Wm. (Carnarvonshire)
Jordan, Jeremiah
Kay-Shuttleworth, RtHnSirU
Kearley, Hudson E.
Kilbride, Denis
Kinloch, Sir John George S.
Kitson, Sir James
Langley, Batty
Lawson, Sir Wilfrid (Cumber.)
Leng, Sir John
Leuty, Thomas Richmond
Lewis, John Herbert
Lloyd-George, David
Lough, Thomas
Lyell, Sir Leonard
Macaleese, Daniel
MacNeill, John Gordon Swift
M'Arthur, Wm. (Cornwall)
M'Ewan, William
M'Ghee, Richard
M'Kenna, Reginald
M'Leod, John
Maddison, Fred.
Maden, John Henry
Mellor, Rt. Hn. J. W. (Yorks)
Molloy, Bernard Charles
Morgan, J. L. (Carmarthen)
Morgan, W. P. (Merthyr)
Morley, Charles (Breconshire)
Morris, Samuel
Morton, E. J. C. (Devonport)
Moss, Samuel

Norton, Capt. Cecil William
O'Brien, J. F. X. (Cork)
O'Connor, T. P. (Liverpool)
Oldroyd, Mark
Paulton, James Mellor
Perks, Robert William
Pickard, Benjamin
Power, Patrick Joseph
Price, Robert John
Priestley, Briggs (Yorks)
Reckitt, Harold James
Richardson, J. (Durham, S.E.)
Rickett, J. Compton
Roberts, John Bryn (Eifion)
Roche, John (East Galway)
Samuel, J. (Stockton-on-Tees)
Schwann, Charles E.
Scott, C. Prestwich (Leigh)
Sinclair, Capt. J. (Forfarshire)
Smith, Samuel (Flint)
Spicer, Albert
Steadman, William Charles
Stevenson, Francis S.
Sullivan, Donal (Westmeath)
Sullivan, T. D. (Donegal, W.)
Tennant, Harold John
Thomas, Abel (Carmarthen, E.
Thomas, A. (Glamorgan, E.)
Trevelyan, Charles Philips
Wallace, Robert
Walton, Joseph (Barnsley)
Wedderburn, Sir William
Weir, James Galloway
Whittaker, Thomas Palmer
Williams, John C. (Notts.)
Wilson, H. J. (York, W.R.)
Wilson, John (Durham, Mid.)
Wilson, John (Govan)
Wilson, J. H. (Middlesbrough)
Woodhouse, Sir J. T. (H'dd'rsf'd
Woods, Samel
Young, Samuel (Cavan, East)
Yoxall, James Henry

TELLERS FOR THE AYES—
Mr. Clancy and Mr. Hayden.

NOES.

Aird, John
Allsopp, Hon. George
Anstruther, H. T.
Archdale, Edward Mervyn
Arrol, Sir William
Bagot, Capt. Josceline FitzRoy
Bailey, James (Walworth)
Baird, John Geo. Alexander
Baldwin, Alfred
Banbury, Frederick George
Barry, Rt Hn A H. Smith-(H'nts
Barton, Dunbar Plunkett
Beach, Rt. Hn. Sir M. H. (Bristol)

Begg, Ferdinand Faithfull
Bemrose, Sir Henry Howe
Bethell, Commander
Bhownaggree, Sir M. M.
Bigwood, James
Bill, Charles
Blakiston-Houston, John
Blundell, Colonel Henry
Boulnois, Edmund
Brookfield, A. Montagu
Butcher, John George
Campbell, Rt. Hn. J. A (Glasgow
Cavendish, V. C. W. (Derby.)

Cecil, Evelyn (Hertford, E.)
Clarke, Sir Edward (Plymouth
Clough, Walter Owen
Coddington, Sir William
Coghill, Douglas Harry
Cohen, Benjamin Louis
Collings, Rt. Hon. Jesse
Colston, Chas. Ed. E. Athole
Cooke, C. W. R. (Hereford)
Corbett, A. Cameron (Glasg.)
Courtney, Rt. Hn. Leonard H.
Cripps, Charles Alfred
Cross, Alexander (Glasgow)

Cross, Herb. Sheph'd (Bolton)
Cruddas, William Donaldson
Dalbiac, Col. Philip Hugh
Davies, Sir Hor. D. (Chatham)
Denny, Colonel
Dixon-Hartland, Sir F. Dixon
Donkin, Richard Sim
Dorington, Sir John Edward
Doughty, George
Doxford, William Theodore
Drucker, A.
Duncombe, Hon. Hubert V.
Dyke, Rt. Hon. Sir W. Hart
Egerton, Hon. A. de Tatton
Elliot, Hon. A. Ralph Douglas
Fergusson, Rt. Hn. Sir J. (M'n'r
Field, Admiral (Eastbourne)
Finch, George H.
Finlay, Sir Robert Bannatyne
Firbank, Joseph Thomas
Fisher, William Hayes
Fison, Frederick William
FitzWygram, General Sir F.
Flannery, Sir Fortescue
Fletcher, Sir Henry
Flower, Ernest
Folkestone, Viscount
Garfit, William
Gedge, Sydney
Gibbons, J. Lloyd
Giles, Charles Tyrrell
Goldsworthy, Major-General
Gordon, Hon. John Edward
Goschen, George J. (Sussex)
Goulding, Edward Alfred
Gourley, Sir. E. Temperley
Graham, Henry Robert
Gray, Ernest (West Ham)
Greene, Henry D. (Shrewsb'ry
Gretton, John
Gunter, Colonel
Hall, Rt. Hon. Sir Charles
Hanson, Sir Reginald
Hardy, Laurence
Hare, Thomas Leigh
Heath, James
Helder, Augustus
Hickman, Sir Alfred
Hoare, Ed. Brodie(Hampstead
Hoare, Samuel (Norwich)
Hobhouse, Henry

Howard, Joseph
Hozier, Hon. James Hy. Cecil
Hubbard, Hon. Evelyn
Hutchinson, Capt. G. W. Grice-
Jebb, Richard Claverhouse
Johnston, William (Belfast)
Kenyon, James
Kenyon-Slaney, Col. William
Kimber, Henry
King, Sir Henry Seymour
Knowles, Lees
Labouchere, Henry
Laurie, Lieut.-General
Lawrence, Sir E. Durn'g-(Corn.
Lawson, John Grant (Yorks.)
Leigh-Bennett, Henry Currie
Llewellyn, E. H. (Somerset)
Llewelyn, Sir D. (Swansea)
Loder, Gerald Walter Erskine
Long, Rt. Hn. Walter (L'pool)
Lopes, Henry Yarde Buller
Macdona, John Cumming
MacIver, David (Liverpool)
M'Arthur, Charles (Liverpool)
M'Killop, James
Malcolm, Ian
Marks, Henry Hananel
Mellor, Colonel (Lancashire)
Milward, Colonel Victor
Monk, Charles James
Moon, Edward Robert Pacy
More, Robt. Jasper (Shropsh.)
Morgan, Hon . Fred. (Mon.)
Morrell, George Herbert
Morrison, Walter
Morton, Arthur H. A. (Deptf'd.)
Murray, Rt. Hn. A. G. (Bute)
Murray, Col. Wyndham (Bath)
Myers, William Henry
Newark, Viscount
Nicholson, William Graham
Nicol, Donald Ninian
Orr-Ewing, Charles Lindsay
Palmer, Sir C. M. (Durham)
Parkes, Ebenezer
Pease, h. Pike (Darlington)
Percy, Earl
Pierpoint, Robert
Pilkington, R. (Lancs. Newt'n)
Powell, Sir Francis Sharp
Priestley, Sir W. O. (Edinb.)

Pryce-Jones, Lt.-Col. Edward
Purvis, Robert
Redmond, John E. (Waterford)
Renshaw, Charles Bine
Rentoul, James Alexander
Rothschild, Hon. Lionel Walter
Round, James
Russell, Gen. F. S. (Chelte'm
Russell, T. W. (Tyrone)
Rutherford, John
Sassoon, Sir Edward Albert
Seely, Charles Hilton
Seton-Karr, Henry
Sharpe, William Edward T.
Sidebotham, J. W. (Cheshire)
Sidebottom, Wm. (Derbysh.)
Simeon, Sir Barrington
Smith, Jas. Parker (Lanaks)
Spencer, Ernest
Stanley, Ed. Jas. (Somerset)
Stanley, Henry M. (Lambeth)
Stewart, Sir M. J. M'Taggart
Stirling-Maxwell, Sir J. M.
Stock, James Henry
Thorburn, Walter
Tomlinson, W. Edw. Murray
Tritton, Charles Ernest
Vincent, Col. Sir C. E. H.
Walrond, Rt. Hn. Sir Wm. H.
Warde, Lt.-Col. C. E. (Kent)
Warr, Augustus Frederick
Webster, R. G. (St. Pancras)
Welby, Lieut.-Col. A. C E.
Wentworth, Bruce C. Vernon-
Wharton, Rt. Hon. J. Lloyd
Whiteley, H. (Ashton-und'-L.)
Whitmore, Charles Algernon
Willox, Sir John Archibald
Wilson, J. W. (Worces'hr, N.)
Wodehouse, Rt Hn E. R. (Bath)
Wolff, Gustav Wilhelm
Wortley, Rt. Hon. C. B. S.-
Wylie, Alexander
Wyndham-Quin, Major W. H.
Wyvil, Marmaduke D'Arcy
Young, Com'and'r (Berks, E.)

TELLERS FOR THE NOES—
Sir Blundell Maple and
Captain Jessel.

Question again proposed—

"That those words be there inserted."

Debate arising, and it being after half-past Five of the clock, Mr. Speaker proceeded to interrupt the business.

Whereupon Sir Blundell Maple rose in his place, and claimed to move—

"That the Question be now put."

Question put—

"That the Question be now put."

The House divided : Ayes, 185 ; Noes, 143. (Division List No. 191.)

AYES.

Aird, John
Allen, W. (Newc.-under-Lyme)
Allsopp, Hon. George
Anstruther, H. T.
Archdale, Edward Mervyn
Arnold, Alfred
Arrol, Sir William
Bagot, Capt. J. FitzRoy

Bailey, James (Walworth)
Baird, J. George Alexander
Baldwin, Alfred
Banbury, Frederick George
Barry, Rt. Hon. A. H. S -(Hunts
Barton, Dunbar Plunket
Beach, Rt. Hn. Sir M. H. (Bristol
Begg, Ferdinand Faithfull

Bemrose, Sir H. H.
Bhownaggree, Sir M. M.
Bigwood, James
Bill, Charles
Blakiston-Houston, Charles
Blundell, Colonel Henry
Boulnois, Edmund
Brookfield, A. Montague

Butcher, John George
Campbell, Rt. Hn. A. J. (Glas'w)
Cavendish, V. C. W. (Derb's're)
Cecil, Evelyn (Hertford, E.)
Clarke, Sir Edw. (Plymouth)
Clough, Walter Owen
Coddington, Sir William
Coghill, Douglas Harry
Cohen, Benjamin Louis
Collings, Rt. Hon. Jesse
Colston, Chas. E. H. Athole
Cooke, C. W. R. (Hereford)
Corbett, A. Cameron (Gl'sg'w)
Courtney, Rt. Hon. L. H.
Cripps, Charles Alfred
Cross, Alexander (Glasgow)
Cross, Herbert S. (Bolton)
Cruddas, William Donaldson
Dalbiac, Colonel Philip Hugh
Davies, Sir H. D. (Chatham)
Denny, Colonel
Dixon-Hartland, Sir F. Dixon
Donkin, Richard Sim
Dorington, Sir John Edward
Doughty, George
Doxford, William Theodore
Drucker, A.
Duncombe, Hon. Hubert V.
Dyke, Rt. Hn. Sir William Hart
Egerton, Hon. A. de Tatton
Elliot, Hon. A. Ralph D.
Fergusson, Rt. Hn. Sir J. (Man.)
Field, Admiral (Eastbourne)
Finch, George H.
Finlay, Sir Robert Bannatyne
Firbank, Joseph Thomas
Fisher, William Hayes
Fison, Frederick William
FitzWygram, General Sir F.
Flannery, Sir Fortescue
Fletcher, Sir Henry
Flower, Ernest
Folkestone, Viscount
Garfit, William
Gedge, Sydney
Gibbons, J. Lloyd
Giles, Charles Tyrrell
Goldsworthy, Major-General
Gordon, Hon. John Edward
Goschen, George J. (Sussex)
Goulding, Edward Alfred
Graham, Henry Robert
Gray, Ernest (West Ham)
Greene, H. D. (Shrewsbury)
Gretton, John

Gunter, Colonel
Hall, Rt. Hon. Sir Charles
Hanson, Sir Reginald
Hardy, Laurence
Hare, Thomas Leigh
Heath, James
Helder, Augustus
Hickman, Sir Alfred
Hoare, Edw. B. (Hampstead)
Hoare, Samuel (Norwich)
Hobhouse, Henry
Houldsworth, Sir Wm. Henry
Howard, Joseph
Hozier, Hon. Jas. Henry Cecil
Hubbard, Hon. Evelyn
Hutchinson, Capt. G. W. Grice-
Jebb, Richard Claverhouse
Johnston, William (Belfast)
Kenyon, James
Kenyon-Slaney, Col. William
Kimber, Henry
King, Sir Henry Seymour
Knowles, Lees
Labouchere, Henry
Laurie, Lieut.-General
Lawrence, Sir E. Durn'g-(Corn
Lawson, John Grant (Yorks.)
Leigh-Bennett, Henry Currie
Llewellyn, Evan H. (Somerset)
Llewelyn, Sir Dillwyn-(Sw'ns'a
Loder, Gerald Walter Erskine
Long, Rt. Hn. W. (Liverpool)
Lopes, Henry Yarde Buller
Macdona, John Cumming
MacIver, David (Liverpool)
M'Arthur, Charles (Liverpool)
M'Killop, James
Malcolm, Ian
Marks, Henry Hananel
Mellor, Colonel (Lancashire)
Milward, Colonel Victor
Monk, Charles James
Moon, Edward Robert Pacy
More, Robt. Jasper(Shropshire)
Morgan, Hon. F. (Monm'thsh
Morrell, George Herbert
Morton, A. H. A. (Deptford)
Murray, Rt. Hon. A. G. (Bute)
Murray, Col W. (Bath)
Myers, William Henry
Nicholson, William G.
Nicol, Donald Ninian
Orr-Ewing, Charles Lindsay
Parkes, Ebenezer
Pease, H. P. (Darlington)

Percy, Earl
Pierpoint, Robert
Pilkington, R. (Lancs. Newton)
Powell, Sir Francis Sharp
Price, Robert John
Priestley, Sir W. O. (Edin.)
Pryce-Jones, Lt.-Col. Edward
Purvis, Robert
Renshaw, Charles Bine
Rentoul, James Alexander
Round, James
Russell, Gen. F. S. (Cheltnham)
Russell, T. W. (Tyrone)
Rutherford, John
Sassoon, Sir Edward Albert
Seely, Charles Hilton
Seton-Karr, Henry
Sharpe, William Edward T.
Sidebotham, J. W. (Cheshire)
Sidebottom, W. (Derbyshire)
Simeon, Sir Barrington
Smith, Jas. Parker (Lanarks.)
Spencer, Ernest
Stanley, E. Jas. (Somerset)
Stanley, Henry M. (Lambeth)
Stewart, Sir M. J. M'Taggart
Stirling-Maxwell, Sir John M.
Stock, James Henry
Thorburn, Walter
Tomlinson, Wm. E. Murray
Tritton, Charles Ernest
Vincent, Col. Sir C. E. Howard
Walrond, Rt. Hn. Sir Wm. H.
Warde, Lt.-Col. C. E. (Kent)
Warr, Augustus Frederick
Webster, R. G. (St. Pancras)
Welby, Lieut.-Col. A. C. E.
Wentworth, Bruce C. Vernon-
Wharton, Rt. Hn. John Lloyd
Whiteley, H. (Ashton-under-L)
Whitmore, Charles Algernon
Willox, Sir John Archibald
Wilson, J. W. (Worcestersh., N.)
Wodehouse, Rt. Hn. E. R. (Bath)
Wolff, Gustav Wilhelm
Wortley, Rt. Hon. C. B. Stuart-
Wylie, Alexander
Wyndham-Quin, Major W. H.
Wyvill, Marmaduke D'Arcy
Young, Commander (Berks, E.)

TELLERS FOR THE AYES—
   Sir Blundell Maple and
   Captain Jessel

NOES.

Abraham, William (Rhondda)
Allan, William (Gateshead)
Allison, Robert Andrew
Ashton, Thomas Gair
Baker, Sir John
Barlow, John Emmott
Barry, E. (Cork, S.)
Bayley, Thomas (Derbyshire)
Billson, Alfred
Birrell, Augustine
Broadhurst, Henry
Brunner, Sir John Tomlinson
Buchanan, Thomas Ryburn
Burns, John
Burt, Thomas
Buxton, Sydney Charles
Caldwell, James

Carvill, Patrick Geo. Hamilton
Causton, Richard Knight
Cawley, Frederick
Clancy, John Joseph
Clark, Dr. G. B. (Caithness-sh.)
Colville, John
Commins, Andrew
Crilly, Daniel
Crombie, John William
Curran, T. B. (Donegal)
Dalziel, James Henry
Davies, M. V. (Cardigan)
Davitt, Michael
Dilke, Rt. Hon. Sir Charles
Dillon, John
Donelan, Captain A.
Doogan, P. C.

Duckworth, James
Dunn, Sir William
Evans, Sam. T. (Glamorgan)
Evans, Sir F. H. (South'ton)
Farrell, J. P. (Cavan, W.)
Fenwick, Charles
Ferguson, R. C. M. (Leith)
Ffrench, Peter
Fitzmaurice, Lord Edmond
Flavin, Michael Joseph
Foster, Sir Walter (Derby Co.)
Gibney, James
Gladstone, Rt. Hn. Herbert J.
Goddard, Daniel Ford
Gold, Charles
Gourley, Sir Ed. Temperley
Gurdon, Sir Wm. Brampton

Hammond, John (Carlow)
Harcourt. Rt. H. Sir William
Harwood, George
Hayden, John Patrick
Hayne, Rt. Hon. Chas. Seale-
Hazell, Walter
Haley, Thos. J. (Wexford)
Healy, Timothy M. (N.Louth)
Hedderwick, Thos.Charles H.
Hemphill, Rt. Hon. Chas. H.
Holland, W. H. (York, W. R.)
Horniman, Frederick John
Hutton, Alfred E. (Morley)
Jacoby, James Alfred
Johnson-Ferguson, Jabez E.
Joicey, Sir James
Jones, William (Carnarvon)
Jordan, Jeremiah
Kay-Shuttleworth,RtHn SirU
Kearley, Hudson E.
Kilbride, Denis
Kinloch, Sir J. Geoge Smyth
Kitson, Sir James
Langley, Batty
Lawson, Sir W. (Cumb'land)
Leng, Sir John
Leuty, Thomas Richmond
Lewis, John Herbert
Lloyd-George, David
Lough, Thomas
Lyell, Sir Leonard
Macaleese, Daniel

MacNeill, John Gordon Swift
M'Arthur, William (Corn.)]
M'Ewan, William
M'Ghee, Richard
M'Kenna, Reginald
M'Leod, John
Maddison, Fred.
Maden, John Henry
Mellor, Rt. Hn. J. W.(Yorks.)
Molley, Bernard Charles
Morgan,J. Lloyd(Carmarthen)
Morgan, W. P. (Merthyr)
Morley, Charles (Breconshire)
Morris, Samuel
Morton, Edw. J. C.(Devonp't
Moss, Samuel
Norton, Capt. Cecil William
O'Brien, James F. X. (Cork)
O'Connor, J. (Wicklow, W.)
Oldroyd, Mark
Palmer, Sir C. M. (Durham)
Paulton, James Mellor
Perks, Robert William
Pickark, Benjamin
Power, Patrick Joseph
Priestley, Briggs (Yorks)
Provand, Andrew Dryburgh
Reckitt, Harold James
Richardson, J. (Durham, S.E.)
Rickett, J. Compton
Roberts, John Bryn (Eifion)
Roche, John (East Galway)

Schwann, Charles E.
Sinclair, Capt. J. (Forfarshire
Smith, Samuel (Flint)
Spicer, Albert
Steadman, William Charles
Stevenson, Francis S.
Sullivan, Donal (Westmeath)
Sullivan, T. D. (Donegal, W.)
Tennant, Harold John
Thomas, A. (Carmarthen, E.)
Thomas, A. (Glamorgan, E.)
Trevelyan, Charles Philips
Tully, Jasper
Wallace, Robert
Walton, Joseph (Barnaley)
Wedderburn, Sir William
Weir, James Galloway
Whittaker, Thomas Palmer
Williams, John C. (Notts)
Wilson, Henry J.(York,W.R.)
Wilson, John (Durham, Mid.)
Wilson, John (Govan)
Wilson,Jos.H.(Middlesbrough
Woodhouse,SirJ.T.(Hud'sfield
Woods, Samuel
Young, Samuel (Cavan, East)
Yoxall, James Henry

TELLERS FOR THE NOES—
Mr. Jonathan Samuel and
Mr. Scott.

Question put accordingly.

The House divided: Ayes, 171; Noes, 154. (Division List No. 192.)

AYES.

Aird, John
Allsopp, Hon. George
Anstruther, H. T.
Archdale, Edward Mervyn
Arnold, Alfred
Arrol, Sir William
Bagot, Capt. Jos'line FitzRoy
Bailey, James (Walworth)
Baldwin, Alfred
Banbury, Frederick George
Barry,Rt.Hn.A.H.Smith-(Hts
Barton,'Dunbar Plunket
Beach,Rt.Hn.SirM.H.(Bristol
Begg, Ferdinand Faithfull
Bemrose, Sir Henry Howe
Bhownaggree, Sir M. M.
Bigwood, James
Blakiston-Houston, John
Blundell, Colonel Henry
Boulnois, Edmund
Brookfield, A. Montagu
Butcher, John George
Campbell, Rt. Hn. J.A.(Glas.)
Cavendish, V.C.W.(Derbysh.)
Cecil, Evelyn (Hertford, E.)
Clarke, Sir E. (Plymouth)
Clough, Walter Owen
Coddington, Sir William
Coghill, Douglas Harry
Cohen, Benjamin Louis
Collings, Right Hon. Jesse
Colston, Chas. E. H. Athole
Corbett, A. C. (Glasgow)
Cripps, Charles Alfred
Cross, Alexander (Glasgow)
Cross, H. Shepherd (Bolton)
Cruddas, William Donaldson
Dalbiac, Colonel Philip Hugh

Davies, Sir H. D. (Chatham)
Denny, Colonel
Dixon-Hartland, Sir F. Dixon
Donkin, Richard Sim
Dorington, Sir John Edward
Doughty, George
Doxford, William Theodore
Drucker, A.
Duncombe, Hon. Hubert V.
Dyke, Rt. Hon. Sir W. Hart
Egerton, Hon. A. de Tatton
Elliot, Hon. A. R. Douglas
Fergusson, Rt. H.SirJ.(Man.)
Field, Admiral (Eastbourne)
Finch, George H.
Finlay, Sir Robert Bannatyne
Firbank, Joseph Thomas
Fisher, William Hayes
Fison, Frederick William
FitzWygram, General Sir F.
Flannery, Sir Fortescue
Fletcher, Sir Henry
Flower, Ernest
Folkestone, Viscount
Garfit, William
Gibbons, J. Lloyd
Giles, Charles Tyrrell
Goldsworthy, Major-General
Gordon, Hon. John Edward
Goschen, George J. (Sussex)
Graham, Henry Robert
Gray, Ernest (West Ham)
Greene, Hy. D. (Shrewsbury)
Gretton, John
Gunter, Colonel
Hall, Rt. Hon. Sir Charles
Hanson, Sir Reginald
Hardy, Laurence

Hare, Thomas Leigh
Heath, James
Helder, Augustus
Hickman, Sir Alfred
Hoare, E. Brodie (Hampstead)
Hoare, Samuel (Norwich)
Hobhouse, Henry
Houldsworth, Sir Wm. Henry
Howard, Joseph
Hozier, Hon. James H. Cecil
Hubbard, Hon. Evelyn
Jebb, Richard Claverhouse
Johnson-Ferguson, Jabez E.
Kenyon, James
Kenyon-Slaney, Col. William
King, Sir Henry Seymour
Knowles, Lees
Laurie, Lieut.-General
Lawrence,SirE.Durning-(Corn
Lawson, John Grant (Yorks.)
Leigh-Bennett, Henry Currie
Llewellyn, Evan H.(Somerset)
Llewelyn,SirDillwyn-(Sw'sea)
Loder, Rt. Hon. W. Erskine
Long,Rt.Hn.Walter(Liv'pool)
Lopes, Henry Yarde Buller)
Macdona, John Cumming
MacIver, David (Liverpool)
Maclure, Sir John William
M'Arthur, Chas. (Liverpool)
M'Killop, James
Marks, Henry Hananel
Mellor, Colone* (Lancashire)
Milward, Col .el Victor
Monk, Charles James
Moon, Edward Robert Pacy
More, R. Jasper (Shropshire)
Morgan, Hon. F. Monm'tshn)

Morton, A. H. A. (Deptford)
Murray, Rt. Hon. A.G. (Bute)
Murray, Col. Wyndham (Bath
Myers, William Henry
Nicholson, William Graham
Nicol, Donald Ninian
Orr-Ewing, Charles Lindsay
Parkes, Ebenezer
Percy, Earl
Pierpoint, Robert
Pilkington, R. (Lancs,Newton
Powell, Sir Francis Sharp
Priestley, Sir W. O.
Pryce-Jones, Lt.-Col. (Edin.)
Purvis, Robert Edward
Rasch, Major Frederic Carne
Renshaw, Charles Bine
Rentoul, James Alexander
Round, James
Russell, Gen. F. S. (Chelt'n'm)

Russell, T. W. (Tyrone)
Rutherford, John
Sassoon, Sir Edward Albert
Seton-Karr, Henry
Sharpe, William Edward T.
Sidebotham, J. W. (Cheshire)
Sidebottom, Wm. (Derbysh)
Simeon, Sir Barrington
Smith, Jas. Parker (Lanarks)
Spencer, Ernest
Stanley. Ed. Jas. (Somerset)
Stanley, Henry M. (Lambeth)
Stewart, Sir M. J. M'Taggart
Stirling-Maxwell, Sir John M.
Stock, James Henry
Thornburn, Walter
Tomlinson, W. Ed. Murray
Tritton, Charles Ernest

Vincent Col. Sir. C. E. H.

Walrond, Rt. Hn. Sir W. H.
Warde, Lt.-Col. C. E. (Kent)
Warr, Augustus Frederick
Webster, R. G. (St. Pancras)
Welby, Lieut.-Col. A. C. E.
Wentworth, B. C. Vernon-
Wharton, Rt. Hn. J. Lloyd
Whiteley, H. (Ashton-u.-L.)
Whitmore, Charles Algernon
Willox, Sir John Archibald
Wodehouse, Rt.Hn.E.R.(Bath
Wolff, Gustav Wilhelm
Wortley, Rt. Hon. C. B. Stuart
Wyvill, Marmaduke D'Arcy
Young, Commander (Berks,E)

TELLERS FOR THE AYES—
   Sir Blundell Maple and
   Captain Jessel.

NOES

Abraham, Wm. (Rhondda)
Allan, William (Gateshead)
Allen, W. (Newc.-und.-Lyme)
Allison, Robert Andrew
Ashton, Thomas Gair
Baker, Sir John
Barlow, John Emmott
Barry, E. (Cork, S.)
Bayley, Thomas (Derbyshire)
Billson, Alfred
Birrell, Augustine
Broadhurst, Henry
Brunner, Sir John Tomlinson
Buchanan, Thomas Ryburn
Burt, Thomas.
Buxton, Sydney Charles
Caldwell, James
Carvill, P. Geo. Hamilton
Causton, Richard Knight
Cawley, Frederick
Clancy, John Joseph
Clark, Dr. G.B. (Caithness-sh)
Colville, John
Commins, Andrew
Cooke, C. W. Rad. (Heref'd)
Crombie, John William
Curran, Thomas B. (Donegal)
Dalziel, James Henry
Davies, M. Vaughan-(Cardig'n
Davitt, Michael
Dillon, John
Donelan, Captain A.
Doogan, P. C.
Duckworth, James
Dunn, Sir William
Evans, Samuel T. (Glamorg'n)
Evans, Sir F. H. (S'thampton)
Farrell, James P. (Cavan, W.)
Fenwick, Charles
Ferguson, R. C. Munro (Leith)
Ffrench, Peter
Fitzmaurice, Lord Edmond
Flavin, Michael Joseph
Foster, Sir W. (Derby Co.)
Fox, Dr. Joseph Francis
Gedge, Sydney
Gibney, James
Gladstone, Rt. Hn. Herbert J.
Goddard, Daniel Ford
Gold, Charles
Goulding, Edward Alfred
Gourley, Sir E. Temperley

Gurdon, Sir Wm. Brampton
Hammond, John (Carlow)
Harcourt, Rt. Hon. Sir Wm.
Harwood, George
Hayden, John Patrick
Hayne, Rt. Hon. Ch. Seale-
Hazell, Walter
Healy, Thomas J. (Wexford)
Healy, Timothy M. (N.Louth)
Hedderwick, Thomas C. H.
Hemphill, Rt. Hon. Chas. H.
Holland, W. H. (York, W. R.)
Horniman, Frederick John
Hutton, Alfred E. (Morley)
Jacoby, James Alfred
Johnson-Ferguson, Jabez. E.
Joicey, Sir James
Jones, William (Carnarvons.)
Jordan, Jeremiah
Kay-ShuttleworthRtHnSirU.
Kearley, Hudson, E.
Kilbride, Denis
Kinloch, Sir John George S.
Kitson, Sir James
Labouchere, Henry
Langley, Batty
Lawson, Sir W. (Cumberland)
Leng, Sir John
Leuty, Thomas Richmond
Lewis, John Herbert
Lough, Thomas
Lyell, Sir Leonard
Macaleese, Daniel
MacNeill, John Gordon Swift
M'Arthur, William (Cornwall)
M'Ewan, William
M'Ghee, Richard
M'Kenna, Reginald
M'Leod, John
Maddison, Fred.
Maden, John Henry
Malcom, Ian
Mellor, Rt. Hn. J. W. (Yorks)
Molloy, Bernard Charles
Morgan, J. L. (Carmarthen)
Morgan, W P. (Merthyr)
Morley, Charles (Breconshire)
Morrell, George Herbert
Morris, Samuel
Morton, E. J. C. (Devonport)
Moss, Samuel
Norton, Captain C. William

O'Brien, James F. X. (Cork)
O'Connor,James(Wicklow,W.
O'Connor, T. P. (Liverpool)
Oldroyd, Mark
Palmer, Sir C. M. (Durham)
Paulton, James Mellor
Pease, H. Pike (Darlington)
Perks, Robert William
Pickard, Benjamin
Power, Patrick Joseph
Price, Robert John
Priestley, Briggs (Yorks.)
Provand, Andrew Dryburgh
Rickett, Harold James
Richardson, J. (Durham,S.E.
Reckitt, J. Compton
Roberts, John Bryn (Eifion)
Roche, John (East Galway)
Samuel, J. (Stockton-on-Tees)
Schwann, Charles E.
Scott, C. Prestwich (Leigh)
Seely, Charles Hilton
Sinclair, Capt J (Forfarshire)
Smith, Samuel (Flint)
Spicer, Albert
Steadman, William Charles
Stevenson, Francis S.
Sullivan, Donal (Westmeath)
Sullivan, T. D. (Donegal, W.)
Tennant, Harold John
Thomas, A. (Carmarthen, E.)
Thomas,Alfred (Glamorgan,E.
Trevelyan, Charles Philips
Tully, Jasper
Wallace, Robert
Walton, Joseph (Barnsley)
Wedderburn, Sir William
Weir, James Galloway
Whittaker, Thomas Palmer
Williams,John Carvell (Notts)
Wilson,Henry J.(York, W.R.)
Wilson, John (Durham, Mid.)
Wilson, John (Govan)
Wilson, J. W. (Worcester, N.)
Wilson, Jos. H. (Middlesbro')
Woodhouse, Sir J. T. (H'dsfld.)
Woods, Samuel
Young, Samuel (Cavan, East)
Yoxall, James Henry

TELLERS FOR THE NOES—
   Sir Charles Dilke and Mr.
   Lloyd-George.

Further proceeding on consideration, as amended, adjourned till To-morrow.

And, it being Six of the clock, Mr. Speaker adjourned the House without Question put :

Adjourned at Six o'clock.

HOUSE OF LORDS.

Thursday, 15th June 1899.

PRIVATE BILL BUSINESS.

The LORD CHANCELLOR acquainted the House that the Clerk of the Parliaments had laid upon the Table the Certificate from the Examiners that the further Standing Orders applicable to the following Bill have been complied with :

LONDON AND NORTH-WESTERN RAILWAY (NEW RAILWAYS).

Also the Certificate that no further Standing Orders are applicable to the following Bill :

WEST GLOUCESTER WATER.

And also the Certificate that the further Standing Orders applicable to the following Bill have not been complied with :

LONDON AND NORTH-WESTERN RAILWAY (ADDITIONAL POWERS).

The same were ordered to lie on the Table.

SHIREBROOK AND DISTRICT GAS BILL.

SOUTH STAFFORDSHIRE STIPENDIARY JUSTICE BILL.

NOTTINGHAM CORPORATION BILL.

WOLVERHAMPTON TRAMWAYS BILL. [Lords.]

Committee to meet To-morrow.

BRYNMAWR AND WESTERN VALLEYS RAILWAY BILL.

EDINBURGH CORPORATION BILL.

SOUTH STAFFORDSHIRE TRAMWAYS BILL. [Lords.]

Reported from the Select Committee with Amendments.

SOUTH-EASTERN RAILWAY BILL.

Report from the Select Committee, That the Committee had not proceeded

with the consideration of the Bill, the opposition thereto having been withdrawn ; read, and ordered to lie upon the Table : The orders made on the 1st and 8th instant discharged ; and Bill committed.

BELFAST CORPORATION BILL.
BAKER STREET AND WATERLOO RAILWAY BILL.

Read 2ª, and committed : The Committees to be proposed by the Committee of Selection.

BELFAST AND NORTHERN COUNTIES RAILWAY BILL.

Read 2ª, and committed.

BOOTLE CORPORATION BILL.

Read 2ª, and committed : The Committee to be proposed by the Committee of Selection.

NORTH PEMBROKESHIRE AND FISHGUARD RAILWAY BILL.

Read 3ª, and passed.

SHOTLEY BRIDGE AND CONSETT DISTRICT GAS BILL.

Read 3ª, with the Amendments, and passed, and returned to the Commons.

BROMPTON AND PICCADILLY CIRCUS RAILWAY BILL.

Brought from the Commons ; read 1ª ; and referred to the Examiners.

INFANT ORPHAN ASYLUM BILL. [Lords.]

LONDON HOSPITAL BILL. [Lords.]
STOCKTON AND MIDDLESBROUGH WATER BILL. [Lords.]

Returned from the Commons agreed to.

ILFORD GAS BILL.

Returned from the Commons with the Amendments agreed to.

TRAMWAYS ORDERS CONFIRMATION (No. 1) BILL. [Lords.]

House to be in Committee To-morrow.

EDUCATION DEPARTMENT PROVISIONAL ORDER CONFIRMATION (LONDON) BILL. [Lords.]

Reported from the Select Committee with Amendments, and committed to a Committee of the whole House.

LOCAL GOVERNMENT PROVISIONAL ORDERS (No. 8) BILL (No. 125).

PIER AND HARBOUR PROVISIONAL ORDERS (No. 1) BILL (No. 126).

Brought from the Commons ; Read 1ª ; to be printed ; and referred to the Examiners.

GAS ORDERS CONFIRMATION (No. 1) BILL. [Lords.]

WATER ORDERS CONFIRMATION BILL. [Lords.]

GAS AND WATER ORDERS CONFIRMATION BILL. [Lords.]

Amendments reported (according to order), and Bills to be read 3ª To-morrow.

ELECTRIC LIGHTING PROVISIONAL ORDERS (No 14.) BILL. [Lords.]

Read 3ª (according to order), and passed and sent to the Commons.

ELECTRIC LIGHTING PROVISIONAL ORDERS (No. 12) BILL. [Lords.]

ELECTRIC LIGHTING PROVISIONAL ORDERS (No. 13) BILL. [Lords.]

ELECTRIC LIGHTING PROVISIONAL ORDERS (No. 15) BILL. [Lords.]

Committee of the whole House (which stands appointed for this day) put off till To-morrow.

ELECTRIC LIGHTING PROVISIONAL ORDERS (No. 2) BILL.

Read 2ª (according to order), and committed to a Committee of the whole House To-morrow.

RETURNS, REPORTS, &c.

CHURCH OF ENGLAND (CONFESSIONAL BOXES).

Return respecting : Laid before the House pursuant to Address of the 3rd of March last, and to be printed. (No. 121.)

FISHERY BOARD FOR SCOTLAND.

Reports on the state of the markets for Scottish herrings on the Continent and in the United States of America.

ARMY (SPECIAL PENSIONS).

Return for the year ended 31st March, 1899, of Pensions specially granted under Articles 730, 1170, and 1207 of the Army Pay Warrant.

Trade Reports—
1. Annual Series :
   No. 2287.—Chile (Valparaiso and District) ;
   No. 2288.—Brazil (Pernambuco and District) ;
   No. 2289.—Trade of Malaga and District.

II. Miscellaneous Series :
   No. 504.—Commercial Education in the United States.
   No. 505.—Agricultural Education in France.

WELSH INTERMEDIATE EDUCATION ACT, 1889.

Report of the Charity Commissioners for England and Wales.

Presented (by Command), and ordered to lie on the Table.

RAILWAYS COMPANIES' POWERS ACT, 1864.

Report by the Board of Trade on applications made during the year 1898 under the Railways Companies' Powers Act, 1864, and of the proceedings of the Board of Trade with respect thereto.

MUNICIPAL CORPORATIONS (INCORPORATION OF SMETHWICK).

Charter of Incorporation of the borough of Smethwick, dated 12th June, 1899.

Laid before the House (pursuant to Act), and ordered to lie on the Table.

PETITIONS.

BOARD OF EDUCATION BILL. [Lords.]

Petition in favour of : of the Clerical and Lay Members of the Synod of the Diocese of Salisbury ; read, and ordered to lie on the Table.

ELEMENTARY EDUCATION (DEFECTIVE AND EPILEPTIC CHILDREN) BILL. [Lords.]

A Bill to make better provision for the elementary education of defective and epileptic children in England and Wales ; was presented by the Earl Waldegrave (for the Lord President, D. Devonshire) ; read 1ª ; and to be printed. (No. 120.)

EDUCATION OF CHILDREN BILL (No. 123).

LONDON GOVERNMENT BILL (No. 124).

Brought from the Commons ; read 1ª ; and to be printed,

FINANCE BILL.

Brought from the Commons :—Read 1ᵃ ; to be printed ; and to be read 2ᵃ To-morrow : (*The Lord Privy Seal, V. Cross*), and Standing Order No. 39 to be considered in order to its being dispensed with. (No. 122.)

QUESTIONS.

MALTESE NOBILITY.

VISCOUNT SIDMOUTH: My Lords, I beg to ask Her Majesty's Government if all correspondence referring to a memorial from Mr. G. Apap Testaferrata, between August, 1888, and the present time, can be laid on the Table of the House. I do not wish to enter into a discussion upon this subject, but as I have had the honour of being appointed hon. president of the Maltese Council of Nobility, I desire to ask whether the Papers relating to this case and the correspondence which has taken place can be laid upon the Table.

THE UNDER SECRETARY OF STATE FOR THE COLONIES (The Earl of SELBORNE): My Lords, the claim of Mr. G. Apap Testaferrata to be recognised as one of the Maltese nobility, to which the noble Lord refers, was twice rejected by the Committee of Privileges of the Maltese Nobility. On a third occasion, in 1892, the Committee advised the allowance of the claim, but no fresh reasons were given for the change of view, which was not accepted by the Secretary of State. It does not appear to the Secretary of State that the matter is one of sufficient general interest to justify the publication of the correspondence on the subject.

LONDON GOVERNMENT BILL.

THE EARL OF KIMBERLEY: Before the House adjourns, I should like to know whether any noble Lord opposite can tell the House when the Second Reading of the London Government Bill will be taken.

THE LORD PRIVY SEAL (Viscount CROSS): I think I must ask the noble Earl to repeat the Question to-morrow, as I have had no opportunity of consulting my colleagues on that point.

House adjourned at twenty-five minutes before Five of the clock, till To-morrow, half past Ten of the clock.

HOUSE OF COMMONS.

Thursday, 15th June 1899.

PRIVATE BILL BUSINESS.

PRIVATE BILLS. [Lords.]

(Standing Orders not previously inquired into complied with.)

MR. SPEAKER laid upon the Table Report from one of the Examiners of Petitions for Private Bills—That, in the case of the following Bill, originating in the Lords, and referred on the First Reading thereof, the Standing Orders not previously inquired into, and which are applicable thereto, have been complied with, viz. :

CLYDE NAVIGATION BILL. [Lords.]

Ordered—That the Bill be read a second time.

PPOVISIONAL ORDER BILLS. [Lords.]

(Standing Orders applicable thereto complied with.)

MR. SPEAKER laid upon the Table Report from one of the Examiners of Petitions for Private Bills—That, in the case of the following Bill, originating in the Lords, and referred on the First Reading thereof, the Standing Orders which are applicable thereto have been complied with, viz. :

EDUCATION DEPARTMENT PROVISIONAL ORDER CONFIRMATION (LIVERPOOL) BILL. [Lords.]

Ordered—That the Bill be read a second time To-morrow.

BLACKPOOL IMPROVEMENT BILL.

Read the third time, and passed.

GODALMING CORPORATION WATER BILL. (By Order.)

As amended, considered.

*THE UNDER SECRETARY OF STATE FOR FOREIGN AFFAIRS (Mr. BRODRICK, Surrey, Guildford): I beg to move to leave out Sub section 8 of Clause 54, and insert—

" (8) And any balance remaining in any year shall be divided between the area of the borough and the area outside the borough within the water limits in the proportion of the water rents collected from each of those two areas during each year. The proportion belonging to the outside area shall be applied in reduction of the water rents of the outside area, and the proportion belonging to the area of the borough shall be applied at the discretion of the Corporation either in reduction of the water rents within the area of the borough or carried to the general district fund."

I have to explain to the House the reason why I move to insert this sub-section. The position is as follows. The Godalming Corporation propose to acquire the water-works which supply not merely the Borough of Godalming but also certain districts outside, and it is anticipated that there will be a considerable deficit in the first few years, which it is proposed to meet by a rate of 7½d. in the £ in the Borough of Godalming. The Committee which considered the Bill made various conditions regarding the price of water, and also the manner in which any profit accruing from the undertaking was to be divided. As regards the price of water, the Committee very considerably re-duced the price the Corporation could charge as compared with that the Water Company which they were purchasing was entitled to charge, and a much lower maximum was fixed. The Committee also provided for the pay-ment of interest on the money borrowed for the undertaking, and for the re-organisation of the capital, as well as for the recoupment of any rate that might be raised, and for a small reserve fund if necessary. Having done all that, the Committee put in a clause by which all the profits subsequent to the payment practically of the actual expenses, and the repayment of the rate in aid, should go equally to all water consumers in the form of a reduction of the price of water. The Corporation of Godalming objected to that clause, because, although they were providing the whole of the necessary funds, and were taking the risk of losing the money to be raised as a rate in aid, which in the first year would amount to £1,200, and which would probably continue for several years, the outside districts, which did not risk any money on the undertaking at all, would equally share in the advan-tages. The Corporation felt that that would be a very hard position to be placed in, and it was a position which the Local Government Board found to be entirely without precedent. Therefore there was a strong demand that the clause should be expunged from the Bill. Two days ago the House consented to allow the consideration of the Bill to be ad-journed until to-day, and in the in-terval a compromise has been effected on the following terms: that the profits, should any accrue from the undertaking, be divided into two parts, of which one goes to the Borough of Godalming and the other to the outside consumers of water in the proportion of the water rents collected from each of those two areas during any one year. The outside consumers will receive their share in a reduction in the price of water, and the Corporation will be able to apply their share to the reduction of the general rate or of the price of water. That is to say, part of the benefit is to be confined exclusively to those inside the borough, and may be shared by those who do not take the water, although they may have subscribed to the rate in aid. It is a very fair compromise. I understand it is acceptable to the Committee which considered the Bill. It has been accepted by the Borough of Godalming, and it has been laid before those outside the borough who had previously been in opposition to the Bill, and we have not had any notice that they object. I think the compromise will be found useful in future cases as a precedent. It has been accepted by the Local Government Board, and commends itself, as far as I am aware, to the authorities of the House.

Amendment proposed—

"In Clause 54, page 28, to leave out sub-section (8), and insert: '(8) And any balance remaining in any year shall be divided between the area of the borough and the area outside the borough within the water limits in the proportion of the water rents collected from each of those two areas during each year. The proportion belonging to the outside area shall be applied in reduction of the water rents of the outside area, and the proportion belonging to the area of the borough shall be applied at the discretion of the Corporation either in reduction of the water rents within the area of the borough or carried to the general district fund.'"—(*Mr. Brodrick.*)

Question proposed—

"That Sub-section (8) stand part of the clause."

MR. SCHWANN (Manchester, N.): As Chairman of the Committee which had the audacity to introduce the precedent, perhaps I may be allowed to say that the Committee have not the slightest objec-tion to this Amendment. But I should like to explain that the Committee does not think it fair that any profit that might result from the undertaking should be used for the reduction of the price of gas or the building of a town hall solely for the benefit of the ratepayers of the town of Godalming. We therefore put in a clause that those outside the borough should not be charged a higher rate than those within the borough, and with the additional clause now introduced they will be amply protected. We also thought it our duty to protect the municipality of Godalming from itself, because I have known cities in the North where the profit from gas and water was invested in a large municipal hotel, which cost a great deal of money which the gas and water consumers should have, but which was expended on an undertaking which had practically no result. We did not wish in any way to be hard on the Corporation. My right hon. friend has put forward a very strong case, but he omitted one fact, and that is that the Corporation had one or two heavy responsibilities when they bought the company up. The decision was given in a spirit of conciliation and concession, and some of the onerous responsibilities which would have been laid on the shoulders of the Corporation have been relaxed or entirely removed. With a hope that the Corporation will make a profit which will go to the reduction of the rates, I will support the amendment.

*Mr. J. W. LOWTHER (Cumberland, Penrith): I am glad the parties have come together and have agreed on this matter. It only remains for me to give the arrangement my blessing. If the matter had to be discussed, I think on the whole I should have supported the view of the Committee. They have considered this matter very carefully, not once or twice, but three times; and though it may be said that they inserted a new principle in the Bill, I consider that where a Committee has given so much attention to the matter, and has thoroughly grasped all the facts and arguments, the House ought to support its decision. I think that the agreement which has been arrived at is a very fair one, and I heartily support it.

Question put, and negatived.

Question—
"That those words be here inserted," put, and agreed to.

Bill to be read a third time.

DUBLIN CORPORATION BILL.

Ordered, That Standing Order 207 be suspended, and that the Third Reading of the Dublin Corporation Bill be taken To-morrow, though opposed.—(*Mr. T. M. Healy.*)

BRADFORD TRAMWAYS AND IMPROVEMENT BILL.

Reported, with Amendments; report to lie upon the Table, and to be printed.

AIRDRIE AND COATBRIDGE WATER BILL. [Lords.]

Reported, with Amendments; report to lie upon the Table.

MESSAGE FROM THE LORDS.

That they have agreed to—

Metropolitan Common Scheme (Harrow Weald) Provisional Order Bill, without Amendment.

London, Brighton, and South Coast Railway (Pensions) Bill,

Lisburn Urban District Council Bill (changed from " Lisburn Town Commissioners Bill "), with Amendments.

Amendments to Dumbarton Burgh Bill [Lords], without Amendment.

That they have passed a Bill, intituled, " An Act to confirm certain Provisional Orders made by the Board of Trade, under the Electric Lighting Acts, 1882 and 1888, relating to Camborne, Dukinfield, Fenton, Finchley, Shipley, and Swinton." [Electric Lighting Provisional Orders (No. 10) Bill. [Lords.]

Also, a Bill, intituled, " An Act for authorising the Buenos Ayres and Pacific Railway Company, Limited, to prepare and carry into effect a scheme or schemes of arrangement with their shareholders, or with any class or classes of shareholders; and to increase and consolidate its capital; and for other purposes." [Buenos Ayres and Pacific Railway Company Bill. [Lords.]

And, also, a Bill, intituled, " An Act to give effect to a compromise of opposing claims affecting certain estates of the late Sir James Cockburn, 7th Baronet, deceased, situate in the counties of Pembroke, Cardigan, and Carmarthen, and in the city and county of London." [Yorke Estate Bill. [Lords.]

ELECTRIC LIGHTING PROVISIONAL ORDERS (No. 10) BILL. [Lords.]

Read the first time; referred to the Examiners of Petitions for Private Bills, and to be printed. [Bill 235.]

BUENOS AYRES AND PACIFIC RAIL-WAY COMPANY BILL. [Lords.]
YORKE ESTATE BILL. [Lords.]

Read the first time; and referred to the Examiners of Petitions for Private Bills.

PETITIONS.

COMPANIES ACTS AMENDMENT BILL.

Petition from Redhill and Reigate, against; to lie upon the Table.

LOCAL GOVERNMENT (SCOTLAND) ACT (1894) AMENDMENT BILL.

Petitions in favour;—From Montrose; —and Arbroath; to lie upon the Table.

POOR LAW AMENDMENT (SCOTLAND) ACT, 1845.

Petition from Arbroath, for alteration of Law; to lie upon the Table.

RETURNS, REPORTS, ETC

FISHERY BOARD (SCOTLAND).

Copy presented,—of Reports on the State of the Markets for Scottish-cured Herrings on the Continent, and in the United States of America [by Command]; to lie upon the Table.

TRADE REPORTS (ANNUAL SERIES).

Copies presented,—of Diplomatic and Consular Reports, Annual Series, Nos. 2287 to 2289 [by Command]; to lie upon the Table.

TRADE REPORTS (MISCELLANEOUS SERIES).

Copy presented,—of Diplomatic and Consular Reports, Miscellaneous Series, Nos. 504 and 505 [by Command]; to lie upon the Table.

QUESTIONS.

MOUNTAIN ARTILLERY.

Mr. PRETYMAN (Suffolk, Wood-bridge): I beg to ask the Under-Secre-

tary of State for War whether, now that it has been definitely laid down that the Mountain Artillery forms part of the Royal Garrison Artillery it is intended that officers serving in mountain batteries should draw armament pay in the same way as other officers of the Garrison Artillery.

THE UNDER SECRETARY OF STATE FOR WAR (Mr. WYNDHAM, Dover): The officers of the Mountain Artillery will have no armament under their charge, and it is not therefore proposed to give them any armament pay.

ROYAL ARSENAL, WOOLWICH.

Mr. STEADMAN (Tower Hamlets, Stepney): I beg to ask the Financial Secretary to the War Office if he will state how many men have been dismissed or suspended from employment at the Royal Arsenal, Woolwich, during the last twelve months, the reason for their dismissal, and the number of hours worked overtime during the same period.

THE FINANCIAL SECRETARY TO THE WAR OFFICE (Mr. J. POWELL WILLIAMS, Birmingham, S.): The point raised by the hon. Gentleman is the same as that raised by the hon. Gentleman the Member for Battersea on the 20th March, and I can only repeat the answer I then gave:

"Before men are finally discharged on reduction the authorities at the Arsenal are instructed to ascertain whether men of the same trade are likely to be required within a reasonable time in other departments. The employment of men on work in another department is not at all times possible. The space and machines in the workshops can only accommodate a certain number of men."

The number of men discharged during the period referred to in the question is 1,316, and of the men suspended 2,677; but it would not be possible to state the number of hours worked overtime during the same period without elaborate calculations, which it would require considerable time and labour to complete.

RIOTS IN MADRAS PRESIDENCY.

SIR MANCHERJEE BHOWNAG-GREE (Bethnal Green, N.E.): I beg to ask the Secretary of State for India whether he has received any official particulars regarding the riots which took place in the Tinnevelli district of Madras last Saturday; and, if so, will he state the same to the House; whether he has received any confirmation of the statement that 100 murders have been committed and whole villages sacked; and what steps are taken to quell the disturbances.

THE SECRETARY OF STATE FOR INDIA (Lord G. HAMILTON, Middlesex, Ealing): In reply to my hon. friend's question I will read the telegram which I have to-day received from the Governor of Madras—

"Tinnevelli riots due to dispute between Shanars on the one hand and Maravars on the other, regarding religious privileges of Shanars. Serious riots 6th June, at Sivakasi. Ten Shanars and ten Maravars killed, numerous houses burnt. Disturbance spread to Madura District to some extent, and serious riot reported from Shencottah in Travancore. Seventy persons wounded. Six companies of native troops called out. European magistracy and police strengthened. Active steps being taken to quell disturbances and punish rioters."

I may add that the Shanars and Maravars are castes of low social position, whose occupations and manner of life are such as might readily lead to rioting and fighting. A similar encounter took place between the same two castes about four years ago.

MR. DILLON (Mayo, E.): Will the noble Lord, in view of what took place at Omdurman the other day, consider the desirability of levelling the temples and digging up the remains of the saints——

*MR. SPEAKER: Order, order.

THE FRANCHISE IN INDIA.

SIR WILLIAM WEDDERBURN (Banffshire): I beg to ask the Secretary of State for India what are the conditions under which the franchise is exercised by the inhabitants of the French possessions in India, and how do these conditions compare with those affecting the inhabitants of British India.

LORD G. HAMILTON: I have no information as to the conditions under which the franchise is exercised by the inhabitants of the French possessions in India, the size and nature of which are such that any comparison of the kind suggested in the question would be altogether misleading.

SIR WM. WEDDERBURN: Does the noble Lord think the franchise cannot safely be entrusted to British Indians?

*MR. SPEAKER: Order, order. That is a matter of opinion, and does not arise out of the answer.

BOMBAY CIVIL AND CRIMINAL PROCEDURE.

SIR WILLIAM WEDDERBURN: I beg to ask the Secretary of State for India whether he will grant a Return for the last three years showing the number and nature of the civil and criminal appeals from the decisions of Political Officers in native states disposed of by the Bombay Government; whether he will state what is the procedure followed in the trial of these appeals; whether the parties have an opportunity of being heard in person or by counsel; and whether any member of the Bombay Government is a trained judicial officer qualified to dispose of capital and other cases as a final Court of Appeal.

*LORD G. HAMILTON: The Return for which the hon. Member asks cannot be supplied from information in this country, but I will communicate with the Government of Bombay on the subject. In the case to which he refers, whether civil or criminal, the parties are heard either in person or by counsel in the Political Courts of first instance, and again in the Political Courts of Appeal. In cases where the decisions of these courts are further reviewed by the Government of Bombay, the appeals and rejoinders may be, and generally are, prepared by counsel and submitted in writing; and if it is found necessary that any issue should be argued by the parties in person or by counsel, the case is remanded to the local Court of Appeal for the purpose; but parties and counsel do not appear before the Governor in Council. The Government of Bombay includes one member who has held high office, political and judicial, in Kathiawar; but it considers these matters as a Government, with the assistance of its legal advisers and its judicial department, and does not depend exclusively upon such legal or judicial training as may be possessed by any of its members.

COOPERS HILL COLLEGE.

SIR SEYMOUR KING (Hull, Central): I beg to ask the Secretary of State for India whether a despatch has been sent to India approving special terms of retirement for certain service officers of the Indian Public Works Department from Coopers Hill; and whether, for the convenience of those concerned, the terms may now be published.

*LORD G. HAMILTON : A despatch on the subject of the terms of retirement to be offered to certain officers of the Indian Public Works Department, who were recruited from Coopers Hill College in the years 1874, 1875, and 1876, has been addressed to the Government of India, but has not yet reached them. As soon as they have received it I understand that they will take steps to make its contents known to the local Governments for such action as they may consider desirable.

THE ARMENIAN ARCHBISHOP AND BISHOPS.

MR. STEVENSON (Suffolk, Eye): I beg to ask the Under Secretary of State for Foreign Affairs whether Her Majesty's Government will represent to the Sultan the injury done to the Armenian archbishop and bishops, who are forcibly detained in the monastery of St. James at Jerusalem without trial, and without knowing for what offences they have been exiled from their dioceses; and whether, seeing that those prelates are men of high character, the Secretary of State will communicate on the subject with the Powers which are parties to Articles 61 and 62 of the Berlin Treaty.

*THE UNDER SECRETARY OF STATE FOR WAR (Mr. BRODRICK, Surrey, Guildford): It appears from a despatch received from Her Majesty's Ambassador at Constantinople that the prelates in question are allowed the same liberty as the other inmates of the monastery, and that there is no reason to suppose that they are subjected to any special treatment apart from the punishment of not being allowed to leave their present place of residence. His Excellency understands that an annual stipend is paid to them by the Imperial Government through the Armenian patriarchate at Constantinople. In these circumstances Her Majesty's Government do not propose to make any special representation to the Sultan on the subject.

TURKISH LOAN OF 1855.

MR. DILLON : I beg to ask the Under Secretary of State for Foreign Affairs

when he expects to be able to communicate to the House the papers connected with the concession of the Turkish loan of 1855.

*MR. BRODRICK : No decision has been come to on this question, and I fear I cannot indicate any date for laying Papers.

THE ANSAHS, OF ASHANTI.

MR. J. A. PEASE (Northumberland, Tyneside) : I beg to ask the Secretary of State for the Colonies, with reference to the petition of John Ansah and Albert Ossoo Ansah, princes of the late kingdom of Ashanti, presented to Her Most Gracious Majesty the Queen, setting forth their grievances, whether he is aware that they rendered material assistance to the late Ashanti Expedition in advising the King of Ashanti to submit without resistance to the English forces; that they were arrested and charged with forgery, and were tried and acquitted of those charges, but nevertheless their property and effects were seized and carried away, and whether the house of one of them at Coomassie was levelled to the ground by order of the English authorities; and whether it is the intention of the Government to compensate the Ansahs for any damage done them, and whether they or any one of them will be allowed to resume the possession of any property which they or he may have owned or possessed, before the conquest of Ashanti, within the confines of that kingdom.

THE SECRETARY OF STATE FOR THE COLONIES (Mr. J. CHAMBERLAIN, Birmingham, W.) : I have no information as to the advice which was given by the Messrs. Ansah to the King of Ashanti. It is true that they were tried on a charge of forging their credentials, and acquitted; but Her Majesty's Government refused to entertain their claim for compensation, because, while not impugning the verdict, they considered that there was a case for trial and did not find that any suggestion to the contrary was made when the trial took place. The property found in the house of Mr. John Ansah at Coomassie was taken possession of by the police and handed over to their counsel, Mr. T. Hutton Mills, after the trial. No house was destroyed in connection with this case, but after their arrest certain native huts were removed in order to clear the ground in the vicinity of the fort at Coomassie, and I will inquire whether their house was one of them. Upon the question whether they can now be allowed to return to Coomassie I will consult the Governor of the Gold Coast. I do not know what property, if any, they possess in Ashanti.

WEST AFRICAN LIQUOR TRAFFIC.

MR. W. F. LAWRENCE (Liverpool, Abercromby) : I beg to ask the Secretary of State for the Colonies whether the authorities for the Niger Coast Protectorate and other West African possessions of the Crown have issued notifications of an additional taxation to be placed upon spirits ; and whether in the case of all these colonies the import duties upon spirits were already higher in the British territories than in the adjacent territories under the French and German flag ; and if so, whether he can state what will be the amount of such increase, and the duty on spirits in future to be levied in the British colonies as compared with similar duties levied in the French and German territories.

MR. J. CHAMBERLAIN : The recently signed Convention provides for a minimum duty of about 3s. per proof gallon throughout the Liquor Zone, with an exception in the case of Dahomey and Togoland, where the duty will be about 2s. 6d. per proof gallon. The duties in Lagos and the Niger Coast Protectorate were recently raised, in anticipation of an increase of the general minimum, to 3s. per proof gallon. The duties in Sierra Leone and the greater part of the Gold Coast were already 3s. and 4s. 6d. per proof gallon respectively. In the case of Sierra Leone, Gold Coast, and Lagos, the duties were already higher than in the adjacent territories under the French flag. There is a Customs Union between the Gold Coast District east of the Volta and the adjacent German possession of Togoland, so that in this case the duties are the same. In the case of the Niger Coast Protectorate the duty was less than in the adjoining German possession of the Cameroons. The duties in all the possessions within the Liquor Zone, whether French, German, or English, cannot, of course, fall below the minima fixed by the Convention, but the Convention empowers any of the Govern-

ments interested to raise their duties above those minima, if they so desire ; and it is therefore impossible at present to answer the latter part of the hon. Member's question.

FALSE TRANSVAAL REPORTS.

MR. BRYN ROBERTS (Carnarvonshire, Eifion) : I beg to ask the Secretary of State for the Colonies whether his attention has been drawn to a cablegram from Cape Town stating that there was a report that he was conferring with Mr. Rhodes, and that this has astounded the local community, affecting Dutch opinion deplorably ; whether he is aware that the Municipal Council of Cape Town has recently, by a large majority, refused an address of welcome to Mr. Rhodes ; and, whether, in order to allay the suspicions that appear to exist in South Africa, and to prevent all possible misconstruction, he will refrain from all interviews with Mr. Cecil Rhodes.

MR. J. CHAMBERLAIN : I am obliged to the hon. Gentleman for giving me an opportunity to contradict this falsehood. My attention was drawn to the cablegram referred to, and I have authorised Sir Alfred Milner to state that I have had no communication with Mr. Rhodes on Transvaal affairs since 1896. I may take this opportunity to warn the House against believing without confirmation any of the numerous statements which at a time like the present are invented and circulated for obvious purposes. Perhaps, Sir, in connection with that, I may be allowed to say that I observed in the newspapers two or three days ago a statement that has been repeated in the evening newspapers tonight, with a breadth of detail, as to my having made arrangements to leave this country. The newspapers have been misinformed. There is not a word of truth in any one of the statements that have been made. I have not engaged carriages either in this country or in France, and I have no intention whatever of leaving this country at the present time.

"ANTI-BRITISH" PROPAGANDA.

SIR ELLIS ASHMEAD-BARTLETT (Sheffield, Ecclesall) : I beg to ask the Secretary of State for the Colonies whether Her Majesty's Government have confirmation of the statement that the

Boer Government have spent considerable sums of money upon an anti-British propaganda in Cape Colony.

MR. SWIFT MACNEILL (Donegal, S.): Before this question is answered I should like to draw attention to a matter of form. I submit that this question is grossly out of order. The observation "Anti-British propaganda" is an argumentative expression. It is a mere matter of opinion, and as such the question cannot be asked. It is like saying "Anti-Boer propaganda."

*MR. SPEAKER: I do no see how it could be put otherwise.

MR. J. CHAMBERLAIN: I have no information which I can give to the House.

SHUNTING FATALITY ON THE CHATHAM AND DOVER RAILWAY.

MR. MADDISON (Sheffield, Brightside): I beg to ask the President of the Board of Trade whether his attention has been called to the remarks of Mr. Coroner Troutbeck, in an inquiry into the death of Frederick Goodacre, a shunter in the employ of the London, Chatham, and Dover Railway Company, in which he commented adversely upon the darkness of the shunting yard and the practice of working shunters overtime, and whether he has instructed one of the sub-inspectors to inquire into this fatality.

THE PRESIDENT OF THE BOARD OF TRADE (Mr. RITCHIE, Croydon): Yes, Sir, an inquiry will be ordered into the case. There is some discrepancy about the name of the deceased, but we are in communication with the railway company on the subject.

BEER MATERIALS COMMITTEE.

SIR CUTHBERT QUILTER (Suffolk, Sudbury): I beg to ask Mr. Chancellor of the Exchequer whether, in conformity with the suggestion contained in the Majority Report and the recommendation contained in the Minority Report of the Beer Materials Committee, he will direct the Commissioners of Inland Revenue to require brewers for sale to make separate entry, after the close of the present fiscal year, of all substitutes for hops used, describing accurately the nature of such substitutes; and whether he will further direct the Commissioners to alter the form of the published return relating to brewers' licences, so as to disclose the quantities of malt, substitutes for malt, or unmalted grain, and of hops or substitutes for hops used by each individual brewer.

THE CHANCELLOR OF THE EXCHEQUER (Sir M. HICKS BEACH, Bristol, W.): The majority of the Committee, while they mentioned that hops and hop substitutes might be made the subject of a separate entry, expressed their opinion that no deleterious substitutes were in fact used, and that compulsory declaration of the use of substitutes would serve no useful end. Legislation would be necessary to compel brewers to make such entries, and, in view of the Committee's opinion, I have not seen my way to propose it. The suggestion in the second paragraph was also considered by the Committee, but the opinion of the majority was that it would involve inquisitorial interference with business and a departure from that reticence as to individuals which is an essential feature of our revenue system.

SIR CUTHBERT QUILTER: Seeing that this information is in the hands of a large number of public servants, can the right hon. Gentleman give any reason why it should be withheld from Members of this House?

SIR M. HICKS BEACH: I do not know that it is in the hands of a large number of public servants.

METROPOLITAN STREET OBSTRUCTIONS.

GENERAL LAURIE (Pembroke and Haverford West): I beg to ask the Secretary of State for the Home Department whether his attention has been called to the dismissal by the presiding magistrate at Marylebone Police Court, on the 16th May, 1899, of two summonses against carmen for permitting their vans to stand on the roadway longer than was necessary for loading or unloading, on the ground that it was too trivial, and that such petty prosecutions were an abuse of the statute; whether he is aware that the practice of obstructing the traffic by leaving large vans often in two ranks in the streets, with the horses feeding, and often without anyone in charge, for a considerable time, is causing both a serious obstruction and a serious danger; and whether, in the Bill for regulating the traffic of the metropolis, he will insert such provisions as will enable the police to prevent such obstructions, and will make the enactment so clear that magistrates cannot refuse to convict.

*The UNDER SECRETARY FOR THE HOME OFFICE (Mr. JESSE COLLINGS, Birmingham, Bordesley): The answer to the first paragraph is in the affirmative. The police possess power to deal with—and they do deal with—cases of obstruction arising from vans, &c., standing longer than may be necessary for loading or unloading, and the Secretary of State is not prepared to say that the obstruction or danger arising from the source indicated is unduly in excess of what must inevitably arise from the commercial needs of the metropolis. The Secretary of State does not think it will be necessary to introduce any further provisions for the purpose suggested into the Bill now before the House.

NATURALISATION CERTIFICATES.

MR. SWIFT MacNEILL: I beg to ask the Secretary of State for the Home Department whether the obtaining of a certificate of naturalisation from a Principal Secretary of State as a British subject by an alien is a condition precedent to becoming a naturalised British subject, although the applicant for naturalisation may have resided in the United Kingdom or served under the Crown the period which may render him qualified for naturalisation under the provisions of the Naturalisation Act of 1870; whether the Secretary of State can give or withhold the certificate of naturalisation at his discretion; whether, in the event of refusal to grant the certificate, the Secretary of State is obliged to state the grounds of refusal; and is there any, and, if so, what appeal from the decision of the Secretary of State refusing to grant the certificate of naturalisation as a British subject to an alien who has fulfilled the statutory conditions qualifying him for naturalisation.

MR. JESSE COLLINGS: The answers to all the hon. Member's questions may be put together shortly as follows: An alien who is a male and of full age can only become a naturalised British subject in the United Kingdom under the provisions of a Personal Act of Parliament, or by receiving a certificate from a Secretary of State. Such certificates may be given or refused by the Secretary of State at his discretion, without reasons assigned and without appeal.

ECCLESIASTICAL JUDGES.

MR. CHARLES McARTHUR (Liverpool, Exchange): I beg to ask Mr. Attorney-General whether Sir Arthur Charles has been appointed Dean of Arches; if so, whether the appointment has been made under the Public Worship Regulation Act, and approved by the Crown, as required by that Act, also when such approval was signified; if the appointment has been made otherwise than under the Public Worship Regulation Act, and under what law and by whose authority it has been made.

*MR. JESSE COLLINGS: It has been decided to appoint Sir Arthur Charles to be a Judge of the Provincial Courts of Canterbury and York, pursuant to the Public Worship Regulation Act, 1874, Section 7; and the necessary formal steps for the making of the appointment by the Archbishops, and its approval and ratification by the Crown, are now being carried out. A Dean of Arches is not now appointed.

BRITISH ARTISTS AND THE PARIS EXHIBITION.

MR. COURTNEY (Cornwall, Bodmin): I beg to ask the Secretary to the Treasury what amount of space has been allotted to the exhibition of the works of British artists, past and living, at the forthcoming Paris Exhibition; and what proportion will be appropriated to works of art produced since the last Paris Exhibition, thus securing the primary object of such periodical exhibitions—viz., the illustration of the progress of contemporary art.

THE FINANCIAL SECRETARY TO THE TREASURY (Mr. HANBURY, Preston): The space allotted in the Paris Exhibition for British works of art executed since the 1st May, 1889, consists of three rooms and part of a corridor in the new Palace of Fine Art. These rooms afford 466 feet run of wall space available for hanging paintings, drawings, etc. Sculpture of all nationalities will be distributed throughout the building at the discretion of the French authorities. Works of art may also be exhibited in the British Pavilion on the Quai d'Orsay, but the Royal Commission have decided to reserve this building mainly for the display of works by old masters of the British School.

ASSISTANTS TO SUB-POSTMASTERS.

MR. STEADMAN: I beg to ask the Secretary to the Treasury, as representing the Postmaster-General, if there is any rule or regulation preventing a rural postman performing part of the official duties of a sub-postmaster, provided that the work so performed is checked or supervised by the sub-postmaster.

MR. HANBURY: There is no regulation on the point referred to; but it is thought undesirable that a rural postman should perform any duties in the office of a sub-postmaster, and there are not many cases in which a rural postman would have sufficient time at his disposal to admit of his giving useful service as an assistant in a sub-office.

CENTRAL TELEGRAPH STAFF, LONDON.

MR. M'GHEE (Louth, S.): I beg to ask the Secretary to the Treasury, as representing the Postmaster-General, whether he has received a petition with reference to permanent duties from noon till 8 p.m., forwarded to him in February last by a section of the telegraph staff of the Central Office, London; whether an elected committee of the staff also petitioned him with reference to the Christmas holidays of 1898; and whether replies can now be communicated to the staff.

MR. HANBURY: The petition referred to in the first part of the hon. Member's question was duly received, and an endeavour has been made to comply with it, but at present the circumstances do not admit of this being done. The hours complained of can, however, scarcely be regarded as irksome, and the Postmaster-General does not consider that any hardship will be involved if they have to be maintained for a time. A petition with reference to the Christmas holidays of 1898 was also received, and a reply was given on the 20th December,

that when the state of the work enabled any portion of the staff to be released in either Christmas week, or in the succeeding week, without additional expense or inconvenience to the public, this should be done; and effect was given to this decision as far as possible.

IRELAND—THE BAGOT ESTATE.

MR. HAYDEN (Roscommon, S.): I beg to ask the Chief Secretary to the Lord-Lieutenant of Ireland whether his attention has been drawn to certain proceedings in reference to the Bagot estate, which took place in the Dublin Courts on 26th April; whether he has received copies of resolutions passed recently at a public meeting held in Ballymoe, county Galway, on the subsequent Sunday; whether the Congested Districts Board have been negotiating for the purchase of the said estate, and whether subsequently Sir Nicholas R. O'Conor, British Ambassador at Constantinople, intervened as a possible purchaser; whether any representations on the subject have been or will be made to Sir N. R. O'Conor, with the view of giving to the people the advantage arising from purchase by the Congested Districts Board; and whether that Board will continue its negotiations to secure the estate.

*THE CHIEF SECRETARY FOR IRELAND (Mr. G. W. BALFOUR, Leeds, Central): I am aware of the proceedings taken by the Congested Districts Board in the Land Judge's Court respecting this estate. The Board instructed their solicitor to negotiate for the purchase of portion of the estate, and he appeared before the Land Judge in reference to the matter, but the Land Judge decided to accept the offer of Sir Nicholas O'Conor. The replies to the fourth and fifth paragraphs are in the negative.

IRISH COUNTY INFIRMARIES.

MR. T. M. HEALY (Louth, N.): I beg to ask the Chief Secretary to the Lord Lieutenant of Ireland if he will give a Return showing the proportionate number of governors and members of county councils prescribed by the Local Government Board to manage Irish county infirmaries, and the data as to contribution and property on which the respective numbers were determined; has any, and, if so, what reply been given to the protest of Queen's County Council against the representation they were afforded; and on what basis was this representation arrived at.

*Mr. G. W. BALFOUR: The Return indicated in the question will be laid on the Table of the House as soon as the respective numbers have been finally decided. This has been done in all but five cases, with respect to which the Local Government Board are still in correspondence with the local authorities. Before finally deciding upon the number of representatives to be elected by the county council and the governors, a provisional statement was sent to each council of the proposal of the Local Government Board, and the views of the council were invited. Where the representations made to the Board appeared to demand consideration they have modified their original proposal. In the case of Queen's County, the Board have added five members to the number of the committee formerly fixed to be elected by the County Council. The financial particulars were in each case supplied by the officers of the board of governors and secretaries of county councils; but as the Local Government Board do not audit the accounts of county infirmaries they have no means of checking the particulars furnished by the officers of these institutions.

Mr. T. M. HEALY: Can the right hon. Gentleman say whether he hopes to be able to lay this Return before Thursday or Friday next, when it is proposed to take the Irish Estimates?

Mr. G. W. BALFOUR: I do not think it advisable to lay it in an incomplete form; but I shall be happy, if it is not complete, to let the hon. Member see any information he wishes.

PENALTIES FOR CARRYING FIRE-ARMS IN IRELAND.

Mr. T. M. HEALY: I beg to ask the Chief Secretary to the Lord Lieutenant of Ireland what is the result of his promise to inquire into the breaches of the law of which Thomas Brady, of Ballinaglera, County Leitrim, has been three times convicted, viz. at Carrick Assizes, 5th June, 1898, for firing at the person; at Doura Petty Sessions, on 9th November, 1898, and 12th April, 1899, for carrying arms without an Excise licence; is Brady still in possession of firearms with a licence under the Arms Act; and is it the intention of the authorities to treat this recent conviction as a contravention of his recognisance to be of good behaviour.

*Mr. G. W. BALFOUR: Since I replied to the hon. and learned Member's previous question of the 21st February respecting this man, he has been prosecuted at the suit of the Excise authorities for carrying a gun without a licence, and has been fined in a sum of £2 10s. Brady is not in possession of firearms, nor has he a licence under the Peace Preservation Act. It is believed that the gun which he used on the occasions mentioned belonged to his son, who has a licence, and who has been warned by the police that if he did not take steps to prevent the use of the weapon by his father the question of revoking his licence would have to be considered. The facts of the case have been fully reported upon to my right hon. friend the Attorney-General for Ireland, who has advised that it is not necessary to have Brady brought up for judgment.

Mr. T. M. HEALY: May I ask whether carrying arms without a licence is not only an offence against the Excise but also under the Arms Act. Why was not this man prosecuted and sent to gaol for three months, as the Nationalists were?

*Mr. G. W. BALFOUR: As the hon. Gentleman knows, if the Excise take up a case it is not always necessary to take it before any other court.

Mr. T. M. HEALY: In one court you get a fine, and the other imprisonment.

THE ROSSMORE ESTATE.

*Mr. MACALEESE (Monaghan, S.): I beg to ask the Chief Secretary to the Lord Lieutenant of Ireland is he aware that an eviction party from the Rossmore estate office at Monaghan attended on Saturday, the 3rd instant, at the townland of Cormary, near Newbliss, to evict Francis Finegan and his sister from their farm; that the woman Finegan, who was over 60 years of age, was lying in bed ill when the bailiffs arrived, but that a doctor, not belonging to the district, certified that she was quite fit to be removed, and that Mr. Turner, relieving officer, when he reached the scene with the workhouse ambulance, refused to remove the woman unless upon the certificate of Dr. Henry, the medical officer of this district; that the bailiffs had the greater portion of the furniture and effects thrown out upon the street when Dr. Henry arrived, and that Dr. Henry forbade any further action by the bailiffs when he saw the condition of the woman, who died the following day or the day after; was an inquest held, seeing that her end was accelerated by the action of the bailiffs; who employed the doctor who supplied the certificate of fitness of removal; and will any notice be taken of this case.

*MR. G. W. BALFOUR: The facts are generally as stated in the first paragraph. Dr. Henry did not arrive until 10.20 p.m., after the evicting party had left. The woman, who was not disturbed, died on the morning of the 6th inst. No inquest was held; the deceased had been ailing for the past twelve months, during the last two of which she was confined to bed. The medical man who stated she was fit for removal was employed by the agent to the landlord. No action is called for in the case on the part of the Government.

MR. MACALEESE: Were the furniture and other effects removed?

*MR. G. W. BALFOUR: The furniture was removed.

IRISH LOCAL GOVERNMENT FINANCE.

MR. SWIFT MacNEILL: I beg to ask the Chief Secretary to the Lord Lieutenant of Ireland whether his attention has been directed to resolutions passed by various county councils in Ireland, including the county councils of Cork and Donegal, directing attention to the enormous increase of labour and of expense entailed on the financial departments of the counties under the new rules of the Irish Local Government Board in connection with the extra duties placed on the county councils by reason of copying rate books and the applotments of the poor rate, including the calculations necessary consequent on each special charge being applotted separately; and whether he, as head of the Irish Local Government Board, will take measures

for the amendment of these rules, either by legislation or otherwise.

*MR. G. W. BALFOUR: The Local Government Board have received resolutions from several county councils on the subject mentioned in the first paragraph. In drafting the County Councils Order, 1899, dealing with accounts, every care was taken to minimise the labour necessitated by the Local Government Act in assessing and applotting the rates, and I do not think these accounts could be simplified further. It must be remembered that a good deal of the labour thrown by the Act upon county councils in applotting the rates implies a corresponding relief to the officers of unions. The additional copying of the rate books is rendered necessary by Section 96 of the Act, and this provision merely involves the temporary employment of a few additional clerks.

AGRICULTURAL GRANT TO COUNTY DONEGAL.

MR. SWIFT MacNEILL: I beg to ask the Chief Secretary to the Lord Lieutenant of Ireland whether his attention has been directed to a resolution passed by the Donegal County Council, requesting the Irish Local Government Board to vary their certificate under Section 49 of the Irish Local Government Act, and allow the county the further sum of £1,100 7s. annually, inasmuch as the sums of £787 17s. 11d. and of £912 16s. 4d., received by the Grand Jury of the County of Donegal from the sale of dog licences, and the sum of £500, received from the Belfast Bank as interest on credit balances on foot of such Grand Jury's account, were in the standard year applied by the Grand Jury in aid of the county cess for said year, and were not taken into account in calculating the proportion of the Agricultural Grant to which the county was entitled; and whether he, as head of the Irish Local Government Board, will take steps to secure that effect be given to this resolution.

MR. G. W. BALFOUR: A copy of the resolution referred to has been received by the Local Government Board, and the County Council have been informed that the sums in question were duly taken into account by the Board before they made their certificate under Section 49 of the Local Government Act.

It has also been pointed out to the Coun.-cil that these sums appear in the audited abstracts of the county accounts, which were used by the Board in making the necessary calculations.

MR. T. M. HEALY: May I ask whether it is not a fact that so cumbrous are the arrangements of the Local Government Board with regard to the books that forty clerks are now required by the Cork County Council to do work hitherto accomplished by two clerks, and that the County Council has in vain protested?

*MR. G. W. BALFOUR: I do not see how that arises out of the question.

NEWCASTLE WEST (LIMERICK) CREAMERY.

MR. AUSTIN (Limerick, W.): I beg to ask the Chief Secretary to the Lord Lieutenant of Ireland if steps will be taken by the Local Government Board to enforce the provisions of Section 3 of the Public Health (Amendment) Act, 1890, in Newcastle West, county Limerick, so as to abate the nuisance created by the washings and rancid scourings of the local creamery pouring into the main sewer of the town, which is held to be dangerous to health.

*MR. G. W. BALFOUR: The newly elected Rural District Council has been urged by the Local Government Board to adopt Part 3 of the Public Health Acts Amendment Act of 1890, but it has declined to do so. The Local Government Board have no power to compel a sanitary authority to adopt this section of the Act, but if the Board receive a complaint under Section 15 of the Public Health Act of 1896, they will cause a local inquiry to be held into the matter.

IRISH INTERMEDIATE EDUCATION.

*MR. WILLIAM JOHNSTON (Belfast, S.): I beg to ask the Chief Secretary to the Lord Lieutenant of Ireland when the pamphlet of the Intermediate Education Rules and Programme for 1900 will be published; whether this pamphlet was passed by the Commissioners and sent to the Lord Lieutenant for approval at or before Whitsuntide; and whether he is aware that, as the pamphlet is issued in all years by 1st April, and as the schools mostly break up for the holidays about 21st June, much inconvenience has already been experienced by the teachers in consequence of the prolonged delay.

MR. G. W. BALFOUR: The Rules and Programme for 1900 were submitted yesterday to the Lord Lieutenant for signature, and will be published, when signed, without delay. The pamphlet is usually issued in March or April, but its publication this year has been delayed for the reason already explained to my hon. friend.

*MR. WILLIAM JOHNSTON: Will the right hon. Gentleman see that no such delay occurs in future years?

MR. G. W. BALFOUR: I have already explained that the delay was in connection with the Report of a Commission, which is still sitting, but which is not likely to sit in future years.

DISTURBANCES AT COOKSTOWN.

MR. DOOGAN (Tyrone, E.): I beg to ask the Chief Secretary to the Lord Lieutenant of Ireland whether he is aware that on the 2nd instant another outbreak of stone-throwing by an Orange drumming party took place in Cookstown, who, after breaking the windows of the Foresters' Hall, though not so extensively as the same or a similar party broke them on the 4th of April last, rushed to the Roman Catholic quarter of the town, into which they showered stones which smashed the windows of three Catholic houses, and injured several persons; that Mr. James Mayne was furiously stoned by the crowd, and a young man who accompanied him was struck on the head and rendered insensible; and that Mr. Mayne having brought the injured young man into Mr. Devlin's house, proceeded to cross the street for medical assistance under the protection of Mr. District Inspector Carey, when both were rushed upon in the middle of the street and driven into Dr. Knight's house amidst a volley of stones; and, whether he can state how many arrests were made, how many persons will be prosecuted, and what steps will be taken to prevent the recurrence of these periodic attacks upon peaceable people.

MR. G. W. BALFOUR: One pane of glass was broken in the Foresters' Hall on the 2nd instant. The Orange party did not rush into the Roman Catholic quarter, but they broke the windows in the houses of three Catholic residents. Stones were also thrown at Mr. Mayne and a young man who accompanied him, and the latter was rendered insensible for a time from a blow on the head. Stones were again thrown at Mr. Mayne when in the company of the district inspector, but he was not struck, and the police drove the Orange crowd away from Dr. Knight's house, charging the crowd with truncheons and dispersing them. The district inspector and a number of police were struck with stones. The actual stone-throwers were not detected, as the occurrence took place in the darkness at night time, and no arrests have been made. Every precaution will be taken by the police to prevent, as far as possible, a repetition of this rioting and disturbance in which both parties have participated.

IRISH LAND PURCHASE.

MR. YOUNG (Cavan, E.): I beg to ask the Chief Secretary to the Lord Lieutenant of Ireland, with reference to the delay complained of by the tenants and owners of land in Ireland in carrying out the Land Purchase Acts (Ireland), whether his attention has been called to the estate of Rev. Edward S. Reilly, in Chancery, near Kingscourt; whether he is aware that a number of tenants on that estate have agreed with the landlords to purchase at a price already fixed, and have lodged with the Land Commission the usual affidavits under the Land Purchase Acts, and no Court valuer has since been sent to inspect the holdings; and if he can state the cause of delay or say when the Court valuer will come down to inspect these holdings.

MR. G. W. BALFOUR: The estate referred to is for sale in the Land Judge's Court, and in nine cases, by applications lodged with the Land Commissioners so recently as the 15th of March last, the tenants have applied for advances to enable them to purchase their holdings in that Court. Two similar applications were also lodged on the 27th of the same month. The cases have been referred to one of the Commissioners' inspectors, but owing to the number of cases on his hands he has not yet been able to visit the holdings. This will be done by him at the earliest possible opportunity.

DISTRICT INSPECTOR MEEHAN.

MR. J. P. FARRELL (Cavan, W.): I beg to ask the Chief Secretary to the Lord Lieutenant of Ireland whether a complaint was made to the Inspector-General, Royal Irish Constabulary, as to the conduct of District Inspector Meehan, Carrick-on-Shannon, in threatening to estreat a man's recognisances because he called a local magistrate by his Christian name; and will the inquiry be granted.

MR. G. W. BALFOUR: The reply to the first paragraph is in the affirmative. It appears the man in question was making a practice of calling after the magistrate by his Christian name in an offensive manner every time he passed. The Inspector-General has informed the writer of the complaint that he had inquired into the matter and found it did not call for his further interference.

LONGFORD AND THE AGRI-CULTURAL GRANT.

MR. J. P. FARRELL: I beg to ask the Chief Secretary to the Lord Lieutenant of Ireland on what basis the allotment of the county Longford portion of the Agricultural Grant was fixed. What excluded charges (if any) were taken into account in fixing the amount for the half-year at £4,905 5s.; will he explain why it is that, although the figures on which this calculation was based have been asked for by the County Council, no reply has been vouchsafed; and will he see that the Local Government Board supply full information as desired.

MR. G. W. BALFOUR: The basis on which the Agricultural Grant to Longford, as to other counties, was fixed, is defined in Sections 48, 49, 56, and 57 of the Act of last year. The excluded charges, in the case of Longford, consist of charges for malicious injuries, relief of distress, and special sanitary rates. They affected the grant to the extent of about £90. The information asked for by the County Council was not given by the Local Government Board, but I propose, as already stated, to lay on the Table of the House a general memorandum explaining the methods adopted in order to arrive at the basis on which the amounts of the Grant have been calculated.

MR. J. P. FARRELL: When will it be laid?

MR. G. W. BALFOUR: I hope before the Irish Estimates come on.

RIOTING AT BELFAST.

MR. DILLON: I beg to ask the Chief Secretary to the Lord Lieutenant of Ireland whether he can state what steps have been taken by the employers on the Queen's Island and in other establishments in Belfast, where Roman Catholic workers have been attacked, to protect these workers and preserve the peace ?

MR. G. W. BALFOUR: The managers of Messrs. Harland and Wolffs, Queen's Island, have given notice that they will reduce the hours of work in case of renewed disturbance, and have offered a reward of £500 for proof of assault on Roman Catholic workers in the mills. Quiet generally prevails, and the employers and managers are most anxious to ensure the safety of their Catholic workers.

MR. DILLON: I beg to ask the Chief Secretary to the Lord Lieutenant of Ireland whether he is aware that Roman Catholic girls in several of the mills in Belfast have been attacked, beaten, and driven from their work; whether any public meeting of the respectable Protestants of Belfast, or of the employers of labour, has been held to condemn these proceedings; and whether the Lord Mayor and magistrates of the city have taken any steps to condemn and put a stop to these proceedings.

MR. G. W. BALFOUR: I am aware that assaults were committed, on the 8th instant, on three Roman Catholic girls employed in mills in Belfast, by a crowd of women. Four of the accused have been convicted by the magistrates; two of them were sentenced to a month's imprisonment each, and the remaining two were fined in a sum of £2 each, with costs. I have no information as to the second paragraph. No meeting of the magistrates has been considered necessary by the Lord Mayor, the city having been quiet for some days past.

CLERKS OF IRISH UNIONS.

MR. TULLY (Leitrim, S.): I beg to ask the Chief Secretary to the Lord Lieutenant of Ireland if he is aware that clerks of unions have been always paid, as part of their duties, for checking periodically the rate collectors' accounts; whether it is proposed by the Local Government Board under a recent Order in Council to pay them an additional sum of 5s. per hundred names for checking the collectors' books; and whether he can state on what grounds it is proposed to increase in this way the remuneration of clerks of unions.

MR. G. W. BALFOUR: While the boards of guardians were the rating authorities it was part of the ordinary duty of the clerk of the union to examine periodically the accounts of the poor rate collectors, but no special remuneration was allowed for this work. This duty now devolves upon the secretaries to the county councils. It is obvious that a county secretary will require assistance in the checking of the accounts of the collectors for an entire county, and it was therefore thought desirable to permit the county council to authorise their secretary to appoint these experienced clerks of unions to act as his deputy for this important work. It is optional with county councils to avail themselves of this permission, but if they do so the clerk will be entitled to remuneration at the rate mentioned in the question.

BUSINESS OF THE HOUSE.

MR. J. P. FARRELL: I beg to ask the First Lord of the Treasury whether he will put down the Local Government Vote or the Constabulary Vote in the Irish Estimates for discussion on Friday next, so as to facilitate discussion by Irish Members.

THE FIRST LORD OF THE TREASURY (Mr. A. J. BALFOUR, Manchester, E.): I think the Votes the hon. Gentleman suggests are very important ones, and I think, probably, it would be convenient that they should be put down first. I do not propose to go further than that until I hear what the views of the Members from Ireland are. I assume that "next Friday" in the question is a misprint. I presume the hon. Gentleman means Friday week. The Scotch Estimates are put down for to-morrow.

CAPTAIN DONELAN (Cork, E.): Will the right hon. Gentleman endeavour to arrange for Irish Bills and Irish Estimates to be taken as nearly as possible consecutively ?

MR. A. J. BALFOUR: I am always prepared to do that if I can. My present idea is to give two days consecutively to Irish Supply—Thursday and Friday in next week. I do not make any promise, but if I can arrange that I shall certainly do so, as it would, of course, be for the convenience of Members from Ireland. With regard to Irish Bills, I am afraid I cannot promise that any Irish Bills will be taken next week.

INDIAN TARIFF ACT, 1899.

---

*SIR H. H. FOWLER (Wolverhampton, E.) : I rise to move " That a humble address be presented to Her Majesty praying that Her Majesty will be pleased to disallow the Indian Tariff Act, 1899." That Act provides that the Governor-General in Council may impose upon any article which receives any bounty or grant on its exportation from the country in which it is manufactured an additional duty on its importation into India equal in amount to such bounty or grant. In pursuance of that statute the Governor-General has imposed upon all sugar imported into India from the Argentine Republic, Austria-Hungary, Belgium, Denmark, France, Germany, Holland, and Russia countervailing duties, varying from 10 rupees to 180 rupees per ton, or, taking the rupee at 1s. 4d., from 13s. 4d. per ton to £12 per ton. In respect of the two countries with which India is mainly concerned and from which practically all the European sugar comes to India— namely, Germany and Austria—this duty varies from £1 4s. per ton to £1 15s. 6d. per ton. I may say in passing, in order that there may be no misconception on the point, that though the noble Lord the Secretary for India has been asked questions in regard to it, these duties are in addition to the existing duty of 5 per cent. on all sugar imported into India, which varies from 14s. to 15s. per ton on refined sugar and from 3s. 6d. to 4s. per ton on raw sugar. Before I proceed to discuss the policy of this measure I must notice the objection which has been taken to any interference on the part of this House with the action of what has been called the local authority, and to any dealing differently with the financial policy of India from the manner in which we deal with the financial policy of our self-governing colonies. That objection proceeds on an entire misconception of the constitution of India and of the legislation and practice which defines the relationship between that Government

and the Imperial Parliament. When the Government of India was transferred to the Crown all the powers vested in the Board of Directors of the East India Company and in the Board of Control which represented the Imperial authority were vested in the Secretary for. India, and three years after that transfer took place the India Council Act was passed, which practically regulates the Government of India at the present time. That Council consists of the Viceroy and six other members, and that Council is technically and literally the Government of India. Every member of the Council is appointed by the Crown ; but the Act passed in 1862, and subsequently modified, said that when the Council was assembled for the purpose of making laws and regulations there should be added to it a certain number of additional members. Those additional members must not be less than ten and they must not be more than sixteen ; but in the selection of those members there is no trace of what we call popular representation. Six of the members are officials of the Government of India appointed by the Viceroy, and the remaining ten are non-official members. Of these ten four are nominated by the Provincial Legislature, and one by the Chamber of Commerce of Bengal, but these nominations are again subject to the veto of the Viceroy, and the remaining five are nominated by the Viceroy in such a manner as appears most suitable with reference to the legislative requirements and adequate representation of the different classes of the community. This body has a very limited jurisdiction. No measures affecting finance, taxation, debt, and some other matters with which I need not trouble the House, can be introduced without the Viceroy's consent. Now, I am not in any way criticising this mode of governing India—I believe it has worked wisely and worked well ; but it does not possess either the characteristics or the independent authority of the elected legislatures of our self-governing colonies. It may be said, Be that as it may, it is a legislative body, and, as such, so long as it is a legislative body, may it not be entrusted with the sole control of matters which exclusively apply to India ? That question has been raised more than once, and it has been disposed of by two great Secretaries of State. the Duke of Argyll and the present

Prime Minister, Lord Salisbury. The Duke of Argyll dealt with that question of general legislation on general policy; Lord Salisbury dealt with it on financial matters, and at a time and under conditions which form an almost exactly opposite precedent to the objection to the present situation. Lord Salisbury was called upon to deal with the contention that the Viceroy and his Council should be as independent with respect to the finances of India as the elected legislatures and the responsible Governments of Australia and Canada were. Now, I am not going to trouble the House with any quotations upon the general question, but, as I do think this point may be cleared up at once and finally, I must quote two or three sentences from that very able despatch of Lord Salisbury. He says :

" It is not open to question that Her Majesty's Government are as much responsible to Parliament for the government of India as they are for any of the Crown colonies of the Empire. . . . Nor has any exception been made, either legally or in constitutional practice, in favour of questions of finance, which your predecessor proposes specially to withdraw from the action of the home Government. On the contrary, the vigilance of Parliament is more active and the weight of Parliamentary responsibility more strongly felt in respect to finance than in respect to any other department of Indian government. . . . It necessarily follows that the control exercised by Her Majesty's Government over financial policy must be effective also. . . . In scrutinising the control exercised over the Government of India by Her Majesty's Government, and the grounds for maintaining that control, it must be borne in mind that the superintending authority of Parliament is the reason and the measure of the authority exercised by the responsible Ministers of the Crown, and that if the one power is limited the other must be limited at the same time. It is impossible, therefore, that ' measures affecting Customs and finance can be dealt with on the responsibility of the Government of India,' as your predecessor in Council has suggested. So far as Parliament is concerned, no such responsibility exists. The only responsibility to Parliament is that of Ministers of the Crown. . . . Measures affecting the tariff touch subjects which are not exclusively of Indian concern: They influence the prosperity of trade and industry outside the confines of India, and they relate to matters on which Her Majesty's Government is in constant negotiation with foreign Powers. Such considerations may furnish important elements in considering the expediency of financial proposals, but they are necessarily less fully within the cognisance of the Indian than of the Imperial Government."

*THE SECRETARY OF STATE FOR INDIA (Lord G. HAMILTON, M d .lesex,

Ealing): What is the date of the despatch ?

*SIR H. H. FOWLER : It is the despatch of March 17, 1876. It is the despatch which regulates the relations of the Indian and Imperial Governments. That, Sir, is my justification for asking the House now to review this great change in the tariff of India, and for pointing to what the Finance Minister of India describes as a new chapter in the fiscal history of that country. When the Statute, which is now limited to sugar— although, as the House will notice, it is not confined to sugar, but covers other foreign imports—when the Bill was introduced, the following official statement was made on behalf of the Government of India :

" The present Bill has been prepared with the object of enabling the Government of India to impose countervailing duties, and thus to preserve the sugar cultivation and industries of India."

The first point, therefore, which I shall deal with is the sugar cultivation and the industries of India. Statistics as to the area of land in India which is under sugar cultivation are not complete, but I think the statement that is made in the Blue Book may be taken as practically accurate. The Government of India, in a despatch which I shall have to deal with later on in my speech, stated that the area under sugar-cane in India is about two and a half million acres, but the figures which are given later in the appendix to the Blue Book show that the average land under sugar cultivation for the five years ended 1896 was 2,900,000 acres. That figure went down to 2,651,000 in 1896-97, and to 2,675,000 in 1897-98. There is no record of what the figure is at the present time. But I think the figures are under estimated, and that the number of acres may be safely taken as something like 3,000,000 ; but the House must remember that in this, as in all other Indian matters, things are on a colossal scale. Two million acres in India are a very different thing from 2,000,000 acres in most other countries. The entire area of India is something like 224,000,000 acres, and therefore, however important the sugar crop may be—and I should be the last man to undervalue it—it is well for the House to remember that the land under sugar cultivation is only 1½ per cent. of the whole area under cultivation at the present time. The crop from this acreage is taken by the Government of India—and I do not dispute the figures, though some authorities give it as much larger—at one ton per acre, so that the sugar crop from 3,000,000 acres is 3,000,000 tons of raw sugar. Now, Sir, it is a difficult question, to say the least, as to what proportion of that product of Indian sugar is consumed in the raw state and how much of it is refined. But in the report in this Blue Book of one of the largest districts where sugar is cultivated—the North-West Provinces and Oudh—the official says:

" The best estimate I can give is that one-fifth of the raw sugar produced is refined, and four-fifths consumed in the natural state."

I believe—I am told, and there are gentlemen in the House who will correct me if I am wrong—I believe that a very large quantity of sugar is consumed as cane both as an article of food and enjoyment. The principal method of refining which prevails in India is crushing and boiling down the raw product, and that is the beginning and ending of the refining of a large portion of the sugar in India. The refining, as the word has been used in this controversy, is on a very small scale. The machinery is inadequate, the processes are defective, and when I tell the House that in the return on the moral and material progress of India of, I think, 1896 and 1897, the Government there state that the entire number of what we call sugar factories or refineries, as we understand them in this country, was only thirteen in the whole of India, an increase of two since 1889, they will see that the sugar industry of India was on a very limited scale. India gets its sugar from two sources—European, which is bounty-fed; non-European, which is not bounty-fed, and the bulk of the latter comes from Mauritius. In 1891 the import into India was 147,000 tons—and I mention the year 1891 because it was not until that year that there was any import into India of German or Austrian bounty-fed sugar. That represented the normal conditions of trade. In 1896 it had fallen to 137,000 tons. In 1897 it was 143,000 tons. In 1898, the year on which so many of these controversies turned, and the year after the famine, it rose to 230,000 tons, and for the year ended March 31, 1899, it had fallen to

Sir H. H. Fowler.

203,000 tons. Of the imports in 1898 109,000 tons were bounty-fed, and in 1899 74 000 tons were bounty-bed. I want the House to understand the true meaning of these figures. We are dealing with a native trade which on a most moderate estimate represents 3,000,000 tons. We are dealing with a trade which is threatened with the importation of 200,000 tons, and you are asked to take special precautions, to pass special legislation in order to penalise 74,000 tons. Where does this sugar come from ? In 1896 Austria and Germany sent 36,000 tons ; in 1897 they sent 43,000 tons ; in 1898, 107,000 tons ; and in 1899 it had fallen to 74,000 tons. The Mauritius plays no small part in the supply of sugar to India and in the initiation of this legislation. In 1896 the Mauritius sent 78,000 ; in 1897, 83,000 ; in 1898 and in the year which has closed 105,000 tons. Now these are the facts as to this threatened industry, and I hope the House will not forget that in face of these increased imports the population of India during the period over which these figures run has been increasing at the rate of at least two millions per annum, and therefore there must necessarily be an increased supply and increased consumption. These, as I say, being the facts, I must ask the House to go with me through the history of the legislation which I am asking for an Address to the Crown to disallow ; and I think, so far as Parliamentary history and Ministerial diplomacy are concerned, this is one of the most interesting and instructive Blue Books which has ever been placed on the table of this House. There is nothing in this Blue Book, no document, prior to May 5th, 1898. We do not know what passed between the Government at home and the Government of of India ; but in May, 1898, the Government of India sent home a despatch containing three enclosures. They did not refer to any previous communication from home, and perhaps the noble Lord will tell us whether this was a reply to any communication from the home authorities. At present it looks like a bolt from the blue so far as India is concerned. The Government of India had been approached by the Chamber of Commerce of Bengal as to India being represented at the Brussels Conference on the Sugar Question. They sent a long letter from three great firms in Calcutta, describing the effect of the unrestricted importation of bounty-fed sugar, and asking the Government to take steps to deal with it. The only other official document accompanying this despatch was a letter from the Governor of the North-West Provinces, who appears also to have been approached by the Chamber of Commerce in his district. He said in it that he had no reason to believe that the sugar industry had yet been seriously threatened by the importation of bounty-fed sugar, but the extension of the great industry in this province was a matter which appeared to be of much importance, and that it should receive the attention of the Government, and kept under observation at the Conference. That is the information on which the Government of India proceeded. Now, I must read what that Government says on the subject. First they say that they approve of the suggestion of the Bengal Chamber of Commerce that India should be represented at the Conference. Then they say :

"An examination of the statements in the note on the effect on the sugar-cane industry of India of the unrestricted importation of bounty-fed sugar, which forms one of the enclosures of this despatch, leads us to the conclusion that while the competition of imported sugar (of which three-fifths are cane-sugar) may have reduced the profits of the refining industry, it does not appear to have materially affected the producer. He relies mainly on the demand for unrefined sugar, which constitutes seven-eighths of the trade, and in respect of these seven-eighths there seems to be no reason to apprehend that the producer's profits have been lowered by the increased importation of beet sugar. While, therefore, we adhere to the position stated in the financial despatches of February 14, 1888, and May 14, 1889, and are prepared to press for the abolition of the sugar bounties, and to join in an international convention for that purpose, we are not prepared to levy countervailing duties on sugar imported into India."

There is one point that we have to take into consideration in dealing with this question. The consumption of sugar in India is put at 28lb. per head. That is a large proportion, showing how important a necessary of life sugar is in India. What is the consumption of sugar in European countries ? Let us contrast it with that of India, bearing in mind also the position of the people of India. Well, in Europe we are the highest consumers of sugar ; we are the highest consumers in the world—it is 86lb. per head. In America

it is 66lb., in Denmark it is 44lb., in France it is only 29lb., in Germany 28lb., in Holland 26lb., but in India it is at least 28lb. per head. Therefore any interference with the general consumption of sugar in that country would be a very serious matter. I asked the noble Lord a few nights ago whether there was any dissent from the despatch to which I have referred. As the House knows, every member of the Council has a right to dissent and to send his dissent to the Secretary of State. But in this case there was no dissent sent home. It was signed unanimously, and it was so signed by the Council of India. So on May 5, 1898, it was recorded as the decision of Lord Elgin and his colleagues that they would not levy any countervailing duties on sugar. Their opinion was that the sugar grower in India as against foreign sugar, whether bounty-fed or not, had nothing to fear. Well, the next step is the Brussels Conference, but I need not trouble the House with that. On August 25 the noble Lord replied to this despatch of the Government of India, and he refers to a letter from the Colonial Office, dated July 23, 1898. The noble Lord said :

"I forward for the information of your Government the papers noted in the margin. The letters from the Mauritius urge that India should take steps to protect her own sugar and Mauritius cane-sugar from the competition of bounty-fed sugar. At paragraph 4 of your letter of the 5th of May, 1898, it was stated that you were not prepared to levy countervailing duties on bounty-fed sugar imported into India. I should be glad to receive more fully your views on this proposal, as Her Majesty's Government, now that they are in possession of the views of foreign Governments, must consider during the next few months the course they will pursue."

Following the story in consecutive order the Government of India on October 31 sent a despatch back in reply to the noble Lord, and this despatch the House will bear in mind. On that date a circular was sent out, in which these words occur :

"The Government of India have no clear evidence before them that the increasing sugar imports have had, or are tending to, such serious consequences. The area under sugar-cane in the different provinces has not declined of late years, nor in recent revenue or settlement reports have any observations regarding the unprofitableness of the industry been noticed. The extent to which the refined sugars from abroad compete in the Indian markets with the coarse sugars ordinarily manufactured by native processes and tend to supplant the latter is uncertain. There is probably an increasing demand for sugar in India for domestic consumption and for spirit distilling and sweetmeat making, and, as the sugar-cane area has not expanded of late years, it may be that the increasing imports have not been in excess of the necessary demand, and that the price of Indian sugars has, notwithstanding these imports, been maintained. Lastly, the question whether sugar prices in India have fallen in recent years is one on which it is difficult on existing materials to pronounce, owing to the many varieties of sugar sold in Indian markets, and the failure of the published price returns to clearly distinguish between them."

While this was going on there was a correspondence proceeding between Mauritius and Whitehall and between the Colonial Office and the India Office, and in November, 1898, the Governor of Mauritius addressed the Colonial Secretary with reference to the position of the Mauritius trade, sending enclosures. The Governor of Mauritius asked that they should be exempted from the payment of the 5 per cent. duty, but this was a request which neither the Government of India nor the Home Government could accede to. Therefore he raised this question again in his correspondence with the Secretary of State for the Colonies. He also accompanied that with a petition from the bankers and merchants of Mauritius, stating their case fairly enough, and, from their point of view, putting the strongest arguments they could in favour of receiving this protection. On January 3, 1899, the Secretary of State for the Colonies forwards this communication to the noble Lord at the head of the India Office, and says:

"Mr. Chamberlain concurs in the apprehension of the memorialists that the continued sale of bounty-fed sugar will drive Mauritian sugar out of the Indian market, and will result in ruin and distress to a colony the majority of whose population are natives of India or their descendants. He therefore trusts that this Petition may receive the favourable consideration of Lord George Hamilton, and of his Excellency the Governor-General of India in Council."

The answer of the noble Lord to that communication is not in the Blue Book. But on 7th January the Secretary to the Colonies returns again to the subject. He says:

"There are two questions affecting the prosperity of the sugar-growing colonies, on which correspondence has already passed between this Office and the India Office, and which Mr. Chamberlain would ask Lord

Sir H. H. Fowler.

George Hamilton to bring to the special notice of Lord Curzon of Kedleston, in order that they may receive his attention at the outset of his term of office. . . It seems not improbable that, however well supplied with East Indian labour the sugar planters may be, their industry may be destroyed if the bounty system continues unchecked, and, in the absence of countervailing duties or penal clauses, it is not easy to see from whence the check will come. On this subject Mr. Chamberlain can only express his own personal views, as he has already expressed them in the House of Commons. There is, in his opinion, no valid economic arguments against countervailing duties, and the question is purely one of policy and of expediency."

He closes his despatch by saying:

"He does not presume to suggest to the Government of India what course should be taken in the matter, but he would ask that their most earnest attention should be given to it. He has more than once declined to allow colonial policy on commercial questions to be tied by the policy for the time being of the mother country, and if the Indian Government, in the interests of East Indians, were to see fit to penalise or to countervail bounty-fed sugar, or to give preference to the honestly grown cane sugar of the British colonies, he would welcome the step as likely to strengthen the opposition to bounties and to hasten the collapse of a mischievous and unsound device for ruining an important British industry."

I do not see that the reply of the noble Lord is in the Blue Book, but on January 24 the noble Lord sent this telegram to the Viceroy:

"A despatch is being sent by next mail. . . . Should you now adopt views different from those of your letter of May, 1898, and propose countervailing duties, I shall be ready to consider proposals fully. Recognising that circumstances of Great Britain and India differ, I shall ascribe great importance to views which people of India hold on this matter. I send for information circular showing how countervailing duties are levied in United States."

On January 26 the noble Lord sent that despatch. It is a very interesting despatch, but as it did not arrive until after the decision of the Indian Government had been taken I will not trouble the House with it. But on February 1 the Viceroy—the new Viceroy was now in power—sent this telegram—

"Your telegram of 24th January last. A despatch has been posted by last mail, in which, taking Indian standpoint and irrespectively of Imperial policy in relation to colonies, we arrive at conclusions on the whole favourable to recommendation of Colonial Office. We considered it expedient to send it unaltered. Despatch points out that since 1897-98 imports of beet sugar from Austria and Germany show marked increase, imports from Mauritius remaining stable. The present market price of imported sugars is unusually low. They compete with native sugar, both refined and coarse, and diminish profits of native sugar refineries."

That was a mistake, an unintentional mistake. The imports of Austria and Germany were rapidly decreasing at that moment, and the imports from Mauritius were as rapidly increasing. I ask the House to mark the next words in the telegram:

"We are inquiring how far these effects are likely to be permanent."

On January 26 Lord Curzon sent his despatch, and it is a very interesting document. He says:

"Inquiries have been initiated in our Department of Revenue and Agriculture, and they will be supplemented by inquiries into the prices of both refined and coarse sugar which will be undertaken by the Director-General of Statistics. With these data before us we shall hereafter be in a position to express a final, or at any rate a more confident, opinion on the policy of imposing countervailing duties."

That was the expression of opinion of the Viceroy on January 26th. On February 24th the Secretary of State telegraphs:

"Desire to know if you propose to pass an Act this session imposing countervailing duties?"

At that moment the inquiry that had been directed in August, that had been promised in October 1898, was still proceeding, and at that time the Government of India had no information at all. They had sent a despatch, possibly two despatches, but on February 24th the noble Lord wants to know if there is going to be legislation this session. The Viceroy immediately replies—

"Propose to legislate at once on American model."

Yes, on the model of the Dingley Tariff. On March 1st the noble Lord telegraphs:

"Suggested legislation approved by Her Majesty's Government. When will Indian Government's intentions be announced?"

On March 3rd the Viceroy replies:

"Bill for imposing duties on lines of American law will be brought forward on March 10th and published in newspapers on March 13th."

There was some delay owing to pending contracts, but on March 20th the Bill

received the Viceroy's assent. I should like to give the House a few dates as to these replies. The Viceroy said he was going to consider the matter and to get statistics about prices. There is not a line of statistics in the Blue Book about prices. The first reply was from the North-West Provinces and dated February 15th; that from Ajmere-Merwara, February 17th; Bombay, February 23rd; Berar, February 28th; and the Punjab, March 7th. I do not think I am speaking too strongly when I say that, practically, there was no regard to the special inquiry into this matter, and that the Viceroy had already formed his opinion when he sent home the telegram of January 24. I am not going to trouble the House with all these replies, but I am going to take the two great districts from which replies were given—one of them decidedly favourable to the legislation the noble Lord approved of, and the other unfavourable. If the House will allow me, I will deal first with the North-West Provinces, which are very largely interested in sugar cultivation. The memorandum is made by the Officiating Director of Land Records and Agriculture, and it contains some very important statements. I will only call attention to two or three of the salient points:

"The area sown in 1896-97 fell below the average by 56,131 acres, or 4·4 per cent. This fall could not be due to competition of foreign imports, because this competition had not begun in the spring of 1896, when this crop was sown."

I call the attention of the House to this, because great stress has been laid on land going out of cultivation. There was no doubt a great decrease in one year owing to the famine. There was a decrease of the whole acreage of land in India under cultivation of upwards of 20 millions of acres owing to the famine. The fall in sugar cultivation was about an average of 10 per cent., but in a great many other instances, I think in wheat, it was 16 or 17 per cent. All through India there was a large diminution in sugar cultivation on account of the famine, and in no part of the country was the famine worse than in the North-West Provinces.

"The decrease is, in fact, just what the figures of past years would suggest; a fall was to be expected after the large rise in the previous year, and if the fall is greater by a few thousand acres than might have been foreseen, the reason is to be found in the local scarcity prevailing in Philibhit and elsewhere at the time (the spring of 1896) when this crop was sown. The crop sown in the spring of 1897 showed a further fall, and was 9·6 per cent. below the normal. This is not surprising, for at seed-time almost the whole province was suffering from acute famine, and cultivators naturally put a large proportion of their irrigable land under food crops. On the other hand, the increase in imports was not at that time so marked as to affect the cultivators' calculations."

That is one point. He goes on to say :

"No matter how cheap refined sugar is, the great majority of the people will continue to use *gur*, and will not substitute refined sugar for it. The imports of refined sugar do not, therefore, immediately threaten our whole home production, but only our home refining industry, leaving the demand for three-fourths or four-fifths of our production unaffected."

That is the report from the North-West Provinces. It gives rather interesting figures about the profits of the sugar-refining industry. The Officiating Director shows how they vary from 30 rupees per acre in one district to seven rupees in another, and he adds :

"I know of no crop which, grown on the same scale, would yield such profits.   .   .   . On the whole, then, as far as prices show, the native refiner cannot say that his profits per cent. have vanished."

Summing up the whole matter, this able and distinguished public servant who presides over that district is exceedingly cautious. He does not commit himself to any decided opinion. I now come to Bombay, which is a large trade centre. There are two reports submitted to the Bombay Government by two very distinguished men—the Commissioner of Customs and the Commissioner of Land Revenues. The effect of these reports is this :

"That the importations of European sugars during recent years were altogether abnormal, and that they neither lowered the price of Indian refined sugar consumed in the Bombay Presidency nor checked the cultivation of the cane, or the production of unrefined sugar to which practically the whole of the cane produced in the Presidency is devoted. On the other hand, the production of refined sugar in this Presidency is so far on too insignificant a scale to merit consideration. . . . The Chambers of Commerce, Bombay and Karachi, are clearly of opinion that in the interest of trade countervailing duties against European sugars are uncalled for. . . . On the whole, his Excellency the Governor in Council is of opinion that neither the commercial nor the agricultural interests of this Presidency are injuriously affected by the increasing imports of refined sugar, or call at present for the

Sir H. H. Fowler,

imposition of countervailing duties upon that part of the imported sugar the export of which to this country is aided by bounties."

There is a very able report by Mr. Mallison, the Deputy-Director of Agriculture in the Bombay Presidency, in which he shows how the sugar is cultivated, and says :

"The increasing foreign imports of refined sugar in the Bombay Presidency more than meet the diminished local production of moist sugar and the diminished rail imports from other parts of India. The increasing foreign imports of refined sugar, owing to cheapness and perhaps also owing to a higher standard of living of an increased population, find extended use for household purposes and in the production of superior descriptions of sweetmeats. The habit of tea-drinking has extended to villages in out-districts, and there is no doubt that villagers who used sugar on rare occasions formerly now use it much more freely and oftener."

He draws the inference that foreign imports have yet had no effect on sugar-cane cultivation in the Presidency, and he makes very valuable suggestions with reference to improvements in cultivation. The Governor of Bombay and his Council sum up their opinion as follows :

"On the whole the Governor in Council is of opinion that neither the commercial nor the agricultural interests of this Presidency are injuriously affected by the increasing imports of refined sugar, or call, at present, for the imposition of countervailing duties upon that part of the imported sugar the export of which to this country is aided by bounties."

The information obtained up to that date, and the information which they received after that date, fully confirmed the policy of 1898, and the decision of the Government of that time was supported by all other considerations. You cannot contend, and they did not contend, that the cultivation of 3,000,000 acres was threatened by the importation of 200,000 tons. It was evident that the amount of sugar produced was increasing ; though competition might decrease the profits of the refiner it did not materially affect the Indian producer. What that correspondence shows is that what the Indian sugar industry needed was better and more scientific cultivation and more modern and effective machinery, and the true policy of the Indian Government would have been in that direction. I maintain that if any money was spent in promoting that industry it would have been wisely spent in that direction. Now,

Sir, the right hon. Lord, when asked the other night whether the despatch had been signed by the same members, said that more accurate information very often resulted in change of opinion. What I want the House to do is to see whether the information received between May and February afforded any ground for that change of belief, and I go on that point to the speech of Sir James Westland when he introduced this legislation to the Legislative Council. He was bound to make out a case ; he signed the recommendation in favour of refusing to levy countervailing duties, and he now proposed to reverse that decision. He was perfectly candid. He said he was proposing " to open an entirely new chapter in our fiscal history." In that speech he defined bounties, he explained the differences between England and India, and I am rather surprised that he said there was no chance of countervailing duties ever being made in England. I think he was not very familiar with the state of the question in this country. But the whole of his case rests entirely upon the increase in the importation of foreign sugar into India in the last three or four years. That is his case from first to last. I will not go over the figures again ; the House recollects them. The very highest import of sugar was only 230,000 tons, of which only 109,000 tons were bounty-fed, and that had been not increasing, but steadily decreasing, during the period which was to be the qualifying period for this reversal of policy. All the increase had taken place before May, 1898 ; and the decrease has taken place since May, 1898, and the importation of bounty-fed sugar has steadily decreased. The same remark would apply to the decrease of cultivated area. It is quite evident that, so far as that decrease goes, it is to a great extent in consequence of the famine. But, Sir, I must ask the attention of the House to two items in what I may call the further information which Sir James Westland had received. He dwelt upon Berar, and he dwelt upon the Punjaub. His case is that in Berar the importation of refined sugar had been 1,000 tons ; in each year there had been a steady decline, till in 1897-8 it had decreased to 430 tons ; while there had been an increased amount of foreign refined sugar in the district, it having risen to as much as

4,730 tons. The House will see that that is not sufficient grounds upon which to rest this legislation. But I was rather interested, when I saw this statement, to look into what was the Berar report, which was not quoted in full. After the Resident had given the information of this decrease in cultivation, he says :

"Since we have no sugar refining industry in Berar, the imported refined sugar does not come into competition with the local production. Our requirements are much in excess of our produce. We import unrefined sugar in large amount. Until the cultivation of the sugar-cane in Berar extends sufficiently to satisfy the local demand for unrefined sugar, the question of the competition of refined sugar does not come in."

Then, Sir, as I pointed out, Sir James Westland also referred to the Punjaub. I turned to the Punjaub, where it says :

"Refined sugar has not found its way into the villages to any appreciable extent. There the people are more bound by custom and tradition than the inhabitants of towns, and use *gur* as an article of daily food. *Gur* is sweeter and more adapted to the necessities of the zemindar, and is very much cheaper than refined sugar."

This is the native sugar. Prices vary from 4 or 5 rupees, while imported sugar sells at from 9 rupees to 10. And he says :

"There is certainly no tendency towards a fall in price, so that it cannot be said either that the profits of cultivation are declining, or that refined sugar has yet entered into competition with *gur.*"

No apprehensions were felt as yet as to the future of the sugar-cane cultivation. This, then, is the new information. But there is one district to which he has not alluded. There is no report from the Government of Bengal. There is a report from the Chamber of Commerce of Calcutta, which is a body of gentlemen who have very strong opinions upon these questions, but we have no evidence from the Government of Bengal. In his speech Sir James Westland introduces the case of Mauritius, and he maintains that there is a very strong case between the inhabitants of India and the inhabitants of Mauritius, which justifies, if possible, legislation being proceeded with. That is always the argument in favour of protective legislation. It is just as strong in the case of the agriculturists of this country. If you once admit that argument, I do not know where you are to stop. Then there was another speech made in that debate. I am bound to say that, although tempted very much to criticise that speech, not only my personal respect for the Viceroy, but also the respect which I feel for his high office, restrains my criticisms. Perhaps I should say something which I should hereafter wish I had not said if I said all I am inclined to say. I will only say this of it, that it was an eloquent exposition of inaccurate statistics and exploded economic fallacies. Comment has been made upon the unanimity with which the Council passed this measure, but nobody who is familiar with its constitution would charge the Legislative Council of India with being affected by Free Trade opinions. They are not apostles of Peel or Cobden, Gladstone or Northcote. They hold strong views on Free Trade and Protection, and on other questions besides sugar. I may remind the House of the controversy which took place with regard to the cotton legislation. The argument was that the duties were injuring the manufactures in Lancashire for the benefit of manufactures in India. Now, Sir, when I made my proposals the Legislative Council declined to accept the principle of an Excise duty, which, of course, is the one element to destroy the protective element. They then proposed that, whereas the import Customs duty was fixed at 5 per cent., the Excise duty should be only $3\frac{1}{2}$ per cent. I think my Lancashire friends, who were very angry with me on that occasion, will do me the justice to say that the strain of the controversy from first to last was that the interests of Lancashire were being sacrificed in order to protect the cotton industry of India. That was not correct. The Government, perhaps, have carried out that policy in a more satisfactory manner than I did myself, but they have never differentiated their policy from mine upon that question. No one spoke more strongly than the First Lord of the Treasury upon the absolute necessity of freeing this class of legislation from everything of a protective character. But those proposals did not meet with the approval of the Council, and when my Bill went to the Legislative Council it was only carried by two—the voting was 11 to 9. If the Bill had been thrown out it would have been upon the avowed ground that removing the element of protection would be a discouragement to the cultivator of

Sir H. H. Fowler.

cotton, that it was a menace to the cotton industry. Substitute the word "sugar" for the word "cotton," and you have the argument for these countervailing duties. The introduction of Free Trade legislation in India was by Lord Lytton, the Viceroy, exercising his absolute prerogative to override his Council The Legislative Council of India would not have Free Trade then, and Lord Lytton wisely exercised his prerogative, and practically repealed the protective legislation which led ultimately to the abolition of the whole of the import duties as well as those on cotton. I mention these facts to show that the House must not take it for granted that this question is looked at in the Legislative Council of India on precisely the same lines as we should look upon it here. Now, Sir, I will not keep the House much longer, but just a word or two upon the legislation which is now proposed. It draws a line between bounty-fed imports and non-bounty-fed imports. But all the imports of refined sugar to some extent affect the interests of the Indian refiner, and from that point of view the principle is the same. I am willing to concede that in certain districts bounty-fed sugar may be produced at less than cost price, but before it gets to the consumer it has to bear certain burdens. There is the carriage from Austria to India; the carriage from Bombay or Calcutta to Upper India; and, in addition, there is a 5 per cent. Customs duty. These three elements of protection the Indian producer possesses at present; and the protection afforded by the cost of carriage is one to which he is entitled. But the ultimate object of this measure is to compensate the Indian refiner if you like, and certainly the Mauritius refiner, by increasing the price of sugar. What else would be the advantage of a countervailing duty? Into whose pocket will the increase go? It will be paid by the Indian consumer, and it will go to the refiner, whether at home or abroad. I submit that there is no case stated for this legislation, as far as the general facts are concerned. But I will not shrink from dealing with the statement that the protection is to be given, not against ordinary competition, but against competition which has attached to it an artificial advantage. The Viceroy says that the industry "should be relieved from external competition fortified by an arbitrary advantage." But he does not say what an arbitrary advantage is, and we have no definition of it. There are advantages of climate, soil, taxation, cost of labour and raw material, cost of transport, cost of land, improved processes, and of many kinds of Government assistance, direct and indirect. Who is to say which is arbitrary? What do the planters of Mauritius say with reference to Australia? They say that they have lost the markets of Australia because the planters of Queensland and New Zealand, with the assistance of the money and credit of their Governments and of protective import duties, are producing more sugar than the Australian consumption. No Government can equalise the conditions of production. But you may put the case in a more plausible way, and say that, if a foreign Government throws a disability on the producer of another country, the Government of that country is bound to compensate its own producer to the extent of that disability. But that would cover protective duties as well as bounties, for there is no real difference. Germany gives so much per ton for sugar exported to India, and thereby places the native producer at a disadvantage. The United States puts a duty on British iron imported, and thereby places the British producer at a disadvantage. The Viceroy talks about "the mutterings of the high priests at the Free Trade shrine." I will quote some of those mutterings of the high priests, and I will choose the high priests irrespective of party. I will first quote the Conservative Government of 1876, when Sir Stafford Northcote was at the Exchequer, and Mr. W. H. Smith at the Treasury. What did they say when this very proposal was made to them in 1896?

"The proposal of a countervailing duty rests upon a principle which the Government of this country could not admit without reversing its whole system of commercial policy. If the doctrine was still maintained that the Government should adopt fiscal measures for other than fiscal objects, and should attempt to make such measures an engine for assisting British manufacturers to compete on what may be considered equal terms with their foreign rivals, the present case might undoubtedly be considered a very proper one for the application of such a principle. But it cannot be doubted that if the Government were to act on this doctrine in the present

case, it would soon be called upon to do so in other cases also. Their Lordships are of opinion that the Government ought not to countenance such a step, unless it is proposed to review the whole code of commercial legislation in this country."

The next high priest I will quote is Sir Louis Mallet. In the Report of the Sugar Bounty Committee he is reported as saying that "he was not able to see the difference between countervailing a bounty and giving a bounty against an import duty of a foreign country"; and with respect to countervailing duties on bounty-fed sugar he said:

"I should very strongly deprecate any such policy. I contend that the objections to it in principle are of a most serious character. I think it would lead to a demand from other industries which it would be very difficult in justice to resist. I entertain the opinion that it would be found very difficult to apply it in practice, without imperilling the security of our treaty stipulations, and without involving us in very great difficulties in our relations with foreign countries."

The next high priest I will quote is Mr. Bright. In declining to attend a public meeting at Birmingham on the sugar bounties question in 1881, Mr. Bright wrote:

"Whilst regretting that the bounty system exists, I am quite unable to act with you and your friends in favour of what are called countervailing duties, whether as regards sugar or shipping, or any other article of trade."

There was another Member for Birmingham at that time who was invited to attend the meeting—the present Secretary of State for the Colonies, who wrote:

"If you were unfortunately to succeed in imposing countervailing duties on foreign sugar, the effect would be that the consumers in this country, principally of the working classes, would, according to the figures supplied by the sugar refiners themselves, have to submit to a tax of something like £1,000,000 sterling per annum, in order to put this sum in the pockets of the West Indian planters and a few sugar refiners in the United Kingdom."

That was the opinion of the right hon. Gentleman in his private and personal capacity; and his official deliverance, as President of the Board of Trade, was as follows:

"The general principle which governs the financial policy of this country is that Government shall not interfere with the course of trade either by giving bounties or by imposing duties. To this policy no exception has hitherto been made, whatever the conduct of foreign Governments may have been either in encouraging their own manufacturers or discouraging ours. There are many ways besides bounties in which Governments can and do encourage or discourage particular industries. None of these have hitherto been thought to call for retaliation by her Majesty's Government, yet they are open to the same kind of objection as sugar bounties. If duties are to be imposed to countervail foreign bounties, *a fortiori* ought they to be imposed to countervail protective duties. To impose countervailing duties in order to neutralise the indirect sugar bounties would therefore be to take the first step in reversing that Free Trade policy which was adopted on the clearest ground of argument, and has conferred immense advantages on the industrial classes of this country."

The last high priest whom I shall quote is *The Times.* When the decision of the Board of Trade in regard to sugar bounties in 1880 was announced, *The Times* wrote :

" This is the language of common sense and common honesty. Whatever can be done, consistently with sound principles, to induce foreign Governments to abandon these foolish devices of bounties on the export of sugar, or on the manufacture of sugar, the Government are prepared to do. Beyond this they cannot stir. The truth is that there is not a single argument in favour of countervailing duties which was not advanced long since in favour of the sliding scale—of an 8s. fixed duty and of the navigation laws."

Sir HOWARD VINCENT (Sheffield, Central): What is the date of that article ?

*Sir H. H. FOWLER: The 5th of November, 1880, when the sugar bounty question was under discussion in this country. One word as to the position of Germany. Austria, we know, buys from India precisely the same amount that she sells to India. But Germany buys from India 7½ millions of rupees worth of goods, and sells only 2½ millions worth of sugar. The question of bounties does not enter into the purchases from France and Germany. So far as the object of commerce is concerned, India has only to take care of her imports, the exports will take care of themselves. Therefore this trade is clearly to the advantage of the people of India, to encourage this import trade in every possible way, especially when imports of Germany are sold to India at less than the cost price, while the exports of India to Germany are sold at the full price. The other great bounty country is France. I think that the French bounty is more than double the bounty

Sir H. H. Fowler.

given either in Germany or Austria ; but why do not the French have a monopoly of the market ? In conlusion, I can only say that this policy is a violation of the principle of Free Trade, that it is the first step towards reversing a policy which has been of such advantage to us, and it can confer no benefit on India. If it succeeds it will stereotype antiquated processes of manufacture and machinery, and it will deprive India of that fair competition which is the best stimulus to increased production and manufacture. If it had no other meaning and no ulterior purpose the question would be a very trifling one, although it is not creditable for a Government to reverse the decision which they formed in 1880 ; but can you stop here ? Can India stop here ? The Viceroy has an absolute power to impose protective duties on everything he may consider desirable. Can we stop here ? Because if this policy is good for India it is good for England. If it is right that the sugar planters of Mauritius should be protected in the Indian markets from competition by the sugars from Austria and Germany, it is right that the sugar planters in the West Indies should be protected in the markets of Great Britain from the same competition. I hear no cheers from the Treasury bench. Is that what you mean ?

The SECRETARY FOR THE COLONIES (Mr. J. CHAMBERLAIN, Birmingham, W.): We should not cheer you.

*Sir H. H. FOWLER : No, I dare say not, but no doubt you would sometimes cheer a principle though you despised the man who advocated that principle. If that is what you mean, I say to the Colonial Secretary, "Have the courage of your convictions and act accordingly." Let the First Lord of the Treasury make the announcement that that is the policy of Her Majesty's Government, and I think he would scatter to the winds the listless apathy which we are told prevails in the political world. Let the Chancellor of the Exchequer, as the Finance Minister of Great Britain, say that he accepts the economic doctrines of the Viceroy of India and the hon. Member for Central Sheffield. Let him say that, and he will be within measurable distance of that haven of rest and repose and freedom from official responsibility for which he so feelingly pleaded in his last utterance to his constituents. No, Sir, right hon. Gentlemen do not mean, and will not take, that fatal plunge. I will tell you why. Because they know —and no one knows better than the Colonial Secretary — that the constituencies would not tolerate it. They would not tolerate the legislative raising of the price of a great primary article of daily consumption among the people of this country for the advantage of the planters. I say that what we cannot and what we dare not do for Great Britain we have no right to do in India. The British nation is as responsible for the fiscal policy, for the commercial freedom, for the material progress of India as it is for its civil and military administration. It is our legitimate pride that we have rescued India from anarchy, from internecine strife, from foreign aggression. We have stamped on its government, on its institutions, on its daily life, that marvellous combination of law and order, of individual freedom and inflexible justice, which are the characteristics and glory of British rule the wide world over. We have adopted that policy because we know by dear-bought and long experience that it was best for ourselves, and we believed it to be the best for that great empire which was entrusted to our charge. We have adopted the policy and we have persevered in it, although it has been misrepresented and misunderstood, and at times unpopular. We are bound to apply that principle all the way through, and the test of righteous trusteeship is that you deal with the interests of others on the same lines as you deal with your own interests in similar circumstances. For half a century this country has found it to be to its commercial advantage and to its material interests to have its trade unfettered, that our people should be at liberty, whenever and wherever they pleased, to trade in the best and cheapest markets, and, above all, that we should levy no tax except for the purposes of revenue, and should not benefit one section of the community at the expense of the rest. Our commercial history, our national prosperity, the marvellous improvement in the condition of our people, are proofs of the wisdom of that policy. We know, the House knows, Members on the other side in their hearts know, that the nation would resist to the uttermost any attempt to weaken or reverse that policy ; and I ask the House

to-night to deal with these retrograde, illusory, mischievous proposals of the Indian Government as they would deal with the same proposals if they were made to the people of Great Britain.

*Mr. J. M. MACLEAN (Cardiff): I cannot hope to reach the flights of eloquence which have distinguished the conclusion of the speech of the hon. Gentleman who has just resumed his seat. But there is not a word in that speech from which I dissent, and I felt myself bound in honour to second this motion to-night. I have been told that this is a motion of censure, and that it is wrong for anyone on the Government benches to second a vote of censure on the Government. But the motion has only taken the form of a vote of censure because the Government has resolutely persisted in denying hon. Members an opportunity of raising a debate on the question on its merits during the last three months. Perhaps I have wearied the House with my pertinacity in this matter, but my knowledge of India enables me to appreciate the far-reaching consequences of legislation of this kind. I have persisted in putting questions to the Government day after day, and the Leader of the House, instead of giving me an opportunity to raise the question at a time when perhaps the passing of this legislation might have been stopped altogether—certainly at a time when further inquiry might have been granted by the Government of India—answered me in language of scarcely veiled mockery that he was exceedingly anxious to bring on this Debate, but that really the Government could not find the time for it. What ! Not find time to discuss a subject involving the commercial policy of the British Empire, when hon. Members are dragged to the House day after day and week after week to waste their time on puerilities of legislation which are hardly worth the attention of a serious assembly ! A few weeks ago I sent a message to the Leader of the House through the right hon. Gentleman's private secretary, offering, if the Government desired, to show a way in which the Government could get out of what I looked upon as a grave departmental blunder without casting any discredit on the Viceroy, or involving him in any conflict with this House, or weakening the authority of the Government of India. The right hon.

Gentleman did not take the slightest notice of that communication. I mention this fact in order to show that I am justified in the action now taken. I have not taken this step without consulting those who, after all, are our masters. I refer to my constituents. I have been twice in Cardiff, and I have fully explained my views on the subject. I have addressed the Chamber of Commerce, and from that day to this not a whisper of remonstrance has reached me from any person in Cardiff against the action I am now taking. I am therefore entitled to say that the whole of that constituency, whether Conservative or Liberal, is united as one man in giving me a free hand on this question. I wonder, however, whether that is the case with the hon. Members representing other important constituencies. I wonder what the Leader of the House has to say to the resolution passed within the last day or two by the Manchester Chamber of Commerce. The Chamber of Commerce includes a large number of the right hon. Gentleman's political friends, and the resolution said :

"It is the opinion of the Board that the policy adopted by the Government of India, with the approval of the Government at home, in levying countervailing duties on sugar imported from bounty-giving countries is opposed to the interests of the people of India, constitutes a dangerous precedent calculated to lead to the adoption of a similar policy in the United Kingdom and to demands which cannot be consistently resisted for the establishment of countervailing duties in several other directions, and without a departure from the principle of Free Trade."

I leave the right hon. Gentleman to settle that matter with the constituency which he represents.

THE FIRST LORD OF THE TREASURY (Mr. A. J. BALFOUR, Manchester, E.): I have heard nothing from my constituency.

*MR. J. M. MACLEAN: I am reading a resolution passed by a large public body. I do not believe there is a single Minister—not even the Colonial Secretary, with all his courage for rash enterprises —who, having seen the effect this agitation has had in familiarising the people of England with the true consequences of this policy, would rise in his place and propose countervailing duties in this country. That, at least, is one good thing that the present agitation has done, for countervail-

Mr. J. M. Maclean.

ing duties in England are henceforth as dead as bimetallism. Now it was impossible for me to believe—and for a long time I did not believe, until the publication of the Blue Book—that the Government as a collective body were in favour of the policy inaugurated by the noble Lord the Secretary of State for India. How could I think it possible that the Chancellor of the Exchequer would consent to a measure of this sort ? The Chancellor of the Exchequer was assailed for his lapse from virtue—economical virtue I mean—in tampering with the Sinking Fund, but I remember that not long ago he made an almost impassioned protest against preferential duties of any kind. India has hitherto been the greatest market of the world which has supported the principle of Free Trade, and has been worth more to us in this respect than all the self-governing colonies put together. India has given us the open door which we profess to desire all over the world, and now we are going, by a shabby and discreditable device, to shut that door in India when we are afraid to do it in this country. But as soon as the Blue Book appeared it became perfectly obvious to all the world why this law had been instituted and passed with so much indecent haste by the Council of the Viceroy of India. There is not the slightest doubt that the influence of the Secretary of State for the Colonies supplied the India Office with the motive power which was necessary to pass this legislation. I do not question the noble Lord's sincerity for a moment in this matter, but I do say that the energy with which he pursued this policy only dates from the moment of the intervention of the right hon. Gentleman the Secretary of State for the Colonies.

LORD G. HAMILTON: I may state at once that that statement is absolutely untrue.

*MR. J. M. MACLEAN: I do not think that the right hon. Gentleman has any right to say that, for I am simply going on what is in this Blue Book. I find that the first occasion on which the Secretary for the Colonies interfered was on July 23rd last year. Immediately afterwards —within a month—on August 25th, the Secretary of State for India wrote to Lord Elgin, who had refused to introduce these countervailing duties, to say what he thought ought to be done. Then, of course, we come to the opinion of Lord Elgin ; but what was written to him did not make any impression upon his fixed mind upon this subject. Then there was a change of Viceroys in India, and once more the Secretary of State for the Colonies comes to the front, and writes immediately to the noble Lord to say what he thinks ought to be done in India. I really cannot understand why the right hon. Gentleman should think it necessary to interfere in Indian affairs. Is he pining for new worlds to conquer ? Has he not sufficient spheres of influence already ? Surely Africa itself is large enough to fill the ambition of anyone, however overweening that ambition may be. At all events, one would have thought before the right hon. Gentleman interfered with India he would have settled his little differences with President Kruger, and then he might have rejoiced, but his policy is apparently not so successful at the present moment as he desires. I will now take the despatch written by the right hon. Gentleman and dated the 7th January, and point out the power he wielded at the India Office. In the first paragraph Mr. Chamberlain asked Lord George Hamilton to bring to the special notice of Lord Curzon, who had only just been appointed Viceroy, two important questions affecting the Island of Mauritius. Then the right hon. Gentleman proceeded to say that the industry of the sugar planters in Mauritius may be destroyed. In another part of the despatch he actually speaks of their ruin being probable if some change is not immediately made in the sugar tariff of India. There is absolutely no foundation for a statement of that kind. Statistics show that the sugar industry of Mauritius has never been in the slightest danger since they found an excellent market in India. I am not at all sure that the sugar planters in Mauritius do not themselves get a bounty of some kind from the State. As the right hon. Gentleman the Member for Wolverhampton has said, bounties are of all kinds. I pointed this out the other day to the Governor-General of Queensland, when he told me that if Queensland had fair play it would be able to supply sufficient sugar for the whole of the British Empire. I said to him, "Don't you consider that you had a remarkably big bounty given you when the Imperial Government presented you with immense tracts of fertile country extending over three times the area of the United Kingdom ?" Surely that was a very considerable bounty to give to Queensland, and they ought to be able to produce sugar there as well as the planters in other countries. Even in the West Indies I should say that considerable bounties have been given already, for at the time of the emancipation of the slaves we practically made a present to them of the whole of the properties belonging to individual citizens in this country. Many Members of this House are, perhaps, at the present moment suffering—either themselves or their families are suffering—from the great act of vicarious virtue which England performed when she emancipated the slaves. We then presented the land in fee simple to the emancipated slaves, and all they did was to turn Jamaica, which was once the garden of the world, into a howling wilderness. It is exceedingly difficult to determine when an industry is bounty fed or not. I looked through the Mauritius Administrative Report, and I came across this passage :

" Parcelling out land amongst Indians proceeds on a large scale. In the majority of cases no money passes for the first year or two, except the value of the canes, if there be any ripe enough to cut in the first year. This great settlement of labouring Indians upon the land will undoubtedly lead to a great increase in the production of sugar canes, raise the value of the land, and must ultimately lead to the establishment of central factories and the division of labour."

It seems that land is being parcelled out rent free for a year or two amongst Indian planters in Mauritius so that they may grow sugar at a cost which would enable them to compete with native sugar in India. That is the kind of Protection which we are asked to encourage to-day. The Secretary of State for the Colonies speaks of his own personal views. We have nothing, of course, to do with the right hon. Gentleman's personal views so long as they are not embodied in acts of legislation or administrative proceedings which are likely to bring damage to the Empire, and the right hon. Gentleman is perfectly at liberty to keep them to himself. I am not quite sure what the personal views of the right hon. Gentleman are on many subjects, but I am inclined to think he takes his foreign policy from the hon. Member for the Ecclesall

Division of Sheffield (Sir E. Ashmead-Bartlett) and his political economy from the hon. and gallant Member for the Central Division of Sheffield (Sir Howard Vincent). Those are views which are not likely to commend themselves either to the House of Commons or to the British people. They may be taught in the new University of Birmingham· to the sons of new Liberal Unionist Peers, but I do not think we need concern ourselves about them in the House of Commons. The Secretary of State for the Colonies absolutely forgets that India is not self-governed at all. It is a dependency of the Crown, and as was so well pointed out in that splendid despatch of Lord Salisbury's, which the right hon. Gentleman the Member for Wolverhampton has quoted:

" India is bound more closely and intimately to the House of Commons in matters of commercial policy than any other part of the Empire. It is here that the commercial policy of India has to be decided, and if we are to act in the interests of India, we in this House ought to watch closely and constantly over the application of the principles which we lay down.'

Having received that dispatch from the Secretary of State for the Colonies, the noble Lord again at once took action, and a good deal has been said about the conduct of the Viceroy in this matter. It appears to me that the Viceroy is very much to be pitied in the position in which he has been placed. He has only ·just received one of the highest posts in the gift of the Crown, when a new law is pressed upon him, in a series of telegrams repeated almost day after day, saying:

" When are you going to introduce this? Send us news the moment it is passed. Will telegraph acceptance. Bring it into operation."

Lord Curzon asked at first that he might be given more time to consider the matter, but no time was allowed him ; and then he took up in a loyal spirit the instructions he had received from the Government which had just made him Viceroy, and he proceeded with a great deal of impetuosity to carry out what he conceived to be their wishes, in fact, he gave the Government of India no rest until he had passed this law. It was introduced on the 10th February, passed on the 28th February, before there had been even time—for it was not published in the *Gazette* until the following

Mr. Maclean.

Tuesday—to send the Bill to the different provinces of India and to receive any reply by ordinary post as to the impression it had made on the public. I never heard of such indecent haste to carry a measure which was not at all urgent since Richard III. said he could not go to his breakfast until he had the head of Lord Hastings placed on the table before him. The Viceroy said he could not go to Simla until this Bill had passed, and the Indian Legislature immediately obeyed his orders. We hear a great deal about the Legislative Council of India, and people might imagine that it was a great free assembly, something after the model of the House of Commons. But, of course, it is nothing of the kind. The Viceroy is there surrounded by courtiers, and he, like Cato, " Gives his little Senate laws, And sits attentive to his own applause." Most of the Members there are really courtiers of the stamp of those gentlemen who first of all denounced countervailing duties with Lord Elgin or myself, and then approved of countervailing duties with Lord Curzon. Human nature is pretty much the same in all ages. These gentlemen act as the immortal Vicar of Bray did, who, no matter whichsoever king might reign, would still be Vicar of Bray. No doubt the noticeable change which has taken place in what was once the proud independence of the Indian Civil servants is due to the extremely lavish distribution of honours and decorations conferred upon them. It seems to me that modern governments have found that these honours—as they are called—are a more potent instrument of political corruption and social degradation than Walpole ever dreamed of. That is the type of men who for the most part form the Council of the Viceroy. There are, I admit, some independent members. There is one distinguished barrister who pleaded with the Government not to press the Bill. He said : " Do give us a little time to consider this measure; refer it to a Select Committee ; let it take its usual course." But the Government would not listen to a word of remonstrance of that kind, and insisted that it should be passed immediately and at all hazards, and they thought of having the public opinion of India behind them. The noble Lord boasted in the House of Commons the other day that the whole public opinion of India was demanding this Bill, and extraordinary telegrams were sent from Calcutta pointing out that I stood alone in opposing this law, and that the whole of India was on the side of the Viceroy. I ascertained by telegraph that that statement was absolutely incorrect. The right hon. Gentleman the Member for Wolverhampton has shown that even most of the provincial Governments—who are largely under the control of the Supreme Government—were opposed to the introduction of this law. Mention has been made of Sir Anthony Macdonell. I would most willingly pay attention to anything advised by that distinguished servant of the Crown, but the views he expressed were purely hypothetical. He said if the introduction of bounty-fed sugar were to cause the cultivation of sugar-cane to fall off then the price might be affected. But he has since stated that the cultivation of sugar-cane has not been affected in the slightest degree in India. And anyone who knows anything of the matter knows that the people of India will always consume nine-tenths of the sugar produced in the country. The production of sugar is perfectly enormous in India. In fact, India can grow sugar to supply the world, and would grow it more easily under the stimulus of competition than under protection. I notice that the Viceroy in his speeches and numerous addresses thinks that he has a sort of Divine mission to encourage native industries in India. I can assure him that nothing of the kind is wanted. The Bombay Government took up a strong position on this matter. The Bombay newspapers were good enough to rebuke me for having criticised the noble Lord, and said that I knew nothing of the public opinion of India. But it turns out that the editors of the Bombay newspapers were the only people who knew absolutely nothing of the state of public opinion in India. In Western India not only all the distinguished servants of the Crown, at Poonah, Kurrachee, Berar, etc., and the whole mercantile community, native and European, but the Government itself were entirely opposed to the introduction of these countervailing duties. I call the attention of the noble Lord to a statement which Lord Curzon made on 20th March, in which he assured the Legislative Council that this Bill had been backed up with a weight of opinion which for quality and homogeneousness had never been equalled. I am sure that Lord Curzon is

not a man to make a statement of that kind without believing it to be correct. I won't repeat the offensive phrase used by the noble Lord to me just now when he stated that what I had said was untrue; but I will say that what Lord Curzon stated was absolutely unfounded. There was no homogeneous feeling in India. I assume that Lord Curzon made that statement in Council, not with the intention of deceiving, but because he had never read or seen that despatch of the Bombay Government in which they protested against the introduction of the law. He could not have seen it. He introduced this law before he could possibly receive the despatch of the Bombay Government, which was only written on the 23rd of February, and could not have reached Calcutta before the end of that month. The decision of the Government of India was taken on the 25th of February, long before it could have received the statement of the views of the important Government of Bombay on the subject. This is a sample of the noble Lord's allegation that the public opinion of India was with the Viceroy in this matter. So much for the provincial Governments and the Council. But I would ask what is the real opinion of the Indian Press on this question, because much has been made of the apparent unanimity of the Indian Press in support of the Government. It was my duty to read the articles which have appeared supporting the policy of the Government. They were mostly what are called inspired articles, and inspired articles are generally like the Address to the Throne, which is usually an echo of Her Majesty's speech. These inspired articles are usually an echo of the statements made by Ministers in Council. All the Indian papers which have carefully examined the question have declared against countervailing duties. I could quote the *Indian Daily News,* which has completely gone over to the side of the opponents of the law, and the whole of the native Press is now on the same side. I will quote an extract from a well-known newspaper, the *Times of India,* which arrived here by last mail, and which is well known to be still favourable to the Government of India. The *Times of India* says :

" There has been a wonderful change in the native Press of India. The Government have passed a law at the behest of Mr. Chamberlain for the benefit of the sugar planters of Mauritius, and they must be prepared for a fine avalanche of denunciation by those who have taken all the moralities under their charge. The storm of reproach is already blowing in that direction, and we know what is coming."

That shows what is the present opinion of the majority of the native Press in regard to the law passed by the Government of India. Who were the real authors of this legislation in India? If we look at the Blue Book we find a memorial from a number of sugar refiners in the North-West Provinces. You would naturally look for the names of native merchants, but you find all the gentlemen who signed the petition hail from north of the Tweed. They nearly all belong to the same class of gentlemen who have lately come down from Glasgow and Greenock, and have assured us that we should pass similar legislation for the United Kingdom. A deputation of them waited the other day on the President of the Board of Trade, and then they were good enough to seek an interview with me and discuss the matter with me. They came to me, and said that the President of the Board of Trade had been most sympathetic with them. I asked them if the President of the Board of Trade had promised to do anything for them; and they said "No, but he advised them that they ought to convert public opinion"; and they were good enough to add "We are beginning with you." I advised them to begin with the Chancellor of the Exchequer, to which they replied that "if they could convert me they would have an easy task with the Chancellor of the Exchequer." These gentlemen seemed to me to be exceedingly prosperous, although they complained of being ruined. But it struck me that all they were pushing for was their own interests, and that they cared nothing for the interests of the great consumers of the country. It was much the same sort of gentlemen who sent a petition to the Government of Bengal, and asked that they should be given a monopoly of refined sugar. It would be much easier, by the employment of skilled labour and improved machinery, to turn out a better article than at present and so command the market. But they will never do such a thing until stimulated by foreign competition. We have forced, as I have said, Free Trade on India, but Free Trade has conferred immense benefits on that

Mr. J. M. Maclean.

country as well as on this country. It is not the fact that there is any want of money or enterprise in India, or that when the necessity of finding new markets is forced upon the people they are incapable of rising to the opportunity. Just look at what they have done with their cotton, always under the stimulus of very forced and unrestricted foreign competition. Manchester goods practically killed the hand loom industry of India, famous in all previous ages; but the natives have not been behind in adapting to their own use the machinery and methods of Manchester, and there are no more successful cotton mills in the world than are to be found in Bombay and a number of other places at the present moment. With the goods they have turned out from short staple cotton they have successfully beaten Manchester out of the market. All that was done with Free Trade. Look at the great tea industry of India. It has beaten China out of the English market. Has that trade been built up by Government protection? No, but by the enterprise of free Englishmen knowing what was wanted, and how to apply successfully capital to the production of the article required. Take coal. When I first went to India I remember coal was only used within a few miles of the pits in Bengal from which it was obtained. At the beginning of this year I find that coal is used on all the twenty odd thousand miles of the Indian railway system. It has beaten English coal almost entirely out of the market. It is used on all the steamers running from Bombay to Suez, and but for the heavy duties in the Suez Canal Indian coal would pass into the Mediterranean and compete with English coal there. All this has been done without Government protection, by capital, industry, and enterprise working together with freedom against foreign competition. Then there is the success of Indian beer against the competition of both English and German beer, and there are innumerable other cases in which India has shown itself quite alive to the necessities of modern industries. The most remarkable illustration I could give the House of the really good working of Free Trade is this. In the old days every town in India was lighted with little lamps containing cocoanut oil, and a very disagreeable light it often was. Paraffin oil was introduced by America and sent out in tins and speedily took possession of the market, and it was taken into consumption all over India. Finally, Russia succeeded in beating America out of the market with the help of English capital. Russia invented a system of sending petroleum in tank steamers to Bombay, where it was sold by measure to the people, and the expense of the tins and the long voyage from America was saved. Russia now has nearly the whole trade of lighting India. Would not this have been a magnificent opportunity for a Viceroy who thought he had a mission to save the industries of India to say, "We will not have the immemorial cocoanut-oil lamps extinguished. We must protect our industries, and we will not give this vast trade to our natural enemies the Russians." What has been the result of the introduction of this trade in India? The native growers of oil seeds, being forced to find another market for their products, have discovered that these vegetable oils are the best that can possibly be used in all the great machine works in Europe, and now these oil seeds are in greater demand than ever, and fetch a higher price than before. That is a splendid example of the natural working of Free Trade and the advantage that freedom of trade gives to the people. I thought it right to say this because it seems to me that people adopt a too apologetic tone for forcing Free Trade on India. Free Trade would never have been adopted there by the natives, but if you ask all the more intelligent natives now you will find that they are satisfied that the present system of commerce is the best thing that England could have possibly given them. I shall, I am afraid, weary the House, but I have had this matter much in my mind and I have never been allowed to speak on it in the House before. I should like to say a word upon the constitutional point touched on by the right hon. Gentleman the Member for Wolverhampton. The noble Lord the Secretary of State for India seems to have formed a radically false conception of his powers and his responsibilities to this House. When I put a question to him on this subject he retorted in tones of some asperity—an asperity which might have kindled resentment in my bosom if we, who are below the gangway, were not used by this time to

"The insolence of office, and the spurns
   That patient merit of the unworthy takes."

The noble Lord practically told me that I had better mind my own business.

LORD G. HAMILTON dissented.

*MR. J. M. MACLEAN : I am not giving the noble Lord's exact words, but he said he had told me more than once that he declined to interfere with the expression of opinion and the determination of the Government of India upon a question of this kind.

LORD G. HAMILTON : The hon. Gentleman put a question to me to this effect : Would I lay this Bill on the Table of the House, for the purpose, of course, of founding questions and motions upon it, and as it was under discussion in the Indian Legislature I replied, as every Secretary of State would, that I declined to interfere with the functions of the Indian Government.

*MR. J. M. MACLEAN : That is where the noble Lord makes what I conceive to be a very great mistake. The Indian Legislature has no independent position. It has only delegated powers from this Parliament. What is the position of the noble Lord towards the Indian Government? It is very clearly defined in the despatch written by Lord Salisbury, when Secretary of State for India, in 1875. Lord Hartington had taken off the cotton duties in order to put Manchester and India on an equal footing, and the Indian Government, at the time strongly Protectionist, claimed that they had a right as an independent Legislature to pass any tariff laws they chose. Lord Salisbury absolutely declined to give them this power. One excellent reason he gave was, that unless complete unanimity was assured beforehand between the House of Commons, represented by the Secretary of State, and the Indian Government, there was no security for the maintenance of the Viceroy's authority in India, which would receive rude shocks by the decisions of the Government of India being frequently challenged in this House. It was impossible, said Lord Salisbury, for the House of Commons to part with its control over Indian finance, and therefore the power was specially reserved to the Secretary of State for India by Lord Salisbury to re-

present the House of Commons in tariff matters, and never to let any change in Indian tariff laws be introduced without his assent. It seems to me that that power which was placed in the hands of the Secretary of State imposes upon him a very heavy responsibility, and he ought to take especial care, as is his constitutional duty, that no sudden or rash change in the settled commercial policy of this Empire is introduced into the Legislative Council of India, unless he is assured of the support of the House of Commons whose servant he is. It may be said that the House, if it does not approve of the conduct of a Secretary of State, has the right to remove him, but that is not enough. We know that if we remove him we shall only have another noble lord in his place. I deny that it is any advantage to us, after the Secretary of State has had the opportunity of throwing India into confusion for six months, and of giving a rude shock to the authority of the new Viceroy from which it will never recover, that we should have the privilege of removing him. It was the wisdom of Lord Salisbury that provided that this agreement should be come to beforehand, and what I condemn the noble Lord for is that he never consulted the House of Commons or took any pains to ascertain whether an Act of this kind would be supported in this country. On the contrary, nearly every Minister on the front bench has said that he is quite convinced that public opinion in this country has not been converted on the question of countervailing duties, and that therefore he would not attempt to meddle with them. Is it not a shabby device, then, when they dare not do it in England, to force it on the people of India and impair the authority of the Viceroy? We know that things cannot rest where they are. We know that if this Act is passed for India it will be passed with the deliberate design to introduce preferential duties into every part of the Empire. Is that a policy which commends itself? I would ask my Conservative friends whether they are willing to go to the country two years hence with "Protection" emblazoned on their banners. Some of them may, but not very many. What will be the result of this policy? Was it not a Conservative Chancellor of the Exchequer—Sir Stafford Northcote—who abolished

Mr. Maclean.

the sugar duties twenty-five years ago? He took off the remaining sugar duties because he said that next to cheap corn no greater boon could be given to the people of this country than cheap sugar. He was perfectly right. His policy has been justified by results, and the people of England, knowing what immense industries are now bound up with the existence of cheap sugar, will never suffer that great boon to be taken away from them. I for one unhesitatingly support the motion of the right hon. Gentleman the Member for Wolverhampton, because it is conceived, I believe, in a spirit of fair play for India and Free Trade for the British Empire.

Motion made, and Question proposed—

"That an humble Address be presented to Her Majesty, praying that Her Majesty will be pleased to disallow the Indian Tariff Act, 1899."—(*Sir Henry Fowler.*)

*Lord G. HAMILTON : I rise for the purpose of asking the House to give a direct negative to the motion that has just been made. Since that motion has been on the Table of the House various Amendments to it have been proposed by Members in different parts of the House. I hope those hon. Gentlemen will not move any one of these Amendments. The two speeches which we have heard tonight, as well as the matter to which they refer, give ample material to the House of Commons for a full night's discussion, and if any Amendments such as those that appear on the paper are introduced unquestionably extraneous issues will creep into the discussion. The issue that is raised is a clear issue; let us meet it clearly, and let our Debate to-night be concentrated on the subject of sugar so far as it affects India. The right hon. Gentleman who opened this Debate and the hon. Gentleman who followed him have made two speeches, the summary of which is nothing more or less than a defence of the bounty system as applied to sugar. From beginning to end there was not a solitary allusion to the detrimental effects of the bounty system, and in the name of Free Trade those two hon. Gentlemen get up and publicly support the blackest system of Protection known. The position of Her Majesty's Government is clearly defined. We gave instructions to our delegates at the Congress at Brussels—and, so far as I know, no political Party has challenged the justice of those instructions—to try and secure the suppression of all bounties on sugar, which they considered to be prejudicial to the general interests of the British Empire. Is any one prepared in this House to contradict that proposition ? If nobody is prepared to contradict that proposition in the abstract, then every vote given by hon. Gentlemen in this House for the motion moved to-night will tend to bolster up and infuse new life and strength into this system of bounties on sugar. Either the system is a good one or it is a bad one. If it is a bad system, we are justified in having recourse to strong measures to get rid of it ; but if it is a good system, let us have the courage to say so openly. I am compelled, in consequence of the nature of the speeches that have been made, to indulge in a few elementary but, I think, necessary propositions. I have been a Free Trader all my life. (Laughter.) Hon. Gentlemen laugh, but I think I am the only person now in this House who has introduced legislation in India which went in the direction of Free Trade. There is at the present moment only one protective Act on the Statute-book of India, and that is an Act —I dare say a necessary Act—which was passed by right hon. Gentlemen opposite when they were in office. It puts a 5 per cent. duty on all imports even where the article imported competes with the native production. I do not blame right hon. Gentlemen for doing that, but it is rather curious that the right hon. Gentleman who invites me not to depart from the principles of Free Trade represents a Government which has put on the Statute-book of India the only law which is essentially protective. I believe it to be to the interest of this country and the duty of the Government of this country to promote Free Trade wherever they can, and by Free Trade I mean the principles that were taught us by Mr. Cobden and by Sir Louis Mallet. Free Trade means the freeing of trade from artificial restraint and artificial fostering, from anything that tends to raise the price of an article artificially. An hon. Gentleman laughs, but anything which tends to raise the price of an article artificially by a hostile tariff is contrary to the principles of Free Trade. But the converse is equally true. Anything which tends to lower the price of an article below the cost of production, by bounties or by Government aid, is contrary to the principles

of Free Trade. The two preceding speakers did not seem to thoroughly grasp and analyse the difference between Free Trade and Protection. The essential difference between the two is this, that the object of Free Trade is to try and establish, so far as fiscal arrangements are concerned, equality of conditions, equality of treatment, and equality of opportunity for all producers, in whatever part of the world they may live, and thus, by encouraging production and increasing competition, to benefit the consumer, who gets the advantage of lower prices in consequence of the increased production. The object of Protection is the reverse—it is to establish inequality, so that the home producer always may have a certain advantage to enable him to compete with others. Free Trade and Protection, therefore, are antagonistic : they are irreconcilable. These two fiscal systems are in operation all over the world, fighting one another, and the most aggressive form which Protection can assume is the bounty system as associated with the production of sugar. What does the bounty system do ? In the first place, the foundation of the bounty system is the drawing of an impenetrable barrier round the country in which the bounty is given, so that no sugar from outside can come in and compete with the home production. The open door is permanently and hermetically sealed against imports. But then the door is opened in order that the bounty-fed sugar exporter may go forth and with the resources of a great system of national taxation behind him make war on indigenous industries and on the enterprise of Free Trade nations engaged in the production of sugar. It is nothing more or less than a deliberate act of economic aggression against the principles of Free Trade and free industry. That is admitted. For twenty years past we in this country, I admit, have adopted a policy of inaction in dealing with this system of bounties on sugar. We were misled by those who undertook to lead us. Almost every prediction that they made has been falsified. I have heard to-night all the old arguments—which experience has shown us to be absolutely false—trotted out for our acceptance in the belief that we have forgotten our experiences of the last 20 years. The first argument was— " After all, the disturbance to the Indian industry is very slight, and it is not worth while taking notice of it." That was an argument used 20 years ago about sugar in this country. The next argument was—" After all, it only affects refined sugar." That also was an argument used 20 years ago, but the bounty-fed sugar now affects the price of raw sugar as well as of refined sugar. All the arguments that were used in the past to induce us to assent to the bounty on sugar under the idea that it was merely a phase of Protection and would pass away are revived, and it is expected that, with all our experience of the past 20 years, and the knowledge of these falsified predictions, we should accept them as true, and on that ground censure the Indian Government. The tactics that this country has followed in connection with the bounty on sugar, whether they were right or wrong, have immensely extended and developed that system, and it has assumed enormous proportions. The hon. Member for Cardiff said that the Indian sugar industry would not prosper except under the stimulus of competition. Where has cane sugar prospered under the stimulus of competition with bounty-fed beet sugar? It is proved, I think, beyond dispute that cane sugar can be produced as cheaply as beet sugar. Experts assure me that is so, and the assertion has been put forward and not contradicted. Twenty years ago the sugar duties were abolished in this country, and that change came into full operation in 1877. The amount of sugar imported into this country in that year was 20,000,000cwt., and of that amount about 6,000,000cwt. came from bounty-giving countries and 14,000,000cwt. came from non-bounty-giving countries. Twenty years later, owing to the increase of population and various other causes, the amount of sugar imported into Great Britain was considerably greater, and it attained the dimensions of upwards of 29,000,000cwt. The sugar from bounty-giving countries had then risen to 24,000,000 cwt. and the sugar from non-bounty-giving countries had fallen to 5,000,000 cwt. This is the bounty-fed sugar which is to go to India and is to give a stimulus to cane sugar and largely increase its production. That displacement of cane sugar is unnatural and artificial. I think all persons who watch these economic questions will admit that the displacement of an industry from its natural locality and the diversion of

Lord G. Hamilton.

trade and commerce from its legitimate channels is a great evil to the trade and commerce of the world, because the forces that we are dealing with are what are known as dynamic forces—they are forces constantly on the move, competing with one another—and the displacement and dislocation of a trade or industry often acts and reacts all round the whole trade and commerce of the world, reducing production and limiting exchange of commodities. The result is that we, who are the great international traders of the world, lose by this unnatural displacement. [Opposition cries of dissent.] Hon. Gentlemen have not followed my argument. I am putting on one side any benefit bounty-fed sugar may confer. I say the displacement of trade and of production from its legitimate channels and its natural locality detrimentally affects the whole trade and commerce of the world. That is a proposition which I think nobody will dispute. The material displacement of cane sugar by this bounty-fed sugar detrimentally affects the production of cane sugar. No one with capital would put his money into a business which was subjected to competition not to a fixed bounty, but with a bounty that at any moment might be doubled. Germany doubled their bounty in 1896, France responded, Austria did the same; and our representatives at Brussels pointed out that in all probability, unless some satisfactory solution of the bounty question could be arrived at, the bounties would be still further raised. I venture to say I have shown that the system of bounties is as contrary to the first principle of Free Trade as any system could possibly be. That system absolutely dominates the production and consumption of sugar in Europe. It turned its attention to America, and exported enormous quantites of beet sugar into the United States; and the United States retaliated by countervailing duties. We were warned by our representatives at Brussels that the stoppage of the import of German sugar in America would result in great masses of German sugar being sent to India; and that the one great indigenous industry of India would be threatened. Of the 300 million people who live in India, 80 per cent. depend for the means of subsistence on agriculture; and in the North of India, where the population is more densely packed than in any other part of the world, the sugar industry is the principal industry. Again, a large proportion of the income of the Indian Government is derived from land revenue. The direct amount paid by cane sugar to the revenue is about £1,600,000, but the indirect amount is much greater. The only question the House has to consider is this—Warned as we were of the danger to India, should the Indian Government, ignoring the effect of twenty years' experience, have aggravated the very evil which we wanted to arrest, by the tactics of inaction adopted here? Or should they have recourse to the simpler policy of attempting to frustrate the object for which the bounties are given, and thus lead to the abolition of the bounty system itself? So gigantic is the production of cane sugar in India that it is far more than the production of the rest of the world, excluding China; it employs several millions of people; and the annual crop is estimated to be worth little short of 20 millions sterling. All that is wanted is the application of capital and enterprise to the sugar industry in India. What person would give one or the other if the bounty system is allowed to enter the field? We had to deal with a danger which unquestionably was imminent, and we had to consider very carefully what course we should adopt. A somewhat farcical account has been given by the hon. Member for Cardiff of the relations between myself and my right hon. friend the Colonial Secretary, and of the communications which he assumed passed between the Colonial Office and the India Office. At the beginning of last year Lord Elgin was asked to nominate a delegate to represent India at the Sugar Conference at Brussels. This was the first occasion upon which India had a special delegate of her own. In the despatch in which the Indian Government sanctioned the appointment of the delegate they forwarded certain proposals made by some gentlemen in Bengal amounting to the proposal of countervailing ·duties; but the Indian Government said they were not prepared to sanction that proposal. The Conference met and separated without arriving at any settlement. Mr. Ozanne, the delegate specially selected by Lord Elgin to represent India at the Conference, was asked if he would write a report by the Revenue Secretary of the India Office, acting on my behalf. He replied :—

" I shall, of course, be glad to write a report if you think it is expected of me, or that it would do any good. But, after all, the only point I could press on the Indian Government is the danger which India runs through an immense increase in the volume of imports of beetroot sugar. If this goes on, and it must go on if India does nothing, it seems to me clear that the sugar cultivation of India and the Mauritius will be most seriously and unjustly handicapped. If sugar-cane profits are reduced the whole agriculture of India must be upset."

Recollect that agriculture is not one of many industries in India. It affects the whole industrial system of the country, and therefore, if any blow were struck at what is really the only staple occupation in India, we would be face to face with a tremendous economic difficulty, the satisfactory solution of which would be almost impossible. As soon as the Brussels Conference broke up without having come to any conclusion I addressed a letter to the Government of India enclosing the correspondence in reference to the Conference, and intimating in the clearest way that I was not satisfied with their declaration of opinion against the imposition of countervailing duties, asking them to more fully consider the matter and in the meantime to collect further information. Simultaneously with the receipt of my letter in India the Indian public received the report that the Brussels Conference had broken up without having come to any decision, and simultaneously all over India an agitation sprang up requesting the Government to impose countervailing duties. The Chambers of Commerce petitioned the Government in favour of this policy, and the Indian as well as the European Press of the country assisted in the agitation. Lord Curzon, as you know, was appointed Viceroy towards the close of last session. In the autumn he spent a considerable part of his time in the India Office consulting with various Members of the Indian Council and myself. We discussed the course to be pursued in regard to the sugar question. The House is perhaps not aware, though the mover of this Motion is, that the Council of India have exceptional authority in matters relating to finance and expenditure. I placed myself in communication with the Revenue Committee of that Council, and was glad to find that their views agreed with mine that we should not close the door against countervailing duties if no other remedy could be found to arrest the adverse influence of bounty-fed sugar on agriculture in India. Lord Curzon came to the same view, but, knowing that further information was being collected, he declined to express any opinion on the subject until he had the opportunity of investigating that further information, and also of personally communicating with the members of the Government of India who had signed the despatch objecting to countervailing duties, in order to ascertain whether that opposition was based upon conviction and a thorough knowledge and investigation of the subject in India. In the meantime we got information from the Foreign Office, from which it seemed perfectly clear the Conference would not meet again, and that therefore there was no likelihood of action being taken for the purpose of suppressing or stopping the bounty system in Europe. We had, at the same time, information that there were immense cargoes of German sugar at Hamburg, and that the probability was that this great stock of sugar would be sent out to the Indian market. Therefore on 12th December I sent a note to the Revenue Committee of the Council of India to the effect that, having considered the question from the Indian point of view, I saw no objection to imposing countervailing duties, and that I should be glad to hear their opinion. They replied that they had considered the matter, and that they entirely endorsed my view that the time had arrived for such duties. Accordingly a despatch was ordered to be prepared. Before it was sent to India my right hon. friend the Colonial Secretary forwarded me two letters from Mauritius, referring to the same subject, and as I thought it it was most desirable that the Indian Government should know that the Colonial Office was of the same mind, I had the letter addressed to India altered and enlarged, so as to include the two letters from Mauritius. That, from the beginning to the end, was all the pressure that the Colonial Secretary exercised on me in the matter; and therefore when the hon. Member for Cardiff gave his farcical description of the affair I said there was not a word of truth in it. In consequence of the delay which was caused by this despatch having been kept back Lord Curzon was not likely to have been able to proceed till the beginning of March. Everyone was

Lord G. Hamilton.

agreed that, if it became necessary to legislate, legislation should be proceeded with at once. Three weeks after Lord Curzon received my despatch I telegraphed to him asking if he would be able to legislate this session, because the Legislative Council at Calcutta broke up towards the end of March, and it was desirable, if he thought legislation necessary, that the Bill should be passed before the close of their session. He replied that he and his Council were ready to proceed, the Bill was introduced, and passed rapidly through the Legislative Council, and it has received a greater amount of support in India than any legislation or any act the Government has done for many years past. It is quite true that there was only an interval of three days between the receipt of the announcement of Lord Curzon's intention to legislate and the reply of Her Majesty's Government. But the Council of India had been consulted by me, and is it likely that we should have arrived at what I admit to have been a momentous decision had we not carefully considered in advance the whole question? The reason why we were able to take such prompt action was that the subject had been for months previous before the Government. This, from beginning to end, is the simple history of the procedure in connection with this Bill, and I venture to say that throughout we have been actuated by one motive only — how best to serve the interests of India. The right hon. Gentleman undertook some little time ago the charge of a Committee which was formed to consider matters connected with the finances of India. It required some courage on the part of the right hon. Gentleman to undertake so laborious a part, with the certain knowledge that whatever way the Committee reports he is sure to be abused. Now, my strong impression is that that Committee will establish a stable rate of exchange between England and India which will enable India to take full advantage of her own resources and the great financial resources of England. There is an enormous amount of English capital which can be properly, and legitimately, invested in India, and therefore, if the right hon. Gentleman were to succeed in carrying his motion to-night, and bounty-fed sugar thus allowed to exercise its detrimental effects in India, he would counteract one of the most important results of the Report which I hope he will shortly produce. There is a vast and ever-growing population in India. It is calculated that something like 70,000,000 people have been added to the population during the last 20 years, and the only hope in any way to satisfactorily deal with this enormous population is to do everything possible to induce English capitalists to invest their money in India, and thus extend and multiply industries. Unless we can do so the economic problem is incapable of solution. What is the objection to the legislation which we propose? If the bounty system as applied to sugar be sound in itself, and if, as the right hon. Gentleman and the hon. Member for Cardiff seem to wish, the House expresses its approval of bounties as applied to sugar, they will effectually prevent anybody from taking measures to suppress the system. The staple support of agriculture in India is the sugar industry; it stands in much the same position as the steel and iron industry does in this country. Suppose for a moment that foreign Governments were to apply the bounty system to the manufacture of steel and iron, and, with the long hours which they work and the lower wages, foreign manufacturers were to make a determined attempt upon the mainspring of our industrial supremacy in Europe, and if they were to devote the sums of money they devote at present to sugar bounties, it is perfectly certain that they could make a great inroad on our steel and iron industry. In that case would the right hon. Gentleman like to go down and address his constituents at Wolverhampton, one of the headquarters of the industry, and use the language he has used in connection with bounty-fed sugar? What popular constituency would tolerate the idea that they were to be deprived of their employment, not by fair competition, but by Government subsidies, and to be told that, after all, it was the consumer who had to be consulted, and that there was no remedy whatsoever? If any such condition of things prevailed, I believe that the whole producing population of this country would combine, and insist upon the Government sweeping away the bounties. If, then, you would be forced to take some strong measures to arrest the pernicious development of the bounty system when applied to a staple industry at home, why

not act towards India as you would towards yourselves? But then I am told that countervailing duties are a violation of the principle of Free Trade. I think the two preceding speakers have argued that they are contrary to our fiscal system, which during the past fifty years has brought such extraordinary prosperity to these islands. They seem to forget that countervailing duties have for 50 years past been part and parcel of our fiscal system, and that they have been applied to that particular commodity from which we derive the largest amount of income—namely, spirits and beer. All foreign spirits which are imported into this country pay a duty of 5d. per gallon more than the home product, and there is also a differential duty upon beer. What is the origin of these duties? Who are the black protectionists responsible for them? They bear the names of Cobden, Sir Louis Mallet, and Gladstone. When Cobden negotiated the Treaty with the French in 1860, one of the inducements which was offered the French Government to reduce the duties upon English goods exported to France was the expectation that French spirits should be allowed to come into this country on exactly the same duty as was paid by home-made spirits to the Excise. In the discussion which took place upon the Treaty it transpired that the Excise system in this country was much more rigorous than the French system, and accordingly the French Government to compensate the British distiller, agreed to an additional duty of 2d. being imposed upon all spirits imported from France. The matter affected a large and important industry, and when the terms of the Treaty became known the British distillers got up an agitation and sent a deputation to Mr. Gladstone to point out that an extra duty of 2d. was not sufficient, and to demand that it should be raised to 5d. After some negotiations the extra duty of 5d. was agreed to. The section of the Treaty in which the surtax of 2d. is struck out and fresh terms negotiated is in the following terms:

"Since the ratification of the said Treaty the Government of Her Britannic Majesty have ascertained that the surtax of 2d. a gallon is not sufficient to countervail the charges with which, in consequence of the operation of the laws of Customs and Excise, home-made British spirits have now to contend; and that a surtax limited to the rate of 2d. a gallon would still leave home-made British spirits subject to a differential duty in favour of foreign brandies and spirits. Consequently the Government of Her Britannic Majesty, having represented these circumstances to the Government of His Majesty the Emperor of the French, and His Imperial Majesty having consented that the amount of the said surtax shall be increased, the two high contracting parties to the said treaty of commerce do, by the present additional article, agree that the amount of such surtax shall be 5d. a gallon; and Her Britannic Majesty engages to recommend to Parliament the admission into the United Kingdom of brandies and spirits imported from France at a duty exactly equal to the Excise duty levied upon home-made spirits, with the addition of a surtax of 5d. a gallon."

Therefore you will see our distillers had the advantage of a countervailing duty. I admit there is a little difference between the two cases, but what hon. Gentlemen have to show is that there is such a vital difference be-between a duty which is imposed to countervail the advantage to the foreigner given by our Excise system, and a duty imposed to countervail the advantage to the foreigner given him by his own fiscal system, as to justify them in still calling Gladstone and Cobden Free Traders and Lord Curzon and myself Protectionists. In an eloquent passage at the conclusion of his speech the right hon. Gentleman alluded to the enormous benefits which Free Trade has conferred upon this country, and he referred to the open port or the open door. I quite agree that the object of the open port or open door is to encourage competition and production all over the world by letting traders know that when once they are inside that door they will meet other producers on terms of equality. What is the object of a bounty? It is that a foreigner may proclaim to the whole world that, although the door is wide open, when you get inside, as regards a particular commodity to which the bounty applies, you shall not meet on terms of equality. Therefore to advocate keeping the door open and at the same time to advocate a system of bounties is to set two contrary influences at work which counteract one another. Since this subject has been under discussion I have been the recipient of a very large amount of literature. My hon. friend the Member for Cardiff is quite confident that I have totally misrepresented public opinion in India.

Lord G. Hamilton.

I do not know what authority he will accept as an adequate one upon that subject, but many years ago he made a just reputation as the able and active editor of the *Bombay Gazette.* I do not know whether he will now accept that paper as an accurate representation of Indian opinion?

Mr. J. M. MACLEAN: Oh, dear, no; I have nothing whatever to do with it now.

*Lord G. HAMILTON: Now, let us see what the *Bombay Gazette* says. On the 27th of April it says that Mr. J. Maclean, M.P., ought certainly to seek redress by an action at law against whoever is contending that opinion in Bombay is absolutely opposed to countervailing duties; that never was a shrewd public man more grievously mistaken; that the European and native community of Bombay was in line on this point with the rest of India, and that the unanimity left nothing to be desired. When I turn to English public opinion I do not think there is a single large representative body in this country which has discussed this question, with the single exception of the Manchester Chamber of Commerce, which has not supported the Government in the action they have taken. The Chambers of Commerce of London, Liverpool, Edinburgh, and Glasgow, representing the great commercial interests, have strongly supported us. Manchester is against us. I say frankly that I think Manchester and the Manchester Chamber of Commerce ought to be ashamed of themselves. Three years ago the Chamber of Commerce bombarded me night and day in order that I might give to them as against the Indian cotton spinners equality of treatment. I was not so much influenced by this clamour as I was by my conviction that the request was a just one. I looked with great alarm on the spirit of antagonism which was growing up between two great industrial communities engaged in producing the same commodities—one in Bombay and one in Manchester. I was desirous in the interests of the Empire of establishing conditions under which they could compete on equal terms for the benefit of the consumer. Well, I succeeded in establishing that equality, and met with much obloquy in doing so; and now the Manchester Chamber of

Commerce, having got that which three years ago they demanded as an inherent right, ask me to refuse to the sugar producers of India the very benefit that they asked for themselves. From whatever point of view you look at this question, whether you look at it from the economic, or the Imperial, or the Indian point of view, prudence, expediency, and justice all combine to support the proposals we have made. There are also considerations which may be suggested in connection with Indian public opinion which I think are well worthy of the attention of this House. We are proud of our rule in India and of the splendid work done by our countrymen. But we must recollect that the extraordinary disproportion between the governing classes and the governed constitutes a risk and danger which ever surrounds our authority in India. Though the risk and danger may from time to time assume, as conditions change, a different form, it is always there. We have passed recently through a very troublesome epoch, and it is during these times that the authorities can best gauge and anticipate the nature of the dangers ahead. The weapons which now assail our Empire in India are not those of material force and violence; subtler and more insidious influences are at work. I am afraid that, whatever we do, our government never will be popular in India. I am speaking my own conviction, and I have spent a great part of my official life in the India Office, and I state my deliberate opinion that, do what you like, our government never can be popular in India, but its strength consists in the confidence the people repose in our integrity and our ability to maintain peace, and on the foundation of that peace to promote their moral and material prosperity. But to attack our honesty and impugn our motives is now the object of a certain agitation in India. I speak what I know. The House may not agree with me, but I am speaking with the full sense of responsibility. I say that to impugn our motives is the object of a certain class of agitators in India. Our policy is impugned, and every effort is made to try and associate the action and the policy of the Government with a disregard of Indian public opinion and a selfish regard for our own interests. Sir, I quite admit that at times it is necessary to overrule local opinion in the interests of India and of our Empire. We are compelled—every Secretary of State is at times compelled—to have something done in India which local opinion would not have done or to stop something which local opinion would have done, but the occasions on which this supreme power should be exercised are rare, and are only justified by most exceptional circumstances. I had practically to overrule Indian public opinion in order to secure equality of treatment between Bombay and Manchester. After all, that proposal only affected a limited number of persons, but you are now dealing with a question which comes home to the daily life of an enormous population. The sugar industry practically covers the whole of the North of India. I have had many communications with the Viceroy on the subject. The last I received was a telegram, dated May 27, as follows:

"Superintending Engineer North-Western Provinces reports that since our Bill the area under sugar crop is rising considerably; that every petty farmer and labourer in the provinces was aware of sugar tax within few days of passing of Bill; that next to famine relief works it is the one measure of Government for years past which has been understood and appreciated by the people, and that it was received everywhere with content."

The House is asked to cancel that legislation—and by cancelling it to destroy all the hopes and expectations that have been founded upon it. What for? Why, to give expression to certain economic theories as to the exact definition of which no two persons agree, and in order not to do violence to certain principles which we are supposed to have violated by a measure the principle of which I have shown to be part and parcel of the fiscal system of this country for fifty years past. The House is asked to take this step in the teeth of the advice and opinion of every authority which constitutes the governing power in India. The Executive Council of the Governor-General is unanimous in its support, the Legislative Council is unanimous, and it is supported by a consensus of Indian public opinion such as I have never known in my experience, and older men tell me they have never known in theirs such unanimity. The House would be undertaking the very gravest responsibility if they venture on such flimsy grounds as have been advanced to interfere in so vital a matter. Therefore I commend this legislation to the House. I commend it because the Indian Government by the action they have taken have not only struck a legitimate blow in defence of their own interests, but because their action will, I think, stimulate other Governments to take counsel together in order that they may put an end to one of the most vicious forms of subsidised production against which free enterprise and legitimate trade and industry have ever had to contend.

*MR. LOUGH (Islington, W.) : After the speech which we have had from the rig t hon. Gentleman the Member for Wolverhampton and the speech of the seconder of the Motion, I think it is desirable that some of us from the seclusion of the back benches should say in a few words—the fewer the better—what they think about the great principle which is now being introduced in the proposed legislation which the Government have carried in India. I would like to proceed at once to that, but after the remarkable speech to which we have listened it is impossible for me to do so without saying one or two words on what has fallen from the Indian Secretary. The right hon. Gentleman has made the most grievous confession of failure that I have ever heard fall from the lips of a Minister in this House. He has said that he, the Indian Secretary, does not believe that it will ever be possible to popularise the rule of England in India.

LORD G. HAMILTON : I said that, do what we like, our Government never will be popular in India.

*MR. LOUGH : That is the same thing. He confessed that he believes it would never be possible to make it popular. I go the length of saying, with all deference, that when the Minister for India makes such a confession about his ideas of the work of the India Office, the time has almost come when he should relinquish the high trust which he holds in regard to that country. Is not our rule everywhere based on popular support? And if the Government have come to the conclusion that it can never be based on popular support in India, surely we have arrived at a grave crisis which this House ought to consider. But this is not the only point in the right hon. Gentleman's speech which should be examined. I am sorry to say that

Lord G. Hamilton.

I must charge him with being a little uncandid in his main argument. He stated that there was no new principle introduced in this legislation. He endeavoured to justify this by references to Mr. Gladstone's Treaty with France in 1860. I will not follow all the niggling arguments which were adduced on that point. I venture to say they did not carry conviction to a single mind. The Government ought to be more candid. The Government ought to take the responsibility of its action, and admit that it is introducing a grave and novel departure in the legislation, at any rate, of India, and probably of this country also. The right hon. Gentleman endeavoured to justify the action of the Government by reference to the 5 per cent. import duty which was imposed some years ago in India. He stated that that was really a protective duty. When the right hon. Gentleman reflects on his words, I believe he will see that that is an unfair description. It can only be protective where it applies to the importation of articles which are produced in India. But this duty applies to all imports. It is a fiscal duty, and not a protective duty. All that Free Trade demands is that duties should be imposed for revenue purposes and not for the purpose of protecting trade. The hon. Member for Cardiff complained, and I think very justly, that all this action of the Government was stimulated by the Colonial Office. That appeared to irritate the Secretary of State for India very much. But anyone who reads the Blue Book must admit that the statement is perfectly justified. I would recall the right hon. Gentleman's attention to what he said on that point. He stated that he was impressed by the proceedings of the Brussels Conference, and that immediately he saw the result of that Conference he entered into negotiations with India. When did the Conference take place? In June, 1898, and these dilatory proceedings were stretched out and nothing occurred till January. Yet the right hon. Gentleman wants us to believe that the stimulus for the action of the Government arose in Brussels in June. I will ask permission to refer to one or two of these despatches. He stated that he was writing on January 6th about this Brussels Conference, when he chanced to get a communication from the Colonial Office which he embodied in the letter he was sending. Then he used this strong statement :

"This is the first and all the communications from the Colonial Office upon this point."

I will ask the right hon. Gentleman to refer to page 30——

Lord G. HAMILTON: That preceded it.

*Mr. LOUGH : I am not referring to one which preceded it The right hon. Gentleman said that by chance he received a communication from the Colonial Office on the 6th January, and included it in the letter. I want him to refer to page 30 of the Blue Book, where it appears he sent a long telegram on the 24th January, in which these words occur: "Secretary of State for the Colonies" is "forwarding a petition in favour of countervailing duties." He is of opinion that Mauritius "is likely to be ruined, and requests that the memorial may be favourably considered." This was the second communication from the Colonial Office—one on the 6th January——

Lord G. HAMILTON: It is the same.

*Mr. LOUGH : I beg your pardon. Of course it is the same, the Colonial Secretary always says the same thing until it is carried out. That is the feature of him. That is where he differs from everybody else in the Ministry. My point is that what the Colonial Secretary said on the 6th January was, "Carry out these duties." What the Indian Secretary said was, "We never received any compulsion—no hints, no inducements—from the Colonial Office except on the 6th January." I produce this telegram on the 24th January, which shows that as late as that date the Colonial Secretary says, "What about my countervailing duties? Have you got them on yet?"

*Lord G. HAMILTON: The hont Gentleman must really read the Blue Book intelligently. That telegram is a summary of the despatch sent by me.

*Mr. LOUGH : Quite so ; that is my point. If it was a mere hint from the Colonial Secretary, a chance communication put in with another letter, there

would be no more about it, the Indian Secretary would leave his chance communication to arrive. He states that the telegram is a repetition of the whole despatch. Nothing of the kind. The telegram is bristling with the Colonial Office. On the 24th January the Colonial Secretary returned to the charge, and said, "How about these duties; have you tried to put them through?" That is not all. On the 24th February we have another telegram. (These telegrams are worth the attention of the House ; they are really most interesting.) It says: "My telegram of the 24th January ; desire to know if you propose to pass an Act this session imposing countervailing duties." Cannot the House trace the hand of the Colonial Secretary in this? He gives the order on the 6th January ; he repeats it by telegram on the 24th January ; he says on the 24th February, "I want your answer. Are you going to pass these countervailing duties?" That wakes up the Government of India. There are no dilatory proceedings now. They see the hand of the Colonial Secretary in it. On the 25th February they reply, "Your telegram of the 24th February. Sugar bounties. We propose to legislate at once on American model." Then there is another telegram from the Secretary for India: "Sugar duties. Suggested legislation approved by Her Majesty's Government." That is on the 1st March. I say that a great step in the legislation of a country was never taken more hurriedly than that. I think I have made good the argument of the hon. Member for Cardiff that the whole proceedings emanated from the Colonial Office. Now, I desire, for my own part, to express in a few words my opinion about these transactions. I consider this to be one of the most extraordinary Blue Books ever issued by a Government Department. We have no reliable statistics, no information. The first six or eight pages are filled with a letter from the firm of Begg, Dunlop, and Co., which is a mere Protectionist argument, such as we constantly receive from firms, not only in India, but in this country. But why on earth this communication should be set out in a Blue Book, on which important legislation of this kind is based, I cannot for a moment imagine. The Blue Book contains no argument whatever in favour of the strong step taken by the

Government, the motive of which I believe is the sturdy action of the Colonial Secretary to which I have referred. The Secretary for India stated that the agriculural prosperity of India mainly depended on sugar. That is a most extraordinary statement. There are about 250,000,000 acres in British India, only 2,500,000 of which are under sugar cultivation, some of which is a very low class of cultivation. Therefore I say that sugar is to a very slight extent indeed a staple product of India. The right hon. Gentleman might as well have said that cotton, tea, tobacco, or a dozen other articles were staples. The fact is that the right hon. Gentleman was bound to find arguments, and his whole speech is full of efforts to find arguments to justify the policy which was inaugurated by the Colonial Secretary. I would like to consider for a moment the inspiration that is at the back of the Colonial Secretary in this matter. He is thinking of what he calls the Colonies. What colonies? The West Indies and Mauritius. These are hardly colonies at all; they are not places in which a European population can live healthily. They are really the most unimportant colonies the Empire has, and the prosperity of these colonies may be sought at too great an expense to the rest of the Empire. He has told us that the staple trade of the West Indies has suffered greatly, and that Mauritius is likely to be ruined. I do not understand that statement. We have no statistics from the Indian Secretary to prove that Mauritius has suffered in any respect. The exports from Mauritius in 1898 were larger than in any other year, with perhaps one exception. Therefore up to the present the sugar trade of Mauritius has suffered in no way whatever. But suppose it did suffer. The Colonial Secretary appears to think that we can enjoy the advantages of a Free Trade policy without having any disadvantages. This is the flaw in the position which he takes up in this matter. We have to take the good and the bad both of Free Trade and of Protection, and to reject one or the other after taking all the circumstances in regard to each into consideration. Suppose when the Free Trade policy was introduced in this country we had had a strong Minister like the Colonial Secretary, who would look at the matter from the same standpoint. Think of all the stories that might

Mr. Lough.

have been told of the suffering caused to British agriculture. Did this House pause because British agriculture suffered? No. This House looked at the matter broadly, and said, " We cannot consider the interests of a class; we must consider the interests of the whole nation, and looking at the interests of the whole nation the Free Trade policy is the best we can adopt." I will give one other example. Look at how Ireland suffered by the introduction of the Free Trade policy. The argument of the Indian Secretary appears to be that the production of sugar may be destroyed in India. Has not the production of flour, meal, and, in fact, all the staple products of Ireland been destroyed within the last 50 years? The House has warmed its hands at the blaze which has burned up all Irish industries; yet this House has gone on steadily in the policy because it believed that, on the whole, the policy of Free Trade conferred greater benefit than it inflicted injury. Take the Indian case from the same standpoint. The one argument of the Indian Secretary was that these imports are increasing rapidly. The meaning of that is that the Indian people are welcoming what these other countries are sending. Is not that the best proof that the Indians want it, and that the continuance of this influx of bounty-fed sugar would be a great benefit to the general population of India? There is a statement in the Blue Book that the poor in India do not consume sugar, but I believe that that statement will not stand examination. The consumption of sugar is increasing as rapidly there—perhaps more rapidly—as in most other countries, and the rapid growth of these very imports proves that there are a great many people there who want it, and that a great blow will be struck at the growing industries of the country by the adoption of the policy which the Government has taken up. A great deal has been said about these bounty-giving countries. We cannot hit them; we cannot touch them; we cannot do them any harm. The only people on whom we can lay any burden with regard to this legislation is the people of India. They want something; we refuse to give it to them. They are building up industries in confectionery and so on, just as such industries have grown up in this country, through cheap sugar. We destroy those industries. It has not been denied that cheap sugar confers considerable benefits, but the argument of the Indian Secretary is that it is an illegitimate benefit. But if foreigners are willing to do something for us which is favourable to us, why should we not take the gifts the gods send ? Why be too particular in inquiring whether the most strictly moral and honourable principles have been pursued in their production ? If we did that in regard to all our commerce it would lead us into very considerable difficulties. Who made us a ruler or a judge as to what it may suit other nations to do ? We assume too readily that these bounties are based upon an entirely rotten foundation. I once had an opportunity of visiting one of these sugar factories on the Continent, in Russia, and I was greatly interested in it. I was told that this factory was kept by a Pole and a Jew, and that we must walk carefully through the works as we might be suspected of being spies. We saw production going on in every process, and I thought as I walked away from that factory that in the Caledonian Road in the East End we could buy that sugar at half the price that was paid at a village about half a mile from that factory. Do these people produce this sugar just for the love of the thing ? No, they do it because it pays them and it suits them ; they take the whole transaction broadly, and they find that the giving of these bounties answers their purpose extremely well. Does anybody think that they give us this cheap sugar just for the love of us ? I for one do not believe it, and I am willing to take the sugar as cheap as they can give it to us, for I assume these people know how to manage their own business, and the people in Austria, Germany, and France also know what they are doing. I believe our true policy is that which we have followed for forty or fifty years, and that is to take whatever advantage these countries offer to us without questioning their motives. This question cannot end where it stands to-day. The step which the Government has taken has been borrowed from America. That step is one of the greatest moment, for it threatens the fiscal policy which we have pursued in this country for the last fifty years. Why should we go to America for an ideal ? Have we not our own ideals established by Adam Smith, by Cobden, and by

Bright in this House ? Had we not many stormy debates here before we adopted the principle of Free Trade ? I was sorry to hear the language of the right hon. Gentleman when he spoke of the agitation in India against the policy of the Government. Had we not lively debates all over England before Free Trade was adopted ? And why should the people of India be blamed for carrying on the same discussion ? Such a policy deserves to be attacked just as much in India as in this country; but the point which I desire to make is that this policy which is being pursued in India cannot stay where it stands to-day. Why should we go to America, which is a Protectionist country, for any of our ideals ? We are a Free Trade country, and we should stick to a Free Trade policy and not allow the good heart of the Colonial Secretary to carry us away in this matter. If the right hon. Gentleman desires to prop up the industries of these colonies, he cannot prop them up by Protection. He must allow the winds of adversity to blow about these industries as they blow about all industries, and if they cannot stand against them they cannot stand at all. The Indian Secretary says that it is a great loss for trade to be disturbed from its old channels, but I say this is not so. It is very often a great gain for it to be disturbed, even when it is proceeding in legitimate channels. Was not the tea trade in China a legitimate channel for that trade to flow in, but does it flow in that channel now ? No, it flows in India and Ceylon now to the benefit of this Empire, and to the benefit of everybody who drinks tea. The policy of the Government is a most fallacious doctrine to lay down, for if you draw a ring fence round this industry what will be the effect ? It will be that production will decline, bad methods of manufacture will be protected, and the people will not enjoy those benefits which they otherwise would enjoy if free competition were allowed to play its part. I am extremely sorry to see that on such extremely flimsy pretexts as are laid down in this book, and advanced by the Indian Secretary, that such a great breach should be made in the Free Trade principles of this country.

SIR LEWIS McIVER (Edinburgh, W.): So far as I have been privileged to hear this Debate I have been chiefly

struck with the flimsiness of the attack
on the Government. Without substantial
basis it has been supported by only the
most strained special pleading, buttressed
by the most shadowy arguments, and
padded out by detached lectures on irrelevant subjects. The right hon. Member
for Wolverhampton gave us three most
interesting and detached lectures—one on
the constitution of the Indian Legislature
—very attractive, and to me very welcome as an old friend. Then a second, in
an analysis of the Blue Book. Finally a
dear old friend, the elementary lecture on
Free Trade principles. The hon. Member
for Cardiff followed with a disquisition on
the shortcomings of the Colonial Secretary ; a sweet contribution on the " uses
of adversity," or the blessings of foreign
competition ; and a second edition of the
Free Trade lecture. But very little from
either in support of the motion before the
House. I am not trying to blame the
right hon. Member for Wolverhampton.
He is only an instrument fulfilling a constitutional *rôle*, giving the countenance
of the front bench to the motion, and is
too good for the job. The putative,
the admitted, engineer of the Debate
is the second speaker and lecturer.
It has always seemed to me, Mr. Speaker,
that it would make for our comfort, and
certainly for the speedier despatch of
public business, if the deadly iteration,
within this Chamber, of a well-known
elementary lecture on political economy
—certain familiar parts of which we have
had over again to-night—were invariably
to be ruled out of order from your chair.
It has been printed as often in *Hansard*—
not to mention the local papers—that we
might with advantage have a Sessional
Order to the effect that a copy of it be
laid upon the Table. We all know it by
heart. To the original lecture itself—
the venerable classic of fifty years' standing—I take no objection. It is all true,
none of it is new, and a good deal of it
doesn't signify. But of the modern emen-
dations and glosses without authority—the
amateur and discordant variations inter-
polated in the old score—this can hardly
be said. They may be new, but they are
rarely true. In practical politics these
performances are either out of date
or out of tune. They are not wanted.
We are all Free Traders to-day, and
don't need converting. Of course there
is a gamut of degree in the fervour
of Free Traders. So there is in the

Sir Lewis McIver.

zeal of Christians. The vast majority,
in both cases, take their creed quietly—
with an unmoving and uninquiring
acquiescence, rather than with any very
militant quality of active faith. At
one pole you have the doubters and
the waverers, at the other are the
bigots and zealots and fanatics. In the
economic school these are represented by
the dervishes and fakirs of the Cobden
Club, with whom the identity of two
oblate spheroids, the terrestrial globe
and Bastiat's orange—is a postulate, and
settles the whole question. I hope the
House will understand that I am not
referring to the great bulk of the
members of the Cobden Club, who take a
rational view of Free Trade, but to that
self-appointed priesthood which poses as
the club and takes its name in vain—
those cotton-gloved ghazis of Manchester,
to whom the blessed word " consumer"
is as comforting and conclusive as the
name of Mesopotamia was to another
group of worthy old ladies. To them
Free Trade is a Divine revelation, not to
be understanded of the vulgar. The words
of its Early Fathers are inspired words—
even including, I suppose, some of their
still unfulfilled prophecies. The Book of
the Law and the exclusive gift of authoritative exposition are in the hands of an
inner circle of Lamas, and their extreme
interpretations are of universal application—in all countries, in all circumstances, and in all times. This is esoteric
Free Trade, which, logically translated
into workaday life, would mean very little
trade and practically no freedom. But all
this is as far removed from the business
Free Trade notions of the general
public in this country as is the theoretic
Buddhism of Lhasa from the working
religion of the Singalese coolie or the
Burman boatman ; and this separation—
this growing divergence between the
preachers and the people, between
clerics and the laity—is fraught with
danger to the Free Trade connection. It
creates a situation pregnant with schism
and revolt. Theoretically, with the
Buddhist, to destroy life is a crime ;
ergo, all good Buddhists must be vege-
tarians. And are they ? Not much.
They don't kill cows ; but they keep a
Mohammedan butcher in nearly every
village, and the simple-minded Burman is
a connoisseur of beefsteaks. Buddhism
is still the creed of Ceylon and Burma—
because it suits the people, I suppose.

But if the attempt were made to force the extreme theory of the creed into practice, there would be more trouble in Burma than we have ever yet encountered in that difficult country. And that is precisely the sort of result I fear from the aggressive assertion of that extreme purism of which the right hon. Member is the mouthpiece to-day. As a sincere Free Trader, I am more afraid of the mulish indiscretions of the doctrinaire Free Trader than of the arguments of the professed Protectionist. I am satisfied that at this moment in the blind zeal of the Free Trade fanatic lies more danger to the continuity of our national economic policy than in all outside attack from whatever direction. This country is a Free Trade country. Its inhabitants are mostly professed Free Traders. Just as this is a Christian country and its inhabitants are mostly professed Protestants—and for much the same reason in both cases. We are mostly Protestants and Free Traders because our fathers were. The majority have never inquired much further in either case, but from their childhood have accepted both conditions contentedly. But of those who have even superficially studied the economic question, who have examined the grounds of the faith that is in them, nine out of ten would say that they are Free Traders because they recognise that Free Trade has done wonders for this country in the past, that Free Trade is probably doing pretty well for this country in the present, and because they hope it may continue to satisfy our wants in the future. They like things cheap, if they are not also nasty. They dislike Customs worries— and, on the whole, it might be a dangerous thing to get tinkering with good old Free Trade. That, I take it, is about the average view. It is a practical and strictly mundane view, and very remote from the sacrosanct aspect which the Ritualist—the Manchester Mahatma— insists on presenting. The average Britisher does not take his Free Trade as a Divine revelation, or even credit its doctrines with the permanent infallibility of a mathematical truth. No, Sir, we accept Free Trade for ourselves in a sober, businesslike spirit, because, on balance, it profits the nation, and for so long as it profits the nation. I repeat, it is this arrogant intolerance that jeopardises the fair fame of Free Trade, and gives a handle to the prophets of Protection. It is speech and action like that of to-day that gives real Free Traders cause for new alarm ; and already we have sufficient ground for disquietude. The House must remember that, although the vast majority of people in this country accept our Free Trade system as the best on balance for this country, there have been, from time to time—there are to-day —parts of the country and communities in the country who, for special reasons, do not accept the validity of Free Trade claims with anything like whole-souled enthusiasm. Roughly speaking, our general view of Free Trade is the free exchange of commodities at natural prices ; but the bounty system is a direct and gross violation of that view, and should be met in the gate. I may be told that foreign tariffs are a violation of Free Trade. Well, Mr. Speaker, so they are ; but that is another story. Primarily a tariff is a fiscal matter, and each country is surely entitled to say how it shall raise its necessary revenue. It is exclusively a Government matter, and the legitimate business of a Government. On the other hand, first and last, a bounty is a trade matter, and means that a Government, departing from its primary and, as I view it, legitimate. attitude, gives its support and its money to bolster up a particular trade in competition with the trade of other countries. That, according to my view, is not a justifiable attitude for a Government. And what we contend is that the Government of a country which believes in, and adheres to, Free Trade principles, is bound to take the strongest available measures to neutralise the effect of this illegitimate interference with Free Trade. The hostile tariffs of foreign nations are their affair, their bounties are very largely our affair. Let them protect their interests as much as they like within their own territories ; in most cases we still can tackle them and beat them even then ; and unless the hon. Member for Cardiff has his way, we shall continue to be able to stick to Free Trade and free imports. But when foreign countries transfer their action to inside our borders, when they insidiously attack our beloved doctrines on our own ground, and so shake the faith of the waverers, we are bound to strike back, if only to stiffen the backs of our own weaker brethren. I submit, Sir, that the bounty question is not an aspect of legitimate trade any more than Greek fire or explosive bullets are debatable subjects in the science of legitimate warfare. It belongs rather to the class of such questions as slave trading and piracy. It is an evil thing and an outrage which all honest nations should combine to suppress, to attack tooth and nail, to stamp out ruthlessly. I maintain that not merely in their interests, but in defence of Free Trade, we, as a Free Trade nation, should treat a bounty pirate as an honest citizen would treat an armed burglar in his bedroom—as an honest farmer would treat a dog addicted to sheep-worrying—shoot on sight, and ask questions afterwards. But, Sir, it is a notorious fact that the bounties which the so-called Free Traders are so anxious to maintain—so determined shall be untouched—are on their last legs. We know that most of the bounty-giving countries are sick of the ghastly, futile expenditure which has only led to an unnatural over-production, that they would welcome any tangible excuse for giving them up; and that, any such excuse once given, the other bounty-giving countries would have to fall into line—would have to follow suit. Everybody except Protectionists of this or that industry denounces bounties. What keeps them going still? One thing and one thing alone—the virginal prudery of the Cobden Club. That, Mr. Speaker, is how extremes meet. In the speech of the hon. Member Free Trade and Protection are for the first time running in double harness. In order to protect some sugar importers in India—or, if you transfer the matter home, in order to protect and increase the profits of certain confectionery and jam industries in this country—it is desirable that the bounty system should be maintained. I do not say that that is his object; but that is what practically he is advocating. I do not say the hon. Member is consciously a Protectionist. I do not suggest that evil communications on that bench below the gangway have so far corrupted the purity of his creed—but, all the same, he is fighting the Protectionist battle. Does he approve of bounties? Are they consistent with his Free Trade creed? Does he desire their maintenance? Well, but what is he doing? He knows they are the most flagrant outrage on Free Trade, and he knows that one word from this Government—the mere threat of countervailing duties—would put an end to

Sir Lewis McIver.

bounties without one sixpence of the countervailing duty even being collected, and yet he forbids that word being spoken. "Under which king, Bezonian?" Is that a blow for Free Trade, or for Protection? Whatever the intentions or the beliefs of the hon. Member may be, the whole body of support which he and his doctrinaire associates have behind them in this country on this question is a Protectionist agitation. The only representations from outside which Members of this House have received on the subject have been appeals to do nothing to interfere with bounties, because they bolster a particular trade. And we practical Free Traders—the real Free Traders—in defending Free Trade, in seeking to strike a blow for Free Trade principles, and to get rid of the shackles on Free Trade imposed by this piratical bounty system, find ourselves confronted, not as usual by the right hon. Member for Thanet and the hon. and gallant Member for Sheffield, but by the hon. Member for Cardiff. Sir, if the views for which I have been contending be true, viz., that, if our economic policy is to be maintained on its present sound and profitable lines, that desirable end can only be secured by the frank recognition of the present danger in which it stands, owing to the heretical extravagances of the zealots, by the recognition of the fact that in our national business Free Trade is a commercial, not an academic, policy, and is to be guided by practical principles, not by purblind pedantry—I say, if that view is of force when stated generally, and as applied to the United Kingdom and to our Crown colonies, it is doubly and trebly true when applied to India. When it comes to dealing with India, its revenue, its interests, its welfare, the House has to remember that we are dealing, not with our own property but with one for which we are trustees; and as the House knows, the action of trustees is very properly subject to strict limitations. We cannot deal with the property of our *cestui que trusts* as fancy dictates. We cannot sell it out at pleasure, and reinvest it in wild-cat stock, like Cobden Club debentures. In our trusteeship for India we are bound by equitable considerations, by obligations of honour, and by the solemn and formal declarations of the proclamation of 1859—so often repeated and expanded—to govern India for the Indians, in the interests of India, and, so far as possible, in harmony with the ideas of the people of India. With regard to the interests of the people of India, this House must recollect that the revenue of India is not the revenue of this country. It belongs to the people of India, to be employed for their benefit according to the judgment of experts on the spot. We have been informed to-day that the sugar bounty system is injuring the revenue of India. The different ways in which this happens, and the extent to which it happens, has been told to us in full and authoritative detail by the noble Lord who sits below me. For my part, I am content to take the fact on authority. Whether the loss is chiefly by direct injury to certain trades, or by the cultivation of sugar proving unprofitable, with the consequence that land falls out of cultivation, the fact remains that there is a loss of revenue and primarily, let me say, a loss of land revenue; and the extent of the area thus thrown out of cultivation is a detail. If a single acre has fallen out of cultivation from this unholy cause, we, as trustees for India, are bound to see to it. And for this reason: there is a loss of land revenue; that loss has to be made up, and by whom? By some other wretched cultivator who has already only a thin paper partition between himself and starvation—

"His life is a long-drawn question
Betwixt a crop and a crop,"

and it is our business to see that the question is not made more difficult for him to solve than is avoidable. Again, I will not deal with sugar refining in India, for with that also the Secretary of State has dealt. It is a young industry, and the hon. Member for Cardiff will probably comfort himself with the reflection that babies generally die quite easily and painlessly. In the same way he is, naturally, too humane a man to derive any pleasure from the death-struggles of that industry even in this country. He has possibly consoled himself for the sufferings and losses of the sugar refiners and their workmen and their families with statistics proving that those losses have meant gain to other people. We all know those crusted old figures by heart. It is pointed out triumphantly that if so many thousand odd men in a particular locality were thrown out of work at sugar refining, so many more thousand—probably three or four times as many—men,

women, and children in another locality have been employed in making jam and confectionery. It is something, but it doesn't prove the whole case, to my mind, and it certainly seems a trifle hard on the first group. But, can the hon. Member point to any similar compensation in India? Have the sugar bounties increased the manufacture of lollipops in India? Have they led to any new source of revenue? Have they encouraged any new cultivation? Have they removed the necessity for any new taxation? Has the hon. Member been able to show that, in any one respect, the sugar bounties have benefited India, or that the action of the Government of India in this matter is not in the interests of the people of India, and therefore in redemption of our national pledge to that people? So much, then, for the interests of India. With regard to our Government in India being in harmony with Indian ideas, in harmony with what, so far as can be ascertained, are the wishes of the people of India, the hon. Member for Cardiff has been posing this afternoon as the Voice of India—the fog-horn of mute millions—and has modestly suggested that, in his opinion, the opinion of the people of India is necessarily his opinion; or, conversely, his opinion is necessarily the opinion of the people of India. He claimed recently in public to be a devout reader of newspapers, and as a result of his reading—not a direct result, but after some unknown process of assimilation—he has arrived at a concrete Indian public opinion opposed to the action of the Government of India. How far it is an authorised version of public opinion the House must judge for itself. I will offer the House some material for judging. There are in India 586 newspapers and periodicals, English and vernacular. How many of these has the hon. Member, after weeks of inquiry, been able to press into his service? What is the real fact about the Indian Press? Probably never in the history of that Press has there been so marvellous a case of whole-souled, passionate unanimity in favour of a measure; and European and native papers have vied with one another in extolling its wisdom and justice—its necessity, its statesmanship. From the *Pioneer* and the *Englishman,* from the *Madras Mail* and notably from the *Bombay Gazette,* the *Hindoo Patriot,* the *Amrita Bazaar Patrika,* and all the established

2 Y 2

and reputable Press there is but one voice. I do not say that is conclusive of Indian opinion ; but it is a more than average indication. There are in India 757 municipal councils, containing a large representative element of natives, elected by popular suffrage. There are 730 district or county councils, similarly equipped. There are seven legislative councils, where the flower of native intellect and ability find seats. From which of these bodies — representative and elective as most of them are—does the hon. Member produce, I will not say a memorial or a petition, but even a single word of protest against the action of the Government of India ? Then there is that august body the Indian Congress, which discusses Imperial problems with as much avidity, and as little knowledge, as certain county councils that we wot of. Has the Indian Congress been stirred to its depths ? Has it rushed to the support of the hon. Member ? I don't know that the Government of India would have been much dismayed if it had ; but, as a matter of fact, nothing of the sort has happened. Then, Sir, we must take it from the hon. Member for Cardiff that the existing outlets for the sentiments of the mute millions are, according to the hon. Member for Cardiff, a negligable quantity ; neither the native Press nor the native representatives are to be counted. Well, Sir, we must turn to the European residents in India not connected with the Government. The hon. Member puts out of court those who are interested in sugar refining; they are damned by their private, selfish interests. Well, I don't mind ; but then, to make things equal, we must in the same way damn the other group of selfish interests, the sugar importers of Bombay and Kurrachee, who are the hon. Member's sole clients. They are the whole question, according to the hon Member. They are the voice of India. They are Free Trade. The logic is perfect. One group of the native refiners is not to be heard because it has selfish interests. The other—a handful of European merchants—are the voice of India, because they have selfish interests. No ; I think the two groups will have to be paired—the sugar importers with the sugar refiners ; and exit the voice of India. Leaving out sugar refiners and sugar importers, you have a whole mass of non-official Anglo-Indian opinion passionately in favour of the measure.

Sir Lewis McIver.

There is yet another recognised voice of India. To my mind, the truest and most indisputable representatives of the interests of the people of India are the executive officers of the administration of India—the District Officers of all the services and all the departments, who pass their lives among the people, and who know their needs and wants better than anyone else does. I do not say that the Indian civilian is devoid of prejudice on this or that subject, that he may not have a fad about revenue settlement or a theory about cholera germs ; but in a question of this sort, as to what are the wishes or interests of the people of India, the Indian official is not only the best, the most trustworthy, but the only real authority, and, almost to a man, the District Officers have approved of the measure. Lastly, you have the responsible Government of India, commanding, at first hand, every channel of information and competent advice, deliberately introducing this measure, supported by the whole mass of Indian opinion, official and non-official, British and native, by the entire Press, English and vernacular ; and against all this, as representing the voice of India, you have the hon. Member for Cardiff supported by the Peculiar People section of the Cobden Club and a handful of sugar importers in Bombay. As the House will recognise, long as I have been, with many of the cogent Indian arguments germane to the Government case I have not dealt at all. The 3,000,000 acres under sugar cane whose cultivation is in peril ; the millions of palm trees in southern India exporting half a million cwts. of sugar annually, whose usefulness may disappear ; the scores or hundreds of native refineries closed or closing ; the loss of land revenue ; the interests of some hundred thousands of natives of India, fellow subjects who earn their living in Mauritius—with none of these have I dealt. My object has been, first, as a Free Trader, to protest against the heresies promulgated by the right hon. Gentlemen, and publicly to dissociate myself from a sort of literary forgery which seeks to father on Richard Cobden a pernicious dogma for which nothing in his works written or spoken, affords a sanction. Secondly, to disavow the childish doctrine which the world's experience disproves, that what has been, and I hope will continue to be, good for the country would have been, or necessarily is, good for other countries differently circumstanced. And, thirdly, to protest against a wanton trifling with the interests of India and its 300 millions of people—whose trustees we are—in deference to the extravagant theories of a handful of doctrinaires in this country. Finally, I would invite the House to take stock of the hollowness and the unreality of the attack on the Government, of the irrelevance of the arguments employed, to the real ground and cause of this onslaught. I ask the House to realise seriously that all these proposals have been presented to it, that this much-laboured controversy, this long-advertised Debate, has been thrust upon it, not because sacred doctrines are in danger, not because the interests of India are imperilled, but because the hon. Member for Cardiff, like the President of the Transvaal, does not care much for the Secretary of State for the Colonies.

MR. W. H. HOLLAND : I should like to express my delight with the poetry and imagination of the previous speaker (Sir L. McIver), but I am sorry to say that I cannot agree with the fiscal views which he expressed. I feel as though I am in a unique position in the House in regard to this question, because it happened to be my lot during the last few months to pass through a bye election, and in my address I specifically alluded to the question of countervailing duties, and to an Imperial Zolverein, and I declared myself in favour of Free Trade, on the ground that I believe it to be the best policy to pursue, entirely independent of any course any other nation might undertake, and I am against an Imperial Zolverein and countervailing duties. These views were endorsed by my constituents by a large majority; therefore, I think I have a mandate from them to support the views I gave expression to during the campaign. I observe that the Secretary of State for India claimed that, as the House of Commons had never challenged the instructions to the Berlin Conference, they might be taken as approving those instructions. I do not see why the House should have been expected to disapprove of them, for those instructions expressly disclaimed all idea of imposition of countervailing duties. I also respectfully demur to the statement of the Secretary

of State for India that Free Trade seeks as its chief object to secure equality of opportunity to traders if opportunities were equally bad. It did not seek to secure equality of opportunity, but it seeks to secure it under most favourable conditions, and we, the Free Traders, believe that those conditions are most favourable which are most free. I noticed that the Secretary of State for India thought it worth his while to criticise duties that were imposed by his predecessor at the India Office. He did so on the ground that they were protective in character, but he seemed to overlook entirely the fact that such duties as would otherwise be protective in their character were countervailed by the Excise, and therefore could not be described as protective. I do not think that it lies in the mouth of the Secretary of State for India to twit his predecessor in regard to these duties, because we who come from Lancashire recollect very well that on the eve of the last General Election a removal of these duties was promised, and directly the election was over the Secretary for India went out of his way to justify the action which his predecessor had taken with regard to them. I think he may be excused for expressing his views somewhat strongly in regard to these duties, because he was victimised at the last General Election, because it was by standing by the then Secretary of State for India and voting for him that he suffered at the General Election. I think it was a little unreasonable on the part of the Secretary of State to denounce the Manchester Chamber of Commerce for sticking to its principles of Free Trade. The Secretary of State for India considered that the Manchester Chamber of Commerce ought to be ashamed of itself for passing the resolution it did the other day. Well, I have read this resolution very carefully, and I was present at the meeting, and that resolution was so entirely in harmony with the policy of the Manchester Chamber of Commerce that I do not think that Chamber had anything whatever to be ashamed of. Indeed, I noticed that it was supported by Conservatives as well as Liberals. I feel that those on the Liberal benches, at any rate, need not concern themselves to defend the question of the giving of bounties, because, for the most part, they would never attempt to give them, holding that all bounties are bad in principle. We in this country, and our fellow subjects in India, have been recipients of the advantages of bounties, and it is not the recipients whose province it is to complain, it is the men who pay the bounties who ought to complain; and it is no wonder that the countries at this time who have saddled themselves with these bounties are now groaning under the burden. Bounties are admitted to be blunders, and hence we find that Germany, Austria, Belgium, and Holland are all willing to abolish them if France will do the same. In the case of France, although she is unwilling to abolish them, we find she is reducing them. I find in the report lately issued that the bounties on exports were reduced in 1898 to the extent of 30 per cent. That reduction was not made for the purpose of pleasing us, but because the authorities of France recognise that these bounties are an evil to themselves. When these bounty-giving nations realise the very great burdens they are imposing on themselves I think then, and not till then, they will abandon them. It was clearly recognised at the Brussels Conference that the bounty system was an evil. What did our Commissioners say in their report on the Conference? They said, "The bounty system is now felt to press heavily on the economical resources of those States which have recourse to it." Accordingly, without the help of countervailing duties, I think it is quite clear that the attention of these nations has been called to the bounty system in a very effective way, and that being so it is not likely to last very much longer. What would be the attitude of the iron and steel industries if foreign countries turned their attention to them and extended bounties to them? That is not in the least likely, because it would be a great deal too expensive. The amount already contributed in the case of sugar by these countries is large, but in such important industries as that of iron and steel the amount would be unsupportable indeed. I think it is hard for us to wax indignant about bounties when our working classes benefit by them to the extent of 2¾ millions a year, and while a cottager here can get his sugar at 2d. or 2½d. a pound a cottager in France has to pay 6d. I think that the Blue Book which has recently been published has entirely failed to justify the proposal of the Government. The words of Sir James Westland which were quoted

Mr. W. H. Holland.

by the right hon. Gentleman the Member for Wolverhampton—"I am proposing to open an entirely new chapter in our fiscal history"—practically amount to a fiscal revolution, and I think the House will agree that the *onus probandi* lies at least with those making this proposal. Has a good case been made out in the opinion of this House? In my opinion there never was such a flimsy case. If these countervailing duties had been demanded evidently and clearly by the public opinion of India I am bound to say I should have hesitated before I said a word against them. But nearly every page in the Blue Book shows exactly the contrary. The Blue Book testifies that this policy was hatched in the Colonial Office and forced upon India. The official mind in India knew what was the opinion of the India Office, and it would be very hard indeed to expect an official called upon to report to run counter to the expressed opinion of the India Office. I think it is clear from a perusal of the Blue Book that opinion in India on the present occasion is a manufactured opinion, and there is nothing easier than to manufacture opinion in favour of Protection. Once admit that you are prepared to open the door for the protection of an industry, and it is the easiest thing in the world to make out a case for it. It is easy in India, and it would be easy in this country. India is all the more ready to embark on a policy of retaliation with a light heart, for, unlike this country, she knows nothing of that long and bitter struggle which took place fifty years ago, and which resulted in the triumph of Free Trade principles. Those who will benefit by these countervailing duties are comparatively few in number, and are more or less organised, and to that extent they are able to make their voices heard. But, on the contrary, those who will be penalised by them are the masses of the people, whose voices are dumb, but who are nevertheless entitled to have their views given expression to in this House. Every Member of the House who knows anything of the industries of India knows there are many industries in which sugar stands in the relation of raw material, and it is an axiom of the successful trader that he must be able to buy his raw material in the cheapest market. Is this policy entirely fair to other industries of India? Sugar is not the most important crop in India by any means, and one would imagine that a sense of proportion would give increased prominence to other crops. Nor has the sugar industry suffered the most. We find that the acreage under pulse has declined by 7¼ per cent., and is cultivated over 78,000,000 acres. Rice has reduced 4 per cent., oilseed 18 per cent., wheat 12½ per cent., and sugar only 10 per cent., so that there are other crops in which there has been a more serious diminution of acreage that in the case of sugar. We are told that the refiner in India wants protection, but what manufacturer does not want protection if he can get it ? But whether he needs protection is a much more pertinent question. We have a report in the Blue Book from the North-West Provinces which states that the average profit of sugar refiners has been 10 per cent. I am quite sure there are a good many cotton mills in Bombay who do not earn 10 per cent. over a series of years. Other industries can be found in which the need is greater than the need of the sugar refiners. In the opinion of many people it would be ten thousand times better for sugar refiners to improve their methods, both as regards appliances and the quality of the cane itself, rather than to rely on the advantage of counter-vailing duties. In France very greatly improved machinery has been adopted during the last ten years. From a return furnished a short time ago I find that in sixteen years the number of factories in France has been reduced by 29 per cent., the number of workers in French refineries by 25 per cent., less beet is used and rather less coal, and yet not-withstanding the diminution in all these respects more sugar is being turned out every year. The Indian refiners have already the advantage of a protection of 5 per cent. imposed as import duty. They have that protection against Mauritius and Europe, but they are not satisfied with that advantage. After an extended experience I have never found a pro-tected industry to be satisfied with the amount of protection it obtained. The levying of countervailing duties will yield very little indeed to the Indian revenue, but the consumer will be heavily penalised, because it is not unreasonable to expect an enhancement not only in the price of sugar in India but also in the price of other productions. It is also sought to justify these countervailing

duties because of the condition of Mauritius. But I think that the case of Mauritius was completely given away by the Report issued a short time ago, which showed that there was no injury inflicted on the sugar refining industry, but that on the contrary the exports into India were greater in weight during the eleven months ending December, 1898, than ever they had been before during any preceding twelve months. And in point of value that year was one of the best Mauritius ever had. I notice that Mauritius asks not only for the advantages of the countervailing duties, but also for the remission of the 5 per cent. customs duty. That only shows that Mauritius, like the rest of us, naturally wants to have as much as it can get. The countervailing duties are really not in the interest of Free Trade. I notice they are very strongly supported by the hon. Member for Central Sheffield. I do not think that is a very strong argument that they are favourable to Free Trade, because I am quite sure the hon. Member is not a great lover of Free Trade. Import duties must be for revenue or protection. These duties cannot be for revenue—because the amount is small, and the Indian Revenue does not need assistance at present—but they are for protection. Countervailing duties are as far removed from Free Trade as it is possible for any duty to be, and their effect is exactly opposite to the effect looked for in Free Trade. Their effect will be to restrict international trade, and to raise prices to the consumer, evils which, in the first instance, Free Trade was designed to combat. I think we will all agree that if we restrict inter-national trade we will be impairing inter-national goodwill, and to that extent we will be undoing the work now in progress at the Hague, which, we trust, will be beneficent in its result. By the passing of such legislation we are inflicting a lasting injury on Free Trade, because it suggests to Protectionist countries that there is something inherently weak in Free Trade which can only be combated by countervailing duties, and we thereby postpone the adoption of Free Trade else-where. I think the policy of retaliation which is now recommended by the Govern-ment is childish in the extreme. I deny that by any such legislation we can help Free Trade. I think, on the contrary, Free Trade is helped much more really by the spectacle of a great and prosperous people—the greatest trading nation in the world—standing unflinchingly by Free Trade as by a sheet anchor ; a nation increasing the number of its works, and paying better wages to its workers. That is a spectacle which is likely to be an object lesson to other nations of the earth, and which must ultimately have effect.

*MR. WYLIE (Dumbartonshire) : I had given notice of an Amendment to the Motion of the right hon. Gentleman the Member for Wolverhampton to the effect that—

"In the interests of India and of Free Trade throughout the world this House approves of the Indian Tariff Act, 1899,"

but in deference to the request of my noble friend the Secretary of State for India I do not propose to move it. Speaking in support of a direct negative, I hope, however, to be able to show that this Tariff Act is not only in the interests of India but also of Free Trade. I will begin by saying that I am a thorough supporter of Free Trade in its widest sense. With Ruskin I would like to see trade amongst the nations as frank and free as honesty and the sea winds can make it, and I also accept his definition of Protection, that (among other pernicious functions) it endeavours to enable one country to compete with another in the production of an article at a disadvantage. Now in the pro duction of sugar the radical question at present is whether European countries with beet for the source of production or tropical countries with cane can produce sugar better or cheaper. On this ground there need be no dubiety whatever. Statistics show that the advantage is altogether with the tropical countries. Mr. Martineau, who gives a series of very exhaustive tables of statistics in connection with sugar manufac ture, has come to the conclusion that, speaking generally, the production of beet sugar in Europe costs consider- ably more than £10 per ton, and of cane considerably less than £9 per ton, and it should be remembered that beet sugar has been enormously sub sidised by State protection, ingeniously employed so as to diminish the cost of production, while cane sugar has been subjected to the benumbing influence of a system which has repelled capital,

Mr. W. H. Holland.

because no capitalist will invest money in the production of cane sugar when bounties may crush the industry out altogether. Speaking generally, there fore, if a Free Trade and natural policy prevailed, tropical countries would send to Europe their supplies of sugar and receive in return manufactured articles which Europe is much better able to supply. Under these circumstances the general supporters of Free Trade would say of sugar, as Cobden said of corn :

"We do not seek Free Trade for sugar primarily because we wish to obtain it at a cheaper money value, but because we require it at the natural price of the world's markets."

This, then, is the general aspect of the question from the genuine Free Trade point of view. But several countries of Europe, notably France and Germany, have entered upon a gigantic system of protection, fostering sugar by enormous subsidies at the expense of their other industries : taking large tracts of culti vated land in Europe which might be much better applied to other purposes, and rendering desolate and uncultivated vast tracts in the tropics which are much better fitted for its production. But it may be asked what advantage has the British Empire derived from this protection, maintained at so much cost and sacrifice by Continental countries. The only advantage that can certainly be asserted is that we have got cheaper sugar. The assertion that the jam and confec tionery trades have been created by it is a gross exaggeration. The disadvantages not at first apparent more than counter balances any advantage that may be obtained. It has supplanted a great deal of our more nutritious products, and it has almost destroyed the sugar industry of the West Indies ; the sugar refining industry and manufacture of sugar refining ma chinery in this country. Upon a large body of working men throughout the country— in London, Liverpool, and Bristol, and particularly in Greenock, the chief centre of the sugar refining industry—it has acted with a peculiarly baneful effect. No other country in the world would have stood quietly by and seen its flourishing colonies and successful industries crushed out by an iniquitous system of protection when it had the means ready at hand to prevent it. The same process has begun in India, and the very same arguments and assertions are being applied to India as were applied in connection with the West Indies for more than twenty years, until they were proved to be utterly fallacious and misleading by the inexorable logic of disastrous experience. Now, let us examine the case of India in the light of this experience. The sugar industry of India is one of its most prominent and profitable industries. It covers three million acres, and in the language of the natives is to other tillage as the elephant is to other beasts. It employs two millions of inhabitants, and its annual produce is worth £20,000,000. This industry has been subjected to the baneful competition of protected sugar. In the year 1892-3 the importation of beet sugar amounted to about 285,000 cwts., and for the nine months ending December, 1897, it had increased to about 1,041,000 cwts., about four times that amount. And supposing the production of sugar in the East Indies were rendered as difficult as it has been in the West Indies, a very important industry would be crushed out of the country altogether. But the Government of India has wisely determined not to look quietly on, like the mother country, but has restored the balance to Free Trade by the simple expedient of imposing countervailing duties, In this country there are two classes who oppose countervailing duties The first class recognise the justice of countervailing duties, but they fear they will not stop until they end in a system of Protection altogether. But they may be assured that the principles of Free Trade are so thoroughly understood in this country that countervailing duties will not be pressed further than is necessary to restore an absolutely just balance. The other class believe that bounties benefit this country, and that it does not matter for anything else. Their sentiment is, "Perish the Indies, East and West, as long as we have cheaper sugar and more abundant confections." But the policy of countervailing duties is steadily commending itself to the common sense of this country. Ten years ago people would have been considered rank Protectionists who mentioned countervailing duties. Now, I am pleased to think, not only the Chamber of Commerce of Glasgow, but those of London, Liverpool, and other towns have stated clearly and distinctly that they are in favour of countervailing duties, in order to give this country a fair field and no favour. As a member of the Glasgow Chamber of Commerce, I am very glad to notice the growth of public opinion on this subject. Ten years ago a man who hinted at countervailing duties would have been considered a rank Protectionist. Now the general feeling of the community is in favour of these duties. I may state that countervailing duties have been very successfully imposed in the Cape of Good Hope and Australia, and with the further result that the Mauritius has been able to send to them the half of the production of 100,000 tons, the other half going to India, and that under this system of Free Trade these countries have been able to hold their own very successfully. They have not only supplied their own communities, but have been able to export a very considerable amount of sugar to other countries. The Mauritius has also been in the same position. India has been very fortunate in having at its seat of Government statesmen who have had the courage of their opinions. I congratulate the right hon. Gentleman the Secretary of State for India on having encouraged the Indian Government to take this step. He has wisely resolved that the interests of India shall not be sacrificed, as the interests of a large section of the trade of this country have been, by an iniquitous system of Protection. This step, which marks a new departure in the commercial policy of the British Empire, will enable India to retain a splendid industry within her domains. In approving of the action of the Government in taking this very drastic step, I venture to hope that we shall give our approval a wider significance than that which attaches to India merely.

*Sir CHARLES CAMERON (Glasgow, Bridgeton): I am glad to have the opportunity of taking part in this Debate, because I entirely agree with the action of the Government in this matter, and I should not like to give a vote against a five-line whip issued by my own front bench without showing that I had reasons for so doing. I have listened attentively to all the speeches which have been made, and especially the speech of the right hon. Gentleman the Member for Wolverhampton. What has struck me most in the course of the debate has been the absence of any reference to the ancient history of the question. Twenty years ago I supported the right hon. Gentleman the present President of the Board of Trade in moving for a Select Committee to inquire into the whole of our sugar industries and the best means of remedying their depression, and one of my arguments then was that for years one Government after another had been denouncing these bounties and had been taking every step in their power but the right one to get rid of them. The right hon. Gentleman the Member for Wolverhampton has twitted the members of the Indian Council with being no longer the disciples of various statesmen, and amongst others he mentioned Sir Stafford Northcote. It struck me, however, that in the course of the Debate on the motion for the appointment of a Select Committee Sir Stafford Northcote had expressed himself in a very different manner. I have the report of the Debate, and I find two expressions of Sir Stafford Northcote's opinion. One was a quotation made by the present President of the Board of Trade from a speech by Sir Stafford Northcote in reply to a deputation on the subject of the sugar bounties. This is what he said:

"He knew it had been said—sometimes he had seen it put strongly in the journals—that if foreign countries chose to pay bounties, or anything in the nature of bounties, on the sugar which they exported, and thereby supplied us with an article cheaper than it would otherwise be, we as a nation had nothing to do but to take advantage of their folly, and that we need not trouble ourselves as to the effect it had on this or that particular trade. He wished to say that he entirely dissented from that view. He did not think that we ought to comfort ourselves with arguments such as those. In general, he agreed in principle with what had been said by so many there present. He agreed with what had been so well said by Mr. Sampson Lloyd, that we ought not by any legislative enactment to interfere to prevent other countries making use of their natural advantages to supply us with the products which they could supply more advantageously than we could. But that principle did not apply to a case in which by legislative action on the part of a foreign Government, by any artificial action on their part, they could supply us with an article which, if things were left to their natural courses, we could supply as cheaply, or more cheaply, ourselves."

That was the teaching of Sir Stafford Northcote. Again Sir Stafford Northcote in the course of that Debate, answering the right hon Gentleman the present Member for Bodmin, said:

"The hon. Member for Liskeard (Mr Courtney) laid down the doctrine that we had

Sir Charles Cameron.

nothing to do with questions of that kind, and that the only principle which we were to go on was that we should buy in the cheapest market and sell in the dearest. If that is so, what are the hon. Member for Liskeard and the right hon. Gentleman the Member for the University of London to say of the conduct which the latter and his colleagues have been pursuing for so many years—namely, trying to prevent the country from buying in the cheapest market by endeavouring to induce the French and other Governments to put an end to a system of bounties which was apparently productive of advantage to this country?"

I do not wish to weary the House with quotations from Adam Smith and Ricardo; I will confine myself to one or two of the authorities quoted by the right hon. Gentleman the Member for Wolverhampton. Cobden was mentioned, but here is Cobden's teaching on the subject:

"We do not seek Free Trade in corn primarily for the purpose of purchasing it at a cheaper money rate; we require it at the natural price of the world's market; whether it becomes dearer with Free Trade, or whether it becomes cheaper it matters not to us, provided the people of this country have it at its natural price, and every source of supply is freely open as Nature and Nature's God intended it to be; then, and then only, shall we be satisfied."

Mr. Gladstone also was most emphatic on the subject, and I adhere to the teaching of Mr. Gladstone. What did Mr. Gladstone say in 1866 when he was speaking of the Sugar Convention of 1864 for the Abolition of Bounties? He said:

"Her Majesty's Government could not but perceive that that would be a beneficial arrangement, beneficial alike to importers, refiners, and consumers."

Returning to the matter in 1879, he wrote a letter which the right hon. Gentleman will find in the report of the Select Committee. It runs as follows:

"If, as I understand, the circumstances of the case continue unaltered I think that both the trader and the workman engaged in the business of refining sugar have great reason to complain My desire is that the British consumer should have both sugar and every other commodity at the lowest possible price at which it can be procured without arbitrary favour to any of those engaged in the competition; but I cannot regard with favour any cheapness which is produced by means of the concealed subsidies of a foreign State to a particular industry, and which has the effect of crippling and distressing capitalists and workmen engaged in a lawful branch of British trade."

And again :

"If they were bound to observe the principles of equity towards foreign countries, they were bound to observe the principles of equity towards their own subjects . . . . and not to suffer them to be crushed by the competition of those who were sustained by the long purse of a foreign Government."

These are the teachings of Mr. Gladstone, and they entirely endorse the step which is now being taken. I give the present Government great credit for having at last taken one effective step in this matter in one important part of the Empire. I intend to support them, because I think that this new bounty is giving practical effect to what has for forty years been the theoretical policy of successive Governments. Well, Sir, when the Select Committee was appointed it expressly denied that countervailing duties were any infraction of Free Trade. To quote the exact words of the Report, it was not "in any sense of the term Protection." If we asked for Protection, we should ask that the duty should be imposed against all imported sugar, whether in bounty-fed States or not. If we asked for reciprocity, we should ask that a duty should be imposed on the sugar of any State that imposed a duty on us. But we do not ask for anything of the sort. We say it is a capital thing to give bounties and to give as many bounties as you like; but we ask Government to intercept them for the benefit of the State, and prevent them being utilised for the purpose of crushing any particular industry. That, I think, is a legitimate step to take. The Select Committee would have recommended countervailing duties had it not been that evidence had been given by Mr. Kennedy that the imposition of countervailing duties would interfere with the most favoured nation clause in some of our treaties. Well, Sir, I don't believe it would. I have seen a most elaborate opinion of Mr. Sheldon Amos, a most eminent lawyer, pointing out that the exact contrary would be the effect. But the fact is, that the system of countervailing duties is already a characteristic of our fiscal arrangements. The Secretary of State for India mentioned the case of spirits, and read an article from the French Treaty which showed that they had been expressly imposed as a countervailing duty. But, Sir, that is not a solitary instance. I have in my hand a report of the Commission on Customs, and if any hon. Gentleman will take the trouble to look on pages 18 and 23 of that document he will be able to confirm what I say. Not only have you countervailing duties levied in the case of spirits, but also in the case of home manufactured tobacco as against foreign manufactured tobacco ; in the case of cigars manufactured in this country as against foreign manufactured cigars, and in the case of chicory as against imported chicory. But it may be said that all these are articles that bring in considerable sums to the Revenue. I want to show that these countervailing duties are imposed absolutely irrespective of any considerations of revenue. Let us take the case of chloroform. Chloroform and ether are anæsthetics which relieve an enormous amount of human suffering. If in anything it was desirable to have free trade surely it is desirable that you should have it in the case of chloroform, so that it may be supplied at the cheapest possible price for use in your hospitals and other institutions. But chloroform and ether require alcohol in their preparation, and these are articles which are enormously taxed. In the Cape, for instance, there is no tax on alcohol, and if you allowed free trade in these articles you would have chloroform and ether sent to this country in such a way as to cut out altogether home manufacture. You clap on 3s. 1d. per lb. on chloroform, and you clap on £1 6s. 2d. per gallon on sulphuric ether. Do you know what is got out of this surtax ? 3s. 1d. per lb. levied on imported chloroform brings in a gross revenue of £12 a year, and sulphuric ether at £1 6s. 2d. per gallon brings in a gross revenue of £7. Collodion is another article in the same position. You tax it to the extent of £1 0s. 5d. per gallon. That brings in £12 a year. Iodide of ethyl is taxed at the rate of 13s. 7d. per gallon, and does not bring in a halfpenny to the Revenue ; the duty, in fact, is absolutely prohibitive. Take an article in general use, namely, soap. Surely there can be no particular reason for taxing soap. Cleanliness is next to godliness, and it is most desirable that people in this country should have free choice of any soap that suits their taste or skin. Well, Sir, we levy a tax on transparent soap, in the manufacture of which spirit is used, of 3d. per lb. With what result ; That we get a gross revenue of £114. In confectionery in the manufacture of which spirit has been used we levy a countervailing duty of ½d. per lb. ; this brings in £488 a year. On confectionery containing not more than 50 per cent. of chocolate the amount brought into the Revenue is £59 a year. We levy another countervailing duty upon sweets in the manufacture of which chocolate and spirit have been used, which brings in £153 a year. Now, Sir, I have given a list of items which you will find in the Report of the Customs Commission, which abundantly proves that these countervailing duties are already part of our fiscal system and are levied by us altogether independently of revenue considerations. This country has been too long shilly-shallying in the matter, and "letting I dare not wait upon I would." At last the Government has taken a practical step. The right hon. Gentleman the President of the Board of Trade is one of the original apostles of the movement, and the right hon. Gentleman the Member for West Birmingham is a convert to it now; with such an array of anti-bounty men in the Government I am glad to see that they have at last put their hands to the plough in the case of India, and I trust that the example they have set with regard to that country will be followed by the adoption of something like a definite policy in our own country in order to put an end to a mischief which statesmen for the last 40 years have deplored and protested against.

MR. COURTNEY (Cornwall, Bodmin): At this time of night it is necessary to speak within rather strict limits, and I will, therefore, be as brief as possible. I have heard with a great deal of admiration the very able speech of my noble friend the Secretary of State for India. It had the merit, if I may say so, of being a resolute attempt to grapple with all the elements of the problem. It was a good, thorough argument, addressed to the action which the Government have taken, and if any good argument can prove the excellence of their conduct in instigating and supporting what has been done at Calcutta, my noble friend's speech ought to do it. He began by laying down the principle that bounties and protective duties are alike hostile to Free Trade. That they are both hostile to Free Trade I at once admit, but if the word "alike" means that they are hostile to Free Trade

in the same manner and to the same effect, I differ from my noble friend, and I will venture to say that it is from want of appreciation of the fundamental distinction between the operation of bounties and protective duties that my noble friend has failed in establishing the conclusion he submitted. Both bounties and protective duties do interfere with the natural course of trade; both are hostile to the principle of Free Trade, but they operate in a very distinct and different way. A bounty is something which the Government or nation paying it imposes upon itself, but other countries dealing with that nation in the commodity in respect of which the bounty is given are primarily benefited by it. A protective duty, on the other hand, fails entirely to benefit the country which imposes it or the country hit by it. It punishes both, whereas a bounty is a punishment on the country which imposes it and a benefit to all other countries. A good deal has been said to-night about our past experience. My hon. friend the Member for Bridgeton (Sir C. Cameron) congratulated the Government on having taken an action which, if it had been taken earlier in a similar and analogous manner, would have relieved us of much from which we have suffered. The hon. Member for Dumbarton proceeded in the same way to refer to the action of the past as having imposed losses upon this country. There are many reasons why we have attempted to get nations to do away with bounties; but the action in the past, to which the hon. Member for Dumbarton and the hon. Member for Bridgeton referred, so far from being a burden to this country, has been, in fact, primarily and principally a benefit to it. Anyone who fails to understand that this country has been benefited by the reception of cheap sugar altogether fails to understand the theory of Free Trade. My hon. and gallant friend the Member for Sheffield is strongly opposed to Free Trade in every fashion.

SIR HOWARD VINCENT: Our present Free Trade.

MR. COURTNEY: He is consistent enough in rejoicing over this attack on bounties as an attack on the benefits we have enjoyed in the past. The bringing into a country of a commodity at a

Sir Charles Cameron.

cheaper rate necessarily displaces, as every improvement in production must displace, some previous producer, and those who fail to understand that have never really grasped what Free Trade means. The whole progress of improvement implies a loss imposed upon someone who up to that point has been engaged in the production of the commodity in respect of which the improvement is effected. But because we as a country have benefited by the introduction of cheap sugar through other countries giving bounties in regard thereto, it does not at all follow that we should go and approve of bounties everywhere, and try to bolster up and maintain them. If we get sugar at a cheaper rate, someone who has hitherto supplied it must be hurt. It is a necessary consequence of every movement in favour of Free Trade, and those who object to cheap sugar ought and must object to cheap corn. My hon. and gallant friend says, quite rightly from his point of view, that cheap corn interferes with the agriculturists, cheap flour interferes with the miller, cheap bread interferes with the baker—they are all interfered with, and therefore the nation suffers. Sir, the nation would be benefitted if twopenny loaves could be showered down from heaven. My hon. and gallant friend would then look up to the skies and say: "This is an interference to trade. Really you are destroying the trade of the agriculturists, and interfering with the miller and the baker. The whole process of trade is interfered with because the bread comes with the free bounty of heaven, and therefore it is wrong." The process in itself, the process of cheapening a commodity through bounties, is only a minor illustration of the great process of cheapening every commodity which we can get cheapened through the free course of trade. This is true of our own country; it is true also of India. If it is true that we should be benefited, even though farmers and agriculturists and landowners may pay the penalty as they do, so also will it be true of India, that if the Indian population receive a commodity which they want, they will be benefited by the introduction of the commodity at a cheaper rate. It may be said that we have to regard other things than India. But even if we take in the case of Mauritius, which I think we ought not to do in considering the matter

of India alone—if we could bring Mauritius and lay it alongside of India, making it a part or province of India, under the same government, the fact that the sugar trade of Mauritius would be injured by the introduction of sugar at a cheaper rate would not be an argument in favour of the Government's policy. I have allowed that bounties are an interference with Free Trade, and I am quite willing to allow, in the language of Mr. Gladstone, that we cannot regard bounties with favour. We look upon them with disfavour—not in a national interest, but in a cosmopolitan interest. If you are a lover of the world at large, you see that bounties do interfere with the free course of trade; that they are a penalty paid by another nation for your benefit, which must injure that other nation, and which in a minor and secondary degree injures you. In a cosmopolitan interest you would desire to do away with bounties; in an altruistic spirit for the benefit of other nations, we should get them to do all we could to remove bounties.

SIR HOWARD VINCENT: Hear, hear!

MR. COURTNEY: But not in the spirit of my hon. and gallant friend, who I am afraid really does not understand the very elements of the problem. If we get this pernicious system of bounties removed we do it at a cost to ourselves. We make some little sacrifice in the attempt to get other countries to follow a Free Trade policy in this matter, and as a practical question we are bound to consider that circumstance with any action we may take. Get bounties removed if you can. But how? In what measure? By what means? These are practical questions, which must be considered before taking practical action. In order to consider every one of them successfully we must bear in mind the primary fact that, as far as we are concerned, a nation not giving bounties, we are benefited and not injured by them. Now, in attempting to get rid of bounties what things are to be considered? It is admitted that imposing these retaliatory duties is a grave matter, and it ought not to be done unless there is some considerable interruption of Free Trade on the part of other people, requiring an action which is a voluntary self-sacrificing action involving some loss, on our part. We ought also, before resorting to a method of removing the evil, to be sure that we should not produce a greater evil. If authority goes for anything, the authority of our greatest predecessors is against making the attempt by duties on our part to counteract the advantages which we may receive from the unwisdom, or even the tyranny, of other people. Our great predecessors have refused, practically, to put on these duties to defeat bounties. They have done more. In a case which appears to me to appeal to our moral sense in a far higher degree than these bounties do, our great predecessors in fiscal legislation absolutely refused to make any discrimination in our duties which were urged as being likely to operate in the cure of a great national wrong. I am referring to the question of slave labour. If ever there was a reason for appealing to the conscience of the nation that reason would be found in the fact that we were receiving sugar from countries produced under conditions of slave labour, which caused it to be cheaper than it would have been had it been produced by free labour, and that we ought, by imposing a differential duty, to negative the advantage which slave-owning countries enjoyed from the existence of slavery. But Sir Robert Peel, Lord John Russell, Mr. Cobden, and Mr. Bright—not inferior in morality to any of us—strenuously refused to make any such discrimination; and it appears now that practically they were right, because slave-labour is not cheaper than free labour, and this discrimination would not have corresponded to a real difference in the cost to the country. If these statesmen refused to do it in that case, they certainly would refuse to do it in order to counteract a bounty which is put on by the free action of other countries. In fact we know that they did deliberately refuse to put on these retaliatory duties. The main principle which is suggested by the analogy to which I have referred is that you really cannot measure the practical effect on the price of a commodity of a bounty put on by another country. I know it will be said that our sugar trade is dominated now by bounties; that it is bounties and bounties alone which cause the supplies to come from certain countries; and my noble friend the Secretary of State for India said in his speech that it is proved

Mr. Cowrtney.

that cane sugar can compete, if the terms are equal, with beet sugar. I venture to say no—not meaning that it could not so compete, which I think is an unproved question—but meaning that it has not been proved that cane sugar could on equal terms compete with beet sugar. Therefore, in attempting to discriminate and measure the compensating duty you might altogether fail in securing the effect you want. What is the case. We get a good deal of our sugar from Germany and France. The bounty granted varies from £1 5s. to £2 per ton. What was the argument of the West Indies Commissioners on that point? We have it in their report that the difference was not enough to restore the sugar industry in the greater part of the West Indian islands, although it would be sufficient here and there; in other words, that cane sugar could not compete with beet in the greater part of the West Indian islands, even if the bounty were nullified, and that the attempt to make that nullification would be vain, if you thought thereby to restore the prosperity of the West Indies. About a week ago I got another illustration, which seemed to me to be so remarkable that I venture to repeat it, because I think the House will be struck by its cogency. I met a most intelligent Danish gentleman, and began to talk to him about the Danish West Indian Islands, and about their circumstances, their social condition, their trade, and at last I said, "I suppose you get a good deal of sugar from them?" "Oh, no, we do not," he said. "We do not get any sugar at all from them now; we used to get sugar from them." Where do you get your sugar from," I asked. "Oh, we get it entirely from our own beet." "I suppose there is some difference in duty?" I said. "No, not at all. The rate of duty which we pay on sugar in Denmark is the same whether it comes from cane or from beet." Beet sugar without any bounty in Denmark has beaten cane. That is in a very large measure because with the beet industry you have much more capable, industrious, and energetic employers, men working their own estate on the spot, and not working through inferior labour. You have the greatest ingenuity, and you have what is more than anything else, such a development in the application of the by-products that the cost of the production of the sugar is very much diminished. So that if you think that nullifying the bounties will fully re-establish trade, you will altogether fail. I have said that I myself would be very glad to see bounties abolished, if I could purge the mental confusion of foreign legislators, if I could cure them of what is worse than mental confusion—the international jealousy which underlies all this stealing of trade from one another. But my main objection to this plan of retaliatory duties is that, instead of curing the root of the evil, you intensify it. You make foreign legislatures think that what they have been doing is a good thing, that you are injured by it, and therefore they must gain; and so they go on in the course they have taken. After all, it deals with a very small matter; it deals with it in a way you cannot measure and accurately compensate, and instead of curing foreign nations of the evil system, you will go on making them more inveterate in it. But I must protest against the suggestion which has been made by the hon. Member for Dumbarton, and by my noble friend the Secretary of State, that the agricultural industry is entirely ruined by this supposed interference with the cultivation of sugar. Out of the whole 230,000,000 acres, only 1⅓ per cent. were under sugar. What would be the effect in India, even if the whole were to go? The Indians would be better off, and would cultivate some other commodity. Those who think they would not be better off are of the opinion that we are not better off through cheap sugar and cheap corn. Then there is the political as well as the economical question to be considered. It may, and probably will, be said that my speech on the whole has been that of a complete doctrinaire, but that is always said when the arguments cannot be disproved. I have never looked upon this question as one which could be solved by considerations of Free Trade alone. I recall the case of the cotton duties, not the cotton duties which were dealt with by my right hon. friend opposite three or four years ago, but the agitation of some twenty years ago, when my lamented friend Mr. Fawcett and myself were in the House together, and when Lancashire Members were making an eager attempt to get rid of the cotton duties in India. We were persuaded like the Members for Lancashire that the cotton duties were bad for the people of India; but we were neither of us very keen in the agitation, because we felt that it carried an ugly look to the people of India, that apparently it would be sacrificing India to Lancashire. In the government of India you must have respect to the prejudices—or the errors, if you like to call them so—of the people you are governing. If you are attempting to force upon India, as we were then, the abolition of the cotton duties, in the face of the opposition of the Government of India, and in the face of the general opinion of India, you are engaged in a dangerous enterprise, against which a good deal may be said, and which ought to be approached with very great caution. But in this case we are really not fighting for England. We are approaching the matter from the point of view of India alone. England has nothing in the world to do with it. It is from the point of view of India alone that we are urging the impropriety of this interposition which has been sanctioned by the Government. I know it may be said that the Council is unanimously in favour of these duties. Yes. But the same Council, minus the Head, was unanimously against them last year. They have changed in the meantime owing to superior information, and the fact that a change had been made in the Governor-General. I will not use the word which the hon. Member for Cardiff applied to members of the Council in this connection, but I think that this question precipitates the bringing forward of the grave question which we will have one day to consider, and which I ventured to suggest a few months ago would soon have to be considered, viz., the composition of and character of the Governing Council itself. Under its present organisation you cannot have those elements of independence which are most desirable in the Government of India. This train of thought was pressed upon me most forcibly quite recently in reading the "Letters and Papers of Sir Robert Peel." When Lord Ellenborough went out to India, Sir Robert Peel had his doubts about the wisdom and prudence of that great Governor-General, and communicated them to the Duke of Wellington, saying—

"I think the Council had better keep him in order."

But the Duke of Wellington, in a note which I commend to the House, said—

"Oh, no, no! The Council are no use in this regard. They are gentlemen who have served in India, most of them, for twelve years or more ; they have been trained in offices ; they have gone through an Indian career which leads them always to look up to the Head of the Government, and you will find that a Governor-General — especially one who had been at the Board of Control and made Indian matters his study—will have the Council entirely round his finger."

We sent a Governor-General out there who has made Indian matters a great study, and the recent action of the Council in India loses, to me, very much, if not the whole, of its weight when I consider that within twelve months the same Council was of an entirely different opinion. The change has, in fact, been brought about by the introduction of a new Governor-General. This is a very grave question. If it were a case of England, none of us would approve of countervailing duties. If we are going to look upon India as something under our charge, as England is, we ought to apply to India precisely the same action ; we ought to refuse there what we refuse here. I know it is said that this is a grave matter, that it is a vote of censure. For my part, I do not very seriously regard these threats of a vote of censure. In the first place, it will not be carried—though that is not much to the point ; in the second place, if it were carried, could anyone conceive the Government dissolved on this question and going to the country in favour of keeping up and enhancing the price of sugar in India—a principle which would be represented, and accurately represented, as leading to an enhancement of the price of sugar at home ? The thing is absolutely impossible. I have no fear whatever of the consequences of victory in this matter, even if we could secure it, and I shall vote with my right hon. friend opposite without any fear.

THE SECRETARY OF STATE FOR THE COLONIES (Mr. J. CHAMBERLAIN, Birmingham, W.): Mr. Speaker, it is rather a curious fact that the last two speakers, although their conclusions have been very different, have this at least in common—both of them have spoken against the views of the Party to which they belong. The only difference is that the hon. Baronet the Member for Glasgow performs that operation very infrequently, while with my right hon. friend the Member for Bodmin it is altogether usual.

Mr. Courtney.

I think I shall not shock my right hon. friend if I say that sometimes his speeches cause some irritation to his friends. That is not because he differs from them, that is not because he is a candid friend, because I can assure him he occupies that position so admirably that the Unionist Party is proud to have so conspicuous a specimen of the genus in their midst. But the feeling is due to a different cause—to that cause which operated in the case of the New Zealand medicine man, as to whom the chief of his tribe said that he gave them so much good advice that they were obliged to |put him away. Now, my right hon. friend, in the course of his speech, spoke of his desire—a most natural and creditable desire on his part —to purge the mental confusion of foreign legislatures. That is an extension of his ordinary *role* ; his ordinary *role* is to purge the mental confusion of domestic legislators. Yet, as with so many other great benefactors of his species, I am afraid the people he is supposed to benefit are not sufficiently grateful. The right hon. Gentleman has contended to-night that a bounty differs from a protective duty, that it is not so bad as a protective duty, because a bounty is a benefit to the country receiving it and an injury to the country giving it. I take issue on both those statements. The right hon. Gentleman appears to think that a bounty given by a foreign country to introduce its products where they could not naturally go is equivalent to a rather extreme hypothesis he raised— namely the possibility that Heaven might shower twopenny loaves upon us. There is a difference between Heaven and foreign governments. The bounty of Heaven is more free ; it is less interested. If Heaven ever does shower twopenny loaves upon us it will not be because it has gone into the bakery trade. I think the comparison is altogether unfair. But I take exception to his first statement, that a bounty is a benefit to the country receiving it. It is, I think, a mental confusion on the part of the right hon. Gentleman which I desire to purge, that a bounty is the cause of cheap sugar. No doubt if the fact that sugar at the present time is half the price it was so many years ago were due entirely to the bounty system, I admit we should have to consider very carefully before we did anything to prevent that system. But nothing of the kind is the case. The low price of sugar is due, principally, to the reduction in the cost of production, and the reduction in the price of sugar is not much, if any, greater than the average reduction of other commodities and other necessaries. Therefore it is not due to the bounty, and when I come a little later to consider more carefully the question of cheapness, I think I shall be able to show that very little of the reduction in price, if any, is due to the giving of a bounty. Therefore I deny that the concession of a bounty is an advantage to the country receiving it. It is a distinct disadvantage in this respect—that it artificially destroys trades and occupations which are natural to the country, and which, once destroyed, it is very difficult to replace. But then my right hon friend goes on to say that it is an injury to the country giving it. Does my right hon. friend suggest that every other country is a fool in regard to its own business? I have a sort of idea that some of these countries, at any rate, know their business as well as we do, and if they have given bounties for now something like twenty or thirty years, and if they have continually increased those bounties, per a s they have found some profit in doing it. I would point out to my right hon. friend, as it appears to have escaped his attention, some profits which they have eminently gained thereby. The production of sugar in Germany, for instance, and in France, has been enormously extended and improved owing directly to the bounties. The bounties were given in accordance with the production of sugar per ton of beet, and the result has been that the production, which was for many years 5 or 6 per cent., has now been raised to 11 or 12 per cent. If that stood alone it might be held by foreign economists to be some justification for the expense they had been put to in the production of the sugar. There is one general remark I would make here of the whole argument of my right hon. friend. If bounties are an advantage to the country, why does he want to remove them? I admit I could not quite follow his argument. No doubt hon. Gentlemen opposite were more fortunate than myself, but if I understood him correctly, what he said was that if he considered the matter in the light of the interests of this country he would not wish to abolish bounties, but, as he takes a wide, a general, a

magnificent, a cosmopolitan view of the situation, he wishes that bounties should be removed for the benefit of foreign countries to the injury of his own. I think I have rightly understood my right hon. friend's argument.

MR. COURTNEY: Quite true.

MR. J. CHAMBERLAIN: A philanthropy which takes in the whole world and leaves out of account its own country is one to the heights of which I confess I am quite incapable of attaining. I gather that hon. Members opposite are able to sympathise with my right hon. friend. Whether that may make them more popular in the country to which they belong, but whose interests they are willing to sacrifice to the interests of the whole world—whether their universal philanthropy will really be more acceptable than my commonplace patriotism, I must leave to the House to decide. One other remark about the speech of my right hon. friend. He professed to believe that the prevalence of beet over cane was due to a sort of natural selection and to the fact that beet sugar can be produced more cheaply than cane sugar. That is entirely opposed to the figures of the case which have been submitted to me by the authorities in this matter. The cost of cane sugar under the most favourable circumstances is less than the cost of beet sugar also under the most favourable circumstances, and I would submit to my right hon. friend, who shakes his head—perhaps his knowledge of sugar production is greater than mine—that if it is not as I state there is no occasion for a bounty, for why on earth should foreign countries give a bounty in order to force their beet sugar into our country and other countries if, naturally and without any bounty, beet sugar would be cheaper than cane sugar? It is evident that the course of this Debate has run upon two questions—the question of principle and the question of expediency. The question of principle covers the whole question of bounties. It covers bounties so far as they affect the West Indies, Queensland, and Mauritius; it covers countervailing duties so far as they affect this country as well as the particular question of India. There is also the question of expediency —that is to say, that, granting countervailing duties may be properly applied in particular cases, you would then have to consider the merits of each particular case. There, of course, a distinction might be drawn between the case of the West Indies and the case of India, or of any other country. I trust this Debate will result in a clear issue and a decision, by an undoubted and overwhelming majority, which will give the opinion of, at all events, this Parliament in regard to the question of principle. Our opponents in this Debate, and generally, claim that their principles, which they associate with the doctrine of Free Trade, absolutely preclude the consideration of countervailing duties or prohibition. They base the general view of the situation on the authority of what my right hon. friend the Member for Wolverhampton calls the high priests of the order, among whom, much to my surprise, he names myself. I can assure him he does me too much honour. I was never a high priest at all. It is not my line. But they base this conclusion in the first place on the authority of the high priests, and, in the second place, upon a theory which they, as I shall endeavour to show, have evolved themselves, that Free Trade consists in the doctrine that cheapness, by whatever means obtained, is the great object of our legislation. Now, Sir, we say, on the contrary, that countervailing duties are not opposed to Free Trade. We absolutely deny it, and we allege that bounties are the very worst form of Protection, because they protect the foreigner, not in his own market, for which there might possibly be some sort of justification, at all events in exceptional circumstances, but they protect the foreigner in our market, in which he has no claim whatever to protection. And, Sir, we say, secondly, that cheapness is not, and never was, in the view of the high priests of Free Trade, the primary object of Free Trade, and, accordingly, our contention is that we can counteract bounties by countervailing duties, or secure their abolition by prohibition, without in the slightest degree derogating from our character of orthodox Free Traders. In the course of the last twenty years or so we have discovered a new Liberalism, a new Radicalism, a new trades unionism, and now there is a new Free Trade doctrine of which the originators of Free Trade were absolutely ignorant, and which I believe they would have repudiated. The new Free Trader has changed altogether his ideas as to

Mr. J. Chamberlain.

what Free Trade consists of, and I think he has made a mistake, and I do not believe that the new Free Traders are the true friends of Free Trade. I remember Lord Macaulay, in a very eloquent speech he made on one occasion, warned his hearers not to give the sanction of religion to abuses which were not religious, because, he said, if you do, in the fall of the abuses the religion may go also; and it seems to me that if you connect in the minds of the people the inevitable sequence between the abuses which have followed the proclamation of Free Trade and the original principles of Free Trade, you will be creating the only danger from which Free Trade has ever suffered. It is a dangerous thing, in my opinion, to teach the people of this country that Free Trade is inseparable from gross injustice and from unfair attacks on their employment and occupations. The hon. Member for Cardiff, in the earlier part of the evening, was daring Members of the Government to go to their constituents and say that in given circumstances they would be prepared to propose countervailing duties in this country. I should not be at all afraid to go to my constituents and propose them. I think there is, on the contrary, a growing feeling in the country, which to a certain extent alarms me, that injustices have attended Free Trade which ought not to have attended Free Trade and which are not due to Free Trade; and the pressure of those injustices has to my mind produced so great an impression on the working classes in the manufacturing centres that I am sometimes alarmed lest they should go a great deal further than I do, and lest they should be ready, not only to remove the abuses, but to deny the doctrine and principle of Free Trade. I think that is a real danger and worthy of some consideration. I think Free Trade is therefore, as I have already said, in danger from its friends. Free Trade is a political religion, and it has had to endure the hard fate of all religions, that it has been corrupted. Since it was promulgated in its original purity it has suffered from the work of annotators and commentators and false prophets, and as a result the doctrine of Free Trade has become a dogma and the religion a fetish, and I think we had better go back to the original fount of inspiration and try, if we can, to clear this religion of the corruption which has been imposed upon it and to remove from it all the result of the fanaticism of certain subsequent professors, like my old friend Lord Farrer. It would be absurd to answer in a debate of this kind without alluding to Lord Farrer, who may be said to be the *fons et origo* of it. Every argument used on the other side of the House has been taken from Lord Farrer. He is one of the ablest of our public servants, and, as I have reason to know, he has done more than any other man to maintain bounties and prevent their abolition during the last twenty years. He has been full of arguments and facts and statistics, and I am ready to admit that in 1881, the year in which I made certain utterances quoted by my right hon. friend the Member for Wolverhampton, I was greatly influenced by what he said. [Laughter.] I do not understand why that is a subject of merriment. I am not ashamed, but I am proud, of having been influenced by so able and experienced a public servant, by his statements, by his knowledge, by the facts which he produced ; and I will go further and say that I was led to believe in the predictions he then made, every one of which has been falsified by subsequent events. I am still ready to believe in his facts, I am still ready to believe in his statistics ; but never again will I believe in his prophecy. Lord Farrer represents the extreme of Free Trade fanaticism ; he is the Torquemada of Free Trade, and I believe he would go to the stake himself, and I am afraid he would send my friends and me there too, rather than sacrifice any of his principles. I maintain that there is no justification whatever in the writings or speeches of any of the great Free Traders of the doctrine that countervailing duties are opposed to the principles of Free Trade. That is a challenge. Some quotations which I had noted have already been made to the House, and I will not repeat them. Mr. Cobden gave two definitions of Free Trade. He defined it as being the abolition of protective duties. Countervailing duties are not protective. A countervailing duty, as its name applies, is a duty strictly confined to countervailing the advantage given by a bounty ; it does not go beyond that, and it does not protect the industry to which it applies. Another definition that Mr. Cobden gave was that Free Trade was to enable the consumers in every country to obtain what they

desire in the cheapest and the best market. [Opposition cheers.] Yes, but that is not all. That is where you stop. But Mr. Cobden added "At its natural price," and that is what hon. Members opposite have forgotten. They have remembered the cheapness, but have forgotten the natural price. Now the main object of the great Free Traders was to secure the natural course of production and of exchange. That was the argument again and again elaborated in all their speeches. Their ideal was that each country should produce what it was naturally best fitted to produce and to exchange it without artificial arrangements. The great Free Traders denounced all artificial arrangements which turned their trade into unnatural channels. They disapproved of Protection whenever it turned labour and capital into operations which might be considered to be artificial and unnatural, and which would be unremunerative under ordinary and natural conditions. But they advocated countervailing duties in cases where it was necessary in order to restore equality. Now, I am going back to the original founder of Free Trade—to Adam Smith. Mr. Cobden said to Mr. Bright that he would take Adam Smith in his hand and would go up and down the country preaching, with the "Wealth of Nations" for his text-book, the doctrines of Free Trade, and so convert the nation. Adam Smith in his "Wealth of Nations" argued against protective duties and in favour of Free Trade, but he said there were certain cases in which a nation might impose duties to protect their home industry. The first case has nothing to do with the present discussion. The second case, in which it might be advantageous to lay some burden on the foreigner for the encouragement of domestic industry, is when some tax is imposed at home on the produce of the latter ; in this case it seems reasonable that an equal tax should be imposed upon the like produce of the former. By what reasoning does he arrive at this suggestion ? Adam Smith did not contemplate bounties as we understand them, but you will find his reasoning applies equally to countervailing duties. He says :

" This tax would not give a monopoly of the home market to domestic industry, nor would it turn to a particular employment a greater share of the stock of labour of the country than would naturally go to it."

That is true of countervaling duties. He goes on to say :

"It would only hinder any part of what would naturally go to it from being turned away by the tax into a less natural direction."

Substitute "bounty" for "tax" and you have the exact argument. That is exactly the argument which we have pointed out in the course of this Debate. Reference has been made to the spirit duty and other duties which we impose as compensatory to the home tariff by the hon. Baronet the Member for Glasgow. I do not think it has been noted—it is rather a special point—that we have actually put a countervailing duty upon West Indian rum to prevent the producers of the West Indies from having an advantage in this market, at the same time refusing to West Indian producers to put them on an equality with regard to their other productions. Then again, take the case of the Indian cotton duties. In the case of the Indian cotton duties—the case of a protective duty put on cotton from this country—the right hon. Gentleman opposite avowed it to be his intention and desire to place the cotton industry on exactly equal terms in Bombay and Manchester, and he put on an Excise duty which was intended to produce equality. Then equality is what we are striving at ! But if equality in cotton and in rum, why not in sugar ? Remember that in all these cases the result has been to increase the price to the consumer. If the excise duty on rum were taken away the English consumer of rum would get it 5d. per gallon cheaper, and if the excise duty on Indian cotton were taken off the Indian consumer would get it 5 per cent. cheaper. Therefore, according to the doctrine of the right hon. Member for Bodmin and the inconsistent doctrine of the right hon. Member for East Wolverhampton, these surtaxes ought never to have been imposed, because they add to the price of the consumer and interfere with the privileges of the great god Cheapness, which they all adore. Let us consider this question of cheapness a little more closely. How much does the consumer gain by the bounties in regard to cheapness ? I think he gains very little. I have been considering this

Mr. J. Chamberlain.

question lately in the light of further information, and I think I and others have been mistaken in attributing a large proportion of the reduction in the price of sugar to the influence of the bounties. Now, let me make it clear to the House. Suppose that the cost of cane sugar is £8, and that the cost of German beet sugar is £9. Suppose the German bounty is 30s. That enables the Germans to undersell the cane sugar. In the first place, £1 of the bounty goes to cover the increase of cost of the beet sugar. That leaves 10s. which the German producer has in hand, and he may give it if he likes to the English consumer. But does he give it ? Is he such a fool ? All that is necessary for him is to give a trifle above the cane price. If he can sell his sugar at £7 19s. he would cut out the whole of the sugar which would come in at £8, and all that he has to give away is 1s. a ton. The rest either goes to meet the difference between the natural price between the beet and the cane, or it goes into the pockets of the producer. I challenge my right hon. friend the Member for Bodmin, or anyone else, to prove that, out of a bounty of 30s., more than an infinitesimal proportion ever goes into the pockets of the consumer in this country.

Mr COURTNEY : But the producers compete among themselves.

Mr. J. CHAMBERLAIN : But the competitors are not quite so rabid as my right hon. friend has suggested ; they are not so foolish. No man in competition cuts his price down lower than is necessary. If they can provide the quantity of sugar which is required from foreign producers by excluding cane sugar, they are perfectly satisfied, and they arrange among themselves in such a way as not to cut down the price more than is necessary to fill their mills, and sufficient to enable them to cut out the cane sugar. I wish here to quote Lord Farrer on this question. In his last pamphlet—his pamphlets follow each other very quickly—Lord Farrer said :

"How far the abolition of sugar bounties would raise the price of sugar to the consumer appears to be very doubtful. My own impression is that the effect of the bounties has been much exaggerated."

I think that the effect of the bounties to the consumer has been much exaggerated, but not so in regard to the producer. In spite, however, of his opinion that the difference in price is not much, Lord Farrer still maintains that a certain increase of price will result from legislation in the shape of countervailing duties, and on that ground chiefly he is opposed to it, because he says that cheapness of price to the consumer is the main object to be attained. I think that hon. Members seem here to confuse two things. They divide the community into two classes. On one side are the consumers, and on the other the producers. As a matter of fact, the consumers are generally producers, and the only class of consumers who are not producers—the only class, therefore, benefited by legislation, which is directed solely in the interest of consumers, and as against the interest of producers—is that class which "toil not, neither do they spin." Is it not a scandalous inversion of *roles* that hon. Gentlemen opposite should be directing the whole of their energies to securing special benefit for that extremely limited class? Mr. Cobden has been already quoted by the hon. Baronet the Member for Glasgow in opposition to this theory that cheapness is really the object which Free Traders should have in view. I should have liked to quote Mr. Gladstone to the same effect, but I am afraid of curtailing unduly the time which remains. On the first question of principle, then, I say that our position is that countervailing duties are matters of expediency to be judged in each case on their merits, and that there is nothing in Free Trade which would exclude their consideration. Then I come to a very important matter. I do not like the tone of the hon. Gentlemen opposite with regard to this Indian question. It is entirely an Indian question; and I agree that it is to be considered entirely from the point of view of Indian interests. But that is not the position taken by my right hon. friend the Member for Bodmin and others.

MR. COURTNEY: Yes, it is.

MR. J. CHAMBERLAIN: No, Sir; my right hon. friend is now going to vote practically against the unanimous opinion of the only persons who can properly represent India, and who can deal with the subject in their representative character.

MR. COURTNEY: That is not the point. My right hon. friend says that I do not look at this question from an Indian point of view, but I do.

MR. CHAMBERLAIN: Then my right friend presumes to know better what is good for India than the only persons who are authorised or are in any way qualified to represent Indian opinion, that is, the Indian native Press, the English Press of India, the Council for India in this country, and the Legislative Council in India. My fear is that there is a tendency on the part of some hon. Gentlemen to return to that mercantile system which was the curse of our colonial empire. It was that system which lost us the United States of America and estranged from us many of our most promising colonies. And what was that mercantile system? It was that the interests of our colonies should be subordinated and put on one side in favour of the interests of British consumers and producers. It is based on the subordination of colonial interests and colonial opinion to British interests and British opinion; and it seems now that there are persons who hold that the interests of the East Indies, of the West Indies, of Mauritius, and of Queensland are comparatively of no importance; that the local opinion of these places is to be sneered at; and that when the planters say they are going to be ruined they are to be told that they do not know what they are talking about, and are making fortunes as hard as they can go. That is the line taken in deference to a number of pedantic economists, and in the supposed interests of the working classes. We are told that we should be sane Imperialists. That is not sane Imperialism. That is insane Imperialism, whatever else it is, and it tends to produce a state of feeling between us and the Colonies which I for one exceedingly regret. In the present case, as I have said, the public opinion of India is practically unanimous. I was quite astounded to hear my right hon. friend the Member for Wolverhampton minimise this opinion by saying, what of course is true, that you have not a public opinion in India such as you have in this country. Why, Sir, my right hon. friend came down here some years ago to defend his policy in respect of the cotton duties; and he himself appealed to this opinion of the native Press, the

English Press, and the Council of India, and, above all, he made a most eloquent defence of a particular official, who, he said, was one of the ablest officials India had ever known, and to whose opinion he attached great importance. He complained that my noble friend Lord James of Hereford, then Sir Henry James, had appeared in some way to slight the value of that opinion. Who was this Government official whose opinion was to be taken without criticism? It was Sir James Westland. It was a member of the Legislative Council, who now, in an admirably reasoned speech, has defended these countervailing duties. It is his opinion that my right hon. friend would set aside as of no importance at all in comparison with the views of English economists such as Lord Farrer and the right hon. Gentleman the Member for Bodmin.

SIR H. H. FOWLER: There has been a change of opinion. I have every respect for the opinion expressed by Sir J. Westland in May, 1898, and I believe that everything that has happened since has confirmed that opinion.

MR. J. CHAMBERLAIN: My right hon. friend is not justified in saying that there has been any such change of opinion. Where is the speech of Sir J. Westland in regard to that former decision? All that former decision amounted to was that the Government were not prepared to consider these countervailing duties at that time. It is not a reasoned argument against them, but a decision merely for the moment, which was probably justified. All this local opinion which was appealed to in relation to the cotton duties was expressed in a still more marked degree in favour of the course we have followed. Now it is a strange thing—and I am almost ashamed to refer to it—but the hon. Member for Cardiff made a speech earlier in the evening in which he attacked the Government with considerable feeling, and especially myself. He seemed to think that, whether the Government policy was good or bad, it must certainly be bad if it was advocated by the Colonial Secretary. He has got the Colonial Secretary on the brain; I am to him what King Charles's head was to Mr. Dick's memorial. But I cannot make out why he attacks me with so much violence. He

Mr. J. Chamberlain.

always professes his loyalty to his party, and I am sure he does it with perfect sincerity, yet he never speaks but to attack some representative Member of the Government. For a long time I was totally unable to make out why. I knew it could not be a personal feeling against myself, for I do not think I have ever spoken to the hon. Member, therefore he could not have any quarrel with me. Then I felt it must be some great question of principle, but fortunately the hon. Member himself relieved my mind, for some time ago I observed that some of his constituents were impertinent enough to ask why he, a supporter of the Government, so often attacked members of the Government. Well, he gave them a proper dressing, and he explained afterwards to a reporter in an interview, a report of which appeared in his own newspaper in Cardiff, that he was not actuated by any antagonistic feeling either against the Government or the Colonial Secretary, but that he was in the position of a man who is looking through the keyhole into a banqueting room in which the Liberal Unionist party were eating, enjoying themselves, and making merry. Well, looking through a keyhole is not a very dignified position——

MR. J. M. MACLEAN: I beg the right hon. Gentleman's pardon; let us be accurate. What appeared in the paper was descriptive of the general character of the party, and did not apply to myself in any way.

MR. J. CHAMBERLAIN: I do not know what authority the hon. Gentleman has for applying it to other members of the party; but at any rate I would suggest to the hon. Gentleman that the process which he describes so graphically is apt to produce a distorted vision. Now what is his ' point about the Colonial Secretary? My noble friend has explained with absolute accuracy what took place; but what an extraordinary idea the hon. Member must have of the power of the Colonial Secretary! What is his theory? It is that the Colonial Secretary first forced the hand of the Secretary of State for India, that he then hypnotised Lord Curzon, and by some process of suggestion he influenced the whole of the members of the Council in India, not one of whom he has ever seen; and lastly, for the same reason, in some occult, mysterious, and pernicious way he influenced the Council of India in this country. Well, really the hon. Member pays me a compliment I do not deserve. I am Colonial Secretary, and when a colony appeals to me, as Mauritius did, reporting that its trade is in a parlous state, in a sad condition, and that it will be seriously endangered unless something is done in the shape of legislation in India, it is my duty to convey that information to the Secretary of State for India. I said at the time that the interests of India would dictate the decision of the Secretary of State in Council, but that, so far as I was concerned, I hoped the condition of Mauritius would be sympathetically considered by the Council in India. There are two or three objections taken with which I will deal in a few minutes. It is complained that the Indian Government and Council decided without completing the inquiry which they had then undertaken. Well, as my noble friend has pointed out, in the interval he had information that led him to believe that if he did not act soon his object would be frustrated by a large importation of foreign bounty-fed sugar. But, after all, the inquiry on which he was engaged could not add much information which would affect his decision, because all the inquiry would be to show what was the effect of the importation of sugar up to that time. It is admitted that they interfered before importation had become a matter of great importance. No serious effect was anticipated up to that time. The steps that were taken were preventive steps. Well, then, the same reply also answers the objection that it was unnecessary to interfere because the amount was so small. Yes, it was small up to the time importation took place, but it was growing rapidly, and there was not the slightest doubt that there would have been an enormous introduction of sugar, diverted from the United States and imported into India, if it had not been for the wise policy of the Indian Government. Then, it is said that the true policy of the Indian Government was not to put on countervailing duties, but to encourage better methods of production. That has often been said about the West Indies and other colonies; but it is an absurd argument, and shows entire ignorance of the situation. You cannot encourage better production, you cannot introduce new energy and new

capital, unless you can give stability to the industry. What is my position at this moment? Have I not been for months, I may almost say for two years, considering night and day methods by which the past prosperity of the West Indies might be restored, and by which the fatal effects of bounties might be removed? And my efforts in that direction have been largely bent to securing, among other things, the introduction of fresh capital and fresh energy. I went to people who are interested in the largest undertakings in this country, who have the possession of the largest capital and have shown the greatest energy; and at this moment I have a statement by one of these parties that he would to-morrow engage to invest a million sterling in the production of sugar in the West Indies if the Government would guarantee him against an increase in the bounties that are now given by foreign countries to beet sugar. Now, a last word in regard to Protection. It is said that if we impose countervailing duties foreign countries will retaliate. Sir, they will retaliate, no doubt, if it is to their interest to do so; but it is not to their interest to do so. They take from us nothing now, they take nothing from India, that they can help taking. They take the raw materials for their own manufactures; they would injure themselves much more than India and us if they retaliated by refusing them. They cannot refuse cotton, they cannot refuse tea, they cannot refuse jute, and other products of India to which the hon. Member for Wolverhampton referred; and under these circumstances, in my opinion, there is no practical fear whatever that they would retaliate in any way by the increase of duties. I would say then, in conclusion, that it appears to me the issues before us are simple. In the first place, we have to decide whether or not there is such an overwhelming, over-mastering principle, either in connection with Free Trade or anything else, as to put countervailing duties out of court, and prevent their consideration on their merits. In the second place, we have to decide whether we are willing to overrule the clearly expressed opinion of the authoritative representatives of Indian interests, and whether we are to do that avowedly in the interests—the very indirect interests as I consider—of the British consumer.

These are the two principles, at any rate, that are to be decided by our vote to-night. But I go one step further. I would say also that, in my opinion, even if we thought the policy of the Indian Government to be wrong, we should still hesitate before we over-ruled it. But, Sir, the Government hold, and they are perfectly willing to accept the responsibility for that opinion, that the policy of the Government of India was right. They hold that the Government of India was right in relieving the burden imposed by this most pernicious system of bounties, in securing to one of the staple productions of India equal opportunity with its foreign competitors, and in neutralising the arbitrary advantage which the foreigner is seeking to obtain in a market to which he has no natural claim.

Sir H. CAMPBELL-BANNERMAN (Stirling Burghs): We have listened to two speeches of extreme interest from my right hon. friend, the Member for Bodmin, and from the right hon. Gentleman who has just sat down. They were lectures on the subject of Free Trade, dealing with the theory and the practice of Free Traders, and it will be somewhat of a relief to the House to know, especially with the scanty time at my disposal, that it is not my intention to inflict upon the House a third essay upon that subject. My right hon. friend the Member for Bodmin spoke with his usual warmth and enthusiasm. I cannot rise, myself, quite to the heights of economic philosophy to which my right hon. friend has attained, but in the main I accept his doctrines and agree with his conclusions. The noble Lord the Secretary of State for India, in the early part of the evening, when he rose to address the House, began by asking those of his hon. friends who had put down Amendments to this Motion not to move the Amendments which stood in their names. I heard this appeal without surprise, because on looking at the Paper it was evident that the Amendments showed how far this question reaches — how very far it goes beyond the mere question of India

Mr. J. Chamberlain.

and the Mauritius, and of their relations to the bounty-fed sugar - producing countries, and displayed really the motives and intentions which underlie the policy in the minds of many of those who support it. But I need not have formed this estimate of the noble Lord's motive, because from the moment he began his speech it became apparent, and it became still more apparent in the speech of the right hon. Gentleman who has just sat down, that the main part of their policy, which they are now seeking to apply to India, it is their intention to apply at a more convenient time to this country. The noble Lord invited my right hon. friend to go to the country in defence of the system of bounties ; but the noble Lord must know perfectly well that we are as much opposed to the system of bounties as he is. I agree with my right hon. friend in that I regard bounties as merely another form of protective duties. We need not speculate as to which is the worse of the two. These bounties appear to me to be bad, to disturb trade, to hinder the development of the country, and above all to punish the very nations which employ them. So that I do not know what there is to be said in favour of them. There is no quarrel between us on that score at all. Where we differ is as to the remedy to be applied. The noble Lord spoke of himself as an old Free Trader. The right hon. Gentleman who has just sat down has told us that there are new doctrines of Free Trade, which are altogether heretical. The Secretary of State for the Colonies is a good judge of new doctrines. For my part I prefer, if a doctrine is to be developed, that it should be developed in a forward, rather than in a backward sense ; and if it was a new development of the old Free Trade principle I should not be afraid of it on that account. But when he said that retaliatory duties— what are called countervailing duties, I prefer to call them retaliatory duties— were accepted, and were advocated in certain cases by the old orthodox Free Traders, I cannot but call to mind a maxim which is constantly quoted, and which is, I think, one of the standing maxims on this topic—the words of Sir Robert Peel, when he said that he would "fight hostile tariffs by free imports." That was the way in which old Free Traders, the high priests of Free Trade, intended to deal with such a case as we have before us. I prefer the old method to the new, Mr. Speaker, and when the noble Lord challenges us to go to the country, as he did, as the advocates of bounties, my reply is, in the first place, that we are not advocates of bounties, and, in the second place, I would invite him, on his part, to go to the country with the cry of "Retaliatory tariffs and dear sugar." There is much interest taken in the relations of these two Cabinet Ministers to each other. There was a suspicion engendered by the Blue Book which is before us that the noble Lord the Secretary of State for India has been acted upon, has been driven into this policy, and, in fact, has been obliged to make himself the obedient servant of the Secretary of State for the Colonies. I am bound to say there was nothing in this which seemed to me *a priori* improbable. But one thing cannot be denied, and that is, that from the very moment the Secretary of State for the Colonies appears upon the scene, activity is shown in the India Office in pushing this new policy. Evidently there was no positive action taken until he read this new economic catechism. One thing is certain—and it is a very remarkable fact—that the proposals of these new duties did not originate in India, wherever they did originate. I have not time to go over the list of dates which was given by my hon. friend the Member for Wolverhampton, which proves conclusively that the Government of India not only expressed a contrary opinion a few months before—and that contrary opinion was not an opinion contrary to the adoption of that policy at that particular moment, as the right hon. Gentleman says, but an opinion contrary to it in general terms—but they had also engaged in an elaborate inquiry, which, oddly enough, was initiated by the very Department of the Government over which Sir James Westland presides, which is some proof that he was not so fixed in his opinion as the right hon. Gentleman represented. They engaged in an inquiry to ascertain the opinion of the different provincial Governments and

to obtain the facts from them, and that inquiry was not concluded, and the reports had not been received, at the time the decision of the Government was taken. So that that decision was taken upon English information, and not upon information from India. The noble Lord said, and the right hon. Gentleman repeated it, that they had information which led them to believe that there was serious danger impending. What was that information ? If it was Indian information it must have been in the possession of Lord Curzon when he told us in the month of January that he was himself instituting a fresh inquiry in order to ascertain the effects of the duties. I wish to bring before the House one or two figures which bear upon this supposed danger to the cultivation of sugar in India, and to the sugar industry in India. I will confine myself to the question of imports. It was said that the imports from the beet-sugar countries had reached alarming proportions, and that they were interfering with the imports from Mauritius. What are the figures ? The figures show that in the average for the years from 1890 to 1895 the imports from Mauritius were 71,610 tons; in 1896-97 they were 83,300 tons; in 1897-98 they were 88,900 tons; and in 1898-99 they were 105,280 tons—a steady, wholesome, healthy increase year by year, showing no falling off and no tendency to fluctuate. But from Germany and Austria there came, in the average of 1890 to 1895, 17,800 tons; in 1896-97, 43,750 tons—a very great increase; in 1897-98, 107,550 tons —again a huge increase; but in 1898-99, which is the critical year, they had fallen to 73,490 tons. So that there was actually a falling off in the very imports which are the foundation for this policy of countervailing duties. There are other figures which bear closely on this matter. I have here the figures of the exports of sugar from Germany to the United States during the last three years. They are given in millions of pounds, and are for nine months in each year. In 1897 Germany exported to the United States 778 millions of pounds. Then there were countervailing duties put on by the United States Government, with the result that in 1898 the exports from Germany to the United States, instead of being 778 millions of pounds, were only 40 millions of pounds. (Cheers.) Yes, but in the year which ended a few months the exports amounted to 658 millions of pounds. So that the United States is the quarter to which have been attracted the large over stocks of German sugar which so frightened the noble Lord the Secretary of State for India, and these stocks have gone to America despite those countervailing duties which the noble Lord thinks will work wonders in the case of India.

*SIR EDWARD CLARKE (Plymouth): And the duties were paid upon them.

SIR H. CAMPBELL-BANNERMAN: I pointed out that the quantity exported to the United States, which fell to 40 millions of pounds in 1898, rose again to 658 millions of pounds last year, and this corresponds to the falling off in the exports from Germany to India, so that the relation between the two is clearly proved. The salient facts of the situation, then, are the falling off in the export of sugar from Germany to India, and the steady increase in the export of sugar from Mauritius to India. And therefore I will be content to leave it to the two right hon. Ministers facing me to decide, if by this measure they succeed in excluding bounty-fed sugar from competition, which country is to benefit. Is India, according to the glowing picture of the noble Lord, to develop her sugar industry so as to supply not only her own wants, but the wants of all the world? In that case, what is to become of Mauritius, the prosperity of which is so dear to the Colonial Secretary? On the other hand, if Mauritius is to flood the Indian market with its sugar, where is the benefit to the Indian trade? On the general question of Free Trade it is unnecessary for me to argue just now. But we are opposed to bounties as to protective duties, and what we say is, Do not correct the financial errors of other people by committing financial errors of your own. If the policy of countervailing duties is good for India, it is good for this country or the West Indies. We are opposed to it in both. The Government ought honestly to have said whether they really intend to extend these countervailing duties to this country and to the West Indies. The noble Lord thought he had placed us in a difficulty by bringing up the duty of 5 per cent. on cotton and the surtax on foreign spirits. But the answer is that we have no objection to these duties imposed for revenue purposes. It is to duties imposed for protective purposes that we object. Sir James Westland, who has been referred to in terms to which I quite agree as to his eminence and his great career, has emphatically pronounced in the debate in the Indian Council that this measure opens up an entirely new chapter in our fiscal history. That is why we support the Motion. A new chapter is being opened up, says this great financial authority; but where is that chapter to be closed, how is it to be closed, and what is to be the effect before it is closed? We adhere to the old-fashioned policy under which Great Britain and India also have flourished. It is matter of common knowledge that the nations of Europe are becoming tired of these bounties; that Germany and Austria are willing to abandon them if France would do it at the same time. Let us hope that they will see the mischievous effect of these bounties upon their own people, and by the pursuance of our remonstrance against the course they are maintaining we shall be more likely to achieve our end than by departing from the sound financial practise of this country.

Question put.

The House divided: Ayes, 152 ; noes, 293. (Division List No. 193.)

AYES.

Allan, William (Gateshead)	Burt, Thomas	Davies, M. Vaughan (Cardigan
Allen, W. (Newc. under Lyme)	Buxton, Sydney Charles	Davitt, Michael
Ashton, Thomas Gair	Caldwell, James	Dilke, Rt. Hon. Sir Charles
Asquith, Rt. Hn. Herbert Hen.	Cameron, Robert (Durham)	Dillon, John
Austin, Sir John (Yorkshire)	Campbell-Bannerman, Sir H.	Doogan, P. C.
Barlow, John Emmott	Carvill, P. George Hamilton	Duckworth, James
Bayley, Thomas (Derbyshire)	Causton, Richard Knight	Dunn, Sir William
Billson, Alfred	Channing, Francis Allston	Edwards, Owen Morgan
Birrell, Augustine	Clark, Dr. G. B. (Caithness-sh.)	Ellis, John Edward
Bolton, Thomas Dolling	Clough, Walter Owen	Evans, Samuel T. (Glamorgan)
Broadhurst, Henry	Commins, Andrew	Evans, Sir Francis H. (South'ton
Brunner, Sir John Tomlinson	Courtney, Rt. Hn. Leonard H.	Farquharson, Dr. Robert
Bryce, Rt. Hon. James	Curran, Thomas (Sligo, S.)	Farrell, James P. (Cavan, W.)
Buchanan, Thomas Ryburn	Dalziel, James Henry	Fenwick, Charles

Sir. H. Campbell-Bannerman.

Ferguson, R. C. Munro (Leith)
Fitzmaurice, Lord Edmond
Fowler, Rt. Hon. Sir Henry
Galloway, William Johnson
Gibney, James
Goddard, Daniel Ford
Gold, Charles
Gourley, Sir Edw. Temperley
Grey, Sir Edward (Berwick)
Griffith, Ellis J.
Gurdon, Sir W. Brampton
Haldane, Richard Burdon
Hammond, John (Carlow)
Harwood, George
Hayne, Rt. Hn. C. Seale-
Healy, Maurice (Cork)
Healy, Timothy M. (N. Louth)
Hedderwick, Thomas C. H.
Hemphill, Rt Hon. Chas. H.
Holden, Sir Angus
Holland, Wm. H. (York,W.R.)
Horniman, Frederick John
Hutton, Alfred E. (Morley)
Jacoby, James Alfred
Joicey, Sir James
Jones, W. (Carnarvonshire)
Jordan, Jeremiah
Kearley, Hudson E.
Kenyon, James
Kilbride, Denis
Kinloch,SirJohnGeorgeSmyth
Kitson, Sir James
Langley, Batty
Lawson,SirWilfrid(Cumb'land
Leese,SirJosephF.(Accrington
Leng, Sir John
Leuty, Thomas Richmond
Logan, John William

Lough, Thomas
Lyell, Sir Leonard
MacAleese, Daniel
MacDonnell,DrMA(Queen'sC
Maclean, James Mackenzie
MacNeill, John Gordon Swift
M'Ewan, William
M'Ghee, Richard
M'Laren, Charles Benjamin
M'Leod, John
Maddison, Fred
Maden, John Henry
Mendl, Sigismund Ferdinand
Montagu, Sir S.(Whitechapel)
Morgan, J.Lloyd(Carmarthen)
Morgan, W. P. (Merthyr)
Morley, Charles (Breconshire)
Morley, Rt.Hon.J. (Montrose)
Morton, E. J. C. (Devonport)
Moulton, John Fletcher
Norton, Capt. Cecil William
O'Connor, Arthur (Donegal)
O'Connor, T. P. (Liverpool)
Oldroyd, Mark
O'Malley, William
Palmer, Sir C. M. (Durham)
Palmer, George W. (Reading)
Paulton, James Mellor
Pearson, Sir Weetman D.
Pease, Alfred E. (Cleveland)
Pease, Joseph A. (Northumb.)
Pease, Sir J. W. (Durham)
Perks, Robert William
Pickersgill, Edward Hare
Power, Patrick Joseph
Price, Robert John
Priestley, Briggs (Yorks.)
Provand, Andrew Dryburgh

Reckitt, Harold James
Richardson, J. (Durham, S. E.)
Roberts, John Bryn (Eifion)
Roche, John (East Galway)
Samuel, J. (Stockton-on-Tees)
Schwann, Charles E.
Scott, C. Prestwich (Leigh)
Shaw, Charles Edw. (Stafford)
Shaw, Thomas (Hawick B.)
Sinclair, Capt. J. (Forfarshire)
Smith, Samuel (Flint)
Souttar, Robinson
Spicer, Albert
Stanhope, Hon. Philip J.
Stevenson, Francis S.
Strachey, Edward
Sullivan, Donal (Westmeath)
Sullivan, T. D. (Donegal, W.)
Tennant, Harold John
Thomas, A. (Glamorgan, E.)
Trevelyan, Charles Philips
Wallace, Robert
Walton, John L. (Leeds, S.)
Walton, Joseph (Barnsley)
Wedderburn, Sir William
Whittaker, Thomas Palmer
Williams, J. Carvell (Notts.)
Wills, Sir William Henry
Wilson,FrederickW.(Norfolk)
Wilson, Henry J.(York,W. R.)
Wilson, John (Govan)
Wilson, J. H.(Middlesbrough)
Young, Samuel (Cavan, East)
Yoxall, James Henry
TELLERS FOR THE AYES—
    Mr. Herbert Gladstone and
    Mr. M'Arthur.

NOES.

Allhusen, Augustus Hy. Eden
Allsopp, Hon. George
Anson, Sir William Reynell
Archdale, Edward Mervin
Arnold, Alfred
Arnold-Forster, Hugh O.
Ashmead-Bartlett, Sir Ellis
Atkinson, Rt. Hon. John
Bagot, Capt. J. FitzRoy
Bailey, James (Walworth)
Baillie, J. E. B (Inverness)
Baird, John George Alexander
Balcarres, Lord
Balfour, Rt.Hn.A.J.(Manch'r)
Balfour, Rt. Hon. G.W.(Leeds)
Barnes, Frederic Gorell
Barton, Dunbar Plunket
Bathurst, Hon.AllenBenjamin
Beach, Rt.Hn.SirM.H(Bristol)
Beach, WWBramston(Hants.)
Begg, Ferdinand Faithfull
Bemrose, Sir Henry Howe
Bentinck, Lord Henry C.
Bethell, Commander
Bhownaggree, Sir M. M.
Biddulph, Michael
Bigwood, James
Bill, Charles
Blakiston-Houston, John
Blundell, Colonel Henry
Boscawen, Arthur Griffith-
Bowles,Capt.H.F.(Middlesex)
Brodrick, Rt. Hon. St. John
Brookfield, A. Montagu
Brown, Alexander H.

Brymer, William Ernest
Bullard, Sir Harry
Burdett-Coutts, W.
Butcher, John George
Cameron, Sir Charles (Glasg.)
Campbell, J. H. M. (Dublin)
Carlile, William Walter
Cavendish, V. C. W. (Derbys.)
Cayzer, Sir Charles William
Cecil, Evelyn (Hertford, East)
Cecil, Lord Hugh (Greenwich)
Chaloner, Captain R.G.W.
Chamberlain,Rt.Hon.J.(Birm.
Chamberlain,J.Austen(Worc'r
Chaplin, Rt. Hon. Henry
Charrington, Spencer
Chelsea, Viscount
Clare, Octavius Leigh
Clarke, Sir Edw. (Plymouth)
Cochrane, Hon. T. H. A. E.
Coghill, Douglas Harry
Cohen, Benjamin Louis
Collings, Rt. Hon. Jesse
Colomb, Sir John Charles R.
Colston, Chas. Edw H. A.
Cooke,C. W.Radcliffe(Heref'd)
Corbett,A.Cameron (Glasgow)
Cornwallis,FiennesStanleyW.
Cotton-Jodrell, Col. E. T. D.
Cox, Irwin Edw. Bainbridge
Cranborne, Viscount
Cripps, Charles Alfred
Cross, Alexander (Glasgow)
Cross, H. Shepherd (Bolton)
Cruddas, William Donaldson

Cubitt, Hon. Henry
Curzon, Viscount
Dalbiac, Colonel Philip Hugh
Dalkeith, Earl of
Dalrymple, Sir Charles
Davies, Sir H. D. (Chatham)
Denny, Colonel
Dickson-Poynder, Sir J. P.
Digby, John K. D. W.
Disraeli, Coningsby Ralph
Dixon-Hartland, Sir Fred. D.
Dorington, Sir John Edward
Douglas, Rt. Hon. A. Akers-
Doxford, William Theodore
Duncombe, Hon. Hubert V.
Dyke, Rt. Hon. Sir Wm. Hart
Egerton, Hon. A. de Tatton
Elliot, Hon A. Ralph D.
Fardell, Sir T. George
Fellowes, Hon. A. Edward
Fergusson,Rt.Hn.SirJ.(Man'r)
Field, Admiral (Eastbourne)
Finch, George H.
Finlay, Sir Robert Bannatyne
Firbank, Joseph Thomas
Fisher, William Hayes
FitzGerald, Sir R. Penrose-
Fitz Wygram, General Sir F.
Flannery, Sir Fortescue
Flavin, Michael Joseph
Fletcher, Sir Henry
Flower, Ernest
Folkestone, Viscount
Foster, Colonel (Lancaster)
Gedge, Sydney

Gibbons, J. Lloyd
Gibbs,Hn.A.G.H.(CityofLond
Gibbs, Hon. Vicary(St.Albans)
Gilliat, John Saunders
Goldsworthy, Major-General
Gorst, Rt. Hon. Sir J. Eldon
Goschen, Rt.Hn.G.J.(St.Geo's)
Goschen, George J. (Sussex)
Graham, Henry Robert
Gray, Ernest (West Ham)
Green, Walford D(Wednesbury
Greene, Hy. D. (Shrewsbury)
Gretton, John
Greville, Hon. Ronald
Gunter, Colonel
Hall, Rt. Hon. Sir Charles
Halsey, Thomas Frederick
Hamilton, Rt. Hon. Lord Geo.
Hanbury, Rt. Hon. R. Wm.
Hanson, Sir Reginald
Hardy, Laurence
Hare, Thomas Leigh
Hatch, Ernest Frederick Geo.
Heath, James
Heaton, John Henniker
Helder, Augustus
Henderson, Alexander
Hermon-Hodge, Robt. Trotter
Hickman, Sir Alfred
Hill,Rt.Hn.A.Staveley(Staffs.
Hoare,EdwBrodie(Hampstead
Hoare, Samuel (Norwich)
Holland,Hon. Lionel R. (Bow)
Houldsworth, Sir Wm. Henry
Houston, R. P.
Howard, Joseph
Howell, William Tudor
Howorth, Sir Henry Hoyle
Hozier, Hon. J. H. Cecil
Hubbard, Hon. Evelyn
Hutchinson, Capt.G.W.Grice-
Hutton, John (Yorks. N.R.)
Jackson, Rt. Hon. Wm. Lawies
Jebb, Richard Claverhouse
Jenkins, Sir John Jones
Jessel, Capt. Herbert Merton
Johnston, William (Belfast)
Johnstone, Heywood (Sussex)
Jolliffe, Hon. H. George
Kemp, George
Kennaway, Rt. Hon. Sir J. H.
Kenyon-Slaney, Col. Wm.
Keswick, William
Kimber, Henry
King, Sir Henry Seymour
Knowles, Lees
Laurie, Lieut.-General
Lawrence, Sir. E. D.-(Corn.)
Lawrence, W. F. (Liverpool)
Lawson, John Grant (Yorks.)
Lea, Sir Thos. (Londonderry)
Lecky, Rt. Hon. W. E. H.
Lees, Sir Elliott (Birkenhead)
Leigh-Bennett, Henry Currie

Leighton, Stanley
Llewellyn, E. H. (Somerset)
Llewelyn, Sir D. (Swansea)
Lockwood, Lt.-Col. A. R.
Loder, G. Walter Erskine
Long, Col. C. W. (Evesham)
Long, Rt. Hon. W. (Liverpool)
Lopes, Henry Yarde Buller
Lorne, Marquess of
Lowe, Francis William
Lowles, John
Lowther,RtHnJW(Cumb'land
Loyd, Archie Kirkman
Lyttelton, Hon. Alfred
Macartney. W. G. Ellison
Macdona, John Cumming
MacIver, David (Liverpool)
Maclure, Sir John William
M'Arthur, Charles (Liverpool)
M'Calmont. Col. J. (Antrim,E.
M'Killop, James
Malcolm, Ian
Maple, Sir John Blundell
Martin, Richard Biddulph
Massey-Mainwaring,Hn.W.F.
Maxwell, Rt. Hon. Sir H. E.
Mellor, Colonel (Lancashire)
Melville, Beresford Valentine
Middlemore, J. Throgmorton
Mildmay, Francis Bingham
Milton, Viscount
Milward, Colonel Victor
Monk, Charles James
More, Robert J. (Shropshire)
Morgan, Hn. F. (Monm'thsh.)
Morrell, George Herbert
Morrison, Walter
Morton, A. H. A. (Deptford)
Mount, William George
Muntz, Philip A.
Murray, Rt. Hon. A. G. (Bute)
Murray, Charles J. (Coventry)
Murray, Col. Wyndham(Bath)
Myers, William Henry
Nicholson, William Graham
Nicol, Donald Ninian
Northcote, Hon. Sir H.Stafford
O'Neill, Hon. Robert Torrens
Orr-Ewing, Charles Lindsay
Parkes, Ebenezer
Parnell, John Howard
Penn, John
Percy, Earl
Pilkington, R.(Lancs,Newton
Powell, Sir Francis Sharp
Pretyman, Ernest George
Priestley, Sir W. O. (Edin.)
Pryce-Jones, Lt.-Col. Edward
Purvis, Robert
Quilter, Sir Cuthbert
Rankin, Sir James
Rasch, Major Frederic Carne
Renshaw, Charles Bine
Rentoul, James Alexander

Ridley, Rt. Hn. Sir Matt. W.
Ritchie, Rt. Hon. C. Thomson
Robertson, Herbert(Hackney)
Robinson, Brooke
Rothschild, Hn. Lionel Walt'r
Round, James
Russell, Gen. F. S. (Chelten'm)
Russell, T. W. (Tyrone)
Rutherford, John
Ryder, John Herbert Dudley
Sandys, Lieut.-Col. Thos. M.
Sassoon, Sir Edward Albert
Savory, Sir Joseph
Seely, Charles Hilton
Seton-Karr, Henry
Sharpe, William Edward T.
Sidebotham, J. W. (Cheshire)
Simeon, Sir Barrington
Skewes-Cox, Thomas
Smith, Jas. Parker (Lanarks.)
Smith, Hon. W. F. D. (Strand)
Stanley, Edw. J. (Somerset)
Stanley, Henry M. (Lambeth)
Stanley, Lord (Lancs.)
Stephens, Henry Charles
Stewart, Sir M.J. M'Taggart
Stock, James Henry
Stone, Sir Benjamin
Strauss, Arthur
Sutherland, Sir Thomas
Talbot, Lord Er. (Chichester)
Talbot, Rt.Hn. J.G.(Ox. Univ.
Thorburn, Walter
Thornton, Percy M.
Tollemache, Henry James
Tomlinson, W. E. Murray
Tritton, Charles Ernest
Valentia, Viscount
Vincent, Col.Sir C. E. Howard
Ward, Hon. Robt. A. (Crewe)
Warde, Lieut.-Col. C.E. (Kent)
Warr, Augustus Frederick
Welby, Lieut.-Col. A. C. E.
Wentworth, Bruce C. Vernon-
Wharton, Rt. Hn. John Lloyd
Whiteley, H. (Ashton-u.-L.)
Whitmore, Charles Algernon
Williams, Colonel R. (Dorset)
Williams, Jos. Powell-(Birm.)
Willox, Sir John Archibald
Wilson-Todd, Wm. H.(Yorks.)
Wodehouse,Rt.Hn.E.R.(Bath
Wortley, Rt. Hn. C. B. Stuart-
Wylie, Alexander
Wyndham, George
Wyndham-Quin, Major W. H.
Wyvill, Marmaduke D'Arcy
Yerburgh, Robert Armstrong
Young, Commander(Berks,E)
Younger, William

TELLERS FOR THE NOES—
　Sir William Walrond and
　Mr. Anstruther.

PRIVATE LEGISLATION PROCEDURE (SCOTLAND) [EXPENSES].

Resolution reported—

"That it is expedient to authorise the payment, out of moneys to be provided by Parliament, of any remuneration, allowances, and expenses that may become payable under any Act of the present session to provide for improving and extending the procedure for obtaining Parliamentary powers by way of Provisional Orders in matters relating to Scotland."

Resolution agreed to.

BATHS AND WASHHOUSES ACTS AMENDMENT BILL.

Read a second time, and committed for Monday next.

Adjourned at twenty minutes
after Twelve o'clock.

HOUSE OF LORDS.

Friday, 16th June 1899.

———

PRIVATE BILL BUSINESS.

———

LONDON AND NORTH - WESTERN RAILWAY (ADDITIONAL POWERS) BILL.

Examiner's Certificate of non-compliance with the Standing Orders referred to the Standing Orders Committee on Thursday next.

KENSINGTON AND NOTTING HILL ELECTRIC LIGHTING BILL.

SHIREBROOK AND DISTRICT GAS BILL.

SOUTH STAFFORDSHIRE STIPENDIARY JUSTICE BILL.

NOTTINGHAM CORPORATION BILL. WOLVERHAMPTON TRAMWAYS BILL [Lords].

Reported with Amendments.

FISHGUARD WATER AND GAS BILL.

WETHERBY DISTRICT WATER BILL.

SOUTH EASTERN RAILWAY BILL.

Committee to meet on Monday next.

BARRY RAILWAY BILL.

LANCASHIRE AND YORKSHIRE RAILWAY (NEW RAILWAYS) BILL.

LANCASHIRE AND YORKSHIRE RAILWAY (VARIOUS POWERS) BILL.

Committee to meet on Friday next.

BIRKENHEAD CORPORATION BILL [Lords].

Commons' Amendments considered, and agreed to.

OWENS COLLEGE (MANCHESTER) BILL [Lords].

Committed forthwith; Reported with Amendments.

WOKING WATER AND GAS BILL.

Read 2ª, and committed.

BROOKE'S PARK (LONDONDERRY) BILL [Lords].

Read 3ª, and passed, and sent to the Commons.

BLACKPOOL IMPROVEMENT BILL.

DARWEN CORPORATION BILL.

DUBLIN CORPORATION BILL.

Brought from the Commons; read 1ª, and referred to the Examiners.

GREAT CENTRAL RAILWAY BILL.

The Chairman of Committees informed the House that the opposition to the Bill was withdrawn: The order made on the 1st instant discharged; and Bill committed.

TRAMWAYS ORDERS CONFIRMATION (No. 2) BILL [Lords].

TRAMWAYS ORDERS CONFIRMATION (No. 3) BILL [Lords].

WEST MIDDLESEX WATER BILL.

AIRE AND CALDER NAVIGATION BILL.

EAST LONDON WATER BILL.

MILTON CREEK CONSERVANCY BILL.

GREAT WESTERN RAILWAY BILL.

GREAT WESTERN AND GREAT CENTRAL RAILWAY COMPANIES BILL.

Report from the Committee of Selection, That the following Lords be proposed to the House to form the Select Committee for the consideration of the said Bills; (viz.),

E. Spencer (chairman),
V. Falmouth,
L. Boston,
L. Crofton,
L. Sudley (E. Arran);

agreed to; and the said Lords appointed accordingly: The Committee to meet on Thursday next, at Eleven o'clock; and all petitions referred to the Committee, with leave to the petitioners praying to be heard by counsel against the Bills to be heard as desired, as also counsel for the Bills.

GAS ORDERS CONFIRMATION (No. 1) BILL [Lords].

WATER ORDERS CONFIRMATION BILL [Lords].

GAS AND WATER ORDERS CONFIRMATION BILL [Lords].

Read 3ª (according to order), and passed, and sent to the Commons.

An Asterisk (*) at the commencement of a Speech indicates revision by the Member.

ELECTRIC LIGHTING PROVISIONAL
ORDERS (No. 12) BILL [Lords].

ELECTRIC LIGHTING PROVISIONAL
ORDERS (No. 15) BILL [Lords].

ELECTRIC LIGHTING PROVISIONAL
ORDERS (No. 2) BILL.

House in Committee (according to
order): Bills reported without Amendment: Standing Committee negatived;
and Bills to be read 3' on Monday next.

TRAMWAYS ORDERS CONFIRMATION
(No. 11) BILL [Lords].

House in Committee (according to
order): Amendments made; Standing
Committee negatived; the Report of
Amendments to be received on Monday
next.

ELECTRIC LIGHTING PROVISIONAL
ORDERS (No. 3) BILL.

CENTRAL ELECTRIC SUPPLY BILL.

CENTRAL LONDON RAILWAY BILL.

CHARING CROSS, EUSTON, AND
HAMPSTEAD RAILWAY BILL.

MIDLAND RAILWAY BILL.

GAS LIGHT AND COKE COMPANY
BILL.

LONDON, BRIGHTON, AND SOUTH
COAST RAILWAY (VARIOUS POWERS)
BILL.

Report from the Committee of Selection, that the Lord Brougham and Vaux
be proposed to the House as a member of
the Select Committee on the said Bills in
the place of the Duke of Bedford; and
that the Lord Brougham and Vaux be
chairman of the said Committee; read,
and agreed to.

NORTH STAFFORDSHIRE RAILWAY
BILL [Lords].

LONDON AND SOUTH-WESTERN
RAILWAY BILL [Lords].

Report from the Committee of Selection, that the Lord Amherst of Hackney
be proposed to the House as a member of
the Select Committee on the said Bills in
the place of the Lord Farnham; read,
and agreed to.

RETURNS, REPORTS, &c.

MERCHANT SEAMEN'S FUND.

Account of the receipt and expenditure
under the Seamen's Fund Winding-up

Act, from 1st January to 31st December,
1898; Laid before the House (pursuant
to Act), and ordered to lie on the Table.

LONDON GOVERNMENT BILL.

To be read 2ª on Tuesday next. (*The
Lord President, Duke of Devonshire*).

FINANCE BILL.

(SECOND READING.)

Order of the Day for the Second Reading read.

Read 2ª (according to order); Committee negatived: Then Standing Order
No. XXXIX. considered (according to
order), and dispensed with: Bill read 3ª,
and passed.

TRAWLERS' CERTIFICATES SUSPEN-
SION BILL [Lords].

Amendments reported (according to
order); further Amendments made; and
Bill to be read 3ª on Thursday next.

ELEMENTARY EDUCATION (DEFEC-
TIVE AND EPILEPTIC CHILDREN)
BILL [Lords].

To be read 2ª on Tuesday next.

QUESTIONS.

INDENTURING IN WESTERN
AUSTRALIA.

*LORD STANLEY OF ALDERLEY:
My Lords, I desire to ask the Under
Secretary of State for the Colonies to
explain fully the nature of the indenturing
arrangements in Western Australia, and
to state why the Secretary of State
abolished the Aborigines Protection
Board in that colony without previously
informing Parliament of his intention, as
he had promised should be done; and to
ask what this board is doing now that it
has been made a branch of the Perth
Government, and under what condt ons
J.P.'s are appointed for the outlying parts
of the colony. As I have already informed my noble friend, I have nothing
to add to the notice except to give him
the extract in which Mr. Chamberlain
promised to lay the information before
Parliament. It appears in a Parliamentary

Paper C. 8350, page 138, No. 44, and is as follows :

"MR. CHAMBERLAIN to GOVERNOR SIR GERARD SMITH.

"August 21, 1896.

"I have now, therefore, to request you to inform Sir John Forrest that, after further consideration of the representations which he has made, I am prepared . . . . to lay the correspondence before Parliament with a view to ascertaining the general feeling of the House of Commons on the subject."

THE UNDER SECRETARY OF STATE FOR THE COLONIES (the EARL of SELBORNE): My Lords, the "Indenturing" system is regulated by Part IV. of the Aborigines Protection Act, 1886, from which it appears that a resident magistrate could at that time on the instructions of the board, but now of the Minister, apprentice a native or half-caste child until he reached the age of 21. It is hardly possible within the limits of a reasonable explanation to give all the details of the arrangement with its accompanying regulations, but if the noble Lord desires, I will gladly furnish him with a copy of the Act. I may say that this system of indenturing is not one of entirely recent growth, but has arisen from experience under the system of Crown and Colony Government as well as during the present *régime*. In reply to the second portion of his question, the noble Lord will see, on reference to Blue Book C. 8,350, published in February, 1897, that what Mr. Chamberlain said (August 21st, 1896, page 138) was that he was prepared, if Sir John Forrest would state what arrangements he proposed to make for fixing definitely the responsibility for, &c., to lay the correspondence before Parliament with a view to ascertaining the general feeling of Parliament on the subject. This Sir John Forrest and the legislature did in the resolutions of the legislature of Western Australia of October 26th, 1896 (see Sir G. Smith's despatch of December 4th, 1896, page 141 of the Blue Book), and the correspondence was duly laid before Parliament in February, 1897. As Parliament took no notice of the correspondence, Mr. Chamberlain had no longer any reason for refusing to accept the proposals of the Western Australian Government, and they were so informed on July 10th, 1897, nearly six months after Parliament had been placed in possession of the correspondence. As to the third portion of this question, the noble Lord will see, on reference to

the Papers C. 8,350, that the arrangement' was that the board was to be abolished and its functions discharged by a Government sub-department under the control of a responsible Minister, and that it has, therefore, now ceased to exist. The work is now entirely under a Department of the Government. The answer to the concluding paragraph of the question is that justices of the peace in Western Australia, as elsewhere, are appointed by the Governor on the recommendation of his responsible advisers, and hold office during pleasure. The Agent-General of Western Australia has pointed out to me what must occur to the noble Lord—namely, how extremely difficult it is in sparsely populated community, such as in Western Australia, always to find first-rate men for the office of magistrate. He assures me that the Government do exercise the greatest possible care in making their appointments.

*THE MARQUESS OF RIPON : My Lords, this matter is more important than perhaps might be gathered from the short answer which has been given by the noble Earl the Under Secretary of State, and I hope your Lordships will pardon me, as I was Secretary of State for the Colonies when this question was first raised, if I make a few observations upon it. I do not propose, in the observations I desire to address to the House, to criticise or to raise any objection to the course which has been taken by the right hon. Gentleman the present Secretary of State in the abolition of the Aborigines Protection Board. I think the conclusion to which he has come was, under the circumstances, probably inevitable, but the circumstances of the case are worth considering. When responsible government was first given to Western Australia there was a strong feeling, as I have always understood, in the other House of Parliament with regard to the question of treatment of natives in the colony, and it was made a condition of the granting of responsible government to Western Australia in 1890 that a board should be appointed, the members of which should be nominated by the Governor, not upon the advice of his new responsible Ministers, but upon his own personal authority, and that it should have at its disposal the sum of £5,000 a year to be voted by the Western

Australian Parliament, which sum it should dispose of entirely at its own pleasure, without any reference to the local Government. The people of Western Australia accepted the condition. They passed the Constitution Act with that provision in it, and it was well known and well understood that this was the only means by which the grant of responsible government to the colony would have been accepted at the time by the Imperial Parliament. I think the Act was passed in the year 1890. Two years afterwards, in 1892, just after I became Secretary of State for the Colonies, remonstrances, couched in very strong language, were received at the Colonial Office against the continuance of this board. It did not require much time to see that a board of this kind, composed in this way and spending at its own will and pleasure money voted by the Colonial Parliament without any reference to the Colonial Ministers, was not a board which could be long maintained in the face of the system of responsible government then established in Western Australia. But I am bound to say that, recollecting that the Act of Parliament had only been passed two years, it did seem to me rather a premature proceeding on the part of the colony to demand the abolition of an institution the establishment of which had been part of the understanding upon which responsible government had been granted ; and while I always admitted that the arrangement was necessarily a temporary one, I did not feel myself able to advise at that time that this board should be abolished. I made various proposals, with which I need not trouble your Lordships, to mitigate the objections which were felt in some minor points, but Sir John Forrest and his Government were not willing to accept these suggestions, their objection being to the general principle, and not to matters of detail. They made complaints against the board which they did not, as I thought, establish, but the essence of their objection was that the existence of a board of this kind was inconsistent with the grant of constitutional government to the colony, and when you find that the board, having £5,000 a year at its disposal, spent sometimes not much more than half that sum, and was therefore accumulating in its hands a sum of money, besides the

Marquess of Ripon.

annual grants raised by the colony, it is not surprising, I admit, that a responsible Government and a Colonial Parliament should find an arrangement of that kind very irksome and inconsistent with the acknowledged principles of constitutional government. Therefore, my Lords, I had no hesitation in admitting that the board must be of a temporary kind, and all that has passed since, I imagine, is this, that the present Secretary of State has found that the state of things which I thought difficult to maintain has become still less easy to maintain ; and that after having, as the noble Earl has said, placed certain Papers before Parliament in 1897, he thought himself free, as those Papers had apparently attracted no Parliamentary attention, to consent to the abolition of the board, and I am not inclined to criticise that decision, which must have been arrived at sooner or later. I think the question was raised, as I have said, rather prematurely by the Colonial Government, but that the system could be maintained in the face of the grant of self-government to the colony for any length of time is, I think, a proposal which cannot be upheld. We have in this case a proof of the delicacy and the difficulty of dealing with these questions · of the treatment of natives in colonies possessing responsible self-government by the Government at home. In the case of Crown colonies and colonies administered by chartered companies like the British South Africa Company the difficulty does not arise. In those cases the Government at home has full power, and therefore it is right that it should have complete responsibility. It can order what it pleases and what it thinks right, and, having ordered it, it has the power of enforcing it. But in the case of colonies with responsible government the Colonial Office has no power at all as regards administration. It cannot order anything to be done. It may express an opinion, but that opinion has no practical force whatever except such as may be allotted to it by the Colonial Government out of respect—and I am afraid this does not often occur—to the opinion of the Colonial Secretary. With regard to legislation, no doubt the Secretary of State has the power of advising Her Majesty to withhold her assent from Acts of the Colonial Parliaments to which he thinks there are objections ; but the tendency of the times, growing, I think, from year to year—and necessarily, in my judgment, growing from year to year—is that the Colonial Secretary should not advise the exercise of that power on the part of the Crown except in cases in which an Imperial interest is concerned, or, at all events, in cases where the matter is more than a purely local one. Therefore, practically, my Lords, even in that case the power of the Secretary of State is not great, and the result is this, that the Home Government and the Secretary of State for the Colonies are supposed to be responsible for proceedings over which they have very little control. The responsibility is not real, but to a great extent theoretical, and, although I am not about to advocate the adoption of any general principle or any immediate steps in the matter, I cannot, as the question has been raised, help expressing my belief that the ultimate solution of this question will be found in placing the management of natives in the territories of responsible Governments in the hands of the local governments themselves. They should have the full responsibility – the full responsibility before their own Parliament, and before the public at home—for anything they may do, and the present supposed responsibility of Downing Street should no longer be maintained even in public opinion. It should be admitted that these are questions which must be dealt with by the local responsible Government, and must be dealt with by that Government upon their own responsibility and at their own cost.

THE EARL OF SELBORNE: I hope your Lordships will allow me to say one or two words in reply to the observations of the noble Marquess. I confined my answer to the rather technical points raised in the question of the noble Lord.

THE MARQUESS OF RIPON: I did not mean to make any complaint.

THE EARL OF SELBORNE: The noble Marquess has taken the opportunity of introducing the subject in rather a wider aspect. He has given your Lordships a history of the case as it was up to the moment when the present Government came into office, and with not only that statement of the case—as to which the noble Marquess, of course, must be

the best informed man existing—but also with the impressions that the sequence of events had left in his mind, I have certainly no issue to join with him. We found steady pressure coming from Western Australia to expunge from the Western Australian Constitution Act this particular provision in respect of the Aborigines Board, and I do not think we differed in any degree from the noble Marquess in thinking that the pressure for a change, relating as it did to a provision in the Act which it was agreed could not be permanent, was rather premature. The pressure, nevertheless, continued to increase rather than to diminish in strength. It seemed to the Legislature of Western Australia to be in the nature of a derogation of their full rights of responsible government. Of course, it is not a case in which the Government would wish to enter upon a perfectly useless contest with the Colonial Government, but Mr. Chamberlain felt that it was quite impossible for him, or for the Government by itself, to consent to such a speedy change in a provision that had been specially inserted, after careful deliberation, in an Act of the Imperial Government. He accordingly said that if Sir John Forrest and his Ministry would make their definite proposals for carrying on the work of the board, he would lay those proposals before Parliament, and that if Parliament, which was responsible for the Imperial Act, raised no objection, then the Colonial Office would consent to the change. Sir John Forrest did make his proposals, the Papers were laid before Parliament, Parliament took no notice of them, and accordingly Mr. Chamberlain admitted that there was no further reasonable cause for holding out against the contention of the Government of Western Australia. That, my Lords, is the history of the case carried on from the point at which the noble Marquess left it. It would be presumptuous on my part to deal with those very large questions raised by the noble Marquess in connection with the responsibility of the Secretary of State for the Colonies for the treatment of aborigines in colonies enjoying the full benefit of responsible government. According to my slight experience, what the noble Marquess has said accurately depicts the difficulties of the Colonial Office, but I feel compelled to say that there seems a very imperfect understanding among some sections of the public, and also among sections of the public Press, in this connection. It is not necessary to cite actual cases, but where acts, which I do ·not criticise, and upon which I express no opinion, in relation to aborigines have been carried out by the Government of a self-governing country there have been frantic appeals from philanthropic people in this country to the Colonial Office to interfere with the Government of the co'ony to which responsible government has been fully granted. But that is not a possible situation or a possible solution. When we give self-government to one of our colonies it is given for good or for evil, for a whole and not for a part ; and only when general Imperial considerations come in, affecting the Empire as a whole, is there an opportunity for the Colonial Office to point out to the Government in question how far its Acts or proposed legislation are at variance with the interests of the Empire at large. So far as the internal government of the colony is concerned, whether the supposed Acts refer to white or to black men, it is not an exaggeration to say that the Colonial Office has no power at all ; and I will go further and say that if the Colonial Office attempted to take any share of responsibility on its shoulders in these cases it would produce more evil than good. It would cause immense friction, it would probably fail in producing the effect intended, and any influence that might otherwise be brought to bear, by purely private and unofficial representation, would be rendered useless. Therefore I cannot too strongly say how heartily I agree with the general principle which has been laid down by the noble Marquess.

LONDON GOVERNMENT BILL.

THE PRIME MINISTER AND SECRETARY OF STATE FOR FOREIGN AFFAIRS (The MARQUESS OF SALISBURY): My Lords, before the House adjourns, I think I ought to reply to the question which was asked yesterday by the noble Earl opposite (the Earl of Kimberley) as to the date when the Second Reading of the London Government Bill will be taken. I understand that Tuesday next will suit my noble friend, the Duke of Devonshire, and if it also suits noble Lords opposite I shall be pleased to put the Bill down for Second Reading on that day.

Earl of Selborne.

THE EARL OF KIMBERLEY: Tuesday next will suit us.

THE MARQUESS OF SALISBURY: Then it shall be put down for Tuesday.

House adjourned at five o'clock to Monday next, a quarter before Eleven o'clock.

HOUSE OF COMMONS.

Friday, 16th June 1899.

PRIVATE BILL BUSINESS.

DARWEN CORPORATION BILL.

DUBLIN CORPORATION BILL. (By Order). Read the third time, and passed.

DERBY CORPORATION (TRAMWAYS, ETC.) BILL.
LONDON COUNTY COUNCIL (MONEY) BILL.

As amended, considered ; to be read the third time.

GLASGOW CORPORATION TELEPHONES BILL. (By Order).

Second Reading deferred till Friday June 30th.

EDUCATION DEPARTMENT PROVISIONAL ORDER CONFIRMATION (LIVERPOOL) BILL. [Lords.]

Read a second time, and committed.

RAILWAY BILLS (GROUP 8).

GREENOCK AND PORT GLASGOW TRAMWAYS BILL.

*MR. J. W. LOWTHER (Cumberland, Penrith): I have to move that certain parties be ordered to attend the Committee on the Greenock and Port Glasgow Tramways Bill on Monday. As the circumstances are a little unusual I wish to explain why I make the Motion instead of the hon. Member for Knutsford, who is chairman of the Committee. The fact is that the Committee have adjourned until Monday, and it was only discovered to-day that it would require an Order of the House to enable the gentlemen to attend on that day. In the absence of the hon.

Member for Knutsford I take upon me the responsibility which ordinarily falls on the chairman.

Mr. James William Lowther informed the House that the Committee on Group 8 of Railway and Tramway Bills having adjourned, the parties promoting the Greenock and Port Glasgow Tramways Bill [Lords], which was comprised in the Group, had appeared before him, and proved that the evidence of Robert Cook, of 9, Orangefield Place, Greenock, John Daniel Clink, of 53, Octavia Terrace, Greenock, John Cameron, of 46, Linnart Street, Greenock, Daniel M'Arthur Erskine, of Linnart Grove, Greenock, and Hugh M'Master, of Port Glasgow, was essential to their case; and that their attendance could not be procured without the intervention of the House.

Ordered, that Robert Cook, John Daniel Clink, John Cameron, Daniel M'Arthur Erskine, and Hugh M'Master do attend the Committee on Group 8 of Railway and Tramway Bills upon Monday next, at half-past Eleven of the clock.—(*Mr. James William Lowther.*)

KINGSCOURT, KEADY, AND ARMAGH RAILWAY BILL.

MR. T. M. HEALY (Louth, N.): I understand that the hon. Baronet the Chairman of the Committee on this Bill is not in his place, and that some of the opponents are also not in their places. I beg to postpone my Motion for the re-committal of the Bill till next Friday.

___

LOCAL GOVERNMENT PROVISIONAL ORDERS (No. 2) BILL.

LOCAL GOVERNMENT PROVISIONAL ORDERS (No. 7) BILL.

Reported, with Amendments (Provisional Orders confirmed); Report to lie upon the Table; Bills, as amended, to be considered upon Monday next.

LOCAL GOVERNMENT (IRELAND) PROVISIONAL ORDERS (No. 2) BILL.

LOCAL GOVERNMENT (IRELAND) PROVISIONAL ORDERS (No. 3) BILL.

Reported, without Amendment (Provisional Orders confirmed); Report to lie upon the Table; Bills to be read the third time upon Monday next.

MILITARY LANDS PROVISIONAL ORDER BILL.

Reported, with an Amendment [Provisional Order confirmed]; Report to lie upon the Table.

Bill, as amended, to be considered upon Monday next.

ELECTRIC LIGHTING PROVISIONAL ORDERS (No. 16) BILL.

Reported, with Amendments; [Provisional Orders confirmed]; Report to lie upon the Table.

Bill, as amended, to be considered upon Monday next.

ELECTRIC LIGHTING PROVISIONAL ORDER (No. 18) BILL.

ELECTRIC LIGHTING PROVISIONAL ORDERS (No. 19) BILL.

Reported, without Amendment; [Provisional Orders confirmed]; Report to lie upon the Table.

Bills to be read the third time upon Monday next.

BEXHILL AND ROTHERFIELD RAILWAY BILL.

INVERNESS HARBOUR BILL. [Lords.]

Reported. with Amendments; Reports to lie upon the Table, and to be printed.

WISHAW WATER BILL. [Lords.]

Reported, without Amendment; Report to lie upon the Table, and to be printed.

BARTON-ON-SEA WATER BILL. [Lords.]

Reported, with Amendments; Report to lie upon the Table, and to be printed.

COLONIAL AND FOREIGN BANKS GUARANTEE FUND BILL. [Lords.]

Reported, with Amendments; Report to lie upon the Table.

GLASGOW CORPORATION (GAS AND WATER) BILL. [Lords.]

GAINSBOROUGH URBAN DISTRICT COUNCIL (GAS) BILL. [Lords.]

DUNDEE GAS, STREET IMPROVEMENTS, AND TRAMWAYS BILL. [Lords.]

LANARKSHIRE (MIDDLE WARD DISTRICT) WATER BILL. [Lords.]

LIVERPOOL OVERHEAD RAILWAY BILL. [Lords.]

Reported, with Amendments, Reports to lie upon the Table, and to be printed.

LOCAL GOVERNMENT PROVISIONAL ORDER (No. 13) BILL.

Reported [Provisional Order not confirmed]; Report to lie upon the Table.

WORCESTERSHIRE COUNTY COUNCIL BILL.

Reported, with Amendments; Report to lie upon the Table, and to be printed.

JONES'S DIVORCE BILL. [Lords.]

Reported, from the Select Committee on Divorce Bills, without Amendment; Report to lie upon the Table.

Bill to be read a third time.

JONES'S DIVORCE BILL. [Lords.]

Ordered, That the Minutes of Evidence and Proceedings in the House of Lords on the Second Reading of Jones's Divorce Bill, together with the Documents deposited in the case, be returned to the House of Lords; and that the Clerk do carry the same.—(*Mr. Solicitor-General.*)

DERBY CORPORATION WATER BILL, LEICESTER CORPORATION WATER BILL, AND SHEFFIELD CORPORATION (DERWENT VALLEY) WATER BILL CONSOLIDATED INTO THE "DERWENT VALLEY WATER BILL."

Reported, with Amendments; Report to lie upon the Table, and to be printed.

———

MESSAGE FROM THE LORDS.

That they have agreed to—

FINANCE BILL, NORTH PEMBROKESHIRE AND FISHGUARD RAILWAY BILL,

Without Amendment.

SHOTLEY BRIDGE AND CONSETT DISTRICT GAS BILL,

With Amendments.

That they have passed a Bill, intituled, "An Act to confirm certain Provisional Orders made by the Board of Trade under the Electric Lighting Acts, 1882 and 1888, relating to Crayford, Halesowen, Handsworth, Lye and Wollescote, and Lymington." [Electric Lighting Provisional Orders (No. 14) Bill. [Lords.]

ELECTRIC LIGHTING PROVISIONAL ORDERS (No. 14) BILL. [Lords.]

Read the first time; referred to the Examiners of Petitions for Private Bills, and to be printed. [Bill 237.]

———

PETITIONS.

———

LIQUOR TRAFFIC LOCAL VETO (SCOTLAND) BILL.

Petition from Dumfries and Maxwelltown, in favour; to lie upon the Table.

LOCAL AUTHORITIES SERVANTS' SUPERANNUATION BILL.

Petition from Sheffield, in favour; to lie upon the Table.

LOCAL GOVERNMENT (SCOTLAND) ACT (1894) AMENDMENT BILL.

Petitions in favour, from Dundee;—and Beath; to lie upon the Table.

LOCAL GOVERNMENT (SCOTLAND) ACT (1894) AMENDMENT (No. 2) BILL.

Petition from Dundee, against; to lie upon the Table.

POOR LAW RELIEF (DISFRANCHISEMENT).

Petition from Holbeach, for alteration of Law; to lie upon the Table.

PRIVATE LEGISLATION PROCEDURE (SCOTLAND) BILL.

Petition from St. Andrews, in favour; to lie upon the Table.

SALE OF INTOXICATING LIQUORS ON SUNDAY BILL.

Petitions in favour, from Sawbridgeworth;—Great Yarmouth;—and Wisbech; to lie upon the Table.

———

RETURNS, REPORTS, &c.

———

MERCHANT SEAMEN'S FUND.

Account presented,—of the receipt and expenditure under the Seamen's Fund Winding-up Act from 1st January to 31st December, 1898 [by Act]; to lie upon the Table, and to be printed. [No. 222.]

APPOINTMENTS OPEN TO RETIRED SOLDIERS.

Return ordered, "showing the number of appointments which would be open to reserve and retired Soldiers under the heads enumerated as suitable in Appendix to Report of Select Committee on Retired Soldiers' and Sailors' Employment 1895; the number of Soldiers now holding such appointments; and the number of vacancies which have occurred in such appointments since December 1895, in the following form :—

Employment.	Number of men employed under each head.	Number of ex-Soldiers employed.	Number of Vacacies which have occurred since 31st day of December 1895.

—(*Colonel Long.*)

PUBLIC INCOME AND EXPENDITURE.

Return ordered, "of Net Public Income and Net Public Expenditure under certain specified heads, as represented by Receipts into and Issues out of the Exchequer from 1869-70 to 1898-9, inclusive (in continuation of Parliamentary Paper, No. 344, of Session 1898)."—(*Sir Henry Fowler.*)

LOCAL GOVERNMENT (IRELAND) ACT, 1898 (METHOD OF DETERMINING AMOUNTS TO BE TAKEN AS HAVING BEEN RAISED IN STANDARD YEAR).

Copy ordered, "of Memorandum respecting the method adopted in determining the amounts of poor rate and county cess to be taken as having been raised during the standard financial year under Section 49 of the Local Government (Ireland) Act, 1898."—(*Mr. Gerald Balfour.*)

Copy presented accordingly; to lie upon the Table, and to be printed. [No. 232.]

———

SHOP HOURS ACT (1892) AMENDMENT.

Bill to amend the Shop Hours Act, 1892, ordered to be brought in by Mr. Steadman, Sir Charles Dilke, and Mr. Woods.

SHOP HOURS ACT (1892) AMENDMENT BILL.

"To amend the Shop Hours Act, 1892," presented accordingly, and read the first time; to be read a second time upon Wednesday, 28th June, and to be printed. [Bill 238.]

———

FIRE BRIGADES.

Ordered, That Mr. Alfred Thomas be discharged from the Select Committee on Fire Brigades.

Ordered, That Mr. William Jones be added to the Committee.—(*Mr. Munro Ferguson.*)

———

QUESTIONS.

———

MOUNTAIN AND GARRISON ARTILLERY.

MR. ARNOLD-FORSTER (Belfast, W.): I beg to ask the Under Secretary of State for War whether, in view of the reorganisation of the Royal Regiment of Artillery, the right of officers serving in the mounted and garrison branches respectively will be re-established.

THE UNDER SECRETARY OF STATE FOR WAR (Mr. WYNDHAM, Dover): The practice alluded to was at all times tempered by selection for Horse and Mountain Batteries. It involved an undesirable amount of complicated manipulation, and was therefore abolished in 1891. There is no intention to restore it.

RECRUITS' RATIONS.

MR. HAYDEN (Roscommon, S.): I beg to ask the Under-Secretary of State for War whether a recruit joining at a regimental depôt is put through a severe course of gymnastic and other training, chiefly in the open air, for a period of three months; and whether he is aware that the bread ration, one pound per diem, issued to him is regarded as altogether insufficient; and, having regard to the fact that the recently established "messing allowance" does not apply, would he consider the advisability of establishing an increased bread ration for the recruit during this period.

MR. WYNDHAM: It is true that the "messing allowance" is not given to a recruit, but this only affects his pocket. He shares with his comrades in the additional messing, which includes extra bread. But, in his case, threepence is still stopped out of his pay.

EDWARD LYNCH'S PENSION.

MR. HAYDEN: I beg to ask the Under-Secretary of State for War whether an ex-soldier, named Edward Lynch, who was discharged from the Army in 1881, received no pension until 1894, when a pension was granted and some arrears paid. Will he explain why, since then, the pension has been discontinued. And, whether he will have the case re-considered with a view to the restoration of the pension.

MR. WYNDHAM: Edward Lynch was discharged from the Army in 1882, and at first was refused a pension, in consequence of some informality in his discharge documents. On reconsideration, however, the Commissioners of Chelsea Hospital granted him a pension in 1883. At that time he could not be found; but he again applied in 1894, and was allowed to draw his pension from

January, 1892. The pension has not been discontinued. The question of allowing arrears from 1882 to 1892 is under consideration.

THE CONNAUGHT RANGERS AT MEERUT.

MR. HERBERT ROBERTS (Denbighshire, W.): I beg to ask the Secretary of State for India whether his attention has been drawn to the shooting case in which four privates of the Connaught Rangers came into collision with some natives near Meerut in December last, and which has aroused considerable interest in India; and whether, in view of the frequent occurrence of such conflicts in India, due to the practice of British soldiers carrying firearms whilst off duty, he will consider whether more stringent regulations are required in the interests of the public peace.

THE SECRETARY OF STATE FOR INDIA (Lord G. HAMILTON, Middlesex, Ealing): I have seen with much regret a newspaper report of the occurrence referred to, and have observed that it was found by the High Court of the North-Western Provinces that the soldiers acted in self defence. As regards the second part of the question, the Government of India were consulted by me last year, and were of opinion that there was no ground for special measures. In this opinion I concur. The regulations for the grant to soldiers of shooting passes, which were revised in 1892 and 1895, are already very stringent. The hon. Member is mistaken in supposing that cases of collision between British soldiers and natives are of frequent occurrence.

OUTRAGE BY BRITISH SOLDIERS AT RANGOON.

MR. HERBERT ROBERTS: I beg to ask the Secretary of State for India whether his attention has been called to the disgraceful outrage upon a Burmese lady, which was committed by from twelve to sixteen men of the West Kent Regiment at Rangoon on 2nd April last; whether the civil authorities are powerless to discover the culprits because the soldiers refuse to give evidence; whether he is aware that some forty men were either witnesses of or participants in the outrage, and that the regimental authorities have so far made no arrests; and, whether he will cause an immediate inquiry to be made into the matter. As

the noble Lord answered a similar question last Tuesday, perhaps he will kindly state if any additional facts have transpired.

LORD G. HAMILTON: On Monday last I fully answered this question in reply to the hon. Member for South Mayo, and I must refer the hon. Gentleman to that answer. I stated that every means at the disposal both of the civil and military authorities in Rangoon would be used for the purpose of bringing the perpetrators of this disgraceful outrage to justice.

MR. DAVITT (Mayo, S.): Is it the intention of the Government to allow this regiment to remain at Rangoon after such a cowardly outrage?

LORD G. HAMILTON: I think that question is hardly germane to the question on the paper. A court of inquiry is now investigating the facts, and until its report has been received it is impossible to say what action should be taken; but the occurrence does not reflect well on the state of discipline in the regiment.

MR. DILLON (Mayo, E.): Have none of the culprits been detected?

LORD G. HAMILTON: One man has already been tried, and has been acquitted, the judge concurring in the acquittal. A court of inquiry was directed to be instituted by the Government of India in order to ascertain, if possible, the culprits, who have hitherto escaped detection.

MR. SWIFT MACNEILL (Donegal, S.): Is it a fact that the unfortunate woman who was the victim of this outrage is now dead?

LORD G. HAMILTON: I have not heard that.

CALCUTTA MUNICIPAL BILL.

MR. HERBERT ROBERTS: I beg to ask the Secretary of State for India whether he will state whether the Select Committee of the Bengal Legislative Council have submitted their Report upon the Calcutta Municipal Bill; and, if so, whether any alteration has been made in Section 8 of the Bill, which reduces the representatives of the town to a minority of four in the proposed Executive Committee of twelve; and, whether he will state what course he intends to adopt with respect to the measure.

LORD G. HAMILTON: No report on the subject has yet reached me, and until I receive the report and the views of the Government of India upon the subject I cannot state what course may be taken.

KURDISH ATROCITIES IN ARMENIA.

MR. SCHWANN (Manchester, N.): I beg to ask the Under Secretary of State for Foreign Affairs whether he has seen a telegram from Vienna, dated Sunday last, in which it was stated that the Russian and French Ambassadors have raised a protest against the Kurdish atrocities in Armenia, which are increasing every day, their Excellencies demand energetic measures, otherwise Turkey will be held responsible for the consequences; and, in the affirmative case, will the British Ambassador at Constantinople be instructed to support their remonstrances and representations to the Porte.

*THE UNDER SECRETARY OF STATE FOR FOREIGN AFFAIRS (MR. BRODRICK, Surrey, Guildford): No information to this effect has reached Her Majesty's Government, but Her Majesty's Ambassador is furnished with instructions which would enable him to join in any well-founded representations on the subject.

THE TRANSVAAL OATH OF ALLE-GIANCE.

MR. BRYN ROBERTS (Carnarvonshire, Eifion): I beg to ask the Secretary of State for the Colonies whether the alteration of the form of the Transvaal oath of allegiance by omitting therefrom an express abjuration of all allegiance to any other State, as suggested by Sir Alfred Milner, will enable British subjects to become naturalised in the South African Republic without losing their British nationality; if not, whether he will take steps to let this be known to British subjects in the Transvaal, so that they shall not unwittingly lose their British nationality.

*THE SECRETARY OF STATE FOR THE COLONIES (Mr. J. CHAMBERLAIN, Birmingham, W.): The answer to the first part of the question is in the negative. In answer to the second part I have to say that the Papers which have been published contain full information on the subject.

ANTI-BOER PROPAGANDA.

MR. SWIFT MACNEILL: I beg to ask the Secretary of State for the Colonies whether Her Majesty's Government have confirmation of the statement that a body calling itself the South African Association has spent considerable sums of money upon an anti-Boer propaganda in this country and Cape Colony.

MR. J. CHAMBERLAIN: No, Sir.

THE NEWFOUNDLAND FISHERIES.

SIR T. GIBSON - CARMICHAEL (Edinburgh, Mid-Lothian): I beg to ask the Secretary of State for the Colonies whether the Committee of Inquiry upon the Newfoundland Fisheries, of which Admiral Sir James Erskine was appointed chairman, has yet reported; and whether the desire which exists for the publication of the Report is likely to be gratified at an early date.

MR. J. CHAMBERLAIN: The Commission of Inquiry into the Newfoundland Fisheries, of which Sir John Bramston was Chairman, has reported. It is not desirable to publish the Report until the Departments concerned have had time to make their observations upon the statements and recommendations of the Commissioners, and Her Majesty's Government have arrived at a decision upon them after consultation with the Colonial Government.

MR. GIBSON BOWLES (Lynn Regis): Can the right hon. Gentleman state approximately the time when the Report may be expected?

MR. CHAMBERLAIN: No, Sir; but I fear it will be some considerable time.

ORPHAN HOMES OF SCOTLAND.

SIR CHARLES CAMERON (Glasgow, Bridgeton): I beg to ask the Lord Advocate whether he is aware that some 1,000 children of school age, inmates of the Orphan Homes of Scotland, on which over £200 of school rates were recently paid, have received no education for nearly two months, owing to the refusal of the School Board to receive them; whether want of school accommodation is the reason alleged for this refusal; whether he is aware that ample school accommodation exists in connection with the homes, and the use of it has been offered to the School Board at a very moderate rent ; and, whether the Scottish Education Department intends taking any steps to enforce the Law of Scotland as to the compulsory education of all children of school age.

THE LORD ADVOCATE (Mr. A. G. MURRAY, Buteshire) : The legal questions connected with the matter referred to in the hon. Member's Question are now under consideration, and it is therefore impossible for me at present to make any further statement regarding it.

SCOTTISH EDUCATION GRANT.

DR. CLARK (Caithness) : I beg to ask the Lord Advocate what sum has been paid to the Scottish Education Department, in accordance with the promise of the Chancellor of the Exchequer, to make up the difference between the ⅗ths and 10s. per child, from the passing of the Free Education Act till the change of the system.

MR. A. G. MURRAY : The sum which the Treasury, on the representation of the Scotch Education Department, agreed to pay in order to make up the difference between ⅘ths of the English grant and 10s. per child, in respect of the years 1892 to 1896, was £23,875. Of this £21,000 was voted in 1898-99, and £2,875 appears in the present year's Estimates.

CASE OF SARAH HALE.

MR. STEADMAN (Tower Hamlets, Stepney) had on the paper the following Question : "To ask the Secretary of State for the Home Department whether his attention has been called to the case of a domestic servant, aged 16, named Sarah Hale, who pleaded guilty to having stolen from her mistress some small articles of jewellery, valued at 7s. 6d., when charged with this offence before the Petty Sessions at Moreton-in-Marsh, and was sentenced to three months' imprisonment, although it was stated that she had been in one or two situations previously where there was nothing against her character, and that her father and mother were most respectable people ; and whether, in view of her previous good character, and of the youth of the girl, he could see his way to give her the benefit of the First Offenders Act." On its being called, the hon. Member announced that he had that morning received from the Home Secretary a letter intimating that the sentence

had been reduced to three weeks, and that the woman would be released the next day.

THE NEW ECCLESIASTICAL JUDGE.

LORD BALCARRES (Lancashire, Chorley) : I wish to ask the Under Secretary to the Home Department a Question of which I have given him private notice—whether the answer which the right hon. Gentleman gave to my hon. friend the Member for the Exchange Division of Liverpool yesterday with reference to the appointment of Sir Arthur Charles was accurate.

*THE UNDER SECRETARY OF STATE FOR THE HOME DEPARTMENT (Mr. JESSE COLLINGS, Birmingham, Bordesley) : The answer was not quite correct in one particular—the statement that a Dean of Arches is not now appointed. On further inquiry I find that Sir Arthur Charles has been appointed by the Archbishop of Canterbury to the office of Dean of Arches. In all other respects the answer is correct.

NATIONAL DEBT ANNUITIES.

MR. J. P. SMITH (Lanark, Partick) : I beg to ask Mr. Chancellor of the Exchequer whether he is aware that the Commissioners of the National Debt will not receive applications or payments to increase the amount of existing annuities otherwise than personally ; whether he will give facilities by which payments to increase an existing annuity may be made by post ; and whether he will provide that the proprietor of an annuity may be able to give instructions that the instalment of the annuity shall be retained and applied to increase the amount of the annuity automatically, as in the case of Consols.

THE CHANCELLOR OF THE EXCHEQUER (Sir M. HICKS BEACH, Bristol, W.) : The law requires that the purchase-money for an annuity must be paid by the purchaser or his agent to the cashier of the Bank of England, and, of course, any banker can act as an agent. I could not therefore legally take the course suggested in the second paragraph of the Question. As to the last paragraph, I think that it must be a very rare thing indeed for the proprietor of an annuity to desire to increase it by the application of instalments of the annuity to that purpose, and without some greater evidence of demand for it I should not feel justified in proposing to the Bank of England such an extension of the system of automatic investment of dividends in Consols.

THE INNISKEEN RAILWAY ACCIDENT.

MR. MACALEESE: I beg to ask the President of the Board of Trade whether he can say if the management of the Great Northern Railway (Ireland) has, so far, taken any steps to carry out the suggestions as to improvements on their line near Culloville, made by Lieutenant-Colonel Addison, on the 6th April last, in his report upon the accident to a cattle train at Inniskeen.

THE PRESIDENT OF THE BOARD OF TRADE (Mr. RITCHIE, Croydon): The railway company have not taken any steps, and the Board of Trade are still in communication with them.

ALLEGED OUTRAGE ON THE GREAT WESTERN RAILWAY.

MR. SCHWANN: I beg to ask the President of the Board of Trade whether his attention has been drawn to the out-rage committed by a sailor of H.M.S. *Terrible* on a fellow passenger, travel-ling on the Great Western 9.30 express from Swansea to Paddington, a few days ago, when it is said the communication cord was not in order, and it was there-fore impossible to call the attention of the guard; whether he would communi-cate with the authorities of the Great Western Railway with a view to a more careful scrutiny of communication cords on making up their trains at their respective starting places; and is he aware that a man named Anderson was killed in the same train two days before the assault referred to above.

MR. RITCHIE: I have communicated with the company, and have received a reply in which they state that there is no such train as the 9.30 express from Swan-sea to Paddington; that on the arrival at Swindon at 3.5 a.m., on May 27th, of the 7 p.m. excursion train from New Milford to London, a passenger complained to the inspector on duty that he had been assaulted by a fellow-passenger and that on the police being sent for each passenger preferred a charge of assault against the other. The police thereupon declined to act, and the two men remained at Swindon, ultimately coming to London by the next

train at 6.40 a.m.; that no representation was made to the company that the com-munication cord failed to act, in fact it was tested at Landore and Cardiff during the journey and found to be in good working order; that one of the men who complained had a few scratches on his face, and from the statement made by a passenger in the same compartment the affair was of a trivial character—one man being as much to blame as the other. With regard to the death of the man Anderson it appears that he and two com-panions—all being discharged sailors—were passengers from Cardiff to London by the 6.30 p.m. express from New Mil-ford on May 23rd; that when the tickets were examined at Chepstow nothing was amiss beyond the fact that one of the men could not find his ticket, but that on arrival at Gloucester, Anderson was found to be dead from a wound in the neck; that the men were apparently under the influence of liquor, and that there was no evidence of any disturbance or fight having taken place.

SCOTTISH LIGHTHOUSE KEEPERS.

DR. CLARK: I beg to ask the Lord Advocate if he can state when a reply will be given to the memorial of the Scottish lighthouse keepers; whether it is proposed to have a retiring allowance to the Scottish keepers on the same basis as that given to the Irish and English keepers; and whether the conditions as to holiday leave now obtaining in England and Ireland will be extended to Scotland.

MR. RITCHIE: I am informed by the Commissioners of Northern Lighthouses that a circular intimating increase of pay to the lighthouse keepers was issued last week. The retiring allowance to the Scottish lighthouse keepers is and will continue to be on the same basis as that given to the Irish and English keepers. I have been informed by the Com-missioners that they propose to put their keepers on the same footing in the matter of holidays as the keepers in the sister services are on.

CIRCULAR POSTAGE.

MR. EDWARD BARRY (Cork Co., S.): I beg to ask the Secretary to the Trea-sury, as representing the Postmaster-General, whether the cost of the postage of circulars is the same in Bandon and Clone; and, if not, will steps be taken to make the cost identical in both places.

THE FINANCIAL SECRETARY TO THE TREASURY (Mr. HANBURY, Preston): Circulars which conform to the Book Post Regulations are transmissible at the halfpenny rate of postage throughout the United Kingdom. If a higher rate has been charged at either of the places mentioned this must have been due to some misunderstanding, and the Postmaster-General will be obliged if the hon. Member will furnish him with particulars.

THE MOY POSTMASTERSHIP.

MR. WILLIAM JOHNSTON (Belfast, S.): I beg to ask the Secretary to the Treasury, as representing the Postmaster-General, on what conditions Mr. J. Morrison, Postmaster of Moy, county Tyrone, was granted permission to become a candidate for the Petty Sessions Clerkship of Moy; and whether it is competent for a Civil Servant to hold two Government appointments; and, if so, why, when permission was granted to Mr. Morrison to become a candidate for the Petty Sessions Clerkship, it was not permitted to the Petty Sessions Clerk at Pomeroy to become a candidate for the Post Office, which recently became vacant.

MR. HANBURY: It is the fact that the Postmaster of Moy received permission several years ago to become a candidate for the position of Petty Sessions Clerk, and this permission was recently renewed to him. The permission will not be granted in any future case. As a general rule it is not considered desirable to appoint as Postmaster or Sub-Postmaster persons who hold the position of Petty Sessions Clerk, and the Petty Sessions Clerk at Pomeroy, who was a candidate for the Sub-Postmastership, was not selected for the appointment.

COST OF POSTCARDS.

MR. FLAVIN (Kerry, N.): I beg to ask the Secretary to the Treasury, as representing the Postmaster - General, whether he is aware that the United Kingdom is the only place in which postcards cost more than the stamp they bear; and whether at an early date the original practice of selling postcards at their face value will be put into effect.

MR. HANBURY: The United Kingdom is not the only place in which postcards cost more than the stamp they bear. There are a few other countries in which that is the case. I cannot hold out any hope that it will be possible to make any change in the price of inland postcards in this country.

FERRYBANK POSTMASTERSHIP.

MR. PATRICK O'BRIEN (Kilkenny): I beg to ask the Secretary to the Treasury, as representing the Postmaster-General, whether a post office has yet been selected and a postmaster appointed at Ferrybank, Arklow; whether he can say who has been appointed and where the office is situated; and, whether, before making the selection of the office and appointing a postmaster, due consideration was given to a memorial signed by the principal inhabitants of Ferrybank urging certain premises as most suitable and convenient to the people to be served by the said post office, and in favour of Mr. Patrick Bradford as the most suitable person to have charge of the office.

MR. HANBURY: Arrangements have been made for opening a post-office at the premises of the Arklow Stores, Ferrybank, Arklow, and Mr. E. Seward (manager of the provision department at the stores) has been appointed sub-postmaster. The premises on which the post-office has been placed were reported to be the only ones suitable, and the selection had been already made when the memorial respecting Mr. Patrick Bradford was received.

SUB-POSTMASTERS' PAY.

MR. PATRICK O'BRIEN: I beg to ask the Secretary to the Treasury, as representing the Postmaster-General, if scales of payment are furnished to sub-postmasters; and, if so, are they binding alike on both the Department and sub-postmaster; and whether he is aware of the fact that sub-postmasters have been working the telephone on behalf of the Post Office for over two years, and that they cannot obtain satisfaction as to when payment will be made, or according to what scale; if so, will he take steps to immediately alter this state of affairs.

MR. HANBURY: Scales of payment are furnished to Sub-Postmasters on application. Under ordinary conditions they are binding alike on the Department and the Sub-Postmaster. The Postmaster-General is aware of the fact stated in the second part of the hon. Member's question. The question of the scale of remuneration for telephone work has been under his consideration for some time, and he hopes that he will very shortly be able to arrive at a conclusion which will be satisfactory to the officers concerned.

DUBLIN POSTMEN'S GRIEVANCES.

MR. PATRICK O'BRIEN: I beg to ask the Secretary to the Treasury, as representing the Postmaster-General, whether assistant postmen at Dublin, who were previously of the telegraph messengers' class, and are between the ages of 18 and 21 years, have been dismissed the service because they have failed to reach the fixed standard of weight for appointments; and, whether he would advise the reinstatement of these lads, in consideration of their service (in most cases six years), with a view to their qualification at a future date, when they are fully grown, and that others of this class, who are under notice of dismissal, may be retained for the same purpose.

MR. HANBURY: There have recently been five candidates in Dublin for the situation of postman as to whose physical qualifications doubts have been raised. One of them has been definitely rejected not only on account of his being below the usual standard of weight and height, but on account of deafness. The other cases are still under consideration, and it is hoped that a decision will be arrived at very shortly.

MR. PATRICK O'BRIEN: I beg to ask the Secretary to the Treasury, as representing the Postmaster-General, why the boot allowance and sick pay recommended by the Tweedmouth Committee to all assistant postmen, and to old auxiliaries who were performing five hours' duty previous to 1897, are not being paid in Dublin.

MR. HANBURY: The Postmaster-General finds that through some misunderstanding the allowances in question have not been paid to 12 men attached to the Dublin Office. The matter has now been put right.

MR. PATRICK O'BRIEN: I beg to ask the Secretary to the Treasury, as representing the Postmaster-General, will he explain why old auxiliaries at Dublin,

with a telegraph messenger and postman service ranging as high as 26 years, who have been performing full time duties, have been informed that their services can be dispensed with at any moment, in view of the recommendation of the Tweedmouth Committee, that in making changes in the auxiliary class the rights of existing holders should be carefully preserved.

MR. HANBURY: The men to whom the question is understood to refer are ineligible for appointment to established situations, and they have been informed that they will be allowed to continue as auxiliaries on the understanding that their retention will give them no claim to advancement, and that their services may be dispensed with at any time when the interests of the service require it. The men are, it is true, now performing full time duties, but this is a temporary arrangement, and they will probably soon have to fall back upon their usual short time duties.

SUPERIOR APPOINTMENTS IN THE IRISH POST OFFICE.

MR. PATRICK O'BRIEN: I beg to ask the Secretary to the Treasury, as representing the Postmaster-General, if he can state how many officials of the Post Office service have been appointed since 1st June, 1892, to situations in the Irish Post Office service carrying salaries in excess of £360 a year; and if he can also state how many Irish postal officials have been appointed during the same period to similar situations in the English postal service.

MR. HANBURY: The number of situations in the Post Office service in Ireland carrying salaries in excess of £360 a year to which appointments have been made since 1st June, 1892, is 32. By "Irish postal officials" the hon. Member is understood to mean officers employed in the Post Office in Ireland, and the number of these appointed during the same period to similar situations in the Post Office in England and Scotland is five.

MR. PATRICK O'BRIEN: I beg to ask the Secretary to the Treasury, as representing the Postmaster - General, whether the situation of chief clerk and acting inspector of mails in the General Post Office, Dublin, with a salary rising from £600 to £800 a year, is expected to become shortly vacant; whether, in filling the anticipated vacancy, the qualifications of officers of the Irish branch of the service will be fully considered, and, if these qualifications be found equal to those of other officers not connected with the Irish service, the Irish officers will have the first claim to the vacant appointment; and whether, in view of the discontent existing throughout the Irish Post Office service at the non-promotion of deserving Irish officers to the higher situations in Ireland, the Postmaster-General will lay upon the Table of the House the entire papers on which these appointments have been made since 1st June, 1892.

MR. HANBURY: The answer to the first and second paragraphs of the hon. Member's question is in the affirmative. The Postmaster-General is not prepared to lay upon the Table of the House the papers to which reference is made. Such papers must necessarily be treated as confidential.

BERKHAMPSTEAD NATIONAL SCHOOLS.

MR. TREVELYAN (York, W. R. Elland): I beg to ask the Vice-President of the Committee of Council on Education whether his attention has been called to the fact that on Ascension Day the children and teachers of the National Schools at Berkhampstead were taken to a service in the parish church; whether the service was held during school hours; and, if so, whether the Department has the power to interfere to prevent the practice in future; and whether any attempt was made to obtain the consent of the parents of the scholars to their being taken from school to attend this service.

THE VICE-PRESIDENT OF THE COMMITTEE OF COUNCIL ON EDUCATION (Sir J. GORST, Cambridge University): The answer to the first question is in the negative. With regard to the attendance of children at church services, I have nothing to add to my answer to a similar question on February 23rd.

SOUTH KENSINGTON MUSEUM (ART BRANCH).

MR. MAURICE HEALY (Cork): I beg to ask the Vice-President of the Committee of Council on Education if he will state the name of the gentleman appointed to fill the position of assistant in the South Kensington Museum (Art Branch), following the Civil Service examination held in December last; and if he will inquire of the Civil Service Commissioners why the practice of announcing the result of the examination in the *Gazette* was departed from in such case.

SIR J. GORST: The name of the gentleman appointed was Mr. Herbert Caleb Andrews. I have no authority over the Civil Service Commissioners.

MEAT INSPECTION AT LIVERPOOL.

MR. PATRICK O'BRIEN: On behalf of the hon. Member for the St. Patrick Division of Dublin, I beg to ask the President of the Local Government Board whether he has received a communication from the City of Liverpool and District Butchers' Association remonstrating against the appointment of a meat inspector who is not qualified according to the terms of the Local Government Board circular; and whether he will consider this appointment and communicate with the Corporation of Liverpool.

THE PRESIDENT OF THE LOCAL GOVERNMENT BOARD (Mr. CHAPLIN, Lincolnshire, Sleaford): I have received a communication from the association referred to with regard to the appointment of a meat inspector at Liverpool and I have made inquiry on the subject. I am informed that the officer appointed holds a certificate of competency as a Sanitary Inspector of the Sanitary Institute, and that before making the appointment the Health Committee of the Liverpool City Council satisfied themselves that the officer possessed the necessary knowledge to discharge the duties of the office. It is added that the Medical Officer of Health and the Committee are convinced that his knowledge of the subject of meat inspection is amply sufficient to justify his acting as meat inspector.

STATE AID FOR THE BLIND.

MR. PATRICK O'BRIEN: On behalf of the hon. Member for the St. Patrick Division of Dublin, I beg to ask the President of the Local Government Board whether he will consider the advisability of introducing a measure to grant State aid to the blind upon similar conditions to those afforded by European Governments.

MR. CHAPLIN : I am afraid I can add nothing to the answer given by my right hon. friend the Home Secretary to a similar question on Monday last. Any such measure as that suggested would not come within the province of the Local Government Board.

PUBLIC VACCINATION AT READING.

MR. PALMER (Reading) : I beg to ask the President of the Local Government Board whether he is aware that the Reading Board of Guardians offered provisionally, under the Vaccination Act, 1898, a scale of remuneration to the public vaccinator, to extend over a period of six months, with the object of gathering from experience some idea of the actual amount of work involved under the new regulations, and with the avowed intention, as soon as this experience had been obtained, of revising such scale if found necessary, so as to afford adequate remuneration to the officer, such revised scale to have retrospective effect ; and why the Local Government Board overruled the proposals of the Guardians, and fixed up a scale of remuneration in excess of that which the officer asked the Guardians for, and in the face of the assurance of the Guardians that they were desirous of awarding adequate remuneration to their officer as soon as they were in a reasonable position to gauge the amount of work involved and the probable value of the services rendered.

MR. CHAPLIN : The Guardians of the Reading Union offered a scale of remuneration to the public vaccinator as stated in the question. He declined, however, to accept the fee for successful vaccination which was offered, on the ground that it was insufficient. No agreement having been come to between the Guardians and the public vaccinator, it devolved on the Local Government Board to determine the fees to be paid to him. The Board delined to raise the fees which the Guardians had offered for successful vaccination and re-vaccination. But as regards the remaining fee, it appeared to them, having regard to the default in administering the Vaccination Acts in the Union in the past, that, unless a change took place in this respect, the Public Vaccinator would not be adequately remunerated for the work which he is bound to perform if this fee was fixed at the minimum, and they consequently

VOL. LXXII. [FOURTH SERIES.]

increased it from 1s. to 1s. 8d. If and when the local circumstances which governed the Board's decision as regards this fee have altered the Board will be quite prepared to reconsider the matter.

KILDARE STREET LIBRARY.

MR. PATRICK O'BRIEN : On behalf of the hon. Member for the St. Patrick Division of Dublin, I beg to ask the Chief Secretary to the Lord Lieutenant of Ireland whether the library in Kildare Street is to be handed over to the New Irish Department ; and, if so, whether adequate arrangements regarding finance and exports will be made.

THE CHIEF SECRETARY FOR IRELAND (Mr. G. W. BALFOUR, Leeds, Central) : The library in Kildare Street is at present under the Science and Art Department, and under Section 2 of the Agriculture and Technical Instruction Bill would be transferred to the new Department. I am not sure that I clearly apprehend the last paragraph of the question, but as it appears to refer to details of administration, it would be premature to make any statement on the subject.

ROYAL COLLEGE OF SCIENCE, DUBLIN.

MR. PATRICK O'BRIEN : On behalf of the hon. Member for the St. Patrick Division of Dubiin, I beg to ask the Chief Secretary to the Lord Lieutenant of Ireland whether he can state when the sum allocated for the buildings of the Royal College of Science in Dublin will be available, and when the work will be commenced ; whether the Department will be under Irish control ; and, whether it is intended to be in connection with the proposed Board of Agriculture and Industries.

MR. G. W. BALFOUR : I cannot at present make any statement in reply to the first paragraph, except that I am not aware that any sum has been allocated for the purpose mentioned. If the Agriculture and Technical Instruction Bill becomes law, the Royal College of Science would be transferred to the new Department.

MONAGHAN UNION MEDICAL OFFICER.

MR. MACALEESE (Monaghan, N.) : I beg to ask the Chief Secretary to the

3 B

Lord Lieutenant of Ireland whether he is aware that a misunderstanding, threatening to have serious consequences for the poor, is at present existing between the Monaghan Poor Law Guardians and the Local Government Board regarding the appointment of a doctor to the electoral divisions of Bragan, Derrygorry, and Shanmullagh, recently transferred from the Clogher to the Monaghan Union; and that the Guardians have appointed a temporary doctor for three months; whether, seeing that the Local Government Board insist that there is no vacancy, as Dr. Phillips holds the position of medical officer for the three divisions named, he will state when Dr. Phillips received this appointment, and by whom was he appointed; is he aware that Dr. Phillips resides in Aughnacloy, twelve miles or so of a rough mountainous country divided from one portion of the boundary of the divisions, entailing in many cases a journey of twenty-four miles upon persons requiring the services of the doctor; and that the Rev. P. Callan, the parish priest of the district, has written to the Local Government Board pointing out the extent to which the poor will be sufferers by the proposed plan, and respectfully asking to have the five units of Truagh erected into a dispensary district, with a resident medical officer; and will he endeavour to obtain the permission of the Local Government Board to this proposal.

MR. G. W. BALFOUR: The Aughnacloy dispensary district of the Clogher Union, of which Dr. Phillips has been medical officer since the year 1888, formerly consisted of the three electoral divisions named in the first paragraph, together with the divisions of Aughnacloy and Tullyvar. By an Order of the Local Government Board, dated the 25th of October last, the former three divisions were transferred to the Monaghan Union, whilst the two latter divisions remained in the Clogher Union, and each of these groups of divisions was constituted a separate dispensary district, to continue, as heretofore, in charge of the medical officer, Dr. Phillips. As regards the third paragraph, the arrangements which previously existed with respect to medical attendance on the sick poor throughout these five divisions worked satisfactorily, and these arrangements, as stated, remain unaltered. The Board have been advised

Mr. Macaleese.

that Dr. Phillips continues to hold the medical officership of his former district, notwithstanding that portion of it has been transferred to the Monaghan Union and formed into a separate district, and the Board do not consider that sufficient grounds exist to warrant them in sanctioning the appointment of a second medical officer for the district, and thus place additional expense upon the ratepayers.

MR. T. M. HEALY: In which Union does the doctor now act?

MR. G. W. BALFOUR: In both.

MR. T. M HEALY: And will he be entitled to a pension from each?

No answer was given.

REVISED VALUATIONS.

MR. EDWARD BARRY: I beg to ask the Chief Secretary to the Lord Lieutenant of Ireland whether notices are given to parties whose valuations are revised; and, if not, will steps be taken to facilitate their right of appeal by giving such notices in future.

MR. G. W. BALFOUR: Under the Valuation Acts, as amended by the Local Government (Ireland) Act, it is provided that on the receipt of the revised valuation lists the secretaries of the county councils and clerks of the urban district councils shall give public notice stating where and when these lists may be inspected, and that they will be open for public inspection for twenty-one days.

AGRICULTURAL GRANT FOR CO. ROSCOMMON.

MR. HAYDEN: I beg to ask the Chief Secretary to the Lord Lieutenant of Ireland, whether, in estimating the amount of the Agricultural Grant for the County Roscommon, the Local Government Board took into account the special circumstances brought under its notice by the grand jury of that county in regard to the county cess in the standard year; whether the Suck drainage tax has been treated as an excluded charge, and, if so, under what authority this has been done; whether credit has been given to the county for the county cess relating to the portions of Galway and Mayo added to the administrative County of Roscommon;

and whether he will instruct the Local Government Board to supply the County Council with the facts and figures upon which the calculation was based.

Mr. G. W. BALFOUR: The answer to each of the inquiries in the first paragraph is in the affirmative. The amount deducted under the provision with respect to excluded charges from the Agricultural Grant to Roscommon in respect of the Suck drainage charges was about £100. The Commissioner of Valuation is of opinion that the Suck Drainage Act of 1889, under which these charges arise, comes within the description given in the latter part of Section 57, Sub-section 6 (1) of the Local Government Act of last year. With regard to the second paragraph, I propose, as already stated, to lay on the Table of the House a general memorandum explaining the methods adopted in order to arrive at the basis on which the amounts of the Grant have been calculated.

BALROTHERY COUNTY CESS.

Mr. CLANCY (Dublin County, N.): I beg to ask the Chief Secretary to the Lord Lieutenant of Ireland, whether his attention has been directed to a correspondence which has taken place between the Balrothery Rural District Council, county of Dublin, and the Local Government Board in reference to the standard rate of county cess certified for that district; whether he is aware that the grand jury records show that whereas the standard rate referred to has been certified to be 1s. 11¼d. in the pound, the county cess actually paid in the standard year was considerably higher in three out of the four baronies of which the district consists, reaching in one barony the figure of 3s. 3d. in the pound; and, if so, what is the explanation of the standard rate being so low; and whether the Local Government Board, in view of the duty cast upon it to correct mistakes in its certificates of standard rates in the event of any mistakes being pointed out to it, is entitled to refuse information as to the manner in which it has arrived at the result of which complaint is made.

Mr. G. W. BALFOUR: The Local Government Board have been in correspondence with the Balrothery Rural District Council relative to the statements made by the Council as to county cess in the standard year. The Board have not refused to afford the Council any information; on the contrary, they have explained to the Council that the statements contained in their resolution of the 17th ultimo were incorrect, as the baronies of Balrothery East and West, which comprise three-fifths of the whole valuation of the rural district, had a county cess in the standard year of only 1s. 7¼d. and 1s. 5d. respectively, while the portion of Coolock, of which barony the cess was taken at 3s. 3¼d., had a valuation of only one-seventh of that of the whole district. The standard rate of county cess in the Balrothery rural district is certified by the Board to be 1s. 11¼d.

CELTIC LANGUAGE IN IRISH SCHOOLS.

Mr. FLAVIN: I beg to ask the Chief Secretary to the Lord Lieutenant of Ireland if he is aware that there is a very strong feeling held by public bodies and the people generally against the recent rules of the Intermediate Board of Education, which have reduced the number of works in Celtic from 600 to 500; and whether, owing to the successful efforts now being made in several portions of Ireland to revive the Irish language, the Intermediate Board of Education will place Celtic on the same level as French and German.

*Mr. G. W. BALFOUR: The reduction from 600 to 500 in the number of marks assigned to Celtic was made by the Commissioners of Intermediate Education in the programme of examination for 1897. The reduction was made by the Commissioners after full consideration, and I am not aware that they propose to again modify their rules in the sense indicated in the question. The matter is entirely one for them to decide.

Mr. FLAVIN: May I ask whether the right hon. Gentleman will accept the opinion of the public of Ireland, who think they are being very unfairly treated in this matter?

*Mr. G. W. BALFOUR: I have no authority in the matter.

TITHE RENT-CHARGE REDEMPTION IN IRELAND.

Mr. SMITH-BARRY (Huntingdonshire, Huntingdon): I beg to ask the

Chief Secretary to the Lord Lieutenant of Ireland whether, in cases where the payers of annual instalments in lieu of tithe rent-charge desired to redeem the remaining instalments (or were compelled to do so in sales under the Irish Land Purchase Acts), the redemption price has hitherto been calculated with reference to the capital sum which would ultimately be realised if the instalments of £4 9s. per cent. were paid for 52 years, or with reference to the capital value of the rent-charge estimated at 22½ years' purchase thereof, or how otherwise. At what rate of interest was the sinking fund estimated to have accumulated in such cases; and have the payers of Church perpetuity rents lost their right of periodical revision owing to the recent decision of the Court of Appeal in Ireland in the case of Regina (Metge) v. the Justices of Meath.

*MR. G. W. BALFOUR: In cases where the payers of instalments created in accordance with the provisions of the 7th Section of the Irish Church Act Amendment Act, 1872, apply voluntarily to redeem the outstanding instalments, the redemption money is calculated so as to ascertain the capital value, at the date fixed for redemption, of the instalments then remaining unpaid, the term being taken at 52 years. The section of the statute referred to fixes such annual sum at £4 9s. per cent. on the purchase money of the tithe rent charge ascertained as in the section provided, and an annuity of £4 9s. per cent., payable for 52 years, implies interest at the rate of £3 16s. 3½d. per cent. Where such annuities are redeemed compulsorily in land purchase cases the redemption is now carried out under Section 37 (2) of the Land Law (Ireland) Act of 1896, and the term is taken at 45 years. The rate of interest involved in a term of 45 years is £3 10s. per cent. The case referred to in the last paragraph of the question has, in the opinion of the Land Commission, deprived the payer of Church perpetuity rents of the right of revision.

FAIR RENTS IN COUNTY CAVAN.

MR. J. P. FARRELL (Cavan, W.): I beg to ask the Chief Secretary to the Lord Lieutenant of Ireland whether any complaint has been made to him by tenants in the neighbourhood of Bally-connell and Belturbet, in county Cavan, on the delay in hearing first and second term applications to fix fair rents; when the next Sub-Commission is fixed to sit in Cavan; and whether he will expedite hearings by making representations to the Land Commissioners.

*MR. G. W. BALFOUR: A list containing 215 cases from the Union of Bawnboy, which embraces the electoral division of Ballyconnell, was commenced in December last and completed in the early part of last month. It is probable that a further list for that district will be issued in the course of the next couple of months. A Sub-Commission has been engaged for a considerable time during the past two years in the disposal of cases from the Union of Cavan, within which Belturbet is situate, and sittings will be held at Cavan on the 20th, 21st, and 22nd instant for the hearing of further cases which appear in a list recently issued, and which list contains cases from the locality of Belturbet. Every endeavour is being made to dispose of fair rent cases as rapidly as circumstances will permit.

PROMOTION IN THE ROYAL IRISH CONSTABULARY.

MR. J. P. FARRELL: I beg to ask the Chief Secretary to the Lord Lieutenant of Ireland whether any examination for the promotion of head constables from that rank to district inspectorship in the Royal Irish Constabulary has recently been held; if so, how many candidates were there, and what was the result; whether he is aware that in County Longford two cadets have been, after a very brief training, recently taken from the depôt and placed in charge of important stations; will he state what qualification either possessed for the position, and who nominated them; and will he see that arrangements are made to place in command men who know better the people amongst whom they operate.

*MR. G. W. BALFOUR: No examination of head constables for promotion to the rank of district inspector has recently been held, the full proportion of promotions, that is to say one-half, having been given to men of that rank. There is only one young officer in the County Longford at present. The qualifications of this gentleman, who was nominated by the Government, were tested in the usual manner by examination in literary and professional subjects. The last paragraph seems to be of a controversial character. There is no intention of departing from the existing system in regard to the appointments in question.

SANITARY WORKS IN CASTLEREA AND BALLAGHADEREEN.

MR. HAYDEN : I beg to ask the Chief Secretary to the Lord Lieutenant of Ireland whether he is aware that the Castlerea Board of Guardians, before the recent elections, had urged the Local Government Board to make the cost of executing certain sanitary works in the towns of Castlerea and Ballaghadereen special expenses leviable on those places only, and that a similar recommendation has since been made by the recently elected District Council, with the assent of the representatives of both Castlerea and Ballaghadereen ; whether it is a fact that the opinion of both the old Board of Guardians and the new Council has been disregarded by the Local Government Board, though that body has acted on similar advice in other cases ; and whether, in view of all the circumstances, and of the probability of the progress of sanitation being impeded by making sanitary charges distinct charges, he will advise the Local Government Board to alter its decision as desired by the local authorities.

*MR. G. W. BALFOUR : The reply to the first paragraph is in the affirmative. The only exceptions made by the Local Government Board to the Rural District being the area of charge for special sanitary expenses are those set forth in Articles 1 and 2 of their Order of the 15th of May last. This Order, which was assented to by the majority of the boards of guardians in Ireland, was rendered necessary in consequence of the rating provisions of the Local Government Act of last year.

FEVER IN THE OUGHTERARD UNION.

MR. PATRICK O'BRIEN : On behalf of the hon. Member for the St. Patrick Division of Dublin, I beg to ask the Chief Secretary to the Lord Lieutenant of Ireland whether he can state how many cases of fever have occurred in the Carraroe Division of the Oughterard Union ; whether he is aware that during the distress of 1898 Carraroe was one of the most distressed districts in Ireland ; and whether, considering the recent outbreak of fever in 1899 in this district, he can state what steps the Local Government Board and the Congested Districts Board have taken to improve the material condition of the people of Carraroe, Carna, Gacumma Island, Lettermore Island, and Lettermullen Island.

*MR. G. W. BALFOUR : Six cases of fever occurred in Carraroe since the 1st January last. I am aware that considerable distress existed in that district in 1898. Much has been done by the Congested Districts Board, since its establishment, to improve the material condition of the people in the localities mentioned in the last paragraph. I cannot, within the limits of a reply to a question, enumerate the various steps taken ; but I have forwarded to the hon Member a statement showing what the Board has done.

FISH TRAFFIC ON RAILWAYS

MR. P. O'BRIEN : On behalf of the hon. Member for the St. Patrick Division of Dublin, I beg to ask the Chief Secretary to the Lord Lieutenant of Ireland whether he can state the amount of fish landed in England, the proportion of it carried by English railways ; and also the amount of fish landed in Ireland, and the proportion of it carried by the Irish railways ; and, considering the difference between the proportions carried by English and Irish railways, whether he will have an inquiry made as to the cause of failure of the Irish railways to carry a larger proportion of the fish landed in Ireland.

*MR. G. W. BALFOUR : The statistics required in the first and second paragraphs are fully detailed in a Return recently prepared by the Board of Trade and in the Annual Report of the Inspectors of Irish Fisheries, both of which documents have been presented to Parliament. As regards the second paragraph, I have nothing to add to my reply to the hon. Member's previous question of the 9th May on this subject.

ILLEGAL FISHING IN IRELAND.

MR. PATRICK O'BRIEN : I beg to ask the Chief Secretary to the Lord Lieutenant of Ireland whether his attention was drawn to a prosecution recently brought against Mr. Patrick Comerford, of Kilkenny, by a water bailiff named Joseph Bannon, the charge being that Comerford and a boy were setting night lines to catch trout or eels in the River Nore; whether he is aware that Bannon failed to prove any offence, and the case was dismissed with costs; whether he can say who will pay the costs of this case; and, whether he will see that the Fishery Conservators will require the bailiff Bannon to pay, as a means of restraining him from bringing such prosecutions in future without being able to give proof of the charges.

MR. G. W. BALFOUR: I am informed that in this case the defendant was found with a night line under suspicious circumstances, and that the bailiff having failed to prove that the line had been used by Mr. Comerford, the case wase dismissed. The costs will be paid by the Conservators. As already stated, I have no jurisdiction over the Conservators, and no authority to act as suggested in the last paragraph.

COUNTY CAVAN MAGISTRACY.

MR. J. P. FARRELL: I beg to ask the Chief Secretary to the Lord Lieutenant of Ireland whether he is aware that a vacancy for a justice of the peace in the Petty Sessions District of Arva, county Cavan, was recently created by the death of P. S. O'Reilly, Esq., Gonna; and that an extensively signed petition was sent to the Lord Lieutenant of Cavan, Lord Lanesborough, recommending the appointment of Mr. Eugene M'Manus, of Gonna, in his stead; whether this memorial was brought to the notice of the Lord Chancellor; and will he explain whether the request of the petitioners was refused, and a local Orangeman appointed in room of the deceased Roman Catholic magistrate; and, whether he intends to take any steps to have Mr. M'Manus appointed.

MR. G. W. BALFOUR: I assume that the memorial referred to in the first paragraph was sent to the Lieutenant of the County, though I have no official information on the subject. It is a fact that a memorial was received by the Lord Chancellor, and that a gentleman has been appointed to the Commission of the Peace for the Arva district since the death of Mr. O'Reilly. I have no knowledge with respect to the religious or political opinions of either of these gentlemen. It is the practice of the Lord Chancellor to appoint on the recommendation of the Lieutenant of the County, and I have no power to act as suggested in the third paragraph.

CHAIRMAN OF IRISH TOWN COMMISSIONERS.

MR. MAURICE HEALY: I beg to ask the Chief Secretary to the Lord Lieutenant of Ireland whether a solicitor who becomes chairman of Town Commissioners under the provisions of The Local Government (Ireland) Act, 1898, s. 26, s.s. 2, thereby loses his right to practise at Quarter Sessions in the county under s. 13 of 14 and 15 Vic. c. 57.

MR. G. W. BALFOUR: The question is an abstract one, but the Government are advised that a solicitor would, under the circumstances mentioned, lose his right to practise under the 13th section of the 14 and 15 Vic. c. 57.

STEAM TRAWLING OFF HOWTH.

MR. CLANCY: I beg to ask the Chief Secretary to the Lord Lieutenant of Ireland whether any steps have yet been taken to inquire into the charges brought by the fishermen of Howth, county of Dublin, against the owners or crews of the following steam trawlers—viz, the "Jackdaw" of Hull, and the "Peter Johnston" of Aberdeen; and, if not, will he explain why; and whether he is aware that, owing to the destruction of nets and lines by those and other steam trawlers, the sole means of living of the fishermen referred to have, in several cases, been absolutely destroyed; and, if so, how it is proposed to compensate the victims of the criminal acts mentioned.

MR. G. W. BALFOUR: I am informed that one fisherman whose lines were carried away by the trawler "Peter Johnston" has been compensated by the owner of the trawler. The Inspectors of Fisheries have been in communication with the owner of the trawler "Jackdaw" respecting a complaint made by another fisherman against that vessel, and have supplied the fisherman with a copy of the reply of the owner. There is no doubt that serious damage is often done by these trawlers, but the Government have no fund at its disposal out of which to compensate fishermen for losses incurred by them.

MR. CLANCY: The right hon. Gentleman has not answered that part of my question as to whether the Government have taken any steps to inquire into these charges.

Mr. G. W. BALFOUR: Everything we can do is done.

Mr. CLANCY: But is it not an illegality which the Government are bound to inquire into?

Mr. G. W. BALFOUR: Not necessarily.

Mr. T. M. HEALY: Do not the Government in Scotland offer a reward in such cases?

Mr. CLANCY: Can the Attorney-General for Ireland say whether, if it be possible to detect the owners and crews of these trawlers, they can be prosecuted for the commission of the offence?

*Mr. SPEAKER: Order, order! That is a question of which notice should be given.

Mr. CLANCY: But it arises out of the question on the Paper. Are the Government taking any steps whatever?

Mr. SPEAKER: It is a question of which notice should be given.

Mr. CLANCY: I have had two or three questions on the Paper, so that the Government have had full notice of my intention to raise this question.

LORD DILLON'S ESTATE.

Mr. T. M. HEALY: I beg to ask the Chief Secretary to the Lord Lieutenant of Ireland whether any minute of the Congested Districts Board exists as to the purpose for which they have acquired Lord Dillon's estate; is it intended to resell to the tenants; if so, when; could he state who has charge of the negotiations for sale; what price is Lord Dillon to receive; and what is the gross and net rental of the estate; does the contract for sale include a covenant requiring Lord Dillon to rebuild the mansion house (lately burnt), which is situated in County Roscommon, far away from the principal estate, which is in County Mayo; how do the Board propose to use the mansion house; and, will any Papers be presented to Parliament on the subject.

Mr. G. W. BALFOUR: The Congested Districts Board have purchased Lord Dillon's estate for the purpose of improving and enlarging some of the holdings and of reselling all the holdings to the tenants through the Land Commission, but the Board are not yet in a position to say when the holdings will be resold. The negotiations have been carried on by the Board and the solicitors for Lord Dillon. The price to be paid to Lord Dillon is £290,000; the figures as to the rental were placed before the Board by his solicitors before the sale, but I am sorry I am not in a position to supply them at present. Lord Dillon has nearly rebuilt the house which was lately burnt down, and has undertaken to complete it. The Board have not yet considered the question of the disposal of the house. It is not intended to lay specially on the Table any Papers on the subject except to refer to the matter in the Board's annual report, which no doubt will give full information on the matter.

Mr. T. M. HEALY: Does any minute of the Congested Districts Board exist?

Mr. G. W. BALFOUR: I do not think there is any special minute.

Mr. T. M. HEALY: Do the Board make contracts involving an expenditure of over half a million without entering it on their minutes?

Mr. G. W. BALFOUR was understood to reply that they had followed their usual course in this case.

Mr. T. M. HEALY: Are the minutes of the Board public or private property?

Mr. G. W. BALFOUR: Private, certainly.

———

SUPPLY [14TH ALLOTTED DAY].

Considered in Committee.

(In the Committee.)

CIVIL SERVICES AND REVENUE DEPARTMENTS ESTIMATES, 1899–1900.

CLASS IV.

Motion made, and Question proposed—

"That a sum not exceeding £701,861 be granted to Her Majesty to complete the sum necessary to defray the charge which will come in course of payment during the year ending on the 31st day of March, 1900, for Public Education in Scotland, and for Science and Art in Scotland."

*THE LORD ADVOCATE (Mr. A. G. MURRAY, Buteshire): As has been the custom for several years, I propose briefly to refer generally to the results of our policy in educational matters. Hon. Members will notice that the total of the vote is £1,301,861, an increase of £19,994 on the year. That increase is practically accounted for under four heads. The annual grant to the day schools shows an increase of £11,038; the additional grant to necessitous school boards is £5,475; the Science and Art grant has risen £7,500, and the grant for training colleges has increased by £6,050. As against these increases there is a decrease of £962 for the evening schools and of £11,679 in the relief of fees. As far as the evening schools are concerned the decrease is an estimated one. It does not actually represent a smaller amount paid, because, as a matter of fact, the grant to evening schools paid in 1898 exceeded that of the previous year by £192. And, too, there is nothing to show any falling off or deterioration. The decrease of £11,679 in the grant for the relief of fees is due to the fact that a very large sum was available for this purpose under the Education and Local Taxation Accounts (Scotland) Act, 1892. I shall later on have probably to go more into detail on these financial matters; but for the present I will content myself with reminding hon. Members of the four possible sources of the fee grant: first, the 10s. grant; secondly, the £40,000 under the Act of 1890; thirdly, there are certain arrears which the Chancellor of the Exchequer has promised to make up, and as to which my hon. friend the Member for Caithness has addressed questions to me; and, finally, there is the balance under the Act of 1892. Now I come to the increases. That in the grant for day schools is, of course, due to the natural growth in numbers and efficiency of the schools themselves, and so far the figures, I think, are perfectly satisfactory. The increase of the item for necessitous school boards is due directly to the action of the Education (Scotland) Act, 1897. It proved that the amount estimated for in the first year was insufficient. The increase in the Science and Art grant occurs mainly in

connection with drawing in elementary schools; while as to the larger sum required for the training colleges, that has been made necessary by the increase in the number of students. It was found that the supply of teachers was likely to become inadequate, and accordingly the number of students was raised from 920 to 1,140. This is a subject on which there has been considerable discussion in past years, and as the hon. Member for Mid Lanark has frequently urged the necessity of an increase I suppose we shall have his support on this matter. I now come to another branch of the subject. The attendance in the day schools has increased by about 7,000; it is now 618,319, and it is satisfactory to find that the percentage of older children in attendance shows a slight increase. The results, judging from the returns coming in day by day, are highly satisfactory, and evidently the change we have made in giving prominence to the merit certificate as against the attendance certificate is having the direct effect of inducing parents to keep their children longer at school. In evening schools the average attendance is 52,340, an increase of 373 as compared with the previous year. The average school rate in Scotland in 1897-98 was 9·23d. as against 8·99d. in 1896-97. The total amount raised from the rates was £839,878, of this £410,280 was spent on the maintenance of schools, in the proportion of £392,543 on day schools, and £17,737 on evening schools, and most of the remainder was absorbed in the repayment of capital and interest on loans incurred in providing school accommodation a further sum of £36,685 was raised locally in the form of voluntary subscriptions—£30,938 for day schools, and £5,747 for evening schools. I am glad to think that, although there is a slight decrease, the voluntary subscriptions are fairly maintained, and, whatever may be occurring on the other side of the border, in Scotland they are not appreciably going down. The grants for day and evening schools amounted to £716,415, which, with a further sum of £334,937 in relief of fees, and £12,316 the aid grant for Voluntary schools, give a total contribution from the Imperial Exchequer of £1,063,668, as against a contribution from local sources of £876,563. These figures, however, do not include the grant for science and art instruction in Scotland; and under this heading in 1898-99 the sum paid was £60,826. Now for some details as to the general progress of education. As hon. Members are aware, this year, owing to the sweeping changes made in the Code, and owing to the fact that an educational policy has had to be developed in the matter of spending money on secondary education, has been a somewhat trying one. The new Code practically means the final disappearance of the principle of payment by individual results. I hope hon. Members will keep in view the fact that although that system may be said to be gone for ever, yet they will find in the gradual action of the Department some pledge that it will not be blind to certain risks which are necessarily run by the change. There are, indeed, very few changes made as to which it is not necessary to place something on the other side of the account, and no one can deny that there are certain dangers under the new system. The Department has shown by its reluctance to make the change hurriedly that its eyes are open to these dangers. May I remind hon. Members what the old system was? Under it no child could bring a grant to a school at all unless it made 250 out of 400 possible school attendances in a year. If he failed to make that number he could not be presented for examination, and his grant-earning power ceased. But if he made the qualifying number of attendances he could earn a certain grant for reading, writing, and arithmetic; on the way in which he passed in those subjects depended the amount of grant earned by him for the school. Besides that, there were a number of subsidiary grants for class subjects, such as discipline and elementary science, and these were paid on the average attendance of children in the class subjects; they were judged in the aggregate, and not as individuals. Beyond this, again, there were grants for specific subjects which were intended to cover the ground for higher education. These do not form part of the general work of the school. Each scholar, as he chose, took up two or three subjects, and the payment depended, not upon the stage reached on the subject, and not at all on the position of the subject with the general curriculum, but on the number of subjects that are taken up. Hon. Members will see that this plan, which I have summarised,

had these various advantages—it necessitated individual attention to each child, because no child could well be neglected; if he was, he would not earn any grant at all, and if his progress was not sufficient he diminished the general financial interests of the school. Obviously, therefore, there was a direct incentive to the teachers to be satisfied that the child would pass the examinations. On the other hand, it had certain very obvious defects. It applied a hard and fast rule which took no heed of the variation of circumstances between the different schools. It is very much easier in some places to have educational advantages than it is in others. Then, again, it was more or less a direct incentive to cramming, because the test of the school was the ability of so many children to get through the examination, and anything that got them through achieved the end desired, even if that end was not the best so far as the real progress of the child was concerned, while it ministered to the cramming. It is also rather discreditable to the progress of a clever and more active pupil, because, obviously, if you had a class which you wanted to get through an examination, as soon as you were satisfied that the pupils were well able to pass the examination you would not attempt to take any more trouble; they could be left alone with the knowledge they had already obtained, and the teacher's time would be more profitably, in a pecuniary sense, employed in bringing on the more stupid pupils. The higher education is conducted on the same lines, and necessarily the higher education encouraged rather a multiplicity of subjects than the development of a high standard of general excellence. All these matters have been felt, and accordingly for some time there have been steps taken by which the original system has been restricted. In 1886 individual examination was abolished for infants and the lower standards, and in 1890 the principle was extended to all standards, and remained solely for special subjects. The present code is the coping stone, and now the system of individual examination has been done away with, and grants have been made on average attendances. Besides that, the grants under the present Code are not to be paid in separate sums. The direct result of that will be that there will no longer be any temptation to take up a long list of subjects having regard to the curriculum of the school, and the test of the merit of the school will not be the way in which the scholars acquit themselves in a large variety of subjects ; managers will now begin by considering the curriculum as a whole. They will draw up a curriculum, and that proposed curriculum will be subject to approval. Concurrently with that there has been an effort made to broaden the elementary curriculum, especially in the particular line—I have already drawn attention to it in the figures—namely, the introduction of drawing as a regular subject. Of course, there will be of necessity a minimum prescribed for the curriculum, but beyond this actual minimum circumstances will necessarily vary a great deal having regard to the circumstances of each school. Hon. Members will see that it is quite obvious the scholars are differently situated as they are in town or country, in a scattered or dense population, and it cannot be expected the education can be carried out on the same curriculum. When the curriculum is once fixed the grant is to be a comprehensive grant— a fixed amount on the general efficiency. It is necessary to recognise the course of education varies with proficiency, and accordingly a larger grant must necessarily be allowed in respect of a higher scale. One way will be, of course, to pay it according to the number of children in the higher class ; but if you do that you at once give a direct initiative to the teachers to force the children into the higher class by the mere progress of time, irrespective of the fact of whether they are fit to go in any class other than that in which they are. Accordingly the Department considered the grand result and came to the conclusion that the best way is not to pay on the number actually in the higher class, but to pay in respect to age. Roughly speaking it will to a great extent correspond, although it does not do so exactly. Accordingly the rates have been fixed for children under seven years of age 18s., between seven and ten 20s., and over ten 22s. In order to check what might be the unfortunate result of cramming the grant may be reduced for special deficiency by 6d. or 1s., and may be increased for special excellence by 6d. Further grants are to be allowed for practical, scientific, and mechanical training, which it is not possible for all scholars to attempt, but

that will be encouraged. The Committee will see that in order to carry out this system the arrangements for inspection must be changed, and the Department had very carefully to consider how the inspection had to be carried out. In old days there was always an' annual inspection. It was a fixed day, and it was known when it was coming on, and efforts were made to turn out well for the day. But after it had gone by they were not quite so strenuous in their efforts until another inspection came round. The result was that if a scholar failed to pass his examination he was still kept in his old place. That system is now altered ; the inspector's visits are to occur at various intervals during the year. It will not be necessary when he does come for him to inspect the whole school at one time ; he may inspect one part of the school at one visit and another part at another. He may then see the work going on and not examine himself, or he may if he chooses examine himself. His duty is to confer with the school authorities, and to learn what their difficulties may be, and give them advice. He is to receive a record of the work week by week, and judge so far as he can by the record how far the school has been successful. He will not expect to find under those circumstances pupils keeping step as it were from class to class, but altering their places in the class, the dull scholars remaining behind ; and the efficiency will be judged not by the height which each scholar has reached, but by the keeping of all scholars at suitable work for each of them. Now I have said briefly that there are certain dangers in this, and one result of the new system will be to make very large schools a little lax. Anyone can judge of these matters, and I hope in that matter that the managers will exercise good judgment. Undoubtedly it is the wish and intention of the Department that nothing like laxity is introduced, and schools may be subjected to very severe tests : more severe tests than the ordinary tests may—if necessary be applied. Probably in the first instance it would be sufficient to warn only, but if it is not attended to then it is within the power of the Department, and it is their intention to resort to very vigorous individual examinations. It does not directly affect the grant whether the persons pass on or not, but it has the result that it would be at once

Mr. A. G. Murray.

a very thorough test of whether the individual has been neglected or not under the new system. Now, I trust that, in general, these new provisions of the code will commend themselves to the educational sense of the Committee. In the complete change which has been made in the method of pay it is necessary to walk very warily at first. It is quite obvious that it is not in the power or the right of the Department to greatly alter by this change the burden that is being laid on the Imperial Exchequer. The object is more or less to make the burden the same, with, of course, capacities for expansion that should always exist through persons taking proper advantage of the system. But still I think the Committee will see that to a certain extent the re-fixing of the precise sums which may be earned under this new system is, so to speak, a matter for trial. The Committee will notice that in order to avoid any possible mistake that may have been made, the operation of the new code, so far as the payment is concerned, is postponed for a year, *i.e.*, nobody will be paid under the provisions of the code until after the beginning of 1900, and the department will certainly very carefully watch the statistics of the year, so that before the payment has been actually made, there will, as a matter of fact, be another code. If the Department, through the better statistics they have got by that time, see that, with due regard to the general burden on the Treasury, they can in safety somewhat increase the various grants, then they will certainly do so in the code of next year. But it is absolutely necessary to move cautiously at the first. Then there is another feature of the code of great interest. I mean that which is embraced in chapter 9, dealing with the provisions for the secondary departments in elementary schools. Those provisions are part of the general system put forward by the minute on Secondary Education. The admission to these schools is to be entirely through the portal of the merit certificate. It is the great object of the Department to tempt parents to keep their children at school in order to get the merit certificate, rather than allow them to be content with the labour certificate, and having got that, to think that they have done all they need to go away. Under chapter 9 in these higher-grade departments there are very large grants pro-

posed ranging from £2 10s. to £4 10s. in certain circumstances, and this the Department look upon, from the Treasury point of view, as an equivalent, for Scotland long remained, as England did not, under the 17s. 6d. limit.

Captain SINCLAIR (Forfar): Are these grants subject to the 17s. 6d. limit?

*Mr. A. G. MURRAY : Oh, yes; everything is subject in Scotland to the 17s. 6d. limit. This leads me to the other topic of interest peculiar to this year, viz., the Minute of the 27th of April, 1899, for the disposition of the money under the Local Taxation Act of 1898; and here, in order to make my remarks intelligible, may I remind hon. Members of the history of this secondary matter? They will remember that this £60,000 for secondary education was provided by the Education and Local Taxation Account Act of 1892, to be distributed according to the Minutes of the Education Department. Well, a Minute was accordingly promulgated in August, 1892. That Minute, in brief, provided for the establishment of committees on secondary education—what I may call local committees—and it proposed that these local committees should make reports to the Education Department, and should propose what institution within their bounds should be subsidised out of this money. Well, that, too, had been heralded by a Memorandum, and owing to certain representations made a departmental committee was appointed, of which Lord Elgin was chairman, and the departmental committee reported in favour of that scheme. Accordingly, there having been a change of Government in the meantime, there was a minute promulgated on the 31st of January, 1893, which, for all practical purposes, was just a repetition of the minute of 1892. Then certain representations were made in this House, with the result that the Minute of January, 1893, was superseded, and instead of that there came the Minute of the 1st of May, 1893, and the Minute of July, 1894, the result being that instead of leaving the administration in the hands of the Department it reversed the process, and made the money to be divided among these committees in such proportion as the Department might determine. Afterwards there were the minutes of 1896 and 1897. As hon. Members knew the policy which was initiated in 1893 so far changed the policy of 1892 that the scheme became a committee scheme instead of a departmental scheme. Now, there has been six years' experience of the working of the system, and, speaking generally, certainly one result has been to leave the higher class schools, which were recognised under the Act of 1872, out in the cold, while the money has been taken over by the county and borough committees. I have had no occasion particularly to criticise the action of that committee. Far from it. On the other hand, anyone who considers the position of county and borough committees will see that what they have done was almost necessarily the result of those circumstances, and for one or two reasons. The most obvious reason was, that if you divide the money among various counties and boroughs, the county that gets the money says, "Now, then, where shall we spend it?" Obviously, they say, "We will spend it within our own borders." It might be, and in fact it was in a great many cases, that the county had not within its own borders a proper secondary school at all. Accordingly, in cases like that, it was almost forced to give the money to the higher department of a primary school. Then you have what may be called a more indirect tendency. Suppose a school with a higher department in one county got aid from the county, because there was no proper school to which to give it, and there was another school just over the border and in the jurisdiction of some other county committee, practically constituted exactly as the other school was with a higher department, it was most obvious that that school should say, "Well, why should not we be treated exactly the same as the school over the boundary is treated?" forgetting, very naturally, that very likely the School Board might perhaps with great educational advantage have had all the money instead of practically sharing. There was another natural temptation—that if you concentrate the money you only relieve the School Board in the district in which that money is concentrated; whereas if you diffuse it, you have the effect of relieving a great many more School Boards than one. Accordingly, so far from blaming the county committees, I think the tendency has been for those county committees to show those ten-

Mr. A. G. *Murray.*

dencies which they were bound to show under the circumstances in which they existed. At the same time, I do not think that educationally there can be any great doubt as to the result. The result has undoubtedly been that the money has been delivered practically in driblets, and very often failed to achieve its proper result. The result has also been that one or more very deserving classes of schools for carrying on the secondary education of the country have been left out in the cold—not that they did not get anything at all, because, for instance, those particular schools to which I referred certainly got something, but that they have not got sufficient monetary provision to do all that they might do. Seeing that it is really for the benefit of the secondary education of the country that proper secondary schools should have further assistance the Department in this case felt it necessary not to divide the money upon the principle of the Minute of 1893, but rather to revert practically to the principle of the Minute of 1892. It has been suggested—"Oh, if you think that is the better plan, you might have done away with the Minute of 1893 altogether." That would have been a very strong step, and it would have been one which the Department undoubtedly could have employed. It could have intimated a censure upon the work of the committees, but it recognises that although there may have been some points worthy of criticism, at the same time there has been really good work done by these committees. It seems to be thought by some that this reverting to the Minute of 1892 implies a vote of censure upon the county committees, and that it is minimising their usefulness and not taking advantage of their usefulness. That is certainly not the intention of the Department, nor do I think it is quite a fair inference from the Department's action. I have already tried to show that what I may call the weakness of the present system is a necessary weakness; it is really a corollary of the plan of beginning by dividing the money according to area and valuation and parcelling the money out. So far from casting any slur upon the county committees, this particular Minute with which I am now dealing proposes to utilise the services of these committees, because it proposes that every scheme which is submitted by any educational authority to the Department shall be subject to the suggestions of these committtes, and that accordingly we are to have the result of their experience, they knowing from their own schemes as well as the Department what are the provisions for secondary education in the districts with which they have to do. Before I depart from this, may I inform the Committee that in the Minute of 1899 there was a slip in the phraseology, which we have amended by a new Minute. In paragraph 5 it is said:

" Each such school shall forward before the 1st October, 1899, for the consideration of the Department through the county committee on secondary education, etc."

Now the word "county" will not do, because there are more than one sort of committee. There are county committees and burgh committees. But even "county and burgh" will not do, because sometimes there is a secondary education committee for a parish. Therefore the alteration is this: In the Minute which has been promulgated it is ordered ·that the paragraph should read as if the word " county," wherever occurring, were therefrom omitted. It is quite enough with the word " county," as it is then simply " the committee on secondary education of the district," which is an appropriate reference. That practically ends the remarks I wish to inflict upon the Committee at the present stage. The intention of the Department has been to try with this new money to supply the deficiency which was left by the natural tendency of the administration which has so long existed. It will in future carefully watch the results, both which are got from the existing system and from the new system now inaugurated. From those results we hope the time will come when it will be possible to reorganise the whole system and put it upon a proper basis. But we thought it would be a very foolish plan at this present moment, without the assistance of this experience, either to shut our eyes to the educational disadvantages which are the necessary concomitants of the present system, or, because we felt those educational disadvantages, to have swung so far the other way as to have with a ruthless hand destroyed the present system altogether and swept away the county committees. We think it would be much safer to proceed as we have done in this matter of the Minute of to-day, and leave to the future, with our experience modified and broadened as it will be during the next few years, the putting of the whole system upon what may then perhaps turn out to be a broader and more logical basis.

*MR. THOMAS SHAW (Hawick Burghs): There are three matters to which the Lord Advocate has referred in the statement he has made—a statement certainly not too long for the importance of the topics with which we have to deal. Those are, the promulgation of the Code of this year, the matter of educational finance in Scotland, and the question of secondary education. On the changes in the Code I am bound to say that, so far as my experience goes, I have been led most heartily to approve of the action of the Department. On the subject of the finance, I confess I retain the state of mind that I was in a few years ago, when the whole matter of our educational finance was settled upon a footing which we thought highly unsatisfactory and unfair. On the question of secondary education, and the allocation of these new grants, I confess that, so far as I have seen, my mind is completely hostile to any interference with our existing system as is proposed. It appears to me that the limitation of secondary grants is a limitation which will cut out the recognition financially by the State of the most excellent and highly valued work that is done in large districts in Scotland in the interests of secondary education by secondary departments of ordinary schools in districts where it is utterly impossible, owing to the sparseness of population or other causes, to have fully equipped secondary schools. On these topics the Committee will excuse me if I deal as briefly as I can—and yet at some length—with them in detail. On the matter of the Code, I have already said that I am thoroughly in sympathy with the action of the Department. There are three periods in the history of the subject. Under the old parochial system prior to 1872 the general interests of the. school were apt to suffer for the sake of the schoolmaster's fancy pupils. Then in order to get the better of the fancy system which obtained when the old teacher was lord and master of the whole position, there came the Statute of 1872; and just as the former legislation erred on the side of laxity, so, I fear, the codes subsequent to 1872 erred on the side of undue rigidity, for it was set forth that each child should pass an examination to the satisfaction of the inspector. I entirely approve of what the Lord Advocate has said upon this matter, that under the circumstances the Department were justified in doing what they did. Now the whole system of individual examination is practically at an end, and I must say that I think, in this Committee, we ought, on our own responsibility, to re-echo the remark of the Lord Advocate with regard to the new and very grave responsibilities which now fall upon the inspectors in Scotland in consequence of this great change. I have no reason whatever to distrust the inspectorate in Scotland which has had a most distinguished history. I hope this change will be a success; but it can only be a success if the inspectors in the discharge of their duties recognise that they are the servants of the State, and decline to lean either towards the teacher on the one hand or towards the interests of the ratepayers on the other. They are the servants paid by the Imperial Treasury, and their duty is to make a report which shall be irrespective of local or personal interests, and in accordance with Imperial demands. The State relies upon this being done, and if that result should ensue I think it will practically be a complete educational justification of the change. On the matter of finance I am bound to say that I have not derived very much satisfaction from my right hon. friend's statement, for we have no light thrown upon the subject by him further than is found in the Estimates for the year. What we, as Scotsmen, having in view the requirements of Scotland, are anxious to know is how does this educational budget compare with the English grants given in recent years? I will try to make this point perfectly clear. When the Act of 1897 was before Parliament the Committee will remember that I very strongly challenged by an adverse vote the proposed grant for voluntary schools in Scotland, and the reason for that was that it was the best pronouncement in the way of protest we could make against the deficiency of the amount which was being allotted to Scotland. But time has gone on, and it now appears that the figures I then gave have been more and more justified in succeeding years. I find that the contrast which we then initiated was a contrast between the pro-

Mr. Thomas Shaw.

posed legislation for England under which £800,000 was to be granted to the voluntary schools and the necessitous Board schools in England. Upon the calculation of the equivalent grant to which we have been so long familiar, on the principle confirmed by successive Chancellors of the Exchequer, we were entitled to an equivalent sum of £110,000 a year. Instead of that we got a sum which left a deficit of £52,000 a year due to Scotland. I remarked at the time that Scotland would be in a situation under which she would be deprived by this proposal of a fund which would have fallen to it at the rate of £1,000 per week. I find that the result more than confirms the estimate I then made. Instead of the sum of £800,000 having been given to England, the sum of £833,000 has been paid, which is more than England expected. But so far as I can wade through the figures only £54,000, instead of £110,000, has been awarded to Scotland, while even upon the reckoning of the items embraced by the Lord Advocate in his statement we were promised £80,000. Take one instance only. The Committee will remember that one great point which was made by the Government of the day was that Scotland need not complain because she was to get an allowance which was to make up a capitation grant of 12s. per head per scholar in Scotland instead of 10s., and that under that allowance she would receive the sum of £26,000 a year. Of course we protested strongly against that statement as one in which some incomprehensible fallacy lay, but we were met by an absolute denial on the part of the Government. Now, how do the facts stand on the present estimate? Why, instead of £26,000 which was to come to Scotland, a sum of only £5,000 has been paid over, and Scotland has been deprived of the sum of £21,000 a year upon this single item. I am bound to say that I hope all the Members for Scotland, irrespective of party, will support the view which I venture to lay before the House—that, however you look at the figures, it is manifestly clear that Scotland has been deprived both of what she was led to expect under the doctrine of the equivalent grant and what she was pledged to receive on the statement of the responsible Minister of the Crown in 1897. We had to submit to this, and what I did expect from the Lord Advocate was that, in answer to the questions which have been put to him more than once, he would have made it clear that there was ample justification for this deficit. In point of fact, it rather appears on the whole figures that, instead of there being a deficit of £52,000 a year, the deficit will probably at least be £60,000 a year. So far as I am concerned, I feel bound to denounce the action of the Government for putting Scotland in the position of having to look upon the doctrine of the equivalent grant as hopelessly gone. I say so with the greatest sorrow and regret, for it is perfectly clear that under the present *régime* we have entered upon a period when Scotland can no longer expect the doctrine of the equivalent grant to be applied to her. And it is surely clear that this Government, having done so much for education, is bound to retrieve the fortunes of Scotland in the direction of a generous apportionment in respect of secondary education When that time does come I hope we shall say with one voice that, recognising the abolition by this Government of the doctrine of the equivalent grant, and recognising that notwithstanding that we continue to contribute our full share to the Imperial revenue, Scotland shall be dealt with on a generous and satisfactory scale, and above all that we shall not limit our claims to what obtains under any system existing south of the Tweed. Some years ago when this matter of the equivalent grants came to be dealt with we were all of one mind. The Scotch Education Department were of the same mind as ourselves, and one of the Minutes was to the effect that when the new grants came to be made in England Scotland might justly expect that she would be treated upon the eleven-eightieth scale. But the Scotch Department did not know, apparently, the straits to which the Government would be reduced in the matter of finance, or the scurvy treatment which would be meted out to Scotland when she came to be dealt with. I venture to recommend to my fellow Members that we ought, if possible, to so arrange Scotch educational finance that the secondary, and if possible the university, system should obtain the payment of fees, and that the benefit of this grant should be given to Scotland in this respect . In the views which I have formerly laid before the House I have urged that the merit certificate should crown the free

elementary course and be a passport to free secondary instruction, and I am very glad that the grant has now so far reached that position, because the main features of the changes during the past year were the fixing of the standard of the merit certificate as a satisfactory outcome of an elementary school course. So far we view the action of the Department with satisfaction. But I observe there is a still further step taken on the lines of my own recommendations. I refer to the merit certificate being regarded as a passport to secondary education. Lord Balfour, in a most interesting and powerful address he delivered at Paisley on September 14th, 1898, put the matter very simply when he said that the real aim of the Department was to make the merit certificate open the door to secondary education, and I find in the Report of this year it is stated that, while the merit certificate is to be taken as evidence of the satisfactory completion of an elementary school course, it will also serve for the purposes of an entrance examination for all pupils who propose to enter for higher education, and that it will be regarded as a test of fitness to profit by such instruction. We have now a guarantee that secondary education in Scotland will not be given to dullards and those unfitted to receive it, and that the merit certificate will be the passport to it. My second point has not yet come, but I hope it will before many years. That is that the State should take on itself courageously the responsibility of providing free secondary instruction. My noble friend the Secretary for Scotland has very nearly found salvation in this matter. He is just shivering on the brink, and is only afraid to launch away. He says in his Paisley address :

" We wish to make secondary schools available for all whose circumstances and whose talents make it expedient they should take advantage of them."

That is exactly the position of all parties in this House, and also I hope in another place. Lord Balfour proceeds :

" There is no difference as to the end to be aimed at among those who take an interest in the subject, but there is a difference as to the means. Some, as I have indicated, say that we should do it by making such schools universally free. This is a view not without its attractions. But, looking at it as a practical question, I am not prepared either on behalf of myself or of the Government to give any adhesion to the doctrine of free secondary education."

I am surprised my noble friend treated this as a new doctrine. It is a doctrine three centuries old, and in Scotland we have long been familiar with the idea that secondary education was not to be the privilege of the higher classes in the community, but was to be the privilege of every student in every rank of life. I find that that is the idea of the Secretary for Scotland himself, because in another passage in the address to which I have referred he says:

"We have in late years done much in the way of making education free. Some desire we should go still further."

and in another passage he says:

"Just as in elementary education the State made a limitation of fee a condition of grant long before it made the abolition of fee a condition, it would seem not unreasonable that in secondary education it should be said that one condition of a grant should be a limitation of fee to a sum which can fairly be faced by a middle-class parent."

Why "middle-class parent"? Why should not the humblest in the land who contributes to the Imperial Revenue be able to have secondary education, not by a limitation of the fee, but by the abolition of the fee being made a condition of the grant? I would remind Lord Balfour that in elementary education the first step was limitation, and it was followed by abolition. As regards secondary education he is prepared to go as far as limitation, and with one short step further we should have abolition in the very near future. It is not a question of money, because we would have plenty of money if we had our due, and even with what we have if it were properly administered. I know there is a social prejudice against secondary education, but that prejudice is unworthy of the traditions of Scotland. I would remind the Committee of an utterance of a Lord High Chancellor of England — Lord Brougham. He was a pupil of the High School of Edinburgh. There was not this social prejudice in his time, and the children of the highest and the lowest ranks of society were educated together. That he considered made the school invaluable. This is his own language:

"There they were, sitting side by side, giving and taking places from each other,

Mr. Thomas Shaw.

without the slightest impression on the part of my noble friends of any superiority on their parts to other boys, or any ideas of inferiority on the part of other boys to them."

I hope the mind of Scotland will become familiar with the idea that every class of society is entitled to the privilege of free education, and that we shall not keep the humblest class in the country out of our secondary institutions. There is one other matter to which I wish to refer, and that is that Scotland is, in spite of the slowness of the Education Department, gradually getting free secondary education, because money is being granted for the purpose by the county committees, many of them representing populations of the poorest character. The Elgin and other County Committees give a direct subsidy to certain schools on the condition that free secondary education is given. Over and over again we find county committees out of the slender means at their disposal endeavouring to secure free places all over Scotland in secondary institutions. Now that the Secretary for Scotland is near salvation on the one hand, and the county committees are doing so much on the other, I hope the time is coming when Scotch Members, irrespective of party, will join in urging the Government to reorganise secondary education in Scotland on a generous scale of payment in the interests of the whole country. My last point is, Where is this secondary education to be got? and here I find myself in opposition to the proposals of the Government. On the 27th April, 1899, the Scotch Education Department issued a Minute which stated:

"The remainder of the balance available under this section shall be applied in aid of such high-class secondary and technical schools as are not in receipt of grants under the Scotch Code."

I wondered whether it could really be the intention of Her Majesty's Government to disfranchise so many schools and localities, but it now appears that our construction of the Minute was unhappily only too true. The right hon. Gentleman's explanation is that there is so little money to give, and that there is a tendency to diffuse it by the county committees, and that in many cases where money was given the committees had no proper secondary schools at all. He said further that the Minute was not a vote of censure on the county committees. No, it is not a vote of censure on the county committees, but it is a very severe vote of censure on the schools throughout Scotland of the most excellent kind, particularly in the northern counties, which have secondary departments doing most admirable work for education. The censure is not on the county committees, but on the schools. I hope this Minute is not yet beyond the stage of further consideration. It is impossible in counties such as Ross and Inverness, where the population is extremely sparse, to draw a circle and make in the centre a secondary education school. You are bound to take circumstances as you find them. Large tracts of the country have a very slender population, and, instead of encouraging secondary schools in large centres with more grants of public money, it would be a wiser distribution of money to give greater encouragement to the secondary departments of schools in the poorer and more sparsely populated districts. I hope that this extension will not continue, and that Her Majesty's Government will see to it that this grant is distributed, as in times past, not where inefficient education is given, but wherever efficient education is administered. There are in the elementary schools of Scotland 6,000 children above the age of 15 who all pay fees, except under the county committee arrangement. Why should not the Government have the courage—they have plenty of money—simply to sweep away the payment of fees in all schools whatever, be their character primary, higher grade, secondary, or technical? Everybody in Scotland seems to be agreed upon the subject, and the Educational Institute of Scotland have taken a strong line on the matter. They say that by continuing the grant to the secondary schools an injustice would be inflicted on the higher department of the primary schools, more especially in districts where secondary education is only available in the ordinary public schools. I say that that observation is justifiable, and I hope that the result of this discussion will be that the Government will recede from its absurd position. When one looks through these reports, and turns to the financial statement furnished with them, as to the grants, duplicated and re-duplicated as they are, one finds that in this matter of Scotch education the confusion is almost inextricable; and I do

not wonder that the local authorities, looking through the Minutes of the Department, are hampered in the administration of the moneys which reach them from the Treasury. We must have legislation to endeavour to bring order out of this confusion, under which is concealed the great loss which the nation is annually sustaining even in the matter of pure finance. When that day dawns I hope it will not be forgotten that Scotland has not been treated very handsomely in the grants —equivalent or corresponding, if you like to call it so—in past years. I hope, further, that in any settlement of Scotch education following on this Code the Government will, if possible, keep in its secondary departments the rate of advance which Scotland has had over England in primary education. The contrast between the English and the Scottish system is most striking. In a poor country like Scotland our school teachers are a far better paid class than they are in England. They receive at least £20 per annum more per head than in the richer country of England. Scotland, poor as it is, and sparsely populated, is willing to pay, all over its land valuation, no less than 9¼d. in the pound for its schools. I wish the same could be said of England. Again, in Scotland we have been extremely loyal to the representative system. I would put the contrast thus. For every five Voluntary scholars in England there are four Board scholars. How do the figures stand in regard to Scotland? For every five Voluntary scholars in Scotland there are thirty-three Board scholars. Scotland has been proud and willing to tax itself in order to submit to the representative system. I think it is very hard indeed that when the equivalents were being granted we got such a small allowance, because we had so few Voluntary schools. It was a punishment for our own independence and our loyalty. We should watch the Department very closely, and I repeat that, irrespective of party, when this matter of education has been recast, we should demand that the whole of the children of Scotland, however humble they may be, must be emphatically the inheritors of that free education which has been so successful in the past.

*MR. RENSHAW (Renfrew, W.): I have listened with interest to the statement which has been made by the Lord Advocate, and I am bound to say that the portion with which I was specially concerned—namely, the defence he made of the Minute of 27th April, 1899—seemed to me perhaps the most unsatisfactory part of his speech. The fact of the matter is that the position of secondary education, and the work that has been carried on in connection with it in Scotland at the present time, is involved in so many intricacies and so much difficulty that it is almost impossible to follow it, and to understand what the actual position is. If the House would bear with me for a minute or two, I would ask it to remember what that position is. You have in Scotland various secondary schools, under the management of School Boards. They are called higher class schools. Fees are regularly charged in them, and they are not grant-earning under the Code, but they do receive grants from the Science and Art Department, which are now administered, fortunately, by the Scotch Education Department. Then we have throughout Scotland a large number of higher departments in the elementary schools, which are doing a great deal of good work, and which earn grants under the Code, grants which were somewhat limited under the provisions of the old Code, but which are being largely extended by the provisions of the new Code. Various sums of money are available for the assistance of secondary and technical education. There is the money which came to the counties and burghs of Scotland under the residue grant of 1890. That money is distributed throughout Scotland to the various counties, burghs, and local authorities. On the whole the counties have applied, I think I may say, the whole of that money to technical education, and the burghs have expended some of it, but not nearly so much as the counties, on technical education. An additional grant came to the same spending authorities out of the Local Taxation Account (Scotland) Grant, under the Act of 1892. A Blue Book has been published recently dealing with the method employed in expending the two grants by the various local authorities, and it forms a very interesting record of the work accomplished so far. Looking upon it from the point of view as a county Member, I consider that the County Committees have done their

Mr. Renshaw.

work satisfactorily and well; and I only wish I could say the same in regard to the expenditure in the burghs. Let me point out that one of the great difficulties in regard to the expenditure of these grants in counties, by the County Committees, is that the very parts of the county where the money could best be spent—that is, within the burghs—are the very parts where no money whatever is given by the local authority for the promotion of technical education. Let me give the Committee an instance which will show the great difficulties that exist at the present moment, and how important is the suggestion that has been made by the hon. Member for the Border Burghs in regard to legislation to give effect to the secondary education grants to which he has referred, and also to some of the other money which comes to us. In my own county the whole of the money under the grant of 1890 is devoted to technical education; but in the large burgh of Paisley only £228 out of a grant of £562, and in Port Glasgow £30 out of £105, are devoted to technical education, whilst in Greenock and five other burghs no part of the grant is given for technical education. I refer to that fact, for I want to bring home to the Lord Advocate the fact that as long as those moneys which it was hoped and intended should be devoted to the development of technical and secondary education are dispersed through so many spending authorities it will be impossible to improve the administration of them. That brings me to the question of the amount available under the Special Grant for secondary education. There is a sum of £60,000 under the Act of 1892 which is distributed throughout the various counties and six burghs of Scotland, on the basis of population, under the Minute of June 10th, 1897. The county committees which distribute their quota of the Grant are constituted by the County Council appointing a certain number of members, and by the Chairmen of the School Boards in each county appointing so many additional members. Her Majesty's Inspector of Schools for the district is also added to the committee. The committees sit and consider the whole question of secondary education within their district. They frame a scheme which they have to submit to the Department. The Department sends the scheme to the various School Boards and the managers of secondary schools in the county, and invites criticism upon the scheme under which the money which is to come from the special Grant for secondary education is to be expended in the county. The Department, having received these criticisms, again place themselves in communication with the county committees, who have to reconsider their schemes, if necessary. After having made their explanations and received the sanction of the Department to their schemes, they then proceed to give effect to them. The Minute of 1897 contained a very valuable suggestion, namely, that they should endeavour, wherever possible, to invite the co-operation of the authorities which had the spending of the money under the residue grant of 1890. To a certain extent, I believe, the county committees had the funds under this grant placed at their disposal; but as long as we have so many spending authorities it is impossible to get a general agreement. This difficulty exists, and will continue to exist until we have legislation on the subject. I understand from the remarks of the Lord Advocate to-night, and from the criticism which has been directed from time to time on the work of the county committees, that these have not been so successful as they might have been in promoting secondary education in various parts of the country. I think he said that one result of the administration had been to leave the higher class schools out in the cold. I should just like, on that point, to ask the attention of the Committee to an interesting synopsis at the end of the Education Report this year, as to the work carried on by these county committees. It is there stated that direct subsidies to the extent of £21,000 were paid out of the grants received for secondary education to higher class schools, and that £19,000 was paid in direct subsidies to higher departments of elementary schools. From that I do not think it can be said, in regard to the work done by the county committees, that they have left the higher class schools out in the cold. The right hon. Gentleman went on to say that the county committees seemed to make up their minds that the money was to be spent within their own boundaries, and that they were thus forced to give it, in some cases, to the higher departments of primary schools. No doubt that is the case. There are counties in Scotland

where no secondary schools exist, and it cannot be a matter of blame that the county committees should spend the money in that way. But no one could follow the Reports that have been made in regard to secondary and technical education without being satisfied that every year there has been more concentration going on. I think it is only right to point out that the greatest compliment that has been paid to the work carried on by the county committees has been the production of the new Code this year. It actually recognised the very smallest class of schools to which Grants had been given out of these two funds by the county committees as being worthy now of receiving special grants under the Code. Under Section 21 of the Code this year there is a grant of 50s. per head for the pupils taught in classes of not more than 40. That is a recognition that these schools are doing good work beyond elementary education. Then, under Chapter 9, a provision is made for a special grant in the higher grade schools on the commercial side, of £2 10s. for the first year, of £3 10s. for the second year, and £4 10s. for the third year, to pupils who have taken the merit certificate. I have nothing but praise to express in regard to the provisions in that respect, and I claim that the Code is a recognition of the good work carried on by the county committees. The county committees have been accused of dispersing their money too much abroad, giving too much to small schools, and leaving the higher class schools out in the cold. My own experience of one of these county committees is that they have done nothing of the kind. We are really and truly aiming, not only at giving a secondary education in all parts of the country, but also in supporting the system of secondary schools. But there is a real difficulty in regard to the administration of these Grants in connection with the higher class schools. The higher class schools charge fees in their elementary department and in the higher department. One of the great difficulties which the County Committees will have to face is, how they are fairly to put fee-paying scholars alongside a large number of free scholars coming from all parts of the country, and perhaps belonging to a humbler class than those they are in the habit of associating with in these schools. Then comes the Minute of April 27th, 1899. The County Committees are, under that Minute, placed in a totally different position from that which they occupied previously. They will have still to administer the grant under the Minute of June 10th, 1897; but they will be placed in a different relation to the Department in regard to the secondary schools, and the higher department of the elementary schools by the provisions of the Minute of April 27th, 1899. In regard to the £60,000 grant the Committee frame a scheme, and the Department sends it down to the school managers and the School Boards, and after receiving the sanction of the Department the Committee give effect to the scheme. Under the Minute of April 27th the same work, in fact, is to be accomplished, but in a different way. A sum of £31,000 would be available for the whole of Scotland. The managers of the secondary schools are to have the right to make a statement of the various items connected with school expenditure, and to send that statement, through the county committees, up to the Education Department. When that has been done, the Education Department is to consider the scheme, and to sanction it, or some modification of it, or possibly not to agree to it at all. What will be the position of the unfortunate county committees? They will be called upon to criticise the scheme of the managers of the Secondary Schools, and if they say that the scheme of the managers asks too much for the Secondary Schools, it will be said that they are disloyal to their localities. I do not at all envy the duty of the county committees in criticising these schemes, and I think the confusion will be worse confounded by the different manner in which they will work under the new Minute. I do hope, notwithstanding what the Lord Advocate has stated, that there will be some reconsideration of this matter, and that it will be found possible to deal with the £60,000 grant and the £31,000 grant together. Whatever the plan should be, the £91,000 should be treated as one sum. Under the scheme of 1897 a provision was made that £200 per annum was to be paid to every Secondary School. Under a new scheme which would thoroughly protect higher class

Mr. Renshaw.

schools, instead of a provision of £200 per annum, in larger centres £500 or £600 might be fixed upon, I think the time has come when without further experiment more concentration should take place. Until the County and the Burghs Authorities are united in an endeavour to establish in Scotland a thoroughly sound and effective system of secondary education—legislation will be necessary for that—it will be impossible for us to feel that we are not wasting some of the money that has been and ought to be devoted to the purposes of secondary and technical education.

MR. HALDANE (Haddington): I have listened to the speech of the hon. Member who has just sat down with intense interest. He addresses the House on this topic with great authority, because his knowledge is not only theoretical, but derived from a large experience in practical administration. It is significant that the work of county committees has been done best in the region which the hon. Gentlemen represents. Not only Renfrewshire, but Lanarkshire stands out in a very admirable fashion for the manner in which the county committees have been able to distribute the grants entrusted to them. It is ominous to the Government when the hon. Member who has just sat down and the hon. and learned member for the Border Burghs have agreed in expressing dissatisfaction with the scheme the Government have embodied in the Minute of last April. To this extent I feel sympathy with the Government; that I think the work which was done by the committees to whom the money has been entrusted has not been, in all respects, of a nature so satisfactory as to encourage the Government in the hope that the best results attainable in the disposal of the money have been secured. I agree with the Lord Advocate when he says that something was necessary to be done to give some guarantee that higher education will be obtained, but where I find myself not wholly at one with the Government, and much more in sympathy with their critics this afternoon, is as regards the machinery which they have devised to give effect to their Minutes. I cannot help thinking that the failure of the local committees in Scotland to carry out the purposes which the friends of education seek to attain in regard to higher and technical education arises from the fact that these committees are far too numerous, that in some cases too little money is at their disposal, and that there has often been a frittering away of national resources. Nothing is more striking in this respect than the contrast between Scotland and Wales. My noble friend the Secretary for Scotland, in a recent speech at Paisley, I think, said that Scotland had nothing to learn from Wales in the matter of higher education. I venture to say that Scotland has everything to learn. In Wales they have a system under which the money at the disposal of the local committees has been properly expended for higher educational purposes, but in Scotland small funds are handed over to town councils and local bodies to be frittered away for the reduction of rates and for no useful purpose whatever. You have in Wales a number of local committees which is not out of proportion to the sum you have to expend; and you have a central body, constituted out of the representatives of these committees and other representative Boards, to assist them, which really represents the educational mind of Wales in regard to the educational necessities of the country. I have been convinced for some time that you never will have a better state of things in Scotland until you arouse public attention to the matter. And I do not think that you will bring about that better state of affairs until you have established in Scotland, not only a central educational authority, such as there is in Wales, which will represent the popular mind on the subject, but until you have also brought about such a reform of the system of local committees as shall diminish their number, and leave them in possession of adequate funds. A considerable change is also necessary in regard to the whole system of intermediate education and the administration of the funds devoted to technical and the higher education. Another necessity is that we should bring our intermediate education into some living relation to the Universities. I think on matters of technical and scientific education in our Scottish Universities we are far behind the Universities of England and Wales. We are wholly deficient in technical science, and there is no element in the Scottish university system which brings itself into contact with the schools, or which would

give the schools the position of a stepping-stone to something higher. We are a nation of Philistines as far as technical education is concerned. Compare it with what exists south of the Tweed. If you turn to the Welsh University, with its three colleges, or to the Victoria University, with its colleges at Liverpool, Manchester, and Preston, you find established a sytem of technical and scientific training which is in living contact with the industrial enterprises of the people, and which enables the pupils to obtain that scientific and practical education which fits them for appointments in the industrial world. Take, for instance, the teaching in Scotland of one single branch of science—chemistry. In the University of Edinburgh, which I know best, you have a large number of students in the chemistry class, but only a single professor, and the teaching has no living relation with the practical work of to-day in the industrial world. Contrast that with the University of Zurich in Switzerland, where there are seven professors of chemistry to the same number of students as in Edinburgh, and where the teaching is brought into practical accord with the industrial necessities of the country. I think that the next step that the Government ought to take should be in the direction of the improvement of scientific and technical education in connection with the intermediate schools. Already in Glasgow the mind of the University authorities is being awakened as to what steps should be taken in this direction. Until we have, as in Wales, a link between the elementary schools and the secondary schools, and between these higher class schools and universities, we will not have in Scotland a system which can, in any sense, be described as satisfactory. I am quite prepared to bear testimony to the admirable energy and ability which has been thrown into the reform of the Scotch system of late years; but how is it possible with our system, administered as it is, to obtain thorough efficiency? We have one official here in London, Sir Henry Craik, and in Scotland we have a number of educational bodies without any centre of interest, as in Wales, on which the public attention might become focussed; and the result is that, under the guise of a democratic institution, under the semblance of handing over the educational interests of the country to local authorities, we have got the most complete system of centralisation that can be seen in this country. Our system, centred in Dover House, in London, is conducted with great ability, no doubt, but without that living contact with the people and that knowledge of the necessities of the case which can only be gained if you have the head of the Department living among the people and on the spot. I, for one, despair of the system of Scotch education being brought into a more efficient condition until we have more of the work of central administration done in Scotland than we have at the present time. I feel that the local committees have, in a large measure, failed, though some have managed their business with conspicuous success. It would have been better if the Government had not proceeded on lines of centralisation, but had reformed the local committees, and given them a better system of working. Until they have done that there will be none of that growth of public interest in education in Scotland which is so urgently required, and without which you will make no marked progress in the reform of your educational system.

*COLONEL DENNY (Kilmarnock Burghs): The question which I desire to bring before the Committee is one of those usual struggles between Departments employed to distribute moneys voted by this House and the beneficiaries, who object to the method of distribution. Under the Education (Scotland) Act, 1897, certain funds were placed at the disposal of the Scotch Educational Department, as a complement of the amounts granted for the payment of a certain sum per head to the poor School Boards and Voluntary schools in England. The Bill is a very simple one, and merely states that where the Board is a poor School Board—that is to say. where the yield of a 3d. rate is not 7s. 6d. per child—that Board shall forthwith be entitled to the privileges accorded to poor School Boards and shall receive 4d. per child for every complete penny by which the school rate per £ exceeds 3d. Read as the House of Commons undoubtedly, to my mind, expected this to be read, there is nothing more simple, and the School Board of Port Glasgow in my constituency made its demand in the month of September, 1898, for the grant for that year, amounting to £109 1s. 4d. This was based on the school rate as levied by the Parish Council of 9d. per £.

Mr. Haldane.

This rate was levied as to 4¼d. on owners and 4¾d. on occupiers, in accordance with, I understand, a legal decision given by the Court of Session as to poor rate only, school rate being by Lord Rutherfurd Clark specifically excepted, to the effect that it was not the rate which should be divided equally between owners and occupiers, but the product of the rate; and as occupiers are notoriously less likely to pay regularly than owners, it naturally requires a larger rate upon them than upon the others to produce equal amounts from both classes. I hold, however, that the division between owners and occupiers has nothing whatever to do with the Act of 1897, which clearly specified the School Board rate without any reservation as to how this was divided; in fact, were they to go into the division of the rate I do not see for what reason they fixed the minimum of 3d. per £, without at the same time going into elaborate explanations of how the 3d. in the £ was to be derived from the two classes of ratepayers. However, it ultimately came to this, that the Scotch Education Department fixed a hypothetical rate of their own, for which no reason, to my mind, has ever been adduced. Taking the owners' rate as the more stable, they multiplied that (4¼d.) by two, producing, as I say, a hypothetical rate of 8½d., as against the 9d. which was levied; and as they do not take into consideration anything less than 1d. they take off the ½d., and pay my unfortunate School Board in Port Glasgow on the rate of 8d. instead of 9d.—that is to say, instead of giving them 24d. per child, to which I hold they were clearly entitled under the Act, they have only given them 20d., or a loss of 4d. per child; and as there are 1,636 children in average attendance, that means a loss to them of £26 14s. per annum, which is sufficiently serious even if it were not justified. The School Board at once protested, and a long correspondence ensued with the Scotch Education Department. I was received—as is customary and usual in all Government Departments—most courteously by the officials, and Sir Henry Craik explained to me that the advice of their legal department was that under no circumstances could the rate levied by the Parish Council overhead be taken, but that they must take twice the owners' rate. I have not yet been able to find out, or to gather from the arguments advanced, why this is so, and although I have applied at the Scotch Office to have the opinion, which I think the House is clearly entitled to, of the Law Officers of the Crown, viz., the Lord Advocate and the Solicitor-General for Scotland, this has not been granted, on the principle that the Law Officers of the Crown never give an opinion on law under any circumstances whatever; or if they do, they are never communicated to the public. Now, Sir, what I hold is this, that the Department are taking a highly erroneous view of the Act; that they are reading into it what the House of Commons never gave them any authority to read; and that they are saving a very small amount of money at the cost of a very great deal of friction. To my mind, it appears that common-sense should enter into this thing more than law, in fact this is a case where common-sense is law; and if the school rate, which we always referred to in this House when discussing the Act in question as the real rate, let me call it, taken overhead on owners and occupiers, is to be the basis, then the hypothetical rate, which has no existence anywhere and no authority for use, should be discarded. The Act distinctly says it is to be upon the rateable value. Now in this case, if we divide the total amount levied both on the owners and occupiers by the average value of owners and occupiers, we get a little over 9d. If, on the other hand, we take the produce of the rate levied and divide it absolutely by the owners' rateable value, it comes so little under 9d. as to be negligible—that is to say, something like 8·98d., which shows that the Parish Council were quite correct in expressly fixing the rate at 9d. Then the Statute expressly imposes the duty of fixing the rate on the Parish Council; and by what authority, I would ask, does the Education Department assume the duty of altering the decision —legally and mathematically correct—of the Parish Council? Now, Sir, what I claim this House is entitled to—and I do not think the Lord Advocate will deny it —is a clear legal decision from him on the rights and wrongs of this question. We are not acquainted with, and we have nothing to do with, any private legal advice given by any gentleman, however eminent, to the Scotch Education Department, when that gentleman is not responsible to this House. Personally I may know who it is that gives this legal

advice; officially I have no cognisance of the gentleman whatever. The only man I recognise in the matter is the Lord Advocate, and what I wish him to tell me and this Committee is this—under what construction of the Education (Scotland) Act, 1897, is anything else taken as a basis than the real school rate in this instance of 9d.? If any other rate is to be taken, on what authority is the owners' rate multiplied by two selected as a basis; and, if another than the real rate is to be taken, why should twice the owners' rate be taken in preference to the average rate per £ arrived at by dividing the product of the rate by the average rateable value on owners and occupiers; or, if this pleases the Education Department better, by taking the actual product of the rate and dividing it by the rateable value affected to the owners alone? Sir, this Act was passed for the purpose of assisting poor School Boards, but it appears to be absolutely impossible for any Department to go in for assisting poor people without showing what, I hope I may say without offence, is a certain official meanness. Now, let me acknowledge that there is nothing I admire more in the conduct of all our various Departments than the honest and economical way in which the majority, possibly the whole, of them are conducted; but there is a great difference between honesty and economy and absolute meanness, and I hold in this instance it is the latter feeling which has predominated in the decision of this question. The poor School Boards are deprived of a large proportion of the grant the House of Commons intended to give them, and to this extent the benevolent intentions of the Act are defeated.

MR. BRYCE (Aberdeen, S.): The Lord Advocate has given us a very clear and instructive statement with regard to the motives which guided the Department in the foundation of the new Code. I should like to say that I think the general feeling of hon. Members on this side of the House, so far as I can gather it, has been on the whole to approve of the changes which the present Code shows, and in particular of that very important change which consists in substituting a general report on the condition of the school for the individual examination of the pupils as the basis of payment for grants. As the Lord Advocate has said, the tendency ever since the great reaction in educational policy began has been in the direction of doing away with the exaggerated length to which the system of payment by results, based on individual examination of the scholars, went, and has been moving towards estimating the school as a whole on its general efficiency. I think that educational opinion both in England and Scotland has been certainly moving in that direction for some time, and I am glad that the Scotch Education Department have put the coping stone to that process by the Code which they have issued this year. At the same time, it must be remembered that very great care will be required in applying the principle, and that the Department will be obliged to insist on the inspectors making more frequent and unexpected visits to the schools than before. Everything, in fact, will now depend on the efficiency with which the inspectors do their work, and the amount of care they devote to their reports. I think it is not, therefore, an idle demand that the Department will require to be more than ever careful in the choice of the persons whom they appoint to the office of inspectors, for the success of the experiment will depend more upon the ability, the common-sense, the tact, the judgment and knowledge of the world, of the Inspectors, than ever before. I am glad to see that the Lord Advocate admits that it will be, to some extent, a tentative measure, and that it will not be brought into force until there has been full opportunity of criticism. I take the opportunity, therefore, of offering some criticism which it seems to me is necessary. The School Board of Aberdeen and other leading School Boards think that the re-requirements of the present Code will tend rather to diminish than increase the grants, and that under the requirements of the new Code School Boards will be put to considerable additional expense. I want to put three points to the Lord Advocate and the Education Department. Firstly, the desirability of considering, this year, which way the Code will work, and considering whether they ought not to raise the amount of the grant. The limit between that which the grant will oscillate at present is about one and sixpence, with another shilling added for special excellence, whilst it may be re-

Mr. Bryce.

duced by sixpence for deficiency. I think the Department will find when it comes to consider the matter that that rise will not be sufficient, and it will be necessary to go higher in order to reward real excellence; otherwise there will be an increased expenditure on the part of the School Board, and the rates will suffer, and that progress which the Department desires will be discouraged. The second point is a somewhat minute question, which is also important, which the School Board of Aberdeen is anxious to have addressed to the Department, upon Section 19 F of the new Code, with regard to which the loss a School Board may incur owing to the school being closed by reason of an epidemic. It often happens that the attendance is largely diminished in such a case. In Aberdeen the percentage of absentees rose from 7 per cent. to 18 per cent. during the course of a severe epidemic, and the School Board feels that some allowance ought to be made for the diminution of attendance under such circumstances. This has been recognised by the Department, but to a very inadequate extent. As I understand, the Department will not make any reduction unless the diminution of attendance averages 5 per cent. on the whole year; but what we feel is that the 5 per cent. ought not to be calculated upon the year, but upon the months during which the epidemic has prevailed. A very reasonable plan would be to make an allowance for diminution of attendance over a small period of time, and not on the year as a whole. I ought to add that this allowance will not require any alteration in the terms of the Code, as it is quite compatible with Section 19 M, and the limit such as I ask for we consider should be put in those terms; but all we ask is that the Department should consider this matter. Thirdly, I desire to support the contention which has just been advanced by the hon. Member for Kilmarnock Burghs. The point he has urged with regard to the School Board of that district is a point which concerns many School Boards in other parts of Scotland. It seems to me, looking at the matter as a whole, that the construction he asks for is an admirable one. He asks it on the ground of common-sense; I should ask for it as a point of law, and it will make the practice very simple. The proposal of the Department to take all the rate that is to be levied from the owners and double it, in order to arrive at the construction put upon the Act of 1897, may make considerable difference to the School Boards, and the question becomes one of great importance. Now I come for a moment to the question of the grants. As the Committee knows, we have three grants—the grant of 1890 of £35,000 or £40,000, the equivalent grant of 1892 of £60,000, and the grant of last year of about £35,000. Those three grants are allotted for different purposes, and are administered by different departments, with the result that the whole matter has got into an almost inextricable tangle. There are three different grants for different purposes, with different methods of application. We ask with practical unanimity upon both sides of the House that this tangle should at least be put an end to. Instead of the system of minutes, introducing fresh complications every time a new grant takes place, we should have a Bill brought into this House dealing with the matter *de novo*, and thus give us an effective and consistent system, which would promote the feeling of contentment in Scotland which cannot be brought about by this method of proceeding by minute. If the whole matter were brought before the House we should endeavour to arrange a comprehensive system, and we put this to the Lord Advocate. Scotch opinion is practically unanimous upon this subject. Scotland is tired of being governed by a Department, not that it at all despises the Department, but that it thinks the Department would do better by taking this House and Scotland into its confidence. We also point out that in Scotland we are agreed not only as to the legislation, but as to the points which it should deal with. We also desire that the grant of 1890 should be ear-marked for the purposes of education, and that the Burgh Councils and County Councils should no longer have power to apply that fund to the relief of rates, which everyone will agree is an absolutely useless purpose, and does no good to the ratepayers, and only tends towards the waste of money. Most educationists in Scotland are also agreed that technical and secondary education should be connected. We are further agreed that these three grants ought to be pooled; that is to say, that the three grants should be thrown into one, and placed in the hands of some authority to be administered conjointly. Lastly, we are agreed that all these matters should be consolidated. These are points upon which Scottish opinion is unanimous. Last year we asked the Lord Advocate to give us legislation, and he pointed out that he did so by proceeding by Minute. Now, what has happened has confirmed the prediction we then made; we have had this Minute. I do not for a moment dispute the zeal and public spirit that has animated the Department in its endeavour to deal with this matter. The Lord Advocate has given us a lucid statement of the principle upon which the Department acts. He has pointed out that the money being administered by the Secondary Education Committees was in many cases given in such small sums to so many small schools that it was not producing that effect upon the best schools which in the true interest of education the Department thought necessary. I am not prepared to deny that there is not a good deal in that view, and I agree as to the advisability of not neglecting the higher departments of elementary schools; still there must be a good deal of force in the view that they will essentially affect secondary education if they endeavour in certain places to create strong secondary schools and draw the promising boys from elementary schools to secondary schools instead of spending the money on the higher elementary schools themselves. All I desire to express is that I am not disposed to quarrel with the views of the Department that some of the money might very well go to the stronger schools, and fit them to render better service to secondary education. But what are we presented with? We are presented with a system out of connection altogether with the system under which the previous grant was administered, and county committees are put into a different position to the old county committees, which will perplex them in dealing with the old grants, supposing our suggestions are carried out. The present system of making grants is very complicated and inconvenient. The answer which the Lord Advocate makes is that the Department has not the courage to censure the Committee by altering the arrangements under the Minute of 1893, but must make the new departure by the Minute of 1898. Surely if the Department cannot make up its mind to do off its own bat, so to speak, what ought to be done, because it is afraid that its views or action will be misunderstood, Parliament is not open to any such consideration. Let the Department come and tell us what are the faults of the existing system. If it would like to go back to the old system of 1892, let it say so. I should like the Department to have a little more courage, so as to give us the chance of dealing with the whole question, and of listening to the arguments which are to be advanced. Whether Scotland wants a central authority, as well as a Scotch Education Department in London, is a question I will not now discuss. But we want in Scotland an aggregation of bodies more important and influential, and with more authority than local bodies now possess, and we want those bodies brought into new relationship with the Department here. We want, in fact, something done to stimulate public interest in educational work in Scotland, as it has been stimulated in Wales. My hon. friend the Member for Haddington referred to the question of Scotch universities. I would like to remind him, sympathising as I do entirely with his remarks as to the necessity for strengthening the efficiency of our universities, that we already possess in Scotland points of connection between the shools and the universities of Scotland which do not exist in England, and which are only beginning to exist in Wales. One is the bursaries, which in many Scotch universities have been a most efficient means of bringing the most promising boys from the schools to the universities, particularly of Aberdeen and Glasgow. Scotch universities, to a far greater extent than in England, have prepared men to be teachers in elementary and secondary schools. We should, therefore, endeavour to carry still further that relation between the universities and the schools which my hon. friend the Member for Haddington advocates. But it is not only on the scientific and technical side that the Scotch universities need to be strengthened; they want to be strengthened on the literary and humanistic side. I am sorry, Sir, to have detained the Committee so long. I will only reiterate what seems to me to be the general moral of the whole thing, and that is that the existence of this grant and this Minute, which has created a good deal of dissatisfaction, as the Lord Advocate must gather from the present Debate, makes it

Mr. Bryce.

more than ever necessary that we should have some legislation on the subject, and I hope that legislation will not be long delayed.

SIR MARK STEWART (Kirkcudbright) : I do not propose to trespass at any length upon the attention of the Committee, but I desire to express my views with regard to several questions which have been raised. I will preface my remarks by expressing my admiration for the new Code as a whole. I know it is yet untried, but I believe it is a step in the right direction. Whilst hoping that our inspectors will address themselves to their new work, and prove in every respect efficient, I cannot disregard what has been already suggested to-night, viz., that the Government will have to pay special attention to the class of inspectors appointed. The position of school inspector is a very onerous and responsible one, and calls for the exercise of many qualities quite apart from scholastic learning to enable him to arrive at a right conclusion in regard to schools. In fact, as the matter stands now, I think there is too much responsibility put upon inspectors. In rural districts, for instance, no intimation is given as to when the inspector may arrive. As a consequence of that no member of the School Board knows when to expect a visit, and consequently the inspector is the only individual with an official qualification present at the examination. If the chairman or clerk of the School Board were notified as to the day on which the inspector was coming a few members of the Board could see for themselves the sort of inspection that went on. Several instances have occurred to my knowledge within the last few months in which not a soul was present except the inspector. Of course we do not dispute the good intentions of the inspector, but an inspector may make mistakes like other people, and a school may be condemned for insufficient reasons. There is another point with regard to the same question. In agricultural districts an inspector may arrive during the hay harvest or the turnip-hoeing season—when the children are mostly in the fields —and consequently find a very depleted school. The result would be that he would not come to a right conclusion with regard to the school. Then there is another matter which I should like to press upon the attention of the Lord

Advocate. Old and well trained teachers are sometimes arbitrarily dismissed. They have nobody to appeal to, and I cannot help thinking that the Lord Advocate and his advisers might very easily arrange that an appeal should be allowed to some central authority, so that all the circumstances of the case may be gone into. The teachers would then feel that they were not entirely at the mercy of an arbitrary and possibly tyrannical School Board, but that justice would be done them. Cases of very considerable hardship have arisen during the past year in which the teacher has had no possible appeal against what he has considered unjust treatment. . Passing on to the Minute of the 27th of April, I am bound to say that when I read that Minute, and indeed when I understood its application, I was not disposed to form a hostile opinion with regard to it. But having paid a visit to Scotland at Whitsuntide and become more familiar with the feelings of the county committees, I am bound to tell the Lord Advocate that it is extremely unpopular in certain parts of the country. I think it would be a very wise thing on the part of the Lord Advocate to withdraw the Minute, and in the meantime bring up another very much on the lines which the right hon. Gentleman the Member for Aberdeen has sketched, so as to get the three grants under one head, and either give the county committees other powers or curtail their powers in the direction in which the Department does not wish the money spent. Now, I am quite satisfied that the Education Department would be the last people in the world to encourage such a thing, but there are certain schools in Scotland which have been somewhat neglected. A large amount is given by the Code in various ways to elementary schools, and what ought to be really secondary schools are very much neglected, and I would suggest that by the new rules a way of escape should be provided from this most unfortunate public Minute. I trust the Lord Advocate will listen to the voice of Scotch opinion in condemning this Minute. There is only one other matter on which I should like to say a word. The remarks of the hon. Member for Haddingtonshire with regard to secondary education have my hearty concurrence. Taking the Welsh University as an example, and the Swiss University as a still greater ex-

ample, I think much may be done in consolidating secondary education, so as to bring it more in touch with the elementary schools, and thus provide a ladder by which a boy, as in the days of John Knox, can enter a university.

*Mr. CROMBIE (Kincardineshire): I think the course this Debate has taken has plainly shown that secondary education is a subject of burning interest, and to that I should like to address myself. But before doing so I hope I shall be allowed to refer to one matter which is perfectly different. Last session we passed an Act for the superannuation of teachers, and under this Act a code of rules has been drawn up by the Department. Now, Sir, I observe that under these rules teachers applying for pensions are to have their pecuniary circumstances taken into account. This was not mentioned in the Act, and it seems to me rather a hardship on the teachers. This is not a charity pension; it is a pension to which teachers subscribe, just as they would to an ordinary insurance, and it would seem rather a hard thing if a man, whose health had broken down, could not benefit by his insurance without his pecuniary circumstances being taken into account. Of course I should be out of order in raising the general question of pensions, and I will simply say in passing that I for one should be exceedingly glad if the Department can provide a remedy for the inequality between the pensions of existing and future teachers. Turning to the question of the Minute, I am certainly not going to break up the unanimity which exists in Scotland, and if a Division is taken, I shall vote against the Minute. I rather hope, however, that a Division will not be taken. Of course, we know that we cannot persuade the Government by means of a Division, but I am hopeful that we can persuade the Lord Advocate by means of fair reasoning, and I, for my part, shall be surprised if he can resist the unanimity of opinion which has been expressed by Scotch Members on both sides of the House against the Minute. Now, Sir, it seems to me that the Lord Advocate defended the Minute on two grounds. He seemed to suggest, in the first place, that the higher schools should get the grant because they had been neglected; and he seemed, in the second place, to say that something had been done by means of the Code that gives a sum to the other schools. When the right hon. Gentleman made these statements, I at once turned to the figures which had been brought before the House, and those figures entirely demolish the idea that the higher schools have been neglected; and as to the other schools having had something under the Code, this provision is liable to the 17s. 6d. limit, and, as far as I can see, it is worked out in such a way that school boards will not be able to take the benefit, at all events without putting themselves to an enormous amount of expense. There are only about 74 schools which will benefit by this Minute, and I am told that it will work out to something like £6 per pupil. That seems to me very unfair. But, Sir, we object to this Minute for other reasons, and I think the reason which seems to underlie the speeches of previous speakers is that it adds to the confusion of secondary education in Scotland. This confusion has become an old topic. We have a secondary education branch, a technical educational branch, an agricultural branch, a science and art branch, and another branch under the superintendence of the Department itself. The way in which the whole administration is conducted is such that it is very largely kept out of the purview of Parliament itself. How is Secondary education administered? It is administered by Minutes and Circulars. A great deal has been said about secondary education committees. I think it would be very unfair to say that they have failed in one sense, for they have done admirable work under very difficult circumstances; but the whole position is anomalous, and the fact is that secondary education, as it is administered, is like a bit of a ladder which has neither beginning nor end. We are all unanimous that one of the first things you must do is to use the technical education money practically for secondary education. If you look at the Minute, you will find that everything is made easy for a committee which meets to hand over this money to a secondary education committee. But I maintain that a great proportion of the money that is spent on secondary education is wasted. A great deal of mischief is done in the attempt to give technical education as opposed to other education. How far the idea has gone may be seen by the

Mr. Crombie.

declarations of a great many gentlemen. I listened to the Debates on the Half-Timers Bill, both at the Second Reading and the Committee stages, and I heard Members, for whose opinions in most things I have the greatest respect, actually arguing that these half-time children when they are employed in mills and taught to tie a knot, and that sort of thing, are actually getting technical education. If the idea is abroad that that is the kind of technical education by which Germany has achieved her present commercial eminence, I say it is utterly absurd, and the sooner it is altered the better. I speak with some slight experience of technical education in Germany, because I have had some of it myself. When I went to Germany to learn the language I determined to learn something of the technical education. I found there were two sorts of technical education in Germany. They actually teach a trade or manufacture in a school, and they have another method beside. What I wanted to learn was weaving and dyeing, and I went to a school that taught those subjects. Certainly they did it systematically, but the net result was that everything I learnt as to the technology of my trade in the technical school could be learnt in almost as short a time in the factory. I went to another sort of school, one of the technological colleges of Germany, and there I found quite a different kind of thing. There was a course of lectures in all subjects—not confined solely to a good general education, but lectures in chemistry and physics, very much the same as those I had already passed through in a Scotch University. This is the technical education that makes Germany excel in the commercial world. Why is it? It is because Germany takes those of her citizens who are going in for commerce or manufacture, and passes them through a training almost as high as that which we give to those who are going in for the professions of medicine, teaching or law. These men thoroughly master the subjects of chemistry, physics, electricity, &c., and then go into a factory. They are absolutely ignorant of the technical manufacture, but they soon pick it up, and they are able to apply the science they have learnt to the processes of the manufacture they are engaged in. Not only that, but they have such an admirable scientific education that they are able to follow what is going on in the laboratories of those who are pursuing science in the abstract. They have, in fact, one eye on abstract science and the other eye on practical manufacture, and when any invention is put forward, whether it is the liquefaction of hydrogen or the Röntgen rays, or anything else, they are following what is done, and are able to apply these new abstract improvements in science to the concrete technicalities of their own manufacture. It is that and that alone that has brought Germany to her present position in commerce as far as technical education is concerned. I am sorry to see that the superstition about technical education has to some extent permeated even the Education Department In the Code in these higher grade schools the greatest pains are taken to keep scientific absolutely distinct from general education. Here, for instance, I quote from Circular 231:

"They will require, however, that the science side shall be clearly separated from the classical or language side of such schools, and that not merely shall the pupils following the science course be separately registered, but that they shall receive separate and special instruction in the essential subjects of the prescribed curriculum, even when these happen to be common to both sides of the school. This condition being fulfilled, my Lords will not object to the instruction being given by members of the same staff who possess the necessary qualifications."

Such an attempt as this to bring about a specialisation at an early stage of the school children's curriculum is going in an absolutely wrong direction. What is wanted is that they should be given a thoroughly good education, and then begin their technical or special or scientific education. For these reasons I believe we want, and I hope Her Majesty's Government will carry out, a consolidation of our various departments. At present there is plenty of time for legislation, but if the Government do not think matters are sufficiently concretely before them to enable them to devise a scheme, let a Commission or Committee be appointed. We have Commissions and Committees on almost everything, and I should be very happy to see one added on Scotch education. Scotch educationalists, to whatever party they belong or from wherever they come, all agree that the very first thing we want, and must get before we shall be happy, is legislation for the unification of the whole system of secondary education.

Mr. J. P. SMITH (Lanark, Partick): I wish that a few more English members had been present to hear what a bold step we have taken in the course of this year, a step which I hope will prove to be a right step, viz., the abandonment of individual examinations and the adoption of a general payment based on the work of the school as a whole, which will certainly be much easier for the inspectors, but at the same time make considerable demands upon their capacity. I hope we shall find the inspectors rise to the greater difficulties of the task which is put upon them. The making of so large a normal grant as is now made is a very complete change, and a great many of those who are affected by it feel rather nervous lest that normal grant has been struck somewhat too low. The School Board for Govan, for instance, have gone into the matter, and made as careful calculations as possible, and their anticipation, with which the Associated School Boards in general seem to agree, is that the new system will mean a very decided diminution in the grants to individual schools. One can hardly ask the Government at the present moment to make any change, but I hope they will be very thoroughly alive to that possibility, and that if it is found that a school, although conducted as well as before, is earning less under the new rules, certain relaxations may be given which will enable them to earn as much. That becomes particularly important in view of the various increased requirements—to most of which I do not at all object—which are involved in the present Code, such as greater expense in the maintenance of schools, which the School Boards fear may result in loss of income. The School Boards feel very strongly that there should be more elasticity about the normal grant. Only an extra 6d. can be given for special merit, but if there could be a possible increase of 1s. 6d. or 2s., they consider they might be able to pay their way satisfactorily. I am glad to see that the whole tendency of the Report of the Education Department is to take further steps in reducing the extent to which specific subjects are gone into in an elementary way. We are getting more and more able to differentiate education; we are devoting ourselves more and more to developing the higher part of education, and as we do that we more and more restrict what hitherto has been a great abuse in our schooling—the extent to which children have been carried through the rudimentary stages of specific subjects, with the knowledge that they will be dropped absolutely and forgotten in a short time. We are getting able to insist that only those children should be carried to the higher subjects who have a probability of being able to go far enough in those subjects for the work that is expended upon them to do them some practical good. We have been too apt to think that the mere presence of a child at school is enough, without considering what is being taught to the child, and that as long as the Education Estimates are swelling and more children being sent to school everything is satisfactory. But I am afraid that an enormous amount of both money and time is being wasted in the fact that what is being taught goes out of, almost as quickly as it goes into, the children. While we give clever children every chance of getting on and obtaining a good secondary education, we should not make the mistake that ambitious teachers are so naturally apt to make, viz., that of trying to teach too many subjects in the very short time the children have before them. That is the case particularly with girls. They have been taught a great deal too much of literary subjects, while not enough attention has been given to those subjects that really make the work of their lives, such as domestic training, cooking, and laundry work. These subjects differ very much in their character from the ordinary technical subjects. It is quite true that trades cannot really be taught in schools, but it has to be remembered that domestic work, cooking, and laundry work is work that the girls will have necessarily to carry out in their after-life, and which they will have no opportunity of learning in a factory or workshop, but which they have to pick up for themselves. It is infinitely more important that these subjects should take a place of due prominence in the education of a girl than that she should be taught merely literary subjects which pass completely out of her head after a while. Attendance at school is now enforced; girls are deprived of the opportunities they formerly had of learning these necessary arts at home with their mothers, and very great care should be taken that they have

Mr. J. P. Smith.

every opportunity at school of learning these branches of work. I am glad to see that in the present Code these branches are made considerably more important, and at the same time more stringent conditions are imposed; classes have to be smaller, and the amount of time has to be greater. I hope that that tendency will go a great deal further. But I regret to see that drawing is being made apparently an obligatory subject for girls as well as for boys. Considering the very limited amount of time before the ordinary girl, it is a great pity to throw in an extra subject like drawing, which, while an education of the hand and eye, is not so useful as would be a little more attention to the domestic subjects. The girls ought to be separated from the boys at a much earlier stage. At present they are treated together, with the result that these special girls' subjects get put into a corner. A master naturally does not like his class broken up by the girls going off to one thing and the boys to another, and the classes are apt to be kept working at the subjects which may be regarded as common to both sexes. More differentiation is needed in an earlier period of girls' education, so that the specially feminine subjects may have a much larger place. I am exceedingly glad to see that cookery is being encouraged in some respects. Classes are being made smaller. Hitherto they have been so big that it was almost a waste of time to attempt to teach so many girls by one teacher. I do not quite understand why the rate of payment is reduced also. Hitherto the rate has been 4s. per 40 hours; now it is being reduced to 8s. 4d. per 100 hours, The reduction in the size of the classes will make the teaching of cooking more expensive, and it would have been better if the scale had been raised a little to correspond with the increased requirements. The reduction in the size of the classes is a step in the right direction, but it has not gone far enough; it would be better to reduce the number to about twelve, if it is possible. Another proper step is the general reduction of the size of the classes to 60. But many School Boards lately have built magnificent schools, in which the class-rooms have been so constructed that a larger class can perfectly well be taught and governed from a single spot. I suggest that the absolutely fixed limit of 60 is rather a rigid one, and that in regard to such schools a certain amount of latitude might be given. Then I want to ask the Lord Advocate whether he will give for Scotland the Returns in regard to the employment of school children which have been given in regard to England. I was told a year ago that it was practically impossible to give such a Return; but the impossibility has been accomplished in regard to England, and we have recently had the two halves of that Return. It is a Return for England and Wales, giving the number of children attending elementary schools who are known to be working for wages or employed for profit. There are given the ages, standards, occupations, hours of work, and rates of pay. The facts as to the employment in different parts of England are extremely interesting, even though the Return itself is fragmentary, for reasons which might be avoided in sending out a fresh Circular. A great number of managers of schools did not reply at all. I hope we may have similar facts brought out in regard to Scotland. The second half of the Return is still more interesting. It gives the different classes of employment taken up by boys and girls attending elementary schools in England and Wales on leaving school during a complete year. From that you get a very complete picture of the different occupations of the children in different parts of the country, and you gather a great deal of information as to the useful and proper forms of technical education in different parts of the country. These facts are important from an educational and interesting from a social point of view, and I hope we may have similar information with regard to Scotland. One-half of the Return was marshalled by the Labour Department of the Board of Trade, and the other half by the Education Department; but I think it would be more satisfactory if all the facts in regard to Scotland were worked out by the Scotch Education Department alone. As to the Circular of the 27th April, I entirely agree that there is very great confusion in regard to these secondary education funds, that it is highly desirable in the interests of everyone that they should be put in a more intelligible form, and that legislation is the only way in which it can be done. But I do not concur in the objection to confining the grant to secondary schools. Schools with

higher departments get their advantages under this new Code; they get a very large increase of advantages under the provisions of Chapter 9, and it is only right when they get so much in addition to what they have already under that part of the Code, that the other schools, which take nothing under the Code, should have their share of assistance from public funds. These higher departments press very hardly upon secondary schools. Secondary schools have in many cases lost pupils and support by the development of the higher departments, and in order to maintain them in a state of proper efficiency it is very necessary that they should have some assistance. I entirely differ from the hon. Member opposite as to making higher education free. We should be throwing away a source of income which is not in the least grudged. So long as every facility is given for clever sons of poor parents, by free places and bursaries, to get to the best schools and make their way to the university— and the majority of those who are able to spend a longer time at school, and to advance through the stages of secondary education, are the children of people who are perfectly ready and willing and desirous to pay for them—you are merely gaining a theoretical advantage by seeking to abolish fees in regard to such schools. The hon. Member says that no social feeling ought to exist, but a very strong social feeling does exist, which has to be reckoned with and must not be left out of sight as a part of the problem. The scheme of the Circular of the 27th April makes confusion more confounded. It leaves the scheme we have had hitherto, and strikes out a new scheme for itself. Instead of leaving the drawing up of plans in the hands of the county committees, subject to the criticism of the Department, each individual school is to send up its scheme through the county committees, and the Department is to decide. You have £60,000 dealt with in one way, and £30,000 in the other. That will be most unsatisfactory. I do not see how either party can work independently, or how the county committee can draw up its scheme for spending its share of the £60,000 in complete ignorance of how the £30,000 will be dealt with. On the other hand, if they knew how the £30,000 would be dealt with, and did not approve, it would be very unsatisfactory for the county committee to be cutting down its grant to other schools, on the ground that those schools would be getting too much from the Education Department. The whole ought to be treated in the same way and made one single fund, and proposals should be made by which the county committee will have full knowledge, and the Department should be the controlling power. Another point I desire to raise is as to the fees and the examination for the leaving certificate. These certificates have been an enormous success. In 1888, when they started, only 29 schools went in for them; in 1898 the number was 398 schools. In the same way the number of candidates has risen from less than 1,000 to over 16,000. The examination is accepted by a vast number of important bodies, and the standard in most subjects is very high, and the percentage of passes very satisfactory. Therefore, this system of examinations exercises an enormous control over higher education in Scotland, a control which is entirely in the hands of the Department. The secretary to Sir Henry Craik has reason to be proud of these results, as these leaving examinations have been very completely his work. The growth is such that there ought to be something outside a secretarial department for the management of a system which is exercising such a very great influence over the whole secondary education of Scotland. At present you have a set of anonymous examination papers and a set of anonymous Reports. The only name connected with the whole system is that of Sir Henry Craik. He signs his Report, putting such men as he thinks fit to examine, putting in his report such portions of their reports as he thinks proper, and wonderfully well that system has worked. Still, it seems to me now that this is too important a matter to leave to a single man, and we ought to know who the people are who are examining. Those who have examined into the system ought to know that their reports will be published upon the authority of their own name. You would have, in that way, control over secondary education, and it would be much wider than that which is at present exercised, for it would be exercised not merely by one individual, but by persons whose names as examiners would carry weight, and they would have the opportunity of knowing that what they say in their reports would have influence

Mr. J. P. Smith.

upon public opinion. Then, it appears that there are leaving certificates that the boys and girls go in for again and again, especially with regard to the lower grade of labour certificates. I want to know what the object of all this is. The object in the higher grade we understand, but considering the number of lower grade leaving certificates, I think you are apt to have a great deal too much of the examination element coming in in the education of these children. I think they should pretty frequently go in for an examination, but it should be limited much more to the nature of their career. There is only one other point I have to mention, and that is the method by which you are to calculate the amount earned per head. That was formerly unimportant, but now it becomes of the greatest importance, because, under certain circumstances, the £4 per head depends upon each child being of the school age. I need hardly enter into the technical details, but I think it is very unnecessary to cut down —when we are discussing the matter in this House—the amount that we give to children under certain circumstances, and I think it is extremely unnatural that a technical view of the exact meaning of the words should be taken. I do not see how any question of law could come in, but it seems to me to be a case which ought to be construed to the advantage of the School Board. In conclusion, I think we must all congratulate the Lord Advocate and the Educational Department upon the progress that the Code shows.

CAPTAIN SINCLAIR: I agree with what the hon. Member who has just sat down has said in expressing the hope that this new Code may answer the expectations formed of it. There is one characteristic and symptom which shows itself in connection with the increased powers given to the inspectors—and there is no reason to think that they will not fulfil that responsibility—and that is that this increased power given to the inspectors must be accompanied by largely increased influence and power in regard to the Scotch Education Department itself. That is not peculiar to the Scotch Education Department, for if there is one subject which more than another may benefit from a strong central authority it is the subject of education. There is another thing which I think we ought also to remember, and that is that all of these improvements which are demanded on every side by those interested in education mean increased cost and expenditure. Education every year is getting more costly, and every specialisation, every new departure made in instruction, means an addition to the burdens which the country has to bear in regard to education, and naturally that increases the power of the Department which has to administer the whole subject. Therefore, if there is criticism to be passed, we cannot press too urgently the necessity of carrying public opinion along with us in these matters. It seems to me that, in regard to this Minute about which so much has been said to-night—and in regard to which I wish to support all that has been said—what we really lose sight of is that no Department, however active or however well supplied with information, can have the opportunity of carrying public opinion along with it unless it is possessed of that local knowledge which can only come from energetic and active local administration in the country itself. It is very natural, under those conditions—perhaps with insufficient funds or inefficient administration—that the whole system of education should not carry along with it public opinion. Perhaps it is natural that the education in the towns should be superior to education in the country, and that different claims should be made from different districts one against the other for a larger share of the funds that are available. No doubt it is better to establish centres from which educational influence may radiate, for larger towns would be able to cover a larger district, and the funds at their disposal would be more efficiently expended, and would achieve better results than the system which has been characterised in this Debate as giving the money away in dribblets. After all, I think we must remember that what has happened in recent years is that the State has stepped in, and by its action in aiding and subsidising by money which Parliament placed at the disposal of public authorities the Government have put an end to all private ventures, and have limited the number of private schools which formerly provided education for the various classes of the population who wish to take advantage of what was offered by those schools. There is now a largely reduced

number of all these schools and colleges for middle-class secondary education, dependent simply and purely upon private resources. They all look to the State and to the funds provided by the Government, and just as elementary education is completely in the hands of the Government, so we shall have this higher stage of education purely in the hands of the Government as well. A remark has been made in the course of this Debate, to the effect that it is for the educational authorities to say when the education of certain children should cease ; and that it was for the children to show by their efficiency and ability to learn what they were qualified to do, and if they attained certain standards then and then only were they to have the privileges and advantages of higher education. That is a perfectly fair system, assuming that you kill all other systems. It is a perfectly fair system if you take care to place within the reach of every family and of every child the facilities which he ought to have, and you will not do this if you administer your education from a single Department without that information and knowledge which can only come from local people who live in those particular localities, and who know the wants of those localities. I will give the Committee an illustration. Condemnation has been poured upon the small efforts made in this direction by the County Councils for the purpose of extending this higher secondary education by the action of the Educational Department. The general influence of this action has been, whether rightly or wrongly exercised, to discourage secondary education in the country districts where educational facilities are most needed, and the larger proportion of the money provided by the Government has been spent in the more populous centres. There is a school in the county which I have the honour to represent which claims, under the County Council, to be approved by the Education Department for the training of certain scholars in a specific subject not required by the Code. Now the Education Department, on the ground that the education given to these scholars did not come under the head of contributing effectively to the secondary education of the country, conceived it to be its duty to disallow the grants which the County Council desired to award, and the school, had to go without the grant. But when the facts were pressed home to the Department they relinquished the position they took up, and the grant was allowed. I quote this simply as an instance of the action of the Department in regard to country schools, and I could mention other schools which have suffered in the same way in the same county. There is a country Highland district in Scotland where the children have to attend a school which is nine-and-a-half miles away from the nearest secondary school.

*MR. WEIR (Ross and Cromarty): In my constituency some of the children are 45 miles and upwards from the nearest secondary school.

CAPTAIN SINCLAIR: Now, it is a fact that 90 per cent. of the children who have attended these schools for the last 20 years are the children of crofters and ploughmen, who could not afford to send their children such a distance to attend these schools. The only alternative is for these parents to send their children to lodge in the towns where the secondary schools are held; but it is perfectly absurd to imagine that crofters and ploughmen can bear the expense of sending their children to lodge in towns in order to get the benefit of this secondary education. In this way you are preventing these children learning these specific subjects and you are doing them great damage. No one will deny this who looks at the Papers, and I can quote from the inspectors' annual reports of the Department in two directions; in the first place, to show the value of the education which can be given in these elementary schools if they are allowed to give the higher education to promising pupils in this way; and, in the second place, to show that the influence of the Department has been exercised to stamp out in the small village schools the teaching of specific subjects and the carrying on of the education of pupils beyond what is the maximum of efficiency in education which the Department lays down. I quite see the importance of encouraging this higher education in popular centres, but when the Government kills all private enterprise in secondary education it should place within the reach of every child in the country opportunities for that child getting such further education as the parents desire. In my con-

Captain Sinclair.

stituency I have noticed that the local trains are often crammed with children going to and from the secondary schools. My complaint against the present system is this, that you are preventing a child whose parents would like it to take another year or a couple of years' education from doing so when it would be for the good of the child itself, and would tend to raise the educational tone of the whole country. There is another argument which I will venture to use in connection with this subject, and it is that this system is extremely bad for efficient teaching. I quite agree that the system under which these pupils are learning these specific subjects savours of the grant-earning system, but I confess that I do not see any other alternative if you are not to deprive these children of opportunities of further education. I see no other alternative under the present system between depriving them altogether of opportunities for further instruction and allowing them to have that instruction in specific subjects provided for them in their own localities. The instance which I have quoted is only one of a number of instances which can be quoted from counties in Scotland. I have another instance just as strong from my own county, in which the Department has practically stepped in and said "These children shall not have any further education," and it is owing to the influence of the Department that these children are sent to work earlier than they would otherwise have been. The old problem here is the social difficulty to which my hon. friend has alluded, and I do beg the right hon. Gentleman to notice this point, because I am sure I am justified in drawing the conclusions which I have drawn from the reports of last year and from the facts which I have just put before the Committee and the general trend of the administration of the Department. But there is another bad effect. In the first place, you are drawing a distinction which has never before been drawn in Scotland between certain classes of the population. This has always been against the wishes of Scotland, for she does not wish that our efforts should be confined to elementary education. The School Boards have the power, and their efforts should not be confined to the provision simply of elementary education, for in every parish there should be provision made for secondary education. May I say a word or two about another subject which illustrates my contention that the influence of the Department is not exercised very wisely in this matter, and it is time that we should urge upon the Government that it is necessary to associate local knowledge and local administration with the Department in administering education. It is precisely because this Minute of the 27th of April does not do this that I take objection to it, for, after all, it is a question of policy. I can say perfectly frankly myself that I never expected anything else from the Department than that it would apply this money for education on some such lines as have been adopted. There is no doubt whatever that the effect of this Minute will be to place, as it was intended, more power and more influence in the hands of the Department, and I can perfectly well imagine that the Secretary for Scotland deems that to be the only way in which he can, by gradually exerting influence in one direction and another, create some order out of the chaos into which secondary education has now fallen in Scotland. It is perfectly ligitimate for him to say, " Here I am the head of a strong Department ; I am not going to create any more vested interests ; but I am going to gradually use the money at my disposal as a lever to get the authorities to simplify the confusion that exists, and to create some kind of order out of chaos." Now, it is not necessary to give further illustrations, because more than one honourable Gentleman has shown this afternoon clearly what the state of secondary education is in Scotland. You have over 200 authorities administering one branch, and you have 38 administering another branch, and altogether you get something like 240 different educational authorities in Scotland. The Education Department says that it did not mean the Minute to be a censure on the county committees, and that it was impossible for it to have taken any other action. But I should like to point out, from the very history which the Lord Advocate has laid before us to-day of the various Minutes which were published and withdrawn, that what the Department is doing may not be a censure on the county committees, but it is a censure on the last recorded decision of the House of Commons on the subject. Last session there was a strongly expressed opinion on both sides in favour of urging the Government to be more courageous and to take

the opportunity, not being greatly occupied, to put things in order, and to meet here in this House any difficulties which existed. I hope it is not yet too late to ask the Government to reconsider their decision, and to either introduce legislation or institute an inquiry into the whole subject of secondary education in Scotland. It is a great pity that the Government will not take advantage of the public interest in the matter which now exists. We have here the best experience ; we have men who have sat on educational committees, like my hon. friend the Member for Aberdeen, who has had experience of educational systems in all parts of the world, and they tell you in a friendly manner that they are anxious to help and that you ought to take advantage of this opportunity. There is one other point to which I wish to direct the attention of the right hon. Gentleman, and it is to the gap which now exists in Scotland because of the want of agricultural education. There could not be a better illustration of the present unsatisfactory state of things than the want of any provision for agricultural education in Scotland. As the right hon. Gentleman knows, Secondary Education is given under this Minute, but it is given by a provision of Parliament administered by the National Education Department. Besides that there are funds granted by the County Committees. The hon. Member for Partick mentioned the various itinerary courses given in the counties, such as veterinary instruction and dairy instruction, but they have no communication or dependence upon each other, and are independent of the central educational authority. I do not know whether we will be successful in inducing the Government to reconsider this Minute, but perhaps at any rate they will reconsider how money to be devoted to agricultural instruction is to be spent, and I wish to point out that there is a large district in the east of Scotland where no provision is made in this respect. In all the country up the east coast, from Edinburgh to Aberdeen, there are only four centres to which money is given for the purposes of agricultural instruction. There is, for instance, no provision in Perthshire. I will, however, take another opportunity of submitting that point. I only now wish to press upon the attention of the right hon. Gentleman the Minute of the

27th April, and to enter my protest against the policy of stamping specific subjects, and not providing secondary education for children whose parents cannot afford to pay the fees demanded.

*Sir Wm. WEDDERBURN (Banffshire): I wish to say that there is a very strong feeling in my constituency in regard to the distribution of this £35,000. The County Committee of Secondary Education have met to consider what their action should be with regard to this Minute of the 27th of April, and it appears to them, not that the money coming under that Minute is insufficient, but that no money is coming to them at all. They naturally feel this very greatly, and I believe they are going to send in a protest to the Secretary for Scotland with regard to the working of this Minute. I do not yet know the exact grounds upon which they have gone nor the particulars, but one thing they are correct in considering, and that is that they cannot obtain any grant under this Minute. I have a hazy recollection that a question was put to the Lord Advocate with regard to this grant. He was asked whether the elementary schools teaching secondary subjects could obtain a grant under this Minute, and my impression is that he said there was no objection to a grant being given under this Minute. Perhaps he will explain whether that is the case.

*Mr. A. G. MURRAY : There may be higher grade schools which obtain no grant under the code, and in those cases they would receive money under this Minute. If the hon. Member means can a school with a higher grade department, which is an elementary school, taking money under that head, participate, it obviously cannot under the terms of the Minute itself.

*Sir Wm. WEDDERBURN : Then I am afraid the county committee was right in believing that no money will come to them at all, and they naturally feel that they have a great grievance. The county of Banff has always held a very high educational position among the counties of Scotland. In fact, I think I may say in proportion to its population it has sent more students direct to the University than any other county of Scotland ; and that is mainly owing to the system of giving very good secondary education in the

Captain Sinclair.

elementary schools. They consider it is very hard that they should be penalised, because with the resources at their disposal they have produced such good results. It must be borne in mind that even supposing there is a secondary school in the county it is not specially to the advantage of the poor children, or the parents of the poor children of Banffshire, because they not only have to pay for the education, which they gladly do, and impoverish themselves to do, but they have to board and lodge their children at a distance, which entails a large additional expense upon them. According to our view of the case the system has worked very well under the special conditions of the county. Our record is a good one, and very distinguished men have taught in these parish schools. I have in my recollection at the present time many gentlemen who taught in those schools, Masters of Arts, and men of very superior attainments indeed. I may mention that one of the masters in one of our schools was our lamented friend Dr. Wallace. There are many men of distinction, and they have sent out extremely creditable students to the University. From that point of view my constituents are satisfied with the present arrangement, and do not wish to alter it ; and they do feel it a hardship that when a considerable sum like this is available for secondary education it should not go in that channel in which it is at present found to be so useful. I appreciate the theory on which the present Minute is based—namely, that in reorganising and creating a good system of secondary education it is desirable to strengthen and consolidate really strong schools in particular parts of the country. The theory is good, and I notice that my right hon. friend the Member for Aberdeen particularly appreciates it, perhaps because, as it happens, Aberdeen is almost the only place in the North Country which obtains a single penny under the present Minute. I think Aberdeen and the Academy at Elgin are the only two institutions north of the Grampians who get a share of the money. I must therefore support the protest which comes from the local authorities in this matter. As regards the general question I sympathise with hon. Gentlemen on both sides of this House who wish all the sums that are available for secondary education to be consolidated, and that money shall be used in some reasonable and good and simple way so that it may be understood of the people, which is not the case at present. Special consideration should be given to the scheme of my hon. friend the Member for the Border Burghs, which was put before the country last year, when he showed the way in which the ladder could be completed which would take the ploughman's son from the elementary school up through the secondary school and on to the university, and give him the same opportunity as the son of the richest man in the land. There are two other points to which I should like to allude ; one is the new duties of the inspectors. Under the amended Code it has been pointed out that the duties of the inspectors are much more difficult and responsible, they will not be so mechanical, and a greater exercise of discretion and knowledge will be required than has been under the old system. I think, in order that an inspector should have that familiarity with the subject that would enable him to form a good judgment, it is very important that he should be familiar with the schools themselves, and for that reason it is desirable that the inspectors should be promoted from the ranks of the most successful of the teachers. The inspectors may be very learned men chosen from the outside, but they might have a difficulty in testing and proving the children if they had not been school teachers themselves. The remaining point is the point that the hon. Baronet the member for Kirkcudbrightshire referred to, which was that there needs to be some appeal in the case of teachers dismissed by the school boards. There is no doubt that whether or not the teacher in the position does get justice, he often has the feeling that he does not get it, and it would be very satisfactory to all the teaching profession if there was some reasonable means of appealing from the decisions of the school board. Whether that could be done by having some court of appeal formed by the chairmen of several School Boards, and making those chairmen the court of appeal for that particular group, or whether it could be done in some other way, I think it would be in the interests of the teaching profession that there should be some arrangement of that sort. If the school boards were grouped together there would also be an opportunity of moving a master from one place to another, which might prove very beneficial where a difference between the School Board and the teacher has arisen. In conclusion, I can only say that when I see the protest that is being brought by the County Committee for Secondary Education I shall be in a better position to know their views, but that as at present advised I must join with other hon. Members of this House in saying that this Minute is very unsatisfactory.

MR. MONRO FERGUSON (Leith Burghs) : This Debate has been of unusual interest, partly because of the statement made by the right hon. Gentleman opposite, and partly because of the criticisms which have been directed against the Code. There are two points to which I wish to draw the attention of the Committee, one of which is the fear that has been excited in the minds of some School Boards that they will suffer a loss of revenue under the new Code. The School Board of Leith have made representations to the effect that they feared they would suffer considerable loss. I do not know that I have ever before had to present a local grievance to the House, but the School Board of Leith represent that the schools of that district would sustain a diminution in the amount of the grant. The expenses of education have gone up very considerably, and while the grants have been increased the expenses have increased to a very much greater extent, and under the new Code it will not be possible for schools to earn so much as formerly if every school and every division of the school succeeded in obtaining the maximum grant. Unless some kind of addition is made to the revenue of the schools in some way, the School Board of Leith will be placed in very considerable difficulty. Their experience is that, after providing for the Government requirements, and taking everything into consideration, including assistance and rate grants, the result during the last ten years has been that they have only just paid, and they are afraid that the state of things cannot be maintained under the new Code, and that they will suffer loss. The School Board rate in Leith has gone up during the last ten or eleven years from 6d. to 1s. 2d., and a very great strain has been put upon the community in order to carry out the requirements of the Education Department. Representation has been made, and it has been considered, but the balance has not been made up by the Department. I mention this case as being one that may be taken as an example of the many difficulties which may be anticipated under the new Code. A new school has been opened quite recently, and that school is not in receipt of any grant under the Code, and this is regarded as a great hardship A new high school has been opened, and it is feared its efficiency cannot be maintained if the grants fall so far short of what has been expected. Therefore, this question of the effect which may follow on the reduction of the grants, will have to receive consideration. Of course it is felt all the more because we have not received the additional sums which have been recently voted for education in the United Kingdom. There is one other question that I will refer to for one brief moment, and that is the grant towards agricultural education. Scotch counties have far less money for that purpose than English counties. I need not go into the details of the case, because the right hon. Gentleman knows them better than I do, but the fact remains that there is much less money available for agricultural education in Scotland, and it consequently becomes almost impossible to obtain anything like the facilities for education which have been provided by such a school as that established by the Bedfordshire County Council or the Northumberland County Council. In France and Germany agricultural schools are established and maintained by the State. Well, as the county councils in Scotland have not the requisite funds to establish such schools, and the education allowance falls considerably below that made to England, it may be fairly urged that Government must give a more generous allowance than £2,000 towards the cost of agricultural education in Scotland. We believe that the present institutions might be improved, and suggest that there should be in Scotland some Government farm where experiments could be carried on. In Germany there are Government establishments where the science of forestry is thoroughly gone into, to the great advantage of the State. In Scotland our

Mr. Monro Ferguson.

farmers are perfectly well qualified by their education to derive the full benefit from such establishments, and considering the falling-off in the Government allowance in the matter of education we are at least entitled to ask that a few more pounds a year should be applied to the furtherance of the great agricultural industry in Scotland.

MR. CALDWELL (Lanarkshire, Mid): The most satisfactory thing in connection with Scotch education is the high rate of the school attendance. The statistics show that the parents have been co-operating with the School Boards in seeing that their children are kept at school. I find that there is only one district where the inspectors complain under this head, and that is in a northern division. As regards school attendance, I observe that the percentage of the total population of Scotland on the school register, which was 15·96 in 1886-7, rose to 17·23 in 1897-8. That is the highest point which has ever been reached. The average attendance is equally satisfactory. The average attendance, which was 12·41 of the population in 1886-7, rose to 14·53 per cent. in 1897-8, or a rise of 2·12 per cent. on the total population, with the result that the average attendance compared with the register, which was 77·77 in 1886-7, has increased to the high point of 84·32 in 1897-8, or a rise of 6·65 per cent. This shows at once that the parents of Scotland have been doing their duty as regards sending their children to school. Complaints have been made that the children have been taken away at too early an age. Now I find, if we take the number of children at school over 13 years of age in 1898, there is an increase compared with the preceding year of 2,655, or 4·36 per cent., as against 1·24 per cent. increase on the total school register. There are no statistics for Scotland except in respect of the State-aided schools, but we have, fortunately the statistics for Glasgow, and the results are very instructive. The total number of children in Glasgow between eleven and twelve years of age on the roll is 12,319, and the number in attendance is 11,767, or a deficiency of only 552. Between ten and eleven years of age only 457 of those on the roll have failed to attend, so that up to twelve years of age there is practically a complete attendance. Between twelve and thirteen we have this remarkable result; that there are 12,626 children in Glasgow, and 9,754 on the register, a deficiency of only 2,872. Now I have gone into these figures minutely because they have an important bearing on the next point that I am going to call attention to, and that is the decrease in the upper standards. The children are going as early to school as ever, are remaining longer, and are attending with greater regularity. What are the educational results? In 1898 there was an increase of 2,251 children over the number presented to the inspector in the previous year. Now we find, notwithstanding this increase, that the number of children who were presented in the upper standards, *i.e.*, Standards IV., V., and VI., shows a decrease of 1,757. The contention of the Scotch Education Department is that they have effected a change in the examination, with the result that the children are now being pushed forward instead of being kept back, but the statistics given by the Department show the extraordinary fact that whilst the number sent to the inspector last year amounted to an increase of 2,251, the numbers presented in Standards IV., V., and VI. actually showed a decrease of 1,757. Now, I venture to say that this result is due to the change of policy of the Department as regards the examinations. As has been pointed out, in 1872, when School Boards were established, there was individual examination, and that had a most important effect, no payment being given except for an actual pass. That was intended to be—and in point of fact was—a protection to the poorest child in the country. The object Parliament had in view was to get at the lowest stratum of the population. The State is interested more in the lower strata of the population than in the upper, so far as regards matters of that kind. However, individual examination at any rate ensured that no payment would be given for any child unless the inspector should pass that child as having been efficiently educated in a particular standard, and that was a great protection to the poorest children. Then came the change of policy which established collective instead of individual examinations. We all know how that change of policy was brought about. It was due to the pressure of the teachers, who felt that they had a great deal of work to do in order to

get the less educated children to pass the examinations. The inspectors approved the change, because it was very worrying work for them to examine every child individually. You consequently find that teachers and inspectors, backed up by the School Boards, advocating the change, but there is not a voice to be heard in favour of the poor parent, who wishes to secure that his child should pass his examination with the other children. We were told that the result of the change of policy would be that the clever children would be pushed forward. But the statistics show that instead of there being more children in the upper standards there are fewer. I have investigated this matter ever since the policy was changed, and I find in the case of Glasgow, where the statistics are nearer completion than in the case of other schools in Scotland, that the children in the junior departments take a longer time to get into the senior departments. The teachers, finding themselves relieved of the pressure that existed under the previous system, are taking things more easily, and it is their policy now to keep the children as long as possible at school, because the result of the Code is that the more schools keep back children the more money they will earn, the payment being based on average attendance. Now the Department are making an important change as regards the carrying out of the law of compulsory attendance. The Education Act of 1872 prescribes that a parent should not be prosecuted for the non-attendance of his child at school if he passed the inspector's examination. That examination, which is prescribed under Section 73 of the Education Act, is a very simple one, the subjects to be taken being reading, writing, and elementary arithmetic. Then we come to the Act of 1883, which prescribes that the certificate to be given by the inspector should not be given unless Standard V. is passed. Now for years the inspectors have been passing under the Code of Standard V., and even half-timers have been able to pass. But now you are practically saying to the inspectors that they are to put every possible obstacle in the way of children receiving the labour certificate, with a view of compelling them to remain at school longer than the law practically enjoins. Let us see what those standards were. Some inspectors pointed out that the standards were such that a child could easily pass two standards in one year, so that even Standard V. might be reached at eleven years of age. You are now making examination more severe than the Act of Parliament authorises. Nothing could be worse than a policy of this kind, because hitherto the parent has loyally co-operated with the School Board. If you want to make a change in the law, do it by legislation in the usual way; don't discourage a child who has attended for several years at school from getting his certificate. Formerly a parent knew if his child did not pass a particular standard. Now he does not know until the child is 13, when he wants to get a labour certificate, and then he discovers that the child's education has been neglected, and that he is not able to pass Standard V. I think that that is an exceeding hardship in the case of the poorer class of the community. If you insist on keeping a child at school till he is 14 years of age, and his widowed mother is only paid 1s. or 1s. 6d. a week from the parochial board, look at the misery your policy entails. It may be in the interest of education, but I question very much, if you continue that child at school after 13, when he has made no educational progress, whether he will do anything more than mark time. The effect of that policy has been that you are alienating sympathy so far as a great many parents are concerned, who have been anxious to co-operate as far as they possibly could. You are adopting every means to keep children at school, but you are not adopting any means to see that the children are being educated. Another subject to which I would call attention is the neglect to meet the demand for certificated teachers. I willingly recognise the improvement that has been made. But will the Lord Advocate say that the improvement is anything like the improvement that ought to be made? It is impossible to get a sufficient number of certificated teachers, because you won't educate in your training colleges as many teachers as are qualified to enter. The demand of the country is for certificated teachers, and you are making, and seeking to maintain, a monopoly of the teaching profession. There are only one or two other matters which I am going to refer to. If there is any money available for secondary education you ought, in the first place, to give it to those schools which hitherto have

Mr. Caldwell.

been getting money for charitable endowments. When money is coming in to be available for secondary education, the claim of the charities to be relieved ought to be considered. I refer in this instance to the case of Hutchisons' Hospital, and there are also cases in the town of Stirling. I think the claims of those charities which bear the brunt of secondary education when no other funds are available ought to be considered, because it may be that their income has largely decreased of late years. Another matter that I would refer to—and it has been before the Department already—is the education of tinker children. The Lord Advocate knows that it is very difficult to get that class educated, because they migrate from place to place. But whether they are the children of tinkers or not, something ought to be done to ensure their education. Another point for consideration is that some children—probably the children of shepherds—are living a long distance from the schools. It would be an expensive matter to establish a school of teachers to "take" one, or perhaps two, children at a great distance, and it has been suggested that the School Board ought to be authorised to make an allowance for the expense of educating them at the regular parish school, which would be both better for the children, and, at the same time, cheaper as far as the School Board was concerned. With regard to the secondary education scheme, all I have to observe is, that the state in which secondary education finds itself in Scotland is the result very much of the policy of the Department. The first thing the Department did was to reduce the efficiency of secondary education in the schools, and to endeavour, by every means in their power, to attract children from the private schools. Take, for instance, the City of Glasgow. There are only 601 children who have not been attracted either to a State-aided school or an endowed school, and half of these come from the surrounding districts. The policy of the Department is to set up secondary departments, and then they kill the secondary schools, and then, having encouraged the elementary schools to set up secondary departments, they are going to turn round and kill the elementary schools.

Sir CHARLES CAMERON (Glasgow, Bridgeton): I wish to call attention to a case in which in a small parish 900 children of school age are at present not in attendance at school, and the Department will take no steps to compel the School Board to provide for their education. That is a matter urgently requiring the attention of this House. What is the use of talking about secondary education or going into these elaborate statistics when here you have a mass of children left, so far as the Department is concerned, without any education whatever? I have asked repeated questions in this House about the matter. I refer to the case of children in the Orphan Homes of Scotland. These schools have been doing a great national service. I am not going to speak on my own authority; I take the testimony of two public documents. Here is what is said about them in the Report of the Departmental Committee of the Scotch Office, over which I had the honour to preside, which among its members numbered the Permanent Under Secretary for Scotland. The Report says:

"We must not pass from the subject of reformatory and industrial institutions without a reference to the excellent work done at Mr. Quarrier's Orphan Homes. These homes, a magnificent range of buildings situated at the Bridge of Weir, have been constructed and are maintained by voluntary contributions. Although, if Mr. Quarrier chose, he might claim a handsome donation from the Education Grant, he informed us that he prefers to keep himself entirely free from Government interference and control. The average daily number of children resident at the homes is about 1,200, while that in the reformatory schools in Scotland is 872, and in the industrial schools, 4,873—together 5,745."

I will not read the entire extract, but the Report says that, although this work is conducted at no cost whatever to the State, a much better result is shown in the children sent out from these schools than in the case of the children sent out from reformatory or industrial schools. An institute that does such work as that, and deals, without any cost whatever to the State, with about one-fourth of the children dealt with in the reformatory and industrial schools, deserves well of the country. Nor is that the only testimony. In the Report of the Board of Supervision for 1887-88 there is a memorandum from one of the inspectors highly approving the work done by these schools, and suggesting that Parochial Boards should be allowed to give subscriptions to them, in order to enable them to do their work more efficiently and more cheaply. The Board of Supervision regret that it would not be legal for that course to be adopted, but express the opinion that an extension of the provisions of the Poor Law Act of 1845 to other institutions than those therein specified would, under proper control, be very beneficial. The Government have not paid any heed to that recommendation. On the contrary, any attempts on the part of the Parochial Board to give donations in support of these schools has been surcharged. Until very recently these homes had not been assessed for rates. The schools being maintained by the generosity of the public, and Mr. Quarrier not asking for any assistance from public funds, no rates were levied on the schools. Recently the legality of that was tested, and the Court of Session held that it was illegal to grant the exemption. That being the law, when Mr. Quarrier found that his homes were to be assessed for education and other rates he considered that he was entitled to claim for the children in his homes the rights of a ratepayer, and have them educated at the public expense, as are children elsewhere. So far back as April he asked the School Board to provide education for them, but they declined. He wrote to the Scotch Education Department as to what steps should be taken, and on the advice of the Secretary of the Department he wrote to the School Board asking them to take over the education of these children. The clerk wrote back refusing to do so. On the receipt of that letter Mr. Quarrier again wrote to the Education Department, who replied that they could not deal with the question until they were assured that the children had been refused admission on "other than reasonable grounds." What the reasonable grounds are Mr. Quarrier could not understand, and until this day he has never had any information with regard to it. Later on Mr. Quarrier made a formal application and received an official refusal. He gave notice that he would bring his children to the school and demand admission. He did so, and the clerk formally, on behalf of the School Board, refused to admit them. Mr. Quarrier naturally lays stress on the fact that he has educated a very large number of children belonging to the parish, thereby largely relieving the rates. He has now been obliged to pay education and poor rates for four years back; he had to pay over £200 in the matter of education rates, and altogether he has had to pay about £1,000 in local rates. Under these circumstances, I say he is entitled to the same rights as any other ratepayer. On the 25th April I asked the Lord Advocate a question on the subject; and he told me that as a matter of fact no child had been refused admission. On the 19th May, the formal application having been refused, I again asked the Lord Advocate a question, and he told me it was undesirable to make any statement beyond that the matters would receive the careful attention of the Department. I then suggested that if the right hon. Gentleman and the Department would not enforce the education of the children by the School Board, would it not be possible to pass some legislation as recommended by the Board of Supervision, or to legalise the exemption of such an institution from the rates? I did not get any answer to that question. The matter is always under consideration. What is the insuperable crux of the legal difficulty in this case that it requires two months to solve? Does or does not the Department intend to enforce upon the School Board the education of these children? As a matter of fact the accommodation belonging to the School Board is not sufficient for these children. I believe the School Board provides accommodation for 600, and has some 390 in average attendance. But in these Orphan Homes there is ample school accommodation, where the children have been satisfactorily educated. The schools have been praised by the inspectors, and nothing could be better for educational purposes. Mr. Quarrier is perfectly willing to let the School Board have them at a reasonable rent, so that there is no difficulty about accommodation; the accommodation could be had to-morrow. Now, Sir, the rates paid on Mr. Quarrier's Homes work out quite as high as those paid by the working-class population. He has the right which every citizen has of demanding education for the children under his care. It is said that he brings waifs and strays into the parish. As long as he was left alone he was content to look after the waifs and strays and pay for their education, and to relieve the parish of every charge in regard to them. The hon. Member for Renfrewshire has a story about some imbecile child brought up in one of

Sir Charles Cameron.

Mr. Quarrier's Homes having been made chargeable to the parish. As a matter of fact that was the case of an imbecile that, when it grew up, became uncontrollable, and went back to its friends; the friends put it on the parish somewhere in Glasgow, and the Glasgow parish found it had a settlement in Renfrewshire, and sent it down. That was perfectly legal. If I were to take a child which through some misfortune had to go upon the parish, the same thing might occur. But that has nothing whatever to do with the right of a ratepayer to demand free education from the School Board for children while they are living in the district, and are inmates of the house in respect of which rates are demanded. I do not want to labour the question, but I am anxious to find out what excuse may be alleged by the Department for this flagrant neglect of its duty to enforce upon the School Board the provision of education for these children. By way of raising the question in a concrete form I beg to move to reduce the vote before the House by £450, being the amount which is payable under the education grant to the School Board of Kilmalcolm.

Motion made, and Question proposed—

"That a sum, not exceeding £701,411, be granted for the said service."—*(Sir Charles Cameron.)*

*MR. A. G. MURRAY: Perhaps it would be convenient that I should at once answer the point which has been raised by the hon. Member. I do not know how far the Committee are cognisant of the matters affecting Mr. Quarrier's Homes, but I certainly do not think the hon. Baronet is quite correct in some of the terms he has used concerning them. First I may say that I am quite at one with the hon. Baronet in giving a very warm testimony to the benefit that these Homes have been. I have no wish to detract; on the contrary, I have the strongest wish to add my testimony as to the good services and most self-denying industry and zeal that Mr. Quarrier has rendered to the State by doing what he has done for the poor and castaway population. But when one has said that, I deplore that Mr. Quarrier has taken up his present position, and has tried to bring to the test what is really a legal question in a way in which the only sufferers will

be the children themselves. The hon. Baronet more than once used the phrase, "as long as he was left alone." But he is acting upon a mistaken view. An exemption had been made to the Homes in respect of rates, and, as you have been told, the point was brought before the Court of Session, where it was declared that the exemption was illegal. When that was done there was really no room for free action afterwards; the authorities could only enforce the law. If the hon. Baronet thinks that it is a proper thing that homes of this class should be exempt from rates, the present law preventing that exemption, the only thing for him to do is to try to pass a Bill in this House altering that law. I do not mean to say that it would be altogether an easy thing to do, because, really, there are considerations on the other side. It is all very well to think that persons who act in that particular way should be exempt from rates, but there are other considerations, and the same considerations which, in the past, have deterred this House from exempting public buildings of various characters from the payment of rates would also induce many persons to say that even such a noble object as this is not a reason why rateable property should be exempt from rates. It is no good laying any blame upon the local authority for not leaving Mr. Quarrier alone, or because they have simply carried out the decision of the Court of Session. If they had acted otherwise they would have been surcharged, so that they had absolutely no choice in the matter.

*Sir CHARLES CAMERON: I quite admit, and I did admit, that the decision of the Court of Session left the local authority no option in the matter. But Mr. Quarrier having been placed in this legal position demands his legal remedy.

*Mr. A. G. MURRAY: If Mr. Quarrier demands his legal remedy it is a very unfortunate thing that the way in which he tries to obtain what he calls his legal remedy is by leaving suddenly nearly a thousand children uneducated. There are ways of raising legal questions, and if Mr. Quarrier thinks he has a right to the education of these children he would have been better advised to have raised the point by the ordinary process of law. But he does no such thing, He simply says, "I will stop educating these children whom I have educated all these

years, and I will call upon the School Board to educate them instead." Very well, what does the School Board say? The School Board says, "Although we are perfectly willing to provide out of the rates for what may be called the normal population of our parish, we do not see that we should be suddenly called upon to provide education for a set of children who have nothing to do with the parish, but who are simply imported into the parish." The hon. Baronet has all along assumed that Mr. Quarrier has a legal right to call upon the School Board to educate these children. All I can say is that that is a question which has never yet been decided in this form, and that is the question which is under the consideration of the Education Department. I am not going to say to-night in this House precisely what view the Education Department adopt upon the matter, but I am in a position to say that the view of the Education Department will certainly be communicated to Mr. Quarrier without undue delay. I do say, however, that the hon. Baronet must not take it for granted that there is any such legal right as he assumes. The point has not been decided in this particular form, but so far as I can see the decision rather points the other way. I prefer not to say more upon this subject, but it is quite obvious that there are two questions which arise. The first is whether Mr. Quarrier has a right to demand free education for these children. If he has that right it should be vindicated by him in a court of law, and not by leaving these children uneducated. If there is no such right, then a question of discretion may arise, but it cannot well arise until the legal question has been settled one way or another. Therefore I fail to see what the hon. Baronet calls the clear duty of the Department in this case, because undoubtedly the question is a very novel one. It is a very serious one for a parish in Scotland, especially such a parish as this, to be suddenly called upon to provide for the education of a large number of children in this way. The matter, however, is not one which can be put forward as a grievance against the administration of the Department; it is rather owing to the mistaken action of an otherwise very worthy man.

Mr. COLVILLE (Lanarkshire, N.E.): There is a purely equitable question, as well as a legal question, in this matter. Mr. Quarrier has for years conducted a most excellent institution for the orphans of Scotland, and he has until recently been permitted so to do without being chargeable for these rates. Now that the Court of Session has decided that he must pay full rates upon the institution, he very naturally contends that there ought to be a corresponding provision for the education of his children. It will not do for the Lord Advocate to tell us that this is a matter entirely in the discretion of the Education Department. Parliament has surely some control over the Education Department. I do not hesitate to say that if the decision of the Education Department should be contrary to the interests of Mr. Quarrier and the orphan children, it will be very much the worse for the present Government, who are the masters of the Education Department. There is surely a clear point of equity in Mr. Quarrier's claim that, if it is insisted that he shall pay full legal rates upon his buildings, those rates ought to bring with them the right to have his children properly educated, more especially as he has made such a liberal offer to the School Board in regard to the premises he has erected for the purpose of educating these children. I trust that, notwithstanding the remarks of the Lord Advocate, the Education Department will see that their interest, as well as their duty, lies in the direction of making adequate provision for the children in the orphan homes of Scotland.

*Mr. HEDDERWICK (Wick Burghs): I desire to draw the attention of the Lord Advocate to the peculiar position of two very ancient charities in the Burgh of Stirling, known as Cowan's Institution and Spitals Hospital. These charities were founded in the beginning or middle of the 17th century, and their object was to enable the trustees to provide for the decaying members of an institution in Stirling. For something like two centuries these charities were enabled to provide for those requirements, but in 1882, when the income of the charities amounted to £1,400, the Charity Commissioners interfered and deprived the charities of some £700, giving that amount to one of the schools in Stirling for the purposes of education. The position in which the charities stand is a very peculiar and

Mr. Colville.

awkward one, because they have now claims for pensions which they are totally unable to satisfy. In fact, owing to the falling away of the revenues arising from the action in question, a number of persons who otherwise would be provided for by these charities are thrown upon the rates. It seems to me that, inasmuch as Parliament has provided considerable sums for the purpose of supplementing education, this sum of money, which has been diverted from its original use, and given to education at a time when funds which are now available for educational purposes were not available, might be re-funded and re-applied to its original charitable purpose. Now, of course, I may be told by the Lord Advocate that he has no power to dispose of the scheme which has been sanctioned by the Charity Commissioners, but I suggest to the right hon. Gentleman that in the forthcoming Bill for secondary and technical education a clause might be inserted which would restore the deflected £700 to the charities to which the sum originally belonged. Passing from that, I wish to touch upon a question which has caused some discontent in Scotland; I refer to the question of the superannuation of teachers. There is considerable discontent among the existing teachers of Scotland in respect of the Superannuation Act of 1898. I understand that the greatest amount that any teacher can expect to receive under that Act is about £40 per annum. It will be admitted by hon. Members of the Committee that that is a very small sum indeed with which to pension a man who has spent his whole life in the tuition of the young. The discontent which the existing teachers feel is aggravated by the consideration that future teachers will receive double that amount. It might surely be possible in some manner or other for the Lord Advocate to remove a great deal of the discontent. I think it might be possible for him, if he chose, to enable the School Board to supplement the pension which these teachers are promised under the Superannuation Act. That suggestion is strengthened by the reflection that previous to the Act of 1898 the School Boards were enabled to pension their teachers. It would not only be generous but wise to remove that feeling of discontent which undoubtedly exists among the teachers in the schools of Scotland.

With regard to the Minute, I do not wish to detain the House by reiterating arguments that have been pressed on the Lord Advocate from both sides of the House. I will only say, if the minds of the Lord Advocate and the Scotch Department had not been fully made up with regard to the Minute, they must be very much impressed by the unanimity of the Committee upon this point.

*Mr. RENSHAW: I should not have intervened in this discussion had it not been for the remark of the hon. Baronet as to the facts with regard to the rating of this Home. Being a member of the County Council, I feel I should not be doing my duty if I did not state the facts here to-day. For many years every effort has been made to prevent putting up the rates on this Home, and I believe the valuation now is very much lower than if it was an ordinary rateable property. The Kilmalcolm School Board suggests that there is a question as to whether they are liable with regard to the education of the Quarrier Home children. The question is a very simple one, and I should just like to remind the Committee what that question is. The parish is an agricultural one, with a small valuation, and during the last twenty or thirty years villas have been built, and a villa population has come down to settle here. Mr. Quarrier's Homes have been erected in the parish, with 1,200 children, and at the present moment there is in the course of erection a Seamen's Home, open to all Scotland, which will hold 200 or 300 people. I do not suppose that the whole of this subject yields in rates £80 per annum for educational purposes; yet it is suggested that, because 1,400 children are settling down in that parish, that that rural parish is to bear the burden of educating all these children, who come principally from the great towns and centres of Scotland, because the proposal of Mr. Quarrier would compel this parish to educate these children, and place burden upon the parish which is quite out of proportion to the ability of the parish. I believe that the Kilmalcolm School Board is quite within its right in resisting this proposal, and I hope, if Mr. Quarrier takes the course suggested by the Lord Advocate and tries this question in a court of law, that it will be found that no such responsibility rests upon the parish.

*Mr. THOMAS SHAW: I must not be supposed in any sense to be now defending the action of Mr. Quarrier in the matter of assessment. My own opinion is that any institution, be it educational, religious, charitable, or otherwise, if it be heritable property in Scotland, ought to pay its rates along with other heritable property in the country. But the point raised under this Code is a serious one with regard to these parish homes, having regard to the compulsory character of education in Scotland. As I understand the circumstances, these children, from whatever place they come, are resident in the parish of Kilmalcolm, and it is perfectly true it is a great hardship to the parish that it should have to educate them. On the other hand, there are many cases in Scotland of hardship not quite so great, perhaps, but of a similar character. I understand that the Education Department ought to compel the law to be obeyed in the sense that no child shall be allowed to escape compulsory education. If there are financial difficulties in different parishes, then there is a case for the Department to interpose; and if a Statute is required, that is a question which the Government must address itself to. The point with regard to this particular parish is whether the Education Department is to stand in the position of permitting what is a temporary and may be a permanent negation of the compulsory character of education in Scotland. I totally object to have it stated in this House that it is possible in a case of this kind to avoid that rigour which is a most wholesome rigour of the law, and which is necessary to enable the Department to compel the education of these children.

Sir JOHN KINLOCH (Perthshire E.): On behalf of Perthshire I rise to enter into the protest which has been made against the Minute, and to join in the general condemnation brought against the Minute of the 27th of April. The secondary departments of our schools are to be excluded from participating in this grant, and in a county like Perthshire that is a very serious question. The higher class schools in Perthshire cannot meet their difficulties, and Perthshire is a typical example of how this Minute will work. The Committee of the County divide the county into eight divisions, the names of which are familiar to every one of us, and the effect of that arrangement has been that it worked well, and each school got its share. Now, instead of that the schools of Perthshire are snubbed and discouraged by the Minute; but I sincerely hope that even now, after the Lord Advocate has seen the strong opinion of the Committee upon this question, it will not be too late, and that the Education Department will still find time to change their opinion.

Dr. CLARK (Caithness): I wish to move a reduction of this Vote in order to express my dissatisfaction with the Department, and expose the terrible blunders which they have made. In order that the Committee may understand the standpoint from which we view it, I must go back to the year 1887. Up to that year this Committee gave grants for special purposes, but when the County Council Act was brought in, in order that real property might have its burdens lifted, and personal property might bear its share, a great change was made. It was proposed by the then Chancellor of the Exchequer to put an end to all grants, and that in lieu thereof there should be paid over a certain proportion of probate duty and excise. The local boards of England and Scotland got their proportions, both got the same; Scotland got 11-80ths, and England got 8 per cent. The English Poor Law Grant paid all those things which used to be paid by the grant, and there was a very large surplus in England. There was also a surplus in Scotland. In England that surplus was used to reduce local taxation, which was in consequence very much reduced. In Scotland it was used for the purpose of free education. That went on from 1887 to 1892. Then England wanted free education, and a Bill was brought in by the Chancellor of the Exchequer, and from Imperial resources, to which England and Scotland each paid their share, England got free education. Scotland got free education and paid for it herself, and England got free education from the common purse. What we ought to have had then was an equivalent grant, and in 1897 the Government gave us not an equivalent grant, but a new grant which they called a similar grant. If they had given us an equivalent grant we should have had many more thousands of pounds, and now we are only getting that

Sir John Kinloch.

money back bit by bit. Now in Scotland one-seventh of our children are in Voluntary schools, the other six-sevenths are in Board schools. In England four-sevenths are in Voluntary schools, and only three-sevenths are in Board schools. The Government then brought in a Bill to give 5s. a head to every child in the Voluntary schools, and they came to the conclusion that the same thing had to be done for Scotland, and an arrangement was made with the Treasury under which we were again robbed. It was unfair to give us 5s. per head for the children in our Voluntary schools, because we have only one-seventh of our children in those schools, and in England there are four-sevenths. But as a matter of fact they did not give us 5s. a head, they only gave us 3s. All the facts which the Lord Advocate has stated are fallacious, and his statements are mis-statements, as I shall directly demonstrate. The Lord Advocate told us that so far as the Board schools were concerned we should benefit, that instead of getting 11-80ths, we should get 21-80ths, and though we were losing on the Voluntary schools we should make a great deal on the Board schools. He told us that this scheme would require £41,200 for Scotland, and £154,000 for England. The man who was responsible for giving the Lord Advocate that estimate was either grossly ignorant and incompetent, or he had some other thing in view, because for England we voted £200,000, and for Scotland £32,000, so that a gross under-estimate was made for England, and a gross over-estimate for Scotland. Then, two years ago a Bill was brought in by which England got a further £41,000, and its claim has increased under the Vote to £210,000. Instead of our getting a great advantage under this scheme, the advantage is in favour of England. We have 660,000 children to educate, and when the Department brings in an estimate for the money required they only estimate 607,000 children. But these estimates are only figments of the imagination of the persons who gave the Lord Advocate his brief, and I think I have proved that his arguments have been demonstrated to be fallacious, and that we are losing £76,000 a year by the transaction. England is receiving £852,000, and if we were getting our fair share of that we should receive £117,000, and we ought fairly to get that sum. But according to the estimate of the Lord Advocate we only get about £80,000. What have we got this year? We are not talking about what we have had in the past, but about the Estimate for the present year. Under the Estimate you are voting to-day we get £41,000 instead of £117,000, and therefore we are losing £76,000 a year. These are startling facts, and I did expect to hear from the Lord Advocate some reason why the Department had committed this blunder. Let us come now to the question as to how they committed this terrible blunder. Up to the year 1897 we got our 12s. per head, and by the change which has been made, instead of getting that amount, we are now only getting 10s. per head. By an arrangement with the Treasury, and by misrepresentation as to the facts, they got their Bill through. This arrangement was made, and last year we ought to have got £26,000 from the Chancellor of the Exchequer to make up our 12s. per head, but we did not get a single penny. Surely that £26,000 will come to us again. We have demonstrated that, as a result of this system, Scotland has been defrauded, and surely we are going to get this sum or a fair equivalent if we are going to continue under the present system. Are we to go on paying for free education, and is England to go on enjoying that great increase while Scotland forgoes the privilege of having free education. All these estimates and figures upon which the Government brought forward this scheme have been proved to be fallacious, and we are losing £76,000 during the present year. I would like to hear something said on behalf of the Department before I move a reduction in this Vote.

Mr. THOMAS SHAW: May I make a suggestion to the House? There has been raised an important point, and perhaps it is advisable that we should have a general reply upon the whole Debate. I therefore suggest that we might now divide upon the Motion for a reduction moved by the hon. Baronet behind me, and then the general Debate could be resumed. I am sure we shall all be very glad indeed to hear a satisfactory explanation from the Lord Advocate.

Mr. ALEXANDER CROSS (Glasgow, Camlachie): Before the question is put I should like to know whether the Lord Advocate intends to insist upon the Department taking action in this matter. He has stated that if anything was wrong in the law as regards rating it was not his duty to bring in a measure to amend it. But is it not within the scope of his lordship, if the Education Department are in a dilemma, to proceed in the matter? If it is true that so many children in Scotland are absolutely without education, that is a state of things we cannot tolerate, and unless it is made clear that within a certain time this very difficult question which is now before the Education Department will be dealt with I shall be disposed to vote with my hon. friend.

*Mr. A. G. MURRAY: I stated distinctly that the determination of the Education Department would be made known to the House.

Mr. McLEOD (Sutherland): We have been told that this matter has been going on for months, and, while it may be proper to take action before the Court to find out what the law is, we have to deal now with the Education Department. Now that we have got back to this question, I think we ought to have a very definite and absolute assurance from the responsible Minister that within the next few days the Education Department will take such action as will ensure that these children will be brought under the control of the Department, because, however wrong Mr. Quarrier may be, I do not think that this Committee has got anything to do with that. The question we are asked to vote on is as to whether we will permit the Education Department to allow over 1,000 children to go without the necessary education, and we ought to have a very distinct assurance that a definite communication will be made within the next few days, and we should have now some indication of the form of action which the Education Department propose to take.

*Mr. WEIR: In reference to the necessity for altering the law, surely if a Bill is necessary it is for the right hon. Gentleman to take the initiative, and not to expect a private Member to bring in a Bill. I sincerely hope that this matter will be taken in hand at once, for it is clearly a matter for the Education Department, and not for the hon. Baronet who is taking this matter up.

Question put.

The Committee divided : Ayes, 46 ; Noes, 103.   (Division List No. 194.)

AYES.

Asquith, Rt. Hon. H. Henry
Bryce, Rt. Hon. James
Caldwell, James
Channing, Francis Allston
Clark, Dr G. B. (Caithness-sh
Crombie, John William
Donelan, Captain A.
Doogan, P. C.
Douglas, Charles M. (Lanark)
Dunn, Sir William
Evans, Samuel T. (Glamorgan)
Farquharson, Dr. Robert
Farrell, Jas. P. (Cavan, W.)
Ferguson, R. C. M. (Leith)
Flavin, Michael Joseph
Gibney, James
Goddard, Daniel Ford

Grey, Sir Edward (Berwick)
Gurdon, Sir Wm. Brampton
Haldane, Richard Burdon
Hammond, John (Carlow)
Hazell, Walter
Hedderwick, Thomas C. H.
Horniman, Frederick John
Jones, Wm. (Carnarvonshire)
Jordan, Jeremiah
Kilbride, Denis
Kinloch, Sir John George S.
Leng, Sir John
Macaleese, Daniel
M'Ghee, Richard
M'Leod, John
Moore, Arthur (Londonderry)
Morton, E. J. C. (Devonport)

Pearson, Sir Weetman D.
Pease, Joseph A. (Northumb.)
Pinkerton, John
Provand, Andrew Dryburgh
Shaw, Thomas, (Hawick B)
Sinclair, Capt. J. (Forfarshire)
Sullivan, Donal (Westmeath)
Tennant, Harold John
Wedderburn, Sir William
Weir, James Galloway
Williams, John C. (Notts.)
Wilson, John (Govan)

TELLERS FOR THE AYES—
  Sir Charles Cameron and
  Mr. Colville.

NOES.

Archdale, Edward Mervyn
Atkinson, Rt. Hon. John
Baird, John George A.
Balcarres, Lord
Balfour, Rt. Hon. G. W. (Leeds)
Banbury, Fred. George
Barry, Rt. Hn. A. H. S. (Hunts.)
Barton, Dunbar Plunket
Beach, Rt. Hn. Sir. M. H. (Br'st'l)
Bethell, Commander
Bill, Charles
Brodrick, Rt. Hon. St. John
Bullard, Sir Harry
Burns, John
Cavendish, V. C. W. (Derbys)
Cecil, E. (Hertford, East)
Chaloner, Captain R. G. W.
Chamberlain, Rt. Hn. J. (Birm.)
Chamberlain, J. A. (Worc'r)
Chaplin, Rt. Hon. Henry
Cochrane, Hon. T. H. A. E.
Collings, Rt. Hon. Jesse
Colomb, Sir John C. Ready.
Cotton-Jodrell, Col. E. T. D.
Cross, Alexander (Glasgow)
Curzon, Viscount
Dalkeith, Earl of
Dalrymple, Sir Charles
Digby, J. K. D. Wingfield-
Douglas, Rt. Hon. A. Akers-
Duncombe, Hon. Hubert V.
Dyke, Rt. Hon. Sir W. Hart
Fellowes, Hon. A. Edward
Finlay, Sir R. Bannatyne
Fisher, William Hayes
Fletcher, Sir Henry

Flower, Ernest
Galloway, Wm. Johnson
Garfit, William
Gibbons, J. Lloyd
Giles, Charles Tyrrell
Goldsworthy, Major-General
Graham, Henry Robert
Greville, Hon. Ronald
Hamilton, Rt. Hon. Lord Geo.
Hanbury, Rt. Hon. Robert W.
Hoare, Samuel (Norwich)
Holland, Hon. Lionel R. (Bow)
Hozier, Hon. Jas. Henry Cecil
Hubbard, Hon. Evelyn
Johnston, William (Belfast)
Johnstone, Heywood (Sussex)
Kenyon, James
Kenyon-Slaney, Col. Wm.
Lawrence, Sir E. Durning-(Corn
Lawson, John Grant (Yorks.)
Leigh-Bennett, Henry Currie
Llewelyn, Sir Dillwyn-(Sw'ns'a
Long, Col. Chas. W. (Evesham)
Long, Rt. Hn. W. (Liverpool)
Lopes, Henry Yarde Buller
Macdona, John Cumming
MacIver, David (Liverpool)
More, Rbt. Jasper (Shropshire)
Morgan, Hn. F. (Monm'thsh.)
Morrell, George Herbert
Morton, Arthur H.A.(Deptf'd)
Murray, Rt. Hon. A. G. (Bute)
Murray, Charles J. (Coventry)
Murray, Col. Wyndham (Bath)
Nicholson, William Graham
Nicol, Donald Ninian

Orr-Ewing, Charles Lindsay
Pilkington, R. (Lancs. Newton
Platt-Higgins, Frederick
Pretyman, Ernest George
Priestley, Sir. W. O. (Edin.)
Pryce-Jones, Lt.-Col. Edward
Purvis, Robert
Renshaw, Charles Bine
Retoul, James Alexander
Richards, Henry Charles
Ridley, Rt. Hn. Sir Matthew
Ritchie, Rt. Hn. Chas. Thomas
Robertson, Herbert (Hackney
Royds, Clement Molyneux
Ryder, John Herbert Dudley
Skewes-Cox, Thomas
Smith, James Parker (Lanark
Stanley, Lord (Lancs.)
Stephens, Henry Charles
Stewart, Sir Mark J M'Taggart
Stock, James Henry
Thorburn, Walter
Tomlinson, Wm. Edw. Murray
Valentia Viscount
Wentworth, Bruce C. Vernon-
Williams, Colonel R. (Dorset
Williams, J. Powell- (Birm.)
Wilson, J. W. (Worcestersh. N
Wodehouse, Rt. Hn. E. R. (Bath
Wyndham, George
Young, Commander (Berks, E

TELLERS FOR THE NOES—
  Sir William Walrond and
  Mr. Anstruther.

Original Question again proposed.

*Mr. A. G. MURRAY : I think the best course for me to take will be to reply generally to the observations which have been made. I am quite aware that the principal topic which has been dealt with is the Minute, and quite a number of objections have been raised to it. These objections, in my opinion, have not been altogether consistent, nor do I think the some hon. Members have at all considered this matter from the practical point of view of the Government, and they have not indicated what they would have done if they had been in office instead of us.

I will take first of all the point raised by the hon. Member for the Border Burghs. What he objects to is the fact that the Minute does not extend to the higher departments of elementary schools. My answer to that is two-fold. First of all the hon. Member takes the Minute entirely by itself, whereas, I endeavoured, in the statement which I made earlier in the evening, to show that, in our view, the policy of the Department in secondary education should not be taken as being limited to the Minute alone, but it must be taken along with the change made in the Code last year. The hon. Gentleman left out of his criticism all reference to the higher grants. Now I would ask him to consider this—Is it not the case that in regard to a great many schools of the very sort he wishes to favour that, as a matter of fact, they would be pecuniarily very much better off by coming under the provisious of the Code, and getting the higher grants than they would be if they only got their share of the £35,000 ? So that, viewing the matter for the moment in this sense as mere "£ s. d.," I think he will find that there are many schools which are actually benefited by this system, and that they are doing better than if they got their share of the £35,000. The hon. Member has stated that these grants are subject to the 17s. 6d. limit, and he is afraid that a great many schools will not be able to avail themselves of this grant. I know they are subject to this limit, but there, again, it is just one of those cases where they may be able to get timely help from the county committees, because hon. Members are aware that anything which would be paid by the county committees out of the £60,000 would unquestionably be considered as a contribution from a local source. So there is a very easy way of helping schools in the higher department under this Code if they are able to get a contribution from that source. As regards the general merits of the proposals, a good many of the observations which have been made are with me, and the right hon. Gentleman the Member for Aberdeen said frankly that he thought there was a great deal in the view of the Department. It has been hinted by some hon. Members who have spoken from the opposite side that in Aberdeen the right hon. Gentleman who represents that constituency knows there are a particular class of schools which are

just the sort that will be assisted. I do think that is treating the right hon. Gentleman rather unkindly, for I think his observations were dictated by true educational policy, and were not at all due to the fact that there were particular schools in his constituency which might be assisted. There is this point, that, of course, the Education Department have already been doing a good deal for higher education through the action of the councils, where, I think, hon. Members are with me, although they rather misunderstood my expression when I said that private secondary schools had been left out of the Code, and a good many hon. Members took that statement as meaning that those schools had nothing given to them at all. But I did not say so. What I said was that they had not had the amount of money yet which would enable them to form themselves into private educational centres which they might otherwise be, and although the hon. Member for Renfrewshire had, with pride, told us what has been done by the county committees, I think he must admit that all the county committees have not behaved in such a proper manner as his own county has done. There are various other hon. Members who really object to this Minute upon the ground that it cuts out the higher education of the . elementary schools. But there is another class of objection. The objection of the hon. Member for Renfrewshire is not, I think, that the Minute prevents the grant being spread over these schools, but rather because he thinks it casts a very difficult and invidious duty upon the county committees. I confess, as I have said before, that I cannot understand why the county committees should feel that they are an inferior instrument or that it is derogatory to their usefulness to have thrown upon them the consultative action which is put upon them by this Minute. But I confess further that my hon. friend left me in doubt—although I listened to his speech very carefully—whether he really wished the whole of this money to be handed over to the county committees as they stand. I rather think that he did not, because he went on to describe the general state of the provision made for secondary education, and he hinted that the only way out of the difficulty was by legislation. Upon this subject he said one thing to which I should like to make reference. He stated that Article 21 of the Code was a recognition of this subject as the work of the county committee. That is scarcely so, because I think he knows that the Department have often refused to recognise as secondary schools some of the schools to which the county committees have given funds. In furthering the cause of secondary education the Department desire to have a higher standard of schools than some of those to which the county committees have given their money. He further declared that bad use had been made of this money, but in 1898, although the councils had done their duty, the principal offenders were the burghs. Here, again, he thought the only remedy was legislation. That was the principal note of the speeches to-night. Member after member joined in saying that what they really wish for is legislation with a view to consolidating the general system of secondary education and bringing the funds together. The hon. Member for Haddington indulged in some terrible pessimism with regard to Scottish technical education, and one would suppose he had never heard of the Heriot-Watt College or what is done at it. He said we were Philistines as regards secondary education, and his whole admiration on that matter at the present moment seems directed to Wales. It is no part of my duty to decry Wales, but, after all, I do not really think we have very much to fear by comparison with Wales. As a matter of fact, the secondary schools in Wales are little more than what we in Scotland would call higher departments, and the number of pupils examined is comparatively small as compared with the number of pupils who get leaving certificates in Scotland. I understand even as regards the Central Committee, over which the hon. Member waxed so enthusiastic, that there are grave doubts as to whether it should be gone on with, or whether its functions should not be handed over to the Universities. The hon. Member was amongst those who said that legislation was a remedy. It seems to me that is really the greatest justification that can be urged for the present Minute. I do not think almost anybody—there may be a few, perhaps—would say that it would be a good thing to simply add this money to the £60,000, and to let it be distributed under the conditions of the old Minute. If we say

that the real solution of this question must eventually be found in legislation, then I think the Minute is justified, because undoubtedly we will be in a much better position for legislation after we have had an opportunity of watching the experience this Minute will give. It is not a question of inquiry in the sense of having a Commission or a Committee of experts to give an opinion. There is, in one sense, almost nothing to learn. What we do want is experience as to how far secondary education would be practically possible, and what we should be able to do for the first time in giving help to real secondary schools. That has not been possible under the action of the county committees. I have tried very hard to show that I am not blaming these county committees, but hon. Members cannot say that their action has had the effect of fostering proper secondary education. Under this Minute that is possible for the first time. We will have experience and something more. We shall have put schools of this description into a state of efficiency. When we have that experience and when these schools are in an improved condition, as we may fairly hope they will be, then surely will be the time to legislate; to review the secondary education system, and put it on a revised basis which will prevent money being wasted on curious forms of technical education, such as teaching a fife and drum band; to divert money from unremunerative channels and to consolidate the whole system. I think also that this Party would never shrink from putting the schools taken over under local supervision in order to obtain the advantage which everybody feels local supervision extends. Accordingly, I certainly would be giving a quite wrong impression if I gave the Committee to understand that there was any intention on the part of the Government to go back on the Minute. On the other hand, we are very far from looking on the Minute as a final settlement of the secondary education question, but we do say that with a sum of money not much greater than £31,000, it is very much the more reasonable thing to find out the proper secondary schools, to get experience, to put the schools into a proper state of efficiency, and then to consider the problem of the general consolidation of secondary education, which is the object of hon. Members on both sides of the House. The time left me is

Mr. A. J. Murray.

now short, and I must go as rapidly as possible over some of the various other questions raised in the Debate. First, as to finance. The hon. Member for Caithness has often by question and speech brought this subject before the House, but I am afraid he has never done me the honour to learn the import of the speech which I made at the time the Education Act of 1897 was passed. I am quite aware that in his view the amount that Scotland got from the Treasury at that time was not adequate, in this respect, that it was not in the proportion of 11 to 80, or the amount England got for the assistance of the Voluntary schools. But there were really no such blunders or false figures as the hon. Member seems to think. There was one very gross underestimate, but neither I nor any of my special advisers was responsible. The only other question was that of the £36,000.

Dr. CLARK: And also that the new system in Scotland would require £41,000, and you only put down £36,000. Scotland was as shamefully underrated as England was overrated.

*Mr. A. G. MURRAY: My impression of the £41,000 is otherwise. The question of the £36,000 was this. Hon. Members know that we had been paying a 12s. capitation grant, but an arrangement was made with the Treasury that only a 10s. grant should be paid. It was, however, very expedient that we should go on paying the 12s. grant, and we had other sources of supply. We had £40,000 available under the Act of 1890 which would, of course, provide the difference for 400,000 children, and there were also certain arrears which had been promised but not actually paid by the Chancellor of the Exchequer in connection with various extra grants which England had received.

Dr. CLARK: The promise was given to me during the Debate on the Bill by the Chancellor of the Exchequer.

*Mr. A. G. MURRAY: Which promise does the hon. Member mean?

Dr. CLARK: The promise that we should get the difference between 10s. capitation grant and the eleven-eightieths.

*Mr. A. G. MURRAY: I do not think the Chancellor of the Exchequer would give a promise of that description. He promised in the matter of arrears to give the difference between the 10s. grant and the eleven-eightieths. However the money is exhausted. Then he gave another promise in 1897 which undoubtedly was estimated to come to £26,000. It has not come to that sum yet, but it is not now very far from it, and would, had we not had other resources, have amounted in the Estimates for 1899-1900 to £23,000. So far for the figures, but my point is that when you come to the question of education, and where a certain thing is done for England, the equivalent grant does not apply at all. If it did it would be absurd, and the Chancellor of the Exchequer has always been firm in holding that a'though there may be other affairs in which the equivalent grant might come in it should not apply to education, and that each country should have the same educational advantages. As a matter of fact, if the whole thing were taken together, it would be found that Scotland was not badly off as compared with England in the matter of the Educational Grant. If any hon. Member will take the Estimates for the current year, and will add up the total educational payments to England and the total to Scotland, he will find that the totals are in the ratio of 80 to 11·08, so that as a matter of fact—although I do not admit that the grant to Scotland has anything to do with it—measured by this standard Scotland is better off as far as educational Imperial endowment is concerned by ·08· So far for finance. The hon. Member for Kilmarnock Burghs asked me a question about the allowance under the Act of 1897. Well, I am sorry I cannot give the hon. Member a legal opinion of my own at this box, but I can tell him exactly what the views of the Department are. The Act of 1897 proceeded by way of further relief on the Act of 1872. Section 67 of the Act of 1872 stated that, "where in a parish or borough a school rate on the rateable value shall be levied," etc., and the view of the Department was that there could only be one "rateable value." Accordingly, if you take the rateable value you must take the owner's half of the rate, not because it is the owner's but because it is the only rate which includes the whole rateable property in the valuation. That is the view which prevails in the Department. I will propound to any hon. Member, who wishes to exercise his mind on it, a question. Suppose you take the other view and do not take the staple rate, but whatever happens to be the occupier's rate, and add it to the owner's rate, how would that work in a classified parish where you might have four or five occupiers ?

MR. CALDWELL : Let the occupiers make up the half, whatever it may be.

*MR. A. G. MURRAY : That is no answer. The hon. Member for Kilmarnock Burghs said : If you want to find the real rate you must add the owner's rate to the occupier's rate ; but how can that be done in a classified parish ?

MR. CALDWELL : This Act applies to England, and in England it is the occupier's rate which is taken.

*MR. A. G. MURRAY : In England there is no classification, and therefore it does not apply in the case given. I pass next to what was said by various members about the Code. The general attitude of hon. Members towards the Code has been extremely satisfactory, and I am sure the Department will consider and bear in mind the weighty remarks made as to the particular duty cast, not only upon inspectors and itself, but also on the care of selection it ought to exercise. As to the apprehension about the loss of grant, I can only again repeat the assurance which I made earlier in the Debate, that undoubtedly the Department will do its very best during the present year—during which payments under this new Code have to be made—to watch very narrowly the effect of the new scales, and if it can see that the result of the scales as they are would be a diminution of the general grant, then the Department would do its best to make some sort of addition, such as the right hon. Gentleman and other hon. Members suggested. Various other questions were asked. The hon. Member for Partick wanted to know what was the use of leaving certificates in the lower grades. I understand that these certificates are accepted as qualifications for various posts without further examination. As a matter of fact, they are found very useful in that way, and are regarded as a recognised standard. Then I was pressed, especially by the hon. Member for Leith,

Mr. A. G. Murray.

to speak about agricultural education, and the hon. Member pointed to the desirability of founding some sort of central establishment. That is a matter which ought to be kept in mind with a view to future legislation, and to an application to the Treasury ; but I think probably he will agree with me that, with the money at present at our command, anything of that sort would be entirely beyond our power. An hon. Member said that there was no provision for agricultural education on the East coast at all, especially in the County of Perth, but I would remind the hon. Member that the Perthshire County Council have contributed with others to the new college which has been started in the West of Scotland.

SIR JOHN KINLOCH : That is too far away.

*MR. A. G. MURRAY : But it shows that they think it is an institution which their own people can take practical advantage of. As to the question of the dismissal of teachers, that can only be dealt with by legislation, and the question of superanuation must be dealt with in the same way. Although, no doubt, I can quite understand teachers may have a grievance in that matter, I would remind hon. Members that it was debated on the Education Bill, and that there was a good deal of feeling even by hon. Gentlemen opposite, that teachers should not be given a pension by the School Boards as well as by the Treasury. I think I have replied, as far as the time at my disposal would permit, to the various points which have been raised, and I hope the Committee will kindly allow us to take the Vote.

CAPTAIN SINCLAIR : The right hon. Gentleman's reply cannot be regarded as satisfactory with regard to the Minute of the 27th April, and I beg to move the reduction which stands in my name, in order to show the unanimity of opinion in condemnation of it.

It being Midnight, the Chairman left the Chair to make his Report to the House.

Committee report progress ; to sit again upon Monday next.

Adjourned at five minutes after Twelve o'clock, till Monday next.

HOUSE OF LORDS.

Monday, 19th June 1899.

———

PRIVATE BILL BUSINESS.

———

THE LORD CHANCELLOR acquainted the House that the Clerk of the Parliaments had laid upon the Table the Certificates from the Examiners that the Standing Orders applicable to the following Bills have been complied with :

ELECTRIC LIGHTING PROVISIONAL ORDERS (No. 5).

ELECTRIC LIGHTING PROVISIONAL ORDERS (No. 6).

HOUSING OF THE WORKING CLASSES PROVISIONAL ORDER (BORROW-STOUNNESS).

LOCAL GOVERNMENT PROVISIONAL ORDER (HOUSING OF WORKING CLASSES).

Also the Certificates that no further Standing Orders are applicable to the following Bills :

LOCAL GOVERNMENT (IRELAND) PROVISIONAL ORDER (No. 1).

LOCAL GOVERNMENT PROVISIONAL ORDERS (POOR LAW).

And also the Certificates that the further Standing Orders applicable to the following Bills have been complied with :

SHEFFIELD CORPORATION MARKETS.

CITY AND BRIXTON RAILWAY.

LONDON IMPROVEMENTS.

STOCKPORT CORPORATION.

LINCOLN AND EAST COAST RAILWAY AND DOCK.

The same were ordered to lie on the Table.

GREAT EASTERN RAILWAY (GENERAL POWERS) BILL. [Lords.]

The Queen's consent signified ; and Bill reported from the Select Committee with Amendments.

WETHERBY DISTRICT WATER BILL.

Reported with Amendments.

SOUTH-EASTERN RAILWAY BILL.

The Queen's consent signified ; and Bill reported with Amendments.

SOUTHPORT AND LYTHAM TRAMROAD BILL. [Lords.]

Reported from the Select Committee with Amendments.

NORTH STAFFORDSHIRE RAILWAY BILL. [Lords.]

The Queen's consent signified ; and Bill reported from the Select Committee with Amendments.

WEST GLOUCESTERSHIRE WATER BILL.

Read 2ª, and committed.

CALEDONIAN RAILWAY (GENERAL POWERS) BILL. [Lords.]

ABERDEEN JOINT PASSENGER STATION BILL. [Lords.]

SOUTH STAFFORDSHIRE TRAMWAYS BILL. [Lords.]

Read 3ª, and passed, and sent to the Commons.

CARDIFF RAILWAY BILL.

RHONDDA URBAN DISTRICT COUNCIL BILL.

Read 3ª, with the Amendments, and passed, and returned to the Commons.

LOWESTOFT PROMENADE PIER BILL.

GODALMING CORPORATION WATER BILL.

Brought from the Commons; read 1ª ; and referred to the Examiners.

JONES'S DIVORCE BILL. [Lords.]

Minutes of evidence and proceedings before this House on the Second Reading together with the documents deposited in the case, returned from the Commons.

EDUCATION DEPARTMENT PROVISIONAL ORDER CONFIRMATION (LONDON) BILL. [Lords.]

House to be in Committee on Thursday next.

LOCAL GOVERNMENT PROVISIONAL ORDERS (No. 3) BILL.

To be read 2ª on Thursday next.—(*The Lord Harris.*)

3 F

ELECTRIC LIGHTING PROVISIONAL ORDERS (No. 5) BILL.

ELECTRIC LIGHTING PROVISIONAL ORDERS (No. 6) BILL

To be read 2ª To-morrow.—(*The Earl of Dudley.*)

TRAMWAYS ORDERS CONFIRMATION (No. 2) BILL. [Lords.]

TRAMWAYS ORDERS CONFIRMATION (No. 3) BILL. [Lords.]

WEST MIDDLESEX WATER BILL.

AIRE AND CALDER NAVIGATION BILL

EAST LONDON WATER BILL.

MILTON CREEK CONSERVANCY BILL.

GREAT WESTERN RAILWAY BILL.

GREAT WESTERN AND GREAT CENTRAL RAILWAY COMPANIES BILL.

Report from the Committee of Selection, that the Earl of Mansfield be proposed to the House as a member of the Select Committee on the said Bills in the place of the Viscount Falmouth ; read, and agreed to.

ELECTRIC LIGHTING PROVISIONAL ORDERS (No. 12) BILL. [Lords.]

Read 3ª (according to order), and passed, and sent to the Commons.

ELECTRIC LIGHTING PROVISIONAL ORDERS (No. 13) BILL, [Lords]

House in Committee (according to order): Amendments made :, Standing Committee negatived : the report of Amendments to be received To-morrow.

ELECTRIC LIGHTING PROVISIONAL ORDERS) No. 15) BILL [Lords.]

Read 3ª (according to order), and passed, and sent to the Commons.

ELECTRIC LIGHTING PROVISIONAL ORDERS (No. 2) BILL.

Read 3ª (according to order), and passed.

TRAMWAYS ORDERS CONFIRMATION (No 1) BILL. [Lords.]

Amendments reported (according to order), and Bill to be read 3ª To-morrow.

RETURNS, REPORTS, ETC.

EDUCATION (SCOTLAND).

Minute of the Committee of Council on Education in Scotland, dated 15th June 1899, amending the terms of paragraph 5 of the Minute of 27th April 1899, providing for the distribution of the sum available for secondary or technical (including agriculture) education under Section 2, Sub-section (4) of the Local Taxation Account (Scotland) Act, 1898.

ARMY (MILITARY WORKS).

Approximate estimate of expenditure for the year 1899–1900 under existing loans.

COLONIES (ANNUAL).

No. 261. Jamaica. Annual Report for 1897–98 (for report for 1896–97, *see* No. 225).

RAILWAYS (CONTINUOUS BRAKES)

Return by railway companies of the United Kingdom for the six months ending 31st December 1898.

TRADE REPORTS (ANNUAL SERIES.

No. 2290. Japan (Yokohama and District).

No. 2291. Persia (Azerbaijan).

No. 2292. Africa (Congo trade returns).

Presented (by Command), and ordered to lie on the Table.

PUBLIC RECORDS (TREASURY).

Schedule containing a list and particulars of classes of Treasury documents which have been deposited in the Public Record Office, but which are not considered of sufficient public value to justify their preservation therein ; laid before the House (pursuant to Act), and ordered to lie on the Table.

PETITION.

LONDON GOVERNMENT BILL.

Petition for amendment of : of the Vestry of the Parish of St. George, Hanover Square, London ; read, and ordered to lie on the Table.

ANCHORS AND CHAIN CABLES BILL.

House to be in Committee on Thursday next.

EDUCATION OF CHILDREN BILL.

To be read 2ᵃ on Friday the 30th instant. (*The Viscount Knutsford.*)

PUBLIC LIBRARIES BILL. [Lords.]

LORD WINDSOR: My Lords, I understand that the Local Government Board object to several of the clauses in this Bill, and therefore I ask leave to postpone the Second Reading in the hope that some modification may be made which will remove these objections.

Order of the Day for Second Reading read, and discharged.

YOUTHFUL OFFENDERS BILL. [Lords.]

SECOND READING.

Order of the Day for the Second Reading read.

*LORD JAMES OF HEREFORD: My Lords, I trust that it will be only necessary for me to make a very short statement to your Lordships in order to obtain the acceptance of this Bill. Its object is to keep children and young persons out of jail, and I assume that to every one of your Lordships that object will appear to be commendable. Amongst the many incidents that have occurred during the present reign probably there are none that can be looked upon with greater satisfaction than the great diminution which has taken place in our criminal classes. Still, a great deal remains to be done. The diminishing power does not progress as quickly as could be wished, principally in consequence of the difficulty experienced at the present time in dealing with the habitual offender. He is a very difficult person to deal with; severity does not appear to affect him, and clemency seems to have but little effect upon him. The result is that if we are to hope for a continued proportionate increase in the diminution of our criminal classes, we must deal in some way with the class of habitual offenders. The only way probably to deal effectually with that class is to destroy the recruiting power—to deal with the class from which

the habitual offender is recruited, and the only way to do that is to seek the fountain head, and to prevent the child or the youth becoming criminal at all, and in this way cut off the supply to the habitual offender class. As you are aware, my Lords, a great deal has been done of late years to diminish the number of youthful offenders, but, as I have said, a great deal yet remains to be done. Much has been accomplished by the increased power of education, the prosperity of the working classes, the greater sympathy that has been shown—progressively shown—towards those who are poor and towards those who are criminal, which have tended to reduce the number of criminal youthful offenders. Also, too, there has been a progression of humane feeling on the part of those who have to administer the law, and there has been a tendency to deal with the youthful offender in the most merciful manner allowed by law. The Legislature has done something. In the year 1879 my noble friend Viscount Cross introduced the Summary Jurisdiction Act, which no doubt relieved the child from the heavier penalties then being imposed. Later on my right hon. friend Sir William Harcourt took the matter in hand when at the Home Office, and insisted that a return should be made of the committal of every child to prison. Again, my noble and learned friend on the Woolsack has, by two Acts, facilitated the process of admitting persons to bail, and in that way has done much to keep both the young and those more advanced in age out of prison. But whilst all these causes have reduced the number of youthful offenders who are committed to our jails, still the number stands at a considerably higher rate than could be wished. If it will not weary your Lordships I will quote a few figures to show the rate at which the decrease has been taking place during the years from 1893 to 1897. In the year 1893 2,924 young persons under the age of 16 were committed to prison, and of these 150 were children under the age of 12 years. In 1897 the 2,924 was reduced to 1,630, not much more than half, whilst the number of children under 12 committed to prison, instead of being 150 in number, were only 58. But, my Lords, there is unfortunately a cause which is increasing, and may increase still more, the number of young persons committed to prison. We have been extending the powers of

3 F 2

local government, which, of course, give local control, and the control by the local authorities over different localities has to be enforced by means of bye-laws. In order to enforce these bye-laws the magistrates are bound, first, to impose a fine, and, in default of the payment of the fine, to send the person who has been thus summarily dealt with to prison. Your Lordships will well understand that many of the offences which result from a breach of bye-laws do not represent crime as we understand the word. They are venial breaches of regulations rather than acts representing any moral offence. The result is somewhat remarkable, but, before calling your Lordships' attention to those results, I am particularly anxious to make it clear that, specially speaking on behalf of the Home Office for the moment, there is not the slightest desire in anything I say to criticise the action of magistrates in administering the law; it is really the machinery of the law that requires remedying. One's experience shows that what may appear a severe sentence in the first instance is generally capable of some explanation, and when the explanation is given the matter you are considering bears a different aspect; but I have Returns here of the different offences for which children are now sent to prison. Amongst them we find playing football in the highway, throwing stones in the highway, obstructing the highway, and gambling in the highway. We have to deal here with children varying from 11 to 13 years of age. The child is fined, and, of necessity, not being able to pay is sent to prison with hard labour, and bears the same penalty for the period as the person who has committed positive crime against our moral law. That surely is a state of things which is scarcely to be desired. I have in my mind the case of a child of 12 who was charged with begging and fined 16s. 6d. Of course, that beggar child could not pay the fine, and was sent to prison for seven days with hard labour. What does this punishment mean to a child of 11 or 12 ? To keep a child in a cell ny himself, especially during the night, must create a state of terror which is a cruel and frightful punishment, or if he is callous and cares not, he becomes habituated, and the prison ceases henceforth to have any terror for him. I think, however, the first phase—namely,

Lord James of Hereford.

that of great fear—predominates, and I may mention that some defendants who were confined in a jail near London approached the Home Office when they were released and complained that they had been unable to sleep at night in consequence of the great noise caused by the screaming of children who were locked up. The Home Secretary and those who have control of our prisons felt that an alteration was necessary, and the doors of the cells in which children are now placed are allowed to remain open, and the children may spend the night within sight of the warder instead of in the dark cell. The Home Office have thought that something should be done to prevent as much as possible youthful offenders being sent to prison. Of course, we must not take too high a position ; if we do we may defeat the intention of legislation. The punishment of youthful offenders must be fixed with due regard to the age of the child, and the law should be enforced with due regard to the conditions of each case. But, where we are dealing with children so young as 10 years of age, surely in those cases there could be a mitigation of this, to them, terrible punishment of imprisonment. It is under these circumstances that the Government submit this Bill to your Lordships. The object of the Bill is, as I have said, to keep youthful offenders away from prison life, and the course that has been taken has been to invent, within reasonable bounds, machinery to carry out this object. The first section extends the powers of the Summary Jurisdiction Act of 1879. By that Act only the offenders by the crimes mentioned in the schedule can be dealt with summarily, but by this section there will be, in respect of young persons. power given to magistrates to deal with all offences, except homicide, summarily, but, of course, by consent in the case of indictable offences. It would be an evil example to the child in future life if you were to say, "Commit whatever offence you will, there will be no punishment." But if the object of this Bill is to be carried into effect the punishment must be inflicted outside the walls of a prison. The suggestion is that the punishment shall be simply whipping. as distinguished from flogging, and that the whipping shall take place upon a graduated scale, and be of a very mild character. The maximum, where the child is under 12, will be six strokes. The punishment will be administered in the presence of the parent or guardian, and certainly cannot be regarded as one of a cruel character. It will be a domestic treatment, and one which will not be looked upon as being associated with prison life.   Section 3 makes an alteration in the same direction. As your Lordships know, a child who has been convicted must not be sent to an Industrial School, but in this section it is proposed that the conviction, if it be for an offence so slight that whipping is a proper punishment, shall not be regarded as punishment so heavy as to debar the child from entering an Industrial School. I will pass over Section 4, which is rather controversial, and to which I will allude later on.   Clause 5 carries out the object which my noble and learned friend the Lord Chancellor had in view when he endeavoured to place all prisoners in a position where they could be bailed instead of being imprisoned.   In respect of the young child who cannot obtain any person to become bail for him, the magistrate shall have power of selecting some "outdoor" place of detention—some suitable person, say, a married constable, in whose home there will be suitable protection for the child—and, instead of sending him for the seven days during which he may be under remand, to prison, the child shall be sent to the custody of this person, who will be responsible for his appearance when the time of the remand shall have expired.   Although detained in this way out of prison, there will be nearly as much certainty of the child appearing when the case comes on as if he were sent to prison, and the child will have been kept free from contact with prison life.   Section 6, in one sense, does not belong to the Government, but refers to a matter dealt with in a Bill introduced last week by my noble friend Lord Leigh.   My noble friend has been the pioneer in this matter, and has worked hard to secure an alteration in the law whereby children shall not necessarily be sent to prison before they are sent to a Reformatory School.   The object of my noble friend is to make it possible for a child, if the magistrate thinks proper, to go direct to a Reformatory School without being brought into contamination with prison life.   That was rendered permissive in the Act of 1893, but a Departmental Committee in 1896 accepted the view which the noble Lord has all along advocated—namely, that it would be advis-

able to make it obligatory upon magistrates to send children who are to go to Reformatory Schools direct to those schools.   I am afraid that Clause 4, which throws an obligation upon parents and guardians who had not taken proper care of their children, will be somewhat controversial, and if any strong objection is shown to it I should be unwilling to see the Bill stopped by that clause.   At the same time, I must say that I believe it is a most beneficial and useful clause, inasmuch as it endeavours to make parents more careful of their children and take greater care to prevent their committing crime.   I have ventured to occupy your Lordships' time by referring to these sections as they have been framed.   I do not labour them, for I am certain that no one in this House or elsewhere can do other than approve of the objects we have in view, and I certainly hope that the manner in which we have endeavoured to carry out those objects will receive the unanimous sanction of your Lordships.

Moved, "That the Bill be now read 2ª."
—(*Lord James of Hereford.*)

*LORD LEIGH: My Lords, having taken for many years a deep interest in the Reformatory School system, may I be permitted to express the very great pleasure I feel at the action of the Government in introducing this Bill, which I believe to be a very useful one indeed. I had the honour, a few days ago, to introduce a Bill into your Lordships' House dealing expressly with the sending of children direct to Reformatory Schools.   This is a subject to which I have paid considerable attention for the past 46 years, and whenever I have had an opportunity of expressing an opinion upon it I have invariably said that, in my judgment, the Legislature had committed a very great mistake in not making it compulsory upon magistrates to send children to Reformatory Schools direct.   I now most cordially thank the Government for having taken the subject into their consideration, and for introducing this Bill. I earnestly trust that the present session will not end without the Act of 1893 being amended, so that the children may go direct to Reformatories without coming into contact with the gaol.   I have always contended that the sending of children to prisons, preparatory to entering Reformatories, has a most pernicious effect upon them; and I have been informed by superintendents of reformatories, whom I have consulted upon the subject, that the hardest cases they have to deal with are invariably those cases where the children have been confined in gaol. Inasmuch as the Government has in this Bill dealt with the subject I had at heart, I desire to withdraw my Bill in favour of the Bill introduced by Her Majesty's Government.

*Lord NORTON : My Lords, I do not suppose any of your Lordships have had more to do with reformatories than I have, for I have taken considerable part in the administration of them during the past 50 years, and I beg to tender my thanks to the noble and learned Lord who has introduced this Bill for the very material improvements in the existing law which he has proposed. The four main improvements introduced by this Bill in the existing law dealing with youthful offenders are — firstly, the extension of the power of summary treatment of offenders, which I think will be found of very great advantage; secondly, the greater use of moderate corporal punishment for boys, which I regard in every way preferable to shutting them up in a place of detention; thirdly, the increase in the liability of parents for cost of maintenance at reformatories and for neglect of their children, which neglect is the cause of half the child criminality of this country; and, lastly, in providing places for children to be sent to when on remand owing to there being no Reformatory School ready at the moment to receive them. For all these improvements in the existing law I, for one, am very much indebted to the noble and learned Lord, the Chancellor of the Duchy; but there is one clause, which has been especially referred to, to which I should like to call attention. The noble Lord opposite (Lord Leigh) proposes to withdraw his Bill, which is adopted by the clause in this Bill dealing with the admission of children to Reformatory Schools, but upon this Clause I feel compelled to say a few words. I do not think there is anything more dangerous than the habit which Parliament is getting into of legislating by reference to other Acts, and not explaining exactly what the

complete object of a Bill is. This system renders it absolutely impossible for anybody, without assistance of a lawyer, to understand what such Bills mean. I must say it is utterly impossible for any of your Lordships to know what the 6th clause of this Bill means as it stands. It proposes to omit the words "in addition to" out of the Act of 1893. No one can tell whether that would be an advantage or not. I think the noble Lord himself, on reflection, will hardly like to be the author of such a provision, and place upon the Statute Book a clause which says that child-convicts shall, not in addition to, but in lieu of punishment, whatever their crime may be, be sent direct to a Reformatory School. This clause either means entire immunity of children from punishment, or that Reformatory Schools are to be looked upon as penal institutions, and that children sent to them shall be treated as criminals for the whole of their childhood. Can there be anything more monstrous or cruel to a boy than to stigmatise him as a criminal during the whole of his childhood ? If this is allowed, boys will be turned out at the end of their detention without any sense of shame, and with a degrading consciousness that they are criminals. This, of course, will also act as an impediment to their being employed in any industry which they have been trained to in these schools. I cannot conceive anything more dangerous or more cruel than such a provision as this. I can hardly suppose that the noble and learned Lord has himself really seen the drift of the sixth clause of this Bill. What he desires, and what we all desire, is that children should not be punished in prison. We are all agreed upon that point. To shut up a young child in a solitary cell in a prison is gross cruelty, and produces no benefit whatever, but the proposal of the noble and learned Lord goes further, and suggests that for all convicts under sixteen there should be no punishment at all. Under this Bill parents who neglect their children will be punished by having to pay costs and a fine, and to give a security for their future better conduct; but that the children should be sent to school as their only punishment is a proposal which I cannot think the noble Lord opposite (Lord Leigh) would wish himself. What he wants is not to secure that in lieu of any punishment the child shall be sent to school, but that he shall not be sent to prison. All desire to see punishment of a suitable kind adopted, which, in the case of boys, would in almost all instances be corporal punishment. They should afterwards go to a Reformatory, if no other schooling offers itself, and the Reformatory should be treated as a school, and not as a penal institution retaining criminal character throughout education. Indeed, they cannot in practice be treated as penal institutions. They are just the same as other schools, except that they are made so excessively agreeable that there is a danger of a premium being given to bad treatment of children to qualify for Reformatories. I was asked by one woman how she could qualify her child for a Reformatory, and I did not like to tell her by throwing him into the street to pick pockets. As a matter of fact, our Reformatories are the very best publicly supported schools we have in the country ; they are far better than the ordinary National schools, for they give technical as well as intellectual instruction. By treating them as direct modes of punishment more harm must be done than good, both to the child and to the country, and I trust the clause to which I have called attention, as well as the Bill it adopts, will not be allowed to appear on the Statute Book. I hope the noble and learned Lord will tell your Lordships that he will alter the clause so as to achieve what I am sure is his desire as well as mine that children should have proper punishment not in prison. If he will not do so, I am certain the magistrates will adopt the usual course of refusing to act upon a provision which is absolutely absurd.

*Lord JAMES of HEREFORD : May I say, with regard to what Lord Leigh has stated with reference to his desire to withdraw his Bill in view of the provision in this Bill dealing with the same subject, that I hope he will not withdraw his Bill. I hope my noble friend's measure, which is a one-clause Bill, will receive the assent of both Houses of Parliament, and I see no objection to his Bill as well as this Bill progressing. If the noble Lord's Bill passes, then the 6th clause of this Bill can be struck out. It is a well-known axiom that if you wish to secure your game two guns are better than one. The proposal contained in the 6th clause will be discussed at length in

the Standing Committee to-morrow on the Bill of the noble Lord opposite. I will, however, consult the Home Office on the subject, and after hearing, as I have no doubt I shall, the matter discussed in the Standing Committee by my noble friends I will state the view taken by the Home Office.

*Lord LEIGH : My Lords, if it is the wish of the House and of the noble and learned Lord the Chancellor of the Duchy that my Bill should continue I will do my best to push it forward. My only desire is to see the clause which embodies the object I have at heart passed into law, and I trust that this desire will be realised.

On Question, agreed to.

Bill read 2ª accordingly, and committed to a Committee of the Whole House on Tuesday the 27th instant.

BILL INTRODUCED.

LIGHT LOAD LINE BILL. [Lords.]

A Bill to supplement the law relating to load lines on merchant ships was presented by the Lord Muskerry; read 1*a* ; to be printed ; and to be read 2ª on Monday the 26th instant. (No. 127.)

QUESTIONS.

THE ROYAL ACADEMY.

*Lord STANLEY of ALDERLEY : I desire to ask Her Majesty's Government whether they will give effect to the following recommendations of the Select Committee of 1836, and of the Royal Commission of 1863 with respect to the Royal Academy—

1. That the Academy should rest on a wider and more liberal basis, and be viewed as a national institution, and that it should have a Charter in lieu of the Instrument of 1768. (1836 and 1863) :

2. That an annual report should be published of the proceedings of the Academy, with a statement of its income and expenditure, duly audited. (1863) :

3. That all voting for Royal Academicians or Associates should be open. (1863):

4. That the Academicians and Associates now existing should send four works as of right, and never more, and that Associates henceforth elected should send no work as of right, and never more than four. (1863):

5. That the charge for admission should be one shilling as heretofore, but on Mondays it might be raised to a higher sum, and that the Exhibition should be wholly free on Saturdays. (1836 and 1863):

6. That the system of teaching hitherto followed is not satisfactory. (1863):

7. The system of teaching which prevails in France seems well worthy of consideration. (1863):

8. That the annual balance-sheet of the accounts of the Academy should be printed and submitted along with the annual report to the General Assembly. (1863):

And to call the attention of the House to the repudiation by the Royal Academy of their responsibility as bailees for damage to works confided to their custody : also to the sixty thousand pounds of the Chantrey Bequest, of which the Chantrey Trustees give no account.

My Lords, the eight recommendations contained in this notice are all taken from the Reports of the Royal Commission of 1863, and the recommendations which have the date 1836 upon them are those which were also recommended by the Select Committee of the House of Commons. Your Lordships may naturally have wondered why these recommendations were not attended to. I think the probable explanation is that in 1836 Lord Melbourne was Prime Minister, and his maxim was to let things alone, and that in 1863 Lord Palmerston was Prime Minister, and he was then 80 years of age. This explanation is strengthened by the similar neglect of two other Parliamentary recommendations of about the same dates, 1837 and 1862, with respect to first fruits paid by poor benefices. The noble Marquess at the head of the Government may ask me why I expect him to carry out the recommendations of these past and gone Commissions.

Lord Stanley of Alderley.

There are several reasons. In the first place, the subject has been refreshed and revived by the recently published book by Mr. Laidlay, which the Royal Academy has not attempted to answer or contradict in any way ; and, in the second place, discontent of the artists and general public has now reached mid-winter. There is also the noble Marquess's own argument of continuity of Government, since there has been nothing to break it since 1863. The first recommendation was that the Academy should rest on a wider and more liberal basis, and be viewed as a national institution, and that it should have a charter in lieu of the instrument of 1768. I will ask your Lordships to observe that this was recommended by the Select Committee in 1836, and by the Royal Commission in 1863. This recommendation does not require any answer from the noble Marquess, because, supposing he is in favour of reform, it would be a matter for negotiation with the Royal Academy as to the conditions under which a new charter should be given. The same observation applies to Recommendation 8. The General Assembly is not a general assembly of Royal artists, but only of members of the Royal Academy. The junior members of the Royal Academy have very little voice. In any new charter it would be necessary that these matters should be remedied, and the present tyranny removed. The second recommendation is that an annual report should be published of the proceedings of the Academy, with a statement of its income and expenditure duly audited. At present the Academy play fast and loose, sometimes claiming to be a public institution, and at other times a private institution, and they also claim a right to deal with their own funds as they like. The result is that nobody knows how the funds are applied, or where they go. The third recommendation is that all voting for Royal Academicians or Associates should be open. That is very necessary, for at the present nobody knows why they are appointed. A great number are appointed chiefly because they have called for reform ; it is known that once inside the Academy they cease all their further arguments in favour of improvements in administration. The fourth recommendation is that the Academicians and Associates now existing should send four works as of right, and never more, and that Associates henceforth elected should send no work as of right, and never more than four. I have put in these recommendations exactly as they stand in the report, but the general opinion now is that the Academicians should be limited to still fewer works, but that at any rate they should pass a competent jury and not send in pictures which are really of no value. I remember a picture entitled "The Flight into Egypt," in the centre of which was a picture of the Holy Family. This occupied the whole side of the room, and the chief impression produced upon my mind was the greediness of this Academician in taking up so much space at the expense of others. The great complaint made by the public and the artists is that favouritism is displayed in the admission and rejection of pictures. Even supposing there was no favouritism, the enormous number sent in render it absolutely impossible for any jury to devote the necessary time to them. There are too many pictures sent in, and in this case, as Seneca said of the Alexandrian library burned by Julius Cæsar, excess is everywhere prejudicial. The fifth recommendation is that the charge for admission be raised to a higher sum, and that the exhibition should be wholly free on Saturdays. Your Lordships will observe that this recommendation was made in 1836, at a time when there was no attempt at vote-catching or much care for popular amusement, and that the recommendation was made with the idea that it would benefit the people of this country by instilling a love for art. There would be no loss to the Academy by allowing the exhibition to be wholly free on Saturdays, for they could charge 2s. on Mondays. This particular recommendation has attracted a good deal of attention out of doors, and many newspapers have strongly supported it. The sixth recommendation says that the system of teaching hitherto followed is not satisfactory, and the following recommendation is to the effect that the system of teaching which prevails in France seems well worthy of consideration. The present system of teaching is very bad. The teacher is changed every month, the result being that you have a landscape painter recommending almost exclusive attention to colour one day, and another painter recommending exactly opposite the next day. I agree that the system of teaching which prevails in France is well worthy of consideration. This is evident by the number of British students who go to France. Nearly the whole of the United States market for pictures is lost to this country because Americans who go to Paris find the studios full of English students, and naturally conclude that if the Academy teaching is bad, English art must be bad also. This is a question for the Board of Trade : from accounts of duty on pictures imported into the United States, furnished by the U.S. Consul in Paris, for the years 1889–90, 1890–91, and 1891–92, the average sum of £1,600,000 was spent in each of those years in Paris by United States citizens. I now have to call the attention of the House to the repudiation by the Royal Academy of their responsibility as bailee for damage to works confided to their custody ; and also to the £60,000 of the Chantrey Bequest, of which the Chantrey Trustees give no account. The action of the Royal Academy in repudiating responsibility as bailees is against the common law, as is proved by the fact that the Liverpool and Manchester Galleries have both repeatedly paid for damages. At the present time I have been informed of a poor man having been offered £2 10s. by the Academy for damage done to his picture. The Liverpool Academy admits pictures protected by glass, but this the Royal Academy refuses to sanction. Perhaps the bringing of the question before your Lordships' notice may have the effect of shaming the Academy into action. As Mr. Laidlay has said in his book, the Academy can reform itself from within, and do so much better than outsiders can do, but pressure is required if anything is to be done. With regard to the £60,000 of the Chantrey Bequest, Mr. Charles Kains-Jackson has written a letter in the April number of a magazine called *The Windmill*, quoting from Mr. Cook's Handbook to the Tate Gallery, to say that Chantrey left £150,000 to the Academy subject to a life interest to his wife, and that the Academy devote the interest on £90,000 to buying pictures ; but what has become of the remaining £60,000. Mr. Kains-Jackson also points out that the Chantrey Trustees pay more than the market value for the pictures they buy. It would be better if the Charity Commissioners paid some attention to this matter, instead of depriving small parishes of endowments in order to devote the money to secondary education. The noble Marquess at the head of the Government made a speech at the last Academy banquet, and I need not repeat to him his own speech. But I should like to ask him, if I may, whether, when he spoke of Commissions on the right and Commissions on the left, this was merely a reminiscence of Tennyson's "Balaclava Charge," and referred to future Commissions, or whether he was aware that the Royal Academy was already flanked by two Commissions. My first impression of his speech was that he had heard there was to be an attempt to reform the Royal Academy, and his speech was a warning. I am certain the noble Marquess would not wish to imitate Lord Beaconsfield in being a Sphinx and a man of mystery, but his speech certainly had a misleading effect. This is shown by the remarks of the *Morning Post* next day. That journal said :

"Nobody is more given to telling the truth in the guise of a jest than Lord Salisbury. . . . Lord Salisbury foreshadowed a time when the Academy might have to be managed by the Government ; and, though he confessed that he did not think it would then be managed particularly well, we are not at all certain that he did not foretell the thing which is bound to happen sooner or later. The Royal Academy really is a Government Department in all but name. It cannot make a painter, but it can secure the prosperity of any tradesman who has learned the rules of drawing, and can use a brush to put colour on canvas. The man who is scorned by this body is scorned by the vast majority of the picture-buying public. . . . The business of the Academy would probably not be well done if it became a Government Department, but half-a-dozen Civil Service clerks would introduce improvements. Through mere laziness they would put some limit to the number of canvases that may be sent in, and, believing in their ignorance that pictures are exhibited in order that they may be seen, they would arrange the galleries as almost all galleries, save those of the Academy, are arranged."

I begin to have doubts as to whether the noble Marquess does not wish to shelter himself under the *vis inertiæ* of Lord Melbourne and Lord Palmerston. If that is not so, there is a very simple way for the noble Marquess to take action. He need not even write a letter to the Royal Academy. It would be quite sufficient if he were now to say that, until the Academy reformed itself, he and his colleagues would not accept the next invitation to the Academy banquet. This would, of course, be a self-denying ordinance, not for the loss of the dinner, but for the loss on the part of the Government of the opportunity, if I may say so, of blowing its own trumpet. The

Lord Stanley of Alderley.

Members of the Government have two opportunities during the year of doing this—the Lord Mayor's banquet and the Royal Academy banquet. But if the noble Marquess and his colleagues would take the step I have suggested, they would escape the danger they now incur of being charged with insincerity in the matter. In the spring the papers referred to what Lord Beaconsfield said at the Academy. In his speech to the Academicians he praised the paintings he saw about him for their imagination, but immediately afterwards he said to Mr. Browning they showed no imagination whatever. This story shows the danger of the insincerity to which the Academy banquet exposes a Minister. I have nothing more to say, except to make a formal motion for Papers, in case I wish to reply.

THE PRIME MINISTER AND SECRETARY OF STATE FOR FOREIGN AFFAIRS (The MARQUESS OF SALISBURY): My Lords, I will try to give some sort of answer to the question which my noble friend has put on the Paper. He has, as usual, surrounded the question with a graceful haze of irrelevant matter upon which it is not necessary for me to touch. I think, if we once attempt an inquiry as to what any newspaper says in this or that leading article, we shall have a great number of subjects for useless debate. I think that the ground fallacy of my noble friend's speech is the impression which he appears to entertain that the Report of a Commission must always be attended to, and that, as a matter of fact, its Report always is attended to. That is not my experience of public life. I have witnessed the appointment of a great number of Commissions, but my impression is that a very small percentage have received any notice from legislators or from Parliament. My noble friend is a man of very great industry, and if he will devote himself to ascertaining how many Commissions during the last 60 years have reported, and how many of those Reports have given grounds for any action, he will furnish a very important contribution to the history of his time. I think I know several Commissions now pending that have not the slightest probability of any action being taken upon them. But my noble friend appears to look forward to a period, which Lord Wemyss glanced at on a previous occasion, when the Government should undertake the management of the Royal Academy. I confess that I think this undertaking is reserved for bolder hands than mine. I hope that if there is to be an artistic Party in Parliament, which will prescribe for the various artistic bodies what they ought to do, they will organise themselves in some such way that all their recommendations may have a unanimous tendency. I am afraid my noble friend and Lord Wemyss are still far apart in the remedies they recommend for the consideration of Parliament. But the practical point is— Are the Government going to introduce any measure this session to alter the constitution of the Royal Academy? I have had the privilege to hear the exposition of the state of public business which my right hon. friend the Leader of the House of Commons has to-day made before that body. I think that when my noble friend comes to read it he will agree with me that the task of introducing any such thorny and difficult subject as the reform of our artistic institutions is not likely to be undertaken in the two months which yet remain of the session. There is no subject which produces such a healthy difference of opinion as questions which relate to art, and, consequently, there is no subject which is likely to make so great a demand on the time of Parliament. I certainly should think it very imprudent of any Minister to undertake such a task, unless he were driven by very much greater evils and defects than it is possible to show in the present management of the Royal Academy. On the whole, the results appear to me to be quite as good as they are likely to be by introducing the Civil Service element into the management of the Royal Academy, and I doubt whether any large addition of politicians to the governing body of our great art institution will add much to the value and beauty of its work.

*Lord STANLEY of ALDERLEY : My Lords, on the whole I am perfectly satisfied with the answer given by the noble Marquess, because he indicates that at some future time something will be done. I shall find the observations of the noble Marquess with regard to Royal Commissions very useful in dealing with another matter I intend to call your Lordships' attention to, and of which I have given notice.

House adjourned at twenty minutes before Six o'clock, till To-morrow, half past Ten o'clock.

HOUSE OF COMMONS.

Monday, 19th June 1899.

NEW WRIT.

New Writ for the County of York, West Riding (Osgoldcross Division), in the room of Sir John Austin, Baronet (Chiltern Hundreds). — (*Mr. William M'Arthur.*)

PRIVATE BILL BUSINESS.

PRIVATE BILLS. [Lords.]

(Standing Orders not previously inquired into complied with.)

Mr. SPEAKER laid upon the Table Report from one of the Examiners of Petitions for Private Bills, That, in the case of the following Bills, originating in the Lords, and referred on the First Reading thereof, the Standing Orders previously inquired into, and which are applicable thereto, have been complied with, viz.—

BUENOS AYRES AND PACIFIC RAILWAY COMPANY BILL. [Lords.]

TRANSVAAL MORTGAGE, LOAN, AND FINANCE COMPANY BILL. [Lords.]

Ordered, That the Bills be read a second time.

PRIVATE BILLS. [Lords.]

(No Standing Orders applicable.)

Mr. SPEAKER laid upon the Table Report from one of the Examiners of Petitions for Private Bills, That, in the case of the following Bill, originating in the Lords, and referred on the First Reading thereof, no Standing Orders are applicable, viz.—

YORKE ESTATE BILL. [Lords.]

Ordered, That the Bill be read a second time.

PROVISIONAL ORDER BILLS.

(Standing Orders applicable thereto complied with.)

Mr. SPEAKER laid upon the Table Report from one of the Examiners of Petitions for Private Bills, That, in the case of the following Bill, referred on the First Reading thereof, the Standing

Orders which are applicable thereto have been complied with, viz.—

ELECTRIC LIGHTING PROVISIONAL ORDER (No. 20) BILL.

·Ordered, That the Bill be read a second time To-morrow.

PRIVATE BILL. [Lords.]

(Standing Orders not previously in-quired into not complied with.)

MR. SPEAKER laid upon the Table Report from one of the Examiners of Petitions for Private Bills, that, in the case of the following Bill, originating in the Lords, and referred on the First Reading thereof, the Standing Orders not previously inquired into, and which are .applicable thereto, have not been complied with, viz.—

BIRMINGHAM, NORTH WARWICK-SHIRE, AND STRATFORD-UPON-AVON RAILWAY BILL. [Lords].

Ordered, That the Report be referred to the Select Committee on Standing ·Orders.

LONDON, BRIGHTON, AND SOUTH COAST RAILWAY (PENSIONS) BILL.

LISBURN URBAN DISTRICT COUNCIL BILL.

Lords' Amendments considered, and .agreed to.

FRIENDS' PROVIDENT INSTITUTION BILL. [Lords.]

Read the third time, and passed, with .an Amendment.

LOWESTOFT PROMENADE PIER BILL.

(Queen's consent signified.) Read the ·third time, and passed.

·SKIPTON URBAN DISTRICT GAS BILL. [Lords.]

Read the third time, and passed, with Amendments.

·GODALMING CORPORATION WATER BILL.

Read the third time, and passed.

MID-KENT GAS BILL. [Lords.]

Read the third time, and passed, with Amendments.

ABERDEEN CORPORATION BILL. [Lords.]

As amended, considered ; Amendments made ; Bill to be read the third time.

HASTINGS AND ST. LEONARDS GAS BILL. [Lords.]

As amended, considered ; to be read the third time.

WALKER AND WALLSEND UNION GAS (ELECTRIC LIGHTING) BILL.

As amended, considered ; Amendments made ; Bill to be read the third time.

ALL SAINTS CHURCH (CARDIFF) BILL. [Lords.]

To be read a second time upon Thursday.

GREAT GRIMSBY STREET TRAM-WAYS BILL. [Lords.]

LOWESTOFT WATER AND GAS BILL. [Lords.]

MERSEY DOCKS AND HARBOUR BOARD (PILOTAGE) BILL. [Lords.]

MILLWALL DOCK BILL.

NORTH-EASTERN AND HULL AND BARNSLEY RAILWAYS (JOINT DOCK) BILL. [Lords.]

NORTH - EASTERN RAILWAY BILL. [Lords.]

Read a second time, and committed.

ST. NEOTS WATER BILL. [Lords.] (By Order.)

Read a second time, and committed.

LONDON COUNTY COUNCIL (GENERAL POWERS) BILL.

Ordered, That the Minutes of Evidence taken before the Committee on the Great Eastern Railway Bill, in the Session of of 1887, be referred to the Committee on the London County Council (General Powers) (recommitted) Bill.—(*Dr. Farquharson.*)

ELECTRIC LIGHTING PROVISIONAL ORDERS (No. 18) BILL.

ELECTRIC LIGHTING PROVISIONAL ORDERS (No. 19) BILL.

LOCAL GOVERNMENT (Ireland) PRO-VISIONAL ORDERS (No. 2) BILL.

LOCAL GOVERNMENT (IRELAND) PROVISIONAL ORDERS (No. 3) BILL.

Read a third time, and passed.

ELECTRIC LIGHTING PROVISIONAL ORDERS (No. 16) BILL.

LOCAL GOVERNMENT PROVISIONAL ORDERS (No. 2) BILL.

LOCAL GOVERNMENT PROVISIONAL ORDERS (No. 7) BILL.

MILITARY LANDS PROVISIONAL ORDER BILL.

As amended, considered ; to be read the third time To-morrow.

HARROW AND UXBRIDGE RAILWAY BILL.

BRISTOL GAS BILL [Lords.]

Reported, with Amendments ; Reports to lie upon the Table, and to be printed.

MESSAGE FROM THE LORDS.

That they have agreed to—

Amendments to

BIRKENHEAD CORPORATION BILL. [Lords.]

Without Amendment.

That they have passed a Bill, intituled, "An Act to confirm certain Provisional Orders made by the Board of Trade under The Gas and Water Works Facilities Act, 1870, relating to Alton (Hants) Gas, Bedworth Gas, Elstree and Boreham Wood Gas, Limavady Gas, and Wellingborough Gas:" [Gas Orders Confirmation (No. 1) Bill. [Lords.]

Also, a Bill, intituled, "An Act to confirm certain Provisional Orders made by the Board of Trade under The Gas and Water Works Facilities Act, 1870, relating to Burnham and District Water, Harpenden Water, Maidstone Water, Stourbridge Water, and Tilehurst, Pangbourne, and District Water." [Water Orders Confirmation Bill. [Lords.]

Also, a Bill, intituled, "An Act to confirm certain Provisional Orders made by the Board of Trade under The Gas and Water Works Facilities Act, 1870, relating to Herne Bay Gas, Hoylake and West Kirby Gas and Water, Tonbridge Gas, and York Town and Blackwater Gas." [Gas and Water Orders Confirmation Bill. [Lords.]

And, also, a Bill, intituled, "An Act for conferring powers upon the trustees of the will of the late James Hood Brooke to acquire Gwyn's Grounds, Londonderry, and lay out the same as a public park ; and for other purposes." [Brooke's Park (Londonderry) Bill. [Lords.]

GAS ORDERS CONFIRMATION (No. 1) BILL. [Lords.]

Read the first time ; referred to the Examiners of Petitions for Private Bills, and to be printed. [Bill 239.]

WATER ORDERS CONFIRMATION BILL. [Lords.]

Read the first time ; referred to the Examiners of Petitions for Private Bills, and to be printed. [Bill 240.]

GAS AND WATER ORDERS CONFIRMATION BILL. [Lords.]

Read the first time ; referred to the Examiners of Petitions for Private Bills and to be printed. [Bill 241.]

BROOKE'S PARK (LONDONDERRY) BILL. [Lords.]

Read the first time, and referred to the Examiners of Petitions for Private Bills.

PETITIONS.

CHURCH DISCIPLINE BILL.

Petition from Nottingham, in favour ; to lie upon the Table.

LIQUOR TRAFFIC LOCAL VETO (SCOTLAND) BILL.

Petition from Nottingham, in favour ; to lie upon the Table.

LOCAL GOVERNMENT (SCOTLAND) ACT (1894) AMENDMENT BILL.

Petitions, in favour: From Wick and Brechin ; to lie upon the Table.

POOR LAW AMENDMENT (SCOTLAND) ACT, 1845.

Petition from Bothwell, for alteration of Law ; to lie upon the Table.

PRIVATE LEGISLATION PROCEDURE (SCOTLAND) BILL.

Petitions, in favour: From Brechin, Astruther, Easter, and Crail ; to lie upon the Table.

SALE OF INTOXICATING LIQUORS ON SUNDAY BILL

Petitions in favour: From Walton, Glastonbury, Street, Parbrook, Aller, Long Sutton, and Preston (three); to lie upon the Table.

TOWN COUNCILS (SCOTLAND) BILL.

Petition from Selkirk, in favour ; to lie upon the Table.

RETURNS, REPORTS, &c.

TRADE REPORTS (ANNUAL SERIES).

Copies presented,—of Diplomatic and Consular Reports, Annual Series, Nos. 2290 to 2292 [by Command] ; to lie upon the Table.

COLONIAL REPORTS (ANNUAL).

Copy presented,—of Report No. 261 (Jamaica, Annual Report for 1897-8) [by Command] ; to lie upon the Table.

RAILWAYS (CONTINUOUS BRAKES).

Copy presented,—of Return by Railway Companies of the United Kingdom for the six months ending the 31st December 1898 [by Command] ; to lie upon the Table.

LONDON COUNTY COUNCIL.

Copy presented,—of Returns relating to the Council up to 31st March, 1899, with Estimate of Expenditure for the year ending 31st March 1900 [by Act] ; to lie upon the Table, and to be printed. [No. 233.]

SUPERANNUATION ACT, 1887.

Copy presented,—of Treasury Minute, dated 8th June 1899, granting to Mr. Alfred Edgar Clay, Second Division Clerk in the Money Order Office, General Post Office, a Retired Allowance under the Act [by Act] ; to lie upon the Table.

EDUCATION (SCOTLAND).

Copy presented,— of Minute of the Committee of Council of Education in Scotland, dated 15th June, 1899, amending the terms of Paragraph 5 of the Minute of 27th April, 1899, providing for the distribution of the sum available for Secondary or Technical (including Agricultural) Education, under Section 2, Subsection (4), of The Local Taxation Account (Scotland) Act, 1898 [by Command] ; to lie upon the Table.

ARMY (MILITARY WORKS).

Copy presented,—of Approximate Estimate of Expenditure for the year 1899-1900 under existing Loans [by Command] ; to lie upon the Table.

Paper laid upon the Table by the Clerk of the House—

PUBLIC RECORDS (TREASURY).

Copy of Schedule of Documents (of the Treasury) which are not considered of sufficient public value to justify their preservation in the Public Record Office [by Act].

ARMY RIFLE RANGES.

Address for " Return of the Rifle Ranges which have been closed to the firing of full-charge ammunition since the issue of the Lee-Metford rifle, and of new ranges approved during the same period." —(*Mr. Frederick Wilson.*)

QUESTIONS.

ADMIRALTY CONTRACTS.

MR. EDMUND ROBERTSON (Dundee) : I beg to ask the Secretary to the Admiralty when the new form of Admiralty Contract will be laid upon the Table.

THE SECRETARY TO THE ADMIRALTY (Mr. MACARTNEY, Antrim, S.): No date can yet be given, but the form is in draft, and it is hoped that the final revision will not be prolonged.

MR. EDMUND ROBERTSON : Seeing that this question was asked 18 months ago, will the hon. Gentleman undertake to let us have the form before the Shipbuilding Vote is reached ?

MR. MACARTNEY : I cannot give that undertaking.

MR. EDMUND ROBERTSON : I shall raise the question on the Vote.

THE GUARDS' LOST STORES.

SIR JAMES FERGUSSON (Manchester, N.E.) : I beg to ask the Under Secretary of State for War whether a claim made by the 1st Battalion Grenadier Guards for losses of canteen stores, amounting to £340, by the upsetting of boats on the Nile provided by the Egyptian Government, has been refused by the War Office ; whether he is aware that the battalion was ordered to take up the Nile coffee bar goods sufficient to last till the end of September, and that a

Board was held to consider the losses as soon as practicable afterwards; whether the finding of the Board was approved by the General commanding the division, who considered the sum claimed moderate, and recommended its payment, and again approved by the General commanding in Egypt; whether the losses in question fall upon the canteen fund, and consequently upon the rank and file of the battalion; and on what grounds the claim has been refused after eight months' delay.

*THE FINANCIAL SECRETARY TO THE WAR OFFICE (Mr. J. POWELL-WILLIAMS, Birmingham, S.): The matter referred to in the question of the right hon. Gentleman is still under consideration, and no final decision has yet been arrived at.

THE GUERNSEY MILITIA.

MAJOR RASCH (Essex, S.E.): I beg to ask the Under Secretary of State for War whether the Guernsey Militia threw down their arms and accoutrements, and played football with their helmets when on parade; and whether the War Office proposes to take any notice of such mutinous proceedings.

*MR. J. POWELL-WILLIAMS: The Governor has telegraphed that the report is untrue.

MAJOR RASCH: May I ask whether the hon. Gentleman knows that the question is practically taken from a report in *The Times* of Wednesday last?

*MR. J. POWELL-WILLIAMS: Yes, I think that is very likely; but, nevertheless, it is untrue.

MR. R. G. WEBSTER (St. Pancras, E.): Is it true that several officers were cheered on parade and others were hissed?

MR. SPEAKER: I think the hon. Member had better give notice of that question.

THE METROPOLITAN VOLUNTEER REVIEW.

GENERAL RUSSELL (Cheltenham): I beg to ask the Under Secretary of State for War whether it is the intention to provide accommodation for Members of Parliament, so as to enable them to witness the Review at Aldershot by Her Majesty on the 26th instant.

*MR. J. POWELL-WILLIAMS: Perhaps my hon. and gallant friend will allow me to answer this question. It is not proposed to erect any stands, but the General Officer Commanding, Aldershot, will do the best he can to accommodate the carriages of persons desiring to see the Review. Applications for carriage tickets should be made to the Chief Staff Officer, Aldershot.

GENERAL RUSSELL: Will Members who do not possess carriages have accommodation?

*MR. J. POWELL-WILLIAMS: Yes; I understand that standing room will be reserved also, and that application for standing should be made in the same way as for carriages.

JOSEPH DENISTON (LATE OF THE 10TH FOOT).

MR. J. P. FARRELL (Kerry, S.): I beg to ask the Financial Secretary to the War Office whether he can order an inquiry by the military authorities at Longford into the present condition of health of Joseph Deniston, formerly belonging to the 10th Foot; and whether he is aware that Deniston, although having served with good conduct in South Africa and elsewhere for many years, is left without any pension or reward, and is now unable to work to support his family.

*MR. J. POWELL-WILLIAMS: I have nothing to add to what has been stated on previous occasions in this House in regard to this case, and can only refer the hon. Member to my reply to him of the 28th March, 1898. The case had then been considered no less than fifteen times.

CORK MILITARY DISTRICT CONTRACTS.

CAPTAIN DONELAN (Cork, E.): I beg to ask the Financial Secretary to the War Office with reference to the contracts for supplies of groceries, provisions, &c., to the Cork Military District, recently given to the Canteen and Mess Co-operative Society, Limited, whether he is aware that since the commencement of the contract on 1st May, 1899, many complaints have been received at the Cork Head-quarters Office, both as to the quality of the goods supplied and as to irregular delivery, and that in some instances the canteens have been compelled to fall back on the local firms for supplies ; whether he is aware that the contract was given to this society although local firms which have long supplied the district satisfactorily quoted lower prices for articles most largely used or consumed ; and whether, in view of these facts, steps will be taken to terminate the contract and afford an opportunity to local tradesmen.

*Mr. J. POWELL-WILLIAMS: A few complaints as to quality of goods and irregularity of delivery were at first received, but the contract is now working smoothly, and those concerned are well satisfied with it. It is not proposed to interfere in this matter with the responsibility of the General Officer commanding at Cork. Of the four successful contractors three were local firms.

CAPTAIN DONELAN: Is the hon. Gentleman aware that when this question was previously raised in this House, the late Under Secretary for War stated that any change which might be made would be in the direction of enabling canteen committees to manage their own affairs in this matter ?

*Mr. J. POWELL-WILLIAMS: If the hon. Member wants further information I shall be happy to get it for him. He can hardly hold me responsible for any statement made by the late Under Secretary for War.

CAPTAIN DONELAN: Has this new system been adopted at any military station in England ?

*Mr. J. POWELL-WILLIAMS: It is not a new system.

FIGHTING ON THE TURCO-SERVIAN FRONTIER.

MR. STEVENSON (Suffolk, Eye): I beg to ask the Under Secretary of State for Foreign Affairs whether he is able to communicate any information with regard to the reported conflict on the Turco-Servian frontier.

*THE UNDER SECRETARY OF STATE FOR FOREIGN AFFAIRS (Mr. BRODRICK, Surrey, Guildford): Her Majesty's Minister at Belgrade has telegraphed that the frontier between Retkotser and Medewtfi was crossed on June 14th by Albanians

and Turkish Regulars, who tried to raid villages and took two Servian guardhouses. They were opposed by the Servian frontier guards and armed villagers. Servian troops have been moved up to the frontier; the invaders have retired, and it is presumed that the military steps taken by Servia will suffice to maintain order.

SIR W. GARSTIN'S REPORT ON THE SOUDAN.

MR. J. E. ELLIS (Nottingham, Rushcliff): I beg to ask the Under Secretary of State for Foreign Affairs when the Report of Sir W. Garstin, respecting his visit of inspection of the Nile south of Khartoum and the Soudan, specifically alluded to by Lord Cromer in his Report on Egyptian affairs for 1898, will be laid upon the Table and distributed.

*Mr. BRODRICK : Sir W. Garstin's Report is now being prepared for presentation to Parliament. It will be laid and distributed in the course of this week.

SOUTH AFRICAN REPUBLIC—THE MURDER OF MRS. APPLEBE.

MR. WILLIAM JOHNSTON (Belfast, S.): I beg to ask the Secretary of State for the Colonies whether any further information has been received concerning the murder of Mrs. Applebe, wife of the Rev. R. F. Applebe, Wesleyan missionary, reported by Sir Alfred Milner in Serial No. 55, South African Republic, Blue Book, as an act of revenge on the part of the liquor dealers for efforts made by Mr. Applebe and Mr. Wilson to expose their nefarious trade ; and whether any of the perpetrators of the outrage have been punished, or any compensation awarded by the President of the South African Republic.

THE SECRETARY OF STATE FOR THE COLONIES (Mr. J. CHAMBERLAIN, Birmingham, W.): The last information received is contained in Nos. 61 and 63 in the Blue Book. No result has been obtained from the offer of a reward of £500 by the Government, and there is no clue as yet to the perpetrators. I am not aware that compensation has been given.

THE KILLING OF MR. EDGAR BY A BOER POLICEMAN.

MR. DUNCOMBE (Cumberland, Egremont): On behalf of the hon. Member for the Ecclesall Division of Sheffield I beg to ask the Secretary of State for the Colonies whether some compensation will be claimed on behalf of the widow of Mr. Edgar, who was shot dead in his own house by a Boer policeman.

MR. J. CHAMBERLAIN : The answer is in the affirmative ; a claim for compensation has been made on behalf of the widow and child.

THE JAMESON RAID.

MR. C. P. SCOTT (Lancashire, Leigh) : I beg to ask the Secretary of State for the Colonies whether, as stated by Sir Alfred Milner in his dispatch dated 4th May, this country was, just before the so-called Jameson Raid, on the verge of war with the Transvaal ; and, if so, what were the grounds justifying a declaration of war against the Transvaal by this country at that time.

MR. J. CHAMBERLAIN : Sir A. Milner's statement is perfectly correct, and the hon. Member will find full information in Blue Book C. 8474 of May, 1897.

PROMOTION IN THE PRISON SERVICE.

MR. LOUGH (Islington, W.) : I beg to ask the Secretary to the Treasury whether there are seven officials in the Prisons Department who have served forty years and upwards, and who are over sixty years of age ; and, if so, will special facilities be offered to induce their retirement, in view of the large number of juniors who are at the maximum of their class.

*THE SECRETARY OF STATE FOR THE HOME DEPARTMENT (Sir M. WHITE RIDLEY, Lancashire, Blackpool) : I have been asked by my right hon. friend the Secretary to the Treasury to answer this question. There are six, not seven, officers in the Prisons Department who have served forty years and upwards and are over sixty years of age. They will retire under the general rule on reaching sixty-five, and there appear to me to be no grounds for any action in the matter.

GLASGOW BAKERY DISPUTE.

SIR CHARLES CAMERON : (Glasgow, Bridgeton) : I beg to ask the Lord Advocate whether his attention has been called to the case of Angus M'Naughton, baker, of Kinning Park, Glasgow, arrested on the 12th ultimo and locked up for the

night on a charge of persistently following with intent to intimidate certain workmen in a bakery connected with which there was some trade dispute ; whether the police officer arresting him had a warrant for his arrest ; will he explain why the police refused to communicate to his wife the fact of his arrest and detention, also why on the occasion of his being brought before a magistrate on the 13th ultimo, and remanded for 48 hours, bail was offered and refused ; and why, if the charge against him was a serious one, was he liberated on 16th May, after four nights' incarceration, without being called on even to make a declaration before the sheriff to whom his case was remitted.

THE LORD ADVOCATE (MR. A. GRAHAM MURRAY, Buteshire) : Inquiry has been made into the case referred to by the hon. Member. The police officer had no warrant ; the arrest was made under Section 86 of the Burgh Police Act, 1892. My information is that the police did not refuse to communicate to the prisoner's wife the fact of his arrest and detention, and that bail was not offered, and therefore not refused. In reply to the last paragraph, the facts are these : The prisoner was brought before the magistrate on Saturday, the 13th, and the case was remitted to the Sheriff Court for consideration. The police report was made to the Sheriff's Procurator-Fiscal on Monday, the 15th. The case was considered on that day by the Procurator-Fiscal, and was disposed of on Tuesday, the 16th, the prisoner being liberated because the evidence was considered insufficient.

SIR CHARLES CAMERON : Will the right hon. Gentleman make further inquiry on the question of bail, which I am assured was offered ?

MR. A. G. MURRAY : I can only repeat what I have stated. If the bail was offered and refused, application could have been made to the Procurator-Fiscal. That certainly was not done

ABERDEEN CEMETERY SCANDAL.

GENERAL RUSSELL : I beg to ask the Lord Advocate if his attention has been called to the alleged wholesale desecration of graves in a cemetery at Aberdeen ; and whether it is the intention of the Government to institute proceedings against all those concerned in these alleged outrages as well as against the superintendent of the cemetery.

MR. A. G. MURRAY: A full investigation of the circumstances is being made, and the case, in all its bearings, is at present under consideration of Crown counsel. The superintendent has been committed for trial, and is now in prison.

GENERAL RUSSELL: The right hon. Gentleman has not answered the last paragraph.

MR. A. G. MURRAY: Yes; the words "the case is under consideration in all its bearings" obviously cover the point whether other persons are to be prosecuted.

THE DAY SCHOOL CODE.

VISCOUNT CRANBORNE (Rochester): I beg to ask the Vice-President of the Committee of Council on Education whether the additions to Articles 37 and 42 of the Day School Code have been withdrawn in conformity with the Address to the Crown carried in this House; and what steps the Department have taken in order to warn managers that the published Code is in this respect incorrect.

THE VICE-PRESIDENT OF THE COMMITTEE OF COUNCIL ON EDUCATION (Sir J. GORST, Cambridge University): Official intimation of the reply to the address of the House of Commons has not yet been received by the Education Department. Meanwhile, a Minute is prepared, restoring the Articles to the form they had in the Code of 1898. This Minute will be laid on the Table of the House, and published in due course.

CARMARTHEN CHARITIES.

MR. LLOYD MORGAN (Carmarthen, W.): I beg to ask the hon. Member representing the Charity Commissioners whether he can state the reason for the delay in the publication of the Reports of the Assistant Charity Commissioners concerning the charities of the borough of Carmarthen, and of the parish of Trelloch-ar-Bettws in the county of Carmarthen.

THE PARLIAMENTARY CHARITY COMMISSIONER (Mr. GRANT LAWSON, York N.R., Thirsk): The reason

for the delay in the publication of the Report on the Charities in the Borough of Carmarthen is that the application made for the production of certain documents in the case of a grant to one particular charity has not yet been complied with. In all other respects the Report is ready to be laid on the Table of the House. With regard to the charities in the parish of Trelloch-ar-Bettws the Report has been delayed by the difficulty experienced in obtaining full information respecting the administration of the charities. The Report as to this parish was laid on the Table of this House on June 8th.

HYDE PARK—LIGHTING.

GENERAL RUSSELL: I beg to ask the First Commissioner of Works whether his attention has been called to the condition of the main thoroughfares in Hyde Park after dusk; and whether he can see his way, by any improvement in the lighting and more police supervision, to enable respectable people to make more use of this part during the summer evenings than under the present conditions is possible.

THE FIRST COMMISSIONER OF WORKS (MR. AKERS DOUGLAS, Kent. St. Augustine's): I have been gradually improving, as funds will permit, the lighting of the parks; and the improvement in Hyde Park has been generally admitted and appreciated. My policy with regard to lighting the parks was fully stated during the discussion of the Parks Estimate a few weeks ago. The maintenance of order in Hyde Park is in the hands of the police authorities, but in my opinion everything is done that is necessary to maintain order there.

FINTONA SUNDAY MAILS.

MR. DILLON (Mayo, E.): I beg to ask the Secretary to the Treasury, as representing the Postmaster-General, whether he is aware that at Fintona, the largest town in the South Tyrone Parliamentary division of county Tyrone, the mails on Sunday mornings are seldom delivered before 10 a.m., though they have been lying at Omagh, six miles distant, from 3 a.m., whence they are conveyed by a horse and trap; and if there is any reason to prevent their delivery little earlier, so as to enable persons obliged to leave Fintona by the only Sunday train at 9 a.m. to receive their letters before leaving; and, seeing that the only mail from Fintona on Sundays is made up about 4.30 p.m. and sent to head office at Omagh, where it lies untouched till about 10 p.m., whether there is anything to prevent its being dispatched later on Sundays, say at 7 or 8 p.m.

THE FINANCIAL SECRETARY TO THE TREASURY (Mr. HANBURY, Preston): The mails are due at Fintona on Sunday about 9 a.m., and the delivery commences at 9.15 a.m. On weekdays the service to Fintona is by train, but on Sunday no trains are run, and the mails are conveyed by a walking postman, leaving Omagh, where they have been lying, as the hon. Member presumes, for some hours, at 6 a.m. This is the usual hour of departure for rural postmen. The Sunday dispatch from Fintona is at 5.10 p.m. As a rule rural postmen are allowed to return from the terminal point of their journeys on Sundays in the forenoon about one hour after the completion of the delivery. As this postman waits eight hours, the inhabitants of Fintona have the advantage of an exceptionally late despatch.

MR. DILLON: My information is that the mails are conveyed by horse and trap. Cannot the right hon. Gentleman, bearing in mind the importance of this district, expedite matters a bit?

MR. HANBURY was understood to reply in the negative.

NORTH KERRY POSTAL ARRANGEMENTS.

MR. FLAVIN (Kerry, N.): I beg to ask the Secretary to the Treasury, as representing the Postmaster - General, whether a petition very largely signed by the people of Clandouglas, Kilfeighney, Pallace, Leam, and other townlands in North Kerry, asking for a house-to-house delivery of letters, has been received by the Secretary of the General Post Office; whether he was aware that great public inconvenience is caused by the non-delivery of letters in those districts; and whether the request of the petitioners will be granted.

MR. HANBURY: A petition was received some time ago asking for a delivery of letters, and a delivery is now being made throughout the district. At Clandouglas, Kilfeighney, and other places the delivery takes place every week-day, but at some of the townlands it is necessarily restricted to two days a week.

BELFAST POST OFFICE STAFF.

MR. MACALEESE (Monaghan, N.): I beg to ask the Secretary to the Treasury, as representing the Postmaster-General, whether at present there exists on the staff of the Belfast Post Office three vacancies for provincial clerks in charge; could he explain to the House when and under what circumstances these vacancies arose, and what was the date of the notice exhibited in each of the postal and telegraph departments inviting applications for these vacancies; how many applications were received from each department, and with whom does the power of selecting rest; and what is the cause of the delay in making these appointments.

MR. HANBURY: The answer to the first paragraph is in the negative, and that covers all the other paragraphs.

DUNDALK POSTMASTERSHIP.

MR. MACALEESE: I beg to ask the Secretary to the Treasury, as representing the Postmaster-General, with reference to the vacancy that at present exists in the postmastership of Dundalk, could he state when did this vacancy actually arise, and what was the date of the official circular in which a notice appeared intimating the vacancy, and inviting applications for it; what was the cause of the delay that arose from the date of the vacancy arising and this notice appearing, and also the delay that has since taken place in making the appointment; how many candidates responded to the invitation that appeared in the official circular in reference to this vacancy; and whether the individual upon whom the vacancy is conferred will draw the salary of the office from the date of the retirement of the late postmaster, or only from the date of his actual appointment; if only the latter, then can it be stated what sum, if any, will accrue to the Treasury as a saving in respect of the cost of the administration of this office by reason of the delay in filling the vacancy; and, if generally greater expedition can be used in making appointments to such vacancies when they arise in the future.

MR. HANBURY: The vacancy occurred on the 23rd of February. It was notified in the Post Office Circular of the 28th of March. There was no delay, as the pension of the late postmaster was not awarded till the 3rd of March, and the salary had to be revised. There were fifty-seven candidates who applied for the appointment, and it was necessary, as usual in such cases, for the surveyors to investigate and report upon the claims and qualifications of each of them. An appointment has been made, but the new postmaster cannot draw the salary until he actually takes up the duty. The officer acting as postmaster in the meantime will receive half of his own salary and half of the salary of the postmaster, in accordance with the usual rule in such cases. The balance of these salaries will remain undrawn.

BALLYMAHON POSTAL ARRANGEMENTS.

MR. HAYDEN (Ròscommon, S.): I beg to ask the Secretary to the Treasury, as representing the Postmaster-General, whether it is proposed to change the arrangements regarding the mail car which at present runs from Ballymahon (6.35 a.m.) to Castletown Railway Station, Midland and Great Western Railway (8.40 a.m.), and conveys the letters posted in Ballymahon and neighbourhood between 6 p.m. and 10 p.m. on the previous evening, which at present reach Dublin and England on the day after posting, and to substitute therefor a car leaving Ballymahon at 3 p.m., which would catch the limited mail train for Dublin at Castletown, and would land its letters in Dublin late for business that day in wholesale houses, and leave Ballymahon without a post from 6.10 p.m. till 3 p.m. next day, so that letters posted at say 6.30 p.m. would not be dispatched for nearly twelve hours; and whether the present more convenient arrangement could be continued, in accordance with a petition presented some days ago to the Postmaster-General.

MR. HANBURY: It has been decided to continue the present arrangement, as requested in a petition recently addressed to the Postmaster-General.

MAIL TRAIN DELAYS AT LIMERICK JUNCTION.

MR. FLAVIN: I beg to ask the Secretary of the Treasury, as representing the Postmaster-General, whether he is aware that train connections at Limerick Junc-

tion failed no less than 14 times during the months between June and December, 1898, causing a great public inconvenience in the delay of Her Majesty's mails in several portions of the South of Ireland; whether the Waterford and Limerick Railway Company, at the request of the Post Office, have consented to delay the departure of these trains for 20 minutes beyond the usual time, so as to remedy this public grievance; and, whether information can be given as to the number of times during the years 1898 and 1899 the connections at Limerick Junction failed owing to the late arrival of the trains on the Great Southern and Western system.

MR. HANBURY: The Waterford, Limerick and Western Railway Company have agreed to detain their train for 20 minutes, if necessary, to maintain the connection, but the train from Dublin is occasionally more than 20 minutes late in arrival. Between June and December, 1898, the connection failed 17 times. During 1898 the connection failed 19 times, and it has failed six times this year.

ENNISKILLEN POST-OFFICE.

MR. JORDAN (Fermanagh, S.): I beg to ask the Secretary to the Treasury, as representing the Postmaster-General, if the plans and specifications for the new post-office in Enniskillen have yet been finished by the Irish Board of Works and approved by the Postal authorities; if so, have tenders for the erection of the building been taken; and, if not, when will the authorities advertise for such tenders.

MR. HANBURY: The plans of the new post office at Enniskillen have been approved, and the working drawings and specifications have been completed. The quantities are being taken out, and the Board of Public Works expect to be in a position to advertise for tenders in about a month.

WEST CAVAN TRAMWAYS.

MR. J. P. FARRELL: I beg to ask the Secretary to the Treasury whether he is state to the House if any relief has been afforded to the taxpayers of West Cavan by the operation of the Tramway Amendment Act passed in 1895; whether the Board of Works or the Treasury has received the last report of the auditors on this line; and, whether, as the guaran-

given will soon expire, it is the intention of Her Majesty's Government to afford relief to the cesspayers by releasing them from the guarantee.

MR. HANBURY: The Treasury more than three years ago expressed its readiness to commute, under the Act of 1895 referred to, its liability upon the Cavan, Leitrim, and Roscommon line; but we have heard nothing on the subject since then from the company or from the county. Relief has, however, been given to the ratepayers by the cancellation of shares amounting to £13,690 upon redemption of the Government Loan in 1896; and I understand that further relief will be given under Section 58 (4) of the Local Government Act, 1898. We have the audited accounts to 1st November last. The guarantee is perpetual, not terminable.

LANESBOROUGH POSTAL ARRANGE-MENTS.

MR. HAYDEN: I beg to ask the Secretary to the Treasury, as representing the Postmaster-General, whether he is aware that complaints have been received from some of the inhabitants of Lanesborough in reference to the defective postal and telegraphic arrangements, alleging that the arrangements are inferior to those which existed in the place a century ago; and whether he will consider the advisability of improving them by the establishment of a telegraph office and a postal delivery in connection with the mail each morning from either Roscommon or Longford, which would enable English and "Cross Post" local letters to be received on the day after being posted, instead of two days as is the case at present.

MR. HANBURY: I shall be obliged if the hon. Member can give me fuller information as to the better telegraphic arrangements which are stated to have existed in the exceptional village a century ago. A telegraph office was offered under guarantee in November last, and the Postmaster-General will be happy to have the extension carried out as soon as the terms are accepted. The mail car for Lanesborough now leaves Longford at 6 a.m., but it could not be despatched until 9.50 a.m. if it were to await the arrival of the English mail. The later delivery which would result from the later despatch of the car from Longford

would probably give rise to serious complaint on the part of some of the residents, and such an alteration could not be made unless ample evidence were adduced that it would give general satisfaction. The existing post to Lanesborough does not pay its expenses, and for this reason a second service on week days or a Sunday service is not warranted.

BALLYDUFF POSTAL ARRANGE-MENTS.

MR. FLAVIN: I beg to ask the Secretary to the Treasury, as representing the Postmaster-General, whether he is aware that a petition, largely signed by residents in the Ballyduff postal district of the county of Kerry, was presented to the Postmaster-General, praying for a Sunday delivery of letters, a money order office, and either telegraphic or telephonic facilities; and will he explain why, seeing that all the surrounding villages and towns are in the enjoyment of those benefits, the application of the memorialists of the Ballyduff district has been so long delayed from getting equal facilities in Post Office affairs.

MR. HANBURY: A petition was received early last year, asking for a Sunday delivery of letters and a money order office, but there is no trace of any application for the establishment of telegraphic or telephonic facilities. A money order office was established at Ballyduff, under guarantee, about a year ago, but a Sunday post could not be sanctioned, because the existing service on weekdays was found to be unremunerative, and additional expense for affording a Sunday service is therefore not warranted.

MR. FLAVIN: Is not the money order office one merely in imagination? Cannot the right hon. Gentleman consult the convenience of——

MR. SPEAKER: Order, order! The hon. Member is proceeding to argue the question.

IRISH SCHOOL TEACHERS' PENSION FUND.

MR. FLAVIN: I beg to ask the Chief Secretary to the Lord Lieutenant of Ireland on what grounds assistant national school teachers in Ireland are compelled to pay the increased premiums towards the pension fund, although they receive no portion of the arrears fee grant; and whether class salaries will be given to the assistant teachers, in order to enable them to meet the increased premiums which they are compelled to pay.

THE CHIEF SECRETARY FOR IRELAND (MR. G. W. BALFOUR, Leeds Central): The increased premiums now paid by assistant teachers, as well as by principals, have been fixed by the National Teachers' Superannuation Department under rules operative from 1st January, 1898. It is not intended to pay assistant teachers the salaries attaching to their class in order to enable them to meet the higher pension premiums.

IRISH GUARDIANS AND LABOURERS' COTTAGES.

MR. GIBNEY (Meath, N.): I beg to ask the Chief Secretary to the Lord Lieutenant of Ireland under what order the Local Government Board have decided that a district councillor who takes a labourer's cottage from the guardians becomes disqualified; and is a landlord who makes a letting to the guardians also disqualified.

MR. G. W. BALFOUR: The decision referred to in the first paragraph is based on the provisions contained in Section 12, Sub-section 4 (e) of the Application of Enactments Order, 1898. As regards the second paragraph, the reply would be determined by the kind of letting to the guardians.

CARRYING FIREARMS IN IRELAND.

MR. HAYDEN: I beg to ask the Chief Secretary to the Lord Lieutenant of Ireland whether he is aware that a man named Patrick Costello, living in Carmaska, near Strollestown, County of Roscommon, who is under police protection and was recently licensed to use a revolver, wantonly fired at three men in that district on the night of 18th May as they were going to their homes from Strollestown; and whether the Government contemplate taking any action in his case.

MR. G. W. BALFOUR: The occurrence to which the question presumably refers took place at 11 o'clock on the night of 11th May. It appears that Costello, against whom there has been much ill-feeling, and who has received considerable annoyance, found four or five men close to his house, one of whom

threw a stone at Costello, whereupon he discharged a shot in the air from his revolver. These men were unknown to Costello, who reported the occurrence to the police on 13th May. The persons alleged to have been fired at have made no complaint, and are also unknown to the police; but if they will come forward and make statements to the police the matter will be further investigated.

TYRONE COUNTY COUNCIL RATE COLLECTOR.

MR. HEMPHILL (Tyrone, N.): I beg to ask the Chief Secretary to the Lord Lieutenant of Ireland is he aware that William M'Farland, of Glencoppagh, Plumbridge, in the County of Tyrone, in the division of North Tyrone, who has been a paid registration inspector to the North Tyrone Unionist Registration Association for a considerable number of years, has been appointed as rate collector by the Tyrone County Council for the electoral divisions of Lislea, Loughash, Plumbridge, Stranagalivilly, and Moyle, the first four of which was part of his inspection district as such political agent, and that the Local Government Board of Ireland has sanctioned this appointment.

MR. G. W. BALFOUR: The Tyrone County Council have submitted a scheme for the collection of the poor rate in their county, in which they propose to appoint Mr. M'Farland, an existing cess collector, who has expressed his willingness to serve, to collect the rates in the electoral divisions mentioned in the question. The scheme submitted by the County Council requires modification in certain particulars, and has not yet been sanctioned by the Local Government Board. The Board have no information relative to Mr. M'Farland's connection with a political association; but if the facts are as stated they would probably require him to resign the office of registration agent before proceeding to further entertain the question of his appointment as poor rate collector.

JUDICIAL RENTS IN IRELAND.

MR. FLAVIN: I beg to ask the Chief Secretary to the Lord Lieutenant of Ireland if he is aware that average reduction of first and second term judicial rents in Ireland is, roughly speaking, between 30 and 40 per cent. less than the old rents; and whether, seeing that there are a very large number of tenants in Ireland who are in the position of future tenants, either through eviction or from other causes over which they have no control, and that all such tenants are debarred from any benefits under the Land Law (Ireland) Acts, Her Majesty's Government will introduce legislation to give equal treatment to all classes of tenants in Ireland.

MR. G. W. BALFOUR : The figures in the first paragraph are substantially accurate. In reply to the second paragraph, it is not quite correct to say that all such tenants are debarred from any benefits under the Land Law Acts. It is not intended to introduce further legislation as suggested.

MR. FLAVIN : How can a future tenant pay a rent which is 30 per cent. more than that paid by existing tenants ?

THE SPEAKER : Order, order !

DEATH OF ANNE FINEGAN, CORMARY.

MR. MACALEESE : I beg to ask the Chief Secretary to the Lord Lieutenant of Ireland if he can now state the specific grounds upon which it was decided not to hold an inquest in the case of the woman Finegan, who died on the day following certain eviction proceedings at her house at Cormary, near Newbliss, which proceedings were conducted by the agent and bailiffs of Lord Rossmore. Was the doctor employed by Lord Rossmore's agent to certify to the woman's fitness for removal a properly qualified medical man, and, if so, where does he regularly practise ; were any police present, and did the officer in charge remonstrate with Lord Rossmore's agent; and, as the belief is general in the district that the woman's death was hastened by the conduct of the evicting party, will an inquest be yet held in this important case.

MR. G. W. BALFOUR : The question of holding an inquest in this case did not arise for consideration. As I have already pointed out, the woman was not evicted or disturbed by the landlord's agent, and she died, not on the day following the visit of the agent, but three days afterwards. The deceased had been ailing for the past twelve months, during the last two of which she was confined to her bed ; her death had been expected some time previously by her own brother, and the police did not in the circumstances con-

sider it necessary to report the death to the Coroner. I understand that the medical gentleman referred to in the second paragraph is properly qualified. I cannot say where he practises. There were two police present at the time ; the woman was not removed, and they did not remonstrate with the agent. The police have no reason to think that the belief is general in the district that the woman's death was hastened by the action of the agent and his bailiffs. It is not intended to hold an inquest, as suggested.

SYLVESTER DWYER.

MR. FLAVIN : I beg to ask the Chief Secretary to the Lord Lieutenant of Ireland whether he has received a resolution passed unanimously by the Guardians of the Killarney Union, praying for the release of Sylvester Dwyer, a prisoner at present confined in Maryborough Prison ; and whether, seeing that Sylvester Dwyer has now been in prison close on 18 years, Her Majesty's Government could order his release after such a lengthened punishment.

MR. G. W. BALFOUR : The resolution referred to has been received. The case of this prisoner was considered by the Lords Justices so recently as the 15th instant, when it was decided that the law should take its course. The term of penal servitude to which he was sentenced was 18 years, and he completed 11½ years of his sentence on the 6th instant.

MR. FLAVIN : Why was not the same clemency extended to this man as was extended to Lord Kenmare's bailiff ?

MR. G. W. BALFOUR : I cannot add anything to my answer.

RAILWAY COMMUNICATION IN DONEGAL.

MR. T. D. SULLIVAN (Donegal, W.): I beg to ask the Chief Secretary to the Lord Lieutenant of Ireland if he has received a copy of a resolution lately passed by the District Council of Dunfanaghy, county Donegal, in which he is thanked for the interest he has taken in the development of railway communication in that county, and requested to expedite as far as possible the opening of the works on the Letterkenny and Burton Port line, with a view to affording employment to the labouring classes, which is much needed at this time ; and whether he will be pleased to comply with the request of the Council in this matter.

MR. G. W. BALFOUR: I have received a copy of the resolution referred to in the question. I understand that the contractors for the line are on the ground to-day for the purpose of commencing work.

MULLINGAR ASYLUM.

MR. J. P. FARRELL: I beg to ask the Chief Secretary to the Lord Lieutenant of Ireland whether any steps have been taken to ascertain or check the recent expenditure on buildings in Mullingar Asylum; whether in many cases the Governors were never consulted, but simply ordered to get these works done by the Board of Control; and whether, in cases where, under the 76th Section of the Local Government Act, county councils amalgamate unions for the purposes of creating auxiliary asylums, the county which withdraws its pauper lunatics from Mullingar Asylum will still have to continue to pay off the building charges incurred.

MR. G. W. BALFOUR: A financial statement of the expenditure on buildings at the Mullingar Asylum is being prepared, and will be forwarded to the Asylum Committee. The Board of Control has not in any case ordered the Governors to undertake works at this asylum, and in no case have works been carried out without previous conference or consultation with the Governors, and without obtaining their general approval of the works. In the event of a county council establishing an auxiliary asylum under the enactment referred to, such auxiliary asylum would be exclusively appropriated to chronic harmless lunatics. While this arrangement would tend to relieve the congestion of the county asylum and facilitate the classification of curable and incurable cases, it would in no way affect the liability of the county for the maintenance of its county asylum or the debts and liabilities already incurred by the county in respect of the asylum.

GUN LICENCES IN IRELAND.

MR. J. P. FARRELL: I beg to ask the Chief Secretary to the Lord Lieutenant of Ireland whether he is aware that Mr. Francis Egan, of Elfeet Burke, parish of Newtowncashel, county Longford, ap-

plied on three occasions for a gun licence to enable him to keep a gun for the destruction of vermin on his farm; that four local magistrates and the police were in favour of his application, but that Mr. J. M. Kilkelly, the resident magistrate, refused this reasonable request, and continues to refuse it; and whether, in view of the fact that Mr. Egan has recently been elected a county councillor for Longford, and is a man of unblemished character, he will recommend the Lord Lieutenant to issue a licence to him.

MR. G. W. BALFOUR: I have made inquiry into this matter and, so far as I can gather, the facts are not quite as represented in the question. Licences to keep firearms are not issued by the Lord Lieutenant, but I would suggest that if Mr. Egan were to renew his application for a licence the licensing officer would perhaps further consider it.

STEAM TRAWLING OFF THE DUBLIN COAST.

MR. CLANCY (Dublin County, N.): I beg to ask the Attorney-General for Ireland, with reference to the illegal destruction of fishermen's nets and lines by steam trawlers off the Dublin coast, will he institute a prosecution against the owners or crew of the *Jackdaw*, of Hull, and the *Peter Johnston*, of Aberdeen, for that offence, if evidence implicating either is forthcoming.

*THE ATTORNEY GENERAL for Ireland (MR. ATKINSON, Londonderry, N.): The answer to this question is in the affirmative. I may mention, however, that the owner of one of the trawlers compensated a fisherman for damage done to his nets.

THE BOARD OF EDUCATION BILL.

MR. STEVENSON: I beg to ask the First Lord of the Treasury when he intends to proceed with the Board of Education Bill.

THE FIRST LORD OF THE TREASURY (Mr. A. J. BALFOUR, Manchester, E.): I am afraid I can give no pledge at all as to on what day we shall be able to proceed with this Bill.

COLONEL LOCKWOOD (Essex, Epping): Will the right hon. Gentleman be able to give us some idea to-morrow ?

Mr. A. J. BALFOUR : The business for this week is settled. At this stage of the session it is hard to say, looking far ahead, on what particular day a special Bill will be taken.

THE TELEPHONE BILL.

Sir CHARLES CAMERON : I beg to ask the First Lord of the Treasury whether his attention has been called to the fact that the Private Bills relating to telephonic communication introduced at the beginning of the session are still waiting for Second Reading pending proceedings on the Government Telegraphs (Telephonic Communication, &c.) Bill; and whether he can now state when it is proposed to bring on that measure.

Mr. A. J. BALFOUR : If the Private Legislation Procedure (Scotland) Bill is not finished to-night—and I hope it will be—the Bill the hon. Member refers to will be the second Order to-morrow; it will be the first Order if the Scotch Bill is finished to-night.

THE LAKES OF KILLARNEY.

Mr. LOUGH : I beg to ask the First Lord of the Treasury whether £90,600 has been realised by the sale of quit and Crown rents in Ireland between the years 1891 and 1897, and since 1864 nearly a quarter of million has been obtained from this source : and whether these moneys are being used for the purchase of estates in Great Britain; if so, whether the Government would be prepared to appropriate a portion of this Irish fund, which is being withdrawn from Ireland at the rate of about £12,000 a year, for the purchase of the Muckross demesne at Killarney as a national park.

Mr. A. J. BALFOUR : The hon. Gentleman's statement of figures is, I believe, quite correct : but I do not think it is a matter which could be made a question as between the expenditure of Imperial money in Ireland and the expenditure of Imperial money in England. None of the money which has come from the sources referred to by the hon. Gentleman has been expended in England upon public parks, nor has any public money ever been expended, so far as I know, on public parks outside the metropolitan area. The policy of purchasing a public park so far from any great centre of population, and of a character which would probably produce very little value to the public during many of the winter months of the year, is very doubtful indeed.

Mr. SWIFT MacNEILL (Donegal, S.) : Is the right hon. Gentleman aware that a portion of the money referred to has been spent on the stabling of Royal parks ?

Mr. A. J. BALFOUR : No, Sir, I am not aware of that, but it may be true, and I will make inquiries.

CYPRUS.

Mr. PIERPOINT (Warrington) : I beg to ask the First Lord of the Treasury whether, in the Votes in Supply, he will arrange that there shall be an opportunity for discussing Cyprus, Grant in Aid (Civil Services, Class V., Vote 4).

Mr. A. J. BALFOUR : I am afraid I can give no pledge to my hon. friend of the character he desires.

THE HOME OFFICE VOTE.

Mr. TENNANT (Berwickshire) : I beg to ask the First Lord of the Treasury upon what day he proposes to take the Home Office Estimates.

Mr. A. J. BALFOUR : As the hon. Gentleman is aware, the Supply arrangements for next Thursday and Friday have already been communicated to the House. I think it would be inexpedient to go beyond that.

BARRACKS LOAN BILL.

Mr. BUCHANAN (Aberdeenshire, E.) : I beg to ask the First Lord of the Treasury, when the Barracks Loan Bill will be introduced.

Mr. A. J. BALFOUR : I hope to take the resolution required in introducing this Bill on Wednesday, and in fact the Bill itself will be moved by my hon. friend the Under Secretary for War on that day.

BUSINESS OF THE HOUSE (GOVERNMENT BUSINESS).

Mr. A. J. BALFOUR : It certainly will be no matter of surprise, and I hope, too, no matter of regret in any part of the House, that I rise at this accustomed period of the session to ask the House to give the Government further facilities for the conduct of such legislation as it may be enabled to pass during the remainder of the session. All the pressure, indeed, that has reached me has been in the other direction, as the Notice Paper has shown day by day, and even to-day the questions indicate the anxiety of the House to proceed with certain Government Bills which have already been introduced. I have noticed in the newspapers mention of a rumour that there is a sort of general anticipation pervading the House that the session would have an end about July 25, and that at that unprecedented date we would be able to occupy ourselves in a manner more suitable to the season. I am afraid, Sir, that estimate never had any substantial foundation, nor do I think anybody could have conceived it possible that we should anticipate to any serious extent the date on which, during the last four years, we have been able to separate. I hope that date will not be exceeded, but I certainly cannot promise the House that we shall be able to shorten matters so that we shall be able to separate in the course of next month, or even in the first week of August. I do not propose to give an exact programme of what we hope to pass, because that would be impossible; nor has any one in my position, at this period of the session, ever attempted such a task. Nor, again, do I need to read through the list of Government Orders on the Paper, but I may just mention those Bills which are, I think, somewhat loosely defined by the name of departmental measures. Taking the Order Book of to-day, and following the order therein, the first is the Telephone Bill, which has not yet reached the Second Reading, and which, I hope, may reach the Second Reading to-morrow night. There is the Board of Education Bill, which has already passed the Lords and awaits the Second Reading. There is the Private Legislation Procedure (Scotland) Bill, of which, I trust, we may be able to make a finish to-night; in any case, I confidently expect we shall be able to make .very substantial progress with it. There is, next, the Colonial Loans Fund Bill, which ought to pass, and ought to be followed by a Bill based upon it, which will ask the House to consent to loans in particular cases. The House will remember that the Colonial Loans Fund Bill merely lays down the general outlines of the scheme for specific loans, and we think that that Bill ought not only to pass, but, as a

Mr. A. J. Balfour.

matter of fact, there are certain specific loans we ought to have the authority of the House to make before the session closes. There is the Parish Churches (Scotland) Bill, which has passed the Lords and not yet been read a second time ; there is the Small Houses (Acquisition of Ownership) Bill, which has reached the Report stage ; the Sale of Food and Drugs Bill, which has reached the Report stage; and two Irish Bills—the Agriculture and Technical Instruction Bill and the Tithe Rent-charge Bill—which, I am sorry to say, have not yet passed their Second Reading ; and then, finally, there is the Money-Lending Bill, which has already passed the Lords, but has made no progress in this House. I do not believe that this list will be materially added to, except in certain particulars which I will mention. There are three more Bills which, as the House is aware, we mean to introduce and deal with in the course of the session. There is the Military Works Bill, the Clerical Tithe Bill, and the Naval Works Bill. There are also Bills of my right hon. friend the Home Secretary, among them one making further amendments in the Factory Acts. There is, in addition to these, a Bill which has not yet been announced to the House, and which the House, I think, will not describe as contentious, and that is a Bill for completing the arrangements for taking over the Niger Company. The present position of affairs on the Niger has led to many embarrassments which I think ought to be put an end to. The present is a transitional and purely provisional state of things, and ought to be terminated as soon as possible. This measure, therefore, will have to be passed before the end of the session. That is the last item in the list of non-departmental measures which it is very desirable to pass. I do not, of course, say that all these measures will, as a matter of fact, pass into law before we separate, but I hope very substantial progress will be made with the list which I have just read to the House. I do not think I need justify the proposal which enables us to take Tuesdays and Wednesdays henceforth for carrying out this legislation. It has always been anticipated about this period, and even before, that that course will be taken, and I think private Members will be anxious to do all they can to help the Government to deal with the legislation which still remains, and which we can justly claim should be passed. In these circumstances I think. I should be wasting the time of the House if I said more to induce it to pass the Resolution. I beg to move the Resolution which stands in my name.

Motion made and Question proposed, "That for the remainder of the session Government business do have precedence on Tuesday and Wednesday, and that the provisions of Standing Order 56 be extended to all the days of the week."— (*Mr. A. J. Balfour*).

Sir H. CAMPBELL-BANNERMAN (Stirling Burghs) : The Resolution which the right hon. Gentleman has proposed is in accordance with recent practice, and I do not imagine that there will be any large number of Members in the House who will be disposed to refuse to the Government the facilities they ask for in the circumstances. But I think it right to lay down at once what hitherto has always been prescribed as a condition for this provisional facility being given to the Government at this time of the year, and that is, that they should not use the power so allowed to them for the purpose of introducing any fresh contentious measure likely to occupy much time and to raise deep controversies in the House. The list of measures which the right hon. Gentleman has gone over contains many Bills with which we are tolerably familiar, and there are some which there is a general desire to pass with as little trouble as possible. I anticipate that that will be the case with the Scottish Private Procedure Bill, as to which we see some method of arranging the differences of opinion which have hitherto existed. But the right hon. Gentlemen named four new subjects. I think one was called the Barracks Loan Bill—a Bill which is announced in supplement, as it were, of the Army Estimates, and which was promised at the beginning of the session. Well, Sir, the only comment I would make, and the only objection I would raise to the introduction of that Bill is not that it ought not to be introduced now, but that it ought to have been introduced a good many weeks if not months ago, because when it was announced the Government surely must have had not only a general but a very close conception of what the nature of this Bill would be, and I think it is due to the House and to those who take an interest in military questions that they

should have a longer time to consider the details of this Bill than the few weeks which now stand between us and the Prorogation of Parliament. As to the Factories Bill, that will probably be a measure in a direction of which we all approve, but we must wait until we see it. In regard to the Bill for taking over the Niger Company, I would also say that there is a large possibility—I am speaking entirely in the dark as to what the Bill may contain—but I think, if it contains any complications whatever, there is a considerable possibility of a difference of opinion. The right hon. Gentleman named, in a somewhat cool and calm manner, another Bill as if it was an old acquaintance that we were familiar with, and to which we already were committed —namely, the Clerical Tithes Bill. I can only say that if the right hon. Gentleman thinks that a Bill dealing with clerical tithes in any way almost, but especially a Bill relieving them from any burdens to which they are now subject—if he thinks that a Bill of that kind can pass through the House in the few weeks of July and part of August, he is totally mistaken. And there is another particular process which it may be sought to apply to this measure, to which I should, for my part, take great objection. We know that clerical influences are clamouring at the door of the Government. We know that from the papers and other sources. Is it possible that this is a Bill intended to be introduced in order to shut the mouths of the clergy, and at the same time introduced in such a manner that there will be a good excuse for saying to them, "My good gentlemen, we have done all we could for you, but a wicked Opposition and the stupid arrangements for the conduct of Parliamentary business compelled us to forego the infinite pleasure we should have felt in doing something"? I do not think that the House of Commons should be treated to a performance of that sort, and if the right hon. Gentleman brings in a Bill—I do not say I hope it will pass— at least I hope that he will bring it in with the intention of its passing, because I think it would be more befitting his own dignity and the dignity of this House and of Parliament that he should bring it in with that intention. But in any case I should strongly advise the right hon. Gentleman, if he does not wish to keep us sitting here until an advanced period of the year, not to meddle with this measure at all.

It is not only that it would be discussed at great length and with great detail in all its stages, but I am afraid that the fact of its being announced, of its looming on the horizon, may induce hon. Members to take a minute and painstaking interest in all the other business, which would not conduce to the rapid advancement of the legislation of the session. I hope the right hon. Gentleman will take my warning, which is not a mere accidental expression of my own opinion, for I am perfectly certain it conveys not only the feeling but the purpose of nine-tenths of the Members on this side of the House, and possibly of some others. I hope that he will take that into consideration when he thinks of proceeding with this Bill during this session. Otherwise, as I have said, I think he has not proposed anything which is calculated to startle and alarm us, and under the circumstances I am disposed to think that the House ought to afford him the facilities he asks for.

SIR CHARLES DILKE (Gloucester, Forest of Dean) : In every word that has fallen from the Leader of the Opposition I am disposed to concur, but there is one subject as to which I wish to say a few words. It is a matter to which a great deal of attention has been given in this portion of the House—I refer to the Factories and Workshops Bill, which it has been announced is to be introduced at this terribly late period of the session, although it was promised, long before the Queen's Speech was delivered, that it would be one of the principal measures of the session. We had two speeches made by Cabinet Ministers in which they appealed for the confidence of the working classes of the country, on the ground that next to the London Government Bill a Factories and Workshops Bill would be one of the chief measures of the session. I cannot but fear that the fact of keeping back this Bill till so late a period means either that it will not be passed or that it will be cut down to the narrowest possible limits. I am bound to say that I should object more strongly to the latter of the two alternatives than to the former, because if the Bill is only intended to deal with two or three points it will be a great disappointment to the country. If, on the other hand, it is to be a large Bill, then I fear the Government do not intend to go on with it, because they would not have the time

Sir H. Campbell-Bannerman.

necessary to carry it this year; and I, for one, would sooner have from them a distinct and clear promise that they will really make it one of the principal measures next session, instead of cutting it down to a mere shred in order to pass it this year. It has always been spoken of as a very important measure. The Home Secretary has stated that there is a very large Bill in preparation, and has made it an excuse for the delay in producing the annual report of the Chief Inspector of Workshops, with the result that we shall have no material for a Home Office Debate this session. Now I would like to point out that the Standing Committees on Trade and Law have been idle during the greater part of this session. One has had before it the Food and Drugs Bill, and the other has had hardly any work at all. If it is now intended to revive the work of these Committees for the purpose of passing the Factories and Workshops Bill, there will be great difficulty at this period of the session in obtaining a quorum, and I am afraid the result will be that the Bill will have to be cut down to the very narrowest limits. Would it not be better to make the best of a bad job, and have a thoroughly good Bill next year ? There is only one other matter I will touch upon. The Government, during the last three or four years, have steadily declined, under pressure from all parts of the House, to find time at this period of the session for private Members' Bills. But there is a rumour that it is the intention of the Government to give some of the time which we are placing at their disposal to the consideration of a hotly opposed private Members' Bill — the Service Franchise Bill, which was extended into a large measure by an Amendment carried in a very thin House, which Amendment was subsequently defeated in a fairly full House by a majority of only 17. In view of the declarations of Irish Members in regard to this Bill, I think we should have some understanding from the Government that they are not going to devote any time to it.

MR DILLON (Mayo, E.): When a motion of this kind is submitted to the House one is entitled to ask for some satisfactory statement as to what the Government intend to do with the time they ask the House to give them. The list of Bills which the right hon. Gentleman read out, and upon which he based his statement for demanding the time of the House, includes three Irish Bills, all of them very important Bills and raising important questions of principle. I desire to take this opportunity of once more protesting against the conduct of the Government in introducing two of their Irish Bills this session under the Ten-Minutes Rule, especially in view of the fact that the Government have done less business than I ever remember during the 15 years I have been in the House. I think the Irish Members have very good ground for complaining that the Irish business, such as it is this session, has been treated with such scant courtesy up to the present period of the session. I say that no one of those Bills could decently have been introduced under the Ten-Minutes Rule, and that such a course is an outrageous abuse in the case of one of those Bills. The first of the Irish Bills—the Agriculture and Technical Instruction Bill—has been promised every year since the present Government took office. It is a Bill raising very large and very broad issues and issues of various kinds, because it proposes to create a new Irish Minister. Of course, I should not be in order in attempting to deal, even in the most cursory way, with the details of the Bill, but it is a Bill of first-class importance, and yet we have been unable to obtain from the Government the probable date on which it will be taken; and now, when we are within about six weeks of the end of the session, we have not received a hint as to when we may expect this Bill to be submitted for discussion. I think we are entitled to demand from the Government that abundant time shall be given for the discussion of this Bill on Second Reading, and still fuller discussion in Committee. I would infinitely prefer that this Bill should be postponed until next session, and then taken at a proper period of the session, rather than that an attempt should be made to shuffle it through at the tail end of the session and force a totally unsatisfactory settlement of this question. I believe and feel convinced that in that view I have the support of the vast majority of Irishmen of all sections. Turning to the other Bills, I am entitled to ask whether the Charitable Loans Bill—a Bill of vital importance to a very large section of the people of the North of Ireland—is to be dropped out altogether. I think the Government ought to say

frankly whether they propose to go on with that Bill this session or not. Now I come to the third of the Irish Bills, an all-important Bill, and I earnestly and respectfully invite the attention of the Liberal Party to this Bill, and to its connection with the Clerical Tithe Bill, which we are informed the Government intend to introduce. It appears it is impossible for the Government to allow one session to go by without putting their hands into the public purse to scatter largess among their supporters in Great Britain and Ireland. While they are about to propose some measure of relief to the clergy in England, they also intend to seize upon a large portion of the Tithe Fund and distribute it among the landlords in Ireland. As the Leader of the Opposition has indicated that possibly, if the Clerical Tithes Bill is introduced, the Liberal Party may be incited to take a great interest in other Bills, I respectfully invite them to turn their attention to the Irish Tithes Bill. They will find it very contentious as well as interesting, and they will be doing a service to Ireland if they study the subject and give some attention to it. I think we might expect from the Chief Secretary some different treatment to the very curt statement we have received in reference to this Bill up to the present. With reference to Supply, what is the condition of things at the present moment? Twenty days is the number allotted for Supply under the new Rule. On the 19th of June, 14 out of the 20 days had gone, and the Government have taken only 57 out of a total of 147 Votes on Supply. Among the Votes still to be disposed of is the Foreign Office Vote; some of the next most important are the Army and Navy Votes and the Colonial Office Vote. The First Lord has kindly consented to give two days this week for Irish Supply. I have had occasion to point out more than once that those responsible for the time of the House have not dealt favourably with Irish Supply. In the first year of the new Rule four days, and in later years three days, and now only two days. I venture to say that this year Irish Supply will demand more time than in any year since this Government came into office. There is, first of all, the Vote for law charges; then there is the Local Government Board Vote, which, owing to the Act of last year, will have to be discussed at length. There is the Queen's College Vote, which should be discussed at considerable length, inasmuch as no Amendment to the Address was moved on the Catholic University Question. There is, further, the Law Charges Vote and the Constabulary Vote, and then there is a question which will undoubtedly be discussed at considerable length on the Industrial Schools Grant. That Grant used to be passed without a word, but this year it will lead to a long Debate. Then there is the Chief Secretary's Salary, and the Board of Works Vote. Here we have eight Votes in Irish Supply, upon which inevitably there will be very considerable discussion. I desire to point out that, in justice to Irish Members, a fair portion of the time now placed at the disposal of the Government ought to be given for the discussion of the important measures I have mentioned. I further desire to support the demand that time should be allowed for the discussion of the Cyprus Vote. With other hon. Members, I have taken great interest in the condition of Cyprus, and we are anxious there should be a discussion this year, because a Convention is on the eve of being concluded with the Sultan of Turkey for the conversion and settlement of the Debt, to the payment of the interest on which the Cyprus tribute is devoted. We think that those interested should have a fair opportunity of discussing this, because we are anxious that the benefits of the conversion should go to Cyprus, and not to France, Germany, or any other Power.

SIR BLUNDELL MAPLE (Camberwell, Dulwich): I desire to ask the right hon. Gentleman the Leader of the House to give an opportunity for the Service Franchise Bill to pass. The right hon. Gentleman opposite who referred to this Bill has done all that he possibly could to obstruct it. He is, I may say, practically the only Member really obstructing the Bill. On the 25th March the Bill was carried by a majority of 100, 188 voting for the Bill, whereas he and his supporters only numbered 88. The Bill at this moment is in exactly the condition in which it was introduced. It is a very important Bill, and one which will be welcomed by thousands of men who ought to have votes given them. I may say that a worse obstruction than this Bill has met with from the hands of the right hon. Gentleman opposite has never

Sir H. Campbell-Bannerman.

occurred to any Bill. I do not oppose the Government taking next Wednesday, although this Bill would have been first Order on that day, because I feel that the Government will realise the importance of the Bill, and the strong support it has in the country at large. I trust the Government may "star" the Bill, and allow it to be again proceeded with.

MR. BRYCE (Aberdeen, S.): Before the right hon. Gentleman answers the various questions which have been put to him, I should like to ask whether he can state when he proposes to take the Board of Education Bill, and, if he cannot state that now, whether he will give some days' notice before he proposes to take the Second Reading.

MR. GALLOWAY (Manchester, S.W.): There is a notice on the Paper for the appointment of a Select Committee to consider the subject of municipal trading. The right hon. Gentleman did not mention that subject in his remarks, and I wish to ask whether it is the intention of the Government to appoint that Committee, for I understand there will be some opposition to the appointment. If the Government do not intend to appoint it, will the right hon. Gentleman say so now, and have the motion removed from the Order Paper. May I be allowed to join in the appeal of the hon. Member for Dulwich in regard to his Bill. I do not know whether the First Lord of the Treasury is aware of the nature of the opposition which has so far existed to this Bill. The right hon. Gentleman the Member for the Forest of Dean said that this Bill was hotly opposed; therefore I think I shall be in order in pointing out to the right hon. Gentleman how hotly this Bill has been opposed. It was so hotly opposed that, when it was in front of the Bill for raising the age of half-timers the opposition was absolutely withdrawn after ten minutes or a quarter of an hour's discussion, and then this other Bill was taken. And on the following Wednesday after the Bill had been read, then, and then only, did the opposition of the right hon. Gentleman and his friends arise to the Service Franchise Bill. I believe also that several Members are not quite clear as to whether it is the intention of the Government to give a day of Supply for the discussion of the South African Vote as soon as the Papers have arrived about which the Colonial Secretary has spoken.

*Mr. RECKITT (Lincolnshire, Brigg) : There is one point upon which I should like to have an announcement before we go to a Division, and that is the question of the Petroleum Bill. Members of the House who were present on the 15th March will doubtless remember that my Bill would probably have got a Second Reading had it not been for the fact that the Under Secretary for the Home Office asked the House to reject the Bill upon that occasion upon the ground that the Government were about to introduce a Bill of their own upon the subject ; and that not only were they about to introduce a Bill of their own, but the Bill was in a forward state of preparation. After the defeat of my Bill the right hon. Gentleman was asked when this Bill was to be introduced, and he said, "As soon as possible, or shortly after Easter." Another question was asked on 14th April, and we were then told that the Bill would be introduced "very shortly," or at any rate "before the end of the month." I had a conversation with the right hon. Gentleman, and he hoped the Bill would be introduced before Whitsun. But Whitsuntide has gone by, and now the Government are taking the whole time of the House and no mention has been made of the intention of the Government with regard to legislation on petroleum. I think this is a time at which I should ask what their intentions are, because I do feel that when a private Member introduces a Bill in this House and it is conceived necessary for the Government to instruct one of the Under Secretaries to oppose the Bill, and the Bill is practically defeated on those grounds, and on a pledge that a Government Bill would be introduced, that pledge should be redeemed in something like reasonable time. No one can say that it is a reasonable time to introduce a Bill which, while not of a party character, is certainly of a controversial character, at so late a period of the session as that at which we have now arrived. I sincerely hope the right hon. Gentleman will be able to make some statement as to why this Bill has not yet been introduced, because the causes and evils are still going on, the deaths and accidents are still mounting up, but apparently the Government do not wish to take any cognisance of this matter. It

may be put now, I suppose, in the same category as legislation in regard to automatic couplings. I should also like to call the attention of the right hon. Gentleman to another Bill which has not yet been introduced — the Agricultural Holdings Bill. That Bill has been mentioned in every Queen's Speech since 1895, and has always occupied more or less the same lowly position of last on the list ; but the First Lord of the Treasury, when his attention was called to the matter, remarked that it did not necessarily follow that it would not have a very much earlier place when introduced for the purpose of a Second Reading Debate. We have had no mention whatever of the Bill yet, and I doubt whether the solicitude of the Government is sincere in regard to the interests of the farmers from whom they so very often derive the bulk of their support when they appeal to the country. It will, I hope, be an object-lesson to the agriculturists that the Government are in the habit of making these promises, but apparently have not the wish or intention to fulfil them. Unless I have a satisfactory answer to my question in regard to the introduction of the Petroleum Bill I am afraid I shall have to trouble the House to take a Division.

Mr. GIBSON BOWLES (Lynn Regis) : The remark of the right hon. Gentleman opposite that the Government make promises which they are not anxious to fulfil is a little inopportune, because my complaint is that the Government have announced their intention of bringing in a number of Bills which were not mentioned at the beginning of the session. This is always a painful moment when the House is asked to set aside the Standing Orders, and take the time of private Members. But we can scarcely drop a tear over either the Standing Orders or the private Member ; both have been almost wiped out by repeated inroads upon them. The right hon. Gentleman opposite said that this motion is usually made on the ground that unless the whole of the time of the House is taken the Government will not have time in the remaining part of the session to pass all the measures to which they are pledged. But the right hon. Gentleman the Leader of the House has gone a step beyond that, because he has announced three or four Bills of first-class importance which are to be introduced, three of which, at any rate, turn upon money. Take the Military Works Bill. There has been a great deal too much military works; you are trusting too much to bricks and mortar, and whatever these military works are that are now proposed they will mean money. Then there is the Naval Works Bill. One of the great reproaches against the right hon. Gentleman the First Lord of the Admiralty is that, ceasing to trust in ships, he, too, has put his trust in bricks and mortar. Bricks and mortar will be the death of the Navy, unless we stop this constant expenditure upon that kind of defence. But the naval works mean money, and millions have already been spent both on military works and on naval works—millions which have been taken out of the surpluses and diverted from their proper destination. Then there is the Clerical Tithes Bill, which, of course, means money. I wish to ask whether all this money is to come out of further Supplemental Estimates. In the Debates on the Finance Bill I ventured to suggest that the Chancellor of the Exchequer had not reckoned upon any Supplemental Estimates, which, according to our present experience, meant an extra two millions a year; but he interrupted me and said that this year there would be no Supplemental Estimates. But all these Bills, which mean money, mean also Supplemental Estimates; if they do not mean that, they mean loans, so that we shall be in the position, after stopping the repayment of our public debt, of adding further large sums to that debt. The fourth Bill is for taking over the responsibilities of the Niger Company. That is an enormous new departure in policy, which may raise most serious questions. I do hope the Government will not embark upon this Bill in the spirit of the remarks of the right hon. Gentleman—that it will have to be passed by the end of the session. It will be an extremely difficult Bill to pass if it in any way answers to its name. I would make one suggestion for the saving of time, and that is that Her Majesty's Government should announce that they are going to drop the Undersized Fish Bill. No harm will be done by that being left over for another year, and by that time the undersized fish will have got a little larger, and the Government's knowledge of fish generally will have become rather greater. The supply of fish has enormously increased, so that there is no

Mr. Gibson Bowles.

immediate pressure for this Bill, and I would respectfully suggest that it should be dropped, and that the fishing industry should not be worried by the passing of a Bill which will not prevent them catching the fish, but only prevent the sale when they are caught.

MR. EDMUND ROBERTSON (Dundee): I think there is some misconception as to the Naval Works Bill.

MR. GIBSON BOWLES: We have not seen it yet.

MR. EDMUND ROBERTSON: The reason why there is to be a Naval Works Bill is because the money is to be raised by loan. That has been perfectly well understood since the beginning of the session. On this point I trust the right hon. Gentleman the First Lord of the Treasury will give us some more definite information about the state of the Bill than has been furnished. The Naval Works Bill which we have had has simply been a continuation Bill. The Government suspended some of the Standing Orders of this House, and all the Standing Orders of the other House, in order to carry the Army Annual Bill, which was quite unnecessary, and I can see no justification for the delay which has taken place in the introduction of this Bill this year. The whole of the interest is now centred in the schedule, for the principle of it has been asserted over and over again. The schedule is now the only thing to which interest attaches, and, as I understand the First Lord of the Admiralty, the schedule this year will be of special importance because it contains new items. As these items may give rise to a good deal of discussion, I think we are entitled to have from the Government a positive statement that the Bill is ready to be produced, and that all the urgency that can be applied to it will be applied, and that we shall have the Bill printed at the earliest possible date at the convenience of the Government. I hope the right hon. Gentleman will give the House some information as to the intentions of the Government in respect to this important measure.

*MR. WILLIAM JOHNSTON (Belfast, S.): I rise for a moment or two to press upon the right hon. Gentleman the great importance of allowing the Agriculture and Technical Instruction (Ireland) Bill to pass through the House this session. There is scarcely any Bill upon which there is a more unanimous feeling in Ireland in its favour, for it has met with the warmest approval in all quarters. The right hon. Gentleman, in his statement, did not dwell with much warmth on this Bill. I know that the Chief Secretary for Ireland takes a very deep interest in the measure, and the Members of the Belfast Chamber of Commerce are most anxious that it should be passed this session, not only in the interests of agriculture, but also in the interests of the whole of Ireland. I trust that the right hon. Gentleman will give the House a distinct assurance that this measure will receive attention, for it will relieve the minds of many people in Ireland who take a great interest in technical instruction. I will not occupy the time of the House any longer, and I earnestly express the hope that this Bill will be carried to a successful issue this session.

MR. SWIFT MacNEILL (Donegal, S.): I intend to be very brief in the remarks I shall address to the House. I want the right hon. Gentleman to forget for the moment that he is the First Lord of the Treasury, and to look at this question from the point of view of what is honourable between man and man. The subject I am raising is one which commands much sympathy upon both sides of the House. I want to know when the Government intend introducing legislation for the regulation of limited companies. This measure has been promised four times already, and yet a Bill has not been introduced in reference to it, although nearly all the Members of this House have expressed themselves in favour of doing away with the gigantic system of fraud which under the present state of legislation is rendered possible. It is little short of a crying scandal that in the month of March, 1898, the Lord Chief Justice stated that 24,000,000 of money were squandered every year because no amendment had been made in the law, The right hon. Gentleman will recollect the incident when I moved an Amendment to the Address dealing with this very subject, when it received the careful attention of the House, and I may add that, at the time, not a single newspaper took exception to legislation being intro-

duced upon this subject, and if ever there was legislation that was popular—except with guinea pigs and company promoters —it is this. Why has this Bill not been introduced? I would like to see any hon. Member of this House standing before his constituents and saying that he is not in favour of this Bill. Is the influence of the guinea pigs in the Lobby too strong for the Government, or is there a majority of company directors in the Cabinet? I desire to ask for a clear explanation of this. It may be said in reply that legislation has been introduced in another place. I do not know whether that is so or not, but it has not come down to this House yet. I ask the right hon. Gentleman, as a matter of fair dealing between man and man, why has the promise in reference to this measure not been fulfilled? Is it because—as a Tory Member has said—this House is honeycombed and moth-eaten with company promoters? Is the company promoting interest in this House so strong as to prevent legislation being passed to stop a gross system of mean, cowardly, and debasing fraud? Here we have the strongest Government of this century, with a majority of 150 behind them, practically confessing that they are unable to deal with this subject. And why? Is it because they are only in favour of legislation for selfish and guinea-pig interests?

CAPTAIN SINCLAIR (Forfarshire): I should like the right hon. Gentleman to say whether some further opportunity will be given for the discussion of Scotch business. Friday night's discussion elicited a very strong expression of opinion, which was shared upon both sides of the House, upon a point which I need not mention now. That discussion was not ended, and no conclusion was come to. I therefore wish to ask the right hon. Gentleman if he will be good enough to bear in mind, when he is considering the question, the enormous importance of this subject to Scotland, and to state to-day when he will afford a further opportunity for the continuation of the discussion which was carried on on Friday night last. The discussion to which I refer was upon the question of the Education Minute, and both sides of the House then argued very generally and strongly in a direction adverse to the Government upon this point. I may also point out that there are several other Scotch Votes on which there has been no opportunity for discussion. As the Half-timers' Bill has now reached a very forward stage in Parliament, I would remind the right hon. Gentleman that there is a similar measure on the Paper in the name of a private Member. There is a very strong feeling in Scotland that this is a question of much less scope and less difficult to deal with than in England, and I do ask the First Lord of the Treasury to consider the unenviable position which Scotland has been left in with regard to this matter, which is one which has excited a good deal of interest in Scotland.

. MR. COGHILL (Stoke-upon-Trent): I desire to urge upon the Government the necessity of proceeding with the Clerical Tithes Bill. I am surprised at the remarks made by the Leader of the Opposition in regard to this measure, for he seems to have reserved all his opposition for this particular measure. I hope the First Lord of the Treasury will not be frightened by the threats of the Leader of the Opposition, and that he will persist in bringing forward this Bill, which I am sure will give great satisfaction in the country.

MR. CHANNING (Northampton, E.): I have no doubt the measure alluded to by my hon. friend will give great satisfaction in the country, especially to those who wish to see the downfall of the present Ministry. One might have supported the Government at this stage of the session if the right hon. Gentleman had limited his proposals to the measures which were contained in the Queen's Speech, for in regard to some of the very useful measures to which he referred no exception could be taken. We know perfectly well what the present proposal of the Government means. It means that useful Bills, like the Money Lending Bill —which is of great importance to the country—the Sale of Food and Drugs Bill, and other important Bills, will be imperilled in order that the Government may be able to spring a certain Report upon the House of Commons and rush through this House, by the force of their great majority, what is nothing but the appropriation of public money and the rating of other people for the relief of one particular class of their supporters. I hope hon. Members will take a Division against this proposal, if only as a protest against

Captain Sinclair.

the policy of the Government in endeavouring to repeat the experiment which they carried out in reference to the Agricultural Rating Act.

*MR. CARVELL WILLIAMS (Nottingham, Mansfield): I do not rise for the purpose of championing the cause of private Members, for they seem to me to be past praying for. What I wish to point out to the Government is this—if the House passes this Resolution the Government will have a considerable amount of time placed at their disposal. Therefore they could use some of that time in trying to pass a measure which the Home Secretary has stated was practically ready, and which he is anxious to introduce. I refer to the Bill for giving practical effect to the recommendations of the Select Committee on Burial Grounds. The majority of that Committee was composed of Ministerial Members, but both Churchmen and Nonconformists were represented. Now, that Committee has arrived at conclusions which would form the basis of a satisfactory measure. I do not say that the subject is considered to be wholly uncontentious, but it is no longer a Party question. I know hon. Members on the other side are as anxious as we are on this side for an early settlement of the question, and it seems to me that it will be a great pity for the Government to lose so favourable an opportunity of dealing with the subject. If the measure be introduced, it will occupy a great deal less time and cause much less trouble than the Bill to give a large amount of public money to the clergy of the Church of England. I hope the Government will introduce the measure, even if they fail to pass it this session, as I believe it would hasten the close of a very painful and protracted struggle.

MR. LABOUCHERE (Northampton): I am afraid we shall at this time of the session have to leave the dead to bury its dead. Apart from all questions of political differences, it does seem to me a mistake, at the advent of that happy moment when we shall cease to have the pleasure of each others' society, to suddenly spring three or four new Bills on the House. I do not think the Leader of the House ought fairly and honestly to do it unless he can show that it has been rendered necessary by circumstances which now exist, and which are different from those which obtained at the commencement of the session. The Leader of the Opposition did not exaggerate in the least when he said that if this clerical Bill is brought in we shall take a most exhaustive and minute interest in every other Bill, with the deliberate and open intention of defeating this Bill so far as we can possibly do it by effluxion of time. I never conceal the fact when I am obstructing. Under the circumstances, if a Bill of this kind is brought in at the close of the session, we shall have a right to render it, so far as we possibly can, impossible for the Government to pass it. We on this side may differ from the views of the Government, but they have a large majority, and if they brought in a Bill at the commencement of the session I should not attempt to obstruct it; but this Bill was not alluded to in the Queen's Speech, and I certainly gathered from the observations of the Chancellor of the Exchequer to a deputation a little while ago that it was not intended to legislate on this matter this year. As a matter of fact, the Chancellor of the Exchequer said that he would not include the money required for it in his Budget, and he did not give the slightest hint that this Bill was to be brought in. Under these circumstances it does appear to me to be a mistake—and I say it not from any Party feeling—to bring in at this time of the session a Bill of such a very controversial nature. There was one Bill to which the right hon. Gentleman alluded, but he did not say he would attempt to pass it, and that is the Money Lending Bill. That Bill is in a very different position. The subject was referred to a very able Committee last session, many witnesses were heard, and a Report which I believe was unanimous was communicated to the House. The Bill was alluded to in the Queen's Speech. I refer to the matter myself because I very much regret that my hon. friend who took such an active and able interest in it is away. The Bill has already passed the House of Lords, and I do not think it would take a very long time to pass through this House. It would do a very large amount of good, and I hope the right hon. Gentleman will tell us that he is not going to push forward this clerical Bill, of which we know nothing at present, and that he will give facilities—for it is a Government measure—for passing the Money Lending Bill.

*Mr. J. E. ELLIS (Nottinghamshire, Rushcliffe): I wish to ask the right hon. Gentleman with reference to the Board of Education Bill, if he cannot name the time when he proposes to introduce it, whether he would tell us how much notice he will give. I wish also to associate myself with all that has been said as to the undesirability of springing on the House of Commons on this the 19th day of June such a controversial matter as the Clergy Bill. I go further than my right hon. friend the Leader of the Opposition, and say that no really controversial Bill should be announced or brought forward by the Government after Whitsuntide. I yield to no man in my admiration of some of the qualities of the Leader of the House, but I am bound to say that, compared with some of his predecessors, of whom I have seen five or six, he fails sometimes—I say so with all respect — as regards the ordinary, everyday, humdrum business of the House in the matter of procedure. The only way in which we can have that reasonable certainty which everyone desires is for the Government, between Easter and Whitsuntide, to get forward with the Second Readings of their larger Bills and some of their minor Bills, to utilise the Grand Committees in the way suggested by the right hon. Baronet the Member for the Forest of Dean, and then to proceed as rapidly as possible with nothing but Committee work after Whitsuntide. The right hon. Gentleman has given a great measure of reasonable certainty with regard to Supply — I congratulate him very much on it — and he gives us a reasonable notice of a week or ten days as to what Supply is to be taken on Fridays. I would venture to very respectfully suggest whether he would not give us next session a reasonable certainty also in regard to other business. The worst thing any Government can do is to announce in the later days in June a Bill which will be a very controversial measure.

Mr. ARTHUR J. MOORE (Derry City): I desire, before the right hon. Gentleman answers all these questions, to join with the hon. Member for South Belfast in urging on him the extreme necessity of pressing forward the Agriculture and Technical Instruction (Ireland) Bill. This is of the very greatest import ance, and anyone who has any knowledge of the magnificent work done by the hon. Member for South Dublin, without any Government assistance, must see that there is a great future on the same lines which this Bill proposes. I daresay it will be necessary to consider the Bill very closely, and to press on the Government certain modifications in Committee, but I earnestly hope that this Bill may not be abandoned. It is a very important Bill, which is earnestly desired, not only by the large towns, particularly in the North of Ireland, but also by the a;ricultural districts in the West of Ireland. I hope the right hon. Gentleman will be able to assure us that he is in a position to fix an early date for the further consideration of the Bill.

MR. A. J. BALFOUR: I have had a large number of critics—kindly critics I admit—in the course of this Debate, and they belong to various classes. There are gentlemen who think we have brought forward too many Bills, there are gentlemen who think we have not brought forward enough of Bills, and there are gentlemen who think that it is our bounden duty to press through certain Bills in which they are interested, but who at the same time say that the Bills would require very close scrutiny. We all know that that is a House of Commons euphemism for a considerable amount of debate. The hon. Member who spoke last but one —the Member for the Rushcliffe Division —complains of the method in which Government business has been arranged in the course of the present session, and says we have got into a tangle.

*MR. J. E. ELLIS: I said before Easter.

MR. A. J. BALFOUR: I do not remember a session in which Government business was less entangled, and I have less hesitation in making the observation because I attribute none of the credit to myself, and I gladly recognise that both sides of the House have seconded the Government in carrying out the work. The Government business has, as I think both before and after Easter, gone through with remarkable smoothness. The hon. Gentleman further says that all Bills which we hope to make progress with ought to be read a second time before Whitsun, and he specially referred to the

Mr. Arthur J. Moore.

Clerical Tithes Bill of which so much unexpected notice has been taken by hon. Members opposite. I think there might be a good deal to be said for that course, and I might in the innocence of my heart have assented to and easily fallen in with it. But now it appears everything is to be stopped until the Bill is withdrawn, and I therefore congratulate myself that I did not carry out the policy of the hon. Gentleman and read the Bill a second time before Whitsuntide. I am not, of course, discussing the provisions of the Bill, though I must say they loom too largely in the somewhat heated imagination of hon. Gentlemen opposite. But there is one criticism of which I really must complain. Hon. Members talk as if no notice or hint had been given that the Government desired to deal with this question. It was perfectly well known that the Government desired to deal with it, and so well was it known that the right hon. Baronet the Member for the Forest of Dean asked me a question last week on the subject, and I made no concealment, and framed my answer in such a way that anybody listening to me would know that it was one of the subjects which the Government were anxious to introduce. It is a measure not quite of the first importance in a Parliamentary sense, but it is a very much needed act of justice. The hon. Gentleman the Member for East Mayo, and some other hon. Gentlemen also, asked me a great many questions about the distribution of the time for Supply. I do not think that the Debate on this resolution is on modern conditions a very fitting opportunity for discussing the allocation of the time for Supply. It is impossible for the Government to give more time under the Sessional Order than they have given, and I do not think pressure ought to be put upon us in this Debate to distribute such time as we have got more favourably to one section of this House than to another. But I must observe that the hon. Member for East Mayo has chosen this opportunity to raise again the criticisms he has more than once delivered on the introduction by the Government of Bills under the Ten-Minutes Rule. It appears to me that any Bill which is not of a long and complicated character may properly and wisely be introduced under that rule. In common with every private Member in the House, he has the right to introduce a Bill of the greatest conceivable importance and complexity, not only without the amount of discussion and explanation which is avoided under the Ten-Minutes Rule, but without any discussion or explanation at all, and practically without even the power of taking a hostile vote. I maintain that in these circumstances, when the Government are introducing Bills not of great complexity, and which can be easily explained in the compass of the Ten-Minutes Rule, it is really a judicious and wise saving of the time of the House that that Rule should be taken advantage of. I grant, of course, that there may be great constitutional issues—like the London Government Bill—which ought not to be dealt with under that Rule, but, on the whole, I hope the general feeling of the House is in favour of proceeding under that Rule rather than reverting to the more antiquated and complicated procedure which is justified in some cases, but which only should be used when absolutely necessary. The hon. Gentleman has told us what view he takes of the Irish Agriculture and Technical Instruction Bill, and these differ fundamentally from those of other hon. Gentlemen from Ireland who have spoken strongly in favour of it. The Bill is not a large measure, but it is an important one. I believe all classes in Ireland desire that that Bill should be passed except the hon. Member for Mayo.

MR. DILLON : What I said was that the Bill was exceedingly defective, and that it would require very full discussion. I further said that I would rather see a good Bill passed next year than a bad Bill this year.

MR. A. J. BALFOUR : Whether the Bill can be improved or not I will not anticipate. I am sorry the hon. Member takes the view he does, and I am sure that only a small section of House share the hon. Gentleman's opinion.

MR. DILLON : All I ask is reasonable time for the discussion of the Bill.

MR. A. J. BALFOUR : We may differ as to what reasonable time is. The right hon. Gentleman the Member for South Aberdeen and the hon. Gentleman the Member for the Rushcliffe Division of Nottinghamshire asked me a supplemental question to that put to me from this side

of the House in regard to the Secondary Education Bill. I greatly desire to see that Bill passed into law this session, and I will give adequate not ce as to when it comes on. I would not like to pledge myself, however, as to the number of days' notice which I will give when the Bill is to be taken. I do not know that I need discuss the views of the hon. Member for Brigg, who has expressed a desire for the introduction of the departmental Bills, and, still further, that a Bill should be introduced on petroleum. If the hon. Gentleman wants to see the Bill, I might be able to arrange with my right hon. friend.

MR. RECKITT : I only asked that the pledge given at the time by the Under Secretary for the Home Department, who made a speech against the Bill introduced by a private Member, should be redeemed. On more than one occasion, in answer to questions in the House, the promise was made that that pledge would be carried out.

MR. A. J. BALFOUR : I was not aware that a promise had been given, and I should like to see the terms of the promise. But if a promise was made to introduce a Bill in the course of the present session, that, promise of course, must be kept. I certainly cannot undertake to give the time for that "reasonable discussion." which the hon. Member for East Mayo desires for the Irish Bill in which he has expressed an interest. I do not think I need say anything about the Naval Works Bill, except that when criticisms have been passed on the Government for not bringing it in earlier in the session, I would remind the hon. Gentlemen that the later it is brought in the more possible is it to foresee the works which will have to be carried out under the Act when the Bill becomes law. I do not think I need say anything more. We have been told that there is not time to pass the Bills on the Paper, and we have been also pressed to bring in and pass a great many more Bills; but these two criticisms are mutually contradictory. It is impossible, at the present stage of the session, to foresee what amount of business we shall get through. But, in spite of the threat or the gloomy prophecy of the right hon. Gentleman opposite, I hope the House will continue the discussion of the Bills for the remainder of the session in the same business like way it has shown hitherto.

MR. SWIFT MacNEILL: What about the Company Promoters' Bill?

MR. A. J. BALFOUR: That is one of the Bills that I a n urged to introduce by the very Gentleman whose friends tell me that I cannot pass the Bills already on the Paper.

MR. SWIFT MacNEILL: It is in the Lords; why don't you bring it down here?

MR. A. J. BALFOUR: We are now discussing the business of the Commons, and we have neither the right nor the title to go beyond that. My hon. friend and colleague in the representation of Manchester asked me whether we could find time for discussing the Committee on Municipal Trading. I cannot promise to find time for that.

SIR H. CAMPBELL-BANNERMAN: What about Private Members' Bills?

MR. A. J. BALFOUR: It is far too early to consider whether the Government could conceivably take under their protection any Private Members'Bills, and certainly I cannot be betrayed into expressing any view on that subject. Indeed I have not any view upon it; and if I had I should be much too wise to express it at the present stage of the session.

MR. TENNANT (Berwickshire): What does the right hon. Gentleman say about the Factories Bill?

MR. A. J. BALFOUR: The right hon. Baronet the member for the Forest of Dean says he would rather see a large and complete measure introduced next year, or in some subsequent session, than a deficient and incomplete measure this session. I will consult my right hon. friend the Home Secretary on that question; but I may say, in the meantime, that I understood from him that, useful as a Bill dealing with dangerous trades would be, a good deal has been done since last year in framing rules governing these dangerous trades, and that the necessity of introducing a measure is not nearly so pressing as it was when we had a discussion on the subject last July. But I will consult with my right hon. friend whether, after the observations of the right hon. Baronet, anything would be gained by introducing a Bill this session.

MR. GALLOWAY: As the Notice of Motion for the Select Committee on Municipal Trading is put down every day, will the right hon. Gentleman undertake not to take it without giving us notice when he will take it?

MR. A. J. BALFOUR: It seems to me that that is one of those resolutions which the Government are surely justified in taking at any opportunity they have. It is greatly to be regretted that the inquiry is blocked in any part of the House; but I do not think that, in submitting to such an inconvenience, I am called upon to give a day's notice of the time at which the discussion will be brought on.

MR. WALLACE (Perth): Can the right hon. Gentleman tell us when the Clerical Tithes Bill will come on?

MR. A. J. BALFOUR: I think I had better not say anything about that.

Question put.

The House divided: Ayes, 250; Noes, 119. (Division List No. 195.)

AYES.

Acland-Hood, Capt. Sir A. F.
Aird, John
Anson, Sir William Reynell
Atkinson, Rt. Hon. John
Bagot, Capt. J. FitzRoy
Bailey, James (Walworth)
Baillie, J. E. B. (Inverness)
Baird, John George A.
Balcarres, Lord
Balfour, Rt. Hon. A. J.(Man.)
Balfour, Rt.Hon.G.W.(Leeds)
Banbury, Frederick George
Barnes, Frederic Gorell

Barry, Rt.Hn.A.H.S.-(Hunts)
Bartley, George C. T.
Barton, Dunbar Plunket
Bathurst,Hon. AllenBenjamin
Beach,Rt.Hn.SirM.H.(Bristol
Beach, W. W. B. (Hants.)
Beckett, Ernest William
Begg, Ferdinand Faithfull
Beresford, Lord Charles
Bethell, Commander
Bhownaggree, Sir M. M.
Biddulph, Michael
Blakiston-Houston, John

Blundell, Colonel Henry
Bolitho. Thomas Bedford
Bond, Ed vard
Bonser, Henry Cosmo Orme
Boscawen, Arthur Griffith-
Boulnois, Edmund
Bousfield, William Robert
Bowles,T.Gibson (King'sLynn
Brodrick, Rt.Hon. St. John
Brookfield, A. Montague
Brown, Alexander H.
Burdett-Coutts, W.
Butcher, John George

Campbell, RtHnJA.(Glasgow)
Cavendish, R. F- (N. Lancs.)
Cayzer, Sir Charles William
Cecil, Lord H. (Greenwich)
Chaloner, Captain R. G. W.
Chamberlain, RtHonJ (Birm.)
Chamberlain, J. A. (Worc'r)
Chaplin, Rt. Hon. Henry
Charrington, Spencer
Chelsea, Viscount
Clarke, Sir Edw. (Plymouth)
Cochrane, Hon. T. H. A. E.
Coghill, Douglas Harry
Cohen, Benjamin Louis
Collings, Rt. Hon. Jesse
Colston, Chas. E. H. Athole
Compton, Lord Alwyne
Cook, Fred. Lucas (Lambeth)
Corbett, A. C. (Glasgow)
Courtney,Rt. Hon. Leonard H
Cranborne, Viscount
Cripps, Charles Alfred
Cruddas, William Donaldson
Curzon, Viscount

Dalbiac, Colonel Philip Hugh
Dalkeith, Earl of
Dalrymple, Sir Charles
Davies, Sir H. D. (Chatham)
Denny, Colonel
Dickson-Poynder, Sir J. P.
Digby, John K D. Wingfield-
Douglas, Rt. Hon. A. Akers-
Douglas-Pennant, Hon. E. S.
Doxford, William Theodore
Drage, Geoffrey
Duncombe, Hon. Hubert V.

Egerton, Hon. A. de Tatton

Fardell, Sir T. George
Fellowes, Hon. Ailwyn Edw.
Fergusson,Rt Hn SirJ(Manc'r)
Finch, George H.
Finlay, Sir Robert Bannatyne
Firbank, Joseph Thomas
Fisher, William Hayes
FitzGerald, Sir Robt. Penrose-
FitzWygram, General Sir F.
Flannery, Sir Fortescue
Fletcher, Sir Henry
Flower, Ernest
Fry, Lewis

Galloway, William Johnson
Garfit, William
Gibbs, Hon, Vicary(St Albans)
Giles, Charles Tyrrell
Gilliat, John Saunders
Gorst, Rt. Hon. Sir John E.
Goschen,Rt.Hn.G.J.(StGeo.'s)
Goschen, George J. (Sussex)
Gourley,SirEdwardTemperley
Graham, Henry Robert
Gray, Ernest (West Ham)
Green, W. D. (Wednesbury)
Greene, H. D. (Shrewsbury)
Greene, W. Raymond.(Cambs.)
Greville, Hon. Ronald
Gunter, Colonel

Hamilton, Rt. Hon. Lord Geo.
Hanbury, Rt. Hon. Robert W.
Hanson, Sir Reginald
Hare, Thomas Leigh
Heath, James

Heaton, John Henniker
Henderson, Alexander
Hermon-Hodge, R. Trotter
Hoare, E. Brodie (Hamstead)
Hoare, Samuel (Norwich)
Hobhouse, Henry
Holland, Hon. Lionel R.(Bow)
Houldsworth, Sir Wm. Henry
Howard, Joseph
Howell, William Tudor
Howorth, Sir Henry Hoyle
Hozier, Hn.James Henry Cecil
Hubbard, Hon. Evelyn
Hutton, John (Yorks, N.R.)

Jebb, Richard Claverhouse
Jeffreys, Arthur Frederick
Jessel,Captain HerbertMerton
Johnston, William (Belfast)
Johnstone, Heywood (Sussex)
Jolliffe, Hon. H. George

Kennaway, Rt. Hn. Sir J. H.
Kimber, Henry

Laurie, Lieut.-General
Lawrence,SirE.Durning-(Corn
Lawson, John Grant (Yorks.)
Lea, SirThomas(Londonderry)
Lecky,Rt.Hon. William E. H.
Lees, Sir Elliott (Birkenhead)
Leigh-Bennett, Henry Currie
Leighton, Stanley
Llewelyn, Sir D.- (Swansea
Lockwood, Lt.-Col. A. R.
Lodes, Gerald Walter Erskine
Long, Col C. W. (Evesham
Lopes, Henry Yarde Buller
Lorne, Marquess of
Lowe, Francis William
Lubbock, Rt. Hon. Sir John
Lucas-Shadwell, William
Lyell, Sir Leonard
Lyttleton, Hon. Alfred

Macartney, W. G. Ellison
Macdona, John Cumming
M'Arthur, Charles (Liv'rpool)
M'Calmont,Col.J.(Antrim,E)
M'Iver,Sir L (Edinburgh,W.)
Malcolm, Ian
Manners, Lord Edward W. J.
Maple, Sir John Blundell
Marks, Henry Hananel
Martin, Richard Biddulph
Maxwell, Rt. Hon. Sir H. E.
Mellor, Colonel (Lancashire)
Melville, Beresford Valentine
Meysey-Thompson, Sir H. M.
Middlemore, J. Throgmorton
Milbank, Sir Powlett Chas. J.
Mildmay, Francis Bingham
Milner, Sir Frederick George
Milward, Colonel Victor
Monk, Charles James
Montagu, Hn. J. S. (Hants)
Moon, Edward Robert Pacy
Moore, Arthur (Londonderry)
More,Robt.Jasper(Shropshire)
Morgan, Hn.Fred.(Monm'ths.)
Morrison, Walter
Morton, A. H. A. (Deptford)
Mount, William George
Murray, Rt. Hn. A. G. (Bute)
Murray,Col. Wyndham (Bath)
Myers, William Henry

Nicholson, William Graham
Nicol, Donald Ninian
O'Neill, Hon. Robert Torrens
Pease, Herb. Pike(Darlington)
Philpotts, Captain Arthur
Pierpoint, Robert
Pilkington,R. (Lancs,Newton
Platt-Higgins, Frederick
Powell, Sir Francis Sharp
Pretyman, Ernest George
Priestley, Sir W. O. (Edin.)
Pryce-Jones,Lt.-Col.Edward
Purvis, Robert
Pym, C. Guy
Rankin, Sir James
Rasch, Major Frederic Carne
Renshaw, Charles Bine
Rentoul, James Alexander
Ridley,Rt.Hn.SirMatthew W
Ritchie,Rt. Hn.Chas.Thomson
Robertson, Herbert, (Hackney
Rothschild,Hon.LionelWalter
Round, James
Royds, Clement Molyneux
Russell, Gen. F.S.(Chelten'm)
Russell, T. W. (Tyrone)
Rutherford, John

Samuel, H. S. (Limehouse)
Sassoon, Sir Edward Albert
Savory, Sir Joseph
Seely, Charles Hilton
Sharpe, William Edward T.
Simeon, Sir Barrington
Smith, Jas. Parker (Lanarks)
Spencer, Ernest
Stanley, Hon. A. (Ormskirk)
Stanley, Edward J.(Somerset)
Stanley, Lord (Lancs.)
Stirling-Maxwell, Sir John M.
Stock, James Henry
Stone, Sir Benjamin
Strauss, Arthur
Sturt, Hon. Humphrey N.

Thorburn, Walter
Thornton, Percy M.
Tollemache, Henry James
Tomlinson, Wm. Edw.Murray
Tritton, Charles Ernest

Usborne, Thomas

Valentia, Viscount
Verney, Hon. Richard G-
Vincent, Col. Sir C. E. Howard

Ward, Hon. R. A. (Crewe)
Warr, Augustus Frederick
Webster, R.G. (St. Pancras)
Whiteley, George (Stockport)
Whitmore, Charles Algernon
Williams, J. Powell- (Birm.)
Wilson, J. W. (Worcester, N.)
Wilson-Todd, W. H. (Yorks.)
Wodehouse,Rt.Hn.E.R (Bath)
Wolff, Gustav Wilhelm
Woodall, William
Wortley, Rt. Hn. C.B. Stuart-
Wyndham, George
Wyndham-Quin, Major W. H.
Wyvill, Marmaduke D'Arcy
Young, Commander(Berks,E.)

TELLERS FOR THE AYES—
Sir William Walrond and
Mr. Anstruther.

NOES.

Allan, William (Gateshead)
Allison, Robert Andrew
Ambrose, Robert
Austin, M.
Barlow. John Emmott
Beaumont, Wentworth C. B
Billson, Alfred
Blake, Edward
Brunner, Sir John Tomlinson
Caldwell, James
Cameron, SirCharles(Glasgow
Carew, James Laurence
Carvell, Patrick G. Hamilton
Causton, Richard Knight
Cawley, Frederick
Channing, Francis Allston
Clark, Dr. G. B (Caithness-sh.)
Clough, Walter Owen
Commins, Andrew
Crombie. John William
Curran, Thomas (Sligo, S.)
Dalziel, James Henry
Dilke, Rt. Hon. Sir Charles
Dillon, John
Donelan, Captain A.
Doogan, P. C.
Duckworth, James
Dunn, Sir William
Evans, SamuelT. (Glamorgan)
Evans, Sir F. H. (South'ton)
Farquharson, Dr. Robert
Farrell, James P. (Cavan, W.)
Fenwick, Charles
Fitzmaurice, Lord Edmond
Flavin, Michael Joseph
Foster, Sir Walter (Derby Co.)
Fox, Dr. Joseph Francis
Gibney, James
Goddard, Daniel Ford
Gold, Charles
Gurdon, Sir William B.

Hammond, John (Carlow)
Hayne, Rt. Hon. C. Seale-
Hazell, Walter
Healy, Thomas J. (Wexford)
Hedderwick, Thomas C. H.
Hemphill, Rt. Hon. C. H.
Horniman, Frederick John
Jacoby, James Alfred
Johnson-Ferguson, JabezEdw.
Joicey, Sir James
Jordan, Jeremiah
Kearley, Hudson E.
Kinloch, Sir J. George Smyth
Kitson, Sir James
Labouchere, Henry
Langley, Batty
Leese, SirJosephF. (Accrington
Leng, Sir John
Lewis, John Herbert
Lloyd-George, David
Lough, Thomas
MacAleese, Daniel
MacNeill, JohnGordonSwift
M'Ewan, William
M'Ghee, Richard
M Kenna, Reginald
M'Leod, John
Mappin, Sir Frederick Thorpe
Mendl, Sigismund Ferdinand
Montagu, Sir S. (Whitechapel)
Morgan, J Lloyd(Carmarthen)
Morgan, W P. (Merthyr)
Morton, Edw J.C.(Devonport)
Moulton. John Fletcher
Norton, Capt. Cecil Will'am
O'Brien, James F. X. (Cork)
O'Connor, James(Wicklow, W.
O'Connor, T. P. (Liverpool)
Oldroyd, Mark
O'Malley, William
Palmer, SirCharlesM.(Durham

Paulton, James Mellor
Perks, Robert William
Pinkerton, John
Power, Patrick Joseph
Priestley, Briggs (Yorks.)
Provand. Andrew Dryburgh
Richardson, J. (Durham, S.E.)
Roberts, J. H. (Denbighs.)
Robertson, Edm. (Dundee)
Robson, W liam Gordon
Samuel, J. (Stockton-on Tees)
Shaw, Charles E. (Stafford)
Shaw, Thomas (Hawick B.)
Sinclair, Capt. J. (Forfarsh.)
Soames, Arthur Wellesley
Souttar, Robinson
Spicer, Albert
Stanhope, Hon. Philip J.
Steadman, William Charles
Stevenson. Francis F.
Sullivan, Donal (Westmeath)
Sullivan, T. D. (Donegal, W.)
Tennant, Harold John
Thomas, Abel (Carmarthen.E.)
Trevelyan, Charles Philips
Ure, Alexander
Wallace, Robetr
Walton, J. Lawson, (Leeds, S.)
Warner Thos. Courtenay T.
Wedderburn, Sir William
Weir, James Galloway
Whittaker, Thomas Palmer
Williams, JohnCarvell(Notts)
Wills, Sir William Henry
Wilson, H. J. (York, W. R.)
Wilson, John (Govan)
Woods, Samuel

TELLERS FOR THE NOES—Mr. Scott and Mr. Harold Rockitt.

PRIVATE LEGISLATION PROCEDURE (SCOTLAND) BILL.

Considered in Committee.

(In the Committee.)

Clause 2 :—

Amendment again proposed—

" In page 2, line 2, after the word ' Commons' to insert the words ' and two Members of each House of Parliament appointed at the beginning of each session in manner provided by Standing Orders shall be a Standing Committee of the two Houses of Parliament."—(*Dr. Clark.*)

Question again proposed, " That those words be their inserted."

THE LORD ADVOCATE (Mr. A. G. MURRAY, Buteshire): As hon. Members are aware, we have been considering the Amendment of the hon. Gentleman the Member for Caithness. The object of that Amendment and the desire of its mover is that there should be proper control. That wish is reflected by hon. Members on both sides of the House, and I feel very strongly the advisability of having other persons added to the panel. Under the scheme of the Bill as at present drafted there is certain control over this matter; but what we propose to do is to alter our Bill in the sense that in every case it will be necessary to bring the matter before this House so that it will always be possible for this House to consider any Bill and amend it, whether it had been opposed in a former stage at the local inquiry or not. The exact form of the alteration has not yet been decided upon, but we think it might very conveniently arise upon an Amendment which is down on the Paper in the name of the hon. Member for Mid Lanark in Clause 7, page 5, and line 9. The control which he suggests in that Amendment I can assure the Committee we shall accept; but there must be some alteration in the words, and under all the circumstances I hope the hon. Member will not press his Amendment.

Sir H. CAMPBELL-BANNERMAN (Stirling Burghs): I did not hear a part of the right hon. Gentleman's explanations and objections, but I think I substantially know what they amount to, and I recognise that this involves a considerable concession to the views expressed by those who sit both upon this side of the House and the other side. I also understand that in this and in other respects the right hon. Gentleman is ready to meet the views put forward. I understand that the right hon. Gentleman is willing to make considerable alterations to meet the ideas of the vestries, and I think that will be most palatable to the Scottish people as a whole. On these grounds I do not think it would be well for my hon. friend, with whom I entirely sympathise, and whose Amendments I have supported, to press his Amendment at this stage. I may say that I have more than once expressed an opinion that the right hon. Gentleman the Lord Advocate could carry through a Bill for this purpose if anyone on this earth could, and I recognise in the conciliatory manner which he has adopted from first to last the fulfilment of my prediction of his success. I hope it will be understood that we are not foregoing any of our rights to criticise when we think necessary any points that may come before us ; but on the main principle of this part of the scheme of the Bill I think we have had such concessions given to us as to justify us in withdrawing the Amendment now before the House.

Dr. CLARK (Caithness): Under the circumstances, I shall be prepared to withdraw the Amendment.

Amendment, by leave, withdrawn.

Mr. CRIPPS (Gloucester, Stroud): The Amendment which I beg to propose is put down with a desire to make the Bill a practical and good one. Under the Bill as it stands at present there is a statutory obligation placed upon the Chairman of Committees of the House of Lords, and the Chairman of Ways and Means in the House of Commons, which is quite outside Parliamentary practice. I therefore propose as an Amendment that there should not be an obligation of

a statutory character which might be enforced by *mandamus*, but that in the exercise of their discretion under this Bill the Chairmen should be subject in the ordinary way to the rules of the House, and not to any outside tribunal. I hope the Lord Advocate will accept the Amendment, recognising, as I trust he will, that it will put the Bill in better form and make it more in accordance with constitutional precedent.

Amendment proposed—

" In page 2, line 3, to leave out from ' shall' to end of clause, and insert ' if the two Houses of Parliament think fit so to order prescribe all matters of practice and procedure which will enable them to take into consideration the draft Order, and to report thereon to the Secretary for Scotland."— (*Mr. Cripps.*)

Question proposed, "That the words proposed to be left out stand part of the clause."

Mr. A. G. MURRAY : I am quite willing to meet my hon. and learned friend in this matter, by leaving out from the word "shall" down to "the Secretary for Scotland," in order to insert the words he proposes. This, however, will necessitate a small Amendment in the next line, and I therefore propose in line 11, as consequential to this Amendment, to insert after the first word "of" "the Chairman report and." That makes the Amendment perfectly consistent, and at the same time gives effect to what the hon. Member wishes.

*Mr. J. E. ELLIS (Nottingham,. Rushcliffe): I think anyone who is interested in constitutional procedure—and who ought not to be ?—will feel obliged to the hon. Member for bringing this Amendment forward, and we are pleased to acknowledge the attitude of the Lord Advocate with regard to this matter.

Mr. EDMUND ROBERTSON (Dundee) : I think this Amendment would cut out an Amendment which stands in my name. I ought to say that I put down that Amendment, not with a view of pressing it to a Division, but really to understand what the nature of the proposal of the Lord Advocate is. The clause appears to involve two lines of procedure, and I desire to know what the intention of the Government is.

MR. A. G. MURRAY: The genesis of the proviso of the clause is in the proceedings of the Select Committee last year. The proviso is put in so that if the Secretary for Scotland does know where the scheme is opposed he should hand on his knowledge to the Chairman. That is the whole meaning of it.

Amendment, by leave, withdrawn.

The Amendment suggested by the Lord Advocate put, and agreed to.

MR. MOULTON (Cornwall, Launceston): The Amendment that I propose must, I think, be admitted by all who have considered this Bill to be a reasonable one. It is to omit the words "or mainly" in the passage "if it appears . . . that the provisions or some provisions of the draft Order do not relate wholly or mainly to Scotland." The effect of the Amendment is to restrict the operation of this Act to Scotch business. The last clause of the Bill says that this Bill shall apply to Scotland only. It is not only called the Private Legislation Procedure (Scotland) Bill, but the terms of the Bill itself apply only to Scotland. Now, so long as the words "or mainly" appear, there is no Bill relating to England which might not come within its provisions, provided it relates also to Scotland, even though the opinion of the Chairmen is that it applies more to Scotland than to England. It seems to me quite foreign to the intention of the Bill that such should be the effect, but as it is at present drafted so it stands. I want to call the attention of the Committee to what the effect will be if the words "or mainly" are allowed to remain. In the first place, if a Private Bill relates in any way to Scotland it must be brought into the provisions of this Bill. The consequence is that, no matter how much a Bill relates to England, still it must come under the Scotch Procedure Bill if in any part it touches Scotch interests. That, of course, would be grossly unfair to the predominant partner, and I cannot understand why the Government have departed from the plain language in which former Bills, if I remember rightly, were couched, which limited the power to Private Bills which related solely to Scotland.

Amendment proposed—

" In page 2, line 13, to leave out ' or mainly.' "
—(*Mr. Moulton.*)

Question proposed, " That the words ' or mainly ' stand part of the clause."

MR. A. G. MURRAY: I really think that there is no such danger as the hon. Member seems to foresee. The retention of the words is simply to provide for such undertakings as may extend a few yards over the border. Surely the hon. Member might be content to trust the Chairmen in such a matter, for they would never be likely to give a wrong decision in regard to it. After the concessions which I have already made to-day, I hope the Committee will support me in opposing this Amendment, because I think it would be a pity to insert these words.

Amendment put, and negatived.

Amendment proposed—

" In page 2, line 13, after ' Scotland,' to insert ' or do not raise any question of policy or principle not previously determined by Parliament.' "—(*Dr. Clark.*)

Question proposed, " That those words be there inserted."

MR. A. G. MURRAY: I shall be quite happy to accept the hon. Member's Amendment in the form adopted in the 1892 Bill. I therefore beg to move to insert the words—

" Or raise any full question of policy or principles."

The clause will then read—

" If it appeared from such report that the provisions, or some of the provisions of the draft Order do not relate wholly or mainly to Scotland, or are of such a character or magnitude, or raise any such question of policy or principle, that they ought to be dealt with by Private Bill, and not by Provisional Order."

Amendment by leave, withdrawn.

The Amendment suggested by the Lord Advocate put and agreed to.

MR. J. P. SMITH (Lanark, Partick): I should like to ask what the Lord Advocate proposes to do with his Amendment as to measures effecting a change in the general law. We have now got a tribunal that will consider certain Bills for carrying out works, but it is a different matter when we have proposals for dealing with the liberty of the subject, and it is necessary to keep these proposals under the control of Parliament. I beg therefore to move the Amendment standing in my name.

Amendment proposed—

" In page 2, line 13, after 'Scotland,' to insert, 'or effect a change in the general law.' "— (*Mr. J. P. Smith.*)

Question proposed, "That those words be there inserted."

MR. CRIPPS : I think the words of my Amendment which appears further down in the Paper, are very much the same as those in the Amendment of the hon. Member, but slightly more definite in form. The words which I proposed to submit are to insert after "Scotland," " or deviate from, or are repugnant to the general law." What the Lord Advocate proposes is that we should have some control, in the form of a confirmation Bill or some other form. But that is not the same control as sending a Bill to a special Committee, the Police and Sanitary Committee, and getting a special report from that Committee. I do not think it is necessary to argue that we ought to keep this legislative power sufficiently under our own control, and the words which I propose are intended to retain that power in cases of real importance.

MR. CALDWELL (Lanarkshire, Mid) : May I point out to the Lord Advocate that the effect of these Amendments would be to hamper the whole purpose of the Bill, because when you introduce a Bill into this House it means in many cases an alteration of the general law. You could never bring in a Bill for the Corporation of Glasgow, for instance, without some little amendment of the general law, and I cannot conceive of any procedure under this Bill which would not make some such change.

MR. STUART-WORTLEY (Sheffield, Hallam) : If I understand the words of the Lord Advocate, they are not limited to the new cases, but are so wide as to cover the Amendment of the hon. Member. I confess I am a little afraid to put in words which might, by including one class of cases, exclude another. If we adopt the Lord Advocate's words, we shall be able to designate the class of cases referred to by simply passing in each

session a Sessional Order similar to that by which we now refer such cases to the Police and Sanitary Committee.

MR. A. G. MURRAY : The hon. Member for Sheffield has so well stated the case that I have really nothing to add.

Question put, and negatived.

Amendment proposed—

" In page 2, line 13, after 'Scotland,' to insert, 'or which raise any such question of policy or principle.' "—(*The Lord Advocate.*)

Question, "That those words be there inserted," put and agreed to.

Amendment proposed—

" In page 2, line 22, to leave out 'that notices published and served and.' "—(*Captain Sinclair.*)

Question proposed, "That the words proposed to be left out stand part of the clause."

MR. A. G. MURRAY : I may say at once that I propose to pass over all questions of notices till the Report stage. I think the matter may be summarised thus. We discussed the question last time, and the feeling of the Committee was that for the Provisional Order system pure and simple we should, if possible, have rather a less expensive mode of procedure. On the other hand, if the matter has to go on as a Private Bill, it is quite clear we should have to amend the Standing Orders in that sense. There are two plans : either you have to have this question determined before notices are served, or you have to have an alternate notice. What I feel is that one would be in a much better position to give an intelligent consideration to the point when we have the Bill in its final form. Therefore I propose, with the permission of the House, to leave over this question of the notices until the Report stage.

MR. CRIPPS : I think the Amendment which stands in my name will really come within the principle which the Lord Advocate has just stated, but if he desires it to be left over I do not desire to bring it up at the present time. What I want to point out is that nothing in this Bill ought to interfere with the power of this House to deal with its own procedure or its own Standing Orders. My Amendment was only to ensure that that right was preserved. With regard to the intercommunication of procedure, where the procedure under this Bill or the ordinary Private Bill procedure is adopted, it seems to me to be essential, if this Bill is to be a success, that where the Chairman holds that a particular procedure ought to be by Private Bill, and not under the terms of this Act, the notices and so on which have already been given should not be thrown away, but should be applicable to procedure by Private Bill. I may illustrate the point by the procedure in connection with the Light Railways Commissioners, where the entire separation of the procedure has created very great difficulty. I hope before the Report stage the Lord Advocate will see his way to preserve the control of this House over this procedure, and also to make sure that when the Chairman says particular proposals ought to come before this House all the expenditure up to that date in regard to notices and matters of that kind should not be thrown away, but be able to be utilised in connection with the other procedure.

MR. A. G. MURRAY : If I were dealing with this Amendment alone, I should be perfectly happy to take the hon. Member's suggestion, but really I think the whole matter must be considered.

MR. J. P. SMITH: The Amendment standing in my name deals with another small point upon notices, which I am content to leave to the Lord Advocate.

Amendment, by leave, withdrawn.

DR. CLARK: This next Amendment is to leave out the last words of the clause, but I do not think I will move it.

MR. CRIPPS : As I have a similar proposal to this on the Paper, may I say that I hope that under no conditions will these last three lines be inserted. Nor are they in the least necessary. It is a most important proposal affecting the procedure of this House. We deal with this matter by Standing Order. I do not think my right hon. friend can find any instance where by Statute this House disentitles itself to take into consideration any petitions. There is no such case, as far as I know, in constitutional law, and I have hunted through all the books, because this

Mr. Cripps.

proposal seemed to be of an extraordinarily unconstitutional character. The procedure under the Standing Orders of the House will practically arrive at the same result, and if my learned friend will accede to that, and not seek to put a statutory disability upon this House, I am quite content with what he will settle. It is most important that you should not allow the privileges of this House to be controlled even by Statute. I beg to move the omission of these lines.

Amendment proposed—

" In page 2, line 26, to leave out from the word ' Parliament ' to the end of the clause."— (*Mr. Cripps.*)

Question proposed, "That the words proposed to be left out stand part of the clause."

SIR CHARLES CAMERON (Glasgow, Bridgeton) : This appears to me to be a most important subject, and I was rather surprised to hear that the hon. Member for Caithness did not propose to move his Amendment. The importance of the matter is emphasised by the fact that you have Amendments from all quarters of the House to the same effect. The hon. and learned Gentleman who has just spoken has thoroughly well explained the constitutional aspect of the case, and I trust the House will accept this Amendment.

DR. CLARK : I did not move my Amendment because we discussed the point fully on the first clause. The question is whether it should be compulsory or not. I think after the Government have agreed that everything can come before us, and we can have a Report stage where it is necessary, and a Third Reading, we should give way to them on this point, and that is why I did not move. This is merely raising the question again in a bad form.

MR. A. G. MURRAY : The truth is this Amendment is very nearly out of order, because we have already decided, although we did not go to a Division, that when you want anything which in the old days could be got by Private Bill, you should apply for a Provisional Order. It is not quite out of order, because if the Amendment were carried the result would be that we could do either. But my hon. and learned friend's argument, if carried out, would obviously make it impossible to have a Bill to deal with private legislation at all, because all private legislation procedure at the present moment is necessarily an infringement of the Standing Orders of this House; and if his position is right that you never can by Act tie up the powers of this House in regard to anything which is dealt with by Standing Orders, it is quite obvious that you cannot have an Act at all to deal with private legislation procedure. But really this clause, as it stands, does not alter or interfere with the general powers of this House with regard to petitions. It simply carries out what we have already determined in the "may" and "shall" discussion.

SIR F. S. POWELL (Wigan): I do not like to interfere even with one word in the course of a Scotch debate, but I confess I always had a great dislike to the lines now before us. It certainly does appear to me that they impair in the most important manner the liberties and almost the rights of the subject. While I desire to concur in what my hon. and learned friend has said as to the privileges and rights of Parliament, I should greatly regret, having regard to my experience as Chairman of the Police and Sanitary Committee, these lines forming part of this clause.

*MR. RENSHAW (Renfrew, W.): The provision in Clause 1 is so clear that there is really no necessity for this sub-section. I do not think they formed any part of the Bill of last year, and if I remember the proceedings in the Committee rightly they were introduced at the instance of the Lord Advocate. I regret he now proposes to retain them, because, in view of the clear nature of the provision in Clause 1, it is not desirable that these lines should stand.

*MR. J. E. ELLIS (Nottingham, Rushcliffe): I beg to join in everything that has been said as to the inexpediency, not to say danger, of these lines. I am not quite sure that it conduces to the rapid progress of the proceedings of the Committee for the Lord Advocate to say after you, Sir, have put it from the chair, that the Amendment is more or less out of order.

MR. A. G. MURRAY: I did not say it was out of order. I said it was nearly out of order, and I gave my reasons for thinking so.

*MR. J. E. ELLIS: I thought I heard the right hon. Member say it was nearly out of order; if he did not say so I was mistaken. The hon. and learned Member opposite has given very fully the constitutional aspect of the matter, and surely we have no right to limit the power of the House in this way. If the hon. Member presses his Amendment to a Division, I shall support him in the lobby.

MR. CRIPPS: I only want to say one word in answer to what the Lord Advocate has said. His view is that so far as the rights and privileges of this House are concerned they have been settled in Sub-section 1. There I quite agree with him. If his desire is, so far as the individual is concerned, to direct the way in which he should make application in the future, that point we have dealt with already in Sub-section 1. These three lines have no effect upon that, except so far as they detail the duties of this House in matters of procedure. That is to say, this House would be under statutory disabilities as regards entertaining such petitions or petitioners. You may put the disability on the petitioner, but that is entirely a different matter. I hope the Lord Advocate or the First Lord of the Treasury will see that these words are unnecessary.

MR. SOUTTAR (Dumfriesshire): I quite agree that this matter was discussed under the first section of the Bill, but I thought that the decision arrived at was an exceedingly bad decision. Therefore I am very glad it has been brought up again, and that one or two men of eminence have taken the side of the subject in this matter. I feel certain the time will come when hon. Members will realise that they are making a great mistake in parting with a constitutional right of the subject which is almost as important as freedom of speech, and which has existed for many, many centuries. This is not the first time Parliament has attempted to infringe upon that right, but the attempt has not been successful. The Lord Advocate seems to me, in the present case, in these three lines, to be adding insult to injury. If the right has been taken away by the first clause, why repeat the operation here ? I do hope that in so important a matter a Division will be taken, and I should support the Amendment.

MR. A. G. MURRAY: If my hon. and learned friend's objection is to the form of the words, I am perfectly willing to take that into consideration along with the other questions of procedure. As I understand, that is really all he wants to raise, as he recognises that we have settled the whole question in the "may" and "shall" Division. I am not quite certain what the hon. Member for Nottingham meant, because I do not know that he was in the House when the previous decision was come to, and therefore perhaps he has not borne in mind that the House has already decided that it is a necessity that people should come by this method for a Provisional Order, leaving it to the Chairmen to relegate the proposal to the Private Bill procedure if necessary. Perhaps if I agree to consider the form of words he will be satisfied, but the hon. Member cannot expect me to give way on this, seeing that we have already taken the sense of the House upon the question.

MR. CRIPPS : In regard to what the Lord Advocate has said, although I believe I am entirely in accord with the hon. Member for Nottingham, I do not at all want to take up the time of the Committee ; and as the Lord Advocate has promised to consider the question, I ask leave to withdraw the Amendment.

SIR CHARLES CAMERON : I entirely object to the Amendment being withdrawn. I do not see the use of wasting time discussing the question, and then not coming to some definite understanding as to what is going to be done. If the matter has been settled you do not want the words, and there is no use in settling it twice.

MR. ROBERT WALLACE (Perth): It was absolutely settled under Clause 1 of this Bill that it was compulsory to come under this Bill, and at first I must confess I thought the last part of this section was unnecessary. But on consideration I begin to doubt that, and there may possibly be cases where these words would be necessary. There is nothing to prevent them coming in the other way, unless some such words are inserted. As

Mr. Soutar.

I understand, my hon. and learned friend wishes to preserve certain rights of Parliament, and if that can be done better by Standing Order or by some other words, we are all agreed it should be done, but I earnestly trust the Committee will sustain the Lord Advocate in the view he has taken in regard to the necessity of something like this being inserted, and reject the Amendment if it is pressed to a Division.

MR. CALDWELL : Nothing in the words of the first clause would interfere with the right of any person to petition this House in the usual way for leave to bring in a Bill. At the same time there is a constitutional right of this House to listen to petitions, and if these words were retained there would be no power to this House to give leave to introduce a Private Bill notwithstanding the words of Clause 1. We have never yet cut out the right of any person in this country to petition this House, or the right of this House to consent to that petition by giving leave to bring in a Bill. So that, after all, this matter raises not the question of the right of the petitioner, which is involved in Clause 1—we have decided that—but the right of this House, upon a petition being presented to them, to say " We will allow this matter to come in by Private Bill." This House has always kept within its own hands the right of anyone to come to them direct. We are dealing now with the right to come to this House and with the constitutional right of this House to say " Notwithstanding Clause 1 we will allow you to proceed by Private Bill."

MR. COURTNEY (Cornwall, Bodmin): The Lord Advocate has promised to consider this matter, and I would suggest that he might take into account the action of Parliament in reference to two matters which were formally settled by the action of the House. In the first place there was the matter of Divorce Bills, and then the right of electors to come to this House with regard to a controverted election for the decision of the House. Nothing could be more constitutional than the right of this House alone to consider such applications. But by Act of Parliament this House concurred in depriving itself of that right and vested it in a Committee of the House. I would suggest that the Lord Advocate should in considering the matter take these analogous subjects into account.

MR. CRIPPS: In regard to the constitutional principle referred to by the right hon. Gentleman the Member for Bodmin, I should like to say that I should cite both his illustrations in favour of the proposal I have made. In regard to election petitions, the right is preserved to this House, although it would find it very inconvenient to exercise it, to interfere. The judicial part of the inquiry has been sent to a Committee, but a report has to be made to this House.

MR. COURTNEY: But you are bound to accept the decision. My hon. friend will not for a moment urge that this House could controvert the finding of the Court which had unseated a Member. It must act upon that conclusion.

MR. CRIPPS: I think this House preserves its control. The question of divorce is an entirely different point. This House has nothing to do with the matter going before the courts, but until the Divorce Court was instituted there was no legal right for divorce in this country at all, and anybody who wanted a divorce had to come for an Act of Parliament. So far as Ireland is concerned, that procedure holds good to the present day. When the matter was brought for the first time within the area of the law courts you had to pass laws in order to allow divorce to take place without Act of Parliament. There is no analogy between that and what we are dealing with here. I hope my hon. friend will not go to a Division, as I should not be able to support him, seeing that all I desire is that this House should be protected, and the Lord Advocate has promised to consider that between now and the Report stage.

DR. CLARK: This is a thing which could be done either by a section in the Bill, which would equally affect the procedure of both Houses, or it could be done by us under our Standing Orders. I think the wiser course is to do it so that it equally affects both Houses; and this is, I believe, the better form.

Question put.

The Committee divided: Ayes, 206 ; Noes, 72. (Division List No. 196.)

AYES.

Acland-Hood, Capt.SirAlexF.
Asquith, Rt. Hon. Herbt. Hen.
Atkinson, Rt. Hon. John
Bailey, James (Walworth)
Balcarres, Lord
Balfour, Rt. Hn. A.J.(Manch'r)
Balfour, Rt. Hn. G.W. (Leeds)
Banbury, Frederic George
Barnes, Frederic Gorell
Barry, RtHnABSmith-(Hunts
Barton, Dunbar Plunket
Bathurst, Hon. Allen B.
Beach, RtHnSirM. H. (Bristol)
Begg, Ferdinand Faithfull
Beresford, Lord Charles
Bethell, Commander
Bhownaggree, Sir M. M.
Blakiston-Houston, John
Blundell, Colonel Henry
Bond, Edward
Boscawen, Arthur Griffith-
Bousfield, William Robert
Bowles,T.Gibson(King's Lynn
Brodrick, Rt. Hon. St. John
Brookfield, A. Montagu
Bryce, Rt. Hon. James
Butcher, John George
Campell,Rt.Hn.J.A.(Glasgow
Campbell-Bannerman, Sir H.
Carmichael, Sir T. D. Gibson-
Cavendish, F. F. (N. Lancs.)
Cawley, Frederick
Cecil, Lord Hugh (Greenwich)

Chaloner, Captain R. G. W.
Chamberlain,Rt.Hon.J.(Birm.
Chamberlain, J. A. (Worc'r)
Chaplin, Rt. Hon. Henry
Chelsea, Viscount
Clare, Octavius Leigh
Cochrane, Hon Thos. H. A.E.
Coghill, Douglas Harry
Cohen, Benjamin Louis
Collings, Rt. Hon. Jesse
Colston, Chas. E. H. Athole
Corbett, A.Cameron(Glasgow)
Courtney, Rt. Hon. L. H.
Cranborne, Viscount
Cripps, Charles Alfred
Crombie, John William
Cruddas, Wm. Donaldson
Cubitt, Hon. Henry
Curzon, Viscount
Dalkeith, Earl of
Dalrymple, Sir Charles
Digby, John K. D. Wingfield-
Donkin, Richard Sim
Douglas, Rt. Hon. A. Akers-
Doxford, William Theodore
Duncombe, Hon. Hubert V.
Fardell, Sir T. George
Fellowes, Hon. Ailwyn E.
Ferguson, R. C. M. (Leith)
Finlay, Sir Robert B.
Fisher, William Hayes
FitzGerald, Sir R. Penrose-
Fitzmaurice, Lord Edmond

Foster, Harry S. (Suffolk)
Foster, Sir W. (Derby Co.)
Fowler, Rt. Hon. Sir H.
Fry, Lewis
Galloway, Wm. Johnson
Garfit, William
Gedge, Sydney
Giles, Charles Tyrell
Godson, Sir A. Frederick
Goldsworthy, Major-General
Gorst,Rt. Hon. Sir John Eldon
Goulding, Edward Alfred
Gray, Ernest (West Ham)
Green, W. D. (Wednesbury)
Greene, H. D. (Shrewsbury)
Haldane, Richard Burdon
Hamilton,Rt.Hn.Lord George
Hanbury, Sir C. (Newcastle)
Hanbury,Rt.Hon.RobertWm.
Hanson, Sir Reginald
Hatch, Ernest Frederick Geo.
Hayne, Rt. Hon. C. Seale-
Heath, James
Hedderwick, Thomas C H.
Hemphill, Rt.Hon. CharlesH.
Henderson, Alexander
Hoare, Samuel (Norwich)
Hornby, Sir William Henry
Houldsworth, Sir Wm. Henry
Howell, William Tudor
Hubbard, Hon. Evelyn
Humphreys-Owen Arthur C.
Hutton, John (Yorks. N. R.)

Jebb, Richard Claverhouse
Jeffreys, Arthur Frederick
Johnston, William (Belfast)
Jolliffe, Hon. H George
Kearley, Hudson E
Kennaway,Rt. Hon.SirJohnH.
Kimber, Henry
Kin r, Sir Henry Seymour
Kinloch,SirJohnGeorgeSmyth
Laurie, Lieut.-General
Lawson, John Grant (Yorks.)
Leigh-Bennett, Henry Currie
Llewelyn,SirDillwyn(Swansea
Loder, Gerald Walter Erskine
Long,Rt.Hn. Walter (Liverp'l)
Lubbock, Rt. Hon. Sir John
Lucas-Shadwell, William
Lyell, Sir Leonard
Lyttelton, Hon. Alfred
Macartney, W. G. Ellison
Macdona, John Cumming
M'Arthur, Charles (Liverpool)
M'Arthur, William (Cornwall)
M'Ewan, William
M'Iver, SirLewis(Edinb'h),W.
Macolm, Ian
Maple, Sir John Blundell
Mappin, Sir Frederick Thorpe
Martin, Biddulph
Maxwell,Rt. Hn.SirHerbertE.
Mellor, Colonel (Lancashire)
Meysey-Thompson, Sir H. M.
Middlemore, J. Throgmorton
Monk, Charles James
Mildmay, Francis Bingham
Milward, Colonel Victor
Monk, Chas. James

Montagu,Hn.J. Scott (Hants.)
Moon, Edward Robert Pacy
More, Robt. Jasper (Shropsh.)
Morgan, Hon. F.(Monm'thsh.)
Morrell, George Herbert
Morrison, Walter
Morton, Arthur H.A.Deptford
Mount, William George
Murray, RtHnAGraham(Bute
Murray, Col.Wyndham (Bath)
Myers, William Henry
Nicol, Donald Ninian
Palmer, George W. (Reading)
Phillpotts, Captain Arthur
Pilkington,R. (Lancs Newton)
Plat:-Higgins, Frederick
Powell, Sir Francis Sharp
Pretyman, Ernest George
Priestley, Sir W. O. (Edin.)
Pryce-Jones, Lt.-Col. Edward
Purvis, Robert
Pym, C. Guy
Rasch, Major Frederic Carne
Renshaw, Charles Bine
Richardson, J.(Durham, S. E.)
Rickett, J. Compton
Ridley, Rt. Hon. Sir Matt. W.
Ritchie, Rt. Hon. C. Thomson
Robertson, Edmund (Dundee)
Robertson, Herbert (Hackney)
Rothschild, Hon. Lionel W.
Round, James
Russell, Gen. F. S. (Cheltenh.)
Russell, T. W. (Tyrone)
Samuel, H. S. (Limehouse)
Seely, Charles Hilton
Seton-Karr, Henry

Sharpe, William Edward T.
Shaw, Thomas (Hawick, B.)
Smith, James Parker(Lanarks.
Smith, Samuel (Flint)
Smith, Hon. W. F.D. (Strand)
Spencer, Ernest
Stanley, Hon. A. (Ormskirk)
Stanley, Lord (Lancs.)
Stewart, Sir M. J. M'Taggart
Stock, James Henry
Stone, Sir Benjamin
Strutt, Hon. Charles Hedley
Sturt, Hon. Humphry Napier
Tennant, Harold John
Thorburn, Walter
Thornton, Percy M.
Tomlinson, Wm Edw. Murray
Tritton, Charles Ernest
Ure, Alexander
Valentia, Viscount
Wallace, Robert (Perth)
Walton, J. Lawson (Leeds S.)
Warr, Augustus Frederick
Whiteley, George (Stockport)
Williams,JosephPowell-(Birm
Wilson,J. W.(Worcerternb N.)
Wilson-Todd, W m. H. (Yorks.)
Wodehouse,Rt.Hn.E.R.(Bath)
Wolff, Gustav Wilhelm
Woodall, William
Wortley, Rt. Hon. C.B.Stuart-
Wyndham, George
Wyvill, Marmaduke D'Arcy
Young, Commander(Berks,E.)
TELLERS FOR THE AYES—
    Sir William Walrond and
    Mr. Anstruther.

NOES.

Allan, William (Gateshead)
Allison, Robert Andrew
Barlow, John Emmott
Beaumont, Wentworth C. B.
Billson, Alfred
Bolton, Thomas Dolling
Caldwell, James
Carvill, P. George Hamilton
Channing, Francis Allston
Clark,Dr.G.B.(Caithness-sh.)
Clough, Walter Owen
Commins, Andrew
Curran, Thomas (Sligo, S.)
Dalziel, James Henry
Davitt, Michael
Dillon, John
Donelan, Captain A.
Doogan, P. C.
Du kworth, James
Dunn, Sir William
Evans, Samuel T.(Glamorgan)
Farrell, James P. (Cavan, W.)
Fenwick, Charles
Flavin, Michael Joseph
Gibney, James

Goddard, Daniel Ford
Gold, Charles
Gourley, Sir Edward T.
Gurdon, Sir William B.
Hammond, John (Carlow)
Healy, Thomas J. (Wexford)
Holden, Sir Angus
Horniman, Frederick John
Jacoby, James Alfred
Joicey, Sir James
Jordon, Jeremiah
Leng, Sir John
Lewis, John Herbert
Macaleese, Daniel
MacNeil, John Gordon Swift
M'Ghee, Richard
M'Leod, John
Mendl, Sigismund Ferdinand
Molloy, Bernard Charles
O'Connor, Arthur (Donegal)
O'Connor, J. (Wicklow, W.)
O'Connor, T. P. (Liverpool)
Oldroyd, Mark
Palmer,SirCharlesM.(Durham
Paulton, James Mellor

Pinkerton, John
Power, Patrick Joseph
Provand, Andrew Dryburgh
Roberts, John Bryn (Eifion)
Robson, William Snowdon
Samuel, J. (Stockton-on-Tees)
Scott, Chas. Prestwich (Leigh)
Shaw, Charles E. (Stafford)
Sinclair, Capt. J. (Forfarshire)
Spicer, Albert
Steadman, William Charles
Strachey, Edward
Sullivan, Donal (Westmeath)
Sullivan, T. D. (Donegal, W.)
Thomas, David A. (Merthyr)
Weir, James Galloway
Whittaker, Thomas Palmer
Williams, John C. (Notts.)
Wills, Sir William Henry
Wilson, John (Govan)
Wilson, J. H. (Middls'rough
Woods, Samuel
TELLERS FOR THE NOES—
    Sir Charles Cameron and
    Mr. Souttar.

Question proposed, "That Clause 2 as amended, stand part of the Bill."

Mr. EDMUND ROBERTSON: I had put down an Amendment to reject Clause 2, because I did not under-stand it as it stood in the original Bill. The clause has now, however, been so entirely transformed that it would be ridiculous to take the course I had intended. It is clear that the important stage of this Bill will be the Report stage, and therefore a prolonged discussion at this stage of the Bill would be superfluous ; therefore I shall not oppose Clause 2 at this stage, but I wish to reserve my right to deal with it on the Report stage when we know what the Bill really is.

Question put, and agreed to.

Clause, as amended, agreed to.

Clause 3 :—

Mr. J. P. SMITH : The Amendment I propose will make the matter simpler by inserting the words, "If the Chairmen report in favour of," instead of putting it in a negative way.

Amendment proposed—

" In page 2 leave out lines 31 and 32, and insert, ' If the Chairmen report in favour of.' " —(*Mr Parker Smith.*)

Question proposed, "That lines 31 and 32 stand part of the clause."

Mr. A. G. MURRAY : I am afraid that I am not in a position to accept the words of my hon. friend's Amendment.

Mr. CRIPPS : I think the Lord Advocate will agree with me that the Secretary for Scotland should not be allowed to grant a Provisional Order unless he has satisfied the Chairmen of both Houses of Parliament. I think it is a mere question of words, but the Lord Advocate cannot really mean to allow this procedure to be adopted without some intimation to the Chairmen. I hope the right hon. Gentleman will consider whether the words would not allow the Secretary for Scotland to proceed without a Report being made, and whether it is not a proper thing to do to keep within the ordinary procedure of the House.

Mr. CALDWELL : There is no compulsion under the Bill for the Chairman to give a Report at all. Whether this House may insist upon this being done is a matter we have not to deal with now. After the Amendment has been put in the clause there might not be any Report at all made, and the result would be that the whole thing would be at a standstill. In the interest of procedure I do think that the words in the Bill are absolutely necessary.

Mr. J. P. SMITH : If such a case occurs, and no Report is made, it is better that the Bill should come before this House.

Question put, and agreed to.

Mr. THOMAS SHAW (Hawick Burghs) : If there is no opposition to a Bill it appears to me to be a very extraordinary thing that the Secretary for Scotland should put the promoters to the expense of going through the whole of these formalities of bringing up witnesses and engaging counsel on the spot. I beg to move.

Amendment proposed—

" In page 2, line 37, to leave out from ' shall,' to ' direct,' in line 39."—(*Mr. Thomas Shaw.*)

Question proposed—"That the words proposed to be left out stand part of the clause."

Mr. A. G. MURRAY : It appears to me that upon this point my hon. and learned friend and myself must be at cross-purposes. The clause says "shall if there is any opposition." We are all agreed that if there is any opposition the Secretary for Scotland ought to direct an inquiry. The clause also goes on to provide that the Secretary for Scotland may order an inquiry in any case where he thinks that an inquiry is necessary. Does my hon. friend wish to insist upon an inquiry if the Secretary for Scotland considers that an inquiry is unnecessary ? I cannot help thinking that my hon. friend does not really wish that. If there is no opposition, let them have the Bill ; but surely there are a great many cases in which you are not entitled to have your Bill, although nobody objects, for I think the preamble of a Bill should be proved. There are certain facts which ought to be proved in all cases before you get your Bill.

Mr. EDMUND ROBERTSON : I have an Amendment in identical terms to the one which has been moved by my hon. friend. I understand that the local inquiry is to take the place of the inquiry before the Committee. You are proposing to create an inquiry before a panel which will have all the apparatus now in existence, and what we ask ourselves now is, why is it necessary in the case of an unopposed measure under the new system that there should be an inquiry when it is not necessary in the case of an unopposed Bill under the present system ? We desire that there should not be introduced into this Bill as part of the new system a formal inquiry which was found to be unnecessary under the old system.

Mr. A. G. MURRAY: It is quite true that in the case of an unopposed Bill there is no inquiry at present, but then you have opportunities of control which are now possessed by this House. But suppose I put in the words which my hon. friend has suggested. Hon. Members would then be able to get up and say, " It is all very well for this House to do this ; here you are going to allow a tribunal on the spot, under the direction of a Government Department, and is it safe to allow that without an inquiry where there are proper circumstances for an inquiry to be held ? " There is no compulsion put upon the Secretary for Scotland to hold an inquiry, and if he does direct an inquiry and the tribunal reports against it he cannot grant the Order at all. Therefore, so far from increasing his powers this really diminishes them. I should have thought that the general feeling of the House would have been rather in favour of making an inquiry possible wherever there appeared to be a necessity for such inquiry.

Mr. CALDWELL : I quite agree that there is a great deal to be said for the case in which the Secretary for Scotland may direct an inquiry. When a Bill comes into this House unopposed we have the Second Reading stage at which matters of this kind may be referred to. I can myself quite conceive many cases in which it should be possible for the Secretary for Scotland to direct an inquiry. I think the greatest danger to a community often arises in an unopposed Bill, and I think the Secretary for Scotland should have the power where he has the least doubt to direct an inquiry, notwithstanding the fact that no one has appeared in opposition in answer to the notices which have been issued.

mr98J

Mr. COURTNEY : At present in the case of an unopposed Bill there is, under the existing Standing Orders, a provision

Mr. Edmund Robertson.

enabling the Chairman of Ways and Means to recommend to the House in matters of unopposed Bills that they should be treated as opposed Bills if he thinks the reasons are sufficient for him to act upon. So that there is at the present time the possibility of directing that an unopposed Bill shall be treated as an opposed Bill, and that is precisely the power which we desire to see given to the Secretary for Scotland.

*MR. RENSHAW : I think it is desirable that the Secretary for Scotland should have an option in the matter, because it is obvious that in some cases questions might arise as to the desirability of an Act applying to some particular locality powers which had been obtained for another locality, but which, in the public interest it was undesirable should be extended to perhaps a smaller locality, or one differently situated. Difficulties of this sort could be avoided if the Secretary for Scotland exercised this power. I think that is a very important matter.

Sir H. CAMPBELL-BANNERMAN : There is a great deal of force in the hon. Gentleman's observations, but it must be remembered that an inquiry may be necessary although there is no opposition. As my hon. friend behind me said, there may be some public interests involved which may require an inquiry. But where I think there is a great difference between the Lord Advocate and my two hon. friends is that the Lord Advocate appears to look on the Secretary for Scotland as the equivalent for the House of Commons, which he is not. At present an unopposed Bill in its different stages is in the hands of the House of Commons, and there are many opportunities of finding out anything that may be objectionable in it. It is proposed that the Secretary for Scotland should determine whether there should be a further inquiry and a further impediment in the way of an unopposed Bill, but is he the proper person to have that power ? The Secretary for Scotland is a political officer at the head of a public Department, and we cannot always be certain that he will take the same general view of questions as would be taken by the House of Commons or by some Committee of the House to which its powers are delegated I think it would be safer in this respect to enlarge the powers of the Chairmen. Let them have the power of deciding whether a Bill, although unopposed, ought to be the subject of further inquiry. I wish to speak with all respect not only of the present Secretary for Scotland but of all Secretaries for Scotland, but I have a little lurking suspicion that sometimes they may be moved by reasons of their own to take a particular action in reference to a Private Bill, and on that ground I think it would be safer and more in accordance with past practice and constitutional principles if this power of putting a great impediment and great expense on persons promoting a Private Bill should be conferred on the Chairmen, or should be dealt with in some other way to that proposed.

Mr. A. G. MURRAY: I do not wish to introduce a discordant note into the pleasant proceedings of this Committee, but I desire to point out that the Secretary for Scotland would be master of the whole proceedings. He could issue the Order with such observations as he chose, and after all he would be in precisely the same position as the official chief of any other Department which has the power of issuing Provisional Orders, such as the Board of Trade and the Local Government Board. I am not asking any superior position for the Secretary for Scotland, but I am putting him in the ordinary position of a chief of a Department which has power to issue Provisional Orders.

Mr. THOMAS SHAW: I certainly have no desire to put the House to an unnecessary Division. The control that the House will have will ultimately largely depend on the shape in which the Bill emerges from Committee, and I shall accordingly reserve any further action until the Report stage. I am at one with the right hon. Gentleman as regards the expediency on public grounds of having a small supplementary inquiry, but what I desire to avoid is that any officer of State should have the power of turning an unopposed Bill practically into an opposed measure, and inflict expense on the promoters.

Amendment, by leave, withdrawn.

Dr. CLARK: I move the Amendment which stands in my name, in order to get from the Lord Advocate an explanation of the modified proposals of the Government. My proposal is to leave out "Commissioners," in order to insert "a Joint Committee of the two Houses of Parliament appointed by the Standing Joint Committee." That would enable the panel to be composed of Scottish Peers and Scottish Members of Parliament. I should like to hear from the Lord Advocate an explanation of the Amendments which stand in his name.

Amendment proposed—

"In page 3, line 1, to leave out 'Commissioners,' and insert 'a Joint Committee of the two Houses of Parliament appointed by the Standing Joint Committee.'"—(*Dr. Clark.*)

Question proposed, "That the word 'Commissioners' stand part of the clause."

Mr. A. G. MURRAY: The scheme of the Bill as it originally stood was that there should be a panel of 25 persons, the only criterion being that they were to be men of affairs, and Members of Parliament should be nominated on the panel before they could serve on committees of inquiry. During the Debate on the Second Reading an appeal was made by the Leader of the Opposition that we should consider the desirability of having this work done by Members of Parliament, and I told him that I would be glad to meet his views, although I could not go the whole way in the direction indicated. Then I put down the Amendment which stands in my name. I took the bulk of what I consider the very excellent suggestion of my hon. friend the Member for North Ayrshire, namely, that instead of putting Members of Parliament on this panel we should make them eligible as Commissioners, and then have other Commissioners as well, giving a hint to the selecting parties that they should use Members of Parliament whenever they could get them. Since the Amendment appeared on the Paper I have gathered that it would certainly be very agreeable to hon. Members on the other side of the House if I put in words of preferential import, and accordingly that is what I propose to do. Hon. Members will feel that I have gone as far as I can, and that I cannot quite go the length of cutting out other people, because then our scheme might break down. There are practically three schemes on the Paper. The scheme of the hon. Baronet the Member for the Bridgeton Division has no ordinary panel. He does not take outsiders at all, but he takes 50 Peers and 50 Members of the House of Commons, and divides them into 50 groups of two each. Then the hon. Gentleman the Member for the Border Burghs takes all Scotch Members of Parliament and 15 Scotch Members of the House of Lords ; and the hon. Member for Kincardineshire takes 20 Peers, 20 Members of the House of Commons, and 10 other persons, and provides for five Chairmen. The scheme which we propose to submit to the House as a compromise is based on the suggestion of the hon. Member for North Ayrshire. We propose to make Members of both Houses of Parliament eligible as Commissioners, to take 25 other persons, and to put in words of preferential selection. With that explanation I will read exactly how Clauses 4 and 5 will stand if my Amendment is carried. Clause 4 will be as follows :—

" On or before the first day of January next after commencement of this Act there shall be formed a panel of persons (hereinafter referred to as the panel) qualified by experience of affairs to act as Commissioners under this Act. The panel shall be formed in manner following ; that is to say :—(a) The Chairmen, acting jointly with the Secretary for Scotland, after such preliminary inquiries as may be necessary, shall nominate 25 persons qualified as aforesaid to be placed on the panel hereinbefore mentioned. The persons so nominated shall remain on the panel for five years, and any casual vacancy on the panel caused by death, resignation, or disqualification shall be filled up by the chairmen acting jointly with the Secretary for Scotland. (b) At the expiration of every period of five years the panel shall be re-formed in like manner and with the like incidents.

Clause 5 will read :—

" When it is determined that Commissioners shall be appointed for the purpose of inquiring as to the propriety of issuing a Provisional Order or Orders under this Act the Secretary for Scotland, acting jointly with the Chairmen, shall, with due regard to the character and magnitude of the provisions in the proposed Order or Orders, appoint as Commissioners three persons being Members of either House of Parliament, or in default of such Member or Members willing to serve being a person or persons nominated on the panel, and shall at the same time nominate one such person or Member as chairman."

I think I have made it clear that there shall be preferential selection of Members of Parliament, and that at the same time our scheme shall not break down in the event of their not being available.

Mr. A. G. Murray.

*SIR CHARLES CAMERON : The right hon. Gentleman has referred to the various schemes on the Paper, but anyone can see that any of them is infinitely more satisfactory as regards one important point than his scheme. He proceeds on the assumption that the Secretary for Scotland and the Chairmen shall do this work. Why not use the machinery of the House of Commons. If the Secretary for Scotland wants a panel, I am content to have a panel as a stand by, but why should we not have a Committee appointed in the same way as a Committee of this House ? The Chairmen have nothing to do in the appointment of Committees, that work being done by the Committee of Selection. On the Second Reading I moved the rejection of the Bill on the ground that it would practically exclude Scottish Members from considering Scottish Private Bill legislation. There is a long standing rule of the Committee of Selection excluding Scottish Members from the consideration of Scottish Bills. In the Amendment I have placed on the paper I have expressly barred that custom, and my proposal is that in nominating Peers or Members of the House of Commons on the various panels under this Act the Committees of Selection shall not have regard to any precedent or usage excluding Scottish Peers or Members representing Scottish constituencies from serving on committees on Scottish Private Bills, but shall have regard solely to the fact of their having no personal or local interest in orders likely to be proposed in connection with the group of counties in respect of which each panel is nominated. What I consider an essential point is that the Committee of Selection should nominate the panel, and that it should be nominated so as not to exclude Scottish Members. It was urged in the course of the Debate on the Second Reading that there were many considerations for including Scottish Members, and the right hon. Gentleman assented to what was said by the noble Lord the Secretary for Scotland, that if we could get a Parliamentary tribunal it would be eminently satisfactory and would command the confidence of the people of Scotland. The only objection put forward by the noble Lord was that we could not get Members of either House to serve, that it would be extremely inconvenient to have to go down to local inquiries, and that therefore there should be a panel of outside persons. The basis of my proposal is that we should give the Parliamentary panel a chance exactly as the right hon. Gentleman now proposes, and that failing that we should have the fancy panel which the noble Lord the Secretary for Scotland has so elaborately devised, selected in any way he chooses, which would be a supplemental panel to be called on in case Members of Parliament could not be got to serve. I do not believe there will be the smallest difficulty in getting Members of Parliament to serve, but it is necessary that we should place a bar on the exclusion of Scottish Members or Peers. You will get Members to serve if you select a panel large enough, and the Members who will be willing to serve will have a sufficient knowledge of Scottish affairs to make an investigation of the sort proposed a matter, not of drudgery, but of interest. The radical fault of the right hon. Gentleman's proposal appears to me to be that the selection is to be made, not by the tribunal entrusted by this House to select Members to serve on Parliamentary Committees, but by a new tribunal consisting of the Secretary for Scotland and the Chairmen of the two Houses, who have no special knowledge of the subject, and upon whom the duty is imposed for the first time. I must say it is a most invidious function. It is not a matter of principle, but it is a matter of adopting existing machinery instead of the novel and revolutionary machinery proposed by the right hon. Gentleman. We should hand over the selection to the Committee of Selection, and we should ensure that the fact of a Member being a Scottish Member should not be a bar to his serving on the proposed Committees. The work of these Committees would not be hard. There were only twelve Bills brought forward last Session to which this proposal would apply, and the Railway Commissioners dispose of their business at the rate of one measure per day. Accordingly I do not see any chance whatever of the supplemental panel being called on, but I have not the smallest objection to its existence. But the selection of the Parliamentary panel should be made in accordance with Parliamentary practice, and a Committee nominated by the Committees of Selection would command very much more public confidence in Scotland than a Committee selected by the Chairmen of the two Houses, who, from their position, have absolutely no special knowledge as to the qualifications of Members of Parliament.

Sir H. CAMPBELL-BANNERMAN : I presume this is only a preliminary discussion, and that the time will come to consider the whole details of the plan the right hon. Gentleman the Lord Advocate will submit to the Committee. I must say that his proposal seems to meet, to a large extent, the views we have expressed on this side of the House, and I thank the Government and the right hon. Gentleman for going so far in that direction. It would, of course, have been more agreeable to our desires if there had been a possibility of confining the panel to Scotch Members and Scotch Peers. There may be a difficulty in the way of that, but I think that my hon. friend who has just sat down was justified in the hope he expressed that it would be distinctly understood—whether explicitly inserted in the Bill or not—that there would be no bar against Scotch Members sitting on these Committees. I do not believe myself that there is any substantial objection to their sitting even now. It may have been the practice to avoid the appointment of Scotch Members sitting on Scotch Bills lest they should be in some way connected with the interests involved ; but I think it is very necessary that we should know that they are eligible to serve. It is only right that they should be so, because it is from among them that we are most likely to get willing victims for these new duties. There is another little point in regard to the constitution of the Parliamentary panel that I should like cleared up, and that is, Are the Peers and Members of the House of Commons to be mixed up hotch-potch, and is the panel to be made out from them irrespective of what their origin is ? For I think we ought not to have a panel composed entirely of Peers. Each Committee, in my opinion, should be composed of four Members, two being Peers and two Members of the House of Commons. My hon. friend who has just sat down has also taken objection to giving the Secretary for Scotland, even with the assistance of the Chairmen, the power of choosing the Members to serve on these Committees. Well, I think there is a great deal of force in what he said. I think it is rather anomalous to give the head of a public Department the power of choosing the Members to serve, especially when we have a well-constituted machinery in this House and in the House of Lords, in the shape of the Committees of Selection, which has always commanded the complete confidence of the respective Houses. Would it not be possible to introduce their authority in the matter rather than the head of the Scotch Department? These are points well worthy of consideration, and I trust that the right hon. Gentleman will provide for them when we come to discuss his plan in its details. I can only say that while the right hon. Gentleman has not been able to fulfil the patriotic wishes of some Scotch Members to enable Scotland to do work for herself with her own Peers and her own Members of Parliament, nobody else intervening, he has gone so far to meet her views on the subject, and I hope the scheme will be in the main acceptable.

MR. STUART-WORTLEY: I wish to thank the Government for the concession which the right hon. Gentleman has made to the feelings of a large number of hon. Members on both sides of the House. I have a full conviction that there will be no difficulty in getting Members of the House of Commons to accept this important and dignified public service. The objection that this panel is to be fixed by the Secretary for Scotland, together with the Chairmen of Committees, is not particularly relevant. It must be borne in mind that these tribunals may have to be selected when the House is not sitting.

SIR CHARLES CAMERON: I should have explained that I provide in my Amendment for the selection of the Commissioners by the Chairman of Committees when the Committee of Selection is not sitting.

MR. STUART-WORTLEY: That is a matter of detail which can be provided for afterwards. I am disposed to enter a caveat against any limiting or restricting words which will have the effect of limiting the choice to Scotch Members or Scotch Peers. A number of Peers in the House of Lords sit there in a representative character, and others sit as British Peers. Again, a number of distinguished and energetic Members of this House

Sir H. Campbell-Bannerman.

who sit for English constituencies are Scotchmen, and I would not like to see them excluded from serving on these Commissions.

*MR. CROMBIE (Kincardineshire): I congratulate the Government on the position they have taken up. They have met us very fairly. As I understand it, the Lord Advocate has followed to some extent an Amendment I put down. My hon. friend the Member for Glasgow, Bridgeton, has stated that Scotch Members are excluded from Scotch Committees in this House. The best answer to that statement is that all this morning I have been sitting on a purely Scotch Committee, and that there is also a second Scotch Member on it.

SIR CHARLES CAMERON: I can only say that I was a member of the Committee of Selection for a great many years, and the rule was not to elect Scotch Members on Scotch Committees.

*MR. CROMBIE: In the evidence of the late Sir John Mowbray on the subject he said there was no rule on the matter, but the custom had arisen, and the reason was that, for the convenience of hon. Members, Bills were grouped in such a way that Members who sat on the Committees on one group of Bills might be eligible for all the Bills on the group. If a Scotch Bill happens to be grouped with English Bills, a Scotch Member might sit in Committee upon it. I hope that in any case the Lord Advocate will accept some Amendment which will make it perfectly clear that Scotch Members are to be put on such Committees, and that they are to be preferred to other Members. But I am not inclined to press for limiting the composition of the Committees to Scotch Members, as it would be more likely to involve an appeal to the outside panel. At present you work a Bill upstairs with a Committee of four Members, and if appealed to both Houses eight Members; whereas under the procedure proposed by this Bill there will be four Members only employed before the Provisional Order passes through the whole of its course. Therefore it seems to me that you are actually reducing the number of Members of Parliament required. I hope my hon. friend will stick to his Amendment, that the Chairmen of Committees, and not the Scotch Secretary, will elect the panels.

MR. DALZIEL (Kirkcaldy Burghs) : I do not quite so readily accept the concessions made by the Lord Advocate as my hon. friend. I looked upon this Bill as a useful measure because it had a certain Scotch flavour about it, and for the life of me I cannot see why the Lord Advocate should have departed from his original intention. I would rather have had the Bill as it originally stood than in the state in which it at present stands, for except on a very few points we will be practically where we were. Take, for instance, the proposal to bring English Members into the panel, or take again the proposal that the panel may sit in any place they may choose. My idea was that the Committee was to sit in Scotland ; but if English Members are to be on the panel it is a very big order indeed to ask them to go up to Scotland and sit there in judgment on a Scotch Bill.

MR. A. G. MURRAY : I certainly mean that the inquiry shall be made locally, and I propose to accept an Amendment which stands in the name of the hon. and learned Member for the Border Burghs, that the Commissioners should sit in Scotland.

MR. DALZIEL : Well, if we have local inquiry, and if English Members are going to be used in these inquiries, they will have to go down to Scotland to perform their functions. That is a tall order indeed. Although it might be popular if they sat in the middle of August, I do not think that English Members will do their duty with great equanimity if they have to go down to Scotland in the middle of November or December. This Amendment shows weakness on the part of the Government. It is ridiculous that English Members should go up to Scotland in mid-winter to sit on a little Railway Bill. If the right hon. Gentleman will consent to give the preference to Scottish Members and Scotch Peers, I think he will greatly improve the value of the Bill. There is only one other point I wish to enforce, and that is that the appointment of the Committees should be made by the Committees of Selection, and that the panel ought not to be appointed for five years. The panel ought to be appointed every year.

MR. A. G. MURRAY : If the hon Member for Caithness will withdraw his Amendment, all these matters will come up for discussion on the new clause.

CAPTAIN SINCLAIR (Forfar): I do not wish to delay progress, but I want to point out what seems to be one defect of the proposal. Inquiries held under the present Provisional Order system vary according to the importance of the Provisional Orders. Sometimes the inquiry is very important, and in a recent instance the President of the Board of Trade himself presided over the inquiry. But many inquiries are held under the supervision of an inspector or some other Departmental official. That gives an elasticity to the system. It seems to me that one defect of the new proposal is that, no matter what the importance of the subject of inquiry, the same elaborate machinery is to be employed.

DR. CLARK : I ask leave of the House to withdraw my Amendment. There is one point which has not been touched upon. Why I am in favour of the form embodied in my Amendment is that when the system of devolution was tried some years ago, it was given up because of the cost ; for they had a fight in the locality, and then two fights in Parliament, which piled up the expenses. The reason why I am very strongly in favour of having the panel composed of two Peers and two Commoners is that when the Commissioners go down to Scotland to hold the inquiry locally it is not at all likely that there will be an appeal to the House, especially when the appellants may be mulcted in costs.

Amendment, by leave, withdrawn.

Clause 3, as amended, agreed to.

Clause 4 :—

*SIR CHARLES CAMERON : I rise to move the first of a series of Amendments which I have drafted embodying a scheme. My scheme is that, for convenience in distributing the work, the Secretary for Scotland should divide the country into different groups of counties—say three ; and that the Committee of Selection in either House of Parliament should name a number—I suggest fifty, or it may be more or less—fifty Peers and fifty Members of this House, and that these should be divided into as many panels as there are groups of counties. When a Bill is to be referred to or e of these tribunals, I propose that the Committee of Selection shall nominate the Members from the appropriate panel. Further, I propose that the tribunal shall consist of two Members of the House of Lords, and two Members of the House of Commons, the Chairman to be alternately a Member of the House of Lords and of the House of Commons, and to be nominated also by the Committee of Selection. I have contemplated that it might be necessary to elect a tribunal when the Committee of Selection is not sitting. In that case the election will be made by the Chairmen of Committees alone. I think that the present proposals are somewhat crude, and that this is a matter in which you cannot have the Secretary for Scotland kept too much out of the business of selection. It is most important that there should be no suspicion whatever as to any possibility of his packing the Committee. I do not mean to say that the Secretary for Scotland would do so; but if you had him selecting, from all the Members of Parliament, one Member of this House, or two or three Members from the other House, you would have a Committee in which there would be no public confidence at all. The reason why Parliamentary Committees command so much confidence is that they are an impartial tribunal nominated in either House. As compared with the proposal of the Lord Advocate, every one of the schemes placed on the Paper has the merit of being worked out in detail and thoroughly thought out; but I must say that the Lord Advocate's proposal is crude, and has certainly not been worked out so thoroughly as the others. The Leader of the Opposition pointed out that the words the Lord Advocate proposed to embody in the Bill gave us not the slightest inkling as to the proportion of the Members of the House of Lords and of this House to be represented on the Committees. It is a matter of constitutional importance that the Committees appointed under this Measure should be representative of the two Houses, and the obvious way to do that is to have an equal number of Members from each House. I believe the proposal of the Lord Advocate will require to be entirely redrafted. You have no machinery whatever for the representa-

Sir Charles Cameron.

tion of this House or the other House on these Parliamentary tribunals, but the selection is entrusted without any check to the Secretary for Scotland, acting jointly with the Chairmen of Committees. The right hon. Gentleman will find it necessary to give principle of equilibrium to the clause by inserting some machinery for the election of Members of this House and the other House infinitely more elaborate than he has embodied in the Bill. Whether you are going to have such a system of grouping as I propose, or not, it is most important that we should remove the barrier at present existing against Scotch Members sitting on Scotch Committees. It is said that there is no constitutional disability on the part of Scotch Members sitting on Scotch Bills. That is true, but in the whole course of my experience I never knew of the appointment of a Scotch Member upon a group of Scotch Bills. I believe if Scotch Members were placed on these Committees in proportion to their numbers in this House that they would serve where English Members would not. But in order to have an opportunity of serving they must be upon the panel.

Amendment proposed—

"In page 3, line 13, to leave out the words 'a panel,' and insert the word 'panels' instead thereof."—(*Sir Charles Cameron.*)

Question proposed, "That the words 'a panel' stand part of the clause."

MR. A. G. MURRAY: The greater part of the hon. Baronet's remarks are really more appropriate to Clause 5 than Clause 4, because obviously the place to deal with an Amendment of this kind is the last section in Clause 5. All that we have to do at present is to see how we are to deal between the hon. Baronet's scheme and the scheme put forward by the Government. I can assure him he will find that the Government scheme has been very carefully drafted, and I do not think he will find it any more slipshod than any Amendment on the Paper. The only question that arises here is whether we shall have upon the panel members other than Members of Parliament. I have already explained that it is necessary to have other people, and some word or other is necessary to describe other people. I think "panel" is as convenient a word as any other, and the whole scope of this clause is simply to provide for the selection of those people other than Members of Parliament. Under the circumstances I cannot accept the hon. Baronet's Amendment.

MR. DALZIEL : I am sorry that I cannot, in this case, agree with the Amendment of the hon. Baronet, but I think that if his scheme were adopted it would lead to too great a complication, and prejudice the popularity of the measure. With regard to the objections of the Lord Advocate, I might point out that the panel is going to contain 1,200 people already. It is to contain both Houses of Parliament. I think that a great thing in

this matter is to make the Bill as simple as possible.

MR. CALDWELL : In forming the panel, Scotland, I think, should be divided into three or four groups, with the idea of having a wider area from which you could select the panel with reference to any particular Bill, and in that way you would be able to make a selection without any invidious distinctions. When you came to a particular Bill the Committee of Selection would consider the panel, and in that way there would be a certain amount of limitation in the selection. The advantage of a system of this kind would be that there would not be such a continuous appointment of particular persons for special Bills.

The Committee divided : Ayes, 135 ; Noes, 48.   (Division List No. 197.)

AYES.

Ashmead-Bartlett, Sir Ellis
Atkinson, Rt Hon. John
Bailey, James (Walworth)
Balfour, Rt. Hon. G W. (Leeds)
Barnes, Frederic Gorell
Barton, Dunbar Plunkett
Begg, Ferdinand Faithfull
Beresford, Lord Charles
Bethell, Commander
Bhownaggree, Sir M. M.
Blakiston-Houstoo, John
Blundell, Colonel Henry
Bond, Edward
Brodrick, Rt. Hon. St. John
Brookfield, A. Montague
Bryce, Rt. Hon. Jan e.
Carmichael, Sir T. D. Gibson-
Causton, Richard Knight
Chaloner, Captain R. G. W.
Chamberlain, J Austen (Worc'r
Clare, Octavius Leigh
Cochrane, Hon. Thos. H. A E.
Coghill, Douglas Harry
Cohen, Benjamin Louis
Collings, Rt. Hon. Jesse
Colston, Chas. Edw. H. A.
Corbett, A.Cameron(Glasgow)
Crombie, John William
Cross, Alexander (Glasgow)
Cruddas, William Donaldson
Cubitt, Hon. Henry
Curran, Thos. B. (Donegal)
Curzon, Viscount
Dalkeith, Earl of
Donkin, Richard Sim
Douglas, Rt. Hon. A. Akers-
Doxford, William Theodore
Duncombe, Hon. Hubert V.
Fardell, Sir T. George
Fellowes, Hon Ailwyn Edw.
Finlay, Sir Robert Bannatyne
Fisher, William Hayes
Flower, Ernest
Folkestone, Viscount
Fry, Lewis
Garfit, William

Godson, Sir Augustus F.
Goldsworthy, Major-General
Gordon, Hon. John Edward
Gorst, Rt. Hon. Sir John Eldon
Goschen, George J. (Sussex)
Goulding, Edward Alfred
Gray, Ernest (West Ham)
Green, W. D. (Wednesbury)
Hamilton, Rt. Hn. Lord George
Hamond, Sir C. (Newcastle)
Hanbury, Rt. Hon. R. W.
Hedderwick, Thos. Charles H.
Henderson, Alexander
Hornby, Sir William Henry
Howell, William Tudor
Hubbard, Hon. Evelyn
Hutton, John (Yorks N.R.)
Jebb, Richard Claverhouse
Johnston, William (Belfast)
Kennaway, Rt. Hon. Sir. J. H.
Kimber, Henry
Kinloch, Sir John Geo. Smyth
Laurie, Lieut-General
Lawrence, Sir E. Durning-(Corn
Lawson, John Grant (Yorks.)
Leigh-Bennett, Henry Currie
Loder, Gerald Walter Erskine
Long, Rt. Hn. Walter(Liverp'l)
Lorne, Marquess of
Lowe, Francis William
Loyd, Archie Kirkman
Lucas-Shadwell, William
Macartney, W. G. Ellison
Macdona, John Cumming
M'Iver, Sir L. (Edinburgh, W.)
Mellor, Colonel (Lancashire)
Middlemore, J. Throgmorton
Milton, Viscount
Milward, Colonel Victor
Morrell, George Herbert
Morrison, Walter
Morton, A. H. A. (Deptford)
Mount, William George
Murray, Rt. Hn. A C. (Bute)
Murray, Col. Wyndham (Bath
Nicol, Donald Ninian

Phillpotts, Captain Arthur
Pilkington, R. (LancsNewton)
Platt-Higgins, Frederick
Powell, Sir Francis Sharp
Pollock, Harry Frederick
Priestley, Sir W. O. (Edin.)
Purvis, Robert
Pym, C. Guy
Renshaw, Charles Bine
Ritchie, Rt. Hon. C. Thomson
Robertson, Herbert(Hackney)
Round James
Royds, Clement Molyneux
Russell, Gen. F.S.(Cheltenham
Russell, T. W. (Tyrone)
Samuel, H. S. (Limehouse)
Sharpe, William Edward T.
Shaw, Thomas (Hawick B.)
Skewes-Cox, Thomas
Smith, James Parker(Lanarks)
Smith, Hon. W. F. D. (St'nd)
Stanley, Lord (Lancs.)
Stirling-Maxwell, Sir John M.
Stone, Sir Benjamin
Strauss, Arthur
Sturt, Hon. Humphry Napier
Talbot, Rt. Hn. J.G.(Ox.Univ.)
Thorburn, Walter
Thornton, Percy M.
Tritton, Charles Ernest
Ure, Alexander
Valentia, Viscount
Wallace, Robert (Perth)
Warr, Augustus Frederick
Williams, Jos. Powell- (Birm.
Wilson, John (Falkirk)
Wilson,J.W.(Worcestersh.N.)
Wolff, Gustav Wilhelm
Wortley,Rt.Hon.C.B. Stuart-
Wylie, Alexander
Wyndham, George
Wyvill Marmaduke D'Arcy
Young, Commander Berks, E.)
TELLERS FOR THE AYES—
  Sir William Walrond and
  Mr. Anstruther.

NOES.

Allan, William (Gateshead)
Bayley, Thomas (Derbyshire)
Billson, Alfred
Burns, John
Carvill, Patrick George H.
Clark,Dr.G.B. (Caithness-sh.)
Clough, Walter Owen
Commins, Andrew
Curran, Thomas (Sligo, S.)
Davitt, Michael
Doogan, P. C.
Evans, Samuel T.(Glamorgan)
Farrell, James P. (Cavan, W.)
Fenwick, Charles
Flavin, Michael Joseph
Gibney, James
Goddard, Daniel Ford

Gourley, Sir Edw. Temperley
Hammond, John (Carlow)
Harwood, George
Horniman, Frederic John
Humphreys Owen, Arthur C.
Jacoby, James Alfred
Jordan, Jeremiah
Kilbride, Denis
Leng, Sir John
Lewis, John Herbert
MacAleese, Daniel
MacNeill, J. Gordon Swift
M'Ghee, Richard
M'Leod, John
Maddison, Fred
Morgan, J. L. (Carmarthen)
Pinkerton, John

Rickett, J. Compton
Roberts, John Bryn (Eifion)
Souttar, Robinson
Spicer, Albert
Steadman, William Charles
Sullivan, Donal (Westmeath)
Sullivan, T. D. (Donegal, W.)
Thomas, David A. (Merthyr)
Trevelyan, Charles Philips
Wedderburn, Sir William
Weir, James Galloway
Whittaker, Thomas Palmer
Williams, John C. (Notts.)
Wilson, J. H. (Middlesbrough)
TELLERS FOR THE NOES—
   Sir Charles Cameron and
   Mr. Caldwell.

MR. CALDWELL: I notice that the next Amendment is in the name of the hon. Member for Bridgeton, who has not yet returned—to leave out from "panel" to the end of line 15. I do not know whether the Lord Advocate will insist upon those words.

MR. A. G. MURRAY: I really think they are necessary.

SIR CHARLES CAMERON: The last Division I think, settled this question, and I propose to leave the matter with the Lord Advocate.

MR. CALDWELL: The hon. Member for the Hawick Burghs is not here to move his Amendment, but I have no doubt that he feels very strongly that the selection of the 25 members of the outside panel should not be left in the hands of the Chairmen acting jointly with the Secretary for Scotland. In regard to determining whether any part of the Bill should proceed by Provisional Order or by Private Bill, it has already been pointed out that the Chairman had so much work to do that the proposal was imposing very great work upon him. You are here imposing upon him a burden of a kind which is altogether foreign to any experience that he has in this House. In regard to deciding under which method a Bill should proceed, there can be no doubt whatever that the Chairman naturally is the best authority if he had the time for the work, but this is a different matter altogether. What particular knowledge would the Chairman have of people in Scotland? I do not consider that the Chairman has necessarily the requisite experience to select men of the kind desired, and the practical result would be that the selection

would be made by the Secretary for Scotland. I quite admit that very likely this outside panel would not be required to act, as probably from Members of Parliament alone a sufficient panel would be found, and that minimises the point here. I therefore move to leave out the words "the chairmen acting jointly with the Secretary for Scotland" in order to insert "the Committee of Selection of either House."

Amendment proposed—

"In page 3, line 18, to leave out from the first 'The,' to 'Scotland,' in line 19, and insert 'Committee of Selection of either House.'"—(*Mr. Caldwell.*)

Question proposed, "That the words proposed to be left out stand part of the clause."

MR. A. G. MURRAY: I do not think the hon. Member for the Hawick Burghs would have moved this Amendment if he had been here. This clause has simply to do with the selection of the outside Commissioners. I quite agree that perhaps the Chairman has not a great deal of experience on this point. The alternative of the hon. Member is the Committee of Selection. Surely the Committee of Selection are not the people to select an outside body. They have just as little knowledge as the Chairman would have, and have far less flexibility. If I had been drafting the clause myself I should have been inclined to put the Secretary for Scotland alone, because he knows more about the people. But there is a jealousy about the Secretary for Scotland doing anything himself, and I am very anxious to meet that feeling, and I have therefore associated with him the two Chairmen.

MR. THOMAS SHAW: I may explain at once that this Amendment was put down as part of the general scheme of Amendments which I laid before the House. It was appropriate to that scheme, but the substantial purpose of it has been served by the concessions of Her Majesty's Government. I understand now that Section 4 is to be confined to the extra-Parliamentary panel, and by the provisions of Section 5 there is to be proposed a Parliamentary panel, so that Section 4 will only operate if the provisions of Section 5 should fail to come into operation. . Accordingly, I should not myself insist upon the Amendment, because while the Committee of Selection of the House of Commons is most appropriate for the selection of inter-Parliamentary bodies, it is not at all a proper body for selecting this panel, which is only to be, as it were, a *dernier ressort* after the proposals of the Government in regard to the Parliamentary panel have failed.

DR. CLARK : I take it that this panel is not to be limited to Scotch people ; the Secretary for Scotland may appoint an Irishman, or a Welshman, or an American ; there is no limitation. Hence you could not expect the Committee of Selection to know much more about the matter than the two Chairmen and the Secretary for Scotland. I think under the circumstances the hon. Member should withdraw his Amendment and let the Lord Advocate get this portion, if it is only a panel *pis aller*—only to be used if the other cannot be got.

Amendment, by leave, withdrawn.

An Amendment made.

SIR CHARLES CAMERON : I think it will be found that this panel is altogether useless, and if the words "may if they consider it necessary" were inserted it would be optional for future Secretaries for Scotland to appoint a panel or not, as it was found necessary. As the Bill stands all future Secretaries for Scotland would be called upon to appoint these 25 persons. Therefore I propose this Amendment, the object of which is simply to give the opportunity of dropping the machinery if it is found unnecessary.

Amendment proposed—

"In page 3, line 20, to leave out 'shall,' and insert 'may if they consider it necessary.' "— (*Sir Charles Cameron.*)

Question proposed, "That the word 'shall' stand part of clause."

MR. A. G. MURRAY : I hope the Amendment will not be pressed, as I think the words had much better be left as they are.

SIR CHARLES CAMERON : It is not worth dividing upon, and if the hon. Gentleman thinks it will save his face to leave it as it stands, I will not press the Amendment.

DR. CLARK : It seems to me it is not the Secretary for Scotland, but the Chairmen who are to appoint, and they are to ask the Secretary for Scotland to assist them. We take it that the present Chairmen and the present Secretary for Scotland will appoint this committee, and perhaps for the next five, ten or fifteen, years it may be appointed ; but surely if it is found unnecessary you do not want the trouble and expense of forming a panel which is never used. The view is that 1,200 Members of Parliament should form one panel, but if sufficient Members cannot be obtained this other panel is to be called in. If, however, plenty of Members are found, this clause might fall into disuse. Surely it might be left to the discretion of the Chairmen whether the panel should be appointed. At any rate the Amendment can do no harm.

MR. CALDWELL : If experience shows, as I have no doubt it will, that there are plenty of Members to be obtained, it will not be advisable to appoint a panel of this kind. For one thing it is invidious, because when there are certain men appointed on the panel there is the difficulty of selecting particular men. It will also be a very awkward thing to select a panel when you know perfectly well that that panel is not at all likely to be used.

Amendment, by leave, withdrawn.

SIR H. CAMPBELL-BANNERMAN : I do not in the least desire to anticipate anybody else, but I suppose we are now on the number of the panel, which is supposed to be 25. Is not that number excessive, if it is to be a real thing at all, and if those who are put upon the panel are to be capable and competent men ? I do not say that 25 such men will not be found in the kingdom, but still it is rather a large number for the purpose. I would also suggest that they should not hold the exalted position in which they are to be placed for as long as five years. Would not 10 Members appointed for two years be better? Someone referred to the desperately small number of cases that would have to be submitted to this panel, and I really think—with 25 men at the back of 1,200 members, as it was put by a previous speaker, 1,225—that 1,210 would be sufficient to cope with perhaps the half-a-dozen inquiries which would be necessary in the course of the year. I quite appreciate the desire of the Lord Advocate not to be left to the goodwill of Members of Parliament, and that he should have somebody behind them upon whom he could fall back, but I think 10 men appointed for two years would be quite sufficient for the purpose.

Amendment proposed—

"In page 3, line 20, to leave out '25' and insert '10.'"—(*Sir H. Campbell-Bannerman.*)

Question proposed, "That '25' stand part of the clause."

MR. A. G. MURRAY: The reason of fixing the number at 25 was to give a number that would be sufficient to deal perfectly well with the duties to be discharged. I am not bound to the number 25, but, on the other hand, 10 is rather few. The right hon. Gentleman prophesies that 10 would be plenty, but he might be wrong. As to the suggestion about two years, I think it would be a pity that the Committee should have to be re-formed at such short intervals. If the right hon. Gentleman thinks 25 is too many, I should be very glad to make it 20; that would be much safer than 10.

SIR H. CAMPBELL-BANNERMAN: I do not regard it as a question of principle. I do not know whether this would be the time to ask whether these 20 persons are to be paid, and if so, in what way? Our feeling towards these gentlemen would be considerably affected by that fact. I will be perfectly candid. There is always a possibility that if a considerable emolument were attached to being employed on the panel, it might increase the difficulty of finding Members and Peers to act upon it. That may be a Machiavellian, almost Mephistophelian, conception

Sir H. Campbell-Bannerman.

of the state of mind of those employed on this matter, but it is a consideration which must be borne in mind.

MR. A. G. MURRAY: I confess that my first impression was in favour of payment, because I rather felt it might be very valuable to have the services of some persons who could not afford to serve without some emolument. But, at the same time, the Treasury allowances are on so modest and sparing a scale that I do not think they would offer any inducement. It having been brought home to me that there is a very considerable feeling on both sides of the House in regard to the matter, and recognising that feeling, I should be prepared, when the time comes, to accept an Amendment to strike out the italicised clause—that is to say, in other words, to make no payment.

Question put and negatived.

Question, "That '20' be there inserted," put, and agreed to.

An Amendment made.

MR. THOMAS SHAW: I move to substitute the word "two" for the word "four," so that it will read—"shall remain therein until the expiration of two years." The first part of the scheme which the Lord Advocate has foreshadowed to the House is that we shall have a Parliamentary panel. It is perfectly clear that the composition of Parliament changes, and changes rapidly, from time to time, and it would be most unfortunate that we should have a permanent Parliamentary panel lasting for five years, or probably four, after the constitution of Parliament had completely changed.

Amendment proposed—

"In page 3, line 22, to leave out the word 'five,' and insert the word 'two.'"—(*Mr. Thomas Shaw.*)

Question proposed, "That the word 'five' stand part of the clause."

MR. J. P. SMITH: I hope the Lord Advocate will be willing to shorten the period. If it is as long as five years you must provide for filling up casual vacancies, while if the period is reduced to two or three years the casual vacancies will look after themselves. With the prospect of so soon making another panel you would not need to trouble about filling vacancies from time to time.

*Sir JOHN LENG (Dundee): I rather hoped that the hon. and learned Member intended to insert the word "one," because all the panels of this House are appointed for only one year, and I do not see why an innovation should be introduced in a panel outside the House. We should keep within regular lines as far as possible.

Mr. A. G. MURRAY: I think the hon. Member is rather misled by the word "panel." These are merely persons from whom the selection is to be made, and in that sense the panels of the House are not made up every year, but correspond with the duration of Parliament. Really the whole matter is one more of convenience than anything else. I do not think it can be said that casual vacancies would not have to be filled, because there must be occasions when, through some misfortune, the numbers were very much reduced indeed. Therefore it would not be safe to take out the clause with regard to filling casual vacancies. The hon. Member for the Hawick Burghs rather wanted the average life of these extra Commissioners to be the same as that of Parliamentary Commissioners. I suppose four years would not be far away from the average life of Parliament, and therefore the two numbers would be much the same. I want to save the trouble of having this number of gentlemen selected too often.

Sir CHARLES CAMERON: I really appeal to my hon. friend not to be too hard upon the Government. The Secretary for Scotland has set his heart upon this panel. He has had it opposed in all sorts of ways, and now he has got it down to this, and with this he says he will be content. Let him have his panel. It will never be called upon to act. Let him have it for five years. He is like the boy and the soap—he won't be happy till he gets it.

Question put.

The Committee divided : Ayes, 149 ; Noes, 69. (Division list No. 198.)

AYES.

Anson, Sir William Reynell
Ashmead-Bartlett, Sir Ellis
Atkinson, Rt. Hon. John
Bailey, James (Walworth)
Balfour, Rt. Hn.G.W. (Leeds)
Balfour, Rt. Hon. A. J. (Man.)
Banbury, Frederick George
Barnes, Frederic Gorell
Barton, Dunbar Plunket
Beach, Rt. Hn.SirMH (Bristol)
Begg, Ferdinand Faithfull
Bethell, Commander
Bhownaggree, Sir M. M.
Blakiston-Houston, John
Blundell, Colonel Henry
Bolton, Thomas Dolling
Bond, Edward
Boscawen, Arthur Griffith-
Brodrick, Rt. Hon. St. John
Brookfield, A. Montagu
Cawley, Frederick
Chaloner, Captain R. G.W.
Chamberlain, J. A. (Worc'r)
Clare, Octavius Leigh
Cochrane, Hon. T. H. A. E.
Coghill, Douglas Harry
Collings, Rt. Hon. Jesse
Colston, C. E. H. Athole
Corbett, A. Cam'ron(Glasgow)
Cripps, Charles Alfred
Cross, Alexander (Glasgow)
Cruddas, William Donaldson
Cubitt, Hon. Henry
Curzon, Viscount
Dalbiac, Colonel Philip Hugh

Dalkeith, Earl of
Dalrymple, Sir Charles
Denny, Colonel
Douglas, Rt. Hon. A. Akers
Duncombe, Hon. Hubert V.
Egerton, Hon. A. de Tatton
Fardell, Sir T. George
Fellowes,Hon.AilwynEdward
Finlay, Sir Robert Bannatyne
Fisher, William Hayes
FitzGerald,SirRobert Penrose-
Flower, Ernest
Folkestone, Viscount
Fry, Lewis
Garfit, William
Gedge, Sydney
Godson, Sir Augustus Fred.
Goldsworthy, Major-General
Gordon, Hon. John Edward
Gorst, Rt. Hon.Sir JohnEldon
Goschen, RtHnGJ(StGeorge's)
Goschen, George J. (Sussex)
Goulding, Edward Alfred
Gray, Ernest (West Ham)
Green, W. D.(Wednesbury)
Greville, Hon. Ronald
Hamilton, Rt. Hon. Lord Geo.
Hamond, Sir Chas.(Newcastle)
Hanbury,Rt. Hon.RobertWm.
Henderson, Alexander
Hermon-Hodge, Robt. Trotter
Hobhouse, Henry
Hornby, Sir William Hnry
Howell, William Tudor
Hubbard, Hon. Evelyn

Jackson, Rt. Hon.Wm.Lawies
Jebb, Richard Claverhouse
Johnston, William (Belfast)
Johnstone, Heywood (Sussex)
Kennaway, Rt. Hon. Sir J.H.
Lawrence,SirE.Durning-(Corn
Lawson, John Grant (Yorks.)
Leigh-Bennett, Henry Currie-
Lockwood, Lt.-Col. A. R.
Loder, Gerald Walter Erskine-
Long, Right Hon. Walter
Lopes, Henry Yarde Buller
Lorne, Marquess of
Lowe, Francis William
Loyd, Archie Kirkman
Lucas-Shadwell, William
Lyell, Sir Leonard
Macartney, W. G. Ellison
Macdona, John Cumming
M'Iver, SirLewis(Ed'nb'gh,W..
Malcolm, Ian
Mellor, Colonel (Lancashire)
Middlemore, J. Throgmorton.
Mildmay, Francis Bingham
Milton, Viscount
Milward, Colonel Victor
Monk. Charles James
Morrell, George Herbert
Morton, Ar. H. A. (Deptford)
Mount, William George
Murray, Rt. Hn. A. G. (Bute)
Murray, Col. W. (Bath)
Nicol, Donald Ninian
Orr-Ewing, Charles Lindsay
Phillpotts, Captain Arthur

Pilkington, R.(Lancs.Newton)
Platt-Higgins, Frederick
Pollock, Harry Frederick
Powell, Sir Francis Sharp
Priestley, Sir W. O. (Edin.)
Purvis, Robert
Rasch, Major F. Carne
Renshaw, Charles Bine
Richardson, Sir T. Hartlep'l)
Ridley, Rt. Hon. Sir M. W.
Ritchie, Rt. Hon. C. T.
Robertson, Herbert(Hackney)
Round, James
Royds, Clement Molyneux
Russell, Gen. F. S. (Ch'lten'm)
Russell, T. W. (Tyrone)

Samuel, Harry S. (Limehouse)
Sharpe, William Edward T.
Skewes-Cox, Thomas
Smith, Hon. W.F.D. (Strand)
Stanley, Lord (Lancs.)
Stephens, Henry Charles
Strauss, Arthur
Sturt, Hon. Humphry Napier
Sutherland, Sir Thomas
Talbot,Rt.Hn.J.G.(OxfdUni.)
Thorburn, Walter
Thornton, Percy M.
Tomlinson, Wm. Edw. Murray
Tritton, Charles Ernest
Valentia, Viscount
Warr, Augustus Frederick

Whiteley,H.(Ashton-under-L.
Williams, J. Powell-(Birm.)
Wilson, John (Falkirk)
Wilson,J.W.(Worcestersh.N)
Wodehouse,Rt.Hn E.R.(Bath
Wolff, Gustav Wilhelm
Wortley,Rt. Hon. C.B.Stuart-
Wylie, Alexander
Wyndham, George
Wyndham-Quin, Major W. H.
Wyvill, Marmaduke D'Arcy
Young, Com. (Berks, E.)

TELLERS FOR THE AYES—
Sir William Walrond and
Mr. Anstruther.

NOES.

Billson, Alfred
Bryce, Rt. Hon. James
Burns, John
Caldwell, James
Cameron,SirCharles(Glasgow)
Campbell-Bannerman, Sir H.
Carmichael, Sir T. D. Gibson-
Causton, Richard Knight
Channing, Francis Allston
Clark, Dr. G. B (Caithness-sh)
Clough, Walter Owen
Commins, Andrew
Crilly, Daniel
Crombie, John William
Curran, Thomas B. (Donegal)
Davitt, Michael
Dillon, John
Donelan, Captain A.
Doogan, P. C.
Dunn, Sir William
Ellis, John Edward
Evans, S. T. (Glamorgan)
Farrell, James P. (Cavan, W.)
Fenwick, Charles
Flavin, Michael Joseph

Foster, Sir W. (Derby Co.)
Gibney, James
Goddard, Daniel Ford
Hammond, John (Carlow)
Horniman, Frederick John
Humphreys-Owen, Arthur C.
Jordan, Jeremiah
Kearley, Hudson E.
Kilbride, Denis
Kinloch, Sir John George S.
Lawson, Sir W. (Cumberland)
Lewis, John Herbert
Macaleese, Daniel
MacNeill, John Gordon Swift
M'Ghee, Richard
M'Leod, John
Maddison, Fred.
Morgan, J. L. (Carmarthen)
Pease, Joseph A. (Northumb.)
Philipps, John Wynford
Pinkerton, John
Power, Patrick Joseph
Provand, Andrew Dryburgh
Rickett, J. Compton
Roberts, John Bryn (Eifion)

Roberts, John H. (Denbigh.)
Robertson, Edmund (Dundee)
Samuel, J. (Stockton-on-Tees)
Shaw, Thomas (Hawick, B.)
Smith, James P. (Lanarks.)
Souttar, Robinson
Spicer, Albert
Steadman, William Charles
Sullivan, Donal (Westmeath
Sullivan, T. D. (Donegal, W.)
Thomas, David A. (Merthyr)
Trevelyan, Charles Philips
Ure, Alexander
Wallace, Robert
Wedderburn, Sir William
Weir, James Galloway
Whittaker, Thomas Palmer
Williams, John C. (Notts.)
Wilson, J. H.(Middlesbrough

TELLERS FOR THE NOES—
Sir John Leng and Mr.
Hedderwick.

Clause, as amended, agreed to.

Clause 5 :—

*SIR CHARLES CAMERON: The Committee of Selection should appoint these new tribunals, and when Parliament is not sitting they should be selected by the Chairmen from a list of Members nominated by the Committee of Selection for that purpose. There is not the smallest difficulty about it. My Amendment proposes that these Commissioners should be nominated not by the Secretary for Scotland, acting in concert with the Chairmen, but, on the grounds which have been repeatedly set forth in this Debate, that this should be done by the Committee of Selection. I think this is an intelligible proposition, and also an important modification.

Amendment proposed—

"In page 3, line 31, to leave out the words 'Secretary for Scotland acting jointly with the Chairmen,' and insert the words 'Committees of Selection of the Houses of Lords and Commons respectively.'"—(*Sir Charles Cameron.*)

Question proposed, "That the words proposed to be left out stand part of the clause."

MR. A. G. MURRAY: Hon. Members opposite seem to think that this is something far away from the duties of the ordinary Chairman of Committees. They forget, I think, for the moment that the Chairman of Committees in the House of Lords is also Chairman of the Committee of Selection. I am perfectly willing to substitute for the Chairman of Committees in the House of Commons the Chairman of the Committee of Selection of this House. Of course the Committees of Selection themselves would be cumbersome bodies to carry out the intention of this clause, and it would be necessary to make special provision for cases arising during the recess.

Mr. THOMAS SHAW: I hope my hon. friend will agree to the suggestion which has just been made by the right hon. Gentleman, for I think that upon the lines which have just been conceded we have practically gained the point which we desired to achieve. It does appear to me that the argument of my right hón. friend is particularly applicable to these cases of Private Bills.

Dr. CLARK: I should like to ask the Lord Advocate how he proposes to create his Joint Committee ?

*The CHAIRMAN: That question is not in order on this point.

Dr. CLARK: We are now going to appoint the short panel to go down and make the preliminary inquiries. I take it that the Chairman of Committees of the House of Lords will appoint the Peers, and the Chairman of Committees of the House of Commons will appoint the Commoners. I think there ought to be some limitation as to the number, and the arrangement suggested seems to be very unsuitable. If we are going to have a Joint Committee, we ought to have an equal number of Peers and Commoners. Under the present system we have a large panel from which the Committees are taken, and I should like to know if that is the panel from which they are going to be taken in the future.

Mr. A. G. MURRAY: That will be for the House to decide.

Sir H. CAMPBELL-BANNERMAN: The objection which my friends and myself still entertain to the amended panel of the right hon. Gentleman is that we wish the selecting authority to be purely Parliamentary, and we do not wish to have this power exercised by the Secretary for Scotland. In this matter, surely the selection of the Members of the House of Commons, and the Peers also, to serve

in this capacity should be left, as near as we can get, to the ordinary selecting authority of Parliament. The only objection I have heard is that this process may have to be conducted during the recess, when the Committee of Selection is not sitting. What would there be to hinder the Committee of Selection first of all dealing with all the necessities that arose during the session ; and, as to the necessities that may arise during the recess, they might, before Parliament is prorogued, establish a sort of subordinate panel, and ascertain the names of a number of Members who would be available for this purpose when the occasion arose, and a limited number might be appointed for any occasional requirements during the recess, and from these the Chairmen or anybody else might select particular Members. In that way we should keep the whole thing in Parliamentary hands. I think, however much we may recognise the desire of the Lord Advocate to meet us, he still retains the bone of contention, which is the practice of an outside element meddling with Parliamentary matters.

Mr. A. G. MURRAY: As far as the outside element is concerned, I should like to know if the following words will meet the views of hon. and right hon. Gentlemen opposite. Instead of saying " the Secretary for Scotland acting jointly with the Chairmen," I suggest the words " the two Chairmen, after communication with the Secretary for Scotland."

Sir H. CAMPBELL-BANNERMAN: I think that the more the Lord Advocate reflects upon this matter the more he will see that the Secretary for Scotland ought to have nothing to do with it. If it is to be a mixed panel, then let the Committee of Selection appoint all the members that are required, and, if there happens to be one or two short, then let the Secretary for Scotland come on with his 20 eligibles, or his regiment of men, but let us keep the Parliamentary part of it in our hands. I do hope the right hon. Gentleman will see his way to accept this.

Mr. CRIPPS: I hope the Lord Advocate will assent to this proposal. There is no harm in leaving out the Secretary for Scotland in this instance, for he appears in Section 4. As regards any question of local knowledge, the Secretary for Scotland is really quite unnecessary, and why should he have anything to do with the selection of representative Members of this House or of the other House? I think the two Chairmen would be by far the best persons who could be selected, in order that the selection should secure Parliamentary representation, and that would be carrying out the suggestion of the Lord Advocate. Really in this matter the Secretary for Scotland has no *locus standi* at all. Although I do not desire to use the harsh terms used by the Leader of the Opposition, I do hope the Lord Advocate will assent to this Amendment.

*SIR CHARLES CAMERON : I have been on a Committee of Selection, and I know how the thing is worked. At the end of the session I have often seen a Committee run very short. I think it is most essential that the representative character of these Committees should be preserved, and if you are going to have a substitute, then by all means have your Chairman of Committees or your Chairman of the Committee of Selection. Let me tell the right hon. Gentleman that this difficulty has arisen owing to his misuse of the word "panel" in connection with these 25 gentlemen.

*MR. HEDDERWICK (Wick Burghs): I trust that the Lord Advocate will consent to omit the Secretary for Scotland from this clause. There are many reasons for taking this course. It has already been pointed out that the Secretary for Scotland has been inserted in Clause 4. The chief objection of the Lord Advocate is that the Chairmen of the Committees would not have any knowledge of the reserve panel, and therefore that it is necessary to include someone who is likely to have such knowledge ; but the provisions with reference to the Secretary in Clause 4 deprives this objection of its force. On the other hand, however willing the Scotch Members might be, it is quite conceivable that English Members of the House of Commons might object to serve as Commissioners upon the nomination of a Scots Secretary, and the operation of the Bill might thus be seriously impeded, because the difficulty of getting men to serve might be very much increased by insisting on this retention of the Secretary for Scotland. On this side of the House it is felt that if the Secretary for Scotland is made one of three Members who are to nominate these Commissioners, then the power will ultimately rest with the Secretary for Scotland, and the Chairmen of Committees will be merely nominal factors in the matter. I trust, therefore, that the Lord Advocate will leave out the Secretary for Scotland from the clause.

*SIR CHARLES DALRYMPLE (Ipswich): I hope that the Lord Advocate will not leave "the Secretary for Scotland" out of the clause. I particularly object to the proposal to bring forward the Chairman of the Committee of Selection in a matter of this kind. It is quite a novelty to separate the Chairman of the Committee of Selection from his Committee, and I cannot see that there is any fitness in the proposal relating to him.

Question put.

The Committee divided : Ayes, 157 ; Noes, 82. (Division List No. 199.)

AYES.

Acland-Hood, Capt. Sir A. F.	Chaloner, Captain R. G. W.	Denny, Colonel
Allhusen, A. Henry Eden	Chamberlain, Rt.Hn.J.(Birm.)	Digby, John K. D. Wingfield-
Anson, Sir Wm. Reynell	Chamberlain, J. A. (Worc'r)	Dorington, Sir John Edward
Ashmead-Bartlett, Sir Ellis	Chaplin, Rt. Hon. Henry	Douglas, Rt. Hon. A. Akers-
Atkinson, Rt. Hon. John	Clare, Octavius Leigh	Duncombe, Hon. Hubert V.
Bailey, James (Walworth)	Cochrane, Hon. Thos. H. A. E.	Egerton, Hon. A. de Tatton
Balcarres, Lord	Cogbill, Douglas Harry	Fardell, Sir T. George
Balfour,Rt.Hn.A.J.(Manch'r)	Collings, Rt. Hon. Jesse	Fellowes, Hon. Ailwyn E.
Balfour, Rt. Hon.G.W.(Leeds)	Colomb, Sir John Charles R.	Finch, George H.
Banbury, Frederick George	Compton, Lord Alwyne	Finlay, Sir Robert Bannatyne
Barton, Dunbar Plunket	Cooke,C.W.Radcliffe(Heref'd)	Fisher, William Hayes
Beach,Rt.Hn.SirM.H.(Brist'l)	Corbett, A.Cameron(Glasgow)	FitzGerald,SirRobert Penrose
Begg, Ferdinand Faithfull	Cranborne, Viscount	Flower, Ernest
Beresford, Lord Charles	Cubitt, Hon. Henry	Folkestone, Viscount
Boscawen, Arthur Griffith-	Curzon, Viscount	Fry, Lewis
Brodrick, Rt. Hon. St. John	Dalbiac, Colonel Philip Hugh	Garfit, William
Brookfield, A. Montagu	Dalkeith, Earl of	Gedge, Sydney
Cecil, Lord Hugh (Greenwich)	Dalrymple, Sir Charles	Godson, Sir Augustus Fredk.

Goldsworthy, Major-General
Gordon, Hon. John Edward
Gorst, Rt. Hon. Sir John E.
Goschen,Rt.HnG.J.(St Geo.'s
Goschen, George J. (Sussex)
Goulding, Edward Alfred
Gray, Ernest (West Ham)
Green, W. D. (Wednesbury)
Greene, W. R. (Cambs.)
Greville, Hon. Ronald
Hamilton,Rt.Hn. Lord George
Hamond, Sir C. (Newcastle)
Hanbury, Rt. Hn. Robert W.
Henderson, Alexander
Hermon-Hodge, Robt.Trotter
Hobhouse, Henry
Hornby, Sir William Henry
Howell, William Tudor
Jebb, Richard Claverhouse
Johnston, William (Belfast)
Johnstone, Heywood (Sussex)
Kennaway,Rt.Hon.SirJohnH.
Kenyon, James
Kimber, Henry
Lawrence,SirE.Durning-(Corn
Lawrence, Wm. F. (Liverpool)
Lawson, John Grant (Yorks.)
Leigh-Bennett, Henry Currie
Lockwood, Lt.-Col. A. R.
Loder, Gerald Walter Erskine
Long, Col. Chas. W.(Evesham
Long, Rt. Hon. W. (Liverpool)
Lopes, Henry Yarde Buller
Lorne, Marquess of
Lowe, Francis William
Loyd, Archie Kirkman

Lucas-Shadwell, William
Macartney, W. G. Ellison
Macdona, John Cumming
M'Iver, Sir L. (Edinburgh,W)
Malcolm, Ian
Middlemore, J. Throgmorton
Mildmay, Francis Bingham
Milner, Sir Frederick George
Milton, Viscount
Milward, Colonel Victor
Monk, Charles James
Morgan,HnFred.(Monm'thsh.
Morrell, George Herbert
Morton,ArthurH.A.(Deptford
Mount, William George
Murray,RtHnAGraham(Bute
Murray, Col. W. (Bath)
Nicholson, William Graham
Nicol, Donald Ninian
Northcote, Hn. Sir H. Stafford
Orr-Ewing, Charles Lindsay
Pease, Herbert P. (Darling'n)
Phillpotts, Captain Arthur
Pilkington,R.(Lancs, Newton)
Pollock, Harry Frederick
Powell, Sir Francis Sharp
Priestley,SirW.Overend(Edin
Purvis, Robert
Rasch, Major Frederic Carne
Renshaw, Charles Bine
Richardson, Sir T. (Hartlep'l)
Ridley, Rt. Hon. Sir Matt. W.
Ritchie, Rt. Hon. C. Thomson
Robertson, Herbert (Hackney)
Rothschild, Hon. Lionel W.
Round, James

Royds, Clement Molyneux
Russell, Gen. F. S. (Chelt'h'm)
Russell, T. W. (Tyrone)
Samuel, Harry S. (Limehouse)
Sharpe, William Edward T.
Skewes-Cox, Thomas
Smith, Hon. W. F. D.(Strand)
Stanley, Lord (Lancashire)
Stephens, Henry Charles
Strauss, Arthur
Sturt, Hon. Humphry Napier
Sutherland, Sir Thomas
Talbot,Rt.Hn.J.G.(Ox.Univ.)
Thorburn, Walter
Thornton, Percy M.
Tomlinson, Wm. Edw. Murray
Valentia, Viscount
Warr, Augustus Frederick
Whiteley, George (Stockport)
Whiteley, H. (Ashton-und.-L.)
Williams, Jos. Powell-(Birm.
Wilson, John (Falkirk)
Wilson,J.W.(Worcestersh.N.)
Wilson-Todd,Wm.H. (Yorks.)
Wodehouse, RtHnER (Bath)
Wortley,Rt.Hon.C.B. Stuart-
Wylie, Alexander
Wyndham, George
Wyndham-Quin, MajorW. H.
Wyvill, Marmaduke D'Arcy
Young,Commander(Berks, E.)

TELLERS FOR THE AYES—
Sir William Walrond and
Mr. Anstruther.

NOES.

Allison, Robert Andrew
Asquith, Rt. Hon. Herbert H.
Bethell, Commander
Billson, Alfred
Bolton, Thomas Dolling
Bryce, Rt. Hon. James
Caldwell, James
Campbell-Bannerman, Sir H.
Carmichael, Sir T. D. Gibson-
Causton, Richard Knight
Channing, Francis Allston
Clark, Dr.G.B. (Caithness-sh.)
Clough, Walter Owen
Commins, Andrew
Cripps, Charles Alfred
Cross, Alexander (Glasgow)
Curran, Thomas B. (Donegal)
Davitt, Michael
Dillon, John
Donelan, Captain A.
Doogan, P. C.
Dunn, Sir William
Ellis, John Edward
Evans, S. T. (Glamorgan)
Farrell, James P. (Cavan, W.)
Fenwick, Charles
Ferguson, R. C. Munro Leith)
Flavin, Michael Joseph
Foster, Sir Walter (Derby Co.)

Gibney, James
Gladstone, Rt. Hon. H. John
Goddard, Daniel Ford
Hammond, John (Carlow)
Hedderwick, Thomas C. H.
Horniman, Frederick John
Humphreys-Owen, Arthur C.
Hutton, Alfred E. (Morley)
Jordan, Jeremiah
Kearley, Hudson E.
Kilbride, Denis
Kinloch,SirJohnGeorgeSmyth
Lawson, Sir W. (Cumb'land)
Leng, Sir John
Lewis, John Herbert
Lyell, Sir Leonard
Macaleese, Daniel
M'Ewan, William
M'Ghee, Richard
M'Leod, John
Maddison, Fred.
Morgan, J.Lloyd(Carmarthen)
O'Connor, J. (Wicklow,W.)
Pease, Joseph A. (Northumb.)
Philipps, John Wynford
Pinkerton, John
Power, Patrick Joseph
Provand, Andrew Dryburgh
Reckitt, Harold James

Rickett, J. Compton
Roberts, John Bryn (Eifion)
Roberts, John H. (Denbighs.)
Samuel, J. (Stockton-on-Tees)
Shaw, Thomas (Hawick B.)
Smith, Jas. Parker (Lanarks.)
Smith, Samuel (Flint)
Souttar, Robinson
Spicer, Albert
Steadman, William Charles
Sullivan, Donal (Westmeath)
Sullivan, T. D. (Donegal, W.)
Tennant, Harold John
Thomas, D. Alfred (Merthyr)
Trevelyan, Charles Philips
Ure, Alexander
Wallace, Robert
Wedderburn, Sir William
Weir, James Galloway
Whittaker, Thomas Palmer
Williams, J. Carvell (Notts.)
Wilson, John (Govan)
Wilson, Jos. H. (Middlesbro')
Woodhouse,SirJ.T.(H'dd'rsf'd)

TELLERS FOR THE NOES—
Sir Charles Cameron and
Mr. Crombie.

Amendment proposed—

"In page 3, line 33, to leave out from 'Orders,' to 'to act,' in line 34, and insert 'appoint three persons being Members of

VOL. LXXII.   [FOURTH SERIES.]

either House of Parliament, or persons whose names are on the panel.' "—(*The Lord Advocate.*)

Question proposed,   That the words

3 K

proposed to be left out stand part of the clause."

MR. THOMAS SHAW: With regard to this Amendment, we are grateful for the proposal to have a Parliamentary panel, but I think there is a very great objection to the terms of the Amendment now proposed. My reasons can be very briefly stated. There have been several suggestions made by the Lord Advocate with regard to one or two things in which he was willing to make concessions to the Members on this side of the House to a certain extent. We hope that he will stick by what he has stated he was willing to concede, and with that hope I beg to move as an Amendment that there shall be "two persons Members of each House of Parliament." We want the Committee of this House to be quite as strong as the Private Bill Committee is. In the next place I would suggest that as this Bill is now framed, the Secretary for Scotland acting with the two Chairmen can make a selection of Members entirely from the other House. The effect of this proposal will be to leave these three gentlemen in the position of having the power to exclude either House of Parliament according to their own will. They may select three Peers for every Scotch Bill, or the Secretary for Scotland might think that no Lord was competent to sit upon the Committee. I do not think my right hon. friend quite realises that what he proposes would not be a Joint Committee at all; therefore I suggest that he should leave out "three Members of either" and insert "two Members of each."

MR. A. G. MURRAY: The objection to having four Members is twofold. In the first place it would make the tribunal larger than is necessary for the work to be done, but the great difficulty would be to get Peers to carry out the work. I might suggest here that it was never the idea nor is it the desire of the Government that one House should be chosen exclusively of the other. It would be easy to devise words so that the Committee should be composed of two Peers and one commoner or of two commoners and one Peer. I suggest this for the consideration of the Committee.

SIR H. CAMPBELL-BANNERMAN: If we had no precedent there might be a good deal to be said in favour of having three upon the Committee rather than four. But at the same time, all our Committees are composed of four Members. I do not know the reason why they are composed of four, but I should suppose that it was in order to have two Members from each side of this House. That is the position in which we now stand; we want two Members from each House; and four is the established number on House of Commons Committees. I do not see that there is very much in the theory of the Lord Advocate that it will be overweighting the tribunal, and there is no other way in which we can have an equal proportion of the two Houses.

THE FIRST LORD OF THE TREASURY (Mr. A. J. BALFOUR, Manchester, E.): I quite sympathise with the right hon. Gentleman in his desire to preserve a certain symmetry in the existing practice, and I think there is a certain advantage in having a Committee of four instead of three. But the reason for making it three instead of four is a reason of convenience, and I should have thought that the hon. Gentlemen opposite whose desire is to keep this tribunal within the four walls of Parliament would prefer three. If you insist upon having four you may not be able to get two Members from the House of Lords, but there is no special objection to your having four if you desire it, and if this proposal goes against the wishes of hon. Members opposite I see no objection to accepting the Amendment of the hon. Member.

MR. DILLON (Mayo, E.): Looking at this Bill as one which affects Ireland, I do not think, even if the Government accept the Amendment of the hon. Member for the Border Burghs, that it will be satisfactory. Because, instead of having an important Private Bill examined and adjudicated on by this House in the first instance, you would have it relegated to a Committee composed of half Lords and half Commons, and I do not think anything would be so unsatisfactory. I take for example the Dublin Bill of the other day. What chance should we have had of getting this Bill through if this machinery had been in force? It would have been killed at its birth. There is no doubt that some great change is required in Private B.

procedure, and is required for Ireland no less than for Scotland, but I do think that the lines upon which this Bill is drawn are most dangerous lines. While they save some expense, they threaten us with the abrogation of every claim we have.

Mr. CALDWELL : I rather favour the words "and in the event of the Chairman selecting the panel and their not appearing to serve on the panel," than the present wording, and I will move that Amendment in order to obtain a reply from the Lord Advocate. It will prevent the outside panel being called upon until it is known that no Member of either House can be got to serve.

Amendment proposed to the proposed Amendment—

"To leave out all the words after 'panel,' in order to insert the words 'and in the event of the Chairman selecting the panel and their not appearing to serve on the panel.'"—(*Mr. Caldwell.*)

Question proposed, "That those words be there inserted in the proposed Amendment."

Mr. A. G. MURRAY : Obviously the words cannot stand as they are. I propose to amend the Amendment as follows :—

"Appoint as Commissioners two Members of each House of Parliament, or in default of such Member or Members willing to serve, persons then in the panel."

Sir H. CAMPBELL-BANNERMAN : I think it might be made plainer, and instead of "Member or Members willing to serve" it might read, "Member or Members being found willing to serve." I think the right hon. Gentleman is entirely at one with us in the matter. Supposing the tribunal is formed, and one Member is smitten with influenza, then we are not to go to the outside panel, but are still to keep to the Parliamentary reservoir.

Mr. A. J. BALFOUR : As my right hon. friend has explained, our idea is that there should be two Members of the House of Commons and two Members of the House of Lords. If the House of Lords can only produce one Member, then we will try to get three from the House of Commons, and if the House of Lords cannot supply one, then we will have four from the House of Commons. But even if the House of Commons fails, then we will have the panel of which we have heard so much. As both sides are in agreement, I think the exact drafting might be left over to the Report stage.

Amendment to the proposed Amendment, by leave, withdrawn.

Original Amendment again proposed.

Sir CHARLES CAMERON : It will be necessary to make some provision for the appointment of a Chairman. The Chairman should alternately be a Member of either House, and that is a point which ought to be provided for in the Bill.

Mr. A. G. MURRAY : There is an Amendment in my name which raises the point.

Amendment put, and agreed to.

Amendment proposed—

"In page 3, line 35, at end, to insert, 'Any casual vacancy among the Commissioners or in the office of Chairman of the Commissioners caused by death, resignation, or disqualification, or inability to give attendance, such resignation or inability to attend being certified by a writing under the Commissioner's hand addressed to the Secretary for Scotland, shall be filled up by the Secretary for Scotland by appointing a Member of either House or a member of the panel.'"—(*The Lord Advocate.*)

Question proposed—"That those words be there inserted."

Sir CHARLES CAMERON : This is quite contrary to the spirit of what we have agreed to. Vacancies should be filled up in accordance with Parliamentary procedure.

Question put, and agreed to.

Amendment proposed—

" In page 3, line 36, leave out Sub-section (2), and insert : ' If it shall happen that all or any of the Commissioners so appointed are not Members of either House of Parliament, there shall be paid to such of the Commissioners as are not Members of either House of Parliament such remuneration for their services as the Treasury shall determine.' "—(*The Lord Advocate.*)

Agreed to.

MR. J. P. SMITH : I beg to move the omission of Sub-section 3. I think it is perfectly easy, considering the large number we will have to choose from, for hon. Gentlemen to look ahead and see what their engagements are going to be. It was quite a different thing when we had only a panel of 25 Members, a few of whom might be Members of either House. Now we have the two Houses to select from, and I think Members ought to be able to judge how far they may be free to undertake these duties.

Amendment proposed—

" To leave out Sub-section 3."—(*Mr. J. P. Smith.*)

Question proposed, " That Sub-section 3 stand part of the clause."

COMMANDER BETHELL (York E.R., Holderness) : I believe the theory is that either House of Parliament has a prior claim on its own Members.

MR. A. G. MURRAY : I am willing to accept the Amendment.

MR. DALZIEL : There is one question I want to put to the right hon. Gentleman. In the case of an English, Welsh, or Irish Member failing to attend the inquiry in Scotland, can he be reported to the House in the ordinary way ? If there is to be no report, what is the use of appointing a

Sir Charles Cameron.

Member ? What sort of pressure is it proposed to bring to bear on Members to attend ?

MR. DILLON : I think that is a very important question. If a Member did not attend in Scotland, what action would be taken ?

MR. CRIPPS : There is no obligation on any Member to serve ; and if when appointed he did not wish to serve there would be a vacancy and his place would be filled.

MR. CALDWELL : Supposing a Member does not attend an inquiry, where are you to find another Member ? Up here it is easy to find another Member, but how can you find one in Scotland ?

*THE CHAIRMAN : That does not arise on this clause.

MR. DALZIEL : I beg to give notice that I will raise the point later.

Amendment agreed to.

Other Amendments made.

MR. CROMBIE : We have already debated the desirability of Scottish Members not being debarred from serving on these Committees, and to emphasise that point I beg to move the Amendment standing in my name.

Amendment proposed—

" In page 4, line 7, after ' Order,' add ' providing that this will not disqualify Scottish Members of either House of Parliament from acting on Committees which deal with Orders which they have no local or personal interest."—(*Mr. Crombie.*)

Question proposed, " That those words be there added."

MR. JONATHAN SAMUEL (Stockton) : Will English Members representing Scottish constituencies come within the meaning of the Amendment ?

Question put, and agreed to.

Clause 5, as amended, agreed to.

Clause 6 : —

Mr. THOMAS SHAW : I beg to move an Amendment to provide that the inquiry shall take place in Scotland. The object of the Amendment is simply to carry out the purpose of the Bill by making the inquiry local.

Amendment proposed—

"In page 4, line 10, after ' place ' to insert ' in Scotland.' "—(*Mr. Thomas Shaw.*)

Question proposed, " That those words be there inserted."

Mr. CALDWELL : I quite agree that the inquiry should be in Scotland. But more is required. The people of Dundee object to an inquiry being held in Edinburgh ; and the people of Aberdeen would probably prefer to come to London than to go to Edinburgh if they could not get an inquiry in their own locality. The whole object of the Bill is to have a local inquiry, and it should be limited to the county or to the borough concerned. If we only say "in Scotland," it will mean that these inquiries will be held in Edinburgh for the benefit of the Edinburgh lawyers. There can be no question that there would be a tendency to hold the inquiries in Scotland where the Commissioners would get better accommodation. I therefore move to insert after " in " in the Amendment the words " the locality in."

Amendment proposed to the proposed Amendment—

" After the word ' in ' to insert ' the locality in.' "—(*Mr. Caldwell.*)

Question proposed, " That those words be there inserted in the proposed Amendment."

Mr. A. G. MURRAY : The hon. Gentleman would, as far as I can see, have attained his object by moving the words " exclusive of Edinburgh." This Amendment would, however, make the Amendment of the hon. Member for the Border Burghs unintelligible. It is provided in the Bill that the Commissioners shall hold their inquiry "at such place as they may determine with due regard to the subject matter of the proposed Order, and to the locality to which its provisions relate." " Such place " obviously includes every place in Scotland, and the section does everything in the way of showing Commissioners where they ought to hold the inquiry. I really think the Amendment would not improve the Bill.

Question put, and negatived.

Original Amendment put, and agreed to.

*Mr. RENSHAW : I would suggest to the Lord Advocate whether it would not be better to omit the words "maintained at the public expense." If these words are retained it might be impossible to use buildings otherwise available.

Mr. A. G. MURRAY : I really think the sub-section as it stands is better. .

Other Amendments made

Clause 6, as amended, agreed to

Clause 7 :—

Mr. THOMAS SHAW : The Amendment which stands in my name is one of a series which develops a new scheme under this clause. I may tell the House in a few words what my object is. It is that there shall not be an inquiry conducted in London, in accordance with the present practice, after an inquiry has been conducted in Scotland. I think that the success or the failure of this Bill depends on the action of Her Majesty's Government in regard to this Amendment. It appears to me that it would be most unsatisfactory if the Government insist that after this elaborate procedure in

Scotland the whole matter should be thrown into hotch-pot again, and that there should be a further protracted and expensive inquiry in London. What we have now done is to establish the proposition that Parliament shall retain its control over the whole proceedings. All the distance we have gone in regard to the Joint Committees is to change the *locale* of the inquiry. It is out of the question to put the Joint Committee in the undignified position of holding a preliminary inquiry, and then having the real battle in London. Our object in having a local inquiry is that Parliament should come to the spot, and there once and for all settle the matter so far as the Committee's inquiry can do it. I agree that the Confirmation Bill should be lodged and discussed on the Third Reading in the ordinary way. I hope that the Government will consent to the Amendment.

Amendment proposed—

" In page 4, line 31, to leave out all the words from the beginning of the clause, to the word ' after,' in line 32."—(*Mr. Thomas Shaw.*)

Question proposed, " That the words proposed to be left out stand part of the clause."

MR. A. G. MURRAY: The technical position of the Amendment of the hon. and learned Member is such that it is a little difficult to discover what the meaning of it is. I think I can explain to the Committee how it stands. Under the scheme of the Bill and the promises I have made to the House I have had to divide necessarily the Provisional Orders into opposed and unopposed Orders. All along there has been this distinction ; whereas on unopposed Orders there is not to be any inquiry or Committee stage up here in London, yet all along the scheme of the Bill has been that in the case of opposed Orders the possibility of an opponent coming to this House on the Confirmation Bill and opposing it has been kept open. The only distinction between the proposed

Mr. Thomas Shaw.

procedure and that which obtains at present is that the proposal in the Bill is that the inquiry in London shall be by Joint Committee of both Houses, instead of by a separate inquiry before each House. The Amendment of the hon. and learned Member is really with a view of taking out all the provisions I have made in regard to the opponent coming here on the Confirmation Bill. I have always held that it was right in principle that an opponent should have an opportunity of taking the sense of Parliament in regard to a Bill ; I adhere to that view, and I am sure it would be against the great body of opinion in the House if I went back on my promise.

DR. CLARK : I am afraid that, unless the Amendment is adopted, instead of the cost of obtaining a Provisional Order being moderate, as compared with the present system, it would be increased, perhaps doubled or trebled. Why should any petitioner in Scotland who has paid for all his advertisements and notices, and made his deposit, and submitted to an inquiry by a Committee of two Peers and two Commoners, which Committee has decided on the matter—why should such a petitioner have to come to Parliament again, repeat his notices and advertisements and deposit, and appear before other two Peers and two Commoners upstairs, who would not have the advantage of seeing the people to be affected and the spot to which the Bill applies ? This second inquiry is totally unnecessary.

MR. CALDWELL : I am afraid the Lord Advocate has not looked at the proposal thoroughly and the effect of it. The question is whether we should have in this House a Joint Committee after the matter has been inquired into locally in Scotland by another Joint Committee.

MR CRIPPS : The question raised by the hon. Member of the Border Burghs is undoubtedly an important one. If the

Amendment is carried it would be inconsistent with the whole framework of the Bill, would work out unjustly, and would impair the control of the House over these Provisional Orders which we have always insisted upon. It has never been suggested at any stage of the discussion until this moment that a man should not have the right of an ordinary hearing before a Joint Committee appointed by this House and the House of Lords. I hope the Lord Advocate will not consent to this Amendment.

DR. CLARK: There is one point which I omitted. The class of Bills which will come before the Commissioners will be very small Bills; all the important Bills will never leave this House, but will be considered here. The Amendment will only affect very small Orders, the policy and principle of which had already been decided by Parliament. So far as we have been able to modify the Bill at all, it has been to limit the cases which will go before the Commissioners.

MR. HOBHOUSE (Somerset, East): It would be ridiculous, in my opinion, if, after there had been an inquiry by a Parliamentary Committee sitting locally, there should be another inquiry by another Parliamentary Committee sitting here.

MR. A. G. MURRAY: It is curious to me how, in one and the same breath, hon. Members ask that the control of the House over these Orders should be retained, and then they wish to throw that control away in the Bill. We have always promised to give the House control even of unopposed Orders. If this Amendment is passed, the result would be that, whereas the House has always felt that that control should be sparingly exercised at a late stage, if an objector were prevented from coming up here then, undoubtedly, he would in every case incite someone in the House to raise the question in the House itself. An abuse of that kind ought certainly to be guarded against. I am keeping faith with the House in standing by the Bill upon the promises made from the beginning. I never could have faced the discussion after the Second Reading if I were to take away from a practical opponent all power of coming to this House.

MR. THOMAS SHAW: The Lord Advocate says that he is very glad that I have such faith in the tribunal he has set up that I would go much further than himself. I have much confidence in the tribunal which the Committee of the House of Commons has set up. What we have done is that a Parliamentary Committee has been set up to make inquiries on the spot, to inspect the localities, and to have in view all the circumstances which the local authorities can furnish them with. It seems to me the most incredible thing I ever heard of that after a local inquiry the whole thing should be done again in London, and a second Joint Committee of both Houses should sit in review of the operations of the first Joint Committee. The new inquiry was to be cheap, but the Lord Advocate's proposal will obliterate every element of cheapness. There is no analogy between a local inquiry under the old Provisional Order system and one under this Bill. Local inquiry under this Bill is not an inquiry by Departmental Committee at all, but an inquiry by this House and the other House. And I altogether object to the duplication of that. If the Amendment be not adopted, the whole Bill will be cumbersome, unpractical, and unworkable, and its administration most expensive.

It being Midnight, the Chairman left the Chair to make his Report to the House.

Committee report progress ; to sit again to-morrow.

BATHS AND WASHHOUSES ACTS AMENDMENT BILL.

Considered in Committee.

(In the Committee.)

Clause 1 :

Committee report progress ; to sit again this day.

REGULATION OF RAILWAYS BILL.

Order for Second Reading read, and discharged.   Bill withdrawn.

MILITARY WORKS (MONEY).

Committee to consider of authorising the issue, out of the Consolidated Fund, of such sums as may be required for the purpose of Military Works and Services (Queen's Recommendation signified), upon Wednesday.—(*Mr. Wyndham.*)

Adjourned at ten minutes after Twelve o'clock.

[INDEX.

INDEX

TO THE

PARLIAMENTARY DEBATES

[AUTHORISED EDITION].

SEVENTH VOLUME OF SESSION 1899.

MAY 31—JUNE 19.

EXPLANATION OF ARRANGEMENT AND ABBREVIATIONS.

Bills = Read First, Second, or Third Time = 1R., 2R., 3R. [c.] = Commons [l.] = Lords. Amendt. = Amendment. Os. = Observations. Qs. = Questions As. = Answers. Com. = Committee. Con. = Consideration. Rep. = Report S. = Debate in Committee of Supply. Where in the Index * is added with Reading of a Bill, or a Vote in Committee of Supply, it indicates that no Debate took place on that Stage of the Bill, or on that Vote. Subjects discussed in Committee of Supply are entered under their headings, and also under Members' Names, without reference to the actual Vote before the Committee. The abbreviation " S " has been adopted as explanation under the subjects.

ABERAVON.
    Education Department Provisional Order Confirmation [Aberavon, etc.] Bill, see that Title.

ABERDEEN CEMETERY SCANDAL.
    Q. Gen. Russell ; A. Mr. A. G. Murray, June 19, 1486.

Aberdeen Corporation Bill.
    c. Rep.*, June 9, 758.
    con.*, June 19, 1475.

Aberdeen Harbour Bill.
    l. Royal Assent, June 6, 409.

Aberdeen Joint Passenger Station Bill.
    l. Rep.*, June 12, 877.
    3R.*, June 19, 1454.

ABORIGINES PROTECTION BOARD, Western Australia, Abolition of, Debate [l]. June 16, 1321.

ACADEMY, see Royal Academy.

ACCIDENTS.
    Garston, Fatal Accident to Dock Labourer.
    Q. Mr. M'Ghee ; A. Sir M. W. Ridley, June 9, 769.
    Railway Accidents, see that Title.

ACKLAND-HOOD. CAPT. SIR A. [Somerset, Wellington].

Soudan Expedition—Grant to Lord Kitchener, Mahdi's Body, etc., June 5, 388.

ADMIRALTY, see Navy.

ADULTERATION OF FOOD.
    Tea, see that Title.

ADVERTISEMENT ORDERS, STAMPING.
    Q. Mr. Hazell ; A. Sir M. Hicks-Beach, June 2, 183.

AFRICA, CENTRAL.
    Trade Report presented, June 19, 1456.

AFRICA, SOUTH.
    Bechuanaland, Cape of Good Hope, Johannesburg, and Transvaal, see those Titles.
    Cables—Delay in transmission of Sir A. Milner's memorandum.
    Q. Mr. Griffith ; A. Mr. J. Chamberlain ; June 13, 1059.
    Ladysmith Barracks, Insanitary Condition.
    Q. Mr. Buchanan ; A. Mr. Wyndham, June 9, 771.

AFRICA, WEST.
    Liquor Traffic.
    Brussels Conference.
    Q. Capt. Sinclair : A. Mr. J. Chamberlain, June 13. 1063.
    Spirit Duties, Increase.
    Q. Mr. W. F. Lawrence ; A. Mr. J. Chamberlain, June 15, 1181.

VOL. LXXII. | [FOURTH SERIES]   3 L

AFRICA, WEST—cont.
Niger, see that Title.
Sierra Leone—Chalmers', Sir D., Report.
Q. Mr. Hedderwick; A. Mr. J. Chamberlain, June 2, 176.
Waima Incident, Compensation Claims,
S.. June 9, 780, 784, 812, 823, 839, 845, 863, 872.

AGRICULTURAL EDUCATION.
S. June 16, 1418, 1423.
France—Report presented, June 15, 1168.

AGRICULTURAL GRANT [Ireland].
Donegal, Increase—County Council Resolution.
Q. Mr. MacNeill; A. Mr. G. W. Balfour, June 15, 1192.
Kildare Grant Reduction.
Q. Mr. Carew; A. Mr. G. W. Balfour, June 8, 650.
Longford—Excluded Charges.
Qs. Mr. J. P. Farrell; As. Mr. G. W. Balfour, June 13, 1072; June 15, 1196.
Roscommon—Excluded Charges.
Qs. Mr. Tully; As. Mr. G. W. Balfour, June 5, 305; June 8, 652; June 13, 1077.
Q. Mr. Hayden; A. Mr. G. W. Balfour, June 16, 1352.
Roscommon and Leitrim.
Q. Mr. Tully; A. Mr. G. W. Balfour, June 5, 305.

AGRICULTURAL PROPERTY.
Death Duties—Finance Bill, New Clause.
Motion [Mr. Bowles], June 6, 452.

AGRICULTURAL RATES.
Tithe-owning Clergy of England and Wales —Petition, June 8, 597.

AGRICULTURE, BOARD OF
President—Rt. Hon. W. H. Long.

Airdrie and Coatbridge Water Bill.
c. Rep.*, June 15, 1171.

Aire and Calder Navigation Bill.
l. 2R.*, June 8, 594.

AKERS-DOUGLAS, see Douglas.

ALASKA BOUNDARY QUESTION.
Anglo-American Commission, see that Title.

ALDERMEN AND COUNCILLORS—LONDON GOVERNMENT BILL—Qualification of Women, Mr. Courtney's New Clause, June 6, 464- Mr. Elliot's Amendment to Recommit Bill, June 13, 1078.

ALDERSHOT.
Bathing Fatality—Case of Private Jackson.
Q. Mr. Jeffreys; A. Mr. Wyndham, June 8, 640.
Sewage Farm—Inspector's Report.
Q. Mr. J. G. Talbot; A. Mr. Wyndham, June 2, 177.
Report presented, June 2, 170; June 6, 413.

ALDERSHOT—Queen's Birthday Parade, Strength of Troops, etc.
Q. Maj. Rasch; A. Mr. Wyndham, June 12, 899.

ALIENS.
Naturalisation Certificates, Obtaining from Secretary of State.
Q. Mr. MacNeill; A. Mr. J. Collings, June 15, 1185.

All Saints' Church [Cardiff] Bill.
l. 3R.*, June 2, 161.
c. 1R.*, June 5, 326
Standing Order Complied with, Motion for Instruction to Examiners. [Mr. A. D. Thomas], June 8, 619.

ALLAHABAD HIGH COURT, WOMEN BARRISTERS—Miss Sorabji's Application to Practice refused.
Q. Mr. H. Roberts; A. Lord G. Hamilton, June 8, 641.

ALLAN, MR. W. [Gateshead].
Irish Lights—Black Head and Maiden Rocks, June 2, 180.

AMBROSE, DR. [Mayo, West].
Migration of Population of Co. Mayo—County Council Resolution, June 6, 439.
Westport Urban Sanitary Authority, Commissioners' Petition, June 13. 1074.

AMBULANCE FOR THE HOUSES OF PARLIAMENT.
Q. Mr. Tomlinson; A. Mr. Akers-Douglas, June 8, 657.

AMERICA, see United States.

AMOY:—
Trade Report Presented, June 2, 163.

AMSTERDAM:—
Trade Report Presented, June 1, 68.

Anchors and Chain Cables Bill.
l. 2R. June 1, 70.

ANGLO-AMERICAN COMMISSION.
Q. Sir E. Gourley; A. Mr. Brodrick, June 1, 81.
Q. Sir E. Gourley; A. Mr. J. Chamberlain, June 6, 440.
Q. Mr. Hogan; A. Mr. Brodrick, June 13, 1064.
Official Statement.
Q. Sir C. Dilke; A. Mr. Brodrick, June 5, 299.

ANGLO-RUSSIAN AGREEMENT, see China.

ANIMALS.
Diseases of Animals Acts, see that Title.
Experiments on Living Animals, see Vivisection.

ANNALY ESTATE, Purchase of Holdings.
Q. Mr. J. P. Farrell; A. Mr. G. W. Balfour, June 13, 1076.

ANNUITIES—National Debt.
Q. Mr. J. P. Smith; A. Sir M. Hicks-Beach, June 16, 1340.

ANSAHS OF ASHANTI—Compensation, etc.
Q. Mr. J. A. Pease; A. Mr. J. Chamberlain, June 15, 1180.

ANSTRUTHER, MR. H. T. [St. Andrews Burghs].
Army and Navy Officers, Retired—Civil Employment, Return, June 8, 657.
"Mandat-Poste" System, Trial of, in England, suggested, June 8, 659.
Secondary and Technical Schools, June 13, 1069.
Telegraphic Messages, Delay in Transit, June 8, 658.

" ANTI-BRITISH " PROPAGANDA IN CAPE
  COLONY.
    Qs. Sir E. Ashmead-Bartlett, Mr. Mac-
    Neill; As. Mr. J. Chamberlain, June
    15, 1182.
    Q. Mr. MacNeill: A. Mr. J. Chamber-
    lain, June 16, 1338.
APPLEBE. MRS., MURDER OF.
    Q. Mr. W. Johnston; A. Mr. J. Cham-
    berlain, June 19. 1484.

Arbroath Corporation Gas Bill.
    c. Rep.*, June 2, 169.
    3R.*, June 6, 430.
ARCHES, DEAN OF—Appointment of Sir A.
  Charles, see Charles, Sir A.
ARKLOW.
    Ferrybank Post Office
    Q. Mr. P. O'Brien; A. Mr. Hanbury,
    June 16, 1344.
ARMENIA.
    Archbishops and Bishops, Detention of,
    Qs. Mr. Stevenson; As. Mr. Brodrick,
    June 1, 80; June 15, 1179.
    Distress in—Peace Conference.
    Q. Mr. S. Smith; A. Mr. Brodrick,
    June 12, 894.
    Kurdish Atrocities—Russian and French
    Protest.
    Q. Mr. Schwann; A. Mr. Brodrick,
    June 16, 1337.
    Massacres—Compensation Claims.
    Q. Col. Denny; A. Mr. Brodrick, June
    9. 763.
ARMS, see Firearms.
ARMY.
    Secretary of State—Marquess of Lans-
    downe.
    Under-Secretary—Mr. G. Wyndham.
    Financial Secretary—Mr. J. Powell-Wil-
    liams.
    Aldershot, Questions Relating to, see
    Aldershot.
    Artillery, see that Title.
    Bullets, see that Title.
    Connaught Rangers at Meerut—Shooting
    Case.
    Q. Mr. H. Roberts; A. Lord G.
    Hamilton, June 16, 1335.
    Dum-Dum Bullets, see that Title.
    Enfield Small Arms Factory, Divine Wor-
    ship in Government Chapels—Illegal
    Practices.
    Qs. Mr. Channing, Mr. C. Williams;
    As. Mr. Wyndham, June 12, 897.
    Guards—Losses of Stores, Claim for.
    Q. Sir J. Fergusson; A. Mr. J. P.
    Williams. June 19, 1480.
    India, see that Title.
    Ladysmith Barracks, Insanitary State of.
    Q. Mr. Buchanan; A. Mr. Wyndham,
    June 9. 771.
    Length of Service and Ages of Men,
    Returns Ordered [Mr. Arnold Foster],
    June 8, 626, 627.
    Medals. Punjaub War and Tirah Campaign,
    1897-8—Distribution of Medals.
    Q. Mr. H. D. Greene; A. Mr.
    Wyndham. June 1, 81.
    Q. Mr. H. D. Greene: A. Lord G.
    Hamilton, June 6, 443.

ARMY—cont.
    Military Lands Provisional Order Bill, see
    that Title.
    Military Works—Expenditure for 1899-
    1900 under existing loans—Estimate pre-
    sented June 19, 1456. 1479.
    Military Works Loan Bill, see that Title.
    Militia, see that Title.
    Patriotic Fund—Case of Mrs. Lewis.
    Q. Mr. Spicer; A. Mr. G. Wyndham,
    June 8. 632.
    Pensions—Special Pensions, Returns pre-
    sented, June 13, 1056, 1167.
    Prisons, Inspector-General's Report.
    Q. Dr. Farquharson; A. Mr. Wynd-
    ham. June 8, 640.
    Recruits, Bread Rations.
    Q. Mr. Hayden; A. Mr. Wyndham,
    June 16, 1334.
    Retired Officers and Civil Employment—
    Return.
    Q. Capt. Norton; A. Mr. Anstruther,
    June 8, 657.
    Rifle Ranges, see that Title.
    Salisbury Plain, see that Title.
    Soldiers. see that Title.
    Soudan Expedition—Vote of Thanks to
    the Forces, etc., see Soudan.
    Superannuation Act—Employees appointed
    without Certificate. Treasury Minute
    presented, June 2, 163, 170.
    Troops at Aldershot.
    Q. Major Rasch; A. Mr. Wyndham,
    June 12, 899.
    Volunteers, see that Title.
    War Office, see that Title.
    Woolwich Arsenal—Dismissal of Men, etc.
    Q. Mr. Steadman; A. Mr. J. P. Williams,
    June 15, 1176.

ARNOLD, MR. A. [Halifax].
    Half-Timers—Education of Children Bill,
    com., May 31, 24.

ARNOLD-FORSTER, MR. H. O. [Belfast, West].
    Mountain and Garrison Artillery Officers,
    June 16, 1333.
    Soudan Expedition—Grant to Lord Kit-
    chener, June 5, 400.

ARRAN, EARL OF.
    Crime. Incitement to [Ireland]—M'Hale v.
    Sullivan, June 12, 882, 884.

ARSENAL, see Woolwich Arsenal.

ART.
    Paris Exhibition—Space allotted to British
    Works of Art.
    Q. Mr. Courtney; A. Mr. Hanbury,
    June 15, 1186.
    South Kensington Museum—Appointment.
    Q. Mr. M. Healy; A. Sir J. Gorst, June
    16, 1347.

ARTILLERY.
    Garrison and Mountain Artillery, Officers'
    Right, of Fall.
    Q. Mr. Arnold-Forster; A. Mr.
    Wyndham, June 16, 1333.
    Mountain Artillery—Officers' Armament
    Pay.
    Q. Mr. Pretyman; A. Mr. Wyndham,
    June 15, 1175.

ARUNDEL PORT, Account and Report presented, June 9, 753, 761.

ASCROFT, MR. R. [Oldham].
Money-lending Bill, June 8, 659.
Post Office, Administration, etc., June 1, 109.
Telegraphic Messages, Delay in Transit, June 8, 658.

ASHANTI, Ansahs of.
Claim for Compensation, etc.
Q. Mr. J. A. Pease ; A. Mr. J. Chamberlain, June 15, 1180.

ASHMEAD-BARTLETT, SIR E. [Sheffield, Eccleshall].
Anti-British Propaganda in Cape Colony, June 15, 1182.
China—Russian Sphere of Interest, Extension of—Anglo-Russian Agreement, June 13, 1065.
Transvaal—Uitlanders' Grievances, Political Rights, June 13, 1061.

ASIA MINOR—Railway Construction.
British Interests in Persian Gulf.
Q. Mr. Maclean ; A. Mr. Brodrick, June 8, 629.

ASSAM, Tea Plantations—Report.
Q. Mr. Schwann ; A. Lord G. Hamilton. June 12, 897.

ATHERLEY-JONES, MR. L. [Durham, N.W.].
Soudan Expedition—Grant to Lord Kitchener—Treatment of the Mahdi's Body, etc., June 5, 372.

AUSTIN, MR. M. [Limerick, W.].
Emergency Men carrying firearms in Ireland—Case of T. Crawford, June 5, 308.
Glin District School—Conveyance of Children by Waterford Steamship Co., June 12, 902.
Newcastle West [Limerick] Creamery—Sewer Complaint, June 15, 1193.

AUSTRALIA.
Indenturing in Western Australia—Abolition of Aborigines Protection Board, Debate [1], June 16, 1321.
Queensland, see that Title.

Ayr Burgh Bill.
1. 2R., June 6, 410.

AZERBAIJAN.
Trade Report presented, June 19, 1456.

BADEN, GRAND DUCHY OF.
Trade Report presented, June 1, 68.

BAGOT ESTATE, Sale of—Sir N. O'Connor and the Congested Districts Board.
Q. Mr. Hayden ; A. Mr. G. W. Balfour, June 15, 1188.

BAHIA.
Trade Report presented, June 8, 596.

BAILIEBOROUGH.
Land Commission — Sub-Commissioners' Judgments.
Q. Mr. S. Young ; A. Mr. G. W. Balfour, June 8, 647.

Baker Street and Waterloo Railway Bill.
1. 2R*, June 15, 1166.

BAKERY DISPUTE, GLASGOW, Case of A. M'Naughten.
Q. Sir C. Cameron ; A. Mr. A. G. Murray, June 19, 1485.

BALCARRES. LORD [Lancashire, Chorley].
Ecclesiastical Judge—Appointment of Sir A. Charles, June 16. 1340.

BALFOUR, RT. HON. A. J.—First Lord of the Treasury [Manchester, East].
Bloemfontein Conference, June 12, 907.
Board of Education Bill [Secondary Education], June 19. 1500.
Business of the House, June 2. 185 ; June 8, 660 ; June 9, 777 ; June 12, 907 ; June 13, 1078 ; June 15, 1198 ; June 19, 1502.
Government Business, Precedence of—Statement, June 19, 1502, 1523.
Comptroller and Auditor-General—Retirement of Mr. Mills. June 1, 84.
Killarney Lakes—Sale of Muckross Estate, June 19, 1501.
London Government Bill, con. June 6, 461, 463, 464, 486, 488, 490. 509, 511. 514, 517, 520. 521, 522, 526 ; June 8, 704, 707, 711, 730.
Municipal Trading Committee, Appointment of, June 8, 661.
Peace Conference, Dum-Dum Bullet—Prohibition Resolution, June 5, 308.
Peers' Interference at Elections—Southport Election. Breach of Privilege, June 5, 307, 315.
Private Legislation Procedure [Scotland] Bill, com. June 12, 928, 985. 986, 987, 969 ; June 19, 1584, 1586.
St. Michael's, Southampton. Illegal Practices at, June 12. 907.
Soudan Campaign.
Deceased Officers, etc.—Condolence to Relatives. June 8, 698.
Kitchener. Lord, Grant to.
House of Lords. Power of Initiating Money Grants—Question of Privilege. June 5, 322.
Mahdi's Body, etc., June 5, 327, 343, 345.
Method of Procedure, June 2. 187—Mr. Dillon's Explanation. June 5, 310.
Thanks of the House.
Kitchener. Lord, June 8, 663. 675.
Medical Officers Omission, June 8, 678.
Wounded Dervishes. Cruelty to—Charges against the Anglo-Egyptian Army, June 8. 679, 681, 682.
Telegraphs [Telephonic Communication, etc.] Bill, June 19, 1501.

BALFOUR, RT. HON. G. W.—Chief Secretary for Ireland [Leeds, Central].
Agricultural Grant.
Donegal. June 15, 1192.
Kildare, Reduction. June 8, 651.
Leitrim. June 5, 305.
Longford—Excluded Charges, June 13, 1072 ; June 15, 1196.
Roscommon, June 5, 305 ; June 8, 652; June 13, 1077 ; June 16. 1353.
Annaly Estate, Purchase of Holdings, June 13, 1077.
Bagot Estate, Sale of—Sir N. O'Conor and the Congested Districts Board, June 15, 1188.

BALFOUR, RT. HON. G. W.—*cont.*

Balrothery County Cess—Standard Rate, June 16, 1353.

Belfast Riots.
  Nationalist Demonstration, June 1, 96; June 6, 534.
  Queen's Island Workers, Attacks on, June 13, 1073; June 15, 1197.
  Religious Disturbances, June 1, 86, 95; June 8, 653.

Belmullet, Extra Police Force, June 13, 1075.

Castlerea and Ballaghadereen—Sanitary Charges, June 16, 1357.

Castletown Berehaven Pier—Removal of Silt, June 12, 906.

Cavan Co. Magistracy, Vacancy, June 16, 1359.

Cavan and Granard Unions, transfer of Divisions refused by Local Government Board, June 13, 1075.

Celtic Language in Irish Schools, Reduction in number of marks, June 16, 1354.

Clerks of Unions checking Rate Collectors' Accounts—Extra Remuneration, June 15, 1198.

Constabulary.
  Meehan, District Inspector, Conduct of, June 15, 1196.
  Promotion in, June 16, 1356.

Cookstown Orange Riot, June 8, 645; June 15, 1194.

County Councils.
  Contractors as Members of Councils.
    Cork, June 8, 652.
    Kerry, June 13, 1070.
  Election Expenses, June 8, 656.

Dillon's, Lord. Estate—Purchase by the Congested Districts Board, June 16, 1361.

Donegal Railway Communication—County Council Resolution, June 19, 1499.

Dublin Metropolitan Police — Summer Clothing, June 13, 1074.

Dwyer, Sylvester, Case of, June 19, 1498.

Emigration to U.S.A., June 8, 649.

Finegan, A., Death of—Inquest, June 15, 1191; June 19, 1497.

Firearms, Carrying without licence.
  Brady, T., Case of, June 15, 1190.
  Costello, P., Case of, June 19, 1495.
  Emergency Man—Case of T. Crawford, June 5, 308.

Fish Traffic on Railways—English and Irish Railways, June 16, 1358.

Fishing Prosecution—Case of P. Comerford. June 16, 1359.

Glin District School—Conveyance of Children by Waterford Steamship Co., June 12, 902.

Gun Licences—Mr. Egan's Application refused, June 19, 1500.

Industrial Schools.
  Committal of Destitute Children, Circular. June 8, 648.
  School Attendance, Committee's Powers, June 12, 902.

Infirmaries. County. Management of—Representatives elected by County Councils, June 15, 1189.

Intermediate Education.
  Rules and Programme for 1900, June 15, 1193.

BALFOUR, RT. HON. G. W.—*cont.*

Viceregal Commission, June 13, 1071.

Judicial Rents.
  Cavan Co., June 19, 1496.
  Equal Rights of Tenants, June 19, 1496.

Kildare Street Library, handing over to New Irish Department, June 16, 1350.

Labourers' Cottages, Disqualification of District Councillors, etc., June 19, 1495.

Land Commission.
  Assistant Commissioners.
    Bailieborough Commissioners' Judgments, June 8, 647.
  Land Purchase Acts, delay in carrying out, June 8, 650.

Loan Fund Board—Illegalities, June 9, 764.

Local Government Board Orders.
  Printing, etc., June 8, 651.
  Sale—Difficulty in obtaining Copies, June 6, 439.

Local Government Finance, Labour and Expense, increase in under new Rules, June 15, 1192.

Longford, County Council Collector—Case of W. Jones, June 13, 1072.

Magistrates, Resident, Salaries, June 9, 767.

Migration of Population of Co. Mayo—County Council Resolution, June 6, 440.

Monaghan Union Medical Officer, June 16, 1351.

Mullingar Lunatic Asylum.
  Building Expenditure, etc., June 19, 1499.
  Joint Committee—Longford Members, June 13, 1076.

National School Teachers.
  Assistant Teachers and the Pension Fund, June 19, 1495.
  Examinations, June 12, 903.
  Guardians, Teachers as—Case of Mr. Kenny, June 5, 304.
  Salaries, Classification of, June 6, 438.
  Ulster and Connaught, June 13, 1071.

Newcastle West [Limerick] Creamery—Sewer Complaint. June 15, 1193.

O'Donnell, Dominick—Inmate of Belmullet Union, June 13, 1075.

Oughterard Union, Fever Outbreak, June 16, 1358.

Phoenix Park Murderer, Release of, June 5, 299.

Rating, new System—Landlord and Tenant Agreements, June 9, 769.

Salmon Fisheries—Illegal Practices, June 9, 766.

Science, Royal College of, Dublin—Building, Control, etc., June 16, 1350.

Tithe Rent-Charge, Redemption, June 1, 84; June 16, 1355.

Town Commissioners, Chairman of—Solicitor losing right to practise at Quarter Sessions, June 16, 1360.

Trawling off Howth—Compensation to Fishermen, June 16, 1360; June 19, 1500.

Tyrone County Council Rate Collector—Appointment of W. McFarland, June 19, 1496.

Valuation—Fixing Fair Rents, etc., June 8, 647; June 9, 768; June 15, 1195.
  Sligo, June 12, 904.

5

[*Continued*

BALFOUR, RT. HON. G. W.—*cont.*
    Valuation Acts—Revised Valuations, June
        16, 1352.
    Westport Urban Sanitary Authority—Com-
        missioners' Petition, June 13, 1074.

BALFOUR OF BURLEIGH, LORD—Secretary for
    Scotland.
    Congested Districts [Scotland] Act Amend-
        ment Bill, 2R., June 2, 164.
    Electric Lighting Provisional Order Bills,
        June 9, 752.
    Sea Fisheries Bill, 2R., June 8, 611.

BALLAGHADEREEN AND CASTLEREA.
    Sanitary Works in—Expenses.
    Q. Mr. Hayden; A. Mr. G. W. Balfour,
        June 16, 1357.

BALLYDUFF POSTAL FACILITIES
    Q. Mr. Flavin; A. Mr. Hanbury, June 19,
        1494.

BALLYMAHON POSTAL ARRANGEMENTS.
    Q. Mr. Hayden; A. Mr. Hanbury, June
        19, 1491.

BALROTHERY COUNTY CESS, STANDARD RATE.
    Q. Mr. Clancy; A. Mr. G. W. Balfour,
        June 16, 1353.

BANBURY, MR. F. G. [Camberwell, Peckham.]
    London Government Bill, con., June 6,
        482, 492.
    Succession [Scotland] Bill, 2R., June 7,
        591.
    Wine and Beerhouse Acts Amendment
        Bill, 2R., June 7, 577.

BANDON, Cost of Postage of Circulars.
    Q. Mr. E. Barry; A. Mr. Hanbury.
        June 16, 1342.

BANKS.
    Colonial and Foreign Banks Guarantee
        Fund Bill, see that Title.

BARLOW, MR. J. E. [Somerset, Frome].
    China, Affairs of, June 9, 868.

BARRACKS.
    Ladysmith, Insanitary Condition of.
    Q. Mr. Buchanan; A. Mr. Wyndham,
        June 9, 771.
    Military Works Bill, see that Title.

BARRISTERS, WOMEN, PRACTISING IN INDIA.
    Miss Sorabji's Application refused.
    Q. Mr. H. Roberts; A. Lord G. Hamil-
        ton, June 8, 641.

BARRY, MR. E. [Cork Co., S.].
    Circulars, cost of Postage in Bandon and
        Clone, June 16. 1342.
    Valuation Acts, Ireland—Revised Valua-
        tions, June 16, 1352.

BARRY, RT. HON. A. H. S. [Hunts, Hunting-
    don].
    Tithe Rent-Charge, Ireland, Redemption,
        June 16, 1354.

Barry Railway Bill.
    l. com.*, June 9, 749.

Barton-on-Sea Water Bill.
    c. 2R.*, May 31, 2.
    Rep.*, June 16, 1330.

BARTLEY, MR. G. C. T. [Islington, N.].
    Colonial Loans Fund Bill, June 12, 908;
        com., June 8, 743.
    Dublin Corporation Bill, con. June 13,
        1039.
    London Water [Purchase] Bill, 2R., June
        1, 75.
    Municipal Loans, Repayment of, June 2,
        225.
    Municipal Trading Committee, Appoint-
        ment of, June 8, 661.

BATH, Postal Deliveries.
    Q. Col. Welby; A. Mr. Hanbury, June
        5, 302.

BATHING FATALITY, ALDERSHOT.
    Q. Mr. Jeffreys; A. Mr. Wyndham,
        June 8, 640.

Baths and Washhouses Acts Amendment
Bill.
    c. 2R.*, June 12. 991; June 15, 1316.

BATOUM AND DISTRICT—Trade Report pre-
    sented. June 1, 68.

BAWNBOY RURAL POSTMAN'S WAGES.
    Q. Mr. J. P. Farrell; A. Mr. Hanbury,
        June 13, 1068.

BAYLEY, MR. T. [Derbyshire, Chesterfield].
    Salisbury Plain, Rentals of Property—
        Return, June 6, 442; June 13, 1059.
    Vaccination Law, Enforcement of—Local
        Government Board Action, June 2, 215.

BEACH, see Hicks-Beach.

BEAUFORT, DUKE OF—Sat first after the death of
    his father, June 13, 993.

BECHUANALAND RAILWAY EXTENSION.
    Correspondence with Mr. C. J. Rhodes,
        Copy presented, May 31, 7; June 1, 68.

BEER MATERIALS COMMITTEE.
    Brewers' Licences, Substitutions for Hops,
        etc.
        Q. Sir C. Quilter; A. Sir M. Hicks-
            Beach, June 15, 1183.

BEERHOUSES.
    Wine and Beerhouse Acts Amendment Bill,
        see that Title.

BEIRUT AND COAST OF SYRIA—Trade Report
    presented, June 8, 596.

BELFAST.
    Post Office Staff.
    Q. Mr. Schwann; A. Mr. Hanbury,
        June 13, 1069.
    Q. Mr. Macaleese; A. Mr. Hanbury,
        June 19, 1490.
    Riots.
    Nationalist Demonstration.
        Q. Mr. Dillon; A. Mr. G. W. Bal-
            four, June 6, 527.
        Motion [Mr. Dillon], June 1, 87.
    Religious Disturbances.
        Q. Mr. Dillon; A. Mr. G. W. Balfour,
            June 1, 85.
        Qs. Capt. Donelan, Mr. McCartan;
            As. Mr. G. W. Balfour, June 8, 653.

BELFAST—cont.
Motion [Mr. Dillon], June 1, 87.
Queen's Island Workers, Attacks on.
Qs. Mr. Dillon; As. Mr. G. W. Balfour, June 13, 1073; June 15, 1197.

Belfast Corporation Bill.
c. 3R.*, June 1, 73.
l. 1R.*, June 2, 162.
2R.*, June 15. 1166.

Belfast Water Bill.
l. 2R.*, June 9, 751.

Belfast and Northern Counties Railway Bill.
c. con.*, May 31, 1.
3R.*, June 5, 293.
l. 1R.*, June 6, 412.
2R.*, June 15, 1166.

BELMULLET, Extra Police Force.
Q. Mr. Crilly; A. Mr. G. W. Balfour, June 13, 1075.

BEREHAVEN.
Beacon, Lighting—Complaints.
Q. Mr. Field; A. Mr. Ritchie, June 13, 1066.
Pier, Silting.
Q. Mr. P. O'Brien; A. Mr. G. W. Balfour, June 12, 906.

BERESFORD, LORD C. [York].
China.
Northern Railway, British Loan Contract—Russian Protest, June 8, 628.
Open Door Policy v. Spheres of Influence, etc.—Attack on Lord Salisbury's Policy, June 9, 784.
Peace Conference, June 9, 798.
Soudan Campaign.
Deceased Officers—Condolence to Relatives, etc., June 8, 697.
Kitchener. Lord, Grant to, June 5, 359, 369.
Waima Incident—Compensation Claims, June 9, 784.

BERESFORD'S, LORD C., MISSION TO CHINA.
O., Mr. Brodrick, June 9, 800.

BERKHAMPSTEAD NATIONAL SCHOOLS.
Ascension Day—Attendance of Children at Church.
Q. Mr. Trevelyan; A. Sir J. Gorst, June 16, 1347.

BETHELL, COMMANDER G. R. [York, E. R., Holderness].
Half-Timers—Education of Children Bill, com. May 31, 37, 38.
Private Legislation Procedure [Scotland] Bill, com. June 19. 1587.
Telegraph Service, June 1, 132.

BETHNAL GREEN.
Schools, Erection by London School Board.
Q. Mr. T. G. Talbot; A. Sir J. Gorst, June 12, 900.
Working Class Dwellings, Removal of.
Q. Mr. J. G. Talbot; A. Sir M. W. Ridley, June 12, 900.

Bexhill and Rotherfield Railway Bill.
c. Rep.*, June 16, 1330.

Bexhill and St. Leonards Tramroads Bill.
c. 2R.*, June 6, 430.

BHOWNAGGREE, SIR M. M. [Bethnal Green, N.E.].
Indian Expenditure, Royal Commission Report, June 2, 184.
Madras Riots, June 15, 1176.

BIGWOOD, MR. J. [Middlesex, Brentford].
Baths and Washhouses Acts [Amendment] Bill, 2R., June 12, 991.

BILL, MR. C. [Staffordshire, Leek].
Commercial Travellers in Russia, Tax on, June 8, 629.
" Mandat-Poste " System, Trial of, in England, suggested, June 8. 659.
School Teachers' Superannuation, Reformatory and Industrial Schools, June 12, 901.
Waima Incident—Compensation Claims, June 9, 839.

BILLS.
Provisional Order Bills Procedure—Insertion of Names.
Q. Mr. Lloyd-George; A. Mr. Russell, June 2, 175.

Birkenhead Corporation Bill.
c. con.*, June 5. 293.
3R.*, June 12. 889.
l. commons amendts.*, June 13, 994; June 16, 1317.

Birmingham, North Warwickshire, and Stratford-on-Avon Railway Bill.
l. 3R.*, June 2, 162.
c. 1R.*, June 5, 326.

BIRTHS, MARRIAGES. AND DEATHS.
Registrar-General, Vote for, June 1, 159.

BLACK HEAD LIGHTHOUSE.
Q. Mr. Allan; A. Mr. Ritchie, June 2, 180.
Q. Capt. Donelan; A. Mr. Ritchie, June 8, 634.

Blackpool Improvement Bill.
c. Rep. from Select com., June 6, 433.
con.*, June 12, 890.
3R.*, June 15, 1170.
l. 1R.*, June 16, 1318.

BLIND.
State Aid for.
Q. Mr. P. O'Brien; A. Sir M. W. Ridley, June 12. 906.
Q. Mr. P. O'Brien; A. Mr. Chaplin, June 16, 1348.

BLOEMFONTEIN CONFERENCE, see Transvaal— Uitlanders' Grievances.

BLOOD-MONEY—Crimping in United States.
Q. Col. Denny; A. Mr. Brodrick, June 12. 894.

BOARD OF AGRICULTURE AND BOARD OF TRADE,
  see Agriculture and Trade.

Board of Education Bill.
  Qs. Mr. Stevenson, Col. Lockwood; As.
    Mr. A. J. Balfour, June 19, 1500.
  Petition, June 15, 1168.

BOARDING-OUT SYSTEM FOR PAUPER CHILDREN,
  see Poor Law Children.

BOERS, see Transvaal.

BOILERS—Water-tube, on H.M. Ships.—Statement.
  Q. Sir J. Fergusson; A. Mr. Goschen,
    June 8, 633.

BOMBAY.
  Civil and Criminal Appeals in Political
    Courts—Return.
  Q. Sir W. Wedderburn; A. Lord G.
    Hamilton, June 15, 1178.

Bootle Corporation Bill.
  c. con.*, May 31, 1.
  3R.*, June 5, 293.
  l. 1R.*, June 6, 412.
  2R.*, June 15, 1166.

BOROUGH FUNDS ACT, 1872.
  Petitions, June 1, 3, 70, 78; June 2, 163,
    173; June 6, 414; June 7, 537; June 9,
    759, 1055.

BORROWING POWERS OF COUNTY COUNCILS.
  S., June 2, 224.

BOSCAWEN, MR. A. S. T. G. [Kent, Tun-
  bridge].
  Workhouses, Religious Ministrations,
    June 2, 267.

BOTTLED SPIRITS, DUTY ON.
  Finance Bill—Motion [Sir M. Hicks-
    Beach], June 6, 458.

BOULNOIS, MR. E. [Marylebone, E.].
  Life Assurance, Lloyd's Policies, June 8,
    633.
  London Government Bill, June 2, 186.
  Women, Qualification of, June 6, 467.
  London Water Purchase Bill, 2R., June 1,
    76.

BOUSFIELD, MR. W. R. [Hackney, N.].
  London Government Bill, con., June 6,
    519, 520, 523.

BOWLES, MR. T. G. [Lynn Regis].
  Agricultural Land Valuation—Finance Bill,
    new clause, June 6, 452.
  Business of the House—Precedence of
    Government Business, June 19, 1514.
  Death Duties, Aggregation Question—
    Finance Bill, June 6, 450.
  Godalming Corporation Water Bill, con.,
    June 15, 1003.
  Half-timers—Education of Children Bill,
    com., May 31, 28.
  Intoxicating Liquors [Sunday Closing] Bill,
    2R., June 7, 561, 562, 563, 565.
  Newfoundland Fisheries, Report, June 16,
    1338.
  Private Legislation Procedure [Scotland]
    Bill, com., June 12, 946.

BOWLES, MR. T. G.—*cont.*
  Queen Victoria, Southsea Birthday Cele-
    brations—Cancelling of Parade, June 2,
    180.
  Salisbury Plain—Rentals of Property, June
    6, 442.
  Supply—Business of the House, June 12,
    907.
  Undersized Fish Bill, 1R., June 8, 661, 662.
  Wine and Beerhouse Acts Amendment Bill,
    2R., June 7, 575.

**Bradford Tramways and Improvement
Bill.**
  Petition, June 6, 431.

BRADY, T.—Carrying Firearms without licence,
  prosecution.
  Q. Mr. T. M. Healy; A. Mr. G. W.
    Balfour, June 15, 1189.

BRAKES, CONTINUOUS—Return presented, June
  19, 1456, 1479.

BRAZIL.
  Trade Report presented, June 8, 596; June
    15, 1168.

BREWERS' LICENCES—Substitutes for Hops, etc.
  Q. Sir C. Quilter; A. Sir M. Hicks-
    Beach, June 15, 1183.

Brigg Urban District Gas Bill.
  c. Lords Amendts.*, June 2, 167.

Brighton Marine Palace and Pier Bill.
  c. 2R.*, June 7, 537.

Bristol Floods Prevention Bill.
  l. Royal Assent, June 6, 409.

Bristol Gas Bill.
  c. Rep.*, June 19, 1477.

BRITISH COLUMBIA.
  Japanese Immigration.
  Q. Mr. Hogan; A. Mr. J. Chamberlain,
    June 8, 636.

BRITISH NEW GUINEA.
  Papers relating to.
  Q. Sir J. Lubbock; A. Mr. J. Chamber-
    lain, June 6, 440.

BRITISH SOUTH AFRICA COMPANY.
  Bechuanaland Railway Extension—Copy of
    Correspondence presented, May 31, 7;
    June 1, 68.

BRIXTON.
  City and Brixton Railway Bill; see that
    Title.

BRODRICK, RT. HON. W. ST. JOHN—Under
  Secretary for Foreign Affairs [Surrey,
  Guildford].
  Anglo-American Commission, June 1,
    82; June 5, 299; June 13, 1064.
  Armenia.
    Archbishops and Bishops, Detention
     of, June 1, 80; June 15, 1179.
    Distressed Armenians—Peace Confer-
     ence, June 12, 894.
    Kurdish Atrocities — Russian and
     French Protest, June 16, 1337.
    Massacres of 1896 — Compensation
     Claims, June 9, 764.

BRODRICK, RT. HON. W. ST. JOHN—cont.
  Canton, British Traders at—Case of Messrs. Banker and Co., June 2, 176.
  China.
    Affairs of, Lord Salisbury's Policy—Lord C. Beresford's Attack, etc., June 9, 800.
    Anglo-Russian Agreement.
      Pekin and Manchurian Railway, June 1, 82; June 8, 630.
      Russian Sphere of Interest, Extension, June 13, 1065.
    French Claims — Mining Rights in Szechuen, June 2, 183.
    Northern Railway, British Loan Contract—Russian Protest, June 8, 628.
    Rice Exports from Nanking, Prohibition of, June 13, 1065.
    Ta-lien-wan as an Open Port—Russian Cargoes, British Vessels carrying, June 2, 175.
    Yang-tsze Valley, Geographical Definition, etc., June 8, 631.
  Commercial Travellers in Russia, Tax on, June 8, 629.
  Consuls, Foreign. Exemption from Taxation, June 8. 628.
  Crimping in United States—Blood-money, June 12, 894.
  Foreign Service Messengers, June 9, 762.
  Godalming Corporation Water Bill, com., June 13, 1004, 1170.
  Most Favoured Nation Clause—United States Treaties, June 9, 763.
  Muscat Incident, Papers relating to, June 8, 627.
  Persia, Russian Railway Construction—Expiration of Agreement, etc., June 8, 629.
  Persian Gulf, British Trade Interests—Railway Concessions to Germany, June 8. 629.
  Russia, Trade in—
    United States, France and German Activity, June 12, 893.
  Soudan :—
    Fever among Troops, June 2, 180.
    Garstin's, Sir W., Report, June 19, 1484.
    Military Operations, Prospective, June 8, 631.
    Omdurman, Battle of—British Officers with Native Troops, June 8, 631.
    Prisoners, Release of, June 2, 179.
    Sugar Bounties, Abolition of, June 9, 763.
    Tonga—Visit of H.M.S. " Tauranga," etc., June 8, 630; June 13, 1064.
    Turco-Servian Frontier, Fighting on, June 19, 1483.
    Turkish Loan of 1855, June 13, 1064; June 15, 1180.
    Waima Incident—Compensation Claims, June 9, 812.

Brompton and Piccadilly Circus Railway Bill.
  c. con.*, June 9, 756.
  3R.*, June 13, 1002.
  1. 1R.*, June 15, 1166.

Brooke's Park (Londonderry) Bill.
  l. Rep.*, June 13, 993.
    3R.*, June 16, 1317.
  c. 1R.*, June 19, 1478.

Broughty Ferry Gas and Paving Order Bill.
  c. Rep.*, June 2, 168
    3R.*, June 5, 295.
BRUNNER, SIR J. T. [Cheshire, Northwich].
  London Government Bill, con., June 6, 491.
BRUSSELS CONFERENCE,
  West African Liquor Traffic, see Africa, West.
BRYCE, RT. HON. J. [Aberdeen, S.].
  Board of Education Bill—Business of the House, June 19, 1512.
  Education, Scotland, Grants, etc., June 16, 1394.
  London Government Bill, con., June 6, 461.
  Private Legislation Procedure [Scotland] Bill, com., June 12, 935.

Brynmawr and Western Valleys Railway Bill.
  l. Rep. from Select com., June 15, 1165.
BUCHANAN, MR. T. R. [Aberdeenshire, E.].
  Ladysmith Barracks, Insanitary condition, June 9, 771.
  Private Legislation Procedure [Scotland] Bill, com. June 12, 913, 944.
  School Teachers, Scottish, Pensions to, June 9, 773.
  Secondary and Technical Schools, Scotland, June 13, 1069.

BUENOS AYRES.
  Cattle Trade—Hindustan losses.
    Q. Mr. Field; A. Mr. Long, June 13, 1067.

Buenos Ayres and Pacific Railway Company Bill.
  l. Rep.*, June 8, 594.
    3R.*, June 13, 994.
  c. 1R.*, June 15, 1175.

Building Feus and Leases (Scotland) Bill.
  Petitions, June 2, 173; June 5, 296.
BULLETS.
  Dum-Dum Bullet, see that Title.
  India, Report Ordered [Lord G. Hamilton], June 8, 627.
BURIAL GROUNDS, see Cemeteries.
Burley-in-Wharfedale Urban District Water Bill.
  l. Royal Assent, June 6, 409.
BURMESE WOMAN, Outrage on by British Soldiers, see India.
BURNS, MR. J. [Battersea].
  Baths and Washhouses Acts [Amendment] Bill, 2R., June 12, 991.
  London Government Bill, con. June 6, 497; June 8, 708, 727.
  Lunacy Bill, 2R., June 12, 991.

Bury Corporation Water Bill.
c. 2R.*, June 6, 430.

BUSINESS OF THE HOUSE.
Q. Capt. Sinclair, Mr. Boulnois, Mr. Morley, Mr. Dillon, Sir W. Lawson, Mr. J. Redmond, Capt. Pretyman, Mr. Drage; A. Mr. A. J. Balfour, June 2, 185; Qs. Mr. Crombie, Mr. Channing, Sir H. Campbell-Bannerman, Sir C. Cameron; As. Mr. A. J. Balfour, June 8, 660; Qs. Sir C. Cameron, Mr. Bowles, Mr. Channing, Mr. Bartley; As. Mr. A. J. Balfour, June 12, 907; Q. Sir C. Dilke; A. Mr. A. J. Balfour, June 13, 1078; Qs. Mr. J. P. Farrell, Capt. Donelan; As. Mr. A. J. Balfour, June 15, 1198.
Government Business, Precedence of, Motion [Mr. A. J. Balfour] June 19, 1502.

BUXTON, MR. S. C. [Tower Hamlets, Poplar].
Colonial Loans Fund Bill, com. June 8, 740.
London Government Bill, con. June 6, 463, 480, 485, 503, 509, 510; June 8, 710, 715, 730.

BY-ELECTIONS.
Edinburgh [East Division]
New Writ, June 13, 1078.
Edinburgh [South Division].
New Writ, June 9, 762.
Lancashire [Southport]. New Member Sworn, June 1, 87.
Yorkshire, W.-R. [Osgoldcross].
New Writ, June 19, 1474.

CABLES.
Pacific Cable Scheme. see that Title.
South Africa—Delay in transmission of Sir A. Milner's Memorandum.
Q. Mr. Griffith; A. Mr. J. Chamberlain, June 13, 1059.

Calcutta Municipal Bill.
Q. Mr. H. Roberts; A. Lord G. Hamilton, June 16, 1336.

CALDER.
Aire and Calder Navigation Bill, see that Title.

CALDWELL, MR. J. [Lanark, Mid].
Baths and Washhouses Acts [Amendment] Bill, 2R., June 12, 992.
Colonial Loans Fund Bill. com., June 8, 736, 744.
Education, Scotland—Attendance of Children at School, etc., June 16, 1424.
Finance Bill, con., June 6, 459.
Promissory Notes, June 8, 731, 732.
Private Legislation Procedure [Scotland] Bill, com., June 12, 923, 931, 936, 939, 942, 946, 957, 959, 962, 964, 969, 971, 974, 987; June 19, 1537, 1544, 1549, 1551, 1566, 1567, 1570, 1585, 1588, 1589, 1592.
Seats for Shop Assistants [England and Ireland] Bill, com., June 8, 748.

Caledonian Railway [General Powers] Bill.
l. Rep.*, June 12, 877.
3R., June 19, 1454.

Cambridge University and Town Gas Bill.
c. 3R.*, June 1, 73.
l. commons amendts., June 8, 593.

CAMERON, SIR C. [Glasgow, Bridgeton].
Bakery Dispute, Glasgow—Case of A. M'Naughton, June 19, 1485.
Finance Bill—Local Loans, June 8, 732, 733, 734.
Indian Sugar Duties—Tariff Act, 1899, June 15, 1278.
Orphan Homes, Scottish—Education of Children, etc., June 12, 896; June 16, 1338, 1429.
"Parliamentary Debates." Delay in Publication, June 5 [72], 303.
Private Legislation Procedure [Scotland] Bill, com., June 12, 941, 968; June 19, 1540, 1543, 1556, 1560, 1562, 1567, 1569, 1570, 1574, 1575, 1579, 1586.
Telegraphs [Telephonic Communication, etc.] Bill, June 8, 661; June 12, 907; June 19, 1501.

CAMPBELL-BANNERMAN, RT. HON. SIR H. [Stirling Burghs].
Business of the House—Precedence of Government Business, June 19, 1505, 1527.
Death Duties, Aggregation Question—Finance Bill. June 6, 449.
Finance Bill, con., June 6, 458.
Indian Sugar Duties—Tariff Act, 1899, June 15, 1307.
London Government Bill—Qualification of Women, June 13, 1084.
Naval Works Bill, June 8, 660.
Private Legislation Procedure [Scotland] Bill, com., June 12, 914, 920, 925, 938, 976, 979, 984, 988; June 19, 1533, 1552, 1558, 1570, 1571, 1578, 1583, 1585.
Soudan Expedition.
Kitchener, Lord, Grant to.
Mahdi's Body, Treatment of, etc., June 5, 332.
Money Grants, House of Lords initiating—Question of Privilege, June 5, 323.
Thanks of the House to Lord Kitchener, June 8, 667.

CAMPERDOWN, EARL OF.
Transvaal—Uitlanders' Grievances.
Bloemfontein Conference, June 8, 597.

CANADA.
Anglo-American Commission, see that Title.
Pauper Children Emigration, see Poor Law Children.

CANARY ISLANDS.
Trade Report presented, June 1, 68.

CANTON—British Traders' Rights—Case of Messrs. Banher and Co.
Q. Mr. Hatch; A. Mr. Brodrick, June 2, 176.

CAPE COLONY.
Anti-British Propaganda.
Qs. Sir E. Ashmead-Bartlett, Mr. MacNeill; As. Mr. J. Chamberlain, June 15, 1182; Q. Mr. MacNeill; A. Mr. J. Chamberlain, June 16, 1338.
Observatory, Report presented, June 2, 163, 170.

CAPE TO CAIRO RAILWAY SCHEME.
Bechuanaland Extension—Correspondence
with Mr. Rhodes presented, May 31, 7;
June 1, 68.

CARDIFF.
All Saints' Church [Cardiff] Bill, see that
Title.

Cardiff Railway Bill.
1. Rep.*, June 13, 993.
3R., June 19, 1454.

CAREW, MR. J. L. [Dublin, College Green].
Kildare Agricultural Grant, Reduction,
June 8, 650.
Tea, Adulteration of—Inquiry. June 9, 775.

CARMARTHEN—Charities.
Commissioners' Report, Delay in Publica-
tion.
Q. Mr. L. Morgan; A. Mr. G.
Lawson, June 19, 1487.
Return presented, June 8, 626.

CARMEN—Street Obstruction.
Dismissal of Prosecution at Marylebone
Police Station.
Q. Gen. Laurie; A. Mr. Collings,
June 15, 1184.

CARMICHAEL, SIR T. G. G. [Edinburgh, Mid-
lothian].
Newfoundland Fisheries Report, June 16,
1338.

CARNARVON POLLING DISTRICT.
County Council Order presented, June 1,
70, 79.

CARSON, RT. HON. E. [Dublin University].
Dublin Corporation Bill, Con., June 13,
1013, 1018.

CARTER, REV. C. E. J.—Illegal Practices at
Government Factory Chapels.
Qs. Mr. Channing, Mr. C. Williams; As.
Mr. Wyndham, June 12, 897.

CASTLEREA AND BALLAGHADEREEN—Sanitary
Works—Expenses.
Q. Mr. Hayden; A. Mr. G. W. Balfour,
June 16, 1357.

CATTLE TRADE.
Buenos Ayres—Hindustan Losses.
Q. Mr. Field; A. Mr. Long, June 13,
1067.

CAUSTON, MR. R. K. [Southwark, W.]
London Government Bill. Con., June 8, 726.

CAVAN.
Fair Rent applications—Delay in hearing.
Q. Mr. J. P. Farrell; A. Mr. G. W. Bal-
four, June 16, 1355.
Land Commission—Sub-Commissioners'
Judgments.
Q. Mr. S. Young; A. Mr. G. W.
Balfour, June 8, 647.
Local Government Board—Refusal to trans-
fer divisions from Granard to Cavan
Union.
Q. Mr. J. P. Farrell; A. Mr. G. W.
Balfour, June 13, 1075.
Magistracy, Vacancy.
Q. Mr. J. P. Farrell; A. Mr. G. W.
Balfour, June 16, 1359.

CAVAN—cont.
Tramways Act—Relief to Ratepayers.
Q. Mr. J. P. Farrell; A. Mr. Hanbury,
June 19, 1492.

CECIL, LORD H. [Greenwich].
London Government Bill, Con., June 6,
490. 524; June 8, 703, 710.

CELTIC LANGUAGE IN IRISH SCHOOLS.
Reduction in number of marks.
Q. Mr. Flavin; A. Mr. G. W. Balfour,
June 16, 1354.

Cemetries Rating Bill.
Petition, June 5, 296.

CEMETERY SCANDAL, ABERDEEN.
Q. Gen. Russell; A. Mr. A. G. Murray,
June 19, 1486.

CENTRAL TELEGRAPH STAFF, see Telegraphists.

CEYLON.
Waste Land Ordnances—Mr. Le Mesurier's
Complaints. Papers relating to.
Q. Mr. Schwann; A. Mr. J. Chamber-
lain, June 13, 1059.

CHAIN CABLES.
See Anchors and Chain Cables.
Chairman of Committees—Rt. Hon. J. W.
Lowther.

CHALONER, CAPT. R. G. W. [Wilts., Westbury].
London Government Bill, Con., June 6,
521. 523.
Money-lending Bill. June 8, 660.

CHAMBERLAIN, RT. HON. J.—Secretary of State
for the Colonies [Birmingham, W.].
Africa, West, Liquor Trade.
Brussels Conference, June 13, 1063.
Spirit Duties Increase, June 15, 1181.

CHAMBERLAIN, RT. HON. J.
Anglo-American Commission, June 6, 441.
Ansahs of Ashanti—Compensation, etc.,
June 15, 1180.
"Anti-British" Propaganda in Cape
Colony. June 15, 1183; June 16, 1338.
British Columbia—Japanese Immigration,
June 8, 636.
Ceylon Waste Land Ordnances, June 13,
1059.
Imperial Institute and the London Univer-
sity Scheme, June 6, 441.
Indian Sugar Duties—Tariff Act, June 15,
1291.
Mauritius Sugar Industry, June 13, 1063.
Natal, Boers in —Alleged Arming by
Transvaal Government, June 13, 1061.
New Guinea, British—Papers relating to,
June 6, 440.
Newfoundland Fisheries, Report, June 16,
1338.
Pacific Cable Scheme, June 13, 1063.
Sierra Leone—Sir D. Chalmers' Report,
June 2, 177.
Transvaal, Uitlanders' Grievance, etc.
Applebe, Mrs., Murder of, June 19,
1484.
Bloemfontein Conference, June 8, 637.
Arbitration—President Kruger's Pro-
posal, June 13, 1060.
Milner's, Sir A., Memorandum, June
13, 1060.

11

[Continued

CHAMBERLAIN, RT. HON. J.—*cont.*
 Edgar, Mr., Killed by Policeman at
  Johannesburg—Compensation to Mrs.
  Edgar, June 2, 183; June 19, 1485.
 Oath of Allegiance—Naturalisation of
  British Subjects, June 16, 1337.
 Political Rights, June 13, 1061, 1062.
 Rhodes', Mr., Interviews with Mr.
  Chamberlain, Alleged, June 15, 1182.
 Uitlanders' Petition—Signatures, June 5,
  306.
 War, Declaration of, Previous to Jame-
  son Raid, June 19, 1485.

CHANCELLOR OF THE EXCHEQUER—Right Hon.
 Sir M. Hicks-Beach.
 West Indies—Fruit Steamers, Local Duties
  on Rum, etc., June 6, 441.

CHANNEL ISLANDS—From Crown Rights,
 Revenues—Return Ordered [Sir C. Dilke],
 June 12, 893.

CHANNING, MR. F. A. [Northampton, East].
 Adulteration of Food and Drugs Bill—
  Business of the House, June 12, 908.
 Business of the House—Precedence of
  Government Business, June 19, 1519.
 Desborough Level Crossing Fatality, In-
  quest—Board of Trade Representative,
  June 2, 181.
 Divine Service at Enfield Ordnance Factory
  Chapel—Illegal Practices, June 12,
  897.
 Dum-Dum Bullet, issue of, to Troops in
  India, June 5, 301.
 Lunacy Bill, 2R.. June 12, 990.
 "Parliamentary Debates," Delay in Publi-
  cation, June 5, 304.
 Private Legislation Procedure [Scotland]
  —Expenses, June 12, 910.
 Railway Servants, Fatalities Among,
  Number of, June 2, 178.
 Soudan Campaign :—
  Grant to Lord Kitchener, House of
   Lords Initiating Money Grants—Ques-
   tion of Privilege, June 5, 321.
  Thanks of the House — Cruelty to
   Wounded Dervishes, Alleged, June 8,
   676, 681, 682.
  Supply—Business of the House, June 8,
   660.
 Vaccination, June 2, 198, 199, 218.

CHAPLIN, RT. HON. H.—President of the Local
 Government Board [Lincolnshire, Slea-
 ford].
 Blind, State Aid for, June 16, 1349.
 Loans, Municipal, Repayment of, June 2,
  227.
 Local Government Board Inquiries, June
  2, 281.
 Meat Inspection at Liverpool—Appoint-
  ment of Unqualified Inspector, June 16,
  1348.
 Poor Law Children—Education, Barrack
  Schools, etc., June 2, 256.
 Reading Public Vaccinator—Remuneration,
  June 16, 1349.
 Vaccination, Conscientious Objections, etc.,
  June 2, 193, 194, 197, 213, 215.
 Workhouses, Religious Ministration, June
  2, 278.

Charing Cross, Euston and Hampstead
 Railway Bill.
 1. Rep. from com. of Selection, June 12,
  879.

CHARITABLE AND OTHER ALLOWANCES.
 Vote for, com.*, June 1, 157, Rep.*,
  June 2, 288.

CHARITIES AND CHARITY COMMISSION,
 CARMARTHEN.
 Delay in Publication of Report.
  Q. Mr. L. Morgan; A. Mr. G. Law-
   son, June 19, 1487.
 Return Presented, June 8, 626.
 Endowed Schools, Report Presented, June
  8, 596, 625.
 Flint, Inquiry, Paper Presented, May 31,
  7.
 Welsh Intermediate Education Act, Report
  Presented, June 14, 1091, June 15, 1168.
 Yorkshire, West Riding, Return Presented,
  June 8, 626.

CHARLES, SIR A.—Appointment as Dean of
 Arches.
 Q. Mr. C. McArthur; A. Mr. Collings,
  June 15, 1186.
 Q. Lord Balcarres; A. Mr. Collings, June
  16, 1340.

Cheap Trains Bill.
 Petition, June 5, 296.

CHILE.—Trade Report presented, June 15, 1168.

CHILDREN.
 Education, see that Title.
 Half-timers Bill, see Education of
  Children Bill.
 Jam Factories, Labour in.
  Q. Mr. Hedderwick; A. Sir M. W. Rid-
   ley, June 5, 297.
 Poor Law Children, see that Title.
 Sale of Intoxicating Liquors to—Petition
  for alteration of Law, June 12, 892.

CHINA.
 Anglo-Russian Agreement—Russian De-
  mand, Pekin and Manchurian Railway,
  S. June 9, 790, 808, 816, 828, 855, 859,
   867.
  Q. Mr. Provand; A. Mr. Brodrick,
   June 1, 82.
  Q. Mr. Lambert; A. Mr. Brodrick,
   June 8, 630.
 Army Reorganisation, S. June 9, 789,
  801.
 Beresford, Lord C., Mission, S. June 9,
  800.
 Break-up of China, S. June 9, 798, 810.
 British Government Policy—Lord Charles
  Beresford's Protest, etc., S. June 9,
  786, 815, 847, 866.
 British Trade, S. June 9, 785, 903, 843.
 Canton, British Traders in—Case of Messrs.
  Banher and Co.
  Q. Mr. Hatch; A. Mr. Brodrick, June
   2, 176.
 Fiscal Reforms, S. June 9, 802.
 French Claims—Mining Rights in Szechuen.
  Q. Sir E. Sassoon; A. Mr. Brodrick, June
   2, 183.
 Government Reorganisation.
  S. June 9, 801.
 Northern Railway—British Loan Contract
  —Russian Protest.

CHINA—cont.
  Q. Lord C. Beresford; A. Mr. Brod-
    rick, June 8, 628.
Open-Door Policy v. Spheres of Influence,
  S. June 9, 779, 786, 793, 804, 828, 847.
" Pipe-down " Policy.
  O. Lord Charles Beresford, S. June 9,
    799.
Railways, S. June 9, 796.
Rice Exports from Nanking.
  Q. Mr. Provand; A. Mr. Brodrick, June
    13, 1065.
Russian Railway Interests—Correspondence
  presented, June 5, 291, 297.
Russian Sphere of Interest, Extension of—
  Anglo-Russian Agreement.
    Q. Sir E. Ashmead-Bartlett; A. Mr.
      Brodrick, June 13, 1065.
Squadron, British, Visit to China.
  Q. Mr. Hedderwick; A. Mr. Goschen,
    June 9, 776.
Ta-lien-wan as an Open Port—Russian
  Cargoes, British Vessels carrying.
    Q. Sir E. Gourley; A. Mr. Brodrick,
      June 2, 175.
Tientsin Treaty.
  S. June 9, 788, 805, 854.
Trade Report presented, June 2, 163.
Yang-tsze Valley.
  S. June 9, 793, 805, 824, 854, 862, 866.
  Geographical Definition, Railway
    Rates, etc.
      Q. Mr. Lambert; A. Mr. Brodrick,
        June 8, 630.
  " No Man's Land," S. June 9. 842, 856.
CHRISTMAS BOXES, POSTMEN'S.
  O. Mr. Steadman, June 1, 102.

Church Discipline Bill.
  Petition, June 19. 1478.
CHURCH DISCIPLINE AND PUBLIC WORSHIP
  REGULATION, Return presented, June 7, 539.
CHURCH OF ENGLAND.
  Confessional Boxes, Return presented, June
    15, 1167.
  Ritualistic Practices.
    Danbury, Rev.. Illegal Practices at St.
      Michael's, Southampton.
        Q. Mr. S. Smith; A. Mr. A. J.
          Balfour, June 12, 907.
    Enfield Small Arms Factory.
      Ritualistic Practices in Government
        Chapels.
          Qs. Mr. Channing, Mr. C. Wil-
            liams; As. Mr. Wyndham,
            June 12, 898.

Church Stretton Water Bill.
  c. 2R.*, June 6, 430.
CIRCULARS, Postage in Bandon and Clone.
  Q. Mr. F. Barry; A. Mr. Hanbury, June
    16, 1342.

City and Brixton Railway Bill.
  c. Rep.*, June 2, 168.
    con.*, June 7, 537.
    3R.*, June 12, 890.
  l. 1R.*, June 13, 994.
CIVIL EMPLOYMENT—Retired Army and Navy
  Officers.
    Q. Capt. Norton; A. Mr. Anstruther,
      June 8, 657.

CIVIL SERVICE.
  India — Examinations. Regulations pre-
    sented, June 1, 69, 78; May 31, 6.
  Pay Deductions.
    Q. Capt. Norton; A. Mr. Hanbury, June
      2, 177.
CIVIL SERVICE ESTIMATES, see Supply.
CLANCY. MR. J. J. [Dublin County, N.].
  Balrothery County Cess—Standard Rate,
    June 16, 1353.
  Service Franchise Bill, con. June 14, 1154.
  Trawling off Howth—Compensation to
    Fishermen, June 16, 1360; June 19, 1500.
CLAPHAM SORTING OFFICE—Vacancies.
  Q. Mr. Steadman; A. Mr. Hanbury, June
    1, 81.
CLARK, DR. [Caithness].
  Education, Scotland, June 16, 1339, 1439,
    1449.
  Letters—Daily Deliveries, June 1, 125.
  Lighthouse Keepers, Scottish — Retiring
    Allowances. etc., June 16, 1342.
  Pauper Children, Education, etc., June
    2, 249.
  Private Legislation Procedure [Scotland]
    Bill. com., June 12, 920, 928, 931, 938,
    945, 947, 953, 955, 961, 964, 967, 973, 975,
    982; June 19, 1533, 1539, 1546, 1553,
    1562, 1569, 1570, 1577, 1592, 1593.
      Expenses, June 12, 909.
  Vaccination Prosecutions, June 2, 218.
CLARKE, SIR E. [Plymouth].
  London Government Bill, con., June 6, 482,
    491, 506, 514.

Clay Cross Water Bill.
  l. Royal Assent, June 6, 409.
CLERGY.
  Tithe-owning Clergy of England and Wales
    —Agricultural Rates Act Petition, June
    8, 597.
  Tithe Rent-Charge [Rates] Bill, see that
    Title.
CLONE—Postage or Circulars.
  Q. Mr. F. Barry; A. Mr. Hanbury, June
    16, 1342.
CLOUGH, MR. W. O. [Portsmouth].
  London Government Bill, con., June 6,
    523, 524.

Clyde Navigation Bill.
  c. 2R.*, June 15, 1170.

Coalville Urban District Gas Bill.
  l. commons amendts.*, June 2, 161.
  Royal Assent, June 6, 410.
COATBRIDGE.
  Airdrie and Coatbridge Water Bill, see that
    Title.

Cobham Gas Bill.
  l. 3R.*, June 2, 161.
  c. 1R.*, June 5, 326.
    2R.*, June 14, 1089.
COCHRANE, HON. T. H. [Ayrshire, North].
  Private Legislation Procedure [Scotland]
    Bill, com., June 12, 979.
COGHILL, MR. D. H. [Stoke-upon-Trent].
  Clerical Tithes Bill—Business of the House,
    June 19, 1519.

13

COHEN, MR. B. L. [Islington, E.]
London Government Bill, con., June 6, 473.

COINAGE. Expenses of, Vote for, Rep.*, June
1, 158.

COLERIDGE, LORD.
Crime, Incitement to, Ireland—M'Hale v.
Sullivan, June 12, 881, 882, 884.

COLLINGS, RT. HON. J.—Under-Secretary for the
Home Office [Birmingham, Bordesley].
Ecclesiastical Judges—Appointment of Sir
A. Charles, June 15, 1186; June 16,
1340.
Naturalisation Certificates, Obtaining
from Secretary of State, June 15, 1185.
Street Obstruction—Dismissal of Prose-
cution against Carmen, June 15, 1185.
Wine and Beerhouse Acts Amendment
Bill, 2R., June 7, 574, 575. 581.

Colonial Loan Funds Bill.
c. com., 735.

Colonial Loan Funds Bill.
Q. Mr. Dillon; A. Mr. A. J. Balfour,
June 9, 777.

COLONIAL OFFICE.
Secretary of State—Rt. Hon. J. Chamber-
lain.
Parliamentary Secretary—Earl of Selborne.

**Colonial and Foreign Banks Guarantee
Fund Bill.**
c. 2R.*, June 6, 430.
Rep.*, June 16. 1330.

COLONIES.
Annual Reports Presented, June 1, 69;
June 2, 170; June 19, 1456, 1479.
Probates Act, Queensland, Order in Coun-
cil Presented, June 6, 414, 434.

COLVILLE, MR. J. [Lanark, N.E.].
Intoxicating Liquors [Sunday Closing] Bill
2R., June 7, 544.
Private Legislation Procedure [Scotland]
Bill, com., June 12, 928.
Quarrier's Orphan Homes—Education of
Children, June 16, 1434.

COMERFORD, P.—Fishing Prosecution.
Q. Mr. P. O'Brien; A. G. W. Balfour,
June 16, 1358.

COMMERCE, see Trade and Commerce.

COMMERCIAL EDUCATION.
United States, Report Presented, June 15,
1168.
University of London and the Imperial
Institute Scheme, etc.
Q. Sir H. Vincent; A. Mr. Russell,
June 1, 80.

COMMERCIAL TRAVELLERS.
Russia. Tax on British Commercial Travellers in.
Q. Mr. Bill; A. Mr. Broderick, June
8, 629.

COMMERCIAL POST-CARDS.
Q. Sir R. Hanson; A. Mr. Hanbury.
June 12, 904.

COMMERCIAL TREATIES.
Most Favoured Nation Clause—Foreign
Treaties.
Q. Col. Milward; A. Mr. Brodrick,
June 9, 763.

COMMISSIONS.
Prevention of Corruption Bill, see that
Title.

COMPANIES WINDING-UP ORDERS.
Return Ordered [Mr. C. McArthur]. June
13, 1057.

Companies Acts Amendment Bill.
Petition, June 15, 1175.

COMPENSATION TO WORKMEN FOR INJURIES.
See Workmen's Compensation.

COMPTON, LORD A. F. [Beds., Biggleswade].
Death Duties, Aggregation—Finance Bill,
new clause, June 6th, 444, 452.

COMPTROLLER AND AUDITOR-GENERAL.
Retirement of Mr. Mills.
Q. Mr. M'Kenna; A. Mr. A. J. Balfour,
June 1, 83.

CONFECTIONERY, Indian Exports—Return.
Q. Mr. Maclean; A. Mr. Ritchie. June
6, 443.

CONFESSIONAL BOXES—Church of England,
Return Presented, June 15, 1167.

CONGESTED DISTRICTS [IRELAND] BOARD.
Bagot Estate.
Q. Mr. Hayden; A. Mr. G. W. Balfour,
June 15, 1188.
Dillon's, Lord, Estate.
Q. Mr. T. M. Healy; A. Mr. G. W.
Balfour, June 16, 1361.

**Congested Districts (Scotland) Act
Amendment Bill.**
l. 2R., June 2, 164.
Rep.*, June 5, 291.
3R.*, June 6, 429.

CONGO—Trade Returns Presented, June 19,
1456.

CONISBROUGH AND WOODHOUSE RAILWAY.
See Woodhouse and Conisbrough Railway.

CONNAUGHT—National School Teachers.
Q. Mr. Field; A. Mr. G. W. Balfour,
June 13, 1070.

CONNAUGHT RANGERS AT MEERUT.
Shooting Case.
Q. Mr. H. Roberts; A. Lord G.
Hamilton. June 16, 1335.

CONSTABULARY, ROYAL IRISH.
Belmullet, Extra Police Force in.
Q. Mr. Crilly; A. Mr. G. W. Balfour,
June 13, 1075.
Mr. Hale v. Sullivan, Debate [l.]. June 12,
880.
Meehan, District Inspector, Conduct of.
Q. Mr. J. P. Farrell; A. Mr. G. W.
Balfour, June 15, 1195.
Promotion.
Q. Mr. J. P. Farrell; A. Mr. G. W.
Balfour, June 16, 1356.

CONSTANTINOPLE,   Massacres — Compensation
Claims.
  Q. Col. Denny; A. Mr. Brodrick, June
  9, 763.

CONSULS, FOREIGN—Exemption from Taxation.
  Q. Mr. Dillon; A. Mr. Brodrick, June
  8, 627.

CONTAGIOUS DISEASES [ANIMALS], see Diseases
of Animals.

COOKSTOWN ORANGE RIOTS.
  Q. Mr. Dillon; A. Mr. G. W. Balfour,
  June 8, 646.
  Q. Mr. Doogan; A. Mr. G. W. Balfour,
  June 15, 1194.

COOPER'S HILL COLLEGE—Retirement of
Officers.
  Q. Sir S. King; A. Lord G. Hamilton,
  June 15, 1178.

CORK.
  Council Contracts, Disqualification of
  Shareholder as Councillor.
    Q. Mr. Tully; A. Mr. G. W. Balfour,
    June 8, 652.
  Military District—Contracts for Stores,
  Complaints.
    Q. Capt. Donelan; A. Mr. J. P. Wil-
    liams. June 19, 1482.

Cork Corporation (Finance) Bill.
  l. 2R.*, June 8, 594.

CORONERS.
  Lincolnshire Coroners' Bill, see that Title.

CORRUPTION, PREVENTION OF,
  See Prevention of Corruption Bill.

COSTELLO, P., CASE OF.
  Q. Mr. Haydon; A. Mr. G. W. Balfour,
  June 19, 1495.

COUNCILLORS AND ALDERMEN—Qualification
of Women—London Government Bill,
Mr. Courtney's new clause, June 6, 464—
Mr. Elliot's Amendment, June 13, 1078.

COUNTY CESS, IRELAND.
  Balrothery—Standard Rate.
    Q. Mr. Clancy; A. Mr. G. W. Balfour,
    June 16, 1353.

**County Councillors [Qualification of
Women] [Scotland] Bill.**
  Petition, June 2, 173.

COUNTY COUNCILS.
  Borrowing Powers, S., June 2, 224.
  Irish Questions, see Ireland.
  Local Government Board Powers, see
  Local Government Board.

COUNTY COURTS.
  Fees—Proposed Reduction.
    Q. Sir C. Dilke; A. Mr. Hanbury,
    June 5, 299.
  Officers [Ireland] Clerical Assistance, Grant
  for—Return.
    Q. Mr. Engledew; A. Mr. Hanbury,
    June 6, 438.

COURTNEY, RT. HON. L. H. [Cornwall, Bodmin].
  Indian Sugar Duties—Tariff Act, 1899,
  June 15. 1283.
  London Government Bill, con. June 6,
  487, 489.
  Women, Qualification as Aldermen and
  Councillors, June 6, 464.
  Paris Exhibition—British Works of Art,
  June 15, 1186.
  Private Legislation Procedure [Scotland]
  Bill. com. June 19, 1544, 1545, 1551.
  Wine and Beerhouse Acts Amendment Bill,
  2R., June 7, 571.

CRANBORNE. VIS. [Rochester].
  Day School Code—Articles 37 and 42,
  June 19, 1487.
  Half-timers—Education of Children Bill,
  com. May 31, 19, 41, 42.
  London Government Bill, con. June 8,
  705.

CRAWFORD, T., CASE OF.
  Q. Mr. Austin; A. Mr. G. W. Balfour,
  June 5, 308.

CRILLY, MR. D. [Mayo, North].
  Belmullet, Extra Police Force, June 13,
  1075.
  Dublin General Post Office, Officials'
  Grievances. June 2, 284.
  Dublin Metropolitan Police — Summer
  Clothing, June 13, 1074.
  O'Donnell, Dominick—Inmate of Belmul-
  let Union, June 13, 1074.

CRIME, INCITEMENT TO, IRELAND, M'Hale v.
Sullivan, Debate.
  (l.) June 12, 880.

CRIMPING—United States.
  Q. Col. Denny; A. Mr. Brodrick, June
  12, 894.

CRIPPS, MR. C. A. [Gloucester, Stroud].
  Half-timers—Education of Children Bill,
  com. May 31, 40.
  London Government Bill, con. June 6,
  501, 511, 514, 515.
  Private Legislation Procedure [Scotland]
  Bill. com. June 12. 919, 920, 923, 924,
  927, 928, 934, 938. 977, 986, 988; June
  19. 1533. 1537. 1538. 1539. 1542, 1543.
  1545. 1549, 1578. 1588. 1592.

**Crofters' Holdings [Scotland] Act [1886]
Amendment Bill.**
  Petition, June 2. 173.

CROMBIE, MR. J. W. [Kincardineshire].
  Education, Scotland, June 8, 635; June
  16, 1441.
  Private Legislation Procedure [Scotland]
  Bill. com. June 12, 941; June 19, 1560.
  Scotch Estimates—Business of the House,
  June 8, 660.
  Secondary Education, Scotland, June 16,
  1402.
  Universities, Scottish—Number of Stu-
  dents, June 12, 896.

CROSS, MR. A. [Glasgow, Camlachie].
  Private Legislation Procedure [Scotland]
  Bill, com. June 12, 963.

CROSS, VISCOUNT.
  London Government Bill, June 15, 1169.

Crowborough District Gas Bill.
l. Royal Assent, June 6, 409.

Crowborough District Water Bill.
l. 3R.*, June 1, 66.
c. Lords Amendments*, June 9, 756.

CUSTOMS DEPARTMENT.
Boatmen's Grievances, S., June 1, 149.
Goschen Minute, S., June 1, 143, 146.
Officers' Grievances, Debate in com. of
Supply, June 1, 132.
Out-door Officers — Hours of Labour,
Wages, etc.
Q. Mr. Steadman ; A. Mr. Hanbury,
June 6, 436.
Vote for, June 1, 132 ; June 2, 287.
Watchers—Hours of Labour, Wages, etc.
Q. Mr. Steadman ; A. Mr. Hanbury,
June 6, 436.
Pay, S., June 1, 148.

CYPRUS—Grant in Aid.
Q. Mr. Pierpoint ; A. Mr. A. J. Balfour,
June 19, 1502.

DALRYMPLE, SIR C. [Ipswich].
Private Legislation Procedure [Scotland]
Bill, com., June 19, 1580.

DALZIEL, MR. J. H. [Kirkcaldy Burghs].
Colonial Loans Fund Bill, com., June 8, 741.
Customs Department, June 1, 154, 155.
Private Legislation Procedure [Scotland]
Bill, com., June 12, 916, 937, 954, 958,
959, 979, 983 ; June 19, 1561, 1565, 1587,
1588.
Trout Fishing Annual Close Time [Scotland]
Bill, 2R., June 12, 989.
Wine and Beerhouse Acts Amendment Bill,
2R, June 7. 580, 581.

DANBURY, REV.—Illegal Practices at St.
Michael's, Southampton.
Q. Mr. S. Smith ; A. Mr. A. J. Balfour,
June 12, 907.

Darwen Corporation Bill.
c. Rep., from Select Com., June 6, 433.
com.*, June 13, 1002.
3R.*, June 16, 1328.
l. 1R.*, June 16, 1318.

DAVITT, MR. [Mayo, S.].
Colonial Loans' Fund Bill, com., June 8, 742.
Dublin Telegraphists' hours of Duty, June 9,
775.
Intoxicating Liquors [Sunday Closing] Bill,
2R, June 7, 561, 563.
Magistrates, Resident [Ireland], Salaries of,
June 9. 767.
National School Teachers, Examinations,
June 12, 902.
Rangoon Woman, Outrage on, by British
Soldiers in India, June 12, 896 ; June 16,
1336.
Soudan Campaign—Thanks of the House.
Kitchener, Lord. June 8, 668.
Wounded Dervishes, Cruelty to—Conduct
of British Troops, June 8, 674, 680, 697.

DEATH DUTIES.
Aggregation Question—Finance Bill, New
Clause, Motion [Lord A. Compton],
June 6, 444.

DEATH DUTIES—cont.
Indefinite Liability for Estate Duty—Endorsement on Registered Titles, Debate
[l], June 13, 997.

DEBATES, see "Parliamentary Debates."

DEFECTIVE CHILDREN.
Elementary Education [Defective and
Epileptic Children] Bill, see that Title.

DENISTON, J., CASE OF.
Q. Mr. J. P. Farrell ; A. Mr. J. P.
Williams, June 19, 1482.

DENMARK.
Trade Report, presented June 8, 596.

DENNY, COL. J. M. [Kilmarnock Burghs].
Armenian Massacres—Compensation Claims,
June 9, 763.
Crimping in United States—Blood-money,
June 12' 894.
Education, Scotland—Distribution of
Grants, June 16, 1391.
Private Legislation Procedure [Scotland]
Bill, com., June 12, 983.

Derby Corporation [Tramways, etc.] Bill.
c. Rep., from Select Com., June 9, 758.
con.*, June 16, 1328.

Derby Corporation Water Bill.
c. Instruction to com. as to Consolidation of
Bills, June 2, 167.
Rep.*, June 16, 1331.

DERBY DAY AND SUTTON SCHOOL CHILDREN,
S., June 2, 247.

Derwent Valley Water Bill,
formerly
Sheffield Corporation [Derwent Val-
ley] Water Bill.
c. Instruction to com. as to Consolidation
of Bills, June 2, 167.
Rep.*, June 16, 1331.

DESBOROUGH LEVEL CROSSING FATALITY,
Inquest—Board of Trade Representative.
Q. Mr. Channing ; A. Mr. Ritchie, June
2, 181.

DESTITUTE CHILDREN [IRELAND] AND INDUS-
TRIAL SCHOOLS.
Q. Capt. Donelan ; A. Mr. G. W. Balfour,
June 8, 648.

DEVONSHIRE, DUKE OF—Interference in
Southport Election—Breach of Privilege.
Q. Mr. J. Lowther ; A. Mr. A. J. Balfour,
June 5, 307.
Motion [Mr. J. Lowther], 311.

DICKSON-POYNDER, SIR J. [Wilts, Chippenham].
London Government Bill, con., June 8, 717,
719, 720, 728.

DILKE, RT. HON. SIR C. [Gloucester, Forest of
Dean].
Anglo-American Commission — Official
Statement, June 5, 299.
Business of the House, June 13, 1078.

DILKE, RT. HON. SIR C.—cont.
  Government Business, Precedence of,
    June 19, 1507.
  County Court Fees, Proposed Reduction,
    June 5, 299.
  Foreign Affairs—Lord Salisbury's Foreign
    Policy, June 9, 778.
  Foreign Service Messengers, June 9, 762.
  Muscat Incident, Papers relating to,
    June 8, 627.
  Service Franchise Bill, com., June 7, 541;
    con., June 14, 1135. 1147.
  Waima Incident, Compensation Claims,
    etc., June 9, 780.

DILLON, MR. J. [Mayo, E.].
  Belfast Riots.
  National Disturbances, June 1, 85, 87;
    June 6, 527.
  Religious Disturbances, June 1, 85, 87.
  Queen's Island Workers, Attacks on,
    June 13, 1073; June 15, 1197.
  Business of the House—Precedence of
    Government Business, June 19, 1508,
    1525.
  Colonial Loans Fund Bill, June 9, 777;
    com., June 8, 737, 740.
  Consuls, Foreign, Exemption from Tax-
    ation, June 8, 627.
  Cookstown Riots, June 8, 646.
  Dublin Corporation Bill, con., June 13,
    1035.
  Dum-Dum Bullets.
  Peace Conference Resolution, June 5,
    308.
  Troops in India, Issue of Bullets to,
    June 5, 300.
  Fintona Sunday Mails, June 19, 1488.
  Local Government Ireland Board Orders,
    Printing, etc., June 8, 651.
  Pauper Children, Education of, etc., June
    2, 254.
  Post Office—Employment of Naval and
    Military Men, June 1, 128, 129.
  Private Legislation Procedure [Scotland]
    Bill, com., June 12, 980; con., June 19,
    1584.
  Rangoon Woman—Outrage on by British
    Soldiers, June 16, 1336.
  Soudan Campaign.
    Deceased Officers, etc—Compensation
      to Relatives, etc., June 8, 698.
    Kitchener, Lord, Grant to.
    Mahdi's Body, Treatment of, etc.,
      June 5, 389.
    Method of Procedure, June 2, 186.
    Personal Explanation, June 5, 309.
    Money Grants, House of Lords' Power
      of Initiating Question of Privilege,
      June 5, 324.
    Wounded Dervishes, Cruelty to—
      Alleged misconduct of British
      Troops, June 8, 682.
  Transvaal Uitlanders' Grievances—
    Bloemfontein Conference, June 8, 636.
  Turkish Loan 1885, June 13, 1064; June
    15, 1179.
  Vaccination and Board of Guardians—
    Irish System, June 2, 216.

DILLON's, LORD, ESTATE, Purchase by Congested
  Districts Board.
  Q. Mr. T. M. Healy; A. Mr. G. W.
    Balfour, June 16, 1361.

DISEASES OF ANIMALS ACTS.
  Conveyance of Animals by s.s. "Hindustan."
    Prohibition of, Order revoked.
    Q. Mr. Field; A. Mr. Long, June 13,
      1067; copy presented May 31, 5;
      June 1, 69.
    Ireland, Return presented, June 12; 880,
      892.

DISFRANCHISEMENT.
  Poor Law Relief, see that Title.

DISPENSERS—Unqualified in Doctors' Surgeries—Accidents resulting from mistakes.
  Q. Maj. Rasch; A. Sir J. Gorst, June 12,
    900.

DISTRICT COUNCILLORS, IRELAND.
  Labourers' Cottages and Disqualification of
    Councillors.
    Q. Mr. Gibney; A. Mr. G. W. Balfour,
      June 19, 1495.

DIVINE SERVICE.
  Illegal Practices, see Names of Places, such
    as St. Michael's, Southampton, etc.

DIVORCE.
  Jones's Divorce Bill, see that Title.

DOCK LABOURER—Garston, Fatal Accident.
  Q. Mr. M'Ghee; A. Sir M. W. Ridley,
    June 9, 769.

DOMESTIC SERVANTS' WAGES, Board of Trade
  Report presented, June 9, 753, 761.

DONEGAL.
  Agricultural Grant—County Council Reso-
    lution.
    Q. Mr. MacNeill; A. Mr. G. W. Bal-
      four, June 15, 1192.
  Railway Communication—County Council
    Resolution.
    Q. Mr. T. D. Sullivan; A. Mr. G. W.
      Balfour, June 19, 1498.

DONELAN, CAPT. [Cork, East].
  Belfast, Religious Disturbances, June 8,
  Blackhead Lighthouse, June 8, 634.
  Cork Military District—Stores Contracts,
    Complaints, June 19, 1482.
  Emigration, Irish, to United States, June 8,
    649.
  Industrial Schools and Destitute Children—
    Circular, June 8, 648.
  Irish Bills and Irish Estimates—Business of
    the House, June 15, 1198.
  Land Commission.
    Assistant Commissioners, June 8, 648.
    Valuations, June 9, 768.
  Youghal Rifle Range, Repairs, etc., June 9,
    771.

DOOGAN, MR. P. C. [Tyrone, E.].
  Cookstown Orange Riot, June 15, 1194.
  Loan Fund Board, Ireland—Illegalities,
    June 9, 765.
  Mountjoy Postal Arrangements, June 9,
    773.

DORSETSHIRE—Postal Deliveries.
  Q. Col. Welby; A. Mr. Hanbury, June
    5, 302.

DOUGLAS, RT. HON. A. A. [St. Augustine's].
Ambulance for the Houses of Parliament,
June 8, 657.
Hyde Park—Lighting, etc., June 19, 1488.
Metropolitan Volunteer March Past—
Arrangements to view, June 8, 657.

DRAGE, MR. [Derby].
Pauper Children, Education of, etc., June 2,
244.
Small Houses [Acquisition of Ownership]
Bill—Business of the House, June 2, 187.
Transvaal—Uitlanders' Grievances, Bloem-
fontein Conference, June 8, 656.

Drainage Separation Bill.
c. 1R.*, June 13, 1058.

DRAINS.
Metropolitan Sewers and Drains Bill, see
that Title.

DUBLIN.
General Post Office, Officials' Grievances, S.,
June 2, 284.
Kildare Street Library, Handing over to
New Irish Department.
Q. Mr. P. O'Brien; A. Mr. G. W. Bal-
four, June 16, 1350.
Police—Summer Clothing.
Q. Mr. Crilly; A. Mr. G. W. Balfour,
June 13, 1074.
Postmen's Grievances.
Q. Mr. P. O'Brien; A. Mr. Hanbury,
June 16, 1345.
Science, Royal College of—Building Control,
etc.
Q. Mr. P. O'Brien; A. Mr. G. W. Bal-
four, June 16, 1350.
Telegraphists' Hours of Duty.
Q. Mr. Davitt; A. Mr. Hanbury, June 9,
775.
Trawling—Compensation to Fishermen.
Qs. Mr. Clancy; As. Mr. G. W. Bal-
four, June 16, 1360; June 19, 1500.

Dublin Corporation Bill.
c. con., June 13, 1006.
3R.*, June 16, 1328.
1. 1R.*, June 16, 1318.

Dublin Corporation [Markets] Bill.
1. 2R.*, June 9, 750.

**Dublin Improvement [Bull Alley Area]
Bill.**
1. Royal Assent, June 6, 409.

DUCKWORTH, MR. [Lancashire, Middleton].
Half-timers—Education of Children Bill.
con. May 31, 53; 3R. June 14, 1101, 1105.

DUDLEY, EARL OF—Parliamentary Secretary to
Board of Trade.
Anchors and Chain Cables Bill, 2R., June
1, 70.

Dumbarton Burgh Bill.
c. Rep. from Select com., June 2, 169.
con.*, June 8, 624.
3R.*, June 12, 890.
1. commons amendts.*, June 13, 994.

DUM-DUM BULLET.
India.
Qs. Mr. Dillon, Col. Milward, Mr. Chan-
ning; As. Lord G. Hamilton, Mr.
Wyndham, June 5, 300.

DUM-DUM BULLET—*cont.*
Effect of Report ordered [Lord G.
Hamilton], June 8, 62.
Prohibition—Peace Conference Resolution.
Q. Mr. Dillon; A. Mr. A. J. Balfour,
June 5, 308.

DUNDALK, Postmastership Vacancy.
Q. Mr. Macaleese; A. Mr. Hanbury,
June 19, 1490.

DUNCOMBE, HON. H. V. [Cumberland, Egre-
mont].
Dublin Corporation Bill, con., June 13,
1044.
Edgar, Mr., Murder of, in the Transvaal,
June 19, 1484.
Godalming Corporation Water Bill, con.,
June 13, 1003.
London Government Bill—Qualification of
Women, June 13, 1080.
St. Neots Water Bill, 2R., June 13, 1053.
Service Franchise Bill, com., June 7, 541.

**Dundee Gas, Street Improvements, and
Tramways Bill ;**
formerly
**Dundee Gas, Tramways, and Exten-
sion Bill.**
c. 2R., June 5, 294.
Rep.*, June 16, 1330.

DWYER, SYLVESTER, IMPRISONMENT OF.
Commutation of Sentence.
Q. Mr. Flavin; A. Mr. G. W. Balfour,
June 19, 1498.

DYKE, SIR W. H. [Kent, Dartford].
Half-timers—Education of Children Bill,
com., May 31, 33.

EARLY CLOSING OF SHOPS, see Shops.

East London Water Bill.
1. 2R.*, June 8, 594.

Ecclesiastical Assessments [Scotland] Bill.
Petitions, June 2, 173; June 5, 296.

ECCLESIASTICAL JUDGES—Sir A. Charles,
Appointment of.
Q. Mr. C. McArthur; A. Mr. Collings,
June 15, 1186.
Q. Lord Balcarres; A. Mr. Collings, June
16, 1340.

EDGAR, MR., Killed by Policeman at Johannesburg—Compensation to Mrs. Edgar.
Q. Mr. Griffith; A. Mr. J. Chamberlain, June 2, 182.
Q. Mr. Duncombe; A. Mr. J. Chamberlain, June 19, 1484.

EDINBURGH, NEW WRITS.
East Division, June 13, 1078.
South Division, June 9, 762.

Edinburgh Corporation Bill.
1. Rep. from Select com., June 15, 1165.

EDUCATION :
Lord President of the Council—Duke of
Devonshire.
Vice-President of the Council—Rt. Hon.
Sir J. E. Gorst.
Berkhampstead National Schools—Atten-
dance of Children at Church on Ascen-
sion Day.

EDUCATION - cont.
  Q. Mr. Trevelyan; A. Sir J. Gorst,
    June 16, 1347.
  Bethnal Green Schools, see Bethnal
    Green.
  Bills relating to, see their Titles.
  Commercial Education, see that Title.
  Day School Code—Articles 37 and 42.
    Q. Vis. Cranborne; A. Sir J. Gorst,
    June 19, 1487.
  Endowed Schools. Charity Commissioners'
    Report presented, June 8, 596. 625.
  Half-timers.
    Education of Children Bill [Half-
      timers], see that Title.
    Return presented, June 1, 78.
  Intermediate Education, see that Title.
  Irish Questions.
    Celtic Language—Reduction in number
      of Marks.
      Q. Mr. Flavin; A. Mr. G. W. Bal-
        four, June 16, 1354.
    Glin District School — Arrangements
      with Waterford Steamship Co. for
      conveyance of Children.
      Q. Mr. Austin; A. Mr. G. W. Bal-
        four, June 12, 902.
    Intermediate Education, see that Title.
    National School Teachers, see that
      Title.
  Poor Law Children, see that Title.
  Reformatory and Industrial Schools, see
    that Title.
  Scotch Questions.
    Agricultural Instruction, S., June 16,
      1418. 1423.
    Attendance of Children at School, S.,
      June 16, 1424.
    Circulars.
      Q. Mr. Crombie; A. Mr. A. G.
        Murray, June 8, 635.
    Code, S., June 16, 1365, 1374, 1394,
      1422, 1443.
    Domestic Instruction, S., June 16,
      1407.
    Finance, S., June 16. 1363, 1375, 1384,
      1391, 1397, 1410, 1439, 1445.
    Grant.
      Q. Dr. Clark; A. Mr. A. G. Murray,
        June 16, 1339.
    Inspectors, S., June 16, 1395, 1400,
      1406, 1421.
    Orphan Homes, see that Title.
    Secondary Education, see that Title.
    Teachers, see that Title.
    Technical Education, see that Title.
    Vote for, June 16, 1362.
  Secondary Education, see that Title.
  Teachers, see that Title.
  Technical Education, see that Title.
  Voluntary Schools, see that Title.
EDUCATION DEPARTMENT.
  South-Western Division, Report presented,
    June 1, 69.
Education Department Provisional Orders
Confirmation [Aberavon, etc.] Bill.
    c. Rep.*, June 2, 168.
    3R.*, June 5, 295.
Education Department Provisional Order
Confirmation [Liverpool] Bill.
    l. Rep.*, June 5. 290.
    3R.*, June 6, 412.
    c. 1R.*, June 8, 625.
    2R.*, June 16, 1328.

Education Department Provisional Order
Confirmation [London] Bill.
    l. com.*, June 1, 67; June 15, 1166.

Education Department Provisional Order
Confirmation [Swansea] Bill.
    l. Royal Assent*, June 6, 409.

Education of Children Bill.
    c. com., May 31, 8; June 7, 541.
      Con.*, June 8, 747.
      3R., June 14, 1092.
    l. 1R.*, June 15, 1168.
    Petitions, May 31, 3; June 2, 173; June 7,
      538.
EGAN'S, MR., APPLICATION FOR GUN LICENCE
  refused.
    Q. Mr. J. P. Farrell; A. Mr. G. W. Bal-
      four, June 19, 1499.
EGYPTIAN ARMY—Soudan Campaign. Thanks
  of the House. Motions [Marquess of Salis-
  bury], June 8, 599; [Mr. A. J. Balfour],
  663.
EIGHT HOURS.
  Mines [Eight Hours] Bill, see that Title.
ELBA—Trade Report presented, June 1, 68.
ELECTIONS — See Bye-Elections and Parlia-
  mentary Elections.
ELECTRIC LIGHTING.
  City of London, Report presented, June 12,
    880. 892.
  Gateshead, Report presented, June 12, 880,
    892.
  Walker and Wallsend Union Gas Electric
    Lighting Bill, see that Title.

Electric Lighting Provisional Orders
[No. 1] Bill.
    l. Rep.*, June 9, 753.
    3R.*, June 12, 879.

Electric Lighting Provisional Orders
[No. 2] Bill.
    c. 3R.*, May 31, 3.
    l. 2R.*, June 15, 1167.
    Rep.*, June 16, 1319.
    3R.*, June 19, 1455.

Electric Lighting Provisional Orders
[No 3] Bill.
    l. 2R.*, June 6, 413.

Electric Lighting Provisional Orders
[No. 4] Bill.
    l. 2R.*, June 6, 413; June 12, 879.
    Rep.*, June 9, 753.

Electric Lighting Provisional Orders
[No. 5] Bill.
    c. 3R.*, May 31, 3.
    l. 1R.*, June 1, 67.

Electric Lighting Provisional Orders
[No. 6] Bill.
    c. 3R.*, May 31, 3.
    l. 1R.*, June 1, 67.

Electric Lighting Provisional Orders [No. 7] Bill.

  c. Rep.*, June 9, 758.
    3ʀ.*, June 12, 890.
  l. 1ʀ.*, June 13, 995.

Electric Lighting Provisional Orders [No. 8] Bill.

  c. 3ʀ.*, May 31, 3.
  l. 1ʀ.*, June 1, 68.

Electric Lighting Provisional Orders [No. 9] Bill.

  l. Rep.*, June 9, 753.
    3ʀ.*, June 12, 879.
  c. 1ʀ.*, June 13, 1055.
  Memorandum presented, June 14, 1091.

Electric Lighting Provisional Orders [No. 10] Bill.

  l. Rep.*, June 9, 753 ; June 12, 879.
    3ʀ.*, June 13, 994.
  c. 1ʀ.*, June 15, 1175.
  Memorandum presented, June 14, 1091.

Electric Lighting Provisional Orders [No. 11] Bill.

  l. Rep.*, June 9, 753.
    3ʀ.*, June 12, 879.
  c. 1ʀ.*, June 13, 1055.
  Memorandum presented, June 14, 1092.

Electric Lighting Provisional Orders [No. 12] Bill.

  l. 2ʀ.*, June 6, 413.
    com.*, June 13, 995.
    Rep.*, June 16, 1319.
    3ʀ.*, June 19, 1455.
  Memorandum presented, June 14, 1092.

Electric Lighting Provisional Orders [No. 13] Bill.

  l. 2ʀ.*, June 6, 413.
    com.*, June 13, 995 ; June 19, 1455.
  Memorandum presented, June 14, 1092.

Electric Lighting Provisional Orders [No. 14] Bill.

  l. 2ʀ.*, June 2, 162.
    com.*, June 13, 995.
    3ʀ.*, June 15, 1167.
  c. 1ʀ.*· June 16, 1331.
  Memorandum presented, June 14, 1092.

Electric Lighting Provisional Orders [No. 15] Bill.

  l. 2ʀ.*, June 6, 413.
    com.*, June 13, 995.
    Rep.*, June 16, 1319.
    3ʀ.*, June 19. 1455.
  Memorandum presented, June 14, 1092.

Electric Lighting Provisional Orders [No. 16] Bill.

  c. 2ʀ.*, June 5. 296.
    Rep.*, June 16, 1330.
    con.*, June 19, 1477.

Electric Lighting Provisional Orders [No. 17] Bill.

  c. 2ʀ.*, June 6, 431.
  Memorandum presented, May 31, 7.

Electric Lighting Provisional Orders [No. 18] Bill.

  c. 2ʀ.*, June 6. 432.
    Rep.*, June 16, 1330.
    3ʀ.*, June 19, 1476.
  Memorandum presented, May 31, 8.

Electric Lighting Provisional Orders [No. 19] Bill.

  c. 2ʀ.*, June 6. 432.
    Rep.*, June 16, 1330.
    3ʀ.*, June 19. 1476.
  Memorandum presented, May 31, 8.

Electric Lighting Provisional Orders [No. 20] Bill.

  c. 1ʀ.*, June 12. 891.
  Memorandum Ordered [Mr. Ritchie], June 13, 1057.

Electric Lighting Provisional Orders Bills.

  Number of—Course of Procedure.
    Os. Earl of Morley. Lord Balfour of Burleigh, June 9. 751.
  Eʟᴇᴄᴛʀɪᴄ Mᴏᴛᴏʀs ɪɴ ᴛʜᴇ Nᴀᴠʏ, Control of.
    Q. Sir F. Flannery ; A. Mr. Goschen, June 8, 632.

Elementary Education [Defective and Epileptic Children] Bill.

  l. 1ʀ.*, June 15, 1168.

Elementary Education [New Bye Laws] Bill.

  Petition. May 31, 4.

Eʟᴇᴍᴇɴᴛᴀʀʏ Sᴄʜᴏᴏʟ Cʜɪʟᴅʀᴇɴ Wᴏʀᴋɪɴɢ ꜰᴏʀ Wᴀɢᴇs—Return presented, June 1, 78.

Eʟʟɪᴏᴛ, Hon. A. R. D. [Durham].
  London Government Bill—Qualification of Women, June 13, 1078, 1079, 1086.

Eʟʟɪs, Mʀ. J. E. [Nottingham, Rushcliffe].
  Business of the House. Precedence of Government Business. June 19, 1522.
  Dundee Gas. Street Improvements, and Tramways Bill, 2ʀ., June 5, 294.
  Private Legislation Procedure [Scotland] Bill, com., June 19, 1534, 1541, 1542.
  Soudan—Sir W. Garstin's Report, June 19, 1484.

Eᴍɪɢʀᴀᴛɪᴏɴ ᴀɴᴅ Iᴍᴍɪɢʀᴀᴛɪᴏɴ.
  British Columbia—Japanese Immigration.
    Q. Mr. Hogan ; A. Mr. J. Chamberlain, June 8, 636.
  Irish Emigration to America.
    Q. Capt. Donelan ; A. Mr. G. W. Balfour, June 8, 649.
  Poor Law Children, see that Title.

Eɴᴅᴏᴡᴇᴅ Sᴄʜᴏᴏʟs, Charity Commissioners' Report presented, June 8, 596, 625.

Eɴꜰɪᴇʟᴅ Sᴍᴀʟʟ Aʀᴍs Fᴀᴄᴛᴏʀʏ.
  Ritualistic Practices in Government Chapels.
    Qs. Mr. Channing, Mr. C. Williams ; A. Mr. Wyndham, June 12, 898.

ENGLEDEW, MR. C. J. [Kildare, N.].
County Court Officers, Ireland—Grant for Clerical Assistance, Return June 6, 438.

ENNISKILLEN POST OFFICE—Plans and Tenders.
Q. Mr. Jordan; A. Mr. Hanbury, June 19, 1492.

EPILEPTIC CHILDREN.
Elementary Education [Defective and Epileptic Children] Bill, see that Title.

ESTATE DUTY, see Death Duties.

EVANS, SIR F. [Southampton].
Customs—Boatmen's Grievances, June 1, 150.

EVERSHED, MR. S. [Staffordshire, Burton].
Wine and Beerhouse Acts Amendment Bill, 2R., June 7, 583.

EVICTIONS, IRELAND.
Finegan, Anne, Death of, see that Title.

EXCHEQUER AND AUDIT DEPARTMENT.
Comptroller and Auditor-General—Retirement of Mr. Mills.
Q. Mr. M'Kenna; A. Mr. A. J. Balfour, June 1, 83.

Executors [Scotland] Amendment Bill.
Petitions, June 2, 173; June 5, 296.

EXETER, MARQUESS OF—Sat first, after the death of his father, June 2, 161.

Exmouth TRAINING SHIP—Poor Law Children, training on, S., June 2, 245, 265.

EXPERIMENTS ON LIVING ANIMALS, see Vivisection.

EXPLOSIVES.
Annual Report presented, June 13, 996. 1056.
Carbo-Gelatine Explosion near Faversham, Report presented June 13, 996, 1056.
Percussion Caps Explosion near Birmingham, Report presented June 13, 996, 1056.

FACTORIES AND WORKSHOPS.
Jam Factories, Child Labour in.
Q. Mr. Hedderwick; A. Sir M. W. Ridley, June 5, 297.
Whitelead Factories, Special Rules presented, June 1, 70, 79.

FAIR RENTS, see Ireland—Judicial Rents.

Farnley Tyas Marriages Bill.
1. 2R.*, June 6. 429.
Rep.*, June 8. 617.
3R*, June 9, 754.

FARQUHARSON, DR. R. [Aberdeenshire, W.].
Dundee Gas. Street Improvements, and Tramways Bill, 2R, June 5, 294.
Friends Provident Institution Bill—Stamp Duties, June 2, 169; June 5, 293.
Military Prisons, Inspector-General's Report, June 8, 640.
Private Legislation Procedure [Scotland] Bill, com., June 12, 944.
Soudan Campaign, Thanks of the House—Medical Officers, Omission of, June 8, 667, 673, 679.

FARRELL, MR. J. P. [Cavan, West].
Annaly Estate, Purchase of Holdings, June 13, 1076.
Bawnboy Postman, Wages of, June 13, 1068.
Constabulary, Royal Irish, Promotion in, June 16, 1356.
Deniston, J., Case of, June 19, 1482.
Fair Rents in Co. Cavan, June 16, 1355.
Granard and Cavan Unions, Transfer of Divisions refused by Local Government Board, June 13, 1075.
Gun Licences—Mr. Egan's Application refused, June 19, 1499.
Irish Estimates—Business of the House, June 15, 1198.
Longford.
Agricultural Grant—Excluded Charges, June 13, 1072; June 15, 1196.
County Council Collector—Case of W. Jones, June 13, 1071.
Militia Headquarters, Removal to Mullingar, June 13, 1058.
Magistracy in Co. Cavan, Vacancy, June 16, 1359.
Meehan District Inspector, Conduct of, June 15, 1195.
Mullingar Lunatic Asylum Board.
Building Expenditure, etc., June 19, 1499.
Joint Committee—County Council Resolution, June 13, 1076.
Tramways, Cavan—Relief to Ratepayers, June 19, 1492.

FAVERSHAM EXPLOSION, Report presented, June 13, 996, 1056.

FEE GRANT [SCOTLAND].
Return presented, May 31, 5.

FENWICK, MR. C. [Northumberland, Wansbeck].
Newbiggin-by-the-Sea — Destruction of Fishing Gear, etc., by Trawlers, June 8, 635.

FERGUSON, MR. R. C. M. [Leith Burghs].
Education, Scotland—New Code, etc., June 16, 1422.

FERGUSSON, RT. HON. SIR J. [Manchester, N.E.].
Guards—Losses of Stores, Claim, June 19, 1480.
Post Office—Employment of Old Non-Commissioned Officers, June 1, 128.
Seats for Shop Assistants [England and Ireland] Bill, com., June 8, 747.
Soudan Expedition—Grant to Lord Kitchener, June 5, 345.
Con.*, June 19, 1477.
Water-tube Boilers on Naval Ships, June 8, 633.
Wine and Beerhouse Acts Amendment Bill, 2R., June 7, 579.

FERRYBANK POST OFFICE AND POSTMASTERSHIP.
Q. Mr. P. O'Brien; A. Mr. Hanbury, June 16, 1344.

FEUS AND LEASES.
Building Feus and Leases [Scotland] Bill; see that Title.

FEVER OUTBREAK IN OUGHTERARD UNION.
Q. Mr. P. O'Brien; A. Mr. G. W. Balfour, June 16, 1357.

FIELD, MR. W. [Dublin, St. Patrick].
Buenos Ayres Cattle Trade—*Hindustan*
Losses, June 13, 1067.
Intermediate Education, Ireland—Vice-
regal Commission, June 13, 1071.
Kerry County Council—Contractors as
Members of Council, June 13, 1070.
Maiden Rocks, etc., Lighthouse, June 13,
1066.
National School Teachers, Ireland—Ulster
and Connaught, June 13, 1070.

FINANCE.
Indian, Royal Commission Report.
Q. Sir M. Bhownaggree; A. Lord G.
Hamilton, June 2, 184.
Mersey Docks and Harbour Board
[Finance] Bill, see that Title.

Finance Bill.
c. con., June 6, 444; June 8, 731.
3R.*, June 13, 1086.
1. 1R.*, June 15, 1169.
2R.*, and 3R.*, June 16, 1320.

Finance Bill.
Local Loans, Amendments [Sir M. Hicks-
Beach], June 8, 731; [Sir C. Cameron],
734.
Promissory Notes, Amendment [Mr. Cald-
well], June 8, 732.

**Fine or Imprisonment [Scotland and
Ireland] Bill.**
c. 3R.*, May 31, 63.
1. 1R.*, June 1, 71.
Petition, June 2, 173.

FINEGAN, ANNE, DEATH OF—Inquest.
Qs. Mr. Macaleese; As. Mr. G. W. Balfour, June 15, 1190; June 19, 1497.

FINLAY, SIR R. B.—Solicitor-General [Inver-
ness Burghs].
London Government Bill, con., June 6,
462, 479, 495, 501, 502, 510; June 8,
707, 708, 713, 715, 716, 717, 725.
Service Franchise Bill, con. June 14, 1143,
1151.

FINTONA—Sunday Mails.
Q. Mr. Dillon; A. Mr. Hanbury, June
19, 1488.

FIREARMS, CARRYING WITHOUT LICENCE IN
IRELAND.
Brady, T., Prosecution of,
Q. Mr. T. M. Healy; A. Mr. G. W.
Balfour, June 15, 1189.
Costello, P., Case of,
Q. Mr. Hayden; A. Mr. G. W. Balfour,
June 19, 1495.
Emergency Man carrying—Case of T. Craw-
ford.
Q. Mr. Austin; A. Mr. G. W. Balfour,
June 5, 308.

FIRMS, Registration, see Registration of Firms
Bill.

FISH.
Railway Traffic—English and Irish Rail-
ways.
Q. Mr. T. O'Brien; A. Mr. G. W.
Balfour, June 16, 1358.
Undersized Fish Bill, see that Title.

FISHERIES.
Newbiggin-by-the-Sea—Destruction of Fish-
ing Gear by Trawlers, alleged.
Q. Mr. Fenwick; A. Mr. Ritchie,
June 8, 635.
Newfoundland Fisheries Report.
Qs. Sir T. G. Carmichael; Mr. Bowles;
As. Mr. J. Chamberlain, June 16,
1338.
North Sea Fisherman, Return Presented,
June 14, 1091.
Poaching Prosecution in Ireland—Case of
P. Comerford,
Q. Mr. P. O'Brien; A. Mr. G. W.
Balfour, June 16, 1358.
Salmon Fisheries, see that Title.
Scottish Fishery Board, Report Presented,
May 31, 6; June 1, 69.
Scottish Herrings—Markets on the Conti-
nent and United States, Reports Pre-
sented, June 15, 1167, 1175.
Sea Fisheries Bill, see that Title.
Trawling, see that Title.
Trout-fishing Annual Close Time [Scot-
land] Bill, see that Title.

Fishguard Water and Gas Bill.
1. Rep. from com of Selection, June 6, 411.
com.*, June 9, 749.

FISON, MR. F. W. [York, W.R., Doncaster.]
Dublin Corporation Bill, con. June 13,
1031, 1032.

FITZMAURICE, LORD E. G. P. [Wilts, Crick-
lade.]
County Councils, Borrowing Powers, June
2, 224.
Local Government Board, Transferring
Powers to County Councils, June 2, 271.
Pauper Children, Barrack-school System,
June 2, 251.

FLANNERY, SIR J. F. [Yorkshire, Shipley.]
Electric Motors in the Navy, control of,
June 8, 632.
Signalmen, North-Eastern Railway—Hours
of Labour, June 8, 634.

FLASH POINT OF PETROLEUM—LEGISLATION.
Q. Mr. Tully; A. Sir M. W. Ridley, June
9, 770.

FLAVIN, MR. M. J. [Kerry, N.]
Ballyduff Postal Facilities, June 19, 1494.
Celtic Language in Irish Schools—Reduc-
tion in Number of Marks, June 16, 1354.
Dwyer, Sylvester, case of, June 19, 1493.
Judicial Rents—Equal Treatment of
Tenants, Future Tenants, etc., June 19,
1496.
Kerry, North, Letter Deliveries, June 19,
1489.
Limerick Mail Train Delays, June 19, 1491.
National School Teachers—Assistant
Teachers and the Pension Fund, June
19, 1494.
Post Cards, Cost of, June 16, 1343.

FLINT—Charities Inquiry, Paper presented, May
31, 7.

FLOWER, MR. E. [Bradford, W.].
Pauper Children, June 2, 239.

FOREIGN OFFICE.
Secretary of State—Marquess of Salisbury;
Under Secretary—Rt. Hon. W. St. John
Brodrick.
Vote for, com., June 9, 777.

FOREIGN POLICY, LORD SALISBURY'S, S., June
9, 778.

FOREIGN SERVICE MESSENGERS, Appointments.
Q. Sir C. Dilke; A. Mr. Brodrick, June
9, 762.

FOSTER, SIR B. W. [Derby, Ilkeston].
Loans, Municipal, Repayment of, June 2,
226.
Vaccination.
Increase in, etc., June 2. 208.
Officers and Boards of Guardians, June
2, 206.

FOWLER, RT. HON. SIR H. H. [Wolver-
hampton, E.].
Finance Bill. com., June 6, 459.
Indian Sugar Duties—Tariff Act, 1899,
June 15, 1199. 1303.
London Government Bill—Qualification
of Women, June 6, 470.

FRANCE.
Agricultural Education, Report presented,
June 15. 1168.
Armenia Kurdish Atrocities—Protest.
Q. Mr. Schwann; A. Mr. Brodrick,
June 16. 1337.
China, Questions relating to, see China.
Franchise in French Possessions in India.
Q. Sir W. Wedderburn; A. Lord G.
Hamilton. June 15, 1177.
Paris Exhibition, see that Title.
Trade Report presented, June 1, 68; June
8, 596.
Waima Incident. Compensation Claims. S.,
June 9, 780, 784. 812. 823, 839, 845,
863, 872.

FRANCHISE.
India—French Possessions.
Q. Sir W. Wedderburn; A. Lord G.
Hamilton. June 15, 1177.
Poor Law Relief Disfranchisement, see
that Title.
Service Franchise Bill, see that Title.
Women, Qualification of. Petition. June 9,
760.

Friends' Provident Institution Bill.
c. Rep. from Select com., June 9, 758.
con.*, June 14, 1089.
3R.*, June 19. 1475.

Friendly Provident Institution Bill.
Stamp Duties, R. [Dr. Farquharson], June
2, 169; June 5, 293.

FRUIT STEAMERS, West Indies—Commencement of Service.
Q. Mr. Lawrence; A. Mr. J. Chamberlain, June 6, 441.

Furness Railway Bill.
c. 2R.*, June 7. 537.

Gainsborough Urban District Council
[Gas] Bill.
c. 2R.*, June 6, 430.
Rep.*, June 16, 1330.

GALLOWAY, MR. W. J. [Manchester, S.W.].
Bloemfontein Conference, June 12, 907.
Business of the House—Precedence of
Government Business, June 19, 1512,
1528.
Half-timers—Education of Children Bill,
com., May 31, 45.
Intoxicating Liquors [Sunday Closing] Bill,
2R., June 7. 557, 558, 561.

GARSTON'S, SIR W., REPORT ON THE SOUDAN.
Q. Mr. Ellis; A. Mr. Brodrick, June 19,
1484.

GARSTIN—Dock Labourer, Fatal Accident to.
Q. Mr. M'Ghee; A. Sir M. W. Ridley,
June 9, 769.

GAS COMPANIES [Metropolis].
Accounts presented, June 1, 69, 78.

Gas Light and Coke Company Bill.
l. 2R.*, June 1, 65.

Gas Orders Confirmation [No. 1] Bill.
l. com.*, June 1, 67; June 13, 994.
Rep.*, June 15, 1167.
3R.*, June 16, 1318.
c. 1R.*, June 19. 1478.

Gas Orders Confirmation [No. 2] Bill.
l. com.*, June 1, 67.

Gas and Water Orders Confirmation Bill.
l 2R.*, June 2, 162.
com.*, June 13, 995.
Rep.*, June 15, 1167.
3R.*, June 16, 1318.
c. 1R.*, June 19. 1478.

GAS AND WATER WORKS FACILITIES ACT, 1870,
Report presented, May 31, 6; June 1, 69.

GATESHEAD ELECTRIC LIGHTING, Report presented, June 12, 880, 892.

GEDGE, MR. S. [Walsall].
Intoxicating Liquors [Sunday Closing] Bill,
2R, June 7, 553, 556.
London Government Bill, con., June 8, 702,
Soudan Expedition—Grant to Lord Kit-
chener, June 5, 402.

GENOA AND DISTRICT—Trade Report presented,
June 1, 68.

GERMANY.
Persian Gulf, British Trade Interests—Rail-
way Concessions to Germany.
Q. Mr. Maclean; A. Mr. Brodrick,
June 8, 629.
Trade Report presented, June 1, 68.

GIBBS, HON. V. [Herts, St. Albans].
London Government Bill, con., June 8, 701,
705.
Soudan Expedition—Grant to Lord Kitchener, June 5, 382, 384.

GIBNEY, MR. J. [Meath, N.].
Labourers' Cottages, Ireland—Disqualification of District Councillers, etc., June 19,
1495.

GILES, MR. C. T. [Cambridge, Wisbech].
Half-timers—Education of Children Bill,
com., May 31, 45.
Postmen's Pay, Higher Grade Test, June 9,
774.
Tradesmen's Cart and Van Licences, June
9, 776.

GILLINGHAM—Postal Deliveries.
Q. Col. Welby ; A. Mr. Hanbury, June
5, 302.

GLAMORGAN.
Vale of Glamorgan Railway Bill, see that
Title.

GLASGOW.
Bakery Dispute—Case of A· M'Naughton.
Q. Sir C. Cameron ; A. Mr. A. G. Murray,
June 19, 1485.

Glasgow Corporation [Gas and Water] Bill.
c. 2R.*, May 31, 2.
Rep.*, June 16, 1330.

**Glasgow Corporation [Tramways, etc.]
Bill.**
c. 2R.*, May 31, 2.

Glasgow District Subway Bill.
l. Royal Assent, June 6, 409.

Glastonbury Water Bill.
c. 3R.*, June 1, 73.
l. commons amendments*, June 2, 162.
Royal Assent, June 6, 410.

GLENDAD—O'Donnell, Dominick—Inmate of
Belmullet Union.
Q. Mr. Crilly ; A. Mr. G. W. Balfour,
June 13, 1074.

GLIN DISTRICT SCHOOL—Waterford Steamship
Co., arrangements for conveyance of
children.
Q. Mr. Austin ; A. Mr. G. W. Balfour, June 12, 902.

GLOUCESTERSHIRE.
West Gloucestershire Water Bill, see that
Title.

Godalming Corporation Water Bill.
c. com., June 13, 1002, 1170.
3R.*, June 19, 1475.
l. 1R.*, 1454.

GOODACRE, F.—Shunting Fatality on Chatham
and Dover Railway.
Q. Mr. Maddison ; A. Mr. Ritchie, June
15, 1183.

GORST, RT. HON. SIR J. E.—Vice-President
of the Council for Education [Cambridge
University].
Berkhampstead National Schools—
Attendance of Children at Church on
Ascension Day, June 16, 1347.
Bethnal Green, New Board Schools,
June 12, 900.

GORST, RT. HON. SIR J. E.—cont.
Day School Code—Articles 37 and 42,
June 19, 1487.
Dispensers, Unqualified, in Doctors' Sur-
geries—Accidents resulting from mis-
takes, June 12, 901.
Half-timers—Education of Children Bill,
com., May 31, 24, 28, 37, 40, 42, 48,
51 ; 3R., June 14, 1131.
South Kensington Museum Art Branch,
Appointment of Assistant, June 16,
1348.

GOSCHEN, RT. HON. G. J.—First Lord of the
Admiralty [St. George's, Hanover Square].
Electric Motors, Control of, June 8, 632.
Reserve, Number of Men, etc., June 6,
435.
Squadron—Visit to China, June 9, 777.
Water-Tube Boilers on Ships, June 8,
633.

GOULDING, MR. E. A. [Wilts, Devizes].
London Government Bill, com., June 6,
491.
Netheravon House—Non-occupation by the
War Office, June 6, 442.

GOURLEY, SIR E. T. [Sunderland].
Anglo-American Commission, June 1, 81;
June 6, 440.
Naval Reserve, Number of Men, etc., June
6, 438.
Talien-wan as an open port—Russian
Cargoes, British vessels carrying, June
2, 175.

GRAHAM, MR. H. R. [St. Pancras, W.].
Prison Officials, Appointments, Promotions, etc., June 9, 769.

GRANARD—Local Government Board—Refusal
to transfer divisions from Cavan to Granard
Union.
Q. Mr. J. P. Farrell ; A. Mr. G. W.
Balfour, June 13, 1075.

GRAY, MR. E. [West Ham, N.].
Customs Department, Officers' Grievances,
June 1, 132, 145, 153.
Half-timers—Education of Children Bill,
com., May 31, 46.
Loans, Municipal, Repayment of, June 2,
223, 228.

Great Central Railway Bill.
l. 2R.*, June 1, 65.
com.*, June 16, 1318.

**Great Eastern Railway [General Powers]
Bill.**
l. Rep. from Select com., June 19, 1453.

Great Grimsby Street Tramways Bill.
l. 3R.*, June 8, 595.
c. 1R.*, June 9, 759.
2R.*, June 19, 1476.

Great Northern Railway Bill.
l. 3R.*, June 1, 65.
c. 1R.*, June 2, 169.
2R.*, June 12, 890.

Great Southern and Western Railway Bills.

Com.—Attendance of Mr. H. Plews ordered, June 7, 592.
County Councils' Petitions, order for presentation, etc., June 5, 295; June 6, 431.

Great Southern and Western, and Waterford, Limerick, and Railway Companies Amalgamation Bill.

Com.—Attendance of Mr. H. Plews ordered, June 7, 592.
County Councils' Petitions, order for presentation, etc., June 5, 295; June 6, 431.

GREAT WESTERN RAILWAY, Alleged Outrage on.
Q. Mr. Schwann; A. Mr. Ritchie, June 16, 1341.

Great Western and Great Central Railway Companies Bill.

l. 2R.*, June 8, 594.

Great Yarmouth Water Bill.

c. 2R.*, June 6, 430.

GREECE. Trade Report presented, June 1, 68.

GREENE, MR. H. D. [Shrewsbury].
Punjaub War and Tirah Campaign—Distribution of Medals, June 1, 81; June 6, 443.

Greenock and Port Glasgow Tramways Bill.

c. com., Attendance of certain persons ordered, June 16, 1328.

GREENWICH HOSPITAL.
Lynch, Mrs., Special gratuity to, Order in Council presented, June 6, 414, 435.

GREY, SIR E. [Northumberland, Berwick].
China, Affairs of, Anglo, Russian Agreement, etc., June 9, 814.
Waima Incident—Compensation Claims, June 9, 823.

GRIFFITH, MR. E. J. [Anglesey].
Bloemfontein Conference—Sir A. Milner's Memorandum, June 13, 1059.
Edgar, Mr., killed by Policeman at Johannesburg—Compensation to Mrs. Edgar, June 2, 182.

Grocers' Licences [Scotland] Abolition Bill.

Petition, June 5, 296.

Grosvenor Chapel [London] Bill.

l. 3R.*, June 2, 162.
c. 1R.*, June 5, 326.
2R.*, June 14, 1089.

GROUND RENTS [TAXATION BY LOCAL AUTHORITIES].
Petitions, May 31, 4; June 2, 173; June 6, 433; June 7, 538; June 9, 759, 891, 1055.

Ground Values [Taxation] Scotland Bill.

Petitions, June 2, 173; June 5, 296; June 14, 1090.

GUARDS—Losses of Stores—Claim.
Q. Sir J. Fergusson; A. Mr. J. P. Williams, June 19, 1480.

GUERNSEY MILITIA—INSUBORDINATION.
Qs. Maj. Rasch, Mr. R. G. Webster; As. Mr. J. P. Williams, June 19, 1481.

GULL, SIR W. C. [Devonshire. Barnstaple].
Letter-boxes on Trains, Late letter-boxes, June 1, 107, 121.
Postmen's Wages, Scale of, June 1, 106.

GULLY, RT. HON. W. C. [Carlisle], see Speaker.

GUN LICENSES, IRELAND.
Egan's, Mr., Application refused.
Q. Mr. J. P. Farrell; A. Mr. G. W. Balfour, June 19, 1499.
[See also Firearms].

HABITUAL INEBRIATES.
See Inebriates.

HAGUE CONFERENCE.
See Peace Conference.

HALDANE, MR. R. B. [Haddington].
Death Duties, Aggregation Question—Finance Bill, June 6, 451.
Education, Scotland, June 16, 1388.

HALE, SARAH, CASE OF.
O. Mr. Steadman, June 16, 1339.

HALF-TIMERS.
Education of Children Bill, see that Title.
Elementary Schools [Children Working for Wages]. Return presented, June 1, 78.

HALSBURY, EARL OF—Lord Chancellor.
Crime, Incitement to [Ireland]—M'Hale v. Sullivan, June 12, 880, 881, 886.
Death Duties—Indefinite Liability for Estate Duty, Endorsement on Registered Titles, June 13, 1000.
Judges. Additional, Appointment of, June 8, 617.
Prevention of Corruption Bill, 2R., June 6, 421.
Vaccination. Compulsory, Abolition of—Petition, June 2, 163.

HAMBURG, Trade Report presented, June 1, 68.

HAMILTON, RT. HON. LORD G.—Secretary of State for India [Middlesex, Ealing].
Assam Tea Plantations—Report, June 12, 897.
Bombay. Civil and Criminal Appeals. June 15, 1178.
Calcutta Municipal Bill, June 16, 1337.
Connaught Rangers at Meerut—Shooting Case, June 16, 1335.
Cooper's Hill College—Retirement of Officers, June 15, 1179.
Dum-Dum Bullet. Issue of, to Troops in India, June 5, 300.
Finance of India—Royal Commission Report, June 2, 184.
Franchise in French Possessions in India, June 15, 1177.
Legal Education. Control by Private Institutions, June 8, 642.
Madras.
Liquor Trade—Opening of Liquor Shops, June 12, 898.
Riots, June 15, 1177.
Mineral Rights in Hyderabad State—Prospectuses, June 8, 644.

[Continued

HAMILTON, RT. HON. LORD G.—*cont.*
Pasteur Institute—Government Grant, etc., proposed, June 8. 643.
Presbyterian Services for Troops, June 9, 772.
Punjaub War and Tirah Campaign—Distribution of Medals. June 6, 443.
Rangoon—Attack on Burmese Woman, by British Soldiers, June 12, 896; June 16, 1336.
Sugar Duties—Tariff Act. 1899, June 15. 1201, 1224, 1234, 1236, 1253.
Sugar Trade—Returns. June 2, 185; June 8. 644.
Women Barristers—Application of Miss Sorabji refused, June 8. 641.

HAMPSHIRE.
South Hants Water Bill, see that Title.

HAMPSTEAD.
Charing Cross. Euston. and Hampstead Railway Bill. see that Title.

Hampstead Church [Emmanuel. West End] Bill.
c. 2R.*, June 6, 430.

HANBURY, RT. HON. R. W.—Financial Secretary to the Treasury [Preston].
American Mail Service—Return, June 6, 437.
Ballyduff Postal Facilities, June 19, 1494.
Ballymahon Postal Arrangements. June 19, 1491.
Bawnboy Postman's Wages, June 13, 1068.
Belfast Post Office Staff.
Pay, June 13, 1069.
Vacancies, June 19, 1490.
Cavan Tramways—Relief to Ratepayers, June 19, 1493.
Central Telegraph Staff—Petitions, June 15. 1187.
Circulars. Cost of Postage in Bandon and Clone. June 16, 1343.
Civil Service—Pay deductions, June 2, 178.
Clapham Sorting Office Vacancies, June 1, 81.
County Court Fees. Proposed Reduction, June 5. 300.
County Court Officers [Ireland]—Grant for Clerical Assistance, Return, June 6, 438.
Customs Officials' Grievances, etc., June 1, 142. 146 ; June 6. 436.
Daily Deliveries of Letters in Rural Districts. June 1. 126.
Dorsetshire Postal Deliveries. June 5, 302.
Dublin.
Postmen's Grievances, June 16. 1345.
Telegraphists' Hours of Duty, June 9. 775.
Dundalk Postmastership—Vacancy, June 19, 1490.
East Central District Post Office Staff—Petition, June 12. 904.
Enniskillen Post Office—Plans and Tenders. June 19. 1492.
Ferrybank Post Office and Postmastership, June 16, 1344.
Fintona Sunday Mails, June 19, 1489.
Ionian Bank Bill, 2R, June 13, 1053.

HANBURY, RT. HON. R. W.—*cont.*
Irish Post Office—Superior Appointments, June 16, 1346.
Kerry, North. Letter Deliveries, June 19, 1489.
Lanesborough Postal Arrangements, Complaint, June 19, 1493.
Letter-boxes on trains, June 1, 121.
Limerick.
Mail Train, Delays, June 19, 1492.
Sorting Clerks, Dismissal of, June 12, 905.
Lough Rynn Letter Deliveries, Complaint, June 13. 1068.
Lurgan, New Post Office, June 9, 774.
Military and Naval Men, Employment of, in the Post Office, June 1, 128.
Mountjoy Postal Arrangements, June 9, 774.
Moy Postmaster—Candidate for Petty Sessions Clerkship, June 16, 1343.
Newbliss Post Office Messenger, Salary of, June 12, 905.
Paris Exhibition—British Works of Art, June 15, 1186.
"Parliamentary Debates." Delay in Publication, etc., June 5, 303.
Post Cards.
Commercial. June 12, 904.
Cost of, Reduction proposed. June 16, 1343.
Post Office Employees.
Clerks' Salaries, June 6, 437.
Grievances, June 1, 103, 115, 120.
Postmen's Pay—Higher Grade Test, June 9, 774.
Sub-Postmasters.
Rural Postmen assisting, June 15, 1187.
Scales of Payment, June 16, 1344.
Tea, Adulteration of—Inquiry, June 9, 775.
Telegraph Service—Private Wires, etc., June 1, 131. 132.
Tradesmen's Cart and Van Licences, June 9, 776.

HANSON, SIR R. [London].
Post Cards, for Commercial purposes, proposed. June 12, 904.

HARCOURT, RT. HON. SIR W. G. V. [Monmouthshire, W.].
Half-timers—Education of Children Bill, 3R. June 14, 1132.
Vaccination. Increase of, June 2, 215.

Harrow and Uxbridge Railway Bill.
c. Rep.*, June 19, 1477.

HARWICH HARBOUR CONSERVANCY BOARD.
Abstract of Accounts, etc., presented, May 31, 6 ; June 1, 69.

HARWOOD, MR. G. [Bolton].
China, Affairs of—British Commercial Interests, June 9, 843.
Half-Timers—Education of Children's Bill, 3R. June 14, 1121.
London Government Bill, con., June 8, 702, 703.

Hastings and St. Leonards Gas Bill.
c. Rep.*, June 9, 757.
con.*, June 19, 1476.

HATCH, MR. [Lancs., Gorton].
Canton, British Traders at—Case of Messrs. Banher and Co., June 2, 176.

HAYDEN, MR. J. P. [Roscommon, S.].
　Army Recruits, Bread, Rations, etc., June
　　16, 1334.
　Bagot Estate, Sale of—Sir N. O'Conor and
　　the Congested Districts Board, June 15,
　　1188.
　Ballymahon Postal Arrangements, June 19,
　　1491.
　Castlerea and Ballaghadereen—Sanitary
　　Charges, June 16, 1357.
　Firearms, Carrying, in Ireland—Case of P.
　　Costello, June 19, 1495.
　Lanesborough Postal Arrangements, Com-
　　plaint, June 19, 1493.
　Lynch's, E., Pension, June 16, 1334.
　Roscommon Agricultural Grant, June 16,
　　1352.

HAZELL, MR. W. [Leicester].
　Advertisement Orders, Stamping, June 2,
　　183.
　Pauper Children—Expenditure on Orphan
　　Schools, etc., June 2, 248.
　Vaccination, June 2, 206.

HEALY, MR. M. [Cork].
　South Kensington Museum, Art Branch—
　　Appointment of Assistant, June 16, 1347.
　Town Commissioners Chairman—Solicitor
　　losing right to practise at Quarter Ses-
　　sions, June 16, 1360.

HEALY, MR. T. M. [Louth, N.].
　Dillon's, Lord, Estate—Purchase by the Con-
　　gested Districts Board, June 16, 1361.
　Dublin Corporation Bill, con., June 13, 1044.
　Firearms, Carrying without Licence, in
　　Ireland—Case of T. Brady, June 15, 1189.
　Infirmaries, County, Management of—Repre-
　　sentatives elected by County Councils,
　　June 15, 1188.
　Service Franchise Bill, con., June 14, 1138,
　　1147, 1152, 1153.

HEDDERWICK, MR. T. C. H. [Wick Burghs].
　Colonial Loans Fund Bill, com., June 8, 743.
　Cowan's Institution and Spitals Hospital
　　Charities, June 16, 1435.
　India, Presbyterian Services for Troops,
　　June 9, 772.
　Jam Factories, Labour in, etc., June 5, 297.
　Private Legislation Procedure [Scotland]
　　Bill, com., June 12, 936, 981; June 19,
　　1579.
　Sierra Leone—Sir D. Chalmers's Report,
　　June 2, 176.
　Squadron—Visit to China, June 9, 776.

HEMPHILL, RT. HON. C. H. [Tyrone, N.].
　Service Franchise Bill, con., June 14, 1154.
　Tyrone County Council Rate Collector—
　　Appointment of W. M'Farland, June 19,
　　1496.

HENEAGE, LORD.
　Sea Fisheries Bill, 2R., June 8, 610, 612.

Herne Bay Water Bill.
　1. Royal Assent, June 6, 409.

HERRINGS.
　Scottish—Markets on the Continent and in
　　United States, Reports presented, June
　　15, 1167, 1175.

HICKMAN, SIR A. [Wolverhampton, W.].
　Half-timers—Education of Children Bill,
　　com., May 31, 23.

HICKMAN, SIR A.—*cont.*
　Natal, Boers in, Alleged Arming by Trans-
　　vaal Government, June 13, 1061.

HICKS-BEACH, RT. HON. SIR M.—Chancellor of
　the Exchequer [Bristol, W.].
　Advertisement Orders, Stamping, June 2,
　　184.
　Agricultural Land Valuation—Finance
　　Bill, June 6, 455.
　Beer Materials Committee—Substitutes
　　for Hops, etc., June 15, 1184.
　Bottled Spirits, Duty on—Finance Bill,
　　June 6, 458, 459, 460.
　Colonial Loans Fund Bill, com., June 8,
　　739, 742, 745.
　Death Duties Aggregation—Finance Bill,
　　New Clause, June 6, 447.
　London Government Bill, 3R—Qualifica-
　　tion of Women, June 13, 1080.
　National Debt Annuities, June 16, 1340.
　Promissory Notes—Finance Bill, June 8,
　　732, 733.
　Savings Banks, Inquiry, June 8, 645.
　Tea Adulteration—Inquiry, etc., June 8,
　　645.
　Waima Incident—Compensation Claims,
　　June 9, 864.
　Wine Duties, increased, Revenue derived
　　from, June 13, 1068.

HILL, COL. SIR E. S. [Bristol, S.].
　All Saints' Church [Cardiff] Bill—Standing
　　Order complied with, June 8, 623.

"HINDUSTAN," S.S.—Conveyance of Animals.
　See Diseases of Animals Acts.

HOBHOUSE, MR. H. [Somerset, E.].
　Half-timers—Education of Children Bill,
　　3R., June 14, 1116.
　Private Legislation Procedure [Scotland]
　　Bill, com., June 19, 1593.

HOGAN, MR. J. F. [Tipperary, Mid.].
　Anglo-American Commission, June 13, 1064.
　British Columbia—Japanese Immigration,
　　June 8, 636.
　Imperial Institute and the London Uni-
　　versity Scheme, June 6, 441
　Pacific Cable Scheme, June 13, 1063.
　Rio de Janeiro, British Sailors and the
　　Liquor Traffic, June 13, 1066.
　Tonga Islands—H.M.S. "Tauranga's" Mis-
　　sion, June 8, 630; June 13, 1064.

HOLLAND.
　Peace Conference, see that Title.
　Trade Report presented, June 1, 68.

HOLLAND, MR. W. H. [York, W.R., Rother-
　ham].
　Indian Sugar Duties—Tariff Act, 1899,
　　June 15, 1269.
　Mauritius Sugar Industry, June 13, 1063.

HOME OFFICE.
　Secretary of State—Rt. Hon. Sir M. W.
　　Ridley.
　Under-Secretary—Rt. Hon. J. Collings.

Horsforth Urban District Council [Water]
　Bill.
　1. Royal Assent, June 6, 409.

HOULDSWORTH, SIR W. H. [Manchester, N.W.].
　Wine and Beerhouse Acts Amendment Bill,
　　2R., June 7, 586.

HOURS OF LABOUR.
  Jam Factories.
    Q. Mr. Hedderwick; A. Sir M. W.
      Ridley, June 5, 298.
  North-Eastern Railway Signalmen.
    Q. Sir F. Flannery; A. Mr. Ritchie, June
      8, 634.

HOUSES OF PARLIAMENT.
  Ambulance for, proposed.
    Q. Mr. Tomlinson; A. Mr. Akers-Doug-
      las, June 8, 657.

HOUSING OF THE WORKING CLASSES.
  Bethnal Green New Schools—London School
    Board Scheme.
    Q. Mr. J. G. Talbot; A. Sir M. W.
      Ridley, June 12, 900.
  Local Government Provisional Order [Hous-
    ing of Working Classes] Bill, see that
    Title.
  Workmen's Houses Tenure Bill, see that
    Title.

Housing of the Working Classes Provisional Order [Borrow-Stounness] Bill.
    c. 2R.*, May 31, 3.
    Rep.*, June 9, 756.
    3R.*, June 12, 890.
    l. 1R.*, June 13, 995.

HOWTH—Trawling off Coast—Compensation to
  Fishermen.
    Qs. Mr. Clancy; As. Mr. G. W. Bal-
      four, June 15, 1360; June 19, 1500.

HUGHES, COL. E. [Woolwich].
  London Government Bill, con., June 6, 463,
    464; June 8, 726, 730.

HULL.
  North-Eastern, and Hull, and Barnsley
    Railways [Joint-Dock] Bill, see that Title.

Hull, Barnsley, and West Riding Junction Railway and Dock Bill.
    c. con.*, June 1, 74.
    3R.*, June 5, 293.
    l. commons amendts.*, June 8, 593.

Humber Conservancy Bill.
    c. 2R.*, June 6, 430.

HUMPHREYS-OWEN, MR. A. C. [Montgomery].
  Postal and Telegraphic Facilities, June 1,
    126.

HYDE PARK.
  Lighting Improvement, etc.,
    Q. Gen. Russell; A. Mr. A. Douglas, June
      19, 1488.

HYDERABAD STATE, Mineral Rights—Prospectuses.
    Q. Sir A. Scoble; A. Lord G. Hamilton,
      June 8, 643.

ICELAND—Trade Report presented, June 8, 596.

ICHANG.—Trade Report presented, June 2, 163.

Ilford Gas Bill.
    l. 3R.*, June 6, 411.
    c. lords amendts.*, June 14, 1089.
    l. commons amendts.*, June 15, 1166.

Ilford Urban District Council [Rates] Bill.
    l. Royal Assent, June 6, 409.

ILLICIT COMMISSIONS.
  Prevention of Corruption Bill, see that
    Title.

Imbecile [Training Institutions] Bill.
    c. 2R.*, June 2, 288.

IMMIGRATION, see Emigration and Immigration.

IMPERIAL INSTITUTE AND THE LONDON UNI-
  VERSITY.
  Chair of Commercial Education.
    Q. Sir H. Vincent; A. Mr. Russell,
      June 1, 80.
  Conference.
    Q. Mr. Hogan; A. Mr. J. Chamberlain,
      June 6, 441.

IMPRISONMENT.
  Fine or Imprisonment [Scotland and Ireland]
    Bill, see that Title.

INCOME AND EXPENDITURE—Return Ordered [Sir
  H. Fowler], June 16, 1333.

INDENTURING IN WESTERN AUSTRALIA.
  Abolition of Aborigines Protection Board
    Debate [l.], June 16, 1321.

INDIA.
  Secretary of State—Rt. Hon. Lord G.
    Hamilton.
  Army.
    Dum-Dum Bullet, Issue to Troops.
      Effect of Report Ordered [Lord G.
        Hamilton], June 8, 627.
      Qs. Mr. Dillon, Col. Milward, Mr.
        Channing; As. Lord G. Hamilton,
        Mr. Wyndham, June 5, 300.
    Presbyterian Services Accommodation.
      Q. Mr. Hedderwick; A. Lord G. Hamil-
        ton, June 9, 772.
  Assam Tea Plantations—Report.
    Q. Mr. Schwann; A. Lord G. Hamilton,
      June 12, 897.
  Bombay—Civil and Criminal Appeals in
    Political Courts, Return.
    Q. Sir W. Wedderburn; A. Lord G.
      Hamilton, June 15, 1178.
  Burmese Woman—Outrage on, by British
    Soldiers at Rangoon.
    Q. Mr. Davitt; A. Lord G. Hamilton,
      June 12, 896.
    Qs. Mr. H. Roberts, Mr. Davitt, Mr.
      Dillon, Mr. MacNeill.
    As. Lord G. Hamilton, June 16, 1335.
  Ceylon Waste Land Ordinances. Papers re-
    lating to.
    Q. Mr. Schwann; A. Mr. J. Chamber-
      lain, June 13, 1059.
  Civil Service Examinations, Regulations
    presented, May 31, 6; June 1, 69, 78.
  Connaught Rangers at Meerut—Shooting
    Case.
    Q. Mr. H. Roberts; A. Lord G. Hamil-
      ton, June 16, 1335.
  Coopers Hill College—Retirement of
    Officers.
    Q. Sir S. King; A. Lord G. Hamilton,
      June 15, 1178.
  Expenditure, Royal Commission Report.
    Q. Sir M. Bhownaggree; A. Lord G.
      Hamilton, June 2, 184.

INDIA—*cont.*

Franchise in French Possessions.
Q. Sir W. Wedderburn; A. Lord G. Hamilton, June 15, 1177.

Legal Education, Control of by Private Institutions.
Q. Sir W. Wedderburn; A. Lord G. Hamilton, June 8, 641.

Madras, see that Title.

Mineral Rights in Hyderabad State—Prospectuses.
Q. Sir A. Scoble; A. Lord G. Hamilton, June 8, 643.

Pasteur Institute — Government Grant, etc., proposed.
Q. Sir W. Wedderburn; A. Lord G. Hamilton, June 8, 643.

Progress and Condition, copy presented, June 6. 414, 435.

Punjaub War and Tirah Campaign, 1897-8, Distribution of Medals.
Q. Mr. H. D. Greene; A. Mr. Wyndham, June 1, 81; June 6, 443.

Riots in Southern India.
Q. Sir M. Bhownaggree; A. Lord G. Hamilton, June 15, 1176.

Sugar Duties—Tariff Act, 1899.
Motion [Sir H. H. Fowler], June 15, 1199.

Sugar Exports and Imports.
Q. Capt. Sinclair; A. Lord G. Hamilton, June 2, 185; June 8, 644.

Return.
Q. Mr. Maclean; A. Mr. Ritchie, June 6, 443.

Women Barristers—Miss Sorabji's Application refused.
Q. Mr. H. Roberts; A. Lord G. Hamilton. June 8, 641.

INDUSTRIAL SCHOOLS.

See Reformatory and Industrial Schools.

INEBRIATE REFORMATORIES, Management, Rules presented, June 13, 996, 1057.

INEBRIATES ACT.

Petition for Alteration of Law, June 14, 1090.

Infant Orphan Asylum Bill.
.c. Rep.*; June 9, 758.
3R.*, June 13, 1002.

Infectious Disease [Notification] Act [1889] Extension Bill.
l. 3R.*; June 1, 71.
c. Lords Amendts.*, June 5, 297.

INFIRMARIES.

Irish County Infirmaries, Management of—Representatives elected by County Councils.
Q. Mr. T. M. Healy; A. Mr. G. W. Balfour, June 15, 1188.

INLAND REVENUE DEPARTMENT.

Vote for, Rep.*, June 1, 157.

INNISKEEN RAILWAY ACCIDENT.

Culloville Line Improvement.
Q. Mr. Macaleese; A. Mr. Ritchie, June 16, 1341.

INTERMEDIATE EDUCATION.

Ireland.
Examination Places. copy of Rules presented, June 6. 414, 434.

INTERMEDIATE EDUCATION—*cont.*

Rules and Programme for 1900.
Q. Mr. W. Johnston; A. Mr. G. W. Balfour, June 15, 1193.

Viceregal Commission.
Q. Mr. Field; A. Mr. G. W. Balfour, June 13, 1071.

Welsh Intermediate Education Act.
Charity Commissioners' Report presented, June 14, 1091; June 15, 1168.

INTERNATIONAL UNION.

Japan, Accession of, copy of Treaty presented, June 6, 435; June 8, 596.

Montenegro, Withdrawal from, copy of Treaty presented, June 9, 761, 880.

INTOXICATING LIQUORS.

Sale of Intoxicating Liquors on Sunday Bill, see that Title.

Intoxicating Liquors [Sunday Closing] Bill.
c. 2R., June 7, 543.

Inverness Harbour Bill.
c. Rep.*, June 16, 1330.

Ionian Bank Bill.
c. 2R., June 13, 1053.

IONIAN ISLANDS—Trade Report presented, June 1, 68.

IRELAND.

Chief Secretary—Rt. Hon. Gerald W. Balfour.
Attorney-General—Rt. Hon. J. Atkinson.
Solicitor-General—Mr. D. P. Barton.

Agricultural Grant, see that Title.

Annaly Estate, Purchase of holdings.
Q. Mr. J. P. Farrell; A. Mr. G. W. Balfour, June 13, 1076.

Bagot Estate, Sale of—Sir N. O'Conor and the Congested Districts Board.
Q. Mr. Hayden; A. Mr. G. W. Balfour. June 15, 1188.

Ballyduff Postal Facilities.
Q. Mr. Flavin; A. Mr. Hanbury, June 19, 1494.

Ballymahon Postal Arrangements.
Q. Mr. Hayden; A. Mr. Hanbury, June 19, 1491.

Belfast, Cork, Dublin, etc., see those Titles.

Bills, relating to, see their Titles.

Blackhead and Maiden Rocks Lighthouses, see those Titles.

Blind, State Aid for, see Blind.

Castlerea and Ballaghadereen, Sanitary Charges.
Q. Mr. Hayden; A. Mr. G. W. Balfour, June 16, 1357.

Cavan, see that Title.

Circular Postage in Bandon and Clone.
Q. Mr. E. Barry; A. Mr. Hanbury, June 16, 1342.

Clerks of Unions checking Rate Collectors' Accounts—Extra Remuneration.
Q. Mr. Tully; A. Mr. G. W. Balfour, June 15, 1197.

Constabulary, Royal Irish, see that Title.

[*Continued*

IRELAND—cont.

Cookstown, see that Title.
County Cess, Balrothery—Standard Rate.
Q. Mr. Clancy; A. Mr. G. W. Balfour,
June 16, 1353.
County Councils.
Contractors as Members of Councils.
Cork.
Q. Mr. Tully; A. Mr. G. W. Bal-
four, June 8, 652.
Kerry.
Q. Mr. Field; A. Mr. G. W. Bal-
four, June 13, 1070.
Elections Expenses.
Q. Mr. Macaleese; A. Mr. G. W.
Balfour, June 8, 656.
Longford Collector—Case of W. Jones.
Q. Mr. J. P. Farrell; A. Mr. G. W.
Balfour, June 13, 1071.
County Court Officers—Grant for Clerical
Assistance—Return.
Q. Mr. Engledew; A. Mr. Hanbury,
438.
Crime, Incitement to, M'Hale v. Sullivan.
Debate [l.], June 12, 880.
Dillon's Lord, Estate—Purchase by Con-
gested Districts Board.
Q. Mr. T. M. Healy; A. Mr. G. W.
Balfour, June 16, 1361.
Diseases of Animals Act, Return presented,
June 12, 880, 892.
Dundalk Postmastership Vacancy.
Q. Mr. Macaleese; A. Mr. Hanbury,
June 19, 1490.
Dwyer Sylvester, Imprisonment of—Com-
mutation of Sentence.
Q. Mr. Flavin; A. Mr. G. W. Balfour,
June 19, 1498.
Education [For collective Heading, see
Education].
Emigration to America, Increase.
Q. Capt. Donelan; A. Mr. G. W. Bal-
four, June 8, 649.
Enniskillen Post Office, Plans and Tenders.
Q. Mr. Jordan; A. Mr. Hanbury, June
19, 1492.
Fair Rents, see sub-heading Judicial Rents.
Ferrybank Post Office and Postmastership.
Q. Mr. P. O'Brien; A. Mr. Hanbury,
June 16, 1344.
Finegan, Eviction Case.
Qs. Mr. Macaleese; A. Mr. G. W. Bal-
four, June 15, 1190; June 19, 1497.
Fintona Sunday Mails.
Q. Mr. Dilon; A. Mr. Hanbury, June
19, 1488.
Firearms, Carrying, see Firearms.
Fish Traffic on Railways—English and
Irish Railways.
Q. Mr. P. O'Brien; A. Mr. G. W.
Balfour, June 16, 1358.
Fishing Prosecution—Case of P. Comerford.
Q. Mr. P. O'Brien; A. Mr. G. W. Bal-
four, June 16, 1358.
G'in District School—Arrangements with
Waterford Steamship Co. for Convey-
ance of Children.
Q. Mr. Austin; A. Mr. G. W. Bal-
four, June 12, 902.
Gun Licences—Mr. Egan's Application Re-
fused.
Q. Mr. J. P. Farrell; A. Mr. G. W.
Balfour, June 19, 1499.
Industrial Schools, see Reformatory and In-
dustrial Schools.

IRELAND—cont.

Infirmaries, Management of—Representa-
tives elected by County Councils.
Q. Mr. T. M. Healy; A. Mr. G. W.
Balfour, June 15, 1188.
Inniskeen Railway Accident.
Q. Mr. Macaleese; A. Mr. Ritchie, June
16, 1341.
Intermediate Education, see that Title.
Judicial Rents.
Cavan Co.
Q. Mr. J. P. Farrell; A. Mr. G. W.
Balfour, June 16, 1355.
Equal Treatment of Tenants—Future
Tenants, etc.
Q. Mr. Flavin; A. Mr. G. W. Bal-
four, June 19, 1496.
Returns presented, June 6, 413, 434.
Kerry, Longford, Limerick, etc., see those
Titles.
Killarney Lakes—Sale of Muckross Estate.
Qs. Mr. Lough, Mr. MacNeill; As. Mr.
A. J. Balfour, June 19, 1501.
Labourers' Cottages—Disqualification of
District Councillors, etc.
Q. Mr. Gibney; A. Mr. G. W. Balfour,
June 19, 1495.
Land Commission, see that Title.
Land Purchase Acts, Delay in Carrying
out.
Q. Mr. S. Young; A. Mr. G. W. Bal-
four, June 8, 650.
Lanesborough Postal Arrangements, Com-
plaint.
Q. Mr. Hayden; A. Mr. Hanbury,
June 19, 1493.
Lights and Lighthouses, see that Title.
Loan Fund Board—Illegalities.
Qs. Mr. J. O'Connor, Mr. Doogan; A.
Mr. G. W. Balfour, June 9, 764.
Local Government Board Orders, Printing,
etc.
Q. Mr. Dillon; A. Mr. G. W. Bal-
four, June 8, 651.
Local Government Finance—Labour and
Expense, Increase in, under new Rules.
Q. Mr. MacNeill; A. Mr. G. W.
Balfour, June 15, 1191.
Lough Rynn Letter Deliveries Complaint.
Q. Mr. Tully; A. Mr. Hanbury, June
13, 1068.
Lurgan, New Post Office.
Q. Mr. M'Ghee; A. Mr. Hanbury, June
9, 774.
Magistracy, see that Title.
Migration of Population of Co. Mayo—
County Council Resolution.
Q. Dr. Ambrose; A. Mr. G. W.
Balfour, June 6, 439.
Military District, Cork—Stores Contract
Complaints.
Q. Captain Donelan; A. Mr. J. P.
Williams, June 19, 1482.
Monaghan Union Medical Officer.
Q. Mr. Macaleese; A. Mr. G. W.
Balfour, June 16, 1350.
Mountjoy Postal Arrangements.
Q. Mr. Doogan; A. Mr. Hanbury, June 9,
773.
Moy Postmaster—Candidate for Petty
Sessions Clerkship.
Q. Mr. W. Johnston; A. Mr. Hanbury,
June 16, 1343.

IRELAND—*cont.*

Mullingar Lunatic Asylum, see that Title.

National School Teachers, see that Title.

Newbliss Post Office Messenger, Salary of.
Q. Mr. Macaleese; A. Mr. Hanbury,
June 12, 904.

O'Donnell, Dominick—Inmate of Belmullet
Union.
Q. Mr. Crilly; A. Mr. G. W. Balfour,
June 13, 1074.

Oughterard Union, Fever outbreak.
Q. Mr. P. O'Brien; A. Mr. G. W. Balfour,
June 16, 1357.

Phœnix Park Murderer, Release.
Q. Mr. J. Lowther; A. Mr. G. W.
Balfour, June 5, 299.

Post Office—For Collective Heading, see
Post Office.

Railway Communication. Donegal.
Q. Mr. T. D. Sullivan; A. Mr. G. W.
Balfour, June 19, 1498.

Rating, New System—Landlord and Tenant
Agreements.
Q. Mr. Tully; A. Mr. G. W. Balfour,
June 9, 768.

Riots, see Belfast and Cookstown.

Roman Catholic University—Petitions, June
2, 174; June 5, 297; June 9, 760.

Salmon Fisheries—Illegal Practices.
Q. Mr. Seton-Kerr; A. Mr. G. W.
Balfour, June 9, 765.

Science, Royal College of, see Dublin.

Technical Education. Return ordered [Sir
J. E. Gorst], June 9, 761.

Telegraphists', Hours of Duty in Dublin.
Q. Mr. Davitt; A. Mr. Hanbury, June 9,
775.

Tithe-Rent Charge Redemption.
Q. Mr. W. Moore; A. Mr. G. W. Balfour,
June 1, 84. Q. Mr. S. Barry; A. Mr.
G. W. Balfour, June 16, 1354.

Town Commissioners, Chairman—Solicitor
losing right to practise at Quarter
Sessions.
Q. Mr. M. Healy; A. Mr. G. W.
Balfour, June 16, 1360.

Tramways Amendment Act—Relief to Cavan
Ratepayers.
Q. Mr. J. P. Farrell; A. Mr. Hanbury,
June 19, 1492.

Trawling off Howth—Compensation to
Fishermen.
Q. Mr. Clancy; As. Mr. G. W.
Balfour, June 16, 1360; June 19,
1500.

Tyrone, see that Title.

Valuation—Fixing of Fair Rents, etc.
Q. Mr. S. Young; A. Mr. G. W.
Balfour, June 8, 647.
Q. Capt. Donelan; A. Mr. G. W. Balfour,
June 9, 768.
Q. Mr. S. Young; A. Mr. G. W.
Balfour, June 15, 1195.

Sligo.
Q. Mr. P. A. M'Hugh; A. Mr. G. W.
Balfour, June 12, 903.

Valuation Acts—Revised Valuations.
Q. Mr. E. Barry; A. Mr. G. W. Balfour,
June 16, 1352.

Westport Urban Sanitary Authority—Com-
missioners' Petition.
Q. Dr. Ambrose; A. Mr. G. W.
Balfour, June 13, 1074.

IRELAND—*cont.*

Youghal Rifle Range, Repairs, etc.
Q. Capt. Donelan; A. Mr. Wyndham,
June 9, 771.

ITALY—Trade Report presented, June 1, 68.

JACKSON, PRIVATE.—Bathing Fatality at Aldershot.
Q. Mr. Jeffreys; A. Mr. Wyndham, June
8, 640.

JAM FACTORIES, Labour in.
Q. Mr. Hedderwick; A. Sir M. W.
Ridley, June 5, 297.

JAMAICA—Annual Report presented, June 19,
1456, 1479.

JAMES, OF HEREFORD, LORD.
Reformatory Schools Amendment Bill, 2R,
June 8, 614; com., June 12, 886.
Youthful Offenders Bill. 2R, June 19. 1457,
1464.

JAMESON RAID—Indemnity—Correspondence
presented, June 8, 596, 625.

JAPAN.
Accession to Industrial Convention of 1883
—Treaty presented, June 2, 163, 171.
Accession to International Union—Treaty
presented, June 6, 435; June 8, 596.
British Columbia—Japanese Immigration.
Q. Mr. Hogan; A. Mr. J. Chamberlain,
June 8, 636.
Trade Report presented, June 1, 68; June
19, 1456.

JEFFREYS, MR. A. F. [Hants, N.]
Aldershot Bathing Fatality, June 8, 640.
Half-timers—Education of Children Bill,
com., May 31, 27, 36.
Private Legislation Procedure [Scotland]
Bill, com., June 12, 927.

JESSEL, CAPT. H. M. [St. Pancras, South].
London Government Bill, con., June 6, 499.

JOHANNESBURG.
Edgar, Mr., Killed by Policeman—Compensation to Mrs. Edgar.
Q. Mr. Griffith; A. Mr. J. Chamberlain, June 2, 182.
Q. Mr. Duncombe; A. Mr. J. Chamberlain, June 19, 1484.

JOHNSON-FERGUSON, MR. J. E. [Leicester,
Loughborough].
Dublin Corporation Bill, con., June 13,
1022.

JOHNSTON, MR. W. [Belfast, S.].
Agriculture and Technical Instruction
[Ireland] Bill—Business of the House,
June 19, 1516.
Dublin Corporation Bill, con., June 13,
1013.
Intermediate Education, Ireland—Rules and
Programme for 1900. June 15, 1193.
Magistrates [Ireland] Resident, salaries of,
June 9, 767.
Moy Postmaster—Candidate for Petty
Sessions Clerkship, June 16, 1343.
Transvaal—Mrs. Applebe, Murder of,
June 19, 1484.

JOHNSTONE, MR. J. H. [Sussex, Horsham].
  Half-timers—Education of Children Bill,
  3R, June 14, 1120.
  London Government Bill—Qualification of
  Women, con. June 6, 475.
JONES, MR. D. B. [Swansea District].
  All Saints' Church [Cardiff] Bill—Standing
  Order Complied with, June 8, 622.
JONES, MR. W. [Carnarvon, Arfon].
  Poor Law Schools, Education in, June 2,
  242.
Jones's Divorce Bill.
  1. Rep.*, June 1, 70.
     3R.*, June 2, 163.
  c. 1R.*, June 2, 169.
     2R.*, June 9, 756.
     Rep.*, June 16, 1331.
JORDAN, MR. J. [Fermanagh, S.].
  Enniskillen Post Office—Plans and Tenders,
  June 19, 1492.
JUDGES.
  Additional Judges, Appointment of.
  Q. Lord Russell of Killowen; A. Lord
  Halsbury, June 8, 617.
  Ecclesiastical Judge, see that Title.
JUDICIAL RENTS, Ireland.
  See Ireland.
JUSTICE.
  South Staffordshire Stipendiary Justice Bill,
  see that Title.
JUVENILE OFFENDERS.
  Youthful Offenders Bill, see that Title.
KENNY, MR., Case of.
  Q. Mr. Tully; A. Mr. G. W. Balfour, June
  5, 304.
Kensington and Notting Hill Electric
Lighting Bill.
  1. 2R.*, June 2, 161.
     Rep.*, June 16, 1317.
KENT.
  Light Railways Order presented, May
  31, 5; June 1, 69.
  Mid-Kent Gas Bill, see that Title.
KENYON, MR. J. [Lancs., Bury].
  Half-timers—Education of Children Bill,
  3R., June 14, 1125, 1127.
KERRY.
  County Council—Contractors as Members of
  Council.
  Q. Mr. Field; A. Mr. G. W. Balfour,
  June 13, 1070.
  Letter Deliveries in North Kerry.
  Q. Mr. Flavin; A. Mr. Hanbury, June
  19, 1489.
KESWICK, MR. W. [Surrey, Epsom].
  China, Affairs of, June 9, 867.
Kew Bridge Bill.
  c. Rep.*, June 2. 169.
     3R.*, June 6, 430.
KILDARE—Agriculture. Grant Reduction.
  Agricultural Grant Reduction.
  Q. Mr. Carew; A. Mr. G. W. Balfour,
  June 8, 650.

KILDARE STREET LIBRARY, Handing over to
new Irish Department.
  Q. Mr. P. O'Brien; A. Mr. G. W. Bal-
  four, June 16, 1350.
KILLARNEY LAKES—Sale of Muckross Estate.
  Qs. Mr. Lough, Mr. MacNeill; As. Mr.
  A. J. Balfour, June 19, 1501.
KIMBER, MR. H. [Wandsworth].
  London Government Bill, con., June 6, 492.
KIMBERLEY, EARL OF.
  London Government Bill, June 15, 1169.
  Soudan Campaign—Grant to Lord Kit-
  chener, Vote of Thanks to the Forces,
  etc., June 8, 600, 607.
KING, SIR H. S. [Hull, Central].
  Coopers Hill College—Retirement of
  Officers, June 15, 1178.
KINLOCH, SIR J. G. S. [Perthshire, E.].
  Secondary Education, Scotland—Minute of
  April 27, 1899, June 16, 1438.
KITCHENER, LORD, Grant to, see Soudan Cam-
  paign.
KNOWLES, MR. L. [Salford, W.].
  Plumbers' Registration—Legislation, June
  13, 1087.
  Soudan Campaign.
  Kitchener, Lord, Grant to—Treatment of
  the Mahdi's Body, etc., June 5, 374.
  Wounded Dervishes, Cruelty to, alleged—
  Major Luigi Calderari's Letter, June 8,
  686.
KRUGER, PRESIDENT—Conference with Sir A.
  Milner, see Transvaal, Uitlanders' Grievance
  —Bloemfontein Conference.
KURDISH ATROCITIES IN ARMENIA.
  Russian and French Protest.
  Q. Mr. Schwann; A. Mr. Brodrick, June
  16, 1337.
LABOUCHERE, MR. H. [Northampton].
  Bloemfontein Conference, June 13, 1060.
  Business of the House, Precedence of
  Government Business, June 19, 1520.
  China, Affairs of—British Government
  Policy, etc., June 9, 865.
  London Government Bill—Qualification of
  Women, June 6, 473, 474; June 13, 1086.
  Salisbury Plain, Purchase of Land by War
  Office—Finance Bill, June 6, 457.
  Soudan Expedition—Grant to Lord Kit-
  chener—Treatment of the Mahdi's Body,
  etc., June 5, 364.
  Vaccination Law, Enforcement of—Local
  Government Board Action, June 2, 217.
  Vaccination Officers and Boards of Guar-
  dians, June 2, 209.
LABOURERS' COTTAGES, IRELAND.
  Disqualification of District Councillors, etc.
  Q. Mr. Gibney; A. Mr. G. W. Balfour,
  June 19, 1495.
LADYSMITH BARRACKS, Insanitary Condition of.
  Q. Mr. Buchanan; A. Mr. Wyndham,
  June 9, 771.
LAKES OF KILLARNEY, see Killarney Lakes.

LAMBERT, MR. G. [Devon, South Molton].
China.
  Anglo-Russian Agreement—Peking and
    Manchurian Railway, June 8, 630.
  Yang-tsze Valley, Geographical Defini-
    tion, Railway Rates, etc., June 8, 630.
Wine Duties, Increased, Revenue derived
  from, June 13, 1068.

Lanarkshire [Middle Ward District
Water] Bill.
  c. Rep.*, June 16, 1330.

Lancashire and Yorkshire Railway
[Various Powers] Bill.
  l. Rep.*, June 12, 878.

LAND.
  Agricultural Land, Valuation—Finance Bill,
    Motion [Mr. Bowles], June 6, 452.
  Ireland.
    Valuation—Fixing of Fair Rents, etc.
      Q. Mr. S. Young; A. Mr. G. W. Balfour,
        June 8, 647; Q. Capt. Donelan; A. Mr.
        G. W. Balfour, June 9, 768; Q. Mr. S.
        Young; A. Mr. G. W. Balfour, June
        15, 1195.
    Sligo.
      Q. Mr. P. A. M'Hugh; A. Mr. G. W.
        Balfour, June 12, 903.
    Valuation Acts—Revised Valuations.
      Q. Mr. F. Barry; A. Mr. G. W. Balfour,
        June 16, 1352.

LAND COMMISSION [Ireland].
  Assistant Commissioners.
    Q. Capt. Donelan; A. Mr. G. W. Bal-
      four, June 8, 648.
  Bailieborough Sub-Commissioners' Judg-
    ments.
    Q. Mr. S. Young; A. Mr. G. W. Bal-
      four, June 8, 647
  Judicial Rents, see Ireland.
  Rating—new System, Landlord and Tenant
    Agreements.
    Q. Mr. Tully; A. Mr. G. W. Balfour,
      June 9, 768.
  Tithe Rent-Charge Redemption.
    Q. Mr. W. Moore; A. Mr. G. W. Balfour,
      June 1, 84.
    Q. Mr. S. Barry; A. Mr. G. W. Balfour,
      June 16, 1354.

LAND PURCHASE ACTS, IRELAND.
  Delay in Carrying out.
    Q. Mr. S. Young; A. Mr. G. W. Balfour,
      June 8, 650.

LANESBOROUGH POSTAL ARRANGEMENTS, Complaint.
    Q. Mr. Hayden; A. Mr. Hanbury, June
      19, 1493.

LAURIE, LIEUT.-GEN. J. W. [Pembroke and
Haverfordwest].
  Loans, Municipal, June 2, 227.
  Pembroke Dock—Delay in Delivery of
    Letters, June 1, 125, 127.
  Street Obstruction—Prosecution of Car-
    men, Dismissal of Case at Marylebone
    Police Court, June 15, 1184.

LAWRENCE, MR. W. F. [Liverpool, Aber-
cromby].
  Africa, West, Liquor Traffic—Spirit
    Duties, June 15, 1181.
  West Indies—Fruit steamers, Local Duties
    on Rum, etc., June 6, 441.

LAWSON, MR. J. G. [York, N.R., Thirsk].
  Carmarthen Charities—Delay in Publication
    of Report, June 19, 1487.
  Half-timers—Education of Children Bill,
    com., May 31, 38, 41, 53.

LAWSON, SIR W. [Cumberland, Cockermouth].
  Intoxicating Liquors [Sunday Closing] Bill,
    2R., June 7, 553, 554, 557, 558, 562.
  Peers' Interference at Elections—Breach of
    Privilege, June 5, 315.
  Soudan Campaign—Grant to Lord
    Kitchener—Treatment of the Mahdi's
    Body, etc., June 5, 385.
  Wine and Beerhouse Acts Amendment Bill,
    2R., June 7, 569.

LAWYERS—Women Practising in India—Miss
Sorabji's application.
    Q. Mr. H. Roberts; A. Lord G.
      Hamilton, June 8, 641.

LEAD FACTORIES—White Lead Factories, Rules
presented, June 1, 70, 79.

LEESE, SIR J. F. [Lancashire, Accrington].
  Intoxicating Liquors [Sunday Closing] Bill,
    2R., June 7, 566.

LEGAL EDUCATION, INDIA—Control of by
Private Institutions.
    Q. Sir W. Wedderburn; A. Lord G.
      Hamilton, June 8, 641.

Leicester Corporation Water Bill.
  c. Instruction to com. as to consolidation of
    Bills, June 2, 167.
  Rep.*, June 16, 1331.

LEIGH, LORD.
  Reformatory Schools Amendment Bill, 2R,
    June 8, 612; com., June 12, 888.
  Youthful Offenders Bill, 2R, June 19, 1462,
    1466.

Leigh-on-Sea Urban District Council Bill.
  c. 2R.*, June 6, 430.

Leith Harbour and Docks Bill.
  l. 1R.*, June 1, 66.
    2R.*, June 9, 750.

LENG, SIR J. [Dundee].
  American Mail Service—Return, June 6,
    437.
  Colonial Loans Fund Bill, com., June 8, 744.
  Private Legislation Procedure [Scotland]
    Bill, com., June 19, 1573.
  Savings Banks, Inquiry, June 8, 644.

LETTER-BOXES—Late Letter-boxes on trains,
  S. June 1, 106, 121.

LETTERS—Daily Deliveries in Rural Districts,
  S., June 1, 125, 126.

LEVEL CROSSINGS.
Desborough Fatality Inquest—Board of
Trade Representative.
Q. Mr. Channing; A. Mr. Ritchie, June
2, 181.
LEWIS, MR. J. H. [Flint Boroughs].
Wine and Beerhouse Acts Amendment Bill,
2R, June 7, 586.
LEWIS, MRS., CASE OF.
Q. Mr. Spicer; A. Mr. G. Wyndham, June
8, 632.
LIBRARIES.
Kildare Street Library, handing over to
New Irish Department.
Q. Mr. P. O'Brien; A. Mr. G. W.
Balfour, June 16, 1350.
Public Libraries [Scotland] Acts Amendment
Bill, see that Title.
LIFE ASSURANCE—Lloyd's Policies—Returns.
Mail Train delays.
Q. Mr. Boulnois; A. Mr. Ritchie, June 8,
633.
LIGHT RAILWAYS.
Glamorgan and Brecon Counties, Order
Presented, May 31, 5; June 1, 69.
Middlesex Co., Order Presented, May 31,
5; June 1, 69.
Sheppey, Isle of, and Co. of Kent, Order
Presented, May 31, 5; June 1, 69.
Weston-super-Mare, Clevedon, and Portis-
head Tramways Company [Light Railway
Extensions] Bill, see that Title.
LIGHTERMEN.
Watermen's and Lightermen's Acts Amend-
ment Bill, see that Title.
LIGHTING OF HYDE PARK.
Q. Gen. Russell; A. Mr. A. Douglas, June
19, 1488.
LIGHTS AND LIGHTHOUSES.
Black Head.
Q. Mr. Allan; A. Mr. Ritchie, June 2,
180; Q. Capt. Donelan; A. Mr. Ritchie,
June 8, 634.
Lighthouse Keepers' Emoluments.
Q. Mr. Nicol; A. Mr. Ritchie, June 9,
770.
Maiden Rocks.
Q. Mr. Allan; A. Mr. Ritchie, June 2,
634.
Q. Mr. Field; A. Mr. Ritchie, June 13,
1066.
Northern Lighthouses Commissioners—
Increase in Clerical Establishments—Order
in Council Presented, June 6, 413, 434.
Scottish Lighthouse Keepers, Retiring
Allowance.
Q. Dr. Clark; A. Mr. Ritchie, June 16,
1342.
LIMERICK.
Great Southern and Western and Waterford,
Limerick, and Western Railway
Companies Amalgamation Bill, see that
Title.
Mail Train Delays.
Q. Mr. Flavin; A. Mr. Hanbury, June 19,
1491.
Newcastle West Creamery—Sewer Com-
plaint.
Q. Mr. Austin; A. Mr. G. W. Balfour,
June 15, 1193.

LIMERICK—cont.
Sorting Clerks, Dismissal of.
Q. Mr. P. O'Brien; A. Mr. Hanbury,
June 12, 905.
Lincolnshire Coroners Bill.
L. 3R.*, June 9, 754.
c. 1R*, June 14, 1092.
LIQUOR TRAFFIC AND LIQUOR LICENSING LAWS.
Africa, West, see that Title.
Beer Materials Committee—Substitutes for
Hops, etc.
Q. Sir C. Quilter; A. Sir M. Hicks-
Beach, June 15, 1183.
Children, Sale of Liquor to—Petition for
Alteration of Law, June 12, 892.
Grocers' Licences [Scotland] Abolition Bill,
see that Title.
Madras—Opening of Liquor Shops.
Q. Mr. S. Smith; A. Lord G. Hamilton,
June 12, 897.
Rio de Janeiro, British Sailors at.
Q. Mr. Hogan; A. Mr. Ritchie, June 13,
1066.
Sunday Sale of Liquor Bills, see Titles In-
toxicating Liquors [Sunday Closing] Bill,
and Sale of Intoxicating Liquors on Sun-
day Bill.
Wine and Beerhouses Acts Amendment
Bill, see that Title.
Liquor Traffic Local Veto [Scotland] Bill.
Petitions, June 13, 1055; June 16, 1331;
June 19, 1478.
Lisburn Urban District Councils Bill
formerly
Lisburn Town Commissioners Bill
l. Rep.*, June 8, 594.
3R.*, June 13, 996.
c. lords amendments*, June 19, 1478.
"LITTLE ENGLANDER."
O. H. Labouchere, June 9, 865.
LIVERPOOL.
Education Department Provisional Order
Confirmation [Liverpool] Bill, see that
Title.
Meat Inspection—Appointment of Unquali-
fied Inspector.
Q. Mr. P. O'Brien; A. Mr. Chaplin,
June 16, 1348.
LIVERPOOL, BISHOP OF—Peers' Interference at
Southport Election—Breach of Privilege.
Q. Mr. J. Lowther; A. Mr. A. J. Bal-
four, June 5, 307.
Motion [Mr. Lowther], June 5, 311.
Liverpool Overhead Railway Bill.
c. 2R.*., May 31, 2.
Rep.*, June 16, 1330.
LLOYD-GEORGE, MR. D. [Carnarvon, etc.].
Local Government Board, transferring
Powers to County Councils, June 2, 265.
Private Legislation Procedure [Scotland]
Bill, com., June 12, 916.
Provisional Order Bills, Procedure—In-
sertion of Names, June 2, 175.
Wine and Beerhouse Acts Amendment
Bill, 2R., June 7, 567.
LLOYD'S LIFE INSURANCE POLICIES—Returns.
Q. Mr. Boulnois; A. Mr. Ritchie, June 8,
633.

LOAN FUND BOARD, IRELAND—Illegalities.
  Qs. Mr. J. O'Connor, Mr. Doogan; As.
  Mr. G. W. Balfour, June 9, 764.

LOANS.
  Colonial Loans Fund Bill, see that Title.
  Finance Bill, Amendments [Sir M. Hicks-
  Beach], June 8, 731; [Sir C. Cameron],
  734
  Turkish Loan, see that Title.

LOCAL AUTHORITIES.
  Taxation of Ground Rents—Petition, June
  6, 433.
  Technical Education, England, Ireland,
  and Wales. Return Ordered [Sir J. Gorst],
  June 9, 761.

Local Authorities Servants' Superannuation Bill.
  Petition, June 16, 1332.

LOCAL GOVERNMENT BOARD.
  President—Rt. Hon. H. Chaplin.
  Parliamentary Secretary—Mr. T. W.
  Russell.
  Inquiries by, Limitation of, S. June 2, 279,
  280.
  Powers, Transferring to County Councils.
  S. June 2, 265, 271, 274, 276.
  Vote for, June 2, 187.

LOCAL GOVERNMENT BOARD, IRELAND.
  Cavan and Granard Unions—Transfer of
  Divisions refused.
    Q. Mr. J. P. Farrell; A. Mr. G. W.
    Balfour, June 13, 1075.
  Orders, Printing, etc.
    Q. Mr. Dillon; A. Mr. G. W. Balfour,
    June 8, 651.

LOCAL GOVERNMENT [IRELAND] ACT, 1898.
  Method or Determining Amounts to be
  taken as having been raised in standard
  year—Memorandum presented, June 16,
  1333.
  Orders and Rules under—Difficulty in obtaining copies.
    Q Mr. Tully; A. Mr. G. W. Balfour,
    June 6, 439.
  [See also Ireland—Sub-heading County
  Councils].

Local Government [Ireland] Provisional Orders [No. 1] Bill.
  c. 2R.*, June 2, 168.
  Rep.*, June 9, 757.
  3R.*, June 12, 890.
  l. 1R.*, June 13, 995.

Local Government [Ireland] Provisional Orders [No. 2] Bill.
  c. 2R.*, June 5, 296.
  Rep.*, June 16, 1329
  3R*, June 19, 1476.

Local Government [Ireland] Provisional Orders [No. 3] Bill.
  c. 2R.*, June 6, 432.
  Rep.*, June 16, 1329.
  3R.*, June 19, 1476.

Local Government [Ireland] Provisional Orders [No. 4] Bill.
  c. 1R.*, June 1, 77.
    2R.*, June 12, 890.

Local Government [Ireland] Provisional Order [Housing of Working Classes] [No. 2] Bill.
  c. 2R.*, June 12, 890.

Local Government Provisional Orders [No. 1] Bill.
  l. Royal Assent. June 6, 409.

Local Government Provisional Orders [No. 2] Bill.
  c. Rep.*, June 16, 1329.
  con.*, June 19, 1477.

Local Government Provisional Orders [No. 3] Bill.
  l. 1R.*, June 1, 68.

Local Government Provisional Orders [No. 4] Bill.
  c. 2R.*, June 2, 168.

Local Government Provisional Orders [No. 5] Bill.
  c. 2R.*, June 2, 168.
    Rep.*, June 9, 757.
    3R.*, June 12, 890.
  l. 1R.*, June 13, 995.

Local Government Provisional Orders [No. 6] Bill.
  c. 2R.*, June 2, 168.

Local Government Provisional Orders [No. 7] Bill.
  c. 2R.*, June 2, 168.
    Rep.*, June 16, 1329.
    con.*, June 19, 1477.

Local Government Provisional Orders [No. 8] Bill.
  c. 2R.*, June 2, 168.
    Rep.*, June 9, 757.
    con.*, June 12, 890.
    3R.*, June 13, 1054.
  l. 1R.*, June 15, 1166.

Local Government Provisional Orders [No. 9] Bill.
  c. 2R.*, June 6, 432.

Local Government Provisional Orders [No. 10] Bill.
  c. 2R.*, June 6, 432.

Local Government Provisional Orders [No. 11] Bill.
  c. 2R.*, June 6, 432.

Local Government Provisional Orders [No. 12] Bill.
  c. 2R.*, June 6, 432.

Local Government Provisional Orders [No. 13] Bill.
  c. 2R.*, June 6, 432.
  Rep.*, June 16, 1330.

Local Government Provisional Orders [No. 14] Bill.
  c. 2R.*, June 6, 432.

Local Government Provisional Orders [Gas] Bill.
  c. 2ʀ.*, June 2, 168.

Local Government Provisional Orders [Housing of Working Classes] Bill.
  c. 2ʀ.*, June 2, 168; June 6, 432.
  Rep*, June 9, 757.
  3ʀ.*, June 12, 890.
  l. 1ʀ.*, June 13, 995.

Local Government Provisional Orders [Poor Law] Bill.
  c. 2ʀ.*, June 2, 168.
  Rep.*, June 9, 757.
  3ʀ.*, June 12, 890.
  l. 1ʀ.*, June 13, 995.

Local Government [Scotland] Act [1894] Amendment Bill.
  Petitions, June 1, 78; June 2, 174; June 7, 538; June 9, 760, 891, 1055, 1090; June 15, 1175; June 16, 1332; June 19, 1478.

Local Government [Scotland] Act [1894] Amendment [No. 2.] Bill.
  Petitions, June 9, 760; June 16, 1332.

Local Government [Scotland] Bill.
  Petitions, June 2, 174; June 9, 760.

LOCAL LOANS, see Loans.

LOCAL TAXATION—Commission, Minutes of Evidence presented, May 31, 7; June 1, 68.

LOCKWOOD, LIEUT.-COL. A. [Essex, Epping].
  Board of Education Bill, June 19, 1500.
  Half-timers—Education of Children Bill, com. May 31, 47.

LONDON, BISHOP OF.
  Marriages Validity Bill, 2ʀ., June 6, 429.
  Prevention of Corruption Bill [Secret Commissions], 2ʀ., June 6, 416.

London, Brighton, and South Coast Railway [Pensions] Bill.
  l. Rep.*, June 8, 594.
  3ʀ.*, June 13, 996.
  c. lords amendts.*, June 19, 1475.

London, Brighton, and South Coast Railway [Various Powers] Bill.
  l. 2ʀ.*, June 8, 594.

LONDON, CHATHAM, AND DOVER RAILWAY.
  Shunting Fatality
  Q. Mr. Maddison; A. Mr. Ritchie, June 15, 1183.

London, Chatham, and Dover Railway Bill.
  l 2ʀ.*, June 9, 750.

LONDON, CITY OF—Electric Lighting, Report presented, June 12, 880, 892.

LONDON COUNTY COUNCIL.
  Estimate of Expenditure presented, June 19, 1479.

London County Council [General Powers] Bill.
  c. con.*, June 13, 1005.

London County Council [Money] Bill.
  c. Rep.*, June 9, 757.
  con.*, June 16, 1328.

London Government Bill.
  c. con., June 6, 460; June 8, 699.
  re-com., June 13, 1078.
  3ʀ., 1080.
  l. 1ʀ.*, June 15, 1168.

London Government Bill.
  Q. Earl of Kimberley; A. Vis. Cross, June 15, 1169.
  Q. Earl of Kimberley; A. Marquess of Salisbury, June 16, 1327.
  Petitions, June 1, 78; June 19, 1456.
    Women, Qualification of—Mr. Courtney's Motion, June 6, 464; Mr Elliot's Amendt., June 13, 1078.

London Hospital Bill.
  c. 2ʀ.*, May 31, 2.
  Rep.*, June 9, 758.
  3ʀ.*, June 13, 1002.

London Improvements Bill.
  c. con.*, June 7, 537.
  3ʀ.*, June 12, 890.
  l. 1ʀ.*, June 13, 994.

LONDON SCHOOL BOARD.
  Bethnal Green Schools, see that Title.

LONDON UNIVERSITY—Imperial Institute Scheme, see Imperial Institute.

London Water [Purchase] Bill.
  c. 2ʀ, June 1, 74.

LONDON WATER SUPPLY.
  East London Water Bill, see that Title.

London and North-Western [New Railways] Bill.
  c. con.*, June 2, 167.
  3ʀ.*, June 6, 430.
  l. 1ʀ.*, June 8, 595.

LONDONDERRY, MARQUESS OF.
  Prevention of Corruption Bill [Secret Commissions], 2ʀ., June 6, 419, 428.

LONG, RT. HON. W. H.—President of Board of Agriculture [Liverpool, West Derby].
  Buenos Ayres Cattle Trade—"Hindustan" Losses, June 13, 1067.

"LONG SPOON" POLICY.
  O. Mr. Labouchere, June 9, 867.

LONGFORD.
  Agricultural Grant—Excluded Charges.
    Qs. Mr. J. P. Farrell; As. Mr. G. W. Balfour, June 13, 1196.
  Annaly Estate—Purchase of Holdings.
    Q. Mr. J. P. Farrell; A. Mr. G. W. Balfour, June 13, 1076.
  County Council Collector—Case of W. Jones.
    Q. Mr. J. P. Farrell; A. Mr. G. W. Balfour, June 13, 1071.
  Militia, Removal of Headquarters to Mullingar.
    Q Mr. J. P. Farrell; A. Mr. Wyndham, June 13, 1058.

LOUGH, MR. T. [Islington, W.].

Finance Bill, con., June 6, 458.
Indian Sugar Duties—Tariff Act, 1899, June 15, 1251.
Killarney Lakes—Sale of Muckross Estate, June 19. 1501.
London Government Bill, con., June 6, 481, 515.
Prison Officials, Retirement of, June 19, 1485.

LOUGH RYNN—Letter Deliveries, Complaint.

Q. Mr. Tully; A. Mr. Hanbury, June 13, 1068.

Loughborough Corporation Bill.

c. 2R.*, June 9, 756.

Loughborough and Sheepshed Railway Bill.

l. Royal Assent, June 6, 409.

Lowestoft Promenade Pier Bill.

c. Rep.*, June 9, 758.
con.*, June 14, 1089.
3R.*, June 19, 1475.
l. 1R.*, 1454.

Lowestoft Water and Gas Bill.

l. 3R.*, June 6, 411.
1R.*, June 6, 625.
c. 2R.*, June 19, 1476.

LOWLES, MR. J. [Shoreditch, Haggerston].

London Government Bill, con., June 6, 493, 504, 511; June 8, 711, 713, 722.
Pauper Children—Cottage Home System, June 1, 250.

LOWTHER, RT. HON. J. [Kent, Thanet].

Agricultural Land Valuation—Finance Bill, June 6, 456.
Dundee Gas, Street Improvements, and Tramways Bill, 2R., June 5, 294.
Half-timers—Education of Children Bill, com., June 7, 542.
Intoxicating Liquors (Sunday Closing] Bill, 2R., June 7, 545, 548.
Peers' Interference at Southport Election—Breach of Privilege, June 5, 507, 311, 316.
Phœnix Park Murderer, Release of, June 5, 299.
Wine and Beerhouse Acts Amendment Bill, 2R., June 7, 567, 569.

LOWTHER, RT. HON. J. W., Chairman of Committees [Cumberland, Penrith].

All Saints' Church [Cardiff] Bill, Standing Order Complied with, June 8, 621.
Godalming Corporation Water Bill, con., June 15, 1170.
St. Neots Water Bill, 2R., June 13, 1053.

LUBBOCK, RT. HON. SIR J. [London University.]

Half-timers—Education of Children Bill, com. May 31, 40.
New Guinea, British Papers relating to, June 6, 440.

LUNATIC ASYLUMS.

Imbecile [Training Institutions] Bill. See that Title.
Mullingar, See that Title.

37

Lunacy Bill.

c. 1R.*, June 2, 171.
2R., June 12, 990.

LUNACY OFFICE, Vote for, June 1, 158.

LURGAN, New Post Office.

Q. Mr. M'Ghee; A. Mr. Hanbury, June 9, 774.

LYNCH, E.—PENSION.

Q. Mr. Hayden; ; A. Mr. Wyndham, 16, 1334.

MACALEESE, MR. D. [Monaghan, N.]

Belfast Post Office Staff—Vacancies, June 19, 1490.
County Councils, Ireland — Election Expenses, June 8, 656.
Dundalk Postmastership Vacancy, June 19, 1490.
Finegan Eviction Case, June 15, 1190; June 19, 1497.
Inniskeen Railway Accident, June 16, 1341.
Monaghan Union Medical Officer, June 16, 1350.
National School Teachers [Ireland], Classification of Salaries, June 6, 438.
Newbliss Post Office Messenger, Salary of June 12, 904.

MACARTNEY, MR. W. E.—Secretary to the Admiralty [Antrim, S.].

Navy Contracts—New Form, June 19, 1480.

MACHINERY.

Rating of Machinery Bill, see that Title.

MACDONA, MR. J. C. [Southwark, Rotherhithe].

China, Affairs of, June 9, 840.

MACIVER, MR. D. [Liverpool, Kirkdale].

Waima Incident — Compensation Claims, June 9, 872.

MACLEAN, MR. J. M. [Cardiff].

All Saints' Church [Cardiff] Bill, Standing Order complied with, June 8, 623.
Bloemfontein Conference, June 8, 639.
Confectionery, Indian Trade, June 6, 443.
Indian Sugar Duties—Tariff Act, 1899, June 15, 1222, 1234, 1304.
Persia, Russian Railway Construction—Expiration of Agreement, etc., June 8, 628.
Persian Gulf, British Interests—Railway Concessions to Germany, June 8, 629.

MACNEILL, MR. J. G. S. [Donegal, S.].

Anti-British Propaganda in Cape Colony, June 15, 1183; June 16, 1338.
Company Promoters Bill—Business of the House, June 19, 1517, 1527.
Donegal Agricultural Grant, June 15, 1192.
Killarney Lakes—Sale of Muckross Estate, June 19, 1502.
Local Government [Ireland] Finance — Labour and Expense, Increase in, under new Rules, June 15, 1191.
Naturalisation Certificates, obtaining from Secretary of State, June 15, 1185.
Rangoon—Outrage on Burmese Woman by British Soldiers, June 16, 1336.
Soudan Campaign — Grant to Lord Kitchener.
Mahdi's Body, Treatment of, etc., June 5, 401.

Continued

MacNEILL, MR. J. G. S.—*cont.*
Money Grants, House of Lords initiating—Question of Privilege, June 5,
319, 324.
Transvaal—Uitlanders' Grievances, Political Rights, June 13, 1062.

McARTHUR, MR. C. [Liverpool, Exchange].
Ecclesiastical Judge—Appointment of Sir
A. Charles, June 15, 1186.

McCARTAN, MR. M. [Down, S.].
Belfast Religious Disturbances, June 8,
655.
Magistrates [Ireland] Resident, Pay of, June
9, 767.

McIVER, SIR L. [Edinburgh, W.].
Indian Sugar Duties—Tariff Act, 1899, June
15, 1258.

McKENNA, MR. R. [Monmouth. N.].
Comptroller and Auditor General—Retire-
ment of Mr. Mills, June 1, 83.
London Government Bill, con., June 6, 504.
Service Franchise Bill, com., June 7, 539,
541.

McLEOD, MR. J. [Sunderland].
Quarrier's, Mr., Homes — Education of
Children, June 16, 1442.

M'CALMONT, COL. J. [Antrim, E.].
Industrial Schools Act, Ireland — School
Attendance Committees, Powers of, June
12. 901.

M'FARLAND, W.—Tyrone County Council—
Rate Collector Appointment.
Q. Mr. Hemphill; A. Mr. G. W.
Balfour, June 19, 1496.

M'GHEE, MR. R. [Louth, S.].
Central Telegraphic Staff—Petitions, June
15, 1187.
East Central District Post Office Staff—Peti-
tions, June 12, 904.
Garston. Fatal Accident to Dock Labourer,
June 9, 769.
Lurgan, New Post Office, June 9, 774.

M'HALE *v.* SULLIVAN.
Debate [l.], June 12, 880.

M'HUGH, MR. P. A. [Leitrim, N.].
Sligo Land Valuation, June 12, 903.

M'NAUGHTON, A.—Glasgow Bakery Dispute.
Q. Sir C. Cameron ; A. Mr. A. G. Murray,
June 19, 1485.

MADAGASCAR QUESTION.
S., June 9, 778.

MADDISON, MR. F. [Sheffield, Brightside].
Half-timers—Education of Children Bill,
3R., June 14, 1128, 1129.
Post Office.
Buildings, Insanitary Condition, June 1,
112.
Employees' Grievances, June 1, 111.
Shunting Fatality on Chatham and Dover
Railway, June 15, 1183.

MADRAS.
Liquor Trade—Opening of Liquor Shops.
Q. Mr. S. Smith ; A. Lord G. Hamilton,
June 12, 897.
Riots between Shanars and Maravars.
Q. Sir M. Bhownaggree ; A. Lord G.
Hamilton, June 15, 1176.

MAGISTRACY, IRELAND.
Cavan co., Vacancy.
Q. Mr. J. P. Farrell ; A. Mr. G. W
Balfour, June 16, 1359.
Resident Magistrates, Salaries of.
Qs. Mr. McCartan, Mr. Davitt, Mr. W.
Johnston ; As. Mr. G. W. Balfour,
June 9, 767.

MAHDI'S BODY, TREATMENT OF. — Charge
against Lord Kitchener.
Os. Earl of Kimberley, June 8, 600.
Morley's, Mr., Protest ; Debate on Lord
Kitchener's Grant, June 5, 327.

MAIDEN ROCKS LIGHTHOUSE.
Q. Mr. Allen ; A. Mr. Ritchie, June 2, 180
Q. Mr. Field ; A. Mr. Ritchie, June 13,
1066.

MAIL SERVICE.
American—Return.
Q. Sir J. Leng ; A. Mr. Hanbury, June
6, 437.
Late Letter Boxes. Q. Sir W. C. Gull,
June 1, 106.

MAIL TRAIN DELAYS IN LIMERICK.
Q. Mr. Flavin ; A. Mr. Hanbury, June 19,
1491.

MALAGA AND DISTRICT.
Trade Report presented, June 15, 1168.

MALTA.
Nobility—Claim of Mr. G. A. Testaferrata
Q. Vis. Sidmouth ; A. Earl of Selborne.
June 15, 1169.
Political Condition—Despatch Ordered [Mr
M'Iver], June 8, 627.

MANCHESTER.
Owens College, Manchester, Bill. see that
Title.

Manchester Canonries Bill.
l. 1R.*, June 12, 888.

**Manchester Corporation [General Powers]
Bill.**
l. 2R.*, June 8, 595.

MANCHURIAN RAILWAY, see China.

" MANDAT-POSTE " SYSTEM.
Trial of, in England, suggested.
Q. Mr. Bill ; A. Mr. Anstruther, June 8.
659.

MAPLE, SIR J. B. [Camberwell, Dulwich.].
Service Franchise Bill, June 19, 1511 ; com.
June 7, 540 ; con. June 14, 1138, 1147,
1149.
Telegraph Service, Charges, etc., June 1.
130, 131.

MARRIAGE.
Farnley Tyas Marriages Bill, see that Title

Marriages Validity Bill.
l. 2R., June 6, 429.

MARYLEBONE POLICE COURT.
Street Obstruction, Prosecution of Carmen.
Q. Gen. Laurie ; A. Mr. Collings, June
15, 1184.

Maryport Harbour Bill.
l. Rep. from Select Com., June 8, 594.

MAURITIUS.
Sugar Industry.
Q. Mr. W. H. Holland; A. Mr. J. Chamberlain, June 13, 1063.

MAYO COUNTY.
Migration of Population—County Council Resolution.
Q. Dr. Ambrose; A. Mr. G. W. Balfour, June 6, 439.

MEAT INSPECTION AT LIVERPOOL.
Appointment of Unqualified Inspector.
Q. Mr. P. O'Brien; A. Mr. Chaplin, June 16, 1348.

MEDALS.
See Army.

MEDICAL PRACTITIONERS.
Dispensers, Unqualified, Accidents resulting from.
Q. Major Rasch; A. Sir J. Gorst, June 12, 901.

MEEHAN, DISTRICT INSPECTOR, CONDUCT OF.
Q. Mr. J. P. Farrell; A. Mr. G. W. Balfour, June 15, 1195.

MEERUT.
Connaught Rangers—Shooting Case.
Q. Mr. H. Roberts; A. Lord G. Hamilton, June 16, 1335.

MELLOR, COL. [Lancashire, Radcliffe].
Half-timers—Education of Children Bill, Com., May 31, 20, 49, 51, 52; 3R., June 14, 1133.

MENDL, MR. S. F. [Plymouth].
Local Loans, Repayment of, June 2, 231.

MERCHANT SEAMEN, see Seamen.

MERCHANT SEAMEN'S FUND.
Pensions, Vote for, June 1, 157; June 2, 287.
Winding-Up Act, Account presented, June 16, 1319, 1332.

MERCHANT SHIPPING.
Merchant Seamen's Fund, see that Title.
Pinner's Point, Navigation of.
Q. Mr. H. Wilson; A. Mr. Ritchie, June 12, 895.
Progress, Tables showing Progress Ordered [Mr. Ritchie], June 13, 1057.
Seamen, see that Title.

Mersey Docks and Harbour Board [Finance] Bill.
c. 2R.*, June 6, 431.

Mersey Docks and Harbour Board [Pilotage] Bill.
c. Rep. from Select com., June 12, 891.
2R.*, June 19, 1476.

MERTHYR TYDFIL.
Light Railway Order, Copy presented, May 31, 5; June 1, 69.

MESOPOTAMIA.
Railway Construction—British Interests in Persian Gulf.
Q. Mr. Maclean; A. Mr. Brodrick, June 8, 629.

39

MESSENGERS.
Foreign Service Messengers, Appointments.
Q. Sir C. Dilke; A. Mr. Brodrick, June 9, 762.
New Bliss Post Office Messenger, Salary of.
Q. Mr. Macaleese; A. Mr. Hanbury, June 12, 904.

Metropolis Management Acts Amendment [Bye-laws] Bill.
c. 2R.*, May, 31, 63.
Petition, June 5, 296.

Metropolitan Common Scheme [Harrow Weald] Provisional Order Bill.
l. 2R.*, June 9, 752.
Rep.*, June 12, 879.
3R.*, June 13, 994.

METROPOLITAN GAS COMPANIES.
Accounts, Copy presented, June 1, 69, 78.

METROPOLITAN POLICE, see Police.

Metropolitan Police Provisional Order Bill.
l. Royal Assent, June 6, 409.

Metropolitan Sewers and Drains Bill [Mr. J. Stewart, etc.].
c. 1R.*, May 31, 64.

METROPOLITAN STREET OBSTRUCTION.
Marylebone Police Court, Prosecution of Carmen.
Q. General Laurie; A. Mr. Collings, June 15, 1184.

METROPOLITAN VOLUNTEER REVIEW.
See Volunteers.

METROPOLITAN WATER COMPANIES.
Return ordered [Mr. T. W. Russell], June 9, 762.

Metropolitan Water Companies Bill.
l. Royal Assent, June 6, 409.

Mid-Kent Gas Bill.
c. 2R.*, May 31, 2.
Rep.*, June 9, 758.
con.*, June 14, 1089.
3R.*, June 19, 1475.

MIDDLEMORE, MR. [Birmingham, N.].
Half-timers— Education of Children Bill, com., May 31, 20.
Pauper Children—Barrack School System, etc., June 2, 254.

MIDDLESBROUGH.
Stockton and Middlesbrough Water Bill, see that Title.

MIDDLESEX.
Light Railway Order, Copy presented, May 31, 5; June 1, 69.

Midland and South Western Junction Railway Bill.
l. 2R.*, June 2, 161.

MIGRATION OF POPULATION [Ireland].
Mayo Co.—County Council Resolution.
Q. Dr. Ambrose; A. Mr. G. W. Balfour, June 6, 439.

MILITARY, see Army.

MILITARY DISTRICT, CORK.
Stores Contracts, Complaints.
Q. Capt. Donelan; A. Mr. J. P. Williams, June 19, 1482.

Military Lands Provisional Order Bill.
c. 2R.*, June 6, 432.
Rep.*, June 16, 1329.
con.*, June 19, 1477.

MILITARY WORKS.
Expenditure for 1899—1900 under existing Loans, Estimates presented, June 19, 1456, 1479.

MILITIA.
Guernsey Militia -Insubordination.
Qs. Maj. Rasch; Mr. R. G. Webster; As. Mr. J. P. Williams, June 19, 1481.
Longford Headquarters, Removal to Mullingar.
Q. Mr. J. P. Farrell; A. Mr. Wyndham, June 13, 1058.

Millwall Dock Bill.
c. 2R.*, June 19, 1476.

MILNER, SIR A.—Conference with President Kruger, see Transvaal, Uitlanders' Grievances.

MILLS, MR.—Comptroller and Auditor General, Retirement of.
Q. Mr. McKenna; A. Mr. A. J. Balfour, June 1, 83.

Milton Creek Conservancy Bill.
l. 2R.*, June 8, 595.

MILWARD, COL. V. [Warwick, Stratford-upon-Avon].
Dum-Dum Bullet—Issue of to Troops in India, June 5, 301.
Local Government Board, Inquiries, June 2, 280.
" Most Favoured Nation " Clause—United States Treaties, June 9, 763.

MINERAL RIGHTS.
Hyderabad State—Prospectuses.
Q. Sir A. Scoble; A. Lord G. Hamilton, June 8, 643.

Mines [Eight Hours] Bill.
Petitions, May 31, 4; June 1, 78; June 2, 174; June 5, 296; June 6, 433; June 7, 528; June 9, 760, 891.
MINT, Vote for, June 1, 158.

MONAGHAN, Union Medical Officer.
Q. Mr. Macaleese; A. Mr. G. W. Balfour, June 16, 1350.

MONEY BY POST.
" Mandat-Poste " System, Trial of, in England suggested.
Q. Mr. Bill; A. Mr. Anstruther, June 8, 659.

Money-Lending Bill.
Petition, June 5, 296.
Qs. Mr. Ancroft; Capt. Chaloner; As. Mr. A. J. Balfour, June 8, 659.

MONK, MR. C. J. [Gloucester].
Post Office, Employees' Grievances—Committee of Inquiry proposed, June 1, 114.

MONSON, LORD—Sat first, after the Death of his Brother, June 8, 593.

MONTAGU, SIR S. [Tower Hamlets, Whitechapel].
London Government Bill, con., June 8, 708.

MONTENEGRO.
Withdrawal from International Union, Treaty presented, June 9, 761; June 12, 880.

MOON, MR. E. R. P. [St. Pancras, N.].
China, Affairs of, June 9, 842.
London Government Bill, con., June 6, 460, 461.

MOORE, MR. A. J. [Londonderry].
Agriculture and Technical Instruction [Ireland Bill]—Business of the House, June 19, 1522.

MOORE, MR. W. [Antrim, N.].
Dublin Corporation Bill, con., June 13, 1040.
Tithe Rent-Charge, Ireland, Redemption of, June 1, 84.

MORGAN, MR. J. L. [Carmarthen, W.].
Carmarthen Charities—Delay in Publication of Report, June 19, 1487.

MORLEY, EARL OF [Chairman of Committees].
Death Duties—Indefinite Liability for Estate Duty—Endorsements on Registered Titles, June 13, 997.
Electric Lighting Provisional Order Bills—Course of Procedure, June 9, 751.

MORLEY, RT. HON. J. [Montrose, etc.].
Kitchener, Lord, Grant to.
Mahdi's Body, Treatment of, June 5, 337.
Method of Procedure, June 2, 186.

MORRISON, MR.—Moy Postmaster, Candidate for Petty Sessions Clerkship.
Q. Mr. W. Johnston; A. Mr. Hanbury, June 16, 1343.

Moss Side Urban District Council [Tramways] Bill.
l. 3R.*, June 2, 162.
c. 1R.*, June 5, 326.
2R.*, June 14, 1089.

" MOST FAVOURED NATION " CLAUSE—United States Treaties.
Q. Col. Milward; A. Mr. Brodrick, June 9, 763.

MOTORS IN THE NAVY, CONTROL OF.
Q. Sir F. Flannery; A. Mr. Goschen, June 8, 632.

MOULTON, MR. J. F. [Cornwall, Launceston].
Private Legislation Procedure [Scotland] Bill, com., June 19, 1535.

MOUNTAIN ARTILLERY.
Officers—Armament Pay.
Q. Capt. Pretyman; A. Mr. Wyndham, June 15, 1175.

MOUNTAIN ARTILLERY—cont.
Officers' Right of Fall, Re-establishment.
Q. Mr. Arnold-Forster; A. Mr. Wyndham, June 16, 1333.
MOUNTJOY POSTAL ARRANGEMENTS.
Q. Mr. Doogan; A. Mr. Hanbury, June 9, 773.
MOY POSTMASTER—Candidate for Petty Sessions Clerkship.
Q. Mr. W. Johnston; A. Mr. Hanbury, June 16, 1343.
MUCKROSS ESTATE, SALE OF.
Qs. Mr. Lough, Mr. MacNeill; As. Mr. A. J. Balfour, June 19, 1501.
MULLINGAR.
Longford Militia Headquarters, Removal to Mullingar.
Q. Mr. J. P. Farrell; A. Mr. Wyndham, June 13, 1068.
Lunatic Asylum Board.
Building Expenditure, etc.
Q. Mr. J. P. Farrell; A. Mr. G. W. Balfour, June 19, 1499.
Joint Committee.
Q. Mr. J. P. Farrell; A. Mr. G. W. Balfour, June 13, 1076.
MUNICIPAL CORPORATIONS.
Borough Funds Act—Petitions, June 1, 3, 70, 78; June 2, 163, 173; June 6, 414; June 7, 537; June 9, 759; June 13, 1055.
Smethwick, Charter of Incorporation presented, June 14, 1091; June 15, 1168.
MUNICIPAL LOANS, see Loans.
MUNICIPAL TRADING—Appointment of Committee.
Q. Mr. Bartley; A. Mr. A. J. Balfour, June 8, 661.
MURRAY, RT. HON. A. G.—Lord Advocate [Buteshire].
Aberdeen Cemetery Scandal, June 19, 1487.
Education.
Circulars, June 8, 635.
Finance, Secondary Education, etc., June 16, 1419, 1443.
Grant, June 16, 1339.
Orphan Homes.
Education of Children, June 12, 896.
Non-Education of Children, June 16, 1339, 1432.
Pensions to Teachers, June 9, 773.
Glasgow, Bakery Dispute—Case of A. M'Naughton, June 19, 1486.
Private Legislation Procedure [Scotland] Expenses, June 12, 909.
Private Legislation Procedure [Scotland] Bill, com., June 12, 914, 919, 920, 922, 923, 930, 931, 939, 940, 942, 945, 952, 958, 959, 960, 963, 974, 978, 984; June 19, 1531, 1534, 1536, 1538, 1539, 1540, 1542, 1543, 1549, 1550, 1551, 1554, 1562, 1564, 1568, 1570, 1571, 1572, 1573, 1576, 1578, 1583, 1585, 1586, 1589, 1591, 1593.
Succession [Scotland] Bill, 2R., June 7, 591.
Universities—Number of Students, June 12, 896.
MUSCAT INCIDENT.
Papers Relating to.
Q. Sir C. Dilke; A. Mr. Brodrick, June 8, 627.

NANKING.
Rice, Export of, prohibited.
Q. Mr. Provand; A. Mr. Brodrick, June 13, 1065.
NATAL.
Boers, alleged arming by Transvaal Government.
Q. Sir A. Hickman; A. Mr. J. Chamberlain, June 13, 1061.
NATIONAL DEBT.
Annuities, Purchase of.
Q. Mr. J. P. Smith; A. Sir M. Hicks-Beach, June 16, 1340.
Office, Vote for, June 1, 158.
Sinking Fund, Account presented, June 2, 169.
Trustee Savings Banks, see that Title.
NATIONAL PORTRAIT GALLERY.
Report presented, June 7, 539; June 8, 596.
NATIONAL SCHOOL TEACHERS, IRELAND.
Assistant Teachers and the Pension Fund.
Q. Mr. Flavin; A. Mr. G. W. Balfour, June 19, 1494.
Examinations.
Q. Mr. Davitt; A. Mr. G. W. Balfour, June 12, 902.
Guardians, Teachers as—Case of Mr. Kenny.
Q. Mr. Tully; A. Mr. G. W. Balfour, June 5, 304.
Salaries, Classification of.
Q. Mr. Macaleese; A. Mr. G. W. Balfour, June 6, 438.
Ulster and Connaught.
Q. Mr. Field; A. Mr. G. W. Balfour, June 13, 1070.
NATURALISATION.
British Subjects—Transvaal Oath of Allegiance.
Q. Mr. B. Roberts; A. Mr. J. Chamberlain, June 16, 1337.
Certificates, obtaining from Secretary of State.
Q. Mr. MacNeill; A. Mr. J. Collings, June 15, 1185.
NAVIGATION OF MERCHANT VESSELS.
Q. Mr. H. Wilson; A. Mr. Ritchie, June 12, 895.
NAVY.
First Lord—Rt. Hon. G. J. Goschen.
Secretary—Mr. W. E. Macartney.
Boilers, Water-tube.
Q. Sir J. Fergusson; A. Mr. Goschen, June 8, 633.
Contracts—New Form.
Q. Mr. E. Robertson; A. Mr. Macartney, June 19, 1480.
Exmouth Training Ship, see that Title.
Motors, Electric, Control of.
Q. Sir F. Flannery; A. Mr. Goschen, June 8, 632.
Records of not sufficient value to justify their preservation, Schedule presented, June 1, 70.
Reserve, Number of Men, etc.
Q. Sir E. Gourley; A. Mr. Goschen, June 6, 435.

[Continue

NAVY—*cont.*
 Retired Officers and Civil Employment—
 Return.
  Q. Capt. Norton; A. Mr. Anstruther,
  June 8, 657.
 Squadron—Visit to China.
  Q. Mr. Hedderwick; A. Mr. Goschen,
  June 9, 776.

NETHERAVON HOUSE.
 Non-occupation of, by the War Office.
  Q. Mr. Goulding; A. Mr. Wyndham,
  June 6, 442.

NEW GUINEA, BRITISH.
 Papers relating to.
  Q. Sir J. Lubbock; A. Mr. J. Chamber-
  lain, June 6, 440.

NEW MEMBER SWORN.
 Pilkington, Sir G., June 1, 87.

NEW WRITS.
 Edinburgh:
  East Division, June 13, 1078.
  South Division, June 9, 762.
 Yorkshire, W. R. [Osgoldcross], June 19,
  1474.

NEWBIGGIN-BY-THE-SEA FISHERIES.
 Destruction of Fishing Gear, etc., by Trawlers, Alleged.
  Q. Mr. Fenwick; A. Mr. Ritchie, June
  8, 635.

NEWRLISS POST OFFICE—Messenger's Salary.
  Q. Mr. Macaleese; A. Mr. Hanbury, June
  12, 904.

NEWCASTLE WEST CREAMERY, Sewer Com-
 plaint.
  Q. Mr. Austin; A. Mr. G. W. Balfour,
  June 15, 1193.

NEWFOUNDLAND FISHERIES REPORT.
  Qs. Sir T. G. Carmichael, Mr. Bowles;
  As. Mr. J. Chamberlain, June 16, 1338.

NICE AND DISTRICT.
 Trade Report presented, June 8, 596.

NICOL, MR. D. N. [Argyll].
 Lighthouse Keepers' Emoluments, June 9,
 770.

NIGER.
 Annual Report [West African Frontier
 Force] presented, June 1, 69; June 2,
 170.

Norfolk Estuary Bill.
 c. 3R.*, June 2, 167.

North-Eastern Railway Bill.
 l. Rep.*, June 2, 161.
  3R.. June 6, 411.
 c. 1R.*, June 8, 625.
  2R.*, June 19, 1476.

NORTH-EASTERN RAILWAY SIGNALMEN—Hours
 of Labour.
  Q. Sir F. Flannery; A. Mr. Ritchie, June
  8, 634.

**North-Eastern and Hull and Barnsley
 Railways [Joint Dock] Bill.**
 l. Rep.*, June 2, 161.
  3R., June 6, 411.
 c. 1R.*, June 8, 625.
  2R.*, June 19, 1476.

**North Pembrokeshire and Fishguard
 Railway Bill.**
 l. 2R.*, June 8, 595.
  Rep.*, June 12, 877.
  3R.*, June 15, 1166.

NORTH SEA FISHERMEN.
 Return presented, June 14, 1091.

North Staffordshire Railway Bill.
 l. Rep. from Select com., June 19, 1454.

North-West London Railway Bill.
 l. Rep.*, June 12, 878.

Northern Assurance Company Bill.
 l. Royal Assent, June 6, 409.

NORTHERN LIGHTHOUSES, COMMISSIONERS OF.
 Increase in Clerical Establishment—Order
 in Council presented, June 6, 413, 434.

NORTON, CAPT. C. W. [Newington, West].
 Army and Navy Officers, Retired—Civil
 Employment, Return, June 8, 657.
 Civil Service—Pay Deductions, June 2, 177
 London Government Bill, con., June 6. 482
 Metropolitan Police, Recruits, etc., June 8
 640.
 Post Office—Employees' and Telegraphists'
 Grievances, June 1, 104, 120.
 Service Franchise Bill, con., June 14, 1142,
 1143.
 Reformatory Schools Amendment Bill, 2R.,
 June 8, 614.

NORTON, LORD.
 Youthful Offenders Bill, 2R., June 19, 1463.

NOTTING HILL.
 Kensington and Notting Hill Electric Lighting Bill, see that Title.

Nottingham Corporation Bill.
 l. com.*, June 8, 593.
  Rep.*, June 16, 1317.
  Royal Assent, June 6, 409.

NUSSEY, MR. T. W. [Pontefract].
 Intoxicating Liquors [Sunday Closing] Bill,
 2R., June 7, 550.

OATH OF ALLEGIANCE.
 Transvaal — Naturalisation of British Subjects.
  Q. Mr. B. Roberts; A. Mr. J. Chamberlain, June 16, 1337.

O'BRIEN, MR. P. [Kilkenny].
 Blind, State Aid for, June 12, 906; June
 16, 1348.
 Castletown Berehaven Pier, Removal of
 Silt, June 12, 906.
 Dublin Postmen's Grievances, June 16, 1345.
 Ferrybank Post Office and Postmastership,
 June 16, 1344.
 Fish Traffic on Railways—English and Irish
 Railways, June 16, 1358.

O'BRIEN, MR. P.—cont.

Fishing Prosecution in Ireland—Case of P. Comerford, June 16, 1358.
Kildare Street Library, handing over to new department, June 16, 1350.
Limerick Sorting Clerks, dismissal of, June 12, 905.
Meat Inspection at Liverpool—Appointment of Unqualified Inspector, June 16, 1348.
Oughterard Union, Fever Outbreak, June 16, 1357.
Post Office, Irish—Superior Appointments, June 16, 1346.
Science, Royal College of, Dublin—Building Control, etc., June 16, 1350.
Sub-Postmasters, Scale of Payment, June 16, 1344.

O'CONNOR, MR. J. [Wicklow, West].

Loan Fund Board, Ireland—Illegalities, June 9, 764.

O'CONOR, SIR N.—Purchase of the Bagot Estate.

Q. Mr. Hayden; A. Mr. G. W. Balfour, June 15, 1188.

O'DONNELL, DOMINICK—Inmate of Belmullet Union.

Q. Mr. Crilly; A. Mr. G. W. Balfour, June 13, 1074.

Oldham Corporation Bill.

c. 2R.*, May 31, 2.

OLDHAM TELEGRAPHIC MESSAGES—Delay in Transit.

Q. Mr. Ascroft; A. Mr. Anstruther, June 8, 658.

OMAN—Muscat Incident, Papers relating to.

Q. Sir C. Dilke; A. Mr. Brodrick, June 8, 627.

OMDURMAN, BATTLE OF, see Soudan Campaign.

ORDNANCE FACTORY, ENFIELD—Divine Service in Government Chapels — Ritualistic Practices.

Qs. Mr. Channing, Mr. C. Williams; As. Mr. Wyndham, June 12, 898.

ORPHAN HOMES.

Infant Orphan Asylum Bill, see that Title.
Scotland—Education of Children.
Qs. Sir C. Cameron; As. Mr. A. G. Murray, June 12, 896; June 16, 1338.
S. June 16, 1429, 1432, 1434, 1442.
Kilmalcolm School Board, S., June 16, 1437.

OSGOLDCROSS, NEW WRIT FOR, June 19, 1474.

OUGHTERARD UNION—Fever Outbreak.

Q. Mr. P. O'Brien; A. Mr. G. W. Balfour, June 16, 1357.

Owens College, Manchester, Bill.

l. 2R.*, June 8, 595.
Rep.*, June 16, 1317.
Report presented, June 8, 593.

PACIFIC CABLE SCHEME.

Q. Mr. Hogan; A. Mr. J. Chamberlain, June 13, 1063.

43

PACIFIC ISLANDS.

Tonga, see that Title.
Trade Report presented, June 1, 68.

Paisley and Barrhead District Railway Bill.

c. 2R.*, June 7, 537.

PALMER, MR. G. W. [Reading].

Reading Public Vaccinator—Remuneration, June 16, 1349.

PARAGUAY TRADE REPORT PRESENTED, June 1, 68.

PARIS EXHIBITION.

British Works of Art, Space allotted to.
Q. Mr. Courtney; A. Mr. Hanbury, June 15, 1186.

Parish Churches [Scotland] Bill.

Petitions, June 2, 174; June 7, 538.

Parish Councillors [Tenure of Office] Bill.

l. 3R.*, June 2, 164.
Commons Amendts.*, June 9, 754.
c. Lords Amendts.*, June 8, 663.

Parish Councils Association [Scotland] Bill.

Petitions, June 12, 891, 1090.

"PARLIAMENTARY DEBATES."

Delay in Publication—Statement as to new Contract.
Qs. Sir C. Cameron, Mr. R. G. Webster, Mr. Channing; As. Mr. Hanbury, June 5, 303.

Parliamentary Deposits Bill.

Q. Mr. Tomlinson; A. Sir R. Webster, June 5, 306.

PARLIAMENTARY ELECTIONS.

By-Elections, see that Title.
Peers' Interference, see Peers.

PARLIAMENTARY FRANCHISE.

Extension to Women—Petition, June 9, 760.
Poor Law Relief, Disfranchisement, see that Title.

PASTEUR INSTITUTE, INDIA.

Government Grant, etc., proposed.
Q. Sir W. Wedderburn; A. Lord G. Hamilton, June 8, 643.

PATRIOTIC FUND.

Lewis, Mrs., Case of.
Q. Mr. Spicer; A. Mr. G. Wyndham, June 8, 632.

PAUPER CHILDREN, see Poor Law Children.

PEACE CONFERENCE.

O. Lord Charles Beresford, June 9, 798.
Armenians, Distressed.
Q. Mr. S. Smith; A. Mr. Brodrick, June 12, 894.
Dum-Dum Bullet, Prohibition Resolution.
Q. Mr. Dillon; A. Mr. A. J. Balfour, June 5, 308.

PEASE, MR. J. A. [Northumberland, Tyneside].
    Ansahs of Ashanti—Compensation, etc.,
        June 15, 1180.
    Slavery in Zanzibar, June 9, 872.

PEERS—Sat First.
    Beaufort, Duke of, after the death of
        his father, June 13, 993.
    Exeter, Marquess of, after the death of
        his father, June 2, 161.
    Monson, Lord, after the death of his
        brother, June 8, 593.

PEERS' INTERFERENCE AT ELECTIONS.
    Southport Election—Duke of Devonshire,
        etc.
        Q. Mr. J. Lowther; A. Mr. A. J.
            Balfour, June 5, 307.
        Motion [Mr. J. Lowther] June 5. 311.

PEKIN AND MANCHURIAN RAILWAY, see China.

PEMBROKE DOCK—Delay in Delivery of Letters.
    O. Gen. Laurie, June 1, 125.

PENSIONS.
    Army, Special Pensions, Returns pre-
        sented, June 13, 1056, 1167.
    London, Brighton and South Coast Rail-
        way [Pensions] Bill, see that Title.
    Scottish School Teachers.
        Q. Mr. Buchanan; A. Mr. A. G. Murray,
            June 9, 773.

PERCY, EARL [Kensington, South].
    China, Affairs of—British Government
        Policy, etc., June 9, 847.
    London Government Bill. 3R.—Qualifica-
        tion of Women, June 13, 1082.
    Waima Incident—Compensation Claims,
        June 9, 845.

PERNAMBUCO AND DISTRICT.
    Trade Report presented, June 15, 1168.

PERSIA.
    Russian Railway Construction—Expiration
        of Agreement, etc.
        Q. Mr. Maclean; A. Mr. Brodrick,
            June 8, 628.
    Trade Report presented, June 19, 1456.

PERSIAN GULF.
    British Interests—Railway Concessions to
        German Capitalists.
        Q. Mr. Maclean; A. Mr. Brodrick,
            June 8, 629.

PERTH WATER, POLICE, AND GAS BILL.
    l. Royal Assent, June 6, 409.

PETITIONS.
    Committee, Report presented, May 31, 64;
        June 7, 592.
    For Subjects and Bills Petitioned, see their
        Titles.

PETROLEUM—Legislation.
    Q. Mr. Tully; A. Sir M. W. Ridley, June
        9, 770.

PETTY SESSIONS CLERKSHIP OF MOY.
    Candidature of Postmaster.
        Q. Mr. W. Johnston; A. Mr. Hanbury.
            June 16, 1343.

44

PHŒNIX PARK MURDERER, RELEASE.
    Q. Mr. J. Lowther; A. Mr. G. W. Balfour,
        June 5, 299.

PICCADILLY CIRCUS.
    Brompton and Piccadilly Circus Railway
        Bill, see that Title.

PICKERSGILL, MR. E. H. [Bethnal Green,
    S.W.].
    London Government Bill, con., June 6,
        462, 464, 479, 501, 510; June 8, 721.
        729, 730.
    Vaccination—Distribution of. Literature
        of Jenner Society, June 2, 191.
    Vaccination Officers and the Guardians,
        Relations between, June 2, 188.

Pier and Harbour Provisional Orders [No.
    1] Bill.
    c. Rep.*, June 9, 757.
        con.*, June 12, 890.
        3R.*, June 13, 1054.
    l. 1R.*, June 15, 1167.

Pier and Harbour Provisional Order [No.
    2] Bill.
    c. 2R.*, June 2, 168.

PIERPOINT, MR. R. [Warrington].
    Cyprus, Grant in Aid, June 19, 1502.
    Turkish Loan 1885, June 13, 1065.

PILKINGTON, COL. [Lancashire, Newton].
    Half-timers—Education of Children Bill.
        com., May 31, 12, 22, 55.

PILOTAGE.
    Mersey Docks and Harbour Board [Pilot-
        age] Bill, see that Title.

Pilotage Provisional Order Bill.
    l. com.*, June 1, 66.
    Rep.*, June 5, 290.
    3R.*, June 6, 413.

"PINNER'S POINT," ss., NAVIGATION OF.
    Q. Mr. H. Wilson; A. Mr. Ritchie, June
        12, 895.

PIRIE, MR. D. V. [Aberdeen, N.].
    Khartoum Prisoners, release of, June 2,
        178.
    Kitchener, Lord, Grant to—Treatment of
        the Mahdi's Body, etc., June 5, 377.
    Soudanese Troops, Fever among, June 2,
        179.

PLUMBERS' REGISTRATION.
    Legislation.
        Motion [Mr. Knowles], June 13, 1087.

POLICE [IRELAND].
    Constabulary, Royal Irish, see that Title.
    Dublin Metropolitan Police—Summer
        Clothing.
        Q. Mr. Crilly; A. Mr. G. W. Balfour,
            June 13, 1074.

POLICE, METROPOLITAN.
    Metropolitan Police Provisional Order
        Bill, see that Title.
    Recruits, etc.
        Q. Capt. Norton; A. Sir M. W. Ridley.
            June 8, 640.

POLITICAL PRISONERS, IRELAND.

Release of Phœnix Park Murderer.
Q. Mr. J. Lowther; A. Mr. G. W.
Balfour, June 5, 299.

POLLING DISTRICTS.

Carnarvon County—County Council Order
presented, June 1, 70, 79.

POOR LAW AMENDMENT [SCOTLAND] ACT, 1845.

Petition for alteration of Law, June 15, 1175.

POOR LAW CHILDREN.

Barrack School System, etc., S., June 2,
231, 239, 250, 251, 254, 258.
Boarding-out System, S., June 2, 235, 237,
239, 240, 250, 254.
Block System, S., June 1, 239, 262.
Cottage Home System, S., June 2, 250, 253,
259.
Education in Poor Law Schools, S., June 2,
242, 244, 254.
Control under Education Department,
S., June 2, 243, 246, 249, 257.
Q. Mr. Stuart; A. Mr. T. W.
Russell, June 1, 82.
Emigration to Canada, S., June 2, 237, 246,
264.
Orphan Homes, see that Title.
Sutton School Children. Begging on Derby
Day, S., June 2, 247, 256.

POOR LAW GUARDIANS.

Ireland—National School Teachers as
Guardians—Case of Mr. Kenny.
Q. Mr. Tully; A. Mr. G. W. Balfour,
June 5, 304.

POOR LAW MEDICAL OFFICER—Monaghan.

Q. Mr. Macaleese; A. Mr. G. W. Balfour,
June 16, 1350.

Poor Law Officers' Superannuation [Scotland] Bill.

Petitions, June 2, 174; June 7, 538;
June 12, 891.

POOR LAW RELIEF—Disfranchisement.

Petitions for alteration of Law, June 5,
297; June 6, 433; June 8, 625; June 12,
891; June 16, 1332.

POOR LAW SCHOOLS.

Education in, see Poor Law Children.

POOR LAW [SCOTLAND] ACTS.

Petition for Alteration of Law, June 12,
892.

POOR RATE, IRELAND.

New System—Landlord and Tenant Agreement.
Q. Mr. Tully; A. Mr. G. W. Balfour,
June 9, 768.

Port Talbot Railway and Docks Bill.

c. 2R.*, June 6, 431.

PORTRAIT GALLERY, NATIONAL.

Report presented, June 7, 539; June 8, 596.

Portsmouth Corporation Bill.

1. com.*, June 2, 161.

POST CARDS.

Cost of.
Q. Mr. Flavin; A. Mr. Hanbury, June
16, 1343.
Thin Post Cards for Commercial Purposes.
Q. Sir R. Hanson; A. Mr. Hanbury,
June 12, 904.

POST OFFICE.

Postmaster-General—Duke of Norfolk.
American Mail Service—Return.
Q. Sir J. Leng; A. Mr. Hanbury, June 6,
437.
Buildings, Insanitary Condition of.
O. Mr. Maddison, June 1, 112.
Clapham Sorting Office Vacancies.
Q. Mr. Steadman; A. Mr. Hanbury, June
1, 81.
Dorsetshire Deliveries.
Q. Col. Welby; A. Mr. Hanbury, June
5, 302.
East Central District Staff, Petition.
Q. Mr. M'Ghee; A. Mr. Hanbury, June
12, 904.
Employees' Grievances, S., June 1, 99.
Committee of Inquiry proposed, S., June
1, 108, 112, 114, 115.
Irish Questions.
Ballyduff.
Q. Mr. Flavin; A. Mr. Hanbury, June
19, 1494.
Ballymahon Postal Arrangements.
Q. Mr. Hayden; A. Mr. Hanbury, June
19, 1491.
Bawnboy Postman.
Q. Mr. J. P. Farrell; A. Mr. Hanbury,
June 13, 1068.
Belfast Staff.
Q. Mr. Schwann; A. Mr. Hanbury,
June 13, 1069.
Q. Mr. Macaleese; A. Mr. Hanbury,
June 19, 1490.
Dublin General Post Office. Officials'
Grievances, S., June 2, 284.
Enniskillen Post Office — Plans and
Tenders.
Q. Mr. Jordan; A. Mr. Hanbury,
June 19, 1492.
Fintona Sunday Mails.
Q. Mr. Dillon; A. Mr. Hanbury, June
19, 1488.
Kerry, North, Letter Deliveries.
Q. Mr. Flavin; A. Mr. Hanbury, June
19, 1489.
Lanesborough Postal Arrangements, Complaint.
Q. Mr. Hayden; A. Mr. Hanbury,
June 19, 1493.
Limerick Mail Train Delays.
Q. Mr. Flavin; A. Mr. Hanbury, June
19, 1491.
Limerick Sorting Clerks, dismissal of.
Q. Mr. P. O'Brien; A. Mr. Hanbury,
June 12, 905.
Lough Rynn Letter Deliveries, Complaint.
Q. Mr. Tully; A. Mr. Hanbury, June
13, 1068.

[Continued

POST OFFICE—*cont.*

Lurgan New Post Office.
Q. Mr. M'Ghee; A. Mr. Hanbury, June 9, 774.

Mountjoy Evening Collection.
Q. Mr. Doogan; A. Mr. Hanbury, June 9, 773.

Newbliss Messenger, Salary of,
Q. Mr. Macaleese; A. Mr. Hanbury. June 12, 904.

Postmen and Postmasters, see those Titles.

Superior Appointments.
Q. Mr. P. O'Brien; A. Mr. Hanbury, June 16, 1345.

Mail Service, see that Title.

"Mandat-Poste" System, Trial of, in England, suggested.
Q. Mr. Bill; A. Mr. Anstruther, June 8, 659.

Military and Naval Men, Employment of, S., June 1, 127.

Post Cards, Postmen, etc., see those Titles.

Salaries of Clerks.
Q. Mr. Yoxall; A. Mr. Hanbury, June 6, 437.

Telegraphists, see that Title.

Vote for, June 1, 99; June 2, 284.

POST OFFICE PACKET SERVICE.
Vote for, June 1, 130; June 2. 285.

POSTAGE.

Circulars, Cost of Postage in Bandon and Clone.
Q. Mr. E. Barry; A. Mr. Hanbury, June 16, 1342.

POSTMASTERS.

Dundalk Vacancy.
Q. Mr. Macaleese; A. Mr. Hanbury, June 19, 1490.

Ferrybank Postmastership.
Q. Mr. P. O'Brien; A. Mr. Hanbury, June 16, 1344.

Moy Postmaster—Candidate for Petty Sessions Clerkship.
Q. Mr. W. Johnston; A. Mr. Hanbury, June 16, 1343.

Sub-postmasters.

Rural Postmen assisting.
Q. Mr. Steadman; A. Mr. Hanbury, June 15, 1187.

Scale of Payment.
Q. Mr. P. O'Brien; A. Mr. Hanbury, June 16, 1344.

POSTMEN.

Christmas Boxes.
O. Mr. Steadman, June 1, 102.

Irish Questions.

Bawnboy.
Q. Mr. J. P. Farrell; A. Mr. Hanbury, June 13, 1068.

Dublin Postmen's Grievances.
Q. Mr. P. O'Brien; A. Mr. Hanbury, June 16, 1345.

Pay, Higher Grade Test.
Q. Mr. Giles; A. Mr. Hanbury, June 9, 774.

Rural Postmen assisting in Sub-postmaster's Office.
Q. Mr. Steadman; A. Mr. Hanbury, June 15, 1187.

Strikes.
O. Mr. Steadman, June 1, 102.

POSTMEN—*cont.*

Strikes.
O. Mr. Steadman June 1, 101.

Superannuations.
Clay, A. E., Retiring Allowance, Treasury Minute presented, June 19, 1479.
Muspratt, J., Appointment without Certificate—Treasury Minute presented. June 7, 539; June 8, 597.

Wages, Scale of.
O. Sir W. C. Gull, June 1, 106.

POWELL, SIR F. S. [Wigan].

Half-timers—Education of Children Bill, com., May 31, 11, 12, 27; 3R., June 14, 1106.

Loans, Municipal, Repayment of, June 2, 225.

London Government Bill, con., June 6, 505.
Private Legislation Procedure [Scotland] Bill, com., June 19, 1541.

PRESBYTERIAN SERVICES, Accommodation for Troops in.

Q. Mr. Hedderwick; A. Lord G. Hamilton, June 9, 772.

PRETYMAN, CAPT. [Suffolk, Woodbridge].

Business of the House, June 2, 187.
Half-timers—Education of Children Bill. com., May 31, 29, 39, 40. 47.
Mountain Artillery Officers — Armament Pay, June 15, 1175.

Prevention of Corruption Bill.

l. 2R., June 6, 414.
Rep.*, June 8, 617.

PRIMOGENITURE, LAW OF.

Succession [Scotland] Bill, see that Title.

PRISONS.

Military—Inspector-General's Report.
Q. Dr. Farquharson; A. Mr. Wyndham. June 8, 640.

Officials.

Appointments, Age Limit, etc.
Q. Mr. Graham; A. Sir M. W. Ridley, June 9, 769.

Retirement of.
Q. Mr. Lough; A. Sir M. W. Ridley. June 19, 1485.

PRIVATE BILLS [Group B].

Jaffray, W., Attendance on Committee Ordered, June 14, 1089.

PRIVATE LEGISLATION PROCEDURE [SCOTLAND].

EXPENSES, R. in Com. [Sir W. Walrond]. June 12, 908; Amendt. [Mr. T. Shaw], 909; Report, June 15, 1315.

Private Legislation Procedure [Scotland] Bill.

c. com., June 12, 910; June 19, 1531.
Petitions, June 1, 78; June 2, 174; June 6, 433; June 7, 538; June 9, 760, 892; June 14, 1090; June 16, 1332; June 19, 1478.

PRIVILEGES OF THE HOUSE, BREACH OF.

Peers' Interference in Southport Election—Duke of Devonshire, etc.
Q. Mr. J. Lowther; A. Mr. A. J. Balfour, June 5, 307; Motion [Mr. J. Lowther], June 5, 311.

PROMISSORY NOTES.

Finance Bill, Amendt. [Mr. Caldwell], June 8, 732.

PROSECUTION OF OFFENCES ACT, 1879, and 1884.

Return Ordered [Mr. Collings], June 2, 171.

PROVAND, MR. A. D. [Glasgow, Blackfriars].

China, Affairs of, June 1, 82; June 9, 853.
Rice Exports from Nanking, Prohibition of, June 13, 1065.

Provisional Orders Bills.

Procedure—Insertion of Names.
Q. Mr. Lloyd-George; A. Mr. Russell, June 2, 175.

Public Health Acts Amendment Bill.

c. Select Com., Nomination, May 31, 63.
Petitions, May 31, 4; June 1, 78; June 9, 760. 1056.

PUBLIC INCOME AND EXPENDITURE.

See Revenue and Expenditure of the United Kingdom.

PUBLIC LIBRARIES. see Libraries.

Public Libraries [Scotland] Acts Amendment Bill.

l. Royal Assent, June 6, 409.
Petition, June 2, 174.

PUBLIC PETITIONS, see Petitions.

PUBLIC RECORDS, see Records.

PUBLIC WORKS, LOANS FOR, S., June 2, 219, 223, 225, 226, 227, 231.

PUBLIC WORKS LOAN BOARD.

Report presented, June 9, 761, 880.

PUBLIC WORKS LOAN COMMISSIONERS.

Vote for, June 1, 158.

PUBLIC WORKS AND BUILDINGS.

Vote for, June 1, 159.

PUBLIC WORSHIP REGULATION AND CHURCH DISCIPLINE.

Return presented, June 7, 539.

PUNJAUB WAR MEDALS.

Distribution to Bengal Staff Corps.
Q. Mr. H. D. Greene; A. Mr. Wyndham, June 1, 31.
Q. Mr. H. D. Greene; A. Lord G. Hamilton, June 6, 443.

QUARTER SESSIONS.

Town Commissioners, Ireland, Chairman of —Solicitor losing right to practice at Quarter Sessions.
Q. Mr. M. Healy; A. Mr. G. W. Balfour, June 16, 1360.

QUEEN'S BIRTHDAY.

Southsea Celebrations—Cancelling Parade.
Q. Mr. Bowles; A. Mr. Wyndham, June 2, 180.

Queen's Ferry Bridge Bill.

c. 3R.*, June 1, 73.
l. commons amendts.. June 2, 162.
Royal Assent, June 6, 410.

QUEEN'S ISLAND RIOTS, see Belfast.

QUEENSLAND.

Colonial Probates Act, Order in Council presented, June 6, 414, 434.

QUILTER, SIR C. [Suffolk, Sudbury].

Beer Materials Committee—Substitutes for Hops, etc., June 15, 1183.

RAILWAY ACCIDENTS.

Desborough Level Crossing Fatality. Inquest—Board of Trade Representative.
Q. Mr. Channing; A. Mr. Ritchie, June 2, 181.
Fatal Accidents, Number of.
Q. Mr. Channing; A. Mr. Ritchie, June 2, 178.
Inniskeen.
Q. Mr. Macaleese; A. Mr. Ritchie, June 16, 1341.
Shunting Fatality on Chatham and Dover Railway.
Q. Mr. Maddison; A. Mr. Ritchie, June 15, 1183.

RAILWAY AND CANAL TRAFFIC ACT.

Board of Trade Report, June 6, 413, 434.

RAILWAYS:

Applications under Railway Companies' Powers Act, Report presented, June 14, 1091; June 15, 1168.
Bills relating to, see their Titles.
Continuous Brakes, Return presented, June 19, 1456, 1479.
Donegal, Railway Communication—County Council Resolution.
Q. Mr. T. D. Sullivan; A. Mr. G. W. Balfour, June 19, 1498
Fish Traffic—English and Irish Railways.
Q. Mr. P. O'Brien; A. Mr. G. W. Balfour. June 16, 1358.
Foreign Railways, see their Titles, such as Bechuanaland, etc.
Light Railways, see that Title.
Signalmen, North-Eastern Railway—Hours of Labour.
Q. Sir F. Flannery; A. Mr. Ritchie, June 8, 634.
Workmen's Trains, see that Title.

RANGOON, Outrage on Burmese Woman by British Soldiers, see India.

RASCH, MAJOR F. C. [Essex, S.E.].

Aldershot—Strength of the Troops on Queen's Birthday Parade, June 12, 899.
Dispensers, Unqualified, in Doctors' Surgeries—Accidents resulting from mistakes, June 12, 901.
Guernsey Militia—Insubordination, June 19, 1481.
Half-timers—Education of Children Bill, com., May 31, 34, 41; 3R., June 14, 1114.
Soudan Campaign—Thanks to the Forces, June 8, 685.

Rating of Machinery Bill.

Petition, June 7, 538.

[*Continued*

READING.
  Public Vaccinator—Remuneration Scale.
    Q. Mr. Palmer; A. Mr. Chaplin, June
    16, 1349.

RECKITT, MR. H. J. [Lincolnshire, Brigg].
    Business of the House—Precedence of
    Government Business, June 19, 1513,
    1526.

RECORD OFFICE, Vote for, June 1, 158.

RECORDS, PUBLIC.
    Records of not sufficient value to ustify
    their preservation—Schedules presented.
    Admiralty Department, June 1, 70.
    Court of Exchequer, June 12, 761, 880.
    Treasury, June 19, 1456, 1480.

RECRUITS, Bread Rations.
    Q. Mr. Hayden; A. Mr. Wyndham, June
    16, 1334.

Redditch Gas Bill.
    1. 2R.*, June 8, 595.

REDMOND, MR. J. E. [Waterford].
    Dublin Corporation Bill. con., June 13,
    1006, 1013.
    Irish Estimates—Business of the House.
    June 2, 187.

REDMOND, MR. W. H. K. [Clare, E.].
    Dublin Corporation Bill, con., June 13,
    1038.

REFORMATORIES.
    Inebriate Reformatories, see that Title.

Reformatory Schools Amendment Bill.
    1. 1R.*, June 5, 291.
    2R, June 8, 612.
    com., June 12, 888.

REFORMATORY AND INDUSTRIAL SCHOOLS.
    Ireland.
    Destitute Children, Committal of—
    Circular.
        Q. Capt. Donelan; A. Mr. G. W.
        Balfour, June 8, 648.
    School Attendance Committees' Powers.
        Q. Col. M'Calmont; A. Mr. G. W.
        Balfour, June 12, 901.
    Teachers' Superannuation—Extension to
    Masters and Matrons proposed.
    Q. Mr. Bill; A. Sir M. W. Ridley, June 12,
    901.

REGISTRAR-GENERAL OF BIRTHS.
    Vote for, June 1, 159.

Registration of Electors [England] Bill.
    c. 1R*, June 13. 1058.

Registration of Firms Bill.
    Petition, June 6, 433.

REILLY, REV. F. S., ESTATE OF, Delay in
    Sale.
    Q. Mr. S. Young; A. Mr. G. W. Balfour,
    June 15, 1195.

RELIGIOUS MINISTRATION IN WORKHOUSES.
    S., June 2, 267, 273, 274, 278.

RENSHAW, MR. C. B. [Renfrew, W.].
    Private Legislation Procedure [Scotland]
    Bill, com., June 12, 932; June 19, 1541,
    1552, 1590.
    Quarrier's Homes, Education of Children,
    Kilmalcolm School Board, etc., June 16,
    1437.
    Secondary Education, Scotland, June 16.
    1382.

RESERVE, NAVAL, Number of Men, etc.
    Q. Sir E. Gourley; A. Mr. G. J. Goschen,
    June 6, 435.

RETIRED AND DISCHARGED SOLDIERS, see
    Soldiers.

REVENUE AND EXPENDITURE OF THE UNITED
    KINGDOM, Return Ordered [Sir H. Fowler].
    June 16, 1333.

RHODES, MR., AND MR. J. CHAMBERLAIN.
    Q. Mr. B. Roberts; A. Mr. J. Chamber-
    lain, June 15, 1182.

Rhondda Urban District Council Bill.
    1. Rep. from Select Com., June 13. 993.
    3R.*, June 19, 1454.

RICE—Exports from Nanking prohibited.
    Q. Mr. Provand; A. Mr. Brodrick, June
    13, 1065.

RICHARDS, MR. H. C. [Finsbury, E.].
    Private Legislation Procedure [Scotland]
    Bill, com., June 12, 975.
    Wine and Beerhouse Acts Amendment Bill.
    2R, June 7. 582.

RICKMANSWORTH.
    Uxbridge and Rickmansworth Railway Bill.
    see that Title.

RIDLEY, RT. HON. SIR M. W.—Secretary of
    State for Home Department [Lancashire.
    Blackpool].
    Bethnal Green New Board Schools—Re-
    moval of Working Class Dwellings.
    June 12, 900.
    Blind State aid for, June 12, 906.
    Garston, Fatal Accident to Dock
    Labourer, June 9, 770.
    Jam Factories, Labour in, June 5, 298.
    Petroleum Bill, June 9, 770.
    Police. Metropolitan, Recruits, etc., June
    8, 641.
    Prison Officials, Appointments. Pro-
    motions and Retirements, June 9, 769;
    June 19, 1485.
    School Teachers' Superannuation, June
    12, 901.

RIFLE RANGES.

Ranges closed to firing of full-charge ammu-
nition, etc., Address for Return [Mr. F.
Wilson], June 19, 1480.
Youghal, Repairs, etc.
Q. Capt. Donelan; A. Mr. Wyndham,
June 9, 771.

RIO DE JANEIRO.

British Seamen and the Liquor Traffic.
Q. Mr. Hogan; A. Mr. Ritchie, June 13,
1066.
Trade Report presented, June 8, 596.

RIOTS IN IRELAND, see Belfast and Cookstown.

RIPON, MARQUESS OF.

Indenturing in Western Australia—Abolition
of Aborigines Protection Board, June 16,
1322, 1325.

RITCHIE, RT. HON. C. T.—President of the
Board of Trade [Croydon]:
Blackhead Lighthouse, June 2, 180;
June 8, 634.
Desborough Level Crossing Fatality,
Inquest—Board of Trade Representa-
tive, June 2, 181.
Great Western Railway, Alleged Outrage
on, June 16, 1341.
Indian Confectionery Trade, June 6, 443.
Inniskeen Railway Accident, June 16,
1341.
Life Assurance—Lloyd's Policies, June
8, 663.
Lighthouse Keepers.
Emoluments, June 9, 770.
Scottish—Retiring Allowances, etc.,
June 16, 1343.
Maiden Rocks Lighthouse, June 2, 180;
June 13, 1066.
Merchant Vessels, Navigation of—Case of,
s.s. "Pinner's Point," June 12, 895.
Newbiggin-by-the-Sea—Destruction of
Fishing Gear, etc., by Trawlers, June
8, 635.
Railway Servants, Fatalities among,
Number of, June 2, 178.
Rio de Janeiro, British Sailors and the
Liquor Traffic, June 13, 1067.
Shunting Fatality on Cham and Dover
Railway, June 15, 1183.
Signalmen on North-Eastern Railway—
Hours of Labour. June 8, 634.
Undersized Fish Bill, 1R, June 8, 661, 662,
663.

ROBERTS, MR. J. B. [Carnarvonshire, Eifion].

Soudan Campaign—Cruelty to Wounded
Dervishes, Charge against Anglo-Egyptian
Army, June 8, 686.
Transvaal.
Oath of Allegiance—Naturalisation of
British Subjects. June 16, 1337.
Rhodes', Mr., Interviews with Mr.
Chamberlain, alleged, June 15, 1182.
Uitlanders' Petition, June 5, 306.

ROBERTS, MR. J. H. [Denbighshire, W.].

Calcutta Municipal Bill, June 16, 1336.
Connaught Rangers at Meerut—Shooting
Case. June 16, 1335.
Local Government Board, transfer of Powers
to County Councils, June 2, 274.

ROBERTS, MR. J. H.—cont.

Rangoon—Outrage on Burmese Woman by
British Soldiers, June 16, 1335.
Wine and Beerhouse Acts Amendment Bill,
2R, June 7, 575.
Women Barristers practising in India—
Application of Miss Sorabji, June 8,
641.

ROBERTSON, MR. E. [Dundee].

Naval Works Bill—Business of the House,
June 19, 1516.
Navy Contracts—New Form, June 19,
1480.
Post Office—Employment of Old Non-Com-
missioned Officers, June 1, 128.
Private Legislation Procedure [Scotland]
Bill, com., June 12, 918, 919, 920, 937,
949, 952, 954, 978; June 19, 1434, 1547,
1550.
Wine and Beerhouse Acts Amendment Bill,
2R., June 7, 572.

ROBERTSON, MR. H. [Hackney, S.].

London Government Bill, con., June 8, 712.

ROBSON, MR. W. S. [South Shields].

Half-timers—Education of Children Bill,
com., May 31, 27, 29, 41, 50, 52, 60.

ROLLIT, SIR A. K. [Islington, S.].

Half-timers—Education of Children Bill,
com., May 31, 21, 29.
Loans, Municipal, Repayment of, June 2,
219, 228.

ROMAN CATHOLIC UNIVERSITY, IRELAND.

Petitions, June 2, 174; June 5, 297; June
9, 760.

ROSCOMMON AGRICULTURAL GRANT.

Qs. Mr. Tully; As. Mr. G. W. Balfour,
June 5, 305; June 8, 652; June 13,
1077; Q. Mr. Hayden; A. Mr. G. W.
Balfour, June 16, 1352.

ROSSMORE ESTATE—Finegan Eviction Case.

Q. Mr. Macaleese; A. Mr. G. W. Balfour;
June 15, 1190; June 19, 1497.

ROUND, MR. J. [Essex, Harwich].

Imbecile [Training Institutions] Bill, 2R.,
June 2, 288.

ROYAL ACADEMY.

Reforms—Recommendations of Select Committee and Royal Commission.
Os. Lord Stanley of Alderley, Marquess
of Salisbury, June 19, 1466.

ROYAL ARSENAL, see Woolwich Arsenal.

ROYAL IRISH CONSTABULARY, see Constabulary,
Royal Irish.

RUM, Local Colonial Duties on, West Indies—
Return.
Q. Mr. Laurence; A. Mr. J. Chamber-
lain, June 6, 441.

RURAL RATING.

Tithe Rent-Charge [Rates] Bill, see that
Title.

Rushden and Higham Ferrers District Gas Bill.

l. Royal Assent, June 6, 409.

RUSSELL, GEN. F. S. [Cheltenham].

Aberdeen Cemetery Scandal, June 19, 1486.
Hyde Park—Lighting, etc., June 19, 1488.
Metropolitan Volunteer Review—Accommodation for Members, June 19, 1481.

RUSSELL, MR. T. W.—Parliamentary Secretary to Local Government Board [Tyrone, S.]
Commercial Education, June 1, 80.
Dublin Corporation Bill, con., June 13, 1035.
Dundee Gas, Street Improvements, and Tramways Bill, 2R., June 5, 295.
Godalming Corporation Water Bill, con., June 13, 1003.
Intoxicating Liquors [Sunday Closing] Bill, 2R., June 7, 545.
Local Government Board, transfer of Powers to County Councils, June 2, 276.
Lunacy Bill, 2R., June 12, 990.
Poor Law Children—Expenditure on Orphan Schools, June 2, 248.
Poor Law Schools—Education Department, Control, June 1, 83.
Provisional Order Bills, Procedure—Insertion of Names, June 2, 175.

RUSSELL OF KILLOWEN, LORD.

Judges, Additional, appointment of, June 8, 617.
Prevention of Corruption Bill, 2R., June 6, 414, 427, 428.

RUSSIA.

Anglo-Russian Agreement, see China.
Armenia, Kurdish Atrocities—Russian and French Protest.
  Q. Mr. Schwann; A. Mr. Brodrick, June 16, 1337.
China, Questions relating to, see China.
Commercial Travellers, British, Tax on.
  Q. Mr. Bill; A. Mr. Brodrick, June 8, 629.
Railway Construction in Persia—Expiration of Agreement, etc.
  Q. Mr. Maclean; A. Mr. Brodrick, June 8, 628.
Trade, British Interests—United States, France, and German activity.
  Q. Sir H. Vincent; A. Mr. Brodrick, June 12, 893.
Trade Report presented, June 1, 68.

RYDER, MR. J. H. D. [Gravesend].

Customs Officers' Grievances, June 1, 147.

SAIGON, Trade Report presented, June 1, 68.

St. Albans Gas Bill.

c. con.*, June 1, 74.
3R.*, June 5, 293.
l. Commons Amendts*, June 8, 593.

St. Andrews Burgh Provisional Order Confirmation Bill.

l. Royal Assent, June 6, 409.

St. Davids Water and Gas Bill.

l. Royal Assent, June 6, 409.

St. Michael's Church, Southampton.
Ritualistic Practices at.
  Q. Mr. S. Smith; A. Mr. A. J. Balfour, June 12, 907.

St. Neots Water Bill.

c. 2R., June 13, 1053; June 19, 1476.

Sale of Food and Drugs Bill.

Petition, June 9, 760.

Sale of Intoxicating Liquors on Sunday Bill.

Petitions, May 31, 4; June 1, 78; June 2, 174; June 5, 297; June 7, 538; June 12, 892; June 13, 1056; June 14, 1090; June 16, 1332; June 19, 1478.

SALE OF INTOXICATING LIQUORS TO CHILDREN.
Petition for Alteration of Law, June 12, 892.

Salford Corporation Bill.

c. 2R.*, June 6, 431.

SALISBURY, MARQUESS OF—Prime Minister and Secretary of State for Foreign Affairs.
London Government Bill, June 16, 1327.
Royal Academy Reforms, June 19, 1472.
Soudan Campaign—Grant to Lord Kitchener, and Vote of Thanks to the Forces, June 5, 291; June 8, 600, 601, 602.

SALISBURY PLAIN.

Lands, Purchase by War Office—Debate on Finance Bill, June 6, 453, 457.
Rentals of Property—Return.
  Qs. Mr. Bayley, Mr. Bowles; As. Mr. Powell Williams, June 6, 442; June 13, 1059.

SALMON FISHERIES.

Irish—Illegal Practices.
  Q. Mr. Seton-Karr; A. Mr. G. W. Balfour, June 9, 765.
Scotland, Report presented, June 1, 69.

SALONICA, Trade Report presented, June 1, 68.

SAMUEL, MR. H. S. [Tower Hamlets, Limehouse].

Customs Boatmen's Grievances, June 1, 149.
London Government Bill, con., June 8, 710.

SAMUEL, MR. J. [Stockton].

Private Legislation Procedure [Scotland] Bill, con., June 19, 1588.

SANCTION ISLAND.

Castlerea and Ballaghaderreen—Sanitary Charges.
  Q. Mr. Hayden; A. Mr. G. W. Balfour, June 16, 1357.

SASSOON, SIR E. [Hythe].

China, Affairs of.
  Yang-tsze Valley Territory, etc., June 9, 824.
  French Claims—Mining Rights in Szechuen, June 2, 185.

SAUNDERSON, COL., Rt. Hon. E. J. [Armagh, N.].
Dublin Corporation Bill, con., June 13, 1034, 1035, 1039.
Soudan Expedition—Grant to Lord Kitchener, Mahdi's Body, etc., June 5, 394.

SAVINGS BANKS.
Inquiry—Committee.
Q. Sir J. Leng; A. Sir M. H. Beach, June 8, 644.
Trustee Savings Banks, see that Title.

SCHOOLS, see Education.

SCHWANN, MR. C. E. [Manchester, N.].
Armenia, Kurdish Atrocities—Russian and French Protest, June 16, 1337.
Assam Tea Plantations—Report, June 12, 897.
Belfast Post Office Staff Pay, June 13, 1069.
Ceylon Waste Land Ordinances, June 13, 1069.
Godalming Corporation Water Bill, con., June 15, 1170.
Great Western Railway, alleged outrage on, June 16, 1341.
Half-timers—Education of Children Bill, 3R., June 14, 1117.

SCIENCE, ROYAL COLLEGE OF, DUBLIN.
Building, Control, etc.
Q. Mr. P. O'Brien; A. Mr. G. W. Balfour, June 16, 1350.

SCIENCE AND ART.
Scotland, Vote for, June 16; 1362.

SCOBLE, SIR A. R. [Hackney, Central].
Mineral Rights in Hyderabad State—Prospectuses, June 8, 643.

SCOTLAND.
Secretary for Scotland—Lord Balfour of Burleigh.
Lord Advocate—Rt. Hon. A. G. Murray.
Solicitor-General—Mr. C. Scott Dickson.
Aberdeen Cemetery Scandal.
Q. Gen. Russell; A. Mr. A. G. Murray, June 19, 1486.
Agricultural Instruction, S., June 16, 1418, 1423.
Bills Relating to, see their Titles.
Domestic Instruction for Girls, S., June 16, 1407.
Edinburgh, New Writs.
East Division, June 13, 1078.
South Division, June 9, 762.
Education, for collective heading, see Education—Scotch Questions.
Fee Grant, Return presented, May 31, 5.
Fisheries.
Herrings—Markets on the Continent and in United States, Reports presented, June 15, 1167, 1175.
Report presented, May 31, 6; June 1, 69.
Salmon, Report presented, June 1, 69.
Glasgow, see that Title.
Lighthouse Keepers' Retiring Allowance, etc.
Q. Dr. Clark; A. Mr. Ritchie, June 16, 1342.
Orphan Homes, see that Title.
Primogeniture, Law of—Abolition, see Succession [Scotland] Bill.

SCOTLAND—cont.
Science and Art, Vote for, June 16, 1362.
Secondary and Technical Education, see those Titles.
Teachers, see that Title.
Universities, Number of Students.
Q. Mr. Crombie; A. Mr. A. G. Murray, June 12, 896.

SCOTT, MR. C. P. [Lancashire, Leigh].
Soudan, Military Operations, Prospective, June 8, 631.
Soudan Campaign.
Kitchener, Lord, Grant to—Treatment of the Mahdi's Body, etc., June 5, 350, 384.
Omdurman, Battle of—British Officers with Native Troops, June 8, 631.
Transvaal.
Uitlanders' Grievances, June 13, 1062.
Bloemfontein Conference, June 8, 637.
War, Declaration of, previous to Jameson Raid, June 19, 1485.

Sea Fisheries Bill.
1. 1R.*, June 2, 164.
2R.*, June 8, 610.

Sea Fisheries Regulation [Scotland] Act [1895] Amendment Bill.
Petitions, June 9, 760, 892.

SEAMEN, MERCHANT SERVICE.
Accommodation on P. and O. Ships, etc., S., June 2, 282, 286.
Crimping in United States—Blood Money.
Q. Col. Denny; A. Mr. Brodrick, June 12, 894.
Merchant Seamen's Fund, see that Title.
Rio de Janeiro—Liquor Traffic.
Q. Mr. Hogan; A. Mr. Ritchie, June 13, 1066.
Wages, S., June 2, 285.

Seats for Shop Assistants [England and Ireland] Bill.
c. 2R.*, May 31, 63.
com., 74.
con.*, June 9, 876.
Rep.*, June 9, 876.
c. 3R.*, June 9, 876.
1. 1R.*, June 12, 889.
Petition, June 5, 297.

SECONDARY EDUCATION.
Board of Education Bill, see that Title.
Scotland.
Q. Mr. Buchanan; A. Mr. Anstruther, June 13, 1069.
S., June 16, 1369, 1377, 1397, 1402, 1407.
Minute of Committee of Council on Education presented, June 19, 1456, 1479.
Minute of April 27, 1899, S., June 16, 1370, 1383, 1388, 1438, 1443.

SECRET COMMISSIONS.
Prevention of Corruption Bill, see that Title.

SELBORNE, EARL OF—Parliamentary Secretary
to the Colonial Office.
Indenturing in Western Australia, Abolition of Aborigines' Protection Board, June
16, 1321, 1325.
Maltese Nobility—Mr. G. A. Testaferrata's
Claim, June 15, 1169.
Transvaal, Uitlanders' Grievances—Bloemfontein Conference, June 8, 597.

SERVANTS.
Domestic Servants, Wages of—Board of
Trade Report presented, June 9, 753, 761.

SERVIA—Turco-Servian Frontier, fighting on.
Q. Mr. Stevenson ; A. Mr. Brodrick, June
19, 1483.

Service Franchise Bill.
c. com., June 7, 539.
con., June 14, 1135.

SETON-KARR, MR. [St. Helen's].
Half-timers—Education of Children Bill,
com., May 31, 54, 56 ; 3R., June 14, 1092.
Irish Salmon Fisheries—Illegal Practices,
June 9, 765.

SEWAGE FARM AT ALDERSHOT, see Aldershot.

SEWERS.
Metropolitan Sewers and Drains Bill, see
that Title.

SHAW, MR. T. [Hawick Burghs].
Education, Scotland, June 16, 1374, 1438.
Private Legislation Procedure [Scotland]
Expenses, June 12, 909.
Private Legislation Procedure [Scotland]
Bill, com., June 12, 943, 960 ; June 19,
1550, 1553, 1569, 1577, 1589, 1590, 1594.
Succession [Scotland] Bill, 2R., June 7, 589.

Sheffield Corporation Markets Bill.
c. con.*, June 8, 624.
3R.*, June 12, 890.
l. 1R.*, June 13, 994.

**Sheffield Corporation [Derwent Valley]
Water Bill.**
See Derwent Valley Water Bill.

SHEPPEY, ISLE OF—Light Railways, Order
presented, May 31, 5 ; June 1, 69.

SHIPPING, see Merchant Shipping.

Shirebrook and District Gas Bill.
l. 2R.*, June 5, 290.
Rep.*, June 16, 1317.

SHOP ASSISTANTS.
Seats for Shop Assistants [England and Ire-
land] Bill, see that Title.
Service Franchise Bill, see that Title.

Shop Hours Act [1892] Amendment Bill.
c. 1R.*, June 16, 1333.

Shops [Early Closing] Bill.
Petition, June 14, 1090.

52

**Shotley Bridge and Consett District Gas
Bill.**
l. Rep.*, June 9, 750.
3R.*, June 15, 1166.

SHUNTING FATALITY ON CHATHAM AND DOVER
RAILWAY.
Q. Mr. Maddison ; A. Mr. Ritchie, June
15, 1183.

SIDMOUTH, VIS.
Maltese Nobility—Mr. G. A. Testaferrata's
Claim, June 15, 1169.

SIERRA LEONE.
Rising, Sir D. Chalmers's Report.
Q. Mr. Hedderwick ; A. Mr. J. Chamber-
lain, June 2, 176.

SIGNALMEN—Hours of Labour.
Q. Sir F. Flannery ; A. Mr. Ritchie,
June 8, 634.

SINCLAIR, CAPT. J. [Forfar].
Africa, West, Liquor Traffic—Brussels Con-
ference, June 13, 1063.
Business of the House, Precedence of
Government Business, June 19, 1518.
Education, Scotland, June 16, 1412, 1452.
Indian Sugar Trade, June 2, 185 ; June 8,
644.
Private Legislation Procedure [Scotland]
Bill, com., June 12, 910, 912, 955 ; June
19, 1562.
Scotch Estimates—Business of the House,
June 2, 185.

SINKING FUND, Account presented, June 2, 169.

SIRDAR, see Kitchener, Lord.

Skipton Urban District Gas Bill.
c. Rep.*, June 9, 758.
con.*, June 14, 1089.
3R.*, June 19, 1475.

SLAVERY IN ZANZIBAR, S., June 9, 872.

SLIGO, Land Valuation.
Q. Mr. P. A. M'Hugh ; A. Mr. G. W.
Balfour, June 12, 903.

SMALL ARMS FACTORY, ENFIELD.
Divine Service in Government Chapels—
Ritualistic Practices.
Qs. Mr. Channing, Mr. C. Williams ;
As. Mr. Wyndham, June 12, 898.

Small Houses [Scotland] Bill.
Petition, June 14, 1090.

Small Tenants [Scotland] Bill.
Petitions, June 2, 174 ; June 9, 760.

SMETHWICK CHARTER OF INCORPORATION, presented, June 14, 1091 ; June 15, 1168.

SMITH, MR. J. P. [Lanark, Partick].
Education, Scotland, June 16, 1406.
Finance Bill, con., June 8, 731.
National Debt, Annuities, June 16, 1340.
Private Legislation Procedure [Scotland]
Bill, com., June 12, 924, 937, 966, 967,
980 ; June 19, 1536, 1539, 1549, 1572,
1587.
Private Legislation Procedure [Scotland]
Expenses, June 12, 910.

SMITH, MR. S. [Flintshire].
Armenians, Distressed—Peace Conference, June 12, 894.
Half-timers—Education Children Bill, 3R, June 14, 1115.
Madras Liquor Trade—Opening of Liquor Shops, June 12, 897.
Pauper Children, Treatment of—Administration of the Poor Law, etc., June 2, 231.
St. Michael's, Southampton, Ritualistic Practices at, June 12, 907.

SMITH, HON. W. F. D. [Strand, Westminster].
London Government Bill, con., June 8, 706.

SOLDIERS.
Aldershot Bathing Fatality.
Q. Mr. Jeffreys; A. Mr. Wyndham, June 8, 640.
Deniston, J., Case of.
Q. Mr. J. P. Farrell; A. Mr. J. P. Williams, June 19, 1482.
Retired and Discharged Soldiers.
Civil Employment, Return Ordered [Col. Long], June 16, 1332..
Lynch's, E., Pension.
Q. Mr. Hayden; A. Mr. Wyndham, June 16, 1334.
Post office Employment, S., June 1, 127, 128.

Solicitors Bill.
l. Royal Assent, June 6, 409.

SORABJI, MISS.—Application to practise at Allahabad High Court.
Q. Mr. H. Roberts; A. Lord G. Hamilton, June 8, 641.

SOUDAN.
Fever among Troops.
Q. Mr. Pirie; A. Mr. Brodrick, June 2, 179.
Garstin's, Sir W. Report.
Q. Mr. Ellis; A. Mr. Brodrick, June 19, 1484.
Military Operations, Prospective.
Q. Mr. C. P. Scott; A. Mr. Brodrick, June 8, 631.

SOUDAN CAMPAIGN.
Kitchener, Lord, Grant to, June 5, 327; June 8, 747—Notice of Motion [Marquess of Salisbury], June 5, 291; Motion, June 8, 599; Motion [Mr. A. J. Balfour], June 8, 663.
House of Lords, Initiating Money Grants—question of Privilege, Motion [Mr. MacNeill], June 5, 319.
Method of Procedure.
Q. Mr. Dillon; A. Mr. A. J. Balfour, June 2, 186; Personal Explanation, Mr. Dillon, June 5, 309.
Queen's Message, June 2, 166, 171.
Mahdi's Body, Treatment of.
Debate on Lord Kitchener's Grant, June 5, 327.
Os. Earl of Kimberley, June 8, 599.
Marquess of Salisbury, 600.
Omdurman, Battle of.
British Officers with Native Troops, Proportion of.
Q. Mr. C. P. Scott; A. Mr. Brodrick, June 8, 631.
Prisoners released, Number of.
Q. Mr. Pirie; A. Mr. Brodrick, June 2, 178.

SOUDAN CAMPAIGN—cont.
Thanks of the House to Lord Kitchener and the Forces; Notice of Motion [Marquess of Salisbury], June 5, 291; Motion, June 8, 599; Motion [Mr. A. J. Balfour], June 8, 663.
Deceased Officers and Men—Acknowledgment of Services and Condolence to Relatives, Motion [Mr. A. J. Balfour], June 8, 697.
Medical Officers, Omission of.
Os. Dr. Farquharson, June 8, 667, 673; Mr. A. J. Balfour, 678.
Noncommissioned Officers, etc., of Army, Navy, and Royal Marines—Motion [Mr. A. J. Balfour], June 8, 697.
Officers of the Navy, Army, and Royal Marines, Motion [Mr. A. J. Balfour], June 8, 672.
Wounded Dervishes, Cruelty to—Charge against Anglo-Egyptian Army, Debate on, Thanks to the Forces, June 8, 674.

South-Eastern Railway Bill.
l. 2R.*, June 1, 65.
com.*, June 15, 1165.
Rep.*, June 19, 1454.

South-Eastern and London, Chatham, a Dover Railway Companies Bill.
l. 2R.*, June 1, 65.

South-Eastern and London, Chatham, and Dover Railway Companies [New Lines] Bill.
c. 3R.*, June 2, 167.
1R.*, June 5, 290.
2R.*, June 13, 994.

South Hants Water Bill.
c. 2R.*, May 31, 2.

SOUTH KENSINGTON MUSEUM.
Art Branch—Appointment of Assistant.
Q. Mr. M. Healy; A. Sir J. Gorst, June 16, 1347.

South Staffordshire Stipendiary Justice Bill.
c. 3R.*, May 31, 1.
l. 1R.*, June 1, 66.
2R.*, June 8, 595.
Rep.*, June 16, 1317.

South Staffordshire Tramways Bill.
l. Rep., from Select com., June 15, 1165.
3R.*, June 19, 1454.

SOUTHAMPTON.
St. Michael's Church, Ritualistic Practices at.
Q. Mr. S. Smith; A. Mr. A. J. Balfour, June 12, 907.

SOUTHPORT BY-ELECTION.
New Member Sworn, June 1, 87.
Peers' Interference—Breach of Privilege.
Q. Mr. J. Lowther; A. Mr. A. J. Balfour, June 5, 307; Motion [Mr. J. Lowther], June 5, 311.

Southport Tramways Bill.
l. Rep. from Select Committee, June 13, 993.

Southport and Lytham Tramroad Bill.
  1. Rep. from Select com., June 19, 1454.

SOUTHSEA—Queen Victoria's Birthday Celebrations—Cancelling Parade.
  Q. Mr. Bowles; A. Mr. Wyndham, June 2, 180.

SOUTTAR, MR. R. [Dumfriesshire].
  Private Legislation Procedure [Scotland] Bill.. com., June 12, 943, 968, 980; June 19, 1542.

SPAIN—Trade Report presented, June 1, 68.

SPEAKER.—Rt. Hon. W. C. Gully [Carlisle].
  Adjournment of Debate, Motion for—Motion could not be accepted after Bill had been fully discussed, and when there was a prospect of an early division, June 7, 583.
  House of Lords and Money Grants—Grant to Lord Kitchener—Question of Privilege, June 5, 321.
  Irrelevant Observations.
    Liquor Licensing Commission—Intoxicating Liquors [Sunday Closing] Bill, June 7, 548.
  Motion to re-commit a Bill on a particular Clause—Discussion on the whole question would not be in order, June 13, 1079.
  References to Statement made in another Debate, June 8, 702.
  Resolutions [Soudan Expedition], Question relevant to Particular Resolution must be raised upon that Resolution, June 8, 668.
  Royal Commissions not reported to the House—Member of Commission stating views, June 7, 557.

SPICER, MR. A. [Monmouth Boroughs].
  Patriotic Fund—Case of Mrs. Lewis, June 8, 632.
  Post Office, Employees' Grievances—Committee of Inquiry proposed, June 1, 108.

SPIRIT DUTIES.
  Africa, West.
    Q. Mr. W. F. Lawrence; A. Mr. J. Chamberlain, June 15, 1181.
  Bottled Spirits—Finance Bill, Amendt. [Sir M. Hicks-Beach], June 6, 458.

SQUADRON—Visit to China.
  Q. Mr. Hedderwick; A. Mr. Goschen, June 9, 776.

STAFFORDSHIRE.
  Bills relating to, see their Titles.

STAMP DUTY.
  Advertisement Orders exemption.
    Q. Mr. Hazell; A. Sir M. Hicks-Beach, June 2, 183.
  Friends' Provident Institution Bill.
    R. [Dr. Farquharson], June 2, 169; June 5, 293.

STANHOPE, HON. P. J. [Burnley.].
  Bloemfontein Conference, June 8, 636.

STANLEY, HON. A. [Lancashire, Ormskirk].
  Soudan Expedition—Grant to Lord Kit-

STANLEY OF ALDERLEY, LORD.
  Death Duties—Indefinite Liability for Estate Duty—Endorsement on Registered Titles, June 13, 1000.
  Indenturing in Western Australia—Abolition of Aborigines Protection Board, June 16, 132.
  Royal Academy Reforms—Recommendations of Select Committee and Royal Commission, June 19, 1466, 1473.

STEADMAN, MR. W. C. [Tower Hamlets, Stepney].
  Clapham Sorting Office Vacancies, June 1, 81.
  Customs.
    Officials, Hours of Labour, etc., June 6, 436.
  Watchers' Pay, June 1, 148.
  Hale, Sarah, Case of, June 16, 1339.
  London Government Bill, con., June 6, 480; June 8, 710, 711, 714.
  Post Office, Employees' Grievances, June 1, 99.
  Postmen's Strikes, June 1, 102.
  Sub-Postmasters, Rural Postmen assisting, June 15, 1187.
  Telegraphists' Grievances, June 1, 100.
  Woolwich Arsenal—Dismissal of Men, etc., June 15, 1176.

STEVENSON, MR. F. S. [Suffolk, Eye].
  Armenia—Archbishops and Bishops, detention of, June 1, 80; June 15, 1179.
  Board of Education Bill [Secondary Education], June 19, 1500.
  Local Government Board Inquiries, June 2, 279.
  Turco-Servian Frontier, Fighting on, June 19, 1483.

STEWART, SIR M. J. [Kirkcudbright].
  Education, Scotland, June 16, 1400.
  Private Legislation Procedure [Scotland] Bill, com., June 12, 953.

Stockport Corporation Bill.
  c. con.*, June 7, 537.
  3R.*, June 12, 890.
  1.R.*, June 13, 994.

Stockton and Middlesbrough Water Bill.
  c. 2R.*, May 31, 3.
  Rep.*, June 9, 758.
  3R.*, June 13, 1002.

STREET OBSTRUCTION IN THE METROPOLIS.
  Marylebone Police Prosecution.
    Q. Gen. Laurie; A. Mr. Collings, June 15, 1184.

Stretford Gas Bill.
  c. 2R.*, June 6, 431.

Stretford Urban District Council [Tramways] Bill.
  1. 3R.*, June 2, 162.
  c. 1R.*, June 5, 326.
    2R.*, June 14, 1089.

chener—Treatment of the Mahdi's Body, etc., June 5, 371.

STUART, MR. J. [Shoreditch, Hoxton].
　Godalming Corporation Water Bill, con.,
　　June 13, 1004.
　London Government Bill, con., June 6, 487,
　　490, 496, 500, 505, 511, 518, 519; June 8,
　　707, 712, 716, 717, 720, 723.
　London Water [Purchase] Bill, 2R., June 1,
　　74, 75.
　Poor Law Schools, Education Department
　　Control, June 1, 82.

SUB-POSTMASTERS, see Postmasters.

Succession [Scotland] Bill.
　c. 2R.*, June 7, 589.
　Petitions, June 2, 175; June 5, 297.

SUGAR—Bounties, Etc.
　Abolition of, proposed.
　　Q. Sir H. Vincent; A. Mr. Brodrick,
　　　June 9, 763.
　Countervailing Duties, Petition, June 2,
　　173.
　Indian Exports and Imports.
　　Qs. Capt. Sinclair; As. Lord G.
　　　Hamilton, June 2, 185, June 8, 644.
　Confectionery Trade—Return.
　　Q. Mr. Maclean; A. Mr. Ritchie, June 6,
　　　443.
　Indian Tariff Act, 1899, Motion to disallow
　　[Sir H. H. Fowler], June 15, 1199.
　Mauritius Industry.
　　Q. Mr. W. H. Holland; A. Mr. J.
　　　Chamberlain, June 13, 1063.
　Return presented, June 2, 170.

SULLIVAN, MR. T. D. [Donegal, W.].
　Donegal Railway Communication—County
　　Council Resolution, June 19, 1498.

SULLIVAN—M'Hale v.—Debate [l.], June 12,
　880.

SUNDAY SALE OF INTOXICATING LIQUORS.
　Intoxicating Liquors [Sunday Closing] Bill,
　　see that Title.
　Sale of Intoxicating Liquors on Sunday Bill,
　　see that Title.

Sunderland Corporation Bill.
　l. 3R.*, June 1, 66.
　c. 1R.*, June 2, 169.
　　2R.*, June 12, 890.

SUPERANNUATION.
　Brading, C., appointment in Royal Labora-
　　tory without certificate—Treasury Minute
　　presented, June 2, 164, 170.
　Clay, A. E., Retiring Allowance—Treasury
　　Minute presented, June 19, 1479.
　Local Authorities Servants' Superannuation
　　Bill, see that Title.
　Mills, J., appointment in Royal Gun Fac-
　　tory without certificate—Treasury
　　Minute presented, June 2, 163, 170.
　Muspratt, J., appointment as Postman
　　without certificate, Treasury Minute pre-
　　sented, June 7, 539; June 8, 597.
　Poor Law Officers' Superannuation [Scot-
　　land] Bill, see that Title.
　Teachers, see that Title.

SUPERANNUATIONS AND RETIRED ALLOWANCES.
　Vote for, June 1, 157; June 2, 287.

SUPPLY—Civil Service and Revenue Depart-
　ments Estimates.
　Charitable and other Allowances—£785.
　　com.*, June 1, 157; Rep.*, June 2,
　　288.
　Customs Department, £496,600.
　　com., June 1, 132; Rep.*, June 2,
　　287.
　Education and Science and Art, Scotland.
　　—£701, 861, com., June 16, 1362.
　Foreign Office—£49,482, com., June 9,
　　777.
　Inland Revenue Department, £1,316,232.
　　Rep.*, June 1, 157.
　Kitchener, Lord, Grant to, £30,000.
　　com., June 5, 327; Rep.*, June 8, 747
　Local Government Board—£132,732.
　　com., June 2, 187.
　Lunacy Commissioners Offices—£9,446.
　　Rep.*, June 1, 158.
　Merchant Setmen's Fund, Pensions—
　　£2,130, com.*, June 1, 157; Rep.*,
　　June 2, 287.
　Mint, Salaries and Expenses, £267.
　　Rep.*, June 1, 158.
　National Debt Office—£9,274.
　　Rep.*, June 1, 158.
　Post Office—£5,522,885.
　　com., June 1, 99; June 2, 284.
　Post Office Packet Service—£570,915.
　　com.*, June 1, 130; Rep., June 2, 285.
　Public Works and Buildings—£36,393.
　　Rep.*, June 1, 159.
　Public Works' Loan Commissioners' Es-
　　tablishment—£13., Rep.*, June 1, 158.
　Record Office—£14,300, Rep.*, June 1,
　　158.
　Registrar General of Births, etc.—
　　£26,884, Rep.*, June 1, 159.
　Superannuation and Retired Allowances
　　—£287,628, com.*, June 1, 157;
　　Rep.*, June 2, 287.
　Telegraph Service—£2,338,390.
　　com., June 1, 130; Rep.*, June 2, 287.

Supreme Court [Appeals] Bill.
　l. Royal Assent*, June 6, 409.

SUPREME COURT OF JUDICATURE AMENDMENT
　ACT, 1875.
　South-Eastern Circuit, Order in Council
　　presented, June 6, 414, 434.

SUPREME COURT OF JUDICATURE [IRELAND]
　ACT, 1877.
　Orders in Council presented, June 1, 79;
　　June 2, 164.

Surrey Commercial Docks Bill.
　l. Royal Assent, June 6, 409.

SUTTON BARRACK SCHOOLS.
　Children begging on Derby Day.
　　O. Mr. Trevelyan, June 2, 247; O. Mr.
　　　Chaplin, June 2, 256.

SWANSEA.
　Education Department—Provisional Order
　　Confirmation [Swansea] Bill, see that
　　Title.

SWITZERLAND, Trade Report presented, June 4,
　68.

SYRIA, SOUTH COAST, Trade Report presented, June 8, 596.

SZECHUEN, MINING RIGHTS IN—French Claims.
Q. Sir F. Sassoon; A. Mr. Broderick, June 2, 183.

TA-LIEN-WAN AS AN OPEN PORT.
Russian Cargoes, British Vessels carrying.
Q. Sir E. Gourley; A. Mr. Brodrick, June 2, 175.

TAGANROG, Trade Report presented, June 1, 68.

TALBOT, RT. HON. J. G. [Oxford University].
Aldershot Sewage Farm—Inspector's Report, June 2, 177.
Bethnal Green, Election of Schools by London School Board, June 12, 900.
Working Class Dwellings. Removal of. June 12, 900.
London Government Bill, con., June 8, 703, 706.
Workhouses, Religious Ministration in. June 2, 273.

TARIFF ACT, INDIA. 1899—Motion [Sir H. H. Fowler], June 15, 1199.

"TAURANGA," H.M.S., VISIT TO TONGA.
Qs. Mr. Hogan; As. Mr. Brodrick, June 8, 630; June 13, 1064.

TAXATION.
Consuls, Foreign, Exemption from.
Q. Mr. Dillon; A. Mr. Brodrick, June 8, 627.
Local Taxation, see that Title.

TEA.
Adulteration—Inquiry, etc.
Q. Sir F. Flannery; A. Sir M. Hicks-Beach, June 8, 645.
Q. Mr. Carew; A. Mr. Hanbury. June 9, 775.
Assam Plantations—Report.
Q. Mr. Schwann; A. Lord George Hamilton. June 12, 897.

TEACHERS.
National School Teachers, Ireland, see that Title.
Scotland.
Dismissal of Teachers by School Boards—Right of Appeal, S., June 16, 1401, 1421.
Superannuation.
Q. Mr. Buchanan; A. Mr. A. G. Murray, June 9, 773.
S., June 16, 1436.

TECHNICAL EDUCATION.
Local Authorities, England, Ireland, and Wales. Return Ordered [Sir J. Gorst]. June 9, 761.
Scotland.
Q. Mr. Buchanan; Mr. Anstruther. June 13, 1069.
Minute of Committee of Council on Education, presented. June 19, 1456, 1479.
S., June 16, 1403, 1407.

Teinds [Scotland] Bill.
Petitions, June 2, 175; June 14, 1090.

TELEGRAPHISTS.
Central Telegraph Staff—Petitions.
Q. Mr. M'Ghee; A. Mr. Hanbury, June 15, 1187.
Dublin—Hours of Labour.
Q. Mr. Davitt; A. Mr. Hanbury. June 9, 775.
Grievances, S., June 1, 100, 104.

TELEGRAPHS.
Oldham—Delay in Transit of Messages.
Q. Mr. Ascroft; A. Mr. Anstruther, June 8, 658.
Vote for, June 1, 130; June 2, 287.

Telegraphs [Telephonic Communication, etc.], Bill.
Q. Sir C. Cameron; A. Mr. A. J. Balfour, June 19 1501.
Petitions, May 31, 4; June 6, 433; June 7, 538.

TELEPHONE SERVICE.
Private Wires, etc., S., June 1, 130.
Telegraphs [Telephone Communication, etc.] Bill, see that Title.

TENNANT, MR. H. J. [Berwickshire].
Half-timers—Education of Children Bill, com., May 31, 18.

Tenterden Railway Bill.
1. Royal Assent, June 6, 409.

TESTAFERRATA, MR. G. A.—Maltese Nobility claim.
Q. Vis. Sidmouth; A. Earl of Selborne, June 15, 1169.

THOMAS, MR. A. [Carmarthen, E.].
Service Franchise Bill, con., June 14, 1154.

THOMAS, MR. D. A. [Merthyr Tydvil].
All Saints' Church [Cardiff] Bill—Standing Order complied with, June 8, 619, 623.

THORBURN, MR. W. [Peebles and Selkirk].
Private Legislation Procedure [Scotland] Bill, com., June 12, 953.

TIRAH CAMPAIGN, 1897-8.
Medals, etc., Distribution to Bengal Staff Corps.
Q. Mr. H. D. Greene; A. Mr. Wyndham, June 1, 81.
Q. Mr. H. D. Greene; A. Lord G. Hamilton, June 6, 443.

TITHE RENT - CHARGE—Ireland—Redemption, etc.
Q. Mr. W. Moore; A. Mr. G. W. Balfour, June 1, 84.
Q. Mr. S. Bairy; A. Mr. G. W. Balfour, June 16, 1354.

Tithe Rent-Charge [Rates] Bill.
Statement [Mr. A. J. Balfour], June 19, 1504.

TITHE-OWNING CLERGY OF ENGLAND AND WALES.
Petition for Amendment of Agricultural Rates Act, June 8, 597.

TOMLINSON, MR. W. E. M. [Preston].
Ambulance for the Houses of Parliament, June 8, 657.
Half-timers—Education of Children Bill, com., May 31, 10, 18, 24, 25, 28, 29, 41, 51, 3R, June 14, 1110.
Parliamentary Deposits Bill, June 5, 306.
Seats for Shop Assistants [England and Ireland] Bill, com., June 8, 748.
Wine and Beerhouse Acts Amendment Bill, 2R, June 7, 584.

TONGA.
"Tauranga," H.M.S., Visit of, etc.
Qs. Mr. Hogan; As. Mr. Brodrick, June 8, 630; June 13, 1064.
Trade Report presented, June 1, 68.

Totland Water Bill.
c. 2R.*, June 13, 1054.

TOWN COMMISSIONERS, IRELAND.
Chairman—Solicitor losing right to practice at Quarter Session.
Q. Mr. Healy; A. Mr. G. W. Balfour, June 16, 1360.

Town Council [Scotland] Bill.
Petitions, June 2, 175; June 5, 297; June 7, 538; June 9, 760, 892, 1091; June 19, 1479.

TRADE, BOARD OF.
President—Rt. Hon. C. T. Ritchie.
Parliamentary Secretary—Earl of Dudley.

TRADE REPORTS PRESENTED.
Annual Series, May 31, 5, 6; June 1, 68; June 2, 163, 171; June 8, 596, 626; June 15, 1168, 1175; June 19, 1456, 1479.
Miscellaneous Series, June 15, 1168, 1175.

TRADE AND COMMERCE.
China, British Trade in, S., June 9, 785.
Russia—United States, France, and German Activity—British Commercial Interests, etc.
Q. Sir H. Vincent; A. Mr. Brodrick, June 12, 893.
United States Treaties—Most-favoured Nation Clause.
Q. Col. Milward; A. Mr. Brodrick, June 9, 763.

TRADESMEN'S CART AND VAN LICENCES.
Q. Mr. Giles; A. Mr. Hanbury, June 9, 776.

TRAMWAYS, BILLS RELATING TO, see their Titles.

TRAMWAYS ACT—Cavan Ratepayers.
Q. Mr. J. P. Farrell; A. Mr. Hanbury, June 19, 1492.

Tramways Orders Confirmation [No. 1] Bill.
l. 2R.*, June 2, 163.
com.*, June 16, 1319.
Rep.*, June 19, 1455.

Tramways Orders Confirmation [No. 2] Bill.
l. 2R.*, June 6, 413.
com.*, June 13, 995.

Tramways Orders Confirmation [No. 3] Bill.
l. 2R.*, June 2, 163.
com.*, June 9, 752.

TRANSVAAL.
Anti-British Propaganda in Cape Colony.
Qs. Sir E. Ashmead-Bartlett, Mr. S. MacNeill; As. Mr. J. Chamberlain, June 15, 1182.
Q. Mr. MacNeill; A. Mr. J. Chamberlain, June 16, 1338.
Applebe, Mrs., Murder of.
Q. Sir W. Johnston; A. Mr. J. Chamberlain, June 19, 1484.
Boers in Natal, alleged arming.
Q. Sir A. Hickman; A. Mr. J. Chamberlain, June 13, 1061.
Edgar, Mr., Murder of—Compensation to Widow.
Q. Mr. Griffith; A. Mr. J. Chamberlain, June 2, 182.
Q. Mr. Duncombe; A. Mr. J. Chamberlain, June 19, 1484.
Jameson Raid Indemnity—Correspondence presented, June 8, 596, 625.
Oath of Allegiance—Naturalisation of British Subjects.
Q. Mr. B. Roberts; A. Mr. J. Chamberlain, June 16, 1337.
Rhodes, Mr., and Mr. Chamberlain.
Q. Mr. B. Roberts; A. Mr. J. Chamberlain, June 15, 1182.
Uitlanders' Grievances.
Qs. Sir E. Ashmead-Bartlett, Mr. C. P. Scott, Mr. MacNeill; As. Mr. J. Chamberlain, June 13, 1061.
Bloemfontein Conference, Failure of.
Q. Earl of Camperdown; A. Earl of Selborne, June 8, 597.
Qs. Mr. Drage, Mr. Dillon, Mr. Stanhope, Mr. C. P. Scott, Mr. Maclean; As. Mr. J. Chamberlain, June 8, 636.
Q. Mr. Galloway; A. Mr. A. J. Balfour, June 12, 907.
Milner's, Sir A., Message, Delay in Despatch, etc.
Qs. Mr. Griffith, Mr. Labouchere; As. Mr. J. Chamberlain, June 13, 1059.
Papers presented, June 13, 996, 1056.
Petition Signatures, Payment for, etc.
Q. Mr. B. Roberts; A. Mr. J. Chamberlain, June 5, 304.
War, Declaration of, previous to Jameson Raid.
Q. Mr. C. P. Scott; A. Mr. J. Chamberlain, June 19, 1485.

Transvaal Mortgage Loan and Finance Company Bill.
l. Rep., June 6, 410
3R.*, June 12, 878.
c. 1R.*, June 13, 1055.

Trawlers' Certificates Suspension Bill.
l. com.*, June 9, 754; June 12, 888.
Rep.*, June 16, 1320.

TRAWLING.

Newbiggin-by-the-Sea — Destruction of Fishing Gear, alleged.
Q. Mr. Fenwick; A. Mr. Ritchie, June 8, 635.
Steam Trawling off Howth—Compensation to Fishermen.
Qs. Mr. Clancy; As. Mr. G. W. Balfour, June 16, 1360; June 19, 1500.

TREASURY.

Premier—Marquess of Salisbury.
First Lord—Rt. Hon. A. J. Balfour.
Joint Secretary—Rt. Hon. Sir W. H. Walrond.
Financial Secretary—Rt. Hon. R. W. Hanbury.

TREATY SERIES PRESENTED.

June 2, 163, 171; June 6, 435; June 8, 596; June 9. 761; June 12, 880.
[For Names of Countries such as Japan, etc., see their Names.]

TREVELYAN, MR. C. P. [York, W.R., Elland].

Berkhampstead National Schools—Attendance of Children at Church on Ascension Day, June 16, 1347.
Sutton Barrack Schools—Children begging on Derby Day, June 2, 247.

TRIPOLI—Trade Report presented, June 1, 68.

TRITTON, MR. C. E. [Lambeth, Norwood].

Intoxicating Liquors [Sunday Closing] Bill, 2R., June 7, 543, 556.

Trout-fishing Annual Close Time [Scotland] Bill.

c. 2R., June 12, 989.
Petitions, June 2, 175; June 12, 892, 1091.

TRUSTEE SAVINGS BANKS—Balance-sheet presented, June 2, 164, 170; June 5, 291.

Trustee Savings Bank Bill.

c. 1R.*, June 2, 172.

TUBERCULOSIS — Recommendations of Royal Commission.

Petition, June 9, 760.

TULLY, MR. J. [Leitrim, S.].

Clerks of Irish Unions checking Rate Collectors' Accounts—Extra Remuneration, June 15, 1197.
Cork Council Contracts—Disqualification of Shareholder as Councillor, June 8, 652.
Leitrim, Agricultural Grants, June 5, 305.
Local Government [Ireland], Orders and Rules, Difficulty in Obtaining Copies, June 6, 439.
Lough Rynn Letter Deliveries, Complaint, June 13, 1068.
National School Teachers as Guardians— Case of Mr. Kenny, June 5, 304.
Petroleum Bill, June 9, 770.
Rating System in Ireland, New System— Landlord and Tenant Agreements, June 9, 768.
Roscommon Agricultural Grant, June 5, 305; June 8, 652; June 13, 1077.

TUNIS—Trade Report presented, June 2, 163.

TURCO-SERVIAN FRONTIER, FIGHTING ON.

Q. Mr. Stevenson; A. Mr. Brodrick, June 19, 1483.

TURKEY.

Armenia, see that Title.
Trade Report presented, June 1, 68; June 8, 596.

TURKISH LOAN 1885, PAPERS RELATING TO.

Qs. Mr. Dillon, Mr. Pierpoint; As. Mr. Brodrick, June 13, 1064; June 15, 1179.

TYRONE.

County Council Rate Collector—Appointment of W. M. Farland.
Q. Mr. Hemphill; A. Mr. G. W. Balfour, June 19, 1496.
Fintona Sunday Mails.
Q. Mr. Dillon; A. Mr. Hanbury, June 19, 1468.

UITLANDERS' GRIEVANCES, see Transvaal.

ULSTER.

National School Teachers.
Q. Mr. Field; A. Mr. G. W. Balfour, June 13, 1070.

UNDERSIZED FISH BILL.

c. 1R., June 8, 661.

UNION WORKHOUSES, see Workhouses.

UNITED IRISH LEAGUE—M'Hale v. Sullivan, Debate [l.], June 12, 880.

UNITED STATES.

Anglo-American Commission, see that Title.
Commercial Education, Report presented, June 15, 1168.
Commercial Treaties—Most favoured Nation Clause.
Q. Col. Milward; A. Mr. Brodrick, June 9, 763.
Crimping—Blood-money.
Q. Col. Denny; A. Mr. Brodrick, June 12, 894.
Irish Emigration.
Q. Capt. Donelan; A. Mr. G. W. Balfour, June 8, 649.
Mail Service—Return.
Q. Sir J. Leng; A. Mr. Hanbury, June 6, 437.
Scottish Herring Markets. Reports presented, June 15. 1167, 1175.

UNIVERSITIES.

London University and the Imperial Institute, see Imperial Institute.
Scottish—Number of Students.
Q. Mr. Crombie; A. Mr. A. G. Murray, June 12, 896.

URE, MR. A. [Linlithgow].

Private Legislation Procedure [Scotland] Bill, com., June 12, 926.

Uxbridge and Rickmansworth Railway Bill.

l. 2R.*, June 8, 595.

VACCINATION.

Acts 1867 to 1898—Legislation, Petition. May 31, 4.

VACCINATION—*cont.*
Compulsory Vaccination.
Abolition of, Petition, June 2, 163.
Petition for Repeal of Acts, June 9. 754, 761, 892.
Conscience Clause, S., June 2, 194, 197, 199.
Enforcement of the Law—Local Government Board Action, S., June 2, 215, 216, 217.
Increase of Vaccination, since Passing Act of 1898. S., June 2, 198, 201, 206, 215.
Officers, Position of, S., June 2, 188, 189, 193, 202, 206, 210. 213.
Promotion of—Circulation of Literature of Jenner Society, S., June 2, 191, 193, 199.
Prosecutions. S., June 2, 188, 189, 193, 200, 202. 204. 206, 218.
Reading Public Vaccinator—Remuneration. Q. Mr. Palmer ; A. Mr. Chaplin, June 16, 1349.

VAGRANCY, INCREASE OF.
O. Mr. Drage, June 2, 246.

Vale of Glamorgan Railway Bill.
l. Royan Assent, June 6, 409.

VALPARAISO AND DISTRICT—Trade Report presented, June 15, 1168.

VALUATION ACTS, IRELAND—Revised Valuations.
Q. Mr. E. Barry ; A. Mr. G. W. Balfour, June 16, 1352.
[See also Land Commission.]

VEHICLE LICENCES — Tradesmen's Carts and Vans.
Q. Mr. Giles ; A. Mr. Hanbury, June 9, 776.

VINCENT, COL. SIR C. E. H. [Sheffield,Central].
Commercial Education, June 1, 80.
Russian Empire, Trade in, British Interests—United States, France and German Activity, June 12, 893.
Sugar Bounties, Abolition of, Proposed, June 9, 753.
Volunteer Officers, Training, June 1, 79.
Volunteers, Metroprolitan, Review, Accommodation for Members, June 8, 656.

VIVISECTION.
Experiments on Living Animals—Return ordered [Mr. Collings], June 8, 626—presented, 748.
Petition for Prohibition, June 13, 1056.

VOLUNTARY SCHOOLS—Petition for Alteration of Law, June 13, 1056.

VOLUNTARY SCHOOLS ASSOCIATIONS.
Return presented, June 6, 434.

VOLUNTEERS.
Officers, Training, with Regiments near civil duties.
Q. Sir H. Vincent ; A. Mr. Wyndham, June 1, 79.

VOLUNTEERS—*cont.*
Review, Metropolitan Volunteers—Accommodation for Members.
Q. Sir H. Vincent ; A. Mr. Akers Douglas, June 8, 656.
Q. Gen. Russell ; A. Mr. J. P. Williams, June 19, 1481.

WAIMA INCIDENT.
Compensation Claims, S., June 9, 780, 784, 812, 823, 839, 845, 863, 872.

Wakefield Corporation Bill.
c. 2R.*, June 6, 431.

WALES.
Bills relating to, see their Titles.
Carmarthen, see that Title.
Intermediate Education Act — Charity Commissioners' Proceedings, Report presented, June 14, 1091 ; June 15, 1168.

Walker and Wallsend Union Gas [Electric Lighting] Bill.
c. Rep.*., June 9, 758.
con.*, June 19, 1476.

WALLACE, MR. R. [Edinburgh, E.].
Soudan Campaign—Grant to Lord Kitchener, June 5, 398—[Sudden Death of Mr. Wallace, see Note on page 400].

WALLACE, MR. R. [Perth].
Private Legislation Procedure [Scotland] Bill, com., June 12, 934, 945 ; June 19, 1543.
Service Franchise Bill, con., June 14, 1141, 1148, 1149.

Wallasey Tramways and Improvements Bill.
l. Royal Assent, June 6, 409.

WALTON, MR. J. [York, W.R., Barnsley].
China, Affairs of—Anglo-Russian Agreement, etc., June 9, 828.

Walton-on-Thames and Weybridge Gas Bill.
l. Royal Assent, June 6, 409.

WAR OFFICE.
Secretary of State—Marquess of Lansdowne.
Under-Secretary—Mr. Wyndham.
Financial Secretary—Mr. J. P. Williams.

WARNER, MR. T. C. T. [Stafford, Lichfield].
Intoxicating Liquors [Sunday Closing] Bill, 2R., June 7, 551.
Wine and Beerhouse Acts Amendment Bill, 2R., June 7, 578.

WASHHOUSES.
Baths and Washhouses Acts Amendment Bill, see that Title.

WASTE LAND ORDINANCES, CEYLON—See Ceylon.

WATER COMPANIES—See Metropolitan Water Companies.

Water Orders Confirmation Bill.
l. com.*, June 1, 67 ; June 13, 994.
Rep.*, June 15, 1167.
3R.*, June 16, 1318.
c. 1R.*, June 19, 1478.

WATER-TUBE BOILERS ON H.M. SHIPS.
Q. Sir J. Fergusson; A. Mr. Goschen,
June 8, 633.

WATERFORD STEAMSHIP Co.—Glin District
School—Conveyance of 'Children.
Q. Mr. Austin; A. Mr. G. W. Balfour,
June 12, 902.

**Waterford and Central Ireland Railway
Bill.**
c. 2R.*, May 31, 3.
County Councils Petitions, Order for
presentation, etc., June 5, 295 ; June
6, 431.

**Watermen's and Lightermen's Acts
Amendment Bill.**
l. Rep. from Select Com., June 13, 994.

WEBSTER, MR. R. G. [St. Pancras, E.].
Guernsey Militia—Insubordination, June
19, 1481.
London Government Bill, Con., June 6, 498.
Women, Qualification of, June 13, 1085.
"Parliamentary Debates," delay in publica-
tion, June 5, 303.

WEBSTER, SIR R. E., Attorney-General [Isle of
Wight].
London Government Bill, Con., June 6,
498, 500, 513, 516, 518.
Parliamentary Deposits Bill, June 5, 306.

WEDDERBURN, SIR W. [Banffshire].
Bombay, Civil and Criminal Appeals in
Political Courts—Return, June 15, 1178.
Franchise in French Possessions in India,
June 15, 1177.
Legal Education in India. Control by Private
Institutions. June 8, 641.
Pasteur Institute, India — Government
Grant, etc., proposed. June 8, 643.
Secondary Education. Scotland, etc., June
16, 1419.

WEIR, MR. J. G. [Ross and Cromarty].
Colonial Loans Fund Bill, com., June 8,
745, 746.
Education. Scotland. June 16, 1442.

WELBY, LIEUT.-COL. A. C. E. [Taunton].
Post Office Officials—Employment of old
Non-commissioned Officers, etc., June 1,
127.
Postal Deliveries in Dorsetshire, June 5,
302.

West Gloucestershire Water Bill.
c. con.*, June 5, 293.
l. 1R.*, June 9, 751.
2R.*, June 19, 1454.
3R.*, June 8, 624.

West Highland Railway Bill.
l. Commons Amendts., June 12, 878.

WEST INDIES.
Fruit Steamers—Commencement of Service.
Q. Mr. Lawrence; A. Mr. J. Chamber-
lain, June 6, 441.
Rum, Local Duties—Return.
Q. Mr. Lawrence; A. Mr. J. Chamber-
lain, June 6, 441.

West Middlesex Water Bill.
l. 2R.*. June 8, 594.

**Weston-super-Mare, Clevedon, and Ports-
head Tramways Company [Light Railway Extension] Bill.**
l. 3R.*, June 2, 162.
c. 1R.*, June 5, 326.
2R., June 14, 1089.

WESTPORT—Urban Sanitary Authority Commissioners' Petition.
Q. Dr. Ambrose; A. Mr. G. W. Balfour, June 13, 1074.

Wetherby District Water Bill.
l. com.*, June 12, 878.
Rep.*, June 19, 1453.

WHITE LEAD FACTORIES.
Rules presented, June 1, 70, 79.

Whitehaven Corporation Bill.
l. 3R.*, June 2, 162.
c. 1R.*, June 5, 326.
2R.*, June 14, 1089.

WHITELEY, MR. G. [Stockport].
Half-timers, Education of Children Bill,
com., May 31, 8, 15, 24, 38, 42, 48, 51,
52, 59. com., June 7, 542 ; 3R., June 14,
1097, 1105, 1112.

WHITELEY, MR. H. [Ashton-under-Lyne].
Half-timers, Education of Children Bill,
com., May 31, 54.

WHITMORE, MR. [Chelsea].
London Water [Purchase] Bill, 2R., June 1,
74.

Wick and Pulteney Harbours Bill.
c. 2R.*, June 6, 431.

WILLIAMS, MR. J. C. [Notts, Mansfield].
Business of the House, Precedence of
Government Business, June 19, 1520.
Divine Service at Ordnance Factory Chapels
—Ritualistic Practices, June 12, 899.
London Government Bill, con., June 8,
699, 701, 702.
Women, Qualification of, June 6, 474.

WILLIAMS, MR. J. P.—Financial Secretary to
the War Office [Birmingham, S.].
Cork Military District—Stores Contracts
Complaints, June 19, 1483.
Deniston, J., Case of, June 19, 1482.
Guards—Losses of Stores, Claim, June
19, 1481.
Guernsey Militia—Insubordination, June
19, 1481.
Metropolitan Volunteer Review—Ac-
commodation for Members, June 19,
1482.
Salisbury Plain. Rentals of Property—
Return, June 6. 442 ; June 13, 1059.
Woolwich Arsenal—Dismissal of Men,
etc., June 15, 1176.

WILSON, MR. C. H. [Hull, W.].
Customs Boatmen's Grievances, June 1,
151.

WILSON, MR. H. F. [York, W. R., Holmsfirth].
Soudan Campaign—Thanks to the Forces, June 8, 686.

WILSON, MR. J. [Durham, Mid.].
Half-timers—Education of Children Bill, com., May 31, 23.

WILSON, MR. J. H. [Middlesbrough].
Customs Boatmen, Pay, etc., June 1, 152.
Merchant Vessels, Navigation of—Case of ss. *Pinner's Point*, June 12, 895.
Seamen.
Accommodation on P. and O. Ships, etc., June 2, 282, 286.
Wages of, June 2, 285.

WINCHESTER, BISHOP OF.
Prevention of Corruption Bill, 2R, June 6, 422.

WINDING-UP OF COMPANIES.
Returned Ordered [Mr. C. McArthur], June 13, 1057.

WINDOW-CLEANING ACCIDENTS.
Deaths from, Return Ordered [Mr. Collings], June 2, 171.

WINE DUTIES, INCREASE.
Correspondence presented, May 31, 7; June 1, 68.
Revenue derived from.
Q. Mr. Lambert; A. Sir M. Hicks-Beach, June 13, 1068.

Wine and Beerhouse Acts Amendment Bill.
c. 2R., June 7, 567.

Wishaw Water Bill.
c. 2R.*, June 5, 295.
Rep.*, June 16, 1330.

Withington Urban District Council [Tramways] Bill.
l. 3R.*, June 2, 162.
c. 1R.*, June 5, 326.
2R., June 14, 1089.

Woking Water and Gas
c. Con.*, June 5, 293.
3R.*, June 8, 624.
l. 1R.*, June 9, 751.
2R.*, June 16, 1317.

Wolverhampton Tramways Bill.
l. Com.*, June 8, 593.
Rep.*, June 16, 1317.

WOMEN.
Barristers—Miss Sorabji's Application.
Q. Mr. H. Roberts; A. Lord G. Hamilton, June 8, 641.
County Councillors [Qualification of Women] [Scotland] Bill, see that Title.
Parliamentary Franchise, Petition, June 9, 760

WOMEN—*cont.*
Qualification as Aldermen and Councillors—London Government Bill, Mr. Courtney's New Clause, June 6, 464; Mr. Elliot's Amendt. to re-com., June 13, 1078.

Woodhouse and Conisbrough Railway [Abandonment] Bill.
c. Lords Amendmts., May 31, 1.
l. Royal Assent, June 6, 410.

WOOLWICH ARSENAL.
Dismissal of Men, etc.
Q. Mr. Steadman; A. Mr. J. P. Williams, June 15, 1176.

Worcestershire County Council Bill.
c. Rep.*, June 16, 1331.

WORKHOUSES.
Ireland—Clerks of Unions checking Rate Collectors' Accounts—Extra Remuneration.
Q. Mr. Tully; A. Mr. G. W. Balfour, June 15, 1197.
Religious Ministration, S., June 2, 267, 273, 274, 278.

Workington Corporation Water Bill.
l. Rep. from Select Com., June 13, 993.

Workmen's Compensation Act [1897] Amendment Bill.
Petition, June 6, 433.

Workmen's Houses Tenure Bill.
Petition, June 14, 1091.

WORKMEN'S TRAINS.
Cheap Trains Bill, see that Title.
Return Ordered [Mr. Woods], June 8, 626.

WORTLEY, RT. HON. C. B. S. [Sheffield, Hallam].
Private Legislation Procedure [Scotland] Bill, com., June 12, 926, 982; June 19, 1537, 1559.

WYLIE, MR. A. [Dumbartonshire].
Half-timers—Education of Children Bill, com., May 31, 16.
Indian Sugar Duties—Tariff Act 1899, June 15, 1275.

WYNDHAM, MR. G.—Under Secretary for War [Dover].
Aldershot.
Bathing Fatality, June 8, 640.
Sewage Farm—Inspector's Report, June 2, 177.
Strength of Troops on Queen's Birthday Parade, June 12, 899.
Divine Service at Enfield Ordnance Factory Chapel—Ritualistic Practices, June 12, 898.
Dum-Dum Bullet. Issue to troops in India, June 5, 302.
Ladysmith Barracks, Insanitary condition of, June 9, 771.
Longford Militia headquarters, removal to Mullingar, June 13, 1058.
Lynch's, E., Pension, June 16, 1334.

[Continued

WYNDHAM, MR. G.—*cont.*

    Mountain Artillery Officers—Armament Pay, June 15, 1176.

    Mountain and Garrison Artillery—Officers' Right of Fall, June 16, 1334.

    Netheravon House—Non-Occupation by War Office, June 6, 442.

    Patriotic Fund—Case of Mrs. Lewis, June 8, 632.

    Prisons, Inspector-General's Report—June 8, 640.

    Punjaub War and Tirah Campaign—Distribution of Medals, June 1, 81.

    Queen's Birthday Celebrations at Southsea—Cancelling Parade, June 2, 181.

    Recruits' Bread Rations, June 16, 1334.

    Volunteer Officers, Training with Regiments near civil duties, June 1, 79.

    Youghal Rifle Range, Repairs, etc., June 9, 771.

YANG-TSZE VALLEY, see China.

YERBURGH, MR. R. A. [Chester].

    China, Affairs of, June 9, 859.

    Waima Incident, Compensation Claims, June 9, 863.

YOKOHAMA AND DISTRICT.—Trade Report presented, June 19, 1456.

Yorke Estate Bill.

    l. Rep.*, June 8, 594.

    3R.*, June 13, 994.

    c. 1R.*, June 15, 1175.

    2R. June 19, 1474.

YORKSHIRE [WEST RIDING].

    Charities, Return presented, June 8, 626.

    Osgoldcross, New Writ for, June 19, 1474.

YOUGHAL RIFLE RANGE—Repairs, etc.

    Q. Capt. Donelan; A. Mr. Wyndham, June 9, 771.

YOUNG, MR. S. [Cavan, E.].

    Intoxicating Liquors [Sunday Closing] Bill, 2R., June 7, 556, 557.

    Land Commission [Ireland].

        Bailieborough Commissioners' Judgments, June 8, 647.

        Valuation—Fixing of Fair Rents, etc., June 8, 647 ; June 15, 1195.

    Land Purchase Acts, Ireland, Delay in carrying out, June 8, 650.

Youthful Offenders Bill.

    l. 1R.*, June 12, 889.

YOXALL, MR. [Nottingham, W.].

    Half-timers—Education of Children Bill, com., May 31, 36 ; 3R., June 14, 1111, 1112.

    Post Office—Clerks' Salaries, June 6, 437.

ZANZIBAR.

    Slavery in, S., June 9, 872.